# Praise for

# The Complete Guide to Service Learning

***"Service learning expert Cathryn Berger Kaye writes a powerful guide*** to invigorate students, teachers, and youth leaders. The practical service learning strategies and diverse themes will awaken and engage even the most reluctant learners."

—Denise Clark Pope, Lecturer, Stanford University School of Education and author of *"Doing School": How We Are Creating a Generation of Stressed Out, Materialistic, and Miseducated Students*

***"Cathryn Berger Kaye's energy, commitment, knowledge, and compassion are an inspiration.*** *The Complete Guide to Service Learning* captures all of these qualities, along with her practical advice and years of experience in educating the hearts and minds of the young. She connects reading to reality, using literature as a springboard for change. Putting these ideas into action in your classroom will forever change the lives of your students and just might help change the world."

—James Howe, author of *Bunnicula* and *The Misfits*

***"Through combining her love of service with her love of children's literature,*** Cathryn Berger Kaye has given a great gift to classroom teachers everywhere in the publication of this book. Through its innovative approach to service learning, this volume reflects the integrity and compassion we all need to bring alive our classrooms and the world outside."

—James C. Toole, Ph.D., Compass Institute and University of Minnesota

***"This is the resource teachers need*** to make service learning a reality for every kind of learner. This is education at a deeper level."

—Susan Meyers, Ph.D., Dean of College of Education, San Jose State University

# The Complete Guide to Service Learning

## Proven, Practical Ways to Engage Students in Civic Responsibility, Academic Curriculum, & Social Action

*Cathryn Berger Kaye, M.A.*

free spirit
PUBLISHING®

**The Library of Congress has cataloged the previous edition as follows:**
Kaye, Cathryn Berger.
The complete guide to service learning : proven, practical ways to engage students in civic responsibility, academic curriculum, and social action / Cathryn Berger Kaye.
p. cm.
ISBN 1-57542-133-X
1. Student service—United States—Handbooks, manuals, etc. 2. Civics—Study and teaching—United States—Handbooks, manuals, etc. I. Title.
LC220.5.K39 2003
373.119—dc21 2003004437

At the time of this book's publication, all facts and figures cited are the most current available. All telephone numbers, addresses, and Web site URLs are accurate and active; all publications, organizations, Web sites, and other resources exist as described in this book; and all have been verified as of August 2006. The author and Free Spirit Publishing make no warranty or guarantee concerning the information and materials given out by organizations or content found at Web sites, and we are not responsible for any changes that occur after this book's publication. If you find an error or believe that a resource listed here is not as described, please contact Free Spirit Publishing. Parents, teachers, and other adults: We strongly urge you to monitor children's use of the Internet.

Service learning occurs in each of the fifty United States and internationally. While project descriptions and scenarios are not attributed to specific schools or youth groups, some are identified by city, state, or region. All efforts have been made to ensure correct attribution.

Edited by Jennifer Brannen
Cover and interior design by Marieka Heinlen
Index by Ina Gravitz

15 14 13 12 11 10 9 8
Printed in the United States of America

**Free Spirit Publishing Inc.**
217 Fifth Avenue North, Suite 200
Minneapolis, MN 55401-1299
(612) 338-2068
help4kids@freespirit.com
www.freespirit.com

As a member of the Green Press Initiative, Free Spirit Publishing is committed to the three Rs: Reduce, Reuse, Recycle. Whenever possible, we print our books on recycled paper containing a minimum of 30% post-consumer waste. At Free Spirit it's our goal to nurture not only children, but nature too!

green press INITIATIVE

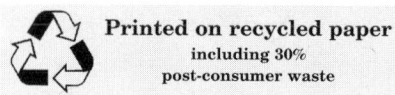

**Printed on recycled paper including 30% post-consumer waste**

## Dedication

With great admiration, to the students and teachers who bring service learning to life every day.


## Acknowledgments

Just as it takes a village to raise a child, a community has contributed to this book. This has been a journey of commitment and passion influenced by many in the service learning world. The following people made exceptional contributions. Truly, I thank you with a full and grateful heart. Many thanks to:

- the authors for their inspiring interviews
- my colleagues for recommendations to the Bookshelf
- Deena Metzger for her encouragement
- Joe Follman, Florida Alliance for Student Service, for his valuable response to my early manuscript and our frequent conversations
- Jill Addison-Jacobson, Youth Service California, for suggestions regarding this book's title and our helpful talks
- Don Hill, Service Learning 2000 at Youth Service California, for book title advice, and the questions that guide reflection on page 27
- Dave Donahue, Mills College, for sharing thoughts about reciprocity
- Betty Berger, my sister, for information essential to the special needs and disabilities chapter
- Madeleine Yates and Luke Frasier, Maryland Student Service Alliance, for service examples and permission to model my curriculum webs on their interdisciplinary service learning webs
- Vicki Lee and Barbara Weiss for urging me to publish the original *Service Learning Bookshelf*
- Children's Book World in Los Angeles for book recommendations
- Judy Galbraith for her vision and the Free Spirit Publishing staff for wholeheartedly embracing this project, especially Nancy Robinson and my editor Jennifer Brannen
- and my wonderful family—husband Barry, and daughters Ariel and Devora—for challenging my thinking, critiquing Bookshelf books, reading these pages, and giving me daily support and love

And to colleagues from across the country:

*California:* Mike Brugh, CalServe; Daphne Dennis and Diane Kahn-Epstein, City of West Hollywood; John Duran, Galt School District; Carolina Goodman and Claire Money, P.S. #1 Elementary School; Kathryn Lee, Prospect Sierra School; Cathleen Micheaelson, East Bay Conservation Corps Charter Elementary School; Lisa Morehouse, Balboa High; Emmy Poling, Fairmeadow Elementary; Donna Ritter, Elementary Community Service Association; Valerie Sorgen, Youth Community Service; Kim Stokely, Adopt-A Watershed; Barbara Thomas, The Willows Community School. *Florida:* Cynthia McCauley, Bay High School; Ossie Hanauer, Miami-Dade College. *Maine:* Fran Rudoff and Barbara Kaufman, Kids Consortium; Glenn Nerbak, Lyman-Moore Middle School. *Maryland:* Judi Bard, The Howard County Office on Aging. *Massachusetts:* Lynn Barclay and Bob Kumin, Hampshire Educational Collaborative; Jenny Lisle, Zoom into Action, PBS Kids; Roberta Sullivan, Sullivan Elementary; Debbie Coyne, North Adams School District. *Minnesota:* Rich Cairn; Nan Peterson, The Blake School. *Oklahoma:* Jessie Craig, Briggs Schools; Donna Gourd, Cherokee Nation Learn and Serve Program; Rebecca Jim, L.E.A.D. Agency; Nancy Scott, Cherokee Nation. *Oregon:* Kate MacPherson, Project Service Leadership. *Texas:* Linda Robinson, Alvin Junior High. *Vermont:* Joe Brooks and Susan Bonthron, Vermont Community Works. *Washington:* John Traynor, Gonzaga Preparatory School. *Wisconsin:* Marcia Applen and Kirk Schneidawind, St. Peter Middle/High School; Janet Levy and Holly Ryan, Cedarburg High School

To students, educators, community groups, and colleagues too numerous to mention by name whose projects inspired the descriptions of service learning scenarios in this book—many thanks.

# CONTENTS


Foreword . . . . . . . . . . ix

Introduction . . . . . . . . . . 1

PART ONE — The Service Learning Handbook . . . . . . . 5

**Chapter 1. What Is Service Learning? . . . . . . 6**

A Definition of Service Learning . . . . . . 7
Before You Start: Frequently Asked Questions . . . . . . 7
The Process of Service Learning: The Big Picture . . . . . . 10
What Makes Service Learning Successful? . . . . . . 12
An Example of Putting It All Together: Service Learning Meets the Canned Food Drive . . . . . . 13
What Next? . . . . . . 15

**Chapter 2. A Blueprint for Service Learning . . . . . . 16**

Getting Started: A Blueprint . . . . . . 16
Beyond the Basics: Advancing Your Service Learning Practice . . . . . . 24
Curve Balls and Stumbling Blocks in Service Learning . . . . . . 30

**Chapter 3. The Theme Chapters and the Service Learning Bookshelf . . . . 52**

Getting Oriented: About the Thematic Chapters . . . . . . 52
About the Service Learning Bookshelf . . . . . . 53
What's on the Shelf? Features of the Service Learning Bookshelf . . . . . . 54
Using the Service Learning Bookshelf . . . . . . 60

PART TWO — Service Learning Themes . . . . . . . . 65

**Chapter 4. AIDS Education and Awareness . . . . . . 66**

Preparation: Getting Ready for Service Learning Involving AIDS Education and Awareness . . . . . . 66
Making Connections Across the Curriculum . . . . . . 68
Service Learning Scenarios: Ideas for Action . . . . . . 68
The AIDS Education and Awareness Bookshelf . . . . . . 71
Interviews with Authors: The Story Behind the Story . . . . . . 73

**Chapter 5. Animals in Danger . . . . 76**

Preparation: Getting Ready for Service Learning Involving Animals in Danger . . . . . . 76
Making Connections Across the Curriculum . . . . . . 77
Service Learning Scenarios: Ideas for Action . . . . . . 79
The Animals in Danger Bookshelf . . . . . . 82
Interviews with Authors: The Story Behind the Story . . . . . . 86

**Chapter 6. Community Safety . . . . 89**

Preparation: Getting Ready for Service Learning Involving Community Safety . . . . . . 89
Making Connections Across the Curriculum . . . . . . 90
Service Learning Scenarios: Ideas for Action . . . . . . 90
The Community Safety Bookshelf . . . . . . 94
Interviews with Authors: The Story Behind the Story . . . . . . 103

**Chapter 7. Elders . . . . . . . . . . . . . 106**

Preparation: Getting Ready for Service Learning Involving Elders . . . . . . . 106
Making Connections Across the Curriculum . . . . . . . . . . . . . . . . . . . 108
Service Learning Scenarios: Ideas for Action . . . . . . . . . . . . . . . . . . . . . . . . 108
The Elders Bookshelf . . . . . . . . . . . . . . . . . . . . . 113
Interviews with Authors: The Story Behind the Story . . . . . . . . . . . . . . 119

**Chapter 8. The Environment . . . . 123**

Preparation: Getting Ready for Service Learning Involving the Environment . . . . . . . 123
Making Connections Across the Curriculum . . . . . . . . . . . . . . . . . . . 124
Service Learning Scenarios: Ideas for Action . . . . . . . . . . . . . . . . . . . . . . . . 126
The Environment Bookshelf . . . . . . . . . . . . . . . . 130
Interviews with Authors: The Story Behind the Story . . . . . . . . . . . . . . 134

**Chapter 9. Gardening . . . . . . . . . . 135**

Preparation: Getting Ready for Service Learning Involving Gardening . . . . . . . . . . . . 135
Making Connections Across the Curriculum . . . . . . . . . . . . . . . . . . . 136
Service Learning Scenarios: Ideas for Action . . . . . . . . . . . . . . . . . . . . . . . . 136
The Gardening Bookshelf . . . . . . . . . . . . . . . . . . 140
Interviews with Authors: The Story Behind the Story . . . . . . . . . . . . . . 144

**Chapter 10. Hunger and Homelessness . . . . . . . . . . . . 146**

Preparation: Getting Ready for Service Learning Involving Hunger and Homelessness . . . . . . . . . . . . . . . . 146
Making Connections Across the Curriculum . . . . . . . . . . . . . . . . . . . 148
Service Learning Scenarios: Ideas for Action . . . . . . . . . . . . . . . . . . . . . . . . 148
The Hunger and Homelessness Bookshelf . . . . . 151
Interviews with Authors: The Story Behind the Story . . . . . . . . . . . . . . 157

**Chapter 11. Immigrants . . . . . . . . 159**

Preparation: Getting Ready for Service Learning Involving Immigrants . . . . . . . . . . . . 159
Making Connections Across the Curriculum . . . . . . . . . . . . . . . . . . . 160
Service Learning Scenarios: Ideas for Action . . . . . . . . . . . . . . . . . . . . . . . . 161
The Immigrants Bookshelf . . . . . . . . . . . . . . . . . 165
Interviews with Authors: The Story Behind the Story . . . . . . . . . . . . . . 171

**Chapter 12. Literacy . . . . . . . . . . 173**

Preparation: Getting Ready for Service Learning Involving Literacy . . . . . 173
Making Connections Across the Curriculum . . . . . . . . . . . . . . . . . . . 175
Service Learning Scenarios: Ideas for Action . . . . . . . . . . . . . . . . . . . . . . . . 175
The Literacy Bookshelf . . . . . . . . . . . . . . . . . . . . 179
Interviews with Authors: The Story Behind the Story . . . . . . . . . . . . . . 184

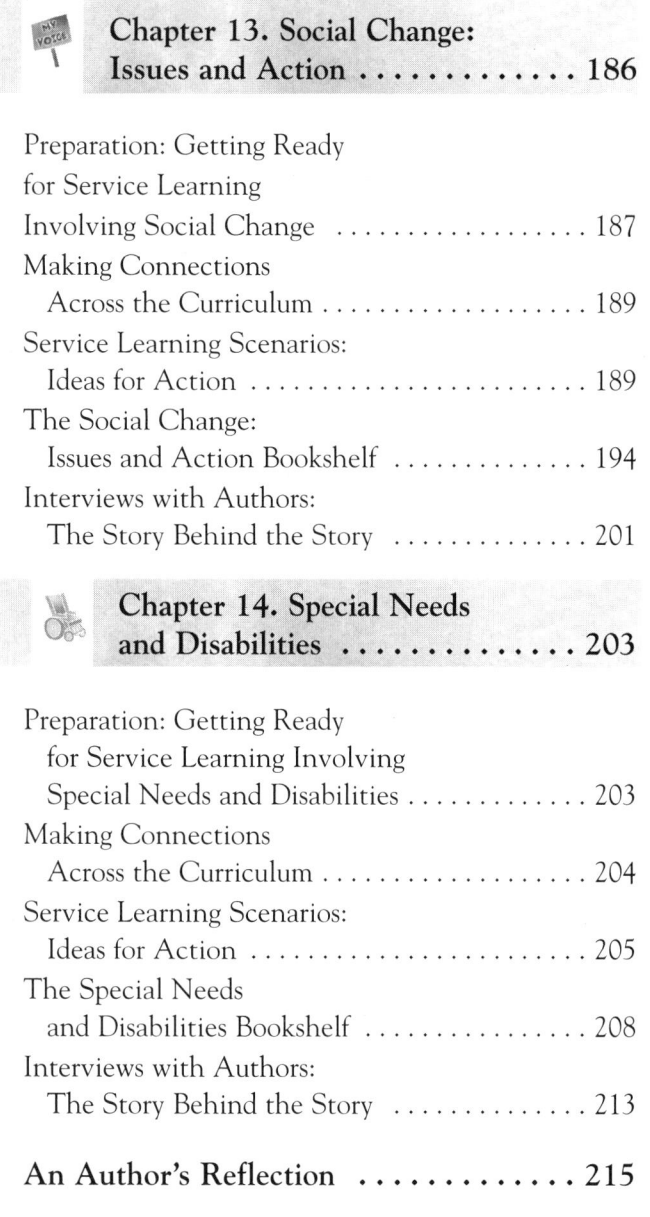

**Chapter 13. Social Change: Issues and Action . . . . . . . . . . . . . 186**

Preparation: Getting Ready for Service Learning Involving Social Change . . . . . . . . . . . . . . . . . . 187
Making Connections Across the Curriculum . . . . . . . . . . . . . . . . . . 189
Service Learning Scenarios: Ideas for Action . . . . . . . . . . . . . . . . . . . . . . . 189
The Social Change: Issues and Action Bookshelf . . . . . . . . . . . . . . 194
Interviews with Authors: The Story Behind the Story . . . . . . . . . . . . . . 201

**Chapter 14. Special Needs and Disabilities . . . . . . . . . . . . . . 203**

Preparation: Getting Ready for Service Learning Involving Special Needs and Disabilities . . . . . . . . . . . . . 203
Making Connections Across the Curriculum . . . . . . . . . . . . . . . . . . 204
Service Learning Scenarios: Ideas for Action . . . . . . . . . . . . . . . . . . . . . . . 205
The Special Needs and Disabilities Bookshelf . . . . . . . . . . . . . . . . 208
Interviews with Authors: The Story Behind the Story . . . . . . . . . . . . . . 213

**An Author's Reflection . . . . . . . . . . . . . 215**

**Resources . . . . . . . . . . . . . . . . . . . . . . . . . 216**

**Index . . . . . . . . . . . . . . . . . . . . . . . . . . . . . 218**

**About the Author . . . . . . . . . . . . . . . . . 228**


## List of Reproducibles


Establishing Curricular Connections: Points of Entry . . . . . . . . . . . . . . . . . . . . . . . . . . 31
Personal Inventory . . . . . . . . . . . . . . . . . . . . . . . . 33
Taking Action in Our Community . . . . . . . . . . . . 34
Service Learning Proposal . . . . . . . . . . . . . . . . . . . 35
The Four Stages of Service Learning . . . . . . . . . . 36
The Essential Elements of Service Learning . . . . 37
Planning for Service Learning . . . . . . . . . . . . . . . 38
Planning for Service Learning: Example (Elementary) . . . . . . . . . . . . . . . . . . . . 39
Planning for Service Learning: Example (Middle School) . . . . . . . . . . . . . . . . . 40
Planning for Service Learning: Example (High School) . . . . . . . . . . . . . . . . . . . 41
Planning for Service Learning: Example (Special Needs) . . . . . . . . . . . . . . . . . 42
Community Contact Information . . . . . . . . . . . . 43
Community Response Form . . . . . . . . . . . . . . . . . 44
Our Service Project . . . . . . . . . . . . . . . . . . . . . . . . 45
Project Promotion—Turning Ideas into Action . . . . . . . . . . . . . . . . . . 46
Sequence for Reflection . . . . . . . . . . . . . . . . . . . . 47
Four Square Reflection Tool . . . . . . . . . . . . . . . . . 48
Assessment for Service Learning: Part One . . . . . 49
Assessment for Service Learning: Part Two . . . . . 50
Student Self-Evaluation . . . . . . . . . . . . . . . . . . . . 51

# FOREWORD

Service learning is emerging as a critical topic in K–12 schools, higher education, and community organizations that work with youth. Why? Studies show, for example, that:

- half of all high schools have service learning projects.
- several million students participate in service learning projects each year.
- students participating in service learning show improvements in academic achievement, career preparation, feelings of self-efficacy, behavior, attendance, and civic engagement.
- students participating in service learning are more likely to continue to volunteer later in life.

Federal, state, and local governments support and encourage service learning projects. Foundations invest millions of dollars each year to initiate, expand, improve, and institutionalize service learning. Service learning earns praise from all points along the political spectrum.

Numbers don't lie, but they also don't explain. They don't explain that service learning is growing in popularity worldwide because it has youth using, through helping others, the knowledge and skills they need to learn. Numbers also don't explain that students and teachers respond positively to learning when it is applied and used in their own communities. Statistical findings don't explain that service learning works and appeals because it brings head and heart together and develops both at the same time. Or that youth are yearning to do good things and service learning allows them to do so *and* have a voice in how and what they contribute.

It is important to state that service learning is not simply a fad or the latest "thing" to come along in education and youth development. I would argue that service learning is not a "thing" at all, or an end in itself that must be added to the countless other "things" educators have to deal with. Service learning is rather a marvelously flexible strategy or tool for educators to better teach students about themselves and the world, while meeting existing goals and objectives. It can be and has been used in every subject and grade level and is equally effective outside the school context.

Service learning, as explained in this invaluable guide, is a relatively new term but not a new idea. Countless teachers over the years have engaged students in experiential activities, many of which provide a real service to other students or to communities. In some cases, these educators have never heard the term, "service learning." In the last several years, however, research and an examination of service learning practice have brought about a consensus on what makes service learning an effective "win-win" proposition—that is, what makes it help both the server and those being served. Understanding these elements and how to apply them are keys to implementing successful service learning and the purpose of the guide.

Cathryn Berger Kaye has been deeply engaged in all aspects of service learning as a teacher; a local, state, and national service learning program developer and advisor; and as one of the nation's leading service learning trainers. She helped shape how service learning is defined and played leading roles in helping us recognize the essential roles that literature and demonstration play in effective projects. I am happy that Cathryn is sharing her knowledge and experience with all of us.

*The Complete Guide to Service Learning* puts all the pieces together in a readable and practical format to help you initiate, expand, improve, and/or sustain your service learning efforts. With its background, wealth of examples, reproducible documents, interdisciplinary approach, links with curricula, and commonsense suggestions, it can give you what you need to take that first, second, or twentieth step in combining service with learning to help improve youth, schools, communities, our nation, and our global society.

Joe Follman
Director, Florida Alliance for Student Service
Florida State University

# INTRODUCTION

At a service learning workshop in the mid-1980s, I asked twelve teachers to think back to their earliest memories of service—of giving service, receiving service, or observing service. They willingly shared images of visiting retirement homes with a youth group, collecting money for UNICEF, working in a hospital as a high school student, and tutoring a young neighbor who was struggling with reading. One woman described living in a rural community with few financial resources. Still, her mother prepared food each week that her father loaded onto the back of their pickup to deliver to families whose needs were more urgent than their own. She described watching this and wondering, "Why are they giving away our food?" She paused, reflecting. Then she said, "Maybe that's why I take care of foster children. Maybe that's why I'm a teacher."

I have continued asking this question over the years and I continue to find a connection between people's early personal experiences and memories of service and their later choice to become teachers or otherwise work with youth. Teachers—along with others who work in service professions—clearly have a natural affinity with service learning. Part of what draws us into this career is the opportunity it offers us to reach children and make a lasting—even profound—difference in their lives. Service learning provides deep and wondrous ways for this to happen.

My own experience with service learning began long before the term was commonly used. I was teaching in a very small school in rural Maine. One morning, a seventh-grade student brought in a newspaper article.

"That's my street," she said, pointing at the photograph. "See that tree? It's two houses away."

"What's wrong with the tree?" another student asked her.

"Dutch Elm Disease."

None of us was familiar with the term, but by the end of the day, we had all learned quite a bit about this disease that threatened the magnificent elms in our neighborhoods. The students wanted to get involved. Before long, they were making phone calls to the state and local departments of agriculture and were directed to a science department at the local university. Within a week, they were trained in assessing elm trees. Clipboards in hand, they traveled from street to street diagnosing and reporting on the condition of each tree.

Suddenly, subjects came alive for our middle and high school students. The study of plant cells took on new meaning. In math classes, record-keeping methods and statistics gained an importance they had not had before. Students described their excitement and frustrations in journals and stories with feedback from other students and teachers. As a culmination of their work, students submitted their findings to state agencies and made a summary presentation to a college class.

The students couldn't save every tree, of course, but they did help to protect some of the majestic elms. Along the way, they learned and practiced scientific reporting methods, became aware of the roles of state officials, and developed partnerships with college students. Motivated by a sense of purpose, our students identified themselves as community activists and came to speak with ease about civic responsibility.

> You should know that the education of the heart is very important. This will distinguish you from others. Educating oneself is easy, but educating ourselves to help other human beings to help the community is much more difficult.
>
> CÉSAR E. CHÁVEZ, SOCIAL ACTIVIST

Since my first experience with service learning, I have worked as a classroom teacher, in program development locally and nationally, and as a leader of educational workshops. *The Complete Guide to Service Learning* reflects my experiences both as an educator, who presents about service learning and develops and refines its concepts and practices, and as a student, who acquires new ideas from the people I meet.

# Why Is Service Learning Important?

You may be coming to service learning for many different reasons—and all of them are valid. Perhaps you're drawn to service learning because of your own experiences as a student or because of personal or community values. You may want to introduce service learning to your classroom or school after hearing about the many ways students become motivated and engaged by this hands-on teaching method. You may approach service learning to respond to specific community needs or concerns or to promote involvement with social justice issues. (Many educators see the direct link between service learning and civic responsibility and character development.) Or perhaps you're responding to school or district requirements on incorporating service learning into curriculum and teaching methods, and you want to maximize the benefits for all involved. Regardless of which scenario seems most familiar to you, you're probably going to find yourself asking—or answering—the question, "Why is service learning important?"

- Service learning provides meaningful ways for students, teachers, administrators, and community agencies and members to move together with deliberate thought and action toward a common purpose that has mutual benefits.
- Students benefit academically, socially, and emotionally; develop skills; explore numerous career options; and may come to appreciate the value of civic responsibility and actively participating in their community.
- Teachers make school and education more relevant for their students, often seeing their students blossom and develop previously untapped strengths in the process; collaborate with their colleagues and community partners to develop exciting curriculum; and may find themselves professionally re-energized.
- School administrators may observe a boost in the morale of staff and students as they achieve desired academic outcomes while seeing the profile of the school raised in a positive way in the community.
- Community partners receive much needed help and may find themselves learning from the students as they teach or interact with them.

By encouraging and supporting thoughtful civic involvement and participation by young people, the entire community benefits. Young people are acknowledged—and see themselves—as resourceful, knowledgeable, and agents of change who can harness their ideas, energy, and enthusiasm to benefit us all.

The beauty of service learning is that something real and concrete is occurring. Learning takes on a new dimension. When students are engaged intellectually and emotionally with a topic, they can light up with a revelation or make a connection between two previously separate ideas. What they've learned in school suddenly matters and engages their minds and their hearts. Teachers also frequently respond to service learning, finding their students' eagerness and curiosity invigorating. Education is relevant in the classroom and in the larger community. Math, science, social studies, languages, literature, the arts—all are applied, used, and placed in contexts where they really matter.

In addition to the educational benefits, our society depends on active participation of its members to thrive. Our acts of service can shape the society we live in. Even young children marvel at how their thinking and planning and doing makes a difference. While it may seem cliché, the truth is, service learning enables

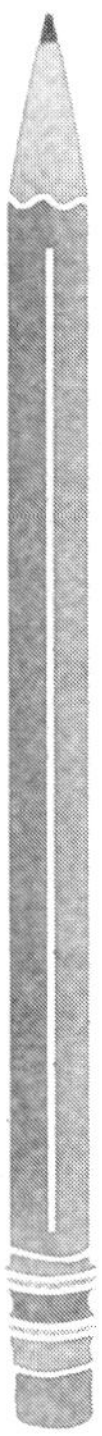

a wealth of "differences" to happen. Relationships develop between people, with an attendant understanding and appreciation for similarities and differences. Eyes become accustomed to looking for needs in the community and are followed by the recognition of possibilities to, yes, make a difference.

Even though service learning can be exciting for teachers as well as students, you may feel daunted by the idea of integrating service learning into an increasingly complicated curricular mix. If so, you're not alone. Often teachers arrive at one of my service learning workshops tired and frustrated by the newest set of mandates to arrive on their desks. Then something happens, as they hear of their colleagues in schools across the country who try service learning and use it again and again. They see that it's really possible to meet the standards, improve literacy, increase test scores, and enjoy their profession while they enhance and strengthen their ability as educators.

# About This Book

This book is designed to help you successfully use service learning in your classroom or youth group. It can also help you sow the seeds for a culture of service learning in your school or community. You will find ideas and strategies to build a strong service learning foundation as well as practical ways to implement service learning with children of all ages. There are thematic chapters that cover a wide variety of issues that are jumping-off points for service learning. Some of the ideas in the themes are probably very familiar, others less so. But all of the issues are important and the concepts and suggestions have all been used in schools around the United States and around the world.

## *How to Use This Book*

This guide has two main parts, and it's designed to be used in a specific order. Part 1 addresses the various elements of service learning, how to get started, and the different ways to use the theme chapters; Part 2 is a series of thematic chapters. By reading Part 1 before moving on to the theme chapters, you will be prepared to apply the principles of service learning.

- **Part 1, The Service Learning Handbook,** includes three chapters that provide definitions and background information on service learning and describe the necessary components for successful service learning in your school, organization, or community. In addition, it includes many reproducible documents and forms to adapt and use as you carry out service learning projects or share ideas with peers. Chapter 1 discusses the nature of service learning in detail. Chapter 2 gives you a blueprint for how to begin using service learning in your classroom and includes reproducible forms to help you. Chapter 3 explains how to use the theme chapters and the service learning bookshelf which appears in each theme chapter.
- **Part 2, Service Learning Themes,** is made up of eleven thematic chapters that give you ideas for specific areas for action, including such themes as "Animals in Danger," "Community Safety," "Hunger and Homelessness," and "Special Needs and Disabilities." Each thematic chapter includes activities, a curriculum web to help you make cross-curricular connections, theme-specific resources, examples of actual service learning projects, and an extensive bookshelf of nonfiction and fiction, including picture books and novels. Each thematic bookshelf is annotated and arranged by topic as well as by theme and identified by level. The books are also cross-referenced where they are applicable to more than one thematic chapter, as noted on an easy-to-reference chart. To help you select books more effectively, each thematic service learning bookshelf is divided into sub-themes. For example, the sub-themes in the Environment chapter bookshelf are "Natural Resources," "Recycling," and "Appreciating Nature."
- **The book concludes with "An Author's Reflection"** and a general resource list to help you explore service learning further.

## About the Bookshelf: The Important Link Between Service Learning and Literature

Books and reading are the basis of all literacy and learning, so it isn't a surprise that they can also be the foundation of service learning. Books and reading can and should be an integral part of the service learning process. Over the years, I have read and gathered many outstanding and memorable books—fiction and nonfiction—that have an authentic connection with service learning themes. A well-chosen book can become the linchpin for an entire service learning project or unit, introducing students to relevant issues as they start working on a project. Compelling books can keep them thinking about the implications of their endeavors during the project and provoke them to reflection throughout. Both teachers and students gravitate toward a well-told story.

When I travel to lead service learning workshops, books pour out of my suitcases. These traveling companions enliven service learning presentations as educators see the relevance and connections between the books, their students, and service that meets genuine community needs. I have included hundreds of my favorite books in the service learning bookshelf sections in the theme chapters of this book.

## Is Service Learning for You?

If you're a teacher, youth worker or group leader, counselor, principal, or administrator who wants to help kids be more engaged and effective learners and take responsibility in their communities, *The Complete Guide to Service Learning* is for you. While this book primarily addresses service learning within a K–12th grade school setting, service learning is also thriving in many colleges and universities. Community organizations, youth groups, and after-school programs also use service learning because it enriches their programs and helps to increase academic achievement and personal growth and development of young people.

Above all, the purpose of this book is to encourage the practice of service learning—to offer a variety of ways you can integrate service learning projects into different curricula so that more young people will reap the benefits. Instilling the concept of civic responsibility and enriching educational opportunities for young people of all ages as they become engaged in social action is a gift to your students, your community, and yourself.

In reading this book, you will find that my commitment to service learning is deep. I am part of a dynamic group of countless educators, community members, writers, social activists, artists, and young people of every age who believe we can repair, improve, and save this world—I stand with those who believe this is perhaps the finest work to be done. Welcome to the group!

*Cathryn Berger Kaye*

# *Part One:* The Service Learning Handbook

CHAPTER 1

# WHAT IS SERVICE LEARNING?

Simply put, service learning connects school-based curriculum with the inherent caring and concern young people have for their world—whether on their school campus, at a local food bank, or in a distant rainforest. The results are memorable, lifelong lessons for students and foster a stronger society for us all.

This is what service learning can look like:

- A teacher reads *A Day at Wood Green Animal Shelter* aloud to her first graders to prepare for a field trip to the local animal humane society. The trip is a central part of their studies about "our community." After discussing the need to care for pets responsibly, the first graders decide to write and illustrate a booklet called "Taking Care of Your Pet" to hand out to students at their school and a nearby preschool.
- On a visit to a local elementary school, high school students demonstrate garden tool safety and soil preparation as they act out *Jack's Garden* for second graders. During the next visit, the older and younger students work together to plant vegetables in a community garden, using math skills to measure and place the seeds appropriately. Follow-up visits include tending the garden and reading *Down to Earth: Garden Secrets! Garden Stories! Garden Projects You Can Do!* The students collaboratively design and paint a garden mural to keep the plants "blooming" year-round. The harvested food is gratefully received by a local food pantry.
- Before students from a middle school English class tutor first through third graders in literacy skills, they read *Thank You, Mr. Falker*. Using the book as a springboard, the class discusses the feelings young children may have when they don't read as well as their peers. The students write personal stories in their journals before and following tutoring sessions.
- A social studies teacher reads *Pink and Say* to her tenth-grade students as part of their study of the Civil War. They discuss social injustice and prejudice and how stories can be lost if they are not handed down to the next generation. Students decide to interview veterans of recent wars to record their stories.
- As part of a school-wide program to eliminate bullying and name-calling, all elementary classes read *Toestomper and the Caterpillars*, *The Hundred Dresses*, or *The Misfits*. After various learning activities, students develop peacemaking strategies to create a safe school environment for everyone.
- A teen youth group decides to learn ballroom dancing and recruits several experienced dancers, men and women who attend a nearby senior activity center. After mastering the basics of the fox trot, waltz, and east coast swing, the young dancers meet with the senior center staff and discuss ways to show their appreciation and gratitude for the lessons. The youth plan and host a "Senior Senior Prom" attended by over 60 dancing seniors.

[ **Note:** Annotated descriptions of all books listed can be found in the subsequent theme chapters. ]

This chapter is designed to give you an overview of service learning from common terms to the criteria that ensure success. An FAQ section will answer key questions to help you get started. You'll be introduced to the process that constitutes the foundation of all service learning activities and how you can maximize the success of your projects and your students. You may find that the questions in this chapter and their answers help you reflect on what service learning means to you and what forms it can take for the young people you work with. For example, you may find yourself considering the meaning of community and how it will need to be defined to best serve your project ideas. Or you might think about what forms of service will be most appealing or effective in your classroom. Of all of these questions, perhaps the most fundamental is: "What exactly is service learning?"

# A Definition of Service Learning

Service learning can be defined in part by what it does for your students. When service learning is used in a structured way that connects classroom content, literature, and skills to community needs, students will:

- apply academic, social, and personal skills to improve the community.
- make decisions that have real, not hypothetical, results.
- grow as individuals, gain respect for peers, and increase civic participation.
- experience success no matter what their ability level.
- gain a deeper understanding of themselves, their community, and society.
- develop as leaders who take initiative, solve problems, work as a team, and demonstrate their abilities while and through helping others.

These important and documented academic and social results have helped validate service learning as a valuable, respected, and widely recognized teaching method. They may be why you're using service learning already or looking for ways to introduce it into your classroom, program, or youth group.

Wherever you plan on using service learning, you'll need a solid definition to guide you in your specific situation. You don't have to start from scratch to create your own definition, though you may need to tailor a general definition of service learning so that it reflects the specific needs of your students, community, and curriculum. While the essential structure and process of service learning stays the same, the resulting activities can take a great variety of forms. In a school context and in other learning situations, ***service learning*** **can be defined as a teaching method where guided or classroom learning is deepened through service to others in a process that provides structured time for reflection on the service experience and demonstration of the skills and knowledge acquired.** This definition also works in nontraditional, less formal educational environments such as after-school programs and youth groups. In these settings, staff find meaningful opportunities to infuse the experience of helping in the community with an acknowledgment of what is also being learned.

# Before You Start:

## Frequently Asked Questions

Defining service learning is only the beginning and it often leads to other important questions that need to be answered before you can start using or refining service learning. These are some common questions that come up in my workshops.

**Q:** ***How is service learning different from community service or volunteer work?***

**A:** Service learning differs from other forms of community service or volunteer work because the education of students and young people is always at its core. Students are actively participating in the process of understanding, integrating, and applying knowledge from various subject areas as they work to improve their communities. The question "Why am I learning this?" disappears as students help older people or register voters or work to restore a fragile ecosystem and see what they've learned in action.

**Q:** ***Can service learning be used with everyone? Or is it only for older kids? Or gifted kids?***

**A:** Service learning works with kindergartners and college students as well as every grade in between. Students of all ages and most ability levels can participate successfully, and almost every subject or skill can be enhanced through the practice of service learning. Because it can be applied to almost every subject area, this naturally encourages cross-curricular integration, which can help students grow and improve in several areas simultaneously.

> Real learning gets to the heart of what it means to be human. Through learning we re-create ourselves. Through learning we become able to do something we never were able to do. Through learning we re-perceive the world and our relationship to it. Through learning we extend our capacity to create, to be part of the generative process of life. There is within each of us a deep hunger for this type of learning.
>
> PETER M. SENGE, EDUCATOR AND AUTHOR

**Q:** ***How can I get my students interested in service learning?***

**A:** An important aspect of service learning is student participation, not only in the actual activity, but in the planning and suggestion phase. When students have a voice in choosing and designing a service project, they are intrinsically more vested emotionally and intellectually. Since projects often utilize student strengths and talents that aren't always apparent in day-to-day lessons, service learning can motivate students to impressive accomplishments both in and out of the classroom. From the primary grades through high school, teachers use this method to do more than meet educational needs and fulfill academic standards but also as a way to excite students and build on their skills and talents.

**Q:** ***Won't service learning just mean more work for me?***

**A:** Initially, as you're learning to use service learning as a teaching method and finding ways to integrate it into your curriculum, you may find that it takes a little more time than regular lesson or activity planning. However, as you become more adept and comfortable with the practice, you'll start to see curricular connections and the possibilities for projects and community partnerships much more easily. More than likely, you'll also find that your own levels of engagement and enthusiasm reflect that of the young people you work with and guide through service learning. The academic results and accomplishments in the community reward the effort for everyone involved.

**Q:** ***Service learning means reaching out to the community. What is community? How do I define it?***

**A:** Any discussion of service learning is going to include many references to community. Service learning helps students to build and improve community, yet sometimes the who or what of community is unclear. *Community* can mean many different things geographically and socially in service learning, so its definition often depends on the nature of the service learning activity or who's doing the defining.

For some schools, service learning activities may be working toward improving interpersonal relationships or safety on the school campus, establishing cross-age tutoring programs, or beautifying the grounds. *Community* in this case may be defined as the school campus and population, which includes the immediate surrounding area, parents, and any outside agencies assisting with the issues being addressed.

Other schools extend their communities geographically and socially to include the surrounding neighborhood, city, or region. Some communities are international in nature, even if students never leave the school grounds. Examples of off-site locations for projects include: a local watershed to help with plant restoration, a refugee center where students assist with child care during adult English-language classes, and a radio station where students record public service announcements. In these situations, *community* usually includes agency partners.

Whatever is included in your definition of *community*, students engaging in service learning will come to know that community develops and builds through interaction, reciprocal relationships, and knowledge of people, places, organizations, governments, and systems. Through service learning, the often elusive idea of "community" takes shape and has a more tangible meaning for all involved. Recognizing and becoming active in a community builds a true foundation for civic responsibility that lasts well beyond the school years.

**Q:** ***I understand what service learning means, but what does service mean?***

**A:** In the context of service learning, "service" is the implementation of a plan, designed or influenced by students, that combines classroom learning with meeting an authentic community need. In some cases, the need is apparent and even urgent—for example, when elementary students rescue duck eggs from a rice field just prior to harvest. In other cases, the students may be supplementing or supporting a larger community effort—for example, by taking dictation of letters for elders in a residential facility. In all cases, service is meant to evoke the spirit of caring in those involved as well as to provide a constructive context for their knowledge.

**Q: *Are there different kinds or categories of service?***

**A:** Service can take many forms. Usually, though, the "service" in service learning can be classified as direct service, indirect service, advocacy, or research.

- *Direct Service*. Students' service directly affects and involves the recipients. The interactions are person-to-person and face-to-face, such as tutoring younger children or working with elders. Students engaged in direct service learn about caring for others who are different in age or experience, developing problem-solving skills, following a sequence from beginning to end, and seeing the "big picture" of a social justice issue. Interacting with animals is also included in direct service.
- *Indirect Service*. Indirect activities do not provide service to individuals but benefit the community or environment as a whole. Examples include restoring a wetland area, constructing park benches, stocking a food pantry, donating picture books to a Head Start program, and collecting clothing for families living in a shelter. Students engaging in indirect service learn about cooperation, working as a team, taking on different roles, organizing, and prioritizing. They will also gain project-specific skills and knowledge that relate to academic content.
- *Advocacy*. The intent of advocacy is to create awareness of or promote action on an issue of public interest. Related activities include writing letters, sponsoring a town meeting, performing a play, and public speaking. Student advocates learn about perseverance; understanding rules, systems, and processes; civic engagement; and working with adults.
- *Research*. Research activities involve students in finding, gathering, and reporting on information in the public interest. For example, students may develop surveys or conduct formal studies, evaluations, experiments, or interviews. They may also test water or soil, or conduct environmental surveys. The students in the Introduction who surveyed local elms for Dutch Elm Disease are a good example of this kind of service. By participating in research-based service learning, students may learn how to gather information, make discriminating judgments, and work systematically. They enhance their skills in organization, assessment, and evaluation as well.

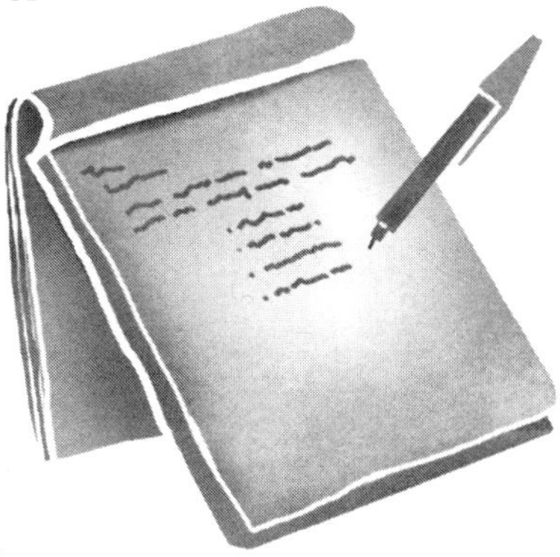

> As you go through life, act in such a way
> as not to deprive others of happiness.
> Avoid giving sorrow to your fellow man,
> but to the contrary, see that you give him joy
> as often as you can.
>
> SIOUX PROVERB

**Q: *Is one type of service learning better than another?***

**A:** Each of the service categories offers its own benefits to the community and to the students. And all types of service raise questions that continue to engage students in study and learning. Students involved in service continually apply and develop their knowledge in ways that meet and enrich the academic curriculum.

**Q: *What do I do if I've been assigned to coordinate service learning for my grade/school/organization?***

**A:** Many of the previous questions and issues are useful jumping-off points for faculty or group discussion. The more people work together to discuss and understand service learning to meet the specific needs of their organization, the more likely they are to believe in the actual process of service learning. Included in this book are forms and information that can guide you and your colleagues and community partners into a quality service learning experience. (See Chapter 2 for more information on this topic.)

# The Process of Service Learning: The Big Picture

At this point, you've thought about what service learning means, how you may choose to define community, and what forms of service might work best for your students. Now it's time to look at the actual process you'll be using. It is the basis of every service learning activity. When the process of service learning is broken down, four essential and interdependent stages emerge:

- Preparation
- Action
- Reflection
- Demonstration

Together these constitute a process that is key to student effectiveness and success. Even though each stage is examined separately, keep in mind that they're linked together and often used simultaneously. It may help to visualize how overlays are used in an anatomy book to reveal what is occurring in the human body system by system. Each stage of service learning in action is like one of these overlays, revealing one part of an interdependent whole.

## *Preparation*

> I cannot predict the wind
> but I can have my sail ready.
> E. F. SCHUMACHER, AUTHOR

All service learning begins with preparation. This covers a wide variety of activities and includes identifying a need, investigating and analyzing it, and making a plan for action. In the preparation phase, the teacher and students work together to set the stage for learning and social action. With guidance from their teacher, students identify a real community need, perhaps with the input of community partners or by conducting their own investigation using surveys, media reports, or other information sources. They go on to research and discuss the subject using books, interviews, the Internet, and field trips. They may examine it through role plays or more complex simulations (such as turning the classroom into an Ellis Island waiting room). In this process of active learning and critical thinking, students grow to understand the underlying problem as well as related subject matter. Investigation, discussion, and analysis lead to plans for action. The class draws on the skills, talents, and interests of individual students as it plans and shapes the service to come. Students may also find and establish partnerships with other teachers and classrooms, local agencies, colleges or universities, or national groups that offer resources.

## *Action*

> If you need a helping hand,
> you will find one at the end of your arm.
> YIDDISH PROVERB

Action is the direct result of preparation. Solid preparation enables students to confidently carry out their plan of action, applying what they have learned to benefit the community. Perhaps they plant flowers to beautify the school grounds, collect school supplies to be sent for use by students in Africa, or create a recycling campaign—the possibilities are almost limitless. The plan may be carried out over the course of an academic year, a semester, two weeks, or a single day. As the students put their plan in motion, they come to recognize vividly how classroom lessons fit into their daily lives and shape the lives of others.

During the action stage, they continue to develop knowledge and resources as they meet new people and interact with their environment in meaningful ways. Over the course of the project, students raise questions that lead to a deeper understanding of the societal context of their efforts. They experience the real results of their actions and observe their strengths and attributes in relation to those of others, which can give them a new appreciation of their classmates and people in the community. By taking action, they identify themselves as community members and stakeholders and, over time, learn how to work within social institutions. Transforming plans into action enables young people to use what is inherently theirs: ideas, energy, talents, skills, knowledge, enthusiasm, and concern for others and their natural surroundings.

## Reflection

> To look backward for a while is to refresh the eye, to restore it, and to render it more fit for its prime function of looking forward.
>
> MARGARET FAIRLESS BARBER, AUTHOR

Reflection is a vital and ongoing process in service learning that integrates learning and experience with personal growth and awareness. Using reflection, students consider how the experience, knowledge, and skills they are acquiring relate to their own lives and their communities. The academic program is often so jam-packed that it's all too easy to miss the meaning behind the details or within the experience. Reflection is a pause button that gives students the time to explore the impact of what they are learning and its effect on their thoughts and future actions.

In the course of reflecting, students put cognitive, social, and emotional aspects of experience into the larger context of self, the community, and the world. This helps them to assess their skills, develop empathy for others, and understand the impact of their actions on others and on themselves. To really work, reflection must go beyond students simply reporting or describing what they are doing or have done. When students can compare their initial assumptions with what they have seen and experienced in the real world, reflection can be a transforming experience. They can ask questions and probe deeper into an issue, leading the class to further levels of investigation and understanding. They can use poetry or music to express a change in feelings that occurred or their appreciation of a classmate. They can also consider what they would change or improve about a particular activity.

While reflection in service learning is structured, with the times and activities usually established by the teacher, reflection also occurs spontaneously, stimulated by a student comment or class discussion of a passage in a novel. Reflection may occur before, during, and after implementation through the use of different approaches and strategies. In all cases, feedback from adults helps students use reflection to elevate their ability to observe, question, and apply their accumulated knowledge to other situations. To be effective, adults who interact with the students must model reflective behaviors. You'll find that soon, students can devise their own strategies for reflection and lead each other through the reflective process.

## Demonstration

> The job of an educator is to teach students to see the vitality in themselves.
>
> JOSEPH CAMPBELL, AUTHOR

The fourth stage of service learning is demonstration, which provides evidence of what students have gained and accomplished through their community involvement. They exhibit their expertise through public presentations—displays, performances, letters to the editor, class lessons—that draw on the preparation, action, and reflection stages of their experience. Presenting what they have learned allows students not only to teach others but also to identify and acknowledge to themselves what they have learned and how they learned it. Students take charge of their own learning as they synthesize and integrate the process through demonstration.

What about celebration and recognition? Descriptions of service learning often list celebration as a key part of the service learning process. Celebrating accomplishments and good work is definitely valuable, but demonstration is more in keeping with the intentions of service learning because students confirm what they have learned and continue the process. It is a significant achievement for students to demonstrate what they've learned clearly and publicly, and celebration can be interwoven with the demonstration. For example, students can invite community members to see their new hiking trail at a nature preserve and also plan a picnic and songfest. Celebration, when planned with thought, can benefit service learning.

While the emphasis should remain on the intrinsic benefits of learning and the satisfaction of helping to meet community needs, recognizing student accomplishment in a public way may show students that the school and community members understand and appreciate their contribution. For many students, this may be the only time their school success is acknowledged.

# What Makes Service Learning Successful?

In order to maximize the value and benefits of each stage in the service learning process, certain elements need to be present. Each one helps students to learn and improves the quality of the service provided. These elements can even be used as criteria for creating successful activities and projects. Is each element always a part of a service learning? Ideally, yes. Experience has shown that when all of the elements are present—the criteria are all met—there is a much greater impact on the students and the community. Service learning is a process, though, and every activity or project is unique. So depending on the project and what approach you take, some of these elements may be more evident than others. However, the more familiar you, your students, and your community partners become with service learning strategies, the more likely it is that all of these elements will be seamlessly integrated into the process.

These are the elements that should be present to ensure a successful service learning project:

***Integrated Learning.*** Students learn skills and content in a variety of ways. Academics come alive and knowledge is applied through interaction, research, practice, literature, discussion, and planning for action. Ideally, the learning and the service weave together and reinforce each other, with the service informing the content and the content informing the service.

***Genuine Needs.*** Students identify, learn about, and articulate a genuine, recognized community need. This is often verified through the media, surveys, observation, or discussion with informed community partners. By addressing an important community need, student actions take on a greater value and importance. They can see their actions making a noticeable difference even as they learn and apply academic skills and knowledge.

***Youth Voice and Choice.*** Young people need ample opportunities to express their ideas and opinions and to make decisions. Service learning gives students the opportunity to take initiative, make decisions, interact with community representatives, learn about the role of government in social issues, develop critical-thinking skills, and put their ideas into action. Students meet significant age-appropriate challenges with tasks that require thinking, initiative, problem solving, and responsibility in an environment safe enough to make mistakes and to succeed.

> No one is born a good citizen; no nation is born a democracy. Rather, both are processes that continue to evolve over a lifetime. Young people must be included from birth. A society that cuts itself off from its youth severs its lifeline.
>
> KOFI ANNAN,
> SECRETARY-GENERAL, UNITED NATIONS

***Collaborative Efforts.*** Students participate in the development of partnerships and share responsibility with community members, parents, organizations, and other students. These relationships give the students opportunities to interact with people of diverse backgrounds in diverse settings. Through these dynamics, students and community members learn about each other, gaining mutual respect, understanding, and appreciation.

***Reciprocity.*** Reciprocity is the mutual exchange of information, ideas, and skills among all participants in the learning and service experience. Reciprocity exists when each person sees the other as having something to share. Everyone is teaching and has the opportunity to learn. This process occurs in personal relationships and also between institutions, as, for example, when the members of a school and a service organization come together to work on a project.

***Civic Responsibility.*** Being "response-able," being "able to respond"—to local and global issues that matter is what develops an active populace. When young people recognize their vital role in improving society, working for social justice, and caring for the environment, then they truly understand the concept of democracy. Students recognize how participation and the ability to respond to authentic needs improves the quality of life in the community, which may lead to a lifelong ethic of service and civic participation.

## An Example of Putting It All Together: Service Learning Meets the Canned Food Drive

So what happens when you put all of the pieces together? A good illustration is to take an activity that you've probably done at some point: a canned food drive. The average canned food drive may be community service, but it isn't actually service learning.

Typically, the way a canned food drive is run ranges from general public-address announcements, such as "Bring in cans of food and put them in the box by the school office," to a contest in which the class contributing the most cans wins a pizza party. Regardless of the form it takes, the motivation to participate is weak and student learning is negligible. In the end, students are no more informed about the issues of hunger in the community than when they began, and the cans collected often don't meet the needs of the receiving agency or the community members who depend on the food bank.

An elementary teacher, "Mr. Baker," describes how a student made a huge difference in one school canned food drive by accidentally introducing the concept of service learning to his school:

> For years, the same procedure had been followed. An announcement on the loud speaker asked students to bring in their cans and place them in the box by the office. Being new to the school, I was placed in charge of delivering the boxes to a local food bank. Jamal, a student known as a "troublemaker," was asked to cart the boxes to my car. Jamal looked inside at the assorted foods: lima beans, pesto sauce, water chestnuts, tomato sauce. Jamal had one comment, "This food stinks." I agreed, adding, "What should we do about it?" Jamal broke into a huge smile and told me his idea. The result? Rather than delivering the boxes, we hosted a luncheon to thank the teachers for helping with the canned food drive. The menu? You guessed it!
>
> After seeing the poor selection from the food drive offered as a meal, the faculty revamped the canned food drive and considered real learning connections in every classroom. Kids began reading books on hunger, doing research about our community, talking with a representative from the local food bank, and creating all sorts of persuasive written materials that got everybody eager to participate. With ideas and leadership from Jamal and other students, we established our most productive and meaningful canned food drive ever. Communication between students and teachers improved as we talked about what we accomplished and shared our experiences and future plans with parents and community partners. Unexpectedly, we found additional ways to collaborate with the food bank throughout the school year.

The new kind of food drive at "Mr. Baker's" school provided opportunities for learning and applying skills that resulted in a significant benefit to the community. During a follow-up discussion, teachers noted that a new group of students had emerged as leaders and that a partnership had been established with a community organization. Student interest in community matters generated classroom conversations about additional local needs and ways in which students could plan and participate. The process of service learning became clear through experience.

What follow are more examples of real-life activities used in effective and meaningful canned food drives. While grade levels are noted, much of the material studied, the resources used, and the actual methods employed are relevant or can be easily adapted for many grade levels.

## First Graders and Uncle Willie

While studying "community," first graders read *Uncle Willie and the Soup Kitchen* to identify the many ways people participate in meaningful service. The class takes a field trip and assembles sack lunches for a local agency which delivers meals to people in need. Back at school, the students plan a drive to collect food that that will help this agency prepare balanced, healthy meals. With assistance from their fourth-grade buddies, they make posters and flyers, which are given to each class; sort collected food into categories, keeping track of quantities on a large graph; and check cans for expired dates and damage. Together, they write reflective stories with illustrations of their experiences and compile the stories into a book. A copy is sent to the partner agency, and one is presented to the school library at an assembly.

## Fourth Graders and The Long March

A fourth-grade teacher reads *Feed the Children First: Irish Memories of the Great Hunger,* a book describing the potato famine, and *The Long March: The Choctaw's Gift to Irish Famine Relief* aloud. The class learns that in 1847, the Choctaw tribe sent $170 (the equivalent of more than $5,000 today) to help the starving Irish. For homework, students ask an adult to describe how people in need of food were helped in times past. As the students continue their study of American Indians, they examine the parallel of Native Americans' loss of lands and displacement onto reservations with the experience of people who lose their homes today because of poverty. When the school's annual canned food drive occurs, students make a presentation to every class about the Irish and their distant Choctaw friends, including information about the meaningful canned food drive. Students keep journals that become part of their portfolios.

## Sixth Grade Initiative

A sixth grader selects *Generation Fix* as a nonfiction book to read to fulfill a language arts assignment. The book tells the story of a student who collected thousands of boxes of cereal for food pantries. The sixth grader asks if the class can design a food drive in the spring to help fill local food banks for the months to come. The teacher revises an essay assignment to mirror the learning, planning, and implementation that follow. At the end of the project, the teacher remarks that student involvement and the writing for this unit are the best of the entire school year.

## Seventh Graders Learn About Social Services

A middle school social studies teacher reads a newspaper article aloud that describes the increased unemployment in the region and the growing strain on local social service agencies, including food banks. Most students are unfamiliar with social service agencies, and this realization begins their research. Students generate questions regarding what social services are available, what circumstances can lead to the need for assistance, and what organizations help in their community. They want to know: Who receives this food? What foods are the staples of this population? Does this population have supplies to open cans and cook the food, or are prepared foods preferred? What nutritional foods or food groups are in short supply? Teams of students take on specific research tasks, including contacting food banks for lists of foods that are needed to meet current demands. They collaborate with the student council to inform the student body about hunger in their community and what they can do to help. At Back-to-School Night, students create a display and serve as docents showing parents and other guests their full program, from research to deliveries to the food bank. The students sign up the families of students to volunteer directly with the food bank during the summer months.

## High School Health

During a ninth-grade health class, students review the foundations of a nutritious diet. They follow up with a guest speaker from the local food bank to learn more about issues of malnutrition, especially how childhood hunger can affect physical growth, learning, and the ability to function. Students then develop a

school-wide marketing plan to promote participation in the canned food drive and emphasize foods that are healthy for kids. They culminate their activities by creating an original coloring book about fruits and vegetables to give to children through the food bank.

### *American History Gets* Nickel and Dimed

An American History class reads *Nickel and Dimed: On (Not) Getting By in America* and draws quotes from the book for discussion. The students are inspired to continue their investigation of poverty in the community through student-designed projects. To learn more, student committees contact local social service agencies to determine their needs and find out about policies that affect low-income and poor people in their community. At the end of three weeks, building on their interests and talents, students present an original video at a chamber of commerce meeting. The video presents their analysis of local, state, and national policies toward homelessness and outlines agency needs and possible community responses. A newspaper runs a student editorial on the class's research and findings. Many letters are printed in response thanking the students for educating the community.

### *High School Electives Participate*

- A drama class responds to an agency request to write a theatrical adaptation of the book *The Can-Do Thanksgiving* for elementary school assemblies to launch a citywide canned food drive.
- Photography students capture images related to the need for food donations. They create a photo display with personal comments that is displayed both at school and at the local public library.
- In a computer class, students create a pamphlet entitled, "Easy Steps to Improve Your Canned Food Drive," post it on a Web site, and send it to all local schools and many agencies.

## What Next?

While you sort through the terms, definitions, and ideas presented here and throughout this book, remember that every teacher has a first service learning activity or project. Most begin with practical, manageable efforts that allow them to become familiar with the process. The following chapter offers guidance and a detailed blueprint for launching your efforts. Over time, as teachers, students, and agency partners gain experience with the value and impact of service learning, the efforts and collaborations may expand. If you've used service learning as a teaching method before, then this book will give you new resources and ideas to work with and may help you refine the practice in your classroom or organization. Advanced service learning teachers continually look for creative ideas and resources and seek out new partnerships, collaborations, and ways to encourage student leadership and initiative. The possibilities and promise of service learning grow with each activity no matter where you are in your service learning career.

# CHAPTER 2

# A BLUEPRINT FOR SERVICE LEARNING

Service learning offers a tremendous array of exciting opportunities, choices, and challenges. If you're considering your first service learning activity, you may ask, "Where do I start?" And even if you're a seasoned veteran, you may wonder how to improve your service learning strategies and methods. This chapter will take you through each step of the service learning process, providing a blueprint to follow as you get started. It will also address issues common to service learning and ways to troubleshoot problems or unexpected situations that may arise both when you're getting started and when you're developing your practice.

> In doing we learn.
> GEORGE HERBERT, POET

## Getting Started: A Blueprint

Getting started with service learning can seem overwhelming because there are many different concerns that you need to address and balance. However, with planning you can establish a solid foundation for your students to build on in their service learning activities. To help you successfully plan out your activity and curricular ties and prepare for different issues you may encounter, use the step-by-step blueprint of the service learning process featured below. This blueprint maps out the service learning process in an easy to follow sequence that you can refer to as you and your students plan and carry out service learning projects. It begins with finding entry points to service learning in your curriculum and closes with the important final step of assessing the overall experience. Each step lists the forms provided in this book that can help you get organized and maximize your resources. You'll also find suggestions in these steps for ways to continue developing your service learning practice as you become more experienced.

[ **Note:** The forms referred to in the blueprint and throughout the text appear at the end of this chapter, starting on page 31. ]

### *An Overview of the Service Learning Blueprint*

The following steps will guide you through the service learning process. Each step includes a reference to useful forms, with page numbers noted in parentheses. Students can assist with and participate in these steps as is appropriate for their age and ability, taking on more responsibility as they gain experience.

***Step One: Points of Entry.*** Think about what you're teaching. What are the underlying skills and content you want your students to come away with? All of these are entry points into service learning and can help you make curricular connections. Ongoing school projects, student-identified needs, and community-identified needs are also good ways to find your entry point into service learning activities.

*Form:* Establishing Curricular Connections: Points of Entry (page 31)

***Step Two: Map Out Your Plans.*** Next get more detailed and start mapping a plan. Identify and write down your service idea. Include in detail the content and skills that will be taught, the cross-curricular connections you can make, the books the students will read, and the community contacts that would be

*continued* ⟶

helpful to find and cultivate. Think about where your students will have their voice in the project. Be specific about your plans for preparation, action, reflection, and demonstration.

*Forms:* The Four Stages of Service Learning (page 36), Planning for Service Learning (page 38)

***Step Three: Clarify Partnerships.*** Here is where you seek out partnerships that will support and enhance the service learning. Establish contact with collaborators—teachers, parents, community members, agency representatives, or others—who you want to participate. Discuss and clarify specific roles and responsibilities for all involved to avoid any confusion once the project is underway.

*Form:* Community Contact Information (page 43)

***Step Four: Review Plans and Gather Resources.*** Review your plans. Determine the kinds of resources you'll need, and start gathering and organizing them. These may include books, newspaper articles, and reference materials from partner agencies. Also, schedule any visits, guest speakers, or field trips. Many of these are good tasks for your students to take on as they gain skills and experience.

*Form:* Planning for Service Learning (page 38)

***Step Five: Begin the Process of Service Learning in Action.*** Now you can begin the process of service learning in your classroom or group. Initiate the four stages of the service learning cycle: preparation, action, reflection, and demonstration. Encourage youth voice and choice as you move through the service learning process. It's important to be flexible for two reasons: Unexpected things can happen and service learning works best when students are able to see their own ideas in action. Continue to look for opportunities for ongoing reflection.

*Forms:* The Essential Elements of Service Learning (page 37), Planning for Service Learning (page 38), Four Square Reflection Tool (page 48)

***Step Six: Assess the Service Learning Experience.*** Once demonstration and closing reflection have been completed, review and assess the learning accomplished, the impact of the service, the planning process, the reciprocal benefits for all involved, and ways to improve for next time. Debrief with all partners, and of course include the students.

*Forms:* Community Response Form (page 44), Assessment for Service Learning Form, Parts One and Two (pages 49 and 50), Student Self-Evaluation (page 51)

As you start following the blueprint, questions often arise. Common ones include:

- How do I come up with ideas for service learning projects that have strong curricular connections?
- How do I ensure that service learning advances student learning?
- How can I plan ahead while leaving room for "youth voice and choice"?
- How can I encourage students to develop a sense of civic responsibility?
- How do I establish partnerships in school *and* in the community?

What follows are the answers to these questions, instructions on how and where to use the forms in this book, and more detailed exploration of the issues common to embarking on service learning. These will all help you to plan your first service activity.

> Even if you are on the right track,
> you'll get run over if you just sit there.
> WILL ROGERS, HUMORIST

## *How do I come up with ideas for service learning projects that have strong curricular connections?*

Where can you get ideas for projects with genuine curricular connections—projects that will truly combine community service with academics? First, think about what skills, content, and themes you're already teaching. Using the Establishing Curricular Connections: Points of Entry form on pages 31–32 may be very helpful to you because it identifies five strategies you can use to generate service learning project ideas complete with sample project ideas and literature resources. Following, each entry point is examined in more detail.

As you think about various ideas for projects, keep in mind that service learning ideas are best developed as a "team sport." Draw others into your planning sessions. Brainstorming possible activities with students, colleagues, and others is a method guaranteed to produce a wealth of options (and excitement). This often leads to collaborative service learning activities: a teacher who has contributed a suggestion is more likely to participate, students whose ideas are taken seriously make a stronger commitment, and agencies become more involved partners.

***Point of Entry #1: Identify an existing program or activity to transform into authentic service learning.*** The familiar canned food drive, mentioned in Chapter 1, can easily become a service learning project. It's a simple matter for teachers, students, and community partners to find related learning opportunities, such as studying nutrition, interviewing the receiving agency to identify what foods are needed, visiting a food bank, and investigating underlying issues of poverty and local housing costs. The learning process can include such books as *The Other America* and *Asphalt Angels*.

***Point of Entry #2: Begin with standard curriculum, content, and skills and find the natural extension into service.*** What are the specific content and skill areas you need to address in the classroom? Fill in those spaces on the Planning for Service Learning form (page 38) first, and consider a service emphasis that extends this classroom learning into a hands-on experience. When students are learning about times of war in American history, for example, and you want them to improve their verbal communication skills, consider having them interview elders about their wartime experiences. This project works as well for elementary students as it does for high school students. Books such as *Growing Older: What Young People Should Know About Aging*, *Hurry Granny Annie*, and *Too Young for Yiddish* can elicit a related discussion about the aging process; and *We Were There, Too! Young People in U.S. History* and *Charlie Wilcox* can add depth to the historical aspects while addressing specific academic standards.

***Point of Entry #3: From a theme or unit of study, identify content and skill connections.*** Most broad themes or topics, such as "interdependence" or "the rainforest," have service implications. Identify the specific content and skill areas to be addressed, and then select a service application that is developmentally appropriate for your students. For example, with the theme "the individual's role in society," students may read nonfiction stories of exemplary acts such as *Rabble Rousers: 20 Women Who Made a Difference* and *Sisters in Strength: American Women Who Made a Difference*. Younger children can dramatize the lives of people they admire, highlighting their civic contributions and sharing the knowledge through performances for other classes, senior citizen groups, or at a community celebration. Older students can research agencies that meet community needs and find ways to provide assistance while studying underlying social issues. After conducting the research, they can produce a series of informative pamphlets on these agencies for young people.

***Point of Entry #4: Start with a student-identified need.*** There are several ways to use student-identified needs as departure points. As a class, identify students' skills, talents, and interests using the Personal Inventory form on page 33. Then have students think about local problems that may be extensions of their interests or talents, identify the causes of the problems, list who is already helping (it might already be a student in your classroom), brainstorm ways in which young people can help, conduct research to learn more, and create an action plan. The Taking

Action in Our Community form on page 34 provides a tool for this process. Next, students can prepare a formal proposal using the Service Learning Proposal form on page 35. Alternatively, students may volunteer ideas and concerns with no prompting. For example, a student may come into class and proclaim that "something has to be done about the empty lot next to the school," and suggest a clean-up or a community garden. Another student might burst into class upset that "the skateboard park is about to be closed" and want to let people know how unfair that is. Or a student could describe how a fire destroyed a neighbor's home and wonder what could be done to help the family. These unpredicted "teachable moments" can initiate the process of clarifying immediate community needs and determining ways to become involved.

***Point of Entry #5: Start with a community-identified need.*** Good news travels fast, and once a school has a reputation for providing service or has established community partnerships, agencies or organizations may ask your students for assistance. Stories in the local media are another common way of identifying community needs. A newspaper article or an evening news report can also make a need apparent to the students. For example, either method could lead to your students providing a day-care center with one-on-one literacy preparation, perhaps with children who do not speak English. Students can create lessons to introduce basic language skills or lead activities in which the younger children make letter shapes with their bodies. Older and younger pairs can enjoy writing and illustrating bilingual books on themes chosen by the younger children. Children can take copies of the books home, and copies can also be donated to the library, a day-care facility, and other places that need books such as health clinics and family shelters. Again, literature (such as *A Movie in My Pillow—Una película en mi almohada* or *La Mariposa*) can be excellent to use in preparation.

**Note:** All of the books mentioned in this chapter can be found in the service learning bookshelves of Part 2.

## *How do I ensure that service learning advances student learning?*

Planning is the answer. Service learning advances and enhances student learning when teachers plan ahead to establish authentic curricular connections.

The Planning for Service Learning form on page 38 helps you map out a service learning project and identify opportunities for learning. On this form, you can write down each step, including specific content, skills to be developed, opportunities for youth voice, literature to be used, and community contacts to be made, as well as curricular connections—all on one page. Many teachers have found that this tool serves as a continuing reference and a reminder of the steps to be followed and the elements to be considered and integrated. As new learning opportunities arise during the service learning process or at the conclusion, you can update this form for documentation and record keeping purposes and to share with others.

To use the form, insert whatever information you have and then use that information to generate ideas, ideally in collaboration with peers, community partners, and students. If you're a single-subject teacher, you may find opportunities for interdisciplinary collaboration as you identify related areas of study.

To give you an idea of the various ways the form can be used, four examples of filled-in forms are provided. The elementary project on page 39 began in one classroom and evolved over four years to include many students and teachers. The environmental theme and activities developed as several teachers exchanged ideas. Each teacher made adjustments for grade level, class needs, and personal teaching style. When implementing the plan, each teacher also made changes as students added or modified ideas and community partnerships were identified. The middle school project on page 40 was a natural extension of a classroom study of immigration. Students' enthusiasm and interest compelled the teacher to engage in community outreach, greatly benefiting the academic achievements of his class while meeting an authentic community need. The high school literacy project on page 41 began as a one-time interaction in which older students were going to read books to younger children. With student leadership, the project evolved into a comprehensive bookmaking activity over three weeks that included extensive preparation and several class visits. Through the fourth project on page 42, children with autism in elementary through middle school grades learned about plants while also being helpful neighbors.

## How can I plan ahead while leaving room for "youth voice and choice"?

It's important to create a service learning framework that provides ample opportunities for student learning to occur. Often this planning occurs well in advance of any service projects. Standards, textbooks, and mandates from many directions usually require you to have a well-thought-out plan for the upcoming year even before the first day of school. The initial framework for service learning projects may be part of this plan. So how can you leave room for genuine decision making by students, for their "voice and choice"—one of the essential elements of service learning? The key is to remain flexible, so that plans can be revised as students and partners introduce new ideas.

Even when the original plan remains intact, there are many opportunities for students to make choices:

- A first-grade teacher decides that having her class paint a mural depicting the local community fits well into her language arts and social studies curriculum. After she leads discussions about what a community is, the class makes field trips to fire stations and food markets, and many books are read aloud, she lets the students determine the content and design of the mural.
- Middle school students interviewing seniors at a retirement community for a social studies project find that many of the older people have extensive experience gardening. Although gardening was not an original focus of the project, students see the need for a change. The students and their senior friends suggest potting plants and writing an intergenerational gardening guide together.
- High school biology students conduct research on water quality using a real-world set of water quality testing methods. They must analyze land use, set their sampling sites to take account of a feedlot or construction project, and collect and analyze the data. They must figure out the best way to apply these methods locally, which offers many opportunities for student input and direction.
- A youth group agrees to learn how to be docents at a children's museum and are given program materials and a script to learn for greeting and guiding the participants. They are asked to review all the documents and make suggestions for improvement. Students recommend both new written text for the museum brochures and ways to make the tours and activity centers more kid-friendly and engaging.

Encouraging youth voice and skill development also involves having students take on clearly defined roles and responsibilities that add to project productivity and efficiency and may, over time, reduce your workload. Students can form teams that have assigned tasks such as:

- Communication Specialists make and keep a project log of phone calls and write correspondence.
- Photographers take pictures that create the visual timeline of memorable moments.
- Publicists learn how to write captivating press releases to send to school board members and media outlets.
- Historians assemble a scrapbook of artifacts—program materials, photographs, news articles—that tell the complete service learning project story.

The teams' success depends upon being prepared for the tasks, which will require lessons and practice activities to hone the skills they require. However, once accomplished, the students build on this foundation through practice, ongoing support, and constructive feedback. Students have been known to compose a guidebook to teach other students about their roles and even lead peer workshops to establish teams in other classes. Students can also help determine what the teams are and rotate jobs so they learn and develop multiple skills. When can you start using this approach? The answer is: Any age when you can match age-appropriate skills that fit the project and plan accordingly. First graders at a rural school formed teams called "The Greeters," "The Appreciators" (they write thank-you notes), and "The Scrapbook Keepers" as part of their school's nature trail project.

The more familiar you become with the service learning process and the unique talents of your students, the earlier you can draw students into the planning process. (For more suggestions on this and other ways to refine this area of your service learning practice, see "Developing Youth Initiative" on pages 24–25.)

> Why not go out on a limb?
> Isn't that where the fruit is?
> FRANK SCULLY, AUTHOR

## How can I encourage students to develop a sense of civic responsibility?

Participation in service learning creates the potential to develop civic knowledge, community awareness, and literacy. Enliven the idea of civic responsibility through activities that promote understanding and knowledge about the different roles that individuals, collaborative efforts, and government all play in a thriving democracy. Consider the following activities as strategies you can use to build a foundation of civic responsibility into your service learning programs.

***Personal Impact.*** Include stories of individuals who have made contributions to the well-being and advancement of society through their initiative and collaborative efforts. Books provide stories such as *The Adventurous Chef: Alex Soyer*, who applied his culinary knowledge to help create soup kitchens in Dublin during the potato blight and famine of the 1840s. Use the book *You Forgot Your Skirt, Amelia Bloomer!* to teach about a suffragette who made a fashion statement with long-term impact. At every age, students also benefit from meeting people within their communities who participate as volunteers, service providers, civic leaders, and elected officials. Students can meet and conduct interviews with people they know or read about in local newspapers who make ongoing contributions through their work, such as police officers, council members, and even teachers. Questions may include, "What do 'service' and 'civic responsibility' mean to you?" "How does your work contribute to our community?" This can lead students to discuss the importance of what an individual can contribute and what each of them hopes to accomplish through service learning.

***Collaborative Experience.*** Introduce anthropologist Margaret Mead's quote, "Never doubt that a small group of citizens can change the world. Indeed it is the only thing that ever has." Have students discuss what this means in small groups, and look for evidence that supports or contradicts this statement. Students can draw from the period of history they are studying or from literature (fiction or nonfiction) to substantiate their perspective.

***The Role of Government.*** Have students identify and contact the government agency associated with their service learning efforts. For younger students, the teacher or a parent may help with this task. For example, there are state agencies that govern the rules and regulations for convalescent facilities. Many states offer free education packets about recycling or toxic waste. City council members or their staff can provide information about services offered for people who are homeless. The role of government becomes more vivid as students gain familiarity with its range of offices, services, and policy. They can make contact through phone calls, the Internet, letters, or visits with city officials. Students can also make presentations at school board meetings, city council meetings, or to the state legislature or just attend simply to learn how the meetings work.

***A Thriving Democracy.*** Have students discuss the foundations and principles of a democratic society. Service learning activities can be developed based on student generated ideas that will support these principles. For example, a fourth-grade class initiated a local campaign to "Vote for America," a nonpartisan effort to increase voter registration and turnout. A middle school social studies class planned and led a town meeting on usage of a town park. A high school Spanish class partnered with an adult education citizenship class to improve their Spanish conversation skills and tutor the adult students about the Constitution.

## *How do I establish partnerships in school and in the community?*

Collaboration can be the lifeblood of service learning. Partners add a variety of perspectives to the process, which can fuel debate and reflection as well as help students gain a better understanding of social issues and generate ideas for civic improvement. Collaboration can provide additional opportunities to acquire knowledge and expertise. Teachers often ask how to set up constructive partnerships with other teachers, community members, and parents.

***Partnerships with Teachers.*** Communicating peer to peer effectively establishes a network of teachers who bring service learning to life within a school. By telling colleagues about the value of service learning, how the basic process works, and any personal experience, you may ignite someone's curiosity or uncover willing partners. Sharing an article from an education journal or an example found on the Internet is another way to stimulate conversation and ideas. Administrative support can also give service learning vital credibility as a teaching method, which can lead to staff development sessions that foster knowledge and faculty interest.

Consider these ideas to bring other teachers on board:

- Even casual discussions often reveal that colleagues are curious about service learning and may be willing to participate. During a lunchtime conversation, for example, one teacher mentions that her second graders want to donate an original picture book to a day-care center. Another teacher suggests that her class could make a companion counting coloring book. A third teacher recommends contacting a friend who teaches Spanish at the local high school. As the result of a simple conversation, the day care receives a bilingual picture book, along with a coloring book and, as a bonus, a relationship between three classrooms in two schools is established.
- More formal meetings can also be used to initiate collaborations. During a small group planning session among fourth-grade teachers, a middle school teaching team, or high school English department, request time to develop an idea for a service learning unit for your class. The Planning for Service Learning form on page 38 can provide a road map that the group can help fill in, and it also helps novices understand the different aspects. Some teachers may be willing to participate, others may want to observe and join in later. Be certain to let your colleagues know how their input impacted the project, and make a point of sharing this information with your students, because they may choose to express appreciation to these teachers verbally or with a written note.
- Are you in search of ideas for cross-curricular collaborations in the middle and high school grades? Brainstorm with students for original ideas. Students can often approach teachers in other subject areas and ask them to help meet specific project needs. Here are some examples: A computer teacher agreed to have her students help a social studies class design a brochure for a local meals on wheels organization; a photography class documents high school science students leading chemistry experiments with fifth graders; and several music students compose background melodies for a family consumer education class' public service announcements on nutrition and exercise.

- Showcase student success! Have students demonstrate their learning and service at a faculty meeting. A creative display of the knowledge acquired, skills developed, and community involvement achieved may encourage other teachers to learn more or to get involved.

> If opportunity doesn't knock, build a door.
>
> MILTON BERLE, COMEDIAN

***Establishing Partnerships in the Community.*** Service Learning offers wonderful opportunities to involve partners from outside the traditional school setting. Everyone concerned benefits in ways that they wouldn't have otherwise. The degree of need and commitment usually dictates the involvement of the partners. A community partner may simply provide written materials to help a class learn about setting up a recycling program at school. Another partner may be more involved; for example, a convalescent facility sends a staff person to lead a simulation about the aging process with a class preparing for a site visit. Sometimes, community partners actually identify learning opportunities within their organizations that match classroom objectives for content or skill development. Always, partnerships are best developed with an explicit purpose and clearly defined roles, responsibilities, and benefits for all involved.

Who can be a partner? Nonprofit organizations, service clubs, businesses, and government offices and agencies are all potential partners in the service learning world. Interacting with youth frequently appeals to members of these groups, especially as they find out about how they enrich student learning and the meaningful contributions made by young people.

Community colleges and universities also make excellent service learning partners. Across the country, colleges and universities are integrating service learning in various curricular areas, and with this trend comes abundant opportunities for collaboration. These might include joint service learning projects; elementary, middle, or high school students demonstrating their expertise to a college class; programs in which classroom teachers provide mentoring in the service learning process to education students (or vice-versa); and cross-age tutoring projects that include service learning as one aspect of the relationship. Many institutions of higher learning have service learning coordinators for general education and are integrating service learning into teacher preparation classes.

Find partners for your project by first identifying the purpose of the relationship: How do the interests of the partners intersect? How will this partnership support and strengthen the learning or service aspect of your project? What are the reciprocal benefits? Teachers and students can come up with lists of potential partners with students getting additional ideas from their families or by interviewing the school principal.

Teachers or parents frequently initiate contact with potential partners. This is a skill that students should learn, too. They will become proficient at finding and interacting with potential community partners when they have ample practice in making phone calls, writing correspondence, and even using telephone or online directories. These skills are valuable in general and are especially helpful as students take more initiative in planning and preparing for service learning. Even very young students can begin developing such skills, though an adult usually calls ahead to provide a general introduction and lay the groundwork for the child.

As contacts are made, the Community Contact Information form on page 43 helps the class or school maintain an ongoing record of interaction that can be used from project to project and year to year. In some schools, students conduct interviews with numerous agencies to create a notebook, directory, or database of willing partners. The directory serves as a useful reference during a given project and in the future.

Once you've identified and established relationships with your partners, keep them informed and appropriately involved at all stages of your service learning efforts. You can include them in reflection as well—the Community Response Form page 44 is designed for just this purpose. The form provides a structure for students to collect feedback and learn more about the impact of their contribution. Often, the community partner also appreciates participating in any public demonstration of the service learning process. Students have made presentations to board of directors of community groups, to local chambers of commerce, at city council meetings, and in other venues with partners in attendance and sometimes participating. When the time comes to express gratitude for the partnership, students can design their own special way of saying, "thank you!" through cards, presentations, skits, songs, or other creative methods.

***Parents as Partners.*** Schools want parents to be involved in the education of their children. In fact, active school-family relationships provide the best educational atmosphere for all children. In terms of service learning, parents can contribute valuable resources, information, and ideas. They can help in the planning and implementation of service learning, identify community partners, assist with group work, join in field trips, collect and prepare supplies, document activities, and help write grants for funding. Even parents who work during the school day may be able to help make phone calls or cut fabric squares for a quilting project.

To find a role for every parent, begin by identifying your parent resources and your program needs. Students in grades 3–12 can survey parents and other family members to develop a database of information: when parents are available to help, their personal hobbies and talents, and their connections and involvement in the community. Some schools even have parent liaisons for service learning. Once parent leaders emerge, they can coordinate parent involvement school-wide, facilitate workshops giving information on service learning and ways to get involved, and even identify opportunities for families to join together outside of school hours to perform service together.

# Beyond the Basics: Advancing Your Service Learning Practice

Perhaps you're so familiar with the basic issues of service learning that addressing them has practically become second nature. If you're looking for ways to enhance your approach to service learning, here are some important areas to focus on:

- developing youth initiative in planning service learning activities
- infusing reflection in preparation, action, and demonstration stages
- assessing student learning and service
- publicizing student activities

## *Developing Youth Initiative*

Why should you work on developing youth initiative in planning service learning activities? Youth initiative means youth involvement. When students play a key role in choosing and defining their service activities, their commitment and satisfaction are intensified. They become more confident in their actions and better able to recognize their impact on the community. If students are truly to grow as individuals and leaders through the service learning experience, they must take this step.

Launching a project that has evolved through student brainstorming and planning may seem risky. Certainly, it can involve a greater sense of the unknown. Your role is still the same—you remain a steadfast guide and mentor. Sometimes you are providing an overall framework, often setting boundaries, giving encouragement, and making sure that the project includes clear academic connections.

**Taking an Inventory of Student Skills and Knowledge**

Every student brings skills, talents, and interests to the class. Finding out what they are is one of your first tasks. Create a class database or chart of this useful information to help you get to know your students and to facilitate them getting to know each other. (Older students can help create this database.) They will frequently discover unexpected commonalities and sometimes fascinating differences.

This information can help the class in a variety of ways. A student who enjoys talking on the phone, for example, with a bit of skill development and practice, can become a group asset by contacting and making arrangements for a service outing. Do you have an "expert shopper" in your midst? Harness that talent for getting items donated or finding the best price on a "must purchase" item. Uncovering a "green thumb" will come in handy, too. What about interests? Knowing that some students have an interest in stopping vandalism or helping animals may set your service learning activity in a particular direction.

Using the Personal Inventory form on page 33, have students interview each other in pairs to reveal abilities and interests that will ultimately be helpful to the group. (For language development, it's enlightening to clarify the terms *skill*, *talent*, and *interest*.) Before the interview process, guide students through steps of active listening, note taking, and asking probing questions so that interviews will yield more detail and useful skills are developed. A student may say he is interested in music. The interviewer could then ask, "Do you play an instrument or listen to music? What kinds of music do you like?" The interviewers record their partners' responses on the form.

The activity should also include having students describe a time when they helped

*continued* ⟶

someone and a time when someone helped them. This develops the recognition of personal reciprocity in the big picture of service learning. By honing their interviewing skills and becoming better acquainted, students are not only preparing for the service learning experience but for other activities outside of school (such as job interviews) as well.

With young children, especially those who aren't writing yet, you can adapt this activity using art. Have the children draw pictures showing their favorite activities and their talents. Alternatively, you can explore skills, talents, and interests through class discussion. In either case, you can develop a list of skills, talents, and interests for the class.

For all age groups, post the list and invite students to add new skills and interests as the year progresses. Refer to this list as you continue to shape your service learning projects.

## *Developing a Plan for Action and a Project Proposal*

Students can use the Taking Action in Our Community form on page 34 to develop a plan, beginning with defining a need and extending through specific ideas for implementation. Using the Taking Action form, students identify, among other things, a problem in the community and an action they can take to help solve it. When possible, community partners should be involved in the process so that students can learn how respectful collaborations are built and maintained.

The Taking Action form provides a guide in the initial planning process; the final description can be recorded on a Service Learning Proposal form found on page 35. When writing a proposal, students clearly articulate their ideas in terms of the need for the action they propose, the purpose of the action, the roles of various partners, the anticipated results, the budget for supplies or transportation, the ways in which the effects of their effort will be measured, and even a timeline for the project. Students may work in committees to perform their designated tasks. While the plans described in the proposal may—and usually do—change during implementation, the document provides an overview and direction as students move forward. The complete document can also be submitted to the school administration for approval, to partners to confirm their participation, and to funding sources if monies or supplies are needed. Students can make changes as required and at the end can use the document as part of their reflection and assessment.

How old do students need to be to participate in making an action plan and writing a proposal? With guidance from their teacher, students in third grade have worked with the Taking Action form and a modified proposal form—Our Service Project, on page 45. Even in the early grades, much can be accomplished through class discussion and by working in small groups. In first and second grades, for example, you can make a chart of ideas for action generated in class discussion. The ideas can lead to concrete plans, to action, and to the rewarding conclusion: We did it!

**Seeking Funds for Service Learning?**

The Service Learning Proposal form on page 35 is based on a standard grant application form. After writing a few proposals, many students have successfully applied their proposal writing skills to apply for service learning project funds, even in the primary grades! Curious about service learning grant opportunities? Several are included in the Resources section (pages 216–217). Also, investigate your own community—older students can do the detective work, too—for financial support through service organizations, businesses, local foundations, city council offices, and even your school district. You may find that funders respond most favorably when they know that students have been part of the grant writing process.

***Identifying Community Resources.*** With your guidance, middle and high school students can become involved in identifying community resources and related tasks. Using the Project Promotion—Turning Ideas into Action form on page 46, students start with an agreed-upon service idea and work in small groups to identify possible new alliances, sources for fundraising (if needed), presentation opportunities, media options, and so forth. Existing community partners may join in the activity, giving students practice in collaboration that leads to community networking.

## Reflecting on Reflection

Reflection is indispensable to the entire service learning process and is what weaves it all together intellectually and emotionally for everyone involved. Through reflection, students can integrate both the learning and the service achieved into their frameworks of experience. Since reflection is so central, how you design and conduct it is important. It is a vital area for you to develop and refine. Understanding what you're trying to achieve with reflection can guide what methods and activities you choose. Do you want students to:

- connect their experience with classroom content and studies?
- integrate their experience with other areas of their life?
- develop a sense of community among the class or with partners?
- clarify misunderstandings, perceptions, or biases?
- improve observation and analytical skills?
- develop an appreciation of others in the group and the community?
- deepen their knowledge and understanding of community and social issues?

Reflection is just as integral for educators as it is for students. You reflect on the process to design meaningful and appropriate reflection activities for your students. Keep these thoughts in mind as you read about weaving reflection into the service learning process, ways to vary your reflection strategies, ideas for using journals, overcoming discussion hazards, the importance of feedback, and opportunities for student leadership. The Sequence for Reflection form on page 47 can help guide your reflection with students or you can use it as a checklist. Maintaining your own reflection over the course of a project can be helpful, too.

## Opportunities for Reflection

As emphasized earlier, reflection occurs both through activities structured by the teacher and spontaneously during all stages of the service learning process. As you plan your service learning strategy, include opportunities for reflection during the preparation, action, and demonstration stages in addition to the actual reflection stage.

***Reflection during preparation.*** Before the service learning process begins, find out what students know. What beliefs, assumptions, and attitudes are already in place? Where and how were they learned? What do students expect will happen? Students can role play situations they imagine will occur to practice and prepare and also to uncover anxieties or misconceptions. Students can consider such questions as, "What will you do if the child you're tutoring won't listen to the story?" "How do you think the convalescent home will look, sound, or smell?" Depending on the situation, you may give students a thought or question to take with them into the service experience. This may encourage them to be more observant or heighten their awareness of a particular need or action being taken.

***Reflection during action.*** As students perform their service, be observant. What do you notice the students paying attention to? What comments do you overhear? What behaviors do you see? Make notes and refer to them later during the reflection that follows the service. As service is actually going on, you may have time to draw students together for on-the-scene reflection and response. Conversation can draw upon your observations. Students can also take the initiative by raising concerns, sharing their excitement, or posing questions. Or you might pose a question such as, "Is there a better way to sort the recycling?" During this on-the-spot reflection, students sometimes have insights or make recommendations that improve their experience and the impact of their contributions right then and there.

***Reflection following service.*** Following the service, use a variety of different methods for reflection: art, poetry, music, role playing, journals, mime, sculpture, drama, movement, photographs. Since people naturally reflect in different ways, you are more likely to elicit a range of responses and involve more students by varying the methods you use. Students can write a recipe for developing youth leadership skills or create a skit that shows a dilemma faced and ask others to step in and respond. Each student can write a haiku to contemplate and describe the experience of a morning spent in a garden. Experiment with less traditional reflection methods as well. For example, have students enter class after a service experience to find their work space covered with butcher paper. In silence, students represent their thoughts and feelings of the experience through art. After drawing for ten minutes, each student finds a private place to sit and write silently for five minutes about the experience. Afterward, discuss both the process and the product. (This method of reflection has been used successfully with groups of all ages.)

***Reflection during demonstration.*** As students prepare their public demonstration—perhaps a presentation to another class or an article for a school newspaper—have them draw upon their reflections, and even use the actual word *reflection*, to concretely explain this essential dynamic to others.

## Journal Writing

Consider having students write their reflections in a journal. Keeping a journal encourages writing and personal expression that's often more unbridled than the formal structure of an essay-writing lesson. Once young people are introduced to keeping a journal, many continue to do so on their own. As one of the strategies for journal entries, consider using The Four Square Reflection Tool on page 48. This approach pushes students to write their responses in four categories:

- *What happened?* This is the cognitive realm, where students can describe what they thought and what they observed.
- *How did you feel?* Students' emotional responses may differ in tone from their cognitive responses. Separating the social and emotional from the cognitive helps students create a more complete picture.
- *What are your ideas?* They may suggest new ways to plan or collaborate with an agency or come up with new service activities that would meet other community needs.
- *What questions do you have?* What do students want to know about as a result of this experience? This question can help guide their own investigation or assist the class in planning the next steps for learning.

Students can refer to these filled-out Four Square forms for discussions, presentations, and other writing assignments based on their service learning experience.

## Reflection Prompts

Whether reflection involves writing poetry or prose, taking photographs, or having a discussion, reflection prompts such as the questions that follow may assist in the process. Questions can be simplified for younger children and adapted to fit the activity. They can be used during preparation and action stages.

- What was special about this activity today?
- What did the experience remind you of?
- What did you learn that you didn't know before? (What you learned might relate to yourself, a peer, the people/place we are helping, or an idea you want to investigate further.)
- How did you feel being at the service site? How did your feelings change from when you first arrived to when you left?
- How did you make a difference today?
- Five years from now, what do you think you will remember about this project?
- Consider the books you read in preparing for this activity. Do you understand the characters better after your personal involvement with service?

> A person's mind stretched to a new idea never goes back to its original dimensions.
> OLIVER WENDELL HOLMES, JURIST AND WRITER

***Beware the "Smelly Elephants."*** Have you ever taken a group of young children to the zoo? After the trip, imagine the students reflecting on their trip through a class discussion. The teacher asks, "What was special about today's activity?" The first child answers, "The smelly elephants," and everyone laughs. Before you know what has happened, every child is describing the smelly elephants, and then the smelly monkeys, and so on until the conversation seems to go in a circle. As in general class discussions, this can be a hazard when students reflect on their service learning experience in a discussion format. The remedy? Have students write down responses to prompts in brief notes before the class starts its discussion, so that they can refer to their written thoughts in conversation. (Young children can draw, instead of writing notes.) This simple act preserves the integrity of each student's experience before it can be influenced by others' impressions and assures that everyone has something to contribute. Many teachers have found this "smelly elephant" remedy so effective, they use it frequently in all sorts of classroom discussions.

***Closing the Loop: Giving Feedback.*** The cycle of student reflection is completed with feedback from you. Your nonjudgmental feedback and response to the students' reflections is important to them individually and to the service learning process as a whole. If journals are kept and you may read them, ask if you can write a response in the journal or on an attached piece of paper. In discussions, listen carefully and ask questions. Either way, it's important that you appreciate what's being revealed and discovered, and that you respond honestly with your own thoughts or with a reflective quote, poem, or passage from a book.

***Student Leadership of Reflection.*** Students can become skilled at creating reflection prompts for their classmates. In some classrooms, pairs of students eagerly accept the assignment of leading reflection. Often, this leads to including music, making links to historical figures the class is studying, creating a gameshow interaction, or some other innovative twist. Even second grade students delight in composing questions for their classmates to think about regarding the value and experience of service. Teachers can always review the plans and give students feedback prior to use.

## Assessing Student Learning and Service

For students, the conclusion to the service learning process is demonstration. For you, it will most likely involve assessing the success of the actual activity, what your students learned, and the effectiveness of your planning and partnerships. This is a perpetual process and may be a little different for every project. Teachers continually look for ways to assess the service learning process to ensure that it has produced appropriate learning for the students and real value for the community. Traditional assessment methods—essays, quizzes, research papers—can be used, along with other forms of inquiry and analysis, including review of documents from student portfolios or of products made, pre- and post-service questionnaires for students and others involved, student presentations or reflective writings, discussions with community partners, and comments from any recipients of the service provided. A conversation with colleagues not directly involved also can help teachers to review and improve the service learning process and find ways to strengthen the teaching methods used.

Whatever the method used, the assessment can focus on the following questions:

- *Student learning.* Were the defined content and skill objectives met? Were there any unforeseen outcomes? Did students show initiative or develop leadership skills? Were students able to reflect and place their experience in the larger context of community or society in general? Could students identify both their cognitive and affective growth?
- *Impact of the service.* Were students able to clearly state the need for and purpose of their service efforts? What contribution was made? Did the service help or hinder community efforts? What did the students accomplish? Is the partner agency or service recipient satisfied with the interaction? Have new relationships been formed? Were planned service programs, activities, or products completed?
- *The process.* How effective was project planning? Do you have ideas for specific areas you'd like to improve? For overall improvement? In future activities, how can students participate more and take greater ownership? How can you continue to develop community partnerships?

The two-part Assessment for Service Learning form on pages 49–50 provides a basic method for reviewing these issues. Part one covers student learning, the impact of the service, and the service learning process. Part two asks you to identify the methods used in each of the four stages and to assess whether each of the essential elements was present. You can select questions from the form to present to students so that they can participate in assessing their service learning experience. The Student Self-Evaluation form on page 51 lets students analyze their learning and contribution. Several service learning organizations have developed more sophisticated instruments for assessment. For more information on these, see the Resources listing (pages 216–217).

> "One can't believe impossible things."
>
> "I daresay you haven't had much practice," said the Queen. "When I was your age, I always did it for half-an-hour a day. Why, sometimes I've believed as many as six impossible things before breakfast."
>
> LEWIS CARROLL,
> *ALICE'S ADVENTURES IN WONDERLAND*

## *Telling Your Service Learning Story*

Service learning has produced media-worthy stories all across the country. The act of publicizing service learning activities contains valuable learning opportunities. Publicizing service learning doesn't just take place at its conclusion—many moments throughout the process provide great stories. Post an attractive student-made flyer about an upcoming field trip to a watershed and other teachers may become inspired to get involved. A student article in a school paper while the project is in process may get other kids wanting to take part in similar "cool" activities and interact with the "real world." A summary news story in a local paper informs the public about what's happening within the school walls and about the positive impact students are having in the community.

Where can you tell your service learning story? Everywhere! Post the story on the Internet through state and national service learning organizations and newsletters (see Resources, pages 216–217). Find opportunities for students to give presentations to other students, to community groups, on cable or local access television, in organization newsletters, or on the radio. Local newspapers often seek good news, and sometimes students actually write the article. *The Kid's Guide to Social Action* (see page 196) includes a section called "Power Media Coverage and Advertising" with tips for getting attention and ways students can promote and publicize their projects both before and after they occur. Your service learning story can be a source of youth and community pride.

**It's Time to Play—Know Your Audience**

This activity can help upper elementary, middle, and high school students consider the best way to promote a project to a particular audience. For example, a tutoring project would be presented very differently to second graders than to a parent group. This activity makes that distinction extremely vivid.

For this role play, select a service project idea, preferably one that the students are enthusiastic about. Create small groups, with each one presenting information about the project to a different audience. Students can get started by brainstorming the reasons for addressing each audience. Here are some suggestions for potential audiences:

- elementary children (specify grade)
- middle school students
- high school parents
- faculty meeting
- community agency
- prospective funding source
- chamber of commerce
- news reporters

As students consider why they're addressing their particular audience, they should start thinking about what methods will present their message most effectively. Encourage students to be creative and dynamic in their presentations, and even to involve their audiences. Students may also use visual aids (posters), skits, or songs to enhance their presentations. After each group makes its presentation, allow time for constructive feedback from the class. The ideas that emerge can be put into practice to inform the broader community about service learning in action.

## Curve Balls and Stumbling Blocks in Service Learning

It happens. After all the planning and collaboration and a phone confirmation just two days ago, your well-prepared fourth-grade students arrive at the senior center to begin their oral history project. A stop at the information desk reveals that your contact person has suddenly resigned and no replacement has been hired. The oral history project? "Sorry, we have nothing in place for you." This situation may seem extreme, but service efforts occasionally go awry. What do you do?

In the case of the "failed" visit to the senior center, the group convened in the parking lot for an emergency discussion. Students asked questions and looked for holes in their thinking and planning. After reviewing their contingency plans, this situation was determined to fall into the category of "truly out of our control." Deterred? No, only delayed. A team of students headed back to the senior center to ask for a brief meeting with the person responsible for scheduling special activities. After describing their plans and exercising their communication skills by using just a little persuasion, they established a new contact and made an agreement to reschedule.

Challenges found in service learning are, not surprisingly, very much like real-life challenges. When students work through these situations, they learn to create options, as well as to develop resiliency, problem-solving skills, persistence, and the concept of having a "plan B"—an important and practical concept. Students of all ages can contribute ideas and strategies that help to repair the moment and often improve the original plan. What better time than while in school to learn about meeting a stumbling block with thoughtfulness and resolve?

> We all want to live in the moment
> but there isn't enough time.
> DAVID ZASLOFF, MUSICIAN

A completely different kind of challenge you may face is aligning other school or organization programs and practices with service learning. For example, in an elementary school with a strong parent-run community service program, several parents resisted a classroom-based service learning program. The remedy was to educate everyone involved about the benefits of service learning and explain how to collaborate in the best interest of the students. In another school, children received stickers and prizes when they were "caught being good." Although the intention was to promote an ethic of service, children were actually refraining from engaging in kind acts unless they were certain an adult was watching and ready to dole out a reward. When administrators came to realize that the appropriate focus of service learning is the intrinsic reward that comes from cooperation and civic responsibility, the program was eliminated and not one child objected.

Some school administrators and teachers claim there is "no time for service learning" because of other priorities, such as improving math scores or creating a safer school climate. Service learning, however, can be an effective strategy to support many, if not most, important school priorities, including improved attendance, higher test scores, academic improvement, parent involvement, character education, and safety at school (reducing bullying, teasing, and name-calling). More information about these proven service learning results can be found throughout this book and in many of the resources on pages 216–217.

Other challenges you may encounter are more systemic. Is the school schedule flexible enough for service learning experiences? Are any funds available for supplies and transportation? Will the district apply for grants to support staff development and other professional opportunities? If the district or school policy requires that students stay on campus, will there be exceptions for classroom-related service learning outings? Many schools and districts with strong commitments to service learning establish advisory groups to unravel these and other issues. Models and prototypes can be found through state and national education agencies, other service learning organizations, and the Internet. Experienced service learning practitioners are usually more than willing to share ideas and resources.

> If you can't make a mistake,
> you can't make anything.
> MARVA N. COLLINS, EDUCATOR

# Establishing Curricular Connections: Points of Entry

**1. Identify an existing program or activity to transform into authentic service learning.**

- Identify an activity or project already existing on campus.
- Examine it for learning opportunities.
- Exchange resources and ideas with teachers, students, and community partners.

***Example: Canned Food Drive***
Before students began bringing in cans of food, teachers integrated meaningful academic activities related to the food drive in their class curriculum. Activities included studying nutrition, contacting the receiving agency to identify what foods were needed, visiting a food bank, encouraging student leadership in identifying the quality and kinds of foods to be provided (in partnership with the agency), having math students graph the food collected, reading books related to hunger and homelessness, and demonstrating to other schools how to connect the canned food drive to academics.

Bookshelf suggestions: *The Can-Do Thanksgiving*, *Soul Moon Soup*, and *The Other America*

**2. Begin with standard curriculum, content, and skills, and find the natural extension into service.**

- Identify the specific content and skill areas to be addressed.
- Select an area of emphasis that supports or adds to classroom learning and addresses learning objectives or state standards.
- Look for additional learning opportunities in other subject areas.

***Example: Learning History through Discussion with Elder Partners***
Teachers wanted students to be better informed about current events and to improve their listening and communication skills. This led to a partnership with a senior center and weekly interactions between students and older adults. Activities included studying recent historical events; learning about aging; practicing interviewing skills; interviewing older people to learn about their knowledge and experiences; collaborating on articles, stories, and photo essays; and displaying the results in the school and public library.

Bookshelf suggestions: *Stranger in the Mirror*, *Growing Older*, and *We Were There, Too! Young People in U.S. History*

**3. From a theme or unit of study, identify content and skill connections.**

- Begin with a broad theme or topic, often with obvious service implications.
- Identify specific content and skill areas.
- Select a service application.

***Example: The Individual's Role in Society***
As teachers identified ways for students to learn about the individual's role in society, they encouraged students to consider how they could participate in social action. Curriculum included reading nonfiction stories of contributions made by adults and young people to their communities, researching the needs of local agencies, providing regular assistance to one of the agencies, and publishing an informative pamphlet on the agency for young people.

Bookshelf suggestions: *Sisters in Strength: American Women Who Make a Difference*, *Generation Fix*, and *Free the Children: A Young Man's Personal Crusade Against Child Labor*

*continued* ⟶

## Establishing Curricular Connections *continued*

**4. Start with a student-identified need.**

- Identify student skills, talents, and interests.
- Students define a problem, a need, and solutions.
- Students lead implementation as teacher facilitates, adding learning opportunities.

***Example: Transform an Empty Lot into a Community Garden***
At the beginning of a class, a student initiated a conversation about starting a community garden in an empty lot near the school. The teacher guided the students in identifying a local government agency to contact about the property, conducting Internet research to find funding sources, partnering with special needs youth at the school to plant and maintain the garden, and donating the harvest to a local shelter.

Bookshelf suggestions: *Seedfolks*, *Just Kids: Visiting a Class for Children with Special Needs*, and *A Kid's Guide to Social Action*

**5. Start with a community-identified need.**

- Community requests assistance, perhaps through an agency that has worked with the school before.
- Teacher, students, and community partners identify learning opportunities.

***Example: Tutoring/literacy***
A school received a flyer inviting the students to participate in a city-wide book collection to benefit local youth service agencies and organizations. Teachers in several grades collaborated on cross-age projects in which older students helped younger children to write and illustrate bilingual books on mutually agreed-on themes. The books were donated to libraries, hospitals, and day-care facilities; and student representatives served on a city committee regarding literacy.

Bookshelf suggestions: *La Mariposa*, *Just Juice*, and *Thank You, Mr. Falker*

# Personal Inventory

Interests, skills, and talents—we all have them. What are they?

***Interests*** are what you think about and what you would like to know more about—for example, outer space, popular music, or a historical event like the Civil War. Are you interested in animals, the movies, mysteries, or visiting faraway places? Do you collect anything?

***Skills and talents*** have to do with things that you like to do or that you do easily or well. Is there an activity you especially like? Do you have a favorite subject in school? Do you sing, play the saxophone, or study ballet? Do you know more than one language? Can you cook? Do you have a garden? Do you prefer to paint pictures or play soccer? Do you have any special computer abilities?

Work with a partner and take turns interviewing each other to identify your interests, skills, and talents and to find out how you have helped and been helped by others.

*Interests:* I like to learn and think about . . .

______________________________________________________________________

______________________________________________________________________

*Skills and talents:* I can . . .

______________________________________________________________________

______________________________________________________________________

*Being helpful:* Describe a time when you helped someone.

______________________________________________________________________

______________________________________________________________________

______________________________________________________________________

*Receiving help:* Describe a time when someone helped you.

______________________________________________________________________

______________________________________________________________________

______________________________________________________________________

# Taking Action in Our Community

***Step 1:*** **Think about the needs in our community.** Make a list.

***Step 2:*** **Identify what you know.**

- Select one community need:
- What is the cause?
- Who is helping?
- What are some ways we can help?

***Step 3:*** **Find out more.**

- What do we need to know about this community need and who is helping?
- How can we find out?

***Step 4:*** **Plan for action.**

- To help our community, we will:
- To make this happen, we will take on these responsibilities:

| **Who** | will do **what** | by **when** | Resources needed |
|---|---|---|---|
| | | | |
| | | | |
| | | | |
| | | | |
| | | | |
| | | | |
| | | | |
| | | | |

# Service Learning Proposal

Student names: ______________________________________________

Teacher: ______________________________________________

School: ______________________________________________

Address: ______________________________________________

Phone: ____________________ Fax: ____________________ Email: ____________________

**Project name:** ______________________________________________

*Need*—Why this plan is needed:

*Purpose*—How this plan will help:

*Participation*—Who will help, and what they will do:

Students: ______________________________________________

Teachers: ______________________________________________

Other adults: ______________________________________________

Organizations or groups: ______________________________________________

*Outcomes*—What we expect to happen as the result of our work:

*How we will check outcomes*—What evidence we will collect and how we will use it:

*Resources*—What we need to get the job done, such as supplies (itemize on back):

Signatures:

# The Four Stages of Service Learning

***Preparation***

With guidance from their teacher, students:

- identify a need.
- draw upon previously acquired skills and knowledge.
- acquire new information through a variety of means and methods.
- analyze the underlying problem.
- collaborate with community partners.
- develop a plan that encourages responsibility.
- recognize the integration of service and learning.
- become ready to provide meaningful service.
- define realistic parameters for implementation.

***Action***

Through direct service, indirect service, research, or advocacy, students take action that:

- has value, purpose, and meaning.
- uses previously learned and newly acquired academic skills and knowledge.
- offers unique learning experiences.
- has real consequences.
- offers a safe environment to learn, to make mistakes, and to succeed.

***Reflection***

During systematic reflection, the teacher or students guide the process using various modalities, such as role play, discussion, and journal writing. Participating students:

- describe what happened.
- examine the difference it made.
- discuss thoughts and feelings.
- place experience in a larger context.
- consider project improvements.
- generate ideas.
- identify questions.
- receive feedback.

***Demonstration***

Students demonstrate skills, insights, and outcomes to an outside group. Methods used might include:

- reporting to peers, faculty, parents, and/or community members.
- writing articles or letters to local newspapers regarding issues of public concern.
- creating a publication or Web site that helps others to learn from the students' experiences.
- making presentations and performances.
- creating visual art forms, such as murals.

# The Essential Elements of Service Learning

*Integrated Learning*

Students **learn** skills and content through varied modalities; the service informs the content, and the content informs the service.

*Meeting Genuine Needs*

Students **identify** and **learn about a recognized community need.** Student actions are **valued** by the community and have **real consequences** while offering opportunities to **apply** newly acquired academic skills and knowledge.

*Youth Voice and Choice*

Students experience **significant age-appropriate challenges** involving tasks that require thinking, initiative, and problem solving as they demonstrate **responsibility** and **decision making** in an environment safe enough to allow them to make mistakes and to succeed.

*Collaborative Efforts*

Students participate in the development of **partnerships** and **share responsibility** with community members, parents, organizations, and other students. These relationships afford **opportunities to interact** with people of diverse backgrounds and experience, resulting in mutual respect, understanding, and appreciation.

*Reciprocity*

Student benefits evolve through **mutual teaching and learning, action, or influence** between all participants in the learning and service experience; this reciprocity extends to relationships between institutions as well as relationships between people.

*Civic Responsibility*

When young people have a role in improving society, working for social justice, and caring for the environment, then they truly understand the **concept of democracy.** Students recognize how participation and the ability to respond to authentic needs improves the quality of life in the community, which may lead to a lifelong **ethic of service and civic engagement.**

# Planning for Service Learning

Grade level: ____________________

CONTENT—LEARNING ABOUT:

SERVICE NEED:

SERVICE IDEA:

PREPARATION:

ACTION:

REFLECTION:

DEMONSTRATION:

YOUTH VOICE and CHOICE:

NOTES:

CURRICULAR CONNECTIONS:

❑ *English/Language Arts:*

❑ *Social Studies/History:*

❑ *Mathematics:*

❑ *Science:*

❑ *Languages:*

❑ *Art and Music:*

❑ *Other:*

SKILL DEVELOPMENT:

BOOKS:

COMMUNITY CONTACTS:

# Planning for Service Learning: *Example (Elementary)*

Grade level: 3

## CONTENT—LEARNING ABOUT:

- Ecology
- Waste reduction
- Composting
- Recycling

**SERVICE NEED:** There is too much waste in our community that could be recycled; if the students and community are informed on options about composting, they can choose to participate.

**SERVICE IDEA: Give It to the Worms**
Promote composting at school and in the community.

**PREPARATION:** Study ecosystems, hear guest speaker from Integrative Waste Management Board, create school map and chart to record waste quantities and reduction, prepare video presentation and talk on ecology and school waste management.

**ACTION:** Install compost and worm bins, monitor school food waste, donate soil from compost to school garden and nearby senior living community (gardening by elder residents), host parent information night with site tour and composting lesson.

**REFLECTION:** Make journals out of recycled paper at school with regular entries, weekly meetings to discuss and review project success, annual discussion and review of progress with partners at IWM (Integrative Waste Management Board).

**DEMONSTRATION:** Distribute monthly copies of newsletter "Warm Ways" to school community, participate in Chinese New Year parade as a giant worm while handing out informational pamphlets on worm bins and composting called "Give It to the Worms!"

**YOUTH VOICE and CHOICE:** Since the project is ongoing, each year students add a new component based on their ideas (for example, making journals, being worm in parade).

**NOTES:** This activity began small with one teacher and grew to involve more; this plan shows what evolved over four years.

## CURRICULAR CONNECTIONS:

☒ *English/Language Arts:* Design a campaign to promote use of school composting and reduce waste at school, write video script, write letter to parents describing project, write "Warm Ways" newsletter, plan and write "Give It to the Worms" brochure

☒ *Social Studies/History:* Study Rachel Carson

☒ *Mathematics:* Graph waste quantities

☒ *Science:* Study life cycles; review ecosystems, waste reduction, and composting; maintain compost and worm bin with signage written by children

☒ *Languages:* Spanish-language signs by compost and worm bin

☒ *Art and Music:* Design poster campaign

☒ *Other:* Video and computer technology

## SKILL DEVELOPMENT:

- Paragraph construction
- Graphing
- Time management

## BOOKS:

*Compost Critters*

*I Want to Be an Environmentalist*

*Compost! Growing Gardens from Your Garbage*

*You Are the Earth: Know the Planet So You Can Make It Better*

*Rachel Carson*

## COMMUNITY CONTACTS:

Integrative Waste Management Board

Chinese New Year Planning Committee

# Planning for Service Learning: *Example (Middle School)*

Grade level: <u>6–7 Social Studies</u>

CONTENT—LEARNING ABOUT:

- Immigration to the United States
- Process of becoming a citizen
- Resettlement of refugees
- Civic involvement

**SERVICE NEED:** Becoming citizens requires dedication and hard work that deserves to be honored by the community; to increase tolerance and understanding between cultures.

**SERVICE IDEA: In Honor of New Citizens**
Sponsoring a citizenship swearing-in ceremony at school.

**PREPARATION:** Meet with Immigration and Naturalization Services (INS), read about countries of origin of people being sworn in, plan the event, get food donations, decorate the auditorium and library, arrange for coverage by educational television channel.

**ACTION:** Set up rooms, greet guests, interview the new citizens, take photographs.

**REFLECTION:** Journal writing, student-led discussion groups, identification of need for written materials and resources for children of these families, letter to INS to share what has been learned and ideas for next time, forms sent to partner agencies for feedback, unsolicited letters received from new citizen families thanking students for meaningful and special event.

**DEMONSTRATION:** Compilation of interviews and photographs for each family; making "welcome kits" for the children of the immigrant families that include: cartoon-style map of the area, places to go for entertainment and sports, lists of after-school and weekend youth activities, translation guide for youth expressions, small journal, and pen.

**YOUTH VOICE and CHOICE:** Develop the idea, establish partnerships, organize into committees, plan interviews, design and make transition kits for children of the families.

**NOTES:** The project evolved from student interest and initiative resulting from an Ellis Island simulation and learning more about their community as a resettlement area for people from all over the world. Partnerships with INS and city offices were essential components.

CURRICULAR CONNECTIONS:

☒ *English/Language Arts:* Writing letters for donations and thank-you letters, keeping journals, reading literature about the immigrant experience, writing press releases, vocabulary

☒ *Social Studies/History:* Participate in Ellis Island simulation, hear guest speaker from INS, research countries of origin of 32 people being sworn in at the ceremony—history, current events, culture (foods, music, traditions), interview immigrants about their transition to citizenship (permission received)

☐ *Mathematics:*

☐ *Science:*

☒ *Languages:* Identify greetings in languages of countries studied, including the correct pronunciations; use greeting on banners

☒ *Art and Music:* Collect music from many cultures, school choral group participates by singing a medley with cultural references

☐ *Other:*

SKILL DEVELOPMENT:

- Organization and planning
- Interviewing
- Teamwork
- Letter writing
- Problem solving

BOOKS:

*The Skirt*
*The Middle of Everywhere: The World's Refugees Come to Our Town* (excerpts)
*Stella: On the Edge of Popularity*
*Behind the Mountains*
*The Whispering Cloth: A Refugee's Story*
*The Kid's Guide to Social Action*
*Immigration: How Should It Be Controlled?*
*A Very Important Day*

COMMUNITY CONTACTS:

Immigration and Naturalization Services
City multicultural program
Educational TV channel
*Portland Press* (newspapers)

# Planning for Service Learning: *Example (High School)*

Grade level: **9 Humanities**

## CONTENT—LEARNING ABOUT:

- Interpersonal relationships
- Civic participation
- Child Psychology
- Bookmaking
- Being role models

**SERVICE NEED:** There is a reciprocal learning that occurs in mentoring relationships between older and younger children with mutual benefits; young children need encouragement to read and write.

**SERVICE IDEA: Book Buddies**
Instruct young children in bookmaking and collaborate on making books for the community.

**PREPARATION:** Write reflections on childhood and favorite books; interactive workshop with child psychologist about learning styles and Howard Gardner's eight types of intelligence; read children's books; in small groups, discuss methods of working with young children; design lessons reflecting different types of intelligence; reach consensus on theme for books ("friendship" chosen to combat bullying); get resources for bookmaking; learn bookbinding techniques; arrange logistics and transportation.

**ACTION:** Visit kindergarten class three times: (1) get acquainted with children and read books, (2) discuss book ideas on theme of friendship and begin story development, (3) write and illustrate story. Copies of books given to children and to school and public libraries.

**REFLECTION:** Students have peer "journal partners" who read entries and respond; teacher reads and gives feedback weekly. Class discussion follows each visit, with role plays and problem solving.

**DEMONSTRATION:** Present project with the elementary children at the school district service learning advisory committee meeting.

**YOUTH VOICE and CHOICE:** Revise project, find partner classroom, write proposal, make phone calls, get donations, design activities.

**NOTES:** This project began as a service requirement of the department. The initial plan to read books to elementary children one time changed, through student initiative and planning, into a three-week comprehensive program. An ongoing relationship was established between the classrooms and the schools.

## CURRICULAR CONNECTIONS:

☒ *English/Language Arts:* Proposal writing; reading and analyzing children's books for content, format, and style; book writing; letter writing for donations or reduced cost for supplies

☒ *Social Studies/History:* Child psychology

☒ *Mathematics:* Budget management for funds received from school, literacy grant

☐ *Science:*

☒ *Languages:* Prepare for working with bilingual children with assistance from a Spanish language teacher; several books are bilingual

☒ *Art and Music:* Advanced art students at school make presentations on illustration to make students aware of various styles; create illustrations with children; bookbinding

☒ *Other:* Computer skills to create a design and template for the book-making process

## SKILL DEVELOPMENT:

- Organization
- Leadership
- Planning
- Writing in different styles—proposals, thank-you letters, stories
- Communication—phone calls for supplies, interaction with elementary teachers, interaction in small planning groups, partnerships with children

## BOOKS:

*The Sissy Duckling*
*Toestomper and the Caterpillars*
*Margarite y Margarita (bilingual)*
*La Mariposa*
*Hey, Little Ant!*

## COMMUNITY CONTACTS:

Will Rogers Elementary School
Kelly Paper Supplies
Service Learning Advisory Committee

# Planning for Service Learning: *Example (Special Needs)*

Grade level: **Preschool–8 Special Needs****

## CONTENT—LEARNING ABOUT:

- Our neighborhood
- Elders
- Acts of kindness and generosity
- Life cycle of plants

**SERVICE NEED:** Two populations are in close proximity with no interaction; this could be mutually beneficial.

**SERVICE IDEA: Being Good Neighbors**
Giving flowering plant pots to older people at a senior residential center

**PREPARATION:** Study about plants, grow plants from seeds to seedlings, paint and decorate pots with glitter and ribbons, work with mainstream teens in high school environmental science class to plant pots.

**ACTION:** Deliver plants, interact with older people at senior residence, give copies of stories to the senior center.

**REFLECTION:** Staff reflect on the activity and discuss each child's level of participation and development. Students write about or give dictation to teachers about their experiences.

**DEMONSTRATION:** The project's success leads to a follow-up activity the next weekend in which the children and their families help plant an outdoor garden in a courtyard at the senior residence. Many seniors and staff help or watch and interact with the children. Most parents noted this was the first time their children had participated in community service.

**YOUTH VOICE and CHOICE:** Making choices is a significant skill for autistic children; this project affords many opportunities: selecting colors, choosing plants to grow, asking to plant pots for their families.

**NOTES:** The program is individualized to student ability. The school is on a high school campus. All of the students with autism visited the environmental science class and the high school students came to their classrooms. Some students requested extra pots to plant for their parents and gave them a book of stories written about their service and learning experience.

## CURRICULAR CONNECTIONS:

☒ *English/Language Arts:* Learn about life cycle of plants through story books and flannel board activities, make sequence books about life cycles of plants, practice what to say with the older people

☒ *Social Studies/History:* Learn about the community (the high school and the senior residential facility); discuss community involvement, service, and generosity

☒ *Mathematics:* Measure plant growth and chart data

☒ *Science:* Plant seedlings in plastic bags to watch seeds sprout, transfer seedlings to soil, draw diagrams of plants

☐ *Languages:*

☒ *Art and Music:* Draw and label pictures, write picture stories

☒ *Other:* Computer skills—typing stories

## SKILL DEVELOPMENT:

- Art—cutting, pasting, tracing
- Handwriting
- Drawing
- Making choices
- Staying on task
- Transitioning from one setting to another
- Social communication and interaction

## BOOKS:

*Jack's Garden*

*Bud*

*A Harvest of Color: Growing a Vegetable Garden*

## COMMUNITY CONTACTS:

High school environmental science teacher

Elder care facility

**Children with autism, assisted in part by high school students grades 10 and 11.

# Community Contact Information

Name of agency: ______________________________

Key individual: ______________________________

Address: ______________________________

Phone: ______________ Fax: ______________ Email: ______________

Location (note proximity to school):

______________________________

Service needs (note ongoing versus short-term):

______________________________

______________________________

Learning opportunities:

______________________________

______________________________

______________________________

Date contact made: ______________________________

Contact made by: ______________________________

Follow-up information (record all calls, visits, etc.; continue on back or new sheet as necessary):

______________________________

______________________________

______________________________

______________________________

______________________________

______________________________

# Community Response Form

Name of agency: ______________________________

Address: ______________________________

Phone: ______________ Fax: ______________ Email: ______________

Contact person: ______________________________

Teacher/class: ______________________________

Date of visit: ______________________________

Purpose of visit: ______________________________

*Please respond to the following questions to help us learn from today's service experience and better meet your agency's needs in the future.*

What were the benefits of today's experience for your agency?

What suggestions do you have for future visits or interactions?

What service needs do you have that our school could assist with in the future?

What did you and others at your agency learn about children and our school that you did not know before?

Additional comments are most appreciated.

Thank you! Please return this form to the teacher listed above at the following address:

# Our Service Project

Our names: ______________________________________________

Teacher: ______________________________________________

School: ______________________________________________

Address: ______________________________________________

Phone: ________________ Fax: ________________ Email: ________________

Project name: ______________________________________________

Our idea: ______________________________________________

This helps others by: ______________________________________________

Student names and jobs:

My name ______________________ My job ______________________

My name ______________________ My job ______________________

My name ______________________ My job ______________________

Others who will help:

Students: ______________________________________________

Teachers: ______________________________________________

Other adults: ______________________________________________

Organizations: ______________________________________________

Supplies needed: ______________________________________________

Our expectations: ______________________________________________

Signatures:

# Project Promotion—Turning Ideas into Action

**What We Already Know**

Service idea:

Need—the community issue:

Community partners:

**New Ideas and Possibilities**

New community alliances: Think outside the box

Evidence: Keeping track of our activities, accomplishments, and outcomes

Donations: What is needed (e.g., flyers, T-shirts, balloons)? Who might donate items?

Media madness: Press releases, radio spots, cable access, news stories

Fund-raising ideas and resources

Presentation opportunities: School and community events, organizations

---

**Follow-up**

Roles and responsibilities: Who will do what?

# Sequence for Reflection

Use this document as a checklist and to record your own reflections.

***In Preparation***

As the service learning process begins, find out what students know: What beliefs and assumptions are already in place? Where and how were they learned? What do students expect to happen? What do they expect to learn, and how do they expect to feel? Depending on the situation, you may give students a thought or question to take with them into the service experience. This may encourage them to be more observant or heighten their awareness of a particular need or action being taken.

*What happened:*

***During Action***

Be observant. What are the students paying attention to? What comments do you overhear? What behaviors do you see? You may make notes and refer to them later, during the reflection that follows the service. During on-the-spot reflection, students sometimes have insights or make recommendations that improve their experience and the impact of their contributions.

*What happened:*

***Following Service***

Vary the reflection methods. As students become more adept, ask them to design a reflection process for themselves and their classmates. Before discussing the service, ask students to first write their responses to discussion prompts. This can protect the integrity of each student's experience and assure that everyone has something to contribute. Have students draw upon their reflections during demonstration of their service learning.

*What happened:*

***Feedback***

Provide *nonjudgmental* feedback. If you may read journals, ask if you can write a response in the journal or on an attached piece of paper. Listen well. Ask questions. Appreciate what is being revealed and discovered.

*What happened:*

# Four Square Reflection Tool

| WHAT HAPPENED? | HOW DO I FEEL? |
|---|---|
| | |
| **IDEAS?** | **QUESTIONS?** |
| | |

# Assessment for Service Learning: *Part One*

***Service Learning Project:*** ______________________________

Respond to the questions that are relevant to your service learning activities.

***Student Learning***

- Were the defined content and skill objectives met?
- Were there any unforeseen outcomes?
- Did students show initiative or develop leadership skills?
- Were students able to reflect and place their experience in the larger context of community or society in general?
- Could students identify both their cognitive and affective growth?

***Impact of the Service***

- Were students able to explicitly state the need and purpose for their service efforts?
- What contribution was made?
- How did the service help or hinder community improvement efforts?
- Is the partner agency satisfied with the interaction?
- Have new relationships been formed?
- Were planned service programs, activities, or products completed?

***Process***

- How did this project affect or change how teachers teach and how children learn?
- How effective was project planning?
- What are your ideas for overall improvement?
- In future activities, how can students take greater ownership?
- How can community partnerships be improved or strengthened?

# Assessment for Service Learning: *Part Two*

***Service Learning Project:*** ______________________________

Identify what methods were used for each stage and whether each element was present.

**Stages of Service Learning**

***Preparation***

- Research
- Literature
- Field trips
- Interviews
- Other:

***Action***

- Direct service
- Indirect service
- Research
- Advocacy

***Reflection***

- Discussion
- Journals
- Role play
- Other:

***Demonstration***

- Presentation
- Performance
- Article
- Other:

**Elements of Service Learning**

- **Integrated learning**
  *Example of curricular connections:*

- **Meeting genuine needs**
  *Example of students verifying need:*

- **Youth voice and choice**
  *Example of student responsibility and decision making:*

- **Collaborative efforts**
  *Example of partnership/shared responsibility:*

- **Reciprocity**
  *Example of reciprocity in relationships between persons and between institutions:*

- **Civic responsibility**
  *Example of students' increased awareness of their role in community improvement and/or students' knowledge of civic institutions:*

# Student Self-Evaluation

Name: ______________________________ Date: ______________

Service Learning Project: ______________________________

*Learning*

- What information did you learn in preparing to do service?
- What skills did you develop through the activities?
- How did this project help you to better understand ideas or subjects we have been studying?
- Through this service learning project, what did you learn about:
  - yourself?
  - working with others, including people in your class?
  - your community?
- How will you use what you learned in this experience?

*Service*

- What was the need for your service effort?
- What contribution did you make?
- What overall contribution was made by your class?
- How did your service affect the community?

*Process*

- How did you and other students help with project planning?
- In what ways did you make decisions and solve problems?
- Were there any differences between the initial project plans and what you actually did?
- What ideas do you have for improving any part of the project?

CHAPTER 3

# The Theme Chapters and the Service Learning Bookshelf

Now that you've learned what service learning is and how you can use it, it's time to get started. You're ready to explore common themes for service and literary resources you can use with your students. Part 2 of this guide consists of chapters on eleven different themes that are commonly selected for service learning activities and were identified through interactions with teachers and students from across the United States. In these theme chapters, you'll find several tools, activities, ideas, and resources that will help you create and tailor service learning projects around a given theme. A primary part of each theme chapter is the Service Learning Bookshelf, which contains a cross-section of books for different ages you can use with your students. This chapter will explain the structure and resources of the theme chapters and how you can use their content and ideas to enhance your service learning activities.

## Getting Oriented:

### About the Thematic Chapters

As you consider designing a service learning project, you may be wondering:

- What social concerns are most often addressed through service learning?
- What activities can help prepare my students for service?
- What are some tried-and-true service learning ideas?
- What books can be used to teach young people, motivate them to read, and inspire them to action?

The thematic chapters answer these questions with a wealth of ideas and resources for service learning in action. The theme chapters address: AIDS awareness and education, animals in danger, community safety, elders, environment, gardening, hunger and homelessness, immigrants, literacy, social change, and special needs and disabilities. For convenience, the topics are arranged alphabetically.

Each thematic chapter includes:

- **Introductory comments** regarding the theme and service learning. This will provide you with basic information about the theme and give you an idea of why it's important.
- **Quotes for inspiration.** These quotes may inspire you or you may find ways to use them with your students.
- **Activities** to help you prepare your students for service learning on the theme. Some provoke preliminary thought and discussion on the theme, while other activities promote learning and skills development related to the theme. The activities usually address all age ranges and many of the activities can be adapted to different grade levels and settings.
- **Organizations and online resources** specific to the content of the theme rather than being general to service learning. They will direct you to reputable organizations or information-rich Web sites that can help you and your students get started on research and planning.
- **A curriculum web** that provides you with a wide sampling of cross-curricular connections you can make specific to the theme.
- **Examples of service learning** that have been successfully carried out by elementary, middle, and high school students. You may find one idea or resource that is just what you've been looking for, or an example might spark another idea that better suits the needs of your students and community. Note that grade levels are given as a reference, but most project ideas transcend age

groups and can be adapted to suit younger or older students.

- **A Service Learning Bookshelf** for each theme. Here, you will find a comprehensive listing of literature that helps to connect classroom learning and literacy with service to the community. These Bookshelves contain more than three hundred book titles that are annotated and categorized for easy identification, reference, and use.

As you use the activities in the theme chapters of Part 2, continue to use Part 1 as a reference, especially if the practice of service learning is relatively new, if you are developing teacher training programs to provide others with service learning knowledge, or simply as a reminder of the four stages and the essential elements of service learning. The reproducible pages at the end of Chapter 2 can give you a jump-start in planning and organizing as you continue to apply the key concepts.

# About the Service Learning Bookshelf

Clear off a shelf and start collecting! The Service Learning Bookshelf in each thematic chapter is filled with nonfiction books, picture books, and novels selected to enhance your service learning activities. Included on each bookshelf are titles that:

- describe the service experiences of others
- introduce important social themes
- tell stories from history
- increase student interest in reading
- promote critical thinking and discussion
- prepare students to interact with diverse populations
- enhance the experiences students have in the community
- inspire students to serve

Whether read aloud or silently, the books included in each bookshelf are guaranteed to make you and your students smile, laugh, cry, think, wonder, dream, plan, hope, and act.

Well-written books such as those in the bookshelf lists provide many benefits. They tap into students' curiosity and desire to know. They can give students the information they need to move to the next level of competency or inspire them to consider important topics. Authors model how to write, how to think creatively, and how to tell one's own story. When the story has at its heart a concern shared by the students, it can give them a range of possibilities for their own actions.

> Reading is to the mind what exercise is to the body.
>
> JOSEPH ADDISON, POET

Reading is clearly the foundation of learning, but books can only go so far. In our classrooms, we want books that inspire students to action—that provide not just knowledge but *motivation* for service. Each book on the Service Learning Bookshelf has been selected with this in mind. The bookshelves hold a myriad of titles that belong in the hands of students and that are resources for teachers, program staff, or family members who want to introduce a topic, expand knowledge, or develop an inquiring mind.

**Books as Catalysts for Action**

Books can lead students to consider many questions:

- What do I have in common with these characters?
- How are the characters' actions changing how the characters think about themselves?
- What actions are making a difference in the lives of others?
- Are any of the problems or conflicts in the story occurring in my life or the lives of people I know or see?
- What questions do I have after reading this book?

*continued* ⟶

- What can we do to address problems in our community that are similar to the ones described in the book?

Use these questions with your students to deepen their relationship with the text, as well as to stimulate their thinking and concern for community needs and issues. You can adapt the questions for writing assignments, discussion groups, or journal entries during reflection. The books listed in the theme bookshelves are ideal for activities that promote critical thinking.

# What's on the Shelf? Features of the Service Learning Bookshelf

Each bookshelf includes the following:

- An annotated bibliography of works related to the chapter theme. The list is arranged under the general categories of nonfiction books, picture books, and fiction. Nonfiction and fiction selections include the book's length and recommended grade levels.
- A quick reference chart that classifies the books according to topics within the theme so you can find the books you want more easily.
- Recommendations made by service learning practitioners, with ideas for service learning activities.
- Author interviews to provide the "story behind the story" and more service connections.

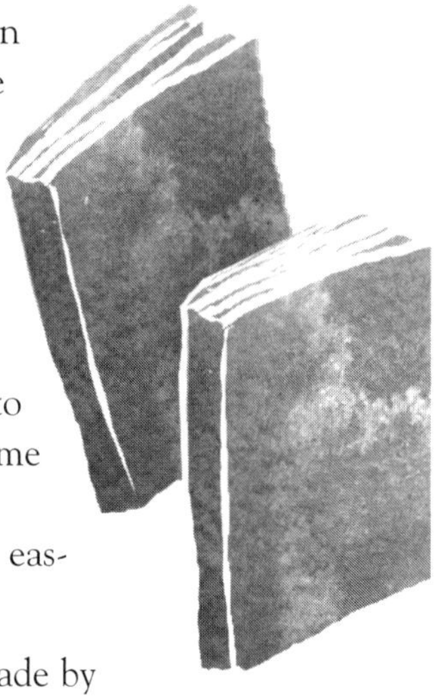

This section will describe these features in more detail and start suggesting ways you can use them. Two other important aspects of titles in the Bookshelves are also discussed: the artwork and illustrations featured in many books and special selections written by young authors.

**A note about bookshelf titles:** Books do go out of print—even our favorites. Almost all of the bookshelf titles listed were in print at the time of publication. A few out-of-print exceptions were included because of their outstanding content and presentation; these books are identified as out of print in the bookshelves. Libraries and used books stores—including those accessible via the Internet—are good sources for these out-of-print gems.

## *Nonfiction Books*

Nonfiction books can cover a wide range of topics, coming in a variety of forms from straightforward narrative prose to songs—with everything in between. They can be collections of plays, songs, and poems such as *Cootie Shots: Theatrical Inoculations Against Bigotry for Kids, Parents and Teachers* (Community Safety Bookshelf), a collection that promotes tolerance. They can be photo essays such as *Rosie, A Visiting Dog's Story* (Special Needs and Disabilities Bookshelf), which is a series of photo essays of a pet bringing joy to infirm children and elders. They can even take the form of a coloring book such as *Conversation Starters As Easy As ABC 123: How to Start Conversations with People Who Have Memory Loss* (Elders Bookshelf).

History is frequently a topic for nonfiction books, and a number of nonfiction books link the study of history with events in the present day. *Orphan Train Rider: One Boy's True Story* (Hunger and Homelessness Bookshelf) describes how orphaned or abandoned children from the eastern states were sent westward on trains to be placed in homes between 1854 and 1929. *Linda Brown, You Are Not Alone: The Brown v. Board of Education Decision* (Social Change Bookshelf) presents different perspectives and insights about a historical event that impacts students' lives in school every day. *When Plague Strikes: The Black Death, Smallpox, AIDS* (AIDS Education and Awareness Bookshelf) shows the parallels linking three epidemics.

Other books describe acts of service, as in *Nights of the Pufflings* (Animals in Danger Bookshelf), which tells how young children rescue small birds from the perils of the city and release them over the ocean waves. Youth activists are profiled in *Generation Fix* (Social Change Bookshelf). And students will be amazed to read how a young activist took on international child labor in *Free the Children: A Young Man's Personal Crusade Against Child Labor* (Social Change Bookshelf).

> Read books. They are good for us.
> NATALIE GOLDBERG, AUTHOR

## *Picture Books*

Picture books can be read and enjoyed by people of all ages. The language and artwork convey messages that transcend age. As a result, picture books can be effective tools for teaching sophisticated concepts and issues at all grade levels. Older students may be surprised to learn that complex social issues and ideas—such as memory loss or the struggles of refugee children forced into manual labor—can be presented to and understood by young children through the medium of picture books.

Most people like to be read to, yet we usually stop reading aloud to students once they reach middle school. Hearing a story read aloud is different from reading to one's self. In a class environment, reading a picture book aloud creates a common experience for discussion and stimulates interest or curiosity regarding an important subject. High school students have been known to sit on the edge of their seats listening to *Too Far Away to Touch* (AIDS Education and Awareness Bookshelf) and *Stranger in the Mirror* (Elders Bookshelf) and laugh out loud when they hear *The Wartville Wizard* (Environment Bookshelf), a hilarious tale of litter flying back to stick to the litterer.

Needless to say, younger children devour picture books, enjoying the pranks of *Stella Louella's Runaway Book* (Literacy Bookshelf) and the thoughtful revelations in *My Diary from Here to There/Mi diario de aquí hasta allá* (Immigrants Bookshelf). These titles also model for students how to write and construct their own stories of service to the community.

Books can also have a direct connection to the service activity. Meeting a young child with spina bifida in *All Kinds of Friends, Even Green!* (Special Needs and Disabilities Bookshelf) is an ideal way to prepare students of any age to interact with special needs youth.

Many picture books provide excellent resources for finding subject matter that engages and motivates children. The importance of preserving our natural habitat, for example, is conveyed in a folktale from India, *The People Who Hugged the Trees* (Environment Bookshelf). There is wonderful storytelling, weaving imagination and reality, in *La Mariposa* (Literacy Bookshelf). These and other titles are useful for tutoring and language development as well as encouraging young people to learn more about their themes.

## *Fiction*

Fiction runs the gamut from easy-to-read beginning chapter books to young adult novels. These selections are well-written stories that challenge and compel the reader. In *Hope Was Here* (Social Change Bookshelf), for example, a teen moves to a new city and finds herself embroiled in a hot political campaign that may rip apart her community. In *Seedfolks* (Gardening Bookshelf), each chapter represents the voice of a different community member bringing his or her seeds and story to a neighborhood garden, acknowledging real struggles and personal dreams. *A Corner of the Universe* (Special Needs and Disabilities Bookshelf) tells the story of a young girl stunned to meet her uncle when he returns after years in a residential program. *Dream Freedom* (Social Change) is a sophisticated interweaving of many lives affected by the slave trade in the Sudan and a classroom of students in the United States working to reach across an ocean to help. Some novels are ideal to read aloud. For example, *Judy Moody Saves the World* (Environment Bookshelf) reinforces the benefits of teamwork. When *Butterflies and Lizards, Beryl and Me* (Gardening Bookshelf) is read to a group of students, it provokes conversations about loneliness, teasing and ridicule, and the needs of elders in the community, all within the metaphor of plants growing. Many of the suggested books integrate English and language arts with other academic subjects and develop awareness, sensitivity, and understanding about the human condition and our society.

While high school reading assignments often neglect the riches to be found in young adult literature, hopefully this list will encourage you to look for—or remind you of—the jewels that can be found in this category of books. "Young adult" literature is so named for a good reason. The stories reflect the challenges, dilemmas, and relationships particularly faced by this age group. They offer the complexity and conflicts that often mirror the situations students observe and experience. Whether you choose *Big Mouth and Ugly Girl* by Joyce Carol Oates (Community Safety Bookshelf) or *Before We Were Free* by Julia Alvarez (Social Change Bookshelf), or one of the many other selections, treat yourself and read a young adult novel. You may be surprised at how compelling you find the story and that the power of the words convinces you to include the book and others like it in your service learning curriculum.

## Looking It Up:

### The Bookshelf Charts

The chart in each bookshelf is arranged by topics commonly associated with the theme and can help you quickly find books that are appropriate for your particular service learning activities. For example, the chart in the Community Safety chapter groups books under the topics of personal safety, bullying, conflict resolution, local violence, hate crimes, the world stage, and community building. The books under the topics generally include a cross-section of nonfiction, picture books, and fiction and encompass a broad range of reading levels. Books that feature young people in service-providing roles are flagged in the chart. Books that can be used for more than one theme are cross-referenced to where they appear in other themes. Out-of-print—but still worthy—titles are also indicated.

## Recommendations from the Field: The Classics and Beyond

"I would like to involve my students in service learning, but we are reading *Romeo and Juliet* this semester. What could I do?"

Substitute any title you like—*Walk Two Moons*, *Tuck Everlasting*, *Fahrenheit 451*—and you have identified a quandary for many teachers: how to connect the required classroom literature with service learning. To address this issue, I asked many service learning colleagues—both adults and youth—from around the country to choose and read a curriculum classic and make recommendations for how it could be used in service learning. Reviewers came from across the service learning spectrum and include a fourth-grade student, a college freshman, parent/child teams, K–12 teachers, university professors, program directors, and policy makers. One high school contributor is autistic.

Most of the books they reviewed are familiar titles, like the kindergarten favorite *Make Way for Ducklings* (Animals in Danger Bookshelf) and the high school classic *Siddhartha* (Community Safety Bookshelf). Other books stretch the idea of "classics" to include more modern literature that tells a significant story in writing of high quality. Book selection occurred in a variety of ways. Based on research, I provided a list of recommended titles. Many reviewers suggested their own favorite books. Several people said this project gave them a chance to pick up a book they had always meant to read. One contributor was relieved to finally finish reading a lengthy novel that had escaped her during high school; she followed up with a letter to her high school teacher saying, "I finally read the book!"

Each of the recommendations provides a summary of the story and offers ideas for service learning connections. Many include questions to initiate discussion regarding service-related themes. Look for these books in most of the thematic chapters, labeled as a "Recommendation from the Field." All of these titles are gathered together for your easy reference in the chart on the next page.

Is one of your favorite books missing? If so, you have a perfect opportunity to create your own service learning classic connection.

# Recommendations from the Field

## *Elementary*


| | | |
|---|---|---|
| Animals in Danger | *Make Way for Ducklings* | (page 85) |
| Community Safety | *Harry Potter and the Sorcerer's Stone* | (page 100) |
| Elders | *The Hundred Penny Box* | (page 117) |
| Environment | *Island of the Blue Dolphins* | (page 133) |
| Immigrants | *The Skirt* | (page 170) |
| Literacy | *A Series of Unfortunate Events* | (page 184) |
| | *The Library Card* | (page 183) |
| Social Change | *The Little Engine That Could* | (page 198) |
| | *Walk Two Moons* | (page 200) |


## *Middle School*


| | | |
|---|---|---|
| Community Safety | *Holes* | (page 101) |
| Elders | *Tuck Everlasting* | (page 118) |
| Immigrants | *Dragonwings* | (page 169) |


## *High School*


| | | |
|---|---|---|
| Community Safety | *Romeo and Juliet* | (page 102) |
| | *Siddhartha* | (page 102) |
| Elders | *The Bonesetter's Daughter* | (page 117) |
| Hunger and Homelessness | *Grapes of Wrath* | (page 155) |
| | *Nickel and Dimed: On (Not) Getting By in America* | (page 154) |
| Literacy | *Fahrenheit 451* | (page 182) |
| Social Change | *In the Time of the Butterflies* | (page 199) |
| Special Needs and Disabilities | *Of Mice and Men* | (page 212) |

## Author Interviews

Have you ever been curious about the story behind the story? Would you sometimes like to pick up the phone, call an author, and ask, "So why did you have the *Wartville Wizard* get the power over trash?" Perhaps you would ask the author to discuss the evolution of the character Nissa in *The Strength of Saints* (Literacy Bookshelf) as she considers consolidating two libraries in a racially divided city. Or perhaps you would ask what caused Richard Michelson to tell the story of sustaining language and tradition in *Too Young for Yiddish* (Elders Bookshelf).

These questions and more are what led to me doing just that—getting in touch with the authors of books I liked and interviewing them. Each interview gives a window into the process that goes into creating a story. Each demonstrates the writer's intelligence and desire to reach others, and their passion for the written word. All of the writers offer thought-provoking insights into the writing process and the subject matter, and some even describe service learning ideas they've heard about from readers.

**Contact Your Favorite Bookshelf Author or Illustrator**

The Internet offers an easy way to contact many authors and illustrators. Some have their own Web sites and welcome notes and letters from readers. For those who do not have personal Web sites, you can write to the book's publisher, who will then forward letters to the author. Many publishers' Web sites also offer guides and supplementary materials for their books on the bookshelf lists.

What to write about? One idea for students is to write about their responses to the book and describe the service learning connection. In their interviews, several authors discussed receiving this kind of correspondence and how appreciative they were and described some wonderful service learning projects!

As the interviews illustrate, there are as many different approaches to writing and reasons for telling a story as there are writers themselves. Francisco Jiménez's memoirs of a young migrant farmworker in *The Circuit* and *Breaking Through* (Immigrants Bookshelf) share the travails faced by his family as they struggled to survive financially. *Hey, Little Ant!* (Community Safety Bookshelf) began as a song written by a father and daughter team, Phillip and Hannah Hoose. In *Wanda's Roses* (Gardening Bookshelf), Pat Brisson wanted to tell of a girl willing to work hard to make her dream come true. The loss of a dear friend inspired Lesléa Newman to write *Too Far Away to Touch* (AIDS Education and Awareness Bookshelf). Through *The Misfits* (Community Safety Bookshelf), James Howe wanted to demonstrate how young people can collaborate to improve peer relationships for an entire school community.

Through the author interviews, teachers and students can enter the writers' worlds. Hopefully, as a result of the interviews, your students will experience added depth when reading the books. Ideally, the interviews will also inspire many young people, and older ones as well, to craft their own experiences, ideas, and feelings into poems, plays, short stories, novels, picture books, memoirs, and nonfiction.

**Using Author Interviews in the Classroom**

You can use an interview for ideas on how to teach and use a book. An interview can provide you with ideas for reflections and questions for class discussions. You start a discussion by asking your students what they think the author wanted to get across in the book, what they think the author's inspiration could have been, or what they think the author was thinking when she wrote a particular plot twist. Interesting discussions can result from these questions and others like them, and the discussions only get better when you read to them what the writer really *was* thinking. Your students may be surprised, amused, touched, or even motivated to write. No matter what their reactions, the class discussion can be enriched by exploring them.

## The Importance of Illustrations and Artwork

Visual images communicate the message of a story as much as text. The bookshelf titles employ innumerable illustration techniques and styles that educate as well as inspire. Illustrations and other artwork show us what happened and where it happened. They also sometimes give information not provided in any other way. For example, in Patricia Polacco's *Chicken Sunday* (Community Safety Bookshelf), one image shows an aged shopkeeper with a number tattooed on his forearm, indicating that he was in a concentration camp during World War II; this fact is never mentioned in the story text. The last picture in *Click, Clack, Moo: Cows That Type* (Social Change Bookshelf), illustrated by Betsy Lewin, reveals the resolution of the ducks' quest for a diving board; no words at all appear on the page.

The bookshelves offer an array of options to students exploring ideas and methods for illustrating original stories or helping younger children create a book. Here is a sampling:

- *Can You Hear a Rainbow? The Story of a Deaf Boy Named Chris* (Special Needs and Disabilities Bookshelf), illustrated by Nicola Simmonds, and *One Day at Wood Green Animal Shelter* (Animals in Danger Bookshelf), by Patricia Casey, mix photographs and art.
- Artist Paul Yalowitz begins the story *Somebody Loves You, Mr. Hatch* (Elders Bookshelf) with dreary colors to match Mr. Hatch's mood. The colors brighten as Mr. Hatch thinks, "Somebody loves me."
- Gerardo Suzán's colorful images in *Butterfly Boy* (Elders Bookshelf) are a mix of representational and modern art.
- In *One Good Apple: Growing Our Food for the Sake of the Earth* (Environment Bookshelf), author-photographer Catherine Paladino presents beautifully composed images to enrich the nonfiction text.
- Tomek Bogacki recreates the colors and the details of his home, the town, and the garden he planted in *My First Garden* (Gardening Bookshelf), which resembles a photo album of art in pastels.
- Ann Arnold uses pen and watercolor illustrations in the information-filled book *The Adventurous Chef: Alexis Soyer* (Hunger and Homelessness Bookshelf) to show the dramatic innovations and inventions made to benefit Irish famine victims and soldiers in the Crimean War; she also shows the actual floor plan of his kitchen.
- Artist and author Susan L. Roth makes collages with photos, fabrics, and other found objects to tell the story *It's Still a Dog's New York: A Book of Healing* (Community Safety Bookshelf).
- In *Jack's Garden* (Gardening Bookshelf), Henry Cole uses sparse, repetitive text in combination with artwork that is dense with information about soil, weather, worms, and seeds.
- Elizabeth Goméz's brilliant use of color and fantastical imagery in *A Movie in My Pillow/Una película en mi almohada* (Immigrants Bookshelf) could inspire murals.
- Lauren Child's *What Planet Are You From, Clarice Bean?* (Environment Bookshelf) integrates text into drawings that form every shape and move in every direction imaginable.
- Two books by Michael J. Rosen, *The Greatest Table: A Banquet to Fight Against Hunger* (Hunger and Homelessness Bookshelf) and *Down to Earth: Garden Secrets! Garden Stories! Garden Projects You Can Do!* (Gardening Bookshelf) include collections of donated artwork by highly regarded children's book illustrators; these are veritable visual feasts.

> Some painters transform the sun into a yellow spot, others transform a yellow spot into the sun.
>
> PABLO PICASSO, ARTIST

## Young Authors at Work

Several of the bookshelf titles were written by authors under the age of twenty. These young authors are models that the young people you work with can draw on for inspiration both for their own creative endeavors and what they can achieve. If you'd like to highlight the achievements and writing of young authors for your students, here are titles on the bookshelves that are written or co-authored by young people:

- *Hey, Little Ant!* (Community Safety Bookshelf), a song-turned-book that ends with the question, "What would you do?"
- *Conversation Starters* (Elders Bookshelf) and *Increase the Peace: The ABCs of Tolerance* (Community Safety Bookshelf), both in ABC formats.
- *Potato: A Tale from the Great Depression* (Hunger and Homelessness Bookshelf), by an eight-year-old, telling a story passed down through her family.
- *We Need to Go to School: Voices of the Rugmark Children* and *Free the Children* (Social Change Bookshelf) about international child labor.

# Using the Service Learning Bookshelf

You can use the Service Learning Bookshelf contents in a remarkable variety of ways throughout your service learning projects. This section will show you how you can use books in every stage of the service learning process, with different partners on a project, and as a source of inspiration for your students. Several charts will help you make quick and easy curricular connections and serve as useful cross-references when you're brainstorming ideas and planning projects. The chart "Connecting the Bookshelf to the Four Stages of Service Learning" suggests ideas for linking reading to each service learning stage. The "Bilingual Books" chart identifies titles you can use in English and Spanish, while the "Historical Content and the Bookshelf" chart lists a selection of bookshelf titles by historical period.

## Connecting the Bookshelf to the Four Stages of Service Learning

***During* Preparation, *use books:***

- to introduce topics.
- for research.
- to enhance understanding of a historical time period through parallel reading of a novel or picture book. (See "Historical Content and the Bookshelf" at the end of this chapter.)
- to show different approaches to or writing styles on a similar theme.

***During* Action, *use books:***

- to begin the service activity with a common experience for all involved.
- to help children learn to read.
- to teach concepts or ideas.
- to dramatize an educational program.

*continued* ⟶

***During* Reflection, *use books:***

- to introduce inspiring thoughts related to the service experience.
- to share the reflective comments of others.
- to show the results of similar service experiences by others.
- in response to a student's expression of thought or feelings.

***During* Demonstration, *use books:***

- in a display to show what books were used as resources for student learning.
- to read aloud and share the impact of a story, similar to what the students experienced in class or in other situations.
- in a choral reading format or selected excerpts to read in presentations to tell the scope of the learning and service experience, and emphasize specific information.
- in a list of recommended reading to help others learn more about the subject.

## Publish, Publish, Publish

The titles in the Service Learning Bookshelf can inspire students to write about their own service experience and serve as templates for good storytelling about significant social issues. Students' stories and books can be donated to hospitals, libraries, family shelters, and other classrooms. With donated time and materials from community partners, students may even be able to publish their book and use it as a fund-raiser. Consider having the students record audiotapes especially for children or elders who are more able to listen than read. Consider, too, translating the stories for multilingual publications.

## Act It Out: The Play's the Thing

Students can also transform favorite stories into plays—or even musicals—that will help the audience learn about social issues. The performance may become an essential part of a service learning activity. The following books are easily adapted into plays and skits:

- *Toestomper and the Caterpillars* (Community Safety Bookshelf) shows how a "rowdy ruffian" is transformed into a kinder fellow by caring for squiggly blue caterpillars.
- *Hey, Little Ant!* (Community Safety Bookshelf) has been staged as an opera and a musical.
- *Pinky and Rex and the Bully* (Community Safety Bookshelf) is about a boy who has to make hard choices about friendships and his identity.
- *Cootie Shots: Theatrical Inoculations Against Bigotry for Kids, Parents and Teachers* (Community Safety Bookshelf) is a ready-to-use collection of plays.
- Even a novel, like *The Misfits* (Community Safety Bookshelf) about middle school kids trying to stop name-calling at school, has been transformed into a play.
- *Somebody Loves You, Mr. Hatch* (Elders Bookshelf) is a heartfelt story perfect for a Valentine's Day theme of valuing all community members, particularly those who are isolated and lonely.
- *The Wartville Wizard* (Environment Bookshelf) is a comical depiction of trash sticking to the people who litter in a small town.
- *The Can-Do Thanksgiving* (Hunger and Homelessness Bookshelf) demonstrates how knowing where the can of food is going can make all the difference.
- Any of the biographical collections can be adapted for "Living History" productions, where students become the people and tell their stories.

## *Library Partnerships*

Books, too, can be a source of community partnerships. Consider all the possible ways you could collaborate with school and public libraries to promote books with service-learning-related themes. Students can set up displays, provide book reviews, or design bookmarks with recommendations. A first-grade class created an attractive calendar for four local libraries featuring books they enjoyed about gardening. Every month, they promoted a new favorite book. Ask your students what they'd like to do—they will have plenty of ideas.

> The future belongs to those who can give the next generation reasons to hope.
>
> PIERRE TEILHARD DECHARDIN, PHILOSOPHER

## *Tutoring Programs*

Many bookshelf titles, particularly ones in the Literacy, Community Safety, and Immigrants Bookshelves, are helpful in various ways during preparation for or implementation of tutoring programs in which elementary, middle, or high school students tutor younger children or peers.

- Nonfiction books such as *Illiteracy* and *Learning Disabilities* (Literacy Bookshelf) provide background information.
- Several books describe the frustrations and embarrassment experienced by challenged readers, like *Just Call Me Stupid* and *Thank You, Mr. Falker* (Literacy Bookshelf). Such books help students learn about how peers may differ by skill, how they are affected by life experience, and how peer teasing and ridicule can present a hurdle.
- Learning English as a second language is hard work and is described in *The Circuit* and *Breaking Through* (Immigrants Bookshelf).
- In *Prairie School* (Literacy Bookshelf), a young boy doesn't see any reason to learn to read, until his persistent aunt comes to visit. A tutor with a particularly reluctant student may find this book inspiring and may even find it helpful to read it to the resistant tutee.
- *My Name Is María Isabel* (Social Change Bookshelf) reminds students and adults of the importance of treating all children with respect, including in classroom settings.
- Skills such as counting can be reinforced by *Ducks Disappearing* and *Cat Up a Tree* (Animals in Danger Bookshelf). These books also tell the stories of individuals teaching adults about our responsibility to care for living creatures.
- Students may find that the love of words can be contagious when they read the humorous *The Bookstore Mouse* (Literacy Bookshelf), a witty fantasy of a mouse with a colorful vocabulary helping a young medieval scribe to rescue storytellers from a dragon.
- In *Dear Whiskers* (Literacy Bookshelf), a young girl expresses frustration with a partner in a cross-age tutoring project, and comes to recognize appreciation for diversity and learning.
- A classroom with a place for every child, including one who is deaf, can be found in *The Year of Miss Agnes* (Literacy Bookshelf).
- *Sahara Special* (Literacy Bookshelf) tells of a girl who resists participating in school yet has a secret talent as a writer. This can inspire tutors to look for and encourage the secret (or not so secret) talents of their tutees (and recognize their own "secret" talents as well).
- If your tutoring program involves students with special needs, *Just Kids: Visiting a Class for Children with Special Needs* (Special Needs and Disabilities Bookshelf) provides an informative and engaging story.
- High school students with low reading skills can develop their own ability while preparing to read quality picture books to younger children.
- Tutors can read books aloud to younger readers to communicate the joy of reading.
- Use the bookshelf to find books of interest to particular tutees. The titles reflect diverse cultures and experiences and should provide something for everyone.

## Bilingual Books

**Community Safety Bookshelf**
*It Doesn't Have to Be This Way: A Barrio Story/No tiene que ser así: Una historia del barrio*

**Elders Bookshelf**
*Remember Me? Alzheimer's Through the Eyes of a Child/¿Te acuerdas de mí? Pensamientos de la enfermedad, Alzheimers a travez de los ojos de un niño*

**Environment Bookshelf**
*Fernando's Gift/El Regalo de Fernando*
*This House Is Made of Mud/Esta casa está hecha de lodo*

**Gardening Bookshelf**
*Gathering the Sun: An Alphabet in Spanish and English*
*Carlos and the Cornfield/Carlos y la milpa de maíz*

**Immigrants Bookshelf**
*A Movie in My Pillow/Una película en mi almohada*
*My Diary from Here to There/Mi diario de aquí hasta allá*

**Social Change Bookshelf**
*¡Sí, Se Puede!/Yes, We Can! Janitor Strike in L.A.*

**Special Needs and Disabilities Bookshelf**
*The Treasure on Gold Street/El tesoro en la calle Oro*

## *School, City, and State Reading Programs*

Programs that promote literacy and community building through reading are growing in popularity. The bookshelf lists are good sources of material for large-scale reading programs. All middle school students in a district, for example, might read *Any Small Goodness* (Immigrants Bookshelf), a chronicle of an adolescent's experience relocating in East Los Angeles. An entire city might be invited to read *Fahrenheit 451* (Literacy Bookshelf) or *To Kill a Mockingbird* (Social Change Bookshelf) and participate in related discussions. A statewide reading program might include *The Grapes of Wrath* (Hunger and Homelessness Bookshelf) among the selections. Community events associated with such programs might include art exhibits on related themes, staged productions of the book, readings, and speakers.

If a citywide or statewide reading program takes place in your community, get involved. If the selection is geared toward adults, recommend an additional book selection appropriate for youth, with follow-up activities at school or the library. Young people can select the book and design worthwhile and exciting learning opportunities. What may begin as a class or school activity could ultimately have city-wide reach.

## *Community Agencies and Organizations*

Although the discussion of the Service Learning Bookshelf focuses on school settings, community agencies and organizations can also make use of the lists. Organizations promoting racial diversity and tolerance can refer to the Social Change Bookshelf when looking for recommended readings for a middle or high school class. A staff member at a retirement home may read a book such as *Sunshine Home* (Elders Bookshelf) aloud to elementary children coming for a service activity as part of an orientation to the facility. Students can compile a list of books to read about special needs (or another theme) for an agency, complete with their original annotations or reviews, and develop analytical and writing skills in the process. Share the booklists with your community partners to find additional ways the resources can be helpful.

# Historical Content and the Bookshelf

Refer to this listing when seeking books depicting a particular period or issue. Dates are approximate. Please note that titles identified as recommendations in the bookshelves are not included in this historical chart.

**The Middle Ages**
*When Plague Strikes: The Black Death, Smallpox, AIDS* (AIDS Education and Awareness)
*Across a Dark and Wild Sea* (Literacy)
*The Bookstore Mouse* (Literacy)

**General United States History**
*Rabble Rousers: 20 Women Who Made a Difference* (Social Change)
*Sisters in Strength: American Women Who Made a Difference* (Social Change)
*We Are the Many: A Picture Book of American Indians* (Social Change)
*We Were There, Too! Young People in U.S. History* (Social Change)

**1845–1852**
*The Adventurous Chef: Alexis Soyer* (Hunger and Homelessness)
*Black Potatoes: The Story of the Great Irish Famine, 1845–1850* (Hunger and Homelessness)
*The Long March: The Choctaw's Gift to Irish Famine Relief* (Hunger and Homelessness)
*Feed the Children First: Irish Memories of the Great Hunger* (Hunger and Homelessness)

**Civil War and Slavery**
*A School for Pompey Walker* (Literacy)
*Pink and Say* (Social Change)

**1870–1910**
*A Different Kind of Hero* (Immigrants)
*Indian School: Teaching the White Man's Way* (Literacy)
*Oranges on Golden Mountain* (Immigrants)
*Prairie School* (Literacy)
*Rodzina* (Hunger and Homelessness)
*They Came from the Bronx: How the Buffalo Were Saved from Extinction* (Animals in Danger)
*A Train to Somewhere* (Hunger and Homelessness)

**World War I**
*After the Dancing Days* (Community Safety)
*Charlie Wilcox* (Community Safety)
*When Christmas Comes Again: The World War I Diary of Simone Spencer* (Community Safety)

**1920s**
*Orphan Train Rider: One Boy's True Story* (Hunger and Homelessness)
*Jemma's Journey* (Social Change)
*White Lilacs* (Social Change)

**The Depression—1930s**
*The Gardener* (Gardening)
*Butterflies and Lizards, Beryl and Me* (Gardening)
*Potato: A Tale from the Great Depression* (Hunger and Homelessness)
*Esperanza Rising* (Immigrants)
*The Strength of Saints* (Literacy)

**World War II**
*The Victory Garden* (Gardening)
*The Yellow Star: The Legend of King Christian X of Denmark* (Community Safety)
*Passage to Freedom: The Sugihara Story* (Social Change)
*Slap Your Sides* (Social Change)
*Boxes for Katje* (Community Safety)
*Bat 6* (Social Change)

**Civil Rights**
*Richard Wright and the Library Card* (Literacy)
*Tomás and the Library Lady* (Literacy)
*Goin' Someplace Special* (Literacy)
*A Bus of Our Own* (Literacy)
*Through My Eyes* (Social Change)
*Linda Brown, You Are Not Alone: The Brown v. Board of Education Decision* (Social Change)

# *Part Two:* Service Learning Themes

# AIDS EDUCATION AND AWARENESS

> I said education was our "basic weapon."
> Actually, it's our only weapon. We've got
> to educate everyone about the disease
> so that each person can take responsibility
> for seeing that it is spread no further.
> C. EVERETT KOOP, FORMER U.S. SURGEON GENERAL

Education is the primary prescription for preventing the spread of HIV and AIDS. With education, we can equip youth for the challenges that confront not only them and their society but our global population. In this continually shrinking world, our neighbors are no longer just the folks down the block; they now include the peoples of Africa, Asia, and South America, where the numbers of people who are HIV positive or living with AIDS are increasing at a staggering rate. Even with medical advances in more affluent countries, the problem is far from being under control. Consider these facts:

- More than 2,000 children are infected with HIV each day worldwide.[1]
- In the United States, it is estimated that two adolescents are infected with HIV each hour.[2]
- More than 6,000 young people between the ages of 15 and 24 become infected with HIV every day. *That is about four young people every minute.*[3]
- There are approximately 11 million children in Africa who have been orphaned by AIDS.[4]
- More than 95 percent of people with HIV live in the developing world.[5]

In our uncertain world, we can help young people deal with facts like these by providing information, resources, and prevention strategies. We can equip them to make healthy personal choices, be advocates for a healthy society, and promote well-being in all parts of the world. We must be involved, continue to create educational opportunities based on current information and resources, help young people separate fact from fiction, and act for prevention.

## Preparation: Getting Ready for Service Learning Involving AIDS Education and Awareness

The following activities can be used in the preparation stage to promote learning and skill development related to HIV and AIDS education and awareness. These activities can be used with different age ranges during preparation to help your students examine key issues through research, analyze community needs, and gain the knowledge they need to effectively contribute to the design of their service plan. Since literature is often an important part of preparation, you can find recommended titles on this theme in the AIDS Education and Awareness Bookshelf later in this chapter.

***Activity: Understanding Leads to Action.*** Providing age-appropriate information helps students gain knowledge that can lead to action. For young children up to third grade, AIDS education is often included with information concerning other health problems. The emphasis is on staying healthy—eating well and getting adequate exercise and sleep.

[1] *Report on the Global HIV/AIDS Epidemic: December 2002,* UNAIDS Joint United Nations Programme on HIV/AIDS
[2] *Youth Report 2000—White House Office of National AIDS Policy*
[3] *Young People and HIV/AIDS: Opportunity in Crisis—A Joint Report by UNICEF, UNAIDS and WHO*
[4] *UNAIDS Fact Sheet 2002, Sub-Saharan Africa,* UNAIDS Joint United Nations Programme on HIV/AIDS
[5] *AIDS Epidemic Update: December 2002,* UNAIDS Joint United Nations Programme on HIV/AIDS

Children are also often taught to differentiate between communicable and noncommunicable diseases. While most children know they can "catch" a cold, young children can be assured that being friends and playing with a child who is HIV positive or living with AIDS is safe.

Young people can also have great empathy for people who are in the hospital or who are taken to emergency rooms or clinics. By revisiting their own experiences with being sick or going to the doctor's office, students can come up with ideas to reach out to others who are affected by HIV or AIDS. Guide your students' empathy with readings from the bookshelf, research, and class discussions. Start looking for organizations in your community that work with people living with HIV or AIDS or who are working to stop the spread of AIDS. Early collaborations with these kinds of agencies can help students develop project ideas that meet real local, or even global, needs. Project ideas that could result include:

- younger students writing "Have a Good Day" greeting cards to be inserted in lunches to be delivered to people living with HIV or AIDS
- making blankets for babies living with HIV or AIDS
- collecting materials for, assembling, and decorating holiday gift baskets for people living with AIDS
- developing programs to replace myths about HIV and AIDS with accurate information
- older students helping to assemble and deliver meals, providing pet care, or participating in other forms of outreach to people living with HIV or AIDS.

***Activity: Discussion and Research.*** Through reading, students can continue to learn about the ever-changing world of education, research, and prevention of AIDS. What is the most current information regarding the spread of HIV and AIDS, strategies for prevention, and the search for a cure? Students can begin by reading one of the nonfiction books listed in this chapter, such as *When Plague Strikes: The Black Death, Smallpox, AIDS*, discussing it in small groups, and generating questions. If needed, you can add any of the following to their list:

- How much funding is allocated to research?
- Do socioeconomic factors affect who is getting treatment for AIDS and what treatments are available?
- How do developing countries cope with the spread of HIV and AIDS?
- What populations are most susceptible to contracting HIV and AIDS?
- What are the resources for children, particularly in developing countries where many have the disease or have been orphaned by it?

In groups, students can use the Internet, newspapers and journals, and local organizations to find answers to these questions and can then share their findings. This research can help students determine what would be a worthwhile and meaningful activity to assist people in the community or in other parts of the world who are affected by HIV or how to educate others to stop the spread of AIDS.

**Find Out More About AIDS Education and Awareness**

To learn more about these issues and to get ideas for service and action, visit these Web sites and organizations online:

***www.nylc.org*** At the National Youth Leadership Council Web site, click on their HIV/AIDS and Service Learning Initiative to promote youth involvement in organizations at home and abroad in finding solutions to this global pandemic.

***www.unicef.org/programme/hiv/overview.htm*** UNICEF works closely with national governments, nongovernmental organizations, and other United Nations agencies to improve the lives of children, youth, and women.

***www.kff.org/worldaidsday*** The Kaiser Family Foundation serves as a resource for information about HIV/AIDS policy, public opinion and knowledge about the disease, and media-based partnerships, plus the annual Worlds AIDS Day.

***www.cdc.gov/hiv/dhap.htm*** The Centers for Disease Control is a good source for current information and statistics on HIV and AIDS. They have a Frequently

*continued* ⟶

Asked Questions section that answers general questions about what causes AIDS, how it's transmitted, and how it can be prevented. It also has a page devoted to debunking common hoaxes and rumors about HIV and AIDS.

# Making Connections Across the Curriculum

Some service learning activities naturally lend themselves to interdisciplinary work and making connections across the curriculum. These connections strengthen and broaden student learning, helping them meet academic standards. More than likely, you'll be looking for these connections and ways to encourage them well before the students ever start working on service learning activities. As with the entire service learning process, it helps to remain flexible, because some connections can be spontaneously generated by the questions raised throughout and by the needs of the project. To help you think about cross-curricular connections and where you can look for them, the Curricular Web for this chapter (page 69) gives examples of many different ways this theme can be used in different academic areas. (The service learning scenarios in the next section of the chapter also demonstrate various ways this theme can be used across the curriculum.)

# Service Learning Scenarios:
## Ideas for Action

Ready to take action? What follows are projects that have been successfully carried out by elementary, middle, or high school students. Most of these scenarios and examples explicitly include some aspects of preparation, action, reflection, and demonstration. These scenarios can be a rich source of project, resource, and curriculum ideas for you to draw upon. While the grade levels are given as a reference, most project ideas can be adapted to suit younger or older students, and many are suitable for cross-age partnerships.

***International Support and Learning: Grades 1–12.*** Through classroom studies, students in Maryland learned about the history, geography, and population of Malawi, a country in southeastern Africa, where approximately 500,000 children under the age of 15 have lost their parents to AIDS. A partnership with the American Red Cross enabled the students to help these children attend school. Attending school in Malawi is free but only possible if you bring your own supplies. The Red Cross provided a list of items needed and an "International School Chest" to fill with paper, pens, markers, jump ropes, and other essentials. Three hundred chests were filled in one state. Students at an alternative high school made jump ropes; they tooled the wood with designs and measured the ropes. At another school, students made a mural about Africa. The result: international awareness and more children in Malawi were able to attend school.

***Blankets for Babies: Grade 4.*** Fourth-grade students took turns bringing in news articles for class discussion. One student brought an article about babies born with AIDS. The class agreed they wanted to help in some way and decided to make baby blankets. They looked at pictures of quilts made by pioneer women and decided to use similar patterns for decoration. Using soft fabric and fabric markers, they worked with geometric patterns in soothing colors. A parent volunteer sewed the edges, and the completed blankets went on "tour" in the school to teach others about this important subject. Students created minilessons to make their classroom presentations interactive. They received a letter of thanks from the organization that received the blankets.

***Teaching Respect: Grade 5.*** After learning about people being mistreated because of illnesses such as AIDS, fifth-grade students considered various ways to get across a message of respect for all people. They decided to create a comic book character who would teach younger children to be thoughtful toward people living with HIV or AIDS. After consulting with a local health organization, students developed several story lines, combined them into one magazine, and made copies for younger children. These were distributed in school and at a community health fair.

***Using the AIDS Memorial Quilt: Grade 7.*** While studying ways to prevent HIV infection and AIDS, two middle school classes in Pennsylvania decided to bring information to the community. After learning about the AIDS Memorial Quilt—an ongoing community art project that includes more than 44,000

# AIDS Education and Awareness Across the Curriculum

### *English/Language Arts*
- Discuss the importance of friendship with children who are living with HIV or AIDS
- Read written material from a clinic offering HIV/AIDS prevention information and adapt to a teen or younger child's version
- Study the impact of media coverage, entertainment, and/or mass marketing campaigns to eliminate misconceptions about people living with HIV or AIDS

### *Social Studies/History*
- Create an AIDS historical timeline
- Study medieval history and the pattern of scapegoating (irrational intolerance toward certain people or groups) during plagues
- Compare approaches to AIDS prevention by different governments

### *Languages*
- Find out how HIV/AIDS impacts countries internationally
- Read HIV/AIDS information in the language being studied as prepared by different countries
- Translate HIV/AIDS prevention information for community organizations and outreach

### *Theater, Music, & Visual Arts*
- Research how theater and storytelling have been used to teach about social issues, including AIDS awareness in the United States and abroad
- Find out how music has influenced HIV/AIDS prevention both through fund-raisers and messages in songs
- Examine how the AIDS Memorial Quilt has grown as an international art project

## AIDS Education and Awareness

### *Math*
- Research the cost of hospital stays for various ailments
- Graph the funds allocated by governments to research and prevent HIV/AIDS
- Review the statistics of HIV and AIDS by age and sex

### *Physical Education*
- Research the role of exercise in healthy living
- Have a physical therapist demonstrate adaptive exercise programs
- Create a simplified exercise protocol for children or teens who have health limitations

### *Computer*
- Design pocket-size information cards with community health resource information
- Create a multimedia presentation on an HIV/AIDS related subject
- Use the Internet to learn how African nations are responding to the AIDS crises

### *Science*
- Learn about the body's regulatory and immune systems and healthy life habits
- Interview doctors at local health clinic about epidemics
- Research the transmission factors that put youth at risk

three-by-six-foot memorial panels, each commemorating a person who has died from AIDS—they wanted to participate. After receiving names and biographies from eleven individuals who died from AIDS and were not yet represented in the quilt, the students made and contributed eleven panels. They mastered sewing, silk screening, and the art of gathering and recycling assorted fabrics and materials. Students proudly displayed their artwork to the community.

***Informational Brochures: Grade 8.*** An English teacher read *Too Far Away to Touch* to his middle school students to stimulate a conversation about HIV and AIDS in our society. This sparked a lengthy discussion of personal experiences involving both losses and new research. Students were allowed to choose a project that would involve developing and using persuasive writing skills, and they decided to help break down some of the myths surrounding AIDS. They found an HIV/AIDS quiz on the Internet and got permission to use it as a teaching tool. Working in small groups, they created brochures, which included the quiz, and informational packets that were used in several schools in their area.

> Once every generation, history brings us
> to an important crossroad. Sometimes in life
> there is that moment when it's possible
> to make a change for the better.
> This is one of those moments.
>
> ELIZABETH GLASER,
> FOUNDER OF THE PEDIATRIC AIDS FOUNDATION

***Building Awareness: Grade 9.*** Using *AIDS: Can This Epidemic Be Stopped?* plus Internet research, high school students in Oakland, California, worked in small groups to plan a series of activities concerning issues affecting people with HIV/AIDS. They conducted an Awareness Day with speakers, in-class workshops, and presentations; prepared a short unit to teach in a ninth-grade health class; and wrote an editorial to the local paper advocating greater respect for persons living with HIV/AIDS.

***Tolerance Campaign: Grade 10.*** Reading *When Plague Strikes: The Black Death, Smallpox, AIDS* as a class text, students in Minnesota learned how people have been blamed for the spread of diseases throughout history. A parallel study emerged of ways in which some teens were scapegoats in their school. Students formed strategy groups to plan campaigns to help eliminate the ridicule and harassment that undermines confidence and isolates their peers. Strategies included public service announcements, meetings with administrators to discuss policy issues, a proposal for "safe school guidelines," and a "teach-in" devoted to music and poetry about building tolerance among teens. The students conducted a survey to find out how the school population was responding to their efforts. The survey indicated that a substantial number of students had become more thoughtful about their actions and were also more likely to interrupt disrespectful actions by their friends.

***Get Cookin': Grade 10.*** A local organization relied on volunteers to prepare and deliver food six days per week to people living with HIV and AIDS. A group of students helped over a holiday break and then decided to recruit their peers to help more often. Eight classes signed up to help on a rotating basis to cook and package the food. They learned about careers in nutrition and food services while discovering there are many people in their community willing to help their neighbors.

***Taking a Stand for Youth Voice: High School.*** Students have a vested interest in participating in developing ideas and strategies to help teens avoid HIV and AIDS. This was the position of high school students in upstate New York as they requested positions on a school district AIDS advisory committee. After making a strong case to the local school board, with a concerted expression of ideas and ways they truly "represent the voice of youth," several students (identified by the youth) were appointed to the advisory group.

***Teams for Understanding: High School.*** High school students who were HIV positive or who were living with AIDS collaborated with uninfected peers to form speaking teams to teach middle and high school youth about the disease. With guidance from professionals, students developed basic scripts and practiced public speaking skills. They rehearsed with their classes how to respond to questions and developed a handout with facts, figures, myths, truths, and Web sites to provide more information.

***Theater Works: High School.*** After research and study, and with guidance from local AIDS activists, high school students in northern Missouri prepared and presented skits depicting youth in situations requiring that choices be made. Because the skits called for audience participation, debate and discussion followed. Through performance, the students hoped to reinforce healthy behavior, give strategies for dealing with peer pressure, and promote community awareness. Ongoing role playing and reflection helped the actors to refine their skills and deal with challenging teaching situations and audience reactions.

***Learning About Policy and Speaking Out: High School.*** Youth activists attended an international AIDS conference to make their voices heard, since 50 percent of new HIV infections worldwide occur among youth ages 15–24*. Through workshops, students learned about policy and current strategies. They returned to their communities to write articles for the school paper, form study groups, and help design an informational brochure about confidential testing for a local AIDS prevention organization.

> A pitcher cries for water to carry
> And a person for work that is real.
> FROM *TO BE OF USE* BY MARGE PIERCY, POET

***A Mural to Remember: High School.*** Fifteen participants in a New York City youth program whose lives had been touched by AIDS designed a mural to face a busy city street. The entire teen group then helped to paint and create this 150-foot long, 10-foot tall masterpiece, unveiled to the community on World AIDS Day. Elected officials, community members, parents, and friends gathered to see the art and hear the poetry written by these young people.

## The AIDS Education and Awareness Bookshelf

The AIDS Education and Awareness Bookshelf contains a modest number of selections compared with other themes. Still, these selections represent a range of opportunities to learn and develop meaningful service connections. To help you find books relevant to your particular projects, the book chart classifies the titles into several topic areas: historical overview, our stories, and relationships.

In general, the bookshelf features:

- An annotated bibliography arranged and alphabetized by title according to the general categories of nonfiction (N), picture books (P), and fiction (F). For nonfiction and fiction, length and recommended grade levels are included. The entries in the picture book category do not include suggested grade levels, since they can be successfully used with all ages.
- A chart organized by topic and category to help you find books relevant to particular projects.
- Recommendations from service learning colleagues and experts that include a book summary and ideas for service learning connections. (The number of recommended books varies in each bookshelf.)

> From what we get, we can make a living;
> what we give, however, makes a life.
> ARTHUR ASHE, ATHLETE

*Listen, Learn, Live! World AIDS Campaign with Children and Young People: Facts and Figures*, UNAIDS Joint United Nations Programme on HIV/AIDS

## AIDS Education and Awareness Bookshelf Topics

| Topics | Books | Category |
|---|---|---|
| ***Historical Overview*** What do we already know about this disease that continues to spread at an alarming rate? | *AIDS* | N |
| | *AIDS: Can This Epidemic Be Stopped?* | N |
| | *A Life Like Mine: How Children Live Around the World* * (see page 196) | N |
| | *People with AIDS* | N |
| | *When Plague Strikes: The Black Death, Smallpox, AIDS* | N |
| ***Our Stories*** The voices of the people living with HIV or AIDS or those close to people who are infected add personal experience to the facts and statistics. | *Be a Friend: Children Who Live with HIV Speak* * | N |
| | *A Small, Good Thing: Stories of Children with HIV and Those Who Care for Them* ‡ | N |
| | *You Can Call Me Willy: A Story for Children About AIDS* | P |
| ***Relationships*** Meaningful relationships demonstrate the caring response of family and community to the AIDS crisis. Learning of these interactions reminds us to reach out and create similar relationships. | *Alex, the Kid with AIDS* | P |
| | *Earthshine* | F |
| | *Far and Beyon'* | F |
| | *Too Far Away to Touch* | P |

Page references are given for books that do not appear in the AIDS Education and Awareness Bookshelf but that can be found in the bookshelf lists of other chapters.

* These books include examples of young people in service-providing roles.

‡ These books are out of print but still worth finding.

## Nonfiction: AIDS Education and Awareness

***AIDS*** by Lori Shein (Lucent Books, 1998). This overview of AIDS from the late 1970s to the late 1990s includes information about its discovery, methods of prevention, testing for HIV infection, the global epidemic, and what the future holds. Includes a glossary and resources. 112pp., young adult

***AIDS: Can This Epidemic Be Stopped?*** by Karen Manning (Henry Holt, 1995). This book provides a history and medical overview of the epidemic. While many advances have been made since publication, the information remains useful for a solid background. Includes resource information and a glossary. 64pp., grades 5–7

***Be a Friend: Children Who Live with HIV Speak*** by Dr. Lori S. Wiener, Aprille Best, and Dr. Phillip A. Pizzo (Albert Whitman, 1994). A moving collection of art and writings by children who are HIV positive or have siblings with AIDS. Each letter uncovers the emotion and courage of young people who just want to be normal and have friends who will stay friends. *All proceeds are donated to the Pediatric AIDS Foundation*. 40pp., all ages

***People with AIDS*** by Gail B. Stewart (Lucent Books, 1996). Following an introduction with facts and a brief overview are four profiles, three of adults and one of an eight-year-old. The candid stories remind us of the people who often get lost with the label. Darrel collects masks and is a popular speaker about AIDS. Cindy unknowingly passed the AIDS virus to her son, who died. Jessica has outlived her mother. Stephen lives "day by day" with support from friends. 96pp., grades 6–12

***A Small, Good Thing: Stories of Children with HIV and Those Who Care for Them*** by Anne Hunsacker Hawkins (W.W. Norton, 2000). Children born with HIV are often an overlooked group. These six portraits, developed through extensive interviews and observations, present both the overwhelming obstacles and the community support provided for these young people. The book is a vivid, life-affirming depiction of the caretakers and the effects of this disease. Out of print, but still worth finding. 286pp., grades 10–12

> Maria and several other children in our clinic have experienced a reversal of fortune, surviving well beyond expectation. But the future for these children—one, three, or seven years hence—is unpredictable and uncertain. . . . The best hope of breaking what seems a cycle of predestined tragedy is that they will come to accept, even embrace, an ethic founded on loving responsibility to others.
>
> FROM *A SMALL, GOOD THING: STORIES OF CHILDREN WITH HIV AND THOSE WHO CARE FOR THEM*

***When Plague Strikes: The Black Death, Smallpox, AIDS*** by James Cross Giblin (HarperCollins, 1995). This compelling study of three deadly epidemics, separated by centuries, shows the similarity of social, political, and cultural reactions. Each disease brought medical advances. At the same time, in each case, blame was placed on people where none was deserved. The insights into the human condition are as provocative as the studies of history and medical advances. 212pp., grades 6–12

## Picture Books:

### AIDS Education and Awareness

***Alex, the Kid with AIDS*** by Linda Walvoord Girard (Albert Whitman, 1991). Michael tells of his growing friendship with Alex, a new kid in fourth grade with AIDS. Alex turns out to be a funny, friendly guy, who learns pretty quickly that their teacher requires proper behavior from everyone in the class.

***Too Far Away to Touch*** by Lesléa Newman (Clarion, 1995). Little Zoe and her Uncle Leonard enjoy adventures together. While at the Planetarium, Zoe asks, "How far away are the stars?" "Too far away to touch, close enough to see," her uncle answers. When Leonard becomes weaker due to AIDS, the message from the Planetarium has special meaning.

***You Can Call Me Willy: A Story for Children About AIDS*** by Joan C. Verniero (Magination Press, 1995). Willy tells about her life with AIDS. She describes the care she receives from her grandmother, her best friend, and other adults. Most of all, she wants to have friends and play baseball.

## Fiction: AIDS Education and Awareness

***Earthshine*** by Theresa Nelson (Orchard, 1994). Twelve-year-old "Slim" has to attend a support group for kids whose parents are living with AIDS. Her adoration for her father, a charismatic actor, is well-deserved. Even as he is dying from AIDS, his charm, humor, and love keep her spirits high at the most fragile of times. Now, Isaiah, a kid in this group, has an idea to head to the mountains for a "cure." Everyone goes for an adventure of a lifetime, and finds "magic." 192pp., young adult

***Far and Beyon'*** by Unity Dow (Aunt Lute Books, 2002). Set in Botswana, this novel draws from the author's experience in the women's rights struggle while sharing a contemporary family's loss due to AIDS. This is a family in conflict, both between and within individuals. At the center is Mora, age 17, who watched her two brothers die, and is torn between her ancestral traditions and the influence of western medicine and culture. After a pregnancy and an abortion, Mora returns to school, only to face the abuse of female students in the corrupt school system. But Mora takes a risk, and joined by other female students, makes a dramatic stand to stop the violence and obtain dignity. 199pp., Grades 9–12

# Interviews with Authors:

## The Story Behind the Story

In the following interviews, we find out the "story behind the story" from James Cross Giblin (*When Plague Strikes: The Black Death, Smallpox, AIDS*) and Lesléa Newman (*Too Far Away to Touch*). James Giblin's book captivated me because of its description of the scapegoating that occurred during three terrible plagues, as well as its depth of information. I was drawn to interview Lesléa Newman after reading *Too Far Away to Touch* aloud to high school students as they began planning an AIDS education project. The students were spellbound by the story and began to talk about their own experiences of loss.

### *James Cross Giblin,*
### *author of* When Plague Strikes: The Black Death, Smallpox, AIDS

I'm probably best known as a writer of nonfiction books for young people, but *When Plague Strikes* came from my work as an editor of children's books. In the mid-1980s, as editor-in-chief of Clarion Books, I knew and worked with two young, talented men, Gary Bargar and Ron

Wegen. Neither man knew the other; they lived in different parts of the country. Both died from AIDS in the summer of 1985. I had published two of Gary's novels and two picture books by Ron and was looking forward to working with both of them again. When they died within two weeks of one another, it struck me as so unfair. I began to think about AIDS in the context of two other plagues that had hit humankind through the centuries. How were they similar, and how did they differ? I realized the book I had in mind would be a major commitment, and I didn't feel ready to start writing it until almost a decade later, in the early 1990s. When it was finally finished I decided to dedicate the book to the two men who had inspired it: Gary and Ron.

Research reveals much that is provocative and surprising. For example, before I researched *When Plague Strikes* I didn't realize how religion had thwarted the development of medicine for centuries. Because the Catholic Church forbade the dissection of human bodies, doctors were stuck with what the Greeks, and to some extent the Arabs, had discovered hundreds of years earlier. Medical advancement was frozen, and this contributed to the spread of awful plagues like the Black Death and smallpox. People were not permitted to study medicine—everything was colored by religious interpretations and prohibitions.

Also, I didn't realize how scapegoating keeps rearing its ugly head when people are confronted with a plague like smallpox or AIDS. Whatever the crisis, people invariably feel the need to blame someone else—a scapegoat. This pattern struck me when I delved into the history of all three diseases.

On the other hand, I met remarkable people in the course of the research—women like Lady Mary Wortley Montague, who took the lead with her own son in testing the effects of inoculation as a protection against smallpox. She was far ahead of her time. Some of the people who surfaced during the AIDS epidemic were outstanding, too—men like Dr. C. Everett Koop, U.S. Surgeon General in the Reagan administration, who surprised his conservative backers when he urged that all kids be educated about AIDS.

Even if I feel emotional about the content, I try in my writing to simply lay out the facts. I would rather have the reader feel the shock and horror of people boarding up their neighbors in their own homes to prevent the spread of a disease than spend a lot of words editorializing about it. I believe a factual approach is far more effective in the long run.

My hope is that *When Plague Strikes* will provoke discussion. We need more thoughtful interchange, especially where social issues are concerned. I would hope a teacher, a parent, a librarian could get a conversation going about these plagues. A dialogue might start with a question: "What stood out for you in the section about smallpox?" for example. Other questions might be as simple as, "What did you find interesting?" or "What did you discover from reading about AIDS that you didn't know before?" Building on the participants' comments, the person leading the discussion could draw them out further.

I have heard of several splendid ideas for using *When Plague Strikes* with students. One imaginative teacher had her kids write poems about grief and examples of prejudice that they had observed in their community. I read one poem by a middle school girl whose favorite teacher had died of AIDS. The poem movingly conveyed her reactions. Another idea was to set up a mock town meeting where students as "townspeople' considered ways to halt the spread of the Black Death. Imagine a student arguing, "We should board up the victims' doors and windows so they won't be able to leave their houses." How would the other students at the gathering respond?

While the book was published in 1995, the foundations of each section are still valid today. But if I were writing about AIDS now, I'd add information about the drug "cocktails" that lessen the assault on the immune system and help to bolster the patient's white blood cell count. I'd expand the section about the tragic spread of AIDS in third world countries, especially in Africa. In the original edition, I refer to thousands of African children orphaned by AIDS, and unfortunately this is even more true now than it was then: Also, I would go further into the spread of AIDS in Eastern Europe, Russia, and Asia—regions of the world where there has been much social and political change. I would also weave in more about today's terrorist threat, including the possibility that disease could be used as a weapon in the wake of September 11. (A good exercise for students after reading the book would be to have them research and write new sections that they would like to see added in a revised edition.)

Above all, I hope the young people who pick up *When Plague Strikes* will find it a compelling read. Every good book, both fiction and nonfiction, contains a story line that unfolds in the natural progression of events. This is what makes a nonfiction book entertaining as well as informative.

I also hope the book's readers will gain a better understanding of how to deal with new threats concerning AIDS and acts of terrorism that employ deadly viruses. In the years to come, they're likely to confront many such threats. Books they've read like *When Plague Strikes* should help them to decide on the best and most intelligent ways to respond.

## Lesléa Newman, *author of*
### Too Far Away to Touch

*Too Far Away to Touch* was written after my friend Gerard died of AIDS. I was inconsolable. We'd been roommates at Naropa Institute in Boulder, Colorado, where we had studied poetics with writer Allen Ginsberg. Gerard was 32 years old.

When I feel such enormous grief, I am moved to a childlike state—a state of being utterly inconsolable and having a huge howl of grief inside. All I could do to console myself was to write a children's story. Something happens to me in the process of writing: I feel better. It also felt very satisfying to put that book into the world, because many children have lost a loved one to AIDS. My friend Gerard had nephews, and this book was read to these children who were so important to him. That was most satisfying for me.

The message of the book? Love never dies. People you love may die, but they will always be inside of you, and as you remember them, you keep them alive in your heart. There is also a message of hope, because Uncle Leonard is still alive at the end of the book. More often than not, characters living with AIDS in children's books die at the end of the story. This book was written in 1992 and published before many of the new drugs and drug combinations were developed. Today, because of these advancements, I am more hopeful. And while in the story Uncle Leonard says there is no cure for AIDS, there is still hope for him and his niece, Zoe.

Another more subtle message in the book concerns Uncle Leonard and his companion, Nathan. I purposely did not make a big deal about this relationship. There is a message here about how Uncle Leonard and Nathan love each other and take care of each other. Clearly, Uncle Leonard and Nathan are part of Zoe's family. Her mom sends her off with them to have an adventure. Inclusion and respect for each other are present in the lives of Zoe's family members; it is not questioned.

I see this book as being particularly meaningful for children who have relatives who are sick or have died from AIDS or any other disease. For children who have no experience with people with AIDS or another serious illness, the story puts a human face on illness: Uncle Leonard is a person with a full life, he loves his niece, and he happens to be sick.

Children can get involved in helping people living with AIDS in many ways. With adult support, children can volunteer with people who need company and who want to be read to. Children can help walk dogs, deliver meals, and provide companionship. For children, this would be a wonderful opportunity to get to know a person who they might not meet otherwise and to do something that is helpful.

CHAPTER 5

# ANIMALS IN DANGER

> Every individual matters. Every individual has a role to play. Every individual makes a difference. And we have a choice: What sort of difference do we want to make?
>
> JANE GOODALL, FROM *THE CHIMPANZEES I LOVE: SAVING THEIR WORLD AND OURS*

Nature is all about balance, and maintaining a desirable balance in nature depends on the survival of a web of species. Yet animals are threatened everywhere by human development that encroaches on natural habitats and disrupts migratory patterns. Honoring the symbiotic relationship among the species requires awareness, education, and action. If we are to prevent extinction and preserve biological diversity, it is important to understand our options while they still exist.

Children seem to be naturally drawn to animals, eager to learn about the Asian elephant, blue whale, and giant armadillo. It often surprises students that animals in their own region may be rare, threatened, vulnerable, or endangered. When they find out about such situations, they are usually eager to get involved. As they observe, compare and contrast, categorize, analyze, and report findings about animals in their own backyards or regions, young people develop scientific inquiry practices and apply their knowledge. The controversies that students may come across in their research can enliven social studies, civics, and government classes and familiarize them with local and national advocacy groups.

## Preparation: Getting Ready for Service Learning Involving Animals in Danger

The following activities can be used in the preparation stage to promote learning and skill development related to endangered animals. These activities can be used with different age ranges during preparation to help your students examine key issues through research, analyze community needs, and gain the knowledge they need to effectively contribute to the design of their service plan. Since literature is often an important part of preparation, you can find recommended titles on this theme in the Animals in Danger Bookshelf later in this chapter.

***Activity: Beginning with the Buffalo.*** Most students are familiar with the majestic buffalo that roamed the plains of the Old West. What students may not know is how these animals were saved from extinction through human intervention. Have students read (or read aloud to students) *They Came from the Bronx: How the Buffalo Were Saved from Extinction* to learn about the American Bison Society, which was established in 1905 at the Bronx Zoo to return a "mother herd" to the wild. Then have students conduct research to find out about the endangered animals in their own region. They can contact government agencies or animal protection groups (such as the ones listed on page 77) and use the Internet to begin their investigation about what animals are at risk and why. In groups, students can then select an animal to study in more detail. They might ask: Why are these animals important? What do they need to survive? What is happening that is harmful to them? How can people protect them? Students can also find out what other young people are doing to help save endangered species. They can share their knowledge with peers, put on displays in public venues such as libraries and community centers, and write articles and editorials for school and local newspapers to tell the public about what they can do to protect the endangered animals.

***Activity: Assisting in Wildlife Rehabilitation.*** Wildlife rehabilitators rescue and care for animals and then release them back to the wild. Young people have been of great assistance to the local nonprofit organizations doing this important work. Students can conduct research in their region to find any such agencies and establish an ongoing relationship with them.

How can youth be involved with wildlife rehabilitation? Author Shannon K. Jacobs, in the book *Healers of the Wild*, offers these suggestions for ways to get started helping rehabilitation centers and protecting animals in the wild:

- Ask for a "wish list" from local rehabilitators. A variety of activities can result when students find out needs and start looking for ways to meet them. They could collect supplies by gathering donated produce daily from grocery stores, picking up fallen fruit under fruit trees and unwanted produce from community gardens, or organizing donations from the community of other supplies the rehabilitation center may need.
- Ask what kinds of help the rehabilitation center needs. They may need help cleaning cages at a rehabilitation center. Or perhaps they might welcome assistance with fundraising and publicity efforts, which could lead to students writing articles, letters to the editor, and press releases, or painting native animals for display or sale. Or perhaps their needs fall into a technical area and they would welcome students setting up and maintaining computer programs that assist with tracking volunteer hours, data about admission/discharge of animals, donations, and the budget.
- Do research and consult with rehabilitation experts, so that students can learn how to design and build birdhouses, bat houses, or cages for mammals.
- Research and consultation could also result in: school presentations and community programs about fascinating native wildlife and how to protect them; the creation of materials to help younger students develop compassion for wildlife; inviting wildlife rehabilitators to speak at school; or the design and organization of a cleanup campaign to pick up litter from schoolyards, parks, and shorelines.

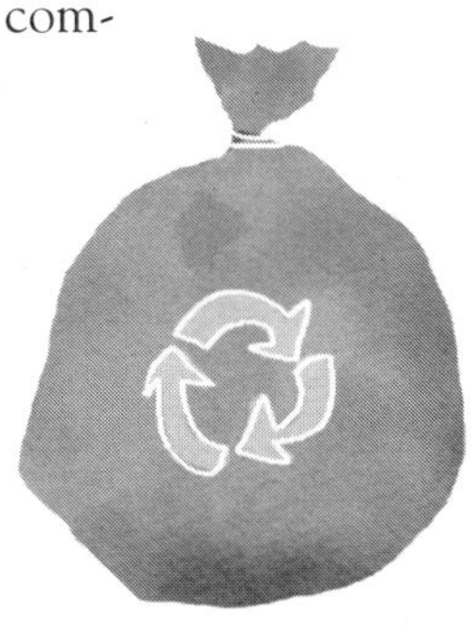

**Find Out More About Animals in Danger**

To learn more about these issues and to get ideas for service and action, visit these Web sites and organizations online:

***www.animaland.org*** This youth-oriented Web site of the American Society for the Prevention of Cruelty to Animals (ASPCA) offers a range of educational information and resources from domestic pet care to lists of endangered animals to "real issues" and ideas for student action.

***www.americanhumane.org/ev-public*** The special events section of the American Humane Society Web site offers resources and opportunities for involvement for both kids and adults.

***www.kidsplanet.org*** Kids' Planet is the youth Web site of Defenders of Wildlife, an organization dedicated to the protection of all native wild animals and plants in their natural communities. At this Web site you will find extensive information about endangered species all over the world.

***www.rootsandshoots.org*** Roots & Shoots is the Jane Goodall Institute's international environmental and humanitarian program for young people. One strand of the program is addressing care and concern for animals locally and globally.

## Making Connections Across the Curriculum

Some service learning activities naturally lend themselves to interdisciplinary work and making connections across the curriculum. These connections strengthen and broaden student learning, helping them meet academic standards. More than likely, you'll be looking for these connections and ways to encourage them well before the students ever start working on service learning activities. As with the entire service learning process, it helps to remain flexible, because some connections can be spontaneously generated by the questions raised throughout and by the needs of the project. To help you think about cross-curricular connections and where you can look for them, the Curricular Web for this chapter (page 78) gives examples of many different ways this theme can be used in different academic areas. (The service learning scenarios in the next section of the chapter also demonstrate ways this theme can be used across the curriculum.)

# Animals in Danger Across the Curriculum

### *English/Language Arts*

- Find books to read to younger children that teach respect for animals
- Create an ABC book of endangered animals and ways to help
- Write essays from the perspective of endangered animals seeking human assistance

### *Social Studies/History*

- Visit an animal shelter or zoo to learn about its role in the community
- Research the government agencies that oversee endangered animals
- Learn about the Progressive Era (1890–1913) and the inception of organizations to protect animals

### *Languages*

- Find out about animal rescue projects run by kids in different countries and correspond by email
- Create multilingual informational brochures about a local endangered animal
- Make presentations to other classes in the language being learned on a topic related to protecting animals

### *Theater, Music, & Visual Arts*

- Write and perform plays with animals as characters teaching about their care or how to protect them
- Learn and perform songs that show respect for animals and nature
- Using drawing, painting, photography, or any visual art medium, create an art show of animals in both dangerous and protected environments

## Animals in Danger

### *Math*

- Develop a budget for the weekly cost of pet care
- Study the math concepts used to build small animal shelters or create a bird habitat
- Compare statistics on changes in the status of an endangered animal

### *Physical Education*

- Do exercises that you've developed or drawn from yoga or other movement systems, that mimic the ways animals naturally move
- Learn how domesticated animals are affected when they don't get exercise
- Conduct research locally to find community needs for animal walkers or runners

### *Computer*

- Find out how computers are used to track migratory patterns
- Create a Web site to help advertise and promote pet adoption
- Research and inform classes about Web sites with information about endangered animals

### *Science*

- Research pet care, including nutrition, physiology, and psychology; also learn about and compare to their relations in the wild
- Learn about endangered animals in your region and groups that work to rescue and restore
- Visit a natural wildlife habitat to make observations, learn about the ecosystems, and ways to protect the animals living there

# Service Learning Scenarios:
## Ideas for Action

Ready to take action? What follows are projects that have been successfully carried out by elementary, middle, or high school students. Most of these scenarios and examples explicitly include some aspects of preparation, action, reflection, and demonstration. These scenarios can be a rich source of project, resource, and curriculum ideas for you to draw upon. While the grade levels are given as a reference, most project ideas can be adapted to suit younger or older students, and many are suitable for cross-age partnerships.

***Animal Care: Kindergarten.*** Most children love animals and enjoy learning about how to provide them with the best possible care. Kindergarten children in Los Angeles listened to many books on animals, including *Nights of the Pufflings* and *One Day at Wood Green Animal Shelter.* An animal specialist and the owner of a hospital companion dog visited their classroom, and the children also took a field trip to visit an animal rescue organization. The children helped to plan and promote a school-wide project to collect old bedding for donation to the rescue group and made dog bandanas to be sold by the local Society for the Prevention of Cruelty to Animals.

***Ducks and Organic Rice: Grade 1 (with High School Partners).*** Wildlife-friendly agriculture in the Central Valley of California led to community partnerships on a river preserve where nearly a thousand acres of organic rice are farmed each year. After the rice is harvested in the fall, the fields are flooded, providing a superb habitat for migrating ducks, swans, geese, and cranes. In spring, ducks nest in the fields before they are plowed and planted. Five first-grade classes integrated a duck egg rescue project into their study of animal life cycles. Students visited the preserve wetlands in the fall, observing shorebirds and waterfowl. Over the next few months, the students learned about the life cycles of many types of animals. In April, just before plowing, the students returned to the preserve. Led by the farmer, with help from preserve staff, volunteers, and a high school biology class, first-grade students walked through the fields, rescuing several nests from the tractor. Eggs were taken back to school and hatched in incubators. Students kept incubation logs, plotted duckling growth and development, and read many duck- and bird-related stories and poems, including *Ducks Disappearing* and *Nights of the Pufflings*, a true story of very young children rescuing baby birds in Iceland. Office and administrative staff volunteered to help with weekend feeding duties. Volunteers working with the state waterfowl association raised the ducks during the summer. The ducks were then banded and released into the wild on the preserve. Not only did students have the opportunity to watch duck eggs hatch in their classrooms, they also participated in an environmental action project.

> If you think you're too small to have an impact, try going to sleep in a room with a mosquito.
>
> ANITA RODDICK, ACTIVIST AND FOUNDER OF THE BODY SHOP

***Zoo Story: Grade 2.*** A second-grade teacher in Santa Monica, California, connected community studies with her science theme of "living things" through a zoo project: students made "brain challenges" for primates. Research shows that animals are healthier when mentally active rather than bored. With student help, animals would be challenged to get food out of containers. The children eagerly agreed to assemble papier-mâché tubes and pine cones stuffed with food for primates. On their first zoo visit, the students learned about primates and zoo life. Back at school, they determined ways to collect supplies: paper tubes, sugar-free cereal, dried fruits, and pine cones. They distributed flyers about their project to school families and neighbors and decorated bins to collect donations at two local

supermarkets. The students researched and wrote reports on primates, made graphs to chart items received and needed, solved mathematical equations about what they could assemble, mimicked body movements of gorillas and lemurs, and determined methods for storing vast quantities of paper tubes. They discussed why they had more donations of recycled goods (tubes and pine cones) than of more costly items (sugar-free cereal and dried fruits). Then, on the second trip to the zoo, they worked with zoo educators to stuff food into paper tubes and cover them with papier-mâché and to put peanut butter and dried fruit into pine cones. Both sets of primates—those at the zoo and the children—mastered brain challenges through this project.

***Turtle Experts: Grade 3.*** Sometimes a teacher shares her passion with her students, and for one teacher in Los Angeles, the passion is turtles. Third-grade students read *Interrupted Journey: Saving Endangered Sea Turtles* and saw turtle videos. A box turtle was their class mascot. On the field trip to, yes, a local turtle museum, the docent admired the students' knowledge and asked them to make a museum kit that could be loaned to other classes before they come to visit. The third graders took the challenge and prepared a variety of teaching tools to help their peers learn about and appreciate turtles. The box containing the tools looked just like a turtle!

***Wildlife Habitat at School: Grade 5.*** As part of their fifth-grade science program, students in Mount Vernon, Washington, learned about the migratory patterns of birds in their region. They constructed bird nesting boxes and feeders to attract and support the birds. Parents joined students on weekends to construct the feeders just outside the classroom. As birds arrived, the students moved quietly to the windows to watch and logged their observations in notebooks. Art projects showed a greater awareness of colors and detail of these feathered guests, as well as a greater appreciation and knowledge of nature.

***Don't Mess with the Lizards: Grade 5.*** When it came time for fifth-grade students in San Angelo, Texas, to select an endangered animal to study, they wanted to learn about something close to their home. They chose the Texas long-horned lizard. After extensive research, students became experts on the subject and were invited to speak to a community college class and appear on local access cable television. To demonstrate their knowledge, they prepared "Don't Mess with the Texas Long-horned Lizard" kits, complete with a lizard constitution (linked to studying government) and ways to protect their green friends. The kits were distributed to every fifth-grade class in their school district.

***Interactive Learning Stations: Grades 6 and 7.*** Middle school students enjoyed a week-long educational experience learning about animal habitats. In small cooperative groups, the students then developed an educational program with interactive learning stations for elementary children. Using puppets, skits, and other attention-getting methods, the middle school "teachers" enjoyed enacting the different situations, such as "I am a salmon and this is what is happening to me!"

***Land and Water Appreciation: Grades 6–8.*** Taking advantage of its rural setting in Middleburg, Florida, a middle school developed environmental service learning projects to teach students personal responsibility and how to take care of natural resources. For example, students worked with the local water management district to maintain and develop a 900-acre nature preserve for public use. The students built an eagle observation site at the preserve so visitors could view an active nest from a safe distance and learn about eagle needs and habits. The experience helped students recognize the necessity for preserving precious land and water resources.

***International Exchange: Grade 7.*** Students visiting the Cosumnes River Preserve in central California in the fall and winter observed magnificent sandhill cranes that travel thousands of miles to winter in these wetlands. As the students learned about cranes and their amazing life story, wetland restoration efforts become even more significant. In class, students read about cranes from around the world, studied crane anatomy and physiology, and wrote stories and poems about the bird, which is a symbol of peace and beauty in many cultures. In collaboration with the International Crane Foundation, the students created over 200 pieces of artwork and poems to be displayed at the Sandhill Crane Festival in Ciego de Avila, Cuba. At the same time, they had the opportunity to contribute much-needed school supplies to Cuban children. Four local biologists and educators visited Cuba to collaborate with Cuban teachers on crane curriculum and to teach lessons on cranes and wetland conservation. Cuban elementary students got involved in service learning, joining biologists in the search for the rare and endangered Cuban sandhill cranes as part of the annual crane census. Students recorded sightings, crane behavior, and calls. (See *When Agnes Caws* on page 85 for a book connection.)

***Animal Enrichment Activities: Grades 7–9.*** Students in Trinidad and Tobago got together with experts from the local zoo to develop enrichment projects for the animals at the zoo. The students worked in teams and selected a variety of animals, from ocelots to otters. The group who chose otters created a feeding ring for a river otter and also purchased a ball for the otter to play with in the water. Students documented the animals' behavior before and after the enrichment activity was introduced. Stories from the book *A Pelican Swallowed My Head—and Other Zoo Stories* provide examples of how zoos help with animal preservation.

***Save Our Species: Grade 8.*** A middle school group focused its efforts on a local species with a declining population—the Channel Island fox, a small canine found on six of the eight California islands. They developed an Island fox sponsorship form, presented educational assemblies, and established an annual Fox Festival at the Santa Barbara Zoo. This dedicated group made a presentation to the school board, received numerous awards, and gained recognition from the city and the National Park Service.

***Lost Animals: Grade 9.*** A ninth-grade English class for remedial readers wrote a book called *What Happens When an Animal Gets Lost?* Working with the county animal shelter and the Society for the Prevention of Cruelty to Animals, the students developed educational materials stressing the importance of licensing and identification tags. They also taught kindergarten and second-grade classes and spoke on local television.

***Writing Children's Books: Grades 9–11.*** For an end-of-term high school biology class project, students have a choice of activities. The most popular was writing a story for children about an endangered or extinct species. The assignment was twofold: research what makes an engaging children's book, and learn enough about the chosen animal to make the book informative. The teacher used *Pipaluk and the Whales* and *Intimate Nature: The Bond Between Women and Animals* to show a variety of storytelling approaches. Students agreed to produce three copies—one to keep and two to donate to local schools or organizations of their choice. In their journals, students described this as a favorite activity.

***Pet Population Control: Grades 9–12.*** High school students described as "at risk" were working on strategies to improve reading and writing. Their teacher introduced them to the world of nonfiction through articles on local community problems related to pet overpopulation. They analyzed the articles to develop questions to help them write a report on the subject without plagiarizing. Questions generated included: Why is there a problem? What can be done? What are the consequences of too many cats and dogs? After practicing social skills, especially how to talk with adults, the students invited two speakers, an animal control officer and a veterinarian, to address the class. The students decided to develop lessons for kindergarten children, with each group focusing on a different problem: dog care, cat care, avoiding dog bites, and being respectful to wildlife. Students wrote and taught five lessons for each theme. To demonstrate what they had learned, students made a presentation with recommendations on pet overpopulation to the city council. Students also assisted at rabies clinics in the area, used Spanish language skills to teach people why they needed to spay or neuter pets, and made public service announcements in Spanish.

> Never doubt that a small group of thoughtful, committed citizens can change the world; indeed, it's the only thing that ever has.
>
> MARGARET MEAD, ANTHROPOLOGIST

***Pet Adoption Program: Grades 9–12.*** As part of a work experience program, developmentally disabled students in Massachusetts walked dogs and cleaned cages at an animal shelter. One student described the work to a high school teacher, who expressed interest in adopting a pet. This initiated a media campaign led by the developmentally disabled students to promote pet adoption within the school. To prepare, they received instruction in photography and videography from a class of students with behavioral and emotional problems. Using these technologies every week to photograph and videotape animals for posters and school cable television enhanced student learning both in skills and vocabulary. Many pets were adopted, and the students expanded the project to inform the broader community about the animal shelter adoption program.

***Science and Government Connections: Grades 10–12.*** What recreational activities threaten our endangered species or disturb sensitive habitats? High school students began to investigate this question in science classes, which led them to approach their government teacher for assistance. Through phone calls and email, students found state officials willing to provide information about state policy. They also partnered with local parks and recreation staff to prepare brochures on safe use of local recreation areas. Students made coloring books about the endangered animals in the area to be given to any young visitors coming to the park.

***Young Scientists: Grades 11 and 12.*** Science students in Crystal River, Florida, conducted surveys and collected data from government agencies regarding animal populations in a wetland area near the school to track the patterns of migratory wildlife. The students analyzed the information and distributed it in a brochure during an open house at school and at community environmental events. Extended activities also included helping with adoption and release of redfish, water protection programs, and demonstration lessons at primary schools. Ongoing partners included state parks, an animal hospital, a mariculture center, and government fish and wildlife agencies.

# The Animals in Danger Bookshelf

The Animals in Danger Bookshelf adds much to the process of finding out about threatened species. Through books such as *ChaseR* and *There's an Owl in the Shower,* students can read about other young people facing dilemmas and choices related to the balance of animals and humans. Other books, such as *Nights of the Pufflings*, make a case for young people's help in restoring that balance. To help you find books relevant to your particular projects, the book chart classifies the titles into several topic areas: for the future, rescue and restore, and caring relationships.

In general, the bookshelf features:

- An annotated bibliography arranged and alphabetized by title according to the general categories of nonfiction (N), picture books (P), and fiction (F). For nonfiction and fiction, length and recommended grade levels are included. The entries in the picture book category do not include suggested grade levels, since they can be successfully used with all ages.
- A chart organized by topic and category to help you find books relevant to particular projects.
- Recommendations from service learning colleagues and experts that include a book summary and ideas for service learning connections. (The number of recommended books varies in each bookshelf.)

## *Nonfiction: Animals in Danger*

***Can We Save Them?*** by David Dobson (Charlesbridge, 1997). Twelve species of endangered animals are featured, from the Florida panther to the Puerto Rican parrot to the ciu-ui fish of Truckee River, Nevada. Learn about present dangers and ways to restore natural environments. Filled with ideas for action. 30pp., grades K–6

***The Chimpanzees I Love: Saving Their World and Ours*** by Jane Goodall (Scholastic, 2001). Jane Goodall's personal narrative describes her many years of coming to know chimpanzees. Photographs show the chimpanzees living within their communities, relationships between mothers and babies, and a glimpse at how chimpanzees think. Strategies presented for taking action include learning about conservation and "showing care and concern: (1) for animals . . . ; (2) for the human community; (3) for the environment we all share." 80pp., all ages

# Animals in Danger Bookshelf Topics

| Topics | Books | Category |
|---|---|---|
| ***For the Future*** Books in this category discuss issues that we must think about as we consider how to protect animals from extinction. | *Can We Save Them?* | N |
| | *Issues in the Environment* (see page 131) | N |
| | *There's an Owl in the Shower* (see page 134) | F |
| ***Rescue and Restore*** Many organizations and individuals actively work to protect, rescue, and save animals from extinction, giving us models for our own work. Notice that young people are included among the activists. | *The Animal Rescue Club* * | F |
| | *Backyard Rescue* * | F |
| | *Cat Up a Tree* | P |
| | *Come Back, Salmon: How a Group of Dedicated Kids Adopted Pigeon Creek and Brought It Back to Life* * | N |
| | *Healers of the Wild* * | N |
| | *Hoot* * | F |
| | *In Good Hands: Behind the Scenes at a Center for Orphaned and Injured Birds* * | N |
| | *Interrupted Journey: Saving Endangered Sea Turtles* * | N |
| | *Nights of the Pufflings* * | N |
| | *Once a Wolf: How Wildlife Biologists Fought to Bring Back the Gray Wolf* | N |
| | *One Day at Wood Green Animal Shelter* * | N |
| | *On the Brink of Extinction: The California Condor* | N |
| | *A Pelican Swallowed My Head—and Other Zoo Stories* | N |
| | *Pipaluk and the Whales* * | P |
| | *Saving Lilly* * | F |
| | *They Came from the Bronx: How the Buffalo Were Saved from Extinction* | P |
| | *Washing the Willow Tree Loon* * | P |
| | *The Wheel on the School* | F |
| ***Caring Relationships*** This category includes stories, fiction and nonfiction, about people whose lives are touched by their animal neighbors. | *ChaseR: a novel in e-mails* | F |
| | *The Chimpanzees I Love: Saving Their World and Ours* | N |
| | *The Deliverance of the Dancing Bears* | P |
| | *Ducks Disappearing* | P |
| | *The Four Ugly Cats in Apartment 3D* * | F |
| | *Hey! Get Off Our Train* | P |
| | *Intimate Nature: The Bond Between Women and Animals* | N |
| | *Make Way for Ducklings* | P |
| | *Mr. Lincoln's Way* * (see page 99) | P |
| | *When Agnes Caws* | P |

Page references are given for books that do not appear in the Animals in Danger Bookshelf but that can be found in the bookshelf lists of other chapters.
* These books include examples of young people in service-providing roles.

***Come Back, Salmon: How a Group of Dedicated Kids Adopted Pigeon Creek and Brought It Back to Life*** by Molly Cone (Sierra Club Books, 1992). With teacher guidance, elementary students clean a stream, stock it with salmon, and preserve it as an unpolluted place where salmon can return to spawn. 48pp., grades 4–8

***Healers of the Wild*** by Shannon K. Jacobs (Johnson Books, 2003). In this comprehensive guide for young people and their families, schools, and communities, we learn about the valuable work of wildlife rehabilitators. As legal caregivers for wild animals, they heal hundreds of sick, orphaned, and injured animals every year and release them back to the wild. Learn more about rascally raccoons, Buddy the bald eagle, and the endangered ridley sea turtle. Find out what young people are doing across the country to assist in rehabilitation. A glossary and reproducible pages are included. 212pp., all ages

***In Good Hands: Behind the Scenes at a Center for Orphaned and Injured Birds*** by Stephen R. Swinburne (Sierra Club, 1998). Hannah, a sixteen-year-old volunteer, cares for injured owls, hawks, eagles, and other birds of prey, as they are nursed back to health and eventually released. 32pp., grades 3–8

***Interrupted Journey: Saving Endangered Sea Turtles*** by Kathryn Lasky (Candlewick Press, 2001). Comprehensive text and photographs depict the dedicated work of volunteers and professionals protecting endangered sea turtles, particularly Kemp's ridley turtles. From ten-year-old Max and his mother, who patrol Cape Cod's beaches, to veterinarians, to a hotel owner who turns his pool into an aquarium, we see people who make a difference in a variety of ways. 48pp., all ages

***Intimate Nature: The Bond Between Women and Animals*** edited by Linda Hogan, Deena Metzger, and Brenda Peterson (Fawcett Columbine, 1998). In this collection of stories, poetry, and essays, women scientists and writers speak out about their kinship with animals. The readings are simultaneously a wake-up call and celebration of this "ancient . . . dialogue between species." The seventy contributors include Barbara Kingsolver, Jane Goodall, Diane Fossey, and Marge Piercy. 455pp., young adult

> She communicated in sign language, using a vocabulary of over 1,000 words. She also understands spoken English, and often carries on "bilingual" conversations, responding in sign to questions asked in English. She is learning the letters of the alphabet, and can read some printed words, including her own name. . . . She laughs at her own jokes and the jokes of others. . . . The person I have described—and she is nothing less than a person to those who are acquainted with her—is Koko, a twenty-year-old lowland gorilla.
>
> FROM "THE CASE FOR THE PERSONHOOD OF GORILLAS" IN *INTIMATE NATURE: THE BOND BETWEEN WOMEN AND ANIMALS*

***Nights of the Pufflings*** by Bruce McMillan (Houghton Mifflin, 1995). Travel to Heimaey Island, Iceland, where children stay up all night when the pufflings are ready to take flight for the first time. Many birds, confused by the village lights, head toward town instead of the open sea. The children rescue the birds from the dangers of cats and cars and set them on their proper course. 32pp., grades K–4

***Once a Wolf: How Wildlife Biologists Fought to Bring Back the Gray Wolf*** by Stephen R. Swinburne (Houghton Mifflin, 1999). With rare and powerful photographs, the reader follows a study that led to heightened appreciation of the magnificent gray wolf and its reintroduction into Yellowstone National Park. 48pp., grades K–3

***One Day at Wood Green Animal Shelter*** by Patricia Casey (Candlewick Press, 2001). The author describes a busy day at this shelter, where volunteers of all ages care for dogs, cats, a curious fox, a gecko, a horse, and a baby pigeon named Roast Potato. The visuals are a mix of art and photo collage—a unique blend to inspire the creative author/illustrator in us all. 29pp., grades K–6

***On the Brink of Extinction: The California Condor*** by Caroline Arnold (Harcourt, 1993). Follow the California Condor Recovery Team as they attempt to restore the North American condor population by breeding these birds in captivity. An easy-to-read story of survival; includes photographs. 48pp., grades 4–8

***A Pelican Swallowed My Head—and Other Zoo Stories*** by Edward Ricciuti (Simon & Schuster, 2002). The Wildlife Conservation Society runs the Bronx Zoo in New York City and has programs to save endangered species in more than fifty countries. These amazing stories explain the work of dedicated individuals at the zoo who create safe sanctuaries and natural habitats for lovable gorillas, Andean condors (the world's largest flying birds), rare and shy okapis, reticulated pythons, mole-rats, and many other animals. This book is filled with photographs and remarkable facts, including how a pelican swallowed a person's head—completely by accident! 222pp., grades 3–8

## Picture Books: Animals in Danger

**Cat Up a Tree** by John and Ann Hassett (Houghton Mifflin, 1998). Nana cries, "Help!" when she sees a cat up a tree, but no help arrives from the firefighters or city hall or anyone else in town. In this counting book with a cause, more and more cats keep coming. Nana cleverly rescues these strays and, in the process, teaches the city about lending a hand.

**The Deliverance of the Dancing Bears** by Elizabeth Stanley (Kane/Miller, 2003). In this contemporary fable, a dancing bear terribly mistreated by her keeper dreams of freedom—wandering in the forests, drinking from mountain streams, catching fish among the rocks. To the keeper's surprise, an old man offers to buy the bear, and with this event comes the bear's taste of freedom.

**Ducks Disappearing** by Phyllis Reynolds Naylor (Atheneum, 1997). Young Willie solves the mystery of disappearing ducks. Most importantly, he explains to the adults how ducks "belong to everyone." A lovely story of a child who pays attention and cares to make a difference.

**Hey! Get Off Our Train** by John Birmingham (Crown, 1989). At bedtime, a young boy takes a trip on his toy train and rescues endangered animals, returning just in time for school. Did the trip really happen? If this was a dream, then why is there a seal in the bathtub?

### Recommendation from the Field
*by Nan Peterson, The Blake School*

*Make Way for Ducklings* by Robert McCloskey (Viking, 1941). Beautiful brown and white drawings illustrate this lovely story of Mr. and Mrs. Mallard looking for a safe place to raise their ducklings. They are met with appreciation, respect, and delight by the citizens of Boston in the Public Garden.

Children can explore service learning themes of respect for nature, park appreciation, animal rights or animal protection, and environmental issues. Students can investigate the needs of the community and the wildlife that lives or migrates through the area. Activities may include:

- Visiting a wildlife center or park, where the need might be to pick up trash, plant annual flowers, dig out invasive plants such as buckthorn or loosestrife, or write a walking guide to the park or center or animals that live in the area.
- Forming a partnership with an animal humane society and collecting needed items like newspapers, leashes, collars, towels, and small rugs.
- Making simple bird feeders or bird baths to give to a senior center or your school.

**Pipaluk and the Whales** by John Himmelman (National Geographic Society, 2002). Never before had Pipaluk and her father seen thousands of whales trapped in a narrow opening of ice. "The whales have helped keep our people alive for many centuries. We owe them too much to slaughter them while they are helpless," he explains. The villagers keep the whales alive, even using their own food supplies. But when the icebreaker ship makes a passage for the whales, they do not move. Pipaluk follows the song in her heart to set the whales free. Based on an event that took place off Russia's Chukchi Peninsula in 1984.

**They Came from the Bronx: How the Buffalo Were Saved from Extinction** by Neil Waldman (Boyds Mills Press, 2001). On an October morning in 1907, a Comanche grandmother and her grandson await a train that carries a herd of buffalo for reintroduction to Oklahoma. Two stories interweave: one that shows the near destruction of this mighty animal, and one that shows the rescue efforts led by concerned conservationists. In the historical note, other efforts to restore the buffalo to their native lands in Canada and the United States are described.

**Washing the Willow Tree Loon** by Jacqueline B. Martin (Simon & Schuster, 1995). When a barge hits a bridge and a thick rush of oil coats the birds of Turtle Bay, people from all walks of life stop their work as bakers, doctors, house painters, and artists to help.

**When Agnes Caws** by Candace Fleming (Aladdin, 2002). Eight-year-old Agnes, who has an extraordinary talent for bird-calling, is sent to locate the elusive pink-headed duck. Little did she suspect that a dastardly bird collector would attempt to use her skill to capture and stuff this precious rare bird. Can Agnes save the duck and herself?

## Fiction: Animals in Danger

**The Animal Rescue Club** by John Himmelman (HarperCollins, 1998). Who can help a squirrel trapped in mud or a baby opossum caught in a drain? The Animal Rescue Club: dedicated kids who work with a wildlife rehabilitator to help the wild animals in their neighborhood. An author's note provides thoughtful advice and safety information. 48pp., grades 2–5

***Backyard Rescue*** by Hope Ryden (Tambourine, 1994). Two ten-year-old friends, Lindsey and Greta, set up a backyard wildlife hospital for wounded animals. They hatch snapping turtle eggs and find a safe home for an injured raccoon. When faced with closure due to Fish and Game laws, they find local resources to protect the animals in their care. 128pp., grades 3–6

***ChaseR: a novel in e-mails*** by Michael J. Rosen (Candlewick Press, 2002). Chase's family has moved from an urban to a rural community, a monumental shift for a teenager. Fortunately, he has his computer and uses email to stay connected with his city friends. Unfortunately, he is caught in a complex dilemma regarding local hunters and their prey. Will Chase come to terms with hunters and hunting? 152pp., young adult

***The Four Ugly Cats in Apartment 3D*** by Marilyn Sachs (Atheneum, 2002). Lily, a ten-year-old latchkey kid, lives near grouchy Mr. Freeman and his four yowling cats. A single gesture of kindness from this crotchety man changes Lily's disposition toward him. When he dies, Lily steps in, determined to "do the right thing" and accomplish the impossible: find the perfect home for the cats that nobody wants. 67pp., grades 3–5

***Hoot*** by Carl Hiaasen (Knopf, 2002). Roy Eberhardt never could have guessed that being bullied by his nemesis Dana Matherson would lead to rescuing small endangered burrowing owls. In fact, every surprising event—seeing potty-trained alligators, meeting a renegade eco-avenger, and making several unexpected friends—leads Roy to think he may enjoy his middle school years after all.

***Saving Lilly*** by Peg Kehret (Simon & Schuster, 2001). After learning about animal abuse, Erin and her friend David create an uproar by refusing to go on the class field trip to the Glitter Tent Circus. Their next challenge is saving Lilly, a mistreated elephant, from being sold to a hunting park. Will sixth graders succeed in standing up to the circus owner's greed and make a difference? 149pp., grades 3–6

> "What are you kids going to do with an elephant?" Mr. Hinkley asked. "They aren't cheap to feed, you know. Lilly weighs two tons and eats a lot of hat every day."
>
> "We're going to send her to an elephant sanctuary in Tennessee," I said.
>
> "Of all the fool ideas I have ever heard," Mr. Hinkley said, "that one takes the cake. Have you thought what you could buy for eight thousand dollars?"
>
> *Yes,* I thought. *I can buy freedom for Lilly.*
>
> FROM *SAVING LILLY*

***The Wheel on the School*** by Meindert Dejong (Harper, 1954). Why did storks stop coming to our town? Lina wonders. Guided by her teacher's words, "sometimes when we wonder, we can make things begin to happen," Lina and her classes infuse the villagers with the challenge and excitement to bring back the storks, renew the environment, and build an inclusive community. 298pp., grades 4–7

# Interviews with Authors:
## The Story Behind the Story

These interviews with Shannon K. Jacobs *(Healers of the Wild: People Who Care for Injured and Orphaned Wildlife)* and Deena Metzger *(Intimate Nature: The Bond Between Women and Animals)* tell the "story behind the story." For many years, I have attended writing classes taught by Deena Metzger, who actually lives with wolves and consistently demonstrates the interconnection between the animal and human worlds by her teaching and actions. In contrast, I learned of Shannon Jacobs's book by accident—a fabulous find that resulted from an Internet search. After speaking with her on the phone for a few minutes, I decided she had a unique story to tell and a definite passion for the well-being of animals.

### *Shannon K. Jacobs, author of* Healers of the Wild: People Who Care for Injured and Orphaned Wildlife

About eight years ago I found a couple of injured birds. One probably had been poisoned by pesticides. I asked everyone I knew, "Who takes care of hurt birds?" No one had an answer. I discovered that most veterinarians and zoos don't treat wildlife because of concern about diseases and because they don't have the expertise to care for native wildlife. Fortunately, someone suggested I take the birds to a wildlife rehabilitator outside of Denver who cares for small mammals and birds. The rehabilitator works full time as a teacher during the school year and cares for wildlife in the summer. She pays for everything herself. I found her work absolutely fascinating. Later, I asked friends what they knew about wildlife rehabilitation. Like me, they knew almost nothing. Quickly my interest turned into a passion to write a book that would provide needed information and a national overview.

Through research I met people from all parts of the country who are committed to taking care of animals that most people don't know about, care about, or even think about. Most have worked intimately with wildlife for many years. These wildlife experts know more about wild animals than many vets and government wildlife people.

Even with good intentions, I would have done everything wrong if I had cared for the sick and injured birds I found. I knew nothing about their natural history. Now I know that all wildlife cannot be treated the same. Each species needs specific care. Some birds eat mainly fruits, others insects, and others eat both. Some have to be taught how to fish or hunt. If the animals don't get proper care, they won't be able to survive in the wild when released. The goal of wildlife rehabilitation, always, is to release healthy animals back to the wild.

Wildlife rehabilitators take care of our neglected native wildlife. No one else does this. Most kids probably know more know about elephants and hippos than about the fascinating crows in their backyards or the raccoon family living in a dead tree. How many students know about opossums, the only marsupials in North America, or about prairie dogs? Prairie dogs are a "keystone" species, meaning that several other species depend on them for survival; we are losing them to development every day.

*Healers of the Wild* integrates two of my favorite interests: native wildlife and helping kids learn about the natural world. I began the book by interviewing wildlife rehabilitators in Colorado, where I live, and branched out to other places in the country. I contacted wildlife rehabilitators in each state to be sure I had information about most regions of the country. I feature a cross-section of wildlife: birds, marine animals, mammals, land mammals, and reptiles.

Since beginning my research, I have volunteered with several wildlife rehabilitators. I fell madly in love with baby birds while feeding and caring for them over a few summers. One day I was in an outside enclosure, putting food and water out for birds soon to be released. In the same enclosure were a pine siskin, a goldfinch, and a meadowlark, and it struck me what an honor it was to be so close to such magnificent wild creatures. Wildlife rehabilitation is the only way to experience truly wild creatures up close.

Find out who your local wildlife rehabilitators are, and then contact the rehabilitators and ask what they need. Most have a "wish list." Usually they need volunteers, supplies, donations, and experts in a variety of areas. Although young people under eighteen typically are not allowed to work directly with animals, they can help in other important ways. For example, they prepare formulas for the babies or chop up fruits and vegetables for the older critters. Kids also build cages.

There is a picture in my book of a Birds of Prey Foundation volunteer holding a Swainson's hawk in a classroom. This is an education bird, kept with a special license because of extensive injuries that would not allow it to survive in the wild. The volunteer and hawk visited a seventh-grade class that had studied raptors and knew about their natural history. The students had raised money to "adopt" the bird. They donate money to the rehabilitation center and receive photos and information about their "adopted" animal. Through the process of helping the center and seeing the bird up close, the students enhance their knowledge and appreciation of these majestic birds.

I hope *Healers of the Wild* conveys the value of our native wildlife. By being better informed, we can learn how to protect our wild neighbors. Since humans cause at least 90 percent of wildlife injuries, we also can learn how to prevent injuries and what to do (and not do) should we find an injured or orphaned animal.

Wildlife rehabilitation has been called "the last frontier of medicine." Interested in becoming a wildlife veterinarian, veterinarian technician, or volunteer? Our native wild creatures need all the help they can get.

### *Deena Metzger, coeditor of* Intimate Nature: The Bond Between Women and Animals

The book *Intimate Nature: The Bond Between Women and Animals* was inspired by the relationship that I have had with animals—I have lived with wolves for seventeen years—and the bond I have felt with women who honor animals as intelligent and sensitive beings. Indigenous peoples have always recognized animals, but most of us no longer remember who animals are. Women have unique relationships with animals because we value the knowledge that comes from intimacy as much as the knowledge that comes from scientific observation. I wanted to be able to document these relationships and their profundity, so that they would be visible to the world.

Animals carry different and varied intelligences. It is possible to have relationships with animals in which we understand and learn about and from each other. The great tragedy is that animals and other species are becoming extinct at a horrendous rate because of diminishing habitats, hunting, poaching, human use, enslavement, and environmental degeneration. Their fate and the fate of the earth are intimately tied. We may not only lose them but ourselves; we may lose the whole world.

*Intimate Nature* reaches out through essays, interviews, stories, and poetry. Some can be read to or told to children who are not yet ready to read themselves. The stories recapitulate real events; they are stories that move and inspire anyone who is ready to learn. The stories open a world that has been closed for a long time in our culture but is a world that children remember. These stories tell of the many faces of animals and the possibility of living in friendship with them. In "The Chimpanzee at Stanford," a short, nonfiction story by Fran Peavey, a chimpanzee recognizes the humans who will be her allies. In "I Acknowledge Mine," Jane Goodall describes visiting a research laboratory where experiments on chimpanzees are being conducted. One chimpanzee recognizes that she is crying for him. This confirms his intelligence, ethical awareness, and spiritual development.

Through *Intimate Nature*, I want to support young people's instinctive love for and camaraderie with animals. I want them to hold on to this basic knowledge without thinking they must outgrow it. There are a thousand ways to support animals, from political activity on behalf of endangered whales, elephants, and wolves, to fighting against cruelty to animals, to stopping use of pesticides that destroy the environment. We can help work with any number of nature preserves for endangered, abandoned, or abused animals. And we can be sure there is enough food and homes for all animals by feeding the birds or rescuing animals from shelters. Let us not injure animals for our entertainment. We can discern which circuses or zoos are inhumane and cruel and insist that the animals be well treated and happy and content in the places they are required to work.

We can all find our own way to honor those animals that are important to us or come to us. And we can find ways—imaginatively and actively—to enter into dialogue with them. Regard your friendships and relationships with animals as being as complex and important as your relationships with human beings.

CHAPTER 6

# COMMUNITY SAFETY

> To be alive, to have freedom to build communities are privileges not to be taken lightly.
>
> NGOAN LE,
> CHICAGO DEPARTMENT OF HUMAN SERVICES

In today's world, everybody is bombarded with issues related to community safety, and unfortunately young people are no exception. On school playgrounds, children wonder how to react to a bully, with teasing and taunting being important issues both for the children who are struggling to stand up for themselves and those who know their behaviors are hurtful. Youth wrestle with peer pressure and worry about exclusion. Gang activity and other acts of violence create fear and feelings of helplessness. Acts of terrorism and war know no national boundaries. Service learning provides an educational strategy for sorting through these challenging and complex issues. Through literature and research, students can learn about the issues at the same time they are discovering new questions to examine. This can help them determine ways to participate in constructive actions.

Whether the concern is safety on a playground, in a neighborhood, or in a war zone, community safety issues offer the opportunity to examine the concept of community. What is community? Is it local or is it global? Although the term is a common one, the actual meaning can be difficult to grasp and define. Each person brings a different understanding based on his or her own experience. One perspective comes from looking at the history of the term itself. The word *community* has roots reaching back to the Indo-European bases *mei*, meaning "change" or "exchange," and *kom*, meaning "with," which combined to produce the word *kommein*: "shared by all."* We might define *community*, then, as a shared change or exchange. This definition shows community in a dynamic state that can be influenced—in this case, by service learning.

## Preparation: Getting Ready for Service Learning Involving Community Safety

The following activities can be used in the preparation stage to promote learning and skill development related to a variety of community safety issues. These activities can be used with different age ranges during preparation to help students examine key issues through research, analyze community needs, and gain the knowledge they need to effectively contribute to the design of their service plan. Since literature is often an important part of preparation, you can find recommended titles on this theme in the Community Safety Bookshelf later in this chapter.

***Activity: Draw Your Community.*** To make the idea of community more concrete, have students present the idea visually. Provide lengths of butcher paper and plenty of markers. Invite students to be absolutely silent as they draw "community." This silence can help maintain the integrity of each student's concept of community, but it also encourages them to collaborate differently and strengthens the reflection that comes after this exercise. Students may work on the same paper or in small groups around smaller sheets as they draw whatever community looks like to them. Following five to ten minutes of art, have students discuss their drawings and their observations. Did the students work individually? Were they aware of what others drew, and did that influence them? What is most apparent in their drawings—people, buildings, animals? Is something missing? Does the art reflect the best of the community or the challenges? What

*This definition was offered by Peter M. Senge, Art Kleiner, Charlotte Roberts, Richard B. Ross, and Bryan J. Smith in *The Fifth Discipline Fieldbook* (Doubleday, 1994).

would they add to improve their community, and how could this be done?

***Activity: A Look at Conflict and Community Building.*** Exploring the nature of conflict can be valuable in examining issues of community safety. Ask a group of people whether conflict is positive or negative, and the majority will probably respond "negative." However, the Latin root of conflict—*confligere*—means "to strike together." This implied friction is an absolute necessity for moving forward and motivating change. Perhaps the personal and collective skills that are key to resolving the conflicts that inevitably occur are more important than the conflicts themselves. Use these ideas to help you explore the nature and importance of conflict with your students.

In class, read aloud any book from the Community Safety Bookshelf, and examine the story line for conflict. Where is it? What is the dilemma facing the characters? Stop the story at any point, and ask, "What would you do?" Have students write the next part of the book. Delve into conflict as the compelling element in all forms of storytelling, including literature, television, film, and song lyrics. Next, have your students identify what the characters in the books do to build community. What ideas do your students have about safety needs, for repairing conflict, and for promoting positive social interaction? How could older students be role models for younger children in promoting healthy, thoughtful behaviors? What shared experiences do they think bring community members together? All of these questions can help you and your students lay the groundwork for a range of different kinds of community safety-based service projects.

**Find Out More About Community Safety**

To learn more about these issues and to get ideas for service and action, visit these Web sites and organizations online:

***nationaltcc.org*** Teens, Crime, and the Community is a national program of the National Crime Prevention Council enabling teens to "get involved in crime prevention to make themselves safer and their communities stronger."

***www.esrnational.org/home.htm*** Educators for Social Responsibility (ESR) helps educators create safe, caring, respectful, and productive learning environments.

***www.nationalsave.org/index.php*** The National Association of S.A.V.E. (Students Against Violence Everywhere) is a student-driven organization encouraging young people to learn about alternatives to violence and practice what they learn through school and community service projects.

## Making Connections Across the Curriculum

Some service learning activities naturally lend themselves to interdisciplinary work and making connections across the curriculum. These connections strengthen and broaden student learning, helping them meet academic standards. More than likely, you'll be looking for these connections and ways to encourage them well before the students ever start working on service learning activities. As with the entire service learning process, it helps to remain flexible, because some connections can be spontaneously generated by the questions raised throughout and by the needs of the project. To help you think about cross-curricular connections and where you can look for them, the Curricular Web for this chapter (page 91) gives examples of many different ways this theme can be used in different academic areas. (The examples in the next section also demonstrate various ways this theme can be used across the curriculum.)

> It is better to be part of a great whole than to be the whole of a small part.
>
> FREDERICK DOUGLASS, ABOLITIONIST

# Service Learning Scenarios:
## Ideas for Action

Ready to take action? What follows are projects that have been successfully carried out by elementary, middle, or high school students. Most of these scenarios and examples explicitly include some aspects of preparation, action, reflection, and demonstration. These scenarios can be a rich source of project, resource, and

# Community Safety Across the Curriculum

**Community Safety**

### *English/Language Arts*

- Write stories or skits that feature characters being bullied or teased and the ways they deal with it
- Make a library display of books that teach about friendship
- Compare coverage of a story on a local act of violence with one about community building

### *Social Studies/History*

- Role-play scenarios that focus on various social skills including how to make friends and stop name-calling
- Research hate crimes and the organizations that intervene
- Follow current events that demonstrate efforts by governments and grassroots organizations to resolve international turmoil; compare strategies and the results

### *Languages*

- Research the symbols used for public safety in different countries
- Learn how to say words related to peace in many languages
- Make multilingual posters that promote peace and peer conflict resolution

### *Theater, Music, & Visual Arts*

- Create and perform skits that illustrate peer mediation skills and problem solving in settings where conflicts often occur, such as in the lunchroom, on the school bus, or on the playground
- Research the origin of and perform songs from different countries about peace
- Find political cartoons that use images to comment about issues related to crime, violence, bullying, or conflict on the world stage

### *Math*

- Research and create a report on local crime statistics
- Monitor the rate of discipline referrals before and after peer mediation or conflict resolution programs are instituted
- Survey students to find out how often they're teased, bullied, and pressured to conform with peers; tabulate and report statistics

### *Physical Education*

- Play noncompetitive games and invent new ones
- Learn strategies for what to do in risky situations; be certain to make these age-appropriate
- Mentor younger children in sports as a means of community building

### *Computer*

- Using the Internet, read about global events as reported by newspapers in different countries or by different participants; compare findings
- Research student-created Web sites that discuss safety issues such as gun safety, peace forums, and anti-bullying campaigns
- Brainstorm ways that computers can be used for community building, i.e., setting up Listservs and sharing information about community events

### *Science*

- Discuss with family and friends the risks associated with smoking or drinking
- Study about human physiological reactions when experiencing strong emotions such as anger, love, hurt, fear, and joy
- Research stories of how community building has occurred through environmental activities such as beach clean-ups, community gardens, and student-led recycling campaigns

curriculum ideas for you to draw upon. While the grade levels are given as a reference, most project ideas can be adapted to suit younger or older students, and many are suitable for cross-age partnerships.

***Peace Keepers Everywhere: Grades K–5.*** An elementary school administration decided to educate youth in ways to reduce bullying and teasing. With faculty and student council agreement, educators from a local nonprofit organization led workshops and trainings on conflict resolution and peer mediation for teachers. Parent information sessions were held and an article was published in the back-to-school newsletter about the new campaign. Education on conflict resolution was carried out in all classrooms. To augment student skills and involvement, eighty children in the third through fifth grades attended workshops to become "peace keepers" and peer mediators on the playground and school buses.

***Reaching Out Across the Globe: Grades K–12.*** Students in schools across the United States have found ways to reach across the globe to war-torn countries and places that have been devastated by natural disasters. They have:

- Made health kits for people who have had to leave their homes because of war. The kits, which can be distributed by relief agencies such as the Red Cross, contain a towel, a toothbrush, and soap.
- Made T-shirts to sell at community fairs to raise money for the Heifer Project. The Heifer Project (*www.heifer.org*) buys cows, sheep, and chickens for families around the world.
- Collected canned goods for earthquake victims.
- Participated in a bike-a-thon to raise money for Bikes not Bombs (*www.bikesnotbombs.org*), which is a group that collects old bikes, fixes them, and gives them to people in other countries who cannot afford them.
- Collected used eyeglasses for "The Gift of Sight," a Lions Clubs (*www.lionsclubs.org*) program that repairs and gives eyeglasses to people in other countries. On Halloween, this program sponsors Sight Night. Children leave signs on their neighbors' doors in late October to let them know that they will be collecting eyeglasses. Then, on Halloween night, they pick up the glasses as they trick-or-treat. Collected eyeglasses are cleaned, repaired, and hand-delivered during optical and medical missions to developing countries.

***A Community Finds Heroes: Grades 1–5.*** As a response to events of September 11, 2001, elementary school children in West Hollywood, California, were invited by their city council to contribute art and poetry based on several themes: "Wishes for the World," "We Give Thanks," and "Our Heroes." Age-appropriate discussion allowed students to share thoughts and feelings and to ask questions of adults. The students' artwork and words were displayed in City Hall. After reviewing the heroes identified by students, teachers and after-school-program specialists scheduled visits to bring these people face-to-face with the kids through field visits. In pairs (a male and female in each set), students interviewed doctors and sheriffs. Firefighters received first-grade visitors at the fire station, and a third-grade class met farmers at the local farmers' market. Students conducted thorough interviews with their heroes and published a series of books, with words and art: *Our Heroes*.

***Slow Down—You Move Too Fast! Grade 3.*** Third-grade students in Wisconsin observed that the speed limit in front of their school was too high and decided to do something about it. They partnered with local police to record the speeds of the cars going by and created a graph showing how fast cars were going. Next, they held a car wash and surveyed adults regarding the speed in front of the school. Finally, they prepared a presentation for the city council requesting that the council immediately lower the speed limit in front of the school. When the students delivered the presentation, the council members were so impressed that they suspended the rules and voted to lower the speed limit that night. The result? A lower speed limit in front of the school and a safer place for the children.

***Spreading the Ideas of Conflict Resolution: Grades 4 and 5.*** In an annual event sponsored by a city government in California, elementary students at two schools meet to celebrate their peer mediation programs. The Conflict Wizards and Peace Patrol groups began with getting-acquainted activities and then role-played common situations they encounter on the playgrounds, such as disagreements over game rules. The groups then created a spiral-bound book together. Previous titles written by the students include *The ABCs of Peer Mediation*, *Poems for Peace* and *Creating Safe Schools for Kids*. These books are distributed to every local school and library and made available to community agencies. As a "thank you" to the students for their dedication, the city awards certificates of merit and presents each young person with a copy of Barbara Lewis's *Kids with Courage: True Stories About Young People Making a Difference*.

> You must be the change
> you wish to see in the world.
> MAHATMA GANDHI, STATESMAN

***Documenting Stories of War and Peace: Grades 4–12.*** Social studies and government teachers have used the parable *Feathers and Fools* to examine issues of combat and coexistence, when teaching about war and conflict. The students drew parallels between the book and the specific dilemmas faced in historical or current events. From this launch pad, students have interviewed war veterans, as well as people who did not serve in the military but felt the impact of war at home. They have asked, for example, questions about how living through times of war has affected how these people have lived in times of peace. Stories have been compiled into books, presented at community gatherings, posted on the Web, used to create a "living museum," and used as the basis for dramatic presentations.

***Building Friendships: Grade 6.*** A sixth-grade English/social studies teacher asked students to write about their earliest experiences of friendship or bullying. Through discussion, the class concluded that elementary children often struggle with both—how to maintain and build strong friendships and how to stand up to bullying behaviors. They identified third grade as a place where they could have an impact and wrote letters to the third-grade classes in a nearby elementary school to verify the need. The project: to lead interactive lessons that model friendship. Using the book *How Humans Make Friends*, the middle school students developed skits and scenarios, which they presented to the younger kids, and made posters, which they left in the classrooms. The students visited three classes weekly for three weeks. Feedback from the third-grade teachers in between visits made the reflection sessions instructive and improved the project and experience for everyone involved.

***A Symposium for Peace: Grades 6–12.*** Bringing students and community together offers an opportunity for learning, community building, and collaborative action. Following the attacks on September 11, 2001, adults and students in St. Cloud, Minnesota, designed a symposium that allowed them to spend time together examining issues of mutual concern. Topics included religious tolerance, dispute resolution, teen suicide, and local refugee programs. Students invited agency representatives to visit classes, and agencies asked youth to participate in community forums and planning meetings.

***Teen Violence: Grades 7 and 10.*** Seventh-grade students read *Making Up Megaboy* as part of their English studies. As the students discussed the multiple points of view represented in the story, they asked questions about real instances of youth violence in their region. With their teacher, they designed a course of study to learn about the issue. Their studies included collecting articles on teen violence from the Internet and inviting a local reporter to their classroom for a discussion of responsible journalism. Based on what they had learned, they developed an educational evening for parents and other students. They read selections from *Megaboy* and discussed ways to maintain ongoing mutually respectful parent-child communication. Later, they documented the resulting recommendations in an article for their school newspaper, which included "Tips on Talking with Your Teen."

A high school teacher who learned of the seventh graders' project replicated it in her tenth-grade class using the book *Give a Boy a Gun*. The high school students discussed the challenges of breaking down cliques and reaching out to students known as "loners" or just "different." They initiated a "Mix-It-Up Day" in which some students agreed to have lunch with randomly assigned people and then to meet with their lunch partners once a week for three weeks. During the second semester, the project was repeated with twice as many students. Later, students even encouraged a similar project for improved teacher-to-teacher interaction. Comments during reflection showed an increase in tolerance and appreciation that extended even to students and faculty who had not taken part.

> Every month, seven percent of eighth graders stay home from school because they are afraid of being bullied by another child.
>
> ELIZABETH RUSCH, *GENERATION FIX: YOUNG IDEAS FOR A BETTER WORLD*

***Oral Histories on Violence: Grade 9.*** After conducting a community needs survey in their study skills class, students in San Francisco chose to study violence. They conducted research on one of the four types of violence—hate crimes, relationship violence, gang violence, and police brutality. Students read biographies, fiction, a play, newspaper articles, and expository text. They formed a coalition with local organizations and planned a community conference to raise issues and have discussions about violence. Also, after conducting a practice interview with a former teacher who had been the victim of police brutality, students conducted interviews with people who had perpetrated or been the target of violence. Their compilation of these people's stories, *I Have Been Strong: Oral Histories on Violence*, has been given to many local agencies and schools.

***Transforming the "Bully": Grades 9 and 10.*** High school students in the Youth Explorers Program in central California worked with local law enforcement to reach out to younger children. They selected *Toestomper and the Caterpillars* as the ideal book for their Friendship Campaign. Students created posters highlighting the key points of the story. At after-school programs, the Explorers held the kids' attention with the humorous story and dramatic effects and led small group discussions about friendship and transforming the "bully" in all of us.

***Lessons from the Middle Ages: Grades 9–12.*** High school teachers in Berkeley used *When Plagues Strike: The Black Death, Smallpox, AIDS* to address issues of tolerance on their campus. The book discusses the issues of intolerance, blame, and scapegoating as they relate to the diseases in the title. Students have used their studies to plan a tolerance campaign at their high school, educating their peers about the perils of scapegoating and the possibilities of creating a more tolerant and inclusive campus.

***The Campaign for "Truth": Grades 9–12.*** Creativity hit a peak when Florida high school students were given a voice in developing "Truth," an antismoking social marketing campaign using tobacco settlement funds. Their candid approach and youthful appeal has reduced smoking by teens in Florida, and now their public service announcements have hit the national airwaves. On the other side of the United States in Hawaii, students used theater to discourage smoking. They conducted pre- and post-tests with their young audiences to find out the impact of their original performances. The results: Similar to their Florida peers, the teens' dramatic efforts have been more effective in making an impact than adult-initiated forms of prevention.

***Rock Out on Tolerance: Grades 11 and 12.*** High school students in Florida used popular culture to send an important message to their peers about tolerance. Tapping their collective creative talents, students wrote an original song addressing three relevant issues of prejudice: race, physical differences, and sexism. Through their campus media center, the students learned the skills necessary to create a rock video that would illustrate the drama of discrimination and cause viewers to think about their personal behavior.

## The Community Safety Bookshelf

The Community Safety Bookshelf covers a broad spectrum of topics, from personal safety and bullying to community building and the world stage. To help you find books relevant to your particular projects, the book chart classifies the titles into several topic areas: personal safety, bullying, conflict resolution, local violence, hate crimes, the world stage, and community building.

In general, the bookshelf features:

- An annotated bibliography arranged and alphabetized by title according to the general categories of nonfiction (N), picture books (P), and fiction (F). For nonfiction and fiction, length and recommended grade levels are included. The entries in the picture book category do not include suggested grade levels, since they can be successfully used with all ages.
- A chart organized by topic and category to help you find books relevant to particular projects.
- Recommendations from service learning colleagues and experts that include a book summary and ideas for service learning connections. (The number of recommended books varies in each bookshelf.)

## Community Safety Bookshelf Topics

| Topics | Books | Category |
|---|---|---|
| ***Personal Safety*** Personal safety involves knowing how to take care of ourselves in a wide variety of situations at home, at school, and in the community. | *50 Ways to a Safer World* | N |
| | *Geography Club* | F |
| | *Handbook for Boys* (see page 117) | F |
| | *Hands Are Not for Hitting* | P |
| | *Holes* | F |
| | *How Humans Make Friends* | P |
| | *The Safe Zone: A Kid's Guide to Personal Safety* ‡ | N |
| | *Smoking: A Risky Business* | N |
| | *Stargirl* | F |
| | *A Step from Heaven* (see page 170) | F |
| ***Bullying*** Inside every child who exhibits bullying behavior on the playground is a child who needs to be reached. These selections look at peer pressure, isolation, and being "different," as well as how to make friends. | *Buddha Boy* | F |
| | *Cowboy Boy* | F |
| | *Don't Laugh at Me* | P |
| | *Harry Potter and the Sorcerer's Stone* | F |
| | *Hey, Little Ant!* | P |
| | *Hoot* (see page 86) | F |
| | *The Hundred Dresses* (see page 156) | F |
| | *I Miss Franklin P. Shuckles* | P |
| | *King of the Kooties* | F |
| | *The Misfits* | F |
| | *Mr. Lincoln's Way* * | P |
| | *Nobody Knew What to Do: A Story About Bullying* | P |
| | *On the Fringe* | F |
| | *Pinky and Rex and the Bully* | F |
| | *The Revealers* | F |
| | *Summer Wheels* * | P |
| | *Thank You, Mr. Falker* (see page 182) | P |
| | *Toestomper and the Caterpillars* | P |
| | *Wings* | P |
| | *Wringer* | F |

*continued* ⟶

| Topics | Books | Category |
|---|---|---|
| **Conflict Resolution**<br>The best defense has nothing to do with hitting, kicking, or punching. Finding the tools of tolerance and peaceful resolution helps to make communities safer. | *Cootie Shots: Theatrical Inoculations Against Bigotry* | N |
| | *Define "Normal"* | F |
| | *Feathers and Fools* | P |
| | *Increase the Peace: The ABCs of Tolerance* | N |
| | *Mole Music* | P |
| | *Siddhartha* | F |
| | *The Sissy Duckling* | P |
| | *The Skirt* (see page 170) | F |
| | *The Summer My Father Was Ten* (see page 143) | P |
| | *We Can Work It Out: Conflict Resolution for Children* | N |
| **Local Violence**<br>Making sense of violence is always a challenge. Books offer a safe haven to investigate what happens in our communities and help us to think about our choices. | *Any Small Goodness* (see page 169) | F |
| | *Bat 6* (see page 198) | F |
| | *Big Mouth and Ugly Girl* | F |
| | *Drive-By* | F |
| | *Give a Boy a Gun* | F |
| | *If You Come Softly* (see page 199) | F |
| | *It Doesn't Have to Be This Way: A Barrio Story/ No tiene que ser así: Una historia del barrio* | P |
| | *Making Up Megaboy* ‡ | F |
| | *Romeo and Juliet* | F |
| | *Shadow of the Dragon* | F |
| | *Smoky Nights* | P |
| | *Stars in the Darkness* * | P |
| | *Your Move* | P |
| **Hate Crimes**<br>Breaking the cycle of hate requires taking a firm stand. When we read about an individual willing to risk personal safety to protect others or about a community that bands together, we are encouraged to stand stronger. | *Chicken Sunday* | P |
| | *The Christmas Menorahs: How a Town Fought Hate* | P |
| | *A Different Kind of Hero* (see page 169) | F |
| | *Passage to Freedom: The Sugihara Story* (see page 198) | P |
| | *When Plagues Strike: The Black Death, Smallpox, AIDS* (see page 73) | N |
| | *The Yellow Star: The Legend of King Christian X of Denmark* | P |
| **The World Stage**<br>Being informed about the challenges faced in other parts of the world develops knowledge and empathy. From Tibet to Ireland to Sudan to New York City, we can learn about others and become citizens of the world. | *After the Dancing Days* | F |
| | *Alloy Peace Book* * | N |
| | *Behind the Mountains* (see page 169) | F |
| | *Boxes for Katje* * | P |
| | *Charlie Wilcox* | F |
| | *The Clay Marble* (see page 169) | F |
| | *Dream Freedom* * (see page 199) | F |
| | *Girl of Kosovo* | F |
| | *Gleam and Glow* | P |

*continued* ⟶

| Topics | Books | Category |
|---|---|---|
| **The World Stage** continued | *It's Still a Dog's New York: A Book of Healing* | P |
| | *A Life Like Mine: How Children Live Around the World* * (see page 196) | N |
| | *The Middle of Everywhere: The World's Refugees Come to Our Town* (see page 167) | N |
| | *Stand Up for Your Rights* * (see page 197) | N |
| | *When Christmas Comes Again: The World War I Diary of Simone Spencer* | F |
| **Community Building** Coming together to build a diverse and thriving community is a memorable experience. Books in this category offer models to examine and stories to emulate. | *DeShawn Days* * | P |
| | *The Green Truck Garden Giveaway* *‡ (see page 142) | P |
| | *Seedfolks* * (see page 143) | F |
| | *Somebody Loves You, Mr. Hatch* (see page 116) | P |
| | *Something Beautiful* * (see page 198) | P |
| | *Wartville Wizard* (see page 133) | P |

Page references are given for books that do not appear in the Community Safety Bookshelf but that can be found in the bookshelf lists of other chapters.
* These books include examples of young people in service-providing roles.
‡ These books are out of print but still worth finding.

## Nonfiction: *Community Safety*

***Alloy Peace Book*** by Tucker Shaw (HarperTrophy, 2002). Written in the aftermath of September 11, 2001, this book examines peace and what it means to young people around the world. A timeline of peace in the twentieth century is outlined; Nobel Peace Prize winners are featured; and young people speak, describing where they were when the September 11 attacks occurred, telling how they responded through social action, and sharing their fears and dreams. 144pp., young adult

***Cootie Shots: Theatrical Inoculations Against Bigotry for Kids, Parents, and Teachers*** by Norma Bowles with Mark E. Rosenthal (Fringe Benefits, 2001). This unique collection of plays, songs, and poems designed for young audiences promotes tolerance and celebrates diversity. 144pp., grades 3–12

***50 Ways to a Safer World*** by Patricia Occhiuzzo Giggans and Barrie Levy (Seal Press, 1997). This compilation of facts, ideas, and resources includes ideas to prevent violence and create a safer community. Among the ideas are tips on raising safety-smart and media-savvy kids, conducting school safety audits, and keeping guns away from children. 144pp., grades 7–12

***Increase the Peace: The ABCs of Tolerance*** by Devora Kaye (ABCD Books, 2002). Written by a high school sophomore, this alphabetical exploration of tolerance includes practical ideas for social activism. The book will inspire students to action and may also inspire them to create their own books. *A percentage of all sales is contributed to a nonprofit organization that supports educational programs for nonviolence.* 29pp., all grades

***The Safe Zone: A Kid's Guide to Personal Safety*** by Donna Chaiet and Francine Russell (Morrow, 1998). This book helps children consider ways to protect themselves without fighting by developing personal awareness, using body language, developing self-esteem, and communicating effectively. The book is filled with activities and ideas and offers plenty of scenarios for classroom discussion and problem solving, including situations that occur in public, at home, and even on the Internet. This book is out of print but still worth finding. 160pp., grades 3–8

***Smoking: A Risky Business*** by Laurence Pringle (Morrow Junior, 1996). Tobacco is a legal product that, when used as directed, causes death. Despite educational and media campaigns to alert the public to the dangers of smoking, people of all ages continue to inhale. This book reviews science, political, media, and health issues related to smoking. Since tobacco companies spend vast amounts to promote smoking, it is vitally important for young people to be informed about the reasons to avoid addiction to tobacco. 124pp., young adult

> In 1604, King James of England wrote that smoking was a "custom lothsome to the eye, hatefull to the Nose, harmefull to the braine, dangerous to the Lungs."
>
> FROM *SMOKING: A RISKY BUSINESS*

***We Can Work It Out: Conflict Resolution for Children*** by Barbara K. Polland (Tricycle Press, 2000). This book includes photographs and questions about conflicts that arise frequently in the lives of young children, along with an introduction for parents and teachers. The book provides a vehicle for discussing a range of topics that can help children become more successful in resolving conflicts. 64pp., grades K–2

## Picture Books: *Community Safety*

***Boxes for Katje*** by Candace Fleming (Farrar, Straus and Giroux, 2003). After World War II, Europe stood in ruins. In the United States, through the Children's Aid Society, many people made charitable contributions of soap, sugar, coats, and other necessary and valued items and sent them overseas. In May of 1945, Katje's family in Holland received such a box and began corresponding with the young girl and family who sent it. As Katje's letters described her family's needs, the American family and their community collected and shipped the goods. One day a box arrived in return—tulips from Holland! Based on a true story of a box sent to Holland by the author's mother.

***Chicken Sunday*** by Patricia Polacco (Philomel, 1992). Three friends plan to surprise Gramma Eula with a special holiday hat. As they approach old Mr. Kodinski at the hat shop, they are mistaken for teens who have vandalized his store. They prove their innocence and make a new friend in the process.

***The Christmas Menorahs: How a Town Fought Hate*** by Janice Cohn (Albert Whitman, 1995). Young Isaac saw a rock shatter his bedroom window and hit his Hanukkah menorah. When this hate crime occurred in Billings, Montana, during the holiday season of 1993, town residents of many races, religions, and backgrounds stood together.

***DeShawn Days*** by Tony Medina (Lee & Low, 2001). Welcome to DeShawn's world. Age ten, DeShawn uses poetry to introduce us to "who I live with—who I love." Mother, uncle, cousin, grandmother, and friends matter to DeShawn. Life in the hood is a mixture of spray paint, magicians, and rap. DeShawn's community extends to people fighting across the globe and "mothers and kids crying," so he asks his teacher if the class can write to children in war-torn countries. The book's afterword shares the author's passion for imagination, reading, and writing and his hope that DeShawn's experiences "will inspire you to write poems, paint pictures, sing songs, and help others, too!"

***Don't Laugh at Me*** by Steve Seskin and Allen Shamblin (Tricycle Press, 2002). The lyrics of the song "Don't Laugh at Me" are told in story form as characters express their dislike for being teased, left out, or chosen last in sports. Especially useful with discussion.

***Feathers and Fools*** by Mem Fox (Voyager Books, 1989). Can peacocks and swans settle their perceived differences peacefully? Or will it take a new generation to learn peaceful coexistence and friendship? A parable for all ages.

***Gleam and Glow*** by Eve Bunting (Harcourt, 2001). As war moves closer to their village, Victor, his little sister, and their mother must escape. Along with the other refugees, they carry their belongings, hoping to find a safe haven. Victor's treasures—his home, books, and two fish—are left behind. And what is much worse, his father is off fighting with the liberation army. How will Papa find them now? This story is inspired by real events.

***Hands Are Not for Hitting*** by Martine Agassi (Free Spirit Publishing, 2000). Hands are for waving hello, playing with friends, helping each other, and definitely not for hitting. The book includes a teaching guide and references to promote nonviolence.

***Hey, Little Ant!*** by Phillip and Hannah Hoose (Tricycle Press, 1998). In this song-turned-book, a boy is about to stomp on an ant when the ant speaks up: "Please, oh please, do not squish me." In the dialogue between boy and ant that follows, the boy wrestles with his conscience, peer pressure, and the logic of this teeny creature. The verdict? Read the book! Sheet music for the song is included.

***How Humans Make Friends*** by Loreen Leedy (Holiday House, 1996). When Dr. Zork Tripork returns to his planet from his expedition to planet Earth, he explains to his fellow aliens just how humans make friends and work out their problems so they can stay friends.

***I Miss Franklin P. Shuckles*** by Ulana Snihura (Annick Press, 1998). To stay popular at school, Molly decides to end her friendship with Franklin because "he has skinny legs and wears funny glasses." She soon misses this genuine friendship and learns the importance of kindness.

***It Doesn't Have to Be This Way: A Barrio Story/No tiene que ser así: Una historia del barrio*** by Luis J. Rodríguez (Children's Book Press/Libros Para Niños, 1999). Reluctantly, a young boy becomes involved in neighborhood gang activity. Then a tragic event forces him to make a choice about the course of his life. In English and Spanish.

***It's Still a Dog's New York: A Book of Healing*** by Susan L. Roth (National Geographic, 2001). In this poignant sequel to *It's a Dog's New York*, Pepper and Rover roam through New York City in the wake of the events of September 11. As they visit each landmark, they consider the tragedy that has occurred and express their sadness and confusion. By sharing their thoughts and feelings, helping others, appreciating the bravery of the rescue workers, and caring for each other, they can begin to heal.

***Mole Music*** by David McPhail (Henry Holt, 1999). Though Mole digs tunnels by day, he has begun to feel that there is something missing in his life. After hearing beautiful music on television, he "wants to make beautiful music, too." With much practice, he learns to play, and his violin echoes through the night. He imagines his music reaching into people's hearts, dissolving anger, and "changing the world." Without knowing it, he does change the world.

***Mr. Lincoln's Way*** by Patricia Polacco (Philomel, 2001). Eugene, a tough kid, always seems angry and picks on his classmates. School principal Mr. Lincoln sees him as a boy in trouble and is determined to reach him. Soon, Mr. Lincoln notices Eugene's interest in birds and a bird sanctuary project. But the trouble is still there. With insightfulness and caring, Mr. Lincoln guides Eugene to be more tolerant of others.

***Nobody Knew What to Do: A Story About Bullying*** by Becky Ray McCain (Albert Whitman, 2001). When Ray is mistreated by his peers, the other children are confused about how to make the bullying behaviors stop. Finally, one child steps forward to enlist the help of a teacher. With adult support, the children learn that they can stand up for fair play and kindness toward all students.

***The Sissy Duckling*** by Harvey Fierstein (Simon & Schuster, 2002). Elmer the duck is teased because he is "different." Bolstered by his mama's belief in his abilities, along with a wealth of creativity and ingenuity, Elmer demonstrates his courage by saving papa duck. What does Elmer ultimately learn? That he's not so different but will always be special!

***Smoky Nights*** by Eve Bunting (Harcourt, 1994). Daniel, his mother, and their neighbors experience civil unrest in Los Angeles—violence, fires, and the loss of homes and businesses. When acts of kindness replace racial prejudice with friendship, new lessons are learned by people both young and old, and by cats, too.

***Stars in the Darkness*** by Barbara Joose (Chronicle, 2002). A boy imagines street sirens to be howling wolves and shots fired by gangs to be stars cracking the darkness. When the brother he loves becomes a "banger," he comes up with a plan to save his brother, unite the neighborhood, and stand for peace. Based on a true story; includes resources for gang prevention.

***Summer Wheels*** by Eve Bunting (Harcourt, 1992). The Bicycle Man offers friendship and the use of fixed-up bikes to neighborhood kids, even to a boy who intentionally does not return the bike. Two other boys set out to get the bike back and resolve this problem.

***Toestomper and the Caterpillars*** by Sharleen Collicott (Houghton Mifflin, 1999). Toestomper and his group of Rowdy Ruffians are mean, and they like it that way. However, once Toestomper begins to care for a family of fuzzy caterpillars, he becomes caring and kind. A humorous story with a message about bullying and friendship.

***Wings*** by Christopher Myers (Scholastic, 2000). Ikarus Jackson is different: He has wings and he can fly. But at school, his wings attract too much attention, and kids think he is "showing off." One girl realizes he must be lonely and resolves to step in and stop the hurtful words coming his way. A challenge to embrace differences and celebrate individuality.

***The Yellow Star: The Legend of King Christian X of Denmark*** by Carmen Agra Deedy (Peachtree, 2000). A compassionate king is determined to protect all of his people during the Nazi occupation of Denmark. The author poses a question to the reader: "What if we could follow that example today against violators of human rights?"

***Your Move*** by Eve Bunting (Harcourt, 1998). When James wants to prove he can be part of a gang, he places himself and his younger brother at risk. But being strong can mean having the courage to say "no."

## Fiction: Community Safety

***After the Dancing Days*** by Margaret I. Rostkowski (HarperTrophy, 1988). It's the end of World War I and Annie feels great relief at her father's return to their home in Kansas City after months away treating wounded soldiers in New York City. But life cannot return to normal. Uncle Paul died during the war in France and now father is a doctor at a local hospital, again treating the wounded. Against her mother's wishes, Annie visits the veterans, befriending an angry, young, disfigured soldier, and helping them all to value the power of friendship and courage. 217pp., young adult

***Big Mouth and Ugly Girl*** by Joyce Carol Oates (HarperCollins, 2002). Matt Donahue sometimes says more than he should, but who would have suspected his words would be taken out of context and cause detectives to question him at school? Never would he have imagined that his friends and the community would turn against him or that high school loner Ursula Riggs would be the only one to stand up for him. This inside look at media frenzy and rumors shows how the temptation of "belonging" can distort reality and destroy relationships. 266pp., young adult

***Buddha Boy*** by Kathe Koja (Farrar, Straus and Giroux, 2003). At Rucher High, the new kid, Jinsen, is called "Buddha Boy" and considered a freak. He dresses in tie-dye shirts, shaves his head, and begs for lunch money in the cafeteria. So when Justin, the book's narrator, has to work with Jinsen on a class project, he hopes to get this over fast. But the discovery of Jinsen's artistic talents leads to a friendship that changes both boys forever. 117pp., young adult

***Charlie Wilcox*** by Sharon E. McKay (Stoddart Kids, 2000). Despite being born with a club foot, Charlie Wilcox, almost fourteen, is determined to work at sea like his father. Following a corrective surgery operation, he defies his parents' plan for his education and future at a university and stows away on a ship, but the wrong ship at that: This ship is headed to World War I! Charlie finds a medical team also from Newfoundland and learns a special courage as he volunteers tending the wounded and dying. 221pp., grades 5–9

***Cowboy Boy*** by James Proimos (Scholastic, 2003). Ricky Smootz is terrified of sixth grade, especially since his friend has warned him of Keanu Dungston's gang of bullies and the wedgies sure to greet him on his first day of school. After two days of wedgies and being framed for throwing spitballs, Ricky feigns sickness to avoid the whole mess and find solace with his grandmother. Her stories of a distant cowboy cousin, courageous Crazy Enzio, gives Ricky a new perspective. Soon he dons a hat, vest, fuzzy pants, and his alter ego—Cowboy Boy—and brings a halt to the bullying varmints at school. 87pp., grades 4–6

***Define "Normal"*** by Julie Anne Peters (Little, Brown and Company, 2000). When she agrees to meet with Jasmine as a peer counselor at their middle school, Antonia, an overachiever, never dreams this "punker" girl with the black lipstick and pierced eyebrow will help her with a serious family problem and become a valued friend. 196pp., grades 6–8

***Drive-By*** by Lynne Ewing (HarperTrophy, 1996). When his family is torn apart by a drive-by shooting, Tito wonders if his dead brother Jimmy was in a gang. Will Tito be forced into a gang to save his mother and sister? 85pp., grades 5–7

***Geography Club*** by Brent Hartinger (HarperCollins, 2003). Russell Middlebrook is convinced he is the only gay student at his high school until he stumbles across a small group of other gay students. United by their secret, they form a club intended to appear so boring that nobody in their right mind would ever join: the Geography Club. The treacherous terrain of high school dynamics and the pull to be popular undermine even their best intentions and threaten every relationship. 226pp., young adult

***Girl of Kosovo*** by Alice Mead (Farrar, Straus and Giroux, 2001). Eleven-year-old Zana appreciates village life in Kosovo with her close-knit Albanian family. She is aware of the growing strife between the Croatians, Bosnians, and Serbs and realizes that danger is coming closer daily. When a resistance leader is murdered, Zana's village is attacked. Zana experiences not only a brutal injury but the loss of loved ones. To survive, she remembers her father's words: "Zana, don't let them fill your heart with hate. Whatever happens." This story is based on the experience of a boy from the Kosovo region. 115pp., grades 5–8

***Give a Boy a Gun*** by Todd Strasser (Simon & Schuster, 2000). After two years of constant harassment and beatings from school jocks, two boys storm a school dance equipped with guns to take their revenge. This book gives voice to the many sides of the school violence issue—school counselors, parents, teens, teachers, and the troubled youth. Along with providing numerous facts about violence in America, the book insists that we consider whether this tragedy could have been prevented and what we can do now. 208pp., grades 7–12

**Recommendation from the Field**

*by Terry Pickeral, Executive Director, National Center for Learning and Citizenship*

*Harry Potter and the Sorcerer's Stone* by J. K. Rowling (Scholastic, 1998). Harry Potter was born a wizard but isn't aware of his birthright until he is sent an invitation to attend Hogwarts School of Wizardry. Harry experiences the wonder of friendship, the joy of discovery, the pain of disappointment, and the courage to face challenges and the unknown. Over the course of the series, Harry learns the skills of wizardry, comes to understand how history shapes his life, and builds a sense of confidence in his own skills.

Students can explore the many feelings and relationships Harry experiences (fear of his extended family, honor from the wizards, jealousy on the part of some of his classmates, and trust from his friends) and identify similarities in their lives. Harry is aided by mentors, people who "show him the way" and help him to understand the complexities of school and life. Similarly, students can become mentors and guides to new students, using the story of Harry to find various themes facing "the new kid." 309pp., grades 4–12

**Recommendation from the Field**

*by Robert Bhaerman, School-Based Program Coordinator, Corporation for National and Community Service*

*Holes* by Louis Sachar (Farrar, Straus and Giroux, 1998). In this humorous yet poignant story, young Stanley Yelnats, falsely arrested for stealing a pair of sneakers, is sentenced to serve time at a juvenile detention facility in the middle of a Texas desert. Having never attended a summer camp, Stanley naively looks on this as a wonderful new opportunity. However, soon he is faced with a group of unhappy campers—inmates—and an evil warden who uses the boys to dig holes in search of buried treasure.

Stanley makes some startling discoveries about himself, the meaning of friendship, and an "ancient curse" that has haunted his family for several generations. In a related story about his great-great grandfather, the mystery of the curse is revealed. In his efforts to help a friend, Stanley now finds himself in control of his own destiny and the fate of his unlucky family.

Connections to service can come through a number of curriculum areas, particularly through social studies, as students discuss issues of juvenile crime and such questions as, "Why is homelessness a major social problem?" Students can provide meaningful service, for example, by working with local organizations to develop materials informing the community as to how these agencies work to combat juvenile crime and help people who are homeless. 233pp., grades 4–7

***King of the Kooties*** by Debbie Dadey (Walker & Company, 1999). Fourth grader Nate is amazed that his new friend Donald has never heard of "kooties." At first Donald doesn't realize he is being insulted when called the "King of the Kooties" by the class bully, Louisa. Nate decides to teach Donald to defend himself—not with his fists but with his wits. 84pp., grades 3–6

***Making Up Megaboy*** by Virginia Walter (Delacorte Press, 1998). What provoked thirteen-year-old Robbie Jones to shoot an old man in the neighborhood store? He isn't talking, but through the voices of people who know Robbie, we may gain insight into this tragic event. Out of print but worth finding. 63pp., grades 5–12

***The Misfits*** by James Howe (Antheneum, 2002). Four students who do not "fit in" at their middle school create a third party for student council elections: the No-Name Party. These good friends laugh together, openly discuss their upsets, and talk about important issues. This "Gang of Five" (they say "five" to keep others off guard) enter the challenging world of adolescent popularity, politics, love, and loss and, on the way, change their school forever. 274pp., grades 4–7

Sticks and stones may break my bones,
but names will never hurt me.

Anybody who believes that has never been called a name. . . . I think that names are a very small way of looking at a person. . . .

Another thing I think about names is that they *do* hurt. They hurt because we believe them. We think they are telling us something true about ourselves, something other people can see even if we don't.

FROM *THE MISFITS*

***On the Fringe*** edited by Donald R. Gallo (Penguin Putnam, 2001). Jeannie is called a boy by her peers because of her short cropped hair and masculine clothes. Lacey knows that standing up for the school "freak" threatens her popularity. Gene brings a loaded rifle to school, fed up with the persistent harassment. These eleven short stories place the outsiders at the center, revealing struggles concerning popularity, nonconformity, hate, and self-acceptance. 221pp., young adult

***Pinky and Rex and the Bully*** by James Howe (Aladdin, 1996). Pinky has a dilemma: his favorite color is pink, his best friend is a girl, and Kevin calls him a sissy. Will he have to give up all his favorite things and his best friend to stop the bullying? 40pp., grades 1–3

***The Revealers*** by Doug Wilhelm (Farrar, Straus and Giroux, 2003). At Parkland Middle School, three middle school students—Elliot, Russell, and Catalina—have had enough of the bullying that plagues their daily lives. By starting an unofficial email forum at school, their collective statements inspire words from other kids who are equally fed up with these harmful acts. Just when the tide seems to be turning for the better, an act of revenge by a few students still bent on bullying others threatens the underground rebellion that has the whole school talking. 207pp., grades 5–8

**Recommendation from the Field**
*by Denise Clark Pope, Lecturer, Stanford University, School of Education*

*Romeo and Juliet* by William Shakespeare (Cambridge University Press, 1999/1595). Romeo and Juliet, two teens whose families are sworn enemies, fall in love. Juliet is supposed to marry Paris but weds Romeo in secret, aided by the Friar. Soon after, while attempting to stop a street fight, Romeo kills Juliet's cousin, which causes his banishment from Verona. The Friar devises a plan to bring the lovers together, but the plan fails. Romeo, believing Juliet is dead, kills himself. Juliet, seeing her dead lover, puts a dagger to her heart. The play ends in tragedy.

To generate ideas for meaningful service, ask students, "What issues from the play are relevant to teens today?" The topic of "families as enemies" can lead to a discussion of friendships, gangs, ethnic strife, or global relations. Another theme is that of teen suicide and love and how tragedy can lead a person to commit suicide. The Friar takes the side of the young people and helps them in deception. Who advocates for teens today, and how far should their role go?

Student service can take several forms. Ideally, students will come up with ideas and strategies. Teens might modernize scenes from *Romeo and Juliet* showing gang problems and perform and discuss the scenes with middle school youth. A high school class could organize a community education night for parents and teens about common causes of suicide. Students, in partnership with local agencies, could also create public service announcements or brochures to distribute on related and relevant themes. 224pp., young adult

***Shadow of the Dragon*** by Sherry Garland (Harcourt, 1993). At sixteen, Danny Vo feels trapped between his American friends and his family's traditions. When Danny's cousin, a recent emigrant, falls in with a Vietnamese gang, hate crimes and violence threaten multiple families, and their lives change forever. 314pp., young adult

**Recommendation from the Field**
*by Ariel Kaye, university student*

*Siddhartha* by Hermann Hesse (Bantam, 1982/1922). Siddhartha leaves his father and a life of privilege to live on his own and determine who he is. During his journey, he meets people who test his virtues and compassion. He gains wealth and experiences passion yet ultimately seeks a life of helping others. He also comes to respect what is found in nature—the beauty of the world. Siddhartha demonstrates the ability to learn from one's experiences and inner struggles as well as from others.

After reading *Siddhartha,* high school students can prepare a guide to help middle school students find their "true selves" in this confusing world, including suggestions for resisting peer pressure and resolving peer conflicts. This guide can include original stories with open-ended questions that stimulate thought and discussion to help younger students approach challenging situations in their lives within a broader context. For the high school authors, this project requires the application of many skills. They will create meaningful text and demonstrate an understanding of philosophy, and they might also lead mutually beneficial discussions with younger students. 152pp., young adult

***Stargirl*** by Jerry Spinelli (Knopf, 2000). Who would guess that Stargirl's arrival at Mica High would make such dramatic changes. With her nonconformist flair, Stargirl sings and strums her ukulele into the minds and hearts of students. Then the unexpected happens: students shun her for all that makes her different. Despite her attempts to be "normal," her individuality shines through. 186pp., grades 6–10

***When Christmas Comes Again: The World War I Diary of Simone Spencer*** by Beth Seidel Levine (Scholastic, 2002). Simone grew up in New York City high society and never expected that World War I would completely alter her life. After her brother volunteers for military service, Simone searches for a meaningful way to join and becomes a "Hello girl," a volunteer switchboard operator for the Army Signal Corps in France. In addition to revealing class issues during this time period, the story describes ways women participated in the war effort. Includes historical notes and photographs. 172pp., grades 5–7

***Wringer*** by Jerry Spinelli (HarperCollins, 1997). In Palmer's hometown, turning ten marks the biggest event of a boy's life: he can be a "wringer" at the annual Pigeon Day, a family festival. But Palmer dreads this day and his new role, which involves actually killing pigeons with his bare hands. An unexpected winged visitor on his windowsill further confirms his opposition to this violent activity and leads him to take a stand for his beliefs. 299pp., grades 4–7

# Interviews with Authors:
## The Story Behind the Story

In the following interviews, we find out the "story behind the story" from Sharleen Collicott (*Toestomper and the Caterpillars*), Phillip Hoose (*Hey, Little Ant!*, *We Were There, Too! Young People in U.S. History*, and *It's Our World, Too! Young People Who Are Making a Difference: How They Do It—How You Can Too*), and James Howe (*The Misfits*, *Pinky and Rex and the Bully*, and *The Drop Dead Inn*).

I have had the pleasure of meeting two of these authors. I attended a concert in Los Angeles where Phillip Hoose and his daughter sang their song "Hey, Little Ant!" for the first time in public. I met James Howe at a bookstore and immediately found we shared an interest in stopping bullying and intolerance in schools (and elsewhere). We have now co-led workshops for teachers and students on the theme "Words That Hurt, Words That Heal, Words That Lead to Social Action." While I have not yet met Sharleen Collicott, her captivating and amusing characters caused me to contact her and say, "Tell me more!"

### *Sharleen Collicott, author of* Toestomper and the Caterpillars

I have a wild imagination. I have many ideas, but putting them down and organizing them is difficult. For me, an idea is more important than being able to draw or write. Develop your idea, that's the main step. If you have one little tiny idea, you can go the next step and think of another. Now, if a child says, "I don't have an idea," I don't believe it! Even a stiff, corny idea is a fine beginning. I would ask, "What's your first idea?" If the child answered, "A butterfly walking across the room," I would ask for the next idea. "The butterfly sits in a chair." I would say, "Fine, and what's next?" And the child would say, "The butterfly flies to the moon!" One idea just leads to the next.

My desire to put my ideas on paper led to my being an author, and I worked hard at my art to accomplish my dream. The first books I wrote were crude; still, my editors liked my art so much they helped. Then I taught myself to write. I draw the pictures first, though not to the point where they are finished. I go over and over the words. I try to let the pictures tell everything, since I do not think of myself as a "writer." I like to write, but I am always learning. I keep in mind that the secret to a good book is the plot.

I create stories, including *Toestomper and the Caterpillars*, for my own pleasure and hope others enjoy the books as well. How did *Toestomper and the Caterpillars* develop? I had about eight different story lines I could follow with my initial drawings of Toestomper and the little caterpillars. He is a bit of a tough guy. I tried to think of a name that was mean but not too mean. In this story, Toestomper changes. First he is mean and hanging with the wrong guys. He changes because of the caterpillars. He becomes a "daddy" or a helper. He gets a little bit better. He also makes the caterpillars a little like him as you can see in the last drawing.

The story will continue with *Toestomper and the Bad Butterflies*. Naturally, the caterpillars turn into butterflies, and of course they are not really that bad. They just overstep their bounds.

I am surprised and pleased that *Toestomper and the Caterpillars* can be used as a teaching tool. I like the fact that this book can help someone learn about bullying and friendship and be used for elementary through high school students. It shows that Toestomper truly has a good side underneath his rough exterior.

## *Phillip Hoose, coauthor of* Hey, Little Ant!

*Hey, Little Ant!* began as a children's song that I cowrote with my daughter Hannah, who was then nine years old. When it occurred to us that the song would make a worthwhile children's book, I thought we would easily find a publisher. Wrong! Even with my track record as an author, finding a publisher for *Hey, Little Ant!* took five years. When editors bothered to respond about why they rejected the book, they usually informed us that children could not accept a book that ended with a question. They said, "Children need resolution." I said, "What about *The Cat in the Hat?*" "Well," they said, "Dr. Seuss is always an exception!"

How did I find a publisher? I asked teachers and performers who use this song to write letters explaining how the story and dialogue worked in their classrooms and onstage. Many people wrote me wonderful, helpful descriptions, so I began sending out large packages to publishing houses and included these letters with the manuscript. I finally received a letter from Tricycle Press saying that our submission had raised quite a debate around their office. But, alas, they still weren't going to buy it. I wrote right back saying they should do themselves and children everywhere a favor and take a chance on this book. To my astonishment it worked! I received a call saying that a consultant had agreed that the open ending was actually a strength. We negotiated a contract, and the publisher found a superb illustrator in Debbie Tilley. Since then, *Hey, Little Ant!* has sold over 35,000 copies and will soon be available in eight different languages: Hebrew, Dutch, Korean, Italian, French, German, Spanish, and English.

How did the story evolve? Basically, one summer day, my daughter Ruby, then two or three, was out in the driveway tromping ants. Hannah, then nine, and I were watching from the porch. Ruby didn't look angry, just bored. I went to her and said, "How would you like to be one of those ants?" "Wouldn't bother me any," she replied. Then I walked away. But Ruby quit stomping. My question and the idea it contained seemed to get to her, and she quit.

Hannah and I were writing songs pretty furiously that summer. Thinking about what had just happened in the driveway, Hannah and I began to script this negotiating session between a child and an ant. As we were wrapping up the song, we said, "How do you want to end it?" We agreed quickly that we did not want to resolve the story at all. The end question was too big for the author to say one way or the other. It's up to the reader. To say how it turns out would weaken the story. The power is in the reader's ability to decide for herself or himself. The story offers a chance for very young people to focus on alternatives to violence at a moment when they have their first opportunity to figure this out: when they're killing bugs. I remember deciding as a very young person my lifelong policy—I won't squish a bug deliberately, but if I do it accidentally I won't let myself feel bad. I believe there is real power in the dialogue between the child and the ant.

In performance, I would crouch down on stage as the ant and Hannah would loom over me with her foot up. Often kids in the audience would ask questions: "What if the bug was a mosquito?" "What if a hundred ants were on your kitchen counter, what would you do?" We would reflect the questions back: "What would *you* do?"

*Hey, Little Ant!* has achieved a reputation as a tool for exploring various things—tolerance, nonviolence, seeing the common worth of all living things. The song/book has been turned into plays, operas, and videos around the world to encourage children to reflect on these very serious questions in ways that are easy for them to think about.

In this story I see two creatures who appear to be very different but who, despite their obvious differences in size and physical power, have a lot in common. I think it is important to look for the common in all of us while we respect and appreciate the differences.

## *James Howe, author of* The Misfits

Writing *The Misfits* had several starting points, with two at the forefront. My daughter had a hard time socially in seventh grade with all the name-calling and ostracism. It brought back my experience during those years and how hard it was for me feeling different from my peers.

The other compelling motivation was that I had recently come out as a gay man after many years in the closet. I wanted to write something that would help young people today not have to go through the experiences of my past. I wanted to write a young gay character who was okay with who he was and could start life on a different foot. While I do think things are changing, we have a long way to go. When I was growing up, being gay was considered an illness or something you did not want to be. Now I realize how much I had lived in fear of what people would think or say to me. "Coming out" made me see what a waste of energy it had been my whole life to not tell the truth. I have developed an impatience with the ways in which we all waste energy and our lives by living in fear, so often of such small things. I wanted to tell this story like it is, as best as I could, to convey the message that we can be part of change. It's possible.

The actual writing of *The Misfits* started with an unfinished short story on the theme of chocolate. I had a setting of a small town and a department store with Bobby selling ties. When I began writing this novel, I thought of Bobby's character and his strong voice that I loved and connected with. From the short story evolved this group of friends. They wrote the book.

Part of my intent in writing, especially for children, is to empower them, to open their minds to think about things in a different way. With *The Misfits*, I was writing a story with characters who, deep in their bones, understand about courage, taking a stand, and telling it like it is. Accepting differences and embracing difference in one's self as a good thing has been central to many of my books. The idea of difference as something we shy away from is a notion that boggles my mind.

That *The Misfits* is told with humor is only natural; humor is part of who I am and also where I come from. My father, a minister and social activist, frequently would wind humor into his sermons, even on serious topics, just as I do in my writing. I want the reader to care! Certainly I do not want readers to feel they are being told what to think. As a reader or audience member, I treasure the times I am laughing one minute and crying the next. Humor and sadness are so connected in life.

The characters in this book grow in their ability to see a larger world. Often, when one is the subject of injustice, it is easier to see there is a larger world. I imagine this book being used to open the reader, the class, the school—whoever is using the book as a community—to build a bridge to the bigger world. This book can open dialogue and suggest creative ways to deal with whatever problems exist. By being direct, and putting yourself out there, you are helping others to do the same.

While I have received very positive responses from kids regarding the book, some say they had a hard time accepting the ending: that two gay characters, Joe and Colin, could express their feelings to each other at the age of twelve and also that a really popular "in" kid would date a less popular kid. Some kids like this sort of "fairy-tale ending." I want the reader to ask, "Why do you think this is unrealistic? Why should it be otherwise?"

One school in California did create a "No Name Day" modeled on *The Misfits* that will be an annual event. Nothing would make me happier than this book being a catalyst to start political action in schools. I didn't start out knowing that this would be so political. But the seed was planted in the book with Addie when she refuses to say the pledge of allegiance. I realized that something larger than the book can come from the book, and that is thrilling.

I hope *The Misfits* opens the minds and hearts of readers. I would like young people to be able to think for themselves—to really consider what it would be like to be in someone else's shoes, how they would feel if they were the object of name-calling. That's a lot right there. I don't think you arbitrarily stop name-calling. I think you develop compassion and an understanding that the other person is a human being.

CHAPTER 7

# ELDERS

> Imagine what a harmonious world it could be if every single person, both young and old, shared a little of what he is good at doing.
>
> QUINCY JONES, MUSICIAN

The intergenerational connection has a long and vibrant history in service learning—young people and older people naturally fit together. Their interactions are often based on shared interests and result in personal growth for everyone involved. Service and learning flow easily in both directions as an older person tutors a child or an adolescent teaches computer skills to a retiree. These partnerships evoke caring and provide an exchange that matters. The two groups often discover similarities more profound than their differences: a love of baseball or gardening, appreciation of music, caring for families, or pleasure in traditions.

Young people benefit from getting to know active elders in their communities as well as those who are infirm or suffering from memory loss. Each of these populations offers unique ways to interact and create meaningful relationships. It is often said that our mobile society separates the generations within families. While the relationships created through service learning are not substitutes, they are rich with their own rewards and exchanges and offer opportunities for contact between generations that might otherwise be missing.

Through intergenerational experiences, young people can explore:

- the learning of life's lessons.
- how different cultures treat older populations.
- how to stay healthy in body and mind.
- the joy of living.
- history related through personal experience and knowledge, which is hard to find in textbooks.
- the mutually beneficial relationships that can be achieved between people of different ages.

When preparing for intergenerational situations and activities, make sure that both your students and the elders are willing participants or recipients. A key purpose of service learning is creating mutually respectful relationships. When combining generations, be particularly attentive to the potential for imbalance or even condescension. It's important to explore and state the value of both the young people and the elders involved in the project and to be sure that the service is directed toward an actual need rather than an assumed one.

## Preparation: Getting Ready for Service Learning Involving Elders

The following activities can be used in the preparation stage to promote learning and skill development related to elders. These activities can be used with different age ranges during preparation to help your students examine key issues through research, analyze community needs, and gain the knowledge they need to effectively contribute to the design of their service plan. Since literature is often an important part of preparation, you can find recommended titles on this theme in the Elders Bookshelf later in this chapter.

***Activity: Coming to Know the Elder Population.*** Who makes up the elder population in your community? How do they spend their time? Answering these questions and others can help generate possibilities for service learning. Sometimes the best way to get the information you need is to go straight to the source. Invite several elder community activists to class—business people, volunteers, educators, historians—and aim for a ratio of one for every five to seven students. To find potential visitors, ask the students or other teachers for referrals, or check with the local volunteer or senior center. Before the visit, ask each of the older community members to submit a brief personal biography or résumé. In small groups, have students read the biographies to prepare questions for an interview session. Each guest may also be asked to prepare a topic for an interactive conversation. You might plan for multiple visits to provide time for both interviews and topic discussions. As a result of these meetings, students and their elder guests may decide to collaborate on social action projects. For younger children, one or two classroom visitors is ample to create a discussion. Have students develop their questions prior to the visit, and be certain every child has a turn to participate.

***Activity: Preparing for Oral History Projects.*** Bringing people together from different generations can be most gratifying, especially when everyone is prepared. For oral history projects, if possible try to colead the activities with an agency partner who has experience with elders. Many books in this chapter's bookshelf also can be helpful, particularly *Growing Older* by George Ancona, which gives samples of oral histories collected from a diverse population. To get your oral history project off to a good start, try the following process.

Begin by meeting separately with the student group and the elders. With the students, ask, "What do you think of older people?" Most students think that elders have a disability. Present information—or have students conduct research—to demonstrate that this is not true. Many seniors are healthy, and even those with infirmities may lead active lives.

Similarly, members of the older group can be asked, "What do you expect from the students?" Often, they expect students to be rude or impolite; they may also express concern about safety issues when visiting a high school. Take this opportunity to present accurate information.

To prepare for the first interaction, students can work in small groups to develop questions to "break the ice." Students can also role-play the initial meetings to practice their personal introductions. Inform the older group that the students will be asking questions to help everyone become acquainted.

Consider this list of questions developed and used by high school students in various projects:

- What should I call you?
- Why did you decide to come today?
- How old are you?
- How many children do you have?
- As a child, what did you want to be when you grew up?
- What was the time of your life that you most enjoyed?
- What are some of your hobbies?
- How did you meet your significant other or others?
- What would you like to change about your life?
- What has changed in the world since you were a teenager?
- What are some major historical events that you lived through/participated in?

Allow time for the interaction and for feedback about the process at the conclusion. Reflection for this initial meeting can be held separately so each group can express any concerns as well as happiness about their new relationships.

Even very young children have successfully created oral histories in collaboration with elder partners. Younger children who cannot yet write may need to dictate their stories for older students or others to transcribe. Sometimes the books take the form of shared histories—for example, "We both like . . . " or "Our favorite animals are . . . " Preparation for these projects also includes getting acquainted with their older student helpers.

### Find Out More About Elders

To learn more about these issues and to get ideas for service and action, visit these Web sites and organizations online:

***www.gu.org*** Elderly United is a national organization promoting intergenerational strategies, programs, and policies.

*continued* ⟶

***www.seniorcorps.org*** Senior Corps, a part of the Corporation of National and Community Service, is a network of programs that tap the experience, skills, and talents of older citizens to meet community challenges, including young and old people serving their communities together.

***www.cps.unt.edu/natla/*** The National Academy for Teaching and Learning About Aging promotes education about aging-related issues and has curriculum and project oriented resources.

## Making Connections Across the Curriculum

Some service learning activities naturally lend themselves to interdisciplinary work and making connections across the curriculum. These connections strengthen and broaden student learning, helping them meet academic standards. More than likely, you'll be looking for these connections and ways to encourage them well before the students ever start working on service learning activities. As with the entire service learning process, it helps to remain flexible, because some connections can be spontaneously generated by the questions raised throughout and by the needs of the project. To help you think about cross-curricular connections and where you can look for them, the Curricular Web for this chapter (page 109) gives examples of many different ways this theme can be used in different academic areas. (The service learning scenarios in the next section of the chapter also demonstrate various ways this theme can be used across the curriculum.)

> The human contribution is the essential ingredient. It is only in the giving of oneself to others that we truly live.
>
> ETHEL PERCY ANDRUS, FOUNDER OF AARP (FORMERLY THE AMERICAN ASSOCIATION OF RETIRED PERSONS)

## Service Learning Scenarios:
### Ideas for Action

Ready to take action? What follows are projects that have been successfully carried out by elementary, middle, or high school students. Most of these scenarios and examples explicitly include some aspects of preparation, action, reflection, and demonstration. These scenarios can be a rich source of project, resource, and curriculum ideas for you to draw upon. While the grade levels are given as a reference, most project ideas can be adapted to suit younger or older students, and many are suitable for cross-age partnerships.

***Shared Moments: Grades 1–3.*** Elder volunteers in Iowa attended a three-part workshop on reading with young children hosted by a local agency (a school district can also sponsor the workshop). The volunteers were then placed in classrooms as Reading Buddies to help students at all levels to advance in their skills and literature appreciation. The students wanted to give back to their buddies, so they wrote special stories, which they read aloud and then gave to their partners. Each story was accompanied by a piece of art showing the buddy and the student together. The elder participants described this experience as a "true exchange between the generations."

***Oral History Projects—Variations on a Worthwhile Theme: Grades 1–12.*** This tried-and-true service learning activity enables young people and other community members to learn from the collective experience of elders. Careful preparation will produce meaningful long-term partnerships. Literature connections can be made through many of the bookshelf titles. The epilogue of *Pink and Say*, for example, attests to the importance of keeping stories alive from generation to generation. *Too Young for Yiddish* illustrates what can be easily lost—or preserved. *Growing Older* presents anecdotal remembrances of older adults with very different backgrounds. Many books explore memory and the beauty of tapping into the stories of our elders.

***First-Grade Historians: Grade 1.*** An elementary teacher in Tennessee described how, for more than twenty years, her first-grade students have documented the lives of local senior citizens and placed the collected stories in the public library. The teacher

# Elders Across the Curriculum

### *English/Language Arts*

- Discuss: Why should younger people care about elders?
- Take dictation and compose letters and other correspondence for elders
- Read and discuss a classic text with an elder partner

### *Social Studies/History*

- Learn about Medicare, social security, and Medicaid
- Establish a current events discussion group with elders at a senior center
- Conduct interviews with older people about community history or significant historical events

### *Languages*

- Contact senior centers to find elders who are fluent in the language being studied to visit and speak with the class
- Compare how elders are regarded by different cultures and countries
- Learn about colloquial expressions or proverbs used by elders in the language

### *Theater, Music, & Visual Arts*

- Create a dramatic reading of passages written by people of all ages
- Learn and perform music enjoyed by a previous generation
- Study and learn to do folk or traditional arts from your community or region

## Elders

### *Math*

- Find out and graph statistics on the population of your region by age
- Learn about tax forms and help prepare tax returns for elders
- Create a "true or false" survey about elders and find out peer group opinions; create a statistical report and use this to teach others

### *Physical Education*

- Learn and teach armchair exercises
- Research athletic programs and competitions for elders; observe and cheer participants
- Arrange for an intergenerational athletic or exercise experience

### *Computer*

- Document elders' memories, pictures, and stories on a Web page
- Conduct Internet research on careers in gerontology and geriatrics
- Survey seniors about their attitudes toward and their uses of technology

### *Science*

- Educate elder people about nutrition
- Study health care and dietary needs of elders; compare with those of youth
- Plan ahead and grow corsage flowers for a "senior senior" prom

and students identified candidates to interview through newspaper stories about contributions made by older community members (read aloud to the class by the teacher) and by publicizing the project on a flyer at the local senior center. The class developed a list of questions and conducted about ten interviews, adding drawings of the older persons and illustrations of their activities. Parents took photographs of the interviews, and a display was mounted in the library when the book was donated. The stories and art are enjoyed and appreciated every year.

***Getting Physical: Grade 3.*** Third graders in West Hollywood, California, got into all sorts of positions while studying yoga, but the ones they enjoyed the most were collaborating with senior citizens. In weekly visits to the local senior center, students shared their yoga skills with the older people, and together, the two groups learned how to modify the yoga positions for people who are less agile. Students used their writing and communication skills to produce "We Love Yoga" brochures for community distribution. To reach more elders, students created a series of public service announcements (PSAs) on exercise for daily broadcast on local cable television. These PSAs were also played occasionally at the senior center.

> No matter what accomplishments you make, somebody helps you.
>
> WILMA RUDOLPH, ATHLETE

***A Poetic Journey: Grade 4.*** Fourth-grade students in Maryland had a long-term, year-round collaboration with older people in the community. At the beginning of the school year, the students gave a "welcoming tea" party. Poetry sessions followed; seniors and students wrote poetry, produced a poetry book, and made poetry posters that were displayed in storefronts. The students and their senior partners had a holiday party, made collages, participated in science experiments with the support of college students, made scrapbooks, and had a storytelling event. The year concluded with a potluck dinner in honor of the senior partners.

***A Gift of Tradition: Grades 4–8.*** More than a hundred students in northeast Oklahoma participated in a cultural event sponsored by the Cherokee Nation. Community volunteers worked with the students as they learned how to craft objects once used in daily life and now viewed as art forms, including stickball sticks and baskets. Students also made corn-husk dolls, traditional Cherokee dolls mothers and grandmothers make as playthings for children. Students met with representatives from the Cherokee Nation to determine appropriate places to donate the corn-husk dolls. Student representatives from every grade level went on field visits to personally give the gifts; one group went to local preschools, and the other went to a local nursing home. At each site, the students demonstrated how the dolls were made. Among the elder recipients were many Cherokee men and women who shared their own recollections of making these and other items.

***Knitting Past and Present Together: Grade 5.*** As part of a unit of study, "Schools of the Past," students in Vermont learned how children helped during World War II by sewing blankets and knitting socks to be sent to soldiers overseas. They decided to learn to knit, which was described as extremely difficult by many children. They also found out that residents of a nearby nursing home had themselves made sweaters and blankets during the war. The class agreed this would be the ideal place to donate their creation, a handmade knitted blanket. The students sent a letter describing their project and asking if the facility would like to receive the blanket and if residents would be willing to meet and discuss their World War II experiences with the class. During a visit to the nursing home, the students listened as the older people described their experiences in the 1940s. Another benefit: The small-motor skills used in knitting improved the students' cursive handwriting.

***Bingo Buttons: Grade 5.*** Fifth graders in New York City who visited a convalescent home each week noticed that while their older friends enjoyed playing bingo, they had difficulty picking up the bingo markers. They brainstormed ways to make the game easier to play. After conferring with the center's staff, they began to collect buttons to replace the traditional bingo chips. When the class initiated a school-wide button collection, the entire school learned about the visits and how much the students enjoyed the time spent in intergenerational activities. The button gathering culminated in an original rap song, a ceremony in which the song was presented to the seniors, and the best bingo game ever.

***A Dance for All Ages: Grade 5.*** Two populations joined together to create a multimedia performance that combined the written word and movement. Elders and fifth graders in Maryland who were interested in movement, writing, and collaboration were recruited for the project. A series of workshops led by a high school dance teacher brought the two groups together. The older people wrote about "what it is like to be old," and the elementary students wrote about "what it might be like to be old." Dances were then created to accompany the written words and the multimedia performance was presented at a school PTA event, the senior center, and a state intergenerational conference.

***Time Online: Grade 6.*** Sixth-grade students read and discussed *Doing Time Online* and reflected on many aspects of the novel: a student required to correspond online with a nursing home resident as the result of a joke that caused harm, the student's original skepticism, and the surprising benefits and relationship that developed. Students talked about finding their own "senior email pals" and began to research possible community sources of such partnerships. They found eight older people who had computers at home and four who regularly went online at the senior center and began to correspond with these elders via email. Sometimes the students or the seniors were slow in responding, and a few of the seniors had to leave the program. Still, there were benefits: companionship, an exchange of experiences, and face-to-face conversations in three gatherings during the school year.

***Holidays of Old: Grade 7.*** A math teacher in Alvin, Texas, brought an idea to a faculty meeting with teachers from the various disciplines that made up the school's seventh-grade teaching team. Having recently visited her elder aunt in a nursing home, she thought that a visit to a similar local facility would make a good addition to the students' learning about "Holidays of Old." Through collaboration, all disciplines participated. Students eagerly contributed ideas and showed leadership. Even a young student with a history of discipline problems "shaped up" so he could go along. English teachers used literature to examine how older people are perceived; in history class, students planned and practiced interviewing so that they could interview residents and learn how holidays were celebrated in the past; health classes found out about residents' dietary restrictions and distributed appropriate recipes to volunteer bakers; math students constructed geometric holiday ornaments for tree decorations; science classes studied the aging process; and art students made papier-mâché picture frames to leave as gifts. Before the visit, residence staff members provided orientations for the students and the elders who chose to participate. The visit far exceeded the expectations of all involved, and the teachers became staunch advocates of service learning.

***A Senior Register: Grade 7.*** Students collected oral histories from older African Americans who attended a church that was being closed. In preparation, students studied the era when the church was built. Interviews were transcribed into stories, and photos were taken of all contributors. Students wrote letters to help get the church placed on the historic register and preserved. At a final celebration, each elder was given a copy of the book. Copies were given to organizations, historical societies, and libraries as well.

***Project Cook 'n' Serve: Grade 7.*** Middle school teachers in Massachusetts were concerned that many of their students lacked the social skills and manners to have appropriate conversations with peers and adults. They decided to build on an existing partnership with a senior center, and Project Cook 'n' Serve was born. Through collaboration between senior center staff and teachers, seventh graders and senior citizens studied nutrition together (this met an academic standard) and took a cooking class together. The students then interviewed their older partners about rules of etiquette, reported their findings in class, and practiced what they had learned. For a finale, the students prepared lunch at the senior center, served the food with proper manners, and had lovely conversations. But the program did not end—the students and seniors decided to collaborate on a community cookbook. After the projects had ended, students maintained communication with their senior friends through frequent emails and occasional visits. Teachers observed an increase in polite and appropriate verbal exchanges student-to-student and student-to-teacher. In their reflection journals, students noted that two of the books they used, *Growing Older: What Young People Should Know About Aging* and *Handbook for Boys* added to their understanding and appreciation for older people and what can be learned through friendships.

***Poetry Partners: Grade 7.*** As the culmination of a poetry unit, middle school students in Wisconsin invited their grandparents and other elders from a local senior center to participate in a poetry event. The students performed poetry, shared music as poetry, and engaged in poetry activities, such as creating the longest alliterative sentence. Then intergenerational "poetry partners" composed collaborative poems: teens wrote on the theme "when I'm old, I'll . . . " and grandparents wrote "looking back on my life." After lunch, some read their poems aloud, and each student presented a previously written poem "Ode to my Grandparent/Grandfriend" to his or her guest.

***Stimulating Conversations: Grade 8.*** Time spent with elders in convalescent centers or day-care facilities for people with memory loss can be designed to provide stimulation and interaction opportunities. After reading *Stranger in the Mirror* and *Conversation Starters: How to Start Conversations with People Who Have Memory Loss*, middle school students raised questions and concerns about working with this population. They learned more about Alzheimer's disease by viewing a video and attending three informational sessions led by staff from the partner day-care facility for people with memory loss. Students had time to develop and try out ideas for helpful activities, including crafts, musical programming for sing-a-longs, and current events discussions. From their journals, the students made a display and booklet for the agency with original poetry and art. They also presented their program to other classes in their school to familiarize students with service learning and to teach about Alzheimer's disease.

***Where Were You When? Grade 8.*** The strategy for a "Where Were You When?" oral history project begins with finding out what subjects interest the senior citizens who will be interviewed. A simple survey of participants at the senior center in Maryland revealed a range of intriguing subjects: a woman who knew Rosa Parks wanted to discuss civil rights, a woman whose brother repaired Charles Lindbergh's airplane had photographs to share, a man wanted to discuss how the Kennedy assassination had affected his life, and a woman was ripe with stories of her experience as a riveter during World War II. Eighth-grade students reviewed the list, and each selected a topic of interest. The students researched their topics to prepare for the first visit, a combination interview and lunch. The preparation created a level of comfort and facilitated exchange for all. During the next visit, the seniors heard the reports written by the students. A compilation of these conversations was given to each participant and the library.

***Intergenerational Technology: Grades 9 and 10.*** What to do with your unwanted computers? A nonprofit organization in Maryland came up with an idea: bring high school students and senior citizens together and provide them with training in repairing and rebuilding computers. A technology center was created at a high school. With skilled volunteer trainers, equipment to repair, and needy recipient agencies and individuals, the center went into operation. Students completing the training program also earned credits toward graduation.

***Intergenerational Learning: Grades 9 and 10.*** Thirty high school students and thirty senior citizens in Maryland formed a mini-university to learn about each other and about topics of mutual interest. Before the groups came together, each had workshops to express concerns about soon-to-be partners, as described in the "Coming to Know the Elder Population" activity on pages 106–107. A committee with representatives from each group selected the topics and planned the workshops, which were usually led by group members. At each monthly class, two topics were presented. For example, in the "Let's Cook" program, participants (1) prepared and brought their favorite recipes to share and (2) watched a cooking demonstration by a local chef. For ESL students and seniors with limited English-speaking skills, the program provided a safe environment for improving conversational abilities. In addition, high school students learned about careers in fields that involve elders.

They also learned grant-writing skills as they sought the funding needed to support the program. The seniors favorably commented on their relationships with their new teen friends. As a result of this project, students developed other service activities, such as a "senior prom," that were greatly appreciated.

***Tennis, Anyone? Grades 9–12.*** Senior citizen tennis players were looking for a good game in preparation for a local tournament, and they found one—at the high school. They became regulars at the school, working out once a week with the tennis team during practice. The high school players became the cheering section at the tournament, and the seniors surprised the young athletes with a donation that helped them get team sweatshirts.

***Tell Me Your Story: Grade 10.*** A tenth-grade "American Experience" class began an oral history project in partnership with a local neighborhood association to record histories of people who had lived in the school's community in Spokane, Washington. To help students prepare, a local news reporter taught them interviewing skills. Through a community meeting, the students identified people who had lived in the neighborhood in the 1930s and 1940s. The students then collected oral histories that reflected community life in those decades. Students recorded the histories, transcribed them, and gave copies of the written histories and recordings to participants. Copies were also kept in the archives of the partnering community organization. Letters from several of the participating older people described their appreciation for the opportunity to share their stories and for having copies of the interview audiotapes to give to their children.

***At the Internet Café: Grades 10–12.*** At the senior citizen center "Internet café," high school students acted as Internet coaches. As the students refined their skills, they helped the elders feel more comfortable going online. The assistance helped many older people stay connected with family members who lived in different regions. The seniors said they especially enjoyed writing to and hearing from their grandchildren.

***A Matter of Health: Grades 10–12.*** High school students who were learning about health sciences took their knowledge and skills directly to the senior citizens in their community of Sarasota, Florida. During six visits, relationships formed between students and their elders as tenth through twelfth graders practiced skills by measuring blood pressure and demonstrating CPR and choking relief measures. Students were well prepared through aging sensitivity training, and extensive research and discussion of aging, the illnesses affecting older people, and death and dying. Time was always made for socializing, which included the young people learning line dancing from their older friends. Students kept journals throughout the year and demonstrated academic competencies beyond the course requirements.

***Remember the Women and Children! Grade 12.*** For an oral history project focusing on World War II, students in a government class divided into groups to interview veterans. Then a student asked, "What about the women?" Responding to this inquiry expanded the activity to include collecting stories from women who were at home during the war as well as adults who were children in the early 1940s. Questions included: "What different roles did you assume?" "What were some unexpected effects of the war?" One result of the project was a unique publication illustrating multiple perspectives on and memories of living through times of war.

> We have to reinvent the wheel every once in a while, not because we need a lot of wheels; but because we need a lot of inventors.
>
> BRUCE JOYCE, EDUCATOR

## The Elders Bookshelf

Our elder generations offer wisdom and insights gained from years of experience. The titles found in the Elders Bookshelf can provide knowledge and support to inspire and sustain intergenerational interactions. To help you find books relevant to your particular projects, the book chart classifies the books into several topic areas: an overview of elders, active elders, intergenerational relationships, and memory loss and/or nursing homes.

In general, the bookshelf features:

- An annotated bibliography arranged and alphabetized by title according to the general categories of nonfiction (N), picture books (P), and fiction (F). For nonfiction and fiction, length and recommended grade levels are included. The entries in the picture book category do not include suggested grade levels, since they can be successfully used with all ages.
- A chart organized by topic and category to help you find books relevant to particular projects.
- Recommendations from service learning colleagues and experts that include a book summary and ideas for service learning connections. (The number of recommended books varies in each bookshelf.)

## Elders Bookshelf Topics

| *Topics* | *Books* | *Category* |
|---|---|---|
| ***An Overview of Elders*** Aging happens, actually, day by day. The "big picture" shows the complexity of aging and includes health concerns, family life, and cultural and societal changes. | *Grandparents Around the World* | N |
| | *Growing Older* ‡ | N |
| | *Growing Older: What Young People Should Know About Aging* ‡ | N |
| ***Active Elders*** Recognizing the many roles played by elders enriches our lives and corrects misconceptions. | *Butterflies and Lizards, Beryl and Me* (see page 143) | F |
| | *The Cay* | F |
| | *A Day's Work* (see page 168) | P |
| | *Edwina Victorious* * (see page 199) | F |
| | *Hurry Granny Annie* | P |
| | *Rainbow Joe and Me* (see page 211) | P |
| | *Tuck Everlasting* | F |
| ***Intergenerational Relationships*** These books continue the theme of active elders but also emphasize the relationships between generations, capturing something special that occurs between young and old. | *Butterfly Boy* | P |
| | *Chicken Sunday* (see page 98) | P |
| | *City Green* * (see page 142) | P |
| | *Dancing with Dziadziu* | P |
| | *Doing Time Online* * | F |
| | *Grandma's Records* | P |
| | *Handbook for Boys* | F |
| | *Happy Birthday Mr. Kang* (see page 168) | P |
| | *The Hundred Penny Box* | F |
| | *Joe's Wish* | P |
| | *Mrs. Katz and Tush* | P |
| | *Petey* * | F |
| | *Somebody Loves You, Mr. Hatch* | P |
| | *The Summer My Father Was Ten* (see page 143) | P |
| | *Too Young for Yiddish* | P |
| | *The War with Grandpa* | F |

*continued* ⟶

| Topics | Books | Category |
|---|---|---|
| **Memory Loss and/or Nursing Homes** With aging can come loss of memory or other conditions leading to a need for assistance. These stories share a range of experience and memories with respect and dignity. | *The Bonesetter's Daughter* | F |
| | *Conversation Starters as Easy as ABC 123: How to Start Conversations with People Who Have Memory Loss* | N |
| | *The Graduation of Jake Moon* | F |
| | *The Memory Box* | P |
| | *Mosaic Moon: Caregiving Through Poetry* | N |
| | *Remember Me? Alzheimer's Through the Eyes of a Child/ ¿Te acuerdas de mí? Pensamientos de la enfermedad, Alzheimers a travez de los ojos de un niño* | P |
| | *Sachiko Means Happiness* | P |
| | *Singing with Momma Lou* | P |
| | *Stranger in the Mirror* | P |
| | *Sunshine Home* | P |
| | *Tiger, Tiger Burning Bright* | F |
| | *Wilfred Gordon McDonald Partridge* | P |
| | *A Window of Time* | P |

Page references are given for books that do not appear in the Elders Bookshelf but that can be found in the bookshelf lists of other chapters.
* These books include examples of young people in service-providing roles.
‡ These books are out of print but still worth finding.

## Nonfiction: Elders

***Conversation Starters As Easy As ABC 123: How to Start Conversations with People Who Have Memory Loss*** by Devora Kaye and Gabi Roussos (ABCD Books, 2000). Written by eighth-grade students, this ABC coloring book is a friendly guide for young people who are interacting with people who have memory loss. 29pp., all ages

***Grandparents Around the World*** by Patricia Lakin (Blackbirch Press, 1999). Text and photographs provide a snapshot of the role that older people, especially grandparents, play in families in various countries, including Canada, Italy, Swaziland, Ecuador, Iraq, and Israel, as well as Native Americans in the United States. 32pp., grades 2–5

***Growing Older*** by George Ancona (Duttons, 1978). In this collection of oral histories, you will meet, among others, an antique dealer from Texas, a woman who travels and gardens, a grandmother from the Yucatán, a Sauk and Fox Indian from Oklahoma, an immigrant from Lithuania, and residents of Nicodemus, Kansas, which began as a settlement of freed slaves. The author recommends, "Ask your grandparents for their stories. If you don't have grandparents nearby, borrow or adopt some, as certain Indian tribes do." Out of print but well worth finding. 48pp., grades 5–12

***Growing Older: What Young People Should Know About Aging*** by John Langone (Little, Brown and Company, 1991). By 2025, American teenagers will be outnumbered two to one by people 65 and older. This book clears up myths and misconceptions about aging and provides information about cultural differences and physical ailments. It also asks, "What kind of old person will you be?" Out of print but worth finding. 162pp., grades 6–12

***Mosaic Moon: Caregiving Through Poetry*** by Frances H. Kakugawa (Watermark Publishing, 2002). For one year, caregivers of people with Alzheimer's disease met each month. This book chronicles their work together and the resulting personal stories and poetry. Suggestions for "how-to" make this a worthwhile resource. 218pp., young adult

## Picture Books: Elders

***Butterfly Boy*** by Virginia Kroll (Boyds Mills Press, 1997). Emilio wheels his *abuelo*—his grandfather—outside each sunny afternoon to watch butterflies flutter around the white garage wall. With limited mobility and no speech, Abuelo brightens up watching the red admirals, a species of butterflies attracted to the color white. As the seasons change, Emilio and his grandfather await the return of the butterflies. But will they return when Papa paints the garage blue?

***Dancing with Dziadziu*** by Susan Campbell Bartoletti (Harcourt, 1997). A young girl shares her ballet dancing and an early Easter celebration with her ill grandmother while the grandmother reminisces about her husband and her immigration from Poland.

***Grandma's Records*** by Eric Velasquez (Walker, 2001). Eric loves summer with Grandma in Spanish Harlem. During the hot days, Grandma fills the apartment with the salsa and merengue music that she grew up with in Puerto Rico. When her nephew Sammy Ayala, a percussionist for Rafael Cortijo's band, "the best band in Puerto Rico," comes to town, Grandma and Eric are special guests at their first New York concert. The performance strengthens the bond between the generations.

Grandma liked all types of music. But one record was very special to her. Whenever she played it, she would put her hand over her heart and close her eyes as she sang along. When it was over, Grandma would sometimes sit quietly, thinking about Grandpa and the old days in Santurce, her hometown.

"Sometimes," Grandma said, "a song can say everything that is in your heart as if it was written just for you."

FROM *GRANDMA'S RECORDS*

***Hurry Granny Annie*** by Arlene Alda (Tricycle Press, 1999). Granny Annie runs so fast the children have to run their hardest to keep up. But they all want to find out what the "something great" is that Annie is determined to catch. Is it a fish, a butterfly, or a baseball? Annie's joy for what is most beautiful is ultimately contagious.

***Joe's Wish*** by James Proimos (Harcourt, 1998). Joe Capri wishes on a star: "Please, I want to be young again." The Something or Other arrives, promising that "tomorrow I will grant your wish." But after a day of play with his grandson, Joe finds that the idea of being young again pales in comparison to the joy of his relationship with his grandson just the way it is.

***The Memory Box*** by Mary Bahr (Albert Whitman, 1992). When Gramps realizes he has the beginnings of Alzheimer's disease, he starts a "memory box" with his young grandson, Zach, to keep memories of all the times they have shared.

***Mrs. Katz and Tush*** by Patricia Polacco (Bantam, 1992). A young African-American boy gives a lonely Jewish widow a kitten named Tush. The cultural and age differences between the boy and the older woman only add to their special friendship, which grows and lasts throughout their lives.

***Remember Me? Alzheimer's Through the Eyes of a Child/¿Te acuerdas de mí? Pensamientos de la enfermedad, Alzheimers a travez de los ojos de un niño*** by Sue Glass (Raven Tree Press, 2003). A young girl is perplexed. She cannot understand why Grandfather no longer remembers her. Did she do something wrong or make him angry or hurt his feelings? When she tells her mother about this problem, her mother explains about Alzheimer's disease. They both learn that sharing the knowledge about what is happening to a family member is better for everyone involved. In English and Spanish.

***Sachiko Means Happiness*** by Kimiko Sakai (Children's Book Press, 1990). Sachiko is upset when her grandmother, who has Alzheimer's disease, no longer recognizes her. Slowly she grows to understand how patience and love help maintain a caring relationship.

***Singing with Momma Lou*** by Linda Jacobs Altman (Lee & Low, 2002). Tamika is frustrated with visiting her grandmother at the nursing home each week, especially now that Alzheimer's disease has robbed Momma Lou of so much memory. When nine-year-old Tamika begins to bring and show her grandmother old photos and yearbooks, and newspaper clippings related to her grandmother's arrest during a civil rights demonstration in her visits, the sparks of memory and relationship are rekindled.

***Somebody Loves You, Mr. Hatch*** by Eileen Spinelli (Aladdin, 1996). An anonymous valentine turns unsociable Mr. Hatch into a friend of everyone in the neighborhood. When he learns the valentine was meant for someone else, Mr. Hatch reverts to his old ways until his true friends come to the rescue. A wonderful book to dramatize with children!

***Stranger in the Mirror*** by Allen Say (Houghton Mifflin, 1995). Sam, an Asian-American boy, does not want to get old like his grandpa, but one morning he awakens with the face of an old man. His family, teacher, and friends treat him as if he is not the same person on the inside. "Who cares what I look like. I am Sam. Nobody can change that." A subtle and perceptive look at societal views on aging.

***Sunshine Home*** by Eve Bunting (Clarion, 1994). Timothy visits his grandmother, who has broken her hip. Timothy and his parents have a hard time leaving Gram at the nursing home. They know that an aging person with physical difficulties still needs love.

***Too Young for Yiddish*** by Richard Michelson (Charlesbridge, 2002). Aaron loves his *zayde* (grandfather), though he is embarrassed by his funny accent and arm-waving gestures. Aaron longs to read Zayde's treasured books, which are written in Yiddish, but Zayde says, "You are too young . . . speak English like everyone else." As the years pass, Aaron and his grandfather realize the importance of preserving family history and culture, agreeing that you are never too young—or old—for Yiddish. Includes a glossary and author's notes.

***Wilfred Gordon McDonald Partridge*** by Mem Fox (Kane/Miller, 1985). A young boy tries to discover the meaning of "memory" so he can help an elder friend.

***A Window of Time*** by Audrey O. Leighton (NADJA, 1995). Grandpa's time machine is "on the fritz." Sometimes he confuses the present with the past—imagining himself riding horses on his farm rather than remembering his current life in the city. His grandson, Shawn, recognizes that Grandpa may forget what he did earlier today but remembers an event from 65 years ago. A sensitive account of the effects of Alzheimer's disease.

## Fiction: Elders

**Recommendation from the Field**
*by Gail M. Kong, President,*
*Asian Pacific Fund*

*The Bonesetter's Daughter* by Amy Tan (Ballantine Books, 2001). Ruth Luyi Young is a busy writer and stepmom, and she tries to be a good daughter by visiting regularly with her mother, LuLing. Lately, LuLing seems more confused and disoriented. Ruth cannot tell if her mother is sick or if they just cannot communicate because Ruth has become Americanized, losing her ability to speak Chinese. As LuLing recalls many vivid details of her childhood in China, Ruth begins to know her mother in a new way even as she accepts that her mother has early-stage Alzheimer's disease.

Students can use the story to discuss how families feel about elder parents or how all elder immigrants might relive the disorientation of coming to America as they age. They can discuss helpful ways to visit with elders. Written against the backdrop of Amy Tan's struggle with her own mother's illness, we see that Alzheimer's disease and dementia are frightening for elders, their families, and other people who care for them. Still, these elders often have important—and accurate—stories to share with us. Writing those stories can be an important service to the families and the elder person. 403pp., young adult

***The Cay*** by Theodore Taylor (Avon, 1969). Phillip, separated from his mother when their ship was torpedoed in 1942, is stranded on a remote cay with an old black man who worked on the ship's deck. Blinded by a blow to his head, Phillip becomes reliant on his elder companion and must confront the racist beliefs he learned from his parents. A story of survival, friendship, and trust. 144pp., grades 4–8

***Doing Time Online*** by Jan Siebold (Albert Whitman, 2002). A "practical joke" that led to an elder woman's injury leaves twelve-year-old Mitchell remorseful. As a consequence of his actions, he is required to participate in a police program involving twice-a-week online chats with a nursing home resident, Wootie Hayes. Despite initial misgivings, Mitchell grows to depend on Wootie for advice, and a valued relationship grows. 90pp., grades 4–7

***The Graduation of Jake Moon*** by Barbara Park (Aladdin, 2000). Fourteen-year-old Jake Moon treasures his relationship with his grandfather, Skelly. The past four years have been difficult, though, because Alzheimer's disease has changed everything. Now roles are reversed, and Jake is a caregiver. Although Jake rebels, his love for his grandfather remains. And when the elder man wanders off, Jake is determined to find him. 115pp., grades 4–7

***Handbook for Boys*** by Walter Dean Myers (HarperCollins, 2002). The wisdom of age becomes apparent to reluctant Jimmy as he meets three elder men. After school, sixteen-year-old Jimmy must spend his afternoons at a barbershop, Duke's Place, in a "community mentorship" program as an alternative to a juvenile facility. As these "old guys" talk about their lives, Jimmy begins to think for himself about staying out of trouble, about making better choices, and about true success. 179pp., grades 6–12

"It's not that you're wrong Jimmy, it's just that your approach needs a lot of work. . . . Too many young people think that because somebody down the road has said you deserve this or deserve that, then all you have to do is wait around until it comes your way. Believe me, it won't."

FROM *HANDBOOK FOR BOYS*

**Recommendation from the Field**
*by Denise Dowell, Program Assistant,*
*Louisiana Learn and Serve America*

*The Hundred Penny Box* by Shannon Bell Mathis (Viking, 1986). One-hundred-year-old

*continued* ⟶

Aunt Dew has come to live with her nephew John, his wife Ruth, and their young son, Michael. John feels responsible for Aunt Dew, since she raised him after his parents drowned when he was a young boy. Ruth, who feels the older lady does not like her, treats Aunt Dew as though she were a child. Michael loves Aunt Dew and promises that even though his mother has burned Aunt Dew's belongings in the furnace, he will keep her hundred penny box safe. This may be a well-used box with a broken lid, but to Aunt Dew it is her life. When she was thirty years old, her husband gave her thirty pennies, each one dated for a year of her life. The tradition of collecting a dated penny continued. For each penny, Aunt Dew remembers important events. Michael and Aunt Dew open the box and talk about the times of life.

Several threads can be discussed after the class reads this book. Students can look at their own families to identify traditions and how they were started. Will those traditions be carried on by their generation? Are they old or new traditions? Also, a discussion of the importance of intergenerational relationships and the care of older people would be appropriate. Although John and Michael love Aunt Dew, Ruth has the role of caregiver. The book can lead students to gather oral histories from elders in their community; the historians could include the topic of family traditions. 47pp., grades 1–4

***Petey*** by Ben Mikaelson (Hyperion, 2000). In 1922, at the age of two, Petey is placed by his parents in the state's insane asylum when he was actually suffering with severe cerebral palsy. His life in institutions continues to age seventy, with brief moments when his caretakers recognize his ability to communicate and his passion for learning and living. In his advancing years, while living at a nursing home, Petey meets Trevor, an eighth grader who is frustrated by a lack of friends and minimal parental attention. The depth of their relationship offers both companionship and much joy. Based on a true story, this book delves into the tragedy of misdiagnosis and inappropriate care. 256pp., grades 5–9

***Tiger, Tiger, Burning Bright*** by Ron Koertge (Orchard, 1994). In a modern-day western setting, Jesse takes the role of protector of his grandfather, Pappy, who loves to ride in the desert and play poker. Pappy's Alzheimer's disease has Jesse's mom looking into a nursing home. Jesse follows a path of deceit to keep his mom from knowing a secret: Pappy sees tiger tracks in the California hills! 179pp., young adult

**Recommendation from the Field**

*by Devora Kaye, high school student*

*Tuck Everlasting* by Natalie Babbitt (Farrar, Straus and Giroux, 1985). After drinking water from the spring of eternal life, the Tuck family wanders from place to place living as inconspicuously as possible. Winnie Foster, a young girl, learns of their secret. The Tucks attempt to explain to her the importance of living life naturally and of regarding age as a gift to be valued. At the same time, though, Winnie is being followed by a man who yearns to sell her this special water!

*Tuck Everlasting* could be used as an introduction to service learning related to elders. It clearly shows the importance of living life day by day and valuing each stage. It can also be used to emphasize the importance of learning from older people and appreciating their knowledge. For a project, students could collaborate on making a book, telling about people of every age from one to a hundred. Each student could find someone of a certain age and write about that person or could write about what he or she knows about that age and what is special about it. Another variation is creating a "decades" book that includes historical information and personal memories about a series of decades. 139pp., grades 5–8

***The War with Grandpa*** by Robert Kimmel Smith (Dell, 1984). Peter likes the idea of Grandpa moving in but he is furious about having to give up his room to relocate to the stuffy third floor. Peter declares war! As a consequence, Grandpa teaches Peter lessons about war, friendship, and family relationships. 140pp., grades 3–6

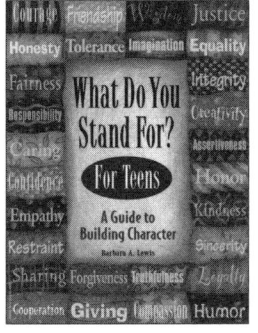

NO POSTAGE
NECESSARY IF
MAILED IN THE
UNITED STATES

BUSINESS REPLY MAIL
FIRST-CLASS MAIL PERMIT NO. 26589 MINNEAPOLIS MN

POSTAGE WILL BE PAID BY ADDRESSEE

free spirit PUBLISHING®
Department 23432
217 Fifth Avenue North, Suite 200
Minneapolis, MN 55401-9776

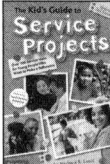

# Interviews with Authors:
## The Story Behind the Story

In the following interviews, we find out the "story behind the story" from Eve Bunting (*Sunshine Home, Gleam and Glow, Smoky Nights, Summer Wheels, Your Move, Someday a Tree, Fly Away Home, A Train to Somewhere, A Day's Work, The Wednesday Surprise*), Richard Michelson (*Too Young for Yiddish*), and Eileen Spinelli (*Somebody Loves You, Mr. Hatch*).

Three authors, three different reasons for their selection. I was familiar with many of Eve Bunting's books, and I wanted to learn why she continuously writes stories on such important social themes. In the case of *Too Young for Yiddish*, Richard Michelson's story of a language nearly lost along with its tradition and history captivated me. And after years of referring to the heartwarming story *Somebody Loves You, Mr. Hatch* in teacher workshops, interviewing Eileen Spinelli, the book's author, was simply a must—and a treat. After the interview, Eileen mailed me the recipe for Mr. Hatch's brownies!

### *Eve Bunting, author of* Sunshine Home, Smoky Nights, A Day's Work, The Wednesday Surprise

I grew up in Northern Ireland, where there was tremendous discrimination. As a Protestant, I was fortunate in that the prejudice was not aimed toward me; Catholics were the targets. Growing up in a small town, I thought all Catholics were poor and begged and had no bathrooms in their homes. I knew no Catholics personally until I was older and attending university. For the first time, I knew Catholics and began to see the intolerance in Ireland.

When my husband and I immigrated to the United States, one important reason was to bring our children away from prejudice and discrimination. However, in this country, we found prejudice of a different kind, and just as much unfairness. At the beginning, I did not understand. We lived next door to a Catholic family. Our children played together, and I was delighted. Then, as months and years passed, I became acutely aware of unfairness against other ethnic groups, people who are homeless, gender inequities.

As an author, I never intended to write about social issues. These stories came out of me; this is in my heart, what interests me and is important to me. Early in my writing career, when reviewers began to talk about my "social issues books," I did not know what they were talking about. Now I fully understand this description

I select a theme for a book from what is going on in my life. Once I identify a subject, I think more deeply, and then a catharsis occurs. Here is an example. My husband's mother came here from Ireland and, at age 86, lived independently in a little apartment near our home. I called her every day, and she often came for meals. One day I called and she did not answer. I rushed over and found her on the rug, where she had fallen and stayed all night with a broken back. We soon learned she would not walk again. Since I could not lift her or provide the care she required, having her live in our home was not an option. We decided to find a place nearby where she would be comfortable, and that was difficult. We did find a place. My book *Sunshine Home* was written out of a need to show her and tell ourselves that sometimes you don't have an option for a beloved family member. As long as the person knows you love them and always will care for them and not abandon them, it will be all right. We all have pangs of guilt when we do this, even though we know it is necessary.

When I am writing a picture book, I think about the story for a very long time. I subconsciously examine the situations from all directions and from all the characters' viewpoints—not thinking in order or logically. Every character has a problem, big or small. I come up with different endings; perhaps this is somewhat deliberate to have an element of surprise. This occurs in *Sunshine Home* when, after saying good-bye to Gram, seven-year old Timmy returns to give her his school picture and finds her in tears. The family gathers to share their true feelings about her living situation and their hopes.

I have had wonderful letters (and I answer each one) about this book. It seems like my words and the illustrations by Diane de Groat capture what most nursing homes look like. Sunshine Home is the generic place. Many letters are from adults (they read picture books, too) saying, "This is just like the nursing home my mother is in. How did you describe this place so accurately?" A man wrote a letter that his wife was living in a similar facility. "Such a comfort," he wrote, "for me to read this book." Children also write me of their visits with grandparents.

For children who want to be writers, I recommend that you read. I was a voracious reader. There was lots of rain in Ireland and no television, and I would stay in and read and read. With the first break in the rainy weather, my mother would say, "Take your nose out of that book and go outside and play!" Also keep a journal. Think of things in your own life that you care about, and write for fun. Remember that words rarely come out right the first time. We all rewrite. Sometimes I bring stacks of different revisions into classrooms, each on a different color paper. The students are in awe over the piles of blue papers, then pink, then yellow—all to show the different stages.

Even though I write young adult novels also, I love to write picture books. They are my favorites. When I get stuck on a novel, I rejoice and go write a picture book and come back to finish the novel. The picture book is the truth being distilled through the economy of words and the economy of thought. When holding one of my newly published picture books, I know that in this tiny little book, I have the essence of truth as I see it.

To be a writer, or a learner of any kind, be open to all experiences and all people. My book that says that best is *Smoky Nights*. This book reminds us to get to *know* other people. You might find out you like them a lot and they may not be so different from you. When we stick with our own kind, we miss a lot.

Sometimes we avoid knowing people because of fear. Being an elder myself, I think that some children are a little bit afraid of older people. We don't have the same kinds of hands as their mothers. Our hair is gray. We can be intimidating to them or appear cranky or bossy. Many children are brought up by grandparents, and that can soften the feelings people have about us. We were young once, and now we, in part, live our lives through the young. I know this from having five grandchildren, whom I adore. When children communicate with older people, there is a mutual advantage. We can give them so much, and they can give to us also. These interactions spark the older people and teach the younger people that they have so much to give to other generations. Examples of this reciprocity can be found in two of my books. In *The Wednesday Surprise*, a child teaches her grandmother to read. In *A Day's Work*, a grandfather teaches his grandson a lesson about honesty. Stories make these wonderful relations apparent. We humanize people by removing the clichés and showing people in all situations and by helping and caring for each other.

## *Richard Michelson*, author of Too Young for Yiddish

I happened to know Aaron Lansky, who started the National Yiddish Book Center. During visits there with my own kids, I began to realize how little they and their friends knew of even recent ancestors' life stories. With both parents often busy and overworked, our society doesn't value the free time when family history is traditionally passed down from generation to generation. Swapping stories nightly around the dinner table is rarely part of the day-to-day routine in our fast-food culture. Even growing up in the fifties, I knew little about my own grandparents' lives. I was too absorbed in the American way of life to care, and they were too busy making a living to share.

When a young person does eventually become curious about his or her family history, there are often only a few relatives with firsthand knowledge still alive. With Eastern and Central European Jews, the situation is especially distressing, because the native Yiddish-speaking world was virtually wiped out by the Nazis during World

War II. A whole link in the chain that reaches backward to teach us where we're coming from is cut off, gone. How can we know the direction in which we are heading? So there is an added immediacy to this situation. The few native speakers of Yiddish who survived the war by escaping to the United States tried hard to fit into the American way of life, abandoning their own language and customs for those of their adopted country. Even that generation is dying off, and we are in danger of an entire culture being lost.

I wanted to write about this, and my first inclination is always to create a story as an avenue for parents and children to start discussing their heritage. In this book, I make reference to the fact that in school we learn about "wars and kings and knights in shining armor." We don't think of history as what happens to real people. Our grandparents lived through history. The record of our own families is as valid as the events we study in school. My children learned French and Spanish, and they know many things—for example, about how the British aristocracy lived—but they've learned almost nothing about Polish *shtetl* life, and it never occurred to them to study Yiddish.

The final spark for the book occurred when my son was doing a school report on the sixties. Reading over what he'd written, I remarked on a section I thought was incorrect. "This is not the way it happened," I insisted, "and I know because I was there!" His response was, "I don't have time to listen to you right now; my assignment is due tomorrow!" In his class, they were already studying an era I'd lived through, but with the pressure-filled high school schedule, our teenagers don't have time to pay attention to our stories when we do offer them. I am hopeful *Too Young for Yiddish* will help inspire a conversation between generations.

Usually, the local community is filled with people eager to tell their stories. Schools should encourage grandparents or other family members to share experiences. In our local area, there is an organization that brings Vietnam veterans into the classroom. This is fascinating for kids and helps to make history come alive. War is something that can tear families apart, affecting our lives and those of our next-door neighbors.

I know that *Too Young for Yiddish* isn't going to change the world, but I hope it plants seeds in the minds of young people. Down the road, they might read another book that interests them on a similar subject. After a while, I hope they develop the curiosity to ask simple questions like, "Did you grow up speaking a different language? What was your neighborhood like?" Recently, I read my book at a reception held at the National Yiddish Book Center. Afterwards, Aaron Lansky's young daughter asked her father, "When are you going to teach me Yiddish?" That is the response I hope for from this book.

## *Eileen Spinelli, author of*
### Somebody Loves You, Mr. Hatch

When I was six years old, I wanted to be a writer. My father gave me his manual typewriter, and I began my career typing with two fingers. I first wrote poetry. After having kids, I began to write picture books. I find picture books to be a form of poetry; they come from the same place. Children's books move on a thread with a sense of focus toward a clear culmination, a lyrical ending, like the punch line of a joke or the last line of a poem.

The story of *Somebody Loves You, Mr. Hatch* began with the idea of kindness being important in life. I have known several people who were standoffish or who seemed stern or not so friendly. I discovered they were either very shy—which can appear unfriendly—or were dealing with a lot of sadness in their lives. This became "Mr. Hatch," who is a little shy and a little different and lonely. He may seem unfriendly, but his heart is friendly. He needs the little spark of love to bloom, which is the way we all are.

Once I had the main character, the idea came to me that he gets a message that someone loves him. How would this happen? I thought of the valentine. Stories arrive in different ways. Some come fast; some come in little pieces that swish inside of you for years and do not come together as easily. I am tickled when the end comes first.

While developing a story I draw on memories of my own. For example, I was trying to think of a humorous place where he could work. I liked shoelaces when I was little. They always fascinated me! So Mr. Hatch works in a shoelace factory. That he eats prunes for dessert just seemed like a funny image.

Like many other writers, I wanted to make a statement that kindness is important, even underrated, and can make a big difference in the world. I was able to say this in a humorous way. Mr. Hatch is endearing, and the art makes him even more so. Artist Paul Yalowitz brings another layer of richness. I would never have thought to change the color of the book from dreary colors to bright cheerful colors so that the pictures and the text work together. The art is inspiring.

How have people responded to *Mr. Hatch?* A businessman in New York read *Mr. Hatch* and began to send flowers anonymously to his employees. He uses *Mr. Hatch* when making presentations and encourages management to honor employees in an anonymous way to create more kindness in the workplace.

One teacher told me that on Valentine's Day she placed a bag of candy at the door of a neighbor who had been giving her a hard time. She told the kids, and they made valentines for classmates they were having a hard time with. I have heard of kids taking brownies and lemonade to the fire department; others have visited nursing homes. They have done things for people who work at school.

Without kindness and love, life is pretty dreary. We have learned that on September 11, 2001, people in danger were not concerned about their bank accounts or revenge. They left phone messages saying, "I love you." This is what life is about.

We can also show kindness even to people we don't know very well. We underestimate what can come from going that extra inch to be nice to the person waiting on the table, to be thoughtful to a new kid at school, or to give a smile to a person you don't know in the cafeteria line. Mr. Hatch is a sweet character who, with just a bit of kindness from others, returns the kindness many times over.

CHAPTER 8

# THE ENVIRONMENT

> When one tugs at a single thing in nature, one finds it attached to the rest of the world.
>
> JOHN MUIR, AUTHOR

Majestic redwood trees, waves cresting near tidal pools, deserts with cacti and coyotes—these are a few images from the diverse landscapes that make up our environment. To define this all-encompassing term, we need only look at the word. At the center of "environment" is the Latin root *viron,* meaning "circle." This simple yet profound image reveals the interconnectedness of air, water, plants, animals, and all of our ecosystems.

At all ages, young people can develop understanding of and respect for our environment. They can acquire a vocabulary that will allow them to participate in conversation and intelligent debate about such topics as acid rain, ozone depletion, alternative energy sources, watersheds, erosion, and composting. They can learn to carefully examine multiple sides of issues and develop informed ideas. Knowing that the earth is dynamic and constantly changing, they can consider which of our human actions protect and preserve and which cause irreparable harm. Knowledge and the ability to respond can join to create a citizenry prepared to ensure a healthy environment for generations to come.

> The frog does not drink up
> the pond in which he lives.
>
> SIOUX PROVERB

## Preparation: Getting Ready for Service Learning Involving the Environment

The following activities can be used in the preparation stage to promote learning and skill development related to the environment. These activities can be used with different age ranges during preparation to help your students examine key issues through research, analyze community needs, and gain the knowledge they need to effectively contribute to the design of their service plan. Since literature is often an important part of preparation, you can find recommended titles on this theme in the Environment Bookshelf later in this chapter.

***Activity: Litter by Litter.*** Young people have been the best advocates for eliminating litter and promoting recycling. How can your school or class join in? Investigating and addressing the issue of litter at school can lead to more complex projects that tackle recycling or even how trash is processed in the community or region. The following suggestions have successfully helped elementary, middle, and high school classes start exploring environmental issues in the world at large by getting them to look at the environment right around them—school.

- Create a school survey to identify litter "hot spots" (usually near the lunch area). Students can walk around the school campus at different times of the day—at breaks or lunch or just after passing periods in middle or high schools—to find out where the trash accumulates. Students can make posters to designate these places as "hot spots" to be cleaned up.
- Establish a litter-free zone in one specific area of the school. Add to the beauty of this area—for example, plant flowers. Students can make signs

and promote this campaign through public-address announcements at school. One litter-free zone can be the start of a litter-free school.

- Use books such as *The Great Trash Bash, The Wartville Wizard* and *I Want to Be an Environmentalist* as resources to develop campaign ideas for cleaning up litter. From these and other books, develop plays or choral readings to educate other students and school community members.
- In a math class, maintain records about the quantities of trash produced by the school—a good way to teach about graphs, statistics, and percentages. Guide students into thinking about how much trash is produced by their community, their city, even their country and what can be done to reduce it. Successful waste reduction at school can lead students into the community to help.

Once the school is on its way to being litter-free, initiate recycling or expand existing efforts using a similar process of education, awareness, promotion, and feedback. Then students can take their expertise into the community, helping other schools and even businesses and government offices to reduce, reuse, and recycle.

***Activity: Take the Challenge.*** What environmental challenges face your community? Are they related to energy conservation? Fire safety? Land use? Using newspapers and the Internet, find a topic that is currently affecting your locale. Learn about all sides of the issue. Plan a debate with invited guests to increase community awareness and understanding of the topics.

> First I thought I was fighting
> for the rubber tappers, then I thought
> I was fighting for the Amazon, then I realized
> I was fighting for humanity.
>
> CHICO MENDEZ, RAIN FOREST ACTIVIST

**Find Out More About the Environment**

To learn more about these issues and to get ideas for service and action, visit these Web sites and organizations online:

***www.earthday.net*** The Earth Day Network includes environmental education curriculum and resources for K–12 teachers and promotes the April 22nd annual Earth Day event that began in 1970.

***www.adopt-a-watershed.org*** Adopt-A-Watershed is a school-community learning experience that uses local watersheds as living laboratories to develop collaborative partnerships and reinforce learning through community service.

***www.earthforce.org*** Earth Force is a youth-driven organization, engaging young people in problem solving to discover and implement lasting solutions to environmental issues in their communities.

***www.arborday.org/kids/kidsdif.cfm*** At the National Arbor Day "Kids Make a Difference" Web site, you can find many activities, plenty of resources, and programs and projects all across the country that encourage tree planting.

***www.nrdc.org*** The National Resources Defense Council has easy-to-read information and photographs on a variety of environmental topics, including wildlife and fish, global warming, energy use, and clean air, water, and oceans.

## Making Connections Across the Curriculum

Some service learning activities naturally lend themselves to interdisciplinary work and making connections across the curriculum. These connections strengthen and broaden student learning, helping them meet academic standards. More than likely, you'll be looking for these connections and ways to encourage them well before the students ever start working on service learning activities. As with the entire service learning process, it helps to remain flexible, because some connections can be spontaneously generated by the questions raised throughout and by the needs of the project. To help you think about cross-curricular connections and where you can look for them, the Curricular Web for this chapter (page 125) gives examples of many different ways this theme can be used in different academic areas. (The

# The Environment Across the Curriculum

## The Environment

### *English/Language Arts*

- Write stories or a collaborative book about a special natural setting in your community
- Read biographies of environmentalists then create a living "wax museum" where students take on the identities of these people and tell their life stories
- Study how classical haiku capture a moment in nature

### *Social Studies/History*

- Study different Native American tribes' relationships with the land they lived on, how they interacted with the environment, and their concepts of "owning" land
- Learn about how Earth Day began as a grassroots event in 1970 and has spread internationally
- Research government policy on an environmentally sensitive area in your region; discuss and debate the issue

### *Languages*

- Find out the words for "reduce, reuse, and recycle" in many languages and create a poster
- Compare the political positions of different countries with U.S. policies on environmental issues
- Compile a book of original poetry in different languages about the environment

### *Theater, Music, & Visual Arts*

- Prepare a skit or play about the environment to be performed in a natural setting
- Create and perform jingles or raps to promote clean schools and playgrounds
- Decorate trash bins at school to make them attractive receptacles

### *Math*

- Present environmental statistics on the public-address system at school each morning
- Analyze the pattern of waste disposal at school
- Review the water or electrical bills at school and develop a conservation program to reduce costs

### *Physical Education*

- Study the effect of pollution on the lungs and overall health
- Create a public service announcement on outdoor activities
- Plan a field trip to a nature reserve or park and hike!

### *Computer*

- Design and make flyers of recycling tips for the community
- Find out what happens to discarded computers in your community and research options for re-use
- Research and discuss: Does computer use result in less paper consumption?

### *Science*

- Learn about and then make recycled paper
- Study science careers in environmental testing and protection
- Compare the effects of composting and recycling with landfills and incinerated waste

service learning scenarios in the next section of the chapter also demonstrate various ways this theme can be used across the curriculum.)

# Service Learning Scenarios:
## Ideas for Action

Ready to take action? What follows are projects that have been successfully carried out by elementary, middle, or high school students. Most of these scenarios and examples explicitly include some aspects of preparation, action, reflection, and demonstration. These scenarios can be a rich source of project, resource, and curriculum ideas for you to draw upon. While the grade levels are given as a reference, most project ideas can be adapted to suit younger or older students, and many are suitable for cross-age partnerships.

***Caring for Earth: Grades K–8.*** At a rural school in Briggs, Oklahoma, students at many grade levels learned the history of Earth Day and decorated 390 grocery bags with environmental slogans such as "Don't Litter!" and "Reduce, Reuse, Recycle." The bags were distributed to the public at the local supermarket on Earth Day.

***From Frogs to Petroglyphs: Grades K and 2.*** Four classes of kindergartners and second graders in El Cerrito, California, set out to learn more about their neighborhood creek and park. Naturalists took the students on nature walks to teach observation skills. They listened to Pacific Chorus frogs singing at dusk, found tiny hummingbird nests, and raised buckeyes, oaks, and willows for creek restoration projects. After discovering a "plucking tree" where Cooper hawks deposit tiny feathers of the birds they hunt and catch, students gathered samples of the feathers and sent them to the Golden Gate Raptor Observatory, where scientists conduct research about what the hawks eat. They studied the petroglyphs etched into the boulder next to the pond and learned some of the history of the area and the people who once lived along the creek. They published an illustrated guidebook—"From the Tops of the Trees to the Bottom of the Pond"—and delivered copies to all the homes in the neighborhood to encourage others to make wonderful discoveries at the creek.

***Oak Forest Sprouts: Grades 2–12.*** Students and other members of one central California community are working together to protect and restore forests of valley oaks, the largest of all oak trees in North America. A local river preserve has the best remaining examples of these oak forests, which once flourished in California's Central Valley. Most of the preserve is left to natural regeneration; however, active restoration efforts are needed in some areas. During one school year, more than a thousand students from four elementary schools and a high school participated in oak forest restoration field trips. Second and third graders gathered over 14,000 acorns. Fifth and sixth graders washed, sorted, counted, and bagged the acorns. Students from all four elementary schools and the high school helped to plant nearly five acres of land that one day will return to oak forest. This project was successful because of the cooperative efforts of the Nature Conservancy, Bureau of Land Management, California Department of Fish and Game, and many parent and community volunteers. In-class lessons that related to the project crossed all curriculum areas, including math, language arts, science, social studies, and fine arts. Several schools also hosted their own tree-planting activities.

> Plant trees. They give us two of the most crucial elements for our survival: oxygen and books.
>
> A. WHITNEY BROWN, WRITER

***Give It to the Worms: Grade 3.*** A composting project that began in one Palo Alto classroom grew over four years to involve many teachers and students and resulted in promoting the benefits of composting to the entire school and its surrounding community. As part of the science curriculum students learned about ecosystems, and after hearing a guest speaker from the Integrative Waste Management Board, students wanted to get involved in a project. They created a chart to record waste at school and brainstormed ideas for waste reduction. They prepared a video presentation and spoke to other classes about ecology, especially how to reduce food waste through composting. The kids became composting and worm bin experts. They collected school food waste and watched as it was transformed into deep, rich soil that they used in their school garden and donated to gardeners who lived in a nearby senior residential facility. The students' next step was community outreach. They hosted a parent information night with a site tour and composting lessons. They distributed monthly copies of their newsletter, "Warm Ways," in the neighborhood and participated in the local Chinese New Year parade, where—costumed as a giant worm—they handed out informational pamphlets on worm bins and composting called "Give It to the Worms!"

***The Mystery of Crabby Kathy: Grades 3 and 6.*** Every year a class of third-grade students at an elementary school in Chico, California, partners with a class of older students on a project where they make a book telling a story about something they've learned. One year the students noticed that a teacher at school was often crabby and wondered why. Through their environmental studies, the children began to look for possibilities in their surroundings to solve this mystery and wrote an entertaining and informative book on their findings. Their story identifies many possible culprits: mold, stinky pens, chemicals used for cleaning, and poor ventilation. With funding from the National Institute of Environmental Health Sciences, copies were made and distributed. The story can be downloaded from the NIEHS Web site at *www.niehs.nih.gov*.

***Lessons from Trash: Grade 4.*** Fourth graders in New Jersey analyzed school trash during a recycling project that included practice computing with fractions and percentages. They determined that 85 percent of the trash could have been recycled. As part of a campaign for awareness and school change, the students put up posters and created PowerPoint presentations to teach others in their school. Learning continued in math as the students tracked and charted their household garbage for a week. In science class, they learned about renewable versus nonrenewable resources. The next step was to compost lunch leftovers, adding earthworms to help. This resulted in newly enriched soil for the vegetable gardens planted by the kindergarten classes.

***Too Much Water, Water Everywhere: Grade 5.*** "How much water do you use?" This question led a class of fifth-grade students to a formidable task: evaluating school and home water usage. In school the students learned to read water bills, and they took a walking tour of the school to identify, with assistance from maintenance staff, ways to conserve water. At home, the students developed a survey to record how much water each family member used per week; they compared the results with the average use (in the United States) of between 80 and 100 gallons of water each day. After hearing a guest speaker describe "water use reduction in the home" and conducting research through literature and the Internet, students created and distributed a family-friendly guide, "Save Water—We Need Every Drop." Their next project? Cutting back on electricity.

***Ancient Egypt and Water Conservation: Grade 6.*** "I'm teaching about ancient Egypt. How can I tie this to service learning?" The response came from another teacher: "I just was in Egypt. Water use and conservation have been huge issues from early times to the present." Students compared methods employed in the past with water use and conservation methods used now. Next, they prepared and distributed literature on water conservation for homes, applied water conservation strategies in the school garden, and also planted drought-resistant plants at a nearby senior center.

***The Lead-Based Paint Project: Grade 7.*** Some environmental materials can make us sick right in our own homes. Middle school science classes began to investigate issues related to toxic materials in homes, such as lead-based paints, and created informative fact sheets. Copies were given to realtors, homeowner associations, and parent groups and made available through local libraries and social service agencies.

***Environmental Heroes: Grades 7–8.*** A middle school teacher in Baton Rouge, Louisiana, initiated a service learning program that aligns environmental education and activities with required state standards and benchmarks. Over four years 1,600 students, teachers, adult volunteers, and partners dedicated 23,000 hours to service projects. Students planted over 1,400 trees, picked up over 600 bags of trash, collected truckloads of junk, and participated in water quality monitoring programs. Over the course of this program middle school students worked alongside community experts to plant trees, perform water quality testing, identify plants, gain hands-on experience with local wildlife, test for soil quality, and learn about the many challenges facing the Louisiana wetlands. The middle school students used this knowledge to lead over 2,000 fifth and sixth graders on wetland trips. One seventh grader reflected on her experience this way: "If the plants and animals could talk, I think they would say we are their heroes. That is what I feel like when we are working in the wetlands."

***Improving the Air We Breathe: Grade 8.*** At the beginning of a science project on air pollution, middle school students in West Palm Beach were described by their teachers as "unaware." The students went on to spend two hours a week investigating air quality issues in their community. They conducted air quality tests and identified pollutants around the school and community, as well as learning about laws, regulations, and practices that made the situation worse. After surveying their peers about transportation-related issues, the students presented a play on environmental pollutants, created posters, and distributed information on alternatives to driving to school.

***Community Revitalization from the Ground Up: Grade 8.*** For four years, every eighth-grade class in rural Ainsworth, Nebraska, has been making improvements to a local nature area. Initially, students formed committees and helped to create a plan for short- and long-term activities. Students draw on art, math, earth science, social studies, English, and technology as they work on trails, bridges, stairs, and picnic areas, help at the information centers, and make project presentations. The teachers continually integrate the idea of community revitalization into the project to increase youth awareness of the broader region and environment.

***The Fractal-Mural-Community Connection: Grades 9 and 10.*** Through service learning, a high school in Spokane, Washington, set out to make new community connections and enrich already established relationships, particularly with a nearby elementary school. By developing a reciprocal relationship with younger students, older students hoped to provide meaningful service to the neighborhood. One immediate need was to reduce or eliminate vandalism and graffiti at a sports field house in a local park. Since murals are proven to be a deterrent to both, planning started to create one for the field house. Students from a high school geometry class taught upper elementary students about the geometry concepts used in fractals, which are reoccurring geometric shapes. While fractals can be extremely complex, the simple rules upon which they are based make them an approachable subject for students of all ages. This service learning activity connected the sometimes esoteric discipline of geometry with an aspect of everyday life. After learning about fractals, the elementary students used their new knowledge to design a mural to decorate the field house and one for their school gymnasium. The geometry students also helped to transfer the younger students' small-scale fractal art plans to the wall murals, then everyone painted. Parents and community volunteers also assisted with the painting or donated supplies.

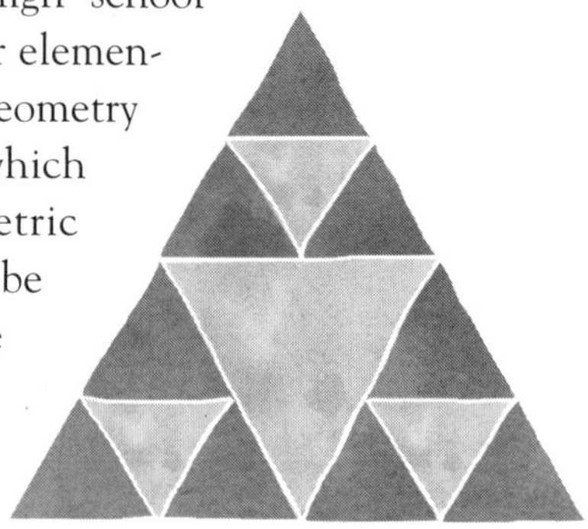

***To Help with Recovery: Grades 9 and 10.*** After a massive local wildfire destroyed more than a hundred homes, a high school biology class in Carlsbad, California, worked alongside elementary school children to plant a native garden at a local park to help demonstrate and study how nature recovers from wildfire.

***A Restorative Process: Grades 9–12.*** During a meeting of their school's environmental club, a teacher asked students to think about issues affecting the future of their community. Students, with input from the local university and the city parks and recreation department, set up a community forum on local environmental issues. Together, they decided that cleaning and restoring the watershed of a nearby creek was crucial to frog and bird habitats. Club members researched previous restoration efforts and brought in environmentalists to discuss what makes a healthy watershed. With a work plan in hand, the students helped to clean and restore five miles on either side of the creek, learning about native and invasive plants in the process. At the conclusion of their project, they made flyers and invited local citizens to discuss how improper disposal of oil and use of pesticides on lawns can impact the watershed and the animal species that depend on it.

***Energy Efficient Teens: Grades 9–12.*** A local energy company contracted with a high school drama class to write and perform a production on energy efficiency. The high school players read literature from the energy company and developed a program with skits, a rap, poetry, and a pop quiz for the audience. The high school players put on assemblies for elementary school audiences to rave reviews.

> This Earth is not ours; it is a treasure
> we hold in trust for future generations.
> AFRICAN PROVERB

***Collaboration for Restoration: Grades 9–12.*** A science teacher in Cedarburg, Wisconsin, initiated a project that—with the help of additional teachers and students—resulted in the restoration of a park to its native woodland habitat. Students determined what had grown in the area before settlers arrived. English students developed an informative pamphlet about the history of the park, highlighting the settlers who were buried there. The art class visited the park, learned about the history of these settling families, and did the graphic design for the project pamphlets. These pamphlets were given to the local preservation committee and the chamber of commerce. A woodshop class constructed benches to replicate those used by the early settlers.

***The Tar Creek Story: Grades 9–12.*** What if you had a toxic creek near your school? Imagine seeing mountains of toxic waste from mining wherever you looked. Students in Miami, Oklahoma, actually live in those surroundings. In fact, their community was so badly polluted it has been identified as a Superfund site. At the local high school, a school counselor and the students took the challenge of educating the community about their hazardous surroundings, including Tar Creek, the most polluted body of water in the United States. More teachers, community members, and national organizations have joined the collaboration every year. Students have become knowledgeable advocates for saving their community—the people and the land. Through their classroom and extracurricular work, students continue to conduct extensive research on a range of topics, including the history of mining in the area, water contamination, and the results of human exposure to toxic heavy metals. Student research papers, poetry, and personal essays have been published in two books that tell the story of "Our Toxic Place." Students have traveled to state and national conferences to lead in-depth workshops. They've given "toxic tours" for students and adults to educate people from the region about this Superfund site. The students also host an annual conference that brings together state and national government officials, leaders of Native American groups, and members of the surrounding community to wrestle with the environmental and personal issues that result from the toxic pollution.

***Adopt a Highway: Grades 10 and 11.*** For several years, high school students in Idaho have participated in the "Adopt a Highway" program. Four times a year, the students picked up litter from their adopted two-mile section of highway. The eight to ten bags of litter collected each time have sparked discussions about wasteful packaging and aesthetic damage to the environment. The students, upset with the amount of trash thrown from vehicles, have been more aware of and conscientious about their surroundings as a result.

***Going Tropical? Grades 11 and 12.*** Students conducted research on products that originate in tropical rain forests and created tools for evaluating the tradeoff between the need for the item and the environmental impact of producing it. The students composed letters to the products' manufacturers to find out about their commitment to conservation of tropical rain forests. Another class made a list of similar products that didn't use rain forest materials, and the product lists were provided during presentations to parent groups and other classes. "Make a choice," students advised, "when buying products, to protect our environment."

> The elders were wise.
> They knew that man's heart, away from nature,
> becomes hard; they knew that lack of respect
> for growing, living things, soon led
> to lack of respect for humans, too."
> CHIEF LUTHER STANDING BEAR
> OF THE LAKOTA SIOUX

# The Environment Bookshelf

It's a big world out there. Clearly, "the environment" covers many aspects of the planet, and this breadth is reflected in the Environment Bookshelf. To help you find books relevant to your particular projects, the book chart classifies the titles into several topic areas: overview of the environment, natural resources, recycling, and appreciation.

In general, the bookshelf features:

- An annotated bibliography arranged and alphabetized by title according to the general categories of nonfiction (N), picture books (P), and fiction (F). For nonfiction and fiction, length and recommended grade levels are included. The entries in the picture book category do not include suggested grade levels, since they can be successfully used with all ages.
- A chart organized by topic and category to help you find books relevant to particular projects.
- Recommendations from service learning colleagues and experts that include a book summary and ideas for service learning connections. (The number of recommended books varies in each bookshelf.)

## The Environment Bookshelf Topics

| *Topics* | *Books* | *Category* |
|---|---|---|
| ***Overview of the Environment*** These "big picture" books cover a range of environmental topics. Ecosystems are highlighted in many of the titles. | *ChaseR* (see page 86) | F |
| | *The Empty Lot* | P |
| | *Issues in the Environment* | N |
| | *I Want to Be an Environmentalist* * | N |
| | *Judy Moody Saves the World* * | F |
| | *A Life Like Mine: How Children Live Around the World* * (see page 196) | N |
| | *The Missing 'Gator of Gumbo Limbo* | F |
| | *One Less Fish* | N |
| | *Saving the Planet* | F |
| | *There's an Owl in the Shower* | F |
| | *What Planet Are You From, Clarice Bean?* * | P |
| | *You Are the Earth: Know the Planet So You Can Make It Better* * | N |
| ***Natural Resources*** These books focus on life-sustaining resources that are at risk—trees, water, and food. | *A Cool Drink of Water* | N |
| | *Fernando's Gift/El Regalo de Fernando* | N |
| | *The Gift of the Tree* | P |
| | *The Great Kapok Tree* | P |
| | *Island of the Blue Dolphins* | F |
| | *One Good Apple: Growing Our Food for the Sake of the Earth* | N |
| | *Our Poisoned Waters* | N |
| | *The People Who Hugged the Trees: An Environmental Folktale* | P |
| | *A River Ran Wild* * | P |

*continued* ⟶

| *Topics* | *Books* | *Category* |
|---|---|---|
| ***Natural Resources*** continued | *The Shape of Betts Meadow: A Wetlands Story* * | P |
| | *Someday a Tree* * | P |
| | *Wildlife Refuge* * | P |
| ***Recycling*** Reduce, reuse, recycle: This is the mantra of the recycling movement. These books tell of the subject from various perspectives. | *Crashed, Smashed, and Mashed: A Trip to Junkyard Heaven* | N |
| | *The Great Trash Bash* * | P |
| | *Recycle Every Day!* * | P |
| | *The Wartville Wizard* | P |
| ***Appreciation*** Taking time to appreciate our planet and our resources is part of the environmental story. | *Be Good to Eddie Lee* (see page 210) | P |
| | *Dear Children of the Earth* | P |
| | *The Table Where Rich People Sit* | P |
| | *This House Is Made of Mud/Esta casa está hecha de lodo* | P |

Page references are given for books that do not appear in the Environment Bookshelf but that can be found in the bookshelf lists of other chapters.
* These books include examples of young people in service-providing roles.

## Nonfiction: The Environment

***A Cool Drink of Water*** by Barbara Kerley (National Geographic Society, 2002). "We live by the grace of water." This photo essay takes us on a global journey to see water stored in clay pots and a burlap bag. We see people drink from a river, a well, and a thin tin cup. We travel from Thailand to Rome to Canada. A note on water conservation gives statistics and strategies for protecting our planet's precious supply of water. 32pp., all ages

***Crashed, Smashed, and Mashed: A Trip to Junkyard Heaven*** by Joyce Slayton Mitchell (Tricycle Press, 2001). Have you ever wondered what happens to the cars headed for the junkyard? Through photographs with text, see an engine that is pulled apart and cars that are shredded. Includes information about recycling. 32pp., grades 1–4

***Fernando's Gift/El Regalo de Fernando*** by Douglas Keister (Sierra Club, 1995). Friends Fernando and Carmina, who live in the rain forest of Costa Rica, discover Carmina's climbing tree has been cut down. What can stop the devastation of the rain forest? Teaching people and planting trees! A bilingual book with photographs. 32pp., grades K–3

***Issues in the Environment*** by Patricia D. Netzley (Lucent Books, 1998). Ready for a book that tackles controversies regarding the environment? Here it is. Controversies discussed include the ozone layer, garbage, endangered species, wilderness protection, and the cost of environmentalism. 94pp., grades 6–12

***I Want to Be an Environmentalist*** by Stephanie Maze (Harcourt, 2000). Meet dedicated people who work hard to protect many different aspects of our environment—botanists, economists, organic farmers, biologists, scuba divers, and more. Includes the history of environmentalism and ways young people are involved. 48pp., all ages

Did you know . . . that tropical forest land shrinks by eighty thousand square miles due to expanding agriculture, logging, and development? . . . . that 55 percent of air pollution in the United States is caused by sources of transportation, such as cars, trucks, buses, and planes? . . . . that recycling a ton of paper saves seventeen trees?

FROM *I WANT TO BE AN ENVIRONMENTALIST*

***One Good Apple: Growing Our Food for the Sake of the Earth*** by Catherine Paladino (Houghton Mifflin, 1999). Apples, strawberries, peaches, corn—foods we love. Yet these foods, and many others, are being sprayed with chemicals that affect living things, from the tiniest organisms to the humans who grow and eat the produce. Through sustainable agriculture, the balance of nature can be maintained, and we can nourish ourselves and the soil we rely on. 48pp., grades 5–12

***One Less Fish*** by Kim Michelle Toft and Allan Sheather. (Charlesbridge, 1998). The informative narrative in this counting book tells how something is wrong in Australia's Great Barrier Reef. As the fish disappear one by one, we learn of the potential hazards of offshore drilling, trash in the ocean, over fishing, and more. Each tropical fish is identified, and a glossary is included. 32pp., grades K–6

***Our Poisoned Waters*** by Edward Dolan (Cobblehill, 1997). Industry and farming waste choke our rivers. Sewage and oil spills damage our coastal waters. Rapidly growing populations deplete our fresh water supply. In this balanced presentation of water use and supply, key questions are raised: How has this occurred? What is the role of governments and private organizations? What can we do as individuals? 128pp., young adult

***You Are the Earth: Know the Planet So You Can Make It Better*** by David Suzuki and Kathy Vanderlinden (Greystone Books, 2001). This book is about what we need to stay alive—clean air, water, soil, ecosystems, and the sun's energy. Information is plentiful in this blend of facts, Native American stories, colorful illustrations, and cartoons. The author also talks about the interdependence of people and animals, plus tells of actions taken by young people to change the world, now! 24pp., grades 4–7

## Picture Books: *The Environment*

***Dear Children of the Earth*** by Schim Schimmel (NorthWord Press, 1994). Mother Earth sends a letter to her children telling of the need to protect the planet and her many wondrous creatures.

***The Empty Lot*** by Dale Fife (Sierra Club Books, 1991). Harry sets out to sell his "empty" lot. "What good is an empty lot?" he wonders while driving to put up a "For Sale" sign. While eating lunch on the lot, he hears a woodpecker tapping and sees baby sparrows in a nest, dragonflies hovering over a stream, and children playing. Harry has a change of heart.

> The earth beneath Harry's feet was alive. Pulsing. Harry watched a line of ants crawl in and out of their ant-mountain home. He thought about beetles and fungi and molds, earthworms and minute bacteria deep in the soil. He wondered how many wild things were watching him, mice and owls and hawks, from the jungle of the nearby blackberry thicket.
>
> And then Harry heard the voices of children.
>
> FROM *THE EMPTY LOT*

***The Gift of the Tree*** by Alvin Tresselt (HarperCollins, 1992). By following a tree's life cycle, we find out about animals that depend on it for shelter and food.

***The Great Kapok Tree*** by Lynne Cherry (Harcourt, 1990). Many different animals living in a great Brazilian kapok tree convince a man with an ax of the importance of the rain forest.

***The Great Trash Bash*** by Loreen Leedy (Holiday House, 1991). When Mayor Hippo has a feeling that "something is wrong in Beaston," he discovers trash on the highway, a polluted swimming hole, and an overloaded landfill. The resident animals decide to make less trash and clean up their town now and for the future.

***The People Who Hugged the Trees: An Environmental Folktale*** by Deborah Lee Rose (Robert Rinehart, 1990). This folktale from India tells of Amtra Devi, who inspired her community to protect the trees because the trees protect the community from the winds.

***Recycle Every Day!*** by Nancy Elizabeth Wallace (Cavendish, 2003). A young bunny named Minna ponders the best way to make a poster about recycling, hoping her art will be selected for a Community Recycling Calendar. Her rabbit family spends the week doing various kinds of recycling as Minna considers many options for her poster. The student calendar is designed to teach lessons about recycling throughout the entire community. Great ideas for service learning!

***A River Ran Wild*** by Lynne Cherry (Harcourt, 1991). The Nashua River, which once provided food to the indigenous people in New England, is polluted by industry and cities. Can a determined local citizen restore the river?

***The Shape of Betts Meadow: A Wetlands Story*** by Meghan Nuttall Sayres (Millbrook Press, 2002). Follow Gunnar Holmquist, a medical doctor who became a "wetland doctor." His efforts restore Betts Meadow, a 140-acre dry pasture, to its original state: a wetland bursting with wildflowers, elk, and tree frogs. Includes a glossary of wetland terms and resources.

***Someday a Tree*** by Eve Bunting (Clarion, 1993). A special oak tree grows near Alice's home—a perfect setting for picnics and gazing through the leaves at the clouds. When the surrounding grass turns yellow, a tree doctor determines that someone has dumped chemicals by the roots. The community unites in trying to save the tree.

***The Table Where Rich People Sit*** by Byrd Baylor (Aladdin, 1998). Young Mountain Girl knows her family doesn't have enough money. Why don't her parents get real "indoor" jobs? As her family sits around their scratched kitchen table, her mother and father say they are "rich." As they determine the value of all they have—being able to see the sky all day, sleeping under stars, viewing the majestic mountains—the girl begins to understand they may be rich after all.

***This House Is Made of Mud/Esta casa está hecha de lodo*** by Ken Buchanan (Northland, 1991). A family's life is interwoven with the natural environment in the Sonoran Desert. Watercolors of azure skies, mountains, giant cacti, and howling coyotes capture the harmony possible when the earth is treasured.

***The Wartville Wizard*** by Don Madden (Aladdin, 1993). A man turns "wizard" to fight a town of litterbugs by making litter stick to the person who dropped it! A memorable and colorful tale of how people learn about the consequences of their actions. Easily adapted to an amusing play with an important message.

***What Planet Are You From, Clarice Bean?*** by Lauren Child (Candlewick Press, 2001). Clarice is wild about her environmental studies at school but not enthusiastic about a project on snails she has to do with her neighbor, Robert. When her brother, granddad, and parents camp beside (and in) a tree scheduled to be chopped down, Clarice and her friends set out to "Free the Tree!"

***Wildlife Refuge*** by Lorraine Ward (Charlesbridge, 1993). Join a classroom of children on a visit to a wildlife refuge, where animals hunt for food, build homes, and defend their territories.

## Fiction: *The Environment*

**Recommendation from the Field**
*by Antoinette C. Rockwell, teacher*

*Island of the Blue Dolphins* by Scott O'Dell (Scott Foresman, 1987/1960). Based on a true story, *Island of the Blue Dolphins* tells of Karana, a Native American, whose tribe escapes by ship after losing a battle with a Russian hunting group. Karana jumps off the ship and swims back to the island to care for her young brother, who missed the boat. When her brother is killed by wild dogs, she blames herself. For eighteen years, Karana lives alone on Saint Nicholas Island off the coast of California, struggling to meet basic needs and facing many difficult choices, such as whether to go against her tribe's rules by making a weapon or killing wildlife for food.

This book can lead to a variety of service learning projects. Students can discuss such questions as: Why are cultural traditions important in our society? Which natural resources should be sustained, how, and to what degree? What survival issues face people who struggle to meet basic needs in our area, and what resources are available?

As one example of a service project, students can study the local natural resources, their use, and any issues surrounding these resources. They can interview community members and resource professionals for some solutions and perform a field study or restoration project that monitors or restores a natural resource on school grounds or in the community. Building bat boxes and planting native plants are restoration project examples. 184pp., grades 4–7

***Judy Moody Saves the World*** by Megan McDonald (Candlewick Press, 2002). When her teacher informs the class about the destruction of the rain forest, endangered species, and recycling, Judy is determined to save the world single-handed. Only after she gets her third-grade class involved does Judy realize that "she no longer had to do it by herself," and the results take root. 145pp., grades 3–6

***The Missing 'Gator of Gumbo Limbo*** by Jean Craighead George (HarperTrophy, 1992). Liza and her mother live in one of the last natural ecosystems, the Florida Everglades. There, with a small community of "woods people" who live on the land, Liza searches for Dajun, the glorious alligator that protects this fragile environment. When a state official arrives to kill Dajun, Liza discovers that the danger extends far beyond the threat to the alligator. Called an "eco mystery," this book provides a wealth of information about the animal and plant world of the Everglades. 144pp., grades 4–6

A group of children in Iowa planted the original prairie grasses in their yards to restore a strand of the prairie ecosystem. . . . A family in Connecticut sowed wild lupine to save an endangered butterfly. . . . And there are millions of young people who know that recycling, planting, protecting, and controlling pollution is the silk that mends the web—and they are enthusiastically reconnecting the strands.

FROM THE FOREWORD,
*THE MISSING 'GATOR OF GUMBO LIMBO*

***Saving the Planet*** by Gail Gauthier (Putnam, 2003). After losing his summer job, sixteen-year-old Michael ends up living and working in Vermont on an environmentalist magazine with Walt and Nora, his grandparents' elder friends. While Michael is trying to become accustomed to vegetarian cuisine, a room filled with recycled Styrofoam, paper and plastic bags, and bicycling to work, he stumbles upon an ecological intrigue and a surprising romance. What a summer! 232pp., grades 6–10

***There's an Owl in the Shower*** by Jean Craighead George (HarperTrophy, 1995). Spotted owls have cost Borden's father, Leon, his job as a logger in the old growth forest of northern California. Intending to kill a spotted owl for revenge, Borden finds an owlet and brings it home. Surprisingly, Leon cares for and about this growing owl. As he learns about the ecological impact of "the ravaging of old growth forests," Leon and his family change their views. 134pp., grades 4–6

# Interviews with Authors:
## The Story Behind the Story

In the following interview, we find out the "story behind the story" from Don Madden (*The Wartville Wizard*). While there are many important and well-written books on the environment, there is one that captures a common desire: to completely rid the planet of litter. Author Don Madden's ingenious book combines art and words to create a hilarious story that jumps off the page and sticks to your memory. Including an interview with the "real" Wartville wizard was simply a must.

### *Don Madden, author of*
### The Wartville Wizard

I am actually "the Wartville Wizard." My home is situated on a road halfway between two fast-food restaurants. When I wrote the book in the early 1980s, people would eat and drive, and they would arrive in front of my driveway as they were finishing their meal. I got really fed up with their trash coming right out the window, landing on my front yard, and cluttering up the roadway. How dare they throw their trash! That really lit my fuse. So I had the idea that all the trash should go back and stick to them. That's what happens in the book. Kids like the illustrations; their favorite seems to be the one with the woman who has a filled trash bag stuck to her backside.

After I wrote the book, I felt better. I got the frustration out of my system. I've received a lot of mail from teachers and kids about *The Wartville Wizard*, as well as from recycling groups who don't seem to mind that I don't tackle recycling in this book. They enjoy the story and get the message.

I would like kids to come away with a feeling of taking care of the environment. I always enjoy hearing about kids getting involved and doing something to help out. I am actually a humanist and that's the message of humanism—to look out for each other. That will make things better for everyone.

I don't notice so much trash on the road anymore. I think some of the laws about bottle returns and so forth have done well in New York state. And I think kids are very aware, and that helps a great deal. Whether our young people will continue to be advocates for our environment, we will have to see. Once you start along those lines, you must continue the work to maintain the improvements.

*The Wartville Wizard* would definitely advocate taking care of the world we live in. It's the only one we've got! So do your part to make this world a better place.

CHAPTER 9

# GARDENING

> You can complain because roses have thorns, or you can rejoice because thorns have roses.
>
> ZIGGY, COMIC STRIP CHARACTER

Sweet peas and cucumbers, tomatoes and daffodils, strawberries and corn. A garden is a place to watch—and help—things grow, where nature's cycles become apparent, and the impact of care and neglect are dramatic lessons in cause and effect. *Planting, growing,* and *transformation* are just a few of the words in a common language used to describe gardening as well as human development and relationships. It's no coincidence that gardens are such an effective way to bring people together and help them grow.

School and community gardens are springing up in many regions, with many hands tending the plants. All ages can work cooperatively to make a garden grow. Even reluctant students or urban youth who have never planted a seed can usually find a connection in the garden with the other gardeners, as well as with the soil, plants, flowers, and produce.

Learning possibilities abound in gardening. Science comes literally alive as students identify the parts of plants in real life and diligently watch as the stages of their garden's life cycle unfold. Students have used computers to design a garden and math skills to measure their plot and estimate the cost of materials. They have serenaded their plants with music and painted murals to keep their garden in bloom year-round. A book such as *The Ugly Vegetables* can lead students to writing their own stories. Harvested food is often shared with shelters and food banks, so the garden can also be used to raise awareness around issues of hunger and poverty in the community and the region. Students come to appreciate and understand how agriculture, farm workers, and environmental issues interconnect through the process of planting and maintaining a garden. Planting, growing, transformation: How will your garden grow?

## Preparation: Getting Ready for Service Learning Involving Gardening

The following activities can be used in the preparation stage to promote learning and skill development related to gardening. These activities can be used with different age ranges during preparation to help your students examine key issues through research, analyze community needs, and gain the knowledge they need to effectively contribute to the design of their service plan. Since literature is often an important part of preparation, you can find recommended titles on this theme in the Gardening Bookshelf later in this chapter.

***Activity: An Old Fashioned Almanac.*** Beginning in 1792, farmers turned to printed almanacs for a variety of information concerning agriculture, including sunrise and sunset tables, planting charts, weather patterns and predictions, and recipes. Students can learn a great deal by reviewing the almanacs available in most libraries. The students can identify topics to research in preparation for creating their own gardens and their own version of an almanac, which can be distributed to community members. The students' almanac could include a planting schedule, tips from gardeners, strategies for dealing with pests, recipes tested by the students, and a problem-solving section. Students could even create short scenes based on their almanac to perform for younger students or community members in (where else?) the garden! *The Green Truck Garden Giveaway: A Neighborhood Story and Almanac,* a picture book in almanac format, and *A Harvest of Color: Growing a Vegetable Garden,* written by very young gardeners, can serve as prototypes for student publications.

***Activity: Community Gardens.*** Community gardens are lovely to look at, and they also provide a valuable resource: fresh produce. Community gardens, like the Victory Gardens of World War II, provide affordable vegetables and fruits to many families, and the surplus is often given to local food shelves or shelters. These are just some of the benefits of a community garden.

Your students can research and learn about local community gardens and their benefits before they start their own garden. There are many different questions that can come up. Does our community already have any community gardens? If so, what are the land use policies in the gardens? How do people reserve or share garden plots? What help is needed to maintain the gardens or to expand the opportunities for participation? Who in the community could benefit from the garden's produce? If there are no community gardens in the area, how could one be started? National and local organizations that support the development of community gardens with funds and expertise are good sources of information for students doing research on many of these questions. In addition to planning their own garden, students can become advocates for garden programs, collaborating with local government agencies and schools. Gardens are not only about seeds, compost, plants, and harvesting, they are also about people and building community.

### Find Out More About Gardening

To learn more about these issues and to get ideas for service and action, visit these Web sites and organizations online:

***www.kidsgardening.com*** KidsGardening!, a program of the National Gardening Association, offers a host of gardening resources including books, curriculum, more Web connections, and grant opportunities.

***www.nwf.org/backyard*** The National Wildlife Federation's Backyard Wildlife Habitat program teaches students about the wildlife right in their own backyard or schoolyard and includes resources to create gardens that are habitat-based learning sites in schoolyards.

***www.abcdbooks.org/curriculum/garden.html*** Visit "How Does Our Garden Grow?" at ABCD Books for gardening curriculum connections you can use in grades 1–5.

## Making Connections Across the Curriculum

Some service learning activities naturally lend themselves to interdisciplinary work and making connections across the curriculum. These connections strengthen and broaden student learning, helping them meet academic standards. More than likely, you'll be looking for these connections and ways to encourage them well before the students ever start working on service learning activities. As with the entire service learning process, it helps to remain flexible, because some connections can be spontaneously generated by the questions raised throughout and by the needs of the project. To help you think about cross-curricular connections and where you can look for them, the Curricular Web for this chapter (page 137) gives examples of many different ways this theme can be used in different academic areas. (The service learning scenarios in the next section of the chapter also demonstrate various ways this theme can be used across the curriculum.)

## Service Learning Scenarios:
### Ideas for Action

Ready to take action? What follows are projects that have been successfully carried out by elementary, middle, or high school students. Most of these scenarios and examples explicitly include some aspects of preparation, action, reflection, and demonstration. These scenarios can be a rich source of project, resource, and curriculum ideas for you to draw upon. While the grade levels are given as a reference, most project ideas can be adapted to suit younger or older students, and many are suitable for cross-age partnerships.

***Gardening Takes Root in an Entire District: Grades K–12.*** In one school district, gardens became an important part of student life at several schools. Students found many different ways to contribute to their gardens and to use the produce that was the result of their efforts. Students at one elementary school began to eat plenty of leafy greens after harvesting certified organic produce from their on-site garden, adding the tastes of bok choy and arugula to the cafeteria food. At another elementary school in the district, students took surplus produce to a

# Gardening Across the Curriculum

### *English/Language Arts*

- Research and write about gardens and herbs
- Write letters soliciting donations for community gardens
- Write poetry about the flowers, fruits, or vegetables (or aspects of the garden) to "plant" or display in the school garden

### *Social Studies/History*

- Research the indigenous plants in your area and Native American gardening methods
- Learn about local gardening organizations
- Study World War II Victory Gardens

### *Languages*

- Learn the vocabulary of gardening in the language of study
- Research fruits and vegetables grown in the country where the language is spoken
- Make multilingual signs for the garden identifying the plants; or translate community gardening materials and distribute them

### *Theater, Music, & Visual Arts*

- Create and perform a dramatization to teach about gardening
- Perform songs about plants and growing
- Design and paint a mural to create a year-round garden

## Gardening

### *Math*

- Create a budget and price list for plants and materials to purchase
- Measure space for planting
- Chart observations of plant growth and change; calculate expected yields and compare to actual harvest

### *Physical Education*

- Prepare a warm-up exercise routine to do before working in the garden
- Research the impact on the body of bending and lifting and other gardening movements, then find the healthiest ways to do these activities
- Plan a garden tour for very young children that includes pretending that they are seeds that grow and grow into a plant

### *Computer*

- Read and research software and literature on garden design
- Create a computer slide show on garden development
- Use the Internet to learn about careers in landscape architecture, horticulture, topiary design, and agriculture

### *Science*

- Identify and compare seeds and plants, then observe and record life cycle of plants
- Examine and test soil
- Study invasive exotic plants

homeless shelter each week. At yet another elementary school with extensive gardens, students progressed through various gardening tasks by grade level, moving from raising berries and vegetables to building ponds and garden structures. Greenhouses at the district middle schools allowed students to start seedlings for the elementary students, and high school students planned nutrition classes and a health fair to teach students across the district about gardening, cooking, and nutrition. The younger students contributed ideas about what to plant, while high school students planned and organized all aspects of the health fair from fund-raising to publicity. Benefits extended in all directions. One school, for example, included a large population of Hmong and Hispanic students, who sometimes had a difficult time sharing expertise at school. The garden provided a way for Hmong and Hispanic families who worked in the agricultural industry to participate. Local businesses (such as nurseries and excavation companies, which provided topsoil) and local nonprofit organizations became collaborators and assisted with the building of garden beds.

***A Giving Garden: Grades 1–3 (with middle and high school helpers).*** Three first- through third-grade classrooms in West Salem, Wisconsin, designed, constructed, planted, maintained, and harvested a garden on school grounds, with help from middle and high school students and community members. After hearing a speaker from the food pantry talk about the pantry and the needs it addressed, the students came up with the idea of planting a garden to help serve their community. The garden was intended to produce vegetables for fifty families per month who used the local food pantry. The project was designed to teach students about community participation by providing opportunities to work with teachers, parents, and other community members. In addition to learning gardening skills, the students learned about the relationships between people, plants, and wildlife and practiced leadership skills in work crews. Students from the junior high constructed benches for the garden, and high school students helped with planting. Classroom reflection included discussion of the concept of community and the reasons a community might need a food pantry, such as job loss and poverty. Students wrote journals throughout the project. And to keep the garden healthy year-round, the students created a weekly schedule for families to work in the garden during the summer.

> It is not enough to be busy; so are the ants.
> The question is: What are we busy about?
> HENRY DAVID THOREAU, PHILOSOPHER

***A Poetic Garden Adds a Mural: Grades 2–4.*** An elementary school garden added beauty to a Los Angeles neighborhood. Students who were planting, tending seedlings, or harvesting would strike up conversations with neighbors passing by. The neighbors commented on the poetry "planted" among the vegetables. Students explained how they had read books about gardening and had been inspired to write poems by the curly pea vines and the large zucchini leaves. Their poems, mounted on boards and laminated, were interspersed with the greenery. During the off-season, however, the area looked pretty dull. The students gathered in their garden to think about what could be done. They designed and received approval to make a garden mural so the beauty of things growing would be present all year long.

***Planting a Butterfly Garden: Grades 2 and 7.*** After elementary students read *Butterfly Boy*, they wanted to create a butterfly garden alongside a local senior center, which was located in a park. The teacher thought the job seemed too large for her class alone, so when she contacted the city parks and recreation department for permission to plant the garden, she also asked for assistance. She was referred to the middle school, and a seventh-grade class at the school offered to help. Their teacher wove the experience into literature by selecting *Butterflies and Lizards, Beryl and Me* for her students to read. Many groups assisted, including the senior citizens, a community college life-sciences class, and a local conservation group. Students conducted research to identify the appropriate plants. The teacher also asked the students for ideas to begin a relationship with members of the senior center. As a result, the students hosted a "butterfly" party at the center and with assistance from the center's art director and the elders who used the center made three-dimensional butterflies to display in the local library.

***To Learn, to Share, to Experience Peace: Grades 3–5.*** Sometimes a garden has many purposes. In Dulles, Oregon, an elementary garden serves three needs. First, the garden offers numerous hands-on learning experiences for children. The students manage the greenhouse, weather station, worm garden, and composting, and grow flowers and vegetables. Second, the produce and flowers are given to people in need within the community. And third, the garden is a place for reflection and peace where students can sit quietly and write in journals or simply enjoy the beauty and peace around them.

***Singing for Plants: Grade 4.*** Students at one Illinois elementary school were interested in planting some native species around their school. To raise money to help them buy the necessary supplies, they decided to do what youngsters do well—sing loudly! They planned a concert and chose songs that pertained to plants and their importance to people, animals, and the earth. The students sold tickets to the concert and used the money they raised to help them buy several varieties of native flowers, vegetables, and herbs. Students not only planted a beautiful garden around their school but also learned how to care for the plants by weeding and watering the garden.

***History That's for the Birds: Grade 5.*** Fifth-grade students in Galt, California, put hammer to nail as they worked on rebuilding a chicken house. While helping the local historical society to develop a living history ranch, they learned construction methods of the past and present. They also planted several acres of pumpkins that were enjoyed by kindergarten classes during fall harvest activities.

***From Worm Bins to Radishes: Grade 5.*** Fifth graders in West Hollywood, California, who began the school year with little, if any, knowledge of gardening had green thumbs by year's end. During science lessons, they planted and cared for seedlings, charting growth and changes. That was just the beginning, then they: read books about gardens, such as *Jack's Garden* and *Wanda's Roses*, to younger students; built compost bins at school and collected appropriate food waste during lunch time; tasted their first radishes; displayed worm bins at the local farmers' market; lead tours for visitors and had them write comments in the guest journal; and published a booklet, "How to Start a Container Garden," for distribution throughout the community. What was left? The next year, the gardeners created a coloring book called "From Apples to Zucchinis: The ABCs of Gardening" to share their expertise and inspire other young gardeners.

***Recipes and Remedies: Grades 5–8.*** Good food grown in gardens may taste even better when used in recipes that teach about culture and tradition. After students in Oklahoma researched traditional plants used by Native Americans for cooking and for herbal remedies, they cooked up a cookbook with art and detailed information to share their new knowledge and recipes for the community.

***Language Skills and Gardens Grow: Grades 6–8.*** Student and adult volunteers in Houston, Texas, created an urban garden with dual objectives: to grow fresh produce for a local food pantry and to learn Spanish related to gardening. In this "speak Spanish" garden, students learned Spanish words for various tools and vegetables and even the vitamins in the produce. The students also learned how to talk to community members in Spanish about why a garden is important and how to get a garden started.

***A Victory Garden: Grade 7.*** As middle school students were preparing to plant a garden, their teacher read aloud essays to them from *Down to Earth: Garden Secrets! Garden Stories! Garden Projects You Can Do!* An essay by Gloria Rand about her father's "Victory Garden" planted during World War II led students to conduct research to learn more about these gardens. Students used history books and conversations with community members who had firsthand experience with Victory gardens to learn more. The students then considered what kind of garden they would like to plant to commemorate an event from their own era. They decided to plant a garden to honor the people who died in the terrorist attacks on September 11. To recognize the fact that people of many different ethnic groups lost their lives, the students included plants from different parts of the world in their peace garden.

***A Neighborly Garden: Grade 8.*** As part of a community cleanup around the school, eighth-grade students in Texas spruced up an elder neighbor's front yard. The invitation to "come back again" began a relationship that grew. Students received permission to create a garden in this new friend's backyard and walked over several times each week to do the necessary work. The students found that their older friend greatly enjoyed their companionship—as well as the produce from the garden, which was also shared with the local food bank. Students helped to deliver and return library books for their neighbor as well.

> All plants are our brothers and sisters. They talk to us and if we listen, we can hear them.
>
> ARAPAHO SAYING

***Two Cultures Growing: Grade 8.*** In partnership with a historical society, an eighth-grade class in Wisconsin created Native American and European gardens to show the difference between the two cultures. Activities expanded with student input to include making Native American tools, writing brochures about the gardens, and creating a display case. During the summer, the gardens were maintained by young students from Somalia who had come to the community as refugees. One outcome of this project was that the Somalis planted their own community garden. For this group, the garden helped in the transition from an agricultural society. (See *Native American Gardening: Stories, Projects and Recipes for Families* in the bookshelf for more about planting a Native American garden.)

***Gardening Partnerships: Grades 9 and 10.*** Environmental biology students stopped building virtual gardens and created a greenhouse on their Santa Monica, California, school campus to try out their ideas and to grow produce for a local shelter. Once the greenhouse was operational, the students addressed the larger challenge of taking what they had practiced into the community. A nearby residential facility for active seniors contacted the high school asking for help in creating an on-site garden. When students visited the facility with their plans, they found a huge flaw: the residents would be unable to bend down to work in a garden. With assistance from shop classes, the students found a solution: raised-bed gardens. This solution led to another dilemma. The elder gardeners wanted to invite elementary classes to visit and receive gardening tips, but the raised-bed gardens where too high for the children! The shop class constructed easy-to-move platforms that would bring the children up to dirt level.

***A Touch Garden: Grades 9–12.*** As part of a dropout prevention program, high school students in Fort Myers, Florida, were given responsibilities and the necessary skills and knowledge to create a "children's touching garden." This required a comprehensive education about planting and plant care, the construction of pathways, and building benches. Students were mentored by master gardeners and other community volunteers. They also created a children's brochure. Once open, thousands of young children had visual and tactile experiences in this colorful and well-planned garden.

***Profits Keep Growing: Grades 9–12.*** Inner-city high school students in Los Angeles transformed themselves into entrepreneurs as they transformed their garden into a business by growing most of the ingredients for a salad dressing. Local business people contributed time and expertise to guide the students in many necessary tasks, from recipe development to promotion. Profits were divided: half goes back into the business and the rest goes to a college scholarship fund. The students have visited many schools to share their knowledge and inspire others.

> A book is like a garden carried in the pocket.
>
> CHINESE PROVERB

## The Gardening Bookshelf

Books from the Gardening Bookshelf can teach us the fundamentals of gardening and frequently show how gardens illuminate many aspects of life and community. Seedlings, like infants, need careful nurturing. By harvest time mature plants can seem like old friends. Bonds can form with the garden and among the people who tend it. The garden can be a source of beauty that grows the soul as well as the produce that feeds the body. To help you find books relevant to your particular projects, the book chart classifies the books into two topic areas: planting and growing, and transformation.

In general, the bookshelf features:

- An annotated bibliography arranged and alphabetized by title according to the general categories of nonfiction (N), picture books (P), and fiction (F). For nonfiction and fiction, length and recommended grade levels are included. The entries in the picture book category do not include suggested grade levels, since they can be successfully used with all ages.
- A chart organized by topic and category to help you find books relevant to particular projects.
- Recommendations from service learning colleagues and experts that include a book summary and ideas for service learning connections. (The number of recommended books varies in each bookshelf.)

## Gardening Bookshelf Topics

| *Topics* | *Books* | *Category* |
|---|---|---|
| ***Planting and Growing*** Methods for planting and providing care are featured in these selections, along with the strong, hardworking people who work the fields. | *Compost! Growing Gardens from Your Garbage* | P |
| | *Compost Critters* | N |
| | *Down to Earth: Garden Secrets! Garden Stories! Garden Projects You Can Do!* ‡ | N |
| | *Gathering the Sun: An Alphabet in Spanish and English* | P |
| | *A Harvest of Color: Growing a Vegetable Garden* | N |
| | *Jack's Garden* | P |
| | *My First Garden* | P |
| | *Native American Gardening: Stories, Projects and Recipes for Families* | N |
| | *The Ugly Vegetables* | P |
| ***Transformation*** In a garden, change happens; a small seed becomes a huge green watermelon or a juicy red tomato. People can change along with the plants. These are their stories. | *Bud* | P |
| | *Butterflies and Lizards, Beryl and Me* | F |
| | *Carlos and the Cornfield/Carlos y la milpa de maíz* | P |
| | *The Chalk Box Kid* | F |
| | *City Green* * | P |
| | *The Gardener* | P |
| | *The Garden of Happiness* * | P |
| | *The Green Truck Garden Giveaway: A Neighborhood Story and Almanac* * | P |
| | *A Place to Grow* (see page 168) | P |
| | *Seedfolks* * | F |
| | *The Summer My Father Was Ten* | P |
| | *The Victory Garden* * | F |
| | *Wanda's Roses* | P |
| | *Xóchitl and the Flowers/Xóchitl, la niña de las flores* | P |

Page references are given for books that do not appear in the Gardening Bookshelf but that can be found in the bookshelf lists of other chapters.
* These books include examples of young people in service-providing roles.
‡ These books are out of print but still worth finding.

> Books are the bees which carry the quickening pollen from one to another mind.
>
> JAMES RUSSELL LOWELL, AUTHOR

## Nonfiction: *Gardening*

***Compost Critters*** by Bianca Lavies (Dutton, 1993). Text and close-up photography give an inside picture of a compost heap and how creatures, from bacteria and mites to millipedes and earthworms, aid in turning compost into humus. 32pp., grades K–8

***Down to Earth: Garden Secrets! Garden Stories! Garden Projects You Can Do!*** edited by Michael J Rosen (Harcourt, 1998). "A garden plot is more than just a piece of land. It's a story." So begins this extraordinary compilation of poetry, stories, artwork, and recipes for successful and creative gardens. Forty-one children's book authors and illustrators contributed their work, with proceeds supporting Share Our Strength, an anti-hunger organization. Out of print but worth finding. 64pp., all ages

***A Harvest of Color: Growing a Vegetable Garden*** by Melanie Eclare (Ragged Bears, 2002). Six young children celebrate the experience of growing five different vegetables. We learn how they measure the plot, thin the seedlings, and come to appreciate worms. Along with the brilliant photographs is a recipe for a vegetable salad. 32pp., grades K–3

> I love carrots because they are sweet and crunchy. And I can share them with my pet rabbit.
>
> I sprinkled seeds into rows as deep as my thumbnail. We planted three rows of carrots, each one as far apart as the distance from my middle finger to my elbow. To be sure the rows were straight, we attached string to two sticks and put them in the soil at each end of the garden bed. . . . In about ten days little plants that looked like ferns showed through the soil.
>
> FROM *A HARVEST OF COLOR: GROWING A VEGETABLE GARDEN*

***Native American Gardening: Stories, Projects and Recipes for Families*** by Michael Caduto and Joseph Bruchac (Fulcrum, 1996). Combining gardening and storytelling, the authors provide information needed to pursue "Three Sisters" gardening: growing the traditional Native garden of corn, beans, and squash. Includes information about the relationships between people and the gardens of Earth, seed preservation, Native diets and meals, natural pest control, and the importance of the Circle of Life. 176pp., all grades

## Picture Books: *Gardening*

***Bud*** by Kevin O'Malley (Walker and Co., 2000). Bud Sweet-William, a young rhinoceros, has a passion for gardening that mystifies his parents. To their surprise, his grandfather also likes to garden. Soon, all are knee deep in dirt and celebration.

***Carlos and the Cornfield/Carlos y la milpa de maíz*** by Jan Romero Stevens (Rising Moon, 1995). Young Carlos tries to rush the planting process when he cares more about the money he will earn than the corn he will grow. His conscience causes him to set things right. *Cosechas lo que siembras*—you reap what you sow. English and Spanish text.

***City Green*** by DyAnne DiSalvo-Ryan (Morrow, 1994). Marcy's plan to turn a vacant lot into a city garden inspires everyone to pitch in, except grouchy, elder Mr. Hammer. Then a few surprises bloom!

***Compost! Growing Gardens from Your Garbage*** by Linda Glaser (Millbrook Press, 1996). A simple story about composting, from adding garbage to using the soil in a garden.

***The Gardener*** by Sarah Stewart (Farrar, Straus and Giroux, 1997). The hard times of the Depression force Lydia to move to an unfamiliar city to stay with her Uncle Jim, a baker with a frown. With determination, she brightens her corner of the world and her uncle's life with flowers.

***The Garden of Happiness*** by Erika Tamar (Harcourt, 1996). Marisol, a young girl, and her diverse neighbors turn a vacant New York City lot into a lush, multicultural garden with a sunflower mural.

***Gathering the Sun: An Alphabet in Spanish and English*** by Alma Flor Ada (HarperCollins, 2001). Twenty-seven poems pay tribute to farm workers and to nature's delicious gifts. Using the Spanish alphabet as a guide, the book takes us into the fields and orchards to learn about people and the pride they carry for their culture. Includes an historical reference to César Chavez. Illustrator Simón Silva grew up in a farm worker's family.

***The Green Truck Garden Giveaway: A Neighborhood Story and Almanac*** by Jacqueline B. Martin (Simon & Schuster, 1997). When two people pass out seeds and gardening supplies, neighbors who claim to have no interest in gardening or their community are transformed. Along with the engaging story, the author offers historical information about plants, recipes, and advice for up-and-coming gardeners. Out of print but worth finding.

***Jack's Garden*** by Henry Cole (Greenwillow, 1995). Text and illustrations show what happens to Jack's garden after he plants his seeds.

***My First Garden*** by Tomek Bogacki (Farrar, Straus and Giroux, 2000). When a young boy hears that a garden used to grow in a courtyard, he sets out to do all the work to make the garden bloom anew. The illustrations in impressionistic pastels return us to the author's small town in Poland and show incisive details of his work and his community.

***The Summer My Father Was Ten*** by Pat Brisson (Boyds Mills Press, 1998). Every year, as the narrator and her father plant their garden, she hears the story "about Mr. Bellavista and the summer my father was ten." What starts as a joke—using a tomato as a baseball—becomes a careless act of vandalism in a neighbor's garden. The elder immigrant neighbor simply asks, "Why?" The next year, to make amends, her father asks to help replant the garden. An act of forgiveness begins a lifelong friendship and a family tradition.

> "Mr. Bellavista?" my father began. "Are you going to plant a garden this year?"
>
> Mr. Bellavista's eyes looked straight into my father's. "So you can destroy again?" he asked.
>
> "No," my father stammered. ". . . I'm sorry about last year, and I thought maybe I could help."
>
> Mr. Bellavista didn't say anything at first. He studied my father for a few minutes, then rubbed his jaw with the back of his hand.
>
> "Tomorrow," he said at last. "Tomorrow we'll make a garden."
>
> FROM *THE SUMMER MY FATHER WAS TEN*

***The Ugly Vegetables*** by Grace Lin (Charlesbridge, 1999). A young girl notices the differences between her mother's garden and the ones planted by her neighbor. The neighbor's flowers are "beautiful" while her mother's Chinese vegetables are "ugly." At harvest, the aroma of the "ugly vegetable soup" attracts everyone to join in the feast. Recipe included.

***Wanda's Roses*** by Pat Brisson (Boyds Mills Press, 1994). When Wanda discovers a thorn bush in an empty lot, she is sure it is a rosebush ready to bloom. She clears away trash and waters her "bush." When no roses appear, her neighbors and friends have a surprising solution.

***Xóchitl and the Flowers/Xóchitl, la niña de las flores*** by Jorge Argueta (Children's Book Press, 2003). Young Xóchitl and her parents, immigrants from El Salvador, work hard to transform a garbage filled backyard into a blooming nursery to provide income for their family. When their landlord tries to stop them, Xóchitl discovers the value of community in her new home in the United States. Based on a true story, this book is written in English and Spanish.

## Fiction: Gardening

***Butterflies and Lizards, Beryl and Me*** by Ruth Lercher Bornstein (Marshall Cavendish, 2002). During the Great Depression in 1936, Charley moves with her mom to a rural town. While her mother works in "the smell cannery," eleven-year-old Charley is drawn to Beryl, an optimistic elder woman, called "crazy" by other children. Together, Charley and Beryl plant a garden. Beryl provides the friendship and encouragement Charley desperately needs. Within this caring relationship, Charley grows like the plants she cherishes. In spite of conflict with her mother, a near tragedy, and a deep loss, Charley finds her heart, her home, and a way to give. 144pp., grades 5–9

***The Chalk Box Kid*** by Clyde Robert Bulla (Random House, 1987). A new neighborhood, a new school, and an unhappy birthday make life hard for nine-year-old Gregory. After he discovers an abandoned chalk factory behind his house, his school assignment of planting a garden develops in a most unusual and creative way. 59pp., grades 2–4

***Seedfolks*** by Paul Fleishman (HarperCollins, 1997). These well-written short stories introduce the people in a diverse urban Cleveland neighborhood. One by one, people of varying ages and backgrounds transform a city lot that is filled with garbage into a productive, beautiful garden. In the process, they are also transformed. 69pp., grades 5–10

***The Victory Garden*** by Lee Kochenderfer. (Delacorte, 2002). Teresa Marks and her entire Kansas town await news that World War II will end soon. Many serve, like her older brother Jess, a fighter pilot. To keep busy, Teresa and her dad, like people all over the United States, plant a victory garden to provide fresh produce so other foods can be sent to troops overseas. In spring, when her neighbor is hospitalized, Teresa rallies her friends to tend his garden. As she tries to raise prize-winning tomatoes, Teresa questions the purpose of gardens and of war. She also finds that her garden grows new friendships. 166pp., grades 6–8

> "Do you ever think about why we were born in this country instead of where the war is?" I asked Maria.
>
> She gave me a strange look, but it was a question I had asked myself over and over.
>
> FROM *THE VICTORY GARDEN*

# Interviews with Authors:
## The Story Behind the Story

In the following interviews, we find out the "story behind the story" from Ruth Lercher Bornstein (*Butterflies and Lizards, Beryl and Me*) and Pat Brisson (*The Summer My Father Was Ten* and *Wanda's Roses*).

Ruth Bornstein's book *Butterflies and Lizards, Beryl and Me* captivated me initially with its title and then with its story. I conducted the interview in Ruth's home and found her to be an accomplished artist as well as a thoughtful writer. I called Pat Brisson to learn more about her protagonist Wanda, a girl with perseverance and creativity. Pat later introduced me to the story of *The Summer My Father Was Ten*, which moved me to tears. Both of her books are included on this bookshelf.

### *Ruth Lercher Bornstein, author of* Butterflies and Lizards, Beryl and Me

Being a dedicated painter, I thought this visual art form would allow me to say what I needed to in this lifetime. But then, in 1970, I found myself drawing little green elephants talking to flowers and rabbits peeking out of the ground. I was creating funny little drawings instead of big serious paintings. I was having fun, so I just let it happen. Then, in 1971, I grew my first vegetable garden and spent more time holding hands with the cucumber vines than I did doing anything in my studio.

By some mysterious, organic process, in November, when the plants began to die and sink into the ground, and feeling that I had experienced the whole span of birth and death in one summer, I began to write. Simple words like *green* and *grow* and *flower* became as real and solid to me as paint. I filled up sketchbook after sketchbook with words and pictures of everything I imagined or loved. My first picture book was published in 1973, and interspersed with periods of painting, I haven't stopped writing since.

In 1987, on a trip to New Zealand, I visited my friend, Beryl, who was dying of cancer. Inspired by her courage—even her humor—in the face of death, I began to write about her on the flight home. I sent the few pages to my editor, Charlotte Zolotow, who wrote back, "Ruth, this is not a picture book. This is a novel."

A novel! How do you write a novel? But somehow I knew she was right, and I continued to jot down feelings, thoughts, memories, ideas. Slowly, through the years and through many, many revisions and rejections, a shape emerged. The story is not autobiographical. A bitter, careworn mother appeared and an absent father, but there are also my own feelings about making art and growing a garden. And, as I worked, I realized that I was telling a story of forgiveness, of being loved, and of learning to give back.

The story takes place during the Great Depression because I needed trains that ran between small towns and a hobo one didn't have to be afraid of. I wanted a "crazy" old woman named Beryl who "grows" butterflies and gives names to lizards and who gives eleven-year-old Charley the gift of the wonder of being alive, the wonder of "all of us poor, beautiful creatures being here together."

Writing this story has given me the chance to be both the child, Charley, and her old woman soul mate, Beryl. It's given me a second chance to grow up, a chance to be able to say with Charley at the end, "the space inside of me is big enough to hold it all."

### *Pat Brisson, author of* The Summer My Father Was Ten *and* Wanda's Roses

I wrote *Wanda's Roses* when winter was almost over but spring hadn't yet arrived. Wanda's longing for something beautiful was mine, too. Of course, this longing is not entirely for roses—it is for something beautiful beyond ourselves, something worth striving for, something we can give our hearts to. I wanted to show a girl who was willing to work hard to make her dream come true. When you share your dream with others, I believe they will do what they can to help you achieve your dream. I often ask students, "What is your dream? What are you willing to work hard at?"

Typically, when I begin writing a book, I don't know how a story will end. With *Wanda's Roses*, I wanted to have a little girl who had a rosebush. As the story developed, I thought, "Oh yes, she will turn this into a blooming bush with paper roses." Wanda's neighbors watch her work hard for a month cleaning the lot and caring for her plant. Wanda's dedication touches the people around her; they sincerely want to help. I've been honored, too, that some students have helped to create beauty by planting rosebushes after reading *Wanda's Roses*.

In *The Summer My Father Was Ten*, a group of boys vandalize a neighbor's garden. When I first read the story to my son, he exclaimed, "Mom, those kids are really bad!" But kids who are not "bad" do "bad" things. The boy who threw one tomato did not intend to destroy a garden. The kids got carried away. While ravaging the garden, they were not considering their actions, only their "fun." How did this happen? Kids can identify with this mistake.

Librarians tell me they can hear a pin drop when reading *The Summer My Father Was Ten* aloud. Sometimes at the end, children express relief saying, "Phew, he got through it." The book is not just about the boy. This would have been a different story if Mr. Bellavista had denied the boy the opportunity to make amends. In the crucial moment when the boy asks to replant the garden, the man thinks, "Do I forgive? Do I give him a chance?" And the boy's life is changed. A true friendship develops. When the boy becomes a father, he is compelled to relate this story every spring to his daughter. Mr. Bellavista's moment of forgiveness affects future generations. The girl now tells us the story. We do not know how one moment of forgiveness will reach distant shores.

Does writing stories come easily to me? I wish I were brimming with ideas for stories that would flow forth as soon as pencil met paper. But for me, writing is work: occasionally frustrating, generally satisfying, but always worth striving for. It is something I believe in, something I have given my heart to, just as Wanda believed in her roses.

My approach is character driven. My interest is in what the characters are thinking and doing and feeling. Keep in mind that people approach the writing process in different ways. Writing requires a kind of problem solving—you figure out what words fit best, how much tension to establish, and the number of characters to include and consider if each character adds to the story or should be eliminated.

People often ask, "Did the book look like you expected?" I am not very visual when writing. I know the tone and feeling of the story. I know who the people are from the inside; sometimes I even hear the character's voice in my head. I may not know what she looks like but I know what she is going through. I am happy if the illustrations match the tone of the story, as they do in these two books.

Do all people respond to my books in the same way? A book exists in relationship to the specific reader or the person listening to the story. Every person brings ideas, experiences, and personality. The reader may see what the author intended and may also find additional meaning. This has happened with a number of my books. For example, I did not write *Wanda's Roses* as a book on ecology or gardening. Only when a teacher described it as "a great ecology book" did I think, "Oh yes, I can see this is also about ecology!"

Literature enables the reader to think, "that could be me" or "that might be me someday." Books allow us to know the reality that exists for others and broadens our limited perspective. A book can also lead the reader to have a change of heart. That is how social action begins, with a change of heart, with the ability to empathize. You don't have to change the whole world. One kind action can change someone's day or someone's life and can in turn help that someone to see people in a fresh way. By tutoring one person or befriending a child who is ignored or teased, you can make a world of difference.

# HUNGER AND HOMELESSNESS

> If you don't like the way the world is,
> you change it. You have an obligation
> to change it. You just do it one step at a time.
> MARIAN WRIGHT EDELMAN,
> FOUNDER, CHILDREN'S DEFENSE FUND

Hunger and homelessness are global problems. They are sometimes considered urban ills, but the reality is they are found in every country and in every community, rural and urban. Hunger and homelessness have many different causes. People throughout history have been uprooted and left without homes because of war or famine. Indigenous groups such as the Native Americans in the United States have been driven from their ancestral lands. Natural disasters also take a toll: floods, droughts, tornados, hurricanes, earthquakes, and fires can all devastate a community or destroy crops. Sometimes, events that do not affect entire communities create havoc in individual lives: People may face poverty and homelessness after losing their jobs or because of unexpected medical expenses.

Children are frequently those most affected by poverty in modern society. Many children live at or below the poverty level. In the United States, almost 12 million children live in poverty.[1] Children account for between 25 percent[2] and 39 percent of the homeless population.[3] (Worldwide nearly 650 million children live in extreme poverty.)[4] Other children may see people living on the streets, in cars, and in shelters and wonder why. During their first years of school, children learn about people's basic needs: food, clothing, shelter. Yet some of the same children lack these basic necessities, and most are cognizant that many people live and struggle without them.

> Peace, in the sense of absence of war, is of little
> value to someone who is dying of hunger or cold.
> Peace can only last where human rights are
> respected, where people are fed, and where
> individuals and nations are free.
> TENZIN GYATSO, THE FOURTEENTH DALAI LAMA

Through service learning, students can examine conditions that cause poverty and lead to hunger and homelessness. They can become familiar with local needs and the services that address them. Studying history through the lenses of hunger, homelessness, and poverty can make it come alive by making it more human and real. Literature, both fiction and nonfiction, can vividly bring these events and the people who were affected by them into students' lives today. Although affecting policy concerning people who are homeless is very challenging, students can work to help shape sustainable programs, can participate in new and existing programs, and can help in many other ways to meet immediate needs.

## Preparation: Getting Ready for Service Learning Involving Hunger and Homelessness

The following activities can be used in the preparation stage to promote learning and skill development related to hunger and homelessness. These activities

[1] *Low Income Children in the United States*, Lu Hsien-Hen (New York: National Center for Children in Poverty, 2003).
[2] *A Status Report on Hunger and Homelessness in America's Cities* (Washington, DC: U.S. Conference of Mayors, 2001).
[3] *A New Look at Homelessness in America* (Washington, DC: The Urban Institute, 2000).
[4] *The Progress of Nations 1999* (New York: UNICEF, 1999).

can be used with different age ranges during preparation to help your students examine key issues through research, analyze community needs, and gain the knowledge they need to effectively contribute to the design of their service plan. Since literature is often an important part of preparation, you can find recommended titles on this theme in the Hunger and Homelessness Bookshelf later in this chapter.

***Activity: What Shape Is Your Pyramid?*** From the four food groups to the food pyramid, is there really one shape for all of us? Ask students to share their families' particular relationship to eating and nutrition. In diverse communities, students will have the opportunity to learn about a range of foods, from bok choy and dal to grits and falafel, and to find out how different cultures and communities address their dietary requirements. This can help students develop appreciation for the diversity in their communities and better analyze and understand the needs of those communities.

***Activity: Learning About the Issues.*** How do we put a face on hunger and homelessness? How do we separate fact from fiction, myth from knowledge? You can try one or all of the following activities to start your students thinking.

- Give each student a piece of drawing paper and a crayon or marker (keep this simple). Ask students to draw a picture of somebody who is hungry. Let them know they can make a simple drawing and that they will have five minutes to finish. Encourage them to work individually and quietly. When everyone is done, ask students to place their drawings where others can see them. Ask the students to describe the person they drew—young, old, single, part of a family, man, woman, child—and how this person portrays hunger.
- Have students work in small groups. Assign each group one population: senior citizens, veterans, immigrants, families with children, unemployed people, people who are homeless. The students will spend five minutes thinking why this particular population might be hungry and might need assistance with food. They will then share their thoughts with classmates, who can ask questions. As a follow up, you or a guest speaker can present facts on these populations (provided by local, state, or national agencies), *and/or* each small group can research its assigned population to gather information about hunger and poverty to be presented to the class.
- Invite a representative from a local agency who works with people who are in need of assistance with food to help answer questions and brainstorm ways the class can provide meaningful assistance.

> The outrage of hunger amidst plenty
> will never be solved by "experts" somewhere.
> It will only be solved when people
> like you and me decide to act.
>
> FRANCES MOORE LAPPE, AUTHOR

**Find Out More About Hunger and Homelessness**

To learn more about these issues and to get ideas for service and action, visit these Web sites and organizations online:

***www.strength.org*** Share Our Strength mobilizes individuals and industries to lend their talents to raise funds and awareness for the fight against hunger and poverty, addressing immediate and long-term solutions. Their Great American Bake Sale program offers educational curriculum and opportunities to work toward eliminating childhood hunger in America.

***www.oxfamamerica.org*** and ***www.oxfam.org*** Both Oxfam America and Oxfam International are dedicated to finding long-term solutions to poverty, hunger, and social injustice around the world. Visit their pages for youth to find ways to become involved.

***www.nationalhomeless.org*** The National Coalition for the Homeless (NCH) engages in public education, policy advocacy, and grassroots organizing. Become educated about homelessness and learn the many ways students can become knowledgeable and involved.

## Making Connections Across the Curriculum

Some service learning activities naturally lend themselves to interdisciplinary work and making connections across the curriculum. These connections strengthen and broaden student learning, helping them meet academic standards. More than likely, you'll be looking for these connections and ways to encourage them well before the students ever start working on service learning activities. As with the entire service learning process, it helps to remain flexible, because some connections can be spontaneously generated by the questions raised throughout and by the needs of the project. To help you think about cross-curricular connections and where you can look for them, the Curricular Web for this chapter (page 149) gives examples of many different ways this theme can be used in different academic areas. (The service learning scenarios in the next section of the chapter also demonstrate various ways this theme can be used across the curriculum.)

## Service Learning Scenarios:
### Ideas for Action

Ready to take action? What follows are projects that have been successfully carried out by elementary, middle, or high school students. Most of these scenarios and examples explicitly include some aspects of preparation, action, reflection, and demonstration. These scenarios can be a rich source of project, resource, and curriculum ideas for you to draw upon. While the grade levels are given as a reference, most project ideas can be adapted to suit younger or older students, and many are suitable for cross-age partnerships.

***A Community Collaboration: Grades K–12.*** Eight hundred public school students in Rhode Island have worked together in a cross-age service learning project to produce food that will feed people who are hungry in their community. The local food bank has received five tons of produce from the students' gardening efforts over four years. While older students teach younger ones about civic involvement, the environment, and how everyone can have a role in ending hunger, both groups enjoy working in the gardens and greenhouse—the latter built through the support of local businesses and volunteers. The broad scale of this project has encouraged the whole community to explore how food, agriculture, abundance, hunger, and society interconnect.

***Quilting: Grade 2.*** In a second-grade class, a teacher read *The Teddy Bear* to initiate conversation about people who are homeless. Students eagerly discussed people they had observed in their semi-rural Washington state community who seemed to have no residence. The children expressed concern and wanted to know who helped people who were homeless in their community. A speaker from a local shelter was invited to answer prepared questions and listen to students' ideas for helping. The class decided to make two quilts that could be used at the shelter. Students applied math and art skills and learned to sew. With parental assistance, they delivered two quilts for permanent use at the shelter.

***Children's Hunger Network: Grades 4 and 5.*** Elementary students in a fourth/fifth-grade combined classroom created a Children's Hunger Network to study national geography, to explore issues of hunger and poverty around the United States, and finally to work on these issues in their own Los Angeles community. To start their geography unit, they identified a school in each of six regions in the United States. Through letters, faxes, and email, they challenged participating classrooms to learn about hunger and homelessness in their communities, find out what organizations were already helping, find a way to make a difference, and report back what they had learned. A local college student helped document the results, and copies were sent to all participating classrooms. For the initiating classroom, U.S. geography came alive as students connected with peers across the country who also wanted to help others. A variety of methods—speakers, field trips, books, and journals—were part of the learning process. The students' direct service included conducting an art exchange with children who lived in a shelter and donating art supplies for their use.

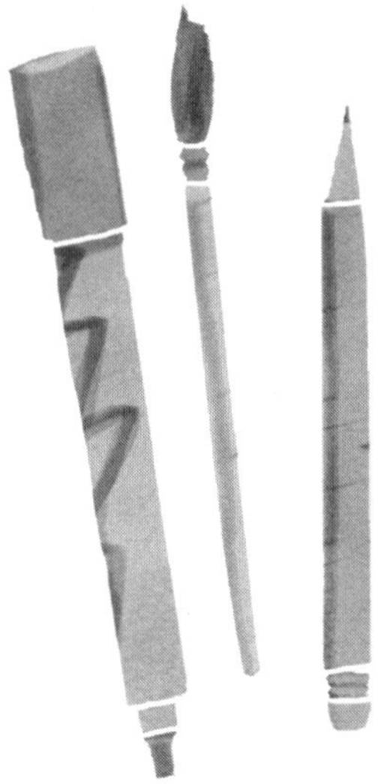

# Hunger and Homelessness Across the Curriculum

## Hunger and Homelessness

### *English/Language Arts*

- Define "home" and its attributes; contrast with "homelessness"
- Research myths and facts about homelessness and use them in a persuasive writing piece to share information
- Find examples of how people who are homeless or living in poverty are depicted in literature

### *Social Studies/History*

- Study historical events that led to hunger or homelessness such as the Irish famine
- Interview a city council member or deputy about the government's role in providing services for people in need
- Conduct a demographic and economic study of people who are hungry or homeless in your community

### *Languages*

- Look at and compare the statistics for poverty and hunger in different countries
- Discuss issues of poverty and government programs in a country where this language is spoken
- Study the different kinds of structures used for homes in different countries and learn the associated vocabulary

### *Theater, Music, & Visual Arts*

- Adapt literature that features a person who is homeless into a performance piece with opportunities for discussion with the audience
- Compose simple songs that teach basic concepts like numbers or colors; record and distribute them to a family shelter
- Research what art supplies are needed at a local shelter and prepare art kits

### *Math*

- Read food labels to find out serving quantities and nutritional values
- Create a statistical chart to compare national and local statistics on hunger; discuss how statistics can be used in a food drive campaign
- Chart how many cans or pounds of food are needed and received by the local food bank in order to serve their target population

### *Physical Education*

- Discuss the effects of malnutrition on physical health and well-being
- Create a child-friendly exercise video for a family shelter
- Visit a food bank and "get physical" while sorting cans and stocking shelves

### *Computer*

- Develop a brochure for a local food shelter
- Type résumés for people who are looking for work and have no computer access
- On the Internet, find slogans and quotes to use in a marketing campaign for a food drive

### *Science*

- Learn about the food pyramid and nutritional needs of children and adults
- Study the effect of hunger on student achievement in school and on adults trying to enter the workforce
- Compare the nutritional value of different foods and the associated costs

***An Art-Full Environment: Grade 6.*** After a food bank relocated, its coordinator visited a class and described how "sterile and unwelcoming" the new waiting area appeared with its rows of chairs and bare white walls. The middle school students made posters and art work to decorate the area and created a child-care area stocked with donated art supplies.

***A Garden That Serves: Grades 6–8.*** What began as a garden for a class science project expanded when students wanted to continue planting, weeding, and harvesting. After five years of year-round participation at school, the students continue to tend an organic garden in a community lot to provide fresh produce for families in need and hundreds of residents of local shelters. A partner agency assists with food distribution.

***What Is Hunger? Grade 7.*** Everyone says it: "I'm hungry!" Is "hungry" a growling stomach before the lunch bell or a longing for an after-school snack? Students in social studies classes discussed hunger and came to understand how the word is experienced by people in poverty. They found out that people who don't eat, or who don't eat regular, nutritionally balanced meals, have impaired immune systems and may get sick more often. Their ability to study or work is reduced, too. These effects can lead to a downward economic spiral unless intervention and assistance are provided. Students partnered with local agencies to prepare written materials for distribution at schools, libraries, youth clubs, and other organizations. The materials provided facts about local hunger, ways in which people can help, and tips for running food and clothing drives.

***Kids Sew for Kids: Grade 8.*** In an eighth-grade home economics class, students working in pairs selected an outfit to make for a child at a homeless shelter. The outfits were color coordinated, and each partner sewed one piece. Outfits ranged from sweat suits to shorts sets. Some students also made backpacks for school. To fund the project, community partnerships were established with local fabric stores.

***Functional Math: Grade 8.*** Middle school students combined math lessons with studies of homelessness to provide community assistance. The students learned about the business math concepts of profit, loss, gross, net, discounts, taxes, and so forth and then applied these skills in a fund-raiser aimed at buying food to make bag lunches for a local soup kitchen. Partnerships were created among the students, the school, community food wholesalers, potential donors, and the soup kitchen itself.

***Monthly Dinners: Grades 8–12.*** In addition to advocating for service learning in schools, a youth service learning advisory board in Maryland plans, buys ingredients for, and prepares dinners for the women and children at a shelter twice each month.

***Shelter Help: Grades 9–11.*** After helping a shelter for women and children with room decorations, students in Maryland asked what else they could do to be helpful. The agency and student representatives met to discuss needs and ideas. Students acted on several ideas, including making journals to give to the young people when they arrive and constructing doll houses for use in play therapy.

***From Activity Center to Family Album: Grades 9–11.*** At a "drop in" agency in San Pedro, California, that helps to find temporary housing, food, and other services for families in need, young children often waited for hours with nothing to do. High school students created an activity center with shelves of games and books. On the day they set up the center, the students played games with and read to the children onsite. One student took photographs, careful not to take pictures of the children because of issues concerning confidentiality. However, one parent approached the photographer, asking, "Can you take a picture of my child? I have no pictures of my children." Students then took the initiative to address this situation. They secured donations of an instant camera and film and returned on a regular basis to keep the games and books in good shape and to take photos of the children to give to their parents.

***"Gotta Feed Them All": Grades 9–12.*** The "Gotta Feed Them All" citywide canned food drive was designed by alternative high school students in southern California and coordinated through their partnerships with city government, schools, and the local food bank. After helping to sort and stock food supplies at a local food bank, the students learned that the food bank is always low on supplies during spring and summer months. The students' campaign, held in April, has become an annual event. It is publicized through street banners and with specially marked containers placed by markets, in schools, and at city hall. This event has been a welcome windfall for the food bank.

> As a result of their homelessness, children are struggling in school, their health is hindered, and they are not getting enough to eat.
>
> HOMES FOR THE HOMELESS, A PROGRAM OF THE INSTITUTE FOR CHILDREN AND POVERTY

***Donated Eggs: Grades 9–12.*** Students raising chickens for an agricultural project found that the local food pantry was an appreciative recipient of their eggs. After learning more about the needs of the community, the students helped to organize and promote the collection of other needed resources.

***A Video Donation: Grade 10.*** Following a tour of a food bank, several students expressed interest in doing more than just "donating food." They worked to develop a video for the agency that featured a video tour of the facility and an interview with a woman who had experienced poverty. The students, with help from their teacher and agency staff, wrote a four-page curriculum with suggestions on how to use the video with upper elementary, middle, and high school classes. This video is now used to educate the local community on poverty and hunger.

***Teaching at a Shelter: Grades 11–12.*** Through research, high school students in Chicago learned that children who live in extreme poverty or are homeless often are ill-prepared for kindergarten. The students contacted a shelter for women and children and prepared educational activities such as workbooks and game boxes for preschoolers. With support from teachers and agency personnel, the high school students led educational lessons with the children while learning valuable skills themselves.

***A Book Club: Grades 11–12.*** Students in a class on contemporary issues read fiction and nonfiction literature about poverty and homelessness. After hearing the director of a shelter for men speak about the facility and the programs available for the residents, the students discussed unmet needs. One student commented on the speaker's remarks about how many of the men spend their evenings reading. The class submitted a proposal to the shelter to start a book group in which the male teens and the men in the facility would read the same fiction and would meet two evenings per month for discussion. The reflective writings of the students showed the respect they developed for the men and their knowledge, courage, and resilience.

> What do we live for, if it is not to make life less difficult for each other.
>
> GEORGE ELIOT, AUTHOR

# The Hunger and Homelessness Bookshelf

Whether describing the past or examining the present, the works in the Hunger and Homelessness Bookshelf show us that these conditions have touched many lives in many places. To help you find books relevant to your particular projects, the book chart classifies the titles into several topic areas: learning from history, communities today, national perspective, and international needs.

In general, the bookshelf features:

- An annotated bibliography arranged and alphabetized by title according to the general categories of nonfiction (N), picture books (P), and fiction (F). For nonfiction and fiction, length and recommended grade levels are included. The entries in the picture book category do not include suggested grade levels, since they can be successfully used with all ages.
- A chart organized by topic and category to help you find books relevant to particular projects.
- Recommendations from service learning colleagues and experts that include a book summary and ideas for service learning connections. (The number of recommended books varies in each bookshelf.)

# Hunger and Homelessness Bookshelf Topics

| Topics | Books | Category |
|---|---|---|
| ***Learning from History*** Is hunger new? Or homelessness? Through the lens of history, find out what occurred in the past and what lessons we can learn. | *The Adventurous Chef: Alexis Soyer* | P |
| | *Black Potatoes: The Story of the Great Irish Famine, 1845–1850* | N |
| | *Feed the Children First: Irish Memories of the Great Hunger* | N |
| | *Grapes of Wrath* | F |
| | *The Long March: The Choctaw's Gift to Irish Famine Relief* * | P |
| | *Orphan Train Rider: One Boy's True Story* | N |
| | *Potato: A Tale from the Great Depression* | P |
| | *Rodzina* | F |
| | *A Train to Somewhere* | P |
| ***Communities Today*** In our own modern times and our own communities, social problems lead too many people into lives of homelessness or hunger. The stories in this category show a variety of situations and needs. | *The Can-Do Thanksgiving* * | P |
| | *A Castle on Viola Street* * | P |
| | *Changing Places: A Kid's View of Shelter Living* | N |
| | *Darnell Rock Reporting* | F |
| | *Drop Dead Inn* | F |
| | *Fly Away Home* | P |
| | *The Greatest Table: A Banquet to Fight Against Hunger* ‡ | P |
| | *Home Is Where We Live: Life at a Shelter through a Young Girl's Eyes* | N |
| | *The House on Mango Street* (see page 199) | F |
| | *The Hundred Dresses* | F |
| | *The King of Dragons* | F |
| | *Money Hungry* | F |
| | *Saily's Journey* | P |
| | *Sam and the Lucky Money* * | P |
| | *Soul Moon Soup* | F |
| | *The Teddy Bear* | P |
| | *Uncle Willie and the Soup Kitchen* * | P |
| | *Where I'd Like to Be* | F |
| ***National Perspective*** How does a nation respond to the needs of people who are homeless? What are the underlying issues, controversies, and possible solutions? As public debate and planning continue, how do people who live on the streets survive? | *Homeless Children* | N |
| | *Homelessness* * | N |
| | *Homelessness: Can We Solve the Problem?* | N |
| | *Homelessness: Whose Problem Is It?* | N |
| | *Nickel and Dimed: On (Not) Getting By in America* | N |
| | *The Other America: Homeless Teens* | N |

*continued* ⟶

| Topics | Books | Category |
|---|---|---|
| ***International Needs*** Hunger and homelessness have no boundaries. These stories take place across the globe. | *Asphalt Angels* | F |
| | *Dream Freedom* * (see page 199) | F |
| | *A Life Like Mine: How Children Live Around the World* * (see page 196) | N |
| | *The Lost Boys of Natinga: A School for Sudan's Young Refugees* | N |

Page references are given for books that do not appear in the Hunger and Homelessness Bookshelf but that can be found in the bookshelf lists of other chapters.
* These books include examples of young people in service-providing roles.
‡ These books are out of print but still worth finding.

## Nonfiction: *Hunger and Homelessness*

***Black Potatoes: The Story of the Great Irish Famine, 1845–1850*** by Susan Campbell Bartoletti (Houghton Mifflin, 2001). The Irish potato famine of 1845–1850 had international repercussions. The Irish people were starving to death. Approximately one million died and two million fled Ireland, with many of those immigrants coming to the United States. The history of this disaster unfolds in vivid text that draws from news reports and first-person narratives. 160pp., grades 6–10

***Changing Places: A Kid's View of Shelter Living*** by Margie Chalofsky, Glen Finland, and Judy Wallace (Gryphon House, 1992). Eight children arrive at a shelter, each with a different story. The first-person narratives help the reader understand the complex situations that arise in families and affect these young people. A preface and an afterword provide a helpful context and include ways to assist at local shelters. 61pp., grades 4–8

***Feed the Children First: Irish Memories of the Great Hunger*** by Mary E. Lyons (Simon & Schuster, 2002). The great Irish potato famine, caused by a fungus that wiped out the staple potato crop, was one of the worst disasters of the nineteenth century. More than a quarter of Ireland's country's eight million people died or emigrated. First-person accounts evoke the time and place, the suffering, and the survival. The introduction includes an overview and examples of the aid received. *The Long March,* also listed in this bookshelf, describes the contribution made by the Choctaw to Irish famine relief. 48pp., grades 4–12

***Home Is Where We Live: Life at a Shelter through a Young Girl's Eyes*** by Bonnie Lee Groth (Cornerstone Press, 1995). "We moved to a shelter this year—Mamma, me, William, and our baby sister, LaTasha." So begins this photo essay about how a young girl acclimates to shelter life and comes to accept the people who help her. 30pp., grades 4–8

***Homeless Children*** by Eleanor H. Ayer (Lucent Books, 1997). What is being done for children who are homeless? Topics include resources provided by agencies and youth-led programs, educational issues, health concerns, and various aspects of daily life. Includes a glossary of terms. 95pp., grades 4–8

***Homelessness*** by Sara Dixon Criswell (Lucent, 1998). Homelessness, a national problem, requires attention from all sectors. This useful book discusses the role of government, charities, nonprofit organizations, and everyday citizens, including youth. In the chapter "Life on the Streets," the subculture of homelessness is described, along with issues of mobility, health care, and self-identity. Education, service providers, and the struggle to turn lives around are candidly presented. 112pp., grades 7–12

***Homelessness: Can We Solve the Problem?*** by Laurie Rozakis (Henry Holt, 1995). The issue of homelessness is presented in a straightforward manner, with chapters on "The Face of Homelessness," "How Do People Become Homeless?" "What Problems Do the Homeless Face?" and "What Can Be Done?" Stereotypes are refuted, and issues such as mental illness, the effects on children, and failures in the social services systems are explored. 64pp., grades 4–6

> All across the United States, citizens are banding together to run soup kitchens, shelters, and neighborhood associations for the homeless. Some fix up abandoned buildings and build new homes for the poor. They pressure local leaders to protect tenants from being unfairly evicted from their apartments.
>
> FROM *HOMELESSNESS: CAN WE SOLVE THE PROBLEM?*

***Homelessness: Whose Problem Is It?*** by Ted Gottfried (Millbrook Press, 1999). Beginning with the history of homelessness in the United States, the author presents a broad and balanced range of issues. Policies, welfare reform, illness, substance abuse, and education, among other topics, are examined. Readers are invited to formulate their own opinions. Organizational resources are included. 128pp., young adult

***The Lost Boys of Natinga: A School for Sudan's Young Refugees*** by Judy Walgren (Houghton Mifflin, 1998). This photo essay takes the reader inside a refugee camp and school for boys, established in 1993 in southern Sudan. Because of the country's civil war, the boys have been forced from their homes. Many came to the camp when they were orphaned or otherwise separated from their families. "Every day these boys struggle to get food, to stay healthy, and to go to school." 44pp., grades 5–8

**Recommendation from the Field**
*by Susan Vermeer, Project Manager,*
*Education Commission of the States*

*Nickel and Dimed: On (Not) Getting By in America* by Barbara Ehrenreich (Metropolitan Books, 2001). *Nickel and Dimed* is an easy and enjoyable yet somewhat painful read about what it takes to survive in modern America on poverty-level wages. In the style of an undercover reporter, Ehrenreich provides an inside view of what it's really like to wait tables, work at Wal-Mart, serve meals in a nursing home, and work at least two jobs simultaneously to survive. Welfare reform, a livable wage, and affordable housing are a few of the societal issues that come to life for the reader.

By reading *Nickel and Dimed,* students can develop empathy and knowledge from this up-close look at what the people they meet might be experiencing. Their perception of low-wage workers will change as they gain a new respect for and understanding of the working poor. This book could prompt significant classroom discussion. It will be powerful when combined with a service learning experience that addresses some of the issues that the working poor must struggle with every day. 221pp., young adult

***Orphan Train Rider: One Boy's True Story*** by Andrea Warren (Houghton Mifflin, 1996). "Children without Homes"—so read the signs announcing the arrival of the Orphan Trains that left New York City heading west. Children on board were orphans or had been abandoned by families who could no longer care for them. Over 200,000 children made such journeys to the Midwest from 1854 to 1929. This book tells the story of one boy, providing an important historical account of societal conditions that predated foster homes and homeless shelters. 80pp., grades 4–8

***The Other America: Homeless Teens*** by Gail B. Stewart (Lucent Books, 1998). "This ruins everything." "We're a close-knit street family." "Sometimes you just feel you're wasting your whole life." "I don't think too many people care." Words from young people, the stories of their plight, and the people who reach out to help turn their lives around are presented. 112pp., young adult

## Picture Books: *Hunger and Homelessness*

***The Adventurous Chef: Alexis Soyer*** by Ann Arnold (Farrar, Straus and Giroux, 2002). In this unique biography, meet Alexis Soyer, flamboyant chef and inventor of kitchen tools, who defied tradition, improved cooking methods, and helped people in need. His philanthropic work led him to create the soup kitchen model in Dublin during the Irish potato famine and to work alongside Florence Nightingale to reform and improve military cooking methods during the Crimean War.

***The Can-Do Thanksgiving*** by Marion Hess Pomeranc (Albert Whitman, 1998). When Dee brings a can of peas to school for the canned food drive, she keeps asking, "Where do my peas go?" Her persistent questioning results in a class project to prepare and serve food for people in need at Thanksgiving. An excellent resource for transforming the traditional canned food drive into a service learning project.

***A Castle on Viola Street*** by DyAnne DiSalvo-Ryan (HarperCollins, 2001). On Viola Street, a family joins Habitat for Humanity volunteers as they restore a home. In time, they learn that another home will be restored for them. As the father says, "Big dreams are built little by little," and many generous hands have helped in the dream building.

***Fly Away Home*** by Eve Bunting (Clarion, 1991). A boy lives in an airport terminal with his father, who continually tries to earn enough money to rent an apartment. The boy wonders when his life will change and gains hope when he watches a bird trapped inside the building find an open window to freedom.

***The Greatest Table: A Banquet to Fight Against Hunger*** edited by Michael J. Rosen (Harcourt, 1994). This is a twelve-foot-long accordion book with artwork contributed by sixteen illustrators. At this great table, there is room for all people who come and plenty of food to share. Out of print but worth finding.

***The Long March: The Choctaw's Gift to Irish Famine Relief*** by Marie-Louise Fitzpatrick (Tricycle Press, 1998). The year is 1847, and Choona, a young Choctaw, has learned of a famine in Ireland. From what precious little they have, the Choctaw collect $170 to help the starving Irish. As Choona learns the terrible truth about his own tribe's long march, he must decide whether to answer another people's faraway cry for help. Based on actual events.

> We have walked the trail of tears.
> The Irish people walk it now. We can help them as we could not help ourselves. Our help will be like an arrow shot through time. It will land many winters from now to wait as a blessing for our unborn generations.
>
> FROM *THE LONG MARCH: THE CHOCTAW'S GIFT TO IRISH FAMINE RELIEF*

***Potato: A Tale from the Great Depression*** by Kate Lied (National Geographic Society, 1997). "This is a story about my grandfather and my grandmother. It is also a story about the Great Depression and how hard things were." A family that has lost their jobs and home turns to farm work. The family members pick potatoes—many, many potatoes—which they eat and also use to barter for other goods, "even a pig." The author wrote this book at age eight to pass on a true family story and to explain why she likes potatoes.

***Saily's Journey*** by Ralph da Costa Nunez (White Tiger Press, 2002). When Saily the Snail loses his shell in a storm, he goes on a journey to find a new home. Along the way, he experiences a range of emotions , including despair, fear, and hope, until he finds the generosity of others that help him find a home once again.

***Sam and the Lucky Money*** by Karen Chinn (Lee & Low Books, 1995). For Chinese New Year, Sam receives lucky money in traditional *leisees*—decorated red envelopes. Sam can buy either sweets or a toy. Near the open market, before the festival lion dances through the street, Sam sees a man who is homeless and barefoot. On this wintry day, Sam considers the best use for his money.

***The Teddy Bear*** by David McPhail (Henry Holt, 2002). A special teddy bear, lost by his little boy, is found and loved by an elder man who lives on the street. Months later, the boy is amazed to find his bear sitting on a park bench. Reunited with his bear at last, the boy hears the cries of a bearded man, "My bear! Where is my bear?" The boy's actions show understanding and compassion.

***A Train to Somewhere*** by Eve Bunting (Clarion, 1996). In 1878, a young girl rides the Orphan Train out west hoping somehow to find her mother, who has abandoned her. With each stop she watches other children being adopted. At the last stop, in the town of Somewhere, she finds a home.

***Uncle Willie and the Soup Kitchen*** by DyAnne DiSalvo-Ryan (Morrow, 1991). When Willie's nephew works at the neighborhood soup kitchen preparing and serving food, he gains admiration for people who lend a hand.

## Fiction: Hunger and Homelessness

***Asphalt Angels*** by Ineke Holtwijk (Front Street, 1995). In Rio de Janeiro, Alex lives among street kids, alone and scared. Thrown out of his house by his stepfather, Alex lives by his wits among "the Asphalt Angels." Although he intends to avoid crime, Alex reluctantly falls into a life of theft and panhandling for survival. 184pp., grades 10–12 (mature themes)

***Darnell Rock Reporting*** by Walter Dean Myers (Delacorte, 1994). Darnell fails his middle school classes and spends too much time in the principal's office for behavior problems. His last opportunity to get his act together is the school newspaper. Encouraged by the librarian and his sudden interest in Sweeby Jones, a veteran who is homeless, Darnell demonstrates initiative and an understanding that everyone needs a second chance. 135pp., grades 4–7

***Dew Drop Dead*** by James Howe (Simon & Schuster, 2000). When Sebastian Barth and his friends decide to sneak into an abandoned inn, the last thing they expect to find is a dead body. The mystery spills over into the new homeless shelter at the church, as evidence suggests a person using the facility might be the murderer. Against this backdrop, the challenges and turmoil of being homeless are revealed, along with the thoughtful response of a caring community. 156pp., grades 4–7

**Recommendation from the Field**

*Nelda Brown, Executive Director, State Education Agency K–12 Service Learning Network*

*The Grapes of Wrath* by John Steinbeck (Penguin, 1939/1992). Service learning can make this classic American novel come alive, particularly in the areas of immigration and hunger and homelessness. After reading about the Joad family's arrival in California and the "Welcome Committee" at the government camp, students can create a "Newcomer's Welcome Guide and Orientation" for families new to this country. Preparing written materials, such as guides, public service announcements,

*continued* ⟶

and role-play scenarios, gives students an opportunity to apply writing skills in a variety of formats. Students can explore immigration issues by researching local trends in new student arrivals. At the same time, they can gain an understanding of and respect for different cultures and experiences. A newcomer orientation project can also welcome students new to the school community and may be especially effective for groups of students transitioning from elementary to middle school or middle to high school. This project also offers a context in which to explore issues of teasing and bullying.

Steinbeck poignantly describes how unpicked fruit rotted and livestock was destroyed while the Oklahoma immigrants starved. After assessing the community's needs, students can research and identify opportunities for "salvaging" food from local restaurants and grocery stores and giving it to food banks or meal assistance programs. Using lessons in persuasive essay- and letter-writing skills and oral presentations, students can work with local grocers, restaurateurs, and human service providers to make unused resources (for example, bread, canned foods, fruits, vegetables, excess meals) available to their neighbors in need. 619pp., young adult

***The Hundred Dresses*** by Eleanor Estes (Harcourt, 1944). Wanda Petronski is teased by classmates for living in a poor part of town and wearing the same dress every day. One girl, Maddie, is confused by the taunting and by Wanda's insistence that she has "one hundred dresses at home." When Wanda's dad moves the family to escape the relentless teasing, Maddie and her friends face up to their behavior and see Wanda's dresses. 80pp., grades 3–7

***The King of Dragons*** by Carol Fenner (McElderry, 1998). Eleven-year-old Ian and his father, a Vietnam veteran, live in a deserted courthouse. Homeless for several years, Ian knows how to stay out of sight and manage on few resources. When his dad does not return to the courthouse and renovations begin to transform the musty halls into a kite museum, Ian finds a unique role as a kite expert to handle his precarious situation. 216pp., grades 4–8

***Money Hungry*** by Sharon G. Flake (Hyperion, 2001). Raspberry Hill is thirteen and knows what it's like to be homeless, and she swears she won't live on the streets again. Her endless schemes at earning money may get her some cash, but not enough to prevent her mother from packing their belongings in plastic bags, leaving the projects, and facing the fears and frustrations of life without a home once again. 188pp., grades 5–8

***Rodzina*** by Karen Cushman (Clarion, 2003). The year is 1881, and Rodzina Clara Jadwiga Anastazya Brodski would rather be anywhere than on an orphan train heading west to an unknown future. Since she is a big girl and already twelve, she is placed in charge of the little children, which only makes her yearn more for her deceased family. What family would want a scruffy orphan from the streets of Chicago? As each child finds a new home, Rodzina's future seems truly unknown. 215pp., grades 4–7

***Soul Moon Soup*** by Lindsay Lee Johnson (Front Street, 2002). In this prose-poem, Phoebe Rose, age eleven, describes life "in the hard poor middle of the city," where she and her mother sleep in shelters or doorways. When her dream of being an artist is torn away, no one notices; she becomes invisible. Only when she is sent to live in the country with her Gram does Phoebe learn, "When things come apart it's your chance to rearrange the pieces." 134pp., grades 7–10

> But lucky days are running out
> in the mean dirty city,
> where the hungry eyes of strangers watch,
> where the quick hands of strangers wait
> to take their chance,
> my chance, my shoes,
> my soul.
>
> FROM *SOUL MOON SOUP*

***Where I'd Like to Be*** by Frances O'Roark Dowell (Simon & Schuster, 2003). After living in her share of foster homes, Maddie, age twelve, moves into the East Tennessee Children's Home. She finds an eclectic group of kids who join together to build a fort, a home of their own. As they fill this structure with their stories and dreams, Maddie wonders whether she will find a place to really call her home—or at least find people who feel like home. 232pp., grades 4–7

# Interviews with Authors:
## The Story Behind the Story

In the following interviews, we find out the "story behind the story" from Lindsay Lee Johnson *(Soul Moon Soup)* and Marion Hess Pomeranc *(The Can-Do Thanksgiving)*. As soon as I read *Soul Moon Soup,* I wanted to call Lindsay Lee Johnson and find out how she could capture so accurately the voice of her protagonist—a young girl grappling with her challenging life. *The Can-Do Thanksgiving* deals with a canned food drive—perhaps the most common community service project. How perfect to find a book on the subject! I had to find out what in particular had inspired author Marion Hess Pomeranc to write the book.

## *Lindsay Lee Johnson,* author of
### Soul Moon Soup

We often talk about a person having a particular "mind-set" to accomplish something. But I credit my desire to write about homelessness and other social justice issues with having a "heart-set" for service. I grew up in a helping family. Whether that meant taking in stray, injured animals or bringing a meal to needy neighbors, it's simply what we did. My father was a doctor and my mother a nurse. Their professional values of caring and helping became our family values.

Later I married a man with similar values, and not surprisingly, our children always seemed to befriend the outsiders and speak up for the "underdogs." However, I don't believe you have to come from a family like this to be drawn to service; this "heart-set" can be contagious and inspired by others. This happens friend to friend, teacher to student, author to reader. Adults and older teens can model behavior that encourages children to seek ways to live that give their lives meaning. The values of compassion and service are not derived from thinking "I ought to help" but from thinking "What can I do to help?"

When I began writing *Soul Moon Soup,* I did not think about "homelessness." I began with a character who has a story to tell. She lived in my mind first, and it's her story, but I believe the story is fed by my personal experience. I focused on words that have emotional currency beyond face value, radioactive words that jump off the page. For instance, the word *home* means much more than a place of residence. In the same way, each word in the book's title resonates with personal as well as universal meaning.

This story began to percolate during my experience as a volunteer baby rocker for a social service agency. These babies had been damaged by abuse or neglect. The moms were in desperate situations, either in jail or facing jail for various reasons. They had to prove their ability to be good caregivers in order to regain custody of their children. These were ordinary women who, for one reason or another, had experienced some catastrophe, and their lives had gone wrong. They were human beings who responded to love and friendship and wanted something better.

As a volunteer at various shelters, again I saw individuals in difficult circumstances, people experiencing homelessness rather than "homeless people" as a group. Labels can stop us from wanting to get involved and take action. People having difficulties certainly don't choose their circumstances. When people experience homelessness, they lose a sense of identity gained by having a place to be themselves, a home. A person can feel lost and have difficulty moving forward. Growing up is hard under the best circumstances, but for children without that "home" in their lives, it is nearly impossible.

Homelessness is a huge and growing problem, especially for children. According to my research, about 40 percent of people who are homeless are children with an average age of six. The best way for me to contribute to people's awareness of this situation is to tell a story, the story of one girl, Phoebe Rose, who lives on the "stoop-sitting, gutter-spitting streets." Her voice spoke to me so clearly and powerfully. I had to pass on what she was telling me, heart to heart and soul to soul.

Phoebe Rose's story is sad in a way, but it also contains hope. Phoebe learns to feed her imagination with art to keep her soul alive. When a child, or anyone, loses imagination and the ability to picture what might come next in life, this is true hopelessness. When Phoebe reclaims her ability to envision her future in the world of art, it is a turning point for her and indicates that she can survive. In writing *Soul Moon Soup* I learned of a nonprofit organization that provides art supplies to children in homeless shelters, along with volunteers to help them explore and express the often unspeakable things in their hearts. It is this sort of service project that inspires me.

As I wrote *Soul Moon Soup*, Phoebe's voice naturally took the form of free verse, with a lyrical poetic quality. I wanted the book to have beautiful language in spite of the harsh realities of the story. Also, I wanted the book to be accessible. For reluctant readers, a book with a lot of text can be off-putting; short lines and sections appear more manageable, like little bites. A more accomplished reader is drawn in to the rhythm and music of the language, the pace of the story. I hope readers of all ages and abilities find their own hearts in these pages and the courage to make connections with people around them who may need something they can give.

While group service projects can be valuable, remember that one-to-one outreach is also important. In one early scene in the book, Phoebe discards a pretty package of soap and shampoo from a girl at school when the girl says, "It's from my mother, I don't care." A true gift, like the gifts Phoebe receives later in the story from Ruby, can only be given with a genuine heart.

I would like to see readers become less fearful of making these honest connections. People want to be treated respectfully, not as projects or special cases. An episode of a lost job or mental illness can suddenly cause people who think they are very secure to end up in trouble.

Phoebe's character demonstrates a strength that will enable her to survive. I imagine her going to art school and becoming a teacher. In the future, I would like to write more about Phoebe. I think she has a lot more to say.

For me, *Soul Moon Soup* is the most meaningful story I have ever written. I hope this is conveyed and that Phoebe's voice is passed along. Then I know I will have accomplished something worthwhile.

## *Marion Hess Pomeranc*, author of The Can-Do Thanksgiving

How did I choose the topic of a canned food drive for my book? I was bringing a can of food into my synagogue's food drive when I thought to myself, "Where do these cans really go?" I realized that kids across the country collect cans of food, and they too want to know where the cans go.

My question turned into action. I began calling different food banks and ended up at a soup kitchen in my neighborhood. It was a cold day, with people lined up outside. When the doors opened, volunteers handed out coffee and breakfast, while men and women sat inside eating their meal. From bringing in a can of food and visiting this kitchen, my story grew.

I want kids to know that whatever you bring to the food banks and kitchens is really going to help. Knowing where the food goes does matter because we need to connect with the places where people get some assistance and with the people who are in need. This helps us remember that whatever we do can make a difference. In my story, Dee saved her own money to buy the can, and her can of peas made a difference.

I would like to see my book inspire canned food drives all year long, because urban children are faced with seeing people in need on the street all the time. When my son was young, he wanted to help the people who were asking for food and money on the streets of New York City. We gave out bagels. I wanted him to view all people, regardless of their need or situation, as part of our human family.

As you read the book, remember we are all like Dee and we are all like Tyler. We will sometimes be in the position to help others, and we will sometimes need help ourselves. The most important thing is to be there for each other.

CHAPTER 11

# IMMIGRANTS

> When we escaped from Cuba,
> all we could carry was our education.
> ALICIA CORO, EDUCATOR

What causes a person to uproot and move to a new country, where language and cultural differences may seem insurmountable? History offers up many reasons: famine, political differences, financial hardships, war, forced relocation, and slavery. Of course, people have immigrated for positive reasons, too, such as a sense of adventure, a hope for better employment or a better education, a promise of streets paved in gold, or simply the expectation of a better life waiting. In today's world, are the reasons for immigration so different?

Immigration means moving somewhere to settle—not a vacation, not passing through. This new place becomes home. Sometimes families who make such moves are separated from loved ones. They face isolation and the challenges of learning a new language while unraveling the mysteries of a foreign culture. Young people in particular may struggle with whether to identify with their culture of origin or to abandon it, even temporarily, in order to fit in with their peers.

Service learning offers opportunities for reaching across differences of language, experience, and culture to learn about these new neighbors and to create an inclusive, diverse community. Kids are naturally curious and want to learn. The challenge is to ensure that their inquisitive minds develop in ways that make them open and thoughtful about others' experiences.

## Preparation: Getting Ready for Service Learning Involving Immigrants

The following activities can be used in the preparation stage to promote learning and skill development related to immigrants. These activities can be used with different age ranges during preparation to help your students examine key issues through research, analyze community needs, and gain the knowledge they need to effectively contribute to the design of their service plan. Since literature is often an important part of preparation, you can find recommended titles on this theme in the Immigrants Bookshelf later in this chapter.

***Activity: Bringing the World Home.*** Where in the world are people coming from? This information is the foundation of any immigrant-based service learning project. You can't help until you know who to help. Conducting a survey is a good way to find out where people lived before coming to your city or town. The survey's target population could be other students, school faculty, or a specific group in the community, such as members of an adult education class. Decide how far back to research. For example, the class could agree to find out the last three places a family responding to the survey has lived. Students may also want to find out the year of each move and the reasons for moving. Remind students that responding to all of the survey questions should be optional for the person completing the survey.

Next, using both world and national maps, track the survey responses using pins or stickers and string to depict the immigration and any other moves visually. Help students to understand the difference between moving within a country and moving between countries. Discuss what immigrants bring to their new home, including language, values, information, skills, ideas, culture, and resources. Identify any stereotypes students may have about immigrant groups in their community, then have speakers from those groups or from agencies that serve immigrant populations address and discuss misinformation and prejudices. Once your students have identified the immigrant groups in the community and have learned more about their cultures, it is much easier to identify ways to reach out and address genuine needs.

***Activity: Who Helps?*** Community agencies that assist immigrant populations can help students learn more about the recent immigrants in the region, find out who helps them become acclimated, bridge potential language or cultural confusion, and identify needs that can be addressed by youth. The following activities are easily tailored to students' abilities, the timeframe for the project, and the course curriculum.

- To encourage students to start thinking about immigration issues, they can read one of the bookshelf titles in this category or have a book read aloud to them. In *My Name Is Yoon,* for example, a young girl changes her name to try to fit in to this new country. *Any Small Goodness* describes an immigrant boy in East Los Angeles, where daily life combines blessings and risk. *Behind the Mountains* tells of a girl moving from Haiti to New York and experiencing an uneasy adjustment. These books can generate conversation regarding the challenges facing young people and their families and what the young people could have done in these stories to mitigate the problems.
- Continuing education is often very important for adult immigrants, so they can learn a new language or other information that will help them adapt to and thrive in their new home. Resources for continued learning can include local and state government offices and the school district, as well as nonprofit agencies. Adult schools may have information about enrollment in classes teaching English as a second language. Students can find out from the school program coordinators what services are offered and if there are needs that can be met through youth involvement. Based on the needs, students can then identify worthwhile projects and collaborate with agencies to carry them out.
- Students can interview other students or adults who are immigrants to learn about their experiences and needs. Preparation for the interview process is important, and professionals who work with immigrant populations can provide extremely useful assistance. Some students who are immigrants themselves or who have relatives who are immigrants may also come forward to volunteer knowledge and guidance.

Interacting with people who are immigrants always offers a multitude of opportunities for exchange and reciprocity that leave everyone richer in knowledge and understanding. Working with people from another culture is not a one-way street with help flowing in a single direction. Again, just as when working with elders, make sure to look for or create activities that make these mutual benefits explicit for everyone involved.

**Find Out More About Immigrants**

To learn more about these issues and to get ideas for service and action, visit these Web sites and organizations online:

***www.uscis.gov*** The Bureau of Citizenship and Immigration Services includes information on naturalization eligibility, the process, forms, news, frequently asked questions, citizenship quizzes, and the *Guide to Naturalization* publication.

***www.theirc.org*** International Rescue Committee is a voluntary agency providing assistance to refugees around the world, including the United States. Many United States cities have local offices and information about the program's involvement.

***www.studycircles.org*** The Study Circles Resource Center is dedicated to finding ways all kinds of people can engage in dialogue and problem solving on critical social and political issues. Their free resource materials for middle and high school grades include a unit on immigration, called "Changing Faces, Changing Communities," that can lead to social action projects.

## Making Connections Across the Curriculum

Some service learning activities naturally lend themselves to interdisciplinary work and making connections across the curriculum. These connections strengthen and broaden student learning, helping them meet academic standards. More than likely, you'll be looking for these connections and ways to encourage them well before the students ever start working on service learning activities. As with the entire service learning process, it helps to remain flexible, because some connections can be spontaneously generated by the questions raised throughout and by the needs of the project. To help you think about cross-curricular connections and where you can look for them, the Curricular Web for this chapter (page 162) gives examples of many different ways this theme can be used in different academic areas. (The service learning scenarios in the next section of the chapter also demonstrate various ways this theme can be used across the curriculum.)

# Service Learning Scenarios:
## Ideas for Action

Ready to take action? What follows are projects that have been successfully carried out by elementary, middle, or high school students. Most of these scenarios and examples explicitly include some aspects of preparation, action, reflection, and demonstration. These scenarios can be a rich source of project, resource, and curriculum ideas for you to draw upon. While the grade levels are given as a reference, most project ideas can be adapted to suit younger or older students, and many are suitable for cross-age partnerships.

***A Good Trade: Grade 2.*** When a teacher in Washington state began to teach origami to her class, she quickly realized that she needed help in guiding all of her students in this hands-on task. A colleague knew of Japanese exchange students attending a local community college through an exchange program. After a few phone calls, six exchange students had volunteered to help the teacher. The volunteers ended up helping nearly every day over a two-week period. They also brought in recent immigrants from Japan who worked with the students on the craft project and told stories about their experiences in Japan and moving to this country. To reciprocate, the children invited the college students and recent immigrants for a special program and presentation. The children taught about important Americans, including men and women of diverse cultures and ethnic groups, who had made contributions to United States society. Each guest received a compilation of these student-written stories as a gift. The exchange students let the children know how much the interaction had helped them learn and practice their English skills.

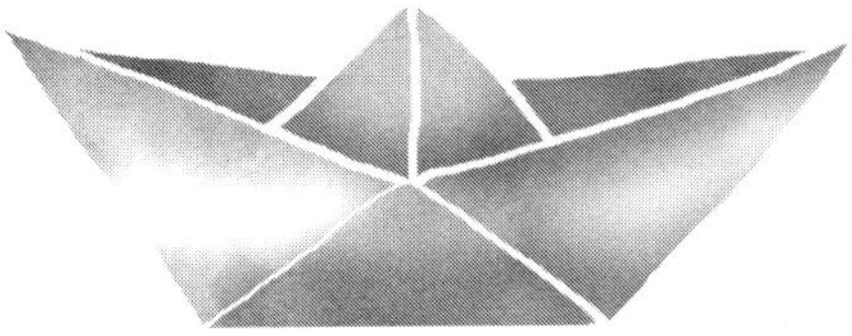

***A Music Fest: Grade 3.*** Third-grade students in a Spanish immersion elementary school in Los Angeles enjoyed learning the rhythms and songs of Latin American music. They performed at a senior center that drew primarily Spanish-speaking elder community members. The elders so appreciated the students' joy in music that they invited the students to come again, this time to be taught dancing by the older people. The younger students returned several times during the school year for singing, dancing, and, of course, cookies.

***Refugee Youth Project: Grades 3–12.*** In Pennsylvania, a service learning collaboration that included the International Rescue Committee and the American Red Cross was formed to meet the needs of young refugees resettled from Africa and the former Yugoslavia. College students tutored refugee students from elementary, middle, and high schools after school. The refugee students then extended their own learning and experience by doing service projects on weekends. These opportunities had multiple benefits for all involved. By helping with community cleanups, working in food shelters, and creating murals depicting their international experience, the students came to know and build community. They learned about community resources, gained skills through volunteering, and became engaged in the civic life of their new country.

***The Story Cloth Museum: Grade 4.*** Fourth-grade classes in central California read *The Whispering Cloth* as a way to become more familiar with Hmong culture and the growing Hmong population in their community. Two parents from Cambodia visited the class and brought Hmong story cloths. Students were fascinated with the artistry and story telling on the fabric. They developed a project to teach the community about Hmong culture by making their own story cloths. After engaging in research, students told some of their family stories through a combination of drawing on fabrics and sewing to give the pictures more depth. The students invited the community to see their museum of story cloths, including Hmong cloths

# Immigrants Across the Curriculum

## Immigrants

### *English/Language Arts*

- Read stories about the personal experiences of immigrating to a new country
- Study interview techniques and practice listening and note taking
- Create English vocabulary books for English as a second language programs

### *Social Studies/History*

- Conduct interviews with immigrants of different ages from the same population and compare their experiences
- Research reasons people leave specific countries and compare how this has changed over recent decades
- Learn about and document the contributions of immigrants in your community in a range of areas—social, political, cultural, and artistic

### *Languages*

- Find words in English that have their roots in the language being studied
- Prepare lessons to tutor immigrants in English language skills
- Translate the school handbook for immigrant populations

### *Theater, Music, & Visual Arts*

- Create collaborative theater events with people from many countries sharing talents
- Listen to world music and invite musicians from other countries into the classroom
- Explore the influence of many cultures on styles of art and architecture

### *Math*

- Compare the decimal system with the metric system used in many parts of the world
- Study and chart statistics reflecting the number of immigrants in your region, where they are coming from, and their reasons for moving
- Make easy-to-use guides to money conversion for new immigrants

### *Physical Education*

- Learn about games and approaches to exercise from different cultures
- Research athletes who are immigrants or children of immigrants who have made and continue to make contributions to sports
- Create a multilingual guide to places in your region for outdoor exercise

### *Computer*

- Create computer-generated lessons on colloquial expressions for teen immigrants
- Research ways the Internet is used for genealogy and country of origin research
- Study language translation programs that can assist students who are learning English

### *Science*

- Research how indigenous gardening techniques have been influenced by immigrants who bring their methods and plants
- Discuss whether or not the food pyramid is an accurate shape to depict the eating and nutrition practices of people from different countries
- Learn about folk traditions and remedies for health concerns used by immigrants from their country of origin

on loan from local families. Serving as docents, the students explained their cultural studies and shared family histories. Much to the students' delight, a local library, bank, and city government offices asked to display the museum pieces.

***Oral History—Across the Decades: Grade 6.*** Using a U.S. Library of Congress collection of interviews and oral histories from the 1930s, students learned about the everyday life of ordinary people who were immigrants. With guidance from teachers, the students then began collecting oral histories from recent immigrants in their own communities. The steps included doing background research, identifying interview subjects, developing interview questions, scheduling and conducting the interviews, and supplementing them with selections of primary source material, including photographs from magazines and from some of the immigrants. Students then wrote papers to compare the experiences of immigrants across the decades. Copies of these comprehensive portfolios were given to the immigrants involved, to support agencies, and to school and local libraries.

***Let's Talk: Grades 6–8.*** Learning English requires practice, practice, and more practice. At one middle school, students learning English are paired with English-speaking students for conversational practice during physical education classes. Both student groups received orientation on the project. The English-speakers worked with counselors and a language specialist to develop skills, such as listening, speaking more slowly, repeating phrases, and answering questions. The English-learners prepared by working with a counselor and developing a document that addressed stereotypes or possible put-downs that could come up in these relationships. Together, both groups of students created a written agreement of how they would work together to be mutually respectful. Then they participated in a getting acquainted activity to identify common interests and topics to talk about, though much of the talking centered on the P.E. class work. As an unexpected benefit, some of the English-learners coached their partners in sports skills!

***Neighborhood Resource Project: Grades 7–8.*** A middle school in New York has students from Cuba, Jamaica, Puerto Rico, Honduras, Mexico, Nicaragua, and Haiti. Many of them have been identified as being at risk, and often their families aren't familiar with the services available through government agencies and other providers. To remedy this, the students collaborated with a local agency to provide the neighborhood population with information regarding available services, including health care, after-school activities, drug prevention programs, adult literacy classes, and language and career training. Based on information acquired from field trips to local government meetings, civic organizations, and guest speakers, the students published a directory of services. The students met several educational objectives: basic awareness of social problems and their solutions, an in-depth study of government, computer literacy, knowledge of the immigrant experience, work skills, and cultural awareness.

> *¡Sí se puede!*
> Yes, it can be done!
> CÉSAR E. CHÁVEZ, SOCIAL ACTIVIST

***In Honor of New Citizens: Grades 7–8.*** After participating in a two-week simulation about immigrants entering this country through Ellis Island, a middle school social studies class in Portland, Maine, wanted to do more. They knew their community was a resettlement area for refugees from around the world. To learn more, they met with staff from Immigration and Naturalization Services (INS), and an idea emerged. The students made a proposal to the INS asking to host a swearing-in ceremony for new citizens at their school. Students found out the countries of origin of the 32 people being sworn in and researched the culture, foods, art, and social and political histories of those countries. They reached out to the community for food donations (including many ethnic treats) and made room decorations. They also arranged for the educational television channel to record and air the event. On the day of the ceremony, they greeted the guests and interviewed the new citizens, compiling their stories (with permission) into books with smiling family photographs. Many of the families wrote letters thanking the students for a most meaningful and memorable event. Still, the students were not finished—they had found another need to fill. They created "welcome kits" for the children of the immigrant families that included cartoon-style maps of the area, places to go for entertainment and sports, lists of after-school and weekend activities, a guide to youth expressions, and a small journal and pen.

***ESL Tutors: Grade 9.*** In Minnesota, several ninth-grade social studies classes spent one class period every two weeks throughout the academic year tutoring new immigrants in English and other basic skills. These freshman linked their experiences to what they were learning about different cultures and current events. Unexpectedly, the teacher noticed that the students' writing skills improved as they began to pay more attention to sentence structure and communicating clearly.

***Beginning with Earthquakes: Grades 9 and 10.*** A high school English-as-a-second-language class in Los Angeles completed an in-depth study of earthquakes. Where to take their knowledge? To a traditional science class. The ESL students developed interactive lessons; each agreed to lead a small-group discussion. The lessons were successful on many levels: The ESL students became more confident in their English skills, students who often kept to their own cultural group became acquainted with others, and the science students agreed to continue the exchange by leading an interactive lesson in return. Although the project was led by a student teacher who was only with the class for a limited time, this reciprocal arrangement continued for the remainder of the school year.

***A Cup of Knowledge: Grades 9–11.*** Enterprising high school students from around the world cooked up language skills as they served coffee. A nonprofit organization north of Los Angeles created a coffee shop, "A Cup of Knowledge/*Taza de Conocimiento*," to connect ESL students with their community. Students in ESL classes plus additional students identified by school counselors worked with representatives from the nonprofit on planning the coffee house including design and marketing. The students suggested ways to make the coffee house more enticing for a teen crowd and along the way learned entrepreneurial and food service skills. The students improved language skills through free classes and workshops they offered for younger students. The older teens also offered bilingual story hours, quilt-making classes, and art classes in the coffee shop to attract families and their children as regular customers. To promote these offerings, students created flyers for community bulletin boards and to send to neighborhood newspapers.

***Welcome Buddies: Grades 9–12.*** New kid in school? Welcome Buddies are there to greet you. Young people designed, improved, and continue to implement this ongoing project at their Los Angeles high school, which registers many immigrant students each semester. Pairs of students drawn from world history and language classes meet, greet, and assist young people coming into their school. Orientation programs are held every few months; special mixers and other activities help students become acclimated and stay involved with positive social and academic activities. "Welcome Buddy" programs can also help students to find their way around campus, supply a buddy to have lunch with, and provide homework helpers.

***Helping to Address Challenges: Grades 10–11.*** A high school in Hawaii with a large number of immigrants recognized the challenges that many students faced attending a new school and living in a new country. High school classes partnered with a local immigration center and became knowledgeable about the services offered and the potential difficulties immigrants in the community could encounter. Students combined this new information with skills learned at school to assist the center in updating the brochures given to new immigrants. This project met the writing, civic, and diversity standards.

***Oral History—An Exchange in Spanish: Grade 11.*** To foster improved community relations and to emphasize the value of being literate in a second language, students in an advanced Spanish class adopted an adult literacy class for recent immigrants. During four visits to the class, held at the local community center, students interviewed the immigrants in Spanish to create written histories of their immigration and life experiences. Using computers at school, students wrote the histories in Spanish, adding photographs and other graphics to produce a book. Copies were presented to the adults at a final gathering. The book was meaningful reading material for the new immigrants and provided a way for students to improve their language skills while acquiring knowledge found outside of their textbooks.

***A World View: Grades 11–12.*** As part of a World Studies class, students in Chicago examined immigration issues. To further students' understanding of the problems facing immigrants, the teacher collaborated with a community organization to work toward a service learning project. The first step was to lead students through team-building activities. Next, guest speakers discussed local issues related to immigration: the problem of work conditions for day laborers and immigrant documentation, specifically referencing a federal initiative that enabled documented immigrants to help family members who were not documented. The students discussed their options and ideas, and decided to work on the documentation issue. With training from lawyers specializing in immigration issues, the students hosted a day to begin the documentation process of immigrants. Two hundred local residents attended on that day and received assistance from students and legal experts. The teacher continually linked the experiences with classroom learning and guided the students in reflection.

***Language in Action: Grades 11 and 12.*** High school advanced language students put their skills to use as "cultural aids." After developing lists of project ideas, students individually or in pairs selected a project that would assist community members. Projects included helping prepare a bilingual brochure for families on how to access local resources, acting as a guide for back-to-school night, helping with health aid programs, translating materials for local agencies, maintaining bilingual information on the school's Web site, and translating school correspondence sent home to parents. Once this program was in place, language teachers saw skill levels rise and classroom discussion became enriched as students brought real-life problems to solve into the classroom.

***Civics with a Purpose: Grade 12.*** A high school civics class established a valuable partnership with a local refugee center, resulting in benefits for all involved. The students applied their classroom knowledge to coach new immigrants who were studying for their citizenship tests. Students came to value their own citizenship as they learned that people sometimes put their lives at risk to move to their new country. Students also provided child care during classes and study groups.

> Reading makes immigrants of us all. It takes us away from home, but more important, it finds homes for us everywhere.
>
> HAZEL ROCHMAN, AUTHOR

## The Immigrants Bookshelf

The books on the Immigrants Bookshelf give us the opportunity to walk, if only for a while, in the shoes of another person. For young people who are immigrants, the books may ease the telling of their own life stories. For others, understanding may encourage empathy and comradeship. To help you find books relevant to your particular projects, the book chart classifies the titles into several topic areas: learning from the past, the story of many, focus on one story, and fitting in.

In general, the bookshelf features:

- An annotated bibliography arranged and alphabetized by title according to the general categories of nonfiction (N), picture books (P), and fiction (F). For nonfiction and fiction, length and recommended grade levels are included. The entries in the picture book category do not include suggested grade levels, since they can be successfully used with all ages.
- A chart organized by topic and category to help you find books relevant to particular projects.
- Recommendations from service learning colleagues and experts that include a book summary and ideas for service learning connections. (The number of recommended books varies in each bookshelf.)

# Immigrants Bookshelf Topics

| Topics | Books | Category |
|---|---|---|
| ***Learning from the Past*** These stories, drawn from the not-so-distant past, shed light on the experience of immigrants and reveal their similarities to today's immigrants. | *The Clay Marble* | F |
| | *A Different Kind of Hero* | F |
| | *Dragonwings* | F |
| | *Esperanza Rising* | F |
| | *Oranges on Golden Mountain* | P |
| | *The Whispering Cloth: A Refugee's Story* | P |
| ***The Story of Many*** These books offer an overview of the issue of immigration, with all of its political, economic, and personal implications. | *Immigration: How Should It Be Controlled?* | N |
| | *The Middle of Everywhere: The World's Refugees Come to Our Town* | N |
| | *A Very Important Day* | P |
| ***Focus on One Story*** From the perspective of one cultural group, what is the story that moves people from one place to another to find a new home? | *The Bonesetter's Daughter* (see page 117) | F |
| | *Breaking Through: Sequel to The Circuit* | N |
| | *The Circuit: Stories from the Life of a Migrant Child* | N |
| | *Dancing with Dziadziu* (see page 115) | P |
| | *A Day's Work* | P |
| | *Dear Whiskers* (see page 182) | F |
| | *The Grapes of Wrath* (see page 155) | F |
| | *Harvest* | N |
| | *Journey of the Sparrows* | F |
| | *Lupita Mañana* | F |
| | *A Movie in My Pillow/Una película en mi almohada* | P |
| | *My Diary from Here to There/Mi diario de aquí hasta allá* | P |
| | *My Name Is Yoon* | P |
| | *A Place to Grow* | P |
| | *The Revealers* (see page 101) | F |
| | *The Skirt* | F |
| | *The Summer My Father Was Ten* (see page 143) | P |
| | *Tangled Threads: A Hmong Girl's Story* | F |
| | *Tomás and the Library Lady* (see page 182) | P |
| | *Too Young for Yiddish* (see page 116) | P |
| | *To Seek a Better World: The Haitian Minority in America* ‡ | N |
| | *Xóchitl and the Flowers/Xóchitl, la Niña de las Flores* (see page 143) | P |
| ***Fitting In*** Books in this category show the challenges experienced by immigrants—coping with a new culture that may clash with family traditions; experiencing loneliness; and struggling for acceptance. | *América Is Her Name* | P |
| | *Any Small Goodness* | F |
| | *Behind the Mountains* | F |
| | *Born Confused* | F |
| | *Children of the River* | F |

*continued* ⟶

| Topics | Books | Category |
|---|---|---|
| **Fitting In** continued | *The Gold-Threaded Dress* | F |
| | *Happy Birthday Mr. Kang* | P |
| | *Miss Happiness and Miss Flower* | F |
| | *Shadow of the Dragon* (see page 102) | F |
| | *Stella: On the Edge of Popularity* | F |
| | *A Step from Heaven* | F |
| | *The Ugly Vegetables* (see page 143) | P |
| | *Uncle Rain Cloud* | P |

Page references are given for books that do not appear in the Immigrants Bookshelf but that can be found in the bookshelf lists of other chapters.
‡ These books are out of print but still worth finding.

## Nonfiction: *Immigrants*

***Breaking Through: Sequel to The Circuit*** by Francisco Jiménez (Houghton Mifflin, 2001). These stories continue the struggles of the Jiménez family through separation, poverty, prejudice, and hope. Each episode reveals the tenacity and fortitude brought by hard work and "the generous people who commit themselves to making a difference in the lives of children and young adults." The family members come alive in Francisco's recounting of his journey toward adulthood. 200pp., young adult

***The Circuit: Stories from the Life of a Migrant Child*** by Francisco Jiménez (University of New Mexico Press, 1997). This autobiography starts with the author as a young boy living in a Mexican village in the late 1940s, who then travels with his family as they enter California illegally to find work. The family moves continuously from picking cotton to topping carrots, from one labor camp to the next, from one school to another. They remain close despite backbreaking work and poverty. These compelling short stories intertwine and paint an intricate picture of the life of migrant *campesinos*. 134pp., young adult

***Harvest*** by George Ancona (Marshall Cavendish, 2001). Photographs, text, and interviews depict the lives of *campesinos*, migrant farm workers who come to the United States from Mexico in search of a better life. In the backbreaking fields, working twelve-hour days, six days a week, they labor under the hot sun, inhaling dust and pesticides. A vivid description of lives that are based on hard work and hope for a better future for their children. 48pp., grades 4–7

***Immigration: How Should It Be Controlled?*** by Meish Goldish (Henry Holt, 1997). This informative survey of issues looks at immigration, primarily into the United States. Stories of people entering legally and illegally and coming as refugees are all included. 64pp., grades 4–6

***The Middle of Everywhere: The World's Refugees Come to Our Town*** by Mary Pipher (Harcourt, 2002). Liem's dad had been a prisoner of war in Vietnam. Two teens lived in northern Bosnia during the war. Two sisters, Shireen and Meena, arrived with their family from Pakistan. From Sierra Leone, Kosovo, Macedonia, from across the globe, refugees arrive in Lincoln, Nebraska, their new home. Their stories enlighten us about the world and about how Americans are perceived by others. 390pp., grades 9 and up

> Most of the refugees who arrive in Lincoln [Nebraska] didn't choose to come to our city. They were handed a plane ticket by INS officials when they got off a plane in New York or Los Angeles. They may know nothing about the Midwest, and they may have been separated from their closest friends. . . . They may have bodies adapted to tropical climates or skills such as deep-sea fishing that they cannot use in the Midwest. They may be moving in to a town where no one speaks their language or even knows where their country is. Most newcomers arrive broke. . . . They have been warned not to trust strangers, yet everyone is a stranger.
>
> FROM *THE MIDDLE OF EVERYWHERE: THE WORLD'S REFUGEES COME TO OUR TOWN*

***To Seek a Better World: The Haitian Minority in America*** by Brent Ashabranner (Cobblehill, 1997). Half a million people from Haiti live in the United States. Where do they live? What do they do? What are their contributions to America? What is happening to those who arrive illegally?

Learn about Haiti's troubled history and its effect on immigrants. Out of print but worth finding. 96pp., grades 5–10

## Picture Books: *Immigrants*

***América Is Her Name*** by Luis J. Rodríguez (Curbstone Press, 1997). América, a Mixteca Indian girl from Oaxaca, Mexico, suffers because of people who insult her background and her life of poverty in a Chicago ghetto. Her love of writing keeps her spirit alive and gives her family hope.

***A Day's Work*** by Eve Bunting (Clarion, 1994). Young Francisco acts as translator for his *abuelo* (grandfather), who recently arrived from Mexico and wants to find a job. Eager to help, Francisco lies to an employer and says that his grandfather, a carpenter by trade, is an able gardener. After ruining the gardening project and learning of Francisco's dishonesty, Abuelo teaches his grandson about integrity and earns the respect of the employer.

***Happy Birthday Mr. Kang*** by Susan L. Roth (National Geographic Society, 2001). Mr. Kang paints poems, reads the *New York Times*, and cares for his hua mei bird as his grandfather did in China. On Sunday, Mr. Kang carries his bird in a bamboo cage to Sara Delano Roosevelt Park in Manhattan, joining other Chinese immigrants with their birds. When his seven-year-old grandson questions whether "a free man should keep a caged bird," Mr. Kang opens the bamboo door. Will the hua mei fly away?

***A Movie in My Pillow/Una película en mi almohada*** by Jorge Argueta (Children's Book Press, 2001). Young Jorge moves to San Francisco from his beloved El Salvador, bringing with him sights, sounds, and smells of his native rural home. He also carries the sorrow of war and of leaving loved ones. To this is added the confusion and joy of reuniting with family in his new urban home. Through Jorge Argueta's poetry and accompanying artwork by Elizabeth Gomez, each story comes alive. In English and Spanish.

Here in the city
there are wonders everywhere
Here mangoes
come in cans
In El Salvador
they grew on trees
Here chickens come
in plastic bags
Over there
they slept beside me

FROM *A MOVIE IN MY PILLOW/ UNA PELÍCULA EN MI ALMOHADA*

***My Diary from Here to There/Mi diario de aquí hasta allá*** by Amada Irma Pérez (Children's Book Press, 2002). Amada writes in her diary, "I overheard Mamá and Papá whispering . . . about leaving our little house in Juárez, Mexico, where we've lived our whole lives, and moving to Los Angeles. . . . Am I the only one scared to leave? What if we're not allowed to speak Spanish? What if I can't learn English?" Young Amada learns she has the strength to survive the exciting and painful move. Through her family and her diary, Amada finds a new home. In English and Spanish, based on the author's experience.

***My Name Is Yoon*** by Helen Recorvits (Farrar, Straus and Giroux, 2003). Yoon's name means "Shining Wisdom." When written in Korean, her name looks happy, but the shapes seem lonely when written in English. Yoon tries out different names—*cat, bird,* even *cupcake*. Only as she finds her place in her new country does she become Yoon again.

***Oranges on Golden Mountain*** by Elizabeth Partridge (Puffin, 2001). During the California gold rush, many Chinese sailed across the Pacific to work and live. When hard times hit Jo Lee's family, he, too, is sent to stay with his uncle in this foreign land called "Gold Mountain." He saves every coin earned by hard work—fishing and growing orange trees—in hopes that his mother and young sister will soon join him.

***A Place to Grow*** by Soyung Pak (Scholastic, 2002). A family, like a seed, needs a safe place to grow. A father uses a blooming garden to tell his daughter why he immigrated to a safe place to raise a family. The story has depth and can provoke discussion of the reasons that people immigrate.

***Uncle Rain Cloud*** by Tony Johnston (Charlesbridge, 2001). Carlos delights in the stories his uncle Tio Tomás tells him of Mexico and the tongue-twister gods, *los dioses trabalenguas*. Sometimes, though, Tomás is stormy, having difficulty adjusting to his life in Los Angeles and his frustration with English. Carlos has his own struggles in third grade. As they forge a partnership, each teaching the other, change comes more easily.

***A Very Important Day*** by Maggie Rugg Herold (Morrow, 1995). All over New York City, families from many countries prepare for the memorable day when they will become citizens. The Patel family from India share breakfast with their neighbors, the Stousos family close their Greek restaurant, and Yujin Zeng's friend gives him a special gift. The event in the courthouse brings all the families together.

***The Whispering Cloth: A Refugee's Story*** by Pegi Deitz Shea (Boyds Mills Press, 1995). Little Mai watches the Hmong women in the refugee camp in Thailand as they stitch stories onto cloth. Traders buy the brightly colored *pa'ndau*. Mai's grandmother shows her how to stitch the border, but only Mai can find the story for her cloth. Mai's cloth whispers the story of her escape, life in the camp, and dreams for a bright future—her cloth is not for sale!

## Fiction: *Immigrants*

***Any Small Goodness*** by Tony Johnston (Scholastic, 2001). Moving from Mexico to Los Angeles with a little English in his pocket, eleven-year-old Arturo Rodriguez struggles to make sense of his world. As his father says, "In life there is *bueno* and *malo*. If you do not find enough good, you must yourself create it." Arturo's journey includes reclaiming his heritage, valuing his teachers and mentors, rescuing the family cat, and living where "what you love is always at risk." His "retaliation" is heartwarming. A glossary translates the Spanish vocabulary used. 128pp., grades 4–8

***Behind the Mountains*** by Edwidge Danticat (Scholastic, 2002). Young Celiane records her life in Haiti in a "sweet little book" given to her by her teacher. We follow her through the fall of 2000, when bombing during the Haitian elections nearly kills her and her mother. Celiane writes of leaving her treasured home in the mountains to join her father in the harsh streets of Brooklyn. This first-person story is marked by love of family and proverbs from the Haitian tradition. 153pp., grades 6–10

***Born Confused*** by Tanuk Desai Hidier (Scholastic, 2002). The art of balancing two cultures is carefully dissected by Dimple Lala, deep in the throes of adolescent self-discovery. While she has great respect for her immigrant parents, Dimple is challenged by how to integrate her language and culture from India with the New York hip scene. After meeting Karsh, a son of Indian friends, Dimple's idea of who is a "suitable" match unravels, and complications arise. 500pp., grades 9–12

***Children of the River*** by Linda Crew (Dell, 1989). Sundara escaped the Khmer Rouge army in Cambodia with her aunt's family and lives in Oregon. Now in high school, she finds that her Cambodian traditions clash with being an American teenager. How will she live up to family expectations if she is drawn to Jonathan, the blonde high school football player? And what of the memories that continue to haunt her? 213pp., young adult

***The Clay Marble*** by Minfong Ho (Farrar, Straus and Giroux, 1991). After fleeing their war-torn Cambodian village, twelve-year-old Dara and her family create makeshift dwellings in refugee camps on the Thai-Cambodian border. The terror is inescapable, as are calamities and tragedies they face in daily life. Separated from her loved ones, Dara discovers the courage and confidence to find her family. 163pp., grades 5–8

***A Different Kind of Hero*** by Ann R. Blakeslee (Cavendish, 1997). Twelve-year-old Renny is not tough enough to please his Irish father, Lon. When Renny befriends and promises to protect a Chinese boy attending school—most unusual in the 1880s—his dad is infuriated. Lon and others are enraged by the presence of Chinese people in this Colorado mining town; they fear that more Chinese families will follow and work for less pay. Renny holds to his commitment to keep his friendship and demonstrates courage even his father comes to admire. 143pp., grades 4–7

**Recommendation from the Field**
*by Carolina Goodman, Curriculum Coordinator*
*P.S. #1 Elementary School*

*Dragonwings* by Lawrence Yep (HarperTrophy, 1975). *Dragonwings* is written from the perspective of a young boy named Moon Shadow, who, in the early 1900s, grows up on a farm in China with his mother and grandmother. At age seven, he journeys across the Pacific to meet his father. Windrider, along with many other Chinese men, had immigrated to the United States to earn money for their families in China. In the course of the novel, we learn about Chinese culture, the Wright brothers' first flight, the San Francisco earthquake, and the prejudice faced by the Chinese in their new country.

There are many curricular connections to be made: comparing Chinese picture writing with the English alphabet; reading and writing poetry; honoring ancestors; comparing lunar and solar calendars; learning the use of an abacus; finding out about the stereopticon, an early 3-D slide projector; learning about aeronautics; and studying earthquakes. Any of these can lead to service activities. For example, after studying earthquakes, students could make safety posters or preparedness brochures and assemble earthquake kits for low-income families. 336pp., grades 5–9

***Esperanza Rising*** by Pan Muñoz Ryan (Scholastic, 2000). Esperanza lives in luxury on her father's ranch in Mexico and assumes that her lifestyle of fancy dresses and servants will last forever. A tragedy on the eve of her birthday in 1930 shatters all she knows. She and her mother escape to California to become migrant farm workers. Esperanza is ill prepared for hard labor and the financial struggles of the Great Depression, but her mother's illness causes her to rise above oppressive circumstances. 262pp., young adult

***The Gold-Threaded Dress*** by Carolyn Marsden (Candlewick Press, 2002). In America, Oy's teacher renames her "Olivia." Having just arrived from Thailand, Oy is unaccustomed to many of the behaviors she encounters in school, from being left out of games to being teased. When the other children learn about her traditional silk dress, they taunt her by promising to be her friend if only she will bring it to school. Will Oy betray her family to fit in? 73pp., grades 3–5

***Journey of the Sparrows*** by Fran Leeper Buss and Daisy Cubias (Lodestar, 1991). Maria, a sixteen-year-old Salvadoran refugee, cares for her siblings during their difficult journey to Chicago. Together, they start a new life with help from their community. 165pp., young adult

***Lupita Mañana*** by Patricia Beatty (Beech Tree, 1981). When her father dies, thirteen-year-old Lupita and her brother leave their Mexican village and head to the United States to earn money. Her struggle is eased by the help of others. 186pp., young adult

***Miss Happiness and Miss Flower*** by Rumer Godden (HarperTrophy, 1960). Eight-year-old Nona longs for her home in sunny India, but instead she lives in a cold English village with her aunt, uncle, and three very British cousins, including Belinda, who hates her. When two Japanese dolls arrive as gifts, Nona wants to build them a proper Japanese house. Over time, and with help from her cousins and new friends, Nona creates a home for the dolls and herself. Includes plans for a Japanese dollhouse. 199pp., grades 3–6

**Recommendation from the Field**

*by Jill Addison-Jacobson, Youth Service California*

*The Skirt* by Gary Soto (Delacorte Press, 1992). On Friday afternoon, Miata leaves her mother's skirt on the bus. She needs that skirt. Her troupe is to dance the *folklorico* on Sunday. If she is the only girl without a costume, her parents, Mexican immigrants living in central California, will "wear sunglasses out of embarrassment." Miata and her friend Ana work together to recover the skirt before her parents discover its absence. The effort leads them to break rules and cooperate with their nemesis—and may end up being unnecessary.

This charming tale raises challenging questions that can lead to service extensions for young readers, especially regarding immigration and conflict resolution. Through discussion, students can generate ideas.

Immigration: Miata and her family are relatively new to central California. Are there ways to help new students at school or new families in your neighborhood? What services in our community help immigrant families? Are there ways you can help these agencies? What services are there for children your age? What do you think is needed?

Conflict Resolution/Peer Counseling: Miata and Ana have trouble on the bus. Ana also seems uncomfortable with their adventure, but goes along. Miata makes choices that would be unacceptable to her parents in order to please her parents. Does your school have or need a conflict resolution program to facilitate problem solving and effective decision making? Where can students go for help with disputes? What activities could students develop to encourage peer interaction or provide ideas to improve parent-child communication? 74pp., grades 4–5

***Stella: On the Edge of Popularity*** by Lauren Lee (Polychrome Publishing, 1994). Seeking acceptance in a seventh-grade clique, Stella follows the direction of the "popular girls" despite their biased attitudes. Her Korean grandmother nags Stella to follow her own cultural traditions, causing her embarrassment. Stella's confusion is intensified when her father is one of a group of men victimized in a racial incident. Will she learn a lesson from her old-fashioned grandmother: "Be who you are"? 178pp., grades 4–8

***A Step from Heaven*** by An Na (Front Street, 2001). Moving from Korea to California is supposed to bring Young Park's family closer to heaven. Instead, learning English, financial hardships, and her father's rage and abuse cause painful difficulties. Each chapter adds to a poignant portrait of a young girl from age four to eighteen striving to turn her dream of finding heaven on earth into a reality. 156pp., young adult

***Tangled Threads: A Hmong Girl's Story*** by Pegi Deitz Shea (Clarion, 2003). After spending ten years in a refugee camp in Thailand, Mai Yang travels to Rhode Island with her grandmother to join the only living relatives—aunts, uncles, and cousins who had gone five years before. The cultural differences are exacerbated by her rebellious cousins, while Mai uses the threads of the traditional *pa'ndau* cloth to help her stay connected to her Hmong heritage. 236pp., grades 4–8

# Interviews with Authors:
## The Story Behind the Story

In the following interview, we find out the "story behind the story" from Francisco Jiménez (*The Circuit, Breaking Through,* and *La Mariposa)*. In *The Circuit* and then *Breaking Through,* Francisco Jiménez created vivid, honest descriptions of life as a migrant farm worker and hope found through love of family and education. He graciously agreed to an interview but needed to postpone it for a week, since he was going to Washington, D.C., to receive an award for these books. Fortuitously, I was also going to be in D.C., so I attended his award ceremony, where I met his brother and sister-in-law, both of whom are important figures in his stories.

### *Francisco Jiménez, author of* The Circuit, Breaking Through, *and* La Mariposa

The inspiration for these books comes from the community of my childhood and my teachers. The migrant families that I grew up with worked and carried courage, tenacity, and hope amidst adversity. These values have been a constant to me in my personal and professional life.

It is important for children and young adults to appreciate farm labor work, the means by which fruits, vegetables, and other foods they have at every meal arrive at their table. We seldom think of the people responsible. I want readers to have a better insight into the hard life that farm workers experience.

Another reason for writing these books is to document the experiences of many migrant families—from the past and the present. For the most part, this sector of society has been ignored. This experience, as painful as it might be, is part of the American experience. To understand the essence of our country, we must learn about different groups that have contributed. Within the Mexican-American community, the farm worker is one of the groups that sustains our agricultural economy.

I wrote *The Circuit* and *Breaking Through* to pay tribute to my teachers. In *The Circuit,* Mr. Lema, my sixth-grade teacher, encouraged me to learn English though I was having difficulty caused by moving from place to place. He valued my Mexican cultural background. During a unit on California geography, he asked me to read aloud the names of the towns and cities on the map because, as he said, "I know you will pronounce them correctly." My native language was being valued. That one small effort on his part made a world of difference in developing my self-concept.

In *Breaking Through,* I mention my sophomore English teacher, Mrs. Bell, who had the class write short essays describing childhood experiences. I began to write of my migrant experiences. She then had me read *The Grapes of Wrath.* For the first time I was able to see the importance of literature in making a connection with one's life. I learned about the power of literature to move hearts and minds. Later, as I thought of writing my own books, I reflected on the importance of children seeing themselves reflected in literature. When growing up, there was hardly any material in school I could relate to regarding my cultural background. I hope to contribute literature that many children can relate to, especially those from similar backgrounds.

In writing the children's book *La Mariposa,* I retold the story "Inside Out" found in *The Circuit.* I realized that not knowing a word of English and the frustration and alienation I felt might be common to many children who enter our school system. The responses I receive from teachers and children indicate I was right.

If you compare the two versions, you will see one significant difference. In *La Mariposa,* the child is prohibited from speaking Spanish. When the teacher has Francisco open the jar and the butterfly emerges, Francisco says, "Hermosa," in a low voice. The teacher translates, saying, "How beautiful." In that moment I used my imagination so the teacher would value the child's language to "break through." Using the metaphor of the butterfly, both are transformed: The child becomes the teacher and the teacher becomes the student.

One of the greatest rewards is hearing how my books affected young people. Letters from teachers point out that after reading the memoirs, students who normally were quiet begin to open up and talk about their experiences. This is one of my intents.

A North Carolina teacher describes using *The Circuit* so students will learn about migrant workers and their difficulties. The teacher had the class connect with a community of migrant workers in their state. The class decided to bring in clothing, food, and books to give to people in the migrant camps. They also made a quilt with squares based on each of the stories in my book and contributed this to the migrant community. The teacher uses the book to help students become more compassionate toward other children who don't have the same socioeconomic background. These actions are meaningful. We must be aware that it is one thing to extend a hand and try to be helpful, to give to others in need. Another is to feel solidarity with them. There is a difference.

My use of Spanish in the books has helped students form a stronger community. Some teachers say that when English-only students come across the Spanish words, they ask the Spanish-speaking students to explain the meaning. This is usually an exchange that has not taken place before and gives value to having a second language.

Overall, these books demonstrate the value of obtaining an education, an important means by which we can improve our lives. Children or young adults are usually told that, "With education you will get a better job." This is true, but equally important is how education enriches our lives in other ways. We enjoy the things that surround us when we have learned about biology or music or art. We can appreciate all that life gives us and makes available to us.

I also want to impart the importance of hard work, respect, and faith in your own talents. Develop these with the help of parents, teachers, and community. People say, "You were able to break through without bilingual education." I respond by saying, "Any success attributed to me is really the success of many people who helped along the way. I made it thanks to many teachers and my family and I will do everything within my power to help others make it as well." In our society we have an overemphasis on individualism that can be a drawback to a commitment to helping others help themselves. In coming from a culture that emphasizes community over individualism, this is what I find more helpful in building a better society.

On a personal level, writing an autobiography is a catharsis; we learn more about ourselves. There is self-discovery as I reflect on my childhood from an adult point of view. I have gained a deeper sense of purpose for the things I do now as a teacher.

CHAPTER 12

# LITERACY

> When I look back, I am so impressed again with the life-giving power of literature. If I were a young person today, trying to gain a sense of myself in the world, I would do that again by reading, just as I did when I was young.
>
> MAYA ANGELOU, AUTHOR

Reading unlocks the door to new worlds. It can provide knowledge and opportunity, excitement and adventure, humor and tragedy. For many, learning to read comes easily, but for others, and for many reasons, reading is a struggle fraught with frustration and embarrassment.

Service learning provides many opportunities to help people who are having difficulty with reading. Tutoring and mentoring activities are the most common; but young people can also help by making books, performing to create enthusiasm for reading, and helping with general language development when the reader's first language is not English.

Preparing for literacy service learning opportunities, especially for tutoring, involves understanding struggling readers' emotions and recognizing how hard reading can be for them. Works listed in the Literacy Bookshelf such as *Thank You, Mr. Falker* and *La Mariposa* can provide insight.

The bookshelf also includes works such as *Richard Wright and the Library Card* and *The Year of Miss Agnes* that are about people whose reading difficulties arose from social and cultural disadvantages rather than reading disabilities or language differences. These books remind us that the opportunity—as well as the ability—to read is closely linked to the rights to life, liberty, and the pursuit of happiness in modern society.

## Preparation: Getting Ready for Service Learning Involving Literacy

The following activities can be used in the preparation stage to promote learning and skill development related to literacy. These activities can be used with different age ranges during preparation to help your students examine key issues through research, analyze community needs, and gain the knowledge they need to effectively contribute to the design of their service plan. Since literature is often an important part of preparation, you can find recommended titles on this theme in the Literacy Bookshelf later in this chapter.

***Activity: Cross-Age Tutoring in Reading Skills.*** Elevate tutoring programs from a casual experience to high-level service learning. Here are some tips to prepare student tutors before they begin and to support continued preparation and skill review for ongoing tutoring relationships.

- Discuss the challenges some students have in learning. Ask students to think of their own challenges. This can be discussed in small groups or written in journals with feedback from the teacher.
- Use fiction and nonfiction from the Literacy Bookshelf to build knowledge and empathy.
- Invite a reading specialist to talk with the class to review the specific needs of the children who will be tutored.
- Ask students to bring in some of their favorite children's books from home or from the library. Discuss what makes a story engaging. Practice reading aloud to each other in pairs or small groups.

- Have tutors get to know their tutees by using the Personal Inventory form (see page 33). The tutors can pair up and practice using the form and the interview process. Discuss ways this can be helpful in getting to know the tutee and identifying high-interest books.
- In pairs or small groups, ask the tutors to design kinesthetic experiences that could help students learn the alphabet, punctuation, or any other writing skill. For example, making letters out of tactile materials or magnets, having students trace over letters with their fingers, or use their bodies to make the shapes of letters. (Simple stretches before a tutoring session can help by removing the "squirmy" factor in learning.)
- Ask students to consider all the reasons why listening skills are essential for the reader and learner. Have students think of ways to reinforce listening—for example, by reading a passage to the tutee and having the child summarize.
- Brainstorm with the tutors ways that quotes might be used with their tutees. Useful quotes are brief, convey an important message, and call for analyzing the meaning of a very short piece of writing or interpreting a metaphor. Some quotes relate directly to the tutoring experience: "No matter what accomplishments you make, somebody helps you" (Wilma Rudolph, athlete). Another metaphorical quote extols the value of reading: "A book is like a garden carried in the pocket" (Chinese proverb). Another removes the pressure of always "getting it right": "If you can't make a mistake, you can't make anything" (Marva N. Collins, educator). Find more quotes throughout this book.
- Since reflection is an important part of the service learning process, suggest that students use reflection with their tutees. For example, the tutor can have the tutee reflect on such ideas as "Today I learned . . . " and "What I want to remember is . . . " Responses can be written down by the tutor and reviewed in the next session to reinforce lessons and skills learned.
- Tutors can involve their tutees in *doing* service learning. Tutees can make alphabet books to demonstrate their skills, write stories or poetry, or create other compilations. Copies can be given to the class or library or exchanged with other students for continued skill development. Many other service learning possibilities exist that often can be linked back to the students' original inventory of interests, skills, and talents.

***Activity: A Right or a Privilege?*** Students generally attend school without considering this question: Is education a right or a privilege? Students can develop research questions to investigate both the history of education and the current struggles to learn for people in many parts of the world. What historical events have made education accessible to the masses? Slavery, women's rights, and child labor laws are part of this story. Where in the world are students now deprived of education because of war, famine, forced child labor, or other factors? In Malawi, for example, as well as other African nations, students can only attend classes if they can afford classroom supplies. In times of war schools close and in refugee camps there may be no schools.

The next step is using this new knowledge and awareness to determine ways to take action. Immigrants locally may need support in order to take full advantage of available opportunities. For example, students could provide free child care during language classes. Advocacy for children in other nations can be accomplished through international organizations such as Oxfam (*www.oxfamamerica.org*), Amnesty International Kids (*www.amnestyusa.org/aikids*), and Peace Corps Kids World (*www.peacecorps.gov/kids*). Collections of school supplies or books may also help.

**Find Out More About Literacy**

To learn more about these issues and to get ideas for service and action, visit these Web sites and organizations online:

***www.nationalservice.org*** The National Service Resource Center, a service of the Corporation for National Service, offers information and many publications, including "Reading Helpers" and "Tutoring Manuals."

***www.ilo.org*** The International Labour Organization has a virtual classroom on child labor—with resources for

*continued* ⟶

elementary and high school students and teachers; includes information on what kids are doing to end child labor and enable all kids to attend schools.

***www.iamfoundation.org*** Million Books for Kids, a project of the I AM Foundation, encourages kids and adults to provide books for children who have none in their homes. Click on "Million Books for Kids Campaign" for more information.

## Making Connections Across the Curriculum

Some service learning activities naturally lend themselves to interdisciplinary work and making connections across the curriculum. These connections strengthen and broaden student learning, helping them meet academic standards. More than likely, you'll be looking for these connections and ways to encourage them well before the students ever start working on service learning activities. As with the entire service learning process, it helps to remain flexible, because some connections can be spontaneously generated by the questions raised throughout and by the needs of the project. To help you think about cross-curricular connections and where you can look for them, the Curricular Web for this chapter (page 176) gives examples of many different ways this theme can be used in different academic areas. (The service learning scenarios in the next section of the chapter also demonstrate various ways this theme can be used across the curriculum.)

## Service Learning Scenarios:
### Ideas for Action

Ready to take action? What follows are projects that have been successfully carried out by elementary, middle, or high school students. Most of these scenarios and examples explicitly include some aspects of preparation, action, reflection, and demonstration. These scenarios can be a rich source of project, resource, and curriculum ideas for you to draw upon. While the grade levels are given as a reference, most project ideas can be adapted to suit younger or older students, and many are suitable for cross-age partnerships.

***Everything You Need to Know About Kindergarten: Kindergarten.*** Think of the big difference between kindergartners on their very first day of school and on the last day of the school year. Kindergarten teachers in Los Angeles have harnessed that growth and transformation into a creative and valued service learning activity. In early spring, the soon-to-be first graders identify what they have learned: how to sit in a circle, where to put their lunches, how to take care of library books, where to recycle paper, and so on. They use their knowledge to produce a booklet, "All About Kindergarten." Students work individually or in pairs to create one page of the book on a selected theme. After drawing illustrations, the students dictate the words to an adult. All work is done in black ink for easy duplication. As parents register their children for the next year's kindergarten, the family receives a copy of "All About Kindergarten." On the first day of school, one parent reported, "My daughter slept with her kindergarten book all summer, it was her security for the transition."

***Collections: Grade 1 (with Grade-6 Helpers).*** First graders focus on literacy as they sponsor an all-school new and "gently used" book drive to support libraries. Counting skills come in to play, as well as writing, since each student writes a book review of one book he or she is donating. With the help of middle school students, the children sort the books into groups according to reading level. The books are personally delivered by the children.

***Original Books for the Community: Grades 1–5.*** So many original books are written by students, but where do they go? Usually home, and that's it. Students at a school in Washington state make two copies of each book (or more if the book is a class collaboration), so one copy can be contributed to a place that needs more books: a library, children's center, after-school program, homeless shelter, hospital, emergency room, or free health clinic. Students learn about the community as they select a place for their books to go and often deliver the books themselves and read them aloud to younger children. Some children have added multiple languages to produce bi- and even tri-lingual books that have a broader community reach.

***Books on Tape: Grade 2.*** Books on tape are welcome in many places. Second graders in a Chicago suburb

# Literacy Across the Curriculum

## Literacy

### *English/Language Arts*

- Discuss: What is your favorite book and why?
- Study stories and practice storytelling techniques, including those from other cultures
- Prepare annotated bibliographies of recommended books for peers

### *Social Studies/History*

- Create and "attend" a classroom environment from the past, e.g., the early 1900s
- Study the Indian Schools established in 1879 by the federal government and its impact on tribal culture then and now
- Learn about pending current legislation that would impact your school and education

### *Languages*

- Learn about education in the countries of the language being studied, and compare to your own
- Create lessons to familiarize younger children with this language and culture
- Identify idioms and slang expressions that would be hard to translate into the language being studied, and find similar kinds of expressions in the language being studied

### *Theater, Music, & Visual Arts*

- Write skits that promote reading as an adventure
- Find and learn contemporary or popular songs that promote learning and education
- Find quotes in books, online, or elsewhere about the wonders of books and reading, then create posters

### *Math*

- Research literacy rates for your state and compare with national statistics
- Prepare "math in a box" kits of basic math concepts with directions and games
- Discuss: What does it mean to be "math literate?" How has this changed with calculators and computers?

### *Physical Education*

- Discuss: How does physical activity help children learn?
- Design an activity to teach the alphabet by having students forms the letters with their bodies either individually on in groups
- Create an annotated list of books about sports or athletes to share with younger children

### *Computer*

- Access the Internet for illiteracy data and local resources and programs
- Make a list of computer terms and meanings in a picture book format
- Research places in the community that need computers for kids, like shelters or community centers, and seek donations from businesses

### *Science*

- Study about learning differences, variations of learning styles, and learning disabilities
- Prepare science lessons for young children that incorporate various learning styles
- Help younger students record science experiments

discovered this fact after taping a choral reading for the Junior Blind organization. Next, they made tapes to donate to emergency waiting rooms, hospitals, and a ward for premature infants, who seemed to do better when listening to the lovely voices of children. Recording original stories also gave students an incentive to improve their writing skills.

***Idioms in Pairs: Grade 2.*** Two schools, two different socioeconomic groups, two languages, and grade-two children: a perfect partnership. Students in West Hollywood, California, met for cultural, recreational, and academic interaction that led to a service learning activity. The project began when one of the schools hosted a Russian storytelling troupe. A second-grade class invited the predominantly Russian-born second-grade students from a nearby school to participate. After social interaction (and lunch), teachers from both schools led activities on idioms, which are very difficult for students learning English as a second language to grasp. Working in pairs, students took an idiom, such as "Don't let the cat out of the bag," and discussed its interpretation and meaning. The students also drew two pictures to illustrate; for example, for "Don't let the cat out of the bag," one picture showed a cat peeking out of a sack, and one showed a child saying "Shh!" The pictures were compiled into a workbook for use in these and other neighboring schools.

***Turn Off the TV! Grades 3–5.*** In a multiage classroom that included grades three through five, the children used a chart to keep track of how much television they each watched in one week's time. For two TV programs, they counted any violent images they saw during the shows or commercials. The next week they recorded how much time they played or read books outside of school. A huge class chart consolidated the data and students compared the amounts. Using information from the TV-Turnoff Network (*www.tvturnoff.org*), the teacher presented information about how violent images impact children and about the "couch potato" syndrome—how inactivity effects children's weight and health. Students decided to educate the rest of the school. They made presentations to other classrooms along with posters and signs announcing "Turn Off the TV Week." Many students in the school pledged to exchange television for books for an entire week, culminating in a read aloud and book exchange project to keep the pages turning, and the television turned off. For more on television versus literature, read *Aunt Chip and the Great Triple Creek Dam Affair* (see page 181).

> I must say that I find television very educational.
> The minute somebody turns it on,
> I go to the library and read a book.
>
> GROUCHO MARX, ACTOR

***Especially for New Parents: Grade 4.*** An elementary teacher in Maine asked her students, "Do you enjoy having your parent or a teacher read you a story?" The response was an overwhelming "Yes!" Students eagerly described what they liked about story times. Later, teachers discussed in a staff meeting the finding that parents in their community didn't spend much time reading to their children. They decided to invite students to address this issue. Children began gift-wrapping original books and writing letters explaining "why it's important to read to your child—and why I like someone to read to me." With assistance from a local community organization, the wrapped books were donated to the local county hospital and given to each new parent as a "welcome baby" gift.

***Tutor Buddies Build Community: Grade 4.*** Entering fourth grade brings a special privilege at one elementary school in Mount Vernon, Washington. Every fourth grader, regardless of skill level, is partnered with a younger student. These "tutor buddies" meet four times a week, twenty minutes each time, and work on the younger children's reading skills. On the fifth day of the week, the tutors continue their training and work on development of their own skills. The school atmosphere has been transformed by these relationships. Every student is valued as having something to offer. Older children have greater empathy for the role of teacher. Younger children look up to their mentors as role models. Service learning is woven into the fabric of this school.

***Math Support: Grade 6.*** Literacy extends to math as well. In one school, sixth graders willingly gave up their usual lunchtime activities to eat with and then tutor their peers in math. The tutors took extra time to learn how to break down a skill into manageable steps and to teach it effectively. Lunch buddy math tutoring became a much sought-after program.

***Kids for Computer Literacy: Grades 6–8.*** The rural community of Kansas, Oklahoma, had no public library to provide access to computers, and many families did not have computers at home. What could middle school kids do to help? They decided to open their school's computer lab on Tuesday evenings and Saturday mornings for instruction and assistance. To prepare, the students practiced creating and leading computer lessons, and learned how to use the résumé templates on the computer. After surveying parents and community members to find out their interests, they also located Web sites that would provide information the community was interested in.

***Giving a Head Start with Reading: Grades 6–8.*** Middle school students in the rural community of London, Kentucky, wanted to write books. They immersed themselves in children's literature, exploring the nuances and writing styles of their favorite books. In further preparation, a communication specialist visited the students and talked about writing short stories. Students took their creative ideas and applied them for a specific audience—preschool children. They used computers and other forms of technology to organize and produce their books. Finally, children from a local Head Start program visited the middle school library, and met the "big kids," who read to them and presented them with a classroom full of original picture books.

***Knowing the Triggers: Grades 7 and 8.*** Confidence, stress reduction, and homework completion are interwoven topics covered by middle school students in Hialeah, Florida. First semester, seventh and eighth graders study stress reduction methods and anger management to overcome tension and anger that can interfere with learning. After learning the triggers for emotional conflict, they apply their knowledge to meet a community need. School counselors had identified third graders as the age where learning good homework habits was most essential in the transition to the upper elementary grades. The middle school students reinforce their own learning by discussing these issues with the counselors, and then writing lessons for mentoring third graders at a nearby elementary school on successful homework strategies. Second semester, the tutoring continues every week.

***A Broad Approach: Grades K–8.*** An independent school in Minnesota takes a broad approach to promote literacy and service learning. All students read books about service to inspire discussions, ideas, and class projects. For example, some fifth-grade students are tutoring beginning readers once a month at a nearby public school while others are sharing book selections with elder friends at a residential facility. At the middle school, students select and read to second graders poetry that can stimulate conversations about making wise choices. Story analysis, discussion and reflection are well-integrated into this schoolwide effort.

***Dependable Tutors: Grades 9–11.*** As part of a high school community service class, students went to a local elementary school for one period daily as tutors for younger students. The high school students had been taught tutoring techniques by a local community college instructor to prepare for the experience. At the end of the semester, they produced a unique reflection piece to present to others—teachers, parents, community members, and peers. Teachers at the elementary school provided regular feedback on the high school students' performance, and skill development was ongoing. Students also learned about dependability. One student wrote: "When I didn't show up on Tuesday, I thought it wouldn't be a big deal. On Thursday, I came in as if everything was normal, and Sara, a little girl I always read to, wouldn't talk to me. Finally, after about twenty minutes, she climbed on my lap with tears in her eyes. 'Where were you? I missed you!' I was speechless. I didn't know she was counting on me."

***Romeo, Romeo! Grade 10.*** In love with Shakespeare? Tenth-grade English students in Alabama discovered an unexpected passion for the great bard, so they decided to share their excitement with younger students. The tenth graders used several strategies. One group performed short versions of the play *A Midsummer Night's Dream* in modern language. Another group made "Shakespeare's Tales" story books. The upper elementary students were delighted with their introduction to Shakespeare.

***A Hero's Journey: Grades 11 and 12.*** For a British literature course, students in South Carolina went on their own "hero's journey" while reading *Beowulf*. Each student found a way to be heroic in the community by providing a service to an individual or organization. The students documented their experiences in language comparable to that used in the epic poem. The culmination of the semester was a video presentation made by several students set to music. Recipients of the service were invited to the presentation and learned how much the students had gained from the experience.

> When I got [my] library card,
> that was when my life began.
> RITA MAE BROWN, AUTHOR

# The Literacy Bookshelf

The ability to read is one part of literacy, and some of the books on the Literacy Bookshelf deal with issues related to this ability. Other stories tell of people yearning for an education, and others describe appreciation of books. To help you find books relevant to your particular projects, the book chart classifies the titles into several topic areas: seeking an education, learning to read, and appreciation of books and reading.

In general, the bookshelf features:

- An annotated bibliography arranged and alphabetized by title according to the general categories of nonfiction (N), picture books (P), and fiction (F). For nonfiction and fiction, length and recommended grade levels are included. The entries in the picture book category do not include suggested grade levels, since they can be successfully used with all ages.
- A chart organized by topic and category to help you find books relevant to particular projects.
- Recommendations from service learning colleagues and experts that include a book summary and ideas for service learning connections. (The number of recommended books varies in each bookshelf.)

## Literacy Bookshelf Topics

| *Topics* | *Books* | *Category* |
|---|---|---|
| ***Seeking an Education*** When social inequities exist, education is usually withheld from some part of the population. These books contain stories of people's struggles simply to be in a place where they can learn, to get to a school, to create a school to be in. | *Breaking Through* (see page 167) | N |
| | *A Bus of Our Own* * | P |
| | *The Circuit* (see page 167) | N |
| | *Indian School: Teaching the White Man's Way* | N |
| | *A Life Like Mine: How Children Live Around the World* (see page 196) | N |
| | *Linda Brown, You Are Not Alone: The Brown v. Board of Education Decision* (see page 196) | N |
| | *The Lost Boys of Natinga: A School for Sudan's Young Refugees* (see page 154) | N |
| | *We Need to Go to School: Voices of the Rugmark Children* (see page 197) | N |

continued ⟶

| Topics | Books | Category |
|---|---|---|
| ***Seeking an Education*** continued | *Richard Wright and the Library Card* | P |
| | *A School for Pompey Walker* | F |
| | *The Strength of Saints* * | F |
| | *The Year of Miss Agnes* | F |
| ***Learning to Read*** Learning to read is not a "one size fits all" proposition. It can be a challenging process for some young people and adults. Language barriers, embarrassment, and lack of resources can be stumbling blocks; community support can make all the difference. | *All Joseph Wanted* | F |
| | *Dear Whiskers* * | F |
| | *The Hard Times Jar* | P |
| | *Illiteracy* | N |
| | *Just Call Me Stupid* | F |
| | *Just Juice* | F |
| | *La Mariposa* | P |
| | *Learning Disabilities* | N |
| | *Once Upon a Time* | P |
| | *Prairie School* | F |
| | *Read for Me, Mama* | P |
| | *Sahara Special* | F |
| | *Thank You, Mr. Falker* | P |
| | *The Wednesday Surprise* * | P |
| ***Appreciation of Books and Reading*** Some people go to great lengths to have books in hand. Appreciation, joy, pleasure, excitement—all to be found within the covers of books and in the libraries where books live. | *Across a Dark and Wild Sea* | P |
| | *Aunt Chip and the Great Triple Creek Dam Affair* | P |
| | *The Bookstore Mouse* | F |
| | *Fahrenheit 451* | F |
| | *Goin' Someplace Special* | P |
| | *The Library Card* | F |
| | *A Series of Unfortunate Events: The Bad Beginning* | F |
| | *Stella Louella's Runaway Book* | P |
| | *Tomás and the Library Lady* | P |
| | *Too Young for Yiddish* (see page 116) | P |

Page references are given for books that do not appear in the Literacy Bookshelf but that can be found in the bookshelf lists of other chapters.
* These books include examples of young people in service-providing roles.

## Nonfiction: Literacy

***Illiteracy*** by Sean M. Grady (Lucent Books, 1994). "Literacy is a skill, a technique of using patterns of letters to preserve ideas." Literacy is highly valued in most societies, but the challenge of learning to read can seem almost insurmountable. Illiteracy in the United States and other nations is profiled in this comprehensive overview, which also discusses how literacy extends beyond "reading and writing." A valuable resource for literacy and tutoring programs. 96pp., grades 6–12

***Indian School: Teaching the White Man's Way*** by Michael L. Cooper (Clarion, 1999). In 1879, eighty-four Sioux boys and girls were forced to leave their tribal homes to attend the Carlisle Indian School. This was the first institution opened by the federal government for the education of Native American children, intending to "civilize" the Indian children and teach them the "white man's way." While a few children succeeded in this setting, for the majority it was an isolating and painful experience in acculturation. 103pp., grades 5–10

***Learning Disabilities*** by Christina M. Girod (Lucent Books, 2001). This book provides a substantial overview of learning disabilities that is useful for a young person engaged in tutoring or other service learning activities with youth or adults with learning disabilities. The many challenges faced both by the struggling reader and by educators are noted. Topics include the history and types of learning disabilities, coping with learning disabilities, and current controversies. 96pp., young adult

## Picture Books: Literacy

***Across a Dark and Wild Sea*** by Don Brown (Millbrook Press, 2002). Columcille lived in a remote part of Ireland in the year 521. As this mixture of legend and history begins to unfold, Columcille develops a love for writing. (Did he really eat a cake filled with alphabet letters?) As a monk and scribe, his fervor grows until he is caught in a dispute over a manuscript he has copied. The resulting battle and loss of life cause him to move abroad. In Scotland, Columcille leaves a legacy that illuminates a corner of the Dark Ages. Includes the uncial alphabet of his time.

***Aunt Chip and the Great Triple Creek Dam Affair*** by Patricia Polacco (Philomel, 1996). In Triple Creek, everyone watches television except Eli's Aunt Chip, who went to bed fifty years ago to protest the library being replaced by a television tower. Yearning for stories, Eli tells his aunt, "Teach me to read!" Soon all the children want to learn to read fables, fairy tales, adventures, and more. In this contemporary fantasy, children restore reading and a librarian to their town.

***A Bus of Our Own*** by Freddi Williams Evans (Albert Whitman, 2001). Mabel Jean wants to attend school, a five-mile walk from home. She tries to find a way for the black children to have a school bus like the white children have. With support from family and friends, she succeeds. Based on real events in 1949.

> "Last week, Lil' Mable Jean asked if I could get a school bus," Cousin Smith told her parents. "I've been figuring on it and decided to buy a bus if enough parents support me. They will have to pay for the children to ride. Now I know we're already paying taxes, and rightly, we should have a bus. It looks like we have to pay twice for our children to get a good learning."
>
> FROM *A BUS OF OUR OWN*

***Goin' Someplace Special*** by Patricia McKissack (Simon & Schuster, 2001). Tricia Ann is on her way to someplace special in the segregated Nashville, Tennessee, of the 1950s. After riding in the "colored section" of the bus, nearly sitting on a "for whites only" park bench, and suffering hurtful words of discrimination, she arrives at the public library where the sign says, "All Are Welcome."

***The Hard Times Jar*** by Ethel Footman Smothers (Farrar, Straus and Giroux, 2003). Although young Emma Turner loves books, she has none at home. The money earned by her family of migrant workers goes strictly for necessities. So Emma works and saves her money until her plans are interrupted: she must attend school! There she finds books, but these cannot be taken home. Will Emma be able to follow the rules?

***La Mariposa*** by Francisco Jiménez (Houghton Mifflin, 1998). Francisco sits in first grade without understanding a word in this English-only school. His desire to learn begins to center on the caterpillar in the jar next to his desk: How does it turn into a butterfly? How long will it take? Through determination and imagination, Francisco overcomes his confusion and isolation and teaches others about tolerance and the love of learning.

***Once Upon a Time*** by Niki Daly (Farrar, Straus and Giroux, 2003). Sarie struggles to read aloud in her South African school. Letters run together and "trip on her tongue," bringing giggles from her classmates. Auntie Anna, Sarie's elder friend, reads Cinderella over and over to the young girl, unlocking the mystery of reading during imaginary trips in a wheel-less car, until the words "pour out [of Sarie] as clear as spring water."

***Read for Me, Mama*** by Vashanti Rahaman (Boyds Mills Press, 1997). Young Joseph loves reading. Each Thursday, he takes home two books from school, one to read himself and "one harder book someone else can read to you." While Mama is "the best storyteller in the world," she asks neighbors to read the "hard books" to Joseph. One evening, Mama admits to Joseph and then to her community, "I have to learn to read." With community support and Joseph's admiration, Mama does learn.

***Richard Wright and the Library Card*** by William Miller (Lee & Low, 1997). Based on a scene from Richard Wright's autobiography, this story tells how seventeen-year-old African American Richard craves books he cannot take from the library because of his race. When a white man at work loans him a library card, Richard can finally read the books he has dreamed about for so long.

***Stella Louella's Runaway Book*** by Lisa Campbell Ernst (Simon & Schuster, 1998). Oh no! Stella cannot find her library book, and it is due at five o'clock today! In her search, she finds that her book has been read and enjoyed by everyone: her brother, the postal carrier, Officer Tim,

Sal who mends chairs, and more. Each person has a different favorite part of the story. Soon the entire town is following Stella to the library to talk to the librarian. A surprising and pleasing ending.

***Thank You, Mr. Falker*** by Patricia Polacco (Philomel, 1998). At first, Trisha loves school, but her difficulty reading makes her feel stupid. Finally, in fifth grade, a teacher helps her overcome her problem. The rest of her odyssey is a learning adventure, and she grows up to write books for children. This semi-autobiographical tale inspires learners, teachers, and tutors!

> But at the new school it was the same.
> When she tried to read, she stumbled over words:
> "the cah, cah. . . cat . . . rrrr, rrr. . . . ran." She was
> reading like a baby in the third grade!
>
> And when her teacher read along with them,
> and called on Trisha for an answer, she gave
> the wrong answer every time.
>
> "Hey dummy!" A boy called out to her on the
> playground, "How come you are so dumb?"
>
> FROM *THANK YOU, MR. FALKER*

***Tomás and the Library Lady*** by Pat Mora (Knopf, 1997). Tomás and his family of migrant workers gather under a tree to hear grandfather's stories. "There are many more in the library," Grande Papa tells young Tomás. Soon Tomás becomes an avid reader and teller of wondrous stories. Based on the real-life story of Tomás Rivera, who became chancellor of the University of California, Riverside.

***The Wednesday Surprise*** by Eve Bunting (Clarion, 1989). A child and her grandmother prepare a special birthday gift, one that involves a commitment to each other and to the joy of being able to read. In this book, the child is the tutor!

## Fiction: Literacy

***All Joseph Wanted*** by Ruth Yaffe Radin (Macmillan, 1991). More than anything, Joseph wants his mother to be able to read. Finally, Joseph reaches for help. 80pp., grades 3–5

***The Bookstore Mouse*** by Peggy Christian (Harcourt, 1995). He lives in a bookstore behind a wall of words. He snacks on letters from cookbooks. He throws sharp words at his enemy. And then one day, this bookstore mouse literally lands right inside one of the books, headed for a great adventure with an unprepared knight as they set out to confront a dragon and free the storytellers. 134pp., grades 4–7

***Dear Whiskers*** by Ann Whitehead Nagda (Holiday House, 2000). During a cross-age school project, fourth-grader Jenny is discouraged because her second-grade pen pal Sameera, a new student from Saudi Arabia, does not speak English. Despite her initial frustrations, Jenny sees the challenges Sameera faces and becomes determined to break the silence. 76pp., grades 2–4

### Recommendation from the Field

*by Christopher Galyean, high school student*

*Fahrenheit 451* by Ray Bradbury (Simon & Schuster, 1953/1993). Guy Montag was a fireman—not a fireman who put out fires but one who started them. Guy and the other firemen were paid to burn books. He never questioned this occupation until one day he met Clarisse, a girl who changed his outlook. The questioning attitude he adopted wasn't favored by his peers, however. One day he saved a book from the fires, hoping to find answers within the book. Instead, he was taken on a journey of self-discovery.

Students can debate whether books are necessary to preserve information now that we have the technology to store everything electronically. Issues of social and political control are also prevalent in the novel, and students can discuss the fairness and effectiveness of the political systems of the world. Finally, they can decide for themselves what would happen if there were no more challenges in the world.

In terms of service, students can select their favorite books from middle or elementary school. They can then arrange for classroom visits to discuss the value of reading in general and these books specifically with the appropriate students. In honor of *Fahrenheit 451*, students could memorize a passage and create a performance piece to encourage appreciation of literature. 190pp., young adult

***Just Call Me Stupid*** by Tom Birdseye (Puffin, 1993). When fifth-grader Patrick tries to read, he remembers his dad calling him stupid, and he freezes. Even his time in the resource room makes him feel as if he is suffocating. Only drawing and medieval fantasies nurture his creative talents. When Celina moves next door, Patrick, for the first time, has a reason to read. 181pp., grades 4–7

***Just Juice*** by Karen Hesse (Scholastic, 1998). Fourth-grader Juice just does not like school. Reading and math are too hard, and she would rather be with her unemployed Pa in his makeshift metal shop. When the family has one last chance to pay back taxes or lose their home, Juice realizes that knowing how to read is more than important—it will help them survive. 138pp., grades 3–6

### Recommendation from the Field
*by Nan Peterson, The Blake School*

*The Library Card* by Jerry Spinelli (Scholastic, 1996). Join the four teenagers featured in this action-packed short story collection of serious, humorous, and exciting adolescent adventures. All the teens are profoundly changed by discoveries found in library books. These adventures feature many themes—literacy, love of learning, poverty, homelessness, parent loss, teenage crime, media addiction, and friendship. Many of the themes can lead to worthwhile activities. Students can investigate issues of hunger and homelessness and the income needed to meet basic needs and pay for transportation, medical costs, and child care. (The book *Nickle and Dimed: On (Not) Getting By in America* can add to this research.) They can study the impact of media on children or teens and promote a "Trade Your TV for a Book" week.

Since *The Library Card* explores, among its themes, the riches found within books, students can consider these questions and add their own: Why do some people not learn to read? Why do some people not enjoy reading? What is the value of reading? What is the value of education? This can lead to a "pay it forward" approach (as described in the book *Pay It Forward* on the Social Change Bookshelf) to instill the love of reading in others. Students can encourage a younger student by reading with the younger child and coauthoring a book that meets that child's particular need. In collaboration with a program for English as a second language, students can read with recent immigrants on a regular basis. Also, many shelters, hospitals, and community centers may appreciate the donation of used books. 148pp., grades 5–8

***Prairie School*** by Avi (Harper, 2001). In 1880, Noah likes working the family farm and roaming the Colorado prairie. He certainly doesn't want to learn to read from his Aunt Dora. What use does he have for reading? Nine-year-old Noah doesn't expect his feisty aunt to have him push her wheelchair so she can explore the prairie and reveal the wealth of book knowledge available for a young boy who can "learn to read and you'll read the prairie." 48pp., grades 2–4

***Sahara Special*** by Esmé Raji Codell (Hyperion, 2003). Sahara intends to be a writer. At home she is a prolific reader, yet at school her hand never seems to raise to answer a question, and doing homework? Never! Is Sahara's obstinacy a reaction to her father leaving, or does she have a learning problem? When Sahara repeats fifth grade, her new teacher, Miss Pointy, uses unusual methods and quiet support to unlock the joy of learning. 175pp., grades 4–7

***A School for Pompey Walker*** by Michael J. Rosen (Harcourt Brace, 1995). "Who would have thought anybody'd applaud a man who spent much of his life a slave, and so much more of it a criminal—at least to some eyes." Pompey Walker stands before children at a school named in his honor, which was on the site of the Sweet Freedom School he had established earlier for black children. Pompey tells of brutalities of slave life and his friendship with Jeremiah Walker, a white abolitionist. Pompey and Jeremiah devised a dangerous plan to gain money from slave owners needed to build the school. As described in the author's note, the incidents are based on recollections of elder freed slaves. 42pp., grades 4–6

You are so blessed, each and every one of you.
Learning and books are yours every day.
First book my eyes knew what to do with,
I was twenty-two years of age.

FROM *A SCHOOL FOR POMPEY WALKER*

**Recommendation from the Field**
*by Terry Pickeral, Executive Director,*
*National Center for Learning and Citizenship*

*A Series of Unfortunate Events: The Bad Beginning* by Lemony Snicket (HarperCollins, 1999). This is the first in a series about three recently orphaned siblings: Violet, Klaus, and Sunny Baudelaire. The book introduces the children and their recent bad luck: their house burned down and their parents perished. The series follows the children as they are introduced to distant relatives, who become responsible for them. Violet is an inventor and Klaus, a reader. Sunny uses her teeth and creates her own language. As the children move from relative to relative, they encounter the strangest streak of bad luck and unfortunate events.

Students put themselves in the place of the Baudelaire orphans and identify how they would handle adversity. In addition, they can identify individuals they consider family and consider why. With regard to service learning activities, students can discuss "worst-case" scenarios and develop problem-solving skills by creating contingency plans. Also, Klaus is always examining language and the meanings of words. Students could create books for younger children to creatively teach about language, words, and meaning. 176pp., grades 4–7

***The Strength of Saints*** by Alexandria LaFaye (Simon & Schuster, 2002). Harper, Louisiana, 1936. Fourteen-year-old Nissa Bergen has a mind and will of her own. As the librarian in a small town with narrow ideas about integration, she has created "separate-but-equal" libraries. Still, she is plagued with a conscience that wants to unite the community. Doing what is right may not be easy, but Nissa's independent spirit and convictions triumph. This third book about Nissa easily stands on its own. 183pp., grades 6–10

***The Year of Miss Agnes*** by Kirkpatrick Hill (Aladdin, 2000). A new teacher arrives in a remote Alaskan town. Frederika, "Fred" for short, age ten, doubts that Miss Agnes will last in this community that smells of fish. But the one-room schoolhouse comes alive as never before with the creative spirit of a dynamic teacher, who reaches out and values every child, including Bokko, Fred's twelve-year-old deaf sister. 113pp., grades 4–8

Miss Agnes used the big map to teach us geography. She pointed out the continents with a yardstick, and then she showed us how to find Alaska every time. . . . Miss Agnes said she was going to teach us every one of the countries on the big map, so we'd know everything about the world. There were places where it was hot all the time and where they had never seen snow. . . . I could hardly wait.

FROM *THE YEAR OF MISS AGNES*

# Interviews with Authors:
## The Story Behind the Story

In the following interview, we find out the "story behind the story" from Alexandria LaFaye (*The Strength of Saints*). The strong character of Nissa caused me to call this author. I wanted to know more about Nissa and found out from her that this book is the third in a series. During the interview, I learned about the author's motivation and her passion for writing. Afterward, I satisfied my desire for more of Nissa by reading *The Year of the Sawdust Man* and *Nissa's Place*.

## *Alexandria LaFaye,* author of
### The Strength of Saints

In *The Year of the Sawdust Man,* we first meet Nissa and follow the story of her mother leaving the family. In the second book, *Nissa's Place,* Nissa has to step out of her mother's shadow to have a life of her own. *The Strength of Saints* is the third book about Nissa. In it, she must discover if she has the strength to do the right thing in a racially divided town.

In my writing process, I don't plan the book ahead of time. I see where the character leads me.

I began writing novels at age twelve. Back then, I started writing with a definite idea of what I wanted people to learn as a result of the book. The books were more like infomercials than literature! One of my college professors said, "You have to get rid of your agenda. You must let the message come out of the story."

Since I wanted to be an actor and a writer, my approach to writing evolved to combine both: I become the characters. I have a strong affinity to my characters. When I think of the story, it all comes out of the character I am following. As a result, I am as surprised as Nissa when she realizes she could not build just one library in this town. She did the best she could in the situation.

While the first two novels come out of Nissa's development as a person and her relationship with her family, *The Strength of Saints* is as much about the society she lives in as it is about her. This was a different experience for me. Nissa's life, before this point, was so insular. She had frequently taken on the role of caretaker for her family. Now she has taken on the role of caretaker for her community. Nissa thinks the two libraries will be appreciated, but there are diverse opinions, especially within the African-American community. There is not one opinion. This, like real life, evolves through story.

One component of creating a character that is fascinating to me as a writer is how multifaceted each character is. The knowledge Nissa gains by creating the library is complex: She learns about herself, her family, her town, and ultimately her country.

In addition to writing, I teach children's literature at the university level. I challenge my students to stop looking at books as teaching tools. A book can't teach a person anything. Reading is a reciprocal process, a relationship between what the book and the teacher have to offer and what the child brings and takes away. What the child takes away will be different for each child and for each time they read the book. A reader once complimented one of my novels, saying, "I didn't realize the book was so funny until I read it a second time." This shows the multilayered nature of a book. The second time, the book is new, yet familiar.

I hope readers carry new things away when they look at or think about any book I've written. I love watching a movie a second time and reading a book a second time. I am glad my books have complexities to review again and again. I hope, too, that reading about Nissa suggests a lot of questions to children about navigating their way in a family, about standing up for what they believe is the right thing to do, and about differences in perspective. Nissa figures out the danger of making assumptions about what is best for others. She begins to look at situations from different angles. Through this act, she gains more respect and understanding for people.

CHAPTER 13

# SOCIAL CHANGE: ISSUES AND ACTION

> If we have learned one thing from our past,
> it is that to live through dramatic events
> is not enough; one has to share them
> and transform them into acts of conscience.
>
> ELIE WIESEL, AUTHOR

Social change by its very nature brings with it a call to action. Change can't happen without awareness, movement, and momentum. The need for social change is frequently rooted in intolerance. This intolerance can be focused on issues of race or ethnicity, religion, sex, poverty, sexual orientation, physical ability, or immigration status among others. It can be rooted in simple ignorance or stereotypes and bloom into prejudice, discrimination, or even hate crimes. In all of its many facets, intolerance is something to recognize, discuss, and finally, address. Sometimes classroom discussion can work wonders at opening minds and eyes alike, but that can be just the beginning.

Social and political action are often the direct result of the need for change. The action can take many forms: raising community awareness through letters to the editor, making public service announcements that air on local cable, and participating in the actual democratic process by speaking at city council meetings or writing letters to Congress. Students have been involved in establishing a much-needed community youth center, working for inclusion in government advisory committees, and even working against unjust actions such as slavery in the Sudan. Social change can be local *and* global in its scope and ambition.

Social change can also be the key to achieving real depth in service learning by driving students to investigate public policy, question the world around them, extend their practice into new areas, and encourage their peers to become active in the civic process. However, there can be some challenges that come with this particular kind of service learning. Results can take time to achieve, and curriculum requirements may push you to move on to the next lesson or activity, leaving opportunities behind.

You may also find yourself working with students who are unaware or disengaged. They may be apathetic or even angry because they feel powerless: "We're just kids. What can we do?" Some students are reluctant. They're told "You need to give back to the community," but they don't believe that they've received much from it yet and think that whatever they have to offer the community doesn't want. Civic engagement and democratic processes also may not seem real to students whose only opportunity to participate in "government" are school elections that are frequently more about popularity than ideas.

You may not face these issues, but they are real challenges for some young people and the educators who work with them. Integrating service learning into your curriculum, extending projects through multiple grades or classes so they are built upon year after year, and making project results visible to the community are all ways to mitigate these challenges.

Your students will find themselves questioning a variety of assumptions as they learn about social change issues. Do people have equal access to vote? Is life in a new country always better for immigrants than the one they left behind? How does economic status impact recreational, educational, and employment opportunities? These questions show that your students are beginning to look at familiar issues in new ways.

More good news is that as students learn about their world—the issues, the problems, the people and programs helping to create social change—they begin to find their own place as social activists. This is as true for reluctant students as it is for enthusiastic ones. Young people of all ages want their beliefs and actions to have value and relevance, and they will respond when offered a challenge, even when it comes with hard work and struggle. Often they are surprised at what they can accomplish when they set their minds and hearts on it.

> Until the great mass of the people shall be filled with the sense of responsibility for each other's welfare, social justice can never be attained.
>
> HELEN KELLER, AUTHOR

## Preparation: Getting Ready for Service Learning Involving Social Change

The following activities can be used in the preparation stage to promote learning and skill development related to social change issues. These activities can be used with different age ranges during preparation to help your students examine key issues through research, analyze community needs, and gain the knowledge they need to effectively contribute to the design of their service plan. Since literature is often an important part of preparation, you can find recommended titles on this theme in the Social Change: Issues and Action Bookshelf later in this chapter.

***Activity: Vocabulary That Matters.*** Prejudice, stereotype, discrimination, tolerance—these are influences that shape our ideas and actions. What do they mean? Even young children can learn these words and concepts, and recognize the behaviors that promote positive ways of interacting with others or stop the negative ways. The following activities can get students thinking about their beliefs and local social issues, so they are better able to design projects that promote communication and tolerance both within the school and the larger community.

- *A Look at Prejudice*. Students can examine and discuss the roots of the word, *pre* and *judge*. How does prejudice happen? How do we learn attitudes about others? Students can discuss the quote, "You can't judge a book by its cover," and then identify the various "covers" or categories they use to judge people. Examples of these "covers" can include: size, race, language ability, athleticism, religion, wealth.
- *Recognizing Stereotypes*. Examine the term beginning with the roots of the word. A stereotype can be defined as an oversimplified generalization about a particular group, race, or sex, which usually carries derogatory implications. Using different forms of media, including television programs, print advertisements, and children's books, students can learn to recognize stereotypes. Create a simple checklist for students to identify tokenism, inaccurate information, favoritism, or ridicule.
- *Discrimination Happens*. Students can look at historical examples of discrimination, particularly with youth. Have students write a list of words or short phrases that describe a time they felt discriminated against as a young person. Then turn these into either collaborative class poetry, short paragraphs, creative nonfiction stories, or essays. Beginning with their own experiences can lead into next examining discrimination against others—ethnic groups, elders, people in poverty, and so on.
- *Teaching Tolerance*. Ask each student to think of a time he or she felt "different." Students often think of wearing glasses, speaking a different language from others, being unable to hit a baseball, or feeling left out of a social gathering. Younger children can share these stories and talk about ways to increase respect and understanding for the experiences of others. Older students can draw an image that represents their experience at the top of a page. Underneath, students can make two columns placing "respecting others" and "knowledge and understanding" at the top of each. In each column, students articulate their thoughts and feelings that emanate under that heading. From these activities, ask students to consider, "What is tolerance?" How can we respect, learn about, and appreciate others who are both similar and different from ourselves?

  Tolerance.org, a Web project of the Southern Poverty Law Center, has interactive pages for kids and teens about issues of tolerance, as well as many teacher resources to assist with and expand these activities. (See Web site resources listed on page 188.)

***Activity: Social Commentary***. Where do we find social commentary in today's media? And how do people get their ideas and opinions into the public arena? These are important questions for students to address and think about as they start preparing to work for social change. There are many different kinds of media that students can explore and learn to use. Consider these options:

- *Fact or Opinion*. Compare two newspaper articles on a similar topic—one that is a standard news story and one that is an editorial. Have students find as many similarities and differences as possible, and then create a chart of do's and don'ts for each category. They can continue their research by reading books that clarify the differences, or having a speaker visit the class. A high school newspaper editor can be an ideal visitor for an elementary or middle school class, or contact your local newspaper.
- *Dear Editor*. Select several letters to the editor for your students to review. Have the students form small groups and give one letter to each group. What is different about this form of writing in comparison to a news article or editorial? Ask each group to write their own sample letter to the editor that conveys an idea, an emotion, or both.
- *Political Cartoons*. Find several political cartoons on different subjects. Depending on the age of the students, have them identify how this medium uses humor or satire to tell a point of view. Are there consistent themes or symbols that appear? (For example, donkeys represent the Democratic Party and elephants represent the Republican Party.) Why are the cartoonists choosing those symbols? Show several to convey the variety of approaches used by these artists.
- *PSAs*. Public service announcements (PSAs) inform people about a variety of issues, including voter registration, eliminating discrimination, gun safety, and the hazards of cigarette smoking. Students can view examples of PSAs on the Internet at Web sites like *www.rockthevote.org*. (Rock the Vote is an organization that mobilizes young people to create positive social and political change and uses media campaigns to increase young voter turnout.) Students can research how PSAs are used on radio, on television, on the Internet, and even in movie theaters to educate and inform. If media facilities are available through the school or community (often through cable access), students can apply what they've learned to create social marketing campaigns that can make a considerable impact. Children as young as second graders have used PSAs as a vehicle to educate the community about important issues, to raise awareness around social action projects, and to invite participation from the community at large.

### Find Out More About Social Change

To learn more about these issues and to get ideas for service and action, visit these Web sites and organizations online:

***www.freethechildren.org*** Free the Children, an organization founded by then teenager Craig Kielburger, works internationally on many issues related to children's rights, including education, health, and youth leadership.

***www.iabolish.com*** The American Anti-Slavery Group includes the S.T.O.P. (Slavery that Oppresses People) Program that educates and empowers students from fourth grade through high school by involving them in abolitionist activities. The site features free curricula and activism guides for teachers.

***www.tolerance.org*** Tolerance.org, a Web project of the Southern Poverty Law Center, promotes and supports anti-bias activism in every venue of American life and includes information and resources for teachers, parents, and children on fighting hate and promoting tolerance. Be sure to check out "Mix It Up at Lunch Day."

***pbskids.org/zoom/action*** Zoom Into Action, a Web site of PBS's Zoom television program, has service learning project examples and resources for kids, teachers, and parents. Young people up to age 12 are invited to share their service learning stories.

***www.kidsvotingusa.org*** Kids Voting USA supplies educational kits and encourages kids to vote with their parents at the polls by casting ballots (similar in content to the official ballot) at Kids Voting USA locations.

***www.amnestyusa.org*** and ***www.amnestyusa.org/aikids*** At Amnesty International and Amnesty International Kids students can learn about and participate in human rights advocacy efforts.

***www.dosomething.org*** Do Something is an organization that helps young people get involved in their communities by identifying the issues they care about and creating projects that turn ideas into action.

# Making Connections Across the Curriculum

Some service learning activities naturally lend themselves to interdisciplinary work and making connections across the curriculum. These connections strengthen and broaden student learning, helping them meet academic standards. More than likely, you'll be looking for these connections and ways to encourage them well before the students ever start working on service learning activities. As with the entire service learning process, it helps to remain flexible, because some connections can be spontaneously generated by the questions raised throughout and by the needs of the project. To help you think about cross-curricular connections and where you can look for them, the Curricular Web for this chapter (page 190) gives examples of many different ways this theme can be used in different academic areas. (The service learning scenarios in the next section of the chapter also demonstrate various ways this theme can be used across the curriculum.)

# Service Learning Scenarios:
## Ideas for Action

Ready to take action? What follows are projects that have been successfully carried out by elementary, middle, or high school students. Most of these scenarios and examples explicitly include some aspects of preparation, action, reflection, and demonstration. These scenarios can be a rich source of project, resource, and curriculum ideas for you to draw upon. While the grade levels are given as a reference, most project ideas can be adapted to suit younger or older students, and many are suitable for cross-age partnerships.

***Young Advocates: Preschool.*** In one Pasadena, California, preschool, a student remarked, "That's not the color of *my* skin!" when he was handed a "flesh-colored" adhesive bandage for a cut. This comment led to an impromptu classroom survey. Each child took a turn to see if the bandage matched her or his skin color. Within this classroom's diverse population, 10 percent more or less matched, 40 percent of the children came close, but 50 percent definitely didn't match. After discussing how melanin contributed to the color of their skin and reading books that featured children of all skin colors, the kids decided to write the bandage company and report their results. They also suggested that the company find a new term to describe the product. The company responded with a thank-you letter and another box of "flesh-colored" bandages! Still, the seeds of activism had been planted.

> Pick battles big enough to matter,
> small enough to win.
> JONATHAN KOZOL, AUTHOR

***Kids that Type: Grade 1.*** After hearing the book *Click, Clack, Moo: Cows That Type* read aloud by their teacher, first-grade students decided they wanted to be "Kids That Type." They decided to look for improvements needed in their surroundings and to write letters to start things changing for the better. First they walked around their school and found several areas on the playground that were in disrepair. They met with the principal to learn more about getting the playground fixed and found out that three requests had already been submitted to the district office. The children composed a letter and visited other first-grade classes, read their letter aloud, and asked for signatures from their peers. The mailed letter was signed by over 100 children. The repair was made within three weeks. For the "Kids That Type," this would be the first of many letters.

***Youth Helping Youth: Grade 3.*** An elementary student saw a television newscast about children living in shelters because they had been victims of domestic violence. The student initiated a discussion of the issue in class, and fellow students wanted to learn more and find ways to help. A social service worker identified by a parent showed the class an age-appropriate video and answered questions. The class generated a range of options for helping and presented their ideas to other classrooms at various grade levels. The students collected needed materials for children living in shelters, including backpacks with school supplies, journals and pens, and current magazines. Letter writing to local businesses assisted in skill development and yielded a substantial quantity of donated goods. Students also discussed showing respect to peers living in a variety of settings, including shelters.

# Social Change Across the Curriculum

## Social Change

### *English/Language Arts*

- Read a biography or autobiography about a person who has worked for social change
- Compare newspaper editorials to learn about methods and styles used to persuade public opinion
- Discuss and write an essay on how young people experience stereotyping and prejudice

### *Social Studies/History*

- Study how each branch of state and federal government directly impacts the life of your community
- Read about Cesar Chavez and the migrant farm worker movement; research current migrant worker issues in your area
- Learn how voting rights were won by suffragettes, during the Civil Rights movement, and in the aftermath of South Africa's apartheid era

### *Languages*

- Create public service videos in different languages about the school, local government, or helpful organizations; distribute through local agencies and cable access
- Learn about opportunities to serve in other countries, including the Peace Corps
- Study the needs and challenges of refugees being resettled in the United States, including language and prejudice

### *Theater, Music, & Visual Arts*

- Adapt a piece of literature about social change for a reader's theater performance
- Find out how folk music has been used as social and political messages, inspiring people to learn and to take action
- Examine murals as expressions of public opinion; include graffiti art in the research

### *Math*

- Create a public opinion poll regarding an issue in the community; survey, tabulate, and report student responses
- Write biographies of famous mathematicians and the impact of their work for society
- Examine the cost and benefits of fund-raising events that aid the community; develop ideas to cut costs and keep records

### *Physical Education*

- Study Title IX of the Educational Amendments of 1972, which bans sex discrimination in schools and especially impacts school athletics
- Research playground safety information and then visit a local public playground; document any needed changes and make recommendations for improvement to the appropriate local government agencies
- Research how physical challenges such as walk-a-thons are designed to engage the community and also benefit social causes

### *Computer*

- Ask local community agencies, such as shelters, meals-on-wheels, or immigrant centers how students can help with computer technology needs
- Create a database of agencies that need student assistance through service learning projects or as volunteers and a database of project ideas and student skills that community agencies can access
- Through the Internet, research careers in public service; create a Web page with links to service agencies and organizations in your community

### *Science*

- Find out how economics impact decisions on environmental issues such as waste disposal, incinerator placement, and toxic site cleanups
- Research community needs of people in low-income housing for safety equipment such as smoke alarms or earthquake emergency kits
- Learn about the connection between science and public relations by researching how social marketing campaigns are used to educate communities about health issues

***Identifying a Female State Hero: Grades 4 and 5.*** While preparing for a visit to their state capitol, fourth graders in Connecticut learned about the state flowers, state song, and state flag. When the time came to tour the capitol building, they found a huge statue of a male "state hero" in the rotunda. The students wondered, "Is there a female state hero?" This observation redirected their course of study. Step by step, the students demonstrated their capabilities as they defined what heroes are and what actions are heroic, researched appropriate female role models from their state, and debated their selection. After learning how a bill becomes a law, they found a state legislator willing to introduce a bill that named their designee, Prudence Crandall, as the Connecticut state heroine because of her stand against prejudice. In spite of the students' informed presentation to the legislature, their bill failed. The kids regrouped. As fifth graders, they created a play about their hero's life and toured the state to gather signatures from the populace in support of their new bill. The second time around, the bill passed; and again, kids made history.

***Creating a Web of Opportunity: Grade 6.*** Middle school students in computer classes found their talents valued. Local nonprofit organizations were in dire straits. Some were being bombarded with more requests than they could handle for youth volunteer opportunities; others were not contacted at all. The need: building kid-friendly, information-rich Web pages for the organizations so young people could learn about specific issues and base their involvement on social concern. At first, students thought they could create dozens of Web pages in a flash, but instead they discovered they had to slow down to learn enough about the issues to create meaningful connections. In the process, the students shared knowledge about the agencies in their English and social studies classes, which led to other service learning activities. Several students began to volunteer their computer skills after school to help with agency needs. The students also made presentations to high school humanities classes, where service learning was part of the curriculum. Feedback from the agencies was extremely positive, and many other agencies wanted to "sign on."

***Turning Dreams into Reality: Grades 5–8.*** Middle school students in Baltimore, Maryland, realized that kids need a place to go after school to keep them off the streets. They decided to accomplish an ambitious plan: raise enough funds to open a youth center. With teacher support and a written agreement to see the project to completion, they went into action. Through a comprehensive letter-writing and phone-calling campaign, students have raised over $250,000 from government, nonprofit, and corporate grants. This money will help buy and renovate a house into a youth center for their neighborhood. Experience and determination have enriched these students with confidence achieved from learning to write grants, make spread sheets, develop budgets, establish community partnerships, and present their ideas to their city council, and most importantly, to work as a team. In the words of one "Youth Dreamer," this is "life-changing for the better."

***Unity and Diversity Week: Grades 6–8.*** "We had been studying about the Civil Rights movement in social studies, and we decided to create a day of school unity. But once we began listing our ideas, the day grew into a week's worth of activities, and we needed more help. Every social studies class in the entire school took part!" The eighth-grade students in this social studies class did not imagine their idea would have such an impact on students, teachers, parents, and the community, but everyone helped turn "possibilities" into "plans." The students wanted to create events that would stimulate ongoing conversation and a veritable buzz of excitement. What occurred? English classes assigned students to read either *If You Come Softly* or *The Circuit* for discussions and writings on social inequalities and racism in society. In social studies, sixth-grade classes used *Through My Eyes*, while seventh- and eighth-grade classes read and discussed selections from *Linda Brown, You Are Not Alone: The Brown v. Board of Education Decision*. Students delivered famous speeches, and choirs sang about peace and harmony at lunch rallies. Every social studies class had guest speakers from community agencies who led workshops on local issues of tolerance related to immigrants, people with special needs, and racial issues. During "Unity Tonight," students and teachers performed music and slam poetry for the invited community. On the last day of the week, the students who had initiated the Unity Week project led reflection sessions in every social studies class. In addition to finding out what was learned, they asked, "What ongoing activities can we establish at school to continue building unity and community?"

***Student Planners: Grades 6–10.*** Students in a university course on facility planning and management worked with the local school district to identify a school in need of remodeling, additions, or new facilities. They surveyed the buildings and grounds; interviewed students, faculty, and administrators; and researched the history of the school and buildings. Then they worked to redesign existing areas they considered to be misused, as well as to design additional space for present or future needs. Middle and high school students became actively engaged in the process, attending university classes, offering feedback and ideas, and preparing drawings and presenting them to the college students, school administrators, and parents. The process allowed students, who are often neglected in the creation of schools and other public places, to become involved, learn community organizing methods, and make decisions.

***A Mural to Honor Social Change: Grade 7.*** A California middle school humanities class wanted to make a mural on an outside school wall. They had been reading biographies and at first wanted to represent their favorite people in the books they had read. A student suggested finding *real* people in the community to honor and the other students decided this was perfect. To find their subjects, they created a public service announcement for the local radio station and wrote a story for the neighborhood newspaper asking for nominations. They selected eight people who represented the community's diversity and had made a variety of different community contributions. Students conducted interviews, made sketches of their honorees, and, with the help of a local artist, completed a ten-foot mural. The students also wrote a booklet of stories about how they selected their mural subjects and what their accomplishments were. The cover of the booklet is the mural.

***Voter Education Project: Grades 7–8.*** To make an impact on voters in the 2000 elections, students in Chicago planned two approaches. First, they developed a voter education guide highlighting the presidential candidates. Then the students researched the candidates and the issues to develop the informational guide, which was distributed to students, parents, and community residents. The second approach was helping register new voters at their school by advertising to parents and unregistered voters in their community. The students teamed up with community organizations to make the registration drive a success. Teachers reported that students followed the election closely and had a true investment in the process. For follow-up, students worked with the high school to make sure each eighteen-year-old received a birthday card with a voter registration form inside. Next step? Students hope to examine school government election procedures and transform "popularity" elections into elections involving substance and issues.

***Taking a Preventive Approach: Grades 7–10.*** A nonprofit organization in Delaware helps teens take a preventive approach to teen pregnancy and drug use. Students complete a series of classes to become mentors for others; to have this responsibility, students must demonstrate the ability to model and communicate ideas and behaviors. Then they form two committees: an action committee that develops programs for local schools and a newsletter committee that creates a quarterly publication to be handed out at schools and low-income housing developments. To make sure the skills being learned are connected to the classroom curriculum, partnerships are maintained between the agency and the schools. Schools are invited to be part of the process by helping to recruit mentors, identifying students who are at-risk academically, advertising school credit for service, integrating the appropriate learning skills into the curriculum, and encouraging students to participate in the Student Action Committee and submit work for newsletter publications.

***Emergency Preparation: Grade 8.*** When earthquakes, tornadoes, or hurricanes occur in their community, students usually learn first-hand the meaning of "being prepared." They may also learn that people of lower socioeconomic groups lack the resources for preparation. In partnership with a social service agency, students in California took part in a countywide survey to find out what natural emergency resources were available for low-income families and elders and what was missing. Their campaign included collecting donated merchandise, preparing emergency kits, and notifying the public of the kits' availability. In language classes, students assisted with translation of promotional flyers and instructions for use of the kits. Presentations were made in adult education programs. Displays were set up at high school sports events. The community response was most favorable.

***A Site to Behold: Grades 9–11.*** Was there really a sacred Native American site on the school campus? The rumor had been floating around for years, but finally an American history class in Los Angeles decided to study the history of the school site and find out whether the story was myth or reality. Students discovered that in fact a stream on the school's site had been important to the indigenous people in the area. In collaboration with local Native American groups, the students set out to restore the area. Overcoming hurdles with the school board and the city took time and skill. The project was eventually handed to the next year's class, so more students became invested in the process. The day the area was permanently restored and opened to the public was a festive community celebration bringing together people of diverse cultures and ages.

***Acting Out: Grades 9–12.*** Community education is a major focus for drama students at a magnet high school for the arts. Students devote several hours per week to developing plays to perform for children. The plays have a variety of themes related to important community topics identified through surveys and community feedback: diversity and tolerance, fire safety, and school violence. Students are sharing their methods through a documentary describing the "how-tos" of using theater as a vehicle for service learning.

***Advocates for Elders: Grades 11–12.*** High school students completely absorbed in reading the state regulations for convalescent homes? While this may not sound "normal," it did occur. After making several visits to a residential care and convalescent facility to conduct interviews, students in Minnesota became upset by what they perceived as poor care. Upon reviewing state regulations and debating interpretations, students composed a letter outlining their concerns and suggesting ways in which they could provide assistance to the facility. They added that they were prepared to send a copy of the letter to the state licensing agency. The response was favorable. The residential care director took the recommendations seriously, outlined a course of action, and even thanked the students, inviting them to return. Two students were hired for summer jobs.

***A School Out of Balance: Grade 12.*** High school seniors wanted to draw attention to what they believed to be educational inequities in their Santa Monica, California, school. After investigating issues of racial discrimination on their campus, they made a proposal to the school administration to plan and lead a one-day summit to address these issues and begin a plan to make significant changes. The event brought together students, parents, faculty, administration, the district superintendent, and community members. The program began with testimonials from African-American and Latino students regarding bias on the part of counselors and teachers. Next, a local education policy expert presented a study of inequities within the school district based on race and socioeconomic background. Finally, in small groups, participants discussed the findings and proposed recommendations and follow-up plans, to be compiled, summarized, and published by the student leadership group. Additional meetings were scheduled to factor this information into the plans for restructuring the high school into smaller learning communities.

> As young people, we have learned that knowledge is power. Child labor is a very complex issue but that is no excuse to ignore the problem. Who better than children to feel and understand the needs of other children?
>
> CRAIG KIELBURGER, AUTHOR

# The Social Change: Issues and Action Bookshelf

The Social Change: Issues and Action Bookshelf is an annotated bibliography of works covering a broad spectrum of topics. To help you find books relevant to your particular projects, the book chart classifies the titles into several topic areas: historical perspectives, planning for action, prejudice and discrimination, and working for change.

In general, the bookshelf features:

- An annotated bibliography arranged and alphabetized by title according to the general categories of nonfiction (N), picture books (P), and fiction (F). For nonfiction and fiction, length and recommended grade levels are included. The entries in the picture book category do not include suggested grade levels, since they can be successfully used with all ages.
- A chart organized by topic and category to help you find books relevant to particular projects.
- Recommendations from service learning colleagues and experts that include a book summary and ideas for service learning connections. (The number of recommended books varies in each bookshelf.)

## Social Change: Issues and Action Bookshelf Topics

| Topics | Books | Category |
|---|---|---|
| ***Historical Perspectives*** The past is a rich source of information and examples of action undertaken by individuals and groups working for the benefit of many. Their stories influence our own. | *Before We Were Free* | F |
| | *Out of Bounds: Seven Stories of Conflict and Hope* | F |
| | *Passage to Freedom: The Sugihara Story* * | P |
| | *Pink and Say* | P |
| | *Sisters in Strength: American Women Who Made a Difference* * | N |
| | *Slap Your Sides* | F |
| | *Spitting Image* | F |
| | *This Land Is My Land* | P |
| | *Through My Eyes* | N |
| | *We Are the Many: A Picture Book of American Indians* * | N |
| | *We Were There, Too! Young People in U.S. History* * | N |
| | *You Forgot Your Skirt, Amelia Bloomer!* | P |
| ***Planning for Action*** Are you ready for action? These books can help with the key stage of preparation. Information, planning tools, ideas, and *The Little Engine That Could* are waiting. | *The Kid's Guide to Service Projects: Over 500 Service Ideas for Young People Who Want to Make a Difference* * | N |
| | *The Kid's Guide to Social Action: How to Solve the Social Problems You Choose—and Turn Creative Thinking into Positive Action* * | N |
| | *The Little Engine That Could* | P |
| | *Stand Up for Your Rights* * | N |
| | *Teen Power Politics: Make Yourself Heard* * | N |

*continued* ⟶

| Topics | Books | Category |
|---|---|---|
| ***Prejudice and Discrimination*** These books delve into such topics as prejudice, stereotypes, discrimination, and racial intolerance. (Many books in other theme bookshelves, especially the Immigrants Bookshelf, address these topics.) The stories also tell us about strength of spirit, character, and resolve to overcome injustice. | *Animal Farm* | F |
| | *Bat 6* | F |
| | *Eagle Song* | F |
| | *The House on Mango Street* | F |
| | *If You Come Softly* | F |
| | *Issues in Racism* | N |
| | *Jemma's Journey* | P |
| | *Linda Brown, You Are Not Alone: The Brown v. Board of Education Decision* | N |
| | *My Name is María Isabel* | F |
| | *Smoky Nights* (see page 99) | P |
| | *To Kill a Mockingbird* | F |
| | *Walk Two Moons* | F |
| | *White Lilacs* | F |
| | ***Also see titles on the Immigrants Bookshelf*** | |
| ***Working for Change*** In *Something Beautiful*, a girl removes one word of graffiti from her front door. A beginning. The path of social change is a long, well-traveled road, and these examples guide us and remind us of what we can accomplish. | *Big Mouth and Ugly Girl* (see page 99) | F |
| | *Click, Clack, Moo: Cows That Type* | P |
| | *Dream Freedom* * | F |
| | *Edwina Victorious* * | F |
| | *Free the Children: A Young Man's Personal Crusade Against Child Labor* * | N |
| | *Generation Fix: Young Ideas for a Better World* * | N |
| | *Hoot* * (see page 86) | F |
| | *Hope Was Here* * | F |
| | *In the Time of the Butterflies* * | F |
| | *It's Our World, Too! Young People Who Are Making a Difference: How They Do It—How You Can Too* * | N |
| | *Kids with Courage: True Stories About Young People Making a Difference* * | N |
| | *A Life Like Mine: How Children Live Around the World* * | N |
| | *Listen to Us: The World's Working Children* * | N |
| | *Pay It Forward* * | F |
| | *Rabble Rousers: 20 Women Who Made a Difference* | N |
| | *¡Sí, Se Puede! Yes, We Can! Janitor Strike in L.A.* * | P |
| | *Something Beautiful* * | P |
| | *Summer Wheels* * (see page 99) | P |
| | *Vote!* * | N |
| | *We Need to Go to School: Voices of the Rugmark Children* * | N |

Page references are given for books that do not appear in the Social Change: Issues and Action Bookshelf but that can be found in the bookshelf lists of other chapters.

* These books include examples of young people in service-providing roles.

> I recognize no rights but human rights—I know nothing of men's rights and women's rights.
>
> ANGELINA E. GRIMKÉ, SUFFRAGETTE

## Nonfiction: Social Change

***Free the Children: A Young Man's Personal Crusade Against Child Labor*** by Craig Kielburger (HarperCollins, 1998). In 1995, at the age of twelve, Craig read a newspaper article about a Pakistani four-year-old who was sold into slavery. Outraged by this child's account of degradation and forced labor, Craig and his friends sought information and later founded Free the Children, a human rights organization. This book chronicles Craig's trips to South Asia to save children forced into labor. 316pp., grades 7–12

***Generation Fix: Young Ideas for a Better World*** by Elizabeth Rusch (Beyond Words Publishing, 2002). As Sol Kelley-Jones, age fourteen, says, "Youth are totally on the front lines of every single movement in history." The stories of twenty young activists who have committed themselves to social action give credibility to this statement. The author provides an informative introduction to each of the book's seven themes, including peace, hunger, and health concerns. A comprehensive list of organizations is included. 176pp., grades 4–12

***Issues in Racism*** by Mary E. Williams (Lucent Books, 2000). Beginning with the torture and murder of James Byrd Jr. in June 1998, this book examines the dynamics of racism. How serious a problem is racism? How does society respond to racial diversity? Is there hope for race relations? This survey presents information and that can stimulate debate and inspire social action. 112pp., young adult

***It's Our World, Too! Young People Who Are Making a Difference: How They Do It—How You Can Too*** by Phillip Hoose (Farrar, Straus and Giroux, 1993). A collection of stories about young people who have made significant contributions, some with the help of a school or organization. Includes "A Handbook for Young Activists." 166pp., all ages

***The Kid's Guide to Service Projects: Over 500 Service Ideas for Young People Who Want to Make a Difference*** by Barbara Lewis (Free Spirit Publishing, 1995). Ideas for both simple and large-scale service projects for young people. 192pp., grades 4–12

***The Kid's Guide to Social Action: How to Solve the Social Problems You Choose—and Turn Creative Thinking into Positive Action*** by Barbara Lewis (Free Spirit Publishing, 1998). What began as a way to help sixth graders address a toxic waste problem became a resource guide for students and teachers to learn social action skills and solve problems on a local, state, and national level. Loaded with ideas and reproducible documents. 224pp., grades 4–12

***Kids with Courage: True Stories About Young People Making a Difference*** by Barbara Lewis (Free Spirit Publishing, 1992). These stories tell how young people are helping our communities and our world by improving the environment, fighting crime, and taking risks. 192pp., grades 4 & up

***A Life Like Mine: How Children Live Around the World*** (DK Publishing and UNICEF, 2002). In this book filled with vivid photographs, we meet eighteen children from around the globe and visit 180 countries. Are the basic needs of water, food, and somewhere to live being met for children? Do children have the right to be safe from war? Does every child deserve the right to play and to know his or her rights? By examining the themes of survival, development, protection, and participation, we see how children pursue a good life for themselves and their communities often amidst seemingly insurmountable challenges. 127pp., grades 4–7

***Linda Brown, You Are Not Alone: The Brown v. Board of Education Decision*** edited by Joyce Carol Thomas (Hyperion, 2003). The Brown v. Board of Education decision affected the life of every child in the United States and provoked a range of reactions. This book includes personal reflections from ten accomplished authors of children and young adult literature. Their essays, stories, and poems capture the many viewpoints from 1954 and encourage us to consider the impact of social change resulting from this historic event. Contributors include Jerry Spinelli, Katherine Paterson, and Leona Nicholas Welch. 114pp., grades 5–8

***Listen to Us: The World's Working Children*** by Jane Springer (Groundwood Books, 1997). "Who says childhood is golden?" The photographs, profiles, and statistics presented in this comprehensive survey of child labor practices expose horrors experienced by young people around the world. Includes "Kids Helping Kids," resources, and glossary. 96pp., grades 5–12

***Rabble Rousers: 20 Women Who Made a Difference*** by Cheryl Harness (Dutton, 2003). Twenty women dared to defy the status quo and pursue their vision for "Life, Liberty, and the Pursuit of Happiness." To others of their time, they appeared "unladylike, dangerous, crazy, and radical" yet they understood that our republic is truly founded on the power that lies in three words: "We the people." 64pp., grades 3–6

***Sisters in Strength: American Women Who Made a Difference*** by Yona Zeldis McDonough (Henry Holt, 2000). Learn about eleven women who shaped history as they triumphed over adversity, made huge sacrifices, and held fast to their beliefs. 48pp., grades 4–8

***Stand Up for Your Rights*** by Peace Child International (World Books, 1998). This book about human rights, written by and for the young people of the world, presents a global vision of needs and activism. It includes a review of the Universal Declaration of Human Rights and poses the question, "What are we doing about it?" Packed with information, resources, and ideas. 96pp., grades 4–8

***Teen Power Politics: Make Yourself Heard*** by Sara Jane Boyers (Millbrook Press, 2000). Wait until adulthood to become involved in politics and make a difference? Not with this book in hand! From the initial list of government decisions that affect youth, through a history of voting rights, to examples of and strategies for youth activism, the ideas and resources are inspiring and motivating. "It's your world. There is no longer any excuse not to be in it." 120pp., young adult

***Through My Eyes*** by Ruby Bridges (Scholastic, 1999). An act of courage by her family led Ruby Bridges to be the first black child to attend an all-white school in New Orleans in the early days of social activism for school integration. Through the eyes of a six-year-old, return to this critical time in American history. 64pp., grades 4–12

***Vote!*** by Eileen Christelow (Clarion, 2003). It's time for a mayoral election, but what does it mean to vote? Does voting matter? How does a person register to vote or campaign for a candidate? What happens if the results are too close to announce a winner? In this mixture of cartoon-style art and text, questions about voting are answered. Also included is a historical timeline of voting rights and a list of resources for additional information. 48pp., grades 1–4

***We Are the Many: A Picture Book of American Indians*** by Doreen Rappaport (HarperCollins, 2002). For thousands of years before Europeans arrived, groups of people now called Indians lived in what is now the United States. "In 1492 more than five hundred languages were spoken." Sixteen men and women, selected from the many American Indians who have made exemplary contributions and achievements, are profiled here, including Tusquantum, Sacajawea, and Maria Tallchief. Each story re-creates a significant moment in the person's life. Includes a pronunciation guide and additional resources. 32pp., grades K–4

***We Need to Go to School: Voices of the Rugmark Children*** by Tanya Roberts-Davis (Groundwood Books, 2001). At age sixteen, the author traveled to Nepal to live with children who had spent years in forced labor in carpet factories. Now in Rugmark rehabilitation centers attending school, these children tell their stories through oral accounts, poetry, and pictures. Opportunities to become active in working to end child labor are included, along with other resources, a glossary, and an overview of Nepal. 48pp., grades 5–12

***We Were There, Too! Young People in U.S. History*** by Phillip Hoose (Farrar, Straus and Giroux, 2001). What role have young people played in American history? How have they made their mark, their contribution? In this comprehensive collection of stories and photographs, we see that young people, from the boys who sailed with Columbus to the young activists of today, have been a significant force in history. An indispensable reference and an inspiring book to read. 264pp., all ages

> In the 1830s, the mill women and girls began to stand up for themselves, organizing strikes for more pay and shorter hours. Eleven-year-old Harriet Hanson, also the daughter of a rooming-house keeper, was one of the fifteen hundred girls who walked out of the Lowell mill in 1836. . . . Harriet never regretted what she did. Many years later she said that leading that walk-out was one of the best moments of her life.
>
> FROM *WE WERE THERE, TOO! YOUNG PEOPLE IN U.S. HISTORY*

## Picture Books: Social Change

***Click, Clack, Moo: Cows That Type*** by Doreen Cronin (Simon & Schuster, 2000). When Farmer Brown's cows find a typewriter in the barn, they start making demands and go "on strike" when the farmer refuses to give them what they want. As the other animals join in, what will the farmer do?

> Dear Farmer Brown,
>
> The barn is very cold at night. We'd like some electric blankets.
>
> Sincerely,
>
> The Cows.
>
> FROM *CLICK, CLACK, MOO: COWS THAT TYPE*

***Jemma's Journey*** by Trevor Romain (Boyds Mills Press, 2002). Grandma kept telling about the "old days" in Ocoee. Ocoee was a town where "peaceful black folk . . . jawed about the lives of people who lived there." Then, on November 2, 1920, two black men tried to vote on election day; riots followed, resulting in many deaths and one lynching. When Jemma hears how the lynching tree was cut down, this young girl sets out to honor her grandmother's memory and reminds us to "always remember to never forget."

**Recommendation from the Field**
*by Don Hill, Youth Service California*

*The Little Engine That Could* by Watty Piper (Grosset and Dunlap, 1930/1978). This is a delightful picture story about a train laden with toys and food for children who live on the other side of a mountain. When the train engine breaks down, the toys, dolls, and clowns become sad because they know how disappointed all the children will be in the morning.

Three times, the toys, dolls, and clowns plead with strong engines that come by to pull their train over the mountain, but the engines are too proud or selfish to waste their time. When hope has almost gone, a small blue engine stops and listens sympathetically to their pleas. Although the blue engine has never gone over the mountain and does not know if it has enough power, it agrees to try. Slowly the little blue engine makes its way up the mountain, saying to itself, "I think I can, I think I can, I think I can" until it reaches the crest and says, "I thought I could, I thought I could, I thought I could."

This simple story offers much for reflection. Why do powerful engines in this story and in life refuse to help others in need? What helped the little blue engine get to the top of the mountain? When you are trying to do things that are difficult, does it make a difference if you say to yourself "I think I can" rather than "I know I can't"? Can people get extra energy when they are doing something to help others?

To identify service possibilities, discuss the following with students: Is there an unmet need in our school or community where we could be like the little blue engine and try to help—even if we are not sure that we can do what is needed?

***Passage to Freedom: The Sugihara Story*** by Ken Mochizuki (Lee & Low, 1997). In 1940, five-year-old Hiroki Sugihara, the son of the Japanese consul in Lithuania, saw hundreds of Jewish refugees from Poland ask in desperation if Consul Sugihara would write visas for them to escape the Nazi threat. When the Japanese government denied Sugihara's request to issue visas, the Sugihara family decided to do what they could to save thousands of lives, even if it placed their own lives at risk.

***Pink and Say*** by Patricia Polacco (Philomel, 1994). The author's great-grandfather Sheldon "Say" Curtis meets Pinkus "Pink" Aylee during the Civil War. Pink, a black Union soldier, brings Say, a wounded white Union soldier, to his mother. Once Say is healed, the boys must return to their units, only to be confronted by Confederate troops. A tribute to telling stories about the people we meet who touch our lives.

***¡Sí, Se Puede!/Yes, We Can! Janitor Strike in L.A.*** by Diana Cohn (Cinco Puentas Press, 2003). Carlitos, a young boy, is proud of his mother who works long hours for low pay as a janitor. In April of 2000, when 8,000 janitors in Los Angeles put down their mops and brooms and went on strike, his mother is among the leaders. Carlitos wants to help and he does: he joins with other children to make posters and join the marchers. The book includes an essay by author Luis J. Rodriguez, whose father was also a janitor. The inside of the dust jacket is an informative poster that explains the role of labor unions and strikes. In English and Spanish.

***Something Beautiful*** by Sharon Dennis Wyeth (Doubleday, 1998). When a little girl searches in her neighborhood for "something beautiful," she finds that through her actions and sense of community, "something beautiful" can happen.

***This Land Is My Land*** by George Littlechild (Children's Book Press, 1993). Through paintings and words, the author shares the history and experiences of native peoples of the Americas to promote cultural understanding.

***You Forgot Your Skirt, Amelia Bloomer!*** by Shana Corey (Scholastic, 2000). Amelia Bloomer was never one to keep quiet about wrongdoing. No surprise she stood up for women's rights and popularized the wearing of a new style of women's wear—bloomers!

## Fiction: Social Change

***Animal Farm*** by George Orwell (Prentice Hall, 1946). The animals on Manor Farm rebel and chase off Farmer Jones and his men. Subsequently, the animals rule themselves, led by the pigs. Eventually, all the revolution's lofty goals are subverted. This classic allegory contains universal themes that can prompt meaningful discussions about power and privilege, propaganda and journalistic integrity, the class system, and real education/learning. 140pp., young adult

***Bat 6*** by Virginia Euwer Wolff (Scholastic, 1998). The sixth-grade girls of Barlow and Bear Creek Ridge eagerly await their chance to play in the annual softball game, Bat

6. Something is different this year, 1949. World War II is over. Aki and her family return after living in Japanese internment camps. Shazaam, whose father was killed at Pearl Harbor, lives here now. Twenty-one girls tell this story of two communities facing prejudice. 230pp., grades 5–9

***Before We Were Free*** by Julia Alvarez (Knopf, 2003). Anita de la Torre never expected her life to be completely turned upside down by the politics in the Dominican Republic. But by her twelfth birthday, most of her relatives had immigrated to the United States, her uncle is in hiding, her father receives mysterious phone calls, and the secret police regularly search her house. Under the dictatorship of General Trujillo no one is safe. 167pp., young adult

***Dream Freedom*** by Sonia Levitin (Harcourt, 2000). Marcus and his fifth-grade classmates learn of tens of thousands of men, women, and children captured and forced into slavery. Even with his own family problems, Marcus joins in raising money to redeem the slaves. Alternate chapters tell the story of the slaves, the people who enslave them, and the people working for their freedom. Based on a true story and contemporary events. Includes historical background, a bibliography, and ways to help. 178pp., young adult

> Peace is no harder to make than war.
> Both need effort and skill.
>
> FROM *DREAM FREEDOM*

***Eagle Song*** by Joseph Bruchac (Dial, 1997). Danny Bigtree's family moves from the Mohawk reservation to New York City, and Danny cannot fit in. He refuses to sacrifice his cultural identity to make friends. His father provides a lesson in courage for Danny and helps Danny's classmates to feel pride in themselves and move toward peace. 80pp., grades 4–7

***Edwina Victorious*** by Susan Bonners (Farrar, Straus and Giroux, 2000). Mayor Granger has been repairing a playground, transforming a vacant lot, and planning a long needed makeover of the zoo, all inspired by letters received from ninety-year-old community activist Edwina Osgood. However, the letters are actually written by young Edwina Osgood posing as her namesake great-aunt! What happens when the truth is revealed? 131pp., grades 3–6

***Hope Was Here*** by Joan Bauer (Puffin, 2000). When sixteen-year-old Hope moves with her aunt from Brooklyn to Mulroney, Wisconsin, to work in a diner, she finds more cooking than expected. To the town's surprise, diner owner G.T. announces his candidacy to oust the corrupt mayor. Hope and other young people rally together, adding the vital ingredient of youth action to the campaign. Recommended for "City Reads" programs. 186pp., young adult

***The House on Mango Street*** by Sandra Cisneros (Vintage Books, 1991). A series of short vignettes tells the story of Esperanza Cordero, her family, her neighborhood, and her aspirations. While they do not follow a linear plot, the novel's vignettes present a compelling narrative that raises important themes of gender, race, and poverty. For example, the chapter "Those Who Don't" describes the fear felt by strangers who stumble into Esperanza's neighborhood, as well as Esperanza's own anxiety about crossing neighborhood boundaries into areas where she is not surrounded by people of her own race. 110pp., young adult

***If You Come Softly*** by Jacqueline Woodson (Putnam, 1998). Teenagers Jeremiah and Ellie, an interracial couple, confront prejudice from family, strangers, and society. In chapters that alternate between first and third person, we get to know these smart and sensitive characters and experience the shocking conclusion. 198pp., young adult

### Recommendation from the Field

*by David M. Donahue, Assistant Professor of Education, Mills College*

*In the Time of the Butterflies* by Julia Alvarez (Plume Books, 1994). Inspired by a true story, Alvarez blends fact and fiction to tell the story of three Mirabal sisters, known as "the butterflies," who became involved in an underground resistance movement to overthrow Rafael Trujillo, dictator of the Dominican Republic. As a consequence of their work against tyranny, they were murdered in 1960 by government security forces. Dede, the fourth and surviving sister, had refused to join her sisters' efforts for fear of losing her husband and her life. The others, headstrong Minerva, religious Patria, and sensitive Maria Teresa, suffered hardship and torture to fight for justice and human rights.

The novel raises provocative questions about the sacrifice required for justice. Service learning projects, such as petitions and letter-writing campaigns to support victims of human rights abuses, can be found through Amnesty International. Check out information about the Urgent Action program and starting a student group. 325pp., grades 9–12

***My Name Is María Isabel*** by Alma Flor Ada (Atheneum, 1993). Third grader María Isabel starts a new school two months after the year begins. All is going well until her teacher begins to call her by the name "Mary." María Isabel's pride in her name and heritage teaches the teacher and the class a lesson about fitting in and respect. Available in English and Spanish. 57pp., grades 3–6

***Out of Bounds: Seven Stories of Conflict and Hope*** by Beverly Naidoo (HarperCollins, 2003). These seven stories, set in South Africa, span the years of apartheid, from 1948 to 2000. Each chronicles the lives of young people as they face restrictions and political upheaval, and the struggle for justice. A timeline provides a social and political context. 175pp., grades 6–10

***Pay It Forward*** by Catherine Ryan Hyde (Simon & Schuster, 1999). Twelve-year-old Trevor takes his social studies assignment to heart: change the world. His inspiring "pay it forward" scheme has far-reaching impact even though his personal attempts seem to fail. Can this young person heal his broken family and create a contagious spirit of community and caring? 311pp., young adult

***Slap Your Sides*** by M. E. Kerr (HarperCollins, 2001). Jubal Shoemaker, fourteen, knows that his family is no longer liked in his town. As friends shun him and sales are cut in half at his father's store, Jubal wonders if he too will follow his brother's choice to be a conscientious objector in World War II. Will the messages of hate painted on the store walls cause him to give up his Quaker beliefs or befriend the teenage perpetrator? 198pp., young adult

***Spitting Image*** by Shutta Crum (Clarion, 2003). During the late 1960s, as part of President Johnson's War on Poverty, a Vista volunteer arrives in Beulah County, Kentucky. Twelve-year-old Jessie sees this as an opportunity to help her best friend get the new eyeglasses he desperately needs. But during this turbulent summer, Jessie's problems keep piling up, caused in part by her out-of-control temper, her desire to find out how her daddy is, and her money-earning plan that completely backfires. 218pp., grades 5–8

***To Kill a Mockingbird*** by Harper Lee (Warner, 1961/1988). Narrated by a six-year-old girl named Scout, Lee's novel portrays small town Southern life in the 1930s, revealing all its prejudices, especially those based on race. Central to the novel's action is the decision by Scout's father, Atticus, to defend an African-American man, Tom Robinson, wrongfully accused of a crime. Knowing the case is hopeless, Atticus defends Robinson because his conscience allows him no alternative. 288pp., young adult

**Recommendation from the Field**

*by Ellen Brahe, Elementary Student, and Kate McPherson, Project Service Leadership*

*Walk Two Moons* by Sharon Creech (HarperTrophy, 1994). Thirteen-year-old Salamanca travels across the country telling her grandparents about her adventures with her best friend, Phoebe Winterbottom. She explains how she has learned not to judge people but has discovered the need to "walk" for two months in someone's moccasins to get to know who the person really is.

Children can use this novel to consider finding what people have in common or experiencing joy in people's differences, all to move toward friendship. After reading this book, upper elementary students could write and illustrate a story about learning to value someone who is different. Then students could share these stories and provide a lesson for second or third graders. The story could also stimulate discussion about stereotypes and assumptions. If read in preparation for service experiences with elders, younger children, or people who are homeless, the book may inspire students to be more open to discovering another person's gifts, concerns, and interests. 280pp., grades 4–5

***White Lilacs*** by Carolyn Meyer (Harcourt, 1993). In 1921, Freedom was a bustling community of black residents surrounded by the white folks in Dillon, Texas. Young Rose Lee expects life to just go on as usual when she overhears a plan to forcibly relocate Freedom's residents to build a park. Can the white community, through city government and intimidation, make this happen? The presence of the Ku Klux Klan and the tarring and feathering of Rose Lee's brother ring all too true. Based on true events in Denton, Texas. 242pp., young adult

# Interviews with Authors:
## The Story Behind the Story

In the following interviews, we find out the "story behind the story" from Sara Jane Boyers (*Teen Power Politics: Make Yourself Heard*) and Sonia Levitin (*Dream Freedom*).

Happenstance played a part in finding the author of *Teen Power Politics: Make Yourself Heard*. A casual conversation with a parent at my daughter's high school became more intriguing when I learned that the woman I was talking with, Sara Jane Boyers, had written a book about teens taking social action. After reading *Dream Freedom*, I was compelled to speak with Sonia Levitin, an author who writes on many issues of social importance—and, in this book, explicitly shows service learning in action.

### *Sara Jane Boyers, author of* Teen Power Politics: Make Yourself Heard

Two key moments inspired me to write this book. First, poor voter turnout (less than 50 percent overall and abysmal for the 18-to-29-year-olds) in the 1994 United States congressional election indicated a lack of participation in the election process and other aspects of our democracy. Second, my preteen son's cogent questions about the election results made it clear that young people are more politically aware and attentive to the issues of our country than most adults realize.

I decided to focus my next book on teens, a large, powerful, questioning, and persuasive group, and write about approaches to social, political, and electoral activism that would address their concerns and help return democracy to the common citizen.

I asked young people their concerns directly. Responses varied from skateboard parks, to juvenile justice, to racial profiling. I learned what teens and youth advocates were doing to promote civic engagement, including stories of people who work toward social change even before they can vote. I looked at creative approaches to engagement used by effective organizations such as Rock the Vote.

How could I put all of this into a book that teens would want to pick up? I wanted to spark youth creativity while making a direct connection between their interests and those of their community and nation. *Teen Power Politics: Make Yourself Heard* is the result. It's a book about civic engagement, using real teen issues and solutions. We often stop short regarding citizen involvement and activism. Yet even if the process takes years, we can make positive social change by using what I call the "toolkit of democracy": service, advocacy, electoral knowledge, and political activism.

Service requires taking from your own time and doing for others. Advocacy involves finding a concern, educating yourself about it, and working toward social change. Electoral knowledge means understanding how we elect others to represent us, elect them wisely, and ensure they work for us. Through political activism we learn how to make change, even on a small, local level, giving people greater options and making societal improvements.

*Teen Power Politics* is a starting point for social activism and a tool to help teens discover their activist voice. In the process, teens can let adults both show them by example and follow them through inspiration to return all of us to active, involved roles in society. I have great faith in our youth in this process. "In chorus with others, you can reshape our world."

### *Sonia Levitin, author of* Dream Freedom

My story begins in February of 1999. I had finished writing *The Cure*, a demanding work because it dealt with the persecution of Jews in the Middle Ages, when they were accused of poisoning the wells. This situation was parallel to what occurred during the Holocaust. I received a notice from the Simon Wiesenthal Center about a symposium on issues of present-day slavery. Normally, I don't have time to attend such events. This day, however, made a significant impact on my life and work. I was overwhelmed with what I heard. The abolitionists who spoke described the genocide that is going on right now in the Sudan. I saw pictures of Sudanese people being brutalized. I met former slaves. I listened to activists dedicated to stopping this horror. I even learned of school children in Colorado who raised funds to free some of the slaves.

I came home depressed. There seemed to be nothing I could do. In the morning I told my husband what I had learned, and of course he agreed that this situation is horrible. On my morning walk, still caught up in the tragedy and frustration, I suddenly realized, of course there is something I can do: I have to write about this subject.

First, I made a phone call to my contact at the Wiesenthal Center to let them know of my intentions. Next, I called my editor and gave her a thumbnail sketch of what I had learned about the Sudan and my idea for a book. I emphasized that this must be published right away, no delay! She agreed. Of course, I hadn't written one word yet.

I decided to write a novel, to use my strength in creating fictional characters out of all I have heard and what I would continue to learn. I wove in the story of the elementary class in Colorado. I included an American child, Marcus, a fifth grader, who is not wealthy and has problems of his own, and had him reach out across the world to a situation more profound and tragic. This was not to compare these sets of problems. We each live with our own concerns. When my family immigrated to this country from Europe, we were desperately poor. Still, my mother was shipping boxes to families in need in her home country. All of us, even those who are seen as underprivileged, have something to give.

For this novel, I wanted to create a feeling of truth and reality for the reader. I did not want to tell a linear story of one enslaved child. I wanted to show that slavery affects everybody, so there are many points of view. I intended to tie the stories together by repeating characters in a subtle way. One of my favorite chapters tells of a boy who goes to work with his father for the first time, his initiation to follow in his father's footsteps. He discovers that his father is a slaveholder and trades in human flesh. We know at the chapter's end that this boy will never inflict pain. He doesn't want to ride with his father. This boy begins a shift. I believe each person can make a change, starting with him or herself.

I did not travel to the Sudan; but I learned about this rich culture and met people who greatly influenced my work and life. I went to Washington, D.C., to meet Dr. Francis Mading Dang, an author and scholar with the Brookings Institute. At one time he was the Sudanese ambassador to Scandinavia. The son of a chief, he has studied all over the world and has written eight books on Sudan's politics and society, and I've read them all.

When traveling to Switzerland, I met John Eibner, Director of Advocacy for the Christian Solidarity International. He goes to the Sudan two or three times annually to bring currency to free slaves at great hazard to himself. The way I described him in the chapter called "Mercy" shows him as he truly is, a most humble person.

Of course I contacted the Colorado teacher, Barbara Vogel, and flew to Denver to meet her class. I also accompanied her fourth- and fifth-grade class to Washington, D.C. The students spoke to members of Congress to ask them to act. On another trip to D.C., the students spoke to the Foreign Relations Committee and read a passage of *Dream Freedom* into the Congressional Record. This is the first time ever that children in our country have lobbied on behalf of children in Africa.

A writer has the opportunity to be a bridge, to reach the reader on an emotional level. Our stories can show how people are the same, with the same needs, the same soul. Our words can fascinate by the differences revealed, including cultural differences. Through fiction, I want to sensitize the reader and show them much more than they would see with a cursory glance. I want to open the reader to understanding other people and caring about them. What they do with that caring is up to them.

In classrooms, the teacher can be the vehicle for the experience: to be sure the story is told, and to have children express their thoughts and feelings and put themselves in someone else's place. Then the action will come from them. When we plant the seed and keep encouraging, children can find what they care about, whether it is the Sudanese slavery issue, local hunger, or abandoned animals. While it is easy to address a problem in a superficial way, we can learn and make the idea of change part of who we are. We can only change ourselves, yet this creates the possibility for others to change as well. Our lives are so much richer when we are involved.

CHAPTER 14

# SPECIAL NEEDS AND DISABILITIES

> We do have to use labels sometimes to give information, but in general, they are silly and sometimes just plain rude.
>
> Kids in this book have disabilities that you cannot easily see—they are hidden in their bodies within the brain and nervous system.
>
> ELLEN SENISI, FROM *JUST KIDS: VISITING A CLASS FOR CHILDREN WITH SPECIAL NEEDS*

The population of children with special needs and disabilities is growing, and chances are you have at least one young person with special needs—or perhaps several—in your classroom or group. Increasingly, that's a fact of life for most people who work with kids and teens. This chapter looks both at how to design service learning projects that address the actual needs of people with disabilities or special needs and at how *everyone* in your classroom or group can participate in and benefit from service learning. Young people with special needs or challenges can take part in service learning and make valuable contributions, regardless of whether you are teaching an inclusive class or one specifically for students with special needs. This is true for theme-based projects of all kinds, including the ones in this chapter. Projects around special needs and disabilities can take a number of different forms: students can lobby for better access for the disabled in the community, donate time and resources to agencies that work with populations with special needs, or work directly with peers with special needs.

A "special need" can be defined as anything that requires care or intervention outside of the norm; it can take the form of a disability, but it doesn't always. Some special needs are fairly visible—using a wheelchair or communicating with sign language. Others are much less obvious—attention deficit disorder or a condition such as lupus, cancer, or asthma. Often the latter are harder to identify for teachers and peers and can be more challenging for young people to understand. Information is available in many forms to teach both educators and students about special needs issues and to help them cultivate mutually respectful relationships with students and people in the community with special needs. As all students learn more about each other, differences become less significant and similarities become more important. Supportive adults can foster increased understanding by providing accurate information, raising awareness, and encouraging open day-to-day interactions.

> Be not afraid of growing slowly;
> be afraid only of standing still.
>
> CHINESE PROVERB

## Preparation: Getting Ready for Service Learning Involving Special Needs and Disabilities

The following activities can be used in the preparation stage to promote learning and skill development related to special needs and disabilities. These activities can be used with different age ranges during preparation to help your students examine key issues through research, analyze community needs, and gain the knowledge they need to effectively contribute to the design of their service plan. Since literature is often an important part of preparation, you can find recommended titles on this theme in the Special Needs and Disabilities Bookshelf later in this chapter.

***Activity: Understanding Dis-Ability.*** This activity explores the idea of differences, challenges, and disability. Start by writing the word *ability* on the board, and ask the students to share their abilities. This usually results in a broad array of different abilities, from playing football to drawing to "I can stand on my head." When students are asked, "What does the word *ability* mean?" the answer usually is "something that a person does well." Ask students to think about the talents of people they know well: "Are they all the same?"

Now add the prefix *dis* to the front of *ability*, and ask your students for a definition. Most often, they will say "something someone cannot do well." This comes from a common societal perception and from turning the word "ability" into a negative, with *ability* meaning "can do" and *disability* meaning "cannot do." Have your students take a closer look; is this really true?

For example, a blind person can't see, so the question you can pose is, "Can a blind person learn to read?" Students usually know that blind people can learn to read using braille. So blind people can learn to read, but they may have to learn in a different way and the task may be more challenging because of the disability. *Disability*, then, means something that a person can do but may do differently or may have more difficulty doing. Can a deaf person learn to speak? Can a person in a wheelchair play basketball? Yes—but with differences.

***Activity: What About a Peanut?*** It may seem simple, but a peanut can be a useful and delicious tool to introduce and discuss the elements of special needs and disabilities. Provide each participant with peanuts still in the shell. Pose the question: "What makes these peanuts similar, and what makes them different?" Write the answers on a two-column chart with the word *peanut* at the top of the chart, *similar* over one column, and *different* over the other. Characteristics could include:

- Similar: basic shape, all have the same thing inside, most people like them.
- Different: appearances and shapes vary, uses vary.

Now cross out the word *peanut*, leaving the letter *p* and write the word *people*. Review the chart to examine how people are alike and different. Most of the characteristics listed will still apply, and new ones can be added. This chart can become quite detailed and cover a wall or two. Include emotions, attitudes, likes, and dislikes in addition to physical attributes.

**Find Out More About Special Needs and Disabilities**

To learn more about these issues and to get ideas for service and action, visit these Web sites and organizations online:

***serviceandinclusion.org*** The National Service Inclusion Project is a training and technical assistance project to increase the participation of people with disabilities in service.

***www.specialolympics.org*** Special Olympics provides year-round sports training and athletic competition to one million people with "mental retardation" in more than 150 countries.

***www.bestbuddies.org*** Best Buddies International is an organization dedicated to enhancing the lives of people with intellectual disabilities by providing opportunities for one-to-one friendships and integrated employment, with programs specifically designed for middle and high schools; also includes an "e-buddies" program accessible at *www.ebuddies.org*.

***www.projectlinus.org*** Project Linus is a volunteer non-profit organization providing a sense of security, warmth, and comfort to children who are seriously ill, traumatized, or otherwise in need through the gifts of new, homemade, washable blankets and afghans, created by volunteer blanketeers.

## Making Connections Across the Curriculum

Some service learning activities naturally lend themselves to interdisciplinary work and making connections across the curriculum. These connections strengthen and broaden student learning, helping them meet academic standards. More than likely, you'll be looking for these connections and ways to encourage them well before the students ever start working on service learning activities. As with the entire service learning process, it helps to remain flexible, because some connections can be spontaneously generated by the questions raised throughout and by the needs of the project. To help you think about cross-curricular connections and where you can look for them, the Curricular Web for this chapter (page 206) gives examples of many different ways this theme can be used in different academic areas. (The service learning scenarios in the next section of the chapter also demonstrate various ways this theme can be used across the curriculum.)

# Service Learning Scenarios:
## Ideas for Action

Ready to take action? What follows are projects that have been successfully carried out by elementary, middle, or high school students. Most of these scenarios and examples explicitly include some aspects of preparation, action, reflection, and demonstration. These scenarios can be a rich source of project, resource, and curriculum ideas for you to draw upon. While the grade levels are given as a reference, most project ideas can be adapted to suit younger or older students, and many are suitable for cross-age partnerships.

***A Child-Friendly Hospital: Kindergarten.*** A kindergarten teacher in North Adams, Massachusetts, listened to her students describe their fears of going to the hospital. They decided this was an important issue and contacted the regional hospital about how they could help children who were sick be more comfortable. The plan: to create a special place for children in one of the emergency treatment rooms. Using math skills and lots of masking tape, students measured off the amount of space they had to fill. They brainstormed a list of things that children would like to have and then began to actualize their ideas. What a wonderful day for hospital staff and the community as the children brought games, a chalkboard, safe toys, decorative murals, and self-portraits to the hospital. They even included an original book with photographs telling the story of how the room was created. A hospital administrator visited the class several months later. She brought a restraining device previously used to strap children down in the emergency room to keep them calm. She reported that since the new child-friendly room had been in use, the restraining device had not been used at all. She also described an elder patient who was quite distraught about his health and was left alone for a while in the special emergency room. When the nurse returned, he was all smiles—busy enjoying the children's portraits and their photo album. What came next? Another year, this teacher's class created a child-friendly waiting room in the emergency registration area.

***Being Good Neighbors: Grades K–8.*** Young students with autism in St. Louis, Missouri, created and then delivered valentines to residents at a senior residential facility next door to the school. In spring, peers from the general population of the school helped their peers with autism paint ceramic pots and plant in them. With parents and teachers, the students hand-delivered the pots to the seniors. The following weekend, parents and siblings of the students with special needs joined with some of the active seniors to plant an outdoor garden at the residence in a courtyard area in desperate need of sprucing up. The nursing staff and many residents came out to watch and compliment the children. A teacher commented, "When the parents stood back and watched their kids planting alongside the elders, some of them started to cry. This was the first time their child had done service for others. Every single parent asked when they could do this again. And the kids were delighted. Anyone who started out skeptical ended up as an advocate of service learning for all kids."

> The best and most beautiful things in the world cannot be seen or even touched. They must be felt with the heart.
>
> HELEN KELLER, AUTHOR

***Increasing Access at School: Grades 2–10.*** Can students improve access for people with disabilities on their school campuses? Second graders were able to create parking for people with disabilities where there had been none at their school. Seventh-grade students worked with a shop teacher to build a portable

# Special Needs and Disabilities Across the Curriculum

## Special Needs and Disabilities

### *English/Language Arts*

- Build vocabulary by learning the current and respectful terms used to describe specific disabilities
- Create child-friendly informational materials for a local organization, agency, or outreach program serving a community with special needs
- Invite someone who reads braille to talk about how they learned it; compare to the process of learning to read for sighted students. What are the similarities? Differences?

### *Social Studies/History*

- Discuss: If money weren't a concern, how could the community be made truly accessible for everyone?
- Study about people with special needs who have been local, national, or international leaders
- Research the Americans with Disabilities Act (1990) and the impact of this and more current legislation

### *Languages*

- Research the laws that impact people with disabilities in the countries that use the language you're learning
- Have a conversation using only picture symbols
- Compare the sign language systems of various countries

### *Theater, Music, & Visual Arts*

- Create a theater performance about people of all abilities and needs in the community as active contributing participants
- Identify music that has repetition and easy rhythms to teach children with developmental disabilities
- Work on art projects with younger students in a special needs class and create an art display for the community

### *Math*

- Create math activities that could be used in math centers for children who need practice identifying shapes, counting, or sorting
- Make a bulletin board of numbers or geometric shapes with each item offering a different tactile experience
- Find out and chart national statistics on disabilities

### *Physical Education*

- Research athletes with disabilities who succeed in a range of sports, including skiing, biking, and skydiving
- Prepare dance lessons for students with special needs
- Play basketball in wheelchairs or "beep baseball" where players have assistance

### *Computer*

- Learn how technology has been adapted to help people with special needs and disabilities be independent
- Compare Web sites that teach American Sign Language (ASL); select one and promote it within the school
- Using the Web, research health and social service careers related to working with people with disabilities

### *Science*

- Assess an outdoor habitat or nature trail for accessibility
- Learn how the human neurological system is affected by different special needs conditions
- Select a special need and learn about recent scientific research that benefits people who have it

ramp for access to a previously inaccessible entrance. And tenth-grade students, concerned about the lack of physical accessibility in school buildings, worked with a local agency to survey the entire campus. A proposal for change was sent to the school board.

***Kids and Canines: Grades 3–5.*** In Tampa, Florida, students who have been identified as being emotionally disturbed take part in an ongoing program by spending two sessions learning about service dogs, their handlers, and their prospective owners. The students also learn about pet care and responsibilities that come with owning a dog. Once a week, an elementary student, a service dog, and a handler visit a nearby nursing home. The interactions help the students develop social skills, empathy, and community awareness through interactions. Preparing for and carrying out basic conversations has given the students more confidence. And the elders enjoy meeting the children and being with the animals.

***Swim Buddies: Grades 4–5.*** In an Anderson, Indiana, elementary school, every fourth- and fifth-grade student learned the skills and knowledge necessary to be an effective and responsible one-on-one swimming instructor for a special needs preschool child. The upper elementary students all received training in water safety and basic child care. Classroom integration continued as disability awareness and sensitivity training were woven into reading, health, computer skills, and civics. Youth voice and choice were evident as the swim buddies found additional ways to interact with the preschool students. They assisted during lunch and recess, and planned additional special events to enjoy their new reciprocal relationships.

***Learning About Independent Living: Grades 7–8.*** Fifteen seventh and eighth graders in Herrin, Illinois, participated in an after-school program at a center for independent living, serving people who have special needs. Students learned about the problems and adaptations made so people with disabilities can live independently. They learned about braille and the computers adapted for this use, and studied American Sign Language. They saw firsthand how people move in wheelchairs or with canine assistance. Twice a month students provided assistance to people who are blind, deaf, and/or otherwise physically challenged. In reflection, students recognized how their ideas about people living with disabilities changed as they grew to be friends and advocates.

***Family Helpers: Grades 9–11.*** After a series of workshops to become familiar with the role of in-home assistance for children with special needs, high school students visited homes identified by their partner agency. Students always worked in pairs. Most often, the activity involved playing with a child who is developmentally disabled whose learning benefits from additional stimulation and interaction. Students had regular meetings with the sponsoring agency for reflection, role playing, and further training.

***Getting Physical: Grades 9–12.*** A squad of cheerleaders took their pep and enthusiasm into a class with teens who have Down syndrome. With teacher guidance and regularly scheduled visits, they taught a series of exercises that grew, over time, to be more complex. In addition to stretches and aerobics, they taught popular dance steps.

***Job Coaching Mentally Challenged Peers: Grades 9–12.*** Leadership and Career Exploration students in a Panama City, Florida, high school provide mentoring for their mentally challenged peers as they prepare to enter the job market. Over the course of the high school years, these students volunteer together for ninety minutes a day in child-care programs, hospitals, humane societies, school and public libraries, rescue missions, teen court, and other community organizations. The mentoring students develop the work and monitor the program. The process begins in ninth grade, when special education students are placed in jobs on the high school campus to learn basic job skills and practices. With their mentors, they work the switchboard, file, make copies, and work in the library. For the next three years, at second period, 120 students on three buses leave campus for ninety minutes; on board is one job mentor for every three special education students. Tenth graders work primarily at child-care centers, and eleventh and twelfth graders are individually placed for student interests and skill levels. Once the special education students can do the jobs independently, the mainstream students take on additional tasks to help the agencies. Recruiting job mentors? Never a problem. This is a popular and well-received program.

> No act of kindness, no matter how small,
> is ever wasted.
>
> AESOP

***Trolley Activists: Grades 9–12.*** The Trolley Project in Panama City, Florida, was a natural outgrowth of the job coaching program described in the preceding scenario. Through observation, class discussion, and reflection, students came to understand that some people want to work but can't because of a lack of confidence, an impairment, difficulty finding employment, or lack of knowledge about how to place themselves in the workforce. Transportation can also be a deciding factor. For example, many community members with special needs use the city's downtown trolley as a primary form of transportation for getting to work, the public library, the senior center, or the technical college. The trolley was also used by many older people who could no longer drive. When the students learned that the downtown trolley, supported by transportation disability funds, would be shut down and the money used elsewhere, they were outraged and began to speak out. In collaboration with other interested groups, they convinced city administrators to keep the trolley running. Students also spoke to groups of older people about how to use the trolley to take outings with their grandchildren. They volunteered to teach senior citizens and students with special needs how to use the trolley. A student-written coloring book that was distributed showed sights to see on the trolley and gave ideas for picnic locations. Almost every day, a school group goes out on the trolley.

***School Clubs: Grades 9–12.*** In many New York high schools, students with and without disabilities meet weekly to share their commonalities and differences. In addition to sharing lunchtime and large group activities, they form pairs or trios and choose a school activity or service project to do together. All students receive orientation and have reflection sessions to ensure that relationships are mutually beneficial and to answer questions as they arise.

***Assistance for Canine Companions: Grades 10–11.*** What are canine companions? They're dogs trained to assist people with disabilities and special needs, including those who are blind, use wheelchairs, or have epilepsy. When the match is ready to be made, the human and the companion dog attend two weeks of "team training," which can be costly. To help with some of the expense, high school students shopped for food, assisted in meal preparation, and served lunch for several days. They improved their skills in comparative shopping, became comfortable interacting with people who have disabilities, and learned more about the animal/human bond and the role of a service dog.

## The Special Needs and Disabilities Bookshelf

The Special Needs and Disabilities Bookshelf provides information that will help students to more ably provide service or serve alongside special needs peers. To help you find books relevant to your particular projects, the book chart classifies the titles into several topic areas: learning about special needs, working with special needs populations, interaction and peer relationships, and animal therapies.

In general, the bookshelf features:

- An annotated bibliography arranged and alphabetized by title according to the general categories of nonfiction (N), picture books (P), and fiction (F). For nonfiction and fiction, length and recommended grade levels are included. The entries in the picture book category do not include suggested grade levels, since they can be successfully used with all ages.
- A chart organized by topic and category to help you find books relevant to particular projects.
- Recommendations from service learning colleagues and experts that include a book summary and ideas for service learning connections. (The number of recommended books varies in each bookshelf.)

# Special Needs and Disabilities Bookshelf Topics

| Topics | Books | Category |
|---|---|---|
| ***Learning About Special Needs*** As we learn more about special needs, we respond more appropriately and effectively. These books increase knowledge and heighten sensitivity about different kinds of special needs. | *All Kinds of Friends, Even Green!* | N |
| | *Can You Hear a Rainbow? The Story of a Deaf Boy Named Chris* | N |
| | *The Cay* (see page 117) | F |
| | *Freak the Mighty* | F |
| | *Just Call Me Stupid* (see page 182) | F |
| | *My Name is Brian* | F |
| | *The Printer* | P |
| | *Seeing Things My Way* | N |
| | *Small Steps: The Year I Got Polio* | N |
| | *The Storm* | P |
| | *We Can Do It!* | P |
| ***Working with Special Needs Populations*** Exchanges between people with differing abilities create experiences in which everyone learns. | *The Acorn People* | N |
| | *Just Kids: Visiting a Class for Children with Special Needs* | N |
| | *The Year of Miss Agnes* (see page 184) | F |
| ***Interaction and Peer Relationships*** Common interactions include: neighbors spending time together, relationships between siblings, friendships at school, and challenges being met and resolved. Reading about these dynamics can assist both in learning about specific disabilities and in recognizing the possibility of forming successful relationships. | *Be Good to Eddie Lee* | P |
| | *Be Quiet, Marina!* | P |
| | *Bluish* | F |
| | *A Corner of the Universe* | F |
| | *Crazy Lady* * | F |
| | *Friends at School* | P |
| | *Ian's Walk: A Story About Autism* | P |
| | *My Brother Sammy* | P |
| | *My Sister Annie* | F |
| | *Of Mice and Men* | F |
| | *Rainbow Joe and Me* | P |
| | *Sosu's Call* | P |
| | *Stoner and Spaz* | F |
| | *The Treasure on Gold Street/El Tesoro en la calle Oro* | P |
| | *Trudi & Pia* | P |
| ***Animal Therapies*** Animals give companionship and assistance to humans. These books show strategies to improve the lives of all community members. | *Dr. White* | P |
| | *Rosie: A Visiting Dog's Story* | N |
| | *Rugby and Rosie* | P |

Page references are given for books that do not appear in the Special Needs and Disabilities Bookshelf but that can be found in the bookshelf lists of other chapters.

* These books include examples of young people in service-providing roles.

## Nonfiction: *Special Needs and Disabilities*

***The Acorn People*** by Ron Jones (Dell, 1976). In this true account of counselors at a summer camp for handicapped and dying youth, everyone is transformed—the counselors learn who the kids are on the inside, and the young people experience joy in their newfound freedom of expression and experience. 79pp., young adult

***All Kinds of Friends, Even Green!*** by Ellen B. Senisi (Woodbine, 2002). "I am lucky because I have so many friends," says Moses, a seven-year-old born with spina bifida and sacral agenesis. In his full inclusion classroom, Moses ponders his assignment to write about friends. Should he write about Jimmy, who shares secrets, or Jocelyn, who also sits in a wheelchair? Moses picks a "green" friend who has "something inside her the same as me." 32pp., grades K–4

***Can You Hear a Rainbow? The Story of a Deaf Boy Named Chris*** by Jamee Riggio Heelan (Peachtree, 2002). Chris, a deaf boy, explains how he uses American Sign Language, hearing aids, and his other senses to communicate. Through a mix of photographs and art, we see Chris playing soccer, attending school, enjoying friends, and performing in a play. 29pp., grades K–5

***Just Kids: Visiting a Class for Children with Special Needs*** by Ellen B. Senisi (Dutton, 1998). Second-grader Cindy is assigned to spend time in a class for children with special needs. Over two weeks, she gains valuable information about autism, Down syndrome, ADHD, learning disabilities, and epilepsy and recognizes how each child learns. She also realizes that they are all "just kids." A resource for teachers and students. 40pp., all ages

***Rosie: A Visiting Dog's Story*** by Stephanie Calmenson (Houghton Mifflin, 1994). Rosie is a dog who makes a difference. After the necessary training, Rosie visits hospitalized children and elders who live in nursing homes. Her manners and friendliness make her well loved. 48pp., grades K–4

***Seeing Things My Way*** by Alden Carter (Albert Whitman, 1998). Second-grader Amanda, who is visually impaired, describes how she learns using different equipment. She also shows how she enjoys sports, sleepovers with friends, and dancing. 32pp., grades K–4

***Small Steps: The Year I Got Polio*** by Peg Kehret (Albert Whitman, 1996). Peg led a normal life until the day in 1949 when she suddenly fell ill. The doctor gave the dreaded diagnosis: polio. At age twelve, Peg was isolated from her family and friends in a hospital with an unknown prognosis. In this memoir, the author chronicles the following eight months, where, aided by doctors and therapists, a supportive family, and courageous roommates, she regains the ability to walk. 179pp., grades 4–8

> I didn't want to have polio; I didn't want to leave my family and go to a hospital one hundred miles from home. . . .
>
> Later that morning, I walked into the isolation ward of the Sheltering Arms Hospital in Minneapolis and went to bed in a private room. No one was allowed in except the doctors and nurses, and they wore masks. My parents stood outside on the grass, waving bravely and blowing kisses through the window. Exhausted, feverish, and scared, I fell asleep.
>
> When I woke up, I was paralyzed.
>
> FROM *SMALL STEPS: THE YEAR I GOT POLIO*

## Picture Books: *Special Needs and Disabilities*

***Be Good to Eddie Lee*** by Virginia Fleming (Philomel, 1993). Christy has no interest in being friends with Eddie Lee, a neighbor who has Down syndrome. Eddie follows her to a pond and reminds her not to take tadpoles from their natural environment. In teaching Christy about friendship, Eddie Lee shows that "It's what's on the inside that counts."

***Be Quiet, Marina!*** by Kirsten DeBear (Star Bright Books, 2001). Marina is four years old, likes to dress up and play on the see-saw, and screams a lot. Marina has cerebral palsy. Moira is also four; she likes to dance, see-saw, and play quietly. She has Down syndrome. At first, the girls cannot play together because of their differences. Now they are best friends. Follow this photo essay of two girls on the journey to friendship.

***Dr. White*** by Jane Goodall (North-South Books, 1999). The pediatric ward of a hospital has a remarkable doctor—Dr. White, a fluffy white dog whose warmth and love work magic on critically ill children. This story is based on actual events at a London hospital. The author's note refers to research supporting the idea that the "love and companionship of animals can contribute to sick people's recovery and rehabilitation."

***Friends at School*** by Rochelle Burnett (Bright Books, 1995). Enter a school where children of all abilities play together. Through photographs, we watch the children in a variety of activities—making snacks, reading books, feeding pets, and interacting with older students who are classroom helpers.

***Ian's Walk: A Story About Autism*** by Laurie Lears (Albert Whitman, 1998). Julie wants to take a walk with her older sister, but her autistic brother Ian insists on coming along. His behaviors irritate and embarrass Julie, until he wanders off on his own and the two girls cannot find him. Once the brother and sisters are reunited, Julie realizes how much she cares for her brother. The book includes a note that addresses siblings' often mixed emotions toward their autistic brothers and sisters.

***My Brother Sammy*** by Becky Edwards (Millbrook Press, 1999). A boy describes some of his many feelings toward his autistic brother, Sammy.

***The Printer*** by Myron Uhlberg (Peachtree, 2003). "As a boy, my father learned to speak with his hands. As a man, he learned to turn lead-type letters into words and sentences. My father loved being a printer." The narrator tells of his deaf father's work and heroism in the printing plant where a daily newspaper was produced. Ignored by hearing coworkers, his father faced a terrible situation when a fire erupted in the noisy pressroom. How would he tell of the danger when they could not hear him? The author's note tells the story of his deaf father and why he became a printer.

***Rainbow Joe and Me*** by Maria Diaz Strom (Lee & Low, 1999). Eloise loves everything about colors. She describes her paintings to her blind neighbor Joe, who has his own way of expressing colors—through music!

***Rugby and Rosie*** by Nan Parson Rossiter (Dutton, 1997). Rugby the dog and his boy are joined by Rosie, a puppy being bred as a guide dog. The threesome become inseparable for a year, until Rosie's departure. Includes information about breeding and training guide dogs.

***Sosu's Call*** by Meshack Asare (Kane/Miller, 2002). Sosu must stay in his parents' house all the time; the villagers think it is "bad luck" to have a boy who cannot walk in the village. So Sosu tends to household chores the best he can and learns to read and write from his siblings who attend school. When a great storm threatens the village, it is Sosu and his dog who risk their own lives to save many.

***The Storm*** by Marc Harshman (Cobblehill, 1995). Ever since the car hit his bicycle, leaving Jonathan in a wheelchair, he has hated feeling different. When a storm threatens his life and his horses, Jonathan proves his abilities and hopes others will now see him more clearly.

***The Treasure on Gold Street/El Tesoro en la calle Oro*** by Lee Merrill Byrd (Cinco Puentas Press, 2003). This is a story about a real person named Isabel, who has mental retardation, and many of the people who live in her neighborhood. Hannah, a young girl, is good friends with Isabel. Hannah likes the fact that Isabel is a grown-up who doesn't criticize and is never in a hurry. On Isabel's birthday, everyone on Gold Street recognizes the neighborhood's true treasure, Isabel. English and Spanish text.

***Trudi & Pia*** by Ursula Hegi (Antheneum, 2003). Trudi, a girl with dwarfism, yearns to know someone "shaped like her, someone whose legs would be short, whose arms could not reach the coat hooks in her classroom." When she visits the circus, to her astonishment, Trudi meets Pia, a woman who is an animal tamer and has dwarfism. Trudi's visit reveals a secret: Feeling you belong begins with loving yourself.

***We Can Do It!*** by Laura Dwight (Star Bright Books, 1997). This book profiles a multiracial group of boys and girls with different conditions: Down syndrome, spina bifida, cerebral palsy, and blindness. These children, all around age five, are shown in color photographs as they play with friends, interact with therapists, and describe how they can "do lots of things." An informative book to help all children learn about similarities and differences.

## Fiction: *Special Needs and Disabilities*

***Bluish*** by Virginia Hamilton (Scholastic, 1999). Natalie is different from other fifth graders in Dreenie's class. She arrives in a wheelchair wearing a wool cap, a dog on her lap, and pale skin with a bluish tint from chemotherapy. Dreenie's journal describes her fears and fascination as she develops a close friendship with a girl struggling with illness and moving toward health. And then there is Tuli, a biracial friend who so wants to be beautiful and be Latina. Most of all, this is a story of three girls who learn, laugh, and grow together. 127pp., grades 4–7

***A Corner of the Universe*** by Ann M. Martin (Scholastic, 2002). It's the summer of 1960: Hattie relishes summer days and her upcoming twelfth birthday. But this summer turns her upside down as she meets her Uncle Adam, who no one has told her about. Hattie sees herself in this developmentally delayed young man, who opens her heart and causes her to defy her parents and grandparents. 191pp., young adult

"Miss Hagerty, what is wrong with Adam?"

Miss Hagerty puts down her teacup and looks at me for a long time. "You know, I'm not sure, Dearie. I don't think anyone has ever told me. He's just . . . funny." Miss Hagerty taps the side of her head. "I believe you would say he is mentally ill."

I sigh. Funny. Mentally ill. I decide not to ask Miss Hagerty if mental illness can run in a family.

FROM *A CORNER OF THE UNIVERSE*

***Crazy Lady*** by Jane Leslie Conly (HarperCollins, 1993). Vernon is suffering because of his mother's death and feels lost in junior high. Then he befriends the "crazy lady," an alcoholic woman in his neighborhood, and comes to know her retarded son, Ronald. Vernon grows to understand the love between these two people. Along the way, he gains self-respect and a purpose: to raise money for Ronald to attend the Special Olympics. 180pp., grades 5–8

***Freak the Mighty*** by Rodman Philbrick (Scholastic, 1993). An unlikely friendship between Kevin, a brilliant twelve-year-old whose birth defect prevents growth, and Max, a gigantic boy with learning disabilities, leads to adventure, risk, and ultimately, shared wisdom. 169pp., grades 4–8

***My Name Is Brian*** by Jeanne Betancourt (Scholastic, 1993). The author draws from her experience with dyslexia to tell about Brian, a boy who forms a club with his friends called "the jokers." Brian's father criticizes his behavior, making him promise to try harder in school. He appears to be joking when he writes "Brain" instead of "Brian," but his teacher realizes he is dyslexic and provides tutoring so he can be a more successful student. 128pp., grades 4–7

***My Sister Annie*** by Bill Dodds (Boyds Mills Press, 1997). Eleven-year-old Charles wants to join a group of tough guys at school. He wants to go to the school dance with Misty. And he wants his older sister Annie, who has Down syndrome, to disappear, at least some of the time. In this humorous and thoughtful story, Charles learns about compassion and meeting life's challenges. 94pp., grades 3–6

**Recommendation from the Field**

*by Betty Berger, Program Director,*
*Giant Steps Integrative Approach to Autism,*
*and Omer Rosenblith, high school student*

*Of Mice and Men* by John Steinbeck (Penguin,1937/1994). This is a story about two men who are completely different but best friends. They travel together planning to work hard, make money, and then buy some land so they can finally be independent. They need each other to make this happen. George, the smart one, tries to protect his friend, makes their plans, and knows how to get away when they get in trouble. Lenny, a very big man who can do hard work, tries to follow his friend's directions but has the mind of a child. He is very loyal to George and has a caring heart. Unfortunately, George cannot save Lenny from tragic events.

Middle and high school students can use this book as a vehicle for understanding friendships between two people with many differences. The students will easily relate to the characters because they are timeless. Use this story to discuss these questions:

- How can differences in people become assets?
- Do you have friends who are different from you? What do you look for in friends?
- Imagine you have a friend with a disability. What would you gain? What would be enjoyable? What would be difficult?
- Could you defend a person that others were ridiculing or teasing?
- How much responsibility do we have to protect others who cannot protect themselves?

For service learning, students can partner with students with special needs on campus or in outside programs. First, the students learn about each other. Then they plan ongoing activities that they would both enjoy, such as swimming, weight lifting, attending sporting events, or acting in plays together. Students can then reflect back to the book and the main characters. What have they learned, gained, and shared? 137pp., young adult

***Stoner and Spaz*** by Ron Koertge (Candlewick, 2002). At age sixteen, Ben, who has cerebral palsy, has no parents, no friends, and no life outside of school and the movies. An unexpected friendship with drugged-out Colleen places him in risky situations that have him making choices for the first time about relationships, engaging in an adolescent world, and letting people know what he has to offer as a thoughtful, humorous, and creative person. 169pp., young adult (mature themes)

# Interviews with Authors:
## The Story Behind the Story

In the following interview, we find out the "story behind the story" from Ellen Senisi (*Just Kids: Visiting a Class for Children with Special Needs* and *All Kinds of Friends, Even Green!*). When I interviewed Ellen, I got more from the conversation than I expected. Of course, I heard how she had photographed the students in *Just Kids: Visiting a Class for Children with Special Needs*, how she had studied disabilities, and how the book had evolved. But I also learned of another book just being published. *All Kinds of Friends, Even Green!* is a story of a special boy with special needs who has so many friends he can't decide which one to describe in a school assignment. I dream of this being the case for every child.

### *Ellen Senisi, author of* Just Kids: Visiting a Class for Children with Special Needs *and* All Kinds of Friends, Even Green!

As a young person, I was drawn to writing. I received training as a teacher and then found photography. I went back to graduate school and studied educational media and technology. Through my books, I bring many aspects of my life together: my experiences as a teacher and a parent, articulating ideas as a writer, and capturing the visual image with my camera. I conceptually design my books using all these elements.

I grew up as the eldest in a family with seven children. My youngest sibling has Down syndrome. People who don't know someone with special needs, especially children, tend to tense up; they don't know how to act or what to do. Through my books, I want to communicate that people with special needs are people just like us. This is a message I particularly want to relate to kids.

I was asked to help special needs students to make books about themselves at Yates School in Schenectady, New York. As I photographed the kids, I really liked how sensitive and helpful they were to each other. The relationships between the kids, and their relationship with their teacher, were special and particularly affectionate. The emotional dynamics were alive in a way that is often missing in a traditional classroom.

I wanted to capture this classroom in a book and had to decide how to approach the story. Should it be fiction or nonfiction? Then the teacher related something that had happened a year earlier, when a girl made a derogatory remark to a special needs child. When I first visited, the girl who had provoked the incident was a volunteer helper in the class twice a week. My editor approved an approach using this scenario. After getting approvals from my publisher, parents of the students, and the school district, I returned to the classroom and began official work on *Just Kids*.

For about seven months, I spent nearly every morning, four to five days a week, in the classroom. I wanted to take time to get to know the kids so I could catch subtle behaviors and interactions. I spent the afternoons reading about autism, learning abilities, Down syndrome, and epilepsy and, in general, gaining an understanding of the basics of neurological impairments. And, of course, I wrote.

The research enriched the time spent with the kids and helped me to notice little things I would have otherwise missed. I learned it was natural for the autistic boy in the class to stare into the distance or not make eye contact, when before I had thought he was just tired, shy, or not paying attention. As a photographer, I learned to be more alert.

In *Just Kids*, special education students are shown in their own classroom, with plenty of interaction with children in traditional classrooms. Many schools now place children with special needs in regular classrooms all day. This is called inclusion, and I show that kind of classroom in *All Kinds of Friends, Even Green!* Zoller School in Schenectady is the setting for this book because the school does an excellent job with inclusion. The particular class photographed for this book, a first-grade class of twenty children, includes a teacher, a half-time special education teacher, and three full-time paraprofessionals. (However, I know of other schools where special needs students are plopped into regular classes and teachers are not given the necessary training or staff support they need to make the inclusion approach effective for all kids.)

The story photographed at Zoller School follows Moses, a child with spina bifida and sacral agenesis, who is thinking about the friends in his life as he works on a writing assignment about friendship. This book was written to help children ages four to seven to begin to understand special needs, so it shows children with easily identifiable disabilities.

I wrote *All Kinds of Friends, Even Green!* in part because once I met Moses, I knew he was exactly the right person for the story I had in mind. Sadly, Moses passed away before he saw this book in print. Still, his story is here for others to learn from.

I hope my books encourage kids to get involved with the kids with special needs who are somewhere in their school. It seems that more inclusion classes and contact between children with and without special needs can be found at the elementary level than at higher levels. In middle and high schools, kids need to be in contact with each other to prevent harmful dynamics, such as the incident I showed at the beginning of the *Just Kids* book. When kids who have special needs are only seen in the hallways of middle and high schools, and they appear "different" from other students, thoughtful interaction is highly unlikely. Yet when kids with and without special needs interact with each other on a regular basis in their environment, whether a special class or an inclusion class, they come to know and understand each other naturally.

Here is an example. In Moses's classroom, a girl with cerebral palsy couldn't hold her hand up for very long when she wanted to answer a question. I noticed how the children sitting next to her would often help her keep her hand up until she was called on. Because the children in that classroom were in daily contact, they knew what to do to help each other; and in the process, they built positive relationships. That's what all schools should be trying to bring about. Schools are a natural place to learn about people who are both similar to and different from us. If we can get kids connected during the school years, wouldn't there be a greater likelihood of this occurring afterwards? The world might then become more inclusive!

# An Author's Reflection

One evening around bedtime, when my daughters were much younger, my eldest asked, "When am I going to have adventures like you?" I turned that question around in my mind for some time, realizing that, like all young people, she longed for the opportunity to extend herself into experiences unknown.

In *Identity: A Novel,* author Milos Kundera defines *adventure* as a way to embrace the world. What a beautiful image, and one I hold for our youth as they maneuver through our educational systems, weaving their own patterns of learning and understanding.

With service learning as an integral part of school life, young people have a greater likelihood of achieving a sense of self through experience. The mystery of "why am I learning this subject?" is replaced with engagement. Studies that once seemed fragmented become interconnected. Learning occurs not only in the classroom but also in the nature preserve, the senior center, the food bank. Young people interact with their community, whether by taking a short walk to read to preschoolers at a Head Start program or by extending their help across the globe as advocates for children who are forced laborers. Wait for adventure? No need. Just enter the world of service learning.

But action is not enough; reflection is essential to service learning. What does reflection look like? In the book *Something Beautiful,* a young girl seeks what is beautiful in a neighborhood filled with trash, where people sleep in doorways and the word "Die" is painted on her front door. She asks her neighbors, "What is beautiful?" and finds a variety of responses: new shoes, a baby, a ripe red apple, a rock carried in a pocket for decades. She sits on her front stoop in reflection, looking at the trash and the graffiti. In this pause, she considers her ideas and her potential for making "something beautiful." Then she stands up, gets the supplies she needs, and scrubs the word "Die" right off her front door.

In a society filled with "busy," finding time for reflection can seem "a chore." Reflection, though, actually gives us a way to sink knee-deep into an experience and find out what it reveals.

Author E. L. Konigsburg draws on an age-old adage to teach about reflection. In her book *From the Mixed-up Files of Mrs. Basil E. Frankweiler,* two children run away from home and spend several nights having an adventure hiding out in the Metropolitan Museum of Art. At the end of their escapade, they meet the eccentric Mrs. Frankweiler and have a conversation asking about the value of learning something new each day. To their surprise, Mrs. Frankweiler disagrees, stating that, ". . . you should also have days when you allow what is already in you to swell up inside of you until it touches everything. And you can feel it inside you. If you never take time out to let that happen, then you just accumulate facts, and they begin to rattle around inside you. You can make noise with them, but never really feel anything with them. It's hollow."*

In service learning lies the balance: the dynamic of combining learning and action with thoughtful integration. A sense of purpose is here to be found, along with self-discovery, knowledge, and the ability to interact and improve our planetary home.

Enjoy the journey—both the adventure and the reflection.

*From *From the Mixed-up Files of* Mrs. *Basil E. Frankweiler* (35th Anniversary Edition) by E. L. Konigsburg (Simon & Schuster, 2002), p.153.

# Resources

These organizations and agencies have made significant contributions to the expanding field of service learning through ongoing research and the development of outstanding materials and information.

**Compass Institute**
P.O. Box 270037
St. Paul, MN 55127
(651) 787-0409
A national leader in service learning, Compass Institute provides research-based professional development opportunities to K–12 educators, education departments, and nonprofit organizations. Topics include service learning, social marketing, brain-based learning, sustaining the service leader, and innovative approaches to implementing programs.

**Constitutional Rights Foundation**
601 South Kingsley Drive
Los Angeles, CA 90005
(213) 487-5590
*www.crf-usa.org*
Offering programs, curricula, and training opportunities designed to engage K–12 youth and teachers in civic participation through service learning activities, this organization also publishes a free quarterly national newsletter, *Service-Learning Network.*

**Council for Service Learning Excellence**
1667 Snelling Avenue North, Suite D300
St. Paul, MN 55108
1-877-572-3924
*www.nslexchange.org*
Under the auspices of the National Youth Leadership Council, this group offers technical assistance and professional development opportunities. It also operates the National Service-Learning Exchange, where staff answer questions about service learning or find you a peer mentor.

**Florida Learn & Serve**
325 John Knox Road
Building F, Suite 210
Tallahassee, FL 32303
1-888-396-6756
*www.fsu.edu/~flserve*
Florida Learn & Serve offers on-site visits, training, and technical assistance at the local, national, and international levels. Publications are available with program descriptions, research on the impact of service learning, and information on linking service learning with state academic standards. The organization offers an exemplary environmental service learning model as well as expertise in youth philanthropy.

**The Giraffe Project**
P.O. Box 759
Langley, WA 98260
(360) 221-7989
*www.giraffe.org*
K–12 service learning and character education curriculum promotes compassion and active citizenship in youth. Kids learn about heroes in their communities and are inspired to make a difference through service learning projects.

**KIDS Consortium**
215 Lisbon Street, Suite 12
Lewiston, ME 04240
(207) 784-0956
*www.kidsconsortium.org*
The KIDS Consortium offers educators and community members ideas for involving students in their own neighborhoods. Trained adults help kids identify, research, and address real community challenges.

**Learn and Serve America**
1201 New York Avenue NW
Washington, DC 20525
(202) 606-5000
*www.learnandserve.org*
Learn and Serve America (a program of the Corporation for National and Community Service) provides grants and scholarships to schools, colleges, and nonprofit groups that participate in community service programs.

**Maryland State Department of Education: Service Learning**
200 West Baltimore Street
Baltimore, MD 21201
(410) 767-0358
*www.mdservice-learning.org*
The Maryland State Department of Education's Service Learning Program creates materials and develops programs designed to strengthen K–12 service learning. Find middle and high school curricula, service learning guides, evaluation rubrics, interdisciplinary service learning webs, and consultation opportunities at their Web site.

**National Center for Learning and Citizenship**
700 Broadway, Suite 1200
Denver, CO 80203
(303) 299-3606
*www.ecs.org/nclc*
This national center for service learning established by the Education Commission of the States works with state and district administrators and educators and promotes service learning opportunities in K–12 education. Publications on a range of service learning topics are available.

**National Dropout Prevention Center**
Clemson University
209 Martin Street
Clemson, SC 29631
(864) 656-2599
*www.dropoutprevention.org*
The center produces publications, videos, and other student resources, as well as organizes conferences and workshops for service learning leaders. Connecting practitioners with peer mentors, the organization also provides independent evaluations of service learning efforts.

**National Service-Learning Clearinghouse**
ETR Associates
4 Carbonero Way
Scotts Valley, CA 95066
1-866-245-7378
*www.servicelearning.org*
At their Web site, users can find materials for all grade levels, submit questions, and access documents about service learning. Funded by the Corporation for National and Community Service, the clearinghouse supports service learning in grades K–12, higher education, community-based initiatives, tribal programs, and programs for the general public.

**National Service-Learning Partnership**
Academy for Educational Development
1825 Connecticut Avenue NW, Suite 800
Washington, DC 20009
(202) 884-8356
*www.service-learningpartnership.org*
Their mission is to make service learning a core element of every K–12 student's education. Members receive news from the service learning community, ideas for strengthening service opportunities in local areas, and access to relevant publications. A free membership is available online.

**National Youth Leadership Council (NYLC)**
1667 Snelling Avenue North
St. Paul, MN 55108
(651) 631-3672
*www.nylc.org*
NYLC provides service learning training and produces publications, videos, and other resources for youth and adults involved in service projects. Contact them for information on the National Service-Learning Conference, the National Teacher Institute for Service Learning, and the National Youth Leadership Camp.

**RMC Research Corporation**
1512 Larimer Street, Suite 540
Denver, CO 80202
1-800-922-3636
*www.rmcdenver.com*
The RMC Research Corporation offers technical assistance, program evaluation, professional development opportunities, and help linking service learning to state and national academic requirements.

**Vermont Community Works**
P.O. Box 2251
South Burlington, VT 05407
(802) 655-5918
*www.vermontcommunityworks.org*
Vermont Community Works provides educators with support for service learning and community-based teaching, a wealth of resources (including curriculum options and teaching tools), technical assistance, and publications on service learning.

**Youth Service America**
1101 15th Street NW, Suite 200
Washington, DC 20005
(202) 296-2992
*www.ysa.org*
Youth Service America is an alliance of organizations committed to increasing opportunities for young Americans to serve locally, nationally, or globally. The organization sponsors National and Global Youth Service Day, which takes place each April, and hosts *SERVEnet.org*, a site with information and resources on service and volunteering.

**Youth Service California**
PO Box 70764
Oakland, CA 94612
(510) 302-0550
*www.yscal.org*
Youth Service California provides free email and phone consultation for educators implementing service learning programs. The professional staff is available for customized on-site training and consultation. Also available are curriculum development institutes and professional development workshops. Curriculum ideas, evaluation tools, and other resource materials are available for purchase.

# Index

f indicates form


## A

ABCD Books gardening curriculum (Web site), 136
*Acorn People, The* (Jones), 210
*Across a Dark and Wild Sea* (Brown), 181
Action
  for AIDS education and awareness, 68–71
  for animals in danger, 79–82
  books as catalysts for, 53–54
  bookshelf use during, 60
  for community safety, 90–94
  description of stage, 10–11, 36
  for elders, 108–110, 139–140, 161, 205, 207
  for environment, 125, 126–129
  for gardening, 136, 138–140, 148, 150
  for hunger and homelessness, 136, 138, 139, 140, 148–151
  for immigrants, 161–165
  for literacy, 108, 175–179
  reflection during, 26
  for social change: issues and action, 189–193
  for special needs and disabilities, 82, 205–208
Activities
  for AIDS education and awareness, 66–68
  for animals in danger, 6, 76–77
  for community safety, 89–90
  for elders, 6, 31, 106–107
  for environment, 123–124
  for gardening, 6, 32, 135–136
  for hunger and homelessness, 13–15, 31, 32, 147
  for immigrants, 159–160
  for literacy, 6, 32, 173–174
  for social change: issues and action, 6, 31, 187–188
  for special needs and disabilities, 204
Ada, Alma Flor, 62, 142, 199–200
Addison, Joseph, 53
Adopt-A-Watershed (Web site), 124
*Adventurous Chef, The* (Arnold), 21, 59, 154
Advocacy as service, 9
Aesop, 208
*After the Dancing Days* (Rostkowski), 99
Agassi, Martine, 98
AIDS education and awareness
  action ideas for, 68–71
  activities for, 66–68
  bookshelf/books for, 71–73
  partnerships for, 68
  statistics, 66
  Web sites for, 67–68
*AIDS* (Manning), 70, 72
*AIDS: Can This Epidemic Be Stopped?* (Shein), 72
Alda, Arlene, 18, 116
*Alex, the Kid with AIDS* (Walvoord), 73
*Alice's Adventures in Wonderland* (Carroll), 29
*All Joseph Wanted* (Radin), 182
*All Kinds of Friends, Even Green!* (Senisi), 55, 210
*Alloy Peace Book* (Shaw), 97
Altman, Linda Jacobs, 116
Alvarez, Julia, 199
*América Is Her Name* (Rodríguez), 168
American Anti-Slavery Group (Web site), 188
American Humane Society (Web site), 77
American Red Cross, 68, 161
American Society for the Prevention of Cruelty to Animals (ASPCA) (Web site), 77
Amnesty International Kids (Web site), 188
Ancona, George, 107, 108, 115, 167
Andrus, Ethel Percy, 108
Angelou, Maya, 173
*Animal Farm* (Orwell), 198
*Animal Rescue Club, The* (Himmelman), 85
Animals in danger
  action ideas for, 79–82
  activities for, 6, 76–77
  bookshelf/books for, 82–86
  partnerships for, 76–77, 80, 81
  Web sites for, 77
Annan, Kofi, 12
*Any Small Goodness* (Johnston), 160, 169
Argueta, Jorge, 19, 59, 143, 168
Arnold, Ann, 21, 59, 154
Arnold, Caroline, 84
Asare, Meshack, 211
Ashabranner, Brent, 167–168
Ashe, Arthur, 71
*Asphalt Angels* (Holtwijk), 18, 155
Assessments
  by community, 44f
  forms for, 49f–51f
  issues to be addressed in, 28–29
  as learning opportunities, 30
*Aunt Chip and the Great Triple Creek Dam Affair* (Polacco), 177, 181
Authors
  interviewed
    Bornstein, 144
    Boyers, 201
    Brisson, 144–145
    Bunting, 119–120
    Collicott, 103–104
    Giblin, 73–75
    Hoose, 104
    Jacobs, 86–88
    Jiménez, 171–172
    Johnson, 157–158
    LaFaye, 184–185
    Levitin, 201–202
    Madden, 134
    Metzger, 88
    Michelson, 120–121
    Newman, 75

Pomeranc, 158
Senisi, 213–214
Spinelli, Eileen, 121–122
using interviews with, 58
young, 59–60
Avi, 62, 183
Ayer, Eleanor H., 153


## B


Babbitt, Nan, 118
*Backyard Rescue* (Ryden), 86
Backyard Wildlife Habitat Program (Web site), 136
Bahr, Mary, 116
Barber, Margaret Fairless, 11
Bartoletti, Susan Campbell, 115–116, 153
*Bat 6* (Wolff), 198–199
Bauer, Joan, 55, 199
Baylor, Byrd, 132
Be a Friend (Weiner), 72
Beatty, Patricia, 170
*Before We Were Free* (Alvarez), 199
*Be Good to Eddie Lee* (Fleming), 210
*Behind the Mountains* (Danticat), 39, 160, 169
*Beowulf*, 179
*Be Quiet, Marina!* (DeBear), 210
Berle, Milton, 22
Best Buddies International (Web site), 204
Betancourt, Jeanne, 212
*Big Mouth and Ugly Girl* (Oates), 99
Bikes not Bombs (Web site), 92
Bilingual books
for community safety, 63, 98
for elders, 63, 116
for environment, 63, 131, 133
for gardening, 63, 142, 143
for hunger and homelessness, 19
for immigrants, 55, 63, 168
for literacy, 41
for social change: issues and action, 63, 198, 199–200
for special needs and disabilities, 63, 211
Birdseye, Tom, 62, 182–183
Birmingham, John, 85
*Black Potatoes* (Bartoletti), 153
Blakeslee, Ann R., 169
*Bluish* (Hamilton), 211
Bogacki, Tomek, 59, 143
*Bonesetter's Daughter, The* (Tan), 117
Bonners, Susan, 199
Bookshelves/books
for AIDS education and awareness, 71–73
for animals in danger, 82–86
charts, 56
for community safety, 94–103
community use of, 63
for elders, 55, 113–118, 135, 143
for environment, 130–134
for gardening, 140–143
with historical content, 64
for hunger and homelessness, 151–156
for immigrants, 165–170
for literacy, 179–184
organization of, 3, 54–56
for social change: issues and action, 181, 184, 194–200
for special needs and disabilities, 181, 208–212
uses in service learning, 4, 53–54, 60–61
*See also* Bilingual books
*Bookstore Mouse, The* (Christian), 62, 182
*Born Confused* (Hidier), 169
Bornstein, Ruth Lercher, 55, 135, 143, 144
Bowles, Norma, 54, 61, 97
*Boxes for Katje* (Fleming), 98
Boyers, Sara Jane, 197, 201
Bradbury, Ray, 182
Brainstorming, 18, 29
*Breaking Through* (Jiménez), 58, 62, 167
Bridges, Ruby, 197
Brisson, Pat, 58, 139, 143, 144–145
Brown, A. Whitney, 126
Brown, Don, 181
Brown, Rita Mae, 179
Bruchac, Joseph, 199
Buchanan, Ken, 133
*Buddha Boy* (Koja), 99–100
*Bud* (O'Malley), 42, 142
Bulla, Clyde Robert, 143
Bullying, 92, 95
*See also* Community safety
Bunting, Eve, 98, 99, 116, 119–120, 132, 154, 155, 168, 182
Bureau of Citizenship and Immigration Services (Web site), 160
Burnett, Rochelle, 210
*Bus of Our Own, A* (Evans), 181
Buss, Fran Leeper, 170
*Butterflies and Lizards, Beryl and Me* (Bornstein), 55, 135, 143
*Butterfly Boy* (Kroll), 59, 115, 138
Byrd, Lee Merrill, 211


## C


Caduto, Michael, 142
Calmenson, Stephanie, 54, 210
Campbell, Joseph, 11
*Can-Do Thanksgiving, The* (Pomeranc), 15, 61, 154, 313
*Can We Save Them?* (Dobson), 82
*Can You Hear a Rainbow?* (Heelan), 59, 210
*Carlos and the Cornfield* (Stevens), 142
Carroll, Lewis, 29
Carter, Alden, 210
Casey, Patricia, 6, 59, 79, 84
*Castle on Viola Street, A* (DiSalvo-Ryan), 154
*Cat Up a Tree* (Hassett), 62, 85
*Cay, The* (Taylor), 117
Celebrations, 11–12
Centers for Disease Control (Web site), 67–68
Chaiet, Donna, 97
*Chalk Box Kid, The* (Bulla), 143
Chalofsky, Margie, 153
*Changing Places* (Chalofsky), 153
*Charlie Wilcox* (McKay), 18, 100
*ChaseR* (Rosen), 86
Chávez, César E., 2, 163
Cherry, Lynne, 132
*Chicken Sunday* (Polacco), 59, 98
Child, Lauren, 59, 133
*Children of the River* (Crew), 169
*Chimpanzees I Love, The* (Goodall), 76, 82
Chinn, Karen, 155
Christelow, Eileen, 197
Christian, Peggy, 62, 182
*Christmas Menorahs, The* (Cohn), 98
*Circuit, The* (Jiménez), 58, 62, 167, 191
Cisneros, Sandra, 199
*City Green* (DiSalvo-Ryan), 142

Civic responsibility
  described, 13
  development of, 12, 21
  as essential element of service learning, 37
*Clay Marble, The* (Ho), 169
*Click, Clack, Moo* (Cronin), 59, 189, 197
Codell, Esmé Raji, 62, 183
Cohn, Diana, 198
Cohn, Janice, 98
Cole, Henry, 6, 42, 59, 139, 143
Collaborative efforts. *See* Partnerships
Collicott, Sharleen, 6, 41, 61, 94, 99, 103–104
Collins, Marva N., 30
*Come Back, Salmon* (Cone), 84
Community
  assessments by, 44f
  benefits to, 1–2
  bookshelves/books and, 63, 97
  concept of, 8, 89
  contact information, 43f
  gardens for, 136
  identifying resources of, 25–26, 46f
  needs of, 12, 18–19
  service in *vs.* service learning, 7
  students as participants in, 11
Community safety
  action ideas for, 90–94
  activities for, 89–90
  bilingual books for, 63, 98
  bookshelf/books for, 94–103
  partnerships for, 92
  Web sites for, 90, 92
Compass Institute, 216
*Compost!* (Glaser), 39, 142
*Compost Critters* (Lavies), 39, 142
Computer activities
  for AIDS education and awareness, 69
  for animals in danger, 77
  for community safety, 91
  for elders, 109, 112, 113
  for environment, 125
  for gardening, 137
  for hunger and homelessness, 15, 149
  for immigrants 162
  for literacy, 176, 178
  for social change: issues and action, 190, 191
  for special needs and disabilities, 206
  *See also* Web sites
Cone, Molly, 84
Conflict resolution, books for, 95
Conly, Leslie, 212
Constitutional Rights Foundation, 216
*Conversation Starters As Easy As ABC 123* (Kaye), 54, 60, 112, 115
*Cool Drink of Water, A* (Kerley), 131
Coordinating Council on Juvenile Justice and Delinquency Prevention (Web site), 204
*Cootie Shots* (Bowles), 54, 61, 97
*Corner of the Universe, A* (Martin), 55, 211
Coro, Alicia, 159
Corporation of National and Community Service (Web site), 108
Cory, Shana, 21, 198
Council for Service Learning Excellence, 216
*Cowboy Boy* (Proimos), 100
*Crashed, Smashed, and Mashed* (Mitchell), 131
*Crazy Lady* (Conly), 212
Creech, Sharon, 200
Crew, Linda, 169
Criswell, Sara Dixon, 153
Cronin, Doreen, 59, 189, 197
Crum, Shutta, 200
Curricular connections
  for AIDS education and awareness, 68, 69
  for animals in danger, 77–78
  for community safety, 90, 91
  developing projects with strong, 18–19, 31–32, 38f–42f
  for elders, 108, 109
  for environment, 1, 124–126
  for gardening, 136, 137
  for hunger and homelessness, 14–15, 48, 149
  for immigrants, 160–161, 162
  for literacy, 175, 176
  with required literature selections, 56–57
  for social change: issues and action, 189, 190
  for special needs and disabilities, 204–205, 206
Cushman, Karen, 156


## D


da Costa Nunez, Ralph, 155
Dadey, Debbie, 101
Daly, Niki, 181
*Dancing with Dziadziu* (Bartoletti), 115–116
Danticat, Edwidge, 39, 160, 169
*Darnell Rock Reporting* (Myers), 155
*Day's Work, A* (Bunting), 168
*Dear Children of the Earth* (Schimmel), 132
*Dear Whiskers* (Nagda), 62, 182
DeBear, Kirsten, 210
DeChardin, Pierre Teilhard, 62
Deedy, Carmen Agra, 99
Defenders of Wildlife (Web site), 77
*Define "Normal"* (Peters), 100
Dejong, Meindert, 86
*Deliverance of the Dancing Bears, The* (Stanley), 82
Demonstration
  bookshelf use during, 61
  description of stage, 11–12
  methods of, 29, 36, 46f
  reflection during, 27
*DeShawn Days* (Medina), 98
*Dew Drop Dead* (Howe), 155
*Different Kind of Hero, A* (Blakeslee), 169
Direct service, 9
Disabilities education and awareness. *See* Special needs and disabilities
DiSalvo-Ryan, DyAnne, 14, 142, 154, 155
Discrimination, 187, 195
  *See also* Social change: issues and action
Dobson, David, 82
Dodds, Bill, 212
*Doing Time Online* (Siebold), 111, 117
Dolan, Edward, 132
*Don't Laugh at Me* (Seskin), 98
Do Something (Web site), 188
Douglass, Frederick, 90
Dow, Unity, 73
Dowell, Frances O'Roark, 156
*Down to Earth* (Rosen), 6, 59, 139, 142
*Dr. White* (Goodall), 210
*Dragonwings* (Yep), 169
*Dream Freedom* (Levitan), 55, 199
*Drive-By* (Ewing), 100
*Ducks Disappearing* (Naylor), 62, 79, 85
Dwight, Laura, 211

## E


*Eagle Song* (Bruchac), 199
Earth Day Network (Web site), 124
Earth Force (Web site), 124
*Earthshine* (Nelson), 73
Eclare, Melanie, 42, 135, 142
Edelman, Marian Wright, 146
Educators for Social Responsibility (ESR), 90
Edwards, Becky, 211
*Edwina Victorious* (Bonners), 199
Ehrenreich, Barbara, 15, 154
Elderly United (Web site), 107
Elders
  action ideas for, 108–110, 139–140, 161, 205, 207
  activities for, 6, 31, 106–107
  bilingual books for, 63, 116
  bookshelf/books for, 55, 113–118, 135, 143
  partnerships for, 106
  Web sites for, 107–109
Eliot, George, 151
*Empty Lot, The* (Fife), 132
Environment
  action ideas for, 125, 126–129
  activities for, 123–124
  bilingual books for, 63, 131, 133
  bookshelf/books for, 130–134
  partnerships for, 126
  Web sites for, 124, 127
Ernst, Lisa Campbell, 55, 181–182
*Esperenza Rising* (Ryan), 169
Estes, Eleanor, 156
Evans, Freddi Williams, 181
Ewing, Lynne, 100


## F


*Fahrenheit 451* (Bradbury), 182
*Far and Beyon'* (Dow), 73
*Feathers and Fools* (Fox), 93, 98
*Feed the Children First* (Lyons), 14, 153
Fenner, Carol, 156
*Fernando's Gift* (Keister), 131
Fiction books, 55–56
  for AIDS education and awareness, 73
  for animals in danger, 85–86
  for community safety, 99–103
  for elders, 117–118
  for environment, 133–134
  for gardening, 143
  for hunger and homelessness, 155–156
  for immigrants, 169–170
  for literacy, 182–184
  for social change: issues and action, 198–200
  for special needs and disabilities, 211–212
Fierstein, Harvey, 41, 99
Fife, Dale, 132
*50 Ways to a Safer World* (Giggans), 97
Fitzpatrick, Marie-Louise, 14, 155
Flake, Sharon G., 156
Fleishman, Paul, 32, 55, 143
Fleming, Candace, 85, 98, 210
Florida Learn & Serve, 216
*Fly Away Home* (Bunting), 154
Forms
  assessment, 44f, 49f–51f
  community contact information, 43f
  community needs identification, 34f
  planning, 38f
    completed examples of, 39–42
  project promotion, 46f
  proposal, 35f, 45f
  for reflection, 47f–48f
  student inventory of skills and knowledge, 33f
*Four Ugly Cats in Apartment 3D, The* (Sachs), 86
Fox, Mem, 93, 98, 117
*Freak the Mighty* (Philbrick), 212
*Free the Children* (Kielburger), 31, 55, 196
Free the Children (Web site), 188
*Friends at School* (Burnett), 210
*From the Mixed-up Files of Mrs. Basil E. Frankweiler* (Konigsburg), 215
Funding, 25, 216


## G


Gallo, Donald R., 101
Gandhi, Mahatma, 93
Gang activity, 94
  *See also* Community safety
*Gardener, The* (Stewart), 142
Gardening
  action ideas for, 136, 138–140, 148, 150
  activities for, 6, 32, 135–136
  bilingual books for, 63, 142, 143
  bookshelf/books for, 140–143
  Web sites for, 136
*Garden of Happiness, The* (Tamar), 142
Garland, Sherry, 102
*Gathering the Sun* (Ada), 142
Gauthier, Gail, 134
*Generation Fix* (Rusch), 14, 31, 196
*Geography Club* (Hartinger), 100
George, Jean Craighead, 133, 134
Giblin, James Cross, 54, 67, 70, 73–75, 94
*Gift of the Tree* (Tresselt), 132
Giggans, Patricia Occhiuzzo, 97
Giraffe Project, The, 216
*Girl of Kosovo* (Mead), 100
Girod, Christina M., 62, 181
*Give a Boy a Gun* (Strasser), 93, 100
Glaser, Elizabeth, 70
Glaser, Linda, 39, 142
Glass, Sue, 116
*Gleam and Glow* (Bunting), 98
Godden, Rumer, 170
*Goin' Someplace Special* (McKissack), 181
Goldberg, Natalie, 55
Goldish, Meish, 39, 167
*Gold-Threaded Dress, The* (Marsden), 170
Goméz, Elizabeth, 59
Goodall, Jane, 76, 82, 210
Gottfried, Ted, 154
*Graduation of Jake Moon, The* (Park), 117
Grady, Sean M., 62, 180
*Grandma's Records* (Velasquez), 116
*Grandparents Around the World* (Lakin), 115
Grant applications, 25, 216
*Grapes of Wrath, The* (Steinback), 155–156
*Greatest Table, The* (Rosen), 59, 154
*Great Kapok Tree, The* (Cherry), 132
*Great Trash Bash, The* (Leedy), 124, 132
*Green Truck Garden Giveaway, The* (Martin), 135, 142
Grimké, Angelina E., 196
Groth, Bonnie Lee, 153
*Growing Older* (Ancona), 107, 108, 115

*Growing Older: What Young People Should Know About Aging* (Langone), 18, 31, 112, 115
Gyatso, Tenzin, 146

## H

Hamilton, Virginia, 211
*Handbook for Boys* (Myers), 112, 117
*Hands Are Not for Hitting* (Agassi), 98
*Happy Birthday Mr. Kang* (Roth), 168
*Hard Times Jar, The* (Smothers), 181
Harness, Cheryl, 18, 196
*Harry Potter and the Sorcerer's Stone* (Rowling), 100
Harshman, Marc, 211
Hartinger, Brent, 100
*Harvest* (Ancona), 167
*Harvest of Color, A* (Eclare), 42, 135, 142
Hassett, Ann, 62, 85
Hate crimes, 94, 95
  *See also* Community safety
Hawkins, Anne Hunsacker, 72–73
*Healers of the Wild* (Jacobs), 77, 84
Heelan, Jamee Riggio, 21059
Hegi, Ursula, 211
Heifer Project (Web site), 92
Herbert, George, 16
Herold, Maggie Rugg, 39, 168
Hesse, Hermann, 102
Hesse, Karen, 32, 183
*Hey, Little Ant!* (Hoose), 41, 58, 60, 61, 98
*Hey! Get Off Our Train* (Birmingham), 85
Hiaasen, Carl, 86
Hidier, Tanuk Desai, 169
Hill, Kirkpatrick, 62, 173, 184
Himmelman, John, 81, 85
HIV. *See* AIDS education and awareness
Ho, Minfong, 169
Hogan, Linda, 81, 84
*Holes* (Sachar), 101
Holmes, Oliver Wendell, 27
Holtwijk, Ineke, 18, 155
*Home Is Where We Live* (Groth), 153
*Homeless Children* (Ayer), 153
Homelessness. *See* Hunger and homelessness
*Homelessness* (Criswell), 153
*Homelessness: Can We Solve the Problem?* (Rozakis), 153
*Homelessness: Whose Problem Is It?* (Gottfried), 154
Homes for the Homeless, 151
Hoose, Philip, 18, 31, 41, 58, 60, 61, 98, 104, 196, 197
*Hoot* (Hiaasen), 86
*Hope Was Here* (Bauer), 55, 199
*House on Mango Street, The* (Cisneros), 199
"How Does Our Garden Grow" (Web site), 136
Howe, James, 6, 58, 61, 101, 103, 105, 155
*How Humans Make Friends* (Leedy), 98
*Hundred Dresses, The* (Estes), 156
*Hundred Penny Box, The* (Mathis), 117–118
Hunger and homelessness
  action ideas for, 136, 138, 139, 140, 148–151
  activities for, 13–15, 31, 32, 147
  bilingual books for, 19
  bookshelf/books for, 151–156
  Web sites for, 147
*Hurry Granny Annie* (Alda), 18, 116
Hyde, Catherine Ryan, 200

## I

I AM Foundation (Web site), 175
*Ian's Walk* (Lears), 211
*Identity* (Kundera), 215
*If You Come Softly* (Woodson), 191, 199
*Illiteracy* (Grady), 62, 180
Illustrators, 58, 59
*I Miss Franklin P. Shuckles* (Snihura), 98
Immigrants
  action ideas for, 161–165
  activities for, 159–160
  bilingual books for, 55, 63, 168
  bookshelf/books for, 165–170
  partnerships for, 163, 165
  Web sites for, 160
  *See also* Social change: issues and action
Immigration and Naturalization Service (INS), 163
*Immigration* (Goldish), 39, 167
*Increase the Peace* (Kaye), 60, 97
*Indian School* (Cooper), 180
Indirect service, 9
*In Good Hands* (Swinburne), 84
Integrated learning, 12
International Crane Foundation, 81
International Labour Organization, 174–175
International Rescue Committee (Web site), 160
Internet
  author/illustrator connections via, 58
  publicizing projects on, 29
  for research, 21
  *See also* Computer activities; Web sites
*Interrupted Journey* (Lasky), 80, 84
Interviews
  with Bornstein, 144
  with Boyers, 201
  with Brisson, 144–145
  with Bunting, 119–120
  with Collicott, 103–104
  with Giblin, 73–75
  with Hoose, 104
  with Jacobs, 86–88
  with Jiménez, 171–172
  with Johnson, 157–158
  with LaFaye, 184–185
  with Levitin, 201–202
  with Madden, 134
  with Michelson, 120–121
  with Newman, 75
  with Pomeranc, 158
  with Senisi, 213–214
  with Spinelli, Eileen, 121–122
  using, 58
*In the Time of the Butterflies* (Alvarez), 199
*Intimate Nature* (Hogan), 81, 84
Intolerance, 94, 186, 187
  *See also* Social change: issues and action
*Island of the Blue Dolphins* (O'Dell), 133
*Issues in Racism* (Williams), 196
*Issues in the Environment* (Netzley), 131
*It Doesn't Have to Be This Way* (Rodríguez), 98
*It's Our World, Too!* (Hoose), 196
*It's Still a Dog's New York* (Roth), 59, 98–99
*I Want to Be an Environmentalist* (Maze), 39, 124, 131

## J

*Jack's Garden* (Cole), 6, 42, 59, 139, 143
Jacobs, Shannon K., 77, 84

Jane Goodall Institute (Web site), 77
*Jemma's Journey* (Romain), 197
Jiménez, Francisco, 32, 41, 55, 58, 62, 167, 171–172, 181, 191
*Joe's Wish* (Proimos), 116
Johnson, Lindsay Lee, 31, 156, 157–158
Johnston, Tony, 160, 168, 169
Jones, Quincy, 106
Jones, Ron, 210
Joose, Barbara, 99
Journal writing, 27, 28, 48f
*Journey of the Sparrows* (Buss), 170
Joyce, Bruce, 113
*Judy Moody Saves the World* (McDonald), 55, 133
*Just Call Me Stupid* (Birdseye), 62, 182–183
*Just Juice* (Hesse), 32, 183
*Just Kids* (Senisi), 32, 62, 203, 210

## K

Kaiser Family Foundation (Web site), 67
Kakugawa, Frances H., 115
Kaye, Devora, 54, 60, 97, 112, 115, 160
Kehret, Peg, 86, 210
Keister, Douglas, 131
Keller, Helen, 187, 205
Kerley, Barbara, 131
Kerr, M. E., 200
KIDS Consortium, 216
KidsGardening! (Web site), 136
*Kid's Guide to Social Action, The* (Lewis), 29, 32, 39, 196
"Kids Make a Difference" (Web site), 124
Kids' Planet (Web site), 77
Kids Voting USA (Web site), 188
*Kids with Courage* (Lewis), 196
Kielburger, Craig, 31, 55, 193, 196
*King of the Dragons* (Fenner), 156
*King of the Kooties* (Dadey), 101
Kochenderfer, Lee, 143
Koertge, Ron, 118, 212
Koja, Kathe, 99–100
Konigsburg, E. L., 215
Koop, C. Everett, 66
Kozol, Jonathan, 189
Kroll, Virginia, 59, 115, 138
Kundera, Milos, 215

## L

LaFaye, Alexandria, 184–185
Lakin, Patricia, 115
*La Mariposa* (Jiménez), 32, 41, 55, 181
Langone, John, 18, 31, 112, 115
Lappe, Frances Moore, 147
Lasky, Kathryn, 80, 84
Lavies, Bianca, 39, 142
Le, Ngoan, 89
Learn and Serve America, 216
*Learning Disabilities* (Girod), 62, 181
Lears, Laurie, 211
Lee, Harper, 200
Lee, Lauren, 39, 170
Leedy, Loreen, 98, 124, 132
Leighton, Audrey O., 117
Levine, Beth Seidel, 102
Levitin, Sonia, 199, 201–202
Lewin, Betsy, 59
Lewis, Barbara, 29, 32, 39, 196
*Library Card, The* (Jerry Spinelli), 183
Lied, Kate, 155
*Life Like Mine* (UNICEF), 196
Lin, Grace, 135, 143
*Linda Brown, You Are Not Alone* (Thomas), 54, 196
Lions Clubs, 92
*Listen to Us* (Springer), 196
Literacy
    action ideas for, 108, 175–179
    activities for, 6, 32, 173–174
    bilingual books for, 41
    bookshelf/books for, 62, 63, 179–184
    Web sites for, 174–175
Littlechild, George, 198
*Little Engine That Could, The* (Piper), 198
*Long March, The* (Fitzpatrick), 14, 155
*Lost Boys of Natinga* (Walgren), 154
Lowell, James Russell, 142
*Lupita Mañana* (Beatty), 170
Lyons, Mary E., 14, 153

## M

Madden, Don, 55, 61, 133
*Make Way for Ducklings* (McCloskey), 85
*Making Up Megaboy* (Walter), 93, 101
Manning, Karen, 70, 72
*Margarite y Margarita*, 41
Marsden, Carolyn, 170
Martin, Ann M., 55, 211
Martin, Jacqueline B., 85, 135, 142
Marx, Groucho, 177
Maryland State Department of Education, 216
Mathis, Shannon Bell, 117–118
Maze, Stephanie, 39, 124, 131
McCain, Becky Ray, 99
McCloskey, Robert, 85
McDonald, Megan, 55, 133
McDonough, Yona Zeldis, 31, 196
McKay, Sharon E., 18, 100
McKissack, Patricia, 181
McMillan, Bruce, 54, 79, 82, 84
McPhail, David, 99, 148, 155
Mead, Alice, 100
Mead, Margaret, 81
Medina, Tony, 98
*Memory Box, The* (Bahr), 116
Mendez, Chico, 124
Metzger, Deena, 86, 88
Meyer, Carolyn, 200
Michelson, Richard, 18, 108, 116, 120–121
Mickaelson, Ben, 118
*Middle of Everywhere* (Pipher), 39, 167
*Midsummer's Night Dream, A* (Shakespeare), 179
Miller, William, 173, 181
Million Books for Kids Campaign (Web site), 175
*Misfits, The* (Howe), 6, 58, 61, 101
*Miss Happiness and Miss Flower* (Godden), 170
*Missing 'Gator of Gumbo Limbo, The* (George), 133
Mitchell, Joyce Slayton, 131
Mochizuki, Ken, 198
*Mole Music* (McPhail), 99
*Money Hungry* (Flake), 156
Mora, Pat, 182
*Mosaic Moon* (Kakugawa), 115
*Movie in My Pillow, A* (Argueta), 19, 59, 168
*Mr. Lincoln's Way* (Polacco), 99
*Mrs. Katz and Tush* (Polacco), 116

Muir, John, 123
*My Brother Sammy* (Edwards), 211
*My Diary from Here to There* (Pérez), 55, 168
Myers, Christopher, 99
Myers, Walter Dean, 112, 117, 155
*My First Garden* (Bogacki), 59, 143
*My Name Is Brian* (Betancourt), 212
*My Name Is María Isabel* (Ada), 62, 199–200
*My Name Is Yoon* (Recorvits), 160, 168
*My Sister Annie* (Dodds), 212

## N

Na, An, 170
Nagda, Ann Whitehead, 182
Naidoo, Beverly, 200
National Academy for Teaching and Learning About Aging (Web site), 108
National Arbor Day "Kids Make a Difference" (Web site), 124
National Association of S.A.V.E. (Students Against Violence Everywhere) (Web site), 90
National Center for Learning and Citizenship, 217
National Coalition for the Homeless (NCH), 147
National Dropout Prevention Center, 217
National Institute of Environmental Health Sciences (Web site), 127
National Resource Defense Council (Web site), 124
National Service Inclusion Project (Web site), 204
National Service-Learning Clearinghouse, 217
National Service-Learning Partnership, 217
National Service Resource Center (Web site), 174
National Wildlife Federation (Web site), 136
National Youth Leadership Council (NYLC), 67, 217
*Native American Gardening* (Caduto), 142
Natural resources/nature appreciation, 130–131
  *See also* Environment
Naylor, Phyllis Reynolds, 62, 79, 85
Nelson, Theresa, 73
Netzley, Patricia D., 131
Newman, Lesléa, 55, 58, 73, 75
*Nickel and Dimed* (Ehrenreich), 15, 154
*Nights of the Pufflings* (McMillan), 54, 79, 82, 84
*Nobody Knew What to Do* (McCain), 99
Nonfiction books, 43–55
  for AIDS education and awareness, 72–73
  for animals in danger, 82, 84
  for community safety, 97–98
  for elders, 115
  for environment, 131–132
  for gardening, 142
  for hunger and homelessness, 153–154
  for immigrants, 167–168
  for literacy, 180–181
  for social change: issues and action, 196–197
  for special needs and disabilities, 210

## O

Oates, Joyce Carol, 99
O'Dell, Scott, 133
*Of Mice and Men* (Steinbeck), 212
O'Malley, Kevin, 42, 142
*Once a Wolf* (Swinburne), 84
*Once Upon a Time* (Daly), 181
*One Day at Wood Green Animal Shelter* (Casey), 6, 59, 79, 84
*One Good Apple* (Paladino), 59, 131
*One Less Fish* (Toft), 132
*On the Brink of Extinction* (Arnold), 84
*On the Fringe* (Gallo), 101
Oral histories, 107, 108, 111, 113, 163
*Oranges on Golden Mountain* (Partridge), 168
*Orphan Train Rider* (Warren), 54, 154
Orwell, George, 198
*Other America, The* (Stewart), 18, 31, 154
*Our Poisoned Waters* (Dolan), 132
*Out of Bounds* (Naidoo), 200
Oxfam America/International (Web site), 147

## P

Pak, Soyung, 168
Paladino, Catherine, 59, 131
Park, Barbara, 117
Partnerships
  for AIDS education and awareness, 68
  for animals in danger, 76–77, 80, 81, 82
  benefits of, 2, 12
  with community organizations, 8, 19, 22–23, 43f, 44f, 62
  for community safety, 92
  for elders, 106
  for environment, 126
  as essential element of service learning, 37
  for immigrants, 161, 163, 165
  with other educators, 22
  with parents, 23–24, 80
  potential organizations for, 23
  for social change: issues and action, 191, 193
  for special needs and disabilities, 205, 207, 208
  students and, 20–21, 23
  success of, 21
  tutoring programs, 62
Partridge, Elizabeth, 168
*Passage to Freedom* (Mochizuki), 198
*Pay It Forward* (Hyde), 200
Peace Child International, 197
*Pelican Swallowed My Head, A* (Riccuti), 81, 84
*People Who Hugged the Trees, The* (Rose), 55, 132
*People with AIDS* (Stewart), 72
Pérez, Amada Irma, 55, 168
Personal safety, 95
  *See also* Community safety
Peters, Julie Anne, 100
*Petey* (Mickaelson), 118
Philbrick, Rodman, 212
Picasso, Pablo, 59
Picture books, 55
  for AIDS education and awareness, 73
  for animals in danger, 85
  for community safety, 98–99
  for elders, 115–117
  for environment, 132–133
  for gardening, 142–143
  for hunger and homelessness, 154–155
  for immigrants, 168
  for literacy, 181–182
  for social change: issues and action, 197–198
  for special needs and disabilities, 210–211
Piercy, Marge, 71
*Pink and Say* (Polacco), 6, 108, 198
*Pinky and Rex and the Bully* (Howe), 61, 101
*Pipaluk and the Whales* (Himmelman), 81, 85
Piper, Watty, 198
Pipher, Mary, 39, 167
*Place to Grow, A* (Pak), 168
Play adaptations, 61
Polacco, Patricia, 6, 32, 59, 62, 98, 99, 108, 116, 177, 181, 182, 198

Pomeranc, Marion Hess, 15, 31, 61, 154, 158
*Potato* (Lied), 155
*Prairie School* (Avi), 62, 183
Prejudice, 187, 195
  *See also* Social change: issues and action
Preparation
  for AIDS education and awareness, 66–68
  for animals in danger, 76–77
  bookshelf use during, 60
  for community safety, 89
  description of, 10, 36
  for elders, 106–107
  for environment, 123–124
  for gardening, 135–136
  for hunger and homelessness, 146–147
  for immigrants, 159–160
  for literacy, 173–174
  reflection during, 26
  for social change: issues and action, 187–188
  for special needs and disabilities, 203–204
Pringle, Laurence, 97
*Printer, The* (Uhlberg), 211
Proimos, James, 100, 116
Project Linus (Web site), 204
Proposal forms, 35f, 45f
Publicity, 29, 46f

## R

*Rabble Rousers* (Harness), 18, 196
*Rachel Carson*, 39
Radin, Ruth Yaffe, 182
Rahaman, Vashanti, 181
*Rainbow Joe and Me* (Strom), 211
Rand, Gloria, 139
*Ran Wild* (Cherry), 132
Rappaport, Doreen, 197
*Read for Me, Mama* (Rahaman), 181
Reciprocity, 12
Recorvits, Helen, 160, 168
*Recycle Every Day!* (Wallace), 132
Recycling, books for, 131, 132, 133
  *See also* Environment
Reflection
  bookshelf use during, 61
  description of stage, 11, 36
  importance of, 26, 215
  prompts for, 27–28
  students leading, 28
  tools for, 27, 28, 47f, 48f
  when to use, 26–27
*Remember Me?* (Glass), 116
Research, 9, 21
*Revealers, The* (Wilhelm), 101
Riccuti, Edward, 81, 84
*Richard Wright and the Library Card* (Miller), 173, 181
RMC Research Corporation, 217
Roberts-Davis, Tanya, 60, 197
Rochman, Hazel, 165
Roddick, Anita, 79
Rodríguez, Luis J., 98, 168
*Rodzina* (Cushman), 156
Rogers, Will, 17
Romain, Trevor, 197
*Romeo and Juliet* (Shakespeare), 102
Roots & Shoots (Web site), 77
Rose, Deborah Lee, 55, 132
Rosen, Michael J., 6, 59, 86, 139, 142, 154, 183
*Rosie* (Calmenson), 54, 210
Rossiter, Nan Pearson, 211
Rostkowski, Margaret J., 99
Roth, Susan L., 59, 98–99, 168
Rowling, J. K., 100
Rozakis, Laurie, 153
Rudolph, Wilma, 110
*Rugby and Rosie* (Rossiter), 211
Rusch, Elizabeth, 14, 31, 196
Ryan, Pan Muñoz, 169
Ryden, Hope, 86

## S

Sachar, Louis, 101
*Sachiko Means Happiness* (Sakai), 116
Sachs, Marilyn, 86
*Safe Zone, The* (Chaiet), 97
*Sahara Special* (Codell), 62, 183
*Saily's Journey* (da Costa Nunez), 155
Sakai, Kimiko, 116
*Sam and the Lucky Money* (Chinn), 155
*Saving Lily* (Kehret), 86
*Saving the Planet* (Gauthier), 134
Say, Allen, 31, 55, 112, 116
Sayres, Meghan Nuttall, 132
Schimmel, Schim, 132
*School for Pompey Walker, A* (Rosen), 183
Schumacher, E. F., 10
Scully, Frank, 21
*Seedfolks* (Fleishman), 32, 55, 143
*Seeing Things My Way* (Carter), 210
Senge, Peter M., 8
Senior citizens. *See* Elders
*Senior Corps* (Web site), 108
Senisi, Ellen B., 32, 55, 62, 203, 210, 213–214
*Series of Unfortunate Events, A* (Snicket), 184
Service learning
  blueprint
    entry points for, 18–19
    overview of, 16–17
    partnerships, 22–24, 38f, 43, 44f
    planning framework, 19–21
    proposals, 25, 35f, 45f
    reflection, 26, 47f, 48f
  definition of, 6, 7
  elements of, 8–9, 12–13, 37
  importance of, 1–3
  lack of time for, 30
  reflection during, 26–27
  stages of, 36 *See also specific stages*
  use by nonschool organizations, 4, 7
Seskin, Steve, 98
*Shadow of the Dragon* (Garland), 102
Shakespeare, William, 102, 179
*Shape of Betts Meadow, The* (Sayres), 132
Share Our Strength (Web site), 147
Shaw, Tucker, 97
Shea, Pegi Deitz, 161, 168, 170
Shein, Lori, 71
*¡Sí, Se Puede!* (Cohn), 198
*Siddhartha* (Hesse), 102
Siebold, Jan, 111, 117

Simmonds, Nicola, 59
*Singing with Mamma Lou* (Altman), 116
*Sissy Duckling, The* (Fierstein), 41, 99
*Sisters in Strength* (McDonough), 31, 196
*Skirt, The* (Soto), 39, 170
*Slap Your Sides* (Kerr), 200
*Small, Good Thing, A* (Hawkins), 72–73
*Small Steps* (Kehret), 210
Smith, Robert Kimmel, 118
*Smoking* (Pringle), 97
*Smoky Nights* (Bunting), 99
Smothers, Ethel Footman, 181
Snicket, Lemony, 184
Snihura, Ulana, 98
Social change: issues and action
  action ideas for, 189–193
  activities for, 6, 31, 187–188
  bilingual books for, 63, 198, 199–200
  bookshelf/books for, 181, 184, 194–200
  unique challenges of, 186
  Web sites for, 188
  *See also* Immigrants; Special needs and disabilities
Society for the Prevention of Cruelty to Animals, 81
*Somebody Loves You, Mr. Hatch* (Eileen Spinelli), 59, 61, 116
*Someday a Tree* (Bunting), 132
*Something Beautiful* (Wyeth), 198, 215
*Sosu's Call* (Asare), 211
Soto, Gary, 39, 170
*Soul Moon Soup* (Johnson), 31, 156
Southern Poverty Law Center (Web site), 187, 188
Special needs and disabilities
  action ideas for, 82, 205–208
  activities for, 204
  bilingual books for, 63, 211
  bookshelf/books for, 181, 208–212
  described, 203
  Web sites for, 204
  *See also* Social change: issues and action
Special Olympics (Web site), 204
Spinelli, Eileen, 59, 61, 116, 121–122
Spinelli, Jerry, 102, 103, 183
*Spitting Image* (Crum), 200
Springer, Jane, 196
Standing Bear, Luther (Lakota Sioux Chief), 129
*Stand Up for Your Rights* (Peace Child International), 197
Stanley, Elizabeth, 82
*Stargirl* (Jerry Spinelli), 102
*Stars in the Darkness* (Joose), 99
Steinbeck, John, 155–156, 212
*Stella* (Lee), 39, 170
*Stella Louella's Runaway Book* (Ernst), 55, 181–182
*Step From Heaven, A* (Na), 170
Stevens, Romero, 142
Stewart, Gail B., 72, 154
Stewart, Sarah, 142
*Stoner and Spaz* (Koertge), 212
S.T.O.P. (Slavery That Oppresses People) (Web site), 188
*Storm, The* (Harshman), 211
*Stranger in the Mirror* (Say), 31, 55, 112, 116
Strasser, Todd, 93, 100
*Strength of Saints* (LaFaye), 184
Strom, Maria Diaz, 211
Students
  assessment by, 28–29, 51f
  benefits to, 1, 2, 7, 10, 13, 215
  choices by, within planning framework, 20
  development of civic responsibility by, 10–11, 21
  ensuring learning opportunities for, 19–20, 38f–42f
  initiating projects, 8, 11, 12, 18–19, 24–25, 34f, 35f
  inventory of skills and knowledge, 24–25, 33f
  partnerships and, 20–21, 23
  reflection and, 26, 28
  writing by, 61
    for AIDS education and awareness, 68, 70, 71
    for animals in danger, 80, 81
    community safety, 92, 93, 94
    for elders, 108, 110–111, 112–113
    for environment, 126, 127, 129
    for gardening, 135, 139
    for hunger and homelessness, 151
    for immigrants, 163, 164–165
    for literacy, 175, 177, 179, 189
    proposals, 25, 35f, 45f
    for social change: issues and action, 189, 191, 192
    for special needs and disabilities, 208
Study Circles Resource Center (Web site), 160
*Summer My Father Was Ten, The* (Brisson), 143
*Summer Wheels* (Bunting), 99
*Sunshine Home* (Bunting), 116
Suzán, Gerardo, 59
Suzuki, David, 39, 132
Swinburne, Stephen R., 84


## T


*Table Where Rich People Sit, The* (Baylor), 132
Tamar, Erika, 142
Tan, Amy, 117
*Tangled Threads* (Shea), 170
Taylor, Theodore, 117
*Teddy Bear, The* (McPhail), 148, 155
*Teen Power Politics* (Boyers), 197
Teens, Crime and the Community (Web site), 90
*Thank You, Mr. Falker* (Polacco), 6, 32, 62, 182
*There's an Owl in the Shower* (George), 134
*They Came from the Bronx* (Waldman), 76, 85
*This House Is Made of Mud* (Buchanan), 133
*This Land Is My Land* (Littlechild), 198
Thomas, Joyce Carol, 54, 196
Thoreau, Henry David, 138
*Through My Eyes* (Bridges), 197
*Tiger, Tiger Burning Bright* (Koertge), 118
*To Be of Use* (Piercy), 71
*Toestomper and the Caterpillars* (Collicott), 6, 41, 61, 94, 99
Toft, Michelle, 132
*To Kill a Mockingbird* (Lee), 200
*Tomás and the Library Lady* (Mora), 182
*Too Far Away to Touch* (Newman), 55, 58, 73
*Too Young for Yiddish* (Michelson), 18, 108, 116
*To Seek a Better World* (Ashabranner), 167–168
*Train to Somewhere, A* (Bunting), 155
*Treasure on Gold Street* (Byrd), 211
Tresselt, Alvin, 132
*Trudi & Pia* (Hegi), 211
*Tuck Everlasting* (Babbitt), 118
Tutoring. *See* Literacy
TV-Turnoff Network (Web site), 177


## U


*Ugly Vegetables, The* (Lin), 135, 143
Uhlberg, Myron, 211
*Uncle Rain Cloud* (Johnston), 168
*Uncle Willie and the Soup Kitchen* (DiSalvo-Ryan), 14, 155
UNICEF (Web site), 67

## V

Velasquez, Eric, 116
Vermont Community Works, 217
Verniero, Joan C., 73
*Very Important Day, A* (Herold), 39, 168
*Victory Garden, The* (Kochenderfer), 143
Volunteer work *vs.* service learning, 7
*Vote!* (Christelow), 197

## W

Waldman, Neil, 76, 85
Walgren, Judy, 154
*Walk Two Moons* (Creech), 200
Wallace, Nancy Elizabeth, 132
Walter, Virginia, 93, 101
Walvoord, Linda, 73
*Wanda's Roses* (Brisson), 58, 139, 143
Ward, Lorraine, 133
Warren, Andrea, 54, 154
*Wartville Wizard, The* (Madden), 55, 61, 133
*War with Grandpa, The* (Smith), 118
*Washing the Willow Tree Loon* (Martin), 85
*We Are the Many* (Rappaport), 197
Web sites
  for AIDS education and awareness, 67–68
  for animals in danger, 77
  for community safety, 90, 92
  for elders, 107–109
  for environment, 124, 127
  for gardening, 136
  for hunger and homelessness, 147
  for immigrants, 160
  for literacy, 174–175
  for social change: issues and action, 188
  for special needs and disabilities, 204
*We Can Do It!* (Dwight), 211
*We Can Work It Out* (Polland), 98
*Wednesday Surprise, The* (Bunting), 182
*We Need to Go to School* (Roberts-Davis), 60, 197
*We Were There, Too!* (Hoose), 18, 31, 197
*What Planet Are You From, Clarice Bean?* (Child), 59, 133
*Wheel on the School Bus, The* (Dejong), 86
*When Agnes Caws* (Fleming), 85
*When Christmas Comes Again* (Levine), 102
*When Plague Strikes* (Giblin), 54, 67, 70, 73, 94
*Where I'd Like to Be* (Dowell), 156
*Whispering Cloth, The* (Shea), 161, 168
*White Lilacs* (Meyer), 200
Wiener, Lori S., 72
Wiesel, Elie, 186
*Wildlife Refuge* (Ward), 133
*Wilfred Gordon McDonald Partidge* (Fox), 117
Wilhelm, Doug, 101
Williams, Mary E., 196
*Window of Time, A* (Leighton), 117
*Wings* (Myers), 99
Wolff, Virginia Euwer, 198–199
Woodson, Jacqueline, 191, 199
*Wringer* (Jerry Spinelli), 103
Wyeth, Sharon Dennis, 198, 215

## X

*Xóchitl and the Flowers* (Argueta), 143

## Y

Yalowitz, Paul, 59
*Year of Miss Agnes, The* (Hill), 62, 173, 184
*Yellow Star, The* (Deedy), 99
Yep, Lawrence, 169
*You Are the Earth* (Suzuki), 39, 132
*You Can Call Me Willy* (Verniero), 73
*You Forgot Your Skirt, Amelia Bloomer!* (Cory), 21, 198
*Your Move* (Bunting), 99
Youth Service America/California, 217

## Z

Zasloff, David, 30
Zoom Into Action (Web site), 188

# About the Author

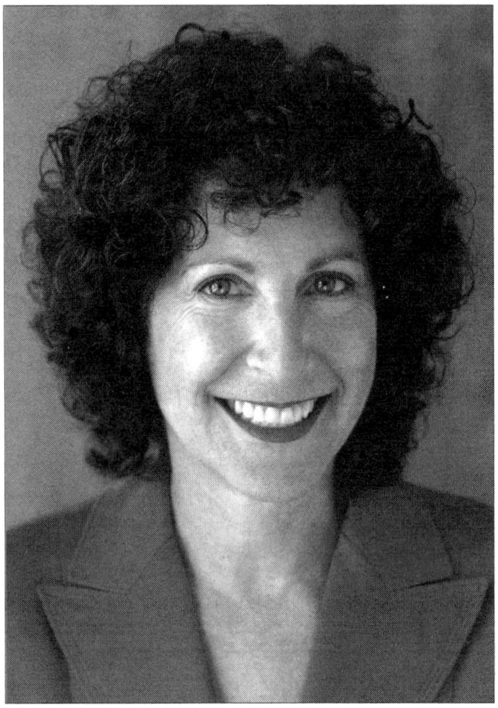

**Cathryn Berger Kaye, M.A.,** enjoys books, nature, theater, writing, and the world of service learning. As a classroom teacher, she worked with grades K–12 in rural, suburban, and urban settings. Cathryn has worked in nonprofit organizations with national outreach developing service learning programs throughout the country. Now, as an international consultant, she is a well-respected and engaging keynote speaker and workshop leader. She assists state departments of education, university faculty and teacher education students, school districts, and classroom teachers and administrators on a variety of issues such as service learning, literacy, civic engagement, youth leadership, and improving school climate and culture.

As an author, Cathryn's publications include *A Kids' Guide to Climate Change & Global Warming*, *A Kids' Guide to Protecting & Caring for Animals*, *A Kids' Guide to Helping Others Read & Succeed*, *A Kids' Guide to Hunger & Homelessness*, *The Service Learning Books: A Bibliography of Fiction & Nonfiction to Inspire Student Learning and Action*, *Service Learning: Raising Service Projects to the Next Level*, and *Parent Involvement in Service Learning*. She has developed a comprehensive curriculum *Strategies for Success with Literacy* integrating literacy development with character education and service learning. Cathryn's articles on improving education appear in magazines and on the Internet. She also writes fiction and nonfiction stories and books for children and adults. She is the author of *Word Works: Why the Alphabet Is a Kid's Best Friend*.

While Cathryn has lived in many places and enjoys traveling, she is glad to feel the ocean breezes at home in Los Angeles. Most of all, she adores her family—her two daughters, Ariel and Devora, and husband, Barry—who inspire her daily.

# Other Great Products from Free Spirit

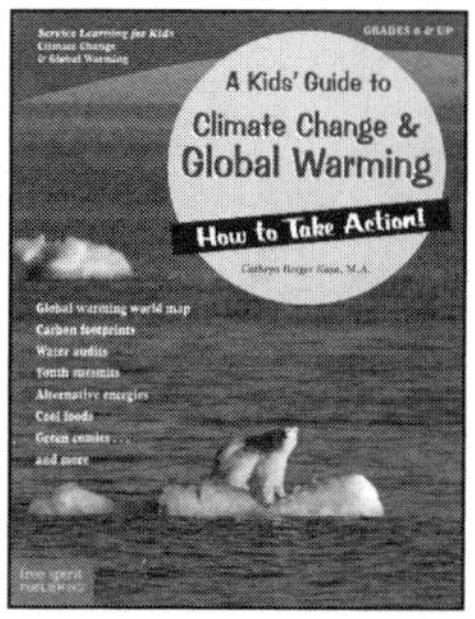


**A Kids' Guide to Climate Change & Global Warming**
How to Take Action!
*by Cathryn Berger Kaye, M.A.*
Current issues presented—carbon footprints, alternative energies, deforestation, water conservation, and more—relate to climate change and global warming. Kids explore how others in the world address the problems, find out what their own community needs, and develop a service project. For grades 6 & up.
*48 pp.; softcover; 8½" x 11"*

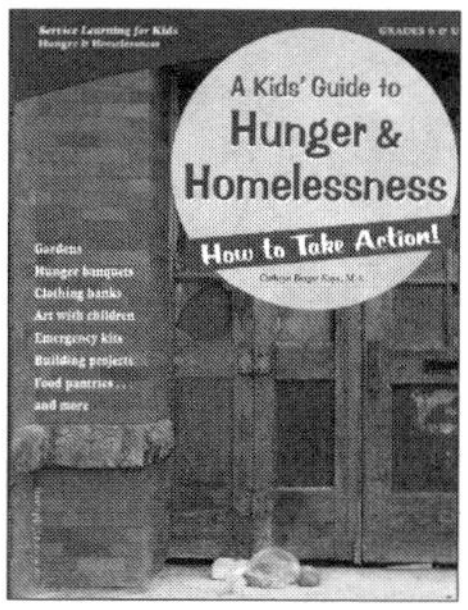


**A Kids' Guide to Hunger & Homelessness**
How to Take Action!
*by Cathryn Berger Kaye, M.A.*
Kids learn about the causes and effects of hunger and homelessness, read about what other people have done and are doing to help, explore what their community needs, and develop a service project. For grades 6 & up.
*48 pp.; softcover; 8½" x 11"*

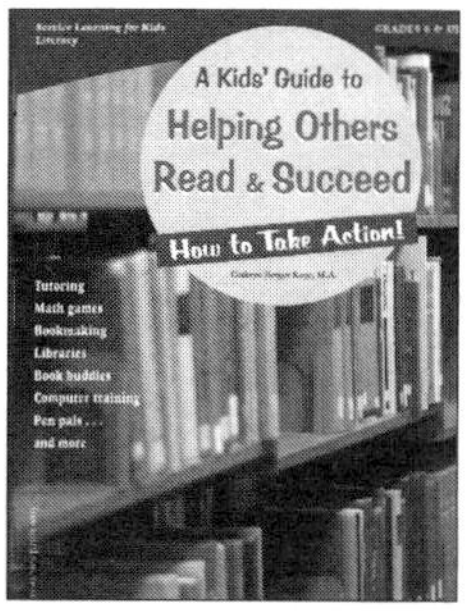


**A Kids' Guide to Helping Others Read & Succeed**
How to Take Action!
*by Cathryn Berger Kaye, M.A.*
Kids learn about literacy—the ability to read, write, and comprehend. They explore ways to improve the literacy of others, read what others (including young people) have done and are doing to help, explore what their community needs, and develop a service project. For grades 6 & up.
*48 pp.; softcover; 8½" x 11"*

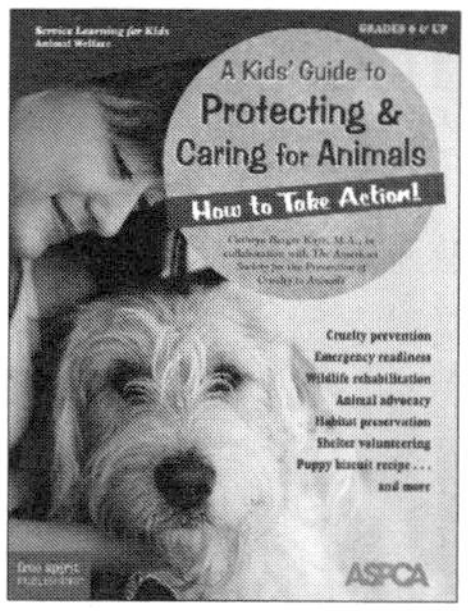


**A Kids' Guide to Protecting & Caring for Animals**
How to Take Action!
*by Cathryn Berger Kaye, M.A., in collaboration with*
*The American Society for the Prevention of Cruelty to Animals*
Kids learn about the welfare of domestic and wild animals around the world. They explore ways to address the needs of animals, such as cruelty prevention, emergency readiness, wildlife rehabilitation, habitat preservation, and shelter volunteering. For grades 6 & up.
*48 pp.; softcover; 8½" x 11"*

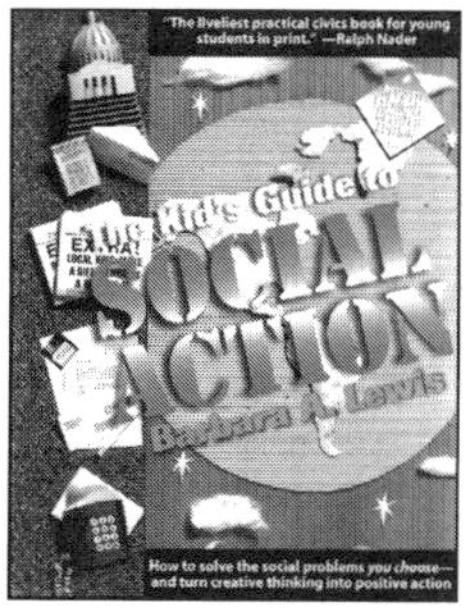


**The Kid's Guide to Social Action**
How to Solve the Social Problems You Choose—and Turn Creative Thinking into Positive Action
*Revised, Expanded, Updated Edition*
*by Barbara A. Lewis*
This exciting, empowering book includes everything kids need to make a difference in the world: step-by-step directions for writing letters, doing interviews, raising funds, getting media coverage, and more. For ages 10 & up.
*224 pp.; softcover; B&W photos and illust.; 8½" x 11"*

*For pricing information, to place an order, or to request a free catalog, contact:*

**Free Spirit Publishing Inc.**
**217 Fifth Avenue North • Suite 200 • Minneapolis, MN 55401-1299**
**toll-free 800.735.7323 • local 612.338.2068 • fax 612.337.5050**
**help4kids@freespirit.com • www.freespirit.com**

# British National Formulary

BNF 51

March 2006

bnf.org

**Published jointly by**
**BMJ Publishing Group Ltd**
Tavistock Square, London WC1H 9JP, UK
and
**RPS Publishing**
RPS Publishing is the wholly-owned publishing organisation of the Royal Pharmaceutical Society of Great Britain
1 Lambeth High Street, London, SE1 7JN, UK



ISBN: 0 85369 668 3

ISSN: 0260-535X

Printed in Germany by Clausen & Bosse, CPI Books, Leck

A catalogue record for this book is available from the British Library.



**Copies may be obtained through any bookseller or direct from:**

RPS Publishing
c/o Turpin Distribution
Stratton Business Park
Pegasus Drive
Biggleswade
Bedfordshire
SG18 8TQ
UK
Tel: +44 (0) 1767 604 971
Fax: +44 (0) 1767 601 640
E-mail: custserv@turpin-distribution.com
www.pharmpress.com

RPS Publishing also supplies the BNF in digital formats suitable for standalone use or for small networks, for use over an intranet and for use on a personal digital assistant (PDA).

**Copies for NHS primary healthcare**
General practitioners and community pharmacies in **England** can telephone the DH Publication Orderline for enquiries concerning the direct mailing of the *British National Formulary*
Tel: 08701 555 455
In **Wales** telephone the Business Services Centre
Tel: 01495 332 000

# Preface

The BNF is a joint publication of the British Medical Association and the Royal Pharmaceutical Society of Great Britain. It is published biannually under the authority of a Joint Formulary Committee which comprises representatives of the two professional bodies and of the UK Health Departments. The Dental Formulary Subcommittee oversees the preparation of advice on the drug management of dental and oral conditions; the Subcommittee includes representatives of the British Dental Association.

The BNF aims to provide prescribers, pharmacists and other healthcare professionals with sound up-to-date information about the use of medicines.

The BNF includes key information on the selection, prescribing, dispensing and administration of medicines. Medicines generally prescribed in the UK are covered and those considered less suitable for prescribing are clearly identified. Little or no information is included on medicines promoted for purchase by the public.

Information on drugs is drawn from the manufacturers' product literature, medical and pharmaceutical literature, regulatory authorities, and professional bodies. Advice is constructed from clinical literature and reflects, as far as possible, an evaluation of the evidence from diverse sources. The BNF also takes account of authoritative national guidelines and emerging safety concerns. In addition, the Joint Formulary Committee takes advice on all therapeutic areas from expert clinicians; this ensures that the BNF's recommendations are relevant to practice. Many individuals and organisations contribute towards the preparation of the BNF.

The BNF is designed as a digest for rapid reference and it may not always include all the information necessary for prescribing and dispensing. Also, less detail is given on areas such as obstetrics, malignant disease, and anaesthesia since it is expected that those undertaking treatment will have specialist knowledge and access to specialist literature. The BNF should be interpreted in the light of professional knowledge and supplemented as necessary by specialised publications and by reference to the product literature. Information is also available from medicines information services (see inside front cover).

It is **vital** to use the most recent edition of the BNF for making clinical decisions. The more important changes for this edition are listed on p. viii.

The BNF on the internet (BNF.org) includes additional information of relevance to healthcare professionals dealing with medicines. Other digital versions of the BNF—including intranet versions—are produced in parallel with the paper version.

The BNF welcomes comments from healthcare professionals. Comments and constructive criticism should be sent to:
Executive Editor, British National Formulary,
Royal Pharmaceutical Society of Great Britain,
1 Lambeth High Street, London SE1 7JN.
Email: editor@bnf.org

# Contents


**Preface** iii
**Acknowledgements** iv
**How to use the BNF** vi
**Changes for this edition** viii
Significant changes viii
Dose changes viii
Classification changes viii
Discontinued preparations ix
New preparations included in this edition ix
Late additions ix
Name changes x
**Guidance on prescribing** 1
General guidance 1
Prescription writing 4
Emergency supply of medicines 6
Controlled drugs and drug dependence 7
Adverse reactions to drugs 10
Prescribing for children 12


For detailed advice on medicines used for children consult *BNF for Children*


Prescribing in palliative care 14
Prescribing for the elderly 18
Prescribing in dental practice 20
Drugs and sport 26
**Emergency treatment of poisoning** 27

**Notes on drugs and Preparations**
1: **Gastro-intestinal system** 37
2: **Cardiovascular system** 69
3: **Respiratory system** 140
4: **Central nervous system** 173
5: **Infections** 266
6: **Endocrine system** 343
7: **Obstetrics, gynaecology, and urinary-tract disorders** 398
8: **Malignant disease and immunosuppression** 427
9: **Nutrition and blood** 463
10: **Musculoskeletal and joint diseases** 504
11: **Eye** 533
12: **Ear, nose, and oropharynx** 550
13: **Skin** 566
14: **Immunological products and vaccines** 611
15: **Anaesthesia** 632

**Appendixes and indices**
Appendix 1: **Interactions** 652
Appendix 2: **Liver disease** 735
Appendix 3: **Renal impairment** 745
Appendix 4: **Pregnancy** 758
Appendix 5: **Breast-feeding** 776
Appendix 6: **Intravenous additives** 789
Appendix 7: **Borderline substances** 801
Appendix 8: **Wound management products and elastic hosiery** 821
Appendix 9: **Cautionary and advisory labels for dispensed medicines** 836
Dental Practitioners' Formulary 851
Nurse Prescribers' Formulary 853
Index of Manufacturers 863
Index 887

# Acknowledgements

The Joint Formulary Committee is grateful to individuals and organisations that have provided advice and information to the BNF.

The principal contributors for this edition were:

I.H. Ahmed-Jushuf, K.W. Ah-See, S.P. Allison, M.N. Badminton, T.P. Baglin, P.R.J. Barnes, D.N. Bateman, D. Bowsher, R.J. Buckley, I.F. Burgess, D.J. Burn, A.J. Camm, D. Chamberlain, R. Dinwiddie, P.N. Durrington, D.A.C. Elliman, T.S.J. Elliott, B.G. Gazzard, A.M. Geretti, A.H. Ghodse, N.J.L. Gittoes, P.J. Goadsby, E.C. Gordon-Smith, I.A. Greer, J. Guillebaud, K.G. Harding, C.H. Hawkes, B.G. Higgins, S.H.D. Jackson, A. Jones, J.R. Kirwan, P.G. Kopelman, T.H. Lee, A.G. Marson, K.E.L. McColl, G.M. Mead, E. Miller, N.S. Morton, J.M. Neuberger, D.J. Nutt, D.J. Oliver, L.P. Ormerod, M. Pirmohamed, P.A. Poole-Wilson, D.J. Rowbotham, P.C. Rubin, P.G. Ryan, J.W. Sander, R.S. Sawers, S. Thomas, D.G. Waller, A. Wilcock.

Expert advice on the management of oral and dental conditions was kindly provided by M. Addy, P Coulthard, A. Crighton, M.A.O. Lewis, J.G. Meechan, N.D. Robb, C. Scully, R.A. Seymour, R. Welbury, and J.M. Zakrzewska.

Members of the British Association of Dermatologists Therapy Guidelines and Audit Subcommittee, H.K. Bell, R.H. Bull, D.J. Eedy, F. Humphreys, S.K. Jones, D. Mitchell, A.D. Ormerod, J. Peters, and M. Donoghue (Secretariat) have provided valuable advice.

Members of the Advisory Committee on Malaria Prevention, B.A. Bannister, R.H. Behrens, P.L. Chiodini, A.D. Green, D. Hill, G. Kassianos, D.G. Lalloo, G. Lea, G. Pasvol, M. Powell, E. Walker, D.A. Warrell, C.J.M. Whitty, P.A. Winstanley, and C.A. Swales (Secretariat) have also provided valuable advice.

The Joint British Societies' Coronary Risk Prediction Charts have been reproduced with the kind permission of P.N. Durrington who has also provided the BNF with access to the computer program for assessing coronary and stroke risk.

Correspondents in the pharmaceutical industry have provided information on new products and commented on products in the BNF. The Prescription Pricing Authority has supplied the prices of products in the BNF.

Numerous doctors, pharmacists, nurses and others have sent comments and suggestions.

The BNF has valuable access to the *Martindale* data banks by courtesy of S. Sweetman and staff.

A. Breewood, E. Carranza-Pitcher, S.G. Coleman, M. Davis, D.T.H. Griffiths, E. Laughton, and A.B. Prasad provided considerable assistance during the production of this edition of the BNF.

Xpage and CSW Informatics Ltd have provided technical assistance with the editorial database and typesetting software.

# Editorial Staff

# Joint Formulary Committee 2005–2006

**Chairman**
Martin J. Kendall
*MB, ChB, MD, FRCP*

**Deputy Chairman**
Nicholas L. Wood
*BPharm, FRPharmS*

**Committee Members**
Nigel S. Baber
*BSc, MB, FRCP, FRCP(Ed), FFPM, DipClinPharmacol*

Alison Blenkinsopp
*PhD, BPharm, FRPharmS*

Michael J. Goodman
*MA, BM, BCh, DPhil, FRCP*

W. Moira Kinnear
*BSc, MSc, MRPharmS*

Frank P. Marsh
*MA, MB, BChir, FRCP*

Roopendra K. Prasad
*MB BS, MS, FRCS, FRCGP*

Gulanar Root
*MRPharmS, DMS*
(from September 2005)

Ewen Sim
*BSc, MB, ChB, DipHlthMgmt*

James Smith
*BPharm, PhD, FRPharmS, MCPP, MIInfSc*
(until August 2005)

**Joint Secretaries**
Vivienne H. Nathanson
*MB, BS*

Philip E. Green
*BSc, MSc, LLM, MRPharmS*

**Executive Secretary**
Tracy L. South
*BTEC*

# Dental Formulary Subcommittee 2005–2006

**Chairman**
Hugh D. Edmondson
*BDS, DDS, LDS, FDS, RCS, MB, ChB, MRCS, LRCP, DARCPS*

**Committee Members**
Christine Arnold
*BDS, DDPHRCS, MCDH*

Simon J. Carruthers
*LDSRCS, BDS, MFGDP(UK)*

Barry Cockcroft
*BDS*

Elizabeth J. Kay
*BDS, MPH, FDSRCPS, PhD, FDSRCS*

Martin J. Kendall
*MB, ChB, MD, FRCP*

Lesley P. Longman
*BSc, BDS, PhD, FDSRCS*

David B. Murphy
*BDS, DGDP(UK)*

D. Gordon Watkins
*MBE, BDS, DGDP(UK), FRSH*

David Wray
*MD, BDS, MB, ChB, FDSRCPS, FDSRCS Ed, F MedSci*

**Joint Secretaries**
Vivienne H. Nathanson
*MB, BS*

Philip E. Green
*BSc, MSc, LLM, MRPharmS*

Claire Lowe
*BSc, DPhil*

**Executive Secretary**
Tracy L. South
*BTEC*

> Advice on dental practice
> The **British Dental Association** has contributed to the advice on medicines for dental practice through its representatives on the Dental Formulary Subcommittee.

# How to use the BNF

## Notes on conditions, drugs and preparations

The main text consists of classified notes on clinical conditions, drugs and preparations. These notes are divided into 15 chapters, each of which is related to a particular system of the body or to an aspect of medical care. Each chapter is then divided into sections which begin with appropriate *notes for prescribers*. These notes are intended to provide information to doctors, dental surgeons, pharmacists, nurses, and other healthcare professionals to facilitate the selection of suitable treatment. Guidance on dental and oral conditions is identified by means of a relevant heading (e.g. Dental and Orofacial pain) in the appropriate sections of the BNF. The notes are followed by details of relevant drugs and preparations. Preparations which can be prescribed by dental surgeons using NHS form FP10D (GP14 in Scotland, WP10D in Wales) are identified within the BNF by means of a note headed Dental Prescribing on NHS.

For information available since publication of this edition see bnf.org

## Guidance on prescribing

This part includes information on prescription writing, controlled drugs and dependence, prescribing for children and the elderly, and prescribing in palliative care. Advice is given on the reporting of adverse reactions. The BNF also includes advice on medical emergencies and other medical problems in dental practice, together with a review of the oral side-effects of drugs.

An index of conditions relevant to dental surgeons is included.

**DRUG NAME** ◢

**Indications** details of uses and indications

**Cautions** details of precautions required (with cross-references to appropriate Appendixes) and also any monitoring required

Counselling Verbal explanation to the patient of specific details of the drug treatment (e.g. posture when taking a medicine)

**Contra-indications** details of any contra-indications to use of drug

**Side-effects** details of common and more serious side-effects

**Dose**

- dose and frequency of administration (max. dose); CHILD and ELDERLY details of dose for specific age group
- By alternative route, dose and frequency

*** Approved Name (Non-proprietary)** PoM

Pharmaceutical form colour, coating, active ingredient and amount in dosage form, net price, pack size = basic NHS price. Label: (as in Appendix 9)

**Proprietary Name® (Manufacturer)** PoM NHS

Pharmaceutical form sugar-free, active ingredient mg/mL, net price, pack size = basic NHS price. Label: (as in Appendix 9)

Excipients includes clinically important excipients or electrolytes

* exceptions to the prescribing status indicated by a footnote.

Note Specific notes about the product e.g. handling

### Preparations

Preparations usually follow immediately after the drug which is their main ingredient.

Preparations are included under a non-proprietary title, if they are marketed under such a title, if they are not otherwise prescribable under the NHS, or if they may be prepared extemporaneously.

If proprietary preparations are of a distinctive colour this is stated.

In the case of compound preparations the indications, cautions, contra-indications, side-effects, and interactions of all constituents should be taken into account for prescribing.

### Drugs

Drugs appear under pharmacopoeial or other non-proprietary titles. When there is an *appropriate current monograph* (Medicines Act 1968, Section 65) preference is given to a name at the head of that monograph; otherwise a British Approved Name (BAN), if available, is used (see also p. x)

The symbol ◢ is used to denote those preparations considered by the Joint Formulary Committee to be less suitable for prescribing. Although such preparations may not be considered as drugs of first choice, their use may be justifiable in certain circumstances.

### Prescription-only medicines PoM

This symbol has been placed against those preparations that are available only on a prescription issued by an appropriate practitioner. For more detailed information see *Medicines, Ethics and Practice*, No. 29, London, Pharmaceutical Press, 2005 (and subsequent editions as available).

The symbol CD indicates that the preparation is subject to the prescription requirements of the Misuse of Drugs Act. For regulations governing prescriptions for such preparations see pages 7–9.

### Preparations not available for NHS prescription NHS

This symbol has been placed against those preparations included in the BNF that are not prescribable under the NHS. Those prescribable only for specific disorders have a footnote specifying the condition(s) for which the preparation remains available. Some preparations which are not *prescribable* by brand name under the NHS may nevertheless be *dispensed* using the brand name providing that the prescription shows an appropriate non-proprietary name.

### Prices

Prices have been calculated from the basic cost used in pricing NHS prescriptions dispensed in September 2005, see p. vii for details.

## Emergency treatment of poisoning

This chapter provides information on the management of acute poisoning when first seen in the home, although aspects of hospital-based treatment are mentioned.

## Appendixes and indexes

The appendixes include information on interactions, liver disease, renal impairment, pregnancy, breast-feeding, intravenous additives, borderline substances, wound management products, and cautionary and advisory labels for dispensed medicines. They are designed for use in association with the main body of the text.

The Dental Practitioners' List and the Nurse Prescribers' List are also included in this section. The indexes consist of the Index of Manufacturers and the Main Index.

## Patient packs

Directive 92/27/EEC specifies the requirements for the labelling of medicines and outlines the format and content of patient information leaflets to be supplied with every medicine; the directive also requires the use of Recommended International Non-proprietary Names for drugs (see p. x).

All medicines have approved labelling and patient information leaflets; anyone who supplies a medicine is responsible for providing the relevant information to the patient (see also Appendix 9).

Many medicines are available in manufacturers' original packs complete with patient information leaflets. Where patient packs are available, the BNF shows the number of dose units in the packs. In particular clinical circumstances, where patient packs need to be split or medicines are provided in bulk dispensing packs, manufacturers will provide additional supplies of patient information leaflets on request.

During the revision of each edition of the BNF careful note is taken of the information that appears on the patient information leaflets. Where it is considered appropriate to alert a prescriber to some specific limitation appearing on the patient information leaflet (for example, in relation to pregnancy) this advice now appears in the BNF.

The patient information leaflet also includes details of all inactive ingredients in the medicine. A list of common E numbers and the inactive ingredients to which they correspond is now therefore included in the BNF (see inside back cover).

## PACT and SPA

PACT (Prescribing Analyses and Cost) and SPA (Scottish Prescribing Analysis) provide prescribers with information about their prescribing.

The *PACT Standard Report*, or in Scotland SPA *Level 1 Report*, is sent to all general practitioners on a quarterly basis. The PACT Standard Report contains an analysis of the practitioner's prescribing and the practice prescribing over the last 3 months, and gives comparisons with the local Primary Care Trust equivalent practice and with a national equivalent. The report also contains details of the practice prescribing for a specific topic; a different topic is chosen each quarter.

The *PACT Catalogue*, or in Scotland SPA *Level 2 Report*, provides a full inventory of the prescriptions issued by a prescriber. The PACT catalogue is available on request for periods between 1 and 24 months. To allow the prescriber to target specific areas of prescribing, a Catalogue may be requested to cover individual preparations, BNF sections, or combinations of BNF chapters.

PACT is also available electronically (ePACT.net). This system gives users on-line access through NHSnet to the 3 years' prescribing data held on the Prescription Pricing Authority's database; tools for analysing the data are also provided.

## Prices in the BNF

Basic **net prices** are given in the BNF to provide an indication of relative cost. Where there is a choice of suitable preparations for a particular disease or condition the relative cost may be used in making a selection. Cost-effective prescribing must, however, take into account other factors (such as dose frequency and duration of treatment) that affect the total cost. The use of more expensive drugs is justified if it will result in better treatment of the patient or a reduction of the length of an illness or the time spent in hospital.

Prices have generally been calculated from the net cost used in pricing NHS prescriptions dispensed in September 2005. Unless an original pack is available these prices are based on the largest pack size of the preparation in use in community pharmacies. The price for an extemporaneously prepared preparation has been omitted where the net cost of the ingredients used to make it would give a misleadingly low impression of the final price. In Appendix 8 prices stated are per dressing or bandage.

The unit of 20 is still sometimes used as a basis for comparison, but where suitable original packs or patient packs are available these are priced instead.

Gross prices vary as follows:

1. Costs to the NHS are greater than the net prices quoted and include professional fees and overhead allowances;
2. Private prescription charges are calculated on a separate basis;
3. Over-the-counter sales are at retail price, as opposed to basic net price, and include VAT.

**BNF prices are NOT, therefore, suitable for quoting to patients seeking private prescriptions or contemplating over-the-counter purchases.**

A fuller explanation of costs to the NHS may be obtained from the Drug Tariff. Separate drug tariffs are applicable to England and Wales, Scotland, and Northern Ireland; prices in the different tariffs may vary.

# Changes for this edition

## Significant changes

The BNF is revised twice yearly and numerous changes are made between issues. All copies of BNF No. 50 (September 2005) should therefore be withdrawn and replaced by BNF No. 51 (March 2006). Significant changes have been made in the following sections for BNF No. 51:

Adult advanced life support algorithm, inside back cover
Emergency supply of medicines, Guidance on prescribing
Prescribing of controlled drugs, Guidance on prescribing
Beta-adrenoceptor blocking drugs [hypertension], section 2.4
Oral anticoagulants, section 2.8.2
Antiplatelet drugs, section 2.9
Lipid-regulating drugs, section 2.12
Omega-3 fatty acid compounds, section 2.12
Selective beta$_2$ agonists [reorganised], section 3.1.1.1
Hyposensitisation, section 3.4.2
Oxygen [new supply arrangements], section 3.6
Changes to prescribing information for amitriptyline and dosulepin, section 4.3.1
Atomoxetine [CSM warning about risk of suicidal ideation], section 4.4
Epilepsy [updated advice on treatment of partial seizures and generalised seizures], section 4.8.1
Nicotine replacement therapy, section 4.10
Suggested treatment of bacterial infections [shigellosis, otitis media, erysipelas, and cellulitis], Table 1, section 5.1
Prevention of secondary case of group A streptococcal infection [new], Table 2, section 5.1
Antibacterial treatment of tuberculosis, section 5.1.9
Prophylaxis of urinary-tract infections in children, section 5.1.13
Antifungal treatment of aspergillosis, section 5.2
Antifungal treatment of cryptococcosis, section 5.2
Treatment of falciparum malaria, section 5.4.1
Malaria prophylaxis [updated advice for Mauritania and South Asia], section 5.4.1
Drug interactions of hormonal contraceptives, section 7.3.1 and section 7.3.2.2
Tumour lysis syndrome [new text], section 8.1
Irinotecan, oxaliplatin, and raltitrexed for advanced colorectal cancer [updated NICE guidance], section 8.1.5
Early breast cancer, section 8.3.4.1
Treatment of hyponatraemia, section 9.2.2.1
Use of plasma and plasma substitutes, section 9.2.2.2
Dental prescribing of fluoride preparations on the NHS, section 9.5.3 and Dental Practitioners' Formulary
Recurrent acute otitis media, section 12.1.2
Desloughing agents, section 13.11.7
BCG vaccines, section 14.4
Hepatitis A vaccine, section 14.4
Hepatitis B vaccine, section 14.4
naesthesia, sedation and resuscitation in dental prac-ice, section 15.1
r intravenous anaesthetics [reorganised], section 1

Changes to the **immunisation schedule** to protect against pneumococcal infection and to extend protection against *Haemophilus influenzae* type b and meningococcal group C infections were announced in February 2006; further details, including the date for introducing the changes, are available from www.dh.gov.uk.

Lists of over-the-counter preparations have been removed. The manufacturer should be consulted for a list of ingredients; preparations with very similar names may contain different ingredients.

## Dose changes

Changes in dose statements introduced into BNF No. 51:

Acenocoumarol, p. 125
*Aerodiol®*, p. 372
*AmBisome®*, p. 310
Atenolol, p. 85
Clindamycin [malaria], p. 329
Clomipramine, p. 198
Co-trimoxazole, p. 296
*Deponit®*, p. 107
Diazepam [anaesthesia], p. 639
Duloxetine [urinary incontinence], p. 420
*Eprex®* [anaemia in adults receiving cancer chemotherapy], p. 469
Ertapenem, p. 284
*Farlutal®*, p. 455
Fluconazole, p. 310
Flucytosine, p. 311
Fluphenazine hydrochloride, p. 184
Gentamicin, p. 288
Heparin, p. 120
Irbesartan, p. 103
*Isoket Retard®*, p. 107
Levetiracetam, p. 242
Levobupivacaine [acute pain, lumbar epidural], p. 650
Levomepromazine [restlessness and confusion in palliative care], p. 17
Levonorgestrel [emergency contraception in patients taking enzyme-inducing drugs], p. 412
Linezolid, p. 294
Metoclopramide, p. 214
Midazolam, p. 639
Nalidixic acid, p. 306
*NeoRecormon®* [anaemia in adults receiving chemotherapy], p. 470
Paroxetine, p. 204
*Phosphate-Sandoz®* [deletion of hypercalcaemia dose], p. 491
Primidone, p. 243
*Rebetol®*, p. 329
Remifentanil, p. 642
Risperidone [depot], p. 192
Ropinirole, p. 256
Rosuvastatin, p. 137
Thiopental, p. 633
Topiramate, p. 244
Valsartan, p. 104
Voriconazole, p. 313

## Classification changes

Classification changes have been made in the following sections for BNF No. 51:

**Section 1.3.6** Other ulcer-healing drugs [section deleted]

**Section 2.5** Hypertension and heart failure [title change]

**Section 2.5.6** Ganglion-blocking drugs [section deleted]

**Section 2.5.7** Tyrosine hydroxylase inhibitors [section deleted—text on metirosine now included under Phaeochromocytoma, section 2.5.4]

**Section 2.6** Nitrates, calcium-channel blockers, and other antianginal drugs [title change]

**Section 2.6.3** Other antianginal drugs [title change]

**Section 2.12** Omega-3 fatty acid compounds [title change]

**Section 3.3** Cromoglicate and related therapy, leukotriene receptor antagonists, and omalizumab [title change]

**Section 3.3.2** Leukotriene receptor antagonists and omalizumab [title change]

**Section 12.2.3** Nasal preparations for infection [title change]

## New names

Name changes introduced into BNF No.51 (see also p. x):

*Anquil®* [formerly *Benquil®*], p. 183

*Flomaxtra® XL* [formerly *Flomax® MR*], p. 418

## Discontinued preparations

Preparations discontinued during the compilation of BNF No. 51:

*Aci-Jel®*
*Acupan®* injection
*Bricanyl®* aerosol inhalation
*Bricanyl®* respirator solution
*Bricanyl SA®*
*Codafen Continus®*
*Colomycin®* powder
*Dermovate-NN®* ointment
*Emeside®* capsules
*Fortovase®*
*Gaviscon®* tablets
*Gynol II®*
*Imazin® XL*
*Intal®* nebuliser solution
*Konakion® Neonatal*
Levocabastine
*Levonelle®-2*
*Lignostab® A*
*Lipofundin N*
*Locabiotal®*
*Microval®*
*Monocor®*
*Monotard®*
*Monovent®*
*Narcan®*
*Narcan® Neonatal*
*Nebcin®*
*Negram®*
*Nutriflex Basal*
*Nutriflex Peri*
*Nutriflex Plus*
*Nutriflex Special*
*Odrik®*
*Orimeten®*
*Phyllocontin Continus® Paediatric*
*Plesmet®*
*Secadrex®*
*Soframycin®* eye ointment
Terfenadine
*Tilade®*
*Tofranil®*
*Tranxene®*
*Ultratard®*
*Zarontin®* capsules

## New preparations included in this edition

Preparations included in the relevant sections of BNF No. 51:

*Acidex®*, p. 40
*Apidra®*, p. 347
*Aptivus®*, p 321
*Atimos Modulite®*, p. 147
*Bonviva®*, p. 390
*BuTrans®*, p. 225
*Ciloxan®* eye ointment, p. 535
*Clarosip®*, p. 291
*Duodopa®*, p. 253
*Fendrix®*, p. 618
*Fosavance®*, p. 388
*Gaviscon® Advance* tablets, p. 40
*Haemaccel®*, p. 481
*Hedrin®*, p. 604
*Levonelle® 1500*, p. 413
*Lysodren®*, p. 443
*Modisal LA®*, p. 108
*Monomil XL®*, p. 108
*Nasofan®*, p. 556
*Octim®*, p. 386
*OliClinomel N5-800E*, p. 486
*OliClinomel N7-1000E*, p. 486
*OliClinomel N8-800*, p. 486
*Pinetarsol®*, p. 583
*Prexige®*, p. 511
*Procoralan®*, p. 115
*Salinum®*, p. 564
*Tarceva®*, p. 442
*Tilade CFC-free Inhaler®*, p. 159
*Voltarol Gel Patch®*, p. 531
*Xolair®*, p. 161
*Zamadol® 24hr*, p. 230

# Late additions

**Negaban®** (Eumedica) PoM

Injection, powder for reconstitution, temocillin (as sodium salt), net price 1-g vial = £25.45
Electrolytes $Na^+$ 4.35 mmol/g
BNF section 5.1.1.2. For the treatment of septicaemia, urinary-tract infections, and lower respiratory-tract infections caused by susceptible Gram-negative bacteria

# Name changes

European Law requires use of the Recommended International Non-proprietary Name (rINN) for medicinal substances. In most cases the British Approved Name (BAN) and rINN were identical. Where the two differed, the BAN was modified to accord with the rINN.

The following list shows those substances for which the former BAN has been modified to accord with the rINN. Former BANs have been retained as synonyms in the BNF.

**Adrenaline and noradrenaline** Adrenaline and noradrenaline are the terms used in the titles of monographs in the European Pharmacopoeia and are thus the official names in the member states. For these substances, BP 2005 shows the European Pharmacopoeia names and the rINNs at the head of the monographs; the BNF has adopted a similar style.

| Former BAN | New BAN |
|---|---|
| adrenaline | *see above* |
| amethocaine | tetracaine |
| aminacrine | aminoacridine |
| amoxycillin | amoxicillin |
| amphetamine | amfetamine |
| amylobarbitone | amobarbital |
| amylobarbitone sodium | amobarbital sodium |
| beclomethasone | beclometasone |
| bendrofluazide | bendroflumethiazide |
| benzhexol | trihexyphenidyl |
| benzphetamine | benzfetamine |
| benztropine | benzatropine |
| busulphan | busulfan |
| butobarbitone | butobarbital |
| carticaine | articaine |
| cephalexin | cefalexin |
| cephradine | cefradine |
| chloral betaine | cloral betaine |
| chlorbutol | chlorobutanol |
| chlormethiazole | clomethiazole |
| chlorpheniramine | chlorphenamine |
| chlorthalidone | chlortalidone |
| cholecalciferol | colecalciferol |
| cholestyramine | colestyramine |
| clomiphene | clomifene |
| colistin sulphomethate sodium | colistimethate sodium |
| corticotrophin | corticotropin |
| cyclosporin | ciclosporin |
| cysteamine | mercaptamine |
| danthron | dantron |
| dexamphetamine | dexamfetamine |
| dibromopropamidine | dibrompropamidine |
| dicyclomine | dicycloverine |
| dienoestrol | dienestrol |
| dimethicone(s) | dimeticone |
| dimethyl sulphoxide | dimethyl sulfoxide |
| dothiepin | dosulepin |
| doxycycline hydrochloride (hemihydrate hemiethanolate) | doxycycline hyclate |
| eformoterol | formoterol |

| Former BAN | New BAN |
|---|---|
| ethamsylate | etamsylate |
| ethinyloestradiol | ethinylestradiol |
| ethynodiol | etynodiol |
| flumethasone | flumetasone |
| flupenthixol | flupentixol |
| flurandrenolone | fludroxycortide |
| frusemide | furosemide |
| guaiphenesin | guaifenesin |
| hexachlorophane | hexachlorophene |
| hexamine hippurate | methenamine hippurate |
| hydroxyurea | hydroxycarbamide |
| indomethacin | indometacin |
| lignocaine | lidocaine |
| lysuride | lisuride |
| methotrimeprazine | levomepromazine |
| methyl cysteine | mecysteine |
| methylene blue | methylthioninium chloride |
| methicillin | meticillin |
| mitozantrone | mitoxantrone |
| nicoumalone | acenocoumarol |
| noradrenaline | *see above* |
| oestradiol | estradiol |
| oestriol | estriol |
| oestrone | estrone |
| oxpentifylline | pentoxifylline |
| phenobarbitone | phenobarbital |
| pipothiazine | pipotiazine |
| polyhexanide | polihexanide |
| pramoxine | pramocaine |
| procaine penicillin | procaine benzylpenicillin |
| prothionamide | protionamide |
| quinalbarbitone | secobarbital |
| riboflavine | riboflavin |
| salcatonin | calcitonin (salmon) |
| sodium calciumedetate | sodium calcium edetate |
| sodium cromoglycate | sodium cromoglicate |
| sodium ironedetate | sodium feredetate |
| sodium picosulphate | sodium picosulfate |
| sorbitan monostearate | sorbitan stearate |
| stibocaptate | sodium stibocaptate |
| stilboestrol | diethylstilbestrol |
| sulphacetamide | sulfacetamide |
| sulphadiazine | sulfadiazine |
| sulphamethoxazole | sulfamethoxazole |
| sulphapyridine | sulfapyridine |
| sulphasalazine | sulfasalazine |
| sulphathiazole | sulfathiazole |
| sulphinpyrazone | sulfinpyrazone |
| tetracosactrin | tetracosactide |
| thiabendazole | tiabendazole |
| thioguanine | tioguanine |
| thiopentone | thiopental |
| thymoxamine | moxisylyte |
| thyroxine sodium | levothyroxine sodium |
| tribavirin | ribavirin |
| trimeprazine | alimemazine |
| urofollitrophin | urofollitropin |

# Guidance on prescribing

## General guidance

Medicines should be prescribed only when they are necessary, and in all cases the benefit of administering the medicine should be considered in relation to the risk involved. This is particularly important during pregnancy where the risk to both mother and fetus must be considered (for further details see Prescribing in Pregnancy, Appendix 4).

It is important to discuss treatment options carefully with the patient to ensure that the patient is content to take the medicine as prescribed (see also Taking Medicines to Best Effect, below). In particular, the patient should be helped to distinguish the side-effects of prescribed drugs from the effects of the medical disorder. Where the beneficial effects of the medicine are likely to be delayed, the patient should be advised of this.

**Taking medicines to best effect** Difficulties in compliance with drug treatment occur regardless of age. Factors contributing to poor compliance with prescribed medicines include:

- Prescription not collected or not dispensed
- Purpose of medicine not clear
- Perceived lack of efficacy
- Real or perceived side-effects
- Patients' perception of the risk and severity of side-effects may differ from that of the prescriber
- Instructions for administration not clear
- Physical difficulty in taking medicines (e.g. with swallowing the medicine, with handling small tablets, or with opening medicine containers)
- Unattractive formulation (e.g. unpleasant taste)
- Complicated regimen

The prescriber and the patient should agree on the health outcomes that the patient desires and on the strategy for achieving them ('concordance'). The prescriber should be sensitive to religious, cultural, and personal beliefs that can affect patients' acceptance of medicines. Further information on concordance is available on the Internet (www.medicines-partnership.org).

Taking the time to explain to the patient (and relatives) the rationale and the potential adverse effects of treatment may improve compliance. Reinforcement and elaboration of the physician's instructions by the pharmacist also helps. Advising the patient of the possibility of alternative treatments may encourage the patient to seek advice rather than merely abandon unacceptable treatment.

Simplifying the drug regimen may help; the need for frequent administration may reduce compliance although there appears to be little difference in compliance between once-daily and twice-daily administration. Combination products reduce the number of drugs taken but this may be at the expense of the ability to titrate individual doses.

**Complementary medicine** An increasing amount of information on complementary ('alternative') medicine is becoming available. However, the BNF's scope is restricted to the discussion of conventional medicines but reference is made to complementary treatments if they affect conventional therapy (e.g. interactions with St John's wort—see Appendix 1). Further information on herbal medicines is available at www.mhra.gov.uk

**Abbreviation of titles** In general, titles of drugs and preparations should be written *in full*. Unofficial abbreviations should not be used as they may be misinterpreted; obsolete titles, such as Mist. Expect. should not be used.

**Non-proprietary titles** Where non-proprietary ('generic') titles are given, they should be used in prescribing. This will enable any suitable product to be dispensed, thereby saving delay to the patient and sometimes expense to the health service. The only exception is where bioavailability problems are so important that the patient should always receive the same brand; in such cases, the brand name or the manufacturer should be stated. Non-proprietary titles should **not** be invented for the purposes of prescribing generically since this can lead to confusion, particularly in the case of compound and modified-release preparations.

Titles used as headings for monographs may be used freely in the United Kingdom but in other countries may be subject to restriction.

Many of the non-proprietary titles used in this book are titles of monographs in the European Pharmacopoeia, British Pharmacopoeia or British Pharmaceutical Codex 1973. In such cases the preparations must comply with the standard (if any) in the appropriate publication, as required by the Medicines Act (Section 65).

**Proprietary titles** Names followed by the symbol® are or have been used as proprietary names in the United Kingdom. These names may in general be applied only to products supplied by the owners of the trade marks.

**Marketing authorisation and BNF advice** In general the *doses, indications, cautions, contra-indications and side-effects* in the BNF reflect those in the manufacturers' data sheets or Summaries of Product Characteristics (SPCs) which, in turn, reflect those in the corresponding Marketing Authorisations (formerly known as Product Licences). The BNF may not include preparations that are not supported by a valid summary of product characteristics or where the marketing authorisation holder has not been able to supply essential information.

Where an unlicensed drug is included in the BNF, this is indicated in brackets after the entry. Where the BNF suggests a use (or route) that is outside the licensed indication of a product ('off-label' use), this too is indicated. Unlicensed use of medicines becomes necessary if the clinical need cannot be met by licensed medicines; such use should be supported by appropriate evidence and experience. When a preparation is available from more than one manufacturer, the BNF reflects advice that is the most clinically relevant regardless of any variation in the marketing authorisations.

The doses stated in the BNF are intended for general guidance and represent, unless otherwise stated, the usual range of doses that are generally regarded as being suitable for adults.

> Prescribing medicines outside the recommendations of their Marketing Authorisation alters (and probably increases) the doctor's professional responsibility.



**Oral syringes** An **oral syringe** is supplied when oral liquid medicines are prescribed in doses other than multiples of 5 mL. The oral syringe is marked in 0.5-mL divisions from 1 to 5 mL to measure doses of less than 5 mL. It is provided with an adaptor and an instruction leaflet. The *5-mL spoon* is used for doses of 5 mL (or multiples thereof).

**Strengths and quantities** The strength or quantity to be contained in capsules, lozenges, tablets, etc. should be stated by the prescriber.

If a pharmacist receives an incomplete prescription for a systemically administered preparation[1] and considers it would not be appropriate for the patient to return to the doctor, the following procedures will apply:

(a) an attempt must always be made to contact the prescriber to ascertain the intention;

(b) if the attempt is successful the pharmacist must, where practicable, subsequently arrange for details of quantity, strength where applicable, and dosage to be inserted by the prescriber on the incomplete form;

(c) where, although the prescriber has been contacted, it has not proved possible to obtain the written intention regarding an incomplete prescription, the pharmacist may endorse the form 'p.c.' (prescriber contacted) and add details of the quantity and strength where applicable of the preparation supplied, and of the dose indicated. The endorsement should be initialled and dated by the pharmacist;

(d) where the prescriber cannot be contacted and the pharmacist has sufficient information to make a professional judgment the preparation may be dispensed. If the quantity is missing the pharmacist may supply sufficient to complete up to 5 days' treatment; except that where a combination pack (i.e. a proprietary pack containing more than one medicinal product) or oral contraceptive is prescribed by name only, the smallest pack shall be dispensed. In all cases the prescription must be endorsed 'p.n.c.' (prescriber not contacted), the quantity, the dose, and the strength (where applicable) of the preparation supplied must be indicated, and the endorsement must be initialled and dated;

(e) if the pharmacist has any doubt about exercising discretion, an incomplete prescription must be referred back to the prescriber.

**Excipients** Oral liquid preparations that do not contain *fructose, glucose* or *sucrose* are described as 'sugar-free' in the BNF. Preparations containing hydrogenated glucose syrup, mannitol, maltitol, sorbitol or xylitol are also marked 'sugar-free' since there is evidence that they do not cause dental caries. Patients receiving medicines containing cariogenic sugars should be advised of appropriate dental hygiene measures to prevent caries. Sugar-free preparations should be used whenever possible.

Where information on the presence of *aspartame, gluten, tartrazine, arachis (peanut) oil* or *sesame oil* is available, this is indicated in the BNF against the relevant preparation.

Information is provided on *selected excipients* in skin preparations (see section 13.1.3), vaccines (see section 14.1), and on *selected preservatives* and *excipients* in eye drops and injections. Pressurised metered aerosols containing *chlorofluorocarbons* (CFCs) have also been identified throughout the BNF (see section 3.1.1.1).

The presence of *benzyl alcohol* and *polyoxyl castor oil* (polyethoxylated castor oil) in injections is indicated in the BNF. Benzyl alcohol has been associated with a fatal toxic syndrome in preterm neonates, and therefore, parenteral preparations containing the preservative should not be used in neonates. Polyoxyl castor oils, used as vehicles in intravenous injections, have been associated with severe anaphylactoid reactions.

The presence of *propylene glycol* in oral or parenteral medicines is indicated in the BNF; it can cause adverse effects if its elimination is impaired, e.g. in renal failure, in neonates and young children, and in slow metabolisers of the substance. It may interact with disulfiram and metronidazole.

> In the absence of information on excipients in the BNF and in the product literature, contact the manufacturer (see Index of Manufacturers) if it is essential to check details.

**Extemporaneous preparation** A product should be dispensed extemporaneously only when no product with a marketing authorisation is available.

The BP direction that a preparation must be *freshly prepared* indicates that it must be made not more than 24 hours before it is issued for use. The direction that a preparation should be *recently prepared* indicates that deterioration is likely if the preparation is stored for longer than about 4 weeks at 15–25° C.

The term **water** used without qualification means either potable water freshly drawn direct from the public supply and suitable for drinking or freshly boiled and cooled purified water. The latter should be used if the public supply is from a local storage tank or if the potable water is unsuitable for a particular preparation (Water for injections, section 9.2.2).

**Drugs and driving** Prescribers should advise patients if treatment is likely to affect their ability to drive motor vehicles. This applies especially to drugs with sedative effects; patients should be warned that these effects are increased by alcohol. General information about a patient's fitness to drive is available from the Driver and Vehicle Licensing Agency at www.dvla.gov.uk (see also Appendix 9).

**Patents** In the BNF, certain drugs have been included notwithstanding the existence of actual or potential patent rights. In so far as such substances are protected

1. With the exception of temazepam, an incomplete prescription is **not** acceptable for controlled drugs in schedules 2 and 3 of the Misuse of Drugs Regulations 2001

by Letters Patent, their inclusion in this Formulary neither conveys, nor implies, licence to manufacture.

**Health and safety** When handling chemical or biological materials particular attention should be given to the possibility of allergy, fire, explosion, radiation, or poisoning. Substances, including corticosteroids, some antimicrobials, phenothiazines, and many cytotoxics, are irritant or very potent and should be handled with caution. Contact with the skin and inhalation of dust should be avoided.

**Safety in the home** Patients must be warned to keep all medicines out of the reach of children. All solid dose and all oral and external liquid preparations must be dispensed in a reclosable *child-resistant container* unless:

- the medicine is in an original pack or patient pack such as to make this inadvisable;
- the patient will have difficulty in opening a child-resistant container;
- a specific request is made that the product shall not be dispensed in a child-resistant container;
- no suitable child-resistant container exists for a particular liquid preparation.

All patients should be advised to dispose of *unwanted medicines* by returning them to a supplier for destruction.

**Name of medicine** The name of the medicine should appear on the label unless the prescriber indicates otherwise.

(a) The strength is also stated on the label in the case of tablets, capsules, and similar preparations that are available in different strengths.

(b) If it is the wish of the prescriber that a description such as 'The Sedative Tablets' should appear on the label, the prescriber should write the desired description on the prescription form.

(c) The arrangement will extend to approved names, proprietary names or titles given in the BP, BPC, BNF, DPF, or NPF. The arrangement does not apply when a prescription is written so that several ingredients are given.

(d) The name written on the label is that used by the prescriber on the prescription.

(e) When a prescription is written other than on an NHS prescription form the name of the prescribed preparation will be stated on the label of the dispensed medicine unless the prescriber indicates otherwise.

(f) The Council of the Royal Pharmaceutical Society advises that the labels of dispensed medicines should indicate the total quantity of the product dispensed in the container to which the label refers. This requirement applies equally to solid, liquid, internal, and external preparations. If a product is dispensed in more than one container, the reference should be to the amount in each container.

> Non-proprietary names of **compound preparations** which appear in the BNF are those that have been compiled by the British Pharmacopoeia Commission or another recognised body; whenever possible they reflect the names of the active ingredients.
> Prescribers should avoid creating their own compound names for the purposes of generic prescribing; such names do not have an approved definition and can be misinterpreted.
> Special care should be taken to avoid errors when prescribing compound preparations; in particular the hyphen in the prefix 'co-' should be retained.
> Special care should also be taken to avoid creating generic names for **modified-release** preparations where the use of these names could lead to confusion between formulations with different lengths of action.

**Security and validity of prescriptions** The Councils of the British Medical Association and the Royal Pharmaceutical Society have issued a joint statement on the security and validity of prescriptions.

In particular, prescription forms should:

- not be left unattended at reception desks;
- not be left in a car where they may be visible; and
- when not in use, be kept in a locked drawer within the surgery and at home.

Where there is any doubt about the authenticity of a prescription, the pharmacist should contact the prescriber. If this is done by telephone, the number should be obtained from the directory rather than relying on the information on the prescription form, which may be false.

**Patient group direction (PGD)** In most cases, the most appropriate clinical care will be provided on an individual basis by a prescriber to a specific individual patient. However, a Patient Group Direction for supply and administration of medicines by other healthcare professionals can be used where it would benefit patient care without compromising safety.

A Patient Group Direction is a written direction relating to supply and administration (or administration only) of a prescription-only medicine by certain classes of healthcare professionals; the Direction is signed by a doctor (or dentist), and by a pharmacist. Further information on Patient Group Directions is available in Health Service Circular HSC 2000/026 (England), HDL (2001) 7 (Scotland), and WHC (2000) 116 (Wales).

**NICE and Scottish Medicines Consortium** Advice issued by the National Institute for Health and Clinical Excellence (NICE) and by the Scottish Medicines Consortium (SMC) is included in the BNF where relevant. Details of the advice together with updates may be obtained from www.nice.org.uk and from www.scottishmedicines.org.uk.

# Prescription writing

**Shared care**
In its guidelines on responsibility for prescribing (circular EL (91) 127) between hospitals and general practitioners, the Department of Health has advised that legal responsibility for prescribing lies with the doctor who signs the prescription.

Prescriptions[1] should be written legibly in ink or otherwise so as to be indelible[2], should be dated, should state the full name and address of the patient, and should be signed in ink by the prescriber[3]. The age and the date of birth of the patient should preferably be stated, and it is a legal requirement in the case of prescription-only medicines to state the age for children under 12 years.

The following should be noted:

(a) The unnecessary use of decimal points should be avoided, e.g. 3 mg, not 3.0 mg.
Quantities of 1 gram or more should be written as 1 g etc.
Quantities less than 1 gram should be written in milligrams, e.g. 500 mg, not 0.5 g.
Quantities less than 1 mg should be written in micrograms, e.g. 100 micrograms, not 0.1 mg.
When decimals are unavoidable a zero should be written in front of the decimal point where there is no other figure, e.g. 0.5 mL, not .5 mL.
Use of the decimal point is acceptable to express a range, e.g. 0.5 to 1 g.

(b) 'Micrograms' and 'nanograms' should **not** be abbreviated. Similarly 'units' should **not** be abbreviated.

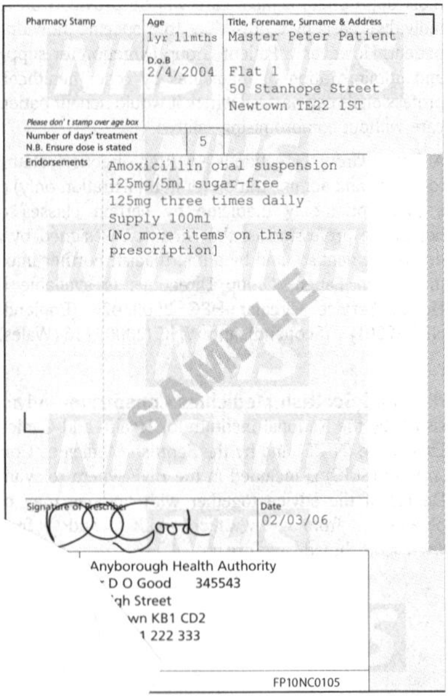
Pharmacy Stamp
Age
1yr 11mths
D.o.B
2/4/2004
Please don't stamp over age box
Title, Forename, Surname & Address
Master Peter Patient
Flat 1
50 Stanhope Street
Newtown TE22 1ST
Number of days' treatment
N.B. Ensure dose is stated
5
Endorsements
Amoxicillin oral suspension
125mg/5ml sugar-free
125mg three times daily
Supply 100ml
[No more items on this prescription]
SAMPLE
Signature of Prescriber
Date
02/03/06
Anyborough Health Authority
D O Good 345543
gh Street
wn KB1 CD2
1 222 333
FP10NC0105

(c) The term 'millilitre' (ml or mL)[4] is used in medicine and pharmacy, and cubic centimetre, c.c., or $cm^3$ should not be used.

(d) Dose and dose frequency should be stated; in the case of preparations to be taken 'as required' a **minimum dose interval** should be specified.
When doses other than multiples of 5 mL are prescribed for *oral liquid preparations* the dose-volume will be provided by means of an **oral syringe**, see p. 2 (except for preparations intended to be measured with a pipette).
Suitable quantities:
Elixirs, Linctuses, and Paediatric Mixtures (5-mL dose), 50, 100, or 150 mL
Adult Mixtures (10-mL dose), 200 or 300 mL
Ear Drops, Eye drops, and Nasal Drops, 10 mL (or the manufacturer's pack)
Eye Lotions, Gargles, and Mouthwashes, 200 mL

(e) For suitable quantities of dermatological preparations, see section 13.1.2.

(f) The names of drugs and preparations should be written clearly and **not** abbreviated, using approved titles **only** (see also advice in box on p. 3 to **avoid** creating generic titles for modified-release preparations).

(g) The quantity to be supplied may be stated by indicating the number of days of treatment required in the box provided on NHS forms. In most cases the exact amount will be supplied. This does not apply to items directed to be used as required—if the dose and frequency are not given the quantity to be supplied needs to be stated.
When several items are ordered on one form the box can be marked with the number of days of treatment provided the quantity is added for any item for which the amount cannot be calculated.

(h) Although directions should preferably be in **English without abbreviation**, it is recognised that some Latin abbreviations are used (for details see Inside Back Cover).

(i) Medical and dental practitioners may prescribe unlicensed medicines (i.e. those without marketing authorisation) or withdrawn medicines. The prescriber should inform the patient or the patient's carer that the product does not have a marketing authorisation.

**Prescribing by dental surgeons** Until new prescribing arrangements are in place for NHS prescriptions dental surgeons should use form FP10D (GP14 in Scotland, WP10D in Wales) to prescribe only those items listed in the Dental Practitioners' Formulary.

1. The above recommendations are acceptable for **prescription-only medicines** (PoM). For items marked CD see also Controlled Drugs and Drug Dependence p. 7.
2. It is permissible to issue carbon copies of NHS prescriptions as long as they are signed in ink.
3. Computer-generated facsimile signatures do not meet the legal requirement.
4. The use of capital 'L' in mL is a printing convention throughout the BNF; both 'mL' and 'ml' are recognised SI abbreviations.

The Act and Regulations do not set any limitations upon the number and variety of substances which the dental surgeon may administer to patients in the surgery or may order by private prescription—provided the relevant legal requirements are observed the dental surgeon may use or order whatever is required for the clinical situation. There is no statutory requirement for the dental surgeon to communicate with a patient's medical practitioner when prescribing for dental use. There are, however, occasions when this would be in the patient's interest and such communication is to be encouraged.

## Computer-issued prescriptions

For computer-issued prescriptions the following advice, based on the recommendations of the Joint GP Information Technology Committee, should also be noted:

1. The computer must print out the date, the patient's surname, one forename, other initials, and address, and may also print out the patient's title and date of birth. The age of children under 12 years and of adults over 60 years must be printed in the box available; the age of children under 5 years should be printed in years and months. A facility may also exist to print out the age of patients between 12 and 60 years.
2. The doctor's name must be printed at the bottom of the prescription form; this will be the name of the doctor responsible for the prescription (who will normally sign it). The doctor's surgery address, reference number, and Primary Care Trust (PCT[1]) are also necessary. In addition, the surgery telephone number should be printed.
3. When prescriptions are to be signed by general practitioner registrars, assistants, locums, or deputising doctors, the name of the doctor printed at the bottom of the form must still be that of the responsible principal.
4. Names of medicines must come from a dictionary held in the computer memory, to provide a check on the spelling and to ensure that the name is written in full. The computer can be programmed to recognise both the non-proprietary and the proprietary name of a particular drug and to print out the preferred choice, but must not print out both names. For medicines not in the dictionary, separate checks are required—the user must be warned that no check was possible and the entire prescription must be entered in the lexicon.
5. The dictionary may contain information on the usual doses, formulations, and pack sizes to produce standard predetermined prescriptions for common preparations, and to provide a check on the validity of an individual prescription on entry.
6. The prescription must be printed in English without abbreviation; information may be entered or stored in abbreviated form. The dose must be in numbers, the frequency in words, and the quantity in numbers in brackets, thus: 40 mg four times daily (112). It must also be possible to prescribe by indicating the length of treatment required, see (h) above.
7. The BNF recommendations should be followed as in (a), (b), (c), (d), and (e) above.
8. Checks may be incorporated to ensure that all the information required for dispensing a particular drug has been filled in. For instructions such as 'as directed' and 'when required', the maximum daily dose should normally be specified.
9. Numbers and codes used in the system for organising and retrieving data must never appear on the form.
10. Supplementary warnings or advice should be written in full, should not interfere with the clarity of the prescription itself, and should be in line with any warnings or advice in the BNF; numerical codes should not be used.
11. A mechanism (such as printing a series of non-specific characters) should be incorporated to cancel out unused space, or wording such as 'no more items on this prescription' may be added after the last item. Otherwise the doctor should delete the space manually.
12. To avoid forgery the computer may print on the form the number of items to be dispensed (somewhere separate from the box for the pharmacist). The number of items per form need be limited only by the ability of the printer to produce clear and well-demarcated instructions with sufficient space for each item and a spacer line before each fresh item.
13. Handwritten alterations should only be made in exceptional circumstances—it is preferable to print out a new prescription. Any alterations must be made in the doctor's own handwriting and countersigned; computer records should be updated to fully reflect any alteration. Prescriptions for drugs used for contraceptive purposes (but which are not promoted as contraceptives) may need to be marked in handwriting with the symbol ♀ (or endorsed in another way to indicate that the item is prescribed for contraceptive purposes).
14. Prescriptions for controlled drugs can be printed from the computer, but the prescriber's signature must be handwritten[2].
15. The strip of paper on the side of the FP10SS[3] may be used for various purposes but care should be taken to avoid including confidential information. It may be advisable for the patient's name to appear at the top, but this should be preceded by 'confidential'.
16. In rural dispensing practices prescription requests (or details of medicines dispensed) will normally be entered in one surgery. The prescriptions (or dispensed medicines) may then need to be delivered to another surgery or location; if possible the computer should hold up to 10 alternatives.
17. Prescription forms that are reprinted or issued as a duplicate should be labelled clearly as such.

1. Health Board in Scotland, Local Health Board in Wales.

2. See Controlled Drugs and Drug Dependence p. 7; the prescriber may use a date stamp.

3. GP10(COMP) and GP10SS in Scotland, WP10SS in Wales

# Emergency supply of medicines

## Emergency supply requested by member of the public

Pharmacists are sometimes called upon by members of the public to make an emergency supply of medicines. The Prescription Only Medicines (Human Use) Order 1997 allows exemptions from the Prescription Only requirements for emergency supply to be made by a person lawfully conducting a retail pharmacy business provided:

(a) that the pharmacist has interviewed the person requesting the prescription-only medicine and is satisfied:

- (i) that there is immediate need for the prescription-only medicine and that it is impracticable in the circumstances to obtain a prescription without undue delay;
- (ii) that treatment with the prescription-only medicine has on a previous occasion been prescribed by a doctor,[1] a supplementary prescriber, a district nurse or health visitor prescriber or an extended formulary nurse prescriber for the person requesting it;
- (iii) as to the dose which it would be appropriate for the person to take;

(b) that no greater quantity shall be supplied than will provide 5 days' treatment except when the prescription-only medicine is:

- (i) insulin, an ointment or cream, or a preparation for the relief of asthma in an aerosol dispenser when the smallest pack can be supplied;
- (ii) an oral contraceptive when a full cycle may be supplied;
- (iii) an antibiotic in liquid form for oral administration when the smallest quantity that will provide a full course of treatment can be supplied;

(c) that an entry shall be made by the pharmacist in the prescription book stating:

- (i) the date of supply;
- (ii) the name, quantity and, where appropriate, the pharmaceutical form and strength;
- (iii) the name and address of the patient;
- (iv) the nature of the emergency;

(d) that the container or package must be labelled to show:

- (i) the date of supply;
- (ii) the name, quantity and, where appropriate, the pharmaceutical form and strength;
- (iii) the name of the patient;
- (iv) the name and address of the pharmacy;
- (v) the words 'Emergency supply';
- (vi) the words 'Keep out of the reach of children' (or similar warning).

1. The doctor must be a UK-registered doctor.

(e) that the prescription-only medicine is not a substance specifically excluded from the emergency supply provision, and does not contain a Controlled Drug specified in schedules 1, 2, or 3 to the Misuse of Drugs Regulations 2001 except for phenobarbital or phenobarbital sodium for the treatment of epilepsy: for details see *Medicines, Ethics and Practice*, No. 29, London, Pharmaceutical Press, 2005 (and subsequent editions as available).

## Emergency supply requested by prescriber

Emergency supply of a prescription-only medicine may also be made at the request of a doctor, a supplementary prescriber, a district nurse or health visitor prescriber, or an extended formulary nurse prescriber provided:

(a) that the pharmacist is satisfied that the prescriber by reason of some emergency is unable to furnish a prescription immediately;

(b) that the prescriber has undertaken to furnish a prescription within 72 hours;

(c) that the medicine is supplied in accordance with the directions of the prescriber requesting it;

(d) that the medicine is not a substance specifically excluded from the emergency supply provision, and does not contain a Controlled Drug specified in schedules 1, 2, or 3 to the Misuse of Drugs Regulations 2001 except for phenobarbital or phenobarbital sodium for the treatment of epilepsy: for details see *Medicines, Ethics and Practice*, No. 29, London, Pharmaceutical Press, 2005 (and subsequent editions as available);

(e) that an entry shall be made in the prescription book stating:

- (i) the date of supply;
- (ii) the name, quantity and, where appropriate, the pharmaceutical form and strength;
- (iii) the name and address of the practitioner requesting the emergency supply;
- (iv) the name and address of the patient;
- (v) the date on the prescription;
- (vi) when the prescription is received the entry should be amended to include the date on which it is received.

## Royal Pharmaceutical Society's Guidelines

1. The pharmacist should consider the medical consequences of *not* supplying a medicine in an emergency.
2. If the pharmacist is unable to make an emergency supply of a medicine the pharmacist should advise the patient how to obtain essential medical care.

For conditions that apply to supplies made at the request of a patient see *Medicines, Ethics and Practice*, No. 29, London Pharmaceutical Press, 2005 (and subsequent editions).

# Controlled drugs and drug dependence

**Prescriptions** Preparations which are subject to the prescription requirements of the Misuse of Drugs Regulations 2001 (and subsequent amendments), i.e. preparations specified in schedules 2 and 3, are distinguished throughout the BNF by the symbol (CD) (Controlled Drugs). The principal legal requirements relating to medical prescriptions are listed below.

Prescriptions for Controlled Drugs, which are subject to prescription requirements must be indelible,[1] and must be *signed* by the prescriber, *be dated,* and specify the prescriber's *address.* The prescription must always state[2]:

- The name and address of the patient;
- In the case of a preparation, the form[3] and where appropriate the strength[4] of the preparation;
- The total quantity of the preparation, or the number of dose units, *in both words and figures;*[5]
- The dose;[6]
- The words 'for dental treatment only' if issued by a dentist.

A prescription may order a Controlled Drug to be dispensed by instalments; the amount of the instalments and the intervals to be observed must be specified.[7] Prescriptions ordering 'repeats' on the same form are **not** permitted. A prescription is valid for 13 weeks from the date stated thereon.

It is an offence for a prescriber to issue an incomplete prescription and a pharmacist is **not** allowed to dispense a Controlled Drug unless all the information required by law is given on the prescription. Failure to comply with the regulations concerning the writing of prescriptions will result in inconvenience to patients and delay in supplying the necessary medicine.

**Temazepam** is subject to the requirement for safe custody of controlled drugs because of problems with abuse, but it is exempt from the prescription requirements for controlled drugs. A prescription for temazepam is valid for 13 weeks from the date stated thereon.

The principal **barbiturates** are Controlled Drugs and must fulfil all controlled drug prescription requirements; for the treatment of epilepsy phenobarbital and phenobarbital sodium are available under the emergency supply regulations (p. 6).

**Cannabis** (Indian hemp) has no approved medicinal use and cannot be prescribed by doctors. Its use is illegal but has become widespread. Cannabis is a mild hallucinogen seldom accompanied by a desire to increase the dose; withdrawal symptoms are unusual. **Lysergide** (lysergic acid diethylamide, LSD) is a much more potent hallucinogen; its use can lead to severe psychotic states in which life may be at risk.

**Prescribing drugs likely to cause dependence or misuse** The prescriber has three main responsibilities:

- To avoid creating dependence by introducing drugs to patients without sufficient reason. In this context, the proper use of the morphine-like drugs is well understood. The dangers of other controlled drugs are less clear because recognition of dependence is not easy and its effects, and those of withdrawal, are less obvious.
- To see that the patient does not gradually increase the dose of a drug, given for good medical reasons, to the point where dependence becomes more likely. This tendency is seen especially with hypnotics and anxiolytics (for CSM advice see section 4.1). The prescriber should keep a close eye on the

**Dependence and misuse** The most serious drugs of addiction are **cocaine**, **diamorphine** (heroin), **morphine**, and the **synthetic opioids**. For arrangements for prescribing of diamorphine, dipipanone or cocaine for addicts, see p. 9.

Despite marked reduction in the prescribing of **amphetamines** there is concern that abuse of illicit amfetamine and related compounds is widespread.

1. A machine-written prescription is acceptable. The prescriber's signature must be handwritten.
2. Does not apply to prescriptions for temazepam.
3. The dosage form (e.g. tablets) must be included on a Controlled Drugs prescription irrespective of whether it is implicit in the proprietary name (e.g. *MST Continus*) or of whether only one form is available.
4. When more than one strength of a preparation exists the strength required must be specified.
5. Does not apply to prescriptions for temazepam.
6. The instruction 'one as directed' constitutes a dose but 'as directed' does not.
7. A total of 14 days' treatment by instalment of any drug listed in Schedule 2 of the Misuse of Drugs Regulations and buprenorphine may be prescribed in England. In *England,* form FP10MDA-SS (blue) or occasionally form FP10MDA (blue) should be used; in hospital, form FP10HP(AD) is being replaced by form FP10MDA-SS. In *Scotland* forms HBP(A) (hospital-based prescribers) or GP10 (general practitioners) should be used. In *Wales* a total of 14 days treatment by instalment of any drug listed in Schedules 2–5 of the Misuse of Drugs Regulations may be prescribed. In Wales form WP10(MDA) or form WP10HP(AD) for hospital prescribers should be used.

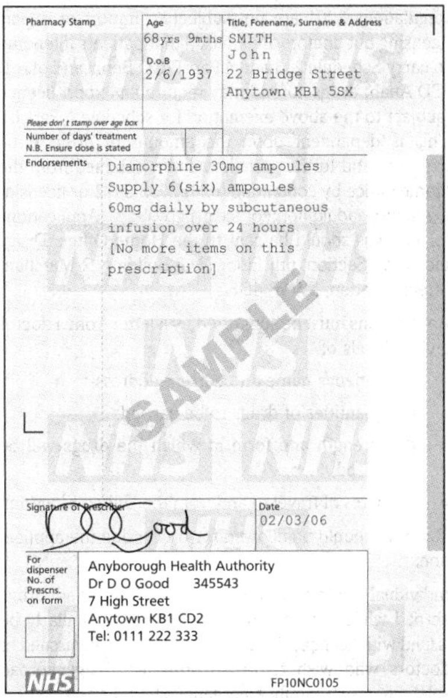
Pharmacy Stamp
Age
68yrs 9mths
D.o.B
2/6/1937
Title, Forename, Surname & Address
SMITH
John
22 Bridge Street
Anytown KB1 5SX
Please don't stamp over age box
Number of days' treatment
N.B. Ensure dose is stated
Endorsements
Diamorphine 30mg ampoules
Supply 6(six) ampoules
60mg daily by subcutaneous
infusion over 24 hours
[No more items on this
prescription]
SAMPLE
Signature of Prescriber
Date
02/03/06
For dispenser No. of Prescns. on form
Anyborough Health Authority
Dr D O Good 345543
7 High Street
Anytown KB1 CD2
Tel: 0111 222 333
NHS
FP10NC0105

amount prescribed to prevent patients from accumulating stocks. A minimal amount should be prescribed in the first instance, or when seeing a new patient for the first time.

- To avoid being used as an unwitting source of supply for addicts. Methods include visiting more than one doctor, fabricating stories, and forging prescriptions.

Patients under temporary care should be given only small supplies of drugs unless they present an unequivocal letter from their own doctors. Doctors should also remember that their own patients may be doing a collecting round with other doctors, especially in hospitals. It is sensible to decrease dosages steadily or to issue weekly or even daily prescriptions for small amounts if it is apparent that dependence is occurring.

The stealing and misuse of prescription forms could be minimised by the following precautions:

- do not leave unattended if called away from the consulting room or at reception desks; do not leave in a car where they may be visible; when not in use, keep in a locked drawer within the surgery and at home;
- draw a diagonal line across the blank part of the form under the prescription;
- write the quantity in words and figures when prescribing drugs prone to abuse; this is obligatory for controlled drugs (see Prescriptions, above);
- alterations are best avoided but if any are made they should be clear and unambiguous; add initials against altered items;
- if prescriptions are left for collection they should be left in a safe place in a sealed envelope.

**Travelling abroad** Prescribed drugs listed in schedule 4 Part II (CD Anab) [only when in the form of a medicinal product and for administration by a person to himself] and schedule 5 of the Misuse of Drugs Regulations 2001 are not subject to import or export licensing but doctors are advised that patients intending to carry Schedule 2, 3 and 4 Part I (CD Benz) and part II (CD Anab) drugs abroad may require an export licence (subject to the above exemption for schedule 4 Part II). This is dependent upon the amount of drug to be exported and further details may be obtained from the Home Office by contacting (020) 7035 0472 or licensing_enquiry.aadu@homeoffice.gsi.gov.uk. Applications for licences should be sent to the Home Office, Drugs Licensing Section, 6th Floor, Peel Building, 2 Marsham Street, London, SW1P 4DF.

Applications must be supported by a letter from a doctor giving details of:

- the patient's name and current address;
- the quantities of drugs to be carried;
- the strength and form in which the drugs will be dispensed;
- the dates of travel to and from the United Kingdom.

Ten days should be allowed for processing the application.

Individual doctors who wish to take Controlled Drugs abroad while accompanying patients may similarly be issued with licences. Licences are not normally issued to doctors who wish to take Controlled Drugs abroad solely in case a family emergency should arise.

These import/export licences for named individuals do not have any legal status outside the UK and are only issued to comply with the Misuse of Drugs Act and facilitate passage through UK Customs and Excise control. For clearance in the country to be visited it would be necessary to approach that country's consulate in the UK.

## Misuse of Drugs Act

The Misuse of Drugs Act, 1971 prohibits certain activities in relation to 'Controlled Drugs', in particular their manufacture, supply, and possession. The penalties applicable to offences involving the different drugs are graded broadly according to the *harmfulness attributable to a drug when it is misused* and for this purpose the drugs are defined in the following three classes:

**Class A** includes: alfentanil, cocaine, diamorphine (heroin), dipipanone, lysergide (LSD), methadone, methylenedioxymethamfetamine (MDMA, 'ecstasy'), morphine, opium, pethidine, phencyclidine, remifentanil, and class B substances when prepared for injection

**Class B** includes: oral amphetamines, barbiturates, codeine, ethylmorphine, glutethimide, pentazocine, phenmetrazine, and pholcodine

**Class C** includes: certain drugs related to the amphetamines such as benzfetamine and chlorphentermine, buprenorphine, cannabis, cannabis resin, diethylpropion, mazindol, meprobamate, pemoline, pipradrol, most benzodiazepines, zolpidem, androgenic and anabolic steroids, clenbuterol, chorionic gonadotrophin (HCG), non-human chorionic gonadotrophin, somatotropin, somatrem, and somatropin

The Misuse of Drugs Regulations 2001 define the classes of person who are authorised to supply and possess controlled drugs while acting in their professional capacities and lay down the conditions under which these activities may be carried out. In the regulations drugs are divided into five schedules each specifying the requirements governing such activities as import, export, production, supply, possession, prescribing, and record keeping which apply to them.

**Schedule 1** includes drugs such as cannabis and lysergide which are not used medicinally. Possession and supply are prohibited except in accordance with Home Office authority.

**Schedule 2** includes drugs such as diamorphine (heroin), morphine, remifentanil, pethidine, secobarbital, glutethimide, amfetamine, and cocaine and are subject to the full controlled drug requirements relating to prescriptions, safe custody (except for secobarbital), the need to keep registers, etc. (unless exempted in schedule 5).

**Schedule 3** includes the barbiturates (except secobarbital, now schedule 2), buprenorphine, diethylpropion, mazindol, meprobamate, pentazocine, phentermine, and temazepam. They are subject to the special prescription requirements (except for temazepam, see p. 7) but not to the safe custody requirements (except for buprenorphine, diethylpropion, and temazepam) nor to the need to keep registers (although there are requirements for the retention of invoices for 2 years).

**Schedule 4** includes in Part I benzodiazepines (except temazepam which is in schedule 3) and zolpidem, which are subject to minimal control. Part II includes androgenic and anabolic steroids, clenbuterol, chorionic gonadotrophin (HCG), non-human chorionic gonadotrophin, somatotropin, somatrem, and somatropin. Controlled drug prescription requirements do not apply and Schedule 4 Controlled Drugs are not subject to safe custody requirements.

**Schedule 5** includes those preparations which, because of their strength, are exempt from virtually all Controlled Drug requirements other than retention of invoices for two years.

## Notification of drug misusers

Doctors are expected to report cases of drug misuse to their regional or national drug misuse database or centre—see below for contact telephone numbers. The National Drugs Treatment Monitoring System (NDTMS) was introduced in England in April 2001; regional (NDTMS) centres replace the Regional Drug Misuse Databases. A similar system has been introduced in Wales.

Notification to regional (NDTMS) or national centre should be made when a patient starts treatment for drug misuse. All types of problem drug misuse should be reported including opioid, benzodiazepine, and CNS stimulant.

The regional (NDTMS) or national centres are now the only national and local source of epidemiological data on people presenting with problem drug misuse; they provide valuable information to those working with drug misusers and those planning services for them. The databases cannot, however be used as a check on multiple prescribing for drug addicts because the data are anonymised.

Enquiries about the regional (NDTMS) or national centres (including information on how to submit data) can be made to one of the centres listed below:

ENGLAND

*Eastern*
Tel: (01223) 597 598
Fax: (01223) 597 601

*South East*
Tel: (01865) 334 725
Fax: (01865) 334 733

*London*
Tel: (020) 7261 8820
Fax: (020) 7261 8883

*North West*
Tel: (0151) 231 4533
Fax: (0151) 231 4515

*North East*
Tel: (0191) 334 0372
Fax: (0191) 334 0391

*Yorkshire and the Humber*
Tel: (0113) 295 3714
Fax: (0113) 295 3720

*South Western*
Tel: (0117) 970 6474 ext 311
Fax: (0117) 970 7021

*East Midlands*
Tel: (0115) 971 2738
Fax: (0115) 971 2740

*West Midlands*
Tel: (0121) 415 8556
Fax: (0121) 414 8197

SCOTLAND
Tel: (0131) 275 6655
Fax: (0131) 275 7511

WALES
Tel: (029) 2050 3343
Fax: (029) 2050 2330

In **Northern Ireland**, the Misuse of Drugs (Notification of and Supply to Addicts) (Northern Ireland) Regulations 1973 require doctors to send particulars of persons whom they consider to be addicted to certain controlled drugs to the Chief Medical Officer of the Department of Health and Social Services. The Northern Ireland contacts are:

Medical contact:

Dr Ian McMaster
C3 Castle Buildings
Belfast BT4 3FQ
Tel: (028) 9052 2421
Fax: (028) 9052 0718

Administrative contact:

Drug & Alcohol Information & Research Unit
Annex 2
Castle Building
Belfast BT4 3SQ
Tel: (028) 9052 2520

The Drug & Alcohol Information & Research Unit also maintains the Northern Ireland Drug Misuse Database (NIDMD) which collects detailed information on those presenting for treatment, on drugs misused and injecting behaviour; participation is not a statutory requirement.

## Prescribing of diamorphine (heroin), dipipanone, and cocaine for addicts

The Misuse of Drugs (Supply to Addicts) Regulations 1997 require that only medical practitioners who hold a special licence issued by the Home Secretary may prescribe, administer or supply diamorphine, dipipanone[1] (*Diconal®*) or cocaine in the treatment of drug addiction; other practitioners must refer any addict who requires these drugs to a treatment centre. Whenever possible the addict will be introduced by a member of staff from the treatment centre to a pharmacist whose agreement has been obtained and whose pharmacy is conveniently sited for the patient. Prescriptions for weekly supplies will be sent to the pharmacy by post and will be dispensed on a daily basis as indicated by the doctor. If any alterations of the arrangements are requested by the addict, the portion of the prescription affected must be represcribed and not merely altered.

General practitioners and other doctors do not require a special licence for prescribing diamorphine, dipipanone, and cocaine for patients (including addicts) for *relieving pain* from organic disease or injury.

For guidance on prescription writing, see p. 7.

1. Dipipanone in *Diconal®* tablets has been much misused by opioid addicts in recent years. Doctors and others should be suspicious of people who ask for the tablets, especially if temporary residents.

# Adverse reactions to drugs

Any drug may produce unwanted or unexpected adverse reactions. Detection and recording of these is of vital importance. Doctors, dentists, coroners, pharmacists and nurses, see also self-reporting below, are urged to help by reporting suspected adverse reactions on yellow cards to:

Medicines and Healthcare products Regulatory Agency
[1]CSM
Freepost
London SW8 5BR
Tel: (0800 731 6789)

Suspected adverse reactions to *any* therapeutic agent should be reported, including drugs (*self-medication* as well as those *prescribed*), blood products, vaccines, radiographic contrast media and herbal products. Prepaid Yellow Cards for reporting are available from the above address and are also bound in this book (inside back cover). Adverse reactions can also be reported at: www.yellowcard.gov.uk.

A 24-hour Freefone service is available to all parts of the UK for advice and information on suspected adverse drug reactions; contact the National Yellow Card Information Service at the MHRA (formerly MCA) on 0800 731 6789. Outside office hours a telephone-answering machine will take messages.

The following regional centres also collect data:

[1]CSM Mersey
Freepost
Liverpool L3 3AB
Tel: (0151) 794 8206

[1]CSM Wales
Freepost
Cardiff CF4 1ZZ
Tel: (029) 2074 4181
(direct line)

[1]CSM Northern & Yorkshire
Freepost 1085
Newcastle upon Tyne NE1 1BR
Tel: (0191) 232 1525
(direct line)

[1]CSM West Midlands
Freepost SW2991
Birmingham B18 7BR
Tel: (0121) 507 5672

[1]CSM Scotland
CARDS
Freepost NAT3271
Edinburgh EH16 4BR
Tel: (0131) 242 2919

The MHRA's Adverse Drug Reactions On-line Information Tracking (ADROIT) facilitates the monitoring of adverse drug reactions.

More detailed information on reporting and a list of products currently under intensive monitoring can be found on the MHRA website: www.mhra.gov.uk.

**Self-reporting** Patients, parents, and carers can also report suspected adverse reactions as part of a pilot scheme. The reports can cover side effects of prescribed medicines as well as of over-the-counter and complementary medicines. For this purpose, patient yellow cards are available from pharmacies, general practice surgeries and other NHS outlets. Reports can also be submitted on-line to www.yellowcard.gov.uk or by telephone on 0808 100 3352.

1. CSM now subsumed under Commission on Human Medicines (CHM).

**Prescription-event monitoring** In addition to the MHRA's Yellow Card scheme, an independent scheme monitors the safety of new medicines using a different approach. The Drug Safety Research Unit identifies patients who have been prescribed selected new medicines and collects data on clinical events in these patients. The data are submitted on a voluntary basis by general practitioners on green forms. More information about the scheme and the Unit's educational material is available from www.dsru.org.

**Newer drugs and vaccines** Only limited information is available from clinical trials on the safety of new medicines. Further understanding about the safety of medicines depends on the availability of information from routine clinical practice.

The black triangle symbol (▼) identifies newly licensed medicines that are monitored intensively by the MHRA. Such medicines include those that have been licensed for administration by a new route or drug delivery system, or for significant new indications which may alter the established risks and benefits of that drug. There is no standard time for which products retain a black triangle; safety data are usually reviewed after 2 years.

Spontaneous reporting is particularly valuable for recognising possible new hazards rapidly. For medicines showing the black triangle symbol, the MHRA asks that **all** suspected reactions (including those considered not to be serious) are reported through the Yellow Card scheme. An adverse reaction should be reported even if it is not certain that the drug has caused it, or if the reaction is well recognised, or if other drugs have been given at the same time.

**Established drugs and vaccines** Doctors, dentists, coroners, pharmacists and nurses are asked to report *all* serious suspected reactions, including those that are fatal, life-threatening, disabling, incapacitating, or which result in or prolong hospitalisation; they should be reported even if the effect is well recognised. Examples include anaphylaxis, blood disorders, endocrine disturbances, effects on fertility, haemorrhage from any site, renal impairment, jaundice, ophthalmic disorders, severe CNS effects, severe skin reactions, reactions in pregnant women, and any drug interactions. Reports of serious adverse reactions are required to enable comparison with other drugs of a similar class. Reports of overdoses (deliberate or accidental) can complicate the assessment of adverse drug reactions, but provides important information on the potential toxicity of drugs.

For established drugs there is no need to report well-known, relatively minor side-effects, such as dry mouth with tricyclic antidepressants or constipation with opioids.

**Adverse reactions to medical devices** Suspected adverse reactions to medical devices including dental or surgical materials, intra-uterine devices and contact lens fluids should be reported. Information on reporting these can be found at: www.mhra.gov.uk

**Side-effects in the BNF** The BNF includes clinically relevant side-effects for most drugs; an exhaustive list is not included for drugs that are used by specialists (e.g. cytotoxics and drugs used in anaesthesia). Side-effects in the manufacturers' literature whose causality has not been established may be omitted from the BNF.

Recognising that hypersensitivity reactions can occur with virtually all medicines, this effect is not generally listed, unless the drug carries an increased risk of such reactions. The BNF also omits effects that are likely to have little clinical consequence (e.g. transient increase in liver enzymes).

Side-effects are generally listed in order of frequency and arranged broadly by body systems. Occasionally a rare side-effect might be listed first if it is considered to be particularly important because of its seriousness.

In the product literature the frequency of side-effects is generally described as follows:

| | |
|---|---|
| *Very common* | greater than 1 in 10 |
| *Common* | 1 in 100 to 1 in 10 |
| *Uncommon* | 1 in 1000 to 1 in 100 |
| *Rare* | 1 in 10 000 to 1 in 1000 |
| *Very rare* | less than 1 in 10 000 |

## Special problems

*Delayed drug effects.* Some reactions (e.g. cancers, chloroquine retinopathy, and retroperitoneal fibrosis) may become manifest months or years after exposure. Any suspicion of such an association should be reported.

*The elderly.* Particular vigilance is required to identify adverse reactions in the elderly.

*Congenital abnormalities.* When an infant is born with a congenital abnormality or there is a malformed aborted fetus doctors are asked to consider whether this might be an adverse reaction to a drug and to report all drugs (including self-medication) taken during pregnancy.

*Children.* Particular vigilance is required to identify and report adverse reactions in children, including those resulting from the unlicensed use of medicines; **all** suspected reactions should be reported (see p. 12).

## Prevention of adverse reactions

Adverse reactions may be prevented as follows:

- never use any drug unless there is a good indication. If the patient is pregnant do not use a drug unless the need for it is imperative;
- allergy and idiosyncrasy are important causes of adverse drug reactions. Ask if the patient had previous reactions;
- ask if the patient is already taking other drugs *including self-medication drugs, health supplements, herbal and complementary therapies*; interactions may occur;
- age and hepatic or renal disease may alter the metabolism or excretion of drugs, so that much smaller doses may be needed. Genetic factors may also be responsible for variations in metabolism, notably of isoniazid and the tricyclic antidepressants;
- prescribe as few drugs as possible and give very clear instructions to the elderly or any patient likely to misunderstand complicated instructions;
- when possible use a familiar drug. With a new drug be particularly alert for adverse reactions or unexpected events;
- if serious adverse reactions are liable to occur warn the patient.

## Oral side-effects of drugs

Drug-induced disorders of the mouth may be due to a local action on the mouth or to a systemic effect manifested by oral changes. In the latter case urgent referral to the patient's medical practitioner may be necessary.

### Oral mucosa

Medicaments left in contact with or applied directly to the oral mucosa can lead to inflammation or ulceration; the possibility of allergy should also be borne in mind.

**Aspirin** tablets allowed to dissolve in the sulcus for the treatment of toothache can lead to a white patch followed by ulceration.

Flavouring agents, particularly **essential oils**, may sensitise the skin, but mucosal swelling is not usually prominent.

The oral mucosa is particularly vulnerable to ulceration in patients treated with cytotoxic drugs, e.g. **methotrexate**. Other drugs capable of causing oral ulceration include **gold**, **nicorandil**, **NSAIDs**, **pancreatin**, **penicillamine**, and **proguanil**. **Captopril** (and other ACE inhibitors) can cause *stomatitis*.

*Erythema multiforme* (including Stevens-Johnson syndrome) may follow the use of a wide range of drugs including **antibacterials**, **sulphonamide derivatives**, and **anticonvulsants**; the oral mucosa may be extensively ulcerated, with characteristic target lesions on the skin. Oral lesions of *toxic epidermal necrolysis* (Lyell's syndrome) have been reported with a similar range of drugs.

*Lichenoid eruptions* are associated with **NSAIDs**, **methyldopa**, **chloroquine**, **oral antidiabetics**, **thiazide diuretics**, and **gold**.

*Candidiasis* can complicate treatment with **antibacterials** and **immunosuppressants** and is an occasional side-effect of **corticosteroid inhalers**, see also p. 154.

### Teeth

*Brown staining* of the teeth frequently follows the use of **chlorhexidine** mouthwash, spray or gel, but can readily be removed by polishing. **Iron** salts in liquid form can stain the enamel black. Superficial staining has been reported rarely with **co-amoxiclav** suspension.

*Intrinsic staining* of the teeth is most commonly caused by **tetracyclines**. They will affect the teeth if given at any time from about the fourth month *in utero* until the age of twelve years; they are contra-indicated in pregnancy, breast-feeding women, and in children under 12 years. All tetracyclines can cause permanent, unsightly staining in children, the colour varying from yellow to grey.

Excessive ingestion of **fluoride** leads to *dental fluorosis* with mottling of the enamel and areas of hypoplasia or pitting; fluoride supplements may occasionally cause mild mottling (white patches) if the dose is too large for the child's age, taking into account the fluoride content of the local drinking water.

### Periodontium

*Gingival overgrowth* (gingival hyperplasia) is a side-effect of **phenytoin** and sometimes of **ciclosporin** or of **nifedipine** (and some other calcium-channel blockers).

*Thrombocytopenia* may be drug related and may cause bleeding at the gingival margins, which may be spontaneous or may follow mild trauma (such as toothbrushing).

### Salivary glands

The most common effect that drugs have on the salivary glands is to *reduce flow* (xerostomia). Patients with a persistently dry mouth may have poor oral hygiene; they may develop increased dental caries, and oral infections (particularly candidiasis). Many drugs have been implicated in xerostomia, particularly **antimuscarinics** (anticholinergics), **antidepressants** (including tricyclic antidepressants, and selective serotonin re-uptake inhibitors), **baclofen**, **bupropion**, **clonidine**, **opioids**, and **tizanidine**. Excessive use of **diuretics** can also result in xerostomia.

Some drugs (e.g. clozapine, neostigmine) can *increase saliva production* but this is rarely a problem unless the patient has associated difficulty in swallowing.

Pain in the salivary glands has been reported with some **antihypertensives** (e.g. clonidine, methyldopa) and with **vinca alkaloids**.

Swelling of the salivary glands can occur with **iodides**, **antithyroid drugs**, **phenothiazines**, **ritodrine**, and **sulphonamides**.

### Taste

There can be *decreased* taste acuity or *alteration* in taste sensation. Drugs implicated include **amiodarone**, **captopril** (and other ACE inhibitors), **carbimazole**, **gold**, **griseofulvin**, **lithium salts**, **metronidazole**, **penicillamine**, **phenindione**, **propafenone**, **terbinafine**, and **zopiclone**.

## Defective medicines

During the manufacture or distribution of a medicine an error or accident may occur whereby the finished product does not conform to its specification. While such a defect may impair the therapeutic effect of the product and could adversely affect the health of a patient, it should **not** be confused with an Adverse Drug Reaction where the product conforms to its specification.

The Defective Medicines Report Centre assists with the investigation of problems arising from licensed medicinal products thought to be defective and co-ordinates any necessary protective action. Reports on suspect defective medicinal products should include the brand or the non-proprietary name, the name of the manufacturer or supplier, the strength and dosage form of the product, the product licence number, the batch number or numbers of the product, the nature of the defect, and an account of any action already taken in consequence.

The Centre can be contacted at:
The Defective Medicines Report Centre
Medicines and Healthcare products Regulatory Agency
Room 18–159
1 Nine Elms Lane
London SW8 5NQ
(020) 7084 2574 (weekdays 9.00 am–5.00 pm)
or (020) 7210 3000 (outside office hours)

# Prescribing for children

For detailed advice on medicines used for children consult *BNF for Children*

Children, and particularly neonates, differ from adults in their response to drugs. Special care is needed in the neonatal period (first 30 days of life) and doses should always be calculated with care. At this age, the risk of toxicity is increased by inefficient renal filtration, relative enzyme deficiencies, differing target organ sensitivity, and inadequate detoxifying systems causing delayed excretion.

Whenever possible, painful intramuscular injections should be **avoided** in children.

Where possible, medicines for children should be prescribed within the terms of the marketing authorisation (product licence) However, many children may require medicines not specifically licensed for paediatric use.

Although medicines cannot be promoted outside the limits of the licence, the Medicines Act does not prohibit the use of unlicensed medicines. It is recognised that the informed use of unlicensed medicines or of licensed medicines for unlicensed applications ('off-label' use) is often necessary in paediatric practice.

**Adverse drug reactions in children** The reporting of all suspected adverse drug reactions in children is **strongly encouraged** through the Yellow Card scheme (see p. 10) even if the intensive monitoring symbol (▼) has been removed, because experience in children may still be limited.

The identification and reporting of adverse reactions to drugs in children is particularly important because:

- the action of the drug and its pharmacokinetics in children (especially in the very young) may be different from that in adults
- drugs are not extensively tested in children
- many drugs are not specifically licensed for use in children and are used 'off-label'
- suitable formulations may not be available to allow precise dosing in children
- the nature and course of illnesses and adverse drug reactions may differ between adults and children.

**Prescription writing** Prescriptions should be written according to the guidelines in Prescription Writing (p. 4) Inclusion of age is a legal requirement in the case of prescription-only medicines for children under 12 years of age, but it is preferable to state the age for **all** prescriptions for children.

It is particularly important to state the strengths of capsules or tablets. Although liquid preparations are particularly suitable for children, they may contain sugar which encourages dental decay. Sugar-free medicines are preferred for long-term treatment.

Many children are able to swallow tablets or capsules and may prefer a solid dose form; involving the child and parents in choosing the formulation is helpful.

When a prescription for a liquid oral preparation is written and the dose ordered is smaller than 5 mL an **oral syringe** will be supplied (for details, see p. 2). Parents should be advised not to add any medicines to the infant's feed, since the drug may interact with the milk or other liquid in it; moreover the ingested dosage may be reduced if the child does not drink all the contents.

Parents must be warned to keep **all** medicines out of reach of children, see Safety in the Home, p. 3

## Rare paediatric conditions

Information on substances such as *biotin* and *sodium benzoate* used in rare metabolic conditions is included in *BNF for Children*; further information can be obtained from:

Alder Hey Children's Hospital
Drug Information Centre
Liverpool L12 2AP
Tel: (0151) 252 5381

Great Ormond Street Hospital for Children
Pharmacy
Great Ormond St
London WC1N 3JH
Tel: (020) 7405 9200

## Dosage in Children

Children's doses in the BNF are stated in the individual drug entries as far as possible, except where paediatric use is not recommended, information is not available, or there are special hazards.

Doses are generally based on body-weight (in kilograms) or the following age ranges:

first month (neonate)

up to 1 year (infant)

1–5 years

6–12 years

Unless the age is specified, the term 'child' in the BNF includes persons aged 12 years and younger.

**Dose calculation** Many children's doses are standardised by **weight** (and therefore require multiplying by the body-weight in kilograms to determine the child's dose); occasionally, the doses have been standardised by **body surface area** (in $m^2$). These methods should be used rather than attempting to calculate a child's dose on the basis of doses used in adults.

For most drugs the adult maximum dose should not be exceeded. For example if the dose is stated as 8 mg/kg (max. 300 mg), a child weighing 10 kg should receive 80 mg but a child weighing 40 kg should receive 300 mg (rather than 320 mg).

Young children may require a higher dose per kilogram than adults because of their higher metabolic rates. Other problems need to be considered. For example, calculation by body-weight in the overweight child may result in much higher doses being administered than necessary; in such cases, dose should be calculated from an ideal weight, related to height and age (see inside back cover).

**Body-surface area (BSA) estimates** are more accurate for calculation of paediatric doses than body-weight since many physiological phenomena correlate better to body-surface area. Body-surface area may be calculated from height and weight by means of a nomogram. For more information, refer to *BNF for Children.*

Where the dose for children is not stated, prescribers should consult *BNF for Children* or seek advice from a medicines information centre.

**Dose frequency** Antibacterials are generally given at regular intervals throughout the day. Some flexibility should be allowed in children to avoid waking them during the night. For example, the night-time dose may be given at the parent's bedtime.

Where new or potentially toxic drugs are used, the manufacturers' recommended doses should be carefully followed.

# Prescribing in palliative care



Palliative care is the active total care of patients whose disease is not responsive to curative treatment. Control of pain, of other symptoms, and of psychological, social and spiritual problems, is paramount to provide the best quality of life for patients and their families. Careful assessment of symptoms and needs of the patient should be undertaken by a multidisciplinary team.

Specialist palliative care is available in most areas as day hospice care, home care teams (often known as Macmillan teams), in-patient hospice care, and hospital teams. Many acute hospitals and teaching centres now have consultative, hospital-based teams.

Hospice care of terminally ill patients has shown the importance of symptom control and psychosocial support of the patient and family. Families should be included in the care of the patient if they wish.

Many patients wish to remain at home with their families. Although some families may at first be afraid of caring for the patient at home, support can be provided by community nursing services, social services, voluntary agencies and hospices together with the general practitioner. The family may be reassured by the knowledge that the patient will be admitted to a hospital or hospice if the family cannot cope.

**Drug treatment** The number of drugs should be as few as possible, for even the taking of medicine may be an effort. Oral medication is usually satisfactory unless there is severe nausea and vomiting, dysphagia, weakness, or coma, in which case parenteral medication may be necessary.

## Pain

Analgesics are more effective in preventing pain than in the relief of established pain; it is important that they are given regularly.

The non-opioid analgesics **paracetamol** or an **NSAID** (section 10.1.1) given regularly will often make the use of opioids unnecessary. The NSAID may also control the pain of *bone secondaries*; if necessary, flurbiprofen or indometacin can be given rectally. Radiotherapy, bisphosphonates (section 6.6.2) and radioactive isotopes of **strontium** (*Metastron*® available from GE Healthcare) may also be useful for pain due to bone metastases.

An opioid such as **codeine** alone or in combination with a non-opioid analgesic at adequate dosage, may be helpful in the control of moderate pain if non-opioids alone are not sufficient. Alternatively, **tramadol** can be considered for moderate pain. If these preparations are not controlling the pain, **morphine** is the most useful opioid analgesic. Alternatives to morphine include **hydromorphone**, **methadone**, **oxycodone** (section 4.7.2) and transdermal **fentanyl** (see below and section 4.7.2); these drugs are best initiated by those with experience in palliative care. Initiation of an opioid analgesic should not be delayed by concern over a theoretical likelihood of psychological dependence (addiction).

### Equivalent single doses of strong analgesics

These equivalences are intended **only** as an approximate guide; patients should be carefully monitored after **any** change in medication and dose titration may be required

| Analgesic | Dose |
|---|---|
| Morphine salts (oral) | 10 mg |
| Diamorphine hydrochloride (intramuscular) | 3 mg |
| Hydromorphone hydrochloride | 1.3 mg |
| Oxycodone (oral) | 5 mg |

**Oral route** Morphine is given *by mouth* as an oral solution or as standard ('immediate release') tablets regularly every 4 hours, the initial dose depending largely on the patient's previous treatment. A dose of 5–10 mg is enough to replace a weaker analgesic (such as paracetamol or co-proxamol), but 10–20 mg or more is required to replace a strong one (comparable to morphine itself). If the first dose of morphine is no more effective than the previous analgesic, the next dose should be increased by 50%, the aim being to choose the lowest dose which prevents pain. The dose should be adjusted with careful assessment of the pain and the use of adjuvant analgesics (such as NSAIDs) should also be considered. Although morphine in a dose of 5–20 mg is usually adequate there should be no hesitation in increasing it stepwise according to response to 100 mg or occasionally up to 500 mg or higher if necessary. It may be possible to omit the overnight dose if double the usual dose is given at bedtime.

If pain occurs between regular doses of morphine ('breakthrough pain'), an additional dose ('rescue dose') should be given. An additional dose should also be given 30 minutes before an activity that causes pain (e.g. wound dressing). Fentanyl lozenges are also licensed for breakthrough pain.

When the pain is controlled and the patient's 24-hour morphine requirement is established, the daily dose can be given as a single dose or in 2 divided doses as a *modified-release preparation.*

Preparations suitable for twice daily administration include *MST Continus*® tablets or suspension, and *Zomorph*® capsules. Preparations that allow administration of the total daily morphine requirement as a single dose include *MXL*® capsules. *Morcap SR*® capsules may be given either twice daily or as a single daily dose.

The starting dose of modified-release morphine preparations designed for twice daily administration is usually 10–20 mg every 12 hours if no other analgesic (or only paracetamol) has been taken previously, but to replace a weaker opioid analgesic (such as co-codamol) the starting dose is usually 20–30 mg every 12 hours. Increments should be made to the dose, not to the frequency of administration, which should remain at every 12 hours.

The effective dose of modified-release preparations can alternatively be determined by giving the oral solution of morphine every 4 hours in increasing doses until the pain has been controlled, and then transferring the patient to the same total 24-hour dose of morphine given as the modified-release preparation (divided into two portions for 12-hourly administration). The first dose of the modified-release preparation is given 4 hours after the last dose of the oral solution.[1]

Morphine, as oral solution or standard formulation tablets, should be prescribed for breakthrough pain; the dose should be about one-sixth of the total daily dose of oral morphine repeated every 4 hours if necessary (review pain management if analgesic required more frequently).

**Parenteral route** If the patient becomes unable to swallow, the equivalent intramuscular dose of morphine is half the oral solution dose; in the case of the modified-release tablets it is half the total 24-hour dose (which is then divided into 6 portions to be given every 4 hours). **Diamorphine** is preferred for injection because, being more soluble, it can be given in a smaller volume. The equivalent intramuscular (or subcutaneous) is approximately a third of the oral dose of morphine. *Subcutaneous infusion* of diamorphine via syringe driver can be useful (for details, see p. 16).

If the patient can resume taking medicines by mouth, then oral morphine may be substituted for subcutaneous infusion of diamorphine; see table of equivalent doses of morphine (p. 17) for equivalences between the two opioids.

**Rectal route** Morphine is also available for *rectal administration* as suppositories; alternatively **oxycodone** suppositories can be obtained on special order.

**Transdermal route** Transdermal preparations of fentanyl are available (section 4.7.2). Careful conversion from oral morphine to transdermal fentanyl is necessary. The following 24-hour doses of morphine are considered to be equivalent to the fentanyl patches shown:

Morphine salt 90 mg daily ≡ fentanyl '25' patch
Morphine salt 180 mg daily ≡ fentanyl '50' patch
Morphine salt 270 mg daily ≡ fentanyl '75' patch
Morphine salt 360 mg daily ≡ fentanyl '100' patch

Morphine (as oral solution or standard formulation tablets) is given for breakthrough pain.

**Gastro-intestinal pain** The pain of *bowel colic* may be reduced by loperamide 2–4 mg 4 times daily. Hyoscine hydrobromide may also be helpful, given sublingually at a dose of 300 micrograms 3 times daily as *Kwells®* (Roche Consumer Health) tablets. For the dose by subcutaneous infusion using a syringe driver, see p. 17).

Gastric distension pain due to pressure on the stomach may be helped by a preparation incorporating an antacid with an antiflatulent (section 1.1.1) and by domperidone 10 mg 3 times daily before meals.

**Muscle spasm** The pain of muscle spasm can be helped by a muscle relaxant such as diazepam 5–10 mg daily or baclofen 5–10 mg 3 times daily.

**Neuropathic pain** Patients with neuropathic pain (section 4.7.3) may benefit from a trial of a tricyclic antidepressant for several weeks. An anticonvulsant may be added or substituted if pain persists; gabapentin and pregabalin (both section 4.8.1) are licensed for neuropathic pain.

Pain due to nerve compression may be reduced by a corticosteroid such as dexamethasone 8 mg daily, which reduces oedema around the tumour, thus reducing compression.

**Nerve blocks** may be considered when pain is localised to a specific area. **Transcutaneous electrical nerve stimulation** (TENS) may also help.

1. Studies have indicated that administration of the last dose of the *oral solution* with the first dose of the *modified-release tablets* is not necessary.

## Miscellaneous conditions

**Non-licensed indications or routes**
Several recommendations in this section involve non-licensed indications or routes.

**Raised intracranial pressure** Headache due to raised intracranial pressure often responds to a high dose of a corticosteroid, such as dexamethasone 16 mg daily for 4 to 5 days, subsequently reduced to 4–6 mg daily if possible; dexamethasone should be given before 6 p.m. to reduce the risk of insomnia.

**Intractable cough** Intractable cough may be relieved by moist inhalations or by regular administration of oral morphine in an initial dose of 5 mg every 4 hours. Methadone linctus should be avoided because it has a long duration of action and tends to accumulate.

**Dyspnoea** Breathlessness at rest may be relieved by regular oral morphine in carefully titrated doses, starting at 5 mg every 4 hours. Diazepam 5–10 mg daily may be helpful for dyspnoea associated with anxiety. A corticosteroid, such as dexamethasone 4–8 mg daily, may also be helpful if there is bronchospasm or partial obstruction.

**Excessive respiratory secretion** Excessive respiratory secretion (death rattle) may be reduced by subcutaneous injection of hyoscine hydrobromide 400–600 micrograms every 4 to 8 hours; care must however be taken to avoid the discomfort of dry mouth. Alternatively glycopyrronium may be given by subcutaneous or intramuscular injection in a dose of 200 micrograms every 4 hours. For the dose by subcutaneous infusion using a syringe driver, see p. 17.

**Restlessness and confusion** Restlessness and confusion may require treatment with haloperidol 1–3 mg by mouth every 8 hours. Levomepromazine (methotrimeprazine) is also used occasionally for restlessness. For the dose by subcutaneous infusion using a syringe driver, see p. 17.

**Hiccup** Hiccup due to gastric distension may be helped by a preparation incorporating an antacid with an antiflatulent (section 1.1). If this fails, metoclopramide 10 mg every 6 to 8 hours by mouth or by subcutaneous or intramuscular injection can be added; if this also fails baclofen 5 mg twice daily, or nifedipine 10 mg three times daily, or chlorpromazine 10–25 mg every 6 to 8 hours can be tried.

**Anorexia** Anorexia may be helped by prednisolone 15–30 mg daily or dexamethasone 2–4 mg daily.

**Constipation** Constipation is a very common cause of distress and is almost invariable after administration of an opioid. It should be prevented if possible by the regular administration of laxatives; a faecal softener with a peristaltic stimulant (e.g. co-danthramer), or lactulose solution with a senna preparation should be used (section 1.6.2 and section 1.6.3).

**Fungating growth** Fungating growth may be treated by regular dressing and oral administration of metronidazole; topical application of metronidazole is also used.

**Capillary bleeding** Capillary bleeding may be reduced by applying gauze soaked in adrenaline (epinephrine) solution 1 mg/mL (1 in 1000).

**Dry mouth** Dry mouth may be relieved by good mouth care and measures such as the sucking of ice or pineapple chunks or the use of artificial saliva (section 12.3.5); dry mouth associated with candidiasis can be treated by oral preparations of nystatin or miconazole (section 12.3.2); alternatively, fluconazole can be given by mouth (section 5.2). Dry mouth may be caused by certain medication including opioids, antimuscarinic drugs (e.g. hyoscine), antidepressants and some anti-emetics; if possible, an alternative preparation should be considered.

**Pruritus** Pruritus, even when associated with obstructive jaundice, often responds to simple measures such as application of emollients (section 13.2.1). In the case of obstructive jaundice, further measures include administration of colestyramine (section 1.9.2).

**Convulsions** Patients with cerebral tumours or uraemia may be susceptible to convulsions. Prophylactic treatment with phenytoin or carbamazepine (section 4.8.1) should be considered. When oral medication is no longer possible, diazepam as suppositories 10–20 mg every 4 to 8 hours, or phenobarbital by injection 50–200 mg twice daily is continued as prophylaxis. For the use of midazolam by subcutaneous infusion using a syringe driver, see below.

**Dysphagia** A corticosteroid such as dexamethasone 8 mg daily may help, temporarily, if there is an obstruction due to tumour. See also under Dry Mouth.

**Nausea and vomiting** Nausea and vomiting are common in patients with advanced cancer. Ideally, the cause should be determined before treatment with an anti-emetic (section 4.6) is started.

Nausea and vomiting may occur with opioid therapy particularly in the initial stages but can be prevented by giving an anti-emetic such as haloperidol or metoclopramide. An anti-emetic is usually necessary only for the first 4 or 5 days and therefore combined preparations containing an opioid with an anti-emetic are not recommended because they lead to unnecessary anti-emetic therapy (and associated side-effects when used long-term).

Metoclopramide has a prokinetic action and is used in a dose of 10 mg 3 times daily by mouth for nausea and vomiting associated with gastritis, gastric stasis, and functional bowel obstruction. Drugs with antimuscarinic effects antagonise prokinetic drugs and, where possible, should not therefore be used concurrently.

Haloperidol is used in a dose of 1.5 mg daily (or twice daily if nausea continues) by mouth for most chemical causes of vomiting (e.g. hypercalcaemia, renal failure).

Cyclizine is given in a dose of 50 mg up to 3 times daily by mouth. It is used for nausea and vomiting due to mechanical bowel obstruction, raised intracranial pressure, and motion sickness.

Anti-emetic therapy should be reviewed every 24 hours; it may be necessary to substitute the anti-emetic or to add another one.

Levomepromazine (methotrimeprazine) may be used if first-line anti-emetics are inadequate; it is given by mouth in a dose of 6–25 mg daily [6-mg tablets available on named-patient basis]. Dexamethasone 8–16 mg daily by mouth may be used as an adjunct.

For the administration of anti-emetics by subcutaneous infusion using a syringe driver, see below.

For the treatment of nausea and vomiting associated with cancer chemotherapy, see section 8.1.

**Insomnia** Patients with advanced cancer may not sleep because of discomfort, cramps, night sweats, joint stiffness, or fear. There should be appropriate treatment of these problems before hypnotics are used. Benzodiazepines, such as temazepam, may be useful (section 4.1.1).

**Hypercalcaemia** See section 9.5.1.2.

## Syringe drivers

Although drugs can usually be administered *by mouth* to control the symptoms of advanced cancer, the parenteral route may sometimes be necessary. If the parenteral route is necessary, repeated administration of *intramuscular injections* can be difficult in a cachectic patient. This has led to the use of a portable syringe driver to give a *continuous subcutaneous infusion*, which can provide good control of symptoms with little discomfort or inconvenience to the patient.

> **Syringe driver rate settings.**
> Staff using syringe drivers should be **adequately trained** and different rate settings should be **clearly identified** and **differentiated**; incorrect use of syringe drivers is a common cause of drug errors.

Indications for the **parenteral route** are:

- the patient is unable to take medicines by mouth owing to *nausea and vomiting, dysphagia, severe weakness,* or *coma;*
- there is *malignant bowel obstruction* in patients for whom further surgery is inappropriate (avoiding the need for an intravenous infusion or for insertion of a nasogastric tube);
- occasionally when the patient *does not wish* to take regular medication by mouth.

**Nausea and vomiting** Haloperidol is given in a *subcutaneous infusion dose* of 2.5–10 mg/24 hours.

Levomepromazine (methotrimeprazine) causes sedation in about 50% of patients; it is given in a *subcutaneous infusion dose* of 25–200 mg/24 hours, although lower doses of 5–25 mg/24 hours may be effective with less sedation.

Cyclizine is particularly liable to precipitate if mixed with diamorphine or other drugs (see under Mixing and Compatibility, below); it is given in a *subcutaneous infusion dose* of 150 mg/24 hours.

Metoclopramide may cause skin reactions; it is given in a *subcutaneous infusion dose* of 30–100 mg/24 hours.

Octreotide (section 8.3.4.3), which stimulates water and electrolyte absorption and inhibits water secretion in the small bowel, can be used by subcutaneous infusion, in a dose of 300–600 micrograms/24 hours to reduce intestinal secretions and vomiting.

**Bowel colic and excessive respiratory secretions** Hyoscine hydrobromide effectively reduces respiratory secretions and is sedative (but occasionally causes paradoxical agitation); it is given in a *subcutaneous infusion dose* of 0.6–2.4 mg/24 hours.

Hyoscine butylbromide is effective in bowel colic, is less sedative than hyoscine hydrobromide, but is not always adequate for the control of respiratory secretions; it is given in a *subcutaneous infusion dose* of 20–60 mg/24 hours (**important:** this dose of *hyoscine butylbromide* must not be confused with the much lower dose of *hyoscine hydrobromide*, above).

Glycopyrronium 0.6–1.2 mg/24 hours may also be used.

**Restlessness and confusion** Haloperidol has little sedative effect; it is given in a *subcutaneous infusion dose* of 5–15 mg/24 hours.

Levomepromazine (methotrimeprazine) has a sedative effect; it is given in a *subcutaneous infusion dose* of 12.5–200 mg/24 hours.

Midazolam is a sedative and an antiepileptic which may be suitable for a very restless patient; it is given in a *subcutaneous infusion dose* of 20–100 mg/24 hours.

**Convulsions** If a patient has previously been receiving an antiepileptic *or* has a primary or secondary cerebral tumour *or* is at risk of convulsion (e.g. owing to uraemia) antiepileptic medication should not be stopped. Midazolam is the benzodiazepine antiepileptic of choice for *continuous subcutaneous infusion*, and it is given intially in a dose of 20–40 mg/24 hours.

**Pain control** Diamorphine is the preferred opioid since its high solubility permits a large dose to be given in a small volume (see under Mixing and Compatibility, below). The table below gives the approximate doses of *morphine by mouth* (as oral solution or standard formulation tablets or as modified-release tablets) equivalent to *diamorphine by injection* (intramuscularly or by subcutaneous infusion).

**Mixing and compatibility** The general principle that injections should be given into separate sites (and should not be mixed) does not apply to the use of syringe drivers in palliative care. Provided that there is evidence of compatibility, selected injections can be mixed in syringe drivers. Not all types of medication can be used in a subcutaneous infusion. In particular, chlorpromazine, prochlorperazine and diazepam are **contra-indicated** as they cause skin reactions at the injection site; to a lesser extent cyclizine and levomepromazine (methotrimeprazine) may also sometimes cause local irritation.

In theory injections dissolved in water for injections are more likely to be associated with pain (possibly owing to their hypotonicity). The use of physiological saline (sodium chloride 0.9%) however increases the likelihood of precipitation when more than one drug is used; moreover subcutaneous infusion rates are so slow (0.1–0.3 mL/hour) that pain is not usually a problem when water is used as a diluent.

Diamorphine can be given by subcutaneous infusion in a strength of up to 250 mg/mL; up to a strength of 40 mg/mL either *water for injections* or *physiological saline* (sodium chloride 0.9%) is a suitable diluent—above that strength only *water for injections* is used (to avoid precipitation).

The following can be mixed with *diamorphine*:

| | |
|---|---|
| Cyclizine[1] | Hyoscine hydrobromide |
| Dexamethasone[2] | Levomepromazine |
| Haloperidol[3] | Metoclopramide[4] |
| Hyoscine butylbromide | Midazolam |

Subcutaneous infusion solution should be monitored regularly both to check for precipitation (and discoloration) and to ensure that the infusion is running at the correct rate

**Problems encountered with syringe drivers** The following are problems that may be encountered with syringe drivers and the action that should be taken:

- if the subcutaneous infusion runs *too quickly* check the rate setting and the calculation;
- if the subcutaneous infusion runs *too slowly* check the start button, the battery, the syringe driver, the cannula, and make sure that the injection site is not inflamed;
- if there is an *injection site reaction* make sure that the site does not need to be changed—firmness or swelling at the site of injection is not in itself an indication for change, but pain or obvious inflammation is.

1. Cyclizine may precipitate at concentrations above 10 mg/mL *or* in the presence of sodium chloride 0.9% *or* as the concentration of diamorphine relative to cyclizine increases; mixtures of diamorphine and cyclizine are also liable to precipitate after 24 hours.
2. Special care is needed to avoid precipitation of dexamethasone when preparing.
3. Mixtures of haloperidol and diamorphine are liable to precipitate after 24 hours if haloperidol concentration is above 2 mg/mL.
4. Under some conditions metoclopramide may become discoloured; such solutions should be discarded.

**Equivalent doses of morphine sulphate by mouth or of diamorphine hydrochloride by intramuscular injection or by subcutaneous infusion**

**These equivalences are approximate only and may need to be adjusted according to response**

| ORAL MORPHINE | | PARENTERAL DIAMORPHINE | |
|---|---|---|---|
| Morphine sulphate oral solution or standard tablets | Morphine sulphate modified-release tablets | Diamorphine hydrochloride by intramuscular injection | Diamorphine hydrochloride by subcutaneous infusion |
| **every 4 hours** | **every 12 hours** | **every 4 hours** | **every 24 hours** |
| 5 mg | 20 mg | 2.5 mg | 15 mg |
| 10 mg | 30 mg | 5 mg | 20 mg |
| 15 mg | 50 mg | 5 mg | 30 mg |
| 20 mg | 60 mg | 7.5 mg | 45 mg |
| 30 mg | 90 mg | 10 mg | 60 mg |
| 40 mg | 120 mg | 15 mg | 90 mg |
| 60 mg | 180 mg | 20 mg | 120 mg |
| 80 mg | 240 mg | 30 mg | 180 mg |
| 100 mg | 300 mg | 40 mg | 240 mg |
| 130 mg | 400 mg | 50 mg | 300 mg |
| 160 mg | 500 mg | 60 mg | 360 mg |
| 200 mg | 600 mg | 70 mg | 400 mg |

If breakthrough pain occurs give a subcutaneous (preferable) or intramuscular injection of diamorphine equivalent to one-sixth of the total 24-hour subcutaneous infusion dose. It is kinder to give an intermittent bolus injection *subcutaneously*—absorption is smoother so that the risk of adverse effects at peak absorption is avoided (an even better method is to use a subcutaneous butterfly needle).
To minimise the risk of infection no individual subcutaneous infusion solution should be used for longer than 24 hours.

# Prescribing for the elderly

Old people, especially the very old, require special care and consideration from prescribers. *Medicines for Older People*, a component document of the National Service Framework for Older People,[1] describes how to maximise the benefits of medicines and how to avoid excessive, inappropriate, or inadequate consumption of medicines by older people.

**Appropriate prescribing** Elderly patients often receive multiple drugs for their multiple diseases. This greatly increases the risk of drug interactions as well as adverse reactions, and may affect compliance (see Taking medicines to best effect under General guidance). The balance of benefit and harm of some medicines may be altered in the elderly. Therefore, elderly patients' medicines should be reviewed regularly and medicines which are not of benefit should be stopped.

Non-pharmacological measures may be more appropriate for symptoms such as headache, sleeplessness and lightheadedness when associated with social stress as in widowhood, loneliness, and family dispersal.

In some cases prophylactic drugs may be inappropriate if they are likely to complicate existing treatment or introduce unnecessary side-effects, especially in elderly patients with poor prognosis or with poor overall health. However, elderly patients should not be denied medicines which may help them, such as anticoagulants or antiplatelet drugs for atrial fibrillation, antihypertensives, statins, and drugs for osteoporosis.

1. Department of Health. National Service Framework for Older People. London: Department of Health, March 2001

**Form of medicine** Frail elderly patients may have difficulty swallowing tablets; if left in the mouth, ulceration may develop. They should always be encouraged to take their tablets or capsules with enough fluid, and whilst in an upright position to avoid the possibility of oesophageal ulceration. It may be helpful to discuss with the patient the possibility of taking the drug as a liquid if available.

**Manifestations of ageing** In the very old, manifestations of normal ageing may be mistaken for disease and lead to inappropriate prescribing. In addition, age-related muscle weakness and difficulty in maintaining balance should not be confused with neurological disease. Disorders such as lightheadedness not associated with postural or postprandial hypotension are unlikely to be helped by drugs.

**Self-medication** Just as in a younger patient self-medication with over-the-counter products or with drugs prescribed for a previous illness (or even for another person) may be an added complication. Discussion with both the patient and relatives as well as a home visit may be needed to establish exactly what is being taken.

**Sensitivity** The ageing nervous system shows increased *susceptibility* to many commonly used drugs, such as opioid analgesics, benzodiazepines, antipsychotics, and antiparkinsonian drugs, all of which must be used with caution. Similarly, other organs may also be more susceptible to the effects of drugs such as antihypertensives and NSAIDs.

## Pharmacokinetics

The most important effect of age is reduction in renal clearance. Many aged patients thus *excrete drugs slowly*, and are *highly susceptible to nephrotoxic drugs*. Acute illness may lead to rapid reduction in renal clearance, especially if accompanied by dehydration. Hence, a patient stabilised on a drug with a narrow margin between the therapeutic and the toxic dose (e.g. digoxin) may rapidly develop adverse effects in the aftermath of a myocardial infarction or a respiratory-tract infection. The metabolism of some drugs may be reduced in the elderly.

Pharmacokinetic changes may markedly increase the tissue concentration of a drug in the elderly, especially in debilitated patients.

## Adverse reactions

Adverse reactions often present in the elderly in a vague and non-specific fashion. *Confusion* is often the presenting symptom (caused by almost any of the commonly used drugs). Other common manifestations are *constipation* (with antimuscarinics and many tranquillisers) and postural *hypotension* and *falls* (with diuretics and many psychotropics).

**Hypnotics** Many hypnotics with long half-lives have serious hangover effects of drowsiness, unsteady gait, and even slurred speech and confusion. Those with short half-lives should be used but they too can present problems (section 4.1.1). Short courses of hypnotics are occasionally useful for helping a patient through an acute illness or some other crisis but every effort must be made to avoid dependence. Benzodiazepines impair balance, which may result in falls.

**Diuretics** Diuretics are overprescribed in old age and should **not** be used on a long-term basis to treat simple gravitational oedema which will usually respond to increased movement, raising the legs, and support stockings. A few days of diuretic treatment may speed the clearing of the oedema but it should rarely need continued drug therapy.

**NSAIDs** Bleeding associated with *aspirin* and *other NSAIDs* is more common in the elderly who are more likely to have a fatal or serious outcome. NSAIDs are also a special hazard in patients with cardiac disease or renal impairment which may again place older patients at particular risk.

Owing to the *increased susceptibilty of the elderly* to the *side-effects of NSAIDs* the following recommendations are made:

- for *osteoarthritis, soft-tissue lesions* and *back pain* first try measures such as weight reduction (if obese), warmth, exercise and use of a walking stick;
- for *osteoarthritis, soft-tissue lesions, back pain* and *pain in rheumatoid arthritis*, paracetamol should be used first and can often provide adequate pain relief;
- alternatively, a low-dose NSAID (e.g. ibuprofen up to 1.2 g daily may be given;
- for pain relief when either drug is inadequate, paracetamol in a full dose plus a low-dose NSAID may be given;
- if necessary, the NSAID dose can be increased or an opioid analgesic given with paracetamol;
- do not give two NSAIDs at the same time.

For advice on prophylaxis of NSAID-induced peptic ulcers if continued NSAID treatment is necessary, see section 1.3.

**Other drugs** Other drugs which commonly cause adverse reactions are *antiparkinsonian drugs, antihypertensives, psychotropics*, and *digoxin*. The usual maintenance dose of digoxin in very old patients is 125 micrograms daily (62.5 micrograms in those with renal disease); lower doses are often inadequate but toxicity is common in those given 250 micrograms daily.

Drug-induced blood disorders are much more common in the elderly. Therefore drugs with a tendency to cause bone marrow depression (e.g. *co-trimoxazole, mianserin*) should be avoided unless there is no acceptable alternative.

The elderly generally require a lower maintenance dose of *warfarin* than younger adults; once again, the outcome of bleeding tends to be more serious.

## Guidelines

Always consider whether a drug is indicated at all.

**Limit range** It is a sensible policy to prescribe from a limited range of drugs and to be thoroughly familiar with their effects in the elderly.

**Reduce dose** Dosage should generally be substantially lower than for younger patients and it is common to start with about 50% of the adult dose. Some drugs (e.g. long-acting antidiabetic drugs such as glibenclamide and chlorpropamide) should be avoided altogether.

**Review regularly** Review repeat prescriptions regularly. In many patients it may be possible to stop some drugs, provided that clinical progress is monitored. It may be necessary to reduce the dose of some drugs as renal function declines.

**Simplify regimens** Elderly patients benefit from simple treatment regimens. Only drugs with a clear indication should be prescribed and whenever possible given once or twice daily. In particular, regimens which call for a confusing array of dosage intervals should be avoided.

**Explain clearly** Write full instructions on every prescription (*including* repeat prescriptions) so that containers can be properly labelled with full directions. Avoid imprecisions like 'as directed'. Child-resistant containers may be unsuitable.

**Repeats and disposal** Instruct patients what to do when drugs run out, and also how to dispose of any that are no longer necessary. Try to prescribe matching quantities.

If these guidelines are followed most elderly people will cope adequately with their own medicines. If not then it is essential to enrol the help of a third party, usually a relative or a friend.

# Prescribing in dental practice

The following is a list of topics of particular relevance to dental surgeons.

> Advice on the drug management of dental and oral conditions has been integrated into the BNF. For ease of access, guidance on such conditions is usually identified by means of a relevant heading (e.g. Dental and Orofacial Pain) in the appropriate sections of the BNF.


**General guidance**

Prescribing by dental surgeons, p. 4
Oral side-effects of drugs, p. 11
Medical emergencies in dental practice, below
Medical problems in dental practice, p. 23

**Drug management of dental and oral conditions**

**Dental and orofacial pain,** p. 217
Neuropathic pain, p. 230
Non-opioid analgesics, p. 218
Opioid analgesics, p. 223
Non-steroidal anti-inflammatory drugs, p. 506

**Oral infections**
Bacterial infections, p. 267
Phenoxymethylpenicillin, p. 273
Broad-spectrum penicillins (amoxicillin and ampicillin), p. 276
Cephalosporins (cefalexin and cefradine), p. 280
Tetracyclines, p. 285
Macrolides (erythromycin and azithromycin) , p. 290
Clindamycin, p. 292
Metronidazole, p. 303
Fusidic acid p. 598
Fungal infections, p. 560
Local treatment, p. 560
Systemic treatment, p. 308
Viral infections
Herpetic gingivostomatitis, local treatment, p. 562
Herpetic gingivostomatitis, systemic treatment, p. 322 and p. 562
Herpes labialis, p. 601

**Anaesthetics, anxiolytics and hypnotics**
Framework for anaesthesia, sedation, and resuscitation in general practice, p. 633
Hypnotics, p. 174
Peri-operative anxiolytics, p. 639
Local anaesthesia, p. 647

**Oral ulceration and inflammation,** p. 558
**Mouthwashes, gargles and dentifrices,** p. 562
**Dry mouth,** p. 564
**Vitamins and minerals**
Fluorides, p. 492
Oral vitamin B complex preparations, p. 493 and p. 495
Ascorbic acid (vitamin C), p. 495
**Antihistamines,** p. 161
**Aromatic inhalations,** p. 170
**Nasal decongestants,** p. 557

**Dental Practitioners' Formulary,** p. 851

**Changes to Dental Practitioners' Formulary,** p. 852


## Medical emergencies in dental practice

This section provides guidelines on the management of the more common medical emergencies which may arise in dental practice. Dental surgeons and their staff should be familiar with standard resuscitation procedures, but in all circumstances it is advisable to summon medical assistance as soon as possible. For an **algorithm** of the procedure for **cardiopulmonary resuscitation**, see inside back cover.

> **The drugs referred to in this section include:**
> Adrenaline Injection (Epinephrine Injection), adrenaline 1 in 1000, (adrenaline 1 mg/mL as acid tartrate), 1-mL amps
> Aspirin Dispersible Tablets 300 mg
> Chlorphenamine Injection (Chlorpheniramine Injection), chlorphenamine maleate 10 mg/mL, 1-mL amps
> Diazepam Injection, diazepam 5 mg/mL, 2-mL amps
> Glucagon Injection, glucagon (as hydrochloride), 1-unit vial (with solvent)
> Glucose Powder
> Glucose Intravenous Infusion, glucose 20% (200 mg/mL), 500-mL pack or glucose 50% (500 mg/mL), 50-mL prefilled syringe
> Glyceryl Trinitrate Tablets and Sprays
> Hydrocortisone Injection, hydrocortisone 100 mg (preferably as sodium succinate vials with 2-mL solvent)
> Oxygen
> Salbutamol Aerosol Inhalation, salbutamol 100 micrograms/metered inhalation
> Salbutamol Injection, salbutamol (as sulphate) 500 micrograms/mL, 1-mL amps

### Adrenal insufficiency

Adrenal insufficiency may be caused by administration of corticosteroids and can persist for years after stopping long-term therapy. A patient with adrenal insufficiency may become hypotensive under the stress of a dental visit (important: see also p. 362 for details of cover for anaesthesia or surgery).

**Management**

- Lay the patient flat
- Give hydrocortisone (as sodium succinate) 100 mg intravenously
- Give oxygen
- Call for medical assistance

### Anaphylaxis

A severe allergic reaction may follow oral or parenteral administration of a drug. Anaphylactic reactions in dentistry may follow the administration of a drug or contact with substances such as latex in surgical gloves. In general, the more rapid the onset of the reaction the more profound it tends to be. Symptoms may develop within minutes and rapid treatment is essential.

Anaphylactic reactions may also be associated with *additives* and *excipients* in foods and medicines (see Excipients, p. 2). Refined arachis (peanut) oil, which may be present in some medicinal products, is unlikely to cause an allergic reaction—nevertheless it is wise to check the full formula of preparations which may contain allergenic fats or oils (including those for topical application, particularly if they are intended for use in the mouth or for application to the nasal mucosa).

**Symptoms and signs**

- Paraesthesia, flushing, and swelling of face
- Generalised itching, especially of hands and feet
- Bronchospasm and laryngospasm (with wheezing and difficulty in breathing)
- Rapid weak pulse together with fall in blood pressure and pallor; finally cardiac arrest

**Management**

First-line treatment includes securing the airway, restoration of blood pressure (laying the patient flat, raising the feet), and administration of **adrenaline** (epinephrine) injection. This is given **intramuscularly** in a dose of 500 micrograms (0.5 mL adrenaline injection 1 in 1000); a preparation delivering a dose of 300 micrograms (0.3 mL adrenaline injection 1 in 1000) is available for immediate *self-administration*. The dose is repeated if necessary at 5-minute intervals according to blood pressure, pulse and respiratory function. **Oxygen** administration is also of primary importance. An antihistamine (e.g. **chlorphenamine** (chlorpheniramine), given by slow intravenous injection in a dose of 10–20 mg, see p. 163) is a useful adjunctive treatment, given after adrenaline injection and continued for 24 to 48 hours to prevent relapse; chlorphenamine can alternatively be given by intramuscular injection. In patients receiving non-cardioselective beta-blockers severe anaphylaxis may not respond to adrenaline injection, calling for administration of **salbutamol** by intravenous injection (alternatively it can be given by intramuscular or subcutaneous injection); adrenaline may also cause severe hypertension in those receiving beta-blockers. Patients on tricyclic antidepressants are considerably more susceptible to cardiac arrhythmias calling for a much reduced dose of adrenaline (for other interactions, see Appendix 1 (sympathomimetics)).

An intravenous corticosteroid e.g. **hydrocortisone** (as sodium succinate) (section 6.3.2) in a dose of 100–300 mg is of secondary value in the initial management of anaphylactic shock because the onset of action is delayed for several hours, but it should be given to prevent further deterioration in severely affected patients.

For further details on the management of anaphylaxis including details of paediatric doses of adrenaline, see p. 165

## Asthma

Patients with asthma may have an attack while at the dental surgery. Most attacks will respond to 2 puffs of the patient's short-acting $beta_2$-adrenoceptor stimulant inhaler such as **salbutamol** 100 micrograms/puff (or **terbutaline** 250 micrograms/puff); further puffs are required if the patient does not respond rapidly. If the patient is unable to use the inhaler effectively further puffs should be given through a large-volume spacer device (or, if not available, through a plastic or paper cup with a hole in the bottom for the inhaler mouthpiece). If the response remains unsatisfactory, or if the patient develops tachycardia, then arrangements should be made to transfer the patient urgently to hospital. Whilst awaiting transfer, **oxygen** should be given with salbutamol 2.5–5 mg by nebuliser. If a nebuliser is unavailable, then 4–6 puffs of salbutamol inhaler or terbutaline inhaler should be given (preferably by a large-volume spacer device), and repeated every 10 minutes if necessary. Hydrocortisone (preferably as sodium succinate) 200 mg may be given by intravenous injection. If asthma is part of a more generalised anaphylactic reaction, an intramuscular injection of **adrenaline** (as detailed under Anaphylaxis above) should be given.

For a table describing the management of Acute Severe Asthma, see p. 142

Patients with severe chronic asthma or whose asthma has deteriorated previously during a dental procedure may require an increase in their prophylactic medication before a dental procedure. This should be discussed with the patient's medical practitioner and may include increasing the dose of inhaled or oral corticosteroid.

## Cardiac emergencies

If there is a history of *angina* the patient will probably carry **glyceryl trinitrate** spray or tablets (or isosorbide dinitrate tablets) and should be allowed to use them. See also Coronary Artery Disease on p. 23.

*Arrhythmias* may lead to a sudden reduction in cardiac output with loss of consciousness. Medical assistance should be summoned. For advice on pacemaker interference, see also Pacemakers, p. 24.

The pain of *myocardial infarction* is similar to that of angina but generally more severe and more prolonged. For general advice see also Coronary Artery Disease on p. 23

**Symptoms and signs of myocardial infarction**

- Progressive onset of severe, crushing pain across front of chest; pain may radiate towards the shoulder and down arm, or into neck and jaw
- Skin becomes pale and clammy
- Nausea and vomiting are common
- Pulse may be weak and blood pressure may fall

**Initial management of myocardial infarction**

Call immediately for medical assistance and an ambulance, as appropriate.

Allow the patient to rest in the position that feels most comfortable; in the presence of breathlessness this is likely to be sitting position, whereas the syncopal patient should be laid flat; often an intermediate position (dictated by the patient) will be most appropriate.

Intramuscular injection of drugs does not provide useful relief of pain because absorption is too slow (particularly when cardiac output is reduced) but a mixture of **nitrous oxide** 50% and **oxygen** 50% can be effective if given continuously; it is safe in this situation.

Reassure the patient as much as possible to relieve further anxiety. If available, aspirin in a single dose of 150–300 mg should be given. A note (to say that aspirin has been given) should be sent with the patient to the hospital. For further details on the initial management of myocardial infarction, see p. 129.

If the patient collapses and loses consciousness attempt standard resuscitation measures. For an **algorithm** of the procedure for **cardiopulmonary resuscitation**, see inside back cover.

## Epileptic seizures

Patients with epilepsy must continue with their normal dosage of anticonvulsant drugs when attending for dental treatment. It is not uncommon for epileptic patients not to volunteer the information that they are epileptic but there should be little difficulty in recognising a tonic-clonic (grand mal) seizure.

### Symptoms and signs

- There may be a brief warning (but variable)
- Sudden loss of consciousness, the patient becomes rigid, falls, may give a cry, and becomes cyanotic (tonic phase)
- After 30 seconds, there are jerking movements of the limbs; the tongue may be bitten (clonic phase)
- There may be frothing from mouth and urinary incontinence
- The seizure typically lasts a few minutes; the patient may then become flaccid but remain unconscious. After a variable time the patient regains consciousness but may remain confused for a while

### Management

During a convulsion try to ensure that the patient is not at risk from injury but make no attempt to put anything in the mouth or between the teeth (in mistaken belief that this will protect the tongue).

Do not attempt to restrain convulsive movements.

After convulsive movements have subsided place the patient in the coma (recovery) position and check the airway.

After the convulsion the patient may be confused ('post-ictal confusion') and may need reassurance and sympathy. The patient should not be sent home until fully recovered but it is not necessary to seek medical attention or transfer to hospital unless the convulsion was atypical, prolonged (or repeated), or if injury occurred.

Medication should only be given if convulsive seizures are prolonged (convulsive movements lasting 5 minutes or longer) or repeated rapidly.

Intravenous administration of **diazepam** 10 mg is often effective but should be used with caution because of the risk of respiratory depression (for further details see p. 248). Alternatively, in prolonged or recurrent seizures, **midazolam** (section 15.1.4.1) can be given intranasally [unlicensed use] in a single dose of 200 micrograms/kg.

Partial seizures similarly need very little active management (in an automatism only a minimum amount of restraint should be applied to prevent injury). Again, the patient should be observed until post-ictal confusion has completely resolved.

## Hypoglycaemia

Insulin-treated diabetic patients attending for dental treatment under general anaesthesia normally require admission to hospital; those only needing local anaesthesia should inject insulin and eat meals as normal. If food is omitted the blood glucose will fall to an abnormally low level (hypoglycaemia). Patients can often recognise the symptoms themselves and this state responds to sugar in water or a few lumps of sugar. Children may not have such prominent changes but may appear unduly lethargic.

### Symptoms and signs

- Shaking and trembling
- Sweating
- 'Pins and needles' in lips and tongue
- Hunger
- Palpitation
- Headache (occasionally)
- Double vision
- Difficulty in concentration
- Slurring of speech
- Confusion
- Change of behaviour; truculence
- Unconsciousness

### Management

Initially glucose 10–20 g is given by mouth either in liquid form or as granulated sugar or sugar lumps. Glucose 10 g is available from 2 teaspoons sugar, 3 sugar lumps, *GlucoGel®* (formerly known as *Hypostop® Gel*; glucose 9.2 g/23-g oral ampoule, available from British BioCell International), and non-diet versions of *Lucozade® Sparkling Glucose Drink* 50–55 mL, *Coca-Cola®* 90 mL, *Ribena® Original* 15 mL (to be diluted). If necessary this may be repeated in 10–15 minutes.

If hypoglycaemia causes unconsciousness, **glucagon** 1 mg (1 unit) should be given by intramuscular (or subcutaneous) injection; a child under 8 years or of body-weight under 25 kg should be given 500 micrograms. If glucagon is ineffective or contra-indicated, 50 mL of **glucose intravenous infusion 20%** can be given (for further details see p. 356). Alternatively, 25 mL of glucose intravenous infusion 50% may be given, but this higher concentration is viscous, making administration difficult; it is also more irritant. Once the patient regains consciousness oral glucose should be administered as above. The patient must be admitted to hospital if hypoglycaemia is caused by an oral antidiabetic drug.

## Syncope

Insufficient blood supply to the brain results in loss of consciousness. The commonest cause is a vasovagal attack or simple faint (syncope) due to emotional stress.

### Symptoms and signs

- Patient feels faint
- Pallor and sweating
- Yawning and slow pulse
- Nausea and vomiting
- Dilated pupils
- Muscular twitching

### Management

- Lay the patient as flat as is reasonably comfortable and, in the absence of associated breathlessness, raise the legs to improve cerebral circulation
- Loosen any tight clothing around the neck
- Once consciousness is regained, give sugar in water or a cup of sweet tea

### Other possible causes

Postural hypotension can be a consequence of rising abruptly or of standing upright for too long; antihypertensive drugs predispose to this. When rising, susceptible patients should take their time. Management is as for a vasovagal attack.

Under stressful circumstances, some patients hyperventilate. This gives rise to feelings of faintness but does not usually result in syncope. In most cases reassurance is all that is necessary; rebreathing from cupped hands or a bag may be helpful but calls for careful supervision.

Adrenal insufficiency or arrhythmias are other possible causes of syncope, see p. 20 and below.

## Medical problems in dental practice

Individuals presenting at the dental surgery may also suffer from an unrelated medical condition; this may require modification to the management of their dental condition. If the patient has systemic disease or is taking other medication, the matter may need to be discussed with the patient's general practitioner or hospital consultant.

For advice on adrenal insufficiency, anaphylaxis, asthma, cardiac emergencies, epileptic seizures, hypoglycaemia and syncope see under Medical Emergencies in Dental Practice.

### Allergy

Patients should be asked about any history of allergy; those with a history of atopic allergy (asthma, eczema, hay fever, etc.) are at special risk. Those with a history of a severe allergy or of anaphylactic reactions are at high risk—it is essential to confirm that they are not allergic to any medication, or to any dental materials or equipment (including latex gloves). See also Anaphylaxis on p. 20.

### Arrhythmias

Patients, especially those who suffer from heart failure or who have sustained a myocardial infarction, may have irregular cardiac rhythm. Atrial fibrillation is a common arrhythmia even in patients with normal hearts and is of little concern except that dental surgeons should be aware that such patients may be receiving anticoagulant therapy. The patient's medical practitioner should be asked whether any special precautions are necessary. Premedication (e.g. with temazepam) may be useful in some instances for very anxious patients.

See also Cardiac emergencies, p. 21 and Dental Anaesthesia, p. 647.

### Breast-feeding

Evidence on the use of medicines during breast-feeding is often inadequate and care is required in choosing appropriate treatment. Appendix 5 includes information on drug treatment and breast-feeding.

### Cardiac prostheses

For an account of the risk of infective endocarditis in patients with prosthetic heart valves and the recommendations of a Working Party of the British Society for Antimicrobial Chemotherapy, see Infective endocarditis, below. For advice on patients receiving anticoagulants, see Thromboembolic disease, below.

### Coronary artery disease

Patients are vulnerable for at least 4 weeks following a myocardial infarction or following any sudden increase in the symptoms of angina. It would be advisable to check with the patient's medical practitioner before commencing treatment. See also Cardiac Emergencies on p. 21.

Treatment with low-dose aspirin (75–300 mg daily), clopidogrel, or dipyridamole should not be stopped routinely nor should the dose be altered before dental procedures.

A Working Party of the British Society for Antimicrobial Chemotherapy has not recommended antibiotic prophylaxis for patients following coronary artery bypass surgery.

### Cyanotic heart disease

Patients with cyanotic heart disease are at risk in the dental chair, particularly if they have pulmonary hypertension. In such patients a syncopal reaction increases the shunt away from the lungs, causing more hypoxia which worsens the syncopal reaction—a vicious circle that may prove fatal. The advice of the cardiologist should be sought on any patient with congenital cyanotic heart disease. Treatment in hospital is more appropriate for some patients with this condition.

### Hypertension

Patients with hypertension are likely to be receiving antihypertensive drugs such as those described in section 2.5. Their blood pressure may fall dangerously low under general anaesthesia, which should only be administered in hospital where appropriate precautions can be taken. See also under Dental Anaesthesia on p. 647.

### Immunosuppression and indwelling intraperitoneal catheters

See Table 2, section 5.1

### Infective endocarditis

Although almost any dental procedure is capable of causing bacteraemia, infective endocarditis is a rare complication even in susceptible patients. It is virtually impossible, therefore, to assess the relative effectiveness of different prophylactic regimens; nevertheless, there is now some consensus among cardiologists and microbiologists. The recommendations of a Working Party of the British Society for Antimicrobial Chemotherapy are reflected in Table 2, section 5.1. Alternative guidelines have been produced and may be in use in some settings.

**Patients at risk** Patients with *cardiac defects* (congenital, rheumatic, etc.) are at risk from infective endocarditis following dental procedures. Those who have a *history of infective endocarditis* in the past are particularly at risk. There is no evidence that patients with *prosthetic heart valves* are any more susceptible to infective endocarditis after dental operations than those with damaged natural valves, but if it develops treatment may be more difficult.

All patients must be questioned about any history of heart defects or rheumatic fever and especially whether they have previously had infective endocarditis. Turbulence around the valves has been identified as a risk factor. Heart murmurs in children are often of no significance but whenever there is any doubt a cardiologist should be consulted. The peak incidence of infective endocarditis is after the sixth decade.

The following patients, who are considered to be at *special risk* should be referred to hospital for endocarditis prophylaxis:

- patients with prosthetic valves who are to have a general anaesthetic;
- patients who are allergic to penicillin who are to have a general anaesthetic;
- patients who have had more than a single dose of a penicillin in the previous month who are to have a general anaesthetic;
- all patients who have had a previous episode of endocarditis.

**Procedures that need cover** Dental procedures that require antibacterial prophylaxis include:

- extractions
- scaling[1]
- surgery involving gingival tissues

**Reduction of oral sepsis** The frequency and severity of bacteraemia is related to the severity of the gingival inflammation. The highest possible standards of oral hygiene in patients at risk reduces:

- need for dental extractions or other surgery;
- chances of severe bacteraemia if dental surgery is needed;
- possibility of 'spontaneous' bacteraemia.

Application of an antiseptic such as chlorhexidine gluconate gel 1% to the dry gingival margin or the use of a chlorhexidine gluconate mouthwash (0.2%) 5 minutes before the dental procedure may reduce the possibility of bacteraemia and may be used to supplement antibiotic prophylaxis in those at risk.

Intraligamentary (periodontal) injection of local anaesthetic solutions may carry a risk of severe bacteraemia and is best avoided in patients susceptible to endocarditis.

**Postoperative care** Patients at risk of endocarditis should be warned to report to the doctor or dental surgeon any minor illness that develops after dental treatment, whether or not antibacterials have been given, because infective endocarditis has an insidious onset and treatment may fail if diagnosis is delayed. If endocarditis develops it is likely to be within a month of dental treatment.

**Patients on anticoagulant therapy** The prophylactic doses of the antibacterials (see Table 2, section 5.1) are unlikely to alter the International Normalised Ratio (INR) in patients receiving oral anticoagulants. Nevertheless, it is prudent to measure the INR again a few days after the procedure especially if a general anaesthetic was used.

For general advice on dental surgery in patients receiving oral anticoagulant therapy see Thromboembolic Disease, below.

1. Prophylaxis is considered appropriate for all scaling and other procedures involving the periodontium

## Joint prostheses

See Table 2, section 5.1

## Liver disease

Liver disease may alter the response to drugs and drug prescribing should be kept to a minimum in patients with severe liver disease. Problems are likely mainly in patients with *jaundice*, *ascites*, or evidence of *encephalopathy*.

For a table of drugs to be avoided or used with caution in liver disease see Appendix 2.

## Pacemakers

Pacemakers prevent asystole or severe bradycardia. Some ultrasonic scalers, electronic apex locators, electro-analgesic devices, and electrocautery devices interfere with the normal function of pacemakers (including shielded pacemakers) and should not be used. The manufacturer's literature should be consulted whenever possible. If severe bradycardia occurs in a patient fitted with a pacemaker, electrical equipment should be switched off and the patient placed supine with the legs elevated. If the patient loses consciousness and the pulse remains slow or is absent, cardiopulmonary resuscitation (see inside back cover) may be needed. Call immediately for medical assistance and an ambulance, as appropriate.

A Working Party of the British Society for Antimicrobial Chemotherapy does not recommend antibacterial prophylaxis for patients with pacemakers.

## Pregnancy

Drugs taken during pregnancy can be harmful to the fetus and should be prescribed only if the expected benefit to the mother is thought to be greater than the risk to the fetus; all drugs should be avoided if possible during the first trimester.

Appendix 4 includes information on drug treatment during pregnancy

## Renal impairment

The use of drugs in patients with reduced renal function can give rise to many problems. Many of these problems can be avoided by reducing the dose or by using alternative drugs.

Special care is required in renal transplantation and immunosuppressed patients; if necessary such patients should be referred to specialists.

For a table of drugs to be avoided or used with caution in renal impairment see Appendix 3.

## Thromboembolic disease

Patients receiving **heparin** or oral anticoagulants such as **warfarin**, **acenocoumarol** (nicoumalone), or **phenindione** may be liable to excessive bleeding after extraction of teeth or other dental surgery. Often dental surgery can be delayed until the anticoagulant therapy has been completed.

For a patient requiring long-term oral anticoagulant therapy, the patient's medical practitioner should be consulted and the International Normalised Ratio (INR) should be assessed preferably no more than 24 hours before the dental procedure (no more than 72 hours beforehand if INR stable). Patients requiring minor dental procedures *without extractions* who have an INR below 4.0 may continue warfarin without dose adjustment. Patients requiring *extractions* and who have an INR below 3.0 may continue warfarin without dose adjustment. If possible, a single extraction should be done first; if this goes well further teeth may be extracted at subsequent visits (two or three at a time). Measures should be taken to minimise bleeding during and after the procedure. Scaling and root planing should initially be restricted to a limited area to assess the potential for bleeding. Some dental surgeons suture the gum over the socket to hold in place a haemostatic such as oxidised cellulose, collagen sponge or resorbable gelatin sponge. For a patient on long-term anticoagulation treatment, the advice of the clinician responsible for the patients's anticoagulation should be sought if:

- the INR is unstable, or if the INR is greater than 4.0, or for minor dental procedures with extractions if the INR is greater than 3.0;
- the patient has thrombocytopenia, haemophilia, or other disorders of haemostasis, or suffers from liver impairment, alcoholism, or renal failure;
- the patient is receiving cytotoxic drugs or radiotherapy.

Intramuscular injections are *contra-indicated* in patients on anticoagulant therapy, and in those with any disorder of haemostasis.

A local anaesthetic containing a vasoconstrictor should be given by infiltration or by intraligamentary injection if possible. If regional nerve blocks cannot be avoided the local anaesthetic should be given cautiously using an aspirating syringe.

Drugs which have potentially serious interactions with anticoagulants include aspirin and other NSAIDs, carbamazepine, imidazole and triazole antifungals (including miconazole), erythromycin, clarithromycin, and metronidazole; for details of these and other interactions with anticoagulants, see Appendix 1 (heparin, phenindione, warfarin and other coumarins). Although studies have failed to demonstrate an interaction, common experience in anticoagulant clinics is that the INR can be altered following a course of an oral broad-spectrum antibiotic, such as ampicillin or amoxicillin.

# Drugs and sport

UK Sport advises that athletes are personally responsible should a prohibited substance be detected in their body. Information and advice, including the status of specific drugs in sport, can be obtained from UK Sport's Drug Information Database at www.didglobal.com. An advice card listing examples of permitted and prohibited substances is available from:



Drug-Free Sport
UK Sport
40 Bernard Street
London WC1N 1ST
Tel: 0800 528 0004
www.uksport.gov.uk
drug-free@uksport.gov.uk

A similar card detailing classes of drugs and doping methods prohibited in football is available from the Football Association.

### General Medical Council's advice

Doctors who prescribe or collude in the provision of drugs or treatment with the intention of improperly enhancing an individual's performance in sport would be contravening the GMC's guidance, and such actions would usually raise a question of a doctor's continued registration. This does not preclude the provision of any care or treatment where the doctor's intention is to protect or improve the patient's health.

# Emergency treatment of poisoning

These notes provide only an overview of the treatment of poisoning and it is strongly recommended that either a **poisons information centre** or **TOXBASE** (see below) be consulted where there is doubt about the degree of risk or about management.

**Hospital admission** All patients who show features of poisoning should generally be admitted to hospital. Patients who have taken poisons with delayed action should also be admitted, even if they appear well. Delayed-action poisons include aspirin, iron, paracetamol, tricyclic antidepressants, co-phenotrope (diphenoxylate with atropine, *Lomotil®*), and paraquat; the effects of modified-release preparations are also delayed. A note of all relevant information including what treatment has been given should accompany the patient to hospital.

## Further information and advice

**TOXBASE**, the primary clinical toxicology database of the National Poisons Information Service, is available on the Internet to registered users at www.spib.axl.co.uk. It provides information about routine diagnosis, treatment and management of patients exposed to drugs, household products, and industrial and agricultural chemicals.

Specialist information and advice on the treatment of poisoning is available from the **UK National Poisons Information Service** through the local poisons information centre on the following number:
Tel: 0870 600 6266

Advice on laboratory analytical services can be obtained from TOXBASE or from a poisons information centre.

Help on identifying capsules or tablets may be available from a regional medicines information centre (see inside front cover).

> The **poisons information centres** (Tel: 0870 600 6266) will provide specialist advice on all aspects of poisoning day and night

## General care

It is often impossible to establish with certainty the identity of the poison and the size of the dose. Fortunately this is not usually important because only a few poisons (such as opioids, paracetamol, and iron) have specific antidotes; few patients require active removal of the poison. In most patients, treatment is directed at managing symptoms as they arise. Nevertheless, knowledge of the type and timing of poisoning can help in anticipating the course of events. All relevant information should be sought from the poisoned individual and from carers or parents. However, such information should be interpreted with care because it may not be complete or entirely reliable. Sometimes symptoms arise from other illnesses and patients should be assessed carefully. Accidents may involve a number of domestic and industrial products (the contents of which are not generally known). A **poisons information centre** should be consulted where there is doubt about any aspect of suspected poisoning.

## Respiration

Respiration is often impaired in unconscious patients. An obstructed airway requires immediate attention. In the absence of trauma, the airway should be opened with simple measures such as chin lift or jaw thrust. An oropharyngeal or nasopharyngeal airway may be useful in patients with reduced consciousness to prevent obstruction, provided ventilation is adequate. Intubation and ventilation should be considered in patients whose airway cannot be protected or who have inadequate ventilation because of respiratory acidosis; such patients should be monitored in a critical care area.

Most poisons that impair consciousness also depress respiration. Assisted ventilation by mouth-to-mouth or *Ambu-bag* inflation may be needed. Oxygen is not a substitute for adequate ventilation, though it should be given in the highest concentration possible in poisoning with carbon monoxide and irritant gases.

Respiratory stimulants do not help and should be **avoided**.

## Blood pressure

Hypotension is common in severe poisoning with central nervous system depressants. A systolic blood pressure of less than 70 mmHg may lead to irreversible brain damage or renal tubular necrosis. Hypotension should be corrected initially by tilting down the head of the bed and administration of either sodium chloride intravenous infusion or a colloidal infusion. Vasoconstrictor sympathomimetics (section 2.7.2) are rarely required and their use may be discussed with a poisons information centre.

Fluid depletion without hypotension is common after prolonged coma and after aspirin poisoning due to vomiting, sweating, and hyperpnoea.

Hypertension, often transient, occurs less frequently than hypotension in poisoning; it may be associated with sympathomimetic drugs such as amphetamines, phencyclidine, and cocaine.

## Heart

Cardiac conduction defects and arrhythmias may occur in acute poisoning, notably with tricyclic antidepressants, some antipsychotics, some antihistamines, and co-proxamol. Arrhythmias often respond to correction of underlying hypoxia, acidosis, or other biochemical abnormalities. Ventricular arrhythmias which are causing serious hypotension require treatment. If the QT interval is prolonged, specialist advice should be sought because the use of some anti-arrhythmic drugs may be inappropriate. Supraventricular arrhythmias are seldom life-threatening and drug treatment is best withheld until the patient reaches hospital.

## Body temperature

Hypothermia may develop in patients of any age who have been deeply unconscious for some hours particularly following overdose with barbiturates or phenothiazines. It may be missed unless core temperature is measured using a low-reading rectal thermometer or by some other means. Hypothermia is best treated by wrapping the patient (e.g. in a 'space blanket') to conserve body heat.

Hyperthermia can develop in patients taking CNS stimulants; children and the elderly are also at risk when taking therapeutic doses of drugs with antimuscarinic properties. Hyperthermia is initially managed by removing all unnecessary clothing and using a fan. Sponging with tepid water will promote evaporation; iced water should **not** be used. Advice should be sought from a poisons information centre on the management of severe hyperthermia resulting from conditions such as the serotonin syndrome.

Both hypothermia and hyperthermia require **urgent** hospitalisation for assessment and supportive treatment.

## Convulsions

Single short-lived convulsions do not require treatment. If convulsions are protracted or recur frequently, lorazepam 4 mg or diazepam (preferably as emulsion) up to 10 mg should be given by slow intravenous injection into a large vein; the benzodiazepines should not be given intramuscularly.

## Removal and elimination

## Removal from the gastro-intestinal tract

Gastric lavage is rarely required and for substances that cannot be removed effectively by other means (e.g. iron), it should be considered only if a life-threatening amount has been ingested within the previous hour. It should be carried out only if the airway can be protected adequately. Gastric lavage is contra-indicated if a corrosive substance or a petroleum distillate has been ingested but it may occasionally be considered in patients who have ingested drugs that are not absorbed by charcoal, such as iron or lithium. Induction of *emesis* (e.g. with ipecacuanha) is **not** recommended because there is no evidence that it affects absorption and it may increase the risk of aspiration.

*Whole bowel irrigation* (by means of a bowel cleansing solution) has been used in poisoning with certain modified-release or enteric-coated formulations, in severe poisoning with iron and lithium salts, and if illicit drugs are carried in the gastro-intestinal tract ('body-packing'). However, it is not clear that the procedure improves outcome and advice should be sought from a poisons information centre.

## Prevention of absorption

Given by mouth, **activated charcoal** can bind many poisons in the gastro-intestinal system, thereby *reducing their absorption*. The **sooner** it is given the **more effective** it is, but it may still be effective up to 1 hour after ingestion of the poison—longer in the case of modified-release preparations or of drugs with antimuscarinic (anticholinergic) properties. It is relatively safe and is particularly useful for the prevention of absorption of poisons which are toxic in small amounts, e.g. antidepressants.

For the use of charcoal in active elimination techniques, see below.

### CHARCOAL, ACTIVATED

**Indications** adsorption of poisons in the gastro-intestinal system; see also active elimination techniques, below

**Cautions** drowsy or comatose patient (risk of aspiration); reduced gastro-intestinal motility (risk of obstruction); **not** for poisoning with petroleum distillates, corrosive substances, alcohols, clofenotane (dicophane, DDT), malathion, and metal salts including iron and lithium salts

**Side-effects** black stools

**Dose**

- See under preparations below

**Actidose-Aqua® Advance** (Cambridge)

Oral suspension, activated charcoal, net price 50-g pack (240 mL) = £11.63

Note The brand name *Actidose-Aqua®* was formerly used

Dose reduction of absorption, 50–100 g; INFANT under 1 year 1 g/kg (approx. 5 mL/kg), CHILD 1–12 years 25–50 g

Active elimination (see below for ADULT dose); INFANT under 1 year, 1 g/kg (approx. 5 mL/kg) every 4–6 hours; CHILD 1–12 years, 25–50 g every 4–6 hours

**Carbomix®** (Meadow)

Powder, activated charcoal, net price 25-g pack = £8.50, 50-g pack = £11.90

Dose reduction of absorption, 50 g, repeated if necessary; CHILD under 12 years 25 g (50 g in severe poisoning)

Active elimination, see below

**Charcodote®** (PLIVA)

Oral suspension, activated charcoal, net price 50-g pack = £11.88

Dose reduction of absorption, 50 g; CHILD under 12 years 25 g (50 g in severe poisoning)

Active elimination, see below

## Active elimination techniques

Repeated doses of **activated charcoal** by mouth *enhance the elimination* of some drugs after they have been absorbed; repeated doses are given after overdosage with:

Carbamazepine
Dapsone
Phenobarbital
Quinine
Theophylline

The usual adult dose of activated charcoal is 50 g initially then 50 g every 4 hours. Vomiting should be treated (e.g. with an anti-emetic drug) since it may reduce the efficacy of charcoal treatment. In cases of intolerance, the dose may be reduced and the frequency increased (e.g. 25 g every 2 hours *or* 12.5 g every hour) but this may compromise efficacy.

Other techniques intended to enhance the elimination of poisons after absorption are only practicable in hospital and are only suitable for a small number of severely poisoned patients. Moreover, they only apply to a limited number of poisons. Examples include:

- haemodialysis for salicylates, phenobarbital, methyl alcohol (methanol), ethylene glycol, and lithium;
- alkanisation of the urine for salicylates and phenoxyacetate herbicides (e.g. 2,4-dichloro-phenoxyacetic acid).

Forced alkaline diuresis is no longer recommended.

## Specific drugs

### Alcohol

Acute intoxication with alcohol (ethanol) is common in adults but also occurs in children. The features include ataxia, dysarthria, nystagmus, and drowsiness, which may progress to coma, with hypotension and acidosis. Aspiration of vomit is a special hazard and hypoglycaemia may occur in children and some adults. Patients are managed supportively with particular attention to maintaining a clear airway and measures to reduce the risk of aspiration of gastric contents. The blood glucose is measured and glucose given if indicated.

The **poisons information centres** (Tel: 0870 600 6266) will provide specialist advice on all aspects of poisoning day and night

### Analgesics (non-opioid)

**Aspirin** The chief features of salicylate poisoning are hyperventilation, tinnitus, deafness, vasodilatation, and sweating. Coma is uncommon but indicates very severe poisoning. The associated acid-base disturbances are complex.

Treatment must be in hospital where plasma salicylate, pH, and electrolytes can be measured; absorption of aspirin may be slow and the plasma-salicylate concentration may continue to rise for several hours, requiring repeated measurement of plasma-salicylate concentration. Fluid losses are replaced and sodium bicarbonate (1.26%) given to enhance urinary salicylate excretion when the plasma-salicylate concentration is greater than:

500 mg/litre (3.6 mmol/litre) in adults *or*

350 mg/litre (2.5 mmol/litre) in children.

Haemodialysis is the treatment of choice for severe salicylate poisoning and should be considered when the plasma-salicylate concentration exceeds 700 mg/litre (5.1 mmol/litre) or in the presence of severe metabolic acidosis.

**NSAIDs** Mefenamic acid has important consequences in overdosage because it can cause convulsions, which if prolonged or recurrent, require treatment with intravenous lorazepam or diazepam.

Ibuprofen may cause nausea, vomiting, and tinnitus, but more serious toxicity is very uncommon. Activated charcoal followed by symptomatic measures are indicated if more than 400 mg/kg has been ingested within the preceding hour, followed by symptomatic measures.

**Paracetamol** As little as 10–15 g (20–30 tablets) or 150 mg/kg of paracetamol taken within 24 hours may cause severe hepatocellular necrosis and, much less frequently, renal tubular necrosis. Nausea and vomiting, the only early features of poisoning, usually settle within 24 hours. Persistence beyond this time, often associated with the onset of right subcostal pain and tenderness, usually indicates development of hepatic necrosis. Liver damage is maximal 3–4 days after ingestion and may lead to encephalopathy, haemorrhage, hypoglycaemia, cerebral oedema, and death.

Therefore, despite a lack of significant early symptoms, patients who have taken an overdose of paracetamol should be transferred to hospital urgently.

Administration of activated charcoal should be considered if paracetamol in excess of 150 mg/kg or 12 g **whichever is the smaller**, is thought to have been ingested within the previous hour.

**Acetylcysteine** protects the liver if infused within 24 hours of ingesting paracetamol. It is most effective if given within 8 hours of ingestion after which effectiveness declines sharply and if more than 24 hours have elapsed advice should be sought from a poisons information centre or from a liver unit on the management of serious liver damage. In remote areas **methionine** (2.5 g) by mouth is an alternative if acetylcysteine cannot be given promptly. Once the patient reaches hospital the need to continue treatment with the antidote will be assessed from the plasma-paracetamol concentration (related to the time from ingestion).

Patients at risk of liver damage and therefore requiring treatment can be identified from a single measurement of the plasma-paracetamol concentration, related to the time from ingestion, provided this time interval is not less than 4 hours; earlier samples may be misleading. The concentration is plotted on a paracetamol treatment graph of a reference line ('normal treatment line') joining plots of 200 mg/litre (1.32 mmol/litre) at 4 hours and 6.25 mg/litre (0.04 mmol/litre) at 24 hours (see below). Those whose plasma-paracetamol concentration is above the *normal treatment line* are treated with acetylcysteine by intravenous infusion (or, if acetylcysteine is not available, with methionine by mouth, provided the overdose has been taken **within 10–12 hours** *and* the patient is not vomiting).

Patients on enzyme-inducing drugs (e.g. carbamazepine, phenobarbital, phenytoin, primidone, rifampicin, alcohol, and St John's wort) or who are malnourished (e.g. in anorexia, in alcoholism, or those who are HIV-positive) may develop toxicity at **lower** plasma-paracetamol concentration and should be treated if the concentration is above the *high-risk treatment line* (which joins plots that are at 50% of the plasma-paracetamol concentrations of the normal treatment line).

The prognostic accuracy of plasma-paracetamol concentration taken after 15 hours is uncertain but a concentration above the relevant treatment line should be regarded as carrying a serious risk of liver damage.

Plasma-paracetamol concentration may be difficult to interpret when paracetamol has been ingested over several hours. If there is doubt about timing or the need for treatment then the patient should be treated with an antidote.

See also Co-proxamol, under Analgesics (opioid).

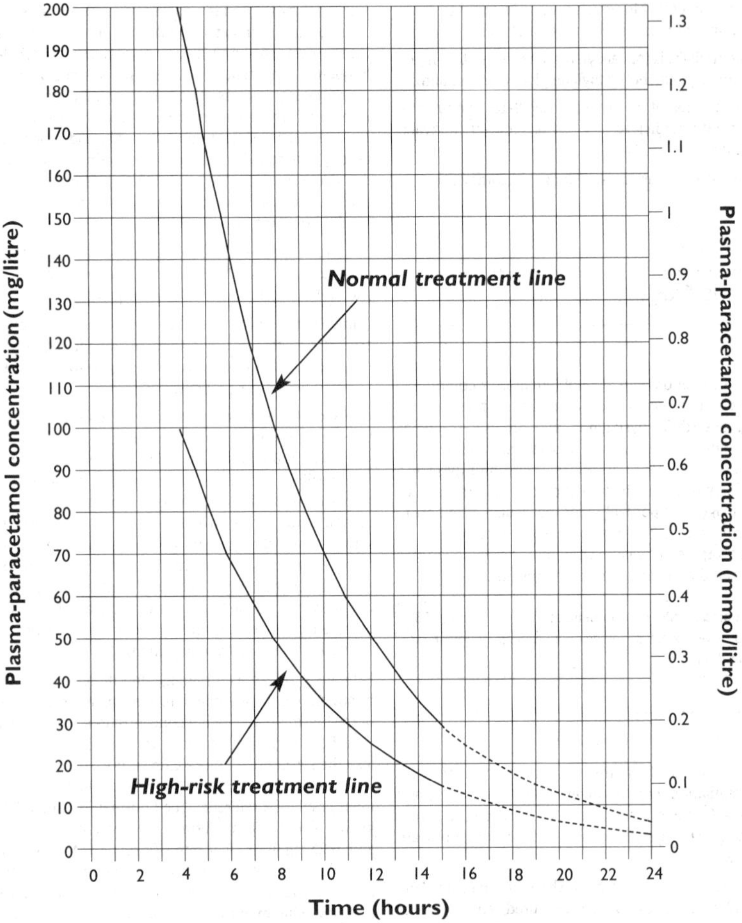


Patients whose plasma-paracetamol concentrations are above the **normal treatment line** should be treated with acetylcysteine by intravenous infusion (or, if acetylcysteine cannot be used, with methionine by mouth, provided the overdose has been taken **within 10–12 hours** and the patient is not vomiting).

Patients on enzyme-inducing drugs (e.g. carbamazepine, phenobarbital, phenytoin, primidone, rifampicin, alcohol, and St John's wort) or who are malnourished (e.g. in anorexia, in alcoholism, or those who are HIV-positive) should be treated if their plasma-paracetamol concentration is above the **high-risk treatment line**.

The prognostic accuracy after 15 hours is uncertain but a plasma-paracetamol concentration above the relevant treatment line should be regarded as carrying a serious risk of liver damage.

Graph reproduced courtesy of University of Wales College of Medicine Therapeutics and Toxicology Centre

## ACETYLCYSTEINE

**Indications** paracetamol overdosage, see notes above

**Cautions** asthma (see side-effects below but do not delay acetylcysteine treatment)

**Side-effects** hypersensitivity-like reactions managed by reducing infusion rate or suspending until reaction settled—contact poisons information centre if reactions severe (rash also managed by giving antihistamine; acute asthma managed by giving nebulised short-acting $beta_2$ agonist)

**Dose**

- By intravenous infusion, ADULT and CHILD, initially 150 mg/kg over 15 minutes, then 50 mg/kg over 4 hours then 100 mg/kg over 16 hours

**Administration** Dilute requisite dose in glucose intravenous infusion 5% as follows: ADULT and CHILD over 12 years, initially 200 mL given over 15 minutes, then 500 mL over 4 hours, then 1 litre over 16 hours; CHILD under 12 years body-weight over 20 kg, initially 100 mL given over 15 minutes, then 250 mL over 4 hours, then 500 mL over 16 hours; CHILD body-weight under 20 kg, initially 3 mL/kg given over 15 minutes, then 7 mL/kg over 4 hours, then 14 mL/kg over 16 hours

**Note** Manufacturer also recommends other infusion fluids, but glucose 5% is preferable

**Acetylcysteine** (Non-proprietary) PoM
Injection, acetylcysteine 200 mg/mL, net price 10-mL amp = £2.50

**Parvolex®** (Celltech) PoM
Injection, acetylcysteine 200 mg/mL, net price 10-mL amp = £2.50

## METHIONINE

**Indications** paracetamol overdosage, see notes above
**Cautions** hepatic impairment (Appendix 2)
**Side-effects** nausea, vomiting, drowsiness, irritability
**Dose**
- ADULT and CHILD over 6 years initially 2.5 g, followed by 3 further doses of 2.5 g every 4 hours, CHILD under 6 years initially 1 g, followed by 3 further doses of 1 g every 4 hours

**Methionine** (Celltech)
Tablets, DL-methionine 250 mg, net price 200-tab pack = £66.05

## Analgesics (opioid)

Opioids (narcotic analgesics) cause coma, respiratory depression, and pinpoint pupils. The specific antidote **naloxone** is indicated if there is coma or bradypnoea. Since naloxone has a shorter duration of action than many opioids, close monitoring and repeated injections are necessary according to the respiratory rate and depth of coma. Where repeated administration of naloxone is required, it may be given by continuous intravenous infusion instead and the rate of infusion adjusted according to vital signs. The effects of some opioids, such as buprenorphine, are only partially reversed by naloxone. Dextropropoxyphene and methadone have very long durations of action; patients may need to be monitored for long periods following large overdoses.

**Co-proxamol** A combination of dextropropoxyphene and paracetamol (co-proxamol) is frequently taken in overdosage and is the most frequent prescription product to cause death. The initial features are those of acute opioid overdosage with coma, respiratory depression, and pinpoint pupils. Patients may die of acute cardiovascular collapse before reaching hospital (particularly if alcohol has also been consumed) unless adequately resuscitated.

**Naloxone** reverses the opioid effects of dextropropoxyphene; the long duration of action of dextropropoxyphene calls for prolonged monitoring and further doses of naloxone may be required. Norpropoxyphene, a metabolite of dextropropoxyphene, also has cardiotoxic effects which may require treatment with **sodium bicarbonate**, or **magnesium sulphate**, or both; arrhythmias may occur for up to 12 hours. Paracetamol hepatotoxicity may develop later and should be anticipated and treated as indicated above.

## NALOXONE HYDROCHLORIDE

**Indications** overdosage with opioids; postoperative respiratory depression (section 15.1.7)
**Cautions** physical dependence on opioids; cardiac irritability; naloxone is short-acting, see notes above
**Dose**
- By intravenous injection, 0.4–2 mg repeated at intervals of 2–3 minutes to a max. of 10 mg if respiratory function does not improve (then question diagnosis); CHILD 10 micrograms/kg; subsequent dose of 100 micrograms/kg if no response
- By subcutaneous *or* intramuscular injection, ADULT and CHILD dose as for intravenous injection but use only if intravenous route not feasible (onset of action slower)
- By continuous intravenous infusion using an infusion pump, 4 mg diluted in 20 mL intravenous infusion solution [unlicensed concentration] at a rate adjusted according to response (initial rate may be set at 60% of initial intravenous injection dose (see above) and infused over 1 hour)

Important Doses used in acute opioid overdosage may not be appropriate for the management of opioid-induced respiratory depression and sedation in those receiving palliative care and in chronic opioid use, see also section 15.1.7 for management of postoperative respiratory depression

[1]**Naloxone** (Non-proprietary) PoM
Injection, naloxone hydrochloride 400 micrograms/mL, net price 1-mL amp = £4.10; 1 mg/mL, 2-mL prefilled syringe = £6.61

[1]**Minijet® Naloxone** (Celltech) PoM
Injection, naloxone hydrochloride 400 micrograms/mL, net price 1-mL disposable syringe = £5.57, 2-mL disposable syringe = £10.71, 5-mL disposable syringe = £10.20

The **poisons information centres** (Tel: 0870 600 6266) will provide specialist advice on all aspects of poisoning day and night

## Antidepressants

**Tricyclic and related antidepressants** Tricyclic and related antidepressants cause dry mouth, coma of varying degree, hypotension, hypothermia, hyperreflexia, extensor plantar responses, convulsions, respiratory failure, cardiac conduction defects, and arrhythmias. Dilated pupils and urinary retention also occur. Metabolic acidosis may complicate severe poisoning; delirium with confusion, agitation, and visual and auditory hallucinations, are common during recovery.

Transfer to hospital is strongly advised in case of poisoning by *tricyclic and related antidepressants* but symptomatic treatment and activated charcoal may be given before transfer. Supportive measures to ensure a clear airway and adequate ventilation during transfer are mandatory. Intravenous lorazepam or intravenous diazepam (preferably in emulsion form) may be required for control of convulsions. Although arrhythmias are worrying, some will respond to correction of hypoxia and acidosis. The use of anti-arrhythmic drugs is best avoided but intravenous infusion of sodium bicarbonate can arrest arrhythmias or prevent them in those with an extended QRS duration. Diazepam given by mouth is usually adequate to sedate delirious patients but large doses may be required.

**Selective serotonin re-uptake inhibitors (SSRIs)** Symptoms of poisoning by selective serotonin re-uptake inhibitors include nausea, vomiting, agitation, tremor, nystagmus, drowsiness, and sinus tachycardia; convulsions may occur. Rarely, severe poisoning could

1. PoM restriction does not apply where administration is for saving life in emergency

result in the serotonin syndrome, with marked neuropsychiatric effects, neuromuscular hyperactivity, and autonomic instability; hyperthermia, rhabdomyolysis, renal failure, and coagulopathies may develop.

Management of SSRI poisoning is supportive. Activated charcoal given within 1 hour of the overdose reduces absorption of the drug. Convulsions may be prevented with lorazepam or diazepam (see p. 28). Contact a poisons information centre for the management of hyperthermia or the serotonin syndrome.

## Antimalarials

Overdosage with chloroquine and hydroxychloroquine is extremely hazardous and difficult to treat. Urgent advice from a poisons information centre is essential. Life-threatening features include arrhythmias (which can have a very rapid onset) and convulsions (which can be intractable). Quinine overdosage is also a severe hazard and calls for urgent advice from a poisons information centre.

## Beta-blockers

Therapeutic overdosages with beta-blockers may cause lightheadedness, dizziness, and possibly syncope as a result of bradycardia and hypotension; heart failure may be precipitated or exacerbated. These complications are most likely in patients with conduction system disorders or impaired myocardial function. Bradycardia is the most common arrhythmia caused by beta-blockers, but sotalol may induce ventricular tachyarrhythmias (sometimes of the torsades de pointes type). The effects of massive overdosage may vary from one beta-blocker to another; propranolol overdosage in particular may cause coma and convulsions.

*Acute massive overdosage* must be managed in hospital and expert advice should be obtained. Maintenance of a clear airway and adequate ventilation is mandatory. An intravenous injection of atropine is required to treat bradycardia and hypotension (3 mg for an adult, 40 micrograms/kg for a child). Cardiogenic shock unresponsive to atropine is probably best treated with an intravenous injection of glucagon 2–10 mg (CHILD 50–150 micrograms/kg) [unlicensed indication and dose] in glucose 5% (with precautions to protect the airway in case of vomiting) followed by an intravenous infusion of 50 micrograms/kg/hour. If glucagon is not available, intravenous isoprenaline [special order only] is an alternative. A cardiac pacemaker may be used to increase the heart rate.

## Calcium-channel blockers

Features of calcium-channel blocker poisoning include nausea, vomiting, dizziness, agitation, confusion, and coma in severe poisoning. Metabolic acidosis and hyperglycaemia may occur. Verapamil and diltiazem have a profound cardiac depressant effect causing hypotension and arrhythmias including complete heart block and asystole. The dihydropyridine calcium-channel blockers cause severe hypotension secondary to profound peripheral vasodilatation.

Activated charcoal is given if the patient presents within 1 hour of overdosage with a calcium-channel blocker; repeated doses of activated charcoal are considered if a modified-release preparation is involved. In patients with significant features of poisoning, calcium chloride or calcium gluconate (section 9.5.1.1) is given by injection; atropine is given to correct symptomatic bradycardia. For the management of hypotension, the choice of inotropic sympathomimetic depends on whether hypotension is secondary to vasodilation or to myocardial depression and advice should be sought from a poisons information centre.

## Hypnotics and anxiolytics

**Benzodiazepines** Benzodiazepines taken alone cause drowsiness, ataxia, dysarthria, and occasionally minor and short-lived depression of consciousness. They potentiate the effects of other central nervous system depressants taken concomitantly. Use of the benzodiazepine antagonist flumazenil can be hazardous, particularly in mixed overdoses involving tricyclic antidepressants or in benzodiazepine-dependent patients. Flumazenil should be used on **expert advice** only.

## Iron salts

Iron poisoning is commonest in childhood and is usually accidental. The symptoms are nausea, vomiting, abdominal pain, diarrhoea, haematemesis, and rectal bleeding. Hypotension, coma, and hepatocellular necrosis occur later. Mortality is reduced with intensive and specific therapy with **desferrioxamine**, which chelates iron. The stomach should be emptied by gastric lavage (with a wide-bore tube) within 1 hour of ingesting a significant quantity of iron or if radiography reveals tablets in the stomach; whole bowel irrigation may be considered in severe poisoning but advice should be sought from a poisons information centre. The serum-iron concentration is measured as an emergency and intravenous desferrioxamine given to chelate absorbed iron in excess of the expected iron binding capacity. In **severe toxicity** intravenous desferrioxamine should be given *immediately* without waiting for the result of the serum-iron measurement (contact a poisons information centre for advice).

### DESFERRIOXAMINE MESILATE
**(Deferoxamine Mesilate)**

**Indications** iron poisoning; chronic iron overload (section 9.1.3)
**Cautions** section 9.1.3
**Side-effects** section 9.1.3
**Dose**
- By continuous intravenous infusion, ADULT and CHILD up to 15 mg/kg/hour; max. 80 mg/kg in 24 hours (in severe cases, higher doses on advice from a poisons information centre)

**Preparations**
Section 9.1.3

## Lithium

Most cases of lithium intoxication occur as a complication of long-term therapy and are caused by reduced excretion of the drug due to a variety of factors including dehydration, deterioration of renal function, infections, and co-administration of diuretics or NSAIDs (or other drugs that interact). Acute deliberate overdoses may also occur with delayed onset of symptoms (12 hours or more) due to slow entry of lithium into the tissues and continuing absorption from modified-release formulations.

The early clinical features are non-specific and may include apathy and restlessness which could be confused with mental changes due to the patient's depressive illness. Vomiting, diarrhoea, ataxia, weakness, dysarthria, muscle twitching, and tremor may follow. Severe poisoning is associated with convulsions, coma, renal failure, electrolyte imbalance, dehydration, and hypotension.

Therapeutic lithium concentrations are within the range of 0.4–1.0 mmol/litre; concentrations in excess of 2.0 mmol/litre are usually associated with serious toxicity and such cases may need treatment with haemodialysis (if there is renal failure). In acute overdosage much higher serum concentrations may be present without features of toxicity and all that is usually necessary is to take measures to increase urine production (e.g. by ensuring adequate fluid intake; but avoid diuretics). Otherwise treatment is supportive with special regard to electrolyte balance, renal function, and control of convulsions. Whole bowel irrigation should be considered for significant ingestion, but advice should be sought from a poisons information centre, p. 27.

## Phenothiazines and related drugs

Phenothiazines cause less depression of consciousness and respiration than other sedatives. Hypotension, hypothermia, sinus tachycardia, and arrhythmias may complicate poisoning. Dystonic reactions can occur with therapeutic doses, (particularly with prochlorperazine and trifluoperazine) and convulsions may occur in severe cases. Arrhythmias may respond to correction of hypoxia, acidosis and other biochemical abnormalities but specialist advice should be sought if arrhythmias result from a prolonged QT interval; the use of some anti-arrhythmic drugs may worsen such arrhythmias. Dystonic reactions are rapidly abolished by injection of drugs such as benzatropine or diazepam (section 4.8.2, emulsion preferred).

## Stimulants

**Amphetamines** These cause wakefulness, excessive activity, paranoia, hallucinations, and hypertension followed by exhaustion, convulsions, hyperthermia, and coma. The early stages can be controlled by diazepam or lorazepam; advice should be sought from a poisons information centre (p. 27) on the management of hypertension. Later, tepid sponging, anticonvulsants, and artificial respiration may be needed.

**Cocaine** Cocaine stimulates the central nervous system, causing agitation, dilated pupils, tachycardia, hypertension, hallucinations, hyperthermia, hypertonia, and hyperreflexia; cardiac effects include chest pain, myocardial infarction, and arrhythmias.

Initial treatment of cocaine poisoning involves intravenous administration of diazepam to control agitation and cooling measures for hyperthermia (see Body temperature, p. 27); hypertension and cardiac effects require specific treatment and expert advice should be sought.

**Ecstasy** Ecstasy (methylenedioxymethamfetamine, MDMA) may cause severe reactions, even at doses that were previously tolerated. The most serious effects are delirium, coma, convulsions, ventricular arrhythmias, hyperpyrexia, rhabdomyolysis, acute renal failure, acute hepatitis, disseminated intravascular coagulation, adult respiratory distress syndrome, hyperreflexia, hypotension and intracerebral haemorrhage; hyponatraemia has also been associated with ecstasy use.

Treatment of methylenedioxymethamfetamine poisoning is supportive, with diazepam to control severe agitation or persistent convulsions and close monitoring including ECG. Self-induced water intoxication should be considered in patients with ecstasy poisoning.

'Liquid ecstacy' is a term used for sodium oxybate (gamma-hydroxybutyrate, GHB), which is a sedative.

## Theophylline

Theophylline and related drugs are often prescribed as modified-release formulations and toxicity may therefore be delayed. They cause vomiting (which may be severe and intractable), agitation, restlessness, dilated pupils, sinus tachycardia, and hyperglycaemia. More serious effects are haematemesis, convulsions, and supraventricular and ventricular arrhythmias. Profound hypokalaemia may develop rapidly.

Repeated doses of activated charcoal can be used to eliminate theophylline even if more than 1 hour has lapsed after ingestion and especially if a modified-release preparation has been taken (see also under Active Elimination Techniques, p. 28). Hypokalaemia is corrected by intravenous infusion of potassium chloride and may be so severe as to require 60 mmol/hour (high doses require ECG monitoring). Convulsions should be controlled by intravenous administration of lorazepam or diazepam (emulsion preferred). Sedation with diazepam may be necessary in agitated patients.

Provided the patient does **not** suffer from asthma, a short-acting beta-blocker (section 2.4) may be administered intravenously to reverse severe tachycardia, hypokalaemia, and hyperglycaemia.

## Other poisons

Consult either a poisons information centre day and night or TOXBASE, see p. 27.

> The **poisons information centres** (Tel: 0870 600 6266) will provide specialist advice on all aspects of poisoning day and night

## Cyanides

Cyanide antidotes include dicobalt edetate, given alone, and sodium nitrite followed by sodium thiosulphate. These antidotes are held for emergency use in hospitals as well as in centres where cyanide poisoning is a risk such as factories and laboratories. The use of sodium nitrite with sodium thiosulphate is preferred over the use of dicobalt edetate because dicobalt edetate itself is toxic and is associated with anaphylactic reactions. Hydroxocobalamin is an alternative antidote but its use should ideally be discussed with a poisons information centre; the usual dose is hydroxocobalamin 70 mg/kg by intravenous infusion (repeated once or twice according to severity). *Cyanokit®*, which provides hydroxocobalamin 2.5 g/bottle, is available but it is not licensed for use in the UK.

## DICOBALT EDETATE

**Indications** acute poisoning with cyanides

**Cautions** owing to toxicity to be used only for definite cyanide poisoning when patient tending to lose, or has lost, consciousness; **not** to be used as a precautionary measure

**Side-effects** hypotension, tachycardia, and vomiting; anaphylactic reactions including facial and laryngeal oedema and cardiac abnormalities

**Dose**

- By intravenous injection, ADULT 300 mg over 1 minute (5 minutes if condition less serious) followed immediately by 50 mL of glucose intravenous infusion 50%; if response inadequate a second dose of both may be given; CHILD consult a poisons information centre

[1]**Dicobalt Edetate** (Cambridge) PoM
Injection, dicobalt edetate 15 mg/mL, net price 20-mL (300-mg) amp = £10.58

## SODIUM NITRITE

**Indications** poisoning with cyanides (used in conjunction with sodium thiosulphate)

**Side-effects** flushing and headache due to vasodilatation

**Dose**

- By intravenous injection over 5–20 minutes (as sodium nitrite injection 30 mg/mL), 300 mg (CHILD 4–10 mg/kg) followed by sodium thiosulphate (as sodium thiosulphate injection 500 mg/mL) by intravenous injection over 10 minutes 12.5 g (CHILD 400 mg/kg)

[1]**Sodium Nitrite** PoM
Injection, sodium nitrite 3% (30 mg/mL) in water for injections
'Special-order' [unlicensed] product: contact Martindale, or regional hospital manufacturing unit

## SODIUM THIOSULPHATE

**Indications** poisoning with cyanides (used in conjunction with sodium nitrite)

**Dose**

- See above under Sodium Nitrite

[1]**Sodium Thiosulphate** PoM
Injection, sodium thiosulphate 50% (500 mg/mL) in water for injections
'Special-order' [unlicensed] product: contact Martindale, or regional hospital manufacturing unit

## Ethylene glycol and methanol

Ethanol (by mouth or by intravenous infusion) is used for the treatment of ethylene glycol or methanol (methyl alcohol) poisoning. Fomepizole (*Antizol®*, available on named-patient basis from IDIS) has also been used for the treatment of ethylene glycol or methanol poisoning. Advice on the treatment of ethylene glycol or methanol poisoning should be obtained from a poisons information centre.

## Heavy metals

Heavy metal antidotes include dimercaprol, penicillamine, and sodium calcium edetate. Other antidotes for heavy metal poisoning include succimer (DMSA) and unithiol (DMPS) [both unlicensed]; their use may be valuable in certain cases and the advice of a poisons information centre should be sought.

## DIMERCAPROL
**(BAL)**

**Indications** poisoning by antimony, arsenic, bismuth, gold, mercury, possibly thallium; adjunct (with sodium calcium edetate) in lead poisoning

**Cautions** hypertension, renal impairment (discontinue or use with extreme caution if impairment develops during treatment), elderly, pregnancy and breast-feeding; **interactions:** Appendix 1 (dimercaprol)

**Contra-indications** not indicated for iron, cadmium, or selenium poisoning; severe hepatic impairment (unless due to arsenic poisoning)

**Side-effects** hypertension, tachycardia, malaise, nausea, vomiting, salivation, lacrimation, sweating, burning sensation (mouth, throat, and eyes), feeling of constriction of throat and chest, headache, muscle spasm, abdominal pain, tingling of extremities; pyrexia in children; local pain and abscess at injection site

**Dose**

- By intramuscular injection, ADULT and CHILD 2.5–3 mg/kg every 4 hours for 2 days, 2–4 times on the third day, then 1–2 times daily for 10 days or until recovery

**Dimercaprol** (Sovereign) PoM
Injection, dimercaprol 50 mg/mL. Net price 2-mL amp = £42.73
Note Contains arachis (peanut) oil as solvent

## PENICILLAMINE

**Indications** lead poisoning

**Cautions** see section 10.1.3

**Contra-indications** see section 10.1.3

**Side-effects** see section 10.1.3

**Dose**

- 1–2 g daily in divided doses before food until urinary lead is stabilised at less than 500 micrograms/day; CHILD 20 mg/kg daily

**Preparations**
Section 10.1.3

## SODIUM CALCIUM EDETATE
**(Sodium Calciumedetate)**

**Indications** poisoning by heavy metals, especially lead

**Cautions** renal impairment

**Side-effects** nausea, diarrhoea, abdominal pain, pain at site of injection, thrombophlebitis if given too rapidly, renal damage particularly in overdosage; hypotension, lacrimation, myalgia, nasal congestion,

1. PoM restriction does not apply where administration is for saving life in emergency

sneezing, malaise, thirst, fever, chills, headache also reported

**Dose**

- By intravenous infusion, ADULT and CHILD up to 40 mg/kg twice daily for up to 5 days, repeated if necessary after 48 hours

**Ledclair®** (Durbin) PoM
Injection, sodium calcium edetate 200 mg/mL, net price 5-mL amp = £7.29

## Noxious gases

**Carbon monoxide** Carbon monoxide poisoning is usually due to inhalation of smoke, car exhaust, or fumes caused by blocked flues or incomplete combustion of fuel gases in confined spaces. Its toxic effects are entirely due to hypoxia.

Immediate treatment of carbon monoxide poisoning is essential. The person should be moved to fresh air, the airway cleared, and **oxygen** 100% administered through a tight-fitting mask with an inflated face seal. Artificial respiration should be given as necessary and continued until adequate spontaneous breathing starts, or stopped only after persistent and efficient treatment of cardiac arrest has failed. The patient should be admitted to hospital because complications may arise after a delay of hours or days. Cerebral oedema should be anticipated in severe poisoning and is treated with an intravenous infusion of mannitol (section 2.2.5). Referral for hyperbaric oxygen treatment should be discussed with the poisons information services if the victim is or has been unconscious, or has psychiatric or neurological features other than a headache, or has myocardial ischaemia or an arrhythmia, or has a blood carboxyhaemoglobin concentration of more than 20%, or is pregnant.

**Sulphur dioxide, chlorine, phosgene, ammonia** All of these gases can cause upper respiratory tract and conjunctival irritation. Pulmonary oedema, with severe breathlessness and cyanosis may develop suddenly up to 36 hours after exposure. Death may occur. Patients are kept under observation and those who develop pulmonary oedema are given oxygen. Assisted ventilation may be necessary in the most serious cases.

## CS Spray

CS spray, which is used for riot control, irritates the eyes (hence 'tear gas') and the respiratory tract; symptoms normally settle spontaneously within 15 minutes. If symptoms persist, the patient should be removed to a well-ventilated area, and the exposed skin washed with soap and water after removal of contaminated clothing. Contact lenses should be removed and rigid ones washed (soft ones should be discarded). Eye symptoms should be treated by irrigating the eyes with physiological saline (or water if saline not available) and advice sought from an ophthalmologist. Patients with features of severe poisoning, particularly respiratory complications, should be admitted to hospital for symptomatic treatment.

## Nerve agents

Treatment of nerve agent poisoning is similar to organophosphorus insecticide poisoning (see below), but advice must be sought from a poisons information centre. The risk of cross-contamination is significant; adequate decontamination and protective clothing for healthcare personnel are essential. In emergencies involving the release of nerve agents, kits ('NAAS pods') which contain **pralidoxime** may be obtained through the Ambulance Service from the National Blood Service (or the Welsh Blood Service in South Wales or designated hospital pharmacies in Northern Ireland and Scotland—see TOXBASE for list of designated centres). In the very rare circumstances where the nerve agent is tabun (GA), **obidoxime** will also be supplied as part of the pod.

> The **poisons information centres** (Tel: 0870 600 6266) will provide specialist advice on all aspects of poisoning day and night

## Pesticides

**Paraquat** Concentrated liquid paraquat preparations (e.g. *Gramoxone®*), available to farmers and horticulturists, contain 10–20% paraquat and are extremely toxic. Granular preparations, for garden use, contain only 2.5% paraquat and have caused few deaths.

Paraquat has local and systemic effects. Splashes in the eyes irritate and ulcerate the cornea and conjunctiva. Copious washing of the eye should aid healing but it may be a long process. Skin irritation, blistering, and ulceration can occur from prolonged contact both with the concentrated and dilute forms. Inhalation of spray, mist, or dust containing paraquat may cause nose bleeding and sore throat but not systemic toxicity.

Ingestion of concentrated paraquat solutions is followed by nausea, vomiting, and diarrhoea. Painful ulceration of the tongue, lips, and fauces may appear after 36 to 48 hours together with renal failure. Some days later there may be dyspnoea with pulmonary fibrosis due to proliferative alveolitis and bronchiolitis.

Treatment should be started immediately. The single most useful measure is oral administration of **activated charcoal**. Vomiting may preclude the use of activated charcoal and an anti-emetic may be required. Gastric lavage is of doubtful value. Intravenous fluids and analgesics are given as necessary. Oxygen therapy should be avoided in the early stages of management since this may exacerbate damage to the lungs, but oxygen may be required in the late stages to palliate symptoms. Measures to enhance elimination of absorbed paraquat are probably valueless but should be discussed with the poisons information centres who will also give guidance on predicting the likely outcome from plasma concentrations. Paraquat absorption can be confirmed by a simple qualitative urine test.

**Organophosphorus insecticides** Organophosphorus insecticides are usually supplied as powders or dissolved in organic solvents. All are absorbed through the bronchi and intact skin as well as through the gut and inhibit cholinesterase activity thereby prolonging and intensifying the effects of acetylcholine. Toxicity between different compounds varies considerably, and onset may be delayed after skin exposure.

Anxiety, restlessness, dizziness, headache, miosis, nausea, hypersalivation, vomiting, abdominal colic, diarrhoea, bradycardia, and sweating are common features of organophosphorus poisoning. Muscle weakness and fasciculation may develop and progress to generalised flaccid paralysis including the ocular and respiratory muscles. Convulsions, coma, pulmonary oedema with copious bronchial secretions, hypoxia, and arrhythmias occur in severe cases. Hyperglycaemia and glycosuria without ketonuria may also be present.

Further absorption of the organophosphorus insecticide should be prevented by moving the patient to fresh air, removing soiled clothing, and washing contaminated skin. In severe poisoning it is vital to ensure a clear airway, frequent removal of bronchial secretions, and adequate ventilation and oxygenation; gastric lavage may be considered provided that the airway is protected. **Atropine** will reverse the muscarinic effects of acetylcholine and is given in a dose of 2 mg (20 micrograms/kg in a child) as atropine sulphate (intramuscularly or intravenously according to the severity of poisoning) every 5 to 10 minutes until the skin becomes flushed and dry, the pupils dilate, and tachycardia develops.

**Pralidoxime mesilate** (P2S), a cholinesterase reactivator, is used as an adjunct to atropine in moderate or severe poisoning. It improves muscle tone within 30 minutes of administration. Repeated doses are required; an intravenous infusion is required in severe cases. Pralidoxime mesilate may be obtained from designated centres, the names of which are held by the poisons information centres (see p. 27).

## PRALIDOXIME MESILATE
(P2S)

**Indications** adjunct to atropine in the treatment of poisoning by organophosphorus insecticide or nerve agent

**Cautions** renal impairment, myasthenia gravis

**Contra-indications** poisoning due to carbamates and to organophosphorus compounds without anti-cholinesterase activity

**Side-effects** drowsiness, dizziness, disturbances of vision, nausea, tachycardia, headache, hyperventilation, and muscular weakness

**Dose**

- By slow intravenous injection (diluted to 10–15 mL with water for injections) over 5–10 minutes, initially 30 mg/kg repeated every 4–6 hours *or* by intravenous infusion, 8 mg/kg/hour; usual max. 12 g in 24 hours

Note Pralidoxime mesilate doses in BNF may differ from those in product literature

[1] **Pralidoxime Mesilate** (PoM)
Injection, pralidoxime mesilate 200 mg/mL
Available as 5-mL amps (from designated centres for organophosphorus insecticide poisoning or from the National Blood Service and the Welsh Blood Service for nerve agent poisoning—see TOXBASE for list of designated centres)

1. (PoM) restriction does not apply where administration is for saving life in emergency

## Snake bites and animal stings

**Snake bites** Envenoming from snake bite is uncommon in the UK. Many exotic snakes are kept, some illegally, but the only indigenous venomous snake is the adder (*Vipera berus*). The bite may cause local and systemic effects. Local effects include pain, swelling, bruising, and tender enlargement of regional lymph nodes. Systemic effects include early anaphylactoid symptoms (transient hypotension with syncope, angio-edema, urticaria, abdominal colic, diarrhoea, and vomiting), with later persistent or recurrent hypotension, ECG abnormalities, spontaneous systemic bleeding, coagulopathy, adult respiratory distress syndrome, and acute renal failure. Fatal envenoming is rare but the potential for severe envenoming must not be underestimated.

Early anaphylactoid symptoms should be treated with **adrenaline (epinephrine)** (section 3.4.3). Indications for antivenom treatment include systemic envenoming, especially hypotension (see above), ECG abnormalities, vomiting, haemostatic abnormalities, and marked local envenoming such that after bites on the hand or foot, swelling extends beyond the wrist or ankle within 4 hours of the bite. For both **adults** and **children**, the contents of one vial (10 mL) of **European viper venom antiserum** (available from Farillon) is given *by intravenous injection* over 10–15 minutes or *by intravenous infusion* over 30 minutes after diluting in sodium chloride intravenous infusion 0.9% (use 5 mL diluent/kg body-weight). The **same dose** should be used for **adults** and **children**. The dose can be repeated in 1–2 hours if symptoms of **systemic envenoming** persist. Adrenaline (epinephrine) injection must be immediately to hand for treatment of anaphylactic reactions to the antivenom (for the management of anaphylaxis see section 3.4.3).

Antivenom is available for certain foreign snakes, spiders and scorpions. For information on identification, management, and supply, telephone:

| | |
|---|---|
| Oxford | (01865) 220 968 |
| | *or* (01865) 221 332 |
| | *or* (01865) 741 166 |
| Liverpool | (0151) 708 9393 |
| Liverpool (Royal Liverpool University Hospital) (emergency supply only) | (0151) 706 2000 |
| London (emergency supply only) | (020) 7771 5394 |

**Insect stings** Stings from ants, wasps, hornets, and bees cause local pain and swelling but seldom cause severe direct toxicity unless many stings are inflicted at the same time. If the sting is in the mouth or on the tongue local swelling may threaten the upper airway. The stings from these insects are usually treated by cleaning the area. Bee stings should be removed as quickly as possible. Anaphylactic reactions require immediate treatment with intramuscular **adrenaline (epinephrine)**; self-administered intramuscular adrenaline (e.g. *EpiPen®*) is the best first-aid treatment for patients with severe hypersensitivity. An inhaled bronchodilator should be used for asthmatic reactions. For the management of anaphylaxis, see section 3.4.3. A short course of an **oral antihistamine** or a **topical corticosteroid** may help to reduce inflammation and relieve itching.

**Marine stings** The severe pain of weeverfish (*Trachinus vipera*) stings can be relieved by immersing the stung area in uncomfortably hot, but not scalding, water (not more than 45° C). People stung by jellyfish and Portuguese man-o'-war around the UK coast should be removed from the sea as soon as possible. Adherent tentacles should be lifted off carefully (wearing gloves or using tweezers) or washed off with seawater. Alcoholic solutions including suntan lotions should **not** be applied because they may cause further discharge of stinging hairs. Ice packs will reduce pain and a slurry of baking soda (sodium bicarbonate), but not vinegar, may be useful for treating stings from UK species.

# 1 Gastro-intestinal system


**1.1 Dyspepsia and gastro-oesophageal reflux disease** 37
1.1.1 Antacids and simeticone 38
1.1.2 Compound alginates and proprietary indigestion preparations 40
**1.2 Antispasmodics and other drugs altering gut motility** 41
**1.3 Ulcer-healing drugs** 43
1.3.1 H2-receptor antagonists 44
1.3.2 Selective antimuscarinics 47
1.3.3 Chelates and complexes 47
1.3.4 Prostaglandin analogues 48
1.3.5 Proton pump inhibitors 48
**1.4 Acute diarrhoea** 51
1.4.1 Adsorbents and bulk-forming drugs 51
1.4.2 Antimotility drugs 51
**1.5 Chronic bowel disorders** 53
**1.6 Laxatives** 57
1.6.1 Bulk-forming laxatives 58
1.6.2 Stimulant laxatives 59
1.6.3 Faecal softeners 61
1.6.4 Osmotic laxatives 61
1.6.5 Bowel cleansing solutions 63
**1.7 Local preparations for anal and rectal disorders** 64
1.7.1 Soothing haemorrhoidal preparations 64
1.7.2 Compound haemorrhoidal preparations with corticosteroids 64
1.7.3 Rectal sclerosants 65
1.7.4 Management of anal fissures 65
**1.8 Stoma care** 66
**1.9 Drugs affecting intestinal secretions** 66
1.9.1 Drugs affecting biliary composition and flow 66
1.9.2 Bile acid sequestrants 67
1.9.3 Aprotinin 67
1.9.4 Pancreatin 67


This chapter includes advice on the drug management of the following:


antibiotic-associated colitis, p. 54
constipation, p. 57
Crohn's disease, p. 53
diverticular disease, p. 54
food allergy, p. 57
*Helicobacter pylori* infection, p. 43
irritable bowel syndrome, p. 53
NSAID-associated ulcers, p. 44
ulcerative colitis, p. 53


## 1.1 Dyspepsia and gastro-oesophageal reflux disease

**1.1.1 Antacids and simeticone**

**1.1.2 Compound alginates and proprietary indigestion preparations**



### Dyspepsia

Dyspepsia covers pain, fullness, early satiety, bloating, and nausea. It can occur with gastric and duodenal ulceration (section 1.3) and gastric cancer but most commonly it is of uncertain origin.

*Helicobacter pylori* may be present in patients with dyspepsia. *H. pylori* eradication therapy (section 1.3) should be considered for dyspepsia if it is ulcer-like. However, most individuals with functional (investigated, non-ulcer) dyspepsia do not benefit symptomatically from *H. pylori* eradication. Urgent investigation is required if the dyspepsia is accompanied by 'alarm features' (e.g. bleeding, dysphagia, recurrent vomiting, and weight loss).

### Gastro-oesophageal reflux disease

Gastro-oesophageal reflux disease (including non-erosive gastro-oesophageal reflux and erosive oesophagitis) is associated with heartburn, acid regurgitation, and sometimes, difficulty in swallowing (dysphagia); oesophageal inflammation (oesophagitis), ulceration, and stricture formation may occur and there is an association with asthma.

The management of gastro-oesophageal reflux disease includes drug treatment, lifestyle changes and, in some cases, surgery. Initial treatment is guided by the severity of symptoms and treatment is then adjusted according to response. The extent of healing depends on the severity of the disease, the treatment chosen, and the duration of therapy.

For *mild symptoms* of gastro-oesophageal reflux disease, initial management may include the use of **antacids** and **alginates**. Alginate-containing antacids form a 'raft' that floats on the surface of the stomach contents to reduce reflux and protect the oesophageal mucosa. **Histamine $H_2$-receptor antagonists** (section 1.3.1) suppress acid secretion. They may relieve symptoms and permit reduction in antacid consumption. For refractory cases, a course of a **proton pump inhibitor** (section 1.3.5) may be considered (as described for severe symptoms, below).

For *severe symptoms* of gastro-oesophageal reflux disease or for patients with a proven or severe pathology (e.g. *oesophagitis, oesophageal ulceration, oesophagopharyngeal reflux, Barrett's oesophagus*), initial management involves the use of a **proton pump inhibitor** (section 1.3.5); patients need to be reassessed if symptoms persist despite treatment for 4–6 weeks with a proton pump inhibitor. When symptoms abate, treatment is titrated down to a level which maintains remission (e.g. by reducing the dose of the proton pump inhibitor or by giving it intermittently, or by substituting treatment with a histamine $H_2$-receptor antagonist). However, for endoscopically confirmed *erosive, ulcerative*, or *stricturing* disease, treatment with a proton pump inhibitor usually needs to be maintained at the minimum effective dose.

A prokinetic drug such as **metoclopramide** (section 4.6) may improve gastro-oesophageal sphincter function and accelerate gastric emptying.

Patients with gastro-oesophageal reflux disease need to be advised about lifestyle changes (avoidance of excess alcohol and of aggravating foods such as fats); other measures include weight reduction, smoking cessation, and raising the head of the bed.

**Children** Gastro-oesophageal reflux disease is common in infancy but most symptoms resolve between 12 and 18 months of age. Mild or moderate reflux without complications can be managed initially by changes in posture and thickening of liquid feeds (see Appendix 7 for suitable products) followed if necessary by treatment with an alginate-containing product (low sodium and low aluminium content for infants). For older children, life-style changes similar to those for adults (see above) may be helpful followed if necessary by treatment with an alginate-containing product.

Children who do not respond to these measures or who have problems such as respiratory disorders or suspected oesophagitis need to be referred to hospital; an $H_2$-receptor antagonist (section 1.3.1) may be needed to reduce acid secretion. If the oesophagitis is resistant to $H_2$-receptor blockade, the proton pump inhibitor omeprazole (section 1.3.5) can be tried.

## 1.1.1 Antacids and simeticone

Antacids (usually containing aluminium or magnesium compounds) can often relieve symptoms in *ulcer dyspepsia* and in *non-erosive gastro-oesophageal reflux* (see also section 1.1); they are also sometimes used in functional (non-ulcer) dyspepsia but the evidence of benefit is uncertain. Antacids are best given when symptoms occur or are expected, usually between meals and at bedtime, 4 or more times daily; additional doses may be required up to once an hour. Conventional doses e.g. 10 mL 3 or 4 times daily of liquid magnesium–aluminium antacids promote ulcer healing, but less well than antisecretory drugs (section 1.3); proof of a relationship between healing and neutralising capacity is lacking. Liquid preparations are more effective than solids.

**Aluminium-** and **magnesium-containing** antacids (e.g. aluminium hydroxide, and magnesium carbonate, hydroxide and trisilicate), being relatively insoluble in water, are long-acting if retained in the stomach. They are suitable for most antacid purposes. Magnesium-containing antacids tend to be laxative whereas aluminium-containing antacids may be constipating; antacids containing both magnesium and aluminium may reduce these colonic side-effects. Aluminium accumulation does not appear to be a risk if renal function is normal (see also Appendix 3).

The acid-neutralising capacity of preparations that contain more than one antacid may be the same as simpler preparations. Complexes such as **hydrotalcite** confer no special advantage.

**Sodium bicarbonate** should no longer be prescribed alone for the relief of dyspepsia but it is present as an ingredient in many indigestion remedies. However, it retains a place in the management of urinary-tract disorders (section 7.4.3) and acidosis (section 9.2.1.3 and section 9.2.2). Sodium bicarbonate should be avoided in patients on salt-restricted diets.

**Bismuth-containing** antacids (unless chelates) are not recommended because absorbed bismuth can be neurotoxic, causing encephalopathy; they tend to be constipating. **Calcium-containing** antacids (section 1.1.2) can induce rebound acid secretion: with modest doses the clinical significance is doubtful, but prolonged high doses also cause hypercalcaemia and alkalosis, and can precipitate the milk-alkali syndrome.

**Simeticone** (activated dimeticone) is added to an antacid as an antifoaming agent to relieve flatulence. These preparations may be useful for the relief of hiccup in palliative care. **Alginates**, added as protectants, may be useful in gastro-oesophageal reflux disease (section 1.1). The amount of additional ingredient or antacid in individual preparations varies widely, as does their sodium content, so that preparations may not be freely interchangeable.

For **preparations** on sale to the public (not prescribable on the NHS), see p. 40.

See also section 1.3 for drugs used in the treatment of peptic ulceration.

**Interactions** Antacids should preferably not be taken at the same time as other drugs since they may impair absorption. Antacids may also damage enteric coatings designed to prevent dissolution in the stomach. See also **Appendix 1** (antacids, calcium salts).

> **Low $Na^+$**
> The words low $Na^+$ added after some preparations indicate a sodium content of less than 1 mmol per tablet or 10-mL dose.

## Aluminium- and magnesium-containing antacids

### ALUMINIUM HYDROXIDE

**Indications** dyspepsia; hyperphosphataemia (section 9.5.2.2)

**Cautions** see notes above; renal impairment (Appendix 3); **interactions:** Appendix 1 (antacids)

**Contra-indications** hypophosphataemia; porphyria (section 9.8.2)

**Side-effects** see notes above

**Aluminium-only preparations**

**Aluminium Hydroxide** (Non-proprietary)
Tablets, dried aluminium hydroxide 500 mg. Net price 20 = 28p
Dose 1–2 tablets chewed 4 times daily and at bedtime or as required
Oral suspension, about 4% w/w $Al_2O_3$ in water, with a peppermint flavour. Net price 200 mL = 41p
Dose antacid, 5–10 mL 4 times daily between meals and at bedtime or as required; CHILD 6–12 years, up to 5 mL 3 times daily

**Alu-Cap®** (3M)
Capsules, green/red, dried aluminium hydroxide 475 mg (low $Na^+$). Net price 120-cap pack = £3.75
Dose antacid, 1 capsule 4 times daily and at bedtime; CHILD not recommended for antacid therapy

**Co-magaldrox**

Co-magaldrox is a mixture of aluminium hydroxide and magnesium hydroxide; the proportions are expressed in the form *x*/*y* where *x* and *y* are the strengths in milligrams per unit dose of magnesium hydroxide and aluminium hydroxide respectively

**Maalox®** (Sanofi-Aventis)
Suspension, sugar-free, co-magaldrox 195/220 (magnesium hydroxide 195 mg, dried aluminium hydroxide 220 mg/5 mL (low $Na^+$)). Net price 500 mL = £2.59
Dose 10–20 mL 20–60 minutes after meals and at bedtime or when required; CHILD under 14 years not recommended

**Mucogel®** (Forest)
Suspension, sugar-free, co-magaldrox 195/220 (magnesium hydroxide 195 mg, dried aluminium hydroxide 220 mg/5 mL (low $Na^+$)). Net price 500 mL = £1.71
Dose 10–20 mL 3 times daily, 20–60 minutes after meals, and at bedtime or when required; CHILD under 12 years not recommended

### MAGNESIUM CARBONATE

**Indications** dyspepsia

**Cautions** renal impairment (Appendix 3); see also notes above; **interactions:** Appendix 1 (antacids)

**Contra-indications** hypophosphataemia

**Side-effects** diarrhoea; belching due to liberated carbon dioxide

**Aromatic Magnesium Carbonate Mixture, BP (Aromatic Magnesium Carbonate Oral Suspension)**
Oral suspension, light magnesium carbonate 3%, sodium bicarbonate 5%, in a suitable vehicle containing aromatic cardamom tincture. Contains about 6 mmol $Na^+$/10 mL. Net price 200 mL = 66p
Dose 10 mL 3 times daily in water

For **preparations** also containing aluminium, see above and section 1.1.2.

### MAGNESIUM TRISILICATE

**Indications** dyspepsia

**Cautions** see under Magnesium Carbonate

**Contra-indications** see under Magnesium Carbonate

**Side-effects** diarrhoea, belching due to liberated carbon dioxide; silica-based renal stones reported on long-term treatment

**Magnesium Trisilicate Tablets, Compound, BP**
Tablets, magnesium trisilicate 250 mg, dried aluminium hydroxide 120 mg
Dose 1–2 tablets chewed when required

**Magnesium Trisilicate Mixture, BP (Magnesium Trisilicate Oral Suspension)**
Oral suspension, 5% each of magnesium trisilicate, light magnesium carbonate, and sodium bicarbonate in a suitable vehicle with a peppermint flavour. Contains about 6 mmol $Na^+$/10 mL
Dose 10 mL 3 times daily in water

For **preparations** also containing aluminium, see above and section 1.1.2.

## Aluminium-magnesium complexes

### HYDROTALCITE

**Aluminium magnesium carbonate hydroxide hydrate**

**Indications** dyspepsia

**Cautions** see notes above; **interactions:** Appendix 1 (antacids)

**Side-effects** see notes above

**Hydrotalcite** (Peckforton)
Suspension, hydrotalcite 500 mg/5 mL (low $Na^+$). Net price 500-mL pack = £1.96
Dose 10 mL between meals and at bedtime; CHILD under 6 years not recommended, 6–12 years 5 mL
Note The brand name *Altacite®* NHS is used for hydrotalcite suspension; for *Altacite Plus®* suspension, see below

## Antacid preparations containing simeticone

**Altacite Plus®** (Peckforton)
Suspension, sugar-free, co-simalcite 125/500 (simeticone 125 mg, hydrotalcite 500 mg)/5 mL (low $Na^+$). Net price 500 mL = £1.96
Dose 10 mL between meals and at bedtime when required; CHILD 8–12 years 5 mL

**Asilone®** (Thornton & Ross)
Suspension, sugar-free, dried aluminium hydroxide 420 mg, simeticone 135 mg, light magnesium oxide 70 mg/5 mL (low $Na^+$). Net price 500 mL = £1.95
Dose 5–10 mL after meals and at bedtime or when required up to 4 times daily; CHILD under 12 years not recommended

**Maalox Plus®** (Sanofi-Aventis)

Suspension, sugar-free, dried aluminium hydroxide 220 mg, simeticone 25 mg, magnesium hydroxide 195 mg/5 mL (low $Na^+$). Net price 500 mL = £2.59

Dose 5–10 mL 4 times daily (after meals and at bedtime or when required); CHILD under 5 years 5 mL 3 times daily, over 5 years appropriate proportion of adult dose

## Simeticone alone

**Simeticone** (activated dimeticone) is an antifoaming agent. It is licensed for infantile colic but evidence of benefit is uncertain.

**Dentinox®** (DDD)

Colic drops (= emulsion), simeticone 21 mg/2.5-mL dose. Net price 100 mL = £1.73

Dose gripes, colic or wind pains, INFANT 2.5 mL with or after each feed (max. 6 doses in 24 hours); may be added to bottle feed

Note The brand name *Dentinox®* is also used for other preparations including teething gel

**Infacol®** (Forest)

Liquid, sugar-free, simeticone 40 mg/mL (low $Na^+$). Net price 50 mL = £2.03 Counselling, use of dropper

Dose gripes, colic or wind pains, INFANT 0.5–1 mL before feeds



# 1.1.2 Compound alginates and proprietary indigestion preparations

**Alginate-containing** antacids form a 'raft' that floats on the surface of the stomach contents to reduce reflux and protect the oesophageal mucosa; they are used in the management of mild symptoms of gastro-oesophageal reflux disease.

## Compound alginate preparations

**Acidex®** (Pinewood)

Liquid, sugar-free, sodium alginate 250 mg, sodium bicarbonate 133.5 mg, calcium carbonate 80 mg/5 mL. Contains about 3 mmol $Na^+$/5 mL. Net price 500 mL (aniseed- or peppermint-flavour) = £1.70

Dose 10–20 mL after meals and at bedtime; CHILD 6–12 years 5–10 mL

**Algicon®** (Sanofi-Aventis)

Suspension, yellow, aluminium hydroxide-magnesium carbonate co-gel 140 mg, magnesium alginate 250 mg, magnesium carbonate 175 mg, potassium bicarbonate 50 mg/5 mL (low $Na^+$). Net price 500 mL (lemon- or mint-flavoured) = £3.07

Dose 10–20 mL 4 times daily (after meals and at bedtime); CHILD under 12 years not recommended

**Gastrocote®** (Thornton & Ross)

Tablets, alginic acid 200 mg, dried aluminium hydroxide 80 mg, magnesium trisilicate 40 mg, sodium bicarbonate 70 mg. Contains about 1 mmol $Na^+$/tablet. Net price 100-tab pack = £3.51

Cautions diabetes mellitus (high sugar content)

Dose 1–2 tablets chewed 4 times daily (after meals and at bedtime); CHILD under 6 years not recommended

Liquid, sugar-free, peach-coloured, dried aluminium hydroxide 80 mg, magnesium trisilicate 40 mg, sodium alginate 220 mg, sodium bicarbonate 70 mg/5 mL. Contains 1.8 mmol $Na^+$/5 mL. Net price 500 mL = £2.67

Dose 5–15 mL 4 times daily (after meals and at bedtime)

**Gaviscon®** (R&C)

Liquid, sugar-free, sodium alginate 250 mg, sodium bicarbonate 133.5 mg, calcium carbonate 80 mg/5 mL. Contains about 3 mmol $Na^+$/5 mL. Net price 600 mL (aniseed- or peppermint-flavour) = £5.12

Dose 10–20 mL after meals and at bedtime; CHILD 2–6 years (on doctor's advice only) and 6–12 years 5–10 mL

**Gaviscon® Advance** (R&C)

Tablets, sugar-free, sodium alginate 500 mg, potassium bicarbonate 100 mg. Contains 2.25 mmol $Na^+$/tablet. Net price 60-tab pack (peppermint-flavoured) = £3.24

Dose ADULT and CHILD over 12 years, 1–2 tablets to be chewed after meals and at bedtime

Suspension, sugar-free, sodium alginate 500 mg, potassium bicarbonate 100 mg/5 mL. Contains 2.3 mmol $Na^+$, 1 mmol $K^+$/5 mL. Net price 500 mL (aniseed- or peppermint-flavour) = £5.40

Dose ADULT and CHILD over 12 years, 5–10 mL after meals and at bedtime

**Gaviscon® Infant** (R&C)

Oral powder, sugar-free, sodium alginate 225 mg, magnesium alginate 87.5 mg, with colloidal silica and mannitol/dose (half dual-sachet). Contains 0.92 mmol $Na^+$/dose. Net price 15 dual-sachets (30 doses) = £2.46

Dose INFANT under 4.5 kg 1 dose (half dual-sachet) mixed with feeds (or water in breast-fed infants) when required; over 4.5 kg 2 doses (1 dual-sachet); CHILD 2 doses (1 dual-sachet) in water after each meal

Note Not to be used in preterm neonates, or where excessive water loss likely (e.g. fever, diarrhoea, vomiting, high room temperature), or if intestinal obstruction. Not to be used with other preparations containing thickening agents

Important Each half of the dual-sachet is identified as 'one dose'. To avoid errors prescribe as 'dual-sachet' with directions in terms of 'dose'

**Peptac®** (IVAX)

Suspension, sugar-free, sodium bicarbonate 133.5 mg, sodium alginate 250 mg, calcium carbonate 80 mg/5 mL. Contains 3.1 mmol $Na^+$/5mL. Net price 500 mL (aniseed- or peppermint-flavoured) = £2.16

Dose 10–20 mL after meals and at bedtime; CHILD 6–12 years 5–10 mL

**Rennie® Duo** (Roche Consumer Health)

Suspension, sugar-free, calcium carbonate 600 mg, magnesium carbonate 70 mg, sodium alginate 150 mg/5 mL. Contains 2.6 mmol $Na^+$/5 mL. Net price 500 mL (mint flavour) = £2.67

Dose ADULT and CHILD over 12 years, 10 mL after meals and at bedtime; an additional 10 mL may be taken between doses for heartburn if necessary, max. 80 mL daily

Excipients include propylene glycol

**Topal®** (Ceuta)

Tablets, alginic acid 200 mg, dried aluminium hydroxide 30 mg, light magnesium carbonate 40 mg with lactose 220 mg, sucrose 880 mg, sodium bicarbonate 40 mg (low $Na^+$). Net price 42-tab pack = £1.67

Cautions diabetes mellitus (high sugar content)

Dose 1–3 tablets chewed 4 times daily (after meals and at bedtime); CHILD half adult dose

### Preparations on sale to the public

**Indigestion preparations** on sale to the public include antacids with other ingredients such as alginates, calcium salts, simeticone, and peppermint oil. To identify the active ingredients in such preparations, consult the product literature or manufacturer.

**Note** The correct proprietary name should be ascertained—many products have similar names but different active ingredients

# 1.2 Antispasmodics and other drugs altering gut motility

Drugs in this section include antimuscarinic compounds and drugs believed to be direct relaxants of intestinal smooth muscle. The smooth muscle relaxant properties of antimuscarinic and other antispasmodic drugs may be useful in *irritable bowel syndrome* and in *diverticular disease*.

The dopamine-receptor antagonists metoclopramide and domperidone (section 4.6) stimulate transit in the gut.

## Antimuscarinics

Antimuscarinics (formerly termed 'anticholinergics') reduce intestinal motility. They are used for the management of *irritable bowel syndrome* and *diverticular disease*. However, their value has not been established and response varies. Other indications for antimuscarinic drugs include arrhythmias (section 2.3.1), asthma and airways disease (section 3.1.2), motion sickness (section 4.6), parkinsonism (section 4.9.2), urinary incontinence (section 7.4.2), mydriasis and cycloplegia (section 11.5), premedication (section 15.1.3) and as an antidote to organophosphorus poisoning (p. 36).

Antimuscarinics that are used for gastro-intestinal smooth muscle spasm include the tertiary amines **atropine sulphate** and **dicycloverine hydrochloride** (dicyclomine hydrochloride) and the quaternary ammonium compounds **propantheline bromide** and **hyoscine butylbromide**. The quaternary ammonium compounds are less lipid soluble than atropine and are less likely to cross the blood–brain barrier; they are also less well absorbed.

Dicycloverine hydrochloride has a much less marked antimuscarinic action than atropine and may also have some direct action on smooth muscle. Hyoscine butylbromide is advocated as a gastro-intestinal antispasmodic, but it is poorly absorbed; the injection is useful in endoscopy and radiology. Atropine and the belladonna alkaloids are outmoded treatments, any clinical virtues being outweighed by atropinic side-effects.

**Cautions** Antimuscarinics should be used with caution in Down's syndrome, in children and in the elderly; they should also be used with caution in gastro-oesophageal reflux disease, diarrhoea, ulcerative colitis, acute myocardial infarction, hypertension, conditions characterised by tachycardia (including hyperthyroidism, cardiac insufficiency, cardiac surgery), pyrexia, pregnancy and breast-feeding. **Interactions:** Appendix 1 (antimuscarinics).

**Contra-indications** Antimuscarinics are contra-indicated in angle-closure glaucoma, myasthenia gravis (but may be used to decrease muscarinic side-effects of anticholinesterases—section 10.2.1), paralytic ileus, pyloric stenosis and prostatic enlargement.

**Side-effects** Side-effects of antimuscarinics include constipation, transient bradycardia (followed by tachycardia, palpitations and arrhythmias), reduced bronchial secretions, urinary urgency and retention, dilatation of the pupils with loss of accommodation, photophobia, dry mouth, flushing and dryness of the skin. Side-effects that occur occasionally include confusion (particularly in the elderly), nausea, vomiting, and giddiness.

### ATROPINE SULPHATE

**Indications** symptomatic relief of gastro-intestinal disorders characterised by smooth muscle spasm; mydriasis and cycloplegia (section 11.5); pre-medication (section 15.1.3); see also notes above

**Cautions** see notes above

**Contra-indications** see notes above

**Side-effects** see notes above

**Atropine** (Non-proprietary) PoM

Tablets, atropine sulphate 600 micrograms. Net price 28-tab pack = £6.60

Available from CP

Dose 0.6–1.2 mg at night

### DICYCLOVERINE HYDROCHLORIDE
(Dicyclomine hydrochloride)

**Indications** symptomatic relief of gastro-intestinal disorders characterised by smooth muscle spasm

**Cautions** see notes above

**Contra-indications** see notes above; infants under 6 months

**Side-effects** see notes above

**Dose**

- 10–20 mg 3 times daily; INFANT 6–24 months 5–10 mg up to 3–4 times daily, 15 minutes before feeds; CHILD 2–12 years 10 mg 3 times daily

[1] **Merbentyl®** (Florizel) PoM

Tablets, dicycloverine hydrochloride 10 mg, net price 20 = £1.01; 20 mg (*Merbentyl 20®*), 84-tab pack = £8.47

Syrup, dicycloverine hydrochloride 10 mg/5 mL, net price 120 mL = £1.84

1. Dicycloverine hydrochloride can be sold to the public provided that max. single dose is 10 mg and max. daily dose is 60 mg

**Compound preparations**

**Kolanticon®** (Peckforton)

Gel, sugar-free, dicycloverine hydrochloride 2.5 mg, dried aluminium hydroxide 200 mg, light magnesium oxide 100 mg, simeticone 20 mg/5 mL, net price 200 mL = £1.69, 500 mL = £1.85

Dose 10–20 mL every 4 hours when required

### HYOSCINE BUTYLBROMIDE

**Indications** symptomatic relief of gastro-intestinal or genito-urinary disorders characterised by smooth muscle spasm

**Cautions** see notes above

**Contra-indications** see notes above; avoid in porphyria (section 9.8.2)

**Side-effects** see notes above

**Dose**

- By mouth (but poorly absorbed, see notes above), 20 mg 4 times daily; CHILD 6–12 years, 10 mg 3 times daily

  Irritable bowel syndrome, 10 mg 3 times daily, increased if required up to 20 mg 4 times daily
- By intramuscular *or* slow intravenous injection, acute spasm and spasm in diagnostic procedures, 20 mg repeated after 30 minutes if necessary (may be repeated more frequently in endoscopy), max. 100 mg daily; CHILD not recommended

**Buscopan®** (Boehringer Ingelheim) PoM

[1]Tablets, coated, hyoscine butylbromide 10 mg. Net price 56-tab pack = £2.59

Injection, hyoscine butylbromide 20 mg/mL. Net price 1-mL amp = 20p

1. Hyoscine butylbromide can be sold to the public provided single dose does not exceed 20 mg, daily dose does not exceed 80 mg, and pack does not contain a total of more than 240 mg; brands include *Buscopan® IBS Relief*

### PROPANTHELINE BROMIDE

**Indications** symptomatic relief of gastro-intestinal disorders characterised by smooth muscle spasm; urinary frequency (section 7.4.2); gustatory sweating (section 6.1.5)

**Cautions** see notes above

**Contra-indications** see notes above

**Side-effects** see notes above

**Dose**

- 15 mg 3 times daily at least 1 hour before meals and 30 mg at night, max. 120 mg daily; CHILD not recommended

**Pro-Banthine®** (Concord) PoM

Tablets, pink, s/c, propantheline bromide 15 mg, net price 112-tab pack = £15.32. Label: 23

## Other antispasmodics

**Alverine**, **mebeverine**, and **peppermint oil** are believed to be direct relaxants of intestinal smooth muscle and may relieve pain in *irritable bowel syndrome* and *diverticular disease*. They have no serious adverse effects but, like all antispasmodics, should be avoided in paralytic ileus. Peppermint oil occasionally causes heartburn.

### ALVERINE CITRATE

**Indications** adjunct in gastro-intestinal disorders characterised by smooth muscle spasm; dysmenorrhoea

**Cautions** pregnancy; breast-feeding (Appendix 5)

**Contra-indications** paralytic ileus; when combined with sterculia, intestinal obstruction, faecal impaction, colonic atony

**Side-effects** nausea, headache, pruritus, rash and dizziness reported

**Dose**

- 60–120 mg 1–3 times daily; CHILD under 12 years not recommended

**Spasmonal®** (Norgine)

Capsules, alverine citrate 60 mg (blue/grey), net price 100-cap pack = £11.95; 120 mg (*Spasmonal® Forte*, blue/grey), 60-cap pack = £13.80

### MEBEVERINE HYDROCHLORIDE

**Indications** adjunct in gastro-intestinal disorders characterised by smooth muscle spasm

**Cautions** pregnancy (Appendix 4); avoid in porphyria (section 9.8.2.)

**Contra-indications** paralytic ileus

**Side-effects** rarely allergic reactions (including rash, urticaria, angioedema)

**Dose**

- ADULT and CHILD over 10 years 135–150 mg 3 times daily preferably 20 minutes before meals

[1]**Mebeverine Hydrochloride** (Non-proprietary) PoM

Tablets, mebeverine hydrochloride 135 mg, net price 20 = £1.34

Oral suspension, mebeverine hydrochloride (as mebeverine embonate) 50 mg/5 mL, net price 300 mL = £107.00

1. Mebeverine hydrochloride can be sold to the public for symptomatic relief of irritable bowel syndrome provided that max. single dose is 135 mg and max. daily dose is 405 mg; for uses other than symptomatic relief of irritable bowel syndrome provided that max. single dose is 100 mg and max. daily dose is 300 mg; proprietary brands on sale to the public include *Colofac IBS®* (135 mg)

**Colofac®** (Solvay) PoM

Tablets, s/c, mebeverine hydrochloride 135 mg. Net price 20 = £1.50

#### Modified release

**Colofac® MR** (Solvay) PoM

Capsules, m/r, mebeverine hydrochloride 200 mg, net price 60-cap pack = £6.67. Label: 25

Dose irritable bowel syndrome, 1 capsule twice daily preferably 20 minutes before meals; CHILD not recommended

#### Compound preparations

[1]**Fybogel® Mebeverine** (R&C) PoM

Granules, buff, effervescent, ispaghula husk 3.5 g, mebeverine hydrochloride 135 mg/sachet. Contains 7 mmol $K^+$/sachet (caution in renal impairment). Net price 60 sachets = £15.00. Label: 13, 22, counselling, see below

Dose irritable bowel syndrome, ADULT, 1 sachet in water, morning and evening 30 minutes before food; an additional sachet may also be taken before the midday meal if necessary; CHILD not recommended

Counselling Preparations that swell in contact with liquid should always be carefully swallowed with water and should not be taken immediately before going to bed

1. 10-sachet pack can be sold to the public

### PEPPERMINT OIL

**Indications** relief of abdominal colic and distension, particularly in irritable bowel syndrome

**Cautions** rarely sensitivity to menthol

**Side-effects** heartburn, perianal irritation; rarely, allergic reactions (including rash, headache, bradycardia, muscle tremor, ataxia)

**Local irritation** Capsules should not be broken or chewed because peppermint oil may irritate mouth or oesophagus

**Colpermin®** (Pharmacia)

Capsules, m/r, e/c, light blue/dark blue, blue band, peppermint oil 0.2 mL. Net price 100-cap pack = £12.05. Label: 5, 25

Excipients include arachis (peanut) oil

Dose 1–2 capsules, swallowed whole with water, 3 times daily for up to 2–3 months if necessary; CHILD under 15 years not recommended

**Mintec®** (Shire)

Capsules, e/c, green/ivory, peppermint oil 0.2 mL. Net price 84-cap pack = £7.04. Label: 5, 22, 25

Dose 1–2 capsules swallowed whole with water, 3 times daily before meals for up to 2–3 months if necessary; CHILD not recommended

## Motility stimulants

**Metoclopramide** and **domperidone** (section 4.6) are dopamine antagonists which stimulate gastric emptying and small intestinal transit, and enhance the strength of oesophageal sphincter contraction. They are used in some patients with *non-ulcer dyspepsia*. Metoclopramide is also used to speed the transit of barium during intestinal follow-through examination, and as accessory treatment for *gastro-oesophageal reflux disease*. Metoclopramide and domperidone are useful in non-specific and in cytotoxic-induced nausea and vomiting. Metoclopramide and occasionally domperidone may induce an acute dystonic reaction, particularly in young women and children—for further details of this and other side-effects, see section 4.6.

# 1.3 Ulcer-healing drugs

1.3.1 H2-receptor antagonists
1.3.2 Selective antimuscarinics
1.3.3 Chelates and complexes
1.3.4 Prostaglandin analogues
1.3.5 Proton pump inhibitors

Peptic ulceration commonly involves the stomach, duodenum, and lower oesophagus; after gastric surgery it involves the gastro-enterostomy stoma.

Healing can be promoted by general measures, stopping smoking and taking antacids and by antisecretory drug treatment, but relapse is common when treatment ceases. Nearly all duodenal ulcers and most gastric ulcers not associated with NSAIDs are caused by *Helicobacter pylori*.

The management of *H. pylori* infection and of NSAID-associated ulcers is discussed below.

## *Helicobacter pylori* infection

Long-term healing of gastric and duodenal ulcers can be achieved rapidly by eradicating *Helicobacter pylori*; it is recommended that the presence of *H. pylori* is confirmed before starting eradication treatment. Acid inhibition combined with antibacterial treatment is highly effective in the eradication of *H. pylori*; reinfection is rare. Antibiotic-induced colitis is an uncommon risk.

One-week triple-therapy regimens that comprise a proton pump inhibitor, amoxicillin, and either clarithromycin or metronidazole, eradicate *H. pylori* in over 90% of cases. There is normally no need to continue antisecretory treatment (with a proton pump inhibitor or $H_2$-receptor antagonist) unless the ulcer is complicated by haemorrhage or perforation. Resistance to clarithromycin or to metronidazole is much more common than to amoxicillin and can develop during treatment. A regimen containing amoxicillin and clarithromycin is therefore recommended for initial therapy and one containing amoxicillin and metronidazole for eradication failure. Ranitidine bismuth citrate may be substituted for a proton pump inhibitor. Other regimens, including those combining clarithromycin and metronidazole are best used in specialist settings. Treatment failure usually indicates antibacterial resistance or poor compliance.

Two-week triple-therapy regimens offer the possibility of higher eradication rates compared to one-week regimens, but adverse effects are common and poor compliance is likely to offset any possible gain.

Two-week dual-therapy regimens using a proton pump inhibitor and a single antibacterial are licensed, but produce low rates of *H. pylori* eradication and are **not** recommended.

A two-week regimen using tripotassium dicitratobismuthate *plus* a proton pump inhibitor *plus* two antibacterials may have a role in the treatment of resistant cases after confirmation of the presence of *H. pylori*.

Tinidazole or tetracycline are also used occasionally for *H. pylori* eradication; they should be used in combination with antisecretory drugs and other antibacterials.

There is insufficient evidence to support eradication therapy in patients infected with *H. pylori* who continue to take NSAIDs.

## Test for *Helicobacter pylori*

$^{13}$C-Urea breath test kits are available for the diagnosis of gastro-duodenal infection with *Helicobacter pylori*. The test involves collection of breath samples before and after ingestion of an oral solution of $^{13}$C-urea; the samples are sent for analysis by an appropriate laboratory. The test should not be performed within 4 weeks of treatment with an antibacterial or within 2 weeks of treatment with an antisecretory drug. A specific $^{13}$C-urea breath test kit for children is available (*Helicobacter Test INFAI for children of the age 3–11®*). However, the appropriateness of testing for *H.pylori* infection in children has not been established.

**diabact UBT®** (MDE) PoM

Tablets, $^{13}$C-urea 50 mg, net price 1 kit (including 1 tablet, 4 breath-sample containers, straws) = £17.55 (analysis included), 10-kit pack (hosp. only) = £74.50 (analysis not included)

**Helicobacter Test Hp-Plus®** (Espire) PoM

Soluble tablets, $^{13}$C-urea 100 mg, net price 1 kit (including 4 breath-sample containers, straws, citric acid test meal) = £19.75 (analysis included)

**Helicobacter Test INFAI®** (Infai) PoM

Oral powder, $^{13}$C-urea 75 mg, net price 1 kit (including 4 breath-sample containers, straws) = £19.20 (spectrometric analysis included), 1 kit (including 2 breath bags) = £14.20 (spectroscopic analysis not included), 50-test set = £855.00 (spectrometric analysis included); 45 mg (*Helicobacter Test INFAI for children of the age 3–11®*), 1 kit (including 4 breath-sample containers, straws) = £19.20 (spectrometric analysis included)

**Pylobactell®** (Torbet) PoM
Soluble tablets, $^{13}$C-urea 100 mg, net price 1 kit (including 6 breath-sample containers, 30-mL mixing and administration vial, straws) = £20.75 (analysis included)

## NSAID-associated ulcers

Gastro-intestinal bleeding and ulceration can occur with NSAID use (section 10.1.1). Wherever possible, NSAIDs should be **withdrawn** if an ulcer occurs.

In those at risk of ulceration a proton pump inhibitor, an $H_2$-receptor antagonist such as ranitidine given at twice the usual dose, or misoprostol may be considered for protection against NSAID-associated gastric and duodenal ulcers; colic and diarrhoea may limit the dose of misoprostol.

NSAID use and *H. pylori* infection are independent risk factors for gastro-intestinal bleeding and ulceration. In patients already on a NSAID, eradication of *H. pylori* is not recommended because it is unlikely to reduce the risk of NSAID-induced bleeding or ulceration. However, in patients about to start long-term NSAID treatment who are *H. pylori* positive and have dyspepsia or a history of gastric or duodenal ulcer, eradication of *H. pylori* may reduce the overall risk of ulceration.

If the *NSAID can be discontinued* in a patient who has developed an ulcer, a proton pump inhibitor usually produces the most rapid healing, but the ulcer can be treated with an $H_2$-receptor antagonist or misoprostol.

If *NSAID treatment needs to continue*, the following options are suitable (see also NICE guidance, section 1.3.5):

- Treat ulcer with a proton pump inhibitor and on healing continue the proton pump inhibitor (dose not normally reduced because asymptomatic ulcer deterioration may occur);
- Treat ulcer with a proton pump inhibitor and on healing switch to misoprostol for maintenance therapy (colic and diarrhoea may limit the dose of misoprostol);
- Treat ulcer with a proton pump inhibitor and switch NSAID to a cyclo-oxygenase-2 selective inhibitor.

## 1.3.1 $H_2$-receptor antagonists

All $H_2$-receptor antagonists heal *gastric and duodenal ulcers* by reducing gastric acid output as a result of histamine $H_2$-receptor blockade; they can also be expected to relieve *gastro-oesophageal reflux disease* (section 1.1). High doses of $H_2$-receptor antagonists have been used in *Zollinger–Ellison syndrome*, but a proton pump inhibitor is preferred.

Maintenance treatment with low doses has largely been replaced in *Helicobacter pylori* positive patients by eradication regimens (section 1.3). Maintenance treatment may occasionally be used for those with frequent severe recurrences and for the elderly who suffer ulcer complications.

Treatment of *undiagnosed dyspepsia* with $H_2$-receptor antagonists may be acceptable in younger patients but care is required in older people because of the possibility of gastric cancer in these patients.

**Recommended regimens for *Helicobacter pylori* eradication**

| Acid suppressant | Antibacterial | | | Price for 7-day course |
|---|---|---|---|---|
| | Amoxicillin | Clarithromycin | Metronidazole | |
| Esomeprazole | 1 g twice daily | 500 mg twice daily | — | £33.31 |
| 20 mg twice daily | — | 500 mg twice daily | 400 mg twice daily | £31.95 |
| Lansoprazole | 1 g twice daily | 500 mg twice daily | — | £35.87 |
| 30 mg twice daily | 1 g twice daily | — | 400 mg twice daily | £15.69 |
| | — | 500 mg twice daily | 400 mg twice daily | £34.51 |
| Omeprazole | 1 g twice daily | 500 mg twice daily | — | £30.23 |
| 20 mg twice daily | 500 mg 3 times daily | — | 400 mg 3 times daily | £10.04 |
| | — | 500 mg twice daily | 400 mg twice daily | £28.87 |
| Pantoprazole | 1 g twice daily | 500 mg twice daily | — | £34.91 |
| 40 mg twice daily | — | 500 mg twice daily | 400 mg twice daily | £33.55 |
| Rabeprazole | 1 g twice daily | 500 mg twice daily | — | £34.64 |
| 20 mg twice daily | — | 500 mg twice daily | 400 mg twice daily | £33.28 |
| Ranitidine bismuth | 1 g twice daily | 500 mg twice daily | — | £36.15 |
| citrate | 1 g twice daily | — | 400 mg twice daily | £15.97 |
| 400 mg twice daily | — | 500 mg twice daily | 400 mg twice daily | £34.79 |

Regimens that include amoxicillin with either clarithromycin or metronidazole are suitable for use in the community. Regimens that combine clarithromycin with metronidazole are best used in specialist settings (see also notes above)

$H_2$-receptor antagonist therapy can promote healing of *NSAID-associated ulcers* (particularly duodenal) (section 1.3).

Treatment has not been shown to be beneficial in haematemesis and melaena, but prophylactic use reduces the frequency of bleeding from *gastroduodenal erosions in hepatic coma*, and possibly in other conditions requiring intensive care. Treatment also reduces the risk of *acid aspiration* in obstetric patients at delivery (Mendelson's syndrome).

**Cautions** $H_2$-receptor antagonists should be used with caution in renal impairment (Appendix 3), pregnancy (Appendix 4), and in breast-feeding (Appendix 5). $H_2$-receptor antagonists might mask symptoms of gastric cancer; particular care is required in those whose symptoms change and in those who are middle-aged or older.

**Side-effects** Side-effects of the $H_2$-receptor antagonists include diarrhoea and other gastro-intestinal disturbances, altered liver function tests (rarely liver damage), headache, dizziness, rash, and tiredness. Rare side-effects include acute pancreatitis, bradycardia, AV block, confusion, depression, and hallucinations particularly in the elderly or the very ill, hypersensitivity reactions (including fever, arthralgia, myalgia, anaphylaxis), blood disorders (including agranulocytosis, leucopenia, pancytopenia, thrombocytopenia), and skin reactions (including erythema multiforme and toxic epidermal necrolysis). There have been occasional reports of gynaecomastia and impotence.

**Interactions** Cimetidine retards oxidative hepatic drug metabolism by binding to microsomal cytochrome P450. It should be avoided in patients stabilised on warfarin, phenytoin, and theophylline (or aminophylline), but other interactions (see **Appendix** 1) may be of less clinical relevance. Famotidine, nizatidine, and ranitidine do not share the drug metabolism inhibitory properties of cimetidine.

## CIMETIDINE

**Indications** benign gastric and duodenal ulceration, stomal ulcer, reflux oesophagitis, Zollinger–Ellison syndrome, other conditions where gastric acid reduction is beneficial (see notes above and section 1.9.4)

**Cautions** see notes above; also preferably avoid intravenous injection (use intravenous infusion) particularly in high dosage and in cardiovascular impairment (risk of arrhythmias); hepatic impairment (Appendix 2); **interactions:** Appendix 1 (histamine $H_2$-antagonists) and notes above

**Side-effects** see notes above; also alopecia; very rarely tachycardia, interstitial nephritis

**Dose**

- By mouth, 400 mg twice daily (with breakfast and at night) *or* 800 mg at night (benign gastric and duodenal ulceration) for at least 4 weeks (6 weeks in gastric ulceration, 8 weeks in NSAID-associated ulceration); when necessary the dose may be increased to 400 mg 4 times daily; INFANT under 1 year 20 mg/kg daily in divided doses has been used; CHILD over 1 year 25–30 mg/kg daily in divided doses

  Maintenance, 400 mg at night *or* 400 mg morning and night

  Reflux oesophagitis, 400 mg 4 times daily for 4–8 weeks

  Zollinger–Ellison syndrome (but see notes above), 400 mg 4 times daily or occasionally more (max. 2.4 g daily)

  Prophylaxis of stress ulceration, 200–400 mg every 4–6 hours

  Gastric acid reduction (prophylaxis of acid aspiration; do not use syrup), obstetrics 400 mg at start of labour, then up to 400 mg every 4 hours if required (max. 2.4 g daily); surgical procedures 400 mg 90–120 minutes before induction of general anaesthesia

  Short-bowel syndrome, 400 mg twice daily (with breakfast and at bedtime) adjusted according to response

  To reduce degradation of pancreatic enzyme supplements, 0.8–1.6 g daily in 4 divided doses 1–1½ hours before meals
- By intramuscular injection, 200 mg every 4–6 hours
- By slow intravenous injection (but see Cautions above) over at least 5 minutes, 200 mg; may be repeated every 4–6 hours; if larger dose needed or if cardiovascular impairment, dilute and give injection over at least 10 minutes (infusion preferable); max. 2.4 g daily
- By intravenous infusion, 200–400 mg (may be repeated every 4–6 hours) *or* by continuous intravenous infusion usually at a rate of 50–100 mg/hour over 24 hours, max. 2.4 g daily; INFANT under 1 year, by slow intravenous injection *or* by intravenous infusion, 20 mg/kg daily in divided doses has been used; CHILD over 1 year, 25–30 mg/kg daily in divided doses

[1]**Cimetidine** (Non-proprietary) PoM

Tablets, cimetidine 200 mg, net price 60-tab pack = £1.98; 400 mg, 60-tab pack = £2.32; 800 mg, 30-tab pack = £2.87

Brands include *Peptimax*®

Oral solution, cimetidine 200 mg/5 mL, net price 300 mL = £14.25

1. Cimetidine can be sold to the public for adults and children over 16 years (provided packs do not contain more than 2 weeks' supply) for the short-term symptomatic relief of heartburn, dyspepsia, and hyperacidity (max. single dose 200 mg, max. daily dose 800 mg), and for the prophylactic management of nocturnal heartburn (single night-time dose 100 mg)

**Dyspamet®** (Goldshield) PoM

Suspension, sugar-free, cimetidine 200 mg/5 mL. Contains sorbitol 2.79 g/5 mL. Net price 600 mL = £24.08

**Tagamet®** (Chemidex) PoM

Tablets, all green, f/c, cimetidine 200 mg, net price 120-tab pack = £19.58; 400 mg, 60-tab pack = £22.62; 800 mg, 30-tab pack = £22.62

Syrup, orange, cimetidine 200 mg/5 mL. Net price 600 mL = £28.49

Excipients include propylene glycol

**Tagamet®** (GSK) PoM

Injection, cimetidine 100 mg/mL. Net price 2-mL amp = 33p

1 Gastro-intestinal system

## FAMOTIDINE

**Indications** see under Dose

**Cautions** see notes above; **interactions:** Appendix 1 (histamine $H_2$-antagonists) and notes above

**Side-effects** see notes above; also very rarely anxiety, anorexia, dry mouth, cholestatic jaundice

**Dose**

- Benign gastric and duodenal ulceration, treatment, 40 mg at night for 4–8 weeks; maintenance (duodenal ulceration), 20 mg at night; CHILD not recommended
- Reflux oesophagitis, 20–40 mg twice daily for 6–12 weeks; maintenance, 20 mg twice daily
- Zollinger–Ellison syndrome (but see notes above), 20 mg every 6 hours (higher dose in those who have previously been receiving another $H_2$-receptor antagonist); up to 800 mg daily in divided doses has been used

[1] **Famotidine** (Non-proprietary) PoM

Tablets, famotidine 20 mg, net price 28-tab pack = £5.00; 40 mg, 28-tab pack = £7.47

1. Famotidine can be sold to the public for adults and children over 16 years (provided packs do not contain more than 2 weeks' supply) for the short-term symptomatic relief of heartburn, dyspepsia, and hyperacidity, and for the prevention of these symptoms when associated with consumption of food or drink including when they cause sleep disturbance (max. single dose 10 mg, max. daily dose 20 mg); proprietary brands on sale to the public include (*Pepcid® AC*; a combination of famotidine and antacids (*Pepcidtwo®*) is also on sale to the public

**Pepcid®** (MSD) PoM

Tablets, f/c, famotidine 20 mg (beige), net price 28-tab pack = £13.37; 40 mg (brown), 28-tab pack = £25.40

## NIZATIDINE

**Indications** see under Dose

**Cautions** see notes above; also avoid rapid intravenous injection (risk of arrhythmias and postural hypotension); hepatic impairment (Appendix 2); **interactions:** Appendix 1 (histamine $H_2$-antagonists) and notes above

**Side-effects** see notes above; also sweating; rarely hyperuricaemia

**Dose**

- By mouth, benign gastric, duodenal or NSAID-associated ulceration, treatment, 300 mg in the evening *or* 150 mg twice daily for 4–8 weeks; maintenance, 150 mg at night; CHILD not recommended

  Gastro-oesophageal reflux disease, 150–300 mg twice daily for up to 12 weeks; CHILD not recommended
- By intravenous infusion, for short-term use in peptic ulcer as alternative to oral route (for hospital inpatients), by intermittent intravenous infusion over 15 minutes, 100 mg 3 times daily, *or* by continuous intravenous infusion, 10 mg/hour; max. 480 mg daily; CHILD not recommended

[1] **Nizatidine** (Non-proprietary) PoM

Capsules, nizatidine 150 mg, net price 30-cap pack = £4.40; 300 mg, 30-cap pack = £7.48

1. Nizatidine can be sold to the public for the prevention and treatment of symptoms of food-related heartburn and meal-induced indigestion in adults and children over 16 years; max. single dose 75 mg, max. daily dose 150 mg for max. 14 days

**Axid®** (Flynn) PoM

Capsules, nizatidine 150 mg (pale yellow/dark yellow), net price 28-cap pack (hosp. only) = £6.87, 30-cap pack = £7.97; 300 mg (pale yellow/brown), 30-cap pack = £15.80

Injection, nizatidine 25 mg/mL. For dilution and use as an intravenous infusion. Net price 4-mL amp = £1.14

## RANITIDINE

**Indications** see under Dose, other conditions where reduction of gastric acidity is beneficial (see notes above and section 1.9.4)

**Cautions** see notes above; also avoid in porphyria (section 9.8.2); **interactions:** Appendix 1 (histamine $H_2$-antagonists) and notes above

**Side-effects** see notes above; also *rarely* tachycardia, agitation, visual disturbances, alopecia, vasculitis ; *very rarely* interstitial nephritis

**Dose**

- By mouth, 150 mg twice daily *or* 300 mg at night for 4 to 8 weeks in benign gastric and duodenal ulceration, up to 6 weeks in chronic episodic dyspepsia, and up to 8 weeks in NSAID-associated ulceration (in duodenal ulcer 300 mg can be given twice daily for 4 weeks to achieve a higher healing rate); CHILD (peptic ulcer) 2–4 mg/kg twice daily, max. 300 mg daily

  Duodenal ulceration associated with *H. pylori,* see eradication regimens on p. 43

  Prophylaxis of NSAID-associated gastric or duodenal ulcer [unlicensed dose], 300 mg twice daily

  Gastro-oesophageal reflux disease, 150 mg twice daily *or* 300 mg at night for up to 8 weeks or if necessary 12 weeks (moderate to severe, 600 mg daily in 2–4 divided doses for up to 12 weeks); long-term treatment of healed gastro-oesophageal reflux disease, 150 mg twice daily

  Zollinger–Ellison syndrome (but see notes above), 150 mg 3 times daily; doses up to 6 g daily in divided doses have been used

  Gastric acid reduction (prophylaxis of acid aspiration) in obstetrics, by mouth, 150 mg at onset of labour, then every 6 hours; surgical procedures, by intramuscular *or* slow intravenous injection, 50 mg 45–60 minutes before induction of anaesthesia (intravenous injection diluted to 20 mL and given over at least 2 minutes), or by mouth, 150 mg 2 hours before induction of anaesthesia and also when possible on the preceding evening
- By intramuscular injection, 50 mg every 6–8 hours
- By slow intravenous injection, 50 mg diluted to 20 mL and given over at least 2 minutes; may be repeated every 6–8 hours
- By intravenous infusion, 25 mg/hour for 2 hours; may be repeated every 6–8 hours

Prophylaxis of stress ulceration, initial slow intravenous injection of 50 mg (as above) then continuous infusion, 125–250 micrograms/kg per hour (may be followed by 150 mg twice daily by mouth when oral feeding commences)

[1] **Ranitidine** (Non-proprietary) PoM
Tablets, ranitidine (as hydrochloride) 150 mg, net price 60-tab pack = £1.86; 300 mg, 30-tab pack = £1.86
Brands include *Ranitic®*, *Rantec®*,

Effervescent tablets, ranitidine (as hydrochloride) 150 mg, net price 60-tab pack = £20.20; 300 mg, 30-tab pack = £20.14. Label: 13
Excipients may include sodium (check with supplier)

Oral solution, ranitidine (as hydrochloride) 75 mg/ 5 mL, net price 300 mL = £22.32

1. Ranitidine can be sold to the public for adults and children over 16 years (provided packs do not contain more than 2 weeks' supply) for the short-term symptomatic relief of heartburn, dyspepsia, and hyperacidity, and for the prevention of these symptoms when associated with consumption of food or drink (max. single dose 75 mg, max. daily dose 300 mg); proprietary brands (*Gavilast-P®*, *Zantac® 75*, *Ranzac®* containing ranitidine (as hydrochloride) 75 mg) are on sale to the public

**Zantac®** (GSK) PoM
Tablets, f/c, ranitidine (as hydrochloride) 150 mg, net price 60-tab pack = £1.30; 300 mg, 30-tab pack = £1.30

Effervescent tablets, pale yellow, ranitidine (as hydrochloride) 150 mg (contains 14.3 mmol $Na^+$/tablet), net price 60-tab pack = £25.94; 300 mg (contains 20.8 mmol $Na^+$/tablet), 30-tab pack = £25.51. Label: 13
Excipients include aspartame (section 9.4.1)

Syrup, sugar-free, ranitidine (as hydrochloride) 75 mg/5 mL. Net price 300 mL = £20.76
Excipients include alcohol 8%

Injection, ranitidine (as hydrochloride) 25 mg/mL. Net price 2-mL amp = 60p

## RANITIDINE BISMUTH CITRATE
**(Ranitidine bismutrex)**

**Indications** see under Dose

**Cautions** see notes above; see also under Tripotassium Dicitratobismuthate; renal impairment (Appendix 3); **interactions:** Appendix 1 (histamine $H_2$-antagonists) and notes above

**Contra-indications** pregnancy (Appendix 4); breast-feeding (Appendix 5); porphyria (section 9.8.2)

**Side-effects** see notes above; may darken tongue or blacken faeces; *rarely* tachycardia, agitation, visual disturbances, erythema multiforme, alopecia; *very rarely* vasculitis

**Dose**

- Benign gastric or duodenal ulceration, 400 mg twice daily, preferably with food, for 8 weeks in benign gastric ulceration or 4–8 weeks in duodenal ulceration; CHILD not recommended
- Eradication of *Helicobacter pylori*, see eradication regimens on p. 43; ranitidine bismuth citrate treatment may be continued for a total of 4 weeks; long-term (maintenance) treatment not recommended (max. total of 16 weeks treatment in any 1 year); CHILD not recommended

Counselling May darken tongue and blacken faeces

**Pylorid®** (GSK) PoM
Tablets, blue, f/c, ranitidine bismuth citrate 400 mg. Net price 14-tab pack = £12.09; Counselling (discoloration of tongue and faeces)

## 1.3.2 Selective antimuscarinics

**Pirenzepine** is a selective antimuscarinic drug which was used for the treatment of gastric and duodenal ulcers. It has been discontinued.

## 1.3.3 Chelates and complexes

**Tripotassium dicitratobismuthate** is a bismuth chelate effective in healing gastric and duodenal ulcers. For the role of tripotassium dicitratobismuthate in a *Helicobacter pylori* eradication regimen for those who have not responded to first-line regimens, see section 1.3.

The bismuth content of tripotassium dicitratobismuthate is low but absorption has been reported; encephalopathy (described with older high-dose bismuth preparations) has not been reported.

Ranitidine bismuth citrate (section 1.3.1) is used in the management of gastric and duodenal ulcers, and in combination with two antibacterials for the eradication of *H. pylori* (section 1.3).

**Sucralfate** may act by protecting the mucosa from acid-pepsin attack in gastric and duodenal ulcers. It is a complex of aluminium hydroxide and sulphated sucrose but has minimal antacid properties. It should be used with caution in patients under intensive care (**important:** reports of bezoar formation, see CSM advice below)

## TRIPOTASSIUM DICITRATOBISMUTHATE

**Indications** benign gastric and duodenal ulceration; see also *Helicobacter pylori* infection, section 1.3

**Cautions** see notes above; **interactions:** Appendix 1 (tripotassium dicitratobismuthate)

**Contra-indications** severe renal impairment; pregnancy (Appendix 4)

**Side-effects** may darken tongue and blacken faeces; nausea and vomiting reported

**De-Noltab®** (Astellas)
Tablets, f/c, tripotassium dicitratobismuthate 120 mg. Net price 112-tab pack = £7.27. Counselling, see below

Dose 2 tablets twice daily *or* 1 tablet 4 times daily; taken for 28 days followed by further 28 days if necessary; maintenance not indicated but course may be repeated after interval of 1 month; CHILD not recommended

Counselling To be swallowed with half a glass of water; twice-daily dosage to be taken 30 minutes before breakfast and main evening meal; four-times-daily dosage to be taken as follows: one dose 30 minutes before breakfast, midday meal and main evening meal, and one dose 2 hours after main evening meal; milk should not be drunk by itself during treatment but small quantities may be taken in tea or coffee or on cereal; antacids should not be taken half an hour before or after a dose; may darken tongue and blacken faeces

## SUCRALFATE

**Indications** see under Dose

**Cautions** renal impairment (avoid if severe, see Appendix 3); pregnancy and breast-feeding; administration of sucralfate and enteral feeds should be separated by 1 hour; **interactions:** Appendix 1 (sucralfate)

Bezoar formation Following reports of bezoar formation associated with sucralfate, the **CSM** has advised caution in seriously ill patients, especially those receiving concomitant enteral feeds or those with predisposing conditions such as delayed gastric emptying

**Side-effects** constipation, diarrhoea, nausea, indigestion, gastric discomfort, dry mouth, rash, hypersensitivity reactions, back pain, dizziness, headache, vertigo and drowsiness, bezoar formation (see above)

**Dose**

- Benign gastric and duodenal ulceration and chronic gastritis, 2 g twice daily (on rising and at bedtime) *or* 1 g 4 times daily 1 hour before meals and at bedtime, taken for 4–6 weeks or in resistant cases up to 12 weeks; max. 8 g daily
- Prophylaxis of stress ulceration, 1 g 6 times daily (max. 8 g daily)
- CHILD not recommended

**Antepsin®** (Chugai) PoM

Tablets, scored, sucralfate 1 g, net price 50-tab pack = £4.37. Label: 5

Counselling Tablets may be dispersed in water

Suspension, sucralfate, 1 g/5 mL, net price 250 mL (aniseed- and caramel-flavoured) = £4.37. Label: 5

# 1.3.4 Prostaglandin analogues

Misoprostol, a synthetic prostaglandin analogue has antisecretory and protective properties, promoting healing of *gastric and duodenal ulcers.* It can prevent NSAID-associated ulcers, its use being most appropriate for the frail or very elderly from whom NSAIDs cannot be withdrawn.

For comment on the use of misoprostol to induce abortion or labour [unlicensed indications], see section 7.1.1.

## MISOPROSTOL

**Indications** see notes above and under Dose

**Cautions** conditions where hypotension might precipitate severe complications (e.g. cerebrovascular disease, cardiovascular disease)

**Contra-indications** pregnancy or planning pregnancy (Appendix 4), (increases uterine tone)—**important:** women of childbearing age, see also below, and breast-feeding (Appendix 5)

Women of childbearing age Manufacturer advises that misoprostol should not be used in women of childbearing age unless the patient requires non-steroidal anti-inflammatory (NSAID) therapy and is at high risk of complications from NSAID-induced ulceration. In such patients it is advised that misoprostol should only be used if the patient takes *effective contraceptive measures* and has been advised of the *risks of taking misoprostol if pregnant.*

**Side-effects** diarrhoea (may occasionally be severe and require withdrawal, reduced by giving single doses not exceeding 200 micrograms and by avoiding magnesium-containing antacids); also reported: abdominal pain, dyspepsia, flatulence, nausea and vomiting, abnormal vaginal bleeding (including intermenstrual bleeding, menorrhagia, and postmenopausal bleeding), rashes, dizziness

**Dose**

- Benign gastric and duodenal ulceration and NSAID-associated ulceration, 800 micrograms daily (in 2–4 divided doses) with breakfast (or main meals) and at bedtime; treatment should be continued for at least 4 weeks and may be continued for up to 8 weeks if required
- Prophylaxis of NSAID-induced gastric and duodenal ulcer, 200 micrograms 2–4 times daily taken with the NSAID
- CHILD not recommended

**Cytotec®** (Pharmacia) PoM

Tablets, scored, misoprostol 200 micrograms, net price 60-tab pack = £10.03, 140-tab pack = £23.40. Label: 21

**With diclofenac or naproxen**

Section 10.1.1

# 1.3.5 Proton pump inhibitors

The proton pump inhibitors **omeprazole**, **esomeprazole**, **lansoprazole**, **pantoprazole** and **rabeprazole** inhibit gastric acid by blocking the hydrogen-potassium adenosine triphosphatase enzyme system (the 'proton pump') of the gastric parietal cell. Proton pump inhibitors are effective short-term treatments for *gastric and duodenal ulcers*; they are also used in combination with antibacterials for the eradication of *Helicobacter pylori* (see p. 43 for specific regimens). An initial short course of a proton pump inhibitor is the treatment of choice in *gastro-oesophageal reflux disease* with severe symptoms; patients with endoscopically confirmed *erosive, ulcerative*, or *stricturing oesophagitis* usually need to be maintained on a proton pump inhibitor (section 1.1).

Proton pump inhibitors are also used in the prevention and treatment of NSAID-associated ulcers (see p. 44 and guidance issued by NICE, below). In patients who need to continue NSAID treatment after an ulcer has healed, the dose of proton pump inhibitor should normally not be reduced because asymptomatic ulcer deterioration may occur.

Omeprazole is effective in the treatment of *Zollinger-Ellison syndrome* (including cases resistant to other treatment); lansoprazole is also indicated for this condition.

**Cautions** Proton pump inhibitors should be used with caution in patients with liver disease (Appendix 2), in pregnancy (Appendix 4) and in breast-feeding (Appendix 5). Proton pump inhibitors may mask the symptoms of gastric cancer; particular care is required in those presenting with 'alarm features' (see p. 37), in such cases gastric malignancy should be ruled out before treatment.

**Side-effects** Side-effects of the proton pump inhibitors include gastro-intestinal disturbances (including nausea, vomiting, abdominal pain, flatulence, diarrhoea, constipation), headache, and dizziness. Less frequent side-effects include dry mouth, insomnia, drowsiness, malaise, blurred vision, rash, and pruritus. Other side-effects reported rarely or very rarely include taste disturbance, liver dysfunction, peripheral oedema, hypersensitivity reactions (including urticaria, angioedema, bronchospasm, anaphylaxis), photosensitivity, fever, sweating, depression, interstitial nephritis, blood disorders (including leucopenia, leucocytosis, pancytopenia, thrombocytopenia), arthralgia, myalgia and skin reactions (including Stevens-Johnson syndrome, toxic epidermal necrolysis, bullous eruption). Proton pump inhibitors, by decreasing gastric acidity, may increase the risk of gastro-intestinal infections.

> **NICE advice (proton pump inhibitors)**
> NICE has provided guidance (July 2000) on the use of proton pump inhibitors for the following indications:
> - Gastro-oesophageal reflux disease—use only for severe symptoms (reduce dose when symptoms abate) and in disease complicated by stricture, ulceration, or haemorrhage (full dose should be maintained);
> - NSAID-associated ulceration in patients who need to continue NSAID treatment—on healing of the ulcer a lower dose of proton pump inhibitor may be used [but see notes above].

## ESOMEPRAZOLE

**Indications** see under Dose

**Cautions** see notes above; renal impairment (Appendix 3); **interactions:** Appendix 1 (proton pump inhibitors)

**Side-effects** see notes above; also reported, dermatitis

**Dose**

- By mouth duodenal ulcer associated with *Helicobacter pylori*, see eradication regimens on p. 43

  NSAID-associated gastric ulcer, 20 mg once daily for 4–8 weeks; prophylaxis in patients with an increased risk of gastroduodenal complications who require continued NSAID treatment, 20 mg daily

  Gastro-oesophageal reflux disease, 40 mg once daily for 4 weeks, continued for further 4 weeks if not fully healed or symptoms persist; maintenance 20 mg daily; symptomatic treatment in the absence of oesophagitis, 20 mg daily for up to 4 weeks, then 20 mg daily when required

  CHILD not recommended

  Counselling Swallow whole *or* disperse in water
- By intravenous injection over at least 3 minutes or by intravenous infusion, gastro-oesophageal reflux disease, 40 mg once daily; symptomatic reflux disease without oesophagitis, 20 mg daily; continue until oral administration possible

  CHILD not recommended

**Nexium®** (AstraZeneca) PoM

Tablets, f/c, esomeprazole (as magnesium trihydrate) 20 mg (light pink), net price 28-tab pack = £18.50 (also 7-tab pack, hosp. only); 40 mg (pink), 28-tab pack = £25.19 (also 7-tab pack, hosp. only). Counselling, administration

Injection ▼, powder for reconstitution, esomeprazole (as sodium salt), net price 40-mg vial = £5.21

## LANSOPRAZOLE

**Indications** see under Dose

**Cautions** see notes above; **interactions:** Appendix 1 (proton pump inhibitors)

**Side-effects** see notes above; also reported, alopecia, paraesthesia, bruising, purpura, petechiae, fatigue, vertigo, hallucinations, confusion; rarely gynaecomastia, impotence

**Dose**

- Benign gastric ulcer, 30 mg daily in the morning for 8 weeks
- Duodenal ulcer, 30 mg daily in the morning for 4 weeks; maintenance 15 mg daily
- NSAID-associated duodenal or gastric ulcer, 15–30 mg once daily for 4 weeks, continued for further 4 weeks if not fully healed; prophylaxis, 15–30 mg once daily
- Eradication of *Helicobacter pylori* associated with duodenal ulcer or ulcer-like dyspepsia, see eradication regimens on p. 43
- Zollinger-Ellison syndrome (and other hypersecretory conditions), initially 60 mg once daily adjusted according to response; daily doses of 120 mg or more given in two divided doses
- Gastro-oesophageal reflux disease, 30 mg daily in the morning for 4 weeks, continued for further 4 weeks if not fully healed; maintenance 15–30 mg daily
- Acid-related dyspepsia, 15–30 mg daily in the morning for 2–4 weeks

**Lansoprazole** (Non-proprietary) PoM

Capsules, enclosing e/c granules, lansoprazole 15 mg, net price 28-cap pack = £12.92; 30 mg, 28-cap pack = £23.63. Label: 5, 25

**Zoton®** (Wyeth) PoM

Capsules, enclosing e/c granules, lansoprazole 15 mg (yellow), net price 28-cap pack = £12.92; 30 mg (lilac/purple), 28-cap pack = £23.63. Label: 5, 25

FasTab® (= orodispersible tablet), lansoprazole 15 mg, net price 28-tab pack = £10.86; 30 mg, 7-tab pack = £4.98, 14-tab pack = £9.94, 28-tab pack = £19.88. Label: 5, counselling, administration

Excipients include aspartame (section 9.4.1)

Counselling Tablets should be placed on the tongue, allowed to disperse and swallowed, or may be swallowed whole with a glass of water; tablets should not be crushed or chewed.

Suspension, pink, powder for reconstitution, lansoprazole 30 mg/sachet (strawberry flavour), net price 28-sachet pack = £33.97. Label: 5, 13

### With antibacterials

For additional cautions, contra-indications and side-effects see Amoxicillin (section 5.1.1), and Clarithromycin (section 5.1.5)

**HeliClear®** (Wyeth) PoM

Triple pack, lansoprazole capsules 30 mg (*Zoton®*), amoxicillin (as trihydrate) capsules 500 mg, clarithromycin tablets 500 mg (*Klaricid®*). Net price 7-day pack (14 × lansoprazole caps, 28 × amoxicillin caps, 14 × clarithromycin tabs) = £35.01. Label: 5, 9, 25

Dose eradication of *Helicobacter pylori* in patients with duodenal ulcer, lansoprazole 30 mg twice daily, clarithromycin 500 mg twice daily, and amoxicillin 1 g twice daily for 7–14 days; CHILD not recommended

## OMEPRAZOLE

**Indications** see under Dose

**Cautions** see notes above; **interactions:** Appendix 1 (proton pump inhibitors)

**Side-effects** see notes above; also reported, paraesthesia, vertigo, alopecia, gynaecomastia, impotence, stomatitis, encephalopathy in severe liver disease; hyponatraemia; reversible confusion, agitation, and hallucinations in the severely ill; visual impairment reported with high-dose injection

**Dose**

- By mouth, benign gastric and duodenal ulcers, 20 mg once daily for 4 weeks in duodenal ulceration or 8 weeks in gastric ulceration; in severe or recurrent cases increase to 40 mg daily; maintenance for recurrent duodenal ulcer, 20 mg once daily; prevention of relapse in duodenal ulcer, 10 mg daily increasing to 20 mg once daily if symptoms return

  NSAID-associated duodenal or gastric ulcer and gastroduodenal erosions, 20 mg once daily for 4 weeks, continued for further 4 weeks if not fully healed; prophylaxis in patients with a history of NSAID-associated duodenal or gastric ulcers, gastroduodenal lesions, or dyspeptic symptoms who require continued NSAID treatment, 20 mg once daily

  Duodenal or benign gastric ulcer associated with *Helicobacter pylori*, see eradication regimens on p. 43

  Zollinger–Ellison syndrome, initially 60 mg once daily; usual range 20–120 mg daily (above 80 mg in 2 divided doses)

  Gastric acid reduction during general anaesthesia (prophylaxis of acid aspiration), 40 mg on the preceding evening then 40 mg 2–6 hours before surgery

  Gastro-oesophageal reflux disease, 20 mg once daily for 4 weeks, continued for further 4–8 weeks if not fully healed; 40 mg once daily has been given for 8 weeks in gastro-oesophageal reflux disease refractory to other treatment; maintenance 20 mg once daily

  Acid reflux disease (long-term management), 10 mg daily increasing to 20 mg once daily if symptoms return

  Acid-related dyspepsia, 10–20 mg once daily for 2–4 weeks according to response

  Severe ulcerating reflux oesophagitis, CHILD over 1 year, body-weight 10–20 kg, 10 mg once daily increased if necessary to 20 mg once daily for 4–12 weeks; body-weight over 20 kg, 20 mg once daily increased if necessary to 40 mg once daily for 4–12 weeks; to be initiated by hospital paediatrician

- By intravenous injection over 5 minutes *or* by intravenous infusion, prophylaxis of acid aspiration, 40 mg completed 1 hour before surgery

  Benign gastric ulcer, duodenal ulcer and gastro-oesophageal reflux, 40 mg once daily until oral administration possible

**Counselling** Swallow whole, *or* disperse *MUPS®* tablets in water, *or* mix capsule contents or *MUPS®* tablets with fruit juice or yoghurt

**Omeprazole** (Non-proprietary) PoM

Capsules, enclosing e/c granules, omeprazole 10 mg, net price 28-cap pack = £5.81; 20 mg, 28-cap pack = £9.67; 40 mg, 7-cap pack = £5.77. Label: 5, counselling, administration

[1]Tablets, e/c, omeprazole 10 mg, net price 28-tab pack = £8.60; 20 mg, 28-tab pack = £19.42; 40 mg, 7-tab pack = £9.77. Label: 25

1. Omeprazole 10 mg tablets can be sold to the public for the short-term relief of reflux-like symptoms (e.g. heartburn) in adults over 18 years, max. daily dose 20 mg for max. 4 weeks, and a pack size of 28 tablets; proprietary brands on sale to the public include *Zanprol®*

**Losec®** (AstraZeneca) PoM

MUPS® (multiple-unit pellet system = dispersible tablets), f/c, omeprazole 10 mg (light pink), net price 28-tab pack = £19.34; 20 mg (pink), 28-tab pack = £29.22; 40 mg (red-brown), 7-tab pack = £14.61. Counselling, administration

Capsules, enclosing e/c granules, omeprazole 10 mg (pink), net price 28-cap pack = £19.34; 20 mg (pink/brown), 28-cap pack = £29.22; 40 mg (brown), 7-cap pack = £14.61. Counselling, administration

Intravenous infusion, powder for reconstitution, omeprazole (as sodium salt), net price 40-mg vial = £5.21

Injection, powder for reconstitution, omeprazole (as sodium salt), net price 40-mg vial (with solvent) = £5.21

## PANTOPRAZOLE

**Indications** see under Dose

**Cautions** see notes above; also renal impairment (Appendix 3); **interactions:** Appendix 1 (proton pump inhibitors)

**Side-effects** see notes above; also reported, raised triglycerides

**Dose**

- By mouth, benign gastric ulcer, 40 mg daily in the morning for 4 weeks, continued for further 4 weeks if not fully healed

  Gastro-oesophageal reflux disease, 20–40 mg daily in the morning for 4 weeks, continued for further 4 weeks if not fully healed; maintenance 20 mg daily, increased to 40 mg daily if symptoms return

  Duodenal ulcer, 40 mg daily in the morning for 2 weeks, continued for further 2 weeks if not fully healed

  Duodenal ulcer associated with *Helicobacter pylori*, see eradication regimens on p. 43

  Prophylaxis of NSAID-associated gastric or duodenal ulcer in patients with an increased risk of gastroduodenal complications who require continued NSAID treatment, 20 mg daily

  Zollinger–Ellison syndrome (and other hypersecretory conditions), initially 80 mg once daily adjusted according to response (ELDERLY max. 40 mg daily); daily doses above 80 mg given in 2 divided doses

  CHILD not recommended

- By intravenous injection over at least 2 minutes *or* by intravenous infusion, duodenal ulcer, gastric ulcer, and gastro-oesophageal reflux, 40 mg daily until oral administration can be resumed

  Zollinger–Ellison syndrome (and other hypersecretory conditions), initially 80 mg (160 mg if rapid acid control required) then 80 mg once daily adjusted according to response; daily doses above 80 mg given in 2 divided doses

  CHILD not recommended

**Protium®** (Altana) PoM
Tablets, yellow, e/c, pantoprazole (as sodium sesquihydrate) 20 mg, net price 28-tab pack = £12.31; 40 mg, 28-tab pack = £21.69. Label: 25
Injection, powder for reconstitution, pantoprazole (as sodium salt), net price 40-mg vial = £5.71

## RABEPRAZOLE SODIUM

**Indications** see under Dose
**Cautions** see notes above; **interactions:** Appendix 1 (proton pump inhibitors)
**Side-effects** see notes above; also reported, cough, pharyngitis, rhinitis, asthenia, influenza-like syndrome; *less commonly* chest pain, sinusitis, nervousness, urinary tract infection; rarely stomatitis, encephalopathy in severe liver disease, anorexia, weight gain
**Dose**
- Benign gastric ulcer, 20 mg daily in the morning for 6 weeks, continued for further 6 weeks if not fully healed
- Duodenal ulcer, 20 mg daily in the morning for 4 weeks, continued for further 4 weeks if not fully healed
- Gastro-oesophageal reflux disease, 20 mg once daily for 4–8 weeks; maintenance 10–20 mg daily; symptomatic treatment in the absence of oesophagitis, 10 mg daily for up to 4 weeks, then 10 mg daily when required
- Duodenal and benign gastric ulcer associated with *Helicobacter pylori*, see eradication regimens on p. 43
- Zollinger–Ellison syndrome, initially 60 mg once daily adjusted according to response (max. 120 mg daily); doses above 100 mg daily given in 2 divided doses
- CHILD not recommended

**Pariet®** (Janssen-Cilag, Eisai) PoM
Tablets, e/c, rabeprazole sodium 10 mg (pink), net price 28-tab pack = £11.56; 20 mg (yellow), 28-tab pack = £21.16. Label: 25

# 1.4 Acute diarrhoea

1.4.1 Adsorbents and bulk-forming drugs
1.4.2 Antimotility drugs

The priority in acute diarrhoea, as in gastro-enteritis, is the prevention or reversal of fluid and electrolyte depletion. This is particularly important in infants and in frail and elderly patients. For details of **oral rehydration preparations**, see section 9.2.1.2. Severe depletion of fluid and electrolytes requires immediate admission to hospital and urgent replacement.

**Antimotility drugs** (section 1.4.2) relieve symptoms of acute diarrhoea. They are used in the management of uncomplicated acute diarrhoea in adults; fluid and electrolyte replacement may be necessary in case of dehydration. However, antimotility drugs are **not** recommended for acute diarrhoea in young children.

Antispasmodics (section 1.2) are occasionally of value in treating abdominal cramp associated with diarrhoea but they should **not** be used for primary treatment. Antispasmodics and antiemetics should be **avoided** in young children with gastro-enteritis because they are rarely effective and have troublesome side-effects.

Antibacterial drugs are generally unnecessary in simple gastro-enteritis because the complaint usually resolves quickly without them, and infective diarrhoeas in the UK often have a viral cause. Systemic bacterial infection does, however, need appropriate systemic treatment; for drugs used in campylobacter enteritis, shigellosis, and salmonellosis, see section 5.1, table 1. **Ciprofloxacin** is occasionally used for prophylaxis against travellers' diarrhoea, but routine use is **not** recommended. Lactobacillus preparations have not been shown to be effective.

**Colestyramine** (cholestyramine, section 1.9.2) and **aluminium hydroxide mixture** (section 1.1.1), bind unabsorbed bile salts and provide symptomatic relief of diarrhoea following ileal disease or resection.

## 1.4.1 Adsorbents and bulk-forming drugs

Adsorbents such as kaolin are **not** recommended for *acute diarrhoeas*. Bulk-forming drugs, such as ispaghula, methylcellulose, and sterculia (section 1.6.1) are useful in controlling faecal consistency in ileostomy and colostomy, and in controlling diarrhoea associated with diverticular disease.

## KAOLIN, LIGHT

**Indications** diarrhoea but see notes above
**Cautions** **interactions:** Appendix 1 (kaolin)

**Kaolin Mixture, BP**
**(Kaolin Oral Suspension)**
Oral suspension, light kaolin or light kaolin (natural) 20%, light magnesium carbonate 5%, sodium bicarbonate 5% in a suitable vehicle with a peppermint flavour.
Dose 10–20 mL every 4 hours

## 1.4.2 Antimotility drugs

Antimotility drugs have a role in the management of uncomplicated *acute diarrhoea* in adults but not in young children; see also section 1.4. However, in severe cases, fluid and electrolyte replacement (section 9.2.1.2) are of primary importance.

For comments on the role of antimotility drugs in *chronic diarrhoea* see section 1.5. For their role in *stoma care* see section 1.8.

## CODEINE PHOSPHATE

**Indications** see notes above; cough suppression (section 3.9.1); pain (section 4.7.2)
**Cautions** see section 4.7.2; also not recommended for children; tolerance and dependence may occur with prolonged use; **interactions:** Appendix 1 (opioid analgesics)
**Contra-indications** see section 4.7.2; also conditions where inhibition of peristalsis should be avoided, where abdominal distension develops, or in acute diarrhoeal conditions such as acute ulcerative colitis or antibiotic-associated colitis
**Side-effects** see section 4.7.2

**Dose**
- See preparations

**Codeine Phosphate** (Non-proprietary) PoM
Tablets, codeine phosphate 15 mg, net price 28 = £1.46; 30 mg, 28 = £1.67; 60 mg, 28 = £2.61. Label: 2
Dose acute diarrhoea, 30 mg 3–4 times daily (range 15–60 mg); CHILD not recommended
Note Travellers needing to take codeine phosphate tablets abroad may require a doctor's letter explaining why they are necessary.

**Kaodene®** (Sovereign) NHS
Suspension, codeine phosphate 5 mg, light kaolin 1.5 g/5 mL. Net price 250 mL = £2.06
Dose 20 mL 3–4 times daily; CHILD under 5 years not recommended, over 5 years 10 mL but see cautions and notes above

## CO-PHENOTROPE

A mixture of diphenoxylate hydrochloride and atropine sulphate in the mass proportions 100 parts to 1 part respectively

**Indications** adjunct to rehydration in acute diarrhoea (but see notes above); chronic mild ulcerative colitis; control of faecal consistency after colostomy or ileostomy (section 1.8)

**Cautions** see under Codeine Phosphate; also young children are particularly susceptible to **overdosage** and symptoms may be delayed and observation is needed for at least 48 hours after ingestion; presence of subclinical doses of atropine may give rise to atropine side-effects in susceptible individuals or in overdosage; **interactions:** Appendix 1 (opioid analgesics)

**Contra-indications** see under Codeine Phosphate; jaundice

**Side-effects** see under Codeine Phosphate, section 4.7.2

**Dose**
- See preparation

[1]**Lomotil®** (Goldshield) PoM
Tablets, co-phenotrope 2.5/0.025 (diphenoxylate hydrochloride 2.5 mg, atropine sulphate 25 micrograms), net price 20 = £1.63
Dose initially 4 tablets, followed by 2 tablets every 6 hours until diarrhoea controlled; CHILD under 4 years not recommended, 4–8 years 1 tablet 3 times daily, 9–12 years 1 tablet 4 times daily, 13–16 years 2 tablets 3 times daily, but see also notes above

1. Co-phenotrope 2.5/0.025 can be sold to the public for adults and adolescents over 16 years (provided packs do not contain more than 20 tablets) as an adjunct to rehydration in acute diarrhoea (max. daily dose 10 tablets); proprietary brands on sale to public include *Dymotil®*

## LOPERAMIDE HYDROCHLORIDE

**Indications** symptomatic treatment of acute diarrhoea; adjunct to rehydration in acute diarrhoea in adults and children over 4 years (but see notes above); chronic diarrhoea in adults only

**Cautions** see notes above; also liver disease; pregnancy (Appendix 4); **interactions:** Appendix 1 (loperamide)

**Contra-indications** conditions where inhibition of peristalsis should be avoided, where abdominal distension develops, or in conditions such as active ulcerative colitis or antibiotic-associated colitis

**Side-effects** abdominal cramps, dizziness, drowsiness, and skin reactions including urticaria; paralytic ileus and abdominal bloating also reported

**Dose**
- Acute diarrhoea, 4 mg initially followed by 2 mg after each loose stool for up to 5 days; usual dose 6–8 mg daily; max. 16 mg daily; CHILD under 4 years not recommended, 4–8 years 1 mg 3–4 times daily for up to *3 days only*, 9–12 years 2 mg 4 times daily for up to 5 days
- Chronic diarrhoea in adults, initially, 4–8 mg daily in divided doses, subsequently adjusted according to response and given in 2 divided doses for maintenance; max. 16 mg daily

[2]**Loperamide** (Non-proprietary) PoM
Capsules, loperamide hydrochloride 2 mg. Net price 30-cap pack = £1.09
Brands include *Norimode®*

[2]**Imodium®** (Janssen-Cilag) PoM
Capsules, green/grey, loperamide hydrochloride 2 mg. Net price 30-cap pack = £1.16
Syrup, red, sugar-free, loperamide hydrochloride 1 mg/5 mL. Net price 100 mL = £1.00

### Compound preparations

**Imodium® Plus** (J&J MSD)
Tablets (chewable), scored, loperamide hydrochloride 2 mg, simeticone 125 mg, net price 6-tab pack = £1.97, 12-tab pack = £3.40, 18-tab pack = £4.54. Label: 24
Caplets (= tablets), loperamide hydrochloride 2 mg, simeticone 125 mg, net price 6-tab pack = £2.14, 12-tab pack = £3.40
Dose acute diarrhoea with abdominal colic, initially 2 tablets or caplets (ADOLESCENT 12–18 years 1 tablet or caplet) then 1 tablet or caplet after each loose stool; max. 4 tablets or caplets daily for up to 2 days; CHILD not recommended

## MORPHINE

**Indications** see notes above

**Cautions** see notes above and under Codeine Phosphate (section 4.7.2)

**Contra-indications** see notes above and under Codeine Phosphate

**Side-effects** see notes above and under Codeine Phosphate (section 4.7.2); sedation and the risk of dependence are greater

**Dose**
- See preparation

**Kaolin and Morphine Mixture, BP**
**(Kaolin and Morphine Oral Suspension)**
Oral suspension, light kaolin or light kaolin (natural) 20%, sodium bicarbonate 5%, and chloroform and morphine tincture 4% in a suitable vehicle. Contains anhydrous morphine 550–800 micrograms/10 mL.
Dose 10 mL every 4 hours in water

2. Loperamide can be sold to the public, for adults and children over 12 years, provided it is licensed and labelled for the treatment of acute diarrhoea; proprietary brands including *Arret®* capsules NHS, *Diasorb®* capsules, *Diocalm Ultra®* capsules NHS, *Imodium®* capsules NHS, *Imodium®* liquid, and *Normaloe®* tablets are on sale to the public

**Preparations on sale to the public**

Preparations on sale to the public for the treatment of diarrhoea contain **morphine**, often combined with **other ingredients**. To identify the active ingredients in such preparations, consult the product literature or manufacturer.

**Note** The correct proprietary name should be ascertained—many products have very similar names but different active ingredients

# 1.5 Chronic bowel disorders

Once tumours are ruled out individual symptoms of chronic bowel disorders need specific treatment including dietary manipulation as well as drug treatment and the maintenance of a liberal fluid intake.

## Irritable bowel syndrome

Irritable bowel syndrome can present with pain, constipation, or diarrhoea. In some patients there may be important psychological aggravating factors which respond to reassurance and possibly specific treatment e.g. with an antidepressant. A laxative (section 1.6) may be needed to relieve constipation. Antimotility drugs such as loperamide (section 1.4.2) may relieve diarrhoea and antispasmodic drugs (section 1.2) may relieve pain. Opioids with a central action such as codeine are better avoided because of the risk of dependence.

## Malabsorption syndromes

Individual conditions need specific management and also general nutritional consideration. Thus coeliac disease (gluten enteropathy) usually needs a gluten-free diet (Appendix 7) and pancreatic insufficiency needs pancreatin supplements (section 1.9.4).

## Inflammatory bowel disease

Chronic inflammatory bowel diseases include *ulcerative colitis* and *Crohn's disease*. Effective management requires drug therapy, attention to nutrition, and in severe or chronic active disease, surgery.

**Aminosalicylates** (balsalazide, mesalazine, olsalazine, and sulfasalazine), and **corticosteroids** (hydrocortisone, budesonide, and prednisolone) form the basis of drug treatment.

**Treatment of acute ulcerative colitis and Crohn's disease** Acute mild to moderate disease affecting the rectum (proctitis) or the recto-sigmoid (distal colitis) is treated initially with local application of a corticosteroid or an aminosalicylate; foam preparations and suppositories are especially useful where patients have difficulty retaining liquid enemas.

Diffuse inflammatory bowel disease or disease that does not respond to local therapy requires oral treatment; mild disease affecting the colon may be treated with an aminosalicylate alone but refractory or moderate disease usually requires adjunctive use of an oral corticosteroid such as **prednisolone** for 4–8 weeks. Modified-release **budesonide** is licensed for Crohn's disease affecting the ileum and the ascending colon; it causes fewer systemic side-effects than oral prednisolone but may be less effective.

Severe inflammatory bowel disease calls for hospital admission and treatment with intravenous corticosteroid; other therapy may include intravenous fluid and electrolyte replacement, blood transfusion, and possibly parenteral nutrition and antibiotics. Specialist supervision is required for patients who fail to respond adequately to these measures. Patients with ulcerative colitis may benefit from a short course of ciclosporin (section 8.2.2) [unlicensed indication]. Patients with unresponsive or chronically active Crohn's disease may benefit from azathioprine (section 8.2.1), mercaptopurine (see below), or once-weekly methotrexate (section 10.1.3) [all unlicensed indications].

**Infliximab** is licensed for the management of severe active Crohn's disease in patients whose condition has not responded adequately to treatment with a corticosteroid and a conventional immunosuppressant or who are intolerant of them. Infliximab is also licensed for the management of refractory fistulating Crohn's disease. Maintenance therapy with infliximab should be considered for patients who respond to the initial induction course; fixed-interval dosing may be superior to intermittent dosing.

**NICE guidance (infliximab for Crohn's disease)**

NICE has recommended (April 2002) that infliximab is used only for the treatment of severe active Crohn's disease (with or without fistulae) when treatment with immunomodulating drugs and corticosteroids has failed or is not tolerated and when surgery is inappropriate. Treatment may be repeated if the condition responded to the initial course but relapsed subsequently. Infliximab should be prescribed only by a gastroenterologist.

**Metronidazole** (section 5.1.11) may be beneficial for the treatment of active Crohn's disease with perianal involvement, possibly through its antibacterial activity. Metronidazole in doses of 0.6–1.5 g daily in divided doses has been used; it is usually given for a month but no longer than 3 months because of concerns about developing peripheral neuropathy. Other antibacterials should be given if specifically indicated (e.g. sepsis associated with fistulas and perianal disease) and for managing bacterial overgrowth in the small bowel.

**Maintenance of remission of acute ulcerative colitis and Crohn's disease** **Aminosalicylates** are of great value in the maintenance of remission of ulcerative colitis. They are of less value in the maintenance of remission of Crohn's disease; an oral formulation of mesalazine is licensed for the long-term management of ileal disease. Corticosteroids are **not** suitable for maintenance treatment because of side-effects. In resistant or frequently relapsing cases either **azathioprine** (section 8.2.1) 2–2.5 mg/kg daily [unlicensed indication] or **mercaptopurine** (section 8.1.3) 1–1.5 mg/kg daily [unlicensed indication], given under close supervision may be helpful; some patients may respond to lower doses of these drugs. Methotrexate (section 10.1.3) is tried in Crohn's disease if azathioprine or mercaptopurine cannot be used [unlicensed indication]; a dose of methotrexate 15 mg *weekly* is used. **Infliximab** is licensed for maintenance therapy in Crohn's disease (but see notes above).

**Adjunctive treatment of inflammatory bowel disease** Due attention should be paid to diet; high-fibre or low-residue diets should be used as appropriate. Irritable bowel syndrome during remission of ulcerative colitis calls for avoidance of a high-fibre diet and possible treatment with an antispasmodic (section 1.2).

Antimotility drugs such as codeine and loperamide, and antispasmodic drugs may precipitate paralytic ileus and megacolon in active ulcerative colitis; treatment of the inflammation is more logical. Laxatives may be required in proctitis. Diarrhoea resulting from the loss of bile-salt absorption (e.g. in terminal ileal disease or bowel resection) may improve with **colestyramine** (section 1.9.2), which binds bile salts.

## Antibiotic-associated colitis

Antibiotic-associated colitis (pseudomembranous colitis) is caused by colonisation of the colon with *Clostridium difficile* which may follow antibiotic therapy. It is usually of acute onset, but may run a chronic course; it is a particular hazard of clindamycin but few antibiotics are free of this side-effect. Oral **vancomycin** (see section 5.1.7) or **metronidazole** (see section 5.1.11) are used as specific treatment; vancomycin may be preferred for very sick patients.

## Diverticular disease

Diverticular disease is treated with a high-fibre diet, **bran supplements**, and **bulk-forming drugs**. **Antispasmodics** may provide symptomatic relief when colic is a problem (section 1.2). **Antibacterials** are used only when the diverticula in the intestinal wall become infected (specialist referral). **Antimotility** drugs which slow intestinal motility, e.g. codeine, diphenoxylate, and loperamide could possibly exacerbate the symptoms of diverticular disease and are **contra-indicated**.

## Aminosalicylates

**Sulfasalazine** is a combination of 5-aminosalicylic acid ('5-ASA') and sulfapyridine; sulfapyridine acts only as a carrier to the colonic site of action but still causes side-effects. In the newer aminosalicylates, **mesalazine** (5-aminosalicylic acid), **balsalazide** (a prodrug of 5-aminosalicylic acid) and **olsalazine** (a dimer of 5-aminosalicylic acid which cleaves in the lower bowel), the sulphonamide-related side-effects of sulfasalazine are avoided, but 5-aminosalicylic acid alone can still cause side-effects including blood disorders (see recommendation below) and lupoid phenomenon also seen with sulfasalazine.

**Cautions** Aminosalicylates should be used with caution in renal impairment (Appendix 3), during pregnancy (Appendix 4) and breast-feeding (Appendix 5); blood disorders can occur (see recommendation below).

> **Blood disorders**
> Patients receiving aminosalicylates should be advised to report any unexplained bleeding, bruising, purpura, sore throat, fever or malaise that occurs during treatment. A blood count should be performed and the drug stopped immediately if there is suspicion of a blood dyscrasia.

**Contra-indications** Aminosalicylates should be avoided in salicylate hypersensitivity.

**Side-effects** Side-effects of the aminosalicylates include diarrhoea, nausea, vomiting, abdominal pain, exacerbation of symptoms of colitis, headache, hypersensitivity reactions (including rash and urticaria); side-effects that occur rarely include acute pancreatitis, hepatitis, myocarditis, pericarditis, lung disorders (including eosinophilia and fibrosing alveolitis), peripheral neuropathy, blood disorders (including agranulocytosis, aplastic anaemia, leucopenia, methaemoglobinaemia, neutropenia, and thrombocytopenia—see also recommendation above), renal dysfunction (interstitial nephritis, nephrotic syndrome), myalgia, arthralgia, skin reactions (including lupus erythematosus-like syndrome, Stevens-Johnson syndrome), alopecia.

### BALSALAZIDE SODIUM

**Indications** treatment of mild to moderate ulcerative colitis and maintenance of remission

**Cautions** see notes above; also history of asthma; **interactions:** Appendix 1 (aminosalicylates)
**Blood disorders** See recommendation above

**Contra-indications** see notes above; also severe hepatic impairment

**Side-effects** see notes above; also cholelithiasis

**Dose**

- Acute attack, 2.25 g 3 times daily until remission occurs or for up to max. 12 weeks
- Maintenance, 1.5 g twice daily, adjusted according to response (max. 6 g daily)
- CHILD not recommended

**Colazide®** (Shire) PoM
Capsules, beige, balsalazide sodium 750 mg. Net price 130-cap pack = £39.00. Label: 21, 25, counselling, blood disorder symptoms (see recommendation above)

### MESALAZINE

**Indications** treatment of mild to moderate ulcerative colitis and maintenance of remission; see also under preparations

**Cautions** see notes above; elderly; with oral preparations, test renal function initially and every 3 months for first year then every 6 months for next 4 years and annually thereafter (risk of serious renal toxicity); **interactions:** Appendix 1 (aminosalicylates)
**Blood disorders** See recommendation above

**Contra-indications** see notes above; also severe hepatic impairment

**Side-effects** see notes above

**Dose**

- See under preparations, below

**Note** The delivery characteristics of enteric-coated mesalazine preparations may vary; these preparations should not be considered interchangeable

**Asacol®** (Procter & Gamble Pharm.) PoM
Foam enema, mesalazine 1 g/metered application, net price 14-application cannister with disposable applicators and plastic bags = £37.82. Counselling,

blood disorder symptoms (see recommendation above)

**Dose** acute attack affecting the rectosigmoid region, 1 metered application (mesalazine 1 g) into the rectum daily for 4–6 weeks; acute attack affecting the descending colon, 2 metered applications (mesalazine 2 g) once daily for 4–6 weeks; CHILD not recommended

Suppositories, mesalazine 250 mg, net price 20-suppos pack = £6.83; 500 mg, 10-suppos pack = £6.83. Counselling, blood disorder symptoms (see recommendation above)

**Dose** 0.75–1.5 g daily in divided doses, with last dose at bedtime; CHILD not recommended

**Asacol® MR** (Procter & Gamble Pharm.) PoM

Tablets, red, e/c, mesalazine 400 mg, net price 90-tab pack = £31.22, 120-tab pack = £41.62. Label: 5, 25, counselling, blood disorder symptoms (see recommendation above)

**Dose** ulcerative colitis, acute attack, 6 tablets daily in divided doses; maintenance of remission of ulcerative colitis and Crohn's ileo-colitis, 3–6 tablets daily in divided doses; CHILD not recommended

**Note** Preparations that lower stool pH (e.g. lactulose) may prevent release of mesalazine

**Ipocol®** (Sandoz) PoM

Tablets, e/c, mesalazine 400 mg, net price 120-tab pack = £35.20. Label: 5, 25, counselling, blood disorder symptoms (see recommendation above)

**Dose** acute attack, 6 tablets daily in divided doses; maintenance of remission, 3–6 tablets daily in divided doses; CHILD not recommended

**Note** Preparations that lower stool pH (e.g. lactulose) may prevent release of mesalazine

**Mesren MR®** (IVAX) PoM

Tablets, red-brown, e/c, mesalazine 400 mg, net price 90-tab pack = £20.29, 120-tab pack = £27.05. Label: 5, 25, counselling, blood disorder symptoms (see recommendation above)

**Dose** acute attack, 6 tablets daily in divided doses; maintenance of remission, 3–6 tablets daily in divided doses; CHILD not recommended

**Note** Preparations that lower stool pH (e.g. lactulose) may prevent release of mesalazine

**Pentasa®** (Ferring) PoM

Slow release tablets, m/r, scored, mesalazine 500 mg (grey), net price 100-tab pack = £25.48. Counselling, administration, see dose, blood disorder symptoms (see recommendation above)

**Dose** acute attack, up to 4 g daily in 2–3 divided doses; maintenance, 1.5 g daily in 2–3 divided doses; tablets may be dispersed in water, but should not be chewed; CHILD under 15 years not recommended

Prolonged release granules, m/r, pale brown, mesalazine 1 g/sachet, net price 50-sachet pack = £30.02. Counselling, administration, see dose, blood disorder symptoms (see recommendation above)

**Dose** acute attack, up to 4 g daily in 2–4 divided doses; maintenance, 2 g daily in 2 divided doses; granules should be placed on tongue and washed down with water or orange juice without chewing; CHILD under 12 years not recommended

Retention enema, mesalazine 1 g in 100-mL pack. Net price 7 enemas = £18.09. Counselling, blood disorder symptoms (see recommendation above)

**Dose** 1 enema at bedtime; CHILD not recommended

Suppositories, mesalazine 1 g. Net price 28-suppos pack = £41.55. Counselling, blood disorder symptoms (see recommendation above)

**Dose** ulcerative proctitis, acute attack, 1 suppository daily for 2–4 weeks; maintenance, 1 suppository daily; CHILD under 15 years not recommended

**Salofalk®** (Dr Falk) PoM

Tablets, e/c, yellow, mesalazine 250 mg. Net price 100-tab pack = £17.40. Label: 5, 25, counselling, blood disorder symptoms (see recommendation above)

**Dose** acute attack, 6 tablets daily in 3 divided doses; maintenance 3–6 tablets daily in divided doses; CHILD not recommended

Granules, m/r, grey, mesalazine 500 mg/sachet, net price 100-sachet pack = £29.30; 1 g/sachet, 50-sachet pack = £29.30. Counselling, administration, see dose, blood disorder symptoms (see recommendation above)

**Excipients** include aspartame (section 9.4.1)

**Dose** acute attack, 0.5–1 g 3 times daily; maintenance, 500 mg 3 times daily; CHILD over 6 years, body-weight under 40 kg half adult dose, body-weight over 40 kg, adult dose; granules should be placed on tongue and washed down with water without chewing

**Note** Preparations that lower stool pH (e.g. lactulose) may prevent release of mesalazine

Suppositories, mesalazine 500 mg. Net price 30-suppos pack = £15.90. Counselling, blood disorder symptoms (see recommendation above)

**Dose** acute attack, 1–2 suppositories 2–3 times daily adjusted according to response; CHILD not recommended

Enema, mesalazine 2 g in 59-mL pack. Net price 7 enemas = £31.20. Counselling, blood disorder symptoms (see recommendation above)

**Dose** acute attack *or* maintenance, 1 enema daily at bedtime; CHILD not recommended

Rectal foam, mesalazine 1 g/metered application, net price 14-application cannister with disposable applicators and plastic bags = £31.10. Counselling, blood disorder symptoms (see recommendation above)

**Dose** mild ulcerative colitis affecting sigmoid colon and rectum, 2 metered applications (mesalazine 2 g) into the rectum at bedtime increased if necessary to 2 metered applications (mesalazine 2 g) twice daily; CHILD not recommended

## OLSALAZINE SODIUM

**Indications** treatment of mild ulcerative colitis and maintenance of remission

**Cautions** see notes above; **interactions**: Appendix 1 (aminosalicylates)

**Blood disorders** See recommendation above

**Contra-indications** see notes above

**Side-effects** see notes above; also watery diarrhoea

**Dose**

- Acute attack, 1 g daily in divided doses after meals increased if necessary over 1 week to max. 3 g daily (max. single dose 1 g)
- Maintenance, 500 mg twice daily after meals
- CHILD not recommended

**Dipentum®** (Celltech) PoM

Capsules, brown, olsalazine sodium 250 mg. Net price 112-cap pack = £20.57. Label: 21, counselling, blood disorder symptoms (see recommendation above)

Tablets, yellow, scored, olsalazine sodium 500 mg. Net price 60-tab pack = £22.04. Label: 21, counselling, blood disorder symptoms (see recommendation above)

## SULFASALAZINE
### (Sulphasalazine)

**Indications** treatment of mild to moderate and severe ulcerative colitis and maintenance of remission; active Crohn's disease; rheumatoid arthritis (section 10.1.3)

**Cautions** see notes above; also history of allergy; hepatic impairment; G6PD deficiency (section 9.1.5); slow acetylator status; risk of haematological and hepatic toxicity (differential white cell, red cell and platelet counts initially and at monthly intervals for first 3 months, liver function tests at monthly intervals for first 3 months); kidney function tests at regular intervals; upper gastro-intestinal side-effects common over 4 g daily; porphyria (section 9.8.2); **interactions:** Appendix 1 (aminosalicylates)
Blood disorders See recommendation above

**Contra-indications** see notes above; also sulphonamide hypersensitivity; CHILD under 2 years of age

**Side-effects** see notes above; also loss of appetite; fever; blood disorders (including Heinz body anaemia, megaloblastic anaemia); hypersensitivity reactions (including exfoliative dermatitis, epidermal necrolysis, pruritus, photosensitisation, anaphylaxis, serum sickness); ocular complications (including periorbital oedema); stomatitis, parotitis; ataxia, aseptic meningitis, vertigo, tinnitus, insomnia, depression, hallucinations; kidney reactions (including proteinuria, crystalluria, haematuria); oligospermia; urine may be coloured orange; some soft contact lenses may be stained

**Dose**

- By mouth, acute attack 1–2 g 4 times daily (but see **cautions**) until remission occurs (if necessary corticosteroids may also be given), reducing to a maintenance dose of 500 mg 4 times daily; CHILD over 2 years, acute attack 40–60 mg/kg daily, maintenance dose 20–30 mg/kg daily
- By rectum, in suppositories, alone or in conjunction with oral treatment 0.5–1 g morning and night after a bowel movement. As an enema, 3 g at night, retained for at least 1 hour

**Sulfasalazine** (Non-proprietary) PoM

Tablets, sulfasalazine 500 mg. Net price 112 = £10.71. Label: 14, counselling, blood disorder symptoms (see recommendation above), contact lenses may be stained
Available from Generics, Hillcross

Tablets, e/c, sulfasalazine 500 mg. Net price 112-tab pack = £8.43. Label: 5, 14, 25, counselling, blood disorder symptoms (see recommendation above), contact lenses may be stained
Available from Alpharma (*Sulazine EC®*)

**Salazopyrin®** (Pharmacia) PoM

Tablets, yellow, scored, sulfasalazine 500 mg. Net price 112-tab pack = £6.97. Label: 14, counselling, blood disorder symptoms (see recommendation above), contact lenses may be stained

EN-Tabs® (= tablets e/c), yellow, f/c, sulfasalazine 500 mg. Net price 112-tab pack = £8.43. Label: 5, 14, 25, counselling, blood disorder symptoms (see recommendation above), contact lenses may be stained

Suspension, yellow, sulfasalazine 250 mg/5 mL. Net price 500 mL = £18.84. Label: 14, counselling, blood disorder symptoms (see recommendation above), contact lenses may be stained

Suppositories, yellow, sulfasalazine 500 mg. Net price 10 = £3.30. Label: 14, counselling, blood disorder symptoms (see recommendation above), contact lenses may be stained

Retention enema, sulfasalazine 3 g in 100-mL single-dose disposable packs fitted with a nozzle. Net price 7× 100 mL = £11.87. Label: 14, counselling, blood disorder symptoms (see recommendation above), contact lenses may be stained

## Corticosteroids

### BUDESONIDE

**Indications** see preparations

**Cautions** see section 6.3.2

**Contra-indications** see section 6.3.2

**Side-effects** see section 6.3.2

**Dose**

- See preparations

**Budenofalk®** (Dr Falk) PoM

Capsules, pink, enclosing e/c pellets, budesonide 3 mg, net price 100-cap pack = £76.70. Label: 5, 10, steroid card, 22, 25
Dose mild to moderate Crohn's disease affecting ileum or ascending colon, chronic diarrhoea due to collagenous colitis, ADULT over 18 years, 3 mg 3 times daily for up to 8 weeks; reduce dose for the last 2 weeks of treatment. See also section 6.3.2

**Entocort®** (AstraZeneca) PoM

CR Capsules, grey/pink, enclosing e/c, m/r granules, budesonide 3 mg, net price 100-cap pack = £99.00. Label: 5, 10, steroid card, 22, 25
Note Dispense in original container (contains dessicant)
Dose mild to moderate Crohn's disease affecting the ileum or ascending colon, 9 mg once daily in the morning before breakfast for up to 8 weeks; reduce dose for the last 2–4 weeks of treatment. See also section 6.3.2
CHILD not recommended

Enema, budesonide 2 mg/100 mL when dispersible tablet reconstituted in isotonic saline vehicle, net price pack of 7 dispersible tablets and bottles of vehicle = £33.00
Dose ulcerative colitis involving rectal and recto-sigmoid disease, 1 enema at bedtime for 4 weeks; CHILD not recommended

### HYDROCORTISONE

**Indications** ulcerative colitis, proctitis, proctosigmoiditis

**Cautions** see section 6.3.2; systemic absorption may occur; prolonged use should be avoided

**Contra-indications** use of enemas and rectal foams in obstruction, bowel perforation, and extensive fistulas; untreated infection

**Side-effects** see section 6.3.2; local irritation

**Dose**

- Rectal, see preparations

**Colifoam®** (Meda) PoM

Foam in aerosol pack, hydrocortisone acetate 10%, net price 14-application cannister with applicator = £8.21
Dose initially 1 metered application (125 mg hydrocortisone acetate) inserted into the rectum once or twice daily for 2–3 weeks, then once on alternate days

## PREDNISOLONE

**Indications** ulcerative colitis, and Crohn's disease; other indications, see section 6.3.2, see also preparations

**Cautions** see under Hydrocortisone and section 6.3.2

**Contra-indications** see under Hydrocortisone and section 6.3.2

**Side-effects** see under Hydrocortisone and section 6.3.2

**Dose**

- By mouth, initially 20–40 mg daily in single or divided doses, until remission occurs, followed by reducing doses
- By rectum, see under preparations

### Oral preparations

Section 6.3.2

### Rectal preparations

**Predenema®** (Forest) PoM

Retention enema, prednisolone 20 mg (as sodium metasulphobenzoate) in 100-mL single-dose disposable pack. Net price 1 (standard tube) = 71p, 1 (long tube) = £1.21

Dose ulcerative colitis, initially 1 enema at bedtime for 2–4 weeks, continued if good response; CHILD not recommended

**Predfoam®** (Forest) PoM

Foam in aerosol pack, prednisolone 20 mg (as metasulphobenzoate sodium)/metered application, net price 14-application cannister with disposable applicators = £6.32

Dose proctitis and distal ulcerative colitis, 1 metered application (20 mg prednisolone) inserted into the rectum once or twice daily for 2 weeks, continued for further 2 weeks if good response; CHILD not recommended

**Predsol®** (Celltech) PoM

Retention enema, prednisolone 20 mg (as sodium phosphate) in 100-mL single-dose disposable packs fitted with a nozzle. Net price 7 = £7.50

Dose rectal and rectosigmoidal ulcerative colitis and Crohn's disease, initially 1 enema at bedtime for 2–4 weeks, continued if good response; CHILD not recommended

Suppositories, prednisolone 5 mg (as sodium phosphate). Net price 10 = £1.40

Dose ADULT and CHILD proctitis and rectal complications of Crohn's disease, 1 suppository inserted night and morning after a bowel movement

## Cytokine inhibitors

**Infliximab** is a monoclonal antibody which inhibits the pro-inflammatory cytokine, tumour necrosis factor α. It should be used by specialists where adequate resuscitation facilities are available.

## INFLIXIMAB

**Indications** see under Inflammatory Bowel Disease above; ankylosing spondylitis, rhematoid arthritis (section 10.1.3)

**Cautions** see section 10.1.3

**Hypersensitivity reactions** Risk of delayed hypersensitivity if drug-free interval exceeds 16 weeks

**Contra-indications** see section 10.1.3

**Side-effects** see section 10.1.3

**Dose**

- By intravenous infusion, severe active Crohn's disease, ADULT over 18 years, initially 5 mg/kg, then if the condition responds within 2 weeks of initial dose, either 5 mg/kg 2 weeks and 6 weeks after initial dose, then 5 mg/kg every 8 weeks *or* after initial dose, further dose of 5 mg/kg if signs and symptoms recur

  Fistulating Crohn's disease, ADULT over 18 years, initially 5 mg/kg, then 5 mg/kg 2 weeks and 6 weeks after initial dose, then if condition has responded, consult literature for guidance on further doses

### Preparations

Section 10.1.3

## Food allergy

Allergy with classical symptoms of vomiting, colic and diarrhoea caused by specific foods such as shellfish should be managed by strict avoidance. The condition should be distinguished from symptoms of occasional food intolerance in those with irritable bowel syndrome. **Sodium cromoglicate** (sodium cromoglycate) may be helpful as an adjunct to dietary avoidance.

## SODIUM CROMOGLICATE
### (Sodium cromoglycate)

**Indications** food allergy (in conjunction with dietary restriction); asthma (section 3.3); allergic conjunctivitis (section 11.4.2); allergic rhinitis (section 12.2.1)

**Side-effects** occasional nausea, rashes, and joint pain

**Dose**

- 200 mg 4 times daily before meals; CHILD 2–14 years 100 mg; capsules may be swallowed whole or the contents dissolved in hot water and diluted with cold water before taking. May be increased if necessary after 2–3 weeks to a max. of 40 mg/kg daily and then reduced according to the response

**Nalcrom®** (Sanofi-Aventis) PoM

Capsules, sodium cromoglicate 100 mg. Net price 100-cap pack = £62.17. Label: 22, counselling, see dose above



# 1.6 Laxatives


1.6.1 Bulk-forming laxatives
1.6.2 Stimulant laxatives
1.6.3 Faecal softeners
1.6.4 Osmotic laxatives
1.6.5 Bowel cleansing solutions


Before prescribing laxatives it is important to be sure that the patient *is* constipated and that the constipation is *not* secondary to an underlying undiagnosed complaint.

It is also important for those who complain of constipation to understand that bowel habit can vary considerably in frequency without doing harm. Some people tend to consider themselves constipated if they do not have a bowel movement each day. A useful definition of constipation is the passage of hard stools less frequently than the patient's own normal pattern and this can be explained to the patient.

Misconceptions about bowel habits have led to excessive laxative use. Abuse may lead to hypokalaemia.

Thus, laxatives should generally be **avoided** except where straining will exacerbate a condition (such as angina) or increase the risk of rectal bleeding as in haemorrhoids. Laxatives are also of value in *drug-induced constipation*, for the expulsion of *parasites* after anthelmintic treatment, and to clear the alimentary tract before *surgery and radiological procedures.* Prolonged treatment of constipation is sometimes necessary.

**Children** The use of laxatives in children should be discouraged unless prescribed by a doctor. Infrequent defaecation may be normal in breast-fed babies or in response to poor intake of fluid or fibre. Delays of greater than 3 days between stools may increase the likelihood of pain on passing hard stools leading to anal fissure, anal spasm and eventually to a learned response to avoid defaecation.

If increased fluid and fibre intake is insufficient, an osmotic laxative such as lactulose or a bulk-forming laxative such as methylcellulose may be effective; methylcellulose is given in a dose of 0.5–1 g twice daily for a child over 7 years [unlicensed use]—an appropriate formulation for a younger child is not readily available. If there is evidence of minor faecal retention, the addition of a stimulant laxative such as senna may overcome withholding but may lead to colic or, in the presence of faecal impaction in the rectum, an increase of faecal overflow. Referral to hospital may be needed unless the child evacuates the impacted mass spontaneously. In hospital, use of a macrogol preparation by mouth or the use of enemas or suppositories may clear the mass but the use of rectal preparations is frequently distressing for the child and may lead to a persistence of withholding. Enemas may be administered under heavy sedation in hospital or alternatively, a bowel cleansing solution (section 1.6.5) may be tried. In severe cases or where the child is afraid, a manual evacuation under anaesthetic may be appropriate.

Long-term use of stimulant laxatives such as senna or sodium picosulfate (sodium picosulphate, section 1.6.2) is essential to prevent recurrence of the faecal impaction. Parents should be encouraged to use them regularly for many months; intermittent use may provoke a series of relapses.

**Pregnancy** If dietary and lifestyle changes fail to control constipation in pregnancy, moderate doses of poorly absorbed laxatives may be used. A bulk-forming laxative should be tried first. An osmotic laxative, such as lactulose, can also be used. Bisacodyl or senna may be suitable, if a stimulant effect is necessary.

> The laxatives that follow have been divided into 5 main groups (sections 1.6.1–1.6.5). This simple classification disguises the fact that some laxatives have a complex action.

## 1.6.1 Bulk-forming laxatives

Bulk-forming laxatives relieve constipation by increasing faecal mass which stimulates peristalsis; patients should be advised that the full effect may take some days to develop.

Bulk-forming laxatives are of particular value in those with small hard stools, but should not be required unless fibre cannot be increased in the diet. A balanced diet, including adequate fluid intake and fibre is of value in preventing constipation.

Bulk-forming laxatives are useful in the management of patients with *colostomy, ileostomy, haemorrhoids, anal fissure, chronic diarrhoea associated with diverticular disease, irritable bowel syndrome*, and as adjuncts in *ulcerative colitis* (section 1.5). Adequate fluid intake must be maintained to avoid intestinal obstruction. Unprocessed wheat **bran**, taken with food or fruit juice, is a most effective bulk-forming preparation. Finely ground bran, though more palatable, has poorer water-retaining properties, but can be taken as bran bread or biscuits in appropriately increased quantities. Oat bran is also used.

**Methylcellulose**, **ispaghula**, and **sterculia** are useful in patients who cannot tolerate bran. Methylcellulose also acts as a faecal softener.

### ISPAGHULA HUSK

**Indications** see notes above; hypercholesterolaemia (section 2.12)

**Cautions** adequate fluid intake should be maintained to avoid intestinal obstruction—it may be necessary to supervise elderly or debilitated patients or those with intestinal narrowing or decreased motility

**Contra-indications** difficulty in swallowing, intestinal obstruction, colonic atony, faecal impaction

**Side-effects** flatulence, abdominal distension, gastro-intestinal obstruction or impaction; hypersensitivity reported

**Dose**

- See preparations below

Counselling Preparations that swell in contact with liquid should always be carefully swallowed with water and should not be taken immediately before going to bed

**Fibrelief®** (Manx)

Granules, sugar- and gluten-free, ispaghula husk 3.5 g/sachet (natural or orange flavour), net price 10 sachets = £1.23, 30 sachets = £2.07. Label: 13, counselling, see above

Excipients include aspartame (section 9.4.1)

Dose 1–6 sachets daily in water in 1–3 divided doses

**Fybogel®** (R&C)

Granules, buff, effervescent, sugar- and gluten-free, ispaghula husk 3.5 g/sachet (low $Na^+$), net price 30 sachets (plain, lemon, or orange flavour) = £2.12, 150 g (orange flavour) = £3.44. Label: 13, counselling, see above

Excipients include aspartame 16 mg/sachet (see section 9.4.1)

Dose 1 sachet or 2 level 5-mL spoonfuls in water twice daily preferably after meals; CHILD (but see section 1.6) 6–12 years ½–1 level 5-mL spoonful (children under 6 years on doctor's advice only)

**Isogel®** (Pfizer Consumer)

Granules, brown, sugar- and gluten-free, ispaghula husk 90%. Net price 200 g = £2.67. Label: 13, counselling, see above

Dose constipation, 2 teaspoonfuls in water once or twice daily, preferably at mealtimes; CHILD (but see section 1.6) 1 teaspoonful

Diarrhoea (section 1.4.1), 1 teaspoonful 3 times daily

**Ispagel Orange®** (LPC)
Granules, beige, effervescent, sugar- and gluten-free, ispaghula husk 3.5 g/sachet, net price 30 sachets = £2.10. Label: 13, counselling, see above
Excipients include aspartame (section 9.4.1)
Dose 1 sachet in water 1–3 times daily; CHILD (but see section 1.6) 6–12 years ½ adult dose (children under 6 years on doctor's advice only)

**Regulan®** (Procter & Gamble)
Powder, beige, sugar- and gluten-free, ispaghula husk 3.4 g/5.85-g sachet (orange or lemon/lime flavour). Net price 30 sachets = £2.12. Label: 13, counselling, see above
Excipients include aspartame (section 9.4.1)
Dose 1 sachet in 150 mL water 1–3 times daily; CHILD (but see section 1.6) 6–12 years 2.5–5 mL

## METHYLCELLULOSE

**Indications** see notes above and section 1.6 [unlicensed dose in children]; adjunct in obesity (but see section 4.5.1)
**Cautions** see under Ispaghula Husk
**Contra-indications** see under Ispaghula Husk; also infective bowel disease
**Side-effects** see under Ispaghula Husk
**Dose**
- See preparations below

Counselling Preparations that swell in contact with liquid should always be carefully swallowed with water and should not be taken immediately before going to bed

**Celevac®** (Shire)
Tablets, pink, scored, methylcellulose '450' 500 mg. Net price 112-tab pack = £2.69. Counselling, see above and dose
Dose constipation and diarrhoea, 3–6 tablets twice daily. In constipation the dose should be taken with at least 300 mL liquid. In diarrhoea, ileostomy, and colostomy control, minimise liquid intake for 30 minutes before and after dose
Adjunct in obesity (but see section 4.5.1), 3 tablets with at least 300 mL warm liquid 30 minutes before food or when hungry

## STERCULIA

**Indications** see notes above
**Cautions** see under Ispaghula Husk
**Contra-indications** see under Ispaghula Husk
**Side-effects** see under Ispaghula Husk
**Dose**
- See under preparations below

Counselling Preparations that swell in contact with liquid should always be carefully swallowed with water and should not be taken immediately before going to bed

**Normacol®** (Norgine)
Granules, coated, gluten-free, sterculia 62%. Net price 500 g = £6.18; 60 × 7-g sachets = £5.19. Label: 25, 27, counselling, see above
Dose 1–2 heaped 5-mL spoonfuls, or the contents of 1–2 sachets, washed down without chewing with plenty of liquid once or twice daily after meals; CHILD (but see section 1.6) 6–12 years half adult dose

**Normacol Plus®** (Norgine)
Granules, brown, coated, gluten-free, sterculia 62%, frangula (standardised) 8%. Net price 500 g = £6.60; 60 × 7 g sachets = £5.56. Label: 25, 27, counselling, see above
Dose constipation and after haemorrhoidectomy, 1–2 heaped 5-mL spoonfuls or the contents of 1–2 sachets washed down without chewing with plenty of liquid once or twice daily after meals

# 1.6.2 Stimulant laxatives

Stimulant laxatives include **bisacodyl** and members of the **anthraquinone** group, **senna** and **dantron** (danthron). The indications for dantron are limited (see below) by its potential carcinogenicity (based on *rodent* carcinogenicity studies) and evidence of genotoxicity. Powerful stimulants such as **cascara** (an anthraquinone) and **castor oil** are obsolete. **Docusate** sodium probably acts both as a stimulant and as a softening agent.

Stimulant laxatives increase intestinal motility and often cause abdominal cramp; they should be avoided in intestinal obstruction. Prolonged use of stimulant laxatives can cause diarrhoea and related effects such as hypokalaemia; however, prolonged use may be justifiable in some circumstances (see section 1.6 for the use of stimulant laxatives in children).

**Glycerol** suppositories act as a rectal stimulant by virtue of the mildly irritant action of glycerol.

The **parasympathomimetics** bethanechol, distigmine, neostigmine, and pyridostigmine (see section 7.4.1 and section 10.2.1) enhance parasympathetic activity in the gut and increase intestinal motility. They are rarely used for their gastro-intestinal effects. Organic obstruction of the gut must first be excluded and they should not be used shortly after bowel anastomosis.

## BISACODYL

**Indications** see under Dose; tablets act in 10–12 hours; suppositories act in 20–60 minutes
**Cautions** see notes above
**Contra-indications** see notes above, acute surgical abdominal conditions, acute inflammatory bowel disease, severe dehydration
**Side-effects** see notes above; tablets, griping; suppositories, local irritation
**Dose**
- Constipation, by mouth, 5–10 mg at night; CHILD (but see section 1.6) 4–10 years (on medical advice only) 5 mg at night, over 10 years, adult dose

  By rectum in suppositories, 10 mg in the morning; CHILD (but see section 1.6) under 10 years (on medical advice only) 5 mg, over 10 years, adult dose
- Before radiological procedures and surgery, by mouth, 10–20 mg the night before procedure and by rectum in suppositories, 10 mg the following morning; CHILD 4–10 years by mouth, 5 mg the night before procedure and by rectum in suppositories, 5 mg the following morning; over 10 years, adult dose

**Bisacodyl** (Non-proprietary)
Tablets, e/c, bisacodyl 5 mg. Net price 20 = 43p. Label: 5, 25

Suppositories, bisacodyl 10 mg. Net price 12 = 77p

Paediatric suppositories, bisacodyl 5 mg. Net price 5 = 94p

Note The brand name *Dulco-lax®* (NHS) (Boehringer Ingelheim) is used for bisacodyl tablets, net price 10-tab pack = 74p; suppositories (10 mg), 10 = £1.57; paediatric suppositories (5 mg), 5 = 94p

The brand names *Dulco-lax® Liquid* and *Dulco-lax Perles®* are used for sodium picosulfate preparations

## DANTRON
(Danthron)

**Indications** only for constipation in terminally ill patients of all ages

**Cautions** see notes above; avoid prolonged contact with skin (as in incontinent patients)—risk of irritation and excoriation; avoid in pregnancy (Appendix 4) and breast-feeding; *rodent* studies indicate potential carcinogenic risk

**Contra-indications** see notes above

**Side-effects** see notes above; urine may be coloured red

**Dose**

- See under preparations

### With poloxamer '188' (as co-danthramer)

Note Co-danthramer suspension 5 mL = one co-danthramer capsule, **but** strong co-danthramer suspension 5 mL = two strong co-danthramer capsules

**Co-danthramer** (Non-proprietary) PoM

Capsules, co-danthramer 25/200 (dantron 25 mg, poloxamer '188' 200 mg). Net price 60-cap pack = £12.86. Label: 14, (urine red)

Dose 1–2 capsules at bedtime; CHILD 1 capsule at bedtime (restricted indications, see notes above)

Strong capsules, co-danthramer 37.5/500 (dantron 37.5 mg, poloxamer '188' 500 mg). Net price 60-cap pack = £15.55. Label: 14, (urine red)

Dose 1–2 capsules at bedtime (restricted indications, see notes above); CHILD under 12 years not recommended

Suspension, co-danthramer 25/200 in 5 mL (dantron 25 mg, poloxamer '188' 200 mg/5 mL). Net price 300 mL = £11.27, 1 litre = £37.57. Label: 14, (urine red)

Dose 5–10 mL at night; CHILD 2.5–5 mL (restricted indications, see notes above)

Brands include *Codalax®* NHS, *Danlax®*

Strong suspension, co-danthramer 75/1000 in 5 mL (dantron 75 mg, poloxamer '188' 1 g/5 mL). Net price 300 mL = £30.13. Label: 14, (urine red)

Dose 5 mL at night (restricted indications, see notes above); CHILD under 12 years not recommended

Brands include *Codalax Forte®* NHS

### With docusate sodium (as co-danthrusate)

**Co-danthrusate** (Non-proprietary) PoM

Capsules, co-danthrusate 50/60 (dantron 50 mg, docusate sodium 60 mg). Net price 63-cap pack = £13.46. Label: 14, (urine red)

Dose 1–3 capsules, usually at night; CHILD 6–12 years 1 capsule at night (restricted indications, see notes above)

Brands include *Capsuvac®*, *Normax®* NHS

Suspension, yellow, co-danthrusate 50/60 (dantron 50 mg, docusate sodium 60 mg/5 mL). Net price 200 mL = £8.75. Label: 14, (urine red)

Dose 5–15 mL at night; CHILD 6–12 years 5 mL at night (restricted indications, see notes above)

Brands include *Normax®*

## DOCUSATE SODIUM
(Dioctyl sodium sulphosuccinate)

**Indications** constipation (oral preparations act within 1–2 days); adjunct in abdominal radiological procedures

**Cautions** see notes above; do not give with liquid paraffin; rectal preparations not indicated if haemorrhoids or anal fissure; pregnancy (Appendix 4); breast-feeding (Appendix 5)

**Contra-indications** see notes above

**Side-effects** see notes above

**Dose**

- By mouth, chronic constipation, up to 500 mg daily in divided doses; CHILD (but see section 1.6) over 6 months 12.5 mg 3 times daily, 2–12 years 12.5–25 mg 3 times daily (use paediatric oral solution only)

  With barium meal, 400 mg

**Dioctyl®** (Schwarz)

Capsules, yellow/white, docusate sodium 100 mg, net price 30-cap pack = £2.40, 100-cap pack = £8.00

Excipients include propylene glycol

**Docusol®** (Typharm)

Adult oral solution, sugar-free, docusate sodium 50 mg/5 mL, net price 300 mL = £2.48

Paediatric oral solution, sugar-free, docusate sodium 12.5 mg/5 mL, net price 300 mL = £1.63

### Rectal preparations

**Norgalax Micro-enema®** (Norgine)

Enema, docusate sodium 120 mg in 10-g single-dose disposable packs. Net price 10-g unit = 60p

Dose ADULT and CHILD (but see section 1.6) over 12 years, 10-g unit

## GLYCEROL
(Glycerin)

**Indications** constipation

**Dose**

- See below

**Glycerol Suppositories, BP**
**(Glycerin Suppositories)**

Suppositories, gelatin 140 mg, glycerol 700 mg, purified water to 1 g. Net price 12 = 81p (infant), 82p (child), £1.83 (adult)

Dose 1 suppository moistened with water before use. The usual sizes are for INFANT under 1 year, small (1-g mould) 1–2 years medium (2-g mould), CHILD medium (2-g mould), ADULT large (4-g mould)

## SENNA

**Indications** constipation; acts in 8–12 hours

**Cautions** see notes above

**Contra-indications** see notes above

**Side-effects** see notes above

**Dose**

- See under preparations

**Senna** (Non-proprietary)

Tablets, total sennosides (calculated as sennoside B) 7.5 mg. Net price 20 = 65p

Dose 2–4 tablets, usually at night; initial dose should be low then gradually increased; CHILD (but see section 1.6) over 6 years, half adult dose in the morning (on doctor's advice only)

Note Lower dose on packs on sale to the public

Brands include *Senokot®* NHS

**Manevac®** (Galen)

Granules, coated, senna fruit 12.4%, ispaghula 54.2%, net price 400 g = £7.45. Label: 25, 27, counselling, see Ispaghula Husk

Dose 1–2 level 5-mL spoonfuls with water or warm drink after supper and, if necessary, before breakfast *or* every 6 hours in resistant cases for 1–3 days; CHILD (but see section 1.6) 5–12 years 1 level 5-mL spoonful daily

Counselling Preparations that swell in contact with liquid should always be carefully swallowed with water and should not be taken immediately before going to bed

**Senokot®** (R&C)

Tablets NHS, see above

Granules, brown, total sennosides (calculated as sennoside B) 15 mg/5 mL or 5.5 mg/g (one 5-mL spoonful = 2.7 g). Net price 100 g = £3.10

Dose 5–10 mL, usually at bedtime; CHILD (but see section 1.6) over 6 years 2.5–5 mL in the morning

Note Lower dose on packs on sale to the public

Syrup, sugar-free, brown, total sennosides (calculated as sennoside B) 7.5 mg/5 mL. Net price 500 mL = £2.69

Dose 10–20 mL, usually at bedtime; CHILD (but see section 1.6) 2–6 years 2.5–5 mL in the morning (doctor's advice only), over 6 years 5–10 mL

Note Lower dose on packs on sale to the public; the brand name *Senokot®* is also used for glycerol suppositories

### SODIUM PICOSULFATE
**(Sodium picosulphate)**

**Indications** constipation; bowel evacuation before abdominal radiological and endoscopic procedures on the colon, and surgery (section 1.6.5); acts within 6–12 hours

**Cautions** see notes above; active inflammatory bowel disease (avoid if fulminant); breast-feeding (Appendix 5)

**Contra-indications** see notes above; severe dehydration

**Side-effects** see notes above

**Dose**

- 5–10 mg at night; CHILD (but see section 1.6) under 4 years 250 micrograms/kg, 4–10 years 2.5–5 mg at night, over 10 years, adult dose

**Sodium Picosulfate** (Non-proprietary)

Elixir, sodium picosulfate 5 mg/5 mL, net price 100 mL = £1.85

Note The brand names *Laxoberal®* NHS and *Dulco-lax® Liquid* (both Boehringer Ingelheim) are used for sodium picosulfate elixir 5 mg/5 mL

**Dulco-lax®** (Boehringer Ingelheim)

Perles® (= capsules), sodium picosulfate 2.5 mg, net price 20-cap pack = £1.93, 50-cap pack = £2.73

Note The brand name *Dulco-lax®* is also used for bisacodyl tablets and suppositories

**Bowel cleansing solutions**

Section 1.6.5

## Other stimulant laxatives

Unstandardised preparations of cascara, frangula, rhubarb, and senna should be **avoided** as their laxative action is unpredictable. Aloes, colocynth, and jalap should be **avoided** as they have a drastic purgative action.

**Preparations on sale to the public**

Many preparations containing **stimulant laxatives** are on sale to the public. To identify the active ingredients in such preparations, consult the product literature or manufacturer.

Note The correct proprietary name should be ascertained—many products have very similar names but different active ingredients

## 1.6.3 Faecal softeners

Liquid paraffin, the traditional lubricant, has disadvantages (see below). Bulk laxatives (section 1.6.1) and non-ionic surfactant 'wetting' agents e.g. docusate sodium (section 1.6.2) also have softening properties. Such drugs are useful for oral administration in the management of haemorrhoids and anal fissure; glycerol (section 1.6.2) is useful for rectal use.

Enemas containing **arachis oil** (ground-nut oil, peanut oil) lubricate and soften impacted faeces and promote a bowel movement.

### ARACHIS OIL

**Indications** see notes above

**Dose**

- See below

**Fletchers' Arachis Oil Retention Enema®** (Forest)

Enema, arachis (peanut) oil in 130-mL single-dose disposable packs. Net price 130 mL = 96p

Dose to soften impacted faeces, 130 mL; the enema should be warmed before use; CHILD (but see section 1.6) under 3 years not recommended; over 3 years reduce adult dose in proportion to body-weight (medical supervision only)

### LIQUID PARAFFIN

**Indications** constipation

**Cautions** Avoid prolonged use; contra-indicated in children under 3 years

**Side-effects** anal seepage of paraffin and consequent anal irritation after prolonged use, granulomatous reactions caused by absorption of small quantities of liquid paraffin (especially from the emulsion), lipoid pneumonia, and interference with the absorption of fat-soluble vitamins

**Dose**

- See under preparation

**Liquid Paraffin Oral Emulsion, BP**

Oral emulsion, liquid paraffin 5 mL, vanillin 5 mg, chloroform 0.025 mL, benzoic acid solution 0.2 mL, methylcellulose-20 200 mg, saccharin sodium 500 micrograms, water to 10 mL

Dose 10–30 mL at night when required

Counselling Should not be taken immediately before going to bed

## 1.6.4 Osmotic laxatives

Osmotic laxatives increase the amount of water in the large bowel, either by drawing fluid from the body into the bowel or by retaining the fluid they were administered with.

**Lactulose** is a semi-synthetic disaccharide which is not absorbed from the gastro-intestinal tract. It produces an osmotic diarrhoea of low faecal pH, and discourages the proliferation of ammonia-producing organisms. It is therefore useful in the treatment of *hepatic encephalopathy*.

**Macrogols** are inert polymers of ethylene glycol which sequester fluid in the bowel; giving fluid with macrogols may reduce the dehydrating effect sometimes seen with osmotic laxatives.

Saline purgatives such as **magnesium hydroxide** are commonly abused but are satisfactory for occasional use; adequate fluid intake should be maintained. **Magnesium salts** are useful where rapid bowel evacuation is required. **Sodium salts** should be avoided as they may give rise to sodium and water retention in susceptible individuals. **Phosphate enemas** are useful in bowel clearance before radiology, endoscopy, and surgery.

## LACTULOSE

**Indications** constipation (may take up to 48 hours to act), hepatic encephalopathy (portal systemic encephalopathy)

**Cautions** lactose intolerance

**Contra-indications** galactosaemia, intestinal obstruction

**Side-effects** flatulence, cramps, and abdominal discomfort

**Dose**

- See under preparations below

**Lactulose** (Non-proprietary)

Solution, lactulose 3.1–3.7 g/5 mL with other ketoses. Net price 500-mL pack = £2.44

Dose constipation, initially 15 mL twice daily, adjusted according to patient's needs; CHILD (but see section 1.6) under 1 year 2.5 mL twice daily, 1–5 years 5 mL twice daily, 5–10 years 10 mL twice daily

Hepatic encephalopathy, 30–50 mL 3 times daily, subsequently adjusted to produce 2–3 soft stools daily

Brands include *Duphalac®* (NHS), *Lactugal®*, *Regulose®*

Note A proprietary brand of lactulose 3.3 g/5 mL (*Regulose®*) is on sale to the public

## MACROGOLS
### (Polyethylene glycols)

**Indications** see preparations below

**Cautions** pregnancy and breast-feeding (Appendix 5); discontinue if symptoms of fluid and electrolyte disturbance

**Contra-indications** intestinal perforation or obstruction, paralytic ileus, severe inflammatory conditions of the intestinal tract (such as Crohn's disease, ulcerative colitis, and toxic megacolon)

**Side-effects** abdominal distension and pain, nausea

**Dose**

- See preparations below

**Idrolax®** (Schwarz)

Oral powder, macrogol '4000' (polyethylene glycol '4000') 10 g/sachet, net price 20-sachet pack (orange-grapefruit flavour) = £4.84. Label: 13

Dose constipation, 1–2 sachets preferably as a single dose in the morning; content of each sachet dissolved in a glass of water; CHILD over 8 years, as adult dose for max. 3 months

**Movicol®** (Norgine)

Oral powder, macrogol '3350' (polyethylene glycol '3350') 13.125 g, sodium bicarbonate 178.5 mg, sodium chloride 350.7 mg, potassium chloride 46.6 mg/sachet, net price 20-sachet pack (lime and lemon flavour) = £4.63, 30-sachet pack = £6.95. Label: 13

Cautions patients with cardiovascular impairment should not take more than 2 sachets in any 1 hour

Dose chronic constipation, 1–3 sachets daily in divided doses usually for up to 2 weeks; content of each sachet dissolved in half a glass (approx. 125 mL) of water; maintenance, 1–2 sachets daily; CHILD not recommended

Faecal impaction, 8 sachets daily dissolved in 1 litre water and drunk within 6 hours, usually for max. 3 days; CHILD not recommended.

After reconstitution the solution should be kept in a refrigerator and discarded if unused after 6 hours

**Movicol®-Half** (Norgine)

Oral powder, macrogol '3350' (polyethylene glycol '3350') 6.563 g, sodium bicarbonate 89.3 mg, sodium chloride 175.4 mg, potassium chloride 23.3 mg/sachet, net price 20-sachet pack (lime and lemon flavour) = £2.78, 30-sachet pack = £4.17. Label: 13

Cautions patients with cardiovascular impairment should not take more than 4 sachets in any 1 hour

Dose chronic constipation, 2–6 sachets daily in divided doses usually for up to 2 weeks; content of each sachet dissolved in quarter of a glass (approx. 60–65 mL) of water; maintenance, 2–4 sachets daily; CHILD not recommended

Faecal impaction, 16 sachets daily dissolved in 1 litre of water and drunk within 6 hours, usually for max. 3 days; CHILD not recommended

After reconstitution the solution should be kept in a refrigerator and discarded if unused after 6 hours

**Movicol® Paediatric Plain** (Norgine) PoM

Oral powder, macrogol '3350' (polyethylene glycol '3350') 6.563 g, sodium bicarbonate 89.3 mg, sodium chloride 175.4 mg, potassium chloride 25.1 mg/sachet, net price 30-sachet pack = £4.63. Label: 13

Contra-indications cardiovascular impairment; renal impairment

Dose chronic constipation and recurrence of faecal impaction, CHILD 2–6 years 1 sachet daily; 7–11 years 2 sachets daily; adjust according to response, max. 4 sachets daily

Faecal impaction, CHILD (taken in divided doses over 12 hours each day until impaction resolves or for max. 7 days) 5–11 years 4 sachets on first day then increased in steps of 2 sachets daily to 12 sachets daily; content of each sachet dissolved in quarter of a glass (approx. 60–65 mL) of water

After reconstitution the solution should be kept in a refrigerator and discarded if unused after 24 hours

## MAGNESIUM SALTS

**Indications** see under preparations below

**Cautions** renal impairment (Appendix 3; risk of magnesium accumulation); hepatic impairment (see Appendix 2); elderly and debilitated; see also notes above; **interactions:** Appendix 1 (antacids)

**Contra-indications** acute gastro-intestinal conditions

**Side-effects** colic

**Dose**

- See under preparations below

### Magnesium hydroxide

**Magnesium Hydroxide Mixture, BP**

Aqueous suspension containing about 8% hydrated magnesium oxide. Do not store in cold place

Dose constipation, 25–50 mL when required

### Magnesium hydroxide with liquid paraffin

**Liquid Paraffin and Magnesium Hydroxide Oral Emulsion, BP**

Oral emulsion, 25% liquid paraffin in aqueous suspension containing 6% hydrated magnesium oxide

Dose constipation, 5–20 mL when required

Note Liquid paraffin and magnesium hydroxide preparations on sale to the public include: *Milpar®* (NHS)

**▲Magnesium sulphate**

**Magnesium Sulphate**

Label: 13, 23

**Dose** rapid bowel evacuation (acts in 2–4 hours) 5–10 g in a glass of water preferably before breakfast

**Note** Magnesium sulphate is on sale to the public as Epsom Salts

**▲Bowel cleansing solutions**

Section 1.6.5

## PHOSPHATES (RECTAL)

**Indications** rectal use in constipation; bowel evacuation before abdominal radiological procedures, endoscopy, and surgery

**Cautions** elderly and debilitated; see also notes above

**Contra-indications** acute gastro-intestinal conditions

**Side-effects** local irritation

**Dose**

- See under preparations

**Carbalax®** (Forest)

Suppositories, sodium acid phosphate (anhydrous) 1.3 g, sodium bicarbonate 1.08 g, net price 12 = £2.01

**Dose** constipation, 1 suppository, inserted 30 minutes before evacuation required; moisten with water before use; CHILD under 12 years not recommended

**Fleet® Ready-to-use Enema** (De Witt)

Enema, sodium acid phosphate 21.4 g, sodium phosphate 9.4 g/118 mL. Net price single-dose pack (standard tube) = 46p

**Dose** ADULT and CHILD (but see section 1.6) over 12 years, 118 mL; CHILD 3–12 years, on doctor's advice only (under 3 years not recommended)

**Fletchers' Phosphate Enema®** (Forest)

Enema, sodium acid phosphate 12.8 g, sodium phosphate 10.24 g, purified water, freshly boiled and cooled, to 128 mL (corresponds to Phosphates Enema Formula B). Net price 128 mL with standard tube = 41p, with long rectal tube = 57p

**Dose** 128 mL; CHILD (but see section 1.6) over 3 years, reduced according to body weight (under 3 years not recommended)

## SODIUM CITRATE (RECTAL)

**Indications** rectal use in constipation

**Cautions** elderly and debilitated; see also notes above

**Contra-indications** acute gastro-intestinal conditions

**Dose**

- See under preparations

**Micolette Micro-enema®** (Pinewood)

Enema, sodium citrate 450 mg, sodium lauryl sulphoacetate 45 mg, glycerol 625 mg, together with citric acid, potassium sorbate, and sorbitol in a viscous solution, in 5-mL single-dose disposable packs with nozzle. Net price 5 mL = 31p

**Dose** ADULT and CHILD over 3 years, 5–10 mL (but see section 1.6)

**Micralax Micro-enema®** (Celltech)

Enema, sodium citrate 450 mg, sodium alkylsulphoacetate 45 mg, sorbic acid 5 mg, together with glycerol and sorbitol in a viscous solution in 5-mL single-dose disposable packs with nozzle. Net price 5 mL = 41p

**Dose** ADULT and CHILD over 3 years, 5 mL (but see section 1.6)

**Relaxit Micro-enema®** (Crawford)

Enema, sodium citrate 450 mg, sodium lauryl sulphate 75 mg, sorbic acid 5 mg, together with glycerol and sorbitol in a viscous solution in 5-mL single-dose disposable packs with nozzle. Net price 5 mL = 32p

**Dose** ADULT and CHILD (but see section 1.6) 5 mL (insert only half nozzle length in child under 3 years)

# 1.6.5 Bowel cleansing solutions

Bowel cleansing solutions are used before colonic surgery, colonoscopy, or radiological examination to ensure the bowel is free of solid contents. They are **not** treatments for constipation.

## BOWEL CLEANSING SOLUTIONS

**Indications** see above

**Cautions** pregnancy; renal impairment(avoid if severe—Appendix 3); heart disease; ulcerative colitis; diabetes mellitus; reflux oesophagitis; impaired gag reflex; unconscious or semiconscious or possibility of regurgitation or aspiration

**Contra-indications** gastro-intestinal obstruction, gastric retention, gastro-intestinal ulceration, perforated bowel, congestive cardiac failure; toxic colitis, toxic megacolon or ileus

**Side-effects** nausea and bloating; less frequently abdominal cramps (usually transient—reduced by taking more slowly); vomiting

**Dose**

- See under preparations

**Citramag®** (Sanochemia)

Powder, effervescent, magnesium carbonate 11.57 g, anhydrous citric acid 17.79 g/sachet, net price 10-sachet pack (lemon and lime flavour) = £14.90. Label: 10, patient information leaflet 13, counselling, see below

**Dose** bowel evacuation for surgery, colonoscopy or radiological examination, on day before procedure, 1 sachet at 8 a.m. and 1 sachet between 2 and 4 p.m.; CHILD 5–9 years one-third adult dose; over 10 years and frail ELDERLY one-half adult dose

**Counselling** The patient information leaflet advises that hot water (200 mL) is needed to make the solution and provides guidance on the timing and procedure for reconstitution; it also mentions need for high fluid, low residue diet beforehand (according to hospital advice), and explains that only clear fluids can be taken after *Citramag®* until procedure completed

**Fleet Phospho-soda®** (De Witt)

Oral solution, sugar-free, sodium dihydrogen phosphate dihydrate 24.4 g, disodium phosphate dodecahydrate 10.8 g/45 mL. Net price 2 × 45-mL bottles = £4.79. Label: 10, patient information leaflet, counselling

**Dose** 45 mL diluted with half a glass (120 mL) of cold water, followed by one full glass (240 mL) of cold water

Timing of doses is dependent on the time of the procedure

For morning procedure, first dose should be taken at 7 a.m. and second at 7 p.m. on day before the procedure

For afternoon procedure, first dose should be taken at 7 p.m. on day before and second dose at 7 a.m. on day of the procedure

Solid food must not be taken during dosing period; clear liquids or water should be substituted for meals

CHILD and ADOLESCENT under 15 years not recommended

**Klean-Prep®** (Norgine)

Oral powder, macrogol '3350' (polyethylene glycol '3350') 59 g, anhydrous sodium sulphate 5.685 g, sodium bicarbonate 1.685 g, sodium chloride 1.465 g, potassium chloride 743 mg/sachet, net price 4 sachets = £8.56. Label: 10, patient information leaflet counselling

Excipients include aspartame (section 9.4.1)

Four sachets when reconstituted with water to 4 litres provides an iso-osmotic solution for bowel cleansing before surgery, colonoscopy or radiological procedures

Dose a glass (approx. 250 mL) of reconstituted solution every 10–15 minutes, or by nasogastric tube 20–30 mL/minute, until 4 litres have been consumed or watery stools are free of solid matter; CHILD not recommended

The solution from all 4 sachets should be drunk within 4–6 hours (250 mL drunk rapidly every 10–15 minutes); flavouring such as clear fruit cordials may be added if required; to facilitate gastric emptying domperidone or metoclopramide may be given 30 minutes before starting.

Alternatively the administration may be divided into two, e.g. taking the solutions from 2 sachets on the evening before examination and the remaining 2 on the morning of the examination

After reconstitution the solution should be kept in a refrigerator and discarded if unused after 24 hours

Note Allergic reactions reported

**Picolax®** (Ferring)

Oral powder, sugar-free, sodium picosulfate 10 mg/sachet, with magnesium citrate (for bowel evacuation before radiological procedure, endoscopy, and surgery), net price 2-sachet pack = £3.53. Label: 10, patient information leaflet, 13, counselling, see below

Dose ADULT and CHILD over 9 years, 1 sachet in water in morning (before 8 a.m.) and a second in afternoon (between 2 and 4 p.m.) of day preceding procedure; CHILD 1–2 years quarter sachet morning and afternoon, 2–4 years half sachet morning and afternoon, 4–9 years 1 sachet morning and half sachet afternoon

Acts within 3 hours of first dose

Note Low residue diet recommended for 2 days before procedure and copious intake of water or other clear fluids recommended during treatment

Counselling. Patients should be warned that heat is generated on addition to water; for this reason the powder should be added initially to 30 mL (2 tablespoonfuls) of water; after 5 minutes (when reaction complete) the solution should be further diluted to 150 mL (approx. half a glass)

# 1.7 Local preparations for anal and rectal disorders


1.7.1 Soothing haemorrhoidal preparations

1.7.2 Compound haemorrhoidal preparations with corticosteroids

1.7.3 Rectal sclerosants

1.7.4 Management of anal fissures


Anal and perianal pruritus, soreness, and excoriation are best treated by application of bland ointments and suppositories (section 1.7.1). These conditions occur commonly in patients suffering from haemorrhoids, fistulas, and proctitis. Cleansing with attention to any minor faecal soiling, adjustment of the diet to avoid hard stools, the use of bulk-forming materials such as bran (section 1.6.1) and a high residue diet are helpful. In proctitis these measures may supplement treatment with corticosteroids or sulfasalazine (see section 1.5).

When necessary topical preparations containing **local anaesthetics** (section 1.7.1) or **corticosteroids** (section 1.7.2) are used provided perianal thrush has been excluded. Perianal thrush is best treated with **nystatin** by mouth and by local application (see section 5.2, section 7.2.2, and section 13.10.2).

For the management of *anal fissures*, see section 1.7.4.

## 1.7.1 Soothing haemorrhoidal preparations

Soothing preparations containing mild astringents such as bismuth subgallate, zinc oxide, and hamamelis may give symptomatic relief in haemorrhoids. Many proprietary preparations also contain lubricants, vasoconstrictors, or mild antiseptics.

**Local anaesthetics** are used to relieve pain associated with *haemorrhoids* and *pruritus ani* but good evidence is lacking. Lidocaine (lignocaine) ointment (section 15.2) is used before emptying the bowel to relieve pain associated with *anal fissure*. Alternative local anaesthetics include tetracaine (amethocaine), cinchocaine, and pramocaine (pramoxine), but they are more irritant. Local anaesthetic ointments can be absorbed through the rectal mucosa therefore excessive application should be **avoided**, particularly in infants and children. They should be used for short periods only (no longer than a few days) since they may cause sensitisation of the anal skin.

### Preparations on sale to the public

Many preparations for the symptomatic relief of haemorrhoids are on sale to the public. To identify the active ingredients in such preparations, consult the product literature or manufacturer.

Note The correct proprietary name should be ascertained—many products have very similar names but different active ingredients

## 1.7.2 Compound haemorrhoidal preparations with corticosteroids

Corticosteroids are often combined with local anaesthetics and soothing agents in preparations for haemorrhoids. They are suitable for occasional short-term use after exclusion of infections, such as herpes simplex; prolonged use can cause atrophy of the anal skin. See section 13.4 for general comments on topical corticosteroids and section 1.7.1 for comment on local anaesthetics.

**Children** Haemorrhoids in children are rare. Treatment is usually symptomatic and the use of a locally applied cream is appropriate for short periods; however, local anaesthetics can cause stinging initially and this may aggravate the child's fear of defaecation.

**Anugesic-HC®** (Pfizer) PoM

Cream, benzyl benzoate 1.2%, bismuth oxide 0.875%, hydrocortisone acetate 0.5%, Peru balsam 1.85%, pramocaine hydrochloride 1%, zinc oxide 12.35%. Net price 30 g (with rectal nozzle) = £3.71

Dose apply night and morning and after a bowel movement; do not use for longer than 7 days; CHILD not recommended

Suppositories, buff, benzyl benzoate 33 mg, bismuth oxide 24 mg, bismuth subgallate 59 mg, hydrocortisone acetate 5 mg, Peru balsam 49 mg, pramocaine hydrochloride 27 mg, zinc oxide 296 mg, net price 12 = £2.69

Dose insert 1 suppository night and morning and after a bowel movement; do not use for longer than 7 days; CHILD not recommended

**Anusol-HC®** (Pfizer Consumer) PoM

Ointment, benzyl benzoate 1.25%, bismuth oxide 0.875%, bismuth subgallate 2.25%, hydrocortisone acetate 0.25%, Peru balsam 1.875%, zinc oxide 10.75%. Net price 30 g (with rectal nozzle) = £3.50

Dose apply night and morning and after a bowel movement; do not use for longer than 7 days; CHILD not recommended

Note A proprietary brand (*Anusol Plus HC®* ointment) is on sale to the public

Suppositories, benzyl benzoate 33 mg, bismuth oxide 24 mg, bismuth subgallate 59 mg, hydrocortisone acetate 10 mg, Peru balsam 49 mg, zinc oxide 296 mg. Net price 12 = £2.46

Dose insert 1 suppository night and morning and after a bowel movement; do not use for longer than 7 days; CHILD not recommended

Note A proprietary brand (*Anusol Plus HC®* suppositories) is on sale to the public

**Perinal®** (Dermal)

Spray application, hydrocortisone 0.2%, lidocaine hydrochloride 1%. Net price 30-mL pack = £6.39

Dose spray twice over the affected area up to 3 times daily; do not use for longer than 1–2 weeks; CHILD under 14 years not recommended

Note Also available as *Germoloids® HC* (Bayer Consumer Care)

**Proctofoam HC®** (Meda) PoM

Foam in aerosol pack, hydrocortisone acetate 1%, pramocaine hydrochloride 1%. Net price 21.2-g pack (approx. 40 applications) with applicator = £5.06

Dose haemorrhoids and proctitis, 1 applicatorful (4–6 mg hydrocortisone acetate, 4–6 mg pramocaine hydrochloride) by rectum 2–3 times daily and after a bowel movement (max. 4 times daily); do not use for longer than 7 days; CHILD not recommended

**Proctosedyl®** (Aventis Pharma) PoM

Ointment, cinchocaine (dibucaine) hydrochloride 0.5%, hydrocortisone 0.5%. Net price 30 g = £7.83 (with cannula)

Dose apply morning and night and after a bowel movement, externally or by rectum; do not use for longer than 7 days

Suppositories, cinchocaine (dibucaine) hydrochloride 5 mg, hydrocortisone 5 mg. Net price 12 = £3.53

Dose insert 1 suppository night and morning and after a bowel movement; do not use for longer than 7 days

**Scheriproct®** (Schering Health) PoM

Ointment, cinchocaine (dibucaine) hydrochloride 0.5%, prednisolone hexanoate 0.19%. Net price 30 g = £3.00

Dose apply twice daily for 5–7 days (3–4 times daily on 1st day if necessary), then once daily for a few days after symptoms have cleared

Suppositories, cinchocaine (dibucaine) hydrochloride 1 mg, prednisolone hexanoate 1.3 mg. Net price 12 = £1.41

Dose insert 1 suppository daily after a bowel movement, for 5–7 days (in severe cases initially 2–3 times daily)

**Ultraproct®** (Meadow) PoM

Ointment, cinchocaine (dibucaine) hydrochloride 0.5%, fluocortolone caproate 0.095%, fluocortolone pivalate 0.092%, net price 30 g (with rectal nozzle) = £4.57

Dose apply twice daily for 5–7 days (3–4 times daily on 1st day if necessary), then once daily for a few days after symptoms have cleared

Suppositories, cinchocaine (dibucaine) hydrochloride 1 mg, fluocortolone caproate 630 micrograms, fluocortolone pivalate 610 micrograms, net price 12 = £2.15

Dose insert 1 suppository daily after a bowel movement, for 5–7 days (in severe cases initially 2–3 times daily) then 1 suppository every other day for 1 week

**Uniroid-HC®** (Chemidex) PoM

Ointment, cinchocaine (dibucaine) hydrochloride 0.5%, hydrocortisone 0.5%. Net price 30 g (with applicator) = £4.23

Dose apply twice daily and after a bowel movement, externally or by rectum; do not use for longer than 7 days; CHILD under 12 years not recommended

Suppositories, cinchocaine (dibucaine) hydrochloride 5 mg, hydrocortisone 5 mg. Net price 12 = £1.91

Dose insert 1 suppository twice daily and after a bowel movement; do not use for longer than 7 days; CHILD under 12 years not recommended

**Xyloproct®** (AstraZeneca) PoM

Ointment (water-miscible), aluminium acetate 3.5%, hydrocortisone acetate 0.275%, lidocaine 5%, zinc oxide 18%, net price 20 g (with applicator) = £2.26

Dose apply several times daily; short-term use only

## 1.7.3 Rectal sclerosants

**Oily phenol injection** is used to inject haemorrhoids particularly when unprolapsed.

### PHENOL

**Indications** see notes above

**Side-effects** irritation, tissue necrosis

**Oily Phenol Injection, BP** PoM

phenol 5% in a suitable fixed oil. Net price 5-mL amp = £5.00

Dose 2–3 mL into the submucosal layer at the base of the pile; several injections may be given at different sites, max. total injected 10 mL at any one time

Available from Celltech

## 1.7.4 Management of anal fissures

The management of *anal fissures* requires stool softening by increasing dietary fibre in the form of bran or by using a bulk-forming laxative. Short-term use of local anaesthetic preparations may help (section 1.7.1). If these measures are inadequate, the patient should be referred for specialist treatment in hospital; surgery or the use of a topical nitrate (e.g. glyceryl trinitrate 0.4% ointment) may be considered.

### GLYCERYL TRINITRATE

**Indications** anal fissure; angina, left ventricular failure (section 2.6.1)

**Cautions** section 2.6.1

**Contra-indications** section 2.6.1

**Side-effects** section 2.6.1; also *less commonly* nausea, vomiting, burning and itching and rectal bleeding

**Dose**

- See preparations

**Rectogesic®** (Strakan) ▼ PoM

Rectal ointment, glyceryl trinitrate 0.4%, net price 30 g = £32.80

Excipients include lanolin, propylene glycol

Dose apply 2.5 cm of ointment to anal canal every 12 hours until pain stops; max. duration of use 8 weeks; CHILD under 18 years not recommended

Note 2.5 cm of ointment contains glyceryl trinitrate 1.5 mg

## 1.8 Stoma care

Prescribing for patients with stoma calls for special care. The following is a brief account of some of the main points to be borne in mind.

*Enteric-coated* and *modified-release* preparations are **unsuitable**, particularly in patients with ileostomies, as there may not be sufficient release of the active ingredient.

*Laxatives.* Enemas and washouts should **not** be prescribed for patients with ileostomies as they may cause rapid and severe loss of water and electrolytes.

Colostomy patients may suffer from constipation and whenever possible should be treated by increasing fluid intake or dietary fibre. **Bulk-forming drugs** (section 1.6.1) should be tried. If they are insufficient, as small a dose as possible of senna (section 1.6.2) should be used.

*Antidiarrhoeals.* Drugs such as **loperamide**, **codeine phosphate**, or **co-phenotrope** (diphenoxylate with atropine) are effective. Bulk-forming drugs (section 1.6.1) may be tried but it is often difficult to adjust the dose appropriately.

**Antibacterials** should **not** be given for an episode of acute diarrhoea.

*Antacids.* The tendency to diarrhoea from magnesium salts or constipation from aluminium salts may be increased in these patients.

*Diuretics* should be used with caution in patients with ileostomies as they may become excessively dehydrated and potassium depletion may easily occur. It is usually advisable to use a **potassium-sparing** diuretic (see section 2.2.3).

*Digoxin.* Patients with a stoma are particularly susceptible to hypokalaemia if on digoxin therapy and potassium supplements or a potassium-sparing diuretic may be advisable (for comment see section 9.2.1.1).

*Potassium supplements.* Liquid formulations are preferred to modified-release formulations (see above).

*Analgesics.* Opioid analgesics (see section 4.7.2) may cause troublesome constipation in colostomy patients. When a non-opioid analgesic is required **paracetamol** is usually suitable but anti-inflammatory analgesics may cause gastric irritation and bleeding.

*Iron preparations* may cause loose stools and sore skin in these patients. If this is troublesome and if iron is definitely indicated an intramuscular iron preparation (see section 9.1.1.2) should be used. Modified-release preparations should be **avoided** for the reasons given above.

Patients are usually given advice about the use of *cleansing agents, protective creams, lotions, deodorants*, or *sealants* whilst in hospital, either by the surgeon or by the health authority stoma care nurses. Voluntary organisations offer help and support to patients with stoma.

## 1.9 Drugs affecting intestinal secretions

1.9.1 Drugs affecting biliary composition and flow
1.9.2 Bile acid sequestrants
1.9.3 Aprotinin
1.9.4 Pancreatin

### 1.9.1 Drugs affecting biliary composition and flow

The use of laparoscopic cholecystectomy and of endoscopic biliary techniques has limited the place of the bile acid **ursodeoxycholic acid** in gallstone disease. Ursodeoxycholic acid is suitable for patients with unimpaired gall bladder function, small or medium-sized radiolucent stones, and whose mild symptoms are not amenable to other treatment; it should be used cautiously in those with liver disease (but see below). Patients should be given dietary advice (including avoidance of excessive cholesterol and calories) and they require radiological monitoring. Long-term prophylaxis may be needed after complete dissolution of the gallstones has been confirmed because they may recur in up to 25% of patients within one year of stopping treatment.

Ursodeoxycholic acid is also used in primary biliary cirrhosis; liver tests improve in most patients but the effect on overall survival is uncertain. Ursodeoxycholic acid has also been tried in primary sclerosing cholangitis [unlicensed indication].

#### URSODEOXYCHOLIC ACID

**Indications** see under Dose and under preparations

**Cautions** see notes above; **interactions:** Appendix 1 (ursodeoxycholic acid)

**Contra-indications** radio-opaque stones, pregnancy (Appendix 4), non-functioning gall bladder, inflammatory diseases and other conditions of the small intestine, colon and liver which interfere with entero-hepatic circulation of bile salts

**Side-effects** nausea, vomiting, diarrhoea; gallstone calcification; pruritus

**Dose**

- Dissolution of gallstones, 8–12 mg/kg daily as a single dose at bedtime *or* in two divided doses, for up to 2 years; treatment is continued for 3–4 months after stones dissolve
- Primary biliary cirrhosis, see under *Ursofalk®*

1 Gastro-intestinal system

**Ursodeoxycholic Acid** (Non-proprietary) PoM
Tablets, ursodeoxycholic acid 150 mg, net price 60-tab pack = £18.51. Label: 21
Capsules, ursodeoxycholic acid 250 mg, net price 60-cap pack = £35.11. Label: 21

**Destolit®** (Norgine) PoM
Tablets, scored, ursodeoxycholic acid 150 mg, net price 60-tab pack = £18.39. Label: 21

**Urdox®** (CP) PoM
Tablets, f/c, ursodeoxycholic acid 300 mg, net price 60-tab pack = £30.24. Label: 21

**Ursofalk®** (Dr Falk) PoM
Capsules, ursodeoxycholic acid 250 mg, net price 60-cap pack = £31.10, 100-cap pack = £32.85. Label: 21
Suspension, sugar-free, ursodeoxycholic acid 250 mg/5 mL, net price 250 mL = £28.50. Label: 21
Dose primary biliary cirrhosis, 10–15 mg/kg daily in 2–4 divided doses
Dissolution of gallstones, see Dose, above

**Ursogal®** (Galen) PoM
Tablets, scored, ursodeoxycholic acid 150 mg, net price 60-tab pack = £17.05. Label: 21
Capsules, ursodeoxycholic acid 250 mg, net price 60-cap pack = £30.50. Label: 21

## Other preparations for biliary disorders

A **terpene** mixture (*Rowachol®*) raises biliary cholesterol solubility. It is not considered to be a useful adjunct.

**Rowachol®** (Rowa) PoM
Capsules, green, e/c, borneol 5 mg, camphene 5 mg, cineole 2 mg, menthol 32 mg, menthone 6 mg, pinene 17 mg in olive oil. Net price 50-cap pack = £7.35. Label: 22
Dose 1–2 capsules 3 times daily before food (but see notes above)
**Interactions:** Appendix 1 (*Rowachol®*)

## 1.9.2 Bile acid sequestrants

**Colestyramine** (cholestyramine) is an anion-exchange resin that is not absorbed from the gastro-intestinal tract. It relieves diarrhoea and pruritus by forming an insoluble complex with bile acids in the intestine. Colestyramine can interfere with the absorption of a number of drugs. Colestyramine is also used in hypercholesterolaemia (section 2.12).

### COLESTYRAMINE
(Cholestyramine)

**Indications** pruritus associated with partial biliary obstruction and primary biliary cirrhosis; diarrhoea associated with Crohn's disease, ileal resection, vagotomy, diabetic vagal neuropathy, and radiation; hypercholesterolaemia (section 2.12)
**Cautions** see section 2.12
**Contra-indications** see section 2.12
**Side-effects** see section 2.12
**Dose**
- Pruritus, 4–8 g daily in water (or other suitable liquid)
- Diarrhoea, after initial introduction over 3–4 week period, 12–24 g daily mixed with water (or other suitable liquid) in 1–4 divided doses, then adjusted as required; max. 36 g daily
- CHILD 6–12 years, consult product literature

**Counselling** Other drugs should be taken at least 1 hour before or 4–6 hours after colestyramine to reduce possible interference with absorption

**Preparations**
Section 2.12

## 1.9.3 Aprotinin

Section 2.11.

## 1.9.4 Pancreatin

Supplements of pancreatin are given by mouth to compensate for reduced or absent exocrine secretion in cystic fibrosis, and following pancreatectomy, gastrectomy, or chronic pancreatitis. They assist the digestion of starch, fat, and protein. Pancreatin may also be necessary if a tumour (e.g. pancreatic cancer) obstructs outflow from the pancreas.

Pancreatin is inactivated by gastric acid therefore pancreatin preparations are best taken with food (or immediately before or after food). Gastric acid secretion may be reduced by giving cimetidine or ranitidine an hour beforehand (section 1.3). Concurrent use of antacids also reduces gastric acidity. Enteric-coated preparations deliver a higher enzyme concentration in the duodenum (provided the capsule contents are swallowed whole without chewing). Higher-strength versions are also available (**important**: see CSM advice below).

Since pancreatin is also inactivated by heat, excessive heat should be avoided if preparations are mixed with liquids or food; the resulting mixtures should not be kept for more than one hour.

Dosage is adjusted according to size, number, and consistency of stools, so that the patient thrives; extra allowance may be needed if snacks are taken between meals.

Pancreatin can irritate the perioral skin and buccal mucosa if retained in the mouth, and excessive doses can cause perianal irritation. The most frequent side-effects are gastro-intestinal, including nausea, vomiting, and abdominal discomfort; hyperuricaemia and hyperuricosuria have been associated with very high doses. Hypersensitivity reactions occur occasionally and may affect those handling the powder.

### PANCREATIN

Note The pancreatin preparations which follow are all of porcine origin

**Indications** see also above
**Cautions** see also above and (for higher-strength preparations) see below
**Side-effects** see also above and (for higher-strength preparations) see below
**Dose**
- See preparations

**Creon® 10 000** (Solvay)
Capsules, brown/clear, enclosing buff-coloured e/c granules of pancreatin, providing: protease 600 units,

lipase 10 000 units, amylase 8000 units. Net price 100-cap pack = £16.66. Counselling, see dose

Dose ADULT and CHILD initially 1–2 capsules with meals either taken whole or contents mixed with fluid or soft food (then swallowed immediately without chewing)

**Creon® Micro** (Solvay)

Gastro-resistant granules, brown, pancreatin, providing: protease 2000 units, lipase 50 000 units, amylase 36 000 units/g, net price 20 g = £31.50 Counselling, see dose

Dose ADULT and CHILD initially 100 mg with meals either taken whole or mixed with acidic fluid or soft food (then swallowed immediately without chewing)

**Nutrizym 10®** (Merck)

Capsules, red/yellow, enclosing e/c minitablets of pancreatin providing minimum of: protease 500 units, lipase 10 000 units, amylase 9000 units. Net price 100 = £14.47. Counselling, see dose

Dose ADULT and CHILD 1–2 capsules with meals and 1 capsule with snacks, swallowed whole or contents taken with water or sprinkled on soft food (then swallowed immediately without chewing); higher doses may be required according to response

**Pancrease®** (Janssen-Cilag)

Capsules, enclosing e/c beads of pancrelipase USP, providing minimum of: protease 330 units, lipase 5000 units, amylase 2900 units. Net price 100 = £16.22. Counselling, see dose

Dose ADULT and CHILD 1–2 (occasionally 3) capsules during each meal and 1 capsule with snacks swallowed whole or contents sprinkled on liquid or soft food (then swallowed immediately without chewing); higher doses may be required according to response

**Pancrex®** (Paines & Byrne)

Granules, pancreatin, providing minimum of: protease 300 units, lipase 5000 units, amylase 4000 units/g. Net price 300 g = £20.39. Label: 25, counselling, see dose

Dose ADULT and CHILD 5–10 g just before meals washed down or mixed with liquid

**Pancrex V®** (Paines & Byrne)

Capsules, pancreatin, providing minimum of: protease 430 units, lipase 8000 units, amylase 9000 units. Net price 300-cap pack = £15.80. Counselling, see dose

Dose ADULT and CHILD over 1 year 2–6 capsules with meals, swallowed whole or sprinkled on food; INFANT up to 1 year 1–2 capsules mixed with feeds

Capsules '125', pancreatin, providing minimum of: protease 160 units, lipase 2950 units, amylase 3300 units. Net price 300-cap pack = £9.72. Counselling, see dose

Dose NEONATE 1–2 capsules with feeds

Tablets, e/c, pancreatin, providing minimum of: protease 110 units, lipase 1900 units, amylase 1700 units. Net price 300-tab pack = £4.51. Label: 5, 25, counselling, see dose

Dose ADULT and CHILD 5–15 tablets before meals

Tablets forte, e/c, pancreatin, providing minimum of: protease 330 units, lipase 5600 units, amylase 5000 units. Net price 300-tab pack = £13.74. Label: 5, 25, counselling, see dose

Dose ADULT and CHILD 6–10 tablets before meals

Powder, pancreatin, providing minimum of: protease 1400 units, lipase 25 000 units, amylase 30 000 units/g. Net price 300 g = £24.28. Counselling, see dose

Dose ADULT and CHILD 0.5–2 g with meals washed down or mixed with liquid; NEONATE 250–500 mg with each feed

**Higher-strength preparations**

The **CSM** has advised of data associating the high-strength pancreatin preparations *Nutrizym 22®* and *Pancreatin HL®* with the development of large bowel strictures (fibrosing colonopathy) in children with cystic fibrosis aged between 2 and 13 years. No association was found with *Creon® 25 000*. The following was recommended:

- *Pancrease HL®*, *Nutrizym 22®*, *Panzytrat® 25 000* [now discontinued] should not be used in children aged 15 years or less with cystic fibrosis;
- the total dose of pancreatic enzyme supplements used in patients with cystic fibrosis should not usually exceed 10 000 units of lipase per kg body-weight daily;
- if a patient on any pancreatin preparation develops new abdominal symptoms (or any change in existing abdominal symptoms) the patient should be reviewed to exclude the possibility of colonic damage.

Possible risk factors are gender (boys at greater risk than girls), more severe cystic fibrosis, and concomitant use of laxatives. The peak age for developing fibrosing colonopathy is between 2 and 8 years.

Counselling It is important to ensure adequate hydration at all times in patients receiving higher-strength pancreatin preparations.

**Creon® 25 000** (Solvay) PoM

Capsules, orange/clear, enclosing brown-coloured e/c pellets of pancreatin, providing: protease (total) 1000 units, lipase 25 000 units, amylase 18 000 units, net price 100-cap pack = £30.03. Counselling, see above and under dose

Dose ADULT and CHILD initially 1 capsule with meals either taken whole or contents mixed with fluid or soft food (then swallowed immediately without chewing)

**Creon® 40 000** (Solvay) PoM

Capsules, brown/clear, enclosing brown-coloured e/c granules of pancreatin, providing: protease (total) 1600 units, lipase 40 000 units, amylase 25 000 units, net price 100-cap pack = £60.00. Counselling, see above and under dose

Dose ADULT and CHILD initially 1–2 capsules with meals either taken whole or contents mixed with fluid or soft food (then swallowed immediately without chewing)

**Nutrizym 22®** (Merck) PoM

Capsules, red/yellow, enclosing e/c minitablets of pancreatin, providing minimum of: protease 1100 units, lipase 22 000 units, amylase 19 800 units. Net price 100-cap pack = £33.33. Counselling, see above and under dose

Dose 1–2 capsules with meals and 1 capsule with snacks, swallowed whole or contents taken with water or sprinkled on soft food (then swallowed immediately without chewing)

CHILD under 15 years not recommended

**Pancrease HL®** (Janssen-Cilag) PoM

Capsules, enclosing light brown e/c minitablets of pancreatin, providing minimum of: protease 1250 units, lipase 25 000 units, amylase 22 500 units. Net price 100 = £34.37. Counselling, see above and under dose

Dose 1–2 capsules during each meal and 1 capsule with snacks swallowed whole or contents sprinkled on liquid or soft food (then swallowed immediately without chewing)

CHILD under 15 years not recommended

# 2 Cardiovascular system


**2.1 Positive inotropic drugs** 69
2.1.1 Cardiac glycosides 69
2.1.2 Phosphodiesterase inhibitors 71
**2.2 Diuretics** 71
2.2.1 Thiazides and related diuretics 72
2.2.2 Loop diuretics 73
2.2.3 Potassium-sparing diuretics and aldosterone antagonists 74
2.2.4 Potassium-sparing diuretics with other diuretics 76
2.2.5 Osmotic diuretics 77
2.2.6 Mercurial diuretics 77
2.2.7 Carbonic anhydrase inhibitors 77
2.2.8 Diuretics with potassium 77
**2.3 Anti-arrhythmic drugs** 77
2.3.1 Management of arrhythmias 77
2.3.2 Drugs for arrhythmias 78
**2.4 Beta-adrenoceptor blocking drugs** 83
**2.5 Hypertension and heart failure** 90
2.5.1 Vasodilator antihypertensive drugs 92
2.5.2 Centrally acting antihypertensive drugs 94
2.5.3 Adrenergic neurone blocking drugs 95
2.5.4 Alpha-adrenoceptor blocking drugs 95
2.5.5 Drugs affecting the renin-angiotensin system 97
2.5.5.1 Angiotensin-converting enzyme inhibitors 97
2.5.5.2 Angiotensin-II receptor antagonists 103
**2.6 Nitrates, calcium-channel blockers, and other antianginal drugs** 105
2.6.1 Nitrates 105
2.6.2 Calcium-channel blockers 109
2.6.3 Other antianginal drugs 115
2.6.4 Peripheral vasodilators and related drugs 115
**2.7 Sympathomimetics** 117
2.7.1 Inotropic sympathomimetics 117
2.7.2 Vasoconstrictor sympathomimetics 118
2.7.3 Cardiopulmonary resuscitation 119
**2.8 Anticoagulants and protamine** 119
2.8.1 Parenteral anticoagulants 119
2.8.2 Oral anticoagulants 124
2.8.3 Protamine sulphate 125
**2.9 Antiplatelet drugs** 126
**2.10 Myocardial infarction and fibrinolysis** 129
2.10.1 Management of myocardial infarction 129
2.10.2 Fibrinolytic drugs 129
**2.11 Antifibrinolytic drugs and haemostatics** 131
**2.12 Lipid-regulating drugs** 133
**2.13 Local sclerosants** 139


This chapter includes advice on the drug management of the following:


- angina, p. 105
- arrhythmias, p. 77
- cardiovascular disease risk, p. 90 and p. 133
- heart failure, p. 97
- hypertension, p. 90
- myocardial infarction, p. 129


## 2.1 Positive inotropic drugs

**2.1.1 Cardiac glycosides**
**2.1.2 Phosphodiesterase inhibitors**

Positive inotropic drugs increase the force of contraction of the myocardium; for sympathomimetics with inotropic activity see section 2.7.1.

### 2.1.1 Cardiac glycosides

Cardiac glycosides increase the force of myocardial contraction and reduce conductivity within the atrioventricular (AV) node. Digoxin is the most commonly used cardiac glycoside.

Cardiac glycosides are most useful in the treatment of supraventricular tachycardias, especially for controlling ventricular response in persistent atrial fibrillation (section 2.3.1). For reference to the role of digoxin in heart failure, see section 2.5.5.

For management of atrial fibrillation the maintenance dose of the cardiac glycoside can usually be determined by the ventricular rate at rest which should not be allowed to fall below 60 beats per minute except in special circumstances, e.g. with the concomitant administration of a beta-blocker.

Digoxin is now rarely used for rapid control of heart rate (see section 2.3 for the management of supraventricular arrhythmias). Even with intravenous administration, response may take many hours; persistence of tachycardia is therefore not an indication for exceeding the recommended dose. The intramuscular route is **not** recommended.

In patients with mild heart failure a loading dose is not required, and a satisfactory plasma-digoxin concentration can be achieved over a period of about a week, using a dose of digoxin 125 to 250 micrograms twice a day which is then reduced.

Digoxin has a long half-life and maintenance doses need to be given only once daily (although higher doses may be divided to avoid nausea). **Digitoxin** also has a long half-life and maintenance doses need to be given only once daily or on alternate days. Renal function is the most important determinant of digoxin dosage, whereas elimination of digitoxin depends on metabolism by the liver.

Unwanted effects depend both on the concentration of the cardiac glycoside in the plasma and on the sensitivity of the conducting system or of the myocardium, which is often increased in heart disease. It may sometimes be difficult to distinguish between toxic effects and clinical deterioration because symptoms of both are similar. Also, the plasma concentration alone cannot indicate toxicity reliably but the likelihood of toxicity increases progressively through the range 1.5 to 3 micrograms/litre for digoxin. Cardiac glycosides should be used with special care in the elderly who may be particularly susceptible to digitalis toxicity.

Regular monitoring of plasma-digoxin concentration during maintenance treatment is not necessary unless problems are suspected. Hypokalaemia predisposes the patient to digitalis toxicity; it is managed by giving a potassium sparing diuretic or, if necessary, potassium supplementation.

Toxicity can often be managed by discontinuing digoxin; serious manifestations require urgent specialist management. **Digoxin-specific antibody fragments** are available for reversal of life-threatening overdosage (see below).

**Children** The dose is based on body-weight; children require a relatively larger dose of digoxin than adults.

## DIGOXIN

**Indications** heart failure (see also section 2.5.5), supraventricular arrhythmias (particularly atrial fibrillation; see also section 2.3.2)

**Cautions** recent infarction; sick sinus syndrome; thyroid disease; reduce dose in the elderly; avoid hypokalaemia or hypomagnesaemia (risk of digitalis toxicity); avoid rapid intravenous administration (nausea and risk of arrhythmias); renal impairment (Appendix 3); pregnancy (Appendix 4); **interactions:** Appendix 1 (cardiac glycosides)

**Contra-indications** intermittent complete heart block, second degree AV block; supraventricular arrhythmias caused by Wolff-Parkinson-White syndrome; ventricular tachycardia or fibrillation; hypertrophic obstructive cardiomyopathy (unless concomitant atrial fibrillation and heart failure—but with caution)

**Side-effects** usually associated with excessive dosage, include: anorexia, nausea, vomiting, diarrhoea, abdominal pain; visual disturbances, headache, fatigue, drowsiness, confusion, dizziness, delirium, hallucinations, depression; arrhythmias, heart block; rarely rash, intestinal ischaemia; gynaecomastia on long-term use; thrombocytopenia reported; see also notes above

**Dose**

- Rapid digitalisation, by mouth, 1–1.5 mg in divided doses over 24 hours; less urgent digitalisation, 250–500 micrograms daily (higher dose may be divided)
- Maintenance, by mouth, 62.5–500 micrograms daily (higher dose may be divided) according to renal function and, in atrial fibrillation, on heart-rate response; usual range, 125–250 micrograms daily (lower dose may be appropriate in elderly)
- Emergency loading dose by intravenous infusion, 0.75–1 mg over at least 2 hours (see also Cautions) then maintenance dose by mouth on the following day

**Note** The above doses may need to be reduced if digoxin (or another cardiac glycoside) has been given in the preceding 2 weeks. Digoxin doses in the BNF may differ from those in product literature. For plasma concentration monitoring, blood should ideally be taken at least 6 hours after a dose

**Digoxin** (Non-proprietary) PoM

Tablets, digoxin 62.5 micrograms, net price 20 = 94p; 125 micrograms, 20 = £1.19; 250 micrograms, 20 = £1.08

Injection, digoxin 250 micrograms/mL, net price 2-mL amp = 70p

Available from Antigen

Paediatric injection, digoxin 100 micrograms/mL

'Special order' [unlicensed] product

**Lanoxin®** (GSK) PoM

Tablets, digoxin 125 micrograms, net price 20 = 32p; 250 micrograms (scored), 20 = 32p

Injection, digoxin 250 micrograms/mL. Net price 2-mL amp = 66p

**Lanoxin-PG®** (GSK) PoM

Tablets, blue, digoxin 62.5 micrograms. Net price 20 = 32p

Elixir, yellow, digoxin 50 micrograms/mL. Do not dilute, measure with pipette. Net price 60 mL = £5.35. Counselling, use of pipette

## DIGITOXIN

**Indications** heart failure, supraventricular arrhythmias (particularly atrial fibrillation)

**Cautions** see under Digoxin; renal impairment (Appendix 3)

**Contra-indications** see under Digoxin

**Side-effects** see under Digoxin

**Dose**

- Maintenance, 100 micrograms daily *or* on alternate days; may be increased to 200 micrograms daily if necessary

**Digitoxin** (Non-proprietary) PoM

Tablets, digitoxin 100 micrograms, net price 20 = £2.66

## Digoxin-specific antibody

**Digoxin-specific antibody fragments** are indicated for the treatment of known or strongly suspected digoxin or digitoxin overdosage, where measures beyond the withdrawal of the cardiac glycoside and correction of any electrolyte abnormality are felt to be necessary (see also notes above).

**Digibind®** (GSK) PoM
Injection, powder for preparation of infusion, digoxin-specific antibody fragments (F(ab)) 38 mg. Net price per vial = £93.97 (hosp. and poisons centres only)
Dose consult product literature

## 2.1.2 Phosphodiesterase inhibitors

**Enoximone** and **milrinone** are selective phosphodiesterase inhibitors which exert most of their effect on the myocardium. Sustained haemodynamic benefit has been observed after administration, but there is no evidence of any beneficial effect on survival.

### ENOXIMONE

**Indications** congestive heart failure where cardiac output reduced and filling pressures increased

**Cautions** heart failure associated with hypertrophic cardiomyopathy, stenotic or obstructive valvular disease or other outlet obstruction; monitor blood pressure, heart rate, ECG, central venous pressure, fluid and electrolyte status, renal function, platelet count, hepatic enzymes; avoid extravasation; renal impairment (Appendix 3); pregnancy (Appendix 4); breast-feeding (Appendix 5)

**Side-effects** ectopic beats; less frequently ventricular tachycardia or supraventricular arrhythmias (more likely in patients with pre-existing arrhythmias); hypotension; also headache, insomnia, nausea and vomiting, diarrhoea; occasionally, chills, oliguria, fever, urinary retention; upper and lower limb pain

**Dose**

- By slow intravenous injection (rate not exceeding 12.5 mg/minute), diluted before use, initially 0.5–1 mg/kg, then 500 micrograms/kg every 30 minutes until satisfactory response or total of 3 mg/kg given; maintenance, initial dose of up to 3 mg/kg may be repeated every 3–6 hours as required
- By intravenous infusion, initially 90 micrograms/kg/minute over 10–30 minutes, followed by continuous or intermittent infusion of 5–20 micrograms/kg/minute

Total dose over 24 hours should not usually exceed 24 mg/kg

**Perfan®** (Myogen) PoM
Injection, enoximone 5 mg/mL. For dilution before use. Net price 20-mL amp = £15.02
Excipients include alcohol, propylene glycol
Note Plastic apparatus should be used; crystal formation if glass used

### MILRINONE

**Indications** short-term treatment of severe congestive heart failure unresponsive to conventional maintenance therapy (not immediately after myocardial infarction); acute heart failure, including low output states, following heart surgery

**Cautions** see under Enoximone; also correct hypokalaemia, monitor renal function; renal impairment (Appendix 3); pregnancy (Appendix 4); breast-feeding (Appendix 5)

**Side-effects** see under Enoximone; also chest pain, tremor, bronchospasm, anaphylaxis and rash reported

**Dose**

- By intravenous injection over 10 minutes, diluted before use, 50 micrograms/kg followed by intravenous infusion at a rate of 375–750 nanograms/kg/minute, usually for up to 12 hours following surgery or for 48–72 hours in congestive heart failure; max. daily dose 1.13 mg/kg

**Primacor®** (Sanofi-Synthelabo) PoM
Injection, milrinone (as lactate) 1 mg/mL. For dilution before use. Net price 10-mL amp = £16.61

## 2.2 Diuretics


2.2.1 Thiazides and related diuretics
2.2.2 Loop diuretics
2.2.3 Potassium-sparing diuretics and aldosterone antagonists
2.2.4 Potassium-sparing diuretics with other diuretics
2.2.5 Osmotic diuretics
2.2.6 Mercurial diuretics
2.2.7 Carbonic anhydrase inhibitors
2.2.8 Diuretics with potassium


**Thiazides** (section 2.2.1) are used to relieve oedema due to chronic heart failure (section 2.5.5) and, in lower doses, to reduce blood pressure.

**Loop diuretics** (section 2.2.2) are used in pulmonary oedema due to left ventricular failure and in patients with chronic heart failure (section 2.5.5).

**Combination diuretic therapy** may be effective in patients with oedema resistant to treatment with one diuretic. Vigorous diuresis, particularly with loop diuretics, may induce acute hypotension; rapid reduction of plasma volume should be avoided.

**Elderly** Lower initial doses of diuretics should be used in the elderly because they are particularly susceptible to the side-effects. The dose should then be adjusted according to renal function. Diuretics should not be used continuously on a long-term basis to treat simple gravitational oedema (which will usually respond to increased movement, raising the legs, and support stockings).

**Potassium loss** Hypokalaemia may occur with both thiazide and loop diuretics. The risk of hypokalaemia depends on the duration of action as well as the potency and is thus greater with thiazides than with an equipotent dose of a loop diuretic.

Hypokalaemia is dangerous in severe coronary artery disease and in patients also being treated with cardiac glycosides. Often the use of potassium-sparing diuretics (section 2.2.3) avoids the need to take potassium supplements.

In hepatic failure, hypokalaemia caused by diuretics can precipitate encephalopathy, particularly in alcoholic cirrhosis; diuretics may also increase the risk of hypomagnesaemia in alcoholic cirrhosis, leading to arrhythmias. Spironolactone, a potassium-sparing diuretic (section 2.2.3), is chosen for oedema arising from cirrhosis of the liver.

Potassium supplements or potassium-sparing diuretics are seldom necessary when thiazides are used in the routine treatment of hypertension (see also section 9.2.1.1).

## 2.2.1 Thiazides and related diuretics

Thiazides and related compounds are moderately potent diuretics; they inhibit sodium reabsorption at the beginning of the distal convoluted tubule. They act within 1 to 2 hours of oral administration and most have a duration of action of 12 to 24 hours; they are usually administered early in the day so that the diuresis does not interfere with sleep.

In the management of *hypertension* a low dose of a thiazide, e.g. bendroflumethiazide (bendrofluazide) 2.5 mg daily, produces a maximal or near-maximal blood pressure lowering effect, with very little biochemical disturbance. Higher doses cause more marked changes in plasma potassium, sodium, uric acid, glucose, and lipids, with little advantage in blood pressure control. For reference to the use of thiazides in chronic heart failure see section 2.5.5.

**Bendroflumethiazide** (bendrofluazide) is widely used for mild or moderate heart failure and for hypertension—alone in the treatment of mild hypertension or with other drugs in more severe hypertension.

**Chlortalidone** (chlorthalidone), a thiazide-related compound, has a longer duration of action than the thiazides and may be given on alternate days to control oedema. It is also useful if acute retention is liable to be precipitated by a more rapid diuresis or if patients dislike the altered pattern of micturition promoted by other diuretics.

Other thiazide diuretics (including benzthiazide, clopamide, cyclopenthiazide, hydrochlorothiazide and hydroflumethiazide) do not offer any significant advantage over bendroflumethiazide and chlortalidone.

**Metolazone** is particularly effective when combined with a loop diuretic (even in renal failure); profound diuresis may occur and the patient should therefore be monitored carefully.

**Xipamide** and **indapamide** are chemically related to chlortalidone. Indapamide is claimed to lower blood pressure with less metabolic disturbance, particularly less aggravation of diabetes mellitus.

### BENDROFLUMETHIAZIDE
(Bendrofluazide)

**Indications** oedema, hypertension (see also notes above)

**Cautions** electrolytes may need to be monitored with high doses or in renal impairment, aggravates diabetes and gout; may exacerbate systemic lupus erythematosus; see also notes above; hepatic impairment (Appendix 2); renal impairment (Appendix 3); pregnancy (Appendix 4); breast-feeding (Appendix 5); **interactions:** Appendix 1 (diuretics)

**Contra-indications** refractory hypokalaemia, hyponatraemia, hypercalcaemia; severe renal and hepatic impairment; symptomatic hyperuricaemia; Addison's disease

**Side-effects** postural hypotension and mild gastro-intestinal effects; impotence (reversible on withdrawal of treatment); hypokalaemia (see also notes above), hypomagnesaemia, hyponatraemia, hypercalcaemia, hypochloraemic alkalosis, hyperuricaemia, gout, hyperglycaemia, and altered plasma lipid concentration; less commonly rashes, photosensitivity; blood disorders (including neutropenia and thrombocytopenia—when given in late pregnancy neonatal thrombocytopenia has been reported); pancreatitis, intrahepatic cholestasis, and hypersensitivity reactions (including pneumonitis, pulmonary oedema, severe skin reactions) also reported

**Dose**
- Oedema, initially 5–10 mg in the morning, daily *or* on alternate days; maintenance 5–10 mg 1–3 times weekly
- Hypertension, 2.5 mg in the morning; higher doses rarely necessary (see notes above)

**Bendroflumethiazide** (Non-proprietary) PoM
Tablets, bendroflumethiazide 2.5 mg, net price 20 = 83p; 5 mg, 20 = 59p
Brands include *Aprinox®*, *Neo-NaClex®*

### CHLORTALIDONE
(Chlorthalidone)

**Indications** ascites due to cirrhosis in stable patients (under close supervision), oedema due to nephrotic syndrome, hypertension (see also notes above), mild to moderate chronic heart failure; diabetes insipidus (see section 6.5.2)

**Cautions** see under Bendroflumethiazide

**Contra-indications** see under Bendroflumethiazide

**Side-effects** see under Bendroflumethiazide; also dizziness; *rarely* jaundice, cardiac arrhythmias, headache, paraesthesia, eosinophilia, and allergic interstitial nephritis

**Dose**
- Oedema, up to 50 mg daily for limited period
- Hypertension, 25 mg in the morning, increased to 50 mg if necessary (but see notes above)
- Heart failure, 25–50 mg in the morning, increased if necessary to 100–200 mg daily (reduce to lowest effective dose for maintenance)

**Hygroton®** (Alliance) PoM
Tablets, yellow, scored, chlortalidone 50 mg, net price 28-tab pack = £1.64

### CYCLOPENTHIAZIDE

**Indications** oedema, hypertension (see also notes above)

**Cautions** see under Bendroflumethiazide

**Contra-indications** see under Bendroflumethiazide

**Side-effects** see under Bendroflumethiazide

**Dose**
- Heart failure, 250–500 micrograms daily in the morning increased if necessary to 1 mg daily (reduce to lowest effective dose for maintenance)
- Hypertension, initially 250 micrograms daily in the

morning, increased if necessary to 500 micrograms daily (but see notes above)
- Oedema, up to 500 micrograms daily for a short period

**Navidrex®** (Goldshield) PoM
Tablets, scored, cyclopenthiazide 500 micrograms. Net price 28-tab pack = £1.27
Excipients include gluten

## INDAPAMIDE

**Indications** essential hypertension

**Cautions** monitor plasma potassium and urate concentrations in elderly, hyperaldosteronism, gout, or with concomitant cardiac glycosides; hyperparathyroidism (discontinue if hypercalcaemia); porphyria (section 9.8.2); hepatic impairment (Appendix 2); renal impairment (Appendix 3—stop if deterioration); pregnancy (Appendix 4); breast-feeding (Appendix 5); **interactions:** Appendix 1 (diuretics)

**Contra-indications** severe hepatic impairment

**Side-effects** hypokalaemia, headache, dizziness, fatigue, muscular cramps, nausea, anorexia, diarrhoea, constipation, dyspepsia, rashes (erythema multiforme, epidermal necrolysis reported); rarely postural hypotension, palpitation, increase in liver enzymes, blood disorders (including thrombocytopenia), hyponatraemia, metabolic alkalosis, hyperglycaemia, increased plasma urate concentrations, paraesthesia, photosensitivity, impotence, renal impairment, reversible acute myopia; diuresis with doses above 2.5 mg daily

**Dose**
- 2.5 mg in the morning

**Indapamide** (Non-proprietary) PoM
Tablets, s/c, indapamide 2.5 mg, net price 28-tab pack = £3.34, 56-tab pack = £5.53
Brands include *Nindaxa 2.5®*

**Natrilix®** (Servier) PoM
Tablets, f/c, indapamide 2.5 mg. Net price 30-tab pack = £4.50, 60-tab pack = £9.00

**Modified release**

**Natrilix SR®** (Servier) PoM
Tablets, m/r, indapamide 1.5 mg. Net price 30-tab pack = £4.50. Label: 25
Dose hypertension, 1 tablet daily, preferably in the morning

## METOLAZONE

**Indications** oedema, hypertension (see also notes above)

**Cautions** see under Bendroflumethiazide; also profound diuresis on concomitant administration with furosemide (monitor patient carefully); porphyria (section 9.8.2)

**Contra-indications** see under Bendroflumethiazide

**Side-effects** see under Bendroflumethiazide

**Dose**
- Oedema, 5–10 mg in the morning, increased if necessary to 20 mg daily in resistant oedema, max. 80 mg daily
- Hypertension, initially 5 mg in the morning; maintenance 5 mg on alternate days

**Metenix 5®** (Borg) PoM
Tablets, blue, metolazone 5 mg. Net price 100-tab pack = £18.94

## XIPAMIDE

**Indications** oedema, hypertension (see also notes above)

**Cautions** see under Bendroflumethiazide; also porphyria (section 9.8.2)

**Contra-indications** see under Bendroflumethiazide

**Side-effects** gastro-intestinal disturbances; mild dizziness; hypokalaemia, more rarely other electrolyte disturbances such as hyponatraemia

**Dose**
- Oedema, initially 40 mg in the morning, increased to 80 mg in resistant cases; maintenance 20 mg in the morning
- Hypertension, 20 mg in the morning

**Diurexan®** (Viatris) PoM
Tablets, scored, xipamide 20 mg. Net price 140-tab pack = £19.46

# 2.2.2 Loop diuretics

Loop diuretics are used in pulmonary oedema due to left ventricular failure; intravenous administration produces relief of breathlessness and reduces pre-load sooner than would be expected from the time of onset of diuresis. Loop diuretics are also used in patients with chronic heart failure. Diuretic-resistant oedema (except lymphoedema and oedema due to peripheral venous stasis or calcium-channel blockers) can be treated with a loop diuretic combined with a thiazide or related diuretic (e.g. bendroflumethiazide 5–10 mg daily or metolazone 5–20 mg daily).

A loop diuretic is sometimes used to lower blood pressure especially in hypertension resistant to thiazide therapy.

Loop diuretics inhibit reabsorption from the ascending limb of the loop of Henlé in the renal tubule and are powerful diuretics. Hypokalaemia may develop, and care is needed to avoid hypotension. If there is an enlarged prostate, urinary retention may occur; this is less likely if small doses and less potent diuretics are used initially.

**Furosemide** (frusemide) and **bumetanide** are similar in activity; both act within 1 hour of oral administration and diuresis is complete within 6 hours so that, if necessary, they can be given twice in one day without interfering with sleep. Following intravenous administration they have a peak effect within 30 minutes. The diuresis associated with these drugs is dose related. In patients with impaired renal function very large doses may occasionally be needed; in such doses both drugs can cause deafness and bumetanide can cause myalgia.

**Torasemide** has properties similar to those of furosemide and bumetanide, and is indicated for oedema and for hypertension.

## FUROSEMIDE
(Frusemide)

**Indications** oedema (see notes above), oliguria due to renal failure

**Cautions** hypotension; correct hypovolaemia before using in oliguria; prostatic enlargement; although manufacturer advises that rate of intravenous administration should not exceed 4 mg/minute, single doses of up to 80 mg may be administered more rapidly; hepatic impairment (Appendix 2); renal impairment (Appendix 3); pregnancy (Appendix 4); **interactions:** Appendix 1 (diuretics)

**Contra-indications** precomatose states associated with liver cirrhosis; renal failure with anuria

**Side-effects** hyponatraemia, hypokalaemia, and hypomagnesaemia (see also section 2.2), hypochloraemic alkalosis, increased calcium excretion, hypotension; less commonly nausea, gastro-intestinal disturbances, hyperuricaemia and gout; hyperglycaemia (less common than with thiazides); temporary increase in plasma cholesterol and triglyceride concentrations; rarely rashes, photosensitivity and bone marrow depression (withdraw treatment), pancreatitis (with large parenteral doses), tinnitus and deafness (usually with large parenteral doses and rapid administration and in renal impairment)

**Dose**

- By mouth, oedema, initially 40 mg in the morning; maintenance 20–40 mg daily, increased in resistant oedema to 80 mg daily or more; CHILD 1–3 mg/kg daily, max. 40 mg daily

  Oliguria, initially 250 mg daily; if necessary larger doses, increasing in steps of 250 mg, may be given every 4–6 hours to a max. of a single dose of 2 g (rarely used)
- By intramuscular injection *or* slow intravenous injection (see Cautions, above), initially 20–50 mg; CHILD 0.5–1.5 mg/kg to a max. daily dose of 20 mg
- By intravenous infusion (by syringe pump if necessary), in oliguria, initially 250 mg over 1 hour (rate not exceeding 4 mg/minute), if satisfactory urine output not obtained in the subsequent hour further 500 mg over 2 hours, then if no satisfactory response within subsequent hour, further 1 g over 4 hours, if no response obtained dialysis probably required; effective dose (up to 1 g) can be repeated every 24 hours

**Furosemide** (Non-proprietary) PoM

Tablets, furosemide 20 mg, net price 28 = 93p; 40 mg, 28-tab pack = £1.05; 500 mg, 28 = £7.72
Brands include *Froop®*, *Frusid®*, *Rusyde®*

Oral solution, sugar-free, furosemide, net price 20 mg/5 mL, 150 mL = £12.07; 40 mg/5 mL, 150 mL = £15.58; 50 mg/5 mL, 150 mL = £16.84
Brands include *Frusol®* (contains alcohol 10%)

Injection, furosemide 10 mg/mL, net price 2-mL amp = 55p; 5-mL amp = 66p

**Lasix®** (Sanofi-Aventis) PoM

Injection, furosemide 10 mg/mL, net price 2-mL amp = 78p

**Note** Large-volume furosemide injections also available; brands include *Minijet®*

## BUMETANIDE

**Indications** oedema (see notes above), oliguria due to renal failure

**Cautions** see under Furosemide; hepatic impairment (Appendix 2); renal impairment (Appendix 3); pregnancy (Appendix 4); breast-feeding (Appendix 5)

**Contra-indications** see under Furosemide

**Side-effects** see under Furosemide; also myalgia

**Dose**

- By mouth, 1 mg in the morning, repeated after 6–8 hours if necessary; severe cases, increased up to 5 mg or more daily; ELDERLY, 500 micrograms daily may be sufficient
- By intravenous injection, 1–2 mg, repeated after 20 minutes; when intramuscular injection considered necessary, 1 mg initially then adjusted according to response
- By intravenous infusion, 2–5 mg over 30–60 minutes

**Bumetanide** (Non-proprietary) PoM

Tablets, bumetanide 1 mg, net price 28-tab pack = £1.42; 5 mg, 28-tab pack = £2.46

Liquid, bumetanide 1 mg/5 mL, net price 150 mL = £15.22

Injection, bumetanide 500 micrograms/mL, net price 4-mL amp = £1.79

**Burinex®** (LEO) PoM

Tablets, both scored, bumetanide 1 mg, net price 28-tab pack = £1.52; 5 mg, 28 = £9.67

## TORASEMIDE

**Indications** oedema (see notes above), hypertension

**Cautions** see under Furosemide; hepatic impairment (Appendix 2); renal impairment (Appendix 3); pregnancy (Appendix 4)

**Contra-indications** see under Furosemide

**Side-effects** see under Furosemide; also dry mouth; rarely limb paraesthesia

**Dose**

- Oedema, 5 mg once daily, preferably in the morning, increased if required to 20 mg once daily; usual max. 40 mg daily
- Hypertension, 2.5 mg daily, increased if necessary to 5 mg once daily

**Torasemide** (Non-proprietary) PoM

Tablets, torasemide 5 mg, net price 28-tab pack = £5.95; 10 mg, 28-tab pack = £8.14

**Torem®** (Roche) PoM

Tablets, torasemide 2.5 mg, net price 28-tab pack = £3.78; 5 mg (scored), 28-tab pack = £5.53; 10 mg (scored), 28-tab pack = £8.14

# 2.2.3 Potassium-sparing diuretics and aldosterone antagonists

**Amiloride** and **triamterene** on their own are weak diuretics. They cause retention of potassium and are therefore used as a more effective alternative to giving potassium supplements with thiazide or loop diuretics. (See section 2.2.4 for compound preparations with thiazides or loop diuretics.)

Potassium supplements must **not** be given with potassium-sparing diuretics. It is also important to bear in mind that administration of a potassium-sparing diuretic to a patient receiving an ACE inhibitor or an angiotensin-II receptor antagonist can cause severe hyperkalaemia.

## AMILORIDE HYDROCHLORIDE

**Indications** oedema, potassium conservation with thiazide and loop diuretics

**Cautions** diabetes mellitus; elderly; renal impairment (Appendix 3); pregnancy (Appendix 4); breast-feeding (Appendix 5); **interactions:** Appendix 1 (diuretics)

**Contra-indications** hyperkalaemia, renal failure

**Side-effects** include gastro-intestinal disturbances, dry mouth, rashes, confusion, postural hypotension, hyperkalaemia, hyponatraemia

**Dose**

- Used alone, initially 10 mg daily *or* 5 mg twice daily, adjusted according to response; max. 20 mg daily
- With other diuretics, congestive heart failure and hypertension, initially 5–10 mg daily; cirrhosis with ascites, initially 5 mg daily

**Amiloride** (Non-proprietary) PoM

Tablets, amiloride hydrochloride 5 mg, net price 28 = £1.21

Oral solution, sugar-free, amiloride hydrochloride 5 mg/5 mL, net price 150 mL = £37.35

Brands include *Amilamont*®

### Compound preparations with thiazide or loop diuretics

See section 2.2.4

## TRIAMTERENE

**Indications** oedema, potassium conservation with thiazide and loop diuretics

**Cautions** see under Amiloride Hydrochloride; may cause blue fluorescence of urine

**Contra-indications** see under Amiloride Hydrochloride

**Side-effects** include gastro-intestinal disturbances, dry mouth, rashes; slight decrease in blood pressure, hyperkalaemia, hyponatraemia; photosensitivity and blood disorders also reported; triamterene found in kidney stones

**Dose**

- Initially 150–250 mg daily, reducing to alternate days after 1 week; taken in divided doses after breakfast and lunch; lower initial dose when given with other diuretics

Counselling Urine may look slightly blue in some lights

**Dytac**® (Goldshield) PoM

Capsules, maroon, triamterene 50 mg. Net price 30-cap pack = £17.35 Label: 14, (see above), 21

### Compound preparations with thiazides or loop diuretics

See section 2.2.4

## Aldosterone antagonists

**Spironolactone** potentiates thiazide or loop diuretics by antagonising aldosterone; it is a potassium-sparing diuretic. It is of value in the treatment of the oedema of cirrhosis of the liver. Low doses of spironolactone are beneficial in severe heart failure, see section 2.5.5.

Spironolactone is also used in primary hyperaldosteronism (Conn's syndrome). It is given before surgery or if surgery is not appropriate, in the lowest effective dose for maintenance.

**Eplerenone** is licensed for use as an adjunct in left ventricular dysfunction and heart failure after a myocardial infarction (see also section 2.5.5 and section 2.10.1). The *Scottish Medicines Consortium* has advised (December 2004) that the use of eplerenone should be restricted to patients who cannot tolerate the hormonal side-effects of spironolactone.

As with potassium-sparing diuretics, potassium supplements must **not** be given with aldosterone antagonists.

## EPLERENONE

**Indications** adjunct in stable patients with left ventricular dysfunction with evidence of heart failure, following myocardial infarction (start therapy within 3–14 days of event)

**Cautions** measure plasma-potassium concentration before treatment, during initiation, and when dose changed; elderly; hepatic impairment (Appendix 2); renal impairment (Appendix 3); pregnancy; breast-feeding (Appendix 5); **interactions**: Appendix 1 (diuretics)

**Contra-indications** hyperkalaemia; concomitant use of potassium-sparing diuretics or potassium supplements

**Side-effects** diarrhoea, nausea; hypotension; dizziness; hyperkalaemia; *less commonly* flatulence, vomiting, atrial fibrillation, postural hypotension, arterial thrombosis, dyslipidaemia, pharyngitis, headache, insomnia, pyelonephritis, hyponatraemia, dehydration, eosinophilia, asthenia, malaise, back pain, leg cramps, impaired renal function, azotaemia, sweating and pruritus

**Dose**

- Initially 25 mg once daily, increased within 4 weeks to 50 mg once daily; CHILD not recommended

**Inspra**® (Pfizer) ▼ PoM

Tablets, yellow, f/c, eplerenone 25 mg, net price 28-tab pack = £42.72; 50 mg, 28-tab pack = £42.72

## SPIRONOLACTONE

**Indications** oedema and ascites in cirrhosis of the liver, malignant ascites, nephrotic syndrome, congestive heart failure (section 2.5.5); primary hyperaldosteronism

**Cautions** potential metabolic products carcinogenic in *rodents*; elderly; monitor electrolytes (discontinue if hyperkalaemia); porphyria (section 9.8.2); hepatic impairment; renal impairment (Appendix 3); pregnancy (Appendix 4); breast-feeding (Appendix 5); **interactions**: Appendix 1 (diuretics)

**Contra-indications** hyperkalaemia, hyponatraemia; Addison's disease

**Side-effects** gastro-intestinal disturbances; impotence, gynaecomastia; menstrual irregularities; lethargy, headache, confusion; rashes; hyperkalaemia (discontinue); hyponatraemia; hepatotoxicity, osteomalacia, and blood disorders reported

**Dose**

- 100–200 mg daily, increased to 400 mg if required; CHILD initially 3 mg/kg daily in divided doses
- Heart failure, see section 2.5.5

**Spironolactone** (Non-proprietary) PoM

Tablets, spironolactone 25 mg, net price 28 = £3.02; 50 mg, 28 = £4.22; 100 mg, 28 = £4.51

Brands include *Spirospare®*

Oral suspensions, sugar-free, spironolactone 5 mg/5 mL, 10 mg/5 mL, 25 mg/5 mL, 50 mg/5 mL and 100 mg/5 mL available from Rosemont (special order)

**Aldactone®** (Searle) PoM

Tablets, all f/c, spironolactone 25 mg (buff), net price 100-tab pack = £8.89; 50 mg (off-white), 100-tab pack = £17.78; 100 mg (buff), 28-tab pack = £9.96

**With thiazides or loop diuretics**

See section 2.2.4

Cardiovascular system 2

## 2.2.4 Potassium-sparing diuretics with other diuretics

Although it is preferable to prescribe thiazides (section 2.2.1) and potassium-sparing diuretics (section 2.2.3) separately, the use of fixed combinations may be justified if compliance is a problem. Potassium-sparing diuretics are not usually necessary in the routine treatment of hypertension, unless hypokalaemia develops. For **interactions**, see Appendix 1 (diuretics).

### Amiloride with thiazides

**Co-amilozide** (Non-proprietary) PoM

Tablets, co-amilozide 2.5/25 (amiloride hydrochloride 2.5 mg, hydrochlorothiazide 25 mg), net price 28-tab pack = £1.85

Brands include *Moduret 25®*

**Dose** hypertension, initially 1 tablet daily, increased if necessary to max. 2 tablets daily

Congestive heart failure, initially 1 tablet daily, increased if necessary to max. 4 tablets daily

Oedema and ascites in cirrhosis of the liver, initially 2 tablets daily, increased if necessary to max. 4 tablets daily; reduce for maintenance if possible

Tablets, co-amilozide 5/50 (amiloride hydrochloride 5 mg, hydrochlorothiazide 50 mg), net price 28 = £1.56

Brands include *Amil-Co®*, *Moduretic®*

**Dose** hypertension, initially ½ tablet daily, increased if necessary to max. 1 tablet daily

Congestive heart failure, initially ½ tablet daily, increased if necessary to max. 2 tablets daily

Oedema and ascites in cirrhosis of the liver, initially 1 tablet daily, increased if necessary to max. 2 tablets daily; reduce for maintenance if possible

**Navispare®** (Goldshield) PoM

Tablets, f/c, orange, amiloride hydrochloride 2.5 mg, cyclopenthiazide 250 micrograms. Net price 28-tab pack = £2.25

**Excipients** include gluten

**Dose** hypertension, 1–2 tablets in the morning

### Amiloride with loop diuretics

**Co-amilofruse** (Non-proprietary) PoM

Tablets, co-amilofruse 2.5/20 (amiloride hydrochloride 2.5 mg, furosemide 20 mg). Net price 28-tab pack = £2.01, 56-tab pack = £2.64

Brands include *Frumil LS®*

**Dose** oedema, 1 tablet in the morning

Tablets, co-amilofruse 5/40 (amiloride hydrochloride 5 mg, furosemide 40 mg). Net price 28-tab pack = £1.47

Brands include *Froop-Co®*, *Fru-Co®*, *Frumil®*, *Lasoride®*

**Dose** oedema, 1–2 tablets in the morning

Tablets, co-amilofruse 10/80 (amiloride hydrochloride 10 mg, furosemide 80 mg). Net price 28-tab pack = £7.43, 56-tab pack = £14.86

Brands include *Aridil®*, *Frumil Forte®*

**Dose** oedema, 1 tablet in the morning

**Burinex A®** (LEO) PoM

Tablets, ivory, scored, amiloride hydrochloride 5 mg, bumetanide 1 mg. Net price 28-tab pack = £2.63

**Dose** oedema, 1–2 tablets daily

### Triamterene with thiazides

**Counselling** Urine may look slightly blue in some lights

**Co-triamterzide** (Non-proprietary) PoM

Tablets, co-triamterzide 50/25 (triamterene 50 mg, hydrochlorothiazide 25 mg), net price 30-tab pack = 95p. Label: 14, (see above), 21

**Dose** hypertension, 1 tablet daily after breakfast, increased if necessary, max. 4 daily

Oedema, 2 tablets daily (1 after breakfast and 1 after midday meal) increased to 3 daily if necessary (2 after breakfast and 1 after midday meal); usual maintenance in oedema, 1 daily or 2 on alternate days; max. 4 daily

Brands include *Triam-Co®*

**Dyazide®** (Goldshield) PoM

Tablets, peach, scored, co-triamterzide 50/25 (triamterene 50 mg, hydrochlorothiazide 25 mg). Net price 30-tab pack = 95p. Label: 14, (see above), 21

**Dose** hypertension, 1 tablet daily after breakfast, increased if necessary, max. 4 daily

Oedema, 2 tablets daily (1 after breakfast and 1 after midday meal) increased to 3 daily if necessary (2 after breakfast and 1 after midday meal); usual maintenance in oedema, 1 daily or 2 on alternate days; max. 4 daily

**Dytide®** (Goldshield) PoM

Capsules, clear/maroon, triamterene 50 mg, benzthiazide 25 mg. Net price 30-cap pack = £17.35. Label: 14, (see above), 21

**Dose** oedema, initially 3 capsules daily (2 after breakfast and 1 after midday meal) for 1 week then 1 or 2 on alternate days

**Kalspare®** (PLIVA) PoM

Tablets, orange, f/c, scored, triamterene 50 mg, chlortalidone 50 mg. Net price 28-tab pack = £3.05. Label: 14, (see above), 21

**Dose** hypertension, oedema, 1–2 tablets in the morning

### Triamterene with loop diuretics

**Counselling** Urine may look slightly blue in some lights

**Frusene®** (Orion) PoM

Tablets, yellow, scored, triamterene 50 mg, furosemide 40 mg. Net price 56-tab pack = £4.54. Label: 14, (see above), 21

**Dose** oedema, ½–2 tablets daily in the morning

**Spironolactone with thiazides**

**Co-flumactone** (Non-proprietary) PoM

Tablets, co-flumactone 25/25 (hydroflumethiazide 25 mg, spironolactone 25 mg). Net price 100-tab pack = £20.23

Brands include *Aldactide 25®*

**Dose** congestive heart failure, initially 4 tablets daily; range 1–8 daily (but not recommended because spironolactone generally given in lower dose)

Tablets, co-flumactone 50/50 (hydroflumethiazide 50 mg, spironolactone 50 mg). Net price 28-tab pack = £10.70

Brands include *Aldactide 50®*

**Dose** congestive heart failure, initially 2 tablets daily; range 1–4 daily (but not recommended because spironolactone generally given in lower dose)

**Spironolactone with loop diuretics**

**Lasilactone®** (Borg) PoM

Capsules, blue/white, spironolactone 50 mg, furosemide 20 mg. Net price 28-cap pack = £8.29

**Dose** resistant oedema, 1–4 capsules daily

## 2.2.5 Osmotic diuretics

Osmotic diuretics are rarely used in heart failure as they may acutely expand the blood volume. **Mannitol** is used in cerebral oedema—a typical dose is 1 g/kg as a 20% solution given by rapid intravenous infusion.

### MANNITOL

**Indications** see notes above; glaucoma (section 11.6)

**Cautions** extravasation causes inflammation and thrombophlebitis

**Contra-indications** congestive cardiac failure, pulmonary oedema

**Side-effects** chills, fever

**Dose**

- Diuresis, by intravenous infusion, 50–200 g over 24 hours, preceded by a test dose of 200 mg/kg by slow intravenous injection
- Cerebral oedema, see notes above

**Mannitol** (Baxter) PoM

Intravenous infusion, mannitol 10% and 20%

## 2.2.6 Mercurial diuretics

Mercurial diuretics are effective but are now almost never used because of their nephrotoxicity.

## 2.2.7 Carbonic anhydrase inhibitors

The carbonic anhydrase inhibitor **acetazolamide** is a weak diuretic and is little used for its diuretic effect. It is used for prophylaxis against mountain sickness [unlicensed indication] but is not a substitute for acclimatisation.

Acetazolamide and eye drops of dorzolamide and brinzolamide inhibit the formation of aqueous humour and are used in glaucoma (section 11.6).

## 2.2.8 Diuretics with potassium

Many patients on diuretics do not need potassium supplements (section 9.2.1.1). For many of those who do, the amount of potassium in combined preparations may not be enough, and for this reason their use is to be discouraged.

Diuretics with potassium and potassium-sparing diuretics should **not** usually be given together.

**Counselling** Modified-release potassium tablets should be swallowed whole with plenty of fluid during meals while sitting or standing

**Burinex K®** (LEO) PoM

Tablets, bumetanide 500 micrograms, potassium 7.7 mmol for modified release. Net price 20 = 80p. Label: 25, 27, counselling, see above

**Centyl K®** (LEO) PoM

Tablets, green, s/c, bendroflumethiazide 2.5 mg, potassium 7.7 mmol for modified release, net price 56-tab pack = £7.50. Label: 25, 27, counselling, see above

**Lasikal®** (Borg) PoM

Tablets, white/yellow, f/c, furosemide 20 mg, potassium 10 mmol for modified release. Net price 100-tab pack = £15.21. Label: 25, 27, counselling, see above

**Neo-NaClex-K®** (Goldshield) PoM

Tablets, pink/white, f/c, bendroflumethiazide 2.5 mg, potassium 8.4 mmol for modified release. Net price 20 = £1.59. Label: 25, 27, counselling, see above



## 2.3 Anti-arrhythmic drugs


2.3.1 Management of arrhythmias
2.3.2 Drugs for arrhythmias


## 2.3.1 Management of arrhythmias

Management of an arrhythmia requires precise diagnosis of the type of arrhythmia, and electrocardiography is essential; underlying causes such as heart failure require appropriate treatment.

**Ectopic beats** If spontaneous with a normal heart, ectopic beats rarely require treatment beyond reassurance. If they are particularly troublesome, beta-blockers are sometimes effective and may be safer than other suppressant drugs.

**Atrial fibrillation** The ventricular rate in atrial fibrillation can be controlled with a beta-blocker, or diltiazem [unlicensed indication], or verapamil. Digoxin is usually effective for controlling the rate at rest; it is also appropriate if atrial fibrillation is accompanied by congestive heart failure. If the rate at rest or during exercise cannot be controlled, diltiazem or verapamil may be combined with digoxin, but care is required if the ventricular function is diminished. In some cases, e.g. acute atrial fibrillation or paroxysmal atrial fibrillation, diltiazem or verapamil or a beta-blocker may be more appropriate than digoxin (see also Paroxysmal Supraventricular Tachycardia and Supraventricular Arrhythmias below). Anticoagulants are indicated especially in valvular or myocardial disease, and in the elderly; in the very elderly the overall benefit and risk needs careful assessment. Younger patients with lone atrial fibrillation in the absence of heart disease probably do not need anticoagulation. Aspirin is less effective than warfarin at preventing emboli but may be appropriate if there are no other risk factors for stroke; aspirin 75 mg may be used.

**Atrial flutter** The ventricular rate at rest can sometimes be controlled with digoxin. Reversion to sinus rhythm (if indicated) may be achieved by appropriately synchronised d.c. shock. Alternatively, amiodarone may be used to restore sinus rhythm, and amiodarone or sotalol to maintain it. If the arrhythmia is long-standing a period of treatment with anticoagulants should be considered before cardioversion to avoid the complication of emboli.

**Paroxysmal supraventricular tachycardia** In most patients this remits spontaneously or can be returned to sinus rhythm by reflex vagal stimulation with respiratory manoeuvres, prompt squatting, or pressure over one carotid sinus (**important:** pressure over carotid sinus should be restricted to monitored patients—it can be dangerous in recent ischaemia, digitalis toxicity, or the elderly).



If vagal stimulation fails, intravenous administration of adenosine is usually the treatment of choice. Intravenous administration of verapamil is useful for patients without myocardial or valvular disease (**important:** never in patients recently treated with beta-blockers, see p. 114). For arrhythmias that are poorly tolerated, synchronised d.c. shock usually provides rapid relief.

In cases of paroxysmal supraventricular tachycardia with block, digitalis toxicity should be suspected. In addition to stopping administration of the cardiac glycoside and giving potassium supplements, intravenous administration of a beta-blocker may be useful. Specific digoxin antibody is available if the toxicity is considered life-threatening (section 2.1.1).

**Arrhythmias after myocardial infarction** In patients with a paroxysmal tachycardia or rapid irregularity of the pulse it is best not to administer an anti-arrhythmic until an ECG record has been obtained. Bradycardia, particularly if complicated by hypotension, should be treated with atropine sulphate, given intravenously in a dose of 0.3–1 mg. If the initial dose is effective it may be repeated if necessary.

**Ventricular tachycardia** Drug treatment is used both for the treatment of ventricular tachycardia and for prophylaxis of recurrent attacks that merit suppression. Ventricular tachycardia requires treatment most commonly in the acute stage of myocardial infarction, but the likelihood of this and other life-threatening arrhythmias diminishes sharply over the first 24 hours after the attack, especially in patients without heart failure or shock. Lidocaine (lignocaine) is the preferred drug for emergency use. Other drugs are best administered under specialist supervision. Very rapid ventricular tachycardia causes profound circulatory collapse and should be treated urgently with d.c. shock.

*Torsades de pointes* is a special form of ventricular tachycardia which tends to occur in the presence of a long QT interval (usually drug induced, but other factors including hypokalaemia, severe bradycardia, and genetic predisposition may also be implicated). The episodes are usually self-limiting, but are frequently recurrent and may cause impairment (or loss) of consciousness. If not controlled, the arrhythmia may progress to ventricular fibrillation. Intravenous infusion of magnesium sulphate (section 9.5.1.3) is usually effective. A beta-blocker (but not sotalol) and atrial (or ventricular) pacing may be considered. Anti-arrhythmics (including lidocaine) may further prolong the QT interval, thus worsening the condition.

## 2.3.2 Drugs for arrhythmias

Anti-arrhythmic drugs can be classified clinically into those that act on supraventricular arrhythmias (e.g. verapamil), those that act on both supraventricular and ventricular arrhythmias (e.g. disopyramide), and those that act on ventricular arrhythmias (e.g. lidocaine (lignocaine)).

They can also be classified according to their effects on the electrical behaviour of myocardial cells during activity:

Class Ia, b, c: membrane stabilising drugs (e.g. quinidine, lidocaine, flecainide respectively)

Class II: beta-blockers

Class III: amiodarone and sotalol (also Class II)

Class IV: calcium-channel blockers (includes verapamil but not dihydropyridines)

This latter classification (the Vaughan Williams classification) is of less clinical significance.

**Cautions** The negative inotropic effects of anti-arrhythmic drugs tend to be additive. Therefore special care should be taken if two or more are used, especially if myocardial function is impaired. Most or all drugs that are effective in countering arrhythmias can also provoke them in some circumstances; moreover, hypokalaemia enhances the arrhythmogenic (pro-arrhythmic) effect of many drugs.

### Supraventricular arrhythmias

**Adenosine** is usually the treatment of choice for terminating paroxysmal supraventricular tachycardia. As it has a very short duration of action (half-life only about 8 to 10 seconds, but prolonged in those taking dipyridamole), most side-effects are short lived. Unlike verapamil, adenosine may be used after a beta-blocker. Verapamil may be preferable to adenosine in asthma.

Oral administration of a **cardiac glycoside** (such as digoxin, section 2.1.1) slows the ventricular response in cases of atrial fibrillation and atrial flutter. However, intravenous infusion of digoxin is rarely effective for rapid control of ventricular rate. Cardiac glycosides are contra-indicated in supraventricular arrhythmias associated with Wolff-Parkinson-White syndrome.

**Verapamil** (section 2.6.2) is usually effective for supraventricular tachycardias. An initial intravenous dose (**important**: serious beta-blocker interaction hazard, see p. 114) may be followed by oral treatment; hypotension may occur with larger doses. It should not be used for tachyarrhythmias where the QRS complex is wide (i.e. broad complex) unless a supraventricular origin has been established beyond reasonable doubt. It is also contra-indicated in atrial fibrillation with pre-excitation (e.g. Wolff-Parkinson-White syndrome). It should not be used in children with arrhythmias without specialist advice; some supraventricular arrhythmias in childhood can be accelerated by verapamil with dangerous consequences.

Intravenous administration of a **beta-blocker** (section 2.4) such as esmolol or propranolol, can achieve rapid control of the ventricular rate.

Drugs for both supraventricular and ventricular arrhythmias include **amiodarone**, **beta-blockers**, **disopyramide**, **flecainide**, **procainamide**, **propafenone** and **quinidine**, see below under Supraventricular and Ventricular Arrhythmias.

## ADENOSINE

**Indications** rapid reversion to sinus rhythm of paroxysmal supraventricular tachycardias, including those associated with accessory pathways (e.g. Wolff-Parkinson-White syndrome); aid to diagnosis of broad or narrow complex supraventricular tachycardias

**Cautions** atrial fibrillation or flutter with accessory pathway (conduction down anomalous pathway may increase); heart transplant (see below); **interactions:** Appendix 1 (adenosine)

**Contra-indications** second- or third-degree AV block and sick sinus syndrome (unless pacemaker fitted); asthma

**Side-effects** include transient facial flush, chest pain, dyspnoea, bronchospasm, choking sensation, nausea, light-headedness; severe bradycardia reported (requiring temporary pacing); ECG may show transient rhythm disturbances

**Dose**

- By rapid intravenous injection into central or large peripheral vein, 3 mg over 2 seconds with cardiac monitoring; if necessary followed by 6 mg after 1–2 minutes, and then by 12 mg after a further 1–2 minutes; increments should not be given if high level AV block develops at any particular dose

**Note** 3-mg dose ineffective in a number of patients, therefore higher initial dose sometimes used but patients with *heart transplant* are **very sensitive** to effects of adenosine, and should **not** receive higher initial dose. Also if essential to give with dipyridamole reduce initial dose to 0.5–1 mg

**Adenocor®** (Sanofi-Synthelabo) PoM

Injection, adenosine 3 mg/mL in physiological saline. Net price 2-mL vial = £4.45 (hosp. only)

**Note** Intravenous infusion of adenosine (*Adenoscan®*, Sanofi Winthrop) may be used in conjunction with radionuclide myocardial perfusion imaging in patients who cannot exercise adequately or for whom exercise is inappropriate—consult product literature

## Supraventricular and ventricular arrhythmias

**Amiodarone** is used in the treatment of arrhythmias particularly when other drugs are ineffective or contra-indicated. It may be used for paroxysmal supraventricular, nodal and ventricular tachycardias, atrial fibrillation and flutter, and ventricular fibrillation. It may also be used for tachyarrhythmias associated with Wolff-Parkinson-White syndrome. It should be initiated only under hospital or specialist supervision. Amiodarone may be given by intravenous infusion as well as by mouth, and has the advantage of causing little or no myocardial depression. Unlike oral amiodarone, intravenous amiodarone may act relatively rapidly.

Intravenous injection of amiodarone may be used in cardiopulmonary resuscitation for ventricular fibrillation or pulseless tachycardia unresponsive to other interventions (section 2.7.3).

Amiodarone has a very long half-life (extending to several weeks) and only needs to be given once daily (but high doses may cause nausea unless divided). Many weeks or months may be required to achieve steady-state plasma-amiodarone concentration; this is particularly important when drug interactions are likely (see also Appendix 1).

Most patients taking amiodarone develop corneal microdeposits (reversible on withdrawal of treatment); these rarely interfere with vision, but drivers may be dazzled by headlights at night. However, if vision is impaired or if optic neuritis or neuropathy occur, amiodarone must be stopped to prevent blindness and expert advice sought. Because of the possibility of phototoxic reactions, patients should be advised to shield the skin from light during treatment and for several months after discontinuing amiodarone; patients should use a wide-spectrum sunscreen (section 13.8.1) to protect against both long ultraviolet and visible light.

Amiodarone contains iodine and can cause disorders of thyroid function; both hypothyroidism and hyperthyroidism may occur. Clinical assessment alone is unreliable, and laboratory tests should be performed before treatment and every 6 months. Thyroxine (T4) may be raised in the absence of hyperthyroidism; therefore tri-iodothyronine (T3), T4, and thyroid-stimulating hormone (thyrotrophin, TSH) should all be measured. A raised T3 and T4 with a very low or undetectable TSH concentration suggests the development of thyrotoxicosis. The thyrotoxicosis may be very refractory, and amiodarone should usually be withdrawn at least temporarily to help achieve control; treatment with carbimazole may be required. Hypothyroidism can be treated with replacement therapy without withdrawing amiodarone if it is essential; careful supervision is required.

Pneumonitis should always be suspected if new or progressive shortness of breath or cough develops in a patient taking amiodarone. Fresh neurological symptoms should raise the possibility of peripheral neuropathy.

Amiodarone is also associated with hepatotoxicity and treatment should be discontinued if severe liver function abnormalities or clinical signs of liver disease develop.

**Beta-blockers** act as anti-arrhythmic drugs principally by attenuating the effects of the sympathetic system on automaticity and conductivity within the heart, for details see section 2.4. For special reference to the role of **sotalol** in ventricular arrhythmias, see also p. 84.

**Disopyramide** may be given by intravenous injection to control arrhythmias after myocardial infarction (including those not responding to lidocaine (lignocaine)), but it impairs cardiac contractility. Oral administration of disopyramide is useful but it has an antimuscarinic effect which limits its use in patients with glaucoma or prostatic hypertrophy.

**Flecainide** belongs to the same general class as lidocaine. It may be of value in serious symptomatic ventricular arrhythmias. It may also be indicated for junctional re-entry tachycardias and for paroxysmal atrial fibrillation. As with quinidine it may precipitate serious arrhythmias in a small minority of patients (including those with otherwise normal hearts).

**Procainamide** is given by intravenous injection to control ventricular arrhythmias.

**Propafenone** is used for the prophylaxis and treatment of ventricular arrhythmias and also for some supraventricular arrhythmias. It has complex mechanisms of action, including weak beta-blocking activity (therefore caution is needed in obstructive airways disease—contra-indicated if severe).

**Quinidine** can suppress supraventricular and ventricular arrhythmias but it may itself precipitate rhythm disorders and is best used on specialist advice; it is rarely used nowadays.

Drugs for supraventricular arrhythmias include **adenosine**, **cardiac glycosides** and **verapamil**, see above under Supraventricular Arrhythmias. Drugs for ventricular arrhythmias include **lidocaine**, **mexiletine**, and **phenytoin**, see below under Ventricular Arrhythmias.



## AMIODARONE HYDROCHLORIDE

**Indications** see notes above (should be initiated in hospital or under specialist supervision)

**Cautions** liver-function and thyroid-function tests required before treatment and then every 6 months (see notes above for tests of thyroid function); hypokalaemia (measure serum-potassium concentration before treatment); chest x-ray required before treatment; heart failure; elderly; severe bradycardia and conduction disturbances in excessive dosage; intravenous use may cause moderate and transient fall in blood pressure (circulatory collapse precipitated by rapid administration or overdosage) or severe hepatocellular toxicity (monitor transaminases closely); porphyria (section 9.8.2); **interactions:** Appendix 1 (amiodarone)

**Contra-indications** sinus bradycardia, sino-atrial heart block; unless pacemaker fitted avoid in severe conduction disturbances or sinus node disease; thyroid dysfunction; iodine sensitivity; avoid *intravenous use* in severe respiratory failure, circulatory collapse (except in cardiac arrest, see section 2.7.3), severe arterial hypotension; avoid bolus injection in congestive heart failure or cardiomyopathy; pregnancy (Appendix 4); breast-feeding (Appendix 5)

**Side-effects** nausea, vomiting, taste disturbances, raised serum transaminases (may require dose reduction or withdrawal if accompanied by acute liver disorders), jaundice; bradycardia (see Cautions); pulmonary toxicity (including pneumonitis and fibrosis); tremor, sleep disorders; hypothyroidism, hyperthyroidism; reversible corneal microdeposits (sometimes with night glare); phototoxicity, persistent slate-grey skin discoloration (see also notes above); *less commonly* onset or worsening of arrhythmia, conduction disturbances (see Cautions), peripheral neuropathy and myopathy (usually reversible on withdrawal); *very rarely* chronic liver disease including cirrhosis, sinus arrest, bronchospasm (in patients with severe respiratory failure), ataxia, benign intracranial hypertension, headache, vertigo, epididymo-orchitis, impotence, haemolytic or aplastic anaemia, thrombocytopenia, rash (including exfoliative dermatitis), hypersensitivity including vasculitis, alopecia, impaired vision due to optic neuritis or optic neuropathy (including blindness), anaphylaxis on rapid injection, also hypotension, respiratory distress syndrome, sweating, and hot flushes

**Dose**

- By mouth, 200 mg 3 times daily for 1 week reduced to 200 mg twice daily for a further week; maintenance, usually 200 mg daily or the minimum required to control the arrhythmia
- By intravenous infusion via central venous catheter, initially 5 mg/kg over 20–120 minutes with ECG monitoring; subsequent infusion given if necessary according to response up to max. 1.2 g in 24 hours
- Ventricular fibrillation or pulseless ventricular tachycardia, by intravenous injection over at least 3 minutes, 300 mg (section 2.7.3)

**Amiodarone** (Non-proprietary) PoM

Tablets, amiodarone hydrochloride 100 mg, net price 28-tab pack = £1.97; 200 mg, 28-tab pack = £2.42. Label: 11

Brands include *Amyben®*

Injection, amiodarone hydrochloride 30 mg/mL, net price 10-mL prefilled syringe = £10.25

Excipients may include benzyl alcohol (avoid in neonates, see Excipients, p. 2)

Sterile concentrate, amiodarone hydrochloride 50 mg/mL, net price 3-mL amp = £1.33, 6-mL amp = £2.86. For dilution and use as an infusion

Excipients may include benzyl alcohol (avoid in neonates, see Excipients, p. 2)

**Cordarone X®** (Sanofi-Synthelabo) PoM

Tablets, both scored, amiodarone hydrochloride 100 mg, net price 28-tab pack = £4.45; 200 mg, 28-tab pack = £7.27. Label: 11

Sterile concentrate, amiodarone hydrochloride 50 mg/mL. Net price 3-mL amp = £1.33. For dilution and use as an infusion

Excipients include benzyl alcohol (avoid in neonates, see Excipients, p. 2)

## DISOPYRAMIDE

**Indications** ventricular arrhythmias, especially after myocardial infarction; supraventricular arrhythmias

**Cautions** discontinue if hypotension, hypoglycaemia, ventricular tachycardia, ventricular fibrillation or torsades de pointes develop; atrial flutter or tachycardia with partial block, bundle branch block, heart failure (avoid if severe); prostatic enlargement; glaucoma; hepatic impairment (Appendix 2); renal impairment (Appendix 3); pregnancy (Appendix 4); breast-feeding (Appendix 5); **interactions**: Appendix 1 (disopyramide)

**Contra-indications** second-and third-degree heart block and sinus node dysfunction (unless pacemaker fitted); cardiogenic shock; severe uncompensated heart failure

**Side-effects** ventricular tachycardia, ventricular fibrillation or torsades de pointes (usually associated with prolongation of QRS complex or QT interval—see Cautions above), myocardial depression, hypotension, AV block; antimuscarinic effects include dry mouth, blurred vision, urinary retention; gastrointestinal irritation; psychosis, cholestatic jaundice, hypoglycaemia also reported (see Cautions above)

**Dose**
- By mouth, 300–800 mg daily in divided doses
- By slow intravenous injection, 2 mg/kg over at least 5 minutes to a max. of 150 mg, with ECG monitoring, followed immediately *either* by 200 mg by mouth, then 200 mg every 8 hours for 24 hours *or* 400 micrograms/kg/hour by intravenous infusion; max. 300 mg in first hour and 800 mg daily

**Disopyramide** (Non-proprietary) PoM
Capsules, disopyramide (as phosphate) 100 mg, net price 20 = £4.97; 150 mg, 20 = £6.37

**Rythmodan®** (Borg) PoM
Capsules, disopyramide 100 mg (green/beige), net price 84-cap pack = £14.71; 150 mg, 84-cap pack = £19.52

Injection, disopyramide (as phosphate) 10 mg/mL, net price 5-mL amp = £2.72

**Modified release**

**Rythmodan Retard®** (Borg) PoM
Tablets, m/r, scored, f/c, disopyramide (as phosphate) 250 mg. Net price 56-tab pack = £28.85. Label: 25
Dose 250–375 mg every 12 hours

## FLECAINIDE ACETATE

**Indications** *Tablets and injection:* AV nodal reciprocating tachycardia, arrhythmias associated with Wolff-Parkinson-White syndrome and similar conditions with accessory pathways, disabling symptoms of paroxysmal atrial fibrillation in patients without left ventricular dysfunction (arrhythmias of recent onset will respond more readily)

*Tablets only:* symptomatic sustained ventricular tachycardia, disabling symptoms of premature ventricular contractions or non-sustained ventricular tachycardia in patients resistant to or intolerant of other therapy

*Injection only:* ventricular tachyarrhythmias resistant to other treatment

**Cautions** patients with pacemakers (especially those who may be pacemaker dependent because stimulation threshold may rise appreciably); avoid in sinus node dysfunction, atrial conduction defects, second-degree or greater AV block, bundle branch block or distal block unless pacing rescue available; atrial fibrillation following heart surgery; elderly (accumulation may occur); hepatic impairment (Appendix 2); renal impairment (monitor plasma-flecainide concentration, see also Appendix 3); pregnancy (Appendix 4); breast-feeding (Appendix 5); **interactions:** Appendix 1 (flecainide)

**Contra-indications** heart failure; history of myocardial infarction and either asymptomatic ventricular ectopics or asymptomatic non-sustained ventricular tachycardia; long-standing atrial fibrillation where conversion to sinus rhythm not attempted; haemodynamically significant valvular heart disease

**Side-effects** nausea, vomiting; pro-arrhythmic effects; dyspnoea; visual disturbances; less commonly gastro-intestinal disturbances, jaundice, hepatic dysfunction, AV block, heart failure, myocardial infarction, hypotension, pneumonitis, hallucinations, depression, convulsions, peripheral neuropathy, paraesthesia, ataxia, dyskinesia, hypoaesthesia, tinnitus, vertigo, reduction in red blood cells, in white blood cells and in platelets, corneal deposits, rashes, alopecia, sweating, urticaria, photosensitivity, increased antinuclear antibodies

**Dose**
- By mouth (initiated under direction of hospital consultant), ventricular arrhythmias, initially 100 mg twice daily (max. 400 mg daily usually reserved for rapid control or in heavily built patients), reduced after 3–5 days if possible

  Supraventricular arrhythmias, 50 mg twice daily, increased if required to max. 300 mg daily
- By slow intravenous injection (in hospital), 2 mg/kg over 10–30 minutes, max. 150 mg, with ECG monitoring; followed if required by infusion at a rate of 1.5 mg/kg/hour for 1 hour, subsequently reduced to 100–250 micrograms/kg/hour for up to 24 hours; max. cumulative dose in first 24 hours, 600 mg; transfer to *oral* treatment, as above

Note Pre-dose ('trough') plasma-flecainide concentration for optimum response 0.2–1 mg/litre

**Flecainide** (Non-proprietary) PoM
Tablets, flecainide acetate 50 mg, net price 60-tab pack = £11.90; 100 mg, 60-tab pack = £15.43

**Tambocor®** (3M) PoM
Tablets, flecainide acetate 50 mg, net price 60-tab pack = £14.46; 100 mg (scored), 60-tab pack = £20.66

Injection, flecainide acetate 10 mg/mL. Net price 15-mL amp = £4.40

## PROCAINAMIDE HYDROCHLORIDE

**Indications** ventricular arrhythmias, especially after myocardial infarction; atrial tachycardia

**Cautions** elderly; asthma, myasthenia gravis; hepatic impairment (Appendix 2); renal impairment (Appendix 3); pregnancy (Appendix 4); **interactions:** Appendix 1 (procainamide)

**Contra-indications** heart block, heart failure, hypotension; systemic lupus erythematosus; not indicated for torsades de pointes (can exacerbate); breast-feeding (Appendix 5)

**Side-effects** nausea, diarrhoea, rashes, fever, myocardial depression, heart failure, lupus erythematosus-like syndrome, agranulocytosis after prolonged treatment; psychosis and angioedema also reported

**Dose**
- By slow intravenous injection, rate not exceeding 50 mg/minute, 100 mg with ECG monitoring, repeated at 5-minute intervals until arrhythmia controlled; max. 1 g
- By intravenous infusion, 500–600 mg over 25–30 minutes with ECG monitoring, followed by maintenance at rate of 2–6 mg/minute, then if necessary oral anti-arrhythmic treatment starting 3–4 hours after infusion

Note Serum procainamide concentration for optimum response 3–10 mg/litre

**Pronestyl®** (Squibb) PoM
Injection, procainamide hydrochloride 100 mg/mL. Net price 10-mL vial = £1.90

## PROPAFENONE HYDROCHLORIDE

**Indications** ventricular arrhythmias; paroxysmal supraventricular tachyarrhythmias which include paroxysmal atrial flutter or fibrillation and paroxysmal re-entrant tachycardias involving the AV node or accessory pathway, where standard therapy ineffective or contra-indicated

**Cautions** heart failure; elderly; pacemaker patients; great caution in obstructive airways disease owing to beta-blocking activity (contra-indicated if severe); hepatic impairment (Appendix 2); renal impairment; pregnancy (Appendix 4); breast-feeding (Appendix 5); **interactions:** Appendix 1 (propafenone)

**Contra-indications** uncontrolled congestive heart failure, cardiogenic shock (except arrhythmia induced), severe bradycardia, electrolyte disturbances, severe obstructive pulmonary disease, marked hypotension; myasthenia gravis; unless adequately paced avoid in sinus node dysfunction, atrial conduction defects, second degree or greater AV block, bundle branch block or distal block

**Side-effects** antimuscarinic effects including constipation, blurred vision, and dry mouth; dizziness, nausea and vomiting, fatigue, bitter taste, diarrhoea, headache, and allergic skin reactions reported; postural hypotension, particularly in elderly; bradycardia, sino-atrial, atrioventricular, or intraventricular blocks; arrhythmogenic (pro-arrhythmic) effect; rarely hypersensitivity reactions (cholestasis, blood disorders, lupus syndrome), seizures; myoclonus also reported

**Dose**

- Body-weight 70 kg and over, initially 150 mg 3 times daily after food under direct hospital supervision with ECG monitoring and blood pressure control (if QRS interval prolonged by more than 20%, reduce dose or discontinue until ECG returns to normal limits); may be increased at intervals of at least 3 days to 300 mg twice daily and, if necessary, to max. 300 mg 3 times daily; body-weight under 70 kg, reduce dose; ELDERLY may respond to lower doses

**Arythmol®** (Abbott) PoM
Tablets, both f/c, propafenone hydrochloride 150 mg, net price 90-tab pack = £8.57; 300 mg (scored), 60-tab pack = £10.86. Label: 21, 25

## QUINIDINE

**Indications** suppression of supraventricular tachycardias and ventricular arrhythmias (see notes above)

**Cautions** 200-mg test dose to detect hypersensitivity reactions; extreme care in uncompensated heart failure, first- or second-degree heart block, myocarditis, severe myocardial damage and in myasthenia gravis; pregnancy (Appendix 4); **interactions:** Appendix 1 (quinidine)

**Contra-indications** heart block

**Side-effects** see under Procainamide Hydrochloride; also ventricular arrhythmias, thrombocytopenia, haemolytic anaemia; rarely granulomatous hepatitis; also cinchonism (see Quinine, section 5.4.1)

**Dose**

- Quinidine sulphate 200–400 mg 3–4 times daily
  Note Quinidine sulphate 200 mg = quinidine bisulphate 250 mg

**Quinidine Sulphate** (Non-proprietary) PoM
Tablets, quinidine sulphate 200 mg, net price 100-tab pack = £32.95

**Modified release**

**Kinidin Durules®** (AstraZeneca) PoM
Tablets, m/r, f/c, quinidine bisulphate 250 mg. Net price 100-tab pack = £11.05. Label: 25
Dose 500 mg every 12 hours, adjusted as required

### Ventricular arrhythmias

**Lidocaine** (lignocaine) is relatively safe when used by slow intravenous injection and should be considered first for emergency use. Though effective in suppressing ventricular tachycardia and reducing the risk of ventricular fibrillation following myocardial infarction, it has not been shown to reduce mortality when used prophylactically in this condition. In patients with cardiac or hepatic failure doses may need to be reduced to avoid convulsions, depression of the central nervous system, or depression of the cardiovascular system.

**Mexiletine** may be given as a slow intravenous injection if lidocaine is ineffective; it has a similar action. Adverse cardiovascular and central nervous system effects may limit the dose tolerated; nausea and vomiting may prevent an effective dose being given by mouth.

**Moracizine** (*Ethmozine®*, Shire) is available on a named-patient basis for the prophylaxis and treatment of serious and life-threatening ventricular arrhythmias for patients already stabilised on moracizine.

Drugs for both supraventricular and ventricular arrhythmias include **amiodarone**, **beta-blockers**, **disopyramide**, **flecainide**, **procainamide**, **propafenone** and **quinidine**, see above under Supraventricular and Ventricular Arrhythmias.

## LIDOCAINE HYDROCHLORIDE
**(Lignocaine hydrochloride)**

**Indications** ventricular arrhythmias, especially after myocardial infarction

**Cautions** lower doses in congestive cardiac failure, and following cardiac surgery; elderly; hepatic impairment (Appendix 2); renal impairment (Appendix 3); pregnancy (Appendix 4); **interactions:** Appendix 1 (lidocaine)

**Contra-indications** sino-atrial disorders, all grades of atrioventricular block, severe myocardial depression; porphyria (see section 9.8.2)

**Side-effects** dizziness, paraesthesia, or drowsiness (particularly if injection too rapid); other CNS effects include confusion, respiratory depression and convulsions; hypotension and bradycardia (may lead to cardiac arrest); hypersensitivity reported

**Dose**

- By intravenous injection, in patients without gross circulatory impairment, 100 mg as a bolus over a few minutes (50 mg in lighter patients or those whose circulation is severely impaired), followed immediately by infusion of 4 mg/minute for 30 minutes, 2 mg/minute for 2 hours, then 1 mg/minute; reduce concentration further if infusion continued beyond 24 hours (ECG monitoring and specialist advice for infusion)
  **Note** Following intravenous injection lidocaine has a short duration of action (lasting for 15–20 minutes). If an intravenous infusion is not immediately available the initial intravenous injection of 50–100 mg can be repeated if necessary once or twice at intervals of not less than 10 minutes

2 Cardiovascular system

**Lidocaine** (Non-proprietary) PoM

Injection 2%, lidocaine hydrochloride 20 mg/mL, net price 2-mL amp = 28p; 5-mL amp = 25p; 10-mL amp = 60p; 20-mL amp = 63p
Available from Braun

Infusion, lidocaine hydrochloride 0.1% (1 mg/mL) and 0.2% (2 mg/mL) in glucose intravenous infusion 5%. 500-mL containers
Available from Baxter

**Minijet® Lignocaine** (Celltech) PoM

Injection, lidocaine hydrochloride 1% (10 mg/mL), net price 10-mL disposable syringe = £4.40; 2% (20 mg/mL), 5-mL disposable syringe = £4.30

## MEXILETINE HYDROCHLORIDE

**Indications** ventricular arrhythmias, especially after myocardial infarction

**Cautions** close monitoring on initiation of therapy (including ECG, blood pressure, etc.); hepatic impairment (Appendix 2); pregnancy (Appendix 4); **interactions:** Appendix 1 (mexiletine)

**Contra-indications** bradycardia, cardiogenic shock; high degree AV block (unless pacemaker fitted)

**Side-effects** nausea, vomiting, constipation; bradycardia, hypotension, atrial fibrillation, palpitation, conduction defects, exacerbation of arrhythmias, torsades de pointes; drowsiness, confusion, convulsions, psychiatric disorders, dysarthria, ataxia, paraesthesia, nystagmus, tremor; jaundice, hepatitis, and blood disorders reported; see also notes above

**Dose**

- By mouth, initial dose 400 mg (may be increased to 600 mg if opioid analgesics also given), followed after 2 hours by 200–250 mg 3–4 times daily
- By intravenous injection, 100–250 mg at a rate of 25 mg/minute with ECG monitoring followed by infusion of 250 mg as a 0.1% solution over 1 hour, 125 mg/hour for 2 hours, then 500 micrograms/minute

**Mexitil®** (Boehringer Ingelheim) PoM

Capsules, mexiletine hydrochloride 50 mg (purple/red), net price 100-cap pack = £4.95; 200 mg (red), 100-cap pack = £11.87

Injection, mexiletine hydrochloride 25 mg/mL. Net price 10-mL amp = £1.49

# 2.4 Beta-adrenoceptor blocking drugs

Beta-adrenoceptor blocking drugs (beta-blockers) block the beta-adrenoreceptors in the heart, peripheral vasculature, bronchi, pancreas, and liver.

Many beta-blockers are now available and in general they are all equally effective. There are, however, differences between them which may affect choice in treating particular diseases or individual patients.

Intrinsic sympathomimetic activity (ISA, partial agonist activity) represents the capacity of beta-blockers to stimulate as well as to block adrenergic receptors. **Oxprenolol**, **pindolol**, **acebutolol** and **celiprolol** have intrinsic sympathomimetic activity; they tend to cause less bradycardia than the other beta-blockers and may also cause less coldness of the extremities.

Some beta-blockers are lipid soluble and some are water soluble. **Atenolol**, **celiprolol**, **nadolol**, and **sotalol** are the most water-soluble; they are less likely to enter the brain, and may therefore cause less sleep disturbance and nightmares. Water-soluble beta-blockers are excreted by the kidneys; they accumulate in renal impairment and dosage reduction is therefore often necessary.

Beta-blockers with a relatively short duration of action have to be given two or three times daily. Many of these are, however, available in modified-release formulations so that administration once daily is adequate for hypertension. For angina twice-daily treatment may sometimes be needed even with a modified-release formulation. Some beta-blockers such as atenolol, bisoprolol, carvedilol, celiprolol, and nadolol have an intrinsically longer duration of action and need to be given only once daily.

Beta-blockers slow the heart and can depress the myocardium; they are contra-indicated in patients with second- or third-degree heart block. Beta-blockers should also be avoided in patients with worsening unstable heart failure; care is required when initiating a beta-blocker in those with stable heart failure (see also section 2.5.5). **Sotalol** may prolong the QT interval, and it occasionally causes life-threatening ventricular arrhythmias (**important:** particular care is required to avoid hypokalaemia in patients taking sotalol).

**Labetalol**, **celiprolol**, **carvedilol** and **nebivolol** are beta-blockers which have, in addition, an arteriolar vasodilating action, by diverse mechanisms, and thus lower peripheral resistance. There is no evidence that these drugs have important advantages over other beta-blockers in the treatment of hypertension.

Beta-blockers may precipitate asthma and this effect can be dangerous. Beta-blockers should be **avoided** in patients with a history of asthma or bronchospasm; if there is no alternative, a cardioselective beta-blocker may be used with extreme caution under specialist supervision. **Atenolol**, **bisoprolol**, **metoprolol**, **nebivolol** and (to a lesser extent) **acebutolol**, have less effect on the $beta_2$ (bronchial) receptors and are, therefore, relatively *cardioselective*, but they are **not** *cardiospecific*. They have a lesser effect on airways resistance but are **not** free of this side-effect.

Beta-blockers are also associated with fatigue, coldness of the extremities (may be less common with those with ISA, see above), and sleep disturbances with nightmares (may be less common with the water-soluble beta-blockers, see above).

Beta-blockers are not contra-indicated in diabetes; however, they can lead to a small deterioration of glucose tolerance and interfere with metabolic and autonomic responses to hypoglycaemia. Cardioselective beta-blockers (see above) may be preferable and beta-blockers should be avoided altogether in those with frequent episodes of hypoglycaemia.

**Hypertension** Beta-blockers are effective for reducing blood pressure (section 2.5), but their mode of action is not understood; they reduce cardiac output, alter baroceptor reflex sensitivity, and block peripheral adrenoceptors. Some beta-blockers depress plasma renin secretion. It is possible that a central effect may also explain their mode of action.

In general, the dose of a beta-blocker does not have to be high; for example, atenolol is given in a dose of 25–50 mg daily and it is rarely necessary to increase the dose to 100 mg.

Although atenolol lowers blood pressure, there is some doubt whether it is as effective as other antihypertensive drugs for reducing the incidence of stroke, myocardial infarction, or cardiovascular mortality.

Beta-blockers can be used to control the pulse rate in patients with *phaeochromocytoma* (section 2.5.4). However, they should never be used alone as beta-blockade without concurrent alpha-blockade may lead to a hypertensive crisis. For this reason phenoxybenzamine should always be used together with the beta-blocker.

**Angina** By reducing cardiac work beta-blockers improve exercise tolerance and relieve symptoms in patients with *angina* (for further details on the management of stable and unstable angina see section 2.6). As with hypertension there is no good evidence of the superiority of any one drug, although occasionally a patient will respond better to one beta-blocker than to another. There is some evidence that sudden withdrawal may cause an exacerbation of angina and therefore gradual reduction of dose is preferable when beta-blockers are to be stopped. There is a risk of precipitating heart failure when beta-blockers and verapamil are used together in established ischaemic heart disease (**important**: see p. 114).

**Myocardial infarction** For advice on the management of myocardial infarction see section 2.10.1.

Several studies have shown that some beta-blockers can reduce the recurrence rate of *myocardial infarction*. However, uncontrolled heart failure, hypotension, bradyarrhythmias, and obstructive airways disease render beta-blockers unsuitable in some patients following a myocardial infarction. **Atenolol** and **metoprolol** may reduce early mortality after intravenous and subsequent oral administration in the acute phase, while **acebutolol**, **metoprolol**, **propranolol**, and **timolol** have protective value when started in the early convalescent phase. The evidence relating to other beta-blockers is less convincing; some have not been tested in trials of secondary protection. It is also not known whether the protective effect of beta-blockers continues after 2–3 years; it is possible that sudden cessation may cause a rebound worsening of myocardial ischaemia.

**Arrhythmias** Beta-blockers act as *anti-arrhythmic drugs* principally by attenuating the effects of the sympathetic system on automaticity and conductivity within the heart. They may be used in conjunction with digoxin to control the ventricular response in atrial fibrillation, especially in patients with thyrotoxicosis. Beta-blockers are also useful in the management of supraventricular tachycardias, and are used to control those following myocardial infarction, see above.

**Esmolol** is a relatively cardioselective beta-blocker with a very short duration of action, used intravenously for the short-term treatment of supraventricular arrhythmias, sinus tachycardia, or hypertension, particularly in the peri-operative period. It may also be used in other situations, such as acute myocardial infarction, where sustained beta blockade might be hazardous.

**Sotalol**, a non-cardioselective beta-blocker with additional class III anti-arrhythmic activity, is used for prophylaxis in paroxysmal supraventricular arrhythmias. It also suppresses ventricular ectopic beats and non-sustained ventricular tachycardia. It has been shown to be more effective than lidocaine (lignocaine) in the termination of spontaneous sustained ventricular tachycardia due to coronary disease or cardiomyopathy. However, it may induce torsades de pointes in susceptible patients.

**Heart failure** Beta-blockers may produce benefit in heart failure by blocking sympathetic activity. **Bisoprolol** and **carvedilol** reduce mortality in any grade of stable heart failure. Treatment should be initiated by those experienced in the management of heart failure (see section 2.5.5 for details on heart failure).

**Thyrotoxicosis** Beta-blockers are used in pre-operative preparation for thyroidectomy. Administration of propranolol can reverse clinical symptoms of *thyrotoxicosis* within 4 days. Routine tests of increased thyroid function remain unaltered. The thyroid gland is rendered less vascular thus making surgery easier (section 6.2.2).

**Other uses** Beta-blockers have been used to alleviate some symptoms of *anxiety*; probably patients with palpitation, tremor, and tachycardia respond best (see also section 4.1.2 and section 4.9.3). Beta-blockers are also used in the *prophylaxis of migraine* (section 4.7.4.2). Betaxolol, carteolol, levobunolol, metipranolol and timolol are used topically in *glaucoma* (section 11.6).

## PROPRANOLOL HYDROCHLORIDE

**Indications** see under Dose

**Cautions** avoid abrupt withdrawal especially in ischaemic heart disease; first-degree AV block; portal hypertension (risk of deterioration in liver function); diabetes; history of obstructive airways disease (introduce cautiously and monitor lung function—see also Bronchospasm below); myasthenia gravis; history of hypersensitivity—may increase sensitivity to allergens and result in more serious hypersensitivity response, also may reduce response to adrenaline (epinephrine) (see also section 3.4.3); see also notes above; reduce dose of oral propranolol in hepatic impairment; renal impairment (Appendix 3); pregnancy (Appendix 4); breast-feeding (Appendix 5); **interactions**: Appendix 1 (beta-blockers), **important**: verapamil interaction, see also p. 114

**Contra-indications** asthma (**important**: see Bronchospasm below), uncontrolled heart failure, Prinzmetal's angina, marked bradycardia, hypotension, sick sinus syndrome, second- or third- degree AV block, cardiogenic shock, metabolic acidosis, severe peripheral arterial disease; phaeochromocytoma (apart from specific use with alpha-blockers, see also notes above)

**Bronchospasm** The CSM has advised that beta-blockers, including those considered to be cardioselective, should not be given to patients with a history of asthma or bronchospasm. However, in rare situations where there is no alternative a cardioselective beta-blocker is given to these patients with extreme caution and under specialist supervision

**Side-effects** bradycardia, heart failure, hypotension, conduction disorders, bronchospasm, peripheral

2 Cardiovascular system

vasoconstriction (including exacerbation of intermittent claudication and Raynaud's phenomenon), gastro-intestinal disturbances, fatigue, sleep disturbances; rare reports of rashes and dry eyes (reversible on withdrawal), sexual dysfunction, and exacerbation of psoriasis; see also notes above; **overdosage:** see Emergency Treatment of Poisoning, p. 32

**Dose**

- By mouth, hypertension, initially 80 mg twice daily, increased at weekly intervals as required; maintenance 160–320 mg daily

  Portal hypertension, initially 40 mg twice daily, increased to 80 mg twice daily according to heart-rate; max. 160 mg twice daily

  Phaeochromocytoma (only with an alpha-blocker), 60 mg daily for 3 days before surgery *or* 30 mg daily in patients unsuitable for surgery

  Angina, initially 40 mg 2–3 times daily; maintenance 120–240 mg daily

  Arrhythmias, hypertrophic obstructive cardiomyopathy, anxiety tachycardia, and thyrotoxicosis (adjunct), 10–40 mg 3–4 times daily

  Anxiety with symptoms such as palpitation, sweating, tremor, 40 mg once daily, increased to 40 mg 3 times daily if necessary

  Prophylaxis after myocardial infarction, 40 mg 4 times daily for 2–3 days, then 80 mg twice daily, beginning 5 to 21 days after infarction

  Migraine prophylaxis and essential tremor, initially 40 mg 2–3 times daily; maintenance 80–160 mg daily

- By intravenous injection, arrhythmias and thyrotoxic crisis, 1 mg over 1 minute; if necessary repeat at 2-minute intervals; max. 10 mg (5 mg in anaesthesia)

  Note Excessive bradycardia can be countered with intravenous injection of atropine sulphate 0.6–2.4 mg in divided doses of 600 micrograms; for **overdosage** see Emergency Treatment of Poisoning, p. 32

**Propranolol** (Non-proprietary) PoM

Tablets, propranolol hydrochloride 10 mg, net price 28 = £1.25; 40 mg, 28 = £1.18; 80 mg, 56 = £1.76; 160 mg, 56 = £2.76. Label: 8

Brands include *Angilol®*

Oral solution, propranolol hydrochloride 5 mg/5 mL, net price 150 mL = £12.50; 10 mg/5 mL, 150 mL = £16.45; 50 mg/5 mL, 150 mL = £19.98

Brands include *Syprol®*

**Inderal®** (AstraZeneca) PoM

Injection, propranolol hydrochloride 1 mg/mL, net price 1-mL amp = 21p

### Modified release

**Half-Inderal LA®** (AstraZeneca) PoM

Capsules, m/r, lavender/pink, propranolol hydrochloride 80 mg. Net price 28-cap pack = £5.40. Label: 8, 25

Note Modified-release capsules containing propranolol hydrochloride 80 mg also available; brands include *Bedranol SR®*, *Half Beta Prograne®*

**Inderal-LA®** (AstraZeneca) PoM

Capsules, m/r, lavender/pink, propranolol hydrochloride 160 mg. Net price 28-cap pack = £6.67. Label: 8, 25

Note Modified-release capsules containing propranolol hydrochloride 160 mg also available; brands include *Bedranol SR®*, *Beta Prograne®*, *Lopranol LA®*, *Slo-Pro®*

## ACEBUTOLOL

**Indications** see under Dose

**Cautions** see under Propranolol Hydrochloride

**Contra-indications** see under Propranolol Hydrochloride

**Side-effects** see under Propranolol Hydrochloride

**Dose**

- Hypertension, initially 400 mg once daily *or* 200 mg twice daily, increased after 2 weeks to 400 mg twice daily if necessary
- Angina, initially 400 mg once daily *or* 200 mg twice daily; 300 mg 3 times daily in severe angina; up to 1.2 g daily has been used
- Arrhythmias, 0.4–1.2 g daily in 2–3 divided doses

**Sectral®** (Winthrop) PoM

Capsules, acebutolol (as hydrochloride) 100 mg (buff/white), net price 84-cap pack = £14.97; 200 mg (buff/pink), 56-cap pack = £19.18. Label: 8

Tablets, f/c, acebutolol 400 mg (as hydrochloride). Net price 28-tab pack = £18.62. Label: 8

## ATENOLOL

**Indications** see under Dose

**Cautions** see under Propranolol Hydrochloride

**Contra-indications** see under Propranolol Hydrochloride

**Side-effects** see under Propranolol Hydrochloride

**Dose**

- By mouth, hypertension, 25–50 mg daily (higher doses rarely necessary)

  Angina, 100 mg daily in 1 or 2 doses

  Arrhythmias, 50–100 mg daily

- By intravenous injection, arrhythmias, 2.5 mg at a rate of 1 mg/minute, repeated at 5-minute intervals to a max. of 10 mg

  Note Excessive bradycardia can be countered with intravenous injection of atropine sulphate 0.6–2.4 mg in divided doses of 600 micrograms; for **overdosage** see Emergency Treatment of Poisoning, p. 32

- By intravenous infusion, arrhythmias, 150 micrograms/kg over 20 minutes, repeated every 12 hours if required

  Early intervention within 12 hours of myocardial infarction (section 2.10.1), by intravenous injection over 5 minutes, 5 mg, then by mouth, 50 mg after 15 minutes, 50 mg after 12 hours, then 100 mg daily

**Atenolol** (Non-proprietary) PoM

Tablets, atenolol 25 mg, net price 28-tab pack = £1.12; 50 mg, 28-tab pack = 84p; 100 mg, 28-tab pack = £1.20. Label: 8

Brands include *Atenix®*

**Tenormin®** (AstraZeneca) PoM

'25' tablets, f/c, atenolol 25 mg. Net price 28-tab pack = £4.41. Label: 8

LS tablets, orange, f/c, scored, atenolol 50 mg. Net price 28-tab pack = £5.11. Label: 8

Tablets, orange, f/c, scored, atenolol 100 mg. Net price 28-tab pack = £6.50. Label: 8

Syrup, sugar-free, atenolol 25 mg/5mL. Net price 300 mL = £8.55. Label: 8

Injection, atenolol 500 micrograms/mL. Net price 10-mL amp = 96p (hosp. only)

**With diuretic**

**Co-tenidone** (Non-proprietary) PoM

Tablets, co-tenidone 50/12.5 (atenolol 50 mg, chlortalidone 12.5 mg), net price 28-tab pack = £2.24; co-tenidone 100/25 (atenolol 100 mg, chlortalidone 25 mg), 28-tab pack = £2.10. Label: 8

Brands include *AtenixCo®*, *Totaretic®*

**Dose** hypertension, 1 tablet daily (but see also under Dose above)

**Kalten®** (BPC 100) PoM

Capsules, red/ivory, atenolol 50 mg, co-amilozide 2.5/25 (anhydrous amiloride hydrochloride 2.5 mg, hydrochlorothiazide 25 mg). Net price 28-cap pack = £8.39. Label: 8

**Dose** hypertension, 1 capsule daily

**Tenoret 50®** (AstraZeneca) PoM

Tablets, brown, f/c, co-tenidone 50/12.5 (atenolol 50 mg, chlortalidone 12.5 mg). Net price 28-tab pack = £5.70. Label: 8

**Dose** hypertension, 1 tablet daily

**Tenoretic®** (AstraZeneca) PoM

Tablets, brown, f/c, co-tenidone 100/25 (atenolol 100 mg, chlortalidone 25 mg). Net price 28-tab pack = £8.12. Label: 8

**Dose** hypertension, 1 tablet daily (but see also under Dose above)

**With calcium-channel blocker**

**Note** Only indicated when calcium-channel blocker or beta-blocker alone proves inadequate

**Beta-Adalat®** (Bayer) PoM

Capsules, reddish-brown, atenolol 50 mg, nifedipine 20 mg (m/r). Net price 28-cap pack = £10.41. Label: 8, 25

**Dose** hypertension, 1 capsule daily, increased if necessary to twice daily; elderly, 1 daily

Angina, 1 capsule twice daily

**Tenif®** (AstraZeneca) PoM

Capsules, reddish-brown, atenolol 50 mg, nifedipine 20 mg (m/r). Net price 28-cap pack = £10.63. Label: 8, 25

**Dose** hypertension, 1 capsule daily, increased if necessary to twice daily; elderly, 1 daily

Angina, 1 capsule twice daily

## BISOPROLOL FUMARATE

**Indications** see under Dose

**Cautions** see under Propranolol Hydrochloride; in heart failure monitor clinical status for 4 hours after initiation (with low dose) and ensure heart failure not worsening before increasing each dose; psoriasis; hepatic impairment (Appendix 2)

**Contra-indications** see under Propranolol Hydrochloride; also acute or decompensated heart failure requiring intravenous inotropes; sino-atrial block

**Side-effects** see under Propranolol Hydrochloride

**Dose**

- Hypertension and angina, usually 10 mg once daily (5 mg may be adequate in some patients); max. 20 mg daily
- Adjunct in stable moderate to severe heart failure (section 2.5.5), initially 1.25 mg once daily (in the morning) for 1 week then, if well tolerated, increased to 2.5 mg once daily for 1 week, then 3.75 mg once daily for 1 week, then 5 mg once daily for 4 weeks, then 7.5 mg once daily for 4 weeks, then 10 mg once daily; max. 10 mg daily

**Bisoprolol Fumarate** (Non-proprietary) PoM

Tablets, bisoprolol fumarate 5 mg, net price 28-tab pack = £2.09; 10 mg, 28-tab pack = £2.11. Label: 8

Brands include *Bipranix®*, *Soloc®*, *Vivacor®*

**Cardicor®** (Merck) ▼ PoM

Tablets, f/c, bisoprolol fumarate 1.25 mg, net price 28-tab pack = £8.56; 2.5 mg (scored), 28-tab pack = £5.90; 3.75 mg (scored, white-yellow), 28-tab pack = £5.90; 5 mg (scored, light yellow), 28-tab pack = £5.90; 7.5 mg (scored, yellow), 28-tab pack = £5.90; 10 mg (scored, orange), 28-tab pack = £5.90. Label: 8

**Emcor®** (Merck) PoM

LS Tablets, yellow, f/c, scored, bisoprolol fumarate 5 mg. Net price 28-tab pack = £9.42. Label: 8

Tablets, orange, f/c, scored, bisoprolol fumarate 10 mg. Net price 28-tab pack = £10.57. Label: 8

## CARVEDILOL

**Indications** hypertension; angina; adjunct to diuretics, digoxin, or ACE inhibitors in symptomatic chronic heart failure

**Cautions** see under Propranolol Hydrochloride; before increasing dose ensure renal function and heart failure not deteriorating; severe heart failure, avoid in acute or decompensated heart failure requiring intravenous inotropes

**Contra-indications** see under Propranolol Hydrochloride; severe chronic heart failure; hepatic impairment

**Side-effects** postural hypotension, dizziness, headache, fatigue, gastro-intestinal disturbances, bradycardia; occasionally diminished peripheral circulation, peripheral oedema and painful extremities, dry mouth, dry eyes, eye irritation or disturbed vision, impotence, disturbances of micturition, influenza-like symptoms; rarely angina, AV block, exacerbation of intermittent claudication or Raynaud's phenomenon; allergic skin reactions, exacerbation of psoriasis, nasal stuffiness, wheezing, depressed mood, sleep disturbances, paraesthesia, heart failure, changes in liver enzymes, thrombocytopenia, leucopenia also reported

**Dose**

- Hypertension, initially 12.5 mg once daily, increased after 2 days to usual dose of 25 mg once daily; if necessary may be further increased at intervals of at least 2 weeks to max. 50 mg daily in single or divided doses; ELDERLY initial dose of 12.5 mg daily may provide satisfactory control
- Angina, initially 12.5 mg twice daily, increased after 2 days to 25 mg twice daily
- Adjunct in heart failure (section 2.5.5) initially 3.125 mg twice daily (with food), dose increased at intervals of at least 2 weeks to 6.25 mg twice daily, then to 12.5 mg twice daily, then to 25 mg twice daily; increase to highest dose tolerated, max. 25 mg twice daily in patients with severe heart failure or body-weight less than 85 kg and 50 mg twice daily in patients over 85 kg

**Carvedilol** (Non-proprietary) PoM

Tablets, carvedilol 3.125 mg, net price 28-tab pack = £6.67; 6.25 mg, 28-tab pack = £7.71; 12.5 mg, 28-tab pack = £8.69; 25 mg, 28-tab pack = £10.56. Label: 8

**Eucardic®** (Roche) PoM

Tablets, all scored, carvedilol 3.125 mg (pink), net price 28-tab pack = £7.57; 6.25 mg (yellow), 28-tab pack = £8.41; 12.5 mg (peach), 28-tab pack = £9.35; 25 mg, 28-tab pack = £11.68. Label: 8

## CELIPROLOL HYDROCHLORIDE

**Indications** mild to moderate hypertension

**Cautions** see under Propranolol Hydrochloride

**Contra-indications** see under Propranolol Hydrochloride

**Side-effects** headache, dizziness, fatigue, nausea and somnolence; also bradycardia, bronchospasm; depression and pneumonitis reported rarely

**Dose**

- 200 mg once daily in the morning, increased to 400 mg once daily if necessary

**Celiprolol** (Non-proprietary) PoM

Tablets, celiprolol hydrochloride 200 mg, net price 28-tab pack = £6.52; 400 mg, 28-tab pack = £16.38. Label: 8, 22

**Celectol®** (Winthrop) PoM

Tablets, both f/c, scored, celiprolol hydrochloride 200 mg (yellow), net price 28-tab pack = £15.99; 400 mg, 28-tab pack = £31.97. Label: 8, 22

## ESMOLOL HYDROCHLORIDE

**Indications** short-term treatment of supraventricular arrhythmias (including atrial fibrillation, atrial flutter, sinus tachycardia); tachycardia and hypertension in peri-operative period

**Cautions** see under Propranolol Hydrochloride; renal impairment

**Contra-indications** see under Propranolol Hydrochloride

**Side-effects** see under Propranolol Hydrochloride; also on infusion venous irritation and thrombophlebitis

**Dose**

- By intravenous infusion, usually within range 50–200 micrograms/kg/minute (consult product literature for details of dose titration and doses during peri-operative period)

**Brevibloc®** (Baxter) PoM

Injection, esmolol hydrochloride 10 mg/mL, net price 10-mL vial = £7.79, 250-mL infusion bag = £81.54

Injection concentrate, esmolol hydrochloride 250 mg/mL (for dilution before infusion), 10-mL amp = £79.08

## LABETALOL HYDROCHLORIDE

**Indications** hypertension (including hypertension in pregnancy, hypertension with angina, and hypertension following acute myocardial infarction); hypertensive crisis (but see section 2.5); controlled hypotension in anaesthesia

**Cautions** see under Propranolol Hydrochloride; interferes with laboratory tests for catecholamines; liver damage (see below)

**Liver damage** Severe hepatocellular damage reported after both short-term and long-term treatment. Appropriate laboratory testing needed at first symptom of liver dysfunction and if laboratory evidence of damage (or if jaundice) labetalol should be stopped and not restarted

**Contra-indications** see under Propranolol Hydrochloride

**Side-effects** postural hypotension (avoid upright position during and for 3 hours after intravenous administration), tiredness, weakness, headache, rashes, scalp tingling, difficulty in micturition, epigastric pain, nausea, vomiting; liver damage (see above); rarely lichenoid rash

**Dose**

- By mouth, initially 100 mg (50 mg in elderly) twice daily with food, increased at intervals of 14 days to usual dose of 200 mg twice daily; up to 800 mg daily in 2 divided doses (3–4 divided doses if higher); max. 2.4 g daily
- By intravenous injection, 50 mg over at least 1 minute, repeated after 5 minutes if necessary; max. total dose 200 mg

  **Note** Excessive bradycardia can be countered with intravenous injection of atropine sulphate 0.6–2.4 mg in divided doses of 600 micrograms; for **overdosage** see Emergency Treatment of Poisoning, p. 32
- By intravenous infusion, 2 mg/minute until satisfactory response then discontinue; usual total dose 50–200 mg, (**not** recommended for phaeochromocytoma, see under Phaeochromocytoma, section 2.5.4)

  Hypertension of pregnancy, 20 mg/hour, doubled every 30 minutes; usual max. 160 mg/hour

  Hypertension following myocardial infarction, 15 mg/hour, gradually increased to max. 120 mg/hour

**Labetalol Hydrochloride** (Non-proprietary) PoM

Tablets, all f/c, labetalol hydrochloride 100 mg, net price, 56 = £6.87; 200 mg, 56 = £10.01; 400 mg, 56 = £15.60. Label: 8, 21

**Trandate®** (Celltech) PoM

Tablets, all orange, f/c, labetalol hydrochloride 50 mg, net price 56-tab pack = £3.79; 100 mg, 56-tab pack = £4.17; 200 mg, 56-tab pack = £6.77; 400 mg, 56-tab pack = £9.42. Label: 8, 21

Injection, labetalol hydrochloride 5 mg/mL. Net price 20-mL amp = £2.12

## METOPROLOL TARTRATE

**Indications** see under Dose

**Cautions** see under Propranolol Hydrochloride; reduce dose in hepatic impairment

**Contra-indications** see under Propranolol Hydrochloride

**Side-effects** see under Propranolol Hydrochloride

**Dose**

- By mouth, hypertension, initially 100 mg daily, increased if necessary to 200 mg daily in 1–2 divided doses; max. 400 mg daily (but high doses rarely necessary)

  Angina, 50–100 mg 2–3 times daily

  Arrhythmias, usually 50 mg 2–3 times daily; up to 300 mg daily in divided doses if necessary

  Migraine prophylaxis, 100–200 mg daily in divided doses

  Hyperthyroidism (adjunct), 50 mg 4 times daily
- By intravenous injection, arrhythmias, up to 5 mg at rate 1–2 mg/minute, repeated after 5 minutes if necessary, total dose 10–15 mg

  **Note** Excessive bradycardia can be countered with intravenous injection of atropine sulphate 0.6–2.4 mg in divided doses of 600 micrograms; for **overdosage** see Emergency Treatment of Poisoning, p. 32

  In surgery, 2–4 mg by slow intravenous injection at induction or to control arrhythmias developing during anaesthesia; 2-mg doses may be repeated to a max. of 10 mg

Early intervention within 12 hours of infarction, 5 mg by intravenous injection every 2 minutes to a max. of 15 mg, followed after 15 minutes by 50 mg by mouth every 6 hours for 48 hours; maintenance 200 mg daily in divided doses

**Metoprolol Tartrate** (Non-proprietary) PoM
Tablets, metoprolol tartrate 50 mg, net price 28 = £1.57; 100 mg, 28 = £2.52. Label: 8

**Betaloc®** (AstraZeneca) PoM
Tablets, both scored, metoprolol tartrate 50 mg, net price 100-tab pack = £3.30; 100 mg, 100-tab pack = £6.13. Label: 8

Injection, metoprolol tartrate 1 mg/mL. Net price 5-mL amp = 42p

**Lopresor®** (Novartis) PoM
Tablets, both f/c, scored, metoprolol tartrate 50 mg (pink), net price 56-tab pack = £2.57; 100 mg (blue), 56-tab pack = £6.68. Label: 8

**Modified release**

**Betaloc-SA®** (AstraZeneca) PoM
Durules® (= tablets, m/r), metoprolol tartrate 200 mg, net price 28-tab pack = £4.56. Label: 8, 25
Dose hypertension, angina, 200 mg daily in the morning, increased to 400 mg daily if necessary; migraine prophylaxis, 200 mg daily

**Lopresor SR®** (Novartis) PoM
Tablets, m/r, yellow, f/c, metoprolol tartrate 200 mg, net price 28-tab pack = £9.80. Label: 8, 25
Dose hypertension, 200 mg daily; angina, 200-400 mg daily; migraine prophylaxis, 200 mg daily

**With diuretic**

**Co-Betaloc®** (Searle) PoM
Tablets, scored, metoprolol tartrate 100 mg, hydrochlorothiazide 12.5 mg, net price 28-tab pack = £5.59. Label: 8
Dose hypertension, 1–3 tablets daily in single or divided doses

## NADOLOL

**Indications** see under Dose

**Cautions** see under Propranolol Hydrochloride

**Contra-indications** see under Propranolol Hydrochloride

**Side-effects** see under Propranolol Hydrochloride

**Dose**

- Hypertension, 80 mg daily, increased at weekly intervals if required; max. 240 mg daily
- Angina, 40 mg daily, increased at weekly intervals if required; usual max. 160 mg daily
- Arrhythmias, initially 40 mg daily, increased to 160 mg if required; reduce to 40 mg if bradycardia occurs
- Migraine prophylaxis, initially 40 mg daily, increased by 40 mg at weekly intervals; usual maintenance dose 80–160 mg daily
- Thyrotoxicosis (adjunct), 80–160 mg daily

**Corgard®** (Sanofi-Synthelabo) PoM
Tablets, blue, scored, nadolol 80 mg, net price 28-tab pack = £5.20. Label: 8

## NEBIVOLOL

**Indications** essential hypertension

**Cautions** see under Propranolol Hydrochloride; reduce dose in renal impairment (Appendix 3); elderly

**Contra-indications** see under Propranolol Hydrochloride; hepatic impairment (Appendix 2)

**Side-effects** see under Propranolol Hydrochloride; oedema, headache, depression, visual disturbances, paraesthesia, impotence

**Dose**

- 5 mg daily; ELDERLY initially 2.5 mg daily, increased if necessary to 5 mg daily

**Nebilet®** (Menarini) PoM
Tablets, scored, nebivolol (as hydrochloride) 5 mg, net price 28-tab pack = £9.23. Label: 8

## OXPRENOLOL HYDROCHLORIDE

**Indications** see under Dose

**Cautions** see under Propranolol Hydrochloride; reduce dose in hepatic impairment

**Contra-indications** see under Propranolol Hydrochloride

**Side-effects** see under Propranolol Hydrochloride

**Dose**

- Hypertension, 80–160 mg daily in 2–3 divided doses, increased as required; max. 320 mg daily
- Angina, 80–160 mg daily in 2–3 divided doses; max. 320 mg daily
- Arrhythmias, 40–240 mg daily in 2–3 divided doses; max. 240 mg daily
- Anxiety symptoms (short-term use), 40–80 mg daily in 1–2 divided doses

**Oxprenolol** (Non-proprietary) PoM
Tablets, all coated, oxprenolol hydrochloride 20 mg, net price 56 = £1.55; 40 mg, 56 = £3.11; 80 mg, 56 = £6.20; 160 mg, 20 = £2.36. Label: 8

**Trasicor®** (Amdipharm) PoM
Tablets, all f/c, oxprenolol hydrochloride 20 mg (contain gluten), net price 56-tab pack = £1.55; 40 mg (contain gluten), 56-tab pack = £3.11; 80 mg (yellow), 56-tab pack = £6.20. Label: 8

**Modified release**

**Slow-Trasicor®** (Amdipharm) PoM
Tablets, m/r, f/c, oxprenolol hydrochloride 160 mg. Net price 28-tab pack = £6.63. Label: 8, 25
Dose hypertension, angina, initially 160 mg once daily; if necessary may be increased to max. 320 mg daily

**With diuretic**

**Trasidrex®** (Goldshield) PoM
Tablets, red, s/c, co-prenozide 160/0.25 (oxprenolol hydrochloride 160 mg (m/r), cyclopenthiazide 250 micrograms). Net price 28-tab pack = £8.88. Label: 8, 25
Dose hypertension, 1 tablet daily, increased if necessary to 2 daily as a single dose

## PINDOLOL

**Indications** see under Dose

**Cautions** see under Propranolol Hydrochloride

**Contra-indications** see under Propranolol Hydrochloride

**Side-effects** see under Propranolol Hydrochloride

**Dose**

- Hypertension, initially 5 mg 2–3 times daily *or* 15 mg once daily, increased as required at weekly intervals; usual maintenance 15–30 mg daily; max. 45 mg daily
- Angina, 2.5–5 mg up to 3 times daily

**Pindolol** (Non-proprietary) PoM
Tablets, pindolol 5 mg, net price 100-tab pack = £7.10. Label: 8

**Visken®** (Amdipharm) PoM
Tablets, both scored, pindolol 5 mg, net price 56-tab pack = £4.88; 15 mg, 28-tab pack = £7.33. Label: 8

**With diuretic**

**Viskaldix®** (Amdipharm) PoM
Tablets, scored, pindolol 10 mg, clopamide 5 mg. Net price 28-tab pack = £6.70. Label: 8
**Dose** hypertension, 1 tablet daily in the morning, increased if necessary to 2 daily; max. 3 daily

## SOTALOL HYDROCHLORIDE

**Indications** *Tablets and injection:* life-threatening arrhythmias including ventricular tachyarrhythmias, symptomatic non-sustained ventricular tachyarrhythmias

*Tablets only:* prophylaxis of paroxysmal atrial tachycardia or fibrillation, paroxysmal AV re-entrant tachycardias (both nodal and involving accessory pathways), paroxysmal supraventricular tachycardia after cardiac surgery, maintenance of sinus rhythm following cardioversion of atrial fibrillation or flutter

*Injection only:* electrophysiological study of inducible ventricular and supraventricular arrhythmias; temporary substitution for tablets

**CSM advice.** The use of sotalol should be limited to the treatment of ventricular arrhythmias or prophylaxis of supraventricular arrhythmias (see above). It should no longer be used for angina, hypertension, thyrotoxicosis or for secondary prevention after myocardial infarction; when stopping sotalol for these indications, the dose should be reduced gradually

**Cautions** see under Propranolol Hydrochloride; reduce dose in renal impairment (avoid if severe); correct hypokalaemia, hypomagnesaemia, or other electrolyte disturbances; severe or prolonged diarrhoea; **interactions:** Appendix 1 (beta-blockers), **important:** verapamil interaction see also p. 114

**Contra-indications** see under Propranolol Hydrochloride; congenital or acquired long QT syndrome; torsades de pointes; renal failure

**Side-effects** see under Propranolol Hydrochloride; arrhythmogenic (pro-arrhythmic) effect (torsades de pointes—increased risk in women)

**Dose**

- By mouth with ECG monitoring and measurement of corrected QT interval, arrhythmias, initially 80 mg daily in 1–2 divided doses increased gradually at intervals of 2–3 days to usual dose of 160–320 mg daily in 2 divided doses; higher doses of 480–640 mg daily for life-threatening ventricular arrhythmias under specialist supervision
- By intravenous injection over 10 minutes, acute arrhythmias, 20–120 mg with ECG monitoring, repeated if necessary with 6-hour intervals between injections

  Diagnostic use, see product literature

**Note** Excessive bradycardia can be countered with intravenous injection of atropine sulphate 0.6–2.4 mg in divided doses of 600 micrograms; for **overdosage** see Emergency Treatment of Poisoning, p. 32

**Sotalol** (Non-proprietary) PoM
Tablets, sotalol hydrochloride 40 mg, net price 56 = £1.34; 80 mg, 56 = £1.99; 160 mg, 28 = £3.84. Label: 8

**Beta-Cardone®** (Celltech) PoM
Tablets, all scored, sotalol hydrochloride 40 mg (green), net price 56-tab pack = £1.34; 80 mg (pink), 56-tab pack = £1.99; 200 mg, 28-tab pack = £2.50. Label: 8

**Sotacor®** (Bristol-Myers Squibb) PoM
Tablets, both scored, sotalol hydrochloride 80 mg, net price 28-tab pack = £3.25; 160 mg, 28-tab pack = £6.41. Label: 8

Injection, sotalol hydrochloride 10 mg/mL. Net price 4-mL amp = £1.76

## TIMOLOL MALEATE

**Indications** see under Dose; glaucoma (section 11.6)

**Cautions** see under Propranolol Hydrochloride; hepatic impairment (Appendix 2)

**Contra-indications** see under Propranolol Hydrochloride

**Side-effects** see under Propranolol Hydrochloride

**Dose**

- Hypertension, initially 5 mg twice daily *or* 10 mg once daily; gradually increased if necessary to max. 60 mg daily (given in divided doses above 20 mg daily)
- Angina, initially 5 mg 2–3 times daily, usual maintenance 35–45 mg daily (range 15–45 mg daily)
- Prophylaxis after myocardial infarction, initially 5 mg twice daily, increased after 2 days to 10 mg twice daily, starting 7 to 28 days after infarction
- Migraine prophylaxis, 10–20 mg once daily

**Betim®** (Valeant) PoM
Tablets, scored, timolol maleate 10 mg. Net price 30-tab pack = £2.08. Label: 8

**With diuretic**

**Moducren®** (MSD) PoM
Tablets, blue, scored, timolol maleate 10 mg, co-amilozide 2.5/25 (amiloride hydrochloride 2.5 mg, hydrochlorothiazide 25 mg). Net price 28-tab pack = £8.00. Label: 8
**Dose** hypertension, 1–2 tablets daily as a single dose

**Prestim®** (Valeant) PoM
Tablets, scored, timolol maleate 10 mg, bendroflumethiazide 2.5 mg. Net price 30-tab pack = £3.49. Label: 8
**Dose** hypertension, 1–2 tablets daily; max. 4 daily

2 Cardiovascular system

# 2.5 Hypertension and heart failure


2.5.1 Vasodilator antihypertensive drugs
2.5.2 Centrally acting antihypertensive drugs
2.5.3 Adrenergic neurone blocking drugs
2.5.4 Alpha-adrenoceptor blocking drugs
2.5.5 Drugs affecting the renin-angiotensin system


Lowering raised blood pressure decreases the frequency of stroke, coronary events, heart failure, and renal failure. Advice on antihypertensive therapy in this section takes into account the recommendations of the British Hypertension Society (Guidelines for management of hypertension: report of the fourth working party of the British Hypertension Society 2004—BHS IV. *J Hum Hypertens* 2004; **18:** 139–85).

Possible causes of hypertension (e.g. renal disease, endocrine causes), contributory factors, risk factors, and the presence of any complications of hypertension, such as left ventricular hypertrophy, should be established. Patients should be given advice on lifestyle changes to reduce blood pressure or cardiovascular risk; these include smoking cessation, weight reduction, reduction of excessive intake of alcohol, reduction of dietary salt, reduction of total and saturated fat, increasing exercise, and increasing fruit and vegetable intake.

**Thresholds and targets for treatment** The following thresholds for treatment[1] are recommended:

- Accelerated (malignant) hypertension (with papilloedema or fundal haemorrhages and exudates) *or* acute cardiovascular complications, admit for **immediate treatment**;
- Where the initial blood pressure is systolic $\geq$ 220 mmHg *or* diastolic $\geq$ 120 mmHg, **treat immediately**;
- Where the initial blood pressure is systolic 180–219 mmHg *or* diastolic 110–119 mmHg, confirm over 1–2 weeks then **treat** if these values are sustained;
- Where the initial blood pressure is systolic 160–179 mmHg *or* diastolic 100–109 mmHg, *and* the patient has cardiovascular complications, target-organ damage (e.g. left ventricular hypertrophy, renal impairment) or diabetes mellitus (type 1 or 2), confirm over 3–4 weeks then **treat** if these values are sustained;
- Where the initial blood pressure is systolic 160–179 mmHg *or* diastolic 100–109 mmHg, but the patient has *no* cardiovascular complications, no target-organ damage, or no diabetes, advise lifestyle changes, reassess weekly initially and **treat** if these values are sustained on repeat measurements over 4–12 weeks;
- Where the initial blood pressure is systolic 140–159 mmHg *or* diastolic 90–99 mmHg *and* the patient has cardiovascular complications, target-organ damage or diabetes, confirm within 12 weeks and **treat** if these values are sustained;
- Where the initial blood pressure is systolic 140–159 mmHg *or* diastolic 90–99 mmHg and *no* cardiovascular complications, no target-organ damage, or no diabetes, advise lifestyle changes and **reassess** monthly; **treat** persistent mild hypertension if the 10-year cardiovascular disease risk is $\geq$ 20%[2].

An optimal target systolic blood pressure < 140 mmHg *and* diastolic blood pressure < 85 mmHg is suggested.[3] In some individuals it may not be possible to reduce blood pressure below the suggested targets despite the use of appropriate therapy.

**Drug treatment of hypertension** No consistent or important differences have been found between the major classes of antihypertensive drugs in terms of antihypertensive efficacy, side-effects or changes to quality of life (but there are differences in response related to age and ethnic group). The choice of antihypertensive drug will depend on the relevant indications or contra-indications for the individual patient; *some* indications and contra-indications for various antihypertensive drugs are shown below (see also under individual drug entries for details):

- **Thiazides** (section 2.2.1)—particularly indicated for hypertension in the elderly (see below); a contra-indication is gout;
- **Beta-blockers** (section 2.4)—indications include myocardial infarction, angina; compelling contra-indications include asthma, heart block;
- **ACE inhibitors** (section 2.5.5.1)—indications include heart failure, left ventricular dysfunction and diabetic nephropathy; contra-indications include renovascular disease (but see section 2.5.5.1) and pregnancy;
- **Angiotensin-II receptor antagonists** (section 2.5.5.2) are alternatives for those who cannot tolerate ACE inhibitors because of persistent dry cough, but they have the same contra-indications as ACE inhibitors;
- **Calcium-channel blockers**. There are important differences between calcium-channel blockers (section 2.6.2). **Dihydropyridine calcium-channel blockers** are valuable in isolated systolic hypertension in the elderly when a low-dose thiazide is contra-indicated or not tolerated (see below). **'Rate-limiting' calcium-channel blockers** (e.g. diltiazem, verapamil) may be valuable in angina; contra-indications include heart failure and heart block;
- **Alpha-blockers** (section 2.5.4)—a possible indication is prostatism; a contra-indication is urinary incontinence.

A single antihypertensive drug is often not adequate and other antihypertensive drugs are usually added in a step-wise manner until control is achieved. Unless it is

1. Thresholds and targets for treatment based on blood pressure measured in clinic may not apply to ambulatory or home blood-pressure monitoring, which usually give lower values.

2. Cardiovascular disease risk may be determined from the chart issued by the British Hypertension Society (*J Hum Hypertens* 2004; **18**: 139–85)—see inside back cover. The Joint British Societies' 'Cardiac Risk Assessor' computer programme may also be used to determine cardiovascular disease risk by adding together the coronary heart disease risk and stroke risk.

3. A lower target for blood pressure should be considered for the secondary prevention of stroke, and for patients with diabetes and renal disease

necessary to lower the blood pressure urgently, an interval of at least 4 weeks should be allowed to determine response.

Where two antihypertensive drugs are needed, an ACE inhibitor *or* an angiotensin-II receptor antagonist *or* a beta-blocker may be combined with *either* a thiazide *or* a calcium-channel blocker.

If control is inadequate with 2 drugs, a thiazide *and* a calcium-channel blocker may be added. In patients at high risk of diabetes it is best to avoid a combination of a beta-blocker and a thiazide. In patients with *primary hyperaldosteronism*, spironolactone (section 2.2.3) is effective.

Response to drug treatment for hypertension may be affected by the patient's age and ethnic background. A beta-blocker or an ACE inhibitor may be the most appropriate initial drug in younger Caucasians; Afro-Caribbean patients respond less well to these drugs and a thiazide or a calcium-channel blocker may be chosen for initial treatment.

**Other measures to reduce cardiovascular risk** **Aspirin** (section 2.9) in a dose of 75 mg daily reduces the risk of cardiovascular events and myocardial infarction; however, concerns about an increased risk of bleeding need to be considered. Unless it is contra-indicated, aspirin is recommended for *secondary prevention* in patients with cardiovascular complications (myocardial infarction, angina, non-haemorrhagic cerebrovascular disease, peripheral vascular disease, or atherosclerotic renovascular disease), and for *primary prevention* in patients aged over 50 years with controlled blood pressure (systolic pressure $< 150$ mmHg and diastolic pressure $< 90$ mmHg) who have end-organ damage, type 2 diabetes, or a cardiovascular disease risk $\geq 20\%$ over 10 years[1].

A **statin** can be of benefit in those at high risk of cardiovascular disease and in those with hypercholesterolaemia (see section 2.12 for details).

**Hypertension in the elderly** Benefit from antihypertensive therapy is evident up to at least 80 years of age, but it is probably inappropriate to apply a strict age limit when deciding on drug therapy. Elderly individuals who have a good outlook for longevity should have their blood pressure lowered if they are hypertensive. The thresholds for treatment are diastolic pressure averaging $\geq 90$ mmHg *or* systolic pressure averaging $\geq 160$ mmHg over 3 to 6 months' observation (despite appropriate non-drug treatment). A low dose of a thiazide is the clear drug of first choice, with addition of another antihypertensive drug when necessary.

**Isolated systolic hypertension** Isolated systolic hypertension (systolic pressure $\geq 160$ mmHg, diastolic pressure $< 90$ mmHg) is associated with an increased cardiovascular disease risk, particularly in those aged over 60 years. Systolic blood pressure averaging 160 mmHg or higher over 3 to 6 months (despite appropriate non-drug treatment) should be lowered in those over 60 years, even if diastolic hypertension is absent.

1. Cardiovascular disease risk may be determined from the chart issued by the British Hypertension Society (*J Hum Hypertens* 2004; **18**: 139–85)—see inside back cover. The Joint British Societies' 'Cardiac Risk Assessor' computer programme may also be used to determine cardiovascular disease risk by adding together the coronary heart disease risk and stroke risk.

Treatment with a low dose of a thiazide, with addition of a beta-blocker when necessary is effective; a long-acting dihydropyridine calcium-channel blocker is recommended when a thiazide is contra-indicated or not tolerated. Patients with severe postural hypotension should not receive blood pressure lowering drugs.

Isolated systolic hypertension in younger patients is uncommon but treatment may be indicated in those with a threshold systolic pressure of 160 mmHg (or less if at increased risk of cardiovascular disease, see above).

**Hypertension in diabetes** For patients with diabetes, the aim should be to maintain systolic pressure $< 130$ mmHg and diastolic pressure $< 80$ mmHg. However, in some individuals, it may not be possible to achieve this level of control despite appropriate therapy. Low-dose thiazides, beta-blockers, ACE inhibitors (or angiotensin-II receptor antagonists) and long-acting dihydropyridine calcium-channel blockers are all beneficial. Most patients require a combination of antihypertensive drugs.

Hypertension is common in type 2 (non-insulin-dependent) diabetes and antihypertensive treatment prevents macrovascular and microvascular complications. In type 1 (insulin-dependent) diabetes, hypertension usually indicates the presence of diabetic nephropathy. An ACE inhibitor (or an angiotensin-II receptor antagonist) may have a specific role in the management of diabetic nephropathy (section 6.1.5); in patients with type 2 diabetes, an ACE inhibitor (or an angiotensin-II receptor antagonist) can delay progression of microalbuminuria to nephropathy.

**Hypertension in renal disease** The threshold for antihypertensive treatment in patients with renal impairment or persistent proteinuria is a systolic blood pressure $\geq 140$ mmHg *or* a diastolic blood pressure $\geq 90$ mmHg. Optimal blood pressure is a systolic blood pressure $< 130$ mmHg and a diastolic pressure $< 80$ mmHg, or lower if proteinuria exceeds 1 g in 24 hours. Thiazides may be ineffective and high doses of loop diuretics may be required. Specific cautions apply to the use of ACE inhibitors in renal impairment, see section 2.5.5.1, but ACE inhibitors may be effective. Dihydropyridine calcium-channel blockers may be added.

**Hypertension in pregnancy** High blood pressure in pregnancy may usually be due to pre-existing essential hypertension or to pre-eclampsia. Methyldopa (section 2.5.2) is safe in pregnancy. Beta-blockers are effective and safe in the third trimester. Modified-release preparations of nifedipine [unlicensed] are also used for hypertension in pregnancy. Intravenous administration of labetalol (section 2.4) can be used to control hypertensive crises; alternatively, hydralazine (section 2.5.1) may be used by the intravenous route. For use of magnesium sulphate in pre-eclampsia and eclampsia, see section 9.5.1.3.

**Accelerated or very severe hypertension** Accelerated (or malignant) hypertension or very severe hypertension (e.g. diastolic blood pressure $> 140$ mmHg) requires urgent treatment in hospital, but it is not an indication for parenteral antihypertensive therapy. Normally treatment should be by mouth with a beta-blocker (atenolol or labetalol) or a long-acting calcium-channel blocker (e.g. amlodipine or modified-release nifedipine). Within the first 24 hours the diastolic blood pressure should be reduced to 100–110 mmHg. Over the next 2 or 3 days blood pressure should be normalised by using beta-blockers, calcium-channel blockers, diuretics, vasodilators, or ACE inhibitors. Very rapid reduction in blood pressure can reduce organ perfusion leading to cerebral infarction and blindness, deterioration in renal function, and myocardial ischaemia. Parenteral antihypertensive drugs are rarely necessary; sodium nitroprusside by infusion is the drug of choice on the rare occasions when parenteral treatment is necessary.

For advice on short-term management of hypertensive episodes in phaeochromocytoma, see under Phaeochromocytoma, section 2.5.4.

## 2.5.1 Vasodilator antihypertensive drugs

These are potent drugs, especially when used in combination with a beta-blocker and a thiazide. **Important:** for a warning on the hazards of a very rapid fall in blood pressure, see section 2.5.

**Diazoxide** has been used by intravenous injection in hypertensive emergencies.

**Hydralazine** given by mouth is a useful adjunct to other treatment, but when used alone causes tachycardia and fluid retention. Side-effects can be few if the dose is kept below 100 mg daily, but systemic lupus erythematosus should be suspected if there is unexplained weight loss, arthritis, or any other unexplained ill health.

**Sodium nitroprusside** is given by intravenous infusion to control severe hypertensive crises on the rare occasions when parenteral treatment is necessary.

**Minoxidil** should be reserved for the treatment of severe hypertension resistant to other drugs. Vasodilatation is accompanied by increased cardiac output and tachycardia and the patients develop fluid retention. For this reason the addition of a beta-blocker and a diuretic (usually furosemide, in high dosage) are mandatory. Hypertrichosis is troublesome and renders this drug unsuitable for women.

Prazosin, doxazosin, and terazosin (section 2.5.4) have alpha-blocking and vasodilator properties.

**Bosentan** and **iloprost** are licensed for the treatment of some types of pulmonary hypertension. **Epoprostenol** (section 2.8.1) is also used for the treatment of pulmonary hypertension.

### BOSENTAN

**Indications** pulmonary arterial hypertension

**Cautions** not to be initiated if systemic systolic blood pressure is below 85 mmHg; monitor liver function before and during treatment (reduce dose or suspend treatment if liver enzymes raised significantly)—discontinue if symptoms of liver impairment; monitor haemoglobin; **interactions:** Appendix 1 (bosentan)

**Contra-indications** hepatic impairment (Appendix 2); **avoid** pregnancy **during** and for **3 months after** treatment (Appendix 4); breast-feeding (Appendix 5)

**Side-effects** dyspepsia, flushing, hypotension, palpitation, fatigue, oedema, anaemia, pruritus, nasopharyngitis, hepatic impairment (see Cautions above)

**Dose**
- Initially 62.5 mg twice daily increased after 4 weeks to 125 mg twice daily; max. 250 mg twice daily

**Tracleer®** (Actelion) ▼ PoM
Tablets, f/c, orange, bosentan (as monohydrate) 62.5 mg, net price 56-tab pack = £1541.00; 125 mg, 56-tab pack = £1541.00

### DIAZOXIDE

**Indications** hypertensive emergency including severe hypertension associated with renal disease (but see section 2.5); hypoglycaemia (section 6.1.4)

**Cautions** ischaemic heart disease; renal impairment (Appendix 3); pregnancy and labour (Appendix 4); **interactions:** Appendix 1 (diazoxide)

**Side-effects** tachycardia, hypotension, hyperglycaemia, sodium and water retention; *rarely* cardiomegaly, hyperosmolar non-ketotic coma, leucopenia, thrombocytopenia, and hirsuitism

**Dose**
- By rapid intravenous injection (less than 30 seconds), 1–3 mg/kg to max. single dose of 150 mg (see below); may be repeated after 5–15 minutes if required

**Note** Single doses of 300 mg have been associated with angina and with myocardial and cerebral infarction

**Eudemine®** (Goldshield) PoM
Injection, diazoxide 15 mg/mL. Net price 20-mL amp = £30.00

Tablets, see section 6.1.4

### HYDRALAZINE HYDROCHLORIDE

**Indications** moderate to severe hypertension (adjunct); heart failure (with long-acting nitrate, but see section 2.5.5); hypertensive crisis (including during pregnancy) (but see section 2.5)

**Cautions** hepatic impairment (Appendix 2); renal impairment (Appendix 3); coronary artery disease (may provoke angina, avoid after myocardial infarction until stabilised), cerebrovascular disease; occasionally blood pressure reduction too rapid even with low parenteral doses; pregnancy (Appendix 4); breast-feeding (Appendix 5); manufacturer advises test for antinuclear factor and for proteinuria every 6 months and check acetylator status before increasing dose above 100 mg daily, but evidence of clinical value unsatisfactory; **interactions:** Appendix 1 (hydralazine)

**Contra-indications** idiopathic systemic lupus erythematosus, severe tachycardia, high output heart failure, myocardial insufficiency due to mechanical obstruction, cor pulmonale, dissecting aortic aneurysm; porphyria (section 9.8.2)

**Side-effects** tachycardia, palpitation, flushing, hypotension, fluid retention, gastro-intestinal disturbances; headache, dizziness; systemic lupus erythematosus-like syndrome after long-term therapy with over 100 mg daily (or less in women and in slow acetylator individuals) (see also notes above); rarely rashes, fever, peripheral neuritis, polyneuritis, paraesthesia, arthralgia, myalgia, increased lacrimation, nasal congestion, dyspnoea, agitation, anxiety, anorexia; blood disorders (including leucopenia, thrombocytopenia, haemolytic anaemia), abnormal liver function, jaundice, raised plasma creatinine, proteinuria and haematuria reported

**Dose**

- By mouth, hypertension, 25 mg twice daily, increased to usual max. 50 mg twice daily (see notes above)
  Heart failure (initiated in hospital) 25 mg 3–4 times daily, increased every 2 days if necessary; usual maintenance dose 50–75 mg 4 times daily
- By slow intravenous injection, hypertension with renal complications and hypertensive crisis, 5–10 mg diluted with 10 mL sodium chloride 0.9%; may be repeated after 20–30 minutes (see Cautions)
- By intravenous infusion, hypertension with renal complications and hypertensive crisis, initially 200–300 micrograms/minute; maintenance usually 50–150 micrograms/minute

**Hydralazine** (Non-proprietary) PoM
Tablets, hydralazine hydrochloride 25 mg, net price 20 = 86p; 50 mg, 20 = £1.37

**Apresoline®** (Sovereign) PoM
Tablets, yellow, s/c, hydralazine hydrochloride 25 mg, net price 84-tab pack = £2.50
Excipients include gluten

Injection, powder for reconstitution, hydralazine hydrochloride. Net price 20-mg amp = £1.64

## ILOPROST

**Indications** primary pulmonary hypertension

**Cautions** unstable pulmonary hypertension with advanced right heart failure; hypotension (do not initiate if systolic blood pressure below 85 mmHg); hepatic impairment (Appendix 2); **interactions:** Appendix 1 (iloprost)

**Contra-indications** unstable angina; within 6 months of myocardial infarction; decompensated cardiac failure (unless under close medical supervision); severe arrhythmias; congenital or acquired heart-valve defects; within 3 months of cerebrovascular events; pulmonary veno-occlusive disease; conditions which increase risk of bleeding; pregnancy (Appendix 4); breast-feeding (Appendix 5)

**Side-effects** vasodilatation, hypotension, syncope, cough, headache, trismus

**Dose**

- By inhalation of nebulised solution, 2.5–5 micrograms 6–9 times daily, adjusted according to response

**Ventavis** (Schering Health) ▼ PoM
Nebuliser solution, iloprost (as trometamol) 10 micrograms/mL, net price 30 x 2 mL (20 microgram) unit-dose vials = £425.00; 100 x 2-mL = £1415.08; 300 x 2-mL = £4243.88. For use with *Prodose®* NHS or *Venta-Neb®* NHS nebuliser

## MINOXIDIL

**Indications** severe hypertension, in addition to a diuretic and a beta-blocker

**Cautions** see notes above; angina; after myocardial infarction (until stabilised); lower doses in dialysis patients; porphyria (section 9.8.2); pregnancy (Appendix 4); **interactions:** Appendix 1 (minoxidil)

**Contra-indications** phaeochromocytoma

**Side-effects** sodium and water retention; weight gain, peripheral oedema, tachycardia, hypertrichosis; reversible rise in creatinine and blood urea nitrogen; occasionally, gastro-intestinal disturbances, breast tenderness, rashes

**Dose**

- Initially 5 mg (elderly, 2.5 mg) daily, in 1–2 doses, increased by 5–10 mg every 3 or more days; max. usually 50 mg daily

**Loniten®** (Pharmacia) PoM
Tablets, all scored, minoxidil 2.5 mg, net price 60-tab pack = £8.88; 5 mg, 60-tab pack = £15.83; 10 mg, 60-tab pack = £30.68

## SODIUM NITROPRUSSIDE

**Indications** hypertensive crisis (but see section 2.5); controlled hypotension in anaesthesia; acute or chronic heart failure

**Cautions** hypothyroidism, hyponatraemia, ischaemic heart disease, impaired cerebral circulation, elderly; hypothermia; monitor blood pressure and blood-cyanide concentration and if treatment exceeds 3 days, also blood-thiocyanate concentration; avoid sudden withdrawal—terminate infusion over 15–30 minutes; hepatic impairment (Appendix 2); renal impairment (Appendix 3); pregnancy (Appendix 4); breast-feeding; **interactions:** Appendix 1 (nitroprusside)

**Contra-indications** severe vitamin $B_{12}$ deficiency; Leber's optic atrophy; compensatory hypertension

**Side-effects** associated with over rapid reduction in blood pressure (reduce infusion rate): headache, dizziness, nausea, retching, abdominal pain, perspiration, palpitation, apprehension, retrosternal discomfort; occasionally reduced platelet count, acute transient phlebitis

Cyanide Side-effects caused by excessive plasma concentration of the cyanide metabolite include tachycardia, sweating, hyperventilation, arrhythmias, marked metabolic acidosis (discontinue and give antidote, see p. 33)

**Dose**

- Hypertensive crisis, by intravenous infusion, initially 0.5–1.5 micrograms/kg/minute, then increased in steps of 500 nanograms/kg/minute every 5 minutes within range 0.5–8 micrograms/kg/minute (lower doses in patients already receiving other anti-hypertensives); stop if response unsatisfactory with max. dose in 10 minutes
  Note Lower initial dose of 300 nanograms/kg/minute has been used
- Maintenance of blood pressure at 30–40% lower than pretreatment diastolic blood pressure, 20–400 micrograms/minute (lower doses for patients being treated with other antihypertensives)
- Controlled hypotension in surgery, by intravenous infusion, max. 1.5 micrograms/kg/minute
- Heart failure, by intravenous infusion, initially 10–15 micrograms/minute, increased every 5–10 minutes as necessary; usual range 10–200 micrograms/minute normally for max. 3 days

**Sodium Nitroprusside** (Mayne) PoM
Intravenous infusion, powder for reconstitution, sodium nitroprusside 10 mg/mL. For dilution and use as an infusion, net price 5-mL vial = £6.64

## 2.5.2 Centrally acting antihypertensive drugs

**Methyldopa** is a centrally acting antihypertensive; it may be used for the management of hypertension in pregnancy. Side-effects are minimised if the daily dose is kept below 1 g.

**Clonidine** has the disadvantage that sudden withdrawal may cause a hypertensive crisis.

**Moxonidine**, a centrally acting drug, is licensed for mild to moderate essential hypertension. It may have a role when thiazides, beta-blockers, ACE inhibitors and calcium-channel blockers are not appropriate or have failed to control blood pressure.

### CLONIDINE HYDROCHLORIDE

**Indications** hypertension; migraine (section 4.7.4.2); menopausal flushing (section 6.4.1.1)

**Cautions** must be withdrawn gradually to avoid hypertensive crisis; Raynaud's syndrome or other occlusive peripheral vascular disease; history of depression; avoid in porphyria (section 9.8.2); pregnancy (Appendix 4); breast-feeding (Appendix 5); **interactions:** Appendix 1 (clonidine)

Driving Drowsiness may affect performance of skilled tasks (e.g. driving); effects of alcohol may be enhanced

**Side-effects** dry mouth, sedation, depression, fluid retention, bradycardia, Raynaud's phenomenon, headache, dizziness, euphoria, nocturnal unrest, rash, nausea, constipation, rarely impotence

**Dose**

- By mouth, 50–100 micrograms 3 times daily, increased every second or third day; usual max. dose 1.2 mg daily
- By slow intravenous injection, 150–300 micrograms; max. 750 micrograms in 24 hours

**Catapres®** (Boehringer Ingelheim) PoM

Tablets, both scored, clonidine hydrochloride 100 micrograms, net price 100-tab pack = £5.60; 300 micrograms, 100-tab pack = £13.04. Label: 3, 8

Injection, clonidine hydrochloride 150 micrograms/mL. Net price 1-mL amp = 29p

**Dixarit®** PoM

(migraine), section 4.7.4.2

### METHYLDOPA

**Indications** hypertension

**Cautions** history of liver impairment (Appendix 2); renal impairment (Appendix 3); blood counts and liver-function tests advised; history of depression; positive direct Coombs' test in up to 20% of patients (may affect blood cross-matching); interference with laboratory tests; **interactions:** Appendix 1 (methyldopa)

Driving Drowsiness may affect performance of skilled tasks (e.g. driving); effects of alcohol may be enhanced

**Contra-indications** depression, active liver disease, phaeochromocytoma; porphyria (section 9.8.2)

**Side-effects** gastro-intestinal disturbances, dry mouth, stomatitis, sialadenitis; bradycardia, exacerbation of angina, postural hypotension, oedema; sedation, headache, dizziness, asthenia, myalgia, arthralgia, paraesthesia, nightmares, mild psychosis, depression, impaired mental acuity, parkinsonism, Bell's palsy; abnormal liver function tests, hepatitis, jaundice; pancreatitis; haemolytic anaemia; bone-marrow depression, leucopenia, thrombocytopenia, eosinophilia; hypersensitivity reactions including lupus erythematosus-like syndrome, drug fever, myocarditis, pericarditis; rashes (including toxic epidermal necrolysis); nasal congestion, failure of ejaculation, impotence, decreased libido, gynaecomastia, hyperprolactinaemia, amenorrhoea

**Dose**

- Initially 250 mg 2–3 times daily, increased gradually at intervals of 2 or more days, max. 3 g daily; ELDERLY initially 125 mg twice daily, increased gradually, max. 2 g daily

**Methyldopa** (Non-proprietary) PoM

Tablets, coated, methyldopa (anhydrous) 125 mg, net price 56-tab pack = £2.87; 250 mg, 56-tab pack = £2.69; 500 mg, 56-tab pack = £4.25. Label: 3, 8

**Aldomet®** (MSD) PoM

Tablets, all yellow, f/c, methyldopa (anhydrous) 250 mg, net price 60 = £1.88; 500 mg, 30 = £1.90. Label: 3, 8

### MOXONIDINE

**Indications** mild to moderate essential hypertension

**Cautions** renal impairment (Appendix 3); avoid abrupt withdrawal (if concomitant treatment with beta-blocker has to be stopped, discontinue beta-blocker first, then moxonidine after few days); **interactions:** see Appendix 1 (moxonidine)

**Contra-indications** history of angioedema; conduction disorders (sick sinus syndrome, sino-atrial block, second- or third-degree AV block); bradycardia; life-threatening arrhythmia; severe heart failure; severe coronary artery disease, unstable angina; severe liver disease or severe renal impairment; also on theoretical grounds: Raynaud's syndrome, intermittent claudication, epilepsy, depression, Parkinson's disease, glaucoma; pregnancy (Appendix 4); breast-feeding (Appendix 5)

**Side-effects** dry mouth; headache, fatigue, dizziness, nausea, sleep disturbance (rarely sedation), asthenia, vasodilatation; rarely skin reactions

**Dose**

- 200 micrograms once daily in the morning, increased if necessary after 3 weeks to 400 micrograms daily in 1–2 divided doses; max. 600 micrograms daily in 2 divided doses (max. single dose 400 micrograms)

**Moxonidine** (Non-proprietary) PoM

Tablets, all f/c, moxonidine 200 micrograms, net price 28-tab pack = £9.49; 300 micrograms, net price 28-tab pack = £11.06; 400 micrograms, net price 28-tab pack = £12.96. Label: 3

**Physiotens®** (Solvay) PoM

Tablets, f/c, moxonidine 200 micrograms (pink), net price 28-tab pack = £9.72; 300 micrograms (red), 28-tab pack = £11.49; 400 micrograms (red), 28-tab pack = £13.26. Label: 3

## 2.5.3 Adrenergic neurone blocking drugs

Adrenergic neurone blocking drugs prevent the release of noradrenaline from postganglionic adrenergic neurones. These drugs do not control supine blood pressure and may cause postural hypotension. For this reason they have largely fallen from use, but may be necessary with other therapy in resistant hypertension.

**Guanethidine**, which also depletes the nerve endings of noradrenaline, is licensed for the rapid control of blood pressure.

### GUANETHIDINE MONOSULPHATE

**Indications** hypertensive crisis (but see section 2.5)

**Cautions** coronary or cerebral arteriosclerosis, asthma, history of peptic ulceration; renal impairment (Appendix 3); pregnancy (Appendix 4); **interactions:** Appendix 1 (adrenergic neurone blockers)

**Contra-indications** phaeochromocytoma, heart failure

**Side-effects** postural hypotension, failure of ejaculation, fluid retention, nasal congestion, headache, diarrhoea, drowsiness

**Dose**

- By intramuscular injection, 10–20 mg, repeated after 3 hours if required

**Ismelin®** (Sovereign) PoM

Injection, guanethidine monosulphate 10 mg/mL. Net price 1-mL amp = £1.56

## 2.5.4 Alpha-adrenoceptor blocking drugs

**Prazosin** has post-synaptic alpha-blocking and vasodilator properties and rarely causes tachycardia. It may, however, cause a rapid reduction in blood pressure after the first dose and should be introduced with caution. **Doxazosin**, **indoramin**, and **terazosin** have properties similar to those of prazosin.

Alpha-blockers may be used with other antihypertensive drugs in the treatment of hypertension.

**Prostatic hyperplasia** Alfuzosin, doxazosin, indoramin, prazosin, tamsulosin and terazosin are indicated for benign prostatic hyperplasia (section 7.4.1).

### DOXAZOSIN

**Indications** hypertension; benign prostatic hyperplasia (section 7.4.1)

**Cautions** care with initial dose (postural hypotension); hepatic impairment (Appendix 2); susceptibility to heart failure; pregnancy (Appendix 4); breast-feeding (Appendix 5); **interactions:** Appendix 1 (alpha-blockers)

**Side-effects** postural hypotension; dizziness, vertigo, headache, fatigue, asthenia, oedema, sleep disturbance, nausea, rhinitis; less frequently abdominal discomfort, diarrhoea, vomiting, agitation, tremor, rash, pruritus; rarely blurred vision, epistaxis, haematuria, thrombocytopenia, purpura, leucopenia, hepatitis, jaundice, cholestasis, and urinary incontinence; isolated cases of priapism and impotence reported

**Dose**

- Hypertension, 1 mg daily, increased after 1–2 weeks to 2 mg once daily, and thereafter to 4 mg once daily, if necessary; max. 16 mg daily

**Doxazosin** (Non-proprietary) PoM

Tablets, doxazosin (as mesilate) 1 mg, net price 28-tab pack = £1.64; 2 mg, 28-tab pack = £2.04; 4 mg, 28-tab pack = £4.23

Brands include *Doxadura®*

**Cardura®** (Pfizer) PoM

Tablets, doxazosin (as mesilate) 1 mg, net price 28-tab pack = £10.56; 2 mg, 28-tab pack = £14.08

**Modified-release**

**Cardura® XL** (Pfizer) PoM

Tablets, m/r, doxazosin (as mesilate) 4 mg, net price 28-tab pack = £6.33; 8 mg, 28-tab pack = £12.67. Label: 25

**Dose** 4 mg once daily, increased to 8 mg once daily after 4 weeks if necessary

### INDORAMIN

**Indications** hypertension; benign prostatic hyperplasia (section 7.4.1)

**Cautions** avoid alcohol (enhances rate and extent of absorption); control incipient heart failure with diuretics and digoxin; hepatic or renal impairment; elderly patients; Parkinson's disease; epilepsy (convulsions in *animal* studies); history of depression; **interactions:** Appendix 1 (alpha-blockers)

**Driving** Drowsiness may affect performance of skilled tasks (e.g. driving); effects of alcohol may be enhanced

**Contra-indications** established heart failure; patients receiving MAOIs

**Side-effects** sedation; also dizziness, depression, failure of ejaculation, dry mouth, nasal congestion, weight gain; rarely exacerbation of Parkinson's disease

**Dose**

- Hypertension, initially 25 mg twice daily, increased by 25–50 mg daily at intervals of 2 weeks; max. daily dose 200 mg in 2–3 divided doses

**Baratol®** (Shire) PoM

Tablets, blue, f/c, indoramin (as hydrochloride) 25 mg, net price 84-tab pack = £9.00. Label: 2

**Prostatic hyperplasia**

**Doralese®** PoM

See section 7.4.1

### PRAZOSIN

**Indications** see under Dose

**Cautions** first dose may cause collapse due to hypotension (therefore should be taken on retiring to bed); elderly; hepatic impairment (Appendix 2); renal impairment (Appendix 3); pregnancy (Appendix 4); breast-feeding (Appendix 5); **interactions:** Appendix 1 (alpha-blockers)

**Contra-indications** not recommended for congestive heart failure due to mechanical obstruction (e.g. aortic stenosis)

**Side-effects** postural hypotension, drowsiness, weakness, dizziness, headache, lack of energy, nausea, palpitation; urinary frequency, incontinence and priapism reported

**Dose**

- Hypertension, 500 micrograms 2–3 times daily for 3–7 days, the initial dose on retiring to bed at night (to avoid collapse, see Cautions); increased to 1 mg 2–3 times daily for a further 3–7 days; further increased if necessary to max. 20 mg daily in divided doses
- Congestive heart failure (but see section 2.5.5), 500 micrograms 2–4 times daily (initial dose at bedtime, see above), increasing to 4 mg daily in divided doses; maintenance 4–20 mg daily in divided doses (but rarely used)
- Raynaud's syndrome (but efficacy not established, see section 2.6.4), initially 500 micrograms twice daily (initial dose at bedtime, see above) increased, if necessary, after 3–7 days to usual maintenance 1–2 mg twice daily
- Benign prostatic hyperplasia, section 7.4.1

**Prazosin** (Non-proprietary) PoM

Tablets, prazosin (as hydrochloride) 500 micrograms, net price 56-tab pack = £2.51; 1 mg, 56-tab pack = £3.23; 2 mg, 56-tab pack = £4.39; 5 mg, 56-tab pack = £8.75. Label: 3, counselling, initial dose

**Hypovase®** (Pfizer) PoM

Tablets, prazosin (as hydrochloride) 500 micrograms, net price 56-tab pack = £2.51; 1 mg (orange, scored), 56-tab pack = £3.23; 2 mg (scored), 56-tab pack = £4.39. Label: 3, counselling, initial dose

## TERAZOSIN

**Indications** mild to moderate hypertension; benign prostatic hyperplasia (section 7.4.1)

**Cautions** first dose may cause collapse due to hypotension (within 30–90 minutes, therefore should be taken on retiring to bed) (may also occur with rapid dose increase); pregnancy (Appendix 4); **interactions:** Appendix 1 (alpha-blockers)

**Side-effects** drowsiness, dizziness, lack of energy, peripheral oedema; urinary frequency and priapism reported; see also section 7.4.1

**Dose**

- Hypertension, 1 mg at bedtime (compliance with bedtime dose important, see Cautions); dose doubled after 7 days if necessary; usual maintenance dose 2–10 mg once daily; more than 20 mg daily rarely improves efficacy

**Terazosin** (Non-proprietary) PoM

Tablets, terazosin (as hydrochloride) 2 mg, net price 28-tab pack = £7.06; 5 mg, 28-tab pack = £12.72; 10 mg, 28-tab pack = £25.97. Label: 3, counselling, see dose above

**Hytrin®** (Abbott) PoM

Tablets, terazosin (as hydrochloride) 2 mg (yellow), net price 28-tab pack = £4.57; 5 mg (tan), 28-tab pack = £8.57; 10 mg (blue), 28-tab pack = £17.14; starter pack (for hypertension) of 7 × 1-mg tabs with 21 × 2-mg tabs = £13.00. Label: 3, counselling, see dose above

## Phaeochromocytoma

Long-term management of phaeochromocytoma involves surgery. Alpha-blockers are used in the short-term management of hypertensive episodes in phaeochromocytoma. Once alpha blockade is established, tachycardia can be controlled by the cautious addition of a beta-blocker (section 2.4); a cardioselective beta-blocker is preferred.

**Phenoxybenzamine**, a powerful alpha-blocker, is effective in the management of phaeochromocytoma but it has many side-effects. **Phentolamine** is a short-acting alpha-blocker used mainly during surgery of phaeochromocytoma; its use for the diagnosis of phaeochromocytoma has been superseded by measurement of catecholamines in blood and urine.

**Metirosine** (*Demser®*, MSD, available on named-patient basis) inhibits the enzyme tyrosine hydroxylase, and hence the synthesis of catecholamines. It is rarely used in the pre-operative management of phaeochromocytoma, and long term in patients unsuitable for surgery; an alpha-adrenoceptor blocking drug may also be required. Metirosine should **not** be used to treat essential hypertension.

## PHENOXYBENZAMINE HYDROCHLORIDE

**Indications** hypertensive episodes in phaeochromocytoma

**Cautions** elderly; congestive heart failure; severe heart disease (see also Contra-indications); cerebrovascular disease (avoid if history of cerebrovascular accident); renal impairment; carcinogenic in *animals*; avoid in porphyria (section 9.8.2); avoid infusion in hypovolaemia; avoid extravasation (irritant to tissues); pregnancy (Appendix 4); breast-feeding (Appendix 5)

**Contra-indications** history of cerebrovascular accident; during recovery period after myocardial infarction (usually 3–4 weeks)

**Side-effects** postural hypotension with dizziness and marked compensatory tachycardia, lassitude, nasal congestion, miosis, inhibition of ejaculation; rarely gastro-intestinal disturbances; decreased sweating and dry mouth after intravenous infusion; idiosyncratic profound hypotension within few minutes of starting infusion

**Dose**

- See under preparations

**Phenoxybenzamine** (Goldshield) PoM

Injection concentrate, phenoxybenzamine hydrochloride 50 mg/mL. To be diluted before use. Net price 3 × 2-mL amp = £94.88 (hosp. only)

Dose by intravenous infusion (preferably through large vein), adjunct in severe shock (but rarely used) and phaeochromocytoma, 1 mg/kg daily over at least 2 hours; do not repeat within 24 hours (intensive care facilities needed)

Caution Owing to risk of contact sensitisation healthcare professionals should avoid contamination of hands

**Dibenyline®** (Goldshield) PoM

Capsules, red/white, phenoxybenzamine hydrochloride 10 mg. Net price 30-cap pack = £10.84

Dose phaeochromocytoma, 10 mg daily, increased by 10 mg daily; usual dose 1–2 mg/kg daily in 2 divided doses

## PHENTOLAMINE MESILATE

**Indications** hypertensive episodes due to phaeochromocytoma e.g. during surgery; diagnosis of phaeochromocytoma

**Cautions** monitor blood pressure (avoid in hypotension), heart rate; renal impairment; gastritis, peptic ulcer; elderly; pregnancy (Appendix 4) and breast-feeding (Appendix 5); **interactions:** Appendix 1 (alpha-blockers)

Asthma Presence of sulphites in ampoules may (especially in patients with asthma) lead to hypersensitivity (with bronchospasm and shock)

**Contra-indications** hypotension; history of myocardial infarction; coronary insufficiency, angina, or other evidence of coronary artery disease

**Side-effects** postural hypotension, tachycardia, dizziness, flushing; nausea and vomiting, diarrhoea, nasal congestion; also acute or prolonged hypotension, angina, chest pain, arrhythmias

**Dose**

- Hypertensive episodes, by intravenous injection, 2–5 mg repeated if necessary
- Diagnosis of phaeochromocytoma, consult product literature

**Rogitine®** (Alliance) PoM
Injection, phentolamine mesilate 10 mg/mL. Net price 1-mL amp = £1.66

# 2.5.5 Drugs affecting the renin-angiotensin system

2.5.5.1 Angiotensin-converting enzyme inhibitors
2.5.5.2 Angiotensin-II receptor antagonists

## Heart failure

The treatment of chronic heart failure aims to relieve symptoms, improve exercise tolerance, reduce the incidence of acute exacerbations and reduce mortality. An **ACE inhibitor** given at an adequate dose[1] generally achieves these aims; a diuretic is also necessary in most patients to reduce symptoms of fluid overload. Digoxin improves symptoms and exercise tolerance and reduces hospitalisation due to acute exacerbations but it does not reduce mortality. Drug treatment of chronic systolic heart failure is covered below; optimal management of diastolic heart failure is less certain but digoxin should probably be avoided.

An ACE inhibitor (section 2.5.5.1) is generally advised for patients with asymptomatic left ventricular dysfunction or symptomatic heart failure. **Angiotensin-II receptor antagonists** (section 2.5.5.2) may be useful alternatives for patients who, because of symptoms such as cough, cannot tolerate ACE inhibtors; a relatively high dose of the angiotensin-II receptor antagonist may be required to produce benefit.

1. For heart failure the dose of the ACE inhibitor is titrated to a 'target' dose (or to the maximum tolerated dose if lower). Target doses for some ACE inhibitors may exceed licensed ones, e.g. captopril (target dose 50 mg three times daily), enalapril (10–20 mg twice daily), lisinopril (30–35 mg daily), ramipril (5 mg twice daily), trandolapril (4 mg daily [unlicensed indication])

Patients with fluid overload should also receive either a loop or a thiazide diuretic (with salt or fluid restriction where appropriate). A **thiazide diuretic** (section 2.2.1) may be of benefit in patients with mild heart failure and good renal function; however, thiazide diuretics are ineffective in patients with poor renal function (estimated creatinine clearance less than 30 mL/minute, see Appendix 3) and a **loop diuretic** (section 2.2.2) is preferred. If diuresis with a single diuretic is insufficient, a combination of a loop diuretic and a thiazide diuretic may be tried; addition of metolazone (section 2.2.1) may also be considered but the resulting diuresis may be profound and care is needed to avoid potentially dangerous electrolyte disturbances.

The aldosterone antagonist **spironolactone** (section 2.2.3) may be considered for patients with severe heart failure who are already receiving an ACE inhibitor and a diuretic; low doses of spironolactone (usually 25 mg daily) reduce symptoms and mortality in these patients. If spironolactone cannot be used, eplerenone (section 2.2.3) may be considered for the management of heart failure after an acute myocardial infarction with evidence of left ventricular dysfunction. Close monitoring of serum creatinine and potassium is necessary with any change in treatment or in the patient's condition.

The **beta-blockers** bisoprolol and carvedilol (section 2.4) are of value in any grade of stable heart failure and left-ventricular systolic dysfunction. Beta-blocker treatment should be started by those experienced in the management of heart failure, at a very low dose and titrated very slowly over a period of weeks or months. Symptoms may deteriorate initially, calling for adjustment of concomitant therapy.

**Digoxin** (section 2.1) is given to patients with atrial fibrillation and also to selected patients in sinus rhythm who remain symptomatic despite treatment with an ACE inhibitor, a diuretic, and a beta-blocker.

Patients who cannot tolerate ACE inhibitors or in whom they are contra-indicated may be given **isosorbide dinitrate** (section 2.6.1) with **hydralazine** (section 2.5.1), but this combination may be poorly tolerated.

## 2.5.5.1 Angiotensin-converting enzyme inhibitors

Angiotensin-converting enzyme inhibitors (ACE inhibitors) inhibit the conversion of angiotensin I to angiotensin II. They are effective antihypertensives and generally well tolerated. The main indications of ACE inhibitors are shown below.

**Heart failure** ACE inhibitors are used in all grades of heart failure, usually combined with a diuretic (section 2.5.5). Potassium supplements and potassium-sparing diuretics should be discontinued before introducing an ACE inhibitor because of the risk of hyperkalaemia. However, a low dose of spironolactone may be beneficial in severe heart failure (section 2.5.5) and can be used with an ACE inhibitor provided serum potassium is monitored carefully. Profound first-dose hypotension may occur when ACE inhibitors are introduced to patients with heart failure who are already taking a high dose of a loop diuretic (e.g. furosemide 80 mg daily or more). Temporary withdrawal of the loop diuretic reduces the risk, but may cause severe rebound pulmonary oedema. Therefore, for patients on high doses of loop diuretics, the ACE inhibitor may need to be initiated under specialist supervision, see below. An ACE inhibitor can be initiated in the community in patients who are receiving a low dose of a diuretic or who are not otherwise at risk of serious hypotension; nevertheless, care is required and a very low dose of the ACE inhibitor is given initially.

**Hypertension** ACE inhibitors should be considered for hypertension when thiazides and beta-blockers are contra-indicated, not tolerated, or fail to control blood pressure; they are particularly indicated for hypertension in insulin-dependent diabetics with nephropathy (see also section 6.1.5). ACE inhibitors may cause very rapid falls of blood pressure in some patients particularly in those receiving diuretic therapy (see Cautions, below); the first dose should preferably be given at bedtime.

**Diabetic nephropathy** For comment on the role of ACE inhibitors in the management of diabetic nephropathy, see section 6.1.5.

**Prophylaxis of cardiovascular events** ACE inhibitors are used in the early and long-term management of patients who have had a myocardial infarction, see section 2.10.1. An ACE inhibitor may also have a role in preventing cardiovascular events and stroke in those at risk because of stable coronary heart disease.

**Initiation under specialist supervision** ACE inhibitors should be initiated under specialist supervision and with careful clinical monitoring in those with severe heart failure or in those:

- receiving multiple or high-dose diuretic therapy (e.g. more than 80 mg of furosemide daily or its equivalent);
- with hypovolaemia;
- with hyponatraemia (plasma-sodium concentration below 130 mmol/litre);
- with pre-existing hypotension (systolic blood pressure below 90 mmHg);
- with unstable heart failure;
- with renal impairment (plasma-creatinine concentration above 150 micromol/litre);
- receiving high-dose vasodilator therapy;
- aged 70 years or more.

**Renal effects** In patients with severe bilateral renal artery stenosis (or severe stenosis of the artery supplying a single functioning kidney), ACE inhibitors reduce or abolish glomerular filtration and are likely to cause severe and progressive renal failure. They are thus contra-indicated in patients known to have these forms of critical renovascular disease.

ACE inhibitor treatment is unlikely to have an adverse effect on overall renal function in patients with severe unilateral renal artery stenosis and a normal contralateral kidney, but glomerular filtration is likely to be reduced (or even abolished) in the affected kidney and the long-term consequences are unknown.

In general, ACE inhibitors are therefore best avoided in patients with known or suspected renovascular disease, unless the blood pressure cannot be controlled by other drugs. If they are used in these circumstances renal function needs to be monitored.

ACE inhibitors should also be used with particular caution in patients who may have undiagnosed and clinically silent renovascular disease. This includes patients with peripheral vascular disease or those with severe generalised atherosclerosis.

Renal function and electrolytes should be checked before starting ACE inhibitors and monitored during treatment (more frequently if features mentioned above present). Although ACE inhibitors now have a specialised role in some forms of renal disease they also occasionally cause impairment of renal function which may progress and become severe in other circumstances (at particular risk are the elderly).

Concomitant treatment with NSAIDs increases the risk of renal damage, and potassium-sparing diuretics (or potassium-containing salt substitutes) increase the risk of hyperkalaemia.

**Cautions** ACE inhibitors need to be initiated with care in patients receiving diuretics (**important:** see Concomitant diuretics, below); first doses may cause hypotension especially in patients taking high doses of diuretics, on a low-sodium diet, on dialysis, dehydrated or with heart failure (see above). They should also be used with caution in peripheral vascular disease or generalised atherosclerosis owing to risk of clinically silent renovascular disease (see also above). Renal function should be monitored before and during treatment, and the dose reduced in renal impairment (see also above and Appendix 3). The risk of agranulocytosis is possibly increased in collagen vascular disease (blood counts recommended). ACE inhibitors should be used with care in patients with severe or symptomatic aortic stenosis (risk of hypotension). They should also be used with care (or avoided) in those with a history of idiopathic or hereditary angioedema. Use ACE inhibitors with caution in breast-feeding (see Appendix 5). **Interactions:** Appendix 1 (ACE inhibitors)

**Anaphylactoid reactions** To prevent anaphylactoid reactions, ACE inhibitors should be avoided during dialysis with high-flux polyacrylonitrile membranes and during low-density lipoprotein apheresis with dextran sulphate; they should also be withheld before desensitisation with wasp or bee venom

**Concomitant diuretics** ACE inhibitors can cause a very rapid fall in blood pressure in volume-depleted patients; treatment should therefore be initiated with very low doses. If the dose of diuretic is greater than 80 mg furosemide or equivalent, the ACE inhibitor should be initiated under close supervision and in some patients the diuretic dose may need to be reduced or the diuretic discontinued at least 24 hours beforehand. If high-dose diuretic therapy cannot be stopped, close observation is recommended after administration of the first dose of ACE inhibitor, for at least 2 hours or until the blood pressure has stabilised.

**Contra-indications** ACE inhibitors are contra-indicated in patients with hypersensitivity to ACE inhibitors (including angioedema) and in known or suspected renovascular disease (see also above). ACE inhibitors should not be used in pregnancy (Appendix 4).

**Side-effects** ACE inhibitors can cause profound hypotension (see Cautions) and renal impairment (see Renal effects above), and a persistent dry cough. They may also cause angioedema (onset may be delayed), rash (which may be associated with pruritus and urticaria), pancreatitis and upper respiratory-tract symptoms such as sinusitis, rhinitis and sore throat. Gastro-intestinal effects reported with ACE inhibitors include nausea, vomiting, dyspepsia, diarrhoea, constipation, and abdominal pain. Altered liver function tests, cholestatic jaundice and hepatitis have been reported. Blood disorders including thrombocytopenia, leucopenia, neutropenia and haemolytic anaemia have also been reported. Other reported side-effects include headache, dizziness, fatigue, malaise, taste disturbance, paraesthesia, bronchospasm, fever, serositis, vasculitis, myalgia, arthralgia, positive antinuclear antibody, raised erythrocyte sedimentation rate, eosinophilia, leucocytosis and photosensitivity.

**Combination products** Products incorporating an ACE inhibitor with a thiazide diuretic are available for the treatment of hypertension. Use of these combination products should be reserved for patients whose blood pressure has not responded to a thiazide diuretic or an ACE inhibitor alone.

Products combining an ACE inhibitor with a calcium-channel blocker are also available for the management of hypertension. Such a combination product should be considered only for those patients who have been stabilised on the individual components in the same proportions.

## CAPTOPRIL

**Indications** mild to moderate essential hypertension alone or with thiazide therapy and severe hypertension resistant to other treatment; congestive heart failure (adjunct—see section 2.5.5); following myocardial infarction, see dose; diabetic nephropathy (microalbuminuria greater than 30 mg/day) in insulin-dependent diabetes

**Cautions** see notes above

**Contra-indications** see notes above

**Side-effects** see notes above; tachycardia, serum sickness, weight loss, stomatitis, maculopapular rash, photosensitivity, flushing and acidosis

**Dose**

- Hypertension, used alone, initially 12.5 mg twice daily; if used in addition to diuretic (see notes above), or in elderly, initially 6.25 mg twice daily (first dose at bedtime); usual maintenance dose 25 mg twice daily; max. 50 mg twice daily (rarely 3 times daily in severe hypertension)
- Heart failure (adjunct), initially 6.25–12.5 mg under close medical supervision (see notes above); usual maintenance dose 25 mg 2–3 times daily (but see section 2.5.5); usual max. 150 mg daily
- Prophylaxis after infarction in clinically stable patients with asymptomatic or symptomatic left ventricular dysfunction (radionuclide ventriculography or echocardiography undertaken before initiation), initially 6.25 mg, starting as early as 3 days after infarction, then increased over several weeks to 150 mg daily (if tolerated) in divided doses
- Diabetic nephropathy, 75–100 mg daily in divided doses; if further blood pressure reduction required, other antihypertensives may be used in conjunction with captopril; in severe renal impairment, initially 12.5 mg twice daily (if concomitant diuretic therapy required, loop diuretic rather than thiazide should be chosen)

**Captopril** (Non-proprietary) PoM
Tablets, captopril 12.5 mg, net price 56-tab pack = £1.02; 25 mg, 56-tab pack = £1.12; 50 mg, 56-tab pack = £1.58
Brands include *Ecopace®*, *Kaplon®*, *Tensopril®*

**Capoten®** (Squibb) PoM
Tablets, captopril 12.5 mg (scored), net price 56-tab pack = £9.82; 25 mg, 56-tab pack = £11.19, 84-tab pack = £16.79; 50 mg (scored), 56-tab pack = £19.07, 84-tab pack = £28.60 (also available as *Acepril®*)

**With diuretic**

**Note** For mild to moderate hypertension in patients stabilised on the individual components in the same proportions

**Co-zidocapt** (Non-proprietary) PoM
Tablets, co-zidocapt 12.5/25 (hydrochlorothiazide 12.5 mg, captopril 25 mg), net price 28-tab pack = £11.00
Brands include *Capto-co®*

Tablets, co-zidocapt 25/50 (hydrochlorothiazide 25 mg, captopril 50 mg), net price 28-tab pack = £14.00
Brands include *Capto-co®*

**Capozide®** (Squibb) PoM
LS tablets, scored, co-zidocapt 12.5/25 (hydrochlorothiazide 12.5 mg, captopril 25 mg). Net price 28-tab pack = £10.46

Tablets, scored, co-zidocapt 25/50 (hydrochlorothiazide 25 mg, captopril 50 mg). Net price 28-tab pack = £13.15 (also available as *Acezide®*)

## CILAZAPRIL

**Indications** essential hypertension; congestive heart failure (adjunct—see section 2.5.5)

**Cautions** see notes above; severe hepatic impairment (Appendix 2)

**Contra-indications** see notes above; ascites

**Side-effects** see notes above; dyspnoea and bronchitis

**Dose**

- Hypertension, initially 1 mg once daily (reduced to 500 micrograms daily in those receiving a diuretic (see notes above), in the elderly, and in renal impairment), then adjusted according to response; usual maintenance dose 2.5–5 mg once daily; max. 5 mg daily
- Heart failure (adjunct), initially 500 micrograms once daily under close medical supervision (see notes above), increased to 1 mg once daily; usual maintenance dose 1–2.5 mg daily; max. 5 mg daily

**Vascace®** (Roche) PoM
Tablets, f/c, cilazapril 500 micrograms (white), net price 28-tab pack = £3.65; 1 mg (yellow), 28-tab pack = £6.01; 2.5 mg (pink), 28-tab pack = £7.64; 5 mg (brown), 28-tab pack = £13.28

## ENALAPRIL MALEATE

**Indications** hypertension; symptomatic heart failure (adjunct—see section 2.5.5); prevention of symptomatic heart failure in patients with left ventricular dysfunction

**Cautions** see notes above; hepatic impairment (Appendix 2)

**Contra-indications** see notes above

**Side-effects** see notes above; also palpitation, arrhythmias, angina, chest pain, Raynaud's syndrome, syncope, cerebrovascular accident, myocardial infarction; dry mouth, peptic ulcer, anorexia, ileus, stomatitis, glossitis, hepatic failure; dermatological side-effects including Stevens-Johnson syndrome, toxic epidermal necrolysis, exfoliative dermatitis and pemphigus; gastro-intestinal angioedema, confusion, depression, nervousness, asthenia, drowsiness, insomnia, dream abnormalities, vertigo, blurred vision, tinnitus, flushing, impotence, gynaecomastia, alopecia, dyspnoea, asthma, pulmonary infiltrates, muscle cramps, and hyponatraemia

**Dose**

- Hypertension, used alone, initially 5 mg once daily; if used in addition to diuretic (see notes above), or in renal impairment, lower initial doses may be required; usual maintenance dose 20 mg once daily; max. 40 mg once daily
- Heart failure (adjunct), asymptomatic left ventricular dysfunction, initially 2.5 mg daily under close medical supervision (see notes above); increased over 2–4 weeks to usual maintenance dose 20 mg daily in 1–2 divided doses (but see section 2.5.5); max. 40 mg daily

**Enalapril Maleate** (Non-proprietary) PoM

Tablets, enalapril maleate 2.5 mg, net price 28-tab pack = 95p; 5 mg, 28-tab pack = £1.28; 10 mg, 28-tab pack = £1.38; 20 mg, 28-tab pack = £1.54

Brands include *Ednyt®*

**Innovace®** (MSD) PoM

Tablets, enalapril maleate 2.5 mg, net price 28-tab pack = £5.35; 5 mg (scored), 28-tab pack = £7.51; 10 mg (red), 28-tab pack = £10.53; 20 mg (peach), 28-tab pack = £12.51

### With diuretic

**Note** For mild to moderate hypertension in patients stabilised on the individual components in the same proportions

**Innozide®** (MSD) PoM

Tablets, yellow, scored, enalapril maleate 20 mg, hydrochlorothiazide 12.5 mg. Net price 28-tab pack = £13.90

**Note** Non-proprietary tablets containing enalapril maleate (20 mg) and hydrochlorothiazide (12.5 mg) are available

## FOSINOPRIL SODIUM

**Indications** hypertension; congestive heart failure (adjunct—see section 2.5.5)

**Cautions** see notes above; hepatic impairment (Appendix 2)

**Contra-indications** see notes above

**Side-effects** see notes above; chest pain; musculoskeletal pain

**Dose**

- Hypertension, initially 10 mg daily, increased if necessary after 4 weeks; usual dose range 10–40 mg (doses over 40 mg not shown to increase efficacy); if used in addition to diuretic see notes above
- Heart failure (adjunct), initially 10 mg daily under close medical supervision (see notes above); if initial dose well tolerated, may be increased to up to 40 mg once daily

**Fosinopril sodium** (Non-proprietary) PoM

Tablets, fosinopril sodium 10 mg, net price 28-tab pack = £8.45; 20 mg, 28-tab pack = £10.13

**Staril®** (Squibb) PoM

Tablets, fosinopril sodium 10 mg, net price 28-tab pack = £11.20; 20 mg, 28-tab pack = £12.09

## IMIDAPRIL HYDROCHLORIDE

**Indications** essential hypertension

**Cautions** see notes above; hepatic impairment (Appendix 2)

**Contra-indications** see notes above

**Side-effects** see notes above; dry mouth, glossitis, ileus; bronchitis, dyspnoea; sleep disturbances, depression, confusion, blurred vision, tinnitus, impotence

**Dose**

- Initially 5 mg daily before food; if used in addition to diuretic (see notes above), in elderly, in patients with heart failure, angina or cerebrovascular disease, or in renal or hepatic impairment, initially 2.5 mg daily; if necessary increase dose at intervals of at least 3 weeks; usual maintenance dose 10 mg once daily; max. 20 mg daily (elderly, 10 mg daily)

**Tanatril** (Trinity) PoM

Tablets, scored, imidapril hydrochloride 5 mg, net price 28-tab pack = £5.65; 10 mg, 28-tab pack = £6.39; 20 mg, 28-tab pack = £7.67

## LISINOPRIL

**Indications** essential and renovascular hypertension (but see notes above); congestive heart failure (adjunct—see section 2.5.5); following myocardial infarction in haemodynamically stable patients; diabetic nephropathy in normotensive insulin-dependent and hypertensive non-insulin-dependent diabetes mellitus

**Cautions** see notes above

**Contra-indications** see notes above

**Side-effects** see notes above; tachycardia, cerebrovascular accident, myocardial infarction; dry mouth, blurred vision, confusion, mood changes, asthenia, sweating, impotence and alopecia

**Dose**

- Hypertension, initially 10 mg daily; if used in addition to diuretic (see notes above) or in renal impairment, initially 2.5–5 mg daily; usual maintenance dose 20 mg once daily; max. 80 mg daily
- Heart failure (adjunct), initially 2.5 mg daily under close medical supervision (see notes above); usual maintenance dose 5–20 mg daily (but see section 2.5.5)
- Prophylaxis after myocardial infarction, systolic blood pressure over 120 mmHg, 5 mg within 24 hours, followed by further 5 mg 24 hours later, then 10 mg after a further 24 hours, and continuing with 10 mg once daily for 6 weeks (or continued if heart failure); systolic blood pressure 100–120 mmHg, initially 2.5 mg, increasing to maintenance dose of 5 mg once daily
  **Note** Should not be started after myocardial infarction if systolic blood pressure less than 100 mmHg; temporarily reduce maintenance dose to 5 mg and if necessary 2.5 mg daily if systolic blood pressure 100 mmHg or less during treatment; withdraw if prolonged hypotension occurs (systolic blood pressure less than 90 mmHg for more than 1 hour)
- Diabetic nephropathy, initially 2.5 mg daily adjusted to achieve a sitting diastolic blood pressure below 75 mmHg in normotensive insulin-dependent dia-

betes and below 90 mmHg in hypertensive non-insulin dependent diabetes; usual dose range 10–20 mg daily

**Lisinopril** (Non-proprietary) PoM
Tablets, lisinopril (as dihydrate) 2.5 mg, net price 28-tab pack = £1.17; 5 mg, 28-tab pack = £1.34; 10 mg, 28-tab pack = £1.70; 20 mg, 28-tab pack = £2.22

**Carace®** (Bristol-Myers Squibb) PoM
Tablets, lisinopril 2.5 mg (blue), net price 28-tab pack = £6.79; 5 mg (scored), 28-tab pack = £8.51; 10 mg (yellow, scored), 28-tab pack = £10.51; 20 mg (orange, scored), 28-tab pack = £11.89

**Zestril®** (AstraZeneca) PoM
Tablets, lisinopril (as dihydrate) 2.5 mg, net price 28-tab pack = £6.26; 5 mg (pink, scored), 28-tab pack = £7.86; 10 mg (pink), 28-tab pack = £9.70; 20 mg (pink), 28-tab pack = £10.97

**With diuretic**

**Note** For mild to moderate hypertension in patients stabilised on the individual components in the same proportions

**Carace Plus®** (Bristol-Myers Squibb) PoM
Carace 10 Plus tablets, blue, lisinopril 10 mg, hydrochlorothiazide 12.5 mg. Net price 28-tab pack = £11.88

Carace 20 Plus tablets, yellow, scored, lisinopril 20 mg, hydrochlorothiazide 12.5 mg. Net price 28-tab pack = £13.44

**Caralpha®** (Alpharma) PoM
Caralpha 10/12.5 mg tablets, peach, lisinopril (as dihydrate) 10 mg, hydrochlorothiazide 12.5 mg, net price 28-tab pack = £10.51

Caralpha 20/12.5 mg tablets, scored, lisinopril (as dihydrate) 20 mg, hydrochlorothiazide 12.5 mg, net price 28-tab pack = £11.89

**Lisicostad®** (Genus) PoM
Lisicostad 10/12.5 mg tablets, scored, lisinopril (as dihydrate) 10 mg, hydrochlorothiazide 12.5 mg, net price 28-tab pack = £10.99

Lisicostad 20/12.5 mg tablets, scored, lisinopril (as dihydrate) 20 mg, hydrochlorothiazide 12.5 mg, net price 28-tab pack = £11.99

**Zestoretic®** (AstraZeneca) PoM
Zestoretic 10 tablets, peach, lisinopril (as dihydrate) 10 mg, hydrochlorothiazide 12.5 mg. Net price 28-tab pack = £13.01

Zestoretic 20 tablets, lisinopril (as dihydrate) 20 mg, hydrochlorothiazide 12.5 mg. Net price 28-tab pack = £14.72

## MOEXIPRIL HYDROCHLORIDE

**Indications** essential hypertension
**Cautions** see notes above; hepatic impairment (Appendix 2)
**Contra-indications** see notes above
**Side-effects** see notes above; arrhythmias, angina, chest pain, syncope, cerebrovascular accident, myocardial infarction; appetite and weight changes; dry mouth, photosensitivity, flushing, nervousness, mood changes, anxiety, drowsiness, sleep disturbance, tinnitus, influenza-like syndrome, sweating and dyspnoea
**Dose**
- Used alone, initially 7.5 mg once daily; if used in addition to diuretic (see notes above), with nifedipine, in elderly, in renal or hepatic impairment, initially 3.75 mg once daily; usual range 15–30 mg once daily; doses above 30 mg daily not shown to increase efficacy

**Perdix®** (Schwarz) PoM
Tablets, f/c, both pink, scored, moexipril hydrochloride 7.5 mg, net price 28-tab pack = £7.55; 15 mg, 28-tab pack = £8.70

## PERINDOPRIL ERBUMINE

**Indications** hypertension (but see notes above); symptomatic heart failure (adjunct—see section 2.5.5)
**Cautions** see notes above; hepatic impairment (Appendix 2)
**Contra-indications** see notes above
**Side-effects** see notes above; asthenia, mood and sleep disturbances
**Dose**
- Hypertension, initially 4 mg daily (before food); if used in addition to diuretic (see notes above), in elderly or in renal impairment, initially 2 mg daily; usual maintenance dose 4 mg once daily; max. 8 mg daily
- Heart failure (adjunct), initial dose 2 mg in the morning under close medical supervision (see notes above); usual maintenance 4 mg once daily (before food)

**Coversyl®** (Servier) PoM
Tablets, perindopril erbumine (= *tert*-butylamine) 2 mg (white), net price 30-tab pack = £10.95; 4 mg (light green, scored), 30-tab pack = £10.95; 8 mg (green), 30-tab pack = £10.95

**With diuretic**

**Note** For hypertension not adequately controlled by perindopril alone

**Coversyl® Plus** (Servier) PoM
Tablets, perindopril erbumine (= *tert*-butylamine) 4 mg, indapamide 1.25 mg, net price 30-tab pack = £13.96

## QUINAPRIL

**Indications** essential hypertension; congestive heart failure (adjunct—see section 2.5.5)
**Cautions** see notes above; hepatic impairment (Appendix 2)
**Contra-indications** see notes above
**Side-effects** see notes above; asthenia, chest pain, oedema, flatulence, nervousness, depression, insomnia, blurred vision, impotence, back pain and myalgia
**Dose**
- Hypertension, initially 10 mg once daily; with a diuretic (see notes above), in elderly, or in renal impairment initially 2.5 mg daily; usual maintenance dose 20–40 mg daily in single or 2 divided doses; up to 80 mg daily has been given
- Heart failure (adjunct), initial dose 2.5 mg under close medical supervision (see notes above); usual maintenance 10–20 mg daily in single or 2 divided doses; up to 40 mg daily has been given

**Quinapril** (Non-proprietary) PoM
Tablets, quinapril (as hydrochloride) 5 mg, net price 28-tab pack = £4.56; 10 mg, 28-tab pack = £4.80; 20 mg, 28-tab pack = £6.03; 40 mg, 28-tab pack = £5.60
Brands include *Quinil*®

**Accupro**® (Pfizer) PoM
Tablets, all brown, f/c, quinapril (as hydrochloride) 5 mg, net price 28-tab pack = £8.60; 10 mg, 28-tab pack = £8.60; 20 mg, 28-tab pack = £10.79; 40 mg, 28-tab pack = £9.75

**With diuretic**
**Note** For hypertension in patients stabilised on the individual components in the same proportions

**Accuretic**® (Pfizer) PoM
Tablets, pink, f/c, scored, quinapril (as hydrochloride) 10 mg, hydrochlorothiazide 12.5 mg. Net price 28-tab pack = £11.75

## RAMIPRIL

**Indications** mild to moderate hypertension; congestive heart failure (adjunct—see section 2.5.5); following myocardial infarction in patients with clinical evidence of heart failure; susceptible patients over 55 years, prevention of myocardial infarction, stroke, cardiovascular death or need of revascularisation procedures (consult product literature)

**Cautions** see notes above; hepatic impairment (Appendix 2)

**Contra-indications** see notes above

**Side-effects** see notes above; arrhythmias, angina, chest pain, syncope, cerebrovascular accident, myocardial infarction, loss of appetite, stomatitis, dry mouth, skin reactions including erythema multiforme and pemphigoid exanthema; precipitation or exacerbation of Raynaud's syndrome; conjunctivitis, onycholysis, confusion, nervousness, depression, anxiety, impotence, decreased libido, alopecia, bronchitis and muscle cramps

**Dose**
- Hypertension, initially 1.25 mg once daily, increased at intervals of 1–2 weeks; usual range 2.5–5 mg once daily; max. 10 mg once daily; if used in addition to diuretic see notes above
- Heart failure (adjunct), initially 1.25 mg once daily under close medical supervision (see notes above), increased if necessary at intervals of 1–2 weeks; max. 10 mg daily (daily doses of 2.5 mg or more may be taken in 1–2 divided doses) (see also section 2.5.5)
- Prophylaxis after myocardial infarction (started in hospital 3 to 10 days after infarction), initially 2.5 mg twice daily, increased after 2 days to 5 mg twice daily; maintenance 2.5–5 mg twice daily
  **Note** If initial 2.5-mg dose not tolerated, give 1.25 mg twice daily for 2 days before increasing to 2.5 mg twice daily, then 5 mg twice daily; withdraw if 2.5 mg twice daily not tolerated
- Prophylaxis of cardiovascular events or stroke, initially 2.5 mg once daily, increased after 1 week to 5 mg once daily, then increased after a further 3 weeks to 10 mg once daily

**Ramipril** (Non-proprietary) PoM
Capsules, ramipril 1.25 mg, net price 28-cap pack = £1.80; 2.5 mg, 28-cap pack = £1.63; 5 mg, 28-cap pack = £2.32; 10 mg, 28-cap pack = £2.68
Brands include *Lopace*®

Tablets, ramipril 1.25 mg, net price 28-tab pack = £2.84; 2.5 mg, 28-tab pack = £3.66; 5 mg, 28-tab pack = £5.23; 10 mg, 28-tab pack = £6.70

**Tritace**® (Aventis Pharma) PoM
Tablets, all scored, ramipril 1.25 mg (white), net price 28-tab pack = £5.30; 2.5 mg (yellow), 28-tab pack = £7.51; 5 mg (red), 28-tab pack = £10.46; 10 mg (white), 28-tab pack = £14.24

Titration pack, capsules, 35-day starter pack of ramipril 7 × 2.5 mg with 21 × 5 mg and 7 × 10 mg, net price = £13.00

**With calcium-channel blocker**
**Note** For hypertension in patients stabilised on the individual components in the same proportions. For cautions, contra-indications and side-effects of felodipine, see section 2.6.2

**Triapin**® (Aventis Pharma) ▼ PoM
Triapin® tablets, f/c, brown, ramipril 5 mg, felodipine 5 mg (m/r), net price 28-tab pack = £24.46. Label: 25

Triapin mite® *tablets*, f/c, orange, ramipril 2.5 mg, felodipine 2.5 mg (m/r), net price 28-tab pack = £19.37. Label: 25

## TRANDOLAPRIL

**Indications** mild to moderate hypertension; following myocardial infarction in patients with left ventricular dysfunction; heart failure [unlicensed] see section 2.5.5

**Cautions** see notes above; hepatic impairment (Appendix 2)

**Contra-indications** see notes above

**Side-effects** see notes above; tachycardia, arrhythmias, angina, transient ischaemic attacks, cerebral haemorrhage, myocardial infarction; ileus, dry mouth; skin reactions including Stevens-Johnson syndrome, toxic epidermal necrolysis, psoriasis-like efflorescence; asthenia, alopecia, dyspnoea and bronchitis

**Dose**
- Hypertension, initially 500 micrograms once daily, increased at intervals of 2–4 weeks; usual range 1–2 mg once daily; max. 4 mg daily; if used in addition to diuretic see notes above
- Prophylaxis after myocardial infarction (starting as early as 3 days after infarction), initially 500 micrograms daily, gradually increased to max. 4 mg once daily
  **Note** If symptomatic hypotension develops during titration, do not increase dose further; if possible, reduce dose of any adjunctive treatment and if this is not effective or feasible, reduce dose of trandolapril

**Gopten**® (Abbott) PoM
Capsules, trandolapril 500 micrograms (red/yellow), net price 14-cap pack = £1.71; 1 mg (red/orange), 28-cap pack = £12.28; 2 mg (red/red), 28-cap pack = £8.39; 4 mg (red/maroon), 28-cap pack = £14.24

**With calcium-channel blocker**
**Note** For hypertension in patients stabilised on the individual components in the same proportions. For cautions, contra-indications and side-effects of verapamil, see section 2.6.2

**Tarka**® (Abbott) ▼ PoM
Capsules, pink, trandolapril 2 mg, verapamil hydrochloride 180 mg (m/r). Net price 28 cap-pack = £17.85. Label: 25

## 2.5.5.2 Angiotensin-II receptor antagonists

**Candesartan**, **eprosartan**, **irbesartan**, **losartan**, **olmesartan**, **telmisartan**, and **valsartan** are angiotensin-II receptor antagonists with many properties similar to those of the ACE inhibitors. However, unlike ACE inhibitors, they do not inhibit the breakdown of bradykinin and other kinins, and thus are unlikely to cause the persistent dry cough which commonly complicates ACE inhibitor therapy. They are therefore a useful alternative for patients who have to discontinue an ACE inhibitor because of persistent cough.

An angiotensin-II receptor antagonist may be used as an alternative to an ACE inhibitor in the management of heart failure (section 2.5.5) or diabetic nephropathy (section 6.1.5).

**Cautions** Angiotensin-II receptor antagonists should be used with caution in renal artery stenosis (see also Renal Effects under ACE Inhibitors, section 2.5.5.1). Monitoring of plasma-potassium concentration is advised, particularly in the elderly and in patients with renal impairment; lower initial doses may be appropriate in these patients. Angiotensin-II receptor antagonists should be used with caution in aortic or mitral valve stenosis and in obstructive hypertrophic cardiomyopathy. Afro-Caribbean patients, particularly those with left ventricular hypertrophy, may not benefit from an angiotensin-II receptor antagonist. **Interactions:** Appendix 1 (angiotensin-II receptor antagonists).

**Contra-indications** Angiotensin-II receptor antagonists, like the ACE inhibitors, should be avoided in pregnancy (see also Appendix 4).

**Side-effects** Side-effects are usually mild. Symptomatic hypotension including dizziness may occur, particularly in patients with intravascular volume depletion (e.g. those taking high-dose diuretics). Hyperkalaemia occurs occasionally; angioedema has also been reported with some angiotensin-II receptor antagonists.

### CANDESARTAN CILEXETIL

**Indications** hypertension; heart failure with impaired left ventricular systolic function (see section 2.5.5)

**Cautions** see notes above; hepatic impairment (Appendix 2); renal impairment (Appendix 3)

**Contra-indications** see notes above; breast-feeding (Appendix 5); cholestasis

**Side-effects** see notes above; also vertigo, headache; *very rarely* nausea, hepatitis, blood disorders, hyponatraemia, back pain, arthralgia, myalgia, rash, urticaria, pruritus

**Dose**

- Hypertension, initially 8 mg (hepatic impairment 2 mg, renal impairment or intravascular volume depletion 4 mg) once daily, increased if necessary at intervals of 4 weeks to max. 32 mg once daily; usual maintenance dose 8 mg once daily
- Heart failure, initially 4 mg once daily, increased at intervals of at least 2 weeks to 'target' dose of 32 mg once daily or to max. tolerated dose

**Amias®** (Takeda) PoM

Tablets, candesartan cilexetil 2 mg, net price 7-tab pack = £2.99; 4 mg (scored), 7-tab pack = £3.24, 28-tab pack = £8.15; 8 mg (pink, scored), 28-tab pack = £9.89; 16 mg (pink, scored), 28-tab pack = £12.72; 32 mg (pink), 28-tab pack = £16.13

### EPROSARTAN

**Indications** hypertension (see also notes above)

**Cautions** see notes above; also renal impairment (Appendix 3); breast-feeding (Appendix 5)

**Contra-indications** see notes above; also severe hepatic impairment (Appendix 2)

**Side-effects** see notes above; also flatulence, arthralgia, rhinitis; hypertriglyceridaemia, rarely anaemia

**Dose**

- 600 mg once daily (elderly over 75 years, mild to moderate hepatic impairment, renal impairment, initially 300 mg once daily); if necessary increased after 2–3 weeks to 800 mg once daily

**Teveten®** (Solvay) PoM

Tablets, f/c, eprosartan (as mesilate) 300 mg, net price 28-tab pack = £11.63; 400 mg (pink), 56-tab pack = £15.77; 600 mg, 28-tab pack = £14.31. Label: 21

### IRBESARTAN

**Indications** hypertension; renal disease in hypertensive type 2 diabetes mellitus (see also notes above)

**Cautions** see notes above

**Contra-indications** see notes above; breast-feeding (Appendix 5)

**Side-effects** see notes above; also nausea, vomiting; fatigue; musculoskeletal pain; *less commonly* diarrhoea, dyspepsia, flushing, tachycardia, chest pain, cough, and sexual dysfunction; *rarely* rash, urticaria; *very rarely* headache, myalgia, arthralgia, tinnitus, taste disturbance, hepatitis, and renal dysfunction

**Dose**

- Hypertension, initially 150 mg once daily, increased if necessary to 300 mg once daily (in haemodialysis or in elderly over 75 years, initial dose of 75 mg once daily may be used); CHILD not recommended
- Renal disease in hypertensive type 2 diabetes mellitus, initially 150 mg once daily, increased according to response to 300 mg once daily (in haemodialysis or in elderly over 75 years, initial dose of 75 mg once daily may be used); CHILD not recommended

**Aprovel®** (Bristol-Myers Squibb, Sanofi-Synthelabo) PoM

Tablets, f/c, irbesartan 75 mg, net price 28-tab pack = £10.29; 150 mg, 28-tab pack = £12.57; 300 mg, 28-tab pack = £16.91

#### With diuretic

**Note** For hypertension not adequately controlled on individual components

**CoAprovel®** (Bristol-Myers Squibb, Sanofi-Synthelabo) PoM

Tablets, f/c, both peach, irbesartan 150 mg, hydrochlorothiazide 12.5 mg, net price 28-tab pack = £12.57; irbesartan 300 mg, hydrochlorothiazide 12.5 mg, 28-tab pack = £16.91

## LOSARTAN POTASSIUM

**Indications** hypertension, including patients with left ventricular hypertrophy; diabetic nephropathy in type 2 diabetes mellitus (see also notes above)

**Cautions** see notes above; hepatic impairment (Appendix 2); renal impairment (Appendix 3)

**Contra-indications** see notes above; breast-feeding (Appendix 5)

**Side-effects** see notes above; diarrhoea, taste disturbance, cough, arthralgia, myalgia, asthenia, fatigue, migraine, vertigo, urticaria, pruritus, rash; *rarely* hepatitis, anaemia (in severe renal disease or following renal transplant), thrombocytopenia, vasculitis (including Henoch-Schönlein purpura)

**Dose**

- Usually 50 mg once daily (intravascular volume depletion, initially 25 mg once daily); if necessary increased after several weeks to 100 mg once daily; ELDERLY over 75 years initially 25 mg daily

**Cozaar®** (MSD) PoM

Tablets, f/c, losartan potassium 25 mg, net price 28-tab pack = £18.09; 50 mg (scored), 28-tab pack = £18.09; 100 mg, 28-tab pack = £24.20

### With diuretic

Note For hypertension not adequately controlled on individual components

**Cozaar-Comp®** (MSD) PoM

Tablets 50/12.5, f/c, yellow, losartan potassium 50 mg, hydrochlorothiazide 12.5 mg, net price 28-tab pack = £18.09

Tablets 100/12.5, f/c, yellow, losartan potassium 100 mg, hydrochlorothiazide 25 mg, net price 28-tab pack = £24.20

## OLMESARTAN MEDOXOMIL

**Indications** hypertension (see also notes above)

**Cautions** see notes above

**Contra-indications** see notes above; hepatic impairment (Appendix 2); moderate to severe renal impairment (Appendix 3); biliary obstruction; breast-feeding (Appendix 5)

**Side-effects** see notes above; also abdominal pain, diarrhoea, dyspepsia, nausea, influenza-like symptoms, cough, pharyngitis, rhinitis, haematuria, urinary-tract infection, peripheral oedema, arthritis, musculoskeletal pain; less commonly angina, vertigo, rash

**Dose**

- Initially 10 mg once daily; if necessary increased to 20 mg once daily; max. 40 mg daily; ELDERLY max. 20 mg daily

**Olmetec®** (Sankyo) PoM

Tablets, f/c, olmesartan medoxomil 10 mg, net price 28-tab pack = £10.95; 20 mg, 28-tab pack = £12.95; 40 mg, 28-tab pack = £17.50

## TELMISARTAN

**Indications** hypertension (see also notes above)

**Cautions** see notes above; hepatic impairment—avoid if severe (Appendix 2); renal impairment (Appendix 3)

**Contra-indications** see notes above; biliary obstruction; breast-feeding (Appendix 5)

**Side-effects** see notes above; also gastro-intestinal disturbances; influenza-like symptoms including pharyngitis and sinusitis; arthralgia, myalgia, back pain, leg cramps; eczema; *less commonly* dry mouth, flatulence, anxiety, vertigo, tendinitis-like symptoms, abnormal vision, increased sweating; *rarely* bradycardia, tachycardia, dyspnoea, insomnia, depression, blood disorders, increase in uric acid, eosinophilia, rash, and pruritus

**Dose**

- Usually 40 mg once daily (but 20 mg may be sufficient), increased if necessary after at least 4 weeks, to max. 80 mg once daily

**Micardis®** (Boehringer Ingelheim) PoM

Tablets, telmisartan 20 mg, net price 28-tab pack = £11.34; 40 mg, 28-tab pack = £11.34; 80 mg, 28-tab pack = £14.18

### With diuretic

Note For patients with hypertension not adequately controlled by telmisartan alone

**Micardis Plus®** (Boehringer Ingelheim) ▼ PoM

Tablets 40/12.5, red/white, telmisartan 40 mg, hydrochlorothiazide 12.5 mg, net price 28-tab pack = £11.34

Tablets 80/12.5, red/white, telmisartan 80 mg, hydrochlorothiazide 12.5 mg, net price 28-tab pack = £14.18

## VALSARTAN

**Indications** hypertension; myocardial infarction with left ventricular failure or left ventricular systolic dysfunction (see section 2.5.5 and section 2.10.1)

**Cautions** see notes above; hepatic impairment (Appendix 2); renal impairment (Appendix 3)

**Contra-indications** see notes above, cirrhosis, biliary obstruction, breast-feeding (Appendix 5)

**Side-effects** see notes above; *rarely* anaemia, neutropenia; *very rarely* taste disturbances, syncope, fatigue, cough, headache, thrombocytopenia, epistaxis, arthralgia, myalgia, and rash

**Dose**

- Hypertension, usually 80 mg once daily (initially 40 mg once daily in intravascular volume depletion); if necessary increased after at least 4 weeks to 160 mg daily; ELDERLY over 75 years, initially 40 mg once daily
- Myocardial infarction, initially 20 mg twice daily increased over several weeks to 160 mg twice daily if tolerated

**Diovan®** (Novartis) PoM

Capsules, valsartan 40 mg (grey), net price 7-cap pack = £3.69; 80 mg (grey/pink), 28-cap pack = £16.44; 160 mg (dark grey/pink), 28-cap pack = £21.66

Tablets, yellow, scored, valsartan 40 mg, net price 7-tab pack = £3.69

### With diuretic

Note For hypertension not adequately controlled by valsartan alone

**Co-Diovan®** (Novartis) ▼ PoM

Tablets 80/12.5, f/c, orange, valsartan 80 mg, hydrochlorothiazide 12.5 mg, net price 28-tab pack = £16.44

2 Cardiovascular system

Tablets 160/12.5, f/c, red, valsartan 160 mg, hydrochlorothiazide 12.5 mg, net price 28-tab pack = £21.66

Tablets 160/25, f/c, brown-orange, valsartan 160 mg, hydrochlorothiazide 25 mg, net price 28-tab pack = £21.66

# 2.6 Nitrates, calcium-channel blockers, and other antianginal drugs

2.6.1 Nitrates
2.6.2 Calcium-channel blockers
2.6.3 Other antianginal drugs
2.6.4 Peripheral vasodilators and related drugs

Nitrates, calcium-channel blockers and potassium-channel activators have a vasodilating effect. Vasodilators are known to act in heart failure either by arteriolar dilatation which reduces both peripheral vascular resistance and left ventricular pressure at systole and results in improved cardiac output, *or* venous dilatation which results in dilatation of capacitance vessels, increase of venous pooling, and diminution of venous return to the heart (decreasing left ventricular end-diastolic pressure).

## Angina

*Stable angina* usually results from atherosclerotic plaques in the coronary arteries, whereas *unstable angina* is usually due to plaque rupture and may occur either in patients with a history of stable angina or in those with previously silent coronary artery disease. It is important to distinguish unstable from stable angina; unstable angina is usually characterised by new onset severe angina or sudden worsening of previously stable angina.

**Stable angina** Acute attacks of stable angina should be managed with sublingual **glyceryl trinitrate**. If attacks occur more than twice a week, regular drug therapy is required and should be introduced in a stepwise manner according to response. **Aspirin** (section 2.9) should be given to patients with angina; a dose of 75 mg daily is suitable. Revascularisation procedures may also be appropriate.

Patients with mild or moderate stable angina who do not have left ventricular dysfunction, may be managed effectively with sublingual glyceryl trinitrate and regular administration of a **beta-blocker** (section 2.4). If necessary a long-acting **dihydropyridine calcium-channel blocker** (section 2.6.2) and then a **long-acting nitrate** (section 2.6.1) may be added. For those without left ventricular dysfunction and in whom beta-blockers are inappropriate, **diltiazem** or **verapamil** may be given (section 2.6.2) and a long-acting nitrate (section 2.6.1) may be added if symptom control is not adequate. For those intolerant of standard treatment, or where standard treatment has failed, nicorandil may be tried.

For patients with left ventricular dysfunction a long-acting nitrate (section 2.6.1) should be used and a long-acting dihydropyridine calcium-channel blocker (section 2.6.2) may be added if necessary.

A **statin** (section 2.12) should be prescribed for those with an elevated plasma-cholesterol concentration.

**Unstable angina** Patients with unstable angina should be admitted to hospital. The aims of management of unstable angina are to provide supportive care and pain relief during the acute attack and to prevent myocardial infarction and death.

**Initial management** **Aspirin** (chewed or dispersed in water) is given for its antiplatelet effect at a dose of 300 mg (section 2.9). If aspirin is given before arrival at hospital, a note saying that it has been given should be sent with the patient.

**Heparin** (section 2.8.1) or the low molecular weight heparins **dalteparin** or **enoxaparin** (section 2.8.1) should also be given.

**Nitrates** (section 2.6.1) are used to relieve ischaemic pain. If sublingual glyceryl trinitrate is not effective, intravenous or buccal glyceryl trinitrate or intravenous isosorbide dinitrate is given.

Patients without contra-indications should receive intravenous or oral **beta-blockers** (section 2.4). In patients without left ventricular dysfunction and in whom beta-blockers are inappropriate, **diltiazem** or **verapamil** may be given (section 2.6.2).

The glycoprotein IIb/IIIa inhibitors **eptifibatide** and **tirofiban** (section 2.9) are recommended (with aspirin and heparin) for unstable angina in patients with a high risk of developing myocardial infarction.

Abciximab, eptifibatide or tirofiban may also be used with aspirin and heparin in patients undergoing percutaneous coronary intervention, to reduce the immediate risk of vascular occlusion.

Revascularisation procedures are often appropriate for patients with unstable angina.

**Long-term management** The importance of life-style changes, especially stopping smoking, should be emphasised. Patients should receive low-dose **aspirin** indefinitely—a dose of 75 mg daily is suitable. A **statin** (section 2.12) should also be prescribed. The need for long-term angina treatment or for coronary angiography should be assessed. If there is continuing ischaemia, standard angina treatment should be continued; if not, antianginal treatment may be withdrawn cautiously at least 2 months after the acute attack.

## 2.6.1 Nitrates

Nitrates have a useful role in *angina* (for details on the management of stable angina, see section 2.6). Although they are potent coronary vasodilators, their principal benefit follows from a reduction in venous return which reduces left ventricular work. Unwanted effects such as flushing, headache, and postural hypotension may limit therapy, especially when angina is severe or when patients are unusually sensitive to the effects of nitrates.

*Sublingual* **glyceryl trinitrate** is one of the most effective drugs for providing rapid symptomatic relief of angina, but its effect lasts only for 20 to 30 minutes; the 300-microgram tablet is often appropriate when glyceryl trinitrate is first used. The *aerosol spray* provides an alternative method of rapid relief of symptoms for those who find difficulty in dissolving sublingual preparations. Duration of action may be prolonged by *modified-release* and *transdermal* preparations (but tolerance may develop, see below).

**Isosorbide dinitrate** is active *sublingually* and is a more stable preparation for those who only require nitrates infrequently. It is also effective by mouth for prophylaxis; although the effect is slower in onset, it may persist for several hours. Duration of action of up to 12 hours is claimed for *modified-release* preparations. The activity of isosorbide dinitrate may depend on the production of active metabolites, the most important of which is isosorbide mononitrate. **Isosorbide mononitrate** itself is also licensed for angina prophylaxis; modified-release formulations (for once daily administration) are available.

Glyceryl trinitrate or isosorbide dinitrate may be tried by *intravenous injection* when the sublingual form is ineffective in patients with chest pain due to myocardial infarction or severe ischaemia. Intravenous injections are also useful in the treatment of acute left ventricular failure.



**Tolerance** Many patients on long-acting or transdermal nitrates rapidly develop tolerance (with reduced therapeutic effects). Reduction of blood-nitrate concentrations to low levels for 4 to 8 hours each day usually maintains effectiveness in such patients. If tolerance is suspected during the use of transdermal patches they should be left off for several consecutive hours in each 24 hours; in the case of modified-release tablets of isosorbide dinitrate (and conventional formulations of isosorbide mononitrate), the second of the two daily doses can be given after about 8 hours rather than after 12 hours. Conventional formulations of isosorbide mononitrate should not usually be given more than twice daily unless small doses are used; modified-release formulations of isosorbide mononitrate should only be given once daily, and used in this way do not produce tolerance.

## GLYCERYL TRINITRATE

**Indications** prophylaxis and treatment of angina; left ventricular failure

**Cautions** hypothyroidism, malnutrition, or hypothermia; head trauma, cerebral haemorrhage; recent history of myocardial infarction; hypoxaemia or other ventilation and perfusion abnormalities; metal-containing transdermal systems should be removed before cardioversion or diathermy; avoid abrupt withdrawal; tolerance (see notes above); severe hepatic impairment; severe renal impairment; pregnancy (Appendix 4); breast-feeding (Appendix 5); **interactions:** Appendix 1 (nitrates)

**Contra-indications** hypersensitivity to nitrates; hypotensive conditions and hypovolaemia; hypertrophic obstructive cardiomyopathy, aortic stenosis, cardiac tamponade, constrictive pericarditis, mitral stenosis; marked anaemia, closed-angle glaucoma

**Side-effects** postural hypotension, tachycardia (but paradoxical bradycardia has occurred); throbbing headache, dizziness; *less commonly* nausea, vomiting, heartburn; flushing; temporary hypoxaemia; rash; application site reactions with patches

Injection Specific side-effects following injection (particularly if given too rapidly) include severe hypotension, diaphoresis, apprehension, restlessness, muscle twitching, retrosternal discomfort, palpitation, abdominal pain, syncope; prolonged administration has been associated with methaemoglobinaemia

**Dose**

- Sublingually, 0.3–1 mg, repeated as required
- By mouth, see under preparations
- By intravenous infusion, 10–200 micrograms/minute
- By transdermal application, see under preparations

### Short-acting tablets and sprays

**Glyceryl Trinitrate** (Non-proprietary)

Sublingual tablets, glyceryl trinitrate 300 micrograms, net price 100 = £2.71; 500 micrograms, 100 = £2.19; 600 micrograms, 100 = £3.79. Label: 16

Note Glyceryl trinitrate tablets should be supplied in glass containers of not more than 100 tablets, closed with a foil-lined cap, and containing no cotton wool wadding; they should be discarded after 8 weeks in use

Aerosol spray, glyceryl trinitrate 400 micrograms/metered dose. Net price 200-dose unit = £3.13

Dose treatment or prophylaxis of angina, spray 1–2 doses under tongue and then close mouth

**Coro-Nitro Pump Spray®** (Ayrton Saunders)

Aerosol spray, glyceryl trinitrate 400 micrograms/metered dose. Net price 200-dose unit = £3.13

Dose treatment or prophylaxis of angina, spray 1–2 doses under tongue and then close mouth

**Glytrin Spray®** (Sanofi-Synthelabo)

Aerosol spray, glyceryl trinitrate 400 micrograms/metered dose. Net price 200-dose unit = £3.49

Dose treatment or prophylaxis of angina, spray 1–2 doses under tongue and then close mouth

*Caution:* flammable

**GTN 300 mcg** (Martindale)

Sublingual tablets, glyceryl trinitrate 300 micrograms. Net price 100 = £2.71. Label: 16

**Nitrolingual Pumpspray®** (Merck)

Aerosol spray, glyceryl trinitrate 400 micrograms/metered dose. Net price 200-dose unit = £3.65; *Duo Pack* (250-dose unit and 75-dose unit) = £4.98

Dose treatment or prophylaxis of angina, spray 1–2 doses under tongue and then close mouth

**Nitromin®** (Egis)

Aerosol spray, glyceryl trinitrate 400 micrograms/metered dose, net price 180-dose unit = £2.63, 200-dose unit = £2.82

Dose treatment or prophylaxis of angina, spray 1–2 doses under tongue and then close mouth

### Longer-acting tablets

**Suscard®** (Forest)

Buccal tablets, m/r, glyceryl trinitrate 2 mg, net price 100-tab pack = £12.70; 3 mg, 100-tab pack = £18.33; 5 mg, 100-tab pack = £24.96. Counselling, see below

Dose treatment of angina, 2 mg as required, increased to 3 mg if necessary; prophylaxis 2–3 mg 3 times daily; 5 mg in severe angina

Unstable angina (adjunct), up to 5 mg with ECG monitoring

Congestive heart failure, 5 mg 3 times daily, increased to 10 mg 3 times daily in severe cases

Acute heart failure, 5 mg repeated until symptoms abate

Counselling Tablets have rapid onset of effect; they are placed between upper lip and gum, and left to dissolve; vary site to reduce risk of dental caries

**Sustac®** (Forest)
Tablets, m/r, all pink, glyceryl trinitrate 2.6 mg, net price 90-tab pack = £4.80; 6.4 mg, 90-tab pack = £6.92. Label: 25
Dose prophylaxis of angina, 2.6–12.8 mg 3 times daily *or* 10 mg 2–3 times daily

### Parenteral preparations
Note Glass or polyethylene apparatus is preferable; loss of potency will occur if PVC is used

**Glyceryl Trinitrate** (Non-proprietary) PoM
Injection, glyceryl trinitrate 5 mg/mL. To be diluted before use. Net price 5-mL amp = £6.49; 10-mL amp = £12.98
Excipients may include ethanol, propylene glycol (see Excipients, p. 2)

**Nitrocine®** (Schwarz) PoM
Injection, glyceryl trinitrate 1 mg/mL. To be diluted before use or given undiluted with syringe pump. Net price 10-mL amp = £7.34; 50-mL bottle = £17.21
Excipients include propylene glycol (see Excipients, p. 2)

**Nitronal®** (Merck) PoM
Injection, glyceryl trinitrate 1 mg/mL. To be diluted before use or given undiluted with syringe pump. Net price 5-mL vial = £1.92; 50-mL vial = £15.67

### Transdermal preparations
**Deponit®** (Schwarz)
Patches, self-adhesive, transparent, glyceryl trinitrate, *'5' patch* (releasing approx. 5 mg/24 hours when in contact with skin), net price 28 = £15.96; *'10' patch* (releasing approx.10 mg/24 hours), 28 = £17.57
Dose prophylaxis of angina, apply one '5' or one '10' patch to lateral chest wall, upper arm, thigh, abdomen, or shoulder; increase to two '10' patches every 24 hours if necessary; replace every 24 hours, siting replacement patch on different area; see also notes above (tolerance)

**Minitran®** (3M)
Patches, self-adhesive, transparent, glyceryl trinitrate, *'5' patch* (releasing approx. 5 mg/24 hours when in contact with skin), net price 30 = £11.62; *'10' patch* (releasing approx. 10 mg/24 hours), 30 = £12.87; *'15' patch* (releasing approx. 15 mg/24 hours), 30 = £14.19
Dose prophylaxis of angina, apply one '5' patch to chest or upper arm; replace every 24 hours, siting replacement patch on different area; adjust dose according to response; see also notes above (tolerance)
Maintenance of venous patency ('5' patch only), consult product literature

**Nitro-Dur®** (Schering-Plough)
Patches, self-adhesive, buff, glyceryl trinitrate, *'0.2 mg/h' patch* (releasing approx. 5 mg/24 hours when in contact with skin), net price 28 = £11.01; *'0.4 mg/h' patch* (releasing approx. 10 mg/24 hours), 28 = £12.18; *'0.6 mg/h' patch* (releasing approx.15 mg/24 hours), 28 = £13.41
Dose prophylaxis of angina, apply one '0.2 mg/h' patch to chest or outer upper arm; replace every 24 hours, siting replacement patch on different area: adjust dose according to response; see also notes above (tolerance)

**Percutol®** (PLIVA)
Ointment, glyceryl trinitrate 2%. Net price 60 g = £9.55. Counselling, see administration below
Excipients include wool fat
Dose prophylaxis of angina, usual dose 1–2 inches of ointment measured on to *Applirule®*, and applied (usually to chest, arm, or thigh) without rubbing in and secured with surgical tape, every 3–4 hours as required; to determine dose, ½ inch on first day then increased by ½ inch/day until headache occurs, then reduced by ½ inch
Note Approx. 800 micrograms/hour absorbed from 1 inch of ointment

**Transiderm-Nitro®** (Novartis)
Patches, self-adhesive, pink, glyceryl trinitrate, *'5' patch* (releasing approx. 5 mg/24 hours when in contact with skin), net price 28 = £21.31; *'10' patch* (releasing approx. 10 mg/24 hours), 28 = £23.43
Dose prophylaxis of angina, apply one '5' or one '10' patch to lateral chest wall; replace every 24 hours, siting replacement patch on different area; max. two '10' patches daily; see also notes above (tolerance)
Prophylaxis of phlebitis and extravasation ('5' patch only), consult product literature

**Trintek®** (Goldshield)
Patches, self-adhesive, glyceryl trinitrate, '5' patch (releasing approx. 5 mg/24 hours when in contact with skin), net price 30 = £11.84; '10' patch (releasing approx. 10 mg/24 hours), net price 30 = £13.10; '15' patch (releasing approx. 15 mg/24 hours), net price 30 = £14.42
Dose prophylaxis of angina, apply one '5' patch to lateral chest wall; replace every 24 hours, siting replacement patch on different area; adjust dose according to response, max one '15' patch daily; see also notes above (tolerance)

## ISOSORBIDE DINITRATE

**Indications** prophylaxis and treatment of angina; left ventricular failure
**Cautions** see under Glyceryl Trinitrate
**Contra-indications** see under Glyceryl Trinitrate
**Side-effects** see under Glyceryl Trinitrate
**Dose**
- By mouth, daily in divided doses, angina 30–120 mg, left ventricular failure 40–160 mg, up to 240 mg if required
- By intravenous infusion, 2–10 mg/hour; higher doses up to 20 mg/hour may be required

### Short-acting tablets and sprays
**Isosorbide Dinitrate** (Non-proprietary)
Tablets, isosorbide dinitrate 10 mg, net price 20 = 76p; 20 mg, 20 = £1.02

**Angitak®** (LPC)
Aerosol spray, isosorbide dinitrate 1.25 mg/metered dose, net price 200-dose unit = £3.95
Dose treatment or prophylaxis of angina, spray 1–3 doses under tongue whilst holding breath; allow 30 second interval between each dose

### Modified-release preparations
**Cedocard Retard®** (Pharmacia)
Retard-20 tablets, m/r, yellow, scored, isosorbide dinitrate 20 mg. Net price 60-tab pack = £6.85. Label: 25
Dose prophylaxis of angina, 1 tablet every 12 hours
Retard-40 tablets, m/r, orange-red, scored, isosorbide dinitrate 40 mg. Net price 60-tab pack = £13.31. Label: 25
Dose prophylaxis of angina, 1–2 tablets every 12 hours

**Isoket Retard®** (Schwarz)
Retard-20 tablets, m/r, scored, isosorbide dinitrate 20 mg. Net price 56-tab pack = £3.23. Label: 25
Retard-40 tablets, m/r, scored, isosorbide dinitrate 40 mg. Net price 56-tab pack = £7.95. Label: 25
Dose prophylaxis of angina, 40 mg daily in 1–2 divided doses, increased if necessary to 60–80 mg daily in 2–3 divided doses

**Parenteral preparations**

**Isoket®** (Schwarz) PoM

Injection 0.05%, isosorbide dinitrate 500 micrograms/mL. To be diluted before use or given undiluted with syringe pump. Net price 50-mL bottle = £8.94

Injection 0.1%, isosorbide dinitrate 1 mg/mL. To be diluted before use. Net price 10-mL amp = £3.37; 50-mL bottle = £16.70; 100-mL bottle = £25.98

**Note** Glass or polyethylene infusion apparatus is preferable; loss of potency if PVC used

## ISOSORBIDE MONONITRATE

**Indications** prophylaxis of angina; adjunct in congestive heart failure

**Cautions** see under Glyceryl Trinitrate

**Contra-indications** see under Glyceryl Trinitrate

**Side-effects** see under Glyceryl Trinitrate

**Dose**

- Initially 20 mg 2–3 times daily *or* 40 mg twice daily (10 mg twice daily in those who have not previously received nitrates); up to 120 mg daily in divided doses if required

**Isosorbide Mononitrate** (Non-proprietary)

Tablets, isosorbide mononitrate 10 mg, net price 56 = £1.10; 20 mg, 56 = £1.33; 40 mg, 56 = £2.42. Label: 25

Brands include *Angeze®*, *Dynamin®*

**Elantan®** (Schwarz)

Elantan 10 tablets, scored, isosorbide mononitrate 10 mg. Net price 56 = £3.31; 84 = £4.97. Label: 25

Elantan 20 tablets, scored, isosorbide mononitrate 20 mg. Net price 56 = £4.32; 84 = £6.13. Label: 25

Elantan 40 tablets, scored, isosorbide mononitrate 40 mg. Net price 56 = £7.03; 84 = £10.56. Label: 25

**Ismo®** (Roche)

Ismo 10 tablets, isosorbide mononitrate 10 mg. Net price 60-tab pack = £3.01. Label: 25

Ismo 20 tablets, scored, isosorbide mononitrate 20 mg. Net price 60-tab pack = £4.42. Label: 25

Ismo 40 tablets, scored, isosorbide mononitrate 40 mg. Net price 60-tab pack = £7.25. Label: 25

**Modified release**

**Chemydur® 60XL** (Sovereign) PoM

Tablets, m/r, scored, ivory, isosorbide mononitrate 60 mg, net price 28-tab pack = £5.99. Label: 25

**Dose** prophylaxis of angina, 1 tablet in the morning (half a tablet for 2–4 days to minimise possibility of headache), increased if necessary to 2 tablets

**Elantan LA®** (Schwarz)

Elantan LA 25 capsules, m/r, brown/white, enclosing white micropellets, isosorbide mononitrate 25 mg. Net price 28-cap pack = £6.59. Label: 25

**Dose** prophylaxis of angina, 1 capsule in the morning, increased if necessary to 2 capsules

Elantan LA 50 capsules, m/r, brown/pink, enclosing white micropellets, isosorbide mononitrate 50 mg. Net price 28-cap pack = £10.54. Label: 25

**Dose** prophylaxis of angina, 1 capsule daily in the morning, increased if necessary to 2 capsules

**Imdur®** (AstraZeneca)

Durules® (= tablets m/r), yellow, f/c, scored, isosorbide mononitrate 60 mg. Net price 28-tab pack = £11.14. Label: 25

**Dose** prophylaxis of angina, 1 tablet in the morning (half a tablet if headache occurs), increased to 2 tablets in the morning if required

**Isib 60XL®** (Ashbourne)

Tablets, m/r, scored, ivory, isosorbide mononitrate 60 mg. Net price 28-tab pack = £8.75. Label: 25

**Dose** prophylaxis of angina, 1 tablet in the morning (half a tablet for 2–4 days if headache occurs), increased if necessary to 2 tablets

**Ismo Retard®** (Roche)

Tablets, m/r, s/c, isosorbide mononitrate 40 mg, net price 30-tab pack = £9.75. Label: 25

**Dose** prophylaxis of angina, 1 tablet daily in morning

**Isodur®** (Galen)

Isodur 25XL capsules, m/r, brown/white, isosorbide mononitrate 25 mg, net price 28-cap pack = £6.05. Label: 25

Isodur 50XL capsules, m/r, brown/pink, isosorbide mononitrate 50 mg, net price 28-cap pack = £9.75. Label: 25

**Dose** prophylaxis of angina, 25–50 mg daily in the morning, increased if necessary to 50–100 mg once daily

**Isotard®** (Strakan)

Isotard 25XL tablets, m/r, ivory, isosorbide mononitrate 25 mg, net price 28-tab pack = £5.95. Label: 25

Isotard 40XL tablets, m/r, ivory, isosorbide mononitrate 40 mg, net price 28-tab pack = £6.78. Label: 25

Isotard 50XL tablets, m/r, ivory, isosorbide mononitrate 50 mg, net price 28-tab pack = £6.78. Label: 25

Isotard 60XL tablets, m/r, ivory, isosorbide mononitrate 60 mg, net price 28-tab pack = £6.78. Label: 25

**Dose** prophylaxis of angina, 25–60 mg daily in the morning (if headache occurs with 60-mg tablet, half a 60-mg tablet may be given for 2–4 days), increased if necessary to 50–120 mg daily

**Modisal LA®** (Schwarz)

Modisal LA25 capsules, m/r, brown/white, isosorbide mononitrate 25 mg, net price 28-cap pack = £6.22. Label: 25

Modisal LA50 capsules, m/r, brown/peach, isosorbide mononitrate 50 mg, net price 28-cap pack = £10.03. Label: 25

**Dose** prophylaxis of angina, 25–50 mg daily in the morning, increased if necessary to 100 mg once daily

**Modisal XL®** (Sandoz)

Tablets, m/r, ivory, isosorbide mononitrate 60 mg. Net price 28-tab pack = £10.36. Label: 25

**Dose** prophylaxis of angina, 1 tablet daily in the morning (half a tablet for first 2–4 days to minimise possibility of headache), increased if necessary to 2 tablets once daily

**Monomax®** (Trinity-Chiesi) PoM

Monomax® SR, capsules, m/r, isosorbide mononitrate 40 mg, net price 28-cap pack = £8.31; 60 mg, 28-cap pack = £6.75. Label: 25

**Dose** prophylaxis of angina, 40–60 mg daily in the morning, increased if necessary to 120 mg daily

**Note** Also available as *Angeze SR®*

Monomax® XL tablets, m/r, isosorbide mononitrate 60 mg, net price 28-tab pack = £6.75. Label: 25

**Dose** prophylaxis of angina, 1 tablet in the morning (half a tablet for first 2–4 days to minimise possibility of headache), increased if necessary to 2 tablets

**Monomil XL®** (IVAX) PoM
Tablets, m/r, isosorbide mononitrate 60 mg, net price 28-tab pack = £4.95. Label: 25
Dose prophylaxis of angina, 1 tablet daily in the morning (half a tablet daily for first 2–4 days to minimise possibility of headache), increased if necessary to 2 tablets once daily

**Monosorb XL 60®** (Dexcel) PoM
Tablets, m/r, f/c, isosorbide mononitrate 60 mg. Net price 28-tab pack = £15.53. Label: 25
Dose prophylaxis of angina, 1 tablet daily in the morning (half a tablet for first 2–4 days to minimise possibility of headache), increased if necessary to 2 tablets
Note Also available as *Monigen® XL, Trangina® XL, Xismox® XL 60*

**Zemon®** (Neolab)
Zemon 40XL tablets, m/r, ivory, isosorbide mononitrate 40 mg, net price 28-tab pack = £14.25. Label: 25
Zemon 60XL tablets, scored, m/r, ivory, isosorbide mononitrate 60 mg, net price 28-tab pack = £11.14. Label: 25
Dose prophylaxis of angina, 40–60 mg daily in the morning (half a 60-mg tablet may be given for 2–4 days to minimise possibility of headache), increased if necessary to 80–120 mg once daily

## 2.6.2 Calcium-channel blockers

Calcium-channel blockers (less correctly called 'calcium-antagonists') interfere with the inward displacement of calcium ions through the slow channels of active cell membranes. They influence the myocardial cells, the cells within the specialised conducting system of the heart, and the cells of vascular smooth muscle. Thus, myocardial contractility may be reduced, the formation and propagation of electrical impulses within the heart may be depressed, and coronary or systemic vascular tone may be diminished.

Calcium-channel blockers differ in their predilection for the various possible sites of action and, therefore, their therapeutic effects are disparate, with much greater variation than those of beta-blockers. There are important differences between verapamil, diltiazem, and the dihydropyridine calcium-channel blockers (amlodipine, felodipine, isradipine, lacidipine, lercanidipine, nicardipine, nifedipine, nimodipine, and nisoldipine). Verapamil and diltiazem should usually be **avoided** in *heart failure* because they may further depress cardiac function and cause clinically significant deterioration.

**Verapamil** is used for the treatment of *angina* (section 2.6), *hypertension*, and *arrhythmias* (section 2.3.2). It is a highly negatively inotropic calcium channel-blocker and it reduces cardiac output, slows the heart rate, and may impair atrioventricular conduction. It may precipitate heart failure, exacerbate conduction disorders, and cause hypotension at high doses and should **not** be used with beta-blockers (see p. 114). Constipation is the most common side-effect.

**Nifedipine** relaxes vascular smooth muscle and dilates coronary and peripheral arteries. It has more influence on vessels and less on the myocardium than does verapamil, and unlike verapamil has no anti-arrhythmic activity. It rarely precipitates heart failure because any negative inotropic effect is offset by a reduction in left ventricular work. Short-acting formulations of nifedipine are not recommended for angina or long-term management of hypertension; their use may be associated with large variations in blood pressure and reflex tachycardia. **Nicardipine** has similar effects to those of nifedipine and may produce less reduction of myocardial contractility. **Amlodipine** and **felodipine** also resemble nifedipine and nicardipine in their effects and do not reduce myocardial contractility and they do not produce clinical deterioration in heart failure. They have a longer duration of action and can be given once daily. Nifedipine, nicardipine, amlodipine, and felodipine are used for the treatment of angina (section 2.6) or hypertension. All are valuable in forms of *angina associated with coronary vasospasm*. Side-effects associated with vasodilatation such as flushing and headache (which become less obtrusive after a few days), and ankle swelling (which may respond only partially to diuretics) are common.

**Isradipine**, **lacidipine**, **lercanidipine** and **nisoldipine** have similar effects to those of nifedipine and nicardipine; isradipine, lacidipine, and lercanidipine are only indicated for *hypertension* whereas nisoldipine is indicated for angina and hypertension.

**Nimodipine** is related to nifedipine but the smooth muscle relaxant effect preferentially acts on cerebral arteries. Its use is confined to prevention of *vascular spasm following aneurysmal subarachnoid haemorrhage.*

**Diltiazem** is effective in most forms of *angina* (section 2.6); the longer-acting formulation is also used for *hypertension*. It may be used in patients for whom beta-blockers are contra-indicated or ineffective. It has a less negative inotropic effect than verapamil and significant myocardial depression occurs rarely. Nevertheless because of the risk of bradycardia it should be used with caution in association with beta-blockers.

**Unstable angina** Calcium-channel blockers do not reduce the risk of myocardial infarction in unstable angina. The use of diltiazem or verapamil should be reserved for patients resistant to treatment with beta-blockers.

**Withdrawal** There is some evidence that sudden withdrawal of calcium-channel blockers may be associated with an exacerbation of angina.

### AMLODIPINE

**Indications** hypertension, prophylaxis of angina
**Cautions** hepatic impairment (Appendix 2); pregnancy (Appendix 4); **interactions:** Appendix 1 (calcium-channel blockers)
**Contra-indications** cardiogenic shock, unstable angina, significant aortic stenosis; breast-feeding (Appendix 5)
**Side-effects** abdominal pain, nausea; palpitation, flushing, oedema; headache, dizziness, sleep disturbances, fatigue; *less commonly* gastro-intestinal disturbances, dry mouth, taste disturbances, hypotension, syncope, chest pain, dyspnoea, rhinitis, mood changes, tremor, paraesthesia, urinary disturbances, impotence, gynaecomastia, weight changes, myalgia, visual disturbances, tinnitus, pruritus, rashes (including isolated reports of erythema multiforme), alopecia, purpura, and skin discolouration; *very rarely* gastritis, pancreatitis, hepatitis, jaundice, cholestasis, gingival hyperplasia, myocardial infarction, arrhythmias, vasculitis, coughing, hyperglycaemia, thrombocytopenia, angioedema, and urticaria

**Dose**

- Hypertension or angina, initially 5 mg once daily; max. 10 mg once daily

**Note** Tables from various suppliers may contain different salts (e.g. amlodipine besilate, amlodipine maleate, and amlodipine mesilate) but the strength is expressed in terms of amlodipine (base); tablets containing different salts are considered interchangeable

**Amlodipine** (Non-proprietary) PoM
Tablets, amlodipine (as maleate or as mesilate) 5 mg, net price 28-tab pack = £5.48; 10 mg, 28-tab pack = £7.96
Brands include *Amlostin®*

**Istin®** (Pfizer) PoM
Tablets, amlodipine (as besilate) 5 mg. Net price 28-tab pack = £13.04; 10 mg, 28-tab pack = £19.47

## DILTIAZEM HYDROCHLORIDE

**Indications** prophylaxis and treatment of angina; hypertension

**Cautions** reduce dose in hepatic and renal impairment; heart failure or significantly impaired left ventricular function, bradycardia (avoid if severe), first degree AV block, or prolonged PR interval; **interactions**: Appendix 1 (calcium-channel blockers)

**Contra-indications** severe bradycardia, left ventricular failure with pulmonary congestion, second- or third-degree AV block (unless pacemaker fitted), sick sinus syndrome; pregnancy; breast-feeding (Appendix 5)

**Side-effects** bradycardia, sino-atrial block, AV block, palpitation, dizziness, hypotension, malaise, asthenia, headache, hot flushes, gastro-intestinal disturbances, oedema (notably of ankles); rarely rashes (including erythema multiforme and exfoliative dermatitis), photosensitivity; hepatitis, gynaecomastia, gum hyperplasia, extrapyramidal symptoms, depression reported

**Dose**

- Angina, 60 mg 3 times daily (elderly initially twice daily); increased if necessary to 360 mg daily
- Longer-acting formulations, see under preparations below

### Standard formulations

**Note** These formulations are licensed as generics and there is no requirement for brand name dispensing. Although their means of formulation has called for the strict designation 'modified-release' their duration of action corresponds to that of tablets requiring administration 3 times daily

**Diltiazem** (Non-proprietary) PoM
Tablets, m/r (but see note above), diltiazem hydrochloride 60 mg. Net price 100 = £3.98. Label: 25
Brands include *Optil®*

**Tildiem®** (Sanofi-Synthelabo) PoM
Tablets, m/r (but see note above), off-white, diltiazem hydrochloride 60 mg. Net price 90-tab pack = £8.28. Label: 25

### Longer-acting formulations

**Note** Different versions of modified-release preparations may not have the same clinical effect. To avoid confusion between these different formulations of diltiazem, prescribers should specify the brand to be dispensed

**Adizem-SR®** (Napp) PoM
Capsules, m/r, diltiazem hydrochloride 90 mg (white), net price 56-cap pack = £8.98; 120 mg (brown/white), 56-cap pack = £9.98; 180 mg (brown/white), 56-cap pack = £14.95. Label: 25
Tablets, m/r, f/c, scored, diltiazem hydrochloride 120 mg. Net price 56-tab pack = £14.72. Label: 25
**Dose** mild to moderate hypertension, usually 120 mg twice daily (dose form not appropriate for initial dose titration)
Angina, initially 90 mg twice daily (elderly, dose form not appropriate for initial dose titration); increased to 180 mg twice daily if required

**Adizem-XL®** (Napp) PoM
Capsules, m/r, diltiazem hydrochloride 120 mg (pink/blue), net price 28-cap pack = £9.66; 180 mg (dark pink/blue), 28-cap pack = £10.96; 200 mg (brown), 28-cap pack = £7.82; 240 mg (red/blue), 28-cap pack = £12.17; 300 mg (maroon/blue), 28-cap pack = £9.66. Label: 25
**Dose** angina and mild to moderate hypertension, initially 240 mg once daily, increased if necessary to 300 mg once daily; in elderly and in hepatic or renal impairment, initially 120 mg daily

**Angitil SR®** (Trinity-Chiesi) PoM
Capsules, m/r, diltiazem hydrochloride 90 mg (white), net price 56-cap pack = £7.86; 120 mg (brown), 56-cap pack = £8.73; 180 mg (brown), 56-cap pack = £14.08. Label: 25
**Dose** angina and mild to moderate hypertension, initially 90 mg twice daily; increased if necessary to 120 mg or 180 mg twice daily
**Note** Also available as *Disogram® SR*

**Angitil XL®** (Trinity-Chiesi) PoM
Capsules, m/r, diltiazem hydrochloride 240 mg (white), net price 28-cap pack = £9.44; 300 mg (yellow), 28-cap pack = £8.57. Label: 25
**Dose** angina and mild to moderate hypertension, initially 240 mg once daily (elderly and in hepatic and renal impairment, dose form not appropriate for initial dose titration); increased if necessary to 300 mg once daily
**Note** Also available as *Disogram® SR*

**Calcicard CR®** (IVAX) PoM
Tablets, m/r, both f/c, diltiazem hydrochloride 90 mg, net price 56-tab pack = £6.33; 120 mg, 56-tab pack = £7.04. Label: 25
**Dose** mild to moderate hypertension, initially 90 mg or 120 mg twice daily; up to 360 mg daily may be required: ELDERLY and in hepatic and renal impairment, initially 120 mg once daily; up to 240 mg daily may be required
Angina, initially 90 mg or 120 mg twice daily; up to 480 mg daily in divided doses may be required; ELDERLY and in hepatic and renal impairment, dose form not appropriate for initial dose titration; up to 240 mg daily may be required
**Note** Also available as *Angiozem CR®*

**Dilcardia SR®** (Generics) PoM
Capsules, m/r, diltiazem hydrochloride 60 mg (pink/white), net price 56-cap pack = £8.31; 90 mg (pink/yellow), 56-cap pack = £10.33; 120 mg (pink/orange), 56-cap pack = £11.49. Label: 25
**Dose** angina and mild to moderate hypertension, initially 90 mg twice daily; increased if necessary to 180 mg twice daily; ELDERLY and in hepatic or renal impairment, initially 60 mg twice daily, max. 90 mg twice daily

**Dilzem SR®** (Zeneus) PoM
Capsules, m/r, all beige, diltiazem hydrochloride 60 mg, net price 56-cap pack = £6.40; 90 mg, 56-cap pack = £9.59; 120 mg, 56-cap pack = £10.95. Label: 25
**Dose** angina and mild to moderate hypertension, initially 90 mg twice daily (elderly 60 mg twice daily); up to 180 mg twice daily may be required

**Dilzem XL®** (Zeneus) PoM
Capsules, m/r, diltiazem hydrochloride 120 mg, net price 28-cap pack = £6.61; 180 mg, 28-cap pack = £9.81; 240 mg, 28-cap pack = £11.70. Label: 25
**Dose** angina and mild to moderate hypertension, initially 180 mg once daily (elderly and in hepatic and renal impairment, 120 mg once daily); if necessary may be increased to 360 mg once daily

**Slozem®** (Merck) PoM
Capsules, m/r, diltiazem hydrochloride 120 mg (pink/clear), net price 28-cap pack = £7.00; 180 mg (pink/clear), 28-cap pack = £7.80; 240 mg (red/clear), 28-cap pack = £8.20; 300 mg (red/white), 28-cap pack = £8.50. Label: 25
**Dose** angina and mild to moderate hypertension, initially 240 mg once daily (elderly and in hepatic and renal impairment, 120 mg once daily); if necessary may be increased to 360 mg once daily

**Tildiem LA®** (Sanofi-Synthelabo) PoM
Capsules, m/r, diltiazem hydrochloride 200 mg (pink/grey, containing white pellets), net price 28-cap pack = £6.66; 300 mg (white/yellow, containing white pellets), 28-cap pack = £7.51. Label: 25
**Dose** angina and mild to moderate hypertension, initially 200 mg once daily before or with food, increased if necessary to 300–400 mg daily, max. 500 mg daily; ELDERLY and in hepatic or renal impairment, initially 200 mg daily, increased if necessary to 300 mg daily

**Tildiem Retard®** (Sanofi-Synthelabo) PoM
Tablets, m/r, diltiazem hydrochloride 90 mg, net price 56-tab pack = £8.55; 120 mg, 56-tab pack = £9.53. Label: 25
**Counselling** Tablet membrane may pass through gastro-intestinal tract unchanged, but being porous has no effect on efficacy
**Dose** mild to moderate hypertension, initially 90 mg or 120 mg twice daily; increased if necessary to 360 mg daily in divided doses; ELDERLY and in hepatic or renal impairment, initially 120 mg once daily; increased if necessary to 120 mg twice daily
Angina, initially 90 mg or 120 mg twice daily; increased if necessary to 480 mg daily in divided doses; ELDERLY and in hepatic or renal impairment, dose form not appropriate for initial titration; up to 120 mg twice daily may be required

**Viazem XL®** (Genus) PoM
Capsules, m/r, diltiazem hydrochloride 120 mg (lavender), net price 28-cap pack = £6.60; 180 mg (white/blue-green), 28-cap pack = £7.36; 240 mg (blue-green/lavender), 28-cap pack = £7.74; 300 mg (white/lavender), 28-cap pack = £8.03; 360 mg (blue-green), 28-cap pack = £14.70. Label: 25
**Dose** angina and mild to moderate hypertension, initially 180 mg once daily, adjusted according to response to 240 mg once daily; max. 360 mg once daily; ELDERLY and in hepatic or renal impairment, initially 120 mg once daily, adjusted according to response

**Zemtard®** (Galen) PoM
Zemtard 120XL capsules, m/r, brown/orange, diltiazem hydrochloride 120 mg, net price 28-cap pack = £6.40. Label: 25
Zemtard 180XL capsules, m/r, grey/pink, diltiazem hydrochloride 180 mg, net price 28-cap pack = £6.50 Label: 25
Zemtard 240XL capsules, m/r, blue, diltiazem hydrochloride 240 mg, net price 28-cap pack = £6.60. Label: 25
Zemtard 300XL capsules, m/r, white/blue, diltiazem hydrochloride 300 mg, net price 28-cap pack = £7.45. Label: 25
**Dose** angina and mild to moderate hypertension, 180–300 mg once daily, increased if necessary to 360 mg once daily in hypertension and to 480 mg once daily in angina; ELDERLY and in hepatic or renal impairment, initially 120 mg once daily

## FELODIPINE

**Indications** hypertension, prophylaxis of angina
**Cautions** withdraw if ischaemic pain occurs or existing pain worsens shortly after initiating treatment or if cardiogenic shock develops; severe left ventricular dysfunction; avoid grapefruit juice (may affect metabolism); reduce dose in hepatic impairment; breast-feeding (Appendix 5); **interactions**: Appendix 1 (calcium-channel blockers)
**Contra-indications** unstable angina, uncontrolled heart failure; significant aortic stenosis; within 1 month of myocardial infarction; pregnancy (Appendix 4)
**Side-effects** flushing, headache, palpitation, dizziness, fatigue, gravitational oedema; rarely rash, pruritus, cutaneous vasculitis, gum hyperplasia, urinary frequency, impotence, fever
**Dose**
- Hypertension, initially 5 mg (elderly 2.5 mg) daily in the morning; usual maintenance 5–10 mg once daily; doses above 20 mg daily rarely needed
- Angina, initially 5 mg daily in the morning, increased if necessary to 10 mg once daily

**Felodipine** (Non-proprietary) PoM
Tablets, m/r felodipine 5 mg, net price 28-tab pack = £8.93; 10 mg, 28-tab pack = £12.01, 30-tab pack = £12.87. Label: 25
Brands include *Cardioplen XL®*, *Felogen XL®*, *Felotens XL®*, *Keloc SR®*, *Neofel XL®*, *Vascalpha®*

**Plendil®** (AstraZeneca) PoM
Tablets, m/r, f/c, felodipine 2.5 mg (yellow), net price 28-tab pack = £6.70; 5 mg (pink), 28-tab pack = £8.93; 10 mg (brown), 28-tab pack = £12.01. Label: 25



## ISRADIPINE

**Indications** hypertension
**Cautions** sick sinus syndrome (if pacemaker not fitted); avoid grapefruit juice (may affect metabolism); reduce dose in hepatic or renal impairment; pregnancy (Appendix 4); **interactions**: Appendix 1 (calcium-channel blockers)
**Contra-indications** cardiogenic shock; symptomatic or tight aortic stenosis; within 1 month of myocardial infarction; unstable angina; breast-feeding (Appendix 5)
**Side-effects** headache, flushing, dizziness, tachycardia and palpitation, localised peripheral oedema; hypotension uncommon; rarely weight gain, fatigue, abdominal discomfort, rashes
**Dose**
- 2.5 mg twice daily (1.25 mg twice daily in elderly, hepatic or renal impairment); increased if necessary after 3–4 weeks to 5 mg twice daily (exceptionally up to 10 mg twice daily); maintenance 2.5 or 5 mg once daily may be sufficient

**Prescal®** (Novartis) PoM
Tablets, yellow, scored, isradipine 2.5 mg. Net price 56-tab pack = £15.04

## LACIDIPINE

**Indications** hypertension
**Cautions** cardiac conduction abnormalities; poor cardiac reserve; withdraw if ischaemic pain occurs shortly after initiating treatment or if cardiogenic

shock develops; avoid grapefruit juice (may affect metabolism); hepatic impairment (Appendix 2); **interactions:** Appendix 1 (calcium-channel blockers)

**Contra-indications** aortic stenosis; avoid within 1 month of myocardial infarction; pregnancy (Appendix 4); breast-feeding (Appendix 5)

**Side-effects** headache, flushing, oedema, dizziness, palpitation; also asthenia, rash (including pruritus and erythema), gastro-intestinal disturbances, gum hyperplasia, muscle cramps, polyuria, chest pain (see Cautions); mood disturbances

**Dose**

- Initially 2 mg as a single daily dose, preferably in the morning; increased after 3–4 weeks to 4 mg daily, then if necessary to 6 mg daily

**Motens®** (Boehringer Ingelheim) PoM
Tablets, both f/c, lacidipine 2 mg, net price 28-tab pack = £9.51; 4 mg (scored), 28-tab pack = £14.23

## LERCANIDIPINE HYDROCHLORIDE

**Indications** mild to moderate hypertension

**Cautions** left ventricular dysfunction; sick sinus syndrome (if pacemaker not fitted); avoid grapefruit juice (may affect metabolism); hepatic impairment (Appendix 2); **interactions:** Appendix 1 (calcium-channel blockers)

**Contra-indications** aortic stenosis; unstable angina, uncontrolled heart failure; within 1 month of myocardial infarction; renal impairment; pregnancy (Appendix 4); breast-feeding

**Side-effects** flushing, peripheral oedema, palpitation, tachycardia, headache, dizziness, asthenia; also gastro-intestinal disturbances, hypotension, drowsiness, myalgia, polyuria, rash

**Dose**

- Initially 10 mg once daily; increased, if necessary, after at least 2 weeks to 20 mg daily

**Zanidip®** (Recordati) PoM
Tablets, yellow, f/c, lercanidipine hydrochloride 10 mg, net price 28-tab pack = £5.80. Label: 22

## NICARDIPINE HYDROCHLORIDE

**Indications** prophylaxis of angina; mild to moderate hypertension

**Cautions** withdraw if ischaemic pain occurs or existing pain worsens within 30 minutes of initiating treatment or increasing dose; congestive heart failure or significantly impaired left ventricular function; elderly; avoid grapefruit juice (may affect metabolism); hepatic impairment (Appendix 2); renal impairment (Appendix 3); pregnancy (Appendix 4); **interactions:** Appendix 1 (calcium-channel blockers)

**Contra-indications** cardiogenic shock; advanced aortic stenosis; unstable or acute attacks of angina; avoid within 1 month of myocardial infarction; breast-feeding (Appendix 5)

**Side-effects** dizziness, headache, peripheral oedema, flushing, palpitation, nausea; also gastro-intestinal disturbances, drowsiness, insomnia, tinnitus, hypotension, rashes, dyspnoea, paraesthesia, frequency of micturition; thrombocytopenia, depression and impotence reported

**Dose**

- Initially 20 mg 3 times daily, increased, after at least three days, to 30 mg 3 times daily (usual range 60–120 mg daily)

**Nicardipine** (Non-proprietary) PoM
Capsules, nicardipine hydrochloride 20 mg, net price 56-cap pack = £7.57; 30 mg, 56-cap pack = £9.38

**Cardene®** (Astellas) PoM
Capsules, nicardipine hydrochloride 20 mg (blue/white), net price 56-cap pack = £8.57; 30 mg (blue/pale blue), 56-cap pack = £9.95

### Modified release

**Cardene SR®** (Astellas) PoM
Capsules, m/r, nicardipine hydrochloride 30 mg, net price 56-cap pack = £10.21; 45 mg (blue), 56-cap pack = £14.86. Label: 25
Dose mild to moderate hypertension, initially 30 mg twice daily; usual effective dose 45 mg twice daily (range 30–60 mg twice daily)

## NIFEDIPINE

**Indications** prophylaxis of angina; hypertension; Raynaud's phenomenon

**Cautions** withdraw if ischaemic pain occurs or existing pain worsens shortly after initiating treatment; poor cardiac reserve; heart failure or significantly impaired left ventricular function (heart failure deterioration observed); severe hypotension; reduce dose in hepatic impairment (Appendix 2); diabetes mellitus; may inhibit labour; pregnancy (Appendix 4); breast-feeding (Appendix 5); avoid grapefruit juice (may affect metabolism); **interactions:** Appendix 1 (calcium-channel blockers)

**Contra-indications** cardiogenic shock; advanced aortic stenosis; within 1 month of myocardial infarction; unstable or acute attacks of angina; porphyria (section 9.8.2)

**Side-effects** headache, flushing, dizziness, lethargy; tachycardia, palpitation; short-acting preparations may induce an exaggerated fall in blood pressure and reflex tachycardia which may lead to myocardial or cerebrovascular ischaemia; gravitational oedema, rash (erythema multiforme reported), pruritus, urticaria, nausea, constipation or diarrhoea, increased frequency of micturition, eye pain, visual disturbances, gum hyperplasia, asthenia, paraesthesia, myalgia, tremor, impotence, gynaecomastia; depression, telangiectasia, cholestasis, jaundice reported

**Dose**

- See preparations below

**Nifedipine** (Non-proprietary) PoM
Capsules, nifedipine 5 mg, net price 84-cap pack = £3.68; 10 mg, 84-cap pack = £3.72
Dose angina prophylaxis (but not recommended, see notes above) and Raynaud's phenomenon, initially 5 mg 3 times daily, adjusted according to response to 20 mg 3 times daily
Hypertension, not recommended therefore no dose stated

**Adalat®** (Bayer) PoM
Capsules, both orange, nifedipine 5 mg, net price 90-cap pack = £6.08; 10 mg, 90-cap pack = £7.74
Dose angina prophylaxis (but not recommended, see notes above) and Raynaud's phenomenon, initially 5 mg 3 times daily, adjusted according to response to 20 mg 3 times daily
Hypertension, not recommended therefore no dose stated

### Modified release

**Note** Different versions of modified-release preparations may not have the same clinical effect. To avoid confusion between these different formulations of nifedipine, prescribers should specify the brand to be dispensed. Modified-release formulations may not be suitable for dose titration in hepatic disease

**Adalat® LA** (Bayer) PoM

LA 20 tablets, m/r, pink, nifedipine 20 mg, net price 28-tab pack = £5.27. Label: 25

LA 30 tablets, m/r, pink, nifedipine 30 mg, net price 28-tab pack = £7.59. Label: 25

LA 60 tablets, m/r, pink, nifedipine 60 mg, net price 28-tab pack = £9.69. Label: 25

**Counselling** Tablet membrane may pass through gastro-intestinal tract unchanged, but being porous has no effect on efficacy

**Dose** hypertension, 20–30 mg once daily, increased if necessary; max. 90 mg once daily

Angina prophylaxis, 30 mg once daily, increased if necessary; max. 90 mg once daily

**Caution** dose form not appropriate for use in hepatic impairment or where there is a history of oesophageal or gastro-intestinal obstruction, decreased lumen diameter of the gastro-intestinal tract, or inflammatory bowel disease (including Crohn's disease)

**Adalat® Retard** (Bayer) PoM

Retard 10 tablets, m/r, pink, nifedipine 10 mg. Net price 56-tab pack = £8.50. Label: 25

Retard 20 tablets, m/r, pink, nifedipine 20 mg. Net price 56-tab pack = £10.20. Label: 25

**Dose** hypertension and angina prophylaxis, 10 mg twice daily, adjusted according to response to 40 mg twice daily

**Adipine® MR** (Trinity-Chiesi) PoM

Tablets, m/r, nifedipine 10 mg (apricot), net price 56-tab pack = £5.96; 20 mg (pink), 56-tab pack = £7.43. Label: 21, 25

**Dose** hypertension and angina prophylaxis, 20 mg twice daily after food (initial titration 10 mg twice daily); max. 40 mg twice daily

**Adipine® XL** (Trinity-Chiesi) PoM

Tablets, m/r, both red, nifedipine 30 mg, net price 28-tab pack = £5.95; 60 mg, 28-tab pack = £8.95.Label: 25

**Dose** hypertension and angina prophylaxis, 30 mg once daily, increased if necessary; max. 90 mg once daily

**Cardilate MR®** (IVAX) PoM

Tablets, m/r, nifedipine 10 mg (pink), net price 56-tab pack = £4.97; 20 mg (brown), net price 100-tab pack = £16.62. Label: 25

**Dose** hypertension and angina prophylaxis, 20 mg twice daily (initial titration 10 mg twice daily); max. 80 mg daily

**Coracten SR®** (Celltech) PoM

Capsules, m/r, nifedipine 10 mg (grey/pink, enclosing yellow pellets), net price 60-cap pack = £4.27; 20 mg (pink/brown, enclosing yellow pellets), 60-cap pack = £5.93. Label: 25

**Dose** hypertension and angina prophylaxis, one 20-mg capsule every 12 hours, adjusted within range 10–40 mg every 12 hours

**Coracten XL®** (Celltech) PoM

Capsules, m/r, nifedipine 30 mg (brown), net price 28-cap pack = £5.89; 60 mg (orange), 28-cap pack = £8.84. Label: 25

**Dose** hypertension and angina prophylaxis, 30 mg once daily, increased if necessary; max. 90 mg once daily

**Fortipine LA 40®** (Goldshield) PoM

Tablets, m/r, red, nifedipine 40 mg, net price 30-tab pack = £8.00. Label: 21, 25

**Dose** hypertension and angina prophylaxis, 40 mg once daily, increased if necessary to 80 mg daily in 1–2 divided doses

**Hypolar® Retard 20** (Sandoz) PoM

Tablets, m/r, red, f/c, nifedipine 20 mg. Net price 56-tab pack = £7.00. Label: 25

**Dose** hypertension and angina prophylaxis, 20 mg twice daily, increased if necessary to 40 mg twice daily

**Nifedipress® MR** (Dexcel) PoM

Tablets, m/r, pink, nifedipine 10 mg, net price 56-tab pack = £9.23. Label: 25

**Dose** hypertension and angina prophylaxis, initially 10 mg twice daily adjusted according to response to 40 mg twice daily

**Nifopress® Retard** (Goldshield) PoM

Tablets, m/r, pink, nifedipine 20 mg, net price 112-tab pack = £10.80. Label: 21, 25

**Dose** mild to moderate hypertension, angina prophylaxis and Raynaud's phenomenon, usually 20 mg twice daily, adjusted according to response to 40 mg twice daily

**Slofedipine®** (Winthrop) PoM

Tablets, m/r, pink, nifedipine 20 mg, net price 56-tab pack = £10.32. Label: 25

**Dose** hypertension and angina prophylaxis, initially 20 mg twice daily adjusted according to response to 40 mg twice daily

**Slofedipine XL®** (Winthrop) PoM

Tablets, m/r, brown, nifedipine 30 mg, net price 28-tab pack = £9.89; 60 mg, 28-tab pack = £14.71. Label: 25

**Dose** hypertension and angina prophylaxis, 30 mg once daily, increased if necessary to 90 mg once daily

*Caution:* dose form not appropriate for use in hepatic impairment or where there is a history of oesophageal or gastro-intestinal obstruction, decreased lumen diameter of the gastro-intestinal tract, or inflammatory bowel disease (including Crohn's disease)

**Tensipine MR®** (Genus) PoM

Tablets, m/r, both pink, nifedipine 10 mg, net price 56-tab pack = £3.75; 20 mg, 56-tab pack = £5.25. Label: 21, 25

**Dose** hypertension and angina prophylaxis, initially 10 mg twice daily adjusted according to response to 40 mg twice daily

### With atenolol

Section 2.4

## NIMODIPINE

**Indications** prevention and treatment of ischaemic neurological deficits following aneurysmal subarachnoid haemorrhage

**Cautions** cerebral oedema or severely raised intracranial pressure; hypotension; avoid concomitant administration of nimodipine tablets and infusion, other calcium-channel blockers, or beta-blockers; concomitant nephrotoxic drugs; avoid grapefruit juice (may affect metabolism); hepatic impairment (Appendix 2); renal impairment (Appendix 3); pregnancy (Appendix 4); **interactions:** Appendix 1 (calcium-channel blockers, alcohol (infusion only))

**Contra-indications** within 1 month of myocardial infarction; unstable angina

**Side-effects** hypotension, variation in heart-rate, flushing, headache, gastro-intestinal disorders, nausea, sweating and feeling of warmth; thrombocytopenia and ileus reported

**Dose**

- Prevention, by mouth, 60 mg every 4 hours, starting within 4 days of aneurysmal subarachnoid haemorrhage and continued for 21 days
- Treatment, by intravenous infusion via central catheter, initially 1 mg/hour (up to 500 micrograms/hour if body-weight less than 70 kg or if blood pres-

sure unstable), increased after 2 hours to 2 mg/hour if no severe fall in blood pressure; continue for at least 5 days (max. 14 days); if surgical intervention during treatment, continue for at least 5 days after surgery; max. total duration of nimodipine use 21 days

**Nimotop®** (Bayer) PoM

Tablets, yellow, f/c, nimodipine 30 mg. Net price 100-tab pack = £38.85

Intravenous infusion, nimodipine 200 micrograms/mL; also contains ethanol 20% and macrogol '400' 17%. Net price 50-mL vial (with polyethylene infusion catheter) = £13.24

Note Polyethylene, polypropylene or glass apparatus should be used; PVC should be avoided

## NISOLDIPINE

**Indications** prophylaxis of angina, mild to moderate hypertension

**Cautions** elderly; hypotension; avoid grapefruit juice (may affect metabolism); **interactions:** Appendix 1 (calcium-channel blockers)

**Contra-indications** cardiogenic shock, aortic stenosis, unstable or acute attacks of angina; within 1 week of myocardial infarction; hepatic impairment (dose form not appropriate); pregnancy (Appendix 4); breast-feeding (Appendix 5)

**Side-effects** gravitational oedema, headache, flushing, tachycardia, palpitation; dizziness, asthenia, gastro-intestinal disturbances (including nausea, constipation); less frequently paraesthesia, myalgia, tremor, hypotension, weakness, dyspnoea, allergic skin reactions, increased frequency of micturition; rarely exacerbation of angina, visual disturbances, gynaecomastia, gum hyperplasia

**Dose**

- Initially 10 mg daily, preferably before breakfast; if necessary increase at intervals of at least 1 week (usual maintenance in angina 20–40 mg once daily); max. 40 mg daily

**Syscor MR®** (Forest) PoM

Tablets, m/r, f/c, yellow, nisoldipine 10 mg, net price 28-tab pack = £8.77. Label: 22, 25

## VERAPAMIL HYDROCHLORIDE

**Indications** see under Dose and preparations

**Cautions** first-degree AV block; acute phase of myocardial infarction (avoid if bradycardia, hypotension, left ventricular failure); patients taking beta-blockers (**important:** see below); hepatic impairment (Appendix 2); children, specialist advice only (section 2.3.2); pregnancy (Appendix 4) and breast-feeding (Appendix 5); avoid grapefruit juice (may affect metabolism); **interactions:** Appendix 1 (calcium-channel blockers)

Verapamil and beta-blockers **Verapamil** injection should not be given to patients recently treated with beta-blockers because of the risk of hypotension and asystole. The suggestion that when verapamil injection has been given first, an interval of 30 minutes before giving a beta-blocker is sufficient has not been confirmed.

It may also be hazardous to give verapamil and a beta-blocker together by mouth (should only be contemplated if myocardial function well preserved).

**Contra-indications** hypotension, bradycardia, second- and third-degree AV block, sick sinus syndrome, cardiogenic shock, sino-atrial block; history of heart failure or significantly impaired left ventricular function, even if controlled by therapy; atrial flutter or fibrillation complicating Wolff-Parkinson-White syndrome; porphyria (section 9.8.2)

**Side-effects** constipation; less commonly nausea, vomiting, flushing, headache, dizziness, fatigue, ankle oedema; rarely allergic reactions (erythema, pruritus, urticaria, angioedema, Stevens-Johnson syndrome); myalgia, arthralgia, paraesthesia, erythromelalgia; increased prolactin concentration; rarely gynaecomastia and gingival hyperplasia after long-term treatment; after intravenous administration or high doses, hypotension, heart failure, bradycardia, heart block, and asystole

**Dose**

- By mouth, supraventricular arrhythmias (but see also Contra-indications), 40–120 mg 3 times daily

  Angina, 80–120 mg 3 times daily

  Hypertension, 240–480 mg daily in 2–3 divided doses
- By slow intravenous injection over 2 minutes (3 minutes in elderly), 5–10 mg (preferably with ECG monitoring); in paroxysmal tachyarrhythmias a further 5 mg after 5–10 minutes if required

**Verapamil** (Non-proprietary) PoM

Tablets, coated, verapamil hydrochloride 40 mg, net price 20 = 47p; 80 mg, 20 = 56p; 120 mg, 20 = £1.12; 160 mg, 20 = £1.69

Oral solution, verapamil hydrochloride 40 mg/5 mL, net price 150 mL = £36.90

Brands include *Zolvera®*

**Cordilox®** (IVAX) PoM

Tablets, all yellow, f/c, verapamil hydrochloride 40 mg, net price 84-tab pack = £1.50; 80 mg, 84-tab pack = £2.05; 120 mg, 28-tab pack = £1.15; 160 mg, 56-tab pack = £2.80

Injection, verapamil hydrochloride 2.5 mg/mL, net price 2-mL amp = £1.11

**Securon®** (Abbott) PoM

Tablets, f/c, verapamil hydrochloride 40 mg, net price 100 = £4.57; 120 mg (scored), 60-tab pack = £6.29

Injection, verapamil hydrochloride 2.5 mg/mL. Net price 2-mL amp = £1.08

### Modified release

**Half Securon SR®** (Abbott) PoM

Tablets, m/r, f/c, verapamil hydrochloride 120 mg. Net price 28-tab pack = £7.50. Label: 25

Dose see *Securon SR®*

**Securon SR®** (Abbott) PoM

Tablets, m/r, pale green, f/c, scored, verapamil hydrochloride 240 mg. Net price 28-tab pack = £6.29. Label: 25

Dose hypertension, 240 mg daily (new patients initially 120 mg), increased if necessary to max. 480 mg daily (doses above 240 mg daily as 2 divided doses)

Angina, 240 mg twice daily (may sometimes be reduced to once daily)

Prophylaxis after myocardial infarction where beta-blockers not appropriate (started at least 1 week after infarction), 360 mg daily in divided doses, given as 240 mg in the morning and 120 mg in the evening *or* 120 mg 3 times daily

**Univer®** (Zeneus) PoM

Capsules, m/r, verapamil hydrochloride 120 mg (yellow/dark blue), net price 28-cap pack = £7.51;

180 mg (yellow), 56-cap pack = £18.15; 240 mg (yellow/dark blue), 28-cap pack = £12.24. Label: 25
Dose hypertension, 240 mg daily, max. 480 mg daily (new patients, initial dose 120 mg); angina, 360 mg daily, max. 480 mg daily

**Verapress MR®** (Dexcel) PoM
Tablets, m/r, pale green, f/c, verapamil hydrochloride 240 mg. Net price 28-tab pack = £9.90. Label: 25
Dose hypertension, 1 tablet daily, increased to twice daily if necessary; angina, 1 tablet twice daily (may sometimes be reduced to once daily)
Note Also available as *Cordilox® MR*

**Vertab® SR 240** (Trinity-Chiesi) PoM
Tablets, m/r, pale green, f/c, scored, verapamil hydrochloride 240 mg, net price 28-tab pack = £8.63. Label: 25
Dose mild to moderate hypertension, 240 mg daily, increased to twice daily if necessary; angina, 240 mg twice daily (may sometimes be reduced to once daily)

## 2.6.3 Other antianginal drugs

**Nicorandil**, a potassium-channel activator with a nitrate component, has both arterial and venous vasodilating properties and is licensed for the prevention and long-term treatment of angina (section 2.6). Nicorandil has similar efficacy to other antianginal drugs in controlling symptoms; it may produce additional symptomatic benefit in combination with other antianginal drugs [unlicensed indication].

**Ivabradine** lowers the heart rate by its action on the sinus node. It is licensed for the treatment of angina in patients with normal sinus rhythm when beta-blockers are contra-indicated or not tolerated.

### IVABRADINE

**Indications** treatment of angina (see notes above)
**Cautions** mild heart failure including asymptomatic left ventricular dysfunction; monitor for atrial fibrillation; hypotension (avoid if severe); retinitis pigmentosa; elderly; hepatic impairment (avoid if severe; Appendix 2); renal impairment (Appendix 3); **interactions**: Appendix 1 (ivabradine)
**Contra-indications** severe bradycardia (do not initiate if heart rate below 60 beats per minute); cardiogenic shock; acute myocardial infarction; acute cerebrovascular accident; sick-sinus syndrome; sino-atrial block; moderate to severe heart failure; patients with pacemaker; unstable angina; second- and third-degree heart block; arrhythmias including atrial fibrillation (ineffective); congenital QT syndrome; pregnancy; breast-feeding
**Side-effects** bradycardia, first-degree heart block, ventricular extrasystoles; headache, dizziness; visual disturbances including phosphenes and blurred vision; *less commonly* nausea, constipation, diarrhoea, palpitations, supraventricular extrasystoles, dyspnoea, vertigo, muscle cramps, eosinophilia, hyperuricaemia, and raised plasma-creatinine concentration
**Dose**
- Initially 5 mg twice daily, increased if necessary after 3–4 weeks to 7.5 mg twice daily (if not tolerated reduce dose to 2.5–5 mg twice daily); ELDERLY initially 2.5 mg twice daily

Note Ventricular rate at rest should not be allowed to fall below 50 beats per minute

**Procoralan®** (Servier) ▼ PoM
Tablets, both pink, f/c, ivabradine (as hydrochloride) 5 mg (scored), net price 56-tab pack = £39.00; 7.5 mg, 56-tab pack = £39.00

### NICORANDIL

**Indications** prophylaxis and treatment of angina
**Cautions** hypovolaemia; low systolic blood pressure; acute pulmonary oedema; acute myocardial infarction with acute left ventricular failure and low filling pressures; pregnancy (Appendix 4); **interactions:** Appendix 1 (nicorandil)
Driving Patients should be warned not to drive or operate machinery until it is established that their performance is unimpaired
**Contra-indications** cardiogenic shock; left ventricular failure with low filling pressures; hypotension; breast-feeding
**Side-effects** headache (especially on initiation, usually transitory); cutaneous vasodilatation with flushing; nausea, vomiting, dizziness, weakness also reported; *rarely* oral ulceration, myalgia, and rash; at high dosage, reduction in blood pressure and/or increase in heart rate; angioedema, hepatic dysfunction, and anal ulceration also reported
**Dose**
- Initially 10 mg twice daily (if susceptible to headache 5 mg twice daily); usual dose 10–20 mg twice daily; up to 30 mg twice daily may be used

**Ikorel®** (Rhône-Poulenc Rorer) PoM
Tablets, both scored, nicorandil 10 mg, net price 60-tab pack = £8.18; 20 mg, 60-tab pack = £15.54

## 2.6.4 Peripheral vasodilators and related drugs

Most serious peripheral vascular disorders, such as *intermittent claudication*, are due to occlusion of vessels, either by spasm or sclerotic plaques. Lifestyle changes including smoking cessation and exercise training are the most important measures in the conservative management of intermittent claudication. Low-dose aspirin (75 mg daily) should be given as long-term prophylaxis against cardiovascular events and a statin (section 2.12) should be considered if serum total cholesterol is raised. **Naftidrofuryl** 200 mg 3 times daily may alleviate symptoms and improve pain-free walking distance in moderate disease, but it is not known whether naftidrofuryl has any effect on the outcome of the disease. Patients receiving naftidrofuryl should be assessed for improvement after 3–6 months. **Cilostazol** is licensed for use in intermittent claudication to improve walking distance in patients without peripheral tissue necrosis and who do not have pain at rest. Inositol nicotinate, pentoxifylline (oxpentifylline) and cinnarizine are not established as being effective.

Management of *Raynaud's syndrome* includes avoidance of exposure to cold and stopping smoking. More severe symptoms may require vasodilator treatment, which is most often successful in primary Raynaud's syndrome.

**Nifedipine** (section 2.6.2) is useful for reducing the frequency and severity of vasospastic attacks. Alternatively, **naftidrofuryl** may produce symptomatic improvement; **inositol nicotinate** (a nicotinic acid derivative) may also be considered. Cinnarizine, pentoxifylline, prazosin and moxisylyte (thymoxamine) are not established as being effective.

Vasodilator therapy is not established as being effective for *chilblains* (section 13.14).

## CILOSTAZOL

**Indications** intermittent claudication in patients without rest pain and no peripheral tissue necrosis

**Cautions** atrial or ventricular ectopy, atrial fibrillation, atrial flutter; diabetes mellitus (higher risk of intraocular bleeding); **interactions:** Appendix 1 (cilostazol)

**Contra-indications** predisposition to bleeding (e.g. active peptic ulcer, haemorrhagic stroke in previous 6 months, surgery in previous 3 months, proliferative diabetic retinopathy, poorly controlled hypertension); history of ventricular tachycardia, of ventricular fibrillation and of multifocal ventricular ectopics, prolongation of QT interval, congestive heart failure; moderate or severe hepatic impairment (Appendix 2); renal impairment (Appendix 3); pregnancy (Appendix 4); breast-feeding (Appendix 5)

**Side-effects** diarrhoea, abnormal stools, and headache are very common; nausea, vomiting, dyspepsia, flatulence, abdominal pain; tachycardia, palpitation, angina, arrhythmia, chest pain; rhinitis; dizziness; ecchymosis; rash, pruritus; oedema, asthenia; less commonly, gastritis, myocardial infarction, congestive heart failure, postural hypotension, insomnia, anxiety, abnormal dreams, dyspnoea, pneumonia, cough, hypersensitivity reactions, diabetes mellitus, anaemia, haemorrhage, thrombocythaemia, myalgia, renal impairment

**Dose**

- 100 mg twice daily (30 minutes before or 2 hours after food)

**Pletal** (Otsuka) ▼ PoM
Tablets, cilostazol 50 mg, net price 56-tab pack = £35.31; 100 mg, 56-tab pack = £35.31

## CINNARIZINE

**Indications** peripheral vascular disease, Raynaud's syndrome

**Cautions** see section 3.4.1

**Contra-indications** see section 3.4.1

**Side-effects** see section 3.4.1; also hypotension with high doses, allergic skin reactions, fatigue; *rarely* extrapyramidal symptoms in elderly on prolonged therapy

**Dose**

- Initially, 75 mg 3 times daily; maintenance, 75 mg 2–3 times daily

**Stugeron Forte®** (Janssen-Cilag)
Capsules, orange/ivory, cinnarizine 75 mg. Net price 100-cap pack = £5.23. Label: 2

**Stugeron®**
See section 4.6

## INOSITOL NICOTINATE

**Indications** peripheral vascular disease; hyperlipidaemia (section 2.12)

**Cautions** cerebrovascular insufficiency, unstable angina

**Contra-indications** recent myocardial infarction, acute phase of a cerebrovascular accident; pregnancy (Appendix 4)

**Side-effects** nausea, vomiting, hypotension, flushing, syncope, oedema, headache, dizziness, paraesthesia, rash

**Dose**

- 3 g daily in 2–3 divided doses; max. 4 g daily

**Hexopal®** (Genus)
Tablets, scored, inositol nicotinate 500 mg. Net price 20 = £4.10

Tablets forte, scored, inositol nicotinate 750 mg. Net price 112-tab pack = £34.02

## MOXISYLYTE
(Thymoxamine)

**Indications** primary Raynaud's syndrome (short-term treatment)

**Cautions** diabetes mellitus

**Contra-indications** active liver disease; pregnancy (Appendix 4)

**Side-effects** nausea, diarrhoea, flushing, headache, dizziness; hepatic reactions including cholestatic jaundice and hepatitis reported to CSM

**Dose**

- Initially 40 mg 4 times daily, increased to 80 mg 4 times daily if poor initial response; discontinue after 2 weeks if no response

**Opilon®** (Concord) PoM
Tablets, yellow, f/c, moxisylyte 40 mg (as hydrochloride). Net price 112-tab pack = £79.98. Label: 21

## NAFTIDROFURYL OXALATE

**Indications** see under Dose

**Side-effects** nausea, epigastric pain, rash, hepatitis, hepatic failure

**Dose**

- Peripheral vascular disease (see notes above), 100–200 mg 3 times daily; cerebral vascular disease, 100 mg 3 times daily

**Naftidrofuryl** (Non-proprietary) PoM
Capsules, naftidrofuryl oxalate 100 mg. Net price 84-cap pack = £6.48. Label: 25, 27

**Praxilene®** (Merck) PoM
Capsules, pink, naftidrofuryl oxalate 100 mg. Net price 84-cap pack = £8.60. Label: 25, 27

## PENTOXIFYLLINE
(Oxpentifylline)

**Indications** peripheral vascular disease; venous leg ulcers [unlicensed indication] (Appendix A8.2.5)

**Cautions** hypotension, coronary artery disease; renal impairment (Appendix 3), severe hepatic impairment; avoid in porphyria (section 9.8.2); **interactions:** Appendix 1 (pentoxifylline)

**Contra-indications** cerebral haemorrhage, extensive retinal haemorrhage, acute myocardial infarction; pregnancy and breast-feeding

**Side-effects** gastro-intestinal disturbances, dizziness, agitation, sleep disturbances, headache; rarely flushing, tachycardia, angina, hypotension, thrombocytopenia, intrahepatic cholestasis, hypersensitivity reactions including rash, pruritus and bronchospasm

**Dose**

- 400 mg 2–3 times daily

**Trental®** (Aventis Pharma) PoM

Tablets, m/r, pink, s/c, pentoxifylline 400 mg. Net price 90-tab pack = £20.48. Label: 21, 25

## Other preparations used in peripheral vascular disease

Rutosides (oxerutins, *Paroven®*) are not vasodilators and are not generally regarded as effective preparations as capillary sealants or for the treatment of cramps; side-effects include headache, flushing, rashes, mild gastro-intestinal disturbances.

**Paroven®** (Novartis Consumer Health)

Capsules, yellow, oxerutins 250 mg. Net price 120-cap pack = £13.05

Dose relief of symptoms of oedema associated with chronic venous insufficiency, 500 mg twice daily

# 2.7 Sympathomimetics

2.7.1 Inotropic sympathomimetics
2.7.2 Vasoconstrictor sympathomimetics
2.7.3 Cardiopulmonary resuscitation

The properties of sympathomimetics vary according to whether they act on alpha or on beta adrenergic receptors. Adrenaline (epinephrine) (section 2.7.3) acts on both alpha and beta receptors and increases both heart rate and contractility (beta$_1$ effects); it can cause peripheral vasodilation (a beta$_2$ effect) or vasoconstriction (an alpha effect).

## 2.7.1 Inotropic sympathomimetics

The cardiac stimulants **dobutamine** and **dopamine** act on beta$_1$ receptors in cardiac muscle, and increase contractility with little effect on rate.

**Dopexamine** acts on beta$_2$ receptors in cardiac muscle to produce its positive inotropic effect; and on peripheral dopamine receptors to increase renal perfusion; it is reported not to induce vasoconstriction.

**Isoprenaline** injection is available on special order only.

**Shock** Shock is a medical emergency associated with a high mortality. The underlying causes of shock such as haemorrhage, sepsis or myocardial insufficiency should be corrected. The profound hypotension of shock must be treated promptly to prevent tissue hypoxia and organ failure. Volume replacement is essential to correct the hypovolaemia associated with haemorrhage and sepsis but may be detrimental in cardiogenic shock. Depending on haemodynamic status, cardiac output may be improved by the use of sympathomimetic inotropes such as adrenaline (epinephrine), dobutamine or dopamine (see notes above). In septic shock, when fluid replacement and inotropic support fail to maintain blood pressure, the vasoconstrictor noradrenaline (norepinephrine) (section 2.7.2) may be considered. In cardiogenic shock peripheral resistance is frequently high and to raise it further may worsen myocardial performance and exacerbate tissue ischaemia.

The use of sympathomimetic inotropes and vasoconstrictors should preferably be confined to the intensive care setting and undertaken with invasive haemodynamic monitoring.

For advice on the management of anaphylactic shock, see section 3.4.3.

### DOBUTAMINE

**Indications** inotropic support in infarction, cardiac surgery, cardiomyopathies, septic shock, and cardiogenic shock

**Cautions** severe hypotension complicating cardiogenic shock; pregnancy; **interactions:** Appendix 1 (sympathomimetics)

**Side-effects** tachycardia and marked increase in systolic blood pressure indicate overdosage; phlebitis; *rarely* thrombocytopenia

**Dose**

- By intravenous infusion, 2.5–10 micrograms/kg/minute, adjusted according to response

**Dobutamine** (Non-proprietary) PoM

Strong sterile solution, dobutamine (as hydrochloride) 12.5 mg/mL. For dilution and use as an intravenous infusion. Net price 20-mL amp = £5.25

### DOPAMINE HYDROCHLORIDE

**Indications** cardiogenic shock in infarction or cardiac surgery

**Cautions** correct hypovolaemia; low dose in shock due to acute myocardial infarction—see notes above; pregnancy (Appendix 4); **interactions:** Appendix 1 (sympathomimetics)

**Contra-indications** tachyarrhythmia, phaeochromocytoma

**Side-effects** nausea and vomiting, peripheral vasoconstriction, hypotension, hypertension, tachycardia

**Dose**

- By intravenous infusion, 2–5 micrograms/kg/minute initially (see notes above)

**Dopamine** (Non-proprietary) PoM

Sterile concentrate, dopamine hydrochloride 40 mg/mL, net price 5-mL amp = £3.88; 160 mg/mL, net price 5-mL amp = £14.75. For dilution and use as an intravenous infusion

Intravenous infusion, dopamine hydrochloride 1.6 mg/mL in glucose 5% intravenous infusion, net price 250-mL container (400 mg) = £11.69; 3.2 mg/mL, 250-mL container (800 mg) = £22.93 (both hosp. only)

**Select-A-Jet® Dopamine** (Celltech) PoM
Strong sterile solution, dopamine hydrochloride 40 mg/mL. Net price 5-mL vial = £4.55; 10-mL vial = £7.32. For dilution and use as an intravenous infusion

## DOPEXAMINE HYDROCHLORIDE

**Indications** inotropic support and vasodilator in exacerbations of chronic heart failure and in heart failure associated with cardiac surgery

**Cautions** myocardial infarction, recent angina, hypokalaemia, hyperglycaemia; correct hypovolaemia before starting and during treatment, monitor blood pressure, pulse, plasma potassium, blood glucose; avoid abrupt withdrawal; pregnancy; **interactions:** Appendix 1 (sympathomimetics)

**Contra-indications** left ventricular outlet obstruction such as hypertrophic cardiomyopathy or aortic stenosis; phaeochromocytoma, thrombocytopenia

**Side-effects** nausea, vomiting; tachycardia, bradycardia, arrhythmias, angina, myocardial infarction; tremor, headache; dyspnoea; reversible thrombocytopenia; sweating

**Dose**

- By intravenous infusion into central or large peripheral vein, 500 nanograms/kg/minute, may be increased to 1 microgram/kg/minute and further increased up to 6 micrograms/kg/minute in increments of 0.5–1 microgram/kg/minute at intervals of not less than 15 minutes

**Dopacard®** (Zeneus) PoM
Strong sterile solution, dopexamine hydrochloride 10 mg/mL (1%). For dilution and use as an intravenous infusion. Net price 5-mL amp = £21.00
**Note** Contact with metal in infusion apparatus should be minimised

## 2.7.2 Vasoconstrictor sympathomimetics

Vasoconstrictor sympathomimetics raise blood pressure transiently by acting on alpha-adrenergic receptors to constrict peripheral vessels. They are sometimes used as an emergency method of elevating blood pressure where other measures have failed (see also section 2.7.1).

The danger of vasoconstrictors is that although they raise blood pressure they do so at the expense of perfusion of vital organs such as the kidney.

Spinal and epidural anaesthesia may result in sympathetic block with resultant hypotension. Management may include intravenous fluids (which are usually given prophylactically), oxygen, elevation of the legs, and injection of a pressor drug such as ephedrine. As well as constricting peripheral vessels **ephedrine** also accelerates the heart rate (by acting on beta receptors). Use is made of this dual action of ephedrine to manage associated bradycardia (although intravenous injection of atropine sulphate 400 to 600 micrograms may also be required if bradycardia persists).

## EPHEDRINE HYDROCHLORIDE

**Indications** see under Dose

**Cautions** hyperthyroidism, diabetes mellitus, ischaemic heart disease, hypertension, angle-closure glaucoma, elderly, pregnancy (Appendix 4); may cause acute urine retention in prostatic hypertrophy; **interactions:** Appendix 1 (sympathomimetics)

**Contra-indications** breast-feeding (Appendix 5)

**Side-effects** nausea, vomiting, anorexia; tachycardia (sometimes bradycardia), arrhythmias, anginal pain, vasoconstriction with hypertension, vasodilation with hypotension, dizziness and flushing; dyspnoea; headache, anxiety, restlessness, confusion, psychoses, insomnia, tremor; difficulty in micturition, urine retention; sweating, hypersalivation; changes in blood-glucose concentration

**Dose**

- Reversal of hypotension from spinal or epidural anaesthesia, by slow intravenous injection of a solution containing ephedrine hydrochloride 3 mg/mL, 3–6 mg (max. 9 mg) repeated every 3–4 minutes according to response to max. 30 mg

**Ephedrine Hydrochloride** (Non-proprietary) PoM
Injection, ephedrine hydrochloride 3 mg/mL, net price 10-mL amp = £2.83; 30 mg/mL, net price 1-mL amp = £1.70

## METARAMINOL

**Indications** acute hypotension (see notes above); priapism (section 7.4.5) [unlicensed indication]

**Cautions** see under Noradrenaline Acid Tartrate; longer duration of action than noradrenaline (norepinephrine), see below; cirrhosis; pregnancy (Appendix 4); breast-feeding (Appendix 5)
**Hypertensive response** Metaraminol has a longer duration of action than noradrenaline, and an excessive vasopressor response may cause a prolonged rise in blood pressure

**Contra-indications** see under Noradrenaline Acid Tartrate

**Side-effects** see under Noradrenaline Acid Tartrate; tachycardia; fatal ventricular arrhythmia reported in Laennec's cirrhosis

**Dose**

- By intravenous infusion, 15–100 mg, adjusted according to response
- In emergency, by intravenous injection, 0.5–5 mg then by intravenous infusion, 15–100 mg, adjusted according to response

**Metaraminol** (Non-proprietary) PoM
Injection, metaraminol 10 mg (as tartrate)/mL.
Available from regional hospital manufacturing unit ('special order')

## NORADRENALINE ACID TARTRATE/ NOREPINEPHRINE BITARTRATE

**Indications** see under dose

**Cautions** coronary, mesenteric, or peripheral vascular thrombosis; following myocardial infarction, Prinzmetal's variant angina, hyperthyroidism, diabetes mellitus; hypoxia or hypercapnia; uncorrected hypovolaemia; elderly; extravasation at injection site may cause necrosis; **interactions:** Appendix 1 (sympathomimetics)

**Contra-indications** hypertension (monitor blood pressure and rate of flow frequently); pregnancy (Appendix 4)

**Side-effects** hypertension, headache, bradycardia, arrhythmias, peripheral ischaemia

**Dose**

- Acute hypotension, by intravenous infusion, via central venous catheter, of a solution containing noradrenaline acid tartrate 80 micrograms/mL (equivalent to noradrenaline base 40 micrograms/mL) at an initial rate of 0.16–0.33 mL/minute, adjusted according to response
- Cardiac arrest, by rapid intravenous *or* intracardiac injection, 0.5–0.75 mL of a solution containing noradrenaline acid tartrate 200 micrograms/mL (equivalent to noradrenaline base 100 micrograms/mL)

**Noradrenaline/Norepinephrine** (Abbott) PoM
Injection, noradrenaline acid tartrate 2 mg/mL (equivalent to noradrenaline base 1 mg/mL). For dilution before use. Net price 2-mL amp = £1.01, 4-mL amp = £1.50, 20-mL amp = £6.35

## PHENYLEPHRINE HYDROCHLORIDE

**Indications** acute hypotension (see notes above); priapism (section 7.4.5) [unlicensed indication]

**Cautions** see under Noradrenaline Acid Tartrate; longer duration of action than noradrenaline (norepinephrine), see below; coronary disease

**Hypertensive response** Phenylephrine has a longer duration of action than noradrenaline, and an excessive vasopressor response may cause a prolonged rise in blood pressure

**Contra-indications** see under Noradrenaline Acid Tartrate; severe hyperthyroidism; pregnancy (Appendix 4)

**Side-effects** see under Noradrenaline Acid Tartrate; tachycardia or reflex bradycardia

**Dose**

- By subcutaneous *or* intramuscular injection, 2–5 mg, followed if necessary by further doses of 1–10 mg
- By slow intravenous injection of a 1 mg/mL solution, 100–500 micrograms repeated as necessary after at least 15 minutes
- By intravenous infusion, initial rate up to 180 micrograms/minute reduced to 30–60 micrograms/minute according to response

**Phenylephrine** (Sovereign) PoM
Injection, phenylephrine hydrochloride 10 mg/mL (1%). Net price 1-mL amp = £5.50

# 2.7.3 Cardiopulmonary resuscitation

The algorithm for cardiopulmonary resuscitation (see inside back cover) reflects the most recent recommendations of the Resuscitation Council (UK). In cardiac arrest **adrenaline (epinephrine)** 1 in 10 000 (100 micrograms/mL) is recommended in a dose of 10 mL by intravenous injection, preferably through a central line. If injected through a peripheral line, the drug must be flushed with at least 20 mL sodium chloride 0.9% injection (to aid entry into the central circulation). Intravenous injection of **amiodarone** 300 mg (from a prefilled syringe *or* diluted in glucose intravenous infusion 5%) should be considered after adrenaline to treat ventricular fibrillation or pulseless ventricular tachycardia in cardiac arrest refractory to defibrillation. **Atropine** 3 mg by intravenous injection (section 15.1.3) as a single dose is also used in cardiopulmonary resuscitation to block vagal activity.

For the management of acute anaphylaxis see section 3.4.3.

## ADRENALINE/EPINEPHRINE

**Indications** see notes above

**Cautions** heart disease, diabetes mellitus, hyperthyroidism, hypertension, arrhythmias, cerebrovascular disease, angle-closure glaucoma, avoid during second stage of labour; **interactions:** Appendix 1 (sympathomimetics)

**Side-effects** anxiety, tremor, tachycardia, headache, cold extremities; in overdosage arrhythmias, cerebral haemorrhage, pulmonary oedema; nausea, vomiting, sweating, weakness, dizziness and hyperglycaemia also reported

**Dose**

- See notes above

**Adrenaline/Epinephrine 1 in 10 000, Dilute** (Non-proprietary) PoM
Injection, adrenaline (as acid tartrate) 100 micrograms/mL. 10-mL amp.
Brands include *Minijet® Adrenaline*

# 2.8 Anticoagulants and protamine

2.8.1 Parenteral anticoagulants
2.8.2 Oral anticoagulants
2.8.3 Protamine sulphate

The main use of anticoagulants is to prevent thrombus formation or extension of an existing thrombus in the slower-moving venous side of the circulation, where the thrombus consists of a fibrin web enmeshed with platelets and red cells. They are therefore widely used in the prevention and treatment of *deep-vein thrombosis in the legs.*

Anticoagulants are of less use in preventing thrombus formation in arteries, for in faster-flowing vessels thrombi are composed mainly of platelets with little fibrin. They are used to prevent thrombi forming on *prosthetic heart valves.*

## 2.8.1 Parenteral anticoagulants

### Heparin

**Heparin** initiates anticoagulation rapidly but has a short duration of action. It is now often referred to as being **standard** or **unfractionated heparin** to distinguish it from the **low molecular weight heparins** (see p. 121), which have a longer duration of action. For patients at high risk of bleeding, heparin is more suitable than low molecular weight heparin because its effect can be terminated rapidly by stopping the infusion.

**Treatment** For the initial treatment of *deep-vein thrombosis and pulmonary embolism* heparin is given as an *intravenous loading dose*, followed by *continuous intravenous infusion* (using an infusion pump) or by *intermittent subcutaneous injection*; the use of *intermittent intravenous injection* is no longer recommended. Alternatively, a low molecular weight heparin is given for initial treatment of deep vein thrombosis and pulmonary embolism. An oral anticoagulant (usually warfarin, section 2.8.2) is started at the same time as the heparin (the heparin needs to be continued for at least 5 days and until the INR has been in the therapeutic range for 2 consecutive days). Laboratory monitoring is essential—preferably on a daily basis, determination of the activated partial thromboplastin time (APTT) being the most widely used technique. Heparin is also used in regimens for the management of *myocardial infarction* to prevent coronary re-occlusion after thrombolysis, or in high risk patients such as those with pulmonary embolism (see also section 2.10.1). It is also used in the management of *unstable angina* (section 2.6), and the management of *acute peripheral arterial occlusion*.

**Prophylaxis** In patients undergoing *general surgery*, low-dose heparin by subcutaneous injection is widely advocated to *prevent postoperative deep-vein thrombosis and pulmonary embolism* in 'high risk' patients (i.e. those with obesity, malignant disease, history of deep-vein thrombosis or pulmonary embolism, patients over 40 years, or those with an established thrombophilic disorder or who are undergoing large or complicated surgical procedures); laboratory monitoring is not required with this *standard prophylactic regimen*.

To combat the increased risk in *major orthopaedic surgery* an *adjusted dose regimen* may be used (with monitoring) or *low molecular weight heparin* (see p. 121), or in patients at high risk of thromboembolism, warfarin may be selected.

**Extracorporeal circuits** Heparin is also used in the maintenance of extracorporeal circuits in *cardiopulmonary bypass* and *haemodialysis*.

**Haemorrhage** If haemorrhage occurs it is usually sufficient to withdraw heparin, but if rapid reversal of the effects of heparin is required, protamine sulphate (section 2.8.3) is a specific antidote (but only partially reverses the effects of low molecular weight heparins).

## HEPARIN

**Indications** see under Dose

**Cautions** elderly; hypersensitivity to low molecular weight heparins; hepatic impairment (Appendix 2); renal impairment (Appendix 3); pregnancy (Appendix 4); **interactions:** Appendix 1 (heparin)

**Heparin-induced thrombocytopenia** Clinically important heparin-induced thrombocytopenia is immune-mediated, and does not usually develop until after 6 to 10 days; it may be complicated by thrombosis. Platelet counts are recommended for patients receiving heparin (including low molecular weight heparins) for longer than 5 days (heparin should be stopped immediately, and not repeated, in those who develop thrombocytopenia or a 50% reduction of platelet count). Patients requiring continued anticoagulation should preferably be given lepirudin or a heparinoid such as danaparoid

**Hyperkalaemia** Inhibition of aldosterone secretion by heparin (including low molecular weight heparins) may result in hyperkalaemia; patients with diabetes mellitus, chronic renal failure, acidosis, raised plasma potassium or those taking potassium-sparing drugs seem to be more susceptible. The risk appears to increase with duration of therapy and the CSM has recommended that plasma potassium should be measured in patients at risk before starting heparin and monitored regularly thereafter, particularly if heparin is to be continued for more than 7 days

**Contra-indications** haemophilia and other haemorrhagic disorders, thrombocytopenia (including history of heparin-induced thrombocytopenia), peptic ulcer, recent cerebral haemorrhage, severe hypertension, severe liver disease (including oesophageal varices), after major trauma or recent surgery to eye or nervous system, acute bacterial endocarditis; spinal or epidural anaesthesia with treatment doses of heparin; hypersensitivity to heparin

**Side-effects** haemorrhage (see notes above), skin necrosis, thrombocytopenia (see Cautions), hyperkalaemia (see Cautions), hypersensitivity reactions (including urticaria, angioedema, and anaphylaxis); osteoporosis after prolonged use (and rarely alopecia)

**Dose**

- Treatment of deep-vein thrombosis and pulmonary embolism, by intravenous injection, loading dose of 5000 units (75 units/kg) followed by continuous infusion of 18 units/kg/hour *or* treatment of deep-vein thrombosis, by subcutaneous injection of 15 000 units every 12 hours (laboratory monitoring essential—preferably on a daily basis, and dose adjusted accordingly); SMALL ADULT OR CHILD, lower loading dose *then*, 15–25 units/kg/hour by intravenous infusion, *or* 250 units/kg every 12 hours by subcutaneous injection
- Unstable angina, acute peripheral arterial occlusion, as intravenous regimen for treatment of deep-vein thrombosis and pulmonary embolism, above
- Prophylaxis in orthopaedic surgery, see notes above
- Prophylaxis in general surgery (see notes above), by subcutaneous injection, 5000 units 2 hours before surgery, then every 8–12 hours for 7 days or until patient is ambulant (monitoring not needed); during pregnancy (with monitoring), 5000–10 000 units every 12 hours (**important**: not intended to cover prevention of prosthetic heart valve thrombosis in pregnancy which calls for separate specialist management)
- Myocardial Infarction, see notes above
- Prevention of clotting in extracorporeal circuits, consult product literature

Note. Doses above reflect the guidelines of the British Society for Haematology; for doses of the low molecular weight heparins, see p. 121

**Heparin** (Non-proprietary) PoM

Injection, heparin sodium 1000 units/mL, net price 1-mL amp = 19p, 5-mL amp = 85p, 5-mL vial = 47p, 10-mL amp = £1.46, 20-mL amp = £2.40; 5000 units/mL, 1-mL amp = 36p, 5-mL amp = £1.00, 5-mL vial = 92p; 25 000 units/mL, 1-mL amp = £1.01, 5-mL vial = £3.68

**Calciparine®** (Sanofi-Synthelabo) PoM

Injection (subcutaneous only), heparin calcium 25 000 units/mL. Net price 0.2-mL syringe = 60p; 0.5-mL syringe = £1.46

**Monoparin®** (CP) PoM

Injection, heparin sodium (mucous) 1000 units/mL, net price 1-mL amp = 19p; 5-mL amp = 52p; 10-mL amp = 69p; 20-mL amp = £1.24; 5000 units/mL, 1-mL amp = 36p; 5-mL amp = £1.00; 25 000 units/mL, 0.2-mL amp = 46p, 1-mL amp = £1.01

**Monoparin Calcium®** (CP) PoM

Injection, heparin calcium 25 000 units/mL. Net price 0.2-mL amp = 48p

**Multiparin®** (CP) PoM

Injection, heparin sodium (mucous) 1000 units/mL, net price 5-mL vial = 47p; 5000 units/mL, 5-mL vial = 92p; 25 000 units/mL, 5-mL vial = £3.68

## Low molecular weight heparins

**Bemiparin**, **dalteparin**, **enoxaparin**, **reviparin**, and **tinzaparin** are low molecular weight heparins. Low molecular weight heparins are as effective and as safe as unfractionated heparin in the *prevention* of venous thrombo-embolism; in orthopaedic practice they are probably more effective. They have a longer duration of action than unfractionated heparin; *once-daily subcutaneous* dosage means that they are convenient to use. The standard prophylactic regimen does not require monitoring.

Some low molecular weight heparins are also used in the *treatment* of deep-vein thrombosis, pulmonary embolism, unstable coronary artery disease (section 2.6) and for the prevention of clotting in extracorporeal circuits. Routine monitoring of anticoagulant effect of the treatment regimen is not usually required, but may be necessary in patients at increased risk of bleeding (e.g. in renal impairment and those who are underweight or overweight)

**Haemorrhage** See under Heparin.

### BEMIPARIN SODIUM

**Indications** see notes above and under preparations

**Cautions** see under Heparin

**Contra-indications** see under Heparin; breast-feeding (Appendix 5)

**Side-effects** see under Heparin

**Dose**

- See under preparations below

**Zibor®** (Amdipharm) ▼ PoM

Injection, bemiparin sodium 12 500 units/mL, net price 0.2-mL (2500-unit) prefilled syringe = £3.39; 17 500 units/mL, 0.2-mL (3500-unit) prefilled syringe = £4.52

Dose prophylaxis of deep-vein thrombosis, by subcutaneous injection, moderate risk, 2500 units 2 hours before or 6 hours after surgery then 2500 units every 24 hours for 7–10 days; high risk, 3500 units 2 hours before or 6 hours after surgery then 3500 units every 24 hours for 7–10 days

Prevention of clotting in extracorporeal circuits, consult product literature

Injection, bemiparin sodium 25 000 units/mL, net price 0.2-mL (5000-unit) prefilled syringe = £6.96, 0.3-mL (7500-unit) prefilled syringe = £8.63, 0.4-mL (10 000-unit) prefilled syringe = £12.60

Dose treatment of deep-vein thrombosis (with or without pulmonary embolism), by subcutaneous injection, 115 units/kg every 24 hours for 5–9 days (and until adequate oral anticoagulation established)

### DALTEPARIN SODIUM

**Indications** see notes above and under preparations

**Cautions** see under Heparin; not known to be harmful in pregnancy

**Contra-indications** see under Heparin

**Side-effects** see under Heparin

**Dose**

- See under preparations below

**Fragmin®** (Pharmacia) PoM

Injection (single-dose syringe), dalteparin sodium 12 500 units/mL, net price 0.2-mL (2500-unit) syringe = £1.86; 25 000 units/mL, 0.2-mL (5000-unit) syringe = £2.82, 0.3-mL (7500-unit) syringe = £4.23, 0.4-mL (10 000-unit) syringe = £5.65, 0.5-mL (12 500-unit) syringe = £7.06, 0.6-mL (15 000-unit) syringe = £8.47, 0.72-mL (18 000-unit) syringe = £10.16

Dose prophylaxis of deep-vein thrombosis, in surgical patients, by subcutaneous injection, moderate risk, 2500 units 1–2 hours before surgery then 2500 units every 24 hours for 5–7 days or longer; high risk, 2500 units 1–2 hours before surgery, then 2500 units 8–12 hours later (*or* 5000 units on the evening before surgery, then 5000 units on the following evening), then 5000 units every 24 hours for 5–7 days or longer (5 weeks in hip replacement)

Prophylaxis of deep-vein thrombosis in medical patients, by subcutaneous injection, 5000 units every 24 hours

Treatment of deep-vein thrombosis and of pulmonary embolism, by subcutaneous injection, as a single daily dose, ADULT body-weight under 46 kg, 7500 units daily; body-weight 46–56 kg, 10 000 units daily; body-weight 57–68 kg, 12 500 units daily; body-weight 69–82 kg, 15 000 units daily; body-weight 83 kg and over, 18 000 units daily, with oral anticoagulant treatment until prothrombin complex concentration in therapeutic range (usually for at least 5 days); monitoring of anti-Factor Xa not usually required; for patients at increased risk of haemorrhage, see below

Injection, dalteparin sodium 2500 units/mL (for subcutaneous or intravenous use), net price 4-mL (10 000-unit) amp = £5.12; 10 000-units/mL (for subcutaneous or intravenous use), 1-mL (10 000-unit) amp = £5.12; 25 000 units/mL (for subcutaneous use only), 4-mL (100 000-unit) vial = £48.66

Dose treatment of deep-vein thrombosis and of pulmonary embolism, by subcutaneous injection, 200 units/kg (max. 18 000 units) as a single daily dose (*or* 100 units/kg twice daily if increased risk of haemorrhage) with oral anticoagulant treatment until prothrombin complex concentration in therapeutic range (usually for at least 5 days)

Note For monitoring, blood should be taken 3–4 hours after a dose (recommended plasma concentration of anti-Factor Xa 0.5–1 unit/mL); monitoring not required for once-daily treatment regimen and not generally necessary for twice-daily regimen

Unstable coronary artery disease, by subcutaneous injection, 120 units/kg every 12 hours (max. 10 000 units twice daily) for 5–8 days

Prevention of clotting in extracorporeal circuits, consult product literature

Injection (graduated syringe), dalteparin sodium 10 000 units/mL, net price 1-mL (10 000-unit) syringe = £5.65

Dose unstable coronary artery disease (including non-ST-segment-elevation myocardial infarction), by subcutaneous injection, 120 units/kg every 12 hours (max. 10 000 units twice daily) for up to 8 days; beyond 8 days (if awaiting angiography or revascularisation) women body-weight less than 80 kg and men less than 70 kg, 5000 units every 12 hours, women body-weight greater than 80 kg and men greater than 70 kg, 7500 units every 12 hours, until day of procedure (max. 45 days)

### ENOXAPARIN SODIUM

**Indications** see notes above and under preparations

**Cautions** see under Heparin; low body-weight (increased risk of bleeding)

**Contra-indications** see under Heparin; breast-feeding (Appendix 5)
**Side-effects** see under Heparin
**Dose**
- See under preparation below

**Clexane®** (Rhône-Poulenc Rorer) PoM
Injection, enoxaparin sodium 100 mg/mL, net price 0.2-mL (20-mg, 2000-units) syringe = £3.15, 0.4-mL (40-mg, 4000-units) syringe = £4.20, 0.6-mL (60-mg, 6000-units) syringe = £4.75, 0.8-mL (80-mg, 8000-units) syringe = £5.40, 1-mL (100-mg, 10 000-units) syringe = £6.69; 150 mg/mL (*Clexane® Forte*), 0.8-mL (120-mg, 12 000-units) syringe = £9.77, 1-mL (150-mg, 15 000-units) syringe = £11.10
Dose prophylaxis of deep-vein thrombosis especially in surgical patients, by subcutaneous injection, *moderate risk*, 20 mg (2000 units) approx. 2 hours before surgery then 20 mg (2000 units) every 24 hours for 7–10 days; *high risk* (e.g. orthopaedic surgery), 40 mg (4000 units) 12 hours before surgery then 40 mg (4000 units) every 24 hours for 7–10 days

Prophylaxis of deep-vein thrombosis in medical patients, by subcutaneous injection, 40 mg (4000 units) every 24 hours for at least 6 days until patient ambulant (max. 14 days)

Treatment of deep-vein thrombosis or pulmonary embolism, by subcutaneous injection, 1.5 mg/kg (150 units/kg) every 24 hours, usually for at least 5 days (and until adequate oral anticoagulation established)

Unstable angina and non-ST-segment-elevation myocardial infarction, by subcutaneous injection, 1 mg/kg (100 units/kg) every 12 hours usually for 2–8 days (minimum 2 days)

Prevention of clotting in extracorporeal circuits, consult product literature

## REVIPARIN SODIUM

**Indications** see notes above and under preparation
**Cautions** see under Heparin; platelet count recommended before treatment, on days 1 and 4 of treatment then twice weekly for first 3 weeks of treatment
**Contra-indications** see under Heparin; pregnancy (Appendix 4)
**Side-effects** see under Heparin
**Dose**
- See under preparation below

**Clivarine®** (Valeant) PoM
Injection, reviparin sodium 1432 units/0.25-mL syringe, net price 1 syringe = £3.63
Dose prophylaxis of deep-vein thrombosis, by subcutaneous injection, 1432 units 2 hours before surgery, then 1432 units every 24 hours for 7 days (or until patient is mobile)

## TINZAPARIN SODIUM

**Indications** see notes above and under preparations
**Cautions** see under Heparin
**Contra-indications** see under Heparin; breast-feeding (Appendix 5)
**Side-effects** see under Heparin
**Dose**
- See under preparations below

**Innohep®** (LEO) PoM
Injection, tinzaparin sodium 10 000 units/mL, net price 2500-unit (0.25-mL) syringe = £2.13, 3500-unit (0.35-mL) syringe = £2.98, 4500-unit (0.45-mL) syringe = £3.83, 20 000-unit (2-mL) vial = £11.36
Dose prophylaxis of deep-vein thrombosis, by subcutaneous injection, general surgery, 3500 units 2 hours before surgery, then 3500 units every 24 hours for 7–10 days; orthopaedic surgery (high risk), 50 units/kg 2 hours before surgery, then 50 units/kg every 24 hours for 7–10 days *or* 4500 units 12 hours before surgery, then 4500 units every 24 hours for 7–10 days

Prevention of clotting in extracorporeal circuits, consult product literature

Injection, tinzaparin sodium 20 000 units/mL, net price 0.5-mL (10 000-unit) syringe = £9.65, 0.7-mL (14 000-unit) syringe = £13.51, 0.9-mL (18 000-unit) syringe = £17.37, 2-mL (40 000-unit) vial = £36.77
Dose treatment of deep-vein thrombosis and of pulmonary embolism, by subcutaneous injection, 175 units/kg once daily for at least 6 days (and until adequate oral anticoagulation established)
Note This treatment regimen does not require anticoagulation monitoring
Asthma Presence of sulphites in formulation may (especially in patients with asthma) lead to hypersensitivity (with bronchospasm and shock)

## Heparinoids

**Danaparoid** is a heparinoid used for prophylaxis of deep-vein thrombosis in patients undergoing general or orthopaedic surgery. Providing there is no evidence of cross-reactivity, it also has a role in patients who develop thrombocytopenia in association with heparin.

## DANAPAROID SODIUM

**Indications** prevention of deep-vein thrombosis in general or orthopaedic surgery; thromboembolic disease in patients with history of heparin-induced thrombocytopenia
**Cautions** recent bleeding or risk of bleeding; antibodies to heparins (risk of antibody-induced thrombocytopenia); body-weight over 90 kg (monitor anti factor Xa activity); hepatic impairment (Appendix 2); renal impairment (Appendix 3); pregnancy (Appendix 4); breast-feeding (Appendix 5)
**Contra-indications** haemophilia and other haemorrhagic disorders, thrombocytopenia (unless patient has heparin-induced thrombocytopenia), recent cerebral haemorrhage, severe hypertension, active peptic ulcer (unless this is the reason for operation), diabetic retinopathy, acute bacterial endocarditis, spinal or epidural anaesthesia with treatment doses of danaparoid
**Side-effects** haemorrhage; hypersensitivity reactions (including rash)
**Dose**
- Prevention of deep-vein thrombosis, by subcutaneous injection, 750 units twice daily for 7–10 days; initiate treatment before operation (with last pre-operative dose 1–4 hours before surgery)
- Thromboembolic disease in patients with history of heparin-induced thrombocytopenia, by intravenous injection, 2500 units (1250 units if body-weight under 55 kg, 3750 units if over 90 kg), followed by intravenous infusion of 400 units/hour for 2 hours, *then* 300 units/hour for 2 hours, *then* 200 units/hour for 5 days

**Orgaran®** (Organon) PoM
Injection, danaparoid sodium 1250 units/mL, net price 0.6-mL amp (750 units) = £29.80

## Hirudins

**Lepirudin**, a recombinant hirudin, is licensed for anticoagulation in patients with Type II (immune) heparin-induced thrombocytopenia who require parenteral antithrombotic treatment. The dose of lepirudin is adjusted according to activated partial thromboplastin time (APTT). **Bivalirudin**, a hirudin analogue, is a thrombin inhibitor which is licensed as an anticoagulant for patients undergoing percutaneous coronary intervention. The *Scottish Medicines Consortium* has advised (March 2005) that bivalirudin is accepted for restricted use for patients undergoing percutaneous coronary intervention who would have been considered for treatment with unfractionated heparin combined with a glycoprotein IIb/IIIa inhibitor; it should not be used alone.

## BIVALIRUDIN

**Indications** anticoagulation for patients undergoing percutaneous coronary intervention

**Cautions** exposure to lepirudin (theoretical risk from lepirudin antibodies); brachytherapy procedures; renal impairment (Appendix 3); pregnancy (Appendix 4); breast-feeding (Appendix 5)

**Contra-indications** severe hypertension; subacute bacterial endocarditis; active bleeding; bleeding disorders

**Side-effects** bleeding (discontinue); *less commonly* nausea, vomiting, tachycardia, bradycardia, hypotension, angina, dyspnoea, allergic reactions (including isolated reports of anaphylaxis), headache, thrombocytopenia, anaemia, back and chest pain, and injection-site reactions; *very rarely* thrombosis

**Dose**

- Initially by intravenous injection, 750 micrograms/kg, then by intravenous infusion of 1.75 mg/kg/hour, for up to 4 hours after procedure complete

**Angiox®** (Nycomed) ▼ PoM
Injection, powder for reconstitution, bivalirudin, net price 250-mg vial = £310.00

## LEPIRUDIN

**Indications** thromboembolic disease requiring parenteral anticoagulation in patients with heparin-induced thrombocytopenia type II

**Cautions** hepatic impairment (Appendix 2); renal impairment (Appendix 3); recent bleeding or risk of bleeding including recent puncture of large vessels, organ biopsy, recent major surgery, stroke, bleeding disorders, severe hypertension, bacterial endocarditis; determine activated partial thromboplastin time 4 hours after start of treatment (or after infusion rate altered) and at least once daily thereafter

**Contra-indications** pregnancy and breast-feeding

**Side-effects** bleeding; reduced haemoglobin concentration without obvious source of bleeding; fever, hypersensitivity reactions (including rash); injection-site reactions

**Dose**

- Initially by slow intravenous injection (of 5 mg/mL solution), 400 micrograms/kg followed by continuous intravenous infusion of 150 micrograms/kg/hour (max. 16.5 mg/hour), adjusted according to activated partial thromboplastin time, for 2–10 days (longer if necessary)

**Refludan®** (Pharmion) PoM
Injection, powder for reconstitution, lepirudin. Net price 50-mg vial = £57.00

## Heparin flushes

For maintaining patency of peripheral venous catheters, sodium chloride injection 0.9% is as effective as heparin flushes.

**Heparin Sodium** (Non-proprietary) PoM
Solution, heparin sodium 10 units/mL, net price 5-mL amp = 25p; 100 units/mL, 2-mL amp = 28p
To maintain patency of catheters, cannulas, etc. 10–200 units flushed through every 4–8 hours. Not for therapeutic use

**Canusal®** (CP) PoM
Solution, heparin sodium 100 units/mL. Net price 2-mL amp = 28p
To maintain patency of catheters, cannulas, etc., 200 units flushed through every 4 hours or as required. Not for therapeutic use

**Hepsal®** (CP) PoM
Solution, heparin sodium 10 units/mL. Net price 5-mL amp = 25p
To maintain patency of catheters, cannulas, etc., 50 units flushed through every 4 hours or as required. Not for therapeutic use

## Epoprostenol

**Epoprostenol** (prostacyclin) can be given to inhibit platelet aggregation during renal dialysis either alone or with heparin. It is also licensed for the treatment of primary pulmonary hypertension resistant to other treatment, usually with oral anticoagulation. Since its half-life is only about 3 minutes it must be given by continuous intravenous infusion. It is a potent vasodilator and therefore its side-effects include flushing, headache, and hypotension.

## EPOPROSTENOL

**Indications** see notes above

**Cautions** anticoagulant monitoring required when given with heparin; haemorrhagic diathesis; dose titration for pulmonary hypertension should be in hospital (risk of pulmonary oedema); pregnancy (Appendix 4)

**Contra-indications** severe left ventricular dysfunction

**Side-effects** see notes above; also bradycardia, tachycardia, pallor, sweating with higher doses; gastro-intestinal disturbances; lassitude, anxiety, agitation; dry mouth, jaw pain, chest pain; also reported, hyperglycaemia and injection-site reactions

**Dose**

- See product literature

**Flolan®** (GSK) PoM
Infusion, powder for reconstitution, epoprostenol (as sodium salt). Net price 500-microgram vial (with diluent) = £64.57; 1.5-mg vial (with diluent) = £130.07

## Fondaparinux

**Fondaparinux sodium** is a synthetic pentasaccharide that inhibits activated factor X. It is licensed for prophylaxis of venous thromboembolism in medical patients and in patients undergoing major orthopaedic surgery of the legs or abdominal surgery. It is also licensed for treatment of deep-vein thrombosis and of pulmonary embolism.

## FONDAPARINUX SODIUM

**Indications** see notes above and under preparations

**Cautions** bleeding disorders, active gastro-intestinal ulcer disease; recent intracranial haemorrhage; brain, spinal, or ophthalmic surgery; spinal or epidural anaesthesia (risk of spinal haematoma—avoid if using treatment doses); low body-weight; elderly patients; concomitant use of drugs that increase risk of bleeding; hepatic impairment (Appendix 2); renal impairment (Appendix 3); pregnancy (Appendix 4); breast-feeding (Appendix 5)

**Contra-indications** active bleeding; bacterial endocarditis

**Side-effects** haemorrhage, purpura, anaemia; *less commonly* gastro-intestinal disturbances, oedema, liver enzyme changes, chest pain, dyspnoea, headache, thrombocytopenia, thrombocythaemia, rash, pruritus; *rarely* hypotension, cough, vertigo, dizziness, hypokalaemia, hyperbilirubinaemia, injection-site reactions

**Dose**

- See under preparation below

**Arixtra®** (GSK) ▼ PoM

Injection, fondaparinux sodium 5 mg/mL, net price 0.5-mL (2.5-mg) prefilled syringe = £6.66

Dose prophylaxis of venous thromboembolism in surgery, by subcutaneous injection, 2.5 mg 6 hours after surgery then 2.5 mg daily for 5–9 days (longer after hip surgery); CHILD under 17 years not recommended

Prophylaxis of venous thromboembolism in medical patients, by subcutaneous injection, 2.5 mg daily usually for 6–14 days; CHILD under 17 years not recommended

Injection, fondaparinux sodium 12.5 mg/mL, net price 0.4-mL (5-mg) prefilled syringe = £12.37, 0.6-mL (7.5-mg) prefilled syringe = £12.37, 0.8-mL (10-mg) prefilled syringe = £12.37

Dose treatment of deep-vein thrombosis and of pulmonary embolism, by subcutaneous injection, ADULT body-weight under 50 kg, 5 mg every 24 hours; body-weight 50–100 kg, 7.5 mg every 24 hours; body-weight over 100 kg, 10 mg every 24 hours; usually for at least 5 days (and until adequate oral anticoagulation established); CHILD under 17 years not recommended

## 2.8.2 Oral anticoagulants

Oral anticoagulants antagonise the effects of vitamin K, and take at least 48 to 72 hours for the anticoagulant effect to develop fully; if an immediate effect is required, heparin must be given concomitantly.

**Uses** The main indication for an oral anticoagulant is *deep-vein thrombosis*. Patients with *pulmonary embolism* should also be treated, as should those with *atrial fibrillation who are at risk of embolisation* (see also section 2.3.1), and those with *mechanical prosthetic heart valves* (to prevent emboli developing on the valves); an antiplatelet drug may also be useful in these patients.

**Warfarin** is the drug of choice; **acenocoumarol** (nicoumalone) and **phenindione** are seldom required.

Oral anticoagulants should not be used in cerebral artery thrombosis or peripheral artery occlusion as first-line therapy; aspirin (section 2.9) is more appropriate for reduction of risk in transient ischaemic attacks.

**Dose** Whenever possible, the base-line prothrombin time should be determined but the initial dose should not be delayed whilst awaiting the result.

The usual adult induction dose of warfarin is 10 mg[1] daily for 2 days (higher doses no longer recommended). The subsequent maintenance dose depends upon the prothrombin time, reported as INR (international normalised ratio). The daily maintenance dose of warfarin is usually 3 to 9 mg (taken at the **same time** each day). The indications and target INRs[2] currently recommended by the British Society for Haematology[3] are:

- INR 2.5 for treatment of deep-vein thrombosis and pulmonary embolism (or for recurrence in patients no longer receiving warfarin), atrial fibrillation, cardioversion, dilated cardiomyopathy, mural thrombus following myocardial infarction, and rheumatic mitral valve disease;
- INR 3.5 for recurrent deep-vein thrombosis and pulmonary embolism (in patients currently receiving warfarin with INR above 2) and mechanical prosthetic heart valves.

**Monitoring** It is essential that the INR be determined daily or on alternate days in early days of treatment, *then* at longer intervals (depending on response[4]) *then* up to every 12 weeks.

**Haemorrhage** The main adverse effect of all oral anticoagulants is haemorrhage. Checking the INR and omitting doses when appropriate is essential; if the anticoagulant is stopped but not reversed, the INR should be measured 2–3 days later to ensure that it is falling. The following recommendations (which take into account the recommendations of the British Society for Haematology[3]) are based on the result of the INR and whether there is major or minor bleeding; the recommendations apply to patients taking warfarin:

- Major bleeding—stop warfarin; give phytomenadione (vitamin $K_1$) 5–10 mg by slow intravenous injection; give prothrombin complex concentrate (factors II, VII, IX and X) 30–50 units/kg *or* (if no concentrate available) fresh frozen plasma 15 mL/kg
- INR > 8.0, no bleeding or minor bleeding—stop warfarin, restart when INR < 5.0; if there are other risk factors for bleeding give phytomenadione (vitamin $K_1$) 500 micrograms by slow intravenous injection or 5 mg by mouth (for partial reversal of anticoagulation give smaller oral doses of phytomenadione e.g. 0.5–2.5 mg using the intravenous preparation orally); repeat dose of phytomenadione if INR still too high after 24 hours

1. First dose less than 10 mg if base-line prothrombin time prolonged, if liver-function tests abnormal, or if patient in cardiac failure, on parenteral feeding, less than average body weight, elderly, or receiving other drugs known to potentiate oral anticoagulants.
2. An INR which is within 0.5 units of the target value is generally satisfactory; larger deviations require dosage adjustment. Target values (rather than ranges) are now recommended.
3. Guidelines on Oral Anticoagulation: third edition. *Br J Haematol* 1998; **101**: 374–87
4. Change in patient's clinical condition, particularly associated with liver disease, intercurrent illness, or drug administration, necessitates more frequent testing. See also **interactions**, Appendix 1 (warfarin). Major changes in diet (especially involving salads and vegetables) and in alcohol consumption may also affect warfarin control.

- INR 6.0–8.0, no bleeding or minor bleeding—stop warfarin, restart when INR < 5.0
- INR < 6.0 but more than 0.5 units above target value—reduce dose or stop warfarin, restart when INR < 5.0
- Unexpected bleeding at therapeutic levels—always investigate possibility of underlying cause e.g. unsuspected renal or gastro-intestinal tract pathology

**Pregnancy** Oral anticoagulants are teratogenic and should not be given in the first trimester of pregnancy. Women at risk of pregnancy should be warned of this danger since stopping warfarin before the sixth week of gestation may largely avoid the risk of fetal abnormality. Oral anticoagulants cross the placenta with risk of placental or fetal haemorrhage, especially during the last few weeks of pregnancy and at delivery. Therefore, if at all possible, oral anticoagulants should be avoided in pregnancy, especially in the first and third trimesters. Difficult decisions may have to be made, particularly in women with prosthetic heart valves, atrial fibrillation, or with a history of recurrent venous thrombosis or pulmonary embolism.

**Treatment booklets** Anticoagulant treatment booklets should be issued to patients, and are available for distribution to local healthcare professionals from Health Authorities and also from:

England and Wales:
Astron
The Causeway
Oldham Broadway
Business Park
Chadderton
Oldham OL9 9XD
(0161) 683 2376

Scotland:
Banner Business Supplies
20 South Gyle Crescent
Edinburgh EH12 9EB
(0131) 479 3279

Northern Ireland:
Central Services Agency
25 Adelaide St
Belfast BT2 8FH
(028) 9053 5652

These booklets include advice for patients on anticoagulant treatment.

### WARFARIN SODIUM

**Indications** prophylaxis of embolisation in rheumatic heart disease and atrial fibrillation; prophylaxis after insertion of prosthetic heart valve; prophylaxis and treatment of venous thrombosis and pulmonary embolism; transient ischaemic attacks

**Cautions** recent surgery; hepatic impairment (Appendix 2); renal impairment (Appendix 3); breast-feeding (Appendix 5); avoid cranberry juice; **interactions:** Appendix 1 (coumarins)

**Contra-indications** peptic ulcer, severe hypertension, bacterial endocarditis; pregnancy (see notes above and Appendix 4)

**Side-effects** haemorrhage—see notes above; other side-effects reported include hypersensitivity, rash, alopecia, diarrhoea, unexplained drop in haematocrit, 'purple toes', skin necrosis, jaundice, hepatic dysfunction; also nausea, vomiting, and pancreatitis

**Dose**

- See notes above

**Warfarin** (Non-proprietary) PoM

Tablets, warfarin sodium 0.5 mg (white), net price 28-tab pack = £1.00; 1 mg (brown), 28 = 90p; 3 mg (blue), 28 = £1.34; 5 mg (pink), 28 = £1.53. Label: 10, anticoagulant card

Brands include *Marevan®*

### ACENOCOUMAROL

**(Nicoumalone)**

**Indications** see under Warfarin Sodium

**Cautions** see under Warfarin Sodium

**Contra-indications** see under Warfarin Sodium

**Side-effects** see under Warfarin Sodium

**Dose**

- 4–12 mg on first day; 4–8 mg on second day; maintenance dose usually 1–8 mg daily

**Sinthrome®** (Alliance) PoM

Tablets, acenocoumarol 1 mg. Net price 20 = 92p. Label: 10, anticoagulant card

### PHENINDIONE

**Indications** prophylaxis of embolisation in rheumatic heart disease and atrial fibrillation; prophylaxis after insertion of prosthetic heart valve; prophylaxis and treatment of venous thrombosis and pulmonary embolism

**Cautions** see under Warfarin Sodium; **interactions:** Appendix 1 (phenindione)

**Contra-indications** see under Warfarin Sodium; breast-feeding (Appendix 5)

**Side-effects** see under Warfarin Sodium; also hypersensitivity reactions including rashes, exfoliative dermatitis, exanthema, fever, leucopenia, agranulocytosis, eosinophilia, diarrhoea, renal and hepatic damage; urine coloured pink or orange

**Dose**

- 200 mg on day 1; 100 mg on day 2; maintenance dose usually 50–150 mg daily

**Phenindione** (Non-proprietary) PoM

Tablets, phenindione 10 mg, net price 100 = £6.80; 25 mg, 100 = £9.50; 50 mg, 100 = £12.10. Label: 10, anticoagulant card, 14, (urine pink or orange)

## 2.8.3 Protamine sulphate

Although protamine sulphate is used to counteract overdosage with heparin, if used in excess it has an anticoagulant effect.

### PROTAMINE SULPHATE

**(Protamine Sulfate)**

**Indications** see above

**Cautions** see above; also if increased risk of allergic reaction to protamine (includes previous treatment with protamine or protamine insulin, allergy to fish, men who are infertile or who have had a vasectomy)

**Side-effects** nausea, vomiting, lassitude, flushing, hypotension, bradycardia, dyspnoea; hypersensitivity reactions (including angioedema, anaphylaxis) reported

**Dose**

- By intravenous injection over approx. 10 minutes, 1 mg neutralises 80–100 units heparin when given within 15 minutes of heparin; if longer time, less protamine required as heparin rapidly excreted; max. 50 mg

**Protamine Sulphate** (Non-proprietary) PoM
Injection, protamine sulphate 10 mg /mL, net price 5-mL amp = £1.14, 10-mL amp = £3.96

**Prosulf®** (CP) PoM
Injection, protamine sulphate 10 mg/mL. Net price 5-mL amp = 96p (glass), £1.20 (polypropylene)

# 2.9 Antiplatelet drugs

Antiplatelet drugs decrease platelet aggregation and may inhibit thrombus formation in the arterial circulation, where anticoagulants have little effect.

A low dose of **aspirin** is used for the *secondary prevention* of thrombotic cerebrovascular or cardiovascular disease. A single dose of aspirin 150–300 mg is given as soon as possible after an ischaemic event, preferably dispersed in water or chewed. The initial dose is followed by maintenance treatment with aspirin 75 mg daily. If aspirin causes dyspepsia or if the patient is at high risk of gastro-intestinal bleeding, a proton pump inhibitor (section 1.3.5) can be added.

A low dose of aspirin is also of benefit in the *primary prevention* of vascular events when the estimated 10-year cardiovascular disease risk is 20% or greater and provided that blood pressure is controlled (section 2.5)[1].

A low dose of aspirin (75 mg daily) is also given following coronary bypass surgery. For details on the use of aspirin in atrial fibrillation see section 2.3.1, for stable angina see section 2.6 and for intermittent claudication see section 2.6.4.

**Clopidogrel** is licensed for the prevention of ischaemic events in patients with a history of symptomatic ischaemic disease. Clopidogrel, in combination with low-dose aspirin, is also licensed for acute coronary syndrome without ST-segment elevation; in these circumstances the combination is given for at least 1 month but usually no longer than 9–12 months. Use of clopidogrel with aspirin increases the risk of bleeding and there is no evidence of benefit beyond 12 months of the last event of acute coronary syndrome without ST-segment elevation.

The *Scottish Medicines Consortium* has advised (February 2004) that clopidogrel be accepted for restricted use for the treatment of confirmed acute coronary syndrome (without ST-segment elevation), in combination with aspirin. Clopidogrel should be initiated in hospital inpatients **only**.

**Dipyridamole** is used by mouth as an adjunct to oral anticoagulation for prophylaxis of thromboembolism associated with prosthetic heart valves. Modified-release preparations are licensed for secondary prevention of ischaemic stroke and transient ischaemic attacks.

1. Cardiovascular disease risk may be determined from the chart issued by the British Hypertension Society (*J Hum Hypertens* 2004; **18**: 139–85)—see inside back cover. The Joint British Societies' 'Cardiac Risk Assessor' computer programme may also be used to determine cardiovascular disease risk by adding together the coronary heart disease risk and stroke risk.

Dipyridamole is also used in combination with low-dose aspirin; this combination may reduce the risk of recurrent stroke but evidence of long-term benefit on cardiovascular mortality has not been established.

**Glycoprotein IIb/IIIa inhibitors** Glycoprotein IIb/IIIa inhibitors prevent platelet aggregation by blocking the binding of fibrinogen to receptors on platelets. **Abciximab** is a monoclonal antibody which binds to glycoprotein IIb/IIIa receptors and to other related sites; it is licensed as an adjunct to heparin and aspirin for the prevention of ischaemic complications in high-risk patients undergoing percutaneous transluminal coronary intervention. Abciximab should be used once only (to avoid additional risk of thrombocytopenia). **Eptifibatide** and **tirofiban** also inhibit glycoprotein IIb/IIIa receptors; they are licensed for use with heparin and aspirin to prevent early myocardial infarction in patients with unstable angina (section 2.6) or non-ST-segment-elevation myocardial infarction. Abciximab, eptifibatide and tirofiban should be used by specialists only.

For use of epoprostenol, see section 2.8.1.

**NICE guidance (glycoprotein IIb/IIIa inhibitors for acute coronary syndromes)**

NICE has recommended (September 2002) that a glycoprotein IIb/IIIa inhibitor (abciximab, eptifibatide, and tirofiban) should be considered in the management of unstable angina or non-ST-segment-elevation myocardial infarction.

A glycoprotein IIb/IIIa inhibitor is recommended for patients at high risk of myocardial infarction or death when early percutaneous coronary intervention is desirable but does not occur immediately; either eptifibatide or tirofiban is recommended in addition to other appropriate drug treatment.

A glycoprotein IIb/IIIa inhibitor is recommended as an adjunct to percutaneous coronary intervention:

- when early percutaneous coronary intervention is indicated but it is delayed;
- in patients with diabetes;
- if the procedure is complex.

**Note** Only abciximab is licensed as an adjunct to percutaneous coronary intervention

## ABCIXIMAB

**Indications** prevention of ischaemic cardiac complications in patients undergoing percutaneous coronary intervention; short-term prevention of myocardial infarction in patients with unstable angina not responding to conventional treatment and who are scheduled for percutaneous coronary intervention (use under specialist supervision)

**Cautions** measure baseline prothrombin time, activated clotting time, activated partial thromboplastin time, platelet count, haemoglobin and haematocrit; monitor haemoglobin and haematocrit 12 hours and 24 hours after start of treatment and platelet count 2–4 hours and 24 hours after start of treatment; concomitant use of drugs that increase risk of bleeding; discontinue if uncontrollable serious bleeding occurs or emergency cardiac surgery needed; consult product literature for details of procedures to minimise bleeding; elderly; hepatic impairment (Appendix 2); renal impairment (Appendix 3); pregnancy (Appendix 4)

**Contra-indications** active internal bleeding; major surgery, intracranial or intraspinal surgery or trauma

2 Cardiovascular system

within last 2 months; stroke within last 2 years; intracranial neoplasm, arteriovenous malformation or aneurysm, severe hypertension, haemorrhagic diathesis, thrombocytopenia, vasculitis, hypertensive retinopathy; breast-feeding (Appendix 5)

**Side-effects** bleeding manifestations; nausea, vomiting, hypotension, bradycardia, chest pain, back pain, headache, fever, puncture site pain, thrombocytopenia; *rarely* cardiac tamponade, adult respiratory distress, hypersensitivity reactions

**Dose**

- ADULT initially by intravenous injection over 1 minute, 250 micrograms/kg, then by intravenous infusion, 125 nanograms/kg/minute (max. 10 micrograms/minute); for prevention of ischaemic complications start 10–60 minutes before percutaneous coronary intervention and continue infusion for 12 hours; for unstable angina start up to 24 hours before possible percutaneous coronary intervention and continue infusion for 12 hours after intervention

**ReoPro®** (Lilly) PoM
Injection, abciximab 2 mg/mL, net price 5-mL vial = £260.40

## ASPIRIN (antiplatelet)
### (Acetylsalicylic Acid)

**Indications** prophylaxis of cerebrovascular disease or myocardial infarction (see section 2.10.1 and notes above)

**Cautions** asthma; uncontrolled hypertension; previous peptic ulceration (but manufacturer's package insert may advise avoidance of low-dose aspirin in history of peptic ulceration); hepatic impairment (Appendix 2); renal impairment (Appendix 3); pregnancy (Appendix 4); **interactions**: Appendix 1 (aspirin)

**Contra-indications** children under 16 years and in breast-feeding (Reye's syndrome, section 4.7.1; Appendix 5); active peptic ulceration; haemophilia and other bleeding disorders

**Side-effects** bronchospasm; gastro-intestinal haemorrhage (occasionally major), also other haemorrhage (e.g. subconjunctival)

**Dose**

- See notes above

[1]**Aspirin** (Non-proprietary) PoM
Dispersible tablets, aspirin 75 mg, net price 20 = 22p; 300 mg, see section 4.7.1. Label: 13, 21, 32

Tablets, e/c, aspirin 75 mg, net price 56-tab pack = £1.39; 300 mg, see section 4.7.1. Label: 5, 25, 32
Brands include *Gencardia®*, *Micropirin®*

**Angettes 75®** (Bristol-Myers Squibb)
Tablets, aspirin 75 mg. Net price 28-tab pack = 94p. Label: 32

**Caprin®** (Sinclair) PoM
Tablets, e/c, pink, aspirin 75 mg, net price 28-tab pack = £1.55, 56-tab pack = £3.08, 100-tab pack = £5.24; 300 mg, see section 4.7.1. Label: 5, 25, 32

**Nu-Seals® Aspirin** (Alliance) PoM
Tablets, e/c, aspirin 75 mg, net price 56-tab pack = £2.60; 300 mg, see section 4.7.1. Label: 5, 25, 32
**Note** Tablets may be chewed at diagnosis for rapid absorption

**With isosorbide mononitrate**
Section 2.6.1

## CLOPIDOGREL

**Indications** see notes above for *Scottish Medicines Consortium* advice; prevention of atherosclerotic events in peripheral arterial disease, or within 35 days of myocardial infarction, or within 6 months of ischaemic stroke, or (given with aspirin—see notes above) in acute coronary syndrome without ST-segment-elevation

**Cautions** patients at risk of increased bleeding from trauma, surgery or other pathological conditions; concomitant use of drugs that increase risk of bleeding; discontinue 7 days before elective surgery if antiplatelet effect not desirable; liver impairment (Appendix 2); renal impairment (Appendix 3); pregnancy (Appendix 4); **interactions**: Appendix 1 (clopidogrel)

**Contra-indications** active bleeding, breast-feeding (Appendix 5)

**Side-effects** dyspepsia, abdominal pain, diarrhoea; bleeding disorders (including gastro-intestinal and intracranial); *less commonly* nausea, vomiting, gastritis, flatulence, constipation, gastric and duodenal ulcers, headache, dizziness, paraesthesia, leucopenia, decreased platelets (very rarely severe thrombocytopenia), eosinophilia, rash, and pruritus; *rarely* vertigo; *very rarely* colitis, pancreatitis, hepatitis, vasculitis, confusion, hallucinations, taste disturbance, blood disorders (including thrombocytopenic purpura, agranulocytosis and pancytopenia), and hypersensitivity-like reactions (including fever, glomerulonephritis, arthralgia, Stevens-Johnson syndrome, lichen planus)

**Dose**

- 75 mg once daily
- Acute coronary syndrome, initially 300 mg then 75 mg daily (with aspirin, but see notes above)

**Plavix®** (Bristol-Myers Squibb, Sanofi-Synthelabo) PoM
Tablets, pink, f/c, clopidogrel (as hydrogen sulphate) 75 mg, net price 28-tab pack = £35.31

## DIPYRIDAMOLE

**Indications** see notes above and under Dose

**Cautions** rapidly worsening angina, aortic stenosis, recent myocardial infarction, heart failure; may exacerbate migraine; hypotension; myasthenia gravis (risk of exacerbation); breast-feeding (Appendix 5); **interactions**: Appendix 1 (dipyridamole)

**Side-effects** gastro-intestinal effects, dizziness, myalgia, throbbing headache, hypotension, hot flushes and tachycardia; worsening symptoms of coronary heart disease; hypersensitivity reactions such as rash, urticaria, severe bronchospasm and angioedema; increased bleeding during or after surgery; thrombocytopenia reported

**Dose**

- By mouth, 300–600 mg daily in 3–4 divided doses before food

  Modified-release preparations, see under preparation below
- By intravenous injection, diagnostic only, consult product literature

**Dipyridamole** (Non-proprietary) PoM
Tablets, coated, dipyridamole 25 mg, net price 20 = 37p; 100 mg, 20 = £1.06; 84 = £4.48. Label: 22
Oral suspension, dipyridamole 50 mg/5 mL, net price 150 mL = £34.00

**Persantin®** (Boehringer Ingelheim) PoM
Tablets, both s/c, dipyridamole 25 mg (orange), net price 84-tab pack = £1.57; 100 mg, 84-tab pack = £4.38. Label: 22
Injection, dipyridamole 5 mg/mL. Net price 2-mL amp = 11p

### Modified release

**Persantin® Retard** (Boehringer Ingelheim) PoM
Capsules, m/r, red/orange containing yellow pellets, dipyridamole 200 mg. Net price 60-cap pack = £8.38. Label: 21, 25
Dose secondary prevention of ischaemic stroke and transient ischaemic attacks (used alone or with aspirin), adjunct to oral anticoagulation for prophylaxis of thromboembolism associated with prosthetic heart valves, 200 mg twice daily preferably with food
Note Dispense in original container (pack contains a desiccant) and discard any capsules remaining 6 weeks after opening

### With aspirin

For cautions, contra-indications and side-effects of aspirin, see under Aspirin, above

**Asasantin® Retard** (Boehringer Ingelheim) PoM
Capsules, red/ivory, aspirin 25 mg, dipyridamole 200 mg (m/r), net price 60-cap pack = £7.80. Label: 21, 25
Dose secondary prevention of ischaemic stroke and transient ischaemic attacks, 1 capsule twice daily
*Note:* Dispense in original container (pack contains a desiccant) and discard any capsules remaining 6 weeks after opening

## EPTIFIBATIDE

**Indications** prevention of early myocardial infarction in patients with unstable angina or non-ST-segment-elevation myocardial infarction and with last episode of chest pain within 24 hours (use under specialist supervision)

**Cautions** risk of bleeding, concomitant drugs that increase risk of bleeding—discontinue immediately if uncontrolled serious bleeding; measure baseline prothrombin time, activated partial thromboplastin time, platelet count, haemoglobin, haematocrit and serum creatinine; monitor haemoglobin, haematocrit and platelets within 6 hours after start of treatment then at least once daily; discontinue if thrombolytic therapy, intra-aortic balloon pump or emergency cardiac surgery necessary; hepatic impairment (Appendix 2); renal impairment (Appendix 3); pregnancy (Appendix 4); breast-feeding (Appendix 5)

**Contra-indications** abnormal bleeding within 30 days, major surgery or severe trauma within 6 weeks, stroke within last 30 days or any history of haemorrhagic stroke, intracranial disease (aneurysm, neoplasm or arteriovenous malformation), severe hypertension, haemorrhagic diathesis, increased prothrombin time or INR, thrombocytopenia, significant hepatic impairment; breast-feeding

**Side-effects** bleeding manifestations; *very rarely* anaphylaxis and rash

**Dose**
- Initially by intravenous injection, 180 micrograms/kg, then by intravenous infusion, 2 micrograms/kg/minute for up to 72 hours (up to 96 hours if percutaneous coronary intervention during treatment)

**Integrilin®** (GSK) PoM
Injection, eptifibatide 2 mg/mL, net price 10-mL (20-mg) vial = £14.45
Infusion, eptifibatide 750 micrograms/mL, net price 100-mL (75-mg) vial = £45.42

## TIROFIBAN

**Indications** prevention of early myocardial infarction in patients with unstable angina or non-ST-segment-elevation myocardial infarction and with last episode of chest pain within 12 hours (use under specialist supervision)

**Cautions** hepatic impairment (avoid if severe; Appendix 2); renal impairment (Appendix 3); major surgery or severe trauma within 3 months (avoid if within 6 weeks); traumatic or protracted cardiopulmonary resuscitation, organ biopsy or lithotripsy within last 2 weeks; risk of bleeding including active peptic ulcer within 3 months; acute pericarditis, aortic dissection, haemorrhagic retinopathy, vasculitis, haematuria, faecal occult blood; severe heart failure, cardiogenic shock, anaemia; puncture of non-compressible vessel within 24 hours; concomitant drugs that increase risk of bleeding (including within 48 hours after thrombolytic); monitor platelet count, haemoglobin and haematocrit before treatment, 2–6 hours after start of treatment and then at least once daily; discontinue if thrombolytic therapy, intra-aortic balloon pump or emergency cardiac surgery necessary; discontinue immediately if serious bleeding uncontrolled by pressure occurs; pregnancy (Appendix 4)

**Contra-indications** abnormal bleeding within 30 days, stroke within 30 days or any history of haemorrhagic stroke, intracranial disease (aneurysm, neoplasm or arteriovenous malformation), severe hypertension, haemorrhagic diathesis, increased prothrombin time or INR, thrombocytopenia; breast-feeding (Appendix 5)

**Side-effects** bleeding manifestations; reversible thrombocytopenia

**Dose**
- By intravenous infusion, initially 400 nanograms/kg/minute for 30 minutes, then 100 nanograms/kg/minute for at least 48 hours (continue during and for 12–24 hours after percutaneous coronary intervention); max. duration of treatment 108 hours

**Aggrastat®** (MSD) PoM
Concentrate for intravenous infusion, tirofiban (as hydrochloride) 250 micrograms/mL. For dilution before use, net price 50-mL (12.5-mg) vial = £146.11
Intravenous infusion, tirofiban (as hydrochloride) 50 micrograms/mL, net price 250-mL *Intravia®* bag = £160.72

# 2.10 Myocardial infarction and fibrinolysis

2.10.1 Management of myocardial infarction
2.10.2 Fibrinolytic drugs

## 2.10.1 Management of myocardial infarction

Local guidelines for the management of myocardial infarction should be followed where they exist

These notes give an overview of the initial and long-term management of myocardial infarction. The aims of management are to provide supportive care and pain relief, to promote revascularisation and to reduce mortality. Oxygen, diamorphine and nitrates provide initial support and pain relief; aspirin and percutaneous coronary intervention or thrombolytics promote revascularisation; long-term use of aspirin, beta-blockers, ACE inhibitors and statins help to reduce mortality further.

**Initial management** **Oxygen** (section 3.6) is administered unless the patient has severe chronic obstructive pulmonary disease.

The pain (and anxiety) of myocardial infarction is managed with slow intravenous injection of **diamorphine** (section 4.7.2); an antiemetic such as metoclopramide (or, if left ventricular function is not compromised, cyclizine) by intravenous injection should also be given (section 4.6).

**Aspirin** (chewed or dispersed in water) is given for its antiplatelet effect (section 2.9); a dose of 150–300 mg is suitable. If aspirin is given before arrival at hospital, a note saying that it has been given should be sent with the patient.

Patency of the occluded artery can be restored by percutaneous coronary intervention or by giving a **thrombolytic drug** (section 2.10.2), unless contra-indicated. Alteplase, reteplase and streptokinase need to be given within 12 hours of a myocardial infarction, ideally within 1 hour; use after 12 hours requires specialist advice. Tenecteplase should be given within 6 hours of a myocardial infarction. Antibodies to streptokinase appear after 4 days and it should not therefore be used again after this time. **Heparin** is used as adjunctive therapy with alteplase, reteplase, and tenecteplase to prevent re-thrombosis; heparin treatment should be continued for at least 24 hours (consult product literature).

**Nitrates** (section 2.6.1) are used to relieve ischaemic pain. If sublingual glyceryl trinitrate is not effective, intravenous glyceryl trinitrate or isosorbide dinitrate is given.

Early intravenous administration of some **beta-blockers** (section 2.4) has been shown to be of benefit and patients without contra-indications should receive **atenolol** by intravenous injection at a dose of 5 mg over 5 minutes, and the dose repeated once after 10–15 minutes; **metoprolol** by intravenous injection is an alternative.

**ACE inhibitors** (section 2.5.5.1) are also of benefit to patients who have no contra-indications; in hypertensive and normotensive patients treatment with an ACE inhibitor can be started within 24 hours of the myocardial infarction and continued for at least 5–6 weeks (see below for long-term treatment).

All patients should be closely monitored for hyperglycaemia; those with diabetes or raised blood-glucose concentration should receive **insulin**.

**Long-term management** Long-term management involves the use of several drugs which should ideally be started before the patient is discharged from hospital.

**Aspirin** (section 2.9) should be given to all patients, unless contra-indicated, at a dose of 75 mg daily. **Warfarin** (with or without aspirin) may confer greater benefit than aspirin alone, but the risk of bleeding is increased.

**Beta-blockers** (section 2.4) should be given to all patients in whom they are not contra-indicated and continued for at least 2–3 years. Acebutolol, metoprolol, propranolol and timolol are suitable; for patients with left ventricular dysfunction, carvedilol, bisoprolol or long-acting metoprolol may be appropriate (section 2.5.5).

**Verapamil** (section 2.6.2) may be useful if a beta-blocker cannot be used; however, other calcium-channel blockers have no place in routine long-term management after a myocardial infarction.

An **ACE inhibitor** (section 2.5.5.1) should be considered for all patients, especially those with evidence of left ventricular dysfunction. If an ACE inhibitor cannot be used, an angiotensin-II receptor antagonist may be used for patients with heart failure. A relatively high dose of either the ACE inhibitor or angiotensin-II receptor antagonist may be required to produce benefit.

**Nitrates** (section 2.6.1) are used for patients with angina.

**Statins** are beneficial in preventing recurrent coronary events (section 2.12).

## 2.10.2 Fibrinolytic drugs

Fibrinolytic drugs act as thrombolytics by activating plasminogen to form plasmin, which degrades fibrin and so breaks up thrombi.

The value of thrombolytic drugs for the treatment of *myocardial infarction* has been established (section 2.10.1). **Streptokinase** and **alteplase** have been shown to reduce mortality. **Reteplase** and **tenecteplase** are also licensed for acute myocardial infarction; they are given by intravenous injection (tenecteplase is given as a bolus injection). Thrombolytic drugs are indicated for any patient with acute myocardial infarction for whom the benefit is likely to outweigh the risk of treatment. Trials have shown that the benefit is greatest in those with ECG changes that include ST segment elevation (especially in those with anterior infarction) and in patients with bundle branch block. Patients should not be denied thrombolytic treatment on account of age alone because mortality in this group is high and the reduction in mortality is the same as in younger patients.

Streptokinase is used in the treatment of *life-threatening venous thrombosis*; alteplase and streptokinase are used in *pulmonary embolism*. Treatment must be started promptly.

**Cautions** Risk of bleeding including that from venepuncture or invasive procedures, external chest compression, pregnancy (Appendix 4), abdominal aneurysm or conditions in which thrombolysis might give rise to embolic complications such as enlarged left atrium with atrial fibrillation (risk of dissolution of clot and subsequent embolisation), diabetic retinopathy (very small risk of retinal bleeding), recent or concurrent anticoagulant therapy.

**Contra-indications** Recent haemorrhage, trauma, or surgery (including dental extraction), coagulation defects, bleeding diatheses, aortic dissection, coma, history of cerebrovascular disease especially recent events or with any residual disability, recent symptoms of possible peptic ulceration, heavy vaginal bleeding, severe hypertension, active pulmonary disease with cavitation, acute pancreatitis, severe liver disease, oesophageal varices; also in the case of streptokinase, previous allergic reactions to either streptokinase or anistreplase (no longer available).

Prolonged persistence of antibodies to streptokinase and anistreplase (no longer available) may reduce the effectiveness of subsequent treatment; therefore, streptokinase should not be used again beyond 4 days of first administration of either streptokinase or anistreplase. Antibodies may also appear after topical use of streptokinase on wounds.

**Side-effects** Side-effects of thrombolytics are mainly nausea and vomiting and bleeding. When thrombolytics are used in myocardial infarction, reperfusion arrhythmias may occur. Hypotension may also occur and can usually be controlled by elevating the patient's legs, or by reducing the rate of infusion or stopping it temporarily. Back pain has been reported. Bleeding is usually limited to the site of injection, but intracerebral haemorrhage or bleeding from other sites may occur. Serious bleeding calls for discontinuation of the thrombolytic and may require administration of coagulation factors and antifibrinolytic drugs (aprotinin or tranexamic acid). Streptokinase may cause allergic reactions (including rash, flushing and uveitis) and anaphylaxis has been reported (for details of management see Allergic Emergencies, section 3.4.3). Guillain-Barré syndrome has been reported rarely after streptokinase treatment.

## ALTEPLASE
### (rt-PA, tissue-type plasminogen activator)

**Indications** acute myocardial infarction (see notes above and section 2.10.1); pulmonary embolism; acute ischaemic stroke (treatment under specialist neurology physician **only**)

**Cautions** see notes above; *in acute stroke*, monitor for intracranial haemorrhage, monitor blood pressure (antihypertensive recommended if systolic above 180 mmHg or diastolic above 105 mmHg); renal impairment (Appendix 3)

**Contra-indications** see notes above; *in acute stroke*, convulsion accompanying stroke, severe stroke, history of stroke in patients with diabetes, stroke in last 3 months, hypoglycaemia, hyperglycaemia

**Side-effects** see notes above; also risk of cerebral bleeding increased in acute stroke

**Dose**

- Myocardial infarction, accelerated regimen (initiated within 6 hours), 15 mg by intravenous injection, followed by intravenous infusion of 50 mg over 30 minutes, then 35 mg over 60 minutes (total dose 100 mg over 90 minutes); lower doses in patients less than 65 kg
- Myocardial infarction, initiated within 6–12 hours, 10 mg by intravenous injection, followed by intravenous infusion of 50 mg over 60 minutes, then 4 infusions each of 10 mg over 30 minutes (total dose 100 mg over 3 hours; max. 1.5 mg/kg in patients less than 65 kg)
- Pulmonary embolism, 10 mg by intravenous injection over 1–2 minutes, followed by intravenous infusion of 90 mg over 2 hours; max. 1.5 mg/kg in patients less than 65 kg
- Acute stroke (treatment **must** begin within 3 hours), by intravenous administration over 60 minutes, 900 micrograms/kg (max. 90 mg); initial 10% of dose by intravenous injection, remainder by intravenous infusion; ELDERLY over 80 years not recommended

**Actilyse®** (Boehringer Ingelheim) PoM
Injection, powder for reconstitution, alteplase 10 mg (5.8 million units)/vial, net price per vial (with diluent) = £135.00; 20 mg (11.6 million units)/vial (with diluent and transfer device) = £180.00; 50 mg (29 million-units)/vial (with diluent, transfer device, and infusion bag) = £300.00

## RETEPLASE

**Indications** acute myocardial infarction (see notes above and section 2.10.1)

**Cautions** see notes above; breast-feeding (Appendix 5)

**Contra-indications** see notes above

**Side-effects** see notes above

**Dose**

- By intravenous injection, 10 units over not more than 2 minutes, followed after 30 minutes by a further 10 units

**Rapilysin®** (Roche) PoM
Injection, powder for reconstitution, reteplase 10 units/vial, net price pack of 2 vials (with 2 prefilled syringes of diluent and transfer device) = £666.11

## STREPTOKINASE

**Indications** acute myocardial infarction (see notes above and section 2.10.1); deep-vein thrombosis, pulmonary embolism, acute arterial thromboembolism, and central retinal venous or arterial thrombosis; topical use (section 13.11.7)

**Cautions** see notes above

**Contra-indications** see notes above

**Side-effects** see notes above

**Dose**

- Myocardial infarction, 1 500 000 units over 60 minutes
- Deep-vein thrombosis, pulmonary embolism, acute arterial thromboembolism, central retinal venous or arterial thrombosis, by intravenous infusion, 250 000 units over 30 minutes, then 100 000 units every hour for up to 12–72 hours according to condition with monitoring of clotting parameters (consult product literature)

**Streptokinase** (Non-proprietary) PoM
Injection, powder for reconstitution, streptokinase, net price 100 000-unit vial = £10.00; 250 000-unit vial = £14.33; 750 000-unit vial = £38.20; 1.5 million-unit vial = £81.18

**Streptase®** (ZLB Behring) PoM
Injection, powder for reconstitution, streptokinase, net price 250 000-unit vial = £17.11; 750 000-unit vial = £44.86; 1.5 million-unit vial = £89.72 (hosp. only)

### TENECTEPLASE

**Indications** acute myocardial infarction (see notes above and section 2.10.1)

**Cautions** see notes above; breast-feeding (Appendix 5)

**Contra-indications** see notes above

**Side-effects** see notes above; also fever

**Dose**

- By intravenous injection over 10 seconds, 30–50 mg according to body-weight (500–600 micrograms/kg)—consult product literature; max. 50 mg

**Metalyse®** (Boehringer Ingelheim) PoM
Injection, powder for reconstitution, tenecteplase, net price 40-mg (8000-unit) vial = £612.50; 50-mg (10 000-unit) vial = £612.50 (both with prefilled syringe of water for injection)

## 2.11 Antifibrinolytic drugs and haemostatics

Fibrin dissolution can be impaired by the administration of **tranexamic acid**, which inhibits fibrinolysis. It may be useful to prevent bleeding (e.g. in prostatectomy and dental extraction in haemophilia) and can be particularly useful in menorrhagia. Tranexamic acid may also be used in hereditary angioedema, epistaxis and in thrombolytic overdose.

**Desmopressin** (section 6.5.2) is used in the management of mild to moderate haemophilia.

**Aprotinin** is a proteolytic enzyme inhibitor acting on plasmin and kallidinogenase (kallikrein). It is indicated for patients at high risk of major blood loss during and after open heart surgery with extracorporeal circulation and for patients in whom optimal blood conservation during open heart surgery is an absolute priority; it is also indicated for the treatment of life-threatening haemorrhage due to hyperplasminaemia (occasionally observed during the mobilisation and dissection of malignant tumours, in acute promyelocytic leukaemia, and following thrombolytic therapy). Aprotinin is also used in liver transplantation [unlicensed].

**Etamsylate** (ethamsylate) reduces capillary bleeding in the presence of a normal number of platelets. It does not act by fibrin stabilisation, but probably by correcting abnormal adhesion.

### APROTININ

**Indications** see notes above

**Cautions** pregnancy (Appendix 4)

**Side-effects** occasionally hypersensitivity reactions and localised thrombophlebitis

**Dose**

- Test dose, by slow intravenous injection *or* infusion, 10 000 units (1 mL) at least 10 minutes before remainder of dose (to detect allergy)
- Open heart surgery, loading dose, by slow intravenous injection *or* infusion over 20 minutes, 2 million units (200 mL) after induction of anaesthesia and before sternotomy; maintenance dose, by intravenous infusion 500 000 units (50 mL) every hour until end of operation (or early postoperative period in septic endocarditis); pump prime, 2 million units (200 mL) in priming volume of extracorporeal circuit (3 million units (300 mL) in septic endocarditis); usual max. 7 million units (700 mL) per treatment course
- Hyperplasminaemia, by slow intravenous injection *or* infusion, initially 0.5–1 million units (50–100 mL) at max. rate 10 mL/minute; followed if necessary by 200 000 units (20 mL) every hour until bleeding stops

**Trasylol®** (Bayer) PoM
Injection, aprotinin 10 000 kallikrein inactivator units/mL. Net price 50-mL vial = £20.53
Note A non-proprietary aprotinin injection containing 10 000 kallikrein inactivator units/mL is also available

### ETAMSYLATE
(Ethamsylate)

**Indications** blood loss in menorrhagia

**Contra-indications** porphyria (see section 9.8.2)

**Side-effects** nausea, headache, rashes

**Dose**

- 500 mg 4 times daily during menstruation

**Dicynene®** (Sanofi-Synthelabo) PoM
Tablets, scored, etamsylate 500 mg, net price 100-tab pack = £8.78

### TRANEXAMIC ACID

**Indications** see notes above

**Cautions** renal impairment (avoid if severe—Appendix 3); massive haematuria (avoid if risk of ureteric obstruction); not for use in disseminated intravascular coagulation; pregnancy (Appendix 4); regular eye examinations and liver function tests in long-term treatment of hereditary angioedema
Note Requirement for regular eye examinations during long-term treatment is based on unsatisfactory evidence

**Contra-indications** severe renal impairment, thromboembolic disease

**Side-effects** nausea, vomiting, diarrhoea (reduce dose); disturbances in colour vision (discontinue) and thromboembolic events reported rarely; giddiness on rapid intravenous injection

**Dose**

- By mouth, local fibrinolysis, 15–25 mg/kg 2–3 times daily

  Menorrhagia (initiated when menstruation has started), 1 g 3 times daily for up to 4 days; max. 4 g daily

  Hereditary angioedema, 1–1.5 g 2–3 times daily
- By slow intravenous injection, local fibrinolysis, 0.5–1 g 3 times daily

**Tranexamic acid** (Non-proprietary) PoM
Tablets, tranexamic acid 500 mg, net price 60-tab pack = £12.28

**Cyklokapron®** (Meda) PoM
Tablets, f/c, scored, tranexamic acid 500 mg. Net price 60-tab pack = £14.30
Injection, tranexamic acid 100 mg/mL. Net price 5-mL amp = £1.55

## Blood products

**NICE guidance (drotrecogin alfa (activated) for severe sepsis)**
NICE has recommended (September 2004) that drotrecogin alfa (activated) should be considered for adults with severe sepsis that has resulted in the failure of two or more major organs and who are receiving optimum intensive care support. Drotrecogin alfa (activated) should be initiated and supervised only by a specialist consultant with intensive care skills and experience in the care of patients with sepsis.

### ANTITHROMBIN III CONCENTRATE

Dried antithrombin III is prepared from human plasma

**Indications** congenital deficiency of antithrombin III
**Side-effects** nausea, flushing, headache; rarely, allergic reactions and fever
Available from BPL (Dried Antithrombin III)

### DROTRECOGIN ALFA (ACTIVATED)
**Recombinant activated protein C**

**Indications** adjunctive treatment of severe sepsis with multiple organ failure
**Cautions** increased risk of bleeding, concomitant use of drugs that increase risk of bleeding; pregnancy (Appendix 4); breast-feeding (Appendix 5); **interactions**: Appendix 1 (drotrecogin alfa)
**Contra-indications** internal bleeding; intracranial neoplasm or cerebral herniation; chronic severe hepatic disease; thrombocytopenia; not recommended for use in children or in single organ failure
**Side-effects** bleeding; headache; ecchymosis; pain
Available from Lilly (*Xigris®*▼)

### FACTOR VIIa (RECOMBINANT)
**Eptacog alfa (activated)**

**Indications** treatment and prophylaxis of haemorrhage in patients with haemophilia A or B with antibodies to factors VIII or IX, acquired haemophilia, factor VII deficiency, or Glanzmann's thrombasthenia
**Cautions** risk of thrombosis or disseminated intravascular coagulation
**Side-effects** *very rarely* nausea, myocardial infarction, cerebrovascular accident, coagulation disorders, fever, pain, and allergic reactions including rash
Available from Novo Nordisk (*NovoSeven®*)

### FACTOR VIII FRACTION, DRIED
**(Human Antihaemophilic Fraction, Dried)**

Dried factor VIII fraction is prepared from human plasma by a suitable fractionation technique

**Indications** treatment and prophylaxis of haemorrhage in haemophilia A
**Cautions** intravascular haemolysis after large or frequently repeated doses in patients with blood groups A, B, or AB—less likely with high potency concentrates
**Side-effects** allergic reactions including chills, fever; hyperfibrinogenaemia occurred after massive doses with earlier products but less likely since fibrinogen content has now been substantially reduced
Available from ZLB Behring (*Beriate® P*; *Haemate® P*), BPL (*Optivate®*, High Purity Factor VIII and von Willebrand factor concentrate; *Replenate®*; *8Y®*), Grifols (*Alphanate®*; *Fanhdi®*), SNBTS (*Liberate®*, High Potency Factor VIII Concentrate)
**Note** Preparation of recombinant human antihaemophilic factor VIII (octocog alfa) available from ZLB Behring (*Helixate® NexGen*), Baxter Bioscience (*Advate®*▼), Bayer (*Kogenate Bayer®*), Wyeth (*ReFacto®*)

### FACTOR VIII INHIBITOR BYPASSING FRACTION

Preparations with factor VIII inhibitor bypassing activity are prepared from human plasma
Human Factor VIII Inhibitor Bypassing Fraction (*FEIBA®*, Baxter Bioscience) is used in patients with factor VIII inhibitors
**Note** A porcine preparation of antihaemophilic factor for patients with inhibitors to human factor VIII is available from Ipsen(*Hyate C®*)

### FACTOR IX FRACTION, DRIED

Dried factor IX fraction is prepared from human plasma by a suitable fractionation technique; it may also contain clotting factors II, VII, and X

**Indications** congenital factor IX deficiency (haemophilia B)
**Cautions** risk of thrombosis—principally with former low purity products
**Contra-indications** disseminated intravascular coagulation
**Side-effects** allergic reactions, including chills, fever
Available from ZLB Behring (*Mononine®*), BPL (*Replenine®-VF*, Dried Factor IX Fraction), Grifols (*AlphaNine®*), SNBTS (*HT Defix®*, Human Factor IX Concentrate, Heat Treated; *Hipfix®*▼, High Purity Factor IX Concentrate)
**Note** Preparation of recombinant coagulation factor IX (nonacog alfa) available from Baxter Bioscience (*BeneFIX®*)

### FACTOR XIII FRACTION, DRIED
**(Human Fibrin-stabilising Factor, Dried)**

**Indications** congenital factor XIII deficiency
**Side-effects** rarely, allergic reactions and fever
Available from ZLB Behring (*Fibrogammin® P*)

### FRESH FROZEN PLASMA

Fresh frozen plasma is prepared from the supernatant liquid obtained by centrifugation of one donation of whole blood

**Indications** to replace coagulation factors or other plasma proteins where their concentration or functional activity is critically reduced, e.g. to reverse warfarin effect

**Cautions** avoid in circulatory overload; need for compatibility

**Side-effects** allergic reactions including chills, fever, bronchospasm; adult respiratory distress syndrome

Available from Regional Blood Transfusion Services and BPL

Note A preparation of solvent/detergent treated human plasma (frozen) is available from Octapharma (*Octaplas*® )

### PROTEIN C CONCENTRATE

Protein C is prepared from human plasma

**Indications** congenital protein C deficiency

**Cautions** hypersensitivity to heparin

**Side-effects** fever, arrhythmia, bleeding and thrombosis reported; rarely allergic reactions

Available from Baxter (*Ceprotin*® ▼)

# 2.12 Lipid-regulating drugs

Lipid-regulating drug therapy must be combined with advice on diet and lifestyle measures to reduce cardiovascular disease risk including, if appropriate, reduction of blood pressure (section 2.5) and use of aspirin (section 2.9).

Lowering the concentration of low density lipoprotein (LDL) cholesterol and raising high density lipoprotein (HDL) cholesterol reduces the progression of atherosclerosis and may even induce regression. Treatment with a lipid-regulating drug should therefore be considered in patients with evidence of cardiovascular disease or at risk of developing it because of risk factors including smoking, hypertension, diabetes mellitus, male sex, age, obesity, and a family history of premature cardiovascular disease.

Treatment with statins (see Statins, below) reduces myocardial infarction, coronary deaths, the risk of stroke, and overall mortality rate and they are the drugs of choice in patients with a high risk of cardiovascular disease.

A number of conditions, some familial, are characterised by very high plasma concentrations of cholesterol, or triglycerides, or both. A statin is the drug of first choice for treating hypercholesterolaemia and moderate hypertriglyceridaemia; a fibrate is added cautiously (see CSM advice below) if triglycerides remain high even after the LDL-cholesterol concentration has been reduced adequately.

Severe hyperlipidaemia not adequately controlled with maximal dose of a statin, may require use of an additional lipid-regulating drug such as ezetimibe or colestyramine; such treatment should generally be under specialist supervision. Nicotinic acid may also be used under specialist supervision to further lower triglycerides or LDL-cholesterol concentration. Combinations of a statin with nicotinic acid or a fibrate carry an increased risk of side-effects (including rhabdomyolysis) and should be used with caution. In particular, concomitant administration of gemfibrozil with a statin may increase the risk of rhabdomyolysis considerably (see also below); gemfibrozil and statins should therefore **not** be used concomitantly.

Patients wth hypothyroidism should receive adequate thyroid replacement therapy before assessing their requirement for lipid-regulating treatment because correction of hypothyroidism itself may resolve the lipid abnormality. Untreated hypothyroidism increases the risk of myositis with lipid-regulating drugs.

> **CSM advice (muscle effects)**
> The CSM has advised that rhabdomyolysis associated with lipid-regulating drugs such as the fibrates and statins appears to be rare (approx. 1 case in every 100 000 treatment years) but may be increased in those with renal impairment and possibly in those with hypothyroidism (see also notes above). Concomitant treatment with drugs that increase plasma-statin concentration increase the risk of muscle toxicity; concomitant treatment with a fibrate and a statin may also be associated with an increased risk of serious muscle toxicity.

## Anion-exchange resins

**Colestyramine** (cholestyramine) and **colestipol** are anion-exchange resins used in the management of hypercholesterolaemia. They act by binding bile acids, preventing their reabsorption; this promotes hepatic conversion of cholesterol into bile acids; the resultant increased LDL-receptor activity of liver cells increases the clearance of LDL-cholesterol. Thus both compounds effectively reduce LDL-cholesterol but can aggravate hypertriglyceridaemia.

**Cautions** Anion-exchange resins interfere with the absorption of fat-soluble vitamins; supplements of vitamins A, D and K may be required when treatment is prolonged. **Interactions:** Appendix 1 (colestyramine and colestipol).

**Side-effects** As colestyramine and colestipol are not absorbed, gastro-intestinal side-effects predominate. Constipation is common, but diarrhoea has occurred, as have nausea, vomiting, and gastro-intestinal discomfort. Hypertriglyceridaemia may be aggravated. An increased bleeding tendency has been reported due to hypoprothrombinaemia associated with vitamin K deficiency.

**Counselling** Other drugs should be taken at least 1 hour (in the case of ezetimibe, at least 2 hours) before or 4–6 hours after colestyramine or colestipol to reduce possible interference with absorption.

### COLESTYRAMINE
**(Cholestyramine)**

**Indications** hyperlipidaemias, particularly type IIa, in patients who have not responded adequately to diet and other appropriate measures; primary prevention of coronary heart disease in men aged 35–59 years with primary hypercholesterolaemia who have not responded to diet and other appropriate measures; pruritus associated with partial biliary obstruction and primary biliary cirrhosis (section 1.9.2); diarrhoeal disorders (section 1.9.2)

**Cautions** see notes above; hepatic impairment (Appendix 2); pregnancy and breast-feeding; **interactions**: Appendix 1 (colestyramine)

**Contra-indications** complete biliary obstruction (not likely to be effective)

**Side-effects** see notes above; hyperchloraemic acidosis reported on prolonged use

**Dose**

- Lipid reduction (after initial introduction over 3–4 weeks) 12–24 g daily in water (or other suitable liquid) in single or up to 4 divided doses; up to 36 g daily if necessary
- Pruritus, see section 1.9.2
- Diarrhoeal disorders, see section 1.9.2
- CHILD 6–12 years, see product literature

**Colestyramine** (Non-proprietary) PoM

Powder, colestyramine (anhydrous) 4 g/sachet, net price 60-sachet pack = £19.23. Label: 13, counselling, avoid other drugs at same time (see notes above)

Excipients include aspartame (section 9.4.1)

**Questran®** (Bristol-Myers Squibb) PoM

Powder, colestyramine (anhydrous) 4 g/sachet. Net price 50-sachet pack = £17.55. Label: 13, counselling, avoid other drugs at same time (see notes above)

Excipients include sucrose 3.79g/sachet

**Questran Light®** (Bristol-Myers Squibb) PoM

Powder, sugar-free, colestyramine (anhydrous) 4 g/sachet, net price 50-sachet pack = £18.43. Label: 13, counselling, avoid other drugs at same time (see notes above)

Excipients include aspartame (section 9.4.1)

## COLESTIPOL HYDROCHLORIDE

**Indications** hyperlipidaemias, particularly type IIa, in patients who have not responded adequately to diet and other appropriate measures

**Cautions** see notes above; pregnancy

**Side-effects** see notes above

**Dose**

- 5 g 1–2 times daily in liquid increased if necessary at intervals of 1–2 months to max. of 30 g daily (in single or 2 divided doses)

**Colestid®** (Pharmacia) PoM

Granules, yellow, colestipol hydrochloride 5 g/sachet. Net price 30 sachets = £15.05. Label: 13, counselling, avoid other drugs at same time (see notes above)

Colestid Orange, granules, yellow/orange, colestipol hydrochloride 5 g/sachet, with aspartame. Net price 30 sachets = £15.05. Label: 13, counselling, avoid other drugs at same time (see notes above)

## Ezetimibe

**Ezetimibe** inhibits the intestinal absorption of cholesterol. It is licensed as adjunctive therapy to dietary manipulation in patients with primary hypercholesterolaemia in combination with a statin or alone (if a statin is inappropriate), in patients with homozygous familial hypercholesterolaemia in combination with a statin, and in patients with homozygous familial sitosterolaemia (phytosterolaemia).

## EZETIMIBE

**Indications** adjunct to dietary measures and statin in primary hypercholesterolaemia and homozygous familial hypercholesterolaemia (statin omitted in primary hypercholesterolaemia if inappropriate or not tolerated); adjunct to dietary measures in homozygous sitosterolaemia

**Cautions** hepatic impairment (avoid if moderate or severe; Appendix 2); pregnancy (Appendix 4); **interactions:** Appendix 1 (ezetimibe)

**Contra-indications** breast-feeding (Appendix 5)

**Side-effects** gastro-intestinal disturbances; headache, fatigue; myalgia; *rarely* hypersensitivity reactions including rash and angioedema, hepatitis; *very rarely* pancreatitis, cholelithiasis, cholecystitis, thrombocytopenia, raised creatine kinase, myopathy, and rhabdomyolysis

**Dose**

- 10 mg once daily; CHILD under 10 years not recommended

**Ezetrol** (MSD, Schering-Plough) ▼ PoM

Tablets, ezetimibe 10 mg, net price 28-tab pack = £26.31

**With simvastatin**

See under Simvastatin

## Fibrates

**Bezafibrate**, **ciprofibrate**, **fenofibrate**, and **gemfibrozil** act mainly by decreasing serum triglycerides; they have variable effects on LDL-cholesterol. Although a fibrate may reduce the risk of coronary heart disease events in those with low HDL-cholesterol or with raised triglycerides, a statin should be used first. Fibrates may be considered first-line therapy in those whose serum-triglyceride concentration is greater than 10 mmol/litre.

Fibrates can cause a myositis-like syndrome, especially in those with impaired renal function. Also, combination of a fibrate with a statin increases the risk of muscle effects (especially rhabdomyolysis) and should be used with caution (see CSM advice on p. 133).

## BEZAFIBRATE

**Indications** hyperlipidaemias of types IIa, IIb, III, IV and V in patients who have not responded adequately to diet and other appropriate measures

**Cautions** correct hypothyroidism before initiating treatment (see p. 133); hepatic impairment (Appendix 2); renal impairment (Appendix 3—see also under Myotoxicity below); **interactions:** Appendix 1 (fibrates)

Myotoxicity Special care needed in patients with renal disease, as progressive increases in serum creatinine concentration or failure to follow dosage guidelines may result in myotoxicity (rhabdomyolysis); discontinue if myotoxicity suspected or creatine kinase concentration increases significantly

**Contra-indications** severe hepatic and renal impairment, hypoalbuminaemia, primary biliary cirrhosis, gall bladder disease, nephrotic syndrome, pregnancy (Appendix 4); breast-feeding (Appendix 5)

**Side-effects** gastro-intestinal disturbances; rash, pruritus; *less commonly*, headache, fatigue, dizziness, insomnia; *rarely* gallstones, hepatomegaly, cholestasis, hypoglycaemia, impotence, anaemia, leucopenia, thrombocytopenia, increased risk of bleeding, alopecia, photosensitivity reactions, raised serum creatinine (unrelated to renal impairment), and myotoxicity (with myasthenia or myalgia)—special risk in renal impairment (see Cautions)

**Dose**

- See preparations below

**Bezafibrate** (Non-proprietary) PoM
Tablets, bezafibrate 200 mg, net price 100-tab pack = £8.62. Label: 21
Dose 200 mg 3 times daily

**Bezalip®** (Roche) PoM
Tablets, f/c, bezafibrate 200 mg. Net price 100-tab pack = £9.15. Label: 21
Dose 200 mg 3 times daily

**Modified release**

**Bezalip® Mono** (Roche) PoM
Tablets, m/r, f/c, bezafibrate 400 mg. Net price 30-tab pack = £8.09. Label: 21, 25
Dose 1 tablet daily (dose form not appropriate in renal impairment)
Note Modified-release tablets containing bezafibrate 400 mg also available; brands include *Zimbacol® XL*

## CIPROFIBRATE

**Indications** hyperlipidaemias of types IIa, IIb, III, and IV in patients who have not responded adequately to diet

**Cautions** see under Bezafibrate

**Contra-indications** see under Bezafibrate

**Side-effects** see under Bezafibrate

**Dose**

- 100 mg daily

**Modalim®** (Sanofi-Synthelabo) PoM
Tablets, scored, ciprofibrate 100 mg. Net price 28-tab pack = £14.72

## FENOFIBRATE

**Indications** hyperlipidaemias of types IIa, IIb, III, IV, and V in patients who have not responded adequately to diet and other appropriate measures

**Cautions** see under Bezafibrate; liver function tests recommended every 3 months for first year (discontinue treatment if significantly raised); renal impairment (avoid if severe; Appendix 3)

**Contra-indications** gall bladder disease; photosensitivity to ketoprofen; severe hepatic impairment (Appendix 2); pregnancy (Appendix 4); breast-feeding (Appendix 5)

**Side-effects** see under Bezafibrate; also *very rarely* hepatitis, pancreatitis, and interstitial pneumopathies

**Dose**

- See preparations below

**Fenofibrate** (Non-proprietary) PoM
Capsules, fenofibrate 200 mg, net price 30-cap pack = £14.75. Label: 21
Dose 1 capsule daily (dose form not appropriate for children or in renal impairment)
Brands include *Fenogal®*

**Lipantil®** (Fournier) PoM
Lipantil® Micro 67 capsules, yellow, fenofibrate (micronised) 67 mg, net price 90-cap pack = £23.30. Label: 21
Dose initially 3 capsules daily in divided doses; usual range 2–4 capsules daily; CHILD 4–15 years 1 capsule/20 kg daily

Lipantil® Micro 200 capsules, orange, fenofibrate (micronised) 200 mg, net price 28-cap pack = £17.95. Label: 21
Dose initially 1 capsule daily (dose form not appropriate for children or in renal impairment)

Lipantil® Micro 267 capsules, orange/cream, fenofibrate (micronised) 267 mg, net price 28-cap pack = £21.75. Label: 21
Dose severe hyperlipidaemia, 1 capsule daily (dose form not appropriate for children or in renal impairment)
Note For an equivalent therapeutic effect, 100 mg previously available non-micronised fenofibrate ≡ 67 mg micronised fenofibrate

**Supralip® 160** (Fournier) PoM
Tablets, f/c, fenofibrate 160 mg, net price 28-tab pack = £14.75. Label: 21, 25
Dose 160 mg daily (dose form not appropriate for children or in renal impairment)

## GEMFIBROZIL

**Indications** hyperlipidaemias of types IIa, IIb, III, IV and V in patients who have not responded adequately to diet and other appropriate measures; primary prevention of cardiovascular disease in men with hyperlipidaemias that have not responded to diet and other appropriate measures

**Cautions** lipid profile, blood counts, and liver-function tests before initiating long-term treatment; preferably avoid use with statins (high risk of rhabdomyolysis); correct hypothyroidism before initiating treatment (see p. 133); elderly; renal impairment (Appendix 3); **interactions**: Appendix 1 (fibrates)

**Contra-indications** alcoholism, biliary-tract disease including gallstones; photosensitivity to fibrates; hepatic impairment (Appendix 2); pregnancy (Appendix 4); breast-feeding (Appendix 5)

**Side-effects** gastro-intestinal disturbances; headache, fatigue, vertigo; eczema, rash; *less commonly* atrial fibrillation; *rarely* pancreatitis, appendicitis, disturbances in liver function including hepatitis and cholestatic jaundice, dizziness, paraesthesia, sexual dysfunction, thrombocytopenia, anaemia, leucopenia, eosinophilia, bone-marrow suppression, myalgia, myopathy, myasthenia, myositis accompanied by increase in creatine kinase (discontinue if raised significantly), blurred vision, exfoliative dermatitis, alopecia, and photosensitivity)

**Dose**

- 1.2 g daily, usually in 2 divided doses; range 0.9–1.2 g daily; CHILD not recommended

**Gemfibrozil** (Non-proprietary) PoM
Capsules, gemfibrozil 300 mg, net price 112-cap pack = £21.76. Label: 22

Tablets, gemfibrozil 600 mg, net price 30-tab pack = £10.57. Label: 22

**Lopid®** (Pfizer) PoM
'300' capsules, white/maroon, gemfibrozil 300 mg. Net price 112-cap pack = £35.57. Label: 22

'600' tablets, f/c, gemfibrozil 600 mg. Net price 56-tab pack = £35.57. Label: 22

## Statins

The statins (**atorvastatin**, **fluvastatin**, **pravastatin**, **rosuvastatin**, and **simvastatin**) competitively inhibit

3-hydroxy-3-methylglutaryl coenzyme A (HMG CoA) reductase, an enzyme involved in cholesterol synthesis, especially in the liver. They are more effective than other classes of drugs in lowering LDL-cholesterol but less effective than the fibrates in reducing triglycerides.

Statins reduce all atherosclerotic cardiovascular disease events, and total mortality. They should be considered for all patients, including the elderly, at risk of cardiovascular disease such as those with coronary heart disease (including history of angina or acute myocardial infarction), occlusive arterial disease (including peripheral vascular disease, non-haemorrhagic stroke or transient ischaemic attacks), or diabetes mellitus.

Statins are also used for the *secondary prevention* of cardiovascular disease events in patients with coronary heart disease (including history of angina or acute myocardial infarction), peripheral artery disease, or a history of stroke. Although statins produce these benefits irrespective of the initial cholesterol concentration, patients with a total serum-cholesterol concentration of 5 mmol/litre or greater are likely to benefit most. Statins also reduce the incidence of non-haemorrhagic stroke when used for secondary prevention in cardiovascular disease.

Statins are also used for the *primary prevention* of cardiovascular disease events in patients at increased risk. Risk of cardiovascular disease events is not accurately predicted from cholesterol concentrations alone and methods that take into account factors such as smoking, hypertension and age should be used to estimate risk. Patients with a 10-year cardiovascular disease risk of ≥ 20%[1] stand to benefit from primary prevention irrespective of the cholesterol concentration, in association with lifestyle measures and other appropriate interventions.

For primary and secondary prevention of cardiovascular disease, statin treatment should be adjusted to achieve a target total cholesterol concentration of less than 5 mmol/litre (or a reduction of 25% if that produces a lower concentration); in terms of LDL-cholesterol, the target should be below 3 mmol/litre (or a reduction of about 30% if that produces a lower concentration).

**Cautions** Statins should be used with caution in those with a history of liver disease or with a high alcohol intake (use should be avoided in active liver disease). Hypothyroidism should be managed adequately before starting treatment with a statin (see p. 133). Liver-function tests should be carried out before and within 1–3 months of starting treatment and thereafter at intervals of 6 months for 1 year, unless indicated sooner by signs or symptoms suggestive of hepatotoxicity. Treatment should be discontinued if serum transaminase concentration rises to, and persists at, 3 times the upper limit of the reference range. Statins should be used with caution in those with risk factors for myopathy or rhabdomyolysis; patients should be advised to report unexplained muscle pain (see Muscle Effects below). Statins should be avoided in porphyria (section 9.8.2) but rosuvastatin thought to be safe. **Interactions:** Appendix 1 (statins).

1. Cardiovascular disease risk may be determined from the chart issued by the British Hypertension Society (*J Hum Hypertens* 2004; **18**: 139–85)—see inside back cover. The Joint British Societies' 'Cardiac Risk Assessor' computer programme may also be used to determine cardiovascular disease risk by adding together the coronary heart disease risk and stroke risk.

**Contra-indications** Statins are contra-indicated in active liver disease (or persistently abnormal liver function tests), in pregnancy (adequate contraception required during treatment and for 1 month afterwards) and breast-feeding (see Appendix 4 and Appendix 5).

**Side-effects** Reversible myositis is a rare but significant side-effect of the statins (see also CSM advice (Muscle Effects), p. 133 and below). The statins also cause headache, altered liver-function tests (rarely, hepatitis), paraesthesia, and gastro-intestinal effects including abdominal pain, flatulence, constipation, diarrhoea, nausea and vomiting. Rash and hypersensitivity reactions (including angioedema and anaphylaxis) have been reported rarely.

**Muscle effects** Myalgia, myositis and myopathy have been reported with the statins; if myopathy is suspected and creatine kinase is markedly elevated (more than 5 times upper limit of normal), or muscular symptoms are severe, treatment should be discontinued; in patients at high risk of muscle effects, a statin should not be started if creatine kinase is elevated. There is an increased incidence of myopathy if the statins are given at high doses or given with a fibrate (see also CSM advice on p. 133), with lipid-lowering doses of nicotinic acid, or with immunosuppressants such as ciclosporin; close monitoring of liver function and, if symptomatic, of creatine kinase is required in patients receiving these drugs. Rhabdomyolysis with acute renal impairment secondary to myoglobinuria has also been reported.

**Counselling** Advise patient to report promptly unexplained muscle pain, tenderness, weakness.

## ATORVASTATIN

**Indications** primary hypercholesterolaemia, heterozygous familial hypercholesterolaemia, homozygous familial hypercholesterolaemia or combined (mixed) hyperlipidaemia in patients who have not responded adequately to diet and other appropriate measures

**Cautions** see notes above

**Contra-indications** see notes above

**Side-effects** see notes above; also chest pain, angina; insomnia, dizziness, hypoaesthesia, arthralgia; back pain; *less commonly* anorexia, malaise, weight gain, amnesia, impotence, thrombocytopenia, tinnitus, and alopecia; *rarely* pancreatitis, peripheral neuropathy, and peripheral oedema; *very rarely* cholestatic jaundice, hypoglycaemia, hyperglycaemia, and Stevens-Johnson syndrome

**Dose**

- Primary hypercholesterolaemia and combined hyperlipidaemia, usually 10 mg once daily; if necessary, may be increased at intervals of at least 4 weeks to max. 80 mg once daily; CHILD 10–17 years usually 10 mg once daily (limited experience with doses above 20 mg daily)
- Familial hypercholesterolaemia, initially 10 mg daily, increased at intervals of at least 4 weeks to 40 mg once daily; if necessary, further increased to max. 80 mg once daily (or 40 mg once daily combined with anion-exchange resin in heterozygous familial hypercholesterolaemia); CHILD 10–17 years up to 20 mg once daily (limited experience with higher doses)

**Lipitor®** (Pfizer) PoM

Tablets, all f/c, atorvastatin (as calcium trihydrate) 10 mg, net price 28-tab pack = £18.03; 20 mg, 28-tab pack = £24.64; 40 mg 28-tab pack = £28.21; 80 mg, 28-tab pack = £28.21. Counselling, muscle effects, see notes above

## FLUVASTATIN

Note The *Scottish Medicines Consortium* has advised (February 2004) that fluvastatin is accepted for restricted use for the secondary prevention of coronary events after percutaneous coronary angioplasty; if the patient has previously been receiving another statin, then there is no need to change the statin

**Indications** adjunct to diet in primary hypercholesterolaemia or combined (mixed) hyperlipidaemia (types IIa and IIb); adjunct to diet to slow progression of coronary atherosclerosis in primary hypercholesterolaemia and concomitant coronary heart disease; prevention of coronary events after percutaneous coronary intervention

**Cautions** see notes above

**Contra-indications** see notes above

**Side-effects** see notes above; also insomnia; *very rarely* dysaesthesia, hypoesthesia, peripheral neuropathy, thrombocytopenia, vasculitis, eczema, dermatitis, bullous exanthema, and lupus erythematosus-like syndrome

**Dose**

- Hypercholesterolaemia or combined hyperlipidaemia, initially 20–40 mg daily in the evening, adjusted at intervals of at least 4 weeks; up to 80 mg daily may be required; CHILD and ADOLESCENT under 18 years, not recommended
- Prevention of progression of coronary atherosclerosis, 40 mg daily in the evening
- Following percutaneous coronary intervention, 80 mg daily

**Lescol®** (Novartis) PoM

Capsules, fluvastatin (as sodium salt) 20 mg (brown/yellow), net price 28-cap pack = £12.72; 40 mg (brown/orange), 28-cap pack = £12.72, 56-cap pack = £25.44. Counselling, muscle effects, see notes above

**Modified release**

**Lescol® XL** (Novartis) PoM

Tablets, m/r, yellow, fluvastatin (as sodium salt) 80 mg, net price 28-tab pack = £16.00. Label: 25, counselling, muscle effects, see notes above

Dose 80 mg once daily (dose form not appropriate for initial dose titration in hypercholesterolaemia or combined hyperlipidaemia)

## PRAVASTATIN SODIUM

**Indications** adjunct to diet for primary hypercholesterolaemia or combined (mixed) hyperlipidaemias in patients who have not responded adequately to dietary control; adjunct to diet to prevent cardiovascular events in patients with hypercholesterolaemia; prevention of cardiovascular events in patients with previous myocardial infarction or unstable angina; reduction of hyperlipidaemia in patients receiving immunosuppressive therapy following solid-organ transplantation

**Cautions** see notes above; renal impairment (Appendix 3)

**Contra-indications** see notes above

**Side-effects** see notes above; *less commonly* fatigue, dizziness, sleep disturbances, abnormal urination (including dysuria, nocturia and frequency), sexual dysfunction, visual disturbances, alopecia, *very rarely* pancreatitis, jaundice, fulminant hepatic necrosis, peripheral neuropathy, lupus erythematosus-like syndrome

**Dose**

- Hypercholesterolaemia or combined hyperlipidaemias, 10–40 mg once daily at night, adjusted at intervals of not less than 4 weeks
- Familial hypercholesterolaemia, CHILD 8–13 years 10–20 mg once daily at night, 14–18 years 10–40 mg once daily at night
- Prevention of cardiovascular events, 40 mg once daily at night
- Post-transplantation hyperlipidaemia, initially 20 mg once daily at night, increased if necessary (under close medical supervision) to max. 40 mg

**Pravastatin** (Non-proprietary) PoM

Tablets, pravastatin sodium 10 mg, net price 28-tab pack = £3.41; 20 mg, 28-tab pack = £4.22; 40 mg, 28-tab pack = £4.59. Counselling, muscle effects, see notes above

**Lipostat®** (Squibb) PoM

Tablets, all yellow, pravastatin sodium 10 mg, net price 28-tab pack = £15.05; 20 mg, 28-tab pack = £27.61; 40 mg, 28-tab pack = £27.61. Counselling, muscle effects, see notes above

## ROSUVASTATIN

**Indications** primary hypercholesterolaemia (type IIa including heterozygous familial hypercholesterolaemia), mixed dyslipidaemia (type IIb), or homozygous familial hypercholesterolaemia in patients who have not responded adequately to diet and other appropriate measures

**Cautions** see notes above; patients of Asian origin (see under Dose); max. dose 20 mg in patients with risk factors for myopathy or rhabdomyolysis (including personal or family history of muscular disorders or toxicity)

**Contra-indications** see notes above; renal impairment (Appendix 3)

**Side-effects** see notes above; also dizziness and asthenia; proteinuria; *rarely* jaundice, arthralgia, and polyneuropathy

**Dose**

- Initially 5–10 mg once daily increased if necessary at intervals of at least 4 weeks to 20 mg once daily; increased after further 4 weeks to 40 mg only in severe hypercholesterolaemia with high cardiovascular risk and under specialist supervision; ELDERLY initially 5 mg once daily; patient of Asian origin, initially 5 mg once daily increased if necessary to max. 20 mg daily

Note Initially 5 mg once daily with concomitant fibrate increased if necessary to max. 20 mg daily

**Crestor®** (AstraZeneca) ▼ PoM

Tablets, f/c, rosuvastatin (as calcium salt) 5 mg (yellow), net price 28-tab pack = £18.03; 10 mg (pink), 28-tab pack = £18.03; 20 mg (pink), 28-tab pack = £29.69; 40 mg (pink), 28-tab pack = £29.69. Counselling, muscle effects, see notes above

## SIMVASTATIN

**Indications** primary hypercholesterolaemia, homozygous familial hypercholesterolaemia or combined (mixed) hyperlipidaemia in patients who have not responded adequately to diet and other appropriate measures; prevention of cardiovascular events in patients with atherosclerotic cardiovascular disease or diabetes mellitus

**Cautions** see notes above; renal impairment (Appendix 3)

**Contra-indications** see notes above

**Side-effects** see notes above; also alopecia, anaemia, dizziness, peripheral neuropathy, asthenia, hepatitis, jaundice, pancreatitis

**Dose**

- Primary hypercholesterolaemia, combined hyperlipidaemia, 10–20 mg daily at night, adjusted at intervals of at least 4 weeks; usual range 10–80 mg once daily at night
- Homozygous familial hypercholesterolaemia, 40 mg daily at night *or* 80 mg daily in 3 divided doses (with largest dose at night)
- Prevention of cardiovascular events, initially 20–40 mg once daily at night, adjusted at intervals of at least 4 weeks; max. 80 mg once daily at night

Note Max. 10 mg daily with concomitant ciclosporin, danazol, fibrate or lipid-lowering dose of nicotinic acid. Max. 20 mg daily with concomitant amiodarone or verapamil. Max. 40 mg daily with diltiazem

[1] **Simvastatin** (Non-proprietary) PoM
Tablets, simvastatin 10 mg, net price 28-tab pack = £1.65, 20 mg, 28-tab pack = £1.48; 40 mg, 28-tab pack = £3.57; 80 mg, 28-tab pack = £20.29. Counselling, muscle effects, see notes above
Brands include *Simvador®*, *Simzal®*

[1] **Zocor®** (MSD) PoM
Tablets, all f/c, simvastatin 10 mg (peach), net price 28-tab pack = £18.03; 20 mg (tan), 28-tab pack = £29.69; 40 mg (red), 28-tab pack = £29.69; 80 mg (red), 28-tab pack = £29.69. Counselling, muscle effects, see notes above

### With ezetimibe

Note For hypercholesterolaemia in patients stabilised on the individual components in the same proportions, or for patients not adequately controlled by statin alone. The *Scottish Medicines Consortium* has advised (June 2005) that Inegy® is accepted for restricted use for patients not adequately controlled with a maximal dose of a statin. For cautions, contra-indications, and side-effects of ezetimibe, see Ezetimibe

**Inegy®** (MSD, Schering-Plough) ▼ PoM
Tablets, simvastatin 20 mg, ezetimibe 10 mg, net price 28-tab pack = £33.42; simvastatin 40 mg, ezetimibe 10 mg, 28-tab pack = £38.98; simvastatin 80 mg, ezetimibe 10 mg, 28-tab pack = £41.21. Counselling, muscle effects, see notes above

## Nicotinic acid group

The value of **nicotinic acid** is limited by its side-effects, especially vasodilatation. In doses of 1.5 to 3 g daily it lowers both cholesterol and triglyceride concentrations by inhibiting synthesis; it also increases HDL-cholesterol. Nicotinic acid is licensed for use with a statin if the statin alone cannot adequately control dyslipidaemia (raised LDL-cholesterol, triglyceridaemia, and low HDL-cholesterol); it can be used alone if the patient is intolerant of statins (for advice on treatment of dyslipidaemia, including use of combination treatment, see p. 133). The *Scottish Medicines Consortium* has advised (April 2004) that *Niaspan®* is not recommended for the treatment of hypercholesterolaemia and mixed dyslipidaemia; this is because of a lack of appropriate studies comparing *Niaspan®* with other lipid-regulating drugs.

**Acipimox** seems to have fewer side-effects than nicotinic acid but may be less effective in its lipid-modulating capabilities.

1. Simvastatin 10 mg tablets can be sold to the public to reduce risk of first coronary event in individuals at moderate risk of coronary heart disease (approx. 10–15% risk of major event in 10 years), max. daily dose 10 mg and pack size of 28 tablets; treatment should form part of a programme to reduce risk of coronary heart disease; a proprietary brand *Zocor Heart-Pro®* is on sale to the public

### ACIPIMOX

**Indications** hyperlipidaemias of types IIa, IIb, and IV in patients who have not responded adequately to diet and other appropriate measures

**Cautions** renal impairment (Appendix 3)

**Contra-indications** peptic ulcer; pregnancy (Appendix 4); breast-feeding (Appendix 5)

**Side-effects** vasodilatation, flushing, itching, rashes, urticaria, erythema; heartburn, epigastric pain, nausea, diarrhoea, headache, malaise, dry eyes; rarely angioedema, bronchospasm, anaphylaxis

**Dose**

- Usually 500–750 mg daily in divided doses

**Olbetam®** (Pharmacia) PoM
Capsules, brown/pink, acipimox 250 mg. Net price 90-cap pack = £46.33. Label: 21

### NICOTINIC ACID

**Indications** adjunct to statin in dyslipidaemia or used alone if statin not tolerated (see also p. 133)

**Cautions** unstable angina, acute myocardial infarction, diabetes mellitus, gout, history of peptic ulceration; hepatic impairment (Appendix 2); renal impairment; pregnancy (Appendix 4); **interactions:** Appendix 1 (nicotinic acid)

**Contra-indications** arterial bleeding; active peptic ulcer disease; breast-feeding

**Side-effects** diarrhoea, nausea, vomiting, abdominal pain, dyspepsia; flushing; pruritus, rash; *less commonly* tachycardia, palpitation, shortness of breath, peripheral oedema, headache, dizziness, increase in uric acid, hypophosphataemia, prolonged prothrombin time, and reduced platelet count; *rarely* hypotension, syncope, rhinitis, insomnia, reduced glucose tolerance, myalgia, myopathy, and myasthenia; *very rarely* anorexia, rhabdomyolysis

Note Prostaglandin-mediated symptoms (such as flushing) can be reduced by low initial doses taken with meals

**Dose**

- Initially 100–200 mg 3 times daily (see above), gradually increased over 2–4 weeks to 1–2 g 3 times daily

Note Doses of standard-release and modified-release formulations are **not** equivalent; when switching formulation initiate treatment with low dose and increase gradually as recommended

[1] **Nicotinic Acid** (Non-proprietary) PoM
Tablets, nicotinic acid 50 mg, net price 100 = £9.25. Label: 21

1. May be sold to the public unless max. daily dose exceeds 600 mg or if intended for treatment of hyperlipidaemia

2 Cardiovascular system

**Modified release**

**Niaspan** (Merck) PoM

Tablets, m/r, nicotinic acid 500 mg, net price 56-tab pack = £17.25; 750 mg, 56-tab pack = £26.25; 1 g, 56-tab pack = £29.50; 21-day starter pack of 7 × 375-mg tab with 7 × 500-mg tab and 7 × 750-mg tab = £14.00. Label: 21, 25

Dose 375 mg once daily at night (after a low-fat snack) for 1 week, then 500 mg once daily at night for 1 week, then 750 mg once daily at night for 1 week, then 1 g once daily at night for 4 weeks, increased if necessary in steps of 500 mg at intervals of at least 4 weeks to max. 2 g daily; usual maintenance dose 1–2 g once daily at night

## Omega-3 fatty acid compounds

Omega-3 fatty acid compounds may be used to reduce triglycerides, as an alternative to a fibrate and in addition to a statin, in patients with combined (mixed) hyperlipidaemia not adequately controlled with a statin alone. A triglyceride concentration exceeding 10 mmol/litre is associated with acute pancreatitis and lowering the concentration reduces this risk. There is little clinical trial evidence that the triglyceride lowering effect decreases the risk of cardiovascular disease.

### OMEGA-3-ACID ETHYL ESTERS

**Indications** adjunct to diet and statin in type IIb or III hypertriglyceridaemia; adjunct to diet in type IV hypertriglyceridaemia; adjunct in secondary prevention after myocardial infarction

**Cautions** haemorrhagic disorders, anticoagulant treatment (bleeding time increased); hepatic impairment (Appendix 2); pregnancy (Appendix 4)

**Contra-indications** breast-feeding (Appendix 5)

**Side-effects** gastro-intestinal disturbances; *less commonly* taste disturbances, dizziness, and hypersensitivity reactions; *rarely* hepatic disorders, headache, hyperglycaemia, acne, and rash; *very rarely* hypotension, nasal dryness, urticaria, and increased white cell count

**Dose**

- See under preparation below

**Omacor®** (Solvay)

Capsules, 1 g of omega-3-acid ethyl esters 90 containing eicosapentaenoic acid 460 mg and docosahexaenoic acid 380 mg, net price 28-cap pack = £13.89, 100-cap pack = £49.60. Label: 21

Dose hypertriglyceridaemia, initially 2 capsules daily with food, increased if necessary to 4 capsules daily

Secondary prevention after myocardial infarction, 1 capsule daily with food

### OMEGA-3-MARINE TRIGLYCERIDES

**Indications** adjunct in the reduction of plasma triglycerides in severe hypertriglyceridaemia

**Cautions** haemorrhagic disorders, anticoagulant treatment; aspirin-sensitive asthma; diabetes mellitus

**Side-effects** occasional nausea and belching

**Dose**

- See under preparations below

**Maxepa®** (Seven Seas)

Capsules, 1 g (approx. 1.1 mL) concentrated fish oils containing eicosapentaenoic acid 170 mg, docosahexaenoic acid 115 mg. Vitamin A content less than 100 units/g, vitamin D content less than 10 units/g, net price 200-cap pack = £27.28. Label: 21

Dose 5 capsules twice daily with food

Liquid, golden-coloured, concentrated fish oils containing eicosapentaenoic acid 170 mg, docosahexaenoic acid 115 mg/g (1.1 mL). Vitamin A content less than 100 units/g, vitamin D content less than 10 units/g, net price 150 mL = £20.46. Label: 21

Dose 5 mL twice daily with food

# 2.13 Local sclerosants

Ethanolamine oleate and sodium tetradecyl sulphate are used in sclerotherapy of varicose veins, and phenol is used in haemorrhoids (section 1.7.3).

### ETHANOLAMINE OLEATE
(Monoethanolamine Oleate)

**Indications** sclerotherapy of varicose veins

**Cautions** extravasation may cause necrosis of tissues

**Contra-indications** inability to walk, acute phlebitis, oral contraceptive use, obese legs

**Side-effects** allergic reactions (including anaphylaxis)

**Ethanolamine Oleate** PoM

Injection, ethanolamine oleate 5%, net price 2-mL amp = £2.62, 5-mL amp = £2.28

Dose by slow injection into empty isolated segment of vein, 2–5 mL divided between 3–4 sites; repeated at weekly intervals

### SODIUM TETRADECYL SULPHATE

**Indications** sclerotherapy of varicose veins

**Cautions** see under Ethanolamine Oleate

**Contra-indications** see under Ethanolamine Oleate

**Side-effects** see under Ethanolamine Oleate

**Fibro-Vein®** (STD Pharmaceutical) PoM

Injection, sodium tetradecyl sulphate 0.2%, net price 5-mL amp = £5.00; 0.5%, 2-mL amp = £2.60; 1%, 2-mL amp = £3.00; 3%, 2-mL amp = £3.70, 5-mL vial = £9.30

Dose by slow injection into empty isolated segment of vein, 0.1–1 mL according to site and condition being treated (consult product literature)

# 3 Respiratory system


**3.1 Bronchodilators** 140
3.1.1 Adrenoceptor agonists 144
3.1.1.1 Selective beta$_2$ agonists 144
3.1.1.2 Other adrenoceptor agonists 148
3.1.2 Antimuscarinic bronchodilators 148
3.1.3 Theophylline 149
3.1.4 Compound bronchodilator preparations 150
3.1.5 Peak flow meters, inhaler devices and nebulisers 151
**3.2 Corticosteroids** 154
**3.3 Cromoglicate and related therapy, leukotriene receptor antagonists, and omalizumab** 159
3.3.1 Cromoglicate and related therapy 159
3.3.2 Leukotriene receptor antagonists and omalizumab 160
**3.4 Antihistamines, hyposensitisation, and allergic emergencies** 161
3.4.1 Antihistamines 161
3.4.2 Hyposensitisation 164
3.4.3 Allergic emergencies 165
**3.5 Respiratory stimulants and pulmonary surfactants** 167
3.5.1 Respiratory stimulants 167
3.5.2 Pulmonary surfactants 167
**3.6 Oxygen** 168
**3.7 Mucolytics** 170
**3.8 Aromatic inhalations** 170
**3.9 Cough preparations** 171
3.9.1 Cough suppressants 171
3.9.2 Expectorant and demulcent cough preparations 172
**3.10 Systemic nasal decongestants** 172


This chapter includes advice on the drug management of the following:


acute severe asthma, p. 143
anaphylaxis, p. 165
angioedema, p. 165
chronic asthma, p. 141
chronic obstructive pulmonary disease, p. 143
croup, p. 143




## 3.1 Bronchodilators


**3.1.1 Adrenoceptor agonists**
**3.1.2 Antimuscarinic bronchodilators**
**3.1.3 Theophylline**
**3.1.4 Compound bronchodilator preparations**
**3.1.5 Peak flow meters, inhaler devices and nebulisers**


### Asthma

Drugs used in the management of asthma include beta$_2$ agonists (section 3.1.1), antimuscarinic bronchodilators (section 3.1.2), theophylline (section 3.1.3), corticosteroids (section 3.2), cromoglicate and nedocromil (section 3.3.1), and leukotriene receptor antagonists (section 3.3.2).

For tables outlining the management of chronic asthma and acute severe asthma see p. 141 and p. 142. For advice on the management of medical emergencies in dental practice, see p. 21.

### Administration of drugs for asthma

**Inhalation** This route delivers the drug directly to the airways; the dose is smaller than that for the drug given by mouth and side-effects are reduced. *Pressurised metered-dose inhalers* are an effective and convenient method of administering many drugs used for asthma. A spacer device (section 3.1.5) may improve drug delivery, particularly for young children and those who have difficulty using a pressurised metered-dose inhaler; spacers also reduce local adverse effects from inhaled corticosteroids. Breath-actuated inhalers and dry powder inhalers are also available.

*Solutions for nebulisation* are available for use in acute severe asthma. They are administered over 5–10 minutes from a nebuliser, usually driven by oxygen in hospital. Electric compressors are best suited to domiciliary use.

**Oral** The oral route is used when administration by inhalation is not possible. Systemic side-effects occur more frequently when a drug is given orally rather than by inhalation. Drugs given by mouth for the treatment of asthma include beta$_2$ agonists, corticosteroids, theophylline and leukotriene receptor antagonists.

**Parenteral** Drugs such as beta$_2$ agonists, corticosteroids, and aminophylline may be given by injection in acute severe asthma when administration by nebulisation is inadequate or inappropriate. If the patient is being treated in the community, urgent transfer to hospital should be arranged.

## MANAGEMENT OF CHRONIC ASTHMA IN ADULTS AND CHILDREN

Start at **step most appropriate** to initial severity

### Chronic asthma: adults and schoolchildren

**Step 1: occasional relief bronchodilators**

Inhaled short-acting $beta_2$ agonist as required (up to once daily)

NOTE. Move to step 2 if needed 3 times a week or more, or if night-time symptoms more than once a week or if exacerbation in the last 2 years requiring systemic corticosteroid or nebulised bronchodilator; check compliance and inhaler technique

**Step 2: regular inhaled preventer therapy**

Inhaled short-acting $beta_2$ agonist as required

*plus*

Regular standard-dose[1] inhaled corticosteroid (alternatives[2] are considerably less effective)

**Step 3: inhaled corticosteroids + long-acting inhaled $beta_2$ agonist**

Inhaled short-acting $beta_2$ agonist as required

*plus*

Regular standard-dose[1] inhaled corticosteroid

*plus*

Regular inhaled long-acting $beta_2$ agonist (salmeterol *or* formoterol) but discontinue long-acting $beta_2$ agonist in the absence of response

*If asthma not controlled*

Increase dose of inhaled corticosteroid to upper end of standard dose[1]

*If asthma still not controlled*

Add one of

- Leukotriene receptor antagonist
- Modified-release oral theophylline
- Modified-release oral $beta_2$ agonist

**Step 4: high-dose inhaled corticosteroids + regular bronchodilators**

Inhaled short-acting $beta_2$ agonist as required

*with*

Regular high-dose[3] inhaled corticosteroid

*plus*

Inhaled long-acting $beta_2$ agonist

*plus*

In adults 6-week sequential therapeutic trial of one or more of

- Leukotriene receptor antagonist
- Modified-release oral theophylline
- Modified-release oral $beta_2$ agonist

**Step 5: regular corticosteroid tablets**

Inhaled short-acting $beta_2$ agonist as required

*with*

Regular high-dose[3] inhaled corticosteroid

*and*

one or more long-acting bronchodilators (see step 4)

*plus*

Regular prednisolone tablets (as single daily dose)

NOTE. In addition to regular prednisolone, continue high-dose inhaled corticosteroid (in exceptional cases may exceed licensed doses); these patients should normally be referred to an asthma clinic

**Stepping down**

Review treatment every 3 months; if control achieved stepwise reduction may be possible; use lowest possible dose of corticosteroid; reduce dose of *inhaled* corticosteroid slowly (consider reduction every 3 months, decreasing dose by up to 50% each time) to the lowest dose which controls asthma

### Chronic asthma: children under 5 years[4]

**Step 1: occasional relief bronchodilators**

Short-acting $beta_2$ agonist as required (not more than once daily)

NOTE. Whenever possible inhaled (less effective and more side-effects when given by mouth); check compliance, technique and that inhaler device is appropriate

Move to step 2 if needed 3 times a week or more, or if night-time symptoms more than once a week or if exacerbation in last 2 years

**Step 2: regular preventer therapy**

Inhaled short-acting $beta_2$ agonist as required

*plus*

*Either* regular standard-dose[1] inhaled corticosteroid

*Or* (if inhaled corticosteroid cannot be used) leukotriene receptor antagonist (alternatives[2] are considerably less effective)

**Step 3: add-on therapy**

**Children 2–5 years:**

Inhaled short-acting $beta_2$ agonist as required

*plus*

Regular inhaled corticosteroid in standard dose[1]

*plus*

Leukotriene receptor antagonist

**Children under 2 years:**

Refer to respiratory paediatrician

**Step 4: persistent poor control**

Refer to respiratory paediatrician

**Stepping down**

Regularly review need for treatment

1. Standard-dose inhaled corticosteroids (given through metered dose inhaler) are beclometasone dipropionate or budesonide 100–400 micrograms (CHILD 100–200 micrograms) twice daily *or* fluticasone propionate 50–200 micrograms (CHILD 50–100 micrograms) twice daily *or* mometasone furoate (given through dry powder inhaler) 200 micrograms twice daily; initial dose according to severity of asthma; use large-volume spacer in children under 5 years
2. Alternatives to inhaled corticosteroid are leukotriene receptor antagonist, theophylline, and in adults, regular cromoglicate, and in children over 5 years, regular nedocromil
3. High-dose inhaled corticosteroids (given through metered dose inhaler) are beclometasone dipropionate or budesonide 0.8–2 mg daily (in divided doses) *or* fluticasone propionate 0.4–1 mg daily (in divided doses) *or* mometasone furoate (given through dry powder inhaler) up to 800 micrograms daily (in 2 divided doses); CHILD 5–12 years, beclometasone dipropionate or budesonide up to 400 micrograms twice daily *or* fluticasone propionate up to 200 micrograms twice daily; use a large-volume spacer
4. Lung-function measurements cannot be used to guide management in those under 5 years

Advice on the management of chronic asthma is based on the recommendations of the British Thoracic Society and Scottish Intercollegiate Guidelines Network (updated November 2005)

## MANAGEMENT OF ACUTE SEVERE ASTHMA IN GENERAL PRACTICE

### Moderate asthma exacerbation

— Peak flow >50–75% of predicted or best
— No features of acute severe asthma
— Increasing symptoms

Treat at home but response to treatment **must** be assessed before doctor leaves

*Treatment:*

High-flow oxygen if available

Salbutamol or terbutaline via large-volume spacer (4–6 puffs each inhaled separately; dose repeated every 10–20 minutes if necessary) or nebuliser

Monitor response 15–30 minutes after nebulisation

Give oral prednisolone 40–50 mg daily for at least 5 days and step up usual treatment

*Follow up*

Monitor symptoms and peak flow

Set up asthma action plan

Review in surgery within 48 hours

Modify treatment at review according to guidelines for chronic asthma (see Management of Chronic Asthma in Adults and Children)

**Important:** regard each emergency consultation as being for **acute severe asthma** until shown otherwise.

**Important:** failure to respond adequately **at any time** requires immediate referral to hospital.

### Acute severe asthma in adults

— Cannot complete sentences in one breath
— Pulse ≥ 110 beats/minute
— Respiration ≥ 25 breaths/minute
— Peak flow 33–50% of predicted or best

Seriously consider hospital admission if more than one of above features present

*Treatment:*

High-flow oxygen if available

Salbutamol or terbutaline via large-volume spacer (4–6 puffs each inhaled separately; dose repeated every 10–20 minutes if necessary) or nebuliser (oxygen driven if available)

Oral prednisolone 40–50 mg daily for at least 5 days (or i/v hydrocortisone 400 mg daily in 4 divided doses)

Monitor response 15–30 minutes after nebulisation

*If any signs of acute asthma persist:*

Arrange hospital admission

While awaiting ambulance repeat nebulised $beta_2$ agonist and give with nebulised ipratropium 500 micrograms

*Alternatively if symptoms have improved, respiration and pulse settling, and peak flow >50% of predicted or best:*

Step up usual treatment *and* continue prednisolone for at least 5 days

*Follow up*

Monitor symptoms and peak flow, set up asthma action plan, review in surgery within 24 hours, modify treatment at review (see Management of Chronic Asthma)

### Life-threatening asthma in adults

— Silent chest
— Cyanosis
— Feeble respiratory effort
— Bradycardia, exhaustion, arrhythmia, hypotension, confusion, or coma
— Peak flow <33% of predicted or best
— Arterial oxygen saturation <92%

Arrange **immediate** hospital admission

*Treatment:*

Oral prednisolone 40–50mg daily for at least 5 days (or i/v hydrocortisone 400 mg daily in 4 divided doses) (immediately)

Oxygen-driven nebuliser in ambulance

Nebulised[1] $beta_2$ agonist with nebulised ipratropium

**Stay with patient until ambulance arrives**

1. If nebuliser not available give 1 puff of $beta_2$ agonist using large-volume spacer and repeat 10–20 times

**Important:** patients with severe or life-threatening attacks may not be distressed and may not have all these abnormalities; the presence of any should alert doctor.

### Acute episodes or exacerbations of asthma in young children in primary care

Mild/moderate episode in young children
– short-acting $beta_2$ agonist from metered dose inhaler *via* large-volume spacer (and face mask in very young), up to 10 puffs; alternatively give by nebuliser
– if favourable response (respiratory rate reduced, reduced use of accessory muscles, improved 'behaviour' pattern), repeat inhaled $beta_2$ agonist as needed
– start short course of oral prednisolone for 3 days (under 2 years 10 mg; 2–5 years 20 mg; over 5 years 30–40 mg daily; those already on prednisolone tablets 2 mg/kg up to max. 60 mg)
– consider i/v hydrocortisone in those who are unable to retain oral prednisolone

If unresponsive or relapse within 3–4 hours:
– immediately refer to hospital
– give nebulised $beta_2$ agonist with nebulised ipratropium 250 micrograms every 20–30 minutes
– give high-flow oxygen *via* face mask

### Signs of acute asthma in children

*Acute severe asthma:*
– too breathless to talk
– too breathless to feed
– respiration >50 breaths/minute (> 30/minute in children over 5 years)
– pulse >130 beats/minute (>120 beats/minute in children over 5 years)
– in younger children, use of accessory muscles of breathing
– in older children, peak flow ≤50% of predicted or best

*Life-threatening features:*
– cyanosis, silent chest, or poor respiratory effort
– exhaustion
– agitation, hypotension, confusion, reduced level of consciousness, or coma
– in older children, peak flow <33% of predicted or best

Advice on the management of acute asthma is based on the recommendations of the British Thoracic Society and Scottish Intercollegiate Guidelines Network (updated November 2005)

## Pregnancy and breast-feeding

It is particularly important that asthma should be well controlled during pregnancy; where this is achieved asthma has no important effects on pregnancy, labour, or on the fetus. Drugs for asthma should preferably be administered by inhalation to minimise exposure of the fetus.

Severe exacerbations of asthma can have an adverse effect on pregnancy and should be treated promptly with conventional therapy, including oral or parenteral administration of a corticosteroid and nebulisation of a $beta_2$ agonist; prednisolone is the preferred corticosteroid for oral administration since very little of the drug reaches the fetus. Oxygen should be given immediately to maintain arterial oxygen saturation above 95% and prevent maternal and fetal hypoxia. Inhaled drugs, theophylline, and prednisolone can be taken as normal during breast-feeding.

## Acute severe asthma

Severe asthma can be fatal and **must** be treated promptly and energetically. It is characterised by persistent dyspnoea poorly relieved by bronchodilators, exhaustion, a high pulse rate (usually over 110/minute), and a very low peak expiratory flow. As asthma becomes more severe, wheezing may be absent. Such patients should be given **oxygen** (if available) and **salbutamol** or **terbutaline** by nebuliser. This should be followed by a large dose of a **corticosteroid** (section 6.3.2)—for adults, prednisolone 30–60 mg by mouth or hydrocortisone 200 mg (preferably as sodium succinate) intravenously; for children, prednisolone 1–2 mg/kg by mouth (1–4 years max. 20 mg, 5–15 years max. 40 mg) or hydrocortisone 100 mg (preferably as sodium succinate) intravenously; if vomiting occurs, the parenteral route may be preferred for the first dose. For a table outlining the management of acute severe asthma, see p. 142.

If there is little response **ipratropium** by nebuliser (section 3.1.2) should be considered. Most patients do not require and do not benefit from the addition of intravenous aminophylline or of a $beta_2$ agonist; both cause more adverse effects than nebulised $beta_2$ agonists. Nevertheless, an occasional patient who has not been taking theophylline, may benefit from a slow intravenous infusion of aminophylline. Patients with severe asthma may be helped by **magnesium sulphate** [unlicensed indication] but evidence of benefit is limited; it may be given by intravenous infusion of magnesium sulphate 1.2–2 g over 20 minutes or by nebulisation of 2.5 mL isotonic magnesium sulphate (60 mg/mL) in 2.5 mL salbutamol nebuliser solution (1 mg/mL).

Treatment of these patients is safer in hospital where resuscitation facilities are immediately available. Treatment should **never** be delayed for investigations, patients should **never** be sedated, and the possibility of a pneumothorax should be considered.

If the patient deteriorates despite appropriate pharmacological treatment, intermittent positive pressure ventilation may be needed.

## Chronic obstructive pulmonary disease

Smoking cessation (section 4.10) reduces the progressive decline in lung function in chronic obstructive pulmonary disease (COPD, chronic bronchitis, or emphysema). Infection can complicate chronic obstructive pulmonary disease and may be prevented by vaccination (pneumococcal vaccine and influenza vaccine, section 14.4).

A trial of a high-dose inhaled corticosteroid *or* an oral corticosteroid is recommended for patients with moderate airflow obstruction to ensure that asthma has not been overlooked.

Chronic obstructive pulmonary disease may be helped by an inhaled **short-acting $beta_2$ agonist** (section 3.1.1.1) or a **short-acting antimuscarinic bronchodilator** (section 3.1.2) used as required.

When the airways obstruction is more severe, a regular inhaled **antimuscarinic bronchodilator** (section 3.1.2) should be added. In those who remain symptomatic or have two or more exacerbations in a year, a **long-acting $beta_2$ agonist** should be added. If symptoms persist despite a trial of short-acting bronchodilators or a long-acting $beta_2$ agonist or a **long-acting antimuscarinic bronchodilator** or if the patient is unable to use inhaled therapy, theophylline (section 3.1.3) can be used.

A mucolytic drug (section 3.7) may be considered for a patient with a chronic productive cough.

In moderate or severe chronic obstructive pulmonary disease, a combination of a long-acting $beta_2$ agonist and an inhaled corticosteroid (section 3.2) should be tried. Combination treatment should be discontinued if there is no benefit after 4 weeks.

Long-term **oxygen** therapy (section 3.6) prolongs survival in patients with severe chronic obstructive pulmonary disease and hypoxaemia.

In an exacerbation of chronic obstructive pulmonary disease, bronchodilator therapy can be administered through a nebuliser if necessary and oxygen given if appropriate. A short course of oral corticosteroid (section 3.2) should be given if increased breathlessness interferes with daily activities. Antibacterial treatment (Table 1, section 5.1) is required when the sputum becomes purulent or if there are other signs of infection.

## Croup

Mild croup requires no specific treatment and can be managed in the community. More severe croup (or mild croup that might cause complications) calls for hospital admission; a single dose of a corticosteroid (e.g. dexamethasone 150 micrograms/kg by mouth, section 6.3.2) may be administered before transfer to hospital. In hospital, dexamethasone 150 micrograms/kg (by mouth or by injection) or budesonide 2 mg (by nebulisation, section 3.2) will often reduce symptoms; the dose may need to be repeated after 12 hours if necessary. For severe croup not effectively controlled with corticosteroid treatment, nebulised adrenaline solution 1 in 1000 (1 mg/mL) may be given with close clinical monitoring in a dose of 400 micrograms/kg (max. 5 mg) repeated after 30 minutes if necessary; the effects of nebulised adrenaline last 2–3 hours and the child needs to be monitored carefully for recurrence of the obstruction.

## 3.1.1 Adrenoceptor agonists (Sympathomimetics)

**3.1.1.1 Selective beta$_2$ agonists**
**3.1.1.2 Other adrenoceptor agonists**

The selective beta$_2$ agonists (selective beta$_2$-adrenoceptor agonists, selective beta$_2$ stimulants) (section 3.1.1.1) such as salbutamol or terbutaline are the safest and most effective short-acting beta$_2$ agonists for asthma. Less selective beta$_2$ agonists such as orciprenaline (section 3.1.1.2) should be avoided whenever possible.

Adrenaline (epinephrine) (which has both alpha- and beta-adrenoceptor agonist properties) is used in the emergency management of allergic and anaphylactic reactions (section 3.4.3) and in the management of croup (see above).

### 3.1.1.1 Selective beta$_2$ agonists

Selective beta$_2$ agonists produce bronchodilation. A short-acting beta$_2$ agonist is used for immediate relief of asthma symptoms while a long-acting beta$_2$ agonist is generally added to an inhaled corticosteroid in patients requiring prophylactic treatment.

**Short-acting beta$_2$ agonists** Mild to moderate symptoms of asthma respond rapidly to the inhalation of a selective short-acting beta$_2$ agonist such as **salbutamol** or **terbutaline**. If beta$_2$ agonist inhalation is needed more often than once daily, prophylactic treatment should be considered, using a stepped approach as outlined on p. 141; regular treatment with a short-acting beta$_2$ agonist provides no clinical benefit.

A short-acting beta$_2$ agonist inhaled immediately before exertion reduces exercise-induced asthma; however, frequent exercise-induced asthma probably reflects poor overall control and calls for reassessment of asthma treatment.

**Long-acting beta$_2$ agonists** **Formoterol** (eformoterol) and **salmeterol** are longer-acting beta$_2$ agonists which are administered by inhalation. Added to regular inhaled corticosteroid treatment, they have a role in the long-term control of chronic asthma (see Chronic Asthma table, p. 141) and they can be useful in nocturnal asthma. Salmeterol should not be used for the relief of an asthma attack; it has a slower onset of action than salbutamol or terbutaline. Formoterol is licensed for short-term symptom relief and for the prevention of exercise-induced bronchospasm; its speed of onset of action is similar to that of salbutamol.

When used without an inhaled corticosteroid, salmeterol has been associated with rare life-threatening attacks of asthma and high doses of formoterol (e.g. 24 micrograms twice daily) may be associated with an increase in severe exacerbation of asthma. Therefore, a long-acting beta$_2$ agonist should be *added* to existing corticosteroid treatment and not replace it. Lower doses of a long-acting beta$_2$ agonist are effective for most patients and should be tried first.

Chronic Asthma table, see p. 141
Acute Severe Asthma table, see p. 142

**Inhalation** *Pressurised-metered dose inhalers* are an effective and convenient method of drug administration in mild to moderate asthma. A spacer device (section 3.1.5) may improve drug delivery. At recommended inhaled doses the duration of action of salbutamol, terbutaline and fenoterol is about 3 to 5 hours and for salmeterol and formoterol 12 hours. The **dose**, the frequency, and the maximum number of inhalations in 24 hours of the beta$_2$ agonist should be **stated explicitly** to the patient. The patient should be advised to seek medical advice when the prescribed dose of beta$_2$ agonist fails to provide the usual degree of symptomatic relief because this usually indicates a worsening of the asthma and the patient may require a prophylactic drug such as an inhaled corticosteroid (see Chronic Asthma table, p. 141).

*Nebuliser (or respirator) solutions* of salbutamol and terbutaline are used for the treatment of acute asthma in hospital or in general practice. Patients with a severe attack of asthma should preferably have oxygen during nebulisation since beta$_2$ agonists can increase arterial hypoxaemia. For the use of nebulisers in chronic obstructive pulmonary disease, see section 3.1.5. The dose given by nebuliser is substantially higher than that given by inhaler. Patients should therefore be warned that it is dangerous to exceed the prescribed dose and they should seek medical advice if they fail to respond to the usual dose of the respirator solution. See also guidelines in section 3.1.5.

**CFC-free inhalers** Chlorofluorocarbon (CFC) propellants in pressurised metered-dose inhalers are being replaced by hydrofluoroalkane (HFA) propellants. Patients receiving CFC-free inhalers should be reassured about the efficacy of the new inhalers and counselled that the aerosol may feel and taste different; any difficulty with the new inhaler should be discussed with the doctor or pharmacist.

**Oral** Oral preparations of beta$_2$ agonists may be used by patients who cannot manage the inhaled route. They are sometimes used for children, but inhaled beta$_2$ agonists are more effective and have fewer side-effects. The longer-acting oral preparations including bambuterol may be of value in nocturnal asthma but they have a limited role and inhaled long-acting beta$_2$ agonists are usually preferred.

**Parenteral** Salbutamol or terbutaline are given by intravenous infusion for severe asthma. The regular use of beta$_2$ agonists by the subcutaneous route is not recommended since the evidence of benefit is uncertain and it may be difficult to withdraw such treatment once started. Patients supplied with a selective beta$_2$ agonist injection for severe attacks should be advised to attend hospital immediately after using the injection, for further assessment. Beta$_2$ agonists may also be given by intramuscular injection.

**Children** Selective beta$_2$ agonists are useful even in children under the age of 18 months. They are most effective by the inhaled route; a pressurised metered-dose inhaler should be used with a spacer device in children under 5 years (see NICE guidance, section 3.1.5). A beta$_2$ agonist may also be given by mouth but administration by inhalation is preferred; a long-acting inhaled beta$_2$ agonist may be used where appropriate (see Chronic Asthma table, p. 141). In severe attacks nebulisation using a selective beta$_2$ agonist or ipratropium is advisable (see also Asthma tables, p. 141 and p. 142).

**Cautions** Beta$_2$ agonists should be used with caution in hyperthyroidism, cardiovascular disease, arrhythmias, susceptibility to QT-interval prolongation, and hypertension. If high doses are needed during pregnancy they should be given by inhalation because a parenteral beta$_2$ agonist can affect the myometrium (section 7.1.3) and possibly cause cardiac problems; see also Pregnancy and Breast-feeding, section 3.1. Beta$_2$ agonists should be used with caution in diabetes—monitor blood glucose (risk of ketoacidosis, especially when beta$_2$ agonist given intravenously). **Interactions:** Appendix 1 (sympathomimetics, beta$_2$)

**Hypokalaemia** The CSM has advised that potentially serious hypokalaemia may result from beta$_2$ agonist therapy. Particular caution is required in severe asthma, because this effect may be potentiated by concomitant treatment with theophylline and its derivatives, corticosteroids, and diuretics, and by hypoxia. Plasma-potassium concentration should therefore be monitored in severe asthma

**Side-effects** Side-effects of the beta$_2$ agonists include fine tremor (particularly in the hands), nervous tension, headache, muscle cramps, and palpitations. Other side-effects include tachycardia and arrhythmias and disturbances of sleep and behaviour in children. Paradoxical bronchospasm, urticaria, angioedema, hypotension, and collapse have also been reported. Beta$_2$ agonists are associated with hypokalaemia after high doses (for CSM advice see under Cautions). Pain may occur on intramuscular injection.

## SALBUTAMOL

**Indications** asthma and other conditions associated with reversible airways obstruction; premature labour (section 7.1.3)

**Cautions** see notes above

**Side-effects** see notes above

**Dose**

- By mouth (but use by inhalation preferred), 4 mg (elderly and sensitive patients initially 2 mg) 3–4 times daily; max. single dose 8 mg (but unlikely to provide much extra benefit or to be tolerated); CHILD under 2 years 100 micrograms/kg 4 times daily [unlicensed]; 2–6 years 1–2 mg 3–4 times daily, 6–12 years 2 mg 3–4 times daily
- By subcutaneous *or* intramuscular injection, 500 micrograms, repeated every 4 hours if necessary
- By slow intravenous injection, 250 micrograms, repeated if necessary
- By intravenous infusion, initially 5 micrograms/minute, adjusted according to response and heart-rate usually in range 3–20 micrograms/minute, or more if necessary; CHILD 1 month–12 years 0.1–1 microgram/kg/minute [unlicensed]
- By aerosol inhalation, 100–200 micrograms (1–2 puffs); for persistent symptoms up to 4 times daily (but see also Chronic Asthma table); CHILD 100 micrograms (1 puff), increased to 200 micrograms (2 puffs) if necessary; for persistent symptoms up to 4 times daily (but see also Chronic Asthma table)

  Prophylaxis in exercise-induced bronchospasm, 200 micrograms (2 puffs); CHILD 100 micrograms (1 puff), increased to 200 micrograms (2 puffs) if necessary
- By inhalation of powder (for *Ventolin Accuhaler®* and *Asmasal®* dose see under preparation), 200–400 micrograms; for persistent symptoms up to 4 times daily (but see also Chronic Asthma table); CHILD 200 micrograms

  Prophylaxis in exercise-induced bronchospasm, 400 micrograms; CHILD 200 micrograms

  **Note** Bioavailability appears to be lower, so recommended doses for dry powder inhalers are twice those in a metered inhaler
- By inhalation of nebulised solution, chronic bronchospasm unresponsive to conventional therapy and severe acute asthma, ADULT and CHILD over 18 months 2.5 mg, repeated up to 4 times daily; may be increased to 5 mg if necessary, but medical assessment should be considered since alternative therapy may be indicated; CHILD under 18 months, [unlicensed] (transient hypoxaemia may occur—consider supplemental oxygen), 1.25–2.5 mg up to 4 times daily but more frequent administration may be needed in severe cases

### Oral

**Salbutamol** (Non-proprietary) PoM

Tablets, salbutamol (as sulphate) 2 mg, net price 28-tab pack = £1.92; 4 mg, 28-tab pack = £2.23

Oral solution, salbutamol (as sulphate) 2 mg/5 mL, net price 150 mL = £1.37

Brands include *Salapin®* (sugar-free)

**Ventmax® SR** (Trinity) PoM

Capsules, m/r, salbutamol (as sulphate) 4 mg (green/grey), net price 56-cap pack = £8.57; 8 mg (white), 56-cap pack = £10.28. Label: 25

Dose 8 mg twice daily; CHILD 3–12 years 4 mg twice daily

**Ventolin®** (A&H) PoM

Syrup, sugar-free, salbutamol (as sulphate) 2 mg/5 mL, net price 150 mL = 60p

**Volmax®** (A&H) PoM

Tablets, m/r, salbutamol (as sulphate) 4 mg, net price 56-tab pack = £9.81; 8 mg, 56-tab pack = £11.77. Label: 25

Dose 8 mg twice daily; CHILD 3–12 years 4 mg twice daily

### Parenteral

**Ventolin®** (A&H) PoM

Injection, salbutamol (as sulphate) 500 micrograms/mL, net price 1-mL amp = 40p

Solution for intravenous infusion, salbutamol (as sulphate) 1 mg/mL. Dilute before use. Net price 5-mL amp = £2.58

### Inhalation

**Counselling** Advise patients not to exceed prescribed dose and to follow manufacturer's directions; if a previously effective dose of inhaled salbutamol fails to provide at least 3 hours relief, a doctor's advice should be obtained as soon as possible.

Patients receiving CFC-free inhalers should be reassured about their efficacy and counselled that aerosol may feel and taste different

**Salbutamol** (Non-proprietary) PoM

Aerosol inhalation, salbutamol 100 micrograms/metered inhalation, net price 200-dose unit = £2.91. Counselling, dose

Excipients include CFC propellants

Aerosol inhalation, salbutamol (as sulphate) 100 micrograms/metered inhalation, net price 200-

dose unit = £2.99. Counselling, dose, change to CFC-free inhaler
Excipients include HFA-134a (a non-CFC propellant), alcohol
Brands include *Salamol®*
Note Can be supplied against a generic prescription but if CFC-free not specified will be reimbursed at price for CFC-containing inhaler

Dry powder for inhalation, salbutamol 100 micrograms/metered inhalation, net price 200-dose unit = £3.46; 200 micrograms/metered inhalation, 100-dose unit = £5.05, 200-dose unit = £6.92. Counselling, dose
Brands include *Easyhaler® Salbutamol, Pulvinal® Salbutamol*

Inhalation powder, *hard capsule* (for use with *Cyclohaler®* device), salbutamol 200 micrograms, net price 120-cap pack = £4.78; 400 micrograms, 120-cap pack = £8.08
Brands include *Salbutamol Cyclocaps®*

Nebuliser solution, salbutamol (as sulphate) 1 mg/mL, net price 20 × 2.5 mL (2.5 mg) = £1.99; 2 mg/mL, 20 × 2.5 mL (5 mg) = £3.98. May be diluted with sterile sodium chloride 0.9%
Brands include *Salamol Steri-Neb®*

**Airomir®** (IVAX) PoM
Aerosol inhalation, salbutamol (as sulphate) 100 micrograms/metered inhalation, net price 200-dose unit = £1.97. Counselling, dose, change to CFC-free inhaler
Excipients include HFA-134a (a non-CFC propellant), alcohol
Note Can be supplied against a generic prescription but if 'CFC-free' not specified will be reimbursed at price for CFC-containing inhaler

Autohaler (breath-actuated aerosol inhalation), salbutamol (as sulphate) 100 micrograms/metered inhalation, net price 200-dose unit = £6.02. Counselling, dose, change to CFC-free inhaler
Excipients include HFA-134a (a non-CFC propellant), alcohol

**Asmasal Clickhaler®** (Celltech) PoM
Dry powder for inhalation, salbutamol (as sulphate) 95 micrograms/metered inhalation, net price 200-dose unit = £5.88. Counselling, dose
Dose acute bronchospasm 1–2 puffs
Persistent symptoms, 2 puffs 3–4 times daily
Prophylaxis in exercise-induced bronchospasm, 2 puffs

**Salamol Easi-Breathe®** (IVAX) PoM
Aerosol inhalation , salbutamol 100 micrograms/metered inhalation, net price 200-dose breath-actuated unit = £1.58 Counselling, dose
Excipients include alcohol, HFA-134a (a non-CFC propellant)

**Ventodisks®** (A&H) PoM
Dry powder for inhalation, disks containing 8 blisters of salbutamol (as sulphate) 200 micrograms/blister, net price 15 disks with *Diskhaler®* device = £6.98, 15-disk refill = £6.45; 400 micrograms/blister, 15 disks with *Diskhaler®* device = £11.83, 15-disk refill = £11.29. Counselling, dose

**Ventolin®** (A&H) PoM
Accuhaler® (dry powder for inhalation), disk containing 60 blisters of salbutamol (as sulphate) 200 micrograms/blister with *Accuhaler®* device, net price = £5.12. Counselling, dose
Dose by inhalation of powder, 200 micrograms; for persistent symptoms up to 4 times daily (but see also Chronic Asthma table); CHILD 200 micrograms
Prophylaxis in allergen- or exercise-induced bronchospasm, 200 micrograms

Evohaler® *aerosol inhalation*, salbutamol (as sulphate) 100 micrograms/metered inhalation, net price 200-dose unit = £1.50. Counselling, dose, change to CFC-free inhaler
Excipients include HFA-134a (a non-CFC propellant)
Note Can be supplied against a generic prescription but if CFC-free not specified will be reimbursed at price for CFC-containing inhaler

Nebules® (for use with nebuliser), salbutamol (as sulphate) 1 mg/mL, net price 20 × 2.5 mL (2.5 mg) = £1.75; 2 mg/mL, 20 × 2.5 mL (5 mg) = £2.95. May be diluted with sterile sodium chloride 0.9% if administration time in excess of 10 minutes is required

Respirator solution (for use with a nebuliser or ventilator), salbutamol (as sulphate) 5 mg/mL. Net price 20 mL = £2.27 (hosp. only). May be diluted with sterile sodium chloride 0.9%

### Compound preparations

For some **compound preparations** containing salbutamol, see section 3.1.4

Chronic Asthma table, see p. 141
Acute Severe Asthma table, see p. 142

## TERBUTALINE SULPHATE

**Indications** asthma and other conditions associated with reversible airways obstruction; premature labour (section 7.1.3)
**Cautions** see notes above
**Side-effects** see notes above
**Dose**
- By mouth, initially 2.5 mg 3 times daily for 1–2 weeks, then up to 5 mg 3 times daily
  CHILD 75 micrograms/kg 3 times daily; 7–15 years 2.5 mg 2–3 times daily
- By subcutaneous, intramuscular, *or* slow intravenous injection, 250–500 micrograms up to 4 times daily; CHILD 2–15 years 10 micrograms/kg to a max. of 300 micrograms
- By continuous intravenous infusion as a solution containing 3–5 micrograms/mL, 1.5–5 micrograms/minute for 8–10 hours; reduce dose for children
- By aerosol inhalation, ADULT and CHILD 250–500 micrograms (1–2 puffs); for persistent symptoms up to 3–4 times daily (but see also Chronic Asthma table)
- By inhalation of powder (*Turbohaler®*), 500 micrograms (1 inhalation); for persistent symptoms up to 4 times daily (but see also Chronic Asthma table)
- By inhalation of nebulised solution, 5–10 mg 2–4 times daily; additional doses may be necessary in severe acute asthma; CHILD, up to 3 years 2 mg, 3–6 years 3 mg; 6–8 years 4 mg, over 8 years 5 mg, 2–4 times daily

### Oral and parenteral

**Bricanyl®** (AstraZeneca) PoM
Tablets, scored, terbutaline sulphate 5 mg. Net price 20 = 82p

Syrup, sugar-free, terbutaline sulphate 1.5 mg/5 mL. Net price 300 mL = £2.60

Injection, terbutaline sulphate 500 micrograms/mL. Net price 1-mL amp = 30p; 5-mL amp = £1.40

**Inhalation**

Counselling Advise patients not to exceed prescribed dose and to follow manufacturer's directions; if a previously effective dose of inhaled terbutaline fails to provide at least 3 hours relief, a doctor's advice should be obtained as soon as possible

**Bricanyl®** (AstraZeneca) PoM

Turbohaler® (= dry powder inhaler), terbutaline sulphate 500 micrograms/metered inhalation. Net price 100-dose unit = £6.92. Counselling, dose

Respules® (= single-dose units for nebulisation), terbutaline sulphate 2.5 mg/mL. Net price 20 × 2-mL units (5-mg) = £4.04

## BAMBUTEROL HYDROCHLORIDE

Note Bambuterol is a pro-drug of terbutaline

**Indications** asthma and other conditions associated with reversible airways obstruction

**Cautions** see notes above; renal impairment (Appendix 3); hepatic impairment (avoid if severe); manufacturer advises avoid in pregnancy

**Side-effects** see notes above

**Dose**

- 20 mg once daily at bedtime if patient has previously tolerated $beta_2$ agonists; other patients, initially 10 mg once daily at bedtime, increased if necessary after 1–2 weeks to 20 mg once daily; CHILD not recommended

**Bambec®** (AstraZeneca) PoM

Tablets, both scored, bambuterol hydrochloride 10 mg, net price 28-tab pack = £12.05; 20 mg, 28-tab pack = £13.14

## FENOTEROL HYDROBROMIDE

**Indications** reversible airways obstruction

**Cautions** see notes above

**Side-effects** see notes above

**Compound preparations**

For **compound preparation** containing fenoterol, see section 3.1.4

## FORMOTEROL FUMARATE
(Eformoterol fumarate)

**Indications** reversible airways obstruction (including nocturnal asthma and prevention of exercise-induced bronchospasm) in patients requiring long-term regular bronchodilator therapy, see also Chronic Asthma table, p. 141; chronic obstructive pulmonary disease

**Cautions** see notes above; severe liver cirrhosis (Appendix 2); pregnancy (Appendix 4 and notes above); breast-feeding (Appendix 5)

**Side-effects** see notes above; oropharyngeal irritation, taste disturbances, rash, insomnia, nausea and pruritus also reported; **important:** potential for paradoxical bronchospasm (calling for discontinuation and alternative therapy)

**Dose**

- See under preparations below

Counselling Advise patients not to exceed prescribed dose, and to follow manufacturer's directions; if a previously effective dose of inhaled formoterol fails to provide adequate relief, a doctor's advice should be obtained as soon as possible

**Atimos Modulite®** (Trinity-Chiesi) ▼ PoM

Aerosol inhalation, formoterol fumerate 10.1 micrograms/metered inhalation, net price 100-dose unit = £31.28. Counselling, dose

Dose by aerosol inhalation, asthma, ADULT and CHILD over 12 years, 10.1 micrograms twice daily, increased to max. 20.2 micrograms twice daily in more severe airways obstruction

Note. Each metered inhalation of *Atimos Modulite® 12* delivers 10.1 micrograms formoterol fumarate

**Foradil®** (Novartis) PoM

Dry powder for inhalation, formoterol fumarate 12 micrograms/capsule, net price 60-dose unit (with inhaler device) = £26.57. Counselling, dose

Dose by inhalation of powder, asthma, ADULT and CHILD over 5 years, 12 micrograms twice daily, increased to 24 micrograms twice daily in more severe airways obstruction

Chronic obstructive pulmonary disease, 12 micrograms twice daily

**Oxis®** (AstraZeneca) PoM

Turbohaler® (= dry powder inhaler), formoterol fumarate 4.5 micrograms/metered inhalation, net price 60-dose unit = £24.80; 9 micrograms/metered inhalation, 60-dose unit = £24.80. Counselling, dose

Dose by inhalation of powder, asthma, 4.5–9 micrograms 1–2 times daily, increased to 18 micrograms twice daily in more severe airways obstruction; for short-term symptom relief (but not acute asthma) additional doses may be taken to max. 54 micrograms daily (max. single dose 27 micrograms); reassess treatment if additional doses required on more than 2 days a week

CHILD over 6 years, 9 micrograms 1–2 times daily, max. 18 micrograms daily

Prevention of exercise-induced bronchospasm ADULT and CHILD over 6 years, 9 micrograms before exercise

Chronic obstructive pulmonary disease, 9 micrograms 1–2 times daily; max. 36 micrograms daily (max. single dose 18 micrograms)

Note Each metered inhalation of *Oxis® 6 Turbohaler®* delivers 4.5 micrograms formoterol fumarate; each metered inhalation of *Oxis® 12 Turbohaler®* delivers 9 micrograms formoterol fumarate

## SALMETEROL

**Indications** reversible airways obstruction (including nocturnal asthma and prevention of exercise-induced bronchospasm) in patients requiring long-term regular bronchodilator therapy, see also Chronic Asthma table, p. 141; chronic obstructive pulmonary disease

Note Not for immediate relief of acute asthma attacks; existing corticosteroid therapy should not be reduced or withdrawn

**Cautions** see notes above

**Side-effects** see notes above; **important:** potential for paradoxical bronchospasm (calling for discontinuation and alternative therapy)

**Dose**

- By inhalation, asthma, 50 micrograms (2 puffs or 1 blister) twice daily; up to 100 micrograms (4 puffs or 2 blisters) twice daily in more severe airways obstruction; CHILD over 4 years, 50 micrograms (2 puffs or 1 blister) twice daily

  Chronic obstructive pulmonary disease 50 micrograms (2 puffs or 1 blister) twice daily

Counselling Advise patients that salmeterol should **not** be used for relief of acute attacks, not to exceed prescribed dose, and to follow manufacturer's directions; if a previously effective dose of inhaled salmeterol fails to provide adequate relief, a doctor's advice should be obtained as soon as possible

**Serevent®** (A&H) PoM

Accuhaler® (dry powder for inhalation), disk containing 60 blisters of salmeterol (as xinafoate) 50 micrograms/blister with *Accuhaler®* device, net price = £29.26. Counselling, dose

Aerosol inhalation, salmeterol (as xinafoate) 25 micrograms/metered inhalation, net price 120-dose unit = £29.26. Counselling, dose
Excipients include CFC propellants

Diskhaler® (dry powder for inhalation), disks containing 4 blisters of salmeterol (as xinafoate) 50 micrograms/blister, net price 15 disks with *Diskhaler®* device = £35.79, 15-disk refill = £35.15. Counselling, dose

### 3.1.1.2 Other adrenoceptor agonists

Ephedrine and the partially selective beta agonist, orciprenaline, are less suitable and less safe for use as bronchodilators than the selective $beta_2$ agonists, because they are more likely to cause arrhythmias and other side-effects. They should be avoided whenever possible.

**Adrenaline (epinephrine) injection** (1 in 1000) is used in the emergency treatment of acute allergic and anaphylactic reactions (section 3.4.3). Adrenaline solution (1 in 1000) is used by nebulisation in the management of severe croup (section 3.1).

#### EPHEDRINE HYDROCHLORIDE

**Indications** reversible airways obstruction, but see notes above

**Cautions** hyperthyroidism, diabetes mellitus, ischaemic heart disease, hypertension, renal impairment, elderly; prostatic hypertrophy (risk of acute retention); interaction with MAOIs a disadvantage; **interactions:** Appendix 1 (sympathomimetics)

**Side-effects** tachycardia, anxiety, restlessness, insomnia common; also tremor, arrhythmias, dry mouth, cold extremities

**Dose**

- 15–60 mg 3 times daily; CHILD up to 1 year 7.5 mg 3 times daily, 1–5 years 15 mg 3 times daily, 6–12 years 30 mg 3 times daily

[1] **Ephedrine Hydrochloride** (Non-proprietary) PoM
Tablets, ephedrine hydrochloride 15 mg, net price 28 = £1.70; 30 mg, 28 = £1.76

1. For exemptions see *Medicines, Ethics and Practice*, No. 29, London, Pharmaceutical Press, 2005 (and subsequent editions as available)

#### ORCIPRENALINE SULPHATE

**Indications** reversible airways obstruction, but see notes above

**Cautions** see section 3.1.1.1 and notes above; **interactions:** Appendix 1 (sympathomimetics)

**Side-effects** see section 3.1.1.1 and notes above

**Dose**

- 20 mg 4 times daily; CHILD up to 1 year 5–10 mg 3 times daily, 1–3 years 5–10 mg 4 times daily, 3–12 years 40–60 mg daily in divided doses

**Alupent®** (Boehringer Ingelheim) PoM
Syrup, sugar-free, orciprenaline sulphate 10 mg/5 mL, net price 300 mL = £6.75

## 3.1.2 Antimuscarinic bronchodilators

**Ipratropium** can provide short-term relief in chronic asthma, but short-acting $beta_2$ agonists act more quickly and are preferred. Ipratropium by nebulisation may be added to other standard treatment in life-threatening asthma or where acute asthma fails to improve with standard therapy (see Acute Severe Asthma table, p. 142).

Antimuscarinic bronchodilators are effective in chronic obstructive pulmonary disease. The aerosol inhalation of ipratropium has a maximum effect 30–60 minutes after use; its duration of action is 3 to 6 hours and bronchodilation can usually be maintained with treatment 3 times a day.

**Tiotropium**, a long-acting antimuscarinic bronchodilator, is licensed for maintenance treatment of chronic obstructive pulmonary disease; it is not suitable for the relief of acute bronchospasm.

**Cautions** Antimuscarinic bronchodilators should be used with caution in glaucoma (see below), prostatic hyperplasia and bladder outflow obstruction; **interactions:** Appendix 1 (antimuscarinics)

Glaucoma *Acute angle-closure glaucoma* reported with nebulised ipratropium, particularly when given with nebulised salbutamol (and possibly other $beta_2$ agonists); care needed to protect patient's eyes from nebulised drug or from drug powder

**Side-effects** The side-effects of antimuscarinic bronchodilators include dry mouth, nausea, constipation, and headache. Tachycardia and atrial fibrillation have also been reported.

#### IPRATROPIUM BROMIDE

**Indications** reversible airways obstruction, particularly in chronic obstructive pulmonary disease

**Cautions** see notes above; also *first dose* of nebulised solution should be inhaled under medical supervision (risk of paradoxical bronchospasm)

**Side-effects** see notes above

**Dose**

- By aerosol inhalation, 20–40 micrograms, 3–4 times daily; CHILD up to 6 years 20 micrograms 3 times daily, 6–12 years 20–40 micrograms 3 times daily
- By inhalation of powder, 40 micrograms 3–4 times daily (may be doubled in less responsive patients); CHILD under 12 years, not recommended
- By inhalation of nebulised solution, reversible airways obstruction in chronic obstructive pulmonary disease, 250–500 micrograms 3–4 times daily

  Acute bronchospasm (see also Acute Asthma table, p. 142), 500 micrograms repeated as necessary; CHILD under 5 years 125–250 micrograms, max. 1 mg daily; 6–12 years 250 micrograms, max. 1 mg daily

  Counselling Advise patient not to exceed prescribed dose and to follow manufacturer's directions

**Ipratropium Bromide** (Non-proprietary) PoM
Nebuliser solution, ipratropium bromide 250 micrograms/mL, net price 20 × 1-mL (250-microgram) unit-dose vials = £6.75, 60 × 1-mL = £21.78; 20 × 2-mL (500-microgram) = £7.43, 60 × 2-mL = £26.97. If dilution is necessary use only sterile sodium chloride 0.9%

3 Respiratory system

**Atrovent®** (Boehringer Ingelheim) PoM

Aerocaps® (dry powder for inhalation; for use with *Atrovent Aerohaler®*), green, ipratropium bromide 40 micrograms, net price pack of 100 caps with *Aerohaler®* = £14.53; 100 caps = £10.53. Counselling, dose

Aerosol inhalation ▼, ipratropium bromide 20 micrograms/metered inhalation, net price 200-dose unit = £4.21. Counselling, dose change to CFC-free inhaler
Excipients include HFA-134a (a non-CFC propellant), alcohol

Nebuliser solution, isotonic, ipratropium bromide 250 micrograms/mL, net price 20 × 1-mL unit-dose vials = £5.18, 60 × 1-mL vials = £15.55; 20 × 2-mL vials = £6.08, 60 × 2-mL vials = £18.24. If dilution is necessary use only sterile sodium chloride 0.9%
Note One *Atrovent Aerocap®* is equivalent to 2 puffs of *Atrovent®* metered aerosol inhalation

**Ipratropium Steri-Neb®** (IVAX) PoM

Nebuliser solution, isotonic, ipratropium bromide 250 micrograms/mL, net price 20 × 1-mL (250-microgram) unit-dose vials = £8.72; 20 × 2-mL (500-microgram) = £9.94. If dilution is necessary use only sterile sodium chloride 0.9%

**Respontin®** (A&H) PoM

Nebuliser solution, isotonic, ipratropium bromide 250 micrograms/mL, net price 20 × 1-mL (250-microgram) unit-dose vials = £5.07; 20 × 2-mL (500-microgram) = £5.95. If dilution is necessary use only sterile sodium chloride 0.9%

**Compound ipratropium preparations**
Section 3.1.4

## TIOTROPIUM

**Indications** maintenance treatment of chronic obstructive pulmonary disease

**Cautions** see notes above; renal impairment (Appendix 3); pregnancy (Appendix 4)

**Side-effects** see notes above; also pharyngitis, sinusitis, candidiasis; rarely difficulty in micturition (urinary retention reported in elderly men with prostatic hyperplasia)

**Dose**

- By inhalation of powder, 18 micrograms once daily, CHILD and ADOLESCENT under 18 years, not recommended

**Spiriva®** (Boehringer Ingelheim) ▼ PoM

Inhalation powder, hard capsule (for use with *HandiHaler®* device), tiotropium (as tiotropium bromide monohydrate) 18 micrograms, net price 30-cap pack with *HandiHaler®* device = £37.62, 30-cap refill = £36.60

# 3.1.3 Theophylline

Theophylline is a bronchodilator used for *asthma* and stable *chronic obstructive pulmonary disease*; it is not generally effective in exacerbations of chronic obstructive pulmonary disease. It may have an additive effect when used in conjunction with small doses of $beta_2$ agonists; the combination may increase the risk of side-effects, including hypokalaemia (for CSM advice see p. 145).

Theophylline is metabolised in the liver; there is considerable variation in plasma-theophylline concentration particularly in smokers, in patients with hepatic impairment or heart failure, or if certain drugs are taken concurrently. The plasma-theophylline concentration is *increased* in heart failure, cirrhosis, viral infections, in the elderly, and by drugs that inhibit its metabolism. The plasma-theophylline concentration is *decreased* in smokers and in chronic alcoholism and by drugs that induce liver metabolism. For other interactions of theophylline see Appendix 1.

Differences in the half-life of theophylline are important because its toxic dose is close to the therapeutic dose; particular care is required when introducing or withdrawing drugs that interact with theophylline. In most individuals a plasma-theophylline concentration of between 10–20 mg/litre is required for satisfactory bronchodilation, although a plasma-theophylline concentration of 10 mg/litre (or less) may be effective. Adverse effects can occur within the range 10–20 mg/litre and both the frequency and severity increase at concentrations above 20 mg/litre.

Theophylline is given by injection as **aminophylline**, a mixture of theophylline with ethylenediamine, which is 20 times more soluble than theophylline alone. Aminophylline injection is needed rarely for severe attacks of asthma. It must be given by **very slow** intravenous injection (over at least 20 minutes); it is too irritant for intramuscular use. Measurement of plasma theophylline concentration may be helpful, and is **essential** if aminophylline is to be given to patients who have been taking theophylline, because serious side-effects such as convulsions and arrhythmias can occasionally precede other symptoms of toxicity.

## THEOPHYLLINE

**Indications** reversible airways obstruction, acute severe asthma; for guidelines see also Asthma tables (p. 141 and p. 142)

**Cautions** cardiac disease, hypertension, hyperthyroidism, peptic ulcer, epilepsy, elderly, fever, hepatic impairment (Appendix 2); pregnancy (Appendix 4) and breast-feeding (Appendix 5); **CSM** advice on hypokalaemia risk, p. 145; avoid in porphyria (section 9.8.2); **interactions:** Appendix 1 (theophylline) and notes above

**Side-effects** tachycardia, palpitations, nausea and other gastro-intestinal disturbances, headache, CNS stimulation, insomnia, arrhythmias, and convulsions especially if given rapidly by intravenous injection; **overdosage:** see Emergency Treatment of Poisoning, p. 33

**Dose**

- See below

Note Plasma-theophylline concentration for optimum response 10–20 mg/litre (55–110 micromol/litre); 4–6 hours after a dose and at least 5 days after starting treatment; narrow margin between therapeutic and toxic dose, see also notes above

> To avoid excessive dosage in obese patients, dose should be calculated on the basis of ideal weight for height

**Modified release**

Note The Council of the Royal Pharmaceutical Society of Great Britain advises pharmacists that if a general practitioner prescribes a modified-release oral theophylline preparation without specifying a brand name, the pharmacist should contact the prescriber and agree the brand to be dispensed. Additionally, it is essential that a patient discharged from hospital should be maintained on the brand on which that patient was stabilised as an in-patient.

**Nuelin SA®** (3M)

SA tablets, m/r, theophylline 175 mg. Net price 60-tab pack = £3.19. Label: 21, 25

Dose 175–350 mg every 12 hours; CHILD over 6 years 175 mg every 12 hours

SA 250 tablets, m/r, scored, theophylline 250 mg. Net price 60-tab pack = £4.46. Label: 21, 25

Dose 250–500 mg every 12 hours; CHILD over 6 years 125–250 mg every 12 hours

**Slo-Phyllin®** (Merck)

Capsules, all m/r, theophylline 60 mg (white/clear, enclosing white pellets), net price 56-cap pack = £2.30; 125 mg (brown/clear, enclosing white pellets), 56-cap pack = £2.90; 250 mg (blue/clear, enclosing white pellets), 56-cap pack = £3.62. Label: 25, or counselling, see below

Dose 250–500 mg every 12 hours; CHILD, every 12 hours, 2–6 years 60–120 mg, 7–12 years 125–250 mg

Counselling Swallow whole with fluid *or* swallow enclosed granules with soft food (e.g. yoghurt)

**Uniphyllin Continus®** (Napp)

Tablets, m/r, all scored, theophylline 200 mg, net price 56-tab pack = £3.13; 300 mg, 56-tab pack = £4.77; 400 mg, 56-tab pack = £5.65. Label: 25

Dose 200 mg every 12 hours increased according to response to 400 mg every 12 hours

May be appropriate to give larger evening or morning dose to achieve optimum therapeutic effect when symptoms most severe; in patients whose night or daytime symptoms persist despite other therapy, who are not currently receiving theophylline, total daily requirement may be added as single evening or morning dose

CHILD 9 mg/kg twice daily; some children with chronic asthma may require 10–16 mg/kg every 12 hours

## AMINOPHYLLINE

**Note** Aminophylline is a stable mixture or combination of theophylline and ethylenediamine; the ethylenediamine confers greater solubility in water

**Indications** reversible airways obstruction, acute severe asthma

**Cautions** see under Theophylline

**Side-effects** see under Theophylline; also allergy to ethylenediamine can cause urticaria, erythema, and exfoliative dermatitis

**Dose**

- See under preparations, below

Note Plasma-theophylline concentration for optimum response 10–20 mg/litre (55–110 micromol/litre); 4–6 hours after dose by mouth and at least 5 days after starting oral treatment; narrow margin between therapeutic and toxic dose, see also notes above

To avoid excessive dosage in obese patients, dose should be calculated on the basis of ideal weight for height

**Aminophylline** (Non-proprietary) PoM

Injection, aminophylline 25 mg/mL, net price 10-mL amp = 67p

Brands include *Minijet® Aminophylline*

Dose deteriorating acute severe asthma **not** previously treated with theophylline, by slow intravenous injection over at least 20 minutes (with close monitoring), 250–500 mg (5 mg/kg), then as for acute severe asthma; CHILD 5 mg/kg, then as for acute severe asthma

Acute severe asthma, by intravenous infusion (with close monitoring), 500 micrograms/kg/hour, adjusted according to plasma-theophylline concentration; CHILD 6 months–9 years 1 mg/kg/hour, 10–16 years 800 micrograms/kg/hour, adjusted according to plasma-theophylline concentration

Note Patients taking oral theophylline or aminophylline should not normally receive intravenous aminophylline unless plasma-theophylline concentration is available to guide dosage

### Modified release

**Note** Advice about modified-release theophylline preparations on p. 149 also applies to modified-release aminophylline preparations

**Phyllocontin Continus®** (Napp)

Tablets, m/r, yellow, f/c, aminophylline hydrate 225 mg. Net price 56-tab pack = £2.54. Label: 25

Dose 1 tablet twice daily initially, increased after 1 week to 2 tablets twice daily; CHILD over 3 years, initially 6 mg/kg twice daily, increased after 1 week to 12 mg/kg twice daily; some children with chronic asthma may require 13–20mg/kg every 12 hours

Note Brands of modified-release tablets containing aminophylline 225 mg include *Amnivent® 225 SR, Norphyllin® SR*

Forte tablets, m/r, yellow, f/c, aminophylline hydrate 350 mg. Net price 56-tab pack = £4.22. Label: 25

Note *Forte* tablets are for smokers and other patients with decreased theophylline half-life (see notes above)

## 3.1.4 Compound bronchodilator preparations

In general, patients are best treated with single-ingredient preparations, such as a selective beta$_2$ agonist (section 3.1.1.1) or ipratropium bromide (section 3.1.2), so that the dose of each drug can be adjusted. This flexibility is lost with combinations. However, a combination product may be appropriate for patients stabilised on individual components in the same proportion.

For **cautions, contra-indications** and **side-effects** see under individual drugs.

**Combivent®** (Boehringer Ingelheim) PoM

Aerosol inhalation, ipratropium bromide 20 micrograms, salbutamol (as sulphate) 100 micrograms/metered inhalation. Net price 200-dose unit = £6.45. Counselling, dose

Excipients include CFC propellants

Dose bronchospasm associated with chronic obstructive pulmonary disease, 2 puffs 4 times daily; CHILD under 12 years not recommended

Nebuliser solution, isotonic, ipratropium bromide 500 micrograms, salbutamol (as sulphate) 2.5 mg/2.5-mL vial, net price 60 unit-dose vials = £25.08

Dose bronchospasm in chronic obstructive pulmonary disease, by inhalation of nebulised solution, 1 vial 3–4 times daily; CHILD under 12 years not recommended

Glaucoma In addition to other potential side-effects acute angle-closure glaucoma has been reported with nebulised ipratropium—for details, see p. 148

**Duovent®** (Boehringer Ingelheim) PoM

Nebuliser solution, isotonic, fenoterol hydrobromide 1.25 mg, ipratropium bromide 500 micrograms/4-mL vial, net price 20 unit-dose vials = £11.00

Dose acute severe asthma or acute exacerbation of chronic asthma, by inhalation of nebulised solution, 1 vial (4 mL); may be repeated up to max. 4 vials in 24 hours; CHILD under 14 years, not recommended

Glaucoma In addition to other potential side-effects acute angle-closure glaucoma has been reported with nebulised ipratropium—for details, see p. 148

# 3.1.5 Peak flow meters, inhaler devices and nebulisers

## Peak flow meters

Measurement of peak flow is particularly helpful for patients who are 'poor perceivers'and hence slow to detect deterioration in their asthma, and for those with moderate or severe asthma.

Standard-range peak flow meters are suitable for both adults and children; low-range peak flow meters are appropriate for severely restricted airflow in adults and children. Patients must be given clear guidelines as to the action they should take if their peak flow falls below a certain level. Patients can be encouraged to adjust some of their own treatment (within specified limits) according to changes in peak flow rate.

**Standard Range Peak Flow Meter**

Conforms to standard EN 13826

MicroPeak®, range 60–800 litres/minute, net price = £6.50, replacement mouthpiece = 38p (Micro Medical)

Mini-Wright®, range 60–800 litres/minute, net price = £6.86, replacement mouthpiece = 38p (Clement Clarke)

Pocketpeak®, range 60–800 litres/minute, net price = £6.53, replacement mouthpiece = 38p (Ferraris)

Vitalograph®, range 50–800 litres/minute, net price = £5.95 (coloured children's version also available), replacement mouthpiece = 40p (Vitalograph)

**Note** Readings from new peak flow meters are often lower than those obtained from old Wright-scale peak flow meters and the correct chart should be used

**Low Range Peak Flow Meter**

Compliant to standard EN 13826 except for reduced measurement range

Mini-Wright®, range 30–400 litres/minute, net price = £6.90, replacement mouthpiece = 38p (Clement Clarke)

Pocketpeak®, range 50–400 litres/minute, net price = £6.53, replacement mouthpiece = 38p (Ferraris)

Vitalograph®, range 50–400 litres/minute, net price = £5.95, replacement mouthpiece = 40p (Vitalograph)

**Note** Readings from new peak flow meters are often lower than those obtained from old Wright-scale peak flow meters and the correct chart should be used

## Drug delivery devices

**Inhaler devices** These include *pressurised metered-dose inhalers, breath-actuated inhalers* and *dry powder inhalers*. Many patients can be taught to use a pressurised metered-dose inhaler effectively but some patients, particularly the elderly and small children, find it difficult to use them. *Spacer devices* (see below) can help such patients because they remove the need to co-ordinate actuation with inhalation and are effective even for children under 5 years. Alternatively, breath-actuated inhalers or dry powder inhalers (which are activated by patient's inhalation) may be used but they are less suitable for young children. On changing from a pressurised metered-dose inhaler to a dry powder inhaler patients may notice a lack of sensation in the mouth and throat previously associated with each actuation. Coughing may also occur.

The patient should be instructed carefully on the use of the inhaler and it is important to check that the inhaler continues to be used correctly because inadequate inhalation technique may be mistaken for a lack of response to the drug.

**NICE guidance (inhaler devices for children with chronic asthma)**

The National Institute for Health and Clinical Excellence has advised that the child's needs, ability to develop and maintain effective technique, and likelihood of good compliance should govern the choice of inhaler and spacer device; only then should cost be considered

For children aged under 5 years:

- corticosteroid and bronchodilator therapy should be delivered by pressurised metered-dose inhaler and spacer device, with a face-mask if necessary;
- if this is not effective, and depending on the child's condition, nebulised therapy may be considered and, in children over 3 years, a dry powder inhaler may also be considered [but see notes above];

For children aged 5–15 years:

- corticosteroid therapy should be routinely delivered by a pressurised metered-dose inhaler and spacer device
- children and their carers should be trained in the use of the chosen device; suitability of the device should be reviewed at least annually. Inhaler technique and compliance should be monitored

**Spacer devices** Spacer devices remove the need for co-ordination between actuation of a pressurised metered-dose inhaler and inhalation. The spacer device reduces the velocity of the aerosol and subsequent impaction on the oropharynx. In addition the device allows more time for evaporation of the propellant so that a larger proportion of the particles can be inhaled and deposited in the lungs. The size of the spacer is important, the larger spacers with a one-way valve (*Nebuhaler*®, *Volumatic*®) being most effective. Spacer devices are particularly useful for patients with poor inhalation technique, for children, for patients requiring higher doses, for nocturnal asthma, and for patients prone to candidiasis with inhaled corticosteroids. It is important to prescribe a spacer device that is compatible with the metered-dose inhaler.

**Use and care of spacer devices** Patients should inhale from the spacer device as soon as possible after actuation because the drug aerosol is very short-lived; single-dose actuation is recommended. Tidal breathing is as effective as single breaths. The device should be cleansed once a month by washing in mild detergent and then allowed to dry in air; the mouthpiece should be wiped clean of detergent before use. More frequent cleaning should be avoided since any electrostatic charge may affect drug delivery. Spacer devices should be replaced every 6–12 months.

**Able Spacer**® (Clement Clarke)

Spacer device, small-volume device. For use with pressurised (aerosol) inhalers, net price standard device = £4.20; with infant, child or adult mask = £6.86

**AeroChamber® Plus** (GSK)

Spacer device, medium-volume device. For use with *Airomir*®, *Alvesco*®, *Atrovent*®, *Atrovent*® *Forte*, *Combivent*®, *Duovent*®, *Salbulin*®, and *Qvar*® inhalers, net price standard device (blue) = £4.36, with mask (blue) = £7.27; infant device (orange) with mask = £4.36; child device (yellow) with mask = £7.27

**Babyhaler®** (A&H) NHS
Spacer device for paediatric use with *Becotide®-50* and *Ventolin®* inhalers. Net price = £11.34

**E-Z Spacer®** (Vitalograph) NHS
Spacer device, large-volume, collapsible device. For use with pressurised (aerosol) inhalers, price (direct from manufacturer) = £23.00

**Haleraid®** (A&H) NHS
Device to place over standard inhalers to aid when strength in hands is impaired (e.g. in arthritis). Available as *Haleraid®-120* for 120-dose inhalers and *Haleraid®-200* for 200-dose inhalers. Net price = 80p

**Nebuchamber®** (AstraZeneca)
Spacer device, for use with *Pulmicort®* aerosol inhalation. Free of charge from manufacturer

**Nebuhaler®** (AstraZeneca)
Spacer device, large-volume device. For use with *Bricanyl®* and *Pulmicort®* inhalers, net price = £4.28; with paediatric mask = £4.28

**PARI Vortex Spacer®** (Pari) NHS
Spacer device, small-volume device. For use with a pressurised (aerosol) inhaler, net price with mouthpiece = £6.07; with mask for infant or child = £7.91; with adult mask = £9.97

**Pocket Chamber®** (Ferraris)
Spacer device, small-volume device. For use with a pressurised (aerosol) inhaler, net price = £4.18; with infant, small, medium, or large mask = £9.75

**Spinhaler®** (Rhône-Poulenc Rorer)
Inhalation device, for use with *Intal Spincaps®*. Net price = £1.92

**Volumatic®** (A&H)
Spacer inhaler, large-volume device. For use with *Becloforte®*, *Becotide®*, *Flixotide®*, *Seretide®*, *Serevent®*, and *Ventolin®* inhalers, net price = £2.75; with paediatric mask = £2.75
Note. Supplies may be difficult to obtain



## Nebulisers

> In England and Wales nebulisers and compressors are not available on the NHS (but they are free of VAT); some nebulisers (but not compressors) are available on form GP10A in Scotland (for details consult Scottish Drug Tariff).

A nebuliser converts a solution of a drug into an aerosol for inhalation. It is used to deliver higher doses of drug to the airways than is usual with standard inhalers. The main indications for use of a nebuliser are:

- to deliver a $beta_2$ agonist or ipratropium to a patient with an *acute exacerbation* of asthma or of chronic obstructive pulmonary disease;
- to deliver a $beta_2$ agonist or ipratropium on a *regular basis* to a patient with severe asthma or reversible airways obstruction who has been shown to benefit from regular treatment with higher doses;
- to deliver *prophylactic medication* such as a corticosteroid to a patient unable to use other inhalational devices (particularly to a young child);
- to deliver an antibiotic (such as colistin) to a patient with chronic purulent infection (as in cystic fibrosis or bronchiectasis);
- to deliver pentamidine for the prophylaxis and treatment of pneumocystis pneumonia.

The proportion of a nebuliser solution that reaches the lungs depends on the type of nebuliser and although it can be as high as 30%, it is more frequently close to 10% and sometimes below 10%. The remaining solution is left in the nebuliser as residual volume or it is deposited in the mouthpiece and tubing. The extent to which the nebulised solution is deposited in the airways or alveoli depends on particle size. Particles with a mass median diameter of 1–5 microns are deposited in the airways and are therefore appropriate for asthma whereas a particle size of 1–2 microns is needed for alveolar deposition of pentamidine to combat pneumocystis infection. The type of nebuliser is therefore chosen according to the deposition required and according to the viscosity of the solution (antibiotic solutions usually being more viscous).

Some jet nebulisers are able to increase drug output during inspiration and hence increase efficiency.

The patient should be aware that the dose of a bronchodilator given by nebulisation is usually **much higher** than that from an aerosol inhaler.

The British Thoracic Society has advised that nebulised bronchodilators may be given to patients with chronic persistent asthma or those with sudden catastrophic severe asthma (brittle asthma). In chronic asthma, nebulised bronchodilators should only be used to relieve persistent daily wheeze (see Chronic Asthma table p. 141). The British Thoracic Society has recommended that the use of nebulisers in chronic persistent asthma should only be considered:

- after a review of the diagnosis;
- if the airflow obstruction is significantly reversible by bronchodilators without unacceptable side-effects;
- after the patient has been using the usual hand-held inhaler correctly;
- after a larger dose of bronchodilator from a hand-held inhaler (with a spacer if necessary) has been tried for at least 2 weeks;
- if the patient is complying with the prescribed dose and frequency of anti-inflammatory treatment including regular use of high-dose inhaled corticosteroid.

Before prescribing a nebuliser, a home trial should preferably be undertaken to monitor peak flow for up to 2 weeks on standard treatment and up to 2 weeks on nebulised treatment. If prescribed, patients must:

- have clear instructions from doctor, specialist nurse or pharmacist on the use of the nebuliser and on peak-flow monitoring;
- be instructed not to treat acute attacks at home without also seeking help;
- receive an education program;
- have regular follow up including peak-flow monitoring and be seen by doctor, specialist nurse or physiotherapist.

### Jet nebulisers

Jet nebulisers are more widely used than ultrasonic nebulisers. Most jet nebulisers require an optimum gas flow rate of 6–8 litres/minute and in hospital can be driven by piped air or oxygen. Domiciliary oxygen cylinders do not provide an adequate flow rate therefore an electrical compressor is required for domiciliary use.

For patients with *chronic obstructive pulmonary disease and hypercapnia*, oxygen can be dangerous and the nebuliser should be driven by air (see also p. 144). In exacerbations of chronic obstructive pulmonary disease, the nebuliser should be driven by compressed air in hypercapnia or acidosis. If oxygen is required, it should be given simultaneously by nasal cannula.

> **Important:** the Department of Health has reminded users of the need to use the correct grade of tubing when connecting a nebuliser to a medical gas supply or compressor.

**Medix Lifecare Nebuliser Chamber®** (Medix) NHS
Jet nebuliser, disposable; for use with bronchodilators, antimuscarinics, corticosteroids, and antibacterials, replacement recommended every 2–3 months if used 4 times a day. Compatible with *AC 2000 Hi Flo®* NHS, *World Traveller Hi Flo®* NHS, and *Econoneb®* NHS, net price = £1.00

**Medix Lifecare Nebuliser System®** (Medix) NHS
Jet nebuliser, consisting of mouthpiece, tubing, and nebuliser chamber, net price = £2.00; mask kits with tubing and nebuliser chamber also available, net price (adult) = £2.00; (child) = £2.10

**PARI LC PLUS FILTER®** (Pari) NHS
Jet nebuliser, closed system, non-disposable, for hospital or home use; for use with bronchodilators, antibacterials and corticosteroids; replacement recommended yearly if used 4 times a day. Compatible with *PARI Turbo BOY'N'®* NHS, *PARI Junior BOY'N'®* NHS and *PARI UNI light mobil®* NHS compressors, net price = £24.80, replacement filters 100 = £35.70

**PARI LC PLUS®** (Pari) NHS
Jet nebuliser, non-disposable, for hospital or home use; for use with bronchodilators, antibacterials, and corticosteroids, replacement recommended yearly if used 4 times a day. Compatible with *PARI Turbo BOY'N'®* NHS, *PARI Junior BOY'N'®* NHS, *PARI UNI light mobil®* NHS and *PARI WALK BOY®* NHS compressors, net price = £15.45

**PARI BABY®** (Pari) NHS
Jet nebuliser, non-disposable, for hospital or home use; for use with bronchodilators, antibacterials and corticosteroids; replacement recommended yearly if used 4 times a day. Compatible with *PARI Turbo BOY'N'®* NHS, *PARI Junior BOY'N'®* NHS, *PARI UNI light mobil®* NHS, *PARI WALK BOY®* NHS compressors. Available separately for children aged less than 1 year, 1–4 years or 4–7 years, net price (with mask and connection tube) = £31.40

**Sidestream Durable®** (Profile Respiratory) NHS
Jet nebuliser, non-disposable, for home use; for use with bronchodilators; yearly replacement recommended if 4 six-minute treatments used per day. Compatible with *Freeway Freedom®* NHS and *Porta-Neb®* NHS, net price year pack = £20.40 (*Porta-Neb®*), £29.00 (*Freeway Freedom®*). *Disposable Sidestream®* NHS nebuliser also available

**Ventstream®** (Profile Respiratory) NHS
Jet nebuliser, closed-system, for use with low flow compressors, compatible with *Porta-Neb®* NHS, and *Freeway Freedom®* NHS compressors; for use with antibacterials, bronchodilators, and corticosteroids, replacement recommended yearly if used 3 times a day, net price year pack with filter = £39.00 (*Porta-Neb®*), £41.00 (*Freeway Freedom®*)

## Home compressors with nebulisers

**AC 2000 HI FLO®** (Medix) NHS
*Home and hospital use*, containing 1 *Jet Nebuliser®* NHS set with mouthpiece, 1 adult and 1 child mask,1 spare inlet filter, filter spanner. Mains operated. Nebulises bronchodilators, corticosteroids, and antibacterials, net price = £117.00; carrying case available

**AC 4000®** (Medix) NHS
*Home and hospital use*, containing 1 *Jet Nebuliser®* NHS set with mouthpiece, 1 adult and 1 child face mask, 1 spare inlet filter, filter spanner. Mains operated. Nebulises bronchodilators, corticosteroids, and antibacterials, net price = £80.10

**Aquilon®** (Henleys) NHS
*Portable, home use*, with 1 adult or 1 child mask and tubing. Mains operated; for use with bronchodilators, corticosteroids and antibacterials, net price = £82.50

**Econoneb®** (Medix) NHS
*Home, clinic and hospital use*, used with 1 *Jet Nebuliser®* NHS set with mouthpiece, 1 adult and 1 child mask, 1 spare inlet filter, filter spanner. Nebulises bronchodilators, corticosteroids, and antibacterials. Mains operated, net price = £99.00

**Freeway Freedom®** (Profile Respiratory) NHS
*Portable*, containing *Sidestream Durable®* NHS nebuliser, 1 adult mask, 1 child mask, 1 angled mouthpiece, 1 coiled *Duratube®*, 4 inlet filters, charger and power lead, net price = £203.20; with *Ventstream®* NHS nebuliser, 1 straight mouthpiece, 1 coiled *Duratube®*, 4 inlet filters, 1 aerosol hose, charger and power lead, net price = £203.20

**PARI Junior BOY'N'®** (Pari) NHS
*Portable, for hospital or home use*, containing *PARI LC PLUS Junior* NHS nebuliser with child mouthpiece, mask, connection tube, and mains cable. Filter replacement recommended every 12 months. Compatible with *PARI LC PLUS®* NHS, *PARI LC PLUS Filter®* NHS, and *PARI Baby®* NHS nebulisers, net price = £70.00

**PARI Turbo BOY'N'®** (Pari) NHS
*Portable, for hospital or home use*, containing *PARI LC PLUS* NHS nebuliser with adult mouthpiece, mask, connection tube and mains cable. Filter replacement recommended every 12 months. Compatible with *PARI LC PLUS®* NHS, *PARI LC PLUS FILTER®* NHS, and *PARI BABY®* NHS nebulisers, net price = £65.00

**PARI UNI light mobil®** (Pari) NHS
*Portable*, containing *PARI LC PLUS®* NHS nebuliser with connection tube, mains cable, rechargeable battery, car battery adaptor, and carrying case. Compatible with *PARI BABY®* NHS, and *PARI LC PLUS FILTER®* NHS nebulisers. Nebulises bronchodilators, corticosteroids, and antibacterials, net price = £180.00

**Porta-Neb®** (Profile Respiratory) NHS
*Portable*, containing *Sidestream Durable®* NHS nebuliser, 1 adult mask, 1 child mask, 1 angled mouthpiece, 1 coiled *Duratube®*, 4 inlet filters. Mains operated, net price = £94.00; with *Ventstream®* NHS nebuliser, 1 straight mouthpiece, 1 coiled *Duratube®*, 4 inlet filters, aerosol hose. Mains operated, net price = £104.80

**De Vilbiss 5650®** (De Vilbiss) NHS
*Home, clinic use*, containing disposable nebuliser set, mouthpiece, mask, mains lead, tubing, thumb-valve. For use with bronchodilators, net price = £142.14

**De Vilbiss 4650®** (De Vilbiss) NHS
*Home, clinic and hospital use*, with mouthpiece. Mains operated, net price = £93.95

**Tourer®** (Henleys) NHS
*Portable, home use*. Mains/car battery operated; for use with bronchodilators, corticosteroids and antibacterials, net price = £101.25

**Ultima®** (Henleys) NHS
*Portable, home use*. Rechargable or mains/car battery operated. Nebulises bronchodilators and corticosteroids, net price = £156.00 (includes case)

**World Traveller HI FLO®** (Medix) NHS
*Portable*, containing 1 *Jet Nebuliser®* NHS set with mouthpiece, 1 adult and 1 child mask, 1 spare inlet filter, filter spanner. Battery, car, and mains operated; rechargeable battery pack available. Nebulises bronchodilators, corticosteroids, and antibacterials, net price excluding battery = £166.00; with battery = £216.00; carrying case available

### Compressors

**Omron CX3®** (Omron) NHS

*Home and hospital use.* Mains operated, net price = £48.75

**Omron compAIR CX^Pro®** (Omron) NHS

*Home and hospital use.* Mains operated, net price = £56.78 (includes 1 adult mask, child mask, 5 spare filters, and carrying case)

**System 22 CR60®** (Profile Respiratory) NHS

*Hospital use,* high flow compressor. Mains operated, net price = £199.90. Also compatible with *System 22 Antibiotic Tee®* NHS for nebulisation of high viscosity drugs such as antibacterials

**Turboneb®** (Medix) NHS

*Hospital use,* high flow compressor. Nebulises bronchodilators, corticosteroids, antibacterials, and pentamidine. Mains operated, net price = £125.00

### Ultrasonic nebulisers

Ultrasonic nebulisers produce an aerosol by ultrasonic vibration of the drug solution and therefore do not require a gas flow

**F16 Wave®** (Parkside) NHS

*Portable,* adjustable delivery rate. Mains/car battery operated or rechargeable battery pack (supplied), net price = £130.00

**Liberty®** (Medix) NHS

*Portable, home and clinic use,* containing disposable mouthpiece and chamber cover. Mains and car battery operated. Nebulises bronchodilators and antibacterials, net price £112.49

**Omron MicroAIR®** (Omron) NHS

*Portable,* battery operated, net price = £149.96 (includes 1 adult mask, 1 child mask, and carrying case; mains adaptor also available)

**Omron NE-U17®** (Omron) NHS

*Clinic and hospital use,* mains operated, net price = £650.17

**Ultra Neb 2000®** (De Vilbiss) NHS

*Hospital, clinic and home use,* delivery rate adjustable. Supplied with stand, net price = £1205.00

## Nebuliser diluent

Nebulisation may be carried out using an undiluted nebuliser solution or it may require dilution beforehand. The usual diluent is sterile sodium chloride 0.9% (physiological saline).

**Sodium Chloride** (Non-proprietary) PoM

Nebuliser solution, sodium chloride 0.9%, net price 20 × 2.5 mL = £5.49

Brands include *Saline Steripoule®*, *Saline Steri-Neb®*

## 3.2 Corticosteroids

Corticosteroids are very effective in *asthma*; they reduce airway inflammation (and hence reduce oedema and secretion of mucus into the airway).

In *chronic obstructive pulmonary disease* inhaled corticosteroid treatment may reduce exacerbations. An inhaled corticosteroid [unlicensed indication] should be considered (in addition to bronchodilator treatment) if the peak flow is worse than 50% of the predicted value and if the patient has had 2 or more exacerbations in a year which require antibacterial treatment or an oral corticosteroid. A trial of an inhaled corticosteroid for about 3 weeks can distinguish patients who have asthma from those who have chronic obstructive pulmonary disease.

**Inhalation** Inhaled corticosteroids are recommended for prophylactic treatment of asthma when patients are using a beta$_2$ agonist more than 3 times a week or if symptoms disturb sleep more than once a week or if the patient has suffered exacerbations in the last 2 years requiring a systemic corticosteroid or a nebulised bronchodilator (see Chronic Asthma table, p. 141). *Regular use* of inhaled corticosteroids reduces the risk of exacerbation of asthma.

Corticosteroid inhalers must be used regularly for maximum benefit; alleviation of symptoms usually occurs 3 to 7 days after initiation. **Beclometasone dipropionate** (beclomethasone dipropionate), **budesonide**, **fluticasone propionate**, and **mometasone furoate** appear to be equally effective. Preparations that combine a corticosteroid with a long-acting beta$_2$ agonist may be helpful for patients stabilised on the individual components in the same proportion.

Doses for CFC-free corticosteroid inhalers may be different from those that contain CFCs.

CFC-free inhalers Chlorofluorocarbon (CFC) propellants in pressurised aerosol inhalers are being replaced by hydrofluoroalkane (HFA) propellants. Patients receiving CFC-free inhalers should be reassured about the efficacy of the new inhalers and counselled that the aerosol may feel and taste different; any difficulty with the new inhaler should be discussed with the doctor or pharmacist.

If the inhaled corticosteroid causes coughing, the use of a beta$_2$ agonist beforehand may help.

Patients taking long-term oral corticosteroids for asthma can often be transferred to an inhaled corticosteroid but the transfer must be slow, with gradual reduction in the dose of the oral corticosteroid, and at a time when the asthma is well controlled.

High-dose corticosteroid inhalers are suitable for patients who respond only partially to standard-dose inhalers and long-acting beta$_2$ agonists or other long-acting bronchodilators (see Chronic Asthma, table, p. 141). High doses should be continued only if there is clear benefit over the lower dose. The recommended maximum dose of an inhaled corticosteroid should not generally be exceeded. However, if higher doses are required (e.g. fluticasone in a dose above 500 micrograms twice daily in an adult or 200 micrograms twice daily in a child aged 4–16 years), then they should be initiated by specialists.

Systemic corticosteroid therapy may be necessary during episodes of infection or if the asthma is worsening, when higher doses are needed and access of inhaled drug to small airways may be reduced; patients may need a reserve supply of tablets.

**Cautions of inhaled corticosteroids** An inhaled corticosteroid should be used cautiously in active or quiescent tuberculosis; systemic therapy may be required during periods of stress or when either airways obstruction or mucus prevent drug access to smaller airways; **interactions:** Appendix 1 (corticosteroids)

Paradoxical bronchospasm The potential for paradoxical bronchospasm (calling for discontinuation and alternative therapy) should be borne in mind—mild bronchospasm may be prevented by inhalation of a short-acting beta$_2$ agonist (or by transfer from an aerosol inhalation to a dry powder inhalation).

**Side-effects of inhaled corticosteroids** Inhaled corticosteroids have considerably fewer systemic effects than oral corticosteroids, but adverse effects have been reported.

Higher doses of inhaled corticosteroids have the potential to induce adrenal suppression (section 6.3.2) and patients on high doses should be given a 'steroid card'; such patients may need corticosteroid cover during an episode of stress (e.g. an operation). Inhaled corticosteroids in children have been associated with adrenal crisis and coma; excessive doses should be **avoided**, particularly of fluticasone, which should be given in a dose of 50–100 micrograms twice daily and the dose should not exceed 200 micrograms twice daily.

Bone mineral density may be reduced following long-term inhalation of higher doses of corticosteroids, predisposing patients to osteoporosis (section 6.6). It is therefore sensible to ensure that the dose of an inhaled corticosteroid is no higher than necessary to keep a patient's asthma under good control. Treatment with an inhaled corticosteroid can usually be stopped after a mild exacerbation as long as the patient knows that it is necessary to reinstate it should the asthma deteriorate or the peak flow rate fall.

In children, growth retardation associated with oral corticosteroid therapy does not seem to be a significant problem with recommended doses of inhaled therapy; although initial growth velocity may be reduced, there appears to be no effect on achieving normal adult height. However, the CSM recommends that the height of children receiving prolonged treatment is monitored; if growth is slowed, referral to a paediatrician should be considered. Large-volume spacer devices should be used for administering inhaled corticosteroids in children under 5 years (see NICE guidance, section 3.1.5); they are also useful in older children and adults, particularly if high doses are required. Spacer devices increase airway deposition and reduce oropharyngeal deposition.

A small increased risk of glaucoma with prolonged high doses of inhaled corticosteroids has been reported; cataracts have also been reported with inhaled corticosteroids. Hoarseness and candidiasis of the mouth or throat have been reported, usually only with large doses (see also below). Hypersensitivity reactions (including rash and angioedema) have been reported rarely.

Candidiasis Candidiasis can be reduced by using spacer, see notes above, and it responds to antifungal lozenges (section 12.3.2) without discontinuation of therapy—rinsing the mouth with water (or cleaning child's teeth) after inhalation of a dose may also be helpful.

**Oral** An acute attack of asthma should be treated with a short course of an oral corticosteroid starting with a high dose, e.g. prednisolone 40–50 mg daily for a few days. Patients whose asthma has deteriorated rapidly usually respond quickly to corticosteroids. The dose can usually be stopped abruptly in a mild exacerbation of asthma (see also Withdrawal of Corticosteroids, section 6.3.2) but it should be reduced gradually in those with poorer asthma control, to reduce the possibility of serious relapse. For use of corticosteroids in the emergency treatment of acute severe asthma see table on p. 142.

In chronic continuing asthma, when the response to other drugs has been inadequate, longer term administration of an oral corticosteroid may be necessary; in such cases high doses of an inhaled corticosteroid should be continued to minimise oral corticosteroid requirements. In chronic obstructive pulmonary disease prednisolone 30 mg daily should be given for 7–14 days; treatment can be stopped abruptly. Prolonged treatment with oral prednisolone is of no benefit and maintenance treatment is not normally recommended.

An oral corticosteroid should normally be taken as a single dose in the morning to reduce the disturbance to circadian cortisol secretion. Dosage should always be titrated to the lowest dose that controls symptoms. Regular peak flow measurements help to optimise the dose.

Alternate-day administration has not been very successful in the management of asthma in adults because control can deteriorate during the second 24 hours. If alternate-day administration is introduced, pulmonary function should be monitored carefully over the 48 hours

**Parenteral** For the use of hydrocortisone injection in the emergency treatment of acute severe asthma, see Acute Severe Asthma table, p. 142.

## BECLOMETASONE DIPROPIONATE
**(Beclomethasone Dipropionate)**

**Indications** prophylaxis of asthma (see also Chronic Asthma table, p. 141)

**Cautions** see notes above

**Side-effects** see notes above

**Dose**

- Standard-dose inhalers

  By aerosol inhalation (for *Qvar®* dose see under preparation), 200 micrograms twice daily *or* 100 micrograms 3–4 times daily (in more severe cases initially 600–800 micrograms daily); CHILD 50–100 micrograms 2–4 times daily

  By inhalation of powder (for *Asmabec®* dose see under preparation), 400 micrograms twice daily *or* 200 micrograms 3–4 times daily; CHILD 100 micrograms 2–4 times daily *or* 200 micrograms twice daily
- High-dose inhalers

  By aerosol inhalation (for *Qvar®* dose see under preparation), 500 micrograms twice daily *or* 250 micrograms 4 times daily; if necessary may be increased to 500 micrograms 4 times daily; CHILD not recommended

  By inhalation of powder (for *Asmabec®* dose see under preparation), 400 micrograms twice daily; if necessary may be increased to 800 micrograms twice daily; CHILD not recommended

### Standard-dose inhalers

**Beclometasone** (Non-proprietary) PoM

Aerosol inhalation, beclometasone dipropionate 50 micrograms/metered inhalation, net price 200-dose unit = £3.97; 100 micrograms/metered inhalation, 200-dose unit = £8.24; 200 micrograms/metered inhalation, 200-dose unit = £8.14. Label: 8, counselling, dose

Excipients include CFC propellants

Brands include *Beclazone®*, *Filair®*

Dry powder for inhalation, beclometasone dipropionate 100 micrograms/metered inhalation, net price 100-dose unit = £5.58; 200 micrograms/

metered inhalation, 100-dose unit = £10.29, 200-dose unit = £15.60. Label: 8, counselling, dose
Brands include *Pulvinal® Beclometasone Dipropionate, Easyhaler® Beclometasone Dipropionate*

Inhalation powder, hard capsule (for use with *Cyclohaler®* device), beclometasone dipropionate 100 micrograms, net price 120-cap pack = £7.59; 200 micrograms, 120-cap pack = £14.41. Label: 8, counselling, dose
Brands include *Beclometasone Cyclocaps®*

**AeroBec®** (3M) PoM

AeroBec 50 Autohaler® (breath-actuated aerosol inhalation), beclometasone dipropionate 50 micrograms/metered inhalation, net price 200-dose unit = £4.04. Label: 8, counselling, dose
**Excipients** include CFC propellants

AeroBec 100 Autohaler® (breath-actuated aerosol inhalation), beclometasone dipropionate 100 micrograms/metered inhalation, net price 200-dose unit = £7.66. Label: 8, counselling, dose
**Excipients** include CFC propellants

**Asmabec Clickhaler®** (Celltech) PoM

Dry powder for inhalation, beclometasone dipropionate 50 micrograms/metered inhalation, net price 200-dose unit = £6.68; 100 micrograms/metered inhalation, 200-dose unit = £9.81. Label: 8, counselling, dose
**Dose** by inhalation of powder, 200–400 micrograms daily, in 2–4 divided doses (in more severe cases initially 0.8–1.6 mg daily, in 2–4 divided doses—see also High-dose inhalers); CHILD 50–100 micrograms 2–4 times daily

**Beclazone Easi-Breathe®** (IVAX) PoM

Aerosol inhalation, beclometasone dipropionate 50 micrograms/metered inhalation, net price 200-dose breath-actuated unit = £3.26; 100 micrograms/metered inhalation, 200-dose breath-actuated unit = £6.18. Label: 8, counselling, dose
**Excipients** include CFC propellants

**Becodisks®** (A&H) PoM

Dry powder for inhalation, disks containing 8 blisters of beclometasone dipropionate 100 micrograms/blister, net price 15 disks with *Diskhaler®* device = £12.00, 15-disk refill = £11.42; 200 micrograms/blister, 15 disks with *Diskhaler®* device = £22.87, 15-disk refill = £22.28. Label: 8, counselling, dose

**Becotide®** (A&H) PoM

Becotide®-50 aerosol inhalation, beclometasone dipropionate 50 micrograms/metered inhalation. Net price 200-dose unit = £1.79. Label: 8, counselling, dose
**Excipients** include CFC propellants

Becotide®-100 aerosol inhalation, beclometasone dipropionate 100 micrograms/metered inhalation. Net price 200-dose unit = £2.79. Label: 8, counselling, dose
**Excipients** include CFC propellants

Becotide®-200 aerosol inhalation, beclometasone dipropionate 200 micrograms/metered inhalation. Net price 200-dose unit = £8.14. Label: 8, counselling, dose, 10, steroid card
**Excipients** include CFC propellants
**Note** *Becotide®-200* not indicated for children

**Qvar®** (IVAX) PoM

Qvar® 50 aerosol inhalation, beclometasone dipropionate 50 micrograms/metered inhalation, net price 200-dose unit = £7.87. Label: 8, counselling, dose

Qvar® 100 aerosol inhalation, beclometasone dipropionate 100 micrograms/metered inhalation, net price 200-dose unit = £17.21. Label: 8, counselling, dose, 10, steroid card

Qvar 50 Autohaler® (breath-actuated aerosol inhalation), beclometasone dipropionate 50 micrograms/metered inhalation, net price 200-dose unit = £7.87. Label: 8, counselling, dose

Qvar 100 Autohaler® (breath-actuated aerosol inhalation), beclometasone dipropionate 100 micrograms/metered inhalation, net price 200-dose unit = £17.21. Label: 8, counselling, dose, 10, steroid card
**Excipients** include HFA-134a (a non-CFC propellant), ethanol

Qvar Easi-Breathe® (breath-actuated aerosol inhalation), beclometasone dipropionate 50 micrograms/metered inhalation, net price 200-dose = £8.24; 100 micrograms/metered inhalation, 200-dose = £18.02. Label: 8, counselling, dose, 10, steroid card
**Excipients** include HFA-134a (a non-CFC propellant), ethanol
**Dose** by aerosol inhalation, 50–200 micrograms twice daily, if necessary may be increased to max. 400 micrograms twice daily; CHILD not recommended
**Note** When transferring a patient from a CFC-containing inhaler (asthma well controlled), initially a 100-microgram metered dose of *Qvar®* should be substituted for:

- 200–250 micrograms of beclometasone dipropionate or budesonide
- 100 micrograms of fluticasone propionate

When transferring a patient from a CFC-containing inhaler (asthma poorly controlled), initially a 100-microgram metered dose of *Qvar®* should be substituted for 100 micrograms of beclometasone dipropionate, budesonide or fluticasone propionate

## High-dose inhalers

**Note** High-dose inhalers not indicated for children

Chronic Asthma table, see p. 141
Acute Severe Asthma table, see p. 142

**Beclometasone** (Non-proprietary) PoM

Aerosol inhalation, beclometasone dipropionate 250 micrograms/metered inhalation, net price 200-dose unit = £12.93. Label: 8, counselling, dose, 10, steroid card
**Excipients** include CFC propellants
Brands include *Beclazone®, Filair Forte®*

Dry powder for inhalation, beclometasone dipropionate 400 micrograms/metered inhalation, net price 100-dose unit = £20.41. Label: 8, counselling, dose, 10, steroid card
Brands include *Pulvinal® Beclometasone Dipropionate*

Inhalation powder, hard capsule (for use with *Cyclohaler®* device), beclometasone dipropionate 400 micrograms, net price 120-cap pack = £27.38. Label: 8, counselling, dose, 10, steroid card
Brands include *Beclometasone 400 Cyclocaps®*

**AeroBec Forte®** (3M) PoM

Aerosol inhalation, beclometasone dipropionate 250 micrograms/metered inhalation, net price 200-inhalation breath-actuated unit (*Autohaler®*) = £16.76. Label: 8, counselling, dose 10, steroid card
**Excipients** include CFC propellants

**Asmabec Clickhaler®** (Celltech) PoM

Dry powder for inhalation, beclometasone dipropionate 250 micrograms/metered inhalation, net price 100-dose unit = £12.31. Label: 8, counselling, dose, 10, steroid card
**Dose** by inhalation of powder, 500 micrograms twice daily *or* 250 micrograms 4 times daily; if necessary may be increased to 500 micrograms 4 times daily; CHILD not recommended

**Beclazone Easi-Breathe®** (IVAX) PoM
Aerosol inhalation, beclometasone dipropionate 250 micrograms/metered inhalation, net price 200-dose breath-actuated unit = £13.52. Label: 8, counselling, dose, 10, steroid card
Excipients include CFC propellants

**Becloforte®** (A&H) PoM
Aerosol inhalation, beclometasone dipropionate 250 micrograms/metered inhalation. Net price 200-dose unit = £6.99. Label: 8, counselling, dose, 10, steroid card
Excipients include CFC propellants

**Becodisks®** (A&H) PoM
Dry powder for inhalation, disks containing 8 blisters of beclometasone dipropionate 400 micrograms/blister, 15 disks with *Diskhaler®* device = £45.14, 15-disk refill = £44.57. Label: 8, counselling, dose, 10, steroid card

**Qvar®** (IVAX) PoM
See under Standard-dose inhalers above

## BUDESONIDE

**Indications** prophylaxis of asthma (see also Chronic Asthma table, p. 141)
**Cautions** see notes above
**Side-effects** see notes above
**Dose**
- See preparations below

**Budesonide** (Non-proprietary) PoM
Inhalation powder, hard capsule (for use with *Cyclohaler®* device), budesonide 200 micrograms, net price 100-cap pack = £15.48; 400 micrograms, 50-cap pack = £15.48. Label: 8, counselling, dose, 10, steroid card
Brands include *Budesonide Cyclocaps®*
Dose 0.2–1.6 mg daily in divided doses adjusted as necessary; CHILD over 6 years 200–400 micrograms daily in divided doses adjusted as necessary (max. 800 micrograms daily)

**Novolizer®** (Viatris) ▼ PoM
Dry powder for inhalation, budesonide 200 micrograms, net price refillable inhaler device and 100-dose cartridge = £14.86; 100-dose refill cartridge = £9.59. Label: 8, counselling, dose, 10, steroid card
Dose 0.2–1.6 mg daily in divided doses adjusted as necessary; CHILD over 6 years 200–400 micrograms daily in divided doses adjusted as necessary (max. 800 micrograms daily)

**Pulmicort®** (AstraZeneca) PoM
LS aerosol inhalation, budesonide 50 micrograms/metered inhalation. Net price 200-dose unit = £7.33. Label: 8, counselling, dose
Excipients include CFC propellants

Aerosol inhalation, budesonide 200 micrograms/metered inhalation. Net price 200-dose unit = £20.90; 100-dose unit = £7.60 (hosp. only; may be difficult to obtain). Label: 8, counselling, dose, 10, steroid card
Excipients include CFC propellants
Dose by aerosol inhalation, 200 micrograms twice daily; may be reduced in well-controlled asthma to not less than 200 micrograms daily; in severe asthma dose may be increased to 1.6 mg daily; CHILD 50–400 micrograms twice daily; in severe asthma may be increased to 800 micrograms daily

*Turbohaler®* (= dry powder inhaler), budesonide 100 micrograms/metered inhalation, net price 200-dose unit = £18.50; 200 micrograms/metered inhalation, 100-dose unit = £18.50; 400 micrograms/metered inhalation, 50-dose unit = £18.50. Label: 8, counselling, dose, 10, steroid card
Dose by inhalation of powder, when starting treatment, during periods of severe asthma, and while reducing or discontinuing oral corticosteroid, 0.2–1.6 mg daily in 2 divided doses; in less severe cases 200–400 micrograms once daily (each evening); patients already controlled on inhaled beclometasone dipropionate or budesonide administered twice daily may be transferred to once-daily dosing (each evening) at the same equivalent total daily dose (up to 800 micrograms once daily); CHILD under 12 years 200–800 micrograms daily in 2 divided doses (800 micrograms daily in severe asthma) *or* 200–400 micrograms once daily (each evening)

Respules® (= single-dose units for nebulisation), budesonide 250 micrograms/mL, net price 20 × 2-mL (500-microgram) unit = £32.00; 500 micrograms/mL, 20 × 2-mL (1-mg) unit = £44.64. May be diluted with sterile sodium chloride 0.9%. Label: 8, counselling, dose, 10, steroid card
Dose by inhalation of nebulised suspension, when starting treatment, during periods of severe asthma, and while reducing or discontinuing oral corticosteroids, 1–2 mg twice daily (may be increased further in very severe asthma); CHILD 3 months–12 years, 0.5–1 mg twice daily
Maintenance, usually half above doses
Croup, 2 mg as a single dose (*or* as two 1-mg doses separated by 30 minutes)

### Compound preparations

**Symbicort®** (AstraZeneca) PoM
Symbicort 100/6 Turbohaler® (= dry powder inhaler), budesonide 80 micrograms, formoterol fumarate 4.5 micrograms/metered inhalation, net price 120-dose unit = £33.00. Label: 8, counselling, dose, 10, steroid card
Note Each metered inhalation of *Symbicort® 100/6* delivers the same quantity of budesonide as a 100-microgram metered inhalation of *Pulmicort Turbohaler®* and of formoterol fumarate as a 4.5-microgram metered inhalation of *Oxis® 6 Turbohaler®*
Dose by inhalation of powder, asthma, 1–2 puffs twice daily increased if necessary to max. 4 puffs twice daily, reduced to 1 puff once daily if control maintained; ADOLESCENT 12–17 years 1–2 puffs twice daily reduced to 1 puff once daily if control maintained; CHILD over 6 years, 2 puffs twice daily reduced to 1 puff once daily if control maintained

Symbicort 200/6 Turbohaler® (=dry powder inhaler), budesonide 160 micrograms, formoterol fumarate 4.5 micrograms/metered inhalation, net price 120-dose unit = £38.00. Label: 8, counselling, dose, 10, steroid card
Note Each metered inhalation of *Symbicort® 200/6* delivers the same quantity of budesonide as a 200-microgram metered inhalation of *Pulmicort Turbohaler®* and of formoterol fumarate as a 4.5-microgram metered inhalation of *Oxis® 6 Turbohaler®*
Dose by inhalation of powder, asthma, 1–2 puffs twice daily increased if necessary to max. 4 puffs twice daily, reduced to 1 puff once daily if control maintained; ADOLESCENT 12–17 years 1–2 puffs twice daily reduced to 1 puff once daily if control maintained; CHILD under 12 years not recommended
Chronic obstructive pulmonary disease, 2 puffs twice daily; CHILD not recommended

Symbicort 400/12 Turbohaler® (=dry powder inhaler), budesonide 320 micrograms, formoterol fumarate 9 micrograms/metered inhalation, net price 60-dose unit = £38.00. Label: 8, counselling, dose, 10, steroid card
Note Each metered inhalation of *Symbicort® 400/12* delivers the same quantity of budesonide as a 400-microgram metered inhalation of *Pulmicort Turbohaler®* and of formoterol fumarate as a 9-microgram metered inhalation of *Oxis® 12 Turbohaler®*
Dose by inhalation of powder, asthma, 1 puff twice daily increased if necessary to max. 2 puffs twice daily, reduced to 1 puff once daily if control maintained; ADOLESCENT 12–17 years 1 puff twice daily reduced to 1 puff once daily if control maintained; CHILD under 12 years not recommended
Chronic obstructive pulmonary disease, 1 puff twice daily; CHILD not recommended

## CICLESONIDE

**Indications** prophylaxis of asthma

**Cautions** see notes above

**Side-effects** see notes above

**Dose**

- By aerosol inhalation, 160 micrograms daily as a single dose reduced to 80 micrograms daily if control maintained; CHILD and ADOLESCENT under 18 years not recommended

**Alvesco®** (Altana) ▼ PoM

Aerosol inhalation, ciclesonide 80 micrograms/metered inhalation, net price 120-dose unit = £28.56; 160 micrograms/metered inhalation, 120-dose unit = £33.60. Label: 8, counselling, dose

Excipients include HFA-134a (a non-CFC propellant), ethanol

## FLUTICASONE PROPIONATE

**Indications** prophylaxis of asthma (see also Chronic Asthma table, p. 141)

**Cautions** see notes above

**Side-effects** see notes above

**Dose**

- See preparations below

**Flixotide®** (A&H) PoM

Accuhaler® (dry powder for inhalation), disk containing 60 blisters of fluticasone propionate 50 micrograms/blister with *Accuhaler®* device, net price = £6.38; 100 micrograms/blister with *Accuhaler®* device = £8.93; 250 micrograms/blister with *Accuhaler®* device = £21.26; 500 micrograms/blister with *Accuhaler®* device = £36.14. Label: 8, counselling, dose; 250- and 500-microgram strengths also label 10, steroid card

Note *Flixotide Accuhaler®* 250 micrograms and 500 micrograms are not indicated for children

Dose by inhalation of powder, ADULT and CHILD over 16 years, 100–250 micrograms twice daily, increased according to severity of asthma to 1 mg twice daily; CHILD 4–16 years, 50–100 micrograms twice daily adjusted as necessary; max. 200 micrograms twice daily

Diskhaler® (dry powder for inhalation), fluticasone propionate 50 micrograms/blister, net price 15 disks of 4 blisters with *Diskhaler®* device = £8.17, 15-disk refill = £7.64; 100 micrograms/blister, 15 disks of 4 blisters with *Diskhaler®* device = £12.71, 15-disk refill = £12.18; 250 micrograms/blister, 15 disks of 4 blisters with *Diskhaler®* device = £24.11, 15-disk refill = £23.58; 500 micrograms/blister, 15 disks of 4 blisters with *Diskhaler®* device = £40.05, 15-disk refill = £39.52. Label: 8, counselling, dose; 250- and 500-microgram strengths also label 10, steroid card

Note *Flixotide Diskhaler®* 250 micrograms and 500 micrograms are not indicated for children

Dose by inhalation of powder, ADULT and CHILD over 16 years, 100–250 micrograms twice daily, increased according to severity of asthma to 1 mg twice daily; CHILD 4–16 years, 50–100 micrograms twice daily adjusted as necessary; max. 200 micrograms twice daily

Evohaler® *aerosol inhalation*, fluticasone propionate 50 micrograms/metered inhalation, net price 120-dose unit = £5.44; 125 micrograms/metered inhalation, 120-dose unit = £21.26; 250 micrograms/metered inhalation, 120-dose unit = £36.14. Label: 8, counselling, dose, change to CFC-free inhaler; 250-microgram strength also label 10, steroid card

Excipients include HFA-134a (a non-CFC propellant)

Note *Flixotide Evohaler®* 125 micrograms and 250 micrograms not indicated for children

Dose by aerosol inhalation, ADULT and CHILD over 16 years, 100–250 micrograms twice daily, increased according to severity of asthma to 1 mg twice daily; CHILD 4–16 years, 50–100 micrograms twice daily adjusted as necessary; max. 200 micrograms twice daily

Nebules® (= single-dose units for nebulisation) fluticasone propionate 250 micrograms/mL, net price 10 × 2-mL (500-microgram) unit = £9.34; 1 mg/mL, 10 × 2-mL (2-mg) unit = £37.35. May be diluted with sterile sodium chloride 0.9%. Label: 8, counselling, dose 10, steroid card

Dose by inhalation of nebulised suspension, ADULT and CHILD over 16 years, 0.5–2 mg twice daily; CHILD 4–16 years, 1 mg twice daily

### Compound preparations

**Seretide®** (A&H) PoM

Seretide 100 Accuhaler® (dry powder for inhalation), disk containing 60 blisters of fluticasone propionate 100 micrograms, salmeterol (as xinafoate) 50 micrograms/blister with *Accuhaler®* device, net price = £31.19. Label: 8, counselling, dose

Dose by inhalation of powder, asthma, ADULT and CHILD over 4 years, 1 blister twice daily, reduced to 1 blister once daily if control maintained

Seretide 250 Accuhaler® (dry powder for inhalation), disk containing 60 blisters of fluticasone propionate 250 micrograms, salmeterol (as xinafoate) 50 micrograms/blister with *Accuhaler®* device, net price = £36.65. Label: 8, counselling, dose, 10, steroid card

Dose by inhalation of powder, asthma, ADULT and CHILD over 12 years, 1 blister twice daily

Seretide 500 Accuhaler® (dry powder for inhalation), disk containing 60 blisters of fluticasone propionate 500 micrograms, salmeterol (as xinafoate) 50 micrograms/blister with *Accuhaler®* device, net price = £40.92. Label: 8, counselling, dose, 10, steroid card

Dose by inhalation of powder, asthma, ADULT and CHILD over 12 years, 1 blister twice daily

Chronic obstructive pulmonary disease, ADULT 1 blister twice daily

Seretide 50 Evohaler® (aerosol inhalation), fluticasone propionate 50 micrograms, salmeterol (as xinafoate) 25 micrograms/metered inhalation, net price 120-dose unit = £19.50. Label: 8, counselling, dose, change to CFC-free inhaler

Excipients include HFA-134a (a non-CFC propellant)

Dose by aerosol inhalation, asthma, ADULT and CHILD over 4 years, 2 puffs twice daily, reduced to 2 puffs once daily if control maintained

Seretide 125 Evohaler® (aerosol inhalation), fluticasone propionate 125 micrograms, salmeterol (as xinafoate) 25 micrograms/metered inhalation, net price 120-dose unit = £39.41. Label: 8, counselling, dose, change to CFC-free inhaler, 10, steroid card

Excipients include HFA-134a (a non-CFC propellant)

Dose by aerosol inhalation, asthma, ADULT and CHILD over 12 years, 2 puffs twice daily

Seretide 250 Evohaler® (aerosol inhalation), fluticasone propionate 250 micrograms, salmeterol (as xinafoate) 25 micrograms/metered inhalation, net

price 120-dose unit = £66.98. Label: 8, counselling, dose, change to CFC-free inhaler, 10, steroid card
**Excipients** include HFA-134a (a non-CFC propellant)
**Dose** by aerosol inhalation, asthma, ADULT and CHILD over 12 years, 2 puffs twice daily

## MOMETASONE FUROATE

**Indications** prophylaxis of asthma (see also Chronic Asthma table, p. 141)
**Cautions** see notes above
**Side-effects** see notes above; also pharyngitis
**Dose**
- By inhalation of powder, 200–400 micrograms as a single dose in the evening or in 2 divided doses; dose increased to 400 micrograms twice daily if necessary; CHILD not recommended

**Asmanex®** (Schering-Plough) ▼ PoM
Twisthaler (= dry powder inhaler), mometasone furoate 200 micrograms/metered inhalation, net price 30-dose unit = £16.00, 60-dose unit = £24.00; 400 micrograms/metered inhalation, 30-dose unit = £22.20, 60-dose unit = £36.75. Label: 8, counselling, dose, 10, steroid card

# 3.3 Cromoglicate and related therapy, leukotriene receptor antagonists, and omalizumab

**3.3.1** Cromoglicate and related therapy
**3.3.2** Leukotriene receptor antagonists and omalizumab

## 3.3.1 Cromoglicate and related therapy

The mode of action of **sodium cromoglicate** and **nedocromil** is not completely understood. They may be of value in asthma with an allergic basis, but, in practice, it is difficult to predict who will benefit; they could probably be given for 4 to 6 weeks to assess response. Dose frequency is adjusted according to response but is usually 3 to 4 times a day initially; this may subsequently be reduced.

In general, *prophylaxis* with sodium cromoglicate is less effective than prophylaxis with corticosteroid inhalations (see Chronic Asthma table, p. 141). There is evidence of efficacy of nedocromil in children aged 5–12 years. Sodium cromoglicate is of no value in the treatment of acute attacks of asthma.

Sodium cromoglicate can prevent exercise-induced asthma. However, exercise-induced asthma may reflect poor overall control and the patient should be assessed.

If inhalation of the dry powder form of sodium cromoglicate causes bronchospasm a selective $beta_2$-adrenoceptor stimulant such as salbutamol or terbutaline should be inhaled a few minutes beforehand. The nebuliser solution is an alternative means of delivery for children who cannot manage the dry powder inhaler or the aerosol.

## SODIUM CROMOGLICATE
(Sodium Cromoglycate)

**Indications** prophylaxis of asthma; food allergy (section 1.5); allergic conjunctivitis (section 11.4.2); allergic rhinitis (section 12.2.1)
**Side-effects** coughing, transient bronchospasm, and throat irritation due to inhalation of powder (see also notes above)
**Dose**
- By aerosol inhalation, ADULT and CHILD, 10 mg (2 puffs) 4 times daily, increased in severe cases or during periods of risk to 6–8 times daily; additional doses may also be taken before exercise; maintenance 5 mg (1 puff) 4 times daily
- By inhalation of powder (*Spincaps®*), ADULT and CHILD, 20 mg 4 times daily, increased in severe cases to 8 times daily; additional doses may also be taken before exercise
- By inhalation of nebulised solution, ADULT and CHILD, 20 mg 4 times daily, increased in severe cases to 6 times daily
**Counselling** Regular use is necessary

**Sodium Cromoglicate** (Non-proprietary) PoM
Aerosol inhalation, sodium cromoglicate 5 mg/metered inhalation. Net price 112-dose unit = £5.92. Label: 8
**Excipients** include CFC propellants
Brands include *Cromogen®*

**Cromogen Easi-Breathe®** (IVAX) PoM
Aerosol inhalation, sodium cromoglicate 5 mg/metered inhalation. Net price 112-dose breath-actuated unit = £13.91. Label: 8
**Excipients** include CFC propellants

**Intal®** (Rhône-Poulenc Rorer) PoM
Aerosol inhalation, sodium cromoglicate 5 mg/metered inhalation. Net price 112-dose unit with large volume spacer inhaler (*Fisonair®*) = £20.52. Label: 8
**Excipients** include CFC propellants
Spincaps®, yellow/clear, sodium cromoglicate 20 mg. Net price 112-cap pack = £15.44. Label: 8
Spinhaler insufflator® (for use with *Intal Spincaps*). Net price = £1.92

## NEDOCROMIL SODIUM

**Indications** prophylaxis of asthma
**Side-effects** see under Sodium Cromoglicate; also headache, nausea, vomiting, dyspepsia and abdominal pain; bitter taste (masked by mint flavour)
**Dose**
- By aerosol inhalation, ADULT and CHILD over 6 years 4 mg (2 puffs) 4 times daily, when control achieved may be possible to reduce to twice daily
**Counselling** Regular use is necessary

**Tilade CFC-free Inhaler®** (Sanofi-Aventis) ▼ PoM
Aerosol inhalation, mint-flavoured, nedocromil sodium 2 mg/metered inhalation. Net price 112-dose unit = £39.94. Label: 8, counselling, change to CFC-free inhaler
**Excipients** include HFA-227 (a non-CFC propellant)

## Related therapy

Antihistamines are of no value in the treatment of bronchial asthma. **Ketotifen** is an antihistamine with an action said to resemble that of sodium cromoglicate, but it has proved ineffective in asthma. Specialists sometimes use it in the management of urticaria [unlicensed indication].

### KETOTIFEN ▲

**Indications** see notes above

**Cautions** previous anti-asthmatic treatment should be continued for a minimum of 2 weeks after initiation of ketotifen treatment; pregnancy (Appendix 4) and breast-feeding (Appendix 5); **interactions:** Appendix 1 (antihistamines)—also, manufacturer advises avoid with oral antidiabetics (fall in thrombocyte count reported)

Driving Drowsiness may affect performance of skilled tasks (e.g. driving); effects of alcohol enhanced

**Side-effects** drowsiness, dry mouth, slight dizziness; CNS stimulation, weight gain also reported

**Dose**

- 1 mg twice daily with food increased if necessary to 2 mg twice daily; initial treatment in readily sedated patients 0.5–1 mg at night; CHILD over 2 years 1 mg twice daily

**Zaditen®** (Novartis) PoM ▲

Tablets, scored, ketotifen (as hydrogen fumarate) 1 mg. Net price 60-tab pack = £9.77. Label: 2, 8, 21

Elixir, ketotifen (as hydrogen fumarate) 1 mg/5 mL. Net price 300 mL = £11.57. Label: 2, 8, 21

3 Respiratory system

## 3.3.2 Leukotriene receptor antagonists and omalizumab

The leukotriene receptor antagonists, **montelukast** and **zafirlukast**, block the effects of cysteinyl leukotrienes in the airways. They are effective in asthma when used alone or with an inhaled corticosteroid (see Chronic Asthma table, p. 141). Montelukast has not been shown to be more effective than a standard dose of inhaled corticosteroid but the two drugs appear to have an additive effect. The leukotriene receptor antagonists may be of benefit in exercise-induced asthma and in those with concomitant rhinitis but they are less effective in those with severe asthma who are also receiving high doses of other drugs.

Churg-Strauss syndrome has occurred very rarely in association with the use of leukotriene receptor antagonists; in many of the reported cases the reaction followed the reduction or withdrawal of oral corticosteroid therapy. The CSM has advised that prescribers should be alert to the development of eosinophilia, vasculitic rash, worsening pulmonary symptoms, cardiac complications, or peripheral neuropathy.

### MONTELUKAST

**Indications** prophylaxis of asthma, see notes above and Chronic Asthma table, p. 141

**Cautions** pregnancy (Appendix 4); breast-feeding (Appendix 5); **interactions:** Appendix 1 (leukotriene antagonists)

**Side-effects** abdominal pain, thirst; hyperkinesia (in young children), headache; *very rarely* dry mouth, diarrhoea, dyspepsia, nausea, vomiting, hepatic disorders, palpitation, oedema, increased bleeding, Churg-Strauss syndrome (see notes above), asthenia, dizziness, hallucinations, paraesthesia, hypoaesthesia, sleep disturbances, abnormal dreams, agitation, aggression, seizures, arthralgia, myalgia, pruritus, and rash

**Dose**

- 10 mg daily in the evening; CHILD 6 months–5 years 4 mg daily in the evening, 6–14 years 5 mg daily in the evening

**Singulair®** (MSD) PoM

Chewable tablets, pink, cherry-flavoured, montelukast (as sodium salt) 4 mg, net price 28-tab pack = £25.69; 5 mg, 28-tab pack = £25.69. Label: 24

Excipients include aspartame equivalent to phenylalanine 674 micrograms/4-mg tablet and 842 micrograms/5-mg tablet (section 9.4.1)

Granules, montelukast (as sodium salt) 4 mg, net price 28-sachet pack = £25.69. Counselling, administration

Counselling Granules may be swallowed or mixed with cold food (but not fluid) and taken immediately

Tablets, beige, f/c, montelukast (as sodium salt) 10 mg, net price 28-tab pack = £26.97

### ZAFIRLUKAST

**Indications** prophylaxis of asthma, see notes above and Chronic Asthma table, p. 141

**Cautions** elderly, pregnancy (Appendix 4), renal impairment (Appendix 3); Churg-Strauss syndrome, see notes above; **interactions:** Appendix 1 (leukotriene antagonists)

Hepatic disorders Patients or their carers should be told how to recognise development of liver disorder and advised to seek medical attention if symptoms or signs such as persistent nausea, vomiting, malaise or jaundice develop

**Contra-indications** hepatic impairment; breast-feeding (Appendix 5)

**Side-effects** gastro-intestinal disturbances, headache, insomnia, malaise; *rarely* bleeding disorders, hypersensitivity reactions including angioedema and skin reactions, arthralgia, myalgia, hepatitis, hyperbilirubinaemia, thrombocytopenia; *very rarely* agranulocytosis; also respiratory-tract infection in the elderly

**Dose**

- 20 mg twice daily; CHILD under 12 years, not recommended

**Accolate®** (AstraZeneca) PoM

Tablets, f/c, zafirlukast 20 mg, net price 56-tab pack = £28.26. Label: 23

## Omalizumab

**Omalizumab** is a monoclonal antibody that binds to immunoglobulin E (IgE). It is licensed for use as additional therapy in individuals with proven IgE-mediated sensitivity to inhaled allergens, whose severe persistent allergic asthma cannot be controlled adequately with high-dose inhaled corticosteroid together with a long-acting $beta_2$ agonist. Omalizumab should be initiated by physicians experienced in the treatment of severe persistent asthma.

## OMALIZUMAB

**Indications** prophylaxis of allergic asthma (see notes above)

**Cautions** autoimmune disease; susceptibility to helminth infection—discontinue if infection does not respond to anthelmintic; hepatic impairment; renal impairment; pregnancy (Appendix 4)

**Contra-indications** breast-feeding (Appendix 5)

**Side-effects** headache; injection-site reactions; *less commonly* nausea, diarrhoea, dyspepsia, postural hypotension, flushing, pharyngitis, cough, fatigue, dizziness, drowsiness, paraesthesia, weight gain, influenza-like symptoms, rash, pruritus, and photosensitivity

**Dose**

- By subcutaneous injection, according to immunoglobulin E concentration and body-weight, consult product literature; CHILD under 12 years, not recommended

**Xolair®** (Novartis) ▼ PoM

Injection, powder for reconstitution, omalizumab, net price 150-mg vial = £256.15 (with solvent)
Excipients include sucrose 108 mg/vial

# 3.4 Antihistamines, hyposensitisation, and allergic emergencies

3.4.1 Antihistamines
3.4.2 Hyposensitisation
3.4.3 Allergic emergencies

## 3.4.1 Antihistamines

All antihistamines are of potential value in the treatment of nasal allergies, particularly seasonal allergic rhinitis (hay fever), and they may be of some value in vasomotor rhinitis. They reduce rhinorrhoea and sneezing but are usually less effective for nasal congestion. Antihistamines are used topically in the eye (section 11.4.2), in the nose (section 12.2.1), and on the skin (section 13.3).

Oral antihistamines are also of some value in preventing urticaria and are used to treat urticarial rashes, pruritus, and insect bites and stings; they are also used in drug allergies. Injections of chlorphenamine (chlorpheniramine) or promethazine are used as an adjunct to adrenaline (epinephrine) in the emergency treatment of anaphylaxis and angioedema (section 3.4.3). For the use of antihistamines (including cinnarizine, cyclizine, and promethazine teoclate) in nausea and vomiting, see section 4.6. Buclizine is included as an anti-emetic in a preparation for migraine (section 4.7.4.1). For reference to the use of antihistamines for occasional insomnia, see section 4.1.1.

Antihistamines differ in their duration of action and incidence of drowsiness and antimuscarinic effects. Many older antihistamines are relatively short acting but some (e.g. promethazine) act for up to 12 hours, while most of the newer non-sedating antihistamines are long acting.

All older antihistamines cause sedation but **alimemazine** (trimeprazine) and **promethazine** may be more sedating whereas **chlorphenamine** and **cyclizine** (section 4.6) may be less so. This sedating activity is sometimes used to manage the pruritus associated with some allergies. There is little evidence that any one of the older, 'sedating' antihistamines is superior to another and patients vary widely in their response.

Non-sedating antihistamines such as **cetirizine**, **desloratadine** (an active metabolite of loratadine), **fexofenadine** (an active metabolite of terfenadine), **levocetirizine** (an isomer of cetirizine), **loratadine**, and **mizolastine** cause less sedation and psychomotor impairment than the older antihistamines because they penetrate the blood brain barrier only to a slight extent.

**Dental surgery** Antihistamines are used widely as anti-emetics (section 4.6) but diazepam is likely to be more effective in patients with an overactive vomiting reflex. See also Anaphylaxis under Medical Emergencies in Dental Practice, p. 20.

**Cautions and contra-indications** Sedating antihistamines have significant antimuscarinic activity and they should therefore be used with caution in prostatic hypertrophy, urinary retention, glaucoma and pyloroduodenal obstruction. Antihistamines should be used with caution in hepatic disease (Appendix 2) and dose reduction may be necessary in renal impairment (Appendix 3). Caution may be required in epilepsy. Children and the elderly are more susceptible to side-effects. Many antihistamines should be avoided in porphyria although some (e.g. chlorphenamine and cetirizine) are thought to be safe (section 9.8.2). **Interactions:** Appendix 1 (antihistamines).

**Side-effects** Drowsiness is a significant side-effect with most of the older antihistamines although paradoxical stimulation may occur rarely, especially with high doses or in children and the elderly. Drowsiness may diminish after a few days of treatment and is considerably less of a problem with the newer antihistamines (see also notes above). Side-effects that are more common with the older antihistamines include headache, psychomotor impairment, and antimuscarinic effects such as urinary retention, dry mouth, blurred vision, and gastro-intestinal disturbances.

Other rare side-effects of antihistamines include hypotension, extrapyramidal effects, dizziness, confusion, depression, sleep disturbances, tremor, convulsions, palpitation, arrhythmias, hypersensitivity reactions (including bronchospasm, angioedema, and anaphylaxis, rashes, and photosensitivity reactions), blood disorders, and liver dysfunction.

### Non-sedating antihistamines

**Driving** Although drowsiness is rare, nevertheless patients should be advised that it can occur and may affect performance of skilled tasks (e.g. driving); excess alcohol should be avoided.

## ACRIVASTINE

**Indications** symptomatic relief of allergy such as hay fever, urticaria

**Cautions** see notes above; pregnancy (Appendix 4) and breast-feeding (Appendix 5)

**Contra-indications** see notes above; also avoid in renal impairment (Appendix 3); hypersensitivity to triprolidine

**Side-effects** see notes above; incidence of sedation and antimuscarinic effects low

**Dose**

- 8 mg 3 times daily; CHILD under 12 years, not recommended; ELDERLY not recommended

**Preparations**

Capsules can be sold to the public for the treatment of hay fever and allergic skin conditions in adults and children over 12 years provided packs do not contain over 10 days' supply (*Benadryl® Allergy Relief*)

## CETIRIZINE HYDROCHLORIDE

**Indications** symptomatic relief of allergy such as hay fever, urticaria

**Cautions** see notes above

**Contra-indications** see notes above; also pregnancy (Appendix 4) and breast-feeding (Appendix 5)

**Side-effects** see notes above; incidence of sedation and antimuscarinic effects low

**Dose**

- ADULT and CHILD over 6 years, 10 mg daily *or* 5 mg twice daily; CHILD 2–6 years, hay fever, 5 mg daily *or* 2.5 mg twice daily

**Cetirizine** (Non-proprietary)

Tablets, cetirizine hydrochloride 10 mg, net price 30-tab pack = £1.46. Counselling, driving

Oral solution, cetirizine hydrochloride 5 mg/5 mL, net price 200 mL = £8.39. Counselling, driving

## DESLORATADINE

Note Desloratadine is a metabolite of loratadine

**Indications** symptomatic relief of allergy such as hay fever, urticaria

**Cautions** see notes above

**Contra-indications** see notes above; also hypersensitivity to loratadine; pregnancy (Appendix 4) and breast-feeding (Appendix 5)

**Side-effects** see notes above; *rarely* myalgia; incidence of sedation and antimuscarinic effects low

**Dose**

- ADULT and ADOLESCENT over 12 years, 5 mg daily; CHILD 1–5 years 1.25 mg daily, 6–11 years 2.5 mg daily

**Neoclarityn®** (Schering-Plough) PoM

Tablets, blue, f/c, desloratadine 5 mg, net price 30-tab pack = £7.04. Counselling, driving

Syrup, desloratadine 2.5 mg/5 mL, net price 100 mL (bubblegum-flavour) = £7.04. Counselling, driving

## FEXOFENADINE HYDROCHLORIDE

Note Fexofenadine is a metabolite of terfenadine

**Indications** see under Dose

**Cautions** see notes above; also pregnancy (Appendix 4)

**Contra-indications** see notes above; also breast-feeding (Appendix 5)

**Side-effects** see notes above; incidence of sedation and antimuscarinic effects low

**Dose**

- Seasonal allergic rhinitis, 120 mg once daily; CHILD 6–11 years, 30 mg twice daily
- Chronic idiopathic urticaria, 180 mg once daily; CHILD under 12 years, not recommended

**Telfast®** (Aventis Pharma) PoM

Tablets, f/c, peach, fexofenadine hydrochloride 30 mg, net price 60-tab pack = £5.68; 120 mg, 30-tab pack = £6.23; 180 mg, 30-tab pack = £7.89. Counselling, driving

## LEVOCETIRIZINE HYDROCHLORIDE

Note Levocetirizine is an isomer of cetirizine

**Indications** symptomatic relief of allergy such as hay fever, urticaria

**Cautions** see notes above; also pregnancy (Appendix 4) and breast-feeding (Appendix 5)

**Contra-indications** see notes above; also severe renal impairment

**Side-effects** see notes above; incidence of sedation and antimuscarinic effects low

**Dose**

- ADULT and CHILD over 6 years, 5 mg daily

**Xyzal®** (UCB Pharma) ▼ PoM

Tablets, f/c, levocetirizine hydrochloride 5 mg, net price 30-tab pack = £7.45. Counselling, driving

## LORATADINE

**Indications** symptomatic relief of allergy such as hay fever, urticaria

**Cautions** see notes above

**Contra-indications** see notes above; also pregnancy (Appendix 4) and breast-feeding (Appendix 5)

**Side-effects** see notes above; incidence of sedation and antimuscarinic effects low

**Dose**

- ADULT and CHILD over 6 years 10 mg daily; CHILD 2–5 years 5 mg daily

**Loratadine** (Non-proprietary)

Tablets, loratadine 10 mg, net price 30-tab pack = £1.73

Syrup, loratadine 5 mg/5 mL, net price 100 mL = £7.57. Counselling, driving

## MIZOLASTINE

**Indications** symptomatic relief of allergy such as hay fever, urticaria

**Cautions** see notes above

**Contra-indications** see notes above; also susceptibility to QT-interval prolongation (including cardiac disease and hypokalaemia); significant hepatic impairment; pregnancy (Appendix 4) and breast-feeding (Appendix 5)

**Side-effects** see notes above; also may cause weight gain; incidence of sedation and antimuscarinic effects low

**Dose**

- 10 mg daily; CHILD under 12 years, not recommended

**Mizollen®** (Schwarz) PoM

Tablets, m/r, f/c, scored, mizolastine 10 mg, net price 30-tab pack = £5.77. Label: 25, Counselling, driving

## Sedating antihistamines

**Driving** Drowsiness may affect performance of skilled tasks (e.g. driving); sedating effects enhanced by alcohol.

### ALIMEMAZINE TARTRATE
(Trimeprazine tartrate)

**Indications** urticaria and pruritus, premedication

**Cautions** see notes above; also pregnancy (Appendix 4); see also section 4.2.1

**Contra-indications** see notes above; also breast-feeding (Appendix 5); see also section 4.2.1

**Side-effects** see notes above; see also section 4.2.1

**Dose**

- Urticaria and pruritus, 10 mg 2–3 times daily, in severe cases up to max. 100 mg daily has been used; ELDERLY 10 mg 1–2 times daily; CHILD over 2 years 2.5–5 mg 3–4 times daily
- Premedication, CHILD 2–7 years up to 2 mg/kg 1–2 hours before operation

**Vallergan®** (Castlemead) PoM

Tablets, blue, f/c, alimemazine tartrate 10 mg, net price 28-tab pack = £3.01. Label: 2

Syrup, straw-coloured, alimemazine tartrate 7.5 mg / 5 mL, net price 100 mL = £3.44. Label: 2

Syrup forte, alimemazine tartrate 30 mg/5 mL, net price 100 mL = £5.32. Label: 2

### CHLORPHENAMINE MALEATE
(Chlorpheniramine maleate)

**Indications** symptomatic relief of allergy such as hay fever, urticaria; emergency treatment of anaphylactic reactions (section 3.4.3)

**Cautions** see notes above; also pregnancy (Appendix 4) and breast-feeding (Appendix 5)

**Contra-indications** see notes above

**Side-effects** see notes above; also exfoliative dermatitis and tinnitus reported; injections may cause transient hypotension or CNS stimulation and may be irritant

**Dose**

- By mouth, 4 mg every 4–6 hours, max. 24 mg daily; INFANT under 1 year not recommended, 1–2 years 1 mg twice daily; CHILD 2–5 years 1 mg every 4–6 hours, max. 6 mg daily; 6–12 years 2 mg every 4–6 hours, max. 12 mg daily
- By subcutaneous *or* intramuscular injection *or* by intravenous injection over 1 minute, 10–20 mg; max. 40 mg in 24 hours; INFANT 1 month–1 year 250 micrograms/kg; CHILD 1–12 years 200 micrograms/kg *or* 1–5 years 2.5–5 mg, 6–12 years 5–10 mg

**Chlorphenamine** (Non-proprietary)

Tablets, chlorphenamine maleate 4 mg, net price 28 = £1.02. Label: 2

Dental prescribing on NHS Chlorphenamine tablets may be prescribed

Oral solution, chlorphenamine maleate 2 mg/5 mL, net price 150 mL = £2.28. Label: 2

Injection PoM[1], chlorphenamine maleate 10 mg/mL, net price 1-mL amp = £1.62

1. PoM restriction does not apply where administration is for saving life in emergency

**Piriton®** (GSK Consumer Healthcare)

Tablets, yellow, scored, chlorphenamine maleate 4 mg, net price 20 = 19p. Label: 2

Syrup, chlorphenamine maleate 2 mg/5 mL, net price 150 mL = £2.28. Label: 2

### CLEMASTINE

**Indications** symptomatic relief of allergy such as hay fever, urticaria

**Cautions** see notes above; also pregnancy (Appendix 4) and breast-feeding (Appendix 5)

**Contra-indications** see notes above

**Side-effects** see notes above

**Dose**

- 1 mg twice daily, increased up to 6 mg daily if required; INFANT under 1 year not recommended, CHILD 1–3 years 250–500 micrograms twice daily; 3–6 years 500 micrograms twice daily; 6–12 years 0.5–1 mg twice daily

**Tavegil®** (Novartis Consumer Health)

Tablets, scored, clemastine (as hydrogen fumarate) 1 mg. Net price 60-tab pack = £2.35. Label: 2

### CYPROHEPTADINE HYDROCHLORIDE

**Indications** symptomatic relief of allergy such as hay fever, urticaria; migraine (section 4.7.4.2)

**Cautions** see notes above; also pregnancy (Appendix 4) and breast-feeding (Appendix 5)

**Contra-indications** see notes above

**Side-effects** see notes above

**Dose**

- Allergy, usual dose 4 mg 3–4 times daily; usual range 4–20 mg daily, max. 32 mg daily; INFANT under 2 years not recommended, CHILD 2–6 years 2 mg 2–3 times daily, max. 12 mg daily; 7–14 years 4 mg 2–3 times daily, max. 16 mg daily
- Migraine, 4 mg with a further 4 mg after 30 minutes if necessary; maintenance, 4 mg every 4–6 hours

**Periactin®** (MSD)

Tablets, scored, cyproheptadine hydrochloride 4 mg. Net price 30 = 86p. Label: 2

### HYDROXYZINE HYDROCHLORIDE

**Indications** pruritus, anxiety (short-term) (section 4.1.2)

**Cautions** see notes above

**Contra-indications** see notes above; also pregnancy (Appendix 4) and breast-feeding (Appendix 5)

**Side-effects** see notes above

**Dose**

- Pruritus, initially 25 mg at night increased if necessary to 25 mg 3–4 times daily; CHILD 6 months–6 years initially 5–15 mg daily increased if necessary to 50 mg daily in divided doses; over 6 years initially 15–25 mg daily increased if necessary to 50–100 mg daily in divided doses
- Anxiety (adults only), 50–100 mg 4 times daily

**Atarax®** (Pfizer) PoM

Tablets, both s/c, hydroxyzine hydrochloride 10 mg (orange), net price 84-tab pack = £1.82; 25 mg (green), 28-tab pack = £1.22. Label: 2

**Ucerax®** (UCB Pharma) PoM

Tablets NHS, f/c, scored, hydroxyzine hydrochloride 25 mg, net price 25-tab pack = 85p. Label: 2

Syrup, hydroxyzine hydrochloride 10 mg/5 mL. Net price 200-mL pack = £1.78. Label: 2

## PROMETHAZINE HYDROCHLORIDE

**Indications** symptomatic relief of allergy such as hay fever, urticaria; premedication; emergency treatment of anaphylactic reactions (section 3.4.3); sedation (section 4.1.1); motion sickness (section 4.6)

**Cautions** see notes above; also pregnancy (Appendix 4) and breast-feeding (Appendix 5)

**Contra-indications** see notes above

**Side-effects** see notes above; intramuscular injection may be painful

**Dose**

- By mouth, 25 mg at night increased to 25 mg twice daily if necessary *or* 10–20 mg 2–3 times daily; CHILD under 2 years not recommended, 2–5 years 5–15 mg daily in 1–2 divided doses, 5–10 years 10–25 mg daily in 1–2 divided doses

  Premedication, CHILD under 2 years not recommended, 2–5 years 15–20 mg, 5–10 years 20–25 mg
- By deep intramuscular injection, 25–50 mg; max. 100 mg; CHILD 5–10 years 6.25–12.5 mg

  Premedication, 25–50 mg 1 hour before operation; CHILD 5–10 years, 6.25–12.5 mg
- By slow intravenous injection in emergencies, 25–50 mg as a solution containing 2.5 mg/mL in water for injections; max. 100 mg

**Phenergan®** (Rhône-Poulenc Rorer)

Tablets, both blue, f/c, promethazine hydrochloride 10 mg, net price 56-tab pack = £1.71; 25 mg, 56-tab pack = £2.55. Label: 2

**Dental prescribing on NHS** May be prescribed as Promethazine Hydrochloride Tablets 10 mg or 25 mg

Elixir, sugar-free, golden, promethazine hydrochloride 5 mg/5 mL. Net price 100 mL = £1.49. Label: 2

**Dental prescribing on NHS** May be prescribed as Promethazine Hydrochloride Oral Solution 5 mg/5 mL

Injection PoM[1], promethazine hydrochloride 25 mg/mL. Net price 1-mL amp = 58p

Promethazine hydrochloride injection 25 mg/mL (1-mL and 2-mL ampoules) also available from Antigen

1. PoM restriction does not apply where administration is for saving life in emergency

# 3.4.2 Hyposensitisation

Immunotherapy using allergen vaccines containing house dust mite, animal dander, or extracts of grass and tree pollen can reduce symptoms of asthma and allergic rhinoconjunctivitis. A vaccine containing extracts of wasp and bee venom is used to reduce the risk of severe anaphylaxis and systemic reactions in individuals with hypersensitivity to wasp and bee stings. Those requiring immunotherapy must be referred to a hospital specialist for accurate diagnosis, assessment, and treatment.

> **CSM advice**
>
> After re-examination of the efficacy and safety of desensitising vaccines, the CSM has concluded that they should only be used for the following indications:
>
> - Seasonal allergic hay fever (which has not responded to anti-allergy drugs) caused by pollens, using licensed products only—patients with *asthma* should not be treated with desensitising vaccines as they are more likely to develop severe adverse reactions.
> - Hypersensitivity to wasp and bee venoms—since reactions can be life-threatening, *asthma* is not an absolute contra-indication.

Desensitising vaccines should be avoided in pregnant women, in children under five years old, and in those taking beta-blockers (adrenaline may be ineffective in case of a hypersensitivity reaction), or ACE inhibitors (risk of severe anaphylactoid reactions).

Hypersensitivity reactions to immunotherapy (especially to wasp and bee venom extracts) can be life-threatening; bronchospasm usually develops within 1 hour and anaphylaxis within 30 minutes of injection. Therefore patients need to be monitored for 1 hour after injection. If symptoms or signs of hypersensitivity develop (e.g. rash, urticaria, bronchospasm, faintness), **even when mild**, the patient should be observed until these have **resolved completely**.

For details of the management of anaphylactic shock, see section 3.4.3.

Each set of allergen extracts usually contains vials for the administration of graded amounts of allergen to patients undergoing hyposensitisation. Maintenance sets containing vials at the highest strength are also available. Product literature must be consulted for details of allergens, vial strengths, and administration.

## BEE AND WASP ALLERGEN EXTRACTS

**Indications** hypersensitivity to wasp or bee venom (see notes above)

**Cautions** see notes above including CSM advice and consult product literature

**CSM advice**. The CSM has advised that facilities for cardiopulmonary resuscitation must be immediately available and patients monitored closely for one hour after each injection, for full details see above.

**Contra-indications** see notes above and consult product literature

**Side-effects** consult product literature

**Dose**

- By subcutaneous injection, consult product literature

3 Respiratory system

**Pharmalgen®** (ALK-Abelló) PoM

Bee venom extract (*Apis mellifera*) or wasp venom extract (*Vespula* spp.). Net price initial treatment set = £59.77 (bee), £73.28 (wasp); maintenance treatment set = £69.54 (bee), £89.45 (wasp)

## GRASS AND TREE POLLEN EXTRACTS

**Indications** treatment of seasonal allergic hay fever due to grass or tree pollen in patients who have failed to respond to anti-allergy drugs (see notes above)

**Cautions** see notes above including CSM advice and consult product literature

**CSM advice.** The CSM has advised that facilities for cardiopulmonary resuscitation must be immediately available and patients must be monitored closely for one hour after each injection, for full details see above.

**Contra-indications** see notes above and consult product literature

**Side-effects** consult product literature

**Dose**

- By subcutaneous injection, consult product literature

**Pollinex®** (Allergy) PoM

Grass or tree pollen extract, net price initial treatment set (3 vials) = £170.00; extension course treatment (1 vial) = £150.00

# 3.4.3 Allergic emergencies

**Adrenaline (epinephrine)** provides physiological reversal of the immediate symptoms (such as laryngeal oedema, bronchospasm, and hypotension) associated with hypersensitivity reactions such as *anaphylaxis* and *angioedema*. See below for full details of adrenaline administration and for adjunctive treatment.

## Anaphylaxis

*Anaphylactic shock* requires prompt energetic treatment of *laryngeal oedema, bronchospasm*, and *hypotension*. Atopic individuals are particularly susceptible. Insect stings are a recognised risk (in particular wasp and bee stings). Certain foods, including eggs, fish, cow's milk protein, peanuts, and nuts may also precipitate anaphylaxis. Medicinal products particularly associated with anaphylaxis include blood products, vaccines, hyposensitising (allergen) preparations, antibacterials, aspirin and other NSAIDs, heparin, and neuromuscular blocking drugs. In the case of drugs, anaphylaxis is more likely after parenteral administration; resuscitation facilities must always be available for injections associated with special risk. Anaphylactic reactions may also be associated with *additives and excipients* in foods and medicines. Refined arachis (peanut) oil, which may be present in some medicinal products, is unlikely to cause an allergic reaction—nevertheless it is wise to check the full formula of preparations which may contain allergenic fats or oils.

*First-line treatment* includes securing the airway, restoration of blood pressure (laying the patient flat, raising the feet), and administration of **adrenaline** (epinephrine) injection. This is given **intramuscularly** in a dose of 500 micrograms (0.5 mL adrenaline injection 1 in 1000); a dose of 300 micrograms (0.3 mL adrenaline injection 1 in 1000) may be appropriate for *immediate self-administration*. The dose is repeated if necessary at 5-minute intervals according to blood pressure, pulse and respiratory function (important: possible need for *intravenous route* using *dilute solution*, see below). **Oxygen** administration is also of primary importance. An antihistamine (e.g. **chlorphenamine** (chlorpheniramine), given by slow intravenous injection in a dose of 10–20 mg, see p. 163) is a useful adjunctive treatment, given after adrenaline injection and continued for 24 to 48 hours to prevent relapse. Patients receiving beta-blockers or those receiving antidepressants require special consideration (see under Adrenaline, p. 166).

*Continuing deterioration* requires further treatment including intravenous fluids (section 9.2.2), intravenous aminophylline (see p. 150) or a nebulised $beta_2$ agonist (such as salbutamol or terbutaline, see p. 145 and p. 146); in addition to oxygen, assisted respiration and possibly emergency tracheotomy may be necessary.

An intravenous corticosteroid e.g. **hydrocortisone** (as sodium succinate) in a dose of 100–300 mg (section 6.3.2) is of secondary value in the initial management of anaphylactic shock because the onset of action is delayed for several hours, but should be given to prevent further deterioration in severely affected patients.

When a patient is so ill that there is doubt as to the adequacy of the circulation, the initial injection of adrenaline may need to be given as a *dilute solution by the intravenous route*, for details of cautions, dose and strength, see under Intravenous Adrenaline (Epinephrine), below.

Some patients with severe allergy to insect stings or foods are encouraged to carry prefilled adrenaline syringes for *self-administration* during periods of risk.

For advice on the management of medical emergencies in dental practice, see p. 20.

## Angioedema

*Angioedema* is dangerous if *laryngeal oedema* is present. In this circumstance adrenaline (epinephrine) injection and oxygen should be given as described under Anaphylaxis (see above); antihistamines and corticosteroids should also be given (see again above). Tracheal intubation may be necessary.

The administration of $C_1$ esterase inhibitor (in fresh frozen plasma or in partially purified form) may terminate acute attacks of *hereditary angioedema*, but is not practical for long-term prophylaxis. **Tranexamic acid** (section 2.11) and **danazol** (section 6.7.2) [unlicensed indication] are used for long-term prophylaxis of hereditary angiodema.

## Intramuscular adrenaline (epinephrine)

The *intramuscular route* is the *first choice route* for the administration of adrenaline (epinephrine) in the management of anaphylactic shock. Adrenaline has a rapid onset of action after intramuscular administration and in the shocked patient its absorption from the intramuscular site is faster and more reliable than from the subcutaneous site (the intravenous route should be reserved for extreme emergency when there is doubt about the adequacy of the circulation; for details of cautions, dose and strength see under Intravenous Adrenaline (Epinephrine), below).

Patients with severe allergy should ideally be instructed in the self-administration of adrenaline by intramuscular injection (for details see under Self-administration of Adrenaline (Epinephrine), below).

*Prompt injection* of adrenaline is of paramount importance. The following adrenaline doses are based on the revised recommendations of the Project Team of the Resuscitation Council (UK).

**Dose of *intramuscular* injection of adrenaline (epinephrine) for anaphylactic shock**

| Age | Dose | Volume of adrenaline **1 in 1000** (1 mg/mL) |
|---|---|---|
| Under 6 months | 50 micrograms | 0.05 mL[1] |
| 6 months–6 years | 120 micrograms | 0.12 mL[1] |
| 6–12 years | 250 micrograms | 0.25 mL |
| Adult and adolescent | 500 micrograms | 0.5 mL |

These doses may be repeated several times if necessary at 5-minute intervals according to blood pressure, pulse and respiratory function.
Subcutaneous injection **not** generally recommended.

1. Use suitable syringe for measuring small volume

## Intravenous adrenaline (epinephrine)

Where the patient is severely ill and there is real doubt about adequacy of the circulation and absorption from the intramuscular injection site, adrenaline (epinephrine) may be given by **slow** *intravenous injection* in a dose of 500 micrograms (5 mL of the dilute 1 in 10 000 adrenaline injection) given at a rate of 100 micrograms (1 mL of the dilute 1 in 10 000 adrenaline injection) per minute, *stopping when a response has been obtained*; children can be given a dose of 10 micrograms/kg (0.1 mL/kg of the dilute 1 in 10 000 adrenaline injection) by **slow** *intravenous injection* over several minutes. Great vigilance is needed to ensure that the *correct strength* is used; anaphylactic shock kits need to make a *very clear distinction* between the 1 in 10 000 strength and the 1 in 1000 strength. It is also important that, where intramuscular injection might still succeed, time should not be wasted seeking intravenous access.

For reference to the use of the intravenous route for *cardiac resuscitation*, see section 2.7.3.

## Self-administration of adrenaline (epinephrine)

Individuals at considerable risk of anaphylaxis need to carry adrenaline (epinephrine) at all times and need to be *instructed in advance* how to inject it. In addition, the packs need to be labelled so that in the case of rapid collapse someone else is able to administer the adrenaline. It is important to ensure that an adequate supply is provided to treat symptoms until medical assistance is available.

Some patients may best cope with a pre-assembled syringe fitted with a needle suitable for very rapid administration (if necessary by a bystander). *Anapen®* and *EpiPen®* consist of a fully assembled syringe and needle delivering a dose of 300 micrograms of adrenaline by *intramuscular injection*; 150-microgram versions (*Anapen® Junior, EpiPen® Jr*) are also available for use in children. Other products for the immediate treatment of anaphylaxis are available but are not licensed for use in the UK. *Ana-Guard®* is a prefilled syringe that delivers two 300-microgram doses of adrenaline *by subcutaneous or intramuscular injection*; it can be adjusted to administer smaller doses for children. *Ana-Kit®* includes a prefilled adrenaline syringe, chewable tablets of chlorphenamine maleate (chlorpheniramine maleate) 2 mg, 2 sterile pads impregnated with 70% isopropyl alcohol, and a tourniquet. *Ana-Guard®* and *Ana-Kit®* are available on a named-patient basis from IDIS.

## ADRENALINE/EPINEPHRINE

**Indications** emergency treatment of acute anaphylaxis; angioedema; cardiopulmonary resuscitation (section 2.7.3); priapism [unlicensed indication] (section 7.4.5)

**Cautions** hyperthyroidism, diabetes mellitus, heart disease, hypertension, arrhythmias, cerebrovascular disease, angle-closure glaucoma, second stage of labour, elderly patients
Interactions Severe anaphylaxis in patients on non-cardioselective beta-blockers may not respond to adrenaline injection calling for intravenous injection of salbutamol (see p. 145); furthermore, adrenaline may cause severe hypertension in those receiving beta-blockers. Patients on tricyclic antidepressants are considerably more susceptible to arrhythmias, calling for a much reduced dose of adrenaline. Other **interactions**, see Appendix 1 (sympathomimetics).

**Side-effects** anxiety, tremor, tachycardia, arrhythmias, headache, cold extremities; also hypertension (risk of cerebral haemorrhage) and pulmonary oedema (on excessive dosage or extreme sensitivity); nausea, vomiting, sweating, weakness, dizziness and hyperglycaemia also reported

**Dose**
- Acute anaphylaxis, by intramuscular injection (preferably midpoint in anterolateral thigh) (*or* by subcutaneous injection) of 1 in 1000 (1 mg/mL) solution, see notes and table above
- Acute anaphylaxis when there is doubt as to the adequacy of the circulation, by slow intravenous injection of 1 in 10 000 (100 micrograms/mL) solution (extreme caution), see notes above
Important Intravenous route should be used with **extreme care**, see notes above

### Intramuscular or subcutaneous

[1]**Adrenaline/Epinephrine 1 in 1000** (Non-proprietary) PoM
Injection, adrenaline (as acid tartrate) 1 mg/mL, net price 0.5-mL amp = 51p; 1-mL amp = 42p
Excipients include sulphites

[1]**Minijet® Adrenaline** (Celltech) PoM
Injection, adrenaline (as hydrochloride) 1 in 1000 (1 mg/mL). Net price 1 mL (with 25 gauge × 0.25 inch needle for subcutaneous injection) = £8.11, 1 mL (with 21 gauge × 1.5 inch needle for intramuscular injection) = £5.00 (both disposable syringes)
Excipients include sulphites

### Intravenous

**Extreme caution**, see notes above

1. PoM restriction does not apply to adrenaline injection 1 mg/mL where administration is for saving life in emergency

3 Respiratory system

**Adrenaline/Epinephrine 1 in 10 000, Dilute** (Non-proprietary) PoM

Injection, adrenaline (as acid tartrate) 100 micrograms/mL, 10-mL amp, 1-mL and 10-mL prefilled syringe
Excipients include sulphites
Brands include *Minijet® Adrenaline*

**Intramuscular injection for self-administration**

**Anapen®** (Celltech) PoM

[1]Anapen® 0.3 mg solution for injection (delivering a single dose of adrenaline 300 micrograms), adrenaline 1 mg/mL (1 in 1000), net price 1.05-mL auto-injector device = £30.67
Excipients include sulphites
Note 0.75 mL of the solution remains in the auto-injector device after use
Dose by intramuscular injection, ADULT and CHILD over 30 kg, 300 micrograms repeated after 10–15 minutes as necessary

Anapen® Junior 0.15 mg solution for injection (delivering a single dose of adrenaline 150 micrograms), adrenaline 500 micrograms/mL (1 in 2000), net price 1.05-mL auto-injector device = £30.67
Excipients include sulphites
Note 0.75 mL of the solution remains in the auto-injector device after use
Dose by intramuscular injection, CHILD 15–30 kg, 150 micrograms repeated after 10–15 minutes as necessary

**EpiPen®** (ALK-Abelló) PoM

[1]EpiPen® Auto-injector 0.3 mg (delivering a single dose of adrenaline 300 micrograms), adrenaline 1 mg/mL (1 in 1000), net price 2-mL auto-injector = £28.05
Excipients include sulphites
Note 1.7 mL of the solution remains in the *Auto-injector* after use
Dose by intramuscular injection, ADULT and CHILD over 30 kg, 300 micrograms repeated after 15 minutes as necessary

Epipen® Jr Auto-injector 0.15 mg (delivering a single dose of adrenaline 150 micrograms), adrenaline 500 micrograms/mL (1 in 2000), net price 2-mL auto-injector = £28.05
Excipients include sulphites
Note 1.7 mL of the solution remains in the *Auto-injector* after use
Dose by intramuscular injection, CHILD 15–30 kg, 150 micrograms (but on the basis of a dose of 10 micrograms/kg, 300 micrograms may be more appropriate for some children) repeated after 15 minutes as necessary

# 3.5 Respiratory stimulants and pulmonary surfactants

3.5.1 Respiratory stimulants
3.5.2 Pulmonary surfactants

## 3.5.1 Respiratory stimulants

Respiratory stimulants (analeptic drugs) have a limited place in the treatment of ventilatory failure in patients with chronic obstructive pulmonary disease. They are effective only when given by intravenous injection or infusion and have a short duration of action. Their use has largely been replaced by ventilatory support including nasal intermittent positive pressure ventilation. However, occasionally when ventilatory support is contra-indicated and in patients with hypercapnic respiratory failure who are becoming drowsy or comatose, respiratory stimulants in the short term may arouse patients sufficiently to co-operate and clear their secretions.

Respiratory stimulants can also be harmful in respiratory failure since they stimulate non-respiratory as well as respiratory muscles. They should only be given under **expert supervision** in hospital and must be combined with active physiotherapy. There is at present no oral respiratory stimulant available for long-term use in chronic respiratory failure.

**Doxapram** is given by continuous intravenous infusion. Frequent arterial blood gas and pH measurements are necessary during treatment to ensure correct dosage.

### DOXAPRAM HYDROCHLORIDE

**Indications** see under Dose

**Cautions** give with oxygen in severe irreversible airways obstruction or severely decreased lung compliance (because of increased work load of breathing); give with $beta_2$ agonist in bronchoconstriction; hypertension (avoid if severe), impaired cardiac reserve; hepatic impairment, pregnancy (compelling reasons only); **interactions**: Appendix 1 (doxapram)

**Contra-indications** severe hypertension, status asthmaticus, coronary artery disease, thyrotoxicosis, epilepsy, physical obstruction of respiratory tract

**Side-effects** perineal warmth, dizziness, sweating, moderate increase in blood pressure and heart rate; side-effects reported in postoperative period (causal effect not established) include muscle fasciculation, hyperactivity, confusion, hallucinations, cough, dyspnoea, laryngospasm, bronchospasm, sinus tachycardia, bradycardia, extrasystoles, nausea, vomiting and salivation

**Dose**

- Postoperative respiratory depression, by intravenous injection over at least 30 seconds, 1–1.5 mg/kg repeated if necessary after intervals of 1 hour *or* alternatively by intravenous infusion, 2–3 mg/minute adjusted according to response; CHILD not recommended
- Acute respiratory failure, by intravenous infusion, 1.5–4 mg/minute adjusted according to response (given concurrently with oxygen and whenever possible monitor with frequent measurement of blood gas tensions); CHILD not recommended

**Dopram®** (Anpharm) PoM

Injection, doxapram hydrochloride 20 mg/mL. Net price 5-mL amp = £2.24

Intravenous infusion, doxapram hydrochloride 2 mg/mL in glucose 5%. Net price 500-mL bottle = £21.33

## 3.5.2 Pulmonary surfactants

Pulmonary surfactants are used in the management of respiratory distress syndrome (hyaline membrane disease) in neonates and preterm neonates. They may also be given prophylactically to those considered at risk of developing the syndrome.

1. PoM restriction does not apply to adrenaline injection 1 mg/mL where administration is for saving life in emergency

3 Respiratory system

**Cautions** Continuous monitoring is required to avoid hyperoxaemia (due to rapid improvement in arterial oxygen concentration).

**Side-effects** Pulmonary haemorrhage, especially in more preterm neonates, is a rare complication of therapy; obstruction of the endotracheal tube by mucous secretions has also been reported.

## BERACTANT

**Indications** treatment of respiratory distress syndrome in neonates over 700 g; prophylaxis of respiratory distress syndrome in preterm neonates
**Cautions** see notes above
**Side-effects** see notes above
**Dose**
- By endotracheal tube, phospholipid 100 mg/kg equivalent to a volume of 4 mL/kg, preferably within 8 hours of birth; may be repeated within 48 hours at intervals of at least 6 hours for up to 4 doses

**Survanta®** (Abbott) PoM
Suspension, beractant (bovine lung extract) providing phospholipid 25 mg/mL, with lipids and proteins, net price 8-mL vial = £306.43

## PORACTANT ALFA

**Indications** treatment of respiratory distress syndrome or hyaline membrane disease in neonates over 700 g; prophylaxis of respiratory distress syndrome in preterm neonates
**Cautions** see notes above
**Side-effects** see notes above
**Dose**
- By endotracheal tube, treatment, 100–200 mg/kg; further doses of 100 mg/kg may be repeated 12 hours later and after further 12 hours if still intubated; max. total dose 300–400 mg/kg; prophylaxis, 100–200 mg/kg soon after birth (preferably within 15 minutes); further doses of 100 mg/kg may be repeated 6–12 hours later and after further 12 hours if still intubated; max. total dose 300–400 mg/kg

**Curosurf®** (Trinity) PoM
Suspension, poractant alfa (porcine lung phospholipid fraction) 80 mg/mL, net price 1.5-mL vial = £382.00; 3-mL vial = £764.00

# 3.6 Oxygen

Oxygen should be regarded as a drug. It is prescribed for hypoxaemic patients to increase alveolar oxygen tension and decrease the work of breathing necessary to maintain a given arterial oxygen tension. The concentration depends on the condition being treated; an inappropriate concentration may have serious or even lethal effects.

*High concentration oxygen therapy*, with concentrations of up to 60%, is safe in conditions such as pneumonia, pulmonary thromboembolism, and fibrosing alveolitis. In such conditions low arterial oxygen ($P_aO_2$) is usually associated with low or normal arterial carbon dioxide ($P_aCO_2$), therefore there is little risk of hypoventilation and carbon dioxide retention.

In acute severe asthma, the arterial carbon dioxide ($P_aCO_2$) is usually subnormal but as asthma deteriorates it may rise steeply (particularly in children). These patients usually require high concentrations of oxygen and if the arterial carbon dioxide ($P_aCO_2$) remains high despite other treatment intermittent positive pressure ventilation needs to be considered urgently. Where facilities for blood gas measurement are not immediately available, for example while transferring the patient to hospital, 40 to 60% oxygen delivered through a high-flow mask is recommended.

*Low concentration oxygen therapy* (controlled oxygen therapy) is reserved for patients with ventilatory failure due to chronic obstructive pulmonary disease or other causes. The concentration should not exceed 28% and in some patients a concentration above 24% may be excessive. The aim is to provide the patient with enough oxygen to correct hypoxaemia but without worsening existing carbon dioxide retention and respiratory acidosis. Treatment should be initiated in hospital because repeated blood gas measurements are required to assess the correct concentration.

**Domiciliary oxygen** Oxygen should only be prescribed for patients in the home after careful evaluation in hospital by respiratory experts; it should never be prescribed on a placebo basis.

Patients should be **advised of the fire risks** when receiving oxygen therapy.

**Air travel** Some patients with arterial hypoxaemia will require supplementary oxygen for air travel. The patient's requirement should be discussed with the airline before travel.

## Intermittent oxygen therapy

Oxygen is occasionally prescribed for intermittent (short-burst) use for episodes of hypoxaemia of short duration, for example asthma. It is important, however, that the patient does not rely on oxygen instead of obtaining medical help or taking more specific treatment.

Alternatively, intermittent oxygen may be prescribed for patients with advanced irreversible respiratory disorders to increase mobility and capacity for exercise and to ease discomfort, for example in chronic obstructive pulmonary disease. Appropriate patients may be prescribed portable equipment through the hospital service, refillable from cylinders in the home.

Under the NHS oxygen may be supplied as **oxygen cylinders**. Oxygen flow can be adjusted as the cylinders are equipped with an oxygen flow meter with 'medium' (2 litres/minute) and 'high' (4 litres/minute) settings.

Patients are supplied with either constant or variable performance masks. The *Intersurgical 010 28%*, *Venticaire Venturi Mask 28%*, or *Ventimask Mk IV 28%* are constant performance masks and provide a nearly constant supply of oxygen (28%) despite variations in oxygen flow rate and the patient's breathing pattern. The variable performance masks include the *Intersurgical 005 Mask* and the *Venticaire Mask*; the concentration of oxygen supplied to the patient varies with the rate of flow of oxygen and with the patient's breathing pattern. If a mask which provides 24% oxygen is required, it may be ordered from BOC Medical.

Giving oxygen by nasal cannula allows the patient to talk and eat but the concentration is not controlled and the method may not be appropriate for acute respiratory failure. When given through a nasal cannula at a rate of 1–2 litres/minute the inspiratory oxygen concentration is usually low, but it varies with ventilation and can be high if the patient is underventilating.

**Portable oxygen cylinders** Medigas and BOC supply a portable oxygen cylinder called 'PD oxygen cylinder', which has the same bull-nose fitting as the normal domiciliary headsets (prescriptions must therefore specify 'PD oxygen cylinder'). The PD oxygen cylinder holds 300 litres of oxygen which will last approximately 2 hours at a standard flow rate of 2 litres/minute.

## Long-term oxygen therapy

*Long-term* administration of oxygen (at least 15 hours daily) prolongs survival in some patients with chronic obstructive pulmonary disease.

The Royal College of Physicians has produced guidelines for oxygen therapy (*Domiciliary oxygen therapy services: Clinical guidelines and advice for prescribers*; June 1999). Assessment for long-term oxygen therapy requires measurement of arterial blood gas tensions. Measurements should be taken on 2 occasions at least 3 weeks apart to demonstrate clinical stability, and not sooner than 4 weeks after an acute exacerbation of the disease. The guidelines recommend that long-term oxygen therapy should be considered for patients with:

- chronic obstructive pulmonary disease with $P_aO_2 < 7.3$ kPa when breathing air during a period of clinical stability;
- chronic obstructive pulmonary disease with $P_aO_2$ 7.3–8 kPa in the presence of secondary polycythaemia, nocturnal hypoxaemia, peripheral oedema or evidence of pulmonary hypertension;
- interstitial lung disease with $P_aO_2 < 8$ kPa and in patients with $P_aO_2 > 8$ kPa with disabling dyspnoea;
- cystic fibrosis when $P_aO_2 < 7.3$ kPa *or* if $P_aO_2$ 7.3–8 kPa in the presence of secondary polycythaemia, nocturnal hypoxaemia, pulmonary hypertension or peripheral oedema;
- pulmonary hypertension, without parenchymal lung involvement when $P_aO_2 < 8$ kPa;
- neuromuscular or skeletal disorders, after specialist assessment;
- obstructive sleep apnoea despite continuous positive airways pressure therapy, after specialist assessment;
- pulmonary malignancy or other terminal disease with disabling dyspnoea;
- heart failure with daytime $P_aO_2 < 7.3$ kPa (on air) or with nocturnal hypoxaemia;
- paediatric respiratory disease, after specialist assessment.

Increased respiratory depression is seldom a problem in patients with stable respiratory failure treated with low concentrations of oxygen although it may occur during exacerbations; patients and relatives should be warned to call for medical help if drowsiness or confusion occur.

**Oxygen concentrators** are more economical for patients requiring oxygen for long periods, and in England and Wales can be ordered on the NHS on a regional tendering basis (see below). A concentrator is recommended for a patient requiring oxygen for more than 8 hours a day (or 21 cylinders per month). Exceptionally, if a higher concentration of oxygen is required the output of 2 oxygen concentrators can be combined using a 'Y' connection.

A nasal cannula is usually preferred for long-term oxygen therapy from an oxygen concentrator. It can, however, produce dermatitis and mucosal drying in sensitive individuals.

## Arrangements for supplying oxygen

The following oxygen services may be ordered in England and Wales:

- emergency oxygen;
- short-burst (intermittent) oxygen therapy;
- long-term oxygen therapy;
- ambulatory oxygen.

The type of oxygen service (or combination of services) should be ordered on a Home Oxygen Order Form (HOOF); the amount of oxygen required (hours per day) and flow rate should be specified. The supplier will determine the appropriate equipment to be provided. Special needs or preferences should be specified on the HOOF.

The clinician should obtain the patient's consent to pass on the patient's details to the supplier and fire brigade. The patient should be informed that the supplier will be in contact to make arrangements for delivery, installation, and maintenance of the equipment. The supplier will also train the patient to use the equipment.

The clinician should send order forms to the supplier by facsimile (see below). A copy of the HOOF should be sent to the Primary Care Trust or Local Health Board. The supplier will continue to provide the service ordered until a revised order or confirmation that a patient no longer requires the home oxygen service is received.

| | |
|---|---|
| Eastern | BOC Medical<br>*to order*:<br>Tel: 0800 136 603<br>Fax: 0800 169 9989 |
| South East London<br>Kent, Surrey and Sussex<br>South West London<br>Thames Valley, Hampshire and Isle of Wight | Allied Respiratory<br>*to order*:<br>Tel: 0500 823 773<br>Fax: 0800 781 4610 |
| North West<br>Yorkshire and Humberside<br>East Midlands<br>West Midlands<br>North London<br>South West<br>Wales | Air Products<br>*to order*:<br>Tel: 0800 373 580<br>Fax: 0800 214 709 |
| North East | Linde Gas UK<br>*to order*:<br>Tel: 0808 202 0999<br>Fax: 0191 497 4340 |

In **Scotland** refer the patient for assessment by a respiratory consultant. Prescriptions for oxygen cylinders and accessories can be dispensed by pharmacies contracted to provide domiciliary oxygen services. If the need for a concentrator is confirmed the consultant will arrange for the provision of a concentrator through the Common Services Agency.

## 3.7 Mucolytics

Mucolytics are prescribed to facilitate expectoration by reducing sputum viscosity. In some patients with chronic obstructive pulmonary disease and a chronic productive cough, mucolytics can reduce exacerbations; mucolytic therapy should be stopped if there is no benefit after a 4-week trial. Steam inhalation with postural drainage is effective in bronchiectasis and in some cases of chronic bronchitis.

Mucolytics should be used with caution in those with a history of peptic ulceration because they may disrupt the gastric mucosal barrier.

For reference to dornase alfa, see below.

### CARBOCISTEINE

**Indications** reduction of sputum viscosity
**Cautions** see notes above
**Contra-indications** active peptic ulceration
**Side-effects** occasional gastro-intestinal irritation, rashes
**Dose**

- Initially 750 mg 3 times daily, then 1.5 g daily in divided doses as condition improves; CHILD 2–5 years 62.5–125 mg 4 times daily, 6–12 years 250 mg 3 times daily

**Carbocisteine** (Beacon) PoM
Capsules, carbocisteine 375 mg. Net price 30-cap pack = £4.17
Brands include *Mucodyne®*

Oral liquid, carbocisteine 125 mg/5 mL, net price 300 mL = £4.57; 250 mg/5 mL, 300 mL = £5.84
Brands include *Mucodyne® Paediatric* 125 mg/5 mL and *Mucodyne®* 250 mg/5 mL

### MECYSTEINE HYDROCHLORIDE
(Methyl Cysteine Hydrochloride)

**Indications** reduction of sputum viscosity
**Cautions** see notes above
**Side-effects** nausea, heartburn
**Dose**

- 200 mg 4 times daily for 2 days, then 200 mg 3 times daily for 6 weeks, then 200 mg twice daily; CHILD over 5 years 100 mg 3 times daily

**Visclair®** (Sinclair)
Tablets, yellow, s/c, e/c, mecysteine hydrochloride 100 mg. Net price 20 = £3.66. Label: 5, 22, 25

### Dornase alfa

Dornase alfa is a genetically engineered version of a naturally occurring human enzyme which cleaves extracellular deoxyribonucleic acid (DNA). It is used in cystic fibrosis and is administered by inhalation using a jet nebuliser (section 3.1.5).

### DORNASE ALFA
Phosphorylated glycosylated recombinant human deoxyribonuclease 1 (rhDNase)

**Indications** management of cystic fibrosis patients with a forced vital capacity (FVC) of greater than 40% of predicted to improve pulmonary function
**Cautions** pregnancy (Appendix 4); breast-feeding (Appendix 5)
**Side-effects** pharyngitis, voice changes, chest pain; occasionally laryngitis, rashes, urticaria, conjunctivitis
**Dose**

- By inhalation of nebulised solution (by jet nebuliser), 2500 units (2.5 mg) once daily (patients over 21 years may benefit from twice daily dosage); CHILD under 5 years not recommended

**Pulmozyme®** (Roche) PoM
Nebuliser solution, dornase alfa 1000 units (1 mg)/mL. Net price 2.5-mL (2500 units) vial = £18.52
Note For use undiluted with jet nebulisers only; ultrasonic nebulisers are unsuitable

## 3.8 Aromatic inhalations

Inhalations containing volatile substances such as eucalyptus oil are traditionally used and although the vapour may contain little of the additive it encourages deliberate inspiration of warm moist air which is often comforting in bronchitis; boiling water should not be used owing to the risk of scalding. Inhalations are also used for the relief of nasal obstruction in acute rhinitis or sinusitis. Menthol and eucalyptus inhalation is used to relieve sinusitis affecting the maxillary antrum (section 12.2.2)

**Children** The use of strong aromatic decongestants (applied as rubs or to pillows) is not advised for infants under the age of 3 months. Carers of young infants in whom nasal obstruction with mucus is a problem can readily be taught appropriate techniques of suction aspiration but sodium chloride 0.9% given as nasal drops is preferred.

**Benzoin Tincture, Compound, BP (Friars' Balsam)**
Tincture, balsamic acids approx. 4.5%. Label: 15
Dose add one teaspoonful to a pint of hot, **not** boiling, water and inhale the vapour

**Menthol and Eucalyptus Inhalation, BP 1980**
Inhalation, racementhol or levomenthol 2 g, eucalyptus oil 10 mL, light magnesium carbonate 7 g, water to 100 mL
Dose add one teaspoonful to a pint of hot, **not** boiling, water and inhale the vapour
Dental prescribing on the NHS Menthol and Eucalyptus Inhalation BP, 1980 may be prescribed

**Karvol®** (Crookes) NHS
Inhalation capsules, levomenthol 35.55 mg, with chlorobutanol, pine oils, terpineol, and thymol, net price 10-cap pack = £2.25; 20-cap pack = £4.06

Inhalation solution, levomenthol 7.9%, with chlorobutanol, pine oils, terpineol, and thymol, net price 12-mL dropper bottle = £1.90
Dose express into handkerchief or add to a pint of hot, **not** boiling, water the contents of 1 capsule or 6 drops of solution; avoid in infants under 3 months

# 3.9 Cough preparations

3.9.1 Cough suppressants
3.9.2 Expectorant and demulcent cough preparations

## 3.9.1 Cough suppressants

Cough is usually a symptom of an underlying disorder e.g. asthma (section 3.1.1), gastro-oesophageal reflux disease (section 1.1), and 'post-nasal drip'; where there is no identifiable cause, cough suppressants may be useful, for example if sleep is disturbed. They may cause sputum retention and this may be harmful in patients with chronic bronchitis and bronchiectasis.

**Codeine** may be effective but it is constipating and can cause dependence; **dextromethorphan** and **pholcodine** have fewer side-effects.

**Sedating antihistamines**, such as diphenhydramine, are used as the cough suppressant component of many compound cough preparations on sale to the public; all tend to cause drowsiness which may reflect their main mode of action.

**Children** The use of cough suppressants containing codeine or similar opioid analgesics is not generally recommended in children and should be avoided altogether in those under 1 year of age.

### CODEINE PHOSPHATE

**Indications** dry or painful cough; diarrhoea (section 1.4.2); pain (section 4.7.2)
**Cautions** asthma; hepatic and renal impairment; history of drug abuse; see also notes above and section 4.7.2; **interactions**: Appendix 1 (opioid analgesics)
**Contra-indications** liver disease, ventilatory failure
**Side-effects** constipation, respiratory depression in sensitive patients or if given large doses

[1] **Codeine Linctus, BP** PoM
Linctus (= oral solution), codeine phosphate 15 mg/5 mL. Net price 100 mL = 40p (diabetic, 73p)
Brands include *Galcodine®*
Dose 5–10 mL 3–4 times daily; CHILD (but not generally recommended) 5–12 years, 2.5–5 mL
Note BP directs that when Diabetic Codeine Linctus is prescribed, Codeine Linctus formulated with a vehicle appropriate for administration to diabetics, whether or not labelled 'Diabetic Codeine Linctus', shall be dispensed or supplied

1. Can be sold to the public provided the maximum single dose does not exceed 5 mL

**Codeine Linctus, Paediatric, BP**
Linctus (= oral solution), codeine phosphate 3 mg/5 mL. Net price 100 mL = 18p
Brands include *Galcodine® Paediatric* (sugar-free)
Dose CHILD (but not generally recommended) 1–5 years 5 mL 3–4 times daily
Note BP directs that Paediatric Codeine Linctus may be prepared extemporaneously by diluting Codeine Linctus with a suitable vehicle in accordance with the manufacturer's instructions

### PHOLCODINE

**Indications** dry or painful cough
**Cautions** see under Codeine Phosphate
**Contra-indications** see under Codeine Phosphate
**Side-effects** see under Codeine Phosphate

**Pholcodine Linctus, BP**
Linctus (= oral solution), pholcodine 5 mg/5 mL in a suitable flavoured vehicle, containing citric acid monohydrate 1%. Net price 100 mL = 24p
Brands include *Pavacol-D®* (sugar-free), *Galenphol®* (sugar-free)
Dose 5–10 mL 3–4 times daily; CHILD (but not generally recommended, see notes above) 5–12 years 2.5–5 mL

**Pholcodine Linctus, Strong, BP**
Linctus (= oral solution), pholcodine 10 mg/5 mL in a suitable flavoured vehicle, containing citric acid monohydrate 2%. Net price 100 mL = 33p
Dose 5 mL 3–4 times daily
Brands include *Galenphol®*

**Galenphol®** (Thornton & Ross)
Paediatric linctus (= oral solution), orange, sugar-free, pholcodine 2 mg/5 mL. Net price 90-mL pack = £1.11
Dose CHILD (but not generally recommended, see notes above) 1–5 years 5–10 mL 3 times daily; 6–12 years 10 mL 3 times daily

### Palliative care

Diamorphine and methadone have been used to control distressing cough in terminal lung cancer although morphine is now preferred (see p. 15). In other circumstances they are contra-indicated because they induce sputum retention and ventilatory failure as well as causing opioid dependence. Methadone linctus should be avoided because it has a long duration of action and tends to accumulate.

### METHADONE HYDROCHLORIDE

**Indications** cough in terminal disease
**Cautions** see notes in section 4.7.2
**Contra-indications** see notes in section 4.7.2
**Side-effects** see notes in section 4.7.2; longer-acting than morphine therefore effects may be cumulative
**Dose**
- See below

**Methadone Linctus** CD
Linctus (= oral solution), methadone hydrochloride 2 mg/5 mL in a suitable vehicle with a tolu flavour. Label: 2
Dose 2.5–5 mL every 4–6 hours, reduced to twice daily on prolonged use

### MORPHINE HYDROCHLORIDE

**Indications** cough in terminal disease (see also Prescribing in Palliative Care p. 15)
**Cautions** see notes in section 4.7.2
**Contra-indications** see notes in section 4.7.2
**Side-effects** see notes in section 4.7.2
**Dose**
- Initially 5 mg every 4 hours

**Preparation**
Section 4.7.2

## 3.9.2 Expectorant and demulcent cough preparations

**Expectorants** are claimed to promote expulsion of bronchial secretions but there is no evidence that any drug can specifically facilitate expectoration. The assumption that sub-emetic doses of expectorants, such as ammonium chloride, ipecacuanha, and squill promote expectoration is a myth. However, a simple expectorant mixture may serve a useful placebo function and has the advantage of being inexpensive.

**Demulcent cough preparations** contain soothing substances such as syrup or glycerol and some patients believe that such preparations relieve a dry irritating cough. Preparations such as **simple linctus** have the advantage of being harmless and inexpensive; **paediatric simple linctus** is particularly useful in children.

**Compound preparations** are on sale to the public for the treatment of cough and colds; the rationale for some is dubious.

**Ammonia and Ipecacuanha Mixture, BP**
Mixture, ammonium bicarbonate 200 mg, liquorice liquid extract 0.5 mL, ipecacuanha tincture 0.3 mL, concentrated camphor water 0.1 mL, concentrated anise water 0.05 mL, double-strength chloroform water 5 mL, water to 10 mL. It should be recently prepared
Dose 10–20 mL 3–4 times daily

**Simple Linctus, BP**
Linctus (= oral solution), citric acid monohydrate 2.5% in a suitable vehicle with an anise flavour. Net price 100 mL = 32p
Dose 5 mL 3–4 times daily
A sugar-free version is also available

**Simple Linctus, Paediatric, BP**
Linctus (= oral solution), citric acid monohydrate 0.625% in a suitable vehicle with an anise flavour. Net price 100 mL = 17p
Dose CHILD 5–10 mL 3–4 times daily
A sugar-free version is also available

**Preparations on sale to the public**

There are many systemic cough and decongestant preparations on sale to the public. To identify the active ingredients in such preparations, consult the product literature or manufacturer.

**Note** The correct proprietary name should be ascertained—many products have very similar names but different active ingredients

## 3.10 Systemic nasal decongestants

Nasal decongestants for administration by mouth may not be as effective as preparations for local application (section 12.2.2) but they do not give rise to rebound nasal congestion on withdrawal. **Pseudoephedrine** is available over-the-counter; it has few sympathomimetic effects.

Systemic decongestants should be used with **caution** in diabetes, hypertension, hyperthyroidism, raised intraocular pressure, prostate hypertrophy, hepatic impairment, renal impairment, and ischaemic heart disease and **avoided** in patients taking monoamine oxidase inhibitors; **interactions:** Appendix 1 (sympathomimetics).

Systemic compound preparations containing pseudoephedrine are shown in the list of cough and decongestant preparations on sale to the public (section 3.9.2). Many preparations also contain antihistamines, which may cause drowsiness and affect the ability to drive or operate machinery.

Preparations containing phenylpropanolamine have been discontinued.

### PSEUDOEPHEDRINE HYDROCHLORIDE

**Indications** see notes above
**Cautions** see notes above
**Side-effects** tachycardia, anxiety, restlessness, insomnia; rarely hallucinations, rash; urinary retention also reported
**Dose**
- See preparations below

**Galpseud®** (Thornton & Ross)
Tablets, pseudoephedrine hydrochloride 60 mg. Net price 20 = 91p
Dose 1 tablet 4 times daily

Linctus, orange, sugar-free, pseudoephedrine hydrochloride 30 mg/5 mL. Net price 100 mL = 69p
Dose 10 mL 3 times daily; CHILD 2–6 years 2.5 mL, 6–12 years 5 mL

**Sudafed®** (Warner Lambert)
Tablets, red, f/c, pseudoephedrine hydrochloride 60 mg. Net price 24 = £2.12
Dose 1 tablet every 4–6 hours (up to 4 times daily)

Elixir, red, pseudoephedrine hydrochloride 30 mg/5 mL. Net price 100 mL = £1.48
Dose 10 mL every 4–6 hours (up to 4 times daily); CHILD 2–5 years 2.5 mL, 6–12 years 5 mL

# 4 Central nervous system


**4.1 Hypnotics and anxiolytics 173**
4.1.1 Hypnotics 174
4.1.2 Anxiolytics 177
4.1.3 Barbiturates 180
**4.2 Drugs used in psychoses and related disorders 181**
4.2.1 Antipsychotic drugs 181
4.2.2 Antipsychotic depot injections 191
4.2.3 Antimanic drugs 193
**4.3 Antidepressant drugs 195**
4.3.1 Tricyclic and related antidepressant drugs 196
4.3.2 Monoamine-oxidase inhibitors 200
4.3.3 Selective serotonin re-uptake inhibitors 202
4.3.4 Other antidepressant drugs 204
**4.4 CNS stimulants and other drugs used for attention deficit hyperactivity disorder 206**
**4.5 Drugs used in the treatment of obesity 208**
4.5.1 Anti-obesity drugs acting on the gastro-intestinal tract 209
4.5.2 Centrally acting appetite suppressants 209
**4.6 Drugs used in nausea and vertigo 210**
**4.7 Analgesics 217**
4.7.1 Non-opioid analgesics 218
4.7.2 Opioid analgesics 222
4.7.3 Neuropathic pain 230
4.7.4 Antimigraine drugs 231
4.7.4.1 Treatment of the acute migraine attack 231
4.7.4.2 Prophylaxis of migraine 235
4.7.4.3 Cluster headache 236
**4.8 Antiepileptics 236**
4.8.1 Control of epilepsy 236
4.8.2 Drugs used in status epilepticus 247
4.8.3 Febrile convulsions 250
**4.9 Drugs used in parkinsonism and related disorders 250**
4.9.1 Dopaminergic drugs used in parkinsonism 250
4.9.2 Antimuscarinic drugs used in parkinsonism 257
4.9.3 Drugs used in essential tremor, chorea, tics, and related disorders 258
**4.10 Drugs used in substance dependence 259**
**4.11 Drugs for dementia 264**


## 4.1 Hypnotics and anxiolytics


**4.1.1 Hypnotics**
**4.1.2 Anxiolytics**
**4.1.3 Barbiturates**


Most anxiolytics ('sedatives') will induce sleep when given at night and most hypnotics will sedate when given during the day. Prescribing of these drugs is widespread but dependence (both physical and psychological) and tolerance occurs. This may lead to difficulty in withdrawing the drug after the patient has been taking it regularly for more than a few weeks (see Dependence and Withdrawal, below). Hypnotics and anxiolytics should therefore be reserved for short courses to alleviate acute conditions after causal factors have been established.

Benzodiazepines are the most commonly used anxiolytics and hypnotics; they act at benzodiazepine receptors which are associated with gamma-aminobutyric acid (GABA) receptors. Older drugs such as meprobamate and barbiturates (section 4.1.3) are **not** recommended—they have more side-effects and interactions than benzodiazepines and are much more dangerous in overdosage.

**Paradoxical effects** A paradoxical increase in hostility and aggression may be reported by patients taking benzodiazepines. The effects range from talkativeness and excitement, to aggressive and antisocial acts. Adjustment of the dose (up or down) usually attenuates the impulses. Increased anxiety and perceptual disorders are other paradoxical effects. Increased hostility and aggression after barbiturates and alcohol usually indicates intoxication.

**Driving** Hypnotics and anxiolytics may impair judgement and increase reaction time, and so affect ability to drive or operate machinery; they increase the effects of alcohol. Moreover the hangover effects of a night dose may impair driving on the following day. See also Drugs and Driving under General Guidance, p. 2.

**Dependence and withdrawal** Withdrawal of a benzodiazepine should be gradual because abrupt withdrawal may produce confusion, toxic psychosis, convulsions, or a condition resembling delirium tremens. Abrupt withdrawal of a barbiturate (section 4.1.3) is even more likely to have serious effects.

The benzodiazepine withdrawal syndrome may develop at any time up to 3 weeks after stopping a long-acting benzodiazepine, but may occur within a few hours in the case of a short-acting one. It is characterised by insomnia, anxiety, loss of appetite and of body-weight, tremor, perspiration, tinnitus, and perceptual disturbances. These symptoms may be similar to the original complaint and encourage further prescribing; some symptoms may continue for weeks or months after stopping benzodiazepines.

A benzodiazepine can be withdrawn in steps of about one-eighth (range one-tenth to one-quarter) of the daily dose every fortnight. A suggested withdrawal protocol for patients who have difficulty is as follows:

1. Transfer patient to equivalent daily dose of diazepam[1] preferably taken at night
2. Reduce diazepam dose every 2–3 weeks in steps of 2 or 2.5 mg; if withdrawal symptoms occur, maintain this dose until symptoms improve
3. Reduce dose further, if necessary in smaller steps[2]; it is better to reduce too slowly rather than too quickly
4. Stop completely; time needed for withdrawal can vary from about 4 weeks to a year or more

Counselling may help; beta-blockers should **only** be tried if other measures fail; antidepressants should be used **only** for clinical depression or for panic disorder; **avoid** antipsychotics (which may aggravate withdrawal symptoms).



**CSM advice**

1. Benzodiazepines are indicated for the short-term relief (two to four weeks only) of anxiety that is severe, disabling or subjecting the individual to unacceptable distress, occurring alone or in association with insomnia or short-term psychosomatic, organic or psychotic illness.
2. The use of benzodiazepines to treat short-term 'mild' anxiety is inappropriate and unsuitable.
3. Benzodiazepines should be used to treat insomnia only when it is severe, disabling, or subjecting the individual to extreme distress.

## 4.1.1 Hypnotics

Before a hypnotic is prescribed the cause of the insomnia should be established and, where possible, underlying factors should be treated. However, it should be noted that some patients have unrealistic sleep expectations, and others understate their alcohol consumption which is often the cause of the insomnia.

*Transient insomnia* may occur in those who normally sleep well and may be due to extraneous factors such as noise, shift work, and jet lag. If a hypnotic is indicated one that is rapidly eliminated should be chosen, and only one or two doses should be given.

*Short-term insomnia* is usually related to an emotional problem or serious medical illness. It may last for a few weeks and may recur; a hypnotic can be useful but should not be given for more than three weeks (preferably only one week). Intermittent use is desirable with omission of some doses. A rapidly eliminated drug is generally appropriate.

*Chronic insomnia* is rarely benefited by hypnotics and is more often due to mild dependence caused by injudicious prescribing. Psychiatric disorders such as anxiety, depression, and abuse of drugs and alcohol are common causes. Sleep disturbance is very common in depressive illness and early wakening is often a useful pointer. The underlying psychiatric complaint should be treated, adapting the drug regimen to alleviate insomnia. For example, clomipramine or mirtazapine prescribed for depression will also help to promote sleep if taken at night. Other causes of insomnia include daytime cat-napping and physical causes such as pain, pruritus, and dyspnoea.

Hypnotics should **not** be prescribed indiscriminately and routine prescribing is undesirable. They should be reserved for short courses in the acutely distressed. Tolerance to their effects develops within 3 to 14 days of continuous use and long-term efficacy cannot be assured. A major drawback of long-term use is that withdrawal causes rebound insomnia and precipitates a withdrawal syndrome (section 4.1).

Where prolonged administration is unavoidable hypnotics should be discontinued as soon as feasible and the patient warned that sleep may be disturbed for a few days before normal rhythm is re-established; broken sleep with vivid dreams and increased REM (rapid eye movement) sleep may persist for several weeks.

**Children** The prescribing of hypnotics to children, except for occasional use such as for night terrors and somnambulism (sleep-walking), is not justified.

**Elderly** Hypnotics should be avoided in the elderly, who are at risk of becoming ataxic and confused and so liable to fall and injure themselves.

**Dental procedures** Some anxious patients may benefit from the use of a hypnotic for 1 to 3 nights before the dental appointment. Hypnotics do not relieve pain, and if pain interferes with sleep an appropriate analgesic should be given. **Diazepam** (section 4.1.2), **nitrazepam** or **temazepam** are used at night for dental patients. Temazepam is preferred when it is important to minimise any residual effect the following day. For information on anxiolytics for dental procedures, see section 15.1.4.1.

### Benzodiazepines

Benzodiazepines used as hypnotics include **nitrazepam** and **flurazepam** which have a prolonged action and may give rise to residual effects on the following day; repeated doses tend to be cumulative.

**Loprazolam**, **lormetazepam**, and **temazepam** act for a shorter time and they have little or no hangover effect. Withdrawal phenomena are more common with the short-acting benzodiazepines.

1. Approximate equivalent doses, diazepam 5 mg
≡chlordiazepoxide 15 mg
≡loprazolam 0.5–1 mg
≡lorazepam 500 micrograms
≡lormetazepam 0.5–1 mg
≡nitrazepam 5 mg
≡oxazepam 15 mg
≡temazepam 10 mg
2. Steps may be adjusted according to initial dose and duration of treatment and can range from diazepam 500 micrograms (one-quarter of a 2-mg tablet) to 2.5 mg

If insomnia is associated with daytime anxiety then the use of a long-acting benzodiazepine anxiolytic such as **diazepam** given as a single dose at night may effectively treat both symptoms.

For general guidelines on benzodiazepine prescribing see section 4.1.2 and for benzodiazepine withdrawal see section 4.1.

## NITRAZEPAM

**Indications** insomnia (short-term use)

**Cautions** respiratory disease, muscle weakness and myasthenia gravis, history of drug or alcohol abuse, marked personality disorder, pregnancy (Appendix 4), breast-feeding (Appendix 5); reduce dose in elderly and debilitated, and in hepatic impairment (avoid if severe; Appendix 2) and renal impairment (Appendix 3); avoid prolonged use (and abrupt withdrawal thereafter); porphyria (section 9.8.2); **interactions**: Appendix 1 (anxiolytics and hypnotics)

Driving Drowsiness may persist the next day and affect performance of skilled tasks (e.g. driving); effects of alcohol enhanced

**Contra-indications** respiratory depression; marked neuromuscular respiratory weakness including unstable myasthenia gravis; acute pulmonary insufficiency; severe hepatic impairment; sleep apnoea syndrome; not for use alone to treat depression (or anxiety associated with depression) or chronic psychosis

**Side-effects** drowsiness and lightheadedness the next day; confusion and ataxia (especially in the elderly); amnesia may occur; dependence; see also under Diazepam (section 4.1.2); **overdosage**: see Emergency Treatment of Poisoning, p. 32

**Dose**

- 5–10 mg at bedtime; ELDERLY (or debilitated) 2.5–5 mg; CHILD not recommended

**Nitrazepam** (Non-proprietary) PoM

Tablets, nitrazepam 5 mg, net price 20 = £1.16. Label: 19

Brands include *Mogadon*® NHS, *Remnos*® NHS

Dental prescribing on NHS Nitrazepam Tablets may be prescribed

Oral suspension, nitrazepam 2.5 mg/5 mL. Net price 150 mL = £5.30. Label: 19

Brands include *Somnite*® NHS

## FLURAZEPAM

**Indications** insomnia (short-term use)

**Cautions** see under Nitrazepam

**Contra-indications** see under Nitrazepam

**Side-effects** see under Nitrazepam

**Dose**

- 15–30 mg at bedtime; ELDERLY (or debilitated) 15 mg; CHILD not recommended

**Dalmane**® (Valeant) PoM NHS

Capsules, flurazepam (as hydrochloride), 15 mg (grey/yellow), net price 30-cap pack = £5.44; 30 mg (black/grey), 30-cap pack = £6.98. Label: 19

## LOPRAZOLAM

**Indications** insomnia (short-term use)

**Cautions** see under Nitrazepam

**Contra-indications** see under Nitrazepam

**Side-effects** see under Nitrazepam; shorter acting

**Dose**

- 1 mg at bedtime, increased to 1.5 or 2 mg if required; ELDERLY (or debilitated) 0.5 or 1 mg; CHILD not recommended

**Loprazolam** (Non-proprietary) PoM

Tablets, loprazolam 1 mg (as mesilate). Net price 28-tab pack = £4.46. Label: 19

## LORMETAZEPAM

**Indications** insomnia (short-term use)

**Cautions** see under Nitrazepam

**Contra-indications** see under Nitrazepam

**Side-effects** see under Nitrazepam; shorter acting

**Dose**

- 0.5–1.5 mg at bedtime; ELDERLY (or debilitated) 500 micrograms; CHILD not recommended

**Lormetazepam** (Non-proprietary) PoM

Tablets, lormetazepam 500 micrograms, net price 30-tab pack = £6.02; 1 mg, 30-tab pack = £7.29. Label: 19

## TEMAZEPAM

**Indications** insomnia (short-term use); see also section 15.1.4.1 for peri-operative use

**Cautions** see under Nitrazepam

**Contra-indications** see under Nitrazepam

**Side-effects** see under Nitrazepam; shorter acting

**Dose**

- 10–20 mg at bedtime, exceptional circumstances 30–40 mg; ELDERLY (or debilitated) 10 mg at bedtime, exceptional circumstances 20 mg; CHILD not recommended

[1] **Temazepam** (Non-proprietary) CD

Tablets, temazepam 10 mg, net price 28-tab pack = 92p; 20 mg, 28-tab pack = £1.52. Label: 19

Oral solution, temazepam 10 mg/5 mL, net price 300 mL = £9.95. Label: 19

Note Sugar-free versions are available and can be ordered by specifying 'sugar-free' on the prescription

Dental prescribing on NHS Temazepam Tablets or Oral Solution may be prescribed

1. See p. 7 for prescribing requirements for temazepam

## Zaleplon, zolpidem, and zopiclone

**Zaleplon**, **zolpidem** and **zopiclone** are non-benzodiazepine hypnotics, but they act at the benzodiazepine receptor. Zolpidem and zopiclone have a short duration of action; zaleplon is very short acting. All three drugs are not licensed for long-term use; dependence has been reported in a small number of patients.

## ZALEPLON

**Indications** insomnia (short-term use—up to 2 weeks)

**Cautions** respiratory insufficiency (avoid if severe); hepatic impairment (avoid if severe; Appendix 2); history of drug or alcohol abuse; avoid prolonged use (and abrupt withdrawal thereafter); pregnancy (Appendix 4); not for use alone to treat depression

**Contra-indications** sleep apnoea syndrome, myasthenia gravis; not for use alone to treat psychosis; breast-feeding (Appendix 5)

**Side-effects** amnesia, paraesthesia, drowsiness, asthenia; nausea, incoordination, confusion, impaired concentration, dizziness, hallucinations, disturbances of hearing, smell, speech, and vision, photosensitivity; dependence; paradoxical effects (discontinue—see also section 4.1)

**Dose**

- 10 mg at bedtime or after going to bed if difficulty falling asleep; ELDERLY 5 mg; CHILD under 18 years not recommended

Note Patients should be advised not to take a second dose during a single night

**Sonata®** (Wyeth) PoM

Capsules, zaleplon 5 mg (white/light brown), net price 14-cap pack = £3.12; 10 mg (white), 14-cap pack = £3.76. Label: 2

## ZOLPIDEM TARTRATE

**Indications** insomnia (short-term use—up to 4 weeks)

**Cautions** depression, history of drug or alcohol abuse, hepatic impairment (avoid if severe; Appendix 2); renal impairment; elderly; avoid prolonged use (and abrupt withdrawal thereafter); **interactions:** Appendix 1 (anxiolytics and hypnotics)

Driving Drowsiness may persist the next day and affect performance of skilled tasks (e.g. driving); effects of alcohol enhanced

**Contra-indications** obstructive sleep apnoea, acute or severe respiratory depression, myasthenia gravis, severe hepatic impairment, psychotic illness, pregnancy, breast-feeding (Appendix 5)

**Side-effects** diarrhoea, nausea, vomiting, vertigo, dizziness, headache, drowsiness, asthenia, amnesia; dependence, memory disturbances, nightmares, nocturnal restlessness, depression, confusion, perceptual disturbances or diplopia, tremor, ataxia, falls, skin reactions, changes in libido; paradoxical effects—see section 4.1

**Dose**

- 10 mg at bedtime; ELDERLY (or debilitated) 5 mg; CHILD not recommended

**Zolpidem** (Non-proprietary) PoM

Tablets, zolpidem tartrate 5 mg, net price 28-tab pack = £2.83; 10 mg, 28-tab pack = £3.05. Label: 19

**Stilnoct®** (Sanofi-Synthelabo) PoM

Tablets, both f/c, zolpidem tartrate 5 mg, net price 28-tab pack = £3.08; 10 mg, 28-tab pack = £4.48. Label: 19

## ZOPICLONE

**Indications** insomnia (short-term use—up to 4 weeks)

**Cautions** hepatic impairment (avoid if severe; Appendix 2) and renal impairment (Appendix 3); elderly; history of drug abuse, psychiatric illness; avoid prolonged use (and abrupt withdrawal thereafter); **interactions:** Appendix 1 (anxiolytics and hypnotics)

Driving Drowsiness may persist the next day and affect performance of skilled tasks (e.g. driving); effects of alcohol enhanced

**Contra-indications** myasthenia gravis, respiratory failure, severe sleep apnoea syndrome, severe hepatic impairment; pregnancy and breast-feeding (Appendix 5)

**Side-effects** bitter or metallic taste; gastro-intestinal disturbances including nausea and vomiting, dry mouth, aggression; irritability, confusion, depressed mood; drowsiness, dizziness, lightheadedness, and incoordination, headache; dependence; hypersensitivity reactions reported (including urticaria and rashes); hallucinations, nightmares, amnesia reported

**Dose**

- 7.5 mg at bedtime; ELDERLY initially 3.75 mg at bedtime increased if necessary; CHILD not recommended

**Zopiclone** (Non-proprietary) PoM

Tablets, zopiclone 3.75 mg, net price 28-tab pack = £2.82; 7.5 mg, 28-tab pack = £2.62. Label: 19

Brands include *Zileze®*

**Zimovane®** (Rhône-Poulenc Rorer) PoM

Tablets, f/c, zopiclone 3.75 mg (*Zimovane® LS*, blue), net price 28-tab pack = £2.33; 7.5 mg, 28-tab pack = £3.39. Label: 19

## Chloral and derivatives

**Chloral hydrate** and derivatives were formerly popular hypnotics for children (but the use of hypnotics in children is not usually justified). There is no convincing evidence that they are particularly useful in the elderly and their role as hypnotics is now very limited. **Triclofos** causes fewer gastro-intestinal disturbances than chloral hydrate.

## CHLORAL HYDRATE

**Indications** insomnia (short-term use)

**Cautions** respiratory disease, history of drug or alcohol abuse, marked personality disorder; reduce dose in elderly and debilitated; avoid prolonged use (and abrupt withdrawal thereafter); avoid contact with skin and mucous membranes; hepatic impairment (avoid if severe—Appendix 2); **interactions:** Appendix 1 (anxiolytics and hypnotics)

Driving Drowsiness may persist the next day and affect performance of skilled tasks (e.g. driving); effects of alcohol enhanced

**Contra-indications** severe cardiac disease, gastritis, severe hepatic impairment, severe renal impairment; pregnancy; breast-feeding (Appendix 5); porphyria (section 9.8.2)

**Side-effects** gastric irritation (nausea and vomiting reported), abdominal distention and flatulence; also ataxia, confusion, rashes, headache, lightheadedness, ketonuria, excitement, nightmares, delirium (especially on abrupt withdrawal); dependence (may be associated with gastritis and renal damage) on prolonged use

**Dose**

- See under preparations below

**Chloral Mixture, BP 2000** PoM
**(Chloral Oral Solution)**

Mixture, chloral hydrate 500 mg/5 mL in a suitable vehicle. Extemporaneous preparations should be recently prepared according to the following formula: chloral hydrate 1 g, syrup 2 mL, water to 10 mL. Net price 100 mL = 53p. Label: 19, 27

Dose 5–20 mL; CHILD 1–5 years 2.5–5 mL, 6–12 years 5–10 mL, taken well diluted with water at bedtime

**Chloral Elixir, Paediatric, BP 2000** PoM
**(Chloral Oral Solution, Paediatric)**

Elixir, chloral hydrate 4% in a suitable vehicle with a black currant flavour. Extemporaneous preparations should be recently prepared according to the following formula: chloral hydrate 200 mg, water 0.1 mL, black currant syrup 1 mL, syrup to 5 mL. Net price 100 mL = £1.02. Label: 1, 27

**Dose** up to 1 year 5 mL, taken well diluted with water at bedtime

Cloral betaine

**Welldorm®** (Alphashow) PoM

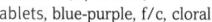

Tablets, blue-purple, f/c, cloral betaine 707 mg (≡ chloral hydrate 414 mg). Net price 30-tab pack = £2.43. Label: 19, 27

**Dose** 1–2 tablets with water or milk at bedtime, max. 5 tablets (2 g chloral hydrate) daily

Elixir, red, chloral hydrate 143.3 mg/5 mL. Net price 150-mL pack = £2.05. Label: 19, 27

**Dose** 15–45 mL (0.4–1.3 g chloral hydrate) with water or milk, at bedtime, max. 70 mL (2 g chloral hydrate) daily; CHILD 1–1.75 mL/kg (30–50 mg/kg chloral hydrate), max. 35 mL (1 g chloral hydrate) daily

### TRICLOFOS SODIUM

**Indications** insomnia (short-term use)

**Cautions** see Chloral Hydrate

**Contra-indications** see Chloral Hydrate

**Side-effects** see Chloral Hydrate but less gastric irritation

**Dose**

- See under preparation below

**Triclofos Oral Solution, BP** PoM
**(Triclofos Elixir)**

Oral solution, triclofos sodium 500 mg/5 mL. Net price 300 mL = £27.83. Label: 19

**Dose** 10–20 mL (1–2 g triclofos sodium) at bedtime; CHILD up to 1 year 25–30 mg/kg, 1–5 years 2.5–5 mL (250–500 mg triclofos sodium), 6–12 years 5–10 mL (0.5–1 g triclofos sodium)

## Clomethiazole

**Clomethiazole** (chlormethiazole) may be a useful hypnotic for elderly patients because of its freedom from hangover but, as with all hypnotics, routine administration is undesirable and dependence occurs. It is licensed for use as a hypnotic only in the elderly (and for *very short-term use* in younger adults to attenuate alcohol withdrawal symptoms, see section 4.10).

### CLOMETHIAZOLE
(Chlormethiazole)

**Indications** see under Dose; alcohol withdrawal (section 4.10)

**Cautions** cardiac and respiratory disease (confusional state may indicate hypoxia); history of drug abuse; marked personality disorder; elderly; excessive sedation may occur (particularly with higher doses); hepatic impairment (especially if severe because sedation can mask hepatic coma; Appendix 2); renal impairment (Appendix 3); avoid prolonged use (and abrupt withdrawal thereafter); **interactions**: Appendix 1 (anxiolytics and hypnotics)

**Driving.** Drowsiness may persist the next day and affect performance of skilled tasks (e.g. driving); effects of alcohol enhanced

**Contra-indications** acute pulmonary insufficiency; alcohol-dependent patients who continue to drink

**Side-effects** nasal congestion and irritation (increased nasopharyngeal and bronchial secretions), conjunctival irritation, headache; rarely, paradoxical excitement, confusion, dependence, gastro-intestinal disturbances, rash, urticaria, bullous eruption, anaphylaxis, alterations in liver enzymes

**Dose**

- Severe insomnia in the elderly (short-term use), 1–2 capsules (*or* 5–10 mL syrup) at bedtime; CHILD not recommended
- Restlessness and agitation in the elderly, 1 capsule (*or* 5 mL syrup) 3 times daily
- Alcohol withdrawal, initially 2–4 capsules, if necessary repeated after some hours; day 1 (first 24 hours), 9–12 capsules in 3–4 divided doses; day 2, 6–8 capsules in 3–4 divided doses; day 3, 4–6 capsules in 3–4 divided doses; then gradually reduced over days 4–6; total treatment for not more than 9 days

**Note** For an equivalent therapeutic effect 1 capsule ≡ 5 mL syrup

**Heminevrin®** (AstraZeneca) PoM

Capsules, grey-brown, clomethiazole base 192 mg in an oily basis. Net price 60-cap pack = £4.78. Label: 19

Syrup, sugar-free, clomethiazole edisilate 250 mg/5 mL. Net price 300-mL pack = £4.00. Label: 19

## Antihistamines

Some **antihistamines** (section 3.4.1) such as diphenhydramine and promethazine are on sale to the public for occasional insomnia; their prolonged duration of action may often lead to drowsiness the following day. The sedative effect of antihistamines may diminish after a few days of continued treatment; antihistamines are associated with headache, psychomotor impairment and antimuscarinic effects.

Promethazine is also popular for use in children, but the use of hypnotics in children is not usually justified.

### PROMETHAZINE HYDROCHLORIDE

**Indications** night sedation and insomnia (short-term use); other indications (section 3.4.1, section 4.6)

**Cautions** section 3.4.1

**Contra-indications** section 3.4.1

**Side-effects** section 3.4.1

**Dose**

- By mouth, 25 mg at bedtime increased to 50 mg if necessary; CHILD under 2 years not recommended, 2–5 years 15–20 mg, 5–10 years 20–25 mg, at bedtime

Preparations

Section 3.4.1

## Alcohol

**Alcohol** is a poor hypnotic because its diuretic action interferes with sleep during the latter part of the night. With chronic use, alcohol disturbs sleep patterns and causes insomnia; **interactions:** Appendix 1 (alcohol).

## 4.1.2 Anxiolytics

**Benzodiazepine** anxiolytics can be effective in alleviating anxiety states. Although these drugs are often prescribed to almost anyone with stress-related symptoms, unhappiness, or minor physical disease, their use in many situations is unjustified. In particular, they are not appropriate for treating depression or chronic psychosis. In bereavement, psychological adjustment may be inhibited by benzodiazepines. In children anxiolytic treatment should be used only to relieve acute anxiety (and related insomnia) caused by fear (e.g. before surgery).

Anxiolytic treatment should be limited to the lowest possible dose for the shortest possible time (see CSM advice, section 4.1). Dependence is particularly likely in patients with a history of alcohol or drug abuse and in patients with marked personality disorders.

Anxiolytics, particularly the benzodiazepines, have been termed 'minor tranquillisers'. This term is misleading because not only do they differ markedly from the antipsychotic drugs ('major tranquillisers') but their use is by no means minor. Antipsychotics, in low doses, are also sometimes used in severe anxiety for their sedative action but long-term use should be avoided in view of a possible risk of tardive dyskinesia (section 4.2.1).

Some antidepressants (section 4.3) are licensed for use in anxiety and related disorders; see section 4.3 for a comment on their role in chronic anxiety, generalised anxiety disorder, and panic disorders. The use of antihistamines (e.g. hydroxyzine, section 3.4.1) for their sedative effect in anxiety is not considered to be appropriate.



## Benzodiazepines

**Benzodiazepines** are indicated for the *short-term relief of severe anxiety* but long-term use should be avoided (see p. 173). Diazepam, alprazolam, chlordiazepoxide, and clobazam have a sustained action. Shorter-acting compounds such as **lorazepam** and **oxazepam** may be preferred in patients with hepatic impairment but they carry a greater risk of withdrawal symptoms.

In *panic disorders* (with or without agoraphobia) resistant to antidepressant therapy (section 4.3), a benzodiazepine (lorazepam 3–5 mg daily or clonazepam 1–2 mg daily (section 4.8.1) [both unlicensed]) may be used; alternatively, a benzodiazepine may be used as short-term adjunctive therapy at the start of antidepressant treatment to prevent the initial worsening of symptoms.

Diazepam or lorazepam are very occasionally administered intravenously for the *control of panic attacks*. This route is the most rapid but the procedure is not without risk (section 4.8.2) and should be used only when alternative measures have failed. The intramuscular route has no advantage over the oral route.

For guidelines on benzodiazepine withdrawal, see p. 173.

### DIAZEPAM

**Indications** short-term use in anxiety or insomnia, adjunct in acute alcohol withdrawal; status epilepticus (section 4.8.2); febrile convulsions (section 4.8.3); muscle spasm (section 10.2.2); peri-operative use (section 15.1.4.1)

**Cautions** respiratory disease, muscle weakness and myasthenia gravis, history of drug or alcohol abuse, marked personality disorder, pregnancy (Appendix 4), breast-feeding (Appendix 5); reduce dose in elderly and debilitated, and in hepatic impairment (avoid if severe; Appendix 2), renal impairment (Appendix 3); avoid prolonged use (and abrupt withdrawal thereafter); special precautions for intravenous injection (section 4.8.2); porphyria (section 9.8.2); when given parenterally, close observation required until full recovery from sedation; **interactions:** Appendix 1 (anxiolytics and hypnotics)

Driving Drowsiness may affect performance of skilled tasks (e.g. driving); effects of alcohol enhanced

**Contra-indications** respiratory depression; marked neuromuscular respiratory weakness including unstable myasthenia gravis; acute pulmonary insufficiency; sleep apnoea syndrome; severe hepatic impairment; not for chronic psychosis; should not be used alone in depression or in anxiety with depression; avoid injections containing benzyl alcohol in neonates (see under preparations below)

**Side-effects** drowsiness and lightheadedness the next day; confusion and ataxia (especially in the elderly); amnesia; dependence; paradoxical increase in aggression (see also section 4.1); muscle weakness; *occasionally:* headache, vertigo, hypotension, salivation changes, gastro-intestinal disturbances, visual disturbances, dysarthria, tremor, changes in libido, incontinence, urinary retention; blood disorders and jaundice reported; skin reactions; on intravenous injection, pain, thrombophlebitis, and rarely apnoea; **overdosage**: see Emergency Treatment of Poisoning, p. 32

**Dose**

- By mouth, anxiety, 2 mg 3 times daily increased if necessary to 15–30 mg daily in divided doses; ELDERLY (or debilitated) half adult dose

  Insomnia associated with anxiety, 5–15 mg at bedtime

  CHILD night terrors and somnambulism, 1–5 mg at bedtime
- By intramuscular injection *or* slow intravenous injection (into a large vein, at a rate of not more than 5 mg/minute), for severe acute anxiety, control of acute panic attacks, and acute alcohol withdrawal, 10 mg, repeated if necessary after not less than 4 hours

  Note Only use intramuscular route when oral and intravenous routes not possible; special precautions for intravenous injection see section 4.8.2
- By intravenous infusion—section 4.8.2
- By rectum as rectal solution, acute anxiety and agitation, 500 micrograms/kg repeated after 12 hours as required; ELDERLY 250 micrograms/kg; CHILD not recommended

  CHILD febrile convulsions, see p. 250

  As suppositories, anxiety when oral route not appropriate, 10–30 mg (higher dose divided); dose form not appropriate for less than 10 mg

**Diazepam** (Non-proprietary) PoM

Tablets, diazepam 2 mg, net price 20 = 65p; 5 mg, 20 = 68p; 10 mg, 20 = 95p. Label: 2 or 19

Brands include *Rimapam*® NHS, *Tensium*® NHS

Oral solution, diazepam 2 mg/5 mL, net price 100 mL = £1.75. Label: 2 or 19

Brands include *Dialar*® NHS

Strong oral solution, diazepam 5 mg/5 mL, net price 100-mL pack = £6.38. Label: 2 or 19 NHS

Brands include *Dialar*® NHS

Injection (solution), diazepam 5 mg/mL. Do not dilute (except for intravenous infusion). Net price 2-mL amp = 32p

Excipients may include benzyl alcohol (avoid in neonates, see Excipients, p. 2), ethanol, propylene glycol

Injection (emulsion), diazepam 5 mg/mL. For intravenous injection or infusion. Net price 2-mL amp = 84p
Brands include *Diazemuls*®

Rectal tubes (= rectal solution), diazepam 2 mg/mL, net price 1.25-mL (2.5-mg) tube = 90p, 2.5-mL (5-mg) tube = £1.27; 4 mg/mL, 2.5-mL (10-mg) tube = £1.34
Brands include *Diazepam Rectubes*®, *Stesolid*®

Suppositories, diazepam 10 mg, net price 6 = £10.20. Label: 2 or 19
Brands include *Valclair*®

**Dental prescribing on NHS** Diazepam Tablets or Diazepam Oral Solution 2 mg/5 mL may be prescribed

## ALPRAZOLAM

**Indications** anxiety (short-term use)
**Cautions** see under Diazepam
**Contra-indications** see under Diazepam
**Side-effects** see under Diazepam
**Dose**
- 250–500 micrograms 3 times daily (elderly or debilitated 250 micrograms 2–3 times daily), increased if necessary to a total of 3 mg daily; CHILD not recommended

**Xanax**® (Pharmacia) PoM NHS
Tablets, both scored, alprazolam 250 micrograms, net price 60-tab pack = £3.18; 500 micrograms (pink), 60-tab pack = £6.09. Label: 2

## CHLORDIAZEPOXIDE HYDROCHLORIDE

**Indications** anxiety (short-term use); adjunct in acute alcohol withdrawal (section 4.10)
**Cautions** see under Diazepam
**Contra-indications** see under Diazepam
**Side-effects** see under Diazepam
**Dose**
- Anxiety, 10 mg 3 times daily increased if necessary to 60–100 mg daily in divided doses; ELDERLY (or debilitated) half adult dose; CHILD not recommended

**Chlordiazepoxide** (Non-proprietary) PoM
Capsules, chlordiazepoxide hydrochloride 5 mg, net price 20 = 81p; 10 mg, 20 = £1.08. Label: 2
Brands include *Librium*® NHS, *Tropium*® NHS

**Chlordiazepoxide Hydrochloride** (Non-proprietary) PoM
Tablets, chlordiazepoxide hydrochloride 5 mg, net price 20 = 79p; 10 mg, 20 = £1.09. Label: 2

## LORAZEPAM

**Indications** short-term use in anxiety or insomnia; status epilepticus (section 4.8.2); peri-operative (section 15.1.4.1)
**Cautions** see under Diazepam; short acting; when given parenterally, facilities for managing respiratory depression with mechanical ventilation must be at hand
**Contra-indications** see under Diazepam
**Side-effects** see under Diazepam
**Dose**
- By mouth, anxiety, 1–4 mg daily in divided doses; ELDERLY (or debilitated) half adult dose
  Insomnia associated with anxiety, 1–2 mg at bedtime; CHILD not recommended
- By intramuscular *or* slow intravenous injection (into a large vein), acute panic attacks, 25–30 micrograms/kg (usual range 1.5–2.5 mg), repeated every 6 hours if necessary; CHILD not recommended
  Note Only use intramuscular route when oral and intravenous routes not possible

**Lorazepam** (Non-proprietary) PoM
Tablets, lorazepam 1 mg, net price 28-tab pack = £2.35; 2.5 mg, 28-tab pack = £2.70. Label: 2 or 19

Injection, lorazepam 4 mg/mL. Net price 1-mL amp = 37p
Excipients include benzyl alcohol, propylene glycol (see Excipients, p. 2)
Brands include *Ativan*®
Note For intramuscular injection it should be diluted with an equal volume of water for injections or physiological saline (but only use when oral and intravenous routes not possible)

## OXAZEPAM

**Indications** anxiety (short-term use)
**Cautions** see under Diazepam; short acting
**Contra-indications** see under Diazepam
**Side-effects** see under Diazepam
**Dose**
- Anxiety, 15–30 mg (elderly or debilitated 10–20 mg) 3–4 times daily; CHILD not recommended
- Insomnia associated with anxiety, 15–25 mg (max. 50 mg) at bedtime; CHILD not recommended

**Oxazepam** (Non-proprietary) PoM
Tablets, oxazepam 10 mg, net price 28-tab pack = £1.78; 15 mg, 28-tab pack = £1.77; 30 mg, 20 = 49p. Label: 2

### Buspirone

**Buspirone** is thought to act at specific serotonin ($5HT_{1A}$) receptors. Response to treatment may take up to 2 weeks. It does not alleviate the symptoms of benzodiazepine withdrawal. Therefore a patient taking a benzodiazepine still needs to have the benzodiazepine withdrawn gradually; it is advisable to do this before starting buspirone. The dependence and abuse potential of buspirone is low; it is, however, licensed for short-term use only (but specialists occasionally use it for several months).

## BUSPIRONE HYDROCHLORIDE

**Indications** anxiety (short-term use)
**Cautions** does not alleviate benzodiazepine withdrawal (see notes above); **interactions:** Appendix 1 (anxiolytics and hypnotics)
Driving May affect performance of skilled tasks (e.g. driving); effects of alcohol may be enhanced
**Contra-indications** epilepsy, severe hepatic impairment (Appendix 2), moderate to severe renal impairment (Appendix 3), pregnancy (Appendix 4) and breast-feeding (Appendix 5)
**Side-effects** nausea, dizziness, headache, nervousness, lightheadedness, excitement; rarely tachycardia, palpitations, chest pain, drowsiness, confusion, seizures, dry mouth, fatigue, and sweating
**Dose**
- Initially 5 mg 2–3 times daily, increased as necessary every 2–3 days; usual range 15–30 mg daily in divided doses; max. 45 mg daily; CHILD not recommended

**Buspirone Hydrochloride** (Non-proprietary) PoM
Tablets, buspirone hydrochloride 5 mg, net price 30-tab pack = £9.17; 10 mg, 30-tab pack = £13.45. Counselling, driving

**Buspar®** (Bristol-Myers Squibb) PoM
Tablets, buspirone hydrochloride 5 mg, net price 90-tab pack = £28.08; 10 mg, 90-tab pack = £42.12. Counselling, driving

## Beta-blockers

**Beta-blockers** (e.g. propranolol, oxprenolol) (section 2.4) do not affect psychological symptoms, such as worry, tension, and fear, but they do reduce autonomic symptoms, such as palpitation and tremor; they do not reduce non-autonomic symptoms, such as muscle tension. Beta-blockers are therefore indicated for patients with predominantly somatic symptoms; this, in turn, may prevent the onset of worry and fear. Patients with predominantly psychological symptoms may obtain no benefit.

## Meprobamate

**Meprobamate** is **less effective** than the benzodiazepines, more hazardous in overdosage, and can also induce dependence. It is **not** recommended.

### MEPROBAMATE

**Indications** short-term use in anxiety, but see notes above

**Cautions** respiratory disease, muscle weakness, epilepsy (may induce seizures), history of drug or alcohol abuse, marked personality disorder, pregnancy (Appendix 4); elderly and debilitated; hepatic impairment (Appendix 2), renal impairment (Appendix 3); avoid prolonged use, abrupt withdrawal may precipitate convulsions; **interactions:** Appendix 1 (anxiolytics and hypnotics)
Driving Drowsiness may affect performance of skilled tasks (e.g. driving); effects of alcohol enhanced

**Contra-indications** acute pulmonary insufficiency; respiratory depression; porphyria (section 9.8.2); breast-feeding (Appendix 5)

**Side-effects** see under Diazepam, but incidence greater and drowsiness most common side-effect; also gastro-intestinal disturbances, hypotension, paraesthesia, weakness, CNS effects including headache, paradoxical excitement, disturbances of vision; rarely agranulocytosis and rashes

**Dose**
- 400 mg 3–4 times daily; elderly patients half adult dose or less; CHILD not recommended

**Meprobamate** (Non-proprietary) CD
Tablets, scored, meprobamate 400 mg. Net price 84-tab pack = £19.95. Label: 2

## 4.1.3 Barbiturates

The intermediate-acting **barbiturates** have a place only in the treatment of severe intractable insomnia in patients **already taking** barbiturates; they should be **avoided** in the elderly. The long-acting barbiturate, phenobarbital is still sometimes of value in epilepsy (section 4.8.1) but its use as a sedative is unjustified. The very short-acting barbiturate thiopental is used in anaesthesia (section 15.1.1).

### BARBITURATES

**Indications** severe intractable insomnia **only** in patients already taking barbiturates; see also notes above

**Cautions** avoid use where possible; dependence and tolerance readily occur; abrupt withdrawal may precipitate serious withdrawal syndrome (rebound insomnia, anxiety, tremor, dizziness, nausea, convulsions, delirium, and death); repeated doses are cumulative and may lead to excessive sedation; respiratory disease; renal impairment (Appendix 3); hepatic impairment; **interactions:** Appendix 1 (barbiturates)
Driving Drowsiness may persist the next day and affect performance of skilled tasks (e.g. driving); effects of alcohol enhanced

**Contra-indications** insomnia caused by pain; porphyria (section 9.8.2); severe hepatic impairment; children, young adults, elderly and debilitated patients, also patients with history of drug or alcohol abuse; pregnancy (Appendix 4); breast-feeding (Appendix 5)

**Side-effects** include hangover with drowsiness, dizziness, ataxia, respiratory depression, hypersensitivity reactions, headache, particularly in elderly; paradoxical excitement and confusion occasionally precede sleep

**Dose**
- See under preparations below

**Amytal®** (Flynn) CD
Tablets, amobarbital (amylobarbitone) 50 mg, net price 20 = £1.84. Label: 19
Dose 100–200 mg at bedtime (**important:** but see also contra-indications)

**Sodium Amytal®** (Flynn) CD
Capsules, both blue, amobarbital (amylobarbitone) sodium 60 mg, net price 20 = £3.43; 200 mg, 20 = £6.75. Label: 19
Dose 60–200 mg at bedtime (**important:** but see also contra-indications)

**Soneryl®** (Concord) CD
Tablets, pink, scored, butobarbital (butobarbitone) 100 mg. Net price 56-tab pack = £10.65. Label: 19
Dose 100–200 mg at bedtime (**important:** but see also contra-indications)

**Preparations containing secobarbital (quinalbarbitone)**
Note Secobarbital (quinalbarbitone) is in schedule 2 of the Misuse of Drugs Regulations 2001; receipt and supply must therefore be recorded in the CD register.

**Seconal Sodium®** (Flynn) CD
Capsules, both orange, secobarbital (quinalbarbitone) sodium 50 mg, net price 20 = £5.30; 100 mg, 20 = £6.96. Label: 19
Dose 100 mg at bedtime (**important:** but see also contra-indications)

**Tuinal®** (Flynn) CD
Capsules, orange/blue, a mixture of amobarbital (amylobarbitone) sodium 50 mg, secobarbital (quinalbarbitone) sodium 50 mg. Net price 20 = £3.88. Label: 19
Dose 1–2 capsules at bedtime (**important:** but see also contra-indications)
Note Prescriptions need only specify 'Tuinal capsules'

# 4.2 Drugs used in psychoses and related disorders


4.2.1 Antipsychotic drugs
4.2.2 Antipsychotic depot injections
4.2.3 Antimanic drugs


**Advice of Royal College of Psychiatrists on doses above BNF upper limit.** Unless otherwise stated, doses in the BNF are licensed doses—any higher dose is therefore **unlicensed** (for an explanation of the significance of this, see p. 1).

1. Consider alternative approaches including adjuvant therapy and newer or atypical neuroleptics such as clozapine.
2. Bear in mind risk factors, including obesity—particular caution is indicated in older patients especially those over 70.
3. Consider potential for drug interactions—see **interactions:** Appendix 1 (antipsychotics).
4. Carry out ECG to exclude untoward abnormalities such as prolonged QT interval; repeat ECG periodically and reduce dose if prolonged QT interval or other adverse abnormality develops.
5. Increase dose slowly and not more often than once weekly.
6. Carry out regular pulse, blood pressure, and temperature checks; ensure that patient maintains adequate fluid intake.
7. Consider high-dose therapy to be for limited period and review regularly; abandon if no improvement after 3 months (return to standard dosage).

**Important:** When prescribing an antipsychotic for administration on an emergency basis, the intramuscular dose should be **lower** than the corresponding oral dose (owing to absence of first-pass effect), particularly if the patient is very active (increased blood flow to muscle considerably increases the rate of absorption). The prescription should specify the dose for **each route** and should **not** imply that the same dose can be given by mouth or by intramuscular injection. The dose of antipsychotic for emergency use should be reviewed at least **daily**.

## 4.2.1 Antipsychotic drugs

Antipsychotic drugs are also known as 'neuroleptics' and (misleadingly) as 'major tranquillisers'. Antipsychotic drugs generally tranquillise without impairing consciousness and without causing paradoxical excitement but they should not be regarded merely as tranquillisers. For conditions such as schizophrenia the tranquillising effect is of secondary importance.

In the short term they are used to quieten disturbed patients whatever the underlying psychopathology, which may be schizophrenia, brain damage, mania, toxic delirium, or agitated depression. Antipsychotic drugs are used to alleviate severe anxiety but this too should be a short-term measure.

**Schizophrenia** Antipsychotic drugs relieve florid psychotic symptoms such as thought disorder, hallucinations, and delusions, and prevent relapse. Although they are usually less effective in apathetic withdrawn patients, they sometimes appear to have an activating influence. Patients with acute schizophrenia generally respond better than those with chronic symptoms.

Long-term treatment of a patient with a definite diagnosis of schizophrenia may be necessary even after the first episode of illness in order to prevent the manifest illness from becoming chronic. Withdrawal of drug treatment requires careful surveillance because the patient who appears well on medication may suffer a disastrous relapse if treatment is withdrawn inappropriately. In addition the need for continuation of treatment may not become immediately evident because relapse is often delayed for several weeks after cessation of treatment.

Antipsychotic drugs are considered to act by interfering with dopaminergic transmission in the brain by blocking dopamine $D_2$ receptors, which may give rise to the extrapyramidal effects described below, and also to hyperprolactinaemia. Antipsychotic drugs may also affect cholinergic, alpha-adrenergic, histaminergic, and serotonergic receptors.

**Cautions and contra-indications** Antipsychotics should be used with **caution** in patients with hepatic impairment (Appendix 2), renal impairment (Appendix 3), cardiovascular disease, Parkinson's disease (may be exacerbated by antipsychotics), epilepsy (and conditions predisposing to epilepsy), depression, myasthenia gravis, prostatic hypertrophy, or a personal or family history of angle-closure glaucoma (avoid chlorpromazine, pericyazine and prochlorperazine in these conditions). Caution is also required in severe respiratory disease and in patients with a history of jaundice or who have blood dyscrasias (perform blood counts if unexplained infection or fever develops). Antipsychotics should be used with caution in the elderly, who are particularly susceptible to postural hypotension and to hyper- or hypothermia in very hot or cold weather. Serious consideration should be given before prescribing these drugs for elderly patients. As photosensitisation may occur with higher dosages, patients should avoid direct sunlight.

Antipsychotic drugs may be **contra-indicated** in comatose states, CNS depression, and phaeochromocytoma. Most antipsychotics are best avoided during pregnancy, unless essential (Appendix 4) and it is advisable to discontinue breast-feeding during treatment (Appendix 5); **interactions:** Appendix 1 (antipsychotics)

**Driving** Drowsiness may affect performance of skilled tasks (e.g. driving or operating machinery), especially at start of treatment; effects of alcohol are enhanced

**Withdrawal** Withdrawal of antipsychotic drugs after long-term therapy should always be gradual and closely monitored to avoid the risk of acute withdrawal syndromes or rapid relapse.

**Side-effects** Extrapyramidal symptoms are the most troublesome. They occur most frequently with the piperazine phenothiazines (fluphenazine, perphenazine, prochlorperazine, and trifluoperazine), the butyrophenones (benperidol and haloperidol), and the depot preparations. They are easy to recognise but cannot be predicted accurately because they depend on the dose, the type of drug, and on individual susceptibility.

Extrapyramidal symptoms consist of:

- *parkinsonian symptoms* (including tremor), which may occur more commonly in adults or the elderly and may appear gradually;
- *dystonia* (abnormal face and body movements) and *dyskinesia*, which occur more commonly in children or young adults and appear after only a few doses;
- *akathisia* (restlessness), which characteristically occurs after large initial doses and may resemble an exacerbation of the condition being treated; and
- *tardive dyskinesia* (rhythmic, involuntary movements of tongue, face, and jaw), which usually develops on long-term therapy or with high dosage, but it may develop on short-term treatment with low doses—short-lived tardive dyskinesia may occur after withdrawal of the drug.

*Parkinsonian symptoms* remit if the drug is withdrawn and may be suppressed by the administration of **antimuscarinic** drugs (section 4.9.2). However, routine administration of such drugs is not justified because not all patients are affected and because they may unmask or worsen tardive dyskinesia.

*Tardive dyskinesia* is of particular concern because it may be irreversible on withdrawing therapy and treatment is usually ineffective. However, some manufacturers suggest that drug withdrawal at the earliest signs of tardive dyskinesia (fine vermicular movements of the tongue) may halt its full development. Tardive dyskinesia occurs fairly frequently, especially in the elderly, and treatment must be carefully and regularly reviewed.

*Hypotension and interference with temperature regulation* are dose-related side-effects and are liable to cause dangerous falls and hypothermia or hyperthermia in the elderly.

*Neuroleptic malignant syndrome* (hyperthermia, fluctuating level of consciousness, muscular rigidity, and autonomic dysfunction with pallor, tachycardia, labile blood pressure, sweating, and urinary incontinence) is a rare but potentially fatal side-effect of some drugs. Discontinuation of the antipsychotic is essential because there is no proven effective treatment, but cooling, bromocriptine, and dantrolene have been used. The syndrome, which usually lasts for 5–7 days after drug discontinuation, may be unduly prolonged if depot preparations have been used.

*Other side-effects include:* drowsiness; apathy; agitation, excitement and insomnia; convulsions; dizziness; headache; confusion; gastro-intestinal disturbances; nasal congestion; antimuscarinic symptoms (such as dry mouth, constipation, difficulty with micturition, and blurred vision); cardiovascular symptoms (such as hypotension, tachycardia, and arrhythmias); ECG changes (cases of sudden death have occurred); endocrine effects such as menstrual disturbances, galactorrhoea, gynaecomastia, impotence, and weight gain; blood dyscrasias (such as agranulocytosis and leucopenia), photosensitisation, contact sensitisation and rashes, and jaundice (including cholestatic); corneal and lens opacities, and purplish pigmentation of the skin, cornea, conjunctiva, and retina.

**Overdosage:** for poisoning with phenothiazines and related compounds, see Emergency Treatment of Poisoning, p. 33.

**Classification of antipsychotics** The **phenothiazine** derivatives can be divided into 3 main groups.

*Group 1:* chlorpromazine, levomepromazine (methotrimeprazine), and promazine, generally characterised by pronounced sedative effects and moderate antimuscarinic and extrapyramidal side-effects.

*Group 2:* pericyazine and pipotiazine, generally characterised by moderate sedative effects, marked antimuscarinic effects, but fewer extrapyramidal side-effects than groups 1 or 3.

*Group 3:* fluphenazine, perphenazine, prochlorperazine, and trifluoperazine, generally characterised by fewer sedative effects, fewer antimuscarinic effects, but more pronounced extrapyramidal side-effects than groups 1 and 2.

Drugs of other chemical groups tend to resemble the phenothiazines of *group 3*. They include the **butyrophenones** (benperidol and haloperidol); **diphenylbutylpiperidines** (pimozide); **thioxanthenes** (flupentixol and zuclopenthixol); and the **substituted benzamides** (sulpiride).

For details of the newer antipsychotic drugs amisulpride, clozapine, olanzapine, quetiapine, risperidone, sertindole, and zotepine, see under Atypical Antipsychotics, p. 187.

**Choice** As indicated above, the various drugs differ somewhat in predominant actions and side-effects. Selection is influenced by the degree of sedation required and the patient's susceptibility to extrapyramidal side-effects. However, the differences between antipsychotic drugs are less important than the great variability in patient response; moreover, tolerance to secondary effects such as sedation usually develops. The atypical antipsychotics may be appropriate if extrapyramidal side-effects are a particular concern (see under Atypical Antipsychotics, below). Clozapine is used for schizophrenia when other antipsychotics are ineffective or not tolerated.

Prescribing of more than one antipsychotic at the same time is **not** recommended; it may constitute a hazard and there is no significant evidence that side-effects are minimised.

**Chlorpromazine** is still widely used despite the wide range of adverse effects associated with it. It has a marked sedating effect and is useful for treating violent patients without causing stupor. Agitated states in the elderly can be controlled without confusion, a dose of 10 to 25 mg once or twice daily usually being adequate.

**Flupentixol** (flupenthixol) and **pimozide** (see CSM advice p. 185) are less sedating than chlorpromazine.

**Sulpiride** in high doses controls florid positive symptoms, but in lower doses it has an alerting effect on apathetic withdrawn schizophrenics.

**Fluphenazine**, **haloperidol**, and **trifluoperazine** are also of value but their use is limited by the high incidence of extrapyramidal symptoms. Haloperidol may be preferred for the rapid control of hyperactive psychotic states; it causes less hypotension than chlorpromazine and is therefore also popular for agitation and restlessness in the elderly, despite the high incidence of extrapyramidal side-effects.

**Promazine** is not sufficiently active by mouth to be used as an antipsychotic drug; it has been used to treat agitation and restlessness in the elderly (see Other uses, below).

**Other uses** Nausea and vomiting (section 4.6), choreas, motor tics (section 4.9.3), and intractable hiccup (see under Chlorpromazine Hydrochloride and under Haloperidol). **Benperidol** is used in deviant antisocial sexual behaviour but its value is not established; see also section 6.4.2 for the role of cyproterone acetate.

Psychomotor agitation and, in the elderly, agitation and restlessness, should be investigated for an underlying cause; they can be managed with low doses of chlorpromazine or haloperidol used for short periods. The use of promazine for agitation and restlessness in the elderly has declined. **Olanzapine** and **risperidone** may be effective for agitation and restlessness in the elderly [both unlicensed].

### Equivalent doses of oral antipsychotics

These equivalences are intended **only** as an approximate guide; individual dosage instructions should **also** be checked; patients should be carefully monitored after **any** change in medication

| Antipsychotic | Daily dose |
|---|---|
| Chlorpromazine | 100 mg |
| Clozapine | 50 mg |
| Haloperidol | 2–3 mg |
| Pimozide | 2 mg |
| Risperidone | 0.5–1 mg |
| Sulpiride | 200 mg |
| Trifluoperazine | 5 mg |

**Important**. These equivalences must **not** be extrapolated beyond the max. dose for the drug. Higher doses require careful titration in specialist units and the equivalences shown here may not be appropriate

### Dosage

After an initial period of stabilisation, in most patients, the long half-life of antipsychotic drugs allows the total daily oral dose to be given as a single dose. For the advice of The Royal College of Psychiatrists on doses above the BNF upper limit, see p. 181.

## BENPERIDOL

**Indications** control of deviant antisocial sexual behaviour (but see notes above)

**Cautions** see notes above; also manufacturer advises regular blood counts and liver function tests during long-term treatment

**Contra-indications** see notes above

**Side-effects** see notes above

**Dose**

- 0.25–1.5 mg daily in divided doses, adjusted according to response; ELDERLY (or debilitated) initially half adult dose; CHILD not recommended

**Anquil®** (Concord) PoM

Tablets, scored, benperidol 250 micrograms, net price 112-tab pack = £104.00. Label: 2

**Note** The proprietary name *Benquil®* has been used for benperidol tablets

## CHLORPROMAZINE HYDROCHLORIDE

**Warning** Owing to the risk of contact sensitisation, pharmacists, nurses, and other health workers should avoid direct contact with chlorpromazine; tablets should not be crushed and solutions should be handled with care

**Indications** see under Dose; antiemetic in palliative care (section 4.6)

**Cautions** see notes above; also patients should remain supine and the blood pressure monitored for 30 minutes after intramuscular injection

**Contra-indications** see notes above

**Side-effects** see notes above; also intramuscular injection may be painful, cause hypotension and tachycardia, and give rise to nodule formation

**Dose**

- By mouth, schizophrenia and other psychoses, mania, short-term adjunctive management of severe anxiety, psychomotor agitation, excitement, and violent or dangerously impulsive behaviour initially 25 mg 3 times daily (*or* 75 mg at night), adjusted according to response, to usual maintenance dose of 75–300 mg daily (but up to 1 g daily may be required in psychoses); ELDERLY (or debilitated) third to half adult dose; CHILD (childhood schizophrenia and autism) 1–5 years 500 micrograms/kg every 4–6 hours (max. 40 mg daily); 6–12 years third to half adult dose (max. 75 mg daily)

  Intractable hiccup, 25–50 mg 3–4 times daily
- By deep intramuscular injection, (for relief of acute symptoms but see also Cautions and Side-effects), 25–50 mg every 6–8 hours; CHILD, 1–5 years 500 micrograms/kg every 6–8 hours (max. 40 mg daily); 6–12 years 500 micrograms/kg every 6–8 hours (max. 75 mg daily)

  Induction of hypothermia (to prevent shivering), by deep intramuscular injection, 25–50 mg every 6–8 hours; CHILD 1–12 years, initially 0.5–1 mg/kg, followed by maintenance 500 micrograms/kg every 4–6 hours
- By rectum in suppositories as chlorpromazine base 100 mg every 6–8 hours [unlicensed]

  **Note** For equivalent therapeutic effect 100 mg chlorpromazine base given rectally as a suppository ≡ 20–25 mg chlorpromazine hydrochloride by intramuscular injection ≡ 40–50 mg of chlorpromazine base or hydrochloride by mouth

**Chlorpromazine** (Non-proprietary) PoM

Tablets, coated, chlorpromazine hydrochloride 10 mg, net price 56-tab pack = 66p; 25 mg, 28-tab pack = £1.94; 50 mg, 28-tab pack = £1.71; 100 mg, 28-tab pack = £2.03. Label: 2, 11

Brands include *Chloractil®*

Oral solution, chlorpromazine hydrochloride 25 mg/5 mL, net price 150 mL = £1.35, 100 mg/5 mL, 150 mL = £3.57. Label: 2, 11

Injection, chlorpromazine hydrochloride 25 mg/mL, net price 1-mL amp = 60p; 2-mL amp = 63p

Suppositories, chlorpromazine 100 mg. Label: 2, 11

'Special order' [unlicensed] product; contact Martindale or regional hospital manufacturing unit

**Largactil®** (Hawgreen) PoM

Tablets, all off-white, f/c, chlorpromazine hydrochloride 10 mg. Net price 56-tab pack = 66p; 25 mg, 56-tab pack = 91p; 50 mg, 56-tab pack = £1.91; 100 mg, 56-tab pack = £3.54. Label: 2, 11

Syrup, brown, chlorpromazine hydrochloride 25 mg/5 mL. Net price 100-mL pack = £1.03. Label: 2, 11

Suspension forte, orange, sugar-free, chlorpromazine hydrochloride 100 mg (as embonate)/5 mL. Net price 100-mL pack = £2.38. Label: 2, 11

Injection, chlorpromazine hydrochloride 25 mg/mL. Net price 2-mL amp = 63p

## FLUPENTIXOL
**(Flupenthixol)**

**Indications** schizophrenia and other psychoses, particularly with apathy and withdrawal but not mania or psychomotor hyperactivity; depression (section 4.3.4)

**Cautions** see notes above; avoid in porphyria (section 9.8.2)

**Contra-indications** see notes above; also excitable and overactive patients

**Side-effects** see notes above; less sedating but extrapyramidal symptoms frequent

**Dose**

- Psychosis, initially 3–9 mg twice daily adjusted according to the response; max. 18 mg daily; ELDERLY (or debilitated) initially quarter to half adult dose; CHILD not recommended

**Depixol®** (Lundbeck) PoM

Tablets, yellow, s/c, flupentixol 3 mg (as dihydrochloride). Net price 20 = £2.78. Label: 2

Depot injection (flupentixol decanoate): section 4.2.2

## FLUPHENAZINE HYDROCHLORIDE

**Indications** see under Dose

**Cautions** see notes above

**Contra-indications** see notes above; also marked cerebral atherosclerosis

**Side-effects** see notes above; less sedating and fewer antimuscarinic or hypotensive symptoms, but extrapyramidal symptoms, particularly dystonic reactions and akathisia, more frequent; systemic lupus erythematosus, inappropriate antidiuretic hormone secretion, oedema, also reported

**Dose**

- Schizophrenia and other psychoses, mania, initially 2–10 mg daily in 2–3 divided doses, adjusted according to response to 20 mg daily; doses above 20 mg daily (10 mg in elderly) only with special caution; CHILD not recommended
- Short-term adjunctive management of severe anxiety, psychomotor agitation, excitement, and violent or dangerously impulsive behaviour, initially 1 mg twice daily, increased as necessary to 2 mg twice daily; CHILD not recommended

**Moditen®** (Sanofi-Synthelabo) PoM

Tablets, s/c, fluphenazine hydrochloride 1 mg (pink), net price 20 = £1.06. Label: 2

**Modecate®** PoM

Section 4.2.2

## HALOPERIDOL

**Indications** see under Dose; motor tics (section 4.9.3)

**Cautions** see notes above; also subarachnoid haemorrhage and metabolic disturbances such as hypokalaemia, hypocalcaemia, or hypomagnesaemia

**Contra-indications** see notes above

**Side-effects** see notes above, but less sedating and fewer antimuscarinic or hypotensive symptoms; pigmentation and photosensitivity reactions rare; extrapyramidal symptoms, particularly dystonic reactions and akathisia especially in thyrotoxic patients; rarely weight loss; hypoglycaemia; inappropriate antidiuretic hormone secretion

**Dose**

- By mouth, schizophrenia and other psychoses, mania, short-term adjunctive management of psychomotor agitation, excitement, and violent or dangerously impulsive behaviour, initially 1.5–3 mg 2–3 times daily *or* 3–5 mg 2–3 times daily in severely affected or resistant patients; in resistant schizophrenia up to 30 mg daily may be needed; adjusted according to response to lowest effective maintenance dose (as low as 5–10 mg daily); ELDERLY (or debilitated) initially half adult dose; CHILD initially 25–50 micrograms/kg daily (in 2 divided doses) to max. 10 mg

  Agitation and restlessness in the elderly, initially 0.5–1.5 mg once or twice daily

  Short-term adjunctive management of severe anxiety, 500 micrograms twice daily; CHILD not recommended

  Intractable hiccup, 1.5 mg 3 times daily adjusted according to response; CHILD not recommended

  Nausea and vomiting, 1 mg daily (see also Prescribing in Palliative Care, p. 16)
- By intramuscular *or* by intravenous injection, initially 2–10 mg, then every 4–8 hours according to response to total max. 18 mg daily; severely disturbed patients may require initial dose of up to 18 mg; ELDERLY (or debilitated) initially half adult dose; CHILD not recommended

  Nausea and vomiting, 0.5–2 mg

**Haloperidol** (Non-proprietary) PoM

Tablets, haloperidol 500 micrograms, net price 28-tab pack = 91p; 1.5 mg, 20 = £1.65; 5 mg, 20 = £4.00; 10 mg, 20 = £4.23; 20 mg, 20 = £7.47. Label: 2

**Dozic®** (Rosemont) PoM

Oral liquid, sugar-free, haloperidol 1 mg/mL. Net price 100-mL pack = £6.86. Label: 2

**Haldol®** (Janssen-Cilag) PoM

Tablets, both scored, haloperidol 5 mg (blue), net price 20 = £1.56; 10 mg (yellow), 20 = £3.05. Label: 2

Oral liquid, sugar-free, haloperidol 2 mg/mL. Net price 100-mL pack (with pipette) = £4.83. Label: 2

Injection, haloperidol 5 mg/mL. Net price 1-mL amp = 31p

Depot injection (haloperidol decanoate): section 4.2.2

**Serenace®** (IVAX) PoM

Capsules, green, haloperidol 500 micrograms, net price 30-cap pack = 98p. Label: 2

Tablets, haloperidol 1.5 mg, net price 30-tab pack = £1.73; 5 mg (pink), 30-tab pack = £4.90; 10 mg (pale pink), 30-tab pack = £8.81. Label: 2

Oral liquid, sugar-free, haloperidol 2 mg/mL, net price 500-mL pack = £43.83. Label: 2

Injection, haloperidol 5 mg/mL, net price 1-mL amp = 59p; 10 mg/mL, 2-mL amp = £2.03

## LEVOMEPROMAZINE
(Methotrimeprazine)

**Indications** see under Dose

**Cautions** see notes above; patients receiving large initial doses should remain supine

Elderly Risk of postural hypotension; not recommended for ambulant patients over 50 years unless risk of hypotensive reaction assessed

**Contra-indications** see notes above

**Side-effects** see notes above; occasionally raised erythrocyte sedimentation rate occurs

**Dose**

- By mouth, schizophrenia, initially 25–50 mg daily in divided doses increased as necessary; bedpatients initially 100–200 mg daily usually in 3 divided doses, increased if necessary to 1 g daily; ELDERLY, see Cautions

  Adjunctive treatment in palliative care (including management of pain and associated restlessness, distress, or vomiting), 12.5–50 mg every 4–8 hours, but see also Prescribing in Palliative Care, p. 15 and p. 16
- By intramuscular injection *or* by intravenous injection (by intravenous injection after dilution with an equal volume of sodium chloride 0.9% injection), adjunct in palliative care, 12.5–25 mg (severe agitation up to 50 mg) every 6–8 hours if necessary
- By continuous subcutaneous infusion, adjunct in palliative care (via syringe driver), diluted in a suitable volume of sodium chloride 0.9% injection, see Prescribing in Palliative Care, p. 17; CHILD (experience limited), 0.35–3 mg/kg daily

**Nozinan®** (Link) PoM

Tablets, scored, levomepromazine maleate 25 mg, net price 84-tab pack = £20.26. Label: 2

Injection, levomepromazine hydrochloride 25 mg/mL, net price 1-mL amp = £2.01

## PERICYAZINE
(Periciazine)

**Indications** see under Dose

**Cautions** see notes above

**Contra-indications** see notes above

**Side-effects** see notes above; more sedating; hypotension common when treatment initiated; respiratory depression

**Dose**

- Schizophrenia and other psychoses, initially 75 mg daily in divided doses increased at weekly intervals by steps of 25 mg according to response; usual max. 300 mg daily (elderly initially 15–30 mg daily); CHILD and INFANT over 1 year (schizophrenia or behavioural disorders only), initially, 500 micrograms daily for 10-kg child, increased by 1 mg for each additional 5 kg body-weight to max. total daily dose of 10 mg; dose may be gradually increased according to response but maintenance should not exceed twice initial dose
- Short-term adjunctive management of severe anxiety, psychomotor agitation, and violent or dangerously impulsive behaviour, initially 15–30 mg (elderly 5–10 mg) daily divided into 2 doses, taking the larger dose at bedtime, adjusted according to response; CHILD not recommended

**Neulactil®** (JHC) PoM

Tablets, all yellow, scored, pericyazine 2.5 mg, net price 84-tab pack = £7.15; 10 mg, 84-tab pack = £19.33. Label: 2

Syrup forte, brown, pericyazine 10 mg/5 mL. Net price 100-mL pack = £9.37. Label: 2

## PERPHENAZINE

**Indications** see under Dose; anti-emetic (section 4.6)

**Cautions** see notes above

**Contra-indications** see notes above; also agitation and restlessness in the elderly

**Side-effects** see notes above; less sedating; extrapyramidal symptoms, especially dystonia, more frequent, particularly at high dosage; rarely systemic lupus erythematosus

**Dose**

- Schizophrenia and other psychoses, mania, short-term adjunctive management of anxiety, severe psychomotor agitation, excitement, and violent or dangerously impulsive behaviour, initially 4 mg 3 times daily adjusted according to the response; max. 24 mg daily; ELDERLY quarter to half adult dose (but see Cautions); CHILD under 14 years not recommended

**Fentazin®** (Goldshield) PoM

Tablets, both s/c, perphenazine 2 mg, net price 20 = £3.73; 4 mg, 20 = £4.39. Label: 2

## PIMOZIDE

**Indications** see under Dose

**Cautions** see notes above

**CSM warning** Following reports of sudden unexplained death, the CSM recommends ECG before treatment. The CSM also recommends that patients on pimozide should have an annual ECG (if the QT interval is prolonged, treatment should be reviewed and either withdrawn or dose reduced under close supervision) and that pimozide should **not** be given with other antipsychotic drugs (including depot preparations), tricyclic antidepressants or other drugs which prolong the QT interval, such as certain antimalarials, anti-arrhythmic drugs and certain antihistamines and should **not** be given with drugs which cause electrolyte disturbances (especially diuretics)

**Contra-indications** see notes above; history of arrhythmias or congenital QT prolongation

**Side-effects** see notes above; less sedating; serious arrhythmias reported; glycosuria and, rarely, hyponatraemia reported

**Dose**

- Schizophrenia, initially 2 mg daily, increased according to response in steps of 2–4 mg at intervals of not less than 1 week; usual dose range 2–20 mg daily; ELDERLY half usual starting dose; CHILD not recommended
- Monosymptomatic hypochondriacal psychosis, paranoid psychosis, initially 4 mg daily, increased according to response in steps of 2–4 mg at intervals of not less than 1 week; max. 16 mg daily; ELDERLY half usual starting dose; CHILD not recommended

**Orap®** (Janssen-Cilag) PoM

Tablets, scored, green, pimozide 4 mg, net price 20 = £5.83. Label: 2

## PROCHLORPERAZINE

**Indications** see under Dose; anti-emetic (section 4.6)

**Cautions** see notes above; also hypotension more likely after intramuscular injection

**Contra-indications** see notes above; children, but see section 4.6 for use as anti-emetic

**Side-effects** see notes above; less sedating; extrapyramidal symptoms, particularly dystonias, more frequent; respiratory depression may occur in susceptible patients

**Dose**

- By mouth, schizophrenia and other psychoses, mania, prochlorperazine maleate or mesilate, 12.5 mg twice daily for 7 days adjusted at intervals of 4–7 days to usual dose of 75–100 mg daily according to response; CHILD not recommended

  Short-term adjunctive management of severe anxiety, 15–20 mg daily in divided doses; max. 40 mg daily; CHILD not recommended
- By deep intramuscular injection, psychoses, mania, prochlorperazine mesilate 12.5–25 mg 2–3 times daily; CHILD not recommended
- By rectum in suppositories, psychoses, mania, the equivalent of prochlorperazine maleate 25 mg 2–3 times daily; CHILD not recommended

**Preparations**

Section 4.6

## PROMAZINE HYDROCHLORIDE

**Indications** see under Dose

**Cautions** see notes above; also cerebral arteriosclerosis

**Contra-indications** see notes above

**Side-effects** see notes above; also haemolytic anaemia

**Dose**

- By mouth, short-term adjunctive management of psychomotor agitation, 100–200 mg 4 times daily; CHILD not recommended

  Agitation and restlessness in elderly, 25–50 mg 4 times daily

**Promazine** (Non-proprietary) PoM

Tablets, coated, promazine hydrochloride 25 mg, net price 20 = 73p; 50 mg, 20 = £1.22. Label: 2

Oral solution, promazine hydrochloride 25 mg/5 mL, net price 150 mL = £3.51; 50 mg/5 mL, 150 mL = £3.51. Label: 2

## SULPIRIDE

**Indications** schizophrenia

**Cautions** see notes above; also excited, agitated, or aggressive patients (even low doses may aggravate symptoms)

**Contra-indications** see notes above; also porphyria (section 9.8.2)

**Side-effects** see notes above; also hepatitis

**Dose**

- 200–400 mg twice daily; max. 800 mg daily in predominantly negative symptoms, and 2.4 g daily in mainly positive symptoms; ELDERLY, lower initial dose, increased gradually according to response; CHILD under 14 years not recommended

**Sulpiride** (Non-proprietary) PoM

Tablets, sulpiride 200 mg, net price 30-tab pack = £4.46, 56-tab pack = £4.77; 400 mg, 30-tab pack = £10.81. Label: 2

**Dolmatil®** (Sanofi-Synthelabo) PoM

Tablets, both scored, sulpiride 200 mg, net price 100-tab pack = £13.85; 400 mg (f/c), 100-tab pack = £36.29. Label: 2

**Sulpitil®** (Pharmacia) PoM

Tablets, scored, sulpiride 200 mg. Net price 28-tab pack = £4.29; 112-tab pack = £12.85. Label: 2

**Sulpor®** (Rosemont) PoM

Oral solution, sugar-free, lemon- and aniseed-flavoured, sulpiride 200 mg/5 mL, net price 150 mL = £25.38. Label: 2

## TRIFLUOPERAZINE

**Indications** see under Dose; anti-emetic (section 4.6)

**Cautions** see notes above

**Contra-indications** see notes above

**Side-effects** see notes above; extrapyramidal symptoms more frequent, especially at doses exceeding 6 mg daily; pancytopenia; thrombocytopenia; hyperpyrexia; anorexia

**Dose**

- By mouth (reduce initial doses in elderly by at least half)

  Schizophrenia and other psychoses, short-term adjunctive management of psychomotor agitation, excitement, and violent or dangerously impulsive behaviour, initially 5 mg twice daily, *or* 10 mg daily in modified-release form, increased by 5 mg after 1 week, then at intervals of 3 days, according to the response; CHILD up to 12 years, initially up to 5 mg daily in divided doses, adjusted according to response, age, and body-weight

  Short-term adjunctive management of severe anxiety, 2–4 mg daily in divided doses *or* 2–4 mg daily in modified-release form, increased if necessary to 6 mg daily; CHILD 3–5 years up to 1 mg daily, 6–12 years up to 4 mg daily

**Trifluoperazine** (Non-proprietary) PoM

Tablets, coated, trifluoperazine (as hydrochloride) 1 mg, net price 20 = 42p; 5 mg, 20 = 46p. Label: 2

Oral solution, trifluoperazine (as hydrochloride) 5 mg/5 mL. Net price 200-mL = £11.07. Label: 2

**Stelazine®** (Goldshield) PoM

Tablets, both blue, f/c, trifluoperazine (as hydrochloride) 1 mg, net price 20 = 61p; 5 mg, 20 = 87p. Label: 2

Spansules® (= capsules m/r), all clear/yellow, enclosing dark blue, light blue, and white pellets, trifluoperazine (as hydrochloride) 2 mg, net price 60-cap pack = £4.65; 10 mg, 30-cap pack = £2.83; 15 mg, 30-cap pack = £4.27. Label: 2, 25

**Note** May be difficult to obtain

Syrup, sugar-free, yellow, trifluoperazine (as hydrochloride) 1 mg/5 mL, net price 200-mL pack = £2.95. Label: 2

Oral solution forte, sugar-free, yellow, peach-flavour, trifluoperazine (as hydrochloride) 5 mg/5 mL, net price 200-mL pack = £10.99. Label: 2

## ZUCLOPENTHIXOL ACETATE

**Indications** short-term management of acute psychosis, mania, or exacerbations of chronic psychosis

**Cautions** see notes above; avoid in porphyria (section 9.8.2)

**Contra-indications** see notes above

**Side-effects** see notes above

**Dose**

- By deep intramuscular injection into the gluteal muscle or lateral thigh, 50–150 mg (ELDERLY 50–100 mg), if necessary repeated after 2–3 days (1 additional dose may be needed 1–2 days after the first injection); max. cumulative dose 400 mg per course and max. 4 injections; max. duration of treatment 2 weeks—if maintenance treatment necessary change to an oral antipsychotic 2–3 days after last injection, *or* to a longer acting antipsychotic depot injection given concomitantly with last injection of zuclopenthixol acetate; CHILD not recommended

**Clopixol Acuphase®** (Lundbeck) PoM
Injection (oily), zuclopenthixol acetate 50 mg/mL. Net price 1-mL amp = £4.84; 2-mL amp = £9.33

## ZUCLOPENTHIXOL DIHYDROCHLORIDE

**Indications** schizophrenia and other psychoses, particularly when associated with agitated, aggressive, or hostile behaviour

**Cautions** see notes above; avoid in porphyria (section 9.8.2)

**Contra-indications** see notes above; apathetic or withdrawn states

**Side-effects** see notes above; urinary frequency or incontinence; weight loss (less common than weight gain)

**Dose**

- By mouth, initially 20–30 mg daily in divided doses, increasing to a max. of 150 mg daily if necessary; usual maintenance dose 20–50 mg daily; ELDERLY (or debilitated) initially quarter to half adult dose; CHILD not recommended

**Clopixol®** (Lundbeck) PoM
Tablets, all f/c, pink, zuclopenthixol (as dihydrochloride) 2 mg, net price 20 = 60p; 10 mg, 20 = £1.61; 25 mg, 20 = £3.22. Label: 2

Depot injection (zuclopenthixol decanoate): section 4.2.2

## Atypical antipsychotics

The 'atypical antipsychotics' **amisulpride**, **aripiprazole**, **clozapine**, **olanzapine**, **quetiapine**, **risperidone**, and **zotepine** may be better tolerated than other antipsychotics; extrapyramidal symptoms may be less frequent than with older antipsychotics.

Aripiprazole, clozapine, olanzapine, quetiapine, and sertindole cause little or no elevation of prolactin concentration; when changing from other antipsychotics, a reduction in prolactin may increase fertility.

Clozapine is licensed for the treatment of schizophrenia only in patients unresponsive to, or intolerant of, conventional antipsychotic drugs. It can cause agranulocytosis and its use is restricted to patients registered with a clozapine patient monitoring service (see under preparations, below).

**Sertindole** has been reintroduced following an earlier suspension of the drug because of concerns about arrhythmias; its use is restricted to patients who are enrolled in clinical studies and who are intolerant of at least one other antipsychotic.

### NICE guidance (atypical antipsychotics for schizophrenia)

NICE has recommended (June 2002) that:

- the atypical antipsychotics (amisulpride, olanzapine, quetiapine, risperidone, and zotepine) should be considered when choosing first-line treatment of *newly diagnosed schizophrenia*;
- an atypical antipsychotic is considered the treatment option of choice for managing an *acute schizophrenic episode* when discussion with the individual is not possible;
- an atypical antipsychotic should be considered for an individual who is suffering unacceptable side-effects from a conventional antipsychotic;
- an atypical antipsychotic should be considered for an individual in relapse whose symptoms were previously inadequately controlled;
- changing to an atypical antipsychotic is not necessary if a conventional antipsychotic controls symptoms adequately and the individual does not suffer unacceptable side-effects;
- clozapine should be introduced if schizophrenia is inadequately controlled despite the sequential use of two or more antipsychotics (one of which should be an atypical antipsychotic) each for at least 6–8 weeks.

**Cautions and contra-indications** While atypical antipsychotics have not generally been associated with clinically significant prolongation of the QT interval, they should be used with care if prescribed with other drugs that increase the QT interval. Atypical antipsychotics should be used with caution in patients with cardiovascular disease, or a history of epilepsy; they should be used with caution in the elderly; **interactions**: Appendix 1 (antipsychotics).

### Atypical antipsychotics and stroke

Olanzapine and risperidone are associated with an increased risk of stroke in elderly patients with dementia. The CSM has advised:

- risperidone or olanzapine should **not** be used for treating behavioural symptoms of dementia;
- for acute psychotic conditions in elderly patients with dementia, risperidone should be limited to short-term use under specialist advice; olanzapine is not licensed for acute psychoses;
- the possibility of cerebrovascular events should be considered carefully before treating any patient with a history of stroke or transient ischaemic attack; risk factors for cerebrovascular disease (e.g. hypertension, diabetes, smoking, and atrial fibrillation) should also be considered.

**Driving** Atypical antipsychotics may affect performance of skilled tasks (e.g. driving); effects of alcohol are enhanced.

**Withdrawal** Withdrawal of antipsychotic drugs after long-term therapy should always be gradual and closely monitored to avoid the risk of acute withdrawal syndromes or rapid relapse.

**Side-effects** Side-effects of the atypical antipsychotics include weight gain, dizziness, postural hypotension (especially during initial dose titration) which may be associated with syncope or reflex tachycardia in some patients, extrapyramidal symptoms (usually mild and transient and which respond to dose reduction or to an antimuscarinic drug), and occasionally tardive dyskinesia on long-term administration (discontinue drug on appearance of early signs). Hyperglycaemia and sometimes diabetes can occur, particularly with clozapine and olanzapine; monitoring weight and plasma glucose may identify the development of hyperglycaemia. Neuroleptic malignant syndrome has been reported rarely.

## AMISULPRIDE

**Indications** schizophrenia

**Cautions** see notes above; also Parkinson's disease; renal impairment (Appendix 3)

**Contra-indications** see notes above; also phaeochromocytoma, prolactin-dependent tumours; pregnancy (Appendix 4); breast-feeding (Appendix 5)

**Side-effects** see notes above; also insomnia, anxiety, agitation, drowsiness, gastro-intestinal disorders such as constipation, nausea, vomiting, and dry mouth; hyperprolactinaemia; occasionally bradycardia; *rarely* seizures

**Dose**

- Acute psychotic episode, 400–800 mg daily in 2 divided doses, adjusted according to response; max. 1.2 g daily; CHILD under 15 years not recommended
- Predominantly negative symptoms, 50–300 mg daily; CHILD under 15 years not recommended

**Amisulpride** (Non-proprietary) PoM
Tablets, amisulpride 50 mg, net price 60-tab pack = £17.79; 100 mg, 60-tab pack = £35.59; 200 mg, 60-tab pack = £59.49; 400 mg, 60-tab pack = £118.98. Label: 2

**Solian®** (Sanofi-Synthelabo) PoM
Tablets, scored, amisulpride 50 mg, net price 60-tab pack = £18.36; 100 mg, 60-tab pack = £36.72; 200 mg, 60-tab pack = £61.38; 400 mg, 60-tab pack = £122.76. Label: 2

Solution, 100 mg/mL, net price 60 mL (caramel flavour) = £30.69. Label: 2

## ARIPIPRAZOLE

**Indications** schizophrenia

**Cautions** see notes above; elderly (reduce initial dose); hepatic impairment (Appendix 2); pregnancy (Appendix 4)

**Contra-indications** see notes above; breast-feeding (Appendix 5)

**Side-effects** see notes above; nausea, vomiting, dyspepsia, constipation, insomnia, akathisia, somnolence, tremor, headache, asthenia, blurred vision; *less commonly* tachycardia, seizures; *very rarely* increased salivation, pancreatitis, chest pain, agitation, speech disorder, stiffness, rhabdomyolysis

**Dose**

- 15 mg daily; max. 30 mg daily; CHILD and ADOLESCENT not recommended

**Abilify®** (Bristol-Myers Squibb) ▼ PoM
Tablets, aripiprazole 5 mg (blue), net price 28-tab pack = £101.63; 10 mg (pink), 28-tab pack = £101.63; 15 mg (yellow), 28-tab pack = £101.63; 30 mg (pink), 28-tab pack = £203.26. Counselling, driving

## CLOZAPINE

**Indications** schizophrenia (including psychosis in Parkinson's disease) in patients unresponsive to, or intolerant of, conventional antipsychotic drugs

**Cautions** see notes above; elderly; monitor leucocyte and differential blood counts (see Agranulocytosis, below); prostatic hypertrophy, angle-closure glaucoma; taper off other antipsychotics before starting; close medical supervision during initiation (risk of collapse because of hypotension); hepatic impairment (Appendix 2); pregnancy (Appendix 4)

**Withdrawal** On planned withdrawal reduce dose over 1–2 weeks to avoid risk of rebound psychosis. If abrupt withdrawal necessary observe patient carefully

**Agranulocytosis** Neutropenia and potentially fatal agranulocytosis reported. Leucocyte and differential blood counts must be normal before starting; monitor counts every week for 18 weeks then at least every 2 weeks and if clozapine continued and blood count stable after 1 year at least every 4 weeks (and 4 weeks after discontinuation); if leucocyte count below 3000/mm$^3$ or if absolute neutrophil count below 1500/mm$^3$ discontinue permanently and refer to haematologist. Avoid drugs which depress leucopoiesis; patients should report immediately symptoms of infection, especially influenza-like illness

**Myocarditis and cardiomyopathy** Fatal myocarditis (most commonly in first 2 months) and cardiomyopathy reported. The CSM has advised:

- physical examination and medical history before starting clozapine;
- specialist examination if cardiac abnormalities or history of heart disease found—clozapine initiated only in absence of severe heart disease and if benefit outweighs risk;
- persistent tachycardia especially in first 2 months should prompt observation for other indicators for myocarditis or cardiomyopathy;
- if myocarditis or cardiomyopathy suspected clozapine should be stopped and patient evaluated urgently by cardiologist;
- discontinue permanently in clozapine-induced myocarditis or cardiomyopathy

**Gastro-intestinal obstruction** Reactions resembling gastro-intestinal obstruction reported. Clozapine should be used cautiously with drugs which cause constipation (e.g. antimuscarinic drugs) or in history of colonic disease or bowel surgery. Monitor for constipation and prescribe laxative if required

**Contra-indications** severe cardiac disorders (e.g. myocarditis; see Myocarditis and Cardiomyopathy, above); severe renal impairment; history of neutropenia or agranulocytosis (see Agranulocytosis, above); bone-marrow disorders; paralytic ileus (see Gastro-intestinal Obstruction, above); alcoholic and toxic psychoses; history of circulatory collapse; drug intoxication; coma or severe CNS depression; uncontrolled epilepsy; breast-feeding (Appendix 5)

**Side-effects** see notes above; also constipation (see Gastro-intestinal Obstruction, above), hypersalivation, dry mouth, nausea, vomiting, anorexia; tachycardia, ECG changes, hypertension; drowsiness, headache, tremor, seizures, fatigue, impaired temperature regulation; urinary incontinence and retention; leucopenia, eosinophilia, leucocytosis; blurred vision; sweating; *less commonly* agranulocytosis (**important:** see Agranulocytosis, above); *rarely* dysphagia, hepatitis, cholestatic jaundice, pancreatitis, circulatory collapse, arrhythmia, myocarditis (**important:** see Myocarditis, above), pericarditis, thromboembolism, agitation, confusion, delirium, anaemia; *very rarely* parotid gland enlargement, intestinal obstruction (see Gastro-intestinal Obstruction, above), cardiomyopathy, myocardial infarction, respiratory depression, priapism, interstitial nephritis, thrombocytopenia, thrombocythaemia, hyperlipidaemia, fulminant hepatic necrosis, and skin reactions

**Dose**

- Schizophrenia, ADULT over 16 years, 12.5 mg once or twice (ELDERLY 12.5 mg once) on first day then 25–50 mg (ELDERLY 25–37.5 mg) on second day then increased gradually (if well tolerated) in steps of 25–50 mg daily (ELDERLY max. increment 25 mg daily) over 14–21 days up to 300 mg daily in divided doses (larger dose at night, up to 200 mg daily may be taken as a single dose at bedtime); if necessary may be further increased in steps of 50–100 mg once (preferably) or twice weekly; usual dose 200–450 mg daily (max. 900 mg daily)

  Note *Restarting* after *interval of more than 2 days*, 12.5 mg once or twice on first day (but may be feasible to increase more quickly than on initiation)—extreme caution if previous respiratory or cardiac arrest with initial dosing

- Psychosis in Parkinson's disease, ADULT over 16 years, 12.5 mg at bedtime then increased according to response in steps of 12.5 mg up to twice weekly; usual dose range 25–37.5 mg at bedtime, usual max. 50 mg daily; exceptionally, dose may be increased further in steps of 12.5 mg weekly to max. 100 mg daily in 1–2 divided doses

**Clozaril®** (Novartis) PoM

Tablets, both yellow, clozapine 25 mg (scored), net price 28-tab pack = £6.17, 84-tab pack (hosp. only) = £18.49; 100 mg, 28-tab pack = £24.64, 84-tab pack (hosp. only) = £73.92. Label: 2, 10, patient information leaflet

Note Patient, prescriber, and supplying pharmacist must be registered with the Clozaril Patient Monitoring Service—takes several days to do this

**Denzapine®** (Denfleet) PoM

Tablets, both yellow, scored, clozapine 25 mg, net price 28-tab pack = £6.17, 84-tab pack = £18.49; 100 mg, 28-tab pack = £24.64, 84-tab pack = £73.92. Label: 2, 10, patient information leaflet

Note. Patient, prescriber, and supplying pharmacist must be registered with the Denzapine Patient Monitoring Service—takes several days to do this

**Zaponex®** (IVAX) PoM

Tablets, both yellow, scored, clozapine 25 mg, net price 84-tab pack = £22.17; 100 mg, 84-tab pack = £88.68. Label: 2, 10, patient information leaflet

Note. Patient, prescriber, and supplying pharmacist must be registered with the Zaponex Treatment Access System—takes several days to do this

## OLANZAPINE

**Indications** see under Dose

**Cautions** see notes above (including advice on atypical antipsychotics and stroke); also prostatic hypertrophy, paralytic ileus, diabetes mellitus (risk of exacerbation or ketoacidosis), low leucocyte or neutrophil count, bone-marrow depression, hypereosinophilic disorders, myeloproliferative disease, Parkinson's disease; hepatic impairment (Appendix 2); renal impairment (Appendix 3); pregnancy (Appendix 4); **interactions:** Appendix 1 (antipsychotics)

CNS and respiratory depression Blood pressure, pulse and respiratory rate should be monitored for at least 4 hours after intramuscular injection, particularly in those also receiving another antipsychotic or benzodiazepine

**Contra-indications** angle-closure glaucoma; breast-feeding (Appendix 5); *for injection*, acute myocardial infarction, unstable angina, severe hypotension or bradycardia, sick sinus syndrome, recent heart surgery

**Side-effects** see notes above; also mild, transient antimuscarinic effects; drowsiness, speech difficulty, exacerbation of Parkinson's disease, abnormal gait, hallucinations, akathisia, asthenia, increased appetite, increased body temperature, raised triglyceride concentration, oedema, hyperprolactinaemia (but clinical manifestations rare); urinary incontinence; eosinophilia; *less commonly* hypotension, bradycardia, photosensitivity; *rarely* seizures, leucopenia, rash; *very rarely* thromboembolism, hypercholesterolaemia, QT interval prolongation, hypothermia, urinary retention, priapism, thrombocytopenia, neutropenia, rhabdomyolysis, hepatitis, pancreatitis; *with injection*, injection-site reactions, sinus pause, hypoventilation

**Dose**

- Schizophrenia, combination therapy for mania, preventing recurrence in bipolar disorder, by mouth, ADULT over 18 years, 10 mg daily adjusted to usual range of 5–20 mg daily; doses greater than 10 mg daily only after reassessment; max. 20 mg daily
- Monotherapy for mania, by mouth, ADULT over 18 years, 15 mg daily adjusted to usual range of 5–20 mg daily; doses greater than 15 mg only after reassessment; max. 20 mg daily
- Control of agitation and disturbed behaviour in schizophrenia or mania, by intramuscular injection, ADULT over 18 years, initially 5–10 mg (usual dose 10 mg) as a single dose followed by 5–10 mg after 2 hours if necessary; ELDERLY initially 2.5–5 mg as a single dose followed by 2.5–5 mg after 2 hours if necessary; max. 3 injections daily for 3 days; max. daily combined oral and parenteral dose 20 mg

Note When one or more factors present that might result in slower metabolism (e.g. female gender, elderly, non-smoker) consider lower initial dose and more gradual dose increase

**Zyprexa®** (Lilly) PoM

Tablets, f/c, olanzapine 2.5 mg, net price 28-tab pack = £33.29; 5 mg, 28-tab pack = £48.78; 7.5 mg, 56-tab pack = £146.34; 10 mg, 28-tab pack = £79.45, 56-tab pack = £158.90; 15 mg (blue), 28-tab pack = £146.34. Label: 2

Orodispersible tablet (*Velotab®*), yellow, olanzapine 5 mg, net price 28-tab pack = £56.10; 10 mg, 28-tab pack = £112.19; 15 mg, 28-tab pack = £168.29; 20 mg, 28-tab pack = £182.74. Label: 2, counselling, administration

Excipients include aspartame (section 9.4.1)

Counselling *Velotab®* may be placed on the tongue and allowed to dissolve or dispersed in water, orange juice, apple juice, milk, or coffee

Injection▼, powder for reconstitution, olanzapine 5 mg/mL, net price 10-mg vial = £3.48

## QUETIAPINE

**Indications** schizophrenia; treatment of episodes of mania either alone or with mood stabilisers

**Cautions** see notes above; also pregnancy (Appendix 4), hepatic impairment (Appendix 2), renal impairment (Appendix 3), cerebrovascular disease

**Contra-indications** breast-feeding (Appendix 5)

**Side-effects** see notes above; also drowsiness, dyspepsia, constipation, dry mouth, mild asthenia, rhinitis, tachycardia; leucopenia, neutropenia and occasionally eosinophilia reported; elevated plasma-triglyceride and cholesterol concentrations, reduced plasma-thyroid hormone concentrations; possible QT interval prolongation; rarely oedema; very rarely priapism

**Dose**

- Schizophrenia 25 mg twice daily on day 1, 50 mg twice daily on day 2, 100 mg twice daily on day 3, 150 mg twice daily on day 4, then adjusted according to response, usual range 300–450 mg daily in 2 divided doses; max. 750 mg daily; ELDERLY initially 25 mg daily as a single dose, increased in steps of 25–50 mg daily in 2 divided doses; CHILD and ADOLESCENT not recommended
- Mania, 50 mg twice daily on day 1, 100 mg twice daily on day 2, 150 mg twice daily on day 3, 200 mg twice daily on day 4, then adjusted according to response in steps of up to 200 mg daily to max. 800 mg daily; usual range 400–800 mg daily in 2 divided doses; ELDERLY initially 25 mg daily as a single dose, increased in steps of 25–50 mg daily in 2 divided doses; CHILD and ADOLESCENT not recommended

**Seroquel®** (AstraZeneca) PoM

Tablets, f/c, quetiapine (as fumarate) 25 mg (peach), net price 60-tab pack = £28.20; 100 mg (yellow), 60-tab pack = £113.10; 150 mg (pale yellow), 60-tab pack = £113.10; 200 mg (white), 60-tab pack = £113.10; 300 mg (white), 60-tab pack = £170.00. Label: 2

## RISPERIDONE

**Indications** acute and chronic psychoses, mania

**Cautions** see notes above (including advice on atypical antipsychotics and stroke); Parkinson's disease; pregnancy (Appendix 4); hepatic impairment (Appendix 2), renal impairment (Appendix 3)

**Contra-indications** breast-feeding (Appendix 5)

**Side-effects** see notes above; also insomnia, agitation, anxiety, headache; *less commonly* drowsiness, impaired concentration, fatigue, blurred vision, constipation, nausea and vomiting, dyspepsia, abdominal pain, hyperprolactinaemia (with galactorrhoea, menstrual disturbances, gynaecomastia), sexual dysfunction, priapism, urinary incontinence, tachycardia, hypertension, oedema, rash, rhinitis; cerebrovascular accident, neutropenia and thrombocytopenia have been reported; *rarely* seizures, hyponatraemia, abnormal temperature regulation, and epistaxis

**Dose**

- Psychoses, 2 mg in 1–2 divided doses on first day *then* 4 mg in 1–2 divided doses on second day (slower titration appropriate in some patients); usual dose range 4–6 mg daily; doses above 10 mg daily only if benefit considered to outweigh risk (max. 16 mg daily); ELDERLY (or in hepatic or renal impairment) initially 500 micrograms twice daily increased in steps of 500 micrograms twice daily to 1–2 mg twice daily; CHILD under 15 years not recommended
- Mania, initially 2 mg once daily, increased if necessary in steps of 1 mg daily; usual dose range 1–6 mg daily; ELDERLY (or in hepatic or renal impairment) initially 500 micrograms twice daily increased in steps of 500 micrograms twice daily to 1–2 mg twice daily

**Risperdal®** (Janssen-Cilag) PoM

Tablets, f/c, scored, risperidone 500 micrograms (brown-red), net price 20-tab pack = £7.06; 1 mg (white), 20-tab pack = £11.61, 60-tab pack = £34.84; 2 mg (orange), 60-tab pack = £68.69; 3 mg (yellow), 60-tab pack = £101.01; 4 mg (green), 60-tab pack = £133.34; 6 mg (yellow), 28-tab pack = £94.28. Label: 2

Orodispersible tablets (*Quicklet®*), all pink, risperidone 500 micrograms, net price 28-tab pack = £11.43; 1 mg, 28-tab pack = £18.39; 2 mg, 28-tab pack = £34.66. Label: 2, counselling, administration

Excipients include aspartame (section 9.4.1)

**Counselling** Tablets should be placed on the tongue, allowed to dissolve and swallowed

Liquid, risperidone 1 mg/mL, net price 100 mL = £56.12. Label: 2

**Note** Liquid may be diluted with mineral water, orange juice or black coffee (should be taken immediately)

Depot injection: section 4.2.2

## SERTINDOLE

**Indications** schizophrenia, see also notes above

**Cautions** see notes above; hepatic impairment (Appendix 2); correct hypokalaemia or hypomagnesaemia before treatment; monitor ECG during treatment; monitor blood pressure during dose titration and early maintenance therapy (risk of postural hypotension)

**Contra-indications** see notes above; pregnancy (Appendix 4), breast-feeding (Appendix 5), severe hepatic impairment, QT interval prolongation (ECG required before and during treatment—consult product literature); concomitant administration of drugs which prolong QT interval (see interactions); uncorrected hypokalaemia or hypomagnesaemia

**Side-effects** see notes above; prolonged QT interval, peripheral oedema, dry mouth, rhinitis, nasal congestion, dyspnoea, paraesthesia, abnormal ejaculation (decreased volume); rarely seizures, hyperglycaemia

**Dose**

- Initially 4 mg daily increased in steps of 4 mg at intervals of 4–5 days to usual maintenance of 12–20 mg as a single daily dose; max. 24 mg daily; ELDERLY consider slower dose titration and lower maintenance dose; CHILD and ADOLESCENT not recommended

**Serdolect®** (Lundbeck) ▼ PoM

Tablets, f/c, sertindole 4 mg, 30-tab pack; 12 mg 28-tab pack; 16 mg, 28-tab pack; 20 mg 28-tab pack

Available only on named-patient basis (see notes above)

## ZOTEPINE

**Indications** schizophrenia

**Cautions** see notes above; personal or close family history of epilepsy; withdrawal of concomitantly prescribed CNS depressants; QT interval prolongation—ECG required (before treatment and at each dose increase) in patients at risk of arrhythmias; monitor plasma electrolytes particularly before treatment and at each dose increase; hepatic impairment (Appendix 2); renal impairment (Appendix 3); prostatic hypertrophy, urinary retention, angle-closure glaucoma, paralytic ileus, pregnancy (Appendix 4)

**Contra-indications** acute intoxication with CNS depressants; high doses of concomitantly prescribed antipsychotics; acute gout (avoid for 3 weeks after episode resolves), history of nephrolithiasis; breast-feeding (Appendix 5)

**Side-effects** see notes above; constipation, dyspepsia, dry mouth, tachycardia, QT interval prolongation, rhinitis, agitation, anxiety, depression, asthenia, headache, EEG abnormalities, insomnia, drowsiness, hyperthermia or hypothermia, increased salivation, blood dyscrasias (including leucocytosis, leucopenia), raised erythrocyte sedimentation rate, blurred vision, sweating; less frequently anorexia, diarrhoea, nausea and vomiting, abdominal pain, hypertension, influenza-like syndrome, cough, dyspnoea, confusion, convulsions, decreased libido, speech disorder, vertigo, hyperprolactinaemia, anaemia, thrombocythaemia, increased serum creatinine, hypoglycaemia and hyperglycaemia, hyperlipidaemia, hypouricaemia, oedema, thirst, impotence, urinary incontinence, arthralgia, myalgia, conjunctivitis, acne, dry skin, rash; rarely bradycardia, epistaxis, abdominal enlargement, amnesia, ataxia, coma, delirium, hypaesthesia, myoclonus, thrombocytopenia, abnormal ejaculation, urinary retention, menstrual irregularities, myasthenia, alopecia, photosensitivity

**Dose**

- Initially 25 mg 3 times daily increased according to response at intervals of 4 days to max. 100 mg 3 times daily; ELDERLY initially 25 mg twice daily increased according to response to max. 75 mg twice daily; CHILD and ADOLESCENT under 18 years not recommended

**Zoleptil®** (Orion) PoM
Tablets, s/c, zotepine 25 mg (white), net price 30-tab pack = £14.33, 90-tab pack = £42.98; 50 mg (yellow), 30-tab pack = £19.10, 90-tab pack = £57.30; 100 mg (pink), 30-tab pack = £31.52, 90-tab pack = £94.55. Label: 2

## 4.2.2 Antipsychotic depot injections

Long-acting depot injections are used for maintenance therapy especially when compliance with oral treatment is unreliable. However, depot injections of conventional antipsychotics may give rise to a higher incidence of extrapyramidal reactions than oral preparations; extrapyramidal reactions occur less frequently with atypical antipsychotics such as risperidone.

**Administration** Depot antipsychotics are administered by deep intramuscular injection at intervals of 1 to 4 weeks. When initiating therapy with sustained-release preparations of conventional antipsychotics, patients should first be given a small test-dose as undesirable side-effects are prolonged. In general not more than 2–3 mL of oily injection should be administered at any one site; correct injection technique (including the use of z-track technique) and rotation of injection sites are essential. If the dose needs to be reduced to alleviate side-effects, it is important to recognise that the plasma-drug concentration may not fall for some time after reducing the dose, therefore it may be a month or longer before side-effects subside.

**Dosage** Individual responses to neuroleptic drugs are very variable and to achieve optimum effect, dosage and dosage interval must be titrated according to the patient's response. For the advice of The Royal College of Psychiatrists on doses above the BNF upper limit, see p. 181

**Equivalent doses of depot antipsychotics**

These equivalences are intended **only** as an approximate guide; individual dosage instructions should **also** be checked; patients should be carefully monitored after **any** change in medication

| Antipsychotic | Dose (mg) | Interval |
|---|---|---|
| Flupentixol decanoate | 40 | 2 weeks |
| Fluphenazine decanoate | 25 | 2 weeks |
| Haloperidol (as decanoate) | 100 | 4 weeks |
| Pipotiazine palmitate | 50 | 4 weeks |
| Zuclopenthixol decanoate | 200 | 2 weeks |

**Important**. These equivalences must **not** be extrapolated beyond the max. dose for the drug

**Choice** There is no clear-cut division in the use of the conventional antipsychotics, but **zuclopenthixol** may be suitable for the treatment of agitated or aggressive patients whereas **flupentixol** can cause over-excitement in such patients. The incidence of extrapyramidal reactions is similar for the conventional antipsychotics.

**Cautions** See section 4.2.1. Treatment requires careful monitoring for optimum effect. When transferring from oral to depot therapy, dosage by mouth should be reduced gradually.

**Contra-indications** See section 4.2.1. Do not use in children.

**Side-effects** See section 4.2.1. Pain may occur at injection site and occasionally erythema, swelling, and nodules. For side-effects of specific antipsychotics see under the relevant drug.

### FLUPENTIXOL DECANOATE
**(Flupenthixol Decanoate)**

**Indications** maintenance in schizophrenia and other psychoses

**Cautions** see notes on p. 181 and also under Flupentixol (section 4.2.1) and notes above; an alternative antipsychotic may be necessary if symptoms such as aggression or agitation appear

**Contra-indications** see notes on p. 181 and also under Flupentixol (section 4.2.1) and notes above

**Side-effects** see notes on p. 181 and also under Flupentixol (section 4.2.1) and notes above, but may have a mood elevating effect

**Dose**

- By deep intramuscular injection into the gluteal muscle, test dose 20 mg, then after at least 7 days 20–40 mg repeated at intervals of 2–4 weeks, adjusted

4 Central nervous system

according to response; max. 400 mg weekly; usual maintenance dose 50 mg every 4 weeks to 300 mg every 2 weeks; ELDERLY initially quarter to half adult dose; CHILD not recommended

**Depixol®** (Lundbeck) PoM
Injection (oily), flupentixol decanoate 20 mg/mL. Net price 1-mL amp = £1.52; 2-mL amp = £2.54

**Depixol Conc.®** (Lundbeck) PoM
Injection (oily), flupentixol decanoate 100 mg/mL. Net price 0.5-mL amp = £3.42; 1-mL amp = £6.25

**Depixol Low Volume®** (Lundbeck) PoM
Injection (oily), flupentixol decanoate 200 mg/mL. Net price 1-mL amp = £19.52

## FLUPHENAZINE DECANOATE

**Indications** maintenance in schizophrenia and other psychoses
**Cautions** see notes on p. 181 and also notes above
**Contra-indications** see notes on p. 181 and also notes above
**Side-effects** see notes on p. 181 and also under Fluphenazine Hydrochloride (section 4.2.1) and notes above; also extrapyramidal symptoms usually appear a few hours after injection and continue for about 2 days but may be delayed
**Dose**
- By deep intramuscular injection into the gluteal muscle, test dose 12.5 mg (6.25 mg in elderly), then after 4–7 days 12.5–100 mg repeated at intervals of 14–35 days, adjusted according to response; CHILD not recommended

**Fluphenazine decanoate** (Non-proprietary) PoM
Injection (oily), fluphenazine decanoate 25 mg/mL, net price 1-mL amp = £2.35; 100 mg/mL, 0.5-mL amp = £4.50, 1-mL amp = £8.79
Excipients include sesame oil

**Modecate®** (Sanofi-Synthelabo) PoM
Injection (oily), fluphenazine decanoate 25 mg/mL. Net price 0.5-mL amp = £1.35, 1-mL amp = £2.35, 2-mL amp = £4.62
Excipients include sesame oil

**Modecate Concentrate®** (Sanofi-Synthelabo) PoM
Injection (oily), fluphenazine decanoate 100 mg/mL. Net price 0.5-mL amp = £4.66, 1-mL amp = £9.10
Excipients include sesame oil

## HALOPERIDOL

**Indications** maintenance in schizophrenia and other psychoses
**Cautions** see notes on p. 181 and also under Haloperidol (section 4.2.1) and notes above
**Contra-indications** see notes on p. 181 and also under Haloperidol (section 4.2.1) and notes above
**Side-effects** see notes on p. 181 and also under Haloperidol (section 4.2.1) and notes above
**Dose**
- By deep intramuscular injection into the gluteal muscle, initially 50 mg every 4 weeks, if necessary increasing by 50-mg increments to 300 mg every 4 weeks; higher doses may be needed in some patients; ELDERLY, initially 12.5–25 mg every 4 weeks; CHILD not recommended

Note If 2-weekly administration preferred, doses should be halved

**Haldol Decanoate®** (Janssen-Cilag) PoM
Injection (oily), haloperidol (as decanoate) 50 mg/mL, net price 1-mL amp = £4.13; 100 mg/mL, 1-mL amp = £5.48
Excipients include sesame oil

## PIPOTIAZINE PALMITATE
(Pipothiazine Palmitate)

**Indications** maintenance in schizophrenia and other psychoses
**Cautions** see notes on p. 181 and notes above
**Contra-indications** see notes on p. 181 and notes above
**Side-effects** see notes on p. 181 and notes above
**Dose**
- By deep intramuscular injection into the gluteal muscle, test dose 25 mg, then a further 25–50 mg after 4–7 days, then adjusted according to response at intervals of 4 weeks; usual maintenance range 50–100 mg (max. 200 mg) every 4 weeks; ELDERLY initially 5–10 mg; CHILD not recommended

**Piportil Depot®** (JHC) PoM
Injection (oily), pipotiazine palmitate 50 mg/mL. Net price 1-mL amp = £10.52; 2-mL amp = £17.21
Excipients include sesame oil

## RISPERIDONE

**Indications** schizophrenia and other psychoses in patients tolerant to risperidone by mouth
**Cautions** see under Risperidone (section 4.2.1) and notes above
**Contra-indications** see under Risperidone (section 4.2.1)
**Side-effects** see under Risperidone (section 4.2.1); also depression, tremor; *less commonly* apathy, weight loss, abnormal vision, pruritus; injection-site reactions also reported
**Dose**
- By deep intramuscular injection into the gluteal muscle, patients taking oral risperidone up to 4 mg daily, initially 25 mg every 2 weeks; patients taking oral risperidone over 4 mg daily, initially 37.5 mg every 2 weeks; dose adjusted at intervals of at least 4 weeks in steps of 12.5 mg to max. 50 mg (ELDERLY 25 mg) every 2 weeks; CHILD and ADOLESCENT under 18 years not recommended

Note During initiation risperidone by mouth may need to be continued for 4–6 weeks; risperidone by mouth may also be used during dose adjustment of depot injection

**Risperdal Consta®** (Janssen-Cilag) ▼ PoM
Injection, powder for reconstitution, risperidone 25-mg vial, net price = £82.92; 37.5-mg vial = £115.84; 50-mg vial = £148.55 (all with diluent)

## ZUCLOPENTHIXOL DECANOATE

**Indications** maintenance in schizophrenia and other psychoses, particularly with aggression and agitation
**Cautions** see notes on p. 181 and notes above; avoid in porphyria (section 9.8.2)
**Contra-indications** see notes on p. 181 and notes above
**Side-effects** see notes on p. 181 and notes above

**Dose**

- By deep intramuscular injection into the gluteal muscle, test dose 100 mg, followed after at least 7 days by 200–500 mg or more, repeated at intervals of 1–4 weeks, adjusted according to response; max. 600 mg weekly; ELDERLY quarter to half usual starting dose; CHILD not recommended

**Clopixol®** (Lundbeck) PoM
Injection (oily), zuclopenthixol decanoate 200 mg/mL. Net price 1-mL amp = £3.15

**Clopixol Conc.®** (Lundbeck) PoM
Injection (oily), zuclopenthixol decanoate 500 mg/mL. Net price 1-mL amp = £7.44

# 4.2.3 Antimanic drugs

Drugs are used in mania both to control acute attacks and also to prevent their recurrence.

## Benzodiazepines

Use of benzodiazepines (section 4.1) may be helpful in the initial stages of treatment until lithium achieves its full effect; they should not be used for long periods because of the risk of dependence.

## Antipsychotic drugs

In an acute attack of mania, treatment with an antipsychotic drug (section 4.2.1) is usually required because it may take a few days for lithium to exert its antimanic effect. Lithium may be given concurrently with the antipsychotic drug, and treatment with the antipsychotic gradually tailed off as lithium becomes effective. Alternatively, lithium therapy may be commenced once the patient's mood has been stabilised with the antipsychotic. The adjunctive use of atypical antipsychotics such as olanzapine (section 4.2.1) and risperidone [unlicensed indication] with either lithium or valproic acid may also be of benefit.

High doses of haloperidol, fluphenazine, or flupentixol may be hazardous when used with lithium; irreversible toxic encephalopathy has been reported.

## Carbamazepine

Carbamazepine (section 4.8.1) may be used for the prophylaxis of bipolar disorder (manic-depressive disorder) in patients unresponsive to lithium; it seems to be particularly effective in patients with rapid cycling manic-depressive illness (4 or more affective episodes per year).

## Valproic acid

Valproic acid (as the semisodium salt) is licensed for the treatment of manic episodes associated with bipolar disorder. It may be useful in patients unresponsive to lithium. Sodium valproate (section 4.8.1) has also been used, but it is unlicensed for this indication.

### VALPROIC ACID

**Indications** treatment of manic episodes associated with bipolar disorder

**Cautions** see Sodium Valproate (section 4.8.1); monitor closely if dose greater than 45 mg/kg daily

**Contra-indications** see Sodium Valproate (section 4.8.1)

**Side-effects** see Sodium Valproate (section 4.8.1)

**Dose**

- Initially 750 mg daily in 2–3 divided doses, increased according to response, usual dose 1–2 g daily; CHILD and ADOLESCENT under 18 years not recommended

**Depakote®** (Sanofi-Synthelabo) PoM
Tablets, e/c, valproic acid (as semisodium valproate) 250 mg, net price 90-tab pack = £12.17; 500 mg, 90-tab pack = £24.29. Label: 25

Note Semisodium valproate comprises equimolar amounts of sodium valproate and valproic acid.

## Lithium

Lithium salts are used in the prophylaxis and treatment of mania, in the prophylaxis of bipolar disorder (manic-depressive disorder) and in the prophylaxis of recurrent depression (unipolar illness or unipolar depression). Lithium is unsuitable for children.

The decision to give prophylactic lithium usually requires *specialist advice*, and must be based on careful consideration of the likelihood of recurrence in the individual patient, and the benefit weighed against the risks. In long-term use lithium has been associated with thyroid disorders and mild cognitive and memory impairment. Long-term treatment should therefore be undertaken only with careful assessment of risk and benefit, and with regular monitoring of thyroid function. The need for continued therapy should be assessed regularly and patients should be maintained on lithium after 3–5 years only if benefit persists.

**Serum concentrations** Lithium salts have a narrow therapeutic/toxic ratio and should therefore not be prescribed unless facilities for monitoring serum-lithium concentrations are available. There seem few if any reasons for preferring one or other of the salts of lithium available. Doses are adjusted to achieve serum-lithium concentration of 0.4–1 mmol/litre (lower end of the range for maintenance therapy and elderly patients) on samples taken 12 hours after the preceding dose. It is important to determine the optimum range for each individual patient.

Overdosage, usually with serum-lithium concentration of over 1.5 mmol/litre, may be fatal and toxic effects include tremor, ataxia, dysarthria, nystagmus, renal impairment, and convulsions. If these potentially hazardous signs occur, treatment should be stopped, serum-lithium concentrations redetermined, and steps taken to reverse lithium toxicity. In mild cases withdrawal of lithium and administration of generous amounts of sodium salts and fluid will reverse the toxicity. Serum-lithium concentration in excess of 2 mmol/litre require urgent treatment as indicated under Emergency Treatment of Poisoning, p. 32.

**Interactions** Lithium toxicity is made worse by sodium depletion, therefore concurrent use of diuretics (particularly thiazides) is hazardous and should be avoided. For other **interactions** with lithium, see Appendix 1 (lithium).

**Withdrawal** While there is no clear evidence of withdrawal or rebound psychosis, abrupt discontinuation of lithium increases the risk of relapse. If lithium is to be discontinued, the dose should be reduced gradually over a period of a few weeks and patients should be warned of possible relapse if discontinued abruptly.

> Lithium cards
> A lithium treatment card available from pharmacies tells patients how to take lithium preparations, what to do if a dose is missed, and what side-effects to expect. It also explains why regular blood tests are important and warns that some medicines and illnesses can change serum-lithium concentration
> Cards may be purchased from the National Pharmacy Association.
> Tel: (01727) 858 687
> sales@npa.co.uk

## LITHIUM CARBONATE

**Indications** treatment and prophylaxis of mania, bipolar disorder, and recurrent depression (see also notes above); aggressive or self-mutilating behaviour

**Cautions** measure serum-lithium concentration regularly (every 3 months on stabilised regimens), measure renal function and thyroid function every 6–12 months on stabilised regimens and advise patient to seek attention if symptoms of hypothyroidism develop (women at greater risk) e.g. lethargy, feeling cold; maintain adequate sodium and fluid intake; test renal function before initiating and if evidence of toxicity, avoid in renal impairment (Appendix 3), cardiac disease, and conditions with sodium imbalance such as Addison's disease; reduce dose or discontinue in diarrhoea, vomiting and intercurrent infection (especially if sweating profusely); psoriasis (risk of exacerbation) pregnancy (Appendix 4), breast-feeding (Appendix 5), elderly (reduce dose), diuretic treatment, myasthenia gravis; surgery (section 15.1); avoid abrupt withdrawal (see notes above); **interactions:** Appendix 1 (lithium)

Counselling Patients should maintain adequate fluid intake and avoid dietary changes which reduce or increase sodium intake

**Side-effects** gastro-intestinal disturbances, fine tremor, renal impairment (particularly impaired urinary concentration and polyuria), polydipsia, leucocytosis; also weight gain and oedema (may respond to dose reduction); hyperparathyroidism and hypercalcaemia reported; signs of intoxication are blurred vision, increasing gastro-intestinal disturbances (anorexia, vomiting, diarrhoea), muscle weakness, increased CNS disturbances (mild drowsiness and sluggishness increasing to giddiness with ataxia, coarse tremor, lack of co-ordination, dysarthria), and require withdrawal of treatment; with severe **overdosage** (serum-lithium concentration above 2 mmol/litre) hyperreflexia and hyperextension of limbs, convulsions, toxic psychoses, syncope, renal failure, circulatory failure, coma, and occasionally, death; goitre, raised anti-diuretic hormone concentration, hypothyroidism, hypokalaemia, ECG changes, and kidney changes may also occur; see also Emergency Treatment of Poisoning, p. 32

**Dose**

- See under preparations below, adjusted to achieve a serum-lithium concentration of 0.4–1 mmol/litre 12 hours after a dose on days 4–7 of treatment, then every week until dosage has remained constant for 4 weeks and every 3 months thereafter; doses are initially divided throughout the day, but once daily administration is preferred when serum-lithium concentration stabilised

Note **Preparations vary widely in bioavailability**; changing the preparation requires the same precautions as initiation of treatment

Note Lithium carbonate 200 mg ≡ lithium citrate 509 mg

**Camcolit®** (Norgine) PoM

Camcolit 250® tablets, f/c, scored, lithium carbonate 250 mg ($Li^+$ 6.8 mmol), net price 20 = 64p. Label: 10, lithium card counselling, see above

Camcolit 400® tablets, m/r, f/c, scored, lithium carbonate 400 mg ($Li^+$ 10.8 mmol), net price 20 = 86p. Label: 10, lithium card 25, counselling, see above

Dose (serum monitoring, see above):
Treatment, initially 1–1.5 g daily; prophylaxis, initially 300–400 mg daily; CHILD not recommended

Note *Camcolit 400®* also available as *Lithonate®* (TEVA UK)

**Liskonum®** (GSK) PoM

Tablets, m/r, f/c, scored, lithium carbonate 450 mg ($Li^+$ 12.2 mmol), net price 60-tab pack = £2.88. Label: 10, lithium card, 25, counselling, see above

Dose (serum monitoring, see above):
Treatment, initially 450–675 mg twice daily (elderly initially 225 mg twice daily); prophylaxis, initially 450 mg twice daily (elderly 225 mg twice daily); CHILD not recommended

**Priadel®** (Sanofi-Synthelabo) PoM

Tablets, m/r, both scored, lithium carbonate 200 mg ($Li^+$ 5.4 mmol), net price 20 = 59p; 400 mg ($Li^+$ 10.8 mmol), 20 = 78p. Label: 10, lithium card, 25, counselling, see above

Dose (serum monitoring, see above):
Treatment and prophylaxis, initially 0.4–1.2 g daily as a single dose or in 2 divided doses (elderly or patients less than 50 kg, 400 mg daily); CHILD not recommended

Liquid, see under Lithium Citrate below

## LITHIUM CITRATE

**Indications** see under Lithium Carbonate and notes above

**Cautions** see under Lithium Carbonate and notes above

Counselling Patients should maintain an adequate fluid intake and should avoid dietary changes which might reduce or increase sodium intake; lithium treatment cards are available from pharmacies (see above)

**Side-effects** see under Lithium Carbonate and notes above

**Dose**

- See under preparations below, adjusted to achieve serum-lithium concentration of 0.4–1 mmol/litre as described under Lithium Carbonate

Note **Preparations vary widely in bioavailability**; changing the preparation requires the same precautions as initiation of treatment

Note Lithium carbonate 200 mg ≡ lithium citrate 509 mg

**Li-Liquid®** (Rosemont) PoM

Oral solution, lithium citrate 509 mg/5 mL ($Li^+$ 5.4 mmol/5 mL), yellow, net price 150-mL pack = £5.79; 1.018 g/5 mL ($Li^+$ 10.8 mmol/5 mL), orange,

150-mL pack = £11.58. Label: 10, lithium card, counselling, see above

Dose (plasma monitoring, see above):
Treatment and prophylaxis, initially 1.018–3.054 g daily in 2 divided doses (elderly or patients less than 50 kg, initially 509 mg twice daily); CHILD not recommended

**Priadel®** (Sanofi-Synthelabo) PoM

Tablets, see under Lithium Carbonate, above

Liquid, sugar-free, lithium citrate 520 mg/5 mL (approx. $Li^+$ 5.4 mmol/5 mL), net price 150-mL pack = £5.84. Label: 10, lithium card, counselling, see above

Dose (plasma monitoring, see above):
Treatment and prophylaxis, initially 1.04–3.12 g daily in 2 divided doses (elderly or patients less than 50 kg, 520 mg twice daily); CHILD not recommended

# 4.3 Antidepressant drugs

**4.3.1 Tricyclic and related antidepressant drugs**
**4.3.2 Monoamine-oxidase inhibitors**
**4.3.3 Selective serotonin re-uptake inhibitors**
**4.3.4 Other antidepressant drugs**

Antidepressant drugs are effective in the treatment of major depression of moderate and severe degree including major depression associated with physical illness and that following childbirth; they are also effective for dysthymia (lower grade chronic depression). Antidepressant drugs are not generally effective in milder forms of acute depression but a trial may be considered in cases refractory to psychological treatments.

**Choice** The major classes of antidepressants include the tricyclics and related antidepressants, the selective serotonin re-uptake inhibitors (SSRIs), and the monoamine oxidase inhibitors (MAOIs). A number of antidepressants cannot be accommodated easily into this classification; these are included in section 4.3.4.

Choice of antidepressant should be based on the individual patient's requirements, including the presence of concomitant disease, existing therapy, suicide risk, and previous response to antidepressant therapy.

Either tricyclic and related antidepressants or SSRIs are generally preferred because MAOIs may be less effective and show dangerous interactions with some foods and drugs.

Tricyclic antidepressants may be suitable for many depressed patients. If the potential side-effects of the older tricyclics are of concern, an SSRI or one of the newer classes of antidepressants may be appropriate. Although SSRIs appear to be better tolerated than older drugs, the difference is too small to justify always choosing an SSRI as first-line treatment.

Compared to older **tricyclics** (e.g. amitriptyline), the **tricyclic-related drugs** (e.g. trazodone) have a lower incidence of antimuscarinic side-effects, such as dry mouth and constipation. The tricyclic-related drugs may also be associated with a lower risk of cardiotoxicity in overdosage, but some have additional side-effects (for further details see section 4.3.1).

The **selective serotonin re-uptake inhibitors** (SSRIs) have fewer antimuscarinic side-effects than the older tricyclics and they are also less cardiotoxic in overdosage. Therefore, although no more effective, they are preferred where there is a significant risk of deliberate overdosing or where concomitant conditions preclude the use of other antidepressants. SSRIs are also preferred to tricyclic antidepressants for depression in patients with diabetes. The SSRIs do, however, have characteristic side-effects of their own; gastro-intestinal side-effects such as nausea and vomiting are common and bleeding disorders have been reported.

For severely ill inpatients and those in whom maximising efficacy is of overriding importance, a tricyclic may be more effective than an SSRI or an MAOI. Venlafaxine, at a dose of 150 mg or greater, may also be more effective than SSRIs for major depression of at least moderate severity. Where the depression is very severe electroconvulsive therapy (ECT) may be indicated.

MAOIs may be more effective than tricyclics in non-hospitalised patients with 'atypical depression'; MAOI treatment should be initiated by those experienced in its use.

Although anxiety is often present in depressive illness (and may be the presenting symptom), the use of an antipsychotic or an anxiolytic may mask the true diagnosis. Anxiolytics (section 4.1.2) or antipsychotics (section 4.2.1) should therefore be used with caution in depression but they are useful adjuncts in agitated patients.

See also section 4.2.3 for references to the management of bipolar disorders.

**St John's wort** (*Hypericum perforatum*) is a popular unlicensed herbal remedy for treating mild depression. However, preparations of St John's wort can induce drug metabolising enzymes and a number of important interactions with conventional drugs have been identified, see Appendix 1 (St John's wort). The amount of active ingredient can vary between different preparations of St John's wort and switching from one to another can change the degree of enzyme induction. Furthermore, when a patient stops taking St John's wort, concentrations of interacting drugs may increase, leading to toxicity. Antidepressants should **not** be used with St John's wort because of the potential for interaction.

**Hyponatraemia and antidepressant therapy.** Hyponatraemia (usually in the elderly and possibly due to inappropriate secretion of antidiuretic hormone) has been associated with all types of antidepressants; however, it has been reported more frequently with SSRIs than with other antidepressants. The CSM has advised that hyponatraemia should be considered in all patients who develop drowsiness, confusion, or convulsions while taking an antidepressant.

**Management** Patients should be reviewed every 1–2 weeks at the start of antidepressant treatment. Treatment should be continued for at least 4 weeks (6 weeks in the elderly) before considering whether to switch antidepressant due to lack of efficacy. In cases of partial response, continue for a further 2 weeks (elderly patients may take longer to respond).

Following remission, antidepressant treatment should be continued at the same dose for at least 4–6 months (about 12 months in the elderly). Patients with a history of recurrent depression should continue to receive maintenance treatment (for at least 5 years and possibly indefinitely). Lithium (section 4.2.3) is an effective second-line alternative for maintenance treatment.

Combination of two antidepressants can be dangerous and is rarely justified (except under specialist supervision).

**Failure to respond** Failure to respond to an initial course of antidepressant, may necessitate an increase in the dose, switching to a different antidepressant class, or in patients with 'atypical' major depression, the use of an MAOI. Failure to respond to a second antidepressant may require the addition of an augmenting drug such as lithium or liothyronine (specialist use), psychotherapy, or ECT. Adjunctive therapy with lithium or an MAOI should only be initiated by doctors with special experience of these combinations.

**Withdrawal** Gastro-intestinal symptoms of nausea, vomiting, and anorexia, accompanied by headache, giddiness, 'chills', and insomnia, and sometimes by hypomania, panic-anxiety, and extreme motor restlessness may occur if an antidepressant (particularly an MAOI) is stopped suddenly after regular administration for 8 weeks or more. The dose should preferably be reduced gradually over about 4 weeks, or longer if withdrawal symptoms emerge (6 months in patients who have been on long-term maintenance treatment). SSRIs have been associated with a specific withdrawal syndrome (section 4.3.3).



**Anxiety** Management of *acute anxiety* generally involves the use of a benzodiazepine or buspirone (section 4.1.2). For *chronic anxiety* (of longer than 4 weeks' duration), it may be appropriate to use an antidepressant before a benzodiazepine. *Generalised anxiety disorder* which does not respond to buspirone or to a benzodiazepine is treated with an antidepressant. Antidepressants such as SSRIs and venlafaxine may be effective in specific anxiety disorders.

Compound preparations of an antidepressant and an anxiolytic are not recommended because it is not possible to adjust the dosage of the individual components separately. Whereas antidepressants are given continuously over several months, anxiolytics are prescribed on a short-term basis.

**Panic disorders** Antidepressants are generally used for *panic disorders* and *phobias*; clomipramine (section 4.3.1) is licensed for *obsessional and phobic states*; escitalopram and paroxetine (section 4.3.3) and moclobemide (section 4.3.2) are licensed for the management of social phobia. However, in panic disorders (with or without agoraphobia) resistant to antidepressant therapy, a benzodiazepine may be considered (section 4.1.2).

## 4.3.1 Tricyclic and related antidepressant drugs

This section covers tricyclic antidepressants and also 1-, 2-, and 4-ring structured drugs with broadly similar properties.

These drugs are most effective for treating moderate to severe *endogenous depression* associated with psychomotor and physiological changes such as loss of appetite and sleep disturbances; improvement in sleep is usually the first benefit of therapy. Since there may be an interval of 2 weeks before the antidepressant action takes place electroconvulsive treatment may be required in severe depression when delay is hazardous or intolerable.

Some tricyclic antidepressants are also effective in the management of *panic disorder*.

For reference to the role of some tricyclic antidepressants in some forms of *neuralgia*, see section 4.7.3, and in *nocturnal enuresis* in children, see section 7.4.2.

**Dosage** About 10 to 20% of patients fail to respond to tricyclic and related antidepressant drugs and inadequate dosage may account for some of these failures. It is important to use doses that are sufficiently high for effective treatment but not so high as to cause toxic effects. Low doses should be used for initial treatment in the **elderly** (see under Side-effects, below).

In most patients the long half-life of tricyclic antidepressant drugs allows **once-daily** administration, usually at night; the use of modified-release preparations is therefore unnecessary.

**Choice** Tricyclic and related antidepressant drugs can be roughly divided into those with additional sedative properties and those which are less so. Agitated and anxious patients tend to respond best to the sedative compounds whereas withdrawn and apathetic patients will often obtain most benefit from the less sedating ones. Those with **sedative** properties include amitriptyline, clomipramine, dosulepin (dothiepin), doxepin, maprotiline, mianserin, trazodone, and trimipramine. Those with **less sedative** properties include amoxapine, imipramine, lofepramine, and nortriptyline.

**Imipramine** is well established and relatively safe and effective, but it has more marked antimuscarinic and cardiac side-effects than compounds such as **doxepin**, **mianserin**, and **trazodone**; this may be important in individual patients. **Amitriptyline** and **dosulepin** (dothiepin) are effective but they are particularly dangerous in overdosage (see Overdosage, below). **Lofepramine** also has a lower incidence of antimuscarinic and sedative side-effects and is less dangerous in overdosage; it is, however, infrequently associated with hepatic toxicity. **Amoxapine** is related to the antipsychotic loxapine and its side-effects include tardive dyskinesia.

For a comparison of tricyclic and related antidepressants with SSRIs and related antidepressants and MAOIs, see section 4.3.

**Children and adolescents** Evidence of the efficacy of tricyclic antidepressants for depression in children has not been established; see also CSM advice, p. 202

**Side-effects** *Arrhythmias* and *heart block* occasionally follow the use of tricyclic antidepressants, particularly amitriptyline, and may be a factor in the sudden death of patients with cardiac disease. They are also sometimes associated with *convulsions* (and should be prescribed with special caution in epilepsy as they lower the convulsive threshold); maprotiline has particularly been associated with convulsions. *Hepatic* and *haematological* reactions may occur and have been particularly associated with mianserin.

Other side-effects of tricyclic and related antidepressants include *drowsiness, dry mouth, blurred vision, constipation,* and *urinary retention* (all attributed to antimuscarinic activity), and sweating. The patient should be encouraged to persist with treatment as some tolerance to these side-effects seems to develop. They are reduced if low doses are given initially and then gradually increased, but this must be balanced against the need to obtain a full therapeutic effect as soon as possible. Gradual introduction of treatment is particularly important in the elderly, who, because of the hypotensive effects of these drugs, are prone to attacks of *dizziness* or even *syncope*. Another side-effect to which the elderly are particularly susceptible is *hyponatraemia* (see CSM advice on p. 195).

*Neuroleptic malignant syndrome* (section 4.2.1) may, very rarely, arise in the course of antidepressant treatment.

**Overdosage** Limited quantities of tricyclic antidepressants should be prescribed at any one time because their cardiovascular effects are dangerous in overdosage. In particular, overdosage with dosulepin (dothiepin) and amitriptyline is associated with a relatively high rate of fatality. For advice on **overdosage** see Emergency Treatment of Poisoning, p. 31

**Withdrawal** If possible tricyclic and related antidepressants should be withdrawn slowly (see also section 4.3).

**Interactions** A tricyclic or related antidepressant (or an SSRI or related antidepressant) should not be started until 2 weeks after stopping an MAOI (3 weeks if starting clomipramine or imipramine). Conversely, an MAOI should not be started until at least 7–14 days after a tricyclic or related antidepressant (3 weeks in the case of clomipramine or imipramine) has been stopped. For guidance relating to the reversible monoamine oxidase inhibitor, moclobemide, see p. 201. For other tricyclic antidepressant **interactions**, see Appendix 1 (antidepressants, tricyclic and antidepressants, tricyclic (related)).

## Tricyclic antidepressants

### AMITRIPTYLINE HYDROCHLORIDE

**Indications** depressive illness (but not recommended, see notes above); nocturnal enuresis in children (section 7.4.2)

**Cautions** cardiac disease (particularly with arrhythmias, see Contra-indications below), history of epilepsy, pregnancy (Appendix 4), breast-feeding (Appendix 5), elderly, hepatic impairment (avoid if severe; Appendix 2), thyroid disease, phaeochromocytoma, history of mania, psychoses (may aggravate psychotic symptoms), angle-closure glaucoma, history of urinary retention, concurrent electroconvulsive therapy; if possible avoid abrupt withdrawal; anaesthesia (increased risk of arrhythmias and hypotension, see surgery section 15.1); porphyria (section 9.8.2); see section 7.4.2 for additional nocturnal enuresis warnings; **interactions:** Appendix 1 (antidepressants, tricyclic)

Driving Drowsiness may affect performance of skilled tasks (e.g. driving); effects of alcohol enhanced

**Contra-indications** recent myocardial infarction, arrhythmias (particularly heart block), not indicated in manic phase, severe liver disease

**Side-effects** dry mouth, sedation, blurred vision (disturbance of accommodation, increased intra-ocular pressure), constipation, nausea, difficulty with micturition; cardiovascular side-effects (such as ECG changes, arrhythmias, postural hypotension, tachycardia, syncope, particularly with high doses); sweating, tremor, rashes and hypersensitivity reactions (including urticaria, photosensitivity), behavioural disturbances (particularly children), hypomania or mania, confusion or delirium (particularly elderly), headache, interference with sexual function, blood sugar changes; increased appetite and weight gain (occasionally weight loss); endocrine side-effects such as testicular enlargement, gynaecomastia, galactorrhoea; also convulsions (see also Cautions), movement disorders and dyskinesias, dysarthria, paraesthesia, taste disturbances, tinnitus, fever, agranulocytosis, leucopenia, eosinophilia, purpura, thrombocytopenia, hyponatraemia (may be due to inappropriate antidiuretic hormone secretion) see CSM advice, p. 195, abnormal liver function tests (jaundice); for a general outline of side-effects see also notes above; **overdosage:** see Emergency Treatment of Poisoning, p. 31 (high rate of fatality—see notes above)

**Dose**

- Depression (but not recommended, see notes above), initially 75 mg (elderly and adolescents 30–75 mg) daily in divided doses *or* as a single dose at bedtime increased gradually as necessary to 150–200 mg; CHILD under 16 years not recommended for depression
- Nocturnal enuresis, CHILD 7–10 years 10–20 mg, 11–16 years 25–50 mg at night; max. period of treatment (including gradual withdrawal) 3 months—full physical examination before further course

**Amitriptyline** (Non-proprietary) PoM
Tablets, coated, amitriptyline hydrochloride 10 mg, net price 20 = 71p; 25 mg, 20 = 73p; 50 mg, 20 = 97p. Label: 2

Oral solution, amitriptyline (as hydrochloride) 25 mg/5 mL, net price 200 mL = £16.53; 50 mg/5 mL, 200 mL = £18.00. Label: 2

Compound preparations

**Triptafen®** (Goldshield) PoM
Tablets, pink, s/c, amitriptyline hydrochloride 25 mg, perphenazine 2 mg. Net price 20 = £4.25. Label: 2

**Triptafen-M®** (Goldshield) PoM
Tablets, pink, s/c, amitriptyline hydrochloride 10 mg, perphenazine 2 mg. Net price 20 = £3.80. Label: 2

### AMOXAPINE

**Indications** depressive illness

**Cautions** see under Amitriptyline Hydrochloride

**Contra-indications** see under Amitriptyline Hydrochloride

**Side-effects** see under Amitriptyline Hydrochloride; tardive dyskinesia reported; menstrual irregularities, breast enlargement

**Dose**

- Initially 100–150 mg daily in divided doses *or* as a single dose at bedtime increased as necessary to max. 300 mg daily; ELDERLY initially 25 mg twice daily increased as necessary after 5–7 days to max. 50 mg 3 times daily; CHILD under 16 years not recommended

**Asendis®** (Goldshield) PoM
Tablets, amoxapine 50 mg (orange, scored), net price 84-tab pack = £16.78; 100 mg (blue, scored), 56-tab pack = £18.65. Label: 2

## CLOMIPRAMINE HYDROCHLORIDE

**Indications** depressive illness, phobic and obsessional states; adjunctive treatment of cataplexy associated with narcolepsy

**Cautions** see under Amitriptyline Hydrochloride

**Contra-indications** see under Amitriptyline Hydrochloride

**Side-effects** see under Amitriptyline Hydrochloride; also diarrhoea; hair loss reported

**Dose**

- Depressive illness, initially 10 mg daily, increased gradually as necessary to 30–150 mg daily in divided doses *or* as a single dose at bedtime; max. 250 mg daily; ELDERLY initially 10 mg daily increased carefully over approx. 10 days to 30–75 mg daily; CHILD not recommended
- Phobic and obsessional states, initially 25 mg daily (ELDERLY 10 mg daily) increased over 2 weeks to 100–150 mg daily; max. 250 mg daily; CHILD not recommended
- Adjunctive treatment of cataplexy associated with narcolepsy, initially 10 mg daily, gradually increased until satisfactory response (range 10–75 mg daily)

**Clomipramine** (Non-proprietary) PoM
Capsules, clomipramine hydrochloride 10 mg, net price 28-cap pack = £1.44; 25 mg, 28-cap pack = £1.77; 50 mg, 28-cap pack = £2.85. Label: 2

**Anafranil®** (Novartis) PoM
Capsules, clomipramine hydrochloride 10 mg (yellow/caramel), net price 84-cap pack = £3.23; 25 mg (orange/caramel), 84-cap pack = £6.35; 50 mg (grey/caramel), 56-cap pack = £8.06. Label: 2

**Anafranil SR®** (Novartis) PoM
Tablets, m/r, grey-red, f/c, clomipramine hydrochloride 75 mg. Net price 28-tab pack = £8.83. Label: 2, 25

## DOSULEPIN HYDROCHLORIDE
### (Dothiepin hydrochloride)

**Indications** depressive illness, particularly where sedation is required

**Cautions** see under Amitriptyline Hydrochloride

**Contra-indications** see under Amitriptyline Hydrochloride

**Side-effects** see under Amitriptyline Hydrochloride (high rate of fatality—see notes above)

**Dose**

- Initially 75 mg (ELDERLY 50–75 mg) daily in divided doses *or* as a single dose at bedtime, increased gradually as necessary to 150 mg daily (ELDERLY 75 mg may be sufficient); up to 225 mg daily in some circumstances (e.g. hospital use); CHILD not recommended

**Dosulepin** (Non-proprietary) PoM
Capsules, dosulepin hydrochloride 25 mg, net price 20 = 93p. Label: 2
Brands include *Dothapax®*, *Prepadine®*

Tablets, dosulepin hydrochloride 75 mg, net price 28-tab pack = £1.50. Label: 2
Brands include *Prepadine®*

**Prothiaden®** (Abbott) PoM
Capsules, red/red-brown, dosulepin hydrochloride 25 mg. Net price 20 = £1.11. Label: 2

Tablets, red, s/c, dosulepin hydrochloride 75 mg. Net price 28-tab pack = £2.97. Label: 2

## DOXEPIN

**Indications** depressive illness, particularly where sedation is required; skin (section 13.3)

**Cautions** see under Amitriptyline Hydrochloride

**Contra-indications** see under Amitriptyline Hydrochloride; breast-feeding (Appendix 5)

**Side-effects** see under Amitriptyline Hydrochloride

**Dose**

- Initially 75 mg daily in divided doses *or* as a single dose at bedtime, increased as necessary to max. 300 mg daily in 3 divided doses (up to 100 mg may be given as a single dose); ELDERLY initially 10–50 mg daily, range of 30–50 mg daily may be adequate; CHILD not recommended

**Sinequan®** (Pfizer) PoM
Capsules, doxepin (as hydrochloride) 10 mg (orange), net price 56-cap pack = £1.33; 25 mg (orange/blue), 28-cap pack = 96p; 50 mg (blue), 28-cap pack = £1.57; 75 mg (yellow/blue), 28-cap pack = £2.49. Label: 2

## IMIPRAMINE HYDROCHLORIDE

**Indications** depressive illness; nocturnal enuresis in children (see section 7.4.2)

**Cautions** see under Amitriptyline Hydrochloride

**Contra-indications** see under Amitriptyline Hydrochloride

**Side-effects** see under Amitriptyline Hydrochloride, but less sedating

**Dose**

- Depression, initially up to 75 mg daily in divided doses increased gradually to 150–200 mg (up to 300 mg in hospital patients); up to 150 mg may be given as a single dose at bedtime; ELDERLY initially 10 mg daily, increased gradually to 30–50 mg daily; CHILD not recommended for depression
- Nocturnal enuresis, CHILD 7 years 25 mg, 8–11 years 25–50 mg, over 11 years 50–75 mg at bedtime; max. period of treatment (including gradual withdrawal) 3 months—full physical examination before further course

**Imipramine** (Non-proprietary) PoM
Tablets, coated, imipramine hydrochloride 10 mg, net price 20 = £1.17; 25 mg, 20 = £1.19. Label: 2

## LOFEPRAMINE

**Indications** depressive illness

**Cautions** see under Amitriptyline Hydrochloride

**Contra-indications** see under Amitriptyline Hydrochloride; hepatic and severe renal impairment

**Side-effects** see under Amitriptyline Hydrochloride, but less sedating, lower incidence of antimuscarinic effects and less dangerous in overdosage; hepatic disorders reported

**Dose**

- 140–210 mg daily in divided doses; ELDERLY may respond to lower doses; CHILD not recommended

**Lofepramine** (Non-proprietary) PoM

Tablets, lofepramine 70 mg (as hydrochloride). Net price 56-tab pack = £13.59. Label: 2

Brands include *Feprapax®*

Oral suspension, lofepramine 70 mg/5 mL (as hydrochloride). Net price 150 mL = £22.22. Label: 2

Brands include *Lomont®* (sugar-free)

**Gamanil®** (Merck) PoM

Tablets, f/c, brown-violet, lofepramine 70 mg (as hydrochloride). Net price 56-tab pack = £9.84. Label: 2

## NORTRIPTYLINE

**Indications** depressive illness; nocturnal enuresis in children (section 7.4.2)

**Cautions** see under Amitriptyline Hydrochloride; manufacturer advises plasma-nortriptyline concentration monitoring if dose above 100 mg daily, but evidence of practical value uncertain

**Contra-indications** see under Amitriptyline Hydrochloride

**Side-effects** see under Amitriptyline Hydrochloride, but less sedating

**Dose**

- Depression, low dose initially increased as necessary to 75–100 mg daily in divided doses *or* as a single dose (max. 150 mg daily); ADOLESCENT and ELDERLY 30–50 mg daily in divided doses; CHILD not recommended for depression
- Nocturnal enuresis, CHILD 7 years 10 mg, 8–11 years 10–20 mg, over 11 years 25–35 mg, at night; max period of treatment (including gradual withdrawal) 3 months—full physical examination and ECG before further course

**Allegron®** (King) PoM

Tablets, nortriptyline (as hydrochloride) 10 mg, net price 20 = £2.48; 25 mg (orange, scored), 20 = £4.90. Label: 2

### Compound preparations

**Motival®** (Sanofi-Synthelabo) PoM

Tablets, pink, s/c, fluphenazine hydrochloride 500 micrograms, nortriptyline 10 mg (as hydrochloride). Net price 20 = 67p. Label: 2

## TRIMIPRAMINE

**Indications** depressive illness, particularly where sedation required

**Cautions** see under Amitriptyline Hydrochloride

**Contra-indications** see under Amitriptyline Hydrochloride

**Side-effects** see under Amitriptyline Hydrochloride

**Dose**

- Initially 50–75 mg daily in divided doses *or* as a single dose at bedtime, increased as necessary to 150–300 mg daily; ELDERLY initially 10–25 mg 3 times daily, maintenance half adult dose may be sufficient; CHILD not recommended

**Surmontil®** (Aventis Pharma) PoM

Capsules, green/white, trimipramine 50 mg (as maleate). Net price 28-cap pack = £7.91. Label: 2

Tablets, trimipramine (as maleate) 10 mg, net price 28-tab pack = £3.57, 84-tab pack = £10.69; 25 mg, 28-tab pack = £4.71, 84-tab pack = £14.10. Label: 2

# Related antidepressants

## MAPROTILINE HYDROCHLORIDE

**Indications** depressive illness, particularly where sedation is required

**Cautions** see under Amitriptyline Hydrochloride; **interactions:** Appendix 1 (antidepressants, tricyclic (related))

**Contra-indications** see under Amitriptyline Hydrochloride; history of epilepsy

**Side-effects** see under Amitriptyline Hydrochloride, antimuscarinic effects may occur less frequently but rashes common and increased risk of convulsions at higher dosage

**Dose**

- Initially 25–75 mg (elderly 30 mg) daily in 3 divided doses *or* as a single dose at bedtime, increased gradually as necessary to max. 150 mg daily; CHILD not recommended

**Ludiomil®** (Novartis) PoM

Tablets, all f/c, maprotiline hydrochloride 25 mg (greyish-red), net price 28-tab pack = £2.53; 75 mg (brownish-orange), 28-tab pack = £7.46. Label: 2

Excipients include gluten

## MIANSERIN HYDROCHLORIDE

**Indications** depressive illness, particularly where sedation is required

**Cautions** see under Amitriptyline Hydrochloride; **interactions:** Appendix 1 (antidepressants, tricyclic (related))

Blood counts A full **blood count** is recommended every 4 weeks during the first 3 months of treatment; clinical monitoring should continue subsequently and treatment should be stopped and a full blood count obtained if *fever, sore throat, stomatitis*, or other signs of infection develop.

**Contra-indications** see under Amitriptyline Hydrochloride

**Side-effects** see under Amitriptyline Hydrochloride, fewer and milder antimuscarinic and cardiovascular effects; leucopenia, agranulocytosis and aplastic anaemia (particularly in the elderly); jaundice; arthritis, arthralgia

**Dose**

- Initially 30–40 mg (elderly 30 mg) daily in divided doses *or* as a single dose at bedtime, increased gradually as necessary; usual dose range 30–90 mg; CHILD not recommended

**Mianserin** (Non-proprietary) PoM
Tablets, mianserin hydrochloride 10 mg, net price 28-tab pack = £3.84; 20 mg, 28-tab pack = £4.14; 30 mg, 28-tab pack = £7.69. Label: 2, 25

## TRAZODONE HYDROCHLORIDE

**Indications** depressive illness, particularly where sedation is required; anxiety

**Cautions** see under Amitriptyline Hydrochloride; **interactions:** Appendix 1 (antidepressants, tricyclic (related))

**Contra-indications** see under Amitriptyline Hydrochloride

**Side-effects** see under Amitriptyline Hydrochloride but fewer antimuscarinic and cardiovascular effects; rarely priapism (discontinue immediately)

**Dose**

- Depression, initially 150 mg (elderly 100 mg) daily in divided doses after food *or* as a single dose at bedtime; may be increased to 300 mg daily; hospital patients up to max. 600 mg daily in divided doses
- Anxiety, 75 mg daily, increasing if necessary to 300 mg daily
- CHILD not recommended

**Trazodone** (Non-proprietary) PoM
Capsules, trazodone hydrochloride 50 mg, net price 84-cap pack = £24.46; 100 mg, 56-cap pack = £23.75. Label: 2, 21
Tablets, trazodone hydrochloride 150 mg, net price 28-tab pack = £14.96. Label: 2, 21

**Molipaxin®** (Hoechst Marion Roussel) PoM
Capsules, trazodone hydrochloride 50 mg (violet/green), net price 84-cap pack = £20.74; 100 mg (violet/fawn), 56-cap pack = £24.40. Label: 2, 21
Tablets, pink, f/c, trazodone hydrochloride 150 mg. Net price 28-tab pack = £13.94. Label: 2, 21
Liquid, sugar-free, trazodone hydrochloride 50 mg/5 mL, net price 120 mL = £9.28. Label: 2, 21

## 4.3.2 Monoamine-oxidase inhibitors (MAOIs)

Monoamine-oxidase inhibitors are used much less frequently than tricyclic and related antidepressants, or SSRIs and related antidepressants because of the dangers of dietary and drug interactions and the fact that it is easier to prescribe MAOIs when tricyclic antidepressants have been unsuccessful than vice versa. **Tranylcypromine** is the most **hazardous** of the MAOIs because of its stimulant action. The drugs of choice are **phenelzine** or **isocarboxazid** which are less stimulant and therefore safer.

Phobic patients and depressed patients with atypical, hypochondriacal, or hysterical features are said to respond best to MAOIs. However, MAOIs should be tried in any patients who are refractory to treatment with other antidepressants as there is occasionally a dramatic response. Response to treatment may be delayed for 3 weeks or more and may take an additional 1 or 2 weeks to become maximal.

**Withdrawal** If possible MAOIs should be withdrawn slowly (see also section 4.3).

**Interactions** MAOIs inhibit monoamine oxidase, thereby causing an accumulation of amine neurotransmitters. The metabolism of some amine drugs such as *indirect-acting sympathomimetics* (present in many cough and decongestant preparations, see section 3.10) is also inhibited and their pressor action may be potentiated; the pressor effect of tyramine (in some foods, such as mature cheese, pickled herring, broad bean pods, and *Bovril®*, *Oxo®*, *Marmite®* or any similar meat or yeast extract or fermented soya bean extract) may also be dangerously potentiated. These interactions may cause a dangerous rise in blood pressure. An early warning symptom may be a throbbing headache. Patients should be advised to eat only fresh foods and avoid food that is suspected of being stale or 'going off'. This is especially important with meat, fish, poultry or offal; game should be avoided. The danger of interaction persists for up to 2 weeks after treatment with MAOIs is discontinued. Patients should also avoid alcoholic drinks or de-alcoholised (low alcohol) drinks.

*Other antidepressants* should **not** be started for 2 weeks after treatment with MAOIs has been stopped (3 weeks if starting clomipramine or imipramine). Some psychiatrists use selected tricyclics in conjunction with MAOIs but this is hazardous, indeed potentially lethal, except in experienced hands and there is no evidence that the combination is more effective than when either constituent is used alone. The combination of tranylcypromine with clomipramine is particularly **dangerous**.

Conversely, an MAOI should not be started until at least 7–14 days after a tricyclic or related antidepressant (3 weeks in the case of clomipramine or imipramine) has been stopped.

In addition, an MAOI should not be started for at least 2 weeks after a previous MAOI has been stopped (then started at a reduced dose).

For other interactions with MAOIs including those with opioid analgesics (notably pethidine), see Appendix 1 (MAOIs). For guidance on interactions relating to the reversible monoamine oxidase inhibitor, moclobemide, see p. 201; for guidance on interactions relating to SSRIs, see p. 202.

## PHENELZINE

**Indications** depressive illness

**Cautions** diabetes mellitus, cardiovascular disease, epilepsy, blood disorders, concurrent electroconvulsive therapy; elderly (great caution); monitor blood pressure (risk of postural hypotension and hypertensive responses—discontinue if palpitations or frequent headaches); if possible avoid abrupt withdrawal; severe hypertensive reactions to certain drugs and foods; avoid in agitated patients; porphyria (section 9.8.2); pregnancy (Appendix 4) and breast-feeding; surgery (section 15.1); **interactions:** Appendix 1 (MAOIs)
Driving Drowsiness may affect performance of skilled tasks (e.g. driving)

**Contra-indications** hepatic impairment or abnormal liver function tests (Appendix 2), cerebrovascular disease, phaeochromocytoma; not indicated in manic phase

**Side-effects** commonly postural hypotension (especially in elderly) and dizziness; less common side-effects include drowsiness, insomnia, headache, weakness and fatigue, dry mouth, constipation and other gastro-intestinal disturbances, oedema, myoclonic movement, hyperreflexia, elevated liver enzymes; agitation and tremors, nervousness, euphoria, arrhythmias, blurred vision, nystagmus, difficulty in micturition, sweating, convulsions, rashes, purpura, leucopenia, sexual disturbances, and weight gain with inappropriate appetite may also occur; psychotic episodes with hypomanic behaviour, confusion, and hallucinations may be induced in susceptible persons; jaundice has been reported and, on rare occasions, fatal progressive hepatocellular necrosis; paraesthesia, peripheral neuritis, peripheral neuropathy may be due to pyridoxine deficiency; for CSM advice on possible hyponatraemia, see p. 195

**Dose**

- 15 mg 3 times daily, increased if necessary to 4 times daily after 2 weeks (hospital patients, max. 30 mg 3 times daily), then reduced gradually to lowest possible maintenance dose (15 mg on alternate days may be adequate); CHILD not recommended

**Nardil®** (Concord) PoM
Tablets, orange, f/c, phenelzine (as sulphate) 15 mg, net price 20 = £3.99. Label: 3, 10, patient information leaflet

## ISOCARBOXAZID

**Indications** depressive illness

**Cautions** see under Phenelzine

**Contra-indications** see under Phenelzine

**Side-effects** see under Phenelzine

**Dose**

- Initially 30 mg daily in single or divided doses until improvement occurs (increased after 4 weeks if necessary to max. 60 mg daily for 4–6 weeks under close supervision), then reduced to usual maintenance dose 10–20 mg daily (but up to 40 mg daily may be required); ELDERLY 5–10 mg daily; CHILD not recommended

**Isocarboxazid** (Non-proprietary) PoM
Tablets, pink, scored, isocarboxazid 10 mg. Net price 50 = £27.79. Label: 3, 10, patient information leaflet

## TRANYLCYPROMINE

**Indications** depressive illness

**Cautions** see under Phenelzine

**Contra-indications** see under Phenelzine; hyperthyroidism

**Side-effects** see under Phenelzine; insomnia if given in evening; hypertensive crises with throbbing headache requiring discontinuation of treatment more frequent than with other MAOIs; liver damage less frequent than with phenelzine

**Dose**

- Initially 10 mg twice daily not later than 3 p.m., increasing the second daily dose to 20 mg after 1 week if necessary; doses above 30 mg daily under close supervision only; usual maintenance dose 10 mg daily; CHILD not recommended

**Tranylcypromine** (Non-proprietary) PoM
Tablets, tranylcypromine (as sulphate) 10 mg. Net price 28-tab pack = £5.08. Label: 3, 10, patient information leaflet

## Reversible MAOIs

**Moclobemide** is indicated for major depression and social phobia; it is reported to act by reversible inhibition of monoamine oxidase type A (it is therefore termed a RIMA). It should be reserved as a second-line treatment.

**Interactions** Moclobemide is claimed to cause less potentiation of the pressor effect of tyramine than the traditional (irreversible) MAOIs, but patients should avoid consuming large amounts of tyramine-rich food (such as mature cheese, yeast extracts and fermented soya bean products).

The risk of drug interactions is also claimed to be less but patients still need to avoid sympathomimetics such as ephedrine and pseudoephedrine. In addition, moclobemide should not be given with another antidepressant. Owing to its short duration of action no treatment-free period is required after it has been stopped but it should not be started until at least a week after a tricyclic or related antidepressant or an SSRI or related antidepressant has been stopped (2 weeks in the case of sertraline, and at least 5 weeks in the case of fluoxetine), or for at least a week after an MAOI has been stopped. For other interactions, see Appendix 1 (moclobemide).

## MOCLOBEMIDE

**Indications** depressive illness; social phobia

**Cautions** avoid in agitated or excited patients (or give with sedative for up to 2–3 weeks), thyrotoxicosis, hepatic impairment (Appendix 2), may provoke manic episodes in bipolar disorders, pregnancy (Appendix 4) and breast-feeding (Appendix 5—patient information leaflet advises avoid); **interactions:** see notes above and Appendix 1 (moclobemide)

**Contra-indications** acute confusional states, phaeochromocytoma

**Side-effects** sleep disturbances, dizziness, gastro-intestinal disorders, headache, restlessness, agitation; paraesthesia, dry mouth, visual disturbances, oedema, skin reactions, confusional states reported; rarely raised liver enzymes, galactorrhoea; for CSM advice on possible hyponatraemia, see p. 195

**Dose**

- Depression, initially 300 mg daily usually in divided doses after food, adjusted according to response; usual range 150–600 mg daily; CHILD not recommended
- Social phobia, initially 300 mg daily increased on fourth day to 600 mg daily in 2 divided doses, continued for 8–12 weeks to assess efficacy; CHILD not recommended

**Moclobemide** (Non-proprietary) PoM
Tablets, moclobemide 150 mg, net price 30-tab pack = £6.32; 300 mg, 30-tab pack = £10.70. Label: 10, patient information leaflet 21

**Manerix®** (Roche) PoM
Tablets, yellow, f/c, scored, moclobemide 150 mg, net price 30-tab pack = £9.33; 300 mg, 30-tab pack = £13.99. Label: 10, patient information leaflet 21

## 4.3.3 Selective serotonin re-uptake inhibitors

**Citalopram**, **escitalopram**, **fluoxetine**, **fluvoxamine**, **paroxetine**, and **sertraline** selectively inhibit the re-uptake of serotonin (5-hydroxytryptamine, 5-HT); they are termed selective serotonin re-uptake inhibitors (SSRIs). For a general comment on the management of depression and on the comparison between *tricyclic and related antidepressants* and the *SSRIs and related antidepressants*, see section 4.3.

**CSM advice (depressive illness in children and adolescents).**
The CSM has advised that the balance of risks and benefits for the treatment of depressive illness in individuals under 18 years is considered unfavourable for the SSRIs citalopram, escitalopram, paroxetine, and sertraline, and for mirtazapine and venlafaxine. Clinical trials have failed to show efficacy and have shown an increase in harmful outcomes. However, it is recognised that specialists may sometimes decide to use these drugs in response to individual clinical need; children and adolescents should be monitored carefully for suicidal behaviour, self-harm or hostility, particularly at the beginning of treatment.
Only fluoxetine has been shown in clinical trials to be effective for treating depressive illness in children and adolescents. However, it is possible that, in common with the other SSRIs, it is associated with a small risk of self-harm and suicidal thoughts. Overall, the balance of risks and benefits for fluoxetine in the treatment of depressive illness in individuals under 18 years is considered favourable, but children and adolescents must be carefully monitored as above.

**Cautions** SSRIs should be used with caution in patients with epilepsy (avoid if poorly controlled, discontinue if convulsions develop), concurrent electroconvulsive therapy (prolonged seizures reported with fluoxetine), history of mania, cardiac disease, diabetes mellitus, angle-closure glaucoma, concomitant use of drugs that increase risk of bleeding, history of bleeding disorders (especially gastro-intestinal bleeding), hepatic impairment (Appendix 2), renal impairment (Appendix 3), pregnancy (Appendix 4), and breast-feeding (Appendix 5). The risk of suicidal behaviour is possibly higher in young adults, calling for close monitoring of those receiving SSRIs (see also CSM advice above). SSRIs may also impair performance of skilled tasks (e.g. driving). **Interactions:** see below and Appendix 1 (antidepressants, SSRI).

**Withdrawal** Gastro-intestinal disturbances, headache, anxiety, dizziness, paraesthesia, sleep disturbances, fatigue, influenza-like symptoms, and sweating are the most common features of abrupt withdrawal of an SSRI or marked reduction of the dose; the dose should be tapered over a few weeks to avoid these effects.

**Interactions** An SSRI or related antidepressant should not be started until 2 weeks after stopping an MAOI. Conversely, an MAOI should not be started until at least a week after an SSRI or related antidepressant has been stopped (2 weeks in the case of sertraline, at least 5 weeks in the case of fluoxetine). For guidance relating to the reversible monoamine oxidase inhibitor, moclobemide, see above. For other SSRI antidepressant interactions, see Appendix 1 (antidepressants, SSRI).

**Contra-indications** SSRIs should not be used if the patient enters a manic phase.

**Side-effects** SSRIs are less sedating and have fewer antimuscarinic and cardiotoxic effects than tricyclic antidepressants (section 4.3). Side-effects of the SSRIs include gastro-intestinal effects (dose-related and fairly common—include nausea, vomiting, dyspepsia, abdominal pain, diarrhoea, constipation), anorexia with weight loss (increased appetite and weight gain also reported) and hypersensitivity reactions including rash (consider discontinuation—may be sign of impending serious systemic reaction, possibly associated with vasculitis), urticaria, angioedema, anaphylaxis, arthralgia, myalgia and photosensitivity; other side-effects include dry mouth, nervousness, anxiety, headache, insomnia, tremor, dizziness, asthenia, hallucinations, drowsiness, convulsions (see Cautions above), galactorrhoea, sexual dysfunction, urinary retention, sweating, hypomania or mania (see Cautions above), movement disorders and dyskinesias, visual disturbances, hyponatraemia (may be due to inappropriate antidiuretic hormone secretion—see CSM warning, section 4.3), and bleeding disorders including ecchymoses and purpura. Suicidal ideation has been linked with SSRIs but causality has not been established.

### CITALOPRAM

**Indications** depressive illness, panic disorder
**Cautions** see notes above
**Contra-indications** see notes above
**Side-effects** see notes above; also palpitation, tachycardia, postural hypotension, coughing, yawning, confusion, impaired concentration, malaise, amnesia, migraine, paraesthesia, abnormal dreams, taste disturbance, increased salivation, rhinitis, tinnitus, polyuria, micturition disorders, euphoria; paradoxical increased anxiety during initial treatment of panic disorder (reduce dose)

**Dose**
- See preparations below

**Citalopram** (Non-proprietary) PoM
Tablets, citalopram (as hydrobromide) 10 mg, net price 28-tab pack = £2.80; 20 mg, 28-tab pack = £3.02; 40 mg, 28-tab pack = £5.04. Counselling, driving

**Cipramil®** (Lundbeck) PoM
Tablets, f/c, citalopram (as hydrobromide) 10 mg, net price 28-tab pack = £8.97; 20 mg (scored), 28-tab pack = £14.91; 40 mg, 28-tab pack = £25.20. Counselling, driving
Dose depressive illness, 20 mg daily as a single dose in the morning or evening increased if necessary to max. 60 mg daily (ELDERLY max. 40 mg daily); CHILD and ADOLESCENT under 18 years not recommended (see CSM advice, below)
Panic disorder, initially 10 mg daily increased to 20 mg after 7 days, usual dose 20–30 mg daily; max. 60 mg daily (ELDERLY max. 40 mg daily); CHILD and ADOLESCENT under 18 years not recommended

Oral drops, sugar-free, citalopram (as hydrochloride) 40 mg/mL, net price 15 mL = £20.16. Counselling, driving, administration

**Dose** depressive illness, 16 mg daily as a single dose in the morning or evening increased if necessary to max. 48 mg daily (ELDERLY max. 32 mg daily); CHILD and ADOLESCENT under 18 years not recommended (see CSM advice, p. 202)

Panic disorder, initially 8 mg daily as a single dose increased to 16 mg daily after 7 days, usual dose 16–24 mg daily; max. 48 mg daily; (ELDERLY max. 32 mg daily); CHILD and ADOLESCENT under 18 years not recommended

Excipients include alcohol

**Note** 8 mg (4 drops) Cipramil® oral drops may be considered to be equivalent in therapeutic effect to 10-mg Cipramil® tablet

Mix with water, orange juice, or apple juice before taking

## ESCITALOPRAM

**Note** Escitalopram is an isomer of citalopram

**Indications** see under Dose

**Cautions** see notes above

**Contra-indications** see notes above

**Side-effects** see notes above; also postural hypotension, sinusitis, fatigue, depersonalisation, yawning, pyrexia, taste disturbance reported; paradoxical increased anxiety during initial treatment of panic disorder (reduce dose)

**Dose**

- Depressive illness and generalised anxiety disorder, 10 mg once daily increased if necessary to max. 20 mg daily; ELDERLY initially half adult dose, lower maintenance dose may be sufficient; CHILD and ADOLESCENT under 18 years not recommended (see CSM advice, p. 202)
- Panic disorder, initially 5 mg daily increased to 10 mg daily after 7 days; max. 20 mg daily; ELDERLY initially half adult dose, lower maintenance dose may be sufficient; CHILD and ADOLESCENT under 18 years not recommended
- Social anxiety disorder, initially 10 mg daily adjusted after 2–4 weeks; usual dose 5–20 mg daily; CHILD and ADOLESCENT under 18 years not recommended

**Cipralex®** (Lundbeck) ▼ PoM

Tablets, f/c, escitalopram (as oxalate) 5 mg, net price 28-tab pack = £8.97; 10 mg (scored), 28-tab pack = £14.91; 20 mg (scored), 28-tab pack = £25.20. Counselling, driving

## FLUOXETINE

**Indications** see under Dose

**Cautions** see notes above

**Contra-indications** see notes above

**Side-effects** see notes above; also vasodilatation, postural hypotension, pharyngitis, dyspnoea, chills, taste disturbances, sleep disturbances, euphoria, confusion, yawning, impaired concentration, changes in blood sugar, alopecia, urinary frequency; *rarely* pulmonary inflammation and fibrosis; *very rarely* hepatitis, toxic epidermal necrolysis, and neuroleptic malignant syndrome-like event

**Dose**

- Major depression, 20 mg once daily increased after 3 weeks if necessary, usual dose 20–60 mg (ELDERLY 20–40 mg) once daily; max. 80 mg (ELDERLY max. 60 mg) once daily; CHILD and ADOLESCENT under 18 years not recommended
- Bulimia nervosa, 60 mg once daily; max. 80 mg once daily; CHILD and ADOLESCENT under 18 years not recommended
- Obsessive-compulsive disorder, initially 20 mg once daily increased after two weeks if necessary, usual dose 20–60 mg (ELDERLY 20–40 mg) once daily; max. 80 mg (ELDERLY max. 60 mg) once daily; discontinue if no improvement within 10 weeks; CHILD and ADOLESCENT under 18 years not recommended

**Long duration of action** Consider the long half-life of fluoxetine when adjusting dosage (or in overdosage)

**Fluoxetine** (Non-proprietary) PoM

Capsules, fluoxetine (as hydrochloride) 20 mg, net price 30-cap pack = £1.38; 60 mg, 30-cap pack = £47.61. Counselling, driving

Brands include *Oxactin®*

Liquid, fluoxetine (as hydrochloride) 20 mg/5 mL, net price 70 mL = £10.12. Counselling, driving

**Prozac®** (Dista) PoM

Capsules, fluoxetine (as hydrochloride) 20 mg (green/yellow), net price 30-cap pack = £14.21; 60 mg (yellow), 30-cap pack = £47.61. Counselling, driving

Liquid, fluoxetine (as hydrochloride) 20 mg/5 mL, net price 70 mL = £13.26. Counselling, driving

## FLUVOXAMINE MALEATE

**Indications** depressive illness, obsessive-compulsive disorder

**Cautions** see notes above

**CSM advice** The CSM has advised that concomitant use of fluvoxamine and theophylline or aminophylline should usually be avoided; see also **interactions:** Appendix 1 (antidepressants, SSRIs)

**Contra-indications** see notes above

**Side-effects** see notes above; palpitation, tachycardia (may also cause bradycardia); *rarely* postural hypotension, confusion, ataxia, paraesthesia, malaise, taste disturbance, neuroleptic malignant syndome-like event, abnormal liver function tests, usually symptomatic (discontinue treatment)

**Dose**

- Depression, initially 50–100 mg daily in the evening, increased gradually if necessary to max. 300 mg daily (over 150 mg in divided doses); usual maintenance dose 100 mg daily; CHILD and ADOLESCENT under 18 years not recommended
- Obsessive-compulsive disorder, initially 50 mg in the evening increased gradually if necessary after some weeks to max. 300 mg daily (over 150 mg in divided doses); usual maintenance dose 100–300 mg daily; CHILD over 8 years initially 25 mg daily increased if necessary in steps of 25 mg every 4–7 days to max. 200 mg daily (over 50 mg in divided doses)

**Note** If no improvement in obsessive-compulsive disorder within 10 weeks, treatment should be reconsidered

**Fluvoxamine** (Non-proprietary) PoM

Tablets, fluvoxamine maleate 50 mg, net price 60-tab pack = £9.17; 100 mg, 30-tab pack = £9.65. Counselling, driving

**Faverin®** (Solvay) PoM

Tablets, f/c, scored, fluvoxamine maleate 50 mg, net price 60-tab pack = £17.10; 100 mg, 30-tab pack = £17.10. Counselling, driving

## PAROXETINE

**Indications** major depression, obsessive-compulsive disorder, panic disorder; social phobia; post-traumatic stress disorder; generalised anxiety disorder

**Cautions** see notes above

CSM advice Extrapyramidal reactions (including orofacial dystonias) and withdrawal syndrome are reported to the CSM more commonly with paroxetine than with other SSRIs

**Contra-indications** see notes above

**Side-effects** see notes above; also yawning; *less commonly* arrhythmias, transient changes in blood pressure, confusion; *rarely* panic attacks and paradoxical increased anxiety during initial treatment of panic disorder (reduce dose), depersonalisation, and neuroleptic malignant syndrome-like event; *very rarely* peripheral oedema, acute glaucoma, hepatic disorders (e.g. hepatitis)

**Dose**

- Major depression, social anxiety disorder, post-traumatic stress disorder, generalised anxiety disorder, usually 20 mg each morning, higher doses on specialist advice only (see also CSM advice, below); max. 50 mg daily (ELDERLY 40 mg daily); CHILD and ADOLESCENT under 18 years not recommended (see CSM advice, p. 202)
- Obsessive compulsive disorder, initially 20 mg each morning, increased gradually in steps of 10 mg to usual dose of 40 mg daily, higher doses on specialist advice only (see also CSM advice, below); max. 60 mg daily (ELDERLY 40 mg daily); CHILD and ADOLESCENT under 18 years not recommended
- Panic disorder, initially 10 mg each morning, increased gradually in steps of 10 mg to usual dose of 40 mg daily, higher doses on specialist advice only (see also CSM advice, below); max. 60 mg daily (ELDERLY 40 mg daily); CHILD and ADOLESCENT under 18 years not recommended

CSM advice The recommended dose for the treatment of depression, social anxiety disorder, generalised anxiety disorder, and post-traumatic stress disorder is 20 mg daily and for obsessive-compulsive disorder and panic disorder it is 40 mg daily. There is no evidence that higher doses are more effective.

**Paroxetine** (Non-proprietary) PoM

Tablets, paroxetine (as hydrochloride) 20 mg, net price 30-tab pack = £6.96, 30 mg, 30-tab pack = £35.53. Label: 21, counselling, driving

**Seroxat®** (GSK) PoM

Tablets, both f/c, scored, paroxetine (as hydrochloride) 20 mg, net price 30-tab pack = £13.21; 30 mg (blue), 30-tab pack = £23.18. Label: 21, counselling, driving

Liquid, orange, sugar-free, paroxetine (as hydrochloride) 10 mg/5 mL. Net price 150-mL pack = £9.49. Label: 21, counselling, driving

## SERTRALINE

**Indications** depressive illness, obsessive-compulsive disorder (under specialist supervision in children), post-traumatic stress disorder in women

**Cautions** see notes above

**Contra-indications** see notes above

**Side-effects** see notes above; tachycardia, postural hypotension, confusion, amnesia, aggressive behaviour, psychosis, pancreatitis, hepatitis, jaundice, liver failure, menstrual irregularities, paraesthesia; thrombocytopenia also reported (causal relationship not established)

**Dose**

- Depressive illness, initially 50 mg daily, increased if necessary by increments of 50 mg over several weeks to max. 200 mg daily; usual maintenance dose 50 mg daily; CHILD and ADOLESCENT under 18 years not recommended (see CSM advice, p. 202)
- Obsessive-compulsive disorder, ADULT and ADOLESCENT over 13 years initially 50 mg daily, increased if necessary in steps of 50 mg over several weeks; usual dose range 50–200 mg daily; CHILD 6–12 years initially 25 mg daily, increased to 50 mg daily after 1 week, further increased if necessary in steps of 50 mg at intervals of at least 1 week (max. 200 mg daily); CHILD under 6 years not recommended
- Post-traumatic stress disorder, initially 25 mg daily, increased after 1 week to 50 mg daily; if response is partial and if drug tolerated, dose increased in steps of 50 mg over several weeks to max. 200 mg daily; CHILD and ADOLESCENT under 18 years not recommended

**Sertraline** (Non-proprietary) PoM

Tablets, sertraline (as hydrochloride) 50 mg, net price 28-tab pack = £17.82; 100 mg, 28-tab pack = £29.16. Counselling, driving

**Lustral®** (Pfizer) PoM

Tablets, both f/c, sertraline (as hydrochloride) 50 mg (scored), net price 28-tab pack = £17.82; 100 mg, 28-tab pack = £29.16. Counselling, driving

## 4.3.4 Other antidepressant drugs

**Duloxetine** inhibits the re-uptake of both serotonin and noradrenaline and is licensed to treat major depressive disorder.

The thioxanthene **flupentixol** (*Fluanxol®*) has antidepressant properties, and low doses (1 to 3 mg daily) are given by mouth for this purpose. Flupentixol is also used for the treatment of psychoses (section 4.2.1 and section 4.2.2)

**Mirtazapine**, a presynaptic $\alpha_2$-antagonist, increases central noradrenergic and serotonergic neurotransmission. It has few antimuscarinic effects, but causes sedation during initial treatment.

**Reboxetine**, a selective inhibitor of noradrenaline re-uptake, has been introduced for the treatment of depressive illness.

**Tryptophan** is licensed as adjunctive therapy for depression resistant to standard antidepressants; it has been associated with eosinophilia-myalgia syndrome. Tryptophan should be initiated under specialist supervision.

**Venlafaxine** is a serotonin and noradrenaline re-uptake inhibitor (SNRI); it lacks the sedative and antimuscarinic effects of the tricyclic antidepressants. The CSM has recommended that because of concerns about toxicity in overdose, treatment with venlafaxine should be initiated and maintained under specialist supervision only. The CSM has advised that venlafaxine should not be used in patients with heart disease, electrolyte imbalance and hypertension.

## DULOXETINE

**Indications** major depressive disorder; diabetic neuropathy; stress urinary incontinence (section 7.4.2)

**Cautions** see section 7.4.2; pregnancy (Appendix 4); **interactions:** Appendix 1 (duloxetine)

**Contra-indications** hepatic impairment; renal impairment (Appendix 3); breast-feeding (Appendix 5)

**Side-effects** see section 7.4.2

**Dose**

- Major depression and diabetic neuropathy, 60 mg once daily; CHILD and ADOLESCENT under 18 years not recommended

Note In diabetic neuropathy, discontinue if inadequate response after 2 months

**Cymbalta®** (Lilly) ▼ PoM

Capsules, duloxetine (as hydrochloride) 30 mg (white/blue), net price 28-cap pack = £22.40; 60 mg (green/blue), 28-cap pack = £27.72, 84-cap pack = £83.16. Label: 2

**Yentreve®** (Lilly) ▼ PoM

Section 7.4.2 (stress urinary incontinence)

## FLUPENTIXOL
(Flupenthixol)

**Indications** depressive illness; psychoses (section 4.2.1)

**Cautions** cardiovascular disease (including cardiac disorders and cerebral arteriosclerosis), senile confusional states, parkinsonism, hepatic impairment (Appendix 2), renal impairment (Appendix 3); avoid in excitable and overactive patients; porphyria (section 9.8.2); see also section 4.2.1; **interactions**: Appendix 1 (antipsychotics)

**Side-effects** restlessness, insomnia; hypomania reported; rarely dizziness, tremor, visual disturbances, headache, hyperprolactinaemia, extrapyramidal symptoms

**Dose**

- Initially 1 mg (elderly 500 micrograms) in the morning, increased after 1 week to 2 mg (elderly 1 mg) if necessary; max. 3 mg (elderly 2 mg) daily, doses above 2 mg (elderly 1 mg) being divided in 2 portions, second dose not after 4 p.m. Discontinue if no response after 1 week at max. dosage; CHILD and ADOLESCENT under 18 years not recommended

Counselling Although drowsiness may occur, can also have an alerting effect so should not be taken in the evening

**Fluanxol®** (Lundbeck) PoM

Tablets, both red, s/c, flupentixol (as dihydrochloride) 500 micrograms, net price 60-tab pack = £2.88; 1 mg, 60-tab pack = £4.86. Label: 2, counselling, administration

## MIRTAZAPINE

**Indications** major depression

**Cautions** epilepsy, cardiac disorders, hypotension, history of urinary retention, angle-closure glaucoma, diabetes mellitus, psychoses (may aggravate psychotic symptoms), history of bipolar depression; hepatic impairment; renal impairment; pregnancy (Appendix 4); breast-feeding (Appendix 5); **interactions:** Appendix 1 (mirtazapine)

Blood disorders Patients should be advised to report any fever, sore throat, stomatitis or other signs of infection during treatment. Blood count should be performed and the drug stopped immediately if blood dyscrasia suspected

Withdrawal Nausea, vomiting, dizziness, agitation, anxiety, and headache are most common features of withdrawal if treatment stopped abruptly or if dose reduced markedly; dose should be reduced over several weeks

**Side-effects** increased appetite and weight gain, oedema, sedation; *less commonly* dizziness, headache; *rarely* postural hypotension, abnormal dreams, mania, suicidal ideation, convulsions, tremor, myoclonus, paraesthesia, arthralgia, myalgia, akathisia, rash, and reversible agranulocytosis (see Cautions above)

**Dose**

- Initially 15 mg daily at bedtime increased within 2–4 weeks according to response; max. 45 mg daily as a single dose at bedtime or in 2 divided doses; CHILD and ADOLESCENT under 18 years not recommended (see CSM advice, p. 202)

**Mirtazapine** (Non-proprietary) PoM

Tablets, mirtazapine 15 mg, net price 28-tab pack = £17.49; 30 mg, 28-tab pack = £12.33; 45 mg, 28-tab pack = £17.49. Label: 2, 25

Oral solution, mirtazapine 15 mg/mL, net price 66 mL = £47.00. Label: 2

**Zispin SolTab®** (Organon) PoM

Orodispersible tablets, mirtazapine 15 mg, net price 6-tab pack = £3.84, 30-tab pack = £19.19; 30 mg, 30-tab pack = £19.19; 45 mg, 30-tab pack = £19.19. Label: 2, counselling, administration

Excipients include aspartame

Counselling *Zispin SolTab®* should be placed on the tongue, allowed to disperse and swallowed

## REBOXETINE

**Indications** depressive illness

**Cautions** history of cardiovascular disease and epilepsy; bipolar disorder; urinary retention; prostatic hypertrophy; glaucoma; hepatic impairment (Appendix 2); renal impairment (Appendix 3); **interactions:** Appendix 1 (reboxetine)

**Contra-indications** pregnancy (Appendix 4) and breast-feeding (Appendix 5)

**Side-effects** nausea, dry mouth, constipation, anorexia; tachycardia, palpitation, vasodilation, postural hypotension; headache, insomnia, dizziness; chills; impotence; urinary retention (mainly in men); impaired visual accommodation; sweating; lowering of plasma-potassium concentration on prolonged administration in the elderly; *also reported* vomiting, aggression, cold extremities, and rash

**Dose**

- 4 mg twice daily increased if necessary after 3–4 weeks to 10 mg daily in divided doses, max. 12 mg daily; CHILD and ELDERLY not recommended

**Edronax®** (Pharmacia) PoM

Tablets, scored, reboxetine (as mesilate) 4 mg. Net price 60-tab pack = £18.91. Counselling, driving

## TRYPTOPHAN
(L-Tryptophan)

**Indications** see notes above

**Cautions** eosinophilia-myalgia syndrome has been reported—close monitoring required (withhold treatment if increased eosinophil count, myalgia, arthralgia, fever, dyspnoea, neuropathy, oedema or skin lesions develop until possibility of eosinophilia-myalgia syndrome excluded); pregnancy and breast-feeding; **interactions**: Appendix 1 (tryptophan)

**Contra-indications** history of eosinophilia-myalgia syndrome following use of tryptophan

**Side-effects** drowsiness, nausea, headache, light-headedness; eosinophilia-myalgia syndrome, see Cautions

**Dose**

- 1 g 3 times daily; max. 6 g daily; ELDERLY lower dose may be appropriate especially where renal or hepatic impairment; CHILD not recommended

**Optimax®** (Merck) PoM
Tablets, scored, tryptophan 500 mg. Net price 84-tab pack = £19.56. Label: 3

## VENLAFAXINE

**Indications** moderate to severe depressive illness, generalised anxiety disorder (under specialist supervision, see CSM advice, p. 204)

**Cautions** ECG required before treatment, measure blood pressure before and periodically during treatment; history of epilepsy, angle-closure glaucoma; concomitant use of drugs that increase risk of bleeding, history of bleeding disorders; hepatic impairment (Appendix 2); renal impairment (Appendix 3); **interactions:** Appendix 1 (venlafaxine)

Driving May affect performance of skilled tasks (e.g. driving)

Withdrawal Gastro-intestinal disturbances, headache, anxiety, dizziness, paraesthesia, tremor, sleep disturbances, and sweating are most common features of withdrawal if treatment stopped abruptly or if dose reduced markedly; dose should be reduced over several weeks

**Contra-indications** see CSM advice, p. 202 and p. 204; heart disease, electrolyte disturbance, hypertension; severe hepatic or renal impairment; pregnancy (Appendix 4) and breast-feeding (Appendix 5)

**Side-effects** constipation, nausea; dizziness, dry mouth, insomnia, nervousness, drowsiness, asthenia, headache; sexual dysfunction; sweating; commonly anorexia, weight changes, diarrhoea, dyspepsia, vomiting, abdominal pain; hypertension, palpitation, vasodilatation, changes in serum cholesterol; chills, pyrexia, dyspnoea, yawning; abnormal dreams, agitation, anxiety, confusion, hypertonia, paraesthesia, tremor; urinary frequency, menstrual disturbances; arthralgia, myalgia; visual disturbances, mydriasis; tinnitus; pruritus, rash; *less commonly* apathy, bruxism, taste disturbances, hypotension and postural hypotension, arrhythmias, syndrome of inappropriate antidiuretic hormone secretion (see advice on Hyponatraemia, p. 195), hallucinations, myoclonus, urinary retention, bleeding disorders (including ecchymosis and rarely haemorrhage), alopecia, hypersensitivity reactions including angioedema, urticaria, photosensitivity; *rarely* prolonged QT interval, ataxia, incoordination, speech disorder, extrapyramidal effects, suicidal ideation, mania and hypomania, aggression, seizures, serotonin syndrome and neuroleptic malignant syndrome, increased prolactin concentration, blood dyscrasias, rhabdomyolysis, erythema multiforme, Stevens-Johnson syndrome; hepatitis and pancreatitis reported

**Dose**

- Depression, initially 75 mg daily in 2 divided doses increased if necessary after at least 3–4 weeks to 150 mg daily in 2 divided doses; severely depressed or hospitalised patients, increased further if necessary in steps of up to 75 mg every 2–3 days to max. 375 mg daily then gradually reduced; CHILD and ADOLESCENT under 18 years not recommended (see CSM advice, p. 202)
- Generalised anxiety disorder, see under preparations below

**Efexor®** (Wyeth) PoM
Tablets, all peach, venlafaxine (as hydrochloride) 37.5 mg, net price 56-tab pack = £23.41; 75 mg, 56-tab pack = £39.03. Label: 3, 21, counselling, driving

**Modified release**

**Efexor® XL** (Wyeth) PoM
Capsules, m/r, venlafaxine (as hydrochloride) 75 mg (peach), net price 28-cap pack = £23.41, 150 mg (orange), 28-cap pack = £39.03. Label: 3, 21, 25, counselling, driving

Dose depression, 75 mg daily as a single dose, increased if necessary after at least 2 weeks to 150 mg once daily; max. 225 mg once daily; ADOLESCENT and CHILD under 18 years not recommended (see CSM advice, p. 202)

Generalised anxiety disorder, 75 mg daily as a single dose; discontinue if no response after 8 weeks; ADOLESCENT and CHILD under 18 years not recommended

# 4.4 CNS stimulants and other drugs used for attention deficit hyperactivity disorder

Central nervous system stimulants include the **amphetamines** (notably dexamfetamine) **and related drugs** (e.g. methylphenidate). They have very few indications and in particular, should **not** be used to treat depression, obesity, senility, debility, or for relief of fatigue.

**Caffeine** is a weak stimulant present in tea and coffee. It is included in many analgesic preparations (section 4.7.1) but does not contribute to their analgesic or anti-inflammatory effect. Over-indulgence may lead to a state of anxiety.

The **amphetamines** have a limited field of usefulness and their use should be **discouraged** as they may cause dependence and psychotic states. They have **no place** in the management of **depression** or **obesity**.

Patients with *narcolepsy* may derive benefit from treatment with dexamfetamine.

**Methylphenidate** is used for the management of *attention deficit hyperactivity disorder* (ADHD) in children and adolescents as part of a comprehensive treatment programme. Growth is not generally affected but it is advisable to monitor growth during treatment. **Dexamfetamine** (dexamphetamine) is an alternative in children who do not respond to other drugs. **Atomoxetine**

is licensed for the management of attention deficit hyperactivity disorder in children. Drug treatment of attention deficit hyperactivity disorder should be initiated by a specialist in ADHD but may be continued by general practitioners, under a shared-care arrangement.

**Modafinil** is used for the treatment of daytime sleepiness associated with narcolepsy or obstructive sleep apnoea syndrome; dependence with long-term use cannot be excluded and it should therefore be used with caution.

## ATOMOXETINE

**Indications** attention deficit hyperactivity disorder (initiated by a specialist physician experienced in managing the condition)

**Cautions** cardiovascular disease including hypertension, tachycardia, and postural hypotension; monitor growth in children; hepatic impairment (see Hepatic Disorders below; Appendix 2); pregnancy (Appendix 4); breast-feeding (Appendix 5); **interactions:** Appendix 1 (atomoxetine)

**Hepatic disorders** Following rare reports of hepatic disorders, the CSM has advised that patients and carers should be advised of the risk and be told how to recognise symptoms; prompt medical attention should be sought in case of abdominal pain, unexplained nausea, malaise, darkening of the urine or jaundice

**Suicidal ideation** Following reports of suicidal thoughts and behaviour, the CSM has advised that patients and their carers should be informed about the risk and told to report clinical worsening, suicidal thoughts or behaviour, irritability, agitation, or depression

**Contra-indications** angle-closure glaucoma

**Side-effects** anorexia, dry mouth, nausea, vomiting, abdominal pain, constipation, dyspepsia, flatulence; palpitation, tachycardia, increased blood pressure, postural hypotension, hot flushes; sleep disturbance, dizziness, headache, fatigue, lethargy, depression, anxiety, irritability, tremor, rigors; urinary retention, enuresis, prostatitis, sexual dysfunction, menstrual disturbances; mydriasis, conjunctivitis; dermatitis, pruritus, rash, sweating, weight changes; *less commonly* cold extremities; *very rarely* hepatic disorders (see Hepatic Disorders above) and suicidal ideation

**Dose**

- ADOLESCENT body-weight over 70 kg, initially 40 mg daily for 7 days then increased according to response to usual maintenance dose 80 mg daily; max. 100 mg daily; CHILD over 6 years and ADOLESCENT body-weight up to 70 kg, initially 500 micrograms/kg daily for 7 days then increased according to response to usual maintenance dose 1.2 mg/kg daily

**Note** Total daily dose may be given *either* as a single dose in the morning *or* in 2 divided doses with last dose no later than early evening

**Strattera®** (Lilly) ▼ PoM

Capsules, atomoxetine (as hydrochloride) 10 mg (white), net price 7-cap pack = £13.65, 28-cap pack = £54.60; 18 mg (gold/white), 7-cap pack = £13.65, 28-cap pack = £54.60; 25 mg (blue/white), 7-cap pack = £13.65, 28-cap pack = £54.60; 40 mg (blue), 7-cap pack = £13.65, 28-cap pack = £54.60; 60 mg (blue/gold), 28-cap pack = £54.60. Label: 3

## DEXAMFETAMINE SULPHATE
(Dexamphetamine sulphate)

**Indications** narcolepsy, adjunct in the management of refractory hyperkinetic states in children (under specialist supervision)

**Cautions** mild hypertension (contra-indicated if moderate or severe)—monitor blood pressure; history of epilepsy (discontinue if convulsions occur); tics and Tourette syndrome (use with caution)—discontinue if tics occur; monitor growth in children (see also below); avoid abrupt withdrawal; data on safety and efficacy of long-term use not complete; porphyria (see section 9.8.2); **interactions:** Appendix 1 (sympathomimetics)

**Special cautions in children** Monitor height and weight as growth retardation may occur during prolonged therapy (drug free periods may allow catch-up in growth but withdraw slowly to avoid inducing depression or renewed hyperactivity). In psychotic children may exacerbate behavioural disturbances and thought disorder

**Driving** May affect performance of skilled tasks (e.g. driving); effects of alcohol unpredictable

**Contra-indications** cardiovascular disease including moderate to severe hypertension, hyperexcitability or agitated states, hyperthyroidism, history of drug or alcohol abuse, glaucoma, pregnancy (Appendix 4) and breast-feeding (Appendix 5)

**Side-effects** insomnia, restlessness, irritability and excitability, nervousness, night terrors, euphoria, tremor, dizziness, headache; convulsions (see also Cautions); dependence and tolerance, sometimes psychosis; anorexia, gastro-intestinal symptoms, growth retardation in children (see also under Cautions); dry mouth, sweating, tachycardia (and anginal pain), palpitation, increased blood pressure; visual disturbances; cardiomyopathy reported with chronic use; central stimulants have provoked choreoathetoid movements, tics and Tourette syndrome in predisposed individuals (see also Cautions above); **overdosage:** see Emergency Treatment of Poisoning, p. 33

**Dose**

- Narcolepsy, 10 mg (ELDERLY, 5 mg) daily in divided doses increased by 10 mg (ELDERLY, 5 mg) daily at intervals of 1 week to a max. of 60 mg daily
- Hyperkinesia, CHILD over 6 years 5–10 mg daily, increased if necessary by 5 mg at intervals of 1 week to usual max. 20 mg daily (older children have received max. 40 mg daily)

**Dexedrine®** (Celltech) CD

Tablets, scored, dexamfetamine sulphate 5 mg. Net price 28-tab pack = £3.00. Counselling, driving

## METHYLPHENIDATE HYDROCHLORIDE

**Indications** part of a comprehensive treatment programme for attention-deficit hyperactivity disorder when remedial measures alone prove insufficient (under specialist supervision)

**Cautions** monitor growth (if prolonged treatment), blood pressure and full blood count; history of drug or alcohol dependence; psychosis; epilepsy (discontinue if increased seizure frequency); avoid abrupt withdrawal; pregnancy (Appendix 4); **interactions:** Appendix 1 (sympathomimetics)

**Contra-indications** anxiety or agitation; tics or a family history of Tourette syndrome; hyperthyroidism, severe angina, cardiac arrhythmias, glaucoma; breast-feeding (Appendix 5)

**Side-effects** abdominal pain, nausea, vomiting, dry mouth; tachycardia, palpitation, arrhythmias, changes in blood pressure; insomnia, nervousness, anorexia, headache, drowsiness, dizziness, movement disorders; arthralgia; rash, pruritus, alopecia; *rarely* cerebral arteritis, angina, hyperactivity, convulsions, psychosis, tics including Tourette syndrome, neuroleptic malignant syndrome, tolerance and dependence, growth retardation, reduced weight gain, blood disorders including leucopenia and thrombocytopenia, muscle cramps, visual disturbances, exfoliative dermatitis, erythema multiforme

**Dose**

- CHILD over 6 years, initially 5 mg 1–2 times daily, increased if necessary at weekly intervals by 5–10 mg daily to max. 60 mg daily in divided doses; discontinue if no response after 1 month, also suspend periodically to assess child's condition (usually finally discontinued during or after puberty)

Evening dose If effect wears off in evening (with rebound hyperactivity) a dose at bedtime may be appropriate (establish need with trial bedtime dose)

**Methylphenidate Hydrochloride** (Non-proprietary) CD

Tablets, methylphenidate hydrochloride 5 mg, net price 30-tab pack = £2.78; 10 mg, 30-tab pack = £5.17; 20 mg, 30-tab pack = £9.98

Brands include *Equasym®*

**Ritalin®** (Novartis) CD

Tablets, scored, methylphenidate hydrochloride 10 mg, net price 30-tab pack = £5.57

### Modified release

**Concerta® XL** (Janssen-Cilag) ▼ CD

Tablets, m/r, methylphenidate hydrochloride 18 mg (yellow), net price 30-tab pack = £27.00; 36 mg (white), 30-tab pack = £36.75. Label: 25

Counselling Tablet membrane may pass through gastro-intestinal tract unchanged

Cautions dose form not appropriate for use in dysphagia or where gastro-intestinal lumen restricted

Dose CHILD over 6 years, initially 18 mg once daily (in the morning), increased if necessary in weekly steps of 18 mg according to response, max. 54 mg once daily; discontinue if no response after 1 month; suspend periodically to assess condition (usually finally discontinued during or after puberty)

Note Total daily dose of 15 mg of standard-release formulation is considered equivalent to *Concerta® XL* 18 mg once daily

**Equasym XL®** (UCB Pharma) CD

Capsules, m/r, methylphenidate hydrochloride 10 mg (white/green), net price 30-cap pack = £25.00; 20 mg (white/blue), 30-cap pack = £30.00; 30 mg (white/brown), 30-cap pack = £35.00. Label: 25

Dose CHILD over 6 years, initially 10 mg once daily in the morning before breakfast, increased gradually if necessary to max. 60 mg daily; discontinue if no response after 1 month; suspend periodically to assess condition (usually finally discontinued during or after puberty)

## MODAFINIL

**Indications** daytime sleepiness associated with chronic pathological conditions including narcolepsy, obstructive sleep apnoea syndrome, and chronic shift work

**Cautions** hepatic impairment (Appendix 2); renal impairment (Appendix 3); monitor blood pressure and heart rate in hypertensive patients (but see below); possibility of dependence; **interactions:** Appendix 1 (modafinil)

**Contra-indications** pregnancy (Appendix 4) and breast-feeding (Appendix 5); moderate to severe hypertension; history of left ventricular hypertrophy, cor pulmonale, or of clinically significant signs of CNS stimulant-induced mitral valve prolapse (including ischaemic ECG changes, chest pain and arrhythmias)

**Side-effects** dry mouth, appetite changes, gastro-intestinal disturbances (including nausea, diarrhoea, constipation, and dyspepsia), abdominal pain; tachycardia, vasodilation, chest pain, dyspnoea; headache (uncommonly migraine), anxiety, insomnia, dizziness, depression, confusion, abnormal thinking, paraesthesia, incoordination, hypertonia, asthenia; visual disturbances; less commonly, mouth ulcers, dysphagia, taste disturbances; hypertension, hypotension, arrhythmia, peripheral oedema, hypercholesterolaemia; rhinitis; dyskinesia, amnesia, emotional lability, abnormal dreams, agitation, tremor, vertigo, decreased libido, weight changes, hyperglycaemia; urinary frequency, myasthenia, muscle cramps, menstrual disturbances; eosinophilia, leucopenia; glossitis, pharyngitis, sinusitis, epistaxis; myalgia, arthralgia; acne, sweating, rash, pruritus, dry eye

**Dose**

- Narcolepsy and obstructive sleep apnoea syndrome, initially 200 mg daily, *either* in 2 divided doses morning and at noon *or* as a single dose in the morning, dose adjusted according to response to 200–400 mg daily in 2 divided doses or as a single dose; ELDERLY initiate at 100 mg daily; CHILD not recommended
- Chronic shift work sleep disorder, 200 mg taken 1 hour before the start of the work shift

**Provigil®** (Cephalon) ▼ PoM

Tablets, modafinil 100 mg, net price 30-tab pack = £60.00; 200 mg, 30 tab-pack = £120.00

## Cocaine

**Cocaine** is a drug of addiction which causes central nervous stimulation. Its clinical use is mainly as a topical local anaesthetic (section 15.2). It has been included in analgesic elixirs for the relief of pain in palliative care but this use is obsolete. For management of cocaine poisoning, see p. 33.

# 4.5 Drugs used in the treatment of obesity

4.5.1 Anti-obesity drugs acting on the gastro-intestinal tract
4.5.2 Centrally acting appetite suppressants

Obesity is associated with many health problems including cardiovascular disease, diabetes mellitus, gallstones and osteoarthritis. Factors that aggravate obesity may include depression, other psychosocial problems, and some drugs.

The main treatment of the obese individual is a suitable diet, carefully explained to the individual, with appropriate support and encouragement; the individual should also be advised to increase physical activity. Smoking cessation (while maintaining body weight) may be worthwhile before attempting supervised weight loss since cigarette smoking may be more harmful than obesity. Attendance at groups (e.g. 'weight-watchers') helps some individuals.

Severe obesity should be managed in an appropriate setting by staff who have been trained in the management of obesity; the individual should receive advice on diet and lifestyle modification and be monitored for changes in weight as well as in blood pressure, blood lipids and other associated conditions.

An anti-obesity drug should be considered only for those with a body mass index (BMI, individual's body-weight divided by the square of the individual's height) of 30 kg/m$^2$ or greater in whom at least 3 months of managed care involving supervised diet, exercise and behaviour modification fails to achieve a realistic reduction in weight. In the presence of risk factors (such as diabetes, coronary heart disease, hypertension, and obstructive sleep apnoea), it may be appropriate to prescribe a drug to individuals with a BMI of 27 kg/m$^2$ or greater, provided that such use is permitted by the drug's marketing authorisation. Drugs should **never** be used as the sole element of treatment. The individual should be monitored on a regular basis; drug treatment should be discontinued if weight loss is less than 5% after the first 12 weeks or if the individual regains weight at any time whilst receiving drug treatment.

Drugs specifically licensed for the treatment of obesity are **orlistat** (section 4.5.1) and **sibutramine** (section 4.5.2). There is little evidence to guide selection between the two drugs, but it may be appropriate to choose orlistat for those who have a high intake of fats whereas sibutramine may be chosen for those who cannot control their eating; the cautions, contra-indications and side-effects of the two drugs should also be considered.

Combination therapy involving more than one anti-obesity drug is **contra-indicated** until further information about efficacy and long-term safety is available.

Thyroid hormones have **no** place in the treatment of obesity except in biochemically proven hypothyroid patients. The use of diuretics, chorionic gonadotrophin, or amphetamines is **not** appropriate for weight reduction.

## 4.5.1 Anti-obesity drugs acting on the gastro-intestinal tract

**Orlistat**, a lipase inhibitor, reduces the absorption of dietary fat. It is used in conjunction with a mildly hypocaloric diet in individuals with a body mass index (BMI) of 30 kg/m$^2$ or more *or* in individuals with a BMI of 28 kg/m$^2$ in the presence of other risk factors such as type 2 diabetes, hypertension, or hypercholesterolaemia.

Orlistat should be used in conjunction with other measures to manage obesity (section 4.5). NICE has recommended (March 2001) that treatment with orlistat should be continued beyond 6 months only if at least 10% weight has been lost since the start of treatment.

Some of the weight loss in those taking orlistat probably results from individuals reducing their fat intake to avoid severe gastro-intestinal effects including steatorrhoea. Vitamin supplementation (especially of vitamin D) may be considered if there is concern about deficiency of fat-soluble vitamins. On stopping orlistat, there may be a gradual reversal of weight loss.

The most commonly used bulk-forming drug is **methylcellulose** (section 1.6.1). It is claimed to reduce intake by producing a feeling of satiety but there is little evidence to support its use in the management of obesity.

### ORLISTAT

**Indications** adjunct in obesity (see notes above)

**Cautions** diabetes mellitus; may impair absorption of fat-soluble vitamins; pregnancy (Appendix 4); **interactions:** Appendix 1 (orlistat)

**Multivitamins** If a multivitamin supplement is required, it should be taken at least 2 hours after orlistat dose or at bedtime

**Contra-indications** chronic malabsorption syndrome; cholestasis; breast-feeding (Appendix 5)

**Side-effects** oily leakage from rectum, flatulence, faecal urgency, liquid or oily stools, faecal incontinence, abdominal distension and pain (gastro-intestinal effects minimised by reduced fat intake), tooth and gingival disorders; respiratory infections; anxiety, headache; menstrual disturbances, urinary-tract infection; fatigue; *very rarely* diverticulitis, cholelithiasis, hepatitis, and bullous eruptions

**Dose**

- 120 mg taken immediately before, during, or up to 1 hour after each main meal (up to max. 360 mg daily); continue treatment beyond 12 weeks only if weight loss since start of treatment exceeds 5% (see also notes above); CHILD not recommended

**Note** If a meal is missed or contains no fat, the dose of orlistat should be omitted

**Xenical®** (Roche) PoM
Capsules, turquoise, orlistat 120 mg, net price 84-cap pack = £39.51

## 4.5.2 Centrally acting appetite suppressants

**Sibutramine** inhibits the re-uptake of noradrenaline and serotonin. It is used in the adjunctive management of obesity in individuals with a body mass index (BMI) of 30 kg/m$^2$ or more (and no associated co-morbidity) or in individuals with a BMI of 27 kg/m$^2$ or more in the presence of other risk factors such as type 2 diabetes or hypercholesterolaemia. Sibutramine is not licensed for use longer than 1 year; on stopping it, there may be a reversal of weight loss.

Dexfenfluramine, fenfluramine, and phentermine have been associated with valvular heart disease and the rare but serious risk of pulmonary hypertension.

NICE guidance (sibutramine)
NICE has recommended that sibutramine should be prescribed in accordance with the summary of product characteristics and under the following conditions:

- it should be prescribed only for individuals who have attempted seriously to lose weight by diet, exercise, and other behavioural modification;
- arrangements should exist for appropriate healthcare professionals to offer specific advice, support, and counselling on diet, physical activity, and behavioural strategies to those receiving sibutramine.

## SIBUTRAMINE HYDROCHLORIDE

**Indications** adjunct in obesity (see notes above)

**Cautions** monitor blood pressure and pulse rate (every 2 weeks for first 3 months *then* monthly for 3 months *then* at least every 3 months)—discontinue if blood pressure exceeds 145/90 mmHg or if systolic or diastolic pressure raised by more than 10 mmHg or if pulse rate raised by 10 beats per minute at 2 consecutive visits; sleep apnoea syndrome (increased risk of hypertension); epilepsy; hepatic impairment (avoid if severe; Appendix 2); renal impairment (avoid if severe; Appendix 3); open angle glaucoma, history of ocular hypertension; monitor for pulmonary hypertension; family history of motor or vocal tics, history of depression; predisposition to bleeding, concomitant use of drugs that increase risk of bleeding; **interactions:** Appendix 1 (sibutramine)

Discontinuation of treatment Discontinue treatment if:

- weight loss after 3 months less than 5% of initial body-weight;
- weight loss stabilises at less than 5% of initial body-weight;
- individuals regain 3 kg or more after previous weight loss

In individuals with co-morbid conditions, treatment should be continued only if weight loss is associated with other clinical benefits

**Contra-indications** history of major eating disorders; psychiatric illness, Tourette syndrome; history of coronary artery disease, congestive heart failure, tachycardia, peripheral arterial occlusive disease, arrhythmias, and of cerebrovascular disease; uncontrolled hypertension; hyperthyroidism; prostatic hypertrophy; phaeochromocytoma; angle closure glaucoma; history of drug or alcohol abuse; pregnancy (Appendix 4); breast-feeding (Appendix 5)

**Side-effects** constipation, dry mouth, nausea, taste disturbances, diarrhoea, vomiting; tachycardia, palpitations, hypertension, flushing, insomnia, lightheadedness, paraesthesia, headache, anxiety, depression, seizures; sexual dysfunction, menstrual disturbances, urinary retention; thrombocytopenia; blurred vision, sweating, hypersensitivity reactions including Henoch-Shönlein purpura, rash, urticaria, angioedema and anaphylaxis; interstitial nephritis, glomerulonephritis

**Dose**

- Initially 10 mg daily in the morning, increased if weight loss less than 2 kg after 4 weeks to 15 mg daily; discontinue if weight loss less than 2 kg after 4 weeks at higher dose (see also Discontinuation of Treatment above); max. period of treatment 1 year; CHILD, ADOLESCENT under 18 years, and ELDERLY over 65 years not recommended

**Reductil®** (Abbott) PoM
Capsules, sibutramine hydrochloride 10 mg (blue/yellow), net price 28-cap pack = £41.29; 15 mg (blue/white), 28-cap pack = £45.14

# 4.6 Drugs used in nausea and vertigo

Anti-emetics should be prescribed only when the cause of vomiting is known because otherwise they may delay diagnosis, particularly in children. Anti-emetics are unnecessary and sometimes harmful when the cause can be treated, such as in diabetic ketoacidosis, or in digoxin or antiepileptic overdose.

If anti-emetic drug treatment is indicated, the drug is chosen according to the aetiology of vomiting.

**Antihistamines** are effective against nausea and vomiting resulting from many underlying conditions. There is no evidence that any one antihistamine is superior to another but their duration of action and incidence of adverse effects (drowsiness and antimuscarinic effects) differ.

The **phenothiazines** are dopamine antagonists and act centrally by blocking the chemoreceptor trigger zone. They are of considerable value for the prophylaxis and treatment of nausea and vomiting associated with diffuse neoplastic disease, radiation sickness, and the emesis caused by drugs such as opioids, general anaesthetics, and cytotoxics. **Prochlorperazine**, **perphenazine**, and **trifluoperazine** are less sedating than **chlorpromazine**; severe dystonic reactions sometimes occur with phenothiazines, especially in children. Other antipsychotic drugs including **haloperidol** and **levomepromazine (methotrimeprazine)** (section 4.2.1) are also used for the relief of nausea. Some phenothiazines are available as rectal suppositories, which can be useful in patients with persistent vomiting or with severe nausea; prochlorperazine can also be administered as a buccal tablet which is placed between the upper lip and the gum.

**Metoclopramide** is an effective anti-emetic and its activity closely resembles that of the phenothiazines. Metoclopramide also acts directly on the gastro-intestinal tract and it may be superior to the phenothiazines for emesis associated with gastroduodenal, hepatic, and biliary disease. In postoperative nausea and vomiting, metoclopramide in a dose of 10 mg has limited efficacy. High-dose metoclopramide injection is now less commonly used for cytotoxic-induced nausea and vomiting. As with the phenothiazines, metoclopramide can induce acute dystonic reactions involving facial and skeletal muscle spasms and oculogyric crises. These dystonic effects are more common in the young (especially girls and young women) and the very old; they usually occur shortly after starting treatment with metoclopramide and subside within 24 hours of stopping it. Injection of an antiparkinsonian drug such as procyclidine (section 4.9.2) will abort dystonic attacks.

**Domperidone** acts at the chemoreceptor trigger zone; it is used for the relief of nausea and vomiting, especially when associated with cytotoxic therapy. It has the advantage over metoclopramide and the phenothiazines of being less likely to cause central effects such as sedation and dystonic reactions because it does not readily cross the blood-brain barrier. In Parkinson's disease, it is used to prevent nausea and vomiting during treatment with apomorphine and also to treat nausea caused by other dopaminergic drugs (section 4.9.1). Domperidone is also used to treat vomiting due to emergency hormonal contraception (section 7.3.1).

**Dolasetron**, **granisetron**, **ondansetron**, and **tropisetron** are specific $5HT_3$ antagonists which block $5HT_3$ receptors in the gastro-intestinal tract and in the CNS. They are of value in the management of nausea and vomiting in patients receiving cytotoxics and in postoperative nausea and vomiting. **Palonosetron** is licensed for prevention of nausea and vomiting associated with moderately or highly emetogenic cytotoxic chemotherapy.

**Dexamethasone** (section 6.3.2) has anti-emetic effects and it is used in vomiting associated with cancer chemotherapy. It can be used alone or with metoclopramide, prochlorperazine, lorazepam, or a $5HT_3$ antagonist (see also section 8.1).

**Aprepitant**, a neurokinin 1 receptor antagonist, is licensed for the prevention of acute and delayed nausea and vomiting associated with cisplatin-based cytotoxic chemotherapy; it is given with dexamethasone and a $5HT_3$ antagonist.

**Nabilone** is a synthetic cannabinoid with anti-emetic properties. It may be used for nausea and vomiting caused by cytotoxic chemotherapy that is unresponsive to conventional anti-emetics. Side-effects such as drowsiness and dizziness occur frequently with standard doses.

## Vomiting of pregnancy

Nausea in the first trimester of pregnancy is generally mild and does not require drug therapy. On rare occasions if vomiting is severe, short-term treatment with an antihistamine, such as **promethazine**, may be required. **Prochlorperazine** or **metoclopramide** may be considered as second-line treatments. If symptoms do not settle in 24 to 48 hours then specialist opinion should be sought. Hyperemesis gravidarum is a more serious condition, which requires intravenous fluid and electrolyte replacement and sometimes nutritional support. Supplementation with thiamine must be considered in order to reduce the risk of Wernicke's encephalopathy.

## Postoperative nausea and vomiting

The incidence of postoperative nausea and vomiting depends on many factors including the anaesthetic used, the type and duration of surgery, and the patient's sex. The aim is to prevent postoperative nausea and vomiting from occurring. Drugs used include some **phenothiazines** (e.g. prochlorperazine), **metoclopramide** (but 10-mg dose has limited efficacy and higher parenteral doses associated with greater side-effects), **$5HT_3$ antagonists**, **antihistamines** (such as cyclizine), and **dexamethasone**. A combination of two anti-emetic drugs acting at different sites may be needed in resistant postoperative nausea and vomiting.

## Motion sickness

Anti-emetics should be given to prevent motion sickness rather than after nausea or vomiting develop. The most effective drug for the prevention of motion sickness is **hyoscine**. A transdermal hyoscine patch provides prolonged activity but it needs to be applied several hours before travelling. The sedating antihistamines are slightly less effective against motion sickness, but are generally better tolerated than hyoscine. If a sedative effect is desired **promethazine** is useful, but generally a slightly less sedating antihistamine such as **cyclizine** or **cinnarizine** is preferred. The $5HT_3$ antagonists, domperidone, metoclopramide, and the phenothiazines (except the antihistamine phenothiazine promethazine) are **ineffective** in motion sickness.

## Other vestibular disorders

Management of vestibular diseases is aimed at treating the underlying cause as well as treating symptoms of the balance disturbance and associated nausea and vomiting. Vertigo and nausea associated with Ménière's disease and middle-ear surgery can be difficult to treat.

**Betahistine** is an analogue of histamine and is claimed to reduce endolymphatic pressure by improving the microcirculation. Betahistine is licensed for vertigo, tinnitus, and hearing loss associated with Ménière's disease.

A **diuretic** alone or combined with salt restriction may provide some benefit in vertigo associated with Ménière's disease. **Antihistamines** (such as cinnarizine), and **phenothiazines** (such as prochlorperazine) are effective for prophylaxis and treatment.

For advice to avoid the inappropriate prescribing of drugs (notably phenothiazines) for dizziness in the elderly, see Prescribing for the Elderly, p. 18

## Cytotoxic chemotherapy

For the management of nausea and vomiting induced by cytotoxic chemotherapy, see section 8.1.

## Palliative care

For the management of nausea and vomiting in palliative care, see p. 16 and p. 17

## Migraine

For the management of nausea and vomiting associated with migraine, see p. 235

## Antihistamines

### CINNARIZINE

**Indications** vestibular disorders, such as vertigo, tinnitus, nausea, and vomiting in Ménière's disease; motion sickness; vascular disease (section 2.6.4)

**Cautions** see section 3.4.1; risk of hypotension with high doses

**Contra-indications** see section 3.4.1

**Side-effects** see section 3.4.1
**Dose**
- Vestibular disorders, 30 mg 3 times daily; CHILD 5–12 years half adult dose
- Motion sickness, 30 mg 2 hours before travel then 15 mg every 8 hours during journey if necessary; CHILD 5–12 years half adult dose

**Cinnarizine** (Non-proprietary)
Tablets, cinnarizine 15 mg. Net price 20 = £1.35. Label: 2
Brands include *Cinazière®*

**Stugeron®** (Janssen-Cilag)
Tablets, scored, cinnarizine 15 mg. Net price 20 = 71p. Label: 2

**Stugeron Forte®**
See section 2.6.4

## CYCLIZINE

**Indications** nausea, vomiting, vertigo, motion sickness, labyrinthine disorders
**Cautions** see section 3.4.1; severe heart failure; may counteract haemodynamic benefits of opioids; **interactions:** Appendix 1 (antihistamines)
**Contra-indications** see section 3.4.1
**Side-effects** see section 3.4.1
**Dose**
- By mouth, cyclizine hydrochloride 50 mg up to 3 times daily; CHILD 6–12 years 25 mg up to 3 times daily
- By intramuscular *or* intravenous injection, cyclizine lactate 50 mg 3 times daily

**Valoid®** (Amdipharm)
Tablets, scored, cyclizine hydrochloride 50 mg. Net price 20 = £1.44. Label: 2
Injection (PoM), cyclizine lactate 50 mg/mL. Net price 1-mL amp = 70p

## MECLOZINE HYDROCHLORIDE

**Indications** see under preparations
**Cautions** see section 3.4.1; **interactions:** Appendix 1 (antihistamines)
**Driving** Drowsiness may affect performance of skilled tasks (e.g. driving); effects of alcohol enhanced
**Contra-indications** see section 3.4.1
**Side-effects** see section 3.4.1

**Preparations**
A proprietary brand of meclozine hydrochloride tablets 12.5 mg (*Sea-legs®*) is on sale to the public for motion sickness

## PROMETHAZINE HYDROCHLORIDE

**Indications** nausea, vomiting, vertigo, labyrinthine disorders, motion sickness; other indications (section 3.4.1, section 4.1.1, section 15.1.4.1)
**Cautions** see section 3.4.1; also pregnancy (Appendix 4) and breast-feeding (Appendix 5)
**Contra-indications** see section 3.4.1
**Side-effects** see section 3.4.1 but more sedating; intramuscular injection may be painful
**Dose**
- Motion sickness prevention, 20–25 mg at bedtime on night before travel, repeat following morning if necessary; CHILD under 2 years not recommended, 2–5 years 5 mg at night and following morning if necessary, 5–10 years 10 mg at night and following morning if necessary

**Preparations**
Section 3.4.1

## PROMETHAZINE TEOCLATE

**Indications** nausea, vertigo, labyrinthine disorders, motion sickness (acts longer than the hydrochloride)
**Cautions** see section 3.4.1; also pregnancy (Appendix 4) and breast-feeding (Appendix 5)
**Contra-indications** see section 3.4.1
**Side-effects** see section 3.4.1
**Dose**
- 25–75 mg, max. 100 mg, daily; CHILD 5–10 years, 12.5–37.5 mg daily
- Motion sickness prevention, 25 mg at bedtime on night before travel *or* 25 mg 1–2 hours before travel; CHILD 5–10 years half adult dose
- Severe vomiting in pregnancy, 25 mg at bedtime, increased if necessary to max. 100 mg daily (but see also Vomiting of Pregnancy in notes above)

**Avomine®** (Manx)
Tablets, scored, promethazine teoclate 25 mg. Net price 10-tab pack = £1.13; 28-tab pack = £3.13. Label: 2

# Phenothiazines and related drugs

## CHLORPROMAZINE HYDROCHLORIDE

**Indications** nausea and vomiting of terminal illness (where other drugs have failed or are not available); other indications (section 4.2.1 and section 15.1.4.1)
**Cautions** see Chlorpromazine Hydrochloride, section 4.2.1
**Contra-indications** see Chlorpromazine Hydrochloride, section 4.2.1
**Side-effects** see Chlorpromazine Hydrochloride, section 4.2.1
**Dose**
- By mouth, 10–25 mg every 4–6 hours; CHILD 500 micrograms/kg every 4–6 hours (1–5 years max. 40 mg daily, 6–12 years max. 75 mg daily)
- By deep intramuscular injection initially 25 mg then 25–50 mg every 3–4 hours until vomiting stops; CHILD 500 micrograms/kg every 6–8 hours (1–5 years max. 40 mg daily, 6–12 years max. 75 mg daily)
- By rectum in suppositories, chlorpromazine 100 mg every 6–8 hours [unlicensed]

**Preparations**
Section 4.2.1

## PERPHENAZINE

**Indications** severe nausea, vomiting (see notes above); other indications (section 4.2.1)
**Cautions** see Perphenazine (section 4.2.1)
**Contra-indications** see Perphenazine (section 4.2.1)

**Side-effects** see Perphenazine (section 4.2.1); extrapyramidal symptoms particularly in young adults, elderly, and debilitated

**Dose**

- 4 mg 3 times daily, adjusted according to response; max. 24 mg daily (chemotherapy-induced); ELDERLY quarter to half adult dose; CHILD under 14 years not recommended

**Preparations**

Section 4.2.1

## PROCHLORPERAZINE

**Indications** severe nausea, vomiting, vertigo, labyrinthine disorders (see notes above); other indications section 4.2.1

**Cautions** see under Prochlorperazine (section 4.2.1); oral route only for children (avoid if under 10 kg); elderly (see notes above)

**Contra-indications** see under Prochlorperazine (section 4.2.1)

**Side-effects** see under Prochlorperazine (section 4.2.1); extrapyramidal symptoms, particularly in children, elderly, and debilitated

**Dose**

Note Doses are expressed as prochlorperazine maleate or mesilate; 1 mg prochlorperazine maleate ≡ 1 mg prochlorperazine mesilate

- By mouth, nausea and vomiting, acute attack, 20 mg initially then 10 mg after 2 hours; prevention 5–10 mg 2–3 times daily; CHILD (over 10 kg only) 250 micrograms/kg 2–3 times daily

  Labyrinthine disorders, 5 mg 3 times daily, gradually increased if necessary to 30 mg daily in divided doses, then reduced after several weeks to 5–10 mg daily; CHILD not recommended
- By deep intramuscular injection, nausea and vomiting, 12.5 mg when required followed if necessary after 6 hours by an oral dose, as above; CHILD not recommended
- By rectum in suppositories, nausea and vomiting, 25 mg followed if necessary after 6 hours by oral dose, as above; *or* due to migraine, 5 mg 3 times daily; CHILD not recommended

**Prochlorperazine** (Non-proprietary) PoM

Tablets, prochlorperazine maleate 5 mg, net price 20 = 98p. Label: 2

Brands include *Prozière®*

**Stemetil®** (Castlemead) PoM

Tablets, prochlorperazine maleate 5 mg (off-white), net price 84-tab pack = £6.18; 25 mg (scored), 56-tab pack = £10.91. Label: 2

Syrup, straw-coloured, prochlorperazine mesilate 5 mg/5 mL. Net price 100-mL pack = £3.48. Label: 2

Eff (= effervescent granules), sugar-free, prochlorperazine mesilate 5 mg/sachet. Net price 21-sachet pack = £6.46. Label: 2, 13

Excipients include aspartame (section 9.4.1)

Injection, prochlorperazine mesilate 12.5 mg/mL. Net price 1-mL amp = 54p

Suppositories, prochlorperazine maleate (as prochlorperazine), 5 mg, net price 10 = £8.74; 25 mg, 10 = £11.46. Label: 2

**Buccal preparation**

[1]**Buccastem®** (R&C) PoM

Tablets (buccal), pale yellow, prochlorperazine maleate 3 mg. Net price 5 × 10-tab pack = £5.75. Label: 2, counselling, administration, see under Dose below

Dose 1–2 tablets twice daily; tablets are placed high between upper lip and gum and left to dissolve; CHILD not recommended

1. Prochlorperazine maleate can be sold to the public for adults over 18 years (provided packs do not contain more than 24 mg) for the treatment of nausea and vomiting in previously diagnosed migraine only (max. daily dose 12 mg); a proprietary brand (*Buccastem® M*) is on sale to the public

## TRIFLUOPERAZINE

**Indications** severe nausea and vomiting (see notes above); other indications (section 4.2.1)

**Cautions** see section 4.2.1

**Contra-indications** see section 4.2.1

**Side-effects** see section 4.2.1; extrapyramidal symptoms, particularly in children, elderly, and debilitated

**Dose**

- 2–4 mg daily in divided doses *or* as a single dose of a modified-release preparation; max. 6 mg daily; CHILD 3–5 years up to 1 mg daily, 6–12 years up to 4 mg daily

**Preparations**

Section 4.2.1

# Domperidone and metoclopramide

## DOMPERIDONE

**Indications** nausea and vomiting, dyspepsia, gastro-oesophageal reflux

**Cautions** renal impairment (Appendix 3); pregnancy (Appendix 4) and breast-feeding (Appendix 5); not recommended for routine prophylaxis of post-operative vomiting or for chronic administration; **interactions:** Appendix 1 (domperidone)

**Contra-indications** prolactinoma, hepatic impairment; where increased gastro-intestinal motility harmful

**Side-effects** rarely gastro-intestinal disturbances (including cramps), raised prolactin concentration; extrapyramidal effects and rashes reported

**Dose**

- By mouth, ADULT and ADOLESCENT body-weight over 35 kg, 10–20 mg 3–4 times daily; max. 80 mg daily; CHILD body-weight up to 34 kg, 250–500 micrograms/kg 3–4 times daily; max. 2.4 mg/kg in 24 hours
- By rectum in suppositories, ADULT and ADOLESCENT body-weight over 35 kg, 60 mg twice daily; CHILD 15–34 kg, 30 mg twice daily; CHILD body-weight under 15 kg, not recommended

[1]**Domperidone** (Non-proprietary) PoM

Tablets, 10 mg (as maleate), net price 30-tab pack = £2.47; 100-tab pack = £4.55

1. Domperidone can be sold to the public (provided packs do not contain more than 200 mg) for the relief of postprandial symptoms of excessive fullness, nausea, epigastric bloating and belching occasionally accompanied by epigastric discomfort and heartburn (max. single dose 10 mg, max. daily dose 40 mg); a proprietary brand (*Motilium® 10*) is on sale to the public

**Motilium®** (Sanofi-Synthelabo) PoM

Tablets, f/c, domperidone 10 mg (as maleate). Net price 30-tab pack = £2.35; 100-tab pack = £7.84

Suspension, sugar-free, domperidone 5 mg/5 mL. Net price 200-mL pack = £1.80

Suppositories domperidone 30 mg. Net price 10 = £2.65

**Compound preparations (for migraine)**
section 4.7.4.1

## METOCLOPRAMIDE HYDROCHLORIDE

**Indications** adults, nausea and vomiting, particularly in gastro-intestinal disorders (section 1.2) and treatment with cytotoxics or radiotherapy; migraine (section 4.7.4.1)

**Patients under 20 years.** Use restricted to severe intractable vomiting of known cause, vomiting of radiotherapy and cytotoxics, aid to gastro-intestinal intubation, pre-medication; also, dose should be determined on the basis of body-weight

**Cautions** hepatic impairment (Appendix 2), renal impairment (Appendix 3); elderly, young adults, and children (measure dose accurately, preferably with a pipette); may mask underlying disorders such as cerebral irritation; epilepsy; pregnancy (Appendix 4); porphyria (section 9.8.2); **interactions**: Appendix 1 (metoclopramide)

**Contra-indications** gastro-intestinal obstruction, perforation or haemorrhage; 3–4 days after gastro-intestinal surgery; phaeochromocytoma; breast-feeding (Appendix 5)

**Side-effects** extrapyramidal effects (especially in children and young adults—see p. 210), hyperprolactinaemia, occasionally tardive dyskinesia on prolonged administration; also reported, drowsiness, restlessness, diarrhoea, depression, neuroleptic malignant syndrome, rashes, pruritus, oedema; cardiac conduction abnormalities reported following intravenous administration; rarely methaemoglobinaemia (more severe in G6PD deficiency)

**Dose**

- By mouth *or* by intramuscular injection *or* by intravenous injection over 1–2 minutes, nausea and vomiting, 10 mg (5 mg in young adults 15–19 years under 60 kg) 3 times daily; CHILD up to 1 year (up to 10 kg) 1 mg twice daily, 1–3 years (10–14 kg) 1 mg 2–3 times daily, 3–5 years (15–19 kg) 2 mg 2–3 times daily, 5–9 years (20–29 kg) 2.5 mg 3 times daily, 9–14 years (30 kg and over) 5 mg 3 times daily

  **Note** Daily dose of metoclopramide should not normally exceed 500 micrograms/kg, particularly for children and young adults (restricted use, see above)

  For diagnostic procedures, as a single dose 5–10 minutes before examination, 10–20 mg (10 mg in young adults 15–19 years); CHILD under 3 years 1 mg, 3–5 years 2 mg, 5–9 years 2.5 mg, 9–14 years 5 mg

**Metoclopramide** (Non-proprietary) PoM

Tablets, metoclopramide hydrochloride 10 mg, net price 28-tab pack = £1.36

Oral solution, metoclopramide hydrochloride 5 mg/5 mL, net price 100-mL pack = £2.55

**Note** Sugar-free versions are available and can be ordered by specifying 'sugar-free' on the prescription

Injection, metoclopramide hydrochloride 5 mg/mL, net price 2-mL amp = 26p

**Maxolon®** (Shire) PoM

Tablets, scored, metoclopramide hydrochloride 10 mg, net price 84-tab pack = £5.24

Syrup, sugar-free, metoclopramide hydrochloride 5 mg/5 mL. Net price 200-mL pack = £3.83

Paediatric liquid, sugar-free, metoclopramide hydrochloride 1 mg/mL. Net price 15-mL pack with pipette = £1.51. Counselling, use of pipette

Injection, metoclopramide hydrochloride 5 mg/mL. Net price 2-mL amp = 27p

**High-dose (with cytotoxic chemotherapy only)**

**Maxolon High Dose®** (Shire) PoM

Injection, metoclopramide hydrochloride 5 mg/mL. Net price 20-mL amp = £2.67.

For dilution and use as an intravenous infusion in nausea and vomiting associated with cytotoxic chemotherapy only

**Dose** by continuous intravenous infusion (preferred method), initially (before starting chemotherapy), 2–4 mg/kg over 15–20 minutes, then 3–5 mg/kg over 8–12 hours; max. in 24 hours, 10 mg/kg

By intermittent intravenous infusion, initially (before starting chemotherapy), up to 2 mg/kg over at least 15 minutes then up to 2 mg/kg over at least 15 minutes every 2 hours; max. in 24 hours, 10 mg/kg

**Modified-release preparations**

**Note** All unsuitable for patients under 20 years

**Gastrobid Continus®** (Napp) PoM

Tablets, m/r, metoclopramide hydrochloride 15 mg. Net price 56-tab pack = £7.75. Label: 25

**Dose** patients over 20 years, 1 tablet twice daily

**Maxolon SR®** (Shire) PoM

Capsules, m/r, clear, enclosing white granules, metoclopramide hydrochloride 15 mg. Net price 56-cap pack = £7.01. Label: 25

**Dose** patients over 20 years, 1 capsule twice daily

**Compound preparations (for migraine)**
Section 4.7.4.1

# $5HT_3$ antagonists

## DOLASETRON MESILATE

**Indications** see under Dose

**Cautions** prolonged QT interval, cardiac conduction disorders, concomitant administration of drugs that prolong QT interval, congestive cardiac failure; pregnancy and breast-feeding; **interactions**: Appendix 1 (dolasetron)

**Side-effects** diarrhoea, constipation, dyspepsia, abdominal pain, flatulence, taste disturbances; tachycardia, bradycardia, ECG changes, flushing; fever, shivering; headache, sleep disorder, fatigue, dizziness, drowsiness, anorexia; hypersensitivity reactions including rash, pruritus, urticaria, angioedema and anaphylaxis; rarely intestinal obstruction, pancreatitis, jaundice, seizures, cardiac arrhythmia, injection-site reactions; very rarely severe hypotension and bradycardia following intravenous injection

**Dose**

- Prevention of nausea and vomiting induced by cytotoxic chemotherapy, by mouth, 200 mg one hour before treatment *or* by intravenous injection (over 30 seconds) *or* by intravenous infusion, 100 mg 30 minutes before treatment

- Prevention of delayed nausea and vomiting after chemotherapy cycle, by mouth, 200 mg once daily

**Note** Dolasetron can be used for a maximum of 4 consecutive days in relation to any one chemotherapy cycle

- Prevention of postoperative nausea and vomiting, by mouth, 50 mg before induction of anaesthesia *or* by intravenous injection (over 30 seconds) *or* by intravenous infusion, 12.5 mg at cessation of anaesthesia
- Treatment of postoperative nausea and vomiting, by intravenous injection (over 30 seconds) *or* by intravenous infusion, 12.5 mg
- CHILD not recommended

**Anzemet®** (Amdipharm) ▼ PoM

Tablets, f/c, pink, dolasetron mesilate 50 mg, net price 3-tab pack = £13.50; 200 mg, 3-tab pack = £42.00, 6-tab pack = £84.00

Injection, dolasetron mesilate 20 mg/mL, net price 0.625-mL (12.5-mg) amp = £4.00, 5-mL (100-mg) amp = £13.00

## GRANISETRON

**Indications** see under Dose

**Cautions** pregnancy (Appendix 4) and breast-feeding (Appendix 5)

**Side-effects** constipation, headache, rash; hypersensitivity reactions reported

**Dose**

- Nausea and vomiting induced by cytotoxic chemotherapy or radiotherapy, by mouth, 1–2 mg within 1 hour before start of treatment, then 2 mg daily in 1–2 divided doses during treatment; when intravenous infusion also used, max. combined total 9 mg in 24 hours; CHILD 20 micrograms/kg (max. 1 mg) within 1 hour before start of treatment, then 20 micrograms/kg (max. 1 mg) twice daily for up to 5 days during treatment

  By intravenous injection (diluted in 15 mL sodium chloride 0.9% and given over not less than 30 seconds) *or* by intravenous infusion (over 5 minutes), prevention, 3 mg before start of cytotoxic therapy (up to 2 additional 3-mg doses may be given within 24 hours); treatment, as for prevention (the two additional doses must not be given less than 10 minutes apart); max. 9 mg in 24 hours; CHILD, by intravenous infusion, (over 5 minutes), prevention, 40 micrograms/kg (max. 3 mg) before start of cytotoxic therapy; treatment, as for prevention—one additional dose of 40 micrograms/kg (max. 3 mg) may be given within 24 hours (not less than 10 minutes after initial dose)

- Postoperative nausea and vomiting, by intravenous injection (diluted to 5 mL and given over 30 seconds), prevention, 1 mg before induction of anaesthesia; treatment, 1 mg, given as for prevention; max. 2 mg in one day; CHILD not recommended

**Kytril®** (Roche) PoM

Tablets, f/c, granisetron (as hydrochloride) 1 mg, net price 10-tab pack = £65.49; 2 mg, 5-tab pack = £65.49

Paediatric liquid, sugar-free, granisetron (as hydrochloride) 1 mg/5 mL, net price 30 mL = £39.29

Sterile solution, granisetron (as hydrochloride) 1 mg/mL, for dilution and use as injection or infusion, net price 1-mL amp = £8.60, 3-mL amp = £25.79

## ONDANSETRON

**Indications** see under Dose

**Cautions** pregnancy (Appendix 4) and breast-feeding (Appendix 5); moderate or severe hepatic impairment (Appendix 2); **interactions:** Appendix 1 (ondansetron)

**Side-effects** constipation; headache, sensation of warmth or flushing, hiccups; occasional alterations in liver enzymes; hypersensitivity reactions reported; occasional transient visual disturbances and dizziness following intravenous administration; involuntary movements, seizures, chest pain, arrhythmias, hypotension and bradycardia also reported; suppositories may cause rectal irritation

**Dose**

- Moderately emetogenic chemotherapy or radiotherapy, by mouth, 8 mg 1–2 hours before treatment *or* by rectum, 16 mg 1–2 hours before treatment *or* by intramuscular injection *or* slow intravenous injection, 8 mg immediately before treatment

  *then* by mouth, 8 mg every 12 hours for up to 5 days *or* by rectum, 16 mg daily for up to 5 days; CHILD, by slow intravenous injection *or* by intravenous infusion over 15 minutes, 5 mg/m² immediately before chemotherapy then, 4 mg by mouth every 12 hours for up to 5 days

- Severely emetogenic chemotherapy, by intramuscular injection *or* slow intravenous injection, 8 mg immediately before treatment, where necessary followed by 8 mg at intervals of 2–4 hours for 2 further doses (*or* followed by 1 mg/hour by continuous intravenous infusion for up to 24 hours)

  *then* by mouth, 8 mg every 12 hours for up to 5 days *or* by rectum, 16 mg daily for up to 5 days;

  *alternatively*, by intravenous infusion over at least 15 minutes, 32 mg immediately before treatment *or* by rectum, 16 mg 1–2 hours before treatment

  *then* by mouth, 8 mg every 12 hours for up to 5 days *or* by rectum, 16 mg daily for up to 5 days; CHILD, by slow intravenous injection *or* by intravenous infusion over 15 minutes, 5 mg/m² immediately before chemotherapy then, 4 mg by mouth every 12 hours for up to 5 days

- Prevention of postoperative nausea and vomiting, by mouth, 16 mg 1 hour before anaesthesia *or* 8 mg 1 hour before anaesthesia followed by 8 mg at intervals of 8 hours for 2 further doses

  *alternatively*, by intramuscular *or* slow intravenous injection, 4 mg at induction of anaesthesia; CHILD over 2 years, by slow intravenous injection, 100 micrograms/kg (max. 4 mg) before, during, or after induction of anaesthesia

- Treatment of postoperative nausea and vomiting, by intramuscular *or* slow intravenous injection, 4 mg; CHILD over 2 years, by slow intravenous injection, 100 micrograms/kg (max. 4 mg)

**Zofran®** (GSK) PoM

Tablets, both yellow, f/c, ondansetron (as hydrochloride) 4 mg, net price 30-tab pack = £107.91; 8 mg, 10-tab pack = £71.94

Oral lyophilisates (*Zofran Melt®*), ondansetron 4 mg, net price 10-tab pack = £35.97; 8 mg, 10-tab pack = £71.94. Counselling, administration

**Counselling** Tablets should be placed on the tongue, allowed to disperse and swallowed

**Excipients** include aspartame (section 9.4.1)

Syrup, sugar-free, ondansetron (as hydrochloride) 4 mg/5 mL. Net price 50-mL pack = £35.97

Injection, ondansetron (as hydrochloride) 2 mg/mL, net price 2-mL amp = £5.99; 4-mL amp = £11.99

Suppositories, ondansetron 16 mg. Net price 1 = £14.39

### PALONOSETRON

**Indications** prevention of nausea and vomiting induced by moderately and severely emetogenic chemotherapy

**Cautions** history of constipation; intestinal obstruction; concomitant administration of drugs that prolong QT interval; pregnancy (Appendix 4); breast-feeding (Appendix 5)

Driving Dizziness or drowsiness may affect performance of skilled tasks (e.g. driving)

**Side-effects** diarrhoea, constipation; headache, dizziness; *less commonly* dyspepsia, abdominal pain, dry mouth, flatulence, changes in blood pressure, tachycardia, bradycardia, arrhythmia, myocardial ischaemia, hiccups, drowsiness, asthenia, insomnia, anxiety, euphoria, paraesthesia, peripheral neuropathy, anorexia, motion sickness, influenza-like symptoms, urinary retention, glycosuria, hyperglycaemia, electrolyte disturbance, arthralgia, eye irritation, amblyopia, tinnitus, rash, pruritus

**Dose**

- By intravenous injection (over 30 seconds), 250 micrograms as a single dose 30 minutes before treatment; do not repeat dose within 7 days; CHILD and ADOLESCENT under 18 years not recommended

**Aloxi®** (Cambridge) ▼ PoM

Injection, palonosetron (as hydrochloride) 50 micrograms/mL, net price 5-mL amp = £55.89

### TROPISETRON

**Indications** see under Dose

**Cautions** uncontrolled hypertension (has been aggravated by doses higher than recommended); cardiac conduction disorders; arrhythmias, concomitant administration of drugs that prolong QT interval; pregnancy (Appendix 4), breast-feeding; **interactions**: Appendix 1 (tropisetron)

Driving Dizziness or drowsiness may affect performance of skilled tasks (e.g. driving)

**Side-effects** constipation, diarrhoea, abdominal pain; headache, dizziness, fatigue; hypersensitivity reactions reported (including facial flushing, urticaria, chest tightness, dyspnoea, bronchospasm and hypotension); collapse, syncope, bradycardia, cardiovascular collapse also reported (causal relationship not established)

**Dose**

- Prevention of nausea and vomiting induced by cytotoxic chemotherapy, by slow intravenous injection *or* by intravenous infusion, 5 mg shortly before chemotherapy, then 5 mg by mouth every morning at least 1 hour before food for 5 days; CHILD over 2 years, by intravenous injection over at least 1 minute or by intravenous infusion, 200 micrograms/kg (max. 5 mg) shortly before chemotherapy, then 200 micrograms/kg daily for 4 days; CHILD 25 kg and over, by intravenous injection over at least 1 minute or by intravenous infusion, 5 mg shortly before chemotherapy, then by mouth (preferably) or by intravenous injection over at least 1 minute or by intravenous infusion, 5 mg daily for 5 days
- Postoperative nausea and vomiting, by slow intravenous injection or by intravenous infusion, prevention, 2 mg shortly before induction of anaesthesia; treatment, 2 mg within 2 hours of the end of anaesthesia

**Navoban®** (Novartis) PoM

Capsules, white/yellow, tropisetron (as hydrochloride) 5 mg, net price 5-cap pack = £53.86; 50-cap pack = £538.60. Label: 23

Injection, tropisetron (as hydrochloride), 1 mg/mL, net price 2-mL amp = £4.86, 5-mL amp = £12.16

## Neurokinin receptor antagonist

### APREPITANT

**Indications** adjunct to dexamethasone and a $5HT_3$ antagonist in preventing nausea and vomiting associated with moderately and highly emetogenic chemotherapy

**Cautions** hepatic impairment (Appendix 2); pregnancy (Appendix 4); **interactions**: Appendix 1 (aprepitant)

**Contra-indications** breast-feeding (Appendix 5)

**Side-effects** hiccups, dyspepsia, diarrhoea, constipation, anorexia, asthenia, headache, dizziness; *less commonly* weight changes, dry mouth, colitis, flatulence, stomatitis, abdominal pain, gastro-oesophageal reflux, duodenal ulcer, oedema, bradycardia, cough, disorientation, euphoria, anxiety, confusion, thirst, abnormal dreams, hyperglycaemia, polyuria, anaemia, dysuria, haematuria, myalgia, conjunctivitis, pharyngitis, sneezing, tinnitus, sweating, oily skin, pruritus, rash, acne, photosensitivity, flushing, hyponatraemia

**Dose**

- 125 mg 1 hour before chemotherapy, then 80 mg daily as a single dose for the next 2 days; consult product literature for dose of concomitant corticosteroid and $5HT_3$ antagonist; CHILD and ADOLESCENT under 18 years not recommended

**Emend®** (MSD) ▼ PoM

Capsules, aprepitant 80 mg, net price 2-cap pack = £31.61; 125 mg (white/pink), 5-cap pack = £79.03; 3-day pack of one 125-mg capsule and two 80-mg capsules = £47.42

## Cannabinoid

### NABILONE

**Indications** nausea and vomiting caused by cytotoxic chemotherapy, unresponsive to conventional antiemetics (under close observation, preferably in hospital setting)

**Cautions** history of psychiatric disorder; elderly; hypertension; heart disease; adverse effects on mental state can persist for 48–72 hours after stopping; pregnancy (Appendix 4); **interactions**: Appendix 1 (nabilone)

Driving Drowsiness may affect performance of skilled tasks (e.g. driving); effects of alcohol enhanced

4 Central nervous system

**Contra-indications** severe hepatic impairment; pregnancy and breast-feeding (Appendix 5)

**Side-effects** drowsiness, vertigo, euphoria, dry mouth, ataxia, visual disturbance, concentration difficulties, sleep disturbance, dysphoria, hypotension, headache and nausea; also confusion, disorientation, hallucinations, psychosis, depression, decreased coordination, tremors, tachycardia, decreased appetite, and abdominal pain

Behavioural effects Patients should be made aware of possible changes of mood and other adverse behavioural effects

**Dose**

- Initially 1 mg twice daily, increased if necessary to 2 mg twice daily, throughout each cycle of cytotoxic therapy and, if necessary, for 48 hours after the last dose of each cycle; max. 6 mg daily given in 3 divided doses. The first dose should be taken the night before initiation of cytotoxic treatment and the second dose 1–3 hours before the first dose of cytotoxic drug; ADOLESCENT and CHILD under 18 years not recommended

**Nabilone** (Cambridge) PoM
Capsules, blue/white, nabilone 1 mg. Net price 20-cap pack = £125.84. Label: 2, counselling, behavioural effects

## Hyoscine

### HYOSCINE HYDROBROMIDE
(Scopolamine Hydrobromide)

**Indications** motion sickness; premedication (section 15.1.3)

**Cautions** elderly, urinary retention, cardiovascular disease, gastro-intestinal obstruction, hepatic or renal impairment; porphyria (section 9.8.2); pregnancy (Appendix 4) and breast-feeding (Appendix 5); **interactions:** Appendix 1 (antimuscarinics)

Driving Drowsiness may affect performance of skilled tasks (e.g. driving) and may persist for up to 24 hours or longer after removal of patch: effects of alcohol enhanced

**Contra-indications** closed-angle glaucoma

**Side-effects** drowsiness, dry mouth, dizziness, blurred vision, difficulty with micturition

**Dose**

- Motion sickness, by mouth, 300 micrograms 30 minutes before start of journey followed by 300 micrograms every 6 hours if required; max. 3 doses in 24 hours; CHILD 4–10 years 75–150 micrograms, over 10 years 150–300 micrograms

Note Proprietary brands of hyoscine hydrobromide tablets (*Joy-rides®*, *Kwells®*) are on sale to the public for motion sickness

- Injection, see section 15.1.3

**Scopoderm TTS®** (Novartis Consumer Health) PoM
Patch, self-adhesive, pink, releasing hyoscine approx. 1 mg/72 hours when in contact with skin. Net price 2 = £4.30. Label: 19, counselling, see below

Dose motion sickness prevention, apply 1 patch to hairless area of skin behind ear 5–6 hours before journey; replace if necessary after 72 hours, siting replacement patch behind other ear; CHILD under 10 years not recommended

Counselling Explain accompanying instructions to patient and in particular emphasise advice to wash hands after handling and to wash application site after removing, and to use one patch at a time

Note The brand name *Scopoderm®* is used for a hyoscine patch that is available for sale to the public

## Other drugs for Ménière's disease

Betahistine has been promoted as a specific treatment for Ménière's disease.

### BETAHISTINE DIHYDROCHLORIDE

**Indications** vertigo, tinnitus and hearing loss associated with Ménière's disease

**Cautions** asthma, history of peptic ulcer; pregnancy and breast-feeding; **interactions:** Appendix 1 (betahistine)

**Contra-indications** phaeochromocytoma

**Side-effects** gastro-intestinal disturbances; headache, rashes and pruritus reported

**Dose**

- Initially 16 mg 3 times daily, preferably with food; maintenance 24–48 mg daily; CHILD not recommended

**Betahistine Dihydrochloride** (Non-proprietary) PoM
Tablets, betahistine dihydrochloride 8 mg, net price 120-tab pack = £2.21; 16 mg, 84-tab pack = £3.69. Label: 21

**Serc®** (Solvay) PoM
Tablets, betahistine dihydrochloride 8 mg (*Serc®-8*), net price 120-tab pack = £9.04; 16 mg (*Serc®-16*), 84-tab pack = £12.65 Label: 21

# 4.7 Analgesics

4.7.1 Non-opioid analgesics
4.7.2 Opioid analgesics
4.7.3 Neuropathic pain
4.7.4 Antimigraine drugs

The non-opioid drugs (section 4.7.1), paracetamol and aspirin (and other NSAIDs), are particularly suitable for pain in musculoskeletal conditions, whereas the opioid analgesics (section 4.7.2) are more suitable for moderate to severe pain, particularly of visceral origin.

**Pain in palliative care** For advice on pain relief in palliative care see p. 14.

**Pain in sickle-cell disease** The pain of mild sickle-cell crises is managed with paracetamol, an NSAID, codeine, or dihydrocodeine. Severe crises may require the use of morphine or diamorphine; concomitant use of an NSAID may potentiate analgesia and allow lower doses of the opioid to be used. Pethidine should be avoided if possible because accumulation of a neurotoxic metabolite can precipitate seizures; the relatively short half-life of pethidine necessitates frequent injections.

**Dental and orofacial pain** Analgesics should be used judiciously in dental care as a **temporary** measure until the cause of the pain has been dealt with.

Dental pain of inflammatory origin, such as that associated with pulpitis, apical infection, localised osteitis (dry socket) or pericoronitis is usually best managed by treating the infection, providing drainage, restorative procedures, and other local measures. Analgesics provide temporary relief of pain (usually for about 1 to 7 days) until the causative factors have been brought under control. In the case of pulpitis, intra-osseous infection or abscess, reliance on analgesics alone is usually inappropriate.

Similarly the pain and discomfort associated with acute problems of the oral mucosa (e.g. acute herpetic gingivostomatitis, erythema multiforme) may be relieved by **benzydamine** mouthwash or spray (see p. 559) until the cause of the mucosal disorder has been dealt with. However, where a patient is febrile, the antipyretic action of **paracetamol** (see p. 220) or **ibuprofen** (see p. 507) is often helpful.

The *choice* of an analgesic for dental purposes should be based on its suitability for the patient. Most dental pain is relieved effectively by non-steroidal anti-inflammatory drugs (NSAIDs). NSAIDs that are used for dental pain include **ibuprofen**, **aspirin**, and **diflunisal**; for further details see section 4.7.1 and section 10.1.1. **Paracetamol** has analgesic and antipyretic effects but no anti-inflammatory effect.



Opioid analgesics (section 4.7.2) such as **dihydrocodeine** and **pethidine** act on the central nervous system and are traditionally used for *moderate to severe pain*. However, opioid analgesics are relatively ineffective in dental pain and their side-effects can be unpleasant. Paracetamol, ibuprofen, aspirin, or diflunisal are adequate for most cases of dental pain and an opioid is rarely required.

Combining a non-opioid with an opioid analgesic can provide greater relief of pain than a non-opioid analgesic given alone. However, this applies only when an appropriate dose combination is used. Most combination analgesic preparations have not been shown to provide greater relief of pain than an adequate dose of the non-opioid component given alone. Moreover, combination preparations have the disadvantage of an increased number of side-effects.

Any analgesic given before a dental procedure should have a low risk of increasing postoperative bleeding. In the case of pain after the dental procedure, taking an analgesic before the effect of the local anaesthetic has worn off can improve control. Postoperative analgesia with ibuprofen or aspirin is usually continued for about 24 to 72 hours.

*Temporomandibular dysfunction* can be related to anxiety in some patients who may clench or grind their teeth (bruxism) during the day or night. The muscle spasm (which appears to be the main source of pain) may be treated empirically with an overlay appliance which provides a free sliding occlusion and may also interfere with grinding. In addition, **diazepam** (section 4.1.2), which has muscle relaxant as well as anxiolytic properties, may be helpful but it should only be prescribed on a short-term basis during the acute phase. Analgesics such as aspirin (section 4.7.1) or ibuprofen (section 10.1.1) may also be required.

For the management of neuropathic pain, persistent idiopathic facial pain, and trigeminal neuralgia, see section 4.7.3.

**Dysmenorrhoea** Use of an oral contraceptive prevents the pain of dysmenorrhoea which is generally associated with ovulatory cycles. If treatment is necessary paracetamol or an NSAID (section 10.1.1) will generally provide adequate relief of pain. The vomiting and severe pain associated with dysmenorrhoea in women with endometriosis may call for an antiemetic (in addition to an analgesic). Antispasmodics (such as alverine citrate, section 1.2) have been advocated for dysmenorrhoea but the antispasmodic action does not generally provide significant relief.

## 4.7.1 Non-opioid analgesics

**Aspirin** is indicated for headache, transient musculoskeletal pain, dysmenorrhoea and pyrexia. In inflammatory conditions, most physicians prefer anti-inflammatory treatment with another NSAID which may be better tolerated and more convenient for the patient. Aspirin is used increasingly for its antiplatelet properties (section 2.9). Aspirin tablets or dispersible aspirin tablets are adequate for most purposes as they act rapidly.

Gastric irritation may be a problem; it is minimised by taking the dose after food. Enteric-coated preparations are available, but have a slow onset of action and are therefore unsuitable for single-dose analgesic use (though their prolonged action may be useful for night pain).

Aspirin interacts significantly with a number of other drugs and its interaction with warfarin is a **special hazard**, see **interactions:** Appendix 1 (aspirin).

**Paracetamol** is similar in efficacy to aspirin, but has no demonstrable anti-inflammatory activity; it is less irritant to the stomach and for that reason is now generally preferred to aspirin, particularly in the elderly. **Overdosage** with paracetamol is particularly dangerous as it may cause hepatic damage which is sometimes not apparent for 4 to 6 days (see Emergency Treatment of Poisoning, p. 29).

**Nefopam** may have a place in the relief of persistent pain unresponsive to other non-opioid analgesics. It causes little or no respiratory depression, but sympathomimetic and antimuscarinic side-effects may be troublesome.

**Non-steroidal anti-inflammatory analgesics** (NSAIDs, section 10.1.1) are particularly useful for the treatment of patients with chronic disease accompanied by pain and inflammation. Some of them are also used in the short-term treatment of mild to moderate pain including transient musculoskeletal pain but paracetamol is now often preferred, particularly in the elderly (see also p. 19). They are also suitable for the relief of pain in *dysmenorrhoea* and to treat pain caused by *secondary bone tumours*, many of which produce lysis of bone and release prostaglandins (see Prescribing in Palliative Care, p. 14). Selective inhibitors of cyclo-oxygenase-2 may be used in preference to non-selective NSAIDs for patients at high risk of developing serious gastro-intestinal side-effects. NSAIDs including ketorolac are also used for peri-operative analgesia (section 15.1.4.2).

**Dental and orofacial pain** Most dental pain is relieved effectively by NSAIDs (section 10.1.1). **Aspirin**

is effective against mild to moderate dental pain; dispersible tablets provide a rapidly absorbed form of aspirin suitable for most purposes.

The analgesic effect of **paracetamol** in mild to moderate dental pain is probably less than that of aspirin, but it does not affect bleeding time or interact significantly with warfarin. Moreover, it is less irritant to the stomach. Paracetamol is a suitable analgesic for children; sugar-free versions can be requested by specifying 'sugar-free' on the prescription.

For further information on the management of dental and orofacial pain, see p. 217.

## Compound analgesic preparations

Compound analgesic preparations that contain a simple analgesic (such as aspirin or paracetamol) with an opioid component reduce the scope for effective titration of the individual components in the management of pain of varying intensity.

Compound analgesic preparations containing paracetamol or aspirin with a *low dose* of an opioid analgesic (e.g. 8 mg of codeine phosphate per compound tablet) are commonly used, but the advantages have not been substantiated. The low dose of the opioid may be enough to cause opioid side-effects (in particular, constipation) and can complicate the treatment of **overdosage** (see p. 31) yet may not provide significant additional relief of pain.

**Co-proxamol** (dextropropoxyphene in combination with paracetamol) (p. 221) has little more analgesic effect than paracetamol alone. An important disadvantage of co-proxamol is that overdosage (which may be combined with alcohol) is complicated by respiratory depression and acute heart failure due to the dextropropoxyphene and by hepatotoxicity due to the paracetamol. Rapid treatment is essential (see Emergency Treatment of Poisoning, p. 31). Co-proxamol is to be withdrawn from the market and the CSM has advised that co-proxamol treatment should **no longer** be prescribed; patients who are already receiving it should have their treatment reviewed and another analgesic considered.

A *full dose* of the opioid component (e.g. 60 mg codeine phosphate) in compound analgesic preparations effectively augments the analgesic activity but is associated with the full range of opioid side-effects (including nausea, vomiting, severe constipation, drowsiness, respiratory depression, and risk of dependence on long-term administration). For details of the **side-effects** of opioid analgesics, see p. 222 (**important:** the elderly are particularly susceptible to opioid side-effects and should receive lower doses).

In general, when assessing pain, it is necessary to weigh up carefully whether there is a need for a non-opioid and an opioid analgesic to be taken simultaneously.

For information on the use of combination analgesic preparations in dental and orofacial pain, see p. 218

**Caffeine** is a weak stimulant that is often included, in small doses, in analgesic preparations. It is claimed that the addition of caffeine may enhance the analgesic effect, but the alerting effect, mild habit-forming effect and possible provocation of headache may not always be desirable. Moreover, in excessive dosage or on withdrawal caffeine may itself induce headache.

## ASPIRIN
### (Acetylsalicylic Acid)

**Indications** mild to moderate pain, pyrexia; see also section 10.1.1; antiplatelet (section 2.9)

**Cautions** asthma, allergic disease, hepatic impairment (Appendix 2), renal impairment (Appendix 3), dehydration; preferably avoid during fever or viral infection in adolescents (risk of Reye's syndrome, see below); pregnancy (Appendix 4); elderly; G6PD-deficiency (section 9.1.5); **interactions:** Appendix 1 (aspirin)

**Contra-indications** children and adolescents under 16 years and in breast-feeding (Reye's syndrome, see below; Appendix 5); previous or active peptic ulceration, haemophilia; not for treatment of gout

Hypersensitivity Aspirin and other NSAIDs are **contra-indicated** in patients with a history of hypersensitivity to aspirin or any other NSAID—*which includes those* in whom attacks of *asthma, angioedema, urticaria or rhinitis* have been precipitated by aspirin or any other NSAID

Reye's syndrome Owing to an association with Reye's syndrome, the CSM has advised that aspirin-containing preparations should not be given to children and adolescents under 16 years, unless specifically indicated, e.g. for Kawasaki syndrome.

**Side-effects** generally mild and infrequent but high incidence of gastro-intestinal irritation with slight asymptomatic blood loss, increased bleeding time, bronchospasm and skin reactions in hypersensitive patients. Prolonged administration, see section 10.1.1. **Overdosage:** see Emergency Treatment of Poisoning, p. 29

**Dose**

- By mouth 300–900 mg every 4–6 hours when necessary; max. 4 g daily; CHILD and ADOLESCENT not recommended (see Reye's syndrome above)
- By rectum, see preparations below

**Aspirin** (Non-proprietary)

Tablets PoM[1], aspirin 300 mg. Net price 20 = 21p. Label: 21, 32

Tablets PoM[1], e/c, aspirin 300 mg, net price 100-tab pack = £4.89; 75 mg, see section 2.9. Label: 5, 25, 32

Dispersible tablets PoM[1], aspirin 300 mg, net price 20 = 31p; 75 mg, see section 2.9. Label: 13, 21, 32

Note BP directs that when no strength is stated the 300-mg strength should be dispensed, and that when soluble aspirin tablets are prescribed, dispersible aspirin tablets shall be dispensed.

Dental prescribing on NHS Aspirin Dispersible Tablets 300 mg may be prescribed

Suppositories PoM, aspirin 150 mg, net price 10 = £9.52; 300 mg, 12 = £59.28. Label: 32

Dose 450–900 mg every 4 hours (max. 3.6 g daily); CHILD under 16 years not recommended (see Contra-indications above)

Brands include *Resprin®*

**Caprin®** (Pinewood)

Tablets PoM[1], e/c, f/c, pink, aspirin 300 mg, net price 100-tab pack = £4.89; 75 mg, see section 2.9. Label: 5, 25, 32

**Nu-Seals® Aspirin** (Alliance)

Tablets PoM[1], e/c, aspirin 300 mg, net price 100-tab pack = £3.46; 75 mg, see section 2.9. Label: 5, 25, 32

1. May be sold to the public provided packs contain no more than 32 capsules or tablets; pharmacists can sell multiple packs up to a total quantity of 100 capsules or tablets in justifiable circumstances; for details see *Medicines, Ethics and Practice*, No. 29, London, Pharmaceutical Press, 2005 (and subsequent editions as available)

**With codeine phosphate 8 mg**

[1]**Co-codaprin** (Non-proprietary) PoM

Dispersible tablets, co-codaprin 8/400 (codeine phosphate 8 mg, aspirin 400 mg). Net price 20 = £1.15. Label: 13, 21, 32

**Dose** 1–2 tablets in water every 4–6 hours; max. 8 tablets daily

When co-codaprin tablets or dispersible tablets are prescribed and no strength is stated, tablets or dispersible tablets, respectively, containing codeine phosphate 8 mg and aspirin 400 mg should be dispensed

**Other compound preparations**

**Aspav®** (Alpharma) PoM

Dispersible tablets, aspirin 500 mg, papaveretum 7.71 mg (providing the equivalent of 5 mg of anhydrous morphine). Net price 30-tab pack = £5.98. Label: 2, 13, 21, 32

**Dose** 1–2 tablets in water every 4–6 hours if necessary; max. 8 tablets daily

## PARACETAMOL
(Acetaminophen)

**Indications** mild to moderate pain, pyrexia

**Cautions** hepatic impairment (Appendix 2); renal impairment (Appendix 3), alcohol dependence; **interactions:** Appendix 1 (paracetamol)

**Side-effects** side-effects rare, but rashes, blood disorders (including thrombocytopenia, leucopenia, neutropenia) reported; hypotension also reported on infusion; **important:** liver damage (and less frequently renal damage) following **overdosage**, see Emergency Treatment of Poisoning, p. 29

**Dose**

- By mouth, 0.5–1 g every 4–6 hours to a max. of 4 g daily; CHILD 2 months 60 mg for post-immunisation pyrexia; otherwise under 3 months (on doctor's advice only), 10 mg/kg (5 mg/kg if jaundiced); 3 months–1 year 60–120 mg, 1–5 years 120–250 mg, 6–12 years 250–500 mg; these doses may be repeated every 4–6 hours when necessary (max. of 4 doses in 24 hours)
- By intravenous infusion over 15 minutes, ADULT and CHILD over 50 kg, 1 g every 4–6 hours; max. 4 g daily; ADULT and CHILD 10–50 kg, 15 mg/kg every 4–6 hours; max. 60 mg/kg daily
- By rectum, see preparations

**Note** For full Joint Committee on Vaccination and Immunisation recommendation on post-immunisation pyrexia, see section 14.1

**Paracetamol** (Non-proprietary)

Tablets PoM[1], paracetamol 500 mg. Net price 20 = 31p. Label: 29, 30

Brands include *Panadol®* NHS

Soluble Tablets (= Dispersible tablets) PoM[2], paracetamol 500 mg. Net price 60-tab pack = £4.64. Label: 13, 29, 30

Brands include *Panadol Soluble®* NHS

Paediatric Soluble Tablets (= Paediatric dispersible tablets), paracetamol 120 mg. Net price 16-tab pack = 91p. Label: 13, 30

Brands include *Disprol® Soluble Paracetamol* NHS

Oral Suspension 120 mg/5 mL (= Paediatric Mixture), paracetamol 120 mg/5 mL. Net price 100 mL = 42p. Label: 30

**Note** BP directs that when Paediatric Paracetamol Oral Suspension or Paediatric Paracetamol Mixture is prescribed Paracetamol Oral Suspension 120 mg/5 mL should be dispensed; sugar-free versions can be ordered by specifying 'sugar-free'on the prescription

Brands include *Calpol® Paediatric*, *Calpol® Paediatric* sugar-free, *Disprol® Paediatric*, *Medinol® Paediatric* sugar-free, *Paldesic®*, *Panadol®* sugar-free

Oral Suspension 250 mg/5 mL (= Mixture), paracetamol 250 mg/5 mL. Net price 100 mL = 73p. Label: 30

Brands include *Calpol® 6 Plus* NHS, *Medinol® Over 6* NHS, *Paldesic®*

Suppositories, paracetamol 60 mg, net price 10 = £9.96; 125 mg, 10 = £11.50; 250 mg, 10 = £23.00; 500 mg, 10 = £9.90. Label: 30

**Dose** by rectum, ADULT and CHILD over 12 years 0.5–1 g up to 4 times daily, CHILD 1–5 years 125–250 mg, 6–12 years 250–500 mg

Brands include *Alvedon®*

**Dental prescribing on NHS** Paracetamol Tablets, Paracetamol Soluble Tablets 500 mg, and Paracetamol Oral Suspension may be prescribed

**Perfalgan®** (Bristol-Myers Squibb) ▼ PoM

Intravenous infusion, paracetamol 10 mg/mL, net price 50-mL vial = £1.50, 100-mL vial = £1.50

**Co-codamol 8/500**

When co-codamol tablets, dispersible (or effervescent) tablets, or capsules are prescribed and **no strength is stated**, tablets, dispersible (or effervescent) tablets, or capsules, respectively, containing codeine phosphate **8 mg** and paracetamol **500 mg** should be dispensed.

[2]**Co-codamol 8/500** (Non-proprietary) PoM

Tablets, co-codamol 8/500 (codeine phosphate 8 mg, paracetamol 500 mg) Net price 20 = 90p. Label: 29, 30

Brands include *Panadeine®* NHS

**Dose** 1–2 tablets every 4–6 hours; max. 8 tablets daily; CHILD 6–12 years ½–1 tablet

Effervescent or *dispersible tablets*, co-codamol 8/500 (codeine phosphate 8 mg, paracetamol 500 mg). Net price 20 = £1.48. Label: 13, 29, 30

Brands include *Paracodol®* NHS

**Dose** 1–2 tablets in water every 4–6 hours, max. 8 tablets daily; CHILD 6–12 years ½–1 tablet, max. 4 daily

**Note** The Drug Tariff allows tablets of co-codamol labelled 'dispersible' to be dispensed against an order for 'effervescent' and *vice versa*

Capsules, co-codamol 8/500 (codeine phosphate 8 mg, paracetamol 500 mg). Net price 10-cap pack = £1.10, 20-cap pack = £1.66. Label: 29, 30

Brands include *Paracodol®* NHS

**Dose** 1–2 capsules every 4 hours; max. 8 capsules daily

**Co-codamol 15/500**

When co-codamol tablets, dispersible (or effervescent) tablets, or capsules are prescribed and **no strength is stated**, tablets, dispersible (or effervescent) tablets, or capsules, respectively, containing codeine phosphate **8 mg** and paracetamol **500 mg** should be dispensed (see preparations above).

See warnings and notes on p. 219 (**important:** special care in elderly—reduce dose)

1. May be sold to the public provided packs contain no more than 32 capsules or tablets; pharmacists can sell multiple packs up to a total quantity of 100 capsules or tablets in justifiable circumstances; for details see *Medicines, Ethics and Practice*, No. 29, London, Pharmaceutical Press, 2005 (and subsequent editions as available)
2. May be sold to the public under certain circumstances; for exemptions see *Medicines, Ethics and Practice*, No. 29, London, Pharmaceutical Press, 2005 (and subsequent editions as available)

**Codipar** (Goldshield) PoM
Caplets (= tablets), co-codamol 15/500 (codeine phosphate 15 mg, paracetamol 500 mg). Net price 100-tab pack = £7.50. Label: 2, 29, 30
Dose 1–2 tablets every 4 hours; max. 8 daily; CHILD not recommended

### Co-codamol 30/500

When co-codamol tablets, dispersible (or effervescent) tablets, or capsules are prescribed and **no strength is stated**, tablets, dispersible (or effervescent) tablets, or capsules, respectively, containing codeine phosphate **8 mg** and on paracetamol **500 mg** should be dispensed (see preparations above).

See warnings and notes on p. 219 (**important:** special care in elderly—reduce dose)

**Co-codamol 30/500** (Non-proprietary) PoM
Tablets, co-codamol 30/500 (codeine phosphate 30 mg, paracetamol 500 mg), net price 100-tab pack = £6.01. Label: 2, 29, 30
Dose 1–2 tablets every 4 hours; max. 8 tablets daily; CHILD not recommended

Capsules, co-codamol 30/500 (codeine phosphate 30 mg, paracetamol 500 mg), net price 100-cap pack = £13.22. Label: 2, 29, 30
Brands include *Medocodene®*, *Zapain®*
Dose 1–2 capsules every 4 hours; max. 8 capsules daily; CHILD not recommended

Effervescent tablets, co-codamol 30/500 (codeine phosphate 30 mg, paracetamol 500 mg). Contains $Na^+$ 13.6 mmol/tablet, avoid in *renal impairment*; net price 100-tab pack = £13.22. Label: 2, 13, 29, 30
Brands include *Medocodene®*
Dose 1–2 tablets in water every 4 hours; max. 8 tablets daily; CHILD not recommended

**Kapake®** (Galen) PoM
Tablets, scored, co-codamol 30/500 (codeine phosphate 30 mg, paracetamol 500 mg). Net price 30-tab pack = £2.26 (hosp. only), 100-tab pack = £7.10. Label: 2, 29, 30
Dose 1–2 tablets every 4 hours; max. 8 tablets daily; CHILD not recommended

Capsules, co-codamol 30/500 (codeine phosphate 30 mg, paracetamol 500 mg), net price 100-cap pack = £7.10. Label: 2, 29, 30
Dose 1–2 capsules every 4 hours; max. 8 capsules daily; CHILD not recommended

Effervescent tablets, co-codamol 30/500 (codeine phosphate 30 mg, paracetamol 500 mg). Contains $Na^+$ 16.9 mmol/tablet; avoid in *renal impairment*, net price 100-tab pack = £8.30. Label: 2, 13, 29, 30
Dose 2 tablets in water every 4 hours; max. 8 daily; CHILD not recommended

**Solpadol®** (Sanofi-Synthelabo) PoM
Caplets(= tablets), co-codamol 30/500 (codeine phosphate 30 mg, paracetamol 500 mg). Net price 100-tab pack = £7.54. Label: 2, 29, 30
Dose 2 tablets every 4 hours; max. 8 daily; CHILD not recommended

Capsules, grey/purple, co-codamol 30/500 (codeine phosphate 30 mg, paracetamol 500 mg). Net price 100-cap pack = £7.54. Label: 2, 29, 30
Dose 1–2 capsules every 4 hours; max. 8 capsules daily; CHILD not recommended
Note May be difficult to obtain

Effervescent tablets, co-codamol 30/500 (codeine phosphate 30 mg, paracetamol 500 mg). Contains $Na^+$ 16.9 mmol/tablet; avoid in *renal impairment*. Net price 100-tab pack = £9.05. Label: 2, 13, 29, 30
Dose 2 tablets in water every 4 hours; max. 8 daily; CHILD not recommended

**Tylex®** (Schwarz) PoM
Capsules, co-codamol 30/500 (codeine phosphate 30 mg, paracetamol 500 mg). Net price 100-cap pack = £8.01. Label: 2, 29, 30
Dose 1–2 capsules every 4 hours; max. 8 capsules daily; CHILD not recommended

Effervescent tablets, co-codamol 30/500 (codeine phosphate 30 mg, paracetamol 500 mg). Contains $Na^+$ 13.6 mmol/tablet; avoid in *renal impairment*. Net price 90-tab pack = £7.94. Label: 2, 13, 29, 30
Excipients include aspartame 25 mg/tablet (see section 9.4.1)
Dose 1–2 tablets in water every 4 hours; max. 8 tablets daily; CHILD not recommended

### With methionine (co-methiamol)

A mixture of methionine and paracetamol; methionine has no analgesic activity but may prevent paracetamol-induced liver toxicity if overdose taken

**Paradote®** (Penn)
Tablets, f/c, co-methiamol 100/500 (DL-methionine 100 mg, paracetamol 500 mg). Net price 24-tab pack = £1.05, 96-tab pack = £2.77. Label: 29, 30
Dose 2 tablets every 4 hours; max. 8 tablets daily; CHILD 12 years and under, not recommended

### With dihydrocodeine tartrate 10 mg

See notes on p. 219

**Co-dydramol** (Non-proprietary) PoM
Tablets, scored, co-dydramol 10/500 (dihydrocodeine tartrate 10 mg, paracetamol 500 mg). Net price 20 = 92p. Label: 21, 29, 30
Dose 1–2 tablets every 4–6 hours; max. 8 tablets daily; CHILD not recommended
When co-dydramol tablets are prescribed and no strength is stated tablets containing dihydrocodeine tartrate 10 mg and paracetamol 500 mg should be dispensed.
Note Tablets containing paracetamol 500 mg and dihydrocodeine 7.46 mg (*Paramol®* NHS) are on sale to the public. The name *Paramol®* was formerly applied to a brand of co-dydramol tablets

### With dihydrocodeine tartrate 20 or 30 mg

See warnings and notes on p. 219 (**important:** special care in elderly—reduce dose)

**Remedeine®** (Napp) PoM
Tablets, paracetamol 500 mg, dihydrocodeine tartrate 20 mg. Net price 112-tab pack = £10.21. Label: 2, 21, 29, 30
Dose 1–2 tablets every 4–6 hours; max. 8 tablets daily; CHILD not recommended

Forte tablets, paracetamol 500 mg, dihydrocodeine tartrate 30 mg. Net price 56-tab pack = £6.31. Label: 2, 21, 29, 30
Dose 1–2 tablets every 4–6 hours; max. 8 tablets daily; CHILD not recommended

### Other compound preparations

Patients should not be initiated on co-proxamol therapy; see also notes on p. 219

**Co-proxamol** (Non-proprietary) PoM
Tablets, co-proxamol 32.5/325 (dextropropoxyphene hydrochloride 32.5 mg, paracetamol 325 mg). Net

price 20 = 38p. Label: 2, 10, patient information leaflet (if available) 29, 30

Brands include *Cosalgesic®* (NHS), *Distalgesic®* (NHS)

Dose patients already receiving co-proxamol, 2 tablets 3–4 times daily; max. 8 tablets daily; ADOLESCENT and CHILD under 18 years, not recommended

When co-proxamol tablets are prescribed and no strength is stated tablets containing dextropropoxyphene hydrochloride 32.5 mg and paracetamol 325 mg should be dispensed.

### Preparations on Sale to the Public

Many preparations on sale to the public contain **aspirin** or **paracetamol**, often combined with **other ingredients**. To identify the active ingredients in such preparations, consult the product literature or manufacturer. In **overdose**, contact Poisons Information Service (p. 27).

Note The correct proprietary name should be ascertained—many products have very similar names but different active ingredients

## NEFOPAM HYDROCHLORIDE

**Indications** moderate pain

**Cautions** hepatic or renal disease, elderly, urinary retention; pregnancy (Appendix 4) and breast-feeding; **interactions:** Appendix 1 (nefopam)

**Contra-indications** convulsive disorders; not indicated for myocardial infarction

**Side-effects** nausea, nervousness, urinary retention, dry mouth, lightheadedness; less frequently vomiting, blurred vision, drowsiness, sweating, insomnia, tachycardia, headache; confusion and hallucinations also reported; may colour urine (pink)

**Dose**

- By mouth, initially 60 mg (elderly, 30 mg) 3 times daily, adjusted according to response; usual range 30–90 mg 3 times daily; CHILD not recommended
- By intramuscular injection, 20 mg every 6 hours; CHILD not recommended

Note Nefopam hydrochloride 20 mg by injection ≡ 60 mg by mouth

**Acupan®** (3M) PoM

Tablets, f/c, nefopam hydrochloride 30 mg. Net price 90-tab pack = £11.18. Label: 2, 14

## 4.7.2 Opioid analgesics

Opioid analgesics are usually used to relieve moderate to severe pain particularly of visceral origin. Repeated administration may cause dependence and tolerance, but this is no deterrent in the control of pain in terminal illness, for guidelines see Prescribing in Palliative Care, p. 14. Regular use of a potent opioid may be appropriate for certain cases of chronic non-malignant pain; treatment should be supervised by a specialist and the patient should be assessed at regular intervals.

**Side-effects** Opioid analgesics share many side-effects though qualitative and quantitative differences exist. The most common include nausea, vomiting, constipation, and drowsiness. Larger doses produce respiratory depression and hypotension. **Overdosage**, see Emergency Treatment of Poisoning, p. 31.

**Interactions** See Appendix 1 (opioid analgesics) (**important**: special hazard with *pethidine and possibly other opioids* and MAOIs).

**Driving** Drowsiness may affect performance of skilled tasks (e.g. driving); effects of alcohol enhanced.

**Choice** **Morphine** remains the most valuable opioid analgesic for severe pain although it frequently causes nausea and vomiting. It is the standard against which other opioid analgesics are compared. In addition to relief of pain, morphine also confers a state of euphoria and mental detachment.

Morphine is the opioid of choice for the oral treatment of *severe pain in palliative care*. It is given regularly every 4 hours (or every 12 or 24 hours as modified-release preparations). For guidelines on dosage adjustment in palliative care, see p. 14.

**Buprenorphine** has both opioid agonist and antagonist properties and may precipitate withdrawal symptoms, including pain, in patients dependent on other opioids. It has abuse potential and may itself cause dependence. It has a much longer duration of action than morphine and sublingually is an effective analgesic for 6 to 8 hours. Vomiting may be a problem. Unlike most opioid analgesics, the effects of buprenorphine are only partially reversed by naloxone.

**Codeine** is effective for the relief of mild to moderate pain but is too constipating for long-term use.

**Diphenoxylate** (in combination with atropine, as co-phenotrope) is used in acute diarrhoea (see section 1.4.2).

**Dipipanone** used alone is less sedating than morphine but the only preparation available contains an anti-emetic and is therefore not suitable for regular regimens in palliative care.

**Diamorphine** (heroin) is a powerful opioid analgesic. It may cause less nausea and hypotension than morphine. In *palliative care* the greater solubility of diamorphine allows effective doses to be injected in smaller volumes and this is important in the emaciated patient.

**Dihydrocodeine** has an analgesic efficacy similar to that of codeine. The dose of dihydrocodeine by mouth is usually 30 mg every 4 hours; doubling the dose to 60 mg may provide some additional pain relief but this may be at the cost of more nausea and vomiting. A 40-mg tablet is now also available.

**Alfentanil**, **fentanyl** and **remifentanil** are used by injection for intra-operative analgesia (section 15.1.4.3); fentanyl is available in a transdermal drug delivery system as a self-adhesive patch which is changed every 72 hours.

**Meptazinol** is claimed to have a low incidence of respiratory depression. It has a reported length of action of 2 to 7 hours with onset within 15 minutes.

**Methadone** is less sedating than morphine and acts for longer periods. In prolonged use, methadone should not be administered more often than twice daily to avoid the risk of accumulation and opioid overdosage. Methadone may be used instead of morphine in the occasional patient who experiences excitation (or exacerbation of pain) with morphine.

**Oxycodone** has an efficacy and side-effect profile similar to that of morphine. It is used primarily for control of *pain in palliative care*. It is used as the pectinate in suppositories (special order from BCM Specials).

**Papaveretum** is rarely used; morphine is easier to prescribe and less prone to error with regard to the strength and dose.

**Pentazocine** has both agonist and antagonist properties and precipitates withdrawal symptoms, including pain in patients dependent on other opioids. By injection it is more potent than dihydrocodeine or codeine, but hallucinations and thought disturbances may occur. It is not recommended and, in particular, should be avoided after myocardial infarction as it may increase pulmonary and aortic blood pressure as well as cardiac work.

**Pethidine** produces prompt but short-lasting analgesia; it is less constipating than morphine, but even in high doses is a less potent analgesic. It is not suitable for severe continuing pain. It is used for analgesia in labour; however, other opioids, such as morphine or diamorphine, are often preferred for obstetric pain.

**Tramadol** produces analgesia by two mechanisms: an opioid effect and an enhancement of serotonergic and adrenergic pathways. It has fewer of the typical opioid side-effects (notably, less respiratory depression, less constipation and less addiction potential); psychiatric reactions have been reported.

**Dose** The dose of opioids in the BNF may need to be **adjusted individually** according to the degree of analgesia and side-effects; patients' response to opioids varies widely.

**Postoperative analgesia** The use of intra-operative opioids affects the prescribing of postoperative analgesics and in many cases delays the need for a postoperative analgesic. A postoperative opioid analgesic should be given with care since it may potentiate any residual respiratory depression (for the treatment of opioid-induced respiratory depression, see section 15.1.7). Non-opioid analgesics are also used for postoperative pain (section 15.1.4.2).

**Morphine** is used most widely. **Tramadol** is not as effective in severe pain as other opioid analgesics. **Buprenorphine** may antagonise the analgesic effect of previously administered opioids and is generally not recommended. **Pethidine** is metabolised to norpethidine which may accumulate, particularly in renal impairment; norpethidine stimulates the central nervous system and may cause convulsions. **Meptazinol** is rarely used.

Opioids are also given epidurally [unlicensed route] in the postoperative period but are associated with side-effects such as pruritus, urinary retention, nausea and vomiting; respiratory depression can be delayed, particularly with morphine.

For details of patient-controlled analgesia (PCA) to relieve postoperative pain, consult hospital protocols. Formulations specifically designed for PCA are available (*Pharma-Ject® Morphine Sulphate*).

**Dental and orofacial pain** Opioid analgesics are **relatively ineffective** in dental pain. Like other opioids, **dihydrocodeine** often causes nausea and vomiting which limits its value in dental pain; if taken for more than a few doses it is also liable to cause constipation. Dihydrocodeine is not very effective in postoperative dental pain.

**Pethidine** can be taken by mouth, but for optimal effect, it needs to be given by injection. Its efficacy in postoperative dental pain is not proven and its use in dentistry is likely to be minimal. The side-effects of pethidine are similar to those of dihydrocodeine and, apart from constipation, pethidine is also more likely to cause them. Dependence is unlikely if very few tablets are prescribed on very few occasions; nevertheless, dental surgeons need to be aware of the possibility that addicts may seek to acquire supplies.

For the management of dental and orofacial pain, see p. 217.

**Addicts** Although caution is necessary, addicts (and ex-addicts) may be treated with analgesics in the same way as other people when there is a real clinical need. Doctors do not require a special licence to prescribe opioid analgesics for addicts for relief of pain due to organic disease or injury.

## MORPHINE SALTS

**Indications** see notes above and under Dose; acute diarrhoea (section 1.4.2); cough in terminal care (section 3.9.1)

**Cautions** hypotension, hypothyroidism, asthma (avoid during attack) and decreased respiratory reserve, prostatic hypertrophy; pregnancy (Appendix 4), breast-feeding (Appendix 5); may precipitate coma in hepatic impairment (reduce dose or avoid but many such patients tolerate morphine well); reduce dose or avoid in renal impairment (see also Appendix 3), elderly and debilitated (reduce dose); convulsive disorders, dependence (severe withdrawal symptoms if withdrawn abruptly); use of cough suppressants containing opioid analgesics not generally recommended in children and should be avoided altogether in those under at least 1 year; **interactions:** Appendix 1 (opioid analgesics)

Palliative care In the control of pain in terminal illness these cautions should not necessarily be a deterrent to the use of opioid analgesics

**Contra-indications** avoid in acute respiratory depression, acute alcoholism and where risk of paralytic ileus; also avoid in raised intracranial pressure or head injury (affects pupillary responses vital for neurological assessment); avoid injection in phaeochromocytoma (risk of pressor response to histamine release)

**Side-effects** nausea and vomiting (particularly in initial stages), constipation, and drowsiness; larger doses produce respiratory depression, hypotension, and muscle rigidity; other side-effects include difficulty with micturition, ureteric or biliary spasm, dry mouth, sweating, headache, facial flushing, vertigo, bradycardia, tachycardia, palpitation, postural hypotension, hypothermia, hallucinations, dysphoria, mood changes, dependence, miosis, decreased libido or potency, rashes, urticaria and pruritus; **overdosage:** see Emergency Treatment of Poisoning, p. 31; for reversal of opioid-induced respiratory depression, see section 15.1.7.

**Dose**

- Acute pain, by subcutaneous injection (not suitable for oedematous patients) *or* by intramuscular injection, 10 mg every 4 hours if necessary (15 mg for heavier well-muscled patients); NEONATE up to 1 month 150 micrograms/kg; INFANT 1–12 months 200 micrograms/kg; CHILD 1–5 years 2.5–5 mg; CHILD 6–12 years 5–10 mg

  By slow intravenous injection, quarter to half corresponding intramuscular dose
- Premedication, by subcutaneous *or* intramuscular injection, up to 10 mg 60–90 minutes before opera-

tion; CHILD, by intramuscular injection, 150 micrograms/kg

- Postoperative pain, by subcutaneous *or* intramuscular injection, 10 mg every 2–4 hours if necessary (15 mg for heavier well-muscled patients); NEONATE up to 1 month 150 micrograms/kg; INFANT 1–12 months 200 micrograms/kg; CHILD 1–5 years 2.5–5 mg; CHILD 6–12 years 5–10 mg
  Note In the postoperative period, the patient should be closely monitored for pain relief as well as for side-effects especially respiratory depression
- Patient controlled analgesia (PCA), consult hospital protocols
- Myocardial infarction, by slow intravenous injection (2 mg/minute), 10 mg followed by a further 5–10 mg if necessary; elderly or frail patients, reduce dose by half
- Acute pulmonary oedema, by slow intravenous injection (2 mg/minute) 5–10 mg
- Chronic pain, by mouth *or* by subcutaneous injection (not suitable for oedematous patients) *or* by intramuscular injection, 5–20 mg regularly every 4 hours; dose may be increased according to needs; oral dose should be approx. double corresponding intramuscular dose and approximately triple corresponding intramuscular *diamorphine* dose (see also Prescribing in Palliative Care, p. 14) by rectum, as suppositories, 15–30 mg regularly every 4 hours
  Note The doses stated above refer equally to morphine hydrochloride, sulphate, and tartrate; see below for doses of **modified-release** preparations.

### Oral solutions

Note For advice on transfer from oral solutions of morphine to modified-release preparations of morphine, see Prescribing in Palliative Care, p. 14

**Morphine Oral Solutions**
PoM or CD
Oral solutions of morphine can be prescribed by writing the formula:
Morphine hydrochloride 5 mg
Chloroform water to 5 mL
Note The proportion of morphine hydrochloride may be altered when specified by the prescriber; if above 13 mg per 5 mL the solution becomes **CD**. For sample prescription see Controlled Drugs and Drug Dependence, p. 7. It is usual to adjust the strength so that the dose volume is 5 or 10 mL.

**Oramorph®** (Boehringer Ingelheim)
Oramorph® oral solution PoM, morphine sulphate 10 mg/5 mL. Net price 100-mL pack = £1.87; 300-mL pack = £5.21; 500-mL pack = £7.86. Label: 2

Oramorph® Unit Dose Vials 10 mg PoM (oral vials), sugar-free, morphine sulphate 10 mg/5-mL vial, net price 20 vials = £2.65. Label: 2

Oramorph® Unit Dose Vials 30 mg CD (oral vials), sugar-free, morphine sulphate 30 mg/5-mL vial, net price 20 vials = £7.44. Label: 2

Oramorph® concentrated oral solution CD, sugar-free, morphine sulphate 100 mg/5 mL. Net price 30-mL pack = £5.24; 120-mL pack = £19.57 (both with calibrated dropper). Label: 2

Oramorph® Unit Dose Vials 100 mg CD (oral vials), sugar-free, morphine sulphate 100 mg/5-mL vial, net price 20 vials = £24.80. Label: 2

### Tablets

**Sevredol®** (Napp) CD
Tablets, f/c, scored, morphine sulphate 10 mg (blue), net price 56-tab pack = £5.61; 20 mg (pink), 56-tab pack = £11.21; 50 mg (pale green), 56-tab pack = £28.02. Label: 2
Dose severe pain uncontrolled by weaker opioid, 10–50 mg every 4 hours (dose adjusted according to response); CHILD 3–5 years, 5 mg every 4 hours; 6–12 years, 5–10 mg

### Modified-release oral preparations

**Morcap® SR** (Mayne) CD
Capsules, m/r, clear enclosing ivory and brown pellets, morphine sulphate 20 mg, net price 60-cap pack = £10.80; 50 mg, 60-cap pack = £26.40; 100 mg, 60-cap pack = £50.10. Label: 2, counselling, see below
Dose every 12 or 24 hours, dose adjusted according to daily morphine requirements, for further advice on determining dose, see Prescribing in Palliative Care, p. 14; dosage requirements should be reviewed if the brand is altered
Counselling Swallow whole or open capsule and sprinkle contents on soft food
Note Prescription must also specify 'capsules' (i.e. 'Morcap SR capsules')

**Morphgesic® SR** (Amdipharm) CD
Tablets, m/r, f/c, morphine sulphate 10 mg (buff), net price 60-tab pack = £4.09; 30 mg (violet), 60-tab pack = £9.81; 60 mg (orange), 60-tab pack = £19.15; 100 mg (grey), 60-tab pack = £30.30. Label: 2, 25
Dose every 12 hours, dose adjusted according to daily morphine requirements, for further advice on determining dose, see Prescribing in Palliative Care, p. 14; dosage requirements should be reviewed if the brand is altered
Note. Prescriptions must also specify 'tablets' (i.e. Morphgesic SR tablets)

**MST Continus®** (Napp) CD
Tablets, m/r, f/c, morphine sulphate 5 mg (white), net price 60-tab pack = £3.29; 10 mg (brown), 60-tab pack = £5.48; 15 mg (green), 60-tab pack = £9.61; 30 mg (purple), 60-tab pack = £13.17; 60 mg (orange), 60-tab pack = £25.69; 100 mg (grey), 60-tab pack = £40.66; 200 mg (green), 60-tab pack = £81.34. Label: 2, 25

Suspension (= sachet of granules to mix with water), m/r, pink, morphine sulphate 20 mg/sachet, net price 30-sachet pack = £24.58; 30 mg/sachet, 30-sachet pack = £25.54; 60 mg/sachet, 30-sachet pack = £51.09; 100 mg/sachet, 30-sachet pack = £85.15; 200 mg/sachet pack, 30-sachet pack = £170.30. Label: 2, 13
Dose every 12 hours, dose adjusted according to daily morphine requirements, for further advice on determining dose, see Prescribing in Palliative Care, p. 14; dosage requirements should be reviewed if the brand is altered
Note Prescriptions must also specify 'tablets' or 'suspension' (i.e. 'MST Continus tablets' or 'MST Continus suspension')

**MXL®** (Napp) CD
Capsules, m/r, morphine sulphate 30 mg (light blue), net price 28-cap pack = £10.91; 60 mg (brown), 28-cap pack = £14.95; 90 mg (pink), 28-cap pack = £22.04; 120 mg (green), 28-cap pack = £29.15; 150 mg (blue), 28-cap pack = £36.43; 200 mg (red-brown), 28-cap pack = £46.15. Label: 2, counselling, see below
Dose every 24 hours, dose adjusted according to daily morphine requirements, for further advice on determining dose, see Prescribing in Palliative Care, p. 14; dosage requirements should be reviewed if the brand is altered
Counselling Swallow whole or open capsule and sprinkle contents on soft food
Note Prescriptions must also specify 'capsules' (i.e. 'MXL capsules')

**Zomorph®** (Link) CD
Capsules, m/r, morphine sulphate 10 mg (yellow/clear enclosing pale yellow pellets), net price 60-cap pack = £4.08; 30 mg (pink/clear enclosing pale yellow pellets), 60-cap pack = £9.77; 60 mg (orange/clear

enclosing pale yellow pellets), 60-cap pack = £19.06; 100 mg (white/clear enclosing pale yellow pellets), 60-cap pack = £30.18; 200 mg (clear enclosing pale yellow pellets), 60-cap pack = £60.35. Label: 2, counselling, see below

Dose every 12 hours, dose adjusted according to daily morphine requirements, for further advice on determining doses, see Prescribing in Palliative Care, p. 14; dosage requirements should be reviewed if the brand is altered

Counselling Swallow whole or open capsule and sprinkle contents on soft food

Note Prescriptions must also specify 'capsules' (i.e. 'Zomorph capsules')

### Suppositories

**Morphine** (Non-proprietary) CD

Suppositories, morphine hydrochloride or sulphate 10 mg, net price 12 = £7.24; 15 mg, 12 = £7.14; 20 mg, 12 = £8.92; 30 mg, 12 = £10.40. Label: 2

Available from Aurum, Martindale

Note Both the strength of the suppositories and the morphine salt contained in them must be specified by the prescriber

### Injections

**Morphine Sulphate** (Non-proprietary) CD

Injection, morphine sulphate 10, 15, 20, and 30 mg/mL, net price 1- and 2-mL amp (all) = 72p–£1.09; 10 mg/mL, 1-mL prefilled syringe = £5.00

Intravenous infusion, morphine sulphate 1 mg/mL, net price 50-mL vial = £5.00; 2 mg/mL, 50-mL vial = £5.10

**Minijet® Morphine Sulphate** (Celltech) CD

Injection, morphine sulphate 1 mg/mL, net price 10-mL disposable syringe = £7.36

### Injection with anti-emetic

Caution In myocardial infarction cyclizine may aggravate severe heart failure and counteract the haemodynamic benefits of opioids, see section 4.6. **Not recommended** in palliative care, see Nausea and Vomiting, p. 16

**Cyclimorph®** (Amdipharm) CD

Cyclimorph-10® Injection, morphine tartrate 10 mg, cyclizine tartrate 50 mg/mL. Net price 1-mL amp = £1.34

Dose moderate to severe pain (short-term use only) by subcutaneous, intramuscular, or intravenous injection, 1 mL, repeated not more often than every 4 hours, with not more than 3 doses in any 24-hour period

Cyclimorph-15® Injection, morphine tartrate 15 mg, cyclizine tartrate 50 mg/mL. Net price 1-mL amp = £1.39

Dose moderate to severe pain (short-term use only) by subcutaneous, intramuscular, or intravenous injection, 1 mL, repeated not more often than every 4 hours, with not more than 3 doses in any 24-hour period

## BUPRENORPHINE

**Indications** moderate to severe pain; peri-operative analgesia; opioid dependence (section 4.10)

**Cautions** see under Morphine Salts and notes above; effects only partially reversed by naloxone; **interactions:** Appendix 1 (opioid analgesics)

Fever or external heat Monitor patients using patches for increased side-effects if fever present (increased absorption possible); avoid exposing application site to external heat (may also increase absorption)

**Contra-indications** see under Morphine Salts and notes above

**Side-effects** see under Morphine Salts and notes above; can give rise to mild withdrawal symptoms in patients dependent on opioids; hiccups, dyspnoea; with patches, local reactions such as erythema and pruritus; delayed local allergic reactions with severe inflammation—discontinue treatment

**Dose**

- Moderate to severe pain, by sublingual administration, initially 200–400 micrograms every 8 hours, increasing if necessary to 200–400 micrograms every 6–8 hours; CHILD over 6 years, 16–25 kg, 100 micrograms every 6–8 hours; 25–37.5 kg, 100–200 micrograms every 6–8 hours; 37.5–50 kg, 200–300 micrograms every 6–8 hours

  By intramuscular *or* slow intravenous injection, 300–600 micrograms every 6–8 hours; CHILD over 6 months 3–6 micrograms/kg every 6–8 hours (max. 9 micrograms/kg)
- Premedication, by sublingual administration, 400 micrograms

  By intramuscular injection, 300 micrograms
- Intra-operative analgesia, by slow intravenous injection, 300–450 micrograms

**BuTrans®** (Napp) CD

Patches, self-adhesive, beige, buprenorphine, '5' patch (releasing 5 micrograms/hour for 7 days), net price 4 = £9.00; '10' patch (releasing 10 micrograms/hour for 7 days), 4 = £32.72; '20' patch (releasing 20 micrograms/hour for 7 days), 4 = £59.59. Label: 2

Dose moderate to severe pain unresponsive to non-opioid analgesics, ADULT over 18 years, initially one '5 micrograms/hour' patch; apply to dry, non-irritated, non-hairy skin on upper torso, removing after 7 days and siting replacement patch on a different area (avoid same area for at least 3 weeks)

Dose adjustment When starting, analgesic effect should **not** be evaluated until the system has been worn for **72 hours** (to allow for gradual increase in plasma-buprenorphine concentration)—if necessary, dose should be adjusted at 3-day intervals using a patch of the next strength or 2 patches of the same strength (applied at *same time* to avoid confusion). Max. 2 patches can be used at any one time

**Temgesic®** (Schering-Plough) CD

Tablets (sublingual), buprenorphine (as hydrochloride), 200 micrograms, net price 50-tab pack = £5.33; 400 micrograms, 50-tab pack = £10.66. Label: 2, 26

Injection, buprenorphine (as hydrochloride) 300 micrograms/mL, net price 1-mL amp = 49p

**Transtec®** (Napp) CD

Patches, self-adhesive, skin-coloured, buprenorphine, '35' patch (releasing 35 micrograms/hour for 72 hours), net price 5 = £28.97; '52.5' patch (releasing 52.5 micrograms/hour for 72 hours), 5 = £43.46; '70' patch (releasing 70 micrograms/hour for 72 hours), 5 = £57.94. Label: 2

Dose moderate to severe pain unresponsive to non-opioid analgesics, ADULT over 18 years, apply to dry, non-irritated, non-hairy skin on upper torso, removing after 72 hours and siting replacement patch on a different area (avoid same area for at least 6 days). Patients who have not previously received strong opioid analgesic, initially, one '35 micrograms/hour' patch replaced after 72 hours; patients who have received strong opioid analgesic, initial dose based on previous 24-hour opioid requirement, consult product literature

Dose adjustment When starting, analgesic effect should **not** be evaluated until the system has been worn for **24 hours** (to allow for gradual increase in plasma-buprenorphine concentration)—if necessary, dose should be adjusted at 72-hour intervals using a patch of the next strength *or* using 2 patches of the same strength (applied at *same time* to avoid confusion). Max. 2 patches can be used at any one time. For breakthrough pain, consider 200–400 micrograms buprenorphine sublingually. **Important:** it may take approx. 30 hours for the plasma-buprenorphine concentration to decrease by 50% after patch is removed

Long duration of action In view of the long duration of action, patients who have severe side-effects should be monitored for up to 30 hours after removing patch

## CODEINE PHOSPHATE

**Indications** mild to moderate pain; diarrhoea (section 1.4.2); cough suppression (section 3.9.1)

**Cautions** see under Morphine Salts and notes above; use of cough suppressants containing codeine or similar opioid analgesics not generally recommended in children and should be avoided altogether in those under 1 year; **interactions:** Appendix 1 (opioid analgesics)

**Contra-indications** see under Morphine Salts and notes above

**Side-effects** see under Morphine Salts and notes above

**Dose**

- By mouth, 30–60 mg every 4 hours when necessary, to a max. of 240 mg daily; CHILD 1–12 years, 3 mg/kg daily in divided doses
- By intramuscular injection, 30–60 mg every 4 hours when necessary

**Codeine Phosphate** (Non-proprietary)

Tablets PoM, codeine phosphate 15 mg, net price 28 = £1.46; 30 mg, 28 = £1.67; 60 mg, 28 = £2.61. Label: 2

Note As for schedule 2 controlled drugs, travellers needing to take codeine phosphate preparations abroad may require a doctor's letter explaining why they are necessary

Syrup PoM, codeine phosphate 25 mg/5 mL. Net price 100 mL = 90p. Label: 2

Injection CD, codeine phosphate 60 mg/mL. Net price 1-mL amp = £2.37

**Codeine Linctuses** Section 3.9.1

Note Codeine is an ingredient of some compound analgesic preparations, section 4.7.1 and section 10.1.1 (*Codafen Continus®*)

## DIAMORPHINE HYDROCHLORIDE
### (Heroin Hydrochloride)

**Indications** see notes above; acute pulmonary oedema

**Cautions** see under Morphine Salts and notes above; **interactions:** Appendix 1 (opioid analgesics)

**Contra-indications** see under Morphine Salts and notes above

**Side-effects** see under Morphine Salts and notes above

**Dose**

- Acute pain, by subcutaneous *or* intramuscular injection, 5 mg repeated every 4 hours if necessary (up to 10 mg for heavier well-muscled patients); by slow intravenous injection, quarter to half corresponding intramuscular dose
- Myocardial infarction, by slow intravenous injection (1 mg/minute), 5 mg followed by a further 2.5–5 mg if necessary; elderly or frail patients, reduce dose by half
- Acute pulmonary oedema, by slow intravenous injection (1 mg/minute) 2.5–5 mg
- Chronic pain, by mouth *or* by subcutaneous *or* intramuscular injection, 5–10 mg regularly every 4 hours; dose may be increased according to needs; intramuscular dose should be approx. half corresponding oral dose, and approx. one third corresponding oral *morphine* dose—see also Prescribing in Palliative Care, p. 14; by subcutaneous infusion (using syringe driver), see Prescribing in Palliative Care, p. 17

**Diamorphine** (Non-proprietary) CD

Tablets, diamorphine hydrochloride 10 mg. Net price 100-tab pack = £12.30. Label: 2

Injection, powder for reconstitution, diamorphine hydrochloride. Net price 5-mg amp = £1.18, 10-mg amp = £1.36, 30-mg amp = £1.62, 100-mg amp = £4.50, 500-mg amp = £20.68

## DIHYDROCODEINE TARTRATE

**Indications** moderate to severe pain

**Cautions** see under Morphine Salts and notes above; **interactions:** Appendix 1 (opioid analgesics)

**Contra-indications** see under Morphine Salts and notes above

**Side-effects** see under Morphine Salts and notes above

**Dose**

- By mouth, 30 mg every 4–6 hours when necessary (see also notes above); CHILD over 4 years 0.5–1 mg/kg every 4–6 hours
- By deep subcutaneous *or* intramuscular injection, up to 50 mg repeated every 4–6 hours if necessary; CHILD over 4 years 0.5–1 mg/kg every 4–6 hours

**Dihydrocodeine** (Non-proprietary)

Tablets PoM, dihydrocodeine tartrate 30 mg. Net price 20 = £1.39. Label: 2, 21

Dental prescribing on NHS Dihydrocodeine Tablets 30 mg may be prescribed

Oral solution PoM, dihydrocodeine tartrate 10 mg/5 mL. Net price 150 mL = £3.08. Label: 2, 21

Injection CD, dihydrocodeine tartrate 50 mg/mL. Net price 1-mL amp = £2.29

**DF 118 Forte®** (Martindale) PoM

Tablets, dihydrocodeine tartrate 40 mg. Net price 100-tab pack = £11.51. Label: 2, 21

Dose severe pain, 40–80 mg 3 times daily; max. 240 mg daily; CHILD not recommended

### Modified release

**DHC Continus®** (Napp) PoM

Tablets, m/r, dihydrocodeine tartrate 60 mg, net price 56-tab pack = £5.50; 90 mg, 56-tab pack = £8.66; 120 mg, 56-tab pack = £11.57. Label: 2, 25

Dose chronic severe pain, 60–120 mg every 12 hours; CHILD not recommended

Note Dihydrocodeine is an ingredient of some compound analgesic preparations, see section 4.7.1

## DIPIPANONE HYDROCHLORIDE

**Indications** moderate to severe pain

**Cautions** see under Morphine Salts and notes above; **interactions:** Appendix 1 (opioid analgesics)

**Contra-indications** see under Morphine Salts and notes above

**Side-effects** see under Morphine Salts and notes above

**Dose**

- See preparation below

**Diconal®** (Amdipharm) CD
Tablets, pink, scored, dipipanone hydrochloride 10 mg, cyclizine hydrochloride 30 mg. Net price 50-tab pack = £8.57. Label: 2

Dose *acute pain*, 1 tablet gradually increased to 3 tablets every 6 hours; CHILD not recommended

Caution **Not recommended** in palliative care, see Nausea and vomiting p. 17

## FENTANYL

**Indications** breakthrough pain in patients already receiving opioid therapy for chronic cancer pain (lozenges); chronic intractable pain (patches), other indications (section 15.1.4.3)

**Cautions** see under Morphine Salts and notes above; **interactions:** Appendix 1 (opioid analgesics)

Fever or external heat Monitor patients using patches for increased side-effects if fever present (increased absorption possible); avoid exposing application site to external heat (may also increase absorption)

**Contra-indications** see under Morphine Salts and notes above

**Side-effects** see under Morphine Salts and notes above; with patches, local reactions such as rash, erythema and itching reported

**Dose**

- See under preparations, below

Conversion (from oral morphine to transdermal fentanyl), see Prescribing in Palliative Care, p. 15

**Actiq®** (Cephalon) CD
Lozenge, (with oromucosal applicator), fentanyl (as citrate) 200 micrograms, net price 3 = £18.58, 30 = £185.80; 400 micrograms, 3 = £18.58, 30 = £185.80; 600 micrograms, 3 = £18.58, 30 = £185.80; 800 micrograms, 3 = £18.58, 30 = £185.80; 1.2 mg, 3 = £18.58, 30 = £185.80; 1.6 mg, 3 = £18.58, 30 = £185.80. Label: 2

Dose initially 200 micrograms (over 15 minutes) repeated if necessary 15 minutes after first dose (no more than 2 dose units for each pain episode); adjust dose according to response; max. 4 dose units daily

Note If more than 4 episodes of breakthrough pain each day, adjust dose of background analgesic

**Durogesic® DTrans®** (Janssen-Cilag) CD
Patches, self-adhesive, transparent, fentanyl, '12' patch (releasing approx. 12 micrograms/hour for 72 hours), net price 5 = £19.26; '25' patch (releasing approx. 25 micrograms/hour for 72 hours), 5 = £27.52; '50' patch (releasing approx. 50 micrograms/hour for 72 hours), 5 = £51.40; '75' patch (releasing approx. 75 micrograms/hour for 72 hours), 5 = £71.66; '100' patch (releasing approx. 100 micrograms/hour for 72 hours), 5 = £88.32. Label: 2

Note Prescriptions must also specify 'patches' (i.e. 'Durogesic DTrans patches')

Dose apply to dry, non-irritated, non-irradiated, non-hairy skin on torso or upper arm, removing after 72 hours and siting replacement patch on a different area (avoid using the same area for several days). Patients who have not previously received a strong opioid analgesic, initial dose, one '25 micrograms/hour' patch replaced after 72 hours; patients who have received a strong opioid analgesic, initial dose based on previous 24-hour opioid requirement (oral morphine sulphate 90 mg over 24 hours is approximately equivalent to one '25 micrograms/hour' patch, consult product literature for details); CHILD not recommended

Dose adjustment When starting, evaluation of the analgesic effect should **not** be made before the system has been worn for **24 hours** (to allow for the gradual increase in plasma-fentanyl concentration)—previous analgesic therapy should be phased out gradually from time of first patch application; if necessary dose should be adjusted at 72-hour intervals in steps of 12–25 micrograms/hour. More than one patch may be used at a time for doses greater than 100 micrograms/hour (but applied at *same time* to avoid confusion)—consider additional or alternative analgesic therapy if dose required exceeds 300 micrograms/hour (**important:** it may take 22 hours or longer for the plasma-fentanyl concentration to decrease by 50%—replacement opioid therapy should be initiated at a low dose, increasing gradually).

Long duration of action In view of the long duration of action, patients who have had severe side-effects should be monitored for up to 24 hours after patch removal

Note Prescriptions for fentanyl patches can be written to show the strength in terms of the release rate and it is acceptable to write '*Fentanyl 25 patches*' to prescribe patches that release fentanyl 25 micrograms per hour. The dosage should be expressed in terms of the interval between applying a patch and replacing it with a new one, e.g. '*one patch to be applied every 72 hours*'. The total quantity of patches should be written in words and figures.

## HYDROMORPHONE HYDROCHLORIDE

**Indications** severe pain in cancer

**Cautions** see Morphine Salts and notes above; **interactions:** Appendix 1 (opioid analgesics)

**Contra-indications** see Morphine Salts and notes above

**Side-effects** see Morphine Salts and notes above

**Dose**

- See under preparations below

**Palladone®** (Napp) CD
Capsules, hydromorphone hydrochloride 1.3 mg (orange/clear), net price 56-cap pack = £8.82; 2.6 mg (red/clear), 56-cap pack = £17.64. Label: 2, counselling, see below

Dose 1.3 mg every 4 hours, increased if necessary according to severity of pain; CHILD under 12 years not recommended

Counselling Swallow whole or open capsule and sprinkle contents on soft food

### Modified release

**Palladone® SR** (Napp) CD
Capsules, m/r, hydromorphone hydrochloride 2 mg (yellow/clear), net price 56-cap pack = £20.98; 4 mg (pale blue/clear), 56-cap pack = £28.75; 8 mg (pink/clear), 56-cap pack = £56.08; 16 mg (brown/clear), 56-cap pack = £106.53; 24 mg (dark blue/clear), 56-cap pack = £159.82. Label: 2, counselling, see below

Dose 4 mg every 12 hours, increased if necessary according to severity of pain; CHILD under 12 years not recommended

Counselling Swallow whole or open capsule and sprinkle contents on soft food

## MEPTAZINOL

**Indications** moderate to severe pain, including postoperative and obstetric pain and renal colic; perioperative analgesia, see section 15.1.4.3

**Cautions** see under Morphine Salts and notes above; effects only partially reversed by naloxone; **interactions:** Appendix 1 (opioid analgesics)

**Contra-indications** see under Morphine Salts and notes above

**Side-effects** see under Morphine Salts and notes above

**Dose**

- By mouth, 200 mg every 3–6 hours as required; CHILD not recommended
- By intramuscular injection, 75–100 mg every 2–4 hours if necessary; obstetric analgesia, 100–150 mg according to patient's weight (2 mg/kg); CHILD not recommended

- By slow intravenous injection, 50–100 mg every 2–4 hours if necessary; CHILD not recommended

**Meptid®** (Shire) PoM

Tablets, orange, f/c, meptazinol 200 mg, net price 112-tab pack = £22.11. Label: 2

Injection, meptazinol 100 mg (as hydrochloride)/mL, net price 1-mL amp = £1.92

## METHADONE HYDROCHLORIDE

**Indications** severe pain, see notes above; cough in terminal disease (section 3.9.1); adjunct in treatment of opioid dependence (section 4.10)

**Cautions** see under Morphine Salts and notes above; **interactions:** Appendix 1 (opioid analgesics)

**Contra-indications** see under Morphine Salts and notes above

**Side-effects** see under Morphine Salts and notes above

**Dose**

- By mouth *or* by subcutaneous *or* intramuscular injection, 5–10 mg every 6–8 hours, adjusted according to response; on prolonged use not to be given more frequenly than every 12 hours; CHILD not recommended

**Methadone** (Non-proprietary) CD

Tablets, methadone hydrochloride 5 mg. Net price 50 = £2.97. Label: 2

Brands include *Physeptone®*

Injection ▼, methadone hydrochloride, 10 mg/mL, net price 1-mL amp = 86p, 2-mL amp = £1.45, 3.5-mL amp = £1.78, 5-mL amp = £1.92

Brands include *Physeptone®*, *Synastone®*

## OXYCODONE HYDROCHLORIDE

**Indications** moderate to severe pain in patients with cancer; postoperative pain; severe pain

**Cautions** see under Morphine Salts and notes above; avoid in porphyria (section 9.8.2); **interactions:** Appendix 1 (opioid analgesics)

**Contra-indications** see under Morphine Salts and notes above; moderate to severe hepatic impairment; severe renal impairment

**Side-effects** see under Morphine Salts and notes above

**Dose**

- By mouth, initially, 5 mg every 4–6 hours, increased if necessary according to severity of pain, usual max. 400 mg daily, but some patients may require higher doses; CHILD under 18 years not recommended
- By slow intravenous injection, 1–10 mg every 4 hours when necessary
- By subcutaneous injection, initially 5 mg every 4 hours when necessary
- By subcutaneous infusion, initially 7.5 mg/24 hours adjusted according to response
- Patient controlled analgesia (PCA), consult hospital protocols

**Note** 2 mg oral oxycodone is approximately equivalent to 1 mg parenteral oxycodone

**OxyNorm®** (Napp) CD

Capsules, oxycodone hydrochloride 5 mg (orange/beige), net price 56-cap pack = £11.09; 10 mg (white/beige), 56-cap pack = £22.18; 20 mg (pink/beige), 56-cap pack = £44.35. Label: 2

Liquid (= oral solution), sugar-free, oxycodone hydrochloride 5 mg/5 mL, net price 250 mL = £9.43. Label: 2

Concentrate (= concentrated oral solution), sugar-free, oxycodone hydrochloride 10 mg/mL, net price 120 mL = £45.25. Label: 2

Injection ▼, oxycodone hydrochloride 10 mg/mL, net price 1-mL amp = £1.47, 2-mL amp = £2.94

**Note** The *Scottish Medicines Consortium* has advised (October 2004) that *OxyNorm®* injection is used only in patients with cancer who have difficulty in tolerating morphine or diamorphine

### Modified release

**OxyContin®** (Napp) CD

Tablets, f/c, m/r, oxycodone hydrochloride 5 mg (blue), net price 28-tab pack = £12.16; 10 mg (white), 56-tab pack = £24.30; 20 mg (pink), 56-tab pack = £48.60; 40 mg (yellow), 56-tab pack = £97.22; 80 mg (green), 56-tab pack = £194.44. Label: 2, 25

**Dose** initially, 10 mg every 12 hours, increased if necessary according to severity of pain, usual max. 200 mg every 12 hours, but some patients may require higher doses; CHILD under 18 years not recommended

## PAPAVERETUM

**Important** Do **not** confuse with papaverine (section 7.4.5)

A mixture of 253 parts of morphine hydrochloride, 23 parts of papaverine hydrochloride and 20 parts of codeine hydrochloride

The CSM has advised that to avoid confusion the figures of 7.7 mg/ml or 15.4 mg/ml should be used for prescribing purposes

**Indications** premedication; enhancement of anaesthesia (but see section 15.1.4.3); postoperative analgesia; severe chronic pain

**Cautions** see Morphine Salts and notes above

**Contra-indications** see Morphine Salts and notes above

**Side-effects** see Morphine Salts and notes above

**Dose**

- By subcutaneous, intramuscular, *or* intravenous injection, 7.7–15.4 mg repeated every 4 hours if necessary (ELDERLY initially 7.7 mg); CHILD up to 1 month 115 micrograms/kg, 1–12 months 154 micrograms/kg, 1–5 years 1.93–3.85 mg, 6–12 years, 3.85–7.7 mg

**Intravenous dose** In general the intravenous dose should be 25–50% of the corresponding subcutaneous or intramuscular dose

**Papaveretum** (Non-proprietary) CD

Injection, papaveretum 15.4 mg/mL (providing the equivalent of 10 mg of anhydrous morphine/mL), net price 1-mL amp = £1.36

**Note** The name *Omnopon®* was formerly used for papaveretum preparations

### With hyoscine

**Papaveretum and Hyoscine Injection** (Non-proprietary) CD

Injection, papaveretum 15.4 mg (providing the equivalent of 10 mg of anhydrous morphine), hyoscine hydrobromide 400 micrograms/mL. Net price 1-mL amp = £2.98

**Dose** premedication, by subcutaneous or intramuscular injection, 0.5–1 mL

### With aspirin

Section 4.7.1

## PENTAZOCINE

**Indications** moderate to severe pain, but see notes above

**Cautions** see under Morphine Salts and notes above; avoid in porphyria (section 9.8.2); **interactions:** Appendix 1 (opioid analgesics)

**Contra-indications** see under Morphine Salts and notes above; patients dependent on opioids; arterial or pulmonary hypertension, heart failure

**Side-effects** see under Morphine Salts and notes above; occasional hallucinations

**Dose**

- By mouth, pentazocine hydrochloride 50 mg every 3–4 hours preferably after food (range 25–100 mg); max. 600 mg daily; CHILD 6–12 years 25 mg
- By subcutaneous, intramuscular, *or* intravenous injection, moderate pain, pentazocine 30 mg, severe pain 45–60 mg every 3–4 hours when necessary; CHILD over 1 year, by subcutaneous *or* intramuscular injection, up to 1 mg/kg, by intravenous injection up to 500 micrograms/kg
- By rectum in suppositories, pentazocine 50 mg up to 4 times daily; CHILD not recommended

**Pentazocine** (Non-proprietary) CD

Capsules, pentazocine hydrochloride 50 mg. Net price 28-cap pack = £4.06. Label: 2, 21
Brands include *Fortral®* NHS

Tablets, pentazocine hydrochloride 25 mg. Net price 28-tab pack = £2.09. Label: 2, 21
Brands include *Fortral®* NHS

Injection, pentazocine 30 mg (as lactate)/mL. Net price 1-mL amp = £1.67; 2-mL amp = £3.21
Brands include *Fortral®* NHS

Suppositories, pentazocine 50 mg (as lactate). Net price 20 = £19.93. Label: 2
Brands include *Fortral®* NHS

## PETHIDINE HYDROCHLORIDE

**Indications** moderate to severe pain, obstetric analgesia; peri-operative analgesia

**Cautions** see under Morphine Salts and notes above; not suitable for severe continuing pain; **interactions:** Appendix 1 (opioid analgesics)

**Contra-indications** see under Morphine Salts and notes above; severe renal impairment

**Side-effects** see under Morphine Salts and notes above; convulsions reported in **overdosage**

**Dose**

- Acute pain, by mouth, 50–150 mg every 4 hours; CHILD 0.5–2 mg/kg

  By subcutaneous *or* intramuscular injection, 25–100 mg, repeated after 4 hours; CHILD, by intramuscular injection, 0.5–2 mg/kg

  By slow intravenous injection, 25–50 mg, repeated after 4 hours
- Obstetric analgesia, by subcutaneous *or* intramuscular injection, 50–100 mg, repeated 1–3 hours later if necessary; max. 400 mg in 24 hours
- Premedication, by intramuscular injection, 25–100 mg 1 hour before operation; CHILD 0.5–2 mg/kg
- Postoperative pain, by subcutaneous *or* intramuscular injection, 25–100 mg, every 2–3 hours if necessary; CHILD, by intramuscular injection, 0.5–2 mg/kg

  **Note** In the postoperative period, the patient should be closely monitored for pain relief as well as for side-effects especially respiratory depression

**Pethidine** (Non-proprietary) CD

Tablets, pethidine hydrochloride 50 mg, net price 20 = £1.97. Label: 2

Dental prescribing on NHS Pethidine Tablets may be prescribed

Injection, pethidine hydrochloride 50 mg/mL, net price 1-mL amp = 53p, 2-mL amp = 56p; 10 mg/mL, 5-mL amp = £2.06, 10-mL amp = £2.18

**Pamergan P100®** (Martindale) CD

Injection, pethidine hydrochloride 50 mg, promethazine hydrochloride 25 mg/mL. Net price 2-mL amp = 70p

Dose by intramuscular injection, premedication, 2 mL 60–90 minutes before operation; CHILD 8–12 years 0.75 mL, 13–16 years 1 mL

Obstetric analgesia, 1–2 mL every 4 hours if necessary

Severe pain, 1–2 mL every 4–6 hours if necessary

Note Although usually given intramuscularly, may be given intravenously after dilution to at least 10 mL with water for injections

## TRAMADOL HYDROCHLORIDE

**Indications** moderate to severe pain

**Cautions** see under Morphine Salts and notes above; history of epilepsy (convulsions reported, usually after rapid intravenous injection); manufacturer advises avoid in pregnancy (Appendix 4) and breast-feeding (Appendix 5); not suitable as substitute in opioid-dependent patients; **interactions:** Appendix 1 (opioid analgesics)

**General anaesthesia** Not recommended for analgesia during potentially very light planes of general anaesthesia (possibly increased operative recall reported)

**Contra-indications** see under Morphine Salts and notes above

**Side-effects** see under Morphine Salts and notes above; also abdominal discomfort, diarrhoea, hypotension and occasionally hypertension; paraesthesia, anaphylaxis, and confusion reported

**Dose**

- By mouth, 50–100 mg not more often than every 4 hours; total of more than 400 mg daily by mouth not usually required; CHILD not recommended
- By intramuscular injection *or* by intravenous injection (over 2–3 minutes) *or* by intravenous infusion, 50–100 mg every 4–6 hours

  Postoperative pain, 100 mg initially then 50 mg every 10–20 minutes if necessary during first hour to total max. 250 mg (including initial dose) in first hour, *then* 50–100 mg every 4–6 hours; max. 600 mg daily; CHILD not recommended

**Tramadol Hydrochloride** (Non-proprietary) PoM

Capsules, tramadol hydrochloride 50 mg. Net price 30-cap pack = £2.19, 100-cap pack = £4.10. Label: 2
Brands include *Tramake®*

Injection, tramadol hydrochloride 50 mg/mL. Net price 2-mL amp = £1.15

**Tramake Insts®** (Galen) PoM

Sachets, effervescent powder, sugar-free, lemon-flavoured, tramadol hydrochloride 50 mg (contains $Na^+$ 9.7 mmol/sachet), net price 60-sachet pack = £8.75;

100 mg (contains Na$^+$ 14.6 mmol/sachet), 60-sachet pack = £17.00. Label: 2, 13
Excipients include aspartame (section 9.4.1)

**Zamadol®** (Viatris) PoM
Capsules, tramadol hydrochloride 50 mg, net price 100-cap pack = £8.00. Label: 2

Orodispersible tablets (*Zamadol Melt®*), tramadol hydrochloride 50 mg, net price 60-tab pack = £7.12, 100-tab pack = £11.88. Label: 2, counselling, administration
Excipients include aspartame

Counselling *Zamadol Melt®* should be sucked and then swallowed. May also be dispersed in water

Injection, tramadol hydrochloride 50 mg/mL, net price 2-mL amp = £1.10

**Zydol®** (Grünenthal) PoM
Capsules, green/yellow, tramadol hydrochloride 50 mg. Net price 100-cap pack = £16.91. Label: 2

Soluble tablets, tramadol hydrochloride 50 mg, net price 20-tab pack = £3.05, 100-tab pack = £15.23. Label: 2, 13

Injection, tramadol hydrochloride 50 mg/mL. Net price 2-mL amp = £1.24

**Modified release**

**Dromadol® SR** (IVAX) PoM
Tablets, m/r, tramadol hydrochloride 100 mg (white), net price 60-tab pack = £16.00; 150 mg (beige), 60-tab pack = £24.00; 200 mg (orange), 60-tab pack = £32.00. Label: 2, 25
Dose initially 100 mg twice daily increased if necessary; usual max. 200 mg twice daily; CHILD under 12 years not recommended

**Larapam® SR** (Sandoz) PoM
Tablets, m/r, tramadol hydrochloride 100 mg, net price 60-tab pack = £18.25; 150 mg, 60-tab pack = £27.35; 200 mg, 60-tab pack = £36.50. Label: 2, 25
Dose initially 100 mg twice daily increased if necessary; usual max. 200 mg twice daily; CHILD under 12 years not recommended

**Zamadol® 24hr** (Viatris) PoM
Tablets, all f/c, all m/r, tramadol hydrochloride 150 mg, net price 28-tab pack = £10.70; 200 mg, 28-tab pack = £14.26; 300 mg, 28-tab pack = £21.39; 400 mg, 28-tab pack = £28.51. Label: 2, 25
Dose 150 mg once daily increased if necessary; max. 400 mg once daily; CHILD under 12 years not recommended

**Zamadol® SR** (Viatris) PoM
Capsules, m/r, tramadol hydrochloride 50 mg (green), net price 60-cap pack = £7.64; 100 mg, net price 60-cap pack = £15.28; 150 mg (dark green), 60-cap pack = £22.92; 200 mg (yellow), 60-cap pack = £30.55. Label: 2, 25
Dose 50–100 mg twice daily increased if necessary to 150–200 mg twice daily; total of more than 400 mg daily not usually required; CHILD under 12 years not recommended
Counselling Swallow whole or open capsule and swallow contents immediately without chewing

**Zydol SR®** (Grünenthal) PoM
Tablets, m/r, f/c, tramadol hydrochloride 100 mg, net price 60-tab pack = £18.26; 150 mg (beige), 60-tab pack = £27.39; 200 mg (orange), 60-tab pack = £36.52. Label: 2, 25
Dose 100 mg twice daily increased if necessary to 150–200 mg twice daily; total of more than 400 mg daily not usually required; CHILD not recommended

**Zydol XL®** (Grünenthal) PoM
Tablets, m/r, f/c, tramadol hydrochloride 150 mg, net price 30-tab pack = £15.22; 200 mg, 30-tab pack = £20.29; 300 mg, 30-tab pack = £30.44; 400 mg, 30-tab pack = £40.59. Label: 2, 25
Dose 150 mg daily increased if necessary; more than 400 mg once daily not usually required; CHILD not recommended

**With paracetamol**

**Tramacet®** (Janssen-Cilag) ▼ PoM
Tablets, f/c, yellow, tramadol hydrochloride 37.5 mg, paracetamol 325 mg, net price 60-tab pack = £10.07. Label: 2, 25, 29, 30
Dose 2 tablets not more than every 6 hours; max. 8 tablets daily; CHILD under 12 years not recommended

## 4.7.3 Neuropathic pain

Neuropathic pain, which occurs as a result of damage to neural tissue, includes *postherpetic neuralgia, phantom limb pain, complex regional pain syndrome* (reflex sympathetic dystrophy, causalgia) *compression neuropathies, peripheral neuropathies* (e.g. due to diabetes, haematological malignancies, rheumatoid arthritis, alcoholism, drug misuse), *trauma, central pain* (e.g. pain following stroke, spinal cord injury and syringomyelia) and *idiopathic neuropathy*. The pain occurs in an area of sensory deficit and may be described as burning, shooting or scalding and is often accompanied by pain that is evoked by a non-noxious stimulus (allodynia).

*Trigeminal neuralgia* is also caused by dysfunction of neural tissue, but its management is distinct from other forms of neuropathic pain.

Neuropathic pain generally requires psychological management as well as the use of a tricyclic antidepressant and certain antiepileptic drugs. Neuropathic pain may respond only partially to opioid analgesics. Of the opioids, methadone, tramadol, and oxycodone are probably the most effective for neuropathic pain and they may be considered when other measures fail. Nerve blocks, transcutaneous electrical nerve stimulation (TENS) and, in selected cases, central electrical stimulation may help. Many patients with chronic neuropathic pain require multidisciplinary management, including physiotherapy and psychological support.

**Amitriptyline** is prescribed most frequently [unlicensed indication], initially at 10–25 mg each night. The dose may be increased gradually to about 75 mg daily if required (higher doses under specialist supervision); **nortriptyline**, a metabolite of amitriptyline, also given at an initial dose of 10–25 mg at night may produce fewer side-effects. **Gabapentin** and **pregabalin** (section 4.8.1) are licensed for the treatment of neuropathic pain.

**Capsaicin** (section 10.3.2) is licensed for neuropathic pain (but the intense burning sensation during initial treatment may limit use). **Ketamine** (section 15.1.1), an NMDA antagonist, or **lidocaine (lignocaine)** by intravenous infusion may also be useful in some forms of neuropathic pain [both unlicensed indication; specialist use only].

A **corticosteroid** may help to relieve pressure in compression neuropathy and thereby reduce pain. The management of trigeminal neuralgia and postherpetic neuralgia are outlined below; for the management of neuropathic pain in *palliative care* see p. 15; for the management of diabetic neuropathy, see section 6.1.5.

## Trigeminal neuralgia

Surgery may be the treatment of choice in many patients; a neurological assessment will identify those who stand to benefit. **Carbamazepine** (section 4.8.1) taken during the acute stages of trigeminal neuralgia, reduces the frequency and severity of attacks. It is very effective for the severe pain associated with trigeminal neuralgia and (less commonly) glossopharyngeal neuralgia. Blood counts and electrolytes should be monitored when high doses are given. Small doses should be used initially to reduce the incidence of side-effects e.g. dizziness. **Oxcarbazepine** [unlicensed indication] is an alternative to carbamazepine. **Gabapentin** and **lamotrigine** [unlicensed indication] are also used in trigeminal neuralgia. Some cases respond to **phenytoin** (section 4.8.1); the drug may be given by intravenous infusion (possibly as fosphenytoin) in a crisis (specialist use only).

## Postherpetic neuralgia

Postherpetic neuralgia follows acute herpes zoster infection (shingles), particularly in the elderly. If **amitriptyline** fails to manage the pain adequately, **gabapentin** may improve control. A topical analgesic preparation containing **capsaicin** 0.075% (section 10.3.2) is licensed for use in postherpetic neuralgia. Application of topical local anaesthetic preparations may be helpful in some patients.

## Chronic facial pain

Chronic oral and facial pain including persistent idiopathic facial pain (less correctly termed 'atypical facial pain') and temporomandibular dysfunction (previously termed temporomandibular joint pain dysfunction syndrome) may call for prolonged use of analgesics or for other drugs. Tricyclic antidepressants (section 4.3.1) may be useful for facial pain [unlicensed indication], but are not on the Dental Practitioners' List. Long-term prescribing for disorders of this type should follow a full investigation and usually involves specialists. Patients on long-term therapy need to be monitored both for progress and for side-effects.

# 4.7.4 Antimigraine drugs


4.7.4.1 Treatment of the acute migraine attack
4.7.4.2 Prophylaxis of migraine
4.7.4.3 Cluster headache


## 4.7.4.1 Treatment of the acute migraine attack

Treatment of a migraine attack should be guided by response to previous treatment and the severity of the attacks. A **simple analgesic** such as aspirin, paracetamol (preferably in a soluble or dispersible form) or an NSAID is often effective; concomitant **anti-emetic** treatment may be required. If treatment with an analgesic is inadequate, an attack may be treated with a specific antimigraine compound such as a **$5HT_1$ agonist** ('triptan'). **Ergot alkaloids** are rarely required now; oral and rectal preparations are associated with many side-effects and they should be avoided in cerebrovascular or cardiovascular disease.

Frequent and prolonged use of analgesics for migraine (opioid and non-opioid analgesics, $5HT_1$ agonists, and ergotamine) is associated with medication-overuse headache (analgesic-induced headache); therefore, increasing consumption of these medicines needs careful management.

## Analgesics

Most migraine headaches respond to analgesics such as **aspirin** or **paracetamol** (section 4.7.1) but because peristalsis is often reduced during migraine attacks the medication may not be sufficiently well absorbed to be effective; dispersible or effervescent preparations are therefore preferred.

The NSAID **tolfenamic acid** is licensed specifically for the treatment of an acute attack of migraine; **diclofenac potassium**, **flurbiprofen**, **ibuprofen**, and **naproxen sodium** (section 10.1.1) are also licensed for use in migraine.

### ANALGESICS

**Aspirin**
Section 4.7.1

**Paracetamol**
Section 4.7.1

**Non-steroidal anti-inflammatory drugs (NSAIDs)**
Section 10.1.1

**With anti-emetics**

**Domperamol®** (Servier) PoM
Tablets, f/c, paracetamol 500 mg, domperidone (as maleate) 10 mg, net price 16-tab pack = £6.51. Label: 17, 30
Dose 2 tablets at onset of attack then up to every 4 hours; max. 8 tablets daily; CHILD not recommended

**Migraleve®** (Pfizer Consumer)
Tablets, all f/c, *pink tablets*, buclizine hydrochloride 6.25 mg, paracetamol 500 mg, codeine phosphate 8 mg; *yellow tablets*, paracetamol 500 mg, codeine phosphate 8 mg. Net price 48-tab *Migraleve* PoM (32 pink + 16 yellow) = £5.10; 48 pink (*Migraleve Pink*) = £5.56; 48 yellow (*Migraleve Yellow*) = £4.70. Label: 2, (*Migraleve Pink*) 17, 30
Dose 2 pink tablets at onset of attack, or if it is imminent, then 2 yellow tablets every 4 hours if necessary; max. in 24 hours 2 pink and 6 yellow; CHILD under 10 years, only under close medical supervision; 10–14 years, half adult dose

**MigraMax®** (Zeneus) PoM
Oral powder, aspirin (as lysine acetylsalicylate) 900 mg, metoclopramide hydrochloride 10 mg/sachet, net price 6-sachet pack = £7.00, 20-sachet pack = £23.33. Label: 13, 21, 32
Dose ADULT over 20 years 1 sachet in water at onset of attack, repeated after 2 hours if necessary (max. 3 sachets in 24 hours); YOUNG ADULT (under 20 years) and CHILD not recommended
Important Metoclopramide can cause **severe extrapyramidal effects**, particularly in children and young adults (for further details, see p. 210)
Excipients include aspartame (section 9.4.1)

**Paramax®** (Sanofi-Synthelabo) PoM
Tablets, scored, paracetamol 500 mg, metoclopramide hydrochloride 5 mg. Net price 42-tab pack = £6.69. Label: 17, 30

Sachets, effervescent powder, sugar-free, the contents of 1 sachet = 1 tablet; to be dissolved in ¼ tumblerful of liquid before administration. Net price 42-sachet pack = £8.69. Label: 13, 17, 30

Dose (tablets or sachets): 2 at onset of attack then every 4 hours when necessary to max. of 6 in 24 hours; YOUNG ADULT 12–19 years, 1 at onset of attack then 1 every 4 hours when necessary to max. of 3 in 24 hours (max. dose of metoclopramide 500 micrograms/kg daily)

Important Metoclopramide can cause **severe extrapyramidal effects**, particularly in children and young adults (for further details, see p. 210)

## TOLFENAMIC ACID

**Indications** treatment of acute migraine attacks
**Cautions** see NSAIDs, section 10.1.1
**Contra-indications** see NSAIDs, section 10.1.1
**Side-effects** see NSAIDs, section 10.1.1; also dysuria (most commonly in men), tremor, euphoria, and fatigue reported
**Dose**
- 200 mg at onset repeated once after 1–2 hours if necessary

**Clotam®** (Provalis) PoM
Rapid Tablets, tolfenamic acid 200 mg. Net price 10-tab pack = £15.00

## $5HT_1$ agonists

A $5HT_1$ agonist is of considerable value in the treatment of an acute migraine attack. The $5HT_1$ agonists ('triptans') act on the 5HT (serotonin) 1B/1D receptors and they are therefore sometimes referred to as $5HT_{1B/1D}$-receptor agonists. A $5HT_1$ agonist may be used during the established headache phase of an attack and is the preferred treatment in those who fail to respond to conventional analgesics.

The $5HT_1$ agonists available for treating migraine are **almotriptan**, **eletriptan**, **frovatriptan**, **naratriptan**, **rizatriptan**, **sumatriptan**, and **zolmitriptan**. Sumatriptan is also of value in cluster headache (section 4.7.4.3).

**Cautions** $5HT_1$ agonists should be used with caution in conditions which predispose to coronary artery disease (pre-existing cardiac disease, see Contra-indications below); hepatic impairment (see Appendix 2); pregnancy (see Appendix 4) and breast-feeding (see Appendix 5). $5HT_1$ agonists are recommended as monotherapy and should not be taken concurrently with other therapies for acute migraine; see also **interactions**: Appendix 1 ($5HT_1$ agonists). Little information is available on the use of these drugs in the elderly (over 65 years).

**Contra-indications** $5HT_1$ agonists should not be used for prophylaxis and they are contra-indicated in ischaemic heart disease, previous myocardial infarction, coronary vasospasm (including Prinzmetal's angina), and uncontrolled or severe hypertension.

**Side-effects** Side-effects of the $5HT_1$ agonists include sensations of tingling, heat, heaviness, pressure, or tightness of any part of the body (including throat and chest—discontinue if intense, may be due to coronary vasoconstriction or to anaphylaxis; see also CSM advice under Sumatriptan); flushing, dizziness, feeling of weakness; fatigue; nausea and vomiting also reported.

## ALMOTRIPTAN

**Indications** treatment of acute migraine attacks
**Cautions** see under $5HT_1$ agonists above; sensitivity to sulphonamides; hepatic impairment (avoid if severe—Appendix 2); renal impairment (Appendix 3); **interactions:** Appendix 1 ($5HT_1$ agonists)
**Contra-indications** see under $5HT_1$ agonists above; previous cerebrovascular accident or transient ischaemic attack; peripheral vascular disease
**Side-effects** see under $5HT_1$ agonists above; also transient increase in blood pressure, drowsiness; *less commonly* diarrhoea, dyspepsia, dry mouth, chest pain, palpitation, paraesthesia, headache, myalgia, bone pain, tinnitus; *very rarely* myocardial infarction, and tachycardia
**Dose**
- 12.5 mg as soon as possible after onset repeated after 2 hours if migraine recurs (patient not responding should not take second dose for same attack); max. 25 mg in 24 hours; CHILD and ADOLESCENT under 18 years not recommended

**Almogran®** (Organon) PoM
Tablets, f/c, almotriptan (as hydrogen malate) 12.5 mg, net price 3-tab pack = £9.07; 6-tab pack = £18.14; 9-tab pack = £27.20. Label: 3

## ELETRIPTAN

**Indications** treatment of acute migraine attacks
**Cautions** see under $5HT_1$ agonists above; hepatic impairment (avoid if severe); renal impairment (avoid if severe—Appendix 3); **interactions**: Appendix 1 ($5HT_1$ agonists)
**Contra-indications** see under $5HT_1$ agonists above; previous cerebrovascular accident or transient ischaemic attack; peripheral vascular disease
**Side-effects** see under $5HT_1$ agonists above; also dry mouth, dyspepsia, abdominal pain, tachycardia, asthenia, drowsiness, ataxia, speech impairment, myasthenia, myalgia, pharyngitis, sweating; less commonly diarrhoea, anorexia, glossitis, thirst, oedema, increased urinary frequency, transient increase in blood pressure, insomnia, depression, confusion, tremor, agitation, euphoria, malaise, arthralgia, dyspnoea, rhinitis, rash, pruritus, visual disturbances, taste disturbance, tinnitus; rarely bradycardia
**Dose**
- 40 mg as soon as possible after onset repeated after 2 hours if migraine recurs (patient not responding should not take second dose for same attack); increase to 80 mg for subsequent attacks if 40-mg dose inadequate; max. 80 mg in 24 hours; CHILD and ADOLESCENT under 18 years not recommended

**Relpax®** (Pfizer) ▼ PoM
Tablets, f/c, orange, eletriptan (as hydrobromide) 20 mg, net price 6-tab pack = £22.50; 40 mg, 6-tab pack = £22.50. Label: 3

## FROVATRIPTAN

**Indications** treatment of acute migraine attacks

**Cautions** see under $5HT_1$ agonists above; **interactions:** Appendix 1 ($5HT_1$ agonists)

**Contra-indications** see under $5HT_1$ agonists above; severe hepatic impairment; previous cerebrovascular attack or transient ischaemic attack; peripheral vascular disease

**Side-effects** see under $5HT_1$ agonists above; also dry mouth, dyspepsia, abdominal pain, palpitation, paraesthesia, drowsiness, visual disturbances, sweating; *less commonly* diarrhoea, constipation, dysphagia, flatulence, tachycardia, hypertension, rhinitis, pharyngitis, sinusitis, laryngitis, tremor, anxiety, insomnia, confusion, nervousness, impaired concentration, euphoria, depression, depersonalisation, taste disturbances, fever, micturition disorders, thirst, arthralgia, muscle weakness, tinnitus, pruritus; *rarely* gastro-oesophageal reflux, hiccup, peptic ulcer, stomatitis, bradycardia, syncope, hyperventilation, amnesia, abnormal dreams, hypertonia, hypotonia, hypocalcaemia, hypoglycaemia, bilirubinaemia, epistaxis, urticaria, and purpura

**Dose**

- 2.5 mg as soon as possible after onset repeated after 2 hours if migraine recurs (patient not responding should not take second dose for same attack); max. 5 mg in 24 hours; CHILD and ADOLESCENT under 18 years not recommended

**Migard®** (Menarini) PoM
Tablets, f/c, frovatriptan (as succinate) 2.5 mg, net price 6-tab pack = £16.67. Label: 3

## NARATRIPTAN

**Indications** treatment of acute migraine attacks

**Cautions** see under $5HT_1$ agonists above; renal impairment (Appendix 3); sensitivity to sulphonamides; **interactions:** Appendix 1 ($5HT_1$ agonists)
**Driving** Drowsiness may affect performance of skilled tasks (e.g. driving)

**Contra-indications** see under $5HT_1$ agonists above; previous cerebrovascular accident or transient ischaemic attack; peripheral vascular disease

**Side-effects** see under $5HT_1$ agonists above, bradycardia or tachycardia; visual disturbances; ischaemic colitis reported

**Dose**

- 2.5 mg as soon as possible after onset; if migraine recurs after initial response, dose may be repeated after 4 hours (patient not responding should not take second dose for same attack); max. 5 mg in 24 hours; CHILD and ADOLESCENT under 18 years not recommended

**Naramig®** (GSK) PoM
Tablets, f/c, green, naratriptan (as hydrochloride) 2.5 mg, net price 6-tab pack = £24.55, 12-tab pack = £49.10. Label: 3

## RIZATRIPTAN

**Indications** treatment of acute migraine attacks

**Cautions** see under $5HT_1$ agonists above; renal impairment (Appendix 3); **interactions:** Appendix 1 ($5HT_1$ agonists)
**Driving** Drowsiness may affect performance of skilled tasks (e.g. driving)

**Contra-indications** see under $5HT_1$ agonists above; previous cerebrovascular accident or transient ischaemic attack; peripheral vascular disease

**Side-effects** see under $5HT_1$ agonists above; drowsiness, palpitation, tachycardia, dry mouth, diarrhoea, dyspepsia, thirst, pharyngeal discomfort, dyspnoea, headache, paraesthesia, decreased alertness, insomnia, tremor, ataxia, nervousness, vertigo, confusion, myalgia and muscle weakness, sweating, urticaria, pruritus, blurred vision; rarely syncope, hypertension; hypersensitivity reactions (including rash, angioedema, and toxic epidermal necrolysis) and taste disturbance reported

**Dose**

- 10 mg as soon as possible after onset repeated after 2 hours if migraine recurs (patient not responding should not take second dose for same attack); max. 20 mg in 24 hours; CHILD and ADOLESCENT under 18 years not recommended

**Note** Halve dose in patients taking propranolol; not to be taken within 2 hours of taking propranolol

**Maxalt®** (MSD) PoM
Tablets, pink, rizatriptan (as benzoate) 5 mg, net price 6-tab pack = £26.74; 10 mg, 3-tab pack = £13.37, 6-tab pack = £26.74. Label: 3

Wafers (*Maxalt® Melt*), rizatriptan (as benzoate) 10 mg, net price 3-wafer pack = £13.37, 6-wafer pack = £26.74. Label: 3, counselling, administration
**Counselling** *Maxalt® Melt* wafers should be placed on the tongue and allowed to dissolve
**Excipients** include aspartame equivalent to phenylalanine 2.1 mg (section 9.4.1)

## SUMATRIPTAN

**Indications** treatment of acute migraine attacks; cluster headache (subcutaneous injection only)

**Cautions** see under $5HT_1$ agonists above; history of seizures; renal impairment; sensitivity to sulphonamides; **interactions:** Appendix 1 ($5HT_1$ agonists)
**Driving** Drowsiness may affect performance of skilled tasks (e.g. driving)

**Contra-indications** see under $5HT_1$ agonists above; previous cerebrovascular accident or transient ischaemic attack; peripheral vascular disease; moderate and severe hypertension

**Side-effects** see under $5HT_1$ agonists above; drowsiness, transient increase in blood pressure, hypotension, bradycardia or tachycardia, visual disturbances, ischaemic colitis, Raynaud's syndrome, seizures reported; erythema at injection site; nasal irritation and taste disturbance with nasal spray
**CSM advice.** Following reports of chest pain and tightness (coronary vasoconstriction) CSM has emphasised that sumatriptan should **not** be used in ischaemic heart disease or Prinzmetal's angina, and that use with ergotamine should be **avoided** (see also Cautions).

**Dose**

- By mouth, 50 mg (some patients may require 100 mg) as soon as possible after onset (patient not responding should not take second dose for same attack); dose may be repeated after not less than 2 hours if migraine recurs; max. 300 mg in 24 hours; CHILD and ADOLESCENT under 18 years not recommended

- By subcutaneous injection using auto-injector, 6 mg as soon as possible after onset (patients not responding should not take second dose for same attack); dose may be repeated once after not less than 1 hour if migraine recurs; max. 12 mg in 24 hours; CHILD and ADOLESCENT under 18 years not recommended

Important **Not** for intravenous injection which may cause coronary vasospasm and angina

- Intranasally, 10–20 mg (ADOLESCENT 12–17 years 10 mg) into one nostril as soon as possible after onset (patient not responding should not take a second dose for same attack); dose may be repeated once after not less than 2 hours if migraine recurs; max. 40 mg (ADOLESCENT 12–17 years 20 mg) in 24 hours; CHILD under 12 years not recommended

**Imigran®** (GSK) PoM

Tablets, f/c, sumatriptan (as succinate) 50 mg, net price 6-tab pack = £27.62, 12-tab pack = £52.48; 100 mg, 6-tab pack = £44.64, 12-tab pack = £89.28. Label: 3, 10, patient information leaflet

Injection, sumatriptan (as succinate) 12 mg/mL (= 6 mg/0.5-mL syringe), net price, treatment pack (2 × 0.5-mL prefilled syringes and auto-injector) = £44.19; refill pack 2 × 0.5-mL prefilled cartridges = £42.05; 6 × 0.5-mL prefilled cartridges = £126.13. Label: 3, 10, patient information leaflet

Nasal spray, sumatriptan 10 mg/0.1-mL actuation, net price 2 unit-dose spray device = £12.28; 20 mg/0.1-mL actuation, 2 unit-dose spray device = £12.28, 6 unit-dose spray device = £36.83. Label: 3, 10, patient information leaflet

**Imigran® RADIS** (GSK) PoM

Tablets, f/c, sumatriptan (as succinate) 50 mg (pink), net price 6-tab pack = £24.87, 12-tab pack = £49.77; 100 mg (white), 6-tab pack = £44.64, 12-tab pack = £89.28. Label: 3, 10, patient information leaflet

## ZOLMITRIPTAN

**Indications** treatment of acute migraine attacks

**Cautions** see under $5HT_1$ agonists above; should not be taken within 12 hours of any other $5HT_1$ agonist; **interactions:** Appendix 1 ($5HT_1$ agonists)

**Contra-indications** see under $5HT_1$ agonists above; Wolff-Parkinson-White syndrome or arrhythmias associated with accessory cardiac conduction pathways; previous cerebrovascular accident or transient ischaemic attack

**Side-effects** see under $5HT_1$ agonists above; also dry mouth, drowsiness, paraesthesia, myalgia, muscle weakness; *rarely* palpitation, tachycardia, angioedema, headache, urticaria; *very rarely* abdominal pain, gastro-intestinal and splenic infarction, ischaemic colitis, angina, myocardial infarction, polyuria, transient increase in blood pressure; taste disturbance and nasal discomfort with nasal spray

**Dose**

- By mouth, 2.5 mg as soon as possible after onset repeated after not less than 2 hours if migraine persists or recurs (increase to 5 mg for subsequent attacks in patients not achieving satisfactory relief with 2.5-mg dose); max. 10 mg in 24 hours; CHILD not recommended
- Intranasally, 5 mg (1 spray) into one nostril as soon as possible after onset repeated after not less than 2 hours if migraine persists or recurs; max. 10 mg in 24 hours; CHILD not recommended

**Zomig®** (AstraZeneca) PoM

Tablets, f/c, yellow, zolmitriptan 2.5 mg, net price 6-tab pack = £24.00, 12-tab pack = £48.00

Orodispersible tablets (*Zomig Rapimelt®*), zolmitriptan 2.5 mg, net-price 6-tab pack = £24.00; 5 mg, 6-tab pack = £26.16 Counselling, administration

Counselling *Zomig Rapimelt®* should be placed on the tongue, allowed to disperse and swallowed

Excipients include aspartame equivalent to phenylalanine 2.81 mg/tablet (section 9.4.1)

Nasal spray▼, zolmitriptan 5 mg/0.1-mL unit-dose spray device, net price 6 unit-dose sprays = £40.50

## Ergot alkaloids

The value of **ergotamine** for migraine is limited by difficulties in absorption and by its side-effects, particularly nausea, vomiting, abdominal pain, and *muscular cramps*; it is best avoided. The recommended doses of ergotamine preparations should **not** be exceeded and treatment should **not** be repeated at intervals of less than 4 days.

To avoid habituation the frequency of administration of ergotamine should be limited to **no more than** twice a month. It should **never** be prescribed prophylactically but in the management of cluster headache a low dose (e.g. ergotamine 1 mg at night for 6 nights in 7) is occasionally given for 1 to 2 weeks [unlicensed indication].

## ERGOTAMINE TARTRATE

**Indications** treatment of acute migraine attacks and migraine variants unresponsive to analgesics

**Cautions** risk of peripheral vasospasm (see advice below); elderly; dependence (see Ergot alkaloids above), should not be used for migraine prophylaxis; **interactions:** Appendix 1 (ergot alkaloids) and under Sumatriptan (Cautions), below

Peripheral vasospasm Warn patient to stop treatment immediately if numbness or tingling of extremities develops and to contact doctor.

**Contra-indications** peripheral vascular disease, coronary heart disease, obliterative vascular disease and Raynaud's syndrome, temporal arteritis, hepatic impairment (Appendix 2), renal impairment (Appendix 3), sepsis, severe or inadequately controlled hypertension, hyperthyroidism, pregnancy (Appendix 4), breast-feeding (Appendix 5), porphyria (section 9.8.2)

**Side-effects** nausea, vomiting, vertigo, abdominal pain, diarrhoea, muscle cramps, and occasionally headache provoked (usually because of prolonged excessive dosage or abrupt withdrawal); precordial pain, myocardial and intestinal ischaemia, rarely myocardial infarction; repeated high dosage may cause ergotism with gangrene and confusion; pleural, peritoneal and heart-valve fibrosis may occur with excessive use; rectal or anal stricture or ulceration and rectovaginal fistula reported with prolonged use of suppositories

**Dose**

- See under preparations below

**Cafergot®** (Alliance) PoM

Tablets, ergotamine tartrate 1 mg, caffeine 100 mg. Net price 30-tab pack = £5.02. Label: 18, counselling, dosage

Dose 1–2 tablets at onset; max. 4 tablets in 24 hours; not to be repeated at intervals of less than 4 days; max. 8 tablets in one week (but see also notes above); CHILD not recommended

Suppositories, ergotamine tartrate 2 mg, caffeine 100 mg. Net price 30 = £10.13. Label: 18, counselling, dosage

Dose 1 suppository at onset; max. 2 in 24 hours; not to be repeated at intervals of less than 4 days; max. 4 suppositories in one week (but see also notes above); CHILD not recommended

**Migril®** (CP) PoM

Tablets, scored, ergotamine tartrate 2 mg, cyclizine hydrochloride 50 mg, caffeine hydrate 100 mg. Net price 20 = £11.67. Label: 2, 18, counselling, dosage

Dose 1 tablet at onset, followed after 30 minutes by ½–1 tablet, repeated every 30 minutes if necessary; max. 4 tablets per attack and 6 tablets in one week (but see also notes above); CHILD not recommended

## Anti-emetics

Anti-emetics (section 4.6), such as **metoclopramide** or **domperidone**, or phenothiazine and antihistamine anti-emetics, relieve the nausea associated with migraine attacks. Anti-emetics may be given by intramuscular injection or rectally if vomiting is a problem. Metoclopramide and domperidone have the added advantage of promoting gastric emptying and normal peristalsis; a single dose should be given at the onset of symptoms. Oral analgesic preparations containing metoclopramide or domperidone are a convenient alternative (**important:** for warnings relating to extrapyramidal effects of metoclopramide particularly in children and young adults, see p. 210).

## Other drugs for migraine

**Isometheptene mucate** (in combination with paracetamol) is licensed for the treatment of acute attacks of migraine; other more effective treatments are available.

### ISOMETHEPTENE MUCATE

**Indications** treatment of acute migraine attacks

**Cautions** cardiovascular disease, hepatic and renal impairment, diabetes mellitus, hyperthyroidism; **interactions:** Appendix 1 (sympathomimetics)

**Contra-indications** glaucoma, severe cardiac, hepatic and renal impairment, severe hypertension, pregnancy and breast-feeding; porphyria (section 9.8.2)

**Side-effects** dizziness, circulatory disturbances, rashes, blood disorders also reported

[1]**Midrid®** (Manx) PoM

Capsules, red, isometheptene mucate 65 mg, paracetamol 325 mg. Net price 30-cap pack = £5.50. Label: 30, counselling, dosage

Dose migraine, 2 capsules at onset of attack, followed by 1 capsule every hour if necessary; max. 5 capsules in 12 hours; CHILD not recommended

1. A pack containing 15 capsules may be sold to the public

## 4.7.4.2 Prophylaxis of migraine

Where migraine attacks are frequent, possible provoking factors such as stress, irregular life-style (e.g. lack of sleep), or chemical triggers (e.g. alcohol and nitrates) should be sought; combined oral contraceptives may also provoke migraine, see section 7.3.1 for advice.

Preventative treatment for migraine should be considered for patients who:

- suffer at least two attacks a month;
- suffer an increasing frequency of headaches;
- suffer significant disability despite suitable treatment for migraine attacks;
- cannot take suitable treatment for migraine attacks.

Prophylaxis is also necessary in some rare migraine subtypes and those at risk of migrainous infarction.

**Pizotifen** is an antihistamine and serotonin antagonist structurally related to the tricyclic antidepressants. It affords good prophylaxis but may cause weight gain. To avoid undue drowsiness treatment may be started at 500 micrograms at night and gradually increased to 3 mg; it is rarely necessary to exceed this dose.

The **beta-blockers** propranolol, metoprolol, nadolol, and timolol (section 2.4) are all effective. Propranolol is the most commonly used in an initial dose of 40 mg 2 to 3 times daily by mouth. Beta-blockers may also be given as a single daily dose of a long-acting preparation. The value of beta-blockers is limited by their contra-indications (section 2.4) and also by their interactions (see Appendix 1, beta-blockers).

**Topiramate** (section 4.8.1) is effective for migraine prophylaxis. Treatment should be supervised by a specialist.

**Amitriptyline** (section 4.3.1) [unlicensed indication] may usefully be prescribed in a dose of 10 mg at night, increasing to a maintenance dose of 50–75 mg at night.

**Sodium valproate** (section 4.8.1) may be effective for migraine prophylaxis [unlicensed indication] in a starting dose of 300 mg twice daily, increased if necessary to 1.2 g daily in divided doses. **Valproic acid** (as semisodium valproate) (section 4.2.3) is similarly effective [unlicensed indication] in a starting dose of 250 mg twice daily, increased if necessary to 1 g daily in divided doses.

**Cyproheptadine** (section 3.4.1), an antihistamine with serotonin-antagonist and calcium channel-blocking properties, may also be tried in refractory cases.

**Clonidine** (*Dixarit®*) is **not** recommended and may aggravate depression or produce insomnia. **Methysergide**, a semi-synthetic ergot alkaloid, has dangerous side-effects (retroperitoneal fibrosis and fibrosis of the heart valves and pleura); **important:** it should only be administered under hospital supervision.

### PIZOTIFEN

**Indications** prevention of vascular headache including classical migraine, common migraine, and cluster headache

**Cautions** urinary retention; angle-closure glaucoma, renal impairment; pregnancy and breast-feeding (Appendix 5); **interactions:** Appendix 1 (pizotifen)

**Driving** Drowsiness may affect performance of skilled tasks (e.g. driving); effects of alcohol enhanced

**Side-effects** antimuscarinic effects, drowsiness, increased appetite and weight gain; occasionally nausea, dizziness; rarely anxiety, aggression, and depression; CNS stimulation may occur in children

**Dose**

- 1.5 mg at night *or* 500 micrograms 3 times daily (but see also notes above), adjusted according to response; max. single dose 3 mg, max. daily dose 4.5 mg; CHILD over 2 years, up to 1.5 mg daily in divided doses; max. single dose at night 1 mg

**Pizotifen** (Non-proprietary) PoM
Tablets, pizotifen (as hydrogen malate), 500 micrograms, net price 28-tab pack = £1.96; 1.5 mg, 28-tab pack = £4.34. Label: 2

**Sanomigran®** (Novartis) PoM
Tablets, both ivory-yellow, s/c, pizotifen (as hydrogen malate), 500 micrograms, net price 60-tab pack = £2.57; 1.5 mg, 28-tab pack = £4.28. Label: 2
Elixir, pizotifen (as hydrogen malate) 250 micrograms/5 mL, net price 300 mL = £4.51. Label: 2

## CLONIDINE HYDROCHLORIDE

**Indications** prevention of recurrent migraine (but see notes above), vascular headache, menopausal flushing; hypertension (section 2.5.2)

**Cautions** depressive illness, concurrent antihypertensive therapy; porphyria (section 9.8.2); **interactions:** Appendix 1 (alpha$_2$-adrenoceptor stimulant)

**Side-effects** dry mouth, sedation, dizziness, nausea, nocturnal restlessness; occasionally rashes

**Dose**

- 50 micrograms twice daily, increased after 2 weeks to 75 micrograms twice daily if necessary; CHILD not recommended

**Clonidine** (Non-proprietary) PoM
Tablets, clonidine hydrochloride 25 micrograms. Net price 112-tab pack = £9.43

**Dixarit®** (Boehringer Ingelheim) PoM
Tablets, blue, s/c, clonidine hydrochloride 25 micrograms. Net price 112-tab pack = £7.11

**Catapres®** PoM
Section 2.5.2 (hypertension)

## METHYSERGIDE

**Indications** prevention of severe recurrent migraine, cluster headache and other vascular headaches in patients who are refractory to other treatment and whose lives are seriously disrupted (**important:** hospital supervision only, see notes above); diarrhoea associated with carcinoid syndrome

**Cautions** history of peptic ulceration; avoid abrupt withdrawal of treatment; after 6 months withdraw (gradually over 2 to 3 weeks) for reassessment for at least 1 month (see also notes above); **interactions:** Appendix 1 (ergot alkaloids)

**Contra-indications** renal, hepatic, pulmonary, and cardiovascular disease, severe hypertension, collagen disease, cellulitis, urinary-tract disorders, cachectic or septic conditions, pregnancy, breast-feeding

**Side-effects** nausea, vomiting, heartburn, abdominal discomfort, drowsiness, and dizziness occur frequently in initial treatment; mental and behavioural disturbances, insomnia, oedema, weight gain, rashes, loss of scalp hair, cramps, arterial spasm (including coronary artery spasm with angina and possible myocardial infarction), paraesthesias of extremities, postural hypotension, and tachycardia also occur; retroperitoneal and other abnormal fibrotic reactions may occur on prolonged administration, requiring immediate withdrawal of treatment

**Dose**

- Initially 1 mg at bedtime, increased gradually over about 2 weeks to 1–2 mg 3 times daily with food (see notes above); CHILD not recommended
- Diarrhoea associated with carcinoid syndrome, usual range, 12–20 mg daily (hospital supervision); CHILD not recommended

**Deseril®** (Alliance) PoM
Tablets, s/c, methysergide (as maleate) 1 mg, net price 60-tab pack = £13.46. Label: 2, 21

### 4.7.4.3 Cluster headache

Cluster headache rarely responds to standard analgesics. **Sumatriptan** given by subcutaneous injection is the drug of choice for the *treatment* of cluster headache. Alternatively, 100% **oxygen** at a rate of 7–12 litres/minute is useful in aborting an attack.

*Prophylaxis* of cluster headache is considered if the attacks are frequent, or last over 3 weeks, or if the attacks cannot be treated effectively. **Verapamil** or **lithium** [both unlicensed use] are used for prophylaxis. **Ergotamine**, used on an intermittent basis is an alternative for patients with short bouts, but it should **not** be used for prolonged periods. **Methysergide** is effective but must be used with extreme caution (see section 4.7.4.2) and only if other drugs cannot be used or if they are not effective.

# 4.8 Antiepileptics

4.8.1 Control of epilepsy
4.8.2 Drugs used in status epilepticus
4.8.3 Febrile convulsions

## 4.8.1 Control of epilepsy

The object of treatment is to prevent the occurrence of seizures by maintaining an effective dose of one or more antiepileptic drugs. Careful adjustment of doses is necessary, starting with low doses and increasing gradually until seizures are controlled or there are significant adverse effects.

The frequency of administration is often determined by the plasma half-life, and should be kept as low as possible to encourage better patient compliance. Most antiepileptics, when used in average dosage, may be given twice daily. Phenobarbital and sometimes phenytoin, which have long half-lives, may often be given as a daily dose at bedtime. However, with large doses, some antiepileptics may need to be administered 3 times daily to avoid adverse effects associated with high peak plasma concentrations. Young children metabolise antiepileptics more rapidly than adults and therefore require more frequent doses and a higher amount per kilogram body-weight.

**Combination therapy** Therapy with two or more antiepileptic drugs concurrently may be necessary; it should preferably only be used when monotherapy with suitable alternative drugs has proved ineffective. Combination therapy enhances toxicity and drug interactions may occur between antiepileptics (see below).

**Interactions** Interactions between antiepileptics are complex and may enhance toxicity without a corresponding increase in antiepileptic effect. Interactions are usually caused by *hepatic enzyme induction* or *hepatic enzyme inhibition*; *displacement from protein binding sites* is not usually a problem. These interactions are highly variable and unpredictable.

Significant interactions that occur **between antiepileptics** themselves are as follows:

> **Note** Check under each drug for possible interactions when two or more antiepileptic drugs are used

**Carbamazepine**

*often lowers* plasma concentration of *clobazam, clonazepam, lamotrigine, an active metabolite of oxcarbazepine,* and of *phenytoin* (but may also raise phenytoin concentration), *tiagabine, topiramate, valproate,* and *zonisamide*

*sometimes lowers* plasma concentration of *ethosuximide, and primidone* (but tendency for corresponding increase in phenobarbital level)

**Ethosuximide**

*sometimes raises* plasma concentration of *phenytoin*

**Gabapentin**

no interactions with gabapentin reported

**Lamotrigine**

*sometimes raises* plasma concentration of *an active metabolite of carbamazepine* (but evidence is conflicting)

*sometimes raises* plasma concentration of *an active metabolite of oxcarbazepine*

**Levetiracetam**

no interactions with levetiracetam reported

**Oxcarbazepine**

*sometimes lowers* plasma concentration of *carbamazepine* (but may raise concentration of *an active metabolite of carbamazepine*)

*often lowers* plasma concentration of *lamotrigine*

*sometimes raises* plasma concentration of *phenytoin*

*often raises* plasma concentration of *phenobarbital*

**Phenobarbital** ***or*** *Primidone*

*often lowers* plasma concentration of *carbamazepine, clonazepam, lamotrigine, an active metabolite of oxcarbazepine,* and of *phenytoin* (but may also raise phenytoin concentration), *tiagabine, valproate,* and *zonisamide*

*sometimes lowers* plasma concentration of *ethosuximide*

**Phenytoin**

*often lowers* plasma concentration of *clonazepam, carbamazepine, lamotrigine, an active metabolite of oxcarbazepine,* and of *tiagabine, topiramate, valproate,* and *zonisamide*

*often raises* plasma concentration of *phenobarbital*

*sometimes lowers* plasma concentration of *ethosuximide, and primidone* (by increasing conversion to phenobarbital)

**Pregabalin**

no interactions with pregabalin reported

**Topiramate**

*sometimes raises* plasma concentration of *phenytoin*

**Valproate**

*sometimes lowers* plasma concentration of *an active metabolite of oxcarbazepine*

*often raises* plasma concentration of *an active metabolite of carbamazepine,* and of *lamotrigine, primidone, phenobarbital, and phenytoin* (but may also lower)

*sometimes raises* plasma concentration of *ethosuximide, and primidone* (and tendency for significant increase in phenobarbital level)

**Vigabatrin**

*often lowers* plasma concentration of *phenytoin*

*sometimes lowers* plasma concentration of *phenobarbital, and primidone*

**Zonisamide**

*sometimes increases* plasma concentration of *carbamazepine* (but may also lower carbamazepine concentration)

For other important interactions see **Appendix 1**, and for FPA guidelines on enzyme-inducing antiepileptics and **oral contraceptives**, see section 7.3.1.

**Withdrawal** Abrupt withdrawal of antiepileptics, particularly the barbiturates and benzodiazepines, should be avoided, as this may precipitate severe rebound seizures. Reduction in dosage should be carried out in stages and, in the case of the barbiturates, the withdrawal process may take months. The changeover from one antiepileptic drug regimen to another should be made cautiously, withdrawing the first drug only when the new regimen has been largely established.

The decision to withdraw all antiepileptics from a seizure-free patient, and its timing, is often difficult and may depend on individual patient factors. Even in patients who have been seizure-free for several years, there is a significant risk of seizure recurrence on drug withdrawal.

In patients receiving several antiepileptic drugs, only one drug should be withdrawn at a time.

**Driving** Patients suffering from epilepsy may drive a motor vehicle (but not a heavy goods or public service vehicle) provided that they have had a seizure-free period of one year or, if subject to attacks only while asleep, have established a 3-year period of asleep attacks without awake attacks. Patients affected by drowsiness should not drive or operate machinery.

Guidance issued by the Drivers Medical Unit of the Driver and Vehicle Licensing Agency (DVLA) recommends that patients should be advised not to drive during withdrawal of antiepileptic drugs, or for 6 months afterwards (see also Drugs and Driving under General Guidance, p. 2).

**Pregnancy and breast-feeding** During pregnancy, total plasma concentrations of antiepileptics (particularly of phenytoin) may fall, particularly in the later stages but free plasma concentrations may remain the same (or even rise). There is an increased risk of teratogenicity associated with the use of antiepileptic drugs (reduced if treatment is limited to a single drug). In view of the increased risk of neural tube and other defects associated, in particular, with **carbamazepine**, **oxcarbazepine**, **phenytoin** and **valproate** women taking antiepileptic drugs who *may become pregnant* should be **informed of the possible consequences**. Those who *wish to become pregnant* should be referred to an appropriate specialist for advice. Women who become pregnant should be **counselled** and offered **antenatal screening** (alpha-fetoprotein measurement and a second trimester ultrasound scan).

To counteract the risk of neural tube defects adequate folate supplements are advised for women before and during pregnancy; to prevent recurrence of neural tube defects, women should receive folic acid 5 mg daily (section 9.1.2)—this dose may also be appropriate for women receiving antiepileptic drugs.

In view of the risk of neonatal bleeding associated with carbamazepine, phenobarbital and phenytoin, prophylactic vitamin $K_1$ (section 9.6.6) is recommended for the mother before delivery (as well as for the neonate).

Breast-feeding is acceptable with all antiepileptic drugs, taken in normal doses, with the possible exception of the barbiturates, and also some of the more recently introduced ones, see Appendix 5.



## Partial seizures with or without secondary generalisation

**Carbamazepine**, **lamotrigine**, **sodium valproate**, **topiramate**, and **oxcarbazepine** are effective as monotherapy for secondarily generalised tonic-clonic seizures and for partial (focal) seizures; alternatively, **phenytoin** monotherapy can be used. **Phenobarbital** (phenobarbitone) and **primidone** are also effective but they are more sedating and are not used as first-line drugs.

Where a single drug has failed to control the seizures, combination therapy can be tried with the above drugs or with additional drugs, such as gabapentin, tiagabine, levetiracetam, or clobazam; alternatives include acetazolamide, clonazepam, and vigabatrin.

## Generalised seizures

**Tonic-clonic seizures (grand mal)** The drugs of choice for tonic-clonic seizures are **carbamazepine**, **lamotrigine**, **phenytoin**, and **sodium valproate**. For those patients who have tonic-clonic seizures as part of the syndrome of primary generalised epilepsy, **sodium valproate** is the drug of choice. **Phenobarbital** and **primidone** are also effective but may be more sedating.

**Absence seizures (petit mal)** **Ethosuximide** and **sodium valproate** are the drugs of choice in simple absence seizures; alternatives include clobazam, clonazepam, and topiramate. Sodium valproate is also highly effective in treating the tonic-clonic seizures which may co-exist with absence seizures in primary generalised epilepsy. **Lamotrigine** may also be effective [unlicensed indication].

**Myoclonic seizures** Myoclonic seizures (myoclonic jerks) occur in a variety of syndromes, and response to treatment varies considerably. **Sodium valproate** is the drug of choice and **clonazepam** or **lamotrigine** may be used. Alternatives include clobazam, levetiracetam, and topiramate. For reference to the adjunctive use of piracetam, see section 4.9.3.

**Atypical absence, atonic, and tonic seizures** These seizure types are usually seen in childhood, in specific epileptic syndromes, or associated with cerebral damage or mental retardation. They may respond poorly to the traditional drugs. **Phenytoin**, **sodium valproate**, **lamotrigine**, **clonazepam**, **ethosuximide**, and **phenobarbital** may be tried. Second-line antiepileptic drugs that are occasionally helpful include **acetazolamide**, **clobazam**, and **topiramate**.

## Carbamazepine and oxcarbazepine

**Carbamazepine** is a drug of choice for simple and complex partial seizures and for tonic-clonic seizures secondary to a focal discharge. It has a wider therapeutic index than phenytoin and the relationship between dose and plasma-carbamazepine concentration is linear, but monitoring of plasma-carbamazepine concentrations may be helpful in determining optimum dosage. It has generally fewer side-effects than phenytoin or the barbiturates, but reversible blurring of vision, dizziness, and unsteadiness are dose-related, and may be dose-limiting. These side-effects may be reduced by altering the timing of medication; use of modified-release tablets also significantly lessens the incidence of dose-related side-effects. It is essential to initiate carbamazepine therapy at a low dose and build this up slowly with increments of 100–200 mg every two weeks.

**Oxcarbazepine** is licensed for the treatment of partial seizures with or without secondarily generalised tonic-clonic seizures. Oxcarbazepine induces hepatic enzymes to a lesser extent than carbamazepine.

### CARBAMAZEPINE

**Indications** partial and secondary generalised tonic-clonic seizures, some primary generalised seizures; trigeminal neuralgia; prophylaxis of bipolar disorder unresponsive to lithium

**Cautions** hepatic impairment (Appendix 2) or renal impairment; cardiac disease (see also Contra-indications), skin reactions (see also Blood, hepatic or skin disorders below and under Side-effects), history of haematological reactions to other drugs; manufacturer recommends blood counts and hepatic and renal function tests (but evidence of practical value unsatisfactory); glaucoma; pregnancy (**important:** see above and Appendix 4 (neural tube screening)), breast-feeding (see above and Appendix 5); avoid abrupt withdrawal; **interactions:** see p. 237 and Appendix 1 (carbamazepine)

**Blood, hepatic or skin disorders** Patients or their carers should be told how to recognise signs of blood, liver, or skin disorders, and advised to seek immediate medical attention if symptoms such as fever, sore throat, rash, mouth ulcers, bruising, or bleeding develop. Leucopenia which is severe, progressive or associated with clinical symptoms requires withdrawal (if necessary under cover of suitable alternative).

**Contra-indications** AV conduction abnormalities (unless paced); history of bone marrow depression, porphyria (section 9.8.2)

**Side-effects** nausea and vomiting, dizziness, drowsiness, headache, ataxia, confusion and agitation (elderly), visual disturbances (especially double vision and often associated with peak plasma concentrations); constipation or diarrhoea, anorexia; mild transient generalised erythematous rash may occur in a large number of patients (withdraw if worsens or is accompanied by other symptoms); leucopenia and other blood disorders (including thrombocytopenia, agranulocytosis and aplastic anaemia); other side-effects include cholestatic jaundice, hepatitis and acute renal failure, Stevens-Johnson syndrome, toxic epidermal necrolysis, alopecia, thromboembolism, arthralgia, fever, proteinuria, lymph node enlargement, cardiac conduction disturbances (sometimes arrhythmias), dyskinesias, paraesthesia, depression, impotence (and impaired fertility), gynaecomastia, galactorrhoea, aggression, activation of psychosis; photosensitivity, pulmonary hypersensitivity (with dyspnoea and pneumonitis), hyponatraemia, oedema, and disturbances of bone metabolism (with osteomalacia) also reported; suppositories may cause occasional rectal irritation

**Dose**

- By mouth, epilepsy, initially, 100–200 mg 1–2 times daily, increased slowly (see notes above) to usual dose of 0.8–1.2 g daily in divided doses; in some cases 1.6–2 g daily may be needed; ELDERLY reduce initial dose; CHILD daily in divided doses, up to 1 year 100–200 mg, 1–5 years 200–400 mg, 5–10 years 400–600 mg, 10–15 years 0.6–1 g

  Trigeminal neuralgia, initially 100 mg 1–2 times daily (but some patients may require higher initial dose), increased gradually according to response; usual dose 200 mg 3–4 times daily, up to 1.6 g daily in some patients

  Prophylaxis of bipolar disorder unresponsive to lithium (see also section 4.2.3), initially 400 mg daily in divided doses increased until symptoms controlled; usual range 400–600 mg daily; max. 1.6 g daily

- By rectum, as suppositories, see below

**Note** Plasma concentration for optimum response 4–12 mg/litre (20–50 micromol/litre)

**Carbamazepine** (Non-proprietary) PoM

Tablets, carbamazepine 100 mg, net price 20 = £1.42; 200 mg, 20 = £1.70; 400 mg, 20 = £3.47. Label: 3, 8, counselling, blood, hepatic or skin disorder symptoms (see above), driving (see notes above)

Brands include *Epimaz®*

**Note** Different preparations may vary in bioavailability; to avoid reduced effect or excessive side-effects, it may be prudent to avoid changing the formulation (see also notes above on how side-effects may be reduced)

**Dental prescribing on NHS** Carbamazepine Tablets may be prescribed

**Tegretol®** (Novartis) PoM

Tablets, all scored, carbamazepine 100 mg, net price 84-tab pack = £2.43; 200 mg, 84-tab pack = £4.50; 400 mg, 56-tab pack = £5.90. Label: 3, 8, counselling, blood, hepatic or skin disorder symptoms (see above), driving (see notes above)

Chewtabs, orange, carbamazepine 100 mg, net price 56-tab pack = £3.54; 200 mg, 56-tab pack = £6.59. Label: 3, 8, 21, 24, counselling, blood, hepatic or skin disorder symptoms (see above), driving (see notes above)

Liquid, sugar-free, carbamazepine 100 mg/5 mL. Net price 300-mL pack = £6.86. Label: 3, 8, counselling, blood, hepatic or skin disorder symptoms (see above), driving (see notes above)

Suppositories, carbamazepine 125 mg, net price 5 = £9.00; 250 mg, 5 = £12.00. Label: 3, 8, counselling, blood, hepatic or skin disorder symptoms (see above), driving (see notes above)

**Dose** epilepsy, for short-term use (max. 7 days) when oral therapy temporarily not possible; suppositories of 125 mg may be considered to be approximately equivalent in therapeutic effect to tablets of 100 mg but final adjustment should always depend on clinical response (plasma concentration monitoring recommended); max. by rectum 1 g daily in 4 divided doses

### Modified release

**Carbagen® SR** (Generics) PoM

Tablets, m/r, f/c, both scored, carbamazepine 200 mg, net price 56-tab pack = £4.88; 400 mg, 56-tab pack = £9.63. Label: 3, 8, 25, counselling, blood, hepatic or skin disorder symptoms (see above), driving (see notes above)

**Dose** epilepsy (ADULT and CHILD over 5 years), as above; trigeminal neuralgia, as above; total daily dose given in 1–2 divided doses; bipolar disorder, as above

**Tegretol® Retard** (Novartis) PoM

Tablets, m/r, both scored, carbamazepine 200 mg (beige-orange), net price 56-tab pack = £5.26; 400 mg (brown-orange), 56-tab pack = £10.34. Label: 3, 8, 25, counselling, blood, hepatic or skin disorder symptoms (see above), driving (see notes above)

**Dose** epilepsy (ADULT and CHILD over 5 years), as above; trigeminal neuralgia, as above; total daily dose given in 2 divided doses

## OXCARBAZEPINE

**Indications** monotherapy and adjunctive treatment of partial seizures with or without secondarily generalised tonic-clonic seizures; trigeminal neuralgia [unlicensed indication] (section 4.7.3)

**Cautions** hypersensitivity to carbamazepine; avoid abrupt withdrawal; hyponatraemia (monitor plasma-sodium concentration in patients at risk), heart failure (monitor body-weight), cardiac conduction disorders; avoid in porphyria (section 9.8.2); hepatic impairment (Appendix 2); renal impairment (Appendix 3); pregnancy (see p. 238 and Appendix 4); breast-feeding (Appendix 5); **interactions:** Appendix 1 (oxcarbazepine)

**Blood, hepatic or skin disorders** Patients or their carers should be told how to recognise signs of blood, liver, or skin disorders, and advised to seek immediate medical attention if symptoms such as lethargy, confusion, muscular twitching, fever, sore throat, rash, blistering, mouth ulcers, bruising, or bleeding develop

**Side-effects** nausea, vomiting, constipation, diarrhoea, abdominal pain; dizziness, headache, drowsiness, agitation, amnesia, asthenia, ataxia, confusion, impaired concentration, depression, tremor; hyponatraemia; acne, alopecia, rash, nystagmus, visual disorders including diplopia; *less commonly* urticaria, leucopenia; *very rarely* hepatitis, pancreatitis, arrhythmias, hypersensitivity reactions, thrombocytopenia, systemic lupus erythematosus, Stevens-Johnson syndrome, and toxic epidermal necrolysis

**Dose**

- Initially 300 mg twice daily increased according to response in steps of up to 600 mg daily at weekly intervals; usual dose range 0.6–2.4 g daily in divided doses; CHILD over 6 years, 8–10 mg/kg daily in 2 divided doses increased according to response in steps of up to 10 mg/kg daily at weekly intervals (in adjunctive therapy, maintenance dose approx. 30 mg/kg daily); max. 46 mg/kg daily in divided doses

Note In adjunctive therapy, the dose of concomitant anti-epileptics may need to be reduced when using high doses of oxcarbazepine

**Trileptal®** (Novartis) PoM

Tablets, f/c, scored, oxcarbazepine 150 mg (green), net price 50-tab pack = £10.00; 300 mg (yellow), 50-tab pack = £20.00; 600 mg (pink), 50-tab pack = £40.00. Label: 3, 8, counselling, blood, hepatic or skin disorders (see above), driving (see notes above)

Oral suspension, sugar-free, oxcarbazepine 300 mg/5 mL, net price 250 mL (with oral syringe) = £40.00. Label: 3, 8, counselling, blood, hepatic or skin disorders (see above), driving (see notes above)

Excipients include propylene glycol

## Ethosuximide

**Ethosuximide** is sometimes used in simple absence seizures; it may also be used in myoclonic seizures and in atypical absence, atonic, and tonic seizures.

### ETHOSUXIMIDE

**Indications** absence seizures

**Cautions** see notes above; hepatic and renal impairment; manufacturer recommends blood counts and hepatic and renal function tests (but evidence of practical value unsatisfactory); pregnancy (see p. 238 and Appendix 4) and breast-feeding (Appendix 5); avoid sudden withdrawal; porphyria (see section 9.8.2); **interactions:** Appendix 1 (ethosuximide)

Blood disorders Patients or their carers should be told how to recognise signs of blood disorders, and advised to seek immediate medical attention if symptoms such as fever, sore throat, mouth ulcers, bruising or bleeding develop

**Side-effects** gastro-intestinal disturbances, weight loss, drowsiness, dizziness, ataxia, dyskinesia, hiccup, photophobia, headache, depression, and mild euphoria. Psychotic states, rashes, hepatic and renal changes (see Cautions), and haematological disorders such as agranulocytosis and aplastic anaemia occur rarely (blood counts required if signs or symptoms of infection); systemic lupus erythematosus and erythema multiforme (Stevens-Johnson syndrome) reported; other side-effects reported include gum hypertrophy, swelling of tongue, irritability, hyperactivity, sleep disturbances, night terrors, inability to concentrate, aggressiveness, increased libido, myopia, vaginal bleeding

**Dose**

- ADULT and CHILD over 6 years initially, 500 mg daily, increased by 250 mg at intervals of 4–7 days to usual dose of 1–1.5 g daily; occasionally up to 2 g daily may be needed; CHILD up to 6 years initially 250 mg daily, increased gradually to usual dose of 20 mg/kg daily

Note Plasma concentration for optimum response 40–100 mg/litre (300–700 micromol/litre)

**Emeside®** (Chemidex) PoM

Syrup, black currant, ethosuximide 250 mg/5 mL. Net price 200-mL pack = £6.60. Label: 8, counselling, blood disorders (see above), driving (see notes above)

**Zarontin®** (Parke-Davis) PoM

Syrup, yellow, ethosuximide 250 mg/5 mL. Net price 200-mL pack = £4.48. Label: 8, counselling, blood disorders (see above), driving (see notes above)

## Gabapentin and pregabalin

**Gabapentin** and **pregabalin** can be given as adjunctive therapy in partial epilepsy with or without secondary generalisation. They are also licensed for the treatment of neuropathic pain (section 4.7.3).

### GABAPENTIN

**Indications** adjunctive treatment of partial seizures with or without secondary generalisation not satisfactorily controlled with other antiepileptics; neuropathic pain (section 4.7.3); trigeminal neuralgia [unlicensed indication] (section 4.7.3)

**Cautions** avoid sudden withdrawal (may cause anxiety, insomnia, nausea, pain and sweating—taper off over at least 1 week); history of psychotic illness, elderly (may need to reduce dose), renal impairment (Appendix 3), diabetes mellitus, false positive readings with some urinary protein tests; pregnancy (see p. 238 and Appendix 4) and breast-feeding (see p. 238 and Appendix 5); **interactions:** Appendix 1 (gabapentin)

**Side-effects** diarrhoea, dry mouth, dyspepsia, nausea, vomiting; peripheral oedema; dizziness, drowsiness, anxiety, abnormal gait, amnesia, ataxia, nystagmus, tremor, asthenia, paraesthesia, emotional lability, hyperkinesia; weight gain; dysarthria, arthralgia; diplopia, amblyopia; rash, purpura; *less commonly* constipation, flatulence, dyspnoea, confusion, impotence, and leucopenia; *rarely* pancreatitis, depression, psychosis, headache, myalgia, and urinary incontinence; hepatitis, jaundice, chest pain, palpitation, movement disorders, thrombocytopenia, tinnitus, acute renal failure, and alopecia also reported

**Dose**

- Epilepsy, 300 mg on day 1, then 300 mg twice daily on day 2, then 300 mg 3 times daily (approx. every 8 hours) on day 3, then increased according to response in steps of 300 mg daily (in 3 divided doses) to max. 2.4 g daily, usual range 0.9–1.2 g daily; CHILD 6–12 years (specialist use only) 10 mg/kg on day 1, then 20 mg/kg on day 2, then 25–35 mg/kg daily (in 3 divided doses approx. every 8 hours), maintenance 900 mg daily (body-weight 26–36 kg) or 1.2 g daily (body-weight 37–50 kg)
- Neuropathic pain, ADULT over 18 years, 300 mg on day 1, then 300 mg twice daily on day 2, then 300 mg 3 times daily (approx. every 8 hours) on day 3, then increased according to response in steps of 300 mg daily (in 3 divided doses) to max. 1.8 g daily

**Gabapentin** (Non-proprietary) PoM

Capsules, gabapentin 100 mg, net price 100-cap pack = £22.92; 300 mg, 100-cap pack = £50.18; 400 mg, 100-cap pack = £53.60. Label: 3, 5, 8, counselling, driving (see notes above)

Tablets, gabapentin 600 mg, net price 100-tab pack = £106.00; 800 mg, 100-tab pack = £121.48. Label: 3, 5, 8, counselling, driving (see notes above)

**Neurontin®** (Pfizer) PoM

Capsules, gabapentin 100 mg (white), net price 100-cap pack = £22.86; 300 mg (yellow), 100-cap pack = £53.00; 400 mg (orange), 100-cap pack = £61.33; titration pack of 40 × 300-mg (yellow) capsules with 10 × 600-mg tablets = £31.80. Label: 3, 5, 8, counselling, driving (see notes above)

Tablets, f/c, gabapentin 600 mg, net price 100-tab pack = £106.00; 800 mg, 100-tab pack = £122.66. Label: 3, 5, 8, counselling, driving (see notes above)

## PREGABALIN

**Indications** peripheral neuropathic pain; adjunctive therapy for partial seizures with or without secondary generalisation

**Cautions** avoid abrupt withdrawal (taper-off over at least 1 week); renal impairment (Appendix 3); pregnancy (Appendix 4)

**Contra-indications** breast-feeding (Appendix 5)

**Side-effects** dry mouth, constipation, vomiting, flatulence; oedema; dizziness, drowsiness, attention disturbance, disturbances in muscle control and movement, memory impairment, speech disorder, paraesthesia, euphoria, confusion, fatigue, appetite changes, weight gain; changes in sexual function; visual disturbances and ocular disorders (including blurred vision, diplopia, eye strain and eye irritation); *less commonly* abdominal distension, increased salivation, gastro-oesophageal reflux disease, taste disturbance, thirst, hot flushes, tachycardia, syncope, dyspnoea, chest tightness, nasal dryness, stupor, depersonalisation, depression, insomnia, hallucinations, agitation, mood swings, panic attacks, apathy, dysuria, urinary incontinence, thrombocytopenia, joint swelling, muscle cramp, myalgia, arthralgia, sweating, and rash; *rarely* ascites, dysphagia, pancreatitis, hypotension, hypertension, cold extremities, first-degree AV block, arrhythmia, bradycardia, nasopharyngitis, cough, epistaxis, rhinitis, parosmia, pyrexia, rigors, disinhibition, weight loss, hypoglycaemia or hyperglycaemia, renal failure, menstrual disturbances, breast pain, breast discharge, breast hypertrophy, neutropenia, rhabdomyolysis, hyperacusis, hypokalaemia, and leucocytosis

**Dose**

- Neuropathic pain, initially 150 mg daily in 2–3 divided doses, increased if necessary after 3–7 days to 300 mg daily in 2–3 divided doses, increased further if necessary after 7 days to max. 600 mg daily in 2–3 divided doses; CHILD and ADOLESCENT not recommended
- Epilepsy, initially 150 mg daily in 2–3 divided doses, increased if necessary after 7 days to 300 mg daily in 2–3 divided doses, increased further if necessary after 7 days to max. 600 mg daily in 2–3 divided doses; CHILD and ADOLESCENT not recommended

**Lyrica®** (Pfizer) ▼ PoM

Capsules, pregabalin 25 mg (white), net price 56-cap pack = £64.40, 84-cap pack = £96.60; 50 mg (white), 84-cap pack = £96.60; 75 mg (white/orange), 56-cap pack = £64.40; 100 mg (orange), 84-cap pack = £96.60; 150 mg (white), 56-cap pack = £64.40; 200 mg (orange), 84-cap pack = £96.60; 300 mg (white/orange), 56-cap pack = £64.40. Label: 3, 8, counselling, driving (see notes above)

## Lamotrigine

**Lamotrigine** is an antiepileptic for partial seizures and primary and secondarily generalised tonic-clonic seizures. It is also used for myoclonic seizures and may be tried for atypical absence, atonic, and tonic seizures in the Lennox-Gastaut syndrome. Lamotrigine may cause serious skin rash especially in children; dose recommendations should be adhered to closely.

Lamotrigine is used either as sole treatment or as an adjunct to treatment with other antiepileptic drugs. Valproate increases plasma-lamotrigine concentration whereas the enzyme inducing antiepileptics reduce it; care is therefore required in choosing the appropriate initial dose and subsequent titration. Where the potential for interaction is not known, treatment should be initiated with lower doses such as those used with valproate.

## LAMOTRIGINE

**Indications** monotherapy and adjunctive treatment of partial seizures and primary and secondarily generalised tonic-clonic seizures; seizures associated with Lennox-Gastaut syndrome; trigeminal neuralgia [unlicensed indication] (section 4.7.3)

**Cautions** closely monitor (including hepatic, renal and clotting function) and consider withdrawal if rash, fever, or other signs of hypersensitivity syndrome develop; avoid abrupt withdrawal (taper off over 2 weeks or longer) unless serious skin reaction occurs; hepatic impairment (Appendix 2); renal impairment (Appendix 3); pregnancy (Appendix 4); breast-feeding (Appendix 5); **interactions:** see p. 237 and Appendix 1 (lamotrigine)

**Blood disorders** The CSM has advised prescribers to be alert for symptoms and signs suggestive of bone-marrow failure such as anaemia, bruising, or infection. Aplastic anaemia, bone-marrow depression and pancytopenia have been associated rarely with lamotrigine.

**Side-effects** rash (see Skin reactions below); hypersensitivity syndrome (possibly including rash, fever, lymphadenopathy, hepatic dysfunction, blood disorders, disseminated intravascular coagulation and multi-organ dysfunction); nausea, vomiting, diarrhoea, hepatic dysfunction; headache, fatigue, dizziness, sleep disturbances, tremor, movement disorders, agitation, confusion, hallucinations; blood disorders (including leucopenia, thrombocytopenia, pancytopenia); lupus erythematosus-like effect; photosensitivity; nystagmus, diplopia, blurred vision, conjunctivitis

**Skin reactions** Serious skin reactions including Stevens-Johnson syndrome and toxic epidermal necrolysis (rarely with fatalities) have developed especially in children; most rashes occur in the first 8 weeks. Rash is sometimes associated with hypersensitivity syndrome (see Side-effects above). Consider withdrawal if rash or signs of hypersensitivity syndrome develop. The CSM has advised that factors associated with increased risk of serious skin reactions include concomitant use of valproate, initial lamotrigine dosing higher than recommended, and more rapid dose escalation than recommended.

**Counselling** Warn patients to see their doctor immediately if rash or signs or symptoms of hypersensitivity syndrome develop

**Dose**

Important Do not confuse the different combinations; see also notes above

- *Monotherapy*, initially 25 mg daily for 14 days, increased to 50 mg daily for further 14 days, then increased by max. of 50–100 mg daily every 7–14 days; usual maintenance as monotherapy, 100–200 mg daily in 1–2 divided doses (up to 500 mg daily has been required)
- Adjunctive therapy *with valproate*, initially 25 mg every other day for 14 days then 25 mg daily for further 14 days, thereafter increased by max. of 25–50 mg daily every 7–14 days; usual maintenance, 100–200 mg daily in 1–2 divided doses
- Adjunctive therapy (with enzyme inducing drugs) *without valproate*, initially 50 mg daily for 14 days then 50 mg twice daily for further 14 days, thereafter increased by max. of 100 mg daily every 7–14 days; usual maintenance 200–400 mg daily in 2 divided doses (up to 700 mg daily has been required)
- CHILD under 12 years, *monotherapy*, not recommended
- CHILD 2–12 years, adjunctive therapy *with valproate*, initially 150 micrograms/kg daily for 14 days (those weighing under 13 kg may receive 2 mg on alternate days for first 14 days) then 300 micrograms/kg daily for further 14 days, thereafter increased by max. of 300 micrograms/kg daily every 7–14 days; usual maintenance 1–5 mg/kg daily in 1–2 divided doses
- CHILD 2–12 years adjunctive therapy (with enzyme inducing drugs) *without valproate*, initially 600 micrograms/kg daily in 2 divided doses for 14 days then 1.2 mg/kg daily in 2 divided doses for further 14 days, thereafter increased by max. of 1.2 mg/kg daily every 7–14 days; usual maintenance 5–15 mg/kg daily in 2 divided doses

**Lamotrigine** (Non-proprietary) PoM

Tablets, lamotrigine 25 mg, net price 56-tab pack = £17.35; 50 mg, 56-tab pack = £29.50; 100 mg, 56-tab pack = £50.88; 200 mg, 30-tab pack = £46.34, 56-tab pack = £86.50. Label: 8, counselling, driving (see notes above), skin reactions

Dispersible tablets, lamotrigine 5 mg, net price 28-tab pack = £8.04; 25 mg, 56-tab pack = £20.31; 100 mg, 56-tab pack = £59.76. Label: 8, 13, counselling, driving (see notes above), skin reactions

**Lamictal®** (GSK) PoM

Tablets, all yellow, lamotrigine 25 mg, net price 21-tab pack (*'Valproate Add-on therapy' Starter Pack*) = £7.65, 42-tab pack (*'Monotherapy' Starter Pack*) = £15.30, 56-tab pack = £20.41; 50 mg, 42-tab pack (*'Non-valproate Add-on therapy' Starter Pack*) = £26.02, 56-tab pack = £34.70; 100 mg, 56-tab pack = £59.86; 200 mg, 56-tab pack = £101.76. Label: 8, counselling, driving (see notes above), skin reactions

Dispersible tablets, chewable, lamotrigine 2 mg, net price 30-tab pack = £8.71; 5 mg, 28-tab pack = £8.14; 25 mg, 56-tab pack = £20.41; 100 mg, 56-tab pack = £59.86. Label: 8, 13, counselling, driving (see notes above), skin reactions

## Levetiracetam

**Levetiracetam** is licensed for the adjunctive treatment of partial seizures.

### LEVETIRACETAM

**Indications** adjunctive treatment of partial seizures with or without secondary generalisation

**Cautions** avoid sudden withdrawal; hepatic impairment (Appendix 2); renal impairment (Appendix 3); pregnancy (see p. 238 and Appendix 4); breast-feeding (Appendix 5)

**Side-effects** nausea, vomiting, dyspepsia, diarrhoea; cough; drowsiness, asthenia, amnesia, ataxia, convulsions, dizziness, headache, tremor, hyperkinesia, depression, emotional lability, insomnia, anxiety, anorexia,; diplopia; rash; *also reported* confusion, irritability, psychosis, suicidal ideation, leucopenia, pancytopenia, thrombocytopenia, and alopecia

**Dose**

- ADULT and ADOLESCENT over 12 years, body-weight over 50 kg, initially 1 g daily in 2 divided doses, adjusted in steps of 1 g every 2 to 4 weeks; max. 3 g daily in 2 divided doses; CHILD and ADOLESCENT 4–18 years, body-weight under 50 kg, initially 20 mg/kg daily in 2 divided doses, adjusted in steps not exceeding 20 mg/kg every 2 weeks; max. 60 mg/kg in 2 divided doses

**Keppra®** (UCB Pharma) ▼ PoM

Tablets, f/c, levetiracetam 250 mg (blue), net price 60-tab pack = £29.70; 500 mg (yellow), 60-tab pack = £52.30; 750 mg (orange) 60-tab pack = £89.10; 1 g (white), 60-tab pack = £101.10. Label: 8

Oral solution, sugar-free, levetiracetam 100 mg/mL, net price 300 mL = £71.00. Label: 8

## Phenobarbital and other barbiturates

**Phenobarbital** (phenobarbitone) is effective for tonic-clonic and partial seizures but may be sedative in adults and cause behavioural disturbances and hyperkinesia in children. It may be tried for atypical absence, atonic, and tonic seizures. Rebound seizures may be a problem on withdrawal. Monitoring plasma concentrations is less useful than with other drugs because tolerance occurs.

**Primidone** is largely converted to phenobarbital and this is probably responsible for its antiepileptic action. A small starting dose of primidone (125 mg) is essential, and the drug should be introduced over several weeks.

### PHENOBARBITAL
(Phenobarbitone)

**Indications** all forms of epilepsy except absence seizures; status epilepticus (section 4.8.2)

**Cautions** elderly, debilitated, children, hepatic impairment (Appendix 2), renal impairment (Appendix 3), respiratory depression (avoid if severe), pregnancy (Appendix 4) and breast-feeding (Appendix 5) (see notes above); avoid sudden withdrawal; see also notes above; avoid in porphyria (see section 9.8.2); **interactions**: see p. 237 and Appendix 1 (barbiturates)

**Side-effects** drowsiness, lethargy, mental depression, ataxia and allergic skin reactions; paradoxical excitement, restlessness and confusion in the elderly and hyperkinesia in children; megaloblastic anaemia (may be treated with folic acid)

**Dose**

- By mouth, 60–180 mg at night; CHILD 5–8 mg/kg daily

Note For therapeutic purposes phenobarbital and phenobarbital sodium may be considered equivalent in effect. Plasma-phenobarbital concentration for optimum response 15–40 mg/litre (60–180 micromol/litre)

**Phenobarbital** (Non-proprietary) CD

Tablets, phenobarbital 15 mg, net price 28-tab pack = 63p; 30 mg, 28-tab pack = 65p; 60 mg, 28-tab pack = 71p. Label: 2, 8, counselling, driving (see notes above)

Elixir, phenobarbital 15 mg/5 mL in a suitable flavoured vehicle, containing alcohol 38%, net price 100 mL = 77p. Label: 2, 8, counselling, driving (see notes above)

Note Some hospitals supply **alcohol-free** formulations of varying phenobarbital strengths

**Injection**

Section 4.8.2

## PRIMIDONE

**Indications** all forms of epilepsy except absence seizures; essential tremor (also section 4.9.3)

**Cautions** see under Phenobarbital; **interactions:** see p. 237 and Appendix 1 (primidone)

**Side-effects** see under Phenobarbital; also nausea and visual disturbances; *less commonly* vomiting, headache, and dizziness; *rarely* personality changes, arthralgia, and osteomalacia

**Dose**

- Epilepsy, ADULT and CHILD over 9 years, initially 125 mg daily at bedtime, increased by 125 mg every 3 days to 500 mg daily in 2 divided doses then increased according to response by 250 mg every 3 days to max. 1.5 g daily in 2 divided doses; CHILD under 9 years, initially 125 mg daily at bedtime, increased by 125 mg every 3 days according to response; usual maintenance, CHILD under 2 years, 250–500 mg daily in 2 divided doses; 2–5 years, 500–750 mg daily in 2 divided doses; 6–9 years 0.75–1 g daily in 2 divided doses
- Essential tremor, initially 62.5 mg daily increased gradually over 2–3 weeks according to response; max. 750 mg daily

Note Monitor plasma concentrations of derived phenobarbital. Optimum range as for phenobarbital. Primidone doses in BNF may differ from those in product literature

**Mysoline®** (Acorus) PoM

Tablets, scored, primidone 250 mg, net price 100-tab pack = £12.60. Label: 2, 8, counselling, driving (see notes above)

## Phenytoin

**Phenytoin** is effective in tonic-clonic and partial seizures. It has a narrow therapeutic index and the relationship between dose and plasma concentration is non-linear; small dosage increases in some patients may produce large rises in plasma concentrations with acute toxic side-effects. Monitoring of plasma concentration greatly assists dosage adjustment. A few missed doses or a small change in drug absorption may result in a marked change in plasma concentration.

Phenytoin may cause coarse facies, acne, hirsutism, and gingival hyperplasia and so may be particularly undesirable in adolescent patients.

When only parenteral administration is possible, **fosphenytoin** (section 4.8.2), a pro-drug of phenytoin, may be convenient to give. Whereas phenytoin can be given intravenously only, fosphenytoin may also be given by intramuscular injection.

## PHENYTOIN

**Indications** all forms of epilepsy except absence seizures; trigeminal neuralgia if carbamazepine inappropriate (see also section 4.7.3)

**Cautions** hepatic impairment (reduce dose), pregnancy (**important**: see notes above and Appendix 4), breast-feeding (see notes above and Appendix 5); avoid sudden withdrawal; manufacturer recommends blood counts (but evidence of practical value unsatisfactory); avoid in porphyria (section 9.8.2); see also notes above; **interactions:** see p. 237 and Appendix 1 (phenytoin)

Blood or skin disorders Patients or their carers should be told how to recognise signs of blood or skin disorders, and advised to seek immediate medical attention if symptoms such as fever, sore throat, rash, mouth ulcers, bruising, or bleeding develop. Leucopenia which is severe, progressive or associated with clinical symptoms requires withdrawal (if necessary under cover of suitable alternative)

**Side-effects** nausea, vomiting, mental confusion, dizziness, headache, tremor, transient nervousness, insomnia occur commonly; rarely dyskinesias, peripheral neuropathy; ataxia, slurred speech, nystagmus and blurred vision are signs of overdosage; rashes (discontinue; if mild re-introduce cautiously but discontinue immediately if recurrence), gingival hypertrophy and tenderness, coarse facies, acne and hirsutism, fever and hepatitis; lupus erythematosus, Stevens-Johnson syndrome, toxic epidermal necrolysis, polyarteritis nodosa; lymphadenopathy; rarely haematological effects, including megaloblastic anaemia (may be treated with folic acid), leucopenia, thrombocytopenia, agranulocytosis, and aplastic anaemia; plasma-calcium concentration may be lowered (rickets and osteomalacia)

**Dose**

- By mouth, initially 3–4 mg/kg daily *or* 150–300 mg daily (as a single dose *or* in 2 divided doses) increased gradually as necessary (with plasma-phenytoin concentration monitoring); usual dose 200–500 mg daily (exceptionally, higher doses may be used); CHILD initially 5 mg/kg daily in 2 divided doses, usual dose range 4–8 mg/kg daily (max. 300 mg)
- By intravenous injection—section 4.8.2

Note Plasma concentration for optimum response 10–20 mg/litre (40–80 micromol/litre)

Counselling Take preferably with or after food

**Phenytoin** (Non-proprietary) PoM

Tablets, coated, phenytoin sodium 100 mg, net price 28-tab pack = £3.23. Label: 8, counselling, administration, blood or skin disorder symptoms (see above), driving (see notes above)

Note On the basis of single dose tests there are no clinically relevant differences in bioavailability between available phenytoin sodium tablets and capsules but there may be a pharmacokinetic basis for maintaining the same brand of phenytoin in some patients

**Epanutin®** (Pfizer) PoM

Capsules, phenytoin sodium 25 mg (white/purple), net price 28-cap pack = 66p; 50 mg (white/pink), 28-cap pack = 67p; 100 mg (white/orange), 20-cap pack = 67p; 300 mg (white/green), 20-cap pack = £2.02. Label: 8, counselling, administration, blood or skin disorder symptoms (see above), driving (see notes above)

Infatabs® (= chewable tablets), yellow, scored, phenytoin 50 mg. Net price 20 = £1.32. Label: 8, 24, counselling, blood or skin disorder symptoms (see above), driving (see notes above)

Note Contain phenytoin 50 mg (as against phenytoin sodium) therefore care is needed on changing to capsules or tablets containing phenytoin sodium

Suspension, red, phenytoin 30 mg/5 mL. Net price 100 mL = 85p. Label: 8, counselling, administration, blood or skin disorder symptoms (see above), driving (see notes above)

Note Suspension of phenytoin 90 mg in 15 mL may be considered to be approximately equivalent in therapeutic effect to capsules or tablets containing phenytoin sodium 100 mg, but nevertheless care is needed in making changes

## Tiagabine

**Tiagabine** is used as adjunctive treatment for partial seizures, with or without secondary generalisation.

### TIAGABINE

**Indications** adjunctive treatment for partial seizures with or without secondary generalisation not satisfactorily controlled with other antiepileptics

**Cautions** avoid in porphyria (section 9.8.2); hepatic impairment (Appendix 2); avoid abrupt withdrawal; **interactions:** Appendix 1 (tiagabine)

Driving May impair performance of skilled tasks (e.g. driving)

**Side-effects** diarrhoea, dizziness, tiredness, nervousness, tremor, concentration difficulties, emotional lability, speech impairment; rarely, confusion, depression, drowsiness, psychosis; leucopenia reported

**Dose**

- Adjunctive therapy, with *enzyme-inducing* drugs, 5 mg twice daily for 1 week, then increased at weekly intervals in steps of 5–10 mg daily; usual maintenance dose 30–45 mg daily (doses above 30 mg given in 3 divided doses); in patients receiving *non-enzyme-inducing* drugs, initial maintenance dose should be 15–30 mg daily; CHILD under 12 years not recommended

**Gabitril®** (Cephalon) PoM

Tablets, f/c, scored, tiagabine (as hydrochloride) 5 mg, net price 100-tab pack = £43.37; 10 mg, 100-tab pack = £86.74; 15 mg, 100-tab pack = £130.11. Label: 21

## Topiramate

**Topiramate** can be given alone or as adjunctive treatment in generalised tonic-clonic seizures or partial seizures with or without secondary generalisation. It can also be used as adjunctive treatment for seizures associated with Lennox-Gastaut syndrome. Topiramate is also licensed for prophylaxis of migraine (section 4.7.4.2).

### TOPIRAMATE

**Indications** monotherapy and adjunctive treatment of generalised tonic-clonic seizures or partial seizures with or without secondary generalisation; adjunctive treatment of seizures in Lennox-Gastaut syndrome; migraine prophylaxis (under specialist supervision)

**Cautions** avoid abrupt withdrawal; ensure adequate hydration (especially if predisposition to nephrolithiasis or in strenuous activity or warm environment); avoid in porphyria (section 9.8.2); hepatic impairment (Appendix 2); renal impairment (Appendix 3); pregnancy (see notes above and Appendix 4); **interactions:** see p. 237 and Appendix 1 (topiramate)

**CSM advice** Topiramate has been associated with acute myopia with secondary angle-closure glaucoma, typically occurring within 1 month of starting treatment. Choroidal effusions resulting in anterior displacement of the lens and iris have also been reported. The CSM advises that if raised intra-ocular pressure occurs:

- seek specialist ophthalmological advice;
- use appropriate measures to reduce intra-ocular pressure;
- stop topiramate as rapidly as feasible

**Contra-indications** breast-feeding (Appendix 5)

**Side-effects** nausea, abdominal pain, dyspepsia, diarrhoea, dry mouth, taste disturbance, weight loss, anorexia; paraesthesia, hypoaesthesia, headache, fatigue, dizziness, speech disorder, drowsiness, insomnia, impaired memory and concentration, anxiety, depression; visual disturbances; *less commonly* suicidal ideation; *rarely* reduced sweating mainly in children, and metabolic acidosis; serious skin reactions reported rarely

**Dose**

- Monotherapy, initially 25 mg daily at night for 1 week *then* increased in steps of 25–50 mg daily at intervals of 1–2 weeks taken in 2 divided doses; usual dose 100 mg daily in 2 divided doses; max. 400 mg daily; CHILD 6–16 years, initially 0.5–1 mg/kg daily at night for 1 week *then* increased in steps of 0.5–1 mg/kg daily at intervals of 1–2 weeks taken in 2 divided doses; usual dose 3–6 mg/kg daily in 2 divided doses; max. 16 mg/kg daily
- Adjunctive therapy, initially 25 mg daily for 1 week *then* increased in steps of 25–50 mg daily at intervals of 1–2 weeks taken in 2 divided doses; usual dose 200–400 mg daily in 2 divided doses; max. 800 mg daily; CHILD 2–16 years, initially 25 mg daily at night for one week *then* increased in steps of 1–3 mg/kg daily at intervals of 1–2 weeks taken in 2 divided doses; recommended dose range 5–9 mg/kg daily in 2 divided doses; max. 30 mg/kg daily
- Migraine prophylaxis ADULT and CHILD over 16 years, initially 25 mg daily at night for 1 week *then* increased in steps of 25 mg daily at intervals of 1 week; usual dose 50–100 mg daily in 2 divided doses

Note If patient cannot tolerate titration regimens recommended above then smaller steps or longer interval between steps may be used

**Topamax®** (Janssen-Cilag) ▼ PoM

Tablets, f/c, topiramate 25 mg, net price 60-tab pack = £20.92; 50 mg (light yellow), 60-tab pack = £34.36; 100 mg (yellow), 60-tab pack = £61.56; 200 mg (salmon), 60-tab pack = £119.54. Label: 3, 8, counselling, driving (see notes above)

Sprinkle capsules, topiramate 15 mg, net price 60-cap pack = £16.04; 25 mg, 60-cap pack = £24.05; 50 mg, 60-cap pack = £39.52. Label: 3, 8, counselling, administration, driving (see notes above)

Counselling Swallow whole or open capsule and sprinkle contents on soft food

## Valproate

**Sodium valproate** is effective in controlling tonic-clonic seizures, particularly in primary generalised epilepsy.

It is a drug of choice in primary generalised epilepsy, generalised absences and myoclonic seizures, and may be tried in atypical absence, atonic, and tonic seizures. Controlled trials in partial epilepsy suggest that it has similar efficacy to that of carbamazepine and phenytoin. Plasma-valproate concentrations are not a useful index of efficacy, therefore routine monitoring is unhelpful. The drug has widespread metabolic effects, and may have dose-related side-effects.

**Valproic acid** (as semisodium valproate) (section 4.2.3) is licensed for acute mania associated with bipolar disorder.

## SODIUM VALPROATE

**Indications** all forms of epilepsy

**Cautions** monitor liver function before therapy and during first 6 months especially in patients most at risk (see also below); measure full blood count and ensure no undue potential for bleeding before starting and before surgery; systemic lupus erythematosus; false-positive urine tests for ketones; avoid abrupt withdrawal; renal impairment (Appendix 3); pregnancy (**important** see notes above and Appendix 4 (neural tube screening)); breast-feeding (Appendix 5); **interactions:** see p. 237 and Appendix 1 (valproate)

Liver toxicity Liver dysfunction (including fatal hepatic failure) has occurred in association with valproate (especially in children under 3 years and in those with metabolic or degenerative disorders, organic brain disease or severe seizure disorders associated with mental retardation) usually in first 6 months and usually involving multiple antiepileptic therapy. Raised liver enzymes during valproate treatment are usually transient but patients should be reassessed clinically and liver function (including prothrombin time) monitored until return to normal—discontinue if abnormally prolonged prothrombin time (particularly in association with other relevant abnormalities). Any concomitant use of salicylates should be stopped.

Blood or hepatic disorders Patients or their carers should be told how to recognise signs and symptoms of blood or liver disorders and advised to seek immediate medical attention if symptoms develop.

Pancreatitis Patients or their carers should be told how to recognise signs and symptoms of pancreatitis and advised to seek immediate medical attention if symptoms such as abdominal pain, nausea and vomiting develop; discontinue if pancreatitis is diagnosed

**Contra-indications** active liver disease, family history of severe hepatic dysfunction, porphyria (section 9.8.2)

**Side-effects** nausea, gastric irritation, diarrhoea; increased appetite, weight gain; hyperammonaemia, thrombocytopenia; transient hair loss (regrowth may be curly); *less frequently* increased alertness, aggression, hyperactivity, behavioural disturbances, ataxia, tremor, and vasculitis; *rarely* hepatic dysfunction (see under Cautions; withdraw treatment immediately if persistent vomiting and abdominal pain, anorexia, jaundice, oedema, malaise, drowsiness, or loss of seizure control), lethargy, drowsiness, confusion, stupor, hallucinations, menstrual disturbances, anaemia, leucopenia, pancytopenia, and rash; *very rarely* pancreatitis (see under Cautions), peripheral oedema, increase in bleeding time, extrapyramidal symptoms, dementia, encephalopathy, coma, gynaecomastia, Fanconi's syndrome, hirsutism, acne, toxic epidermal necrolysis, and Stevens-Johnson syndrome

**Dose**

- By mouth, initially 600 mg daily in 2 divided doses, preferably after food, increased by 200 mg daily every 3 days to max. 2.5 g daily in divided doses, usual maintenance dose 1–2 g daily (20–30 mg/kg daily); CHILD body-weight up to 20 kg, initially 20 mg/kg daily in divided doses, may be increased provided plasma concentration monitored (dose above 40 mg/kg daily also monitor clinical chemistry and haematological parameters); CHILD body-weight over 20 kg, initially 400 mg daily in divided doses increased according to response (usual range 20–30 mg/kg daily); max. 35 mg/kg daily
- By intravenous injection (over 3–5 minutes) or by intravenous infusion, continuation of valproate treatment, same as current dose by oral route

  Initiation of valproate therapy, by intravenous injection (over 3–5 minutes), 400–800 mg (up to 10 mg/kg) followed by intravenous infusion up to max. 2.5 g daily; CHILD, usually 20–30 mg/kg daily, may be increased provided plasma concentration monitored (dose above 40 mg/kg daily also monitor clinical chemistry and haematological parameters)

**Sodium Valproate** (Non-proprietary) PoM

Tablets (crushable), scored, sodium valproate 100 mg, net price 20 = 78p. Label: 8, counselling, blood or hepatic disorder symptoms (see above), driving (see notes above)

Tablets, e/c, sodium valproate 200 mg, net price 20 = £1.29; 500 mg, 20 = £3.02. Label: 5, 8, 25, counselling, blood or hepatic disorder symptoms (see above), driving (see notes above)

Brands include *Orlept®*

Oral solution, sodium valproate 200 mg/5 mL, net price 300 mL = £8.00. Label: 8, counselling, blood or hepatic disorder symptoms (see above), driving (see notes above)

Brands include *Orlept®* sugar-free

**Epilim®** (Sanofi-Synthelabo) PoM

Tablets (crushable), scored, sodium valproate 100 mg, net price 20 = 78p. Label: 8, counselling, blood or hepatic disorder symptoms (see above), driving (see notes above)

Tablets, both e/c, lilac, sodium valproate 200 mg, net price 20 = £1.28; 500 mg, 20 = £3.21. Label: 5, 8, 25, counselling, blood or hepatic disorder symptoms (see above), driving (see notes above)

Liquid, red, sugar-free, sodium valproate 200 mg/ 5 mL, net price 300-mL pack = £6.48. Label: 8, counselling, blood or hepatic disorder symptoms (see above), driving (see notes above)

Syrup, red, sodium valproate 200 mg/5 mL, net price 300-mL pack = £6.48. Label: 8, counselling, blood or hepatic disorder symptoms (see above), driving (see notes above)

**Epilim® Intravenous** (Sanofi-Synthelabo) PoM

Injection, powder for reconstitution, sodium valproate, net price 400-mg vial (with 4-mL amp water for injections) = £9.65

### Modified release

**Epilim Chrono®** (Sanofi-Synthelabo) PoM

Tablets, m/r, all lilac, sodium valproate 200 mg (as sodium valproate and valproic acid), net price 100-tab pack = £8.09; 300 mg, 100-tab pack = £12.13; 500 mg, 100-tab pack = £20.21. Label: 8, 25, counselling, blood or hepatic disorder symptoms (see above), driving (see notes above)

**Dose** ADULT and CHILD over 20 kg, as above, total daily dose given in 1–2 divided doses

### ▲Valproic acid

**Convulex®** (Pharmacia) PoM

Capsules, e/c, valproic acid 150 mg, net price 100-cap pack = £3.68; 300 mg, 100-cap pack = £7.35; 500 mg, 100-cap pack = £12.25. Label: 8, 25, counselling, blood or hepatic disorder symptoms (see above), driving (see notes above)

**Dose** ADULT and CHILD as for sodium valproate, in 2–4 divided doses

**Equivalence to sodium valproate** Manufacturer advises that *Convulex®* has a 1:1 dose relationship with products containing sodium valproate, but nevertheless care is needed in making changes.

## Vigabatrin

For partial epilepsy with or without secondary generalisation, **vigabatrin** is given in combination with other antiepileptic treatment; its use is restricted to patients in whom all other combinations are inadequate or are not tolerated. It can be used as sole therapy in the management of infantile spasms in West's syndrome.

About one-third of patients treated with vigabatrin have suffered visual field defects; counselling and **careful monitoring** for this side-effect are required (see also Visual Field Defects under Cautions below). Vigabatrin has prominent behavioural side-effects in some patients.



### VIGABATRIN

**Indications** initiated and supervised by appropriate specialist, adjunctive treatment of partial seizures with or without secondary generalisation not satisfactorily controlled with other antiepileptics; monotherapy for management of infantile spasms (West's syndrome)

**Cautions** renal impairment (Appendix 3); elderly; closely monitor neurological function; avoid sudden withdrawal (taper off over 2–4 weeks); history of psychosis, depression or behavioural problems; pregnancy (see p. 238 and Appendix 4) and breast-feeding (Appendix 5); absence seizures (may be exacerbated); **interactions:** see p. 237 and Appendix 1 (vigabatrin)

**Visual field defects** Vigabatrin is associated with visual field defects. The CSM has advised that onset of symptoms varies from 1 month to several years after starting. In most cases, visual field defects have persisted despite discontinuation. Product literature advises visual field testing before treatment and at 6-month intervals; a procedure for testing visual fields in those with a developmental age of less than 9 years is available from the manufacturers. Patients should be warned to report any new visual symptoms that develop and those with symptoms should be referred for an urgent ophthalmological opinion. Gradual withdrawal of vigabatrin should be considered.

**Contra-indications** visual field defects

**Side-effects** drowsiness (rarely, encephalopathic symptoms consisting of marked sedation, stupor, and confusion with non-specific slow wave EEG—reduce dose or withdraw), fatigue, visual field defects (see also under Cautions), dizziness, nervousness, irritability, behavioural effects such as excitation and agitation especially in children; depression, abnormal thinking, headache, nystagmus, ataxia, tremor, paraesthesia, impaired concentration; less commonly confusion, aggression, psychosis, mania, memory disturbance, visual disturbance (e.g. diplopia); also weight gain, oedema, gastro-intestinal disturbances, alopecia, rash; less commonly, urticaria, occasional increase in seizure frequency (especially if myoclonic), decrease in liver enzymes, slight decrease in haemoglobin; photophobia and retinal disorders (e.g. peripheral retinal atrophy); optic neuritis, optic atrophy, hallucinations also reported

**Dose**

- With current antiepileptic therapy, initially 1 g daily in single or 2 divided doses then increased according to response in steps of 500 mg at weekly intervals; usual range 2–3 g daily (max. 3 g daily); CHILD initially 40 mg/kg daily in single or 2 divided doses then adjusted according to body-weight 10–15 kg, 0.5–1 g daily; body-weight 15–30 kg, 1–1.5 g daily; body-weight 30–50 kg, 1.5–3 g daily; body-weight over 50 kg, 2–3 g daily
- Infantile spasms (West's syndrome), *monotherapy*, 50 mg/kg daily, adjusted according to response over 7 days; up to 150 mg/kg daily used with good tolerability

**Sabril®** (Aventis Pharma) PoM

Tablets, f/c, scored, vigabatrin 500 mg, net price 100-tab pack = £30.84. Label: 3, 8, counselling, driving (see notes above)

Powder, sugar-free, vigabatrin 500 mg/sachet. Net price 50-sachet pack = £17.08. Label: 3, 8, 13, counselling, driving (see notes above)

**Note** The contents of a sachet should be dissolved in water or a soft drink immediately before taking

## Zonisamide

**Zonisamide** can be used as adjunctive treatment for refractory partial seizures with or without secondary generalisation.

### ZONISAMIDE

**Indications** adjunctive therapy for partial seizures with or without secondary generalisation

**Cautions** elderly; ensure adequate hydration (especially if predisposition to nephrolithiasis or in strenuous activity or warm environment); concomitant use of drugs that increase risk of hyperthermia or nephrolithiasis; avoid abrupt withdrawal; hepatic impairment (avoid if severe—Appendix 2); renal impairment (Appendix 3); pregnancy (Appendix 4); **interactions:** see p. 237 and Appendix 1 (zonisamide)

**Contra-indications** hypersensitivity to sulphonamides; breast-feeding (Appendix 5)

**Side-effects** nausea, diarrhoea, gastro-intestinal pain; drowsiness, dizziness, confusion, agitation, irritability, depression, ataxia, speech disorder, impaired memory and attention, anorexia and weight loss, pyrexia; diplopia; rash (consider withdrawal); *less commonly* vomiting, cholelithiasis, cholecystitis, convulsions, psychosis, urinary calculus, hypokalaemia; *very rarely* dyspnoea, hallucinations, insomnia, suicidal ideation, amnesia, coma, myasthenic syndrome, neuroleptic malignant syndrome, heat stroke, hydronephrosis, renal impairment, metabolic acidosis, blood disorders, rhabdomyolysis, impaired sweating, pruritus, Stevens-Johnson syndrome, hepatitis, pancreatitis

**Dose**

- Initially 50 mg daily in 2 divided doses, increased after 7 days to 100 mg daily in 2 divided doses; then increase if necessary by 100 mg every 7 days; usual maintenance 300–500 mg daily in 1–2 divided doses; CHILD and ADOLESCENT under 18 years not recommended

**Zonegran®** (Eisai) ▼ PoM

Capsules, zonisamide 25 mg (white), net price 14-cap pack = £8.82; 50 mg (white/grey), 56-cap pack = £47.04; 100 mg (white/red), 56-cap pack = £62.72. Label: 3

## Benzodiazepines

**Clonazepam** is occasionally used in tonic-clonic or partial seizures, but its sedative side-effects may be prominent. **Clobazam** may be used as adjunctive therapy in the treatment of epilepsy (section 4.1.2), but the effectiveness of these and other **benzodiazepines** may wane considerably after weeks or months of continuous therapy.

### CLOBAZAM

**Indications** adjunct in epilepsy; anxiety (short-term use)

**Cautions** see under Diazepam (section 4.1.2)

**Contra-indications** see under Diazepam (section 4.1.2)

**Side-effects** see under Diazepam (section 4.1.2)

**Dose**

- Epilepsy, 20–30 mg daily; max. 60 mg daily; CHILD over 3 years, not more than half adult dose
- Anxiety, 20–30 mg daily in divided doses or as a single dose at bedtime, increased in severe anxiety (in hospital patients) to a max. of 60 mg daily in divided doses; ELDERLY (or debilitated) 10–20 mg daily

[1]**Clobazam** (Non-proprietary) PoM NHS

Tablets, clobazam 10 mg. Net price 30-tab pack = £9.74. Label: 2 or 19, 8, counselling, driving (see notes above)

Brands include *Frisium®* NHS

1. NHS except for epilepsy and endorsed 'SLS'

### CLONAZEPAM

**Indications** all forms of epilepsy; myoclonus; status epilepticus (section 4.8.2)

**Cautions** see notes above; elderly and debilitated, respiratory disease, spinal or cerebellar ataxia; history of alcohol or drug abuse, depression or suicidal ideation; avoid sudden withdrawal; myasthenia gravis; porphyria (section 9.8.2); hepatic impairment (avoid if severe; Appendix 2); renal impairment; pregnancy (see notes above and Appendix 4); breast-feeding (see notes above and Appendix 5); **interactions:** Appendix 1 (anxiolytics and hypnotics)

Driving Drowsiness may affect performance of skilled tasks (e.g. driving); effects of alcohol enhanced

**Contra-indications** respiratory depression; acute pulmonary insufficiency; sleep apnoea syndrome; marked neuromuscular respiratory weakness including unstable myasthenia gravis

**Side-effects** drowsiness, fatigue, dizziness, muscle hypotonia, co-ordination disturbances; also poor concentration, restlessness, confusion, amnesia, dependence, and withdrawal; salivary or bronchial hypersecretion in infants and small children; *rarely* gastro-intestinal symptoms, respiratory depression, headache, paradoxical effects including aggression and anxiety, sexual dysfunction, urinary incontinence, urticaria, pruritus, reversible hair loss, skin pigmentation changes; dysarthria, and visual disturbances on long-term treatment; blood disorders reported; **overdosage:** see Emergency Treatment of Poisoning, p. 32

**Dose**

- 1 mg (ELDERLY 500 micrograms) initially at night for 4 nights, increased according to response over 2–4 weeks to usual maintenance dose of 4–8 mg daily in 3–4 divided doses; may be given as a single daily dose in the evening once maintenance dose established; max. 20 mg daily; CHILD up to 1 year, initially 250 micrograms increased as above to usual maintenance dose of 0.5–1 mg, 1–5 years, initially 250 micrograms increased as above to 1–3 mg, 5–12 years, initially 500 micrograms increased as above to 3–6 mg

**Rivotril®** (Roche) PoM

Tablets, both scored, clonazepam 500 micrograms (beige), net price 100 = £3.92; 2 mg (white), 100 = £5.23. Label: 2, 8, counselling, driving (see notes above)

Injection, section 4.8.2

## Other drugs

**Acetazolamide** (section 11.6), a carbonic anhydrase inhibitor, is a second-line drug for both tonic-clonic and partial seizures. It is occasionally helpful in atypical absence, atonic, and tonic seizures.

**Piracetam** (section 4.9.3) is used as adjunctive treatment for cortical myoclonus.

## 4.8.2 Drugs used in status epilepticus

Initial management of status epilepticus includes positioning the patient to avoid injury, supporting respiration including the provision of oxygen, maintaining blood pressure, and the correction of any hypoglycaemia. The use of parenteral **thiamine** should be considered if alcohol abuse is suspected; **pyridoxine** should be administered if the status epilepticus is caused by pyridoxine deficiency.

Major status epilepticus should be treated initially with intravenous **lorazepam**. Intravenous **diazepam** is effective but it is associated with a high risk of thrombophlebitis (reduced by using an emulsion formulation). Alternatively, in prolonged or recurrent seizures, a single dose of **midazolam** (section 15.1.4.1) can be given [unlicensed use] by the buccal route (in a dose of 10 mg) or intranasally (200 micrograms/kg).

Where facilities for resuscitation are not immediately available, small doses of lorazepam or diazepam can be given intravenously, or diazepam can be administered as a rectal solution. Absorption from intramuscular injection or from suppositories is too slow for treatment of status epilepticus.

**Clonazepam** can also be used as an alternative.

If seizures recur or fail to respond after 30 minutes, phenytoin sodium, fosphenytoin, or phenobarbital sodium should be used.

**Phenytoin sodium** may be given by slow intravenous injection, with ECG monitoring, followed by the maintenance dosage. Intramuscular use of phenytoin is not recommended (absorption is slow and erratic).

Alternatively, **fosphenytoin**, a pro-drug of phenytoin, can be given more rapidly and when given intravenously causes fewer injection site reactions compared to phenytoin. Intravenous administration requires ECG monitoring. Although it can also be given intramuscularly, absorption is too slow by this route for treatment of status epilepticus. Doses of fosphenytoin should be expressed in terms of phenytoin sodium.

Alternatively, **phenobarbital sodium** can be given by intravenous injection.

**Paraldehyde** also remains a valuable drug. Given rectally it causes little respiratory depression and is therefore useful where facilities for resuscitation are poor.

If the above measures fail to control seizures, anaesthesia with thiopental (section 15.1.1) or in adults, a non-barbiturate anaesthetic such as propofol [unlicensed indication] (section 15.1.1), should be instituted with full intensive care support.

For advice on the management of medical emergencies in dental practice, see p. 20



## DIAZEPAM

**Indications** status epilepticus; convulsions due to poisoning (see Emergency Treatment of Poisoning); other indications (section 4.1.2, section 10.2.2, and section 15.1.4.1)

**Cautions** see section 4.1.2; when given intravenously facilities for reversing respiratory depression with mechanical ventilation must be at hand (but see also notes above)

Special cautions for intravenous infusion Intravenous infusion of diazepam is potentially hazardous (especially if prolonged), calling for close and constant observation and best carried out in specialist centres with intensive care facilities. Prolonged infusion may lead to accumulation and delay recovery

**Contra-indications** see section 4.1.2

**Side-effects** see section 4.1.2; hypotension and apnoea

**Dose**

- Status epilepticus (but see notes above) and convulsions due to poisoning, by intravenous injection, 10–20 mg at a rate of 0.5 mL (2.5 mg) per 30 seconds, repeated if necessary after 30–60 minutes; may be followed by intravenous infusion to max. 3 mg/kg over 24 hours; CHILD 200–300 micrograms/kg *or* 1 mg per year of age

  By rectum as rectal solution, ADULT and CHILD over 10 kg 500 micrograms/kg, up to max. 30 mg (ELDERLY 250 micrograms/kg, up to max. 15 mg); repeated after 12 hours if necessary

**Diazepam** (Non-proprietary) PoM

Injection (solution), diazepam 5 mg/mL. See Appendix 6. Net price 2-mL amp = 32p

Excipients may include benzyl alcohol (avoid in neonates, see Excipients, p. 2), ethanol, propylene glycol

Injection (emulsion), diazepam 5 mg/mL (0.5%). See Appendix 6. Net price 2-mL amp = 84p

Brands include *Diazemuls®*

Rectal tubes (= rectal solution), diazepam 2 mg/mL, net price 1.25-mL (2.5-mg) tube = 90p, 2.5-mL (5-mg) tube = £1.27; 4 mg/mL, 2.5-mL (10-mg) tube = £1.34

Brands include *Diazepam Rectubes®*, *Stesolid®*

**Oral preparations**

Section 4.1.2

## CLONAZEPAM

**Indications** status epilepticus; other forms of epilepsy, and myoclonus (section 4.8.1)

**Cautions** see section 4.8.1; facilities for reversing respiratory depression with mechanical ventilation must be at hand (but see also notes above)

Intravenous infusion Intravenous infusion of clonazepam is potentially hazardous (especially if prolonged), calling for close and constant observation and best carried out in specialist centres with intensive care facilities. Prolonged infusion may lead to accumulation and delay recovery

**Contra-indications** see section 4.8.1; avoid injections containing benzyl alcohol in neonates (see under preparations below)

**Side-effects** see section 4.8.1; hypotension and apnoea

**Dose**

- By intravenous injection into a large vein (over at least 2 minutes) *or* by intravenous infusion, 1 mg, repeated if necessary; CHILD all ages, 500 micrograms

**Rivotril®** (Roche) PoM

Injection, clonazepam 1 mg/mL in solvent, for dilution with 1 mL water for injections immediately before injection or as described in Appendix 6. Net price 1-mL amp (with 1 mL water for injections) = 63p

Excipients include benzyl alcohol (avoid in neonates, see Excipients, p. 2), ethanol, propylene glycol

**Oral preparations**

Section 4.8.1

## FOSPHENYTOIN SODIUM

Note Fosphenytoin is a pro-drug of phenytoin

**Indications** status epilepticus; seizures associated with neurosurgery or head injury; when phenytoin by mouth not possible

**Cautions** see Phenytoin Sodium; liver impairment (Appendix 2); renal impairment (Appendix 3); resuscitation facilities must be available; **interactions:** see p. 237 and Appendix 1 (phenytoin)

**Contra-indications** see Phenytoin Sodium

**Side-effects** see Phenytoin Sodium

CSM advice Intravenous infusion of fosphenytoin has been associated with severe cardiovascular reactions including asystole, ventricular fibrillation, and cardiac arrest. Hypotension, bradycardia, and heart block have also been reported. The CSM advises:

- monitor heart rate, blood pressure, and respiratory function for duration of infusion
- observe patient for at least 30 minutes after infusion
- if hypotension occurs, reduce infusion rate or discontinue
- reduce dose or infusion rate in elderly, and in renal or hepatic impairment.

**Dose**

> Note Prescriptions for fosphenytoin sodium should state the dose in terms of phenytoin sodium equivalent (PE); fosphenytoin sodium 1.5 mg ≡ phenytoin sodium 1 mg

- Status epilepticus, by intravenous infusion (at a rate of 100–150 mg(PE)/minute), initially 15 mg(PE)/kg then by intramuscular injection or by intravenous infusion (at a rate of 50–100 mg(PE)/minute), 4–5 mg(PE)/kg daily in 1–2 divided doses, dose adjusted according to response and trough plasma-phenytoin concentration

  CHILD 5 years and over, by intravenous infusion (at a rate of 2–3 mg(PE)/kg/minute), initially 15 mg(PE)/kg then by intravenous infusion (at a rate of 1–2 mg(PE)/kg/minute), 4–5 mg(PE)/kg daily in 1–4 divided doses, dose adjusted according to response and trough plasma-phenytoin concentration
- Prophylaxis or treatment of seizures associated with neurosurgery or head injury, by intramuscular injection or by intravenous infusion (at a rate of 50–100 mg(PE)/minute), initially 10–15 mg(PE)/kg then by intramuscular injection or by intravenous infusion (at a rate of 50–100 mg(PE)/minute), 4–5 mg(PE)/kg daily (in 1–2 divided doses), dose adjusted according to response and trough plasma-phenytoin concentration

  CHILD 5 years and over, by intravenous infusion (at a rate of 1–2 mg(PE)/kg/minute), initially 10–15 mg(PE)/kg then 4–5 mg(PE)/kg daily in 1–4 divided doses, dose adjusted according to response and trough plasma-phenytoin concentration
- Temporary substitution for oral phenytoin, by intramuscular injection or by intravenous infusion (at a rate of 50–100 mg(PE)/minute), same dose and dosing frequency as oral phenytoin therapy; CHILD 5 years and over, by intravenous infusion (at a rate of 1–2 mg(PE)/kg/minute), same dose and dosing frequency as oral phenytoin therapy

Note ELDERLY consider 10–25% reduction in dose or infusion rate

**Pro-Epanutin®** (Pfizer) PoM

Injection, fosphenytoin sodium 75 mg/mL (equivalent to phenytoin sodium 50 mg/mL), net price 10-mL vial = £40.00

Electrolytes phosphate 3.7 micromol/mg fosphenytoin sodium (phosphate 5.6 micromol/mg phenytoin sodium)

## LORAZEPAM

**Indications** status epilepticus; other indications (section 4.1.2)

**Cautions** see section 4.1.2

**Contra-indications** see under Diazepam (section 4.1.2)

**Side-effects** see under Diazepam (section 4.1.2)

**Dose**

- By intravenous injection (into large vein), 4 mg; CHILD 2 mg

**Preparations**

Section 4.1.2

## PARALDEHYDE

**Indications** status epilepticus

**Cautions** bronchopulmonary disease, hepatic impairment; pregnancy (Appendix 4) and breast-feeding (Appendix 5); **interactions**: Appendix 1 (paraldehyde)

**Contra-indications** gastric disorders; rectal administration in colitis

**Side-effects** rashes; rectal irritation after enema

**Dose**

- By rectum, usually 10–20 mL; CHILD up to 3 months 0.5 mL, 3–6 months 1 mL, 6–12 months 1.5 mL, 1–2 years 2 mL, 3–5 years 3–4 mL, 6–12 years 5–6 mL

  Administration Administer as an enema containing 1 part paraldehyde diluted with 9 parts physiological saline (some centres mix paraldehyde with an equal volume of arachis (peanut) oil instead)

  Note Do not use paraldehyde if it has a brownish colour or an odour of acetic acid. Avoid contact with rubber and plastics.

**Paraldehyde** (Non-proprietary) PoM

Injection, sterile paraldehyde, net price 5-mL amp = £9.49

## PHENOBARBITAL SODIUM
### (Phenobarbitone sodium)

**Indications** status epilepticus; other forms of epilepsy except absence seizures (section 4.8.1)

**Cautions** see under Phenobarbital (section 4.8.1)

**Side-effects** see under Phenobarbital (section 4.8.1)

**Dose**

- Status epilepticus, by intravenous injection (dilute injection 1 in 10 with water for injections), 10 mg/kg at a rate of not more than 100 mg/minute; max. 1 g
- Control of acute seizures, by intramuscular injection, 200 mg, repeated after 6 hours if necessary; CHILD 15 mg/kg as a single dose

  Note For therapeutic purposes phenobarbital and phenobarbital sodium may be considered equivalent in effect

**Phenobarbital** (Non-proprietary) CD

Injection, phenobarbital sodium 200 mg/mL, net price 1-mL amp = £1.82

Excipients include propylene glycol 90%

Note. Must be diluted before intravenous administration (see under Dose)

**Oral preparations**

Section 4.8.1

## PHENYTOIN SODIUM

**Indications** status epilepticus; seizures in neurosurgery; arrhythmias, but now obsolete (section 2.3.2)

**Cautions** hypotension and heart failure; resuscitation facilities must be available; injection solutions alkaline (irritant to tissues); see also p. 243; **interactions**: see p. 237 and Appendix 1 (phenytoin)

**Contra-indications** sinus bradycardia, sino-atrial block, and second- and third-degree heart block; Stokes-Adams syndrome; porphyria (section 9.8.2)

**Side-effects** intravenous injection may cause cardiovascular and CNS depression (particularly if injection too rapid) with arrhythmias, hypotension, and cardiovascular collapse; alterations in respiratory function (including respiratory arrest); see also p. 243

**Dose**

- By slow intravenous injection *or* infusion (with blood pressure and ECG monitoring), status epilepticus, 15 mg/kg at a rate not exceeding 50 mg per minute, as a loading dose (see also notes above); maintenance doses of about 100 mg should be given thereafter at intervals of every 6–8 hours, monitored by measurement of plasma concentrations; rate and dose reduced according to weight; CHILD 15 mg/kg as a loading dose (neonate 15–20 mg/kg at rate of 1–3 mg/kg/minute)

  Ventricular arrhythmias (but use now obsolete), by intravenous injection via caval catheter, 3.5–5 mg/kg at a rate not exceeding 50 mg/minute, with blood pressure and ECG monitoring; repeat once if necessary

  Note Phenytoin is licensed for administration by intravenous infusion (at the same rate of administration as the injection—not exceeding 50 mg/minute, for further details of the infusion, see Appendix 6). To avoid local venous irritation each injection or infusion should be preceded and followed by an injection of sterile physiological saline through the same needle or catheter
- By intramuscular injection, not recommended (see notes above)

**Phenytoin** (Non-proprietary) PoM

Injection, phenytoin sodium 50 mg/mL with propylene glycol 40% and alcohol 10% in water for injections, net price 5-mL amp = £3.40

**Epanutin® Ready-Mixed Parenteral** (Pfizer) PoM

Injection, phenytoin sodium 50 mg/mL with propylene glycol 40% and alcohol 10% in water for injections. Net price 5-mL amp = £4.88

**Oral preparations**

Section 4.8.1

## 4.8.3 Febrile convulsions

*Brief febrile convulsions* need only simple treatment such as tepid sponging or bathing, or antipyretic medication, e.g. **paracetamol** (section 4.7.1). *Prolonged febrile convulsions* (those lasting 15 minutes or longer), *recurrent convulsions*, or those occurring in a child at known risk must be treated more actively, as there is the possibility of resulting brain damage. **Diazepam** is the drug of choice given either by slow intravenous injection in a dose of 250 micrograms/kg (section 4.8.2) or preferably rectally in solution (section 4.8.2) in a dose of 500 micrograms/kg (max. 10 mg), repeated if necessary. The rectal route is preferred as satisfactory absorption is achieved within minutes and administration is much easier. Suppositories are not suitable because absorption is too slow.

Intermittent prophylaxis (i.e. the anticonvulsant administered at the onset of fever) is possible in only a small proportion of children. Again **diazepam** is the treatment of choice, orally or rectally.

The exact role of continuous prophylaxis in children at risk from prolonged or complex febrile convulsions is controversial. It is probably indicated in only a small proportion of children, including those whose first seizure occurred at under 14 months or who have pre-existing neurological abnormalities or who have had previous prolonged or focal convulsions. Thus long-term anticonvulsant prophylaxis is rarely indicated.

# 4.9 Drugs used in parkinsonism and related disorders

4.9.1 Dopaminergic drugs used in parkinsonism
4.9.2 Antimuscarinic drugs used in parkinsonism
4.9.3 Drugs used in essential tremor, chorea, tics, and related disorders

In idiopathic Parkinson's disease, the progressive degeneration of pigmented neurones in the substantia nigra leads to a deficiency of the neurotransmitter dopamine. The resulting neurochemical imbalance in the basal ganglia causes the characteristic signs and symptoms of the illness. Drug therapy does not prevent disease progression, but it improves most patients' quality of life.

When initiating treatment, patients should be advised about its limitations and possible side-effects. About 5–10% of patients with Parkinson's disease respond poorly to treatment.

Symptoms resembling Parkinson's disease can occur in diseases such as progressive supranuclear palsy and multiple system atrophy, but they do not normally respond to the drugs used in the treatment of idiopathic Parkinson's disease.

**Elderly** Antiparkinsonian drugs can cause confusion in the elderly. It is particularly important to initiate treatment with low doses and to increase the dose gradually.

## 4.9.1 Dopaminergic drugs used in parkinsonism

Treatment for Parkinson's disease should be initiated under the supervision of a physician specialising in Parkinson's disease. Treatment is usually not started until symptoms cause significant disruption of daily activities.

The dopamine receptor agonists, **bromocriptine**, **cabergoline**, **lisuride** (lysuride), **pergolide**, **pramipexole**, and **ropinirole**, have a direct action on dopamine receptors. The treatment of new patients is often started with dopamine receptor agonists. They are also used with levodopa in more advanced disease.

When used alone, dopamine receptor agonists cause fewer motor complications in long-term treatment compared with levodopa treatment but their improvement on overall motor performance is slightly less. The dopamine receptor agonists are associated with more neuropsychiatric side-effects than levodopa. The ergot-derived dopamine receptor agonists, bromocriptine, cabergoline, lisuride, and pergolide have been associated with fibrotic reactions (see notes below).

Doses of dopamine receptor agonists should be increased slowly according to response and tolerability. They should also be withdrawn gradually.

**Apomorphine** is a dopamine receptor agonist that is used in advanced disease (see below).

**Fibrotic reactions**

The CSM has advised that ergot-derived dopamine receptor agonists, bromocriptine, cabergoline, lisuride, and pergolide have been associated with pulmonary, retroperitoneal, and pericardial fibrotic reactions. Before starting treatment with these ergot derivatives it may be appropriate to measure the erythrocyte sedimentation rate and serum creatinine and to obtain a chest X-ray. Patients should be monitored for dyspnoea, persistent cough, chest pain, cardiac failure, and abdominal pain or tenderness. If long-term treatment is expected, then lung-function tests may also be helpful.

**Levodopa**, the amino-acid precursor of dopamine, acts by replenishing depleted striatal dopamine; it is given with an extracerebral **dopa-decarboxylase inhibitor** that reduces the peripheral conversion of levodopa to dopamine, thereby limiting side-effects such as nausea, vomiting and cardiovascular effects. Additionally, effective brain-dopamine concentrations can be achieved with lower doses of levodopa. The extracerebral dopa-decarboxylase inhibitors used with levodopa are benserazide (in **co-beneldopa**) and carbidopa (in **co-careldopa**).

Levodopa, in combination with a dopa-decarboxylase inhibitor, is useful in the elderly or frail, in patients with other significant illnesses, and in those with more severe symptoms. It is effective and well tolerated in the majority of patients.

Levodopa therapy should be initiated at a low dose and increased in small steps; the final dose should be as low as possible. Intervals between doses should be chosen to suit the needs of the individual patient.

**Note** When co-careldopa is used, the total daily dose of carbidopa should be at least 70 mg. A lower dose may not achieve full inhibition of extracerebral dopa-decarboxylase, with a resultant increase in side-effects.

Nausea and vomiting with co-beneldopa or co-careldopa are rarely dose-limiting but domperidone (section 4.6) may be useful in controlling these effects.

Levodopa treatment is associated with the development of potentially troublesome motor complications including response fluctuations and dyskinesias. Response fluctuations are characterised by large variations in motor performance, with normal function during the 'on' period, and weakness and restricted mobility during the 'off' period. 'End-of-dose' deterioration also occurs, where the duration of benefit after each dose becomes progressively shorter. Modified-release preparations may help with 'end-of-dose' deterioration or nocturnal immobility and rigidity. Motor complications are particularly problematic in young patients treated with levodopa.

**Selegiline** is a monoamine-oxidase-B inhibitor used in conjunction with levodopa to reduce 'end-of-dose' deterioration in advanced Parkinson's disease. Early treatment with selegiline alone may delay the need for levodopa therapy for some months but other more effective drugs are preferred. When combined with levodopa, selegiline should be avoided or used with great caution in postural hypotension.

**Rasagiline**, a monoamine-oxidase B inhibitor, is licensed for the management of Parkinson's disease used alone or as an adjunct to levodopa for 'end-of-dose' fluctuations.

**Entacapone** and **tolcapone** prevent the peripheral breakdown of levodopa, by inhibiting catechol-*O*-methyltransferase, allowing more levodopa to reach the brain. They are licensed for use as an adjunct to co-beneldopa or co-careldopa for patients with Parkinson's disease who experience 'end-of-dose' deterioration and cannot be stabilised on these combinations. Due to the risk of hepatotoxicity, tolcapone should be prescribed under specialist supervision only, when other catechol-*O*-methyltransferase inhibitors combined with co-beneldopa or co-careldopa are ineffective.

**Amantadine** has modest antiparkinsonian effects. It improves mild bradykinetic disabilities as well as tremor and rigidity. It may also be useful for dyskinesias in more advanced disease. Tolerance to its effects may develop and confusion and hallucinations may occasionally occur. Withdrawal of amantadine should be gradual irrespective of the patient's response to treatment.

**Apomorphine** is a potent dopamine agonist that is sometimes helpful in advanced disease for patients experiencing unpredictable 'off' periods with levodopa treatment. For the treatment of Parkinson's disease it is only available for parenteral administration. Apomorphine is highly emetogenic; patients must receive domperidone for at least 2 days before starting treatment. Specialist supervision is advisable throughout apomorphine treatment.

**Sudden onset of sleep**

Excessive daytime sleepiness and sudden onset of sleep can occur with co-careldopa, co-beneldopa, and the dopamine receptor agonists.

Patients starting treatment with these drugs should be warned of the possibility of these effects and of the need to exercise caution when driving or operating machinery.

Patients who have suffered excessive sedation or sudden onset of sleep, should refrain from driving or operating machines, until those effects have stopped recurring.

## LEVODOPA

**Indications** parkinsonism (but not drug-induced extrapyramidal symptoms), see notes above

**Cautions** pulmonary disease, peptic ulceration, cardiovascular disease, diabetes mellitus, osteomalacia, open-angle glaucoma, history of skin melanoma (risk of activation), psychiatric illness (avoid if severe); warn patients about excessive drowsiness (see notes above); in prolonged therapy, psychiatric, hepatic, haematological, renal, and cardiovascular surveillance is advisable; warn patients to resume normal activities gradually; avoid abrupt withdrawal; **interactions:** Appendix 1 (levodopa)

**Contra-indications** closed-angle glaucoma; pregnancy (Appendix 4) and breast-feeding (Appendix 5)

**Side-effects** anorexia, nausea and vomiting, insomnia, agitation, postural hypotension (rarely labile hypertension), dizziness, tachycardia, arrhythmias, reddish discoloration of urine and other body fluids, rarely hypersensitivity; abnormal involuntary movements and psychiatric symptoms which include hypomania and psychosis may be dose-limiting; depression, drowsiness, headache, flushing, sweating, gastro-intestinal bleeding, peripheral neuropathy, taste disturbance, pruritus, rash, and liver enzyme changes also reported; syndrome resembling neuroleptic malignant syndrome reported on withdrawal

**Dose**

- Initially 125–500 mg daily in divided doses after meals, increased according to response (but rarely used alone, see notes above)

**Levodopa** (Non-proprietary) PoM

Tablets—product discontinued

## CO-BENELDOPA

A mixture of benserazide hydrochloride and levodopa in mass proportions corresponding to 1 part of benserazide and 4 parts of levodopa

**Indications** see under Levodopa and notes above

**Cautions** see under Levodopa and notes above

**Contra-indications** see under Levodopa

**Side-effects** see under Levodopa and notes above

**Dose**

- Expressed as levodopa, initially 50 mg 3–4 times daily (100 mg 3 times daily in advanced disease), increased by 100 mg once or twice weekly according to response; usual maintenance dose 400–800 mg daily in divided doses after meals; ELDERLY initially 50 mg once or twice daily, increased by 50 mg every 3–4 days according to response

  Note When transferring patients from other levodopa preparations, it is recommended that the previous preparation should be discontinued 12 hours beforehand (although interval can be shorter); 3 capsules co-beneldopa 25/100 (*Madopar 125®*) should be substituted for 2 g levodopa; if transferring from another levodopa/dopa-decarboxylase inhibitor preparation, initial dose, expressed as levodopa, should be 50 mg 3–4 times daily

**Madopar®** (Roche) PoM

Capsules 62.5, blue/grey, co-beneldopa 12.5/50 (benserazide 12.5 mg (as hydrochloride), levodopa 50 mg). Net price 100-cap pack = £6.20. Label: 14, counselling, driving, see notes above

Capsules 125, blue/pink, co-beneldopa 25/100 (benserazide 25 mg (as hydrochloride), levodopa 100 mg). Net price 100-cap pack = £8.64. Label: 14, counselling, driving, see notes above

Capsules 250, blue/caramel, co-beneldopa 50/200 (benserazide 50 mg (as hydrochloride), levodopa 200 mg). Net price 100-cap pack = £14.73. Label: 14, counselling, driving, see notes above

Dispersible tablets 62.5, scored, co-beneldopa 12.5/50 (benserazide 12.5 mg (as hydrochloride), levodopa 50 mg). Net price 100-tab pack = £7.37. Label: 14, counselling, administration, see below, driving see notes above

Dispersible tablets 125, scored, co-beneldopa 25/100 (benserazide 25 mg (as hydrochloride) levodopa 100 mg). Net price 100-tab pack = £13.06. Label: 14, counselling, administration, see below, driving see notes above

Note The tablets may be dispersed in water or orange squash (not orange juice) or swallowed whole

### Modified release

**Madopar® CR** (Roche) PoM

Capsules 125, m/r, dark green/light blue, co-beneldopa 25/100 (benserazide 25 mg (as hydrochloride), levodopa 100 mg). Net price 100-cap pack = £15.96. Label: 5, 14, 25, counselling, driving, see notes above

Dose Patients not receiving levodopa therapy, initially 1 capsule 3 times daily (max. initial dose 6 capsules daily) Fluctuations in response related to plasma-levodopa concentration or to timing of dose, initially 1 capsule substituted for every 100 mg of levodopa and given at same dosage frequency, subsequently increased every 2–3 days according to response; average increase of 50% needed over previous levodopa dose and titration may take up to 4 weeks

Supplementary dose of conventional *Madopar®* may be needed with first morning dose; if response still poor to total daily dose of *Madopar® CR* plus *Madopar®* corresponding to 1.2 g levodopa, consider alternative therapy

## CO-CARELDOPA

A mixture of carbidopa and levodopa; the proportions are expressed in the form *x*/*y* where *x* and *y* are the strengths in milligrams of carbidopa and levodopa respectively

**Indications** see under Levodopa and notes above

**Cautions** see under Levodopa and notes above

**Contra-indications** see under Levodopa

**Side-effects** see under Levodopa and notes above

**Dose**

- See preparations

  Note Carbidopa 70–100 mg daily is necessary to achieve full inhibition of peripheral dopa-decarboxylase

**Sinemet®** (Bristol-Myers Squibb) PoM

Sinemet-62.5® *tablets*, yellow, scored, co-careldopa 12.5/50 (carbidopa 12.5 mg (as monohydrate), levodopa 50 mg), net price 90-tab pack = £7.03. Label: 14, counselling, driving, see notes above

Note 2 tablets *Sinemet-62.5®* ≡ 1 tablet *Sinemet Plus®*; *Sinemet-62.5®* previously known as *Sinemet LS®*

Sinemet-110® *tablets*, blue, scored, co-careldopa 10/100 (carbidopa 10 mg (as monohydrate), levodopa 100 mg), net price 90-tab pack = £6.84. Label: 14, counselling, driving, see notes above

Sinemet-Plus® *tablets*, yellow, scored, co-careldopa 25/100 (carbidopa 25 mg (as monohydrate), levodopa 100 mg), net price 90-tab pack = £10.05. Label: 14, counselling, driving, see notes above

Note The daily dose of carbidopa required to achieve full inhibition of extracerebral dopa-decarboxylase is 75 mg; co-careldopa 25/100 provides an adequate dose of carbidopa when low doses of levodopa are needed

Sinemet-275® *tablets*, blue, scored, co-careldopa 25/250 (carbidopa 25 mg (as monohydrate), levodopa 250 mg), net price 90-tab pack = £14.28. Label: 14, counselling, driving, see notes above

Dose expressed as levodopa, initially 100 mg (with carbidopa 25 mg, as *Sinemet-Plus®*) 3 times daily, increased by 50–100 mg (with carbidopa 12.5–25 mg, as *Sinemet-62.5®* or *Sinemet-Plus®*) daily or on alternate days according to response, up to 800 mg (with carbidopa 200 mg) daily in divided doses

Alternatively, initially 50–100 mg (with carbidopa 10–12.5 mg, as *Sinemet-62.5®* or *Sinemet-110®*) 3–4 times daily, increased by 50–100 mg daily or on alternate days according to response, up to 800 mg (with carbidopa 80–100 mg) daily in divided doses

Alternatively, initially 125 mg (with carbidopa 12.5 mg, as ½ tablet of *Sinemet-275®*) 1–2 times daily, increased by 125 mg (with carbidopa 12.5 mg) daily or on alternate days according to response

Note When transferring patients from levodopa, 1 tablet co-careldopa 25/250 (*Sinemet-275®*) 3–4 times daily should be substituted for patients receiving more than 1.5 g levodopa daily; 1 tablet co-careldopa 25/100 (*Sinemet-Plus®*) 3–4 times daily should be substituted for patients receiving less than 1.5 g levodopa daily; levodopa should be discontinued 12 hours beforehand

**For use with enteral tube**

**Duodopa®** (Solvay) ▼ PoM

Intestinal gel, co-careldopa 5/20 (carbidopa 5mg as monohydrate, levodopa 20mg)/mL, net price 100 mL cassette (for use with *Duodopa®* portable pump) = £77.00. Label: 14, counselling, driving, see notes above

Dose Severe Parkinson's disease inadequately controlled by other preparations, consult product literature

**Modified release**

**Half Sinemet® CR** (Bristol-Myers Squibb) PoM

Tablets, m/r, pink, co-careldopa 25/100 (carbidopa 25 mg (as monohydrate), levodopa 100 mg), net price 60-tab pack = £12.07. Label: 14, 25, counselling, driving, see notes above

Dose for fine adjustment of *Sinemet® CR* dose (see below)

**Sinemet® CR** (Bristol-Myers Squibb) PoM

Tablets, m/r, peach, co-careldopa 50/200 (carbidopa 50 mg (as monohydrate), levodopa 200 mg), net price 60-tab pack = £12.07. Label: 14, 25, counselling, driving, see notes above

Dose initial treatment or fluctuations in response to conventional levodopa therapy, 1 *Sinemet® CR* tablet twice daily; both dose and interval then adjusted according to response at intervals of not less than 3 days; if transferring from existing levodopa therapy withdraw 8 hours beforehand; 1 tablet *Sinemet® CR* twice daily can be substituted for a daily dose of levodopa 300–400 mg in conventional *Sinemet®* tablets

**Tilolec®** (Tillomed) PoM

Tilolec® *100/25 tablets*, m/r, orange-brown, co-careldopa 25/100 (carbidopa 25 mg (as monohydrate), levodopa 100 mg), net price 60-tab pack = £18.90. Label: 14, 25, counselling, driving, see notes above

Tilolec® *200/50 tablets*, m/r, orange-brown, co-careldopa 50/200 (carbidopa 50 mg (as monohydrate), levodopa 200 mg), net price 60-tab pack = £22.15. Label: 14, 25, counselling, driving, see notes above

Dose initiation of treatment, 1 tablet *Tilolec® 100/25* twice daily or 1 tablet *Tilolec® 200/50* twice daily (initial max. 3 tablets *Tilolec® 200/50* daily in 2–3 divided doses) adjusting dose and frequency according to response at intervals of at least 2 days; max. 8 tablets *Tilolec® 200/50* daily in divided doses

Switching from immediate-release co-careldopa, withdraw existing treatment 12 hours beforehand then substitute *Tilolec® 100/25* 1 tablet twice daily for levodopa 100–200 mg daily or *Tilolec® 200/50* 1 tablet twice daily for levodopa 300–400 mg daily, then adjust dose and frequency according to response at intervals of at least 3 days; max. 8 tablets *Tilolec® 200/50* daily in divided doses

**With entacapone**

Note For Parkinson's disease and end-of-dose motor fluctuations not adequately controlled with levodopa and dopa-decarboxylase inhibitor treatment

**Stalevo®** (Orion) ▼ PoM

Stalevo 50 mg/12.5 mg/200 mg tablets, f/c, brown, levodopa 50 mg, carbidopa 12.5 mg, entacapone 200 mg, net price 30-tab pack = £21.72, 100-tab pack = £72.40. Label: 14 (urine reddish-brown), 25, counselling, driving, see notes above

Stalevo 100 mg/25 mg/200 mg tablets, f/c, brown, levodopa 100 mg, carbidopa 25 mg, entacapone 200 mg, net price 30-tab pack = £21.72, 100-tab pack = £72.40. Label: 14 (urine reddish-brown), 25, counselling, driving, see notes above

Stalevo 150 mg/37.5 mg/200 mg tablets, f/c, brown, levodopa 150 mg, carbidopa 37.5 mg, entacapone 200 mg, net price 30-tab pack = £21.72, 100-tab pack = £72.40. Label: 14 (urine reddish-brown), 25, counselling, driving, see notes above

Dose only 1 tablet of *Stalevo®* to be taken for each dose

Patients receiving standard-release co-careldopa or co-beneldopa alone, initiate *Stalevo®* at a dose that provides similar (or slightly lower) amount of levodopa

Patients with dyskinesia or receiving more than 800 mg levodopa daily, introduce entacapone before transferring to *Stalevo®* (levodopa dose may need to be reduced by 10–30% initially)

Patients receiving entacapone and standard-release co-careldopa or co-beneldopa, initiate *Stalevo®* at a dose that provides similar (or slightly higher) amount of levodopa

## AMANTADINE HYDROCHLORIDE

**Indications** Parkinson's disease (but not drug-induced extrapyramidal symptoms); antiviral (section 5.3.4)

**Cautions** hepatic, or renal impairment (Appendix 3), congestive heart disease (may exacerbate oedema), confused or hallucinatory states, elderly; avoid abrupt discontinuation in Parkinson's disease; **interactions:** Appendix 1 (amantadine)

Driving May affect performance of skilled tasks (e.g. driving)

**Contra-indications** epilepsy, history of gastric ulceration, severe renal impairment; pregnancy (Appendix 4), breast-feeding (Appendix 5)

**Side-effects** anorexia, nausea, nervousness, inability to concentrate, insomnia, dizziness, convulsions, hallucinations or feelings of detachment, blurred vision, gastro-intestinal disturbances, livedo reticularis and peripheral oedema; rarely leucopenia, rashes

**Dose**

- Parkinson's disease, 100 mg daily increased after one week to 100 mg twice daily, usually in conjunction with other treatment; some patients may require higher doses, max. 400 mg daily; ELDERLY 65 years and over, 100 mg daily adjusted according to response
- Post-herpetic neuralgia, 100 mg twice daily for 14 days, continued for a further 14 days if necessary

**Symmetrel®** (Alliance) PoM

Capsules, red-brown, amantadine hydrochloride 100 mg. Net price 56-cap pack = £16.88. Counselling, driving

Syrup, amantadine hydrochloride 50 mg/5 mL. Net price 150-mL pack = £5.55. Counselling, driving

**Lysovir®** (Alliance) PoM

See p. 327

## APOMORPHINE HYDROCHLORIDE

**Indications** refractory motor fluctuations in Parkinson's disease ('off' episodes) inadequately controlled by levodopa or other dopaminergics (for capable and motivated patients under specialist supervision); erectile dysfunction (section 7.4.5)

**Cautions** pulmonary or cardiovascular disease, history of postural hypotension (special care on initiation); hepatic, haemopoietic, renal, and cardiovascular monitoring; *on administration with levodopa* test initially and every 6 months for haemolytic anaemia (development calls for specialist haematological care with dose reduction and possible discontinuation); renal impairment; **interactions:** Appendix 1 (apomorphine)

**Contra-indications** respiratory depression, hypersensitivity to opioids; neuropsychiatric problems or dementia; not suitable if 'on' response to levodopa marred by severe dyskinesia, hypotonia or psychiatric effects; hepatic impairment; pregnancy; breast-feeding; not for intravenous administration

**Side-effects** nausea, vomiting (see below under Dose); drowsiness, confusion, hallucinations, injection-site reactions (including nodule formation and ulceration)—change injection sites in rotation; *less commonly* postural hypotension, breathing difficulties, dykinesias during 'on' periods (may require discontinuation), haemolytic anaemia with levodopa (see Cautions); *rarely* eosinophilia

**Dose**

- By subcutaneous injection, usual range (after initiation as below) 3–30 mg daily in divided doses; subcutaneous infusion may be preferable in those requiring division of injections into more than 10 doses daily; max. single dose 10 mg; CHILD and ADOLESCENT under 18 years not recommended
- By continuous subcutaneous infusion (those requiring division into more than 10 injections daily) initially 1 mg/hour daily increased according to response (not more often than every 4 hours) in max. steps of 500 micrograms/hour, to usual rate of 1–4 mg/hour (14–60 micrograms/kg/hour); change infusion site every 12 hours and give during waking hours only (24-hour infusions not advised unless severe night-time symptoms)—intermittent bolus boosts also usually needed; CHILD and ADOLESCENT under 18 years not recommended

Note Total daily dose by either route (or combined routes) max. 100 mg

Requirements for initiation *Hospital admission* and at least 2 days of pretreatment with domperidone for nausea and vomiting, *after* at least 3 days withhold existing antiparkinsonian medication overnight to provoke 'off' episode, *determine* threshold dose, *re-establish* other antiparkinsonian drugs, *determine* effective apomorphine regimen, *teach* to administer by subcutaneous injection into lower abdomen or outer thigh at first sign of 'off' episode, *discharge* from hospital, *monitor* frequently and *adjust* dosage regimen as appropriate (domperidone may normally be withdrawn over several weeks or longer)—for full details of initiation requirements, consult product literature

**APO-go®** (Britannia) PoM

Injection, apomorphine hydrochloride 10 mg/mL, net price 2-mL amp = £7.59, 5-mL amp = £14.62

Excipients include sulphites

Injection (APO-go® Pen), apomorphine hydrochloride 10 mg/mL, net price 3-mL pen injector = £24.78

Excipients include sulphites

Injection (APO-go® PFS), apomorphine hydrochloride 5 mg/mL, net price 10-mL prefilled syringe = £14.62

Excipients include sulphites

## BROMOCRIPTINE

**Indications** parkinsonism (but not drug-induced extrapyramidal symptoms); endocrine disorders, section 6.7.1

**Cautions** section 6.7.1; fibrotic reactions—see CSM advice in notes above

Hypotensive reactions Hypotensive reactions in some patients may be disturbing during the first few days of treatment and particular care should be exercised when driving or operating machinery; tolerance may be reduced by alcohol

**Contra-indications** section 6.7.1

**Side-effects** section 6.7.1

**Dose**

- First week 1–1.25 mg at night, second week 2–2.5 mg at night, third week 2.5 mg twice daily, fourth week 2.5 mg 3 times daily then increasing by 2.5 mg every 3–14 days according to response to a usual range of 10–40 mg daily; taken with food

**Preparations**

Section 6.7.1

## CABERGOLINE

**Indications** adjunct to levodopa (with dopa-decarboxylase inhibitor) in Parkinson's disease; endocrine disorders (section 6.7.1)

**Cautions** section 6.7.1; fibrotic reactions—see CSM advice in notes above

Hypotensive reactions Hypotensive reactions in some patients may be disturbing during the first few days of treatment; tolerance may be reduced by alcohol

**Contra-indications** section 6.7.1

**Side-effects** section 6.7.1

**Dose**

- Initially 1 mg daily, increased by increments of 0.5–1 mg at 7 or 14 day intervals; usual range 2–6 mg daily

Note Concurrent dose of levodopa may be decreased gradually while dose of cabergoline is increased

**Cabaser®** (Pharmacia) PoM

Tablets, all scored, cabergoline 1 mg, net price 20-tab pack = £83.00; 2 mg, 20-tab pack = £83.00; 4 mg, 16-tab pack = £75.84. Label: 21, counselling, hypotensive reactions, driving, see notes above

Note Dispense in original container (contains desiccant)

## ENTACAPONE

**Indications** adjunct to levodopa with dopa-decarboxylase inhibitor in Parkinson's disease and 'end-of-dose' motor fluctuations

**Cautions** concurrent levodopa dose may need to be reduced by about 10–30%; **interactions:** Appendix 1 (entacapone)

**Contra-indications** pregnancy (Appendix 4) and breast-feeding (Appendix 5); hepatic impairment; phaeochromocytoma; history of neuroleptic malignant syndrome or non-traumatic rhabdomyolysis

**Side-effects** nausea, vomiting, abdominal pain, constipation, diarrhoea, urine may be coloured reddish-brown, dry mouth, dyskinesias; dizziness; rarely hepatitis

**Dose**

- 200 mg with each dose of levodopa with dopa-decarboxylase inhibitor; max. 2 g daily

**Comtess®** (Orion) PoM

Tablets, f/c, brown/orange, entacapone 200 mg, net price 30-tab pack = £18.00, 100-tab pack = £60.00. Label: 14, (urine reddish-brown), counselling, driving, see notes above

## LISURIDE MALEATE

### (Lysuride maleate)

**Indications** Parkinson's disease, used alone or as an adjunct to levodopa

**Cautions** history of pituitary tumour; history of psychotic disturbance; pregnancy; porphyria (section

9.8.2); fibrotic reactions—see CSM advice in notes above; **interactions:** Appendix 1 (lisuride)

Hypotensive reactions Hypotensive reactions in some patients may be disturbing during the first few days of treatment and particular care should be exercised when driving or operating machinery

**Contra-indications** severe disturbances of peripheral circulation; coronary insufficiency

**Side-effects** see notes above; nausea and vomiting; dizziness; headache, lethargy, malaise, drowsiness, psychotic reactions (including hallucinations); occasionally severe hypotension, rashes; rarely abdominal pain and constipation; Raynaud's phenomenon reported

**Dose**

- Initially 200 micrograms at bedtime with food increased as necessary at weekly intervals to 200 micrograms twice daily (midday and bedtime) then to 200 micrograms 3 times daily (morning, midday, and bedtime); further increases made by adding 200 micrograms each week first to the bedtime dose, then to the midday dose and finally to the morning dose; max. 5 mg daily in 3 divided doses after food

**Lisuride Maleate** (Non-proprietary) PoM

Tablets, scored, lisuride maleate 200 micrograms. Net price 100-tab pack = £45.27. Label: 21, counselling, hypotensive reactions

## PERGOLIDE

**Indications** alone or as adjunct to levodopa in Parkinson's disease where dopamine receptor agonists other than ergot derivative not appropriate

**Cautions** arrhythmias or underlying cardiac disease; before treatment assess for asymptomatic valvular disease (see notes above—Fibrotic Reactions); history of confusion or hallucinations, dyskinesia (may exacerbate); increase dose gradually and avoid abrupt withdrawal; porphyria (section 9.8.2); pregnancy (Appendix 4); breast-feeding (Appendix 5); **interactions:** Appendix 1 (pergolide)

Hypotensive reactions Hypotensive reactions in some patients may be disturbing during the first few days of treatment and particular care should be exercised when driving or operating machinery

**Contra-indications** history of fibrotic disorders; cardiac valve disease

**Side-effects** see notes above; hallucinations, confusion, dizziness, dyskinesia, drowsiness, abdominal pain, nausea, vomiting, dyspepsia, diplopia, rhinitis, dyspnoea, pleuritis, pleural effusion, pleural fibrosis, pericarditis, pericardial effusion, cardiac valvulopathy, and retroperitoneal fibrosis, insomnia, constipation or diarrhoea, hypotension, syncope, tachycardia and atrial premature contractions, rash, fever, Raynaud's phenomenon reported; neuroleptic malignant syndrome also reported

**Dose**

- Monotherapy, 50 micrograms at night on day 1, then 50 micrograms twice daily on days 2–4, then increased by 100–250 micrograms daily every 3–4 days (given in 3 divided doses) up to a daily dose of 1.5 mg at day 28; after day 30, further increases of up to 250 micrograms twice a week; usual maintenance dose approx. 2–2.5 mg daily; max. 5 mg daily
- Adjunctive therapy with levodopa, 50 micrograms daily for 2 days, increased gradually by 100–150 micrograms every 3 days over next 12 days, usually given in 3 divided doses; further increases of 250 micrograms every 3 days; usual maintenance dose 3 mg daily; max. 5 mg daily; during pergolide titration levodopa dose may be reduced cautiously

**Pergolide** (Non-proprietary) PoM

Tablets, pergolide (as mesilate) 50 micrograms, net price 100-tab pack = £16.06; 250 micrograms, 100-tab pack = £18.46; 1 mg, 100-tab pack = £53.75. Counselling, hypotensive reactions, driving, see notes above

**Celance®** (Lilly) PoM

Tablets, all scored, pergolide (as mesilate) 50 micrograms (ivory), net price 100-tab pack = £32.44; 250 micrograms (green), 100-tab pack = £48.92; 1 mg (pink), 100-tab pack = £176.58. Counselling, hypotensive reactions, driving, see notes above

## PRAMIPEXOLE

**Indications** Parkinson's disease, used alone or as adjunct to levodopa

**Cautions** psychotic disorders; ophthalmological testing recommended (risk of visual disorders); severe cardiovascular disease; avoid abrupt withdrawal (risk of neuroleptic malignant syndrome); renal impairment (Appendix 3); pregnancy (Appendix 4); **interactions:** Appendix 1 (pramipexole)

Hypotensive reactions Hypotensive reactions may be disturbing in some patients during the first few days of treatment

**Contra-indications** breast-feeding (Appendix 5)

**Side-effects** see notes above; also nausea, constipation, confusion, drowsiness (including sudden onset of sleep) and insomnia, dizziness, hallucinations (mostly visual), dyskinesia during initial dose titration (more frequent in women—reduce levodopa dose), peripheral oedema; changes in libido also reported

**Dose**

- Initially, 264 micrograms daily in 3 divided doses, doubling the dose every 5–7 days to 1.08 mg daily in 3 divided doses; further increased if necessary by 540 micrograms daily at weekly intervals; max. 3.3 mg daily in 3 divided doses

Note During pramipexole dose titration and maintenance, levodopa dose may be reduced

Important Doses and strengths are stated in terms of pramipexole (base); equivalent strengths in terms of pramipexole dihydrochloride monohydrate (salt) are as follows: 88 micrograms base ≡ 125 micrograms salt; 180 micrograms base ≡ 250 micrograms salt; 700 micrograms base ≡ 1 mg salt

**Mirapexin®** (Boehringer Ingelheim) PoM

Tablets, pramipexole (as hydrochloride) 88 micrograms, net price 30-tab pack = £9.25; 180 micrograms (scored), 30-tab pack = £18.50, 100-tab pack = £61.67; 700 micrograms (scored), 30-tab pack = £58.89, 100-tab pack = £196.32. Counselling, hypotensive reactions, driving, see notes above

## RASAGILINE

**Indications** Parkinson's disease, used alone or as adjunct to levodopa

**Cautions** hepatic impairment (Appendix 2); pregnancy (Appendix 4); breast-feeding (Appendix 5); **interactions:** Appendix 1 (rasagiline)

**Side-effects** dry mouth, dyspepsia, constipation; angina; headache, depression, anorexia, weight loss, abnormal dreams, vertigo; influenza-like symptoms;

urinary urgency; leucopenia; arthralgia; conjunctivitis; rash; *less commonly* myocardial infarction, and cerebrovascular accident

**Dose**

- 1 mg daily

**Azilect®** (Teva) ▼ PoM

Tablets, rasagiline (as mesilate) 1 mg, net price 28-tab pack = £70.72

## ROPINIROLE

**Indications** Parkinson's disease, either used alone or as an adjunct to levodopa; see also notes above

**Cautions** hepatic impairment (Appendix 2); renal impairment (Appendix 3); severe cardiovascular disease, major psychotic disorders, avoid abrupt withdrawal; **interactions:** Appendix 1 (ropinirole)

**Contra-indications** pregnancy and breast-feeding

**Side-effects** see notes above; nausea, drowsiness (including sudden onset of sleep), leg oedema, abdominal pain, vomiting and syncope; dyskinesia, hallucinations and confusion reported in adjunctive therapy; occasionally severe hypotension and bradycardia

**Dose**

- Initially 750 micrograms daily in 3 divided doses, increased by increments of 750 micrograms at weekly intervals to 3 mg daily; further increased by increments of up to 3 mg at weekly intervals according to response; usual range 9–16 mg daily (but higher doses may be required if used with levodopa); max. 24 mg daily

Note When administered as adjunct to levodopa, concurrent dose of levodopa may be reduced by approx. 20%; ropinirole doses in the BNF may differ from those in product literature

**Requip®** (GSK) PoM

Tablets, f/c, ropinirole (as hydrochloride) 1 mg (green), net price 84-tab pack = £47.26; 2 mg (pink), 84-tab pack = £94.53; 5 mg (blue), 84-tab pack = £163.27; 28-day starter pack of 42 × 250-microgram (white) tablets, 42 × 500-microgram (yellow) tablets, and 21 × 1-mg (green) tablets = £40.10; 28-day follow-on pack of 42 × 500-microgram (yellow) tablets, 42 × 1-mg (green) tablets, and 63 × 2-mg (pink) tablets = £74.40. Label: 21, counselling, driving, see notes above

## SELEGILINE HYDROCHLORIDE

**Indications** Parkinson's disease, used alone or as adjunct to levodopa

**Cautions** gastric and duodenal ulceration (avoid in active ulceration), uncontrolled hypertension, arrhythmias, angina, psychosis, side-effects of levodopa may be increased, concurrent levodopa dosage may need to be reduced by 10–50%; **interactions:** Appendix 1 (selegiline)

**Contra-indications** pregnancy (Appendix 4); breast-feeding (Appendix 5)

**Side-effects** nausea, constipation, diarrhoea, dry mouth; postural hypotension; dyskinesia, vertigo, sleeping disorders, confusion, hallucinations; arthralgia, myalgia; mouth ulcers with oral lyophilisate; *rarely* arrhythmias, agitation, headache, micturition difficulties, skin reactions; also reported chest pain

**Dose**

- 10 mg in the morning, or 5 mg at breakfast and midday; ELDERLY see below

Elderly To avoid initial confusion and agitation, it may be appropriate to start treatment with a dose of 2.5 mg daily, particularly in the elderly

**Selegiline Hydrochloride** (Non-proprietary) PoM

Tablets, selegiline hydrochloride 5 mg, net price 56-tab pack = £4.30; 10 mg, 30-tab pack = £3.59

**Eldepryl®** (Orion) PoM

Tablets, both scored, selegiline hydrochloride 5 mg, net price 60-tab pack = £10.35; 10 mg, 30-tab pack = £10.10

Oral liquid, selegiline hydrochloride 10 mg/5 mL, net price 200 mL = £18.72

### Oral lyophilisate

**Zelapar®** (Zeneus) PoM

Oral lyophilisates (= freeze-dried tablets), yellow, selegiline hydrochloride 1.25 mg, net price 30-tab pack = £59.95. Counselling, administration

Excipients include aspartame (section 9.4.1)

Dose initially 1.25 mg daily before breakfast

Counselling Tablets should be placed on the tongue and allowed to dissolve. Advise patient not to drink, rinse, or wash mouth out for 5 minutes after taking the tablet

Note Patients receiving 10 mg conventional selegiline hydrochloride tablets can be switched to *Zelapar®* 1.25 mg

## TOLCAPONE

**Indications** adjunct to levodopa with dopa-decarboxylase inhibitor in Parkinson's disease and 'end-of-dose' motor fluctuations if another inhibitor of peripheral catechol-*O*-methyltransferase inappropriate (under specialist supervision)

**Cautions** most patients receiving more than 600 mg levodopa daily require reduction of levodopa dose; pregnancy (Appendix 4); **interactions:** Appendix 1 (tolcapone)

Hepatotoxicity Potentially life-threatening hepatotoxicity including fulminant hepatitis reported rarely, usually in first 6 months; test liver function before treatment, and monitor every 2 weeks for first year, every 4 weeks for next 6 months and every 8 weeks thereafter (restart monitoring schedule if dose increased); discontinue if abnormal liver function tests or symptoms of liver disorder (counselling, see below); do not re-introduce tolcapone once discontinued

Counselling Patients should be told how to recognise signs of liver disorder and advised to seek immediate medical attention if symptoms such as anorexia, nausea, vomiting, fatigue, abdominal pain, dark urine, or pruritus develop

**Contra-indications** hepatic impairment or raised liver enzymes (see Hepatotoxicity above), severe dyskinesia, phaeochromocytoma, previous history of neuroleptic malignant syndrome, rhabdomyolysis, or hyperthermia; breast-feeding (Appendix 5)

**Side-effects** diarrhoea, constipation, dyspepsia, abdominal pain, xerostomia, hepatotoxicity (see above); chest pain; confusion; intensification of urine colour; increase in levodopa-related side-effects; neuroleptic malignant syndrome reported on dose reduction or withdrawal

**Dose**

- 100 mg 3 times daily, leave 6 hours between each dose; max. 200 mg 3 times daily in exceptional circumstances; first daily dose should be taken at the same time as levodopa with dopa-decarboxylase inhibitor

Note Continue beyond 3 weeks **only** if substantial improvement

**Tasmar®** (Valeant) ▼ PoM
Tablets, f/c, yellow, tolcapone 100 mg, net price 100-tab pack = £95.20. Label: 14, 25

## 4.9.2 Antimuscarinic drugs used in parkinsonism

Antimuscarinic drugs exert their antiparkinsonian action by reducing the effects of the central cholinergic excess that occurs as a result of dopamine deficiency. Antimuscarinic drugs are useful in drug-induced parkinsonism, but they are generally not used in idiopathic Parkinson's disease because they are less effective than dopaminergic drugs and they are associated with cognitive impairment.

The antimuscarinic drugs, **benzatropine**, **orphenadrine**, **procyclidine**, and **trihexyphenidyl** (benzhexol), reduce the symptoms of parkinsonism induced by antipsychotic drugs, but there is no justification for giving them routinely in the absence of parkinsonian side-effects. Tardive dyskinesia is not improved by antimuscarinic drugs and may be made worse.

In idiopathic Parkinson's disease, antimuscarinic drugs reduce tremor and rigidity but they have little effect on bradykinesia. They may be useful in reducing sialorrhoea.

No important differences exist between the antimuscarinic drugs, but some patients tolerate one better than another.

Benzatropine may be given parenterally and it is effective emergency treatment for acute drug-induced dystonic reactions which may be severe.

### BENZATROPINE MESILATE
(Benztropine mesylate)

**Indications** see Trihexyphenidyl Hydrochloride
**Cautions** see Trihexyphenidyl Hydrochloride
**Contra-indications** see Trihexyphenidyl Hydrochloride; avoid in children under 3 years
**Side-effects** see Trihexyphenidyl Hydrochloride, but causes sedation rather than stimulation; also reported tachycardia, dizziness, depression, hyperthermia
**Dose**
- By intramuscular *or* intravenous injection, 1–2 mg, repeated if symptoms reappear; ELDERLY preferably lower end of range

**Cogentin®** (MSD) PoM
Injection, benzatropine mesilate 1 mg/mL. Net price 2-mL amp = 92p

### ORPHENADRINE HYDROCHLORIDE

**Indications** see Trihexyphenidyl Hydrochloride
**Cautions** see Trihexyphenidyl Hydrochloride
**Contra-indications** see Trihexyphenidyl Hydrochloride; porphyria (section 9.8.2)
**Side-effects** see Trihexyphenidyl Hydrochloride; may cause insomnia
**Dose**
- 150 mg daily in divided doses, increased gradually; max. 400 mg daily; ELDERLY preferably lower end of range

**Orphenadrine Hydrochloride** (Non-proprietary) PoM
Tablets, orphenadrine hydrochloride 50 mg, net price 20 = £1.03. Counselling, driving
Oral solution, orphenadrine hydrochloride 50 mg/5 mL. Net price 200 mL = £9.47. Counselling, driving

**Biorphen®** (Alliance) PoM
Elixir, sugar-free, orphenadrine hydrochloride 25 mg/5 mL. Net price 200 mL = £7.07. Counselling, driving

**Disipal®** (Astellas) PoM
Tablets, yellow, s/c, orphenadrine hydrochloride 50 mg. Net price 20 = 69p. Counselling, driving
Excipients include tartrazine

### PROCYCLIDINE HYDROCHLORIDE

**Indications** see Trihexyphenidyl Hydrochloride
**Cautions** see Trihexyphenidyl Hydrochloride
**Contra-indications** see Trihexyphenidyl Hydrochloride
**Side-effects** see Trihexyphenidyl Hydrochloride
**Dose**
- By mouth, 2.5 mg 3 times daily, increased gradually if necessary; usual max. 30 mg daily (60 mg daily in exceptional circumstances); ELDERLY preferably lower end of range
- By intramuscular *or* intravenous injection, acute dystonia, 5–10 mg (occasionally more than 10 mg), usually effective in 5–10 minutes but may need 30 minutes for relief

**Procyclidine** (Non-proprietary) PoM
Tablets, procyclidine hydrochloride 5 mg. Net price 20 = £1.17. Counselling, driving

**Arpicolin®** (Rosemont) PoM
Syrup, sugar-free, procyclidine hydrochloride 2.5 mg/5 mL, net price 150 mL = £4.22; 5 mg/5 mL, 150 mL pack = £7.54. Counselling, driving

**Kemadrin®** (GSK) PoM
Tablets, scored, procyclidine hydrochloride 5 mg. Net price 20 = 94p. Counselling, driving

**Kemadrin®** (Auden Mckenzie) PoM
Injection, procyclidine hydrochloride 5 mg/mL, net price 2-mL amp = £1.49

### TRIHEXYPHENIDYL HYDROCHLORIDE
(Benzhexol hydrochloride)

**Indications** parkinsonism; drug-induced extrapyramidal symptoms (but not tardive dyskinesia, see notes above)
**Cautions** cardiovascular disease, glaucoma, gastro-intestinal obstruction, prostatic hypertrophy; elderly; avoid abrupt withdrawal; liable to abuse; hepatic impairment; renal impairment; pregnancy; breast-feeding; **interactions**: Appendix 1 (antimuscarinics)
Driving May affect performance of skilled tasks (e.g. driving)
**Side-effects** constipation, dry mouth; blurred vision; *less commonly* nausea, vomiting, agitation, confusion, hallucinations, euphoria, insomnia, restlessness, urinary retention; paranoid delusions and impaired memory also reported

**Dose**

- 1 mg daily, increased gradually; usual maintenance dose 5–15 mg daily in 3–4 divided doses (max. 20 mg daily); ELDERLY preferably lower end of range; CHILD not recommended

**Trihexyphenidyl** (Non-proprietary) PoM

Tablets, trihexyphenidyl hydrochloride 2 mg, net price 20 = 52p; 5 mg, 20 = 79p. Counselling, before or after food (see notes above), driving

**Broflex®** (Alliance) PoM

Syrup, pink, trihexyphenidyl hydrochloride 5 mg/5 mL. Net price 200 mL = £6.20. Counselling, before or after food (see notes above), driving

## 4.9.3 Drugs used in essential tremor, chorea, tics, and related disorders

**Tetrabenazine** is mainly used to control movement disorders in Huntington's chorea and related disorders. It may act by depleting nerve endings of dopamine. It has useful action in only a proportion of patients and its use may be limited by the development of depression.

**Haloperidol** may be useful in improving motor tics and symptoms of Gilles de la Tourette syndrome and related choreas. **Pimozide** (see section 4.2.1 for CSM warning), **clonidine** (section 4.7.4.2) and **sulpiride** (section 4.2.1) are also used in Gilles de la Tourette syndrome. **Trihexyphenidyl** (**benzhexol**) (section 4.9.2) at high dosage may also improve some movement disorders; it is sometimes necessary to build the dose up over many weeks, to 20 to 30 mg daily or higher. **Chlorpromazine** and **haloperidol** are used to relieve intractable hiccup (section 4.2.1).

**Propranolol** or another beta-adrenoceptor blocking drug (section 2.4) may be useful in treating essential tremor or tremors associated with anxiety or thyrotoxicosis. Propranolol is given in a dosage of 40 mg 2 or 3 times daily, increased if necessary; 80 to 160 mg daily is usually required for maintenance.

**Primidone** (section 4.8.1) in some cases provides relief from benign essential tremor; the dose is increased slowly to reduce side-effects.

**Piracetam** is used as an adjunctive treatment for myoclonus of cortical origin.

**Riluzole** is used to extend life or the time to mechanical ventilation in patients with motor neurone disease who have amyotrophic lateral sclerosis.

> **NICE guidance (riluzole)**
> NICE has recommended (January 2001) riluzole to treat individuals with the amyotrophic lateral sclerosis (ALS) form of motor neurone disease (MND). Treatment should be initiated by a specialist in MND but it can then be supervised under a shared-care arrangement involving the general practitioner.

### HALOPERIDOL

**Indications** motor tics, adjunctive treatment in choreas and Gilles de la Tourette syndrome; other indications, section 4.2.1

**Cautions** section 4.2.1

**Contra-indications** section 4.2.1

**Side-effects** section 4.2.1

**Dose**

- By mouth, 0.5–1.5 mg 3 times daily adjusted according to the response; 10 mg daily or more may occasionally be necessary in Gilles de la Tourette syndrome; CHILD, Gilles de la Tourette syndrome up to 10 mg daily

**Preparations**

Section 4.2.1

### PIRACETAM

**Indications** adjunctive treatment of cortical myoclonus

**Cautions** avoid abrupt withdrawal; elderly; haemostasis, major surgery, or severe haemorrhage; renal impairment (avoid if severe; Appendix 3)

**Contra-indications** cerebral haemorrhage; hepatic impairment; pregnancy; breast-feeding

**Side-effects** weight gain, nervousness, hyperkinesia; *less commonly* drowsiness, depression, asthenia,; *also reported* abdominal pain, nausea, vomiting, diarrhoea, headache, anxiety, confusion, hallucination, vertigo, ataxia, insomnia, and rash

**Dose**

- Initially 7.2 g daily in 2–3 divided doses, increased according to response by 4.8 g daily every 3–4 days to max. 20 g daily (subsequently, attempts should be made to reduce dose of concurrent therapy); CHILD under 16 years not recommended

Oral solution Follow the oral solution with a glass of water (or soft drink) to reduce bitter taste.

**Nootropil®** (UCB Pharma) PoM

Tablets, f/c, scored, piracetam 800 mg, net price 90-tab pack = £14.69; 1.2 g, 60-tab pack = £13.71. Label: 3

Oral solution, piracetam, 333.3 mg/mL, net price 300-mL pack = £20.39. Label: 3

### RILUZOLE

**Indications** to extend life or the time to mechanical ventilation for patients with amyotrophic lateral sclerosis, initiated by specialists experienced in the management of motor neurone disease

**Cautions** history of abnormal hepatic function (consult product literature for details)

Blood disorders Patients or their carers should be told how to recognise signs of neutropenia and advised to seek immediate medical attention if symptoms such as fever occur; white blood cell counts should be determined in febrile illness; neutropenia requires discontinuation of riluzole

Driving Dizziness or vertigo may affect performance of skilled tasks (e.g. driving)

**Contra-indications** hepatic and renal impairment (Appendix 3); pregnancy (Appendix 4) and breast-feeding (Appendix 5)

**Side-effects** nausea, vomiting, asthenia, tachycardia, somnolence, headache, dizziness, vertigo, abdominal pain, circumoral paraesthesia, alterations in liver function tests

**Dose**

- 50 mg twice daily; CHILD not recommended

**Rilutek®** (Aventis Pharma) PoM

Tablets, f/c, riluzole 50 mg. Net price 56-tab pack = £179.37. Counselling, blood disorders, driving

## TETRABENAZINE

**Indications** see under Dose

**Cautions** pregnancy (Appendix 4); avoid in breast-feeding; **interactions:** Appendix 1 (tetrabenazine)

Driving May affect performance of skilled tasks (e.g. driving)

**Side-effects** drowsiness, gastro-intestinal disturbances, depression, extrapyramidal dysfunction, hypotension; rarely parkinsonism; neuroleptic malignant syndrome reported

**Dose**

- Movement disorders due to Huntington's chorea, hemiballismus, senile chorea, and related neurological conditions, initially 12.5 mg twice daily (elderly 12.5 mg daily) gradually increased to 12.5–25 mg 3 times daily; max. 200 mg daily
- Moderate to severe tardive dyskinesia, initially 12.5 mg daily, gradually increased according to response

**Xenazine® 25** (Cambridge) PoM

Tablets, pale yellow-buff, scored, tetrabenazine 25 mg. Net price 112-tab pack = £100.00. Label: 2

# Torsion dystonias and other involuntary movements

## BOTULINUM A TOXIN

**Indications** focal spasticity, including arm symptoms in conjunction with physiotherapy, dynamic equinus foot deformity caused by spasticity in ambulant paediatric cerebral palsy patients over 2 years, and hand and wrist disability associated with stroke; blepharospasm; hemifacial spasm; spasmodic torticollis; severe hyperhidrosis of axillae (all specialist use only)

**Cautions** history of dysphagia; pregnancy (Appendix 4); breast-feeding (Appendix 5)

Specific cautions for blepharospasm or hemifacial spasm Caution if risk of angle-closure glaucoma; reduced blinking can lead to corneal exposure, persistent epithelial defect and corneal ulceration (especially in those with VIIth nerve disorders)—careful testing of corneal sensation in previously operated eyes, avoidance of injection in lower lid area to avoid ectropion, and vigorous treatment of epithelial defect needed

**Contra-indications** generalised disorders of muscle activity (e.g. myasthenia gravis)

**Side-effects** increased electrophysiologic jitter in some distant muscles; misplaced injections may paralyse nearby muscle groups and excessive doses may paralyse distant muscles; influenza-like symptoms; *rarely* arrhythmias, myocardial infarction, seizures, hypersensitivity reactions including rash, pruritus and anaphylaxis, antibody formation (substantial deterioration in response), and injection-site reactions

Specific side-effects in blepharospasm or hemifacial spasm Ptosis; keratitis, lagophthalmos, dry eye, irritation, photophobia, lacrimation; facial oedema; *less commonly* facial weakness (including drooping), dizziness, tiredness, ectropion, entropion, diplopia, visual disturbances; *rarely* eyelid bruising and swelling (minimised by applying gentle pressure at injection site immediately after injection); *very rarely* angle-closure glaucoma, corneal ulceration

Specific side-effects in paediatric cerebral palsy Drowsiness, paraesthesia, urinary incontinence, myalgia

Specific side-effects in torticollis Dysphagia and pooling of saliva (occurs most frequently after injection into sternomastoid muscle), nausea, dry mouth, rhinitis, drowsiness, headache, dizziness, hypertonia, stiffness; *less commonly* dyspnoea, voice alteration, diplopia, and ptosis; *rarely* respiratory difficulties (associated with high doses); CSM has warned of persistent dysphagia and sequelae (including death)—**important**

Specific side-effects in axillary hyperhidrosis Non-axillary sweating, hot flushes; *less commonly* myalgia and joint pain

Specific side-effects in focal upper-limb spasticity associated with stroke Dysphagia; hypertonia; *less commonly* arthralgia and bursitis

**Dose**

- Consult product literature (**important:** specific to **each individual preparation** and **not interchangeable**)

**Botox®** (Allergan) PoM

Injection, powder for reconstitution, botulinum A neurotoxin complex, net price 100-unit vial = £128.93

**Dysport®** (Ipsen) PoM

Injection, powder for reconstitution, botulinum A toxin-haemagglutinin complex, net price 500-unit vial = £153.21

## BOTULINUM B TOXIN

**Indications** spasmodic torticollis (cervical dystonia)—specialist use only

**Cautions** inadvertent injection into a blood vessel; tolerance may occur

**Contra-indications** neuromuscular or neuromuscular junctional disorders; pregnancy (Appendix 4) and breast-feeding (Appendix 5)

**Side-effects** increased electrophysiologic jitter in some distant muscles; dry mouth, dysphagia; also dyspepsia, worsening torticollis, neck pain, myasthenia, voice changes, taste disturbances

**Dose**

- By intramuscular injection, initially 5000–10 000 units divided between 2–4 most affected muscles; adjust dose and frequency according to response; **important: not** interchangeable with other botulinum toxin preparations

**NeuroBloc®** (Zeneus) PoM

Injection, botulinum B toxin 5000 units/mL, net price 0.5-mL vial = £111.20; 1-mL vial = £148.27; 2-mL vial = £197.69

Note May be diluted with sodium chloride 0.9%

# 4.10 Drugs used in substance dependence

This section includes drugs used in alcohol dependence, cigarette smoking, and opioid dependence.

The health departments of the UK have produced a report, *Drug Misuse and Dependence* which contains guidelines on clinical management.

*Drug Misuse and Dependence*, London, The Stationery Office, 1999 can be obtained from:

The Publications Centre
PO Box 276
London, SW8 5DT
Tel: (087) 0600 5522
Fax: (087) 0600 5533

*or* from The Stationery Office bookshops and through all good booksellers.

It is **important** to be aware that *people who misuse drugs* may be at risk not only from the intrinsic toxicity of the drug itself but also from the practice of injecting preparations intended for administration by mouth. Excipients used in the production of oral dose forms are usually insoluble and may lead to *abscess formation at the site of injection*, or even to *necrosis and gangrene*; moreover, deposits in the heart or lungs may lead to *severe cardiac or pulmonary toxicity*. Additional hazards include *infection* following the use of a dirty needle or an unsterilised diluent.

## Alcohol dependence

**Disulfiram** is used as an adjunct to the treatment of alcohol dependence. It gives rise to extremely unpleasant systemic reactions after the ingestion of even a small amount of alcohol because it leads to accumulation of acetaldehyde in the body. Reactions include flushing of the face, throbbing headache, palpitation, tachycardia, nausea, vomiting, and, with large doses of alcohol, arrhythmias, hypotension, and collapse. Small amounts of alcohol included in many oral medicines may be sufficient to precipitate a reaction (even toiletries and mouthwashes that contain alcohol should be avoided). It may be advisable for patients to carry a card warning of the danger of administration of alcohol.

Long-acting **benzodiazepines** (section 4.1) are used to attenuate withdrawal symptoms but they also have a dependence potential. To minimise the risk of dependence, administration should be for a limited period only (e.g. **chlordiazepoxide** 10–50 mg 4 times daily, gradually reducing over 7–14 days). Benzodiazepines should not be prescribed if the patient is likely to continue drinking alcohol.

**Clomethiazole** (chlormethiazole) (section 4.1.1) should be used for the management of withdrawal in an **in-patient setting only**. It is associated with a risk of dependence and should not be prescribed if the patient is likely to continue drinking alcohol.

**Acamprosate**, in combination with counselling, may be helpful in maintaining abstinence in alcohol-dependent patients. It should be initiated as soon as possible *after* abstinence has been achieved and should be maintained if the patient relapses. Continued alcohol abuse, however, negates the therapeutic benefit of acamprosate.

### ACAMPROSATE CALCIUM

**Indications** maintenance of abstinence in alcohol dependence

**Cautions** continued alcohol abuse (risk of treatment failure)

**Contra-indications** renal and severe hepatic impairment; pregnancy and breast-feeding

**Side-effects** diarrhoea, nausea, vomiting, abdominal pain, pruritus, occasionally maculopapular rash, rarely bullous skin reactions; fluctuation in libido

**Dose**

- ADULT 18–65 years, 60 kg and over, 666 mg 3 times daily; less than 60 kg, 666 mg at breakfast, 333 mg at midday and 333 mg at night
  Treatment course Treatment should be initiated as soon as possible after alcohol withdrawal period and maintained if patient relapses; recommended treatment period 1 year

**Campral EC®** (Merck) PoM
Tablet, e/c, acamprosate calcium 333 mg. Net price 168-tab pack = £28.92. Label: 21, 25
Electrolytes $Ca^{2+}$ 0.8 mmol/tablet

### DISULFIRAM

**Indications** adjunct in the treatment of chronic alcohol dependence (under specialist supervision)

**Cautions** ensure that alcohol not consumed for at least 24 hours before initiating treatment; see also notes above; alcohol challenge **not** recommended on routine basis (if considered essential—specialist units only with resuscitation facilities); hepatic or renal impairment, respiratory disease, diabetes mellitus, epilepsy; **interactions:** Appendix 1 (disulfiram)
Alcohol reaction Patients should be warned of unpredictable and occasionally severe nature of disulfiram-alcohol interactions. Reactions can occur within 10 minutes and last several hours (may require intensive supportive therapy—oxygen should be available). Patients should not ingest alcohol at all and should be warned of possible presence of alcohol in liquid medicines, remedies, tonics, foods and even in toiletries (alcohol should also be avoided for at least 1 week after stopping)

**Contra-indications** cardiac failure, coronary artery disease, history of cerebrovascular accident, hypertension, psychosis, severe personality disorder, suicide risk, pregnancy (Appendix 4), breast-feeding (Appendix 5)

**Side-effects** initially drowsiness and fatigue; nausea, vomiting, halitosis, reduced libido; rarely psychotic reactions (depression, paranoia, schizophrenia, mania), allergic dermatitis, peripheral neuritis, hepatic cell damage

**Dose**

- 800 mg as a single dose on first day, reducing over 5 days to 100–200 mg daily; should not be continued for longer than 6 months without review; CHILD not recommended

**Antabuse®** (Alpharma) PoM
Tablets, scored, disulfiram 200 mg. Net price 50-tab pack = £26.28. Label: 2, counselling, alcohol reaction

## Cigarette smoking

Smoking cessation interventions are a cost-effective way of reducing ill health and prolonging life. Smokers should be advised to stop and offered help if interested in doing so, with follow-up where appropriate.

Where possible, smokers should have access to a smoking cessation clinic for behavioural support. **Nicotine replacement therapy** and **bupropion** are effective aids to smoking cessation for those smoking more than 10 cigarettes a day. Bupropion has been used as an antidepressant but its mode of action in smoking cessation is not clear and may involve an effect on noradrenaline and dopamine neurotransmission. Nicotine replacement therapy is regarded as the pharmacological treatment of choice in the management of smoking cessation.

Cigarette smoking should stop completely before starting a smoking cessation regimen including nicotine replacement therapy. If complete smoking cessation is not possible some nicotine preparations are licensed for use as part of a programme to reduce smoking before stopping completely; the smoking cessation regimen can be followed during a quit attempt.

**NICE guidance (nicotine replacement therapy and bupropion for smoking cessation)**
NICE has recommended (March 2002) that nicotine replacement therapy or bupropion should be prescribed only for a smoker who commits to a target stop date. The smoker should be offered advice and encouragement to aid smoking cessation.
Therapy to aid smoking cessation is chosen according to the smoker's likely compliance, availability of counselling and support, previous experience of smoking-cessation aids, contra-indications and adverse effects of the products, and the smoker's preferences.
Initial supply of the prescribed smoking-cessation therapy should be sufficient to last only 2 weeks after the target stop date; normally this will be 2 weeks of nicotine replacement therapy or 3–4 weeks of bupropion. A second prescription should be issued only if the smoker demonstrates a continuing attempt to stop smoking.
If an attempt to stop smoking is unsuccessful, the NHS should not normally fund a further attempt within 6 months.
There is currently insufficient evidence to recommend the combined use of nicotine replacement therapy and bupropion.

**CSM advice (bupropion).** The CSM has issued a reminder that bupropion is contra-indicated in patients with a history of seizures or of eating disorders, a CNS tumour, or who are experiencing acute symptoms of alcohol or benzodiazepine withdrawal. Bupropion should not be prescribed to patients with other risk factors for seizures unless the potential benefit of smoking cessation clearly outweighs the risk. Factors that increase the risk of seizures include concomitant administration of drugs that can lower the seizure threshold (e.g. antidepressants, antimalarials [such as mefloquine and chloroquine], antipsychotics, quinolones, sedating antihistamines, systemic corticosteroids, theophylline, tramadol), alcohol abuse, history of head trauma, diabetes, and use of stimulants and anorectics.

## BUPROPION
(Amfebutamone)

**Indications** adjunct to smoking cessation in combination with motivational support

**Cautions** elderly; hepatic impairment (Appendix 2, avoid in severe hepatic cirrhosis), renal impairment (Appendix 3); predisposition to seizures (see CSM advice above); measure blood pressure before and during treatment (monitor weekly if used with nicotine products); **interactions**: Appendix 1 (bupropion)

Driving May impair performance of skilled tasks (e.g. driving)

**Contra-indications** history of seizures, of eating disorders (see CSM advice above) and of bipolar disorder; pregnancy (Appendix 4); breast-feeding (Appendix 5)

**Side-effects** dry mouth, gastro-intestinal disturbances, insomnia (reduced by avoiding dose at bedtime), tremor, impaired concentration, headache, dizziness, depression, agitation, anxiety, rash, pruritus, sweating, hypersensitivity reactions (may resemble serum sickness), fever, taste disturbances; *less commonly* chest pain, asthenia, tachycardia, hypertension, flushing, confusion, anorexia, tinnitus, visual disturbances; *rarely* palpitations, postural hypotension, vasodilation, hallucinations, depersonalisation, seizures, abnormal dreams, memory impairment, paraesthesia, irritability, incoordination, urinary retention, urinary frequency, Stevens-Johnson syndrome, jaundice, hepatitis, blood-glucose disturbances, exacerbation of psoriasis

**Dose**

- Start 1–2 weeks before target stop date, initially 150 mg daily for 6 days then 150 mg twice daily (max. single dose 150 mg, max. daily dose 300 mg; minimum 8 hours between doses); max. period of treatment 7–9 weeks; discontinue if abstinence not achieved at 7 weeks; consider max. 150 mg daily in patients with risk factors for seizures (see CSM advice above); ELDERLY max. 150 mg daily; CHILD and ADOLESCENT under 18 years not recommended

**Zyban®** (GSK) ▼ PoM
Tablets, m/r, f/c, bupropion (as hydrochloride) 150 mg, net price 60-tab pack = £39.85. Label: 25

## NICOTINE

**Indications** adjunct to smoking cessation

**Cautions** cardiovascular disease (avoid if severe); peripheral vascular disease; hyperthyroidism; diabetes mellitus; phaeochromocytoma, history of gastritis and peptic ulcers; should not use nicotine replacement products in combination; hepatic impairment (Appendix 2); renal impairment; pregnancy (Appendix 4); breast-feeding (Appendix 5); *patches*, exercise may increase absorption and side-effects, skin disorders (patches should not be placed on broken skin)

**Contra-indications** severe cardiovascular disease (including severe arrhythmias or immediate post-myocardial infarction period); recent cerebrovascular accident (including transient ischaemic attacks)

Note Most warnings under Cautions and Contra-indications also apply to continuation of cigarette smoking

**Side-effects** nausea, dizziness, headache and cold and influenza-like symptoms, palpitations, dyspepsia and other gastro-intestinal disturbances, hiccups, insomnia, vivid dreams, myalgia; other side-effects reported include chest pain, blood pressure changes, anxiety and irritability, drowsiness and impaired concentration, abnormal hunger, dysmenorrhoea, rash; *with patches*, skin reactions (discontinue if severe)—vasculitis also reported; *with spray*, nasal irritation, nose bleeds, watering eyes, ear sensations; *with gum, lozenges, sublingual tablets* or *inhalator*, aphthous ulceration (sometimes with swelling of tongue); *with spray, inhalator, lozenges, sublingual tablets* or *gum*, throat irritation; *with inhalator*, cough, rhinitis, pharyngitis, stomatitis, sinusitis, dry mouth; *with lozenges* or *sublingual tablets*, unpleasant taste

**Dose**

- See under preparations, below

**Nicorette®** (Pharmacia)

Nicorette Microtab (sublingual), nicotine (as a cyclodextrin complex) 2 mg, net price starter pack of 2 × 15-tablet discs with dispenser = £3.57; refill pack of 7 × 15-tablet discs = £9.84. Label: 26

Dose smoking cessation, individuals smoking 20 cigarettes or less daily, sublingually, 2 mg each hour; for patients who fail to stop smoking or have significant withdrawal symptoms, consider increasing to 4 mg each hour

Individuals smoking more than 20 cigarettes daily, sublingually, 4 mg each hour

Max. 80 mg daily; treatment should be continued for at least 3 months followed by a gradual reduction in dose; review treatment if abstinence not achieved in 9 months; ADOLESCENT 12–18 years, treatment continued for up to 8 weeks followed by gradual reduction over 4 weeks; review treatment if abstinence not achieved in 3 months

Nicorette chewing gum, sugar-free, nicotine (as resin) 2 mg, net price pack of 15 = £1.71, pack of 30 = £3.25, pack of 105 = £8.89; 4 mg, net price pack of 15 = £2.11, pack of 30 = £3.99, pack of 105 = £10.83

Note Also available in mint and freshmint flavours

Dose smoking cessation, individuals smoking 20 cigarettes or fewer daily, initially chew one 2-mg piece slowly for approx. 30 minutes, when urge to smoke occurs; individuals smoking more than 20 cigarettes daily or needing more than 15 pieces of 2-mg gum daily may need the 4-mg strength; max. 15 pieces of 4-mg strength daily; withdraw gradually after 3 months; review treatment if abstinence not achieved in 9 months; ADOLESCENT 12–18 years, treatment continued for up to 8 weeks followed by gradual reduction over 4 weeks; review treatment if abstinence not achieved in 3 months

Smoking reduction, chew one piece when urge to smoke occurs between smoking episodes; reduce smoking within 6 weeks and attempt smoking cessation within 6 months; review treatment if abstinence not achieved within 9 months

Nicorette patches, self-adhesive, all beige, nicotine, *'5 mg' patch* (releasing approx. 5 mg/16 hours), net price 7 = £9.07; *'10 mg' patch* (releasing approx. 10 mg/16 hours), 7 = £9.07; *'15 mg' patch* (releasing approx. 15 mg/16 hours), 2 = £2.85, 7 = £9.07

Dose smoking cessation, apply on waking to dry, non-hairy skin on hip, chest or upper arm, removing after approx. 16 hours, usually when retiring to bed; site next patch on different area (avoid using same area on consecutive days); initially '15-mg' patch for 16 hours daily for 8 weeks then if abstinence achieved '10-mg' patch for 16 hours daily for 2 weeks then '5-mg' patch for 16 hours daily for 2 weeks; review treatment if abstinence not achieved in 3 months—further courses may be given if considered beneficial

Nicorette nasal spray, nicotine 500 micrograms/metered spray. Net price 200-spray unit = £10.99

Dose smoking cessation, apply 1 spray into each nostril as required to max. twice an hour for 16 hours daily (max. 64 sprays daily) for 8 weeks, then reduce gradually over next 4 weeks (reduce by half at end of first 2 weeks, stop altogether at end of next 2 weeks); review treatment if abstinence not achieved in 3 months

Nicorette inhalator (nicotine-impregnated plug for use in inhalator mouthpiece), nicotine 10 mg/cartridge. Net price 6-cartridge (starter) pack = £3.39, 42-cartridge (refill) pack = £11.37

Dose smoking cessation, inhale when urge to smoke occurs; initially use between 6 and 12 cartridges daily for up to 8 weeks, then reduce number of cartridges used by half over next 2 weeks and then stop altogether at end of further 2 weeks; review treatment if abstinence not achieved in 3 months

Smoking reduction, inhale when urge to smoke occurs between smoking episodes; reduce smoking within 6 weeks and attempt smoking cessation within 6 months; review treatment if abstinence not achieved within 9 months

**Nicotinell®** (Novartis Consumer Health)

Chewing gum, sugar-free, nicotine 2 mg, net price pack of 12 = £1.59, pack of 24 = £3.01, pack of 96 = £8.26; 4 mg, pack of 12 = £1.70, pack of 24 = £3.30, pack of 96 = £10.26

Note Also available in fruit, liquorice and mint flavours

Dose smoking cessation, initially one 2-mg or 4-mg piece chewed slowly for approx. 30 minutes, when urge to smoke occurs; max. 60 mg daily; withdraw gradually after 3 months; max. period of treatment should not usually exceed 6 months

Nicotinell mint lozenge, sugar-free, nicotine (as bitartrate) 1 mg, net price pack of 12 = £1.71, pack of 36 = £4.27, pack of 96 = £9.12; 2 mg, net price pack of 12 = £1.99, pack of 36 = £4.95, pack of 96 = £10.60. Label: 24

Excipients include aspartame (section 9.4.1)

Dose smoking cessation, initially 1 lozenge every 1–2 hours, when urge to smoke occurs; max. 30 mg daily; withdraw gradually after 3 months; max. period of treatment should not usually exceed 6 months

TTS Patches, self-adhesive, all yellowish-ochre, nicotine, *'10' patch* (releasing approx. 7 mg/24 hours), net price 7 = £9.12; *'20' patch* (releasing approx. 14 mg/24 hours), net price 2 = £2.57, 7 = £9.40; *'30' patch* (releasing approx. 21 mg/24 hours), net price 2 = £2.85, 7 = £9.97, 21 = £24.51

Dose smoking cessation, apply to dry, non-hairy skin on trunk or upper arm, removing after 24 hours and siting replacement patch on a different area (avoid using the same area for several days); individuals smoking 20 cigarettes daily or fewer, initially '20' patch daily; individuals smoking more than 20 cigarettes daily, initially '30' patch daily; withdraw gradually, reducing dose every 3–4 weeks; review treatment if abstinence not achieved in 3 months

**NiQuitin CQ®** (GSK Consumer Healthcare)

Chewing gum, sugar-free, mint-flavour, nicotine 2 mg, net price pack of 12 = £1.71, pack of 24 = £2.85, pack of 96 = £8.55; 4 mg, net price pack of 12 = £1.71, pack of 24 = £2.85, pack of 96 = £8.55

Dose smoking cessation, initially 1 piece chewed slowly for approx. 30 minutes, when urge to smoke occurs; max. 15 pieces daily; withdraw gradually after 3 months

Lozenges, sugar-free, nicotine (as polacrilex) 2 mg, net price pack of 36 = £5.12, pack of 72 = £9.97; 4 mg, pack of 36 = £5.12, pack of 72 = £9.97. Contains 0.65 mmol $Na^+$/lozenge

Excipients include aspartame (section 9.4.1)

Dose smoking cessation, initially 1 lozenge every 1–2 hours (when urge to smoke occurs) (max. 15 lozenges daily) for 6 weeks, then 1 lozenge every 2–4 hours for 3 weeks, then 1 lozenge every 4–8 hours for 3 weeks; withdraw gradually after 3 months; max. period of treatment should not exceed 6 months

Patches, self-adhesive, pink/beige, nicotine *'7 mg' patch* (releasing approx. 7 mg/24 hours), net price 7 = £9.97; *'14 mg' patch* (releasing approx. 14 mg/24 hours), 7 = £9.97; *'21 mg' patch* (releasing approx. 21 mg/24 hours), 7 = £9.97, 14 = £18.79

Note Also available as a clear patch

Dose smoking cessation, apply on waking to dry, non-hairy skin site, removing after 24 hours and siting replacement patch on different area (avoid using same area for 7 days); individuals smoking 10 or more cigarettes daily, initially '21-mg' patch daily for 6 weeks then '14-mg' patch daily for 2 weeks then '7-mg' patch daily for 2 weeks; review treatment if abstinence not achieved in 10 weeks

Individuals smoking less than 10 cigarettes daily, initially '14-mg' patch daily for 6 weeks then '7-mg' patch daily for 2 weeks

Note Patients using the '21-mg' patch who experience excessive side-effects, which do not resolve within a few days, should change to '14-mg' patch for the remainder of the initial 6 weeks before switching to the '7-mg' patch for the final 2 weeks

## Opioid dependence

The management of opioid dependence requires medical, social, and psychological treatment; access to a multidisciplinary team is valuable. Treatment with opioid substitutes or with naltrexone is best initiated under the supervision of an appropriately qualified physician.

**Methadone**, an opioid *agonist*, can be substituted for opioids such as diamorphine, preventing the onset of withdrawal symptoms; it is itself addictive and should only be prescribed for those who are physically dependent on opioids. It is administered in a single daily dose usually as methadone oral solution 1 mg/mL. The dose is adjusted according to the degree of dependence.

**Buprenorphine** is an opioid partial agonist. Because of its abuse and dependence potential it should be prescribed only for those who are already physically dependent on opioids. It can be used as substitution therapy for patients with moderate opioid dependence. In patients dependent on high doses of opioids, buprenorphine may precipitate withdrawal due to its partial antagonist properties; in these patients, the daily opioid dose should be reduced gradually before initiating therapy with buprenorphine.

**Naltrexone**, an opioid *antagonist*, blocks the action of opioids and precipitates withdrawal symptoms in opioid-dependent subjects. Because the euphoric action of opioid agonists is blocked by naltrexone it is given to former addicts as an aid to prevent relapse.

**Lofexidine** is used for the alleviation of symptoms in individuals whose opioid use is well controlled and are undergoing opioid withdrawal. Like clonidine it is an alpha-adrenergic agonist and appears to act centrally to produce a reduction in sympathetic tone, but reduction in blood pressure is less marked.

## BUPRENORPHINE

**Indications** adjunct in the treatment of opioid dependence; premedication, peri-operative analgesia, analgesia in other situations (section 4.7.2)

**Cautions** see section 4.7.2 and notes above; effects only partially reversed by naloxone

**Contra-indications** see section 4.7.2; breast-feeding (Appendix 5)

**Side-effects** see section 4.7.2

**Dose**

- By sublingual administration, initially, 0.8–4 mg as a single daily dose, adjusted according to response; max. 32 mg daily; withdraw gradually; CHILD under 16 years not recommended

Note In those who have not undergone opioid withdrawal, buprenorphine should be administered at least 4 hours after last use of opioid or when signs of craving appear
For those receiving methadone, dose of methadone should be reduced to max. 30 mg daily before starting buprenorphine

**Subutex®** (Schering-Plough) CD

Tablets (sublingual), buprenorphine (as hydrochloride) 400 micrograms, net price 7-tab pack = £1.60; 2 mg, 7-tab pack = £6.72; 8 mg, 7-tab pack = £20.16. Label: 2, 26

## LOFEXIDINE HYDROCHLORIDE

**Indications** management of symptoms of opioid withdrawal

**Cautions** severe coronary insufficiency, recent myocardial infarction, cerebrovascular disease, marked bradycardia (monitor pulse rate frequently); history of QT prolongation; concomitant administration of drugs that prolong QT interval; renal impairment; history of depression (on longer treatment); pregnancy and breast-feeding; withdraw gradually over 2–4 days (or longer) to minimise risk of rebound hypertension and associated symptoms; **interactions**: Appendix 1 (lofexidine)

**Side-effects** drowsiness, dry mucous membranes (particularly dry mouth, throat and nose), hypotension, bradycardia, rebound hypertension on withdrawal (see Cautions); sedation and coma in overdosage

**Dose**

- Initially, 200 micrograms twice daily, increased as necessary in steps of 200–400 micrograms daily to max. 2.4 mg daily; recommended duration of treatment 7–10 days if no opioid use (but longer may be required); withdraw gradually over 2–4 days or longer; CHILD not recommended

**BritLofex®** (Britannia) PoM

Tablets, peach, f/c, lofexidine hydrochloride 200 micrograms. Net price 60-tab pack = £61.79. Label: 2

## METHADONE HYDROCHLORIDE

**Indications** adjunct in treatment of opioid dependence, see notes above; analgesia (section 4.7.2); cough in terminal disease (section 3.9.1)

**Cautions** section 4.7.2

**Contra-indications** section 4.7.2

**Side-effects** section 4.7.2; **overdosage**: see Emergency Treatment of Poisoning, p. 31

Important Methadone, even in low doses is a **special hazard** for children; non-dependent adults are also at risk of toxicity; dependent adults are at risk if tolerance is incorrectly assessed during induction

Incompatibility Syrup preserved with hydroxybenzoate (parabens) esters may be incompatible with methadone hydrochloride.

**Dose**

- Initially 10–40 mg daily, increased by up to 10 mg daily (max. weekly increase 30 mg) until no signs of withdrawal or intoxication; usual dose range 60–120 mg daily; CHILD not recommended (see also important note above)

Note Methadone hydrochloride doses in the BNF may differ from those in the product literature

**Methadone** (Non-proprietary) CD

Oral solution 1 mg/mL, methadone hydrochloride 1 mg/mL, net price 30 mL = 44p, 50 mL = 73p, 100 mL = £1.35, 500 mL = £7.59. Label: 2

Brands include *Metharose®* (sugar-free), *Physeptone* (also as sugar-free)

Important This preparation is 2½ times the strength of Methadone Linctus; many preparations of this strength are licensed for opioid drug addiction only but some are also licensed for analgesia in severe pain

Injection ▼, methadone hydrochloride 25 mg/mL, net price 2-mL amp = £2.05; 50 mg/mL, 1-mL amp = £2.05

Brands include *Synastone®*

**Methadose®** (Rosemont) CD

Oral concentrate, methadone hydrochloride 10 mg/mL (blue), net price 150 mL = £12.01; 20 mg/mL (brown), 150 mL = £24.02. Label: 2

Note The final strength of the methadone mixture to be dispensed to the patient must be specified on the prescription

Important Care is required in prescribing and dispensing the **correct strength** since any confusion could lead to an overdose; this preparation should be dispensed only **after dilution** as appropriate with *Methadose® Diluent* (life of diluted solution 3 months) and is for drug dependent persons (see also p. 7)

## NALTREXONE HYDROCHLORIDE

**Indications** adjunct to prevent relapse in detoxified formerly opioid-dependent patients (who have remained opioid-free for at least 7–10 days)

**Cautions** hepatic and renal impairment; liver function tests needed before and during treatment; test for opioid dependence with naloxone; avoid concomitant use of opioids but increased dose of opioid analgesic may be required for pain (monitor for opioid intoxication); pregnancy, breast-feeding

Warning for patients Patients need to be warned that an attempt to overcome the block could result in acute opioid intoxication

**Contra-indications** patients currently dependent on opioids; acute hepatitis or liver failure

**Side-effects** nausea, vomiting, abdominal pain; anxiety, nervousness, sleeping difficulty, headache, reduced energy; joint and muscle pain; less frequently, loss of appetite, diarrhoea, constipation, increased thirst; chest pain; increased sweating and lacrimation; increased energy, 'feeling down', irritability, dizziness, chills; delayed ejaculation, decreased potency; rash; occasionally, liver function abnormalities; reversible idiopathic thrombocytopenia reported

**Dose**

- (Initiate in specialist clinics only) 25 mg initially then 50 mg daily; the total weekly dose may be divided and given on 3 days of the week for improved compliance (e.g. 100 mg on Monday and Wednesday, and 150 mg on Friday); CHILD not recommended

**Nalorex®** (Bristol-Myers Squibb) PoM

Tablets, yellow, f/c, scored, naltrexone hydrochloride 50 mg. Net price 28-tab pack = £42.51

# 4.11 Drugs for dementia

Acetylcholinesterase inhibiting drugs are used in the treatment of Alzheimer's disease, specifically for mild to moderate disease. The evidence to support the use of these drugs relates to their cognitive enhancement.

Treatment with drugs for dementia should be initiated and supervised only by a specialist experienced in the management of dementia.

Benefit is assessed by repeating the cognitive assessment at around 3 months. Such assessment cannot demonstrate how the disease may have progressed in the absence of treatment but it can give a good guide to response. Up to half the patients given these drugs will show a slower rate of cognitive decline. The drug should be discontinued in those thought not to be responding. Many specialists repeat the cognitive assessment 4 to 6 weeks after discontinuation to assess deterioration; if significant deterioration occurs during this short period, consideration should be given to restarting therapy.

**Donepezil** is a reversible inhibitor of acetylcholinesterase that can be given once daily. **Galantamine** is a reversible inhibitor of acetylcholinesterase and it also has nicotinic receptor agonist properties. It is given twice daily. **Rivastigmine** is a reversible non-competitive inhibitor of acetylcholinesterases, which is given twice daily.

Acetylcholinesterase inhibitors can cause unwanted dose-related cholinergic effects and should be started at a low dose and the dose increased according to response and tolerability.

**Memantine** is a NMDA-receptor antagonist that affects glutamate transmission; it is licensed for treating moderate to severe Alzheimer's disease.

### NICE guidance (Alzheimer's disease)

NICE has recommended (January 2001) that, for the adjunctive treatment of mild and moderate Alzheimer's disease in those whose mini mental-state examination (MMSE) score is above 12 points, donepezil, galantamine, and rivastigmine should be available under the following conditions:

- Alzheimer's disease must be diagnosed in a specialist clinic; the clinic should also assess cognitive, global and behavioural functioning, activities of daily living, and the likelihood of compliance with treatment;
- treatment should be initiated by specialists but may be continued by general practitioners under a shared-care protocol;
- the carers' views of the condition should be sought before and during drug treatment;
- the patient should be assessed 2–4 months after maintenance dose is established; drug treatment should continue only if MMSE score has improved or has not deteriorated *and* if behavioural or functional assessment shows improvement;
- the patient should be assessed every 6 months and drug treatment should normally continue only if MMSE score remains above 12 points and if treatment is considered to have a worthwhile effect on the global, functional and behavioural condition.

## DONEPEZIL HYDROCHLORIDE

**Indications** mild to moderate dementia in Alzheimer's disease

**Cautions** sick sinus syndrome or other supraventricular conduction abnormalities; susceptibility to peptic ulcers; asthma, chronic obstructive pulmonary disease; may exacerbate extrapyramidal symptoms; hepatic impairment; **interactions:** Appendix 1 (parasympathomimetics)

**Contra-indications** pregnancy and breast-feeding

**Side-effects** nausea, vomiting, anorexia, diarrhoea, fatigue, insomnia, headache, dizziness, syncope, psychiatric disturbances, muscle cramps, urinary incontinence, rash, pruritus; less frequently, bradycardia, convulsions, gastric and duodenal ulcers, gastro-intestinal haemorrhage; rarely, sino-atrial block, AV block, hepatitis reported; potential for bladder outflow obstruction

**Dose**

- 5 mg once daily at bedtime, increased if necessary after one month to 10 mg daily; max. 10 mg daily

**Aricept®** (Pfizer, Eisai) PoM

Tablets, f/c, donepezil hydrochloride 5 mg, net price 28-tab pack = £63.54; 10 mg (yellow), 28-tab pack = £89.06.

## GALANTAMINE

**Indications** mild to moderate dementia in Alzheimer's disease

**Cautions** cardiac disease (including sick sinus syndrome or other supraventricular conduction abnormalities, unstable angina, congestive heart failure); electrolyte disturbances; susceptibility to peptic ulcers; asthma, chronic obstructive pulmonary disease, pulmonary infection; avoid in urinary retention and gastro-intestinal obstruction; hepatic impairment (Appendix 2—avoid if severe); pregnancy (Appendix 4); **interactions:** Appendix 1 (parasympathomimetics)

**Contra-indications** severe renal impairment; breast-feeding (Appendix 5)

**Side-effects** nausea, vomiting, diarrhoea, abdominal pain, dyspepsia; syncope; rhinitis; sleep disturbances, dizziness, confusion, depression, headache, fatigue, anorexia, tremor; fever; weight loss; *less commonly* arrythmias, palpitation, myocardial infarction, cerebrovascular disease, paraesthesia, tinnitus, and leg cramps; *rarely* bradycardia, seizures, hallucinations, agitation, aggression, dehydration, hypokalaemia, and rash; *very rarely* gastrointestinal bleeding, dysphagia, hypotension, exacerbation of Parkinson's disease, and sweating

**Dose**

- Initially 4 mg twice daily for 4 weeks increased to 8 mg twice daily for 4 weeks; maintenance 8–12 mg twice daily

**Reminyl®** (Shire) PoM

Tablets, all f/c, galantamine (as hydrobromide) 4 mg (white), net price 56-tab pack = £54.60; 8 mg (pink), 56-tab pack = £68.32; 12 mg (orange-brown), 56-tab pack = £84.00 Label: 3, 21

Oral solution, galantamine (as hydrobromide) 4 mg/mL, net price 100 mL with pipette = £120.00. Label: 3, 21

### Modified release

**Reminyl® XL** (Shire) PoM

Capsules, m/r, galantamine (as hydrobromide) 8 mg (white), net price 28-cap pack = £54.60; 16 mg (pink), 28-cap pack = £68.32; 24 mg (beige), 28-cap pack = £84.00. Label: 3, 21, 25

Dose initially 8 mg once daily for 4 weeks increased to 16 mg once daily for 4 weeks; maintenance 16–24 mg daily

## MEMANTINE HYDROCHLORIDE

**Indications** moderate to severe dementia in Alzheimer's disease

**Cautions** history of convulsions; renal impairment (avoid if severe—Appendix 3); pregnancy (Appendix 4); **interactions:** Appendix 1 (memantine)

**Contra-indications** breast-feeding

**Side-effects** constipation; headache, dizziness, drowsiness; *less commonly* vomiting, confusion, fatigue, hallucinations, and abnormal gait; *very rarely* seizures

**Dose**

- Initially 5 mg in the morning, increased in steps of 5 mg at intervals of 1 week up to max. 10 mg twice daily

**Ebixa®** (Lundbeck) ▼ PoM

Tablets, f/c, scored, memantine hydrochloride 10 mg, net price 28-tab pack = £34.50, 56-tab pack = £69.01, 112-tab pack = £138.01

Oral drops, memantine hydrochloride 10 mg/g, net price 50 g = £61.61, 100 g = £123.23

Note 5 mg ≡ 10 drops of memantine hydrochloride oral drops

## RIVASTIGMINE

**Indications** mild to moderate dementia in Alzheimer's disease

**Cautions** renal impairment, mild to moderate hepatic impairment (Appendix 2); sick sinus syndrome, conduction abnormalities; gastric or duodenal ulcers (and those at risk of developing ulcers); history of asthma or chronic obstructive pulmonary disease; history of seizures, bladder outflow obstruction, pregnancy (Appendix 4); may exacerbate extrapyramidal symptoms (including worsening of Parkinson's disease); monitor body-weight; **interactions:** Appendix 1 (parasympathomimetics)

Note If treatment interrupted for more than several days, re-introduce with initial dose and increase gradually (see Dose)

**Contra-indications** breast-feeding (Appendix 5)

**Side-effects** nausea, vomiting, diarrhoea, dyspepsia, anorexia, abdominal pain; dizziness, headache, drowsiness, tremor, asthenia, malaise, agitation, confusion; sweating; less commonly, syncope, depression, insomnia; rarely gastric or duodenal ulceration, gastro-intestinal haemorrhage, pancreatitis, angina pectoris, arrhythmias, bradycardia, hypertension, convulsions, hallucinations, urinary infection, rash

Note Gastro-intestinal side-effects may occur more commonly in women

**Dose**

- Initially 1.5 mg twice daily, increased in steps of 1.5 mg twice daily at intervals of at least 2 weeks according to response and tolerance; usual range 3–6 mg twice daily; max. 6 mg twice daily

**Exelon®** (Novartis) PoM

Capsules, rivastigmine (as hydrogen tartrate) 1.5 mg (yellow), net price 28-cap pack = £34.02, 56-cap pack = £68.04; 3 mg (orange), 28-cap pack = £34.02, 56-cap pack = £68.04; 4.5 mg (red), 28-cap pack = £34.02, 56-cap pack = £68.04; 6 mg (red/orange), 28-cap pack = £34.02, 56-cap pack = £68.04. Label: 21, 25

Oral solution, rivastigmine (as hydrogen tartrate) 2 mg/mL, net price 120 mL (with oral syringe) = £116.64. Label: 21

# 5 Infections


| | | |
|---|---|---|
| **5.1** | **Antibacterial drugs** | **266** |
| 5.1.1 | Penicillins | 273 |
| 5.1.1.1 | Benzylpenicillin and phenoxymethylpenicillin | 273 |
| 5.1.1.2 | Penicillinase-resistant penicillins | 274 |
| 5.1.1.3 | Broad-spectrum penicillins | 275 |
| 5.1.1.4 | Antipseudomonal penicillins | 278 |
| 5.1.1.5 | Mecillinams | 279 |
| 5.1.2 | Cephalosporins and other beta-lactams | 279 |
| 5.1.3 | Tetracyclines | 285 |
| 5.1.4 | Aminoglycosides | 287 |
| 5.1.5 | Macrolides | 289 |
| 5.1.6 | Clindamycin | 291 |
| 5.1.7 | Some other antibacterials | 292 |
| 5.1.8 | Sulphonamides and trimethoprim | 296 |
| 5.1.9 | Antituberculous drugs | 297 |
| 5.1.10 | Antileprotic drugs | 302 |
| 5.1.11 | Metronidazole and tinidazole | 302 |
| 5.1.12 | Quinolones | 304 |
| 5.1.13 | Urinary-tract infections | 307 |
| **5.2** | **Antifungal drugs** | **308** |
| **5.3** | **Antiviral drugs** | **314** |
| 5.3.1 | HIV infection | 314 |
| 5.3.2 | Herpesvirus infections | 322 |
| 5.3.2.1 | Herpes simplex and varicella–zoster infection | 322 |
| 5.3.2.2 | Cytomegalovirus infection | 324 |
| 5.3.3 | Viral hepatitis | 326 |
| 5.3.4 | Influenza | 326 |
| 5.3.5 | Respiratory syncytial virus | 328 |
| **5.4** | **Antiprotozoal drugs** | **329** |
| 5.4.1 | Antimalarials | 329 |
| 5.4.2 | Amoebicides | 337 |
| 5.4.3 | Trichomonacides | 337 |
| 5.4.4 | Antigiardial drugs | 337 |
| 5.4.5 | Leishmaniacides | 338 |
| 5.4.6 | Trypanocides | 338 |
| 5.4.7 | Drugs for toxoplasmosis | 338 |
| 5.4.8 | Drugs for pneumocystis pneumonia | 338 |
| **5.5** | **Anthelmintics** | **340** |
| 5.5.1 | Drugs for threadworms | 340 |
| 5.5.2 | Ascaricides | 341 |
| 5.5.3 | Drugs for tapeworm infections | 341 |
| 5.5.4 | Drugs for hookworms | 341 |
| 5.5.5 | Schistosomicides | 341 |
| 5.5.6 | Filaricides | 342 |
| 5.5.7 | Drugs for cutaneous larva migrans | 342 |
| 5.5.8 | Drugs for strongyloidiasis | 342 |


This chapter includes advice on the drug management of the following:


- anthrax, p. 304
- bacterial infections (summary of treatment and prophylaxis), pp. 268–73
- Lyme disease, p. 276
- MRSA, p. 274
- oral infections, p. 267, p. 270, p. 273, p. 276, p. 280, p. 285, p. 290, p. 292, p. 303, p. 308


## Notifiable diseases

Doctors must notify the Proper Officer of the local authority (usually the consultant in communicable disease control) when attending a patient suspected of suffering from any of the diseases listed below; a form is available from the Proper Officer.

| | |
|---|---|
| Anthrax | Ophthalmia neonatorum |
| Cholera | Paratyphoid fever |
| Diphtheria | Plague |
| Dysentery (amoebic or bacillary) | Poliomyelitis, acute |
| | Rabies |
| Encephalitis, acute | Relapsing fever |
| Food poisoning | Rubella |
| Haemorrhagic fever (viral) | Scarlet fever |
| Hepatitis, viral | Smallpox |
| Leprosy | Tetanus |
| Leptospirosis | Tuberculosis |
| Malaria | Typhoid fever |
| Measles | Typhus |
| Meningitis | Whooping cough |
| Meningococcal septicaemia (without meningitis) | Yellow fever |
| Mumps | |

**Note** It is good practice for doctors to also inform the consultant in communicable disease control of instances of other infections (e.g. psittacosis) where there could be a public health risk.

## 5.1 Antibacterial drugs

**Choice of a suitable drug** Before selecting an antibacterial the clinician must first consider two factors—the patient and the known or likely causative organism. Factors related to the patient which must be considered include history of allergy, renal and hepatic function, susceptibility to infection (i.e. whether immunocompromised), ability to tolerate drugs by mouth, severity of illness, ethnic origin, age, whether taking other medication and, if female, whether pregnant, breast-feeding or taking an oral contraceptive.

The known or likely organism and its antibacterial sensitivity, in association with the above factors, will suggest one or more antibacterials, the final choice depending on the microbiological, pharmacological, and toxicological properties.

An example of a rational approach to the selection of an antibacterial is treatment of a urinary-tract infection in a patient complaining of nausea in early pregnancy. The organism is reported as being resistant to ampicillin but sensitive to nitrofurantoin (can cause nausea), gentamicin (can be given only by injection and best avoided in pregnancy), tetracycline (causes dental discoloration) and trimethoprim (folate antagonist therefore theoretical teratogenic risk), and cefalexin. The safest antibiotics in pregnancy are the penicillins and cephalosporins; therefore, cefalexin would be indicated for this patient.

The principles involved in selection of an antibacterial must allow for a number of variables including changing renal and hepatic function, increasing bacterial resistance, and new information on side-effects. Duration of therapy, dosage, and route of administration depend on site, type and severity of infection and response.

**Antibacterial policies** Local policies often limit the antibacterials that may be used to achieve reasonable economy consistent with adequate cover, and to reduce the development of resistant organisms. A policy may indicate a range of drugs for general use, and permit other drugs only on the advice of the microbiologist or physician responsible for the control of infectious diseases.

**Before starting therapy** The following precepts should be considered before starting:

- Viral infections should not be treated with antibacterials. However, antibacterials are occasionally helpful in controlling secondary bacterial infection (e.g. acute necrotising ulcerative gingivitis secondary to herpes simplex infection);
- Samples should be taken for culture and sensitivity testing; **'blind'** antibacterial prescribing for unexplained pyrexia usually leads to further difficulty in establishing the diagnosis;
- Knowledge of **prevalent organisms** and their current sensitivity is of great help in choosing an antibacterial before bacteriological confirmation is available;
- The **dose** of an antibacterial varies according to a number of factors including age, weight, hepatic function, renal function, and severity of infection. The prescribing of the so-called 'standard' dose in serious infections may result in failure of treatment or even death of the patient; therefore it is important to prescribe a dose appropriate to the condition. An inadequate dose may also increase the likelihood of antibacterial resistance. On the other hand, for an antibacterial with a narrow margin between the toxic and therapeutic dose (e.g. an aminoglycoside) it is also important to avoid an excessive dose and the concentration of the drug in the plasma may need to be monitored;
- The **route** of administration of an antibacterial often depends on the severity of the infection. Life-threatening infections require intravenous therapy. Whenever possible painful intramuscular injections should be avoided in children;
- **Duration** of therapy depends on the nature of the infection and the response to treatment. Courses should not be unduly prolonged because they encourage resistance, they may lead to side-effects and they are costly. However, in certain infections such as tuberculosis or chronic osteomyelitis it is necessary to treat for prolonged periods. Conversely a single dose of an antibacterial may cure uncomplicated urinary-tract infections.

**Oral bacterial infections** Antibacterial drugs should only be prescribed for the *treatment* of oral infections on the basis of defined need. They may be used in conjunction with (but not as an alternative to) other appropriate measures, such as providing drainage or extracting a tooth.

The 'blind' prescribing of an antibacterial for unexplained pyrexia, cervical lymphadenopathy, or facial swelling can lead to difficulty in establishing the diagnosis. Bacteriological sampling should always be carried out in severe oral infections.

Oral infections which call for antibacterial treatment include acute suppurative pulpitis, acute periapical or periodontal abscess, cellulitis, oral-antral fistula (and acute sinusitis), severe pericoronitis, localised osteitis, acute necrotising ulcerative gingivitis, and destructive forms of chronic periodontal disease. Most of these infections are readily resolved by the early establishment of drainage and removal of the cause (typically an infected necrotic pulp). Antibacterials may be indicated if treatment has to be delayed and they are essential in immunocompromised patients or in those with conditions such as diabetes or Paget's disease. Certain rarer infections including bacterial sialadenitis, osteomyelitis, actinomycosis, and infections involving fascial spaces such as Ludwig's angina, require antibiotics and specialist hospital care.

Antibacterial drugs may also be useful after dental surgery in some cases of spreading infection. Infection may spread to involve local lymph nodes, to fascial spaces (where it can cause airway obstruction), or into the bloodstream (where it can lead to cavernous sinus thrombosis and other serious complications). Extension of an infection can also lead to maxillary sinusitis; osteomyelitis is a complication, which usually arises when host resistance is reduced.

If the oral infection fails to respond to antibacterial treatment within 48 hours the antibacterial should be changed, preferably on the basis of bacteriological investigation. Failure to respond may also suggest an incorrect diagnosis, lack of essential additional measures (such as drainage), poor host resistance, or poor patient compliance.

Combination of a penicillin (or erythromycin) with metronidazole may sometimes be helpful for the treatment of severe or resistant oral infections.

See also **Penicillins** (section 5.1.1), **Cephalosporins** (section 5.1.2), **Tetracyclines** (section 5.1.3), **Macrolides** (section 5.1.5), **Clindamycin** (section 5.1.6), **Metronidazole** (section 5.1.11), **Fusidic acid** (section 13.10.1.2).

**Superinfection** In general, broad-spectrum antibacterial drugs such as the cephalosporins are more likely to be associated with adverse reactions related to the selection of resistant organisms e.g. *fungal infections* or *antibiotic-associated colitis* (pseudomembranous colitis); other problems associated with superinfection include vaginitis and pruritus ani.

**Therapy** Suggested treatment is shown in table 1. When the pathogen has been isolated treatment may be changed to a more appropriate antibacterial if necessary. If no bacterium is cultured the antibacterial can be continued or stopped on clinical grounds. Infections for which prophylaxis is useful are listed in table 2.

## Table 1. Summary of antibacterial therapy

If treating a patient suspected of suffering from a notifiable disease, the consultant in communicable disease control should be informed (see p. 266)

### Gastro-intestinal system

**Gastro-enteritis**
Antibacterial not usually indicated
Frequently self-limiting and may not be bacterial

**Campylobacter enteritis**
Ciprofloxacin *or* erythromycin

**Invasive salmonellosis**
Ciprofloxacin *or* cefotaxime
Includes severe infections which may be invasive

**Shigellosis**
Ciprofloxacin *or* trimethoprim *or* ceftriaxone
Antibacterial not indicated for mild cases. Ciprofloxacin should be used for trimethoprim-resistant strains

**Typhoid fever**
Ciprofloxacin *or* cefotaxime
Infections from Indian subcontinent, Middle-East, and South-East Asia may be multiple-antibacterial-resistant and sensitivity should be tested; azithromycin [unlicensed indication] may be an option in mild or moderate disease caused by multiple antibacterial-resistant organisms

**Antibiotic-associated colitis (pseudomembranous colitis)**
Oral metronidazole *or* oral vancomycin
Give metronidazole by intravenous infusion if oral treatment inappropriate

**Biliary-tract infection**
A cephalosporin *or* gentamicin

**Peritonitis**
A cephalosporin (*or* gentamicin) + metronidazole (*or* clindamycin)

**Peritoneal dialysis-associated peritonitis**
*Either* vancomycin[1] + ceftazidime added to dialysis fluid *or* vancomycin added to dialysis fluid + ciprofloxacin by mouth
Treat for 14 days or longer

### Cardiovascular system

**Endocarditis: initial 'blind' therapy**
Flucloxacillin (*or* benzylpenicillin if symptoms less severe) + gentamicin
Substitute flucloxacillin (or benzylpenicillin) with vancomycin + rifampicin if cardiac prostheses present, or if penicillin-allergic, or if meticillin-resistant *Staphylococcus aureus* suspected

1. Where vancomycin is suggested teicoplanin may be used.

**Endocarditis caused by staphylococci**
Flucloxacillin (*or* vancomycin + rifampicin if penicillin-allergic or if meticillin-resistant *Staphylococcus aureus*)
Treat for at least 4 weeks; treat prosthetic valve endocarditis for at least 6 weeks and if using flucloxacillin add rifampicin for at least 2 weeks

**Endocarditis caused by streptococci** (e.g. viridans streptococci)
Benzylpenicillin (*or* vancomycin[1] if penicillin- allergic or highly penicillin-resistant) + gentamicin
Treat endocarditis caused by fully sensitive streptococci with benzylpenicillin or vancomycin alone for 4 weeks *or* (if no cardiac or embolic complications) with benzylpenicillin + gentamicin for 2 weeks; treat more resistant organisms for 4–6 weeks (stopping gentamicin after 2 weeks for organisms moderately sensitive to penicillin); if aminoglycoside cannot be used and if streptococci moderately sensitive to penicillin, treat with benzylpenicillin alone for 4 weeks; treat prosthetic valve endocarditis for at least 6 weeks (stopping gentamicin after 2 weeks if organisms fully sensitive to penicillin)

**Endocarditis caused by enterococci** (e.g. *Enterococcus faecalis*)
Amoxicillin[2] (*or* vancomycin[1] if penicillin-allergic or penicillin-resistant) + gentamicin
Treat for at least 4 weeks (at least 6 weeks for prosthetic valve endocarditis); if gentamicin-resistant, substitute gentamicin with streptomycin

**Endocarditis caused by haemophilus, actinobacillus, cardiobacterium, eikenella, and kingella species** ('HACEK' organisms)
Amoxicillin[2] (*or* ceftriaxone if amoxicillin-resistant) + low-dose gentamicin
Treat for 4 weeks (6 weeks for prosthetic valve endocarditis); stop gentamicin after 2 weeks

### Respiratory system

***Haemophilus influenzae* epiglottitis**
Cefotaxime *or* chloramphenicol
Give intravenously

**Exacerbations of chronic bronchitis**
Amoxicillin[2] *or* tetracycline (*or* erythromycin[3])
Some pneumococci and *Haemophilus influenzae* strains tetracycline-resistant; 15% *H. influenzae* strains amoxicillin-resistant

**Uncomplicated community-acquired pneumonia**
Amoxicillin[2] (*or* benzylpenicillin if previously healthy chest *or* erythromycin[3] if penicillin-allergic)
Add flucloxacillin if staphylococci suspected, e.g. in influenza or measles (or vancomycin[1] if meticillin-resistant *Staphylococcus aureus* suspected); treat for 7 days (14–21 days for infections caused by staphylococci); pneumococci with decreased penicillin sensitivity being isolated but not yet common in UK; add erythromycin[3] if atypical pathogens suspected

**Severe community-acquired pneumonia of unknown aetiology**
Cefuroxime (or cefotaxime) + erythromycin[3]
Add flucloxacillin if staphylococci suspected (or vancomycin[1] if meticillin-resistant *Staphylococcus aureus* suspected); treat for 10 days (14–21 days if staphylococci, legionella, or Gram-negative enteric bacilli suspected)

**Pneumonia possibly caused by atypical pathogens**
Erythromycin[3]
Severe Legionella infections may require addition of rifampicin; tetracycline is an alternative for chlamydial and mycoplasma infections; treat for at least 14 days (14–21 days for legionella)

2. Where amoxicillin is suggested ampicillin may be used.
3. Where erythromycin is suggested another macrolide (e.g. azithromycin or clarithromycin) may be used.

### Hospital-acquired pneumonia
A broad-spectrum cephalosporin (e.g. cefotaxime or ceftazidime) *or* an antipseudomonal penicillin or another antipseudomonal beta-lactam

An aminoglycoside may be added in severe illness

## Central nervous system

### Meningitis: initial 'blind' therapy
- Transfer patient urgently to hospital.
- If bacterial meningitis and especially if *meningococcal disease* suspected, general practitioners should give benzylpenicillin (see p. 274 for dose) before urgent transfer to hospital; cefotaxime (section 5.1.2) may be an alternative in penicillin allergy; chloramphenicol (section 5.1.7) may be used if history of anaphylaxis to penicillin or to cephalosporins
- Consider adjunctive treatment with dexamethasone (particularly if pneumococcal meningitis suspected in adults) starting before or with first dose of antibacterial; avoid dexamethasone in septic shock, meningococcal disease, or if immunocompromised, or in meningitis following surgery

### Meningitis caused by meningococci
Benzylpenicillin *or* cefotaxime

Treat for at least 5 days; substitute chloramphenicol if history of anaphylaxis to penicillin or to cephalosporins; to eliminate nasopharyngeal carriage give rifampicin for 2 days to patients treated with benzylpenicillin or chloramphenicol

### Meningitis caused by pneumococci
Cefotaxime

Treat for 10–14 days; substitute benzylpenicillin if organism penicillin-sensitive; if organism highly penicillin- and cephalosporin-resistant, add vancomycin and if necessary rifampicin; consider early adjunctive treatment with dexamethasone (but may reduce penetration of vancomycin into cerebrospinal fluid; section 6.3.2)

### Meningitis caused by *Haemophilus influenzae*
Cefotaxime

Treat for at least 10 days; substitute chloramphenicol if history of anaphylaxis to penicillin or to cephalosporins or if organism resistant to cefotaxime; consider early adjunctive treatment with dexamethasone (section 6.3.2); for *H. influenzae* type b give rifampicin for 4 days before hospital discharge

### Meningitis caused by Listeria
Amoxicillin[1] + gentamicin

Treat for 10–14 days

## Urinary tract

### Acute pyelonephritis
A broad-spectrum cephalosporin *or* a quinolone

Treat for 14 days; longer treatment may be necessary in complicated pyelonephritis

### Acute prostatitis
A quinolone *or* trimethoprim

Treat for 28 days; in severe infection, start treatment with a high dose broad-spectrum cephalosporin (e.g. cefuroxime or cefotaxime) + gentamicin

### 'Lower' urinary-tract infection
Trimethoprim *or* amoxicillin[1] *or* nitrofurantoin *or* oral cephalosporin

Treat for 7 days but a short course (e.g. 3 days) of trimethoprim or amoxicillin is usually adequate for uncomplicated urinary-tract infections in women

## Genital system

### Syphilis
Procaine benzylpenicillin [unlicensed] *or* doxycycline *or* erythromycin

Treat early syphilis for 14 days (10 days with procaine benzylpenicillin); treat late latent syphilis (asymptomatic infection of more than 2 years) with procaine benzylpenicillin for 17 days (or with doxycycline for 28 days); treat asymptomatic contacts of patients with infectious syphilis with doxycycline for 14 days; contact tracing recommended

### Uncomplicated gonorrhoea
Cefixime [unlicensed indication] *or* ciprofloxacin

Single-dose treatment in uncomplicated infection; choice depends on locality where infection acquired; pharyngeal infection requires treatment with ceftriaxone; use ciprofloxacin only if organism sensitive; contact-tracing recommended; remember chlamydia

### Uncomplicated genital chlamydial infection, non-gonococcal urethritis and non-specific genital infection
Doxycycline *or* azithromycin

Treat with doxycycline for 7 days or with azithromycin as a single dose; alternatively, treat with erythromycin for 14 days; contact tracing recommended

### Pelvic inflammatory disease
Ofloxacin + metronidazole

Treat for at least 14 days; in severely ill patients substitute initial treatment with doxycycline + ceftriaxone + metronidazole, then switch to oral treatment with doxycycline + metronidazole to complete 14 days' treatment; contact tracing recommended; remember gonorrhoea

## Blood

### Community-acquired septicaemia
A broad-spectrum antipseudomonal penicillin (e.g. *Tazocin®*, *Timentin®*) *or* a broad-spectrum cephalosporin (e.g. ceftazidime, cefotaxime)

Add aminoglycoside if pseudomonas suspected, or if severe sepsis, or if patient recently discharged from hospital; add vancomycin[2] if meticillin-resistant *Staphylococcus aureus* suspected; add metronidazole to broad-spectrum cephalosporin if anaerobic infection suspected

### Hospital-acquired septicaemia
A broad-spectrum antipseudomonal beta-lactam antibacterial (e.g. ceftazidime, *Tazocin®*, *Timentin®*, imipenem (with cilastatin as *Primaxin®*) *or* meropenem)

Add aminoglycoside if pseudomonas suspected, or if multiple-resistant organisms suspected, or if severe sepsis; add vancomycin[2] if meticillin-resistant *Staphylococcus aureus* suspected; add metronidazole to broad-spectrum cephalosporin if anaerobic infection suspected

### Septicaemia related to vascular catheter
Vancomycin[2]

Add an aminoglycoside + a broad-spectrum antipseudomonal beta-lactam if Gram-negative sepsis suspected, especially in the immunocompromised; consider removing vascular catheter, particularly if infection caused by *Staphylococcus aureus*, pseudomonas, or candida

### Meningococcal septicaemia
Benzylpenicillin *or* cefotaxime

If meningococcal disease suspected, general practitioners advised to give a single dose of benzylpenicillin (see p. 274 for dose) before urgent transfer to hospital; cefotaxime (section 5.1.2) may be an alternative in penicillin allergy; chloramphenicol may be used if history of anaphylaxis to penicillin or to cephalosporins; give rifampicin for 2 days to patients treated with benzylpenicillin or chloramphenicol

## Musculoskeletal system

### Osteomyelitis
Flucloxacillin *or* clindamycin if penicillin-allergic (*or* vancomycin[2] if resistant *Staphylococcus epidermidis* or meticillin-resistant *Staph. aureus*)

Treat acute infection for 4–6 weeks and chronic infection for at least 12 weeks; combine vancomycin[2] with either fusidic acid or rifampicin if prostheses present or if life-threatening condition

1. Where amoxicillin is suggested ampicillin may be used.

2. Where vancomycin is suggested teicoplanin may be used.

**Septic arthritis**
Flucloxacillin + fusidic acid *or* clindamycin alone if penicillin-allergic (*or* vancomycin[1] if resistant *Staphylococcus epidermidis* or meticillin-resistant *Staph. aureus*) (*or* cefotaxime if gonococcal arthritis or Gram-negative infection)

Treat for 6–12 weeks (2 weeks if gonococcal); combine vancomycin[1] with either fusidic acid or rifampicin if prostheses present or if life-threatening condition

## Eye

**Purulent conjunctivitis**
Chloramphenicol *or* gentamicin eye-drops

## Ear, nose, and oropharynx

**Pericoronitis**
Metronidazole *or* amoxicillin

Antibacterial required only in presence of systemic features of infection or of trismus or persistent swelling despite local treatment; treat for 3 days or until symptoms resolve

**Acute necrotising ulcerative gingivitis**
Metronidazole *or* amoxicillin

Antibacterial required only if systemic features of infection; treat for 3 days or until symptoms resolve

**Periapical or periodontal abscess**
Amoxicillin *or* metronidazole

Antibacterial required only in severe disease with cellulitis or if systemic features of infection; treat for 5 days

**Periodontitis**
Metronidazole *or* doxycycline

Antibacterial required for severe disease or disease unresponsive to local treatment

**Throat infections**
Phenoxymethylpenicillin (*or* erythromycin[2] if penicillin-allergic)

Most throat infections are caused by viruses and many do not require antibiotic therapy; prescribe antibacterial for beta-haemolytic streptococcal pharyngitis (treat for 10 days), if history of valvular heart disease, if marked systemic upset, if peritonsillar cellulitis or if at increased risk from acute infection (e.g. in immunosuppression, diabetes); **avoid** amoxicillin if possibility of glandular fever, see section 5.1.1.3; initial parenteral therapy (in severe infection) with benzylpenicillin, then oral therapy with phenoxymethylpenicillin *or* amoxicillin[3]

**Sinusitis**
Amoxicillin[3] *or* doxycycline *or* erythromycin[2]

Antibacterial should usually be used only for persistent symptoms and purulent discharge lasting at least 7 days or if severe symptoms; treat for 7–10 days

**Otitis externa**
Flucloxacillin (*or* erythromycin[2] if penicillin-allergic)

Use ciprofloxacin (or an aminoglycoside) if pseudomonas suspected, see section 12.1.1

**Otitis media**
Amoxicillin[3] (*or* erythromycin[2] if penicillin-allergic)

Many infections caused by viruses; most uncomplicated cases resolve without antibacterial treatment; in children without systemic features, antibacterial treatment may be started after 72 hours if no improvement (earlier in immunocompromised patients, children under 2 years, or if deterioration); treat for 5 days (longer if severely ill); initial parenteral therapy in severe infections; consider co-amoxiclav or ceftriaxone if no improvement after 24–48 hours

1. Where vancomycin is suggested teicoplanin may be used.
2. Where erythromycin is suggested another macrolide (e.g. azithromycin or clarithromycin) may be used.
3. Where amoxicillin is suggested ampicillin may be used.

## Skin

**Impetigo**
Topical fusidic acid (*or* mupirocin if meticillin-resistant *Staphylococcus aureus*); oral flucloxacillin *or* erythromycin[2] if widespread

Topical treatment for 7 days usually adequate; max. duration of topical treatment 10 days; seek local microbiology advice before using topical treatment in hospital; oral treatment for 7 days; add phenoxymethylpenicillin to flucloxacillin if streptococcal infection suspected

**Erysipelas**
Phenoxymethylpenicillin (*or* erythromycin[2] if penicillin-allergic)

Treat for at least 7 days; add flucloxacillin to phenoxymethylpenicillin if staphylococcus suspected; substitute benzylpenicillin for phenoxymethylpenicillin if parenteral treatment required

**Cellulitis**
Benzylpenicillin + flucloxacillin (*or* erythromycin[2] alone if penicillin-allergic)

Substitute phenoxymethylpenicillin for benzylpenicillin if oral treatment appropriate; discontinue flucloxacillin if streptococcal infection confirmed; substitute treatment with broad-spectrum antibacterials if Gram-negative bacteria or anaerobes suspected

**Animal and human bites**
Co-amoxiclav alone (*or* doxycycline + metronidazole if penicillin-allergic)

Cleanse wound thoroughly; for tetanus-prone wound, give human tetanus immunoglobulin (with a tetanus-containing vaccine if necessary, according to immunisation history and risk of infection), see under Tetanus Vaccines, section 14.4; consider rabies prophylaxis (section 14.4) for bites from animals in endemic countries; assess risk of blood-borne viruses

**Acne**
See section 13.6

## Table 2. Summary of antibacterial prophylaxis

### Prevention of secondary case of *meningococcal meningitis*[4]

Rifampicin 600 mg every 12 hours for 2 days; CHILD 10 mg/kg (under 1 year, 5 mg/kg) every 12 hours for 2 days

*or* ciprofloxacin [not licensed for this indication] 500 mg as a single dose; CHILD 5–12 years 250 mg

*or* i/m ceftriaxone [not licensed for this indication] 250 mg as a single dose; CHILD under 12 years 125 mg

### Prevention of secondary case of *Haemophilus influenzae type b disease*[4]

Rifampicin 600 mg once daily for 4 days (regimen of choice for adults); CHILD 1–3 months 10 mg/kg once daily for 4 days, over 3 months 20 mg/kg once daily for 4 days (max. 600 mg daily)

4. For details of those who should receive chemoprophylaxis contact a consultant in communicable disease control (or a consultant in infectious diseases or the local Health Protection Agency laboratory). Unless there has been mouth-to-mouth contact (or direct exposure to infectious droplets from a patient with meningococcal disease), healthcare workers do not generally require chemoprophylaxis.

## Prevention of *endocarditis*[1] in patients with heart-valve lesion, septal defect, patent ductus, prosthetic valve, or history of endocarditis

**Dental procedures**[2] *under local or no anaesthesia*, patients who have not received more than a single dose of a penicillin[3] in the previous month, including those with a prosthetic valve (but not those who have had endocarditis), oral amoxicillin 3 g 1 hour before procedure; CHILD under 5 years quarter adult dose; 5–10 years half adult dose

patients who are penicillin-allergic or have received more than a single dose of a penicillin[3] in the previous month, oral clindamycin[4] 600 mg 1 hour before procedure; CHILD under 5 years clindamycin[4] 150 mg *or* azithromycin[5] 200 mg; 5–10 years clindamycin[4] 300 mg *or* azithromycin[5] 300 mg

patients who have had endocarditis, amoxicillin + gentamicin, as under general anaesthesia

**Dental procedures**[2] *under general anaesthesia*,

*no special risk* (including patients who have not received more than a single dose of a penicillin in the previous month),
*either* i/v amoxicillin 1 g at induction, then oral amoxicillin 500 mg 6 hours later; CHILD under 5 years quarter adult dose; 5–10 years half adult dose
*or* oral amoxicillin 3 g 4 hours before induction then oral amoxicillin 3 g as soon as possible after procedure; CHILD under 5 years quarter adult dose; 5–10 years half adult dose

*special risk* (patients with a prosthetic valve or who have had endocarditis), i/v amoxicillin 1 g + i/v gentamicin 120 mg at induction, then oral amoxicillin 500 mg 6 hours later; CHILD under 5 years amoxicillin quarter adult dose, gentamicin 2 mg/kg; 5–10 years amoxicillin half adult dose, gentamicin 2 mg/kg

patients who are penicillin-allergic or who have received more than a single dose of a penicillin in the previous month,
*either* i/v vancomycin 1 g over at least 100 minutes then i/v gentamicin 120 mg at induction or 15 minutes before procedure; CHILD under 10 years vancomycin 20 mg/kg, gentamicin 2 mg/kg
*or* i/v teicoplanin 400 mg + gentamicin 120 mg at induction or 15 minutes before procedure; CHILD under 14 years teicoplanin 6 mg/kg, gentamicin 2 mg/kg
*or* i/v clindamycin[4] 300 mg over at least 10 minutes at induction or 15 minutes before procedure then oral or i/v clindamycin 150 mg 6 hours later; CHILD under 5 years quarter adult dose; 5–10 years half adult dose

**Upper respiratory-tract procedures**, as for dental procedures; post-operative dose may be given parenterally if swallowing is painful

**Genito-urinary procedures**, as for *special risk* patients undergoing dental procedures under general anaesthesia except that clindamycin is not given, see above; if urine infected, prophylaxis should also cover infective organism

**Obstetric, gynaecological and gastro-intestinal procedures** (prophylaxis required for patients with prosthetic valves or those who have had endocarditis only), as for genito-urinary procedures

### Joint prostheses and dental treatment

Advice of a Working Party of the British Society for Antimicrobial Chemotherapy is that patients with prosthetic joint implants (including total hip replacements) do not require antibiotic prophylaxis for dental treatment. The Working Party considers that it is unacceptable to expose patients to the adverse effects of antibiotics when there is no evidence that such prophylaxis is of any benefit, but that those who develop any intercurrent infection require prompt treatment with antibiotics to which the infecting organisms are sensitive.
The Working Party has commented that joint infections have rarely been shown to follow dental procedures and are even more rarely caused by oral streptococci.

### Dermatological procedures

Advice of a Working Party of the British Society for Antimicrobial Chemotherapy is that patients who undergo dermatological procedures[6] do not require antibacterial prophylaxis against endocarditis.

### Immunosuppression and indwelling intraperitoneal catheters

Advice of a Working Party of the British Society for Antimicrobial Chemotherapy is that patients who are immunosuppressed (including transplant patients) and patients with indwelling intraperitoneal catheters do not require antibiotic prophylaxis for dental treatment provided there is no other indication for prophylaxis.
The Working Party has commented that there is little evidence that dental treatment is followed by infection in immunosuppressed and immunodeficient patients nor is there evidence that dental treatment is followed by infection in patients with indwelling intraperitoneal catheters.

1. Advice on the prevention of endocarditis reflects the recommendations of a Working Party of the British Society for Antimicrobial Chemotherapy, *Lancet*, 1982, **2**, 1323–26; *idem*, 1986, **1**, 1267; *idem*, 1990, **335**, 88–9; *idem*, 1992, **339**, 1292–93; *idem*, 1997, **350**, 1100; also *J Antimicrob Chemother*, 1993; **31**, 437–8
2. Dental procedures that require antibacterial prophylaxis are, *extractions*, *scaling*, and *surgery involving gingival tissues* (see also p. 23). Antibiotic prophylaxis for dental procedures may be supplemented with *chlorhexidine gluconate gel 1%* or *chlorhexidine gluconate mouthwash 0.2%*, used 5 minutes before procedure. Oral antibacterial should be taken in the presence of a dental surgeon or a dental nurse
3. For multistage procedures a max. of 2 single doses of a penicillin may be given in a month; alternative drugs should be used for further treatment and the penicillin should not be used again for 3–4 months
4. If **clindamycin** is used, periodontal or other multistage procedures should not be repeated at intervals of less than 2 weeks; clindamycin is not licensed for use in endocarditis prophylaxis but it is recommended by the Endocarditis Working Party
5. Azithromycin is not licensed for use in endocarditis prophylaxis but it is recommended by the Endocarditis Working Party
6. The British Association of Dermatologists Therapy Guidelines and Audit Subcommittee advise that such dermatological procedures include skin biopsies and excision of moles or of malignant lesions

### Prevention of recurrence of *rheumatic fever*

Phenoxymethylpenicillin 250 mg twice daily *or* sulfadiazine 1 g daily (500 mg daily for patients under 30 kg)

### Prevention of secondary case of group A streptococcal infection

Phenoxymethylpenicillin 250–500 mg every 6 hours for 10 days; CHILD under 1 year 62.5 mg every 6 hours, 1–5 years 125 mg every 6 hours, 6–12 years 250 mg every 6 hours

*or* erythromycin[1] (if penicillin-allergic) ADULT and CHILD over 8 years, 250–500 mg every 6 hours for 10 days; CHILD under 2 years 125 mg every 6 hours, 2–8 years 250 mg every 6 hours

### Prevention of secondary case of *diphtheria* in non-immune patient

Erythromycin 500 mg every 6 hours for 7 days; CHILD up to 2 years 125 mg every 6 hours, 2–8 years 250 mg every 6 hours

Treat for further 10 days if nasopharyngeal swabs positive after first 7 days' treatment

### Prevention of secondary case of *pertussis* in non-immune patient or partially immune patient

Erythromycin[1] ADULT and CHILD over 8 years, 250–500 mg every 6 hours for 7 days; CHILD under 2 years 125 mg every 6 hours, 2–8 years 250 mg every 6 hours

### Prevention of *pneumococcal infection* in asplenia or in patients with sickle cell disease

Phenoxymethylpenicillin 500 mg every 12 hours; CHILD under 5 years 125 mg every 12 hours, 6–12 years 250 mg every 12 hours—if cover also needed for *H. influenzae* in CHILD give amoxicillin instead (under 5 years 125 mg every 12 hours, over 5 years 250 mg every 12 hours)

**Note** Antibiotic prophylaxis is not fully reliable; for vaccines in asplenia see p. 612

### Prevention of *gas-gangrene* in high lower-limb amputations or following major trauma

Benzylpenicillin 300–600 mg every 6 hours for 5 days *or* if penicillin-allergic metronidazole 400–500 mg every 8 hours

### Prevention of *tuberculosis* in susceptible close contacts or those who have become tuberculin positive[2]

Isoniazid 300 mg daily for 6 months; CHILD 5–10 mg/kg daily (max. 300 mg daily)

*or* isoniazid 300 mg daily + rifampicin 600 mg daily (450 mg if less than 50 kg) for 3 months; CHILD isoniazid 5–10 mg/kg daily (max. 300 mg daily) + rifampicin 10 mg/kg daily (max. 600 mg daily)

1. Where erythromycin is suggested another macrolide (e.g. azithromycin or clarithromycin) may be used.

### Prevention of infection in *gastro-intestinal* procedures

Operations on stomach or oesophagus for carcinoma

Single dose[3] of i/v gentamicin *or* i/v cefuroxime

Open biliary surgery

Single dose[3] of i/v cefuroxime + i/v metronidazole[4] *or* i/v gentamicin + i/v metronidazole[4]

Resections of colon and rectum for carcinoma, and resections in inflammatory bowel disease, and appendicectomy

Single dose[3] of i/v gentamicin + i/v metronidazole[4] *or* i/v cefuroxime + i/v metronidazole[4] *or* i/v co-amoxiclav alone

Endoscopic retrograde cholangiopancreatography

Single dose of i/v gentamicin *or* oral or i/v ciprofloxacin

Prophylaxis particularly recommended if bile stasis, pancreatic pseudocyst, previous cholangitis or neutropenia

### Prevention of infection in *orthopaedic* surgery

Joint replacement including hip and knee and management of fractures

Single dose[3] of i/v cefuroxime or i/v flucloxacillin

Substitute i/v vancomycin if history of allergy to penicillins or to cephalosporins; use cefuroxime + metronidazole for complex open fractures with extensive soft-tissue damage; prophylaxis continued for 24 hours in open fractures (longer if complex open fractures)

### Prevention of infection in *urological* procedures

Transrectal prostate biopsy

Single dose[3] of i/v cefuroxime + i/v metronidazole[4] *or* i/v gentamicin + i/v metronidazole[4]

Transurethral resection of prostate

Single dose[3] of oral ciprofloxacin *or* i/v gentamicin *or* i/v cefuroxime

2. The Joint Tuberculosis Committee recommends chemoprophylaxis for patients with documented recent tuberculin conversion, for some tuberculin-positive children identified in BCG schools programme, for children under 2 years in close contact with smear-positive tuberculosis (including those previously vaccinated with BCG but now showing strongly positive tuberculin test), for children under 16 years showing a positive tuberculin test at new immigrant or contact screening; chemoprophylaxis should be considered in immigrant adults 16–34 years without a BCG scar but with strongly positive tuberculin test. See also section 5.1.9, for advice on immunocompromised patients and on prevention of tuberculosis
3. Additional intra-operative or postoperative doses of antibacterial may be given for prolonged procedures or if there is major blood loss
4. Metronidazole may alternatively be given by suppository but to allow adequate absorption, it should be given 2 hours before surgery

### Prevention of infection in *obstetric* and *gynaecological* surgery

Caesarean section

Single dose[1] of i/v cefuroxime

Administer immediately after umbilical cord is clamped; substitute i/v clindamycin if history of allergy to penicillins or cephalosporins

Hysterectomy

Single dose[1] of i/v cefuroxime + i/v metronidazole[2] *or* i/v gentamicin + i/v metronidazole[2] *or* i/v co-amoxiclav alone

Termination of pregnancy

Single dose[1] of oral metronidazole

If genital chlamydial infection cannot be ruled out, give doxycycline (section 5.1.3) postoperatively

### Prevention of infection in *vascular* surgery

Reconstructive arterial surgery of abdomen, pelvis or legs

Single dose[1] of i/v cefuroxime *or* i/v gentamicin

Add i/v metronidazole for patients at risk from anaerobic infections including those with diabetes, gangrene, or undergoing amputation; substitute i/v vancomycin for cefuroxime or gentamicin if high risk of meticillin-resistant *Staphylococcus aureus*

## 5.1.1 Penicillins

5.1.1.1 Benzylpenicillin and phenoxymethylpenicillin
5.1.1.2 Penicillinase-resistant penicillins
5.1.1.3 Broad-spectrum penicillins
5.1.1.4 Antipseudomonal penicillins
5.1.1.5 Mecillinams

The penicillins are bactericidal and act by interfering with bacterial cell wall synthesis. They diffuse well into body tissues and fluids, but penetration into the cerebrospinal fluid is poor except when the meninges are inflamed. They are excreted in the urine in therapeutic concentrations.

The most important side-effect of the penicillins is hypersensitivity which causes rashes and anaphylaxis and can be fatal. Allergic reactions to penicillins occur in 1–10% of exposed individuals; anaphylactic reactions occur in fewer than 0.05% of treated patients. Patients with a history of atopic allergy (e.g. asthma, eczema, hay fever) are at a higher risk of severe anaphylactic reactions to penicillins. Individuals with a history of anaphylaxis, urticaria, or rash immediately after penicillin administration are at risk of immediate hypersensitivity to a penicillin; these individuals should not receive a penicillin, a cephalosporin or another beta-lactam antibiotic. Patients who are allergic to one penicillin will be allergic to all because the hypersensitivity is related to the basic penicillin structure. Individuals with a history of a minor rash (i.e. non-confluent rash restricted to a small area of the body) or a rash that occurs more than 72 hours after penicillin administration are probably not allergic to penicillin and in these individuals a penicillin should not be withheld unnecessarily for serious infections; the possibility of an allergic reaction should, however, be borne in mind.

A rare but serious toxic effect of the penicillins is encephalopathy due to cerebral irritation. This may result from excessively high doses or in patients with severe renal failure. The penicillins should **not** be given by intrathecal injection because they can cause encephalopathy which may be fatal.

Another problem relating to high doses of penicillin, or normal doses given to patients with renal failure, is the accumulation of electrolyte since most injectable penicillins contain either sodium or potassium.

Diarrhoea frequently occurs during oral penicillin therapy. It is most common with broad-spectrum penicillins, which can also cause antibiotic-associated colitis.

1. Additional intra-operative or postoperative doses of antibacterial may be given for prolonged procedures or if there is major blood loss
2. Metronidazole may alternatively be given by suppository but to allow adequate absorption, it should be given 2 hours before surgery

### 5.1.1.1 Benzylpenicillin and phenoxymethylpenicillin

**Benzylpenicillin** (Penicillin G) remains an important and useful antibiotic but is inactivated by bacterial beta-lactamases. It is effective for many streptococcal (including pneumococcal), gonococcal, and meningococcal infections and also for anthrax (section 5.1.12), diphtheria, gas-gangrene, leptospirosis, and treatment of Lyme disease (section 5.1.1.3) in children. Pneumococci, meningococci, and gonococci which have decreased sensitivity to penicillin have been isolated; benzylpenicillin is no longer the drug of first choice for pneumococcal meningitis. Although benzylpenicillin is effective in the treatment of tetanus, metronidazole (section 5.1.11) is preferred. Benzylpenicillin is inactivated by gastric acid and absorption from the gut is low; therefore it is best given by injection.

**Procaine benzylpenicillin** (procaine penicillin) (available on a named-patient basis from IDIS) is used for the treatment of early syphilis and late latent syphilis; it is given in a dose of 600 mg daily by intramuscular injection.

**Phenoxymethylpenicillin** (Penicillin V) has a similar antibacterial spectrum to benzylpenicillin, but is less active. It is gastric acid-stable, so is suitable for oral administration. It should not be used for serious infections because absorption can be unpredictable and plasma concentrations variable. It is indicated principally for respiratory-tract infections in children, for streptococcal tonsillitis, and for continuing treatment after one or more injections of benzylpenicillin when clinical response has begun. It should not be used for meningococcal or gonococcal infections. Phenoxymethylpenicillin is used for prophylaxis against streptococcal infections following rheumatic fever and against pneumococcal infections following splenectomy or in sickle-cell disease.

**Oral infections** Phenoxymethylpenicillin is effective for dentoalveolar abscess.

## BENZYLPENICILLIN
(Penicillin G)

**Indications** throat infections, otitis media, endocarditis, meningococcal disease, pneumonia, cellulitis (Table 1, section 5.1); anthrax; prophylaxis in limb amputation (Table 2, section 5.1); see also notes above

**Cautions** history of allergy; false-positive urinary glucose (if tested for reducing substances); renal impairment (Appendix 3); **interactions:** Appendix 1 (penicillins)

**Contra-indications** penicillin hypersensitivity

**Side-effects** hypersensitivity reactions including urticaria, fever, joint pains, rashes, angioedema, anaphylaxis, serum sickness-like reaction; *rarely* CNS toxicity including convulsions (especially with high doses or in severe renal impairment), interstitial nephritis, haemolytic anaemia, leucopenia, thrombocytopenia, and coagulation disorders; also reported diarrhoea (including antibiotic-associated colitis)

**Dose**
- By intramuscular *or* by slow intravenous injection *or* by infusion, 2.4–4.8 g daily in 4 divided doses, increased if necessary in more serious infections (single doses over 1.2 g intravenous route only; see also below); PRETERM NEONATE and NEONATE under 1 week, 50 mg/kg daily in 2 divided doses; NEONATE 1–4 weeks, 75 mg/kg daily in 3 divided doses; CHILD 1 month–12 years, 100 mg/kg daily in 4 divided doses (higher doses may be required, see also below); intravenous route recommended in neonates and infants
- Endocarditis (in combination with another antibacterial if necessary, see Table 1, section 5.1), by slow intravenous injection *or* by infusion, 7.2 g daily in 6 divided doses, increased if necessary (e.g. in enterococcal endocarditis or if benzylpenicillin used alone) to 14.4 g daily in 6 divided doses
- Anthrax (in combination with other antibacterials, see also section 5.1.12), by slow intravenous injection or by infusion, 2.4 g every 4 hours; CHILD 150 mg/kg daily in 4 divided doses
- Intrapartum prophylaxis against group B streptococcal infection, by slow intravenous injection *or* by infusion, initially 3 g then 1.5 g every 4 hours until delivery
- Meningococcal disease, by slow intravenous injection *or* by infusion, 2.4 g every 4 hours; PRETERM NEONATE and NEONATE under 1 week, 100 mg/kg daily in 2 divided doses; NEONATE 1–4 weeks, 150 mg/kg daily in 3 divided doses; CHILD 1 month–12 years, 180–300 mg/kg daily in 4–6 divided doses

  **Important.** If bacterial meningitis and especially if meningococcal disease is suspected general practitioners are advised to give a single injection of benzylpenicillin by intravenous injection (or by intramuscular injection) before transferring the patient urgently to hospital. Suitable doses are: ADULT 1.2 g; INFANT under 1 year 300 mg; CHILD 1–9 years 600 mg, 10 years and over as for adult. In **penicillin allergy**, cefotaxime (section 5.1.2) may be an alternative; chloramphenicol may be used if there is a history of anaphylaxis to penicillins
- By intrathecal injection, **not** recommended

**Note** Benzylpenicillin doses in BNF may differ from those in product literature

**Crystapen®** (Britannia) PoM
Injection, powder for reconstitution, benzylpenicillin sodium (unbuffered), net price 600-mg vial = 43p, 2-vial 'GP pack' = £1.90; 1.2-g vial = 87p
Electrolytes $Na^+$ 1.68 mmol/600-mg vial; 3.36 mmol/1.2-g vial

## PHENOXYMETHYLPENICILLIN
(Penicillin V)

**Indications** oral infections (see notes above); tonsillitis, otitis media, erysipelas, cellulitis; rheumatic fever and pneumococcal infection prophylaxis (Table 2, section 5.1)

**Cautions** see under Benzylpenicillin; **interactions:** Appendix 1 (penicillins)

**Contra-indications** see under Benzylpenicillin

**Side-effects** see under Benzylpenicillin

**Dose**
- 500 mg every 6 hours increased up to 1 g every 6 hours in severe infections; CHILD up to 1 year 62.5 mg every 6 hours, increased up to 12.5 mg/kg every 6 hours in severe infections; 1–5 years, 125 mg every 6 hours, increased up to 12.5 mg/kg every 6 hours in severe infections; 6–12 years, 250 mg every 6 hours, increased up to 12.5 mg/kg every 6 hours in severe infections

**Note** Phenoxymethylpenicillin doses in the BNF may differ from those in product literature

**Phenoxymethylpenicillin** (Non-proprietary) PoM
Tablets, phenoxymethylpenicillin (as potassium salt) 250 mg, net price 28-tab pack = £1.67. Label: 9, 23

Oral solution, phenoxymethylpenicillin (as potassium salt) for reconstitution with water, net price 125 mg/5 mL, 100 mL = £1.59; 250 mg/5 mL, 100 mL = £2.22. Label: 9, 23

**Dental prescribing on NHS** Phenoxymethylpenicillin Tablets and Oral Solution may be prescribed

## 5.1.1.2 Penicillinase-resistant penicillins

Most staphylococci are now resistant to benzylpenicillin because they produce penicillinases. **Flucloxacillin**, however, is not inactivated by these enzymes and is thus effective in infections caused by penicillin-resistant staphylococci, which is the sole indication for its use. Flucloxacillin is acid-stable and can, therefore, be given by mouth as well as by injection.

Flucloxacillin is well absorbed from the gut. For CSM warning on hepatic disorders see under Flucloxacillin.

**MRSA** *Staphylococcus aureus* strains resistant to meticillin [now discontinued] (meticillin-resistant *Staph. aureus*, MRSA) and to flucloxacillin have emerged; some of these organisms may be sensitive to vancomycin or teicoplanin (section 5.1.7). Strains may be susceptible to rifampicin, sodium fusidate, tetracyclines, aminoglycosides, macrolides, and clindamycin. Rifampicin or sodium fusidate should not be used alone because resistance may develop rapidly. Trimethoprim alone may be used for urinary-tract infections caused by some MRSA strains. Linezolid (section 5.1.7) and the combination of the streptogramin antibiotics quinupristin and dalfopristin (section 5.1.7) are active against MRSA but these antibacterial drugs should be reserved for organisms resistant to treatment with other antibacterials or for patients who cannot tolerate other antibacterial drugs. Treatment is guided by the sensitivity of the infecting strain. For eradication of nasal carriage of MRSA see section 12.2.3.

## FLUCLOXACILLIN

**Indications** infections due to beta-lactamase-producing staphylococci including otitis externa; adjunct in pneumonia, impetigo, cellulitis, osteomyelitis and in staphylococcal endocarditis (Table 1, section 5.1)

**Cautions** see under Benzylpenicillin (section 5.1.1.1); also hepatic impairment (see CSM advice below); risk of kernicterus in jaundiced neonates when high doses given parenterally

**CSM advice (hepatic disorders)**
CSM has advised that very rarely cholestatic jaundice and hepatitis may occur up to several weeks after treatment with flucloxacillin has been stopped. Administration for more than 2 weeks and increasing age are risk factors. CSM has reminded that:

- flucloxacillin should not be used in patients with a history of hepatic dysfunction associated with flucloxacillin;
- flucloxacillin should be used with caution in patients with hepatic impairment;
- careful enquiry should be made about hypersensitivity reactions to beta-lactam antibacterials.

**Contra-indications** see under Benzylpenicillin (section 5.1.1.1)

**Side-effects** see under Benzylpenicillin (section 5.1.1.1); also gastro-intestinal disturbances; *very rarely* hepatitis and cholestatic jaundice (see also CSM advice above)

**Dose**

- By mouth, 250–500 mg every 6 hours, at least 30 minutes before food; CHILD under 2 years quarter adult dose; 2–10 years half adult dose
- By intramuscular injection, 250–500 mg every 6 hours; CHILD under 2 years quarter adult dose; 2–10 years half adult dose
- By slow intravenous injection *or* by intravenous infusion, 0.25–2 g every 6 hours; CHILD under 2 years quarter adult dose; 2–10 years half adult dose

Endocarditis (in combination with another antibacterial, see Table 1, section 5.1), body-weight under 85 kg, 8 g daily in 4 divided doses; body-weight over 85 kg, 12 g daily in 6 divided doses

Osteomyelitis (see Table 1, section 5.1), up to 8 g daily in 3–4 divided doses

**Note** Flucloxacillin doses in BNF may differ from those in product literature

**Flucloxacillin** (Non-proprietary) PoM

Capsules, flucloxacillin (as sodium salt) 250 mg, net price 20 = £2.17; 500 mg, 20 = £3.78. Label: 9, 23
Brands include *Flucломix®*, *Galfloxin®*, *Ladropen®*

Oral solution (= elixir or syrup), flucloxacillin (as sodium salt) for reconstitution with water, 125 mg/5 mL, net price 100 mL = £3.88; 250 mg/5 mL, 100 mL = £6.97. Label: 9, 23
Brands include *Ladropen®*

Injection, powder for reconstitution, flucloxacillin (as sodium salt). Net price 250-mg vial = 91p; 500-mg vial = £1.81; 1-g vial = £3.63

**Floxapen®** (GSK) PoM

Capsules, both black/caramel, flucloxacillin (as sodium salt) 250 mg, net price 28-cap pack = £6.31; 500 mg, 28-cap pack = £12.66. Label: 9, 23

Syrup, tutti-frutti-and menthol-flavoured, flucloxacillin (as magnesium salt) for reconstitution with water, 125 mg/5 mL, net price 100 mL = £3.25; 250 mg/5 mL, 100 mL = £6.48. Label: 9, 23
Excipients include sucrose

Injection, powder for reconstitution, flucloxacillin (as sodium salt). Net price 250-mg vial = 91p; 500-mg vial = £1.81; 1-g vial = £3.63
Electrolytes $Na^+$ 0.57 mmol/250-mg vial, 1.13 mmol/500-mg vial, 2.26 mmol/1-g vial

### 5.1.1.3 Broad-spectrum penicillins

**Ampicillin** is active against certain Gram-positive and Gram-negative organisms but is inactivated by penicillinases including those produced by *Staphylococcus aureus* and by common Gram-negative bacilli such as *Escherichia coli*. Almost all staphylococci, 50% of *E. coli* strains and 15% of *Haemophilus influenzae* strains are now resistant. The likelihood of resistance should therefore be considered before using ampicillin for the 'blind' treatment of infections; in particular, it should not be used for hospital patients without checking sensitivity.

Ampicillin is well excreted in the bile and urine. It is principally indicated for the treatment of exacerbations of chronic bronchitis and middle ear infections, both of which may be due to *Streptococcus pneumoniae* and *H. influenzae*, and for urinary-tract infections (section 5.1.13).

Ampicillin can be given by mouth but less than half the dose is absorbed, and absorption is further decreased by the presence of food in the gut.

Maculopapular rashes commonly occur with ampicillin (and amoxicillin) but are not usually related to true penicillin allergy. They almost always occur in patients with glandular fever; broad-spectrum penicillins should not therefore be used for 'blind' treatment of a sore throat. Rashes are also common in patients with acute or chronic lymphocytic leukaemia or in cytomegalovirus infection.

**Amoxicillin** (amoxycillin) is a derivative of ampicillin and has a similar antibacterial spectrum. It is better absorbed than ampicillin when given by mouth, producing higher plasma and tissue concentrations; unlike ampicillin, absorption is not affected by the presence of food in the stomach. Amoxicillin is used for endocarditis prophylaxis (section 5.1, table 2); it may also be used for the treatment of Lyme disease [not licensed], see below.

**Co-amoxiclav** consists of amoxicillin with the beta-lactamase inhibitor clavulanic acid. Clavulanic acid itself has no significant antibacterial activity but, by inactivating beta-lactamases, it makes the combination active against beta-lactamase-producing bacteria that are resistant to amoxicillin. These include resistant strains of *Staph. aureus*, *E. coli*, and *H. influenzae*, as well as many *Bacteroides* and *Klebsiella* spp. Co-amoxiclav should be reserved for infections likely, or known, to be caused by amoxicillin-resistant beta-lactamase-producing strains; for CSM warning on cholestatic jaundice see under Co-amoxiclav.

A combination of ampicillin with flucloxacillin (as co-fluampicil) is available to treat infections involving either streptococci or staphylococci (e.g. cellulitis).

**Lyme disease** Lyme disease should generally be treated by those experienced in its management. **Doxycycline** is the antibacterial of choice for *early Lyme disease*. **Amoxicillin** [unlicensed indication], **cefuroxime axetil**, or **azithromycin** [unlicensed indication] are alternatives if doxycycline is contra-indicated. Intravenous administration of **cefotaxime**, **ceftriaxone**, or **benzylpenicillin** is recommended for Lyme disease associated with moderate to severe *cardiac* or neurological abnormalities, *late Lyme disease*, and *Lyme arthritis*. The duration of treatment is generally 2–4 weeks; Lyme arthritis requires longer treatment with oral antibacterial drugs.

**Oral infections** Amoxicillin or ampicillin are as effective as phenoxymethylpenicillin (section 5.1.1.1) but they are better absorbed; however, they may encourage emergence of resistant organisms. Like phenoxymethylpenicillin, amoxicillin and ampicillin are ineffective against bacteria that produce beta-lactamases. Amoxicillin may be useful for short-course oral regimens. Amoxicillin is also used for prophylaxis of endocarditis (Table 2, section 5.1).

## AMOXICILLIN
(Amoxycillin)

**Indications** see under Ampicillin; oral infections (see notes above); also endocarditis prophylaxis (Table 2, section 5.1) and treatment (Table 1, section 5.1); anthrax (section 5.1.12); adjunct in listerial meningitis (Table 1, section 5.1); *Helicobacter pylori* eradication (section 1.3)

**Cautions** see under Ampicillin; maintain adequate hydration with high doses (particularly during parenteral therapy)

**Contra-indications** see under Ampicillin

**Side-effects** see under Ampicillin

**Dose**

- By mouth, 250 mg every 8 hours, doubled in severe infections; CHILD up to 10 years, 125 mg every 8 hours, doubled in severe infections

  Otitis media, 1 g every 8 hours; CHILD 40 mg/kg daily in 3 divided doses (max. 3 g daily)

  Pneumonia, 0.5–1 g every 8 hours

  Anthrax (treatment and post-exposure prophylaxis—see also section 5.1.12), 500 mg every 8 hours; CHILD body-weight under 20 kg, 80 mg/kg daily in 3 divided doses, body-weight over 20 kg, adult dose
- Short-course oral therapy

  Dental abscess, 3 g repeated after 8 hours

  Urinary-tract infections, 3 g repeated after 10–12 hours
- By intramuscular injection, 500 mg every 8 hours; CHILD, 50–100 mg/kg daily in divided doses
- By intravenous injection *or* infusion, 500 mg every 8 hours increased to 1 g every 6 hours in severe infections; CHILD, 50–100 mg/kg daily in divided doses
- Listerial meningitis (in combination with another antibiotic, see Table 1, section 5.1), by intravenous infusion, 2 g every 4 hours for 10–14 days
- Endocarditis (in combination with another antibiotic if necessary, see Table 1, section 5.1), by intravenous infusion, 2 g every 6 hours, increased to 2 g every 4 hours e.g. in enterococcal endocarditis or if amoxicillin used alone

**Note** Amoxicillin doses in BNF may differ from those in product literature

**Amoxicillin** (Non-proprietary) PoM

Capsules, amoxicillin (as trihydrate) 250 mg, net price 21 = £1.29; 500 mg, 21 = £1.69. Label: 9

Brands include *Amix®*, *Amoram®*, *Amoxident®*, *Galenamox®*, *Rimoxallin®*

Oral suspension, amoxicillin (as trihydrate) for reconstitution with water, 125 mg/5 mL, net price 100 mL = £1.23; 250 mg/5 mL, 100 mL = £1.75. Label: 9

**Note** Sugar-free versions are available and can be ordered by specifying 'sugar-free' on the prescription

Brands include *Amix®*, *Amoram®*, *Galenamox®*, *Rimoxallin®*

Sachets, sugar-free, amoxicillin (as trihydrate) 3 g/sachet, net price 2-sachet pack = £5.12, 14-sachet pack = £31.94. Label: 9, 13

Injection, powder for reconstitution, amoxicillin (as sodium salt), net price 250-mg vial = 32p; 500-mg vial = 58p; 1-g vial = £1.16

**Dental prescribing on NHS** Amoxicillin Capsules and Oral Suspension may be prescribed. Amoxicillin Sachets may be prescribed as Amoxicillin Oral Powder

**Amoxil®** (GSK) PoM

Capsules, both maroon/gold, amoxicillin (as trihydrate), 250 mg, net price 21-cap pack = £3.59; 500 mg, 21-cap pack = £7.19. Label: 9

Syrup SF, both sugar-free, peach- strawberry- and lemon-flavoured, amoxicillin (as trihydrate) for reconstitution with water, 125 mg/5 mL, net price 100 mL = 59p; 250 mg/5 mL, 100 mL = 59p. Label: 9

Paediatric suspension, amoxicillin 125 mg (as trihydrate)/1.25 mL when reconstituted with water, net price 20 mL (peach- strawberry- and lemon-flavoured) = £3.38. Label: 9, counselling , use of pipette

Excipients include sucrose 600 mg/1.25 mL

Sachets SF, powder, sugar-free, amoxicillin (as trihydrate) 3 g/sachet, 2-sachet pack (peach- strawberry- and lemon-flavoured) = £2.99. Label: 9, 13

Injection, powder for reconstitution, amoxicillin (as sodium salt), net price 500-mg vial = 58p; 1-g vial = £1.16

Electrolytes $Na^+$ 3.3 mmol/g

## AMPICILLIN

**Indications** urinary-tract infections, otitis media, sinusitis, oral infections (see notes above), bronchitis, uncomplicated community-acquired pneumonia (Table 1, section 5.1), *Haemophilus influenzae* infections, invasive salmonellosis; listerial meningitis (Table 1, section 5.1)

**Cautions** history of allergy; renal impairment (Appendix 3); erythematous rashes common in glandular fever, cytomegalovirus infection, and acute or chronic lymphocytic leukaemia (see notes above); **interactions**: Appendix 1 (penicillins)

**Contra-indications** penicillin hypersensitivity

**Side-effects** nausea, vomiting, diarrhoea; rashes (discontinue treatment); rarely, antibiotic-associated colitis; see also under Benzylpenicillin (section 5.1.1.1)

**Dose**

- By mouth, 0.25–1 g every 6 hours, at least 30 minutes before food; CHILD under 10 years, half adult dose

5 Infections

Urinary-tract infections, 500 mg every 8 hours; CHILD under 10 years, half adult dose

- By intramuscular injection *or* intravenous injection *or* infusion, 500 mg every 4–6 hours; CHILD under 10 years, half adult dose
- Endocarditis (in combination with another antibiotic if necessary), by intravenous infusion, 2 g every 6 hours, increased to 2 g every 4 hours e.g. in enterococcal endocarditis or if ampicillin used alone
- Listerial meningitis (in combination with another antibiotic), by intravenous infusion, 2 g every 4 hours for 10–14 days; NEONATE 50 mg/kg every 6 hours; INFANT 1–3 months, 50–100 mg/kg every 6 hours; CHILD 3 months–12 years, 100 mg/kg every 6 hours (max. 12 g daily)

**Note** Ampicillin doses in BNF may differ from those in product literature

**Ampicillin** (Non-proprietary) PoM

Capsules, ampicillin 250 mg, net price 20 = £2.30; 500 mg, 20 = £3.15. Label: 9, 23
Brands include *Rimacillin®*

Oral suspension, ampicillin 125 mg/5 mL when reconstituted with water, net price 100 mL = £2.63; 250 mg/5 mL, 100 mL = £4.56. Label: 9, 23
Brands include *Rimacillin®*

Injection, powder for reconstitution, ampicillin (as sodium salt), net price 500-mg vial = 68p

**Dental prescribing on NHS** Ampicillin Capsules and Oral Suspension may be prescribed

**Penbritin®** (Chemidex) PoM

Capsules, grey/red, ampicillin (as trihydrate) 250 mg, net price 28-cap pack = £2.10; 500 mg, 28-cap pack = £5.28.Label: 9, 23

**With flucloxacillin**

See Co-fluampicil

## CO-AMOXICLAV

A mixture of amoxicillin (as the trihydrate or as the sodium salt) and clavulanic acid (as potassium clavulanate); the proportions are expressed in the form $x/y$ where $x$ and $y$ are the strengths in milligrams of amoxicillin and clavulanic acid respectively

**Indications** infections due to beta-lactamase-producing strains (where amoxicillin alone not appropriate) including respiratory-tract infections, genito-urinary and abdominal infections, cellulitis, animal bites, severe dental infection with spreading cellulitis

**Cautions** see under Ampicillin and notes above; also caution in hepatic impairment (monitor hepatic function), pregnancy; maintain adequate hydration with high doses (particularly during parenteral therapy)

**Cholestatic jaundice** CSM has advised that cholestatic jaundice can occur either during or shortly after the use of co-amoxiclav. An epidemiological study has shown that the risk of acute liver toxicity was about 6 times greater with co-amoxiclav than with amoxicillin. Cholestatic jaundice is more common in patients above the age of 65 years and in men; these reactions have only rarely been reported in children. Jaundice is usually self-limiting and very rarely fatal. The duration of treatment should be appropriate to the indication and should not usually exceed 14 days

**Contra-indications** penicillin hypersensitivity, history of co-amoxiclav-associated or penicillin-associated jaundice or hepatic dysfunction

**Side-effects** see under Ampicillin; hepatitis, cholestatic jaundice (see above); Stevens-Johnson syndrome, toxic epidermal necrolysis, exfoliative dermatitis, vasculitis reported; rarely prolongation of bleeding time, dizziness, headache, convulsions (particularly with high doses or in renal impairment); superficial staining of teeth with suspension, phlebitis at injection site

**Dose**

- By mouth, expressed as amoxicillin, 250 mg every 8 hours, dose doubled in severe infections; CHILD see under preparations below (under 6 years *Augmentin® '125/31 SF'* suspension; 6–12 years *Augmentin® '250/62 SF'* suspension *or* for short-term treatment with twice daily dosage in CHILD 2 months–12 years *Augmentin-Duo® 400/57* suspension)

  Severe dental infections (but not generally first-line, see notes above), expressed as amoxicillin, 250 mg every 8 hours for 5 days
- By intravenous injection over 3–4 minutes *or* by intravenous infusion, expressed as amoxicillin, 1 g every 8 hours increased to 1 g every 6 hours in more serious infections; INFANTS up to 3 months 25 mg/kg every 8 hours (every 12 hours in the perinatal period and in premature infants); CHILD 3 months–12 years, 25 mg/kg every 8 hours increased to 25 mg/kg every 6 hours in more serious infections

  Surgical prophylaxis, expressed as amoxicillin, 1 g at induction; for high risk procedures (e.g. colorectal surgery) up to 2–3 further doses of 1 g may be given every 8 hours

**Co-amoxiclav** (Non-proprietary) PoM

Tablets, co-amoxiclav 250/125 (amoxicillin 250 mg as trihydrate, clavulanic acid 125 mg as potassium salt), net price 21-tab pack = £4.47. Label: 9

Tablets, co-amoxiclav 500/125 (amoxicillin 500 mg as trihydrate, clavulanic acid 125 mg as potassium salt), net price 21-tab pack = £11.30. Label: 9

Oral suspension, co-amoxiclav 125/31 (amoxicillin 125 mg as trihydrate, clavulanic acid 31.25 mg as potassium salt)/5 mL when reconstituted with water, net price 100 mL = £4.18. Label: 9

Oral suspension, co-amoxiclav 250/62 (amoxicillin 250 mg as trihydrate, clavulanic acid 62.5 mg as potassium salt)/5 mL when reconstituted with water, net price 100 mL = £5.48. Label: 9

Injection 500/100, powder for reconstitution, co-amoxiclav 500/100 (amoxicillin 500 mg as sodium salt, clavulanic acid 100 mg as potassium salt), net price per vial = £1.49

Injection 1000/200, powder for reconstitution, co-amoxiclav 1000/200 (amoxicillin 1 g as sodium salt, clavulanic acid 200 mg as potassium salt), net price per vial = £2.97

**Augmentin®** (GSK) PoM

Tablets 375 mg, f/c, co-amoxiclav 250/125 (amoxicillin 250 mg as trihydrate, clavulanic acid 125 mg as potassium salt), net price 21-tab pack = £4.45. Label: 9

Tablets 625 mg, f/c, co-amoxiclav 500/125 (amoxicillin 500 mg as trihydrate, clavulanic acid 125 mg as potassium salt). Net price 21-tab pack = £8.49. Label: 9

Dispersible tablets, sugar-free, co-amoxiclav 250/125 (amoxicillin 250 mg as trihydrate, clavulanic acid 125 mg as potassium salt). Net price 21-tab pack = £10.22. Label: 9, 13

Suspension '125/31 SF', sugar-free, co-amoxiclav 125/31 (amoxicillin 125 mg as trihydrate, clavulanic

acid 31 mg as potassium salt)/5 mL when reconstituted with water. Net price 100 mL (raspberry-and orange-flavoured) = £4.25. Label: 9
Excipients include aspartame 12.5 mg/5 mL (section 9.4.1)
**Dose** CHILD 1–6 years (10–18 kg) 5 mL every 8 hours *or* INFANT and CHILD up to 6 years 0.8 mL/kg daily in 3 divided doses; in severe infections dose increased to 1.6 mL/kg daily in 3 divided doses

Suspension '250/62 SF', sugar-free, co-amoxiclav 250/62 (amoxicillin 250 mg as trihydrate, clavulanic acid 62 mg as potassium salt)/5 mL when reconstituted with water. Net price 100 mL (raspberry-and orange-flavoured) = £5.97. Label: 9
Excipients include aspartame 12.5 mg/5 mL (section 9.4.1)
**Dose** CHILD 6–12 years (18–40 kg) 5 mL every 8 hours *or* 0.4 mL/kg daily in 3 divided doses; in severe infections dose increased to 0.8 mL/kg daily in 3 divided doses

Injection 600 mg, powder for reconstitution, co-amoxiclav 500/100 (amoxicillin 500 mg as sodium salt, clavulanic acid 100 mg as potassium salt). Net price per vial = £1.38
Electrolytes $Na^+$ 1.35 mmol, $K^+$ 0.5 mmol/600-mg vial

Injection 1.2 g, powder for reconstitution, co-amoxiclav 1000/200 (amoxicillin 1 g as sodium salt, clavulanic acid 200 mg as potassium salt). Net price per vial = £2.76
Electrolytes $Na^+$ 2.7 mmol, $K^+$ 1 mmol/1.2-g vial

**Augmentin-Duo®** (GSK) PoM
Suspension '400/57', sugar-free, strawberry-flavoured, co-amoxiclav 400/57 (amoxicillin 400 mg as trihydrate, clavulanic acid 57 mg as potassium salt)/5 mL when reconstituted with water. Net price 35 mL = £4.38, 70 mL = £6.15. Label: 9
Excipients include aspartame 12.5 mg/5 mL (section 9.4.1)
**Dose** CHILD 2 months–2 years 0.15 mL/kg twice daily, 2–6 years (13–21 kg) 2.5 mL twice daily, 7–12 years (22–40 kg) 5 mL twice daily, doubled in severe infections



## CO-FLUAMPICIL

A mixture of equal parts by mass of flucloxacillin and ampicillin

**Indications** mixed infections involving beta-lactamase-producing staphylococci

**Cautions** see under Ampicillin and Flucloxacillin

**Contra-indications** see under Ampicillin and Flucloxacillin

**Side-effects** see under Ampicillin and Flucloxacillin

**Dose**

- By mouth, co-fluampicil, 250/250 every 6 hours, dose doubled in severe infections; CHILD under 10 years half adult dose, dose doubled in severe infections
- By intramuscular *or* slow intravenous injection *or* by intravenous infusion, co-fluampicil 250/250 every 6 hours, dose doubled in severe infections; CHILD under 2 years quarter adult dose, 2–10 years half adult dose, dose doubled in severe infections

**Co-fluampicil** (Non-proprietary) PoM
Capsules, co-fluampicil 250/250 (flucloxacillin 250 mg as sodium salt, ampicillin 250 mg as trihydrate), net price 28-cap pack = £5.04. Label: 9, 22
Brands include *Flu-Amp®*

**Magnapen®** (CP) PoM
Capsules, black/turquoise, co-fluampicil 250/250 (flucloxacillin 250 mg as sodium salt, ampicillin 250 mg as trihydrate), net price 20-cap pack = £6.15. Label: 9, 22

Syrup, co-fluampicil 125/125 (flucloxacillin 125 mg as magnesium salt, ampicillin 125 mg as trihydrate)/5 mL when reconstituted with water, net price 100 mL = £4.99. Label: 9, 22
Excipients include sucrose 3.14 g/5 mL

Injection 500 mg, powder for reconstitution, co-fluampicil 250/250 (flucloxacillin 250 mg as sodium salt, ampicillin 250 mg as sodium salt), net price per vial = £1.33
Electrolytes $Na^+$ 1.3 mmol/vial

## 5.1.1.4 Antipseudomonal penicillins

The carboxypenicillin, **ticarcillin**, is principally indicated for serious infections caused by *Pseudomonas aeruginosa* although it also has activity against certain other Gram-negative bacilli including *Proteus* spp. and *Bacteroides fragilis*.

Ticarcillin is now available only in combination with clavulanic acid (section 5.1.1.3); the combination (*Timentin®*) is active against beta-lactamase-producing bacteria resistant to ticarcillin.

*Tazocin®* contains the ureidopenicillin **piperacillin** with the beta-lactamase inhibitor tazobactam. Piperacillin is more active than ticarcillin against *Ps. aeruginosa*. The spectrum of activity of *Tazocin®* is comparable to that of the carbapenems, imipenem and meropenem (section 5.1.2).

For pseudomonas septicaemias (especially in neutropenia or endocarditis) these antipseudomonal penicillins should be given with an aminoglycoside (e.g. gentamicin or netilmicin, section 5.1.4) since they have a synergistic effect. Penicillins and aminoglycosides must not, however, be mixed in the same syringe or infusion.

Owing to the sodium content of many of these antibiotics, high doses may lead to hypernatraemia.

## PIPERACILLIN

**Indications** see preparations

**Cautions** see under Benzylpenicillin (section 5.1.1.1); renal impairment (Appendix 3); pregnancy (Appendix 4); breast-feeding (Appendix 5)

**Contra-indications** see under Benzylpenicillin (section 5.1.1.1)

**Side-effects** see under Benzylpenicillin (section 5.1.1.1); also nausea, vomiting, diarrhoea; *less commonly* stomatitis, dyspepsia, constipation, jaundice, hypotension, headache, insomnia, and injection-site reactions; *rarely* abdominal pain, hepatitis, oedema, fatigue, and eosinophilia; *very rarely* hypoglycaemia, hypokalaemia, pancytopenia, Stevens-Johnson syndrome, and toxic epidermal necrolysis

**Dose**

- See preparations

### With tazobactam

**Tazocin®** (Lederle) PoM
Injection 2.25 g, powder for reconstitution, piperacillin 2 g (as sodium salt), tazobactam 250 mg (as sodium salt). Net price per vial = £7.96
Electrolytes $Na^+$ 4.69 mmol/2.25-g vial

Injection 4.5 g, powder for reconstitution, piperacillin 4 g (as sodium salt), tazobactam 500 mg (as sodium salt). Net price per vial = £15.79
Electrolytes $Na^+$ 9.37 mmol/4.5-g vial

Dose lower respiratory-tract, urinary-tract, intra-abdominal and skin infections, and septicaemia, ADULT and CHILD over 12 years, by intravenous injection over 3–5 minutes *or* by intravenous infusion, 2.25–4.5 g every 6–8 hours, usually 4.5 g every 8 hours

Complicated appendicitis, by intravenous injection over 3–5 minutes or by intravenous infusion, CHILD 2–12 years, 112.5 mg/kg every 8 hours (max. 4.5 g every 8 hours) for 5–14 days; CHILD under 2 years, not recommended

Infections in neutropenic patients (in combination with an aminoglycoside), by intravenous injection over 3–5 minutes *or* by intravenous infusion, ADULT and CHILD over 50 kg, 4.5 g every 6 hours; CHILD less than 50 kg, 90 mg/kg every 6 hours

## TICARCILLIN

**Indications** infections due to *Pseudomonas* and *Proteus* spp, see notes above

**Cautions** see under Benzylpenicillin (section 5.1.1.1)

**Contra-indications** see under Benzylpenicillin (section 5.1.1.1)

**Side-effects** see under Benzylpenicillin (section 5.1.1.1); also nausea, vomiting, coagulation disorders, haemorrhagic cystitis (more frequent in children), injection-site reactions, Stevens-Johnson syndrome, toxic epidermal necrolysis, hypokalaemia, eosinophilia

**Dose**
- See under preparation

### With clavulanic acid

**Note** For a CSM warning on cholestatic jaundice possibly associated with clavulanic acid, see under Co-amoxiclav p. 277.

**Timentin** (GSK) PoM

Injection 3.2 g, powder for reconstitution, ticarcillin 3 g (as sodium salt), clavulanic acid 200 mg (as potassium salt). Net price per vial = £5.66
Electrolytes $Na^+$ 16 mmol, $K^+$ 1 mmol /3.2-g vial

Dose by intravenous infusion, 3.2 g every 6–8 hours increased to every 4 hours in more severe infections; CHILD 80 mg/kg every 6–8 hours (every 12 hours in neonates)

## 5.1.1.5 Mecillinams

**Pivmecillinam** has significant activity against many Gram-negative bacteria including *Escherichia coli*, klebsiella, enterobacter, and salmonellae. It is not active against *Pseudomonas aeruginosa* or enterococci. Pivmecillinam is hydrolysed to mecillinam, which is the active drug.

## PIVMECILLINAM HYDROCHLORIDE

**Indications** see under Dose below

**Cautions** see under Benzylpenicillin (section 5.1.1.1); also liver and renal function tests required in long-term use; avoid in porphyria (section 9.8.2); pregnancy; **interactions:** Appendix 1 (penicillins)

**Contra-indications** see under Benzylpenicillin (section 5.1.1.1); also carnitine deficiency, oesophageal strictures, gastro-intestinal obstruction, infants under 3 months

**Side-effects** see under Benzylpenicillin (section 5.1.1.1); nausea, vomiting, dyspepsia; also reduced serum and total body carnitine (especially with long-term or repeated use)

**Dose**
- Acute uncomplicated cystitis, ADULT and CHILD over 40 kg, initially 400 mg then 200 mg every 8 hours for 3 days
- Chronic or recurrent bacteriuria, ADULT and CHILD over 40 kg, 400 mg every 6–8 hours
- Urinary-tract infections, CHILD under 40 kg, 20–40 mg/kg daily in 3–4 divided doses
- Salmonellosis, not recommended therefore no dose stated

Counselling Tablets should be swallowed whole with plenty of fluid during meals while sitting or standing

**Selexid®** (LEO) PoM

Tablets, f/c, pivmecillinam hydrochloride 200 mg, net price 10-tab pack = £4.50. Label 9, 21, 27, counselling, posture (see Dose above)

# 5.1.2 Cephalosporins and other beta-lactams

Antibiotics in this section include the **cephalosporins**, such as cefotaxime, ceftazidime, cefuroxime, cefalexin and cefradine, the **monobactam**, aztreonam, and the **carbapenems**, imipenem (a thienamycin derivative) and meropenem.

## Cephalosporins

The cephalosporins are broad-spectrum antibiotics which are used for the treatment of septicaemia, pneumonia, meningitis, biliary-tract infections, peritonitis, and urinary-tract infections. The pharmacology of the cephalosporins is similar to that of the penicillins, excretion being principally renal. Cephalosporins penetrate the cerebrospinal fluid poorly unless the meninges are inflamed; cefotaxime is a suitable cephalosporin for infections of the CNS (e.g meningitis).

The principal side-effect of the cephalosporins is hypersensitivity and about 10% of penicillin-sensitive patients will also be allergic to the cephalosporins.

**Cefradine** (cephradine) has generally been replaced by the newer cephalosporins.

**Cefuroxime** is a 'second generation' cephalosporin that is less susceptible than the earlier cephalosporins to inactivation by beta-lactamases. It is, therefore, active against certain bacteria which are resistant to the other drugs and has greater activity against *Haemophilus influenzae* and *Neisseria gonorrhoeae*.

**Cefotaxime**, **ceftazidime** and **ceftriaxone** are 'third generation' cephalosporins with greater activity than the 'second generation' cephalosporins against certain Gram-negative bacteria. However, they are less active than cefuroxime against Gram-positive bacteria, most notably *Staphylococcus aureus*. Their broad antibacterial spectrum may encourage superinfection with resistant bacteria or fungi.

**Ceftazidime** has good activity against pseudomonas. It is also active against other Gram-negative bacteria.

**Ceftriaxone** has a longer half-life and therefore needs to be given only once daily. Indications include serious infections such as septicaemia, pneumonia, and meningitis. The calcium salt of ceftriaxone forms a precipitate in the gall bladder which may rarely cause symptoms but these usually resolve when the antibiotic is stopped.

**Cefpirome** is licensed for urinary-tract, lower respiratory-tract and skin infections, bacteraemia, and infections associated with neutropenia.

**Orally active cephalosporins** The orally active 'first generation' cephalosporins, **cefalexin** (cephalexin), **cefradine**, and **cefadroxil** and the 'second generation' cephalosporins, **cefaclor** and **cefprozil**, have a similar antimicrobial spectrum. They are useful for urinary-tract infections which do not respond to other drugs or which occur in pregnancy, respiratory-tract infections, otitis media, sinusitis, and skin and soft-tissue infections. Cefaclor has good activity against *H. influenzae*, but it is associated with protracted skin reactions especially in children. Cefadroxil has a long duration of action and can be given twice daily; it has poor activity against *H. influenzae*. **Cefuroxime axetil**, an ester of the 'second generation' cephalosporin cefuroxime, has the same antibacterial spectrum as the parent compound; it is poorly absorbed.

**Cefixime** has a longer duration of action than the other cephalosporins that are active by mouth. It is only licensed for acute infections.

**Cefpodoxime proxetil** is more active than the other oral cephalosporins against respiratory bacterial pathogens and it is licensed for upper and lower respiratory-tract infections.

For treatment of Lyme disease, see section 5.1.1.3.



**Oral infections** The cephalosporins offer little advantage over the penicillins in dental infections, often being less active against anaerobes. Infections due to oral streptococci (often termed viridans streptococci) which become resistant to penicillin are usually also resistant to cephalosporins. This is of importance in the case of patients who have had rheumatic fever and are on long-term penicillin therapy. Cefalexin and cefradine have been used in the treatment of oral infections.

## CEFACLOR

**Indications** infections due to sensitive Gram-positive and Gram-negative bacteria, but see notes above

**Cautions** sensitivity to beta-lactam antibacterials (avoid if history of immediate hypersensitivity reaction); renal impairment (Appendix 3); pregnancy and breast-feeding (but appropriate to use); false positive urinary glucose (if tested for reducing substances) and false positive Coombs' test; **interactions**: Appendix 1 (cephalosporins)

**Contra-indications** cephalosporin hypersensitivity

**Side-effects** diarrhoea and rarely antibiotic-associated colitis (CSM has warned both more likely with higher doses), nausea and vomiting, abdominal discomfort, headache; allergic reactions including rashes, pruritus, urticaria, serum sickness-like reactions with rashes, fever and arthralgia, and anaphylaxis; Stevens-Johnson syndrome, toxic epidermal necrolysis reported; disturbances in liver enzymes, transient hepatitis and cholestatic jaundice; other side-effects reported include eosinophilia and blood disorders (including thrombocytopenia, leucopenia, agranulocytosis, aplastic anaemia and haemolytic anaemia); reversible interstitial nephritis, hyperactivity, nervousness, sleep disturbances, hallucinations, confusion, hypertonia, and dizziness

**Dose**

- 250 mg every 8 hours, doubled for severe infections; max. 4 g daily; CHILD over 1 month, 20 mg/kg daily in 3 divided doses, doubled for severe infections, max. 1 g daily; *or* 1 month–1 year, 62.5 mg every 8 hours; 1–5 years, 125 mg; over 5 years, 250 mg; doses doubled for severe infections

**Cefaclor** (Non-proprietary) PoM

Capsules, cefaclor (as monohydrate) 250 mg, net price 21-cap pack = £5.69; 500 mg 50-cap pack = £26.27. Label: 9

Brands include *Keftid*®

Suspension, cefaclor (as monohydrate) for reconstitution with water, 125 mg/5 mL, net price 100 mL = £4.23; 250 mg/5 mL, 100 mL = £7.38. Label: 9

Note Sugar-free versions are available and can be ordered by specifying 'sugar-free' on the prescription

Brands include *Keftid*®

**Distaclor**® (Flynn) PoM

Capsules, cefaclor (as monohydrate) 500 mg (violet/grey), net price 20 = £17.33. Label: 9

Suspension, both pink, cefaclor (as monohydrate) for reconstitution with water, 125 mg/5 mL, net price 100 mL = £4.13; 250 mg/5 mL, 100 mL = £8.26. Label: 9

**Distaclor MR**® (Flynn) PoM

Tablets, m/r, both blue, cefaclor (as monohydrate) 375 mg. Net price 14-tab pack = £6.93. Label: 9, 21, 25

Dose 375 mg every 12 hours with food, dose doubled for pneumonia

Lower urinary-tract infections, 375 mg every 12 hours with food

## CEFADROXIL

**Indications** see under Cefaclor; see also notes above

**Cautions** see under Cefaclor

**Contra-indications** see under Cefaclor

**Side-effects** see under Cefaclor

**Dose**

- Patients over 40 kg, 0.5–1 g twice daily; skin, soft tissue, and simple urinary-tract infections, 1 g daily; CHILD under 1 year, 25 mg/kg daily in divided doses; 1–6 years, 250 mg twice daily; over 6 years, 500 mg twice daily

**Cefadroxil** (Non-proprietary) PoM

Capsules, cefadroxil (as monohydrate) 500 mg, net price 20-cap pack = £5.64. Label: 9

**Baxan**® (Bristol-Myers Squibb) PoM

Capsules, cefadroxil (as monohydrate) 500 mg, net price 20-cap pack = £5.64. Label: 9

Suspension, cefadroxil (as monohydrate) for reconstitution with water, 125 mg/5 mL, net price 60 mL = £1.75; 250 mg/5 mL, 60 mL = £3.48; 500 mg/5 mL, 60 mL = £5.21. Label: 9

## CEFALEXIN
### (Cephalexin)

**Indications** see under Cefaclor

**Cautions** see under Cefaclor

**Contra-indications** see under Cefaclor

**Side-effects** see under Cefaclor

**Dose**

- 250 mg every 6 hours *or* 500 mg every 8–12 hours increased to 1–1.5 g every 6–8 hours for severe infections; CHILD 25 mg/kg daily in divided doses, doubled for severe infections, max. 100 mg/kg daily; *or* under 1 year 125 mg every 12 hours, 1–5 years 125 mg every 8 hours, 6–12 years 250 mg every 8 hours
- Prophylaxis of recurrent urinary-tract infection, ADULT 125 mg at night

**Cefalexin** (Non-proprietary) PoM

Capsules, cefalexin 250 mg, net price 28-cap pack = £2.68; 500 mg, 21-cap pack = £3.29. Label: 9

Tablets, cefalexin 250 mg, net price 28-tab pack = £2.20; 500 mg, 21-tab pack = £3.88. Label: 9

Oral suspension, cefalexin for reconstitution with water, 125 mg/5 mL, net price 100 mL = £1.89; 250 mg/5 mL, 100 mL = £2.74. Label: 9

**Dental prescribing on NHS** Cefalexin Capsules, Tablets, and Oral Suspension may be prescribed

**Ceporex®** (Galen) PoM

Capsules, both caramel/grey, cefalexin 250 mg, net price 28-cap pack = £4.02; 500 mg, 28-cap pack = £7.85. Label: 9

Tablets, all pink, f/c, cefalexin 250 mg, net price 28-tab pack = £4.02; 500 mg, 28-tab pack = £7.85. Label: 9

Syrup, all orange, cefalexin for reconstitution with water, 125 mg/5 mL, net price 100 mL = £1.43; 250 mg/5 mL, 100 mL = £2.87; 500 mg/5 mL, 100 mL = £5.57. Label: 9

**Keflex®** (Flynn) PoM

Capsules, cefalexin 250 mg (green/white), net price 28-cap pack = £1.76; 500 mg (pale green/dark green), 21-cap pack = £2.66. Label: 9

Tablets, both peach, cefalexin 250 mg, net price 28-tab pack = £2.09; 500 mg (scored), 21-tab pack = £2.47. Label: 9

Suspension, cefalexin for reconstitution with water, 125 mg/5 mL, net price 100 mL = 88p; 250 mg/5 mL, 100 mL = £1.51. Label: 9

## CEFIXIME

**Indications** see under Cefaclor (acute infections only); gonorrhoea [unlicensed indication] (Table 1, section 5.1)

**Cautions** see under Cefaclor

**Contra-indications** see under Cefaclor

**Side-effects** see under Cefaclor

**Dose**

- ADULT and CHILD over 10 years, 200–400 mg daily in 1–2 divided doses; CHILD over 6 months 8 mg/kg daily in 1–2 divided doses *or* 6 months–1 year 75 mg daily; 1–4 years 100 mg daily; 5–10 years 200 mg daily
- Gonorrhoea [unlicensed indication], 400 mg as a single dose

**Suprax®** (Rhône-Poulenc Rorer) PoM

Tablets, f/c, scored, cefixime 200 mg. Net price 7-tab pack = £13.23. Label: 9

Paediatric oral suspension, cefixime 100 mg/5 mL when reconstituted with water, net price 50 mL (with double-ended spoon for measuring 3.75 mL or 5 mL since dilution not recommended) = £10.53, 100 mL = £18.91. Label: 9

## CEFOTAXIME

**Indications** see under Cefaclor; gonorrhoea; surgical prophylaxis; Haemophilus epiglottitis and meningitis (Table 1, section 5.1); see also notes above

**Cautions** see under Cefaclor

**Contra-indications** see under Cefaclor

**Side-effects** see under Cefaclor; rarely arrhythmias following rapid injection reported

**Dose**

- By intramuscular *or* intravenous injection *or* by intravenous infusion, 1 g every 12 hours increased in severe infections (e.g. meningitis) to 8 g daily in 4 divided doses; higher doses (up to 12 g daily in 3–4 divided doses) may be required; NEONATE 50 mg/kg daily in 2–4 divided doses increased to 150–200 mg/kg daily in severe infections; CHILD 100–150 mg/kg daily in 2–4 divided doses increased up to 200 mg/kg daily in very severe infections

  Gonorrhoea, 500 mg as a single dose

**Important.** If bacterial meningitis and especially if meningococcal disease is suspected the patient should be transferred urgently to hospital. If benzylpenicillin cannot be given (e.g. because of an allergy), a single dose of cefotaxime may be given (if available) before urgent transfer to hospital. Suitable doses of cefotaxime by intravenous injection (or by intramuscular injection) are ADULT and CHILD over 12 years 1 g; CHILD under 12 years 50 mg/kg; chloramphenicol (section 5.1.7) may be used if there is a history of anaphylaxis to penicillins or cephalosporins

**Cefotaxime** (Non-proprietary) PoM

Injection, powder for reconstitution, cefotaxime (as sodium salt), net price 500-mg vial = £2.14; 1-g vial = £4.31; 2-g vial = £8.57

**Claforan®** (Aventis Pharma) PoM

Injection, powder for reconstitution, cefotaxime (as sodium salt), net price 500-mg vial = £2.14; 1-g vial (with or without infusion connector) = £4.31; 2-g vial (with or without infusion connector) = £8.57

Electrolytes $Na^+$ 2.09 mmol/g

## CEFPIROME

**Indications** see under Cefaclor and notes above

**Cautions** see under Cefaclor; interference with creatinine assays using picrate method

**Contra-indications** see under Cefaclor

**Side-effects** see under Cefaclor; taste disturbance shortly after injection reported

**Dose**

- By intravenous injection *or* infusion, complicated upper and lower urinary-tract, skin and soft-tissue infections, 1 g every 12 hours increased to 2 g every 12 hours in very severe infections

  Lower respiratory-tract infections, 1–2 g every 12 hours

  Severe infections including bacteraemia and septicaemia and infections in neutropenic patients, 2 g every 12 hours
- CHILD under 12 years not recommended

**Cefrom®** (Hoechst Marion Roussel) PoM

Injection, powder for reconstitution, cefpirome (as sulphate), net price 1-g vial = £10.75; 2-g vial = £21.50

## CEFPODOXIME

**Indications** see under Dose

**Cautions** see under Cefaclor

5 Infections

**Contra-indications** see under Cefaclor
**Side-effects** see under Cefaclor
**Dose**
- Upper respiratory-tract infections (but in pharyngitis and tonsillitis reserved for infections which are recurrent, chronic, or resistant to other antibacterials), 100 mg twice daily (200 mg twice daily in sinusitis); CHILD 15 days–6 months 4 mg/kg every 12 hours, 6 months–2 years 40 mg every 12 hours, 3–8 years 80 mg every 12 hours, over 9 years 100 mg every 12 hours
- Lower respiratory-tract infections (including bronchitis and pneumonia), 100–200 mg twice daily; CHILD 15 days–6 months 4 mg/kg every 12 hours, 6 months–2 years 40 mg every 12 hours, 3–8 years 80 mg every 12 hours, over 9 years 100 mg every 12 hours
- Skin and soft tissue infections, 200 mg twice daily; CHILD 15 days–6 months 4 mg/kg every 12 hours, 6 months–2 years 40 mg every 12 hours, 3–8 years 80 mg every 12 hours, over 9 years 100 mg every 12 hours
- Uncomplicated urinary-tract infections, 100 mg twice daily (200 mg twice daily in uncomplicated upper urinary-tract infections); CHILD 15 days–6 months 4 mg/kg every 12 hours, 6 months–2 years 40 mg every 12 hours, 3–8 years 80 mg every 12 hours, over 9 years 100 mg every 12 hours
- Uncomplicated gonorrhoea, 200 mg as a single dose

**Orelox®** (Hoechst Marion Roussel) PoM
Tablets, f/c, cefpodoxime 100 mg (as proxetil), net price 10-tab pack = £10.18. Label: 5, 9, 21
Oral suspension, cefpodoxime (as proxetil) for reconstitution with water, 40 mg/5 mL, net price 100 mL = £11.97. Label: 5, 9, 21
Excipients include aspartame (section 9.4.1)

## CEFPROZIL

**Indications** see under Dose
**Cautions** see under Cefaclor
**Contra-indications** see under Cefaclor
**Side-effects** see under Cefaclor
**Dose**
- Upper respiratory-tract infections and skin and soft tissue infections, 500 mg once daily usually for 10 days; CHILD 6 months–12 years, 20 mg/kg (max. 500 mg) once daily
- Acute exacerbation of chronic bronchitis, 500 mg every 12 hours usually for 10 days
- Otitis media, CHILD 6 months–12 years, 20 mg/kg (max. 500 mg) every 12 hours

**Cefzil®** (Bristol-Myers Squibb) PoM
Tablets, cefprozil, 250 mg (orange), net price 20-tab pack = £14.95; 500 mg, 10-tab pack = £14.95. Label: 9
Suspension, cefprozil, 250 mg/5 mL when reconstituted with water, net price 100 mL = £15.22. Label: 9
Excipients include aspartame equivalent to phenylalanine 28 mg/5 mL (section 9.4.1)

## CEFRADINE
(Cephradine)

**Indications** see under Cefaclor; surgical prophylaxis
**Cautions** see under Cefaclor
**Contra-indications** see under Cefaclor
**Side-effects** see under Cefaclor
**Dose**
- By mouth, 250–500 mg every 6 hours *or* 0.5–1 g every 12 hours; up to 1 g every 6 hours in severe infections; CHILD, 25–50 mg/kg daily in 2–4 divided doses
- By deep intramuscular injection *or* by intravenous injection over 3–5 minutes *or* by intravenous infusion, 0.5–1 g every 6 hours, increased to 8 g daily in severe infections; CHILD 50–100 mg/kg daily in 4 divided doses
- Surgical prophylaxis, by deep intramuscular injection *or* by intravenous injection over 3–5 minutes, 1–2 g at induction

**Cefradine** (Non-proprietary) PoM
Capsules, cefradine 250 mg, net price 20-cap pack = £4.26; 500 mg, 20-cap pack = £7.92. Label: 9
Brands include *Nicef®*
Dental prescribing on NHS Cefradine Capsules may be prescribed

**Velosef®** (Squibb) PoM
Capsules, cefradine 250 mg (orange/blue), net price 20-cap pack = £3.55; 500 mg (blue), 20-cap pack = £7.00. Label: 9
Syrup, cefradine 250 mg/5 mL when reconstituted with water. Net price 100 mL = £4.22. Label: 9
Dental prescribing on NHS *Velosef®* syrup may be prescribed as Cefradine Oral Solution
Injection, powder for reconstitution, cefradine. Net price 500-mg vial = 99p; 1-g vial = £1.95

## CEFTAZIDIME

**Indications** see under Cefaclor; see also notes above
**Cautions** see under Cefaclor
**Contra-indications** see under Cefaclor
**Side-effects** see under Cefaclor
**Dose**
- By deep intramuscular injection *or* intravenous injection *or* infusion, 1 g every 8 hours *or* 2 g every 12 hours; 2 g every 8–12 hours *or* 3 g every 12 hours in severe infections; single doses over 1 g intravenous route only; ELDERLY usual max. 3 g daily; CHILD, up to 2 months 25–60 mg/kg daily in 2 divided doses, over 2 months 30–100 mg/kg daily in 2–3 divided doses; up to 150 mg/kg daily (max. 6 g daily) in 3 divided doses if immunocompromised or meningitis; intravenous route recommended for children

  Urinary-tract and less serious infections, 0.5–1 g every 12 hours

  Pseudomonal lung infection in cystic fibrosis, ADULT 100–150 mg/kg daily in 3 divided doses; CHILD up to 150 mg/kg daily (max. 6 g daily) in 3 divided doses; intravenous route recommended for children

  Surgical prophylaxis, prostatic surgery, 1 g at induction of anaesthesia repeated if necessary when catheter removed

**Ceftazidime** (Non-proprietary) PoM
Injection, powder for reconstitution, ceftazidime (as pentahydrate), with sodium carbonate, net price 1-g vial = £8.50; 2-g vial = £17.00

**Fortum®** (GSK) PoM
Injection, powder for reconstitution, ceftazidime (as pentahydrate), with sodium carbonate, net price 250-mg vial = £2.20, 500-mg vial = £4.40, 1-g vial = £8.79, 2-g vial (for injection and for infusion, both) = £17.59, 3-g vial (for injection or infusion) = £25.76; *Monovial*, 2 g vial (with transfer needle) = £17.59
Electrolytes $Na^+$ 2.3 mmol/g

**Kefadim®** (Flynn) PoM

Injection, powder for reconstitution, ceftazidime (as pentahydrate), with sodium carbonate, net price 1-g vial = £7.92; 2-g vial = £15.84

Electrolytes $Na^+$ 2.3 mmol/g

## CEFTRIAXONE

**Indications** see under Cefaclor and notes above; surgical prophylaxis; prophylaxis of meningococcal meningitis [unlicensed indication] (Table 2, section 5.1)

**Cautions** see under Cefaclor; severe renal impairment (Appendix 3); hepatic impairment if accompanied by renal impairment (Appendix 2); premature neonates; may displace bilirubin from serum albumin, administer over 60 minutes in neonates (see also Contra-indications); treatment longer than 14 days, renal failure, dehydration, or concomitant total parenteral nutrition—risk of ceftriaxone precipitation in gall bladder

**Contra-indications** see under Cefaclor; neonates with jaundice, hypoalbuminaemia, acidosis or impaired bilirubin binding

**Side-effects** see under Cefaclor; calcium ceftriaxone precipitates in urine (particularly in very young, dehydrated or those who are immobilised) or in gall bladder—consider discontinuation if symptomatic; rarely prolongation of prothrombin time, pancreatitis

**Dose**

- By deep intramuscular injection, *or* by intravenous injection over at least 2–4 minutes, *or* by intravenous infusion, 1 g daily; 2–4 g daily in severe infections; intramuscular doses over 1 g divided between more than one site; single intravenous doses above 1 g by intravenous infusion only

  NEONATE by intravenous infusion over 60 minutes, 20–50 mg/kg daily (max. 50 mg/kg daily) INFANT and CHILD under 50 kg, by deep intramuscular injection, *or* by intravenous injection over 2–4 minutes, *or* by intravenous infusion, 20–50 mg/kg daily; up to 80 mg/kg daily in severe infections; doses of 50 mg/kg and over by intravenous infusion only; 50 kg and over, adult dose
- Endocarditis caused by haemophilus, actinobacillus, cardiobacterium, eikenella, and kingella species ('HACEK organisms') (in combination with another antibacterial, see Table 1, section 5.1; [unlicensed indication]), by intravenous infusion, 2–4 g daily
- Uncomplicated gonorrhoea, by deep intramuscular injection, 250 mg as a single dose
- Surgical prophylaxis, by deep intramuscular injection *or* by intravenous injection over at least 2–4 minutes, 1 g at induction; colorectal surgery, by deep intramuscular injection *or* by intravenous infusion, 2 g at induction; intramuscular doses over 1 g divided between more than one site

**Ceftriaxone** (Non-proprietary) PoM

Injection, powder for reconstitution, ceftriaxone (as sodium salt), net price 1-g vial = £10.17; 2-g vial = £20.36

**Rocephin®** (Roche) PoM

Injection, powder for reconstitution, ceftriaxone (as sodium salt), net price 250-mg vial = £2.55; 1-g vial = £10.17; 2-g vial = £20.36

Electrolytes $Na^+$ 3.6 mmol /g

## CEFUROXIME

**Indications** see under Cefaclor; surgical prophylaxis; more active against *Haemophilus influenzae* and *Neisseria gonorrhoeae*; Lyme disease

**Cautions** see under Cefaclor

**Contra-indications** see under Cefaclor

**Side-effects** see under Cefaclor

**Dose**

- By mouth (as cefuroxime axetil), 250 mg twice daily in most infections including mild to moderate lower respiratory-tract infections (e.g. bronchitis); doubled for more severe lower respiratory-tract infections or if pneumonia suspected

  Urinary-tract infection, 125 mg twice daily, doubled in pyelonephritis

  Gonorrhoea, 1 g as a single dose

  CHILD over 3 months, 125 mg twice daily, if necessary doubled in child over 2 years with otitis media

  Lyme disease, ADULT and CHILD over 12 years, 500 mg twice daily for 20 days
- By intramuscular injection *or* intravenous injection *or* infusion, 750 mg every 6–8 hours; 1.5 g every 6–8 hours in severe infections; single doses over 750 mg intravenous route only

  CHILD usual dose 60 mg/kg daily (range 30–100 mg/kg daily) in 3–4 divided doses (2–3 divided doses in neonates)
- Gonorrhoea, 1.5 g as a single dose by intramuscular injection (divided between 2 sites)
- Surgical prophylaxis, 1.5 g by intravenous injection at induction; up to 3 further doses of 750 mg may be given by intramuscular *or* intravenous injection every 8 hours for high-risk procedures
- Meningitis, 3 g intravenously every 8 hours; CHILD, 200–240 mg/kg daily (in 3–4 divided doses) reduced to 100 mg/kg daily after 3 days or on clinical improvement; NEONATE, 100 mg/kg daily reduced to 50 mg/kg daily

**Zinacef®** (GSK) PoM

Injection, powder for reconstitution, cefuroxime (as sodium salt). Net price 250-mg vial = 94p; 750-mg vial = £2.34; 1.5-g vial = £4.70

Electrolytes $Na^+$ 1.8 mmol/750-mg vial

**Zinnat®** (GSK) PoM

Tablets, both f/c, cefuroxime (as axetil) 125 mg, net price 14-tab pack = £4.84; 250 mg, 14-tab pack = £9.67. Label: 9, 21, 25

Suspension, cefuroxime (as axetil) 125 mg/5 mL when reconstituted with water, net price 70 mL (tutti-frutti-flavoured) = £5.52. Label: 9, 21

Excipients include aspartame (section 9.4.1)

## Other beta-lactam antibiotics

**Aztreonam** is a monocyclic beta-lactam ('monobactam') antibiotic with an antibacterial spectrum limited to Gram-negative aerobic bacteria including *Pseudomonas aeruginosa*, *Neisseria meningitidis*, and *Haemophilus influenzae*; it should not be used alone for 'blind' treatment since it is not active against Gram-positive organisms. Aztreonam is also effective against *Neisseria gonorrhoeae* (but not against concurrent chlamydial infection). Side-effects are similar to those of the other beta-lactams although aztreonam may be less likely to cause hypersensitivity in penicillin-sensitive patients.

**Imipenem**, a carbapenem, has a broad spectrum of activity which includes many aerobic and anaerobic Gram-positive and Gram-negative bacteria. Imipenem is partially inactivated in the kidney by enzymatic activity and is therefore administered in combination with **cilastatin**, a specific enzyme inhibitor, which blocks its renal metabolism. Side-effects are similar to those of other beta-lactam antibiotics; neurotoxicity has been observed at very high dosage or in renal failure.

**Meropenem** is similar to imipenem but is stable to the renal enzyme which inactivates imipenem and therefore can be given without cilastatin. Meropenem has less seizure-inducing potential and can be used to treat central nervous system infection.

**Ertapenem** has a broad spectrum of activity that covers Gram-positive and Gram-negative organisms and anaerobes. It is licensed for treating abdominal and gynaecological infections and for community-acquired pneumonia, but it is not active against atypical respiratory pathogens and it has limited activity against penicillin-resistant pneumococci. Unlike imipenem and meropenem, ertapenem is not active against *Pseudomonas* or against *Acinetobacter* spp.



## AZTREONAM

**Indications** Gram-negative infections including *Pseudomonas aeruginosa*, *Haemophilus influenzae*, and *Neisseria meningitidis*

**Cautions** hypersensitivity to beta-lactam antibiotics; hepatic impairment; renal impairment (Appendix 3); breast-feeding (Appendix 5); **interactions:** Appendix 1 (aztreonam)

**Contra-indications** aztreonam hypersensitivity; pregnancy (Appendix 4)

**Side-effects** nausea, vomiting, diarrhoea, abdominal cramps; mouth ulcers, altered taste; jaundice and hepatitis; flushing; hypersensitivity reactions; blood disorders (including thrombocytopenia and neutropenia); rashes, injection-site reactions; rarely hypotension, seizures, asthenia, confusion, dizziness, headache, halitosis, and breast tenderness; very rarely antibiotic-associated colitis, gastro-intestinal bleeding, and toxic epidermal necrolysis

**Dose**

- By deep intramuscular injection *or* by intravenous injection over 3–5 minutes *or* by intravenous infusion, 1 g every 8 hours *or* 2 g every 12 hours; 2 g every 6–8 hours for severe infections (including systemic *Pseudomonas aeruginosa* and lung infections in cystic fibrosis); single doses over 1 g intravenous route only

  Urinary-tract infections, 0.5–1 g every 8–12 hours
- CHILD over 1 week, by intravenous injection *or* infusion, 30 mg/kg every 6–8 hours increased in severe infections for child of 2 years or older to 50 mg/kg every 6–8 hours; max. 8 g daily
- Gonorrhoea, cystitis, by intramuscular injection, 1 g as a single dose

**Azactam®** (Squibb) PoM

Injection, powder for reconstitution, aztreonam. Net price 500-mg vial = £4.48; 1-g vial = £8.95; 2-g vial = £17.90

## ERTAPENEM

**Indications** abdominal infections; acute gynaecological infections; community-acquired pneumonia

**Cautions** sensitivity to beta-lactam antibacterials (avoid if history of immediate hypersensitivity reaction); renal impairment (Appendix 3); pregnancy (Appendix 4); **interactions:** Appendix 1 (ertapenem)

**Contra-indications** breast-feeding (Appendix 5)

**Side-effects** diarrhoea, nausea, vomiting, headache, injection-site reactions, rash, pruritus, raised platelet count; *less commonly* dry mouth, taste disturbances, dyspepsia, abdominal pain, anorexia, constipation, melaena, antibiotic-associated colitis, hypotension, chest pain, oedema, pharyngeal discomfort, dyspnoea, dizziness, sleep disturbances, confusion, asthenia, seizures, vaginitis, raised glucose, petechiae; *rarely* dysphagia, cholecystitis, liver disorder (including jaundice), arrhythmia, increase in blood pressure, syncope, nasal congestion, cough, wheezing, anxiety, depression, agitation, tremor, pelvic peritonitis, renal impairment, muscle cramp, scleral disorder, blood disorders (including neutropenia, thrombocytopenia, haemorrhage), hypoglycaemia, electrolyte disturbances; *very rarely* hallucinations

**Dose**

- By intravenous infusion, ADULT and ADOLESCENT over 13 years, 1 g once daily; CHILD 3 months–13 years, 15 mg/kg every 12 hours (max. 1 g daily)

**Invanz®** (MSD) ▼ PoM

Intravenous infusion, powder for reconstitution, ertapenem (as sodium salt), net price 1-g vial = £31.65

Electrolytes $Na^+$ 6 mmol/1-g vial

## IMIPENEM WITH CILASTATIN

**Indications** aerobic and anaerobic Gram-positive and Gram-negative infections; surgical prophylaxis; hospital-acquired septicaemia (Table 1, section 5.1); not indicated for CNS infections

**Cautions** sensitivity to beta-lactam antibacterials (avoid if history of immediate hypersensitivity reaction); renal impairment (Appendix 3); CNS disorders (e.g. epilepsy); pregnancy (Appendix 4); breast-feeding (Appendix 5); **interactions:** Appendix 1 (imipenem with cilastatin)

**Side-effects** nausea, vomiting, diarrhoea (antibiotic-associated colitis reported), taste disturbances, tooth or tongue discoloration, hearing loss; blood disorders, positive Coombs' test; allergic reactions (with rash, pruritus, urticaria, Stevens-Johnson syndrome, fever, anaphylactic reactions, rarely toxic epidermal necrolysis, exfoliative dermatitis); myoclonic activity, convulsions, confusion and mental disturbances reported; slight increases in liver enzymes and bilirubin reported, rarely hepatitis; increases in serum creatinine and blood urea; red coloration of urine in children reported; local reactions: erythema, pain and induration, and thrombophlebitis

**Dose**

- By deep intramuscular injection, mild to moderate infections, in terms of imipenem, 500–750 mg every 12 hours
- By intravenous infusion, in terms of imipenem, 1–2 g daily (in 3–4 divided doses); less sensitive organisms, up to 50 mg/kg daily (max. 4 g daily) in 3–4 divided

doses; CHILD 3 months and older, 60 mg/kg (up to max. of 2 g) daily in 4 divided doses; over 40 kg, adult dose

- Surgical prophylaxis, by intravenous infusion, 1 g at induction repeated after 3 hours, supplemented in high risk (e.g. colorectal) surgery by doses of 500 mg 8 and 16 hours after induction

**Primaxin®** (MSD) PoM

Intramuscular injection, powder for reconstitution, imipenem (as monohydrate) 500 mg with cilastatin (as sodium salt) 500 mg, net price per vial = £12.00
Electrolytes $Na^{+}$ 1.47 mmol/vial

Intravenous infusion, powder for reconstitution, imipenem (as monohydrate) 500 mg with cilastatin (as sodium salt) 500 mg, net price per vial = £12.00; *Monovial* (vial with transfer needle) = £12.00
Electrolytes $Na^{+}$ 1.72 mmol/vial

## MEROPENEM

**Indications** aerobic and anaerobic Gram-positive and Gram-negative infections

**Cautions** sensitivity to beta-lactam antibacterials (avoid if history of immediate hypersensitivity reaction); hepatic impairment (monitor liver function; Appendix 2); renal impairment (Appendix 3); pregnancy (Appendix 4); breast-feeding (Appendix 5); **interactions:** Appendix 1 (meropenem)

**Side-effects** nausea, vomiting, diarrhoea (antibiotic-associated colitis reported), abdominal pain; disturbances in liver function tests; thrombocytopenia (reduction in partial thromboplastin time reported), positive Coombs' test, eosinophilia, leucopenia, neutropenia; headache, paraesthesia; hypersensitivity reactions including rash, pruritus, urticaria, angioedema, and anaphylaxis; also reported, convulsions, Stevens-Johnson syndrome and toxic epidermal necrolysis; local reactions including pain and thrombophlebitis at injection site

**Dose**

- By intravenous injection over 5 minutes *or* by intravenous infusion, 500 mg every 8 hours, dose doubled in hospital-acquired pneumonia, peritonitis, septicaemia and infections in neutropenic patients; CHILD 3 months–12 years [not licensed for infection in neutropenia] 10–20 mg/kg every 8 hours, over 50 kg body weight adult dose

  Meningitis, 2 g every 8 hours; CHILD 3 months–12 years 40 mg/kg every 8 hours, over 50 kg body weight adult dose

  Exacerbations of chronic lower respiratory-tract infection in cystic fibrosis, up to 2 g every 8 hours; CHILD 4–18 years 25–40 mg/kg every 8 hours

**Meronem®** (AstraZeneca) PoM

Injection, powder for reconstitution, meropenem (as trihydrate), net price 500-mg vial = £14.33; 1-g vial = £28.65
Electrolytes $Na^{+}$ 3.9 mmol/g

# 5.1.3 Tetracyclines

The tetracyclines are broad-spectrum antibiotics whose value has decreased owing to increasing bacterial resistance. They remain, however, the treatment of choice for infections caused by chlamydia (trachoma, psittacosis, salpingitis, urethritis, and lymphogranuloma venereum), rickettsia (including Q-fever), brucella (doxycycline with either streptomycin or rifampicin), and the spirochaete, *Borrelia burgdorferi* (Lyme disease—see section 5.1.1.3). They are also used in respiratory and genital mycoplasma infections, in acne, in destructive (refractory) periodontal disease, in exacerbations of chronic bronchitis (because of their activity against *Haemophilus influenzae*), and for leptospirosis in penicillin hypersensitivity (as an alternative to erythromycin).

Microbiologically, there is little to choose between the various tetracyclines, the only exception being **minocycline** which has a broader spectrum; it is active against *Neisseria meningitidis* and has been used for meningococcal prophylaxis but is no longer recommended because of side-effects including dizziness and vertigo (see section 5.1, table 2 for current recommendations). *Deteclo®* (a combination of tetracycline, chlortetracycline and demeclocycline) does not have any advantages over preparations containing a single tetracycline.

**Oral infections** In adults, tetracyclines can be effective against oral anaerobes but the development of resistance (especially by oral streptococci) has reduced their usefulness for the treatment of acute oral infections; they may still have a role in the treatment of destructive (refractory) forms of periodontal disease. Doxycycline has a longer duration of action than tetracycline or oxytetracycline and need only be given once daily; it is reported to be more active against anaerobes than some other tetracyclines.

For the use of doxycycline in the treatment of recurrent aphthous ulceration, oral herpes, or as an adjunct to gingival scaling and root planing for periodontitis, see section 12.3.1 and section 12.3.2.

**Cautions** Tetracyclines should be used with caution in patients with hepatic impairment (Appendix 2) or those receiving potentially hepatotoxic drugs. Tetracyclines may increase muscle weakness in patients with myasthenia gravis, and exacerbate systemic lupus erythematosus. Antacids, and aluminium, calcium, iron, magnesium and zinc salts decrease the absorption of tetracyclines; milk also reduces the absorption of demeclocycline, oxytetracycline, and tetracycline. Other **interactions:** Appendix 1 (tetracyclines).

**Contra-indications** Deposition of tetracyclines in growing bone and teeth (by binding to calcium) causes staining and occasionally dental hypoplasia, and they should **not** be given to children under 12 years, or to pregnant (Appendixes 4) or breast-feeding women (Appendix 5). However, doxycycline may be used in children for treatment and post-exposure prophylaxis of anthrax when an alternative antibacterial cannot be given [unlicensed indication]. With the exception of **doxycycline** and **minocycline**, the tetracyclines may exacerbate renal failure and should **not** be given to patients with kidney disease (Appendix 3).

**Side-effects** Side-effects of the tetracyclines include nausea, vomiting, diarrhoea (antibiotic-associated colitis reported occasionally), dysphagia, and oesophageal irritation. Other rare side-effects include hepatotoxicity, pancreatitis, blood disorders, photosensitivity (particularly with demeclocycline), and hypersensitivity reactions (including rash, exfoliative dermatitis, Stevens-

Johnson syndrome, urticaria, angioedema, anaphylaxis, pericarditis). Headache and visual disturbances may indicate benign intracranial hypertension (discontinue treatment); bulging fontanelles have been reported in infants.

## TETRACYCLINE

**Indications** see notes above; acne vulgaris, rosacea (section 13.6)

**Cautions** see notes above

**Contra-indications** see notes above

**Side-effects** see notes above; also acute renal failure, skin discoloration

**Dose**

- 250 mg every 6 hours, increased in severe infections to 500 mg every 6–8 hours
- Acne, see section 13.6.2
- Non-gonococcal urethritis, 500 mg every 6 hours for 7–14 days (21 days if failure or relapse after first course)

Counselling Tablets should be swallowed whole with plenty of fluid while sitting or standing

**Tetracycline** (Non-proprietary) PoM

Tablets, coated, tetracycline hydrochloride 250 mg, net price 28-tab pack = £1.91. Label: 7, 9, 23, counselling, posture

Dental prescribing on NHS Tetracycline Tablets may be prescribed

### Compound preparations

**Deteclo®** (Goldshield) PoM

Tablets, blue, f/c, tetracycline hydrochloride 115.4 mg, chlortetracycline hydrochloride 115.4 mg, demeclocycline hydrochloride 69.2 mg, net price 14-tab pack = £1.83. Label: 7, 9, 11, 23, counselling, posture

Dose 1 tablet every 12 hours; 3–4 tablets daily in more severe infections

## DEMECLOCYCLINE HYDROCHLORIDE

**Indications** see notes above; also inappropriate secretion of antidiuretic hormone, section 6.5.2

**Cautions** see notes above, but photosensitivity more common (avoid exposure to sunlight or sun lamps)

**Contra-indications** see notes above

**Side-effects** see notes above; also reversible nephrogenic diabetes insipidus, acute renal failure

**Dose**

- 150 mg every 6 hours *or* 300 mg every 12 hours

**Ledermycin®** (Goldshield) PoM

Capsules, red, demeclocycline hydrochloride 150 mg, net price 28-cap pack = £6.94. Label: 7, 9, 11, 23

## DOXYCYCLINE

**Indications** see notes above; chronic prostatitis; sinusitis, syphilis, pelvic inflammatory disease (Table 1, section 5.1); treatment and prophylaxis of anthrax [unlicensed indication]; malaria treatment and prophylaxis (section 5.4.1); recurrent aphthous ulceration, adjunct to gingival scaling and root planing for periodontitis (section 12.3.1); oral herpes simplex (section 12.3.2); rosacea [unlicensed indication], acne vulgaris (section 13.6)

**Cautions** see notes above, but may be used in renal impairment; alcohol dependence; photosensitivity reported (avoid exposure to sunlight or sun lamps); avoid in porphyria (section 9.8.2)

**Contra-indications** see notes above

**Side-effects** see notes above; also anorexia, flushing, and tinnitus

**Dose**

- 200 mg on first day, then 100 mg daily; severe infections (including refractory urinary-tract infections), 200 mg daily
- Early syphilis, 100 mg twice daily for 14 days; late latent syphilis 200 mg twice daily for 28 days
- Uncomplicated genital chlamydia, non-gonococcal urethritis, 100 mg twice daily for 7 days (14 days in pelvic inflammatory disease, see also Table 1, section 5.1)
- Anthrax (treatment or post-exposure prophylaxis; see also section 5.1.12), 100 mg twice daily; CHILD (only if alternative antibacterial cannot be given) [unlicensed dose] 5 mg/kg daily in 2 divided doses (max. 200 mg daily)

Counselling Capsules should be swallowed whole with plenty of fluid during meals while sitting or standing

Note Doxycycline doses in BNF may differ from those in product literature

**Doxycycline** (Non-proprietary) PoM

Capsules, doxycycline (as hyclate) 50 mg, net price 28-cap pack = £3.47; 100 mg, 8-cap pack = £1.71. Label: 6, 9, 11, 27, counselling, posture

Brands include *Doxylar®*

Dental prescribing on NHS Doxycycline Capsules 100 mg may be prescribed

**Vibramycin®** (Pfizer) PoM

Capsules, doxycycline (as hyclate) 50 mg (green/ivory), net price 28-cap pack = £7.74. Label: 6, 9, 11, 27, counselling, posture

**Vibramycin-D®** (Pfizer) PoM

Dispersible tablets, yellow, scored, doxycycline 100 mg, net price 8-tab pack = £4.91. Label: 6, 9, 11, 13

## LYMECYCLINE

**Indications** see notes above

**Cautions** see notes above

**Contra-indications** see notes above

**Side-effects** see notes above

**Dose**

- 408 mg every 12 hours, increased to 1.224–1.632 g daily in severe infections
- Acne, 408 mg daily for at least 8 weeks

**Tetralysal 300®** (Galderma) PoM

Capsules, red/yellow, lymecycline 408 mg (= tetracycline 300 mg), net price 28-cap pack = £7.16, 56-cap pack = £14.26. Label: 6, 9

## MINOCYCLINE

**Indications** see notes above; meningococcal carrier state; acne vulgaris (section 13.6.2)

**Cautions** see notes above, but may be used in renal impairment; if treatment continued for longer than 6 months, monitor every 3 months for hepatotoxicity, pigmentation and for systemic lupus erythematosus—

discontinue if these develop or if pre-existing systemic lupus erythematosus worsens

**Contra-indications** see notes above

**Side-effects** see notes above; also anorexia, dizziness, tinnitus and vertigo (more common in women), acute renal failure; pigmentation (sometimes irreversible), discoloration of conjunctiva, tears and sweat, systemic lupus erythematosus

**Dose**

- 100 mg twice daily
- Acne, see section 13.6.2 and under preparations, below
- Prophylaxis of asymptomatic meningococcal carrier state (but no longer recommended, see notes above), 100 mg twice daily for 5 days usually followed by rifampicin

Counselling Tablets or capsules should be swallowed whole with plenty of fluid while sitting or standing

**Minocycline** (Non-proprietary) PoM

Capsules, minocycline (as hydrochloride) 50 mg, net price 56-cap pack = £17.20; 100 mg, 28-cap pack = £14.74. Label: 6, 9, counselling, posture

Brands include *Aknemin*®

Tablets, minocycline (as hydrochloride) 50 mg, net price 28-tab pack = £7.59, 84-tab pack = £16.20 100 mg, 28-tab pack = £11.78. Label: 6, 9, counselling, posture

**Minocin MR**® (Lederle) PoM

Capsules, m/r, orange/brown (enclosing yellow and white pellets), minocycline (as hydrochloride) 100 mg. Net price 56-cap pack = £21.14. Label: 6, 25

Dose acne, 1 capsule daily

**Sebomin MR**® (Alpharma) PoM

Capsules, m/r, orange, minocycline (as hydrochloride) 100 mg, net price 56-cap pack = £21.14. Label: 6, 25

Dose acne, 1 capsule daily

## OXYTETRACYCLINE

**Indications** see notes above; acne vulgaris, rosacea (section 13.6)

**Cautions** see notes above; porphyria (section 9.8.2)

**Contra-indications** see notes above

**Side-effects** see notes above

**Dose**

- 250–500 mg every 6 hours
- Acne, see section 13.6.2

**Oxytetracycline** (Non-proprietary) PoM

Tablets, coated, oxytetracycline dihydrate 250 mg, net price 28-tab pack = £1.26. Label: 7, 9, 23

Brands include *Oxymycin*®, *Oxytetramix*®

**Dental prescribing on NHS** Oxtetracycline Tablets may be prescribed

# 5.1.4 Aminoglycosides

These include amikacin, gentamicin, neomycin, netilmicin, streptomycin, and tobramycin. All are bactericidal and active against some Gram-positive and many Gram-negative organisms. Amikacin, gentamicin, and tobramycin are also active against *Pseudomonas aeruginosa*; streptomycin is active against *Mycobacterium tuberculosis* and is now almost entirely reserved for tuberculosis (section 5.1.9).

The aminoglycosides are not absorbed from the gut (although there is a risk of absorption in inflammatory bowel disease and liver failure) and must therefore be given by injection for systemic infections.

Excretion is principally via the kidney and accumulation occurs in renal impairment.

Most side-effects of this group of antibiotics are dose-related therefore care must be taken with dosage and whenever possible treatment should not exceed 7 days. The important side-effects are ototoxicity, and nephrotoxicity; they occur most commonly in the elderly and in patients with renal failure.

If there is impairment of renal function (or high pre-dose serum concentrations) the interval between doses must be increased; if the renal impairment is severe the dose itself should be reduced as well.

Aminoglycosides may impair neuromuscular transmission and should not be given to patients with myasthenia gravis; large doses given during surgery have been responsible for a transient myasthenic syndrome in patients with normal neuromuscular function.

Aminoglycosides should preferably not be given with potentially ototoxic diuretics (e.g. furosemide (frusemide)); if concurrent use is unavoidable administration of the aminoglycoside and of the diuretic should be separated by as long a period as practicable.

**Serum concentrations** Serum concentration monitoring avoids both excessive and subtherapeutic concentrations thus preventing toxicity and ensuring efficacy. In patients with normal renal function, aminoglycoside concentrations should be measured after 3 or 4 doses of a multiple daily dose regimen; patients with renal impairment may require earlier and more frequent measurement of aminoglycoside concentration.

For multiple daily dose regimens, blood samples should be taken approximately 1 hour after intramuscular or intravenous administration ('peak' concentration) and also just before the next dose ('trough' concentration). For once daily dose regimens, consult local guidelines on serum concentration monitoring.

Serum aminoglycoside concentrations should be measured in all patients and **must** be determined in infants, in the elderly, in obesity, and in cystic fibrosis, *or* if high doses are being given, *or* if there is renal impairment.

**Once daily dosage** Although aminoglycosides are generally given in 2–3 divided doses during the 24 hours, *once daily administration* is more convenient (while ensuring adequate serum concentration) but local guidelines on dosage and serum concentrations should be consulted.

**Endocarditis** **Gentamicin** is used in combination with other antibiotics for the treatment of bacterial endocarditis (Table 1, section 5.1). Serum-gentamicin concentration should be determined twice each week (more often in renal impairment). **Streptomycin** may be used as an alternative in gentamicin-resistant enterococcal endocarditis.

**Gentamicin** is the aminoglycoside of choice in the UK and is used widely for the treatment of serious infections. It has a broad spectrum but is inactive against anaerobes and has poor activity against haemolytic streptococci and pneumococci. When used for the 'blind' therapy of undiagnosed serious infections it is usually given in conjunction with a penicillin or metronidazole (or both). Gentamicin is used together with another antibiotic for the treatment of endocarditis (see above and Table 1, section 5.1).

Loading and maintenance doses of gentamicin may be calculated on the basis of the patient's weight and renal function (e.g. using a nomogram); adjustments are then made according to serum-gentamicin concentrations. High doses are occasionally indicated for serious infections, especially in the neonate or the immunocompromised patient. Whenever possible treatment should not exceed 7 days.

**Amikacin** is more stable than gentamicin to enzyme inactivation. Amikacin is used in the treatment of serious infections caused by gentamicin-resistant Gram-negative bacilli.

**Netilmicin** has similar activity to gentamicin, but may cause less ototoxicity in those needing treatment for longer than 10 days. Netilmicin is active against a number of gentamicin-resistant Gram-negative bacilli but is less active against *Ps. aeruginosa* than gentamicin or tobramycin.

**Tobramycin** has similar activity to gentamicin. It is slightly more active against *Ps. aeruginosa* but shows less activity against certain other Gram-negative bacteria. Tobramycin may be administered by nebuliser on a cyclical basis (28 days of tobramycin followed by a 28-day tobramycin-free interval) for the treatment of chronic pulmonary *Ps. aeruginosa* infection in cystic fibrosis; however, resistance may develop and some patients do not respond to treatment.

**Neomycin** is too toxic for parenteral administration and can only be used for infections of the skin or mucous membranes or to reduce the bacterial population of the colon prior to bowel surgery or in hepatic failure. Oral administration may lead to malabsorption. Small amounts of neomycin may be absorbed from the gut in patients with hepatic failure and, as these patients may also be uraemic, cumulation may occur with resultant ototoxicity.



## GENTAMICIN

**Indications** septicaemia and neonatal sepsis; meningitis and other CNS infections; biliary-tract infection, acute pyelonephritis or prostatitis, endocarditis (see notes above); pneumonia in hospital patients, adjunct in listerial meningitis (Table 1, section 5.1); eye (section 11.3.1); ear (section 12.1.1)

**Cautions** pregnancy (Appendix 4), renal impairment, neonates, infants and elderly (adjust dose and monitor renal, auditory and vestibular function together with serum gentamicin concentrations); avoid prolonged use; conditions characterised by muscular weakness; obesity (use ideal body-weight to calculate dose and monitor serum-gentamicin concentration closely); see also notes above; **interactions:** Appendix 1 (aminoglycosides)

**Contra-indications** myasthenia gravis

**Side-effects** vestibular and auditory damage, nephrotoxicity; rarely, hypomagnesaemia on prolonged therapy, antibiotic-associated colitis, stomatitis; also reported, nausea, vomiting, rash, blood disorders; see also notes above

**Dose**

- By intramuscular *or* by slow intravenous injection over at least 3 minutes *or* by intravenous infusion, 3–5 mg/kg daily (in divided doses every 8 hours), see also notes above; NEONATE up to 2 weeks, 3 mg/kg every 12 hours; CHILD 2 weeks–12 years, 2 mg/kg every 8 hours

  Endocarditis (in combination with other antibacterials, see Table 1, section 5.1), ADULT 1 mg/kg every 8 hours

  Endocarditis prophylaxis, Table 2, section 5.1
- By intrathecal injection, seek specialist advice, 1 mg daily (increased if necessary to 5 mg daily)

Note For multiple daily dose regimen, one-hour ('peak') serum concentration should be 5–10 mg/litre (3–5 mg/litre for endocarditis); pre-dose ('trough') concentration should be less than 2 mg/litre (less than 1 mg/litre for endocarditis)

- Once daily dose regimen, by intravenous infusion, initially 5–7 mg/kg, then adjusted according to serum-gentamicin concentration

**Gentamicin** (Non-proprietary) PoM

Injection, gentamicin (as sulphate), net price 40 mg/mL, 1-mL amp = £1.40, 2-mL amp = £1.54, 2-mL vial = £1.48

Paediatric injection, gentamicin (as sulphate) 10 mg/mL, net price 2-mL vial = £1.80

Intrathecal injection, gentamicin (as sulphate) 5 mg/mL, net price 1-mL amp = 74p

**Cidomycin®** (Beacon) PoM

Injection, gentamicin (as sulphate) 40 mg/mL. Net price 2-mL amp or vial = £1.48

**Genticin®** (Roche) PoM

Injection, gentamicin (as sulphate) 40 mg/mL. Net price 2-mL amp = £1.40

**Isotonic Gentamicin Injection** (Baxter) PoM

Intravenous infusion, gentamicin (as sulphate) 800 micrograms/mL in sodium chloride intravenous infusion 0.9%. Net price 100-mL (80-mg) *Viaflex®* bag = £1.61

Electrolytes $Na^+$ 15.4 mmol/100-mL bag

## AMIKACIN

**Indications** serious Gram-negative infections resistant to gentamicin

**Cautions** see under Gentamicin

**Contra-indications** see under Gentamicin

**Side-effects** see under Gentamicin

**Dose**

- By intramuscular *or* by slow intravenous injection *or* by infusion, 15 mg/kg daily in 2 divided doses, increased to 22.5 mg/kg daily in 3 divided doses in severe infections; max. 1.5 g daily for up to 10 days (max. cumulative dose 15 g); CHILD 15 mg/kg daily in 2 divided doses; NEONATE loading dose of 10 mg/kg then 15 mg/kg daily in 2 divided doses

  Note One-hour ('peak') serum concentration should not exceed 30 mg/litre; pre-dose ('trough') concentration should be less than 10 mg/litre

**Amikacin** (Non-proprietary) PoM

Injection, amikacin (as sulphate) 250 mg/mL. Net price 2-mL vial = £10.14

Electrolytes $Na^+$ 0.56 mmol/500-mg vial

**Amikin®** (Bristol-Myers Squibb) PoM

Injection, amikacin (as sulphate) 250 mg/mL. Net price 2-mL vial = £10.14
Electrolytes $Na^+$ < 0.5 mmol/vial

Paediatric injection, amikacin (as sulphate) 50 mg/mL. Net price 2-mL vial = £2.36
Electrolytes $Na^+$ < 0.5 mmol/vial

## NEOMYCIN SULPHATE

**Indications** bowel sterilisation before surgery, see also notes above

**Cautions** see under Gentamicin but too toxic for systemic use, see notes above

**Contra-indications** see under Gentamicin; intestinal obstruction

**Side-effects** see under Gentamicin but poorly absorbed on oral administration; increased salivation, stomatitis, impaired intestinal absorption with steatorrhoea and diarrhoea

**Dose**

- By mouth, pre-operative bowel sterilisation, 1 g every hour for 4 hours, then 1 g every 4 hours for 2–3 days

  Hepatic coma, up to 4 g daily in divided doses usually for max. 14 days

**Neomycin** (Non-proprietary) PoM

Tablets, neomycin sulphate 500 mg. Net price 20 = £3.44
Brands include *Nivemycin®*

## NETILMICIN

**Indications** serious Gram-negative infections resistant to gentamicin

**Cautions** see under Gentamicin

**Contra-indications** see under Gentamicin

**Side-effects** see under Gentamicin

**Dose**

- By intramuscular injection *or* by intravenous injection over 3–5 minutes *or* by intravenous infusion, 4–6 mg/kg daily, as a single daily dose or in divided doses every 8 or 12 hours; in severe infections, up to 7.5 mg/kg daily in divided doses every 8 hours (reduced as soon as clinically indicated, usually within 48 hours); PRETERM NEONATE and NEONATE up to 1 week, 3 mg/kg every 12 hours; INFANT 1 week–1 year, 2.5–3 mg/kg every 8 hours; CHILD over 1 year, 2–2.5 mg/kg every 8 hours

  Urinary-tract infection, 150 mg as a single daily dose for 5 days

  **Note** For divided daily dose regimens, one-hour ('peak') serum concentration should not exceed 12 mg/litre; pre-dose ('trough') concentration should be less than 2 mg/litre

**Netillin®** (Schering-Plough) PoM

Injection, netilmicin (as sulphate) 10 mg/mL, net price 1.5-mL (15-mg) amp = £1.42; 50 mg/mL, 1-mL (50-mg) amp = £2.11; 100 mg/mL, 1-mL (100-mg) amp = £2.75; 1.5-mL (150-mg) amp = £3.92, 2-mL (200-mg) amp = £5.09

## TOBRAMYCIN

**Indications** see under Gentamicin and notes above

**Cautions** see under Gentamicin

**Specific cautions for inhaled treatment** Other inhaled drugs should be administered before tobramycin; monitor for bronchospasm with initial dose, measure peak flow before and after nebulisation—if bronchospasm occurs, repeat test using bronchodilator; monitor renal function before treatment and then annually; severe haemoptysis

**Contra-indications** see under Gentamicin

**Side-effects** see under Gentamicin; *on inhalation*, mouth ulcers, voice alteration, cough, bronchospasm (see Cautions)

**Dose**

- By intramuscular injection *or* by slow intravenous injection *or* by intravenous infusion, 3 mg/kg daily in divided doses every 8 hours, see also notes above; in severe infections up to 5 mg/kg daily in divided doses every 6–8 hours (reduced to 3 mg/kg as soon as clinically indicated); NEONATE 2 mg/kg every 12 hours; CHILD over 1 week 2–2.5 mg/kg every 8 hours
- Urinary-tract infection, by intramuscular injection, 2–3 mg/kg daily as a single dose

  **Note** One-hour ('peak') serum concentration should not exceed 10 mg/litre; pre-dose ('trough') concentration should be less than 2 mg/litre

**Tobramycin** (Non-proprietary) PoM

Injection, tobramycin (as sulphate) 40 mg/mL, net price 1-mL (40-mg) vial = £2.73, 2-mL (80-mg) vial = £4.16, 6-mL (240-mg) vial = £12.47

**Tobi®** (Chiron) PoM

Nebuliser solution, tobramycin 60 mg/mL, net price 56 × 5-mL (300-mg) unit = £1540.00

**Dose** chronic pulmonary *Pseudomonas aeruginosa* infection in cystic fibrosis patients, by inhalation of nebulised solution, ADULT and CHILD over 6 years, 300 mg every 12 hours for 28 days, courses repeated after 28-day interval

# 5.1.5 Macrolides

**Erythromycin** has an antibacterial spectrum that is similar but not identical to that of penicillin; it is thus an alternative in penicillin-allergic patients.

Indications for erythromycin include respiratory infections, whooping cough, legionnaires' disease, and campylobacter enteritis. It is active against many penicillin-resistant staphylococci but some are now also resistant to erythromycin; it has poor activity against *Haemophilus influenzae*. Erythromycin is also active against chlamydia and mycoplasmas.

Erythromycin causes nausea, vomiting, and diarrhoea in some patients; in mild to moderate infections this can be avoided by giving a lower dose (250 mg 4 times daily) but if a more serious infection, such as Legionella pneumonia, is suspected higher doses are needed.

**Azithromycin** is a macrolide with slightly less activity than erythromycin against Gram-positive bacteria but enhanced activity against some Gram-negative organisms including *H. influenzae*. Plasma concentrations are very low but tissue concentrations are much higher. It has a long tissue half-life and once daily dosage is recommended. For treatment of Lyme disease, see section 5.1.1.3. Azithromycin is also used in the treatment of trachoma [unlicensed indication] (section 11.3.1).

**Clarithromycin** is an erythromycin derivative with slightly greater activity than the parent compound. Tissue concentrations are higher than with erythromycin. It is given twice daily.

Azithromycin and clarithromycin cause fewer gastro-intestinal side-effects than erythromycin.

**Spiramycin** is also a macrolide (section 5.4.7).

The ketolide **telithromycin** is a derivative of erythromycin. The antibacterial spectrum of telithromycin is similar to that of macrolides and it is also active against penicillin- and erythromycin-resistant *Streptococcus pneumoniae*.

**Oral infections** Erythromycin is an alternative for oral infections in penicillin-allergic patients or where a beta-lactamase producing organism is involved. However, many organisms are now resistant to erythromycin or rapidly develop resistance; its use should therefore be limited to short courses. Metronidazole (section 5.1.11) may be preferred as an alternative to a penicillin.

For prophylaxis of infective endocarditis in patients allergic to penicillin, a single-dose of oral clindamycin is used; see Table 2, section 5.1. Single-dose azithromycin is used for prophylaxis of endocarditis in those unable to take clindamycin [unlicensed indication].

## ERYTHROMYCIN

**Indications** alternative to penicillin in hypersensitive patients; oral infections (see notes above); campylobacter enteritis, syphilis, non-gonococcal urethritis, respiratory-tract infections (including legionnaires' disease), skin infections (Table 1, section 5.1); chronic prostatitis; diphtheria and whooping cough prophylaxis (Table 2, section 5.1); acne vulgaris and rosacea (section 13.6)

**Cautions** neonate under 2 weeks (risk of hypertrophic pyloric stenosis); predisposition to QT interval prolongation (including electrolyte disturbances, concomitant use of drugs that prolong QT interval); avoid in porphyria (section 9.8.2); hepatic impairment (Appendix 2); renal impairment (Appendix 3); pregnancy (not known to be harmful) and breast-feeding (only small amounts in milk); **interactions**: Appendix 1 (macrolides)

Arrhythmias Avoid concomitant administration with pimozide [other interactions, Appendix 1]

**Side-effects** nausea, vomiting, abdominal discomfort, diarrhoea (antibiotic-associated colitis reported); less frequently urticaria, rashes and other allergic reactions; reversible hearing loss reported after large doses; cholestatic jaundice, pancreatitis, cardiac effects (including chest pain and arrhythmias), myasthenia-like syndrome, Stevens-Johnson syndrome, and toxic epidermal necrolysis also reported

**Dose**

- By mouth, ADULT and CHILD over 8 years, 250–500 mg every 6 hours *or* 0.5–1 g every 12 hours (see notes above); up to 4 g daily in severe infections; CHILD up to 2 years 125 mg every 6 hours, 2–8 years 250 mg every 6 hours, doses doubled for severe infections

  Early syphilis, 500 mg 4 times daily for 14 days

  Uncomplicated genital chlamydia, non-gonococcal urethritis, 500 mg twice daily for 14 days
- By intravenous infusion, ADULT and CHILD severe infections, 50 mg/kg daily by continuous infusion *or* in divided doses every 6 hours; mild infections (oral treatment not possible), 25 mg/kg daily; NEONATE 30–45 mg/kg daily in 3 divided doses

**Erythromycin** (Non-proprietary) PoM

Capsules, enclosing e/c microgranules, erythromycin 250 mg, net price 28-cap pack = £4.92. Label: 5, 9, 25

Brands include *Tiloryth*®

Tablets, e/c, erythromycin 250 mg, net price 20 = £1.92. Label: 5, 9, 25

Brands include *Rommix*®

Dental prescribing on NHS Erythromycin Tablets e/c may be prescribed

**Erythromycin Ethyl Succinate** (Non-proprietary) PoM

Oral suspension, erythromycin (as ethyl succinate) for reconstitution with water 125 mg/5 mL, net price 100 mL = £2.20; 250 mg/5 mL, 100 mL = £2.72; 500 mg/5 mL, 100 mL = £4.44. Label: 9

Note Sugar-free versions are available and can be ordered by specifying 'sugar-free' on the prescription

Brands include *Primacine*®

Dental prescribing on NHS Erythromycin Ethyl Succinate Oral Suspension may be prescribed

**Erythromycin Lactobionate** (Non-proprietary) PoM

Intravenous infusion, powder for reconstitution, erythromycin (as lactobionate), net price 1-g vial = £9.98

**Erymax**® (Zeneus) PoM

Capsules, opaque orange/clear orange, enclosing orange and white e/c pellets, erythromycin 250 mg, net price 28-cap pack = £5.95, 112-cap pack = £23.80. Label: 5, 9, 25

Dose 1 capsule every 6 hours *or* 2 capsules every 12 hours; acne, 1 capsule twice daily for 1 month then 1 capsule daily

**Erythrocin**® (Abbott) PoM

Tablets, both f/c, erythromycin (as stearate), 250 mg, net price 20 = £2.92; 500 mg, 20 = £6.01. Label: 9

Dental prescribing on NHS May be prescribed as Erythromycin Stearate Tablets

**Erythroped**® (Abbott) PoM

Suspension SF, sugar-free, banana-flavoured, erythromycin (as ethyl succinate) for reconstitution with water, 125 mg/5 mL (*Suspension PI SF*), net price 140 mL = £3.18; 250 mg/5 mL, 140 mL = £6.20; 500 mg/5 mL (*Suspension SF Forte*), 140 mL = £10.99. Label: 9

**Erythroped A**® (Abbott) PoM

Tablets, yellow, f/c, erythromycin 500 mg (as ethyl succinate). Net price 28-tab pack = £8.29. Label: 9

Dental prescribing on NHS May be prescribed as Erythromycin Ethyl Succinate Tablets

## AZITHROMYCIN

**Indications** respiratory-tract infections; otitis media; skin and soft-tissue infections; uncomplicated genital chlamydial infections and non-gonococcal urethritis (Table 1, section 5.1); mild or moderate typhoid due to multiple-antibacterial-resistant organisms [unlicensed indication]; prophylaxis of endocarditis in children [unlicensed indication] (Table 2, section 5.1)

**Cautions** see under Erythromycin; pregnancy (Appendix 4) and breast-feeding (Appendix 5); **interactions**: Appendix 1 (macrolides)

**Contra-indications** hepatic impairment

**Side-effects** see under Erythromycin; also anorexia, dyspepsia, flatulence, constipation, pancreatitis, hepatitis, syncope, dizziness, headache, drowsiness, agitation, anxiety, hyperactivity, asthenia, paraesthesia, convulsions, mild neutropenia, thrombocytopenia, interstitial nephritis, acute renal failure, arthralgia, photosensitivity; *rarely* taste disturbances, tongue discoloration, and hepatic failure

**Dose**

- 500 mg once daily for 3 days; CHILD over 6 months 10 mg/kg once daily for 3 days; *or* body-weight 15–25 kg, 200 mg once daily for 3 days; body-weight 26–35 kg, 300 mg once daily for 3 days; body-weight 36–45 kg, 400 mg once daily for 3 days
- Uncomplicated genital chlamydial infections and non-gonococcal urethritis, 1 g as a single dose
- Typhoid [unlicensed indication], 500 mg once daily for 7 days

**Zithromax®** (Pfizer) PoM

Capsules, azithromycin (as dihydrate) 250 mg, net price 4-cap pack = £8.95, 6-cap pack = £13.43. Label: 5, 9, 23

Oral suspension, cherry/banana-flavoured, azithromycin (as dihydrate) 200 mg/5 mL when reconstituted with water. Net price 15-mL pack = £5.08, 22.5-mL pack = £7.62, 30-mL pack = £13.80. Label: 5, 9

**Dental prescribing on NHS** May be prescribed as Azithromycin Oral Suspension 200 mg/5 mL

## CLARITHROMYCIN

**Indications** respiratory-tract infections, mild to moderate skin and soft tissue infections, otitis media; *Helicobacter pylori* eradication (section 1.3)

**Cautions** see under Erythromycin; renal impairment (Appendix 3); pregnancy (Appendix 4); breast-feeding (Appendix 5); **interactions:** Appendix 1 (macrolides)

**Arrhythmias** Avoid concomitant administration with pimozide [other interactions, Appendix 1]

**Side-effects** see under Erythromycin; also dyspepsia, tooth and tongue discoloration, smell and taste disturbances, stomatitis, glossitis, and headache; *less commonly* hepatitis, arthralgia, and myalgia; *rarely* tinnitus; *very rarely* pancreatitis, dizziness, insomnia, nightmares, anxiety, confusion, psychosis, paraesthesia, convulsions, hypoglycaemia, renal failure, leucopenia, and thrombocytopenia; on intravenous infusion, local tenderness, phlebitis

**Dose**

- By mouth, 250 mg every 12 hours for 7 days, increased in severe infections to 500 mg every 12 hours for up to 14 days; CHILD body-weight under 8 kg, 7.5 mg/kg twice daily; 8–11 kg (1–2 years), 62.5 mg twice daily; 12–19 kg (3–6 years), 125 mg twice daily; 20–29 kg (7–9 years), 187.5 mg twice daily; 30–40 kg (10–12 years), 250 mg twice daily
- By intravenous infusion into larger proximal vein, 500 mg twice daily; CHILD safety and efficacy not established

**Clarithromycin** (Non-proprietary) PoM

Tablets, clarithromycin 250 mg, net price 14-tab pack = £10.94; 500 mg, 14-tab pack = £21.90. Label: 9

**Clarosip** (Grünenthal) PoM

Granules, clarithromycin 125 mg/straw, net price 14-straw pack = £6.70; 187.5 mg/straw, 14-straw pack = £9.70; 250 mg/straw, 14-straw pack = £12.70. Label: 9, counselling, administration

**Counselling** Place straw in cold or warm drink such as water, carbonated drink, or tea (but **not** full fat milk, milk-shake, or drink with solid particles) and sip drink through straw; several sips may be required to obtain full dose

**Klaricid®** (Abbott) PoM

Tablets, both yellow, f/c, clarithromycin 250 mg, net price 14-tab pack = £10.94; 500 mg, 14-tab pack = £21.90, 20-tab pack = £31.29. Label: 9

Paediatric suspension, clarithromycin for reconstitution with water 125 mg/5 mL, net price 70 mL = £5.58, 100 mL = £9.60; 250 mg/5 mL, 70 mL = £11.16. Label: 9

Granules, clarithromycin 250 mg/sachet, net price 14-sachet pack = £11.68. Label: 9, 13

Intravenous infusion, powder for reconstitution, clarithromycin. Net price 500-mg vial = £11.46

Electrolytes $Na^+ < 0.5$ mmol/500-mg vial

**Klaricid XL®** (Abbott) PoM

Tablets, m/r, yellow, clarithromycin 500 mg, net price 7-tab pack = £9.90, 14-tab pack = £19.81. Label: 9, 21, 25

Dose 500 mg once daily (doubled in severe infections) for 7–14 days

## TELITHROMYCIN

**Indications** community-acquired pneumonia; exacerbation of chronic bronchitis; sinusitis; beta-haemolytic streptococcal pharyngitis or tonsillitis when beta-lactam antibiotics are inappropriate

**Cautions** hepatic impairment; renal impairment (Appendix 3); pregnancy (Appendix 4); coronary heart disease, ventricular arrhythmias, bradycardia, hypokalaemia, hypomagnesaemia—risk of QT interval prolongation; concomitant administration of drugs that prolong QT-interval; myasthenia gravis (risk of exacerbation—use only if no other alternative); **interactions:** Appendix 1 (telithromycin)

**Contra-indications** breast-feeding (Appendix 5); prolongation of QT interval; congenital or family history of QT interval prolongation (if not excluded by ECG)

**Arrhythmias** Avoid concomitant administration with pimozide [other interactions, Appendix 1]

**Side-effects** diarrhoea, nausea, vomiting, flatulence, abdominal pain, taste disturbances; dizziness, headache; *less commonly* constipation, stomatitis, anorexia, flushing, palpitations, drowsiness, insomnia, nervousness, eosinophilia, blurred vision, rash, urticaria, and pruritus; *rarely* cholestatic jaundice, arrhythmias, hypotension, loss of consciousness, paraesthesia, and diplopia; *very rarely* antibiotic-associated colitis, hepatitis, pancreatitis, altered sense of smell, muscle cramp, erythema multiforme

**Dose**

- 800 mg once daily for 5 days for sinusitis or exacerbation of chronic bronchitis *or* for 7–10 days in community-acquired pneumonia; CHILD under 18 years safety and efficacy not established
- Beta-haemolytic streptococcal pharyngitis or tonsillitis, ADULT and CHILD over 12 years, 800 mg once daily for 5 days

**Ketek®** (Aventis Pharma) ▼ PoM

Tablets, orange, f/c, telithromycin 400 mg, net price 10-tab pack = £19.31.Label: 9

# 5.1.6 Clindamycin

Clindamycin has only a limited use because of serious side-effects. Its most serious toxic effect is antibiotic-associated colitis (section 1.5) which may be fatal and is most common in middle-aged and elderly women, especially following operation. Although antibiotic-associated colitis can occur with most antibacterials it occurs more frequently with clindamycin. Patients should therefore discontinue treatment immediately if diarrhoea develops.

Clindamycin is active against Gram-positive cocci, including penicillin-resistant staphylococci and also against many anaerobes, especially *Bacteroides fragilis*. It is well concentrated in bone and excreted in bile and urine.

Clindamycin is recommended for staphylococcal joint and bone infections such as osteomyelitis, and intra-abdominal sepsis.

Clindamycin is used for prophylaxis of endocarditis in patients allergic to penicillin [unlicensed indication], see Table 2, section 5.1.

**Oral infections** Clindamycin should not be used routinely for the treatment of oral infections because it may be no more effective than penicillins against anaerobes and there may be cross-resistance with erythromycin-resistant bacteria. Clindamycin can be used for the treatment of dentoalveolar abscess that has not responded to penicillin or to metronidazole.

### CLINDAMYCIN

**Indications** see notes above; staphylococcal bone and joint infections, peritonitis; endocarditis prophylaxis [unlicensed indication], table 2, section 5.1

**Cautions** discontinue immediately if diarrhoea or colitis develops; hepatic impairment (Appendix 2); renal impairment; monitor liver and renal function on prolonged therapy and in neonates and infants; pregnancy (Appendix 4); breast-feeding (Appendix 5); avoid rapid intravenous administration; avoid in porphyria (section 9.8.2); **interactions:** Appendix 1 (clindamycin)

**Contra-indications** diarrhoeal states; avoid injections containing benzyl alcohol in neonates (see under preparations below)

**Side-effects** diarrhoea (discontinue treatment), abdominal discomfort, oesophagitis, nausea, vomiting, antibiotic-associated colitis; jaundice; leucopenia, eosinophilia, and thrombocytopenia reported; rash, pruritus, urticaria, anaphylactoid reactions, Stevens-Johnson syndrome, exfoliative and vesiculobullous dermatitis reported; pain, induration, and abscess after intramuscular injection; thrombophlebitis after intravenous injection

**Dose**

- By mouth, 150–300 mg every 6 hours; up to 450 mg every 6 hours in severe infections; CHILD, 3–6 mg/kg every 6 hours

  **Counselling** Patients should discontinue immediately and contact doctor if diarrhoea develops; capsules should be swallowed with a glass of water.

- By deep intramuscular injection *or* by intravenous infusion, 0.6–2.7 g daily (in 2–4 divided doses); life-threatening infection, up to 4.8 g daily; single doses above 600 mg by intravenous infusion only; single doses by intravenous infusion not to exceed 1.2 g; CHILD over 1 month, 15–40 mg/kg daily in 3–4 divided doses; severe infections, at least 300 mg daily regardless of weight

**Clindamycin** (Non-proprietary) PoM

Capsules, clindamycin (as hydrochloride) 150 mg, net price 24-cap pack = £13.72. Label: 9, 27, counselling, see above (diarrhoea)

**Dental prescribing on NHS** Clindamycin Capsules may be prescribed

**Dalacin C®** (Pharmacia) PoM

Capsules, clindamycin (as hydrochloride) 75 mg (lavender), net price 24-cap pack = £7.45; 150 mg, (lavender/maroon), 24-cap pack = £13.72. Label: 9, 27, counselling, see above (diarrhoea)

**Dental prescribing on NHS** May be prescribed as Clindamycin Capsules

Injection, clindamycin (as phosphate) 150 mg/mL, net price 2-mL amp = £6.20; 4-mL amp = £12.35

**Excipients** include benzyl alcohol (avoid in neonates, see Excipients, p. 2)

## 5.1.7 Some other antibacterials

Antibacterials discussed in this section include chloramphenicol, fusidic acid, glycopeptide antibiotics (vancomycin and teicoplanin), linezolid, the streptogramins (quinupristin and dalfopristin) and the polymyxin, colistin.

### Chloramphenicol

**Chloramphenicol** is a potent broad-spectrum antibiotic; however, it is associated with serious haematological side-effects when given systemically and should therefore be reserved for the treatment of life-threatening infections, particularly those caused by *Haemophilus influenzae*, and also for typhoid fever.

Chloramphenicol eye drops (section 11.3.1) and chloramphenicol ear drops (section 12.1.1) are also available.

### CHLORAMPHENICOL

**Indications** see notes above

**Cautions** avoid repeated courses and prolonged treatment; reduce doses in hepatic impairment (Appendix 2); renal impairment (Appendix 3); blood counts required before and periodically during treatment; monitor plasma-chloramphenicol concentration in neonates (see below); **interactions:** Appendix 1 (chloramphenicol)

**Contra-indications** pregnancy (Appendix 4), breast-feeding (Appendix 5), porphyria (section 9.8.2)

**Side-effects** blood disorders including reversible and irreversible aplastic anaemia (with reports of resulting leukaemia), peripheral neuritis, optic neuritis, headache, depression, urticaria, erythema multiforme, nausea, vomiting, diarrhoea, stomatitis, glossitis, dry mouth; nocturnal haemoglobinuria reported; grey syndrome (abdominal distension, pallid cyanosis, circulatory collapse) may follow excessive doses in neonates with immature hepatic metabolism

**Dose**

- By mouth *or* by intravenous injection *or* infusion, 50 mg/kg daily in 4 divided doses (exceptionally, can be doubled for severe infections such as septicaemia and meningitis, providing high doses reduced as soon as clinically indicated); CHILD, haemophilus epiglottitis and pyogenic meningitis, 50–100 mg/kg daily in divided doses (high dosages decreased as soon as clinically indicated); NEONATE under 2 weeks 25 mg/kg daily (in 4 divided doses); INFANT 2 weeks–1 year 50 mg/kg daily (in 4 divided doses)

  **Note** Plasma concentration monitoring required in neonates and preferred in those under 4 years of age, in the elderly, and in hepatic impairment; recommended peak plasma concentration (approx. 1 hour after intravenous injection or infusion) 15–25 mg/litre; pre-dose ('trough') concentration should not exceed 15 mg/litre

**Chloramphenicol** (Non-proprietary) PoM

Capsules, chloramphenicol 250 mg. Net price 60 = £377.00

**Kemicetine®** (Pharmacia) PoM

Injection, powder for reconstitution, chloramphenicol (as sodium succinate). Net price 1-g vial = £1.39

Electrolytes $Na^+$ 3.14 mmol/g

## Fusidic acid

**Fusidic acid** and its salts are narrow-spectrum antibiotics. The only indication for their use is in infections caused by penicillin-resistant staphylococci, especially osteomyelitis, as they are well concentrated in bone; they are also used for staphylococcal endocarditis. A second antistaphylococcal antibiotic is usually required to prevent emergence of resistance.

### SODIUM FUSIDATE

**Indications** penicillin-resistant staphylococcal infection including osteomyelitis; staphylococcal endocarditis in combination with other antibacterials (Table 1, section 5.1)

**Cautions** monitor liver function with high doses, on prolonged therapy or in hepatic impairment (Appendix 2); elimination may be reduced in hepatic impairment or biliary disease or biliary obstruction; pregnancy (Appendix 4); breast-feeding (Appendix 5); **interactions:** Appendix 1 (fusidic acid)

**Side-effects** nausea, vomiting, reversible jaundice, especially after high dosage or rapid infusion (withdraw therapy if persistent); rarely hypersensitivity reactions, acute renal failure (usually with jaundice), blood disorders

**Dose**

- See under Preparations, below

**Sodium fusidate** (LEO) PoM

Intravenous infusion, powder for reconstitution, sodium fusidate 500 mg (= fusidic acid 480 mg), with buffer, net price per vial (with diluent) = £70.04

Electrolytes $Na^+$ 3.1 mmol/vial when reconstituted with buffer

**Dose** as sodium fusidate, by intravenous infusion, ADULT over 50 kg, 500 mg 3 times daily; ADULT under 50 kg and CHILD, 6–7 mg/kg 3 times daily

**Fucidin®** (LEO) PoM

Tablets, f/c, sodium fusidate 250 mg, net price 10-tab pack = £6.02. Label: 9

**Dose** as sodium fusidate, 500 mg every 8 hours, doubled for severe infections

Skin infection, as sodium fusidate, 250 mg every 12 hours for 5–10 days

Suspension, off-white, banana- and orange-flavoured, fusidic acid 250 mg/5 mL, net price 50 mL = £6.73. Label: 9, 21

**Dose** as fusidic acid, ADULT 750 mg every 8 hours; CHILD up to 1 year 50 mg/kg daily (in 3 divided doses), 1–5 years 250 mg every 8 hours, 5–12 years 500 mg every 8 hours

**Note** Fusidic acid is incompletely absorbed and doses recommended for suspension are proportionately higher than those for sodium fusidate tablets

## Vancomycin and teicoplanin

The glycopeptide antibiotics vancomycin and teicoplanin have bactericidal activity against aerobic and anaerobic Gram-positive bacteria including multi-resistant staphylococci. However, there are reports of *Staphylococcus aureus* with reduced susceptibility to glycopeptides. There are increasing reports of glycopeptide-resistant enterococci.

**Vancomycin** is used *by the intravenous route* in the prophylaxis and treatment of endocarditis and other serious infections caused by Gram-positive cocci. It has a relatively long duration of action and can therefore be given every 12 hours. Vancomycin (added to dialysis fluid) is also used in the treatment of peritonitis associated with peritoneal dialysis [unlicensed route] (Table 1 section 5.1).

Vancomycin given *by mouth* is effective in the treatment of antibiotic-associated colitis (pseudomembranous colitis, see also section 1.5); a dose of 125 mg every 6 hours for 7 to 10 days is considered adequate (higher dose may be considered if the infection fails to respond or if it is severe). Vancomycin should **not** be given by mouth for systemic infections since it is not significantly absorbed.

**Teicoplanin** is very similar to vancomycin but has a significantly longer duration of action allowing once-daily administration. Unlike vancomycin, teicoplanin can be given by intramuscular as well as by intravenous injection; it is not given by mouth.

### VANCOMYCIN

**Indications** see notes above

**Cautions** avoid rapid infusion (risk of anaphylactoid reactions, see Side-effects); rotate infusion sites; renal impairment (Appendix 3); elderly; avoid if history of deafness; all patients require plasma-vancomycin measurement (after 3 or 4 doses if renal function normal, earlier if renal impairment), blood counts, urinalysis, and renal function tests; monitor auditory function in elderly or if renal impairment; pregnancy (Appendix 4) and breast-feeding (Appendix 5); systemic absorption may follow oral administration especially in inflammatory bowel disorders or following multiple doses; **interactions:** Appendix 1 (vancomycin)

**Side-effects** after parenteral administration: nephrotoxicity including renal failure and interstitial nephritis; ototoxicity (discontinue if tinnitus occurs); blood disorders including neutropenia (usually after 1 week or cumulative dose of 25 g), rarely agranulocytosis and thrombocytopenia; nausea; chills, fever; eosinophilia, anaphylaxis, rashes (including exfoliative dermatitis, Stevens-Johnson syndrome, toxic epidermal necrolysis, and vasculitis); phlebitis (irritant to tissue); on rapid infusion, severe hypotension (including shock and cardiac arrest), wheezing, dyspnoea, urticaria, pruritus, flushing of the upper body ('red man' syndrome), pain and muscle spasm of back and chest

**Dose**

- By mouth, antibiotic-associated colitis, 125 mg every 6 hours for 7–10 days, see notes above; CHILD 5 mg/kg every 6 hours, over 5 years, half adult dose

  **Note** Oral paediatric dose is lower than that on product literature but is adequate

- By intravenous infusion, 500 mg every 6 hours *or* 1 g every 12 hours; ELDERLY over 65 years, 500 mg every 12 hours *or* 1 g once daily; NEONATE up to 1 week, 15 mg/kg initially then 10 mg/kg every 12 hours; 1–4 weeks, 15 mg/kg initially then 10 mg/kg every 8 hours; CHILD over 1 month, 10 mg/kg every 6 hours

Endocarditis prophylaxis, section 5.1, table 2

**Note** Plasma concentration monitoring required; pre-dose ('trough') concentration should be 5–10 mg/litre (10–15 mg/litre in endocarditis); vancomycin doses in BNF may differ from those in product literature

**Vancomycin** (Non-proprietary) PoM

Capsules, vancomycin (as hydrochloride) 125 mg, net price 28-cap pack = £66.23; 250 mg, 28-cap pack = £132.47. Label: 9

Injection, powder for reconstitution, vancomycin (as hydrochloride), for use as an infusion, net price 500-mg vial = £8.05; 1-g vial = £16.11

**Note** Can be used to prepare solution for oral administration

**Vancocin®** (Flynn) PoM

Injection, powder for reconstitution, vancomycin (as hydrochloride), for use as an infusion, net price 500-mg vial = £8.05; 1-g vial = £16.11

**Note** Can be used to prepare solution for oral administration

### TEICOPLANIN

**Indications** potentially serious Gram-positive infections including endocarditis, dialysis-associated peritonitis, and serious infections due to *Staphylococcus aureus*; prophylaxis in endocarditis [unlicensed indication] and in orthopaedic surgery at risk of infection with Gram-positive organisms

**Cautions** vancomycin sensitivity; blood counts and liver and kidney function tests required; renal impairment (Appendix 3)—monitor renal and auditory function on prolonged administration or if other nephrotoxic or neurotoxic drugs given; pregnancy (Appendix 4) and breast-feeding; **interactions:** Appendix 1 (teicoplanin)

**Side-effects** nausea, vomiting, diarrhoea; rash, pruritus, fever, bronchospasm, rigors, urticaria, angioedema, anaphylaxis; dizziness, headache; blood disorders including eosinophilia, leucopenia, neutropenia, and thrombocytopenia; disturbances in liver enzymes, transient increase of serum creatinine, renal failure; tinnitus, mild hearing loss, and vestibular disorders also reported; rarely exfoliative dermatitis, Stevens-Johnson syndrome, toxic epidermal necrolysis; local reactions include erythema, pain, thrombophlebitis, injection site abscess and rarely flushing with infusion

**Dose**

- By intramuscular injection *or* by intravenous injection *or* infusion, initially 400 mg (for severe infections, by intravenous injection *or* infusion, initially 400 mg every 12 hours for 3 doses), then 200 mg daily (400 mg daily for severe infections); higher doses may be required in patients of over 85 kg and in severe burns or endocarditis (consult product literature)
- CHILD over 2 months by intravenous injection *or* infusion, initially 10 mg/kg every 12 hours for 3 doses, subsequently 6 mg/kg daily (severe infections or in neutropenia, 10 mg/kg daily); subsequent doses can be given by intramuscular injection (but intravenous administration preferred in children); NEONATE by intravenous infusion, initially a single dose of 16 mg/kg, subsequently 8 mg/kg daily
- Orthopaedic surgery prophylaxis, by intravenous injection, 400 mg at induction of anaesthesia
- Endocarditis prophylaxis [unlicensed indication], section 5.1, table 2

**Targocid®** (Aventis Pharma) PoM

Injection, powder for reconstitution, teicoplanin, net price 200-mg vial (with diluent) = £17.58; 400-mg vial (with diluent) = £35.62

Electrolytes $Na^+ < 0.5$ mmol/200- and 400-mg vial

## Linezolid

**Linezolid**, an oxazolidinone antibacterial, is active against Gram-positive bacteria including meticillin-resistant *Staphylococcus aureus* (MRSA), and vancomycin-resistant enterococci. Resistance to linezolid can develop with prolonged treatment or if the dose is less than that recommended. Linezolid should be reserved for infections resistant to other antibacterials or when other antibacterials are not tolerated. Linezolid is not sufficiently active against common Gram-negative organisms.

### LINEZOLID

**Indications** pneumonia, complicated skin and soft-tissue infections caused by Gram-positive bacteria (initiated under expert supervision)

**Cautions** monitor full blood count (including platelet count) weekly (see also CSM Advice below); unless close observation and blood-pressure monitoring possible, avoid in uncontrolled hypertension, phaeochromocytoma, carcinoid tumour, thyrotoxicosis, bipolar depression, schizophrenia, or acute confusional states; hepatic impairment (Appendix 2); renal impairment (Appendix 3); pregnancy (Appendix 4); **interactions:** Appendix 1 (MAOIs)

**CSM advice**

Haematopoietic disorders (including thrombocytopenia, anaemia, leucopenia, and pancytopenia) have been reported in patients receiving linezolid. It is recommended that full blood counts are monitored weekly. Close monitoring is recommended in patients who:

- receive treatment for more than 10–14 days;
- have pre-existing myelosuppression;
- are receiving drugs that may have adverse effects on haemoglobin, blood counts, or platelet function;
- have severe renal impairment.

If significant myelosuppression occurs, treatment should be stopped unless it is considered essential, in which case intensive monitoring of blood counts and appropriate management should be implemented.

**Monoamine oxidase inhibition** Linezolid is a reversible, non-selective monoamine oxidase inhibitor (MAOI). Patients should avoid consuming large amounts of tyramine-rich foods (such as mature cheese, yeast extracts, undistilled alcoholic beverages, and fermented soya bean products). In addition, linezolid should not be given with another MAOI or within 2 weeks of stopping another MAOI. Unless close observation and blood-pressure monitoring is possible, avoid in those receiving SSRIs, $5HT_1$ agonists ('triptans'), tricyclic antidepressants, sympathomimetics, dopaminergics, buspirone, pethidine and possibly other opioid analgesics. For other interactions see Appendix 1 (MAOIs)

**Contra-indications** breast-feeding (Appendix 5); see also Monoamine oxidase inhibition above

**Side-effects** diarrhoea (antibiotic-associated colitis reported), nausea, vomiting, taste disturbances; headache; *less commonly* thirst, dry mouth, glossitis, stomatitis, tongue discoloration, abdominal pain, dyspepsia, gastritis, constipation, pancreatitis, hypertension, fever, fatigue, dizziness, insomnia, hypoaesthesia, paraesthesia, tinnitus, polyuria, anaemia, leucopenia, thrombocytopenia, eosinophilia, electrolyte disturbances, blurred vision, rash, pruritus, diaphoresis, and injection-site reactions; *very rarely* transient ischaemic attacks, renal failure, pancytopenia and Stevens-Johnson syndrome; peripheral and optic neuropathy reported on prolonged therapy

**Dose**

- By mouth, ADULT over 18 years, 600 mg every 12 hours for 10–14 days; CHILD [unlicensed] 1 week–12 years, 10 mg/kg every 8 hours; 12–18 years, adult dose
- By intravenous infusion over 30–120 minutes, ADULT over 18 years, 600 mg every 12 hours; CHILD [unlicensed] 1 week–12 years, 10 mg/kg every 8 hours; 12–18 years, adult dose

**Zyvox** (Pharmacia) ▼ PoM

Tablets, f/c, linezolid 600 mg, net price 10-tab pack = £445.00. Label: 9, 10, patient information leaflet

Suspension, yellow, linezolid 100 mg/5 mL when reconstituted with water, net price 150 mL (orange-flavoured) = £222.50. Label: 9, 10 patient information leaflet

Excipients include aspartame 20 mg/5 mL (section 9.4.1); $Na^+ < 0.5$ m-mmol/5 mL

Intravenous infusion, linezolid 2 mg/mL, net price 300-mL *Excel®* bag = £44.50

Excipients include $Na^+$ 5 mmol/300-mL bag, glucose 13.71 g/300-mL bag

## Quinupristin and dalfopristin

A combination of the streptogramin antibiotics, **quinupristin** and **dalfopristin** (as *Synercid®*) is licensed for infections due to Gram-positive bacteria. The combination should be reserved for treating infections which have failed to respond to other antibacterials (e.g. meticillin-resistant *Staphylococcus aureus*, MRSA) or for patients who cannot be treated with other antibacterials. Quinupristin and dalfopristin are not active against *Enterococcus faecalis* and they need to be given in combination with other antibacterials for mixed infections which also involve Gram-negative organisms.

### QUINUPRISTIN WITH DALFOPRISTIN

**A mixture of quinupristin and dalfopristin (both as mesilate salts) in the proportions 3 parts to 7 parts**

**Indications** serious Gram-positive infections where no alternative antibacterial is suitable including hospital-acquired pneumonia, skin and soft-tissue infections, infections due to vancomycin-resistant *Enterococcus faecium*

**Cautions** hepatic impairment (avoid if severe; Appendix 2); pregnancy (Appendix 4); predisposition to cardiac arrhythmias (including congenital QT syndrome, concomitant use of drugs that prolong QT interval, cardiac hypertrophy, dilated cardiomyopathy, hypokalaemia, hypomagnesaemia, bradycardia); **interactions**: Appendix 1 (quinupristin with dalfopristin)

**Contra-indications** plasma-bilirubin concentration greater than 3 times upper limit of reference range; breast-feeding (Appendix 5)

**Side-effects** nausea, vomiting, diarrhoea, headache, arthralgia, myalgia, asthenia, rash, pruritus, anaemia, leucopenia, eosinophilia, raised urea and creatinine; injection-site reactions on peripheral venous administration; less frequently oral candidiasis, stomatitis, constipation, abdominal pain, antibiotic-associated colitis, anorexia, peripheral oedema, hypotension, chest pain, arrhythmias, dyspnoea, hypersensitivity reactions (including anaphylaxis and urticaria), insomnia, anxiety, confusion, dizziness, paraesthesia, hypertonia, hepatitis, jaundice, pancreatitis, gout; also reported, thrombocytopenia, pancytopenia, electrolyte disturbances

**Dose**

**Note** Expressed as a combination of quinupristin and dalfopristin (in a ratio of 3:7)

- ADULT over 18 years, by intravenous infusion into central vein, 7.5 mg/kg every 8 hours for 7 days in skin and soft-tissue infections; for 10 days in hospital-acquired pneumonia; duration of treatment in *E. faecium* infection depends on site of infection

**Note** In emergency, first dose may be administered *via* peripheral line until central venous catheter in place

**Synercid®** (Aventis Pharma) PoM

Intravenous infusion, powder for reconstitution, quinupristin (as mesilate) 150 mg, dalfopristin (as mesilate) 350 mg, net price 500-mg vial = £37.00

Electrolytes $Na^+$ approx. 16 mmol/500-mg vial

## Polymyxins

The polymyxin antibiotic, **colistin**, is active against Gram-negative organisms, including *Pseudomonas aeruginosa*. It is **not** absorbed by mouth and thus needs to be given by injection to obtain a systemic effect; however, it is toxic and has few, if any, indications for systemic use.

Colistin is used by mouth in bowel sterilisation regimens in neutropenic patients (usually with nystatin); it is **not** recommended for gastro-intestinal infections. It is also given by inhalation of a nebulised solution as an adjunct to standard antibacterial therapy in patients with cystic fibrosis.

Both colistin and polymyxin B are included in some preparations for topical application.

### COLISTIN

**Indications** see notes above

**Cautions** renal impairment (Appendix 3); porphyria (section 9.8.2); risk of bronchospasm on inhalation—may be prevented or treated with a selective $beta_2$ agonist; **interactions:** Appendix 1 (polymyxins)

**Contra-indications** myasthenia gravis; pregnancy (Appendix 4); breast-feeding (Appendix 5)

**Side-effects** neurotoxicity reported especially with excessive doses (including apnoea, perioral and peripheral paraesthesia, vertigo; rarely vasomotor instability, slurred speech, confusion, psychosis, visual disturbances); nephrotoxicity; hypersensitivity reactions including rash; injection-site reactions; inhalation may cause sore throat, sore mouth, cough, bronchospasm

**Dose**

- By mouth, bowel sterilisation, 1.5–3 million units every 8 hours
- By intravenous injection into a totally implantable venous access device, *or* by intravenous infusion (but see notes above), ADULT and CHILD body-weight under

60 kg, 50 000–75 000 units/kg daily in 3 divided doses; body-weight over 60 kg, 1–2 million units every 8 hours

**Note** Plasma concentration monitoring required in neonates, renal impairment, and in cystic fibrosis; recommended 'peak' plasma-colistin concentration (approx. 30 minutes after intravenous injection or infusion) 10–15 mg/litre (125–200 units/mL)

- By inhalation of nebulised solution, ADULT and CHILD over 2 years, 1–2 million units every 12 hours; CHILD under 2 years, 0.5–1 million units every 12 hours

**Colomycin®** (Forest) PoM

Tablets, scored, colistin sulphate 1.5 million units. Net price 50 = £58.28

Syrup, colistin sulphate 250 000 units/5 mL when reconstituted with water. Net price 80 mL = £3.48

Injection, powder for reconstitution, colistimethate sodium (colistin sulphomethate sodium). Net price 500 000-unit vial = £1.14; 1 million-unit vial = £1.68; 2 million-unit vial = £3.09

Electrolytes (before reconstitution) $Na^+ < 0.5$ mmol/500 000-unit, 1 million-unit, and 2 million-unit vial

**Note** *Colomycin®* Injection (dissolved in physiological saline) may be used for nebulisation

**Promixin** (Profile) PoM

Powder for nebuliser solution, colistimethate sodium (colistin sulphomethate sodium), net price 1 million-unit vial = £4.60. For use with *Prodose®* NHS nebuliser

Injection, powder for reconstitution, colistimethate sodium (colistin sulphomethate sodium), net price 1 million unit-vial = £2.30

Electrolytes (before reconstitution) $Na^+ < 0.5$ mmol/1 million-unit vial

## 5.1.8 Sulphonamides and trimethoprim

The importance of the sulphonamides has decreased as a result of increasing bacterial resistance and their replacement by antibacterials which are generally more active and less toxic.

Sulfamethoxazole (sulphamethoxazole) and trimethoprim are used in combination (as **co-trimoxazole**) because of their synergistic activity. However, co-trimoxazole is associated with rare but serious side-effects (e.g. Stevens-Johnson syndrome and blood dyscrasias, notably bone marrow depression and agranulocytosis) especially in the elderly (see CSM recommendations below).

**CSM recommendations.** Co-trimoxazole should be limited to the role of drug of choice in *Pneumocystis carinii* (*Pneumocystis jiroveci*) pneumonia; it is also indicated for *toxoplasmosis* and *nocardiasis*. It should now only be considered for use in *acute exacerbations of chronic bronchitis* and *infections of the urinary tract* when there is good bacteriological evidence of sensitivity to co-trimoxazole and good reason to prefer this combination to a single antibacterial; similarly it should only be used in *acute otitis media in children* when there is good reason to prefer it.

**Trimethoprim** can be used alone for urinary- and respiratory-tract infections and for prostatitis, shigellosis, and invasive salmonella infections. Trimethoprim has side-effects similar to co-trimoxazole but they are less severe and occur less frequently.

For *topical preparations* of sulphonamides used in the treatment of burns see section 13.10.1.1.

### CO-TRIMOXAZOLE

A mixture of trimethoprim and sulfamethoxazole in the proportions of 1 part to 5 parts

**Indications** see CSM recommendations above

**Cautions** maintain adequate fluid intake; avoid in blood disorders (unless under specialist supervision); monitor blood counts on prolonged treatment; discontinue immediately if blood disorders or rash develop; predisposition to folate deficiency or hyperkalaemia; elderly (see CSM recommendations above); asthma; G6PD deficiency (section 9.1.5); avoid in infants under 6 weeks (except for treatment or prophylaxis of pneumocystis pneumonia); hepatic impairment (avoid if severe); renal impairment (avoid if severe; Appendix 3); pregnancy (Appendix 4); breast-feeding (Appendix 5); **interactions:** Appendix 1 (trimethoprim, sulfamethoxazole)

**Contra-indications** porphyria (section 9.8.2)

**Side-effects** nausea, diarrhoea; headache; rash (very rarely including Stevens-Johnson syndrome, toxic epidermal necrolysis, photosensitivity)—discontinue immediately; *less commonly* vomiting; *very rarely* glossitis, stomatitis, anorexia, liver damage (including jaundice and hepatic necrosis), pancreatitis, antibiotic-associated colitis, myocarditis, cough and shortness of breath, pulmonary infiltrates, aseptic meningitis, depression, convulsions, peripheral neuropathy, ataxia, tinnitus, vertigo, hallucinations, hypoglycaemia, blood disorders (including leucopenia, thrombocytopenia, megaloblastic anaemia, eosinophilia), hyperkalaemia, hyponatraemia, renal disorders including interstitial nephritis, arthralgia, myalgia, vasculitis, and systemic lupus erythematosus

**Dose**

- By mouth, 960 mg every 12 hours; CHILD, every 12 hours, 6 weeks–5 months, 120 mg; 6 months–5 years, 240 mg; 6–12 years, 480 mg
- By intravenous infusion, 960 mg every 12 hours increased to 1.44 g every 12 hours in severe infections; CHILD 36 mg/kg daily in 2 divided doses increased to 54 mg/kg daily in severe infections
- Treatment of *Pneumocystis carinii* (*Pneumocystis jiroveci*) infections (undertaken where facilities for appropriate monitoring available—consult microbiologist and product literature), by mouth *or* by intravenous infusion, ADULT and CHILD over 4 weeks, 120 mg/kg daily in 2–4 divided doses for 14 days
- Prophylaxis of *Pneumocystis carinii* (*Pneumocystis jiroveci*) infections, by mouth, 960 mg once daily (may be reduced to 480 mg once daily to improve tolerance) *or* 960 mg on alternate days (3 times a week) *or* 960 mg twice daily on alternate days (3 times a week); CHILD 6 weeks–5 months, 120 mg twice daily on 3 consecutive or alternate days per week *or* on 7 days per week; 6 months–5 years, 240 mg; 6–12 years, 480 mg

**Note** 480 mg of co-trimoxazole consists of sulfamethoxazole 400 mg and trimethoprim 80 mg

**Co-trimoxazole** (Non-proprietary) PoM

Tablets, co-trimoxazole 480 mg, net price 28-tab pack = £5.19, 960 mg, 20 = £4.69. Label: 9
Brands include *Fectrim®*, *Fectrim® Forte*

Paediatric oral suspension, co-trimoxazole 240 mg/5 mL, net price 100 mL = £1.12. Label: 9

Oral suspension, co-trimoxazole 480 mg/5 mL. Net price 100 mL = £4.41. Label: 9

Strong sterile solution, co-trimoxazole 96 mg/mL. For dilution and use as an intravenous infusion. Net price 5-mL amp = £1.58, 10-mL amp = £3.06

**Septrin®** (GSK) PoM

Tablets, co-trimoxazole 480 mg. Net price 20 = £3.10. Label: 9

Forte tablets, scored, co-trimoxazole 960 mg. Net price 20 = £4.69. Label: 9

Adult suspension, co-trimoxazole 480 mg/5 mL. Net price 100 mL (vanilla-flavoured) = £4.41. Label: 9

Paediatric suspension, sugar-free, co-trimoxazole 240 mg/5 mL. Net price 100 mL (banana- and vanilla-flavoured) = £2.45. Label: 9

Intravenous infusion, co-trimoxazole 96 mg/mL. To be diluted before use. Net price 5-mL amp = £1.48
**Excipients** include propylene glycol, sulphites

## SULFADIAZINE
(Sulphadiazine)

**Indications** prevention of rheumatic fever recurrence, toxoplasmosis [unlicensed]—see section 5.4.7

**Cautions** see under Co-trimoxazole; renal impairment (avoid if severe; Appendix 3); pregnancy (Appendix 4); breast-feeding (Appendix 5); **interactions:** Appendix 1 (sulphonamides)

**Contra-indications** see under Co-trimoxazole

**Side-effects** see under Co-trimoxazole

**Dose**

- Prevention of rheumatic fever, by mouth, 1 g daily (500 mg daily for patients less than 30kg)

**Sulfadiazine** (Non-proprietary) PoM

Tablets, sulfadiazine 500 mg, net price 56-tab pack = £17.60. Label: 9, 27

Injection, sulfadiazine (as sodium salt) 250 mg/mL, net price 4-mL amp = £4.97

## TRIMETHOPRIM

**Indications** urinary-tract infections, acute and chronic bronchitis

**Cautions** renal impairment (Appendix 3); pregnancy (Appendix 4); breast-feeding (Appendix 5); predisposition to folate deficiency; elderly; manufacturer recommends blood counts on long-term therapy (but evidence of practical value unsatisfactory); neonates (specialist supervision required); porphyria (section 9.8.2); **interactions:** Appendix 1 (trimethoprim)

**Blood disorders** On long-term treatment, patients and their carers should be told how to recognise signs of blood disorders and advised to seek immediate medical attention if symptoms such as fever, sore throat, rash, mouth ulcers, purpura, bruising or bleeding develop

**Contra-indications** blood dyscrasias

**Side-effects** gastro-intestinal disturbances including nausea and vomiting, pruritus, rashes, hyperkalaemia, depression of haematopoiesis; rarely erythema multiforme, toxic epidermal necrolysis, photosensitivity and other allergic reactions including angioedema and anaphylaxis; aseptic meningitis reported

**Dose**

- Acute infections, 200 mg every 12 hours; CHILD, every 12 hours, 6 weeks–5 months 25 mg, 6 months–5 years 50 mg, 6–12 years 100 mg
- Chronic infections and prophylaxis, 100 mg at night; CHILD 1–2 mg/kg at night

**Trimethoprim** (Non-proprietary) PoM

Tablets, trimethoprim 100 mg, net price 20 = 73p; 200 mg, 14-tab pack = 99p. Label: 9
Brands include *Trimopan®*

Suspension, trimethoprim 50 mg/5 mL, net price 100 mL = £1.77. Label: 9

**Monotrim®** (Solvay) PoM

Suspension, sugar-free, trimethoprim 50 mg/5 mL. Net price 100 mL = £1.77. Label: 9

## 5.1.9 Antituberculous drugs

Tuberculosis is treated in two phases—an *initial phase* using at least three drugs and a *continuation phase* using two drugs in fully sensitive cases. Treatment requires specialised knowledge, particularly where the disease involves resistant organisms or non-respiratory organs.

The regimens given below are recommended for the treatment of tuberculosis in the UK; variations occur in other countries. Either the unsupervised regimen or the supervised regimen described below should be used; the two regimens should **not** be used concurrently.

**Initial phase** The concurrent use of 4 drugs during the initial phase is designed to reduce the bacterial population as rapidly as possible and to prevent the emergence of drug-resistant bacteria. The drugs are best given as combination preparations unless one of the components cannot be given because of resistance or intolerance. The treatment of choice for the initial phase is the daily use of isoniazid, rifampicin, pyrazinamide and ethambutol. Streptomycin is rarely used in the UK but it may be used in the initial phase of treatment if resistance to isoniazid has been established before therapy is commenced. The initial phase drugs should be continued for 2 months. Where a positive culture for *M. tuberculosis* has been obtained, but susceptibility results are not available after 2 months, treatment with pyrazinamide and ethambutol should be continued until full susceptibility is confirmed, even if this is for longer than 2 months.

**Continuation phase** After the initial phase, treatment is continued for a further 4 months with isoniazid and rifampicin (preferably given as a combination preparation). Longer treatment is necessary for meningitis and for resistant organisms which may also require modification of the regimen.

**Unsupervised treatment** The following regimen should be used for patients who are likely to take antituberculous drugs reliably **without supervision**. Patients who are unlikely to comply with daily administration of antituberculous drugs should be treated with the regimen described under Supervised Treatment.

*Recommended dosage for standard unsupervised 6-month treatment*

***Rifater®*** [rifampicin, isoniazid, and pyrazinamide] (for 2-month initial phase only)
ADULT under 40 kg 3 tablets daily, 40–49 kg 4 tablets daily, 50–64 kg 5 tablets daily, over 65 kg 6 tablets daily

**Ethambutol** (for 2-month initial phase only)
ADULT AND CHILD 15 mg/kg daily

***Rifinah®*** or ***Rimactazid®*** [rifampicin and isoniazid] (for 4-month continuation phase following initial treatment with *Rifater®*)
ADULT under 50 kg 3 tablets daily of *Rifinah®-150*, 50 kg and over, 2 tablets daily of *Rifinah®-300* or *Rimactazid®-300*

*or* (if combination preparations not appropriate):

**Isoniazid** (for 2-month initial and 4-month continuation phases)
ADULT 300 mg daily; CHILD 5–10 mg/kg (max. 300 mg) daily

**Rifampicin** (for 2-month initial and 4-month continuation phases)
ADULT under 50 kg 450 mg daily, 50 kg and over 600 mg daily; CHILD 10 mg/kg (max. 600 mg) daily

**Pyrazinamide** (for 2-month initial phase only)
ADULT under 50 kg 1.5 g daily, 50 kg and over 2 g daily; CHILD 35 mg/kg daily

**Ethambutol** (for 2-month initial phase only)
ADULT AND CHILD 15 mg/kg daily

**Pregnancy and breast-feeding** The standard regimen (above) may be used during pregnancy and breast-feeding. Streptomycin should not be given in pregnancy.

**Children** Children are given isoniazid, rifampicin, pyrazinamide, and ethambutol for the first 2 months followed by isoniazid and rifampicin during the next 4 months. However, care is needed in young children receiving ethambutol because of the difficulty in testing eyesight and in obtaining reports of visual symptoms (see below).

**Supervised treatment** Drug administration needs to be **fully supervised** (directly observed therapy, DOT) in patients who cannot comply reliably with the treatment regimen. These patients are given isoniazid, rifampicin, pyrazinamide and ethambutol (or streptomycin) 3 times a week under supervision for the first 2 months followed by isoniazid and rifampicin 3 times a week for a further 4 months.

*Recommended dosage for intermittent supervised 6-month treatment*

**Isoniazid** (for 2-month initial and 4-month continuation phases)
ADULT AND CHILD 15 mg/kg (max. 900 mg) 3 times a week

**Rifampicin** (for 2-month initial and 4-month continuation phases)
ADULT 600–900 mg 3 times a week; CHILD 15 mg/kg (max. 900 mg) 3 times a week

**Pyrazinamide** (for 2-month initial phase only)
ADULT under 50 kg 2 g 3 times a week, 50 kg and over 2.5 g 3 times a week; CHILD 50 mg/kg 3 times a week

**Ethambutol** (for 2-month initial phase only)
ADULT AND CHILD 30 mg/kg 3 times a week

**Immunocompromised patients** Multi-resistant *Mycobacterium tuberculosis* may be present in immunocompromised patients. The organism should always be cultured to confirm its type and drug sensitivity. Confirmed *M. tuberculosis* infection sensitive to first-line drugs should be treated with a standard 6-month regimen; after completing treatment, patients should be closely monitored. The regimen may need to be modified if infection is caused by resistant organisms, and specialist advice is needed.

Specialist advice should be sought about tuberculosis treatment or chemoprophylaxis in a HIV-positive individual; care is required in choosing the regimen and in avoiding potentially hazardous interactions. Starting antiretroviral treatment in the first 2 months of antituberculosis treatment increases the risk of immune reconstitution syndrome.

Infection may also be caused by other mycobacteria e.g. *M. avium* complex in which case specialist advice on management is needed.

**Prevention of tuberculosis** Some individuals may develop tuberculosis owing to reactivation of previously latent disease. Chemoprophylaxis may be required in those who have evidence of latent tuberculosis and are receiving treatment with immunosuppressants (including cytotoxics and possibly long-term treatment with systemic corticosteroids). In these cases, isoniazid chemoprophylaxis may be given for 6 months; longer chemoprophylaxis is not recommended.

For prevention of tuberculosis in susceptible close contacts or those who have become tuberculin-positive, see Table 2, section 5.1. For advice on immunisation against tuberculosis, see section 14.4

**Monitoring** Since isoniazid, rifampicin and pyrazinamide are associated with liver toxicity (see Appendix 2), *hepatic function* should be checked before treatment with these drugs. Those with pre-existing liver disease or alcohol dependence should have frequent checks particularly in the first 2 months. If there is no evidence of liver disease (and pre-treatment liver function is normal), further checks are only necessary if the patient develops fever, malaise, vomiting, jaundice or unexplained deterioration during treatment. In view of the need to comply fully with antituberculous treatment on the one hand and to guard against serious liver damage on the other, patients and their carers should be informed carefully how to recognise signs of liver disorders and advised to discontinue treatment and seek **immediate** medical attention should symptoms of liver disease occur.

*Renal function* should be checked before treatment with antituberculous drugs and appropriate dosage adjustments made. Streptomycin or ethambutol should preferably be avoided in patients with renal impairment, but if used, the dose should be reduced and the plasma-drug concentration monitored.

*Visual acuity* should be tested before ethambutol is used (see below).

> Major causes of treatment failure are incorrect prescribing by the physician and inadequate compliance by the patient. Monthly tablet counts and urine examination (rifampicin imparts an orange-red coloration) may be useful indicators of compliance with treatment. Avoid both excessive and inadequate dosage. Treatment should be supervised by a specialist physician.

**Isoniazid** is cheap and highly effective. Like rifampicin it should always be included in any antituberculous regimen unless there is a specific contra-indication. Its only common side-effect is peripheral neuropathy which is more likely to occur where there are pre-existing risk factors such as diabetes, alcohol dependence, chronic renal failure, malnutrition and HIV infection. In these circumstances pyridoxine 10 mg daily (or 20 mg daily if suitable product not available) (section 9.6.2) should be given prophylactically from the start of treatment. Other side-effects such as hepatitis (important: see Monitoring above) and psychosis are rare.

**Rifampicin**, a rifamycin, is a key component of any antituberculous regimen. Like isoniazid it should always be included unless there is a specific contra-indication.

During the first two months ('initial phase') of rifampicin administration transient disturbance of liver function with elevated serum transaminases is common but generally does not require interruption of treatment. Occasionally more serious liver toxicity requires a change of treatment particularly in those with pre-existing liver disease (important: see Monitoring above).

On intermittent treatment six toxicity syndromes have been recognised—influenza-like, abdominal, and respiratory symptoms, shock, renal failure, and thrombocytopenic purpura—and can occur in 20 to 30% of patients.

Rifampicin induces hepatic enzymes which accelerate the metabolism of several drugs including oestrogens, corticosteroids, phenytoin, sulphonylureas, and anticoagulants; **interactions:** Appendix 1 (rifamycins). **Important:** the effectiveness of hormonal contraceptives is reduced and alternative family planning advice should be offered (section 7.3.1).

**Rifabutin**, a newly introduced rifamycin, is indicated for *prophylaxis* against *M. avium* complex infections in patients with a low CD4 count; it is also licensed for the *treatment* of non-tuberculous mycobacterial disease and pulmonary tuberculosis. **Important:** as with rifampicin it induces hepatic enzymes and the effectiveness of hormonal contraceptives is reduced requiring alternative family planning methods.

**Pyrazinamide** [unlicensed] is a bactericidal drug only active against intracellular dividing forms of *Mycobacterium tuberculosis*; it exerts its main effect only in the first two or three months. It is particularly useful in tuberculous meningitis because of good meningeal penetration. It is not active against *M. bovis*. Serious liver toxicity may occasionally occur (important: see Monitoring above).

**Ethambutol** is included in a treatment regimen if isoniazid resistance is suspected; it can be omitted if the risk of resistance is low.

Side-effects of ethambutol are largely confined to visual disturbances in the form of loss of acuity, colour blindness, and restriction of visual fields. These toxic effects are more common where excessive dosage is used or if the patient's renal function is impaired. The earliest features of ocular toxicity are subjective and patients should be advised to discontinue therapy immediately if they develop deterioration in vision and promptly seek further advice. Early discontinuation of the drug is almost always followed by recovery of eyesight. Patients who cannot understand warnings about visual side-effects should, if possible, be given an alternative drug. In particular, ethambutol should be used with caution in children until they are at least 5 years old and capable of reporting symptomatic visual changes accurately.

Visual acuity should be tested by Snellen chart before treatment with ethambutol.

**Streptomycin** [unlicensed] is now rarely used in the UK except for resistant organisms. It is given intramuscularly in a dose of 15 mg/kg (max. 1 g) daily; the dose is reduced in those under 50 kg, those over 40 years or those with renal impairment. Plasma-drug concentration should be measured in patients with impaired renal function in whom streptomycin must be used with great care. Side-effects increase after a cumulative dose of 100 g, which should only be exceeded in exceptional circumstances.

Drug-resistant tuberculosis should be treated by a specialist physician with experience in such cases, and where appropriate facilities for infection-control exist. Second-line drugs available for infections caused by resistant organisms, or when first-line drugs cause unacceptable side-effects, include amikacin, capreomycin, cycloserine, newer macrolides (e.g. azithromycin and clarithromycin), moxifloxacin and protionamide (prothionamide) (no longer on UK market).

## CAPREOMYCIN

**Indications** in combination with other drugs, tuberculosis resistant to first-line drugs

**Cautions** hepatic impairment; renal impairment (Appendix 3); auditory impairment; monitor renal, hepatic, auditory, and vestibular function and electrolytes; pregnancy (teratogenic in *animals*; Appendix 4) and breast-feeding (Appendix 5); **interactions:** Appendix 1 (capreomycin)

**Side-effects** hypersensitivity reactions including urticaria and rashes; leucocytosis or leucopenia, rarely thrombocytopenia; changes in liver function tests; nephrotoxicity, electrolyte disturbances; hearing loss with tinnitus and vertigo; neuromuscular block after large doses, pain and induration at injection site

**Dose**

- By deep intramuscular injection, 1 g daily (not more than 20 mg/kg) for 2–4 months, then 1 g 2–3 times each week

**Capastat®** (King) PoM
Injection, powder for reconstitution, capreomycin sulphate 1 million units (= capreomycin approx. 1 g). Net price per vial = £16.01

## CYCLOSERINE

**Indications** in combination with other drugs, tuberculosis resistant to first-line drugs

**Cautions** reduce dose in renal impairment (avoid if severe); monitor haematological, renal, and hepatic function; pregnancy (Appendix 4); breast-feeding (Appendix 5); **interactions:** Appendix 1 (cycloserine)

**Contra-indications** severe renal impairment, epilepsy, depression, severe anxiety, psychotic states, alcohol dependence, porphyria (section 9.8.2)

**Side-effects** mainly neurological, including headache, dizziness, vertigo, drowsiness, tremor, convulsions, confusion, psychosis, depression (discontinue or reduce dose if symptoms of CNS toxicity); rashes, allergic dermatitis (discontinue or reduce dose);

megaloblastic anaemia; changes in liver function tests; heart failure at high doses reported

**Dose**

- Initially 250 mg every 12 hours for 2 weeks increased according to blood concentration and response to max. 500 mg every 12 hours; CHILD initially 10 mg/kg daily adjusted according to blood concentration and response

  **Note** Blood concentration monitoring required especially in renal impairment or if dose exceeds 500 mg daily or if signs of toxicity; blood concentration should not exceed 30 mg/litre

**Cycloserine** (King) PoM

Capsules, red/grey cycloserine 250 mg, net price 100-cap pack = £220.69. Label: 2, 8

## ETHAMBUTOL HYDROCHLORIDE

**Indications** tuberculosis, in combination with other drugs

**Cautions** reduce dose in renal impairment and if creatinine clearance less than 30 mL/minute, also monitor plasma-ethambutol concentration (Appendix 3); elderly; pregnancy; test visual acuity before treatment and warn patients to report visual changes—see notes above; young children (see notes above)—routine ophthalmological monitoring recommended

**Contra-indications** optic neuritis, poor vision

**Side-effects** optic neuritis, red/green colour blindness, peripheral neuritis, rarely rash, pruritus, urticaria, thrombocytopenia

**Dose**

- See notes above

  **Note** 'Peak' concentration (2–2.5 hours after dose) should be 2–6 mg/litre (7–22 micromol/litre); 'trough' (pre-dose) concentration should be less than 1 mg/litre (4 micromol/litre); for advice on laboratory assay of ethambutol contact the Poisons Unit at New Cross Hospital (Tel (020) 7771 5360)

**Ethambutol** (Non-proprietary) PoM

Tablets, ethambutol hydrochloride 100 mg (yellow), net price 56-tab pack = £11.50; 400 mg (grey), 56-tab pack = £42.73. Label: 8

## ISONIAZID

**Indications** tuberculosis, in combination with other drugs; prophylaxis—Table 2, section 5.1

**Cautions** hepatic impairment (Appendix 2; see also below); renal impairment (Appendix 3); slow acetylator status (increased risk of side-effects); epilepsy; history of psychosis; alcohol dependence, malnutrition, diabetes mellitus, HIV infection (risk of peripheral neuritis); pregnancy (Appendix 4) and breast-feeding (Appendix 5); porphyria (section 9.8.2); **interactions:** Appendix 1 (isoniazid)

**Hepatic disorders** Patients or their carers should be told how to recognise signs of liver disorder, and advised to discontinue treatment and seek immediate medical attention if symptoms such as persistent nausea, vomiting, malaise or jaundice develop

**Contra-indications** drug-induced liver disease

**Side-effects** nausea, vomiting, constipation, dry mouth; peripheral neuritis with high doses (pyridoxine prophylaxis, see notes above), optic neuritis, convulsions, psychotic episodes, vertigo; hypersensitivity reactions including fever, erythema multiforme, purpura; blood disorders including agranulocytosis, haemolytic anaemia, aplastic anaemia; hepatitis (especially over age of 35 years); systemic lupus erythematosus-like syndrome, pellagra, hyperreflexia, difficulty with micturition, hyperglycaemia, and gynaecomastia reported

**Dose**

- By mouth *or* by intramuscular *or* intravenous injection, see notes above

**Isoniazid** (Non-proprietary) PoM

Tablets, isoniazid 50 mg, net price 56-tab pack = £5.78; 100 mg, 28-tab pack = £5.77. Label: 8, 22

Elixir (BPC), isoniazid 50 mg, citric acid monohydrate 12.5 mg, sodium citrate 60 mg, concentrated anise water 0.05 mL, compound tartrazine solution 0.05 mL, glycerol 1 mL, double-strength chloroform water 2 mL, water to 5 mL. Label: 8, 22

'Special order' [unlicensed] product; contact Martindale, Rosemont, or regional hospital manufacturing unit

Injection, isoniazid 25 mg/mL, net price 2-mL amp = £7.39

## PYRAZINAMIDE

**Indications** tuberculosis in combination with other drugs

**Cautions** pregnancy (Appendix 4); hepatic impairment (monitor hepatic function, see also below and Appendix 2); diabetes; gout (avoid in acute attack); **interactions:** Appendix 1 (pyrazinamide)

**Hepatic disorders** Patients or their carers should be told how to recognise signs of liver disorder, and advised to discontinue treatment and seek immediate medical attention if symptoms such as persistent nausea, vomiting, malaise or jaundice develop

**Contra-indications** porphyria (section 9.8.2)

**Side-effects** hepatotoxicity including fever, anorexia, hepatomegaly, splenomegaly, jaundice, liver failure; nausea, vomiting, flushing, dysuria, arthralgia, sideroblastic anaemia, rash and occasionally photosensitivity

**Dose**

- See notes above

**Pyrazinamide** (Non-proprietary) PoM

Tablets, scored, pyrazinamide 500 mg. Label: 8

Available on named-patient basis from IDIS

## RIFABUTIN

**Indications** see under Dose

**Cautions** see under Rifampicin; hepatic impairment (Appendix 2); renal impairment (Appendix 3); pregnancy (Appendix 4); breast-feeding (Appendix 5); porphyria (section 9.8.2)

**Side-effects** nausea, vomiting; leucopenia, thrombocytopenia, anaemia, rarely haemolysis; raised liver enzymes, jaundice, rarely hepatitis; uveitis following high doses or administration with drugs which raise plasma concentration—see also **interactions:** Appendix 1 (rifamycins); arthralgia, myalgia, influenza-like syndrome, dyspnoea; also hypersensitivity reactions including fever, rash, eosinophilia, bronchospasm, shock; skin, urine, saliva and other body secretions coloured orange-red; asymptomatic corneal opacities reported with long-term use

**Dose**

- Prophylaxis of *Mycobacterium avium* complex infections in immunosuppressed patients with low CD4 count (see product literature), 300 mg daily as a single dose

- Treatment of non-tuberculous mycobacterial disease, in combination with other drugs, 450–600 mg daily as a single dose for up to 6 months after cultures negative
- Treatment of pulmonary tuberculosis, in combination with other drugs, 150–450 mg daily as a single dose for at least 6 months
- CHILD not recommended

**Mycobutin®** (Pharmacia) PoM
Capsules, red-brown, rifabutin 150 mg. Net price 30-cap pack = £90.38. Label: 8, 14, counselling, lenses, see under Rifampicin

## RIFAMPICIN

**Indications** see under Dose

**Cautions** hepatic impairment (Appendix 2; liver function tests and blood counts in hepatic disorders, alcohol dependence, and on prolonged therapy, see also below); renal impairment (if above 600 mg daily); pregnancy and breast-feeding (see notes above and Appendix 4 and Appendix 5); porphyria (section 9.8.2); **important:** advise patients on hormonal contraceptives to use additional means (see also section 7.3.1); discolours soft contact lenses; see also notes above; **interactions:** Appendix 1 (rifamycins)

Note If treatment interrupted re-introduce with low dosage and increase gradually; discontinue permanently if serious side-effects develop

Hepatic disorders Patients or their carers should be told how to recognise signs of liver disorder, and advised to discontinue treatment and seek immediate medical attention if symptoms such as persistent nausea, vomiting, malaise or jaundice develop

**Contra-indications** jaundice

**Side-effects** gastro-intestinal symptoms including anorexia, nausea, vomiting, diarrhoea (antibiotic-associated colitis reported); headache, drowsiness; those occurring mainly on intermittent therapy include influenza-like symptoms (with chills, fever, dizziness, bone pain), respiratory symptoms (including shortness of breath), collapse and shock, haemolytic anaemia, acute renal failure, and thrombocytopenic purpura; alterations of liver function, jaundice; flushing, urticaria, and rashes; other side-effects reported include oedema, muscular weakness and myopathy, exfoliative dermatitis, toxic epidermal necrolysis, pemphigoid reactions, leucopenia, eosinophilia, menstrual disturbances; urine, saliva, and other body secretions coloured orange-red; thrombophlebitis reported if infusion used for prolonged period

**Dose**

- Brucellosis, legionnaires' disease, endocarditis and serious staphylococcal infections, in combination with other drugs, by mouth *or* by intravenous infusion, 0.6–1.2 g daily (in 2–4 divided doses)
- Tuberculosis, in combination with other drugs, see notes above
- Leprosy, section 5.1.10
- Prophylaxis of meningococcal meningitis and *Haemophilus influenzae* (type b) infection, section 5.1, table 2

**Rifampicin** (Non-proprietary) PoM
Capsules, rifampicin 150 mg, net price 20 = £5.27.; 300 mg, 20 = £10.16. Label: 8, 14, 22, counselling, see lenses above

**Rifadin®** (Aventis Pharma) PoM
Capsules, rifampicin 150 mg (blue/red), net price 20 = £3.81; 300 mg (red), 20 = £7.62. Label: 8, 14, 22, counselling, see lenses above

Syrup, red, rifampicin 100 mg/5 mL (raspberry-flavoured). Net price 120 mL = £3.70. Label: 8, 14, 22, counselling, see lenses above

Intravenous infusion, powder for reconstitution, rifampicin. Net price 600-mg vial (with solvent) = £7.98
Electrolytes $Na^+$ < 0.5 mmol/vial

**Rimactane®** (Sandoz) PoM
Capsules, rifampicin 150 mg (red), net price 60-cap pack = £11.35; 300 mg (red/brown), 60-cap pack = £22.69. Label: 8, 14, 22, counselling, see lenses above

### Combined preparations

**Rifater®** (Aventis Pharma) PoM
Tablets, pink, s/c, rifampicin 120 mg, isoniazid 50 mg, pyrazinamide 300 mg. Net price 20 = £4.39. Label: 8, 14, 22, counselling, see lenses above
Dose initial treatment of pulmonary tuberculosis, patients up to 40 kg 3 tablets daily preferably before breakfast, 40–49 kg 4 tablets daily, 50–64 kg 5 tablets daily, 65 kg or more, 6 tablets daily; not suitable for use in children

**Rifinah 150®** (Aventis Pharma) PoM
Tablets, pink, s/c, rifampicin 150 mg, isoniazid 100 mg, net price 84-tab pack = £16.55. Label: 8, 14, 22, counselling, see lenses above
Dose ADULT under 50 kg, 3 tablets daily, preferably before breakfast

**Rifinah 300®** (Aventis Pharma) PoM
Tablets, orange, s/c, rifampicin 300 mg, isoniazid 150 mg, net price 56-tab pack = £21.87. Label: 8, 14, 22, counselling, see lenses above
Dose ADULT 50 kg and over, 2 tablets daily, preferably before breakfast

**Rimactazid 300®** (Sandoz) PoM
Tablets, orange, s/c, rifampicin 300 mg, isoniazid 150 mg, net price 60-tab pack = £38.77. Label: 8, 14, 22, counselling, see lenses above
Dose ADULT 50 kg and over, 2 tablets daily, preferably before breakfast

## STREPTOMYCIN

**Indications** tuberculosis, in combination with other drugs; adjunct to doxycycline in brucellosis; enterococcal endocarditis (Table 1, section 5.1)

**Cautions** see under Aminoglycosides, section 5.1.4; **interactions:** Appendix 1 (aminoglycosides)

**Contra-indications** see under Aminoglycosides, section 5.1.4

**Side-effects** see under Aminoglycosides, section 5.1.4; also hypersensitivity reactions, paraesthesia of mouth

**Dose**

- By deep intramuscular injection, tuberculosis, see notes above; brucellosis, expert advice essential

Note One-hour ('peak') concentration should be 15–40 mg/litre; pre-dose ('trough') concentration should be less than 5 mg/litre (less than 1 mg/litre in renal impairment or in those over 50 years)

**Streptomycin Sulphate** (Non-proprietary) PoM
Injection, powder for reconstitution, streptomycin (as sulphate), net price 1-g vial = £8.25
Available on named-patient basis from Celltech

## 5.1.10 Antileprotic drugs

Advice from a member of the Panel of Leprosy Opinion is essential for the treatment of leprosy (Hansen's disease). Details of the Panel can be obtained from the Department of Health telephone (020) 7972 4480.

The World Health Organization has made recommendations to overcome the problem of dapsone resistance and to prevent the emergence of resistance to other antileprotic drugs. Drugs recommended are **dapsone**, **rifampicin** (section 5.1.9), and **clofazimine**. Other drugs with significant activity against *Mycobacterium leprae* include ofloxacin, minocycline and clarithromycin, but none of these are as active as rifampicin; at present they should be reserved as second-line drugs for leprosy.

A three-drug regimen is recommended for *multibacillary leprosy* (lepromatous, borderline-lepromatous, and borderline leprosy) and a two-drug regimen for *paucibacillary leprosy* (borderline-tuberculoid, tuberculoid, and indeterminate). The following regimens are widely used throughout the world (with minor local variations):

*Multibacillary leprosy (3-drug regimen)*

| | |
|---|---|
| Rifampicin | 600 mg once-monthly, supervised (450 mg for adults weighing less than 35 kg) |
| Dapsone | 100 mg daily, self-administered (50 mg daily or 1–2 mg/kg daily for adults weighing less than 35 kg) |
| Clofazimine | 300 mg once-monthly, supervised, *and* 50 mg daily (or 100 mg on alternate days), self-administered |

Multibacillary leprosy should be treated for at least 2 years. Treatment should be continued unchanged during both type I (reversal) or type II (erythema nodosum leprosum) reactions. During reversal reactions neuritic pain or weakness can herald the rapid onset of permanent nerve damage. Treatment with prednisolone (initially 40–60 mg daily) should be instituted at once. Mild type II reactions may respond to aspirin or chloroquine. Severe type II reactions may require corticosteroids; thalidomide [unlicensed] is also useful in men and post-menopausal women who have become corticosteroid dependent, but it should be used under **specialist supervision** and it should **never** be used in women of child-bearing potential (significant teratogenic risk—for CSM guidance on prescribing, see *Current Problems in Pharmacovigilance* 1994; **20**, 8). Increased doses of clofazimine 100 mg 3 times daily for the first month with subsequent reductions, are also useful but may take 4–6 weeks to attain full effect.

*Paucibacillary leprosy (2-drug regimen)*

| | |
|---|---|
| Rifampicin | 600 mg once-monthly, supervised (450 mg for those weighing less than 35 kg) |
| Dapsone | 100 mg daily, self-administered (50 mg daily or 1–2 mg/kg daily for adults weighing less than 35 kg) |

Paucibacillary leprosy should be treated for 6 months. If treatment is interrupted the regimen should be recommenced where it was left off to complete the full course.

Neither the multibacillary nor the paucibacillary antileprosy regimen is sufficient to treat tuberculosis.



### DAPSONE

**Indications** leprosy, dermatitis herpetiformis; *Pneumocystis carinii* (*Pneumocystis jiroveci*) pneumonia (section 5.4.8)

**Cautions** cardiac or pulmonary disease; anaemia (treat severe anaemia before starting); susceptibility to haemolysis including G6PD deficiency (section 9.1.5)—susceptible breast-feeding infants also at risk (Appendix 5); pregnancy (Appendix 4); avoid in porphyria (section 9.8.2); **interactions**: Appendix 1 (dapsone)

**Blood disorders** On long-term treatment, patients and their carers should be told how to recognise signs of blood disorders and advised to seek immediate medical attention if symptoms such as fever, sore throat, rash, mouth ulcers, purpura, bruising or bleeding develop

**Side-effects** (dose-related and uncommon at doses used for leprosy), haemolysis, methaemoglobinaemia, neuropathy, allergic dermatitis (rarely including toxic epidermal necrolysis and Stevens-Johnson syndrome), anorexia, nausea, vomiting, tachycardia, headache, insomnia, psychosis, hepatitis, agranulocytosis; dapsone syndrome (rash with fever and eosinophilia)—discontinue immediately (may progress to exfoliative dermatitis, hepatitis, hypoalbuminaemia, psychosis and death)

**Dose**

- Leprosy, 1–2 mg/kg daily, see notes above
- Dermatitis herpetiformis, see specialist literature

**Dapsone** (Non-proprietary) PoM
Tablets, dapsone 50 mg, net price 28-tab pack = £3.12; 100 mg, 28-tab pack = £4.23. Label: 8

### CLOFAZIMINE

**Indications** leprosy

**Cautions** hepatic and renal impairment; pregnancy and breast-feeding; may discolour soft contact lenses; avoid if persistent abdominal pain and diarrhoea

**Side-effects** nausea, vomiting (hospitalise if persistent), abdominal pain; headache, tiredness; brownish-black discoloration of lesions and skin including areas exposed to light; reversible hair discoloration; dry skin; red discoloration of faeces, urine and other body fluids; also rash, pruritus, photosensitivity, acne-like eruptions, anorexia, eosinophilic enteropathy, bowel obstruction, dry eyes, dimmed vision, macular and subepithelial corneal pigmentation; elevation of blood sugar, weight loss, splenic infarction, lymphadenopathy

**Dose**

- Leprosy, see notes above
- Lepromatous lepra reactions, dosage increased to 300 mg daily for max. of 3 months

**Clofazimine** (Non-proprietary) PoM
Capsules, clofazimine 100 mg. Label: 8, 14, 21
Available on named-patient basis

## 5.1.11 Metronidazole and tinidazole

**Metronidazole** is an antimicrobial drug with high activity against anaerobic bacteria and protozoa; indications include trichomonal vaginitis (section 5.4.3), bacterial vaginosis (notably *Gardnerella vaginalis* infections), and *Entamoeba histolytica* and *Giardia lamblia* infections (section 5.4.2). It is also used for surgical and gynaecological sepsis in which its activity against colonic anaerobes, especially *Bacteroides fragilis*, is important. Metronidazole is also effective in the treatment of antibiotic-associated colitis (pseudomembranous colitis, see also section 1.5). Metronidazole by the rectal route is an effective alternative to the intravenous route when oral administration is not possible. Intravenous metronidazole is used for the treatment of established cases of tetanus; diazepam (section 10.2.2) and tetanus immunoglobulin (section 14.5) are also used.

Topical metronidazole (section 13.10.1.2) reduces the odour produced by anaerobic bacteria in fungating tumours; it is also used in the management of rosacea (section 13.6).

**Tinidazole** is similar to metronidazole but has a longer duration of action.

**Oral infections** Metronidazole is an alternative to a penicillin for the treatment of many oral infections where the patient is allergic to penicillin or the infection is due to beta-lactamase-producing anaerobes (Table 1, section 5.1). It is the drug of first choice for the treatment of acute necrotising ulcerative gingivitis (Vincent's infection) and pericoronitis; suitable alternatives are amoxicillin (section 5.1.1.3) and erythromycin (section 5.1.5). For these purposes metronidazole in a dose of 200 mg 3 times daily for 3 days is sufficient, but the duration of treatment may need to be longer in pericoronitis. Tinidazole is licensed for the treatment of acute ulcerative gingivitis.

## METRONIDAZOLE

**Indications** anaerobic infections (including dental), see under Dose below; protozoal infections (section 5.4.2); *Helicobacter pylori* eradication (section 1.3); skin (section 13.10.1.2)

**Cautions** disulfiram-like reaction with alcohol, hepatic impairment and hepatic encephalopathy (Appendix 2); pregnancy (Appendix 4) and breast-feeding (Appendix 5); avoid in porphyria (section 9.8.2); clinical and laboratory monitoring advised if treatment exceeds 10 days; **interactions:** Appendix 1 (metronidazole)

**Side-effects** gastro-intestinal disturbances (including nausea and vomiting), taste disturbances, furred tongue, oral mucositis, anorexia; *very rarely* hepatitis, jaundice, pancreatitis, drowsiness, dizziness, headache, ataxia, psychotic disorders, darkening of urine, thrombocytopenia, pancytopenia, myalgia, arthralgia, visual disturbances, rash, pruritus, and erythema multiforme; on prolonged or intensive therapy peripheral neuropathy, transient epileptiform seizures, and leucopenia

**Dose**

- Anaerobic infections (usually treated for 7 days and for 10 days in antibiotic-associated colitis), by mouth, *either* 800 mg initially then 400 mg every 8 hours *or* 500 mg every 8 hours, CHILD 7.5 mg/kg every 8 hours; by rectum, 1 g every 8 hours for 3 days, then 1 g every 12 hours, CHILD every 8 hours for 3 days, then every 12 hours, age up to 1 year 125 mg, 1–5 years 250 mg, 5–10 years 500 mg, over 10 years, adult dose; by intravenous infusion over 20 minutes, 500 mg every 8 hours; CHILD 7.5 mg/kg every 8 hours
- Leg ulcers and pressure sores, by mouth, 400 mg every 8 hours for 7 days
- Bacterial vaginosis, by mouth, 400–500 mg twice daily for 5–7 days *or* 2 g as a single dose
- Pelvic inflammatory disease (see also Table 1, section 5.1), by mouth, 400 mg twice daily for 14 days
- Acute ulcerative gingivitis, by mouth, 200–250 mg every 8 hours for 3 days; CHILD 1–3 years 50 mg every 8 hours for 3 days; 3–7 years 100 mg every 12 hours; 7–10 years 100 mg every 8 hours
- Acute oral infections, by mouth, 200 mg every 8 hours for 3–7 days (see also notes above); CHILD 1–3 years 50 mg every 8 hours for 3–7 days; 3–7 years 100 mg every 12 hours; 7–10 years 100 mg every 8 hours
- Surgical prophylaxis, by mouth, 400–500 mg 2 hours before surgery; up to 3 further doses of 400–500 mg may be given every 8 hours for high-risk procedures; CHILD 7.5 mg/kg 2 hours before surgery; up to 3 further doses of 7.5 mg/kg may be given every 8 hours for high-risk procedures

  By rectum, 1 g 2 hours before surgery; up to 3 further doses of 1 g may be given every 8 hours for high-risk procedures; CHILD 5–10 years 500 mg 2 hours before surgery; up to 3 further doses of 500 mg may be given every 8 hours for high-risk procedures

  By intravenous infusion (if rectal administration inappropriate), 500 mg at induction; up to 3 further doses of 500 mg may be given every 8 hours for high-risk procedures; CHILD 7.5 mg/kg at induction; up to 3 further doses of 7.5 mg/kg may be given every 8 hours for high-risk procedures

**Note** Metronidazole doses in BNF may differ from those in product literature

**Metronidazole** (Non-proprietary) PoM

Tablets, metronidazole 200 mg, net price 21-tab pack = £1.17; 400 mg, 21-tab pack = £1.41. Label: 4, 9, 21, 25, 27

Brands include *Vaginyl®*

Tablets, metronidazole 500 mg, net price 21-tab pack = £5.36. Label: 4, 9, 21, 25, 27

Suspension, metronidazole (as benzoate) 200 mg/ 5 mL. Net price 100 mL = £7.70. Label: 4, 9, 23

Brands include *Norzol®*

Intravenous infusion, metronidazole 5 mg/mL. Net price 20-mL amp = £1.53, 100-mL container = £3.41

**Dental prescribing on NHS** Metronidazole Tablets and Oral Suspension may be prescribed

**Flagyl®** (Winthrop) PoM

Tablets, both f/c, ivory, metronidazole 200 mg, net price 21-tab pack = £3.62; 400 mg, 14-tab pack = £5.12. Label: 4, 9, 21, 25, 27

Suppositories, metronidazole 500 mg, net price 10 = £12.25; 1 g, 10 = £18.60. Label: 4, 9

**Flagyl®** (Aventis Pharma) PoM

Intravenous infusion, metronidazole 5 mg/mL, net price 100-mL *Viaflex®* bag = £3.41

Electrolytes $Na^+$ 13.6 mmol/100-mL bag

**Flagyl S®** (Winthrop) PoM

Suspension, orange- and lemon-flavoured, metronidazole (as benzoate) 200 mg/5 mL. Net price 100 mL = £9.01. Label: 4, 9, 23

**Metrolyl®** (Sandoz) PoM

Intravenous infusion, metronidazole 5 mg/mL, net price 100-mL Steriflex® bag = £1.22

Electrolytes $Na^+$ 14.53 mmol/100-mL bag

Suppositories, metronidazole 500 mg, net price 10 = £12.34; 1 g, 10 = £18.34. Label: 4, 9

## TINIDAZOLE

**Indications** anaerobic infections, see under Dose below; protozoal infections (section 5.4.2); *Helicobacter pylori* eradication (section 1.3)

**Cautions** see under Metronidazole; pregnancy (manufacturer advises avoid in first trimester); avoid in porphyria (section 9.8.2); **interactions:** Appendix 1 (tinidazole)

**Side-effects** see under Metronidazole

**Dose**

- Anaerobic infections, 2 g initially, followed by 1 g daily *or* 500 mg twice daily, usually for 5–6 days
- Bacterial vaginosis and acute ulcerative gingivitis, a single 2-g dose
- Abdominal surgery prophylaxis, a single 2-g dose approximately 12 hours before surgery

**Fasigyn®** (Pfizer) PoM

Tablets, f/c, tinidazole 500 mg. Net price 20-tab pack = £13.80. Label: 4, 9, 21, 25

# 5.1.12 Quinolones

**Nalidixic acid** and **norfloxacin** are effective in uncomplicated urinary-tract infections.

**Ciprofloxacin** is active against both Gram-positive and Gram-negative bacteria. It is particularly active against Gram-negative bacteria, including salmonella, shigella, campylobacter, neisseria, and pseudomonas. Ciprofloxacin has only moderate activity against Gram-positive bacteria such as *Streptococcus pneumoniae* and *Enterococcus faecalis*; it should not be used for pneumococcal pneumonia. It is active against chlamydia and some mycobacteria. Most anaerobic organisms are not susceptible. Uses for ciprofloxacin include infections of the respiratory tract (but not for pneumococcal pneumonia) and of the urinary tract, and of the gastro-intestinal system (including typhoid fever), and gonorrhoea and septicaemia caused by sensitive organisms.

**Ofloxacin** is used for urinary-tract infections, lower respiratory-tract infections, gonorrhoea, and non-gonococcal urethritis and cervicitis.

**Levofloxacin** is active against Gram-positive and Gram-negative organisms. It has greater activity against pneumococci than ciprofloxacin. Levofloxacin is licensed for community-acquired pneumonia but it is considered to be **second-line treatment** for this indication.

Although ciprofloxacin, levofloxacin and ofloxacin are licensed for skin and soft-tissue infections, many staphylococci are resistant to the quinolones and their use should be avoided in MRSA infections.

**Moxifloxacin** should be used for treating acute exacerbations of chronic bronchitis **only** if conventional treatment has failed or is contra-indicated, and for **second-line treatment** of community-acquired pneumonia. Moxifloxacin is active against Gram-positive and Gram-negative organisms. It has greater activity against Gram-positive organisms including pneumococci than ciprofloxacin. Moxifloxacin is not active against *Pseudomonas aeruginosa* or meticillin-resistant *Staphylococcus aureus* (MRSA).

**Anthrax** *Inhalation* or *gastro-intestinal anthrax* should be treated initially with either **ciprofloxacin** or **doxycycline** [unlicensed indication] (section 5.1.3) combined with one or two other antibacterials (such as amoxicillin, benzylpenicillin, chloramphenicol, clarithromycin, clindamycin, imipenem with cilastatin, rifampicin [unlicensed indication], and vancomycin). When the condition improves and the sensitivity of the *Bacillus anthracis* strain is known, treatment may be switched to a single antibacterial. Treatment should continue for 60 days because germination may be delayed.

*Cutaneous anthrax* should be treated with either ciprofloxacin [unlicensed indication] or doxycycline [unlicensed indication] (section 5.1.3) for 7 days. Treatment may be switched to amoxicillin (section 5.1.1.3) if the infecting strain is susceptible. Treatment may need to be extended to 60 days if exposure is due to aerosol. A combination of antibacterials for 14 days is recommended for cutaneous anthrax with systemic features, extensive oedema, or lesions of the head or neck.

Ciprofloxacin or doxycycline may be given for *post-exposure prophylaxis*. If exposure is confirmed, antibacterial prophylaxis should continue for 60 days. Antibacterial prophylaxis may be switched to amoxicillin after 10–14 days if the strain of *B. anthracis* is susceptible. Vaccination against anthrax (section 14.4) may allow the duration of antibacterial prophylaxis to be shortened.

**Cautions** Quinolones should be used with caution in patients with a history of epilepsy or conditions that predispose to seizures, in G6PD deficiency (section 9.1.5), myasthenia gravis (risk of exacerbation), in renal impairment (Appendix 3); pregnancy (Appendix 4), during breast-feeding (Appendix 5), and in children or adolescents (arthropathy has developed in weight-bearing joints in young *animals*—see below). Exposure to excessive sunlight should be avoided (discontinue if photosensitivity occurs). The CSM has warned that quinolones may induce **convulsions** in patients with or without a history of convulsions; taking NSAIDs at the same time may also induce them. Other **interactions:** Appendix 1 (quinolones).

**Use in children** Quinolones cause arthropathy in the weight-bearing joints of immature *animals* and are therefore generally not recommended in children and growing adolescents. However, the significance of this effect in humans is uncertain and in some specific circumstances short-term use of a quinolone in children may be justified. Nalidixic acid is used for urinary-tract infections in children over 3 months of age. Ciprofloxacin is licensed for pseudomonal infections in cystic fibrosis (for children above 5 years of age), and for treatment and prophylaxis of inhalational anthrax.

**CSM advice (tendon damage)**

Tendon damage (including rupture) has been reported rarely in patients receiving quinolones. Tendon rupture may occur within 48 hours of starting treatment. The CSM has reminded that:

- quinolones are contra-indicated in patients with a history of tendon disorders related to quinolone use;
- elderly patients are more prone to tendinitis;
- the risk of tendon rupture is increased by the concomitant use of corticosteroids;
- if tendinitis is suspected, the quinolone should be discontinued immediately.

**Side-effects** Side-effects of the quinolones include nausea, vomiting, dyspepsia, abdominal pain, diarrhoea (rarely antibiotic-associated colitis), headache, dizziness, sleep disorders, rash (rarely Stevens-Johnson syndrome and toxic epidermal necrolysis), and pruritus. Less frequent side-effects include anorexia, increase in blood urea and creatinine; drowsiness, restlessness, asthenia, depression, confusion, hallucinations, convulsions, tremor, paraesthesia, hypoaesthesia; photosensitivity, hypersensitivity reactions including fever, urticaria, angioedema, arthralgia, myalgia, and anaphylaxis; blood disorders (including eosinophilia, leucopenia, thrombocytopenia); disturbances in vision, taste, hearing and smell. Also isolated reports of tendon inflammation and damage (especially in the elderly and in those taking corticosteroids, see also CSM advice above). Other side-effects that have been reported include haemolytic anaemia, renal failure, interstitial nephritis, and hepatic dysfunction (including hepatitis and cholestatic jaundice). The drug should be **discontinued** if psychiatric, neurological or hypersensitivity reactions (including severe rash) occur.

## CIPROFLOXACIN

**Indications** see notes above and under Dose; eye infections (section 11.3.1)

**Cautions** see notes above; avoid excessive alkalinity of urine and ensure adequate fluid intake (risk of crystalluria); **interactions:** Appendix 1 (quinolones)

**Driving** May impair performance of skilled tasks (e.g. driving); effects enhanced by alcohol

**Side-effects** see notes above; also flatulence, dysphagia, pancreatitis, tachycardia, hypotension, oedema, hot flushes, sweating, movement disorders, tinnitus, vasculitis, tenosynovitis, erythema nodosum, haemorrhagic bullae, petechiae and hyperglycaemia; pain and phlebitis at injection site

**Dose**

- By mouth, respiratory-tract infections, 250–750 mg twice daily

  Urinary-tract infections, 250–500 mg twice daily (100 mg twice daily for 3 days in acute uncomplicated cystitis in women)

  Chronic prostatitis, 500 mg twice daily for 28 days

  Gonorrhoea, 500 mg as a single dose

  Pseudomonal lower respiratory-tract infection in cystic fibrosis, 750 mg twice daily; CHILD 5–17 years (see Cautions above), up to 20 mg/kg twice daily (max. 1.5 g daily)

  Most other infections, 500–750 mg twice daily

  Surgical prophylaxis, 750 mg 60–90 minutes before procedure

  Prophylaxis of meningococcal meningitis [not licensed], Table 2, section 5.1

- By intravenous infusion (over 30–60 minutes; 400 mg over 60 minutes), 200–400 mg twice daily

  Pseudomonal lower respiratory-tract infection in cystic fibrosis, 400 mg twice daily; CHILD 5–17 years (see Cautions above), up to 10 mg/kg 3 times daily (max. 1.2 g daily)

  Urinary-tract infections, 100 mg twice daily

  Gonorrhoea, 100 mg as a single dose

- CHILD not recommended (see Cautions above) but where benefit outweighs risk, by mouth, 10–30 mg/kg daily in 2 divided doses *or* by intravenous infusion, 8–16 mg/kg daily in 2 divided doses

- Anthrax (treatment and post-exposure prophylaxis, see notes above), by mouth, 500 mg twice daily; CHILD 30 mg/kg daily in 2 divided doses (max. 1g daily)

  By intravenous infusion, 400 mg twice daily; CHILD 20 mg/kg daily in 2 divided doses (max. 800 mg daily)

**Ciprofloxacin** (Non-proprietary) PoM

Tablets, ciprofloxacin (as hydrochloride) 100 mg, net price 6-tab pack = £1.50; 250 mg, 10-tab pack = £1.75, 20-tab pack = £2.32; 500 mg, 10-tab pack = £2.05, 20-tab pack = £2.47; 750 mg, 10-tab pack = £3.00. Label: 7, 9, 25, counselling, driving

**Ciproxin®** (Bayer) PoM

Tablets, all f/c, ciprofloxacin (as hydrochloride) 100 mg, net price 6-tab pack = £2.80; 250 mg (scored), 10-tab pack = £7.50, 20-tab pack = £15.00; 500 mg (scored), 10-tab pack = £14.20, 20-tab pack = £28.40; 750 mg, 10-tab pack = £20.00. Label: 7, 9, 25, counselling, driving

Suspension, strawberry-flavoured, ciprofloxacin for reconstitution with diluent provided, 250 mg/5 mL, net price 100 mL = £15.00. Label: 7, 9, 25, counselling, driving

Intravenous infusion, ciprofloxacin (as lactate) 2 mg/mL, in sodium chloride 0.9%, net price 50-mL bottle = £8.65, 100-mL bottle = £16.89, 200-mL bottle = £25.70

Electrolytes $Na^+$ 15.4 mmol/100-mL bottle

## LEVOFLOXACIN

**Indications** see under Dose

**Cautions** see notes above; **interactions:** Appendix 1 (quinolones)

**Driving** May impair performance of skilled tasks (e.g. driving)

**Side-effects** see notes above; rarely anxiety, tachycardia, hypotension, hypoglycaemia, pneumonitis, rhabdomyolysis; local reactions and transient hypotension reported with infusion

**Dose**

- By mouth, acute sinusitis, 500 mg daily for 10–14 days

  Exacerbation of chronic bronchitis, 250–500 mg daily for 7–10 days

  Community-acquired pneumonia, 500 mg once or twice daily for 7–14 days

  Urinary-tract infections, 250 mg daily for 7–10 days (for 3 days in uncomplicated infection)

  Chronic prostatitis, 500 mg once daily for 28 days

  Skin and soft tissue infections, 250 mg daily *or* 500 mg once or twice daily for 7–14 days

- By intravenous infusion (over at least 60 minutes for 500 mg), community-acquired pneumonia, 500 mg once or twice daily

  Complicated urinary-tract infections, 250 mg daily, increased in severe infections

  Skin and soft tissue infections, 500 mg twice daily

**Tavanic®** (Hoechst Marion Roussel) PoM

Tablets, yellow-red, f/c, scored, levofloxacin 250 mg, net price 5-tab pack = £7.23, 10-tab pack = £14.45; 500 mg, 5-tab pack = £12.93, 10-tab pack = £25.85. Label: 6, 9, 25, counselling, driving

Intravenous infusion, levofloxacin 5 mg/mL, net price 100-mL bottle = £26.40

Electrolytes $Na^+$ 15.4 mmol/100-mL bottle

## MOXIFLOXACIN

**Indications** community-acquired pneumonia; exacerbation of chronic bronchitis; sinusitis

**Cautions** see notes above; conditions pre-disposing to arrhythmias, including myocardial ischaemia; **interactions:** Appendix 1 (quinolones)

Driving May impair performance of skilled tasks (e.g. driving)

**Contra-indications** see notes above; severe hepatic impairment; history of QT-interval prolongation, bradycardia, history of symptomatic arrhythmias, heart failure with reduced left ventricular ejection fraction, electrolyte disturbances, concomitant use with other drugs known to prolong QT-interval

**Side-effects** see notes above; also dry mouth, stomatitis, glossitis, flatulence, constipation, arrhythmias, palpitations, peripheral oedema, angina, blood pressure changes, dyspnoea, anxiety, and sweating; *rarely* hypotension, hyperlipidaemia, agitation, abnormal dreams, incoordination, hyperglycaemia, and dry skin

**Dose**

- 400 mg once daily for 10 days in community-acquired pneumonia, for 5–10 days in exacerbation of chronic bronchitis, for 7 days in sinusitis

**Avelox** (Bayer) ▼ PoM

Tablets, red, f/c, moxifloxacin (as hydrochloride) 400 mg, net price 5-tab pack = £10.95. Label: 6, 9, counselling, driving

## NALIDIXIC ACID

**Indications** urinary-tract infections

**Cautions** see notes above; avoid in porphyria (section 9.8.2); liver disease; false positive urinary glucose (if tested for reducing substances); monitor blood counts, renal and liver function if treatment exceeds 2 weeks; **interactions:** Appendix 1 (quinolones)

**Side-effects** see notes above; also reported toxic psychosis, increased intracranial pressure, cranial nerve palsy, metabolic acidosis

**Dose**

- 900 mg every 6 hours for 7 days, reduced in chronic infections to 600 mg every 6 hours; CHILD over 3 months max. 50 mg/kg daily in divided doses; reduced in prolonged therapy to 30 mg/kg daily

**Uriben®** (Rosemont) PoM

Suspension, pink, nalidixic acid 300 mg/5 mL, net price 150 mL (raspberry- and strawberry-flavoured) = £11.42. Label: 9, 11

Excipients include sucrose 450 mg/5mL

## NORFLOXACIN

**Indications** see under Dose

**Cautions** see notes above; **interactions:** Appendix 1 (quinolones)

Driving May impair performance of skilled tasks (e.g. driving)

**Side-effects** see notes above; also euphoria, anxiety, tinnitus, polyneuropathy, exfoliative dermatitis, pancreatitis, vasculitis

**Dose**

- Urinary-tract infections, 400 mg twice daily for 7–10 days (for 3 days in uncomplicated lower urinary-tract infections)
- Chronic relapsing urinary-tract infections, 400 mg twice daily for up to 12 weeks; may be reduced to 400 mg once daily if adequate suppression within first 4 weeks
- Chronic prostatitis, 400 mg twice daily for 28 days

**Norfloxacin** (Non-proprietary) PoM

Tablets, norfloxacin 400 mg, net price 6-tab pack = £2.41, 14-tab pack = £5.96. Label: 7, 9, 23, counselling, driving

**Utinor®** (MSD) PoM

Tablets, scored, norfloxacin 400 mg. Net price 6-tab pack = £2.19, 14-tab pack = £5.11. Label: 7, 9, 23, counselling, driving

## OFLOXACIN

**Indications** see under Dose

**Cautions** see notes above; hepatic impairment (Appendix 2); history of psychiatric illness; **interactions:** Appendix 1 (quinolones)

Driving May affect performance of skilled tasks (e.g. driving); effects enhanced by alcohol

**Side-effects** see notes above; also tachycardia, transient hypotension, anxiety, unsteady gait, neuropathy, extrapyramidal symptoms, psychotic reactions (discontinue treatment—see notes above); *very rarely* changes in blood sugar and vasculitic reactions; isolated cases of pneumonitis; on intravenous infusion, hypotension and local reactions (including thrombophlebitis)

**Dose**

- By mouth, urinary-tract infections, 200–400 mg daily preferably in the morning, increased if necessary in upper urinary-tract infections to 400 mg twice daily

  Chronic prostatitis, 200 mg twice daily for 28 days

  Lower respiratory-tract infections, 400 mg daily preferably in the morning, increased if necessary to 400 mg twice daily

  Skin and soft-tissue infections, 400 mg twice daily

  Uncomplicated gonorrhoea, 400 mg as a single dose

  Uncomplicated genital chlamydial infection, non-gonococcal urethritis, 400 mg daily in single or divided doses for 7 days

  Pelvic inflammatory disease (see also section 5.1, table 1), 400 mg twice daily for 14 days
- By intravenous infusion (over at least 30 minutes for each 200 mg), complicated urinary-tract infection, 200 mg daily

  Lower respiratory-tract infection, 200 mg twice daily

  Septicaemia, 200 mg twice daily

  Skin and soft-tissue infections, 400 mg twice daily

  Severe or complicated infections, dose may be increased to 400 mg twice daily

**Ofloxacin** (Non-proprietary) PoM

Tablets, ofloxacin 200 mg, net price 10-tab pack = £11.01; 400 mg, 5-tab pack = £11.52, 10-tab pack = £11.84. Label: 6, 9, 11, counselling, driving

**Tarivid®** (Aventis Pharma) PoM

Tablets, f/c, scored, ofloxacin 200 mg, net price 10-tab pack = £7.84, 20-tab pack = £15.66; 400 mg (yellow), 5-tab pack = £7.82, 10-tab pack = £15.60. Label: 6, 9, 11, counselling, driving

Intravenous infusion, ofloxacin (as hydrochloride) 2 mg/mL, net price 100-mL bottle = £16.82 (hosp. only)

## 5.1.13 Urinary-tract infections

Urinary-tract infection is more common in women than in men; when it occurs in men there is frequently an underlying abnormality of the renal tract. Recurrent episodes of infection are an indication for radiological investigation especially in children in whom untreated pyelonephritis may lead to permanent kidney damage.

*Escherichia coli* is the most common cause of urinary-tract infection; *Staphylococcus saprophyticus* is also common in sexually active young women. Less common causes include Proteus and Klebsiella spp. *Pseudomonas aeruginosa* infections usually occur in the hospital setting and may be associated with functional or anatomical abnormalities of the renal tract. *Staphylococcus epidermidis* and *Enterococcus faecalis* infection may complicate catheterisation or instrumentation.

> Whenever possible a specimen of urine should be collected for culture and sensitivity testing before starting antibacterial therapy. The antibacterial chosen should reflect current local bacterial sensitivity to antibacterials.

*Uncomplicated lower urinary-tract infections* often respond to amoxicillin, nalidixic acid, nitrofurantoin, or trimethoprim given for 7 days (3 days of trimethoprim or amoxicillin may be adequate for infections in women); those caused by fully sensitive bacteria respond to two 3-g doses of amoxicillin (section 5.1.1.3). Widespread bacterial resistance, especially to ampicillin, amoxicillin, and trimethoprim has increased the importance of urine culture before therapy. Alternatives for resistant organisms include co-amoxiclav (amoxicillin with clavulanic acid), an oral cephalosporin, pivmecillinam, or a quinolone.

Long-term low dose therapy may be required in selected patients to prevent *recurrence of infection*; indications include frequent relapses and significant kidney damage. Trimethoprim, nitrofurantoin and cefalexin have been recommended for long-term therapy.

**Methenamine** (hexamine) should **not** generally be used because it requires an acidic urine for its antimicrobial activity and it is ineffective for upper urinary-tract infections; it may, however, have a role in chronic bacteriuria particularly in infection caused by highly resistant Gram-negative bacteria or by yeasts.

*Acute pyelonephritis* can lead to septicaemia and is best treated initially by injection of a broad-spectrum antibacterial such as cefuroxime or a quinolone especially if the patient is severely ill; gentamicin can also be used.

*Prostatitis* can be difficult to cure and requires treatment for several weeks with an antibacterial which penetrates prostatic tissue such as trimethoprim, or some quinolones.

Where infection is localised and associated with an indwelling *catheter* a bladder instillation is often effective (section 7.4.4).

Patients with *heart-valve lesions* undergoing instrumentation of the urinary tract should be given a parenteral antibiotic to prevent bacteraemia and endocarditis (section 5.1, table 2).

Urinary-tract infection in *pregnancy* may be asymptomatic and requires prompt treatment to prevent progression to acute pyelonephritis. Penicillins and cephalosporins are suitable for treating urinary-tract infection during pregnancy. Nitrofurantoin may also be used but it should be avoided at term. Sulphonamides, quinolones, and tetracyclines should be avoided during pregnancy; trimethoprim should also preferably be avoided particularly in the first trimester.

In *renal failure* antibacterials normally excreted by the kidney accumulate with resultant toxicity unless the dose is reduced. This applies especially to the aminoglycosides which should be used with great caution; tetracyclines, methenamine, and nitrofurantoin should be avoided altogether.

**Children** Urinary-tract infections in children require prompt antibacterial treatment to minimise the risk of renal scarring. For the first infection, treatment may be initiated with trimethoprim or co-amoxiclav and the choice of antibacterial is reviewed when sensitivity results are available; full doses of the antibacterial drug should be given for 5–7 days. Antibacterial prophylaxis with low doses of trimethoprim or nitrofurantoin should then be given if further investigations are considered necessary. Antibacterial prophylaxis should be continued until investigations are complete; long-term prophylaxis may be necessary in some cases (e.g. vesicoureteric reflux or renal scarring).

*Children under 3 months or seriously unwell children over 3 months* should be transferred to hospital and treated initially with intravenous antibacterial drugs such as ampicillin with gentamicin or cefotaxime alone until the infection responds; full doses of oral antibacterials are then given for a further period. Antibacterial prophylaxis should then be given as above.

### NITROFURANTOIN

**Indications** urinary-tract infections

**Cautions** anaemia; diabetes mellitus; electrolyte imbalance; vitamin B and folate deficiency; pulmonary disease; hepatic impairment; monitor lung and liver function on long-term therapy, especially in the elderly (discontinue if deterioration in lung function); susceptibility to peripheral neuropathy; false positive urinary glucose (if tested for reducing substances); urine may be coloured yellow or brown; **interactions:** Appendix 1 (nitrofurantoin)

**Contra-indications** renal impairment (Appendix 3); infants less than 3 months old, G6PD deficiency (including pregnancy at term, and breast-feeding of affected infants, see section 9.1.5 and Appendix 4 and Appendix 5), porphyria (section 9.8.2)

**Side-effects** anorexia, nausea, vomiting, and diarrhoea; acute and chronic pulmonary reactions (pulmonary fibrosis reported; possible association with lupus erythematosus-like syndrome); peripheral neuropathy; also reported, hypersensitivity reactions (including angioedema, anaphylaxis, sialadenitis, urticaria, rash and pruritus); rarely, cholestatic jaundice, hepatitis, exfoliative dermatitis, erythema multiforme, pancreatitis, arthralgia, blood disorders (including agranulocytosis, thrombocytopenia, and aplastic anaemia), benign intracranial hypertension, and transient alopecia

**Dose**

- Acute uncomplicated infection, 50 mg every 6 hours with food for 7 days; CHILD over 3 months, 3 mg/kg daily in 4 divided doses
- Severe chronic recurrent infection, 100 mg every 6 hours with food for 7 days (dose reduced or discontinued if severe nausea)
- Prophylaxis (but see Cautions), 50–100 mg at night; CHILD over 3 months, 1 mg/kg at night

**Nitrofurantoin** (Non-proprietary) PoM

Tablets, nitrofurantoin 50 mg, net price 20 = £1.65; 100 mg, 20 = £3.04. Label: 9, 14, 21

Oral suspension, nitrofurantoin 25 mg/5 mL, net price 300 mL = £65.00. Label: 9, 14, 21

**Furadantin®** (Goldshield) PoM

Tablets, all yellow, scored, nitrofurantoin 50 mg, net price 20 = £1.96; 100 mg, 20 = £3.62. Label: 9, 14, 21

**Macrobid®** (Goldshield) PoM

Capsules, m/r, blue/yellow, nitrofurantoin 100 mg (as nitrofurantoin macrocrystals and nitrofurantoin monohydrate). Net price 14-cap pack = £4.89. Label: 9, 14, 21, 25

Dose uncomplicated urinary-tract infection, 1 capsule twice daily with food

Genito-urinary surgical prophylaxis, 1 capsule twice daily on day of procedure and for 3 days after

**Macrodantin®** (Goldshield) PoM

Capsules, nitrofurantoin 50 mg (yellow/white), net price 30-cap pack = £3.05; 100 mg (yellow/white), 20 = £3.84. Label: 9, 14, 21



## METHENAMINE HIPPURATE

**(Hexamine hippurate)**

**Indications** prophylaxis and long-term treatment of chronic or recurrent lower urinary-tract infections

**Cautions** pregnancy; avoid concurrent administration with sulphonamides (risk of crystalluria) or urinary alkalinising agents; **interactions:** Appendix 1 (methenamine)

**Contra-indications** hepatic impairment, severe renal impairment, severe dehydration, gout, metabolic acidosis

**Side-effects** gastro-intestinal disturbances, bladder irritation, rash

**Dose**

- 1 g every 12 hours (may be increased in patients with catheters to 1 g every 8 hours); CHILD 6–12 years 500 mg every 12 hours

**Hiprex®** (3M)

Tablets, scored, methenamine hippurate 1 g. Net price 60-tab pack = £6.58. Label: 9

# 5.2 Antifungal drugs

## Treatment of fungal infections

The systemic treatment of common fungal infections is outlined below; specialist treatment is required in most forms of systemic or disseminated fungal infections. For local treatment of fungal infections, see section 7.2.2 (genital), section 7.4.4 (bladder), section 11.3.2 (eye), section 12.1.1 (ear), section 12.3.2 (oropharynx), and section 13.10.2 (skin).

**Aspergillosis** Aspergillosis most commonly affects the respiratory tract but in severely immunocompromised patients, invasive forms can affect the sinuses, heart, brain, and skin. **Voriconazole** is the drug of choice; **amphotericin** (liposomal formulation preferred if toxicity or renal impairment are concerns) and **itraconazole** are alternatives in patients in whom initial treatment has failed. Itraconazole is also used as an adjunct in the treatment of allergic bronchopulmonary aspergillosis [unlicensed indication]. **Caspofungin** is licensed for invasive aspergillosis unresponsive to amphotericin or to itraconazole, or in patients who cannot tolerate amphotericin or itraconazole. The *Scottish Medicines Consortium* (March 2003) does not recommend the use of caspofungin because of a lack of robust data on efficacy and safety in the treatment of invasive aspergillosis.

**Candidiasis** Many superficial candidal infections including infections of the skin (section 13.10.2) are treated locally; widespread or intractable infection requires systemic antifungal treatment. Vaginal candidiasis (section 7.2.2) may be treated with locally acting antifungals or with fluconazole given by mouth; for resistant organisms, itraconazole can be given by mouth.

*Oropharyngeal candidiasis* generally responds to topical therapy (section 12.3.2); fluconazole is given by mouth for unresponsive infections; it is effective and is reliably absorbed. Itraconazole may be used for fluconazole-resistant infections.

For *deep and disseminated candidiasis*, **amphotericin** by intravenous infusion is used alone or with **flucytosine** by intravenous infusion; an alternative is **fluconazole** given alone for *Candida albicans* infection, particularly in AIDS patients. **Voriconazole** is licensed for infections caused by fluconazole-resistant *Candida* spp. (including *C. krusei*). The use of **caspofungin** should be restricted to treating fluconazole-resistant Candida infections that have not responded to amphotericin or in patients intolerant of amphotericin.

**Cryptococcosis** Cryptococcosis is uncommon but infection in the immunocompromised, especially in AIDS patients, can be life-threatening; cryptococcal meningitis is the most common form of fungal meningitis. The treatment of choice in cryptococcal meningitis is **amphotericin** by intravenous infusion with **flucytosine** by intravenous infusion for 2 weeks, followed by **fluconazole** by mouth for 8 weeks. In cryptococcosis, **fluconazole** given alone is an alternative in AIDS patients with no disturbances of consciousness. Following successful treatment, fluconazole can be used for prophylaxis against relapse until immunity recovers.

**Histoplasmosis** Histoplasmosis is rare in temperate climates; it can be life-threatening, particularly in HIV-infected persons. **Itraconazole** can be used for the treatment of immunocompetent patients with indolent non-meningeal infection including chronic pulmonary histoplasmosis; **ketoconazole** is an alternative in immunocompetent patients. **Amphotericin** by intravenous infusion is preferred in patients with fulminant or severe infections. Following successful treatment, itraconazole can be used for prophylaxis against relapse.

**Skin and nail infections** Mild localised fungal infections of the skin (including tinea corporis, tinea cruris, and tinea pedis) respond to topical therapy (section

13.10.2). Systemic therapy (itraconazole, fluconazole, or terbinafine) is appropriate if topical therapy fails, if many areas are affected, or if the site of infection is difficult to treat such as in infections of the nails (onychomycosis) and of the scalp (tinea capitis).

**Griseofulvin** is used for tinea capitis in adults and children; it was used extensively in tinea of various other sites but it has largely been replaced by newer antifungals. Oral imidazole or triazole antifungals (particularly **itraconazole**) and **terbinafine** are used more commonly because they have a broader spectrum of activity and require a shorter duration of treatment. The role of terbinafine in the management of *Microsporum* species (cat or dog ringworm) is uncertain.

Pityriasis versicolor (section 13.10.2) may be treated with **itraconazole** by mouth if topical therapy is ineffective; **fluconazole** by mouth is an alternative. Oral **terbinafine** is **not** effective for pityriasis versicolor.

**Terbinafine** and **itraconazole** have largely replaced griseofulvin for the systemic treatment of onychomycosis, particularly of the toenail; terbinafine is considered to be the drug of choice. Itraconazole can be administered as intermittent 'pulse' therapy.

**Immunocompromised patients** Immunocompromised patients are at particular risk of fungal infections and may receive antifungal drugs prophylactically; oral imidazole or triazole antifungals are the drugs of choice for prophylaxis. **Fluconazole** is more reliably absorbed than itraconazole and ketoconazole and is considered less toxic than ketoconazole on long-term use.

Amphotericin by intravenous infusion is used for the empirical *treatment* of serious fungal infections. Fluconazole is used for treating *Candida albicans* infection. Caspofungin is licensed for the empirical treatment of systemic fungal infections (such as those involving *Candida* spp. or *Aspergillus* spp.) in patients with neutropenia.

## Drugs used in fungal infections

**Polyene antifungals** The polyene antifungals include amphotericin and nystatin; neither drug is absorbed when given by mouth. They are used for oral, oropharyngeal, and perioral infections by local application in the mouth (section 12.3.2).

**Amphotericin** by intravenous infusion is used for the treatment of systemic fungal infections and is active against most fungi and yeasts. It is highly protein bound and penetrates poorly into body fluids and tissues. When given parenterally amphotericin is toxic and side-effects are common. Lipid formulations of amphotericin (*Abelcet®*, *AmBisome®*, and *Amphocil®*) are significantly less toxic and are recommended when the conventional formulation of amphotericin is contra-indicated because of toxicity, especially nephrotoxicity or when response to conventional amphotericin is inadequate; lipid formulations are more expensive.

**Nystatin** is used principally for *Candida albicans* infections of the skin and mucous membranes, including oesophageal and intestinal candidiasis.

**Imidazole antifungals** The imidazole antifungals include clotrimazole, econazole, ketoconazole, sulconazole, and tioconazole. They are used for the local treatment of vaginal candidiasis (section 7.2.2) and for dermatophyte infections (section 13.10.2).

**Ketoconazole** is better absorbed by mouth than other imidazoles. It has been associated with fatal hepatotoxicity; the CSM has advised that prescribers should weigh the potential benefits of ketoconazole treatment against the risk of liver damage and should carefully monitor patients both clinically and biochemically. It should not be used by mouth for superficial fungal infections.

**Miconazole** can be used locally for oral infections; it is also effective in intestinal infections. Systemic absorption may follow use of miconazole oral gel and may result in significant drug interactions.

**Triazole antifungals** **Fluconazole** is very well absorbed after oral administration. It also achieves good penetration into the cerebrospinal fluid to treat fungal meningitis.

**Itraconazole** is active against a wide range of dermatophytes. Itraconazole capsules require an acid environment in the stomach for optimal absorption.

Itraconazole has been associated with liver damage and should be avoided or used with caution in patients with liver disease; fluconazole is less frequently associated with hepatotoxicity.

**Voriconazole** is a broad-spectrum antifungal drug which is licensed for use in life-threatening infections.

**Other antifungals** **Caspofungin** is active against *Aspergillus* spp. and *Candida* spp. It is given by intravenous infusion for invasive infection. **Flucytosine** is often used with amphotericin in a synergistic combination. Bone marrow depression can occur which limits its use, particularly in AIDS patients; weekly blood counts are necessary during prolonged therapy. Resistance to flucytosine can develop during therapy and sensitivity testing is essential before and during treatment.

**Griseofulvin** is effective for widespread or intractable dermatophyte infections but has been superseded by newer antifungals, particularly for nail infections. It is the drug of choice for trichophyton infections in children. Duration of therapy is dependent on the site of the infection and may be required for a number of months.

**Terbinafine** is the drug of choice for fungal nail infections and is also used for ringworm infections where oral treatment is considered appropriate.



### AMPHOTERICIN
**(Amphotericin B)**

**Indications** See under Dose

**Cautions** when given parenterally, toxicity common (close supervision necessary and test dose required); renal impairment (Appendix 3); hepatic and renal-function tests, blood counts, and plasma electrolyte (including plasma-potassium and magnesium concentration) monitoring required; corticosteroids (avoid except to control reactions); pregnancy (Appendix 4); breast-feeding (Appendix 5); avoid rapid infusion (risk of arrhythmias); **interactions:** Appendix 1 (amphotericin)

**Anaphylaxis** The CSM has advised that anaphylaxis occurs rarely with any intravenous amphotericin product and a test dose is advisable before the first infusion; the patient should be carefully observed for at least 30 minutes after the test dose. Prophylactic antipyretics or hydrocortisone should only be used in patients who have previously experienced acute adverse reactions (in whom continued treatment with amphotericin is essential)

**Side-effects** when given parenterally, anorexia, nausea and vomiting, diarrhoea, epigastric pain; febrile reactions, headache, muscle and joint pain; anaemia; disturbances in renal function (including hypokalaemia and hypomagnesaemia) and renal toxicity; also cardiovascular toxicity (including arrhythmias), blood disorders, neurological disorders (including hearing loss, diplopia, convulsions, peripheral neuropathy), abnormal liver function (discontinue treatment), rash, anaphylactoid reactions (see Anaphylaxis, above); pain and thrombophlebitis at injection site

**Dose**
- By mouth, intestinal candidiasis, 100–200 mg every 6 hours; INFANT and CHILD, 100 mg 4 times daily
  Prophylaxis NEONATE 100 mg once daily
  Oral and perioral infections, see section 12.3.2
- By intravenous infusion, see under preparations, below

**Fungilin®** (Squibb) PoM
Tablets, yellow, scored, amphotericin 100 mg, Net price 56-tab pack = £7.74. Label: 9

Suspension, yellow, sugar-free, amphotericin 100 mg/mL, net price 12 mL = £2.15. Label: 9, counselling, use of pipette

**Fungizone®** (Squibb) PoM
Intravenous infusion, powder for reconstitution, amphotericin (as sodium deoxycholate complex). Net price 50-mg vial = £3.16
Electrolytes $Na^{+}$ < 0.5 mmol/vial
Dose by intravenous infusion, systemic fungal infections, initial test dose of 1 mg over 20–30 minutes then 250 micrograms/kg daily, gradually increased if tolerated to 1 mg/kg daily; max. (severe infection) 1.5 mg/kg daily or on alternate days
Note Prolonged treatment usually necessary; if interrupted for longer than 7 days recommence at 250 micrograms/kg daily and increase gradually

### Lipid formulations

**Abelcet®** (Zeneus) PoM
Intravenous infusion, amphotericin 5 mg/mL as lipid complex with L-α-dimyristoylphosphatidylcholine and L-α-dimyristoylphosphatidylglycerol. Net price 20-mL vial = £82.13 (hosp. only)
Dose severe invasive candidiasis; severe systemic fungal infections in patients not responding to conventional amphotericin or to other antifungal drugs or where toxicity or renal impairment precludes conventional amphotericin, including invasive aspergillosis, cryptococcal meningitis and disseminated cryptococcosis in HIV patients, by intravenous infusion, ADULT and CHILD, initial test dose 1 mg over 15 minutes then 5 mg/kg daily for at least 14 days

**AmBisome®** (Gilead) PoM
Intravenous infusion, powder for reconstitution, amphotericin 50 mg encapsulated in liposomes. Net price 50-mg vial = £96.69
Electrolytes $Na^{+}$ < 0.5 mmol/vial
Excipients include sucrose 900 mg/vial
Dose severe systemic or deep mycoses where toxicity (particularly nephrotoxicity) precludes use of conventional amphotericin, by intravenous infusion, ADULT and CHILD initial test dose 1 mg over 10 minutes then 1 mg/kg daily as a single dose increased gradually if necessary to 3 mg/kg daily as a single dose; max. 5 mg/kg daily [unlicensed dose]
Infections in febrile neutropenic patients unresponsive to broad-spectrum antibacterials, ADULT and CHILD, initial test dose 1 mg over 10 minutes then 3 mg/kg daily as a single dose until afebrile for 3 consecutive days; max. period of treatment 42 days; max. 5 mg/kg daily [unlicensed dose]
Visceral leishmaniasis, see section 5.4.5 and product literature
Note *Ambisome®* doses in BNF may differ from those in product literature

**Amphocil®** (Cambridge) PoM
Intravenous infusion, powder for reconstitution, amphotericin as a complex with sodium cholesteryl sulphate. Net price 50-mg vial = £96.81, 100-mg vial = £190.05
Electrolytes $Na^{+}$ < 0.5 mmol/vial
Dose severe systemic or deep mycoses where toxicity or renal failure preclude use of conventional amphotericin, by intravenous infusion, ADULT and CHILD initial test dose 2 mg over 10 minutes then 1 mg/kg daily as a single dose increased gradually if necessary to 3–4 mg/kg daily as a single dose; max.6 mg/kg daily

## CASPOFUNGIN

**Indications** invasive aspergillosis either unresponsive to amphotericin or itraconazole or in patients intolerant of amphotericin or itraconazole; invasive candidiasis (see notes above); empirical treatment of systemic fungal infections in patients with neutropenia

**Cautions** hepatic impairment (Appendix 2); pregnancy (Appendix 4); **interactions:** Appendix 1 (caspofungin)

**Contra-indications** breast-feeding (Appendix 5)

**Side-effects** nausea, vomiting, abdominal pain, diarrhoea; tachycardia, flushing; dyspnoea; fever, headache; anaemia, decrease in serum potassium, hypomagnesaemia; rash, pruritus, sweating; injection-site reactions; *less commonly* hypercalcaemia; also reported, hepatic dysfunction, oedema, adult respiratory distress syndrome, hypersensitivity reactions (including anaphylaxis)

**Dose**
- By intravenous infusion, ADULT over 18 years, 70 mg on first day then 50 mg once daily (70 mg once daily if body-weight over 80 kg)

**Cancidas®** (MSD) PoM
Intravenous infusion, powder for reconstitution, caspofungin (as acetate), net price 50-mg vial = £327.67; 70-mg vial = £416.78

## FLUCONAZOLE

**Indications** see under Dose

**Cautions** renal impairment (Appendix 3); pregnancy (Appendix 4) and breast-feeding (Appendix 5); monitor liver function—discontinue if signs or symptoms of hepatic disease (risk of hepatic necrosis); susceptibility to QT interval prolongation; **interactions:** Appendix 1 (antifungals, triazole)

**Side-effects** nausea, abdominal discomfort, diarrhoea, flatulence, headache, rash (discontinue treatment or monitor closely if infection invasive or systemic); less frequently dyspepsia, vomiting, taste disturbance, hepatic disorders, hypersensitivity reactions, anaphylaxis, dizziness, seizures, alopecia, pruritus, toxic epidermal necrolysis, Stevens-Johnson syndrome (severe cutaneous reactions more likely in AIDS patients), hyperlipidaemia, leucopenia, thrombocytopenia, and hypokalaemia reported

**Dose**
- Vaginal candidiasis (see also Recurrent Vulvovaginal Candidiasis, section 7.2.2) and candidal balanitis, by mouth, a single dose of 150 mg
- Mucosal candidiasis (except genital), by mouth, 50 mg daily (100 mg daily in unusually difficult infections) given for 7–14 days in oropharyngeal candidiasis (max. 14 days except in severely immunocompromised patients); for 14 days in atrophic oral candi-

diasis associated with dentures; for 14–30 days in other mucosal infections (e.g. oesophagitis, candiduria, non-invasive bronchopulmonary infections); CHILD by mouth *or* by intravenous infusion, 3–6 mg/kg on first day then 3 mg/kg daily (every 72 hours in NEONATE up to 2 weeks old, every 48 hours in neonate 2–4 weeks old)

- Tinea pedis, corporis, cruris, pityriasis versicolor, and dermal candidiasis, by mouth, 50 mg daily for 2–4 weeks (for up to 6 weeks in tinea pedis); max. duration of treatment 6 weeks
- Invasive candidal infections (including candidaemia and disseminated candidiasis) and cryptococcal infections (including meningitis), by mouth *or* intravenous infusion, 400 mg daily (400 mg initially then 200 mg daily in invasive candidal infections, increased if necessary to 400 mg daily); treatment continued according to response (at least 8 weeks for cryptococcal meningitis); CHILD 6–12 mg/kg daily (every 72 hours in NEONATE up to 2 weeks old, every 48 hours in NEONATE 2–4 weeks old); max. 400 mg daily
- Prevention of relapse of Cryptococcal meningitis in AIDS patients after completion of primary therapy, by mouth, 200 mg daily *or* by intravenous infusion, 100–200 mg daily
- Prevention of fungal infections in immunocompromised patients, by mouth *or* by intravenous infusion, 50–400 mg daily adjusted according to risk; 400 mg daily if high risk of systemic infections e.g. following bone-marrow transplantation; commence treatment before anticipated onset of neutropenia and continue for 7 days after neutrophil count in desirable range; CHILD according to extent and duration of neutropenia, 3–12 mg/kg daily (every 72 hours in NEONATE up to 2 weeks old, every 48 hours in NEONATE 2–4 weeks old); max. 400 mg daily

**Fluconazole** (Non-proprietary) PoM

[1]Capsules, fluconazole 50 mg, net price 7-cap pack = £2.89; 150 mg, single-capsule pack = £1.65; 200 mg, 7-cap pack = £5.39. Label: 9, (50 and 200 mg)

**Dental prescribing on NHS** Fluconazole Capsules 50 mg may be prescribed

Intravenous infusion, fluconazole 2 mg/mL, net price 25-mL bottle = £7.32; 100-mL bottle = £29.28

**Diflucan®** (Pfizer) PoM

[1]Capsules, fluconazole 50 mg (blue/white), net price 7-cap pack = £16.61; 150 mg (blue), single-capsule pack = £7.12; 200 mg (purple/white), 7-cap pack = £66.42. Label: 9, (50 and 200 mg)

Oral suspension, orange-flavoured, fluconazole for reconstitution with water, 50 mg/5 mL, net price 35 mL = £16.61; 200 mg/5 mL, 35 mL = £66.42. Label: 9

**Dental prescribing on NHS** May be prescribed as Fluconazole Oral Suspension 50 mg/5 mL

Intravenous infusion, fluconazole 2 mg/mL in sodium chloride intravenous infusion 0.9%, net price 25-mL bottle = £7.32; 100-mL bottle = £29.28

**Electrolytes** $Na^+$ 15 mmol/100-mL bottle

1. Capsules can be sold to the public for vaginal candidiasis and associated candidal balanitis in those aged 16–60 years, in a container or packaging containing not more than 150 mg and labelled to show a max. dose of 150 mg; proprietary brands on sale to the public include *Canesten® Oral, Diflucan® One*

## FLUCYTOSINE

**Indications** systemic yeast and fungal infections; adjunct to amphotericin (or fluconazole) in cryptococcal meningitis (see Cryptococcosis, p. 308), adjunct to amphotericin in severe systemic candidiasis and in other severe or long-standing infections

**Cautions** renal impairment (Appendix 3); elderly; blood disorders; liver- and kidney-function tests and blood counts required (weekly in renal impairment or blood disorders); pregnancy (Appendix 4), breast-feeding (Appendix 5); **interactions**: Appendix 1 (flucytosine)

**Side-effects** nausea, vomiting, diarrhoea, rashes; less frequently cardiotoxicity, confusion, hallucinations, convulsions, headache, sedation, vertigo, alterations in liver function tests (hepatitis and hepatic necrosis reported), and toxic epidermal necrolysis; blood disorders including thrombocytopenia, leucopenia, and aplastic anaemia reported

**Dose**

- By intravenous infusion over 20–40 minutes, ADULT and CHILD, 200 mg/kg daily in 4 divided doses usually for not more than 7 days; extremely sensitive organisms, 100–150 mg/kg daily may be sufficient; treat for 2 weeks in cryptococcal meningitis (see Cryptococcosis, p. 308 [unlicensed dose])

**Note** For plasma concentration monitoring blood should be taken shortly before starting the next infusion; plasma concentration for optimum response 25–50 mg/litre (200–400 micromol/litre)—should not be allowed to exceed 80 mg/litre (620 micromol/litre)

**Ancotil®** (Valeant) PoM

Intravenous infusion, flucytosine 10 mg/mL. Net price 250-mL infusion bottle = £30.33 (hosp. only)

**Electrolytes** $Na^+$ 34.5 mmol/250-mL bottle

**Note** Flucytosine tablets may be available on a named-patient basis from Bell and Croyden

## GRISEOFULVIN

**Indications** dermatophyte infections of the skin, scalp, hair and nails where topical therapy has failed or is inappropriate

**Cautions** **interactions**: Appendix 1 (griseofulvin)

**Driving** May impair performance of skilled tasks (e.g. driving); effects of alcohol enhanced

**Contra-indications** severe liver disease; systemic lupus erythematosus (risk of exacerbation); porphyria (section 9.8.2); pregnancy (**avoid** pregnancy **during** and for **1 month after** treatment (Appendix 4); men should not father children within 6 months of treatment); breast-feeding (Appendix 5)

**Side-effects** nausea, vomiting, diarrhoea; headache; less frequently hepatotoxicity, dizziness, confusion, fatigue, sleep disturbances, impaired co-ordination, peripheral neuropathy, leucopenia, systemic lupus erythematosus, rash (including rarely erythema multiforme, toxic epidermal necrolysis), and photosensitivity

**Dose**

- 500 mg daily in divided doses or as a single dose, in severe infection dose may be doubled, reducing when response occurs; CHILD, 10 mg/kg daily in divided doses or as a single dose

**Griseofulvin** (Non-proprietary) PoM

Tablets, griseofulvin 125 mg, net price 20 = £6.76; 500 mg, 20 = £17.52. Label: 9, 21, counselling, driving

**Grisovin®** (Chemidex) PoM

Tablets, both f/c, griseofulvin 125 mg, net price 20 = 48p; 500 mg, 20 = £1.79. Label: 9, 21, counselling, driving

## ITRACONAZOLE

**Indications** see under Dose

**Cautions** absorption reduced in AIDS and neutropenia (monitor plasma-itraconazole concentration and increase dose if necessary); susceptibility to congestive heart failure (see also CSM advice, below); renal impairment (Appendix 3); pregnancy (Appendix 4) and breast-feeding (Appendix 5); **interactions:** Appendix 1 (antifungals, triazole)

Hepatotoxicity Potentially life-threatening hepatotoxicity reported very rarely. Monitor liver function—discontinue if signs of hepatitis develop; avoid or use with caution if history of hepatotoxicity with other drugs or in active liver disease (Appendix 2); use with caution in patients receiving other hepatotoxic drugs

Counselling Patients should be told how to recognise signs of liver disorder and advised to seek immediate medical attention if symptoms such as anorexia, nausea, vomiting, fatigue, abdominal pain or dark urine develop

**CSM advice (heart failure)**

Following rare reports of heart failure, the CSM has advised caution when prescribing itraconazole to patients at high risk of heart failure. Those at risk include:

- patients receiving high doses and longer treatment courses;
- older patients and those with cardiac disease;
- patients receiving treatment with negative inotropic drugs, e.g. calcium channel blockers.

**Side-effects** *very rarely* nausea, vomiting, dyspepsia, abdominal pain, diarrhoea, constipation, jaundice, hepatitis (see also Hepatotoxicity above), heart failure (see CSM advice above), pulmonary oedema, headache, dizziness, peripheral neuropathy (discontinue treatment), menstrual disorder, hypokalaemia, rash, pruritus, Stevens-Johnson syndrome, and alopecia; *with intravenous injection, very rarely* hypertension and hyperglycaemia

**Dose**

- By mouth, oropharyngeal candidiasis, 100 mg daily (200 mg daily in AIDS or neutropenia) for 15 days; see also under *Sporanox®* oral liquid below

  Vulvovaginal candidiasis, 200 mg twice daily for 1 day

  Pityriasis versicolor, 200 mg daily for 7 days

  Tinea corporis and tinea cruris, *either* 100 mg daily for 15 days *or* 200 mg daily for 7 days

  Tinea pedis and tinea manuum, *either* 100 mg daily for 30 days *or* 200 mg twice daily for 7 days

  Onychomycosis, *either* 200 mg daily for 3 months *or* course ('pulse') of 200 mg twice daily for 7 days, subsequent courses repeated after 21-day interval; fingernails 2 courses, toenails 3 courses

  Histoplasmosis, 200 mg 1–2 times daily

  Systemic aspergillosis, candidiasis and cryptococcosis including cryptococcal meningitis where other antifungal drugs inappropriate or ineffective, 200 mg once daily (candidiasis 100–200 mg once daily) increased in invasive or disseminated disease and in cryptococcal meningitis to 200 mg twice daily

  Maintenance in AIDS patients to prevent relapse of underlying fungal infection and prophylaxis in neutropenia when standard therapy inappropriate, 200 mg once daily, increased to 200 mg twice daily if low plasma-itraconazole concentration (see Cautions)

  Prophylaxis in patients with haematological malignancy or undergoing bone-marrow transplant, see under *Sporanox®* oral liquid below
- By intravenous infusion, systemic aspergillosis, candidiasis and cryptococcosis including cryptococcal meningitis where other antifungal drugs inappropriate or ineffective, histoplasmosis, 200 mg every 12 hours for 2 days, then 200 mg once daily for max. 12 days
- CHILD and ELDERLY safety and efficacy not established

**Sporanox®** (Janssen-Cilag) PoM

Capsules, blue/pink, enclosing coated beads, itraconazole 100 mg, net price 4-cap pack = £3.98; 15-cap pack = £14.93; 28-cap pack (*Sporanox®-Pulse*) = £27.88; 60-cap pack = £59.75. Label: 5, 9, 21, 25

Oral liquid, sugar-free, itraconazole 10 mg/mL, net price 150 mL (with 10-mL measuring cup) = £49.67. Label: 9, 23, counselling, administration

Dose oral or oesophageal candidiasis in HIV-positive or other immunocompromised patients, 20 mL (2 measuring cups) daily in 1–2 divided doses for 1 week (continue for another week if no response)

Fluconazole-resistant oral or oesophageal candidiasis, 10–20 mL (1–2 measuring cups) twice daily for 2 weeks (continue for another 2 weeks if no response; the higher dose should not be used for longer than 2 weeks if no signs of improvement)

Prophylaxis of deep fungal infections (when standard therapy is inappropriate) in patients with haematological malignancy or undergoing bone-marrow transplantation who are expected to become neutropenic, 5 mg/kg daily in 2 divided doses; starting before transplantation or before chemotherapy (taking care to avoid interaction with cytotoxic drugs) and continued until neutrophil count recovers; CHILD and ELDERLY safety and efficacy not established

Counselling Do not take with food; swish around mouth and swallow, do not rinse afterwards

Concentrate for intravenous infusion, itraconazole 10 mg/mL. For dilution before use. Net price 25-mL amp (with infusion bag and filter) = £67.86

Excipients include propylene glycol

## KETOCONAZOLE

**Indications** systemic mycoses, serious chronic resistant mucocutaneous candidiasis, serious resistant gastro-intestinal mycoses, chronic resistant vaginal candidiasis, resistant dermatophyte infections of skin or finger nails (not toe nails); prophylaxis of mycoses in immunosuppressed patients

**Cautions** monitor liver function clinically and biochemically—for treatment lasting longer than 14 days perform liver function tests before starting, 14 days after starting, then at monthly intervals (for details consult product literature)—for CSM advice see p. 309; avoid in porphyria (section 9.8.2); **interactions:** Appendix 1 (antifungals, imidazole)

**Contra-indications** hepatic impairment; pregnancy (Appendix 4) and breast-feeding

**Side-effects** nausea, vomiting, abdominal pain; headache; rashes, urticaria, pruritus; rarely angioedema, thrombocytopenia, paraesthesia, photophobia, dizziness, alopecia, gynaecomastia and oligospermia; fatal liver damage—see also under Cautions, risk of developing hepatitis greater if given for longer than 14 days

**Dose**

- 200 mg once daily with food, usually for 14 days; if response inadequate after 14 days continue until at least 1 week after symptoms have cleared and cultures negative; max. 400 mg (ELDERLY 200 mg) daily; CHILD 3 mg/kg daily

- Chronic resistant vaginal candidiasis, 400 mg once daily with food for 5 days
- Prophylaxis and maintenance treatment in immunosuppressed patients, 200 mg daily

**Nizoral®** (Janssen-Cilag) PoM
Tablets, scored, ketoconazole 200 mg. Net price 30-tab pack = £14.91. Label: 5, 9, 21

## MICONAZOLE

**Indications** see under Dose

**Cautions** pregnancy (Appendix 4); breast-feeding; avoid in porphyria (section 9.8.2); **interactions:** Appendix 1 (antifungals, imidazole)

**Contra-indications** hepatic impairment

**Side-effects** nausea and vomiting, diarrhoea (usually on long-term treatment); rarely allergic reactions; isolated reports of hepatitis

**Dose**

- Prevention and treatment of oral and intestinal fungal infections, 5–10 mL in the mouth after food 4 times daily; retain near lesions before swallowing; CHILD under 2 years, 2.5 mL twice daily, 2–6 years, 5 mL twice daily, over 6 years, 5 mL 4 times daily
- Localised lesions, smear on affected area with clean finger (dental prostheses should be removed at night and brushed with gel); treatment continued for 48 hours after lesions have resolved

**Note** Not licensed for use in NEONATE

[1]**Daktarin®** (Janssen-Cilag) PoM
Oral gel, sugar-free, orange-flavoured, miconazole 24 mg/mL (20 mg/g). Net price 15-g tube = £2.45, 80-g tube = £4.75. Label: 9, counselling advised, hold in mouth, after food

1. 15-g tube can be sold to public

## NYSTATIN

**Indications** candidiasis; vaginal infection (section 7.2.2); oral infection (section 12.3.2); skin infection (section 13.10.2)

**Side-effects** nausea, vomiting, diarrhoea at high doses; oral irritation and sensitisation; rash (including urticaria) and rarely Stevens-Johnson syndrome reported

**Dose**

- By mouth, intestinal candidiasis 500 000 units every 6 hours, doubled in severe infections; CHILD 100 000 units 4 times daily

  Prophylaxis, 1 million units once daily; NEONATE 100 000 units once daily

  **Note** Unlicensed for treatment of candidiasis in NEONATE

**Nystatin** (Non-proprietary) PoM
Oral suspension, nystatin 100 000 units/mL. Net price 30 mL = £2.05. Label: 9, counselling, use of pipette
Brands include *Nystamont®*

**Nystan®** (Squibb) PoM
Tablets, brown, s/c, nystatin 500 000 units, net price 56-tab pack = £4.70. Label: 9

Suspension, yellow, nystatin 100 000 units/mL, net price 30 mL with pipette = £2.05. Label: 9, counselling, use of pipette

## TERBINAFINE

**Indications** dermatophyte infections of the nails, ringworm infections (including tinea pedis, cruris, and corporis) where oral therapy appropriate (due to site, severity or extent)

**Cautions** hepatic impairment (Appendix 2) and renal impairment (Appendix 3); pregnancy (Appendix 4), breast-feeding (Appendix 5); psoriasis (risk of exacerbation); autoimmune disease (risk of lupus-erythematosus-like effect); **interactions:** Appendix 1 (terbinafine)

**Side-effects** abdominal discomfort, anorexia, nausea, diarrhoea; headache; rash and urticaria occasionally with arthralgia or myalgia; *less commonly* taste disturbance; *rarely* liver toxicity (including jaundice, cholestasis and hepatitis)—discontinue treatment, angioedema, dizziness, malaise, paraesthesia, hypoaesthesia, photosensitivity, serious skin reactions (including Stevens-Johnson syndrome and toxic epidermal necrolysis) —discontinue treatment if progressive skin rash; *very rarely* psychiatric disturbances, blood disorders (including leucopenia and thrombocytopenia), lupus erythematosus-like effect, and exacerbation of psoriasis

**Dose**

- By mouth, 250 mg daily usually for 2–6 weeks in tinea pedis, 2–4 weeks in tinea cruris, 4 weeks in tinea corporis, 6 weeks–3 months in nail infections (occasionally longer in toenail infections); CHILD [unlicensed] usually for 2 weeks, tinea capitis, over 1 year, body-weight 10–20 kg, 62.5 mg once daily; body-weight 20–40 kg, 125 mg once daily; body-weight over 40 kg, 250 mg once daily

**Terbinafine** (Non-proprietary) PoM
Tablets, terbinafine (as hydrochloride) 250 mg, net price 14-tab pack = £23.15, 28- tab pack = £44.65. Label: 9

**Lamisil®** (Novartis) PoM
Tablets, off-white, scored, terbinafine (as hydrochloride) 250 mg, net price 14-tab pack = £23.16, 28-tab pack = £44.66. Label: 9

## VORICONAZOLE

**Indications** invasive aspergillosis; serious infections caused by *Scedosporium* spp., *Fusarium* spp., or invasive fluconazole-resistant *Candida* spp. (including *C. krusei*); candidaemia

**Cautions** monitor liver function before treatment and during treatment; haematological malignancy (increased risk of hepatic reactions); hepatic impairment (Appendix 2); monitor renal function; renal impairment (Appendix 3); pregnancy (ensure effective contraception during treatment—Appendix 4); electrolyte disturbances, cardiomyopathy, bradycardia, symptomatic arrhythmias, history of QT interval prolongation, concomitant use with other drugs that prolong QT interval; avoid exposure to sunlight; **interactions:** Appendix 1 (antifungals, triazole)

**Contra-indications** breast-feeding (Appendix 5)

**Side-effects** gastro-intestinal disturbances (including nausea, vomiting, abdominal pain, diarrhoea), jaundice; oedema, hypotension, chest pain; respiratory distress syndrome, sinusitis; headache, dizziness, asthenia, anxiety, depression, confusion, agitation, hallucinations, paraesthesia, tremor; influenza-like symptoms; hypoglycaemia; haematuria; blood disorders (including anaemia, thrombocytopenia, leucopenia, pancytopenia), acute renal failure, hypokalaemia; visual disturbances including altered perception, blurred vision, and photophobia; rash, pruritus, photosensitivity, alopecia, cheilitis; injection-site reactions; *less commonly* taste disturbances, cholecystitis, pancreatitis, hepatitis, constipation, arrhythmias (including QT interval prolongation), syncope, raised serum cholesterol, hypersensitivity reactions (including flushing), ataxia, nystagmus, hypoaesthesia, adrenocortical insufficiency, arthritis, blepharitis, optic neuritis, scleritis, glossitis, gingivitis, psoriasis, and Stevens-Johnson syndrome; *rarely* pseudomembranous colitis, sleep disturbances, tinnitus, hearing disturbances, extrapyramidal effects, hypertonia, hypothyroidism, hyperthyroidism, discoid lupus erythematosus, toxic epidermal necrolysis, retinal haemorrhage, and optic atrophy

**Dose**

- By mouth, ADULT and ADOLESCENT over 12 years, body-weight over 40 kg, 400 mg every 12 hours for 2 doses then 200 mg every 12 hours, increased if necessary to 300 mg every 12 hours; body-weight under 40 kg, 200 mg every 12 hours for 2 doses then 100 mg every 12 hours, increased if necessary to 150 mg every 12 hours; CHILD 2–12 years, (oral suspension recommended) 200 mg every 12 hours
- By intravenous infusion, 6 mg/kg every 12 hours for 2 doses, then 4 mg/kg every 12 hours (reduced to 3 mg/kg every 12 hours if not tolerated) for max. 6 months; CHILD 2–12 years, 7 mg/kg every 12 hours (reduced to 4 mg/kg every 12 hours if not tolerated)

**Vfend®** (Pfizer) PoM

Tablets, f/c, voriconazole 50 mg, net price 28-tablet pack = £227.84; 200 mg, 28-tab pack = £911.36. Label: 11, 23

Oral suspension, voriconazole 200 mg/5 mL when reconstituted with water, net price 75 mL (orange-flavoured) = £501.25. Label: 11, 23

Intravenous infusion, powder for reconstitution, voriconazole, net price 200-mg vial = £77.14
Excipients include sulphobutylether beta cyclodextrin sodium (risk of accumulation in renal impairment)
Electrolytes $Na^{+}$ 9.62 mmol/vial

# 5.3 Antiviral drugs

5.3.1 HIV infection
5.3.2 Herpesvirus infections
5.3.3 Viral hepatitis
5.3.4 Influenza
5.3.5 Respiratory syncytial virus

The majority of virus infections resolve spontaneously in immunocompetent subjects. A number of specific treatments for viral infections are available, particularly for the immunocompromised. This section includes notes on herpes simplex and varicella-zoster, human immunodeficiency virus, cytomegalovirus, respiratory syncytial virus, viral hepatitis and influenza.

## 5.3.1 HIV infection

There is no cure for infection caused by the human immunodeficiency virus (HIV) but a number of drugs slow or halt disease progression. Drugs for HIV infection (antiretrovirals) increase life expectancy considerably but they are toxic. Treatment should be undertaken only by those experienced in their use.

**Principles of treatment** Treatment is aimed at reducing the plasma viral load as much as possible and for as long as possible; it should be started before the immune system is irreversibly damaged. The need for early drug treatment should, however, be balanced against the development of toxicity. Commitment to treatment and strict adherence over many years are required; the regimen chosen should take into account convenience and patient tolerance. The development of drug resistance is reduced by using a combination of drugs; such combinations should have synergistic or additive activity while ensuring that their toxicity is not additive. It is recommended that viral sensitivity to antiretroviral drugs is established before starting treatment or before switching drugs if the infection is not responding.

**Initiation of treatment** The optimum time for initiating antiretroviral treatment depends primarily on the CD4 cell count; the plasma viral load and clinical symptoms may also help. The timing and choice of treatment should also take account of the possible effects of antiretroviral drugs on factors such as the risk of cardiovascular events. Initiating treatment with a combination of drugs ('highly active antiretroviral therapy' which includes 2 nucleoside reverse transcriptase inhibitors with *either* a non-nucleoside reverse transcriptase inhibitor *or* a boosted protease inhibitor) is recommended.

**Switching therapy** Deterioration of the condition (including clinical and virological changes) may require either switching therapy or adding another antiretroviral drug. The choice of an alternative regimen depends on factors such as the response to previous treatment, tolerance and the possibility of cross-resistance.

**Pregnancy and breast-feeding** Treatment of HIV infection in pregnancy aims to reduce the risk of toxicity to the fetus (although the teratogenic potential of most antiretroviral drugs is unknown), to minimise the viral load and disease progression in the mother, and to prevent transmission of infection to the neonate. **All treatment options require careful assessment by a specialist**. Zidovudine monotherapy reduces transmission of infection to the neonate. However, combination antiretroviral therapy maximises the chance of preventing transmission and represents optimal therapy for the mother.

Breast-feeding by HIV-positive mothers may cause HIV infection in the infant and should be avoided.

**Post-exposure prophylaxis** Prophylaxis with antiretroviral drugs [unlicensed indication] may be appropriate following exposure to HIV-contaminated material. Immediate expert advice should be sought in such cases; national guidelines on post-exposure prophylaxis for healthcare workers have been developed (by the Chief Medical Officer's Expert Advisory Group on AIDS) and local ones may also be available. Antiretrovirals for prophylaxis are chosen on the basis of efficacy and potential for toxicity.

**Drugs used for HIV infection** **Zidovudine**, a nucleoside reverse transcriptase inhibitor (or 'nucleoside analogue'), was the first anti-HIV drug to be introduced. Other nucleoside reverse transcriptase inhibitors include **abacavir**, **didanosine**, **emtricitabine**, **lamivudine**, **stavudine**, **tenofovir**, and **zalcitabine**. Stavudine, especially with didanosine, is associated with a higher risk of lipodystrophy and lactic acidosis and should be used only if alternative regimens are not suitable.

The protease inhibitors include **amprenavir**, **atazanavir**, **fosamprenavir** (a pro-drug of amprenavir), **indinavir**, **lopinavir**, **nelfinavir**, **ritonavir**, **saquinavir**, and **tipranavir**. Ritonavir in low doses boosts the activity of amprenavir, atazanavir, indinavir, lopinavir, saquinavir, and tipranavir increasing the persistence of plasma concentrations of these drugs; at such a low dose, ritonavir has no intrinsic antiviral activity. A combination of lopinavir with low-dose ritonavir is available. The protease inhibitors are metabolised by cytochrome P450 enzyme systems and therefore have a significant potential for drug interactions. Protease inhibitors are associated with lipodystrophy and metabolic effects (see below).

The non-nucleoside reverse transcriptase inhibitors **efavirenz** and **nevirapine** are active against the subtype HIV-1 but not HIV-2, a subtype prevalent mainly in Africa. These drugs may interact with a number of drugs metabolised in the liver. Nevirapine is associated with a high incidence of rash (including Stevens-Johnson syndrome) and occasionally fatal hepatitis. Rash is also associated with efavirenz but it is usually milder. Efavirenz treatment has also been associated with an increased plasma cholesterol concentration.

**Enfuvirtide**, which inhibits HIV from fusing to the host cell, is licensed for managing infection that has failed to respond to a regimen of other antiretroviral drugs; enfuvirtide should be combined with other potentially active antiretroviral drugs.

Improvement in immune function as a result of antiretroviral treatment may provoke an inflammatory reaction against residual opportunistic organisms.

**Lipodystrophy syndrome** Metabolic effects associated with antiretroviral treatment include *fat redistribution*, *insulin resistance* and *dyslipidaemia*; collectively these have been termed *lipodystrophy syndrome*.

Fat redistribution (with loss of subcutaneous fat, increased abdominal fat, 'buffalo hump' and breast enlargement) is associated with regimens containing protease inhibitors and nucleoside reverse transcriptase inhibitors.

Dyslipidaemia (with adverse effects on body lipids) is associated with antiretroviral treatment, particularly with protease inhibitors. Protease inhibitors are associated with insulin resistance and hyperglycaemia. Plasma lipids, blood glucose and the usual risk factors for atherosclerotic disease should be taken into account before prescribing regimens containing a protease inhibitor; patients receiving protease inhibitors should be monitored for changes in plasma lipids and blood glucose.

## Nucleoside reverse transcriptase inhibitors

**Cautions** Nucleoside reverse transcriptase inhibitors should be used with caution in patients with chronic hepatitis B or C (greater risk of hepatic side-effects), in hepatic impairment (see also Lactic Acidosis below and Appendix 2), in renal impairment (Appendix 3), and in pregnancy (see also p. 314 and Appendix 4).

**Lactic acidosis** Life-threatening lactic acidosis associated with hepatomegaly and hepatic steatosis has been reported with nucleoside reverse transcriptase inhibitors. They should be used with caution in patients (particularly obese women) with hepatomegaly, hepatitis (especially hepatitis C treated with interferon alfa and ribavirin), liver-enzyme abnormalities and with other risk factors for liver disease and hepatic steatosis (including alcohol abuse). Treatment with the nucleoside reverse transcriptase inhibitor should be **discontinued** in case of symptomatic hyperlactataemia, lactic acidosis, progressive hepatomegaly or rapid deterioration of liver function.

**Side-effects** Side-effects of the nucleoside reverse transcriptase inhibitors include gastro-intestinal disturbances (such as nausea, vomiting, abdominal pain, flatulence and diarrhoea), anorexia, pancreatitis, liver damage (see also Lactic Acidosis, above), dyspnoea, cough, headache, insomnia, dizziness, fatigue, blood disorders (including anaemia, neutropenia, and thrombocytopenia), myalgia, arthralgia, rash, urticaria, and fever. See notes above for metabolic effects and lipodystrophy (Lipodystrophy Syndrome).

### ABACAVIR

**Indications** HIV infection in combination with other antiretroviral drugs

**Cautions** see notes above; **interactions:** Appendix 1 (abacavir)

**Hypersensitivity reactions** Life-threatening hypersensitivity reactions reported—characterised by fever or rash and possibly nausea, vomiting, diarrhoea, abdominal pain, dyspnoea, cough, lethargy, malaise, headache, and myalgia; less frequently mouth ulceration, oedema, hypotension, sore throat, acute respiratory distress syndrome, anaphylaxis, paraesthesia, arthralgia, conjunctivitis, lymphadenopathy, lymphocytopenia and renal failure (CSM has identified hypersensitivity reactions presenting as sore throat, influenza-like illness, cough and breathlessness); rarely myolysis; laboratory abnormalities may include raised liver function tests (see below) and creatine phosphokinase; symptoms usually appear in the first 6 weeks, but may occur at any time; monitor for symptoms every 2 weeks for 2 months; discontinue immediately if any symptom of hypersensitivity develops and do not rechallenge (risk of more severe hypersensitivity reaction); discontinue if hypersensitivity cannot be ruled out, even when other diagnoses possible—if rechallenge necessary it must be carried out in hospital setting; if abacavir is stopped for any reason other than hypersensitivity, exclude hypersensitivity reaction as the cause and rechallenge only if medical assistance is readily available; care needed with concomitant use of drugs which cause skin toxicity

**Counselling** Patients should be told the importance of regular dosing (intermittent therapy may increase the risk of sensitisation), how to recognise signs of hypersensitivity, and advised to seek immediate medical attention if symptoms develop or before re-starting treatment; patients should be advised to keep Alert card with them at all times

**Contra-indications** breast-feeding (Appendix 5)

**Side-effects** see notes above; also hypersensitivity reactions (see above); *very rarely* Stevens-Johnson syndrome and toxic epidermal necrolysis; rash and gastro-intestinal disturbances more common in children

**Dose**

- 600 mg daily in 1–2 divided doses; CHILD 3 months–12 years, 8 mg/kg every 12 hours (max. 600 mg daily)

**Ziagen®** (GSK) PoM

Tablets, yellow, f/c, abacavir (as sulphate) 300 mg, net price 60-tab pack = £221.81. Counselling, hypersensitivity reactions

Oral solution, sugar-free, banana and strawberry flavoured, abacavir (as sulphate) 20 mg/mL, net price 240-mL = £59.15. Counselling, hypersensitivity reactions

**With lamivudine**

For **cautions**, **contra-indications** and **side-effects** see under individual drugs

**Kivexa** (GSK) ▼ PoM

Tablets, orange, f/c, abacavir (as sulphate) 600 mg, lamivudine 300 mg, net price 30-tab pack = £373.94. Counselling, hypersensitivity reactions

**Dose** ADULT and CHILD over 12 years, body-weight over 40 kg, 1 tablet once daily

**With lamivudine and zidovudine**

**Note** For patients stabilised (for 6–8 weeks) on the individual components in the same proportions. For **cautions**, **contra-indications** and **side-effects** see under individual drugs

**Trizivir®** (GSK) PoM

Tablets, blue-green, f/c, abacavir (as sulphate) 300 mg, lamivudine 150 mg, zidovudine 300 mg, net price 60-tab pack = £540.40. Counselling, hypersensitivity reactions

**Dose** ADULT over 18 years, 1 tablet twice daily

## DIDANOSINE
(ddI, DDI)

**Indications** HIV infection in combination with other antiretroviral drugs

**Cautions** see notes above; also history of pancreatitis (preferably avoid, otherwise extreme caution, see also below); peripheral neuropathy or hyperuricaemia (see under Side-effects); dilated retinal examinations recommended (especially in children) every 6 months, or if visual changes occur; **interactions**: Appendix 1 (didanosine)

**Pancreatitis** Suspend treatment if serum lipase raised (even if asymptomatic) or if symptoms of pancreatitis develop; discontinue if pancreatitis confirmed. Whenever possible avoid concomitant treatment with other drugs known to cause pancreatic toxicity (e.g. intravenous pentamidine isetionate); monitor closely if concomitant therapy unavoidable. Since significant elevations of triglycerides cause pancreatitis monitor closely if elevated

**Contra-indications** breast-feeding (Appendix 5)

**Side-effects** see notes above; also pancreatitis (see also under cautions), liver failure, anaphylactic reactions, peripheral neuropathy—suspend (reduced dose may be tolerated when symptoms resolve), diabetes mellitus, hypoglycaemia, acute renal failure, rhabdomyolysis, dry eyes, retinal and optic nerve changes (especially in children), dry mouth, parotid gland enlargement, sialadenitis, alopecia, hyperuricaemia (suspend if raised significantly)

**Dose**

- ADULT under 60 kg 250 mg daily in 1–2 divided doses, 60 kg and over 400 mg daily in 1–2 divided doses; CHILD over 3 months (under 6 years *Videx®* tablets only), 240 mg/m² daily (180 mg/m² daily in combination with zidovudine) in 1–2 divided doses

**Videx®** (Bristol-Myers Squibb) PoM

Tablets, both with calcium and magnesium antacids, didanosine 25 mg, net price 60-tab pack = £26.60; 200 mg, 60-tab pack = £163.68. Label: 23, counselling, administration, see below

**Excipients** include aspartame equivalent to phenylalanine 36.5 mg per tablet (section 9.4.1)

**Note** Antacids in formulation may affect absorption of other drugs—see **interactions**: Appendix 1 (antacids)

**Counselling** To ensure sufficient antacid, each dose to be taken as 2 tablets (CHILD under 1 year 1 tablet) chewed thoroughly, crushed or dispersed in water; clear apple juice may be added for flavouring; tablets to be taken 2 hours after atazanavir with ritonavir

Videx® EC capsules, enclosing e/c granules, didanosine 125 mg, net price 30-cap pack = £51.15; 200 mg, 30-cap pack = £81.84; 250 mg, 30-cap pack = £102.30; 400 mg, 30-cap pack = £163.68. Label: 25, counselling, administration, see below

**Counselling** Capsules to be taken at least 2 hours before or 2 hours after food

## EMTRICITABINE

**Indications** HIV infection in combination with other antiretroviral drugs

**Cautions** see notes above; also on discontinuation, monitor patients with hepatitis B (risk of exacerbation of hepatitis); **interactions**: Appendix 1 (emtricitabine)

**Contra-indications** breast-feeding (Appendix 5)

**Side-effects** see notes above; also abnormal dreams, pruritus, and hyperpigmentation

**Dose**

- See preparations

**Emtriva®** (Gilead) ▼ PoM

Capsules, white/blue, emtricitabine 200 mg, net price 30-cap pack = £163.50

**Dose** ADULT and CHILD body-weight over 33 kg, 200 mg once daily

Oral solution, orange, emtricitabine 10 mg/mL, net price 170-mL pack = £46.50

**Dose** ADULT and CHILD body-weight over 33 kg, 240 mg once daily; CHILD 4 months–18 years, body-weight under 33 kg, 6 mg/kg once daily

**Note** 240 mg oral solution ≡ 200 mg capsule; where appropriate the capsule may be used instead of the oral solution

**With tenofovir**

See under Tenofovir

## LAMIVUDINE
(3TC)

**Indications** see preparations below

**Cautions** see notes above; **interactions**: Appendix 1 (lamivudine)

**Chronic Hepatitis B** Recurrent hepatitis in patients with chronic hepatitis B may occur on discontinuation of lamivudine. When treating chronic hepatitis B with lamivudine, monitor liver function tests at least every 3 months and serological markers of hepatitis B every 6 months, more frequently in patients with advanced liver disease or following transplantation (monitoring to continue after discontinuation)—consult product literature

**Contra-indications** breast-feeding (Appendix 5)

**Side-effects** see notes above; also peripheral neuropathy, muscle disorders including rhabdomyolysis, nasal symptoms, alopecia

**Dose**

- See preparations below

**Epivir®** (GSK) PoM

Tablets, f/c, lamivudine 150 mg (white), net price 60-tab pack = £152.14; 300 mg (grey), 30-tab pack = £167.21

Oral solution, banana- and strawberry-flavoured, lamivudine 50 mg/5 mL, net price 240-mL pack = £41.41

Excipients include sucrose 1 g/5 mL

Dose HIV infection in combination with other antiretroviral drugs, 150 mg every 12 hours *or* 300 mg once daily; CHILD 3 months–12 years, 4 mg/kg every 12 hours; max. 300 mg daily

**Zeffix®** (GSK) PoM

Tablets, brown, f/c, lamivudine 100 mg, net price 28-tab pack = £78.09

Oral solution, banana and strawberry flavoured, lamivudine 25 mg/5 mL, net price 240-mL pack = £22.79

Excipients include sucrose 1 g/5 mL

Dose chronic hepatitis B infection with *either* compensated liver disease (with evidence of viral replication and histology of active liver inflammation or fibrosis), *or* decompensated liver disease, 100 mg daily; CHILD [unlicensed indication] 2–11 years, 3 mg/kg once daily (max. 100 mg daily); 12–17 years, adult dose; patients receiving lamivudine for concomitant HIV infection should continue to receive lamivudine in a dose appropriate for HIV infection

### With abacavir

See under Abacavir

### With zidovudine

See under Zidovudine

### With abacavir and zidovudine

See under Abacavir

## STAVUDINE
### (d4T)

**Indications** HIV infection in combination with other antiretroviral drugs

**Cautions** see notes above; also history of peripheral neuropathy (see below); history of pancreatitis or concomitant use with other drugs associated with pancreatitis; **interactions:** Appendix 1 (stavudine)

Peripheral neuropathy Suspend if peripheral neuropathy develops—characterised by persistent numbness, tingling or pain in feet or hands; if symptoms resolve satisfactorily on withdrawal and if stavudine needs to be continued, resume treatment at half previous dose

**Contra-indications** breast-feeding (Appendix 5)

**Side-effects** see notes above; also peripheral neuropathy, abnormal dreams, cognitive dysfunction, drowsiness, depression, pruritus; *less commonly* anxiety, gynaecomastia

**Dose**

- ADULT under 60 kg, 30 mg every 12 hours preferably at least 1 hour before food; 60 kg and over, 40 mg every 12 hours; CHILD over 3 months, under 30 kg, 1 mg/kg every 12 hours; 30 kg and over, adult dose

**Zerit®** (Bristol-Myers Squibb) PoM

Capsules, stavudine 15 mg (yellow/red), net price 56-cap pack = £143.10; 20 mg (brown), 56-cap pack = £148.05; 30 mg (light orange/dark orange), 56-cap pack = £155.25; 40 mg (dark orange), 56-cap pack = £159.94 (all hosp. only)

Oral solution, cherry-flavoured, stavudine for reconstitution with water, 1 mg/mL, net price 200 mL = £24.35

## TENOFOVIR DISOPROXIL

**Indications** HIV infection in combination with other antiretroviral drugs

**Cautions** see notes above; also test renal function and serum phosphate before treatment, then every 4 weeks (more frequently if at increased risk of renal impairment) for 1 year and then every 3 months, interrupt treatment if renal function deteriorates or serum phosphate decreases; **interactions:** Appendix 1 (tenofovir)

**Contra-indications** breast-feeding (Appendix 5)

**Side-effects** see notes above; also hypophosphataemia, reduced bone density, polyuria, and renal failure

**Dose**

- ADULT over 18 years, 245 mg once daily

**Viread®** (Gilead) ▼ PoM

Tablets, f/c, blue, tenofovir disoproxil (as fumarate) 245 mg, net price 30-tab pack = £255.00. Label: 21, counselling, administration

Counselling Patients with swallowing difficulties may disperse tablet in half a glass of water, grape juice, or orange juice

### With emtricitabine

For **cautions**, **contra-indications** and **side-effects** see under individual drugs

**Truvada®** (Gilead) ▼ PoM

Tablets, blue, f/c, tenofovir disoproxil (as fumarate) 245 mg, emtricitabine 200 mg, net price 30-tab pack = £418.50. Label: 21, counselling, administration

Counselling Patients with swallowing difficulties may disperse tablet in half a glass of water, orange juice, or grape juice

Dose ADULT over 18 years, 1 tablet once daily

## ZALCITABINE
### (ddC, DDC)

**Indications** HIV infection in combination with other antiretroviral drugs

**Cautions** see notes above; also patients at risk of developing peripheral neuropathy (see below); pancreatitis (see also below)—monitor serum amylase in those with history of elevated serum amylase, pancreatitis, alcohol abuse, or receiving parenteral nutrition; monitor full blood count; cardiomyopathy, history of congestive cardiac failure; **interactions:** Appendix 1 (zalcitabine)

Peripheral neuropathy Discontinue immediately if peripheral neuropathy develops—characterised by numbness and burning dysaesthesia possibly followed by sharp shooting pains or severe continuous burning and potentially irreversible pain; extreme caution and close monitoring required in those at risk of peripheral neuropathy (especially those with low CD4 cell count for whom risk is greater and those receiving another drug known to cause peripheral neuropathy)

Pancreatitis Discontinue permanently if clinical pancreatitis develops; suspend if raised serum amylase associated with dysglycaemia, rising triglyceride, decreasing serum calcium or other signs of impending pancreatitis until pancreatitis excluded; suspend if treatment required with another drug known to cause pancreatic toxicity (e.g. intravenous pentamidine isetionate); caution and close monitoring if history of pancreatitis (or of elevated serum amylase) or if at risk of pancreatitis

**Contra-indications** peripheral neuropathy (see also above); breast-feeding (Appendix 5)

**Side-effects** see notes above; also oral ulcers, dysphagia, oesophageal ulcers (suspend zalcitabine if no response to treatment for specific organisms), pancreatitis (see also Cautions), rectal ulcers, flushing, hypertension, chest pain, cardiomyopathy, congestive heart failure, tachycardia, palpitation, syncope, pharyngitis, hypersensitivity reactions, peripheral neuropathy (discontinue immediately, see also Cautions), convulsions, tremor, movement disorders, mood changes, anxiety, sleep disturbances, weight loss, hypoglycaemia, hyperglycaemia, acute renal failure, gout, dry mouth, pruritus, sweating, alopecia, electrolyte disturbances, taste, hearing and visual disturbances

**Dose**
- 750 micrograms every 8 hours; CHILD under 13 years safety and efficacy not established

**Hivid®** (Roche) PoM
Tablets, both f/c, zalcitabine 375 micrograms (beige), net price 100-tab pack = £92.54; 750 micrograms (grey), 100-tab pack = £140.96

## ZIDOVUDINE
### (Azidothymidine, AZT)

**Note** The abbreviation AZT which is sometimes used for zidovudine has also been used for another drug

**Indications** HIV infection in combination with other antiretroviral drugs; prevention of maternal-fetal HIV transmission (see notes above under Pregnancy and Breast-feeding)

**Cautions** see notes above; also haematological toxicity particularly with high dose and advanced disease (blood tests at least every 2 weeks for first 3 months then at least once a month, early disease with good bone marrow reserves may require less frequent tests e.g. every 1–3 months); vitamin $B_{12}$ deficiency (increased risk of neutropenia); reduce dose or interrupt treatment according to product literature if anaemia or myelosuppression; elderly; **interactions**: Appendix 1 (zidovudine)

**Contra-indications** abnormally low neutrophil counts or haemoglobin values (consult product literature); neonates with hyperbilirubinaemia requiring treatment other than phototherapy, or with raised transaminase (consult product literature); breast-feeding (Appendix 5)

**Side-effects** see notes above; also anaemia (may require transfusion), taste disturbance, chest pain, influenza-like symptoms, paraesthesia, neuropathy, convulsions, dizziness, drowsiness, insomnia, anxiety, depression, loss of mental acuity, myopathy, gynaecomastia, urinary frequency, sweating, pruritus, pigmentation of nails, skin and oral mucosa

**Dose**
- By mouth, 500–600 mg daily in 2–3 divided doses; CHILD over 3 months 360–480 mg/m² daily in 3–4 divided doses; max. 200 mg every 6 hours
- Prevention of maternal-fetal HIV transmission, seek specialist advice (combination therapy preferred)
- Patients temporarily unable to take zidovudine by mouth, by intravenous infusion over 1 hour, 1–2 mg/kg every 4 hours (approximating to 1.5–3 mg/kg every 4 hours by mouth) usually for not more than 2 weeks; CHILD 80–160 mg/m² every 6 hours (120 mg/m² every 6 hours approximates to 180 mg/m² every 6 hours by mouth)

**Retrovir®** (GSK) PoM
Capsules, zidovudine 100 mg (white/blue band), net price 100-cap pack = £110.98; 250 mg (blue/white/dark blue band), 40-cap pack = £110.98

Oral solution, sugar-free, strawberry-flavoured, zidovudine 50 mg/5 mL, net price 200-mL pack with 10-mL oral syringe = £22.20

Injection, zidovudine 10 mg/mL. For dilution and use as an intravenous infusion. Net price 20-mL vial = £11.14

**With lamivudine**
For cautions, contra-indications, and side-effects of lamivudine, see Lamivudine

**Combivir®** (GSK) PoM
Tablets, f/c, zidovudine 300 mg, lamivudine 150 mg, net price 60-tab pack = £318.60
**Dose** 1 tablet twice daily

**With abacavir and lamivudine**
See under Abacavir

## Protease inhibitors

**Cautions** Protease inhibitors are associated with hyperglycaemia and should be used with caution in diabetes (see also notes above under Lipodystrophy Syndrome). Caution is also needed in patients with haemophilia who may be at increased risk of bleeding. Protease inhibitors should be used with caution in hepatic impairment (Appendix 2); the risk of hepatic side-effects is increased in patients with chronic hepatitis B or C. Atazanavir, fosamprenavir, and tipranavir may be used at usual doses in patients with renal impairment, but other protease inhibitors should be used with caution in renal impairment (Appendix 3). Protease inhibitors should also be used with caution during pregnancy (Appendix 4).

**Side-effects** Side-effects of the protease inhibitors include gastro-intestinal disturbances (including diarrhoea, nausea, vomiting, abdominal pain, flatulence), anorexia, hepatic dysfunction, pancreatitis; blood disorders including anaemia, neutropenia, and thrombocytopenia; sleep disturbances, fatigue, headache, dizziness, paraesthesia, myalgia, myositis, rhabdomyolysis; taste disturbances; rash, pruritus, Stevens-Johnson syndrome, hypersensitivity reactions including anaphylaxis; see also notes above for lipodystrophy and metabolic effects.

## AMPRENAVIR

**Indications** HIV infection in combination with other antiretroviral drugs in patients previously treated with other protease inhibitors

**Cautions** see notes above; **interactions**: Appendix 1 (amprenavir)
Rash Rash may occur, usually in the second week of therapy; discontinue permanently if severe rash with systemic or allergic symptoms or, mucosal involvement; if rash mild or moderate, may continue without interruption—rash usually resolves within 2 weeks and may respond to antihistamines

**Contra-indications** breast-feeding (Appendix 5)

**Side-effects** see notes above; also reported, rash including rarely Stevens-Johnson syndrome (see also above); tremors, oral or perioral paraesthesia, mood disorders including depression

**Dose**
- See preparations below

**Agenerase®** (GSK) PoM

Capsules, ivory, amprenavir 50 mg, net price 480-cap pack = £139.50. Label: 5

Excipients include vitamin E 36 units/50 mg amprenavir (avoid vitamin E supplements)

Dose ADULT and ADOLESCENT over 12 years, body-weight over 50 kg, 1.2 g every 12 hours; ADULT and ADOLESCENT over 12 years, body-weight under 50 kg and CHILD 4–12 years, 20 mg/kg every 12 hours (max. 2.4 g daily)

With low-dose ritonavir, ADULT and ADOLESCENT over 12 years, body-weight over 50 kg, amprenavir 600 mg every 12 hours with ritonavir 100 mg every 12 hours

Oral solution, grape-bubblegum- and peppermint-flavoured, amprenavir 15 mg/mL, net price 240-mL pack = £33.48. Label: 4, 5

Excipients include vitamin E 46 units/mL (avoid vitamin E supplements), propylene glycol 550 mg/mL (see Excipients, p. 2)

Dose ADULT and CHILD over 4 years, 17 mg/kg every 8 hours (max. 2.8 g daily); CHILD under 4 years not recommended

Note The bioavailability of *Agenerase®* oral solution is lower than that of capsules; the two formulations are **not** interchangeable on a milligram-for-milligram basis

## ATAZANAVIR

**Indications** HIV infection in combination with other antiretroviral drugs in patients previously treated with antiretrovirals

**Cautions** see notes above; also concomitant use with drugs that prolong PR interval; cardiac conduction disorders; **interactions:** Appendix 1 (atazanavir)

**Contra-indications** breast-feeding (Appendix 5)

**Side-effects** see notes above; also mouth ulcers, jaundice, hepatosplenomegaly, hypertension, oedema, palpitation, syncope, chest pain, dyspnoea, peripheral neurological symptoms, abnormal dreams, amnesia, depression, anxiety, gynaecomastia, weight changes, increased appetite, nephrolithiasis, urinary frequency, haematuria, proteinuria, arthralgia, alopecia

**Dose**

- With low-dose ritonavir and food, ADULT over 18 years, 300 mg once daily with ritonavir 100 mg once daily

**Reyataz®** (Bristol-Myers Squibb) ▼ PoM

Capsules, atazanavir (as sulphate) 100 mg (dark blue/white), net price 60-cap pack = £315.69; 150 mg (dark blue/light blue), 60-cap pack = £315.69; 200 mg (dark blue), 60-cap pack = £315.69. Label: 5, 21

## FOSAMPRENAVIR

Note Fosamprenavir is a pro-drug of amprenavir

**Indications** HIV infection in combination with other antiretroviral drugs

**Cautions** see notes above and under Amprenavir

**Contra-indications** breast-feeding (Appendix 5)

**Side-effects** see notes above and under Amprenavir

**Dose**

- With low-dose ritonavir, ADULT over 18 years, 700 mg twice daily

  Note 700 mg fosamprenavir is equivalent to approx. 600 mg amprenavir

**Telzir®** (GSK) ▼ PoM

Tablets, f/c, pink, fosamprenavir (as calcium) 700 mg, net price 60-tab pack = £274.92

Oral suspension, fosamprenavir (as calcium) 50 mg/mL, net price 225-mL pack (grape-bubblegum-and peppermint-flavoured) (with 10-mL oral syringe) = £73.31. Label: 23

## INDINAVIR

**Indications** HIV infection in combination with nucleoside reverse transcriptase inhibitors

**Cautions** see notes above; also ensure adequate hydration (risk of nephrolithiasis especially in children); patients at risk of nephrolithiasis (monitor for nephrolithiasis); avoid in porphyria (section 9.8.2); **interactions:** Appendix 1 (indinavir)

**Contra-indications** breast-feeding (Appendix 5)

**Side-effects** see notes above; also reported, dry mouth, hypoaesthesia, dry skin, hyperpigmentation, alopecia, paronychia, interstitial nephritis (with medullary calcification and cortical atrophy in asymptomatic severe leucocyturia), nephrolithiasis (may require interruption or discontinuation; more frequent in children), dysuria, haematuria, crystalluria, proteinuria, pyuria (in children); haemolytic anaemia

**Dose**

- 800 mg every 8 hours; CHILD and ADOLESCENT 4–17 years, 500 mg/m² every 8 hours (max. 800 mg every 8 hours); CHILD under 4 years, safety and efficacy not established

**Crixivan®** (MSD) PoM

Capsules, indinavir (as sulphate), 200 mg, net price 360-cap pack = £226.28; 400 mg, 90-cap pack = £113.15, 180-cap pack = £226.28. Label: 27, counselling, administration

Counselling Administer 1 hour before or 2 hours after a meal; may be administered with a low-fat light meal; in combination with didanosine tablets, allow 1 hour between each drug (antacids in didanosine tablets reduce absorption of indinavir); in combination with low dose ritonavir give with food

Note Dispense in original container (contains dessicant)

## LOPINAVIR WITH RITONAVIR

**Indications** HIV infection in combination with other antiretroviral drugs

**Cautions** see notes above; concomitant use with drugs that prolong QT interval; pancreatitis (see below); **interactions:** Appendix 1 (lopinavir, ritonavir)

Pancreatitis Signs and symptoms suggestive of pancreatitis (including raised serum amylase and lipase) should be evaluated—discontinue if pancreatitis diagnosed

**Contra-indications** breast-feeding (Appendix 5, *Kaletra®*)

**Side-effects** see notes and Cautions above; also electrolyte disturbances in children; *less commonly* dysphagia, appetite changes, weight changes, cholecystitis, hypertension, myocardial infarction, palpitation, thrombophlebitis, vasculitis, chest pain, oedema, dyspnoea, cough, agitation, anxiety, amnesia, ataxia, hypertonia, confusion, depression, abnormal dreams, extrapyramidal effects, neuropathy, influenza-like syndrome, Cushing's syndrome, hypothyroidism, menorrhagia, sexual dysfunction, breast enlargement, dehydration, hypercalciuria, lactic acidosis, arthralgia, hyperuricaemia, abnormal vision, otitis media, tinnitus, dry mouth, sialadenitis, mouth ulceration, periodontitis, acne, alopecia, dry skin, sweating, skin discoloration, nail disorders, *rarely* prolonged PR interval

**Dose**

- See preparations below

**Kaletra®** (Abbott) PoM

Capsules, orange, lopinavir 133.3 mg, ritonavir 33.3 mg, net price 180-cap pack = £307.39. Label: 21

Dose ADULT and CHILD over 2 years with body surface area of 1.4 m² or greater, 3 capsules twice daily with food; CHILD over 2 years with body surface area less than 1.4 m², oral solution preferred; if oral solution inappropriate and body surface area 0.4–0.75 m², 1 capsule twice daily, body surface area 0.8–1.3 m², 2 capsules twice daily

Oral solution, lopinavir 400 mg, ritonavir 100 mg/5 mL, net price 5×60-mL packs = £307.39. Label: 21

Excipients include propylene glycol 153 mg/mL (see Excipients, p. 2), alcohol 42%

Dose ADULT and ADOLESCENT, 5 mL twice daily with food; CHILD over 2 years 2.9 mL/m² twice daily with food, max. 5 mL twice daily; CHILD under 2 years, safety and efficacy not established

Note 5 mL oral solution ≡ 3 capsules; where appropriate, capsules may be used instead of oral solution

## NELFINAVIR

**Indications** HIV infection in combination with other antiretroviral drugs

**Cautions** see notes above; **interactions:** Appendix 1 (nelfinavir)

**Contra-indications** breast-feeding (Appendix 5)

**Side-effects** see notes above; also reported, fever

**Dose**

- 1.25 g twice daily *or* 750 mg 3 times daily; CHILD 3–13 years, initially 50–55 mg/kg twice daily (max. 1.25 g twice daily) *or* 25–30 mg/kg 3 times daily (max. 750 mg 3 times daily)

**Viracept®** (Roche) PoM

Tablets, f/c, nelfinavir (as mesilate) 250 mg, net price 300-tab pack = £273.16. Label: 21

Oral powder, nelfinavir (as mesilate) 50 mg/g. Net price 144 g (with 1-g and 5-g scoop) = £28.72. Label: 21, counselling, administration

Excipients include aspartame (section 9.4.1)

Counselling Powder may be mixed with water, milk, formula feeds or pudding; it should **not** be mixed with acidic foods or juices owing to its taste

## RITONAVIR

**Indications** HIV infection in combination with nucleoside reverse transcriptase inhibitors; low doses used to increase effect of some protease inhibitors

**Cautions** see notes above; avoid in porphyria (section 9.8.2); pancreatitis (see below); **interactions:** Appendix 1 (ritonavir)

Pancreatitis Signs and symptoms suggestive of pancreatitis (including raised serum amylase and lipase) should be evaluated—discontinue if pancreatitis diagnosed

**Contra-indications** breast-feeding (Appendix 5)

**Side-effects** see notes and Cautions above; also reported, diarrhoea (may impair absorption—close monitoring required), throat irritation, vasodilatation, syncope, hypotension; drowsiness, circumoral and peripheral paraesthesia, hyperaesthesia, seizures, raised uric acid, dry mouth and ulceration, cough, anxiety, fever, decreased blood thyroxine concentration, menorrhagia, sweating, electrolyte disturbances, increased prothrombin time

**Dose**

- Initially 300 mg every 12 hours for 3 days, increased in steps of 100 mg every 12 hours over not longer than 14 days to 600 mg every 12 hours; CHILD over 2 years initially 250 mg/m² every 12 hours, increased by 50 mg/m² at intervals of 2–3 days to 350 mg/m² every 12 hours (max. 600 mg every 12 hours)
- Low-dose booster to increase effect of other protease inhibitors, 100–200 mg once or twice daily

**Norvir®** (Abbott) PoM

Capsules, ritonavir 100 mg, net price 336-cap pack = £377.39. Label 21

Excipients include alcohol 12%

Oral solution, sugar-free, ritonavir 400 mg/5 mL, net price 5 × 90-mL packs (with measuring cup) = £403.20. Label: 21, counselling, administration

Counselling Oral solution contains 43% alcohol; bitter taste can be masked by mixing with chocolate milk; do not mix with water, measuring cup must be dry

**With lopinavir**

See under Lopinavir with ritonavir

## SAQUINAVIR

**Indications** HIV infection in combination with other antiretroviral drugs

**Cautions** see notes above; concomitant use of garlic (avoid garlic capsules—reduces plasma-saquinavir concentration); **interactions:** Appendix 1 (saquinavir)

**Contra-indications** breast-feeding (Appendix 5)

**Side-effects** see notes above; also buccal and mucosal ulceration, chest pain, peripheral neuropathy, mood changes, fever, changes in libido, verruca, nephrolithiasis

**Dose**

- With low-dose ritonavir, ADULT and ADOLESCENT over 16 years, 1 g every 12 hours within 2 hours after a meal

Note To avoid confusion between the different formulations of saquinavir, prescribers should specify the brand to be dispensed; absorption from *Fortovase®* [now discontinued] is much greater than from *Invirase®*.

**Invirase®** (Roche) PoM

Capsules, brown/green, saquinavir (as mesilate) 200 mg, net price 270-cap pack = £240.06. Label: 21

Tablets, orange, f/c, saquinavir (as mesilate) 500 mg, net price 120-tab pack = £266.73. Label: 21

## TIPRANAVIR

**Indications** HIV infection resistant to other protease inhibitors, in combination with other antiretroviral drugs in patients previously treated with antiretrovirals

**Cautions** see notes above; **interactions:** Appendix 1 (tipranavir)

Hepatotoxicity Potentially life-threatening hepatotoxicity reported; monitor liver function before treatment then on weeks 2, 4 and 8 of treatment, then every 2–3 months (every 2 weeks for first 3 months then monthly in those with hepatic impairment (Appendix 2)). Discontinue if signs or symptoms of hepatitis develop or if liver-function abnormality develops (consult product literature)

**Contra-indications** breast-feeding (Appendix 5)

**Side-effects** see notes above; also dyspnoea, anorexia, peripheral neuropathy, influenza-like symptoms, renal impairment and photosensitivity; *rarely* dehydration

**Dose**

- With low-dose ritonavir 500 mg twice daily; CHILD safety and efficacy not established

5 Infections

**Aptivus®** (Boehringer Ingelheim) ▼ PoM
Capsules, pink, tipranavir 250 mg, net price 120-cap pack = £490.00. Label: 5, 21
**Excipients** include ethanol 100 mg per capsule

## Non-nucleoside reverse transcriptase inhibitors

### EFAVIRENZ

**Indications** HIV infection in combination with other antiretroviral drugs

**Cautions** chronic hepatitis B or C (greater risk of hepatic side-effects), hepatic impairment (avoid if severe; Appendix 2); severe renal impairment (Appendix 3); pregnancy (Appendix 4); elderly; history of mental illness or seizures; **interactions:** Appendix 1 (efavirenz)

**Rash** Rash, usually in the first 2 weeks, is the most common side-effect; discontinue if severe rash with blistering, desquamation, mucosal involvement or fever; if rash mild or moderate, may continue without interruption—rash usually resolves within 1 month

**Psychiatric disorders** Patients or their carers should be advised to seek immediate medical attention if symptoms such as severe depression, psychosis or suicidal ideation occur

**Contra-indications** breast-feeding (Appendix 5)

**Side-effects** rash including Stevens-Johnson syndrome (see Rash above); abdominal pain, diarrhoea, nausea, vomiting; anxiety, depression, sleep disturbances, abnormal dreams, dizziness, headache, fatigue, impaired concentration (administration at bedtime especially in first 2–4 weeks reduces CNS effects); pruritus; *less commonly* pancreatitis, hepatitis, psychosis, mania, suicidal ideation, amnesia, ataxia, convulsions, and blurred vision; also reported hepatic failure, raised serum cholesterol, gynaecomastia, photosensitivity

**Dose**

- See preparations below

**Sustiva** (Bristol-Myers Squibb) PoM
Capsules, efavirenz 50 mg (yellow/white), net price 30-cap pack = £17.41; 100 mg (white), 30-cap pack = £34.77; 200 mg (yellow), 90-cap pack = £208.40
**Dose** ADULT and CHILD over 3 years, body-weight 13–14 kg, 200 mg once daily; body-weight 15–19 kg, 250 mg once daily; body-weight 20–24 kg, 300 mg once daily; body-weight 25–32.4 kg, 350 mg once daily; body-weight 32.5–39 kg, 400 mg once daily; body-weight 40 kg and over, 600 mg once daily

Tablets, f/c, yellow, efavirenz 600 mg, net price 30-tab pack = £208.40. Label: 23
**Dose** ADULT and ADOLESCENT over 12 years, body-weight over 40 kg, 600 mg once daily

Oral solution, sugar-free, strawberry and mint flavour, efavirenz 30 mg/mL, net price 180-mL pack = £56.02
**Dose** ADULT and CHILD over 5 years, body-weight 13–14 kg, 270 mg once daily; body-weight 15–19 kg, 300 mg once daily; body-weight 20–24 kg, 360 mg once daily; body-weight 25–32.4 kg, 450 mg once daily; body-weight 32.5–39 kg, 510 mg once daily; body-weight 40 kg and over, 720 mg once daily; CHILD 3–4 years, body-weight 13–14 kg, 360 mg once daily; body-weight 15–19 kg, 390 mg once daily; body-weight 20–24 kg, 450 mg once daily; body-weight 25–32.4 kg, 510 mg once daily

**Note** The bioavailability of *Sustiva®* oral solution is lower than that of the capsules and tablets; the oral solution is **not** interchangeable with either capsules or tablets on a milligram-for-milligram basis

### NEVIRAPINE

**Indications** progressive or advanced HIV infection, in combination with at least two other antiretroviral drugs

**Cautions** hepatic impairment (see below and Appendix 2); chronic hepatitis B or C, high CD4 cell count, and women (all at greater risk of hepatic side-effects—manufacturer advises avoid in women with CD4 cell count greater than 250 cells/mm$^3$ or in men with CD4 cell count greater than 400 cells/mm$^3$ unless potential benefit outweighs risk); pregnancy (Appendix 4); **interactions:** Appendix 1 (nevirapine)

**Hepatic disease** Potentially life-threatening hepatotoxicity including fatal fulminant hepatitis reported usually in first 6 weeks; close monitoring required during first 18 weeks; monitor liver function before treatment then every 2 weeks for 2 months then after 1 month and then regularly; discontinue permanently if abnormalities in liver function tests accompanied by hypersensitivity reaction (rash, fever, arthralgia, myalgia, lymphadenopathy, hepatitis, renal impairment, eosinophilia, granulocytopenia); suspend if severe abnormalities in liver function tests but no hypersensitivity reaction—discontinue permanently if significant liver function abnormalities recur; monitor patient closely if mild to moderate abnormalities in liver function tests with no hypersensitivity reaction

**Note** If treatment interrupted for more than 7 days reintroduce with 200 mg daily (CHILD 4 mg/kg daily) and increase dose cautiously

**Rash** Rash, usually in first 6 weeks, is most common side-effect; incidence reduced if introduced at low dose and dose increased gradually; monitor closely for skin reactions during first 18 weeks; discontinue permanently if severe rash or if rash accompanied by blistering, oral lesions, conjunctivitis, facial oedema, general malaise or hypersensitivity reactions; if rash mild or moderate may continue without interruption but dose should not be increased until rash resolves

**Counselling** Patients should be told how to recognise hypersensitivity reactions and advised to discontinue treatment and seek immediate medical attention if symptoms of hepatitis, severe skin reaction or hypersensitivity reactions develop

**Contra-indications** breast-feeding (Appendix 5); severe hepatic impairment; post-exposure prophylaxis

**Side-effects** rash including Stevens-Johnson syndrome and rarely, toxic epidermal necrolysis (see also Cautions above); nausea, hepatitis (see also Hepatic Disease above), headache; less commonly vomiting, abdominal pain, fatigue, fever, and myalgia; rarely diarrhoea, angioedema, anaphylaxis, hypersensitivity reactions (may involve hepatic reactions and rash, see Hepatic Disease above), arthralgia, anaemia, and granulocytopenia (more frequent in children); very rarely neuropsychiatric reactions

**Dose**

- 200 mg once daily for first 14 days then (if no rash present) 200 mg twice daily; CHILD 2 months–8 years, 4 mg/kg once daily for first 14 days then (if no rash present) 7 mg/kg twice daily (max. 400 mg daily); 8–16 years (but under 50 kg), 4 mg/kg once daily for first 14 days then (if no rash present) 4 mg/kg twice daily (max. 400 mg daily); over 50 kg, adult dose

**Viramune®** (Boehringer Ingelheim) PoM
Tablets, nevirapine 200 mg, net price 60-tab pack = £160.00. Counselling, hypersensitivity reactions

Suspension, nevirapine 50 mg/5 mL, net price 240-mL pack = £50.40. Counselling, hypersensitivity reactions

## Other antiretrovirals

### ENFUVIRTIDE

**Indications** HIV infection in combination with other antiretroviral drugs for resistant infection or for patients intolerant to other antiretroviral regimens

**Cautions** chronic hepatitis B or C (possibly greater risk of hepatic side-effects); hepatic impairment (Appendix 2); renal impairment (Appendix 3); pregnancy (Appendix 4)

Hypersensitivity reactions Hypersensitivity reactions including rash, fever, nausea, vomiting, chills, rigors, low blood pressure, respiratory distress, glomerulonephritis, and raised liver enzymes reported; discontinue immediately if any signs or symptoms of systemic hypersensitivity develop and do not rechallenge

Counselling Patients should be told how to recognise signs of hypersensitivity, and advised to discontinue treatment and seek immediate medical attention if symptoms develop

**Contra-indications** breast-feeding (Appendix 5)

**Side-effects** injection-site reactions; pancreatitis, gastro-oesophageal reflux disease, anorexia, weight loss; hypertriglyceridaemia; peripheral neuropathy, asthenia, tremor, anxiety, nightmares, irritability, impaired concentration, vertigo; pneumonia, sinusitis, influenza-like illness; diabetes mellitus; haematuria; renal calculi, lymphadenopathy; myalgia; conjuctivitis; dry skin, acne, erythema, skin papilloma; *less commonly* hypersensitivity reactions (see Cautions)

**Dose**

- By subcutaneous injection, ADULT and ADOLESCENT over 16 years, 90 mg twice daily; CHILD 6–15 years, 2 mg/kg twice daily (max. 90 mg twice daily)

**Fuzeon®** (Roche) ▼ PoM

Injection, powder for reconstitution, enfuvirtide 108 mg (= enfuvirtide 90 mg/mL when reconstituted with 1.1 mL water for injections), net price 108-mg vial = £19.13 (with solvent, syringe, and alcohol swabs). Counselling, hypersensitivity reactions

## 5.3.2 Herpesvirus infections

### 5.3.2.1 Herpes simplex and varicella–zoster infection

The two most important herpesvirus pathogens are herpes simplex virus (herpesvirus hominis) and varicella–zoster virus.

**Herpes simplex infections** Herpes infection of the mouth and lips and in the eye is generally associated with herpes simplex virus serotype 1 (HSV-1); other areas of the skin may also be infected, especially in immunodeficiency. Genital infection is most often associated with HSV-2 and also HSV-1. Treatment of herpes simplex infection should start as early as possible and usually within 5 days of the appearance of the infection.

In individuals with good immune function, mild infection of the eye (ocular herpes, section 11.3.3) and of the lips (herpes labialis or cold sores, section 13.10.3) is treated with a topical antiviral drug. Primary herpetic gingivostomatitis is managed by changes to diet and with analgesics (section 12.3.2). Severe infection, neonatal herpes infection or infection in immunocompromised individuals requires treatment with a systemic antiviral drug. Primary or recurrent genital herpes simplex infection is treated with an antiviral drug given by mouth. Persistence of a lesion or recurrence in an immunocompromised patient may signal the development of resistance.

Specialist advice should be sought for systemic treatment of herpes simplex infection in pregnancy.

**Varicella–zoster infections** Regardless of immune function and the use of any immunoglobulins, neonates with *chickenpox* should be treated with a parenteral antiviral to reduce the risk of severe disease. Chickenpox in otherwise healthy children between 1 month and 12 years is usually mild and antiviral treatment is not usually required.

Chickenpox is more severe in adolescents and adults than in children; antiviral treatment started within 24 hours of the onset of rash may reduce the duration and severity of symptoms in otherwise healthy adults and adolescents. Antiviral treatment is generally recommended in immunocompromised patients and those at special risk (e.g. because of severe cardiovascular or respiratory disease or chronic skin disorder); an antiviral is given for 10 days with at least 7 days of parenteral treatment.

Pregnant women who develop severe chickenpox may be at risk of complications, especially varicella pneumonia. Specialist advice should be sought for the treatment of chickenpox during pregnancy.

In *herpes zoster* (shingles) systemic antiviral treatment can reduce the severity and duration of pain, reduce complications, and reduce viral shedding. Treatment with the antiviral should be started within 72 hours of the onset of rash and is usually continued for 7–10 days.

Immunocompromised patients at high risk of disseminated or severe infection should be treated with a parenteral antiviral drug. Chronic pain which persists after the rash has healed (postherpetic neuralgia) requires specific management (section 4.7.3).

Those who have been exposed to chickenpox and are at special risk of complications may require prophylaxis with varicella-zoster immunoglobulin (see under Specific Immunoglobulins, section 14.5).

**Choice** **Aciclovir** is active against herpesviruses but does not eradicate them. Uses of aciclovir include systemic treatment of varicella–zoster and the systemic and topical treatment of herpes simplex infections of the skin (section 13.10.3) and mucous membranes (section 7.2.2). It is used by mouth for severe herpetic stomatitis (see also p. 562). Aciclovir eye ointment (section 11.3.3) is used for herpes simplex infections of the eye; it is combined with systemic treatment for ophthalmic zoster.

**Famciclovir**, a prodrug of penciclovir, is similar to aciclovir and is licensed for use in herpes zoster and genital herpes. Penciclovir itself is used as a cream for herpes simplex labialis (section 13.10.3).

**Valaciclovir** is an ester of aciclovir, licensed for herpes zoster and herpes simplex infections of the skin and mucous membranes (including genital herpes); it is also licensed for preventing cytomegalovirus disease following renal transplantation. Famciclovir or valaciclovir are suitable alternatives to aciclovir for oral lesions associated with herpes zoster. Valaciclovir once daily may reduce the risk of transmitting genital herpes to heterosexual partners—specialist advice should be sought.

**Idoxuridine** (section 13.10.3) has been used topically for treating herpes simplex infections of the skin and external genitalia with variable results. Its value in the treatment of shingles is unclear.

**Inosine pranobex** has been used by mouth for herpes simplex infections; its effectiveness remains unproven.

## ACICLOVIR
(Acyclovir)

**Indications** herpes simplex and varicella–zoster (see also under Dose)

**Cautions** maintain adequate hydration (especially with infusion or high doses); renal impairment (Appendix 3); pregnancy (Appendix 4); breast-feeding (Appendix 5); **interactions:** Appendix 1 (aciclovir)

**Side-effects** nausea, vomiting, abdominal pain, diarrhoea, headache, fatigue, rash, urticaria, pruritus, photosensitivity; *very rarely* hepatitis, jaundice, dyspnoea, neurological reactions (including dizziness, confusion, hallucinations, convulsions and drowsiness), acute renal failure, anaemia, thrombocytopenia and leucopenia; on *intravenous infusion*, severe local inflammation (sometimes leading to ulceration), and *very rarely* agitation, tremors, psychosis and fever

**Dose**

- By mouth, herpes simplex, treatment, 200 mg (400 mg in the immunocompromised or if absorption impaired) 5 times daily, usually for 5 days (longer if new lesions appear during treatment or if healing incomplete); CHILD under 2 years, half adult dose, over 2 years, adult dose

  Herpes simplex, prevention of recurrence, 200 mg 4 times daily *or* 400 mg twice daily possibly reduced to 200 mg 2 or 3 times daily and interrupted every 6–12 months

  Herpes simplex, prophylaxis in the immunocompromised, 200–400 mg 4 times daily; CHILD under 2 years, half adult dose, over 2 years, adult dose

  Varicella and herpes zoster, treatment, 800 mg 5 times daily for 7 days; CHILD, varicella, 20 mg/kg (max. 800 mg) 4 times daily for 5 days *or* under 2 years 200 mg 4 times daily, 2–5 years 400 mg 4 times daily, over 6 years 800 mg 4 times daily

  Attenuation of chickenpox (if varicella–zoster immunoglobulin not indicated) [unlicensed use], ADULT and CHILD 40 mg/kg daily in 4 divided doses for 7 days starting 1 week after exposure

- By intravenous infusion, treatment of herpes simplex in the immunocompromised, severe initial genital herpes, and varicella–zoster, 5 mg/kg every 8 hours usually for 5 days, doubled to 10 mg/kg every 8 hours in varicella–zoster in the immunocompromised and in simplex encephalitis (usually given for at least 10 days in encephalitis, possibly for 14–21 days); prophylaxis of herpes simplex in the immunocompromised, 5 mg/kg every 8 hours

  **Note** To avoid excessive dosage in obese patients, parenteral dose should be calculated on the basis of ideal body-weight

  NEONATE and INFANT up to 3 months, with disseminated herpes simplex, 20 mg/kg every 8 hours for 14 days (21 days if CNS involvement); varicella–zoster [unlicensed use] 10–20 mg/kg every 8 hours for at least 7 days; CHILD 3 months–12 years, herpes simplex or varicella–zoster, 250 mg/m² every 8 hours usually for 5 days, doubled to 500 mg/m² every 8 hours for varicella–zoster in the immunocompromised and in simplex encephalitis (usually given for at least 10 days in encephalitis, possibly for 14–21 days)

- By topical application, see sections 13.10.3 (skin) and 11.3.3 (eye)

**Aciclovir** (Non-proprietary) PoM

Tablets, aciclovir 200 mg, net price 25-tab pack = £4.01; 400 mg, 56-tab pack = £7.31; 800 mg, 35-tab pack = £9.53. Label: 9

Brands include *Virovir*®

**Dental prescribing on NHS** Aciclovir Tablets 200 mg may be prescribed

Dispersible tablets, aciclovir 200 mg, net price 25-tab pack = £2.82; 400 mg, 56-tab pack = £8.30; 800 mg, 35-tab pack = £9.53. Label: 9

Intravenous infusion, powder for reconstitution, aciclovir (as sodium salt). Net price 250-mg vial = £10.91; 500-mg vial = £20.22

Electrolytes $Na^+$ 1.1 mmol/250-mg vial

Intravenous infusion, aciclovir (as sodium salt), 25 mg/mL, net price 10-mL (250-mg) vial = £10.37; 20-mL (500-mg) vial = £19.21; 40-mL (1-g) vial = £40.44

Electrolytes $Na^+$ 1.16 mmol/250-mg vial

**Zovirax®** (GSK) PoM

Tablets, all dispersible, f/c, aciclovir 200 mg (blue), net price 25-tab pack = £18.80; 400 mg (pink), 56-tab pack = £68.98; 800 mg (scored, *Shingles Treatment Pack*), 35-tab pack = £69.85. Label: 9

Suspension, both off-white, sugar-free, aciclovir 200 mg/5 mL (banana-flavoured), net price 125 mL = £29.56; 400 mg/5 mL (*Double Strength Suspension*, orange-flavoured) 100 mL = £33.02. Label: 9

**Dental prescribing on NHS** May be prescribed as Aciclovir 200 mg/5 mL oral Suspension

Intravenous infusion, powder for reconstitution, aciclovir (as sodium salt). Net price 250-mg vial = £10.15; 500-mg vial = £18.81

Electrolytes $Na^+$ 1.1 mmol/250-mg vial

## FAMCICLOVIR

**Note** Famciclovir is a pro-drug of penciclovir

**Indications** treatment of herpes zoster, acute genital herpes simplex and suppression of recurrent genital herpes

**Cautions** hepatic impairment (Appendix 2); renal impairment (Appendix 3); pregnancy (Appendix 4) and breast-feeding (Appendix 5); **interactions:** Appendix 1 (famciclovir)

**Side-effects** *rarely* nausea, headache, confusion; *very rarely* vomiting, jaundice, dizziness, drowsiness, hallucinations, rash, and pruritus; abdominal pain and fever have been reported in immunocompromised patients

**Dose**

- Herpes zoster, 250 mg 3 times daily for 7 days *or* 750 mg once daily for 7 days (in immunocompromised, 500 mg 3 times daily for 10 days)
- Genital herpes, first episode, 250 mg 3 times daily for 5 days (longer if new lesions appear during treatment or if healing incomplete); recurrent infection, 125 mg twice daily for 5 days (in immunocompromised, all episodes, 500 mg twice daily for 7 days)
- Genital herpes, suppression, 250 mg twice daily (in HIV patients, 500 mg twice daily) interrupted every 6–12 months
- CHILD not recommended

**Famvir®** (Novartis) PoM
Tablets, all f/c, famciclovir 125 mg, net price 10-tab pack = £30.93; 250 mg, 15-tab pack = £92.79, 21-tab pack = £129.89; 56-tab pack = £346.39; 500 mg, 14-tab pack = £173.22, 30-tab pack = £371.07, 56-tab pack = £692.88; 750 mg, 7-tab pack = £123.99. Label: 9

## INOSINE PRANOBEX

**Indications** see under Dose
**Cautions** renal impairment (Appendix 3); history of gout or hyperuricaemia
**Contra-indications** pregnancy
**Side-effects** reversible increase in serum and urinary uric acid; *less commonly* nausea, vomiting, epigastric discomfort, headache, vertigo, fatigue, arthralgia, rashes and itching; *rarely* diarrhoea, constipation, anxiety, sleep disturbances, and polyuria
**Dose**
- Mucocutaneous herpes simplex, 1 g 4 times daily for 7–14 days
- Adjunctive treatment of genital warts, 1 g 3 times daily for 14–28 days
- Subacute sclerosing panencephalitis, 50–100 mg/kg daily in 6 divided doses

**Imunovir®** (Ardern) PoM
Tablets, inosine pranobex 500 mg. Net price 100 = £39.50. Label: 9

## VALACICLOVIR

Note Valaciclovir is a pro-drug of aciclovir

**Indications** treatment of herpes zoster; treatment of initial and suppression of recurrent herpes simplex infections of skin and mucous membranes including initial and recurrent genital herpes; prevention of cytomegalovirus disease following renal transplantation
**Cautions** see under Aciclovir; hepatic impairment (Appendix 2); renal impairment (Appendix 3)
**Side-effects** see under Aciclovir but neurological reactions more frequent with high doses
**Dose**
- Herpes zoster, 1 g 3 times daily for 7 days
- Herpes simplex, first episode, 500 mg twice daily for 5 days (longer if new lesions appear during treatment or if healing incomplete); recurrent infection, 500 mg twice daily for 5 days
- Herpes simplex, suppression, 500 mg daily in 1–2 divided doses (in immunocompromised, 500 mg twice daily)
- Prevention of cytomegalovirus disease following renal transplantation (preferably starting within 72 hours of transplantation), 2 g 4 times daily usually for 90 days
- CHILD not recommended

**Valtrex®** (GSK) PoM
Tablets, f/c, valaciclovir (as hydrochloride) 500 mg, net price 10-tab pack = £21.86, 42-tab pack = £91.61. Label: 9

## 5.3.2.2 Cytomegalovirus infection

Recommendations for the optimum maintenance therapy of cytomegalovirus (CMV) infections and the duration of treatment are subject to rapid change.

**Ganciclovir** is related to aciclovir but it is more active against cytomegalovirus; it is also much more toxic than aciclovir and should therefore be prescribed only when the potential benefit outweighs the risks. Ganciclovir is administered by intravenous infusion for the *initial treatment* of CMV retinitis. Ganciclovir causes profound myelosuppression when given with zidovudine; the two should not normally be given together particularly during initial ganciclovir therapy. The likelihood of ganciclovir resistance increases in patients with a high viral load or in those who receive the drug over a long duration; cross-resistance to cidofovir is common.

**Valaciclovir** (see above) is licensed for prevention of cytomegalovirus disease following renal transplantation.

**Valganciclovir** is an ester of ganciclovir which is licensed for the *initial treatment* and *maintenance treatment* of CMV retinitis in AIDS patients. Valganciclovir is also licensed for preventing CMV disease following solid organ transplantation from a cytomegalovirus-positive donor.

**Foscarnet** is also active against cytomegalovirus; it is toxic and can cause renal impairment.

**Cidofovir** is given in combination with probenecid for CMV retinitis in AIDS patients when ganciclovir and foscarnet are contra-indicated. Cidofovir is nephrotoxic.

For local treatment of CMV retinitis, see section 11.3.3.

## CIDOFOVIR

**Indications** cytomegalovirus retinitis in AIDS patients for whom other drugs are inappropriate
**Cautions** monitor renal function (serum creatinine and urinary protein) and neutrophil count within 24 hours before each dose; co-treatment with probenecid and prior hydration with intravenous fluids necessary to minimise potential nephrotoxicity (see below); diabetes mellitus (increased risk of ocular hypotony); **interactions:** Appendix 1 (cidofovir)
Nephrotoxicity Do not initiate treatment in renal impairment (assess creatinine clearance and proteinuria—consult product literature); discontinue treatment and give intravenous fluids if renal function deteriorates—consult product literature
Ocular disorders Regular ophthalmological examinations recommended; iritis and uveitis have been reported which may respond to a topical corticosteroid with or without a cycloplegic drug—discontinue cidofovir if no response to topical corticosteroid or if condition worsens, or if iritis or uveitis recurs after successful treatment
**Contra-indications** renal impairment (creatinine clearance 55 mL/minute or less); concomitant administration of potentially nephrotoxic drugs (discontinue potentially nephrotoxic drugs at least 7 days before starting cidofovir); pregnancy (avoid pregnancy during and for 1 month after treatment, men should not father a child during or within 3 months of treatment; Appendix 4), breast-feeding (Appendix 5)
**Side-effects** nephrotoxicity (see Cautions above); neutropenia, fever, asthenia, alopecia, nausea, vomiting, hypotony, decreased intra-ocular pressure, iritis, uveitis (see Cautions above)
**Dose**
- Initial (induction) treatment, by intravenous infusion over 1 hour, 5 mg/kg once weekly for 2 weeks (give probenecid and intravenous fluids with each dose, see below); CHILD not recommended
- Maintenance treatment, beginning 2 weeks after completion of induction, by intravenous infusion over

1 hour, 5 mg/kg once every 2 weeks (give probenecid and intravenous fluids with each dose, see below)
Probenecid co-treatment By mouth (preferably after food), probenecid 2 g 3 hours before cidofovir infusion followed by probenecid 1 g at 2 hours and 1 g at 8 hours after the end of cidofovir infusion (total probenecid 4 g); for cautions, contra-indications and side-effects of probenecid see section 10.1.4
Prior hydration Sodium chloride 0.9%, by intravenous infusion, 1 litre over 1 hour immediately before cidofovir infusion (if tolerated an additional 1 litre may be given over 1–3 hours, starting at the same time as the cidofovir infusion or immediately afterwards)

**Vistide®** (Pharmacia) PoM
Intravenous infusion, cidofovir 75 mg/mL, net price 5-mL vial = £653.22
Caution in handling Cidofovir is toxic and personnel should be adequately protected during handling and administration; if solution comes into contact with skin or mucosa, wash off immediately with water

## GANCICLOVIR

**Indications** life-threatening or sight-threatening cytomegalovirus infections in immunocompromised patients only; prevention of cytomegalovirus disease during immunosuppressive therapy following organ transplantation; local treatment of CMV retinitis (section 11.3.3)

**Cautions** close monitoring of full blood count (severe deterioration may require correction and possibly treatment interruption); history of cytopenia; low platelet count; potential carcinogen and teratogen; renal impairment (consult product literature); radiotherapy; ensure adequate hydration during intravenous administration; vesicant—infuse into vein with adequate flow preferably using plastic cannula; children (possible risk of long-term carcinogenic or reproductive toxicity—not for neonatal or congenital cytomegalovirus disease); **interactions:** Appendix 1 (ganciclovir)

**Contra-indications** pregnancy (ensure effective contraception during treatment and barrier contraception for men during and for at least 90 days after treatment; Appendix 4); breast-feeding; hypersensitivity to ganciclovir or aciclovir; abnormally low haemoglobin, neutrophil, or platelet counts (consult product literature)

**Side-effects** diarrhoea, nausea, vomiting, dyspepsia, abdominal pain, constipation, flatulence, dysphagia, hepatic dysfunction; dyspnoea, chest pain, cough; headache, insomnia, convulsions, dizziness, neuropathy, depression, anxiety, confusion, abnormal thinking, fatigue, weight loss, anorexia; infection, fever, night sweats; anaemia, leucopenia, thrombocytopenia, pancytopenia, renal impairment; myalgia, arthralgia; macular oedema, retinal detachment, vitreous floaters, eye pain; ear pain, taste disturbance; dermatitis, pruritus; injection-site reactions; less commonly mouth ulcers, pancreatitis, arrhythmias, hypotension, anaphylactic reactions, psychosis, tremor, male infertility, haematuria, disturbances in hearing and vision, and alopecia

**Dose**
- By intravenous infusion, initially (induction) 5 mg/kg every 12 hours for 14–21 days for treatment or for 7–14 days for prevention; maintenance (for patients at risk of relapse of retinitis) 6 mg/kg daily on 5 days per week *or* 5 mg/kg daily until adequate recovery of immunity; if retinitis progresses initial induction treatment may be repeated

**Cymevene®** (Roche) PoM
Intravenous infusion, powder for reconstitution, ganciclovir (as sodium salt). Net price 500-mg vial = £31.60
Electrolytes $Na^+$ 2 mmol/500-mg vial
Caution in handling Ganciclovir is toxic and personnel should be adequately protected during handling and administration; if solution comes into contact with skin or mucosa, wash off immediately with soap and water

## FOSCARNET SODIUM

**Indications** cytomegalovirus retinitis in AIDS patients; mucocutaneous herpes simplex virus infections unresponsive to aciclovir in immunocompromised patients

**Cautions** renal impairment (reduce dose or avoid if severe); monitor electrolytes, particularly calcium and magnesium; monitor serum creatinine every second day during induction and every week during maintenance; ensure adequate hydration; avoid rapid infusion; **interactions:** Appendix 1 (foscarnet)

**Contra-indications** pregnancy; breast-feeding (Appendix 5)

**Side-effects** nausea, vomiting, diarrhoea (occasionally constipation and dyspepsia), abdominal pain, anorexia; changes in blood pressure and ECG; headache, fatigue, mood disturbances (including psychosis), asthenia, paraesthesia, convulsions, tremor, dizziness, and other neurological disorders; rash; impairment of renal function including acute renal failure; hypocalcaemia (sometimes symptomatic) and other electrolyte disturbances; abnormal liver function tests; decreased haemoglobin concentration, leucopenia, granulocytopenia, thrombocytopenia; thrombophlebitis if given undiluted by peripheral vein; genital irritation and ulceration (due to high concentrations excreted in urine); isolated reports of pancreatitis

**Dose**
- CMV retinitis, by intravenous infusion, induction 60 mg/kg every 8 hours for 2–3 weeks then maintenance, 60 mg/kg daily, increased to 90–120 mg/kg if tolerated; if retinitis progresses on maintenance dose, repeat induction regimen
- Mucocutaneous herpes simplex infection, by intravenous infusion, 40 mg/kg every 8 hours for 2–3 weeks or until lesions heal

**Foscavir®** (AstraZeneca) PoM
Intravenous infusion, foscarnet sodium hexahydrate 24 mg/mL, net price 250-mL bottle = £34.49

## VALGANCICLOVIR

Note Valganciclovir is a pro-drug of ganciclovir

**Indications** induction and maintenance treatment of cytomegalovirus retinitis in AIDS patients; prevention of cytomegalovirus disease following solid organ transplantation from a cytomegalovirus-positive donor.

**Cautions** see under Ganciclovir

**Side-effects** see under Ganciclovir

**Dose**
- CMV retinitis, induction, 900 mg twice daily for 21 days then 900 mg once daily; induction regimen may be repeated if retinitis progresses
- Prevention of cytomegalovirus disease following solid organ transplantation (starting within 10 days of

transplantation), 900 mg once daily for 100 days
- CHILD and ADOLESCENT not recommended

**Note** Oral valganciclovir 900 mg twice daily is equivalent to intravenous ganciclovir 5 mg/kg twice daily

**Valcyte®** (Roche) ▼ PoM
Tablets, pink, f/c, valganciclovir (as hydrochloride) 450 mg, net price 60-tab pack = £1148.05. Label: 21
**Caution in handling** Valganciclovir is a potential teratogen and carcinogen and caution is advised for handling of broken tablets; if broken tablets come into contact with skin or mucosa, wash off immediately with water

## 5.3.3 Viral hepatitis

Treatment for viral hepatitis should be initiated by a specialist. The management of uncomplicated acute viral hepatitis is largely symptomatic. Early treatment of acute hepatitis C with interferon alfa [unlicensed indication] may reduce the risk of chronic infection. Hepatitis B and hepatitis C viruses are major causes of chronic hepatitis. For details on immunisation against hepatitis A and B infections, see section 14.4 (active immunisation) and section 14.5 (passive immunisation).

**Chronic Hepatitis B** **Interferon alfa** (section 8.2.4) is used in the treatment of chronic hepatitis B but its use is limited by a response rate of less than 50%, and relapse is frequent. If no improvement occurs after 3–4 months of treatment, interferon alfa should be discontinued. Interferon alfa is contra-indicated in patients receiving immunosuppressant treatment (or who have received it recently). The manufacturers of interferon alfa contra-indicate its use in decompensated liver disease but low doses can be used with great caution in these patients. **Peginterferon alfa-2a** is also licensed for the treatment of chronic hepatitis B and may be preferable to interferon alfa.

**Lamivudine** (see p. 316) is used for the initial treatment of chronic hepatitis B. It can also be used in patients with decompensated liver disease. Treatment should be continued if there is no loss of efficacy and until seroconversion is adequate (consult product literature); it is continued long-term in decompensated liver disease. Hepatitis B viruses with reduced susceptibility to lamivudine have emerged following extended therapy. In patients infected with HIV and hepatitis B, lamivudine should be given only as part of combination antiretroviral therapy and in a dose appropriate for treating HIV; the use of lamivudine alone is likely to result in lamivudine-resistant HIV.

**Adefovir dipivoxil** is licensed for the treatment of chronic hepatitis B. It is effective in lamivudine-resistant chronic hepatitis B. Treatment should be continued, if there is no loss in efficacy, until adequate seroconversion has occurred (consult product literature); it is continued long-term in patients with decompensated liver disease or cirrhosis.

**Chronic Hepatitis C** Before starting treatment, the genotype of the infecting hepatitis C virus should be determined and the viral load measured as this may affect choice of treatment regimen. A combination of **ribavirin** (see p. 328) and **peginterferon alfa** (section 8.2.4) is used for the treatment of chronic hepatitis C (see NICE guidance, below). The combination of ribavirin and interferon alfa is less effective than the combination of peginterferon alfa and ribavirin. Peginterferon alfa alone should be used if ribavirin is contra-indicated or not tolerated. Ribavirin monotherapy is ineffective.

**NICE guidance (peginterferon alfa, interferon alfa, and ribavirin for chronic hepatitis C).**

NICE has recommended (January 2004) that the combination of peginterferon alfa and ribavirin should be used for treating moderate to severe chronic hepatitis C in patients aged over 18 years:
- not previously treated with interferon alfa or peginterferon alfa;
- treated previously with interferon alfa alone or in combination with ribavirin;
- whose condition did not respond to peginterferon alfa alone or responded but subsequently relapsed.

Peginterferon alfa alone should be used if ribavirin is contra-indicated or not tolerated. Interferon alfa for either monotherapy or combined therapy should be used only if neutropenia and thrombocytopenia are a particular risk. Patients receiving interferon alfa may be switched to peginterferon alfa.
The duration of treatment depends on genotype and viral load (full guidance available at www.nice.org.uk/TA075).

### ADEFOVIR DIPIVOXIL

**Indications** chronic hepatitis B infection with *either* compensated liver disease with evidence of viral replication, and histologically documented active liver inflammation and fibrosis *or* decompensated liver disease

**Cautions** monitor liver function and viral, and serological markers for hepatitis B every 6 months; discontinue if deterioration in liver function, hepatic steatosis, progressive hepatomegaly or unexplained lactic acidosis; recurrent hepatitis may occur on discontinuation; monitor renal function every 3 months, more frequently in renal impairment (Appendix 3) or in patients receiving nephrotoxic drugs; pregnancy (Appendix 4); elderly; HIV infection (particularly if uncontrolled—theoretical risk of HIV resistance)

**Contra-indications** breast-feeding (Appendix 5)

**Side-effects** nausea, dyspepsia, abdominal pain, flatulence, diarrhoea; asthenia, headache; renal failure; also reported, rash and pruritus

**Dose**
- ADULT over 18 years, 10 mg once daily

**Hepsera** (Gilead) ▼ PoM
Tablets, adefovir dipivoxil 10 mg, net price 30-tab pack = £315.00

## 5.3.4 Influenza

For advice on immunisation against influenza, see section 14.4.

**Oseltamivir** and **zanamivir** reduce replication of influenza A and B viruses by inhibiting viral neuraminidase. They are most effective for the treatment of influenza if started within a few hours of the onset of symptoms; they are licensed for use within 48 hours of the first symptoms. In otherwise healthy individuals they reduce the duration of symptoms by about 1–1.5 days. The effect of oseltamivir or zanamivir on hospitalisation or on mortality is not clear in those at risk of serious complications from influenza. Oseltamivir is also licensed for prophylaxis when used within 48 hours of exposure to influenza and when influenza is circulating in the community; it is also licensed for use in exceptional circumstances (e.g. when vaccination does not cover the infecting strain) to prevent influenza in an epidemic. Where prophylaxis against influenza A or B is required and oseltamivir cannot be used, zanamivir 10 mg once daily by inhalation, is an alternative [unlicensed indication].

**NICE guidance (oseltamivir, zanamivir, and amantadine for prophylaxis and treatment of influenza)**

NICE has recommended (February and September 2003) that the drugs described here are not a substitute for vaccination, which remains the most effective way of preventing illness from influenza. When influenza A or influenza B is circulating in the community:

- amantadine is **not** recommended for post-exposure prophylaxis, seasonal prophylaxis, or treatment of influenza;
- oseltamivir and zanamivir are **not** recommended for seasonal prophylaxis against influenza;
- oseltamivir or zanamivir are **not** recommended for post-exposure prophylaxis, or treatment of otherwise healthy individuals with influenza;
- oseltamivir is recommended for post-exposure prophylaxis in at-risk adults and adolescents over 13 years who are not effectively protected by influenza vaccine and who can commence oseltamivir within 48 hours of close contact with someone suffering from influenza-like illness; prophylaxis is also recommended for residents in care establishments (regardless of influenza vaccination) who can commence oseltamivir within 48 hours if influenza-like illness is present in the establishment;
- oseltamivir and zanamivir are recommended (in accordance with UK licensing) to treat at-risk adults who can start treatment within 48 hours of the onset of symptoms; oseltamivir is recommended for at-risk children who can start treatment within 48 hours of the onset of symptoms;

At-risk patients include those aged over 65 years *or* those who have one or more of the following conditions:

- chronic respiratory disease (including chronic obstructive pulmonary disease and asthma) [but see cautions under Zanamivir below];
- significant cardiovascular disease (excluding hypertension);
- chronic renal disease;
- immunosuppression;
- diabetes mellitus.

Community-based virological surveillance schemes including those run by the Health Protection Agency and the Royal College of General Practitioners should be used to indicate when influenza is circulating in the community.

**Amantadine** is licensed for prophylaxis and treatment of influenza A but it is no longer recommended (see NICE guidance).

## AMANTADINE HYDROCHLORIDE

**Indications** see under Dose; parkinsonism (section 4.9.1)

**Cautions** see section 4.9.1

**Contra-indications** see section 4.9.1

**Side-effects** see section 4.9.1

**Dose**

- Influenza A (see also notes above), ADULT and CHILD over 10 years, treatment, 100 mg daily for 4–5 days; prophylaxis, 100 mg daily usually for 6 weeks *or* with influenza vaccination for 2–3 weeks after vaccination; ELDERLY 100 mg daily

**Lysovir®** (Alliance) PoM

Capsules, red-brown, amantadine hydrochloride 100 mg, net price 5-cap pack = £2.40, 14-cap pack = £4.80. Counselling, driving

**Symmetrel®** (Alliance) PoM

Section 4.9.1

## OSELTAMIVIR

**Indications** see notes above

**Cautions** renal impairment (Appendix 3); pregnancy (Appendix 4); breast-feeding (Appendix 5)

**Side-effects** nausea, vomiting, abdominal pain, dyspepsia, diarrhoea; headache, fatigue, insomnia, dizziness; conjunctivitis, epistaxis; rash; *rarely* hypersensitivity reactions; *very rarely* hepatitis, Stevens-Johnson syndrome

**Dose**

- Prevention of influenza, ADULT and ADOLESCENT over 13 years, 75 mg once daily for at least 7 days for post-exposure prophylaxis; for up to 6 weeks during an epidemic
- Treatment of influenza, 75 mg every 12 hours for 5 days; CHILD over 1 year, body-weight 15 kg or under, 30 mg every 12 hours, body-weight 16–23 kg, 45 mg every 12 hours, body-weight 24–40 kg, 60 mg every 12 hours, body-weight over 40 kg, adult dose

[1]**Tamiflu®** (Roche) ▼ PoM

Capsules, grey/yellow, oseltamivir (as phosphate) 75 mg, net price 10-cap pack = £16.36. Label: 9

Suspension, sugar-free, tutti-frutti-flavoured, oseltamivir (as phosphate) for reconstitution with water, 60 mg/5 mL, net price 75 mL = £16.36. Label: 9

Excipients include sorbitol 1.71 g/5 mL

1. NHS except for the treatment and prophylaxis of influenza as indicated in the notes above and NICE guidance; endorse prescription 'SLS'

## ZANAMIVIR

**Indications** see notes above

**Cautions** asthma and chronic pulmonary disease (risk of bronchospasm—short-acting bronchodilator should be available; avoid in severe asthma unless close monitoring possible and appropriate facilities available to treat bronchospasm); uncontrolled chronic illness; other inhaled drugs should be administered before zanamivir; pregnancy (Appendix 4)

**Contra-indications** breast-feeding (Appendix 5)

**Side-effects** *very rarely*, bronchospasm, respiratory impairment, angioedema, urticaria, and rash

**Dose**

- By inhalation of powder, 10 mg twice daily for 5 days, CHILD under 12 years not recommended

[1]**Relenza®** (GSK) PoM

Dry powder for inhalation disks containing 4 blisters of zanamivir 5 mg/blister, net price 5 disks with *Diskhaler®* device = £24.55

1. NHS except for the treatment of influenza as indicated in the notes above and NICE guidance; endorse prescription 'SLS'

## 5.3.5 Respiratory syncytial virus

**Ribavirin** (tribavirin) inhibits a wide range of DNA and RNA viruses. It is licensed for administration by inhalation for the treatment of severe bronchiolitis caused by the respiratory syncytial virus (RSV) in infants, especially when they have other serious diseases. However, there is no clear evidence that ribavirin produces clinically relevant benefit in RSV bronchiolitis. Ribavirin is given by mouth with peginterferon alfa or interferon alfa for the treatment of chronic hepatitis C infection (see Viral Hepatitis, p. 326). Ribavirin is also effective in Lassa fever [unlicensed indication].

**Palivizumab** is a monoclonal antibody indicated for the prevention of serious respiratory disease following respiratory syncytial virus infection in infants at high risk of infection; it should be prescribed under specialist supervision and on the basis of the likelihood of hospitalisation. It is licensed for monthly use during the RSV season; the first dose should be administered before the start of the RSV season.

### PALIVIZUMAB

**Indications** see notes above; prevention of serious respiratory disease following infection with respiratory syncytial virus during infectious season in infant under 6 months born at less than 35 weeks gestation, *and* in child under 2 years treated in last 6 months for bronchopulmonary dysplasia, *and* in child under 2 years with haemodynamically significant heart disease

**Cautions** moderate to severe acute infection or febrile illness; thrombocytopenia; serum-palivizumab concentration may be reduced after cardiac surgery

**Contra-indications** hypersensitivity to humanised monoclonal antibodies

**Side-effects** fever, injection-site reactions, nervousness; *less commonly* diarrhoea, vomiting, constipation, haemorrhage, rhinitis, cough, wheeze, pain, drowsiness, asthenia, hyperkinesia, leucopenia, and rash; *rarely* apnoea, hypersensitivity reactions (including anaphylaxis)

**Dose**

- By intramuscular injection (preferably in anterolateral thigh), 15 mg/kg once a month during season of RSV risk (children undergoing cardiac bypass surgery, 15 mg/kg as soon as stable after surgery, then at monthly intervals during season of risk); injection volume over 1 mL should be divided between more than one site

**Synagis®** (Abbott) ▼ PoM
Injection, powder for reconstitution, palivizumab, net price 50-mg vial = £360.40; 100-mg vial = £600.10

### RIBAVIRIN
(Tribavirin)

**Indications** severe respiratory syncytial virus bronchiolitis in infants and children; in combination with peginterferon alfa or interferon alfa for chronic hepatitis C not previously treated in patients without liver decompensation, or for relapse following previous response to interferon alfa (see also section 5.3.3)

**Cautions**
Specific cautions for inhaled treatment Maintain standard supportive respiratory and fluid management therapy; monitor electrolytes closely; monitor equipment for precipitation; pregnant women (and those planning pregnancy) should avoid exposure to aerosol
Specific cautions for oral treatment Exclude pregnancy before treatment; effective contraception essential during treatment and for 6 months after treatment in women and in men; routine monthly pregnancy tests recommended; condoms must be used if partner of male patient is pregnant (ribavirin excreted in semen); renal impairment (Appendix 3); cardiac disease (assessment including ECG recommended before and during treatment—discontinue if deterioration); gout; determine full blood count, platelets, electrolytes, serum creatinine, liver function tests and uric acid before starting treatment and then on weeks 2 and 4 of treatment, then as indicated clinically—adjust dose if adverse reactions or laboratory abnormalities develop (consult product literature); check thyroid function before treatment and then every 3 months in children

**Interactions:** Appendix 1 (Ribavirin)

**Contra-indications** pregnancy (**important teratogenic risk**: see Cautions and Appendix 4); breast-feeding
Specific contra-indications for oral treatment Severe cardiac disease, including unstable or uncontrolled cardiac disease in previous 6 months; haemoglobinopathies; severe debilitating medical conditions; severe hepatic dysfunction or decompensated cirrhosis (Appendix 2); autoimmune disease (including autoimmune hepatitis); uncontrolled severe psychiatric condition; history of severe psychiatric condition in children

**Side-effects**
Specific side-effects for inhaled treatment Worsening respiration, bacterial pneumonia, and pneumothorax reported; rarely non-specific anaemia and haemolysis
Specific side-effects for oral treatment Haemolytic anaemia (anaemia may be improved by epoetin); also reported (in combination with peginterferon alfa or interferon alfa) nausea, vomiting, dry mouth, stomatitis, glossitis, dyspepsia, abdominal pain, gastritis, peptic ulcer, flatulence, diarrhoea, constipation, pancreatitis, anorexia, weight loss; chest pain, tachycardia, palpitation, syncope, peripheral oedema, flushing; dyspnoea, cough, rhinitis, pharyngitis, interstitial pneumonitis; sleep disturbances, asthenia, impaired concentration and memory, irritability, aggression, anxiety, depression, suicidal ideation (more frequent in children), dizziness, tremor, hypertonia, myalgia, arthralgia, paraesthesia, peripheral neuropathy, influenza-like symptoms, headache; thyroid disorders, menstrual disturbances, reduced libido, impotence; micturition disorders; rash, pruritus, urticaria, photosensitivity, alopecia, dry skin, increased sweating; taste disturbance, eye changes including blurred vision, tinnitus; neutropenia, thrombocytopenia, aplastic anaemia, lymphadenopathy, hyperuricaemia; in children also growth retardation, Raynaud's disease, hypertriglyceridaemia, hyperkinesia, testicular pain, virilism, and skin discoloration

**Dose**

- See preparations below

**Copegus** (Roche) PoM
Tablets, f/c, pink, ribavirin 200 mg, net price 42-tab pack = £115.62, 112-tab pack = £308.31, 168-tab pack = £462.47. Label: 21
Dose chronic hepatitis C (in combination with interferon alfa or peginterferon alfa), ADULT over 18 years, body-weight under 75 kg, 400 mg in the morning and 600 mg in the evening; body-weight 75 kg and over, 600 mg twice daily
Note Chronic hepatitis C genotype 2 or 3, or patients infected with HIV and hepatitis C require a lower dose of *Copegus®* (in combination with peginterferon alfa), usual dose 400 mg twice daily

5 Infections

**Rebetol®** (Schering-Plough) PoM

Capsules, ribavirin 200 mg, net price 84-cap pack = £275.65, 140-cap pack = £459.42, 168-cap pack = £551.30. Label: 21

**Dose** chronic hepatitis C, ADULT over 18 years (in combination with interferon alfa or peginterferon alfa), body-weight under 65 kg, 400 mg twice daily; body-weight 65–85 kg, 400 mg in the morning and 600 mg in the evening; body-weight over 85 kg, 600 mg twice daily; CHILD AND ADOLESCENT 3–17 years (in combination with interferon alfa-2b), body-weight under 47 kg, 15 mg/kg daily in 2 divided doses; body-weight 47–49 kg, 200 mg in the morning and 400 mg in the evening; body-weight 50–65 kg, 400 mg twice daily; body-weight over 65kg, as adult

**Virazole®** (Valeant) PoM

Inhalation, ribavirin 6 g for reconstitution with 300 mL water for injections. Net price 3 × 6-g vials = £349.00

**Dose** bronchiolitis, by aerosol inhalation *or* nebulisation (via small particle aerosol generator) of solution containing 20 mg/mL for 12–18 hours for at least 3 days; max. 7 days

# 5.4 Antiprotozoal drugs

**5.4.1 Antimalarials**
**5.4.2 Amoebicides**
**5.4.3 Trichomonacides**
**5.4.4 Antigiardial drugs**
**5.4.5 Leishmaniacides**
**5.4.6 Trypanocides**
**5.4.7 Drugs for toxoplasmosis**
**5.4.8 Drugs for pneumocystis pneumonia**

Advice on specific problems available from:

**Advice for healthcare professionals**

| | |
|---|---|
| HPA (Health Protection Agency) Malaria Reference Laboratory | (020) 7636 3924 (prophylaxis only) |
| National Travel Health Network and Centre | 0845 602 6712 |
| Scottish Centre for Infection and Environmental Health (registered users of Travax only) www.travax.scot.nhs.uk (for registered users of the NHS Travax website only) | (0141) 300 1130 (weekdays 2–4 p.m. only) |
| Birmingham | (0121) 424 0357 |
| Liverpool | (0151) 708 9393 |
| London | 0845 155 5000 (treatment) |
| Oxford | (01865) 225 430 |

**Advice for travellers**

| | |
|---|---|
| HPA Malaria Reference Laboratory | |
| Recorded advice for Travellers (£1.00/minute standard rate) | 09065 508 908 |
| Hospital for Tropical Diseases Travel Healthline (50p/minute) | 09061 337 733 |

www.fitfortravel.scot.nhs.uk

WHO advice on international travel and health www.who.int/ith

## 5.4.1 Antimalarials

Recommendations on the prophylaxis and treatment of malaria reflect guidelines agreed by UK malaria specialists.

The centres listed above should be consulted for advice on special problems.

### Treatment of malaria

If the infective species is **not known**, or if the infection is **mixed**, initial treatment should be as for *falciparum malaria* with quinine, *Malarone®* (proguanil with atovaquone), or *Riamet®* (artemether with lumefantrine). Falciparum malaria can progress rapidly in unprotected individuals and antimalarial treatment should be considered in those with features of severe malaria and possible exposure, even if the initial blood tests for the organism are negative.

### Falciparum malaria (treatment)

Falciparum malaria (malignant malaria) is caused by *Plasmodium falciparum*. In most parts of the world *P. falciparum* is now resistant to chloroquine which should not therefore be given for treatment.

**Quinine**, ***Malarone®*** (proguanil with atovaquone), or ***Riamet®*** (artemether with lumefantrine) can be given *by mouth* if the patient can swallow and retain tablets and there are no serious manifestations (e.g. impaired consciousness); quinine should be given *by intravenous infusion* (see below) if the patient is seriously ill or unable to take tablets. Mefloquine is now rarely used for treatment because of concerns about resistance. Specialist advice should be sought in difficult cases since other drugs such as **artesunate** (given intravenously) and intramuscular **artemether** may be available for 'named-patient use'.

*Oral.* The adult dosage regimen for **quinine** *by mouth* is:
600 mg (of quinine salt[1]) every 8 hours for 5–7 days
*followed by*
*either* **doxycycline** 200 mg daily (as a single dose or in 2 divided doses) for at least 7 days
*or* **clindamycin** 450 mg 3 times daily for 5 days.
If the parasite is likely to be sensitive, *Fansidar®* 3 tablets as a single dose may be given after a course of quinine.

Alternatively, ***Malarone®*** or ***Riamet®*** may be given instead of quinine. It is not necessary to give doxycycline, clindamycin or *Fansidar®* after *Malarone®* or *Riamet®* treatment.

The adult dose of ***Malarone®*** *by mouth* is:
4 ('standard') tablets once daily for 3 days.

The dose of ***Riamet®*** *by mouth* for adult with body-weight of over 35 kg is:
4 tablets initially, followed by 5 further doses of 4 tablets each given at 8, 24, 36, 48, and 60 hours (total 24 tablets over 60 hours).

1. Valid for quinine hydrochloride, dihydrochloride, and sulphate; not valid for quinine bisulphate which contains a correspondingly smaller amount of quinine.

*Parenteral.* If the patient is seriously ill, **quinine** should be given *by intravenous infusion.* The adult dosage regimen for quinine *by infusion* is:

loading dose[1] of 20 mg/kg[2] (up to maximum 1.4 g) of quinine salt[3] infused over 4 hours *then after 8 hours* maintenance dose of 10 mg/kg[4] (up to maximum 700 mg) of quinine salt[3] infused over 4 hours every 8 hours (until patient can swallow tablets to complete the 7-day course) *followed by either Fansidar® or* doxycycline as above.

### Children

*Oral.* **Quinine** is well tolerated by children although the salts are bitter. The dosage regimen for quinine *by mouth* for children is:

10 mg/kg (of quinine salt[3]) every 8 hours for 7 days *then either*

*Fansidar®* as a single dose: up to 4 years ½ tablet, 5–6 years 1 tablet, 7–9 years 1½ tablets, 10–14 years 2 tablets

*or* clindamycin 20–40 mg/kg daily in 3 divided doses for 5 days [unlicensed indication]

Alternatively ***Malarone®*** or ***Riamet®*** may be given instead of quinine; it is not necessary to give clindamycin or *Fansidar®* after *Malarone®*, or *Riamet®* treatment. The dose regimen for *Malarone® by mouth* for children over 40 kg is the same as for adults (see above); the dose regimen for *Malarone®* for smaller children is reduced as follows:

body-weight under 11 kg, no suitable dose form

body-weight 11–20 kg, 1 ('standard') tablet daily for 3 days; body-weight 21–30 kg, 2 ('standard') tablets daily for 3 days; body-weight 31–40 kg, 3 ('standard') tablets daily for 3 days.

The dose regimen of *Riamet® by mouth* for children over 12 years and body-weight over 35 kg is the same as for adults (see above).

*Parenteral.* The dose regimen for quinine *by intravenous infusion* for children is calculated on a mg/kg basis as for adults (see above).

**Pregnancy** Falciparum malaria is particularly dangerous in pregnancy, especially in the last trimester. The adult treatment doses of oral and intravenous quinine given above (including the loading dose) can safely be given to pregnant women. Clindamycin, 450 mg every 8 hours for 5 days [unlicensed indication] should be given after quinine. Doxycycline should be avoided in pregnancy (affects teeth and skeletal development); *Fansidar®*, *Malarone®* and *Riamet®* are also best avoided until more information is available.

1. In intensive care units the loading dose can alternatively be given as quinine salt[3] 7 mg/kg infused over 30 minutes followed immediately by 10 mg/kg over 4 hours then (after 8 hours) maintenance dose as described.
2. **Important:** the loading dose of 20 mg/kg should **not** be used if the patient has received quinine (or quinidine) or mefloquine during the previous 24 hours
3. Valid for quinine hydrochloride, dihydrochloride, and sulphate; not valid for quinine bisulphate which contains a correspondingly smaller amount of quinine.
4. Maintenance dose should be reduced to 5–7 mg/kg of salt in patients with renal impairment or if parenteral treatment is required for more than 48 hours.

## Benign malarias (treatment)

Benign malaria is usually caused by *Plasmodium vivax* and less commonly by *P. ovale* and *P. malariae.* **Chloroquine**[5] is the drug of choice for the treatment of benign malarias (but chloroquine-resistant *P. vivax* infection has been reported from New Guinea and some adjacent islands).

The adult dosage regimen for **chloroquine** *by mouth* is:

initial dose of 600 mg (of base) *then*

a single dose of 300 mg after 6 to 8 hours *then*

a single dose of 300 mg daily for 2 days

(approximate total cumulative dose of 25 mg/kg of base)

Chloroquine alone is adequate for *P. malariae* infections but in the case of *P. vivax* and *P. ovale*, a *radical cure* (to destroy parasites in the liver and thus prevent relapses) is required. This is achieved with **primaquine**[6] given after chloroquine; in *P. vivax* infection primaquine is given in an adult dosage of 30 mg daily for 14 days and for *P. ovale* infection it is given in an adult dosage of 15 mg daily for 14 days.

**Children** The dosage regimen of chloroquine for benign malaria in children is:

initial dose of 10 mg/kg (of base) *then*

a single dose of 5 mg/kg after 6–8 hours *then*

a single dose of 5 mg/kg daily for 2 days

For a *radical cure* children are then given primaquine[6] in a dose of 250 micrograms/kg daily.

**Pregnancy** The adult treatment doses of chloroquine can be given for benign malaria. In the case of *P. vivax* or *P. ovale*, however, the radical cure with primaquine should be **postponed** until the pregnancy is over; instead chloroquine should be continued at a dose of 600 mg each week during the pregnancy.

## Prophylaxis against malaria

The recommendations on prophylaxis reflect guidelines agreed by UK malaria specialists; the advice is aimed at residents of the UK who travel to endemic areas. The choice of drug for a particular individual should take into account:

risk of exposure to malaria;

extent of drug resistance;

efficacy of the recommended drugs;

side-effects of the drugs;

patient-related factors (e.g. age, pregnancy, renal or hepatic impairment).

5. Alternatives to chloroquine for the treatment of benign malaria are *Malarone®* [unlicensed indication], quinine, mefloquine, or *Riamet®* [unlicensed indication]; as with chloroquine, primaquine should be given for radical cure.
6. Before starting primaquine blood should be tested for glucose-6-phosphate dehydrogenase (G6PD) activity since the drug can cause haemolysis in G6PD-deficient patients. In G6PD deficiency primaquine, in a dose for adults of 30 mg once a week (children 500–750 micrograms/kg once a week) for 8 weeks, has been found useful and without undue harmful effects.

**Protection against bites** **Prophylaxis is not absolute**, and breakthrough infection can occur with any of the drugs recommended. Personal protection against being bitten is very important. Mosquito nets impregnated with permethrin provide the most effective barrier protection against insects; coils, mats and vaporised insecticides are also useful. Diethyltoluamide (DEET) in lotions, sprays or roll-on formulations is safe and effective when applied to the skin but the protective effect only lasts for a few hours. Long sleeves and trousers worn after dusk also provide protection.

**Length of prophylaxis** In order to determine tolerance and to establish habit, prophylaxis should generally be started one week (preferably 2½ weeks in the case of mefloquine) before travel into an endemic area (or if not possible at earliest opportunity up to 1 or 2 days before travel); *Malarone®* prophylaxis should be started 1–2 days before travel. Prophylaxis should be continued for **4 weeks after leaving** (except for *Malarone®* prophylaxis which should be stopped 1 week after leaving).

In those requiring long-term prophylaxis, chloroquine and proguanil may be used for periods of over 5 years. Mefloquine is licensed for up to 1 year (although it has been used for up to 3 years without undue problems). Doxycycline can be used for up to 2 years while *Malarone®* is licensed for up to 28 days but can be used safely for up to 3 months (and possibly 6 months or longer). Specialist advice should be sought for long-term prophylaxis.

**Return from malarial region** It is important to be aware that **any illness** that occurs within 1 year and **especially within 3 months of return might be malaria** even if all recommended precautions against malaria were taken. Travellers should be **warned** of this and told that if they develop any illness **particularly within 3 months** of their return they should go **immediately** to a doctor and specifically mention their exposure to malaria.

**Children** Prophylactic doses are based on guidelines agreed by UK malaria experts and may differ from advice in product literature. Weight is a better guide than age. If in doubt telephone centres listed on p. 329.

**Epilepsy** Both chloroquine and mefloquine are unsuitable for malaria prophylaxis in individuals with a history of epilepsy. In areas *without chloroquine resistance* proguanil 200 mg daily alone is recommended; in areas *with chloroquine resistance*, doxycycline or *Malarone®* may be considered; the metabolism of doxycycline may be influenced by antiepileptics (see **interactions:** Appendix 1 (tetracyclines)).

**Asplenia** Asplenic individuals (or those with severe splenic dysfunction) are at particular risk of severe malaria. If travel to malarious areas is unavoidable, rigorous precautions are required against contracting the disease.

**Renal impairment** Avoidance (or dosage reduction) of proguanil is recommended since it is excreted by the kidneys. *Malarone®* should not be used for prophylaxis in patients with creatinine clearance less than 30 mL/minute. Chloroquine is only partially excreted by the kidneys and reduction of the dose for prophylaxis is not required except in severe impairment. Mefloquine is considered to be appropriate to use in renal impairment and does not require dosage reduction. Doxycycline is also considered to be appropriate.

**Pregnancy** Travel to malarious areas should be avoided during pregnancy; if travel is unavoidable, effective prophylaxis must be used. Chloroquine and proguanil may be given in usual doses in areas where *P. falciparum* strains are sensitive; in the case of proguanil, folic acid 5 mg daily should be given. The manufacturer advises that prophylaxis with mefloquine should be avoided as a matter of principle but studies of mefloquine in pregnancy (including use in the first trimester) indicate that it can be considered for travel to chloroquine-resistant areas. Doxycycline is contra-indicated during pregnancy. *Malarone®* should be avoided during pregnancy unless there is no suitable alternative. The centres listed on p. 329 should be consulted for advice on prophylaxis in resistant areas.

**Breast-feeding** Prophylaxis is required in **breast-fed infants**; although antimalarials are present in milk, the amounts are too variable to give reliable protection.

## Specific recommendations

Where a journey requires two regimens, the regimen for the higher risk area should be used for the whole journey. Those travelling to remote or little-visited areas may require expert advice.

> Risk may vary in different parts of a country—check under all risk levels

> **Warning** Settled immigrants (or long-term visitors) to the UK may be unaware that they will have **lost some of their immunity** and also that the areas where they previously lived **may now be malarious**

### North Africa, the Middle East, and Central Asia

**Very low risk** Risk *very low* in Algeria, Egypt (tourist areas malaria-free), Georgia (south-east, July–October), Kyrgystan (but *Low Risk* in south-west, see below), Libya, rural Morocco, most tourist areas of Turkey, Uzbekistan (extreme south-east only):

> chemoprophylaxis not recommended but avoid mosquito bites and consider malaria if fever presents

**Low risk** Risk *low* in Armenia (June–October), Azerbaijan (southern border areas, June–September), Egypt (El Fayoum only, June–October), rural north Iraq and Basrah Province (May–November), Kyrgystan (south-west, May–October), north border of Syria (May–October), Turkey (plain around Adana, Side, south-east Anatolia, March–November), Turkmenistan (south-east only, June–October):

**preferably**

> chloroquine *or* (if chloroquine not appropriate) proguanil hydrochloride

**Risk** Risk *present* and *chloroquine resistance present* in Afghanistan (below 2000 m, May–November), Iran, Oman (remote rural areas only), Saudi Arabia (except northern, eastern and central provinces, Asir plateau, and western border cities where very little risk, no risk in Mecca), Tajikistan (June–October), Yemen (no risk in Sana'a):

> chloroquine + proguanil hydrochloride *or* (if chloroquine + proguanil not appropriate) doxycyline

## Sub-Saharan Africa

*No chemoprophylaxis recommended* for Cape Verde and non-rural areas of Mauritius (but avoid mosquito bites and consider malaria if fever presents); *chloroquine prophylaxis* appropriate for rural areas of **Mauritius**

**Very high risk** Risk *very high* (or *locally very high*) and *chloroquine resistance very widespread* in Angola, Benin, Botswana (northern half, November–June), Burkina Faso, Burundi, Cameroon, Central African Republic, Chad, Comoros, Congo, Democratic Republic of the Congo (formely Zaïre), Djibouti, Equatorial Guinea, Eritrea, Ethiopia (below 2200 m; no risk in Addis Ababa), Gabon, Gambia, Ghana, Guinea, Guinea-Bissau, Ivory Coast, Kenya, Liberia, Madagascar, Malawi, Mali, Mauritania (all year in south; July–November in north), Mozambique, Namibia (all year along Kavango and Kunene rivers; November–June in northern third), Niger, Nigeria, Principe, Rwanda, São Tomé, Senegal, Sierra Leone, Somalia, South Africa (Kruger Park, north-east, low-altitude areas of Northern Province and Mpumalanga, and north-east KwaZulu-Natal as far south as Tugela river), Sudan, Swaziland, Tanzania, Togo, Uganda, Zambia, Zimbabwe (all year in Zambezi valley; November–June in other areas below 1200 m; risk negligible in Harare and Bulawayo):

> mefloquine *or* doxycycline *or* *Malarone®*

**Note** In Zimbabwe and neighbouring countries, pyrimethamine with dapsone (also known as *Deltaprim®*) prophylaxis is used by local residents (sometimes with chloroquine).

## South Asia

**Variable risk** Risk *variable* and *chloroquine resistance usually moderate* in Bangladesh (except in Chittagong Hill Tracts, see below; no risk in Dhaka city), southern districts of Bhutan, India (no risk in parts of mountain states of north; *High Risk* in Assam), Nepal (below 1500 m, especially Terai districts; no risk in Kathmandu), Pakistan (below 2000 m), Sri Lanka (no risk in and just south of Colombo):

> chloroquine + proguanil hydrochloride *or* (if chloroquine + proguanil not appropriate) mefloquine *or* doxycycline *or* *Malarone®*

**High risk** Risk *high* and *chloroquine resistance high* in Bangladesh (only in Chittagong Hill Tracts), India (Assam only):

> mefloquine *or* doxycycline *or* *Malarone®*

## South-East Asia

**Very low risk** Risk *very low* in Bali, main tourist areas of China (but *substantial risk* in Yunnan and Hainan, see below; *chloroquine prophylaxis* appropriate for other remote areas), Hong Kong, Korea (both Democratic People's Republic and Republic), Malaysia (but *substantial risk* in Sabah, and *variable risk* in deep forests, see below), Sarawak (but *variable risk* in deep forests, see below), Thailand (Bangkok, main tourist centres—**important:** regional risk exists, see under *Great risk*, below):

> chemoprophylaxis not recommended but avoid mosquito bites and consider malaria if fever presents

**Variable risk** Risk *variable* and *some chloroquine resistance* in Indonesia (very low risk in Bali, and cities but *substantial risk* in Irian Jaya [West Papua] and Lombok, see below), rural Philippines below 600 m (no risk in cities, Cebu, Bohol, and Catanduanes), deep forests of peninsular Malaysia and Sarawak (but *substantial risk* in Sabah, see below):

> chloroquine + proguanil hydrochloride *or* (if chloroquine + proguanil not appropriate) mefloquine *or* *Malarone®*

**Substantial risk** Risk *substantial* and *drug resistance common* in Cambodia (no risk in Phnom Penh; for western provinces, see below), China (Yunnan and Hainan; *chloroquine prophylaxis* appropriate for other remote areas), East Timor, Irian Jaya [West Papua], Laos (no risk in Vientiane), Lombok, Malaysia (Sabah; see also *Very low risk* and *Variable risk* above), Myanmar (formerly Burma; see also *Great risk* below), Vietnam (no risk in cities, Red River delta area, coastal plain north of Nha Trang):

> mefloquine *or* doxycycline *or* *Malarone®*

**Great risk and drug resistance present** Risk *great and mefloquine resistance present* in western provinces of Cambodia, borders of Thailand with Cambodia and Myanmar, and Ko Chang, Myanmar (eastern Shan State):

> doxycycline *or* *Malarone®*

## Oceania

**Risk** Risk *high* and *chloroquine resistance high* in Papua New Guinea (below 1800 m), Solomon Islands, Vanuatu:

> doxycycline *or* mefloquine *or* *Malarone®*

5 Infections

### Central and South America and the Caribbean

**Variable to low risk** Risk *variable to low* in Argentina (rural areas along northern borders only), rural Belize (except Belize district), rural Costa Rica (below 500 m), Dominican Republic, El Salvador (Santa Ana province in west), Guatemala (below 1500 m), Haiti, Honduras, some rural areas of Mexico (not regularly visited by tourists), Nicaragua, Panama (west of Panama Canal but *variable to high risk* east of Panama Canal, see below), rural Paraguay:

chloroquine *or* (if chloroquine not appropriate) proguanil hydrochloride

**Variable to high risk** Risk *variable to high* and *chloroquine resistance present* in rural areas of Bolivia (below 2500 m), Ecuador (below 1500 m; no malaria in Galapagos Islands and Guayaquil; see below for Esmeraldas Province), Panama (east of Panama Canal), rural areas of Peru (below 1500 m; see below for Amazon basin area), rural areas of Venezuela (except on coast, Caracas free of malaria):

chloroquine + proguanil hydrochloride *or* (if chloroquine + proguanil not appropriate) mefloquine *or* doxycycline *or Malarone®*

**High risk** Risk *high* and *marked chloroquine resistance* in Bolivia (Amazon basin area), Brazil (throughout 'Legal Amazon' area which includes the Amazon basin area, Mato Grosso and Maranhao only; elsewhere *very low risk*—no chemoprophylaxis), Colombia (most areas below 800 m), Ecuador (Esmeraldas Province), French Guiana, all interior regions of Guyana, Peru (Amazon basin area), Surinam (except Paramaribo and coast), Venezuela (Amazon basin area):

mefloquine *or* doxycycline *or Malarone®*

### Standby treatment

Adults travelling for prolonged periods to areas of chloroquine-resistance who are unlikely to have easy access to medical care should carry a standby treatment course. Self-medication should be **avoided** if medical help is accessible; prophylaxis should be continued during and after the attack.

In order to avoid excessive self-medication, the traveller should be provided with **written instructions** that urgent medical attention should be sought if fever (38°C or more) develops 7 days (or more) after arriving in a malarious area and that self-treatment is indicated if medical help is not immediately available or the condition is worsening.

In view of the continuing emergence of resistant strains and of the different regimens required for different areas expert advice should be sought on the best treatment course for an individual traveller.

A drug used for chemoprophylaxis should not be considered for standby treatment for the same traveller.

## Artemether with lumefantrine

Artemether with lumefantrine is licensed for the *treatment of acute uncomplicated falciparum malaria.*

### ARTEMETHER WITH LUMEFANTRINE

**Indications** treatment of acute uncomplicated falciparum malaria; treatment of benign malaria [unlicensed indication]

**Cautions** electrolyte disturbances, concomitant use with other drugs known to cause QT-interval prolongation; hepatic impairment (Appendix 2); renal impairment (Appendix 3); pregnancy (Appendix 4); monitor patients unable to take food (greater risk of recrudescence); **interactions:** Appendix 1 (artemether with lumefantrine)

Driving Dizziness may affect performance of skilled tasks (e.g. driving)

**Contra-indications** history of arrhythmias, of clinically relevant bradycardia, and of congestive heart failure accompanied by reduced left ventricular ejection fraction; family history of sudden death or of congenital QT interval prolongation; breast-feeding (Appendix 5)

**Side-effects** abdominal pain, anorexia, diarrhoea, vomiting, nausea; palpitation; cough; headache, dizziness, sleep disturbances, asthenia; arthralgia, myalgia; pruritus, rash

**Dose**

- See notes above

**Riamet®** (Novartis) ▼ PoM

Tablets, yellow, artemether 20 mg, lumefantrine 120 mg, net price 24-tab pack = £22.50. Label: 21, counselling, driving

## Chloroquine

Chloroquine is used for the *prophylaxis of malaria* in areas of the world where the *risk of chloroquine-resistant falciparum malaria is still low*. It is also used with proguanil when chloroquine-resistant falciparum malaria is present but this regimen may not give optimal protection (see specific recommendations by country, p. 331).

Chloroquine is **no longer recommended** for the *treatment of falciparum malaria* owing to widespread resistance, nor is it recommended if the infective species is *not known* or if the infection is *mixed*; in these cases treatment should be with quinine, *Malarone®*, or *Riamet®* (for details, see p. 329). It is still recommended for the *treatment of benign malarias* (for details, see p. 330).

### CHLOROQUINE

**Indications** chemoprophylaxis and treatment of malaria, see notes above; rheumatoid arthritis and lupus erythematosus (section 10.1.3)

**Cautions** renal impairment (see notes above), pregnancy (but for malaria benefit outweighs risk, see Appendix 4, Antimalarials), may exacerbate psoriasis, neurological disorders (avoid for prophylaxis if history of epilepsy, see notes above), may aggravate myasthenia gravis, severe gastro-intestinal disorders, G6PD deficiency (see section 9.1.5); ophthalmic examination and long-term therapy, see under Chloroquine, section 10.1.3; avoid concurrent therapy with hepatotoxic drugs—other **interactions:** Appendix 1 (chloroquine and hydroxychloroquine)

**Side-effects** gastro-intestinal disturbances, headache; also hypotension, convulsions, visual disturbances, depigmentation or loss of hair, skin reactions (rashes, pruritus); rarely, bone-marrow suppression, hypersensitivity reactions such as urticaria and angioedema; other side-effects (not usually associated with malaria prophylaxis or treatment), see under Chloroquine, section 10.1.3; very toxic in **overdosage**—immediate advice from poisons centres essential (see also p. 32)

**Dose**

Note Doses expressed as chloroquine base

- Prophylaxis of malaria, preferably started 1 week before entering endemic area and continued for 4 weeks after leaving (see notes above), 300 mg once weekly; INFANT up to 12 weeks body-weight under 6 kg, 37.5 mg once weekly; 12 weeks–11 months body-weight 6–10 kg, 75 mg once weekly; CHILD 1–3 years body-weight 10–16 kg, 112.5 mg once weekly; 4–7 years body-weight 16–25 kg, 150 mg once weekly; 8–12 years body-weight 25–45 kg, 225 mg once weekly; over 13 years body-weight over 45 kg, adult dose
- Treatment of malaria, see notes above

Counselling Warn travellers about **importance** of avoiding mosquito bites, **importance** of taking prophylaxis regularly, and **importance** of immediate visit to doctor if ill within 1 year and **especially** within 3 months of return. For details, see notes above

Note Chloroquine doses in BNF may differ from those in product literature

5 Infections

**Chloroquine sulphate** (Beacon) PoM

Injection, chloroquine sulphate 54.5 mg/mL (≡ chloroquine base 40 mg/mL), net price 5-mL amp = 79p

[1]**Avloclor®** (AstraZeneca) PoM

Tablets, scored, chloroquine phosphate 250 mg (≡ chloroquine base 155 mg). Net price 20-tab pack = £1.22. Label: 5, counselling, prophylaxis, see above

**Malarivon®** (Wallace Mfg) PoM

Syrup, chloroquine phosphate 80 mg/5 mL (≡ chloroquine base 50 mg/5 mL), net price 75 mL = £3.35. Label: 5, counselling, prophylaxis, see above

[1]**Nivaquine®** (Beacon)

Tablets, f/c, yellow, chloroquine sulphate 200 mg (≡ chloroquine base 150 mg), net price 28-tab pack = £2.16. Label: 5, counselling, prophylaxis, see above

Syrup, golden, chloroquine sulphate 68 mg/5 mL (≡ chloroquine base 50 mg/5 mL), net price 100 mL = £5.15. Label: 5, counselling, prophylaxis, see above

**With proguanil**

For cautions and side-effects of proguanil see Proguanil; for dose see notes above

**Paludrine/Avloclor®** (AstraZeneca)

Tablets, travel pack of 14 tablets of chloroquine phosphate 250 mg (≡ chloroquine base 155 mg) and 98 tablets of proguanil hydrochloride 100 mg, net price 112-tab pack = £8.79. Label: 5, 21, counselling, prophylaxis, see above

1. Can be sold to the public provided it is licensed and labelled for the prophylaxis of malaria. Drugs for malaria prophylaxis not prescribable on the NHS; health authorities may investigate circumstances under which antimalarials are prescribed

## Mefloquine

Mefloquine is used for the *prophylaxis of malaria* in areas of the world where there is a *high risk of chloroquine-resistant falciparum malaria* (for details, see specific recommendations by country, p. 331).

Mefloquine is now rarely used for the *treatment of falciparum malaria* because of increased resistance. It is effective for the *treatment of benign malarias*, but is not required as chloroquine is usually effective. Mefloquine should not be used for treatment if it has been used for prophylaxis.

The CSM has advised that travellers should be informed about adverse reactions of mefloquine and, if they occur, medical advice should be sought on alternative antimalarials before the next dose is due; the patient information leaflet, which describes adverse reactions should always be provided when dispensing mefloquine.

### MEFLOQUINE

**Indications** chemoprophylaxis of malaria, treatment of chloroquine-resistant vivax malaria, see notes above

**Cautions** pregnancy (see notes under Prophylaxis against malaria; Appendix 4)—manufacturer advises **avoid** pregnancy during and for 3 months after; breast-feeding (Appendix 5); avoid for chemoprophylaxis in severe hepatic impairment; cardiac conduction disorders; epilepsy (avoid for prophylaxis); not recommended in infants under 3 months (5 kg); **interactions:** Appendix 1 (mefloquine)

Driving Dizziness or a disturbed sense of balance may affect performance of skilled tasks (e.g. driving); effects may persist for up to 3 weeks

**Contra-indications** history of neuropsychiatric disorders, including depression, or convulsions; hypersensitivity to quinine

**Side-effects** nausea, vomiting, diarrhoea, abdominal pain; dizziness, loss of balance, headache, sleep disorders (insomnia, drowsiness, abnormal dreams); also neuropsychiatric reactions (including sensory and motor neuropathies, tremor, ataxia, anxiety, depression, suicidal ideation, panic attacks, agitation, hallucinations, psychosis, convulsions), tinnitus and vestibular disorders, visual disturbances, circulatory disorders (hypotension and hypertension), chest pain, tachycardia, bradycardia, cardiac conduction disorders, dyspnoea, muscle weakness, myalgia, arthralgia, rash, urticaria, pruritus, alopecia, asthenia, malaise, fatigue, fever, loss of appetite, leucopenia or leucocytosis, thrombocytopenia; rarely Stevens-Johnson syndrome, AV block, encephalopathy and anaphylaxis

**Dose**

- Prophylaxis of malaria, preferably started 2½ weeks before entering endemic area and continued for 4 weeks after leaving (see notes above), ADULT and CHILD body-weight over 45 kg, 250 mg once weekly; body-weight 6–16 kg, 62.5 mg once weekly; body-weight 16–25 kg, 125 mg once weekly; body-weight 25–45 kg, 187.5 mg once weekly
- Treatment of malaria, see notes above

Counselling See CSM advice in notes above. Also warn travellers about **importance** of avoiding mosquito bites, **importance** of taking prophylaxis regularly, and **importance** of immediate visit to doctor if ill within 1 year and **especially** within 3 months of return. For details, see notes above

Note Mefloquine doses in BNF may differ from those in product literature

[1]**Lariam®** (Roche) PoM
Tablets, scored, mefloquine (as hydrochloride) 250 mg. Net price 8-tab pack = £14.53. Label: 21, 25, 27, counselling, driving, prophylaxis, see above

## Primaquine

Primaquine is used to eliminate the liver stages of *P. vivax or P. ovale following chloroquine treatment* (for details, see p. 330).

### PRIMAQUINE

**Indications** adjunct in the treatment of *Plasmodium vivax* and *P. ovale* malaria (eradication of liver stages)

**Cautions** G6PD deficiency (test blood, see under Benign Malarias (treatment) above); systemic diseases associated with granulocytopenia (e.g. rheumatoid arthritis, lupus erythematosus); pregnancy (Appendix 4) and breast-feeding; **interactions:** Appendix 1 (primaquine)

**Side-effects** nausea, vomiting, anorexia, abdominal pain; less commonly methaemoglobinaemia, haemolytic anaemia especially in G6PD deficiency, leucopenia

**Dose**

- See notes above

**Primaquine** (Non-proprietary)
Tablets, primaquine (as phosphate) 7.5 mg or 15 mg
Available on a named-patient basis from Durbin, IDIS

## Proguanil

Proguanil is used (usually *with chloroquine*, but occasionally *alone*) for the *prophylaxis of malaria*, (for details, see specific recommendations by country, p. 331).

Proguanil used alone is not suitable for the *treatment of malaria*; *Malarone®* (a combination of atovaquone with proguanil) is, however, licensed for the treatment of acute uncomplicated falciparum malaria. *Malarone®* is also used for the *prophylaxis of falciparum malaria* in areas of *widespread mefloquine or chloroquine resistance*. *Malarone®* is also used as an alternative to mefloquine or doxycycline. *Malarone®* is particularly suitable for short trips to highly chloroquine-resistant areas because it needs to be taken only for 7 days after leaving an endemic area.

### PROGUANIL HYDROCHLORIDE

**Indications** chemoprophylaxis of malaria

**Cautions** renal impairment (see notes under Prophylaxis against malaria and Appendix 3); pregnancy (folate supplements needed); **interactions:** Appendix 1 (proguanil)

**Side-effects** mild gastric intolerance, diarrhoea and constipation; occasionally mouth ulcers and stomatitis; *very rarely* cholestasis, vasculitis, skin reactions and hair loss

**Dose**

- Prophylaxis of malaria, preferably started 1 week before entering endemic area and continued for 4 weeks after leaving (see notes above), 200 mg once daily; INFANT up to 12 weeks body-weight under 6 kg, 25 mg once daily; 12 weeks–11 months body-weight 6–10 kg, 50 mg once daily; CHILD 1–3 years body-weight 10–16 kg, 75 mg once daily; 4–7 years body-weight 16–25 kg, 100 mg once daily; 8–12 years, body-weight 25–45 kg, 150 mg once daily; over 13 years body-weight over 45 kg, adult dose

**Counselling** Warn travellers about **importance** of avoiding mosquito bites, **importance** of taking prophylaxis regularly, and **importance** of immediate visit to doctor if ill within 1 year and **especially** within 3 months of return. For details, see notes above

**Note** Proguanil doses in BNF may differ from those in product literature

[1]**Paludrine®** (AstraZeneca)
Tablets, scored, proguanil hydrochloride 100 mg. Net price 98-tab pack = £7.43. Label: 21, counselling, prophylaxis, see above

**With chloroquine**
See under Chloroquine

### PROGUANIL HYDROCHLORIDE WITH ATOVAQUONE

**Indications** treatment of acute uncomplicated falciparum malaria and prophylaxis of falciparum malaria, particularly where resistance to other antimalarial drugs suspected; treatment of benign malaria [unlicensed indication]

**Cautions** renal impairment (Appendix 3), diarrhoea or vomiting (reduced absorption of atovaquone), pregnancy (Appendix 4) and breast-feeding (Appendix 5); efficacy not evaluated in cerebral or complicated malaria (including hyperparasitaemia, pulmonary oedema or renal failure); **interactions:** see Appendix 1 (proguanil, atovaquone)

**Side-effects** nausea, vomiting, mouth ulcers and stomatitis, diarrhoea, abdominal pain, anorexia, fever; headache, dizziness, abnormal dreams, insomnia, cough, visual disturbances, pruritus, rash, blood disorders, hyponatraemia, and hair loss reported

**Dose**

- See under preparation

**Counselling** Warn travellers about **importance** of avoiding mosquito bites, **importance** of taking prophylaxis regularly, and **importance** of immediate visit to doctor if ill within 1 year and **especially** within 3 months of return. For details, see notes above

[1]**Malarone®** (GSK) PoM
Tablets ('standard'), pink, f/c, proguanil hydrochloride 100 mg, atovaquone 250 mg. Net price 12-tab pack = £22.92. Label: 21, counselling, prophylaxis, see below

**Dose** prophylaxis of malaria, started 1–2 days before entering endemic area and continued for 1 week after leaving, ADULT and CHILD over 40 kg, 1 tablet daily

Treatment of malaria, ADULT and CHILD body-weight over 40 kg, 4 tablets once daily for 3 days; CHILD body-weight 11–20 kg 1 tablet daily for 3 days; body-weight 21–30 kg 2 tablets once daily for 3 days; body-weight 31–40 kg 3 tablets once daily for 3 days

[1]**Malarone® Paediatric** (GSK) ▼ PoM
Paediatric tablets, pink, f/c proguanil hydrochloride 25 mg, atovaquone 62.5 mg, net price 12-tab pack = £7.64. Label: 21, counselling, prophylaxis, see above

**Dose** prophylaxis of malaria, started 1–2 days before entering endemic area and continued for 1 week after leaving, CHILD body-weight 11–20 kg, 1 tablet once daily; body-weight 21–30 kg, 2 tablets once daily; body-weight 31–40 kg, 3 tablets once daily; body-weight over 40 kg use *Malarone®* ('standard') tablets

1. Drugs for malaria prophylaxis not prescribable on the NHS; health authorities may investigate circumstances under which antimalarials prescribed

## Pyrimethamine

Pyrimethamine should not be used alone, but is used with sulfadoxine (in *Fansidar®*).

**Fansidar®** is not recommended for the *prophylaxis of malaria,* but it is used in the treatment of *falciparum malaria* and can be used *with (or following) quinine.*

### PYRIMETHAMINE

**Indications** malaria (but used only in combined preparations incorporating sulfadoxine); toxoplasmosis—section 5.4.7

**Cautions** hepatic or renal impairment, pregnancy (Appendix 4); breast-feeding (Appendix 5); blood counts required with prolonged treatment; history of seizures—avoid large loading doses; **interactions:** Appendix 1 (pyrimethamine)

**Side-effects** depression of haematopoiesis with high doses, rashes, insomnia

**Dose**

- Malaria, no dose stated because not recommended alone
- Toxoplasmosis, section 5.4.7

**Daraprim®** (GSK) PoM
Tablets, scored, pyrimethamine 25 mg. Net price 30-tab pack = £2.17



### PYRIMETHAMINE WITH SULFADOXINE

**Indications** adjunct to quinine in treatment of *Plasmodium falciparum* malaria (see notes above); **not** recommended for prophylaxis

**Cautions** see under Pyrimethamine and under Co-trimoxazole (section 5.1.8); pregnancy (Appendix 4); breast-feeding (Appendix 5); not recommended for prophylaxis (severe side-effects on long-term use); **interactions:** Appendix 1 (pyrimethamine, sulphonamides)

**Contra-indications** see under Pyrimethamine and under Co-trimoxazole (section 5.1.8); sulphonamide allergy

**Side-effects** see under Pyrimethamine and under Co-trimoxazole (section 5.1.8); pulmonary infiltrates (e.g. eosinophilic or allergic alveolitis) reported—discontinue if cough or shortness of breath

**Dose**

- Treatment, see notes above
- Prophylaxis, not recommended by UK malaria experts

**Fansidar®** (Roche) PoM
Tablets, scored, pyrimethamine 25 mg, sulfadoxine 500 mg, net price 3-tab pack = 74p

## Quinine

Quinine is not suitable for the *prophylaxis of malaria.*

Quinine is used for the *treatment of falciparum malaria* or if the infective species is *not known* or if the infection is *mixed* (for details see p. 329).

1. Drugs for malaria prophylaxis not prescribable on the NHS; health authorities may investigate circumstances under which antimalarials prescribed

### QUININE

**Indications** falciparum malaria; nocturnal leg cramps, see section 10.2.2

**Cautions** atrial fibrillation, conduction defects, heart block, pregnancy (but appropriate for treatment of malaria; Appendix 4); monitor blood glucose and electrolyte concentration during parenteral treatment; G6PD deficiency (see section 9.1.5); **interactions:** Appendix 1 (quinine)

**Contra-indications** haemoglobinuria, myasthenia gravis, optic neuritis

**Side-effects** cinchonism, including tinnitus, headache, hot and flushed skin, nausea, abdominal pain, rashes, visual disturbances (including temporary blindness), confusion; hypersensitivity reactions including angioedema, blood disorders (including thrombocytopenia and intravascular coagulation), and acute renal failure; hypoglycaemia (especially after parenteral administration); cardiovascular effects (see Cautions); very toxic in **overdosage**—immediate advice from poisons centres essential (see also p. 32)

**Dose**

- See notes above

Note Quinine (anhydrous base) 100 mg ≡ quinine bisulphate 169 mg ≡ quinine dihydrochloride 122 mg ≡ quinine hydrochloride 122 mg ≡ quinine sulphate 121 mg. Quinine bisulphate 300-mg tablets are available but provide less quinine than 300 mg of the dihydrochloride, hydrochloride, or sulphate

**Quinine Sulphate** (Non-proprietary) PoM
Tablets, coated, quinine sulphate 200 mg, net price 28-tab pack = £2.13; 300 mg, 28-tab pack = £2.20

**Quinine Dihydrochloride** (Non-proprietary) PoM
Injection, quinine dihydrochloride 300 mg/mL. For dilution and use as an infusion. 1- and 2-mL amps
'Special order' product; contact Martindale or specialist centres (see p. 329)
Note Intravenous injection of quinine is so hazardous that it has been superseded by infusion

## Tetracyclines

**Doxycycline** (section 5.1.3) is used for the *prophylaxis of malaria* in areas of *widespread mefloquine or chloroquine resistance.* Doxycycline is also used as an alternative to mefloquine or *Malarone®* (for details, see specific recommendations by country, p. 331).

**Doxycycline** is also used as an *adjunct to quinine in the treatment of falciparum malaria* (for details see p. 329).

### DOXYCYCLINE

**Indications** prophylaxis of malaria; adjunct to quinine in treatment of *Plasmodium falciparum* malaria; see also section 5.1.3

**Cautions** section 5.1.3

**Contra-indications** section 5.1.3

**Side-effects** section 5.1.3

**Dose**

- Prophylaxis of malaria, preferably started 1 week before entering endemic area and continued for 4 weeks after leaving (see notes above), 100 mg once daily
- Treatment of falciparum malaria, see notes above

**Preparations**
Section 5.1.3

## 5.4.2 Amoebicides

**Metronidazole** is the drug of choice for *acute invasive amoebic dysentery* since it is very effective against vegetative forms of *Entamoeba histolytica* in ulcers; it is given in an adult dose of 800 mg three times daily for 5 days. **Tinidazole** is also effective. Metronidazole and tinidazole are also active against amoebae which may have migrated to the liver. Treatment with metronidazole (or tinidazole) is followed by a 10-day course of diloxanide furoate.

**Diloxanide furoate** is the drug of choice for asymptomatic patients with *E. histolytica* cysts in the faeces; metronidazole and tinidazole are relatively ineffective. Diloxanide furoate is relatively free from toxic effects and the usual course is of 10 days, given alone for chronic infections or following metronidazole or tinidazole treatment.

For *amoebic abscesses* of the liver **metronidazole** is effective in doses of 400 mg 3 times daily for 5–10 days; tinidazole is an alternative. The course may be repeated after 2 weeks if necessary. Aspiration of the abscess is indicated where it is suspected that it may rupture or where there is no improvement after 72 hours of metronidazole; the aspiration may need to be repeated. Aspiration aids penetration of metronidazole and, for abscesses with more than 100 mL of pus, if carried out in conjunction with drug therapy, may reduce the period of disability.

Diloxanide furoate is not effective against hepatic amoebiasis, but a 10-day course should be given at the completion of metronidazole or tinidazole treatment to destroy any amoebae in the gut.

### DILOXANIDE FUROATE

**Indications** see notes above; chronic amoebiasis and as adjunct to metronidazole or tinidazole in acute amoebiasis

**Contra-indications** pregnancy (Appendix 4), breast-feeding (Appendix 5)

**Side-effects** flatulence, vomiting, urticaria, pruritus

**Dose**

- 500 mg every 8 hours for 10 days; CHILD over 25 kg, 20 mg/kg daily in 3 divided doses for 10 days
  See also notes above

**Diloxanide** (Sovereign) PoM
Tablets, diloxanide furoate 500 mg, net price 30-tab pack = £32.95. Label: 9

### METRONIDAZOLE

**Indications** see under Dose below; anaerobic infections, section 5.1.11

**Cautions** section 5.1.11

**Side-effects** section 5.1.11

**Dose**

- By mouth, invasive intestinal amoebiasis, 800 mg every 8 hours for 5 days; CHILD 1–3 years 200 mg every 8 hours; 3–7 years 200 mg every 6 hours; 7–10 years 400 mg every 8 hours
  Extra-intestinal amoebiasis (including liver abscess) and symptomless amoebic cyst passers, 400–800 mg every 8 hours for 5–10 days; CHILD 1–3 years 100–200 mg every 8 hours; 3–7 years 100–200 mg every 6 hours; 7–10 years 200–400 mg every 8 hours
  Urogenital trichomoniasis, 200 mg every 8 hours for 7 days *or* 400–500 mg every 12 hours for 5–7 days, *or* 2 g as a single dose; CHILD 1–3 years 50 mg every 8 hours for 7 days; 3–7 years 100 mg every 12 hours; 7–10 years 100 mg every 8 hours
  Giardiasis, 2 g daily for 3 days *or* 400 mg 3 times daily for 5 days *or* 500 mg twice daily for 7–10 days; CHILD 1–3 years 500 mg daily for 3 days; 3–7 years 600–800 mg daily; 7–10 years 1 g daily

**Preparations**
Section 5.1.11

### TINIDAZOLE

**Indications** see under Dose below; anaerobic infections, section 5.1.11

**Cautions** section 5.1.11

**Side-effects** section 5.1.11

**Dose**

- Intestinal amoebiasis, 2 g daily for 2–3 days; CHILD 50–60 mg/kg daily for 3 days
- Amoebic involvement of liver, 1.5–2 g daily for 3–6 days; CHILD 50–60 mg/kg daily for 5 days
- Urogenital trichomoniasis and giardiasis, single 2 g dose; CHILD single dose of 50–75 mg/kg (repeated once if necessary)

**Preparations**
Section 5.1.11



## 5.4.3 Trichomonacides

**Metronidazole** (section 5.4.2) is the treatment of choice for *Trichomonas vaginalis* infection. Contact tracing is recommended and sexual contacts should be treated simultaneously. If metronidazole is ineffective, **tinidazole** (section 5.4.2) may be tried.

## 5.4.4 Antigiardial drugs

**Metronidazole** (section 5.4.2) is the treatment of choice for *Giardia lamblia* infections, given by mouth in a dosage of 2 g daily for 3 days or 400 mg every 8 hours for 5 days.

Alternative treatments are **tinidazole** (section 5.4.2) 2 g as a single dose or **mepacrine hydrochloride** 100 mg every 8 hours for 5–7 days [unlicensed indication].

### MEPACRINE HYDROCHLORIDE

**Indications** giardiasis; discoid lupus erythematosus (Antimalarials, section 10.1.3)

**Cautions** hepatic impairment, elderly, history of psychosis; avoid in psoriasis; **interactions:** Appendix 1 (mepacrine)

**Side-effects** gastro-intestinal disturbances; dizziness, headache; with large doses nausea, vomiting and occasionally transient acute toxic psychosis and CNS stimulation; on prolonged treatment yellow discoloration of skin and urine, chronic dermatoses (including severe exfoliative dermatitis), hepatitis, aplastic anaemia; also reported blue/black discoloration of palate and nails and corneal deposits with visual disturbances

**Dose**

- Giardiasis, 100 mg every 8 hours for 5–7 days; CHILD 2 mg/kg every 8 hours

**Mepacrine Hydrochloride**

Tablets, mepacrine hydrochloride 100 mg. Label: 4, 9, 14, 21

Available from BCM Specials [unlicensed—special order]

## 5.4.5 Leishmaniacides

Cutaneous leishmaniasis frequently heals spontaneously but if skin lesions are extensive or unsightly, treatment is indicated, as it is in visceral leishmaniasis (kala-azar).

**Sodium stibogluconate**, an organic pentavalent antimony compound, is the treatment of choice for visceral leishmaniasis. The dose is 20 mg/kg daily (max. 850 mg) for at least 20 days by intramuscular or intravenous injection; the dosage varies with different geographical regions and expert advice should be obtained. Skin lesions are treated for 10 days.

**Amphotericin** is used with or after an antimony compound for visceral leishmaniasis unresponsive to the antimonial alone; side-effects may be reduced by using liposomal amphotericin (*AmBisome®*—section 5.2) at a dose of 1–3 mg/kg daily for 10–21 days to a cumulative dose of 21–30 mg/kg. Other lipid formulations of amphotericin (*Abelcet®* and *Amphocil®*) are also likely to be effective but less information is available.

**Pentamidine isetionate** (pentamidine isethionate) (section 5.4.8) has been used in antimony-resistant visceral leishmaniasis, but although the initial response is often good, the relapse rate is high; it is associated with serious side-effects. Other treatments include paromomycin (available on named-patient basis from IDIS).

### SODIUM STIBOGLUCONATE

**Indications** leishmaniasis

**Cautions** hepatic impairment; pregnancy; intravenous injections must be given slowly over 5 minutes (to reduce risk of local thrombosis) and stopped if coughing or substernal pain; mucocutaneous disease (see below); monitor ECG before and during treatment; heart disease (withdraw if conduction disturbances occur); treat intercurrent infection (e.g. pneumonia)

Mucocutaneous disease Successful treatment of mucocutaneous leishmaniasis may induce severe inflammation around the lesions (may be life-threatening if pharyngeal or tracheal involvement)—may require corticosteroid

**Contra-indications** significant renal impairment; breast-feeding

**Side-effects** anorexia, nausea, vomiting, abdominal pain, diarrhoea; ECG changes; coughing (see Cautions); headache, lethargy; arthralgia, myalgia; *rarely* jaundice, flushing, bleeding from nose or gum, substernal pain (see Cautions), vertigo, fever, sweating, and rash; also reported pancreatitis and anaphylaxis; pain and thrombosis on intravenous administration, intramuscular injection also painful

**Dose**

- See notes above

**Pentostam®** (GSK) PoM

Injection, sodium stibogluconate equivalent to pentavalent antimony 100 mg/mL. Net price 100-mL bottle = £66.43

## 5.4.6 Trypanocides

The prophylaxis and treatment of trypanosomiasis is difficult and differs according to the strain of organism. Expert advice should therefore be obtained.

## 5.4.7 Drugs for toxoplasmosis

Most infections caused by *Toxoplasma gondii* are self-limiting, and treatment is not necessary. Exceptions are patients with eye involvement (toxoplasma choroidoretinitis), and those who are immunosuppressed. Toxoplasmic encephalitis is a common complication of AIDS. The treatment of choice is a combination of pyrimethamine and sulfadiazine (sulphadiazine), given for several weeks (expert advice **essential**). Pyrimethamine is a folate antagonist, and adverse reactions to this combination are relatively common (folinic acid supplements and weekly blood counts needed). Alternative regimens use combinations of pyrimethamine with clindamycin or clarithromycin or azithromycin. Long-term secondary prophylaxis is required after treatment of toxoplasmosis in AIDS.

If toxoplasmosis is acquired in pregnancy, transplacental infection may lead to severe disease in the fetus. Spiramycin (available on named-patient basis from IDIS) may reduce the risk of transmission of maternal infection to the fetus.

## 5.4.8 Drugs for pneumocystis pneumonia

Pneumonia caused by *Pneumocystis carinii (Pneumocystis jiroveci)* occurs in immunosuppressed patients; it is a common cause of pneumonia in AIDS. Pneumocystis pneumonia should generally be treated by those experienced in its management. Blood gas measurement is used to assess disease severity.

## Treatment

**Mild to moderate disease** **Co-trimoxazole** (section 5.1.8) in high dosage is the drug of choice for the treatment of mild to moderate pneumocystis pneumonia.

**Atovaquone** is licensed for the treatment of mild to moderate pneumocystis infection in patients who cannot tolerate co-trimoxazole. A combination of **dapsone** 100 mg daily (section 5.1.10) with **trimethoprim** 5 mg/kg every 6–8 hours (section 5.1.8) is given by mouth for the treatment of mild to moderate disease [unlicensed indication].

A combination of **clindamycin** 600 mg by mouth every 8 hours (section 5.1.6) and **primaquine** 30 mg daily by mouth (section 5.4.1) is used in the treatment of mild to moderate disease [unlicensed indication]; this combination is associated with considerable toxicity.

Inhaled **pentamidine isetionate** is sometimes used for mild disease. It is better tolerated than parenteral pentamidine but systemic absorption may still occur.

**Severe disease** **Co-trimoxazole** (section 5.1.8) in high dosage, given by mouth or by intravenous infusion, is the drug of choice for the treatment of severe pneumocystis pneumonia. **Pentamidine isetionate** given by intravenous infusion is an alternative for patients who cannot tolerate co-trimoxazole, or who have not responded to it. Pentamidine isetionate is a potentially toxic drug that can cause severe hypotension during or immediately after infusion.

Corticosteroid treatment can be lifesaving in those with severe pneumocystis pneumonia (see Adjunctive Therapy below).

**Adjunctive therapy** In moderate to severe infections associated with HIV infection, prednisolone 50–80 mg daily is given by mouth for 5 days (alternatively, hydrocortisone may be given parenterally); the dose is then reduced to complete 21 days of treatment. Corticosteroid treatment should ideally be started at the same time as the anti-pneumocystis therapy and certainly no later than 24–72 hours afterwards. The corticosteroid should be withdrawn before anti-pneumocystis treatment is complete.

## Prophylaxis

Prophylaxis against pneumocystis pneumonia should be given to all patients with a history of the infection. Prophylaxis against pneumocystis pneumonia should also be considered for severely immunocompromised patients. Prophylaxis should continue until immunity recovers sufficiently. It should not be discontinued if the patient has oral candidiasis, continues to lose weight, or is receiving cytotoxic therapy or long-term immunosuppressant therapy.

**Co-trimoxazole** by mouth is the drug of choice for prophylaxis against pneumocystis pneumonia. It is given in a dose of 960 mg daily or 960 mg on alternate days (3 times a week); the dose may be reduced to co-trimoxazole 480 mg daily to improve tolerance.

Intermittent inhalation of **pentamidine isetionate** is used for prophylaxis against penumocystis pneumonia in patients unable to tolerate co-trimoxazole. It is effective but patients may be prone to extrapulmonary infection. Alternatively, **dapsone** 100 mg daily (section 5.1.10) can be used. **Atovaquone** 750 mg twice daily has also been used for prophylaxis [unlicensed indication].

### ATOVAQUONE

**Indications** treatment of mild to moderate *Pneumocystis carinii (Pneumocystis jiroveci)* pneumonia in patients intolerant of co-trimoxazole

**Cautions** initial diarrhoea and difficulty in taking with food may reduce absorption (and require alternative therapy); other causes of pulmonary disease should be sought and treated; elderly; hepatic impairment (Appendix 2); renal impairment (Appendix 3); pregnancy (Appendix 4); avoid breast-feeding (Appendix 5); **interactions:** Appendix 1 (atovaquone)

**Side-effects** nausea, rash; commonly diarrhoea, vomiting, headache, insomnia; fever, anaemia, neutropenia, hyponatraemia

**Dose**

- 750 mg twice daily with food (particularly high fat) for 21 days; CHILD not recommended

**Wellvone®** (GSK) PoM

Suspension, sugar-free, fruit-flavoured, atovaquone 750 mg/5 mL, net price 210 mL = £405.31. Label: 21

**With proguanil hydrochloride**

See section 5.4.1

### PENTAMIDINE ISETIONATE

**Indications** see under Dose (should only be given by specialists)

**Cautions** risk of severe hypotension following administration (establish baseline blood pressure and administer with patient lying down; monitor blood pressure closely during administration, and at regular intervals, until treatment concluded); hypokalaemia, hypomagnesaemia, coronary heart disease, bradycardia, history of ventricular arrhythmias, concomitant use with other drugs which prolong QT-interval; hypertension or hypotension; hyperglycaemia or hypoglycaemia; leucopenia, thrombocytopenia, or anaemia; carry out laboratory monitoring according to product literature; care required to protect personnel during handling and administration; hepatic impairment; renal impairment (Appendix 3); pregnancy (Appendix 4); breast-feeding (Appendix 5); **interactions:** Appendix 1 (pentamidine isetionate)

**Side-effects** severe reactions, sometimes fatal, due to hypotension, hypoglycaemia, pancreatitis, and arrhythmias; also leucopenia, thrombocytopenia, acute renal failure, hypocalcaemia; also reported: azotaemia, abnormal liver-function tests, anaemia, hyperkalaemia, nausea and vomiting, dizziness, syncope, flushing, hyperglycaemia, rash, and taste disturbances; Stevens-Johnson syndrome reported; on inhalation, bronchoconstriction (may be prevented by prior use of bronchodilators), cough, and shortness of breath; discomfort, pain, induration, abscess formation, and muscle necrosis at injection site

**Dose**

- *Pneumocystis carinii (Pneumocystis jiroveci)* pneumonia, by intravenous infusion, 4 mg/kg daily for at least 14 days (reduced according to product literature in renal impairment)

  By inhalation of nebulised solution (using suitable equipment—consult product literature) 600 mg pentamidine isetionate daily for 3 weeks; secondary prevention, 300 mg every 4 weeks *or* 150 mg every 2 weeks
- Visceral leishmaniasis (kala-azar, section 5.4.5), by deep intramuscular injection, 3–4 mg/kg on alternate days to max. total of 10 injections; course may be repeated if necessary
- Cutaneous leishmaniasis, by deep intramuscular injection, 3–4 mg/kg once or twice weekly until condition resolves (but see also section 5.4.5)
- Trypanosomiasis, by deep intramuscular injection *or* intravenous infusion, 4 mg/kg daily or on alternate days to total of 7–10 injections

  **Note** Direct intravenous injection should be avoided whenever possible and **never** given rapidly; intramuscular injections should be deep and preferably given into the buttock

**Pentacarinat®** (JHC) PoM

Injection, powder for reconstitution, pentamidine isetionate, net price 300-mg vial = £30.45

Nebuliser solution, pentamidine isetionate, net price 300-mg bottle = £32.15

**Caution in handling** Pentamidine isetionate is toxic and personnel should be adequately protected during handling and administration—consult product literature

# 5.5 Anthelmintics


**5.5.1 Drugs for threadworms**
**5.5.2 Ascaricides**
**5.5.3 Drugs for tapeworm infections**
**5.5.4 Drugs for hookworms**
**5.5.5 Schistosomicides**
**5.5.6 Filaricides**
**5.5.7 Drugs for cutaneous larva migrans**
**5.5.8 Drugs for strongyloidiasis**


Advice on prophylaxis and treatment of helminth infections is available from:

| | |
|---|---|
| Birmingham | (0121) 424 0357 |
| Scottish Centre for Infection and Environmental Health (registered users of Travax only) | (0141) 300 1130 (weekdays 2–4 p.m. only) |
| Liverpool | (0151) 708 9393 |
| London | (020) 7387 9300 (treatment) |

## 5.5.1 Drugs for threadworms (pinworms, Enterobius vermicularis)

Anthelmintics are effective in threadworm infections, but their use needs to be combined with hygienic measures to break the cycle of auto-infection. All members of the family require treatment.

Adult threadworms do not live for longer than 6 weeks and for development of fresh worms, ova must be swallowed and exposed to the action of digestive juices in the upper intestinal tract. Direct multiplication of worms does not take place in the large bowel. Adult female worms lay ova on the perianal skin which causes pruritus; scratching the area then leads to ova being transmitted on fingers to the mouth, often via food eaten with unwashed hands. Washing hands and scrubbing nails before each meal and after each visit to the toilet is essential. A bath taken immediately after rising will remove ova laid during the night.

**Mebendazole** is the drug of choice for treating threadworm infection in patients of all ages over 2 years. It is given as a single dose; as reinfection is very common, a second dose may be given after 2 weeks.

**Piperazine** is available in combination with sennosides as a single-dose preparation.

### MEBENDAZOLE

**Indications** threadworm, roundworm, whipworm, and hookworm infections

**Cautions** pregnancy (toxicity in *rats*); breast-feeding (Appendix 5); **interactions:** Appendix 1 (mebendazole)

**Note** The package insert in the *Vermox®* pack includes the statement that it is not suitable for women known to be pregnant or children under 2 years

**Side-effects** *very rarely* abdominal pain, diarrhoea, convulsions (in infants) and rash (including Stevens-Johnson syndrome and toxic epidermal necrolysis)

**Dose**

- Threadworms, ADULT and CHILD over 2 years, 100 mg as a single dose; if reinfection occurs second dose may be needed after 2 weeks; CHILD under 2 years, not yet recommended
- Whipworms, ADULT and CHILD over 2 years, 100 mg twice daily for 3 days; CHILD under 2 years, not yet recommended
- Roundworms—section 5.5.2
- Hookworms—section 5.5.4

[1]**Mebendazole** (Non-proprietary) PoM

Tablets, chewable, mebendazole 100 mg

1. Can be sold to the public if supplied for oral use in the treatment of enterobiasis in adults and children over 2 years provided its container or package is labelled to show a max. single dose of 100 mg and it is supplied in a container or package containing not more than 800 mg; proprietary brands on sale to the public include *Boots Threadworm Tablets 2 Years Plus®*, *Ovex®* and *Pripsen® Mebendazole*

**Vermox®** (Janssen-Cilag) PoM

Tablets, orange, scored, chewable, mebendazole 100 mg. Net price 6-tab pack = £1.45

Suspension, mebendazole 100 mg/5 mL. Net price 30 mL = £1.68

## PIPERAZINE

**Indications** threadworm and roundworm infections

**Cautions** liver impairment (Appendix 2); renal impairment (Appendix 3); epilepsy; pregnancy (Appendix 4); packs on sale to the general public carry a warning to avoid in epilepsy, or in liver or kidney disease, and to seek medical advice in pregnancy; breast-feeding (Appendix 5)

**Side-effects** nausea, vomiting, colic, diarrhoea, allergic reactions including urticaria, bronchospasm, and rare reports of arthralgia, fever, Stevens-Johnson syndrome and angioedema; rarely dizziness, muscular incoordination ('worm wobble'); drowsiness, nystagmus, vertigo, blurred vision, confusion and clonic contractions in patients with neurological or renal abnormalities

**Dose**

- See under Preparation, below

**Piperazine Citrate** (Non-proprietary)

Syrup, piperazine hydrate 750 mg/5 mL (as citrate)
Brands include *Ascalix®*
Dose consult product literature

Syrup, piperazine hydrate 4 g/30 mL (as citrate)
Brands include *Ascalix®*
Dose consult product literature

### With sennosides

For cautions, contra-indications, side-effects of senna see section 1.6.2

**Pripsen®** (Thornton & Ross)

Oral powder, piperazine phosphate 4 g, total sennosides (calculated as sennoside B) 15.3 mg/sachet. Net price two-dose sachet pack = £1.36. Label: 13

Dose threadworms, stirred into milk or water, ADULT and CHILD over 6 years, content of 1 sachet as a single dose (bedtime in adults or morning in children), repeated after 14 days; INFANT 3 months–1 year, 1 level 2.5-mL spoonful in the morning, repeated after 14 days; CHILD 1–6 years, 1 level 5-mL spoonful in the morning, repeated after 14 days

Roundworms, first dose as for threadworms; repeat at monthly intervals for up to 3 months if reinfection risk

## 5.5.2 Ascaricides (common roundworm infections)

**Levamisole** (available on named-patient basis from IDIS) is very effective against *Ascaris lumbricoides* and is generally considered to be the drug of choice. It is very well tolerated; mild nausea or vomiting has been reported in about 1% of treated patients; it is given as a single dose of 120–150 mg in adults.

**Mebendazole** (section 5.5.1) is also active against ascaris; the usual dose is 100 mg twice daily for 3 days. **Piperazine** may be given in a single adult dose, see Piperazine, above.

## 5.5.3 Drugs for tapeworm infections

### Taenicides

**Niclosamide** (available on named-patient basis from IDIS) is the most widely used drug for tapeworm infections and side-effects are limited to occasional gastro-intestinal upset, lightheadedness, and pruritus; it is not effective against larval worms. Fears of developing cysticercosis in *Taenia solium* infections have proved unfounded. All the same, it is wise to anticipate this possibility by using an anti-emetic on wakening.

**Praziquantel** (available on named-patient basis from Merck (*Cysticide®*)) is as effective as niclosamide and is given as a single dose of 10–20 mg/kg after a light breakfast (a single dose of 25 mg/kg for *Hymenolepis nana*).

### Hydatid disease

Cysts caused by *Echinococcus granulosus* grow slowly and asymptomatic patients do not always require treatment. Surgical treatment remains the method of choice in many situations. **Albendazole** (available on named-patient basis from IDIS (*Zentel®*)) is used in conjunction with surgery to reduce the risk of recurrence or as primary treatment in inoperable cases. Alveolar echinococcosis due to *E. multilocularis* is usually fatal if untreated. Surgical removal with albendazole cover is the treatment of choice, but where effective surgery is impossible, repeated cycles of albendazole (for a year or more) may help. Careful monitoring of liver function is particularly important during drug treatment.



## 5.5.4 Drugs for hookworms (ancylostomiasis, necatoriasis)

Hookworms live in the upper small intestine and draw blood from the point of their attachment to their host. An iron-deficiency anaemia may thereby be produced and, if present, effective treatment of the infection requires not only expulsion of the worms but treatment of the anaemia.

**Mebendazole** (section 5.5.1) has a useful broad-spectrum activity, and is effective against hookworms; the usual dose is 100 mg twice daily for 3 days.

## 5.5.5 Schistosomicides (bilharziasis)

Adult *Schistosoma haematobium* worms live in the genito-urinary veins and adult *S. mansoni* in those of the colon and mesentery. *S. japonicum* is more widely distributed in veins of the alimentary tract and portal system.

**Praziquantel** (available on named-patient basis from Merck (*Cysticide*®)) is effective against all human schistosomes. The dose is 40 mg/kg in 2 divided doses 4–6 hours apart on one day (60 mg/kg in 3 divided doses on one day for *S. japonicum* infections). No serious toxic effects have been reported. Of all the available schistosomicides, it has the most attractive combination of effectiveness, broad-spectrum activity, and low toxicity.

Hycanthone, lucanthone, niridazole, oxamniquine, and sodium stibocaptate have now been superseded.

## 5.5.6 Filaricides

**Diethylcarbamazine** (not on UK market) is effective against microfilariae and adults of *Loa loa*, *Wuchereria bancrofti*, and *Brugia malayi*. To minimise reactions treatment is commenced with a dose of diethylcarbamazine citrate 1 mg/kg on the first day and increased gradually over 3 days to 6 mg/kg daily in divided doses; this dosage is maintained for 21 days and usually gives a radical cure for these infections. Close medical supervision is necessary particularly in the early phase of treatment.

In heavy infections there may be a febrile reaction, and in heavy *Loa loa* infection there is a small risk of encephalopathy. In such cases treatment must be given under careful in-patient supervision and stopped at the first sign of cerebral involvement (and specialist advice sought).

**Ivermectin** (available on named-patient basis from IDIS) is very effective in *onchocerciasis* and it is now the drug of choice. A single dose of 150 micrograms/kg by mouth produces a prolonged reduction in microfilarial levels. Retreatment at intervals of 6 to 12 months depending on symptoms must be given until the adult worms die out. Reactions are usually slight and most commonly take the form of temporary aggravation of itching and rash. Diethylcarbamazine or suramin should no longer be used for onchocerciasis because of their toxicity.

## 5.5.7 Drugs for cutaneous larva migrans (creeping eruption)

Dog and cat hookworm larvae may enter human skin where they produce slowly extending itching tracks usually on the foot. Single tracks can be treated with topical tiabendazole (no commercial preparation available). Multiple infections respond to **ivermectin** (available on named-patient basis from IDIS), **albendazole** (available on named-patient basis from IDIS (*Zentel*®)) or **tiabendazole** (thiabendazole) (available on a named-patient basis from IDIS (*Mintezol*®, *Triasox*®)) by mouth.

## 5.5.8 Drugs for strongyloidiasis

Adult *Strongyloides stercoralis* live in the gut and produce larvae which penetrate the gut wall and invade the tissues, setting up a cycle of auto-infection. **Tiabendazole** (thiabendazole) (available on a named-patient basis from IDIS (*Mintezol*®, *Triasox*®)) is the drug of choice for adults (but side-effects are much more marked in the elderly); it is given at a dosage of 25 mg/kg (max. 1.5 g) every 12 hours for 3 days. **Albendazole** is an alternative (available on named-patient basis from IDIS (*Zentel*®)) with fewer side-effects; it is given in a dose of 400 mg twice daily for 3 days, repeated after 3 weeks if necessary. **Ivermectin** (available on named-patient basis from IDIS) in a dose of 200 micrograms/kg daily for 2 days may be the most effective drug for chronic *Strongyloides* infection.

# 6 Endocrine system


| | | |
|---|---|---|
| **6.1** | **Drugs used in diabetes** | **343** |
| 6.1.1 | Insulins | 344 |
| 6.1.1.1 | Short-acting insulins | 346 |
| 6.1.1.2 | Intermediate- and long-acting insulins | 347 |
| 6.1.1.3 | Hypodermic equipment | 350 |
| 6.1.2 | Oral antidiabetic drugs | 351 |
| 6.1.2.1 | Sulphonylureas | 351 |
| 6.1.2.2 | Biguanides | 353 |
| 6.1.2.3 | Other antidiabetics | 354 |
| 6.1.3 | Diabetic ketoacidosis | 355 |
| 6.1.4 | Treatment of hypoglycaemia | 356 |
| 6.1.5 | Treatment of diabetic nephropathy and neuropathy | 357 |
| 6.1.6 | Diagnostic and monitoring agents for diabetes mellitus | 357 |
| **6.2** | **Thyroid and antithyroid drugs** | **359** |
| 6.2.1 | Thyroid hormones | 359 |
| 6.2.2 | Antithyroid drugs | 360 |
| **6.3** | **Corticosteroids** | **361** |
| 6.3.1 | Replacement therapy | 361 |
| 6.3.2 | Glucocorticoid therapy | 362 |
| **6.4** | **Sex hormones** | **367** |
| 6.4.1 | Female sex hormones | 367 |
| 6.4.1.1 | Oestrogens and HRT | 367 |
| 6.4.1.2 | Progestogens | 375 |
| 6.4.2 | Male sex hormones and antagonists | 377 |
| 6.4.3 | Anabolic steroids | 379 |
| **6.5** | **Hypothalamic and pituitary hormones and anti-oestrogens** | **379** |
| 6.5.1 | Hypothalamic and anterior pituitary hormones and anti-oestrogens | 379 |
| 6.5.2 | Posterior pituitary hormones and antagonists | 384 |
| **6.6** | **Drugs affecting bone metabolism** | **386** |
| 6.6.1 | Calcitonin and teriparatide | 387 |
| 6.6.2 | Bisphosphonates and other drugs affecting bone metabolism | 388 |
| **6.7** | **Other endocrine drugs** | **391** |
| 6.7.1 | Bromocriptine and other dopaminergic drugs | 391 |
| 6.7.2 | Drugs affecting gonadotrophins | 393 |
| 6.7.3 | Metyrapone and trilostane | 396 |


This chapter includes advice on the drug management of the following:


- Adrenal suppression during illness, trauma or surgery, p. 362
- Serious infections in patients taking corticosteroids, p. 363
- Osteoporosis, p. 386
- Breast pain (mastalgia), p. 396


## 6.1 Drugs used in diabetes


**6.1.1 Insulins**
**6.1.2 Oral antidiabetic drugs**
**6.1.3 Diabetic ketoacidosis**
**6.1.4 Treatment of hypoglycaemia**
**6.1.5 Treatment of diabetic nephropathy and neuropathy**
**6.1.6 Diagnostic and monitoring agents for diabetes mellitus**


Diabetes mellitus occurs because of a lack of insulin or resistance to its action. It is diagnosed by measuring fasting or random blood-glucose concentration (and occasionally by glucose tolerance test). Although there are many subtypes, the two principal classes of diabetes are type 1 diabetes and type 2 diabetes.

*Type 1 diabetes*, also referred to as insulin-dependent diabetes mellitus (IDDM), occurs as a result of a deficiency of insulin following autoimmune destruction of pancreatic beta cells. Patients with type 1 diabetes require administration of insulin.

*Type 2 diabetes*, also referred to as non-insulin-dependent diabetes (NIDDM), is due either to reduced secretion of insulin or to peripheral resistance to the action of insulin. Although patients may be controlled on diet alone, many also require oral antidiabetic drugs or insulin (or both) to maintain satisfactory control. In overweight individuals, type 2 diabetes may be prevented by losing weight and increasing physical activity; use of drugs such as orlistat (section 4.5.1) or sibutramine (section 4.5.2) may be considered in obese patients.

Treatment of all forms of diabetes should be aimed at alleviating symptoms and minimising the risk of long-term complications (see below); tight control of diabetes is essential.

Diabetes is a strong risk factor for cardiovascular disease. Other risk factors for cardiovascular disease such as smoking (section 4.10), hypertension (section 2.5), obesity (section 4.5), and hyperlipidaemia (section 2.12) should be addressed. The use of an ACE inhibitor (section 2.5.5.1), of low-dose aspirin (section 2.9) and of a lipid-regulating drug (section 2.12) can be beneficial in patients with diabetes and a high cardiovascular risk.

**Prevention of diabetic complications** Optimal glycaemic control in both type 1 diabetes and type 2 diabetes reduces, in the long term, the risk of microvascular complications including retinopathy, development of proteinuria and to some extent neuropathy. However, a temporary deterioration in established diabetic retinopathy may occur when normalising blood-glucose concentration. For reference to the use of an ACE inhibitor or an angiotensin-II receptor antagonist in the management of diabetic nephropathy, see section 6.1.5.

A measure of the total glycated (or glycosylated) haemoglobin ($HbA_1$) or a specific fraction ($HbA_{1c}$) provides a good indication of long-term glycaemic control. The ideal $HbA_{1c}$ concentration is between 6.5 and 7.5% but this cannot always be achieved, and those on insulin may have significantly increased risks of severe hypoglycaemia. Tight control of blood pressure in hypertensive patients with type 2 diabetes reduces mortality and protects visual acuity (by reducing considerably the risks of maculopathy and retinal photocoagulation) (see also section 2.5).

## 6.1.1 Insulins


6.1.1.1 Short-acting insulins
6.1.1.2 Intermediate- and long-acting insulins
6.1.1.3 Hypodermic equipment


Insulin plays a key role in the regulation of carbohydrate, fat, and protein metabolism. It is a polypeptide hormone of complex structure. There are differences in the amino-acid sequence of animal insulins, human insulins and the human insulin analogues. Insulin may be extracted from pork pancreas and purified by crystallisation; it may also be extracted from beef pancreas, but beef insulins are now rarely used. Human sequence insulin may be produced semisynthetically by enzymatic modification of porcine insulin (emp) or biosynthetically by recombinant DNA technology using bacteria (crb, prb) or yeast (pyr).

All insulin preparations are to a greater or lesser extent immunogenic in man but immunological resistance to insulin action is uncommon. Preparations of human sequence insulin should theoretically be less immunogenic, but no real advantage has been shown in trials.

Insulin is inactivated by gastro-intestinal enzymes, and must therefore be given by injection; the subcutaneous route is ideal in most circumstances. Insulin is usually injected into the upper arms, thighs, buttocks, or abdomen; absorption from a limb site may be increased if the limb is used in strenuous exercise after the injection. Generally subcutaneous insulin injections cause few problems; fat hypertrophy does, however, occur but can be minimised by using different injection sites in rotation. Local allergic reactions are rare.

Insulin is needed by all patients with ketoacidosis, and it is likely to be needed by most patients with:

- rapid onset of symptoms;
- substantial loss of weight;
- weakness;
- ketonuria.

If the condition worsens, vomiting can occur and patients may rapidly develop ketoacidosis. Insulin is required by almost all children with diabetes. It is also needed for type 2 diabetes when other methods have failed to achieve good control, and temporarily in the presence of intercurrent illness or peri-operatively. Pregnant women with type 2 diabetes should be treated with insulin when diet alone fails.

**Management of diabetes with insulin** The aim of treatment is to achieve the best possible control of blood-glucose concentration without making the patient obsessional and to avoid disabling hypoglycaemia; close co-operation is needed between the patient and the medical team since good control reduces the risk of complications. Mixtures of insulin preparations may be required and appropriate combinations have to be determined for the individual patient. For patients with acute-onset diabetes, treatment should be started with soluble insulin given 3 times daily with medium-acting insulin at bedtime. For those less severely ill, treatment is usually started with a mixture of premixed short- and medium-acting insulins (most commonly in a proportion of 30% soluble insulin and 70% isophane insulin) given twice daily; 8 units twice daily is a suitable initial dose for most ambulant patients. The proportion of the short-acting soluble component can be increased in those with excessive postprandial hyperglycaemia.

The dose of insulin is adjusted on an individual basis, by gradually increasing the dose but avoiding troublesome hypoglycaemic reactions.

There are 3 main types of insulin preparations:

- those of **short** duration which have a relatively rapid onset of action, namely soluble insulin, insulin lispro and insulin aspart;
- those with an **intermediate** action, e.g. isophane insulin and insulin zinc suspension; and
- those whose action is slower in onset and lasts for **long** periods, e.g. insulin zinc suspension.

The duration of action of a particular type of insulin varies considerably from one patient to another, and needs to be assessed individually.

### Examples of recommended insulin regimens

- Short-acting insulin mixed with intermediate-acting insulin: twice daily (before meals)
- Short-acting insulin mixed with intermediate-acting insulin: before breakfast
  Short-acting insulin: before evening meal
  Intermediate-acting insulin: at bedtime
- Short-acting insulin: three times daily (before breakfast, midday, and evening meal)
  Intermediate-acting insulin: at bedtime
- Intermediate-acting insulin with or without short-acting insulin: once daily either before breakfast or at bedtime suffices for some patients with type 2 diabetes who need insulin, sometimes in combination with oral hypoglycaemic drugs

Insulin requirements may be increased by infection, stress, accidental or surgical trauma, puberty, and during the second and third trimesters of pregnancy. Requirements may be decreased in patients with renal impairment (Appendix 3) or hepatic impairment and in those with some endocrine disorders (e.g. Addison's disease, hypopituitarism) or coeliac disease. In pregnancy insulin requirements should be assessed frequently by an experienced diabetes physician.

**Insulin administration** Insulin is generally given by *subcutaneous injection*. Injection devices ('pens') (section 6.1.1.3) which hold the insulin in a cartridge and meter the required dose are convenient to use. The conventional syringe and needle is still the preferred method of insulin administration by many and is also required for insulins not available in cartridge form.

For intensive insulin regimens multiple subcutaneous injections (3 to 4 times daily) are usually recommended.

Short-acting insulins (soluble insulin, insulin aspart and insulin lispro) can also be given by *continuous subcutaneous infusion* using a portable infusion pump. This device delivers a continuous basal insulin infusion and patient-activated bolus doses at meal times. This technique is appropriate only for patients who suffer recurrent hypoglycaemia or marked morning rise in blood-glucose concentration despite optimised multiple-injection regimens. NICE (February 2003) has also recommended continuous subcutaneous infusion as an option in those who suffer repeated or unpredictable hypoglycaemia despite optimal multiple-injection regimens (including the use of insulin glargine where appropriate). Patients on subcutaneous insulin infusion must be highly motivated, able to monitor their blood-glucose concentration, and have expert training, advice and supervision from an experienced healthcare team.

Soluble insulin by the *intravenous route* is reserved for urgent treatment, and for fine control in serious illness and in the perioperative period (see under Diabetes and Surgery, below).

**Units** The word 'unit' should **not** be abbreviated.

**Monitoring** Many patients now monitor their own blood-glucose concentrations (section 6.1.6). Since blood-glucose concentrations vary substantially throughout the day, 'normoglycaemia' cannot always be achieved throughout a 24-hour period without causing damaging hypoglycaemia. It is therefore best to recommend that patients should maintain a blood-glucose concentration of between 4 and 9 mmol/litre for most of the time (4–7 mmol/litre before meals and less than 9 mmol/litre after meals), while accepting that on occasions, for brief periods, it will be above these values; strenuous efforts should be made to prevent the blood-glucose concentration from falling below 4 mmol/litre. Patients should be advised to look for 'peaks' and 'troughs' of blood glucose, and to adjust their insulin dosage only once or twice weekly. Overall it is ideal to aim for an $HbA_{1c}$ (glycosylated haemoglobin) concentration of 6.5–7.5% or less (reference range 4–6%) but this is not always possible without causing disabling hypoglycaemia; in those at risk of arterial disease, the aim should be to maintain the $HbA_{1c}$ concentration at 6.5% or less. $HbA_{1c}$ should be measured every 3–6 months. Fructosamine can also be used for assessment of control; this is simpler and cheaper but the measurement of $HbA_{1c}$ is generally a more reliable method.

The intake of energy and of simple and complex carbohydrates should be adequate to allow normal growth and development but obesity must be avoided. The carbohydrate intake needs to be regulated and should be distributed throughout the day. Fine control of plasma glucose can be achieved by moving portions of carbohydrate from one meal to another without altering the total intake.

**Hypoglycaemia** Hypoglycaemia is a potential problem with insulin therapy. All patients must be carefully instructed on how to avoid it.

Loss of warning of hypoglycaemia is common among insulin-treated patients and can be a serious hazard, especially for drivers and those in dangerous occupations. Very tight control of diabetes lowers the blood-glucose concentration needed to trigger hypoglycaemic symptoms; increase in the frequency of hypoglycaemic episodes reduces the warning symptoms experienced by the patient. Beta-blockers can also blunt hypoglycaemic awareness (and also delay recovery).

To restore the warning signs, episodes of hypoglycaemia must be minimised; this involves appropriate adjustment of insulin type, dose and frequency together with suitable timing and quantity of meals and snacks.

Some patients have reported loss of hypoglycaemia warning after transfer to human insulin. Clinical studies do not confirm that human insulin decreases hypoglycaemia awareness. If a patient believes that human insulin is responsible for the loss of warning it is reasonable to revert to animal insulin and essential to educate the patient about avoiding hypoglycaemia. Great care should be taken to specify whether a human or an animal preparation is required.

Few patients are now treated with beef insulins; when undertaking conversion from beef to human insulin, the total dose should be reduced by about 10% with careful monitoring for the first few days. When changing between pork and human sequence insulins, a dose change is not usually needed, but careful monitoring is still advised.

**Driving** Drivers treated with insulin or oral antidiabetic drugs are required to notify the Driver and Vehicle Licensing Agency of their condition, as are drivers of Group 2 vehicles (heavy goods vehicles or public service vehicles) whose diabetes is controlled by diet alone; the Agency's Drivers Medical Unit provides guidance on eligibility to drive. Driving is not permitted when hypoglycaemic awareness is impaired.

Drivers need to be particularly careful to avoid hypoglycaemia (see also above) and should be warned of the problems. Drivers treated with insulin should normally check their blood-glucose concentration before driving and, on long journeys, at 2-hour intervals; these precautions may also be necessary for drivers taking oral antidiabetic drugs who are at particular risk of hypoglycaemia. Drivers treated with insulin should ensure that a supply of sugar is always available in the vehicle and they should avoid driving if they are late for a meal. If hypoglycaemia occurs, or warning signs develop, the driver should:

- stop the vehicle in a safe place;
- switch off the ignition;
- eat or drink a suitable source of sugar;
- wait until recovery is complete before continuing journey; recovery may take 15 minutes or longer and should preferably be confirmed by checking blood-glucose concentration.

**Diabetes and surgery** The following regimen is suitable when surgery in a patient with type 1 diabetes requires intravenous infusion of insulin for 12 hours or longer.

- Give an injection of the patient's usual insulin on the night before the operation.
- Early on the day of the operation, start an intravenous infusion of glucose 5% or 10% containing potassium chloride 10 mmol/litre (provided that the patient is not hyperkalaemic) and infuse at a con-

stant rate appropriate to the patient's fluid requirements (usually 125 mL per hour); make up a solution of soluble insulin 1 unit/mL in sodium chloride 0.9% and infuse intravenously using a syringe pump piggy-backed to the intravenous infusion.

- The rate of the insulin infusion should normally be:
  Blood glucose < 4 mmol/litre, give 0.5 units/hour
  Blood glucose 4–15 mmol/litre, give 2 units/hour
  Blood glucose 15–20 mmol/litre, give 4 units/hour
  Blood glucose > 20 mmol/litre, review.

In resistant cases (such as patients who are in shock or severely ill or those receiving corticosteroids or sympathomimetics) 2–4 times these rates or even more may be needed.

If a syringe pump is not available soluble insulin 16 units/litre should be added to the intravenous infusion of glucose 5% or 10% containing potassium chloride 10 mmol per litre (provided the patient is not hyperkalaemic) and the infusion run at the rate appropriate to the patient's fluid requirements (usually 125 mL per hour) with the insulin dose adjusted as follows:

Blood glucose < 4 mmol/litre, give 8 units/litre
Blood glucose 4–15 mmol/litre, give 16 units/litre
Blood glucose 15–20 mmol/litre, give 32 units/litre
Blood glucose > 20 mmol/litre, review.

The rate of intravenous infusion depends on the volume depletion, cardiac function, age, and other factors. Blood-glucose concentration should be measured preoperatively and then hourly until stable, thereafter every 2 hours. The duration of action of intravenous insulin is only a few minutes and the infusion must not be stopped unless the patient becomes overtly hypoglycaemic (blood glucose < 3 mmol/litre) in which case it should be stopped for up to 30 minutes. The amount of potassium chloride required in the infusion needs to be assessed by regular measurement of plasma electrolytes. Sodium chloride 0.9% infusion should replace glucose 5% or 10% if the blood glucose is persistently above 15 mmol/litre.

Once the patient starts to eat and drink, give subcutaneous insulin before breakfast and stop intravenous insulin 30 minutes later; the dose may need to be 10–20% more than usual if the patient is still in bed or unwell. If the patient was not previously receiving insulin, an appropriate initial dose is 30–40 units daily in four divided doses using soluble insulin before meals and intermediate-acting insulin at bedtime and the dose adjusted from day to day. Patients with hyperglycaemia often relapse after conversion back to subcutaneous insulin calling for one of the following approaches:

- additional doses of soluble insulin at any of the four injection times (before meals or bedtime) *or*
- temporary addition of intravenous insulin infusion (while continuing the subcutaneous regimen) until blood-glucose concentration is satisfactory *or*
- complete reversion to the intravenous regimen (especially if the patient is unwell).

## 6.1.1.1 Short-acting insulins

**Soluble insulin** is a short-acting form of insulin. For maintenance regimens it is usual to inject it 15 to 30 minutes before meals.

Soluble insulin is the most appropriate form of insulin for use in diabetic emergencies and at the time of surgery. It can be given intravenously and intramuscularly, as well as subcutaneously.

When injected subcutaneously, soluble insulin has a rapid onset of action (30 to 60 minutes), a peak action between 2 and 4 hours, and a duration of action of up to 8 hours.

When injected intravenously, soluble insulin has a very short half-life of only about 5 minutes and its effect disappears within 30 minutes.

The human insulin analogues, **insulin aspart**, **insulin glulisine**, and **insulin lispro** have a faster onset and shorter duration of action than soluble insulin; as a result, compared to soluble insulin, fasting and preprandial blood-glucose concentration is a little higher, postprandial blood-glucose concentration is a little lower, and hypoglycaemia occurs slightly less frequently. Subcutaneous injection of insulin analogues may be convenient for those who wish to inject shortly before or, when necessary, shortly after a meal. They may also help those prone to pre-lunch hypoglycaemia and those who eat late in the evening and are prone to nocturnal hypoglycaemia. They may also be administered by subcutaneous infusion.

### SOLUBLE INSULIN
**(Insulin Injection; Neutral Insulin)**

A sterile solution of insulin (i.e. bovine or porcine) or of human insulin; pH 6.6–8.0

**Indications** diabetes mellitus; diabetic ketoacidosis (section 6.1.3)

**Cautions** see notes above; reduce dose in renal impairment (Appendix 3); **interactions:** Appendix 1 (antidiabetics)

**Side-effects** see notes above; transient oedema; local reactions and fat hypertrophy at injection site; rarely hypersensitivity reactions including urticaria, rash; overdose causes hypoglycaemia

**Dose**
- By subcutaneous, intramuscular, *or* intravenous injection *or* intravenous infusion, according to requirements

Counselling Show container to patient and confirm that patient is expecting the version dispensed

**Highly purified animal**

**Hypurin® Bovine Neutral** (CP) PoM
Injection, soluble insulin (bovine, highly purified) 100 units/mL. Net price 10-mL vial = £18.48; cartridges (for *Autopen®* devices) 5 × 1.5 mL = £13.86, 5 × 3 mL = £27.72

**Hypurin® Porcine Neutral** (CP) PoM
Injection, soluble insulin (porcine, highly purified) 100 units/mL. Net price 10-mL vial = £16.80; cartridges (for *Autopen®* devices) 5 × 1.5 mL = £12.60, 5 × 3 mL = £25.20

**Pork Actrapid®** (Novo Nordisk) PoM
Injection, soluble insulin (porcine, highly purified) 100 units/mL. Net price 10-mL vial = £4.00
Note Not recommended for use in subcutaneous insulin infusion pumps—may precipitate in catheter or needle

**Human sequence**

**Actrapid®** (Novo Nordisk) PoM
Injection, soluble insulin (human, pyr) 100 units/mL. Net price 10-mL vial = £7.48
Note Not recommended for use in subcutaneous insulin infusion pumps—may precipitate in catheter or needle

**Velosulin®** (Novo Nordisk) PoM
Injection, soluble insulin (human, pyr) 100 units/mL. Net price 10-mL vial = £7.48

**Humulin S®** (Lilly) PoM
Injection, soluble insulin (human, prb) 100 units/mL. Net price 10-mL vial = £15.00; 5 × 3-mL cartridge (for most *Autopen®* devices or *HumaPen®*) = £25.56

**Insuman® Rapid** (Aventis Pharma) ▼ PoM
Injection, soluble insulin (human, crb) 100 units/mL, net price 5 × 3-mL cartridge (for *OptiPen® Pro 1* NHS) = £23.43; 5 × 3-mL *Insuman® Rapid OptiSet®* prefilled disposable injection devices (range 2–40 units, allowing 2-unit dosage adjustment) = £27.90
Note Not recommended for use in subcutaneous insulin infusion pumps

**Mixed preparations**

See Biphasic Isophane Insulin (section 6.1.1.2)

## INSULIN ASPART
**(Recombinant human insulin analogue)**

**Indications** diabetes mellitus

**Cautions** see under Soluble Insulin; children (use only if benefit likely compared to soluble insulin)

**Side-effects** see under Soluble Insulin

**Dose**
- By subcutaneous injection, immediately before meals or when necessary shortly after meals, according to requirements
- By subcutaneous infusion, intravenous injection *or* intravenous infusion, according to requirements

Counselling Show container to patient and confirm that patient is expecting the version dispensed

**NovoRapid®** (Novo Nordisk) PoM
Injection, insulin aspart (recombinant human insulin analogue) 100 units/mL, net price 10-mL vial = £17.27; *Penfill®* cartridge (for *Innovo®* and *NovoPen®* devices) 5 × 3-mL = £29.43; 5 × 3-mL *FlexPen®* prefilled disposable injection devices (range 1–60 units, allowing 1-unit dosage adjustment) = £32.00

## INSULIN GLULISINE
**(Recombinant human insulin analogue)**

**Indications** diabetes mellitus

**Cautions** see under Soluble Insulin

**Side-effects** see under Soluble Insulin

**Dose**
- By subcutaneous injection, immediately before meals or when necessary shortly after meals, according to requirements
- By subcutaneous infusion, according to requirements
- CHILD and ADOLESCENT not recomended

Counselling Show container to patient and confirm that patient is expecting the version dispensed

**Apidra®** (Sanofi-Aventis) ▼ PoM
Injection, insulin glulisine (recombinant human insulin analogue) 100 units/mL, net price 10-mL vial = £17.27; 5× 3-mL cartridge (for *OptiPen® Pro 1* NHS) =£29.45

## INSULIN LISPRO
**(Recombinant human insulin analogue)**

**Indications** diabetes mellitus

**Cautions** see under Soluble Insulin; children (use only if benefit likely compared to soluble insulin)

**Side-effects** see under Soluble Insulin

**Dose**
- By subcutaneous injection shortly before meals or when necessary shortly after meals, according to requirements
- By subcutaneous infusion, *or* intravenous injection, *or* intravenous infusion, according to requirements

Counselling Show container to patient and confirm that patient is expecting the version dispensed

**Humalog®** (Lilly) PoM
Injection, insulin lispro (recombinant human insulin analogue) 100 units/mL. Net price 10-mL vial = £17.28; 5 × 3-mL cartridge (for most *Autopen®* devices or *HumaPen®* ) = £29.46; 5 × 3-mL *Humalog®-Pen* prefilled disposable injection devices (range 1–60 units, allowing 1-unit dosage adjustment) = £29.46

## 6.1.1.2 Intermediate- and long-acting insulins

When given by subcutaneous injection, intermediate- and long-acting insulins have an onset of action of approximately 1–2 hours, a maximal effect at 4–12 hours, and a duration of 16–35 hours. Some are given twice daily in conjunction with short-acting (soluble) insulin, and others are given once daily, particularly in elderly patients. Soluble insulin can be mixed with intermediate and long-acting insulins (except insulin detemir and insulin glargine) in the syringe, essentially retaining the properties of the two components, although there may be some blunting of the initial effect of the soluble insulin component (especially on mixing with protamine zinc insulin, see below).

**Isophane insulin** is a suspension of insulin with protamine which is of particular value for initiation of twice-daily insulin regimens. Patients usually mix isophane with soluble insulin but ready-mixed preparations may be appropriate (**biphasic isophane insulin**, **biphasic insulin aspart**, or **biphasic insulin lispro**).

**Insulin zinc suspension (crystalline)** has a more prolonged duration of action; it may be used independently or in **insulin zinc suspension** (30% amorphous, 70% crystalline).

**Protamine zinc insulin** is usually given once daily with short-acting (soluble) insulin. It has the drawback of binding with the soluble insulin when mixed in the same syringe, and is now rarely used.

**Insulin glargine** and **insulin detemir** are both human insulin analogues with a prolonged duration of action; insulin glargine is given once daily and insulin detemir is given once or twice daily.

**NICE guidance (insulin glargine)**

NICE has recommended (December 2002) that insulin glargine should be available as an option for patients with type 1 diabetes.

Insulin glargine is **not** recommended for routine use in patients with type 2 diabetes who require insulin, but it may be considered in type 2 diabetes for those:

- who require assistance with injecting their insulin; *or*
- whose lifestyle is significantly restricted by recurrent symptomatic hypoglycaemia; *or*
- who would otherwise need twice-daily basal insulin injections in combination with oral anti-diabetic drugs

## INSULIN DETEMIR

**(Recombinant human insulin analogue—long acting)**

**Indications** diabetes mellitus

**Cautions** see under Soluble Insulin (section 6.1.1.1); pregnancy (Appendix 4)

**Side-effects** see under Soluble Insulin (section 6.1.1.1)

**Dose**

- By subcutaneous injection, ADULT and CHILD over 6 years, according to requirements

Counselling Show container to patient and confirm that patient is expecting the version dispensed

**Levemir®** (Novo Nordisk) ▼ PoM

Injection, insulin detemir (recombinant human insulin analogue) 100 units/mL, net price 5 × 3-mL cartridge (for *NovoPen®* devices) = £39.00; 5 × 3-mL *FlexPen®* prefilled disposable injection device (range 1–60 units, allowing 1-unit dosage adjustment) = £39.00.

## INSULIN GLARGINE

**(Recombinant human insulin analogue—long acting)**

**Indications** diabetes mellitus

**Cautions** see under Soluble Insulin (section 6.1.1.1); pregnancy (Appendix 4)

**Side-effects** see under Soluble Insulin (section 6.1.1.1)

**Dose**

- By subcutaneous injection, ADULT and CHILD over 6 years, according to requirements

Counselling Show container to patient and confirm that patient is expecting the version dispensed

**Lantus®** (Aventis Pharma) ▼ PoM

Injection, insulin glargine (recombinant human insulin analogue) 100 units/mL, net price 10-mL vial = £26.00; 5 × 3-mL cartridge (for *OptiPen® Pro 1*) = £39.00; 5 × 3-mL *Lantus® OptiSet®* prefilled disposable injection devices (range 2–40 units, allowing 2-unit dosage adjustment) = £39.00

## INSULIN ZINC SUSPENSION

**(Insulin Zinc Suspension (Mixed); I. Z. S.—long acting)**

A sterile neutral suspension of bovine and/or porcine insulin or of human insulin in the form of a complex obtained by the addition of a suitable zinc salt; consists of rhombohedral crystals (10–40 microns) and of particles of no uniform shape (not exceeding 2 microns)

**Indications** diabetes mellitus

**Cautions** see under Soluble Insulin (section 6.1.1.1)

**Side-effects** see under Soluble Insulin (section 6.1.1.1)

**Dose**

- By subcutaneous injection, according to requirements

Counselling Show container to patient and confirm that patient is expecting the version dispensed

**Highly purified animal**

**Hypurin® Bovine Lente** (CP) PoM

Injection, insulin zinc suspension (bovine, highly purified) 100 units/mL. Net price 10-mL vial = £18.48

## ISOPHANE INSULIN

**(Isophane Insulin Injection; Isophane Protamine Insulin Injection; Isophane Insulin (NPH)—intermediate acting)**

A sterile suspension of bovine or porcine insulin or of human insulin in the form of a complex obtained by the addition of protamine sulphate or another suitable protamine

**Indications** diabetes mellitus

**Cautions** see under Soluble Insulin (section 6.1.1.1)

**Side-effects** see under Soluble Insulin (section 6.1.1.1); protamine may cause allergic reactions

**Dose**

- By subcutaneous injection, according to requirements

Counselling Show container to patient and confirm that patient is expecting the version dispensed

**Highly purified animal**

**Hypurin® Bovine Isophane** (CP) PoM

Injection, isophane insulin (bovine, highly purified) 100 units/mL. Net price 10-mL vial = £18.48; cartridges (for *Autopen®* devices) 5 × 1.5 mL = £13.86, 5 × 3 mL = £27.72

**Hypurin® Porcine Isophane** (CP) PoM

Injection, isophane insulin (porcine, highly purified) 100 units/mL. Net price 10-mL vial = £16.80; cartridges (for *Autopen®* devices) 5 × 1.5 mL = £12.60, 5 × 3 mL = £25.20

**Pork Insulatard®** (Novo Nordisk) PoM

Injection, isophane insulin (porcine, highly purified) 100 units/mL. Net price 10-mL vial = £4.00

**Human sequence**

**Insulatard®** (Novo Nordisk) PoM

Injection, isophane insulin (human, pyr) 100 units/mL. Net price 10-mL vial = £7.48; *Insulatard Penfill®* cartridge (for *Innovo®*, or *Novopen®* devices) 5 × 3 mL = £20.08; 5 × 3-mL *Insulatard InnoLet®* prefilled disposable injection devices (range 1–50 units, allowing 1-unit dosage adjustment) = £20.40

**Humulin I®** (Lilly) PoM

Injection, isophane insulin (human, prb) 100 units/mL. Net price 10-mL vial = £15.00; 5 × 3-mL cartridge (for most *Autopen®* devices or *HumaPen®*) = £27.22; 5 × 3-mL *Humulin I-Pen®* prefilled disposable injection devices (range 1–60 units, allowing 1-unit dosage adjustment) = £27.22

**Insuman® Basal** (Aventis Pharma) ▼ PoM

Injection, isophane insulin (human, crb) 100 units/mL, net price 5-mL vial = £5.84; 5 × 3-mL cartridge (for *OptiPen® Pro 1* NHS) = £23.43; 5 × 3-mL *Insuman® Basal OptiSet®* prefilled disposable injection devices (range 2–40 units, allowing 2-unit dosage adjustment) = £27.90

◢Mixed preparations
See Biphasic Isophane Insulin (below)

## PROTAMINE ZINC INSULIN
### (Protamine Zinc Insulin Injection—long acting)

A sterile suspension of insulin in the form of a complex obtained by the addition of a suitable protamine and zinc chloride; this preparation was included in BP 1980 but is not included in BP 1988

**Indications** diabetes mellitus

**Cautions** see under Soluble Insulin (section 6.1.1.1); see also notes above

**Side-effects** see under Soluble Insulin (section 6.1.1.1); protamine may cause allergic reactions

**Dose**

- By subcutaneous injection, according to requirements
  Counselling Show container to patient and confirm that patient is expecting the version dispensed

**Hypurin® Bovine Protamine Zinc** (CP) PoM
Injection, protamine zinc insulin (bovine, highly purified) 100 units/mL. Net price 10-mL vial = £18.48

## Biphasic insulins

## BIPHASIC INSULIN ASPART
### (Intermediate-acting insulin)

**Indications** diabetes mellitus

**Cautions** see under Soluble Insulin and Insulin Aspart (section 6.1.1.1)

**Side-effects** see under Soluble Insulin (section 6.1.1.1); protamine may cause allergic reactions

**Dose**

- By subcutaneous injection, up to 10 minutes before or soon after a meal, according to requirements
  Counselling Show container to patient and confirm that patient is expecting the version dispensed; the proportions of the two components should be checked **carefully** (the order in which the proportions are stated may not be the same in other countries)

**NovoMix® 30** (Novo Nordisk) PoM
Injection, biphasic insulin aspart (recombinant human insulin analogue), 30% insulin aspart, 70% insulin aspart protamine, 100 units/mL, net price 5 × 3-mL *Penfill®* cartridges (for *Innovo®* and *NovoPen®* devices) = £29.43; 5 × 3-mL *FlexPen®* prefilled disposable injection devices (range 1–60 units, allowing 1-unit dosage adjustment) = £32.00

## BIPHASIC INSULIN LISPRO
### (Intermediate-acting insulin)

**Indications** diabetes mellitus

**Cautions** see under Soluble Insulin and Insulin Lispro (section 6.1.1.1)

**Side-effects** see under Soluble Insulin (section 6.1.1.1); protamine may cause allergic reactions

**Dose**

- By subcutaneous injection, up to 15 minutes before or soon after a meal, according to requirements
  Counselling Show container to patient and confirm that patient is expecting the version dispensed; the proportions of the two components should be checked **carefully** (the order in which the proportions are stated may not be the same in other countries)

**Humalog® Mix25** (Lilly) PoM
Injection, biphasic insulin lispro (recombinant human insulin analogue), 25% insulin lispro, 75% insulin lispro protamine, 100 units/mL, net price 5 × 3-mL cartridge (for most *Autopen®* devices or *HumaPen®*) = £29.46; 5 × 3-mL prefilled disposable injection devices (range 1–60 units, allowing 1-unit dosage adjustment) = £30.98

**Humalog® Mix50** (Lilly) PoM
Injection, biphasic insulin lispro (recombinant human insulin analogue), 50% insulin lispro, 50% insulin lispro protamine, 100 units/mL, net price 5 × 3-mL prefilled disposable injection devices (range 1–60 units, allowing 1-unit dosage adjustment) = £30.98

## BIPHASIC ISOPHANE INSULIN
### (Biphasic Isophane Insulin Injection—intermediate acting)

A sterile buffered suspension of either porcine or human insulin complexed with protamine sulphate (or another suitable protamine) in a solution of insulin of the same species

**Indications** diabetes mellitus

**Cautions** see under Soluble Insulin (section 6.1.1.1)

**Side-effects** see under Soluble Insulin (section 6.1.1.1); protamine may cause allergic reactions

**Dose**

- By subcutaneous injection, according to requirements
  Counselling Show container to patient and confirm that patient is expecting the version dispensed; the proportions of the two components should be checked **carefully** (the order in which the proportions are stated may not be the same in other countries)

◢Highly purified animal

**Hypurin® Porcine 30/70 Mix** (CP) PoM
Injection, biphasic isophane insulin (porcine, highly purified), 30% soluble, 70% isophane, 100 units/mL. Net price 10-mL vial = £16.80; cartridges (for *Autopen®* devices) 5 × 1.5 ml = £12.60, 5 × 3 mL = £25.20

**Pork Mixtard 30®** (Novo Nordisk) PoM
Injection, biphasic isophane insulin (porcine, highly purified), 30% soluble, 70% isophane, 100 units/mL. Net price 10-mL vial = £4.00

◢Human sequence

**Mixtard® 10** (Novo Nordisk) PoM
Injection, biphasic isophane insulin (human, pyr), 10% soluble, 90% isophane, 100 units/mL. Net price *Mixtard 10 Penfill®* cartridge (for *Innovo®* or *Novopen®* devices) 5 × 3 mL = £20.08

**Mixtard® 20** (Novo Nordisk) PoM
Injection, biphasic isophane insulin (human, pyr), 20% soluble, 80% isophane, 100 units/mL. Net price *Mixtard 20 Penfill®* cartridge (for *Innovo®* or *Novopen®* devices) 5 × 3 mL = £20.08

**Mixtard® 30** (Novo Nordisk) PoM
Injection, biphasic isophane insulin (human, pyr), 30% soluble, 70% isophane, 100 units/mL. Net price

10-mL vial = £7.48; *Mixtard 30 Penfill*® cartridge (for *Innovo*® or *Novopen*® devices) 5 × 3 mL = £20.08; 5 × 3-mL *Mixtard 30 InnoLet*® prefilled disposable injection devices (range 1–50 units allowing 1-unit dosage adjustment) = £19.87

**Mixtard® 40** (Novo Nordisk) PoM
Injection, biphasic isophane insulin (human, pyr), 40% soluble, 60% isophane, 100 units/mL. Net price *Mixtard 40 Penfill*® cartridge (for *Innovo*® or *Novopen*® devices) 5 × 3 mL = £20.08

**Mixtard® 50** (Novo Nordisk) PoM
Injection, biphasic isophane insulin (human, pyr), 50% soluble, 50% isophane, 100 units/mL. Net price *Mixtard 50 Penfill*® cartridge (for *Innovo*® or *Novopen*® devices) 5 × 3 mL = £20.08

**Humulin M3®** (Lilly) PoM
Injection, biphasic isophane insulin (human, prb), 30% soluble, 70% isophane, 100 units/mL. Net price 10-mL vial = £15.00; 5 × 3-mL cartridge (for most *Autopen*® devices or *HumaPen*®) = £25.56

**Insuman® Comb 15** (Aventis Pharma) ▼ PoM
Injection, biphasic isophane insulin (human, crb), 15% soluble, 85% isophane, 100 units/mL, net price 5 × 3-mL *Insuman*® *Comb 15 OptiSet*® prefilled disposable injection devices (range 2–40 units, allowing 2-unit dosage adjustment) = £27.90

**Insuman® Comb 25** (Aventis Pharma) ▼ PoM
Injection, biphasic isophane insulin (human, crb), 25% soluble, 75% isophane, 100 units/mL, net price 5-mL vial = £5.84; 5 × 3-mL cartridge (for *OptiPen*® *Pro 1* NHS) = £23.43; 5 × 3-mL *Insuman*® *Comb 25 OptiSet*® prefilled disposable injection devices (range 2–40 units, allowing 2-unit dosage adjustment) = £27.90

**Insuman® Comb 50** (Aventis Pharma) ▼ PoM
Injection, biphasic isophane insulin (human, crb), 50% soluble, 50% isophane, 100 units/mL, net price 5 × 3-mL cartridge (for *OptiPen*® *Pro 1* NHS) = £23.43; 5 × 3-mL *Insuman*® *Comb 50 OptiSet*® prefilled disposable injection devices (range 2–40 units, allowing 2-unit dosage adjustment) = £27.90

## 6.1.1.3 Hypodermic equipment

Patients should be advised on the safe disposal of lancets, single-use syringes, and needles. Suitable arrangements for the safe disposal of contaminated waste must be made before these products are prescribed for patients who are carriers of infectious diseases.

### Injection devices

**Autopen®** (Owen Mumford)
Injection device, *Autopen*® *24* (for use with Aventis 3-mL insulin cartridges), allows adjustments of dosage in multiples of 1 unit, max. 21 units (single-unit version) *or* 2 units, max. 42 units (2 unit version), net price (both) = £14.70; *Autopen*® *Classic*, *Autopen*® *Special Edition*, and *Autopen*® *Junior* (for use with Lilly 3-mL insulin cartridges), all allow adjustment of dosage in multiples of 1 unit, max. 21 units (single-unit version) *or* 2 units, max. 42 units (2-unit version), net price (all) = £14.92

**HumaPen® Ergo** (Lilly)
Injection device, for use with *Humulin*® and *Humalog*® 3-mL cartridges; allows adjustment of dosage in multiples of 1 unit, max. 60 units, net price = £22.39 (available in burgundy and teal)

**HumaPen® Luxura** (Lilly)
Injection device, for use with *Humulin*® and *Humalog*® 3-mL cartridges; allows adjustment of dosage in multiples of 1 unit, max. 60 units, net price = £26.36

**Innovo®** (Novo Nordisk)
Injection device, for use with 3-mL *Penfill*® insulin cartridges; allows adjustment of dosage in multiples of 1 unit, max. 70 units, net price = £26.88 (available in green or orange)

**mhi-500®** (Medical House)
Needle-free insulin delivery device NHS for use with any 10-mL vial *or* any 3-mL cartridge of insulin (except the Novo Nordisk 3 mL penfills), allows adjustment of dosage in multiples of 0.5 units, max. 50 units, net price *starter pack* NHS for 10-mL adaptor (*mhi-500*® device, 5 nozzles, 2 insulin vial adaptors) = £122.12, for 3-mL adaptor = (*mhi-500*® device, 5 nozzles, 2 insulin cartridge adaptors) = £120.00; *3-month consumables pack* for 10-mL adaptor (13 nozzles, 5 insulin vial adaptors) = £22.54, for 3-mL adaptor (13 nozzles, 5 insulin cartridge adaptors) = £34.45; *vial adaptor pack* (6 insulin vial adaptors) = £7.51, *cartridge adaptor pack* (6 insulin cartridge adaptors) = £7.38; *nozzle pack* (6 nozzles) = £7.51

**NovoPen®** (Novo Nordisk)
Injection device; for use with *Penfill*® insulin cartridges; *NovoPen*® *Junior* (for 3-mL cartridges), allows adjustment of dosage in multiples of 0.5 units, max. 35 units, net price = £23.66; *NovoPen*® *3 Demi* (for 3-mL cartridges), allows adjustment of dosage in multiples of 0.5 units, max. 35 units, net price = £24.07; *NovoPen*® *3 Classic* or *Fun* (for 3-mL cartridges), allows adjustment of dosage in multiples of 1 unit, max. 70 units, net price = £24.07

**OptiPen® Pro 1** (Aventis Pharma)
Injection device, for use with *Insuman*® insulin cartridges; allows adjustment of dosage in multiples of 1 unit, max. 60 units, net price = £22.00

### Lancets

**Lancets—sterile, single use** (Drug Tariff)
*Ascensia Microlet*® 100 = £3.55, 200 = £6.76; *BD Micro-Fine*®+ 100 = £3.16, 200 = £6.13; *Cleanlet Fine*® 100 = £3.19, 200 = £6.13; *Finepoint*® 100 = £3.48; *FreeStyle*® 200 = £6.50; *GlucoMen*® Fine 100 = £3.42, 200 = £6.61; *Hypoguard Supreme*® 100 = £2.75; *MediSense Thin*® 200 = £6.63; *Milward Steri-Let*®, 23 gauge, 100 = £3.00, 200 = £5.70, 28 gauge, 100 = £3.00, 200 = £5.70; *Monolet*® 100 = £3.28, 200 = £6.24; *Monolet Extra* 100 = £3.28; *One Touch UltraSoft*® 100 = £3.49; [1] *Softclix*® 200 = £6.93; [1] *Softclix XL*® 50 = £1.73; [2] *Unilet ComforTouch*® 100 = £3.40, 200 = £6.44; [2] *Unilet General Purpose*® 100 = £3.47, 200 = £6.59; [2] *Unilet General Purpose Superlite*® 100 = £3.46, 200 = £6.56; [3] *Unilet Superlite*® 100 = £3.46, 200 = £6.56; *Vitrex Soft*®, 23-gauge, 100 = £3.00, 200 = £5.70; *Vitrex Gentle*® 28-gauge, 100 = £3.19, 200 = £6.13

Compatible finger-pricking devices (unless indicated otherwise, see footnotes), all NHS: *B-D Lancer*®, *Glucolet*®, *Monojector*®, *Penlet II*®, *Soft Touch*®

1. Use NHS *Softclix*® finger-pricking device
2. NHS *Autolet*® and NHS *Autolet Impression*® are also compatible finger-pricking devices
3. Use NHS *Autolet*®, or NHS *Glucolet*® finger-pricking devices

### Needles

**Hypodermic Needle, Sterile single use** (Drug Tariff)
For use with reusable glass syringe, sizes 0.5 mm (25G), 0.45 mm (26G), 0.4 mm (27G). Net price 100-needle pack = £2.53

Brands include *Microlance*®, *Monoject*®

**Needles for Prefilled and Reusable Pen Injectors** (Drug Tariff)
Screw on, needle length 6.1 mm or less, net price 100-needle pack = £12.08; 6.2–9.9 mm, 100-needle pack = £8.57; 10 mm or more, 100-needle pack = £8.57

Brands include *BD Micro-Fine*®+, *NovoFine*®, *Unifine*® *Pentips*

Snap on, needle length 6.1 mm or less, net price 100-needle pack = £11.82; 6.2–9.9 mm, 100-needle pack = £8.38; 10 mm or more, 100-needle pack = £8.38

Brands include *Penfine*®

### Syringes

**Hypodermic Syringe** (Drug Tariff)

Calibrated glass with Luer taper conical fitting, for use with U100 insulin. Net price 0.5 mL and 1 mL = £15.18

Brands include *Abcare®*

**Pre-Set U100 Insulin Syringe** (Drug Tariff)

Calibrated glass with Luer taper conical fitting, supplied with dosage chart and strong box, for blind patients. Net price 1 mL = £21.99

**U100 Insulin Syringe with Needle** (Drug Tariff)

Disposable with fixed or separate needle for single use or single patient-use, colour coded orange. Needle length 8 mm, diameters 0.33 mm (29G), 0.3 mm (30G), net price 10 (with needle), 0.3 mL = £1.27, 0.5 mL = £1.23; needle length 12 mm, diameters 0.45 mm (26G), 0.4 mm (27G), 0.36 mm (28G), 0.33 mm (29G), net price 10 (with needle), 0.3 mL = £1.37; 0.5 mL = £1.32; 1 mL = £1.33

Brands include *BD Micro-Fine®+*, *Clinipak®*, *Insupak®*, *Monoject® Ultra*, *Omnikan®*, *Plastipak®*, *Unifine®*

### Accessories

**Needle Clipping (Chopping) Device** (Drug Tariff)

Consisting of a clipper to remove needle from its hub and container from which cut-off needles cannot be retrieved; designed to hold 1200 needles, not suitable for use with lancets. Net price = £1.24

Brands include *BD Safe-Clip®*

**Sharpsbin** (Drug Tariff)

Net price 1-litre sharpsbin = 85p

## 6.1.2 Oral antidiabetic drugs

**6.1.2.1 Sulphonylureas**
**6.1.2.2 Biguanides**
**6.1.2.3 Other antidiabetics**

Oral antidiabetic drugs are used for the treatment of type 2 (non-insulin-dependent) diabetes mellitus. They should be prescribed only if the patient fails to respond adequately to at least 3 months' restriction of energy and carbohydrate intake and an increase in physical activity. They should be used to augment the effect of diet and exercise, and not to replace them.

For patients not adequately controlled by diet and oral hypoglycaemic drugs, insulin may be added to the treatment regimen or substituted for oral therapy. When insulin is added to oral therapy, it is generally given at bedtime as isophane insulin, and when insulin replaces an oral regimen it is generally given as twice-daily injections of a biphasic insulin (or isophane insulin mixed with soluble insulin). Weight gain and hypoglycaemia may be complications of insulin therapy but weight gain may be reduced if the insulin is given in combination with metformin.

### 6.1.2.1 Sulphonylureas

The sulphonylureas act mainly by augmenting insulin secretion and consequently are effective only when some residual pancreatic beta-cell activity is present; during long-term administration they also have an extrapancreatic action. All may cause hypoglycaemia but this is uncommon and usually indicates excessive dosage. Sulphonylurea-induced hypoglycaemia may persist for many hours and must always be treated in hospital.

Sulphonylureas are considered for patients who are not overweight, or in whom metformin is contra-indicated or not tolerated. Several sulphonylureas are available and choice is determined by side-effects and the duration of action as well as the patient's age and renal function. The long-acting sulphonylureas **chlorpropamide** and **glibenclamide** are associated with a greater risk of hypoglycaemia; for this reason they should be avoided in the elderly and shorter-acting alternatives, such as **gliclazide** or **tolbutamide**, should be used instead. Chlorpropamide also has more side-effects than the other sulphonylureas (see below) and therefore it is no longer recommended.

When the combination of strict diet and sulphonylurea treatment fails other options include:

- combining with metformin (section 6.1.2.2) (reports of increased hazard with this combination remain unconfirmed);
- combining with acarbose (section 6.1.2.3), which may have a small beneficial effect, but flatulence can be a problem;
- combining with pioglitazone or rosiglitazone, but see section 6.1.2.3;
- combining with bedtime isophane insulin (section 6.1.1) but weight gain and hypoglycaemia can occur.

Insulin therapy should be instituted temporarily during intercurrent illness (such as myocardial infarction, coma, infection, and trauma). Sulphonylureas should be omitted on the morning of surgery; insulin is required because of the ensuing hyperglycaemia in these circumstances.

**Cautions** Sulphonylureas can encourage weight gain and should be prescribed only if poor control and symptoms persist despite adequate attempts at dieting; metformin (section 6.1.2.2) is considered the drug of choice in obese patients. Caution is needed in the elderly and in those with mild to moderate hepatic (Appendix 2) and renal impairment (Appendix 3) because of the hazard of hypoglycaemia. The short-acting tolbutamide may be used in renal impairment, as may gliquidone and gliclazide which are principally metabolised in the liver, but careful monitoring of blood-glucose concentration is essential; care is required to choose the smallest possible dose that produces adequate control of blood glucose.

**Contra-indications** Sulphonylureas should be avoided where possible in severe hepatic (Appendix 2) and renal (Appendix 3) impairment and in porphyria (section 9.8.2). They should not be used while breast-feeding and insulin therapy should be substituted during pregnancy (see also Appendix 4). Sulphonylureas are contra-indicated in the presence of ketoacidosis.

**Side-effects** Side-effects of sulphonylureas are generally mild and infrequent and include gastro-intestinal disturbances such as nausea, vomiting, diarrhoea and constipation.

Chlorpropamide has appreciably more side-effects, mainly because of its very prolonged duration of action and the consequent hazard of hypoglycaemia and it should no longer be used. It may also cause facial flushing after drinking alcohol; this effect does not normally occur with other sulphonylureas. Chlorpropamide may also enhance antidiuretic hormone secretion and very rarely cause hyponatraemia (hyponatraemia is also reported with glimepiride and glipizide).

Sulphonylureas can occasionally cause a disturbance in liver function, which may rarely lead to cholestatic jaundice, hepatitis and hepatic failure. Hypersensitivity reactions can occur, usually in the first 6–8 weeks of therapy, they consist mainly of allergic skin reactions which progress rarely to erythema multiforme and exfoliative dermatitis, fever and jaundice; photosensitivity has rarely been reported with chlorpropamide and glipizide. Blood disorders are also rare but may include leucopenia, thrombocytopenia, agranulocytosis, pancytopenia, haemolytic anaemia, and aplastic anaemia.

## CHLORPROPAMIDE

**Indications** type 2 diabetes mellitus (for use in diabetes insipidus, see section 6.5.2)

**Cautions** see notes above; **interactions:** Appendix 1 (antidiabetics)

**Contra-indications** see notes above

**Side-effects** see notes above

**Dose**

- Initially 250 mg daily with breakfast (ELDERLY 100–125 mg but avoid—see notes above), adjusted according to response; max. 500 mg daily

**Chlorpropamide** (Non-proprietary) PoM

Tablets, chlorpropamide 100 mg, net price 20 = £1.70; 250 mg, 20 = £2.00. Label: 4

## GLIBENCLAMIDE

**Indications** type 2 diabetes mellitus

**Cautions** see notes above; **interactions:** Appendix 1 (antidiabetics)

**Contra-indications** see notes above

**Side-effects** see notes above

**Dose**

- Initially 5 mg daily with or immediately after breakfast (ELDERLY 2.5 mg, but avoid—see notes above), adjusted according to response; max. 15 mg daily

**Glibenclamide** (Non-proprietary) PoM

Tablets, glibenclamide 2.5 mg, net price 28-tab pack = 78p; 5 mg, 28-tab pack = 95p

**Daonil®** (Hoechst Marion Roussel) PoM

Tablets, scored, glibenclamide 5 mg. Net price 28-tab pack = £2.69

**Semi-Daonil®** (Hoechst Marion Roussel) PoM

Tablets, scored, glibenclamide 2.5 mg. Net price 28-tab pack = £1.73

**Euglucon®** (Aventis Pharma) PoM

Tablets, glibenclamide 2.5 mg, net price 28-tab pack = £1.72

## GLICLAZIDE

**Indications** type 2 diabetes mellitus

**Cautions** see notes above; **interactions:** Appendix 1 (antidiabetics)

**Contra-indications** see notes above

**Side-effects** see notes above

**Dose**

- Initially, 40–80 mg daily, adjusted according to response; up to 160 mg as a single dose, with breakfast; higher doses divided; max. 320 mg daily

**Gliclazide** (Non-proprietary) PoM

Tablets, scored, gliclazide 80 mg, net price 28-tab pack = £1.62, 60-tab pack = £1.87

Brands include *DIAGLYK®*

**Diamicron®** (Servier) PoM

Tablets, scored, gliclazide 80 mg, net price 60-tab pack = £6.51

### Modified release

**Diamicron® MR** (Servier) PoM

Tablets, m/r, gliclazide 30 mg, net price 28-tab pack = £4.40, 56-tab pack = £8.80. Label: 25

Dose initially 30 mg daily with breakfast, adjusted according to response every 4 weeks (after 2 weeks if no decrease in blood glucose); max. 120 mg daily

Note *Diamicron® MR* 30 mg may be considered to be approximately equivalent in therapeutic effect to standard formulation *Diamicron®* 80 mg

## GLIMEPIRIDE

**Indications** type 2 diabetes mellitus

**Cautions** see notes above; manufacturer recommends regular hepatic and haematological monitoring but limited evidence of clinical value; **interactions:** Appendix 1 (antidiabetics)

**Contra-indications** see notes above

**Side-effects** see notes above

**Dose**

- Initially 1 mg daily, adjusted according to response in 1-mg steps at 1–2 week intervals; usual max. 4 mg daily (exceptionally, up to 6 mg daily may be used); taken shortly before or with first main meal

**Amaryl®** (Hoechst Marion Roussel) PoM

Tablets, all scored, glimepiride 1 mg (pink), net price 30-tab pack = £4.51; 2 mg (green), 30-tab pack = £7.42; 3 mg (yellow), 30-tab pack = £11.19; 4 mg (blue), 30-tab pack = £14.82

## GLIPIZIDE

**Indications** type 2 diabetes mellitus

**Cautions** see notes above; **interactions:** Appendix 1 (antidiabetics)

**Contra-indications** see notes above

**Side-effects** see notes above; also dizziness, drowsiness

**Dose**

- Initially 2.5–5 mg daily shortly before breakfast or lunch, adjusted according to response; max. 20 mg daily; up to 15 mg may be given as a single dose; higher doses divided

**Glipizide** (Non-proprietary) PoM

Tablets, glipizide 5 mg, 56-tab pack = £3.94

**Glibenese®** (Pfizer) PoM

Tablets, scored, glipizide 5 mg. Net price 56-tab pack = £4.36

**Minodiab®** (Pharmacia) PoM

Tablets, glipizide 2.5 mg, net price 28-tab pack = £1.48; 5 mg (scored), 28-tab pack = £1.26

## GLIQUIDONE

**Indications** type 2 diabetes mellitus

**Cautions** see notes above; **interactions:** Appendix 1 (antidiabetics)

**Contra-indications** see notes above

**Side-effects** see notes above

**Dose**

- Initially 15 mg daily before breakfast, adjusted to 45–60 mg daily in 2 or 3 divided doses; max. single dose 60 mg, max. daily dose 180 mg

**Glurenorm®** (Sanofi-Synthelabo) PoM

Tablets, scored, gliquidone 30 mg. Net price 100-tab pack = £17.54

## TOLBUTAMIDE

**Indications** type 2 diabetes mellitus

**Cautions** see notes above; **interactions:** Appendix 1 (antidiabetics)

**Contra-indications** see notes above

**Side-effects** see notes above; also headache, tinnitus

**Dose**

- 0.5–1.5 g (max. 2 g) daily in divided doses (see notes above); with or immediately after breakfast

**Tolbutamide** (Non-proprietary) PoM

Tablets, tolbutamide 500 mg. Net price 28-tab pack = £1.70

## 6.1.2.2 Biguanides

**Metformin**, the only available biguanide, has a different mode of action from the sulphonylureas, and is not interchangeable with them. It exerts its effect mainly by decreasing gluconeogenesis and by increasing peripheral utilisation of glucose; since it acts only in the presence of endogenous insulin it is effective only if there are some residual functioning pancreatic islet cells.

Metformin is the drug of first choice in overweight patients in whom strict dieting has failed to control diabetes, if appropriate it may also be considered as an option in patients who are not overweight. It is also used when diabetes is inadequately controlled with sulphonylurea treatment. When the combination of strict diet and metformin treatment fails, other options include:

- combining with acarbose (section 6.1.2.3), which may have a small beneficial effect, but flatulence can be a problem;
- combining with insulin (section 6.1.1) but weight gain and hypoglycaemia can be problems (weight gain minimised if insulin given at night);
- combining with a sulphonylurea (section 6.1.2.1) (reports of increased hazard with this combination remain unconfirmed);
- combining with pioglitazone or rosiglitazone (section 6.1.2.3);
- combining with repaglinide or nateglinide (section 6.1.2.3).

Insulin treatment is almost always required in medical and surgical emergencies; insulin should also be substituted before elective surgery (omit metformin on the morning of surgery and give insulin if required).

Hypoglycaemia does not usually occur with metformin; other advantages are the lower incidence of weight gain and lower plasma-insulin concentration. It does not exert a hypoglycaemic action in non-diabetic subjects unless given in overdose.

Gastro-intestinal side-effects are initially common with metformin, and may persist in some patients, particularly when very high doses such as 3 g daily are given.

Metformin may provoke lactic acidosis which is most likely to occur in patients with renal impairment; it should not be used in patients with even mild renal impairment.

Metformin is used for the symptomatic management of polycystic ovary syndrome [unlicensed indication]; it improves insulin sensitivity, may aid weight reduction, helps to normalise menstrual cycle (increasing the rate of spontaneous ovulation), and may improve hirsutism.

## METFORMIN HYDROCHLORIDE

**Indications** diabetes mellitus (see notes above); polycystic ovary syndrome [unlicensed indication]

**Cautions** see notes above; determine renal function (using an appropriately sensitive method) before treatment and once or twice annually (more frequently in the elderly or if deterioration suspected); **interactions:** Appendix 1 (antidiabetics)

**Contra-indications** renal impairment (Appendix 3), ketoacidosis, withdraw if tissue hypoxia likely (e.g. sepsis, respiratory failure, recent myocardial infarction, hepatic impairment (Appendix 2)), use of iodine-containing X-ray contrast media (do not restart metformin until renal function returns to normal) and use of general anaesthesia (suspend metformin on the morning of surgery and restart when renal function returns to normal), pregnancy (Appendix 4) and breast-feeding (Appendix 5)

**Side-effects** anorexia, nausea, vomiting, diarrhoea (usually transient), abdominal pain, metallic taste; *rarely* lactic acidosis (withdraw treatment), decreased vitamin-$B_{12}$ absorption, erythema, pruritus and urticaria; hepatitis also reported

**Dose**

- Diabetes mellitus, ADULT and CHILD over 10 years initially 500 mg with breakfast for at least 1 week then 500 mg with breakfast and evening meal for at least 1 week then 500 mg with breakfast, lunch and evening meal; usual max. 2 g daily in divided doses
- Polycystic ovary syndrome [unlicensed], initially 500 mg with breakfast for 1 week, then 500 mg with breakfast and evening meal for 1 week, then 1.5–1.7 g daily in 2–3 divided doses

**Note** Metformin doses in the BNF may differ from those in the product literature

**Metformin** (Non-proprietary) PoM

Tablets, coated, metformin hydrochloride 500 mg, net price 28-tab pack = £1.31, 84-tab pack= £1.78; 850 mg, 56-tab pack = £1.88. Label: 21

**Glucophage®** (Merck) PoM

Tablets, f/c, metformin hydrochloride 500 mg, net price 84-tab pack = £2.40; 850 mg, 56-tab pack = £2.67. Label: 21

### Modified release

**Glucophage® SR** (Merck) PoM

Tablets, m/r, metformin hydrochloride 500 mg, net price 28 tab-pack = £2.67, 56 tab-pack = £5.34. Label: 21, 25

**Dose** initially 500 mg once daily, increased every 10–15 days, max. 2 g once daily with evening meal; if control not achieved use

6 Endocrine system

1 g twice daily with meals and if control still not achieved change to standard-release tablets

Note Patients taking less than 2 g daily of the standard-release metformin may start with the same daily dose of *Glucophage® SR*; not suitable if dose of standard release tablets more than 2 g daily

**With rosiglitazone**

See section 6.1.2.3

## 6.1.2.3 Other antidiabetics

**Acarbose**, an inhibitor of intestinal alpha glucosidases, delays the digestion and absorption of starch and sucrose. It has a small but significant effect in lowering blood glucose and is used either on its own or as an adjunct to metformin or to sulphonylureas when they prove inadequate. Postprandial hyperglycaemia in type 1 (insulin-dependent) diabetes can be reduced by acarbose, but it has been little used for this purpose. Flatulence deters some from using acarbose although this side-effect tends to decrease with time.

**Nateglinide** and **repaglinide** stimulate insulin release. Both drugs have a rapid onset of action and short duration of activity, and should be administered shortly before each main meal. Repaglinide may be given as monotherapy for patients who are not overweight or for those in whom metformin is contra-indicated or not tolerated, or it may be given in combination with metformin. Nateglinide is licensed only for use with metformin.

The thiazolidinediones, **pioglitazone** and **rosiglitazone**, reduce peripheral insulin resistance, leading to a reduction of blood-glucose concentration. Either drug may be used alone or in combination with metformin or with a sulphonylurea (if metformin inappropriate); the combination of a thiazolidinedione plus metformin is preferred to a thiazolidinedione plus sulphonylurea, particularly for obese patients. Inadequate response to a combination of metformin and sulphonylurea may indicate failing insulin release; the introduction of pioglitazone or rosiglitazone has a limited role in these circumstances and insulin treatment should not be delayed. Blood-glucose control may deteriorate temporarily when a thiazolidinedione is substituted for an oral antidiabetic drug that is being used in combination with another. Long-term benefits of the thiazolidinediones have not yet been demonstrated.

**NICE guidance (pioglitazone and rosiglitazone for type 2 diabetes mellitus)**

NICE has advised (August 2003) that the use of a thiazolidinedione (pioglitazone or rosiglitazone) as second-line therapy added to either metformin or a sulphonylurea is **not** recommended [see also notes above], except for:

- patients who are unable to tolerate metformin and sulphonylurea in combination therapy, *or*
- patients in whom either metformin or a sulphonylurea is contra-indicated. In such cases, the thiazolidinedione should replace whichever drug in the combination is poorly tolerated or contra-indicated.

### ACARBOSE

**Indications** diabetes mellitus inadequately controlled by diet or by diet with oral antidiabetic drugs

**Cautions** monitor liver function; may enhance hypoglycaemic effects of insulin and sulphonylureas (hypoglycaemic episodes may be treated with oral glucose but not with sucrose); **interactions:** Appendix 1 (antidiabetics)

**Contra-indications** pregnancy (Appendix 4); breast-feeding (Appendix 5); inflammatory bowel disease (e.g. ulcerative colitis, Crohn's disease), partial intestinal obstruction (or predisposition); hepatic impairment, severe renal impairment; hernia, history of abdominal surgery

**Side-effects** flatulence, soft stools, diarrhoea (may need to reduce dose or withdraw), abdominal distention and pain; rarely nausea, abnormal liver function tests and skin reactions; ileus, oedema, jaundice and hepatitis reported

Note Antacids not recommended for treating side-effects (unlikely to be beneficial)

**Dose**

- 50 mg daily initially (to minimise side-effects) increased to 50 mg 3 times daily, then increased if necessary after 6–8 weeks to 100 mg 3 times daily; max. 200 mg 3 times daily; CHILD and ADOLESCENT under 18 years not recommended

Counselling Tablets should be chewed with first mouthful of food or swallowed whole with a little liquid immediately before food. To counteract possible hypoglycaemia, patients receiving insulin or a sulphonylurea as well as acarbose need to carry glucose (not sucrose—acarbose interferes with sucrose absorption)

**Glucobay®** (Bayer) PoM

Tablets, acarbose 50 mg, net price 90-tab pack = £6.60; 100 mg (scored), 90-tab pack = £12.51. Counselling, administration

### NATEGLINIDE

**Indications** type 2 diabetes mellitus in combination with metformin when metformin alone inadequate

**Cautions** substitute insulin during intercurrent illness (such as myocardial infarction, coma, infection, and trauma) and during surgery (omit on morning of surgery and recommence when eating and drinking normally); debilitated and malnourished patients; moderate hepatic impairment (avoid if severe—Appendix 2); **interactions:** Appendix 1 (antidiabetics)

**Contra-indications** ketoacidosis; pregnancy (Appendix 4) and breast-feeding (Appendix 5)

**Side-effects** hypoglycaemia; hypersensitivity reactions including pruritus, rashes and urticaria

**Dose**

- Initially 60 mg 3 times daily within 30 minutes before main meals, adjusted according to response up to max. 180 mg 3 times daily; CHILD and ADOLESCENT under 18 years not recommended

**Starlix®** (Novartis) PoM

Tablets, f/c, nateglinide 60 mg (pink), net price 84-tab pack = £19.75; 120 mg (yellow), 84-tab pack = £22.50; 180 mg (red), 84-tab pack = £22.50

### PIOGLITAZONE

**Indications** type 2 diabetes mellitus (alone or combined with metformin or a sulphonylurea—see also notes above)

**Cautions** monitor liver function (see below); cardiovascular disease (risk of heart failure); **interactions**: Appendix 1 (antidiabetics)

Liver toxicity Rare reports of liver dysfunction; monitor liver function before treatment, then every 2 months for 12 months and periodically thereafter; advise patients to seek immediate medical attention if symptoms such as nausea, vomiting, abdominal pain, fatigue and dark urine develop; discontinue if jaundice occurs

**Contra-indications** hepatic impairment, history of heart failure, combination with insulin (risk of heart failure), pregnancy (Appendix 4), breast-feeding (Appendix 5)

**Side-effects** gastro-intestinal disturbances, weight gain, oedema, anaemia, headache, visual disturbances, dizziness, arthralgia, hypoaesthesia, haematuria, impotence; less commonly hypoglycaemia, fatigue, insomnia, vertigo, sweating, altered blood lipids, proteinuria; see also Liver Toxicity above

**Dose**

- Initially 15–30 mg once daily increased to 45 mg once daily according to response

**Actos®** (Takeda) PoM

Tablets, pioglitazone (as hydrochloride) 15 mg, net price 28-tab pack = £24.14; 30 mg, 28-tab pack = £33.54; 45 mg, 28-tab pack = £36.96

## REPAGLINIDE

**Indications** type 2 diabetes mellitus (as monotherapy or in combination with metformin when metformin alone inadequate)

**Cautions** substitute insulin during intercurrent illness (such as myocardial infarction, coma, infection, and trauma) and during surgery (omit on morning of surgery and recommence when eating and drinking normally); debilitated and malnourished patients; renal impairment; **interactions**: Appendix 1 (antidiabetics)

**Contra-indications** ketoacidosis; severe hepatic impairment; pregnancy (Appendix 4) and breast-feeding (Appendix 5)

**Side-effects** abdominal pain, diarrhoea, constipation, nausea, vomiting; *rarely* hypoglycaemia, hypersensitivity reactions including pruritus, rashes, vasculitis, urticaria, and visual disturbances

**Dose**

- Initially 500 micrograms within 30 minutes before main meals (1 mg if transferring from another oral hypoglycaemic), adjusted according to response at intervals of 1–2 weeks; up to 4 mg may be given as a single dose, max. 16 mg daily; CHILD and ADOLESCENT under 18 years and ELDERLY over 75 years, not recommended

**NovoNorm®** (Novo Nordisk) PoM

Tablets, repaglinide 500 micrograms, net price 30-tab pack = £3.92, 90-tab pack = £11.76; 1 mg (yellow), 30-tab pack = £3.92, 90-tab pack = £11.76; 2 mg (peach), 90-tab pack = £11.76

## ROSIGLITAZONE

**Indications** type 2 diabetes mellitus (alone *or* combined with metformin *or* with a sulphonylurea *or* with both—see also notes above)

**Cautions** monitor liver function (see below); cardiovascular disease (risk of heart failure), renal impairment (Appendix 3); **interactions**: Appendix 1 (antidiabetics)

Liver toxicity Rare reports of liver dysfunction reported; monitor liver function before treatment and periodically thereafter; advise patients to seek immediate medical attention if symptoms such as nausea, vomiting, abdominal pain, fatigue, anorexia and dark urine develop; discontinue if jaundice occurs or liver enzymes significantly raised

**Contra-indications** hepatic impairment, history of heart failure, combination with insulin (risk of heart failure), pregnancy (Appendix 4), breast-feeding (Appendix 5)

**Side-effects** gastro-intestinal disturbances, headache, anaemia, altered blood lipids, weight gain, oedema, hypoglycaemia; less commonly increased appetite, heart failure, fatigue, paraesthesia, alopecia, dyspnoea; *rarely* pulmonary oedema; *very rarely* angioedema, urticaria; see also Liver Toxicity above

**Dose**

- Initially 4 mg daily; if used alone or in combination with metformin may increase to 8 mg daily (in 1 or 2 divided doses) after 8 weeks according to response; CHILD and ADOLESCENT under 18 years not recommended

**Avandia®** (GSK) ▼ PoM

Tablets, f/c, rosiglitazone (as maleate) 4 mg (orange), net price 28-tab pack = £24.74, 56-tab pack = £49.48; 8 mg (red/brown), 28-tab pack = £50.78

### With metformin

For cautions, contra-indications and side-effects of metformin see section 6.1.2.2

**Avandamet** (GSK) ▼ PoM

Avandamet® 2 mg/500 mg tablets, f/c, pink, rosiglitazone (as maleate) 2 mg, metformin hydrochloride 500 mg, net price 112-tab pack = £52.45.Label: 21

Avandamet® 2 mg/1 g tablets, f/c, yellow, rosiglitazone (as maleate) 2 mg, metformin hydrochloride 1 g, net price 56-tab pack = £27.71. Label: 21

Avandamet® 4 mg/1 g tablets, f/c, pink, rosiglitazone (as maleate) 4 mg, metformin hydrochloride 1 g, net price 56-tab pack = £52.45. Label: 21

Dose type 2 diabetes mellitus not controlled by metformin alone, initially one *Avandamet®* 2 mg/1 g twice daily, increased after 8 weeks according to response up to two *Avandamet®* 2 mg/500 mg tablets twice daily or one *Avandamet®* 4 mg/1 g tablet twice daily; max. 8 mg rosiglitazone and 2 g metformin hydrochloride daily; CHILD and ADOLESCENT under 18 years not recommended

Note Titration with the individual components (rosiglitazone and metformin) may be desirable before initiation of *Avandamet®*

## 6.1.3 Diabetic ketoacidosis

**Soluble insulin**, used intravenously, is the most appropriate form of insulin for the management of diabetic ketoacidotic and hyperosmolar non-ketotic coma. It is preferable to use the type of soluble insulin that the patient has been using previously. It is necessary to achieve and to maintain an adequate plasma-insulin concentration until the metabolic disturbance is brought under control.

Insulin is best given by intravenous infusion, using an infusion pump, and diluted to 1 unit/mL (care in mixing, see Appendix 6). Adequate plasma-insulin concentration can usually be maintained with infusion rates of 6 units/hour for adults and 0.1 units/kg/hour for children. Blood glucose is expected to decrease by about

5 mmol/litre/hour; if the response is inadequate the infusion rate can be doubled or quadrupled. When the blood-glucose concentration has fallen to 10 mmol/litre the infusion rate can be reduced to 3 units/hour for adults (about 0.05 units/kg/hour for children) and continued until the patient is ready to take food by mouth. The insulin infusion should not be stopped before subcutaneous insulin has been started.

No matter how large, a bolus intravenous injection of insulin can provide an adequate plasma concentration for a short time only; therefore if facilities for intravenous infusion are not available the insulin is given by *intramuscular injection*. An initial loading dose of 20 units intramuscularly is followed by 6 units intramuscularly every hour until the blood-glucose concentration falls to 10 mmol/litre; intramuscular injections are then given every 2 hours. Although absorption of insulin is usually rapid after intramuscular injection, it may be impaired in the presence of hypotension and poor tissue perfusion; moreover insulin may accumulate during treatment and late hypoglycaemia should be watched for and treated appropriately.

Intravenous replacement of fluid and electrolytes (section 9.2.2) with **sodium chloride** intravenous infusion is an essential part of the management of ketoacidosis; **potassium chloride** is included in the infusion as appropriate to prevent the hypokalaemia induced by the insulin. **Sodium bicarbonate** infusion (1.26% or 2.74%) is used only in cases of extreme acidosis and shock since the acid-base disturbance is normally corrected by the insulin. When the blood glucose has fallen to approximately 10 mmol/litre **glucose** 5% is infused (maximum 2 litres in 24 hours), but insulin infusion must continue.



## 6.1.4 Treatment of hypoglycaemia

Initially glucose 10–20 g is given by mouth either in liquid form or as granulated sugar or sugar lumps. Approximately 10 g of glucose is available from 2 teaspoons of sugar, 3 sugar lumps, *GlucoGel*® (formerly known as *Hypostop Gel*®; glucose 9.2 g/23-g oral ampoule, available from British BioCell International), and non-diet versions of *Lucozade*® *Sparkling Glucose Drink* 50–55 mL, *Coca-Cola*® 90 mL, *Ribena*® *Original* 15 mL (to be diluted). If necessary this may be repeated in 10–15 minutes.

Hypoglycaemia which causes unconsciousness is an emergency. **Glucagon**, a polypeptide hormone produced by the alpha cells of the islets of Langerhans, increases plasma-glucose concentration by mobilising glycogen stored in the liver. In hypoglycaemia, if sugar cannot be given by mouth, glucagon can be given by injection. Carbohydrates should be given as soon as possible to restore liver glycogen; glucagon is not appropriate for chronic hypoglycaemia. It may be issued to close relatives of insulin-treated patients for emergency use in hypoglycaemic attacks. It is often advisable to prescribe on an 'if necessary' basis to hospitalised insulin-treated patients, so that it may be given rapidly by the nurses during an hypoglycaemic emergency. If not effective in 10 minutes intravenous glucose should be given.

Alternatively, 50 mL of **glucose intravenous infusion 20%** (section 9.2.2) may be given intravenously into a large vein through a large-gauge needle; care is required since this concentration is irritant especially if extravasation occurs. Alternatively, 25 mL of glucose intravenous infusion 50% may be given, but this higher concentration is more irritant and viscous making administration difficult. Glucose intravenous infusion 10% may also be used but larger volumes are needed. Close monitoring is necessary in the case of an overdose with a long-acting insulin because further administration of glucose may be required. Patients whose hypoglycaemia is caused by an oral antidiabetic drug should be transferred to hospital because the hypoglycaemic effects of these drugs may persist for many hours.

For advice on the emergency management of hypoglycaemia in dental practice, see p. 22

### GLUCAGON

**Indications** see notes above and under Dose

**Cautions** see notes above, insulinoma, glucagonoma; ineffective in chronic hypoglycaemia, starvation, and adrenal insufficiency

**Contra-indications** phaeochromocytoma

**Side-effects** nausea, vomiting, abdominal pain, hypokalaemia, hypotension, rarely hypersensitivity reactions

**Dose**

- Insulin-induced hypoglycaemia, by subcutaneous, intramuscular, *or* intravenous injection, ADULT and CHILD over 8 years (or body-weight over 25 kg), 1 mg; CHILD under 8 years (or body-weight under 25 kg), 500 micrograms; if no response within 10 minutes intravenous glucose must be given
- Diagnostic aid, consult product literature
- Beta-blocker poisoning, see p. 32

**Note** 1 unit of glucagon = 1 mg of glucagon

[1]**GlucaGen® HypoKit** (Novo Nordisk) PoM

Injection, powder for reconstitution, glucagon (rys) as hydrochloride with lactose, net price 1-mg vial with prefilled syringe containing water for injection = £11.52

1. PoM restriction does not apply where administration is for saving life in emergency

## Chronic hypoglycaemia

**Diazoxide**, administered by mouth, is useful in the management of patients with chronic hypoglycaemia from excess endogenous insulin secretion, either from an islet cell tumour or islet cell hyperplasia. It has no place in the management of acute hypoglycaemia.

### DIAZOXIDE

**Indications** chronic intractable hypoglycaemia (for use in hypertensive crisis see section 2.5.1)

**Cautions** ischaemic heart disease, pregnancy (Appendix 4), labour, impaired renal function (Appendix 3); haematological examinations and blood pressure monitoring required during prolonged treatment; growth, bone, and developmental checks in children; **interactions**: Appendix 1 (diazoxide)

**Side-effects** anorexia, nausea, vomiting, hyperuricaemia, hypotension, oedema, tachycardia, arrhythmias, extrapyramidal effects; hypertrichosis on prolonged treatment

**Dose**

- By mouth, ADULT and CHILD, initially 5 mg/kg daily in 2–3 divided doses

**Eudemine®** (Celltech) PoM

Tablets, diazoxide 50 mg. Net price 20 = £9.29

Injection, see section 2.5.1

# 6.1.5 Treatment of diabetic nephropathy and neuropathy

## Diabetic nephropathy

Regular review of diabetic patients should include an annual test for urinary protein (using *Albustix®*) and serum creatinine measurement. If the urinary protein test is negative, the urine should be tested for microalbuminuria (the earliest sign of nephropathy). If reagent strip tests (*Micral-Test II®* NHS or *Microbumintest®* NHS) are used and prove positive, the result should be confirmed by laboratory analysis of a urine sample. Provided there are no contra-indications, all diabetic patients with nephropathy causing proteinuria or with established microalbuminuria (at least 3 positive tests) should be treated with an ACE inhibitor (section 2.5.5.1) or an angiotensin-II receptor antagonist (section 2.5.5.2) even if the blood pressure is normal; in any case, to minimise the risk of renal deterioration, blood pressure should be carefully controlled (section 2.5).

ACE inhibitors may potentiate the hypoglycaemic effect of insulin and oral antidiabetic drugs; this effect is more likely during the first weeks of combined treatment and in patients with renal impairment.

For the treatment of hypertension in diabetes, see section 2.5.

## Diabetic neuropathy

Optimal diabetic control is beneficial for the management of *painful neuropathy* in patients with type 1 diabetes (see also section 4.7.3). **Paracetamol** or a **non-steroidal anti-inflammatory drug** such as ibuprofen (section 10.1.1) may relieve *mild to moderate pain.*

The **tricyclic antidepressants** amitriptyline and nortriptyline (section 4.3.1) are the drugs of choice for painful diabetic neuropathy [unlicensed use]; amitriptyline is given in a dose of 25–75 mg daily (higher doses under specialist supervision). Other classes of antidepressants do not appear to be effective. **Gabapentin** (section 4.8.1) is licensed for the treatment of neuropathic pain and is an effective alternative to a tricyclic antidepressant.

**Duloxetine** (section 4.3.4) is licensed for the treatment of diabetic neuropathic pain.

**Carbamazepine** and **phenytoin** [both unlicensed] (section 4.8.1) may be useful for shooting or stabbing pain, but adverse effects are common; carbamazepine 200–800 mg daily in divided doses has been used.

**Capsaicin** cream 0.075% (section 10.3.2) is licensed for painful diabetic neuropathy and may have some effect, but it produces an intense burning sensation during the initial treatment period.

Neuropathic pain may respond partially to some **opioid analgesics**, such as methadone, oxycodone and tramadol, and they may have a role when other treatments have failed.

In *autonomic neuropathy* diabetic diarrhoea can often be managed by 2 or 3 doses of **tetracycline** 250 mg [unlicensed use] (section 5.1.3). Otherwise **codeine phosphate** (section 1.4.2) is the best drug, but other antidiarrhoeal preparations can be tried. An **antiemetic** which promotes gastric transit, such as metoclopramide or domperidone (section 4.6), is helpful for gastroparesis. In rare cases when an antiemetic does not help, erythromycin (especially when given intravenously) may be beneficial but this needs confirmation.

For the management of erectile dysfunction, see section 7.4.5.

In *neuropathic postural hypotension* increased salt intake and the use of the **mineralocorticoid** fludrocortisone 100–400 micrograms daily [unlicensed use] (section 6.3.1) help by increasing plasma volume, but uncomfortable oedema is a common side-effect. Fludrocortisone can also be combined with **flurbiprofen** (section 10.1.1) and **ephedrine hydrochloride** (section 3.1.1.2) [both unlicensed]. **Midodrine** [unlicensed], an alpha agonist, may also be useful in postural hypotension.

*Gustatory sweating* can be treated with an **antimuscarinic** such as propantheline bromide (section 1.2); side-effects are common. For the management of hyperhidrosis, see section 13.12.

In some patients with *neuropathic oedema*, **ephedrine hydrochloride** [unlicensed use] 30–60 mg 3 times daily offers effective relief.

# 6.1.6 Diagnostic and monitoring agents for diabetes mellitus

## Blood glucose monitoring

Blood glucose monitoring gives a direct measure of the glucose concentration at the time of the test and can detect hypoglycaemia as well as hyperglycaemia. Patients should be properly trained in the use of blood glucose monitoring systems and to take appropriate action on the results obtained. Inadequate understanding of the normal fluctuations in blood glucose may lead to confusion and inappropriate action. It is ideal for patients to observe the 'peaks' and 'troughs' of blood glucose over 24 hours and make adjustments of their insulin no more than once or twice weekly. Daily alterations to the insulin dose are highly undesirable (except during illness).

Blood glucose monitoring is best carried out by means of a meter. Visual colour comparison is sometimes used but is much less satisfactory. Meters give a more precise reading and are useful for patients with poor eyesight or who are colour blind.

**Note** In the UK blood-glucose concentration is expressed in mmol/litre and Diabetes UK advises that these units should be used for self-monitoring of blood glucose. In other European countries units of mg/100 mL (or mg/dL) are commonly used. It is advisable to check that the meter is pre-set in the correct units.

### Test strips

**Active®** (Roche Diagnostics)
Reagent strips, for blood glucose monitoring, range 0.6–33.3 mmol/litre, for use with *Glucotrend®* and *Accu-Chek® Active* NHS meters only. Net price 50-strip pack = £16.13

**Advantage Plus®** (Roche Diagnostics)
Reagent strips, for blood glucose monitoring, range 0.6–33.3 mmol/litre, for use with *Accu-Chek® Advantage* NHS meter only. Net price 50-strip pack = £16.13

**Ascensia® Autodisc** (Bayer Diagnostics)
Sensor discs, for blood glucose monitoring, range 0.6–33.3 mmol/litre, for use with *Ascensia Breeze®* NHS and *Ascensia Esprit® 2* NHS meters only. Net price 5 × 10-disc pack = £15.67

**Ascensia® Glucodisc** (Bayer Diagnostics) NHS
Sensor discs, for blood glucose monitoring, range 0.6–33.3 mmol/L, for use with *Ascensia Esprit®* 2 NHS meter only. Net price 5 × 10-disc pack = £15.53

**Ascensia® Microfill** (Bayer Diagnostics)
Sensor strips, for blood glucose monitoring, range 0.6–33.3 mmol/litre, for use with *Ascensia® Contour* NHS meter only. Net price 50-strip pack = £15.55

**BM-Accutest®** (Roche Diagnostics)
Reagent strips, for blood glucose monitoring, range 1.1–33.3 mmol/litre, for use with *Accutrend®* NHS meters only. Net price 50-strip pack = £15.64

**Compact®** (Roche Diagnostics)
Reagent strips, for blood glucose monitoring, range 0.6–33.3 mmol/litre, for use with *Accu-Chek® Compact* and *Accu-Chek® Compact Plus* NHS meters only. Net price 3 × 17-strip pack = £16.26

**FreeStyle®** (TheraSense)
Reagent strips, for blood glucose monitoring, range 1.1–27.8 mmol/litre, for use with *FreeStyle®* NHS meter only. Net price 50-strip pack = £15.67

**GlucoMen®** (Menarini Diagnostics)
Sensor strips, for blood glucose monitoring, range 1.1–33.3 mmol/litre, for use with *GlucoMen® Glycó* NHS meter only. Net price 50-strip pack = £14.94

**Glucotide®** (Bayer Diagnostics) NHS
Reagent strips, for blood glucose monitoring, range 0.6–33.3 mmol/litre, for use with *Glucometer® 4* NHS meter only. Net price 50-strip pack = £15.33

**Hypoguard® Supreme** (Hypoguard)
Reagent strips, for blood glucose monitoring, range 2.2–27.7 mmol/litre, for use with *Hypoguard® Supreme* NHS meters. Net price 50-strip pack = £13.64

**Hypoguard® Supreme Spectrum** (Hypoguard)
Reagent strips, for blood glucose monitoring, visual range 2.2–27.8 mmol/litre. Net price 50-strip pack = £10.34

**MediSense G2®** (MediSense)
Sensor strips, for blood glucose monitoring, range 1.1–33.3 mmol/litre. for use with *MediSense Card®* NHS or *MediSense Pen®* NHS meters only. Net price 50-strip pack = £14.40

**MediSense® Optium Plus** (MediSense)
Sensor strips, for blood glucose monitoring, range 1.1–27.7 mmol/litre, for use with *MediSense® Optium* NHS meter only. Net price 50-strip pack = £15.30

**MediSense® Soft-Sense** (MediSense)
Sensor strips, for blood glucose monitoring, range 1.7–25 mmol/litre, for use with *MediSense® Soft-Sense* meter only. Net price 50-strip pack = £15.55

**One Touch®** (LifeScan)
Reagent strips, for blood glucose monitoring, range 0–33.3 mmol/litre, for use with *One Touch® II, Profile* and *Basic* NHS meters only. Net price 50-strip pack = £15.41

**One Touch® Ultra** (LifeScan)
Reagent strips, for blood glucose monitoring, range 1.1–33.3 mmol/litre, for use with *One Touch® Ultra* meter only. Net price 50-strip pack = £15.57

**PocketScan®** (LifeScan)
Reagent strips, for blood glucose monitoring, range 1.1–33.3 mmol/litre, for use with *PocketScan®* NHS meter only. Net price 50-strip pack = £15.21

**Prestige® Smart System** (DiagnoSys)
Reagent strips, for blood glucose monitoring, range 1.4–33.3 mmol/litre, for use with *Prestige® Smart System* NHS meter only. Net price 50-strip pack = £15.29

### Meters

**Accu-Chek® Active** (Roche Diagnostics) NHS
Meter, for blood glucose monitoring (for use with *Active®* test strips). *Accu-Chek® Active* system = £7.79

**Accu-Chek® Advantage** (Roche Diagnostics) NHS
Meter, for blood glucose monitoring (for use with *Advantage Plus®* test strips). *Accu-Chek® Advantage* system = £7.00

**Accu-Chek® Compact Plus** (Roche Diagnostics) NHS
Meter, for blood glucose monitoring (for use with *Compact®* test strips). *Accu-Chek® Compact Plus* system = £7.79

**Ascensia Breeze®** (Bayer Diagnostics) NHS
Meter, for blood glucose monitoring (for use with *Ascensia® Autodisc* test sensor discs)

**Ascensia Contour®** (Bayer Diagnostics) NHS
Meter, for blood glucose monitoring (for use with *Ascensia® Microfill* sensor strips) = £19.97

**Ascensia Esprit® 2** (Bayer Diagnostics) NHS
Meter, for blood glucose monitoring (for use with *Ascensia® Glucodisc* test sensor discs) = £17.49

**FreeStyle®** (TheraSense) NHS
Meter for blood glucose monitoring (for use with *FreeStyle®* test strips) = £25.00

**GlucoMen® Glycó** (Menarini Diagnostics) NHS
Meter, for blood glucose monitoring (for use with *GlucoMen®* sensor strips)

**GlucoMen® PC** (Menarini Diagnostics) NHS
Meter, for blood glucose monitoring (for use with *GlucoMen®* sensor strips)

**Hypoguard® Supreme** (Hypoguard) NHS
Meters, for blood glucose monitoring (for use with *Hypoguard® Supreme* test strips). *Hypoguard® Supreme Plus* meter = £35.00; *Hypoguard® Supreme Extra* meter = £45.00

**MediSense®** (MediSense) NHS
Meters (Sensor), for blood glucose monitoring. *MediSense Card* = £15.31, *MediSense®* card starter pack = £17.50, *MediSense®* Pen = £30.63, *MediSense®* pen starter pack = £39.38, *MediSense® Precision QID* starter pack = £12.00 (all for use with *MediSense G2®* test strips); *MediSense® Optium* starter pack (for use with *MediSense® Optium* test strips) = £17.50; *MediSense® Soft-Sense* meter (for use with *MediSense® Soft-Sense* test strips)

**One Touch®** (LifeScan) NHS
Meters, for blood glucose monitoring (for use with *One Touch®* test strips). *One Touch® Basic* system pack = £9.38, *One Touch® Profile* system pack = £18.38

**One Touch® Ultra** (LifeScan) NHS
Meter, for blood glucose monitoring (for use with *One Touch® Ultra* test strips) = £10.00

**PocketScan®** (LifeScan) NHS
Meter, for blood glucose monitoring (for use with *PocketScan®* test strips). *Complete PocketScan® System* = £17.50

**Prestige® Smart System** (DiagnoSys) NHS
Meter, for blood glucose monitoring (for use with *Prestige® Smart System* test strips) = £5.63

## Urinalysis

Urine testing for glucose is useful in patients who find blood glucose monitoring difficult. Tests for glucose range from reagent strips specific to glucose to reagent tablets which detect all reducing sugars. Few patients still use *Clinitest*®; *Clinistix*® is suitable for screening purposes only. Tests for ketones by patients are rarely required unless they become unwell.

Microalbuminuria can be detected with *Micral-Test II*® NHS or *Microbumintest*® NHS but this should be followed by confirmation in the laboratory, since false positive results are common.

### Glucose

**Clinistix**® (Bayer Diagnostics)
Reagent strips, for detection of glucose in urine. Net price 50-strip pack = £3.18

**Clinitest**® (Bayer Diagnostics) NHS
Reagent tablets, for detection of glucose and other reducing substances in urine. Pocket set (test tube, dropper and 36 tablets), net price = £4.02, 36-tab pack = £2.00, 6-test tube pack = £3.70, 6-dropper pack = £3.80

**Diabur-Test 5000**® (Roche Diagnostics)
Reagent strips, for detection of glucose in urine. Net price 50-strip pack = £2.69

**Diastix**® (Bayer Diagnostics)
Reagent strips, for detection of glucose in urine. Net price 50-strip pack = £2.71

**Medi-Test® Glucose** (BHR)
Reagent strips, for detection of glucose in urine. Net price 50-strip pack = £2.17

### Ketones

**Ketostix**® (Bayer Diagnostics)
Reagent strips, for detection of ketones in urine. Net price 50-strip pack = £2.87

**Ketur Test**® (Roche Diagnostics)
Reagent strips, for detection of ketones in urine. Net price 50-strip pack = £2.58

### Protein

**Albustix**® (Bayer Diagnostics)
Reagent strips, for detection of protein in urine. Net price 50-strip pack = £3.94

**Medi-Test® Protein 2** (BHR)
Reagent strips, for detection of protein in urine. Net price 50-strip pack = £3.03

### Other reagent strips available for urinalysis include:

*Combur-3 Test*® NHS (glucose and protein—Roche Diagnostics), *Clinitek Microalbumin*® NHS (albumin and creatinine—Bayer Diagnostics), *Ketodiastix*® NHS (glucose and ketones—Bayer Diagnostics), *Medi-Test Combi 2*® NHS (glucose and protein—BHR), *Micral-Test II*® NHS (albumin—Roche Diagnostics), *Microalbustix*® NHS (albumin and creatinine—Bayer Diagnostics), *Microbumintest*® NHS (albumin—Bayer Diagnostics), *Uristix*® NHS (glucose and protein—Bayer Diagnostics)

## Glucose tolerance test

The **glucose** tolerance test is now rarely needed for the diagnosis of diabetes when symptoms of hyperglycaemia are present, though it is still required to establish the presence of gestational diabetes. This generally involves giving anhydrous glucose 75 g (equivalent to Glucose BP 82.5 g) by mouth to the fasting patient, and measuring blood-glucose concentrations at intervals.

The appropriate amount of glucose should be given with 200–300 mL fluid. Anhydrous glucose 75 g may alternatively be given as 113 mL *Polycal*® (Nutricia Clinical) with extra fluid to administer a total volume of 200–300 mL.

# 6.2 Thyroid and antithyroid drugs

6.2.1 Thyroid hormones
6.2.2 Antithyroid drugs

## 6.2.1 Thyroid hormones

Thyroid hormones are used in hypothyroidism (myxoedema), and also in diffuse non-toxic goitre, Hashimoto's thyroiditis (lymphadenoid goitre), and thyroid carcinoma. Neonatal hypothyroidism requires prompt treatment for normal development.

**Levothyroxine sodium** (thyroxine sodium) is the treatment of choice for *maintenance* therapy. The initial dose should not exceed 100 micrograms daily, preferably before breakfast, or 25 to 50 micrograms in elderly patients or those with cardiac disease, increased by 25 to 50 micrograms at intervals of at least 4 weeks. The usual maintenance dose to relieve hypothyroidism is 100 to 200 micrograms daily which can be administered as a single dose.

In infants and children doses of thyroxine, for congenital hypothyroidism and juvenile myxoedema, should be titrated according to clinical response, growth assessment, and measurements of plasma thyroxine and thyroid-stimulating hormone.

**Liothyronine sodium** has a similar action to levothyroxine but is more rapidly metabolised and has a more rapid effect; 20 micrograms is equivalent to 100 micrograms of levothyroxine. Its effects develop after a few hours and disappear within 24 to 48 hours of discontinuing treatment. It may be used in *severe hypothyroid states* when a rapid response is desired.

Liothyronine by intravenous injection is the treatment of choice in *hypothyroid coma*. Adjunctive therapy includes intravenous fluids, hydrocortisone, and treatment of infection; assisted ventilation is often required.



### LEVOTHYROXINE SODIUM
(Thyroxine sodium)

**Indications** hypothyroidism

**Cautions** panhypopituitarism or predisposition to adrenal insufficiency (initiate corticosteroid therapy before starting levothyroxine), elderly, cardiovascular disorders (myocardial insufficiency or myocardial infarction, see Initial Dosage below), long-standing hypothyroidism, diabetes insipidus, diabetes mellitus (dose of antidiabetic drugs including insulin may need to be increased); pregnancy (Appendix 4) and breast-feeding (Appendix 5); **interactions:** Appendix 1 (thyroid hormones)

**Initial dosage** A pre-therapy ECG is valuable as changes induced by hypothyroidism may be confused with evidence of ischaemia. If metabolism increases too rapidly (causing diarrhoea, nervousness, rapid pulse, insomnia, tremors and sometimes anginal pain where there is latent myocardial ischaemia), reduce dose or withhold for 1–2 days and start again at a lower dose

**Contra-indications** thyrotoxicosis

**Side-effects** usually at excessive dosage (see Initial Dosage above) include anginal pain, arrhythmias, palpitation, skeletal muscle cramps, tachycardia, diarrhoea, vomiting, tremors, restlessness, excitability, insomnia, headache, flushing, sweating, fever, heat intolerance, excessive loss of weight and muscular weakness

**Dose**

- ADULT, initially 50–100 micrograms (50 micrograms for those over 50 years) daily, preferably before breakfast, adjusted in steps of 50 micrograms every 3–4 weeks until metabolism normalised (usually 100–200 micrograms daily); in cardiac disease, initially 25 micrograms daily *or* 50 micrograms on alternate days, adjusted in steps of 25 micrograms every 4 weeks
- Congenital hypothyroidism and juvenile myxoedema, NEONATE up to 1 month initially 5–10 micrograms/kg daily, CHILD over 1 month initially 5 micrograms/kg daily adjusted in steps of 25 micrograms every 2–4 weeks until mild toxic symptoms appear then reduce dose slightly

**Levothyroxine** (Non-proprietary) PoM

Tablets, levothyroxine sodium 25 micrograms, net price 28-tab pack = 93p; 50 micrograms, 28-tab pack = £1.17; 100 micrograms, 28-tab pack = £1.04

Brands include *Eltroxin®*

## LIOTHYRONINE SODIUM
(L-Tri-iodothyronine sodium)

**Indications** see notes above

**Cautions** see under Levothyroxine Sodium; pregnancy (Appendix 4); breast-feeding (Appendix 5); **interactions:** Appendix 1 (thyroid hormones)

**Contra-indications** see under Levothyroxine Sodium

**Side-effects** see under Levothyroxine Sodium

**Dose**

- By mouth, initially 10–20 micrograms daily gradually increased to 60 micrograms daily in 2–3 divided doses; ELDERLY smaller initial doses; CHILD, adult dose reduced in proportion to body-weight
- By slow intravenous injection, hypothyroid coma, 5–20 micrograms repeated every 12 hours or as often as every 4 hours if necessary; alternatively 50 micrograms initially then 25 micrograms every 8 hours reducing to 25 micrograms twice daily

**Tertroxin®** (Goldshield) PoM

Tablets, scored, liothyronine sodium 20 micrograms, net price 100-tab pack = £15.92

**Triiodothyronine** (Goldshield) PoM

Injection, powder for reconstitution, liothyronine sodium (with dextran). Net price 20-microgram amp = £37.92

# 6.2.2 Antithyroid drugs

Antithyroid drugs are used for hyperthyroidism either to prepare patients for thyroidectomy or for long-term management. In the UK carbimazole is the most commonly used drug. Propylthiouracil may be used in patients who suffer sensitivity reactions to carbimazole as sensitivity is not necessarily displayed to both drugs. Both drugs act primarily by interfering with the synthesis of thyroid hormones.

> **CSM warning (neutropenia and agranulocytosis)**
>
> Doctors are reminded of the importance of recognising bone marrow suppression induced by carbimazole and the need to stop treatment promptly.
>
> 1. Patient should be asked to report symptoms and signs suggestive of infection, especially sore throat.
> 2. A white blood cell count should be performed if there is any clinical evidence of infection.
> 3. Carbimazole should be stopped promptly if there is clinical or laboratory evidence of neutropenia.

**Carbimazole** is given in a dose of 15 to 40 mg daily; occasionally a larger dose may be required. This dose is continued until the patient becomes euthyroid, usually after 4 to 8 weeks and the dose is then gradually reduced to a maintenance dose of 5 to 15 mg. Therapy is usually given for 12 to 18 months. Children may be given carbimazole in an initial dose of 250 micrograms/kg three times daily, adjusted according to response; treatment in children should be undertaken by a specialist. Rashes and pruritus are common but they can be treated with antihistamines without discontinuing therapy; alternatively propylthiouracil may be substituted. All patients should be advised to report any sore throat immediately because of the rare complication of agranulocytosis (see CSM warning, above).

**Propylthiouracil** is given in a dose of 200 to 400 mg daily in adults and this dose is maintained until the patient becomes euthyroid; the dose may then be gradually reduced to a maintenance dose of 50 to 150 mg daily.

Antithyroid drugs only need to be given once daily because of their prolonged effect on the thyroid. Overtreatment can result in the rapid development of hypothyroidism and should be avoided particularly during pregnancy because it can cause fetal goitre.

A combination of carbimazole, 40 to 60 mg daily with levothyroxine, 50 to 150 micrograms daily, may be used in a *blocking-replacement regimen*; therapy is usually given for 18 months. The blocking-replacement regimen is **not** suitable during pregnancy.

**Iodine** has been used as an adjunct to antithyroid drugs for 10 to 14 days before partial thyroidectomy; however, there is little evidence of a beneficial effect. Iodine should not be used for long-term treatment because its antithyroid action tends to diminish.

Radioactive sodium iodide ($^{131}I$) solution is used increasingly for the treatment of thyrotoxicosis at all ages, particularly where medical therapy or compliance is a problem, in patients with cardiac disease, and in patients who relapse after thyroidectomy.

**Propranolol** is useful for rapid relief of thyrotoxic symptoms and may be used in conjunction with antithyroid drugs or as an adjunct to radioactive iodine. Beta-blockers are also useful in neonatal thyrotoxicosis and in supraventricular arrhythmias due to hyperthyroidism. Propranolol has been used in conjunction with iodine to prepare mildly thyrotoxic patients for surgery but it is preferable to make the patient euthyroid with carbimazole. Laboratory tests of thyroid function are not altered by beta-blockers. Most experience in treating thyrotoxicosis has been gained with propranolol but **nadolol** is also used. For doses and preparations of beta-blockers see section 2.4.

*Thyrotoxic crisis* ('thyroid storm') requires emergency treatment with intravenous administration of fluids, propranolol (5 mg) and hydrocortisone (100 mg every 6 hours, as sodium succinate), as well as oral iodine solution and carbimazole or propylthiouracil which may need to be administered by nasogastric tube.

**Pregnancy and breast-feeding** Radioactive iodine therapy is contra-indicated during pregnancy. Propylthiouracil and carbimazole can be given but the blocking-replacement regimen (see above) is **not** suitable. Both propylthiouracil and carbimazole cross the placenta and in high doses may cause fetal goitre and hypothyroidism—the lowest dose that will control the hyperthyroid state should be used (requirements in Graves' disease tend to fall during pregnancy). Rarely, carbimazole has been associated with aplasia cutis of the neonate.

Carbimazole and propylthiouracil appear in breast milk but this does not preclude breast-feeding as long as neonatal development is closely monitored and the lowest effective dose is used.

### CARBIMAZOLE

**Indications** hyperthyroidism

**Cautions** liver disorders, pregnancy, breast-feeding (see notes above)

**Side-effects** nausea, mild gastro-intestinal disturbances, headache, rashes and pruritus, arthralgia; rarely myopathy, alopecia, bone marrow suppression (including pancytopenia and agranulocytosis, see **CSM warning** above), jaundice

**Dose**

- See notes above

Counselling Warn patient to tell doctor **immediately** if sore throat, mouth ulcers, bruising, fever, malaise, or non-specific illness develops

**Neo-Mercazole®** (Roche) PoM

Tablets, both pink, carbimazole 5 mg, net price 100-tab pack = £5.05; 20 mg, 100-tab pack = £18.75. Counselling, blood disorder symptoms

### IODINE AND IODIDE

**Indications** thyrotoxicosis (pre-operative)

**Cautions** pregnancy, children; not for long-term treatment

**Contra-indications** breast-feeding

**Side-effects** hypersensitivity reactions including coryza-like symptoms, headache, lacrimation, conjunctivitis, pain in salivary glands, laryngitis, bronchitis, rashes; on prolonged treatment depression, insomnia, impotence; goitre in infants of mothers taking iodides

**Aqueous Iodine Oral Solution**

(Lugol's Solution), iodine 5%, potassium iodide 10% in purified water, freshly boiled and cooled, total iodine 130 mg/mL. Net price 100 mL = £1.19. Label: 27

Dose 0.1–0.3 mL 3 times daily well diluted with milk or water

### PROPYLTHIOURACIL

**Indications** hyperthyroidism

**Cautions** see under Carbimazole; hepatic impairment (Appendix 2), renal impairment (Appendix 3)

**Side-effects** see under Carbimazole; leucopenia; rarely cutaneous vasculitis, thrombocytopenia, aplastic anaemia, hypoprothrombinaemia, hepatitis, encephalopathy, hepatic necrosis, nephritis, lupus erythematous-like syndromes

**Dose**

- See notes above

**Propylthiouracil** (Non-proprietary) PoM

Tablets, propylthiouracil 50 mg. Net price 56-tab pack = £24.92

# 6.3 Corticosteroids

6.3.1 Replacement therapy
6.3.2 Glucocorticoid therapy

## 6.3.1 Replacement therapy

The adrenal cortex normally secretes hydrocortisone (cortisol) which has glucocorticoid activity and weak mineralocorticoid activity. It also secretes the mineralocorticoid aldosterone.

In deficiency states, physiological replacement is best achieved with a combination of **hydrocortisone** (section 6.3.2) and the mineralocorticoid **fludrocortisone**; hydrocortisone alone does not usually provide sufficient mineralocorticoid activity for complete replacement.

In *Addison's disease* or following adrenalectomy, **hydrocortisone** 20 to 30 mg daily by mouth is usually required. This is given in 2 doses, the larger in the morning and the smaller in the evening, mimicking the normal diurnal rhythm of cortisol secretion. The optimum daily dose is determined on the basis of clinical response. Glucocorticoid therapy is supplemented by fludrocortisone 50 to 300 micrograms daily.

In *acute adrenocortical insufficiency*, **hydrocortisone** is given intravenously (preferably as sodium succinate) in doses of 100 mg every 6 to 8 hours in sodium chloride intravenous infusion 0.9%.

In *hypopituitarism* glucocorticoids should be given as in adrenocortical insufficiency, but since the production of aldosterone is also regulated by the renin-angiotensin system a mineralocorticoid is not usually required. Additional replacement therapy with levothyroxine (section 6.2.1) and sex hormones (section 6.4) should be given as indicated by the pattern of hormone deficiency.

### FLUDROCORTISONE ACETATE

**Indications** mineralocorticoid replacement in adrenocortical insufficiency

**Cautions** section 6.3.2; **interactions:** Appendix 1 (corticosteroids)

**Contra-indications** section 6.3.2

**Side-effects** section 6.3.2

**Dose**

- 50–300 micrograms daily; CHILD 5 micrograms/kg daily

**Florinef®** (Squibb) PoM

Tablets, pink, scored, fludrocortisone acetate 100 micrograms. Net price 56-tab pack = £2.50. Label: 10, steroid card

## 6.3.2 Glucocorticoid therapy

In comparing the relative potencies of corticosteroids in terms of their anti-inflammatory (glucocorticoid) effects it should be borne in mind that high glucocorticoid activity in itself is of no advantage unless it is accompanied by relatively low mineralocorticoid activity (see Disadvantages of Corticosteroids below). The mineralocorticoid activity of **fludrocortisone** (section 6.3.1) is so high that its anti-inflammatory activity is of no clinical relevance. The table below shows equivalent anti-inflammatory doses.

### Equivalent anti-inflammatory doses of corticosteroids

This table takes no account of mineralocorticoid effects, nor does it take account of variations in duration of action

| | |
|---|---|
| Prednisolone 5 mg | |
| ≡ | Betamethasone 750 micrograms |
| ≡ | Cortisone acetate 25 mg |
| ≡ | Deflazacort 6 mg |
| ≡ | Dexamethasone 750 micrograms |
| ≡ | Hydrocortisone 20 mg |
| ≡ | Methylprednisolone 4 mg |
| ≡ | Triamcinolone 4 mg |

The relatively high mineralocorticoid activity of **cortisone** and **hydrocortisone**, and the resulting fluid retention, make them unsuitable for disease suppression on a long-term basis. However, they can be used for adrenal replacement therapy (section 6.3.1); hydrocortisone is preferred because cortisone requires conversion in the liver to hydrocortisone. Hydrocortisone is used on a short-term basis by intravenous injection for the emergency management of some conditions. The relatively moderate anti-inflammatory potency of hydrocortisone also makes it a useful topical corticosteroid for the management of inflammatory skin conditions because side-effects (both topical and systemic) are less marked (section 13.4); cortisone is not active topically.

**Prednisolone** has predominantly glucocorticoid activity and is the corticosteroid most commonly used by mouth for long-term disease suppression.

**Betamethasone** and **dexamethasone** have very high glucocorticoid activity in conjunction with insignificant mineralocorticoid activity. This makes them particularly suitable for high-dose therapy in conditions where fluid retention would be a disadvantage.

Betamethasone and dexamethasone also have a long duration of action and this, coupled with their lack of mineralocorticoid action makes them particularly suitable for conditions which require suppression of corticotropin (corticotrophin) secretion (e.g. congenital adrenal hyperplasia). Some esters of betamethasone and of **beclometasone** (beclomethasone) exert a considerably more marked topical effect (e.g. on the skin or the lungs) than when given by mouth; use is made of this to obtain topical effects whilst minimising systemic side-effects (e.g. for skin applications and asthma inhalations).

**Deflazacort** has a high glucocorticoid activity; it is derived from prednisolone.

## Disadvantages of corticosteroids

Overdosage or prolonged use may exaggerate some of the normal physiological actions of corticosteroids leading to mineralocorticoid and glucocorticoid side-effects.

**Mineralocorticoid** side-effects include hypertension, sodium and water retention and potassium loss. They are most marked with fludrocortisone, but are significant with cortisone, hydrocortisone, corticotropin, and tetracosactide (tetracosactrin). Mineralocorticoid actions are negligible with the high potency glucocorticoids, betamethasone and dexamethasone, and occur only slightly with methylprednisolone, prednisolone, and triamcinolone.

**Glucocorticoid** side-effects include diabetes and osteoporosis (section 6.6), which is a danger, particularly in the elderly, as it may result in osteoporotic fractures for example of the hip or vertebrae; in addition high doses are associated with avascular necrosis of the femoral head. Mental disturbances may occur; a serious paranoid state or depression with risk of suicide may be induced, particularly in patients with a history of mental disorder. Euphoria is frequently observed. Muscle wasting (proximal myopathy) may also occur. Corticosteroid therapy is also weakly linked with peptic ulceration (the potential advantage of soluble or enteric-coated preparations to reduce the risk is speculative only).

High doses of corticosteroids may cause Cushing's syndrome, with moon face, striae, and acne; it is usually reversible on withdrawal of treatment, but this must always be gradually tapered to avoid symptoms of acute adrenal insufficiency (**important**: see also Adrenal Suppression, below).

In children, administration of corticosteroids may result in suppression of growth. For the effect of corticosteroids given in pregnancy, see Pregnancy and Breast-feeding, below.

### Adrenal Suppression

During prolonged therapy with corticosteroids, adrenal atrophy develops and may persist for years after stopping. Abrupt withdrawal after a prolonged period may lead to acute adrenal insufficiency, hypotension or death (see Withdrawal of Corticosteroids, below). Withdrawal may also be associated with fever, myalgia, arthralgia, rhinitis, conjunctivitis, painful itchy skin nodules and weight loss.

To compensate for a diminished adrenocortical response caused by prolonged corticosteroid treatment, any significant intercurrent illness, trauma, or surgical procedure requires a temporary increase in corticosteroid dose, or if already stopped, a temporary re-introduction of corticosteroid treatment. Anaesthetists **must** therefore know whether a patient is taking or has been taking a corticosteroid, to avoid a precipitous fall in blood pressure during anaesthesia or in the immediate postoperative period. A suitable regimen for corticosteroid replacement, in patients who have taken more than 10 mg prednisolone daily (or equivalent) within 3 months of surgery, is:

- *Minor surgery under general anaesthesia*—usual oral corticosteroid dose on the morning of surgery or hydrocortisone 25–50 mg (usually the sodium succinate) intravenously at induction; the usual oral corticosteroid dose is recommenced after surgery

- *Moderate or major surgery*—usual oral corticosteroid dose on the morning of surgery and hydrocortisone 25–50 mg intravenously at induction, followed by hydrocortisone 25–50 mg 3 times a day by intravenous injection for 24 hours after moderate surgery or for 48–72 hours after major surgery; the usual pre-operative oral corticosteroid dose is recommenced on stopping hydrocortisone injections

Patients on long-term corticosteroid treatment should carry a Steroid Treatment Card (see below) which gives guidance on minimising risk and provides details of prescriber, drug, dosage and duration of treatment.

## Infections

Prolonged courses of corticosteroids increase susceptibility to infections and severity of infections; clinical presentation of infections may also be atypical. Serious infections e.g. *septicaemia* and *tuberculosis* may reach an advanced stage before being recognised, and *amoebiasis* or *strongyloidiasis* may be activated or exacerbated (exclude before initiating a corticosteroid in those at risk or with suggestive symptoms). Fungal or viral *ocular infections* may also be exacerbated (see also section 11.4.1).

**Chickenpox** Unless they have had chickenpox, patients receiving oral or parenteral corticosteroids for purposes other than replacement should be regarded as being *at risk of severe chickenpox* (see Steroid Treatment Card). Manifestations of fulminant illness include pneumonia, hepatitis and disseminated intravascular coagulation; rash is not necessarily a prominent feature.

Passive immunisation with varicella–zoster immunoglobulin (section 14.5) is needed for exposed non-immune patients receiving systemic corticosteroids or for those who have used them within the previous 3 months; varicella–zoster immunoglobulin should preferably be given within 3 days of exposure and no later than 10 days. Confirmed chickenpox warrants specialist care and urgent treatment (section 5.3.2.1). Corticosteroids should not be stopped and dosage may need to be increased.

Topical, inhaled or rectal corticosteroids are less likely to be associated with an increased risk of severe chickenpox.

**Measles** Patients taking corticosteroids should be advised to take particular care to avoid exposure to measles and to seek immediate medical advice if exposure occurs. Prophylaxis with intramuscular normal immunoglobulin (section 14.5) may be needed.

> Following concern about severe chickenpox associated with systemic corticosteroids, the CSM has issued a notice that **every** patient prescribed a *systemic* corticosteroid should receive the patient information leaflet supplied by the manufacturer.

> Steroid treatment cards (see below) should also be issued where appropriate. Doctors and pharmacists can obtain supplies of the card from:
> England and Wales
> NHS Customer Services, Astron
> Causeway Distribution Centre, Oldham Broadway Business Park, Chadderton
> Oldham, OL9 9XD
> Tel: (0161) 683 2376/2382
> Fax: (0161) 683 2396
> Scotland
> Banner Business Supplies
> 20 South Gyle Crescent
> Edinburgh, EH12 9EB
> Tel: (01506) 448 440
> Fax: (01256) 448 400

For other references to the adverse effects of corticosteroids see section 11.4 (eye) and section 13.4 (skin).

**STEROID TREATMENT CARD**

I am a patient on STEROID treatment which must not be stopped suddenly

- If you have been taking this medicine for more than three weeks, the dose should be reduced gradually when you stop taking steroids unless your doctor says otherwise.
- Read the patient information leaflet given with the medicine.
- Always carry this card with you and show it to anyone who treats you (for example a doctor, nurse, pharmacist or dentist). For one year after you stop the treatment, you must mention that you have taken steroids.
- If you become ill, or if you come into contact with anyone who has an infectious disease, consult your doctor promptly. If you have never had chickenpox, you should avoid close contact with people who have chickenpox or shingles. If you do come into contact with chickenpox, see your doctor urgently.
- Make sure that the information on the card is kept up to date.

## Use of corticosteroids

Dosage of corticosteroids varies widely in different diseases and in different patients. If the use of a corticosteroid can save or prolong life, as in exfoliative dermatitis, pemphigus, acute leukaemia or acute transplant rejection, high doses may need to be given, because the complications of therapy are likely to be less serious than the effects of the disease itself.

When long-term corticosteroid therapy is used in some chronic diseases, the adverse effects of treatment may become greater than the disabilities caused by the disease. To minimise side-effects the maintenance dose should be kept as low as possible.

When potentially less harmful measures are ineffective corticosteroids are used topically for the treatment of inflammatory conditions of the skin (section 13.4). Corticosteroids should be avoided or used only under specialist supervision in psoriasis (section 13.5).

Corticosteroids are used both topically (by rectum) and systemically (by mouth or intravenously) in the management of ulcerative colitis and Crohn's disease (section 1.5 and section 1.7.2).

Use can be made of the mineralocorticoid activity of fludrocortisone to treat postural hypotension in autonomic neuropathy (section 6.1.5).

Although very high doses of corticosteroids have been given by intravenous injection in septic shock, a study of high-dose methylprednisolone sodium succinate did not demonstrate efficacy and, moreover, suggested a higher mortality in some subsets of patients given the high-dose corticosteroid therapy. However, there is evidence that administration of lower doses of hydrocortisone (50 mg intravenously every 6 hours) and fludrocortisone (50 micrograms daily by mouth) is of benefit in patients who have adrenocortical insufficiency as a consequence of septic shock.



Dexamethasone and betamethasone have little if any mineralocorticoid action and their long duration of action makes them particularly suitable for suppressing corticotropin secretion in congenital adrenal hyperplasia where the dose should be tailored to clinical response and by measurement of adrenal androgens and 17-hydroxyprogesterone. In common with all glucocorticoids their suppressive action on the hypothalamic-pituitary-adrenal axis is greatest and most prolonged when they are given at night. In most normal subjects a single dose of 1 mg of dexamethasone at night, is sufficient to inhibit corticotropin secretion for 24 hours. This is the basis of the 'overnight dexamethasone suppression test' for diagnosing Cushing's syndrome.

Betamethasone and dexamethasone are also appropriate for conditions where water retention would be a disadvantage.

A corticosteroid may be used in the management of raised intracranial pressure or cerebral oedema that occurs as a result of malignancy (see also p. 15); high doses of betamethasone or dexamethasone are generally used. However, a corticosteroid should **not** be used for the management of head injury or stroke because it is unlikely to be of benefit and may even be harmful

In acute hypersensitivity reactions such as angioedema of the upper respiratory tract and anaphylactic shock, corticosteroids are indicated as an adjunct to emergency treatment with adrenaline (epinephrine) (section 3.4.3). In such cases hydrocortisone (as sodium succinate) by intravenous injection in a dose of 100 to 300 mg may be required.

Corticosteroids are preferably used by inhalation in the management of asthma (section 3.2) but systemic therapy in association with bronchodilators is required for the emergency treatment of severe acute asthma (section 3.1.1).

Corticosteroids may also be useful in conditions such as auto-immune hepatitis, rheumatoid arthritis and sarcoidosis; they may also lead to remissions of acquired haemolytic anaemia (section 9.1.3), and some cases of the nephrotic syndrome (particularly in children) and thrombocytopenic purpura (section 9.1.4).

Corticosteroids can improve the prognosis of serious conditions such as systemic lupus erythematosus, temporal arteritis, and polyarteritis nodosa; the effects of the disease process may be suppressed and symptoms relieved, but the underlying condition is not cured, although it may ultimately remit. It is usual to begin therapy in these conditions at fairly high dose, such as 40 to 60 mg prednisolone daily, and then to reduce the dose to the lowest commensurate with disease control.

For other references to the use of corticosteroids see Prescribing in Palliative Care, section 8.2.2 (immunosuppresion), section 10.1.2 (rheumatic diseases), section 11.4 (eye), section 12.1.1 (otitis externa), section 12.2.1 (allergic rhinitis), and section 12.3.1 (aphthous ulcers).

## Pregnancy and breast-feeding

Following a review of the data on the safety of systemic corticosteroids used in pregnancy and breast-feeding the CSM has concluded:

- corticosteroids vary in their ability to cross the placenta; betamethasone and dexamethasone cross the placenta readily while 88% of prednisolone is inactivated as it crosses the placenta;
- there is no convincing evidence that systemic corticosteroids increase the incidence of congenital abnormalities such as cleft palate or lip;
- when administration is prolonged or repeated during pregnancy, systemic corticosteroids increase the risk of intra-uterine growth restriction; there is no evidence of intra-uterine growth restriction following short-term treatment (e.g. prophylactic treatment for neonatal respiratory distress syndrome);
- any adrenal suppression in the neonate following prenatal exposure usually resolves spontaneously after birth and is rarely clinically important;
- prednisolone appears in small amounts in breast milk but maternal doses of up to 40 mg daily are unlikely to cause systemic effects in the infant; infants should be monitored for adrenal suppression if the mothers are taking a higher dose.

See also Appendix 4.

## Administration

Whenever possible *local treatment* with creams, intra-articular injections, inhalations, eye-drops, or enemas should be used in preference to *systemic treatment*. The suppressive action of a corticosteroid on cortisol secretion is least when it is given as a single dose in the morning. In an attempt to reduce pituitary-adrenal suppression further, the total dose for two days can sometimes be taken as a single dose on alternate days; alternate-day administration has not been very successful in the management of asthma (section 3.2). Pituitary-adrenal suppression can also be reduced by means of intermittent therapy with short courses. In some conditions it may be possible to reduce the dose of corticosteroid by adding a small dose of an immunosuppressive drug (section 8.2.1).

## Withdrawal of corticosteroids

The CSM has recommended that *gradual* withdrawal of systemic corticosteroids should be considered in those whose disease is unlikely to relapse and have

- recently received repeated courses (particularly if taken for longer than 3 weeks)
- taken a short course within 1 year of stopping long-term therapy
- other possible causes of adrenal suppression
- received more than 40 mg daily prednisolone (or equivalent)
- been given repeat doses in the evening
- received more than 3 weeks' treatment

Systemic corticosteroids may be stopped abruptly in those whose disease is unlikely to relapse *and* who have received treatment for 3 weeks or less *and* who are not included in the patient groups described above.

During corticosteroid withdrawal the dose may be reduced rapidly down to physiological doses (equivalent to prednisolone 7.5 mg daily) and then reduced more slowly. Assessment of the disease may be needed during withdrawal to ensure that relapse does not occur.

## PREDNISOLONE

**Indications** suppression of inflammatory and allergic disorders; see also notes above; inflammatory bowel disease, section 1.5; asthma, section 3.2; immunosuppression, section 8.2.2; rheumatic disease, section 10.1.2

**Cautions** adrenal suppression and infection (see notes above), children and adolescents (growth retardation possibly irreversible), elderly (close supervision required particularly on long-term treatment); frequent monitoring required if history of tuberculosis (or X-ray changes), hypertension, recent myocardial infarction (rupture reported), congestive heart failure, liver failure (Appendix 2), renal impairment, diabetes mellitus including family history, osteoporosis (postmenopausal women at special risk), glaucoma (including family history), corneal perforation, severe affective disorders (particularly if history of steroid-induced psychosis), epilepsy, peptic ulcer, hypothyroidism, history of steroid myopathy; pregnancy (Appendix 4) and breast-feeding (Appendix 5) (see also notes above); **interactions**: Appendix 1 (corticosteroids)

**Contra-indications** systemic infection (unless specific antimicrobial therapy given); avoid live virus vaccines in those receiving immunosuppressive doses (serum antibody response diminished)

**Side-effects** minimised by using lowest effective dose for minimum period possible;

*gastro-intestinal effects* include dyspepsia, peptic ulceration (with perforation), abdominal distension, acute pancreatitis, oesophageal ulceration and candidiasis; *musculoskeletal effects* include proximal myopathy, osteoporosis, vertebral and long bone fractures, avascular osteonecrosis, tendon rupture; *endocrine effects* include adrenal suppression, menstrual irregularities and amenorrhoea, Cushing's syndrome (with high doses, usually reversible on withdrawal), hirsutism, weight gain, negative nitrogen and calcium balance, increased appetite; increased susceptibility to and severity of infection; *neuropsychiatric effects* include euphoria, psychological dependence, depression, insomnia, increased intracranial pressure with papilloedema in children (usually after withdrawal), psychosis and aggravation of schizophrenia, aggravation of epilepsy; *ophthalmic effects* include glaucoma, papilloedema, posterior subcapsular cataracts, corneal or scleral thinning and exacerbation of ophthalmic viral or fungal disease; *other side-effects* include impaired healing, skin atrophy, bruising, striae, telangiectasia, acne, myocardial rupture following recent myocardial infarction, fluid and electrolyte disturbance, leucocytosis, hypersensitivity reactions (including anaphylaxis), thromboembolism, nausea, malaise, hiccups

**Dose**

- By mouth, initially, up to 10–20 mg daily (severe disease, up to 60 mg daily), preferably taken in the morning after breakfast; can often be reduced within a few days but may need to be continued for several weeks or months

  Maintenance, usual range, 2.5–15 mg daily, but higher doses may be needed; cushingoid side-effects increasingly likely with doses above 7.5 mg daily
- By intramuscular injection, prednisolone acetate (section 10.1.2.2), 25–100 mg once or twice weekly

**Prednisolone** (Non-proprietary) PoM

Tablets, prednisolone 1 mg, net price 28-tab pack = £1.26; 5 mg, 28-tab pack = £1.36; 25 mg, 56-tab pack = £9.67. Label: 10, steroid card, 21

Tablets, both e/c, prednisolone 2.5 mg (brown), net price 30-tab pack = 31p; 5 mg (red), 30-tab pack = 51p. Label: 5, 10, steroid card 25

Brands include *Deltacortril Enteric®*

Soluble tablets, prednisolone 5 mg (as sodium phosphate), net price 30-tab pack = £2.20. Label: 10, steroid card, 13, 21

Injection, see section 10.1.2.2

## BETAMETHASONE

**Indications** suppression of inflammatory and allergic disorders; congenital adrenal hyperplasia; see also notes above; ear (section 12.1.1); eye (section 11.4.1); nose (section 12.2.1)

**Cautions** see notes above and under Prednisolone; transient effect on fetal movements and heart rate

**Contra-indications** see notes above and under Prednisolone

**Side-effects** see notes above and under Prednisolone

**Dose**

- By mouth, usual range 0.5–5 mg daily; see also Administration (above)
- By intramuscular injection *or* slow intravenous injection *or* infusion, 4–20 mg, repeated up to 4 times in 24 hours; CHILD, by slow intravenous injection, up to 1 year 1 mg, 1–5 years 2 mg, 6–12 years 4 mg

**Betnelan®** (Celltech) PoM

Tablets, scored, betamethasone 500 micrograms. Net price 100-tab pack = £4.39. Label: 10, steroid card, 21

**Betnesol®** (Celltech) PoM

Soluble tablets, pink, scored, betamethasone 500 micrograms (as sodium phosphate). Net price 100-tab pack = £5.17. Label: 10, steroid card, 13, 21

Injection, betamethasone 4 mg (as sodium phosphate) /mL. Net price 1-mL amp = £1.22. Label: 10, steroid card

## CORTISONE ACETATE

**Indications** see under Dose but now superseded, see also notes above

**Cautions** see notes above and under Prednisolone

**Contra-indications** see notes above and under Prednisolone

**Side-effects** see notes above and under Prednisolone

**Dose**

- For replacement therapy, 25–37.5 mg daily in divided doses

**Cortisone** (Non-proprietary) PoM

Tablets, cortisone acetate 25 mg, net price 56-tab pack = £10.92. Label: 10, steroid card, 21

## DEFLAZACORT

**Indications** suppression of inflammatory and allergic disorders

**Cautions** see notes above and under Prednisolone

**Contra-indications** see notes above and under Prednisolone

**Side-effects** see notes above and under Prednisolone

**Dose**

- Usual maintenance 3–18 mg daily (acute disorders, initially up to 120 mg daily); see also Administration (above)

  CHILD 0.25–1.5 mg/kg daily (or on alternate days); see also Administration (above)

**Calcort®** (Shire) PoM

Tablets, deflazacort 1 mg, net price 100-tab pack = £8.00; 6 mg, 60-tab pack = £16.46; 30 mg, 30-tab pack = £22.80. Label: 5, 10, steroid card

## DEXAMETHASONE

**Indications** suppression of inflammatory and allergic disorders; diagnosis of Cushing's disease, congenital adrenal hyperplasia; cerebral oedema associated with malignancy; croup (section 3.1); nausea and vomiting with chemotherapy (section 8.1); rheumatic disease (section 10.1.2); eye (section 11.4.1); see also notes above

**Cautions** see notes above and under Prednisolone

**Contra-indications** see notes above and under Prednisolone

**Side-effects** see notes above and under Prednisolone; perineal irritation may follow intravenous administration of the phosphate ester

**Dose**

- By mouth, usual range 0.5–10 mg daily; CHILD 10–100 micrograms/kg daily; see also Administration (above)
- By intramuscular injection *or* slow intravenous injection *or* infusion (as dexamethasone phosphate), initially 0.5–24 mg; CHILD 200–400 micrograms/kg daily

  Cerebral oedema (as dexamethasone phosphate), by intravenous injection, 10 mg initially, then 4 mg by intramuscular injection every 6 hours as required for 2–4 days then gradually reduced and stopped over 5–7 days

  Adjunctive treatment of bacterial meningitis, (started with antibacterial treatment, as dexamethasone phosphate) [unlicensed indication], by intravenous injection, 10 mg every 6 hours for 4 days; CHILD 150 micrograms/kg every 6 hours for 4 days

  **Note** Dexamethasone 1 mg ≡ dexamethasone phosphate 1.2 mg ≡ dexamethasone sodium phosphate 1.3 mg

**Dexamethasone** (Non-proprietary) PoM

Tablets, dexamethasone 500 micrograms, net price 20 = 67p; 2 mg, 20 = £2.42. Label: 10, steroid card, 21
Available from Organon

Oral solution, sugar-free, dexamethasone (as dexamethasone sodium phosphate) 2 mg/5 mL, net price 150-mL = £42.30. Label: 10, steroid card, 21
Brands include *Dexsol®*

Injection, dexamethasone phosphate (as dexamethasone sodium phosphate) 4 mg/mL, net price 1-mL amp = £1.00, 2-mL vial = £1.98; 24 mg/mL, 5-mL vial = £16.66. Label: 10, steroid card
Available from Mayne

Injection, dexamethasone (as dexamethasone sodium phosphate) 4 mg/mL, net price 1-mL amp = 83p, 2-mL vial = £1.27. Label: 10, steroid card
Available from Organon

## HYDROCORTISONE

**Indications** adrenocortical insufficiency (section 6.3.1); shock; see also notes above; hypersensitivity reactions e.g. anaphylactic shock and angioedema (section 3.4.3); inflammatory bowel disease (section 1.5); haemorrhoids (section 1.7.2); rheumatic disease (section 10.1.2); eye (section 11.4.1); skin (section 13.4)

**Cautions** see notes above and under Prednisolone

**Contra-indications** see notes above and under Prednisolone

**Side-effects** see notes above and under Prednisolone; phosphate ester associated with paraesthesia and pain (particularly in the perineal region)

**Dose**

- By mouth, replacement therapy, 20–30 mg daily in divided doses—see section 6.3.1; CHILD 10–30 mg
- By intramuscular injection *or* slow intravenous injection *or* infusion, 100–500 mg, 3–4 times in 24 hours or as required; CHILD by slow intravenous injection up to 1 year 25 mg, 1–5 years 50 mg, 6–12 years 100 mg

[1] **Efcortesol®** (Sovereign) PoM

Injection, hydrocortisone 100 mg (as sodium phosphate)/mL, net price 1-mL amp = 75p, 5-mL amp = £3.40. Label: 10, steroid card

**Note** Paraesthesia and pain (particularly in the perineal region) may follow intravenous injection of the phosphate ester

1. PoM restriction does not apply where administration is for saving life in emergency

**Hydrocortone®** (MSD) PoM

Tablets, scored, hydrocortisone 10 mg, net price 30-tab pack = 70p; 20 mg, 30-tab pack = £1.07. Label: 10, steroid card, 21

[1] **Solu-Cortef®** (Pharmacia) PoM

Injection, powder for reconstitution, hydrocortisone (as sodium succinate). Net price 100-mg vial = 92p, 100-mg vial with 2-mL amp water for injections = £1.16. Label: 10, steroid card

1. PoM restriction does not apply where administration is for saving life in emergency

## METHYLPREDNISOLONE

**Indications** suppression of inflammatory and allergic disorders; cerebral oedema associated with malignancy; see also notes above; rheumatic disease (section 10.1.2); skin (section 13.4)

**Cautions** see notes above and under Prednisolone; rapid intravenous administration of large doses associated with cardiovascular collapse

**Contra-indications** see notes above and under Prednisolone

**Side-effects** see notes above and under Prednisolone

**Dose**

- By mouth, usual range 2–40 mg daily; see also Administration (above)
- By intramuscular injection *or* slow intravenous injection *or* infusion, initially 10–500 mg; graft rejection, up to 1 g daily by intravenous infusion for up to 3 days

**Medrone®** (Pharmacia) PoM
Tablets, scored, methylprednisolone 2 mg (pink), net price 30-tab pack = £3.23; 4 mg, 30-tab pack = £6.19; 16 mg, 30-tab pack = £17.17; 100 mg (blue), 20-tab pack = £48.32. Label: 10, steroid card 21

**Solu-Medrone®** (Pharmacia) PoM
Injection, powder for reconstitution, methylprednisolone (as sodium succinate) (all with solvent). Net price 40-mg vial = £1.58; 125-mg vial = £4.75; 500-mg vial = £9.60; 1-g vial = £17.30; 2-g vial = £32.86. Label: 10, steroid card

### Intramuscular depot

**Depo-Medrone®** (Pharmacia) PoM
Injection (aqueous suspension), methylprednisolone acetate 40 mg/mL. Net price 1-mL vial = £2.87; 2-mL vial = £5.15; 3-mL vial = £7.47. Label: 10, steroid card
**Dose** by deep intramuscular injection into gluteal muscle, 40–120 mg, a second injection may be given after 2–3 weeks if required

## TRIAMCINOLONE

**Indications** suppression of inflammatory and allergic disorders; see also notes above; rheumatic disease, section 10.1.2; mouth, section 12.3.1; skin, section 13.4

**Cautions** see notes above and under Prednisolone; high dosage may cause proximal myopathy, avoid in chronic therapy

**Contra-indications** see notes above and under Prednisolone

**Side-effects** see notes above and under Prednisolone

**Dose**

- By deep intramuscular injection, into gluteal muscle, 40 mg of acetonide for depot effect, repeated at intervals according to the patient's response; max. single dose 100 mg

**Kenalog® Intra-articular/Intramuscular** (Squibb) PoM
Injection (aqueous suspension), triamcinolone acetonide 40 mg/mL, net price 1-mL vial = £1.70; 1-mL prefilled syringe = £2.11; 2-mL prefilled syringe = £3.66. Label: 10, steroid card
**Note** Intramuscular needle with prefilled syringe should be replaced for intra-articular injection

# 6.4 Sex hormones

6.4.1 Female sex hormones
6.4.2 Male sex hormones and antagonists
6.4.3 Anabolic steroids

## 6.4.1 Female sex hormones

6.4.1.1 Oestrogens and HRT
6.4.1.2 Progestogens

### 6.4.1.1 Oestrogens and HRT

Oestrogens are necessary for the development of female secondary sexual characteristics; they also stimulate myometrial hypertrophy with endometrial hyperplasia.

In terms of oestrogenic activity *natural oestrogens* (estradiol (oestradiol), estrone (oestrone), and estriol (oestriol)) have a more appropriate profile for hormone replacement therapy (HRT) than *synthetic oestrogens* (ethinylestradiol (ethinyloestradiol) and mestranol). Tibolone has oestrogenic, progestogenic and weak androgenic activity.

Oestrogen therapy is given cyclically or continuously for a number of gynaecological conditions. If long-term therapy is required a progestogen should normally be added to reduce the risk of cystic hyperplasia of the endometrium (or of endometriotic foci in women who have had a hysterectomy) and possible transformation to cancer.

Oestrogens are no longer used to *suppress lactation* because of their association with thromboembolism.



#### Hormone replacement therapy

Hormone replacement therapy (HRT) with small doses of an oestrogen (together with a progestogen in women with an intact uterus) is appropriate for alleviating menopausal symptoms such as *vaginal atrophy* or *vasomotor instability*. Oestrogen given systemically in the perimenopausal and postmenopausal period or tibolone given in the postmenopausal period also diminish *postmenopausal osteoporosis* (section 6.6.1) but other drugs (section 6.6) are preferred. Menopausal atrophic vaginitis may respond to a short course of a topical vaginal oestrogen preparation (section 7.2.1) used for a few weeks and repeated if necessary.

Systemic therapy with an oestrogen or drugs with oestrogenic properties alleviates the symptoms of oestrogen deficiency such as *vasomotor symptoms*. Tibolone combines oestrogenic and progestogenic activity with weak androgenic activity; it is given continuously, without cyclical progestogen.

HRT increases the risk of *venous thromboembolism*, of *stroke* and, after some years of use, *endometrial cancer* (reduced by a progestogen) and of *breast cancer* (see below). The CSM advises that the minimum effective dose should be used for the shortest duration. Treatment should be reviewed at least annually and for osteoporosis alternative treatments considered (section

6.6). HRT does not prevent coronary heart disease or protect against a decline in cognitive function and it should **not** be prescribed for these purposes. Experience of treating women over 65 years with HRT is limited.

Clonidine (section 2.5.2 andsection 4.7.4.2) may be used to reduce vasomotor symptoms in women who cannot take an oestrogen, but clonidine may cause unacceptable side-effects.

HRT may be used in women with *early natural or surgical menopause (before age 45 years)*, since they are at high risk of osteoporosis. For early menopause, HRT can be given until the approximate age of natural menopause (i.e. until age 50 years). Alternatives to HRT should be considered if osteoporosis is the main concern (section 6.6).

In women with an intact uterus, the addition of a progestogen reduces the risk of endometrial cancer but this should be weighed against the increased risk of breast cancer.

For the treatment of menopausal symptoms the benefits of short-term HRT outweigh the risks in the majority of women, especially in those aged under 60 years.

**Risk of breast cancer** The CSM has estimated that using *all* types of HRT, including tibolone, increases the risk of breast cancer within 1–2 years of initiating treatment. The increased risk is related to the duration of HRT use (but not to the age at which HRT is started) and this excess risk disappears within about 5 years of stopping.

About 14 in every 1000 women aged 50–64 years not using HRT have breast cancer diagnosed over 5 years. In those using *oestrogen-only HRT* for 5 years, breast cancer is diagnosed in about 1.5 extra cases in 1000. In those using *combined HRT* for 5 years, breast cancer is diagnosed in about 6 extra cases in 1000. About 31 in every 1000 women aged 50–79 years not using HRT have breast cancer diagnosed over 5 years. In those using oestrogen-only HRT for 5 years no extra cases are diagnosed, but in those using *combined HRT* for 5 years, breast cancer is diagnosed in about 4 extra cases in 1000.

Tibolone increases the risk of breast cancer but to a lesser extent than with *combined HRT*.

**Risk of venous thromboembolism** Women on combined or oestrogen-only HRT are at an increased risk of deep vein thrombosis and of pulmonary embolism especially in the first year.

The CSM has estimated that about 10 in every 1000 *women aged 50–59 years* not using HRT develop venous thromboembolism over 5 years; this figure rises by about 1 extra case in 1000 in those using oestrogen-only HRT and about 4 extra cases in 1000 in those using combined HRT for 5 years. About 20 in every 1000 *women aged 60–69 years* not using HRT develop venous thromboembolism over 5 years; this figure rises by about 4 extra cases in 1000 in those using oestrogen-only HRT and about 9 extra cases in 1000 in those using combined HRT for 5 years. It is not known if tibolone increases the risk of venous thromboembolism.

In *women who have predisposing factors* (such as a personal or family history of deep vein thrombosis or pulmonary embolism, severe varicose veins, obesity, trauma, or prolonged bed-rest) it may be prudent to review the need for HRT as in some cases the risks of HRT may exceed the benefits. See below for advice on surgery.

*Travel* involving prolonged immobility further increases the risk of deep vein thrombosis, see under Travel in section 7.3.1.

**Other risks** Combined HRT or oestrogen-only HRT slightly increases the risk of *stroke*. The CSM has estimated that about 3 in every 1000 *women aged 50–59 years* not using HRT have a stroke over 5 years; this figure rises by about 2 extra cases in 1000 in those using oestrogen-only HRT and by about 1 extra case in those using combined HRT for 5 years. About 26 in every *1000 women aged 60–69 years* not using HRT have a stroke over 5 years; this figure rises by about 6 extra cases in 1000 in those using oestrogen-only HRT and by about 4 extra cases in those using combined HRT for 5 years.

HRT does not prevent *coronary heart disease* and should not be prescribed for this purpose. HRT possibly increases the risk of coronary heart disease in the first year.

The CSM has estimated that about 3 in every 1000 women aged 50–69 years not using HRT have *endometrial cancer* diagnosed over 5 years; in those using *oestrogen-only HRT* for 5 years endometrial cancer is diagnosed in about 5 extra cases in 1000. The risk of endometrial cancer cannot be reliably estimated in those using combined HRT because the addition of progestogen for at least 12 days per month greatly reduces the additional risk. The risk of endometrial cancer may be different for sequential and continuous combined HRT. The risk of endometrial cancer with tibolone is not known.

The CSM has estimated that about 3 in every 1000 women aged 50–69 years not using HRT have *ovarian cancer* diagnosed over 5 years; this figure rises by about 1 extra case in 1000 in those using *oestrogen-only HRT* for 5 years; the risks in women using combined HRT are unknown.

**Choice** The choice of HRT for an individual depends on an overall balance of indication, risk, and convenience. A woman with an intact uterus normally requires oestrogen with cyclical progestogen for the last 12 to 14 days of the cycle *or* a preparation which involves continuous administration of an oestrogen and a progestogen (*or* one which provides both oestrogenic and progestogenic activity in a single preparation). Continuous combined preparations or tibolone are **not suitable** for use in the *perimenopause* or within 12 months of the last menstrual period; women who use such preparations may bleed irregularly in the early stages of treatment—if bleeding continues endometrial abnormality should be ruled out and consideration given to changing to cyclical HRT.

An oestrogen alone is suitable for continuous use in women without a uterus. However, in endometriosis, endometrial foci may remain despite hysterectomy and the addition of a progestogen should be considered in these circumstances.

An oestrogen may be given by mouth or it may be given by subcutaneous or transdermal administration, which avoids first-pass metabolism. In the case of subcutaneous implants, recurrence of vasomotor symptoms at supraphysiological plasma concentrations may occur; moreover, there is evidence of prolonged endometrial stimulation after discontinuation (calling for continued cyclical progestogen). For the use of topical HRT preparations see section 7.2.1.

**Contraception** HRT does **not** provide contraception and a woman is considered potentially fertile for *2 years after her last menstrual period* if she is *under 50 years*, and for *1 year* if she is *over 50 years*. A woman who is under 50 years and free of all risk factors for venous and arterial disease can use a low-oestrogen combined oral contraceptive pill (section 7.3.1) to provide both *relief of menopausal symptoms* and *contraception*; it is recommended that the oral contraceptive be stopped at 50 years of age since there are more suitable alternatives. If any potentially fertile woman needs HRT, *non-hormonal contraceptive measures* (such as condoms, or by this age, contraceptive foam, section 7.3.3) are necessary.

Measurement of follicle-stimulating hormone can help to determine fertility, but high measurements alone (particularly in women aged under 50 years) do not necessarily preclude the possibility of becoming pregnant.

**Surgery** Major surgery under general anaesthesia, including orthopaedic and vascular leg surgery, is a predisposing factor for venous thromboembolism and it may be prudent to stop HRT 4–6 weeks before surgery (see Risk of Venous Thromboembolism, above); it should be restarted only after full mobilisation. If HRT is continued or if discontinuation is not possible (e.g. in non-elective surgery), prophylaxis with heparin and graduated compression hosiery is advised. Oestrogenic activity may persist after removing an estradiol implant (see above).

**Reasons to stop HRT** For circumstances in which HRT should be stopped, see p. 409.

## OESTROGENS FOR HRT

**Note** Relates only to small amounts of oestrogens given for hormone replacement therapy

**Indications** see notes above and under preparations

**Cautions** prolonged exposure to unopposed oestrogens may increase risk of developing endometrial cancer (see notes above); migraine (or migraine-like headaches); diabetes (increased risk of heart disease); history of breast nodules or fibrocystic disease—closely monitor breast status (risk of breast cancer, see notes above); risk factors for oestrogen-dependent tumours (e.g. breast cancer in first-degree relative); uterine fibroids may increase in size, symptoms of endometriosis may be exacerbated; factors predisposing to thromboembolism (see notes above); presence of antiphospholipid antibodies (increased risk of thrombotic events); increased risk of gall-bladder disease reported; hypophyseal tumours; porphyria (see section 9.8.2); **interactions:** Appendix 1 (oestrogens)

**Other conditions** The product literature advises caution in other conditions including hypertension, renal disease, asthma, epilepsy, sickle-cell disease, melanoma, otosclerosis, multiple sclerosis, and systemic lupus erythematosus (but care required if antiphospholipid antibodies present, see above). Evidence for caution in these conditions is unsatisfactory and many women with these conditions may stand to benefit from HRT.

**Contra-indications** pregnancy; oestrogen-dependent cancer, history of breast cancer, active thrombophlebitis, active or recent arterial thromboembolic disease (e.g. angina or myocardial infarction), venous thromboembolism, or history of recurrent venous thromboembolism (unless already on anticoagulant treatment), liver disease (where liver function tests have failed to return to normal), Dubin-Johnson and Rotor syndromes (or monitor closely), untreated endometrial hyperplasia, undiagnosed vaginal bleeding, breast-feeding

**Side-effects** see notes above for risks of long-term use; nausea and vomiting, abdominal cramps and bloating, weight changes, breast enlargement and tenderness, premenstrual-like syndrome, sodium and fluid retention, cholestatic jaundice, glucose intolerance, altered blood lipids–may lead to pancreatitis, rashes and chloasma, changes in libido, depression, mood changes, headache, migraine, dizziness, leg cramps (rule out venous thrombosis), vaginal candidiasis, contact lenses may irritate; transdermal delivery systems may cause contact sensitisation (possible severe hypersensitivity reaction on continued exposure), and headache has been reported on vigorous exercise; nasal spray may cause local irritation, rhinorrhoea and epistaxis

**Withdrawal bleeding** Cyclical HRT (where a progestogen is taken for 12–14 days of each 28-day oestrogen treatment cycle) usually results in *regular withdrawal bleeding* towards the end of the progestogen. The aim of continuous combined HRT (where a combination of oestrogen and progestogen is taken, usually in a single tablet, throughout each 28-day treatment cycle) is to avoid bleeding, but *irregular bleeding* may occur during the early treatment stages (if it continues endometrial abnormality should be excluded and consideration given to cyclical HRT instead)

**Dose**

- See under preparations

**Counselling on patches** Patch should be removed after 3–4 days (or once a week in case of 7-day patch) and replaced with fresh patch on slightly different site; recommended sites: clean, dry, unbroken areas of skin on trunk below waistline; not to be applied on or near breasts or under waistband. If patch falls off in bath allow skin to cool before applying new patch

### Conjugated oestrogens with progestogen

**Premique®** (Wyeth) PoM

Premique® Low Dose tablets, s/c, ivory, conjugated oestrogen (equine) 300 micrograms and medroxyprogesterone acetate 1.5 mg, net price 3 × 28-tab pack = £29.85

**Dose** menopausal symptoms in women with an intact uterus, 1 tablet daily continuously

Premique® tablets, s/c, blue, conjugated oestrogen (equine) 625 micrograms and medroxyprogesterone acetate 5 mg. Net price 3 × 28-tab pack = £27.14

**Dose** menopausal symptoms and osteoporosis prophylaxis (see section 6.6), in women with intact uterus, 1 tablet daily continuously (starting on day 1 of menstruation if cycles have not ceased)

Premique® Cycle Calendar pack, all s/c, 14 white tablets, conjugated oestrogens (equine) 625 micrograms; 14 green tablets, conjugated oestrogens (equine) 625 micrograms and medroxyprogesterone acetate 10 mg, net price 3 × 28-tab pack = £24.87

**Dose** menopausal symptoms and osteoporosis prophylaxis (see section 6.6), 1 white tablet daily for 14 days, starting on day 1 of menstruation (or at any time if cycles have ceased or are infrequent) then 1 green tablet daily for 14 days; subsequent courses are repeated without interval

**Prempak-C®** (Wyeth) PoM

Prempak C® 0.625 Calendar pack, s/c, 28 maroon tablets, conjugated oestrogens (equine) 625 micrograms; 12 light brown tablets, norgestrel 150 micrograms (≡ levonorgestrel 75 micrograms). Net price 3 × 40-tab pack = £17.67

**Dose** menopausal symptoms and osteoporosis prophylaxis (see section 6.6), in women with intact uterus, 1 maroon tablet daily continuously, starting on day 1 of menstruation (or at any time if cycles have ceased or are infrequent), and 1 brown tablet daily on days 17–28 of each 28-day treatment cycle; subsequent courses are repeated without interval

Prempak C® 1.25 Calendar pack, s/c, 28 yellow tablets, conjugated oestrogens (equine) 1.25 mg; 12 light brown tablets, norgestrel 150 micrograms (≡ levonorgestrel 75 micrograms). Net price 3 × 40-tab pack = £17.67

**Dose** see under 0.625 Calendar pack, but taking 1 yellow tablet daily continuously (instead of 1 maroon tablet) if symptoms not fully controlled with lower strength

## Estradiol with progestogen

**Angeliq®** (Schering Health) ▼ PoM

Tablets, f/c, red, estradiol 1mg, drospirenone 2 mg. Net price 3 x 28-tab pack = £25.80

**Dose** menopausal symptoms and osteoporosis prophylaxis (see section 6.6), in women with intact uterus, 1 tablet daily continuously (if changing from cyclical HRT begin treatment the day after finishing oestrogen plus progestogen phase)

**Cautions** use with care if an increased concentration of potassium might be hazardous; renal impairment (Appendix 3)

**Note** Unsuitable for use in perimenopausal women or within 12 months of last menstrual period—see choice above

**Climagest®** (Novartis) PoM

Climagest® 1-mg tablets, 16 grey-blue, estradiol valerate 1 mg; 12 white, estradiol valerate 1 mg and norethisterone 1 mg. Net price 28-tab pack = £4.78; 3 × 28-tab pack = £13.91

**Dose** menopausal symptoms, 1 grey-blue tablet daily for 16 days, starting on day 1 of menstruation (or at any time if cycles have ceased or are infrequent) then 1 white tablet for 12 days; subsequent courses are repeated without interval

Climagest® 2-mg tablets, 16 blue, estradiol valerate 2 mg; 12 yellow, estradiol valerate 2 mg and norethisterone 1 mg. Net price 28-tab pack = £4.78; 3 × 28-tab pack = £13.91

**Dose** see *Climagest® 1-mg*, but starting with 1 blue tablet daily (instead of 1 grey-blue tablet) if symptoms not controlled with lower strength

**Climesse®** (Novartis) PoM

Tablets, pink, estradiol valerate 2 mg, norethisterone 700 micrograms. Net price 1 × 28-tab pack = £8.62; 3 × 28-tab pack = £25.86

**Dose** menopausal symptoms and osteoporosis prophylaxis (see section 6.6), in women with intact uterus, 1 tablet daily continuously

**Note** Unsuitable for use in perimenopausal women or within 12 months of last menstrual period—see Choice above

**Cyclo-Progynova®** (Viatris) PoM

Cyclo-Progynova® 1-mg tablets, all s/c, 11 beige, estradiol valerate 1 mg; 10 brown, estradiol valerate 1 mg and levonorgestrel 250 micrograms. Net price per pack = £3.11

**Dose** menopausal symptoms, in women with intact uterus, 1 beige tablet daily for 11 days, starting on day 5 of menstruation (or at any time if cycles have ceased or are infrequent), then 1 brown tablet daily for 10 days, followed by a 7-day interval

Cyclo-Progynova® 2-mg tablets, all s/c, 11 white, estradiol valerate 2 mg; 10 brown, estradiol valerate 2 mg and norgestrel 500 micrograms (≡ levonorgestrel 250 micrograms). Net price per pack = £3.11

**Dose** menopausal symptoms and osteoporosis prophylaxis (see section 6.6) as *Cyclo-Progynova® 1-mg*, but starting with 1 white tablet daily for 11 days, then 1 brown tablet daily for 10 days, followed by a 7-day interval

**Elleste-Duet®** (Pharmacia) PoM

Elleste-Duet® 1-mg tablets, 16 white, estradiol 1 mg; 12 green, estradiol 1 mg and norethisterone acetate 1 mg. Net price 3 × 28-tab pack = £9.72

**Dose** menopausal symptoms, 1 white tablet daily for 16 days starting on day 1 of menstruation (or at any time if cycles have ceased or are infrequent), then 1 green tablet daily for 12 days; subsequent courses are repeated without interval

Elleste-Duet® 2-mg tablets, 16 orange, estradiol 2 mg; 12 grey, estradiol 2 mg, norethisterone acetate 1 mg. Net price 3 × 28-tab pack = £9.72

**Dose** menopausal symptoms and osteoporosis prophylaxis (see section 6.6), 1 orange tablet daily for 16 days, starting on day 1 of menstruation (or at any time if cycles have ceased or are infrequent) then 1 grey tablet daily for 12 days; subsequent courses are repeated without interval

Elleste-Duet Conti® tablets, f/c, grey, estradiol 2 mg, norethisterone acetate 1 mg. Net price 3 × 28-tab pack = £17.97

**Dose** menopausal symptoms and osteoporosis prophylaxis (see section 6.6), in women with intact uterus, 1 tablet daily on a continuous basis (if changing from cyclical HRT begin treatment at the end of scheduled bleed)

**Note** Unsuitable for use in perimenopausal women or within 12 months of last menstrual period—see Choice above

**Estracombi®** (Novartis) PoM

Combination pack, self-adhesive patches of *Estraderm TTS® 50* (releasing estradiol approx. 50 micrograms/24 hours) and of *Estragest TTS®* (releasing estradiol approx. 50 micrograms/24 hours and norethisterone acetate 250 micrograms/24 hours); net price 1-month pack (4 of each) = £11.14, 3-month pack (12 of each) = £33.42. Counselling, administration

**Dose** menopausal symptoms and osteoporosis prophylaxis (see section 6.6), in women with intact uterus, starting within 5 days of onset of menstruation (or any time if cycles have ceased or are infrequent), 1 *Estraderm TTS® 50* patch to be applied twice weekly for 2 weeks followed by 1 *Estragest TTS®* patch twice weekly for 2 weeks; subsequent courses are repeated without interval

**Evorel®** (Janssen-Cilag) PoM

Evorel® Conti patches, self-adhesive, (releasing estradiol approx. 50 micrograms/24 hours and norethisterone acetate approx. 170 micrograms/24 hours), net price 8-patch pack = £12.26, 24-patch pack = £36.77. Counselling, administration

**Dose** menopausal symptoms and osteoporosis prophylaxis (see section 6.6), in women with intact uterus, 1 patch to be applied twice weekly continuously

Evorel® Pak calendar pack, 8 self-adhesive patches (releasing estradiol approx. 50 micrograms/24 hours) and 12 tablets, norethisterone 1 mg, net price per pack = £8.03. Counselling, administration

**Dose** menopausal symptoms and osteoporosis prophylaxis (see section 6.6), in women with intact uterus, apply 1 patch twice weekly continuously (increased if necessary for menopausal symptoms to 2 patches twice weekly after first month) and take 1 tablet daily on days 15–26 of each 28-day treatment cycle

Evorel® Sequi combination pack, 4 self-adhesive patches of *Evorel® 50* (releasing estradiol approx. 50 micrograms/24 hours) and 4 self-adhesive patches of *Evorel® Conti* (releasing estradiol approx. 50 micrograms/24 hours and norethisterone acetate approx.

170 micrograms/24 hours), net price 8-patch pack = £10.45. Counselling, administration

Dose menopausal symptoms and osteoporosis prophylaxis (see section 6.6), in women with intact uterus, 1 *Evorel® 50* patch to be applied twice weekly for 2 weeks followed by 1 *Evorel® Conti* patch twice weekly for 2 weeks; subsequent courses are repeated without interval

**Femapak®** (Solvay) PoM

Femapak® 40 combination pack of 8 self-adhesive patches of *Fematrix® 40* (releasing estradiol approx. 40 micrograms/24 hours) and 14 tablets of *Duphaston®* (dydrogesterone 10 mg). Net price per pack = £7.61. Counselling, administration

Dose see under *Femapak® 80*

Femapak® 80 combination pack of 8 self-adhesive patches of *Fematrix® 80* (releasing estradiol approx. 80 micrograms/24 hours) and 14 tablets of *Duphaston®* (dydrogesterone 10 mg). Net price per pack = £8.06. Counselling, administration

Dose menopausal symptoms (and osteoporosis prophylaxis (see section 6.6) in case of *Femapak® 80* **only**), in women with intact uterus, starting within 5 days of onset of menstruation (or any time if cycles have ceased or are infrequent), apply 1 patch twice weekly continuously and take 1 tablet daily on days 15–28 of each 28-day treatment cycle; therapy should be initiated with *Femapak® 40* in those with menopausal symptoms, prolonged oestrogen deficiency or anticipated intolerance to higher strengths, subsequently adjusted to lowest effective dose

**Femoston®** (Solvay) PoM

Femoston® 1/10 tablets, both f/c, 14 white, estradiol 1 mg; 14 grey, estradiol 1 mg, dydrogesterone 10 mg. Net price 3 × 28-tab pack = £13.47

Dose menopausal symptoms and osteoporosis prophylaxis (see section 6.6), in women with intact uterus, 1 white tablet daily for 14 days, starting within 5 days of onset of menstruation (or any time if cycles have ceased or are infrequent) then 1 grey tablet for 14 days; subsequent courses repeated without interval

Femoston® 2/10 tablets, both f/c, 14 red, estradiol 2 mg; 14 yellow, estradiol 2 mg, dydrogesterone 10 mg. Net price 3 × 28-tab pack = £13.47

Dose menopausal symptoms and osteoporosis prophylaxis (see section 6.6), in women with intact uterus, 1 red tablet daily for 14 days, starting within 5 days of onset of menstruation (or any time if cycles have ceased or are infrequent) then 1 yellow tablet daily for 14 days; subsequent courses repeated without interval; where therapy required for menopausal symptoms alone, *Femoston® 1/10* given initially and *Femoston® 2/10* substituted if symptoms not controlled

Femoston®-conti tablets, f/c, salmon, estradiol 1 mg, dydrogesterone 5 mg, net price 3 × 28-tab pack = £22.44

Dose menopausal symptoms and osteoporosis prophylaxis (see section 6.6), in women with intact uterus, 1 tablet daily continuously (if changing from cyclical HRT begin treatment the day after finishing oestrogen plus progestogen phase)

Note Unsuitable for use in perimenopausal women or within 12 months of last menstrual period—see Choice above

**FemSeven® Conti** (Merck) PoM

Patches, self-adhesive (releasing estradiol approx. 50 micrograms/24 hours and levonorgestrel approx. 7 micrograms/24 hours); net price 4-patch pack = £12.90, 12-patch pack = £ 36.77. Counselling, administration

Dose menopausal symptoms in women with intact uterus, 1 patch to be applied once a week continuously

Note Unsuitable for use in perimenopausal women or within 12 months of last menstrual period—see Choice above

**FemSeven® Sequi** (Merck) PoM

Combination pack, self-adhesive patches of *FemSeven® Sequi Phase 1* (releasing estradiol approx. 50 micrograms/24 hours) and of *FemSeven® Sequi Phase 2* (releasing estradiol approx. 50 micrograms/24 hours and levonorgestrel approx. 10 micrograms/24 hours); net price 1-month pack (2 of each) = £10.98, 3-month pack (6 of each) = £31.28. Counselling, administration

Dose menopausal symptoms in women with intact uterus, 1 *Phase 1* patch applied once a week for 2 weeks followed by 1 *Phase 2* patch once a week for 2 weeks; subsequent courses are repeated without interval

**FemTab® Sequi** (Merck) PoM

Tablets, both s/c, 16 white, estradiol valerate 2 mg; 12 pink, estradiol valerate 2 mg, levonorgestrel 75 micrograms, net price 3 × 28-tab pack = £15.15

Dose menopausal symptoms and osteoporosis prophylaxis (see section 6.6), in women with intact uterus, 1 white tablet daily for 16 days, starting on day 5 of menstruation (or any time if cycles have ceased or are infrequent) then 1 pink tablet daily for 12 days; subsequent courses are repeated without interval

**Indivina®** (Orion) PoM

Indivina® 1 mg/2.5 mg tablets, estradiol valerate 1 mg, medroxyprogesterone acetate 2.5 mg, net price 3 × 28-tab pack = £21.49

Indivina® 1 mg/5 mg tablets, estradiol valerate 1 mg, medroxyprogesterone acetate 5 mg, net price 3 × 28-tab pack = £21.49

Indivina® 2 mg/5 mg tablets, estradiol valerate 2 mg, medroxyprogesterone acetate 5 mg, net price 3 × 28-tab pack = £21.49

Dose menopausal symptoms and osteoporosis prophylaxis (see section 6.6), in women with intact uterus, 1 tablet daily continuously; initiate therapy with *Indivina®* 1 mg/2.5 mg tablets and adjust according to response; start at end of scheduled bleed if changing from cyclical HRT

Note Less suitable for use in perimenopausal women or within 3 years of last menstrual period—see Choice above

**Kliofem®** (Novo Nordisk) PoM

Tablets, f/c yellow, estradiol 2 mg, norethisterone acetate 1 mg. Net price 3 × 28-tab pack = £11.43

Dose menopausal symptoms and osteoporosis prophylaxis (see section 6.6), in women with intact uterus, 1 tablet daily continuously; start at end of scheduled bleed if changing from cyclical HRT

Note Unsuitable for use in perimenopausal women or within 12 months of last menstrual period—see Choice above

**Kliovance®** (Novo Nordisk) PoM

Tablets, f/c, estradiol 1mg, norethisterone acetate 500 micrograms, net price 3 × 28-tab pack = £14.67

Dose menopausal symptoms and osteoporosis prophylaxis (see section 6.6), in women with intact uterus, 1 tablet daily continuously; start at end of scheduled bleed if changing from cyclical HRT

Note Unsuitable for use in perimenopausal women or within 12 months of last menstrual period—see Choice above

**Novofem** (Novo Nordisk) PoM

Tablets, f/c, 16 red, estradiol 1 mg; 12 white, estradiol 1 mg, norethisterone acetate 1 mg, net price 3 × 28-tab pack = £13.50

Dose menopausal symptoms and osteoporosis prophylaxis (see section 6.6), in women with intact uterus, 1 red tablet daily for 16 days then 1 white tablet daily for 12 days; subsequent courses are repeated without interval; start treatment with red tablet at any time or if changing from cyclical HRT, start treatment the day after finishing oestrogen plus progestogen phase

**Nuvelle®** (Schering Health) PoM

Nuvelle® tablets, all s/c, 16 white, estradiol valerate 2 mg; 12 pink, estradiol valerate 2 mg and levonorgestrel 75 micrograms. Net price 3 × 28-tab pack = £12.87

Dose menopausal symptoms and osteoporosis prophylaxis (see section 6.6), in women with intact uterus, 1 white tablet daily for 16 days, starting on day 5 of menstruation (or any time if cycles have ceased or are infrequent) then 1 pink tablet daily for 12 days; subsequent courses are repeated without interval

Nuvelle® Continuous tablets, f/c, pink, estradiol 2 mg, norethisterone acetate 1 mg, net price 3 × 28-tab pack = £16.85

**Dose** menopausal symptoms and osteoporosis prophylaxis (see section 6.6), in women with intact uterus, 1 tablet daily continuously; start at end of scheduled bleed if changing from cyclical HRT

**Note** Unsuitable for use in perimenopausal women or within 12 months of last menstrual period—see Choice above

**Tridestra®** (Orion) PoM

Tablets, 70 white, estradiol valerate 2 mg; 14 blue, estradiol valerate 2 mg and medroxyprogesterone acetate 20 mg; 7 yellow, inactive. Net price 91-tab pack = £21.40

**Dose** menopausal symptoms and osteoporosis prophylaxis (see section 6.6), in women with intact uterus, 1 white tablet daily for 70 days, then 1 blue tablet daily for 14 days, then 1 yellow tablet daily for 7 days; subsequent courses are repeated without interval

**Trisequens®** (Novo Nordisk) PoM

Tablets, 12 blue, estradiol 2 mg; 10 white, estradiol 2 mg, norethisterone acetate 1 mg; 6 red, estradiol 1 mg, net price 3 × 28-tab pack = £11.10

**Dose** menopausal symptoms and osteoporosis prophylaxis (see section 6.6), in women with intact uterus, 1 blue tablet daily, starting on day 5 of menstruation (or at any time if cycles have ceased or are infrequent), then 1 tablet daily in sequence (without interruption)

## Conjugated oestrogens only

**Premarin®** (Wyeth) PoM

Tablets, all s/c, conjugated oestrogens (equine) 625 micrograms (maroon), net price 3 × 28-tab pack = £9.72; 1.25 mg (yellow), 3 × 28-tab pack = £13.19

**Dose** menopausal symptoms and osteoporosis prophylaxis (see section 6.6), (with progestogen for 12–14 days per cycle in women with intact uterus), 0.625–1.25 mg daily

## Estradiol only

**Estradiol Implants** (Organon) PoM

Implant, estradiol 25 mg, net price each = £11.27; 50 mg, each = £20.12

**Dose** by implantation, oestrogen replacement, and osteoporosis prophylaxis (see section 6.6) (with cyclical progestogen for 12–14 days of each cycle in women with intact uterus, see notes above), 25–100 mg as required (usually every 4–8 months) according to oestrogen levels—check before each implant

**Note** On cessation of treatment or if implants are removed from those with intact uterus, cyclical progesterone should be continued until withdrawal bleed stops

**Aerodiol®** (Servier) PoM

Nasal spray, estradiol 150 micrograms/metered spray, net price 4.2-mL unit (60 metered sprays) = £7.41

**Dose** menopausal symptoms, initially 1 spray into one nostril daily at the same time each day *either* continuously *or* for 21–28 days followed by a 2–7 day treatment-free interval; daily dose adjusted according to response to 1–4 sprays daily in divided doses; usual maintenance dose, 1 spray into each nostril once daily; with cyclical progestogen for at least 12 days of each cycle in women with intact uterus; not to be used immediately after nasal corticosteroid or nasal vasoconstrictor

**Note** If patient has a severely blocked nose, *Aerodiol®* may be temporarily administered into the mouth between the cheek and the gum above the upper teeth; in this situation the normal dose should be doubled

**Climaval®** (Novartis) PoM

Tablets, estradiol valerate 1 mg (grey-blue), net price 1 × 28-tab pack = £2.55, 3 × 28-tab pack = £7.66; 2 mg (blue), 1 × 28-tab pack = £2.55, 3 × 28-tab pack = £7.66

**Dose** menopausal symptoms (if patient has had a hysterectomy), 1–2 mg daily

**Elleste-Solo®** (Pharmacia) PoM

Elleste-Solo® 1-mg tablets, estradiol 1 mg. Net price 3 × 28-tab pack = £5.34

**Dose** menopausal symptoms, with cyclical progestogen for 12–14 days of each cycle in women with intact uterus, 1 mg daily starting on day 1 of menstruation (or at any time if cycles have ceased or are infrequent)

Elleste-Solo® 2-mg tablets, orange, estradiol 2 mg. Net price 3 × 28-tab pack = £5.34

**Dose** menopausal symptoms not controlled with lower strength and osteoporosis prophylaxis (see section 6.6), with cyclical progestogen for 12–14 days of each cycle in women with intact uterus, 2 mg daily starting on day 1 of menstruation (or at any time if cycles have ceased or are infrequent)

**Elleste Solo® MX** (Pharmacia) PoM

Patches, self-adhesive, estradiol, *MX 40 patch* (releasing approx. 40 micrograms/24 hours), net price 8-patch pack = £5.19; *MX 80 patch* (releasing approx. 80 micrograms/24 hours), 8-patch pack = £5.99. Counselling, administration.

**Dose** menopausal symptoms (and osteoporosis prophylaxis in case of *Elleste Solo MX 80®* **only**; see section 6.6), 1 patch to be applied twice weekly continuously starting within 5 days of onset of menstruation (or at any time if cycles have ceased or are infrequent); with cyclical progestogen for 12–14 days of each cycle in women with intact uterus; therapy should be initiated with *MX 40* in those with menopausal symptoms, prolonged oestrogen deficiency or anticipated intolerance to higher strength, dosage may be increased if required, subsequently adjusted to lowest effective dose

**Estraderm MX®** (Novartis) PoM

Patches, self-adhesive, estradiol, *MX 25 patch* (releasing approx. 25 micrograms/24 hours), net price 8-patch pack = £5.20, 24-patch pack = £15.59; *MX 50 patch* (releasing approx. 50 micrograms/24 hours), 8-patch pack = £5.22, 24-patch pack = £15.65, 20-patch pack (hosp. only) = £13.04; *MX 75 patch* (releasing approx. 75 micrograms/24 hours), 8-patch pack = £6.08, 24-patch pack = £18.25; *MX 100 patch* (releasing approx. 100 micrograms/24 hours), 8-patch pack = £6.31, 24-patch pack = £18.94. Counselling, administration

**Dose** menopausal symptoms (and osteoporosis prophylaxis in case of *Estraderm MX® 50* and *75* **only**; see section 6.6), 1 patch to be applied twice weekly continuously, with cyclical progestogen for 12 days of each cycle in women with intact uterus; therapy should be initiated with *MX 50* for first month, subsequently adjusted to lowest effective dose

**Estraderm TTS®** (Novartis) PoM

Patches, self-adhesive, estradiol, *TTS 25 patch* (releasing approx. 25 micrograms/24 hours), net price, 8-patch pack = £6.21, 24-patch pack = £18.63; *TTS 50 patch* (releasing approx. 50 micrograms/24 hours), 8-patch pack = £6.23, 24-patch pack = £18.69; *TTS 100 patch* (releasing approx. 100 micrograms/24 hours), 8-patch pack = £7.52, 24-patch pack = £22.63, 20-patch pack (hosp. only) = £16.76. Counselling, administration

**Dose** menopausal symptoms (and osteoporosis prophylaxis in case of *Estraderm TTS® 50* **only**; see section 6.6), 1 patch to be applied twice weekly continuously, with cyclical progestogen for 12 days of each cycle in women with intact uterus; therapy should be initiated with *TTS 50* for first month, subsequently adjusted to lowest effective dose

**Estradot®** (Novartis) PoM

Patches, self-adhesive, estradiol, *'25' patch* (releasing approx. 25 micrograms/24 hours), net price 8-patch pack = £5.20; *'37.5' patch* (releasing approx. 37.5 micrograms/24 hours), 8-patch pack = £5.21; *'50' patch* (releasing approx. 50 micrograms/24 hours), 8-patch pack = £5.22; *'75' patch* (releasing approx. 75 micrograms/24 hours), 8-patch pack = £6.08; *'100' patch* (releasing approx. 100 micrograms/24 hours), 8-patch pack = £6.31. Counselling, administration

Dose menopausal symptoms (all strengths) and osteoporosis prophylaxis (*Estradot® '50'*, *'75'*, and *'100'* **only**; see section 6.6), 1 patch to be applied twice weekly continuously, with cyclical progestogen for 12 days of each cycle in women with intact uterus; for osteoporosis prophylaxis therapy should be initiated with *'50' patch*

**Evorel®** (Janssen-Cilag) PoM

Patches, self-adhesive, estradiol, *'25' patch* (releasing approx. 25 micrograms/24 hours), net price 8-patch pack = £2.92; *'50' patch* (releasing approx. 50 micrograms/24 hours), 8-patch pack = £3.31, 24-patch pack = £9.93; *'75' patch* (releasing approx. 75 micrograms/24 hours), 8-patch pack = £3.52; *'100' patch* (releasing approx. 100 micrograms/24 hours), 8-patch pack = £3.65. Counselling, administration

Dose menopausal symptoms and osteoporosis prophylaxis (except *Evorel® 25*; see section 6.6), 1 patch to be applied twice weekly continuously, with cyclical progestogen for at least 12 days of each cycle in women with intact uterus; therapy should be initiated with *'50' patch* for first month, subsequently adjusted to lowest effective dose

**Fematrix®** (Solvay) PoM

Fematrix® 40 patch, self-adhesive, estradiol, *'40' patch* (releasing approx. 40 micrograms/24 hours). Net price 8-patch pack = £4.95. Counselling, administration

Dose menopausal symptoms, 1 patch to be applied twice weekly continuously starting within 5 days of onset of menstruation (or at any time if cycles have ceased or are infrequent), with cyclical progestogen for 12–14 days of each cycle in women with intact uterus; *'80' patch* may be used if required (subsequently adjusted to lowest effective dose)

Fematrix® 80 patch, self-adhesive, estradiol (releasing approx. 80 micrograms/24 hours). Net price 8-patch pack = £5.40. Counselling, administration

Dose menopausal symptoms and osteoporosis prophylaxis (see section 6.6), as for *Fematrix® 40*; therapy should be initiated with *Fematrix® 40* in those with menopausal symptoms, prolonged oestrogen deficiency or anticipated intolerance to higher strength

**FemSeven®** (Merck) PoM

Patches, self-adhesive, estradiol, *'50' patch* (releasing approx. 50 micrograms/24 hours), net price 4-patch pack = £5.03, 12-patch pack = £15.02; *'75' patch* (releasing approx. 75 micrograms/24 hours), net price 4-patch pack = £5.82; *'100' patch* (releasing approx. 100 micrograms/24 hours), net price 4-patch pack = £6.07. Counselling, administration

Dose menopausal symptoms and osteoporosis prophylaxis (see section 6.6), 1 patch to be applied once a week continuously, with cyclical progestogen for at least 10 days of each cycle in women with intact uterus; therapy should be initiated with *FemSeven® 50* patches for the first few months, subsequently adjusted according to response

**FemTab®** (Merck) PoM

Tablets, s/c, estradiol valerate 1 mg, net price 3 × 28-tab pack = £7.72; 2 mg, 3 × 28-tab pack = £7.72

Dose menopausal symptoms, 1–2 mg daily continuously; osteoporosis prophylaxis (see section 6.6), 2 mg daily continuously; with cyclical progestogen for 12 days of each cycle in women with intact uterus

**Menoring® 50** (Galen) PoM

Vaginal ring, releasing estradiol approx. 50 micrograms/24 hours, net price 1-ring pack = £29.50. Label: 10, patient information leaflet

Dose for postmenopausal vasomotor and urogenital symptoms in women without a uterus, to be inserted into upper third of vagina and worn continuously; replace after 3 months

**Oestrogel®** (Hoechst Marion Roussel) PoM

Gel, estradiol 0.06%, net price 64-dose pump pack = £7.39. Counselling, administration

Dose menopausal symptoms and osteoporosis prophylaxis (see section 6.6), 2 measures (estradiol 1.5 mg) to be applied over an area twice that of the template provided once daily continuously, starting within 5 days of menstruation (or anytime if cycles have ceased or are infrequent), with cyclical progestogen for 12 days of each cycle in women with intact uterus; for menopausal symptoms may be increased if necessary after 1 month to max. 4 measures daily

Counselling Apply gel to clean, dry, intact skin such as arms, shoulders or inner thighs and allow to dry for 5 minutes before covering with clothing. Not to be applied on or near breasts or on vulval region. Avoid skin contact with another person (particularly male) and avoid other skin products or washing the area for at least 1 hour after application

**Progynova®** (Schering Health) PoM

Tablets, both s/c, estradiol valerate 1 mg (beige), net price 3 × 28-tab pack = £6.56; 2 mg (blue), 3 × 28-tab pack = £6.56

Dose menopausal symptoms, 1–2 mg daily continuously; osteoporosis prophylaxis (see section 6.6), 2 mg daily continuously; with cyclical progestogen for 12 days of each cycle in women with intact uterus

**Progynova® TS** (Schering Health) PoM

Patches, self-adhesive, *Progynova® TS 50* (releasing estradiol approx. 50 micrograms/24 hours), net price 12-patch pack = £16.71; *Progynova® TS 100* (releasing estradiol approx. 100 micrograms/24 hours), 12-patch pack = £18.39. Counselling, administration

Dose menopausal symptoms, 1 patch to be applied once a week on a continuous or cyclical basis (1 patch per week for three weeks followed by a 7-day patch-free interval); therapy should be initiated with *Progynova®* TS *50* and adjusted to lowest effective dose; osteoporosis prophylaxis (see section 6.6), 1 *Progynova®* TS *50* patch to be applied once a week on a continuous basis (with cyclical progestogen for 10–14 days of each cycle in women with intact uterus)

Note Women receiving *Progynova®* TS *100* patches for menopausal symptoms may continue with this strength for osteoporosis prophylaxis (see section 6.6)

**Sandrena®** (Organon) PoM

Gel, estradiol (0.1%), 500 microgram/500 mg sachet, net price 28-sachet pack = £5.28, 1 mg/1 g sachet, 28-sachet pack = £6.08. Counselling, administration

Excipients include propylene glycol (see section 13.1.3)

Dose menopausal symptoms, estradiol 1 mg (1 g gel) to be applied once daily over area 1–2 times size of hand; with cyclical progestogen for 12–14 days of each cycle in women with intact uterus; dose may be adjusted after 2–3 cycles to a usual dose of estradiol 0.5–1.5 mg (0.5–1.5 g gel) daily

Counselling Apply gel to intact areas of skin such as lower trunk or thighs, using right and left sides on alternate days. Wash hands after application. Not to be applied on the breasts or face and avoid contact with eyes. Allow area of application to dry for 5 minutes and do not wash area for at least 1 hour

**Zumenon®** (Solvay) PoM

Tablets, f/c, estradiol 1 mg, net price 84-tab pack = £6.89; 2 mg (red), 84-tab pack = £6.89

Dose menopausal symptoms, initially 1 mg daily starting on day 5 of menstruation (or any time if cycles have ceased or are infrequent) adjusted to 1–4 mg daily according to response; osteoporosis prophylaxis (see section 6.6), 2 mg daily; with cyclical progestogen for 10–14 days of each cycle in women with intact uterus

### Estradiol, estriol and estrone

**Hormonin®** (Shire) PoM

Tablets, pink, estradiol 600 micrograms, estriol 270 micrograms, estrone 1.4 mg. Net price 84-tab pack = £6.61

Dose menopausal symptoms and osteoporosis prophylaxis (see section 6.6), 1–2 tablets daily, with cyclical progestogen for 12–14 days of each cycle in women with intact uterus

Note *Hormonin®* tablets can be given continuously or cyclically (21 days out of 28)

### Estriol only

**Ovestin®** (Organon) PoM

Tablets, scored, estriol 1 mg. Net price 30-tab pack = £3.91. Label: 25

Dose genito-urinary symptoms associated with oestrogen-deficiency states, 0.5–3 mg daily, as single dose, for up to 1 month, then 0.5–1 mg daily until restoration of epithelial integrity (short-term use); infertility due to poor cervical penetration, 0.25–1 mg daily on days 6–15 of cycle

### Estropipate only

**Harmogen®** (Pharmacia) PoM

Tablets, peach, scored, estropipate 1.5 mg. Net price 28-tab pack = £3.77

Dose menopausal symptoms and osteoporosis prophylaxis (see section 6.6), 1.5 mg daily continuously (with cyclical progestogen for 10–13 days of each cycle in women with intact uterus); up to 3 mg daily (in single or divided doses) for vasomotor symptoms and menopausal vaginitis



## TIBOLONE

**Indications** short-term treatment of symptoms of oestrogen deficiency (including women being treated with gonadotrophin releasing hormone analogues); osteoporosis prophylaxis in women at risk of fractures (second-line)

**Cautions** see notes above and under Oestrogens for HRT; renal impairment, history of liver disease (Appendix 2), epilepsy, migraine, diabetes mellitus, hypercholesterolaemia; withdraw if signs of thromboembolic disease, abnormal liver function tests or cholestatic jaundice; see also Note below; **interactions:** Appendix 1 (tibolone)

**Contra-indications** see notes above and under Oestrogens for HRT; hormone-dependent tumours, history of cardiovascular or cerebrovascular disease (e.g. thrombophlebitis, thromboembolism), uninvestigated vaginal bleeding, severe liver disease, pregnancy, breast-feeding

**Side-effects** see notes above; weight changes, oedema, dizziness, nausea, seborrhoeic dermatitis, vaginal bleeding, leucorrhoea, headache, abdominal pain, gastro-intestinal disturbances, increased facial hair; depression, arthralgia, myalgia, migraine, breast cancer (see notes above and section 6.4.1.1), visual disturbances, liver-function changes, rash and pruritus also reported

**Dose**

- 2.5 mg daily

Note Unsuitable for use in the premenopause (unless being treated with gonadotrophin-releasing hormone analogue) and as (or with) an oral contraceptive; also unsuitable for use within 12 months of last menstrual period (may cause irregular bleeding); induce withdrawal bleed with progestogen if transferring from another form of HRT

**Livial®** (Organon) PoM

Tablets, tibolone 2.5 mg. Net price 28-tab pack = £10.77; 3 × 28-tab pack = £32.29

## Ethinylestradiol

Ethinylestradiol (ethinyloestradiol) is licensed for short-term treatment of symptoms of oestrogen deficiency, for osteoporosis prophylaxis if other drugs (section 6.6) cannot be used and for the treatment of female hypogonadism and menstrual disorders.

Ethinylestradiol is occasionally used under **specialist supervision** for the management of *hereditary haemorrhagic telangiectasia* (but evidence of benefit is limited). Side-effects include nausea, fluid retention, and thrombosis. Impotence and gynaecomastia have been reported in men.

For use in prostate cancer, see section 8.3.1.

## ETHINYLESTRADIOL
(Ethinyloestradiol)

**Indications** see notes above

**Cautions** cardiovascular disease (sodium retention with oedema, thromboembolism), hepatic impairment (jaundice), see also under Combined Hormonal Contraceptives (section 7.3.1) and under Oestrogen for HRT (above)

**Contra-indications** see under Combined Hormonal Contraceptives (section 7.3.1) and under Oestrogen for HRT (above)

**Side-effects** feminising effects in men; see also under Combined Hormonal Contraceptives (section 7.3.1) and under Oestrogen for HRT (above)

**Dose**

- Menopausal symptoms and osteoporosis prophylaxis, (with progestogen for 12–14 days per cycle in women with intact uterus), 10–50 micrograms daily for 21 days, repeated after 7-day tablet-free period
- Female hypogonadism, 10–50 micrograms daily, usually on cyclical basis; initial oestrogen therapy should be followed by combined oestrogen and progestogen therapy
- Menstrual disorders, 20–50 micrograms daily from day 5 to 25 of each cycle, with progestogen added either throughout the cycle or from day 15 to 25

**Ethinylestradiol** (Non-proprietary) PoM

Tablets, ethinylestradiol 10 micrograms, net price 21-tab pack = £12.86; 50 micrograms, 21-tab pack = £15.16; 1 mg, 28-tab pack = £28.85

## Raloxifene

**Raloxifene** is licensed for the treatment and prevention of *postmenopausal osteoporosis*; unlike hormone replacement therapy, raloxifene does not reduce menopausal vasomotor symptoms.

Raloxifene may reduce the incidence of oestrogen-receptor-positive breast cancer but its role in established breast cancer is not yet clear. The manufacturer advises avoiding its use during treatment for breast cancer.

## RALOXIFENE HYDROCHLORIDE

**Indications** treatment and prevention of postmenopausal osteoporosis

**Cautions** risk factors for venous thromboembolism (discontinue if prolonged immobilisation); breast cancer (see notes above); history of oestrogen-induced hypertriglyceridaemia (monitor serum triglycerides); **interactions:** Appendix 1 (raloxifene)

**Contra-indications** history of venous thromboembolism, undiagnosed uterine bleeding, endometrial cancer, hepatic impairment, cholestasis, severe renal impairment; pregnancy and breast-feeding

**Side-effects** venous thromboembolism, thrombophlebitis, hot flushes, leg cramps, peripheral oedema, influenza-like symptoms; rarely rashes, gastro-intestinal disturbances, hypertension, headache (including migraine), breast discomfort

**Dose**

- 60 mg once daily

**Evista®** (Lilly) PoM

Tablets, f/c, raloxifene hydrochloride 60 mg, net price 28-tab pack = £19.86; 84-tab pack = £59.59

## 6.4.1.2 Progestogens

There are two main groups of progestogen, *progesterone and its analogues* (dydrogesterone and medroxyprogesterone) and *testosterone analogues* (norethisterone and norgestrel). The newer progestogens (desogestrel, norgestimate, and gestodene) are all derivatives of norgestrel; levonorgestrel is the active isomer of norgestrel and has twice its potency. Progesterone and its analogues are less androgenic than the testosterone derivatives and neither progesterone nor dydrogesterone causes virilisation.

Where *endometriosis* requires drug treatment, it may respond to a progestogen, e.g. norethisterone, administered on a continuous basis. Danazol, gestrinone, and gonadorelin analogues are also available (section 6.7.2).

Although oral progestogens have been used widely for *menorrhagia* they are relatively ineffective compared with tranexamic acid (section 2.11) or, particularly where dysmenorrhoea is also a factor, mefenamic acid (section 10.1.1); the levonorgestrel-releasing intra-uterine system (section 7.3.2.3) may be particularly useful for women also requiring contraception. Oral progestogens have also been used for *severe dysmenorrhoea*, but where contraception is also required in younger women the best choice is a combined oral contraceptive (section 7.3.1).

Progestogens have also been advocated for the alleviation of *premenstrual symptoms*, but no convincing physiological basis for such treatment has been shown.

Progestogens have been used for the prevention of spontaneous abortion in women with a history of *recurrent miscarriage* (habitual abortion) but there is no evidence of benefit and they are **not** recommended for this purpose. In pregnant women with antiphospholipid antibody syndrome who have suffered recurrent miscarriage, administration of low-dose aspirin (section 2.9) and a prophylactic dose of a low molecular weight heparin (section 2.8.1) may decrease the risk of fetal loss (use under specialist supervision only).

**Hormone replacement therapy** In women with a uterus a progestogen needs to be added to *long-term oestrogen therapy for hormone replacement*, to prevent cystic hyperplasia of the endometrium and possible transformation to cancer; it can be added on a cyclical or a continuous basis (see section 6.4.1.1). Combined packs incorporating suitable progestogen tablets are available, see p. 369.

**Oral contraception** Desogestrel, etynodiol (ethynodiol), gestodene, levonorgestrel, norethisterone, and norgestimate are used in *combined oral contraceptives* and in *progestogen-only contraceptives* (section 7.3.1 and section 7.3.2).

**Cancer** Progestogens also have a role in *neoplastic disease* (section 8.3.2).

**Cautions** Progestogens should be used with caution in conditions that may worsen with fluid retention e.g. epilepsy, hypertension, migraine, asthma, cardiac or renal dysfunction, and in those susceptible to thromboembolism (particular caution with high dose). Care is also required in liver impairment (avoid if severe), and in those with a history of depression. Progestogens can decrease glucose tolerance and diabetes should be monitored closely. For **interactions** see Appendix 1 (progestogens).

**Contra-indications** Progestogens should be avoided in patients with a history of liver tumours, and in severe liver impairment. They are also contra-indicated in those with genital or breast cancer (unless progestogens are being used in the management of these conditions), severe arterial disease, undiagnosed vaginal bleeding and porphyria (section 9.8.2). Progestogens should not be used if there is a history during pregnancy of idiopathic jaundice, severe pruritus, or pemphigoid gestationis.

**Side-effects** Side-effects of progestogens include menstrual disturbances, premenstrual-like syndrome (including bloating, fluid retention, breast tenderness), weight gain, nausea, headache, dizziness, insomnia, drowsiness, depression; also skin reactions (including urticaria, pruritus, rash, and acne), hirsutism and alopecia. Jaundice and anaphylactoid reactions have also been reported.

### DYDROGESTERONE

**Indications** see under Dose and notes above

**Cautions** see notes above; breast-feeding (Appendix 5)

**Contra-indications** see notes above

**Side-effects** see notes above

**Dose**

- Endometriosis, 10 mg 2–3 times daily from day 5 to 25 of cycle or continuously
- Infertility, irregular cycles, 10 mg twice daily from day 11 to 25 for at least 6 cycles (but not recommended)
- Recurrent miscarriage, 10 mg twice daily from day 11 to 25 of cycle until conception, then continuously until week 20 of pregnancy and then gradually reduced (but not recommended, see notes above)
- Dysfunctional uterine bleeding, 10 mg twice daily (together with an oestrogen) for 5–7 days to arrest bleeding; 10 mg twice daily (together with an oestrogen) from day 11 to 25 of cycle to prevent bleeding
- Dysmenorrhoea (but see notes above), 10 mg twice daily from day 5 to 25 of cycle
- Amenorrhoea, 10 mg twice daily from day 11 to 25 of cycle with oestrogen therapy from day 1 to 25 of cycle

- Premenstrual syndrome, 10 mg twice daily from day 12 to 26 of cycle increased if necessary (but not recommended, see notes above)
- Hormone replacement therapy, with continuous oestrogen therapy, see under *Duphaston® HRT* below

**Duphaston®** (Solvay) PoM
Tablets, scored, dydrogesterone 10 mg. Net price 60-tab pack = £4.04

**Duphaston® HRT** (Solvay) PoM
Tablets, scored, dydrogesterone 10 mg. Net price 42-tab pack = £2.83
Dose 10 mg daily on days 15–28 of each 28-day oestrogen HRT cycle, increased to 10 mg twice daily if withdrawal bleed is early or endometrial biopsy shows inadequate progestational response

## MEDROXYPROGESTERONE ACETATE

**Indications** see under Dose; contraception (section 7.3.2.2); malignant disease (section 8.3.2)
**Cautions** see notes above; breast-feeding (Appendix 5)
**Contra-indications** see notes above; pregnancy (Appendix 4)
**Side-effects** see notes above; indigestion
**Dose**
- By mouth, 2.5–10 mg daily for 5–10 days beginning on day 16 to 21 of cycle, repeated for 2 cycles in dysfunctional uterine bleeding and 3 cycles in secondary amenorrhoea
- Mild to moderate endometriosis, 10 mg 3 times daily for 90 consecutive days, beginning on day 1 of cycle
- Progestogenic opposition of oestrogen HRT, 10 mg daily for the last 14 days of each 28-day oestrogen HRT cycle

**Provera®** (Pharmacia) PoM
Tablets, all scored, medroxyprogesterone acetate 2.5 mg (orange), net price 30-tab pack = £1.84; 5 mg (blue), 10-tab pack = £1.23; 10 mg (white), 10-tab pack = £2.47, 90-tab pack = £22.16

**Combined preparations**
Section 6.4.1.1

## NORETHISTERONE

**Indications** see under Dose; HRT (section 6.4.1.1); contraception (section 7.3.1 and section 7.3.2); malignant disease (section 8.3.2)
**Cautions** see notes above; breast-feeding (Appendix 5)
**Contra-indications** see notes above; pregnancy (Appendix 4)
**Side-effects** see notes above
**Dose**
- Endometriosis, 10–15 mg daily for 4–6 months or longer, starting on day 5 of cycle (if spotting occurs increase dose to 20–25 mg daily, reduced once bleeding has stopped)
- Dysfunctional uterine bleeding, menorrhagia (but see notes above), 5 mg 3 times daily for 10 days to arrest bleeding; to prevent bleeding 5 mg twice daily from day 19 to 26
- Dysmenorrhoea (but see notes above), 5 mg 3 times daily from day 5 to 24 for 3–4 cycles
- Premenstrual syndrome, 5 mg 2–3 times daily from day 19 to 26 for several cycles (but not recommended, see notes above)
- Postponement of menstruation, 5 mg 3 times daily starting 3 days before anticipated onset (menstruation occurs 2–3 days after stopping)
- Progestogenic opposition of menopausal oestrogen HRT, see under *Micronor® HRT* , below

**Tablets of 5 mg**

**Norethisterone** (Non-proprietary) PoM
Tablets, norethisterone 5 mg, net price 30-tab pack = £2.69

**Primolut N®** (Schering Health) PoM
Tablets, norethisterone 5 mg. Net price 30-tab pack = £2.01

**Utovlan®** (Pharmacia) PoM
Tablets, norethisterone 5 mg, net price 30-tab pack = £1.40, 90-tab pack = £4.21

**Tablets of 1 mg for HRT**

**Micronor® HRT** (Janssen-Cilag) PoM
Tablets, norethisterone 1 mg. Net price 3 × 12-tab pack = £3.56
Dose 1 tablet daily on days 15–26 of each 28-day oestrogen HRT cycle

**Combined preparations**
Section 6.4.1.1

## PROGESTERONE

**Indications** see under preparations
**Cautions** see notes above; breast-feeding (Appendix 5)
**Contra-indications** see notes above; missed or incomplete abortion
**Side-effects** see notes above; injection-site reactions; pain, diarrhoea and flatulence can occur with rectal administration

**Crinone®** (Serono) PoM
Vaginal gel, progesterone 90 mg/application (8%), 15 = £32.73
Dose by vagina, infertility due to inadequate luteal phase, insert 1 applicatorful daily starting either after documented ovulation or on day 18–21 of cycle. *In vitro* fertilisation, daily application continued for 30 days after laboratory evidence of pregnancy

**Cyclogest®** (Alpharma) PoM
Pessaries, progesterone 200 mg, net price 15 = £7.46; 400 mg, 15 = £10.80
Dose by vagina *or* rectum, premenstrual syndrome and post-natal depression, 200 mg daily to 400 mg twice daily; for premenstrual syndrome start on day 12–14 and continue until onset of menstruation (but not recommended, see notes above); rectally if barrier methods of contraception are used, in patients who have recently given birth or in those who suffer from vaginal infection or recurrent cystitis

**Gestone®** (Nordic) PoM
Injection, progesterone 50 mg/mL, 1-mL amp = 57p, 2-mL amp = 75p
Dose by deep intramuscular injection into buttock, dysfunctional uterine bleeding, 5–10 mg daily for 5–10 days until 2 days before expected onset of menstruation

Recurrent miscarriage due to inadequate luteal phase (but not recommended, see notes above) or following *in vitro* fertilisation *or* gamete intra-fallopian transfer, 25–100 mg 2–7 times a week from day 15, or day of embryo *or* gamete transfer, until 8–16 weeks of pregnancy; max. 200 mg daily

## 6.4.2 Male sex hormones and antagonists

Androgens cause masculinisation; they may be used as replacement therapy in castrated adults and in those who are hypogonadal due to either pituitary or testicular disease. In the normal male they inhibit pituitary gonadotrophin secretion and depress spermatogenesis. Androgens also have an anabolic action which led to the development of anabolic steroids (section 6.4.3).

Androgens are useless as a treatment of impotence and impaired spermatogenesis unless there is associated hypogonadism; they should not be given until the hypogonadism has been properly investigated. Treatment should be under expert supervision.

When given to patients with hypopituitarism they can lead to normal sexual development and potency but not to fertility. If fertility is desired, the usual treatment is with gonadotrophins or pulsatile gonadotrophin-releasing hormone (section 6.5.1) which will stimulate spermatogenesis as well as androgen production.

Caution should be used when androgens or chorionic gonadotrophin are used in treating boys with delayed puberty since the fusion of epiphyses is hastened and may result in short stature.

Intramuscular depot preparations of **testosterone esters** are preferred for replacement therapy. Testosterone enantate, propionate or undecanoate, or alternatively *Sustanon®*, which consists of a mixture of testosterone esters and has a longer duration of action, may be used. Satisfactory replacement therapy can sometimes be obtained with 1 mL of *Sustanon 250®*, given by intramuscular injection once a month, although more frequent dose intervals are often necessary. Implants of testosterone can be used for hypogonadism; the implants are replaced every 4 to 5 months. Menopausal women are also sometimes given implants of testosterone (in a dose of 50–100 mg every 4–8 months) as an adjunct to hormone replacement therapy.

### TESTOSTERONE AND ESTERS

**Indications** see under preparations

**Cautions** cardiac, renal, or hepatic impairment (Appendix 2), elderly, ischaemic heart disease, hypertension, epilepsy, migraine, diabetes mellitus, skeletal metastases (risk of hypercalcaemia), undertake regular examination of the prostate and breast during treatment; pre-pubertal boys (see notes above and under Side-effects); **interactions:** Appendix 1 (testosterone)

**Contra-indications** breast cancer in men, prostate cancer, history of primary liver tumours, hypercalcaemia, pregnancy (Appendix 4), breast-feeding (Appendix 5), nephrotic syndrome

**Side-effects** prostate abnormalities and prostate cancer, headache, depression, gastro-intestinal bleeding, nausea, cholestatic jaundice, changes in libido, gynaecomastia, polycythaemia, anxiety, asthenia, paraesthesia, hypertension, electrolyte disturbances including sodium retention with oedema and hypercalcaemia, weight gain; increased bone growth; androgenic effects such as hirsutism, male-pattern baldness, seborrhoea, acne, pruritus, excessive frequency and duration of penile erection, precocious sexual development and premature closure of epiphyses in pre-pubertal males, suppression of spermatogenesis in men and virilism in women; *rarely* liver tumours; sleep apnoea also reported; *with patches, buccal tablets, and gel*, local irritation and allergic reactions, bitter taste with *buccal tablets*

#### Oral

**Restandol®** (Organon) PoM
Capsules, red-brown, testosterone undecanoate 40 mg in oily solution. Net price 28-cap pack = £8.30; 56-cap pack = £16.60. Label: 21, 25
**Dose** androgen deficiency, 120–160 mg daily for 2–3 weeks; maintenance 40–120 mg daily

#### Buccal

**Striant® SR** (Ardana) PoM
Mucoadhesive buccal tablets, m/r, testosterone 30 mg, net price 60-tab pack = £45.84. Counselling, see under Dose below
**Dose** hypogonadism, 30 mg every 12 hours; CHILD and ADOLESCENT under 18 years not recommended
**Counselling** Place rounded side of tablet on gum above front teeth and hold lip firmly over the gum for 30 seconds. If tablet detaches within 4 hours of next dose, replace with new tablet which is considered the second dose for the day.

#### Intramuscular

**Testosterone Enantate** (Cambridge) PoM
Injection (oily), testosterone enantate 250 mg/mL. Net price 1-mL amp = £8.33
**Dose** by slow intramuscular injection, hypogonadism, initially 250 mg every 2–3 weeks; maintenance 250 mg every 3–6 weeks
Breast cancer, 250 mg every 2–3 weeks

**Nebido®** (Schering Health) ▼ PoM
Injection (oily), testosterone undecanoate 250 mg/mL. Net price 4-mL amp = £76.70
**Dose** by deep intramuscular injection, hypogonadism in men over 18 years, 1 g every 10–14 weeks; if necessary, second dose may be given after 6 weeks to achieve rapid steady state plasma testosterone levels and then every 10–14 weeks

**Sustanon 100®** (Organon) PoM
Injection (oily), testosterone propionate 20 mg, testosterone phenylpropionate 40 mg, and testosterone isocaproate 40 mg/mL. Net price 1-mL amp = £1.09
**Excipients** include arachis (peanut) oil, benzyl alcohol (see Excipients p. 2)
**Dose** by deep intramuscular injection, androgen deficiency, 1 mL every 2 weeks

**Sustanon 250®** (Organon) PoM
Injection (oily), testosterone propionate 30 mg, testosterone phenylpropionate 60 mg, testosterone isocaproate 60 mg, and testosterone decanoate 100 mg/mL. Net price 1-mL amp = £2.55
**Excipients** include arachis (peanut) oil, benzyl alcohol (see Excipients p. 2)
**Dose** by deep intramuscular injection, androgen deficiency, 1 mL usually every 3 weeks

**Virormone®** (Nordic) PoM
Injection, testosterone propionate 50 mg/mL. Net price 2-mL amp = 59p
**Dose** by intramuscular injection, androgen deficiency, 50 mg 2–3 times weekly
Delayed puberty, 50 mg weekly
Breast cancer in women, 100 mg 2–3 times weekly

### Implant

**Testosterone** (Organon) PoM

Implant, testosterone 100 mg, net price = £7.40; 200 mg = £13.79

Dose by implantation, male hypogonadism, 100–600 mg; 600 mg usually maintains plasma-testosterone concentration within the normal range for 4–5 months

Menopausal women, see notes above

### Transdermal preparations

**Andropatch®** (GSK) PoM

Patches, self-adhesive, releasing testosterone approx. 2.5 mg/24 hours, net price 60-patch pack = £49.10; releasing testosterone approx. 5 mg/24 hours, net price 30-patch pack = £49.10. Counselling, administration

Dose androgen deficiency in men (over 15 years) associated with primary or secondary hypogonadism, apply to clean, dry, unbroken skin on back, abdomen, upper arms or thighs, removing after 24 hours and siting replacement patch on a different area (with an interval of 7 days before using the same site); initially apply patches equivalent to testosterone 5 mg/24 hours (2.5 mg/24 hours in non-virilised patients) at night (approx. 10 p.m.), then adjust to 2.5 mg to 7.5 mg every 24 hours according to plasma-testosterone concentration (those with a body-weight over 130 kg may require 7.5 mg every 24 hours)

**Testim®** (Ipsen) ▼ PoM

Gel, testosterone 50 mg/5 g tube, net price 30-tube pack = £33.00. Counselling, administration

Excipients include propylene glycol (see section 13.1.3)

Dose hypogonadism due to testosterone deficiency in men (over 18 years), 50 mg testosterone (5 g gel) applied once daily; subsequent application adjusted according to response; max. 100 mg (10 g gel) daily

Counselling Squeeze entire content of tube on to one palm and apply as a thin layer on clean, dry, healthy skin of shoulder or upper arm, preferably in the morning after washing or bathing (if 2 tubes required use 1 per shoulder or upper arm); rub in and allow to dry before putting on clothing to cover site; wash hands with soap after application; avoid washing application site for at least 6 hours

Avoid skin contact with application sites to prevent testosterone transfer to other people, especially pregnant women and children—consult product literature

**Testogel®** (Schering Health) PoM

Gel, testosterone 50 mg/5 g sachet, net price 30-sachet pack = £33.00. Counselling, administration

Dose hypogonadism due to androgen deficiency in men (over 18 years), 50 mg testosterone (5 g gel) to be applied once daily; subsequent application adjusted according to response in 25-mg (2.5 g gel) increments to max. 100 mg (10 g gel) daily

Counselling Apply thin layer of gel on clean, dry, healthy skin such as shoulders, arms or abdomen, immediately after sachet is opened. Not to be applied on genital area as high alcohol content may cause local irritation. Allow to dry for 3–5 minutes before dressing. Wash hands with soap and water after applying gel, avoid shower or bath for at least 6 hours

Avoid skin contact with gel application sites to prevent testosterone transfer to other people, especially pregnant women and children—consult product literature

## MESTEROLONE

**Indications** see under Dose

**Cautions** see under Testosterone and Esters

**Contra-indications** see under Testosterone and Esters

**Side-effects** see under Testosterone and Esters but spermatogenesis unimpaired

**Dose**

- Androgen deficiency and male infertility associated with hypogonadism, 25 mg 3–4 times daily for several months, reduced to 50–75 mg daily in divided doses for maintenance; CHILD not recommended

**Pro-Viron®** (Schering Health) PoM

Tablets, scored, mesterolone 25 mg. Net price 30-tab pack = £4.44

## Anti-androgens

### Cyproterone acetate

**Cyproterone acetate** is an anti-androgen used in the treatment of severe hypersexuality and sexual deviation in the male. It inhibits spermatogenesis and produces reversible infertility (but is not a male contraceptive); abnormal sperm forms are produced. Fully informed consent is recommended and an initial spermatogram. As hepatic tumours have been produced in *animal* studies, careful consideration should be given to the risk/benefit ratio before treatment. Cyproterone acetate is also used as an adjunct in prostatic cancer (section 8.3.4.2) and in the treatment of acne and hirsutism in women (section 13.6.2).

## CYPROTERONE ACETATE

**Indications** see notes above; prostate cancer (section 8.3.4.2)

**Cautions** ineffective for male hypersexuality in chronic alcoholism (relevance to prostate cancer not known); blood counts initially and throughout treatment; monitor hepatic function regularly (liver function tests should be performed before treatment, see also under Side-effects below); monitor adrenocortical function regularly; diabetes mellitus (see also Contra-indications)

Driving Fatigue and lassitude may impair performance of skilled tasks (e.g. driving)

**Contra-indications** (do not apply in prostate cancer) hepatic disease (Appendix 2), severe diabetes (with vascular changes); sickle-cell anaemia, malignant or wasting disease, severe depression, history of thrombo-embolic disorders; youths under 18 years (may arrest bone maturation and testicular development)

**Side-effects** fatigue and lassitude, breathlessness, weight changes, reduced sebum production (may clear acne), changes in hair pattern, gynaecomastia (rarely leading to galactorrhoea and benign breast nodules); rarely hypersensitivity reactions, rash and osteoporosis; inhibition of spermatogenesis (see notes above); hepatotoxicity reported (including jaundice, hepatitis and hepatic failure usually in men given 200–300 mg daily for prostatic cancer, see section 8.3.4.2 for details and warnings)

**Dose**

- Male hypersexuality, 50 mg twice daily after food

**Cyproterone Acetate** (Non-proprietary) PoM

Tablets, cyproterone acetate 50 mg, net price 56-tab pack = £31.54. Label: 21 counselling, driving

**Androcur®** (Schering Health) PoM

Tablets, scored, cyproterone acetate 50 mg. Net price 56-tab pack = £25.89. Label: 21 counselling, driving

### Dutasteride and finasteride

**Dutasteride** and **finasteride** are specific inhibitors of the enzyme 5α-reductase, which metabolises testosterone into the more potent androgen, dihydrotestosterone. This inhibition of testosterone metabolism leads to reduction in prostate size, with improvement in urinary flow rate and in obstructive symptoms. Dutasteride and finasteride are alternatives to alpha-blockers (section 7.4.1) particularly in men with a significantly enlarged prostate. Finasteride is also licensed for use with doxazosin in the management of benign prostatic hyperplasia.

A low strength of finasteride is licensed for treating male-pattern baldness in men (section 13.9).

**Cautions** Dutasteride and finasteride decrease serum concentration of prostate cancer markers such as prostate-specific antigen; reference values may need adjustment. Both dutasteride and finasteride are excreted in semen and use of a condom is recommended if sexual partner is pregnant or likely to become pregnant. Women of childbearing potential should avoid handling crushed or broken tablets of finasteride and leaking capsules of dutasteride.

**Contra-indications** Dutasteride and finasteride are contra-indicated in women, children, and adolescents.

**Side-effects** The side-effects of dutasteride and finasteride include impotence, decreased libido, ejaculation disorders, and breast tenderness and enlargement.

### DUTASTERIDE

**Indications** benign prostatic hyperplasia
**Cautions** see notes above; **interactions:** Appendix 1 (dutasteride)
**Contra-indications** see notes above; also severe hepatic impairment
**Side-effects** see notes above
**Dose**
- 500 micrograms daily (may require 6 months' treatment before benefit is obtained)

**Avodart®** (GSK) PoM
Capsules, yellow, dutasteride 500 micrograms, net price 30-cap pack = £24.81. Label: 25

### FINASTERIDE

**Indications** benign prostatic hyperplasia; male-pattern baldness in men (section 13.9)
**Cautions** see notes above; also obstructive uropathy
**Side-effects** see notes above; also testicular pain, hypersensitivity reactions (including lip and face swelling, pruritus and rash)
**Dose**
- 5 mg daily, review treatment after 6 months (may require several months' treatment before benefit is obtained)

**Proscar®** (MSD) PoM
Tablets, blue, f/c, finasteride 5 mg. Net price 28-tab pack = £13.94

## 6.4.3 Anabolic steroids

Anabolic steroids have some androgenic activity but they cause less virilisation than androgens in women. They are used in the treatment of some *aplastic anaemias* (section 9.1.3). Anabolic steroids have been given for osteoporosis in women but they are no longer advocated for this purpose.

The protein-building properties of anabolic steroids have not proved beneficial in the clinical setting. Their use as body builders or tonics is quite unjustified; some athletes abuse them.

### NANDROLONE

**Indications** osteoporosis in postmenopausal women (but not recommended, see notes above); aplastic anaemia (section 9.1.3)
**Cautions** cardiac and renal impairment, hepatic impairment (Appendix 2), hypertension, diabetes mellitus, epilepsy, migraine; monitor skeletal maturation in young patients; skeletal metastases (risk of hypercalcaemia); **interactions:** Appendix 1 (anabolic steroids)
**Contra-indications** severe hepatic impairment, prostate cancer, male breast cancer, pregnancy (Appendix 4) and breast-feeding, porphyria (section 9.8.2)
**Side-effects** acne, sodium retention with oedema, virilisation with high doses including voice changes (sometimes irreversible), amenorrhoea, inhibition of spermatogenesis, premature epiphyseal closure; abnormal liver-function tests reported with high doses; liver tumours reported occasionally on prolonged treatment with anabolic steroids
**Dose**
- See below

**Deca-Durabolin®** (Organon) PoM ▲
Injection (oily), nandrolone decanoate 50 mg/mL, net price 1-mL amp = £3.29
Excipients include arachis (peanut) oil, benzyl alcohol (see Excipients, p. 2)
Dose by deep intramuscular injection, 50 mg every 3 weeks

## 6.5 Hypothalamic and pituitary hormones and anti-oestrogens

**6.5.1** Hypothalamic and anterior pituitary hormones and anti-oestrogens
**6.5.2** Posterior pituitary hormones and antagonists

Use of preparations in these sections requires detailed prior investigation of the patient and *should be reserved for specialist centres.*

## 6.5.1 Hypothalamic and anterior pituitary hormones and anti-oestrogens

### Anti-oestrogens

The anti-oestrogens **clomifene** (clomiphene) and **tamoxifen** (section 8.3.4.1) are used in the treatment of female infertility due to oligomenorrhoea or secondary amenorrhoea (e.g. associated with polycystic ovarian disease). They induce gonadotrophin release by occupying oestrogen receptors in the hypothalamus, thereby interfering with feedback mechanisms; chorionic gonadotrophin is sometimes used as an adjunct. Patients should be warned that there is a risk of multiple pregnancy (*rarely* more than twins).

## CLOMIFENE CITRATE
(Clomiphene Citrate)

**Indications** anovulatory infertility—see notes above

**Cautions** see notes above; polycystic ovary syndrome (cysts may enlarge during treatment), ovarian hyperstimulation syndrome, uterine fibroids, ectopic pregnancy, incidence of multiple births increased (consider ultrasound monitoring), visual symptoms (discontinue and initiate ophthalmological examination); breast-feeding (Appendix 5)

**CSM Advice**. The CSM has recommended that clomifene should not normally be used for longer than 6 cycles (possibly increased risk of ovarian cancer)

**Contra-indications** hepatic disease (Appendix 2), ovarian cysts, hormone dependent tumours or abnormal uterine bleeding of undetermined cause, pregnancy (exclude before treatment; Appendix 4)

**Side-effects** visual disturbances (withdraw), ovarian hyperstimulation (withdraw), hot flushes, abdominal discomfort, occasionally nausea, vomiting, depression, insomnia, breast tenderness, headache, intermenstrual spotting, menorrhagia, endometriosis, convulsions, weight gain, rashes, dizziness, hair loss

**Dose**
- 50 mg daily for 5 days, starting within about 5 days of onset of menstruation (preferably on 2nd day) or at any time (normally preceded by a progestogen-induced withdrawal bleed) if cycles have ceased; second course of 100 mg daily for 5 days may be given in absence of ovulation; most patients who are going to respond will do so to first course; 3 courses should constitute adequate therapeutic trial; long-term cyclical therapy not recommended—see CSM advice, above

**Clomifene** (Non-proprietary) PoM
Tablets, clomifene citrate 50 mg, net price 30-tab pack = £11.25

**Clomid®** (Aventis Pharma) PoM
Tablets, yellow, scored, clomifene citrate 50 mg. Net price 30-tab pack = £8.80

## Anterior pituitary hormones

### Corticotrophins

**Tetracosactide** (tetracosactrin), an analogue of corticotropin (ACTH), is used to test adrenocortical function; failure of the plasma cortisol concentration to rise after administration of tetracosactide indicates adrenocortical insufficiency.

Both corticotropin and tetracosactide were formerly used as alternatives to corticosteroids in conditions such as Crohn's disease or rheumatoid arthritis; their value was limited by the variable and unpredictable therapeutic response and by the waning of their effect with time.

## TETRACOSACTIDE
(Tetracosactrin)

**Indications** see notes above

**Cautions** as for corticosteroids, section 6.3.2; **important**: risk of anaphylaxis (medical supervision; consult product literature); **interactions**: Appendix 1 (corticosteroids)

**Contra-indications** as for corticosteroids, section 6.3.2; avoid injections containing benzyl alcohol in neonates (see under preparations)

**Side-effects** as for corticosteroids, section 6.3.2

**Dose**
- See under preparations below

**Synacthen®** (Alliance) PoM
Injection, tetracosactide 250 micrograms (as acetate)/mL. Net price 1-mL amp = £2.93
**Dose** diagnostic (30-minute test), by intramuscular *or* intravenous injection, 250 micrograms as a single dose

**Synacthen Depot®** (Alliance) PoM
Injection (aqueous suspension), tetracosactide acetate 1 mg/mL, with zinc phosphate complex. Net price 1-mL amp = £4.18
**Excipients** include benzyl alcohol (avoid in neonates, see Excipients p. 2)
**Dose** diagnostic (5-hour test), by intramuscular injection, 1 mg as a single dose
**Note** Formerly used therapeutically by intramuscular injection, in an initial dose of 1 mg daily (or every 12 hours in acute cases); reduced to 1 mg every 2–3 days, then 1 mg weekly (or 500 micrograms every 2–3 days) but value was limited (see notes above)

### Gonadotrophins

Follicle-stimulating hormone (FSH) and luteinising hormone (LH) together (as in **human menopausal gonadotrophin**), follicle-stimulating hormone alone (as in **follitropin**), or chorionic gonadotrophin, are used in the treatment of infertility in women with proven hypopituitarism or who have not responded to clomifene, or in superovulation treatment for assisted conception (such as *in vitro* fertilisation).

The gonadotrophins are also occasionally used in the treatment of hypogonadotrophic hypogonadism and associated oligospermia. There is no justification for their use in primary gonadal failure.

Chorionic gonadotrophin has also been used in delayed puberty in the male to stimulate endogenous testosterone production, but has little advantage over testosterone (section 6.4.2).

## CHORIONIC GONADOTROPHIN
(Human Chorionic Gonadotrophin; HCG)

A preparation of a glycoprotein fraction secreted by the placenta and obtained from the urine of pregnant women having the action of the pituitary luteinising hormone

**Indications** see notes above

**Cautions** cardiac or renal impairment, asthma, epilepsy, migraine; prepubertal boys (risk of premature epiphyseal closure or precocious puberty)

**Contra-indications** androgen-dependent tumours

**Side-effects** oedema (particularly in males—reduce dose), headache, tiredness, mood changes, gynaecomastia, local reactions; may aggravate ovarian hyperstimulation, multiple pregnancy

**Dose**
- By subcutaneous *or* intramuscular injection, according to patient's response

**Choragon®** (Ferring) PoM
Injection, powder for reconstitution, chorionic gonadotrophin. Net price 5000-unit amp (with solvent) = £3.26. For intramuscular injection

**Pregnyl®** (Organon) PoM
Injection, powder for reconstitution, chorionic gonadotrophin. Net price 1500-unit amp = £2.20; 5000-unit amp = £3.27 (both with solvent). For subcutaneous or intramuscular injection

## CHORIOGONADOTROPIN ALFA
### (Human chorionic gonadotropin)

**Indications** see notes above

**Cautions** rule out infertility caused by hypothyroidism, adrenocortical deficiency, hyperprolactinaemia, tumours of the pituitary or hypothalamus

**Contra-indications** ovarian enlargement or cyst (unless caused by polycystic ovarian disease); ectopic pregnancy in previous 3 months; active thromboembolic disorders; hypothalamus, pituitary, ovarian, uterine or mammary malignancy

**Side-effects** nausea, vomiting, abdominal pain; headache, tiredness; injection-site reactions; ovarian hyperstimulation syndrome; rarely diarrhoea, depression, irritability, breast pain; ectopic pregnancy and ovarian torsion reported

**Dose**
- By subcutaneous injection, according to patient's response

**Ovitrelle®** (Serono) ▼ PoM
Injection, choriogonadotropin alfa, net price 6500-unit/0.5 mL (250-micrograms/0.5 mL) prefilled syringe = £33.31

## FOLLITROPIN ALFA and BETA
### (Recombinant human follicle stimulating hormone)

**Indications** see notes above

**Cautions** see under Human Menopausal Gonadotrophins

**Contra-indications** see under Human Menopausal Gonadotrophins

**Side-effects** see under Human Menopausal Gonadotrophins

**Dose**
- By subcutaneous *or* intramuscular injection, according to patient's response

### Follitropin alfa

**Gonal-F®** (Serono) PoM
Injection, powder for reconstitution, follitropin alfa. Net price 75-unit amp = £22.31; 450 units/0.75 mL, multidose vial = £133.86; 1050 units/1.75 mL, multidose vial = £312.34 (all with diluent). For subcutaneous injection

Injection, prefilled pen, follitropin alfa 600 units/mL, net price 0.5 mL (300 units) = £97.08, 0.75 mL (450 units) = £145.62, 1.5 mL (900 units) = £291.24. For subcutaneous injection

### Follitropin beta

**Puregon®** (Organon) PoM
Injection, follitropin beta 100 units/mL, net price 0.5-mL (50-unit) vial = £18.74; 200 units/mL, 0.5-mL (100-unit) vial = £37.48; 300 units/mL, 0.5-mL (150-unit) vial = £50.62; 400 units/mL, 0.5-mL (200-unit) vial = £67.49; 0.36-mL (300-unit) cartridge = £101.23, 0.72-mL (600-unit) cartridge = £202.47, 1.08-mL (900-unit) cartridge = £303.66, (cartridges for use with *Puregon®* pen). For subcutaneous (cartridges and vials) or intramuscular injection (vials)
Excipients may include neomycin and streptomycin

## HUMAN MENOPAUSAL GONADOTROPHINS

Purified extract of human post-menopausal urine containing follicle-stimulating hormone (FSH) and luteinising hormone (LH); the relative *in vivo* activity is designated as a ratio; the 1:1 ratio is also known as menotrophin

**Indications** see notes above

**Cautions** rule out infertility caused by adrenal or thyroid disorders, hyperprolactinaemia or tumours of the pituitary or hypothalamus

**Contra-indications** ovarian cysts (not caused by polycystic ovarian syndrome); tumours of breast, uterus, ovaries, testes or prostate; vaginal bleeding of unknown cause; pregnancy and breast-feeding

**Side-effects** ovarian hyperstimulation, increased risk of multiple pregnancy and miscarriage, hypersensitivity reactions, nausea, vomiting, joint pain, fever, injection site reactions, very rarely thromboembolism; gynaecomastia, acne, and weight gain reported in men

**Dose**
- By deep intramuscular *or* subcutaneous injection, according to patient's response

**Menogon®** (Ferring) PoM
Injection, powder for reconstitution, menotrophin as follicle-stimulating hormone 75 units, luteinising hormone 75 units, net price per amp (with solvent) = £9.50. For intramuscular injection

**Menopur®** (Ferring) PoM
Injection, powder for reconstitution, menotrophin as follicle-stimulating hormone 75 units, luteinising hormone 75 units, net price per amp (with solvent) = £13.65. For intramuscular or subcutaneous injection

## LUTROPIN ALFA
### (Recombinant human luteinising hormone)

**Indications** see notes above

**Cautions** rule out infertility caused by hypothyroidism, adrenocortical deficiency, hyperprolactinaemia, tumours of the pituitary or hypothalamus

**Contra-indications** ovarian enlargement or cyst (unless caused by polycystic ovarian disease); undiagnosed vaginal bleeding; tumours of hypothalamus and pituitary; ovarian, uterine or mammary carcinoma

**Side-effects** nausea, vomiting, abdominal and pelvic pain; headache, somnolence; injection-site reactions; ovarian hyperstimulation syndrome, ovarian cyst, breast pain, ectopic pregnancy; thromboembolism, adnexal torsion, and haemoperitoneum

**Dose**
- By subcutaneous injection, in conjunction with follicle-stimulating hormone, according to response

**Luveris®** (Serono) PoM
Injection, powder for reconstitution, lutropin alfa, net price 75-unit vial = £33.31 (with solvent)

## Growth hormone

Growth hormone is used to treat deficiency of the hormone in children and in adults (see NICE guidance below). In children it is used in Prader-Willi syndrome, Turner's syndrome and in chronic renal insufficiency; growth hormone has also recently been licensed for use in short children considered small for gestational age at birth.

Growth hormone of human origin (HGH; somatotrophin) has been replaced by a growth hormone of human sequence, **somatropin**, produced using recombinant DNA technology.

### NICE guidance (somatropin in children with growth failure)

NICE has recommended (May 2002) treatment with somatropin for children with:

- proven growth-hormone deficiency;
- Turner's syndrome;
- Prader-Willi syndrome;
- chronic renal insufficiency before puberty.

Treatment should be initiated and monitored by a paediatrician with expertise in managing growth-hormone disorders; treatment can be continued under a shared-care protocol by a general practitioner.

Treatment should be discontinued if the response is poor (i.e. an increase in growth velocity of less than 50% from baseline) in the first year of therapy. In children with chronic renal insufficiency, treatment should be stopped after renal transplantation and not restarted for at least a year

### NICE guidance (somatropin for adults with growth hormone deficiency)

NICE has recommended (August 2003) somatropin in adults **only** if the following 3 criteria are fulfilled:

- Severe growth hormone deficiency, established by an appropriate method,
- Impaired quality of life, measured by means of a specific questionnaire,
- Already receiving treatment for another pituitary hormone deficiency.

Somatropin treatment should be discontinued if the quality of life has not improved sufficiently by 9 months.

Severe growth hormone deficiency developing after linear growth is complete but before the age of 25 years should be treated with growth hormone; treatment should continue until adult peak bone mass has been achieved. Treatment for adult-onset growth hormone deficiency should be stopped only when the patient and the patient's physician consider it appropriate.

Treatment with somatropin should be initiated and managed by a physician with expertise in growth hormone disorders; maintenance treatment can be prescribed in the community under a shared-care protocol.

## SOMATROPIN
### (Synthetic Human Growth Hormone)

**Indications** see under Dose

**Cautions** diabetes mellitus (adjustment of antidiabetic therapy may be necessary), papilloedema (see under Side-effects), relative deficiencies of other pituitary hormones (notably hypothyroidism—manufacturers recommend periodic thyroid function tests but limited evidence of clinical value), history of malignant disease, disorders of the epiphysis of the hip (monitor for limping), resolved intracranial hypertension (monitor closely), initiation of treatment close to puberty not recommended in child born small for gestational age; Silver-Russell syndrome; rotate subcutaneous injection sites to prevent lipoatrophy; breast-feeding (Appendix 5); **interactions**: Appendix 1 (somatropin)

**Contra-indications** evidence of tumour activity (complete antitumour therapy and ensure intracranial lesions inactive before starting); not to be used after renal transplantation or for growth promotion in children with closed epiphyses (or near closure in Prader-Willi syndrome); severe obesity or severe respiratory impairment in Prader-Willi syndrome; pregnancy (interrupt treatment if pregnancy occurs, Appendix 4)

**Side-effects** headache, funduscopy for papilloedema recommended if severe or recurrent headache, visual problems, nausea and vomiting occur—if papilloedema confirmed consider benign intracranial hypertension (rare cases reported); fluid retention (peripheral oedema), arthralgia, myalgia, carpal tunnel syndrome, paraesthesia, antibody formation, hypothyroidism, insulin resistance, hyperglycaemia, hypoglycaemia, reactions at injection site; leukaemia in children with growth hormone deficiency also reported

**Dose**

- Gonadal dysgenesis (Turner's syndrome), by subcutaneous injection, 45–50 micrograms/kg daily *or* 1.4 mg/m$^2$ daily
- Deficiency of growth hormone in children, by subcutaneous *or* intramuscular injection, 23–39 micrograms/kg daily *or* 0.7–1 mg/m$^2$ daily
- Growth disturbance in short children born small for gestational age, by subcutaneous injection, 35 micrograms/kg daily or 1 mg/m$^2$ daily
- Prader-Willi syndrome, by subcutaneous injection in children with growth velocity greater than 1 cm/year, in combination with energy-restricted diet, 35 micrograms/kg daily *or* 1 mg/m$^2$ daily; max. 2.7 mg daily
- Chronic renal insufficiency in children (renal function decreased to less than 50%), by subcutaneous injection, 45–50 micrograms/kg daily *or* 1.4 mg/m$^2$ daily (higher doses may be needed) adjusted if necessary after 6 months
- Adult growth hormone deficiency, by subcutaneous injection, initially 150–300 micrograms daily, gradually increased if required to max. 1 mg daily; use minimum effective dose (requirements may decrease with age)

**Note** Dose formerly expressed in units; somatropin 1 mg ≡ 3 units

**Genotropin®** (Pharmacia) PoM

Injection, two-compartment cartridge containing powder for reconstitution, somatropin (rbe) and diluent, net price 5.3-mg (16-unit) cartridge = £122.87, 12-mg (36-unit) cartridge = £278.20. For use with *Genotropin® Pen* NHS device (available free of charge from clinics). For subcutaneous injection

MiniQuick injection, two-compartment single-dose syringe containing powder for reconstitution, somatropin (rbe) and diluent, net price 0.2-mg (0.6-unit)

syringe = £4.64; 0.4-mg (1.2-unit) syringe = £9.27; 0.6-mg (1.8-unit) syringe = £13.91; 0.8-mg (2.4-unit) syringe = £18.55; 1-mg (3-unit) syringe = £23.18; 1.2-mg (3.6-unit) syringe = £27.82; 1.4-mg (4.2-unit) syringe = £32.46; 1.6-mg (4.8-unit) syringe = £37.09; 1.8-mg (5.4-unit) syringe = £41.73; 2-mg (6-unit) syringe = £46.37. For subcutaneous injection

**Humatrope®** (Lilly) PoM
Injection, powder for reconstitution, somatropin (rbe), net price 6-mg (18-unit) cartridge = £137.25; 12-mg (36-unit) cartridge = £274.50; 24-mg (72-unit) cartridge = £549.00; all supplied with diluent. For subcutaneous or intramuscular injection; cartridges for subcutaneous injection

**Norditropin®** (Novo Nordisk) PoM
SimpleXx injection, somatropin (epr) 3.3 mg (10 units)/mL, net price 1.5-mL (5-mg, 15-unit) cartridge = £115.90; 6.7 mg (20 units)/mL, 1.5-mL (10-mg, 30-unit) cartridge = £231.80; 10 mg (30 units)/mL, 1.5-mL (15-mg, 45-unit) cartridge = £347.70. For use with appropriate *NordiPen®* NHS device (available free of charge from clinics). For subcutaneous injection

**NutropinAq®** (Ipsen) PoM
Injection, somatropin (rbe), net price 10 mg (30 units) 2-ml cartridge = £215.57. For use with *NutropinAq® Pen* NHS device (available free of charge from clinics). For subcutaneous injection

**Saizen®** (Serono) PoM
Injection, powder for reconstitution, somatropin (rmc), net price 1.33-mg (4-unit) vial (with diluent) = £29.28; 3.33-mg (10-unit) vial (with diluent) = £73.20. For subcutaneous or intramuscular injection

Click.easy®, powder for reconstitution, somatropin (rmc), net price 8-mg (24-unit) vial (in *Click.easy®* device with diluent) = £175.68. For use with *One.click®* NHS autoinjector device *or Cool.Click®* NHS needle-free device (both available free of charge from clinics). For subcutaneous injection

**Zomacton®** (Ferring) PoM
Injection, powder for reconstitution, somatropin (rbe), net price 4-mg (12-unit) vial (with diluent) = £81.32. For use with *ZomaJet® 2* NHS needle-free device or with *Auto-Jector®* NHS (both available free of charge from clinics) or with needles and syringes. For subcutaneous injection

## Growth hormone receptor antagonists

**Pegvisomant** is a genetically modified analogue of human growth hormone and is a highly selective growth hormone receptor antagonist. Pegvisomant is licensed for the treatment of acromegaly in patients with inadequate response to surgery, radiation, or both, and to treatment with somatostatin analogues. Pegvisomant should be initiated only by physicians experienced in the treatment of acromegaly.

### PEGVISOMANT

**Indications** see notes above

**Cautions** liver disease (monitor liver enzymes every 4–6 weeks for 6 months or if symptoms of hepatitis develop); diabetes mellitus (adjustment of antidiabetic therapy may be necessary); possible increase in female fertility

**Contra-indications** pregnancy and breast-feeding

**Side-effects** diarrhoea, constipation, nausea, vomiting, abdominal distension, dyspepsia, flatulence, elevated liver enzymes; hypertension; headache, asthenia, dizziness, drowsiness, tremor, sleep disturbances; influenza-like syndrome, weight gain, hyperglycaemia, hypoglycaemia; arthralgia, myalgia; injection-site reactions, sweating, pruritus, rash; fatigue; hypercholesterolaemia; less commonly thrombocytopenia, leucopenia, leucocytosis, bleeding tendency

**Dose**

- By subcutaneous injection, initially 80 mg, then 10 mg daily, increased in steps of 5 mg daily according to response; max. 30 mg daily; CHILD not recommended

**Somavert®** (Pfizer) ▼ PoM
Injection, powder for reconstitution, pegvisomant, net price 10-mg vial = £50.00; 15-mg vial = £75.00; 20-mg vial = £100.00 (all with solvent)

## Thyrotrophin

**Thyrotropin alfa** is a recombinant form of thyrotrophin (thyroid stimulating hormone). It is licensed for use with or without radioiodine imaging, together with serum thyroglobulin testing, for the detection of thyroid remnants and thyroid cancer in post-thyroidectomy patients.

### THYROTROPIN ALFA
**(Recombinant human thyroid stimulating hormone, rhTSH)**

**Indications** detection of thyroid remnants and thyroid cancer in post-thyroidectomy patients

**Cautions** presence of thyroglobulin autoantibodies may give false negative results

**Contra-indications** pregnancy and breast-feeding; hypersensitivity to bovine or human thyrotrophin

**Side-effects** nausea, vomiting; headache, dizziness, asthenia, paraesthesia; pain (including pain at site of metastases), chills, fever, influenza-like symptoms; injection site reactions include urticaria, pruritus and rash

**Dose**

- By intramuscular injection into the gluteal muscle, 900 micrograms every 24 hours for 2 doses, consult product literature

**Thyrogen®** (Genzyme) PoM
Injection, powder for reconstitution, thyrotropin alfa 900 micrograms/vial, net price = £232.50

## Hypothalamic hormones

**Gonadorelin** when injected intravenously in normal subjects leads to a rapid rise in plasma concentrations of both luteinising hormone (LH) and follicle-stimulating hormone (FSH). It has not proved to be very helpful, however, in distinguishing hypothalamic from pituitary lesions. **Gonadorelin analogues** are indicated in endometriosis and infertility (section 6.7.2) and in breast and prostate cancer (section 8.3.4).

**Protirelin** is a hypothalamic releasing hormone which stimulates the release of thyrotrophin from the pituitary. It is licensed for the diagnosis of mild hyperthyroidism or hypothyroidism, but its use has been superseded by immunoassays for thyroid-stimulating hormone.

**Sermorelin**, an analogue of growth hormone releasing hormone (somatorelin, GHRH), is licensed as a diagnostic test for secretion of growth hormone.

## GONADORELIN
### (Gonadotrophin-releasing hormone; GnRH; LH–RH)

**Indications** see preparations below

**Cautions** pituitary adenoma

**Side-effects** rarely, nausea, headache, abdominal pain, increased menstrual bleeding; rarely, hypersensitivity reaction on repeated administration of large doses; irritation at injection site

**Dose**

- See under preparations

**HRF®** (Intrapharm) PoM
Injection, powder for reconstitution, gonadorelin. Net price 100-microgram vial (with diluent) = £13.72 (hosp. only)
Excipients include benzyl alcohol (avoid in neonates, see Excipients p. 2)
Dose for assessment of pituitary function (adults), by subcutaneous *or* intravenous injection, 100 micrograms

## PROTIRELIN
### (Thyrotrophin-releasing hormone; TRH)

**Indications** assessment of thyroid function and thyroid stimulating hormone reserve

**Cautions** severe hypopituitarism, myocardial ischaemia, bronchial asthma and obstructive airways disease, pregnancy, breast-feeding (Appendix 5)

**Side-effects** after rapid intravenous administration desire to micturate, flushing, dizziness, nausea, strange taste; transient increase in pulse rate and blood pressure; rarely bronchospasm

**Dose**

- By intravenous injection, 200 micrograms; CHILD under 12 years 1 microgram/kg

**Protirelin** (Cambridge) PoM
Injection, protirelin 100 micrograms/mL. Net price 2-mL amp = £9.03

## SERMORELIN

**Indications** see notes above

**Cautions** epilepsy; discontinue growth hormone therapy 1–2 weeks before test; untreated hypothyroidism, antithyroid drugs; obesity, hyperglycaemia, elevated plasma fatty acids; avoid preparations which affect release of growth hormone (includes those affecting release of somatostatin, insulin or glucocorticoids and cyclo-oxygenase inhibitors such as aspirin and indometacin)

**Contra-indications** pregnancy and breast-feeding

**Side-effects** occasional facial flushing and pain at injection site

**Dose**

- By intravenous injection, 1 microgram/kg in the morning after an overnight fast

**Geref 50®** (Serono) PoM
Injection, powder for reconstitution, sermorelin 50 micrograms (as acetate). Net price per amp (with solvent) = £48.85

# 6.5.2 Posterior pituitary hormones and antagonists

## Posterior pituitary hormones

**Diabetes insipidus** **Vasopressin** (antidiuretic hormone, ADH) is used in the treatment of *pituitary* ('cranial') *diabetes insipidus* as is its analogue **desmopressin**. Dosage is tailored to produce a slight diuresis every 24 hours to avoid water intoxication. Treatment may be required for a limited period only in diabetes insipidus following trauma or pituitary surgery.

Desmopressin is more potent and has a longer duration of action than vasopressin; unlike vasopressin it has no vasoconstrictor effect. It is given by mouth or intranasally for maintenance therapy, and by injection in the postoperative period or in unconscious patients. Desmopressin is also used in the differential diagnosis of diabetes insipidus. Following a dose of 2 micrograms intramuscularly or 20 micrograms intranasally, restoration of the ability to concentrate urine after water deprivation confirms a diagnosis of cranial diabetes insipidus. Failure to respond occurs in nephrogenic diabetes insipidus.

In *nephrogenic* and *partial pituitary diabetes insipidus* benefit may be gained from the paradoxical antidiuretic effect of thiazides (section 2.2.1) e.g. chlortalidone 100 mg twice daily reduced to maintenance dose of 50 mg daily.

Chlorpropamide (section 6.1.2.1) is also useful in partial pituitary diabetes insipidus, and probably acts by sensitising the renal tubules to the action of remaining endogenous vasopressin; it is given in doses of up to 350 mg daily in adults and 200 mg daily in children, care being taken to avoid hypoglycaemia. Carbamazepine (section 4.8.1) is also sometimes useful (in a dose of 200 mg once or twice daily) [unlicensed]; its mode of action may be similar to that of chlorpropamide.

**Other uses** Desmopressin is also used to boost factor VIII concentration in mild to moderate haemophilia and in von Willebrand's disease; it is also used to test fibrinolytic response. For a comment on use of desmopressin in nocturnal enuresis see section 7.4.2.

Vasopressin infusion is used to control variceal bleeding in portal hypertension, prior to more definitive treatment and with variable results. Terlipressin, a derivative of vasopressin, is used similarly.

Oxytocin, another posterior pituitary hormone, is indicated in obstetrics (section 7.1.1).

## VASOPRESSIN

**Indications** pituitary diabetes insipidus; bleeding from oesophageal varices

**Cautions** heart failure, hypertension, asthma, epilepsy, migraine or other conditions which might be aggravated by water retention; renal impairment (see also Contra-indications); pregnancy (Appendix 4); avoid fluid overload

**Contra-indications** vascular disease (especially disease of coronary arteries) unless extreme caution, chronic nephritis (until reasonable blood nitrogen concentrations attained)

**Side-effects** fluid retention, pallor, tremor, sweating, vertigo, headache, nausea, vomiting, belching, abdominal cramps, desire to defaecate, hypersensitivity reactions (including anaphylaxis), constriction of coronary arteries (may cause anginal attacks and myocardial ischaemia), peripheral ischaemia and rarely gangrene

**Dose**

- By subcutaneous *or* intramuscular injection, diabetes insipidus, 5–20 units every four hours
- By intravenous infusion, initial control of variceal bleeding, 20 units over 15 minutes

### Synthetic vasopressin

**Pitressin®** (Goldshield) PoM

Injection, argipressin (synthetic vasopressin) 20 units/mL. Net price 1-mL amp = £17.14 (hosp. only)

## DESMOPRESSIN

**Indications** see under Dose

**Cautions** see under Vasopressin; less pressor activity, but still considerable caution in renal impairment (Appendix 3), in cardiovascular disease and in hypertension (not indicated for nocturnal enuresis or nocturia in these circumstances); elderly (avoid for nocturnal enuresis and nocturia in those over 65 years); also considerable caution in cystic fibrosis; in nocturia and nocturnal enuresis limit fluid intake to minimum from 1 hour before dose until 8 hours afterwards; in nocturia periodic blood pressure and weight checks needed to monitor for fluid overload; pregnancy (Appendix 4) **interactions:** Appendix 1 (desmopressin)

**Hyponatraemic convulsions** The CSM has advised that patients being treated for primary nocturnal enuresis should be warned to avoid fluid overload (including during swimming) and to stop taking desmopressin during an episode of vomiting or diarrhoea (until fluid balance normal). The risk of hyponatraemic convulsions can also be minimised by keeping to the recommended starting doses and by avoiding concomitant use of drugs which increase secretion of vasopressin (e.g. tricyclic antidepressants)

**Contra-indications** cardiac insufficiency and other conditions treated with diuretics; psychogenic polydipsia and polydipsia in alcohol dependence

**Side-effects** fluid retention, and hyponatraemia (in more serious cases with convulsions) on administration without restricting fluid intake; stomach pain, headache, nausea, vomiting, allergic reactions, and emotional disturbance in children also reported; epistaxis, nasal congestion, rhinitis with nasal spray

**Dose**

- By mouth

  Diabetes insipidus, treatment, ADULT and CHILD initially 300 micrograms daily (in 3 divided doses); maintenance, 300–600 micrograms daily in 3 divided doses; range 0.2–1.2 mg daily

  Primary nocturnal enuresis (if urine concentrating ability normal), ADULT (under 65 years) and CHILD over 5 years (preferably over 7 years) 200 micrograms at bedtime, only increased to 400 micrograms if lower dose not effective (**important:** see also Cautions); withdraw for at least 1 week for reassessment after 3 months

  Postoperative polyuria or polydipsia, adjust dose according to urine osmolality

- Intranasally

  Diabetes insipidus, diagnosis, ADULT and CHILD 20 micrograms (limit fluid intake to 500 mL from 1 hour before to 8 hours after administration)

  Diabetes insipidus, treatment, ADULT 10–40 micrograms daily (in 1–2 divided doses); CHILD 5–20 micrograms daily; infants may require lower doses

  Primary nocturnal enuresis (if urine concentrating ability normal), ADULT (under 65 years) and CHILD over 5 years (preferably over 7 years) initially 20 micrograms at bedtime, only increased to 40 micrograms if lower dose not effective (**important:** see also Cautions); withdraw for at least 1 week for reassessment after 3 months

  Nocturia associated with multiple sclerosis (when other treatments have failed), ADULT (under 65 years) 10–20 micrograms at bedtime (**important:** see also Cautions), dose not to be repeated within 24 hours

  Renal function testing (empty bladder at time of administration and limit fluid intake to 500 mL from 1 hour before until 8 hours after administration), ADULT 40 micrograms; INFANT under 1 year 10 micrograms (restrict fluid intake to 50% at next 2 feeds to avoid fluid overload), CHILD 1–15 years 20 micrograms

  Mild to moderate haemophilia and von Willebrand's disease, ADULT 300 micrograms (one 150-microgram spray into each nostril) 30 minutes before surgery or when bleeding; may be repeated at intervals of 12 hours (or at intervals of at least 3 days if self-administered)

  Fibrinolytic response testing, ADULT 300 micrograms (one 150-microgram spray into each nostril); blood sampled after 1 hour for fibrinolytic activity

- By injection

  Diabetes insipidus, diagnosis (subcutaneous *or* intramuscular), ADULT and CHILD 2 micrograms (limit fluid intake to 500 mL from 1 hour before to 8 hours after administration)

  Diabetes insipidus, treatment (subcutaneous, intramuscular *or* intravenous), ADULT 1–4 micrograms daily; INFANT and CHILD 400 nanograms

  Renal function testing (empty bladder at time of administration and limit fluid intake to 500 mL from 1 hour before until 8 hours after administration) (subsubcutaneous *or* intramuscular), ADULT and CHILD 2 micrograms; INFANT 400 nanograms (restrict fluid intake to 50% at next 2 feeds)

  Mild to moderate haemophilia and von Willebrand's disease, (subcutaneous *or* intravenous), ADULT and CHILD over 1 month 300 nanograms/kg as a single dose immediately before surgery or after trauma; may be repeated at intervals of 12 hours

  Fibrinolytic response testing, (subcutaneous *or* intravenous), ADULT and CHILD 300 nanograms/kg; blood sampled after 20 minutes for fibrinolytic activity

  Lumbar-puncture-associated headache, consult product literature

**Desmopressin acetate** (Non-proprietary) PoM

Nasal spray, desmopressin acetate 10 micrograms/metered spray, net price 6-mL unit (60 metered sprays) = £26.04. Counselling, fluid intake, see above

Brands include *Presinex®*

**Note** Children requiring dose of less than 10 micrograms should be given *DDAVP®* intranasal solution

6 Endocrine system

**DDAVP®** (Ferring) PoM
Tablets, both scored, desmopressin acetate 100 micrograms, net price 90-tab pack = £45.48; 200 micrograms, 90-tab pack = £90.96. Counselling, fluid intake, see above

Intranasal solution, desmopressin acetate 100 micrograms/mL. Net price 2.5-mL dropper bottle and catheter = £9.72. Counselling, fluid intake, see above

Injection, desmopressin acetate 4 micrograms/mL. Net price 1-mL amp = £1.10

**Desmotabs®** (Ferring) PoM
Tablets, scored, desmopressin acetate 200 micrograms, net price 30-tab pack = £30.34. Counselling, fluid intake, see above

**Desmospray®** (Ferring) PoM
Nasal spray, desmopressin acetate 10 micrograms/metered spray. Net price 6-mL unit (60 metered sprays) = £26.04. Counselling, fluid intake, see above
Note Children requiring dose of less than 10 micrograms should be given *DDAVP® intranasal solution*

**Nocutil®** (Norgine) PoM
Nasal spray, desmopressin acetate 10 micrograms/metered spray, net price 5-mL unit (50 metered sprays) = £19.69. Counselling, fluid intake, see above

**Octim®** (Ferring) PoM
Nasal spray, desmopressin acetate 150 micrograms/metered spray, net price 2.5-mL unit (25 metered sprays) = £600.00. Counselling, fluid intake, see above

Injection, desmopressin acetate 15 micrograms/mL, net price 1-mL amp = £20.00

### TERLIPRESSIN

**Indications** bleeding from oesophageal varices

**Cautions** see under Vasopressin

**Contra-indications** see under Vasopressin

**Side-effects** see under Vasopressin, but effects milder

**Dose**
- By intravenous injection, 2 mg followed by 1 or 2 mg every 4 to 6 hours until bleeding is controlled, for up to 72 hours

**Glypressin®** (Ferring) PoM
Injection, terlipressin, powder for reconstitution. Net price 1-mg vial with 5 mL diluent = £19.44 (hosp. only)

## Antidiuretic hormone antagonists

**Demeclocycline** (section 5.1.3) may be used in the treatment of hyponatraemia resulting from inappropriate secretion of antidiuretic hormone. It is thought to act by directly blocking the renal tubular effect of antidiuretic hormone. Initially 0.9 to 1.2 g is given daily in divided doses, reduced to 600–900 mg daily for maintenance.

# 6.6 Drugs affecting bone metabolism

**6.6.1** Calcitonin and teriparatide
**6.6.2** Bisphosphonates and other drugs affecting bone metabolism

See also calcium (section 9.5.1.1), phosphorus (section 9.5.2), vitamin D (section 9.6.4), and oestrogens in postmenopausal osteoporosis (section 6.4.1.1).

## Osteoporosis

Osteoporosis occurs most commonly in postmenopausal women and in those taking long-term oral corticosteroids (glucocorticosteroids). Other risk factors for osteoporosis include low body weight, cigarette smoking, excess alcohol intake, lack of physical activity, family history of osteoporosis, and early menopause.

> Those at risk of osteoporosis should maintain an adequate intake of **calcium and vitamin D** and any deficiency should be corrected by increasing dietary intake or taking supplements.

Elderly patients, especially those who are housebound or live in residential or nursing homes, are at increased risk of calcium and vitamin D deficiency and may benefit from supplements (section 9.5.1.1 and section 9.6.4). Reversible secondary causes of osteoporosis such as hyperthyroidism, hyperparathyroidism, osteomalacia or hypogonadism should be excluded, in both men and women, before treatment for osteoporosis is initiated.

**Postmenopausal osteoporosis** The **bisphosphonates** (alendronic acid, disodium etidronate, and risedronate, section 6.6.2) are effective for preventing postmenopausal osteoporosis. **Hormone replacement therapy** (HRT section 6.4.1.1) is an option where other therapies are contra-indicated, cannot be tolerated, or if there is a lack of response. The CSM has advised that HRT should **not** be considered first-line therapy for long-term prevention of osteoporosis in women over 50 years of age. HRT is of most benefit for the prophylaxis of postmenopausal osteoporosis if started early in menopause and continued for up to 5 years, but bone loss resumes (possibly at an accelerated rate) on stopping HRT. **Calcitonin** (section 6.6.1) may be considered for those at high risk of osteoporosis for whom a bisphosphonate is unsuitable. Women of Afro-Caribbean origin appear to be less susceptible to osteoporosis than those who are white or of Asian origin.

Postmenopausal osteoporosis may be *treated* with a **bisphosphonate** (section 6.6.2). The bisphosphonates (such as alendronate, etidronate, and risedronate) decrease the risk of vertebral fracture; alendronate and risedronate have also been shown to reduce non-vertebral fractures. If bisphosphonates are unsuitable **calcitriol** (section 9.6.4), **calcitonin** or **strontium ranelate** (section 6.6.2) may be considered. Calcitonin [unlicensed indication] may also be useful for pain relief for up to 3 months after a vertebral fracture if other analgesics are ineffective. **Teriparatide** (section 6.6.1) has been introduced for the treatment of postmenopausal oestoporosis.

**Raloxifene** (section 6.4.1.1) is licensed for the *prophylaxis* and *treatment* of vertebral fractures in postmenopausal women.

**NICE guidance (bisphosphonates, selective oestrogen receptor modulators and parathyroid hormone for secondary prevention of osteoporotic fragility fractures in postmenopausal women).**

NICE has recommended (January 2005) **bisphosphonates** as treatment options for the secondary prevention of osteoporotic fractures in susceptible postmenopausal women. In women who cannot take a bisphosphonate or who have suffered a fragility fracture despite treatment for a year and whose bone mineral density declines below the pretreatment level, the selective oestrogen receptor modulator **raloxifene** is an alternative. The parathyroid hormone fragment **teriparatide** is recommended for women over 65 years who cannot take a bisphosphonate (or in whom bisphosphonate has failed to prevent a fracture) and have:

- either an extremely low bone mineral density
- or a very low bone mineral density, suffered more than 2 fractures, and have other risk factors for fractures (e.g. body mass index under 19 $kg/m^2$, premature menopause, prolonged immobility, history of maternal hip fracture under the age of 75 years).

**Corticosteroid-induced osteoporosis** To reduce the risk of osteoporosis doses of oral corticosteroids should be as low as possible and courses of treatment as short as possible. The risk of osteoporosis may be related to cumulative dose of corticosteroids; even intermittent courses can therefore increase the risk. The greatest rate of bone loss occurs during the first 6–12 months of corticosteroid use and so early steps to prevent the development of osteoporosis are important. Long-term use of high-dose inhaled corticosteroids may also contribute to corticosteroid-induced osteoporosis(- section 3.2).

Patients taking (or who are likely to take) the equivalent of prednisolone 7.5 mg or more each day for 3 months or longer should be assessed and where necessary given prophylactic treatment; those aged over 65 years are at greater risk. Patients taking oral corticosteroids who have sustained a low-trauma fracture should receive treatment for osteoporosis. The therapeutic options for *prophylaxis* and *treatment* of corticosteroid-induced osteoporosis are the same:

- a bisphosphonate such as alendronate, etidronate or risedronate;
- calcitriol.
- hormone replacement (HRT in women, (section 6.4.1) testosterone in men (section 6.4.2))

## 6.6.1 Calcitonin and teriparatide

Calcitonin is involved with parathyroid hormone in the regulation of bone turnover and hence in the maintenance of calcium balance and homoeostasis. **Calcitonin (salmon)** (**salcatonin**, synthetic or recombinant salmon calcitonin) is used to lower the plasma-calcium concentration in some patients with hypercalcaemia (notably when associated with malignant disease). Calcitonin is licensed for treatment of Paget's disease of bone. It can also be used in the prevention and treatment of postmenopausal osteoporosis (see section 6.6).

**Teriparatide**, a recombinant, fragment of parathyroid hormone, has been introduced for the treatment of postmenopausal osteoporosis. *The Scottish Medicines Consortium* has advised (December 2003) that teriparatide should be initiated by specialists experienced in the treatment of osteoporosis.

**Cinacalcet** (section 9.5.1.2) is licensed for the treatment of hypercalcaemia in parathyroid carcinoma.

### CALCITONIN (SALMON)/ SALCATONIN

**Indications** see under Dose

**Cautions** history of allergy (skin test advised); renal impairment; heart failure; pregnancy (Appendix 4), breast-feeding (Appendix 5)

**Contra-indications** hypocalcaemia

**Side-effects** nausea, vomiting, diarrhoea, abdominal pain; flushing; dizziness, headache, taste disturbances; musculoskeletal pain; with nasal spray nose and throat irritation, rhinitis, sinusitis and epistaxis; *less commonly* diuresis, oedema, cough, visual disturbances, injection-site reactions, rash, hypersensitivity reactions including pruritus

**Dose**

- Hypercalcaemia of malignancy (see also section 9.5.1.2), ADULT over 18 years, by subcutaneous *or* intramuscular injection, 100 units every 6–8 hours adjusted according to response; max. 400 units every 6–8 hours; in severe or emergency cases, by intravenous infusion, up to 10 units/kg over at least 6 hours
- Paget's disease of bone, ADULT over 18 years, by subcutaneous *or* intramuscular injection, 50 units 3 times weekly to 100 units daily adjusted according to response
- Postmenopausal osteoporosis to reduce risk of vertebral fractures, intranasally, 200 units (1 spray) into one nostril daily, with dietary calcium and vitamin D supplements (section 9.5.1.1 and section 9.6.4)
- Prevention of acute bone loss due to sudden immobility, ADULT over 18 years, by subcutaneous *or* intramuscular injection, 100 units daily in 1–2 divided doses for 2–4 weeks, reduced to 50 units daily at start of mobilisation and continued until fully mobile

**Miacalcic®** (Novartis) PoM

Nasal spray▼, calcitonin (salmon) 200 units/metered spray, net price 2-mL unit (approx. 14 metered sprays) = £20.99

Injection, calcitonin (salmon) 50 units/mL, net price 1-mL amp = £4.27; 100 units/mL, 1-mL amp = £8.55; 200 units/mL, 2-mL vial = £30.75

For subcutaneous or intramuscular injection and for dilution and use as an intravenous infusion

### TERIPARATIDE

**Indications** treatment of postmenopausal osteoporosis (initiated by specialist—see notes above)

**Cautions** moderate renal impairment (avoid if severe)

**Contra-indications** pre-existing hypercalcaemia, metabolic bone diseases, including Paget's disease

6 Endocrine system

and hyperparathyroidism, unexplained raised levels of alkaline phosphatase, previous radiation therapy to the skeleton, pregnancy and breast-feeding

**Side-effects** gastro-intestinal disorders (including nausea, reflux and haemorrhoids); postural hypotension; dysponea; depression, dizziness, vertigo; urinary disorders, polyuria; muscle cramps, sciatica; increased sweating; injection-site reactions

**Dose**

- By subcutaneous injection, 20 micrograms daily; max. duration of treatment 18 months

**Forsteo®** (Lilly) ▼ PoM

Injection, teriparatide 250 micrograms/mL, net price 3-mL prefilled pen = £271.88

Note 3-ml prefilled pen intended for 28 doses

## 6.6.2 Bisphosphonates and other drugs affecting bone metabolism

Bisphosphonates are adsorbed onto hydroxyapatite crystals in bone, slowing both their rate of growth and dissolution, and therefore reducing the rate of bone turnover. Bisphosphonates have an important role in the prophylaxis and treatment of osteoporosis and corticosteroid-induced osteoporosis; **alendronic acid** or **risedronate sodium** are considered the drugs of choice for these conditions, but **disodium etidronate** may be considered if these drugs are unsuitable or not tolerated (see also section 6.6).

Bisphosphonates are also used in the treatment of *Paget's disease*, hypercalcaemia of malignancy (section 9.5.1.2). and in bone metastases in breast cancer (section 8.3.4.1). Disodium etidronate can impair bone mineralisation when used continuously or in high doses (such as in the treatment of *Paget's disease*).

**Strontium ranelate** stimulates bone formation and reduces bone resorption. It is licensed for the treatment of postmenopausal osteoporosis. The *Scottish Medicines Consortium* has advised (July 2005) that strontium ranelate should be restricted to use when bisphosphonates are contra-indicated or not tolerated and then only in women aged over 75 years with a previous fracture and low bone mineral density or in other women at equivalent risk

### ALENDRONIC ACID

**Indications** see under Dose

**Cautions** upper gastro-intestinal disorders (dysphagia, symptomatic oesophageal disease, gastritis, duodenitis, or ulcers—see also under Contra-indications and Side-effects); history (within 1 year) of ulcers, active gastro-intestinal bleeding, or surgery of the upper gastro-intestinal tract; renal impairment (manufacturer advises avoid if creatinine clearance is less than 35 mL/minute); correct disturbances of calcium and mineral metabolism (e.g. vitamin-D deficiency, hypocalcaemia) before starting and monitor serum calcium during treatment; exclude other causes of osteoporosis; **interactions**: Appendix 1 (bisphosphonates)

**Contra-indications** abnormalities of oesophagus and other factors which delay emptying (e.g. stricture or achalasia), hypocalcaemia, pregnancy (Appendix 4) and breast-feeding (Appendix 5)

**Side-effects** oesophageal reactions (see below), abdominal pain and distension, dyspepsia, regurgitation, melaena, diarrhoea or constipation, flatulence, musculoskeletal pain, headache; *rarely* rash, pruritus, erythema, photosensitivity, uveitis, scleritis, transient decrease in serum calcium and phosphate; nausea, vomiting, gastritis, peptic ulceration, and hypersensitivity reactions (including urticaria and angioedema) also reported; myalgia, malaise and fever at initiation of treatment; *very rarely* severe skin reactions (including Stevens-Johnson syndrome)

**Oesophageal reactions** Severe oesophageal reactions (oesophagitis, oesophageal ulcers, oesophageal stricture and oesophageal erosions) have been reported; patients should be advised to stop taking the tablets and to seek medical attention if they develop symptoms of oesophageal irritation such as dysphagia, new or worsening heartburn, pain on swallowing or retrosternal pain

**Dose**

- Treatment of postmenopausal osteoporosis and osteoporosis in men, 10 mg daily *or* (in postmenopausal osteoporosis) 70 mg once weekly
- Prevention of postmenopausal osteoporosis, 5 mg daily
- Prevention and treatment of corticosteroid-induced osteoporosis, 5 mg daily (postmenopausal women not receiving hormone replacement therapy, 10 mg daily)

**Counselling** Tablets should be swallowed whole with plenty of water while sitting or standing; to be taken on an empty stomach at least 30 minutes before breakfast (or another oral medicine); patient should stand or sit upright for at least 30 minutes after taking tablet

**Fosamax®** (MSD) PoM

Tablets, alendronic acid (as sodium alendronate) 5 mg, net price 28-tab pack = £25.43; 10 mg, 28-tab pack = £23.12. Counselling, administration

**Fosamax® Once Weekly** (MSD) PoM

Tablets, alendronic acid (as sodium alendronate) 70 mg, net price 4-tab pack = £22.80. Counselling, administration

**With colecalciferol**

For cautions, contra-indications, and side-effects of colecalciferol, see section 9.6.4

**Fosavance®** (MSD) ▼ PoM

Tablets, alendronic acid (as sodium alendronate) 70 mg, colecalciferol 70 micrograms (2 800 units), net price 4-tab pack = £22.80. Counselling, administration

**Dose** treatment of postmenopausal osteoporosis in women at risk of vitamin D deficiency, 1 tablet once weekly

**Counselling** Tablets should be swallowed whole with plenty of water while sitting or standing; to be taken on an empty stomach at least 30 minutes before breakfast (or another oral medicine); patient should stand or sit upright for at least 30 minutes after taking tablet

### DISODIUM ETIDRONATE

**Indications** see under Dose

**Cautions** renal impairment (Appendix 3); **interactions**: Appendix 1 (bisphosphonates)

**Contra-indications** moderate to severe renal impairment; pregnancy (Appendix 4) and breast-feeding (Appendix 5); not indicated for osteoporosis in presence of hypercalcaemia or hypercalciuria or for osteomalacia

**Side-effects** nausea, diarrhoea or constipation, abdominal pain; increased bone pain in Paget's disease, also increased risk of fractures with high doses in Paget's disease (discontinue if fractures occur); rarely exacerbation of asthma, skin reactions (including angioedema, rash, urticaria and pruritus), transient hyperphosphataemia, headache, paraesthesia, peripheral neuropathy reported; blood disorders (including leucopenia, agranulocytosis and pancytopenia) also reported

**Dose**

- Paget's disease of bone, by mouth, 5 mg/kg as a single daily dose for up to 6 months; doses above 10 mg/kg daily for up to 3 months may be used with caution but doses above 20 mg/kg daily are not recommended; after interval of not less than 3 months may be repeated where evidence of reactivation—including biochemical indices (avoid premature retreatment)

  Monitoring Serum phosphate, serum alkaline phosphatase and (if possible) urinary hydroxyproline should be measured before starting and at intervals of 3 months—consult product literature for further details
- Osteoporosis, see under *Didronel PMO*®

  Counselling Avoid food for at least 2 hours before and after oral treatment, particularly calcium-containing products e.g.milk; also avoid iron and mineral supplements and antacids

**Didronel**® (Procter & Gamble Pharm.) PoM

Tablets, disodium etidronate 200 mg. Net price 60-tab pack = £20.68. Counselling, food and calcium (see above)

**With calcium carbonate**

For cautions and side-effects of calcium carbonate see section 9.5.1.1

**Didronel PMO**® (Procter & Gamble Pharm.) PoM

Tablets, 14 white, disodium etidronate 400 mg; 76 pink, effervescent, calcium carbonate 1.25 g (*Cacit*®). Net price per pack = £22.29. Label: 10, patient information leaflet, counselling, food and calcium (see above)

Dose treatment of osteoporosis, prevention of bone loss in postmenopausal women (particularly if hormone replacement therapy inappropriate), and prevention and treatment of corticosteroid-induced osteoporosis, given in 90-day cycles, 1 *Didronel*® tablet daily for 14 days, then 1 *Cacit*® tablet daily for 76 days

## DISODIUM PAMIDRONATE

Disodium pamidronate was formerly called aminohydroxypropylidenediphosphonate disodium (APD)

**Indications** see under Dose

**Cautions** renal impairment (Appendix 3); assess renal function before each dose; hepatic impairment (Appendix 2); cardiac disease (especially in elderly); previous thyroid surgery (risk of hypocalcaemia); monitor serum electrolytes, calcium and phosphate—possibility of convulsions due to electrolyte changes; avoid concurrent use with other bisphosphonates; **interactions:** Appendix 1 (bisphosphonates)

Osteonecrosis of the jaw Osteonecrosis of the jaw reported in cancer patients being treated with bisphosphonate; consider dental examination and preventative treatment before initiating bisphosphonate; avoid invasive dental procedures during treatment

Driving Patients should be warned against driving or operating machinery immediately after treatment (somnolence or dizziness may occur)

**Contra-indications** pregnancy (Appendix 4) and breast-feeding (Appendix 5)

**Side-effects** hypophosphataemia, fever and influenza-like symptoms (sometimes accompanied by malaise, rigors, fatigue and flushes); nausea, vomiting, anorexia, abdominal pain, diarrhoea, constipation; symptomatic hypocalcaemia (paraesthesia, tetany), hypomagnesaemia, headache, insomnia, drowsiness; hypertension; anaemia, thrombocytopenia, lymphocytopenia; rash; arthralgia, myalgia; rarely muscle cramps, dyspepsia, agitation, confusion, dizziness, lethargy; leucopenia, hypotension, pruritus, hyperkalaemia or hypokalaemia, and hypernatraemia; osteonecrosis (see also Cautions above), isolated cases of seizures, hallucinations, haematuria, acute renal failure, deterioration of renal disease, conjunctivitis and other ocular symptoms; reactivation of herpes simplex and zoster also reported; also injection-site reactions

**Dose**

- By slow intravenous infusion (via cannula in a relatively large vein), see also Appendix 6
- Hypercalcaemia of malignancy, according to serum calcium concentration 15–60 mg in single infusion or in divided doses over 2–4 days; max. 90 mg per treatment course
- Osteolytic lesions and bone pain in bone metastases associated with breast cancer or multiple myeloma, 90 mg every 4 weeks (or every 3 weeks to coincide with chemotherapy in breast cancer)
- Paget's disease of bone, 30 mg once a week for 6 weeks (total dose 180 mg) *or* 30 mg in first week then 60 mg every other week (total dose 210 mg); max. total 360 mg (in divided doses of 60 mg) per treatment course; may be repeated every 6 months
- CHILD not recommended

  Calcium and vitamin d supplements Oral supplements are advised for those with Paget's disease at risk of calcium or vitamin D deficiency (e.g. through malabsorption or lack of exposure to sunlight) to minimise potential risk of hypocalcaemia

**Disodium pamidronate** (Non-proprietary) PoM

Concentrate for intravenous infusion, disodium pamidronate 3 mg/mL, net price 5-mL vial = £27.50, 10-mL vial = £55.00; 6 mg/mL, 10-mL vial = £110.00; 9 mg/mL, 10-mL vial = £165.00

**Aredia Dry Powder**® (Novartis) PoM

Injection, powder for reconstitution, disodium pamidronate, for use as an infusion. Net price 15-mg vial = £29.83; 30-mg vial = £59.66; 90-mg vial = £170.45 (all with diluent)

## IBANDRONIC ACID

**Indications** see under Dose

**Cautions** renal impairment (Appendix 3); monitor renal function and serum calcium, phosphate and magnesium; cardiac disease (avoid fluid overload); breast-feeding (Appendix 5); **interactions:** Appendix 1 (bisphosphonates)

**Contra-indications** pregnancy (Appendix 4)

**Side-effects** hypocalcaemia, hypophosphataemia, influenza-like symptoms (including fever, chills, and muscle pain), bone pain; oesophageal reactions (see below), diarrhoea, nausea, vomiting, abdominal pain, dyspepsia, pharyngitis; headache, asthenia; rarely anaemia, hypersensitivity reactions (pruritus, bronchospasm and angioedema reported)

Oesophageal reactions Severe oesophageal reactions reported with all **oral** bisphosphonates; patients should be

6 Endocrine system

advised to stop tablets and seek medical attention for symptoms of oesophageal irritation such as dysphagia, pain on swallowing, retrosternal pain, or heartburn

**Dose**

- Reduction of bone damage in bone metastases in breast cancer, by mouth, 50 mg daily, *or* by intravenous infusion, 6 mg every 3–4 weeks
- Hypercalcaemia of malignancy by intravenous infusion, according to serum calcium concentration, 2–4 mg in single infusion
- Treatment of postmenopausal osteoporosis, by mouth, 150 mg once a month
- CHILD not recommended

**Counselling** Tablets should be swallowed whole with plenty of water while sitting or standing; to be taken on an empty stomach at least 1 hour before breakfast (or another oral medicine); patient should stand or sit upright for at least 1 hour after taking tablet

**Bondronat®** (Roche) ▼ PoM
Tablets, f/c, ibandronic acid 50 mg, net price 28-tab pack = £195.00. Counselling, administration

Concentrate for intravenous infusion, ibandronic acid 1 mg/mL, net price 2-mL amp = £94.86, 6-mL vial = £195.00

**Bonviva®** (Roche) ▼ PoM
Tablets, f/c, ibandronic acid 150 mg, net price 1-tab pack = £21.45, 3-tab pack = £64.35. Counselling, administration

## RISEDRONATE SODIUM

**Indications** see under Dose

**Cautions** oesophageal abnormalities and other factors which delay transit or emptying (e.g. stricture or achalasia—see also under Side-effects); renal impairment (Appendix 3); correct hypocalcaemia before starting, correct other disturbances of bone and mineral metabolism (e.g. vitamin-D deficiency) at onset of treatment; **interactions:** Appendix 1 (bisphosphonates)

**Contra-indications** hypocalcaemia (see Cautions above), pregnancy (Appendix 4) and breast-feeding (Appendix 5)

**Side-effects** gastro-intestinal disturbances (including abdominal pain, dyspepsia, nausea, diarrhoea, constipation); dizziness, headache; influenza-like symptoms, musculoskeletal pain; *rarely* oesophageal stricture, oesophagitis, oesphageal ulcer, dysphagia, gastritis, duodenitis, glossitis, peripheral oedema, weight loss, myasthenia, arthralgia, apnoea, bronchitis, sinusitis, rash, nocturia, ambylopia, corneal lesion, dry eye, tinnitus, iritis; *very rarely* hypersensitivity reactions including angioedema

**Dose**

- Paget's disease of bone, 30 mg daily for 2 months; may be repeated if necessary after at least 2 months
- Treatment of postmenopausal osteoporosis to reduce risk of vertebral or hip fractures, 5 mg daily *or* 35 mg once weekly
- Prevention of osteoporosis (including corticosteroid-induced osteoporosis) in postmenopausal women, 5 mg daily
- CHILD not recommended

**Counselling** Swallow tablets whole with full glass of water; on rising, take on an empty stomach at least 30 minutes before first food or drink of the day **or**, if taking at any other time of the day, avoid food and drink for at least 2 hours before or after risedronate (particularly avoid calcium-containing products e.g. milk, also avoid iron and mineral supplements and antacids); stand or sit upright for at least 30 minutes; do not take tablets at bedtime or before rising

**Actonel®** (Procter & Gamble Pharm.) PoM
Tablets, f/c, risedronate sodium 5 mg (yellow), net price 28-tab pack = £19.10; 30 mg (white), 28-tab pack = £152.81. Counselling, administration, food and calcium (see above)

**Actonel Once a Week®** (Procter & Gamble Pharm.) PoM
Tablets, f/c, risedronate sodium 35 mg (orange), net price 4-tab pack = £20.30. Counselling, administration, food and calcium (see above)

## SODIUM CLODRONATE

**Indications** see under Dose

**Cautions** monitor renal and hepatic function and white cell count; also monitor serum calcium and phosphate periodically; renal dysfunction reported in patients receiving concomitant NSAIDs; maintain adequate fluid intake during treatment; **interactions:** Appendix 1 (bisphosphonates)

**Contra-indications** moderate to severe renal impairment; pregnancy (Appendix 4) and breast-feeding (Appendix 5)

**Side-effects** nausea, diarrhoea; skin reactions

**Dose**

- Osteolytic lesions, hypercalcaemia and bone pain associated with skeletal metastases in patients with breast cancer or multiple myeloma, by mouth, 1.6 g daily in single or 2 divided doses increased if necessary to a max. of 3.2 g daily

  **Counselling** Avoid food for 1 hour before and after treatment, particularly calcium-containing products e.g. milk; also avoid iron and mineral supplements and antacids; maintain adequate fluid intake
- Hypercalcaemia of malignancy, by slow intravenous infusion, 300 mg daily for max. 7–10 days *or* by single-dose infusion of 1.5 g

**Bonefos®** (Schering Health) PoM
Capsules, yellow, sodium clodronate 400 mg. Net price 30-cap pack = £40.49, 120-cap pack = £161.97. Counselling, food and calcium

Tablets, f/c, scored, sodium clodronate 800 mg. Net price 10-tab pack = £28.27; 60-tab pack = £169.62. Counselling, food and calcium

Concentrate (= intravenous solution), sodium clodronate 60 mg/mL, for dilution and use as infusion. Net price 5-mL amp = £12.82

**Loron®** (Roche) PoM
Loron 520® tablets, f/c, scored, sodium clodronate 520 mg. Net price 60-tab pack = £161.99. Label: 10, patient information leaflet counselling, food and calcium

Dose 2 tablets daily in single or two divided doses; may be increased to max. 4 tablets daily

## STRONTIUM RANELATE

**Indications** treatment of postmenopausal osteoporosis to reduce risk of vertebral and hip fractures

**Cautions** predisposition to thromboembolism; interferes with colorimetric measurements of calcium in blood and urine; renal impairment (Appendix 3); **interactions**: Appendix 1 (strontium ranelate)

**Contra-indications** pregnancy, breast-feeding

**Side-effects** nausea, diarrhoea; venous thromboembolism; headache; dermatitis, eczema

**Dose**

- 2 g once daily in water, preferably at bedtime
  Counselling Avoid food for 2 hours before and after taking granules, particularly calcium-containing products e.g. milk; also preferably avoid concomitant antacids containing aluminium and magnesium hydroxides for 2 hours after taking granules

**Protelos®** (Servier) ▼ PoM
Granules, yellow, strontium ranelate, 2 g/sachet, net price 28-sachets = £25.60. Label: 5, 13, counselling, food and calcium
Excipients include aspartame (section 9.4.1)

## TILUDRONIC ACID

**Indications** Paget's disease of bone

**Cautions** renal impairment (monitor renal function regularly, see under Contra-indications); correct disturbances of calcium metabolism (e.g. vitamin D deficiency, hypocalcaemia) before starting; avoid concomitant use of indometacin; **interactions:** Appendix 1 (bisphosphonates)

**Contra-indications** severe renal impairment, juvenile Paget's disease, pregnancy (Appendix 4) and breast-feeding (Appendix 5)

**Side-effects** stomach pain, nausea, diarrhoea; rarely asthenia, dizziness, headache and skin reactions

**Dose**

- 400 mg daily as a single dose for 12 weeks; may be repeated if necessary after 6 months
  Counselling Avoid food for 2 hours before and after treatment, particularly calcium-containing products e.g. milk; also avoid antacids

**Skelid®** (Sanofi-Synthelabo) PoM
Tablets, tiludronic acid (as tiludronate disodium) 200 mg. Net price 28-tab pack = £99.00. Counselling, food and calcium

## ZOLEDRONIC ACID

**Indications** see under Dose

**Cautions** monitor serum electrolytes, calcium, phosphate and magnesium; assess renal function before each dose; ensure adequate hydration; renal impairment (Appendix 3); severe hepatic impairment (Appendix 2); cardiac disease (avoid fluid overload); **interactions:** Appendix 1 (bisphosphonates)
osteonecrosis of the jaw Osteonecrosis of the jaw reported in cancer patients being treated with bisphosphonate; consider dental examination and preventative treatment before initiating bisphosphonate; avoid invasive dental procedures during treatment

**Contra-indications** pregnancy (Appendix 4), breast-feeding (Appendix 5)

**Side-effects** hypophosphataemia, anaemia, influenza-like symptoms including bone pain, myalgia, arthralgia, fever and rigors; gastro-intestinal disturbances; headache, conjunctivitis, renal impairment (rarely acute renal failure); *less commonly* taste disturbance, dry mouth, stomatitis, chest pain, hypertension, dyspnoea, cough, dizziness, paraesthesia, tremor, anxiety, sleep disturbance, blurred vision, weight gain, pruritus, rash, sweating, muscle cramps, haematuria, proteinuria, hypersensitivity reactions (including angioedema), asthenia, peripheral oedema, thrombocytopenia, leucopenia, hypomagnesaemia, hypokalaemia, also injection-site reactions; *rarely* bradycardia, confusion, hyperkalaemia, hypernatraemia, pancytopenia, osteonecrosis of the jaw (*see also* Cautions above); *very rarely* uveitis and episcleritis

**Dose**

- Reduction of bone damage in advanced malignancies involving bone (with calcium and vitamin D supplement), by intravenous infusion, 4 mg every 3–4 weeks
- Hypercalcaemia of malignancy, by intravenous infusion, 4 mg as a single dose
- CHILD not recommended

**Zometa®** (Novartis) PoM
Concentrate for intravenous infusion, zoledronic acid, 800 micrograms/mL, net price 5-mL (4-mg) vial = £195.00

# 6.7 Other endocrine drugs

6.7.1 Bromocriptine and other dopaminergic drugs
6.7.2 Drugs affecting gonadotrophins
6.7.3 Metyrapone and trilostane

## 6.7.1 Bromocriptine and other dopaminergic drugs

**Bromocriptine** is a stimulant of dopamine receptors in the brain; it also inhibits release of prolactin by the pituitary. Bromocriptine is used for the treatment of galactorrhoea and cyclical benign breast disease, and for the treatment of prolactinomas (when it reduces both plasma prolactin concentration and tumour size). Bromocriptine also inhibits the release of growth hormone and is sometimes used in the treatment of acromegaly, but somatostatin analogues (such as octreotide, section 8.3.4.3) are more effective.

**Cabergoline** has actions and uses similar to those of bromocriptine, but its duration of action is longer. Its side-effects appear to differ from that of bromocriptine and patients intolerant of bromocriptine may be able to tolerate cabergoline (and *vice versa*).

> **Fibrotic reactions**
> The CSM has advised that ergot-derived dopamine-receptor agonists, bromocriptine, cabergoline, lisuride, and pergolide have been associated with pulmonary, retroperitoneal, and pericardial fibrotic reactions.
> Before starting treatment with these ergot derivatives it may be appropriate to measure the erythrocyte sedimentation rate and serum creatinine and to obtain a chest X-ray. Patients should be monitored for dyspnoea, persistent cough, chest pain, cardiac failure, and abdominal pain or tenderness. If long-term treatment is expected, then lung-function tests may also be helpful.

**Quinagolide** has actions and uses similar to those of ergot-derived dopamine agonists, but its side-effects differ slightly.

**Suppression of lactation** Although bromocriptine and cabergoline are licensed to suppress lactation, they are **not** recommended for routine suppression (or for the relief of symptoms of postpartum pain and engorgement) that can be adequately treated with simple analgesics and breast support. If a dopamine-receptor agonist is required, cabergoline is preferred. Quinagolide is not licensed for the suppression of lactation.

> **Sudden onset of sleep**
> Excessive daytime sleepiness and sudden onset of sleep can occur with dopaminergic drugs.
> Patients starting treatment with these drugs should be warned of the possibility of these effects and of the need to exercise caution when driving or operating machinery.
> Patients who have suffered excessive sedation or sudden onset of sleep, should refrain from driving or operating machines, until those effects have stopped recurring.

## BROMOCRIPTINE

**Indications** see notes above and under Dose; parkinsonism (section 4.9.1)

**Cautions** specialist evaluation—monitor for pituitary enlargement, particularly during pregnancy, annual gynaecological assessment (postmenopausal, every 6 months), monitor for peptic ulceration in acromegalic patients; contraceptive advice if appropriate (oral contraceptives may increase prolactin concentration); avoid breast-feeding for about 5 days if lactation prevention fails; history of serious mental disorders (especially psychotic disorders) or cardiovascular disease or Raynaud's syndrome; monitor for retroperitoneal fibrosis (see Fibrotic Reactions in notes above); porphyria (section 9.8.2); hepatic impairment (Appendix 2); **interactions:** Appendix 1 (bromocriptine)

Hypotensive reactions Hypotensive reactions may be disturbing in some patients during the first few days of treatment and particular care should be exercised when driving or operating machinery; tolerance may be reduced by alcohol

**Contra-indications** hypersensitivity to bromocriptine or other ergot alkaloids; toxaemia of pregnancy and hypertension in postpartum women or in puerperium (see also below)

Postpartum or puerperium Should not be used postpartum or in puerperium in women with high blood pressure, coronary artery disease or symptoms (or history) of serious mental disorder; monitor blood pressure carefully (especially during first few days) in postpartum women. Very rarely hypertension, myocardial infarction, seizures or stroke (both sometimes preceded by severe headache or visual disturbances) and mental disorders have been reported in postpartum women given bromocriptine for lactation suppression—caution with antihypertensive therapy and avoid other ergot alkaloids. Discontinue immediately if hypertension, unremitting headache or signs of CNS toxicity develop

**Side-effects** nausea, constipation, headache, drowsiness (see also notes above on Sudden Onset of Sleep), nasal congestion; *less commonly* vomiting, postural hypotension, fatigue, dizziness, dyskinesia, dry mouth, leg cramps; also, particularly with *high doses*, confusion, psychomotor excitation, hallucinations; *rarely* constrictive pericarditis, pericardial effusion, pleural effusion (may necessitate discontinuation), retroperitoneal fibrosis reported (monitoring required)–see Fibrotic Reactions in notes above, hair loss, and allergic skin reactions; *very rarely* gastro-intestinal bleeding, gastric ulcer, vasospasm of fingers and toes particularly in patients with Raynaud's syndrome, and effects like neuroleptic malignant syndrome on withdrawal

**Dose**

- Prevention or suppression of lactation (but see notes above and under Cautions), 2.5 mg on day 1 (prevention) or daily for 2–3 days (suppression); then 2.5 mg twice daily for 14 days
- Hypogonadism, galactorrhoea, infertility, initially 1–1.25 mg at bedtime, increased gradually; usual dose 7.5 mg daily in divided doses, increased if necessary to max. 30 mg daily, usual dose in infertility without hyperprolactinaemia, 2.5 mg twice daily
- Cyclical benign breast disease (see also Breast Pain, section 6.7.2) and cyclical menstrual disorders (particularly breast pain), 1–1.25 mg at bedtime, increased gradually; usual dose 2.5 mg twice daily
- Acromegaly, initially 1–1.25 mg at bedtime, increase gradually to 5 mg every 6 hours
- Prolactinoma, initially 1–1.25 mg at bedtime; increased gradually to 5 mg every 6 hours (occasional patients may require up to 30 mg daily)
- CHILD under 15 years, not recommended

**Bromocriptine** (Non-proprietary) PoM
Tablets, bromocriptine (as mesilate) 2.5 mg, net price 30-tab pack = £6.03. Label: 21, counselling, hypotensive reactions driving, see notes above

**Parlodel®** (Novartis) PoM
Tablets, both scored, bromocriptine (as mesilate) 1 mg, net price 100-tab pack = £9.90; 2.5 mg, 30-tab pack = £5.78. Label: 21, counselling, hypotensive reactions, driving, see notes above

Capsules, bromocriptine (as mesilate) 5 mg (blue/white), net price 100-cap pack = £37.57; 10 mg (white), 100-cap pack = £69.50. Label: 21, counselling, hypotensive reactions driving, see notes above

## CABERGOLINE

**Indications** see notes above and under Dose

**Cautions** see under Bromocriptine; peptic ulcer, gastro-intestinal bleeding; severe hepatic impairment (Appendix 2); fibrotic lung disease (see Fibrotic Reactions in notes above); monthly pregnancy tests during the amenorrhoeic period; advise non-hormonal contraception if pregnancy not desired (see also Contra-indications); avoid in porphyria (section 9.8.2); **interactions**: Appendix 1 (cabergoline)

Hypotensive reactions Hypotensive reactions may be disturbing in some patients during the first few days of treatment and particular care should be exercised when driving or operating machinery; tolerance may be reduced by alcohol

**Contra-indications** see under Bromocriptine; exclude pregnancy before starting and discontinue 1 month before intended conception (ovulatory cycles persist for 6 months)—discontinue if pregnancy occurs during treatment (specialist advice needed; Appendix 4); avoid breast-feeding if lactation prevention fails (Appendix 5)

**Side-effects** see under Bromocriptine; also dyspepsia, epigastric and abdominal pain, syncope, breast pain, palpitation, angina, epistaxis, peripheral oedema, hemianopia, asthenia, paraesthesia, erythromelalgia, hot flushes, depression

**Dose**

- Prevention of lactation (but see notes above and under Contra-indications), during first day postpartum, 1 mg as a single dose; suppression of established lactation (but see notes above) 250 micrograms every 12 hours for 2 days
- Hyperprolactinaemic disorders, 500 micrograms weekly (as a single dose *or* as 2 divided doses on separate days) increased at monthly intervals in steps of 500 micrograms until optimal therapeutic response (usually 1 mg weekly, range 0.25–2 mg weekly) with monthly monitoring of serum prolactin levels; reduce initial dose and increase more gradually if patient intolerant; over 1 mg weekly give as divided doses; up to 4.5 mg weekly has been used in hyperprolactinaemic patients
- Parkinsonism, section 4.9.1
- CHILD under 16 years, not recommended

**Dostinex®** (Pharmacia) PoM
Tablets, scored, cabergoline 500 micrograms. Net price 8-tab pack = £30.04. Label: 21, counselling, hypotensive reactions, driving, see notes above

## QUINAGOLIDE

**Indications** see notes above and under Dose

**Cautions** see under Bromocriptine; advise non-hormonal contraception if pregnancy not desired; discontinue if pregnancy occurs during treatment (specialist advice needed; Appendix 4); **interactions:** Appendix 1 (quinagolide)

**Hypotensive reactions** Hypotensive reactions may be disturbing in some patients during the first few days of treatment—monitor blood pressure for a few days after starting treatment and following dosage increases; particular care should be exercised when driving or operating machinery; tolerance may be reduced by alcohol

**Contra-indications** see under Bromocriptine; hypersensitivity to quinagolide (but not ergot alkaloids); hepatic impairment (Appendix 2); renal impairment (Appendix 3); breast-feeding (Appendix 5)

**Side-effects** nausea, vomiting, headache, dizziness, fatigue; less frequently anorexia, abdominal pain, constipation or diarrhoea, oedema, flushing, hypotension, nasal congestion, insomnia; rarely sudden onset of sleep (see notes above), psychosis

**Dose**

- Hyperprolactinaemia, 25 micrograms at bedtime for 3 days; increased at intervals of 3 days in steps of 25 micrograms to usual maintenance dose of 75–150 micrograms daily; for doses higher than 300 micrograms daily increase in steps of 75–150 micrograms at intervals of not less than 4 week; CHILD not recommended

**Norprolac®** (Ferring) PoM
Tablets, quinagolide (as hydrochloride) 75 micrograms (white), net price 30-tab pack = £30.00; starter pack of 3 × 25-microgram tabs (pink) with 3 × 50-microgram tabs (blue) = £2.50. Label: 21, counselling, hypotensive reactions

# 6.7.2 Drugs affecting gonadotrophins

**Danazol** inhibits pituitary gonadotrophins; it combines androgenic activity with antioestrogenic and antiprogestogenic activity. It is licensed for the treatment of *endometriosis* and for the relief of severe pain and tenderness in *benign fibrocystic breast disease* where other measures have proved unsatisfactory. It may also be effective in the long-term management of *hereditary angioedema* [unlicensed indication].

**Gestrinone** has general actions similar to those of danazol and is indicated for the treatment of endometriosis.

**Cetrorelix** and **ganirelix** are luteinising hormone releasing hormone antagonists, which inhibit the release of gonadotrophins (luteinising hormone and follicle-stimulating hormone). They are used in the treatment of infertility by assisted reproductive techniques.

## CETRORELIX

**Indications** adjunct in the treatment of female infertility (under specialist supervision)

**Contra-indications** pregnancy, breast-feeding (Appendix 5), moderate renal impairment (Appendix 3), moderate hepatic impairment (Appendix 2)

**Side-effects** nausea, headache, injection site reactions; rarely hypersensitivity reactions

**Dose**

- By subcutaneous injection into the lower abdominal wall,
  *either* 250 micrograms in the morning, starting on day 5 or 6 of ovarian stimulation with gonadotrophins (*or* each evening starting on day 5 of ovarian stimulation); continue throughout administration of gonadotrophin including day of ovulation induction (*or* evening before ovulation induction)
  *or* 3 mg on day 7 of ovarian stimulation with gonadotrophins; if ovulation induction not possible on day 5 after 3-mg dose, additional 250 micrograms once daily until day of ovulation induction

**Cetrotide®** (Serono) PoM
Injection, powder for reconstitution, cetrorelix (as acetate), net price 250-micrograms vial = £24.00; 3-mg vial = £168.00 (both with solvent)

## DANAZOL

**Indications** see notes above and under Dose

**Cautions** cardiac, hepatic, or renal impairment (avoid if severe), elderly, polycythaemia, epilepsy, diabetes mellitus, hypertension, migraine, lipoprotein disorder, history of thrombosis or thromboembolic disease; withdraw if virilisation (may be irreversible on continued use); non-hormonal contraceptive methods should be used, if appropriate; **interactions:** Appendix 1 (danazol)

**Contra-indications** pregnancy (Appendix 4), ensure that patients with amenorrhoea are not pregnant; breast-feeding (Appendix 5); severe hepatic, renal or cardiac impairment; thromboembolic disease; undiagnosed genital bleeding; androgen-dependent tumours; porphyria (section 9.8.2)

**Side-effects** nausea, dizziness, skin reactions including rashes, photosensitivity and exfoliative dermatitis, fever, backache, nervousness, mood changes, anxiety, changes in libido, vertigo, fatigue, epigastric and pleuritic pain, headache, weight gain; menstrual disturbances, vaginal dryness and irritation, flushing and reduction in breast size; musculo-skeletal spasm, joint pain and swelling, hair loss; androgenic effects including acne, oily skin, oedema, hirsutism, voice changes and rarely clitoral hypertrophy (see also Cautions); temporary alteration in lipoproteins and other metabolic changes, insulin resistance; thrombotic events; leucopenia, thrombocytopenia, eosinophilia, reversible erythrocytosis or polycythaemia reported; headache and visual disturbances may indicate benign intracranial hypertension; rarely cholestatic jaundice, pancreatitis, peliosis hepatis and benign hepatic adenomata

**Dose**

- In women of child-bearing potential, treatment should start during menstruation, preferably on day 1
- Endometriosis, 200–800 mg daily in up to 4 divided doses, adjusted to achieve amenorrhoea, usually for 3–6 months
- Severe pain and tenderness in benign fibrocystic breast disease not responding to other treatment, 300 mg daily in divided doses usually for 3–6 months
- Hereditary angioedema [unlicensed indication], intially 200 mg 2–3 times daily, then reduced according to response

**Danazol** (Non-proprietary) PoM
Capsules, danazol 100 mg, net price 60-cap pack = £18.18; 200 mg, net price 56-cap pack = £29.34

**Danol®** (Sanofi-Synthelabo) PoM
Capsules, danazol 100 mg (grey/white), net price 60-cap pack = £17.04; 200 mg (pink/white), 60-cap pack = £33.75

## GANIRELIX

**Indications** adjunct in the treatment of female infertility (under specialist supervision)

**Contra-indications** pregnancy (Appendix 4), breast-feeding (Appendix 5); moderate renal impairment (Appendix 3); moderate hepatic impairment (Appendix 2)

**Side-effects** nausea, headache, injection site reactions; dizziness, asthenia and malaise also reported

**Dose**

- By subcutaneous injection preferably into the upper leg (rotate injection sites to prevent lipoatrophy), 250 micrograms in the morning (or each afternoon) starting on day 6 of ovarian stimulation with gonadotrophins; continue throughout administration of gonadotrophins including day of ovulation induction (if administering in afternoon, give last dose in afternoon *before* ovulation induction)

**Orgalutran®** (Organon) PoM
Injection, ganirelix, 500 micrograms/mL, net price 0.5-mL prefilled syringe = £22.32

## GESTRINONE

**Indications** endometriosis

**Cautions** cardiac and renal impairment; **interactions:** Appendix 1 (gestrinone)

**Contra-indications** pregnancy (use non-hormonal method of contraception); breast-feeding (Appendix 5); severe cardiac, renal impairment or hepatic impairment; metabolic or vascular disorders associated with previous sex hormone treatment

**Side-effects** spotting; acne, oily skin, fluid retention, weight gain, hirsutism, voice change; liver enzyme disturbances; headache; gastro-intestinal disturbances; change in libido, flushing, decrease in breast size; nervousness, depression, change in appetite; muscle cramp

**Dose**

- 2.5 mg twice weekly starting on first day of cycle with second dose 3 days later, repeated on same two days preferably at same time each week; duration of treatment usually 6 months

  **Missed doses** One missed dose—2.5 mg as soon as possible and maintain original sequence; two or more missed doses—discontinue, re-start on first day of new cycle (following negative pregnancy test)

**Dimetriose®** (Florizel) PoM
Capsules, gestrinone 2.5 mg, net price 8-cap pack = £103.91

## Gonadorelin analogues

Administration of **gonadorelin analogues** produces an initial phase of stimulation; continued administration is followed by down-regulation of gonadotrophin-releasing hormone receptors, thereby reducing the release of gonadotrophins (follicle stimulating hormone and luteinising hormone) which in turn leads to inhibition of androgen and oestrogen production.

Gonadorelin analogues are used in the treatment of endometriosis, precocious puberty, infertility, anaemia due to uterine fibroids (together with iron supplementation), breast cancer (section 8.3.4.1), prostate cancer (section 8.3.4.2) and before intra-uterine surgery. Use of leuprorelin and triptorelin for 3 to 4 months before surgery reduces the uterine volume, fibroid size and associated bleeding. For women undergoing hysterectomy or myomectomy, a vaginal procedure is made more feasible following the use of a gonadorelin analogue.

**Cautions** Non-hormonal, barrier methods of contraception should be used during entire treatment period with gonadorelin analogues; also use with caution in patients with metabolic bone disease because decrease in bone mineral density can occur.

**Contra-indications** Gonadorelin analogues are contra-indicated for use longer than 6 months (do not repeat), where there is undiagnosed vaginal bleeding, in pregnancy (Appendix 4; exclude pregnancy—also give first injection during menstruation or shortly afterwards *or* use barrier contraception for 1 month beforehand) and in breast-feeding.

**Side-effects** Side-effects of the gonadorelin analogues related to the inhibition of oestrogen production include menopausal-like symptoms (e.g. hot flushes, increased sweating, vaginal dryness, dyspareunia and loss of libido) and a decrease in trabecular bone density; these effects can be reduced by hormone replacement (e.g. with an oestrogen and a progestogen or with tibolone). Side-effects of gonadorelin analogues also include headache (rarely migraine) and hypersensitivity reactions including urticaria, pruritus, rash, asthma and anaphylaxis; when treating uterine fibroids, bleeding associated with fibroid degeneration can occur; spray formulations can cause irritation of the nasal mucosa including nose bleeds; local reactions at injection site can occur; other side-effects also reported with some gonadorelin analogues include palpitation, hypertension, ovarian cysts (may require withdrawal), changes in breast size, musculoskeletal pain or weakness, visual disturbances, paraesthesia, changes in scalp and body hair, oedema of the face and extremities, weight changes, and mood changes including depression.

## BUSERELIN

**Indications** see under Dose; prostate cancer (section 8.3.4.2)

**Cautions** see notes above; polycystic ovarian disease, depression, hypertension, diabetes

**Contra-indications** see notes above; hormone-dependent tumours

**Side-effects** see notes above; initially withdrawal bleeding and subsequently breakthrough bleeding, leucorrhoea; nausea, vomiting, constipation, diarrhoea; anxiety, memory and concentration disturbances, sleep disturbances, nervousness, dizziness, drowsiness; breast tenderness, lactation; abdominal pain; fatigue; increased thirst, changes in appetite; acne, dry skin, splitting nails, dry eyes; altered blood lipids, leucopenia, thrombocytopenia; hearing disturbances; reduced glucose tolerance

**Dose**

- Endometriosis, intranasally, 300 micrograms (one 150-microgram spray in each nostril) 3 times daily (starting on days 1 or 2 of menstruation); max. duration of treatment 6 months (do not repeat)
- Pituitary desensitisation before induction of ovulation by gonadotrophins for *in vitro* fertilisation (under specialist supervision), by subcutaneous injection, 200–500 micrograms daily given as a single injection (occasionally up to 500 micrograms twice daily may be needed) starting in early follicular phase (day 1) *or*, after exclusion of pregnancy, in midluteal phase (day 21) and continued until down-regulation achieved (usually about 1–3 weeks) then maintained during gonadotrophin administration (stopping gonadotrophin and buserelin on administration of chorionic gonadotrophin at appropriate stage of follicular development)

  Intranasally, 150 micrograms (one spray in one nostril) 4 times daily during waking hours (occasionally up to 300 micrograms 4 times daily may be needed) starting in early follicular phase (day 1) *or*, after exclusion of pregnancy, in midluteal phase (day 21) and continued until down-regulation achieved (usually about 2–3 weeks) then maintained during gonadotrophin administration (stopping gonadotrophin and buserelin on administration of chorionic gonadotrophin at appropriate stage of follicular development)

  Counselling Avoid use of nasal decongestants before and for at least 30 minutes after treatment

**Suprecur®** (Aventis Pharma) PoM

Nasal spray, buserelin (as acetate) 150 micrograms/metered spray. Net price 2 × 100-dose pack (with metered dose pumps) = £75.43. Counselling, nasal decongestants

Injection, buserelin (as acetate) 1mg/mL. Net price 5.5-mL vial = £11.85

## GOSERELIN

**Indications** see under Dose; prostate cancer (section 8.3.4.2); early and advanced breast cancer (section 8.3.4.1)

**Cautions** see notes above; polycystic ovarian disease

**Contra-indications** see notes above

**Side-effects** see notes above; withdrawal bleeding

**Dose**

- By subcutaneous injection into anterior abdominal wall, endometriosis, 3.6 mg every 28 days; max. duration of treatment 6 months (do not repeat); endometrial thinning before intra-uterine surgery, 3.6 mg (may be repeated after 28 days if uterus is large or to allow flexible surgical timing); before surgery in women who have anaemia due to uterine fibroids, 3.6 mg every 28 days (with supplementary iron); max. duration of treatment 3 months
- Pituitary desensitisation before induction of ovulation by gonadotrophins for *in vitro* fertilisation (under specialist supervision), after exclusion of pregnancy, 3.6 mg to achieve pituitary down-regulation (usually 1–3 weeks) then gonadotrophin is administered (stopping gonadotrophin on administration of chorionic gonadotrophin at appropriate stage of follicular development)

**Preparation**

Section 8.3.4.2

## LEUPRORELIN ACETATE

**Indications** see under Dose; prostate cancer (section 8.3.4.2)

**Cautions** see notes above; family history of osteoporosis; chronic use of other drugs which reduce bone density including alcohol and tobacco; diabetes

**Contra-indications** see notes above

**Side-effects** see notes above; breast tenderness; nausea, vomiting, diarrhoea, anorexia; fever, chills; sleep disturbances, dizziness, fatigue, leucopenia, thrombocytopenia, altered blood lipids, pulmonary embolism; spinal fracture, paralysis, hypotension and worsening of depression also reported

**Dose**

- By subcutaneous *or* intramuscular injection

  Endometriosis, 3.75 mg as a single dose in first 5 days of menstrual cycle then every month for max. 6 months (course not to be repeated)

  Endometrial thinning before intra-uterine surgery, 3.75 mg as a single dose (given between days 3 and 5 of menstrual cycle) 5–6 weeks before surgery

  Reduction of size of uterine fibroids and of associated bleeding before surgery, 3.75 mg as a single dose every month usually for 3–4 months (max. 6 months)

**Preparation**

Section 8.3.4.2

## NAFARELIN

**Indications** see under Dose

**Cautions** see notes above

**Contra-indications** see notes above

**Side-effects** see notes above; acne

**Dose**

- Women over 18 years, endometriosis, 200 micrograms twice daily as one spray in one nostril in the morning and one spray in the other nostril in the evening (starting on days 2–4 of menstruation), max. duration of treatment 6 months (do not repeat)
- Pituitary desensitisation before induction of ovulation by gonadotrophins for *in vitro* fertilisation (under specialist supervision), 400 micrograms (one spray in each nostril) twice daily starting in early follicular phase (day 2) or, after exclusion of pregnancy, in midluteal phase (day 21) and continued until down-regulation achieved (usually within 4 weeks) then maintained (usually for 8–12 days) during gonadotrophin administration (stopping gonadotrophin and nafarelin on administration of chorionic gonadotrophin at follicular maturity); discontinue if down-regulation not achieved within 12 weeks

  Counselling Avoid use of nasal decongestants before and for at least 30 minutes after treatment; repeat dose if sneezing occurs during or immediately after administration

**Synarel®** (Pharmacia) PoM

Nasal spray, nafarelin (as acetate) 200 micrograms/metered spray. Net price 30-dose unit = £32.28; 60-dose unit = £55.66. Label: 10, patient information leaflet, counselling, see above

### TRIPTORELIN

**Indications** advanced prostate cancer, endometriosis, precocious puberty, reduction in size of uterine fibroids (section 8.3.4.2)

**Cautions** see notes above

**Contra-indications** see notes above

**Side-effects** see notes above; asthenia

**Dose**

- See section 8.3.4.2

Preparations

Section 8.3.4.2

## Breast pain (mastalgia)

Once any serious underlying cause for breast pain has been ruled out, most women will respond to reassurance and reduction in dietary fat; withdrawal of an oral contraceptive or of hormone replacement therapy may help to resolve the pain.

Mild, non-cyclical breast pain is treated with simple analgesics (section 4.7.1); moderate to severe pain, cyclical pain or symptoms that persist for longer than 6 months may require specific drug treatment. **Bromocriptine** (section 6.7.1) is used in the management of breast pain but is associated with unpleasant side-effects; it acts within 2 months.

**Danazol** (section 6.7.2) is licensed for the relief of severe pain and tenderness in benign fibrocystic breast disease which has not responded to other treatment.

**Tamoxifen** (section 8.3.4.1) may be a useful adjunct in the treatment of mastalgia [unlicensed indication] especially when symptoms can definitely be related to cyclic oestrogen production; it may be given on the days of the cycle when symptoms are predicted.

Treatment for breast pain should be reviewed after 6 months and continued if necessary. Symptoms recur in about 50% of women within 2 years of withdrawal of therapy but may be less severe.

## 6.7.3 Metyrapone and trilostane

**Metyrapone** is a competitive inhibitor of 11β-hydroxylation in the adrenal cortex; the resulting inhibition of cortisol (and to a lesser extent aldosterone) production leads to an increase in ACTH production which, in turn, leads to increased synthesis and release of cortisol precursors. It may be used as a test of anterior pituitary function.

Although most types of *Cushing's syndrome* are treated surgically, that which occasionally accompanies carcinoma of the bronchus is not usually amenable to surgery. Metyrapone has been found helpful in controlling the symptoms of the disease; it is also used in other forms of Cushing's syndrome to prepare the patient for surgery. The dosages used are either low, and tailored to cortisol production, or high, in which case corticosteroid replacement therapy is also needed.

**Trilostane** reversibly inhibits 3β-hydroxysteroid dehydrogenase /delta 5-4 isomerase in the adrenal cortex; the resulting inhibition of the synthesis of mineralocorticoids and glucocorticoids may be useful in *Cushing's syndrome* and *primary hyperaldosteronism*. Trilostane appears to be less effective than metyrapone for Cushing's syndrome (where it is tailored to corticosteroid production). It also has a minor role in postmenopausal breast cancer that has relapsed following initial oestrogen antagonist therapy (corticosteroid replacement therapy is also required). **Ketoconazole** (section 5.2) is also used by specialists for the management of *Cushing's syndrome* [unlicensed indication].

### METYRAPONE

**Indications** see notes above and under Dose (specialist supervision in hospital)

**Cautions** gross hypopituitarism (risk of precipitating acute adrenal failure); hypertension on long-term administration; hypothyroidism or hepatic impairment (delayed response); many drugs interfere with diagnostic estimation of steroids; avoid in porphyria (section 9.8.2)

Driving Drowsiness may affect the performance of skilled tasks (e.g. driving)

**Contra-indications** adrenocortical insufficiency (see Cautions); pregnancy (Appendix 4), breast-feeding (Appendix 5)

**Side-effects** occasional nausea, vomiting, dizziness, headache, hypotension, sedation; rarely abdominal pain, allergic skin reactions, hypoadrenalism, hirsutism

**Dose**

- Differential diagnosis of ACTH-dependent Cushing's syndrome, 750 mg every 4 hours for 6 doses; CHILD 15 mg/kg (minimum 250 mg) every 4 hours for 6 doses
- Management of Cushing's syndrome, range 0.25–6 g daily, tailored to cortisol production; see notes above
- Resistant oedema due to increased aldosterone secretion in cirrhosis, nephrotic syndrome, and congestive heart failure (with glucocorticoid replacement therapy) 3 g daily in divided doses

6 Endocrine system

**Metopirone®** (Alliance) PoM
Capsules, ivory, metyrapone 250 mg. Net price 100-tab pack = £41.44. Label: 21, counselling, driving

## TRILOSTANE

**Indications** see notes above and under Dose (specialist supervision)

**Cautions** breast cancer (concurrent corticosteroid replacement therapy needed, see under Dose), adrenal cortical hyperfunction (tailored to cortisol and electrolytes, concurrent corticosteroid therapy may be needed, see under Dose); hepatic and renal impairment; **interactions:** Appendix 1 (trilostane)

**Contra-indications** pregnancy (use non-hormonal method of contraception; Appendix 4); breast-feeding; children

**Side-effects** flushing, tingling and swelling of mouth, rhinorrhoea, nausea, vomiting, diarrhoea, and rashes reported; rarely granulocytopenia

**Dose**

- Adrenal cortical hyperfunction, 240 mg daily in divided doses for at least 3 days then tailored according to response with regular monitoring of plasma electrolytes and circulating corticosteroids (both mineralocorticoid and glucocorticoid replacement therapy may be needed); usual dose: 120–480 mg daily (may be increased to 960 mg)
- Postmenopausal breast cancer (with glucocorticoid replacement therapy) following relapse to initial oestrogen receptor antagonist therapy, initially 240 mg daily increased every 3 days in steps of 240 mg to a maintenance dose of 960 mg daily (720 mg daily if not tolerated)

**Modrenal®** (Bioaccelerate) PoM
Capsules, trilostane 60 mg (pink/black), net price 100-cap pack = £49.50; 120 mg (pink/yellow), 100-cap pack = £98.50. Label: 21

# 7 Obstetrics, gynaecology, and urinary-tract disorders




**7.1 Drugs used in obstetrics** 398
7.1.1 Prostaglandins and oxytocics 398
7.1.1.1 Ductus arteriosus 401
7.1.2 Mifepristone 402
7.1.3 Myometrial relaxants 402
**7.2 Treatment of vaginal and vulval conditions** 404
7.2.1 Preparations for vaginal atrophy 404
7.2.2 Vaginal and vulval infections 405
**7.3 Contraceptives** 407
7.3.1 Combined hormonal contraceptives 407
7.3.2 Progestogen-only contraceptives 413
7.3.2.1 Oral progestogen-only contraceptives 413
7.3.2.2 Parenteral progestogen-only contraceptives 414
7.3.2.3 Intra-uterine progestogen-only device 415
7.3.3 Spermicidal contraceptives 415
7.3.4 Contraceptive devices 416
**7.4 Drugs for genito-urinary disorders** 417
7.4.1 Drugs for urinary retention 417
7.4.2 Drugs for urinary frequency, enuresis, and incontinence 419
7.4.3 Drugs used in urological pain 422
7.4.4 Bladder instillations and urological surgery 422
7.4.5 Drugs for erectile dysfunction 423


This chapter includes advice on the drug management of the following:


- emergency contraception, p. 412
- induction of abortion, p. 398
- induction and augmentation of labour, p. 398
- nocturnal enuresis, p. 421
- premature labour, p. 402
- prevention and treatment of post-partum haemorrhage, p. 399
- priapism, p. 423


For hormonal therapy of gynaecological disorders see section 6.4.1, section 6.5.1 and section 6.7.2.

## 7.1 Drugs used in obstetrics

**7.1.1 Prostaglandins and oxytocics**
**7.1.2 Mifepristone**
**7.1.3 Myometrial relaxants**

Because of the complexity of dosage regimens in obstetrics, in all cases **detailed specialist literature** should be consulted.

### 7.1.1 Prostaglandins and oxytocics

Prostaglandins and oxytocics are used to induce abortion or induce or augment labour and to minimise blood loss from the placental site. They include oxytocin, ergometrine, and the prostaglandins. All induce uterine contractions with varying degrees of pain according to the strength of contractions induced.

**Induction of abortion** **Gemeprost**, administered vaginally as pessaries is the preferred prostaglandin for the medical induction of late therapeutic abortion. Gemeprost ripens and softens the cervix before surgical abortion, particularly in primigravida. The prostaglandin **misoprostol** is given by mouth or by vaginal administration to induce medical abortion [unlicensed indication]; intravaginal use ripens the cervix before surgical abortion [unlicensed indication]. Extra-amniotic **dinoprostone** is rarely used nowadays.

Pre-treatment with **mifepristone** (section 7.1.2) can facilitate the process of medical abortion. It sensitises the uterus to subsequent administration of a prostaglandin and, therefore, abortion occurs in a shorter time and with a lower dose of prostaglandin.

**Induction and augmentation of labour** **Dinoprostone** is available as vaginal tablets, pessaries and vaginal gels for the induction of labour. The intravenous solution is rarely used; it is associated with more side-effects.

**Oxytocin** (*Syntocinon®*) is administered by slow intravenous infusion, using an infusion pump, to induce or augment labour, usually in conjunction with amniotomy. Uterine activity must be monitored carefully and hyperstimulation avoided. Large doses of oxytocin may result in excessive fluid retention.

**Misoprostol** is given orally or vaginally for the induction of labour [unlicensed indication].

**NICE guidance (induction of labour)**

NICE has recommended (June 2001) that:

- dinoprostone is preferable to oxytocin for induction of labour in women with intact membranes, regardless of parity or cervical favourability;
- dinoprostone or oxytocin are equally effective for the induction of labour in women with ruptured membranes, regardless of parity or cervical favourability;
- oxytocin should not be started for 6 hours following administration of vaginal prostaglandins;
- when used to induce labour, the recommended dose of oxytocin by intravenous infusion[1] is initially 0.001–0.002 units/minute increased at intervals of at least 30 minutes until a maximum of 3–4 contractions occur every 10 minutes (0.012 units/minute is often adequate); the maximum recommended rate is 0.032 units/minute (licensed max. 0.02 units/minute)

1. Oxytocin should be used in standard dilutions of 10 units/500 mL (infusing 3 mL/hour delivers 0.001 unit/minute) or, for higher doses, 30 units/500 mL (infusing 1 mL/hour delivers 0.001 unit/minute).

**Prevention and treatment of haemorrhage** Bleeding due to incomplete abortion can be controlled with **ergometrine** and **oxytocin** (*Syntometrine®*) given intramuscularly, the dose is adjusted according to the patient's condition and blood loss. This is commonly used before surgical evacuation of the uterus, particularly when surgery is delayed. Oxytocin and ergometrine combined are more effective in early pregnancy than either drug alone.

For the routine management of the third stage of labour ergometrine 500 micrograms with oxytocin 5 units (*Syntometrine®* 1 mL) is given by intramuscular injection on delivery of the anterior shoulder or, at the latest, immediately after the baby is delivered. If ergometrine is inappropriate (e.g. in pre-eclampsia), oxytocin may be given by intramuscular injection [unlicensed indication].

In excessive uterine bleeding, any placental products remaining in the uterus should be removed. In bleeding caused by uterine atony oxytocic drugs are used in turn as follows:

- oxytocin 5–10 units by intravenous injection
- ergometrine 250–500 micrograms by intravenous injection
- oxytocin 5–30 units in 500 mL infusion fluid given by intravenous infusion at a rate that controls uterine atony

**Carboprost** has an important role in severe postpartum haemorrhage unresponsive to ergometrine and oxytocin.

Mild secondary postpartum haemorrhage has been treated in domiciliary practice with ergometrine by mouth, but it is rarely used now.

## CARBOPROST

**Indications** postpartum haemorrhage due to uterine atony in patients unresponsive to ergometrine and oxytocin

**Cautions** history of glaucoma or raised intra-ocular pressure, asthma, hypertension, hypotension, anaemia, jaundice, diabetes, epilepsy; uterine scars; excessive dosage may cause uterine rupture; **interactions:** Appendix 1 (prostaglandins)

**Contra-indications** untreated pelvic infection; cardiac, renal, pulmonary, or hepatic disease

**Side-effects** nausea, vomiting and diarrhoea, hyperthermia and flushing, bronchospasm; less frequent effects include raised blood pressure, dyspnoea, and pulmonary oedema; chills, headache, diaphoresis, dizziness; cardiovascular collapse also reported; erythema and pain at injection site reported

**Dose**

- By deep intramuscular injection, 250 micrograms repeated if necessary at intervals of 1½ hours (in severe cases the interval may be reduced but should not be less than 15 minutes); total dose should not exceed 2 mg (8 doses)

**Hemabate®** (Pharmacia) PoM

Injection, carboprost as trometamol salt (tromethamine salt) 250 micrograms/mL, net price 1-mL amp = £18.20 (hosp. only)

## DINOPROSTONE

**Indications** see notes above and under preparations below

**Cautions** history of asthma, glaucoma and raised intra-ocular pressure; cardiac, hepatic or renal impairment; hypertension; history of epilepsy; uterine scarring; monitor uterine activity and fetal status (particular care if history of uterine hypertony); uterine rupture; see also notes above; effect of oxytocin enhanced (care needed in monitoring uterine activity when used in sequence)—see also under *Propess®* and **interactions:** Appendix 1 (prostaglandins)

**Contra-indications** active cardiac, pulmonary, renal or hepatic disease; placenta praevia or unexplained vaginal bleeding during pregnancy, ruptured membranes, major cephalopelvic disproportion or fetal malpresentation, history of caesarean section or major uterine surgery, untreated pelvic infection, fetal distress, grand multiparas and multiple pregnancy, history of difficult or traumatic delivery; avoid extra-amniotic route in cervicitis or vaginitis

**Side-effects** nausea, vomiting, diarrhoea; other side-effects include uterine hypertonus, severe uterine contractions, pulmonary or amniotic fluid embolism, abruptio placenta, fetal distress, maternal hypertension, bronchospasm, rapid cervical dilation, fever, backache; uterine hypercontractility with or without fetal bradycardia, low Apgar scores; cardiac arrest, uterine rupture, stillbirth or neonatal death also reported; vaginal symptoms (warmth, irritation, pain); after intravenous administration—flushing, shivering, headache, dizziness, temporary pyrexia and raised white blood cell count; also local tissue reaction and erythema after intravenous administration and possibility of infection after extra-amniotic administration

**Dose**

- See under preparations, below

**Important** Do not confuse dose of *Prostin E2®* vaginal **gel** with that of *Prostin E2®* vaginal **tablets**—not bioequivalent.

**Propess®** (Ferring) PoM

Pessaries (within retrieval system), releasing dinoprostone approx. 5 mg over 12 hours. Net price 1-pessary pack = £30.00

Dose by vagina, cervical ripening and induction of labour at term, 1 pessary inserted high into posterior fornix; if cervical ripening insufficient, remove pessary 8–12 hours later and replace with a second pessary (which should also be removed not more than 12 hours later); max. 2 consecutive pessaries

Important Effect of oxytocin enhanced—particular care needed to monitor uterine activity when oxytocin used in sequence (remove pessary beforehand)

**Prostin E2®** (Pharmacia) PoM

Intravenous solution ▲, for dilution and use as an infusion, dinoprostone 1 mg/mL, net price 0.75-mL amp = £8.52; 10 mg/mL, 0.5-mL amp = £18.40 (both hosp. only; rarely used, consult product literature for dose and indications)

Extra-amniotic solution ▲, dinoprostone 10 mg/mL. Net price 0.5-mL amp (with diluent) = £18.40 (hosp. only; less commonly used nowadays, consult product literature for dose and indications)

Vaginal gel, dinoprostone 400 micrograms/mL, net price 2.5 mL (1 mg) = £15.25; 800 micrograms/mL, 2.5 mL (2 mg) = £16.80

Dose by vagina, induction of labour, inserted high into posterior fornix (avoid administration into cervical canal), 1 mg (unfavourable primigravida 2 mg), followed after 6 hours by 1–2 mg if required; max. [gel] 3 mg (unfavourable primigravida 4 mg)

Vaginal tablets, dinoprostone 3 mg. Net price 8-vaginal tab pack = £78.05

Dose by vagina, induction of labour, inserted high into posterior fornix, 3 mg, followed after 6–8 hours by 3 mg if labour is not established; max. 6 mg [vaginal tablets]

Note *Prostin E2 Vaginal Gel* and *Vaginal Tablets* are **not** bioequivalent

## ERGOMETRINE MALEATE

**Indications** see notes above

**Cautions** cardiac disease, hypertension, multiple pregnancy; porphyria (section 9.8.2); hepatic impairment (Appendix 2); renal impairment (Appendix 3); **interactions:** Appendix 1 (ergot alkaloids)

**Contra-indications** induction of labour, first and second stages of labour, vascular disease, severe cardiac disease, severe hepatic and renal impairment, sepsis, severe hypertension, eclampsia

**Side-effects** nausea, vomiting, headache, dizziness, tinnitus, abdominal pain, chest pain, palpitation, dyspnoea, bradycardia, transient hypertension, vasoconstriction; stroke, myocardial infarction and pulmonary oedema also reported

**Dose**

- See notes above

**Ergometrine** (Non-proprietary) PoM

Tablets ▲, ergometrine maleate 500 micrograms, net price 21-tab pack = £25.00

Injection, ergometrine maleate 500 micrograms/mL. Net price 1-mL amp = 60p

▲**With oxytocin**

**Syntometrine®** (Alliance) PoM

Injection, ergometrine maleate 500 micrograms, oxytocin 5 units/mL. Net price 1-mL amp = £1.31

Dose by intramuscular injection, 1 mL; by intravenous injection, no longer recommended

## GEMEPROST

**Indications** see under Dose

**Cautions** obstructive airways disease, cardiovascular insufficiency, raised intra-ocular pressure, cervicitis or vaginitis; **interactions:** Appendix 1 (prostaglandins)

Important For warnings relating to use of gemeprost in a patient undergoing induction of abortion with mifepristone, see under Mifepristone and Note below

**Contra-indications** unexplained vaginal bleeding

**Side-effects** vaginal bleeding and uterine pain; nausea, vomiting, or diarrhoea; headache, muscle weakness, dizziness, flushing, chills, backache, dyspnoea, chest pain, palpitation and mild pyrexia; uterine rupture reported (most commonly in multiparas or if history of uterine surgery or if given with intravenous oxytocics); also reported severe hypotension, coronary artery spasm and myocardial infarction

**Dose**

- By vagina in pessaries, softening and dilation of the cervix to facilitate transcervical operative procedures in first trimester, inserted into posterior fornix, 1 mg 3 hours before surgery
- Second trimester abortion, inserted into posterior fornix, 1 mg every 3 hours for max. of 5 administrations; second course may begin 24 hours after start of treatment (if treatment fails pregnancy should be terminated by another method)
- Second trimester intra-uterine death, inserted into posterior fornix, 1 mg every 3 hours for max. of 5 administrations only; monitor for coagulopathy

Note If used in combination with mifepristone, carefully monitor blood pressure and pulse for 6 hours

**Gemeprost** (Beacon) PoM

Pessaries, gemeprost 1 mg. Net price 5-pessary pack = £215.00

## OXYTOCIN

**Indications** see under Dose and notes above

**Cautions** particular caution needed when given for *induction or enhancement of labour* in presence of borderline cephalopelvic disproportion (avoid if significant), mild or moderate pregnancy-induced hypertension or cardiac disease, women over 35 years or with history of lower-uterine segment caesarean section (see also under Contra-indications below); if fetal death *in utero* or meconium-stained amniotic fluid avoid tumultuous labour (may cause amniotic fluid embolism); water intoxication and hyponatraemia—avoid large infusion volumes and restrict fluid intake by mouth (see also Appendix 6); effects enhanced by concomitant prostaglandins (very careful monitoring), caudal block anaesthesia (may enhance hypertensive effects of sympathomimetic vasopressors), see also **interactions:** Appendix 1 (oxytocin)

**Contra-indications** hypertonic uterine contractions, mechanical obstruction to delivery, fetal distress; any condition where spontaneous labour or vaginal delivery inadvisable; avoid prolonged administration in oxytocin-resistant uterine inertia, severe pre-eclamptic toxaemia or severe cardiovascular disease

**Side-effects** uterine spasm (may occur at low doses), uterine hyperstimulation (usually with excessive doses—may cause fetal distress, asphyxia and death, or may lead to hypertonicity, tetanic contractions, soft-tissue damage or uterine rupture); water intoxication and hyponatraemia associated with high doses with large infusion volumes of electrolyte-free fluid (see also under Dose below); also nausea, vomiting, arrhythmias; rashes and anaphylactoid reactions (with dyspnoea, hypotension or shock) also reported; placental abruption and amniotic fluid embolism also reported on overdose

**Dose**

- Induction of labour for medical reasons or stimulation of labour in hypotonic uterine inertia, by intravenous infusion, see NICE guidance above; max. 5 units in 1 day (may be repeated next day starting again at 0.001–0.002 units/minute)

  Important Careful monitoring of fetal heart rate and uterine motility essential for dose titration (**avoid** intravenous injection during labour); discontinue immediately in uterine hyperactivity or fetal distress
- Caesarean section, by slow intravenous injection immediately after delivery, 5 units
- Prevention of postpartum haemorrhage, after delivery of placenta, by slow intravenous injection, 5 units (if infusion used for induction or enhancement of labour, increase rate during third stage and for next few hours)

  Note May be given in a dose of 10 units by intramuscular injection [unlicensed route] instead of oxytocin with ergometrine (*Syntometrine®*), see notes above
- Treatment of postpartum haemorrhage, by slow intravenous injection, 5–10 units, followed in severe cases by intravenous infusion of 5–30 units in 500 mL infusion fluid at a rate sufficient to control uterine atony

  Important Avoid rapid intravenous injection (may transiently reduce blood pressure); prolonged administration, see warning below
- Incomplete, inevitable or missed abortion, by slow intravenous injection, 5 units followed if necessary by intravenous infusion, 0.02–0.04 units/minute or faster

  Important Prolonged intravenous administration at high doses with large volume of fluid (as possible in inevitable or missed abortion or postpartum haemorrhage) may cause water intoxication with hyponatraemia. To avoid: use electrolyte-containing diluent (i.e. not glucose), increase oxytocin concentration to reduce fluid, restrict fluid intake by mouth; monitor fluid and electrolytes

  Note Oxytocin doses in the BNF may differ from those in the product literature

**Syntocinon®** (Alliance) PoM

Injection, oxytocin, net price 5 units/mL, 1-mL amp = 89p; 10 units/mL, 1-mL amp = £1.01

**With ergometrine**

See Syntometrine®, p. 400

## 7.1.1.1 Ductus arteriosus

### Maintenance of patency

**Alprostadil** (prostaglandin $E_1$) is used to maintain patency of the ductus arteriosus in neonates with congenital heart defects, prior to corrective surgery in centres where intensive care is immediately available.

### ALPROSTADIL

**Indications** congenital heart defects in neonates prior to corrective surgery; erectile dysfunction (section 7.4.5)

**Cautions** see notes above; history of haemorrhage, avoid in hyaline membrane disease, monitor arterial pressure; **interactions:** Appendix 1 (prostaglandins)

**Side-effects** apnoea (particularly in neonates under 2 kg), flushing, bradycardia, hypotension, tachycardia, cardiac arrest, oedema, diarrhoea, fever, convulsions, disseminated intravascular coagulation, hypokalaemia; cortical proliferation of long bones and weakening of the wall of the ductus arteriosus and of pulmonary artery may follow prolonged use; gastric-outlet obstruction reported

**Dose**

- By intravenous infusion, initially 50–100 nanograms/kg/minute, then decreased to lowest effective dose [but lower dose such as 10 nanograms/kg/minute may be effective and safer]

**Prostin VR®** (Pharmacia) PoM

Intravenous solution, alprostadil 500 micrograms/mL in alcohol. For dilution and use as an infusion. Net price 1-mL amp = £75.19 (hosp. only)

### Closure of ductus arteriosus

**Indometacin** (indomethacin) is used to close a patent ductus arteriosus in premature babies, probably by inhibiting prostaglandin synthesis.

### INDOMETACIN
(Indomethacin)

**Indications** patent ductus arteriosus in premature babies (under specialist supervision in neonatal intensive care unit); rheumatoid disease (section 10.1.1)

**Cautions** may mask symptoms of infection; may reduce urine output by 50% or more (monitor carefully—see also under Anuria or Oliguria, below) and precipitate renal impairment especially if extracellular volume depleted, heart failure, sepsis, or hepatic impairment, or if receiving nephrotoxic drugs; may induce hyponatraemia; monitor renal function and electrolytes; inhibition of platelet aggregation (monitor for bleeding); **interactions:** Appendix 1 (NSAIDs)

Anuria or oliguria If anuria or marked oliguria (urinary output less than 0.6 mL/kg/hour) at time of scheduled second or third dose, delay until renal function returns to normal

**Contra-indications** untreated infection, bleeding (especially with active intracranial haemorrhage or gastro-intestinal bleeding); thrombocytopenia, coagulation defects, necrotising enterocolitis, renal impairment

**Side-effects** haemorrhagic, renal, gastro-intestinal (including necrotising enterocolitis), metabolic, and coagulation disorders; pulmonary hypertension, intracranial bleeding, fluid retention, and exacerbation of infection

**Dose**

- By intravenous injection, over 20–30 minutes (using a suitable syringe driver), 3 doses at intervals of 12–24 hours (provided urine output remains adequate), age less than 48 hours, 200 micrograms/kg then 100 micrograms/kg then 100 micrograms/kg; age 2–7 days, 200 micrograms/kg then 200 micrograms/kg then 200 micrograms/kg; age over 7 days, 200 micrograms/kg then 250 micrograms/kg then 250 micrograms/kg; solution prepared with 1–2 mL sodium chloride 0.9% or water for injections (not glucose and no preservatives)

If ductus arteriosus reopens a second course of 3 injections may be given 48 hours after first course

**Indocid PDA®** (MSD) PoM

Injection, powder for reconstitution, indometacin (as sodium trihydrate). Net price 3 × 1-mg vials = £22.50 (hosp. only)



## 7.1.2 Mifepristone

**Mifepristone**, an antiprogestogenic steroid, sensitises the myometrium to prostaglandin-induced contractions and it softens and dilates the cervix. For the termination of pregnancy, a single dose of mifepristone is followed by vaginal administration of the prostaglandin gemeprost. Although mifepristone is licensed for use in a dose of 600 mg, for medical abortion, a dose of 200 mg is effective for gestation of up to 24 weeks. Guidelines of the Royal College of Obstetricians and Gynaecologists (September 2004) include the following [unlicensed] regimens for inducing medical abortion:

- For gestation up to 9 weeks, mifepristone 200 mg by mouth followed 1–3 days later by misoprostol 800 micrograms vaginally; in women at more than 7 weeks gestation (49–63 days), if the abortion has not occurred 4 hours after misoprostol, a further dose of misoprostol 400 micrograms may be given vaginally or by mouth
- For gestation between 9 and 13 weeks, mifepristone 200 mg by mouth followed 36–48 hours later by misoprostol 800 micrograms vaginally followed if necessary by a maximum of 4 further doses at 3-hourly intervals of misoprostol 400 micrograms vaginally or by mouth
- For gestation between 13 and 24 weeks, mifepristone 200 mg by mouth followed 36–48 hours later by misoprostol 800 micrograms vaginally then a maximum of 4 further doses at 3-hourly intervals of misoprostol 400 micrograms by mouth

### MIFEPRISTONE

**Indications** see under dose

**Cautions** asthma (avoid if severe); haemorrhagic disorders and anticoagulant therapy; prosthetic heart valve or history of endocarditis (prophylaxis recommended, see section 5.1 table 2); smokers aged over 35 years (increased risk of cardiovascular events); adrenal suppression (may require corticosteroid); not recommended in hepatic or renal impairment; breast-feeding (Appendix 5); avoid aspirin and NSAIDs for analgesia; **interactions**: Appendix 1 (mifepristone)

Important For warnings relating to use of gemeprost in a patient undergoing induction of abortion with mifepristone, see under Gemeprost

**Contra-indications** uncontrolled severe asthma; suspected ectopic pregnancy (use other specific means of termination); chronic adrenal failure, porphyria (section 9.8.2)

**Side-effects** nausea, vomiting, gastro-intestinal cramps; uterine contractions, vaginal bleeding (sometimes severe) may occur between administration of mifepristone and surgery (and rarely abortion may occur before surgery); *less commonly* hypersensitivity reactions including rash, urticaria, and facial oedema; *rarely* malaise, headache, fever, hot flushes, dizziness, chills

**Dose**

- Medical termination of intra-uterine pregnancy of up to 63 days gestation, by mouth, mifepristone 600 mg as a single dose under medical supervision, followed 36–48 hours later (unless abortion already complete) by gemeprost 1 mg by vagina and observed for at least 6 hours (or until bleeding or pain at acceptable level) with follow-up visit 10–14 days later to verify complete expulsion (if treatment fails essential that pregnancy be terminated by another method)
- Softening and dilatation of cervix before mechanical cervical dilatation for termination of pregnancy, 36–48 hours before procedure, by mouth, mifepristone 600 mg as a single dose under medical supervision
- Termination of pregnancy of 13–24 weeks gestation (in combination with gemeprost), by mouth, mifepristone 600 mg as a single dose under medical supervision followed 36–48 hours later by gemeprost 1 mg by vagina every 3 hours up to max. 5 mg; if abortion does not occur, 24 hours after start of treatment repeat course of gemeprost 1 mg by vagina up to max. 5 mg (if treatment fails pregnancy should be terminated by another method); follow-up visit after appropriate interval to assess vaginal bleeding recommended

  Note Careful monitoring essential for 6 hours after administration of gemeprost pessary (risk of profound hypotension)
- Labour induction in fetal death *in utero*, by mouth, mifepristone 600 mg daily as a single dose for 2 days under medical supervision; if labour not started within 72 hours of first dose, another method should be used

**Mifegyne®** (Exelgyn) PoM

Tablets, yellow, mifepristone 200 mg. Net price 3-tab pack = £41.83 (supplied to NHS hospitals and premises approved under Abortion Act 1967). Label: 10, patient information leaflet

## 7.1.3 Myometrial relaxants

Tocolytic drugs postpone *premature labour* and they are used with the aim of reducing harm to the child. However, there is no satisfactory evidence that the use of these drugs reduces mortality. The greatest benefit is gained by using the delay to administer corticosteroid therapy or to implement other measures which improve perinatal health (including transfer to a unit with neonatal intensive care facility).

The oxytocin receptor antagonist, **atosiban**, is licensed for the inhibition of uncomplicated premature labour *between 24 and 33 weeks* of gestation. Atosiban may be preferable to a beta$_2$ agonist because it has fewer side-effects.

The dihydropyridine calcium-channel blocker **nifedipine** (section 2.6.2) also has fewer side-effects than a beta$_2$ agonist. Nifedipine [unlicensed indication] can be given initially in a dose of 20 mg followed by 10–20 mg 3–4 times daily adjusted according to uterine activity.

A beta$_2$ agonist (**ritodrine**, **salbutamol** or **terbutaline**) is used for inhibiting uncomplicated premature labour between 24 and 33 weeks of gestation and it may permit a delay in delivery of at least 48 hours. Prolonged therapy should be avoided since risks to the mother increase after 48 hours and there is a lack of evidence of benefit from further treatment; maintenance treatment is therefore **not recommended**.

Indometacin (indomethacin) (section 10.1.1), a cyclo-oxygenase inhibitor, also inhibits labour [unlicensed indication] and it may be useful in situations where a $beta_2$ agonist is not appropriate; however, there are concerns about neonatal complications such as transient impairment of renal function and premature closure of ductus arteriosus.

## ATOSIBAN

**Indications** uncomplicated premature labour (see notes above)

**Cautions** monitor blood loss after delivery; intra-uterine growth restriction; abnormal placental site; hepatic impairment (Appendix 2); renal impairment (Appendix 3)

**Contra-indications** eclampsia and severe pre-eclampsia, intra-uterine infection, intra-uterine fetal death, antepartum haemorrhage (requiring immediate delivery), placenta praevia, abruptio placenta, intra-uterine growth restriction with abnormal fetal heart rate, premature rupture of membranes after 30 weeks' gestation

**Side-effects** nausea, vomiting, tachycardia, hypotension, headache, dizziness, hot flushes, hyperglycaemia, injection-site reaction; *less commonly* pruritus, rash, fever, insomnia

**Dose**

- By intravenous injection, initially 6.75 mg over 1 minute, then by intravenous infusion 18 mg/hour for 3 hours, then 6 mg/hour for up to 45 hours; max. duration of treatment 48 hours

**Tractocile®** (Ferring) PoM

Injection, atosiban (as acetate) 7.5 mg/mL, net price 0.9-mL (6.75-mg) vial = £18.60

Concentrate for intravenous infusion, atosiban (as acetate) 7.5 mg/mL, net price 5-mL vial = £53.35

## RITODRINE HYDROCHLORIDE

**Indications** uncomplicated premature labour (see notes above)

**Cautions** suspected cardiac disease (physician experienced in cardiology to assess), hypertension, hyperthyroidism, hypokalaemia (special risk with potassium-depleting diuretics), diabetes mellitus (closely monitor blood glucose during intravenous treatment), mild to moderate pre-eclampsia, monitor blood pressure and pulse rate (should not exceed 140 beats per minute) and avoid over-hydration (Appendix 6); **important**: closely monitor state of hydration (discontinue immediately and institute diuretic therapy if pulmonary oedema occurs); concomitant beta-blocker treatment; drugs likely to enhance sympathomimetic side-effects or induce arrhythmias, see also **interactions**, Appendix 1 (sympathomimetics *and* sympathomimetics, $beta_2$)

**Contra-indications** cardiac disease, eclampsia and severe pre-eclampsia, intra-uterine infection, intra-uterine fetal death, antepartum haemorrhage (requires immediate delivery), placenta praevia, cord compression

**Side-effects** nausea, vomiting, flushing, sweating, tremor; hypokalaemia, tachycardia, palpitation, and hypotension (left lateral position throughout infusion to minimise risk), uterine bleeding (may be reversed with a non-selective beta-blocker); pulmonary oedema (see below and under Cautions); chest pain or tightness (with or without ECG changes) and arrhythmias reported; salivary gland enlargement also reported; on prolonged administration (several weeks) leucopenia and agranulocytosis reported; liver function abnormalities (including increased transaminases and hepatitis) reported

**Dose**

- By intravenous infusion (**important:** minimum fluid volume, see below), initially 50 micrograms/minute, increased gradually according to response by 50 micrograms/minute every 10 minutes until contractions stop or maternal heart rate reaches 140 beats per minute; continue for 12–48 hours after contractions cease (usual rate 150–350 micrograms/minute); max. rate 350 micrograms/minute; or by intramuscular injection, 10 mg every 3–8 hours continued for 12–48 hours after contractions have ceased; then by mouth (but see notes above), 10 mg 30 minutes before termination of intravenous infusion, repeated every 2 hours for 24 hours, followed by 10–20 mg every 4–6 hours, max. oral dose 120 mg daily

Important Manufacturer states that although *fatal pulmonary oedema* associated with ritodrine infusion is almost certainly multifactorial in origin, evidence suggests that **fluid overload** may be the most important single factor. The volume of infusion should therefore be kept to a minimum; for further guidance see Appendix 6. For specific guidance on infusion rates, consult product literature

**Yutopar®** (Durbin) PoM

Tablets, yellow, scored, ritodrine hydrochloride 10 mg. Net price 90-tab pack = £25.55

Injection, ritodrine hydrochloride 10 mg/mL. Net price 5-mL amp = £2.98

## SALBUTAMOL

**Indications** uncomplicated premature labour (see notes above); asthma (section 3.1.1)

**Cautions** see under Ritodrine Hydrochloride; **interactions:** Appendix 1 (sympathomimetics, $beta_2$)

**Contra-indications** see under Ritodrine Hydrochloride

**Side-effects** see under Ritodrine Hydrochloride; headache, rarely muscle cramps; hypersensitivity reactions including bronchospasm, urticaria, and angioedema reported

**Dose**

- By intravenous infusion, initially 10 micrograms/minute, rate increased gradually according to response at 10-minute intervals until contractions diminish then increase rate slowly until contractions cease (max. rate 45 micrograms/minute); maintain rate for 1 hour after contractions have stopped, then gradually reduce by 50% every 6 hours; then by mouth (but see notes above), 4 mg every 6–8 hours

**Preparations**

Section 3.1.1.1

## TERBUTALINE SULPHATE

**Indications** uncomplicated premature labour (see notes above); asthma (section 3.1.1)

**Cautions** see under Ritodrine Hydrochloride; **interactions:** Appendix 1 (sympathomimetics, $beta_2$)

**Contra-indications** see under Ritodrine Hydrochloride

**Side-effects** see under Ritodrine Hydrochloride

**Dose**

- By intravenous infusion, 5 micrograms/minute for 20 minutes, increased every 20 minutes in steps of 2.5 micrograms/minute until contractions have ceased (more than 10 micrograms/minute should **seldom** be given—20 micrograms/minute should **not** be exceeded), continue for 1 hour then decrease every 20 minutes in steps of 2.5 micrograms/minute to lowest dose that maintains suppression, continue at this level for 12 hours then by mouth (but see notes above), 5 mg every 8 hours for as long as is desirable to prolong pregnancy (or alternatively follow the intravenous infusion by subcutaneous injection 250 micrograms every 6 hours for a few days then by mouth as above)

**Preparations**
Section 3.1.1.1

# 7.2 Treatment of vaginal and vulval conditions

7.2.1 Preparations for vaginal atrophy
7.2.2 Vaginal and vulval infections

Symptoms are often restricted to the vulva, but infections almost invariably involve the vagina which should also be treated. Applications to the vulva alone are likely to give only symptomatic relief without cure.

*Aqueous medicated douches* may disturb normal vaginal acidity and bacterial flora.

*Topical anaesthetic agents* give only symptomatic relief and may cause sensitivity reactions. They are indicated only in cases of pruritus where specific local causes have been excluded.

*Systemic drugs* are required in the treatment of infections such as gonorrhoea and syphilis (section 5.1).

## 7.2.1 Preparations for vaginal atrophy

### Topical HRT

A cream containing an oestrogen may be applied on a short-term basis to improve the vaginal epithelium in *menopausal atrophic vaginitis*. It is **important** to bear in mind that topical oestrogens should be used in the **smallest effective** amount to minimise systemic effects. Modified-release vaginal tablets and an impregnated vaginal ring are now also available.

The risk of endometrial hyperplasia and carcinoma is increased when *systemic* oestrogens are administered alone for prolonged periods (section 6.4.1.1). The endometrial safety of long-term or repeated use of *topical* vaginal oestrogens is uncertain; treatment should be reviewed at least annually, with special consideration given to any symptoms of endometrial hyperplasia or carcinoma.

Topical oestrogens are also used in postmenopausal women before vaginal surgery for prolapse when there is epithelial atrophy.

For a general comment on hormone replacement therapy, including the role of topical oestrogens, see section 6.4.1.1.

### OESTROGENS, TOPICAL

**Indications** see notes above

**Cautions** see notes above; see also Oestrogens for HRT (section 6.4.1.1); interrupt treatment periodically to assess need for continued treatment

**Contra-indications** see notes above; see also Oestrogens for HRT (section 6.4.1.1); pregnancy and breast-feeding

**Side-effects** see notes above; see also Oestrogens for HRT (section 6.4.1.1); local irritation

**Ortho-Gynest®** (Janssen-Cilag) PoM

Intravaginal cream, estriol 0.01%. Net price 80 g with applicator = £2.58

Excipients include arachis (peanut) oil

Condoms damages latex condoms and diaphragms

Dose insert 1 applicatorful daily, preferably in evening; reduced to 1 applicatorful twice a week; attempts to reduce or discontinue should be made at 3–6 month intervals with re-examination

Pessaries, estriol 500 micrograms. Net price 15 pessaries = £5.03

Excipients include butylated hydroxytoluene

Condoms damages latex condoms and diaphragms

Dose insert 1 pessary daily, preferably in the evening, until improvement occurs; maintenance 1 pessary twice a week; attempts to reduce or discontinue should be made at 3–6 month intervals with re-examination

**Ovestin®** (Organon) PoM

Intravaginal cream, estriol 0.1%. Net price 15 g with applicator = £4.63

Excipients include cetyl alcohol, polysorbates, stearyl alcohol

Condoms effect on latex condoms and diaphragms not yet known

Dose insert 1 applicator-dose daily for 2–3 weeks, then reduce to twice a week (discontinue every 2–3 months for 4 weeks to assess need for further treatment); vaginal surgery, 1 applicator-dose daily for 2 weeks before surgery, resuming 2 weeks after surgery

**Premarin®** (Wyeth) PoM

Vaginal cream, conjugated oestrogens (equine) 625 micrograms/g. Net price 42.5 g with calibrated applicator = £2.19

Excipients include cetyl alcohol, propylene glycol

Condoms effect on latex condoms and diaphragms not yet known

Dose insert 1–2 g daily starting on day 5 of cycle (or at any time if cycles have ceased) for 3 weeks, repeated after a 1-week interval

**Vagifem®** (Novo Nordisk) PoM

Vaginal tablets, f/c, m/r, estradiol 25 micrograms in disposable applicators. Net price 15-applicator pack = £7.28

Excipients none as listed in section 13.1.3

Condoms no evidence of damage to latex condoms and diaphragms

Dose insert 1 tablet daily for 2 weeks then reduce to 1 tablet twice weekly; discontinue after 3 months to assess need for further treatment

**Vaginal ring**

**Estring®** (Pharmacia) PoM

Vaginal ring, releasing estradiol approx. 7.5 micrograms/24 hours. Net price 1-ring pack = £31.42. Label: 10, patient information leaflet

Dose for postmenopausal urogenital conditions (not suitable for vasomotor symptoms or osteoporosis prophylaxis), to be inserted into upper third of vagina and worn continuously; replace after 3 months; max. duration of continuous treatment 2 years

## Non-hormonal preparations

*Replens MD®* is an acidic, non-hormonal vaginal preparation that provides a high moisture content for up to 3 days.

# 7.2.2 Vaginal and vulval infections

Effective specific treatments are available for the common vaginal infections.

## Fungal infections

*Candidal vulvitis* can be treated locally with cream but is almost invariably associated with vaginal infection which should also be treated. *Vaginal candidiasis* is treated primarily with antifungal pessaries or cream inserted high into the vagina (including during menstruation). Single-dose preparations offer an advantage when compliance is a problem. Local irritation may occur on application of vaginal antifungal products.

**Imidazole** drugs (clotrimazole, econazole, and miconazole) are effective against candida in short courses of 3 to 14 days according to the preparation used. Vaginal applications may be supplemented with antifungal cream for vulvitis and to treat other superficial sites of infection.

One or two pessaries of **nystatin** are inserted for 14 to 28 nights; a cream is also used in cases of vulvitis and infection of other superficial sites. Nystatin stains clothing yellow.

Oral treatment of vaginal infection with **fluconazole** or **itraconazole** (section 5.2) is also effective; oral ketoconazole has been associated with fatal hepatotoxicity (see section 5.2 for CSM warning).

**Recurrent vulvovaginal candidiasis** Recurrence of vulvovaginal candidiasis is particularly likely if there are predisposing factors such as antibacterial therapy, pregnancy, diabetes mellitus and possibly oral contraceptive use. Reservoirs of infection may also lead to recontamination and should be treated; these include other skin sites such as the digits, nail beds, and umbilicus as well as the gastro-intestinal tract and the bladder. The partner may also be the source of re-infection and, if symptomatic, should be treated with cream at the same time.

Treatment against candida may need to be extended for 6 months in recurrent vulvovaginal candidiasis. Some recommended regimens [all unlicensed] include:

- fluconazole (section 5.2) by mouth 100 mg (as a single dose) every week for 6 months
- clotrimazole vaginally 500-mg pessary (as a single dose) every week for 6 months
- itraconazole (section 5.2) by mouth 400 mg (as 2 divided doses on one day) every month for 6 months.

### PREPARATIONS FOR VAGINAL AND VULVAL CANDIDIASIS

**Side-effects** occasional local irritation

**Clotrimazole** (Non-proprietary)

Cream (topical), clotrimazole 1%, net price 20 g = £2.29, 50 g = £3.80
Condoms effect on latex condoms and diaphragms not yet known
Dose apply to anogenital area 2–3 times daily

Pessary, clotrimazole 500 mg, net price 1 pessary with applicator = £3.26
Dose insert 1 at night as a single dose

**Canesten®** (Bayer Consumer Care)

Cream (topical), clotrimazole 1%. Net price 20 g = £2.14; 50 g = £3.80
Excipients include benzyl alcohol, cetostearyl alcohol, polysorbates
Condoms damages latex condoms and diaphragms
Dose apply to anogenital area 2–3 times daily

Thrush Cream (topical), clotrimazole 2%, net price 20 g = £3.42
Excipients include benzyl alcohol, cetostearyl alcohol, polysorbates
Condoms damages latex condoms and diaphragms
Dose apply to anogenital area 2–3 times daily

Vaginal cream (*10% VC®*) PoM, clotrimazole 10%. Net price 5-g applicator pack = £4.50
Excipients include benzyl alcohol, cetostearyl alcohol, polysorbates
Condoms damages latex condoms and diaphragms
Dose insert 5 g at night as a single dose; may be repeated once if necessary
Note Brands for sale to the public include *Canesten® Internal Cream*

Pessaries, clotrimazole 100 mg, net price 6 pessaries with applicator = £3.30; 200 mg, 3 pessaries with applicator = £3.30
Condoms damages latex condoms and diaphragms
Dose insert 200 mg for 3 nights *or* 100 mg for 6 nights

Pessary, clotrimazole 500 mg. Net price 1 with applicator = £3.25
Excipients none as listed in section 13.1.3
Condoms damages latex condoms and diaphragms
Dose insert 1 at night as a single dose

Combi, clotrimazole 500-mg pessary and cream (topical) 2%. Net price 1 pessary and 10 g cream = £4.74
Condoms damages latex condoms and diaphragms

**Ecostatin®** (Squibb)

Cream (topical), econazole nitrate 1%. Net price 15 g = £1.49; 30 g = £2.75
Excipients include butylated hydroxyanisole, fragrance
Condoms damages latex condoms and diaphragms
Dose apply to anogenital area twice daily

Pessaries PoM, econazole nitrate 150 mg. Net price 3 with applicator = £3.35
Excipients none as listed in section 13.1.3
Condoms damages latex condoms and diaphragms
Dose insert 1 pessary for 3 nights

Pessary (*Ecostatin 1®*) PoM, econazole nitrate 150 mg, formulated for single-dose therapy. Net price 1 pessary with applicator = £3.35
Excipients none as listed in section 13.1.3
Condoms damages latex condoms and diaphragms
Dose insert 1 pessary at night as a single dose

Twinpack PoM, econazole nitrate 150-mg pessaries and cream 1%. Net price 3 pessaries and 15 g cream = £4.35
Condoms damages latex condoms and diaphragms

**Gyno-Daktarin®** (Janssen-Cilag) PoM

Intravaginal cream, miconazole nitrate 2%. Net price 78 g with applicators = £4.70
Excipients include butylated hydroxyanisole
Condoms damages latex condoms and diaphragms
Dose insert 5-g applicatorful once daily for 10–14 days *or* twice daily for 7 days; topical, apply to anogenital area twice daily

Pessaries, miconazole nitrate 100 mg. Net price 14 = £3.18
Excipients none as listed in section 13.1.3
Condoms damages latex condoms and diaphragms
Dose insert 1 pessary daily for 14 days or 1 pessary twice daily for 7 days

Combipack, miconazole nitrate 100-mg pessaries and cream (topical) 2%. Net price 14 pessaries and 15 g cream = £4.13
Condoms damages latex condoms and diaphragms

Ovule (= vaginal capsule) (*Gyno-Daktarin 1*®), miconazole nitrate 1.2 g in a fatty basis. Net price 1 ovule (with finger stall) = £3.18
Excipients include hydroxybenzoates (parabens)
Condoms damages latex condoms and diaphragms
Dose insert 1 ovule at night as a single dose

**Gyno-Pevaryl®** (Janssen-Cilag) PoM
Cream, econazole nitrate 1%. Net price 15 g = £1.43; 30 g = £3.28
Excipients none as listed in section 13.1.3
Condoms damages latex condoms and diaphragms
Dose insert 5-g applicatorful intravaginally and apply to vulva at night for at least 14 nights

Pessaries, econazole nitrate 150 mg. Net price 3 pessaries = £3.01
Excipients none as listed in section 13.1.3
Condoms damages latex condoms and diaphragms
Dose ADULT and ADOLESCENT over 16 years, insert 1 pessary for 3 nights

Pessary (*Gyno-Pevaryl 1*®), econazole nitrate 150 mg, formulated for single-dose therapy. Net price 1 pessary with applicator = £3.20
Excipients none as listed in section 13.1.3
Condoms damages latex condoms and diaphragms
Dose ADULT and ADOLESCENT over 16 years, insert 1 pessary at night as a single dose

Combipack, econazole nitrate 150-mg pessaries, econazole nitrate 1% cream. Net price 3 pessaries and 15 g cream = £4.13
Condoms damages latex condoms and diaphragms

CP pack (*Gyno-Pevaryl 1*®), econazole nitrate 150-mg pessary, econazole nitrate 1% cream. Net price 1 pessary and 15 g cream = £4.13
Condoms damages latex condoms and diaphragms

**Nizoral®** (Janssen-Cilag) PoM
Cream (topical), ketoconazole 2%. Net price 30 g = £3.62
Excipients include polysorbates, propylene glycol, stearyl alcohol
Dose apply to anogenital area once or twice daily

**Nystan®** (Squibb) PoM
Cream and *Ointment*, see section 13.10.2

Vaginal cream, nystatin 100 000 units/4-g application. Net price 60 g with applicator = £2.77
Excipients include benzyl alcohol, propylene glycol
Condoms damages latex condoms and diaphragms
Dose insert 1–2 applicatorfuls at night for at least 14 nights

Pessaries, yellow, nystatin 100 000 units. Net price 28-pessary pack = £1.96
Excipients none as listed in section 13.1.3
Condoms no evidence of damage to latex condoms and diaphragms
Dose insert 1–2 pessaries at night for at least 14 nights

**Pevaryl®** (Janssen-Cilag)
Cream, econazole nitrate 1%. Net price 30 g = £2.65
Excipients include butylated hydroxyanisole, fragrance
Condoms effect on latex condoms and diaphragms not yet known
Dose apply to anogenital area twice daily

## Other infections

Vaginal preparations intended to restore normal acidity may prevent recurrence of vaginal infections and permit the re-establishment of the normal vaginal flora.

*Trichomonal infections* commonly involve the lower urinary tract as well as the genital system and need systemic treatment with metronidazole or tinidazole (section 5.1.11).

*Bacterial infections* with Gram-negative organisms are particularly common in association with gynaecological operations and trauma. Metronidazole is effective against certain Gram-negative organisms, especially *Bacteroides* spp. and may be used prophylactically in gynaecological surgery.

Topical vaginal products containing povidone–iodine can be used to treat vaginitis due to candidal, trichomonal, non-specific or mixed infections; they are also used for the pre-operative preparation of the vagina. Clindamycin cream and metronidazole gel are also indicated for bacterial vaginosis; *Sultrin*® cream is licensed for the treatment of infections due to *Haemophilus vaginalis* only.

The antiviral drugs aciclovir, famciclovir and valaciclovir may be used in the treatment of genital infection due to *herpes simplex virus*, the HSV type 2 being a major cause of genital ulceration. They have a beneficial effect on virus shedding and healing, generally giving relief from pain and other symptoms. See section 5.3.2.1 for systemic preparations, and section 13.10.3 for topical preparations.

### PREPARATIONS FOR OTHER VAGINAL INFECTIONS

**Betadine®** (Medlock)
Cautions avoid in pregnancy (Appendix 4) (also if planned) and in breast-feeding (Appendix 5); renal impairment (Appendix 3); avoid regular use in thyroid disorders
Side-effects rarely sensitivity; may interfere with thyroid function

Vaginal Cleansing Kit, solution, povidone-iodine 10%. Net price 250 mL with measuring bottle and applicator = £2.79
Excipients include fragrance
Condoms effect on latex condoms and diaphragms not yet known
Dose to be diluted and used once daily, preferably in the morning; may be used with *Betadine*® pessaries or vaginal gel

Pessaries, brown, povidone-iodine 200 mg. Net price 28 pessaries with applicator = £6.06
Condoms effect on latex condoms and diaphragms not yet known

**Dalacin®** (Pharmacia) PoM
Cream, clindamycin 2% (as phosphate). Net price 40-g pack with 7 applicators = £10.86
Excipients include benzyl alcohol, cetostearyl alcohol, polysorbates, propylene glycol
Condoms damages latex condoms and diaphragms
Side-effects irritation, cervicitis and vaginitis; poorly absorbed into the blood—very low likelihood of systemic effects (section 5.1.6)
Dose bacterial vaginosis, insert 5-g applicatorful at night for 3–7 nights

**Sultrin®** (Janssen-Cilag) PoM ▲
Cream, sulfathiazole 3.42%, sulfacetamide 2.86%, sulfabenzamide 3.7%. Net price 80 g with applicator = £3.31
Excipients include arachis (peanut) oil, cetyl alcohol, hydroxybenzoates (parabens), propylene glycol, wool fat
Condoms damages latex condoms and diaphragms

7 Obstetrics, gynaecology, and urinary-tract disorders

**Cautions** absorption of sulphonamides may produce systemic effects
**Contra-indications** pregnancy and breast-feeding; hypersensitivity to peanuts
**Side-effects** sensitivity
**Dose** bacterial vaginosis, insert 1 applicatorful of cream twice daily for 10 days, then once daily if necessary (but see also notes above)

**Zidoval®** (3M) PoM
Vaginal gel, metronidazole 0.75%. Net price 40-g pack with 5 applicators = £4.31
**Excipients** include disodium edetate, hydroxybenzoates (parabens), propylene glycol
**Cautions** not recommended during menstruation; some absorption may occur, see section 5.1.11 for systemic effects
**Side-effects** local effects including irritation, candidiasis, abnormal discharge, pelvic discomfort
**Dose** bacterial vaginosis, insert 5-g applicatorful at night for 5 nights

# 7.3 Contraceptives

**7.3.1 Combined hormonal contraceptives**
**7.3.2 Progestogen-only contraceptives**
**7.3.3 Spermicidal contraceptives**
**7.3.4 Contraceptive devices**

**Hormonal contraception** is the most effective method of fertility control, but has major and minor side-effects, especially for certain groups of women.

**Intra-uterine devices** are a highly effective method of contraception but may produce undesirable local side-effects. They are most suitable for older parous women, but less appropriate for younger nulliparous women and for those with an increased risk of pelvic inflammatory disease.

**Barrier methods** alone (condoms, diaphragms, and caps) are less effective but can be very reliable for well-motivated couples if used in conjunction with a **spermicide**. Occasionally sensitivity reactions occur. A female condom (*Femidom®*) is also available; it is prelubricated but does not contain a spermicide.

## 7.3.1 Combined hormonal contraceptives

Oral contraceptives containing an oestrogen and a progestogen ('combined oral contraceptives') are the most effective preparations for general use. Advantages of combined oral contraceptives include:

- reliable and reversible;
- reduced dysmenorrhoea and menorrhagia;
- reduced incidence of premenstrual tension;
- less symptomatic fibroids and functional ovarian cysts;
- less benign breast disease;
- reduced risk of ovarian and endometrial cancer;
- reduced risk of pelvic inflammatory disease, which may be a risk with intra-uterine devices.

Combined oral contraceptives containing a fixed amount of an oestrogen and a progestogen in each active tablet are termed 'monophasic'; those with varying amounts of the two hormones according to the stage of the cycle are termed 'biphasic' and 'triphasic'. A transdermal patch containing an oestrogen with a progestogen is also available.

**Choice** The oestrogen content of combined oral contraceptives ranges from 20 to 40 micrograms and generally a preparation with the lowest oestrogen and progestogen content which gives good cycle control and minimal side-effects in the individual woman is chosen.

- *Low strength preparations* (containing ethinylestradiol 20 micrograms) are particularly appropriate for women with risk factors for circulatory disease, provided a combined oral contraceptive is otherwise suitable. It is recommended that the combined oral contraceptive is not continued beyond 50 years of age since more suitable alternatives exist.
- *Standard strength preparations* (containing ethinylestradiol 30 or 35 micrograms or in 30–40 microgram *phased* preparations) are appropriate for standard use—but see Risk of Venous Thromboembolism below. Phased preparations are generally reserved for women who *either* do not have withdrawal bleeding *or* who have breakthrough bleeding with monophasic products.

The progestogens desogestrel, drospirenone, and gestodene (in combination with ethinylestradiol) may be considered for women who have side-effects (such as acne, headache, depression, weight gain, breast symptoms, and breakthrough bleeding) with other progestogens. However, women should be advised that desogestrel and gestodene have also been associated with an increased risk of *venous thromboembolism*. Drospirenone, a derivative of spironolactone, has anti-androgenic and anti-mineralocorticoid activity; it should be used with care if an increased concentration of potassium might be hazardous. The progestogen norelgestromin is combined with ethinylestradiol in a transdermal patch.

**Risk of venous thromboembolism** There is an increased risk of venous thromboembolic disease (particularly during the first year) in users of oral contraceptives but this risk is considerably smaller than that associated with pregnancy (about 60 cases of venous thromboembolic disease per 100 000 pregnancies). In all cases the risk of venous thromboembolism increases with age and in the presence of other risk factors for venous thromboembolism (e.g. obesity). The risk of venous thromboembolism with transdermal patches is not yet known.

The incidence of venous thromboembolism in healthy, non-pregnant women who are not taking an oral contraceptive is about 5 cases per 100 000 women per year. For those using combined oral contraceptives containing second-generation progestogens e.g. levonorgestrel, this incidence is about 15 per 100 000 women per year of use. Some studies have reported a greater risk of venous thromboembolism in women using preparations containing the third-generation progestogens desogestrel and gestodene; the incidence in these women is about 25 per 100 000 women per year of use.

The absolute risk of venous thromboembolism in women using combined oral contraceptives containing these third-generation progestogens remains very small and well below the risk associated with pregnancy. Provided that women are informed of the relative risks of venous thromboembolism and accept them, the choice of oral contraceptive is for the woman together with the prescriber jointly to make in light of her individual medical history and any contra-indications.

**Travel** Women taking oral contraceptives, or using the patch are at an increased risk of deep-vein thrombosis during travel involving long periods of immobility (over 5 hours). The risk may be reduced by appropriate exercise during the journey and possibly by wearing elastic hosiery.

**Missed pill** The critical time for loss of contraceptive protection is when a pill is omitted at the *beginning* or *end* of a cycle (which lengthens the pill-free interval).

If a woman forgets to take a pill, it should be taken as soon as she remembers, and the next one taken at the normal time. If the delay is 24 hours or longer with any pill (especially the first in the packet) the pill may not work. As soon as she remembers, she should continue taking the pill normally. However, she will not be protected for the next 7 days and must either not have sex or she should use another method of contraception such as a condom. If these 7 days run beyond the end of the packet, the next packet should be started at once, omitting the pill-free interval (or, in the case of *everyday* (ED) pills, omitting the 7 inactive tablets).

Emergency contraception is recommended if more than 2 combined oral contraceptive tablets are missed from the first 7 tablets in a packet.

**Delayed application or detached patch** If a patch is partly detached for less than 24 hours, reapply to the same site or replace with a new patch immediately; no additional contraception is needed and the next patch should be applied on the usual change day. If a patch remains detached for more than 24 hours or if the user is not aware when the patch became detached then stop the current contraceptive cycle and start a new cycle by applying a new patch, giving a new 'Day 1'; an additional non-hormonal contraceptive must be used concurrently for the first 7 days of the new cycle.

If application of a new patch at the start of a new cycle is delayed, contraceptive protection is lost. A new patch should be applied as soon as remembered giving a new 'Day 1'; additional non-hormonal methods of contraception should be used for the first 7 days of the new cycle. If intercourse has occurred during this extended patch-free interval, a possibility of fertilisation should be considered. If application of a patch in the middle of the cycle is delayed (i.e. the patch is not changed on day 8 or day 15):

- for up to 48 hours, apply a new patch immediately; next patch change day remains the same and no additional contraception is required.
- for more than 48 hours, contraceptive protection may have been lost. Stop the current cycle and start a new 4-week cycle immediately by applying a new patch giving a new 'Day 1'; additional non-hormonal contraception should be used for the first 7 days of the new cycle.

If the patch is not removed at the end of the cycle (day 22), remove it as soon as possble and start the next cycle on the usual 'change day', after day 28; no additional contraception is required.

**Diarrhoea and vomiting** Vomiting within 2 hours of taking an oral contraceptive *or* very severe diarrhoea can interfere with its absorption. Additional precautions should therefore be used during and for 7 days after recovery (see also under Missed Pill, above). If the vomiting and diarrhoea occurs during the last 7 tablets, the next pill-free interval should be omitted (in the case of ED tablets the inactive ones should be omitted).

**Interactions** The effectiveness of both *combined* and *progestogen-only* oral contraceptives may be considerably reduced by interaction with drugs that induce hepatic enzyme activity (e.g. **carbamazepine**, **griseofulvin**, **modafinil**, **nelfinavir**, **nevirapine**, **oxcarbazepine**, **phenytoin**, **phenobarbital**, **ritonavir**, **topiramate**, and, above all, **rifabutin** and **rifampicin**). A condom together with a long-acting method such as injectable contraceptive, may be more suitable for patients with HIV infection or at risk of HIV infection and advice on the possibility of interaction with antiretroviral drugs should be sought from HIV specialists.

For a *short course of an enzyme-inducing drug*, the dose of combined oral contraceptives should be adjusted to provide ethinylestradiol 50 micrograms or more daily [unlicensed use]; furthermore, additional contraceptive precautions should be taken whilst taking the enzyme-inducing drug and for 4 weeks after stopping it. If breakthrough bleeding occurs, the dose of ethinylestradiol may be increased further.

Women requiring a *prolonged course of an enzyme-inducing drug* should be encouraged to consider a contraceptive method that is unaffected by the interacting drug. In women unable to use an alternative method of contraception (for rifampicin and rifabutin see also below), a combination of combined oral contraceptives should be taken to provide a daily intake of ethinylestradiol 50 micrograms or more [unlicensed use]; 'tricycling' (i.e. taking 3 or 4 packets of monophasic tablets without a break followed by a short tablet-free interval of 4 days) is recommended (but women should be warned of uncertainty about the effectiveness of this regimen). **Rifampicin** and **rifabutin** are such potent enzyme-inducing drugs that an alternative method of contraception (such as an IUD) is **always** recommended. Since enzyme activity does not return to normal for several weeks after stopping an enzyme-inducing drug, appropriate contraceptive measures are required for 4 to 8 weeks after stopping.

The effectiveness of contraceptive patches may also be reduced by drugs that induce hepatic enzyme activity. Additional contraceptive precautions are required whilst taking the enzyme-inducing drug and for 4 weeks after stopping. If concomitant administration runs beyond the 3 weeks of patch treatment, a new treatment cycle should be started immediately without a patch-free break. For women taking a prolonged course of an enzyme-inducing drug, another method of contraception should be considered.

Some antibacterials that do not induce liver enzymes (e.g. ampicillin, doxycycline) may reduce the efficacy of *combined* oral contraceptives by impairing the bacterial flora responsible for recycling ethinylestradiol from the large bowel. Additional contraceptive precautions should be taken whilst taking a short course of an antibacterial that is not enzyme-inducing and for 7 days after stopping. If these 7 days run beyond the end of a packet the next packet should be started immediately without a break (in the case of ED tablets the inactive ones should be omitted). If the antibacterial course *exceeds 3 weeks*, the bacterial flora develop antibacterial resistance and additional precautions become unnecessary unless a new antibacterial is prescribed; additional precautions are also unnecessary if a woman starting a *combined* oral contraceptive has been on a course of antibacterial for 3 weeks or more.

It is possible that some antibacterials affect the efficacy of contraceptive patches. Additional contraceptive precautions are recommended during concomitant use and for 7 days after discontinuation of an antibacterial that is not enzyme-inducing (except tetracycline). If concomitant administration runs beyond the 3 weeks of patch treatment, a new treatment cycle should be started immediately without a patch-free break. If the antibacterial course exceeds 3 weeks, additional precautions become unnecessary unless a new antibacterial is prescribed; additional precautions are also unnecessary if a woman starting a contraceptive patch has been on a course of antibacterial for 3 weeks or more.

**Surgery** Oestrogen-containing contraceptives should preferably be discontinued (and adequate alternative contraceptive arrangements made) 4 weeks before major elective surgery and all surgery to the legs or surgery which involves prolonged immobilisation of a lower limb; they should normally be recommenced at the first menses occurring at least 2 weeks after full mobilisation. A depot injection of a progestogen-only contraceptive may be offered and the oestrogen-containing contraceptive restarted later—if preferred before the next injection would be due. When discontinuation of an oestrogen-containing contraceptive is not possible, e.g. after trauma or if a patient admitted for an elective procedure is still on an oestrogen-containing contraceptive, thromboprophylaxis (with heparin and graduated compression hosiery) is advised. These recommendations do not apply to minor surgery with short duration of anaesthesia, e.g. laparoscopic sterilisation or tooth extraction, or to women using oestrogen-free hormonal contraceptives (whether by mouth or by injection).

**Reason to stop immediately** Combined hormonal contraceptives or hormone replacement therapy (HRT) should be stopped (pending investigation and treatment), if any of the following occur:

- sudden severe chest pain (even if not radiating to left arm);
- sudden breathlessness (or cough with blood-stained sputum);
- unexplained severe pain in calf of one leg;
- severe stomach pain;
- serious neurological effects including unusual severe, prolonged headache especially if first time or getting progressively worse *or* sudden partial or complete loss of vision *or* sudden disturbance of hearing or other perceptual disorders *or* dysphasia *or* bad fainting attack or collapse *or* first unexplained epileptic seizure *or* weakness, motor disturbances, very marked numbness suddenly affecting one side or one part of body;
- hepatitis, jaundice, liver enlargement;
- blood pressure above systolic 160 mmHg and diastolic 100 mmHg;
- detection of a risk factor see Cautions and Contra-indications under Combined Hormonal Contraceptives;
- prolonged immobility after surgery or leg injury.

## COMBINED HORMONAL CONTRACEPTIVES

**Indications** contraception; menstrual symptoms (section 6.4.1.2)

**Cautions** risk factors for venous thromboembolism (see below and also notes above), arterial disease and migraine, see below; hyperprolactinaemia (seek specialist advice); history of severe depression especially if induced by hormonal contraceptive, sickle-cell disease, inflammatory bowel disease including Crohn's disease; **interactions:** see above and Appendix 1 (oestrogens, progestogens)

Risk factors for venous thromboembolism See also notes above. Use with **caution** if any of following factors present but **avoid** if two or more factors present:

- *family history of venous thromboembolism* in first-degree relative aged under 45 years (avoid contraceptive containing desogestrel or gestodene, *or* if known prothrombotic coagulation abnormality e.g. factor V Leiden or antiphospholipid antibodies (including lupus anticoagulant));
- *obesity*—body mass index above 30 kg/m$^2$ (avoid if body mass index above 39 kg/m$^2$);
- *long-term immobilisation* e.g. in a wheelchair (avoid if confined to bed or leg in plaster cast);
- *varicose veins* (avoid during sclerosing treatment or where definite history of thrombosis).

Risk factors for arterial disease Use with **caution** if any one of following factors present but **avoid** if two or more factors present:

- *family history of arterial disease* in first degree relative aged under 45 years (avoid if atherogenic lipid profile);
- *diabetes mellitus* (avoid if diabetes complications present);
- *hypertension*—blood pressure above *systolic 140 mmHg* and *diastolic 90 mmHg* (avoid if blood pressure above *systolic 160 mmHg* and *diastolic 100 mmHg*);
- *smoking* (avoid if smoking 40 or more cigarettes daily);
- *age* over 35 years (avoid if over 50 years);
- *obesity* (avoid if body mass index above 39 kg/m$^2$);
- *migraine*—see below.

Migraine Women should report any increase in headache frequency or onset of focal symptoms (discontinue immediately and refer urgently to neurology expert if focal neurological symptoms not typical of aura persist for more than 1 hour—see also Reason to stop immediately in notes above); **contra-indicated** in

- migraine with typical focal aura,
- severe migraine regularly lasting over 72 hours despite treatment,
- migraine treated with ergot derivatives;

use with **caution** in

- migraine without focal aura,
- migraine controlled with 5HT$_1$ agonist (section 4.7.4.1).

**Contra-indications** pregnancy (Appendix 4); personal history of venous or arterial thrombosis, severe or multiple risk factors for arterial disease or for venous thromboembolism (see above), heart disease associated with pulmonary hypertension or risk of embolus; migraine (see above), transient cerebral ischaemic attacks without headaches; liver disease including disorders of hepatic excretion (e.g. Dubin-Johnson or Rotor syndromes), infective hepatitis (until liver function returns to normal); systemic lupus erythematosus; porphyria (section 9.8.2); liver adenoma; gallstones; after evacuation of hydatidiform mole (until return to normal of urine and plasma gonadotrophin concentration); history of haemolytic uraemic syndrome or history during pregnancy of pruritus, cholestatic jaundice, chorea or deterioration of otosclerosis, pemphigoid gestationis; breast or genital-tract carcinoma; undiagnosed vaginal bleeding; breast-feeding (until weaning or for 6 months after birth—Appendix 5)

**Side-effects** nausea, vomiting, headache, breast tenderness, changes in body weight, fluid retention, thrombosis (more common when factor V Leiden present or in blood groups A, B, and AB; see also notes above), changes in libido, depression, chorea, skin reactions, chloasma, hypertension, contact lenses may irritate, impairment of liver function, hepatic tumours, reduced menstrual loss, 'spotting' in early cycles, absence of withdrawal bleeding; rarely photosensitivity

Breast cancer There is a small increase in the risk of having breast cancer diagnosed in women taking the combined oral contraceptive pill; this relative risk may be due to an earlier diagnosis. In users of combined oral contraceptive pills the cancers are more likely to be localised to the breast. The most important factor for diagnosing breast cancer appears to be the age at which the contraceptive is stopped rather than the duration of use; any increase in the rate of diagnosis diminishes gradually during the 10 years after stopping and disappears by 10 years. The CSM has advised that a possible small increase in the risk of breast cancer should be weighed against the benefits and evidence of the protective effect against cancers of the ovary and endometrium

**Dose**

- By mouth, each tablet should be taken at approximately same time each day; if delayed by longer than 24 hours contraceptive protection may be lost

*21-day combined (monophasic) preparations*, 1 tablet daily for 21 days; subsequent courses repeated after a 7-day interval (during which withdrawal bleeding occurs); first course usually started on day 1 of cycle—if starting on day 4 of cycle or later additional precautions (barrier methods) necessary during first 7 days

*Every day (ED) combined (monophasic) preparations*, 1 *active* tablet starting on day 1 of cycle (see also under preparations below)—if starting on day 4 of cycle or later additional precautions (barrier methods) necessary during first 7 days; withdrawal bleeding occurs when *inactive* tablets being taken; subsequent courses repeated without interval

*Biphasic and triphasic preparations*, see under individual preparations below

Changing to combined preparation containing different progestogen *21-day combined preparations:* continue current pack until last tablet and start first tablet of new brand the next day. If a 7-day break is taken before starting new brand, additional precautions (barrier methods) should be used during first 7 days of taking the new brand.

*Every Day (ED) combined preparations:* start the new brand (first tablet of a *21-day preparation* or the first *active* tablet of an *ED preparation*) the day after taking the last *active* tablet of previous brand (omitting the *inactive* tablets).

Changing from progestogen-only tablet Start on day 1 of menstruation or any day if amenorrhoea present and pregnancy has been excluded.

Secondary amenorrhoea (exclude pregnancy) Start any day, additional precautions (barrier methods) necessary during first 7 days.

After childbirth (not breast-feeding) Start 3 weeks after birth (increased risk of thrombosis if started earlier); later than 3 weeks postpartum additional precautions (barrier methods) necessary for first 7 days.

Not recommended if woman breast-feeding—oral progestogen-only contraceptive preferred.

After abortion or miscarriage Start same day.

- By transdermal application, apply first patch on day 1 of cycle, change patch on days 8 and 15; remove third patch on day 22 and apply new patch after 7-day patch-free interval to start subsequent contraceptive cycle

Changing from combined oral contraceptive Apply patch on the first day of withdrawal bleeding; if no withdrawal bleeding within 5 days of taking last *active* tablet, rule out pregnancy before applying first patch. Unless patch is applied on first day of withdrawal bleeding, additional precautions (barrier methods) should be used concurrently for first 7 days

Changing from progestogen-only method From an implant, apply first patch on the day implant removed; from an injection, apply first patch when next injection due; from oral progestogen, first patch may be started on any day after stopping pill. For all methods additional precautions (barrier methods) should be used concurrently for first 7 days

After childbirth (not breast-feeding) Start 4 weeks after birth; if started later than 4 weeks after birth additional precautions (barrier methods) should be used for first 7 days

After abortion or miscarriage Before 20 weeks' gestation start immediately; no additional contraception required if started immediately. After 20 weeks' gestation start on day 21 after abortion or on the first day of first spontaneous menstruation; additional precautions (barrier methods) should be used for first 7 days after applying the patch

## Low strength (oral)

### ▲Ethinylestradiol with Norethisterone

**Loestrin 20®** (Galen) PoM

Tablets, norethisterone acetate 1 mg, ethinylestradiol 20 micrograms. Net price 3 × 21-tab pack = £2.70

Dose 1 tablet daily for 21 days; subsequent courses repeated after 7-day tablet-free interval (during which withdrawal bleeding occurs); for starting routines see under Dose above

### ▲Ethinylestradiol with Desogestrel

See Risk of Venous Thromboembolism in notes above before prescribing

**Mercilon®** (Organon) PoM

Tablets, desogestrel 150 micrograms, ethinylestradiol 20 micrograms. Net price 3 × 21-tab pack = £7.97

Dose 1 tablet daily for 21 days; subsequent courses repeated after 7-day tablet-free interval (during which withdrawal bleeding occurs); for starting routines see under Dose above

### ▲Ethinylestradiol with Gestodene

See Risk of Venous Thromboembolism in notes above before prescribing

**Femodette®** (Schering Health) PoM

Tablets, s/c, gestodene 75 micrograms, ethinylestradiol 20 micrograms, net price 3 × 21-tab pack = £9.00

Dose 1 tablet daily for 21 days; subsequent courses repeated after 7-day tablet-free interval (during which withdrawal bleeding occurs); for starting routines see under Dose above

## Low strength (transdermal)

### ▲Ethinylestradiol with Norelgestromin

**Evra®** (Janssen-Cilag) ▼ PoM

Patches, self-adhesive (releasing ethinylestradiol approx. 20 micrograms/24 hours and norelgestromin approx. 150 micrograms/24 hours); net price 9-patch pack = £16.26. Counselling, administration

Dose 1 patch to be applied once weekly for three weeks, followed by a 7-day patch-free interval; subsequent courses repeated after 7-day patch-free interval (during which withdrawal bleeding occurs); for starting routines see under Dose above

Note Adhesives or bandages should not be used to hold patch in place. If patch no longer sticky do not reapply but use a new patch.

The *Scottish Medicines Consortium* has advised (September 2003) that *Evra®* patches should be restricted for use in women who are likely to comply poorly with combined oral contraceptives

## Standard strength

### Ethinylestradiol with Levonorgestrel

**Logynon®** (Schering Health) PoM

6 light brown tablets, ethinylestradiol 30 micrograms, levonorgestrel 50 micrograms;

5 white tablets, ethinylestradiol 40 micrograms, levonorgestrel 75 micrograms;

10 ochre tablets, ethinylestradiol 30 micrograms, levonorgestrel 125 micrograms.

Net price 3 × 21-tab pack = £3.92

Dose 1 tablet daily for 21 days, starting with light brown tablet marked 1 on day 1 of cycle; repeat after 7-day tablet-free interval

**Logynon ED®** (Schering Health) PoM

6 light brown tablets, ethinylestradiol 30 micrograms, levonorgestrel 50 micrograms;

5 white tablets, ethinylestradiol 40 micrograms, levonorgestrel 75 micrograms;

10 ochre tablets, ethinylestradiol 30 micrograms, levonorgestrel 125 micrograms;

7 white, inactive tablets.

Net price 3 × 28-tab pack = £3.92

Dose 1 tablet daily for 28 days, starting on day 1 of cycle with active tablet (withdrawal bleeding occurs when inactive tablets being taken); subsequent courses repeated without interval; for starting routines see under Dose above

**Microgynon 30®** (Schering Health) PoM

Tablets, s/c, levonorgestrel 150 micrograms, ethinylestradiol 30 micrograms. Net price 3 × 21-tab pack = £2.82

Dose 1 tablet daily for 21 days; subsequent courses repeated after 7-day tablet-free interval (during which withdrawal bleeding occurs); for starting routines see under Dose above

**Microgynon 30 ED®** (Schering Health) PoM

Tablets, beige, levonorgestrel 150 micrograms, ethinylestradiol 30 micrograms, white inactive tablets. Net price 3 × 28-tab (7 are inactive) pack = £2.56

Dose 1 tablet daily for 28 days starting on day 1 of cycle with active tablet (withdrawal bleeding occurs when inactive tablets being taken); subsequent courses repeated without interval; for starting routines see also under Dose above

**Ovranette®** (Wyeth) PoM

Tablets, levonorgestrel 150 micrograms, ethinylestradiol 30 micrograms. Net price 3 × 21-tab pack = £2.29

Dose 1 tablet daily for 21 days; subsequent courses repeated after 7-day tablet-free interval (during which withdrawal bleeding occurs); for starting routines see under Dose above

**Trinordiol®** (Wyeth) PoM

6 light brown tablets, ethinylestradiol 30 micrograms, levonorgestrel 50 micrograms;

5 white tablets, ethinylestradiol 40 micrograms, levonorgestrel 75 micrograms;

10 ochre tablets, ethinylestradiol 30 micrograms, levonorgestrel 125 micrograms.

Net price 3 × 21-tab pack = £4.04

Dose 1 tablet daily for 21 days, starting with light brown tablet marked 1 on day 1 of cycle; repeat after 7-day tablet-free interval

### Ethinylestradiol with Norethisterone

**BiNovum®** (Janssen-Cilag) PoM

7 white tablets, ethinylestradiol 35 micrograms, norethisterone 500 micrograms;

14 peach tablets, ethinylestradiol 35 micrograms, norethisterone 1mg.

Net price 3 × 21-tab pack = £2.13

Dose 1 tablet daily for 21 days, starting with white tablet on day 1 of cycle; repeat after 7-day tablet-free interval

**Brevinor®** (Pharmacia) PoM

Tablets, blue, norethisterone 500 micrograms, ethinylestradiol 35 micrograms. Net price 3 × 21-tab pack = £1.99

Dose 1 tablet daily for 21 days; subsequent courses repeated after 7-day tablet-free interval (during which withdrawal bleeding occurs); for starting routines see under Dose above

**Loestrin 30®** (Galen) PoM

Tablets, norethisterone acetate 1.5 mg, ethinylestradiol 30 micrograms. Net price 3 × 21-tab pack = £3.90

Dose 1 tablet daily for 21 days; subsequent courses repeated after 7-day tablet-free interval (during which withdrawal bleeding occurs); for starting routines see under Dose above

**Norimin®** (Pharmacia) PoM

Tablets, norethisterone 1 mg, ethinylestradiol 35 micrograms. Net price 3 × 21-tab pack = £2.28

Dose 1 tablet daily for 21 days; subsequent courses repeated after 7-day tablet-free interval (during which withdrawal bleeding occurs); for starting routines see under Dose above

**Ovysmen®** (Janssen-Cilag) PoM

Tablets, norethisterone 500 micrograms, ethinylestradiol 35 micrograms. Net price 3 × 21-tab pack = £1.62

Dose 1 tablet daily for 21 days; subsequent courses repeated after 7-day tablet-free interval (during which withdrawal bleeding occurs); for starting routines see under Dose above

**Synphase®** (Pharmacia) PoM

7 blue tablets, ethinylestradiol 35 micrograms, norethisterone 500 micrograms;

9 white tablets, ethinylestradiol 35 micrograms, norethisterone 1 mg;

5 blue tablets, ethinylestradiol 35 micrograms, norethisterone 500 micrograms.

Net price 21-tab pack = £1.20

Dose 1 tablet daily for 21 days, starting with blue tablet marked 1 on day 1 of cycle; repeat after 7-day tablet-free interval

**TriNovum®** (Janssen-Cilag) PoM

7 white tablets, ethinylestradiol 35 micrograms, norethisterone 500 micrograms;

7 light peach tablets, ethinylestradiol 35 micrograms, norethisterone 750 micrograms;

7 peach tablets, ethinylestradiol 35 micrograms, norethisterone 1 mg.

Net price 3 × 21-tab pack = £2.95

Dose 1 tablet daily for 21 days, starting with white tablet on day 1 of cycle; repeat after 7-day tablet-free interval

### Ethinylestradiol with Norgestimate

**Cilest®** (Janssen-Cilag) PoM

Tablets, blue, norgestimate 250 micrograms, ethinylestradiol 35 micrograms. Net price 3 × 21-tab pack = £6.10, 6 × 21-tab pack = £12.20

Dose 1 tablet daily for 21 days; subsequent courses repeated after 7-day tablet-free interval (during which withdrawal bleeding occurs); for starting routines see under Dose above

### Ethinylestradiol with Desogestrel

See Risk of Venous Thromboembolism in notes above before prescribing

**Marvelon®** (Organon) PoM

Tablets, desogestrel 150 micrograms, ethinylestradiol 30 micrograms. Net price 3 × 21-tab pack = £6.70

Dose 1 tablet daily for 21 days; subsequent courses repeated after 7-day tablet-free interval (during which withdrawal bleeding occurs); for starting routines see under Dose above

### Ethinylestradiol with Drospirenone

**Yasmin®** (Schering Health) PoM

Tablets, f/c, yellow, drospirenone 3 mg, ethinylestradiol 30 micrograms. Net price 3 × 21-tab pack = £14.70

**Dose** 1 tablet daily for 21 days; subsequent courses repeated after 7-day tablet-free interval (during which withdrawal bleeding occurs); for starting routines see under Dose above

The *Scottish Medicines Consortium* has advised (March 2003) that *Yasmin®* is not recommended

### Ethinylestradiol with Gestodene

See Risk of Venous Thromboembolism in notes above before prescribing

**Femodene®** (Schering Health) PoM

Tablets, s/c, gestodene 75 micrograms, ethinylestradiol 30 micrograms. Net price 3 × 21-tab pack = £6.84

**Dose** 1 tablet daily for 21 days; subsequent courses repeated after 7-day tablet-free interval (during which withdrawal bleeding occurs); for starting routines see under Dose above

**Femodene® ED** (Schering Health) PoM

Tablets, s/c, gestodene 75 micrograms, ethinylestradiol 30 micrograms. Net price 3 × 28-tab (7 are inactive) pack = £6.84

**Dose** 1 tablet daily for 28 days, starting on day 1 of cycle with active tablet (withdrawal bleeding occurs when inactive tablets being taken); subsequent courses repeated without interval; for starting routines see under Dose above

**Minulet®** (Wyeth) PoM

Tablets, gestodene 75 micrograms, ethinylestradiol 30 micrograms. Net price 3 × 21-tab pack = £6.36

**Dose** 1 tablet daily for 21 days; subsequent courses repeated after 7-day tablet-free interval (during which withdrawal bleeding occurs); for starting routines see under Dose above

**Triadene®** (Schering Health) PoM

6 beige tablets, ethinylestradiol 30 micrograms, gestodene 50 micrograms;

5 dark brown tablets, ethinylestradiol 40 micrograms, gestodene 70 micrograms;

10 white tablets, ethinylestradiol 30 micrograms, gestodene 100 micrograms.

Net price 3 × 21-tab pack = £9.54

**Dose** 1 tablet daily for 21 days, starting with beige tablet marked 'start' on day 1 of cycle; repeat after 7-day tablet-free interval

**Tri-Minulet®** (Wyeth) PoM

6 beige tablets, ethinylestradiol 30 micrograms, gestodene 50 micrograms;

5 dark brown tablets, ethinylestradiol 40 micrograms, gestodene 70 micrograms;

10 white tablets, ethinylestradiol 30 micrograms, gestodene 100 micrograms.

Net price 3 × 21-tab pack = £8.87

**Dose** 1 tablet daily for 21 days, starting with beige tablet marked '1' on day 1 of the cycle; repeat after 7-day tablet-free interval

### Mestranol with Norethisterone

**Norinyl-1®** (Pharmacia) PoM

Tablets, norethisterone 1 mg, mestranol 50 micrograms. Net price 3 × 21-tab pack = £2.19

**Dose** 1 tablet daily for 21 days; subsequent courses repeated after 7-day tablet-free interval (during which withdrawal bleeding occurs); for starting routines see under Dose above

### Ethinylestradiol with cyproterone acetate

See Co-cyprindiol (section 13.6.2)

## Emergency contraception

### Hormonal methods

Hormonal emergency contraception involves the use of **levonorgestrel**. It is effective if dose is taken within 72 hours (3 days) of unprotected intercourse; taking the dose as soon as possible increases efficacy. Levonorgestrel may also be used between 72 and 120 hours after unprotected intercourse [unlicensed use] but efficacy decreases with time. Hormonal emergency contraception is less effective than insertion of an intra-uterine device (see below).

If vomiting occurs within 3 hours of taking levonorgestrel, a replacement dose can be given. If an anti-emetic is required domperidone is preferred.

When prescibing hormonal emergency contraception the doctor should explain:

- that the next period may be early or late;
- that a barrier method of contraception needs to be used until the next period;
- the need to return promptly if any lower abdominal pain occurs because this could signify an ectopic pregnancy (and also in 3 to 4 weeks if the subsequent menstrual bleed is abnormally light, heavy or brief, or is absent, or if she is otherwise concerned).

**Intra-uterine pregnancy** despite treatment: see Appendix 4 (levonorgestrel).

**Interactions** The effectiveness of hormonal emergency contraception is reduced by enzyme-inducing drugs; a copper intra-uterine device may be offered or, otherwise, the dose of levonorgestrel should be increased to a total of 3 mg (1.5 mg taken immediately and 1.5 mg taken 12 hours later) [unlicensed dose—advise women accordingly]. There is no need to increase the dose for emergency contraception if the patient is taking antibacterials that are not enzyme inducers.

## LEVONORGESTREL

**Indications** emergency contraception

**Cautions** see notes above; past ectopic pregnancy, severe malabsorption syndromes, severe liver disease (Appendix 2), pregnancy (see notes above and Appendix 4); breast-feeding (Appendix 5); **interactions**: see notes above and Appendix 1 (progestogens)

**Contra-indications** porphyria (section 9.8.2)

**Side-effects** menstrual irregularities (see also notes above), nausea, low abdominal pain, fatigue, headache, dizziness, breast tenderness, vomiting

**Dose**

- 1.5 mg as a single dose as soon as possible after coitus (preferably within 12 hours but no later than after 72 hours)

[1]**Levonelle® One Step** (Schering Health)

Tablets, levonorgestrel 1.5 mg, net price 1-tab pack = £13.83

1. Can be sold to women over 16 years when supplying emergency contraception to the public, pharmacists should refer to guidance issued by the Royal Pharmaceutical Society of Great Britain

7 Obstetrics, gynaecology, and urinary-tract disorders

**Levonelle® 1500** (Schering Health) PoM
Tablets, levonorgestrel 1.5 mg, net price 1-tab pack = £5.11

## Intra-uterine device

Insertion of an intra-uterine device is more effective than the hormonal methods of emergency contraception. A copper intra-uterine contraceptive device (section 7.3.4) can be inserted up to 120 hours (5 days) after unprotected intercourse; sexually transmitted diseases should be tested for and insertion of the device should usually be covered by antibacterial prophylaxis (e,g, azithromycin 1 g as a single dose). If intercourse has occurred more than 5 days previously, the device can still be inserted up to 5 days after the earliest likely calculated ovulation (i.e. within the minimum period before implantation).

# 7.3.2 Progestogen-only contraceptives

**7.3.2.1** Oral progestogen-only contraceptives
**7.3.2.2** Parenteral progestogen-only contraceptives
**7.3.2.3** Intra-uterine progestogen-only device

## 7.3.2.1 Oral progestogen-only contraceptives

Oral progestogen-only preparations may offer a suitable alternative when oestrogens are contra-indicated (including those patients with venous thrombosis or a past history or predisposition to venous thrombosis), but have a higher failure rate than combined preparations. They are suitable for older women, for heavy smokers, and for those with hypertension, valvular heart disease, diabetes mellitus, and migraine. Menstrual irregularities (oligomenorrhoea, menorrhagia) are more common but tend to resolve on long-term treatment.

**Interactions** Effectiveness of oral progestogen-only preparations is not affected by antibacterials that do not induce liver enzymes. The efficacy of oral progesterone-only preparations is, however, reduced by enzyme-inducing drugs and an additional or alternative contraceptive method is recommended during treatment with an enzyme-inducing drug and for at least 4 weeks afterwards—see p. 408 and Appendix 1 (progestogens).

**Surgery** All progestogen-only contraceptives (including those given by injection) are suitable for use as an alternative to combined oral contraceptives before major elective surgery, before all surgery to the legs, or before surgery which involves prolonged immobilisation of a lower limb.

**Starting routine** One tablet daily, on a continuous basis, starting on day 1 of cycle and taken at the same time each day (if delayed by longer than 3 hours contraceptive protection may be lost). Additional contraceptive precautions are not necessary when initiating treatment.

**Changing from a combined oral contraceptive:** start on the day following completion of the combined oral contraceptive course without a break (or in the case of ED tablets omitting the inactive ones).

**After childbirth:** start any time after 3 weeks postpartum (increased risk of breakthrough bleeding if started earlier)—lactation is not affected.

**Missed pill** The following advice is now recommended by family planning organisations:

> 'If you forget a pill, take it as soon as you remember and carry on with the next pill at the right time. If the pill was more than 3 hours (12 hours for *Cerazette®*) overdue you are not protected. Continue normal pill-taking but you must also use another method, such as the condom, for the next 2 days.'

The Faculty of Family Planning and Reproductive Health Care recommends emergency contraception (see p. 412) if one or more progestogen-only contraceptive tablets are missed or taken more than 3 hours late and intercourse has occurred before 2 further tablets have been correctly taken.

**Diarrhoea and vomiting** Vomiting within 2 hours after taking an oral contraceptive *or* very severe diarrhoea can interfere with its absorption. Additional precautions should be used during and for 2 days after recovery.

### ORAL PROGESTOGEN-ONLY CONTRACEPTIVES
**(Progestogen-only pill, 'POP')**

**Indications** contraception

**Cautions** heart disease, sex-steroid dependent cancer, past ectopic pregnancy, malabsorption syndromes, functional ovarian cysts, active liver disease, recurrent cholestatic jaundice, history of jaundice in pregnancy; **interactions:** p. 408 and Appendix 1 (progestogens)
Other conditions The product literature advises caution in patients with history of thromboembolism, hypertension, diabetes mellitus and migraine; evidence for caution in these conditions is unsatisfactory

**Contra-indications** pregnancy, undiagnosed vaginal bleeding; severe arterial disease; liver adenoma, porphyria (section 9.8.2); after evacuation of hydatidiform mole (until return to normal of urine and plasma gonadotrophin values); history of breast cancer but may be used after 5 years if no evidence of current disease

**Side-effects** menstrual irregularities (see also notes above); nausea, vomiting, headache, dizziness, breast discomfort, depression, skin disorders, disturbance of appetite, weight changes, changes in libido
Breast cancer There is a small increase in the risk of having breast cancer diagnosed in women using, or who have recently used, a progestogen-only contraceptive pill; this relative risk may be due to an earlier diagnosis. The most important risk factor appears to be the age at which the contraceptive is stopped rather than the duration of use; the risk disappears gradually during the 10 years after stopping and there is no excess risk by 10 years. The CSM has advised that a possible small increase in the risk of breast cancer should be weighed against the benefits

**Dose**
- 1 tablet daily at same time each day, starting on day 1 of cycle then continuously; if administration delayed for 3 hours (12 hours for *Cerazette®*) or more it should be regarded as a 'missed pill', see notes above

**Cerazette®** (Organon) PoM
Tablets, f/c, desogestrel 75 micrograms. Net price 3 × 28-tab pack = £8.85
The *Scottish Medicines Consortium* has advised (September 2003) that *Cerazette®* should be restricted for use in women who cannot tolerate oestrogen-containing contraceptives or in whom these preparations are contra-indicated

**Femulen®** (Pharmacia) PoM
Tablets, etynodiol diacetate 500 micrograms. Net price 3 × 28-tab pack = £3.31

**Micronor®** (Janssen-Cilag) PoM
Tablets, norethisterone 350 micrograms. Net price 3 × 28-tab pack = £1.80

**Norgeston®** (Schering Health) PoM
Tablets, s/c, levonorgestrel 30 micrograms. Net price 35-tab pack = 98p

**Noriday®** (Pharmacia) PoM
Tablets, norethisterone 350 micrograms. Net price 3 × 28-tab pack = £2.10



## 7.3.2.2 Parenteral progestogen-only contraceptives

**Medroxyprogesterone acetate** (*Depo-Provera®*) is a long-acting progestogen given by intramuscular injection; it is as effective as the combined oral preparations but because of its prolonged action it should never be given without *full counselling backed by the patient information leaflet*. It may be used as a short-term or long-term contraceptive for women who have been counselled about the likelihood of menstrual disturbance and the potential for a delay in return to full fertility. Delayed return of fertility and irregular cycles may occur after discontinuation of treatment but there is no evidence of permanent infertility. Heavy bleeding has been reported in patients given medroxyprogesterone acetate in the immediate puerperium (the first dose is best delayed until 6 weeks after birth). If the woman is not breast-feeding, the first injection may be given within 5 days postpartum (she should be warned that the risk of heavy or prolonged bleeding may be increased).

Reduction in bone mineral density and, rarely, osteoporosis and osteoporotic fractures have also been reported with medroxyprogesterone acetate. The reduction in bone mineral density occurs in the first 2–3 years of use and then stabilises. See also CSM advice below.

> **CSM advice**
> The CSM has advised that:
> - in adolescents, medroxyprogesterone acetate (*Depo-Provera®*) be used only when other methods of contraception are inappropriate;
> - in all women, benefits of using medroxyprogesterone acetate beyond 2 years should be evaluated against risks;
> - in women with risk factors for osteoporosis a method of contraception other than medroxyprogesterone acetate should be considered.

**Norethisterone enantate** (*Noristerat®*) is a long-acting progestogen given as an oily injection which provides contraception for 8 weeks; it is used as short-term interim contraception e.g. before vasectomy becomes effective. The **cautions** and **contra-indications** of oral progestogen-only contraceptives apply except that because the injection also reliably inhibits ovulation, it protects against ectopic pregnancy and functional ovarian cysts.

An **etonogestrel-releasing implant** (*Implanon®*), consisting of a single flexible rod, is also available; the rod is inserted subdermally into the lower surface of the upper arm and it provides effective contraception for up to 3 years. In women with a body mass index greater than 35 kg/m², blood etonogestrel concentrations are lower and therefore the implant may not provide effective contraception during the third year; earlier replacement should be considered in such patients. Local reactions such as bruising and itching may occur at the insertion site. The **cautions**, **contra-indications** and **side-effects** of oral preparations apply; the contraceptive effect of *Implanon®* is rapidly reversed on removal of the implant. *The doctor or nurse administering (or removing) the system should be fully trained in the technique and should provide full counselling backed by the patient information leaflet.*

**Interactions** Effectiveness of parenteral progestogen-only contraceptives is not affected by antibacterials that do not induce liver enzymes. However, effectiveness of norethisterone and etonogestrel (but not medroxyprogesterone acetate) may be reduced by enzyme-inducing drugs; additional contraceptive precautions should be taken whilst taking the enzyme-inducing drug and for 4 weeks after stopping it *or* an alternative contraceptive method should be considered if *long-term* use of the enzyme-inducing drug is contemplated.

## PARENTERAL PROGESTOGEN-ONLY CONTRACEPTIVES

**Indications** contraception, see also notes above and under preparations (roles vary according to preparation)

**Cautions** see notes above and under preparations; possible risk of breast cancer, see oral progestogen-only contraceptives (section 7.3.2.1); history during pregnancy of pruritus or of deterioration of otosclerosis, disturbances of lipid metabolism; **interactions:** see notes above and Appendix 1 (progestogens)
Counselling Full counselling backed by *patient information leaflet* required before administration

**Contra-indications** see notes above; history of breast cancer

**Side-effects** see notes above; injection-site reactions

**Dose**
- See under preparations

### Injectable preparations

**Depo-Provera®** (Pharmacia) PoM
Injection (aqueous suspension), medroxyprogesterone acetate 150 mg/mL, net price 1-mL prefilled syringe = £5.01, 1-mL vial = £5.01. Counselling, see patient information leaflet
Dose by deep intramuscular injection, 150 mg within first 5 days of cycle or within first 5 days after parturition (delay until 6 weeks after parturition if breast-feeding); for long-term contraception, repeated every 12 weeks (if interval greater than 12 weeks and 5 days, rule out pregnancy before next injection and advise patient to use additional contraceptive measures (e.g. barrier) for 14 days after the injection)

**Noristerat®** (Schering Health) PoM
Injection (oily), norethisterone enantate 200 mg/mL. Net price 1-mL amp = £3.59. Counselling, see patient information leaflet
**Dose** by deep intramuscular injection given very slowly *into gluteal muscle*, short-term contraception, 200 mg within first 5 days of cycle or immediately after parturition (duration 8 weeks); may be repeated once after 8 weeks (withhold breast-feeding for neonates with severe or persistent jaundice requiring medical treatment)

**Implants**

**Implanon®** (Organon) PoM
Implant, containing etonogestrel 68 mg in each flexible rod, net price = £90.00. Counselling, see patient information leaflet
**Dose** by subdermal implantation, no previous hormonal contraceptive, 1 implant inserted during first 5 days of cycle; parturition or abortion in second trimester, 1 implant inserted between days 21–28 after delivery or abortion (if inserted after 28 days additional precautions necessary for next 7 days); abortion in first trimester, 1 implant inserted immediately; changing from an oral contraceptive, consult product literature; remove within 3 years of insertion

## 7.3.2.3 Intra-uterine progestogen-only device

The progestogen-only intra-uterine system, *Mirena®*, releases **levonorgestrel** directly into the uterine cavity. It is licensed for use as a contraceptive, for the treatment of primary menorrhagia and for the prevention of endometrial hyperplasia during oestrogen replacement therapy. This may therefore be a contraceptive method of choice for women who have excessively heavy menses. The effects of the intra-uterine system are mainly local and hormonal including prevention of endometrial proliferation, thickening of cervical mucus, and suppression of ovulation in some women (in some cycles). In addition to the progestogenic activity, the intra-uterine system itself may contribute slightly to the contraceptive effect. Return of fertility after removal is rapid and appears to be complete. Advantages over copper intra-uterine devices are that there may be an improvement in any dysmenorrhoea and a reduction in blood loss; there is also evidence that the frequency of pelvic inflammatory disease may be reduced (particularly in the youngest age groups who are most at risk).

In primary menorrhagia, menstrual bleeding is reduced significantly within 3–6 months of inserting the levonogestrel intra-uterine system, probably because it prevents endometrial proliferation. Another treatment should be considered if menorrhagia does not improve within this period (section 6.4.1.2).

Generally the **cautions** and **contra-indications** for levonorgestrel intra-uterine system are as for standard intra-uterine devices (section 7.3.4) but the risk of ectopic pregnancy is considerably smaller. Moreover, since levonorgestrel is released close to the site of the main contraceptive action (on cervical mucus and endometrium) progestogenic side-effects and interactions are less likely; in particular, enzyme-inducing drugs are unlikely to significantly reduce the contraceptive effect and additional contraceptive precautions are not required. Initially, changes in the pattern and duration of menstrual bleeding (spotting or prolonged bleeding) are common; endometrial disorders should be ruled out before insertion and the patient should be fully counselled (and provided with a patient information leaflet). Improvement in progestogenic side-effects, such as mastalgia and mood changes, and in the bleeding pattern usually occurs a few months after insertion and bleeding may often become very light or absent. Functional ovarian cysts (usually asymptomatic) may occur and usually resolve spontaneously (ultrasound monitoring recommended).

### INTRA-UTERINE PROGESTOGEN-ONLY SYSTEM

**Indications** see under Dose

**Cautions** see notes above; in case of pregnancy—remove system (teratogenicity cannot be excluded); advanced uterine atrophy; not suitable for emergency contraception; **interactions:** see notes above and Appendix 1 (progestogens)

**Contra-indications** see notes above

**Side-effects** see notes above; also abdominal pain; peripheral oedema; nervousness; salpingitis and pelvic inflammatory disease; pelvic pain, back pain; *rarely* hirsutism, hair loss, pruritus, migraine, rash

**Mirena®** (Schering Health) PoM
Intra-uterine system, T-shaped plastic frame (impregnated with barium sulphate and with threads attached to base) with polydimethylsiloxane reservoir releasing levonorgestrel 20 micrograms/24 hours. Net price = £83.16. Counselling, see patient information leaflet
**Dose** Contraception and menorrhagia, insert into uterine cavity within 7 days of onset of menstruation (anytime if replacement) or immediately after first-trimester termination by curettage; postpartum insertions should be delayed until 6 weeks after delivery; effective for 5 years.
Prevention of endometrial hyperplasia during oestrogen replacement therapy, insert during last days of menstruation or withdrawal bleeding or anytime if amenorrhoeic; effective for 4 years

## 7.3.3 Spermicidal contraceptives

Spermicidal contraceptives are useful additional safeguards but do **not** give adequate protection if used alone except where fertility is already significantly diminished (section 6.4.1.1); they are suitable for use with barrier methods. They have two components: a spermicide and a vehicle which itself may have some inhibiting effect on sperm activity.

> **CSM advice**
> Products such as petroleum jelly (*Vaseline®*), baby oil and oil-based vaginal and rectal preparations are likely to damage condoms and contraceptive diaphragms made from latex rubber, and may render them less effective as a barrier method of contraception and as a protection from sexually transmitted diseases (including HIV).

*Condoms:* no evidence of harm to latex condoms and diaphragms with the products listed below

**Ortho-Creme®** (Janssen-Cilag)
Cream, nonoxinol '9' 2% in a water-miscible basis. Net price 70 g = £2.44; applicator = 75p
**Excipients** include cetyl alcohol, hydroxybenzoates (parabens), propylene glycol, sorbic acid, fragrance

**Orthoforms®** (Janssen-Cilag)
Pessaries, nonoxinol '9' 5% in a water-soluble basis. Net price 15 pessaries = £2.40
Excipients none as listed in section 13.1.3

## 7.3.4 Contraceptive devices

### Intra-uterine devices

The intra-uterine device (IUD) is suitable for older parous women and as a second-line contraceptive in young nulliparous women who should be carefully screened because they have an increased background risk of pelvic inflammatory disease.

Smaller devices have been introduced to minimise side-effects; these consist of a plastic carrier wound with copper wire or fitted with copper bands; some also have a central core of silver to prevent fragmentation of the copper. Fertility declines with age and therefore a copper intra-uterine device which is fitted in a woman over the age of 40, may remain in the uterus until menopause. The intra-uterine device *Gyne-T 380®* (Janssen-Cilag) is no longer available, but some women may have the device in place until 2009. The intra-uterine devices *Multiload® Cu250* and *Multiload® Cu250 Short* (Organon) have been discontinued, but some women may have the devices in place until 2011.

A frameless, copper-bearing intra-uterine device (*GyneFix®*) has been introduced recently. It consists of a knotted, polypropylene thread with 6 copper sleeves; the device is anchored in the uterus by inserting the knot into the uterine fundus. *The healthcare professional inserting (or removing) the device should be fully trained in the technique and should provide full counselling backed by the patient information leaflet.*

The timing and technique of fitting an intra-uterine device are critical for its subsequent performance and call for proper training and experience. Devices should not be fitted during the heavy days of the period; they are best fitted after the end of menstruation and before the calculated time of implantation. The main excess risk of infection occurs in the first 20 days after insertion and is believed to be related to existing carriage of a sexually transmitted disease, therefore pre-screening (at least for chlamydia) should ideally be performed. The woman should be advised to attend *as an emergency* if she experiences sustained pain during the next 20 days.

An intra-uterine device should not be removed in mid-cycle unless an additional contraceptive was used for the previous 7 days. If removal is essential post-coital contraception should be considered.

If an intra-uterine device fails and the woman wishes to continue to full-term the device should be removed in the first trimester if possible.

### INTRA-UTERINE CONTRACEPTIVE DEVICES

**Indications** see notes above

**Cautions** anaemia, menorrhagia (progestogen intra-uterine system might be preferable, section 7.3.2.3), endometriosis, severe primary dysmenorrhoea, history of pelvic inflammatory disease, history of ectopic pregnancy or tubal surgery, diabetes, fertility problems, nulliparity and young age, severely scarred uterus (including after endometrial resection) or severe cervical stenosis; valvular heart disease or history of endocarditis (antibacterial cover needed at insertion—Table 2, section 5.1); drug- or disease-induced immunosuppression (risk of infection—avoid if marked immunosuppression); epilepsy; increased risk of expulsion if inserted before uterine involution; gynaecological examination before insertion, 6–8 weeks after then annually but counsel women to see doctor promptly in case of significant symptoms, especially pain; anticoagulant therapy (avoid if possible); remove if pregnancy occurs; if pregnancy occurs, increased likelihood that it may be ectopic

**Contra-indications** pregnancy, severe anaemia, recent sexually transmitted infection (if not fully investigated and treated), unexplained uterine bleeding, distorted or small uterine cavity, genital malignancy, active trophoblastic disease, pelvic inflammatory disease, established or marked immunosuppression; *copper devices:* copper allergy, Wilson's disease, medical diathermy

**Side-effects** uterine or cervical perforation, displacement, expulsion; pelvic infection may be exacerbated, menorrhagia, dysmenorrhoea, allergy; *on insertion*: pain (alleviated by NSAID such as ibuprofen 30 minutes before insertion) and bleeding, occasionally epileptic seizure and vasovagal attack

**Flexi-T® 300** (FP)
Intra-uterine device, copper wire, surface area approx. 300 mm² wound on vertical stem of T-shaped plastic carrier, impregnated with barium sulphate for radio-opacity, monofilament thread attached to base of vertical stem; preloaded in inserter, net price = £8.95
For uterine length over 5 cm; replacement every 5 years (see also notes above)

**GyneFix®** (FP)
Intra-uterine device, 6 copper sleeves with surface area of 330 mm² on polypropylene thread, net price = £25.19
Suitable for all uterine sizes; replacement every 5 years

**Load® 375** (Durbin)
Intra-uterine device, copper wire wound on vertical stem of U-shaped plastic carrier, surface area approx. 375 mm², impregnated with barium sulphate for radio-opacity, monofilament thread attached to base of vertical stem; preloaded in inserter, net price = £8.00
For uterine length over 7 cm; replacement every 5 years (see also notes above)

**Multiload® Cu375** (Organon)
Intra-uterine device, as above, with copper surface area approx. 375 mm² and vertical stem length 3.5 cm, net price = £9.24
For uterine length 6–9 cm; replacement every 5 years (see notes above)

**Nova-T® 380** (Schering Health)
Intra-uterine device, copper wire with silver core, surface area approx. 380 mm² wound on vertical stem of T-shaped plastic carrier, impregnated with barium sulphate for radio-opacity, threads attached to base of vertical stem, net price = £13.50
For uterine length 6.5–9 cm; replacement every 5 years (see notes above)

**T-Safe® CU 380 A** (FP)
Intra-uterine device, copper wire, wound on vertical stem of T-shaped plastic carrier with copper collar on the distal portion of each arm, total surface area approx. 380 mm², impregnated with barium sulphate for radio-opacity, threads attached to base of vertical stem, net price = £9.73
For uterine length 6.5–9 cm; replacement every 8 years (see notes above)

7 Obstetrics, gynaecology, and urinary-tract disorders

**TT 380 Slimline®** (Durbin)
Intra-uterine device, copper wire wound on vertical stem of T-shaped plastic carrier, total surface area approx. 380 mm², impregnated with barium sulphate for radio-opacity, with copper sleeves fitted flush on to distal portion of each horizontal arm, thread attached to base of vertical stem; easy-loading system, no capsule, net price = £11.70
For uterine length over 7 cm; replacement every 10 years (see also notes above)

**UT 380 Short®** (Durbin)
Intra-uterine device, copper wire wound on vertical stem of T-shaped plastic carrier, total surface area approx. 380 mm², impregnated with barium sulphate for radio-opacity, thread attached to base of vertical stem; net price = £10.53
For uterine length less than 7 cm; replacement every 5 years (see also notes above)

**UT 380 Standard®** (Durbin)
Intra-uterine device, copper wire wound on vertical stem of T-shaped plastic carrier, total surface area approx. 380 mm², impregnated with barium sulphate for radio-opacity, thread attached to base of vertical stem; net price = £10.53
For uterine length over 7 cm; replacement every 5 years (see also notes above)

## Other contraceptive devices

### Contraceptive caps

**Type A contraceptive pessary**
Opaque rubber, sizes 1 to 5 (55–75 mm rising in steps of 5 mm), net price = £7.26
Brands include *Dumas Vault Cap®*

**Type B contraceptive pessary**
Opaque rubber, sizes 22 to 31 mm (rising in steps of 3 mm), net price = £8.46
Brands include *Prentif Cavity Rim Cervical Cap®*

**Type C contraceptive pessary**
Opaque rubber, sizes 1 to 3 (42, 48 and 54 mm), net price = £7.26
Brands include *Vimule Cap®*

### Contraceptive diaphragms

**Type A Diaphragm with flat metal spring**
Transparent rubber with flat metal spring, sizes 55–95 mm (rising in steps of 5 mm), net price = £5.78
Brands include *Reflexions®*

**Type B Diaphragm with coiled metal rim**
Opaque rubber with coiled metal rim, sizes 60–95 mm (rising in steps of 5 mm), net price = £6.35
Brands include *Ortho®*

**Type C Arcing Spring Diaphragm**
Opaque rubber with arcing spring, sizes 60–95 mm (rising in steps of 5 mm), net price = £7.23
Brands include *All-Flex®*

### Fertility thermometer

**Fertility (Ovulation) Thermometer** (Zeal)
Mercury in glass thermometer, range 35 to 39°C (graduated in 0.1°C), net price = £1.83
For monitoring ovulation for the fertility awareness method of contraception

# 7.4 Drugs for genito-urinary disorders

7.4.1 Drugs for urinary retention
7.4.2 Drugs for urinary frequency, enuresis, and incontinence
7.4.3 Drugs used in urological pain
7.4.4 Bladder instillations and urological surgery
7.4.5 Drugs for erectile dysfunction

For drugs used in the treatment of urinary-tract infections see section 5.1.13.

## 7.4.1 Drugs for urinary retention

*Acute retention* is painful and is treated by catheterisation.

*Chronic retention* is painless and often long-standing. Catheterisation is unnecessary unless there is deterioration of renal function. After the cause has initially been established and treated, drugs may be required to increase detrusor muscle tone.

*Benign prostatic hyperplasia* is treated either surgically or medically with alpha-blockers (see below) or with the anti-androgen finasteride (section 6.4.2).

### Alpha-blockers

The selective alpha-blockers, **alfuzosin**, **doxazosin**, **indoramin**, **prazosin**, **tamsulosin** and **terazosin** relax smooth muscle in benign prostatic hyperplasia producing an increase in urinary flow-rate and an improvement in obstructive symptoms.

**Cautions** Since selective alpha-blockers reduce blood pressure, patients receiving antihypertensive treatment may require reduced dosage and specialist supervision. Caution may be required in the elderly and in patients with hepatic impairment (Appendix 2) and severe renal impairment (Appendix 3). For **interactions** see Appendix 1 (alpha-blockers).

**Contra-indications** Alpha-blockers should be avoided in patients with a history of postural hypotension and micturition syncope.

**Side-effects** Side-effects of selective alpha-blockers include drowsiness, hypotension (notably postural hypotension), syncope, asthenia, depression, headache, dry mouth, gastro-intestinal disturbances (including nausea, vomiting, diarrhoea, constipation), oedema, blurred vision, rhinitis, erectile disorders (including priapism), tachycardia, and palpitations. Hypersensitivity reactions including rash, pruritus and angioedema have also been reported.

## ALFUZOSIN HYDROCHLORIDE

**Indications** see notes above

**Cautions** see notes above

**Contra-indications** see notes above; severe liver impairment

**Side-effects** see notes above; flushes, chest pain

**Dose**

- 2.5 mg 3 times daily, max. 10 mg daily; ELDERLY initially 2.5 mg twice daily

  First dose effect First dose may cause collapse due to hypotensive effect (therefore should be taken on retiring to bed). Patient should be warned to lie down if symptoms such as dizziness, fatigue or sweating develop, and to remain lying down until they abate completely

**Xatral®** (Sanofi-Synthelabo) PoM

Tablets, f/c, alfuzosin hydrochloride 2.5 mg, net price 60-tab pack = £21.20. Label: 3, counselling, see dose above

### Modified release

**Xatral® XL** (Sanofi-Synthelabo) PoM

Tablets, m/r, yellow/white, alfuzosin hydrochloride 10 mg, net price 10-tab pack = £4.42, 30-tab pack = £13.28. Label: 3, 21, 25, counselling, see above

Dose benign prostatic hyperplasia 10 mg once daily

Acute urinary retention associated with benign prostatic hyperplasia in men over 65 years, 10 mg once daily for 2–3 days during catheterisation and for one day after removal; max. 4 days

## DOXAZOSIN

**Indications** see notes above and section 2.5.4

**Cautions** see notes above and section 2.5.4

**Contra-indications** see notes above

**Side-effects** see notes above and section 2.5.4

**Dose**

- Initially 1 mg daily; dose may be doubled at intervals of 1–2 weeks according to response, up to max. 8 mg daily; usual maintenance 2–4 mg daily

### Preparations

Section 2.5.4

## INDORAMIN

**Indications** see notes above and section 2.5.4

**Cautions** see notes above and section 2.5.4

**Contra-indications** see notes above and section 2.5.4

**Side-effects** see notes above and section 2.5.4

**Dose**

- 20 mg twice daily; increased if necessary by 20 mg every 2 weeks to max. 100 mg daily in divided doses; ELDERLY, 20 mg at night may be adequate

**Doralese®** (GSK) PoM

Tablets, yellow, f/c, indoramin 20 mg, net price 60-tab pack = £11.44. Label: 2

## PRAZOSIN HYDROCHLORIDE

**Indications** see notes above and section 2.5.4

**Cautions** see notes above and section 2.5.4

**Contra-indications** see notes above and section 2.5.4

**Side-effects** see notes above and section 2.5.4; paraesthesia, arthralgia, epistaxis, nervousness, dyspnoea, hallucinations, alopecia

**Dose**

- Initially 500 micrograms twice daily for 3–7 days, subsequently adjusted according to response; usual maintenance (and max.) 2 mg twice daily; ELDERLY initiate with lowest possible dose

  First dose effect First dose may cause collapse due to hypotensive effect (therefore should be taken on retiring to bed). Patient should be warned to lie down if symptoms such as dizziness, fatigue or sweating develop, and to remain lying down until they abate completely

### Preparations

Section 2.5.4

## TAMSULOSIN HYDROCHLORIDE

**Indications** see notes above

**Cautions** see notes above

**Contra-indications** see notes above; severe liver impairment

**Side-effects** see notes above

**Dose**

- 400 micrograms daily as a single dose

**Flomaxtra® XL** (Astellas) ▼ PoM

Tablets, m/r, tamsulosin hydrochloride 400 micrograms. Net price 30-tab pack = £17.55. Label: 25

## TERAZOSIN

**Indications** see notes above and section 2.5.4

**Cautions** see notes above and section 2.5.4

**Contra-indications** see notes above

**Side-effects** see notes above and section 2.5.4; weight gain, paraesthesia, dyspnoea, thrombocytopenia, nervousness, decreased libido, back pain and pain in extremities

**Dose**

- Initially 1 mg at bedtime; if necessary dose may be doubled at intervals of 1–2 weeks according to response, up to max. 10 mg once daily; usual maintenance 5–10 mg daily

  First dose effect First dose may cause collapse due to hypotensive effect (therefore should be taken on retiring to bed). Patient should be warned to lie down if symptoms such as dizziness, fatigue or sweating develop, and to remain lying down until they abate completely

**Terazosin** (Non-proprietary) PoM

Tablets, terazosin (as hydrochloride) 2 mg, net price 28-tab pack = £5.64; 5 mg, 28-tab pack = £9.59; 10 mg, 28-tab pack = £20.16. Label: 3, counselling, see dose above

**Hytrin®** (Abbott) PoM

Tablets, terazosin (as hydrochloride) 2 mg (yellow) net price, 28-tab pack = £8.07; 5 mg (tan), 28-tab pack = £13.07; 10 mg (blue), 28-tab pack = £26.59; starter pack (for benign prostatic hyperplasia) of 7 × 1-mg tab with 14 × 2-mg tab and 7 × 5-mg tab = £10.97. Label: 3, counselling, see dose above

## Parasympathomimetics

The parasympathomimetic **bethanechol** increases detrusor muscle contraction. However, it has only a limited role in the relief of urinary retention; its use has been superseded by catheterisation.

**Distigmine** inhibits the breakdown of acetylcholine. It may help patients with an upper motor neurone neurogenic bladder.

**Cautions and contra-indications** Parasympathomimetics should be used with caution or avoided in hyperthyroidism or in cardiac disorders including bradycardia, arrhythmias and recent myocardial infarction. They are contra-indicated in intestinal or urinary obstruction or where increased motility of the gastro-intestinal or urinary tract could be harmful. Parasympathomimetics should also be avoided in gastro-intestinal ulceration, asthma, hypotension, epilepsy, parkinsonism, pregnancy, and breast-feeding. **Interactions**: Appendix 1 (parasympathomimetics)

**Side-effects** Parasympathomimetic side-effects such as nausea, vomiting, intestinal colic, bradycardia, blurred vision, and sweating may occur, particularly in the elderly.

### BETHANECHOL CHLORIDE

**Indications** urinary retention, but see notes above
**Cautions** see notes above
**Contra-indications** see notes above
**Side-effects** see notes above
**Dose**
- 10–25 mg 3–4 times daily half an hour before food

**Myotonine®** (Glenwood) PoM
Tablets, both scored, bethanechol chloride 10 mg, net price 20 = £1.01; 25 mg, 20 = £1.30 Label: 22

### DISTIGMINE BROMIDE

**Indications** postoperative urinary retention (see notes above), neurogenic bladder; myasthenia gravis (section 10.2.1)
**Cautions** see notes above; also pregnancy (Appendix 4); breast-feeding
**Contra-indications** see notes above; also severe postoperative shock, serious circulatory insufficiency
**Side-effects** see notes above, but action slower than bethamecol chloride (therefore side-effects less acute; see also Neostigmine (section 10.2.1); also dyspnoea, muscle twitching, and urinary frequency
**Dose**
- Urinary retention, 5 mg daily, half an hour before breakfast
- Neurogenic bladder, 5 mg daily or on alternate days, half an hour before breakfast

**Ubretid®** (Rhône-Poulenc Rorer) PoM
Tablets, scored, distigmine bromide 5 mg. Net price 30-tab pack = £31.26. Label: 22

## 7.4.2 Drugs for urinary frequency, enuresis, and incontinence

### Urinary incontinence

Incontinence in adults which arises from detrusor instability is managed by combining drug therapy with conservative methods for managing urge incontinence such as pelvic floor exercises and bladder training; stress incontinence is generally managed by non-drug methods. **Duloxetine**, an inhibitor of serotonin and noradrenaline re-uptake can be added and is licensed for the treatment of moderate to severe stress incontinence in women; it may be more effective when used as an adjunct to pelvic floor exercises.

Involuntary detrusor contractions cause urgency and urge incontinence, usually with frequency and nocturia. Antimuscarinic drugs reduce these contractions and increase bladder capacity. **Oxybutynin** also has a direct relaxant effect on urinary smooth muscle. Side-effects limit the use of oxybutynin but they may be reduced by starting at a lower dose. A modified-release preparation of oxybutynin is effective and has fewer side-effects; a transdermal patch is also available. The efficacy and side-effects of **tolterodine** are comparable to those of modified-release oxybutynin. **Flavoxate** has less marked side-effects but it is also less effective. **Propiverine**, **solifenacin** and **trospium** are newer antimuscarinic drugs licensed for urinary frequency, urgency, and incontinence. The need for continuing antimuscarinic drug therapy should be reviewed after 3–6 months.

Propantheline and tricyclic antidepressants were used for urge incontinence but they are little used now because of their side-effects. The use of imipramine is limited by its potential to cause cardiac side-effects.

Purified bovine collagen implant (*Contigen®*, Bard) is indicated for *urinary incontinence* caused by intrinsic sphincter deficiency (poor or non-functioning bladder outlet mechanism). The implant should be inserted only by surgeons or physicians trained in the technique for injection of the implant.

**Cautions** Antimuscarinic drugs should be used with caution in the elderly (especially if frail) and in those with autonomic neuropathy. They should also be used with caution in hiatus hernia with reflux oesophagitis, and in hepatic impairment (Appendix 2; avoid propiverine) and renal impairment (Appendix 3). Antimuscarinics may worsen hyperthyroidism, coronary artery disease, congestive heart failure, hypertension, prostatic hypertrophy, arrhythmias and tachycardia. For **interactions** see Appendix 1 (antimuscarinics).

**Contra-indications** Antimuscarinic drugs should be avoided in patients with myasthenia gravis, angle closure glaucoma, significant bladder outflow obstruction or urinary retention, severe ulcerative colitis, toxic megacolon, and in gastro-intestinal obstruction or intestinal atony.

**Side-effects** Side-effects of antimuscarinic drugs include dry mouth, gastro-intestinal disturbances including constipation, blurred vision, dry eyes, drowsiness, difficulty in micturition (less commonly urinary retention), palpitation, and skin reactions (including dry skin, rash, and photosensitivity); also headache, diarrhoea, angioedema, arrhythmias and tachycardia. Central nervous system stimulation, such as restlessness, disorientation, hallucination and convulsion may occur; children are at higher risk of these effects. Antimuscarinic drugs may reduce sweating leading to heat sensations and fainting in hot environments or in patients with fever.

## DULOXETINE

**Indications** moderate to severe stress urinary incontinence in women; major depressive disorder (section 4.3.4); diabetic neuropathy (section 4.3.4)

**Cautions** elderly, cardiac disease, hypertension; history of mania; history of seizures; raised intra-ocular pressure, acute angle-closure glaucoma; bleeding disorders or concomitant use of drugs that increase risk of bleeding; suicidal thoughts or behaviour; avoid abrupt withdrawal; **interactions**: Appendix 1 (duloxetine)

**Contra-indications** hepatic impairment; pregnancy (Appendix 4); breast-feeding (Appendix 5)

**Side-effects** nausea, vomiting, dyspepsia, constipation, diarrhoea, dry mouth; hot flushes; insomnia or drowsiness, anxiety, headache, dizziness, tremor, nervousness, anorexia; sexual dysfunction; thirst; fatigue, lethargy, weakness; blurred vision; sweating, pruritus; *rarely* urinary retention and hyponatraemia

**Dose**

- 40 mg twice daily, assessed after 2–4 weeks and reduced to 20 mg twice daily if side-effects troublesome; CHILD and ADOLESCENT under 18 years not recommended

**Note** Initial dose of 20 mg twice daily can be used to minimise side-effects

**Yentreve®** (Lilly) ▼ PoM
Capsules, duloxetine (as hydrochloride) 20 mg (blue), net price 28-cap pack = £15.40, 56-cap pack = £30.80; 40 mg (orange/blue), 56-cap pack = £30.80. Label: 2

**Cymbalta®** (Lilly) ▼ PoM
Section 4.3.4 (major depressive episode)

## FLAVOXATE HYDROCHLORIDE

**Indications** urinary frequency and incontinence, dysuria, urgency; bladder spasms due to catheterisation

**Cautions** see notes above; pregnancy (Appendix 4), breast-feeding (Appendix 5)

**Contra-indications** see notes above; gastro-intestinal haemorrhage

**Side-effects** see notes above; also vertigo, fatigue, eosinophilia

**Dose**

- 200 mg 3 times daily; CHILD under 12 years not recommended

**Urispas 200®** (Shire) PoM
Tablets, f/c, flavoxate hydrochloride 200 mg, net price 90-tab pack = £11.87

## OXYBUTYNIN HYDROCHLORIDE

**Indications** urinary frequency, urgency and incontinence, neurogenic bladder instability and nocturnal enuresis

**Cautions** see notes above; pregnancy (Appendix 4), porphyria (section 9.8.2)

**Contra-indications** see notes above; breast-feeding (Appendix 5)

**Side-effects** see notes above; also anorexia, facial flushing (more marked in children) and dizziness; application site reactions with *patches*

**Dose**

- Initially 2.5–5 mg 2–3 times daily increased if necessary to max. 5 mg 4 times daily; ELDERLY initially 2.5–3 mg twice daily, increased to 5 mg twice daily according to response and tolerance; CHILD over 5 years, neurogenic bladder instability, 2.5–3 mg twice daily increased to 5 mg twice daily (max. 5 mg 3 times daily); nocturnal enuresis (preferably over 7 years, see notes below), 2.5–3 mg twice daily increased to 5 mg 2–3 times daily (last dose before bedtime)

**Oxybutynin Hydrochloride** (Non-proprietary) PoM
Tablets, oxybutynin hydrochloride 2.5 mg, net price 56-tab pack = £5.04; 3 mg, 56-tab pack = £9.15; 5 mg, 56-tab pack = £10.26, 84-tab pack = £3.21. Label: 3

**Cystrin®** (Sanofi-Synthelabo) PoM
Tablets, oxybutynin hydrochloride 3 mg, net price 56-tab pack = £9.15; 5 mg (scored), 84-tab pack = £22.88. Label: 3

**Ditropan®** (Sanofi-Synthelabo) PoM
Tablets, both blue, scored, oxybutynin hydrochloride 2.5 mg, net price 84-tab pack = £6.86; 5 mg, 84-tab pack = £13.34. Label: 3
Elixir, oxybutynin hydrochloride 2.5 mg/5 mL. Net price 150-mL pack = £4.78. Label: 3

### Modified release

**Lyrinel® XL** (Janssen-Cilag) PoM
Tablets, m/r, oxybutynin hydrochloride 5 mg (yellow), net price 30-tab pack = £12.34; 10 mg (pink), 30-tab pack = £24.68. Label: 3, 25

**Dose** ADULT over 18 years, initially 5 mg daily, adjusted according to response in 5-mg steps at weekly intervals; max. 20 mg daily taken as a single dose

**Note** Patients taking immediate-release oxybutynin may be transferred to the nearest equivalent daily dose of *Lyrinel® XL*

### Transdermal preparations

**Kentera®** (UCB Pharma) PoM
Patches, self-adhesive, oxybutynin 36 mg (releasing oxybutynin approx. 3.9 mg/24 hours), net price 8-patch pack = £27.20. Label: 3, counselling, administration

**Dose** urinary frequency, urgency and incontinence, apply 1 patch twice weekly to clean, dry, unbroken skin on abdomen, hip or buttock, remove after every 3–4 days and site replacement patch on a different area (avoid using same area for 7 days); CHILD and ADOLESCENT not recommended

The *Scottish Medicines Consortium* has advised (July 2005) that *Kentera®* should be restricted for use in patients who benefit from oral oxybutynin but cannot tolerate its side-effects

## PROPANTHELINE BROMIDE

**Indications** adult enuresis

**Cautions** see notes above; ulcerative colitis, pregnancy (Appendix 4) and breast-feeding (Appendix 5)

**Contra-indications** see notes above

**Side-effects** see notes above; also facial flushing

**Dose**

- Initially 15 mg 3 times daily at least one hour before food and 30 mg at bedtime, subsequently adjusted according to response (max. 120 mg daily)

### Preparations

Section 1.2

## PROPIVERINE HYDROCHLORIDE

**Indications** urinary frequency, urgency and incontinence; neurogenic bladder instability

**Cautions** see notes above

**Contra-indications** see notes above; pregnancy (Appendix 4) and breast-feeding (Appendix 5)

**Side-effects** see notes above

**Dose**

- 15 mg 1–3 times daily, increased if necessary to max. 15 mg 4 times daily; CHILD not recommended

**Detrunorm®** (Amdipharm) PoM

Tablets, pink, s/c, propiverine hydrochloride 15 mg, net price 56-tab pack = £24.45. Label: 3

## SOLIFENACIN SUCCINATE

**Indications** urinary frequency, urgency and urge incontinence

**Cautions** see notes above; neurogenic bladder disorder; pregnancy (Appendix 4)

**Contra-indications** see notes above; haemodialysis; breast-feeding (Appendix 5)

**Side-effects** see notes above; gastro-oesophageal reflux, altered taste; fatigue; oedema

**Dose**

- 5 mg daily, increased if necessary to 10 mg once daily; CHILD not recommended

Note Max. 5 mg daily with concomitant itraconazole, ketoconazole, nelfinavir or ritonavir

**Vesicare®** (Astellas) ▼ PoM

Tablets, f/c, solifenacin succinate 5 mg (yellow), net price 30-tab pack = £27.62; 10 mg (pink), 30-tab pack = £35.91. Label: 3

## TOLTERODINE TARTRATE

**Indications** urinary frequency, urgency and incontinence

**Cautions** see notes above

**Contra-indications** see notes above; pregnancy (Appendix 4) and breast-feeding (Appendix 5)

**Side-effects** see notes above; also dyspepsia, fatigue, flatulence, chest pain, dry eyes, peripheral oedema, paraesthesia

**Dose**

- 2 mg twice daily; reduce to 1mg twice daily if necessary to minimise side-effects; CHILD not recommended

**Detrusitol®** (Pharmacia) PoM

Tablets, f/c, tolterodine tartrate 1 mg, net price 56-tab pack = £29.03; 2 mg, 56-tab pack = £30.56

### Modified release

**Detrusitol® XL** (Pharmacia) PoM

Capsules, blue, m/r, tolterodine tartrate 4 mg, net price 28-cap pack = £29.03. Label: 25

Dose 4 mg once daily (dose form not appropriate for hepatic and renal impairment)

## TROSPIUM CHLORIDE

**Indications** urinary frequency, urgency and incontinence

**Cautions** see notes above; pregnancy (Appendix 4); breast-feeding (Appendix 5)

**Contra-indications** see notes above

**Side-effects** see notes above; also flatulence, chest pain, dyspnoea, rash and asthenia

**Dose**

- 20 mg twice daily before food; CHILD not recommended

**Regurin®** (Galen) PoM

Tablets, brown, f/c, trospium chloride 20 mg, net price 60-tab pack = £26.00. Label: 23

## Nocturnal enuresis

*Nocturnal enuresis* is a common occurrence in young children but persists in as many as 5% by 10 years of age. Treatment is not appropriate in children under 5 years and it is usually not needed in those aged under 7 years and in cases where the child and parents are not anxious about the bedwetting; however, children over 10 years usually require prompt treatment. An **enuresis alarm** should be first-line treatment for well-motivated children aged over 7 years because it may achieve a more sustained reduction of enuresis than use of drugs. Use of an alarm may be combined with drug therapy if either method alone is unsuccessful.

Drug therapy is not usually appropriate for children under 7 years of age; it can be used when alternative measures have failed, preferably on a short-term basis, to cover periods away from home for example. The possible side-effects of the various drugs should be borne in mind when they are prescribed.

**Desmopressin** (section 6.5.2), an analogue of vasopressin, is used for nocturnal enuresis; it is given intranasally or it may be given by mouth as tablets. Particular care is needed to avoid fluid overload and treatment should not be continued for longer than 3 months without stopping for a week for full re-assessment.

Tricyclics (section 4.3.1) such as **amitriptyline**, **imipramine**, and less often **nortriptyline** are also used but behaviour disturbances may occur and relapse is common after withdrawal. Treatment should not normally exceed 3 months unless a full physical examination is given and the child is fully re-assessed; toxicity following overdosage with tricyclics is of particular concern.

## 7.4.3 Drugs used in urological pain

The acute pain of *ureteric colic* may be relieved with **pethidine** (section 4.7.2). **Diclofenac** by injection or as suppositories (section10.1.1) is also effective and compares favourably with pethidine; other non-steroidal anti-inflammatory drugs are occasionally given by injection.

**Lidocaine (lignocaine) gel** is a useful topical application in *urethral pain* or to relieve the discomfort of catheterisation (section 15.2).

### Alkalinisation of urine

*Alkalinisation* of urine may be undertaken with **potassium citrate**. The alkalinising action may relieve the discomfort of *cystitis* caused by lower urinary tract infections. **Sodium bicarbonate** is used as a urinary alkalinising agent in some metabolic and renal disorders (section 9.2.1.3).

#### POTASSIUM CITRATE

**Indications** relief of discomfort in mild urinary-tract infections; alkalinisation of urine

**Cautions** renal impairment, cardiac disease; elderly; **interactions**: Appendix 1 (potassium salts)

**Side-effects** hyperkalaemia on prolonged high dosage, mild diuresis

**Potassium Citrate Mixture BP (Potassium Citrate Oral Solution)**

Oral solution, potassium citrate 30%, citric acid monohydrate 5% in a suitable vehicle with a lemon flavour. Extemporaneous preparations should be recently prepared according to the following formula: potassium citrate 3 g, citric acid monohydrate 500 mg, syrup 2.5 mL, quillaia tincture 0.1 mL, lemon spirit 0.05 mL, double-strength chloroform water 3 mL, water to 10 mL. Contains about 28 mmol $K^+$/10 mL. Label: 27

Dose 10 mL 3 times daily well diluted with water

Note Concentrates for preparation of Potassium Citrate Mixture BP are available from Hillcross

Proprietary brands of potassium citrate on sale to the public for the relief of discomfort in mild urinary-tract infections include *Cystopurin®* and *Effercitrate®*

#### SODIUM BICARBONATE

**Indications** relief of discomfort in mild urinary-tract infections; alkalinisation of urine

**Cautions** hepatic impairment (Appendix 2); renal impairment (Appendix 3), cardiac disease, pregnancy; patients on sodium-restricted diet; elderly; avoid prolonged use; **interactions:** Appendix 1 (antacids)

**Side-effects** belching, alkalosis on prolonged use

**Dose**

- 3 g in water every 2 hours until urinary pH exceeds 7; maintenance of alkaline urine 5–10 g daily

**Preparations**

Section 9.2.1.3

#### SODIUM CITRATE

**Indications** relief of discomfort in mild urinary-tract infections

**Cautions** renal impairment, cardiac disease, hypertension, pregnancy, patients on a sodium-restricted diet; elderly

**Side-effects** mild diuresis

Note Proprietary brands of sodium citrate on sale to the public for the relief of discomfort in mild urinary-tract infections include *Boots Cystitis Relief Sachets* and *Tablets*, *Canesten® Oasis* and *Cymalon®*.

### Acidification of urine

*Urine acidification* is difficult; it is very occasionally used in the management of recurrent urinary-tract infections and to prevent renal stone formation, especially in patients with paraplegia or with a neurogenic bladder. Methenamine (section 5.1.13) requires acid urine for its antimicrobial activity.

**Ammonium chloride** may be used for urinary acidification but tolerance can develop rapidly. Vomiting and, with large doses, hypokalaemia and acidosis can also occur. Ammonium chloride oral solution needs to be prepared extemporaneously and may not be readily available. **Ascorbic acid** is less suitable for urine acidification because it is not always reliable and high doses, which can lead to renal stones in those with hyperoxaluria, are required.

For pH-modifying solutions for the maintenance of indwelling urinary catheters, see section 7.4.4.

### Other preparations for urinary disorders

A terpene mixture (*Rowatinex®*) is claimed to be of benefit in *urolithiasis* for the expulsion of calculi.

**Rowatinex®** (Rowa) PoM

Capsules, yellow, e/c, anethol 4 mg, borneol 10 mg, camphene 15 mg, cineole 3 mg, fenchone 4 mg, pinene 31 mg. Net price 50 = £7.35. Label: 25

Dose 1–2 capsules 3–4 times daily before food; CHILD not recommended

## 7.4.4 Bladder instillations and urological surgery

**Bladder infection** Various solutions are available as irrigations or washouts.

Aqueous **chlorhexidine** (section 13.11.2) may be used in the management of common infections of the bladder but it is ineffective against most *Pseudomonas* spp. Solutions containing chlorhexidine 1 in 5000 (0.02%) are used but they may irritate the mucosa and cause burning and haematuria (in which case they should be discontinued); sterile **sodium chloride solution 0.9%** (physiological saline) is usually adequate and is preferred as a mechanical irrigant.

Continuous bladder irrigation with **amphotericin** 50 micrograms/mL (section 5.2) may be of value in mycotic infections.

**Dissolution of blood clots** Clot retention is usually treated by irrigation with sterile **sodium chloride solution 0.9%** but sterile **sodium citrate solution for bladder irrigation 3%** may also be helpful. **Streptokinase-streptodornase** (*Varidase Topical®*, section 13.11.7) is an alternative.

**Bladder cancer** Bladder instillations of **doxorubicin** (section 8.1.2), **mitomycin** (section 8.1.2), and **thiotepa** (section 8.1.1) are used for recurrent superficial bladder tumours. Such instillations reduce systemic side-effects; adverse effects on the bladder (e.g. micturition disorders and reduction in bladder capacity) may occur.

Instillation of **epirubicin** (section 8.1.2) is used for treatment and prophylaxis of certain forms of superficial bladder cancer; instillation of **doxorubicin** (section 8.1.2) is also used for some papillary tumours.

Instillation of **BCG** (Bacillus Calmette-Guérin), a live attenuated strain derived from *Mycobacterium bovis* (section 8.2.4), is licensed for the treatment of primary or recurrent bladder carcinoma *in-situ* and for the prevention of recurrence following transurethral resection.

**Interstitial cystitis** **Dimethyl sulfoxide** (dimethyl sulphoxide) may be used for symptomatic relief in patients with interstitial cystitis (Hunner's ulcer). 50 mL of a 50% solution (*Rimso-50®*—available on named-patient basis from Britannia) is instilled into the bladder, retained for 15 minutes, and voided by the patient. Treatment is repeated at intervals of 2 weeks. Bladder spasm and hypersensitivity reactions may occur and long-term use requires ophthalmic, renal, and hepatic assessment at intervals of 6 months.

### SODIUM CITRATE

**Indications** bladder washouts, see notes above

**Sterile Sodium Citrate Solution for Bladder Irrigation**
sodium citrate 3%, dilute hydrochloric acid 0.2%, in purified water, freshly boiled and cooled, and sterilised

## Urological surgery

There is a high risk of fluid absorption from the irrigant used in endoscopic surgery within the urinary tract; if this occurs in excess, hypervolaemia, haemolysis, and renal failure may result. **Glycine irrigation solution 1.5%** is the irrigant of choice for transurethral resection of the prostate gland and bladder tumours; **sterile sodium chloride solution 0.9%** (physiological saline) is used for percutaneous renal surgery.

### GLYCINE

**Indications** bladder irrigation during urological surgery; see notes above
**Cautions** see notes above
**Side-effects** see notes above

**Glycine Irrigation Solution** (Non-proprietary)
Irrigation solution, glycine 1.5% in water for injections

## Maintenance of indwelling urinary catheters

The deposition which occurs in catheterised patients is usually chiefly composed of phosphate and to minimise this the catheter (if latex) should be changed at least as often as every 6 weeks. If the catheter is to be left for longer periods a silicone catheter should be used together with the appropriate use of catheter maintenance solutions. Repeated blockage usually indicates that the catheter needs to be changed.

### CATHETER PATENCY SOLUTIONS

**Chlorhexidine 0.02%**
Brands include *Uriflex C®*, 100-mL sachet = £2.40; *Uro-Tainer Chlorhexidine®*, 100-mL sachet = £2.60

**Sodium chloride 0.9%**
Brands include *OptiFlo S®*, 50- and 100-mL sachets = £3.10; *Uriflex S®*, 100-mL sachet = £2.40; *Uriflex SP®*, with integral drug additive port, 100-mL sachet = £2.40; *Uro-Tainer Sodium Chloride®*, 50- and 100-mL sachets = £2.99; *Uro-Tainer M®*, with integral drug additive port, 50- and 100-mL sachets = £2.90

**Solution G**
Citric acid 3.23%, magnesium oxide 0.38%, sodium bicarbonate 0.7%, disodium edetate 0.01%. Brands include *OptiFlo G®*, 50- and 100-mL sachets = £3.29; *Uriflex G®*, 100-mL sachet = £2.40; *Uro-Tainer® Twin Suby G*, 2 × 30-mL = £4.10

**Solution R**
Citric acid 6%, gluconolactone 0.6%, magnesium carbonate 2.8%, disodium edetate 0.01%. Brands include *OptiFlo R®*, 50- and 100-mL sachets = £3.29; *Uriflex R®*, 100-mL sachet = £2.40; *Uro-Tainer® Twin Solutio R*, 2 × 30-mL = £4.10

## 7.4.5 Drugs for erectile dysfunction

Reasons for failure to produce a satisfactory erection include *psychogenic, vascular, neurogenic,* and *endocrine abnormalities*; impotence can also be drug-induced. Intracavernosal injection or urethral application of vasoactive drugs under careful medical supervision is used for both diagnostic and therapeutic purposes.

Erectile disorders may also be treated with drugs given by mouth which increase the blood flow to the penis. Drugs should be used with caution if the penis is deformed (e.g. in angulation, cavernosal fibrosis, and Peyronie's disease).

**Priapism** If priapism occurs with alprostadil, treatment should not be delayed more than 6 hours and is as follows:

Initial therapy by penile aspiration—using aseptic technique a 19–21 gauge butterfly needle inserted into the corpus cavernosum and 20–50 mL of blood aspirated; if necessary the procedure may be repeated on the opposite side.

If initial aspiration is unsuccessful a second 19-21 gauge butterfly needle can be inserted into the opposite corpus cavernosum and sterile physiological saline introduced through the first needle and drained through the second.

If aspiration and lavage of corpora are unsuccessful, *cautious* intracavernosal injection of a sympathomimetic (section 2.7.2) with action on alpha-adrenergic receptors, continuously monitoring blood pressure and pulse (*extreme caution:* coronary heart disease, hypertension, cerebral ischaemia or if taking antidepressant) as follows:

- intracavernosal injections of phenylephrine 100–200 micrograms (0.5–1 mL of a 200 microgram/mL solution) every 5–10 minutes; max. total dose 1 mg [unlicensed indication] [*important:* if suitable strength of phenylephrine injection not available may be specially prepared by diluting 0.1 mL of the phenylephrine 1% (10 mg/mL) injection (section 2.7.2) to 5 mL with sodium chloride 0.9%];
  *alternatively*
- intracavernosal injections of adrenaline 10–20 micrograms (0.5–1mL of a 20 microgram/mL solution) every 5–10 minutes; max. total dose 100 micrograms [unlicensed indication] [*important:* if suitable strength of adrenaline not available may be specially prepared by diluting 0.1 mL of the adrenaline 1 in 1000 (1 mg/mL, section 3.4.3) injection to 5 mL with sodium chloride 0.9%];
  *alternatively*
- intracavernosal injection of metaraminol (*caution: has been associated with fatal hypertensive crises*); metaraminol 1 mg (0.1 mL of 10 mg/mL metaraminol injection, section 2.7.2) is diluted to 50 mL with sodium chloride injection 0.9% and given carefully by slow injection into the corpora in 5-mL injections every 15 minutes [unlicensed indication].

If necessary the sympathomimetic injections can be followed by further aspiration of blood through the same butterfly needle.

If sympathomimetics unsuccessful, urgent surgical referral for management (possibly including shunt procedure).

**Prescribing on the NHS** Drug treatments for erectile dysfunction may only be prescribed on the NHS under certain circumstances (see individual preparations). The Department of Health (England) has recommended that treatment should also be available from specialist services (commissioned by Health Authorities and Primary Care Groups, and operating under local agreement) when the condition is causing severe distress; specialist centres should use form FP10(HP) or form HBP in Scotland or form WP10HP in Wales and endorse them 'SLS' if the treatment is to be dispensed in the community. The following criteria should be considered when assessing distress:

- significant disruption to normal social and occupational activities;
- a marked effect on mood, behaviour, social and environmental awareness;
- a marked effect on interpersonal relationships.

## Alprostadil

**Alprostadil** (prostaglandin $E_1$) is given by intracavernosal injection or intraurethral application for the management of erectile dysfunction (after exclusion of treatable medical causes); it is also used as a diagnostic test.

### ALPROSTADIL

**Indications** erectile dysfunction (including aid to diagnosis); neonatal congenital heart defects (section 7.1.1.1)

**Cautions** priapism—patients should be instructed to report any erection lasting 4 hours or longer—for management, see section 7.4.5; anatomical deformations of penis (painful erection more likely)—follow up regularly to detect signs of penile fibrosis (consider discontinuation if angulation, cavernosal fibrosis or Peyronie's disease develop); **interactions:** Appendix 1 (prostaglandins)

**Contra-indications** predisposition to prolonged erection (as in sickle cell anaemia, multiple myeloma or leukaemia); not for use with other agents for erectile dysfunction, in patients with penile implants or when sexual activity medically inadvisable; urethral application also contra-indicated in urethral stricture, severe hypospadia, severe curvature, balanitis, urethritis

**Side-effects** penile pain, priapism (see section 7.4.5 and under Cautions); reactions at injection site include haematoma, haemosiderin deposits, penile rash, penile oedema, penile fibrosis, haemorrhage, inflammation; other local reactions include urethral burning and bleeding, penile warmth, numbness, penile or urinary-tract infection, irritation, sensitivity, phimosis, pruritus, erythema, venous leak, abnormal ejaculation; systemic effects reported include testicular pain and swelling, scrotal disorders, changes in micturition (including haematuria), nausea, dry mouth, fainting, hypotension (very rarely circulatory collapse) or hypertension, rapid pulse, vasodilatation, chest pain, supraventricular extrasystole, peripheral vascular disorder, dizziness, weakness, localised pain (buttocks, legs, genital, perineal, abdominal), headache, pelvic pain, back pain, influenza-like syndrome, swelling of the leg veins

**Dose**

- See under preparations below

#### Intracavernosal injection

[1]**Caverject**® (Pharmacia) PoM NHS

Injection, powder for reconstitution, alprostadil, net price 5-microgram vial = £7.73; 10-microgram vial = £9.24; 20-microgram vial = £11.94; 40-microgram vial = £21.58 (all with diluent-filled syringe, needles and swabs)

1. NHS except to treat erectile dysfunction in men who:

- have diabetes, multiple sclerosis, Parkinson's disease, poliomyelitis, prostate cancer, severe pelvic injury, single gene neurological disease, spina bifida or spinal cord injury;
- are receiving dialysis for renal failure;
- have had radical pelvic surgery, prostatectomy, or kidney transplant;
- were receiving *Caverject*®, *Erecnos*®, *MUSE*®, *Viagra*® or *Viridal*® for erectile dysfunction, at the expense of the NHS, on 14 September 1998;
- are suffering severe distress as a result of impotence (prescribed in specialist centres only, see notes above).

The prescription must be endorsed 'SLS'.

Caverject® Dual Chamber, double-chamber cartridges (containing alprostadil and diluent), net price 10-microgram cartridge (for doses 2.5–10 micrograms) = £7.35; 20-microgram cartridge (for doses 5–20 micrograms) = £9.50 (both with needles)

**Dose** by direct intracavernosal injection, erectile dysfunction, first dose 2.5 micrograms, second dose 5 micrograms (if some response to first dose) *or* 7.5 micrograms (if no response to first dose), increasing in steps of 5–10 micrograms to obtain dose suitable for producing erection not lasting more than 1 hour (neurological dysfunction, first dose 1.25 micrograms, second dose 2.5 micrograms, third dose 5 micrograms, increasing in steps of 5 micrograms to obtain suitable dose); if no response to dose then next higher dose can be given within 1 hour, if there is a response the next dose should not be given for at least 24 hours; usual range 5–20 micrograms; max. 60 micrograms (max. frequency of injection not more than once daily and not more than 3 times in any 1 week)

**Note** The first dose must be given by medically trained personnel; self-administration may only be undertaken after proper training

Aid to diagnosis, 20 micrograms as a single dose (where evidence of neurological dysfunction, initially 5 micrograms and max. 10 micrograms)—consult product literature for details

[1]**Viridal® Duo** (Schwarz) PoM NHS

Starter Pack (hosp. only), contents as for *Continuation Pack* below plus *Duoject* applicator, 10-microgram starter pack = £20.13, 20-microgram starter pack = £24.54, 40-microgram starter pack = £29.83; *Continuation Pack*, 2 double-chamber cartridges (containing alprostadil and diluent), 2 needles, swabs, 10-microgram continuation pack = £16.55, 20-microgram continuation pack = £21.39, 40-microgram continuation pack = £27.22; *Duoject®* applicator available free of charge from Schwarz

**Dose** by direct intracavernosal injection, erectile dysfunction, initially 2.5 micrograms (1.25 micrograms in neurogenic erectile dysfunction) increasing in steps of 2.5–5 micrograms to obtain dose suitable for producing erection not lasting more than 1 hour; usual range 10–20 micrograms; max. 40 micrograms (max. frequency of injection not more than 2–3 times per week with at least 24 hour interval between injections); erection lasting longer than 2 hours—re-titrate dose; patient should report to doctor erection lasting longer than 4 hours

**Note** The first dose must be given by medically trained personnel; self-administration may only be undertaken after proper training

### Urethral application

**Counselling** If partner pregnant barrier contraception should be used

[1]**MUSE®** (Meda) PoM NHS

Urethral application, alprostadil, net price 125-microgram single-use applicator = £9.89, 250-microgram single-use applicator = £10.76, 500-microgram single-use applicator = £10.76, 1-mg single-use applicator = £11.01 (all strengths also available in packs of 6 applicators)

**Condoms** no evidence of harm to latex condoms and diaphragms

**Dose** by direct urethral application, erectile dysfunction, initially 250 micrograms adjusted according to response (usual range 0.125–1 mg); max. 2 doses in 24 hours and 7 doses in 7 days)

**Note** The first dose must be given by medically trained personnel; self-administration may only be undertaken after proper training

Aid to diagnosis, 500 micrograms as a single dose

## Apomorphine

**Apomorphine** is licensed for the treatment of erectile dysfunction; it is given as sublingual tablets. Compared to subcutaneous injection, absorption from the sublingual site is limited.

### APOMORPHINE HYDROCHLORIDE

**Indications** erectile dysfunction; Parkinson's disease (section 4.9.1)

**Cautions** hepatic impairment (Appendix 2), renal impairment (Appendix 3); uncontrolled hypertension, hypotension; elderly; anatomical deformation of penis (e.g. angulation, cavernosal fibrosis, Peyronie's disease); not recommended for use in combination with other treatments for erectile dysfunction; **interactions:** Appendix 1 (apomorphine)

**Driving** May impair performance of skilled tasks (e.g. driving)

**Contra-indications** recent myocardial infarction; severe unstable angina, severe heart failure or hypotension; conditions where sexual activity is medically inadvisable

**Side-effects** nausea, dyspepsia, headache, dizziness, yawning, drowsiness, rhinitis, pharyngitis, cough, flushing, taste disturbance, sweating; vasovagal syndrome; less frequently syncope, stomatitis, mouth ulcers; rarely hypersensitivity reactions including angioedema

**Dose**

- By sublingual administration, initially 2 mg approx. 20 minutes before sexual activity, subsequent doses may be increased to 3 mg if necessary; minimum of 8 hours between doses

[1]**Uprima®** (Abbott) PoM NHS

Sublingual tablets, both red, apomorphine hydrochloride 2 mg, net price 2-tab pack = £7.47; 3 mg, 4-tab pack = £14.94. Counselling, driving

## Phosphodiesterase type-5 inhibitors

**Sildenafil**, **tadalafil** and **vardenafil** are phosphodiesterase type-5 inhibitors licensed for the treatment of erectile dysfunction; they are not recommended for use with other treatments for erectile dysfunction. The patient should be assessed appropriately before prescribing sildenafil, tadalafil or vardenafil. Since these drugs are given by mouth there is a potential for drug interactions.

**Cautions** Sildenafil, tadalafil and vardenafil should be used with caution in cardiovascular disease, anatomical deformation of the penis (e.g. angulation, cavernosal fibrosis, Peyronie's disease), and in those with a predis-

1. NHS except to treat erectile dysfunction in men who:

- have diabetes, multiple sclerosis, Parkinson's disease, poliomyelitis, prostate cancer, severe pelvic injury, single gene neurological disease, spina bifida or spinal cord injury;
- are receiving dialysis for renal failure;
- have had radical pelvic surgery, prostatectomy, or kidney transplant;
- were receiving *Caverject®*, *Erecnos®*, *MUSE®*, *Viagra®* or *Viridal®* for erectile dysfunction, at the expense of the NHS, on 14 September 1998;
- are suffering severe distress as a result of impotence (prescribed in specialist centres only, see notes above).

The prescription must be endorsed 'SLS'.

position to prolonged erection (e.g. in sickle-cell disease, multiple myeloma, or leukaemia).

**Contra-indications** Sildenafil, tadalafil and vardenafil are contra-indicated in patients receiving nitrates, in patients in whom vasodilation or sexual activity are inadvisable, or in patients with a previous history of non-arteritic anterior ischaemic optic neuropathy. In the absence of information, manufacturers contra-indicate these drugs in hypotension, recent stroke, unstable angina, and myocardial infarction.

**Side-effects** The side-effects of sildenafil, tadalafil and vardenafil include dyspepsia, vomiting, headache, flushing, dizziness, myalgia, visual disturbances (non-arteritic anterior ischaemic optic neuropathy has been reported), raised intra-ocular pressure, and nasal congestion. Hypersensitivity reactions (including rash), priapism, and painful red eyes have been reported.



## SILDENAFIL

**Indications** erectile dysfunction

**Cautions** see notes above; also hepatic impairment (Appendix 2—avoid if severe); renal impairment (Appendix 3); bleeding disorders or active peptic ulceration; **interactions:** Appendix 1 (sildenafil)

**Contra-indications** see notes above; also hereditary degenerative retinal disorders

**Side-effects** see notes above; also serious cardiovascular events reported

**Dose**

- ADULT over 18 years initially 50 mg approx. 1 hour before sexual activity, subsequent doses adjusted according to response to 25–100 mg as a single dose as needed; max. 1 dose in 24 hours (max. single dose 100 mg)

  Note Onset of effect may be delayed if taken with food

[1]**Viagra®** (Pfizer) PoM NHS

Tablets, all blue, f/c, sildenafil (as citrate), 25 mg, net price 4-tab pack = £16.59, 8-tab pack = £33.19; 50 mg, 4-tab pack = £19.34, 8-tab pack = £38.67; 100 mg, 4-tab pack = £23.50, 8-tab pack = £46.99

## TADALAFIL

**Indications** erectile dysfunction

**Cautions** see notes above; also hepatic impairment (Appendix 2); renal impairment (Appendix 3); **interactions:** Appendix 1 (tadalafil)

**Contra-indications** see notes above; also moderate heart failure, uncontrolled arrhythmias, uncontrolled hypertension

**Side-effects** see notes above; also back pain

**Dose**

- Initially 10 mg at least 30 minutes before sexual activity, subsequent doses adjusted according to response to 20 mg as a single dose; max. 1 dose in 24 hours (but daily use not recommended)

  Note Effect may persist for longer than 24 hours

[1]**Cialis®** (Lilly) ▼ PoM NHS

Tablets, f/c, tadalafil 10 mg (light yellow), net price 4-tab pack = £23.40; 20 mg (yellow), 4-tab pack = £23.40; 8-tab pack = £46.79

## VARDENAFIL

**Indications** erectile dysfunction

**Cautions** see notes above; also hepatic impairment (Appendix 2—avoid if severe); renal impairment (Appendix 3); bleeding disorders or active peptic ulceration; susceptibility to prolongation of QT interval (including concomitant use of drugs which prolong QT interval); **interactions:** Appendix 1 (vardenafil)

**Contra-indications** see notes above; also hereditary degenerative retinal disorders

**Side-effects** see notes above; also *less commonly* drowsiness, hypotension, hypertension, tachycardia, palpitation, epistaxis, dyspnoea, back pain, increased lacrimation, and facial oedema; *rarely* myocardial ischaemia, anxiety, hypertonia, angina, and laryngeal oedema

**Dose**

- Initially 10 mg (ELDERLY 5 mg) approx. 25–60 minutes before sexual activity, subsequent doses adjusted according to response up to max. 20 mg as a single dose (max. 5 mg if concomitant stable alpha-blocker therapy); max. 1 dose in 24 hours

  Note Onset of effect may be delayed if taken with high-fat meal

[1]**Levitra®** (Bayer) ▼ PoM NHS

Tablets, all orange, f/c, vardenafil (as hydrochloride trihydrate) 5 mg, net price 4-tab pack = £16.58, 8-tab pack = £33.19; 10 mg, 4-tab pack = £19.34, 8-tab pack = £38.67; 20 mg, 4-tab pack = £23.50, 8-tab pack = £46.99

## Papaverine and phentolamine

Although not licensed the smooth muscle relaxant **papaverine** has also been given by intracavernosal injection for erectile dysfunction. Patients with neurological or psychogenic impotence are more sensitive to the effect of papaverine than those with vascular abnormalities. **Phentolamine** is added if the response is inadequate [unlicensed indication].

Persistence of the erection for longer than 4 hours is an emergency, see advice in section 7.4.5.

1. NHS except to treat erectile dysfunction in men who:

- have diabetes, multiple sclerosis, Parkinson's disease, poliomyelitis, prostate cancer, severe pelvic injury, single gene neurological disease, spina bifida or spinal cord injury;
- are receiving dialysis for renal failure;
- have had radical pelvic surgery, prostatectomy, or kidney transplant;
- were receiving *Caverject®*, *Erecnos®*, *MUSE®*, *Viagra®* or *Viridal®* for erectile dysfunction, at the expense of the NHS, on 14 September 1998;
- are suffering severe distress as a result of impotence (prescribed in specialist centres only, see notes above).

The prescription must be endorsed 'SLS'.

# 8 Malignant disease and immunosuppression


| | | |
|---|---|---|
| **8.1** | **Cytotoxic drugs** | **427** |
| **8.1.1** | Alkylating drugs | 430 |
| **8.1.2** | Cytotoxic antibiotics | 432 |
| **8.1.3** | Antimetabolites | 435 |
| **8.1.4** | Vinca alkaloids and etoposide | 438 |
| **8.1.5** | Other antineoplastic drugs | 439 |
| **8.2** | **Drugs affecting the immune response** | **447** |
| **8.2.1** | Antiproliferative immunosuppressants | 447 |
| **8.2.2** | Corticosteroids and other immunosuppressants | 448 |
| **8.2.3** | Rituximab and alemtuzumab | 451 |
| **8.2.4** | Other immunomodulating drugs | 452 |
| **8.3** | **Sex hormones and hormone antagonists in malignant disease** | **455** |
| **8.3.1** | Oestrogens | 455 |
| **8.3.2** | Progestogens | 455 |
| **8.3.3** | Androgens | 456 |
| **8.3.4** | Hormone antagonists | 456 |
| **8.3.4.1** | Breast cancer | 456 |
| **8.3.4.2** | Prostate cancer and gonadorelin analogues | 458 |
| **8.3.4.3** | Somatostatin analogues | 461 |


## 8.1 Cytotoxic drugs


**8.1.1** Alkylating drugs
**8.1.2** Cytotoxic antibiotics
**8.1.3** Antimetabolites
**8.1.4** Vinca alkaloids and etoposide
**8.1.5** Other antineoplastic drugs


The chemotherapy of cancer is complex and should be confined to specialists in oncology. Cytotoxic drugs have both anti-cancer activity and the potential to damage normal tissue. Chemotherapy may be given with a curative intent or it may aim to prolong life or to palliate symptoms. In an increasing number of cases chemotherapy may be combined with radiotherapy or surgery or both as either neoadjuvant treatment (initial chemotherapy aimed at shrinking the primary tumour, thereby rendering local therapy less destructive or more effective) or as adjuvant treatment (which follows definitive treatment of the primary disease, when the risk of sub-clinical metastatic disease is known to be high). All chemotherapy drugs cause side-effects and a balance has to be struck between likely benefit and acceptable toxicity.

**CRM guidelines on handling cytotoxic drugs:**

1. Trained personnel should reconstitute cytotoxics;
2. Reconstitution should be carried out in designated areas;
3. Protective clothing (including gloves) should be worn;
4. The eyes should be protected and means of first aid should be specified;
5. Pregnant staff should not handle cytotoxics;
6. Adequate care should be taken in the disposal of waste material, including syringes, containers, and absorbent material.

**Intrathecal chemotherapy**

A Health Service Circular (HSC 2003/010) provides guidance on the introduction of safe practice in NHS Trusts where intrathecal chemotherapy is administered. Support for training programmes is also available.

Copies, and further information may be obtained from:

Department of Health
PO Box 777
London SE1 6XH
Fax: 01623 724524

It is also available from the Department of Health website (www.dh.gov.uk)

Combinations of cytotoxic drugs are frequently more toxic than single drugs but have the advantage in certain tumours of enhanced response, reduced development of drug resistance and increased survival. However for some tumours, single-agent chemotherapy remains the treatment of choice.

> Most cytotoxic drugs are teratogenic and all may cause life-threatening toxicity; administration should, where possible, be confined to those experienced in their use.
> Because of the complexity of dosage regimens in the treatment of malignant disease, dose statements have been omitted from some of the drug entries in this chapter. *In all cases detailed specialist literature should be consulted.*
> Prescriptions should **not** be repeated except on the instructions of a specialist.

Cytotoxic drugs fall into a number of classes, each with characteristic antitumour activity, sites of action, and toxicity. A knowledge of sites of metabolism and excretion is important because impaired drug handling as a result of disease is not uncommon and may result in enhanced toxicity.



## Side-effects of cytotoxic drugs

Side-effects common to most cytotoxic drugs are discussed below whilst side-effects characteristic of a particular drug or class of drugs (e.g. neurotoxicity with vinca alkaloids) are mentioned in the appropriate sections. Manufacturers' product literature should be consulted for full details of side-effects associated with individual drugs.

**Extravasation of intravenous drugs** A number of cytotoxic drugs will cause severe local tissue necrosis if leakage into the extravascular compartment occurs. To reduce the risk of extravasation injury it is recommended that cytotoxic drugs are administered by appropriately trained staff. For information on the prevention and management of extravasation injury see section 10.3.

**Oral mucositis** A sore mouth is a common complication of cancer chemotherapy; it is most often associated with fluorouracil, methotrexate, and the anthracyclines. It is best to prevent the complication. Good mouth care (rinsing the mouth frequently and effective brushing of the teeth with a soft brush 2–3 times daily) is probably beneficial. For fluorouracil, sucking ice chips during short infusions of the drug is also helpful.

Once a sore mouth has developed, treatment is much less effective. Saline mouthwashes should be used but there is no good evidence to support the use of antiseptic or anti-inflammatory mouthwashes. In general, mucositis is self-limiting but with poor oral hygiene it can be a focus for blood-borne infection.

**Tumour lysis syndrome** Tumour lysis syndrome can occur as a result of massive cell breakdown following treatment of cancer sensitive to the chemotherapy. Features include hyperkalaemia, hyperuricaemia (see below), and hyperphosphataemia with hypocalcaemia; renal damage and arrhythmias can follow.

**Hyperuricaemia** Hyperuricaemia, which may be present in high-grade lymphoma and leukaemia, can be markedly worsened by chemotherapy and is associated with acute renal failure. Allopurinol (section 10.1.4) should be started 24 hours before treating such tumours and patients should be adequately hydrated. The dose of mercaptopurine or azathioprine should be reduced if allopurinol needs to be given concomitantly (see Appendix 1).

Rasburicase (section 10.1.4), a recombinant urate oxidase, is licensed for hyperuricaemia in patients with haematological malignancy, for details, see p. 525. It rapidly reduces plasma uric acid and may be of particular value in reducing complications following treatment of leukaemias or bulky lymphomas.

**Nausea and vomiting** Nausea and vomiting cause considerable distress to many patients who receive chemotherapy and, to a lesser extent, abdominal radiotherapy; it may lead to refusal of further treatment. Symptoms may be acute (occurring within 24 hours of treatment), delayed (first occurring more than 24 hours after treatment) or anticipatory (occurring prior to subsequent doses). Delayed and anticipatory symptoms are more difficult to control than acute symptoms and require different management.

Patients vary in their susceptibility to drug-induced nausea and vomiting; those affected more often include women, patients under 50 years of age, anxious patients, and those who experience motion sickness. Susceptibility also increases with repeated exposure to the cytotoxic drug.

Drugs may be divided according to their emetogenic potential and some examples are given below, but the symptoms vary according to the dose, to other drugs administered and to individual susceptibility.

*Mildly emetogenic treatment*—fluorouracil, etoposide, methotrexate (less than 100 mg/m$^2$), the vinca alkaloids, and abdominal radiotherapy.

*Moderately emetogenic treatment*—doxorubicin, intermediate and low doses of cyclophosphamide, mitoxantrone (mitozantrone), and high doses of methotrexate (0.1–1.2 g/m$^2$).

*Highly emetogenic treatment*—cisplatin, dacarbazine, and high doses of cyclophosphamide.

**Prevention of acute symptoms**. For patients at *low risk of emesis*, pretreatment with domperidone or, in adults over 20 years, with metoclopramide, continued for up to 24 hours after chemotherapy, is often effective (section 4.6). If metoclopramide or domperidone are not sufficiently effective, additional drugs such as dexamethasone (6–10 mg by mouth) or lorazepam (1–2 mg by mouth) may be used.

For patients at *high risk of emesis* or when other treatment is inadequate, a specific ($5HT_3$) serotonin antagonist (section 4.6), usually given by mouth, is often highly effective, particularly when used with dexamethasone; adding the neurokinin receptor antagonist, aprepitant (section 4.6) can improve control of cisplatin-related nausea and vomiting.

**Prevention of delayed symptoms**. Dexamethasone, given by mouth, is the drug of choice for preventing delayed symptoms; it is used alone or with metoclopramide or prochlorperazine. The $5HT_3$ antagonists may be less effective for delayed symptoms.

**Prevention of anticipatory symptoms**. Good symptom control is the best way to prevent anticipatory symptoms. The addition of lorazepam to antiemetic therapy is helpful because of its amnesic, sedative and anxiolytic effects.

**Bone-marrow suppression** All cytotoxic drugs except vincristine and bleomycin cause bone-marrow depression. This commonly occurs 7 to 10 days after administration, but is delayed for certain drugs, such as carmustine, lomustine, and melphalan. Peripheral blood counts must be checked before each treatment, and doses should be reduced or therapy delayed if bone-marrow has not recovered.

Fever in a neutropenic patient (neutrophil count less than $1.0 \times 10^9$/litre) requires immediate broad-spectrum antibacterial therapy. Patients at low risk (those receiving chemotherapy for solid tumours, lymphoma or chronic leukaemia) can be treated with oral ciprofloxacin with or without co-amoxiclav (initially in hospital). All other patients should receive parenteral broad-spectrum antibacterial therapy. Appropriate bacteriological investigations should be conducted as soon as possible.

In selected patients, the duration and the severity of neutropenia can be reduced by the use of bone marrow growth factors (colony stimulating factors, section 9.1.6).

Symptomatic anaemia is usually treated with red blood cell transfusions. Epoetin administered subcutaneously is also effective but not widely used.

**Alopecia** Reversible hair loss is a common complication, although it varies in degree between drugs and individual patients. No pharmacological methods of preventing this are available.

**Reproductive function** Most cytotoxic drugs are teratogenic and should not be administered during pregnancy, especially during the first trimester.

Contraceptive advice should be offered where appropriate before cytotoxic therapy begins (and should cover the duration of contraception required after therapy has ended). Regimens that do not contain an alkylating drug may have less effect on fertility, but those with an alkylating drug carry the risk of causing permanent male sterility (there is no effect on potency). Pre-treatment counselling and consideration of sperm storage may be appropriate. Women are less severely affected, though the span of reproductive life may be shortened by the onset of a premature menopause. No increase in fetal abnormalities or abortion-rate has been recorded in patients who remain fertile after cytotoxic chemotherapy.

**Thromboembolism** Venous thromboembolism can be a complication of cancer itself, but chemotherapy can also increase the risk. Prophylaxis against thromboembolism may be considered for those receiving chemotherapy.

## Drugs for cytotoxic-induced side-effects

### Methotrexate-induced mucositis and myelosuppression

**Folinic acid** (given as calcium folinate) is used to counteract the folate-antagonist action of methotrexate and thus speed recovery from methotrexate-induced mucositis or myelosuppression. It is generally given 24 hours after the methotrexate, in a dose of 15 mg by mouth every 6 hours, for 2–8 doses (depending on the dose of methotrexate). It does not counteract the antibacterial activity of folate antagonists such as trimethoprim.

When folinic acid and fluorouracil are used together in metastatic colorectal cancer the response-rate improves compared to that with fluorouracil alone.

The calcium salt of **levofolinic acid**, a single isomer of folinic acid, is also used for rescue therapy following methotrexate administration and for use with fluorouracil for colorectal cancer. The dose of calcium levofolinate is generally half that of calcium folinate.

The disodium salt of folinic acid is also licensed for rescue therapy following methotrexate therapy and for use with fluorouracil for colorectal cancer.

### CALCIUM FOLINATE
(Calcium leucovorin)

**Indications** see notes above

**Cautions** avoid simultaneous administration of methotrexate; **not** indicated for pernicious anaemia or other megaloblastic anaemias due to vitamin $B_{12}$ deficiency; pregnancy (Appendix 4) and breast-feeding (Appendix 5); **interactions**: Appendix 1 (folates)
Important Intrathecal injection **contra-indicated**

**Side-effects** hypersensitivity reactions; rarely pyrexia after parenteral use

**Dose**

Note Doses expressed as folinic acid

- As an antidote to methotrexate (usually started 24 hours after the beginning of methotrexate infusion), usually up to 120 mg in divided doses over 12–24 hours by intramuscular *or* intravenous injection *or* by intravenous infusion, followed by 12–15 mg intramuscularly *or* 15 mg by mouth every 6 hours for the next 48–72 hours
- Suspected methotrexate overdosage, immediate administration of folinic acid at a rate not exceeding 160 mg/minute in a dose equal to (or higher than) the dose of methotrexate
- Adjunct to fluorouracil in colorectal cancer, consult product literature

**Calcium Folinate** (Non-proprietary) PoM

Tablets, scored, folinic acid (as calcium salt) 15 mg, net price 10-tab pack = £40.50, 30-tab pack = £85.74
Brands include *Refolinon®*
Note Not all strengths and pack sizes are available from all manufacturers

Injection, folinic acid (as calcium salt) 3 mg/mL, net price 1-mL amp = £2.28, 10-mL amp = £4.62; 7.5 mg/mL, net price 2-mL amp = £7.80; 10 mg/mL, net price 5-mL vial = £19.41, 10-mL vial = £35.09, 30-mL vial = £94.69, 35-mL vial = £90.98
Brands include *Lederfolin®*
Note Not all strengths and pack sizes are available from all manufacturers

Injection, powder for reconstitution, folinic acid (as calcium salt), net price 15-mg vial = £4.46; 30-mg vial = £8.36

### CALCIUM LEVOFOLINATE
(Calcium levoleucovorin)

**Indications** see notes above

**Cautions** see Calcium Folinate

**Side-effects** see Calcium Folinate

**Dose**

Note Doses expressed as levofolinic acid

- As an antidote to methotrexate (usually started 24 hours after the beginning of methotrexate infusion), usually 7.5 mg, by intramuscular injection, *or* by intravenous injection *or* by intravenous infusion every 6 hours for 10 doses
- Suspected methotrexate overdosage, immediate administration of levofolinic acid at a rate not exceeding 160 mg/minute in a dose which is at least 50% of the dose of methotrexate
- Adjunct to fluorouracil in colorectal cancer, consult product literature

**Isovorin®** (Wyeth) ▼ PoM

Injection, levofolinic acid (as calcium salt) 10 mg/mL, net price 2.5-mL vial = £12.09, 5-mL vial = £26.00, 17.5-mL vial = £84.63

## DISODIUM FOLINATE

**Indications** see notes above

**Cautions** see Calcium Folinate

**Side-effects** see Calcium Folinate

**Dose**

- As an antidote to methotrexate, see Calcium Folinate
- Adjunct to fluorouracil in colorectal cancer, consult product literature

**Sodiofolin®** (Medac) PoM

Injection, folinic acid (as disodium salt) 50 mg/mL, net price 2-mL vial = £35.09, 8-mL vial = £126.25, 18-mL vial = £284.07

### Urothelial toxicity

Haemorrhagic cystitis is a common manifestation of urothelial toxicity which occurs with the oxazaphosphorines, cyclophosphamide and ifosfamide; it is caused by the metabolite acrolein. **Mesna** reacts specifically with this metabolite in the urinary tract, preventing toxicity. Mesna is used routinely (preferably by mouth) in patients receiving ifosfamide, and in patients receiving cyclophosphamide by the intravenous route at a high dose (e.g. more than 2 g) or in those who experienced urothelial toxicity when given cyclophosphamide previously.

## MESNA

**Indications** see notes above

**Contra-indications** hypersensitivity to thiol-containing compounds

**Side-effects** nausea, vomiting, colic, diarrhoea, fatigue, headache, limb and joint pains, depression, irritability, rash, hypotension and tachycardia; rarely hypersensitivity reactions (more common in patients with auto-immune disorders)

**Dose**

Note Doses calculated according to oxazaphosphorine (cyclophosphamide or ifosfamide) treatment—for details consult product literature

- By mouth, dose is given 2 hours *before* oxazaphosphorine treatment and repeated 2 and 6 hours *after* treatment
- By intravenous injection, dose is given *with* oxazaphosphorine treatment and repeated 4 and 8 hours *after* treatment

**Uromitexan®** (Baxter) PoM

Tablets, f/c, mesna 400 mg, net price 10-tab pack = £21.10; 600 mg, 10-tab pack = £27.40

Injection, mesna 100 mg/mL. Net price 4-mL amp = £1.95; 10-mL amp = £4.38

Note For oral administration contents of ampoule are taken in a flavoured drink such as orange juice or cola which may be stored in a refrigerator for up to 24 hours in a sealed container

# 8.1.1 Alkylating drugs

Extensive experience is available with these drugs, which are among the most widely used in cancer chemotherapy. They act by damaging DNA, thus interfering with cell replication. In addition to the side-effects common to many cytotoxic drugs (section 8.1), there are two problems associated with prolonged usage. Firstly, gametogenesis is often severely affected (section 8.1). Secondly, prolonged use of these drugs, particularly when combined with extensive irradiation, is associated with a marked increase in the incidence of acute non-lymphocytic leukaemia.

**Cyclophosphamide** is widely used in the treatment of chronic lymphocytic leukaemia, the lymphomas, and solid tumours. It is given by mouth or intravenously and is inactive until metabolised by the liver. A urinary metabolite of cyclophosphamide, acrolein, may cause haemorrhagic cystitis; this is a rare but very serious complication. An increased fluid intake, for 24–48 hours after intravenous injection, will help avoid this complication. When high-dose therapy (e.g. more than 2 g intravenously) is used or when the patient is considered to be at high risk of cystitis (e.g. previous pelvic irradiation) mesna (given initially intravenously then by mouth) will also help prevent this—see under Urothelial toxicity (section 8.1).

**Ifosfamide** is related to cyclophosphamide and is given intravenously; mesna (section 8.1) is routinely given with it to reduce urothelial toxicity.

**Chlorambucil** is used to treat chronic lymphocytic leukaemia, non-Hodgkin's lymphoma, Hodgkin's disease, and Waldenstrom's macroglobulinaemia. It is given by mouth. Side-effects, apart from bone-marrow suppression, are uncommon. However, patients occasionally develop severe widespread rashes which can progress to Stevens-Johnson syndrome or to toxic epidermal necrolysis. If a rash occurs further chlorambucil is contra-indicated and cyclophosphamide is substituted.

**Melphalan** is licensed for the treatment of multiple myeloma, advanced ovarian adenocarcinoma, advanced breast cancer, childhood neuroblastoma, and polycythaemia vera. Melphalan is also licensed for regional arterial perfusion in localised malignant melanoma of the extremities and localised soft-tissue sarcoma of the extremities. Interstitial pneumonitis and life-threatening pulmonary fibrosis are associated with melphalan.

**Busulfan** (busulphan) is given by mouth to treat chronic myeloid leukaemia. Busulphan given intravenously, followed by cyclophosphamide, is also licensed as conditioning treatment before haematopoietic stem-cell transplantation in adults. Frequent blood tests are necessary because excessive myelosuppression may result in irreversible bone-marrow aplasia. Rarely, progressive pulmonary fibrosis is associated with busulfan. Skin hyperpigmentation is a common side-effect of oral therapy.

**Lomustine** is a lipid-soluble nitrosourea and is given by mouth. It is mainly used to treat Hodgkin's disease and certain solid tumours. Bone marrow toxicity is delayed, and the drug is therefore given at intervals of 4 to 6 weeks. Permanent bone marrow damage may occur with prolonged use. Nausea and vomiting are common and moderately severe.

**Carmustine** given intravenously has similar activity to lomustine; it is given to patients with multiple myeloma, non-Hodgkin's lymphomas, and brain tumours. Cumulative renal damage and delayed pulmonary fibrosis may occur with intravenous use. Carmustine implants are licensed for intralesional use in adults for the treatment of recurrent glioblastoma multiforme as an adjunct to surgery. Carmustine implants are also licensed for high-grade malignant glioma as adjunctive treatment to surgery and radiotherapy.

**Estramustine** is a combination of an oestrogen and chlormethine used predominantly in prostate cancer. It is given by mouth and has both an antimitotic effect and (by reducing testosterone concentration) a hormonal effect.

**Treosulfan** is given by mouth or intravenously and is used to treat ovarian cancer. Skin pigmentation is a common side-effect and allergic alveolitis, pulmonary fibrosis and haemorrhagic cystitis occur rarely.

**Thiotepa** is usually used as an intracavitary drug for the treatment of malignant effusions or bladder cancer (section 7.4.4). It is also occasionally used to treat breast cancer, but requires parenteral administration.

**Mitobronitol** is occasionally used to treat chronic myeloid leukaemia; it is available on a named-patient basis only (as *Myelobromol*®, Durbin).

## BUSULFAN
(Busulphan)

**Indications** see notes above

**Cautions** see section 8.1 and notes above; avoid in porphyria (section 9.8.2); **interactions:** Appendix 1 (busulfan)

**Contra-indications** pregnancy (Appendix 4); breast-feeding

**Side-effects** see section 8.1 and notes above

**Dose**

- By mouth, chronic myeloid leukaemia, induction of remission, 60 micrograms/kg to max. 4 mg daily; maintenance, 0.5–2 mg daily
- By intravenous infusion, consult product literature

**Busilvex®** (Fabre) ▼ PoM
Concentrate for intravenous infusion, busulfan 6 mg/mL, net price 10-mL vial = £201.25

**Myleran®** (GSK) PoM
Tablets, f/c, busulfan 2 mg, net price 25-tab pack = £5.20

## CARMUSTINE

**Indications** see notes above

**Cautions** see section 8.1 and notes above

**Contra-indications** pregnancy (Appendix 4), breast-feeding

**Side-effects** see section 8.1 and notes above; irritant to tissues

**BiCNU®** (Bristol-Myers Squibb) PoM
Injection, powder for reconstitution, carmustine. Net price 100-mg vial (with diluent) = £12.50

**Gliadel®** (Link) PoM
Implant, carmustine 7.7 mg, net price = £650.38

## CHLORAMBUCIL

**Indications** see notes above

**Cautions** see section 8.1 and notes above; hepatic impairment (Appendix 2); avoid in porphyria (section 9.8.2)

**Contra-indications** pregnancy (Appendix 4), breast-feeding

**Side-effects** see section 8.1 and notes above

**Dose**

- Hodgkin's disease, used alone, 200 micrograms/kg daily for 4–8 weeks
- Non-Hodgkin's lymphoma, used alone, initially 100–200 micrograms/kg daily for 4–8 weeks then dose reduced or given intermittently
- Chronic lymphocytic leukaemia, initially 150 micrograms/kg daily until leucocyte count sufficiently reduced; maintenance (started 4 weeks after end of first course) 100 micrograms/kg daily
- Waldenstrom's macroglobulinaemia, 6–12 mg daily until leucopenia occurs, then reduce to 2–8 mg daily

**Leukeran®** (GSK) PoM
Tablets, f/c, brown, chlorambucil 2 mg, net price 25-tab pack = £8.36

## CYCLOPHOSPHAMIDE

**Indications** see notes above; rheumatoid arthritis (section 10.1.3)

**Cautions** see section 8.1 and notes above; hepatic impairment (Appendix 2); renal impairment (Appendix 3); avoid in porphyria (section 9.8.2); **interactions:** Appendix 1 (cyclophosphamide)

**Contra-indications** pregnancy (Appendix 4), breast-feeding (Appendix 5)

**Side-effects** see section 8.1 and notes above

**Cyclophosphamide** (Non-proprietary) PoM
Tablets, s/c, cyclophosphamide (anhydrous) 50 mg, net price 20 = £2.12. Label: 27

Injection, powder for reconstitution, cyclophosphamide, net price 500-mg vial = £2.88; 1-g vial = £5.04

**Endoxana®** (Baxter) PoM
Tablets, s/c, cyclophosphamide 50 mg, net price 100-tab pack = £12.00. Label: 27

Injection, powder for reconstitution, cyclophosphamide. Net price 200-mg vial = £1.86; 500-mg vial = £3.25; 1-g vial = £5.67

## ESTRAMUSTINE PHOSPHATE

**Indications** prostate cancer

**Cautions** see section 8.1; hepatic impairment (Appendix 2); renal impairment (Appendix 3)

**Contra-indications** peptic ulceration, cardiac disease

**Side-effects** see section 8.1; also gynaecomastia, altered liver function, cardiovascular disorders (angina and rare reports of myocardial infarction)

**Dose**

- 0.14–1.4 g daily in divided doses (usual initial dose 560 mg daily)
  Counselling Each dose should be taken not less than 1 hour before or 2 hours after meals and should not be taken with dairy products

**Estracyt®** (Pharmacia) PoM
Capsules, estramustine phosphate 140 mg (as disodium salt). Net price 100-cap pack = £171.28. Label: 23, counselling, see above

## IFOSFAMIDE

**Indications** see notes above

**Cautions** see section 8.1 and notes above; renal impairment (Appendix 3); **interactions:** Appendix 1 (ifosfamide)

**Contra-indications** hepatic impairment; pregnancy (Appendix 4), breast-feeding

**Side-effects** see section 8.1 and notes above

**Mitoxana®** (Baxter) PoM
Injection, powder for reconstitution, ifosfamide. Net price 1-g vial = £24.57; 2-g vial = £45.49 (hosp. only)

## LOMUSTINE

**Indications** see notes above

**Cautions** see section 8.1 and notes above

**Side-effects** see section 8.1 and notes above

**Dose**

- Used alone, 120–130 mg/m$^2$ body-surface every 6–8 weeks

**Lomustine** (Medac) PoM
Capsules, blue/clear, lomustine 40 mg. Net price 20-cap pack = £344.51
Note The brand name *CCNU®* has been used for lomustine capsules

## MELPHALAN

**Indications** see notes above

**Cautions** see section 8.1 and notes above; renal impairment (Appendix 3); **interactions:** Appendix 1 (melphalan)

**Contra-indications** pregnancy (Appendix 4); breast-feeding

**Side-effects** see section 8.1 and notes above

**Dose**

- By mouth, multiple myeloma, dose may vary according to regimen; typical dose 150 micrograms/kg daily for 4 days, repeated every 6 weeks
  Ovarian adenocarcinoma, 200 micrograms/kg daily for 5 days, repeated every 4–8 weeks
  Advanced breast cancer, 150 micrograms/kg daily for 5 days, repeated every 6 weeks
  Polycythaemia vera, initially, 6–10 mg daily reduced after 5–7 days to 2–4 mg daily until satisfactory response then further reduce to 2–6 mg **per week**
- By intravenous injection *or* infusion and regional arterial perfusion, consult product literature

**Alkeran®** (GSK) PoM
Tablets, melphalan 2 mg, net price 25 = £11.46

Injection, powder for reconstitution, melphalan 50 mg (as hydrochloride). Net price 50-mg vial (with solvent-diluent) = £27.61

## THIOTEPA

**Indications** see notes above and section 7.4.4

**Cautions** see section 8.1; **interactions:** Appendix 1 (thiotepa)

**Contra-indications** pregnancy (Appendix 4); breast-feeding

**Side-effects** see section 8.1

**Thiotepa** (Goldshield) PoM
Injection, powder for reconstitution, thiotepa, net price 15-mg vial = £5.20

## TREOSULFAN

**Indications** see notes above

**Cautions** see section 8.1

**Contra-indications** pregnancy; breast-feeding

**Side-effects** see section 8.1 and notes above

**Dose**

- By mouth, courses of 1–2 g daily in 3–4 divided doses to provide total dose of 21–28 g over initial 8 weeks (with treatment-free intervals during this period—consult product literature)
- By intravenous injection *or* by intraperitoneal administration, consult product literature

**Treosulfan** (Medac) PoM
Capsules, treosulfan 250 mg. Net price 20 = £67.25 Label: 25

Injection, powder for reconstitution, treosulfan. Net price 1 g = £39.44; 5 g = £152.41 (both in infusion bottle with transfer needle)

# 8.1.2 Cytotoxic antibiotics

Drugs in this group are widely used. Many cytotoxic antibiotics act as radiomimetics and simultaneous use of radiotherapy should be **avoided** as it may result in markedly enhanced toxicity.

Daunorubicin, doxorubicin, epirubicin and idarubicin are anthracycline antibiotics. Mitoxantrone (mitozantrone) is an anthracycline derivative.

**Doxorubicin** is used to treat the acute leukaemias, lymphomas, and a variety of solid tumours. It is given by injection into a fast-running infusion, commonly at 21-day intervals. Extravasation can cause severe tissue necrosis. Doxorubicin is largely excreted by the biliary tract, and an elevated bilirubin concentration is an indication for reducing the dose. Supraventricular tachycardia related to drug administration is an uncommon complication. Higher cumulative doses are associated with cardiomyopathy and it is usual to limit total cumulative doses to 450 mg/m$^2$ because symptomatic and potentially fatal heart failure is common above this dose. Patients with cardiac disease, the elderly, and those who have received myocardial irradiation should be treated cautiously. Cardiac monitoring may assist in determining safe dosage. Some evidence suggests that weekly low-dose administration may be less cardiotoxic. Doxorubicin is also given by bladder instillation for the treatment of transitional cell carcinoma, papillary bladder tumours and carcinoma *in-situ*.

Liposomal formulations of doxorubicin for intravenous use are also available. They may reduce the incidence of cardiotoxicity and lower the potential for local necrosis, but infusion reactions, sometimes severe, may occur. Hand-foot syndrome (painful, macular reddening skin eruptions) occurs commonly with liposomal doxorubicin and may be dose limiting. It can occur after 2–3 treatment cycles and may be prevented by cooling hands and feet and avoiding socks, gloves, or tight-fitting footwear for 4–7 days after treatment.

The *Scottish Medicines Consortium* has advised (December 2003) that pegylated liposomal doxorubicin is **not** recommended for metastatic breast cancer.

> **NICE guidance (paclitaxel, pegylated liposomal doxorubicin and topotecan for second-line or subsequent treatment of advanced ovarian cancer)**
> See p. 443

**Epirubicin** is structurally related to doxorubicin and clinical trials suggest that it is as effective in the treatment of breast cancer. A maximum cumulative dose of 0.9–1 $g/m^2$ is recommended to help avoid cardiotoxicity. Like doxorubicin it is given intravenously and by bladder instillation.

**Idarubicin** has general properties similar to those of doxorubicin. It is given intravenously and it may also be given by mouth.

**Daunorubicin** also has general properties similar to those of doxorubicin. It should be given by intravenous infusion and is indicated for acute leukaemias. A liposomal formulation for intravenous use is licensed for AIDS-related Kaposi's sarcoma.

> **Use with trastuzumab**
> Concomitant use of anthracyclines with trastuzumab (section 8.1.5) is associated with cardiotoxicity; for details, see p. 446.

**Mitoxantrone** (**mitozantrone**) is structurally related to doxorubicin; it is used for metastatic breast cancer. Mitoxantrone is also licensed for use in the treatment of non-Hodgkin's lymphoma and adult non-lymphocytic leukaemia. It is given intravenously and is well tolerated but myelosuppression and dose-related cardiotoxicity occur; cardiac examinations are recommended after a cumulative dose of 160 $mg/m^2$.

**Bleomycin** is given intravenously or intramuscularly to treat metastatic germ cell cancer and, in some regimens, non-Hodgkin's lymphoma. It causes little bone-marrow suppression but dermatological toxicity is common and increased pigmentation particularly affecting the flexures and subcutaneous sclerotic plaques may occur. Mucositis is also relatively common and an association with Raynaud's phenomenon is reported. Hypersensitivity reactions manifest by chills and fevers commonly occur a few hours after drug administration and may be prevented by simultaneous administration of a corticosteroid, for example hydrocortisone intravenously. The principal problem associated with the use of bleomycin is progressive pulmonary fibrosis. This is dose-related, occurring more commonly at cumulative doses greater than 300 000 units (see Bleomycin, below) and in the elderly. Basal lung crepitations or suspicious chest X-ray changes are an indication to stop therapy with this drug. Patients who have received extensive treatment with bleomycin (e.g. cumulative dose more than 100 000 units—see Bleomycin below) may be at risk of developing respiratory failure if a general anaesthetic is given with high inspired oxygen concentrations. Anaesthetists should be warned of this.

**Dactinomycin** is principally used to treat paediatric cancers; it is given intravenously. Its side-effects are similar to those of doxorubicin, except that cardiac toxicity is not a problem.

**Mitomycin** is given intravenously to treat upper gastro-intestinal and breast cancers and by bladder instillation for superficial bladder tumours. It causes delayed bone-marrow toxicity and therefore it is usually administered at 6-weekly intervals. Prolonged use may result in permanent bone-marrow damage. It may also cause lung fibrosis and renal damage.

## BLEOMYCIN

**Indications** squamous cell carcinoma; see also notes above

**Cautions** see section 8.1 and notes above; renal impairment (Appendix 3); caution in handling—irritant to tissues

**Contra-indications** pregnancy (Appendix 4); breast-feeding

**Side-effects** see section 8.1 and notes above

**Bleomycin** (Non-proprietary) PoM
Injection, powder for reconstitution, bleomycin (as sulphate). Net price 15 000-unit vial = £15.56
**Note** To conform to the European Pharmacopoeia vials previously labelled as containing '15 units' of bleomycin are now labelled as containing 15 000 units. The amount of bleomycin in the vial has not changed.
Brands include *Bleo-Kyowa*®

## DACTINOMYCIN
(Actinomycin D)

**Indications** see notes above

**Cautions** see section 8.1 and notes above; caution in handling—irritant to tissues

**Contra-indications** pregnancy (Appendix 4); breast-feeding

**Side-effects** see section 8.1 and notes above

**Cosmegen Lyovac®** (MSD) PoM
Injection, powder for reconstitution, dactinomycin, net price 500-microgram vial = £1.50

## DAUNORUBICIN

**Indications** see notes above

**Cautions** see section 8.1 and notes above; hepatic impairment (Appendix 2), renal impairment (Appendix 3); caution in handling—irritant to tissues

**Contra-indications** pregnancy (Appendix 4); breast-feeding

**Side-effects** see section 8.1 and notes above

**Daunorubicin** (Non-proprietary) PoM
Injection, powder for reconstitution, daunorubicin (as hydrochloride), net price 20-mg vial = £39.26
**Note** The brand name *Cerubidin*® was formerly used.

**Lipid formulation**

**DaunoXome®** (Gilead) PoM

Concentrate for intravenous infusion, daunorubicin encapsulated in liposomes. For dilution before use. Net price 50-mg vial = £137.67

For advanced AIDS-related Kaposi's sarcoma

## DOXORUBICIN HYDROCHLORIDE

**Indications** see notes above and section 7.4.4

**Cautions** see section 8.1 and notes above; hepatic impairment (Appendix 2); caution in handling—irritant to tissues; **interactions:** Appendix 1 (doxorubicin)

**Contra-indications** pregnancy (Appendix 4); breast-feeding

**Side-effects** see section 8.1 and notes above

**Doxorubicin Rapid Dissolution** (Pharmacia) PoM

Injection, powder for reconstitution, doxorubicin hydrochloride, net price 10-mg vial = £18.72; 50-mg vial = £93.60

Note This preparation has replaced *Adriamycin®*

**Doxorubicin Solution for Injection** (Pharmacia) PoM

Injection, doxorubicin hydrochloride 2 mg/mL, net price 5-mL vial = £20.60, 25-mL vial = £103.00, 100-mL vial = £412.00

**Lipid formulation**

**Caelyx®** (Schering-Plough) PoM

Concentrate for intravenous infusion, pegylated doxorubicin hydrochloride 2 mg/mL encapsulated in liposomes. For dilution before use. Net price 10-mL vial = £382.51, 25-mL vial = £813.49

For AIDS-related Kaposi's sarcoma in patients with low CD4 count and extensive mucocutaneous or visceral disease, for advanced ovarian cancer when platinum-based chemotherapy has failed, and as monotherapy for metastatic breast cancer with increased cardiac risk

**Myocet®** (Zeneus) ▼ PoM

Injection, powder for reconstitution, doxorubicin hydrochloride (as doxorubicin–citrate complex) encapsulated in liposomes, net price 50-mg vial (with vials of liposomes and buffer) = £464.50

For use with cyclophosphamide for metastatic breast cancer

## EPIRUBICIN HYDROCHLORIDE

**Indications** see notes above and section 7.4.4

**Cautions** see section 8.1 and notes above; hepatic impairment (Appendix 2); caution in handling—irritant to tissues; **interactions:** Appendix 1 (epirubicin)

**Contra-indications** pregnancy (Appendix 4); breast-feeding

**Side-effects** see section 8.1 and notes above

**Pharmorubicin® Rapid Dissolution** (Pharmacia) PoM

Injection, powder for reconstitution, epirubicin hydrochloride. Net price 10-mg vial = £19.31; 20-mg vial = £38.62; 50-mg vial = £96.54

**Pharmorubicin® Solution for Injection** (Pharmacia) PoM

Injection, epirubicin hydrochloride 2 mg/mL, net price 5-mL vial = £19.31, 25-mL vial = £96.54, 100-mL vial = £386.16

## IDARUBICIN HYDROCHLORIDE

**Indications** advanced breast cancer after failure of first-line chemotherapy (not including anthracyclines); acute leukaemias—see notes above

**Cautions** see section 8.1 and notes above; hepatic impairment (Appendix 2); renal impairment (Appendix 3); caution in handling—irritant to tissues

**Contra-indications** pregnancy (Appendix 4); breast-feeding

**Side-effects** see section 8.1 and notes above

**Dose**

- By mouth, acute non-lymphocytic leukaemia, 30 mg/m² daily for 3 days alone *or* 15–30 mg/m² daily for 3 days in combination therapy

  Advanced breast cancer, 45 mg/m² alone, as a single dose *or* divided over 3 consecutive days; repeat every 3–4 weeks

  Note Max. cumulative dose by mouth (for all indications) 400 mg/m²
- By intravenous administration, consult product literature

**Zavedos®** (Pharmacia) PoM

Capsules, idarubicin hydrochloride, 5 mg (red), net price 1-cap pack = £34.56; 10 mg (red/white), 1-cap pack = £69.12; 25 mg (white), 1-cap pack = £172.80. Label: 25

Injection, powder for reconstitution, idarubicin hydrochloride, net price 5-mg vial = £87.36; 10-mg vial = £174.72

## MITOMYCIN

**Indications** see notes above and section 7.4.4

**Cautions** see section 8.1 and notes above; caution in handling—irritant to tissues

**Contra-indications** pregnancy (Appendix 4); breast-feeding

**Side-effects** see section 8.1 and notes above

**Mitomycin C Kyowa®** (Kyowa Hakko) PoM

Injection, powder for reconstitution, mitomycin. Net price 2-mg vial = £5.88; 10-mg vial = £19.37; 20-mg vial = £36.94; 40-mg vial = £73.88 (hosp. only)

## MITOXANTRONE
**(Mitozantrone)**

**Indications** see notes above

**Cautions** see section 8.1 and notes above; intrathecal administration not recommended

**Contra-indications** pregnancy (Appendix 4); breast-feeding

**Side-effects** see section 8.1 and notes above

**Mitoxantrone** (Non-proprietary) PoM

Concentrate for intravenous infusion, mitoxantrone (as hydrochloride) 2 mg/mL, net price 10-mL vial = £100.00

**Novantrone®** (Lederle) PoM

Concentrate for intravenous infusion, mitoxantrone (as hydrochloride) 2 mg/mL, net price 10-mL vial = £139.90, 12.5-mL vial = £174.89, 15-mL vial = £209.81

**Onkotrone®** (Baxter) PoM

Concentrate for intravenous infusion, mitoxantrone (as hydrochloride) 2 mg/mL, net price 10-mL vial = £135.39, 12.5-mL vial = £169.25, 15-mL vial = £203.04

## 8.1.3 Antimetabolites

Antimetabolites are incorporated into new nuclear material or combine irreversibly with vital cellular enzymes, preventing normal cellular division.

**Methotrexate** inhibits the enzyme dihydrofolate reductase, essential for the synthesis of purines and pyrimidines. It is given by mouth, intravenously, intramuscularly, or intrathecally.

Methotrexate is used as maintenance therapy for childhood acute lymphoblastic leukaemia. Other uses include choriocarcinoma, non-Hodgkin's lymphoma, and a number of solid tumours. Intrathecal methotrexate is used in the CNS prophylaxis of childhood acute lymphoblastic leukaemia, and as a therapy for established meningeal cancer or lymphoma.

Methotrexate causes myelosuppression, mucositis, and rarely pneumonitis. It is **contra-indicated** in significant renal impairment because it is excreted primarily by the kidney. It is also contra-indicated in patients with severe hepatic impairment. It should also be **avoided** in the presence of significant pleural effusion or ascites because it can accumulate in these fluids, and its subsequent return to the circulation may cause myelosuppression. Systemic toxicity may follow intrathecal administration and blood counts should be carefully monitored.

Folinic acid (section 8.1) following methotrexate administration helps to prevent methotrexate-induced mucositis or myelosuppression.

**Capecitabine**, which is metabolised to fluorouracil, is given by mouth. It is used as monotherapy for metastatic colorectal cancer; it has been shown to be of similar efficacy as a combination of fluorouracil and folinic acid. Capecitabine is also licensed for adjuvant treatment of advanced colon cancer following surgery. It is also licensed for second-line treatment of locally advanced or metastatic breast cancer either in combination with docetaxel (where previous therapy included an anthracycline) or alone (after failure of a taxane and anthracycline regimen or where further anthracycline treatment is not indicated).

**NICE guidance (capecitabine and tegafur with uracil for metastatic colorectal cancer)**
NICE has recommended (May 2003) capecitabine or tegafur with uracil (in combination with folinic acid) as an option for the first-line treatment of metastatic colorectal cancer.

**NICE guidance (capecitabine for locally advanced or metastatic breast cancer)**
NICE has recommended (May 2003) capecitabine in combination with docetaxel in preference to docetaxel monotherapy for locally advanced or metastatic breast cancer in people for whom anthracycline-containing regimens are unsuitable or have failed.
Capecitabine monotherapy is recommended as an option for people with locally advanced or metastatic breast cancer who have not previously received capecitabine in combination therapy and for whom anthracycline and taxane-containing regimens have failed or further anthracycline therapy is contra-indicated.

**Cytarabine** acts by interfering with pyrimidine synthesis. It is given subcutaneously, intravenously, or intrathecally. Its predominant use is in the induction of remission of acute myeloblastic leukaemia. It is a potent myelosuppressant and requires careful haematological monitoring. A liposomal formulation of cytarabine for intrathecal use is licensed for lymphomatous meningitis.

**Fludarabine** is licensed for the initial treatment of advanced B-cell chronic lymphocytic leukaemia (CLL) or after first-line treatment in patients with sufficient bone-marrow reserves; it is given by mouth or by intravenous injection or by intravenous infusion. Fludarabine is generally well tolerated but it does cause myelosuppression, which may be cumulative. Immunosuppression is also common (see panel on cladribine and fludarabine below) and co-trimoxazole is often used to prevent pneumocystis infection. Immune-mediated haemolytic anaemia, thrombocytopenia, and neutropenia are less common side-effects.

**NICE guidance (fludarabine)**
NICE has recommended (September 2001) oral fludarabine as second-line therapy for B-cell chronic lymphocytic leukaemia (CLL) for patients who have either failed, or are intolerant of, first-line chemotherapy.

**Cladribine** is an effective but potentially toxic drug given by intravenous infusion for the treatment of hairy cell leukaemia. It is also licensed for chronic lymphocytic leukaemia in patients who have failed to respond to standard regimens containing an alkylating agent; it is given by intravenous infusion. Myelosuppression may be severe and serious neurotoxicity has been reported rarely.

**Cladribine** and **fludarabine** have a potent and prolonged immunosuppressive effect and only irradiated blood products should be administered to prevent potentially fatal graft-versus-host reaction. Prescribers should consult specialist literature when using highly immunosuppressive drugs.

**Gemcitabine** is used intravenously; it is given alone for palliative treatment or with cisplatin as a first-line treatment for locally advanced or metastatic non-small cell lung cancer. It is also used in the treatment of locally advanced or metastatic pancreatic cancer. Combined with cisplatin, gemcitabine is also licensed for the treatment of advanced bladder cancer. It is generally well tolerated but may cause mild gastro-intestinal side-effects and rashes; renal impairment, pulmonary toxicity and influenza-like symptoms have also been reported. Haemolytic uraemic syndrome has been reported rarely and gemcitabine should be discontinued if signs of microangiopathic haemolytic anaemia occur.

**NICE guidance (gemcitabine)**
NICE has recommended (May 2001) that gemcitabine is an option for first-line chemotherapy for patients with advanced or metastatic adenocarcinoma of the pancreas and a Karnofsky score of at least 50 [Karnofsky score is a measure of the ability to perform ordinary tasks].
Gemcitabine is not recommended for patients who can have potentially curative surgery. There is insufficient evidence about its use for second-line treatment of pancreatic adenocarcinoma.

**NICE guidance (docetaxel, paclitaxel, gemcitabine and vinorelbine for non-small cell lung cancer)**
NICE has recommended (June 2001) that chemotherapy should be considered for non-small cell lung cancer in patients who are unsuitable for curative treatment or who are unlikely to respond to such treatment.
Gemcitabine, paclitaxel, or vinorelbine should be considered as first-line chemotherapy for advanced non-small cell lung cancer. Combination of each of these drugs with platinum-based chemotherapy, where tolerated, is likely to be most effective.
Docetaxel monotherapy should be considered for locally advanced or metastatic non-small cell lung cancer which relapses after previous chemotherapy.

**Fluorouracil** is usually given intravenously because absorption following oral administration is unpredictable. It is used to treat a number of solid tumours, including gastro-intestinal tract cancers and breast cancer. It is commonly used with folinic acid in advanced colorectal cancer. It may also be used topically for certain malignant and pre-malignant skin lesions. Toxicity is unusual, but may include myelosuppression, mucositis, and rarely a cerebellar syndrome. On prolonged infusion, a desquamative hand–foot syndrome may occur.

**Pemetrexed** inhibits thymidylate transferase and other folate-dependent enzymes. It is licensed for use with cisplatin for the treatment of unresectable malignant pleural mesothelioma which has not previously been treated with chemotherapy; it is given by intravenous infusion. Pemetrexed used alone is also licensed for the treatment of locally advanced or metastatic non-small cell lung cancer which has previously been treated with chemotherapy. Common adverse effects include myelosuppression, gastro-intestinal toxicity, and skin disorders.

**Raltitrexed**, a thymidylate synthase inhibitor, is given intravenously for palliation of advanced colorectal cancer when fluorouracil and folinic acid cannot be used. It is probably of similar efficacy to fluorouracil. Raltitrexed is generally well tolerated, but can cause marked myelosuppression and gastro-intestinal side-effects.

**NICE guidance (irinotecan, oxaliplatin and raltitrexed for advanced colorectal cancer)**
See p. 443

**Mercaptopurine** is used as maintenance therapy for the acute leukaemias and in the management of ulcerative colitis and Crohn's disease (section 1.5). Azathioprine, which is metabolised to mercaptopurine, is generally used as an immunosuppressant (section 8.2.1 and section 10.1.3). The dose of both drugs should be reduced if the patient is receiving allopurinol since it interferes with their metabolism.

**Tegafur** (in combination with uracil) is given by mouth, together with calcium folinate, in the management of metastatic colorectal cancer. Tegafur is a prodrug of fluorouracil; uracil inhibits the degradation of fluorouracil. Tegafur (with uracil) has been shown to be of similar efficacy as a combination of fluorouracil and folinic acid for metastatic colorectal cancer. For NICE guidance on capecitabine and tegafur with uracil for metastatic colorectal cancer, see above.

**Tioguanine** (thioguanine) is given by mouth to induce remission in acute myeloid leukaemia.

## CAPECITABINE

**Indications** see notes above

**Cautions** see section 8.1; **interactions**: Appendix 1 (fluorouracil)

**Contra-indications** hepatic impairment (Appendix 2), renal impairment (Appendix 3); pregnancy (Appendix 4); breast-feeding

**Side-effects** see section 8.1 and notes above; hand–foot (desquamative) syndrome

**Dose**

- ADULT over 18 years, 1.25 g/m$^2$ twice daily for 14 days; subsequent courses repeated after a 7-day interval

**Xeloda®** (Roche) ▼ PoM
Tablets, f/c, peach, capecitabine 150 mg, net price 60-tab pack = £44.47; 500 mg, 120-tab pack = £295.06. Label: 21

## CLADRIBINE

**Indications** see notes above

**Cautions** see section 8.1 and notes above; use irradiated blood only; hepatic impairment (Appendix 2); renal impairment (Appendix 3)

**Contra-indications** pregnancy (Appendix 4); breast-feeding

**Side-effects** see section 8.1 and notes above

**Leustat®** (Janssen-Cilag) PoM
Injection, cladribine 1 mg/mL. For dilution and use as an infusion, net price 10-mL vial = £173.18

## CYTARABINE

**Indications** see notes above

**Cautions** see section 8.1 and notes above; hepatic impairment (Appendix 2); **interactions**: Appendix 1 (cytarabine)

**Contra-indications** pregnancy (Appendix 4); breast-feeding

**Side-effects** see section 8.1 and notes above

**Cytarabine** (Non-proprietary) PoM
Injection (for intravenous, subcutaneous or intrathecal use), cytarabine 20 mg/mL, net price 5-mL vial (Mayne) = £4.00

Injection (for intravenous or subcutaneous use), cytarabine 20 mg/mL, net price 5-mL vial (Pharmacia) = £3.90, 25-mL vial (Pharmacia) = £19.50

Injection (for intravenous or subcutaneous use), cytarabine 100 mg/mL, net price 1-mL vial (Mayne) = £4.00; 5-mL vial (Mayne) = £20.00; 10-mL vial (Mayne) = £40.00, (Pharmacia) = £39.00; 20-mL vial (Mayne) = £79.00, (Pharmacia) = £77.50; 20-mL *Onco-vial®* (Mayne) = £79.00

**Lipid formulation for intrathecal use**

**DepoCyte®** (Napp) ▼ PoM
Intrathecal injection, cytarabine encapsulated in liposomes, net price 50-mg vial = £1250.00
For lymphomatous meningitis

## FLUDARABINE PHOSPHATE

**Indications** see notes above

**Cautions** see section 8.1 and notes above; use irradiated blood only; renal impairment (Appendix 3) **interactions:** Appendix 1 (fludarabine)

**Contra-indications** haemolytic anaemia, pregnancy (Appendix 4); breast-feeding

**Side-effects** see section 8.1 and notes above; also peripheral neuropathy

**Dose**

- By mouth, ADULT 40 mg/m$^2$ for 5 days every 28 days usually for 6 cycles
- By intravenous injection *or* infusion, consult product literature

**Fludara®** (Schering Health) PoM

Tablets▼, f/c, pink, fludarabine phosphate 10 mg, net price 15-tab pack = £279.00, 20-tab pack = £372.00

Injection, powder for reconstitution, fludarabine phosphate. Net price 50-mg vial = £156.00

## FLUOROURACIL

**Indications** see notes above

**Cautions** see section 8.1 and notes above; caution in handling—irritant to tissues; hepatic impairment (Appendix 2); **interactions:** Appendix 1 (fluorouracil)

**Contra-indications** pregnancy (Appendix 4); breast-feeding

**Side-effects** see section 8.1 and notes above; also local irritation with topical preparation

**Dose**

- By mouth, maintenance 15 mg/kg weekly; max. in one day 1 g
- By intravenous injection *or* infusion *or* by intra-arterial infusion, consult product literature

**Fluorouracil** (Non-proprietary) PoM

Capsules, fluorouracil 250 mg.
Available from Cambridge on a named-patient basis

Injection, fluorouracil (as sodium salt) 25 mg/mL, net price 10-mL vial = £3.20, 20-mL vial = £6.40, 100-mL vial = £32.00; 50 mg/mL, 10-mL vial = £6.40, 20-mL vial = £12.80, 50-mL vial = £32.00, 100-mL vial = £64.00

### Topical preparations

**Efudix®** (Valeant) PoM

Cream, fluorouracil 5%. Net price 20 g = £17.72
Excipients include hydroxybenzoates (parabens)

Dose malignant and pre-malignant skin lesions, apply thinly to the affected area once or twice daily; cover with occlusive dressing in malignant conditions; max. area of skin treated at one time, 500 cm$^2$; usual duration of initial therapy, 3–4 weeks

## GEMCITABINE

**Indications** see notes above

**Cautions** see section 8.1 and notes above; hepatic impairment (Appendix 2); renal impairment (Appendix 3)

**Contra-indications** pregnancy (Appendix 4); breast-feeding

**Side-effects** see section 8.1 and notes above

**Gemzar®** (Lilly) PoM

Injection, powder for reconstitution, gemcitabine (as hydrochloride), net price 200-mg vial = £32.55; 1-g vial = £162.76 (both hosp. only)

## MERCAPTOPURINE

**Indications** acute leukaemias; inflammatory bowel disease [unlicensed indication] (section 1.5)

**Cautions** see section 8.1 and notes above; monitor liver function—hepatic impairment (Appendix 2); renal impairment (Appendix 3); **interactions:** Appendix 1 (mercaptopurine)

**Contra-indications** pregnancy (Appendix 4); breast-feeding

**Side-effects** see section 8.1 and notes above; also hepatotoxicity; rarely pancreatitis

**Dose**

- Initially 2.5 mg/kg daily

**Puri-Nethol®** (GSK) PoM

Tablets, yellow, scored, mercaptopurine 50 mg, net price 25-tab pack = £18.78

## METHOTREXATE

**Indications** see notes above and under Dose; rheumatoid arthritis (section 10.1.3); psoriasis (section 13.5.3)

**Cautions** see section 8.1, notes above and section 10.1.3; hepatic impairment (Appendix 2); renal impairment (Appendix 3); **interactions:** Appendix 1 (methotrexate)

**Contra-indications** pregnancy (Appendix 4); breast-feeding

**Side-effects** see section 8.1, notes above and section 10.1.3

**Dose**

- By mouth, leukaemia in children (maintenance), 15 mg/m$^2$ weekly in combination with other drugs

> **Important**
> Note that the above dose is a **weekly** dose. The CSM has received reports of prescription and dispensing errors including fatalities. Attention should be paid to the **strength** of methotrexate tablets prescribed and the **frequency** of dosing

- By intravenous injection *or* infusion, by intra-arterial infusion, *or* by intramuscular injection, *or* intrathecal administration, consult product literature

**Methotrexate** (Non-proprietary) PoM

Injection, methotrexate 2.5 mg (as sodium salt)/mL. Net price 2-mL vial (Mayne) = £1.68

Injection, methotrexate 25 mg (as sodium salt)/mL. Net price 2-mL vial (Mayne) = £4.58, (Goldshield) = £2.62; 8-mL vial (Goldshield) = £10.02; 20-mL vial (Mayne) = £39.09, (Goldshield) = £25.07; 40-mL vial (Goldshield) = £44.57; 200-mL vial (Goldshield) = £200.57

Injection, methotrexate 100 mg/mL (not for intrathecal use). Net price 10-mL vial (Mayne) = £78.33; 50-mL vial (Mayne) = £380.07

### Oral preparations

Section 10.1.3

## PEMETREXED

**Indications** see notes above

**Cautions** see section 8.1 and notes above; prophylactic folic acid and vitamin-$B_{12}$ supplementation required (consult product literature)

**Contra-indications** pregnancy (Appendix 4); breast-feeding (Appendix 5)

**Side-effects** see section 8.1 and notes above

**Dose**

- Consult product literature

**Alimta®** (Lilly) ▼ PoM
Injection, powder for reconstitution, pemetrexed 500 mg (as disodium), net price 500-mg vial = £800.00

## RALTITREXED

**Indications** see notes above

**Cautions** see section 8.1 and notes above; hepatic impairment (Appendix 2); renal impairment (Appendix 3)

**Contra-indications** pregnancy (Appendix 4); breast-feeding

**Side-effects** see section 8.1 and notes above

**Tomudex®** (AstraZeneca) PoM
Injection, powder for reconstitution, raltitrexed. Net price 2-mg vial = £121.86

## TEGAFUR WITH URACIL

**Indications** see notes above

**Cautions** see section 8.1; cardiac disease; renal impairment; hepatic impairment (avoid if severe—Appendix 2); **interactions:** Appendix 1 (fluorouracil)

**Contra-indications** pregnancy (Appendix 4); breast-feeding

**Side-effects** see section 8.1 and notes above

**Dose**

- ADULT, tegafur 300 mg/m$^2$ (with uracil 672 mg/m$^2$) daily in 3 divided doses for 28 days; subsequent courses repeated after 7-day interval; for dose adjustment due to toxicity, consult product literature

**Uftoral®** (Bristol-Myers Squibb) ▼ PoM
Capsules, tegafur 100 mg, uracil 224 mg, net price 21-cap pack = £79.88, 28-cap pack = £106.51, 35-cap pack = £133.14, 42-cap pack = £159.77. Label: 23

## TIOGUANINE
(Thioguanine)

**Indications** acute leukaemias; chronic myeloid leukaemia

**Cautions** see section 8.1 and notes above; renal impairment (Appendix 3); **interactions:** Appendix 1 (tioguanine)

**Contra-indications** pregnancy (Appendix 4); breast-feeding

**Side-effects** see section 8.1 and notes above

**Dose**

- Induction, 100–200 mg/m$^2$ in 1–2 divided doses for 5–20 days; maintenance, usually 60–200 mg/m$^2$ daily

**Lanvis®** (GSK) PoM
Tablets, yellow, scored, tioguanine 40 mg. Net price 25-tab pack = £45.41

# 8.1.4 Vinca alkaloids and etoposide

The vinca alkaloids, **vinblastine**, **vincristine**, and **vindesine**, are used to treat a variety of cancers including leukaemias, lymphomas, and some solid tumours (e.g. breast and lung cancer). **Vinorelbine** is a semi-synthetic vinca alkaloid, it is given intravenously for the treatment of advanced breast cancer (see also NICE guidance below) and for advanced non-small cell lung cancer (see also NICE guidance, p. 436). An oral preparation of vinorelbine is also licensed to treat advanced non-small cell lung cancer.

Neurotoxicity, usually as peripheral or autonomic neuropathy, occurs with all vinca alkaloids and is a limiting side-effect of vincristine; it occurs less often with vindesine, vinblastine, and vinorelbine. Patients with neurotoxicity commonly have peripheral paraesthesia, loss of deep tendon reflexes, abdominal pain, and constipation; ototoxicity has been reported. If symptoms of neurotoxicity are severe, doses should be reduced. Motor weakness can also occur, and increasing motor weakness calls for discontinuation of these drugs. Recovery from neurotoxic effects is usually slow but complete.

Myelosuppression is the dose-limiting side-effect of vinblastine, vindesine, and vinorelbine; vincristine causes negligible myelosuppression. The vinca alkaloids may cause reversible alopecia. They cause severe local irritation and care must be taken to avoid extravasation.

> Vinblastine, vincristine, vindesine, and vinorelbine are for **intravenous administration only**. Inadvertent intrathecal administration can cause severe neurotoxicity, which is usually fatal.

> **NICE guidance (vinorelbine for advanced breast cancer)**
> NICE has recommended (December 2002) that vinorelbine be considered as an option for the second-line (or subsequent) treatment of advanced breast cancer where anthracycline-based regimens have failed or are unsuitable.
> Vinorelbine monotherapy is not recommended as first-line treatment for advanced breast cancer.
> Insufficient information is available to recommend the routine use of vinorelbine in combination with other therapies for advanced breast cancer.

**Etoposide** may be given orally or by slow intravenous infusion, the oral dose being double the intravenous dose. A preparation containing etoposide phosphate can be given by intravenous injection or infusion. Etoposide is usually given daily for 3–5 days and courses should not be repeated more frequently than at intervals of 21 days. It has particularly useful activity in small cell carcinoma of the bronchus, the lymphomas, and testicular cancer. Toxic effects include alopecia, myelosuppression, nausea, and vomiting.

## ETOPOSIDE

**Indications** see notes above

**Cautions** see section 8.1 and notes above; renal impairment (Appendix 3); **interactions:** Appendix 1 (etoposide)

**Contra-indications** see section 8.1 and notes above; severe hepatic impairment; pregnancy (Appendix 4); breast-feeding

**Side-effects** see section 8.1 and notes above; irritant to tissues

**Dose**

- By mouth, 120–240 mg/m² daily for 5 days
- By intravenous infusion, consult product literature

**Etoposide** (Non-proprietary) PoM

Concentrate for intravenous infusion, etoposide 20 mg/mL, net price 5-mL vial = £12.15, 10-mL vial = £29.00, 25-mL vial = £60.75

Note Prices from different suppliers can vary

Brands include *Eposin®*

**Etopophos®** (Bristol-Myers Squibb) PoM

Injection, powder for reconstitution, etoposide (as phosphate), net price 100-mg vial = £29.87 (hosp. only)

**Vepesid®** (Bristol-Myers Squibb) PoM

Capsules, both pink, etoposide 50 mg, net price 20 = £105.97; 100 mg, 10-cap pack = £92.60 (hosp. only). Label: 23

Concentrate for intravenous infusion, etoposide 20 mg/mL, net price 5-mL vial = £13.56 (hosp. only)

Excipients include benzyl alcohol (avoid in neonates, see Excipients, p. 2)

## VINBLASTINE SULPHATE

**Indications** see notes above

**Cautions** see section 8.1 and notes above; hepatic impairment (Appendix 2); caution in handling; **interactions:** Appendix 1 (vinblastine)

**Contra-indications** see section 8.1 and notes above; pregnancy (Appendix 4); breast-feeding

Important Intrathecal injection **contra-indicated**

**Side-effects** see section 8.1 and notes above; irritant to tissues

**Vinblastine** (Non-proprietary) PoM

Injection, vinblastine sulphate 1 mg/mL. Net price 10-mL vial = £13.09

**Velbe®** (Genus) PoM

Injection, powder for reconstitution, vinblastine sulphate. Net price 10-mg amp = £14.15

## VINCRISTINE SULPHATE

**Indications** see notes above

**Cautions** see section 8.1 and notes above; hepatic impairment (Appendix 2); neuromuscular disease; caution in handling; **interactions:** Appendix 1 (vincristine)

**Contra-indications** see section 8.1 and notes above; pregnancy (Appendix 4); breast-feeding

Important Intrathecal injection **contra-indicated**

**Side-effects** see section 8.1 and notes above; irritant to tissues

**Vincristine** (Non-proprietary) PoM

Injection, vincristine sulphate 1 mg/mL. Net price 1-mL vial = £10.92; 2-mL vial = £21.17; 5-mL vial = £44.16

**Oncovin®** (Genus) PoM

Injection, vincristine sulphate 1 mg/mL, net price 1-mL vial = £14.18; 2-mL vial = £28.05

## VINDESINE SULPHATE

**Indications** see notes above

**Cautions** see section 8.1 and notes above; hepatic impairment (Appendix 2); neuromuscular disease; caution in handling

**Contra-indications** see section 8.1 and notes above; pregnancy (Appendix 4); breast-feeding

Important Intrathecal injection **contra-indicated**

**Side-effects** see section 8.1 and notes above; irritant to tissues

**Eldisine®** (Genus) PoM

Injection, powder for reconstitution, vindesine sulphate, net price 5-mg vial = £78.30 (hosp. only)

## VINORELBINE

**Indications** see notes above

**Cautions** see section 8.1 and notes above; hepatic impairment (Appendix 2); caution in handling

**Contra-indications** see section 8.1 and notes above; pregnancy (Appendix 4); breast-feeding

Important Intrathecal injection **contra-indicated**

**Side-effects** see section 8.1 and notes above; irritant to tissues

**Dose**

- By mouth, 60 mg/m² once weekly for 3 weeks, increased if tolerated to 80 mg/m² once weekly; max. 160 mg once weekly
- By intravenous injection *or* infusion, consult product literature

**Navelbine®** (Fabre) PoM

Concentrate for intravenous infusion, vinorelbine (as tartrate) 10 mg/mL. Net price 1-mL vial = £29.75; 5-mL vial = £139.98

Capsules ▼, vinorelbine (as tartrate) 20 mg (brown), net price 1-cap pack = £43.98; 30 mg (pink), 1-cap pack = £65.98. Label: 21, 25

# 8.1.5 Other antineoplastic drugs

### Amsacrine

**Amsacrine** has an action and toxic effects similar to those of doxorubicin (section 8.1.2) and is given *intravenously*. It is occasionally used in acute myeloid leukaemia. Side-effects include myelosuppression and mucositis; electrolytes should be monitored as fatal arrhythmias have occurred in association with hypokalaemia.

## AMSACRINE

**Indications** see notes above

**Cautions** see section 8.1 and notes above; reduce dose in renal or hepatic impairment; also caution in handling—irritant to skin and tissues

**Contra-indications** pregnancy (Appendix 4); breast-feeding

**Side-effects** see section 8.1 and notes above

**Amsidine®** (Goldshield) PoM
Concentrate for intravenous infusion, amsacrine 5 mg (as lactate)/mL, when reconstituted by mixing two solutions. Net price 1.5-mL (75-mg) amp with 13.5-mL diluent vial = £49.17 (hosp. only)
Note Use glass apparatus for reconstitution

## Arsenic trioxide

**Arsenic trioxide** is licensed for acute promyelocytic leukaemia in patients who have relapsed or failed to respond to previous treatment with a retinoid and chemotherapy.

### ARSENIC TRIOXIDE

**Indications** see notes above

**Cautions** see section 8.1; correct electrolyte abnormalities before treatment; ECG required before and during treatment—consult product literature; avoid concomitant administration with drugs causing QT interval prolongation, hypokalaemia, and hypomagnesaemia; previous treatment with anthracyclines (increased risk of QT interval prolongation); renal impairment (Appendix 3)

**Contra-indications** pregnancy (Appendix 4); breast-feeding

**Side-effects** see section 8.1; leucocyte activation syndrome (requires immediate treatment—consult product literature); hyperglycaemia, hypokalaemia, leucocytosis, QT interval prolongation, atrial fibrillation, atrial flutter, haemorrhage, dyspnoea, pleuritic pain, musculoskeletal pain, paraesthesia, fatigue

**Trisenox®** (Cell Therapeutics) ▼ PoM
Concentrate for intravenous infusion, arsenic trioxide 1 mg/mL, net price 10-mL amp = £250.90

## Bevacizumab

**Bevacizumab** is an inhibitor of vascular endothelial growth factor. It is licensed for first-line treatment of metastatic colorectal cancer with a combination *either* of fluorouracil and folinic acid *or* of fluorouracil, folinic acid, and irinotecan. Bevacizumab is given by intravenous infusion.

### BEVACIZUMAB

**Indications** see notes above

**Cautions** see section 8.1; intra-abdominal inflammation (risk of gastro-intestinal perforation); withhold treatment for elective surgery and avoid for at least 28 days after major surgery or until wound fully healed; history of hypertension (increased risk of proteinuria—discontinue if nephrotic syndrome); uncontrolled hypertension; monitor blood pressure during treatment; history of arterial thromboembolism; elderly (increased risk of cardiovascular events)

**Contra-indications** pregnancy (Appendix 4); breast-feeding (Appendix 5); untreated CNS metastases

**Side-effects** see section 8.1; mucocutaneous bleeding; gastro-intestinal perforation; impaired wound healing; arterial thromboembolism; hypertension (see also Cautions); proteinuria

**Avastin®** (Roche) ▼ PoM
Concentrate for intravenous infusion, bevacizumab 25 mg/mL, net price 100-mg vial = £242.66; 400-mg vial = £924.40

## Bexarotene

**Bexarotene** is an agonist at the retinoid X receptor, which is involved in the regulation of cell differentiation and proliferation. It is generally well tolerated and is associated with little myelosuppression or immunosuppression. Bexarotene can cause regression of cutaneous T-cell lymphoma. The main adverse effects are hyperlipidaemia, hypothyroidism, leucopenia, headache, rash, and pruritus.

### BEXAROTENE

**Indications** skin manifestations of cutaneous T-cell lymphoma refractory to previous systemic treatment

**Cautions** see section 8.1 and notes above; hyperlipidaemia (avoid if uncontrolled), hypothyroidism (avoid if uncontrolled); hypersensitivity to retinoids; **interactions:** Appendix 1 (bexarotene)

**Contra-indications** see section 8.1 and notes above; history of pancreatitis, hypervitaminosis A, hepatic impairment; pregnancy (Appendix 4); breast-feeding

**Side-effects** see section 8.1 and notes above

**Dose**

- Initially 300 mg/m² daily as a single dose with a meal; adjust dose according to response

**Targretin®** (Zeneus) ▼ PoM
Capsules, bexarotene 75 mg in a liquid suspension, net price 100-cap pack = £937.50

## Bortezomib

**Bortezomib**, a proteasome inhibitor, is licensed for multiple myeloma which has progressed despite the use of at least one therapy, and where the patient has already had bone-marrow transplantation or cannot have it. It is given by intravenous injection. Peripheral neuropathy, thrombocytopenia, gastro-intestinal disturbances, pyrexia, postural hypotension, and fatigue are among the most common side-effects.

### BORTEZOMIB

**Indications** see notes above

**Cautions** see section 8.1 and notes above; hepatic impairment (avoid if severe; Appendix 2); renal impairment (Appendix 3); pregnancy (Appendix 4); monitor blood-glucose concentration in patients on oral antidiabetics

**Contra-indications** breast-feeding

**Side-effects** see section 8.1 and notes above

**Velcade®** (Ortho Biotech) ▼ PoM
Injection, powder for reconstitution, bortezomib (as mannitol boronic ester), net price 3.5-mg vial = £762.38

## Cetuximab

**Cetuximab** is licensed, in combination with irinotecan, for the treatment of metastatic colorectal cancer in patients with tumours expressing epidermal growth factor receptor in whom previous chemotherapy, that has included irinotecan, has failed.

Cetuximab is given by intravenous infusion. Resuscitation facilities should be available and treatment should be initiated by a specialist.

### CETUXIMAB

**Indications** see notes above and product literature

**Cautions** cardiopulmonary disease, pulmonary disease; pregnancy (Appendix 4)

**Contra-indications** breast-feeding (Appendix 5)

**Side-effects** infusion-related side-effects including chills, fever, hypersensitivity reactions such as rash, urticaria, airway obstruction, dyspnoea (possibly delayed onset), hypotension; skin reactions including acne, nail disorders; conjunctivitis; also reported, hypomagnesaemia

**Erbitux®** (Merck) ▼ PoM
Intravenous infusion, cetuximab 2 mg/mL, net price 50-mL vial = £136.50

## Crisantaspase

**Crisantaspase** is the enzyme asparaginase produced by *Erwinia chrysanthemi*. It is given *intramuscularly*, *intravenously*, or *subcutaneously* almost exclusively in acute lymphoblastic leukaemia. Facilities for the management of anaphylaxis should be available. Side-effects also include nausea, vomiting, fever, pancreatitis, CNS depression, neurotoxicity, liver function changes, coagulation disorders, and blood lipid changes; careful monitoring is therefore necessary and the urine is tested for glucose because of a risk of hyperglycaemia.

### CRISANTASPASE

**Indications** see notes above

**Cautions** see notes above

**Contra-indications** pregnancy (Appendix 4); breast-feeding

**Side-effects** see notes above

**Erwinase®** (OPi) PoM
Injection, powder for reconstitution, crisantaspase. Net price 10 000-unit vial = £194.77

## Dacarbazine and temozolomide

**Dacarbazine** is used to treat metastatic melanoma and, in combination therapy, soft tissue sarcomas. It is also a component of a commonly used combination for Hodgkin's disease (ABVD—doxorubicin [previously *Adriamycin*®], bleomycin, vinblastine, and dacarbazine). It is given *intravenously*. The predominant side-effects are myelosuppression and severe nausea and vomiting.

**Temozolomide** is structurally related to dacarbazine. It is given by mouth and is licensed for the initial treatment of glioblastoma multiforme (in combination with radiotherapy) and for second-line treatment of malignant glioma.

> **NICE guidance (temozolomide)**
> NICE has recommended (April 2001) that temozolomide may be considered for the treatment of recurrent malignant glioma, which has not responded to first-line chemotherapy.

### DACARBAZINE

**Indications** see notes above

**Cautions** see section 8.1; hepatic impairment (Appendix 2); renal impairment (Appendix 3); caution in handling

**Contra-indications** pregnancy (Appendix 4)

**Side-effects** see section 8.1 and notes above; rarely liver necrosis due to hepatic vein thrombosis; irritant to skin and tissues

**Dacarbazine** (Non-proprietary) PoM
Injection, powder for reconstitution, dacarbazine (as citrate), net price 100-mg vial = £5.11 (Medac) or £5.05 (Pliva); 200-mg vial = £7.24 (Medac) or £7.50 (Mayne) or £7.16 (Pliva); 500-mg vial = £16.50 (Medac); 600-mg vial = £22.50 (Mayne); 1-g vial = £31.80 (Medac)

**DTIC-Dome®** (Bayer) PoM
Injection, powder for reconstitution, dacarbazine. Net price 200-mg vial = £7.40

### TEMOZOLOMIDE

**Indications** see notes above

**Cautions** see section 8.1; severe hepatic impairment and renal impairment; **interactions:** Appendix 1 (temozolomide)

**Contra-indications** pregnancy (Appendix 4); breast-feeding

**Side-effects** see section 8.1

**Dose**

- Consult product literature; CHILD under 3 years not recommended

**Temodal®** (Schering-Plough) PoM
Capsules, temozolomide 5 mg, net price 5-cap pack = £17.30; 20 mg, 5-cap pack = £69.20; 100 mg, 5-cap pack = £346.00; 250 mg, 5-cap pack = £865.00. Label: 23, 25

## Erlotinib

**Erlotinib**, a tyrosine kinase inhibitor, is licensed for the treatment of locally advanced or metastatic non-small cell lung cancer after failure of previous chemotherapy.

### ERLOTINIB

**Indications** see notes above

**Cautions** see section 8.1; hepatic impairment (Appendix 2); renal impairment (Appendix 3); **interactions:** Appendix 1 (erlotinib)

**Contra-indications** pregnancy (Appendix 4); breast-feeding (Appendix 5)

**Side-effects** see section 8.1; diarrhoea, anorexia, gastro-intestinal bleeding; keratitis; rash; *less commonly* interstitial lung disease—discontinue if unexplained symptoms such as dyspnoea, cough or fever occur

**Dose**

- By mouth, 150 mg daily

**Tarceva®** (Roche) ▼ PoM

Tablets, f/c, white-yellow, erlotinib (as hydrochloride) 100 mg, net price 30-tab pack = £1324.14; 150 mg, 30-tab pack = £1631.53. Label: 23

## Hydroxycarbamide

**Hydroxycarbamide** (hydroxyurea) is an orally active drug used mainly in the treatment of chronic myeloid leukaemia. It is occasionally used for polycythaemia (the usual treatment is venesection). Myelosuppression, nausea, and skin reactions are the most common toxic effects.

### HYDROXYCARBAMIDE
(Hydroxyurea)

**Indications** see notes above

**Cautions** see section 8.1 and notes above

**Contra-indications** pregnancy (Appendix 4); breast-feeding

**Side-effects** see section 8.1 and notes above

**Dose**

- 20–30 mg/kg daily *or* 80 mg/kg every third day

**Hydroxycarbamide** (Non-proprietary) PoM

Capsules, hydroxycarbamide 500 mg, net price 20 = £17.20

**Hydrea®** (Squibb) PoM

Capsules, pink/green, hydroxycarbamide 500 mg. Net price 20 = £2.39

## Imatinib

**Imatinib** is a protein-tyrosine kinase inhibitor, which is licensed for the treatment of newly diagnosed chronic myeloid leukaemia where bone marrow transplantation is not considered first-line treatment and for chronic myeloid leukaemia in chronic phase after failure of interferon alfa, or in accelerated phase, or in blast crisis. It is also licensed for Kit-positive unresectable or metastatic malignant gastro-intestinal stromal tumours (GIST). The most frequent side-effects of imatinib are nausea, vomiting, diarrhoea, oedema, abdominal pain, fatigue, myalgia, headache, and rash; gynaecomastia because of reduced testosterone has been reported.

The *Scottish Medicines Consortium* has advised (March 2002) that imatinib should be used for chronic myeloid leukaemia only under specialist supervision in accordance with British Society of Haematology guidelines (November 2001).

> **NICE guidance (imatinib for chronic myeloid leukaemia)**
>
> NICE has recommended (October 2003) imatinib as first-line treatment for Philadelphia-chromosome-positive chronic myeloid leukaemia in the chronic phase and as an option for patients presenting in the accelerated phase or with blast crisis, provided that imatinib has not been used previously.
>
> Where imatinib has failed to stop disease progression from chronic phase to accelerated phase or blast crisis, continued use is recommended only as part of further clinical study.

### IMATINIB

**Indications** see notes above

**Cautions** consult product literature; pregnancy (Appendix 4 and section 8.1); **interactions:** Appendix 1 (imatinib)

**Contra-indications** breast-feeding

**Side-effects** see section 8.1 and notes above

**Dose**

- Consult product literature

**Glivec®** (Novartis) ▼ PoM

Tablets, f/c, imatinib (as mesilate) 100 mg (yellow-brown, scored), net price 60-tab pack = £778.68; 400 mg, (yellow), 30-tab pack = £1557.36

## Mitotane

**Mitotane** selectively inhibits the activity of the adrenal cortex; it is licensed for the symptomatic treatment of advanced or inoperable adrenocortical carcinoma. Gastro-intestinal side-effects such as anorexia, nausea, and vomiting are very common, and neurotoxicity occurs in many patients.

### MITOTANE

**Indications** see notes above

**Cautions** see section 8.1; suspend treatment and administer corticosteroid in case of shock, severe trauma, or infection; hepatic impairment (Appendix 2); renal impairment (Appendix 3); pregnancy (Appendix 4); **interactions**: Appendix 1 (mitotane)

Driving CNS effects may affect performance of skilled tasks (e.g. driving)

Counselling Warn patient to contact doctor immediately if injury, infection or illness occurs

**Contra-indications** breast-feeding

**Side-effects** see section 8.1 and notes above; *also* autoimmune hepatitis, hypercholesterolaemia, hypertriglyceridaemia, gynaecomastia, increased bleeding time, rash; *rarely* hypertension, orthostatic hypotension, flushing, haematuria, proteinuria, haemorrhagic cystitis, hypouricaemia, visual disturbances and ocular disorders; cognitive impairment reported with prolonged high doses

**Dose**

- Initially 2–3 g daily in 2–3 divided doses, reduced to 1–2 g daily after 2 months (cumulative dose 200 g) or if signs of toxicity (higher doses used if plasma-mitotane concentration monitoring available—consult product literature)

**Lysodren®** (HRA Pharma) PoM
Tablets, scored, mitotane 500 mg, net price 100-tab pack = £460.40. Label: 2, 21, counselling, driving adrenal suppression

## Pentostatin

**Pentostatin** is highly active in hairy cell leukaemia. It is given *intravenously* on alternate weeks and is capable of inducing prolonged complete remission. It is potentially toxic, causing myelosuppression, immunosuppression and a number of other side-effects which may be severe. Its use is probably best confined to specialist centres.

### PENTOSTATIN

**Indications** see notes above

**Cautions** see section 8.1 and notes above; **interactions**: Appendix 1 (pentostatin)

**Contra-indications** pregnancy (Appendix 4); breast-feeding

**Side-effects** see section 8.1 and notes above

**Nipent®** (Lederle) PoM
Injection, powder for reconstitution, pentostatin. Net price 10-mg vial = £863.78

## Platinum compounds

**Carboplatin** is widely used in the treatment of advanced ovarian cancer and lung cancer (particulary the small cell type). It is given *intravenously*. The dose of carboplatin is determined according to renal function rather than body surface area. Carboplatin can be given on an outpatient basis and is better tolerated than cisplatin; nausea and vomiting are reduced in severity and nephrotoxicity, neurotoxicity, and ototoxicity are much less of a problem than with cisplatin. It is, however, more myelosuppressive than cisplatin.

**Cisplatin** is used alone or in combination for the treatment of testicular, lung, cervical, bladder, head and neck, and ovarian cancer (but carboplatin is preferred for ovarian cancer). It is given *intravenously*. Cisplatin requires intensive intravenous hydration and treatment may be complicated by severe nausea and vomiting. Cisplatin is toxic, causing nephrotoxicity (monitoring of renal function is essential), ototoxicity, peripheral neuropathy, hypomagnesaemia and myelosuppression. It is, however, increasingly given in a day-care setting.

**Oxaliplatin** is licensed in combination with fluorouracil and folinic acid, for the treatment of metastatic colorectal cancer and as adjuvant treatment of colon cancer after resection of the primary tumour; it is given by intravenous infusion. Neurotoxic side-effects (including sensory peripheral neuropathy) are dose limiting. Other side-effects include gastro-intestinal disturbances, ototoxicity, and myelosuppression. Manufacturers advise renal function monitoring in moderate impairment.

**NICE guidance (irinotecan, oxaliplatin, and raltitrexed for advanced colorectal cancer)**
NICE has recommended (August 2005) that a combination of fluorouracil and folinic acid with either irinotecan or oxaliplatin are options for first-line treatment for advanced colorectal cancer.
Irinotecan alone or fluorouracil and folinic acid with oxaliplatin are options for patients who have failed to respond to first-line treatment.
Raltitrexed is **not** recommended for the treatment of advanced colorectal cancer. Its use should be confined to clinical studies.

**NICE guidance (paclitaxel for ovarian cancer)**
NICE has recommended (January 2003) that *either* paclitaxel in combination with a platinum compound (cisplatin or carboplatin) *or* a platinum compound alone be used for the first-line treatment of ovarian cancer (usually following surgery).

**NICE guidance (paclitaxel, pegylated liposomal doxorubicin, and topotecan for second-line or subsequent treatment of advanced ovarian cancer)**
NICE has recommended (May 2005) that paclitaxel, combined with a platinum compound, is an option for advanced cancer that relapses 6 months or more after completing initial platinum-based chemotherapy. Paclitaxel alone is an option for advanced ovarian cancer that does not respond to, or relapses within 6 months of completing initial platinum-based chemotherapy.
Pegylated liposomal doxorubicin is an option for advanced ovarian cancer that does not respond to, or relapses within 12 months of completing initial platinum-based chemotherapy.
Paclitaxel alone or pegylated liposomal doxorubicin are options for advanced ovarian cancer in patients who are allergic to platinum compounds. Topotecan alone is an option only for advanced ovarian cancer that does not respond to, or relapses within 6 months of completing initial platinum-based chemotherapy or in those allergic to platinum compounds *and* for whom paclitaxel alone or pegylated liposomal doxorubicin are inappropriate.

### CARBOPLATIN

**Indications** see notes above

**Cautions** see section 8.1 and notes above; renal impairment (Appendix 3); **interactions**: Appendix 1 (platinum compounds)

**Contra-indications** pregnancy (Appendix 4); breast-feeding

**Side-effects** see section 8.1 and notes above

**Carboplatin** (Non-proprietary) PoM
Injection, carboplatin 10 mg/mL, net price 5-mL vial = £22.04, 15-mL vial = £56.29, 45-mL vial = £168.85, 60-mL vial = £260.00
Note Prices from different suppliers can vary
Brands include *Onco-vial®*

**Paraplatin®** (Bristol-Myers Squibb) PoM
Concentrate for intravenous infusion, carboplatin 10 mg/mL, net price 5-mL vial = £21.26, 15-mL vial = £61.22, 45-mL vial = £183.66, 60-mL vial = £244.88

## CISPLATIN

**Indications** see notes above

**Cautions** see section 8.1 and notes above; renal impairment (Appendix 3); **interactions:** Appendix 1 (platinum compounds)

**Contra-indications** pregnancy (Appendix 4); breast-feeding

**Side-effects** see section 8.1 and notes above

**Cisplatin** (Non-proprietary) PoM

Injection, cisplatin 1 mg/mL, net price 10-mL vial = £5.85, 50-mL vial = £25.37, 100-mL vial = £50.22

Note Prices from different suppliers can vary

Brands include *Platinex®*

Injection, powder for reconstitution, cisplatin, net price 50-mg vial = £17.00

## OXALIPLATIN

**Indications** metastatic colorectal cancer in combination with fluorouracil and folinic acid; colon cancer—see notes above

**Cautions** see section 8.1 and notes above; renal impairment (Appendix 3); **interactions:** Appendix 1 (platinum compounds)

**Contra-indications** see section 8.1; peripheral neuropathy with functional impairment; pregnancy (Appendix 4); breast-feeding

**Side-effects** see section 8.1 and notes above

**Eloxatin®** (Sanofi-Synthelabo) PoM

Injection, powder for reconstitution, oxaliplatin, net price 50-mg vial = £165.00, 100-mg vial = £330.00

### Porfimer sodium and temoporfin

**Porfimer sodium** and **temoporfin** are used in the photodynamic treatment of various tumours. The drugs accumulate in malignant tissue and are activated by laser light to produce a cytotoxic effect.

Porfimer sodium is licensed for photodynamic therapy of non-small cell lung cancer and obstructing oesophageal cancer. Temoporfin is licensed for photodynamic therapy of advanced head and neck cancer.

The *Scottish Medicines Consortium* has advised (May 2004) that temoporfin is **not** recommended for the palliative treatment of advanced head and neck cancer.

## PORFIMER SODIUM

**Indications** non-small cell lung cancer; oesophageal cancer; see notes above

**Cautions** see section 8.1; avoid exposure of skin and eyes to direct sunlight or bright indoor light for at least 30 days

**Contra-indications** see section 8.1; severe hepatic impairment; tracheo-oesophageal or broncho-oesophageal fistula; porphyria (section 9.8.2); pregnancy (Appendix 4); breast-feeding (Appendix 5)

**Side-effects** see section 8.1; photosensitivity (see Cautions above—sunscreens offer no protection), constipation

**Dose**

- By intravenous injection over 3–5 minutes, 2 mg/kg

Note For further information on administration and light activation, consult product literature

**Photofrin** (Sinclair) ▼ PoM

Injection, powder for reconstitution, porfimer sodium, net price 15-mg vial = £154.00; 75-mg vial = £770.00

## TEMOPORFIN

**Indications** advanced head and neck squamous cell carcinoma refractory to, or unsuitable for, other treatments

**Cautions** see section 8.1; avoid exposure of skin and eyes to direct sunlight or bright indoor light for at least 15 days after administration; **interactions:** Appendix 1 (temoporfin)

**Contra-indications** see section 8.1; porphyria (section 9.8.2) or other diseases exacerbated by light; elective surgery or ophthalmic slit-lamp examination for 30 days after administration; existing photosensitising treatment; pregnancy; breast-feeding

**Side-effects** see section 8.1; photosensitivity (see Cautions above—sunscreens offer no protection), constipation, local haemorrhage, facial pain and oedema, scarring, dysphagia

**Dose**

- By intravenous injection over at least 6 minutes, ADULT 150 microgram/kg

Note For use undiluted; for further information on administration and light activation, consult product literature

**Foscan®** (Biolitec) ▼ PoM

Injection, temoporfin 4 mg/mL, net price 5-mL vial = £4400.00

### Procarbazine

**Procarbazine** is most often used in Hodgkin's disease, for example in MOPP (chlormethine (mustine), vincristine [*Oncovin®*], procarbazine, and prednisolone) chemotherapy. It is given *by mouth*. Toxic effects include nausea, myelosuppression, and a hypersensitivity rash preventing further use of this drug. It is a mild monoamine-oxidase inhibitor but dietary restriction is not considered necessary. Alcohol ingestion may cause a disulfiram-like reaction.

## PROCARBAZINE

**Indications** see notes above

**Cautions** see section 8.1 and notes above; hepatic impairment—avoid if severe; renal impairment—avoid if severe; **interactions:** Appendix 1 (procarbazine)

**Contra-indications** pregnancy (Appendix 4); breast-feeding

**Side-effects** see section 8.1 and notes above

**Dose**

- Used alone, initially 50 mg daily, increased by 50 mg daily to 250–300 mg daily in divided doses; maintenance (on remission) 50–150 mg daily to cumulative total of at least 6 g

**Procarbazine** (Cambridge) PoM

Capsules, ivory, procarbazine (as hydrochloride) 50 mg, net price 50-cap pack = £37.44. Label: 4

## Taxanes

**Paclitaxel** is a member of the taxane group of drugs. It is given by *intravenous infusion*. Paclitaxel given with carboplatin or cisplatin is used for the treatment of ovarian cancer (see NICE guidance p. 443); the combination is also considered appropriate for women whose ovarian cancer is initially considered inoperable. Paclitaxel is also used in the secondary treatment of metastatic breast cancer (see NICE guidance below). There is limited evidence to support its use in non-small cell lung cancer. Routine premedication with a corticosteroid, an antihistamine and a histamine $H_2$-receptor antagonist is recommended to prevent severe hypersensitivity reactions; hypersensitivity reactions may occur rarely despite premedication, although more commonly only bradycardia or asymptomatic hypotension occur.

Other side-effects of paclitaxel include myelosuppression, peripheral neuropathy, and cardiac conduction defects with arrhythmias (which are nearly always asymptomatic). It also causes alopecia and muscle pain; nausea and vomiting is mild to moderate.

**Docetaxel** is licensed for use in locally advanced or metastatic breast cancer and non-small cell lung cancer resistant to other cytotoxic drugs (see NICE guidance on breast cancer, below) or for initial chemotherapy in combination with other cytotoxic drugs. It is also licensed for hormone-resistant prostate cancer and for use with other cytotoxic drugs for adjuvant treatment of operable node-positive breast cancer. Its side-effects are similar to those of paclitaxel but persistent fluid retention (commonly as leg oedema that worsens during treatment) can be resistant to treatment; hypersensitivity reactions also occur. Dexamethasone by mouth is recommended for reducing fluid retention and hypersensitivity reactions.

> **NICE guidance (paclitaxel, pegylated liposomal doxorubicin and topotecan for second-line or subsequent treatment of advanced ovarian cancer)**
> See p. 443

> **NICE guidance (breast cancer)**
> NICE has recommended (September 2001) that both docetaxel and paclitaxel should be available for the treatment of advanced breast cancer where initial cytotoxic chemotherapy (including an anthracycline) has failed or is inappropriate. The use of taxanes for adjuvant treatment of early breast cancer or for the first-line treatment of advanced breast cancer should be limited to clinical trials [but see notes above].

> **NICE guidance (docetaxel, paclitaxel, gemcitabine and vinorelbine for non-small cell lung cancer)**
> See p. 436

### DOCETAXEL

**Indications** adjuvant treatment of operable node-positive breast cancer, in combination with doxorubicin and cyclophosphamide; with doxorubicin for initial chemotherapy of advanced or metastatic breast cancer; alone or with capecitabine for advanced or metastatic breast cancer where cytotoxic chemotherapy with anthracycline or alkylating drug has failed; with trastuzumab for initial chemotherapy of metastatic breast cancer; advanced or metastatic non-small cell lung cancer where first-line chemotherapy has failed; with cisplatin for unresectable, advanced or metastatic non-small cell lung cancer; with prednisolone for hormone-refractory metastatic prostate cancer

**Cautions** see section 8.1 and notes above; hepatic impairment (Appendix 2); **interactions:** Appendix 1 (docetaxel)

**Contra-indications** pregnancy (Appendix 4); breast-feeding

**Side-effects** see section 8.1 and notes above

**Taxotere®** (Sanofi-Aventis) PoM
Concentrate for intravenous infusion, docetaxel 40 mg/mL. Net price 0.5-mL vial = £162.75, 2-mL vial = £534.75 (both with diluent) (hosp. only)

### PACLITAXEL

**Indications** ovarian cancer (advanced or residual disease following laparotomy) in combination with cisplatin; metastatic ovarian cancer where platinum-containing therapy has failed; locally advanced or metastatic breast cancer (in combination with other cytotoxics or alone if other cytotoxics have failed or are inappropriate); adjuvant treatment of node-positive breast cancer following treatment with anthracycline and cyclophosphamide; non-small cell lung cancer (in combination with cisplatin) when surgery or radiotherapy not appropriate; advanced AIDS-related Kaposi's sarcoma where liposomal anthracycline therapy has failed

**Cautions** see section 8.1 and notes above; **interactions:** Appendix 1 (paclitaxel)

**Contra-indications** see section 8.1 and notes above; severe hepatic impairment; pregnancy (Appendix 4); breast-feeding

**Side-effects** see section 8.1 and notes above

**Paclitaxel** (Non-proprietary) PoM
Concentrate for intravenous infusion, paclitaxel 6 mg/mL, net price 5-mL vial = £112.20, 16.7-mL vial = £336.60, 25-mL vial = £561.00, 50-mL vial = £1009.80
Excipients include polyoxyl castor oil (risk of anaphylaxis, see Excipients, p. 2)

**Taxol®** (Bristol-Myers Squibb) PoM
Concentrate for intravenous infusion, paclitaxel 6 mg/mL, net price 5-mL vial = £116.05, 16.7-mL vial = £347.82, 25-mL vial = £521.73, 50-mL vial = £1043.46 (hosp. only)
Excipients include polyoxyl castor oil (risk of anaphylaxis, see Excipients, p. 2)

## Topoisomerase I inhibitors

Irinotecan and topotecan inhibit topoisomerase I, an enzyme involved in DNA replication.

**Irinotecan** is licensed for metastatic colorectal cancer in combination with fluorouracil and folinic acid or as monotherapy when treatment containing fluorouracil has failed; it is given by intravenous infusion.

> **NICE guidance (irinotecan, oxaliplatin and raltitrexed for advanced colorectal cancer)**
> See p. 443

**Topotecan** is given by intravenous infusion in metastatic ovarian cancer when first-line or subsequent therapy has failed.

In addition to dose-limiting myelosuppression, side-effects of irinotecan and topotecan include gastro-intestinal effects (delayed diarrhoea requiring prompt treatment may follow irinotecan treatment), asthenia, alopecia, and anorexia.

> **NICE guidance (paclitaxel, pegylated liposomal doxorubicin and topotecan for second-line or subsequent treatment of advanced ovarian cancer)**
> See p. 443

## IRINOTECAN HYDROCHLORIDE

**Indications** metastatic colorectal cancer in combination with fluorouracil and folinic acid or where treatment containing fluorouracil has failed

**Cautions** see section 8.1 and notes above; raised plasma-bilirubin concentration (see under Contra-indications and Appendix 2)

**Contra-indications** see section 8.1 and notes above, also chronic inflammatory bowel disease, bowel obstruction; plasma bilirubin concentration more than 1.5 times the upper limit of reference range; avoid conception for at least 3 months after cessation of treatment (Appendix 4); breast-feeding

**Side-effects** see section 8.1 and notes above; also acute cholinergic syndrome (with early diarrhoea) and delayed diarrhoea (consult product literature)

**Campto®** (Pfizer) PoM
Concentrate for intravenous infusion, irinotecan hydrochloride 20 mg/mL, net price 2-mL vial = £53.00; 5-mL vial = £130.00

## TOPOTECAN

**Indications** metastatic ovarian cancer where first-line or subsequent therapy has failed

**Cautions** see section 8.1 and notes above; renal impairment (avoid if severe—Appendix 3)

**Contra-indications** see section 8.1 and notes above; severe hepatic impairment; pregnancy (Appendix 4); breast-feeding

**Side-effects** see section 8.1 and notes above

**Hycamtin®** (Merck) PoM
Intravenous infusion, powder for reconstitution, topotecan (as hydrochloride), net price 1-mg vial = £97.65; 4-mg vial = £290.62

### Trastuzumab

**Trastuzumab** is licensed, in combination with paclitaxel, for metastatic breast cancer in patients with tumours overexpressing the human epidermal growth factor receptor 2 (HER2) who have not received chemotherapy for metastatic breast cancer and in whom anthracycline treatment is inappropriate; trastuzumab is also licensed for use with docetaxel.

Trastuzumab is also licensed as monotherapy for metastatic breast cancer in patients with tumours that over-express HER2 who have received at least 2 chemotherapy regimens including, where appropriate, an anthracycline and a taxane; women with oestrogen-receptor-positive breast cancer should also have received hormonal therapy.

Trastuzumab is given by intravenous infusion. Resuscitation facilities should be available and treatment should be initiated by a specialist.

> **NICE guidance (trastuzumab for advanced breast cancer)**
> NICE has recommended (March 2002) that trastuzumab, used in accordance with the licensed indications for *Herceptin®*, is an option in the management of metastatic breast cancer.

**Use with anthracyclines** Concomitant use of trastuzumab with anthracyclines (section 8.1.2) is associated with cardiotoxicity. The EMEA has advised that the use of anthracyclines even after stopping trastuzumab may carry a higher risk of cardiotoxicity and if possible should be avoided for up to 22 weeks. If anthracyclines need to be used, cardiac function should be monitored.

## TRASTUZUMAB

**Indications** see notes above and product literature

**Cautions** see section 8.1 and notes above; symptomatic heart failure, history of hypertension, coronary artery disease; pregnancy (Appendix 4)

**Cardiotoxicity** Monitor cardiac function of all patients before and during treatment—for details of monitoring and managing cardiotoxity, consult product literature

**Contra-indications** see section 8.1 and notes above; severe dyspnoea at rest; breast-feeding (Appendix 5)

**Side-effects** infusion-related side-effects including chills, fever, hypersensitivity reactions such as anaphylaxis, urticaria and angioedema, pulmonary events (possibly delayed onset); cardiotoxicity (see also above); gastro-intestinal symptoms, asthenia, headache, chest pains, arthralgia, myalgia, hypotension

**Herceptin®** (Roche) ▼ PoM
Injection, powder for reconstitution, trastuzumab, net price 150-mg vial = £407.40. For intravenous infusion

### Tretinoin

**Tretinoin** is licensed for the induction of remission in acute promyelocytic leukaemia. It is used in previously untreated patients as well as in those who have relapsed after standard chemotherapy or who are refractory to it.

## TRETINOIN

**Note** Tretinoin is the acid form of vitamin A

**Indications** see notes above; acne (section 13.6.1); photodamage (section 13.8.1)

**Cautions** exclude pregnancy before starting treatment and avoid pregnancy during and for at least 1 month after treatment; monitor haematological and coagulation profile, liver function, serum calcium and plasma lipids before and during treatment; increased risk of thrombo-embolism during first month of treatment; hepatic impairment (Appendix 2); renal impairment (Appendix 3); **interactions**: Appendix 1 (retinoids)

**Contra-indications** pregnancy (**important teratogenic risk**: see Cautions and Appendix 4) and breast-feeding

**Side-effects** retinoic acid syndrome (fever, dyspnoea, acute respiratory distress, pulmonary infiltrates, pleural effusion, hyperleukocytosis, hypotension, oedema, weight gain, hepatic, renal and multi-organ failure) requires immediate treatment—consult product literature; gastro-intestinal disturbances, pancreatitis; arrhythmias, flushing, oedema; headache, benign intracranial hypertension (mainly in children—consider dose reduction if intractable headache in children), shivering, dizziness, confusion, anxiety, depression, insomnia, paraesthesia, visual and hearing disturbances; raised liver enzymes, serum creatinine and lipids; bone and chest pain, alopecia, erythema, rash, pruritus, sweating, dry skin and mucous membranes, cheilitis; thromboembolism, hypercalcaemia, and genital ulceration reported

**Dose**

- ADULT and CHILD 45 mg/m² daily in 2 divided doses, max. duration of treatment 90 days (consult product literature for details of concomitant chemotherapy)

**Vesanoid®** (Roche) PoM

Capsules, yellow/brown, tretinoin 10 mg. Net price 100-cap pack = £170.52. Label: 21

# 8.2 Drugs affecting the immune response


8.2.1 Antiproliferative immunosuppressants
8.2.2 Corticosteroids and other immunosuppressants
8.2.3 Rituximab and alemtuzumab
8.2.4 Other immunomodulating drugs


## Immunosuppressant therapy

Immunosuppressants are used to suppress rejection in organ transplant recipients and to treat a variety of chronic inflammatory and autoimmune diseases. Solid organ transplant patients are usually maintained on a corticosteroid combined with a calcineurin inhibitor (ciclosporin or tacrolimus), *or* with an antiproliferative drug (azathioprine or mycophenolate mofetil), *or* with both. Specialist management is required and other immunomodulators may be used to initiate treatment or to treat rejection.

**Impaired immune responsiveness** Modification of tissue reactions caused by corticosteroids and other immunosuppressants may result in the rapid *spread of infection*. Corticosteroids may suppress clinical signs of infection and allow diseases such as septicaemia or tuberculosis to reach an advanced stage before being recognised—**important**: for advice on measles and chickenpox (varicella) exposure, see Immunoglobulins (section 14.5). For advice on the use of live vaccines in individuals with impaired immune response, see section 14.1. For general comments and warnings relating to corticosteroids and immunosuppressants see section 6.3.2 (under Prednisolone).

**Pregnancy** Transplant patients immunosuppressed with azathioprine should not discontinue it on becoming pregnant; there is no evidence that azathioprine is teratogenic. However, there have been reports of premature birth and low birth-weight following exposure to azathioprine, particularly in combination with corticosteroids. Spontaneous abortion has been reported following maternal or paternal exposure.

There is less experience of ciclosporin in pregnancy but it does not appear to be any more harmful than azathioprine. The use of these drugs during pregnancy needs to be supervised in specialist units.

Manufacturers contra-indicate the use of tacrolimus and mycophenolate in pregnancy (Appendix 4).

## 8.2.1 Antiproliferative immunosuppressants

**Azathioprine** is widely used for transplant recipients and it is also used to treat a number of auto-immune conditions, usually when corticosteroid therapy alone provides inadequate control. It is metabolised to mercaptopurine, and doses should be reduced when allopurinol is given concurrently.

Blood tests and monitoring for signs of myelosuppression are essential in long-term treatment with azathioprine. The enzyme thiopurine methyltransferase (TPMT) metabolises azathioprine; the risk of myelosuppression is increased in those with a low activity of the enzyme, particularly in the very few individuals who are homozygous for low TPMT activity.

**Mycophenolate mofetil** is metabolised to mycophenolic acid which has a more selective mode of action than azathioprine. It is licensed for the prophylaxis of acute rejection in renal or cardiac transplantation when used in combination with ciclosporin and corticosteroids. There is evidence that compared with similar regimens incorporating azathioprine, mycophenolate mofetil reduces the risk of acute rejection episodes; the risk of opportunistic infections (particularly due to tissue-invasive cytomegalovirus) and the occurrence of blood disorders such as leucopenia may be higher.

Cyclophosphamide (section 8.1.1) is less commonly prescribed as an immunosuppressant.

### AZATHIOPRINE

**Indications** see notes above; also rheumatoid arthritis (section 10.1.3)

**Cautions** monitor for toxicity throughout treatment; monitor full blood count weekly (more frequently with higher doses or if hepatic or renal impairment) for first 4 weeks (manufacturer advises weekly monitoring for 8 weeks but evidence of practical value unsatisfactory), thereafter reduce frequency of monitoring to at least every 3 months; hepatic impairment (Appendix 2); renal impairment (Appendix 3); reduce dose in elderly; pregnancy (see section 8.2)—treatment should not generally be initiated during pregnancy; **interactions**: Appendix 1 (azathioprine)

Bone marrow suppression Patients should be warned to report immediately any signs or symptoms of bone marrow suppression e.g. inexplicable bruising or bleeding, infection

**Contra-indications** hypersensitivity to azathioprine or mercaptopurine; breast-feeding

**Side-effects** hypersensitivity reactions (including malaise, dizziness, vomiting, diarrhoea, fever, rigors, myalgia, arthralgia, rash, hypotension and interstitial nephritis—calling for immediate withdrawal); dose-related bone marrow suppression (see also Cautions); liver impairment, cholestatic jaundice, hair loss and increased susceptibility to infections and colitis in patients also receiving corticosteroids; nausea; rarely pancreatitis, pneumonitis, hepatic veno-occlusive disease

**Dose**

- By mouth, *or* (if oral administration not possible—intravenous solution very irritant, see below) by intravenous injection over at least 1 minute (followed by 50 mL sodium chloride intravenous infusion), *or* by intravenous infusion

  Autoimmune conditions, 1–3 mg/kg daily, adjusted according to response (consider withdrawal if no improvement in 3 months)

  Suppression of transplant rejection, initially up to 5 mg/kg then 1–4 mg/kg daily according to response

Note Intravenous injection is alkaline and very irritant, intravenous route should therefore be used **only** if oral route not feasible, see also Appendix 6

**Azathioprine** (Non-proprietary) PoM

Tablets, azathioprine 25 mg, net price 28-tab pack = £7.88; 50 mg, 56-tab pack = £7.90. Label: 21

Brands include *Azamune®*, *Immunoprin®*

**Imuran®** (GSK) PoM

Tablets, both f/c, azathioprine 25 mg (orange), net price 100-tab pack = £10.99; 50 mg (yellow), 100-tab pack = £7.99. Label: 21

Injection, powder for reconstitution, azathioprine (as sodium salt). Net price 50-mg vial = £15.38

## MYCOPHENOLATE MOFETIL

**Indications** prophylaxis of acute renal, cardiac, or hepatic transplant rejection (in combination with ciclosporin and corticosteroids) under specialist supervision

**Cautions** full blood counts every week for 4 weeks then twice a month for 2 months then every month in the first year (possibly interrupt treatment if neutropenia develops); elderly (increased risk of infection, gastro-intestinal haemorrhage and pulmonary oedema); children (higher incidence of side-effects may call for temporary reduction of dose or interruption); active serious gastro-intestinal disease (risk of haemorrhage, ulceration and perforation); delayed graft function; increased susceptibility to skin cancer (avoid exposure to strong sunlight); **interactions**: Appendix 1 (mycophenolate mofetil)

Bone marrow suppression Patients should be warned to report immediately any signs or symptoms of bone marrow suppression e.g. infection and inexplicable bruising or bleeding

**Contra-indications** pregnancy (exclude before starting and avoid for 6 weeks after discontinuation) (Appendix 4); breast-feeding (Appendix 5)

**Side-effects** diarrhoea, abdominal discomfort, gastritis, nausea, vomiting, constipation; cough, influenza-like syndrome; headache; infections (viral, bacterial, and fungal); increased blood creatinine; leucopenia, anaemia, thrombocytopenia; *less commonly* gastro-oesophageal reflux, gastro-intestinal ulceration and bleeding, pancreatitis, abnormal liver function tests, hepatitis, tachycardia, blood pressure changes, oedema, dyspnoea, tremor, insomnia, dizziness, hyperglycaemia, increased risk of malignancies, disturbances of electrolytes and blood lipids, renal tubular necrosis, arthralgia, alopecia, acne

**Dose**

- Renal transplantation, by mouth, 1 g twice daily starting within 72 hours of transplantation *or* by intravenous infusion, 1 g twice daily starting within 24 hours of transplantation for up to max. 14 days (then transfer to oral therapy); CHILD and ADOLESCENT 2–18 years (and body-surface area over 1.25 $m^2$) 600 mg/$m^2$ twice daily (max. 2 g daily)

  Note Tablets and capsules not appropriate for dose titration in young children
- Cardiac transplantation, by mouth, 1.5 g twice daily starting within 5 days of transplantation
- Hepatic transplantation, by intravenous infusion, 1 g twice daily starting within 24 hours of transplantation for 4 days (up to max. 14 days), then by mouth, 1.5 g twice daily as soon as is tolerated

**CellCept®** (Roche) PoM

Capsules, blue/brown, mycophenolate mofetil 250 mg, net price 100-cap pack = £87.33

Tablets, lavender, mycophenolate mofetil 500 mg, net price 50-tab pack = £87.33

Oral suspension, mycophenolate mofetil 1 g/5 mL when reconstituted with water, net price 175 mL = £122.25

Intravenous infusion, powder for reconstitution, mycophenolate mofetil (as hydrochloride), net price 500-mg vial = £9.69

### Mycophenolic acid

**Myfortic®** (Novartis) PoM

Tablets, e/c, mycophenolic acid (as mycophenolate sodium) 180 mg (green), net price 120-tab pack = £122.49; 360 mg (orange), 120-tab pack = £244.97. Label: 25

Dose renal transplantation, 720 mg twice daily starting within 72 hours of transplantation

Equivalence to mycophenolate mofetil Mycophenolic acid 720 mg is approximately equivalent to mycophenolate mofetil 1 g but avoid unnecessary switching because of pharmacokinetic differences

## 8.2.2 Corticosteroids and other immunosuppressants

**Prednisolone** (section 6.3.2) is widely used in oncology. It has a marked antitumour effect in acute lymphoblastic leukaemia, Hodgkin's disease, and the non-Hodgkin lymphomas. It has a role in the palliation of symptomatic end-stage malignant disease when it may enhance appetite and produce a sense of well-being (see also Prescribing in Palliative Care, p. 16).

The corticosteroids are also powerful immunosuppressants. They are used to prevent organ transplant rejection, and in high dose to treat rejection episodes.

**Ciclosporin** (cyclosporin), a calcineurin inhibitor, is a potent immunosuppressant which is virtually non-myelotoxic but markedly nephrotoxic. It has an important role in organ and tissue transplantation, for prevention of graft rejection following bone marrow, kidney, liver, pancreas, heart, lung, and heart-lung transplantation, and for prophylaxis and treatment of graft-versus-host disease.

**Tacrolimus** is also a calcineurin inhibitor. Although not chemically related to ciclosporin it has a similar mode of action and side-effects, but the incidence of neurotoxicity and nephrotoxicity appears to be greater; cardiomyopathy has also been reported. Disturbance of glucose metabolism also appears to be significant; hypertrichosis appears to be less of a problem than with ciclosporin.

**Sirolimus** is a potent non-calcineurin inhibiting immunosuppressant introduced recently for renal transplantation. It can cause hyperlipidaemia.

**Basiliximab** and **daclizumab** are monoclonal antibodies that prevent T-lymphocyte proliferation; they are used for prophylaxis of acute rejection in allogenic renal transplantation. They are given with ciclosporin and corticosteroid immunosuppression regimens; their use should be confined to specialist centres.

**Thalidomide** [unlicensed drug] should **always** be given under specialist supervision because of its teratogenic potential. It has immunomodulatory and anti-inflammatory activity; it is used in the treatment of refractory myeloma and can delay progression of early disease. It is used alone or in combination with a corticosteroid and an alkylating drug. Thalidomide can cause drowsiness, constipation, and on prolonged use, peripheral neuropathy. It should **never** be given to women of child-bearing potential.

### NICE guidance (immunosuppressive therapy for adult renal transplantation)

NICE has recommended (September 2004) that for induction therapy in the prophylaxis of organ rejection, either basiliximab or daclizumab are options for combining with a calcineurin inhibitor. For each individual, ciclosporin or tacrolimus is chosen as the calcineurin inhibitor on the basis of side-effects.

Mycophenolate mofetil [mycophenolic acid now also available, see p. 448] is recommended as part of an immunosuppressive regimen only if:

- the calcineurin inhibitor is not tolerated, particularly if nephrotoxicity endangers the transplanted kidney; *or*
- there is very high risk of nephrotoxicity from the calcineurin inhibitor, requiring a reduction in the dose of the calcineurin inhibitor or its avoidance.

Sirolimus is recommended as a component of immunosuppressive regimen **only if** intolerance necessitates the withdrawal of a calcineurin inhibitor.

These recommendations may not be consistent with the marketing authorisation of some of the products.

## BASILIXIMAB

**Indications** see notes above

**Contra-indications** pregnancy (Appendix 4) and breast-feeding

**Side-effects** *rarely* severe hypersensitivity reactions; cytokine release syndrome also reported; for side-effects of regimen see under Ciclosporin (below) and Prednisolone (section 6.3.2)

**Dose**

- By intravenous injection *or* by intravenous infusion, 20 mg within 2 hours before transplant surgery and 20 mg 4 days after surgery; CHILD and ADOLESCENT under 35 kg, 10 mg within 2 hours before transplant surgery and 10 mg 4 days after surgery; withhold second dose if severe hypersensitivity or graft loss occurs

**Simulect®** (Novartis) PoM

Injection, powder for reconstitution, basiliximab, net price 10-mg vial = £758.69, 20-mg vial = £842.38 (both with water for injections). For intravenous infusion

## CICLOSPORIN
(Cyclosporin)

**Indications** see notes above, and under Dose; atopic dermatitis and psoriasis (section 13.5.3); rheumatoid arthritis (section 10.1.3)

**Cautions** monitor kidney function—dose dependent increase in serum creatinine and urea during first few weeks may necessitate dose reduction in transplant patients (exclude rejection if kidney transplant) or discontinuation in non-transplant patients; monitor liver function (dosage adjustment based on bilirubin and liver enzymes may be needed); monitor blood pressure—discontinue if hypertension develops that cannot be controlled by antihypertensives; hyperuricaemia; monitor serum potassium especially in renal dysfunction (risk of hyperkalaemia); monitor serum magnesium; measure blood lipids before treatment and thereafter as appropriate; pregnancy (see p. 447) and breast-feeding (Appendix 5); porphyria (section 9.8.2); use with tacrolimus specifically contra-indicated and apart from specialist use in transplant patients preferably avoid other immunosuppressants with the exception of corticosteroids (increased risk of infection and lymphoma); **interactions:** Appendix 1 (ciclosporin)

Additional cautions in nephrotic syndrome ***Contra-indicated*** in uncontrolled hypertension, uncontrolled infections, and malignancy; reduce dose by 25–50% if serum creatinine more than 30% above baseline on more than one measurement; in renal impairment initially 2.5 mg/kg daily; in long-term management, perform renal biopsies at yearly intervals

Additional cautions Atopic Dermatitis and Psoriasis, section 13.5.3; Rheumatoid Arthritis, section 10.1.3

**Side-effects** dose-dependent increase in serum creatinine and urea during first few weeks (see also under Cautions); less commonly renal structural changes on long-term administration; also hypertrichosis, headache, tremor, hypertension (especially in heart transplant patients), hepatic dysfunction, fatigue, gingival hypertrophy, gastro-intestinal disturbances, burning sensation in hands and feet (usually during first week); *occasionally* rash (possibly allergic), mild anaemia, hyperkalaemia, hyperuricaemia, gout, hypomagnesaemia, hypercholesterolaemia, hyperglycaemia, weight increase, oedema, pancreatitis, neuropathy, confusion, paraesthesia, convulsions, benign intracranial hypertension (discontinue), dysmenorrhoea or amenorrhoea; myalgia, muscle weakness, cramps, myopathy, gynaecomastia (in patients receiving concomitant spironolactone), colitis and cortical blindness also reported; thrombocytopenia (sometimes with haemolytic uraemic syndrome) also reported; incidence of malignancies and lymphoproliferative disorders similar to that with other immunosuppressive therapy

**Dose**

- Organ transplantation, used alone, ADULT and CHILD over 3 months 10–15 mg/kg by mouth 4–12 hours before transplantation followed by 10–15 mg/kg daily for 1–2 weeks postoperatively then reduced gradually to 2–6 mg/kg daily for maintenance (dose should be adjusted according to blood-ciclosporin concentration and renal function); dose lower if given concomitantly with other immunosuppressant therapy (e.g. corticosteroids); if necessary one-third corresponding oral dose can be given by intravenous infusion over 2–6 hours
- Bone-marrow transplantation, prevention and treatment of graft-versus-host disease, ADULT and CHILD over 3 months 3–5 mg/kg daily by intravenous infusion over 2–6 hours from day before transplantation to 2 weeks postoperatively (or 12.5–15 mg/kg daily by mouth) then 12.5 mg/kg daily by mouth for 3–6 months then tailed off (may take up to a year after transplantation)
- Nephrotic syndrome, by mouth, 5 mg/kg daily in 2 divided doses; CHILD 6 mg/kg daily in 2 divided doses; maintenance treatment reduce to lowest effective dose according to proteinuria and serum creatinine measurements; discontinue after 3 months if no improvement in glomerulonephritis or glomerulosclerosis (after 6 months in membranous glomerulonephritis)

Conversion Any conversion between brands should be undertaken very carefully and the manufacturer contacted for further information. Currently only *Neoral*® remains available for oral use; *Sandimmun*® capsules and oral solution and *SangCya*® oral solution are available on named-patient basis only for patients who cannot be transferred to another brand of oral ciclosporin

> Because of differences in bioavailability, the brand of ciclosporin to be dispensed should be specified by the prescriber

**Neoral**® (Novartis) PoM

Capsules, ciclosporin 10 mg (yellow/white), net price 60-cap pack = £16.44; 25 mg (blue/grey), 30-cap pack = £12.00; 50 mg (yellow/white), 30-cap pack = £26.50; 100 mg (blue/grey), 30-cap pack = £50.00. Counselling, administration

Oral solution, yellow, sugar-free, ciclosporin 100 mg/mL, net price 50 mL = £82.00. Counselling, administration

Counselling Total daily dose should be taken in 2 divided doses. Avoid grapefruit or grapefruit juice for 1 hour before dose

Mix solution with orange juice (or squash) or apple juice (to improve taste) or with water immediately before taking (and rinse with more to ensure total dose). Do not mix with grapefruit juice. Keep medicine measure away from other liquids (including water)

**Sandimmun**® (Novartis) PoM

Concentrate for intravenous infusion (oily), ciclosporin 50 mg/mL. To be diluted before use. Net price 1-mL amp = £1.94; 5-mL amp = £9.17

Excipients include polyoxyl castor oil (risk of anaphylaxis, see Excipients, p. 2)

Note Observe for at least 30 minutes after starting infusion and at frequent intervals thereafter

## DACLIZUMAB

**Indications** see notes above

**Contra-indications** pregnancy and breast-feeding

**Side-effects** severe hypersensitivity reactions reported rarely; for side-effects of regimen see under Ciclosporin (above) and Prednisolone (section 6.3.2)

**Dose**

- By intravenous infusion, ADULT and CHILD, 1 mg/kg within the 24-hour period before transplantation, then 1 mg/kg every 14 days for a total of 5 doses

**Zenapax**® (Roche) ▼ PoM

Concentrate for intravenous infusion, daclizumab 5 mg/mL, net price 5-mL = £223.68

## SIROLIMUS

**Indications** prophylaxis of organ rejection in kidney allograft recipients (initially in combination with ciclosporin and corticosteroid, then with corticosteroid only); see also under Dose

**Cautions** monitor kidney function when given with ciclosporin; Afro-Caribbean patients may require higher doses; hepatic impairment (Appendix 2; renal impairment (Appendix 3); food may affect absorption (administer at the same time with respect to food); **interactions:** Appendix 1 (sirolimus)

**Contra-indications** pregnancy (Appendix 4); breast-feeding (Appendix 5)

**Side-effects** lymphocele, oedema, abdominal pain, diarrhoea, tachycardia, anaemia, fever, thrombocytopenia, neutropenia, leucopenia, thrombotic thrombocytopenic purpura, hyperlipidaemias (including hypercholesterolaemia, hypertriglyceridaemia), increase in serum creatinine in patients also receiving ciclosporin, hypokalaemia, arthralgia, acne; less commonly, venous thromboembolism, epistaxis, interstitial lung disease, impaired healing, increased susceptibility to infection, stomatitis, haemolytic uraemia, bone necrosis, rash, pyelonephritis; rarely, pancreatitis, susceptibility to lymphoma and other malignancies particularly of the skin, pancytopenia, hepatic necrosis, hypersensitivity reactions including anaphylaxis

**Dose**

- Initially 6 mg, after surgery, then 2 mg once daily (dose adjusted according to blood-sirolimus concentration) in combination with ciclosporin and corticosteroid for 2–3 months (sirolimus given 4 hours after ciclosporin); ciclosporin should then be withdrawn over 4–8 weeks (if not possible, sirolimus should be discontinued and an alternate immunosuppressive regimen used)

Note Pre-dose ('trough') blood-sirolimus concentration (using chromatographic assay) when used with ciclosporin should be 4–12 micrograms/litre; after withdrawal of ciclosporin pre-dose blood-sirolimus concentration should be 12–20 micrograms/litre; close monitoring of blood-sirolimus concentration required in hepatic impairment, during

treatment with potent inducers or inhibitors of metabolism and after discontinuing them
When changing between oral solution and tablets, measurement of serum 'trough' blood-sirolimus concentration after 1–2 weeks is recommended

**Rapamune** (Wyeth) ▼ PoM
Tablets, coated, sirolimus 1 mg, net price 30-tab pack = £90.00; 2 mg, 30-tab pack = £180.00

Oral solution, sirolimus 1 mg/mL, net price 60 mL = £169.00. Counselling, administration
Counselling Mix solution with at least 60 mL water or orange juice in a glass or plastic container immediately before taking; refill container with at least 120 mL and drink immediately (to ensure total dose). Do not mix with any other liquids

## TACROLIMUS

**Indications** primary immunosuppression in liver and kidney allograft recipients and allograft rejection resistant to conventional immunosuppressive regimens, see also notes above; moderate to severe atopic eczema (section 13.5.3)

**Cautions** see under Ciclosporin; also monitor ECG (**important:** also echocardiography, see CSM warning below), visual status, blood glucose, haematological and neurological parameters; **interactions:** Appendix 1 (tacrolimus)
Driving May affect performance of skilled tasks (e.g. driving)

**Contra-indications** hypersensitivity to macrolides; pregnancy (exclude before starting—if contraception needed non-hormonal methods should be used, Appendix 4); breast-feeding (Appendix 5); avoid concurrent administration with ciclosporin (care if patient has previously received ciclosporin)

**Side-effects** include gastro-intestinal disturbances including dyspepsia, and inflammatory and ulcerative disorders; hepatic dysfunction, jaundice, bile-duct and gall-bladder abnormalities; hypertension (less frequently hypotension), tachycardia, angina, arrhythmias, thromboembolic and ischaemic events, rarely myocardial hypertrophy, cardiomyopathy (**important:** see CSM warning below); dyspnoea, pleural effusion, tremor, headache, insomnia, paraesthesia, confusion, depression, dizziness, anxiety, convulsions, incoordination, encephalopathy, psychosis; visual and hearing abnormalities; haematological effects including anaemia, leucocytosis, leucopenia, thrombocytopenia, coagulation disorders; altered acid-base balance and glucose metabolism, electrolyte disturbances including hyperkalaemia (less frequently hypokalaemia); altered renal function including increased serum creatinine; hypophosphataemia, hypercalcaemia, hyperuricaemia; muscle cramps, arthralgia; pruritus, alopecia, rash, sweating, acne, photosensitivity; susceptibility to lymphoma and other malignancies particularly of the skin; less commonly ascites, pancreatitis, atelectasis, kidney damage and renal failure, myasthenia, hirsutism, rarely Stevens-Johnson syndrome
CSM warning Cardiomyopathy has been reported in children given tacrolimus after transplantation. Patients should be monitored carefully by echocardiography for hypertrophic changes; dose reduction or discontinuation should be considered if these occur

**Dose**
- Liver transplantation, starting 6 hours after transplantation, by mouth, 100–200 micrograms/kg daily in 2 divided doses *or* by intravenous infusion over 24 hours, 10–50 micrograms/kg; CHILD by mouth, 300 micrograms/kg daily in 2 divided doses *or* by intravenous infusion over 24 hours, 50 micrograms/kg
- Renal transplantation, starting within 24 hours of transplantation, by mouth, 150–300 micrograms/kg daily in 2 divided doses *or* by intravenous infusion over 24 hours, 50–100 micrograms/kg; CHILD by mouth, 300 micrograms/kg daily in 2 divided doses *or* by intravenous infusion over 24 hours, 100 micrograms/kg
- Maintenance treatment, dose adjusted according to response

**Prograf®** (Astellas) PoM
Capsules, tacrolimus 500 micrograms (yellow), net price 50-cap pack = £65.69; 1 mg (white), 50-cap pack = £85.22, 100-cap pack = £170.43; 5 mg (greyish-red), 50-cap pack = £314.84. Label: 23, counselling, driving

Concentrate for intravenous infusion, tacrolimus 5 mg/mL. To be diluted before use. Net price 1-mL amp = £62.05
Excipients include polyoxyl castor oil (risk of anaphylaxis, see Excipients, p. 2)

## 8.2.3 Rituximab and alemtuzumab

**Rituximab**, a monoclonal antibody which causes lysis of B lymphocytes, is licensed for the treatment of chemotherapy-resistant advanced follicular lymphoma (see NICE guidance below) and for diffuse large B-cell non-Hodgkin's lymphoma in combination with other chemotherapy (see NICE guidance below). Rituximab has recently been licensed for the treatment of previously untreated advanced follicular lymphoma in combination with other chemotherapy. Full resuscitation facilities should be at hand and as with other cytotoxics, treatment should be undertaken under the close supervision of a specialist.

Rituximab should be used with caution in patients receiving cardiotoxic chemotherapy or with a history of cardiovascular disease because exacerbation of angina, arrhythmia, and heart failure have been reported. Transient hypotension occurs frequently during infusion and antihypertensives may need to be withheld for 12 hours before infusion.

Infusion-related side-effects (including cytokine release syndrome) are reported commonly with rituximab and occur predominantly during the first infusion; they include fever and chills, nausea and vomiting, allergic reactions (such as rash, pruritus, angioedema, bronchospasm and dyspnoea), flushing and tumour pain. Patients should be given an analgesic and an antihistamine before each dose of rituximab to reduce these effects. Premedication with a corticosteroid should also be considered. The infusion may have to be stopped temporarily and the infusion-related effects treated—consult product literature for appropriate management. Evidence of pulmonary infiltration and features of tumour lysis syndrome should be sought if infusion-related effects occur.

Fatalities following **severe** cytokine release syndrome (characterised by severe dyspnoea) and associated with features of tumour lysis syndrome have occurred 1–2 hours after infusion of rituximab. Patients with a high tumour burden as well as those with pulmonary insufficiency or infiltration are at increased risk and should be monitored **very closely** (and a slower rate of infusion considered).

> **NICE guidance (rituximab for follicular non-Hodgkin's lymphoma)**
> NICE has recommended (March 2002) that for stage III or IV follicular lymphoma, rituximab is used only if the disease is resistant to other chemotherapy or if the patient cannot tolerate such treatment. In these circumstances rituximab should be used as part of a prospective study.

> **NICE guidance (rituximab for aggressive non-Hodgkin's lymphoma)**
> NICE has recommended (September 2003) rituximab, in combination with cyclophosphamide, doxorubicin, vincristine and prednisolone, for first-line treatment of CD20-positive diffuse large-B-cell lymphoma at clinical stage II, III or IV.
> The use of rituximab for localised (stage I) disease should be limited to clinical trials.

**Alemtuzumab**, another monoclonal antibody that causes lysis of B lymphocytes, is licensed for use in patients with chronic lymphocytic leukaemia which has failed to respond to treatment with an alkylating drug, or which has remitted for only a short period (less than 6 months) following fludarabine treatment. In common with rituximab, it causes infusion-related side-effects including cytokine release syndrome (see above) and premedication with an analgesic, an antihistamine, and a corticosteroid is recommended.



### ALEMTUZUMAB

**Indications** see notes above

**Cautions** see notes above—for full details (including monitoring) consult product literature

**Contra-indications** pregnancy (Appendix 4) and breast-feeding (Appendix 5); for full details consult product literature

**Side-effects** see notes above—for full details (including monitoring and management of side-effects) consult product literature

**Dose**

- Consult product literature

**MabCampath®** (Schering Health) ▼ PoM
Concentrate for intravenous infusion, alemtuzumab 30 mg/mL, net price 1-mL vial = £274.83

### RITUXIMAB

**Indications** see notes above

**Cautions** see notes above—for full details (including monitoring) consult product literature; pregnancy (Appendix 4)

**Contra-indications** breast-feeding

**Side-effects** see notes above—but for full details (including monitoring and management of side-effects) consult product literature

**MabThera®** (Roche) PoM
Concentrate for intravenous infusion, rituximab 10 mg/mL, net price 10-mL vial = £174.63, 50-mL vial = £873.15

## 8.2.4 Other immunomodulating drugs

### Interferon alfa

**Interferon alfa** has shown some antitumour effect in certain lymphomas and solid tumours. Interferon alfa preparations are also used in the treatment of chronic hepatitis B, and chronic hepatitis C ideally in combination with ribavirin (section 5.3.3). Side-effects are dose-related, but commonly include anorexia, nausea, influenza-like symptoms, and lethargy. Ocular side-effects and depression (including suicidal behaviour) have also been reported. Myelosuppression may occur, particularly affecting granulocyte counts. Cardiovascular problems (hypotension, hypertension, and arrhythmias), nephrotoxicity and hepatotoxicity have been reported. Hypertriglyceridaemia, sometimes severe, has been observed; monitoring of lipid concentration is recommended. Other side-effects include hypersensitivity reactions, thyroid abnormalities, hyperglycaemia, alopecia, psoriasiform rash, confusion, coma and seizures (usually with high doses in the elderly).

Polyethylene glycol-conjugated ('pegylated') derivatives of interferon alfa (**peginterferon alfa-2a** and **peginterferon alfa-2b**) are available; pegylation increases the persistence of the interferon in the blood. The peginterferons are licensed for the treatment of chronic hepatitis C, ideally in combination with ribavirin (see section 5.3.3).

### INTERFERON ALFA

**Indications** see under preparations

**Cautions** consult product literature; **interactions:** Appendix 1 (interferons)

**Contra-indications** consult product literature; avoid injections containing benzyl alcohol in neonates (see under preparations below)

**Side-effects** see notes above and consult product literature

**Dose**

- Consult product literature

**IntronA®** (Schering-Plough) PoM
Injection, interferon alfa-2b (rbe) 10 million units/mL, net price 2.5-mL vial = £108.00. For subcutaneous or intravenous injection

Injection, powder for reconstitution, interferon alfa-2b (rbe), net price 10-million unit vial (with injection equipment and water for injections) = £43.17. For subcutaneous or intravenous injection

Injection pen, interferon alfa-2b (rbe), net price 15 million units/mL, 1.5-mL cartridge = £77.76; 25 million units/mL, 1.5-mL cartridge = £129.60; 50 million units/mL, 1.5-mL cartridge = £259.20. For subcutaneous injection

Note Each 1.5-mL multidose cartridge delivers 6 doses of 0.2 mL i.e. a total of 1.2 mL

For chronic myelogenous leukaemia (as monotherapy or in combination with cytarabine), hairy cell leukaemia, follicular lymphoma, lymph or liver metastases of carcinoid tumour, chronic hepatitis B, chronic hepatitis C, adjunct to surgery in malignant melanoma and maintenance of remission in multiple myeloma

**Roferon-A®** (Roche) PoM

Injection, interferon alfa-2a (rbe). Net price 6 million units/mL, 0.5-mL (3 million-unit) prefilled syringe = £15.07; 9 million units/mL, 0.5-mL (4.5 million-unit) prefilled syringe = £22.60; 12 million units/mL, 0.5-mL (6 million-unit) prefilled syringe = £30.12; 18 million units/mL, 0.5-mL (9 million-unit) prefilled syringe = £45.19 36 million units/mL, 0.5-mL (18 million-unit) prefilled syringe = £90.39; 30 million units/mL, 0.6-mL (18 million-unit) cartridge = £90.39, for use with *Roferon* pen device. For subcutaneous injection (cartridges, vials, and prefilled syringes) and intramuscular injection (cartridges and vials)

Excipients include benzyl alcohol (avoid in neonates, see Excipients, p. 2)

For AIDS-related Kaposi's sarcoma, hairy cell leukaemia, chronic myelogenous leukaemia, recurrent or metastatic renal cell carcinoma, progressive cutaneous T-cell lymphoma, chronic hepatitis B and chronic hepatitis C, follicular non-Hodgkin's lymphoma, adjunct to surgery in malignant melanoma

**Viraferon®** (Schering-Plough) PoM

Injection, interferon alfa-2b (rbe) 6 million units/mL, net price 3-mL vial = £90.40. For subcutaneous injection

Injection pen, interferon alfa-2b (rbe), net price 15 million units/mL, 1.5-mL cartridge = £90.40. For subcutaneous injection

Note 1.5-mL multidose cartridge delivers 6 doses of 0.2 mL each

For chronic hepatitis B and chronic hepatitis C

## PEGINTERFERON ALFA

**Indications** see under preparations

**Cautions** consult product literature; **interactions:** Appendix 1 (interferons)

**Contra-indications** consult product literature

**Side-effects** see notes above and consult product literature

**Dose**

- Consult product literature

**Pegasys®** (Roche) ▼ PoM

Injection, peginterferon alfa-2a, net price 135-microgram prefilled syringe = £114.39, 180-microgram prefilled syringe = £132.06. For subcutaneous injection

Combined with ribavirin for chronic hepatitis C; as monotherapy for chronic hepatitis C if ribavirin not tolerated or contra-indicated (see section 5.3.3); as monotherapy for chronic hepatitis B

**PegIntron®** (Schering-Plough) PoM

Injection, powder for reconstitution, peginterferon alfa-2b (rbe), net price 50-microgram vial = £62.78, 80-microgram vial = £108.00, 100-microgram vial = £125.55, 120-microgram vial = £162.00, 150-microgram vial = £202.50 (all with injection equipment and water for injections). For subcutaneous injection

Combined with ribavirin for chronic hepatitis C; as monotherapy for chronic hepatitis C if ribavirin not tolerated or contra-indicated (see section 5.3.3)

**ViraferonPeg®** (Schering-Plough) PoM

Injection, powder for reconstitution, peginterferon alfa-2b (rbe), net price 50-microgram vial = £62.78, 80-microgram vial = £100.44, 100-microgram vial = £125.55, 120-microgram vial = £150.66, 150-microgram vial = £188.33 (all with injection equipment and water for injections). For subcutaneous injection

Injection, prefilled pen, powder for reconstitution, peginterferon alfa-2b (rbe), net price 50-microgram pen = £69.05, 80-microgram pen = £118.80, 100-microgram pen = £138.11, 120-microgram pen = £165.73, 150-microgram pen = £207.16 (all with needles and swabs). For subcutaneous injection

Combined with ribavirin for chronic hepatitis C; as monotherapy for chronic hepatitis C if ribavirin not tolerated or contra-indicated (see section 5.3.3)

## Interferon beta

**Interferon beta** is licensed for use in patients with *relapsing, remitting multiple sclerosis* (characterised by at least two attacks of neurological dysfunction over the previous 2 or 3 years, followed by complete or incomplete recovery) who are able to walk unaided. Not all patients respond and a deterioration in the bouts has been observed in some. Interferon beta-1b is also licensed for use in patients with *secondary progressive multiple sclerosis* but its role in this condition has not been confirmed.

Interferon beta should not be used in those with a history of severe depressive illness (or of suicidal ideation), in those with inadequately controlled epilepsy, or in decompensated hepatic impairment; caution is advised in those with a history of these conditions or with cardiac disorders or myelosuppression. Side-effects reported most frequently include irritation at injection site (including inflammation, hypersensitivity, necrosis) and influenza-like symptoms (fever, chills, myalgia, or malaise) but these decrease over time; nausea and vomiting occur occasionally. Other side-effects include hypersensitivity reactions (including anaphylaxis and urticaria), blood disorders, menstrual disorders, mood and personality changes, suicide attempts, confusion and convulsions; alopecia, hepatitis, and thyroid dysfunction have been reported rarely with interferon beta-1b.

### NICE guidance (interferon beta and glatiramer for multiple sclerosis)

NICE does not recommend (January 2002) either interferon beta or glatiramer acetate for the treatment of multiple sclerosis in the NHS in England and Wales.

Patients who are currently receiving interferon beta or glatiramer acetate for multiple sclerosis, whether as routine therapy or as part of a clinical trial, should have the option to continue treatment until they and their consultant consider it appropriate to stop, having regard to the established criteria for withdrawal from treatment.

### Provision of disease-modifying therapies for multiple sclerosis

The Department of Health, the National Assembly for Wales, the Scottish Executive, the Northern Ireland Department of Health, Social Services & Public Safety, and the manufacturers have reached agreement on a risk-sharing scheme for the NHS supply of interferon beta and glatiramer acetate for multiple sclerosis. Health Service Circular (HSC 2002/004) explains how patients can participate in the scheme. It is available on the Department of Health website (www.dh.gov.uk)

## INTERFERON BETA

**Indications** see notes above

**Cautions** see notes above and consult product literature

**Contra-indications** consult product literature; pregnancy (Appendix 4—advise contraceptive measures if appropriate), breast-feeding (Appendix 5)

**Side-effects** see notes above and consult product literature

**Dose**

- Consult product literature

**Interferon beta-1a**

**Avonex®** (Biogen) PoM
Injection, interferon beta-1a 60 micrograms (12 million units)/mL, net price 0.5-mL (30-microgram, 6 million-unit) prefilled syringe = £163.50. For intramuscular injection

**Rebif®** (Serono) PoM
Injection, interferon beta-1a, net price 22-microgram (6 million-unit) prefilled syringe = £54.18; 44-microgram (12 million-unit) prefilled syringe = £71.94. For subcutaneous injection

**Interferon beta-1b**

**Betaferon®** (Schering Health) PoM
Injection, powder for reconstitution, interferon beta-1b. Net price 300-microgram (9.6 million-unit) vial with diluent = £39.78. For subcutaneous injection
Note An autoinjector device (*Betaject® Light*) is available from Schering Health

## Aldesleukin

**Aldesleukin** (recombinant interleukin-2) is licensed for metastatic renal cell carcinoma; it is usually given by subcutaneous injection. It is now rarely given by intravenous infusion because of an association with a capillary leak syndrome, which can cause pulmonary oedema and hypotension. Aldesleukin produces tumour shrinkage in a small proportion of patients, but it has not been shown to increase survival. Bone-marrow, hepatic, renal, thyroid, and CNS toxicity is common. It is for use in **specialist units only**. **Interactions:** Appendix 1 (aldesleukin)

**Proleukin®** (Chiron) PoM
Injection, powder for reconstitution, aldesleukin. Net price 18-million unit vial = £112.00. For subcutaneous injection

Injection, powder for reconstitution, aldesleukin. Net price 18-million unit vial = £112.00. For intravenous infusion but see notes above

For metastatic renal cell carcinoma, **excluding** patients in whom all three of the following prognostic factors are present: performance status of Eastern Co-operative Oncology Group of 1 or greater, more than one organ with metastatic disease sites, and a period of less than 24 months between initial diagnosis of primary tumour and date of evaluation of treatment.

## BCG bladder instillation

**BCG (Bacillus Calmette-Guérin)** is a live attenuated strain derived from *Mycobacterium bovis*. It is licensed as a bladder instillation for the treatment of primary or recurrent bladder carcinoma and for the prevention of recurrence following transurethral resection.

## BACILLUS CALMETTE-GUÉRIN

**Indications** see notes above; BCG immunisation (section 14.4)

**Cautions** screen for active tuberculosis (contra-indicated if tuberculosis confirmed); traumatic catheterisation or urethral or bladder injury (delay administration until mucosal damage healed)

**Contra-indications** impaired immune response, HIV infection, urinary-tract infection, severe haematuria, tuberculosis, fever of unknown origin; pregnancy and breast-feeding

**Side-effects** cystitis, dysuria, urinary frequency, haematuria, malaise, fever, influenza-like syndrome; also systemic BCG infection (with fatalities)—consult product literature; rarely hypersensitivity reactions (such as arthralgia and rash), orchitis, transient urethral obstruction, bladder contracture, renal abscess; ocular symptoms reported

**Dose**

- Consult product literature

**ImmuCyst®** (Cambridge) PoM
Bladder instillation, freeze-dried powder containing attenuated *Mycobacterium bovis* prepared from the Connaught strain of bacillus of Calmette and Guérin, net price 81-mg vial = £89.00

**OncoTICE®** (Organon) PoM
Bladder instillation, freeze-dried powder containing attenuated *Mycobacterium bovis* prepared from the TICE strain of bacillus of Calmette and Guérin, net price 12.5-mg vial = £80.00

## Glatiramer acetate

**Glatiramer** is an immunomodulating drug comprising synthetic polypeptides. It is licensed for reducing the frequency of relapses in ambulatory patients with relapsing-remitting multiple sclerosis who have had at least 2 clinical relapses in the past 2 years. Initiation of treatment with glatiramer should be supervised by a specialist.

**NICE guidance (interferon beta and glatiramer for multiple sclerosis)**
See p. 453

**Provision of disease-modifying therapies for multiple sclerosis**
See p. 453

## GLATIRAMER ACETATE

**Indications** see notes above

**Cautions** cardiac disorders; renal impairment (Appendix 3); breast-feeding (Appendix 5)

**Contra-indications** pregnancy (Appendix 4)

**Side-effects** flushing, chest pain, palpitation, tachycardia, and dyspnoea may occur within minutes of injection; nausea, constipation, diarrhoea; syncope, anxiety, asthenia, depression, dizziness, headache, tremor, sweating; oedema, lymphadenopathy; hypertonia, back pain, arthralgia, influenza-like symptoms; injection-site reactions, rash; *rarely* convulsions, hypersensitivity reactions

**Dose**

- By subcutaneous injection, ADULT over 18 years, 20 mg daily

**Copaxone®** (Teva) PoM
Injection, glatiramer acetate 20 mg/mL, net price 1-mL prefilled syringe = £19.49

## 8.3 Sex hormones and hormone antagonists in malignant disease

8.3.1 Oestrogens
8.3.2 Progestogens
8.3.3 Androgens
8.3.4 Hormone antagonists

Hormonal manipulation has an important role in the treatment of breast, prostate, and endometrial cancer, and a more marginal role in the treatment of hypernephroma. These treatments are not curative, but may provide excellent palliation of symptoms in selected patients, sometimes for a period of years. Tumour response, and treatment toxicity should be carefully monitored and treatment changed if progression occurs or side-effects exceed benefit.

### 8.3.1 Oestrogens

**Diethylstilbestrol** (stilboestrol) is rarely used to treat prostate cancer because of its side-effects. It is occasionally used in postmenopausal women with breast cancer. Toxicity is common and dose-related side-effects include nausea, fluid retention, and venous and arterial thrombosis. Impotence and gynaecomastia always occur in men, and withdrawal bleeding may be a problem in women. Hypercalcaemia and bone pain may also occur in breast cancer.

**Ethinylestradiol** (ethinyloestradiol) is the most potent oestrogen available; unlike other oestrogens it is only slowly metabolised in the liver. Ethinylestradiol is licensed for the palliative treatment of prostate cancer.

#### DIETHYLSTILBESTROL
(Stilboestrol)

**Indications** see notes above
**Cautions** cardiovascular disease
**Contra-indications** hepatic impairment (Appendix 2)
**Side-effects** sodium retention with oedema, thromboembolism, jaundice, feminising effects in men; see also notes above
**Dose**

- Breast cancer, 10–20 mg daily
- Prostate cancer, 1–3 mg daily

**Diethylstilbestrol** (Non-proprietary) PoM
Tablets, diethylstilbestrol 1 mg, net price 28 = £26.40; 5 mg, 28 = £51.73

#### ETHINYLESTRADIOL
(Ethinyloestradiol)

**Indications** see notes above; other indications (section 6.4.1.1)
**Cautions** see section 6.4.1.1; **interactions:** Appendix 1 (oestrogens)
**Contra-indications** see section 6.4.1.1
**Side-effects** see section 6.4.1.1
**Dose**

- Prostate cancer (palliative), 0.15–1.5 mg daily

Preparations
Section 6.4.1.1

### 8.3.2 Progestogens

Progestogens have a role in the treatment of endometrial cancer; their use in breast cancer and renal cell cancer has declined. Progestogens are now rarely used to treat prostate cancer. **Medroxyprogesterone** or **megestrol** are usually chosen and can be given orally; high-dose or parenteral treatment cannot be recommended. Side-effects are mild but may include nausea, fluid retention, and weight gain.

#### MEDROXYPROGESTERONE ACETATE

**Indications** see notes above; contraception (section 7.3.2.2); other indications (section 6.4.1.2)
**Cautions** see section 6.4.1.2 and notes above; **interactions:** Appendix 1 (progestogens)
**Contra-indications** see section 6.4.1.2 and notes above
**Side-effects** see section 6.4.1.2 and notes above; glucocorticoid effects at high dose may lead to a cushingoid syndrome
**Dose**

- See preparations below

**Farlutal®** (Pharmacia) PoM
Injection, medroxyprogesterone acetate 200 mg/mL. Net price 2.5-mL vial = £13.26
Dose by deep intramuscular injection into the gluteal muscle, breast carcinoma, initially 0.5–1 g daily for 4 weeks; maintenance, 500 mg twice a week
Endometrial or renal cell carcinoma, initially 0.4–1 g weekly; maintenance, 400 mg monthly may be sufficient
Prostatic carcinoma, initially 500 mg twice weekly for 3 months; maintenance, 500 mg weekly

**Provera®** (Pharmacia) PoM
Tablets, medroxyprogesterone acetate 100 mg (scored), net price 60-tab pack = £29.98, 100-tab pack = £49.94; 200 mg (scored), 30-tab pack = £29.65, 400 mg, 30-tab pack = £58.67
Dose endometrial and renal cell cancer, 200–400 mg daily; breast cancer, 400–800 mg daily
Tablets, medroxyprogesterone acetate 2.5 mg, 5 mg and 10 mg, see section 6.4.1.2

#### MEGESTROL ACETATE

**Indications** see notes above
**Cautions** see under Medroxyprogesterone acetate (section 6.4.1.2) and notes above; **interactions:** Appendix 1 (progestogens)

**Contra-indications** see under Medroxyprogesterone acetate (section 6.4.1.2) and notes above

**Side-effects** see under Medroxyprogesterone acetate (section 6.4.1.2) and notes above

**Dose**

- Breast cancer, 160 mg daily in single or divided doses
- Endometrial cancer, 40–320 mg daily in divided doses

**Megace®** (Bristol-Myers Squibb) PoM
Tablets, both scored, megestrol acetate 40 mg, net price 20 = £5.08; 160 mg (off-white), 30-tab pack = £29.30

## NORETHISTERONE

**Indications** see notes above; other indications (section 6.4.1.2)

**Cautions** see section 6.4.1.2 and notes above; **interactions:** Appendix 1 (progestogens)

**Contra-indications** see section 6.4.1.2 and notes above

**Side-effects** see section 6.4.1.2 and notes above

**Dose**

- Breast cancer, 40 mg daily, increased to 60 mg daily if required

**Preparations**
Section 6.4.1.2

## 8.3.3 Androgens

Testosterone esters (section 6.4.2) have largely been superseded by other drugs for breast cancer.

## 8.3.4 Hormone antagonists

### 8.3.4.1 Breast cancer

The management of patients with breast cancer involves surgery, radiotherapy, drug therapy, or a combination of these.

**Early breast cancer** All women should be considered for adjuvant therapy following surgical removal of the tumour. Adjuvant therapy is used to eradicate the micrometastases that cause relapses. Choice of adjuvant treatment is determined by the risk of recurrence, oestrogen-receptor status of the primary tumour, and menopausal status.

Adjuvant therapy comprises either cytotoxic chemotherapy or hormone-antagonist therapy. Women with oestrogen-receptor-positive breast cancer are considered for hormone-antagonist therapy (preceded by cytotoxic chemotherapy if necessary) whilst women with oestrogen-receptor-negative breast cancer should be considered for cytotoxic chemotherapy.

The oestrogen-receptor antagonist **tamoxifen** is effective in premenopausal, perimenopausal, and postmenopausal women. The aromatase inhibitors **anastrozole**, **exemestane**, and **letrozole** are effective in postmenopausal women **only**. Adjuvant hormone antagonist therapy reduces the risk of cancer in the other breast and should generally be continued for 5 years following removal of the tumour. In those considered for extended adjuvant therapy, 5 years of tamoxifen is followed by an aromatase inhibitor such as letrozole for a further 3 years.

Premenopausal women may also benefit from treatment with a gonadorelin analogue or ovarian ablation.

**Advanced breast cancer** Tamoxifen is used in postmenopausal women with oestrogen-receptor-positive tumours, long disease-free interval following treatment for early breast cancer, and disease limited to bone or soft tissues. However, aromatase inhibitors, such as anastrozole or letrozole, may be more effective and are regarded as preferred treatment in postmenopausal women. Ovarian ablation or a gonadorelin analogue (section 8.3.4.2) should be considered in premenopausal women.

Progestogens such as medroxyprogesterone acetate continue to have a role in postmenopausal women with advanced breast cancer. They are as effective as tamoxifen, but they are not as well tolerated; they are less effective than the aromatase inhibitors.

Cytotoxic chemotherapy is preferred for advanced oestrogen-receptor-negative tumours and for aggressive disease, particularly where metastases involve visceral sites (e.g. the liver) or where the disease-free interval following treatment for early breast cancer is short.

**Chemoprevention** Recent evidence suggests that tamoxifen prophylaxis can reduce breast cancer in women at high risk of the disease. However, the adverse effects of tamoxifen preclude its routine use in most women.

**Cytotoxic drugs used in breast cancer** The most common cytotoxic chemotherapy regimen for both adjuvant use and metastatic disease has been cyclophosphamide (section 8.1.1), methotrexate and fluorouracil (both section 8.1.3). However, anthracycline-containing regimens are now increasingly used and should be regarded as standard therapy unless contra-indicated (e.g. in cardiac disease).

**Metastatic disease**. The choice of chemotherapy regimen will be influenced by whether the patient has previously received adjuvant treatment and the presence of any co-morbidity.

For women who have not previously received chemotherapy, *either* cyclophosphamide, methotrexate and fluorouracil *or* an anthracycline-containing regimen is the standard initial therapy for metastatic breast disease.

Patients with anthracycline-refractory or resistant disease should be considered for treatment with a taxane (section 8.1.5) either alone or in combination with trastuzumab if they have tumours that overexpress HER2 (human epidermal growth factor-2). Other cytotoxic drugs with activity against breast cancer include capecitabine (section 8.1.3), mitoxantrone, mitomycin (both section 8.1.2), and vinorelbine (section 8.1.4). In cancers that overexpress HER2, trastuzumab (section 8.1.5) is an option for chemotherapy-resistant disease.

**Oestrogen-receptor antagonists** **Tamoxifen** is an oestrogen-receptor antagonist that is licensed for breast cancer and anovulatory infertility (section 6.5.1).

**Fulvestrant** is licensed for the treatment of oestrogen-receptor-positive metastatic or locally advanced breast cancer in postmenopausal women in whom disease progresses or relapses while on, or after, other anti-oestrogen therapy.

**Toremifene** is licensed for hormone-dependent metastatic breast cancer in postmenopausal women, but it is not often used.

**Aromatase inhibitors** Aromatase inhibitors act predominantly by blocking the conversion of androgens to oestrogens in the peripheral tissues. They do not inhibit ovarian oestrogen synthesis and should not be used in premenopausal women.

**Anastrozole** and **letrozole** are non-steroidal aromatase inhibitors; **exemestane** is a steroidal aromatase inhibitor. Anastrozole and letrozole are at least as effective as tamoxifen for first-line treatment of metastatic breast cancer in postmenopausal women. However, it is not yet known whether the benefits of aromatase inhibitors persist over the long term.

**Gonadorelin analogues** **Goserelin** (section 8.3.4.2), a gonadorelin analogue is licensed for the management of advanced breast cancer in premenopausal women.

**Other drugs used in breast cancer** **Trilostane** (section 6.7.3) is licensed for postmenopausal breast cancer. It is quite well tolerated but diarrhoea and abdominal discomfort may be a problem. Trilostane causes adrenal hypofunction and corticosteroid replacement therapy is needed.

The use of **bisphosphonates** (section 6.6.2) in patients with metastatic breast cancer may prevent skeletal complications of bone metastases.

## TAMOXIFEN

**Indications** see under Dose and notes above; mastalgia [unlicensed indication] (section 6.7.2)

**Cautions** occasional cystic ovarian swellings in premenopausal women; increased risk of thromboembolic events when used with cytotoxics (see also below); breast-feeding (Appendix 5); endometrial changes (**important:** see below); porphyria (section 9.8.2); **interactions:** Appendix 1 (tamoxifen)

**Endometrial changes** Increased endometrial changes, including hyperplasia, polyps, cancer, and uterine sarcoma reported; prompt investigation required if abnormal vaginal bleeding including menstrual irregularities, vaginal discharge, and pelvic pain or pressure in those receiving (or who have received) tamoxifen.

**Contra-indications** pregnancy (exclude before commencing and advise non-hormonal contraception if appropriate—Appendix 4)

**Side-effects** hot flushes, vaginal bleeding and vaginal discharge (**important:** see also Endometrial Changes under Cautions), suppression of menstruation in some premenopausal women, pruritus vulvae, gastro-intestinal disturbances, headache, light-headedness, tumour flare, decreased platelet counts; occasionally oedema, hypercalcaemia if bony metastases, alopecia, rashes, uterine fibroids; also visual disturbances (including corneal changes, cataracts, retinopathy); leucopenia (sometimes with anaemia and thrombocytopenia), rarely neutropenia; hypertriglyceridaemia reported (sometimes with pancreatitis); thromboembolic events reported (see below); liver enzyme changes (rarely fatty liver, cholestasis, hepatitis); rarely interstitial pneumonitis, hypersensitivity reactions including angioedema, Stevens-Johnson syndrome, bullous pemphigoid; see also notes above

**Risk of thromboembolism** Tamoxifen can increase the risk of thromboembolism particularly during and immediately after major surgery or periods of immobility. Patients should be made aware of the symptoms of thromboembolism and advised to report sudden breathlessness and any pain in the calf of one leg

**Dose**

- Breast cancer, 20 mg daily

  **CSM advice** The CSM has advised that tamoxifen in a dose of 20 mg daily substantially increases survival in early breast cancer, and that no further benefit has been demonstrated with higher doses. Patients should be told of the small risk of endometrial cancer (see under Cautions above) and encouraged to report relevant symptoms early. They can, however, be reassured that the benefits of treatment far outweigh the risks
- Anovulatory infertility, 20 mg daily on days 2, 3, 4 and 5 of cycle; if necessary the daily dose may be increased to 40 mg then 80 mg for subsequent courses; if cycles irregular, start initial course on any day, with subsequent course starting 45 days later *or* on day 2 of cycle if menstruation occurs

**Tamoxifen** (Non-proprietary) PoM

Tablets, tamoxifen (as citrate) 10 mg, net price 30-tab pack = £1.59; 20 mg, 30-tab pack = £2.39; 40 mg, 30-tab pack = £4.90

Oral solution, tamoxifen (as citrate) 10 mg/5 mL, net price 150 mL = £29.61

Brands include *Soltamox®*

**Nolvadex-D®** (AstraZeneca) PoM

Tablets, tamoxifen (as citrate) 20 mg, net-price 30-tab pack = £8.71

## ANASTROZOLE

**Indications** adjuvant treatment of oestrogen-receptor-positive early breast cancer in postmenopausal women; advanced breast cancer in postmenopausal women which is oestrogen-receptor positive or responsive to tamoxifen

**Cautions** laboratory test for menopause if doubt; susceptibility to osteoporosis (assess bone mineral density before treatment and at regular intervals)

**Contra-indications** pregnancy and breast-feeding; moderate or severe hepatic disease; moderate or severe renal impairment; not for premenopausal women

**Side-effects** hot flushes, vaginal dryness, vaginal bleeding, hair thinning, anorexia, nausea, vomiting, diarrhoea, headache, arthralgia, bone fractures, rash (including Stevens-Johnson syndrome); asthenia and drowsiness—may initially affect ability to drive or operate machinery; slight increases in total cholesterol levels reported; very rarely allergic reactions including angioedema and anaphylaxis

**Dose**

- 1 mg daily

**Arimidex®** (AstraZeneca) PoM

Tablets, f/c, anastrozole 1 mg. Net price 28-tab pack = £68.56

## EXEMESTANE

**Indications** adjuvant treatment of oestrogen-receptor-positive early breast cancer in postmenopausal women following 2–3 years of tamoxifen therapy;

advanced breast cancer in postmenopausal women in whom anti-oestrogen therapy has failed

**Cautions** hepatic impairment (Appendix 2); renal impairment (Appendix 3); **interactions:** Appendix 1 (exemestane)

**Contra-indications** pregnancy and breast-feeding; not indicated for premenopausal women

**Side-effects** nausea, vomiting, abdominal pain, dyspepsia, constipation, anorexia; dizziness, fatigue, headache, depression, insomnia; hot flushes, sweating; alopecia, rash; *less commonly* drowsiness, asthenia, and peripheral oedema; *rarely* thrombocytopenia, leucopenia

**Dose**

- 25 mg daily

**Aromasin®** (Pharmacia) PoM

Tablets, s/c, exemestane 25 mg, net price 30-tab pack = £88.80, 90-tab pack = £266.40. Label: 21

## FULVESTRANT

**Indications** treatment of oestrogen-receptor-positive metastatic or locally advanced breast cancer in postmenopausal women in whom disease progresses or relapses while on, or after, other anti-oestrogen therapy

**Cautions** hepatic impairment (avoid if severe; Appendix 2)

**Contra-indications** pregnancy (Appendix 4); breast-feeding (Appendix 5)

**Side-effects** hot flushes, nausea, vomiting, diarrhoea, anorexia, headache, back pain, rash, asthenia, venous thromboembolism, injection-site reactions, urinary-tract infections; less commonly vaginal haemorrhage, vaginal candidiasis, leucorrhoea, hypersensitivity reactions including angioedema, urticaria

**Dose**

- By deep intramuscular injection, 250 mg into gluteal muscle every 4 weeks

**Faslodex®** (AstraZeneca) ▼ PoM

Injection (oily), fulvestrant 50 mg/mL, net price 5-mL (250-mg) prefilled syringe = £348.27

## LETROZOLE

**Indications** adjuvant treatment of oestrogen-receptor-positive early breast cancer in postmenopausal women; advanced breast cancer in postmenopausal women (including those in whom other anti-oestrogen therapy has failed); early invasive breast cancer in postmenopausal women after standard adjuvant tamoxifen therapy; pre-operative treatment in postmenopausal women with localised hormone-receptor-positive breast cancer to allow subsequent breast conserving surgery

**Cautions** severe renal impairment

**Contra-indications** severe hepatic impairment; not indicated for premenopausal women; pregnancy and breast-feeding

**Side-effects** hot flushes, nausea, vomiting, fatigue, dizziness, headache, dyspepsia, constipation, diarrhoea, depression, anorexia, appetite increase, hypercholesterolaemia, alopecia, increased sweating, rash, peripheral oedema, musculoskeletal pain, osteoporosis, bone fracture; *less commonly* hypertension, palpitation, tachycardia, dyspnoea, drowsiness, insomnia, anxiety, memory impairment, dysaesthesia, taste disturbance, pruritus, dry skin, urticaria, thrombophlebitis, abdominal pain, urinary frequency, urinary-tract infection, vaginal bleeding, vaginal discharge, breast pain, pyrexia, mucosal dryness, stomatitis, cataract, eye irritation, blurred vision, tumour pain, leucopenia, general oedema; *rarely* pulmonary embolism, arterial thrombosis, cerebrovascular infarction

**Dose**

- 2.5 mg daily

**Femara®** (Novartis) ▼ PoM

Tablets, f/c, letrozole 2.5 mg. Net price 14-tab pack = £41.58, 28-tab pack = £83.16

## TOREMIFENE

**Indications** hormone-dependent metastatic breast cancer in postmenopausal women

**Cautions** hypercalcaemia may occur (especially if bone metastases and usually at beginning of treatment); **interactions:** Appendix 1 (toremifene)

Endometrial changes There is a risk of increased endometrial changes including hyperplasia, polyps and cancer. Abnormal vaginal bleeding including menstrual irregularities, vaginal discharge and symptoms such as pelvic pain or pressure should be promptly investigated

**Contra-indications** endometrial hyperplasia, severe hepatic impairment (Appendix 2), history of severe thromboembolic disease; pregnancy and breast-feeding

**Side-effects** hot flushes, vaginal bleeding or discharge (**important**: see also Cautions), dizziness, oedema, sweating, nausea, vomiting, chest or back pain, fatigue, headache, skin discoloration, weight increase, insomnia, constipation, dyspnoea, paresis, tremor, vertigo, pruritus, anorexia, corneal opacity (reversible), asthenia; thromboembolic events reported; rarely dermatitis, alopecia, emotional lability, depression, jaundice, stiffness

**Dose**

- 60 mg daily

**Fareston®** (Orion) PoM

Tablets, toremifene (as citrate) 60 mg. Net price 30-tab pack = £30.37

## 8.3.4.2 Prostate cancer and gonadorelin analogues

Metastatic cancer of the prostate usually responds to hormonal treatment aimed at androgen depletion. Standard treatments include bilateral subcapsular orchidectomy or use of a gonadorelin analogue (**buserelin**, **goserelin**, **leuprorelin**, or **triptorelin**). Response in most patients lasts for 12 to 18 months. No entirely satisfactory therapy exists for disease progression despite this treatment (hormone-refractory prostate cancer), but occasional patients respond to other hormone manipulation e.g. with an anti-androgen. Bone disease can often be palliated with irradiation or, if widespread, with strontium or prednisolone (section 6.3.2).

## Gonadorelin analogues

Gonadorelin analogues are as effective as orchidectomy or **diethylstilbestrol** (section 8.3.1) but are expensive and require parenteral administration, at least initially. They cause initial stimulation then depression of luteinising hormone release by the pituitary. During the initial stage (1–2 weeks) increased production of testosterone may be associated with progression of prostate cancer. In susceptible patients this tumour 'flare' may cause spinal cord compression, ureteric obstruction or increased bone pain. When such problems are anticipated, alternative treatments (e.g. orchidectomy) or concomitant use of an anti-androgen such as cyproterone acetate or flutamide (see below) are recommended; anti-androgen treatment should be started 3 days before the gonadorelin analogue and continued for 3 weeks. Gonadorelin analogues are also used in women for breast cancer (section 8.3.4.1) and other indications (section 6.7.2).

**Cautions** Men at risk of tumour 'flare' (see above) should be monitored closely during the first month of therapy. Caution is required in women with metabolic bone disease because decreases in bone mineral density may occur. The injection site should be rotated.

**Side-effects** The gonadorelin analogues cause side-effects similar to the menopause in women and orchidectomy in men and include hot flushes and sweating, sexual dysfunction, vaginal dryness or bleeding, and gynaecomastia or changes in breast size. Signs and symptoms of prostate or breast cancer may worsen initially (managed in prostate cancer with anti-androgens, see above). Other side-effects include hypersensitivity reactions (rashes, pruritus, asthma, and rarely anaphylaxis), injection site reactions (see Cautions), headache (rarely migraine), visual disturbances, dizziness, arthralgia and possibly myalgia, hair loss, peripheral oedema, gastro-intestinal disturbances, weight changes, sleep disorders, and mood changes.

## Anti-androgens

**Cyproterone acetate**, **flutamide** and **bicalutamide** are anti-androgens that inhibit the tumour 'flare' which may occur after commencing gonadorelin analogue administration. Cyproterone acetate and flutamide are also licensed for use alone in patients with metastatic prostate cancer refractory to gonadorelin analogue therapy. Bicalutamide is used for prostate cancer either alone or as an adjunct to other therapy, according to the clinical circumstances.

### BICALUTAMIDE

**Indications** advanced prostate cancer in combination with a gonadorelin analogue or surgical castration; locally advanced prostate cancer either alone or as adjuvant treatment

**Cautions** hepatic impairment (Appendix 2), also consider periodic liver function tests; **interactions**: Appendix 1 (bicalutamide)

**Side-effects** nausea, vomiting, diarrhoea, asthenia, gynaecomastia, breast tenderness, hot flushes, pruritus, dry skin, alopecia, hirsutism, decreased libido, impotence, weight gain; less commonly hypersensitivity reactions including angioneurotic oedema and urticaria, interstitial lung disease; rarely abdominal pain, cardiovascular disorders (including angina, heart failure and arrhythmias), depression, dyspepsia, haematuria, cholestasis, jaundice, thrombocytopenia

**Dose**
- Advanced prostate cancer, with orchidectomy or gonadorelin therapy, 50 mg daily (in gonadorelin therapy, started 3 days beforehand, see also notes above)
- Locally advanced prostate cancer, 150 mg once daily

Note The CSM has advised (October 2003) that bicalutamide should no longer be used for the treatment of localised prostate cancer

**Casodex®** (AstraZeneca) PoM
Tablets, f/c, bicalutamide 50 mg, net price 28-tab pack = £128.00; 150 mg, 28-tab pack = £240.00

### BUSERELIN

**Indications** advanced prostate cancer; other indications (section 6.7.2)

**Cautions** depression, see also notes above

**Side-effects** see notes above; worsening hypertension, palpitation, glucose intolerance, altered blood lipids, thrombocytopenia, leucopenia, nervousness, fatigue, memory and concentration disturbances, anxiety, increased thirst, hearing disorders, musculoskeletal pain; nasal irritation, nose bleeds and altered sense of taste and smell (spray formulation only)

**Dose**
- By subcutaneous injection, 500 micrograms every 8 hours for 7 days, then intranasally, 1 spray into each nostril 6 times daily (see also notes above)

Counselling Avoid use of nasal decongestants before and for at least 30 minutes after treatment.

**Suprefact®** (Aventis Pharma) PoM
Injection, buserelin (as acetate) 1 mg/mL. Net price 2 × 5.5-mL vial = £23.69

Nasal spray, buserelin (as acetate) 100 micrograms/metered spray. Net price treatment pack of 4 × 10-g bottle with spray pump = £87.68. Counselling, see above

### CYPROTERONE ACETATE

**Indications** prostate cancer, see under Dose and also notes above; other indications, see section 6.4.2

**Cautions** in prostate cancer, blood counts initially and throughout treatment; hepatic impairment (Appendix 2; see also under side-effects below); monitor hepatic function (liver function tests should be performed before treatment, see also under Side-effects below); monitor adrenocortical function regularly; risk of recurrence of thromboembolic disease; diabetes mellitus, sickle-cell anaemia, severe depression (in other indications some of these are contra-indicated, see section 6.4.2)

Driving Fatigue and lassitude may impair performance of skilled tasks (e.g. driving)

**Contra-indications** none in prostate cancer; for contra-indications relating to other indications see section 6.4.2

**Side-effects** see section 6.4.2

Hepatotoxicity Direct hepatic toxicity including jaundice, hepatitis and hepatic failure have been reported (usually after several months) in patients treated with cyproterone acetate 200–300 mg daily. Liver function tests should be performed before and regularly during treatment and whenever symptoms suggestive of hepatotoxicity occur—if confirmed cyproterone should normally be withdrawn unless the hepatotoxicity can be explained by another cause such as metastatic disease (in which case cyproterone should be continued only if the perceived benefit exceeds the risk)

**Dose**

- Flare with initial gonadorelin therapy, 300 mg daily in 2–3 divided doses, reduced to 200 mg daily in 2–3 divided doses if necesssary
- Long-term palliative therapy where gonadorelin analogues or orchidectomy contra-indicated, not tolerated, or where oral therapy preferred, 200–300 mg daily in 2–3 divided doses
- Hot flushes with gonadorelin therapy or after orchidectomy, initially 50 mg daily, adjusted according to response to 50–150 mg daily in 1–3 divided doses

**Cyproterone Acetate** (Non-proprietary) PoM
Tablets, cyproterone acetate 50 mg, net price 56-tab pack = £31.54; 100 mg, 84-tab pack = £91.39. Label: 21, counselling, driving

**Cyprostat®** (Schering Health) PoM
Tablets, scored, cyproterone acetate 50 mg, net price 168-tab pack = £77.68; 100 mg, 84-tab pack = £77.68. Label: 21, counselling, driving

## FLUTAMIDE

**Indications** advanced prostate cancer, see also notes above

**Cautions** cardiac disease (oedema reported); hepatic impairment, also liver function tests, monthly for first 4 months, periodically thereafter and at the first sign or symptom of liver disorder (e.g. pruritus, dark urine, persistent anorexia, jaundice, abdominal pain, unexplained influenza-like symptoms); avoid excessive alcohol consumption; **interactions:** Appendix 1 (flutamide)

**Side-effects** gynaecomastia (sometimes with galactorrhoea); nausea, vomiting, diarrhoea, increased appetite, insomnia, tiredness; other side-effects reported include decreased libido, reduced sperm count, gastric and chest pain, hypertension, headache, dizziness, oedema, blurred vision, thirst, rash, pruritus, haemolytic anaemia, systemic lupus erythematosus-like syndrome, and lymphoedema; hepatic injury (with transaminase abnormalities, cholestatic jaundice, hepatic necrosis, hepatic encephalopathy and occasional fatality) reported

**Dose**

- 250 mg 3 times daily (see also notes above)

**Flutamide** (Non-proprietary) PoM
Tablets, flutamide 250 mg. Net price 84-tab pack = £18.60

**Drogenil®** (Schering-Plough) PoM
Tablets, yellow, scored, flutamide 250 mg, net price 84-tab pack = £65.10

## GOSERELIN

**Indications** prostate cancer; advanced breast cancer; oestrogen-receptor positive early breast cancer (section 8.3.4.1); other indications (section 6.7.2)

**Cautions** see notes above; breast-feeding (Appendix 5)

**Contra-indications** pregnancy (Appendix 4); undiagnosed vaginal bleeding

**Side-effects** see notes above; also transient changes in blood pressure, paraesthesia, rarely hypercalcaemia (in patients with metastatic breast cancer)

**Dose**

- See under preparations below

**Zoladex®** (AstraZeneca) PoM
Implant, goserelin 3.6 mg (as acetate) in *SafeSystem®* syringe applicator. Net price each = £84.14
Dose breast cancer and prostate cancer by subcutaneous injection into anterior abdominal wall, 3.6 mg every 28 days (see also notes above)

**Zoladex® LA** (AstraZeneca) PoM
Implant, goserelin 10.8 mg (as acetate) in *SafeSystem®* syringe applicator. Net price each = £267.48
Dose prostate cancer, by subcutaneous injection into anterior abdominal wall, 10.8 mg every 12 weeks (see also notes above)

## LEUPRORELIN ACETATE

**Indications** advanced prostate cancer; other indications (section 6.7.2)

**Cautions** see notes above and section 6.7.2

**Side-effects** see notes above and section 6.7.2; also fatigue, muscle weakness, paraesthesia, hypertension, palpitation, alteration of glucose tolerance and of blood lipids; hypotension, jaundice, thrombocytopenia and leucopenia reported

**Dose**

- See under preparations below

**Prostap® SR** (Wyeth) PoM
Injection (microsphere powder for reconstitution), leuprorelin acetate, net price 3.75-mg vial with 1-mL vehicle-filled syringe = £125.40
Dose advanced prostate cancer, by subcutaneous *or* by intramuscular injection, 3.75 mg every 4 weeks (see also notes above)

**Prostap® 3** (Wyeth) PoM
Injection (microsphere powder for reconstitution), leuprorelin acetate, net price 11.25-mg vial with 2-mL vehicle-filled syringe = £376.20
Dose advanced prostate cancer, by subcutaneous injection, 11.25 mg every three months (see also notes above)

## TRIPTORELIN

**Indications** advanced prostate cancer; endometriosis, precocious puberty, reduction in size of uterine fibroids (section 6.7.2)

**Cautions** see notes above

**Side-effects** see notes above; transient hypertension, dry mouth, paraesthesia, increased dysuria, gynaecomastia

**Dose**

- See under preparations below

**Decapeptyl® SR** (Ipsen) PoM
Injection (powder for suspension), m/r, triptorelin (as acetate), net price 4.2-mg vial (with diluent) = £69.00
Dose by intramuscular injection, advanced prostate cancer, 3 mg every 4 weeks
Endometriosis and reduction in size of uterine fibroids, 3 mg every 4 weeks starting during first 5 days of menstrual cycle; for uterine fibroids continue treatment for at least 3 months; max. duration of treatment 6 months (do not repeat)
Note Each 4.2-mg vial includes an overage to allow administration of a 3-mg dose

Injection (powder for suspension), m/r, triptorelin (as acetate), net price 15-mg vial (with diluent) = £207.00

Dose by intramuscular injection, advanced prostate cancer, 11.25 mg every 3 months (see also notes above)

Note Each 15-mg vial includes an overage to allow administration of an 11.25-mg dose

**Gonapeptyl Depot®** (Ferring) PoM

Injection (powder for suspension), triptorelin (as acetate), net price 3.75-mg prefilled syringe (with prefilled syringe of vehicle) = £85.00

Dose by subcutaneous *or* deep intramuscular injection, advanced prostate cancer, 3.75 mg every 4 weeks (see also notes above)

Endometriosis and reduction in size of uterine fibroids, 3.75 mg every 4 weeks starting during first 5 days of menstrual cycle; for uterine fibroids continue treatment for 3 or 4 months; max. duration of treatment 6 months (do not repeat)

Precocious puberty (girls under 9 years, boys under 10 years), initially 3.75 mg every 2 weeks for 3 doses then every 3–4 weeks; dose reduced to 1.875 mg if body-weight under 20 kg or to 2.5 mg if body-weight 20–30 kg; discontinue when bone maturation consistent with age over 12 years in girls or over 13 years in boys

## 8.3.4.3 Somatostatin analogues

**Octreotide** and **lanreotide** are analogues of the hypothalamic release-inhibiting hormone somatostatin. They are indicated for the relief of symptoms associated with neuroendocrine (particularly carcinoid) tumours and acromegaly. Additionally, lanreotide is licensed for the treatment of thyroid tumours and octreotide is also licensed for the prevention of complications following pancreatic surgery; octreotide may also be valuable in reducing vomiting in palliative care (see p. 17) and in stopping variceal bleeding [unlicensed indication]—see also vasopressin and terlipressin (section 6.5.2).

**Cautions** Growth hormone-secreting pituitary tumours can expand causing serious complications; during treatment with somatostatin analogues patients should be monitored for signs of tumour expansion (e.g. visual field defects). Ultrasound examination of the gallbladder is recommended before treatment and at intervals of 6–12 months during treatment (avoid abrupt withdrawal of short-acting octreotide—see Side-effects below). In insulinoma an increase in the depth and duration of hypoglycaemia may occur (observe patients when initiating treatment and changing doses); in diabetes mellitus, insulin or oral antidiabetic requirements may be reduced.

**Side-effects** Gastro-intestinal disturbances including anorexia, nausea, vomiting, abdominal pain and bloating, flatulence, diarrhoea, and steatorrhoea may occur. Postprandial glucose tolerance may be impaired and rarely persistent hyperglycaemia occurs with chronic administration; hypoglycaemia has also been reported. Gallstones have been reported after long-term treatment (abrupt withdrawal of subcutaneous octreotide is associated with biliary colic and pancreatitis). Pain and irritation may occur at the injection site and sites should be rotated. Rarely, pancreatitis has been reported shortly after administration.

### OCTREOTIDE

**Indications** see under Dose

**Cautions** see notes above; hepatic impairment; pregnancy (Appendix 4); breast-feeding (Appendix 5); monitor thyroid function on long-term therapy; **interactions**: Appendix 1 (octreotide)

**Side-effects** see notes above; rarely altered liver function tests, hepatitis and transient alopecia

**Dose**

- Symptoms associated with carcinoid tumours With features of carcinoid syndrome, VIPomas, glucagonomas, by subcutaneous injection, initially 50 micrograms once or twice daily, gradually increased according to response to 200 micrograms 3 times daily (higher doses required exceptionally); maintenance doses variable; in carcinoid tumours discontinue after 1 week if no effect; if rapid response required, initial dose by intravenous injection (with ECG monitoring and after dilution to a concentration of 10–50% with sodium chloride 0.9% injection)
- Acromegaly, short-term treatment before pituitary surgery *or* long-term treatment in those inadequately controlled by other treatment *or* until radiotherapy becomes fully effective by subcutaneous injection, 100–200 micrograms 3 times daily; discontinue if no improvement within 3 months
- Prevention of complications following pancreatic surgery, consult product literature

**Sandostatin®** (Novartis) PoM

Injection, octreotide (as acetate) 50 micrograms/mL, net price 1-mL amp = £3.47; 100 micrograms/mL, 1-mL amp = £6.53; 200 micrograms/mL 5-mL vial = £65.10; 500 micrograms/mL, 1-mL amp = £31.65

**Depot preparation**

**Sandostatin Lar®** (Novartis) PoM

Injection (microsphere powder for aqueous suspension), octreotide (as acetate) 10-mg vial = £637.50; 20-mg vial = £850.00; 30-mg vial = £1062.50 (all supplied with 2.5-mL diluent-filled syringe)

Dose acromegaly (test dose by subcutaneous injection 50–100 micrograms if subcutaneous octreotide not previously given), neuroendocrine (particularly carcinoid) tumour adequately controlled by subcutaneous octreotide, by deep intramuscular injection into gluteal muscle, initially 20 mg every 4 weeks for 3 months then adjusted according to response; max. 30 mg every 4 weeks

For acromegaly, start depot octreotide 1 day after the last dose of subcutaneous octreotide (for pituitary surgery give last dose of depot octreotide at least 3 weeks before surgery); for neuroendocrine tumours, continue subcutaneous octreotide for 2 weeks after first dose of depot octreotide

### LANREOTIDE

**Indications** see notes above

**Cautions** see notes above; pregnancy (Appendix 4); breast-feeding (Appendix 5); **interactions**: Appendix 1 (lanreotide)

**Side-effects** see notes above; also reported asthenia, fatigue, raised bilirubin; less commonly skin nodule, hot flushes, leg pain, malaise, headache, tenesmus, decreased libido, drowsiness, pruritus, increased sweating; rarely hypothyroidism (monitor as necessary)

**Dose**

- See under preparations

**Somatuline® LA** (Ipsen) PoM

Injection (copolymer microparticles for aqueous suspension), lanreotide (as acetate) 30-mg vial (with vehicle) = £310.85

Dose by intramuscular injection, acromegaly and neuroendocrine (particularly carcinoid) tumours, initially 30 mg every 14 days, frequency increased to every 7–10 days according to response

Thyroid tumours, 30 mg every 14 days, frequency increased to every 10 days according to response

**Somatuline Autogel®** (Ipsen)

Injection, prefilled syringe, lanreotide (as acetate) 60 mg = £525.00; 90 mg = £699.00; 120 mg = £902.00

**Dose** by deep subcutaneous injection into the gluteal region, acromegaly (if somatostatin analogue not given previously), initially 60 mg every 28 days, adjusted according to response; for patients treated previously with somatostatin analogue, consult product literature for initial dose

Neuroendocrine (particularly carcinoid) tumours, initially 60–120 mg every 28 days, adjusted according to response

# 9 Nutrition and blood


**9.1 Anaemias and some other blood disorders 463**
9.1.1 Iron-deficiency anaemias 463
9.1.1.1 Oral iron 463
9.1.1.2 Parenteral iron 466
9.1.2 Drugs used in megaloblastic anaemias 466
9.1.3 Drugs used in hypoplastic, haemolytic, and renal anaemias 468
9.1.4 Drugs used in platelet disorders 471
9.1.5 G6PD deficiency 472
9.1.6 Drugs used in neutropenia 472
**9.2 Fluids and electrolytes 474**
9.2.1 Oral preparations for fluid and electrolyte imbalance 474
9.2.1.1 Oral potassium 474
9.2.1.2 Oral sodium and water 476
9.2.1.3 Oral bicarbonate 477
9.2.2 Parenteral preparations for fluid and electrolyte imbalance 477
9.2.2.1 Electrolytes and water 477
9.2.2.2 Plasma and plasma substitutes 480
**9.3 Intravenous nutrition 482**
**9.4 Oral nutrition 487**
9.4.1 Foods for special diets 487
9.4.2 Enteral nutrition 488
**9.5 Minerals 488**
9.5.1 Calcium and magnesium 488
9.5.1.1 Calcium supplements 488
9.5.1.2 Hypercalcaemia and hypercalciuria 489
9.5.1.3 Magnesium 490
9.5.2 Phosphorus 491
9.5.2.1 Phosphate supplements 491
9.5.2.2 Phosphate-binding agents 491
9.5.3 Fluoride 492
9.5.4 Zinc 493
**9.6 Vitamins 493**
9.6.1 Vitamin A 494
9.6.2 Vitamin B group 494
9.6.3 Vitamin C 495
9.6.4 Vitamin D 496
9.6.5 Vitamin E 497
9.6.6 Vitamin K 498
9.6.7 Multivitamin preparations 498
**9.7 Bitters and tonics 499**
**9.8 Metabolic disorders 499**
9.8.1 Drugs used in metabolic disorders 499
9.8.2 Acute porphyrias 502


## 9.1 Anaemias and some other blood disorders


**9.1.1 Iron-deficiency anaemias**
**9.1.2 Drugs used in megaloblastic anaemias**
**9.1.3 Drugs used in hypoplastic, haemolytic, and renal anaemias**
**9.1.4 Drugs used in platelet disorders**
**9.1.5 G6PD deficiency**
**9.1.6 Drugs used in neutropenia**


Before initiating treatment for anaemia it is essential to determine which type is present. Iron salts may be harmful and result in iron overload if given alone to patients with anaemias other than those due to iron deficiency.

## 9.1.1 Iron-deficiency anaemias


**9.1.1.1 Oral iron**
**9.1.1.2 Parenteral iron**


*Treatment* with an iron preparation is justified only in the presence of a demonstrable iron-deficiency state. Before starting treatment, it is important to exclude any serious underlying cause of the anaemia (e.g. gastric erosion, gastro-intestinal cancer).

*Prophylaxis* with an iron preparation is justifiable in individuals who have additional risk factors for iron deficiency (e.g. poor diet). Prophylaxis may also be appropriate in malabsorption, menorrhagia, pregnancy, after subtotal or total gastrectomy, in haemodialysis patients, and in the management of low birth-weight infants such as preterm neonates.

### 9.1.1.1 Oral iron

Iron salts should be given by mouth unless there are good reasons for using another route.

Ferrous salts show only marginal differences between one another in efficiency of absorption of iron, but ferric salts are much less well absorbed. Haemoglobin regeneration rate is little affected by the type of salt used provided sufficient iron is given, and in most patients the speed of response is not critical. Choice of preparation is thus usually decided by incidence of side-effects and cost.

The oral dose of elemental iron for deficiency should be 100 to 200 mg daily. It is customary to give this as dried **ferrous sulphate**, 200 mg (≡ 65 mg elemental iron) three times daily; a dose of ferrous sulphate 200 mg once or twice daily may be effective for prophylaxis or for mild iron deficiency.

**Iron content of different iron salts**

| Iron salt | Amount | Content of ferrous iron |
|---|---|---|
| Ferrous fumarate | 200 mg | 65 mg |
| Ferrous gluconate | 300 mg | 35 mg |
| Ferrous sulphate | 300 mg | 60 mg |
| Ferrous sulphate, dried | 200 mg | 65 mg |

**Therapeutic response** The haemoglobin concentration should rise by about 100–200 mg/100 mL (1–2 g/litre) per day *or* 2 g/100 mL (20 g/litre) over 3–4 weeks. When the haemoglobin is in the normal range, treatment should be continued for a further 3 months to replenish the iron stores. Epithelial tissue changes such as atrophic glossitis and koilonychia are usually improved, but the response is often slow.

**Side-effects** Gastro-intestinal irritation may occur with iron salts. Nausea and epigastric pain are dose-related but the relationship between dose and altered bowel habit (constipation or diarrhoea) is less clear. Oral iron, particularly modified-release preparations, may exacerbate diarrhoea in patients with inflammatory bowel disease; care is also needed in patients with intestinal strictures and diverticular disease.

Iron preparations taken orally may be constipating, particularly in older patients, occasionally leading to faecal impaction.

If side-effects occur, the dose may be reduced; alternatively, another iron salt may be used but an improvement in tolerance may simply be a result of a lower content of elemental iron. The incidence of side-effects due to ferrous sulphate is no greater than with other iron salts when compared on the basis of equivalent amounts of elemental iron.

Iron preparations are a common cause of accidental overdose in children. For the treatment of **iron overdose**, see Emergency Treatment of Poisoning, p. 32.

**Compound preparations** Some oral preparations contain ascorbic acid to aid absorption of the iron but the therapeutic advantage of such preparations is minimal and cost may be increased.

There is no justification for the inclusion of other ingredients, such as the B group of vitamins (except folic acid for pregnant women, see Iron and Folic Acid, p. 465 and on p. 467).

**Modified-release preparations** Modified-release preparations of iron are licensed for once-daily dosage, but have no therapeutic advantage and should not be used. These preparations are formulated to release iron gradually; the low incidence of side-effects may reflect the small amounts of iron available for absorption as the iron is carried past the first part of the duodenum into an area of the gut where absorption may be poor.

## FERROUS SULPHATE

**Indications** iron-deficiency anaemia

**Cautions** pregnancy (see section 9.1.1); **interactions:** Appendix 1 (iron)

**Side-effects** see notes above

**Dose**

- See under preparations below and notes above

Counselling Although iron preparations are best absorbed on an empty stomach they may be taken after food to reduce gastro-intestinal side-effects; they may discolour stools

**Ferrous Sulphate** (Non-proprietary)

Tablets, coated, dried ferrous sulphate 200 mg (65 mg iron), net price 28-tab pack = £1.59

Dose prophylactic, 1 tablet daily; therapeutic, 1 tablet 2–3 times daily

**Ironorm® Drops** (Wallace Mfg)

Oral drops, ferrous sulphate 625 mg (125 mg iron)/5 mL. Net price 15-mL = £3.35

Dose ADULT and CHILD over 6 years, 0.6 mL daily; INFANT and CHILD up to 6 years, 0.3 mL daily

**Modified-release preparations**

**Feospan®** (Intrapharm) NHS

Spansule® (= capsules m/r), clear/red, enclosing green and brown pellets, dried ferrous sulphate 150 mg (47 mg iron). Net price 30-cap pack = £1.43. Label: 25

Dose 1–2 capsules daily; CHILD over 1 year, 1 capsule daily; can be opened and sprinkled on food

**Ferrograd®** (Abbott)

Tablets, f/c, m/r, red, dried ferrous sulphate 325 mg (105 mg iron). Net price 30-tab pack = 54p. Label: 25

Dose ADULT and CHILD over 12 years, 1 tablet daily before food

## FERROUS FUMARATE

**Indications** iron-deficiency anaemia

**Cautions** pregnancy (see section 9.1.1); **interactions:** Appendix 1 (iron)

**Side-effects** see notes above

**Dose**

- See under preparations below and notes above

**Fersaday®** (Goldshield)

Tablets, brown, f/c, ferrous fumarate 322 mg (100 mg iron). Net price 28-tab pack = 66p

Dose prophylactic, 1 tablet daily; therapeutic, 1 tablet twice daily

**Fersamal®** (Goldshield)

Tablets, brown, ferrous fumarate 210 mg (68 mg iron). Net price 20 = 29p

Dose 1–2 tablets 3 times daily

Syrup, brown, ferrous fumarate approx. 140 mg (45 mg iron)/5 mL. Net price 200 mL = £3.00

Dose 10–20 mL twice daily; PRETERM NEONATE 0.6–2.4 mL/kg daily; CHILD up to 6 years 2.5–5 mL twice daily

**Galfer®** (Thornton & Ross)

Capsules, red/green, ferrous fumarate 305 mg (100 mg iron). Net price 20 = 36p

Dose 1 capsule 1–2 times daily before food

Syrup, brown, sugar-free ferrous fumarate 140 mg (45 mg iron)/5 mL. Net price 300 mL = £4.86

Dose 10 mL 1–2 times daily before food; CHILD (full-term infant and young child) 2.5–5 mL 1–2 times daily

## FERROUS GLUCONATE

**Indications** iron-deficiency anaemia

**Cautions** pregnancy (see section 9.1.1); **interactions:** Appendix 1 (iron)

**Side-effects** see notes above

**Dose**

- See under preparation below and notes above

**Ferrous Gluconate** (Non-proprietary)

Tablets, red, coated, ferrous gluconate 300 mg (35 mg iron). Net price 20 = 73p

Dose prophylactic, 2 tablets daily before food; therapeutic, 4–6 tablets daily in divided doses before food; CHILD 6–12 years, prophylactic and therapeutic, 1–3 tablets daily

## POLYSACCHARIDE-IRON COMPLEX

**Indications** iron-deficiency anaemia

**Cautions** pregnancy (see section 9.1.1); **interactions:** Appendix 1 (iron)

**Side-effects** see notes above

**Dose**

- See under preparation below and notes above

**Niferex®** (Tillomed)

Elixir, brown, sugar-free, polysaccharide-iron complex equivalent to 100 mg of iron/5 mL. Net price 240-mL pack = £6.06; NHS[1] 30-mL dropper bottle for paediatric use = £2.16. Counselling, use of dropper

Dose prophylactic, 2.5 mL daily; therapeutic, 5 mL 1–2 times daily (once daily if required during second and third trimester of pregnancy); PRETERM NEONATE, NEONATE, and INFANT (from dropper bottle) 1 drop (approx. 500 micrograms iron) per 450 g body-weight 3 times daily; CHILD 2–6 years 2.5 mL daily, 6–12 years 5 mL daily

1. except 30 mL paediatric dropper bottle for prophylaxis and treatment of iron deficiency in infants born prematurely; endorse prescription 'SLS'

## SODIUM FEREDETATE
### (Sodium ironedetate)

**Indications** iron-deficiency anaemia

**Cautions** pregnancy (see section 9.1.1); **interactions:** Appendix 1 (iron)

**Side-effects** see notes above

**Dose**

- See under preparation below and notes above

**Sytron®** (Link)

Elixir, sugar-free, sodium feredetate 190 mg equivalent to 27.5 mg of iron/5 mL. Net price 100 mL = 89p

Dose 5 mL increasing gradually to 10 mL 3 times daily; PRETERM NEONATE, NEONATE, and INFANT under 1 year 2.5 mL twice daily (smaller doses should be used initially); CHILD 1–5 years 2.5 mL 3 times daily, 6–12 years 5 mL 3 times daily

## Iron and folic acid

These preparations are used during pregnancy in women who are at high risk of developing iron and folic acid deficiency; they should be distinguished from those used for the prevention of neural tube defects in women planning a pregnancy (see p. 467).

It is important to note that the small doses of folic acid contained in these preparations are inadequate for the treatment of megaloblastic anaemias.

**Fefol®** (Intrapharm) NHS ▲

Spansule® (= capsules m/r), clear/green, enclosing brown, yellow, and white pellets, dried ferrous sulphate 150 mg (47 mg iron), folic acid 500 micrograms. Net price 30-cap pack = £1.69. Label: 25

Dose 1 capsule daily

**Ferrograd Folic®** (Abbott) ▲

Tablets, f/c, red/yellow, dried ferrous sulphate 325 mg (105 mg iron) for sustained release, folic acid 350 micrograms. Net price 30-tab pack = 60p. Label: 25

Dose ADULT and CHILD over 12 years, 1 tablet daily before food

**Galfer FA®** (Thornton & Ross)

Capsules, red/yellow, ferrous fumarate 305 mg (100 mg iron), folic acid 350 micrograms. Net price 30-cap pack = £1.10

Dose 1 capsule daily before food

**Lexpec with Iron-M®** (Rosemont) PoM

Syrup, brown, sugar-free, ferric ammonium citrate equivalent to 80 mg iron, folic acid 500 micrograms/ 5 mL. Net price 150 mL = £4.09

Dose 5–10 mL daily before food

Note *Lexpec with Iron-M®* contains five times less folic acid than *Lexpec with Iron®*

**Pregaday®** (Celltech)

Tablets, brown, f/c, ferrous fumarate equivalent to 100 mg iron, folic acid 350 micrograms. Net price 28-tab pack =£1.25

Dose 1 tablet daily

### ▲Higher folic acid content

Appropriate in context of prevention of *recurrence of neural tube defects*, see recommendations on p. 467

*Cautions:* theoretical possibility of masking anaemia due to vitamin-$B_{12}$ deficiency (which could allow vitamin-$B_{12}$ neuropathy to develop).

**Ferfolic SV®** (Durbin) PoM NHS

Tablets, pink, ferrous gluconate 250 mg (30 mg iron), folic acid 4 mg, ascorbic acid 10 mg. Net price 100-tab pack = £2.50

Dose anaemia, 1–3 tablets daily after food

Prophylaxis of neural tube defects in women known to be at risk, 1 tablet daily started before conception and continued for at least first trimester; see also recommendations on p. 467

**Lexpec with Iron®** (Rosemont) PoM

Syrup, brown, sugar-free, ferric ammonium citrate equivalent to 80 mg iron, folic acid 2.5 mg/5 mL. Net price 150 mL = £4.09

Dose 5–10 mL daily before food

Note *Lexpec with Iron®* contains five times as much folic acid as *Lexpec with Iron-M®*

## Compound iron preparations

There is no justification for prescribing compound iron preparations, except for preparations of iron and folic acid for prophylactic use in pregnancy (see above).

**Ferrograd C®** (Abbott) NHS ▲

Tablets, f/c, red, dried ferrous sulphate 325 mg (105 mg iron) for sustained release, ascorbic acid 500 mg (as sodium salt). Net price 30-tab pack = £1.71. Label: 25

Dose ADULT and CHILD over 12 years, 1 tablet daily before food

**Givitol®** (Galen) NHS ▲

Capsules, red/maroon, ferrous fumarate 305 mg (100 mg iron) with vitamins B group and C. Net price 20 = 88p

Dose 1 capsule daily before food

## 9.1.1.2 Parenteral iron

Iron may be administered parenterally as iron dextran, or iron sucrose. Parenteral iron is generally reserved for use when oral therapy is unsuccessful because the patient cannot tolerate oral iron, or does not take it reliably, or if there is continuing blood loss, or in malabsorption.

Also, many patients with chronic renal failure who are receiving haemodialysis (and some who are receiving peritoneal dialysis) require iron by the intravenous route on a regular basis (see also Erythropoietin, section 9.1.3).

With the exception of patients with severe renal failure receiving haemodialysis, parenteral iron does not produce a faster haemoglobin response than oral iron provided that the oral iron preparation is taken reliably and is absorbed adequately.

**Iron dextran**, a complex of ferric hydroxide with dextrans, and **iron sucrose**, a complex of ferric hydroxide with sucrose, are used for the parenteral administration of iron. Anaphylactoid reactions can occur with parenteral administration of iron complexes and patients should be given a small test dose initially.



### IRON DEXTRAN

A complex of ferric hydroxide with dextran containing 5% (50 mg/mL) of iron

**Indications** iron-deficiency anaemia, see notes above

**Cautions** facilities for cardiopulmonary resuscitation must be at hand; increased risk of allergic reaction in immune or inflammatory conditions; oral iron not to be given until 5 days after last injection; hepatic impairment (Appendix 2); renal impairment (Appendix 3); pregnancy (Appendix 4)

**Contra-indications** history of allergic disorders including asthma and eczema; infection; active rheumatoid arthritis

**Side-effects** nausea, vomiting, abdominal pain; flushing, anaphylactoid reactions, dyspnoea, numbness, fever, urticaria, rash, arthralgia, myalgia; blurred vision; injection-site reactions including phlebitis; rarely diarrhoea, arrhythmias, hypotension, chest pain, seizures, tremor, dizziness, fatigue, sweating

**Dose**

- By deep intramuscular injection into the gluteal muscle or by slow intravenous injection or by intravenous infusion, calculated according to body-weight and iron deficit, consult product literature

  CHILD under 14 years, not recommended

**CosmoFer®** (Vitaline) ▼ PoM

Injection, iron (as iron dextran) 50 mg/mL, net price 2-mL amp = £7.97

### IRON SUCROSE

A complex of ferric hydroxide with sucrose containing 2% (20 mg/mL) of iron

**Indications** iron-deficiency anaemia, see notes above

**Cautions** oral iron therapy should not be given until 5 days after last injection; facilities for cardiopulmonary resuscitation must be at hand; pregnancy (Appendix 4)

**Contra-indications** history of allergic disorders including asthma, eczema and anaphylaxis; liver disease; infection

**Side-effects** taste disturbance; *less commonly* nausea, vomiting, abdominal pain, diarrhoea, chest pain, headache, dizziness, fever, myalgia, hypersensitivity reactions such as hypotension, tachycardia, palpitation, flushing, bronchospasm, dyspnoea, pruritus, urticaria, rash; injection-site reactions including phlebitis; *rarely* peripheral oedema, paraesthesia, fatigue, anaphylactoid reactions

**Dose**

- By slow intravenous injection or by intravenous infusion, calculated according to body-weight and iron deficit, consult product literature; CHILD not recommended

**Venofer®** (Syner-Med) PoM

Injection, iron (as iron sucrose) 20 mg/mL, net price 5-mL amp = £8.50

## 9.1.2 Drugs used in megaloblastic anaemias

Most megaloblastic anaemias result from a lack of either vitamin $B_{12}$ or folate, and it is essential to establish in every case which deficiency is present and the underlying cause. In emergencies, where delay might be dangerous, it is sometimes necessary to administer both substances after the bone marrow test while plasma assay results are awaited. Normally, however, appropriate treatment should be instituted only when the results of tests are available.

One cause of megaloblastic anaemia in the UK is *pernicious anaemia* in which lack of gastric intrinsic factor resulting from an auto-immune gastritis causes malabsorption of vitamin $B_{12}$.

Vitamin $B_{12}$ is also needed in the treatment of megaloblastosis caused by *prolonged nitrous oxide anaesthesia*, which inactivates the vitamin, and in the rare syndrome of *congenital transcobalamin II deficiency*.

Vitamin $B_{12}$ should be given prophylactically after *total gastrectomy* or *total ileal resection* (or after *partial gastrectomy* if a vitamin $B_{12}$ absorption test shows vitamin $B_{12}$ malabsorption).

Apart from dietary deficiency, all other causes of vitamin-$B_{12}$ deficiency are attributable to malabsorption. There is little place for the use of low-dose vitamin $B_{12}$ orally and none for vitamin $B_{12}$ intrinsic factor complexes given by mouth. Vitamin $B_{12}$ in larger oral doses of 1–2 mg daily [unlicensed] may be effective.

**Hydroxocobalamin** has completely replaced cyanocobalamin as the form of vitamin $B_{12}$ of choice for therapy; it is retained in the body longer than cyanocobalamin and thus for maintenance therapy can be given at intervals of up to 3 months. Treatment is generally initiated with frequent administration of intramuscular injections to replenish the depleted body stores. Thereafter, maintenance treatment, which is usually for life, can be instituted. There is no evidence that doses larger than those recommended provide any additional benefit in vitamin-$B_{12}$ neuropathy.

**Folic acid** has few indications for long-term therapy since most causes of folate deficiency are self-limiting or will yield to a short course of treatment. It should not be used in undiagnosed megaloblastic anaemia unless vitamin $B_{12}$ is administered concurrently otherwise neuropathy may be precipitated (see above).

In *folate-deficient megaloblastic anaemia* (e.g. because of poor nutrition, pregnancy, or antiepileptics), standard treatment to bring about a haematological remission and replenish body stores, is oral administration of folic acid 5 mg daily for 4 months; up to 15 mg daily may be necessary in malabsorption states. In pregnancy, folic acid 5 mg is continued to term.

For *prophylaxis in chronic haemolytic states or in renal dialysis*, it is sufficient to give folic acid 5 mg daily or even weekly, depending on the diet and the rate of haemolysis.

For *prophylaxis in pregnancy* the dose of folic acid is 200–500 micrograms daily (see Iron and Folic Acid, section 9.1.1.1). See also Prevention of Neural Tube Defects below.

**Folinic acid** is also effective in the treatment of folate-deficient megaloblastic anaemia but it is generally used in association with cytotoxic drugs (see section 8.1); it is given as calcium folinate.

**Prevention of neural tube defects** Recommendations of an expert advisory group of the Department of Health include the advice that:

> To prevent *recurrence of neural tube defect* (in a child of a man or woman with spina bifida or if there is a history of neural tube defect in a previous child) women who wish to become pregnant (or who are at risk of becoming pregnant) should be advised to take folic acid supplements at a dose of 5 mg daily (reduced to 4 mg daily if a suitable preparation becomes available); supplementation should continue until week 12 of pregnancy. Women receiving antiepileptic therapy need individual counselling by their doctor before starting folic acid.
>
> To prevent *first occurrence of neural tube defect* women who are planning a pregnancy should be advised to take folic acid as a medicinal or food supplement at a dose of 400 micrograms daily before conception and during the first 12 weeks of pregnancy. Women who have not been taking supplements and who suspect they are pregnant should start at once and continue until week 12 of pregnancy.

There is **no** justification for prescribing multiple-ingredient vitamin preparations containing vitamin $B_{12}$ or folic acid.

## HYDROXOCOBALAMIN

**Indications** see under dose below

**Cautions** should not be given before diagnosis fully established but see also notes above

**Side-effects** nausea, headache, dizziness; fever, hypersensitivity reactions including rash and pruritus; injection-site pain; hypokalaemia during initial treatment

**Dose**

- By intramuscular injection, pernicious anaemia and other macrocytic anaemias without neurological involvement, initially 1 mg 3 times a week for 2 weeks then 1 mg every 3 months

  Pernicious anaemia and other macrocytic anaemias with neurological involvement, initially 1 mg on alternate days until no further improvement, then 1 mg every 2 months

  Prophylaxis of macrocytic anaemias associated with vitamin-$B_{12}$ deficiency, 1 mg every 2–3 months

  Tobacco amblyopia and Leber's optic atrophy, initially 1 mg daily for 2 weeks, then 1 mg twice weekly until no further improvement, thereafter 1 mg every 1–3 months

  CHILD doses as for adult

**Hydroxocobalamin** (Non-proprietary) PoM

Injection, hydroxocobalamin 1 mg/mL. Net price 1-mL amp = £2.46

Note The BP directs that when vitamin $B_{12}$ injection is prescribed or demanded hydroxocobalamin injection shall be dispensed or supplied

Brands include *Cobalin-H®* NHS, *Neo-Cytamen®* NHS

## CYANOCOBALAMIN

**Indications** see notes above

**Dose**

- By mouth, vitamin-$B_{12}$ deficiency of dietary origin, 50–150 micrograms or more daily taken between meals; CHILD 50–105 micrograms daily in 1–3 divided doses
- By intramuscular injection, initially 1 mg repeated 10 times at intervals of 2–3 days, maintenance 1 mg every month, but see notes above

**Cyanocobalamin** (Non-proprietary)

[1]Tablets NHS, cyanocobalamin 50 micrograms. Net price 50-tab pack = £3.04

Brands include *Cytacon®* NHS

Liquid NHS, cyanocobalamin 35 micrograms/5 mL. Net price 200 mL = £2.77

Brands include *Cytacon®* NHS

Injection PoM, cyanocobalamin 1 mg/mL. Net price 1-mL amp = £1.67

Brands include *Cytamen®* NHS

Note The BP directs that when vitamin $B_{12}$ injection is prescribed or demanded hydroxocobalamin injection shall be dispensed or supplied

1. NHS except to treat or prevent vitamin-$B_{12}$ deficiency in a patient who is a vegan or who has a proven vitamin-$B_{12}$ deficiency of dietary origin; endorse prescription 'SLS'

## FOLIC ACID

**Indications** see notes above

**Cautions** should never be given alone for pernicious anaemia and other vitamin-$B_{12}$ deficiency states (may precipitate subacute combined degeneration of the spinal cord); **interactions:** Appendix 1 (folates)

**Dose**

- By mouth, initially, 5 mg daily for 4 months (see notes above); maintenance, 5 mg every 1–7 days depending on underlying disease; CHILD up to 1 year, 500 micrograms/kg daily; over 1 year, as adult dose

  Prevention of neural tube defects, see notes above

[1]**Folic Acid** (Non-proprietary) PoM

Tablets, folic acid 400 micrograms, net price = 90-tab pack = £2.24; 5 mg, 28-tab pack = £1.10

Syrup, folic acid 2.5 mg/5 mL, net price 150 mL = £9.16; 400 micrograms/5 mL, 150 mL = £1.40

Brands include *Folicare®*, *Lexpec®* (sugar-free)

Injection, folic acid 15 mg, net price 1-mL amp = £1.34

'Special order' [unlicensed] product; contact BCM Specials

1. Can be sold to the public provided daily doses do not exceed 500 micrograms; brands include *Preconceive®*

## 9.1.3 Drugs used in hypoplastic, haemolytic, and renal anaemias

Anabolic steroids (section 6.4.3), pyridoxine, antilymphocyte immunoglobulin, and various corticosteroids are used in hypoplastic and haemolytic anaemias.

**Antilymphocyte globulin** given intravenously through a central line over 12–18 hours each day for 5 days produces a response in about 50% of cases of acquired *aplastic anaemia*; the response rate may be increased when ciclosporin is given as well. Severe reactions are common in the first 2 days and profound immunosuppression can occur; antilymphocyte globulin should be given under specialist supervision with appropriate resuscitation facilities. Alternatively, oxymetholone tablets (available on named-patient basis from Cambridge) may be used in aplastic anaemia at a dose of 1–5 mg/kg daily for 3 to 6 months.

It is unlikely that dietary deprivation of **pyridoxine** (section 9.6.2) produces clinically relevant haematological effects. However, certain forms of *sideroblastic anaemia* respond to pharmacological doses, possibly reflecting its role as a co-enzyme during haemoglobin synthesis. Pyridoxine is indicated in both *idiopathic acquired* and *hereditary sideroblastic anaemias.* Although complete cures have not been reported, some increase in haemoglobin may occur; the dose required is usually high, up to 400 mg daily. *Reversible sideroblastic anaemias* respond to treatment of the underlying cause but in pregnancy, haemolytic anaemias, and alcohol dependence, or during isoniazid treatment, pyridoxine is also indicated.

**Hydroxycarbamide** (hydroxyurea, section 8.1.5) can reduce the frequency of crises in *sickle-cell disease* and reduce the need for blood transfusions [unlicensed indication].

**Corticosteroids** (see section 6.3) have an important place in the management of a wide variety of haematological disorders. They include conditions with an immune basis such as *autoimmune haemolytic anaemia, immune thrombocytopenias* and *neutropenias*, and *major transfusion reactions.* They are also used in chemotherapy schedules for many types of *lymphoma, lymphoid leukaemias*, and *paraproteinaemias*, including *multiple myeloma.*

### Erythropoietin

**Epoetin** (recombinant human erythropoietin) is used for the anaemia associated with erythropoietin deficiency in chronic renal failure, to increase the yield of autologous blood in normal individuals and to shorten the period of anaemia in patients receiving cytotoxic chemotherapy. The clinical efficacy of epoetin alfa and epoetin beta is similar. Epoetin beta is also used for the prevention of anaemia in preterm neonates of low birth-weight.

**Darbepoetin**, is a hyperglycosylated derivative of epoetin which has a longer half-life and may be administered less frequently than epoetin.

Other factors which contribute to the anaemia of chronic renal failure such as iron or folate deficiency should be corrected before treatment and monitored during therapy. Supplemental iron may improve the response in resistant patients. Aluminium toxicity, concurrent infection or other inflammatory disease may impair the response to erythropoietin.

> **CSM advice**
> There have been very rare reports of pure red cell aplasia in patients treated with epoetin alfa. The CSM has advised that in patients developing epoetin alfa failure with a diagnosis of pure red cell aplasia, treatment with epoetin alfa must be discontinued and testing for erythropoietin antibodies considered. Patients who develop pure red cell aplasia should **not** be switched to another erythropoietin.

### DARBEPOETIN ALFA

**Indications** see under Dose below

**Cautions** see Epoetin; hepatic disease (Appendix 2); pregnancy (Appendix 4); **interactions:** Appendix 1 (epoetin)

**Contra-indications** see Epoetin; breast-feeding (Appendix 5)

**Side-effects** see Epoetin; also, peripheral oedema, injection-site pain; isolated reports of pure red cell aplasia (discontinue therapy)—see also CSM advice above

**Dose**

- Anaemia associated with chronic renal failure in patients on dialysis, ADULT and CHILD over 11 years, by subcutaneous *or* intravenous injection, initially 450 nanograms/kg once weekly, adjusted according to response by approx. 25% of initial dose at intervals of at least 4 weeks; maintenance dose (when haemoglobin concentration of 11 g/100 mL achieved), given once weekly *or* once every 2 weeks
- Anaemia associated with chronic renal failure in patients not on dialysis, ADULT and CHILD over 11 years, by subcutaneous *or* intravenous injection, initially 450 nanograms/kg once weekly *or* by subcutaneous injection, initially 750 nanograms/kg once every 2 weeks; adjusted according to response by approx. 25% of initial dose at intervals of at least 4 weeks; maintenance dose (when haemoglobin concentration of at least 11 g/100 mL achieved), given once weekly *or* once every 2 weeks *or* once every month

**Note** Reduce dose by 25–50% if haemoglobin rise exceeds 2.5 g/100 mL per month; suspend if haemoglobin exceeds 14 g/100 mL until it falls below 13 g/100 mL and then restart with dose at 25% below previous dose. When changing route give same dose then adjust according to weekly or fortnightly haemoglobin measurements. Adjust doses at 2-week intervals during maintenance treatment

- Anaemia in adults with non-myeloid malignancies receiving chemotherapy, by subcutaneous injection, initially 6.75 micrograms/kg once every 3 weeks (if response inadequate after 9 weeks further treatment may not be effective) *or* 2.25 micrograms/kg once weekly (if appropriate rise in haemoglobin not achieved after 4 weeks, double initial dose; if response remains inadequate after 4 weeks at higher dose further treatment may not be effective); haemoglobin should not exceed 13 g/100 mL; if adequate response obtained or if rise in haemoglobin greater than 2 g/100 mL in 4 weeks, reduce dose by 25–50%; continue for approx. 4 weeks after chemotherapy

**Aranesp®** (Amgen) ▼ PoM

Injection, prefilled syringe, darbepoetin alfa, 25 micrograms/mL, net price 0.4 mL (10 micrograms) = £15.59; 40 micrograms/mL, 0.375 mL (15 micrograms) = £23.38, 0.5 mL (20 micrograms) = £31.17; 100 micrograms/mL, 0.3 mL (30 micrograms) = £46.76, 0.4 mL (40 micrograms) = £62.34, 0.5 mL (50 micrograms) = £77.93; 200 micrograms/mL, 0.3 mL (60 micrograms) = £93.51, 0.4 mL (80 micrograms) = £124.68, 0.5 mL (100 micrograms) = £155.85; 500 micrograms/mL, 0.3 mL (150 micrograms) = £233.78, 0.6 mL (300 micrograms) = £467.55, 1 mL (500 micrograms) = £779.25

**Aranesp® SureClick** (Amgen) ▼ PoM

Injection, prefilled disposable injection device, darbepoetin alfa, 40 micrograms/mL, net price 0.5 mL (20 micrograms) = £31.17; 100 micrograms/mL, net price 0.4 mL (40 micrograms) = £62.34; 200 micrograms/mL, net price 0.3 mL (60 micrograms) = £93.51, 0.4 mL (80 micrograms) = £124.68, 0.5 mL (100 micrograms) = £155.85; 500 micrograms/mL, net price 0.3 mL (150 micrograms) = £233.78, 0.6 mL (300 microrgrams) = £467.55, 1 mL (500 micrograms) = £779.25

## EPOETIN ALFA and BETA
### (Recombinant human erythropoietins)

Note Although epoetin alfa and beta are clinically indistinguishable the prescriber must specify which is required

**Indications** see under preparations, below

**Cautions** inadequately treated or poorly controlled blood pressure (monitor closely blood pressure, reticulocyte counts, haemoglobin, and electrolytes), interrupt treatment if blood pressure uncontrolled; sudden stabbing migraine-like pain is warning of hypertensive crisis; sickle-cell disease (lower target haemoglobin concentration may be appropriate), exclude other causes of anaemia (e.g. folic acid or vitamin $B_{12}$ deficiency) and give iron supplements if necessary (see also notes above); ischaemic vascular disease; thrombocytosis (monitor platelet count for first 8 weeks); epilepsy; malignant disease; chronic liver failure (Appendix 2); increase in heparin dose may be needed; risk of thrombosis may be increased when used for anaemia in adults receiving cancer chemotherapy; risk of thrombosis may be increased when used for anaemia before orthopaedic surgery—avoid in cardiovascular disease including recent myocardial infarction or cerebrovascular accident ; pregnancy (Appendix 4) and breast-feeding (Appendix 5); **interactions**: Appendix 1 (epoetin)

**Contra-indications** pure red cell aplasia following erythropoietin (see also CSM advice above); uncontrolled hypertension; patients unable to receive thromboprophylaxis; avoid injections containing benzyl alcohol in neonates (see under preparations, below)

**Side-effects** dose-dependent increase in blood pressure or aggravation of hypertension; in isolated patients with normal or low blood pressure, hypertensive crisis with encephalopathy-like symptoms and generalised tonic-clonic seizures requiring immediate medical attention; headache; dose-dependent increase in platelet count (but thrombocytosis rare) regressing during treatment; influenza-like symptoms (may be reduced if intravenous injection given over 5 minutes); thromboembolic events; shunt thrombosis especially if tendency to hypotension or arteriovenous shunt complications; very rarely sudden loss of response because of pure red cell aplasia, particularly following subcutaneous administration in patients with chronic renal failure (discontinue erythropoietin therapy)—see also CSM advice above, hyperkalaemia, and skin reactions

**Dose**

- Aimed at increasing haemoglobin concentration at rate not exceeding 2 g/100 mL/month to stable level of 10–12 g/100 mL (9.5–11 g/100 mL in children); see under preparations, below

### Epoetin alfa

**Eprex®** (Janssen-Cilag) PoM

Injection, epoetin alfa 40 000 units/mL, net price 1-mL (40 000-unit) vial = £318.44

Injection, prefilled syringe, epoetin alfa, net price 1000 units = £7.96; 2000 units = £15.92; 3000 units = £23.88; 4000 units = £31.84; 5000 units = £39.81; 6000 units = £47.77; 8000 units = £63.69; 10 000 units = £79.61. An auto-injector device is available for use with 10 000-units prefilled syringes

Dose anaemia associated with chronic renal failure in patients on haemodialysis, by intravenous injection over 1–5 minutes, initially 50 units/kg 3 times weekly adjusted according to response in steps of 25 units/kg 3 times weekly at intervals of at least 4 weeks; maintenance dose (when haemoglobin concentration of 10–12 g/100 mL achieved), usually a total of 75–300 units/kg weekly (as a single dose or in divided doses); CHILD initially as for adults; maintenance dose (when haemoglobin concentration of 9.5–11 g/100 mL achieved), body-weight under 10 kg usually 75–150 units/kg 3 times weekly, body-weight 10–30 kg usually 60–150 units/kg 3 times weekly, body-weight over 30 kg usually 30–100 units/kg 3 times weekly

Important Subcutaneous injection **contra-indicated** in patients with chronic renal failure

Anaemia associated with chronic renal failure in adults on peritoneal dialysis, by intravenous injection over 1–5 minutes, initially 50 units/kg twice weekly; maintenance dose (when haemoglobin concentration of 10–12 g/100 mL achieved), 25–50 units/kg twice weekly

Important Subcutaneous injection **contra-indicated** in patients with chronic renal failure

Severe symptomatic anaemia of renal origin in adults with renal insufficiency not yet on dialysis, by intravenous injection over 1–5 minutes, initially 50 units/kg 3 times weekly increased according to response in steps of 25 units/kg 3 times weekly at intervals of at least 4 weeks; maintenance dose (when haemoglobin concentration of 10–12 g/100 mL achieved), 17–33 units/kg 3 times weekly; max. 200 units/kg 3 times weekly;

Important Subcutaneous injection **contra-indicated** in patients with chronic renal failure

Anaemia in adults receiving cancer chemotherapy, by subcutaneous injection (max. 1 mL per injection site), initially 150 units/kg 3 times weekly, increased if appropriate rise in haemoglobin (or reticulocyte count) not achieved after 4 weeks to 300 units/kg 3 times weekly; discontinue if inadequate response after 4 weeks at higher dose; reduce dose by 25–50% if haemoglobin rise exceeds 2 g/100 mL per month; suspend if haemoglobin exceeds 13 g/100 mL until it falls to 12 g/100 mL and reinstate with dose at 25% below previous dose; continue epoetin for 1 month after end of chemotherapy

To increase yield of autologous blood (to avoid homologous blood) in predonation programme in moderate anaemia *either* when large volume of blood required *or* when sufficient blood cannot be saved for elective major surgery, by intravenous injection over 1–5 minutes, 600 units/kg twice weekly for 3 weeks before surgery; consult product literature for details and advice on ensuring high iron stores

Moderate anaemia (haemoglobin concentration 10–13 g/100 mL) before elective orthopaedic surgery in adults with expected moderate blood loss to reduce exposure to allogeneic transfusion or if autologous transfusion unavailable, by subcutaneous injection (max. 1 mL per injection site), 600 units/kg every week for 3 weeks before surgery and on day of surgery *or* 300 units/kg daily for 15 days starting 10 days before surgery; consult product literature for details

### Epoetin beta

**NeoRecormon®** (Roche) PoM

Injection, prefilled syringe, epoetin beta, net price 500 units = £3.90; 1000 units = £7.79; 2000 units = £15.59; 3000 units = £23.38; 4000 units = £31.17; 5000 units = £38.97; 6000 units = £46.76; 10 000 units = £77.93; 20 000 units = £155.87; 30 000 units = £233.81

**Excipients** include phenylalanine up to 300 micrograms/syringe (section 9.4.1)

Multidose injection, powder for reconstitution, epoetin beta, net price 50 000-unit vial = £419.01; 100 000-unit vial = £838.01 (both with solvent)

**Excipients** include phenylalanine up to 5 mg/vial (section 9.4.1), benzyl alcohol (avoid in neonates, see Excipients p. 2)

**Note** Avoid contact of reconstituted injection with glass; use only plastic materials

Reco-Pen, (for subcutaneous use), double-chamber cartridges (containing epoetin beta and solvent), net price 10 000-unit cartridge = £77.93; 20 000-unit cartridge = £155.87; 60 000-unit cartridge = £467.61; for use with *Reco-Pen* injection device and needles (both available free from Roche)

**Excipients** include phenylalanine up to 500 micrograms/cartridge (section 9.4.1), benzyl alcohol (avoid in neonates, see Excipients, p. 2)

**Dose** anaemia associated with chronic renal failure in dialysis patients, symptomatic anaemia of renal origin in patients not yet on dialysis, ADULT and CHILD

By subcutaneous injection, initially 60 units/kg weekly (in 1–7 divided doses) for 4 weeks, increased according to response at intervals of 4 weeks in steps of 60 units/kg; maintenance dose (when haemoglobin concentration of 10–12 g/100 mL achieved), initially reduce dose by half then adjust according to response at intervals of 1–2 weeks; max. 720 units/kg weekly

By intravenous injection over 2 minutes, initially 40 units/kg 3 times weekly for 4 weeks, increased according to response to 80 units/kg 3 times weekly with further increases if needed at intervals of 4 weeks in steps of 20 units/kg 3 times weekly; maintenance dose (when haemoglobin concentration of 10–12 g/100 mL achieved), initially reduce dose by half then adjust according to response at intervals of 1–2 weeks; max. 720 units/kg weekly

Prevention of anaemia of prematurity in neonates with birth-weight of 0.75–1.5 kg and gestational age of less than 34 weeks, by subcutaneous injection (of single-dose, unpreserved injection), 250 units/kg 3 times weekly preferably starting within 3 days of birth and continued for 6 weeks

Anaemia in adults with solid tumours receiving chemotherapy with haemoglobin concentration not more than 11 g/100 mL, by subcutaneous injection, initially 450 units/kg weekly (in 3–7 divided doses), increased if appropriate rise in haemoglobin not achieved after 4 weeks to 900 units/kg weekly (in 3–7 divided doses); reduce dose by 25–50% if haemoglobin rise exceeds 2 g/100 mL per month; once target haemoglobin concentration achieved, adjust dose to ensure concentration does not exceed 13 g/100 mL; continue for up to 3 weeks after end of chemotherapy

**Note** If haemoglobin concentration falls by more than 1 g/100 mL in the first cycle of chemotherapy despite treatment with epoetin beta, further treatment may not be effective

Anaemia in adults with multiple myeloma, low-grade non-Hodgkin's lymphoma or chronic lymphocytic leukaemia receiving chemotherapy, by subcutaneous injection, initially 450 units/kg weekly (as a single dose or in 3–7 divided doses), increased if rise in haemoglobin of at least 1 g/100 mL not achieved after 4 weeks to 900 units/kg weekly (in 2–7 divided doses); reduce dose by 25–50% if haemoglobin rise exceeds 2 g/100 mL per month; once target haemoglobin concentration achieved, adjust dose to ensure concentration does not exceed 13 g/100 mL; max. 900 units/kg weekly; continue for up to 4 weeks after end of chemotherapy

**Note** Discontinue treatment if haemoglobin concentration does not increase by at least 1 g/100 mL after 8 weeks of therapy

To increase yield of autologous blood (to avoid homologous blood) in predonation programme in moderate anaemia when blood-conserving procedures are insufficient or unavailable, consult product literature

## Iron overload

Severe tissue iron overload may occur in aplastic and other refractory anaemias, mainly as the result of repeated blood transfusions. It is a particular problem in refractory anaemias with hyperplastic bone marrow, especially *thalassaemia major*, where excessive iron absorption from the gut and inappropriate iron therapy may add to the tissue siderosis.

Iron overload associated with haemochromatosis may be treated with repeated venesection. Venesection may also be used for patients who have received multiple transfusions and whose bone marrow has recovered. Where venesection is contra-indicated, the long-term administration of the iron chelating compound **desferrioxamine mesilate** is useful. Subcutaneous infusions of desferrioxamine are given over 8–12 hours, 3–7 times a week. The dose should reflect the degree of iron overload. For children starting therapy (and who have low iron overload) the dose should not exceed 30 mg/kg. For established overload the dose is usually between 20 and 50 mg/kg daily. Desferrioxamine (up to 2 g per unit of blood) may also be given at the time of blood transfusion, provided that the desferrioxamine is **not** added to the blood and is **not** given through the same line as the blood (but the two may be given through the same cannula).

Iron excretion induced by desferrioxamine is enhanced by administration of ascorbic acid (vitamin C, section 9.6.3) in a dose of 200 mg daily (100 mg in infants); it should be given separately from food since it also enhances iron absorption. Ascorbic acid should not be given to patients with cardiac dysfunction; in patients with normal cardiac function ascorbic acid should be introduced 1 month after starting desferrioxamine.

Infusion of desferrioxamine may be used to treat *aluminium overload* in dialysis patients; theoretically 100 mg of desferrioxamine binds with 4.1 mg of aluminium.

**Deferiprone**, an oral iron chelator, is licensed for the treatment of iron overload in patients with thalassaemia major in whom desferrioxamine is contra-indicated or is not tolerated. Blood dyscrasias, particularly agranulocytosis, have been reported with deferiprone.

### DEFERIPRONE

**Indications** see notes above

**Cautions** monitor neutrophil count weekly and discontinue treatment if neutropenia develops; monitor plasma-zinc concentration; hepatic impairment (Appendix 2); renal impairment (Appendix 3); limited experience in children 6–10 years

**Blood disorders** Patients or their carers should be told how to recognise signs of neutropenia and advised to seek immediate medical attention if symptoms such as fever or sore throat develop

**Contra-indications** pregnancy (contraception advised in women of child-bearing potential; *important terato-*

*genic risk*: see Appendix 4) and breast-feeding (Appendix 5)

**Side-effects** gastro-intestinal disturbances (reducing dose and increasing gradually may improve tolerance); red-brown urine discoloration; neutropenia, agranulocytosis; zinc deficiency; arthropathy

**Dose**

- ADULT and CHILD over 6 years 25 mg/kg (to the nearest 250 mg) 3 times daily (max. 100 mg/kg daily); CHILD under 6 years not recommended

**Ferriprox®** (Swedish Orphan) PoM

Tablets, f/c, scored, deferiprone 500 mg, net price 100-tab pack = £152.39. Label: 14, counselling, blood disorders

## DESFERRIOXAMINE MESILATE
(Deferoxamine Mesilate)

**Indications** see notes above; iron poisoning, see Emergency Treatment of Poisoning

**Cautions** renal impairment; eye and ear examinations before treatment and at 3-month intervals during treatment; monitor body-weight and height in children at 3-month intervals—risk of growth retardation with excessive doses; aluminium-related encephalopathy (may exacerbate neurological dysfunction); pregnancy (Appendix 4), breast-feeding (Appendix 5); **interactions:** Appendix 1 (desferrioxamine)

**Side-effects** hypotension (especially when given too rapidly by intravenous injection), disturbances of hearing and vision (including lens opacity and retinopathy); injection site reactions, gastro-intestinal disturbances, asthma, fever, headache, arthralgia and myalgia; very rarely anaphylaxis, acute respiratory distress syndrome, neurological disturbances (including dizziness, neuropathy and paraesthesia), Yersinia and mucormycosis infections, rash, renal impairment, and blood dyscrasias

**Dose**

- See notes above; iron poisoning, see Emergency Treatment of Poisoning

  **Note** For full details and warnings relating to administration, consult product literature

**Desferrioxamine mesilate** (Non-proprietary) PoM

Injection, powder for reconstitution, desferrioxamine mesilate, net price 500-mg vial = £4.26; 2-g vial = £17.05

**Desferal®** (Novartis) PoM

Injection, powder for reconstitution, desferrioxamine mesilate, net price 500-mg vial = £4.44, 2-g vial = £17.77

# 9.1.4 Drugs used in platelet disorders

It is usual to treat autoimmune (idiopathic) thrombocytopenic purpura with a **corticosteroid**, e.g. prednisolone 1 mg/kg daily, gradually reducing the dose over several weeks. Splenectomy is considered if a satisfactory platelet count is not achieved or if there is a relapse on reducing the dose of corticosteroid or withdrawing it.

**Immunoglobulin** preparations (section 14.5), are also used in autoimmune thrombocytopenic purpura or where a temporary rapid rise in platelets is needed, as in pregnancy or pre-operatively; they are also used for children often in preference to a corticosteroid. **Anti-D ($Rh_0$) immunoglobulin** (section 14.5) is effective in raising the platelet count in about 80% of unsplenectomised rhesus-positive individuals; its effects may last longer than normal immunoglobulin for intravenous use, but further doses are usually required. In autoimmune thrombocytopenic purpura refractory to corticosteroid treatment or in chronic cases where splenectomy is inappropriate, **danazol** (section 6.7.2) may be used [unlicensed indication], particularly in older patients. Danazol may also allow the dose of corticosteroid to be reduced.

Other therapy that has been tried in refractory autoimmune thrombocytopenic purpura includes azathioprine (section 8.2.1), cyclophosphamide (section 8.1.1), vincristine (section 8.1.4), and ciclosporin (section 8.2.2). Rituximab (section 8.2.3) may also be effective and in some cases induces prolonged remission. For patients with chronic severe thrombocytopenia refractory to other therapy, tranexamic acid (section 2.11) may be given to reduce the severity of haemorrhage.

**Anagrelide** reduces platelets in primary thrombocythaemia and in thrombocythaemia secondary to myeloproliferative disorders.

## ANAGRELIDE

**Indications** primary thrombocythaemia in at risk patients who have not responded adequately to other therapy or who are intolerant of it (initiated under specialist supervision)

**Cautions** cardiac disease; assess cardiac function before and during treatment; concomitant aspirin in patients with a history of haemorrhage or severely raised platelet count; monitor full blood count (monitor platelet count every 2 days for 1 week, then weekly until maintenance dose established), liver function, serum creatinine and urea; hepatic impairment (Appendix 2); renal impairment (Appendix 3); **interactions:** Appendix 1 (anagrelide)

**Driving** Dizziness may affect performance of skilled tasks (e.g. driving)

**Contra-indications** pregnancy (Appendix 4); breast-feeding (Appendix 5)

**Side-effects** gastro-intestinal disturbances; palpitation, tachycardia, fluid retention; headache, dizziness, fatigue; anaemia; rash; *less commonly* pancreatitis, gastro-intestinal haemorrhage, congestive heart failure, hypertension, arrhythmias, syncope, chest pain, dyspnoea, sleep disturbances, paraesthesia, hypoaesthesia, depression, confusion, amnesia, fever, weight changes, impotence, blood disorders, myalgia, arthralgia, epistaxis, dry mouth, alopecia, skin discoloration, and pruritus; *rarely* gastritis, colitis, postural hypotension, myocardial infarction, vasodilatation, pulmonary infiltrates, impaired co-ordination, dysarthria, asthenia, tinnitus, renal failure, nocturia, visual disturbances, and gingival bleeding

**Dose**

- Initially 500 micrograms twice daily adjusted according to response in steps of 500 micrograms daily at weekly intervals to max. 10 mg daily (max. single dose 2.5 mg); usual dose range 1–3 mg daily in divided doses

**Xagrid®** (Shire) ▼ PoM
Capsules, anagrelide (as hydrochloride), 500 micrograms, net price 100-cap pack = £337.14. Counselling, driving, see above

## 9.1.5 G6PD deficiency

Glucose 6-phosphate dehydrogenase (G6PD) deficiency is highly prevalent in individuals originating from most parts of Africa, from most parts of Asia, from Oceania, and from Southern Europe; it can also occur, rarely, in any other individuals.

Individuals with G6PD deficiency are susceptible to developing acute haemolytic anaemia on taking a number of common drugs. They are also susceptible to developing acute haemolytic anaemia upon ingestion of fava beans (broad beans, *Vicia faba*); this is termed *favism* and can be more severe in children or when the fresh fava beans are eaten raw.

When prescribing drugs for patients with G6PD deficiency, the following three points should be kept in mind:

- G6PD deficiency is genetically heterogeneous; susceptibility to the haemolytic risk from drugs varies; thus, a drug found to be safe in some G6PD-deficient individuals may not be equally safe in others;
- manufacturers do not routinely test drugs for their effects in G6PD-deficient individuals;
- the risk and severity of haemolysis is almost always dose-related.

The lists below should be read with these points in mind. Ideally, information about G6PD deficiency should be available before prescribing a drug listed below. However, in the absence of this information, the possibility of haemolysis should be considered, especially if the patient belongs to a group in which G6PD deficiency is common.

A very few G6PD-deficient individuals with chronic non-spherocytic haemolytic anaemia have haemolysis even in the absence of an exogenous trigger. These patients must be regarded as being at high risk of severe exacerbation of haemolysis following administration of any of the drugs listed below.

**Drugs with definite risk of haemolysis in most G6PD-deficient individuals**

Dapsone and other sulphones (higher doses for dermatitis herpetiformis more likely to cause problems)
Methylthioninium chloride (methylene blue)
Niridazole [not on UK market]
Nitrofurantoin
Pamaquin [not on UK market]
Primaquine (30 mg weekly for 8 weeks has been found to be without undue harmful effects in African and Asian people, see section 5.4.1)
Quinolones (including ciprofloxacin, moxifloxacin, nalidixic acid, norfloxacin, and ofloxacin)
Sulphonamides (including co-trimoxazole; some sulphonamides, e.g. sulfadiazine, have been tested and found not to be haemolytic in many G6PD-deficient individuals)

**Drugs with possible risk of haemolysis in some G6PD-deficient individuals**

Aspirin (acceptable up to a dose of at least 1 g daily in most G6PD-deficient individuals)
Chloroquine (acceptable in acute malaria)
Menadione, water-soluble derivatives (e.g. menadiol sodium phosphate)
Probenecid [not on UK market]
Quinidine (acceptable in acute malaria)
Quinine (acceptable in acute malaria)

Note Naphthalene in mothballs also causes haemolysis in individuals with G6PD-deficiency.

## 9.1.6 Drugs used in neutropenia

Recombinant human granulocyte-colony stimulating factor (rhG-CSF) stimulates the production of neutrophils and may reduce the duration of chemotherapy-induced neutropenia and thereby reduce the incidence of associated sepsis; there is as yet no evidence that it improves overall survival. **Filgrastim** (unglycosylated rhG-CSF) and **lenograstim** (glycosylated rhG-CSF) have similar effects; both have been used in a variety of clinical settings but they do not have any clear-cut routine indications. In congenital neutropenia filgrastim usually elevates the neutrophil count with appropriate clinical response. Prolonged use may be associated with an increased risk of myeloid malignancy. **Pegfilgrastim** is a polyethylene glycol-conjugated ('pegylated') derivative of filgrastim; pegylation increases the duration of filgrastim activity.

Treatment with recombinant human growth factors should only be prescribed by those experienced in their use.

**Cautions** Recombinant human growth factors should be used with caution in patients with pre-malignant or malignant myeloid conditions. Full blood counts including differential white cell and platelet counts should be monitored. Treatment should be withdrawn in patients who develop signs of pulmonary infiltration. Splenic rupture following administration of granulocyte-colony stimulating factors has been reported; monitor spleen size. Recombinant human growth factors are not recommended in pregnancy (Appendix 4) or breast-feeding (Appendix 5).

**Side-effects** Side-effects of granulocyte-colony stimulating factors include gastro-intestinal disturbances (including nausea, vomiting, and diarrhoea), anorexia, headache, asthenia, fever, musculoskeletal pain, bone pain, rash, alopecia, injection-site reactions, and leucocytosis. Less frequent side-effects include chest pain, hypersensitivity reactions (including anaphylaxis and bronchospasm) and arthralgia. There have been reports of pulmonary infiltrates leading to acute respiratory distress syndrome.

## FILGRASTIM

**(Recombinant human granulocyte-colony stimulating factor, G-CSF)**

**Indications** (specialist use only) reduction in duration of neutropenia and incidence of febrile neutropenia in cytotoxic chemotherapy for malignancy (except chronic myeloid leukaemia and myelodysplastic syndromes); reduction in duration of neutropenia (and associated sequelae) in myeloablative therapy followed by bone-marrow transplantation; mobilisation of peripheral blood progenitor cells for harvesting and subsequent autologous or allogeneic infusion; severe congenital neutropenia, cyclic neutropenia, or idiopathic neutropenia and history of severe or recurrent infections (distinguish carefully from other haematological disorders, consult product literature); persistent neutropenia in advanced HIV infection

**Cautions** see notes above; also reduced myeloid precursors; regular morphological and cytogenetic bone-marrow examinations recommended in severe congenital neutropenia (possible risk of myelodysplastic syndromes or leukaemia); secondary acute myeloid leukaemia, sickle-cell disease; monitor spleen size (risk of rupture); osteoporotic bone disease (monitor bone density if given for more than 6 months); **interactions:** Appendix 1 (filgrastim)

**Contra-indications** severe congenital neutropenia (Kostman's syndrome) with abnormal cytogenetics

**Side-effects** see notes above; also splenic enlargement, hepatomegaly, transient hypotension, epistaxis, urinary abnormalities (including dysuria, proteinuria, and haematuria), osteoporosis, exacerbation of rheumatoid arthritis, cutaneous vasculitis, thrombocytopenia, anaemia, transient decrease in blood glucose, raised uric acid

**Dose**

- Cytotoxic-induced neutropenia, preferably by subcutaneous injection *or* by intravenous infusion (over 30 minutes), ADULT and CHILD, 500 000 units/kg daily started not less than 24 hours after cytotoxic chemotherapy, continued until neutrophil count in normal range, usually for up to 14 days (up to 38 days in acute myeloid leukaemia)
- Myeloablative therapy followed by bone-marrow transplantation, by intravenous infusion over 30 minutes or over 24 hours *or* by subcutaneous infusion over 24 hours, 1 million units/kg daily, started not less than 24 hours following cytotoxic chemotherapy (and within 24 hours of bone-marrow infusion), then adjusted according to absolute neutrophil count (consult product literature)
- Mobilisation of peripheral blood progenitor cells for autologous infusion, used alone, by subcutaneous injection *or* by subcutaneous infusion over 24 hours, 1 million units/kg daily for 5–7 days; used following adjunctive myelosuppressive chemotherapy (to improve yield), by subcutaneous injection, 500 000 units/kg daily, started the day after completion of chemotherapy and continued until neutrophil count in normal range; for timing of leucopheresis consult product literature
- Mobilisation of peripheral blood progenitor cells in normal donors for allogeneic infusion, by subcutaneous injection, ADULT under 60 years and ADOLESCENT over 16 years, 1 million units/kg daily for 4–5 days; for timing of leucopheresis consult product literature
- Severe chronic neutropenia, by subcutaneous injection, ADULT and CHILD, in severe congenital neutropenia, initially 1.2 million units/kg daily in single or divided doses (initially 500 000 units/kg daily in idiopathic or cyclic neutropenia), adjusted according to response (consult product literature)
- Persistent neutropenia in HIV infection, by subcutaneous injection, initially 100 000 units/kg daily, increased as necessary until absolute neutrophil count in normal range (usual max. 400 000 units/kg daily), then adjusted to maintain absolute neutrophil count in normal range (consult product literature)

**Neupogen®** (Amgen) PoM

Injection, filgrastim 30 million-units (300 micrograms)/mL, net price 1-mL vial = £68.41

Injection (Singleject®), filgrastim 60 million-units (600 micrograms)/mL, net price 0.5-mL prefilled syringe = £68.41; 96 million-units (960 micrograms)/mL, 0.5-mL prefilled syringe = £109.11

## LENOGRASTIM

**(Recombinant human granulocyte-colony stimulating factor, rHuG-CSF)**

**Indications** (specialist use only) reduction in the duration of neutropenia and associated complications following bone-marrow transplantation for non-myeloid malignancy or following treatment with cytotoxic chemotherapy associated with a significant incidence of febrile neutropenia; mobilisation of peripheral blood progenitor cells for harvesting and subsequent infusion

**Cautions** see notes above; also pre-malignant myeloid conditions; reduced myeloid precursors; sickle cell disease; monitor spleen size (risk of rupture)

**Side-effects** see notes above; also splenic rupture, cutaneous vasculitis, Sweet's syndrome, toxic epidermal necrolysis

**Dose**

- Following bone-marrow transplantation, by intravenous infusion, ADULT and CHILD over 2 years 19.2 million units/$m^2$ daily started the day after transplantation, continued until neutrophil count stable in acceptable range (max. 28 days)
- Cytotoxic-induced neutropenia, by subcutaneous injection, ADULT 19.2 million units/$m^2$ daily started the day after completion of chemotherapy, continued until neutrophil count stable in acceptable range (max. 28 days)
- Mobilisation of peripheral blood progenitor cells, used alone, by subcutaneous injection, ADULT 1.28 million units/kg daily for 4–6 days (5–6 days in healthy donors); used following adjunctive myelosuppressive chemotherapy (to improve yield), by subcutaneous injection, 19.2 million units/$m^2$ daily, started the day after completion of chemotherapy and continued until neutrophil count in acceptable range; for timing of leucopheresis consult product literature

**Granocyte®** (Chugai) PoM

Injection, powder for reconstitution, lenograstim, net price 13.4 million-unit (105-microgram) vial = £42.00; 33.6 million-unit (263-microgram) vial = £67.95 (both with 1-mL prefilled syringe water for injections)

## PEGFILGRASTIM

**(Pegylated recombinant methionyl human granulocyte-colony stimulating factor)**

**Indications** (specialist use only) reduction in duration of neutropenia and incidence of febrile neutropenia in cytotoxic chemotherapy for malignancy (except chronic myeloid leukaemia and myelodysplastic syndromes)

**Cautions** see notes above; also acute leukaemia and myelosuppressive chemotherapy; sickle-cell disease; monitor spleen size (risk of rupture); **interactions:** Appendix 1 (filgrastim)

**Side-effects** see notes above; also *rarely* thrombocytopenia; *very rarely* acute febrile neutrophilic dermatosis and splenic rupture

**Dose**

Note Dose expressed as filgrastim

- By subcutaneous injection, ADULT over 18 years, 6 mg (0.6 mL) for each chemotherapy cycle, starting 24 hours after chemotherapy

**Neulasta®** (Amgen) ▼ PoM

Injection, pegfilgrastim (expressed as filgrastim) 10 mg/mL, net price 0.6-mL (6-mg) prefilled syringe = £714.24; *SureClick®* prefilled disposable injection device 0.6 mL (6 mg) = £714.24



# 9.2 Fluids and electrolytes


9.2.1 Oral preparations for fluid and electrolyte imbalance

9.2.2 Parenteral preparations for fluid and electrolyte imbalance


The following tables give a selection of useful electrolyte values:

**Electrolyte concentrations—intravenous fluids**

| Intravenous infusion | Millimoles per litre: $Na^+$ | $K^+$ | $HCO_3^-$ | $Cl^-$ | $Ca^{2+}$ |
|---|---|---|---|---|---|
| *Normal plasma values* | 142 | 4.5 | 26 | 103 | 2.5 |
| Sodium Chloride 0.9% | 150 | — | — | 150 | — |
| Compound Sodium Lactate (Hartmann's) | 131 | 5 | 29 | 111 | 2 |
| Sodium Chloride 0.18% and Glucose 4% | 30 | — | — | 30 | — |
| Potassium Chloride 0.3% and Glucose 5% | — | 40 | — | 40 | — |
| Potassium Chloride 0.3% and Sodium Chloride 0.9% | 150 | 40 | — | 190 | — |
| *To correct metabolic acidosis* | | | | | |
| Sodium Bicarbonate 1.26% | 150 | — | 150 | — | — |
| Sodium Bicarbonate 8.4% for cardiac arrest | 1000 | — | 1000 | — | — |
| Sodium Lactate (m/6) | 167 | — | 167 | — | — |

**Electrolyte content —gastro-intestinal secretions**

| Type of fluid | Millimoles per litre: $H^+$ | $Na^+$ | $K^+$ | $HCO_3^-$ | $Cl^-$ |
|---|---|---|---|---|---|
| Gastric | 40–60 | 20–80 | 5–20 | — | 100–150 |
| Biliary | — | 120–140 | 5–15 | 30–50 | 80–120 |
| Pancreatic | — | 120–140 | 5–15 | 70–110 | 40–80 |
| Small bowel | — | 120–140 | 5–15 | 20–40 | 90–130 |

Faeces, vomit, or aspiration should be saved and analysed where possible if abnormal losses are suspected; where this is impracticable the approximations above may be helpful in planning replacement therapy

## 9.2.1 Oral preparations for fluid and electrolyte imbalance


9.2.1.1 Oral potassium

9.2.1.2 Oral sodium and water

9.2.1.3 Oral bicarbonate


Sodium and potassium salts, which may be given by mouth to prevent deficiencies or to treat established deficiencies of mild or moderate degree, are discussed in this section. Oral preparations for removing excess potassium and preparations for oral rehydration therapy are also included here. Oral bicarbonate, for metabolic acidosis, is also described in this section.

For reference to calcium, magnesium, and phosphate, see section 9.5.

### 9.2.1.1 Oral potassium

Compensation for potassium loss is especially necessary:

- in those taking digoxin or anti-arrhythmic drugs, where potassium depletion may induce arrhythmias;
- in patients in whom secondary hyperaldosteronism occurs, e.g. renal artery stenosis, cirrhosis of the liver, the nephrotic syndrome, and severe heart failure;
- in patients with excessive losses of potassium in the faeces, e.g. chronic diarrhoea associated with intestinal malabsorption or laxative abuse.

Measures to compensate for potassium loss may also be required in the elderly since they frequently take inadequate amounts of potassium in the diet (but see below for **warning** on **renal insufficiency**). Measures may also be required during long-term administration of drugs known to induce potassium loss (e.g. corticosteroids). Potassium supplements are **seldom required** with the small doses of diuretics given to treat hypertension; **potassium-sparing diuretics** (rather than potassium supplements) are recommended for prevention of hypokalaemia due to diuretics such as furosemide (frusemide) or the thiazides when these are given to eliminate oedema.

**Dosage** If potassium salts are used for the *prevention of hypokalaemia*, then doses of potassium chloride 2 to 4 g (approx. 25 to 50 mmol) daily by mouth are suitable in patients taking a normal diet. *Smaller doses* must be used if there is *renal insufficiency (common in the elderly)* otherwise there is **danger of hyperkalaemia**. Potassium salts cause nausea and vomiting therefore poor compliance is a major limitation to their effectiveness; where appropriate, potassium-sparing diuretics are preferable (see also above). When there is *established potassium depletion* larger doses may be necessary, the quantity depending on the severity of any continuing potassium loss (monitoring of plasma-potassium concentration and specialist advice would be required). Potassium depletion is frequently associated with chloride depletion and with metabolic alkalosis, and these disorders require correction.

**Administration** Potassium salts are preferably given as a liquid (or effervescent) preparation, rather than modified-release tablets; they should be given as the chloride (the use of effervescent potassium tablets BPC 1968 should be restricted to *hyperchloraemic states*, section 9.2.1.3).

**Salt substitutes.** A number of salt substitutes which contain significant amounts of potassium chloride are readily available as health food products (e.g. *LoSalt®* and *Ruthmol®*). These should not be used by patients with renal failure as potassium intoxication may result.

## POTASSIUM CHLORIDE

**Indications** potassium depletion (see notes above)

**Cautions** elderly, mild to moderate renal impairment (close monitoring required), intestinal stricture, history of peptic ulcer, hiatus hernia (for sustained-release preparations); **important**: special hazard if given with drugs liable to raise plasma potassium concentration such as potassium-sparing diuretics, ACE inhibitors, or ciclosporin, for other **interactions**: Appendix 1 (potassium salts)

**Contra-indications** severe renal impairment, plasma potassium concentrations above 5 mmol/litre

**Side-effects** nausea and vomiting (severe symptoms may indicate obstruction), oesophageal or small bowel ulceration

**Dose**

- See notes above

Note Do not confuse Effervescent Potassium Tablets BPC 1968 (section 9.2.1.3) with effervescent potassium chloride tablets. Effervescent Potassium Tablets BPC 1968 do not contain chloride ions and their use should be restricted to hyperchloraemic states (section 9.2.1.3). Effervescent Potassium Chloride Tablets BP are usually available in two strengths, one containing 6.7 mmol each of $K^+$ and $Cl^-$ (corresponding to *Kloref®*), the other containing 12 mmol $K^+$ and 8 mmol $Cl^-$ (corresponding to *Sando-K®*). Generic prescriptions must specify the strength required.

**Kay-Cee-L®** (Geistlich)
Syrup, red, sugar-free, potassium chloride 7.5% (1 mmol/mL each of $K^+$ and $Cl^-$). Net price 500 mL = £3.74. Label: 21

**Kloref®** (Alpharma)
Tablets, effervescent, betaine hydrochloride, potassium benzoate, bicarbonate, and chloride, equivalent to potassium chloride 500 mg (6.7 mmol each of $K^+$ and $Cl^-$). Net price 50 = £2.71. Label: 13, 21
Note May be difficult to obtain

**Sando-K®** (HK Pharma)
Tablets, effervescent, potassium bicarbonate and chloride equivalent to potassium 470 mg (12 mmol of $K^+$) and chloride 285 mg (8 mmol of $Cl^-$). Net price 20 = £1.53. Label: 13, 21

### Modified-release preparations
Avoid unless effervescent tablets or liquid preparations inappropriate

**Slow-K®** (Alliance)
Tablets, m/r, orange, s/c, potassium chloride 600 mg (8 mmol each of $K^+$ and $Cl^-$). Net price 20 = 54p. Label: 25, 27, counselling, swallow whole with fluid during meals while sitting or standing

## Potassium removal

Ion-exchange resins may be used to remove excess potassium in *mild hyperkalaemia* or in *moderate hyperkalaemia* when there are no ECG changes; intravenous therapy is required in emergencies (section 9.2.2).

## POLYSTYRENE SULPHONATE RESINS

**Indications** hyperkalaemia associated with anuria or severe oliguria, and in dialysis patients

**Cautions** children (impaction of resin with excessive dosage or inadequate dilution); monitor for electrolyte disturbances (stop if plasma-potassium concentration below 5 mmol/litre); pregnancy and breast-feeding; sodium-containing resin in congestive heart failure, hypertension, renal impairment, and oedema; **interactions:** Appendix 1 (sodium polystyrene sulphonate)

**Contra-indications** obstructive bowel disease; oral administration or reduced gut motility in neonates; avoid calcium-containing resin in hyperparathyroidism, multiple myeloma, sarcoidosis, or metastatic carcinoma

**Side-effects** rectal ulceration following rectal administration; colonic necrosis reported following enemas containing sorbitol; sodium retention, hypercalcaemia, gastric irritation, anorexia, nausea and vomiting, constipation (discontinue treatment—avoid magnesium-containing laxatives), diarrhoea; calcium-containing resin may cause hypercalcaemia (in dialysed patients and occasionally in those with renal impairment), hypomagnesaemia

**Dose**

- By mouth, 15 g 3–4 times daily in water (not fruit squash which has a high potassium content) or as a paste; CHILD 0.5–1 g/kg daily in divided doses
- By rectum, as an enema, 30 g in methylcellulose solution, retained for 9 hours followed by irrigation to remove resin from colon; NEONATE and CHILD, 0.5–1 g/kg daily

**Calcium Resonium®** (Sanofi-Synthelabo)
Powder, buff, calcium polystyrene sulphonate. Net price 300 g = £47.55. Label: 13

**Resonium A®** (Sanofi-Synthelabo)
Powder, buff, sodium polystyrene sulphonate. Net price 454 g = £58.53. Label: 13

## 9.2.1.2 Oral sodium and water

Sodium chloride is indicated in states of sodium depletion and usually needs to be given intravenously (section 9.2.2). In chronic conditions associated with mild or moderate degrees of sodium depletion, e.g. in salt-losing bowel or renal disease, oral supplements of sodium chloride or sodium bicarbonate (section 9.2.1.3), according to the acid-base status of the patient, may be sufficient.

### SODIUM CHLORIDE

**Indications** sodium depletion—see also 9.2.2.1; nebuliser diluent (section 3.1.5); eye (section 11.8.1); oral hygiene (section 12.3.4); wound irrigation (section 13.11.1)

**Slow Sodium®** (HK Pharma)

Tablets, m/r, sodium chloride 600 mg (approx. 10 mmol each of $Na^+$ and $Cl^-$). Net price 100-tab pack = £6.05. Label: 25

**Dose** prophylaxis of sodium chloride deficiency 4–8 tablets daily with water (in severe depletion up to max. 20 tablets daily)

Chronic renal salt wasting, up to 20 tablets daily with appropriate fluid intake

CHILD, according to requirements

## Oral rehydration therapy (ORT)

As a worldwide problem *diarrhoea* is by far the most important indication for fluid and electrolyte replacement. Intestinal absorption of sodium and water is enhanced by glucose (and other carbohydrates). Replacement of fluid and electrolytes lost through diarrhoea can therefore be achieved by giving solutions containing sodium, potassium, and glucose or another carbohydrate such as rice starch.

Oral rehydration solutions should:

- enhance the absorption of water and electrolytes;
- replace the electrolyte deficit adequately and safely;
- contain an alkalinising agent to counter acidosis;
- be slightly hypo-osmolar (about 250 mmol/litre) to prevent the possible induction of osmotic diarrhoea;
- be simple to use in hospital and at home;
- be palatable and acceptable, especially to children;
- be readily available.

It is the policy of the World Health Organization (WHO) to promote a single oral rehydration solution but to use it flexibly (e.g. by giving extra water between drinks of oral rehydration solution to moderately dehydrated infants).

Oral rehydration solutions used in the UK are lower in sodium (50–60 mmol/litre) than the WHO formulation since, in general, patients suffer less severe sodium loss.

Rehydration should be rapid over 3 to 4 hours (except in hypernatraemic dehydration in which case rehydration should occur more slowly over 12 hours). The patient should be reassessed after initial rehydration and if still dehydrated rapid fluid replacement should continue.

Once rehydration is complete further dehydration is prevented by encouraging the patient to drink normal volumes of an appropriate fluid and by replacing continuing losses with an oral rehydration solution; in infants, breast-feeding or formula feeds should be offered between oral rehydration drinks.

For intravenous rehydration see section 9.2.2.

### ORAL REHYDRATION SALTS (ORS)

**Indications** fluid and electrolyte loss in diarrhoea, see notes above

**Dose**

- According to fluid loss, usually 200–400 mL solution after every loose motion; INFANT 1–1½ times usual feed volume; CHILD 200 mL after every loose motion

#### UK formulations

**Note** After reconstitution any unused solution should be discarded no later than 1 hour after preparation unless stored in a refrigerator when it may be kept for up to 24 hours.

**Dioralyte®** (Sanofi-Aventis)

Effervescent tablets, sodium chloride 117 mg, sodium bicarbonate 336 mg, potassium chloride 186 mg, citric acid anhydrous 384 mg, anhydrous glucose 1.62 g. Net price 10-tab pack (black currant- or citrus-flavoured) = £1.42

**Dose** reconstitute 2 tablets with 200 mL of water (only for adults and for children over 1 year)

**Note** Ten tablets when reconstituted with 1 litre of water provide $Na^+$ 60 mmol, $K^+$ 25 mmol, $Cl^-$ 45 mmol, citrate 20 mmol, and glucose 90 mmol

Oral powder, sodium chloride 470 mg, potassium chloride 300 mg, disodium hydrogen citrate 530 mg, glucose 3.56 g/sachet, net price 6-sachet pack = £2.02, 20-sachet pack (black currant- or citrus-flavoured or natural) = £6.19

**Dose** reconstitute one sachet with 200 mL of water (freshly boiled and cooled for infants)

**Note** Five sachets reconstituted with 1 litre of water provide $Na^+$ 60 mmol, $K^+$ 20 mmol, $Cl^-$ 60 mmol, citrate 10 mmol, and glucose 90 mmol

**Dioralyte® Relief** (Sanofi-Aventis)

Oral powder, sodium chloride 350 mg, potassium chloride 300 mg, sodium citrate 580 mg, cooked rice powder 6 g/sachet, net price 6-sachet pack (apricot-, black currant- or raspberry-flavoured) = £2.26, 20-sachet pack (apricot-flavoured) = £7.42

**Dose** reconstitute one sachet with 200 mL of water (freshly boiled and cooled for infants)

**Note** 5 sachets when reconstitued with 1 litre of water provide $Na^+$ 60 mmol, $K^+$ 20 mmol, $Cl^-$ 50 mmol and citrate 10 mmol; contains aspartame (section 9.4.1)

**Electrolade®** (Thornton & Ross)

Oral powder, sodium chloride 236 mg, potassium chloride 300 mg, sodium bicarbonate 500 mg, anhydrous glucose 4 g/sachet (banana-, black currant-, lemon and lime-, or orange-flavoured). Net price 6-sachet (plain or multiflavoured) pack = £1.33, 20-sachet (single- or multiflavoured) pack = £4.99

**Dose** reconstitute one sachet with 200 mL of water (freshly boiled and cooled for infants)

**Note** Five sachets when reconstituted with 1 litre of water provide $Na^+$ 50 mmol, $K^+$ 20 mmol, $Cl^-$ 40 mmol, $HCO_3^-$ 30 mmol, and glucose 111 mmol

**Rapolyte®** (Provalis)

Oral powder, sodium chloride 350 mg, potassium chloride 300 mg, sodium citrate 600 mg, anhydrous glucose 4 g, net price 20-sachet pack (black currant- or raspberry-flavoured) = £4.28

Dose reconstitute one sachet with 200 mL of water (freshly boiled and cooled for infants)

Note Five sachets when reconstituted with 1 litre of water provide $Na^+$ 60 mmol, $K^+$ 20 mmol, $Cl^-$ 50 mmol, citrate 10 mmol, and glucose 110 mmol

WHO formulation

**Oral Rehydration Salts** (Non-proprietary)

Oral powder, sodium chloride 2.6 g, potassium chloride 1.5 g, sodium citrate 2.9 g, anhydrous glucose 13.5 g. To be dissolved in sufficient water to produce 1 litre (providing $Na^+$ 75 mmol, $K^+$ 20 mmol, $Cl^-$ 65 mmol, citrate 10 mmol, glucose 75 mmol/litre)

Note Recommended by the WHO and the United Nations Children's Fund but not commonly used in the UK.

### 9.2.1.3 Oral bicarbonate

**Sodium bicarbonate** is given by mouth for *chronic acidotic states* such as uraemic acidosis or renal tubular acidosis. The dose for correction of metabolic acidosis is not predictable and the response must be assessed; sodium bicarbonate 4.8 g daily (57 mmol each of $Na^+$ and $HCO_3^-$) or more may be required. For severe metabolic acidosis, sodium bicarbonate can be given intravenously (section 9.2.2).

Sodium bicarbonate may also be used to increase the pH of the urine (see section 7.4.3); for use in dyspepsia see section 1.1.1.

Sodium supplements may increase blood pressure or cause fluid retention and pulmonary oedema in those at risk; hypokalaemia may be exacerbated.

Where *hyperchloraemic acidosis* is associated with potassium deficiency, as in some renal tubular and gastro-intestinal disorders it may be appropriate to give oral **potassium bicarbonate**, although acute or severe deficiency should be managed by intravenous therapy.

#### SODIUM BICARBONATE

**Indications** see notes above

**Cautions** see notes above; avoid in respiratory acidosis; **interactions**: Appendix 1 (antacids)

**Dose**

- See notes above

**Sodium Bicarbonate** (Non-proprietary)

Capsules, sodium bicarbonate 500 mg (approx. 6 mmol each of $Na^+$ and $HCO_3^-$). Net price 20 = £5.36

Tablets, sodium bicarbonate 600 mg, net price 100 = £2.48

Important Oral solutions of sodium bicarbonate are required occasionally; these need to be obtained on special order and the strength of sodium bicarbonate should be stated on the prescription

#### POTASSIUM BICARBONATE

**Indications** see notes above

**Cautions** cardiac disease, renal impairment (Appendix 3); **interactions**: Appendix 1 (potassium salts)

**Contra-indications** hypochloraemia; plasma potassium concentration above 5 mmol/litre

**Side-effects** nausea and vomiting

**Dose**

- See notes above

**Potassium Tablets, Effervescent** (Non-proprietary)

Effervescent tablets, potassium bicarbonate 500 mg, potassium acid tartrate 300 mg, each tablet providing 6.5 mmol of $K^+$. To be dissolved in water before administration. Net price 56 = £6.03. Label: 13, 21

Note These tablets do not contain chloride; for effervescent tablets containing potassium and chloride, see under Potassium Chloride, section 9.2.1.1

## 9.2.2 Parenteral preparations for fluid and electrolyte imbalance

9.2.2.1 Electrolytes and water
9.2.2.2 Plasma and plasma substitutes

### 9.2.2.1 Electrolytes and water

Solutions of electrolytes are given intravenously, to meet normal fluid and electrolyte requirements or to replenish substantial deficits or continuing losses, when the patient is nauseated or vomiting and is unable to take adequate amounts by mouth. When intravenous administration is not possible, fluid (as sodium chloride 0.9% or glucose 5%) can also be given subcutaneously by hypodermoclysis.

In an individual patient the nature and severity of the electrolyte imbalance must be assessed from the history and clinical and biochemical examination. Sodium, potassium, chloride, magnesium, phosphate, and water depletion can occur singly and in combination with or without disturbances of acid-base balance; for reference to the use of magnesium and phosphates, see section 9.5.

Isotonic solutions may be infused safely into a peripheral vein. Solutions more concentrated than plasma, e.g. 20% glucose, are best given through an indwelling catheter positioned in a large vein.

#### Intravenous sodium

**Sodium chloride** in isotonic solution provides the most important extracellular ions in near physiological concentration and is indicated in *sodium depletion* which may arise from such conditions as gastro-enteritis, diabetic ketoacidosis, ileus, and ascites. In a severe deficit of from 4 to 8 litres, 2 to 3 litres of isotonic sodium chloride may be given over 2 to 3 hours; thereafter infusion can usually be at a slower rate. Excessive administration should be avoided; the jugular venous pressure should be assessed, the bases of the lungs should be examined for crepitations, and in elderly or seriously ill patients it is often helpful to monitor the right atrial (central) venous pressure.

Chronic hyponatraemia arising from inappropriate secretion of antidiuretic hormone should ideally be corrected by fluid restriction. However, if sodium chloride is required for acute or chronic hyponatraemia, regardless of the cause, the deficit should be corrected slowly to avoid the risk of osmotic demyelination syndrome and the rise in plasma-sodium concentration should not exceed 10 mmol/litre in 24 hours. In severe hyponatraemia, sodium chloride 1.8% may be used cautiously.

**Compound sodium lactate** (Hartmann's solution) can be used instead of isotonic sodium chloride solution during surgery or in the initial management of the injured or wounded.

**Sodium chloride and glucose** solutions are indicated when there is combined *water and sodium depletion.* A 1:1 mixture of isotonic sodium chloride and 5% glucose allows some of the water (free of sodium) to enter body cells which suffer most from dehydration while the sodium salt with a volume of water determined by the normal plasma $Na^+$ remains extracellular. Maintenance fluid should accurately reflect daily requirements and close monitoring is required to avoid fluid and electrolyte imbalance. Illness or injury increase the secretion of anti-diuretic hormone and therefore the ability to excrete excess water may be impaired. Injudicious use of solutions such as sodium chloride 0.18% and glucose 4% may also cause dilutional hyponatraemia especially in children and the elderly; if necessary, guidance should be sought from a clinician experienced in the management of fluid and electrolytes.

Combined sodium, potassium, chloride, and water depletion may occur, for example, with severe diarrhoea or persistent vomiting; replacement is carried out with sodium chloride intravenous infusion 0.9% and glucose intravenous infusion 5% with potassium as appropriate.



## SODIUM CHLORIDE

**Indications** electrolyte imbalance—see also section 9.2.1.2; nebuliser diluent (section 3.1.5); eye (section 11.8.1); oral hygiene (section 12.3.4); wound irrigation (section 13.11.1)

**Cautions** restrict intake in impaired renal function, cardiac failure, hypertension, peripheral and pulmonary oedema, toxaemia of pregnancy

**Side-effects** administration of large doses may give rise to sodium accumulation, oedema, and hyperchloraemic acidosis

**Dose**

- See notes above

**Sodium Chloride Intravenous Infusion** (Non-proprietary) PoM

Intravenous infusion, usual strength sodium chloride 0.9% (9 g, 150 mmol each of $Na^+$ and $Cl^-$/litre), this strength being supplied when normal saline for injection is requested. Net price 2-mL amp = 24p; 5-mL amp = 33p; 10-mL amp = 36p; 20-mL amp = £1.04; 50-mL amp = £2.01

In hospitals, 500- and 1000-mL packs, and sometimes other sizes, are available

**Note** The term 'normal saline' should **not** be used to describe sodium chloride intravenous infusion 0.9%; the term 'physiological saline' is acceptable but it is preferable to give the composition (i.e. sodium chloride intravenous infusion 0.9%).

### With other ingredients

**Sodium Chloride and Glucose Intravenous Infusion** (Non-proprietary) PoM

Intravenous infusion, sodium chloride 0.18% ($Na^+$ and $Cl^-$ each 30 mmol/litre), glucose 4%

In hospitals, usually 500-mL packs and sometimes other sizes are available

Intravenous infusion, sodium chloride 0.9% ($Na^+$ and $Cl^-$ each 150 mmol/litre), glucose 5%

In hospitals, usually 500-mL packs and sometimes other sizes are available

Intravenous infusion, sodium chloride 0.45% ($Na^+$ and $Cl^-$ each 75 mmol/litre), glucose 5%

In hospitals, usually 500-mL packs and sometimes other sizes are available

Intravenous infusion, sodium chloride 0.45% ($Na^+$ and $Cl^-$ each 75 mmol/litre), glucose 2.5%

In hospitals, usually 500-mL packs and sometimes other sizes are available

**Note** See above for warning on hyponatraemia especially in children and elderly

**Ringer's Solution for Injection** PoM

Calcium chloride (dihydrate) 322 micrograms, potassium chloride 300 micrograms, sodium chloride 8.6 mg/mL, providing the following ions (in mmol/litre), $Ca^{2+}$ 2.2, $K^+$ 4, $Na^+$ 147, $Cl^-$ 156

In hospitals, 500- and 1000-mL packs, and sometimes other sizes, are available

**Sodium Lactate Intravenous Infusion, Compound** (Non-proprietary) PoM

**(Hartmann's Solution for Injection; Ringer-Lactate Solution for Injection)**

Intravenous infusion, sodium chloride 0.6%, sodium lactate 0.25%, potassium chloride 0.04%, calcium chloride 0.027% (containing $Na^+$ 131 mmol, $K^+$ 5 mmol, $Ca^{2+}$ 2 mmol, $HCO_3^-$ (as lactate) 29 mmol, $Cl^-$ 111 mmol/litre)

In hospitals, 500- and 1000-mL packs, and sometimes other sizes, are available

## Intravenous glucose

**Glucose** solutions (5%) are mainly used to replace water deficits and should be given alone when there is no significant loss of electrolytes. Average water requirements in a healthy adult are 1.5 to 2.5 litres daily and this is needed to balance unavoidable losses of water through the skin and lungs and to provide sufficient for urinary excretion. Water depletion (dehydration) tends to occur when these losses are not matched by a comparable intake, as may occur in coma or dysphagia or in the elderly or apathetic who may not drink enough water on their own initiative.

Excessive loss of water without loss of electrolytes is uncommon, occurring in fevers, hyperthyroidism, and in uncommon water-losing renal states such as diabetes insipidus or hypercalcaemia. The volume of glucose solution needed to replace deficits varies with the severity of the disorder, but usually lies within the range of 2 to 6 litres.

Glucose solutions are also given in regimens with calcium, bicarbonate, and insulin for the emergency management of *hyperkalaemia.* They are also given, after correction of hyperglycaemia, during treatment of diabetic ketoacidosis, when they must be accompanied by continuing insulin infusion.

## GLUCOSE
### (Dextrose Monohydrate)

Note Glucose BP is the monohydrate but Glucose Intravenous Infusion BP is a sterile solution of anhydrous glucose or glucose monohydrate, potency being expressed in terms of anhydrous glucose

**Indications** fluid replacement (see notes above), provision of energy (section 9.3)

**Side-effects** glucose injections especially if hypertonic may have a low pH and may cause venous irritation and thrombophlebitis

**Dose**

- Water replacement, see notes above; energy source, 1–3 litres daily of 20–50% solution

**Glucose Intravenous Infusion** (Non-proprietary) PoM
Intravenous infusion, glucose or anhydrous glucose (potency expressed in terms of anhydrous glucose), usual strength 5% (50 mg/mL) and 10% (100 mg/mL); 25% solution, net price 25-mL amp = £2.21; 50% solution,[1] 25-mL amp = £3.80, 50-mL amp = £1.63
In hospitals, 500- and 1000-mL packs, and sometimes other sizes and strengths, are available; also available as *Min-I-Jet® Glucose*, 50% in 50-mL disposable syringe[1]

1. PoM restriction does not apply where administration is for saving life in emergency

## Intravenous potassium

**Potassium chloride and sodium chloride** intravenous infusion is the initial treatment for the correction of *severe hypokalaemia* and when sufficient potassium cannot be taken by mouth. Ready-mixed infusion solutions should be used when possible; alternatively, potassium chloride concentrate, as ampoules containing 1.5 g ($K^+$ 20 mmol) in 10 mL, is **thoroughly mixed** with 500 mL of sodium chloride 0.9% intravenous infusion and given slowly over 2 to 3 hours, with specialist advice and ECG monitoring in difficult cases. Higher concentrations of potassium chloride may be given in very severe depletion, but require specialist advice.

Repeated measurements of plasma-potassium concentration are necessary to determine whether further infusions are required and to avoid the development of hyperkalaemia, which is especially likely in renal impairment.

Initial potassium replacement therapy should **not** involve glucose infusions, because glucose may cause a further decrease in the plasma-potassium concentration.

## POTASSIUM CHLORIDE

**Indications** electrolyte imbalance; see also oral potassium supplements, section 9.2.1.1

**Cautions** for intravenous infusion the concentration of solution should not usually exceed 3.2 g (43 mmol)/litre; specialist advice and ECG monitoring (see notes above); **interactions:** Appendix 1 (potassium salts)

**Side-effects** rapid infusion toxic to heart

**Dose**

- By slow intravenous infusion, depending on the deficit or the daily maintenance requirements, see also notes above

**Potassium Chloride and Glucose Intravenous Infusion** (Non-proprietary) PoM
Intravenous infusion, usual strength potassium chloride 0.3% (3 g, 40 mmol each of $K^+$ and $Cl^-$/litre) or 0.15% (1.5 g, 20 mmol each of $K^+$ and $Cl^-$/litre) with 5% of anhydrous glucose
In hospitals, 500- and 1000-mL packs, and sometimes other sizes, are available

**Potassium Chloride and Sodium Chloride Intravenous Infusion** (Non-proprietary) PoM
Intravenous infusion, usual strength potassium chloride 0.15% (1.5 g/litre) with sodium chloride 0.9% (9 g/litre), containing $K^+$ 20 mmol, $Na^+$ 150 mmol, and $Cl^-$ 170 mmol/litre *or* potassium chloride 0.3% (3 g/litre) with sodium chloride 0.9% (9 g/litre), containing $K^+$ 40 mmol, $Na^+$ 150 mmol, and $Cl^-$ 190 mmol/litre
In hospitals, 500- and 1000-mL packs, and sometimes other sizes, are available

**Potassium Chloride, Sodium Chloride, and Glucose Intravenous Infusion** (Non-proprietary) PoM
Intravenous infusion, sodium chloride 0.45% (4.5 g, $Na^+$ 75 mmol/litre) with 5% of anhydrous glucose and usually sufficient potassium chloride to provide $K^+$ 10–40 mmol/litre (to be specified by the prescriber)
In hospitals, 500- and 1000-mL packs, and sometimes other sizes, are available

Intravenous infusion, sodium chloride 0.18% (1.8 g, $Na^+$ 30 mmol/litre) with 4% of anhydrous glucose and usually sufficient potassium chloride to provide $K^+$ 10–40 mmol/litre (to be specified by the prescriber)
In hospitals, 500- and 1000-mL packs, and sometimes other sizes, are available

**Potassium Chloride Concentrate, Sterile** (Non-proprietary) PoM
Sterile concentrate, potassium chloride 15% (150 mg, approximately 2 mmol each of $K^+$ and $Cl^-$/mL). Net price 10-mL amp = 48p
**Important** Must be diluted with **not less** than 50 times its volume of sodium chloride intravenous infusion 0.9% or other suitable diluent and **mixed well**
Solutions containing 10 and 20% of potassium chloride are also available in both 5- and 10-mL ampoules

## Bicarbonate and lactate

**Sodium bicarbonate** is used to control severe *metabolic acidosis* (as in renal failure). Since this condition is usually attended by sodium depletion, it is reasonable to correct this first by the administration of isotonic sodium chloride intravenous infusion, provided the kidneys are not primarily affected and the degree of acidosis is not so severe as to impair renal function. In these circumstances, isotonic sodium chloride alone is usually effective as it restores the ability of the kidneys to generate bicarbonate. In renal acidosis or in severe metabolic acidosis of any origin (for example, blood pH < 7.1) sodium bicarbonate (1.26%) may be infused with isotonic sodium chloride when the acidosis remains unresponsive to correction of anoxia or fluid depletion; a total volume of up to 6 litres (4 litres of sodium chloride and 2 litres of sodium bicarbonate) may be necessary in the adult. In severe shock due for example to cardiac arrest (see section 2.7), metabolic acidosis may develop without sodium depletion; in these circumstances sodium bicarbonate is best given in a small volume of hypertonic solution, such as 50 mL of

8.4% solution intravenously; plasma pH should be monitored.

Sodium bicarbonate infusion is also used in the emergency management of *hyperkalaemia* (see also under Glucose).

**Sodium lactate** intravenous infusion is obsolete in metabolic acidosis, and carries the risk of producing lactic acidosis, particularly in seriously ill patients with poor tissue perfusion or impaired hepatic function.

## SODIUM BICARBONATE

**Indications** metabolic acidosis

**Dose**

- By slow intravenous injection, a strong solution (up to 8.4%), or by continuous intravenous infusion, a weaker solution (usually 1.26%), an amount appropriate to the body base deficit (see notes above)

**Sodium Bicarbonate Intravenous Infusion** PoM

Usual strength sodium bicarbonate 1.26% (12.6 g, 150 mmol each of $Na^+$ and $HCO_3^-$/litre); various other strengths available

In hospitals, 500- and 1000-mL packs, and sometimes other sizes, are available

**Min-I-Jet® Sodium Bicarbonate** (Celltech) PoM

Intravenous injection, sodium bicarbonate in disposable syringe, net price 4.2%, 10 mL = £5.29; 8.4%, 10 mL = £5.71, 50 mL = £7.75

## SODIUM LACTATE

**Indications** see notes above

**Sodium Lactate** (Non-proprietary) PoM

Intravenous infusion, sodium lactate M/6, contains the following ions (in mmol/litre), $Na^+$ 167, $HCO_3^-$ (as lactate) 167

## Water

**Water for Injections** PoM

Net price 1-mL amp = 18p; 2-mL amp = 17p; 5-mL amp = 28p; 10-mL amp = 31p; 20-mL amp = 55p; 50-mL amp = £1.91; 100-mL vial = 23p

## 9.2.2.2 Plasma and plasma substitutes

Plasma and plasma substitutes ('colloids') contain large molecules that do not readily leave the intravascular space where they exert osmotic pressure to maintain circulatory volume. Compared to fluids containing electrolytes such as sodium chloride and glucose ('crystalloids'), a smaller volume of colloid is required to produce the same expansion of blood volume, thereby reducing salt and water overload of the extravascular space. If resuscitation requires a volume of fluid that exceeds the maximum dose of the colloid then crystalloids are also given together with packed red cells as necessary.

**Albumin solutions**, prepared from whole blood, contain soluble proteins and electrolytes but no clotting factors, blood group antibodies, or plasma cholinesterases; they may be given without regard to the recipient's blood group.

Albumin should usually be used after the acute phase of illness, to correct a plasma-volume deficit in patients with salt and water retention and oedema; hypoalbuminaemia itself is not an appropriate indication. The use of albumin solutions in acute plasma or blood loss may be wasteful; plasma substitutes are more appropriate. Concentrated albumin solutions may also be used to obtain a diuresis in hypoalbuminaemic patients (e.g. in hepatic cirrhosis).

Recent evidence does not support the previous view that the use of albumin increases mortality.

> Plasma and plasma substitutes are often used in very ill patients whose condition is unstable. Therefore, close monitoring is required and fluid and electrolyte therapy should be adjusted according to the patient's condition at all times.

## ALBUMIN SOLUTION
### (Human Albumin Solution)

A solution containing protein derived from plasma, serum, or normal placentas; at least 95% of the protein is albumin. The solution may be isotonic (containing 4–5% protein) or concentrated (containing 15–25% protein).

**Indications** see under preparations, and also notes above

**Cautions** history of cardiac or circulatory disease (administer slowly to avoid rapid rise in blood pressure and cardiac failure, and monitor cardiovascular and respiratory function); increased capillary permeability; correct dehydration when administering concentrated solution

**Contra-indications** cardiac failure; severe anaemia

**Side-effects** hypersensitivity reactions (including anaphylaxis) with nausea, vomiting, increased salivation, fever, tachycardia, hypotension and chills reported

**Isotonic solutions**

*Indications:* acute or sub-acute loss of plasma volume e.g. in burns, pancreatitis, trauma, and complications of surgery; plasma exchange

Available as: *Human Albumin Solution 4.5%* (50-, 100-, 250- and 400-mL bottles—Baxter Bioscience); *Human Albumin Solution 5%* (100-, 250- and 500-mL bottles—Grifols); *ALBA® 4.5%* (100- and 400-mL bottles—SNBTS); *Albutein® 5%* (250- and 500-mL bottles—Grifols); *Octalbin® 5%* (100- and 200-mL bottles—Octapharm); *Zenalb® 4.5%* (50-, 100-, 250-, and 500-mL bottles—BPL)

**Concentrated solutions (20–25%)**

*Indications:* severe hypoalbuminaemia associated with low plasma volume and generalised oedema where salt and water restriction with plasma volume expansion are required; adjunct in the treatment of hyperbilirubinaemia by exchange transfusion in the newborn; paracentesis of large volume ascites associated with portal hypertension

Available as: *Human Albumin Solution 20%* (50- and 100-mL vials—Baxter Bioscience); *Human Albumin Solution 20%* (50- and 100-mL bottles—Grifols); *ALBA® 20%* (50-mL vials—SNBTS); *Albutein® 20%* (50- and 100-mL bottles—Grifols); *Albutein® 25%* (20-, 50-, and 100-mL vials—Grifols); *Octalbin® 20%* (50- and 100-mL bottles—Octapharm); *Zenalb® 20%* (50- and 100-mL bottles—BPL)

## Plasma substitutes

**Dextrans**, **gelatin**, and the etherified starches, **hexastarch**, **hydroxyethyl starch** and **pentastarch** are macromolecular substances which are metabolised slowly; they may be used at the outset to expand and maintain blood volume in shock arising from conditions such as burns or septicaemia. Plasma substitutes may be used as an immediate short-term measure to treat haemorrhage until blood is available. They are rarely needed when shock is due to sodium and water depletion because, in these circumstances, the shock responds to water and electrolyte repletion. See also section 2.7.1 for the management of shock.

Plasma substitutes should **not** be used to maintain plasma volume in conditions such as burns or peritonitis where there is loss of plasma protein, water and electrolytes over periods of several days or weeks. In these situations, plasma or plasma protein fractions containing large amounts of albumin should be given.

Large volumes of *some* plasma substitutes can increase the risk of bleeding through depletion of coagulation factors; however, the risk is reduced if 1–2 litres of a substitute such as hexastarch is used.

Dextran 70 by intravenous infusion is used predominantly for volume expansion. Dextran 40 intravenous infusion is used in an attempt to improve peripheral blood flow in ischaemic disease of the limbs. Dextrans 40 and 70 have also been used in the prophylaxis of thromboembolism but are now rarely used for this purpose.

Dextrans may interfere with blood group cross-matching or biochemical measurements and these should be carried out before infusion is begun.

> Plasma and plasma substitutes are often used in very ill patients whose condition is unstable. Therefore, close monitoring is required and fluid and electrolyte therapy should be adjusted according to the patient's condition at all times.

**Cautions** Plasma substitutes should be used with caution in patients with cardiac disease, liver disease, or renal impairment; urine output should be monitored. Care should be taken to avoid haematocrit concentration from falling below 25–30% and the patient should be monitored for hypersensitivity reactions.

**Side-effects** Hypersensitivity reactions may occur including, rarely, severe anaphylactoid reactions. Transient increase in bleeding time may occur.

### DEXTRAN 40

Dextrans of weight average molecular weight about '40 000'

**Indications** conditions associated with peripheral local slowing of the blood flow; prophylaxis of post-surgical thromboembolic disease (but see notes above)

**Cautions** see notes above; can interfere with some laboratory tests (see also above); correct dehydration beforehand, give adequate fluids during therapy and, where possible, monitor central venous pressure; pregnancy (Appendix 4)

**Side-effects** see notes above

**Dose**

- By intravenous infusion, initially 500–1000 mL; further doses are given according to the patient's condition (see notes above)

**Dextran 40®** (Baxter) PoM

Intravenous infusion, dextran 40 intravenous infusion in glucose intravenous infusion 5% or in sodium chloride intravenous infusion 0.9%. Net price 500-mL bag (both) = £4.56

### DEXTRAN 70

Dextrans of weight average molecular weight about '70 000'

**Indications** short-term blood volume expansion; prophylaxis of post-surgical thromboembolic disease (but see notes above)

**Cautions** see notes above; can interfere with some laboratory tests (see also above); where possible, monitor central venous pressure; pregnancy (Appendix 4)

**Side-effects** see notes above

**Dose**

- By intravenous infusion, after moderate to severe haemorrhage or in the shock phase of burn injury (initial 48 hours), 500–1000 mL rapidly initially followed by 500 mL later if necessary (see also notes above); total dosage should not exceed 20 mL/kg during initial 24 hours; CHILD total dosage should not exceed 20 mL/kg

**Dextran 70®** (Baxter) PoM

Intravenous infusion, dextran 70 intravenous infusion in glucose intravenous infusion 5% or in sodium chloride intravenous infusion 0.9%. Net price 500-mL bag (both) = £4.56

**Hypertonic solution**

**RescueFlow®** (Vitaline) PoM

Intravenous infusion, dextran 70 intravenous infusion 6% in sodium chloride intravenous infusion 7.5%. Net price 250-mL bag = £28.50

Cautions see notes above; severe hyperglycaemia and hyperosmolality

Dose initial treatment of hypovolaemia with hypotension induced by traumatic injury, by intravenous infusion over 2–5 minutes, 250 mL, followed immediately by administration of isotonic fluids

### GELATIN

**Note** The gelatin is partially degraded

**Indications** low blood volume

**Cautions** see notes above

**Side-effects** see notes above

**Dose**

- By intravenous infusion, initially 500–1000 mL of a 3.5–4% solution (see notes above)

**Gelofusine®** (Braun) PoM

Intravenous infusion, succinylated gelatin (modified fluid gelatin, average molecular weight 30 000) 40 g (4%), $Na^+$ 154 mmol, $Cl^-$ 120 mmol/litre, net price 500-mL *Ecobag®* = £4.63, 1-litre *Ecobag®* = £9.45

**Haemaccel®** (Syner-Med) PoM

Intravenous infusion, polygeline (gelatin derivative, average molecular weight 30 000) 35 g (3.5%), $Na^+$ 145 mmol, $K^+$ 5.1 mmol, $Ca^{2+}$ 6.25 mmol, $Cl^-$ 145 mmol/litre net price 500–mL bottle = £5.00

**Volplex®** (Cambridge) PoM
Intravenous infusion, succinylated gelatin (modified fluid gelatin, average molecular weight 30 000) 40 g (4%), $Na^+$ 154 mmol, $Cl^-$ 125 mmol/litre, net price 500-mL bag = £5.05
Cautions see notes above; also diabetes
Dose by intravenous injection over 2–5 minutes, 4 mL/kg as a single dose, followed immediately by administration of appropriate replacement fluids

## ETHERIFIED STARCH

A starch composed of more than 90% of amylopectin that has been etherified with hydroxyethyl groups; hetastarch has a higher degree of etherification than pentastarch

**Indications** low blood volume

**Cautions** see notes above; children

**Side-effects** see notes above; also pruritus, raised serum amylase

**Dose**

- See under preparations below

### Hexastarch

**eloHAES®** (Fresenius Kabi) PoM
Intravenous infusion, hexastarch (weight average molecular weight 200 000) 6% in sodium chloride intravenous infusion 0.9%. Net price 500-mL *Steriflex®* bag = £12.50
Dose by intravenous infusion, 500–1000 mL; usual daily max. 1500 mL (see notes above)

### Pentastarch

**HAES-steril®** (Fresenius Kabi) PoM
Intravenous infusion, pentastarch (weight average molecular weight 200 000), net price (both in sodium chloride intravenous infusion 0.9%) 6%, 500 mL = £10.50; 10%, 500 mL = £16.50
Dose by intravenous infusion, pentastarch 6%, up to 2500 mL daily; pentastarch 10%, up to 1500 mL daily (see notes above)

**Hemohes®** (Braun) PoM
Intravenous infusion, pentastarch (weight average molecular weight 200 000), net price (both in sodium chloride intravenous infusion 0.9%) 6%, 500 mL = £12.50; 10%, 500 mL = £16.50
Cautions see notes above
Dose by intravenous infusion, pentastarch 6%, up to 2500 mL daily; pentastarch 10%, up to 1500 mL daily (see notes above)

**Infukoll®** (Beacon) PoM
Intravenous infusion, pentastarch (hydroxyethyl starch, weight average molecular weight 200 000) 6% in sodium chloride intravenous infusion 0.9%, net price 500-mL bag = £10.00
Dose by intravenous infusion, up to 2 500 mL daily (see notes above)

### Tetrastarch

**Voluven®** (Fresenius Kabi) PoM
Intravenous infusion, hydroxyethyl starch (weight average molecular weight 130 000) 6% in sodium chloride intravenous infusion 0.9%, net price 500-mL bag = £12.50
Dose by intravenous infusion, up to 50 mL/kg daily (see notes above)

### Hypertonic solution

**HyperHAES®** (Fresenius Kabi) PoM
Intravenous infusion, hydroxyethyl starch (weight average molecular weight 200 000) 6% in sodium chloride intravenous infusion 7.2%, net price 250-mL bag = £28.00

# 9.3 Intravenous nutrition

When adequate feeding through the alimentary tract is not possible, nutrients may be given by intravenous infusion. This may be in addition to ordinary oral or tube feeding—**supplemental parenteral nutrition**, or may be the sole source of nutrition—**total parenteral nutrition** (TPN). Indications for this method include preparation of undernourished patients for surgery, chemotherapy, or radiation therapy; severe or prolonged disorders of the gastro-intestinal tract; major surgery, trauma, or burns; prolonged coma or refusal to eat; and some patients with renal or hepatic failure. The composition of proprietary preparations available is given in the table below.

Total parenteral nutrition requires the use of a solution containing amino acids, glucose, fat, electrolytes, trace elements, and vitamins. This is now commonly provided by the pharmacy in the form of a 3-litre bag. A single dose of vitamin $B_{12}$, as hydroxocobalamin, is given by intramuscular injection; regular vitamin $B_{12}$ injections are not usually required unless total parenteral nutrition continues for many months. Folic acid is given in a dose of 15 mg once or twice each week, usually in the nutrition solution. Other vitamins are usually given daily; they are generally introduced in the parenteral nutrition solution. Alternatively, if the patient is able to take small amounts by mouth, vitamins may be given orally.

The nutrition solution is infused through a central venous catheter inserted under full surgical precautions. Alternatively infusion through a peripheral vein may be used for supplementary as well as total parenteral nutrition for periods of up to a month, depending on the availability of peripheral veins; factors prolonging cannula life and preventing thrombophlebitis include the use of soft polyurethane paediatric cannulas and use of feeds of low osmolality and neutral pH. Only nutritional fluids should be given by the dedicated intravenous line.

Before starting, the patient should be well oxygenated with a near normal circulating blood volume and attention should be given to renal function and acid-base status. Appropriate biochemical tests should have been carried out beforehand and serious deficits corrected. Nutritional and electrolyte status must be monitored throughout treatment.

Complications of long-term TPN include gall bladder sludging, gall stones, cholestasis and abnormal liver function tests. For details of the prevention and management of TPN complications, specialist literature should be consulted.

**Protein** is given as mixtures of essential and non-essential synthetic L-amino acids. Ideally, all essential amino acids should be included with a wide variety of non-essential ones to provide sufficient nitrogen together with electrolytes (see also section 9.2.2). Solutions vary in their composition of amino acids; they often contain an energy source (usually glucose) and electrolytes.

**Energy** is provided in a ratio of 0.6 to 1.1 megajoules (150–250 kcals) per gram of protein nitrogen. Energy requirements must be met if amino acids are to be utilised for tissue maintenance. A mixture of carbohydrate and fat energy sources (usually 30–50% as fat) gives better utilisation of amino acids than glucose alone.

**Glucose** is the preferred source of carbohydrate, but if more than 180 g is given per day frequent monitoring of blood glucose is required, and insulin may be necessary. Glucose in various strengths from 10 to 50% must be infused through a central venous catheter to avoid thrombosis.

In total parenteral nutrition regimens, it is necessary to provide adequate phosphate in order to allow phosphorylation of the glucose; between 20 and 30 mmol of phosphate is required daily.

Fructose and sorbitol have been used in an attempt to avoid the problem of hyperosmolar hyperglycaemic non-ketotic acidosis but other metabolic problems may occur, as with xylitol and ethanol which are now rarely used.

**Fat** emulsions have the advantages of a high energy to fluid volume ratio, neutral pH, and iso-osmolarity with plasma, and provide essential fatty acids. Several days of adaptation may be required to attain maximal utilisation. Reactions include occasional febrile episodes (usually only with 20% emulsions) and rare anaphylactic responses. Interference with biochemical measurements such as those for blood gases and calcium may occur if samples are taken before fat has been cleared. Daily checks are necessary to ensure complete clearance from the plasma in conditions where fat metabolism may be disturbed. **Additives may only be mixed with fat emulsions where compatibility is known**.

**Administration**. Because of the complex requirements relating to parenteral nutrition full details relating to administration have been omitted. In all cases *product literature and other specialist literature should be consulted.*

## Supplementary preparations

Compatibility with the infusion solution must be ascertained before adding supplementary preparations.

**Addiphos®** (Fresenius Kabi) PoM
Solution, sterile, phosphate 40 mmol, $K^+$ 30 mmol, $Na^+$ 30 mmol/20 mL. For addition to *Vamin®* solutions and glucose intravenous infusions. Net price 20-mL vial = £1.44

**Additrace®** (Fresenius Kabi) PoM
Solution, trace elements for addition to *Vamin®* solutions and glucose intravenous infusions, traces of $Fe^{3+}$, $Zn^{2+}$, $Mn^{2+}$, $Cu^{2+}$, $Cr^{3+}$, $Se^{4+}$, $Mo^{6+}$, $F^-$, $I^-$. For adults and children over 40 kg. Net price 10-mL amp = £2.18

**Cernevit®** (Baxter) PoM
Solution, *dl*-alpha tocopherol 11.2 units, ascorbic acid 125 mg, biotin 69 micrograms, colecalciferol 220 units, cyanocobalamin 6 micrograms, folic acid 414 micrograms, glycine 250 mg, nicotinamide 46 mg, pantothenic acid (as dexpanthenol) 17.25 mg, pyridoxine hydrochloride 5.5 mg, retinol (as palmitate) 3500 units, riboflavin (as dihydrated sodium phosphate) 4.14 mg, thiamine (as cocarboxylase tetrahydrate) 3.51 mg. Dissolve in 5 mL water for injections. Net price per vial = £2.90

**Decan®** (Baxter) PoM
Solution, trace elements for addition to infusion solutions, $Fe^{2+}$, $Zn^{2+}$, $Cu^{2+}$, $Mn^{2+}$, $F^-$, $Co^{2+}$, $I^-$, $Se^{4+}$, $Mo^{6+}$, $Cr^{3+}$. For adults and children over 40 kg. Net price 40-mL vial = £2.00

**Dipeptiven®** (Fresenius Kabi) PoM
Solution, *N*(2)-L-alanyl-L-glutamine 200 mg/mL (providing L-alanine 82 mg, L-glutamine 134.6 mg). For addition to infusion solutions containing amino acids. Net price 50 mL = £15.90, 100 mL = £29.60
Dose amino acid supplement for hypercatabolic or hypermetabolic states, 300–400 mg/kg daily; max. 400 mg/kg daily, dose not to exceed 20% of total amino acid intake

**Glycophos® Sterile Concentrate** (Fresenius Kabi) PoM
Solution, sterile, phosphate 20 mmol, $Na^+$ 40 mmol/20 mL. For addition to *Vamin®* and *Vaminolact®* solutions, and glucose intravenous infusions. Net price 20-mL vial = £4.25

**Peditrace®** (Fresenius Kabi) PoM
Solution, trace elements for addition to *Vaminolact®*, *Vamin® 14 Electrolyte-Free* solutions and glucose intravenous infusions, traces of $Zn^{2+}$, $Cu^{2+}$, $Mn^{2+}$, $Se^{4+}$, $F^-$, $I^-$. For use in neonates (when kidney function established, usually second day of life), infants, and children. Net price 10-mL vial = £3.88
Cautions reduced biliary excretion especially in cholestatic liver disease or in markedly reduced urinary excretion (careful biochemical monitoring required); total parenteral nutrition exceeding 1 month (measure serum manganese concentration and check liver function before commencing treatment and regularly during treatment)—discontinue if manganese concentration raised or if cholestasis develops

**Solivito N®** (Fresenius Kabi) PoM
Solution, powder for reconstitution, biotin 60 micrograms, cyanocobalamin 5 micrograms, folic acid 400 micrograms, glycine 300 mg, nicotinamide 40 mg, pyridoxine hydrochloride 4.9 mg, riboflavin sodium phosphate 4.9 mg, sodium ascorbate 113 mg, sodium pantothenate 16.5 mg, thiamine mononitrate 3.1 mg. Dissolve in water for injections or glucose intravenous infusion for adding to glucose intravenous infusion or *Intralipid®*; dissolve in *Vitlipid N®* or *Intralipid®* for adding to *Intralipid®* only. Net price per vial = £2.19

**Vitlipid N®** (Fresenius Kabi) PoM
Emulsion, adult, vitamin A 330 units, ergocalciferol 20 units, *dl*-alpha tocopherol 1 unit, phytomenadione 15 micrograms/mL. For addition to *Intralipid®*. For adults and children over 11 years. Net price 10-mL amp = £2.19

Emulsion, infant, vitamin A 230 units, ergocalciferol 40 units, *dl*-alpha tocopherol 0.7 unit, phytomenadione 20 micrograms/mL. For addition to *Intralipid®*. Net price 10-mL amp = £2.19

## Proprietary Infusion Fluids for Parenteral Feeding

| Preparation | Nitrogen g/litre | [1]Energy kJ/litre | Electrolytes mmol/litre | | | | | Other components/litre |
|---|---|---|---|---|---|---|---|---|
| | | | K⁺ | $Mg^{2+}$ | $Na^{+}$ | Acet⁻ | Cl⁻ | |
| Aminoplasmal 5% E (Braun) Net price 500 mL = £9.02 | 8 | | 25 | 2.6 | 43 | 59 | 29 | dihydrogen phosphate 9 mmol, malic acid 1.01 g |
| Aminoplasmal 10% (Braun) Net price 500 mL = £17.06 | 16 | | | | | | 57 | |
| Aminoven 25 (Fresenius Kabi) Net price 500 mL = £22.00 | 25.7 | | | | | | | |
| Clinimix N9G20E (Baxter) Net price (dual compartment bag of amino acids with electrolytes 1000 mL and glucose 20% with calcium 1000 mL) = £29.00 | 4.55 | 1680 | 30 | 2.5 | 35 | 50 | 40 | $Ca^{2+}$ 2.25 mmol, phosphate 15 mmol, anhydrous glucose 100 g |
| Clinimix N14G30E (Baxter) Net price (dual compartment bag of amino acids with electrolytes 1000 mL and glucose 30% with calcium 1000 mL) = £33.00 | 7 | 2520 | 30 | 2.5 | 35 | 70 | 40 | $Ca^{2+}$ 2.25 mmol, phosphate 15 mmol, anhydrous glucose 150 g |
| ClinOleic 20% (Baxter) Net price 100 mL = £6.28; 250 mL = £10.08; 500 mL = £13.88 | | 8360 | | | | | | purified olive and soya oil 200 g, glycerol 22.5 g, egg phosphatides 12 g |
| Compleven (Fresenius Kabi) Net price (triple compartment bag of amino acids 1000 mL; glucose 1000 mL; lipid emulsion 500 mL) 2500 mL = £67.00 | 4.8 | 3275 | 20 | 2 | 32 | | 32.4 | $Ca^{2+}$ 2 mmol, $Zn^{2+}$ 0.04 mmol, glycerophosphate 8 mmol, anhydrous glucose 96 g, soya oil 40 g, egg lecithin 2.4 g, glycerol 2.4 g |
| Glamin (Fresenius Kabi) Net price 250 mL = £14.16; 500 mL = £26.38 | 22.4 | | | | | 62 | | |
| Hyperamine 30 (Braun) Net price 500 mL = £23.67 | 30 | | | | 5 | | | |
| Intrafusin 11 (Fresenius Kabi) Net price 1000 mL = £17.80 | 11.4 | | 40 | 5 | 80 | | 76 | $Ca^{2+}$ 3 mmol, phosphate 20 mmol, citrate 6 mmol |
| Intrafusin 22 (Fresenius Kabi) Net price 500 mL = £17.80 | 22.8 | | | | | | | |
| Intralipid 10% (Fresenius Kabi) Net price 100 mL = £4.70; 500 mL = £10.30 | | 4600 | | | | | | soya oil 100 g, glycerol 22 g, purified egg phospholipids 12 g, phosphate 15 mmol |
| Intralipid 20% (Fresenius Kabi) Net price 100 mL = £7.05; 250 mL = £11.60; 500 mL = £15.45 | | 8400 | | | | | | soya oil 200 g, glycerol 22 g, purified egg phospholipids 12 g, phosphate 15 mmol |
| Intralipid 30% (Fresenius Kabi) Net price 333 mL = £17.30 | | 12600 | | | | | | soya oil 300 g, glycerol 16.7 g, purified egg phospholipids 12 g, phosphate 15 mmol |
| Ivelip 10% (Baxter) Net price 500 mL = £9.08 | | 4600 | | | | | | soya oil 100 g, glycerol 25 g |
| Ivelip 20% (Baxter) Net price 100 mL = £6.28; 500 mL = £13.88 | | 8400 | | | | | | soya oil 200 g, glycerol 25 g |
| Kabiven (Fresenius Kabi) Net price (triple compartment bag of amino acids and electrolytes 300 mL, 450 mL, 600 mL, or 750 mL; glucose 526 mL, 790 mL, 1053 mL, or 1316 mL; lipid emulsion 200 mL, 300 mL, 400 mL, or 500 mL) 1026 mL = £35.00, 1540 mL = £50.00, 2053 mL = £67.00, 2566 mL = £70.00 | 5.3 | 3275 | 23 | 4 | 31 | 38 | 45 | $Ca^{2+}$ 2 mmol, phosphate 9.7 mmol, anhydrous glucose 97 g, soya oil 39 g |

1. Excludes protein- or amino acid-derived energy
*Note.* 1000 kcal = 4200 kJ; 1000 kJ= 238.8 kcal. All entries are PoM

| Preparation | Nitrogen g/litre | Energy[1] kJ/litre | Electrolytes mmol/litre | | | | | Other components/litre |
|---|---|---|---|---|---|---|---|---|
| | | | $K^+$ | $Mg^{2+}$ | $Na^+$ | $Acet^-$ | $Cl^-$ | |
| **Kabiven Peripheral (Fresenius Kabi)**<br>Net price (triple compartment bag of amino acids and electrolytes 300 mL, 400 mL, or 500 mL; glucose 885 mL, 1180 mL, or 1475 mL; lipid emulsion 255 mL, 340 mL, or 425 mL) 1440 mL = £35.00, 1920 mL = £50.00, 2400 mL = £64.00 | 3.75 | 2625 | 17 | 2.8 | 22 | 27 | 33 | $Ca^{2+}$ 1.4 mmol, phosphate 7.5 mmol, anhydrous glucose 67.5 g, soya oil 35.4 g |
| Lipofundin MCT/LCT 10% (Braun)<br>Net price 100 mL = £7.70; 500 mL = £12.90 | | 4430 | | | | | | soya oil 50 g, medium chain triglycerides 50 g |
| **Lipofundin MCT/LCT 20% (Braun)**<br>Net price 100 mL = £12.51; 250 mL = £11.30; 500 mL = £19.18 | | 8000 | | | | | | soya oil 100 g, medium chain triglycerides 100 g |
| Nutracel 400 (Baxter)<br>Net price 500 mL = £2.43 | | 3400 | | 18 | | 0.16 | 66 | $Ca^{2+}$ 15 mmol, $Mn^{2+}$ 0.01 mmol, $Zn^{2+}$ 0.08 mmol, anhydrous glucose 200 g |
| **Nutracel 800 (Baxter)**<br>Net price 1000 mL = £4.19 | | 3400 | | 9 | | 0.08 | 33 | $Ca^{2+}$ 7.5 mmol, $Mn^{2+}$ 0.005 mmol, $Zn^{2+}$ 0.04 mmol, anhydrous glucose 200 g |
| NuTRIflex Lipid peri (Braun)<br>Net price (triple compartment bag of amino acids 500 mL or 1000 mL; glucose 500 mL or 1000 mL; lipid emulsion 20% 250 mL or 500 mL) 1250 mL = £43.38, 2500 mL = £65.05 | 4.56 | 2664 | 24 | 2.4 | 40 | 32 | 38.4 | $Ca^{2+}$ 2.4 mmol, $Zn^{2+}$ 0.024 mmol, phosphate 6 mmol, anhydrous glucose 64 g, soya oil 20 g, medium chain triglycerides 20 g |
| **NuTRIflex Lipid plus (Braun)**<br>Net price (triple compartment bag of amino acids 500 mL, 750 mL or 1000 mL; glucose 500 mL, 750 mL or 1000 mL; lipid emulsion 20% 250 mL, 375 mL or 500 mL) 1250 mL = £47.17, 1875 mL = £60.23, 2500 mL = £69.27 | 5.44 | 3600 | 28 | 3.2 | 40 | 36 | 36 | $Ca^{2+}$ 3.2 mmol, $Zn^{2+}$ 0.024 mmol, phosphate 12 mmol, anhydrous glucose 120 g, soya oil 20 g, medium chain triglycerides 20 g |
| NuTRIflex Lipid plus without Electrolytes (Braun)<br>Net price (triple compartment bag of amino acids 500 mL, 750 mL or 1000 mL; glucose 500 mL, 750 mL or 1000 mL; lipid emulsion 20% 250 mL, 375 mL or 500 mL) 1250 mL = £47.17, 1875 mL = £60.23, 2500 mL = £69.27 | 5.44 | 3600 | | | | | | anhydrous glucose 120 g, soya oil 20 g, medium chain triglycerides 20 g |
| **NuTRIflex Lipid special (Braun)**<br>Net price (triple compartment bag of amino acids 500 mL, 750 mL or 1000 mL; glucose 500 mL, 750 mL or 1000 mL; lipid emulsion 20% 250 mL, 375 mL or 500 mL) 1250 mL = £57.69, 1875 mL = £75.58, 2500 mL = £89.21 | 8 | 4004 | 37.6 | 4.24 | 53.6 | 48 | 48 | $Ca^{2+}$ 4.24 mmol, $Zn^{2+}$ 0.032 mmol, phosphate 16 mmol, anhydrous glucose 144 g, soya oil 20 g, medium chain triglycerides 20 g |
| NuTRIflex Lipid special without Electrolytes (Braun)<br>Net price (triple compartment bag of amino acids 500 mL, 750 mL or 1000 mL; glucose 500 mL, 750 mL or 1000 mL; lipid emulsion 20% 250 mL, 375 mL or 500 mL) 1250 mL = £57.69, 1875 mL = £75.58, 2500 mL = £89.21 | 8 | 4004 | | | | | | anhydrous glucose 144 g, soya oil 20 g, medium chain triglycerides 20 g |

1. Excludes protein- or amino acid-derived energy
*Note.* 1000 kcal = 4200 kJ; 1000 kJ= 238.8 kcal. All entries are PoM

| Preparation | Nitrogen g/litre | [1]Energy kJ/litre | Electrolytes mmol/litre | | | | | Other components/litre |
|---|---|---|---|---|---|---|---|---|
| | | | $K^+$ | $Mg^{2+}$ | $Na^+$ | Acet⁻ | Cl⁻ | |
| **OliClinomel N4-550E** (Baxter) Net price (triple compartment bag of amino acids with electrolytes 1000 mL; glucose 20% 1000 mL; lipid emulsion 10% 500 mL) 2500 mL = £69.30 | 3.6 | 2184 | 16 | 2.2 | 21 | 30 | 33 | $Ca^{2+}$ 2 mmol, phosphate 8.5 mmol, refined olive and soya oil 20 g, anhydrous glucose 80 g |
| **OliClinomel N4-720E** (Baxter) Net price (triple compartment bag of amino acids with electrolytes 1000 mL; glucose 20% 1000 mL; lipid emulsion 20% 500 mL) 2500 mL = £69.30 | 3.64 | 3024 | 24 | 2 | 28 | 40 | 40 | $Ca^{2+}$ 1.8 mmol, phosphate 8 mmol, refined olive and soya oil 40 g, anhydrous glucose 80 g |
| **OliClinomel N5-800E** (Baxter) Net price (triple compartment bag of amino acids with electrolytes 800 mL or 1000 mL; glucose 25% 800 mL or 1000 mL; lipid emulsion 20% 400 mL or 500 mL) 2000 mL = £60.39, 2500 mL = £65.34 | 4.6 | 3360 | 24 | 2.2 | 32 | 49 | 44 | $Ca^{2+}$ 2 mmol, phosphate 10 mmol, refined olive and soya oil 40 g, anhydrous glucose 100 g |
| **OliClinomel N6-900E** (Baxter) Net price (triple compartment bag of amino acids with electrolytes 800 mL or 1000 mL; glucose 30% 800 mL or 1000 mL; lipid emulsion 20% 400 mL or 500 mL) 2000 mL = £70.40, 2500 mL = £75.90 | 5.6 | 3696 | 24 | 2.2 | 32 | 53 | 46 | $Ca^{2+}$ 2 mmol, phosphate 10 mmol, refined olive and soya oil 40 g, anhydrous glucose 120 g |
| **OliClinomel N7-1000** (Baxter) Net price (triple compartment bag of amino acids with electrolytes 400 mL or 600 mL; glucose 40% 400 mL or 600 mL; lipid emulsion 20% 200 mL or 300 mL) 1000 mL = £28.75, 1500 mL = £43.70 | 6.6 | 4368 | | | | 37 | 16 | phosphate 3 mmol, refined olive and soya oil 40 g, anhydrous glucose 160 g |
| **OliClinomel N7-1000E** (Baxter) Net price (triple compartment bag of amino acids with electrolytes 800 mL; glucose 40% 800 mL; lipid emulsion 20% 400 mL) 2000 mL = £66.33 | 6.6 | 4368 | 24 | 2.2 | 32 | 57 | 48 | $Ca^{2+}$ 2 mmol, phosphate 10 mmol, refined olive and soya oil 40 g, anhydrous glucose 160 g |
| **OliClinomel N8-800** (Baxter) Net price (triple compartment bag of amino acids 800 mL; glucose 31.25% 800 mL; lipid emulsion 15% 400 mL) 2000 mL = £77.10 | 8.25 | 3360 | | | | 42.5 | 20 | phosphate 2.25 mmol, refined olive and soya oil 30 g, anhydrous glucose 125 g |
| **Plasma-Lyte 148 (water)** (Baxter) Net price 1000 mL = £1.59 | | | 5 | 1.5 | 140 | 27 | 98 | gluconate 23 mmol |
| **Plasma-Lyte 148 (dextrose 5%)** (Baxter) Net price 1000 mL = £1.59 | | 840 | 5 | 1.5 | 140 | 27 | 98 | gluconate 23 mmol, anhydrous glucose 50 g |
| **Plasma-Lyte M (dextrose 5%)** (Baxter) Net price 1000 mL = £1.33 | | 840 | 16 | 1.5 | 40 | 12 | 40 | $Ca^{2+}$ 2.5 mmol, lactate 12 mmol, anhydrous glucose 50 g |
| [2]**Primene 10%** (Baxter) Net price 100 mL = £5.78, 250 mL = £7.92 | 15 | | | | | | 19 | |
| **StructoKabiven Electrolyte Free** (Fresenius Kabi) Net price (triple compartment bag of amino acids 750 mL or 1000 mL; glucose 42% 446 mL or 595 mL; lipid emulsion 281 mL or 375 mL) 1477 mL = £69.00, 1970 mL = £74.00 | 8 | 3685 | | | | 74.5 | | phosphate 2.8 mmol, anhydrous glucose 127 g, glycerol 4.23 g, egg phospholipids 4.56 g, purified structured triglyceride 38.5 g (contains coconut oil, palm kernel oil and soya oil trigylcerides) |

1. Excludes protein- or amino acid-derived energy
   *Note.* 1000 kcal = 4200 kJ; 1000 kJ= 238.8 kcal. All entries are PoM
2. For use in neonates and children only
   *Note.* 1000 kcal = 4200 kJ; = 238.8 kcal. All entries are PoM

| Preparation | Nitrogen g/litre | Energy[1] kJ/litre | Electrolytes mmol/litre $K^+$ | $Mg^{2+}$ | $Na^+$ | $Acet^-$ | $Cl^-$ | Other components/litre |
|---|---|---|---|---|---|---|---|---|
| Structolipid 20% (Fresenius Kabi) Net price 500 mL = £16.09 | | 8200 | | | | | | purified structured triglyceride 200 g (contains coconut oil, palm kernel oil, and soya oil triglycerides) |
| Synthamin 9 (Baxter) Net price 500 mL = £6.66; 1000 mL = £12.34 | 9.1 | | 60 | 5 | 70 | 100 | 70 | acid phosphate 30 mmol |
| Synthamin 9 EF (electrolyte-free) (Baxter) Net price 500 mL = £6.66; 1000 mL = £12.34 | 9.1 | | | | | 44 | 22 | |
| Synthamin 14 (Baxter) Net price 500 mL = £9.64; 1000 mL = £17.13; 3000 mL = £48.98 | 14 | | 60 | 5 | 70 | 140 | 70 | acid phosphate 30 mmol |
| Synthamin 14 EF (electrolyte–free) (Baxter) Net price 500 mL = £9.87; 1000 mL = £17.51 | 14 | | | | | 68 | 34 | |
| Synthamin 17 (Baxter) Net price 500 mL = £12.66; 1000 mL = £23.00 | 16.5 | | 60 | 5 | 70 | 150 | 70 | acid phosphate 30 mmol |
| Synthamin 17 EF (electrolyte–free) (Baxter) Net price 500 mL = £12.66; 1000 mL = £23.00 | 16.5 | | | | | 82 | 40 | |
| Vamin 9 (Fresenius Kabi) Net price 500 mL = £7.30; 1000 mL = £12.55 | 9.4 | | 20 | 1.5 | 50 | | 50 | $Ca^{2+}$ 2.5 mmol |
| Vamin 9 Glucose (Fresenius Kabi) Net price 100 mL = £3.80; 500 mL = £7.70; 1000 mL = £13.40 | 9.4 | 1700 | 20 | 1.5 | 50 | | 50 | $Ca^{2+}$ 2.5 mmol, anhydrous glucose 100 g |
| Vamin 14 (Fresenius Kabi) Net price 500 mL = £10.80; 1000 mL = £14.67 | 13.5 | | 50 | 8 | 100 | 135 | 100 | $Ca^{2+}$ 5 mmol, $SO_4^{2-}$ 8 mmol |
| Vamin 14 (Electrolyte-Free) (Fresenius Kabi) Net price 500 mL = £10.80; 1000 mL = £18.30 | 13.5 | | | | | 90 | | |
| Vamin 18 (Electrolyte-Free) (Fresenius Kabi) Net price 500 mL = £13.70; 1000 mL = £26.70 | 18 | | | | | 110 | | |
| Vaminolact (Fresenius Kabi) Net price 100 mL = £4.20; 500 mL = £9.70 | 9.3 | | | | | | | |
| Vitrimix KV (Fresenius Kabi) Net price (combined pack of Intralipid 20% 250 mL and Vamin 9 glucose 750 mL) = £21.00 | 7 | 3340 | 15 | 1.1 | 38 | | 38 | $Ca^{2+}$ 1.9 mmol, anhydrous glucose 75 g, soya oil 50 g, purified egg phospholipids 3 g, glycerol 5.5 g, phosphate 3.75 mmol |

## 9.4 Oral nutrition

**9.4.1** Foods for special diets
**9.4.2** Enteral nutrition

### 9.4.1 Foods for special diets

These are preparations that have been modified to eliminate a particular constituent from a food or are nutrient mixtures formulated as substitutes for the food. They are for patients who either cannot tolerate or cannot metabolise certain common constituents of food.

**Phenylketonuria** Phenylketonuria (phenylalaninaemia), which results from the inability to metabolise phenylalanine, is managed by restricting its dietary intake to a small amount sufficient for tissue building and repair. Aspartame (as a sweetener in some foods and medicines) contributes to the phenylalanine intake and may affect control of phenylketonuria. Where the presence of aspartame is specified in the product literature this is indicated in the BNF against the preparation.

1. Excludes protein- or amino acid-derived energy
*Note.* 1000 kcal = 4200 kJ; 1000 kJ= 238.8 kcal. All entries are PoM

**Coeliac disease** Coeliac disease, which results from an intolerance to gluten, is managed by completely eliminating gluten from the diet.

ACBS
In certain clinical conditions some foods may have the characteristics of drugs and the Advisory Committee on Borderline Substances advises as to the circumstances in which such foods may be regarded as drugs and so can be prescribed in the NHS. Prescriptions for these foods issued in accordance with the advice of this committee and endorsed 'ACBS' will normally not be investigated. See Appendix 7 for details of these foods and a listing by clinical condition (consult Drug Tariff for late amendments).

Preparations
For preparations on the ACBS list see Appendix 7

**Forceval Protein Powder®** (Alliance)
Powder, strawberry, vanilla and natural flavours, protein (calcium caseinate, providing all essential amino acids) 55%, carbohydrate 30%, with vitamins, minerals, trace elements, fat and low electrolytes (lactose- and gluten-free), net price 14 × 30-g sachets = £15.57; chocolate flavour (as above but protein content is 45%), 14 × 36-g sachets = £15.57.
For hypoproteinaemia, malabsorption states and as an adjunct to nutritional support. Not to be prescribed for any CHILD under 2 years or for those with renal or hepatic failure; unsuitable as a sole source of nutrition



## 9.4.2 Enteral nutrition

The body's reserves of protein rapidly become exhausted in severely ill patients, especially during chronic illness or in those with severe burns, extensive trauma, pancreatitis, or intestinal fistula. Much can be achieved by frequent meals and by persuading the patient to take supplementary snacks of ordinary food between the meals.

However, extra calories, protein, other nutrients, and vitamins are often best given by supplementing ordinary meals with sip or tube feeds of one of the nutritionally complete foods.

When patients cannot feed normally at all, for example, patients with severe facial injury, oesophageal obstruction, or coma, a diet composed solely of nutritionally complete foods must be given. This is planned by a dietitian who will take into account the protein and total energy requirement of the patient and decide on the form and relative contribution of carbohydrate and fat to the energy requirements.

There are a number of nutritionally complete foods available and their use reduces an otherwise heavy workload in hospital or in the home. Most contain protein derived from milk or soya. Some contain protein hydrolysates or free amino acids and are only appropriate for patients who have diminished ability to break down protein, as may be the case in inflammatory bowel disease or pancreatic insufficiency.

Even when nutritionally complete feeds are being given it may be important to monitor water and electrolyte balance. Extra minerals (e.g. magnesium and zinc) may be needed in patients where gastro-intestinal secretions are being lost. Additional vitamins may also be needed. Regular haematological and biochemical tests may be needed particularly in the unstable patient.

Some feeds are supplemented with vitamin K; for drug interactions of vitamin K see Appendix 1 (vitamins).

**Children** Infants and young children have special requirements and in most situations liquid feeds prepared for adults are totally unsuitable and should not be given. Expert advice should be sought.

Preparations
See Appendix 7

# 9.5 Minerals

9.5.1 Calcium and magnesium
9.5.2 Phosphorus
9.5.3 Fluoride
9.5.4 Zinc

See section 9.1.1 for iron salts.

## 9.5.1 Calcium and magnesium

9.5.1.1 Calcium supplements
9.5.1.2 Hypercalcaemia and hypercalciuria
9.5.1.3 Magnesium

### 9.5.1.1 Calcium supplements

Calcium supplements are usually only required where dietary calcium intake is deficient. This dietary requirement varies with age and is relatively greater in childhood, pregnancy, and lactation, due to an increased demand, and in old age, due to impaired absorption. In osteoporosis, a calcium intake which is double the recommended amount reduces the rate of bone loss. If the actual dietary intake is less than the recommended amount, a supplement of as much as 40 mmol is appropriate.

In hypocalcaemic tetany an initial intravenous injection of 10 mL (2.25 mmol) of calcium gluconate injection 10% should be followed by the continuous infusion of about 40 mL (9 mmol) daily, but plasma calcium should be monitored. This regimen can also be used immediately to temporarily reduce the toxic effects of hyperkalaemia.

#### CALCIUM SALTS

**Indications** see notes above; calcium deficiency
**Cautions** renal impairment; sarcoidosis; history of nephrolithiasis; avoid calcium chloride in respiratory acidosis or respiratory failure; **interactions:** Appendix 1 (antacids, calcium salts)
**Contra-indications** conditions associated with hypercalcaemia and hypercalciuria (e.g. some forms of malignant disease)

**Side-effects** gastro-intestinal disturbances; bradycardia, arrhythmias; *with injection,* peripheral vasodilatation, fall in blood pressure, injection-site reactions

**Dose**

- By mouth, daily in divided doses, see notes above
- By slow intravenous injection, acute hypocalcaemia, calcium gluconate 1–2 g ($Ca^{2+}$ 2.25–4.5 mmol); CHILD obtain paediatric advice

### Oral preparations

**Calcium Gluconate** (Non-proprietary)

Tablets, calcium gluconate 600 mg (calcium 53.4 mg or $Ca^{2+}$ 1.35 mmol), net price 20 = £1.43. Label: 24

Effervescent tablets, calcium gluconate 1 g (calcium 89 mg or $Ca^{2+}$ 2.25 mmol), net price 28-tab pack = £4.62. Label: 13

**Note** Each tablet usually contains 4.46 mmol $Na^{+}$

**Calcium Lactate** (Non-proprietary)

Tablets, calcium lactate 300 mg (calcium 39 mg or $Ca^{2+}$ 1 mmol), net price 20 = 72p

**Adcal®** (Strakan)

Chewable tablets, calcium carbonate 1.5 g (calcium 600 mg or $Ca^{2+}$ 15 mmol), net price 100-tab pack = £7.25. Label: 24

**Cacit®** (Procter & Gamble Pharm.)

Tablets, effervescent, pink, calcium carbonate 1.25 g, providing calcium citrate when dispersed in water (calcium 500 mg or $Ca^{2+}$ 12.6 mmol), net price 76-tab pack = £16.72. Label: 13

**Calcichew®** (Shire)

Tablets (chewable), calcium carbonate 1.25 g (calcium 500 mg or $Ca^{2+}$ 12.6 mmol), net price 100-tab pack = £9.33

Forte tablets (chewable), scored, calcium carbonate 2.5 g (calcium 1 g or $Ca^{2+}$ 25 mmol), net price 60-tab pack = £13.16. Label: 24

**Excipients** include aspartame

**Calcium-500** (Martindale)

Tablets, pink, f/c, calcium carbonate 1.25 g (calcium 500 mg or $Ca^{2+}$ 12.5 mmol). Net price 100-tab pack = £9.46. Label: 25

**Calcium-Sandoz®** (Alliance)

Syrup, calcium glubionate 1.09 g, calcium lactobionate 727 mg (calcium 108.3 mg or $Ca^{2+}$ 2.7 mmol)/5 mL. Net price 300 mL = £3.39

**Sandocal®** (Novartis Consumer Health)

Sandocal-400 tablets, effervescent, calcium lactate gluconate 930 mg, calcium carbonate 700 mg, anhydrous citric acid 1.189 g, providing calcium 400 mg ($Ca^{2+}$ 10 mmol). Net price 5 × 20-tab pack = £6.87. Label: 13

**Excipients** include aspartame (section 9.4.1)

Sandocal-1000 tablets, effervescent, calcium lactate gluconate 2.327 g, calcium carbonate 1.75 g, anhydrous citric acid 2.973 g providing 1 g calcium ($Ca^{2+}$ 25 mmol). Net price 3 × 10-tab pack = £6.17. Label: 13

**Excipients** include aspartame (section 9.4.1)

### Parenteral preparations

**Calcium Gluconate** (Non-proprietary) PoM

Injection, calcium gluconate 10% (calcium 8.9 mg or $Ca^{2+}$ 220 micromol/mL). Net price 10-mL amp = 60p

**Calcium Chloride** (Non-proprietary) PoM

Injection, calcium chloride (as calcium chloride dihydrate 10%) 75 mg/mL (calcium 27.3 mg or $Ca^{2+}$ 680 micromol/mL). Net price 10-mL disposable syringe = £4.42

Brands include *Minijet® Calcium Chloride 10%*

Injection, calcium chloride (as calcium chloride dihydrate 13.4%) 100 mg/mL (calcium 36 mg or $Ca^{2+}$ 910 micromol/mL). Net price 10-mL amp = £14.94

### With vitamin D

Section 9.6.4

### With disodium etidronate

See section 6.6.2

## 9.5.1.2 Hypercalcaemia and hypercalciuria

**Severe hypercalcaemia** Severe hypercalcaemia calls for urgent treatment before detailed investigation of the cause. Dehydration should be corrected first with intravenous infusion of **sodium chloride 0.9%**. Drugs (such as thiazides and vitamin D compounds) which promote hypercalcaemia, should be discontinued and dietary calcium should be restricted.

If *severe hypercalcaemia persists* drugs which inhibit mobilisation of calcium from the skeleton may be required. The **bisphosphonates** are useful and disodium pamidronate (section 6.6.2) is probably the most effective.

**Corticosteroids** (section 6.3) are widely given, but may only be useful where hypercalcaemia is due to sarcoidosis or vitamin D intoxication; they often take several days to achieve the desired effect.

**Calcitonin** (section 6.6.1) is relatively non-toxic but is expensive and its effect can wear off after a few days despite continued use; it is rarely effective where bisphosphonates have failed to reduce serum calcium adequately.

Intravenous chelating drugs such as **trisodium edetate** are rarely used; they usually cause pain in the limb receiving the infusion and may cause renal damage; trisodium edetate should no longer be used for the management of hypercalcaemia.

After treatment of severe hypercalcaemia the underlying cause must be established. *Further treatment* is governed by the same principles as for initial therapy. Salt and water depletion and drugs promoting hypercalcaemia should be avoided; oral administration of a bisphosphonate may be useful.

**Hyperparathyroidism** **Cinacalcet** is licensed for the treatment of secondary hyperparathyroidism in dialysis patients with end-stage renal disease and for the treatment of hypercalcaemia in parathyroid carcinoma. Cinacalcet reduces parathyroid hormone which leads to a decrease in serum calcium concentrations.

Parathyroidectomy may be indicated for hyperparathyroidism.

**Hypercalciuria** Hypercalciuria should be investigated for an underlying cause, which should be treated. Where a cause is not identified (idiopathic hypercalciuria), the condition is managed by increasing fluid intake and giving bendroflumethiazide in a dose of 2.5 mg daily (a higher dose is not usually necessary). Reducing dietary calcium intake may be beneficial but severe restriction of calcium intake has not proved beneficial and may even be harmful.

## CINACALCET

**Indications** see under Dose

**Cautions** measure serum-calcium concentration within 1 week of starting treatment or adjusting dose, then every 1–3 months; monitor parathyroid hormone concentration; dose adjustment may be necessary if smoking started or stopped during treatment; hepatic impairment (Appendix 2); pregnancy (Appendix 4); **interactions:** Appendix 1 (cinacalcet)

**Contra-indications** breast-feeding (Appendix 5)

**Side-effects** nausea, vomiting; anorexia, dizziness, paraesthesia, asthenia; reduced testosterone concentrations; myalgia; rash; *less commonly* dyspepsia, seizures

**Dose**

- Secondary hyperparathyroidism in patients with end-stage renal disease on dialysis, ADULT over 18 years, 30 mg once daily, adjusted every 2–4 weeks to max. 180 mg daily
- Hypercalcaemia of parathyroid carcinoma, ADULT over 18 years, initially 30 mg twice daily, adjusted every 2–4 weeks according to response up to max. 90 mg 4 times daily

**Mimpara®** (Amgen) ▼ PoM

Tablets, green, f/c, cinacalcet (as hydrochloride) 30 mg, net price 28-tab pack = £126.28; 60 mg, 28-tab pack = £232.96; 90 mg, 28-tab pack = £349.44. Label: 21

## TRISODIUM EDETATE

**Indications** hypercalcaemia (but see notes above); lime burns in the eye (see under preparations)

**Cautions** repeated plasma-calcium determinations important; caution in tuberculosis; avoid rapid infusion, see under Dose

**Contra-indications** impaired renal function (Appendix 3)

**Side-effects** nausea, diarrhoea, cramp; in overdosage renal damage

**Dose**

- Hypercalcaemia, by intravenous infusion over 2–3 hours, up to 70 mg/kg daily; CHILD up to 60 mg/kg daily

Important Ensure rate of infusion and concentration correct (see Appendix 6); too rapid a rate or too high a concentration is extremely hazardous and repeated measurements of plasma calcium concentrations are important for control and maintenance of near normal ionised calcium concentrations. Decrease infusion rate on signs of increased muscle reactivity; discontinue if tetany occurs and restart cautiously only after plasma ionised and total calcium concentrations indicate need for further treatment (and tetany has stopped)

**Limclair®** (Sinclair) PoM

Concentrate for infusion, trisodium edetate 200 mg/mL. Net price 5-mL amp = £7.93

Note For topical use in the eye, dilute 1 mL to 50 mL with sterile purified water

## 9.5.1.3 Magnesium

Magnesium is an essential constituent of many enzyme systems, particularly those involved in energy generation; the largest stores are in the skeleton.

Magnesium salts are not well absorbed from the gastro-intestinal tract, which explains the use of magnesium sulphate (section 1.6.4) as an osmotic laxative.

Magnesium is excreted mainly by the kidneys and is therefore retained in renal failure, but significant *hypermagnesaemia* (causing muscle weakness and arrhythmias) is rare.

**Hypomagnesaemia** Since magnesium is secreted in large amounts in the gastro-intestinal fluid, excessive losses in diarrhoea, stoma or fistula are the most common causes of *hypomagnesaemia*; deficiency may also occur in alcoholism or as a result of treatment with certain drugs. Hypomagnesaemia often causes secondary hypocalcaemia (with which it may be confused) and also hypokalaemia and hyponatraemia.

Symptomatic *hypomagnesaemia* is associated with a deficit of 0.5–1 mmol/kg; up to 160 mmol $Mg^{2+}$ over up to 5 days may be required to replace the deficit (allowing for urinary losses). Magnesium is given initially by intravenous infusion or by intramuscular injection of **magnesium sulphate**; the intramuscular injection is painful. Plasma magnesium concentration should be measured to determine the rate and duration of infusion and the dose should be reduced in renal impairment. To prevent *recurrence of the deficit*, magnesium may be given by mouth in a dose of 24 mmol $Mg^{2+}$ daily in divided doses; a suitable preparation is magnesium glycerophosphate tablets [not licensed, available from IDIS and Special Products]. For maintenance (e.g. in intravenous nutrition), parenteral doses of magnesium are of the order of 10–20 mmol $Mg^{2+}$ daily (often about 12 mmol $Mg^{2+}$ daily).

**Arrhythmias** Magnesium sulphate has also been recommended for the emergency treatment of *serious arrhythmias*, especially in the presence of hypokalaemia (when hypomagnesaemia may also be present) and when salvos of rapid ventricular tachycardia show the characteristic twisting wave front known as *torsades de pointes* (see also section 2.3.1). The usual dose of magnesium sulphate is intravenous injection of 8 mmol $Mg^{2+}$ over 10–15 minutes (repeated once if necessary).

**Myocardial infarction** Evidence suggesting a sustained reduction in mortality in patients with *suspected myocardial infarction* given an initial intravenous injection of magnesium sulphate 8 mmol $Mg^{2+}$ over 20 minutes followed by an intravenous infusion of 65–72 mmol $Mg^{2+}$ over the following 24 hours, has not been borne out by a larger study. Some, however, continue to hold the view that magnesium is beneficial if given immediately (and for as long as there is a likelihood of reperfusion taking place).

**Eclampsia and pre-eclampsia** Magnesium sulphate is the drug of choice for the prevention of recurrent seizures in *eclampsia*; see also Appendix 4. Regimens may vary between hospitals. Calcium gluconate injection is used for the management of magnesium toxicity.

Magnesium sulphate is also of benefit in women with *pre-eclampsia* in whom there is concern about developing eclampsia. The patient should be monitored carefully (see under Magnesium Sulphate).

### MAGNESIUM SULPHATE

**Indications** see notes above; constipation (section 1.6.4); severe acute asthma (section 3.1); paste for boils (section 13.10.5)

**Cautions** see notes above; hepatic impairment (Appendix 2); renal impairment (Appendix 3); in severe hypomagnesaemia administer initially via controlled infusion device (preferably syringe pump); monitor blood pressure, respiratory rate, urinary output and for signs of overdosage (loss of patellar reflexes, weakness, nausea, sensation of warmth, flushing, drowsiness, double vision, and slurred speech); pregnancy (Appendix 4); **interactions**: Appendix 1 (magnesium, parenteral)

**Side-effects** generally associated with hypermagnesaemia, nausea, vomiting, thirst, flushing of skin, hypotension, arrhythmias, coma, respiratory depression, drowsiness, confusion, loss of tendon reflexes, muscle weakness; colic and diarrhoea following oral administration

**Dose**
- Hypomagnesaemia, see notes above
- Prevention of seizure recurrence in eclampsia, initially by intravenous injection over 5–15 minutes, 4 g, followed by intravenous infusion, 1 g/hour for at least 24 hours after last seizure; if seizure recurs, additional dose by intravenous injection, 2 g (4 g if body-weight over 70 kg)
- Prevention of seizures in pre-eclampsia [unlicensed indication], initially by intravenous infusion over 5–15 minutes, 4 g followed by intravenous infusion, 1 g/hour for 24 hours; if seizure occurs, additional dose by intravenous injection, 2 g

Intravenous administration For intravenous injection concentration of magnesium sulphate should not exceed 20% (dilute 1 part of magnesium sulphate injection 50% with at least 1.5 parts of water for injections)

Note Magnesium sulphate 1 g equivalent to $Mg^{2+}$ approx. 4 mmol

**Magnesium Sulphate** (Non-proprietary) PoM
Injection, magnesium sulphate 20% ($Mg^{2+}$ approx. 0.8 mmol/mL), net price 20-mL (4-g) amp = £2.75; 50% ($Mg^{2+}$ approx. 2 mmol/mL), 2-mL (1-g) amp = £2.59, 4-mL (2-g) prefilled syringe = £6.50, 5-mL (2.5-g) amp = £2.50, 10-mL (5-g) amp = £3.35; 10-mL (5-g) prefilled syringe = £4.95
Brands include *Minijet® Magnesium Sulphate 50%*

## 9.5.2 Phosphorus

9.5.2.1 Phosphate supplements
9.5.2.2 Phosphate-binding agents

### 9.5.2.1 Phosphate supplements

Oral phosphate supplements may be required in addition to vitamin D in a small minority of patients with hypophosphataemic vitamin D-resistant rickets. Diarrhoea is a common side-effect and should prompt a reduction in dosage.

Phosphate infusion is occasionally needed in alcohol dependence or in phosphate deficiency arising from use of parenteral nutrition deficient in phosphate supplements; phosphate depletion also occurs in severe diabetic ketoacidosis. For *established hypophosphataemia*, monobasic potassium phosphate may be infused at a maximum rate of 9 mmol every 12 hours. Excessive doses of phosphates may cause hypocalcaemia and metastatic calcification; it is **essential** to monitor closely plasma concentrations of calcium, phosphate, potassium, and other electrolytes.

For phosphate requirements in *total parenteral nutrition* regimens, see section 9.3.

**Phosphates** (Fresenius Kabi) PoM
Intravenous infusion, phosphates (providing $PO_4^{3-}$ 100 mmol/litre), net price 500 mL (*Polyfusor®*) = £3.75.
For the treatment of moderate to severe hypophosphatemia

**Phosphate-Sandoz®** (HK Pharma)
Tablets, effervescent, anhydrous sodium acid phosphate 1.936 g, sodium bicarbonate 350 mg, potassium bicarbonate 315 mg, equivalent to phosphorus 500 mg (phosphate 16.1 mmol), sodium 468.8 mg ($Na^+$ 20.4 mmol), potassium 123 mg ($K^+$ 3.1 mmol). Net price 20 = £3.29. Label: 13
Dose vitamin D-resistant hypophosphataemic osteomalacia, 4–6 tablets daily; CHILD under 5 years 2–3 tablets daily

### 9.5.2.2 Phosphate-binding agents

Aluminium-containing and calcium-containing preparations are used as phosphate-binding agents in the management of hyperphosphataemia complicating renal failure. Calcium-containing phosphate-binding agents are contra-indicated in hypercalcaemia or hypercalciuria. Phosphate-binding agents which contain aluminium may increase plasma aluminium in dialysis patients.

**Sevelamer** is licensed for the treatment of hyperphosphataemia in patients on haemodialysis.

### ALUMINIUM HYDROXIDE

**Indications** hyperphosphataemia; dyspepsia (section 1.1)

**Cautions** hyperaluminaemia; porphyria (section 9.8.2); see also notes above; **interactions**: Appendix 1 (antacids)

**Side-effects** see section 1.1.1

**Aluminium Hydroxide** (Non-proprietary)
Mixture (gel), about 4% w/w $Al_2O_3$ in water. Net price 200 mL = 41p
Dose hyperphosphataemia, 20–100 mL according to requirements of patient

**Alu-Cap®** (3M)
Capsules, green/red, dried aluminium hydroxide 475 mg (low $Na^+$). Net price 120-cap pack = £3.75
Dose phosphate-binding agent in renal failure, 4–20 capsules daily in divided doses with meals

### CALCIUM SALTS

**Indications** hyperphosphataemia

**Cautions** see notes above; **interactions:** Appendix 1 (antacids, calcium salts)

**Side-effects** hypercalcaemia

**Adcal®**, section 9.5.1.1

**Calcichew®**, section 9.5.1.1

**Calcium-500**, section 9.5.1.1

**Phosex®** (Vitaline)
Tablets, yellow, calcium acetate 1 g (calcium 250 mg or $Ca^{2+}$ 6.2 mmol), net price 180-tab pack = £19.79. Label: 25
Dose phosphate-binding agent (with meals) in renal failure, according to the requirements of the patient

## SEVELAMER

**Indications** hyperphosphataemia in patients on haemodialysis

**Cautions** pregnancy (Appendix 4); breast-feeding (Appendix 5); gastro-intestinal disorders

**Contra-indications** bowel obstruction

**Side-effects** intestinal obstruction

**Dose**

- ADULT over 18 years, initially 2.4–4.8 g daily in 3 divided doses with meals, then adjusted according to plasma-phosphate concentration

**Renagel®** (Genzyme) PoM
Tablets, f/c, sevelamer 800 mg, net price 180-tab pack = £122.76. Label: 25, C, with meals

9 Nutrition and blood

# 9.5.3 Fluoride

Availability of adequate fluoride confers significant resistance to dental caries. It is now considered that the topical action of fluoride on enamel and plaque is more important than the systemic effect.

Where the fluoride content of the drinking water is less than 700 micrograms per litre (0.7 parts per million), daily administration of fluoride tablets or drops is a suitable means of supplementation. Systemic fluoride supplements should not be prescribed without reference to the fluoride content of the local water supply. Infants need not receive fluoride supplements until the age of 6 months.

Dentifrices which incorporate sodium fluoride or monofluorophosphate are also a convenient source of fluoride.

Individuals who are either particularly caries prone or medically compromised may be given additional protection by use of fluoride rinses or by application of fluoride gels. Rinses may be used daily or weekly; daily use of a less concentrated rinse is more effective than weekly use of a more concentrated one. High-strength gels must be applied on a regular basis under professional supervision; extreme caution is necessary to prevent the child from swallowing any excess. Less concentrated gels are available for home use. Varnishes are also available and are particularly valuable for young or disabled children since they adhere to the teeth and set in the presence of moisture.

> Fluoride mouthwash, oral drops, tablets and toothpaste are prescribable on form FP10D (GP14 in Scotland, WP10D in Wales; for details see below ). There are also arrangements for health authorities to supply fluoride tablets in the course of pre-school dental schemes, and they may also be supplied in school dental schemes.
> Fluoride gels are not prescribable on form FP10D (GP14 in Scotland, WP10D in Wales).

## FLUORIDES

**Note** Sodium fluoride 2.2 mg provides approx. 1 mg fluoride ion

**Indications** prophylaxis of dental caries—see notes above

**Contra-indications** not for areas where drinking water is fluoridated

**Side-effects** occasional white flecks on teeth with recommended doses; rarely yellowish-brown discoloration if recommended doses are exceeded

**Dose**

**Note** Dose expressed as fluoride ion ($F^-$)

- Water content less than $F^-$ 300 micrograms/litre (0.3 parts per million), CHILD up to 6 months none; 6 months–3 years $F^-$ 250 micrograms daily, 3–6 years $F^-$ 500 micrograms daily, over 6 years $F^-$ 1 mg daily
- Water content between $F^-$ 300 and 700 micrograms/litre (0.3–0.7 parts per million), CHILD up to 3 years none, 3–6 years $F^-$ 250 micrograms daily, over 6 years $F^-$ 500 micrograms daily
- Water content above $F^-$ 700 micrograms/litre (0.7 parts per million), supplements not advised

**Note** These doses reflect the recommendations of the British Dental Association, the British Society of Paediatric Dentistry and the British Association for the Study of Community Dentistry (*Br Dent J* 1997; **182:** 6–7)

### Tablets

**Counselling** Tablets should be sucked or dissolved in the mouth and taken preferably in the evening

**En-De-Kay®** (Manx)
Fluotabs 3–6 years, orange-flavoured, scored, sodium fluoride 1.1 mg ($F^-$ 500 micrograms). Net price 200-tab pack = £1.80

Fluotabs 6+ years, orange-flavoured, scored, sodium fluoride 2.2 mg ($F^-$ 1 mg). Net price 200-tab pack = £1.80

**Dental prescribing on NHS** May be prescribed as Sodium Fluoride Tablets

**Fluor-a-day®** (Dental Health)
Tablets, buff, sodium fluoride 1.1 mg ($F^-$ 500 micrograms), net price 200-tab pack = £1.91; 2.2 mg ($F^-$ 1 mg), 200-tab pack = £1.91
**Dental prescribing on NHS** May be prescribed as Sodium Fluoride Tablets

**FluoriGard®** (Colgate-Palmolive)
Tablets 0.5, purple, grape-flavoured, scored, sodium fluoride 1.1 mg ($F^-$ 500 micrograms). Net price 200-tab pack = £1.91

Tablets 1.0, orange, orange-flavoured, scored, sodium fluoride 2.2 mg ($F^-$ 1 mg). Net price 200-tab pack = £1.91

**Dental prescribing on NHS** May be prescribed as Sodium Fluoride Tablets

**Oral drops**

*Note.* Fluoride supplements not considered necessary below 6 months of age (see notes above)

**En-De-Kay®** (Manx)

Fluodrops® (= paediatric drops), sugar-free, sodium fluoride 550 micrograms ($F^-$ 250 micrograms)/ 0.15 mL. Net price 60 mL = £1.82

Dental prescribing on NHS Corresponds to Sodium Fluoride Oral Drops DPF 0.37% equivalent to sodium fluoride 80 micrograms ($F^-$ 36 micrograms)/drop

**Mouthwashes**

Rinse mouth for 1 minute and spit out

Counselling Avoid eating, drinking, or rinsing mouth for 15 minutes after use

**Duraphat®** (Colgate-Palmolive)

Weekly dental rinse (= mouthwash), blue, sodium fluoride 0.2%. Net price 150 mL = £2.42. Counselling, see above

Dose CHILD 6 years and over, for *weekly* use, rinse with 10 mL

Dental prescribing on NHS May be prescribed as Sodium Fluoride Mouthwash 0.2%

**En-De-Kay®** (Manx)

Daily fluoride mouthrinse (= mouthwash), blue, sodium fluoride 0.05%. Net price 250 mL = £1.51

Dose CHILD 6 years and over, for *daily* use, rinse with 10 mL

Dental prescribing on NHS May be prescribed as Sodium Fluoride Mouthwash 0.05%

Fluorinse (= mouthwash), red, sodium fluoride 2%. Net price 100 mL = £3.97. Counselling, see above

Dose CHILD 8 years and over, for *daily* use, dilute 5 drops to 10 mL of water; for *weekly* use, dilute 20 drops to 10 mL

Dental prescribing on NHS May be prescribed as Sodium Fluoride Mouthwash 2%

**FluoriGard®** (Colgate-Palmolive)

Daily dental rinse (= mouthwash), blue, sodium fluoride 0.05%. Net price 500 mL = £3.11. Counselling, see above

Dose CHILD 6 years and over, for *daily* use, rinse with 10 mL

Dental prescribing on NHS May be prescribed as Sodium Fluoride Mouthwash 0.05%

**Gels**

**FluoriGard®** (Colgate-Palmolive)

Gel-Kam (= gel), stannous fluoride 0.4% in glycerol basis. Net price 100 mL = £3.05. Counselling, see below

Dose ADULT and CHILD 3 years and over, for *daily* use, using a toothbrush, apply onto all tooth surfaces

Counselling Swish between teeth for 1 minute before spitting out. Avoid eating, drinking, or rinsing mouth for at least 30 minutes after use

**Toothpastes**

**Duraphat®** (Colgate-Palmolive) PoM

Toothpaste, sodium fluoride 0.619%. Net price 75 mL = £2.86. Counselling, see below

Dose ADULT and ADOLESCENT over 16 years, apply 1 cm twice daily using a toothbrush

Counselling Brush teeth for 1 minute before spitting out. Avoid drinking or rinsing mouth for 30 minutes after use

Dental prescribing on NHS May be prescribed as Sodium Fluoride Toothpaste 0.619%

## 9.5.4 Zinc

Zinc supplements should be given only when there is good evidence of deficiency (hypoproteinaemia spuriously lowers plasma-zinc concentration) or in zinc-losing conditions. Zinc deficiency can occur as a result of inadequate diet or malabsorption; excessive loss of zinc can occur in trauma, burns and protein-losing conditions. A zinc supplement is given until clinical improvement occurs but it may need to be continued in severe malabsorption, metabolic disease (section 9.8.1) or in zinc-losing states.

Total parenteral nutrition regimens usually include trace amounts of zinc (section 9.3). If necessary, further zinc can be added to intravenous feeding regimens. A suggested dose for intravenous nutrition is elemental zinc 6.5 mg ($Zn^{2+}$ 100 micromol) daily.

### ZINC SULPHATE

**Indications** zinc deficiency or supplementation in zinc-losing conditions

**Cautions** acute renal failure (may accumulate); **interactions:** Appendix 1 (zinc)

**Side-effects** abdominal pain, dyspepsia, nausea, vomiting, diarrhoea, gastric irritation, gastritis; irritability, headache, lethargy

**Dose**

- See preparation below and notes above

**Zinc Sulphate** (Non-proprietary) PoM

Injection, zinc sulphate 14.6 mg/mL (zinc 50 micromol/mL), net price 10 mL vial = £2.50

**Solvazinc®** (Provalis)

Effervescent tablets, yellow-white, zinc sulphate monohydrate 125 mg (45 mg zinc). Net price 30 = £4.32. Label: 13, 21

Dose ADULT and CHILD over 30 kg, 1 tablet in water 1–3 times daily after food; CHILD under 10 kg, ½ tablet daily; 10–30 kg, ½ tablet 1–3 times daily

## 9.6 Vitamins


9.6.1 Vitamin A
9.6.2 Vitamin B group
9.6.3 Vitamin C
9.6.4 Vitamin D
9.6.5 Vitamin E
9.6.6 Vitamin K
9.6.7 Multivitamin preparations


Vitamins are used for the prevention and treatment of specific deficiency states or where the diet is known to be inadequate; they may be prescribed in the NHS to prevent or treat deficiency but not as dietary supplements.

Their use as general 'pick-me-ups' is of unproven value and, in the case of preparations containing vitamin A or D, may actually be harmful if patients take more than the prescribed dose. The 'fad' for mega-vitamin therapy with water-soluble vitamins, such as ascorbic acid and pyridoxine, is unscientific and can be harmful.

Dietary reference values for vitamins are available in the Department of Health publication:

Dietary Reference Values for Food Energy and Nutrients for the United Kingdom: Report of the Panel on Dietary Reference Values of the Committee on Medical Aspects of Food Policy. *Report on Health and Social Subjects 41*. London: HMSO, 1991

**Dental patients** Most patients who develop a nutritional deficiency despite an adequate intake of vitamins have malabsorption and if this is suspected the patient should be referred to a medical practitioner.

It is unjustifiable to treat stomatitis or glossitis with mixtures of vitamin preparations; this delays diagnosis and correct treatment.

## 9.6.1 Vitamin A

Deficiency of vitamin A (retinol) is associated with ocular defects (particularly xerophthalmia) and an increased susceptibility to infections, but deficiency is rare in the UK (even in disorders of fat absorption).

Massive overdose can cause rough skin, dry hair, an enlarged liver, and a raised erythrocyte sedimentation rate and raised serum calcium and serum alkaline phosphatase concentrations.

In view of evidence suggesting that high levels of vitamin A may cause birth defects, women who are (or may become) pregnant are advised not to take vitamin A supplements (including tablets and fish-liver oil drops), except on the advice of a doctor or an antenatal clinic; nor should they eat liver or products such as liver paté or liver sausage.



### VITAMIN A
(Retinol)

**Indications** see notes above
**Cautions** see notes above; **interactions:** Appendix 1 (vitamins)
**Side-effects** see notes above
**Dose**
- See notes above and under preparations

#### Vitamins A and D

**Halibut-liver Oil** (Non-proprietary)
Capsules, vitamin A 4000 units [also contains vitamin D]. Net price 20 = 18p

**Vitamins A and D** (Non-proprietary)
Capsules, vitamin A 4000 units, vitamin D 400 units. Net price 20 = 64p

**Halycitrol®** (LAB) NHS
Emulsion, vitamin A 4600 units, vitamin D 380 units/5 mL. Net price 114 mL = £1.77
Dose 5 mL daily but see notes above

## 9.6.2 Vitamin B group

Deficiency of the B vitamins, other than deficiency of vitamin $B_{12}$ (section 9.1.2), is rare in the UK and is usually treated by preparations containing thiamine ($B_1$), riboflavin ($B_2$), and nicotinamide, which is used in preference to nicotinic acid, as it does not cause vasodilatation. Other members (or substances traditionally classified as members) of the vitamin B complex such as aminobenzoic acid, biotin, choline, inositol, and pantothenic acid or panthenol may be included in vitamin B preparations but there is no evidence of their value.

The severe deficiency states Wernicke's encephalopathy and Korsakoff's psychosis, especially as seen in chronic alcoholism, are best treated initially by the parenteral administration of B vitamins (*Pabrinex®*), followed by oral administration of thiamine in the longer term. Anaphylaxis has been reported with parenteral B vitamins (see CSM advice, below).

As with other vitamins of the B group, pyridoxine ($B_6$) deficiency is rare, but it may occur during isoniazid therapy (section 5.1.9) and is characterised by peripheral neuritis. High doses of pyridoxine are given in some metabolic disorders, such as hyperoxaluria, and it is also used in sideroblastic anaemia (section 9.1.3). There is evidence to suggest that pyridoxine in a dose not exceeding 100 mg daily may provide some benefit in premenstrual syndrome. It has been tried for a wide variety of other disorders, but there is little sound evidence to support the claims of efficacy, and overdosage induces toxic effects.

Nicotinic acid inhibits the synthesis of cholesterol and triglyceride (see section 2.12). Folic acid and vitamin $B_{12}$ are used in the treatment of megaloblastic anaemia (section 9.1.2). Folinic acid (available as calcium folinate) is used in association with cytotoxic therapy (section 8.1).

### RIBOFLAVIN
(Riboflavine, vitamin $B_2$)

**Indications** see notes above

#### Preparations
Injections of vitamins B and C, see under Thiamine

#### Oral vitamin B complex preparations
See below

### THIAMINE
(Vitamin $B_1$)

> **CSM advice**
> Since potentially serious allergic adverse reactions may occur during, or shortly after, parenteral administration, the CSM has recommended that:
> 1. Use be restricted to patients in whom parenteral treatment is essential;
> 2. Intravenous injections should be administered slowly (over 10 minutes);
> 3. Facilities for treating anaphylaxis should be available when administered.

**Indications** see notes above
**Cautions** anaphylactic shock may occasionally follow injection (see CSM advice above)
**Dose**
- Mild chronic deficiency, 10–25 mg daily; severe deficiency, 200–300 mg daily

**Thiamine** (Non-proprietary)
Tablets, thiamine hydrochloride 50 mg, net price 20 = 80p; 100 mg, 20 = £1.23
Brands include *Benerva®* NHS

**Pabrinex®** (Link) PoM
I/M High potency injection, for intramuscular use only, ascorbic acid 500 mg, nicotinamide 160 mg, pyridoxine hydrochloride 50 mg, riboflavin 4 mg, thiamine hydrochloride 250 mg/7 mL. Net price 7 mL (in 2 amps) = £1.96

I/V High potency injection, for intravenous use only, ascorbic acid 500 mg, anhydrous glucose 1 g, nicotinamide 160 mg, pyridoxine hydrochloride 50 mg, riboflavin 4 mg, thiamine hydrochloride 250 mg/10 mL. Net price 10 mL (in 2 amps) = £1.96

Parenteral vitamins B and C for rapid correction of severe depletion or malabsorption (e.g. in alcoholism, after acute infections, postoperatively, or in psychiatric states), maintenance of vitamins B and C in chronic intermittent haemodialysis

Dose see CSM advice above

Coma or delirium from alcohol, from opioids, or from barbiturates, collapse following narcosis, by intravenous injection *or* infusion of *I/V High potency*, 2–3 pairs every 8 hours

Psychosis following narcosis or electroconvulsive therapy, toxicity from acute infections, by intravenous injection *or* infusion of *I/V High potency* or by deep intramuscular injection into the gluteal muscle of *I/M High potency*, 1 pair twice daily for up to 7 days

Haemodialysis, by intravenous infusion of *I/V High potency* (in sodium chloride intravenous infusion 0.9%) 1 pair every 2 weeks

Oral vitamin B complex preparations
See below

## PYRIDOXINE HYDROCHLORIDE
(Vitamin $B_6$)

**Indications** see under Dose

**Cautions** **interactions:** Appendix 1 (vitamins)

**Side-effects** sensory neuropathy reported with high doses given for extended periods

**Dose**
- Deficiency states, 20–50 mg up to 3 times daily
- Isoniazid neuropathy, prophylaxis 10 mg daily [or 20 mg daily if suitable product not available]; therapeutic, 50 mg three times daily
- Idiopathic sideroblastic anaemia, 100–400 mg daily in divided doses
- Premenstrual syndrome, 50–100 mg daily (see notes above)

> Prolonged use of pyridoxine in a dose of 10 mg daily is considered safe but the long-term use of pyridoxine in a dose of 200 mg or more daily has been associated with neuropathy. The safety of long-term pyridoxine supplementation with doses above 10 mg daily has not been established.

**Pyridoxine** (Non-proprietary)
Tablets, pyridoxine hydrochloride 10 mg, net price 20 = 34p; 20 mg, 20 = 34p; 50 mg, 20 = 38p

Injections of vitamins B and C
See under Thiamine

## NICOTINAMIDE

**Indications** see notes above; acne vulgaris, see section 13.6.1

**Nicotinamide** (Non-proprietary)
Tablets, nicotinamide 50 mg. Net price 20 = £1.37

Injections of vitamins B and C
See under Thiamine

## Oral vitamin B complex preparations

Note Other multivitamin preparations are in section 9.6.7.

**Vitamin B Tablets, Compound**
Tablets, nicotinamide 15 mg, riboflavin 1 mg, thiamine hydrochloride 1 mg. Net price 20 = 7p
Dose prophylactic, 1–2 tablets daily

**Vitamin B Tablets, Compound, Strong**
Tablets, brown, f/c or s/c, nicotinamide 20 mg, pyridoxine hydrochloride 2 mg, riboflavin 2 mg, thiamine hydrochloride 5 mg. Net price 28-tab pack = £1.11
Dose treatment of vitamin-B deficiency, 1–2 tablets 3 times daily
Dental prescribing on NHS Vitamin B Tablets, Compound Strong may be prescribed

**Vigranon B®** (Wallace Mfg) NHS
Syrup, thiamine hydrochloride 5 mg, riboflavin 2 mg, nicotinamide 20 mg, pyridoxine hydrochloride 2 mg, panthenol 3 mg/5 mL. Net price 150 mL = £2.41

## Other compounds

**Potassium aminobenzoate** has been used in the treatment of various disorders associated with excessive fibrosis such as scleroderma but its therapeutic value is **doubtful**.

**Potaba®** (Glenwood)
Capsules, potassium aminobenzoate 500 mg. Net price 20 = £1.59. Label: 21

Tablets, potassium aminobenzoate 500 mg. Net price 20 = £1.12. Label: 21

Envules® (= powder in sachets), potassium aminobenzoate 3 g. Net price 40 sachets = £17.21. Label: 13, 21

Dose Peyronie's disease, scleroderma, 12 g daily in divided doses after food

# 9.6.3 Vitamin C
(Ascorbic acid)

Vitamin C therapy is essential in scurvy, but less florid manifestations of vitamin C deficiency are commonly found, especially in the elderly. It is rarely necessary to prescribe more than 100 mg daily except early in the treatment of scurvy.

Severe scurvy causes gingival swelling and bleeding margins as well as petechiae on the skin. This is, however, exceedingly rare and a patient with these signs is more likely to have leukaemia. Investigation should not be delayed by a trial period of vitamin treatment.

Claims that vitamin C ameliorates colds or promotes wound healing have not been proved.

## ASCORBIC ACID

**Indications** prevention and treatment of scurvy

**Dose**
- Prophylactic, 25–75 mg daily; therapeutic, not less than 250 mg daily in divided doses

**Ascorbic Acid** (Non-proprietary)

Tablets, ascorbic acid 50 mg, net price 20 = 84p; 100 mg, 20 = 18p; 200 mg, 20 = 22p; 500 mg (label: 24), 20 = £1.49

Brands include *Redoxon*® NHS

Dental prescribing on NHS Ascorbic Acid Tablets may be prescribed

Injection, ascorbic acid 100 mg/mL. Net price 5-mL amp = £2.51

Available from UCB Pharma

**For children's welfare vitamin drops containing vitamin C with A and D**

See vitamin A

## 9.6.4 Vitamin D

Note The term Vitamin D is used for a range of compounds which possess the property of preventing or curing rickets. They include ergocalciferol (calciferol, vitamin $D_2$), colecalciferol (vitamin $D_3$), dihydrotachysterol, alfacalcidol (1α-hydroxycholecalciferol), and calcitriol (1,25-dihydroxycholecalciferol).

Simple vitamin D deficiency can be prevented by taking an oral supplement of only 10 micrograms (400 units) of ergocalciferol (calciferol, vitamin $D_2$) daily. Vitamin D deficiency can occur in people whose exposure to sunlight is limited and in those whose diet is deficient in vitamin D. In these individuals, ergocalciferol in a dose of 20 micrograms (800 units) daily by mouth can prevent vitamin D deficiency. Since there is no plain tablet of this strength available **calcium and ergocalciferol tablets** can be given (although the calcium is unnecessary).

Vitamin D deficiency caused by *intestinal malabsorption* or *chronic liver disease* usually requires vitamin D in pharmacological doses, such as **calciferol tablets** up to 1 mg (40 000 units) daily; the hypocalcaemia of *hypoparathyroidism* often requires doses of up to 2.5 mg (100 000 units) daily in order to achieve normocalcaemia.

Vitamin D requires hydroxylation by the kidney to its active form therefore the hydroxylated derivatives **alfacalcidol** or **calcitriol** should be prescribed if patients with *severe renal impairment* require vitamin D therapy. Calcitriol is also licensed for the management of postmenopausal osteoporosis.

**Paricalcitol**, a synthetic vitamin D analogue, is licensed for the prevention and treatment of secondary hyperparathyroidism associated with chronic renal failure (see also section 9.5.1.2).

**Important.** All patients receiving pharmacological doses of vitamin D should have the plasma-calcium concentration checked at intervals (initially weekly) and whenever nausea or vomiting are present. Breast milk from women taking pharmacological doses of vitamin D may cause hypercalcaemia if given to an infant.

### ERGOCALCIFEROL
**(Calciferol, Vitamin $D_2$)**

**Indications** see notes above

**Cautions** take care to ensure correct dose in infants; monitor plasma calcium in patients receiving high doses and in renal impairment; **interactions**: Appendix 1 (vitamins)

**Contra-indications** hypercalcaemia; metastatic calcification

**Side-effects** symptoms of overdosage include anorexia, lassitude, nausea and vomiting, diarrhoea, weight loss, polyuria, sweating, headache, thirst, vertigo, and raised concentrations of calcium and phosphate in plasma and urine

**Dose**

- See notes above

**Daily supplements**

Note There is no plain vitamin D tablet available for treating simple deficiency (see notes above). Alternatives include vitamins capsules (see 9.6.7), preparations of vitamins A and D (see 9.6.1), and calcium and ergocalciferol tablets (see below).

**Calcium and Ergocalciferol** (Non-proprietary) **(Calcium and Vitamin D)**

Tablets, calcium lactate 300 mg, calcium phosphate 150 mg (calcium 97 mg or $Ca^{2+}$ 2.4 mmol), ergocalciferol 10 micrograms (400 units). Net price 28-tab pack = £1.43. Counselling, crush before administration or may be chewed

**Adcal-$D_3$®** (Strakan)

Tablets (chewable), calcium carbonate 1.5 g (calcium 600 mg or $Ca^{2+}$ 15.1 mmol), colecalciferol 10 micrograms (400 units), net price 100-tab pack = £7.25. Label: 24

**Cacit® D3** (Procter & Gamble Pharm.)

Granules, effervescent, calcium carbonate 1.25 g (calcium 500 mg or $Ca^{2+}$ 12.6 mmol), colecalciferol 11 micrograms (440 units)/sachet. Net price 30-sachet pack = £5.75. Label: 13

**Calceos®** (Provalis)

Tablets (chewable), calcium carbonate 1.25 g (calcium 500 mg or $Ca^{2+}$ 12.6 mmol), colecalciferol 10 micrograms (400 units). Net price 60-tab pack = £4.74. Label: 24

**Calcichew-$D_3$®** (Shire)

Tablets (chewable), calcium carbonate 1.25 g (calcium 500 mg or $Ca^{2+}$ 12.6 mmol), colecalciferol 5 micrograms (200 units). Net price 100-tab pack = £15.02. Label: 24

Excipients include aspartame (section 9.4.1)

**Calcichew-$D_3$® Forte** (Shire)

Tablets (chewable), calcium carbonate 1.25 g (calcium 500 mg or $Ca^{2+}$ 12.6 mmol), colecalciferol 10 micrograms (400 units). Net price 100-tab pack = £7.50. Label: 24

Excipients include aspartame (section 9.4.1)

**Calfovit D3®** (Trinity) PoM

Powder, calcium phosphate 3.1 g (calcium 1.2 g or $Ca^{2+}$ 30 mmol), colecalciferol 20 micrograms (800 units), net price 30-sachet pack = £4.32. Label: 13, 21

**Pharmacological strengths (see notes above)**

Note The BP directs that when calciferol is prescribed or demanded, colecalciferol or ergocalciferol should be dispensed or supplied

**Ergocalciferol** (Non-proprietary)

Tablets, ergocalciferol 250 micrograms (10 000 units), net price 20 = £4.24; 1.25 mg (50 000 units) may also be available

Important When the strength of the tablets ordered or prescribed is not clear, the intention of the prescriber with respect to the strength (expressed in micrograms or milligrams per tablet) should be ascertained.

Injection, ergocalciferol, 7.5 mg (300 000 units)/mL in oil, net price 1-mL amp = £5.92, 2-mL amp = £7.07

## ALFACALCIDOL
**(1α-Hydroxycholecalciferol)**

**Indications** see notes above
**Cautions** see under Ergocalciferol
**Contra-indications** see under Ergocalciferol
**Side-effects** see under Ergocalciferol
**Dose**
- By mouth *or* by intravenous injection over 30 seconds, ADULT and CHILD over 20 kg, initially 1 microgram daily (elderly 500 nanograms), adjusted to avoid hypercalcaemia; maintenance, usually 0.25–1 microgram daily; NEONATE and PRETERM NEONATE initially 50–100 nanograms/kg daily, CHILD under 20 kg initially 50 nanograms/kg daily

**Alfacalcidol** (Non-proprietary) PoM
Capsules, alfacalcidol 250 nanograms, net price 30-cap pack = £4.78; 500 nanograms 30-cap pack = £8.19; 1 microgram 30-cap pack = £11.49

**One-Alpha®** (LEO) PoM
Capsules, alfacalcidol 250 nanograms (white), net price 30-cap pack = £3.37; 500 nanograms (red), 30-cap pack = £6.27; 1 microgram (brown), 30-cap pack = £8.75
Excipients include sesame oil

Oral drops, sugar-free, alfacalcidol 2 micrograms/mL (1 drop contains approx. 100 nanograms), net price 10 mL = £22.49
Excipients include alcohol
**Note** The concentration of alfacalcidol in *One-Alpha® drops* is **10 times greater** than that of the former presentation *One-Alpha® solution*.

Injection, alfacalcidol 2 micrograms/mL, net price 0.5-mL amp = £2.16, 1-mL amp = £4.11
**Note** Contains propylene glycol and should be used with caution in small preterm neonates

## CALCITRIOL
**(1,25-Dihydroxycholecalciferol)**

**Indications** see notes above
**Cautions** see under Ergocalciferol; monitor plasma calcium, phosphate, and creatinine during dosage titration
**Contra-indications** see under Ergocalciferol
**Side-effects** see under Ergocalciferol
**Dose**
- By mouth, renal osteodystrophy, initially 250 nanograms daily, or on alternate days (in patients with normal or only slightly reduced plasma-calcium concentration), increased if necessary in steps of 250 nanograms at intervals of 2–4 weeks; usual dose 0.5–1 microgram daily; CHILD not established

  Established postmenopausal osteoporosis, 250 nanograms twice daily (monitor plasma-calcium concentration and creatinine, consult product literature)
- By intravenous injection (or injection through catheter after haemodialysis), hypocalcaemia in dialysis patients with chronic renal failure, initially 500 nanograms (approx. 10 nanograms/kg) 3 times a week, increased if necessary in steps of 250–500 nanograms at intervals of 2–4 weeks; usual dose 0.5–3 micrograms 3 times a week; CHILD not established

  Moderate to severe secondary hyperparathyroidism in dialysis patients, initially 0.5–4 micrograms 3 times a week, increased if necessary in steps of 250–500 nanograms at intervals of 2–4 weeks; max. 8 micrograms 3 times a week

**Calcitriol** (Non-proprietary) PoM
Capsules, calcitriol 250 nanograms, net price 30-cap pack = £6.18; 500 nanograms, 30-cap pack = £11.05

**Rocaltrol®** (Roche) PoM
Capsules, calcitriol 250 nanograms (red/white), net price 20 = £3.83; 500 nanograms (red), 20 = £6.85

**Calcijex®** (Abbott) PoM
Injection, calcitriol 1 microgram/mL, net price 1-mL amp = £5.14; 2 micrograms/mL, 1-mL amp = £10.28

## COLECALCIFEROL
**(Cholecalciferol, vitamin $D_3$)**

**Indications** see under Ergocalciferol—alternative to ergocalciferol in calciferol tablets and injection
**Cautions** see under Ergocalciferol
**Contra-indications** see under Ergocalciferol
**Side-effects** see under Ergocalciferol

**With alendronic acid**
See section 6.6.2

## DIHYDROTACHYSTEROL

**Indications** see under Ergocalciferol
**Cautions** see under Ergocalciferol
**Contra-indications** see under Ergocalciferol
**Side-effects** see under Ergocalciferol

**AT 10®** (Intrapharm)
Oral solution, dihydrotachysterol 250 micrograms/mL. Net price 15-mL dropper bottle = £22.87
Excipients include arachis (peanut) oil
Dose acute, chronic, and latent forms of hypocalcaemic tetany due to hypoparathyroidism, consult product literature

## PARICALCITOL

**Indications** see notes above
**Cautions** monitor plasma calcium and phosphate during dose titration and at least monthly when stabilised; monitor parathyroid hormone concentration; pregnancy (Appendix 4); breast-feeding (Appendix 5); **interactions**: Appendix 1 (vitamins)
**Contra-indications** see under Ergocalciferol
**Side-effects** see under Ergocalciferol; also hypercalcaemia, hyperphosphataemia; pruritus; taste disturbance
**Dose**
- By slow intravenous injection—consult product literature; max. initial dose 40 micrograms

**Zemplar®** (Abbott) ▼ PoM
Injection, paricalcitol 5 micrograms/mL, net price 5 × 1-mL amp = £62.00, 5 × 2-mL amp = £124.00
Excipients include propylene glycol

# 9.6.5 Vitamin E
**(Tocopherols)**

The daily requirement of vitamin E has not been well defined but is probably about 3 to 15 mg daily. There is little evidence that oral supplements of vitamin E are essential in adults, even where there is fat malabsorption secondary to cholestasis. In young children with congenital cholestasis, abnormally low vitamin E concentrations may be found in association with neuromuscular abnormalities, which usually respond only to the parenteral administration of vitamin E.

Vitamin E has been tried for various other conditions but there is little scientific evidence of its value.

### ALPHA TOCOPHERYL ACETATE

**Indications** see notes above

**Cautions** predisposition to thrombosis; increased risk of necrotising enterocolitis in neonate weighing less than 1.5 kg

**Side-effects** diarrhoea and abdominal pain with doses more than 1 g daily

**Vitamin E Suspension** (Cambridge)
Suspension, alpha tocopheryl acetate 500 mg/5 mL. Net price 100 mL = £17.23

Dose malabsorption in cystic fibrosis, 100–200 mg daily; CHILD under 1 year 50 mg daily; 1 year and over, 100 mg daily

Malabsorption in abetalipoproteinaemia, ADULT and CHILD 50–100 mg/kg daily

Malabsorption in chronic cholestasis, INFANT 150–200 mg/kg daily

Note Tablets containing tocopheryl acetate 100 mg are available on a named-patient basis from Bell and Croyden (*Ephynal®*)



## 9.6.6 Vitamin K

Vitamin K is necessary for the production of blood clotting factors and proteins necessary for the normal calcification of bone.

Because vitamin K is fat soluble, patients with fat malabsorption, especially in biliary obstruction or hepatic disease, may become deficient. For oral administration to prevent vitamin-K deficiency in malabsorption syndromes, a water-soluble preparation, **menadiol sodium phosphate** must be used; the usual dose is about 10 mg daily.

Oral coumarin anticoagulants act by interfering with vitamin K metabolism in the hepatic cells and their effects can be antagonised by giving vitamin K; for British Society for Haematology Guidelines, see section 2.8.2.

**Vitamin k deficiency bleeding** Neonates are relatively deficient in vitamin K and those who do not receive supplements of vitamin K are at risk of serious bleeds including intracranial bleeding. The Chief Medical Officer and the Chief Nursing Officer have recommended that all newborn babies should receive vitamin K to prevent vitamin K deficiency bleeding (haemorrhagic disease of the newborn). An appropriate regimen should be selected after discussion with parents in the antenatal period.

Vitamin K (as **phytomenadione**) 1 mg may be given by a single intramuscular injection at birth; this prevents vitamin K deficiency bleeding in virtually all babies. Fears about the safety of parenteral vitamin K appear to be unfounded.

Alternatively, vitamin K may be given by mouth, and arrangements must be in place to ensure the appropriate regimen is followed. Two doses of a colloidal (mixed micelle) preparation of phytomenadione 2 mg should be given in the first week. For breast-fed babies, a third dose of phytomenadione 2 mg is given at 1 month of age; the third dose is omitted in formula-fed babies because formula feeds contain vitamin K.

### MENADIOL SODIUM PHOSPHATE

**Indications** see notes above

**Cautions** G6PD deficiency (section 9.1.5) and vitamin E deficiency (risk of haemolysis); **interactions:** Appendix 1 (vitamins)

**Contra-indications** neonates and infants, late pregnancy

**Dose**
- See notes above

**Menadiol Phosphate** (Cambridge)
Tablets, menadiol sodium phosphate equivalent to 10 mg of menadiol phosphate. Net price 100-tab pack = £37.34

### PHYTOMENADIONE
(Vitamin $K_1$)

**Indications** see notes above

**Cautions** intravenous injections should be given very slowly (see also below); pregnancy (Appendix 4); **interactions:** Appendix 1 (vitamins)

**Dose**
- See notes above and section 2.8.2

**Konakion®** (Roche) PoM
Tablets, s/c, phytomenadione 10 mg, net price 10-tab pack = £1.65. To be chewed or allowed to dissolve slowly in the mouth (Label: 24)

**Colloidal formulation**

**Konakion® MM** (Roche) PoM
Injection, phytomenadione 10 mg/mL in a mixed micelles vehicle. Net price 1-mL amp = 40p
Excipients include glycocholic acid 54.6 mg/amp, lecithin

Cautions reduce dose in elderly; liver impairment (glycocholic acid may displace bilirubin); reports of anaphylactoid reactions

Note *Konakion® MM* may be administered by slow intravenous injection or by intravenous infusion in glucose 5% (see Appendix 6); **not** for intramuscular injection

**Konakion® MM Paediatric** (Roche) PoM
Injection, phytomenadione 10 mg/mL in a mixed micelles vehicle. Net price 0.2-mL amp = £1.00
Excipients include glycocholic acid 10.9 mg/amp, lecithin

Cautions parenteral administration in neonate of less than 2.5 kg (increased risk of kernicterus)

Note *Konakion® MM Paediatric* may be administered *by mouth* or *by intramuscular injection* or *by intravenous injection*

## 9.6.7 Multivitamin preparations

**Vitamins**
Capsules, ascorbic acid 15 mg, nicotinamide 7.5 mg, riboflavin 500 micrograms, thiamine hydrochloride 1 mg, vitamin A 2500 units, vitamin D 300 units. Net price 20 = 22p

**Abidec®** (Chefaro UK)
Drops, vitamins A, B group, C, and D. Net price 25 mL (with dropper) = £1.84
Excipients include arachis (peanut) oil

**Dalivit®** (LPC)
Oral drops, vitamins A, B group, C, and D, net price 25 mL = £1.60, 50 mL = £2.85

## Vitamin and mineral supplements and adjuncts to synthetic diets

**Forceval®** (Alliance)
Capsules, brown/red, vitamins (ascorbic acid 60 mg, biotin 100 micrograms, cyanocobalamin 3 micrograms, folic acid 400 micrograms, nicotinamide 18 mg, pantothenic acid 4 mg, pyridoxine 2 mg, riboflavin 1.6 mg, thiamine 1.2 mg, vitamin A 2500 units, vitamin $D_2$ 400 units, vitamin E 10 mg, minerals and trace elements (calcium 100 mg, chromium 200 micrograms, copper 2 mg, iodine 140 micrograms, iron 12 mg, magnesium 30 mg, manganese 3 mg, molybdenum 250 micrograms, phosphorus 77 mg, potassium 4 mg, selenium 50 micrograms, zinc 15 mg). Net price 30-cap pack = £4.94, 45-cap pack = £6.47; 90-cap pack = £11.93
Dose vitamin and mineral deficiency and as adjunct in synthetic diets, 1 capsule daily

Junior capsules, brown, vitamins (ascorbic acid 25 mg, biotin 50 micrograms, cyanocobalamin 2 micrograms, folic acid 100 micrograms, nicotinamide 7.5 mg, pantothenic acid 2 mg, pyridoxine 1 mg, riboflavin 1 mg, thiamine 1.5 mg, vitamin A 1250 units, vitamin $D_2$ 200 units, vitamin E 5 mg, vitamin $K_1$ 25 micrograms), minerals and trace elements (chromium 50 micrograms, copper 1 mg, iodine 75 micrograms, iron 5 mg, magnesium 1 mg, manganese 1.25 mg, molybdenum 50 micrograms, selenium 25 micrograms, zinc 5 mg). Net price 30-cap pack = £3.52, 60-cap pack = £6.69
Dose vitamin and mineral deficiency and as adjunct in synthetic diets, CHILD over 5 years, 2 capsules daily

**Ketovite®** (Paines & Byrne)
Tablets PoM, yellow, ascorbic acid 16.6 mg, riboflavin 1 mg, thiamine hydrochloride 1 mg, pyridoxine hydrochloride 330 micrograms, nicotinamide 3.3 mg, calcium pantothenate 1.16 mg, alpha tocopheryl acetate 5 mg, inositol 50 mg, biotin 170 micrograms, folic acid 250 micrograms, acetomenaphthone 500 micrograms. Net price 100-tab pack = £4.17
Dose prevention of vitamin deficiency in disorders of carbohydrate or amino-acid metabolism and adjunct in restricted, specialised, or synthetic diets, 1 tablet 3 times daily; use with *Ketovite® Liquid* for complete vitamin supplementation

Liquid, pink, sugar-free, vitamin A 2500 units, ergocalciferol 400 units, choline chloride 150 mg, cyanocobalamin 12.5 micrograms/5 mL. Net price 150-mL pack = £2.70
Dose prevention of vitamin deficiency in disorders of carbohydrate or amino-acid metabolism and adjunct in restricted, specialised, or synthetic diets, 5 mL daily; use with *Ketovite® Tablets* for complete vitamin supplementation

**Vivioptal®** (Pharma-Global)
Capsules, brown, vitamins (biotin 50 micrograms, calcium ascorbate 60 mg, colecalciferol 400 units, cyanocobalamin 3 micrograms, dexpanthenol 10 mg, folic acid 400 micrograms, inositol 30 mg, nicotinamide 25 mg, pyridoxine 6.08 mg, riboflavin 3 mg, rutoside 20 mg, thiamine nitrate 5 mg, vitamin A 5000 units, vitamin E 10 mg), minerals and trace elements (calcium hydrogen phosphate 35 mg, cobalt sulphate 100 micrograms, copper sulphate 500 micrograms, iron 3.25 mg, magnesium glycerophosphate 40 mg, manganese sulphate 500 micrograms, potassium sulphate 8 mg, sodium molybdate 80 micrograms, zinc oxide 500 micrograms); also contains adenosine, choline hydrogen tartrate, ethyl linoleate, lecithin, lysine hydrochloride, and orotic acid, net price 30-cap pack = £5.62
Dose vitamin and mineral deficiency and as an adjunct in synthetic diets, 1 capsule daily
Excipients include arachis (peanut) oil

# 9.7 Bitters and tonics

Mixtures containing simple and aromatic bitters, such as alkaline gentian mixture, are traditional remedies for loss of appetite. All depend on suggestion.

**Gentian Mixture, Alkaline, BP (Alkaline Gentian Oral Solution)**
Mixture, concentrated compound gentian infusion 10%, sodium bicarbonate 5% in a suitable vehicle. Extemporaneous preparations should be recently prepared according to the following formula: concentrated compound gentian infusion 1 mL, sodium bicarbonate 500 mg, double-strength chloroform water 5 mL, water to 10 mL
Dose 10 mL 3 times daily in water before meals

**Effico®** (Forest) NHS
Tonic, orange-red, thiamine hydrochloride 180 micrograms, nicotinamide 2.1 mg, caffeine 20.2 mg, compound gentian infusion 0.31 mL/5 mL. Net price 300-mL pack = £2.46, 500-mL pack = £3.13

**Labiton®** (LAB) NHS
Tonic, brown, thiamine hydrochloride 375 micrograms, caffeine 3.5 mg, kola nut dried extract 3.025 mg, alcohol 1.4 mL/5 mL. Net price 200 mL = £2.62

**Metatone®** (W-L) NHS
Tonic, thiamine hydrochloride 500 micrograms, calcium glycerophosphate 45.6 mg, manganese glycerophosphate 5.7 mg, potassium glycerophosphate 45.6 mg, sodium glycerophosphate 22.8 mg/5 mL. Net price 300 mL = £2.79

# 9.8 Metabolic disorders

9.8.1 Drugs used in metabolic disorders
9.8.2 Acute porphyrias

This section covers drugs used in metabolic disorders and not readily classified elsewhere.

## 9.8.1 Drugs used in metabolic disorders

### Wilson's disease

**Penicillamine** (see also section 10.1.3) is used in Wilson's disease (hepatolenticular degeneration) to aid the elimination of copper ions. See below for other indications.

**Trientine** is used for the treatment of Wilson's disease only in patients intolerant of penicillamine; it is **not** an alternative to penicillamine for rheumatoid arthritis or cystinuria. Penicillamine-induced systemic lupus erythematosus may not resolve on transfer to trientine.

**Zinc** prevents the absorption of copper in Wilson's disease. Symptomatic patients should be treated initially with a chelating agent because zinc has a slow onset of action. When transferring from chelating treatment to zinc maintenance therapy, chelating treatment should be co-administered for 2–3 weeks until zinc takes maximum effect.

## PENICILLAMINE

**Indications** see under Dose below
**Cautions** see section 10.1.3
**Contra-indications** see section 10.1.3
**Side-effects** see section 10.1.3
**Dose**
- Wilson's disease, 1.5–2 g daily in divided doses before food; max. 2 g daily for 1 year; maintenance 0.75–1 g daily; ELDERLY 20 mg/kg daily in divided doses, adjusted according to response; CHILD up to 20 mg/kg daily in divided doses, minimum 500 mg daily
- Autoimmune hepatitis (used rarely; after disease controlled with corticosteroids), initially 500 mg daily in divided doses increased slowly over 3 months; usual maintenance dose 1.25 g daily; ELDERLY not recommended
- Cystinuria, therapeutic, 1–3 g daily in divided doses before food, adjusted to maintain urinary cystine below 200 mg/litre; prophylactic (maintain urinary cystine below 300 mg/litre) 0.5–1 g at bedtime; maintain adequate fluid intake (at least 3 litres daily); CHILD and ELDERLY minimum dose to maintain urinary cystine below 200 mg/litre
- Severe active rheumatoid arthritis, section 10.1.3
- Copper and lead poisoning, see Emergency Treatment of Poisoning

**Preparations**
Section 10.1.3

## TRIENTINE DIHYDROCHLORIDE

**Indications** Wilson's disease in patients intolerant of penicillamine
**Cautions** see notes above; pregnancy (Appendix 4); **interactions:** Appendix 1 (trientine)
**Side-effects** nausea, rash; rarely anaemia
**Dose**
- 1.2–2.4 g daily in 2–4 divided doses before food; CHILD initially 0.6–1.5 g daily in 2–4 divided doses before food, adjusted according to response

**Trientine Dihydrochloride** (Univar) PoM
Capsules, trientine dihydrochloride 300 mg. Label: 6, 22
Note The CSM has requested that in addition to the usual CSM reporting request, special records should also be kept by the pharmacist

## ZINC ACETATE

**Indications** Wilson's disease (initiated under specialist supervision)
**Cautions** portal hypertension (risk of hepatic decompensation when switching from chelating agent); monitor full blood count and serum cholesterol; pregnancy (Appendix 4); **interactions:** Appendix 1 (zinc)
**Contra-indications** breast-feeding
**Side-effects** gastric irritation (usually transient; may be reduced if first dose taken mid-morning or with a little protein); *less commonly* sideroblastic anaemia and leucopenia
**Dose**
Note Dose expressed as elemental zinc
- Wilson's disease, 50 mg 3 times daily (max. 50 mg 5 times daily), adjusted according to response; CHILD 1–6 years, 25 mg twice daily; 6–16 years, body-weight under 57 kg, 25 mg 3 times daily, body-weight over 57 kg, 50 mg 3 times daily; ADOLESCENT 16–18 years, 50 mg 3 times daily

**Wilzin**® (Orphan Europe) ▼ PoM
Capsules, zinc (as acetate) 25 mg (blue), net price 250-cap pack = £123.00; 50 mg (orange), 250-cap pack = £233.00. Label: 23

# Carnitine deficiency

**Carnitine** is available for the management of primary carnitine deficiency due to inborn errors of metabolism or of secondary deficiency in haemodialysis patients.

## CARNITINE

**Indications** primary and secondary carnitine deficiency
**Cautions** diabetes mellitus; renal impairment; monitoring of free and acyl carnitine in blood and urine recommended; pregnancy (but appropriate to use—Appendix 4) and breast-feeding
**Side-effects** nausea, vomiting, abdominal pain, diarrhoea, body odour; side-effects may be dose-related—monitor tolerance during first week and after any dose increase
**Dose**
- Primary deficiency, by mouth, up to 200 mg/kg daily in 2–4 divided doses; higher doses of up to 400 mg/kg daily occasionally required; by intravenous injection over 2–3 minutes, up to 100 mg/kg daily in 3–4 divided doses
- Secondary deficiency, by intravenous injection over 2–3 minutes, 20 mg/kg after each dialysis session (dosage adjusted according to carnitine concentration); maintenance, by mouth, 1 g daily

**Carnitor**® (Shire) PoM
Oral liquid, L-carnitine 1 g/10-mL (10%) single-dose bottle. Net price 10 × 10-mL single-dose bottle = £35.00

Paediatric solution, L-carnitine 30% (3 g/10-mL). Net price 20 mL = £21.00
Excipients include sorbitol

Injection, L-carnitine 200 mg/mL. Net price 5-mL amp = £11.90

# Fabry's disease

**Agalsidase beta**, an enzyme produced by recombinant DNA technology, is licensed for long-term enzyme

9 Nutrition and blood

replacement therapy in Fabry's disease (a lysosomal storage disorder caused by deficiency of α-galactosidase).

## AGALSIDASE BETA

**Indications** (specialist use only) Fabry's disease

**Cautions** pregnancy (Appendix 4); breast-feeding (Appendix 5); **interactions:** Appendix 1 (agalsidase beta)

Hypersensitivity reactions Hypersensitivity reactions common, calling for use of antihistamine, antipyretic and corticosteroid; consult product literature for details

**Side-effects** nausea, vomiting, oedema, hypertension, hypersensitivity reactions, fever, headache, tremor, myalgia, injection-site pain; commonly abdominal pain, bradycardia, tachycardia, palpitation, fatigue, drowsiness, paraesthesia, dizziness, anaemia, proteinuria, visual disturbances, and abnormal tear secretion

**Dose**

- By intravenous infusion, ADULT and ADOLESCENT over 16 years 1 mg/kg every 2 weeks

**Fabrazyme®** (Genzyme) ▼ PoM

Intravenous infusion, powder for reconstitution, agalsidase beta, net price 5-mg vial = £325.50; 35-mg vial = £2269.20

## Gaucher's disease

**Imiglucerase**, an enzyme produced by recombinant DNA technology, is administered as enzyme replacement therapy for non-neurological manifestations of type I or type III Gaucher's disease, a familial disorder affecting principally the liver, spleen, bone marrow, and lymph nodes.

**Miglustat**, an inhibitor of glucosylceramide synthase, is licensed for the treatment of mild to moderate type I Gaucher's disease in patients for whom imiglucerase is unsuitable; it is given by mouth.

## IMIGLUCERASE

**Indications** (specialist use only) non-neurological manifestations of type I or type III Gaucher's disease

**Cautions** pregnancy (Appendix 4); breast-feeding (Appendix 5); monitor for imiglucerase antibodies; when stabilised monitor all parameters and response to treatment at intervals of 6–12 months

**Side-effects** hypersensitivity reactions (including urticaria, angioedema, hypotension, flushing, tachycardia); less commonly nausea, vomiting, diarrhoea, abdominal cramps, headache, dizziness, fatigue, fever, injection-site reactions

**Dose**

- By intravenous infusion, initially 60 units/kg once every 2 weeks (2.5 units/kg 3 times a week or 15 units/kg once every 2 weeks may improve haematological parameters and organomegaly, but not bone parameters); maintenance, adjust dose according to response

**Cerezyme®** (Genzyme) PoM

Intravenous infusion, powder for reconstitution, imiglucerase, net price 200-unit vial = £553.35; 400-unit vial = £1106.70

## MIGLUSTAT

**Indications** mild to moderate type I Gaucher's disease (specialist supervision only)

**Cautions** hepatic impairment (Appendix 2); renal impairment (Appendix 3); monitor cognitive and neurological function

**Contra-indications** pregnancy (Appendix 4); men should not father a child during or within 3 months of treatment; breast-feeding (Appendix 5)

**Side-effects** diarrhoea, flatulence, abdominal pain, constipation, nausea, vomiting, weight changes; tremor, dizziness, headache; leg cramps; visual disturbances; commonly dyspepsia, decreased appetite, peripheral neuropathy, cognitive dysfunction

**Dose**

- ADULT over 18 years, 100 mg 3 times daily; reduced if not tolerated to 100 mg 1–2 times daily

**Zavesca®** (Actelion) ▼ PoM

Capsules, miglustat 100 mg, net price 84-cap pack = £4480.00 (hospital only)

## Mucopolysaccharidosis I

**Laronidase**, an enzyme produced by recombinant DNA technology, is licensed for long-term replacement therapy in the treatment of non-neurological manifestations of mucopolysaccharidosis I, a lysosomal storage disorder caused by deficiency of α-L- iduronidase.

## LARONIDASE

**Indications** (specialist use only) non-neurological manifestations of mucopolysaccharidosis I

**Cautions** pregnancy (Appendix 4); breast-feeding (Appendix 5); **interactions:** Appendix 1 (laronidase)

Infusion-related reactions Infusion-related reactions very common, calling for use of antihistamine and antipyretic; recurrent reactions may require corticosteroid; consult product literature for details

**Side-effects** flushing, musculoskeletal pain, rash, headache, abdominal pain

**Dose**

- By intravenous infusion, ADULT and CHILD over 5 years 100 units/kg once weekly

**Aldurazyme®** (Genzyme) ▼ PoM

Concentrate for intravenous infusion, laronidase 100 units/mL, net price 5-mL vial = £460.35

## Nephropathic cystinosis

**Mercaptamine** (cysteamine) is available for the treatment of nephropathic cystinosis.

## MERCAPTAMINE
**(Cysteamine)**

**Indications** (specialist use only) nephropathic cystinosis

**Cautions** leucocyte-cystine concentration and haematological monitoring required—consult product literature; dose of phosphate supplement may need to be adjusted

**Contra-indications** pregnancy and breast-feeding; hypersensitivity to mercaptamine or penicillamine

**Side-effects** breath and body odour, nausea, vomiting, diarrhoea, anorexia, lethargy, fever, rash; also reported dehydration, hypertension, abdominal discomfort, gastroenteritis, drowsiness, encephalopathy, headache, nervousness, depression; anaemia, leucopenia, increases in liver enzymes; rarely gastro-intestinal ulceration and bleeding, seizures, hallucinations, urticaria, interstitial nephritis

**Dose**
- Initial doses should be one-sixth to one-quarter of the expected maintenance dose, increased gradually over 4–6 weeks
- Maintenance, ADULT and CHILD over 50 kg body-weight, 2 g daily in 4 divided doses
  CHILD up to 12 years, 1.3 g/m² (approx. 50 mg/kg) daily in 4 divided doses

**Cystagon®** (Orphan Europe) PoM
Capsules, mercaptamine (as bitartrate) 50 mg, net price 100-cap pack = £44.00; 150 mg, 100-cap pack = £125.00
Note CHILD under 6 years at risk of aspiration, capsules can be opened and contents sprinkled on food (at a temperature suitable for eating); avoid adding to acidic drinks (e.g. orange juice)

## Urea cycle disorders

**Sodium phenylbutyrate** is used in the management of urea cycle disorders. It is indicated as adjunctive therapy in all patients with neonatal-onset disease and in those with late-onset disease who have a history of hyperammonaemic encephalopathy.

**Carglumic acid** is licensed for the treatment of hyperammonaemia due to *N*-acetylglutamate synthase deficiency.

### CARGLUMIC ACID

**Indications** hyperammonaemia due to *N*-acetylglutamate synthase deficiency (initiated under specialist supervision)

**Cautions** pregnancy (Appendix 4) and breast-feeding (Appendix 5)

**Side-effects** occasionally, raised serum transaminases, sweating

**Dose**
- ADULT and CHILD initially 100 mg/kg daily in 2–4 divided doses immediately before food (max. 250 mg/kg daily), adjusted according to plasma–ammonia concentration; maintenance 10–100 mg/kg daily in 2–4 divided doses

**Carbaglu®** (Orphan Europe) ▼ PoM
Dispersible tablets, carglumic acid 200 mg, net price 15-tab pack = £679.00, 60-tab pack = £2685.00. Label: 13

### SODIUM PHENYLBUTYRATE

**Indications** adjunct in long-term treatment of urea cycle disorders (under specialist supervision)

**Cautions** congestive heart failure, hepatic and renal impairment

**Contra-indications** pregnancy (Appendix 4); breast-feeding (Appendix 5)

**Side-effects** amenorrhoea and irregular menstrual cycles, decreased appetite, body odour, taste disturbances; less commonly nausea, vomiting, abdominal pain, peptic ulcer, pancreatitis, rectal bleeding, arrhythmia, oedema, syncope, depression, headache, rash, weight gain, renal tubular acidosis, aplastic anaemia, ecchymoses

**Dose**
- ADULT and CHILD over 20 kg, 9.9–13 g/m² daily in divided doses with meals (max. 20 g daily); CHILD less than 20 kg, 450–600 mg/kg daily in divided doses with meals

**Ammonaps®** (Orphan Europe) PoM
Tablets, sodium phenylbutyrate 500 mg. Contains $Na^+$ 2.7 mmol/tablet. Net price 250-tab pack = £493.00

Granules, sodium phenylbutyrate 940 mg/g. Contains $Na^+$ 5.4 mmol/g. Net price 266-g pack = £860.00
Note Granules should be mixed with food before taking

## 9.8.2 Acute porphyrias

The acute porphyrias (acute intermittent porphyria, variegate porphyria, hereditary coproporphyria and 5-aminolaevulinic acid dehydratase deficiency porphyria) are hereditary disorders of haem biosynthesis; they have a prevalence of about 1 in 10 000 of the population.

Great care must be taken when prescribing for patients with acute porphyria since many drugs can induce acute porphyric crises. Since acute porphyrias are hereditary, relatives of affected individuals should be screened and advised about the potential danger of certain drugs.

Treatment of serious or life-threatening conditions should not be withheld from patients with acute porphyria. Where there is no safe alternative, urinary porphobilinogen excretion should be measured regularly; if it increases or symptoms occur, the drug can be withdrawn and the acute attack treated.

**Haem arginate** is administered by short intravenous infusion as haem replacement in moderate, severe or unremitting acute porphyria crises.

Supplies of haem arginate may be obtained outside office hours from the on-call pharmacist at:

| | |
|---|---|
| St. James's University Hospital, Leeds | (0113) 243 3144 or (0113) 283 7010 |
| St Thomas' Hospital, London | (020) 7188 7188 |

### HAEM ARGINATE
**(Human hemin)**

**Indications** acute porphyrias (acute intermittent porphyria, porphyria variegata, hereditary coproporphyria)

**Cautions** pregnancy (Appendix 4); breast feeding (Appendix 5)

**Side-effects** rarely hypersensitivity reactions and fever; pain and thrombophlebitis at injection site

**Dose**
- By intravenous infusion, ADULT and CHILD 3 mg/kg once daily (max. 250 mg daily) for 4 days; if response inadequate, repeat 4-day course with close biochemical monitoring

**Normosang®** (Orphan Europe) ▼ PoM
Concentrate for intravenous infusion, haem arginate 25 mg/mL, net price 10-mL amp = £281.25

## Drugs unsafe for use in acute porphyrias

The following list contains drugs on the UK market that have been classified as 'unsafe' in porphyria because they have been shown to be porphyrinogenic in animals or *in vitro*, or have been associated with acute attacks in patients. Absence of a drug from the following lists does not necessarily imply that the drug is safe. For many drugs no information about porphyria is available.

Further information may be obtained from:
www.porphyria-europe.com
and also from:

Welsh Medicines Information Centre
University Hospital of Wales
Cardiff, CF14 4XW
Tel: (029) 2074 2979/3877

**Note** Quite modest changes in chemical structure can lead to changes in porphyrinogenicity but where possible general statements have been made about groups of drugs; these should be checked first

## Unsafe Drug groups (check *first*)

| | | | |
|---|---|---|---|
| Amphetamines | Barbiturates[3] | Hormone Replacement Therapy[4] | Statins[6] |
| Anabolic Steroids | Contraceptives, hormonal[4] | Progestogens[4] | Sulphonamides[7] |
| Antidepressants[1] | Ergot Derivatives[5] | | Sulphonylureas[8] |
| Antihistamines[2] | Gold Salts | | |

## Unsafe Drugs (check groups above *first*)

| | | | |
|---|---|---|---|
| Aceclofenac | Diazepam[12] | Mebeverine | Pivmecillinam |
| Alcohol | Diclofenac | Mefenamic Acid[11] | Porfimer |
| Amiodarone | Doxycycline | Meprobamate | Probenecid |
| Baclofen | Econazole | Methyldopa | Pyrazinamide |
| Bromocriptine | Erythromycin | Metoclopramide[11] | Rifabutin[15] |
| Busulfan | Etamsylate | Metolazone | Rifampicin[15] |
| Cabergoline | Ethionamide | Metronidazole[11] | Ritonavir |
| Carbamazepine | Ethosuximide | Metyrapone | Simvastatin |
| Carisoprodol | Etomidate | Miconazole | Spironolactone |
| Chloral Hydrate[9] | Fenfluramine | Mifepristone | Sulfinpyrazone |
| Chlorambucil | Flupentixol | Minoxidil[11] | Sulpiride |
| Chloramphenicol | Griseofulvin | Nalidixic Acid | Tamoxifen |
| Chloroform[10] | Halothane | Nifedipine | Temoporfin |
| Clindamycin | Hydralazine | Nitrofurantoin | Theophylline[16] |
| Clonidine | Hyoscine | Orphenadrine | Tiagabine |
| Cocaine | Indapamide | Oxcarbazepine | Tinidazole |
| Colistin | Indinavir | Oxybutynin | Topiramate |
| Cyclophosphamide[11] | Isometheptene Mucate | Oxycodone | Triclofos[9] |
| Cycloserine | Isoniazid | Oxytetracycline | Trimethoprim |
| Danazol | Ketamine | Pentazocine[14] | Valproate[12] |
| Dapsone | Ketoconazole | Pentoxifylline (oxpentifylline) | Verapamil |
| Dexfenfluramine | Ketorolac | Phenoxybenzamine | Xipamide |
| Dextropropoxyphene | Lidocaine (lignocaine)[13] | Phenytoin | Zuclopenthixol |

1. Includes tricyclic (and related) and MAOIs; fluoxetine thought to be safe.
2. Chlorphenamine, ketotifen, loratadine, and alimemazine (trimeprazine) thought to be safe.
3. Includes primidone and thiopental.
4. Progestogens are more porphyrinogenic than oestrogens; oestrogens may be safe at least in replacement doses. Progestogens should be avoided whenever possible by all women susceptible to acute porphyria; however, where non-hormonal contraception is inappropriate, progestogens may be used with extreme caution if the potential benefit outweighs risk. The risk of an acute attack is greatest in women who have had a previous attack or are aged under 30 years. Long-acting progestogen preparations should never be used in those at risk of acute porphyria.
5. Includes ergometrine (oxytocin probably safe), lisuride and pergolide.
6. Rosuvastatin is thought to be safe.
7. Includes co-trimoxazole and sulfasalazine.
8. Glipizide is thought to be safe.
9. Although evidence of hazard is uncertain, manufacturer advises avoid.
10. Small amounts in medicines probably safe.
11. May be used with caution if safer alternative not available.
12. Status epilepticus has been treated successfully with intravenous diazepam.
13. For local anaesthesia, bupivacaine, lidocaine (lignocaine), and prilocaine are thought to be safe.
14. Buprenorphine, codeine, diamorphine, dihydrocodeine, fentanyl, morphine, and pethidine are thought to be safe.
15. Rifamycins have been used in a few patients without evidence of harm—use with caution if safer alternative not available.
16. Includes aminophylline.

# 10 Musculoskeletal and joint diseases

**10.1 Drugs used in rheumatic diseases and gout** 504
10.1.1 Non-steroidal anti-inflammatory drugs 505
10.1.2 Corticosteroids 514
10.1.2.1 Systemic corticosteroids 514
10.1.2.2 Local corticosteroid injections 515
10.1.3 Drugs which suppress the rheumatic disease process 516
10.1.4 Gout and cytotoxic-induced hyperuricaemia 524
**10.2 Drugs used in neuromuscular disorders** 526
10.2.1 Drugs which enhance neuromuscular transmission 526
10.2.2 Skeletal muscle relaxants 527
**10.3 Drugs for the relief of soft-tissue inflammation** 530
10.3.1 Enzymes 530
10.3.2 Rubefacients and other topical antirheumatics 531

This chapter includes advice on the drug management of the following:
dental and orofacial pain, p. 506
extravasation, p. 530
myasthenia gravis, p. 526
osteoarthritis and soft-tissue disorders, p. 504
rheumatoid arthritis and other inflammatory disorders, p. 504

For treatment of septic arthritis see Table 1, section 5.1.

## 10.1 Drugs used in rheumatic diseases and gout

**10.1.1** Non-steroidal anti-inflammatory drugs
**10.1.2** Corticosteroids
**10.1.3** Drugs which suppress the rheumatic disease process
**10.1.4** Gout and cytotoxic-induced hyperuricaemia

### Rheumatoid arthritis and other inflammatory disorders

A non-steroidal anti-inflammatory drug (NSAID) is indicated for pain and stiffness resulting from inflammatory rheumatic disease. Drugs are also used to influence the disease process itself (section 10.1.3). For rheumatoid arthritis these disease-modifying antirheumatic drugs (DMARDs) include penicillamine, gold salts, antimalarials (chloroquine and hydroxychloroquine), drugs that affect the immune response, and sulfasalazine; corticosteroids may also be of value (section 10.1.2.1). Drugs which may affect the disease process in psoriatic arthritis include sulfasalazine, gold salts, azathioprine, methotrexate (section 10.1.3), and etanercept. For long-term control of gout uricosuric drugs and allopurinol (section 10.1.4) may be used.

### Osteoarthritis and soft-tissue disorders

In osteoarthritis (sometimes called degenerative joint disease or osteoarthrosis) non-drug measures such as weight reduction and exercise should be encouraged. For pain relief in osteoarthritis and soft-tissue disorders, paracetamol (section 4.7.1) is often adequate and should be used first. Alternatively a low-dose of a NSAID (e.g. ibuprofen up to 1.2 g daily) may be used. If pain relief with either drug is inadequate, both paracetamol (in a full dose of 4 g daily) and a low-dose of a NSAID may be required; if necessary the dose of the NSAID may be increased or a low dose of an opioid analgesic given with paracetamol (as co-codamol 8/500 or co-dydramol 10/500).

Topical treatment including application of a NSAID or capsaicin 0.025% (section 10.3.2) may provide some pain relief in osteoarthritis.

Intra-articular corticosteroid injections (section 10.1.2.2) may produce temporary benefit in osteoarthritis, especially if associated with soft-tissue inflammation.

Hyaluronic acid and its derivatives are available for osteoarthritis of the knee. Sodium hyaluronate (*Arthrease®*, *Durolane®*, *Fermathron®*, *Hyalgan®*, *Orthovisc®*, *Ostenil®*, *Suplasyn®*), or hylan G-F 20 (*Synvisc®*) is injected intra-articularly to supplement natural hyaluronic acid in the synovial fluid. These injections may reduce pain over 1–6 months but they are associated with short-term increase in knee inflammation.

## 10.1.1 Non-steroidal anti-inflammatory drugs

In *single doses* non-steroidal anti-inflammatory drugs (NSAIDs) have analgesic activity comparable to that of paracetamol (section 4.7.1), but paracetamol is preferred, particularly in the elderly (see also Prescribing for the Elderly, p. 19).

In regular *full dosage* NSAIDs have both a lasting analgesic and an anti-inflammatory effect which makes them particularly useful for the treatment of continuous or regular pain associated with inflammation. Therefore, although paracetamol often gives adequate pain control in osteoarthritis, NSAIDs are more appropriate than paracetamol or the opioid analgesics in the *inflammatory arthritides* (e.g. rheumatoid arthritis) and in some cases of *advanced osteoarthritis*. They may also be of benefit in the less well defined conditions of *back pain* and *soft-tissue disorders*.

**Choice** Differences in anti-inflammatory activity between different NSAIDs are small, but there is considerable variation in individual patient tolerance and response. About 60% of patients will respond to any NSAID; of the others, those who do not respond to one may well respond to another. Pain relief starts soon after taking the first dose and a full analgesic effect should normally be obtained within a week, whereas an anti-inflammatory effect may not be achieved (or may not be clinically assessable) for up to 3 weeks. If appropriate responses are not obtained within these times, another NSAID should be tried.

The main differences between NSAIDs are in the incidence and type of side-effects. Before treatment is started the prescriber should weigh efficacy against possible side-effects.

NSAIDs vary in their selectivity for inhibiting different types of cyclo-oxygenase; selective inhibition of cyclo-oxygenase-2 improves gastro-intestinal tolerance. A number of other factors also determine susceptibility to gastro-intestinal effects and a NSAID should be chosen on the basis of the incidence of gastro-intestinal and other side-effects.

**Ibuprofen** is a propionic acid derivative with anti-inflammatory, analgesic, and antipyretic properties. It has fewer side-effects than other non-selective NSAIDs but its anti-inflammatory properties are weaker. Doses of 1.6 to 2.4 g daily are needed for rheumatoid arthritis and it is unsuitable for conditions where inflammation is prominent such as acute gout. **Dexibuprofen** is the active enantiomer of ibuprofen. It has similar properties to ibuprofen and is licensed for the relief of mild to moderate pain and inflammation.

Other propionic acid derivatives:

**Naproxen** is one of the first choices because it combines good efficacy with a low incidence of side-effects (but more than ibuprofen, see CSM comment below).

**Fenbufen** is claimed to be associated with less gastro-intestinal bleeding, but there is a high risk of rashes (see p. 510).

**Fenoprofen** is as effective as naproxen, and **flurbiprofen** may be slightly more effective. Both are associated with slightly more gastro-intestinal side-effects than ibuprofen.

**Ketoprofen** has anti-inflammatory properties similar to ibuprofen and has more side-effects (see also CSM comment below). **Dexketoprofen**, an isomer of ketoprofen, has been introduced for the short-term relief of mild to moderate pain.

**Tiaprofenic acid** is as effective as naproxen; it has more side-effects than ibuprofen (**important:** reports of severe cystitis, see CSM advice on p. 513).

Drugs with properties similar to those of propionic acid derivatives:

**Diclofenac** and **aceclofenac** have actions similar to that of naproxen; their side-effects are also similar to naproxen.

**Diflunisal** is an aspirin derivative but its clinical effect more closely resembles that of the propionic acid derivatives than that of its parent compound. Its long duration of action allows twice-daily administration.

**Etodolac** has comparable efficacy to naproxen; it is licensed for symptomatic relief in osteoarthritis and rheumatoid arthritis.

**Indometacin** (indomethacin) has an action equal to or superior to that of naproxen, but with a high incidence of side-effects including headaches, dizziness, and gastro-intestinal disturbances (see also CSM comment below).

**Mefenamic acid** has minor anti-inflammatory properties. Occasionally, it has been associated with diarrhoea and haemolytic anaemia which require discontinuation of treatment.

**Meloxicam** is licensed for the short-term symptomatic relief of osteoarthritis and long-term symptomatic treatment of rheumatoid arthritis and ankylosing spondylitis.

**Nabumetone** is comparable in effect to naproxen.

**Piroxicam** is as effective as naproxen and has a prolonged duration of action which permits once-daily administration. It has more gastro-intestinal side-effects than ibuprofen, especially in the elderly (see also CSM comment below).

**Sulindac** is similar in tolerance to naproxen.

**Tenoxicam** is similar in activity and tolerance to naproxen. Its long half-life allows once-daily administration.

**Tolfenamic acid** is licensed for the treatment of migraine (section 4.7.4.1)

**Ketorolac** and the selective inhibitor of cyclo-oxygenase-2, **parecoxib** are licensed for the short-term management of postoperative pain (section 15.1.4.2).

The selective inhibitors of cyclo-oxygenase-2, **etoricoxib**, **celecoxib**, and **lumiracoxib** are as effective as non-selective NSAIDs such as diclofenac and naproxen. Short-term data indicate that the risk of serious upper gastro-intestinal events is lower with selective inhibitors compared to non-selective NSAIDs; this advantage may be lost in patients who require concomitant low-dose aspirin. There are concerns about the cardiovascular safety of cyclo-oxygenase-2 selective inhibitors (see below).

**Celecoxib** and **etoricoxib** are licensed for symptomatic relief of osteoarthritis and rheumatoid arthritis; **etoricoxib** is also licensed for the relief of pain from acute gout. **Lumiracoxib** is licensed for osteoarthritis and moderate to severe pain.

> **Cyclo-oxygenase-2 inhibitors and cardiovascular events**
> In the light of emerging concerns about cardiovascular safety, cyclo-oxygenase-2 selective inhibitors should be used in preference to non-selective NSAIDs **only** when specifically indicated (i.e. for patients who are at a particularly high risk of developing gastroduodenal ulcer, perforation, or bleeding) *and* after an assessment of cardiovascular risk. Furthermore, the CSM has advised (August 2005) that patients who have ischaemic heart disease or cerebrovascular disease should not receive a cyclo-oxygenase-2 selective inhibitor.

**Dental and orofacial pain** Most mild to moderate dental pain and inflammation is effectively relieved by NSAIDs. Those used for dental pain include **ibuprofen** and **aspirin**. **Diflunisal** is also licensed for dental pain. Postoperative use of diflunisal has been associated with localised osteitis (dry socket) but this remains to be confirmed. Ibuprofen can be used in children.

Like aspirin and diflunisal, ibuprofen causes gastro-intestinal irritation, but in an appraisal of the relative safety of 7 non-selective NSAIDs the CSM has assessed ibuprofen to have the lowest risk of serious gastro-intestinal side-effects (see below).

For further information on the management of dental and orofacial pain, see p. 217.

**Cautions and contra-indications** NSAIDs should be used with caution in the elderly (risk of serious side-effects and fatalities, see also Prescribing for the Elderly p. 19), in allergic disorders (they are **contra-indicated** in patients with a history of hypersensitivity to aspirin or any other NSAID—which includes those in whom attacks of asthma, angioedema, urticaria or rhinitis have been precipitated by aspirin or any other NSAID), during pregnancy and breast-feeding (see Appendix 4 and Appendix 5), and in coagulation defects. Long-term use of some NSAIDs is associated with reduced female fertility which is reversible on stopping treatment.

In patients with renal, cardiac, or hepatic impairment caution is required since NSAIDs may impair renal function (see also under Side-effects, below and Appendix 2 and Appendix 3); the dose should be kept as **low as possible** and renal function should be **monitored**.

All NSAIDs are contra-indicated in severe heart failure. The selective inhibitors of cyclo-oxygenase-2 (celecoxib, etoricoxib, lumiracoxib, and parecoxib) are **contra-indicated** in ischaemic heart disease, cerebrovascular disease, peripheral arterial disease, and moderate or severe heart failure. The selective inhibitors of cyclo-oxygenase-2 should be used with caution in patients with a history of cardiac failure, left ventricular dysfunction, hypertension, in patients with oedema for any other reason, and in patients with risk factors for developing heart disease.

The CSM has advised that non-selective NSAIDs are contra-indicated in patients with previous or active peptic ulceration and that selective inhibitors of cyclo-oxygenase-2 are contra-indicated in active peptic ulceration (see also **CSM advice** below). While it is preferable to avoid NSAIDs in patients with active or previous gastro-intestinal ulceration or bleeding, and to withdraw them if gastro-intestinal lesions develop, nevertheless patients with serious rheumatic diseases (e.g. rheumatoid arthritis) are usually dependent on NSAIDs for effective relief of pain and stiffness. For advice on the prophylaxis and treatment of NSAID-associated peptic ulcers, see section 1.3.

For **interactions** of NSAIDs, see Appendix 1 (NSAIDs)

**Side-effects** Gastro-intestinal discomfort, nausea, diarrhoea, and occasionally bleeding and ulceration occur (see also CSM advice below). Systemic as well as local effects of NSAIDs contribute to gastro-intestinal damage; taking oral formulations with milk or food, or using enteric-coated formulations, or changing the route of administration may only partially reduce symptoms such as dyspepsia. Those at risk of duodenal or gastric ulceration (including the elderly) who need to continue NSAID treatment should receive either a selective inhibitor of cyclo-oxygenase-2 alone, or a non-selective NSAID with gastroprotective treatment (section 1.3).

Other side-effects include hypersensitivity reactions (particularly rashes, angioedema, and bronchospasm—see CSM advice below), headache, dizziness, nervousness, depression, drowsiness, insomnia, vertigo, hearing disturbances such as tinnitus, photosensitivity, and haematuria. Blood disorders have also occurred. Fluid retention may occur (rarely precipitating congestive heart failure); blood pressure may be raised.

Renal failure may be provoked by NSAIDs especially in patients with renal impairment (**important**, see also under Cautions above). Rarely, papillary necrosis or interstitial fibrosis associated with NSAIDs may lead to renal failure.

Hepatic damage, alveolitis, pulmonary eosinophilia, pancreatitis, eye changes, Stevens-Johnson syndrome and toxic epidermal necrolysis are other rare side-effects. Induction of or exacerbation of colitis has been reported. Aseptic meningitis has been reported rarely with NSAIDs; patients with connective-tissue disorders such as systemic lupus erythematosus may be especially susceptible.

**Overdosage:** see Emergency Treatment of Poisoning, p. 29.

**CSM advice (gastro-intestinal side-effects)**

All NSAIDs are associated with serious gastro-intestinal toxicity; the risk is higher in the elderly. Evidence on the relative safety of 7 **non-selective** NSAIDs indicates differences in the risks of serious upper gastro-intestinal side-effects. **Azapropazone** [discontinued] is associated with the *highest risk* and **ibuprofen** with the *lowest*; **piroxicam**, **ketoprofen**, **indometacin**, **naproxen** and **diclofenac** are associated with *intermediate risks* (possibly higher in the case of piroxicam). **Selective inhibitors of cyclo-oxygenase-2** are associated with a *lower risk* of serious upper gastro-intestinal side-effects than non-selective NSAIDs.

Recommendations are that NSAIDs associated with low risk e.g. ibuprofen are *generally preferred*, to start at the *lowest recommended dose, not to use more than one* oral NSAID at a time, and to remember that all NSAIDs (including selective inhibitors of cyclo-oxygenase-2) are *contra-indicated* in patients with active peptic ulceration. The CSM also contra-indicates non-selective NSAIDs in patients with a history of peptic ulceration.

The combination of a NSAID and low-dose aspirin may increase the risk of gastro-intestinal side-effects; this combination should only be used if absolutely necessary and the patient monitored closely

**CSM warning (asthma)**

Any degree of worsening of asthma may be related to the ingestion of NSAIDs, either prescribed or (in the case of ibuprofen and others) purchased over the counter.

## IBUPROFEN

**Indications** pain and inflammation in rheumatic disease (including juvenile arthritis) and other musculoskeletal disorders; mild to moderate pain including dysmenorrhoea; postoperative analgesia; migraine; fever and pain in children; post-immunisation pyrexia (section 14.1)

**Cautions** see notes above; breast-feeding (Appendix 5); **interactions**: Appendix 1 (NSAIDs)

**Contra-indications** see notes above

**Side-effects** see notes above; **overdosage**: see Emergency Treatment of Poisoning, p. 29

**Dose**

- Initially 1.2–1.8 g daily in 3–4 divided doses preferably after food; increased if necessary to max. 2.4 g daily; maintenance dose of 0.6–1.2 g daily may be adequate
- Juvenile rheumatoid arthritis, CHILD over 5 kg body-weight 30–40 mg/kg daily in 3–4 divided doses
- Fever and pain in children, CHILD over 5 kg body-weight 20–30 mg/kg daily in divided doses *or* 3–6 months (body-weight over 5 kg) 50 mg 3 times daily, 6 months–1 year 50 mg 3–4 times daily, 1–3 years 100 mg 3 times daily, 4–6 years 150 mg 3 times daily, 7–9 years 200 mg 3 times daily, 10–12 years 300 mg 3 times daily

**Ibuprofen** (Non-proprietary) PoM

Tablets, coated, ibuprofen 200 mg, net price 84-tab pack = £2.12; 400 mg, 84-tab pack = £2.66; 600 mg, 84-tab pack = £4.10. Label: 21

Brands include *Arthrofen®*, *Ebufac®*, *Rimafen®*

Oral suspension, ibuprofen 100 mg/5 mL, net price 100 mL = £2.15, 150 mL = £2.71, 500 mL = £8.88. Label: 21

Note Sugar-free versions are available and can be ordered by specifying 'sugar-free' on the prescription

Brands include *Calprofen®*, *Fenpaed®*, *Galprofen®*, *Nurofen® for Children*, *Orbifen® for Children*

Dental prescribing on NHS Ibuprofen Tablets and Ibuprofen Oral Suspension Sugar-free may be prescribed

**Brufen®** (Abbott) PoM

Tablets, all magenta, ibuprofen 200 mg (s/c), net price 20 = 82p; 400 mg (s/c), 20 = £1.63; 600 mg (f/c), 20 = £2.45. Label: 21

Syrup, orange, ibuprofen 100 mg/5 mL. Net price 500 mL = £8.07. Label: 21

Granules, effervescent, ibuprofen 600 mg/sachet. Net price 20-sachet pack = £6.80. Label: 13, 21

Note Contains sodium approx. 9 mmol/sachet

### Preparations on sale to the public

Many preparations on sale to the public contain **ibuprofen**. To identify the active ingredients in such preparations consult the product literature or manufacturer.

Note The correct proprietary name should be ascertained—many products have very similar names but different active ingredients.

### Topical preparations

Section 10.3.2

### Modified release

**Brufen Retard®** (Abbott) PoM

Tablets, m/r, f/c, ibuprofen 800 mg, net price 56-tab pack = £6.74. Label: 25, 27

Dose 2 tablets daily as a single dose, preferably in the early evening, increased in severe cases to 3 tablets daily in 2 divided doses; CHILD not recommended

**Fenbid®** (Goldshield) PoM

Spansule® (= capsule m/r), maroon/pink, enclosing off-white pellets, ibuprofen 300 mg. Net price 120-cap pack = £9.64. Label: 25

Dose 1–3 capsules every 12 hours; CHILD not recommended

## ACECLOFENAC

**Indications** pain and inflammation in rheumatoid arthritis, osteoarthritis and ankylosing spondylitis

**Cautions** see notes above; avoid in porphyria (section 9.8.2); breast-feeding (Appendix 5); **interactions**: Appendix 1 (NSAIDs)

**Contra-indications** see notes above

**Side-effects** see notes above

**Dose**

- 100 mg twice daily; CHILD not recommended

**Preservex®** (UCB Pharma) PoM

Tablets, f/c, aceclofenac 100 mg, net price 60-tab pack = £9.63. Label: 21

## ACEMETACIN

**(Glycolic acid ester of indometacin)**

**Indications** pain and inflammation in rheumatic disease and other musculoskeletal disorders; postoperative analgesia

**Cautions** see under Indometacin and notes above; breast-feeding (Appendix 5); **interactions:** Appendix 1 (NSAIDs)

**Driving** Dizziness may affect performance of skilled tasks (e.g. driving)

**Contra-indications** see notes above

**Side-effects** see under Indometacin and notes above

**Dose**

- 120 mg daily in divided doses with food, increased if necessary to 180 mg daily; CHILD not recommended

**Emflex®** (Merck) PoM

Capsules, yellow/orange, acemetacin 60 mg, net price 90-cap pack = £23.50. Label: 21, counselling, driving

## CELECOXIB

**Indications** pain and inflammation in osteoarthritis or rheumatoid arthritis

**Cautions** see notes above; breast-feeding (Appendix 5); **interactions**: Appendix 1 (NSAIDs)

**Contra-indications** see notes above; sulphonamide sensitivity; inflammatory bowel disease

**Side-effects** see notes above; flatulence, insomnia, pharyngitis, sinusitis; less frequently stomatitis, constipation, palpitations, fatigue, paraesthesia, muscle cramps; rarely taste alteration, alopecia; very rarely aggravation of epilepsy

**Dose**

- Osteoarthritis, 200 mg daily in 1–2 divided doses, increased if necessary to max. 200 mg twice daily; CHILD not recommended
- Rheumatoid arthritis, 200–400 mg daily in 2 divided doses; ELDERLY initially 200 mg daily in 2 divided doses; max. 200 mg twice daily; CHILD not recommended

**Celebrex®** (Pharmacia) PoM

Capsules, celecoxib 100 mg (white/blue), net price 60-cap pack = £21.55; 200 mg (white/gold), 30-cap pack = £21.55

## DEXIBUPROFEN

**Indications** pain and inflammation associated with osteoarthritis and other musculoskeletal disorders; mild to moderate pain and inflammation including dysmenorrhoea and dental pain

**Cautions** see notes above; systemic lupus erythematosus and other connective tissue disorders; breast-feeding (Appendix 5); **interactions**: Appendix 1 (NSAIDs)

**Contra-indications** see notes above

**Side-effects** see notes above

**Dose**

- 600–900 mg daily in up to 3 divided doses; increased if necessary to max. 1.2 g daily (900 mg daily for dysmenorrhoea); max. single dose 400 mg (300 mg for dysmenorrhoea); CHILD not recommended

**Seractil®** (Genus) ▼ PoM

Tablets, f/c, dexibuprofen 300 mg, net price 60–tab pack = £9.47; 400 mg (scored) 60–tab pack = £9.47. Label: 21

## DEXKETOPROFEN

**Indications** short-term treatment of mild to moderate pain including dysmenorrhoea

**Cautions** see notes above; breast-feeding (Appendix 5); **interactions**: Appendix 1 (NSAIDs)

**Contra-indications** see notes above

**Side-effects** see notes above

**Dose**

- 12.5 mg every 4–6 hours *or* 25 mg every 8 hours; max. 75 mg daily; ELDERLY initially max. 50 mg daily; CHILD not recommended

**Keral®** (Menarini) PoM

Tablets, f/c, scored, dexketoprofen (as trometamol) 25 mg, net price 20-tab pack = £3.67, 50-tab pack = £9.18. Label: 22

## DICLOFENAC SODIUM

**Indications** pain and inflammation in rheumatic disease (including juvenile arthritis) and other musculoskeletal disorders; acute gout; postoperative pain

**Cautions** see notes above; breast-feeding (Appendix 5); **interactions:** Appendix 1 (NSAIDs)

**Contra-indications** see notes above; porphyria (section 9.8.2)

**Intravenous use** Additional contra-indications include concomitant NSAID or anticoagulant use (including low-dose heparin), history of haemorrhagic diathesis, history of confirmed or suspected cerebrovascular bleeding, operations with high risk of haemorrhage, history of asthma, moderate or severe renal impairment, hypovolaemia, dehydration

**Side-effects** see notes above; suppositories may cause rectal irritation; injection site reactions

**Dose**

- By mouth, 75–150 mg daily in 2–3 divided doses
- By deep intramuscular injection into the gluteal muscle, acute exacerbations of pain and postoperative pain, 75 mg once daily (twice daily in severe cases) for max. of 2 days

  Ureteric colic, 75 mg then a further 75 mg after 30 minutes if necessary
- By intravenous infusion (in hospital setting), 75 mg repeated if necessary after 4–6 hours for max. 2 days

  Prevention of postoperative pain, initially after surgery 25–50 mg over 15–60 minutes then 5 mg/hour for max. 2 days
- By rectum in suppositories, 75–150 mg daily in divided doses
- Max. total daily dose by any route 150 mg
- CHILD 1–12 years, juvenile arthritis, by mouth *or* by rectum, 1–3 mg/kg daily in divided doses (25 mg e/c tablets, 12.5 mg and 25 mg suppositories only)
- CHILD 6–12 years, postoperative pain, by rectum, 1–2 mg/kg daily in divided doses (12.5 mg and 25 mg suppositories only) for max. 4 days

**Diclofenac Sodium** (Non-proprietary) PoM

Tablets, both e/c, diclofenac sodium 25 mg, net price 84-tab pack = £1.52; 50 mg, 84-tab pack = £2.14. Label: 5, 25

**Note** Other brands include *Acoflam®*, *Defenac®*, *Dicloflex®*, *Diclovol®*, *Diclozip®*, *Fenactol®*, *Flamrase®*, *Lofensaid®*, *Volraman®*

Suppositories, diclofenac sodium 100 mg, net price 10 = £3.04

Brands include *Econac®*

Injection, diclofenac sodium 25 mg/mL. Net price 3-mL amp = 74p

**Note** Licensed for intramuscular use

10 Musculoskeletal and joint diseases

**Voltarol®** (Novartis) PoM

Tablets, both e/c, diclofenac sodium 25 mg (yellow), net price 84-tab pack = £3.67; 50 mg (brown), 84-tab pack = £5.71. Label: 5, 25

Dispersible tablets, sugar-free, pink, diclofenac, equivalent to diclofenac sodium 50 mg, net price 21-tab pack = £5.63. Label: 13, 21

Note Voltarol Dispersible tablets are more suitable for **short-term** use in acute conditions for which treatment required for no more than 3 months (no information on use beyond 3 months)

Injection, diclofenac sodium 25 mg/mL. Net price 3-mL amp = 83p

Excipients include benzyl alcohol (see Excipients, p. 2)

Suppositories, diclofenac sodium 12.5 mg, net price 10 = 71p; 25 mg, 10 = £1.26; 50 mg, 10 = £2.07; 100 mg, 10 = £3.70

Emulgel® gel, section 10.3.2

### Diclofenac potassium

**Voltarol® Rapid** (Novartis) PoM

Tablets, s/c, diclofenac potassium 25 mg (red), net price 28-tab pack = £3.67; 50 mg (brown), 28-tab pack = £7.03

Dose rheumatic disease, musculoskeletal disorders, acute gout, post-operative pain, 75–150 mg daily in 2–3 divided doses; CHILD over 14 years, 75–100 mg daily in 2–3 divided doses

Migraine, 50 mg at onset, repeated after 2 hours if necessary then after 4–6 hours; max. 200 mg in 24 hours; CHILD not recommended

### Modified release

**Diclomax SR®** (Provalis) PoM

Capsules, m/r, yellow, diclofenac sodium 75 mg. Net price 56-cap pack = £12.10. Label: 21, 25

Dose 1 capsule 1–2 times daily *or* 2 capsules once daily, preferably with food; CHILD not recommended

**Diclomax Retard®** (Provalis) PoM

Capsules, m/r, diclofenac sodium 100 mg. Net price 28-tab pack = £8.71. Label: 21, 25

Dose 1 capsule daily preferably with food; CHILD not recommended

**Motifene® 75 mg** (Sankyo) PoM

Capsules, e/c, m/r, diclofenac sodium 75 mg (enclosing e/c pellets containing diclofenac sodium 25 mg and m/r pellets containing diclofenac sodium 50 mg). Net price 56-cap pack = £8.00. Label: 25

Dose 1 capsule 1-2 times daily; CHILD not recommended

**Voltarol® 75 mg SR** (Novartis) PoM

Tablets, m/r, pink, diclofenac sodium 75 mg. Net price 28-tab pack = £8.08; 56-tab pack = £16.15. Label: 21, 25

Dose 75 mg 1–2 times daily preferably with food; CHILD not recommended

Note Other brands of modified-release tablets containing diclofenac sodium 75 mg include *Acoflam® 75 SR, Defenac® SR, Dexomon® 75 SR, Dicloflex® 75 SR, Diclovol® SR, Fenactol® 75 mg SR, Flamatak® 75 MR, Flamrase® SR, Flexotard® MR 75, Rheumatac® Retard 75, Rhumalgan® CR, Slofenac® SR, Volsaid® Retard 75*

**Voltarol® Retard** (Novartis) PoM

Tablets, m/r, red, diclofenac sodium 100 mg. Net price 28-tab pack = £11.84. Label: 21, 25

Dose 1 tablet daily preferably with food; CHILD not recommended

Note Other brands of modified-release tablets containing diclofenac sodium 100 mg include *Acoflam® Retard, Defenac® Retard, Dexomon® Retard 100, Dicloflex® Retard, Diclovol® Retard, Fenactol® Retard 100 mg, Flamatak® 100 MR, Flamrase® SR, Rhumalgan® CR, Slofenac® SR, Volsaid® Retard 100*

### With misoprostol

For **cautions**, **contra-indications**, and **side-effects** of misoprostol, see section 1.3.4

**Arthrotec®** (Pharmacia) PoM

Arthrotec® 50 tablets, diclofenac sodium (in e/c core) 50 mg, misoprostol 200 micrograms. Net price 60-tab pack = £13.31; Label: 21, 25

Dose prophylaxis against NSAID-induced gastroduodenal ulceration in patients requiring diclofenac for rheumatoid arthritis or osteoarthritis, 1 tablet 2–3 times daily with food; CHILD not recommended

Arthrotec® 75 tablets, diclofenac sodium (in e/c core) 75 mg, misoprostol 200 micrograms. Net price 60-tab pack = £17.59. Label: 21, 25

Dose prophylaxis against NSAID-induced gastroduodenal ulceration in patients requiring diclofenac for rheumatoid arthritis or osteoarthritis, 1 tablet twice daily with food; CHILD not recommended

## DIFLUNISAL

**Indications** pain and inflammation in rheumatic disease and other musculoskeletal disorders; mild to moderate pain including dysmenorrhoea

**Cautions** see notes above; breast-feeding (Appendix 5); **interactions:** Appendix 1 (NSAIDs)

**Contra-indications** see notes above

**Side-effects** see notes above

**Dose**

- Mild to moderate pain, initially 1 g, then 500 mg every 12 hours (increased to max. 500 mg every 8 hours if necessary); CHILD not recommended
- Osteoarthritis, rheumatoid arthritis, 0.5–1 g daily as a single daily dose *or* in 2 divided doses; CHILD not recommended
- Dysmenorrhoea, initially 1 g, then 500 mg every 12 hours; CHILD not recommended

**Dolobid®** (MSD) PoM

Tablets, both f/c, diflunisal 250 mg (peach), net price 60-tab pack = £5.41; 500 mg (orange), 60-tab pack = £10.82. Label: 21, 25, counselling, avoid aluminium hydroxide

Dental prescribing on NHS May be prescribed as Diflusinal Tablets

## ETODOLAC

**Indications** pain and inflammation in rheumatoid arthritis and osteoarthritis

**Cautions** see notes above; breast-feeding (Appendix 5); **interactions:** Appendix 1 (NSAIDs)

**Contra-indications** see notes above

**Side-effects** see notes above

**Dose**

- 600 mg daily in 1–2 divided doses; CHILD not recommended

**Etodolac** (Non-proprietary) PoM

Capsules, etodolac 300 mg, net price 60-cap pack = £8.14

Brands include *Eccoxolac®*

### Modified release

**Lodine SR®** (Shire) PoM

Tablets, m/r, light-grey, etodolac 600 mg. Net price 30-tab pack = £15.50. Label: 25

Dose 1 tablet daily; CHILD not recommended

## ETORICOXIB

**Indications** pain and inflammation in osteoarthritis and in rheumatoid arthritis; acute gout

**Cautions** see notes above; monitor blood pressure; breast-feeding (Appendix 5); **interactions:** Appendix 1 (NSAIDs)

**Contra-indications** see notes above; inflammatory bowel disease; uncontrolled hypertension

**Side-effects** see notes above; also dry mouth, taste disturbance, mouth ulcers, flatulence, constipation, appetite and weight changes, chest pain, fatigue, paraesthesia, influenza-like syndrome, myalgia

**Dose**

- Osteoarthritis, ADULT and ADOLESCENT over 16 years, 60 mg once daily
- Rheumatoid arthritis, ADULT and ADOLESCENT over 16 years, 90 mg once daily
- Acute gout, ADULT and ADOLESCENT over 16 years, 120 mg once daily

**Arcoxia®** (MSD) ▼ PoM
Tablets, f/c, etoricoxib 60 mg (green), net price 28-tab pack = £22.96; 90 mg (white), 28-tab pack = £22.96; 120 mg (pale green), 7-tab pack = £5.74

## FENBUFEN

**Indications** pain and inflammation in rheumatic disease and other musculoskeletal disorders

**Cautions** see notes above; breast-feeding (Appendix 5); **interactions:** Appendix 1 (NSAIDs)

**Contra-indications** see notes above

**Side-effects** see notes above, but also high risk of rashes especially in seronegative rheumatoid arthritis, psoriatic arthritis and in women (discontinue immediately); erythema multiforme and Stevens-Johnson syndrome reported; also allergic interstitial lung disorders (may follow rashes)

**Dose**

- 300 mg in the morning and 600 mg at bed-time *or* 450 mg twice daily; CHILD under 14 years not recommended

**Fenbufen** (Non-proprietary) PoM
Capsules, fenbufen 300 mg, net price 84-cap pack = £20.71. Label: 21

Tablets, fenbufen 300 mg, net price 84-tab pack = £8.59; 450 mg, 56-tab pack = £10.74. Label: 21

**Lederfen®** (Goldshield) PoM
Capsules, dark blue, fenbufen 300 mg. Net price 84-cap pack = £20.71. Label: 21

Tablets, both light blue, f/c, fenbufen 300 mg, net price 84-tab pack = £20.71; 450 mg, 56-tab pack = £18.83. Label: 21

## FENOPROFEN

**Indications** pain and inflammation in rheumatic disease and other musculoskeletal disorders; mild to moderate pain

**Cautions** see notes above; breast-feeding (Appendix 5); **interactions:** Appendix 1 (NSAIDs)

**Contra-indications** see notes above

**Side-effects** see notes above; upper respiratory-tract infection, nasopharyngitis, and cystitis also reported

**Dose**

- 300–600 mg 3–4 times daily with food; max. 3 g daily; CHILD not recommended

**Fenopron®** (Typharm) PoM
Tablets, both orange, fenoprofen (as calcium salt) 300 mg (*Fenopron®* 300), net price 100-tab pack = £9.45; 600 mg (*Fenopron®* 600, scored), 100-tab pack = £18.29. Label: 21

## FLURBIPROFEN

**Indications** pain and inflammation in rheumatic disease and other musculoskeletal disorders; mild to moderate pain including dysmenorrhoea; migraine; postoperative analgesia; relief of sore throat (section 12.3.1)

**Cautions** see notes above; breast-feeding (Appendix 5); **interactions:** Appendix 1 (NSAIDs)

**Contra-indications** see notes above

**Side-effects** see notes above

**Dose**

- 150–200 mg daily in divided doses, increased in acute conditions to 300 mg daily; CHILD not recommended
- Dysmenorrhoea, initially 100 mg, then 50–100 mg every 4–6 hours; max. 300 mg daily; CHILD not recommended

**Flurbiprofen** (Non-proprietary) PoM
Tablets, flurbiprofen 50 mg, net price 20 = £3.19; 100 mg, 20 = £5.93. Label: 21

**Froben®** (Abbott) PoM
Tablets, both yellow, s/c, flurbiprofen 50 mg, net price 20 = £2.18; 100 mg, 20 = £4.13. Label: 21

### Modified release

**Froben SR®** (Abbott) PoM
Capsules, m/r, yellow, enclosing off-white beads, flurbiprofen 200 mg. Net price 30-cap pack = £7.84. Label: 21, 25

**Dose** rheumatic disease, 1 capsule daily, preferably in the evening; CHILD not recommended

## INDOMETACIN
### (Indomethacin)

**Indications** pain and moderate to severe inflammation in rheumatic disease and other acute musculoskeletal disorders; acute gout; dysmenorrhoea; closure of ductus arteriosus (section 7.1.1.1)

**Cautions** see notes above; also epilepsy, parkinsonism, psychiatric disturbances; during prolonged therapy ophthalmic and blood examinations particularly advisable; avoid rectal administration in proctitis and haemorrhoids; breast-feeding (Appendix 5); **interactions:** Appendix 1 (NSAIDs)

**Driving** Dizziness may affect performance of skilled tasks (e.g. driving)

**Contra-indications** see notes above

**Side-effects** see notes above; frequently gastro-intestinal disturbances (including diarrhoea), headache, dizziness, and light-headedness; also gastro-intestinal ulceration and bleeding; rarely, drowsiness, confusion, insomnia, convulsions, psychiatric disturbances, depression, syncope, blood disorders (particularly thrombocytopenia), hypertension, hyperglycaemia, blurred vision, corneal deposits, peripheral neuropathy, and intestinal strictures; suppositories may cause rectal irritation and occasional bleeding

**Dose**
- By mouth, rheumatic disease, 50–200 mg daily in divided doses, with food; CHILD not recommended
  Acute gout, 150–200 mg daily in divided doses
  Dysmenorrhoea, up to 75 mg daily
- By rectum in suppositories, 100 mg at night and in the morning if required; CHILD not recommended
  Combined oral and rectal treatment, max. total daily dose 150–200 mg

**Indometacin** (Non-proprietary) PoM
Capsules, indometacin 25 mg, net price 20 = £1.26; 50 mg, 20 = £1.06. Label: 21, counselling, driving, see above
Brands include *Rimacid®*

Suppositories, indometacin 100 mg. Net price 10 = £1.20. Counselling, driving, see above

**Modified release**

**Indometacin m/r preparations** PoM
Capsules, m/r, indometacin 75 mg. Label: 21, 25, counselling, driving, see above
Brands include *Indolar SR®*, *Indomax 75 SR®*, *Pardelprin®*, *Rheumacin LA®*, *Slo-Indo®*
Dose 1 capsule 1–2 times daily; CHILD not recommended

**Flexin Continus** (Napp) PoM
Tablets, m/r, indometacin 25 mg (green), net price 56-tab pack = £5.45; 50 mg (red), 28-tab pack = £5.45; 75 mg (yellow), 28-tab pack = £7.79. Label: 21, 25, counselling, driving, see above
Dose initially 75 mg daily, adjusted in steps of 25–50 mg; range 25–200 mg daily in 1–2 divided doses; dysmenorrhoea, up to 75 mg daily; CHILD not recommended

## KETOPROFEN

**Indications** pain and mild inflammation in rheumatic disease and other musculoskeletal disorders, and after orthopaedic surgery; acute gout; dysmenorrhoea
**Cautions** see notes above; breast-feeding (Appendix 5); **interactions:** Appendix 1 (NSAIDs)
**Contra-indications** see notes above
**Side-effects** see notes above; pain may occur at injection site (occasionally tissue damage); suppositories may cause rectal irritation
**Dose**
- By mouth, rheumatic disease, 100–200 mg daily in 2–4 divided doses with food; CHILD not recommended
  Pain and dysmenorrhoea, 50 mg up to 3 times daily; CHILD not recommended
- By rectum in suppositories, rheumatic disease, 100 mg at bedtime; CHILD not recommended
  Combined oral and rectal treatment, max. total daily dose 200 mg
- By deep intramuscular injection into the gluteal muscle, 50–100 mg every 4 hours (max. 200 mg in 24 hours) for up to 3 days; CHILD not recommended

**Ketoprofen** (Non-proprietary) PoM
Capsules, ketoprofen 50 mg, net price 28-cap pack = £6.37; 100 mg, 100-cap pack = £13.55. Label: 21

**Orudis®** (Hawgreen) PoM
Capsules, ketoprofen 50 mg (green/purple), net price 112-cap pack = £16.07; 100 mg (pink), 56-cap pack = £16.12. Label: 21

Suppositories, ketoprofen 100 mg. Net price 10 = £6.92

**Oruvail®** (Hawgreen) PoM
Injection, ketoprofen 50 mg /mL. Net price 2-mL amp = £1.11
Gel, section 10.3.2

**Modified release**

**Oruvail®** (Hawgreen) PoM
Capsules, all m/r, enclosing white pellets, ketoprofen 100 mg (pink/purple), net price 56-cap pack = £24.90; 150 mg (pink), 28-cap pack = £14.21; 200 mg (pink/white), 28-cap pack = £24.82. Label: 21, 25
Dose 100–200 mg once daily with food; CHILD not recommended
Note Other brands of modified-release capsules containing ketoprofen 100 mg and 200 mg include *Ketocid®* 200 mg, *Ketovail®*, *Ketpron XL®* 100 mg, *Ketpron®* 200 mg, *Larafen CR®* 200 mg, *Tiloket® CR*

## LUMIRACOXIB

**Indications** pain and inflammation in osteoarthritis; moderate to severe pain associated with orthopaedic and dental surgery and dysmenorrhoea
**Cautions** see notes above; renal impairment (Appendix 3); breast-feeding (Appendix 5); **interactions:** Appendix 1 (NSAIDs)
**Contra-indications** see notes above; inflammatory bowel disease
**Side-effects** see notes above; also constipation, flatulence, cough, pharyngitis, influenza-like symptoms, respiratory and urinary infections; *less commonly* aphthous ulceration, dry mouth, chest pain, taste disturbances, paraesthesia, appetite changes, and muscle cramps
**Dose**
- Osteoarthritis, ADULT over 18 years, 100 mg once daily
- Moderate to severe pain following surgery, ADULT over 18 years, 400 mg once daily for max. 5 days
- Dysmenorrhoea, ADULT over 18 years, 200 mg once daily for max. 3 days per cycle

**Prexige®** (Novartis) ▼ PoM
Tablets, f/c, red, lumiracoxib 100 mg, net price 28-tab pack = £17.24; 400 mg, 5-tab pack = £3.46

## MEFENAMIC ACID

**Indications** mild to moderate pain in rheumatoid arthritis (including juvenile arthritis), osteoarthritis, and related conditions; postoperative analgesia; mild to moderate pain; dysmenorrhoea and menorrhagia
**Cautions** see notes above; breast-feeding (Appendix 5); porphyria (section 9.8.2); **interactions:** Appendix 1 (NSAIDs)
**Contra-indications** see notes above; inflammatory bowel disease
**Side-effects** see notes above; drowsiness; diarrhoea or rashes (withdraw treatment); thrombocytopenia, haemolytic anaemia (positive Coombs' test), and aplastic anaemia reported; convulsions in overdosage
**Dose**
- 500 mg 3 times daily preferably after food; CHILD over 6 months, 25 mg/kg daily in divided doses for not longer than 7 days, except in juvenile arthritis

**Mefenamic Acid** (Non-proprietary) PoM
Capsules, mefenamic acid 250 mg. Net price 20 = 72p. Label: 21
Tablets, mefenamic acid 500 mg, net price 28-tab pack = £2.93. Label: 21
Paediatric oral suspension, mefenamic acid 50 mg/5 mL. Net price 125 mL = £79.98. Label: 21

**Ponstan®** (Chemidex) PoM
Capsules, blue/white, mefenamic acid 250 mg, net price 100-cap pack = £8.17. Label: 21
Forte tablets, yellow, mefenamic acid 500 mg, net price 100-tab pack = £15.72. Label: 21

## MELOXICAM

**Indications** pain and inflammation in rheumatic disease; exacerbation of osteoarthritis (short-term); ankylosing spondylitis
**Cautions** see notes above; avoid rectal administration in proctitis or haemorrhoids; breast-feeding (Appendix 5); **interactions:** Appendix 1 (NSAIDs)
**Contra-indications** see notes above; renal failure (unless receiving dialysis); severe heart failure
**Side-effects** see notes above
**Dose**
- By mouth, osteoarthritis, 7.5 mg daily with food, increased if necessary to max. 15 mg once daily
  Rheumatoid arthritis, ankylosing spondylitis, 15 mg once daily with food, may be reduced to 7.5 mg daily; ELDERLY 7.5 mg daily
- By rectum, in suppositories, osteoarthritis, 7.5 mg daily, increased if necessary to max. 15 mg once daily
  Rheumatoid arthritis, ankylosing spondylitis, 15 mg once daily, may be reduced to 7.5 mg daily; ELDERLY 7.5 mg daily
- CHILD under 15 years not recommended

**Mobic®** (Boehringer Ingelheim) PoM
Tablets, both yellow, scored, meloxicam 7.5 mg, net price 30-tab pack = £9.30; 15 mg, 30-tab pack = £12.93. Label: 21
Suppositories, meloxicam 7.5 mg, net price 12 = £3.72; 15 mg, 12 = £5.58

## NABUMETONE

**Indications** pain and inflammation in osteoarthritis and rheumatoid arthritis
**Cautions** see notes above; breast-feeding (Appendix 5); **interactions:** Appendix 1 (NSAIDs)
**Contra-indications** see notes above
**Side-effects** see notes above
**Dose**
- 1 g at night, in severe conditions 0.5–1 g in morning as well; elderly 0.5–1 g daily; CHILD not recommended

**Nabumetone** (Non-proprietary) PoM
Tablets, nabumetone 500 mg, net price 56-tab pack = £9.50. Label: 21

**Relifex®** (Meda) PoM
Tablets, red, f/c, nabumetone 500 mg. Net price 56-tab pack = £6.18. Label: 21
Suspension, sugar-free, nabumetone 500 mg/5 mL. Net price 300-mL pack = £24.08. Label: 21

## NAPROXEN

**Indications** pain and inflammation in rheumatic disease (including juvenile arthritis) and other musculoskeletal disorders; dysmenorrhoea; acute gout
**Cautions** see notes above; breast-feeding (Appendix 5); **interactions:** Appendix 1 (NSAIDs)
**Contra-indications** see notes above
**Side-effects** see notes above
**Dose**
- Rheumatic disease, 0.5–1 g daily in 1–2 divided doses; CHILD (over 5 years), juvenile arthritis, 10 mg/kg daily in 2 divided doses
- Acute musculoskeletal disorders and dysmenorrhoea, 500 mg initially, then 250 mg every 6–8 hours as required; max. dose after first day 1.25 g daily; CHILD under 16 years not recommended
- Acute gout, 750 mg initially, then 250 mg every 8 hours until attack has passed; CHILD under 16 years not recommended

**Naproxen** (Non-proprietary) PoM
Tablets, naproxen 250 mg, net price 28-tab pack = 46p; 500 mg, 28-tab pack = £1.60. Label: 21
Brands include *Arthroxen®*
Tablets, e/c, naproxen 250 mg, net price 56-tab pack = £4.15; 375 mg, 56-tab pack = £6.96; 500 mg, 56-tab pack = £6.83. Label: 5, 25

**Naprosyn®** (Roche) PoM
Tablets, all scored, naproxen 250 mg (buff), net price 56-tab pack = £4.55; 500 mg (buff), 56-tab pack = £9.09. Label: 21
Tablets, e/c, (*Naprosyn EC®*), naproxen 250 mg, net price 56-tab pack = £4.55; 375 mg, 56-tab pack = £6.82; 500 mg, 56-tab pack = £9.09. Label: 5, 25

**Synflex®** (Roche) PoM
Tablets, blue, naproxen sodium 275 mg. Net price 60-tab pack = £7.54. Label: 21
Note 275 mg naproxen sodium ≡ 250 mg naproxen
Dose musculoskeletal disorders, postoperative analgesia, 550 mg twice daily when necessary, preferably after food; max. 1.1 g daily; CHILD under 16 years not recommended
Dysmenorrhoea and acute gout, initially 550 mg then 275 mg every 6–8 hours as required; max. of 1.375 g on first day and 1.1 g daily thereafter; CHILD under 16 years not recommended
Migraine, 825 mg at onset, then 275–550 mg at least 30 minutes after initial dose; max. 1.375 g in 24 hours; CHILD under 16 years not recommended

### With misoprostol

For **cautions**, **contra-indications**, and **side-effects** of misoprostol, see section 1.3.4

**Napratec®** (Pharmacia) PoM
Combination pack, 56 yellow scored tablets, naproxen 500 mg; 56 white scored tablets, misoprostol 200 micrograms. Net price = £23.76. Label: 21
Dose patients requiring naproxen for rheumatoid arthritis, osteoarthritis, or ankylosing spondylitis, with prophylaxis against NSAID-induced gastroduodenal ulceration, 1 naproxen 500-mg tablet and 1 misoprostol 200-microgram tablet taken together twice daily with food; CHILD not recommended

## PIROXICAM

**Indications** pain and inflammation in rheumatic disease (including juvenile arthritis) and other musculoskeletal disorders; acute gout

**Cautions** see notes above; avoid in porphyria (section 9.8.2); breast-feeding (Appendix 5); **interactions:** Appendix 1 (NSAIDs)

**Contra-indications** see notes above

**Side-effects** see notes above; pain at injection site (occasionally tissue damage); suppositories may cause rectal irritation and occasional bleeding

**Dose**

- By mouth, rheumatic disease, initially 20 mg daily, maintenance 10–30 mg daily, in single or divided doses; CHILD (over 6 years), juvenile arthritis, under 15 kg, 5 mg daily; 16–25 kg, 10 mg; 26–45 kg, 15 mg; over 46 kg, 20 mg

  Acute musculoskeletal disorders, 40 mg daily in single or divided doses for 2 days, then 20 mg daily for 7–14 days; CHILD not recommended

  Acute gout, 40 mg initially, then 40 mg daily in single or divided doses for 4–6 days; CHILD not recommended
- By deep intramuscular injection into gluteal muscle, for initial treatment of acute conditions, as dose by mouth (on short-term basis); CHILD not recommended

**Piroxicam** (Non-proprietary) PoM

Capsules, piroxicam 10 mg, net price 56-cap pack = £4.40; 20 mg, 28-cap pack = £3.58. Label: 21

Dispersible tablets, piroxicam 10 mg, net price 56-tab pack = £9.33; 20 mg, 28-tab pack = £12.48. Label: 13, 21

**Feldene®** (Pfizer) PoM

Capsules, piroxicam 10 mg (maroon/blue), net price 56-cap pack = £7.20; 20 mg (maroon), 28-cap pack = £7.20. Label: 21

Tablets, (*Feldene Melt®*), piroxicam 20 mg, net price 28-tab pack = £9.83. Label: 10, patient information leaflet, 21

**Excipients** include aspartame equivalent to phenylalanine 140 micrograms/tablet (section 9.4.1)

**Note** *Feldene Melt®* tablets can be taken by placing on tongue or by swallowing

Dispersible tablets, piroxicam 10 mg (scored), net price 56-tab pack = £11.70; 20 mg, 28-tab pack = £11.70. Label: 13, 21

Injection, piroxicam 20 mg/mL. Net price 1-mL amp = 84p

Gel, section 10.3.2

**Brexidol®** (Trinity) PoM

Tablets, yellow, scored, piroxicam (as betadex) 20 mg, net price 30-tab pack = £12.22. Label: 21

**Dose** osteoarthritis, rheumatic disease and acute musculoskeletal disorders, 1 tablet daily (may be halved in elderly); CHILD not recommended

## SULINDAC

**Indications** pain and inflammation in rheumatic disease and other musculoskeletal disorders; acute gout

**Cautions** see notes above; also history of renal stones and ensure adequate hydration; breast-feeding (Appendix 5); **interactions:** Appendix 1 (NSAIDs)

**Contra-indications** see notes above

**Side-effects** see notes above; jaundice with fever, cholestasis, hepatitis, hepatic failure; also urine discoloration occasionally reported

**Dose**

- 200 mg twice daily with food (may be reduced according to response); max. 400 mg daily; acute gout should respond within 7 days; limit treatment of periarticular disorders to 7–10 days; CHILD not recommended

**Sulindac** (Non-proprietary) PoM

Tablets, sulindac 100 mg, net price 56-tab pack = £9.06; 200 mg, 56-tab pack = £16.96. Label: 21

**Clinoril®** (MSD) PoM

Tablets, both yellow, scored, sulindac 100 mg, net price 60-tab pack = £6.73; 200 mg, 60-tab pack = £12.96. Label: 21

## TENOXICAM

**Indications** pain and inflammation in rheumatic disease and other musculoskeletal disorders

**Cautions** see notes above; breast-feeding (Appendix 5); **interactions:** Appendix 1 (NSAIDs)

**Contra-indications** see notes above

**Side-effects** see notes above

**Dose**

- By mouth, rheumatic disease, 20 mg daily; CHILD not recommended

  Acute musculoskeletal disorders, 20 mg daily for 7 days; max. 14 days; CHILD not recommended
- By intravenous *or* intramuscular injection, for initial treatment for 1–2 days, as dose by mouth; CHILD not recommended

**Mobiflex®** (Roche) PoM

Tablets, yellow, f/c, tenoxicam 20 mg. Net price 30-tab pack = £13.42. Label: 21

Injection, powder for reconstitution, tenoxicam 20 mg. Net price per amp (with solvent) = 82p

## TIAPROFENIC ACID

**Indications** pain and inflammation in rheumatic disease and other musculoskeletal disorders

**Cautions** see notes above; breast-feeding (Appendix 5); **interactions:** Appendix 1 (NSAIDs)

**Contra-indications** see notes above; also active bladder or prostate disease (or symptoms) and history of recurrent urinary-tract disorders—if urinary symptoms develop discontinue immediately and perform urine tests and culture; see also CSM advice below

> **CSM advice**
> Following reports of **severe cystitis** CSM has recommended that tiaprofenic acid should not be given to patients with urinary-tract disorders and should be stopped if urinary symptoms develop. Patients should be advised to stop taking tiaprofenic acid and to report to their doctor promptly if they develop urinary-tract symptoms (such as increased frequency, nocturia, urgency, pain on urinating, or blood in urine)

**Side-effects** see notes above

**Dose**

- 600 mg daily in 2–3 divided doses; CHILD not recommended

**Tiaprofenic Acid** (Non-proprietary) PoM

Tablets, tiaprofenic acid 200 mg, net price 84-tab pack = £20.48; 300 mg, 56-tab pack = £20.48. Label: 21

**Surgam®** (Florizel) PoM

Tablets, tiaprofenic acid 200 mg, net price 84-tab pack = £15.56; 300 mg, 56-tab pack = £15.56. Label: 21

**Modified release**

**Surgam SA®** (Aventis Pharma) PoM

Capsules, m/r, maroon/pink enclosing white pellets, tiaprofenic acid 300 mg. Net price 56-cap pack = £15.56. Label: 25

Dose 2 capsules once daily; CHILD not recommended

## Aspirin

**Aspirin** was the traditional first choice anti-inflammatory analgesic but most physicians now prefer to start treatment with another NSAID which may be better tolerated and more convenient for the patient.

In regular high dosage aspirin has about the same anti-inflammatory effect as other NSAIDs. The required dose for active inflammatory joint disease is at least 3.6 g daily. There is little anti-inflammatory effect with less than 3 g daily. Gastro-intestinal side-effects such as nausea, dyspepsia, and gastro-intestinal bleeding may occur with any dosage of aspirin but anti-inflammatory doses are associated with a much higher incidence of side-effects. Anti-inflammatory doses of aspirin may also cause mild chronic salicylate intoxication (salicylism) characterised by dizziness, tinnitus, and deafness; these symptoms may be controlled by reducing the dosage.

### ASPIRIN
(Acetylsalicylic Acid)

**Indications** pain and inflammation in rheumatic disease and other musculoskeletal disorders (including juvenile arthritis); see also section 4.7.1; antiplatelet (section 2.9)

**Cautions** asthma, allergic disease, uncontrolled hypertension, hepatic impairment (Appendix 2), renal impairment—avoid if severe (Appendix 3), dehydration, pregnancy (particularly at term; see also Appendix 4), elderly; preferably avoid during fever or viral infection in adolescents (risk of Reye's syndrome, see below); G6PD-deficiency (section 9.1.5); **interactions:** Appendix 1 (aspirin)

Reye's syndrome Owing to an association with Reye's syndrome the CSM has advised that aspirin-containing preparations should not be given to children and adolescents under 16 years, unless specifically indicated, e.g. for Kawasaki syndrome

**Contra-indications** previous or active peptic ulceration; children and adolescents under 16 years (unless specifically indicated e.g. for Kawasaki syndrome) and breast-feeding—risk of Reye's syndrome (Appendix 5), see above; haemophilia and other bleeding disorders; not for treatment of gout

Hypersensitivity Aspirin and other NSAIDs **contra-indicated** in history of hypersensitivity to aspirin or any other NSAID—which includes those in whom attacks of asthma, angioedema, urticaria or rhinitis have been precipitated by aspirin or any other NSAID

**Side-effects** common with anti-inflammatory doses; gastro-intestinal discomfort or nausea, ulceration with occult bleeding (but occasionally major haemorrhage); also other haemorrhage (e.g. subconjunctival); hearing disturbances such as tinnitus (leading rarely to deafness), vertigo, confusion, hypersensitivity reactions (angioedema, bronchospasm and rashes); increased bleeding time; rarely oedema, blood disorders, particularly thrombocytopenia; **overdosage:** see Emergency Treatment of Poisoning, p. 29

**Dose**
- 0.3–1 g every 4 hours after food; max. in acute conditions 8 g daily; CHILD, juvenile arthritis, up to 80 mg/kg daily in 5–6 divided doses after food, increased in acute exacerbations to 130 mg/kg

Note High doses of aspirin are very rarely required and are now given under specialist supervision only, and with plasma monitoring (especially in children)

**Preparations**

Section 4.7.1

# 10.1.2 Corticosteroids

## 10.1.2.1 Systemic corticosteroids

The general actions and uses of the corticosteroids are described in section 6.3. Treatment with corticosteroids in rheumatic diseases should be reserved for specific indications, e.g. when other anti-inflammatory drugs are unsuccessful. Corticosteroids can induce osteoporosis, and prophylaxis should be considered on long-term treatment (section 6.6).

In severe, possibly life-threatening, situations a high initial dose of corticosteroid is given to induce remission and the dose is then reduced gradually and discontinued altogether. Relapse may occur as the dose of corticosteroid is reduced, particularly if the reduction is too rapid. The tendency is therefore to increase the maintenance dose and consequently the patient becomes dependent on corticosteroids. For this reason pulse doses of corticosteroids (e.g. methylprednisolone up to 1 g intravenously on 3 consecutive days) are used to suppress highly active inflammatory disease while longer-term treatment with a disease-modifying drug is commenced.

**Prednisolone** 7.5 mg daily may reduce the rate of joint destruction in moderate to severe *rheumatoid arthritis* of less than 2 years' duration. The reduction in joint destruction must be distinguished from mere symptomatic improvement (which lasts only 6 to 12 months at this dose) and care should be taken to avoid increasing the dose above 7.5 mg daily. Evidence supports maintenance of this anti-erosive dose for 2–4 years only after which treatment should be tapered off to reduce long-term adverse effects.

*Polymyalgia rheumatica* and *giant cell (temporal) arteritis* are always treated with corticosteroids. The usual initial dose of prednisolone in polymyalgia rheumatica is 10–15 mg daily and in giant cell arteritis 40–60 mg daily (the higher dose being used if visual symptoms occur). Treatment should be continued until remission of disease activity and doses are then reduced gradually to about 7.5–10 mg daily for maintenance. Relapse is common if therapy is stopped prematurely. Many patients require treatment for at least 2 years and in some patients it may be necessary to continue long-term low-dose corticosteroid treatment.

*Polyarteritis nodosa* and *polymyositis* are usually treated with corticosteroids. An initial dose of 60 mg of prednisolone daily is often used and reduced to a maintenance dose of 10–15 mg daily.

*Systemic lupus erythematosus* is treated with corticosteroids when necessary using a similar dosage regimen to that for polyarteritis nodosa and polymyositis (above).

Patients with pleurisy, pericarditis, or other systemic manifestations will respond to corticosteroids. It may then be possible to reduce the dosage; alternate-day treatment is sometimes adequate, and the drug may be gradually withdrawn. In some mild cases corticosteroid treatment may be stopped after a few months. Many mild cases of systemic lupus erythematosus do not require corticosteroid treatment. Alternative treatment with anti-inflammatory analgesics, and possibly chloroquine or hydroxychloroquine, should be considered.

*Ankylosing spondylitis* should not be treated with long-term corticosteroids; rarely, pulse doses may be needed and may be useful in extremely active disease that does not respond to conventional treatment.

## 10.1.2.2 Local corticosteroid injections

Corticosteroids are injected locally for an anti-inflammatory effect. In inflammatory conditions of the joints, particularly in rheumatoid arthritis, they are given by *intra-articular injection* to relieve pain, increase mobility, and reduce deformity in one or a few joints. Full aseptic precautions are essential; infected areas should be avoided. Occasionally an acute inflammatory reaction develops after an intra-articular or soft-tissue injection of a corticosteroid. This may be a reaction to the microcrystalline suspension of the corticosteroid used, but must be distinguished from sepsis introduced into the injection site.

Smaller amounts of corticosteroids may also be injected directly into soft tissues for the relief of inflammation in conditions such as *tennis* or *golfer's elbow* or *compression neuropathies*. In *tendinitis*, injections should be made into the tendon sheath and not directly into the tendon (due to the absence of a true tendon sheath, the Achilles tendon should not be injected). A soluble preparation (e.g. containing betamethasone or dexamethasone sodium phosphate) is preferred for injection into the carpal tunnel.

Hydrocortisone acetate or one of the synthetic analogues is generally used for local injection. Flushing has been reported with intra-articular corticosteroid injections. Charcot-like arthropathies have also been reported (particularly following repeated intra-articular injections). Intra-articular injections may affect the hyaline cartilage and each joint should usually be treated **no more** than 3 times in one year.

Corticosteroid injections are also injected into soft tissues for the treatment of skin lesions (see section 13.4).

### LOCAL CORTICOSTEROID INJECTIONS

**Indications** local inflammation of joints and soft tissues (for details, consult product literature)

**Cautions** see notes above and consult product literature; see also section 6.3.2

**Contra-indications** see notes above and consult product literature

**Side-effects** see notes above and consult product literature

**Dose**

- See under preparations

**Dose calculated as dexamethasone**

**Dexamethasone** (Organon) PoM

Injection, dexamethasone 4 mg/mL (as sodium phosphate) (≡ dexamethasone sodium phosphate 5.2 mg/mL ≡ dexamethasone phosphate 4.8 mg/mL). Net price 1-mL amp = 83p; 2-mL vial = £1.27

**Dose** by intra-articular *or* intrasynovial injection (for details consult product literature), 0.6–3 mg (calculated as dexamethasone) according to size; where appropriate may be repeated at intervals of 3–21 days according to response

**Dose calculated as dexamethasone phosphate**

**Dexamethasone** (Mayne) PoM

Injection, dexamethasone phosphate 4 mg/mL (as sodium phosphate) (≡ dexamethasone 3.3 mg/mL ≡ dexamethasone sodium phosphate 4.4 mg/mL), net price 1-mL amp = £1.00; 2-mL vial = £1.98

**Dose** by intra-articular *or* intrasynovial injection (for details consult product literature), 0.4–4 mg (calculated as dexamethasone phosphate) according to size (soft-tissue infiltration 2–6 mg); where appropriate may be repeated at intervals of 3–21 days

**Hydrocortisone acetate**

**Hydrocortistab®** (Sovereign) PoM

Injection, (aqueous suspension), hydrocortisone acetate 25 mg/mL. Net price 1-mL amp = £4.77

**Dose** by intra-articular *or* intrasynovial injection (for details consult product literature), 5–50 mg according to size; where appropriate may be repeated at intervals of 21 days; not more than 3 joints should be treated on any one day; CHILD 5–30 mg (divided)

**Methylprednisolone acetate**

**Depo-Medrone®** (Pharmacia) PoM

Injection (aqueous suspension), methylprednisolone acetate 40 mg/mL. Net price 1-mL vial = £2.87; 2-mL vial = £5.15; 3-mL vial = £7.47

**Dose** by intra-articular *or* intrasynovial injection (for details consult product literature), 4–80 mg, according to size; where appropriate may be repeated at intervals of 7–35 days; also for intralesional injection

**Depo-Medrone® with Lidocaine** (Pharmacia) PoM

Injection (aqueous suspension), methylprednisolone acetate 40 mg, lidocaine hydrochloride 10 mg/mL. Net price 1-mL vial = £3.28; 2-mL vial = £5.88

**Dose** by intra-articular *or* intrasynovial injection (for details consult product literature), 4–80 mg, according to size; where appropriate may be repeated at intervals of 7–35 days

**Prednisolone acetate**

**Deltastab®** (Sovereign) PoM

Injection (aqueous suspension), prednisolone acetate 25 mg/mL. Net price 1-mL amp = £4.77

**Dose** by intra-articular *or* intrasynovial injection (for details consult product literature), 5–25 mg according to size; not more than 3 joints should be treated on any one day; where appropriate may be repeated when relapse occurs

For intramuscular injection, see section 6.3.2

**Triamcinolone acetonide**

**Adcortyl® Intra-articular/Intradermal** (Squibb) PoM

Injection (aqueous suspension), triamcinolone acetonide 10 mg/mL. Net price 1-mL amp = £1.02; 5-mL vial = £4.14

**Dose** by intra-articular injection *or* intrasynovial injection (for details consult product literature), 2.5–15 mg according to size (for larger doses use *Kenalog®*); where appropriate may be repeated when relapse occurs

By intradermal injection, (for details consult product literature): 2–3 mg; max. 5 mg at any one site (total max. 30 mg); where appropriate may be repeated at intervals of 1–2 weeks

CHILD under 6 years not recommended

**Kenalog® Intra-articular/Intramuscular** (Squibb)
PoM

Injection (aqueous suspension), triamcinolone acetonide 40 mg/mL, net price 1-mL vial = £1.70; 1-mL prefilled syringe = £2.11; 2-mL prefilled syringe = £3.66

**Note** Intramuscular needle with prefilled syringe should be replaced for intra-articular injection

**Dose** by intra-articular *or* intrasynovial injection (for details consult product literature), 5–40 mg according to size; total max. 80 mg (for doses below 5 mg use *Adcortyl® Intra-articular/Intradermal*); where appropriate may be repeated when relapse occurs; CHILD under 6 years not recommended

For intramuscular injection, see section 6.3.2

## 10.1.3 Drugs which suppress the rheumatic disease process

Certain drugs such as those affecting the immune response can suppress the disease process in *rheumatoid arthritis* and *psoriatic arthritis*; gold, penicillamine, hydroxychloroquine, chloroquine, and sulfasalazine can also suppress the disease process in *rheumatoid arthritis* while sulfasalazine and possibly gold can suppress the disease process in *psoriatic arthritis*. Unlike NSAIDs, disease-modifying anti-rheumatic drugs (DMARDs) can affect the progression of disease but they require 4–6 months of treatment for a full therapeutic response. Since in the first few months of treatment, the course of rheumatoid arthritis is unpredictable and the diagnosis uncertain, it is usual to start treatment with an NSAID alone. However, disease-modifying anti-rheumatic drugs should be initiated by specialists as soon as diagnosis, progression, and severity of the disease have been confirmed. Response to a disease-modifying anti-rheumatic drug may allow the dose of the NSAID to be reduced.

Disease-modifying antirheumatic drugs may improve not only the symptoms and signs of inflammatory joint disease but also extra-articular manifestations such as vasculitis. They reduce the erythrocyte sedimentation rate, C-reactive protein, and sometimes the titre of rheumatoid factor. Some (e.g. methotrexate and ciclosporin) are believed to retard erosive damage as judged radiologically.

**Choice** The choice of a disease-modifying anti-rheumatic drug should take into account co-morbidity and patient preference. Sulfasalazine, methotrexate, intramuscular gold and penicillamine are similar in efficacy. However, **sulfasalazine** or **methotrexate** are often used first because they may be better tolerated.

**Penicillamine** and drugs that affect the immune response ('immunomodulators') are also sometimes used in rheumatoid arthritis where there are troublesome extra-articular features such as vasculitis, and in patients who are taking high doses of corticosteroids. Response to the drugs often produces a striking reduction in requirements of both corticosteroids and other drugs. **Gold** and **penicillamine** are effective in *palindromic rheumatism*. *Systemic* and *discoid lupus erythematosus* are sometimes treated with **chloroquine** or **hydroxychloroquine**.

If a disease-modifying anti-rheumatic drug does not lead to an objective benefit within 6 months (or within 3 months for inhibitors of tumour necrosis factor), it should be replaced by a different one.

In some circumstances, and under specialist supervision, combining two or more disease-modifying anti-rheumatic drugs may be considered.

**Juvenile idiopathic arthritis** Many children with *juvenile idiopathic arthritis* (juvenile chronic arthritis) do not require disease-modifying antirheumatic drugs. Methotrexate is effective [unlicensed indication]; sulfasalazine is an alternative [unlicensed indication] but it should be avoided in systemic-onset juvenile idiopathic arthritis. Gold and penicillamine are no longer used. For the role of etanercept in polyarticular-course juvenile idiopathic arthritis, see p. 521

### Gold

**Gold** may be given by intramuscular injection as sodium aurothiomalate or by mouth as auranofin.

**Sodium aurothiomalate** must be given by deep intramuscular injection and the area gently massaged. A test dose of 10 mg must be given followed by doses of 50 mg at weekly intervals until there is definite evidence of remission. Benefit is not to be expected until about 300–500 mg has been given; it should be discontinued if there is no remission after 1 g has been given. In patients who do respond, the interval between injections is then gradually increased to 4 weeks and treatment is continued for up to 5 years after complete remission. If relapse occurs the dosage frequency may be immediately increased to 50 mg weekly and only once control has been obtained again should the dosage frequency be decreased; if no response is seen within 2 months, alternative treatment should be sought. It is important to avoid complete relapse since second courses of gold are not usually effective. Children may be given 1 mg/kg weekly to a maximum of 50 mg weekly, the intervals being gradually increased to 4 weeks according to response; an initial test dose is given corresponding to one-tenth to one-fifth of the calculated dose.

**Auranofin** is given by mouth. If there is no response after 6 months treatment should be discontinued. Auranofin is less effective than parenteral gold.

Gold therapy should be discontinued in the presence of blood disorders, gastro-intestinal bleeding (associated with ulcerative enterocolitis), or unexplained proteinuria (associated with immune complex nephritis) which is repeatedly above 300 mg/litre. Urine tests and full blood counts (including total and differential white cell and platelet counts) must therefore be performed before starting treatment with gold and before each intramuscular injection; in the case of oral treatment the urine and blood tests should be carried out monthly. Rashes with pruritus often occur after 2 to 6 months of intramuscular treatment and may necessitate discontinuation of treatment; the most common side-effect of oral therapy, diarrhoea with or without nausea or abdominal pain, may respond to bulking agents (such as bran) or temporary reduction in dosage.

## SODIUM AUROTHIOMALATE

**Indications** active progressive rheumatoid arthritis, juvenile arthritis

**Cautions** see notes above; hepatic impairment (Appendix 2), renal impairment (Appendix 3), pregnancy (Appendix 4), breast-feeding (Appendix 5); elderly, history of urticaria, eczema, colitis, drugs which cause blood disorders; annual chest X-ray

**Contra-indications** severe renal and hepatic disease (see notes above); history of blood disorders or bone marrow aplasia, exfoliative dermatitis, systemic lupus erythematosus, necrotising enterocolitis, pulmonary fibrosis; porphyria (section 9.8.2)

**Side-effects** severe reactions (occasionally fatal) in up to 5% of patients; mouth ulcers, skin reactions (including, on prolonged parenteral treatment, irreversible pigmentation in sun-exposed areas), proteinuria, blood disorders (sometimes sudden and fatal); rarely colitis, peripheral neuritis, pulmonary fibrosis, hepatotoxicity with cholestatic jaundice, nephrotic syndrome, alopecia

**Dose**

- By deep intramuscular injection, administered on expert advice, see notes above

  Counselling Warn patient to tell doctor immediately if sore throat, fever, infection, non-specific illness, unexplained bleeding and bruising, purpura, mouth ulcers, metallic taste, or rashes develop; also ask patients to report immediately any breathlessness or cough

**Myocrisin®** (JHC) PoM

Injection, sodium aurothiomalate 20 mg/mL, net price 0.5-mL (10-mg) amp = £2.94; 40 mg/mL, 0.5-mL (20-mg) amp = £4.28; 100 mg/mL, 0.5-mL (50-mg) amp = £8.71. Counselling, blood disorder symptoms

## AURANOFIN

**Indications** active progressive rheumatoid arthritis

**Cautions** see under Sodium Aurothiomalate; hepatic impairment (Appendix 2); pregnancy (Appendix 4); breast-feeding (Appendix 5); also inflammatory bowel disease

Blood counts Withdraw if platelet count falls below 100 000/mm$^3$ or if signs and symptoms suggestive of thrombocytopenia occur, see also notes above

**Contra-indications** see under Sodium Aurothiomalate

**Side-effects** diarrhoea most common (reduced by bulking agents such as bran); see also under Sodium Aurothiomalate

**Dose**

- Administered on expert advice, 6 mg daily (initially in 2 divided doses then if tolerated as single dose), if response inadequate after 6 months, increase to 9 mg daily (in 3 divided doses), discontinue if no response after a further 3 months; CHILD not recommended

  Counselling Warn patient to tell doctor immediately if sore throat, fever, infection, non-specific illness, unexplained bleeding and bruising, purpura, mouth ulcers, metallic taste, or rashes develop; also ask patients to report immediately any breathlessness or cough

  Note The package insert for *Ridaura®* also advises that patients must also report immediately if conjunctivitis or hair loss develops

**Ridaura®** (Yamanouchi) PoM

Tablets, yellow, f/c, auranofin 3 mg. Net price 60-tab pack = £25.20. Label: 21, counselling, blood disorder symptoms (see above)

## Penicillamine

**Penicillamine** has a similar action to gold, and more patients are able to continue treatment than with gold but side-effects occur frequently.

Patients should be warned not to expect improvement for at least 6 to 12 weeks after treatment is initiated. Penicillamine should be discontinued if there is no improvement within 1 year.

Blood counts, including platelets, and urine examinations should be carried out before starting treatment and then every 1 or 2 weeks for the first 2 months then every 4 weeks to detect blood disorders and proteinuria (they should also be carried out in the week after any dose increase). A reduction in platelet count calls for discontinuation with subsequent re-introduction at a lower dosage and then, if possible, gradual increase. Proteinuria, associated with immune complex nephritis, occurs in up to 30% of patients, but may resolve despite continuation of treatment; treatment may be continued provided that renal function tests remain normal, oedema is absent, and the 24-hour urinary excretion of protein does not exceed 2 g.

Nausea may occur but is not usually a problem provided that penicillamine is taken before food or on retiring and that low initial doses are used and only gradually increased. Loss of taste may occur about 6 weeks after treatment is started but usually returns 6 weeks later irrespective of whether or not treatment is discontinued; mineral supplements are not recommended. Rashes are a common side-effect. Those which occur in the first few months of treatment disappear when the drug is stopped and treatment may then be re-introduced at a lower dose level and gradually increased. Late rashes are more resistant and often necessitate discontinuation of treatment.

Patients who are hypersensitive to penicillin may react rarely to penicillamine.

## PENICILLAMINE

**Indications** see notes above and under Dose

**Cautions** see notes above; renal impairment (Appendix 3); pregnancy (Appendix 4); concomitant nephrotoxic drugs (increased risk of toxicity); gold treatment (avoid concomitant use if adverse reactions to gold); **interactions:** Appendix 1 (penicillamine)

Blood counts and urine tests See notes above. Longer intervals may be adequate in cystinuria and Wilson's disease. Consider withdrawal if platelet count falls below 120 000/mm$^3$ or white blood cells below 2500/mm$^3$ or if 3 successive falls within reference range (can restart at reduced dose when counts return to within reference range but permanent withdrawal necessary if recurrence of leucopenia or thrombocytopenia)

Counselling Warn patient to tell doctor immediately if sore throat, fever, infection, non-specific illness, unexplained bleeding and bruising, purpura, mouth ulcers, or rashes develop

**Contra-indications** lupus erythematosus; moderate to severe renal impairment

**Side-effects** (see also notes above) initially nausea, anorexia, fever, and skin reactions; taste loss (mineral supplements not recommended); blood disorders including thrombocytopenia, leucopenia, agranulocytosis and aplastic anaemia; proteinuria, rarely haematuria (withdraw immediately); haemolytic anaemia, nephrotic syndrome, lupus erythematosus-like syndrome, myasthenia gravis-like syndrome, polymyositis (rarely with cardiac involvement), dermatomyositis, mouth ulcers, stomatitis, alopecia, bronchiolitis and pneumonitis, pemphigus, Goodpasture's syndrome, and Stevens-Johnson syndrome also reported; male and female breast enlargement reported; in non-rheumatoid conditions rheumatoid arthritis-like syndrome also reported; late rashes (consider withdrawing treatment)

**Dose**

- Severe active rheumatoid arthritis, administered on expert advice, ADULT initially 125–250 mg daily before food for 1 month increased by similar amounts at intervals of not less than 4 weeks to usual maintenance of 500–750 mg daily in divided doses; max. 1.5 g daily; if remission sustained for 6 months, reduction of daily dose by 125–250 mg every 12 weeks may be attempted; ELDERLY initially up to 125 mg daily before food for 1 month increased by similar amounts at intervals of not less than 4 weeks; max. 1 g daily; CHILD maintenance of 15–20 mg/kg daily (initial dose lower and increased at intervals of 4 weeks over a period of 3-6 months)
- Wilson's disease, chronic active hepatitis, and cystinuria, section 9.8.1
- Lead poisoning, see Emergency Treatment of Poisoning, p. 34

**Penicillamine** (Non-proprietary) PoM
Tablets, penicillamine 125 mg, net price 56-tab pack = £8.27; 250 mg, 56-tab pack = £13.29. Label: 6, 22, counselling, blood disorder symptoms (see above)

**Distamine®** (Alliance) PoM
Tablets, all f/c, penicillamine 125 mg, net price 20 = £1.96; 250 mg, 20 = £3.41. Label: 6, 22, counselling, blood disorder symptoms (see above)

## Antimalarials

The antimalarial **hydroxychloroquine** is used to treat rheumatoid arthritis of moderate inflammatory activity; **chloroquine** is also licensed for treating inflammatory disorders but it is used much less frequently and it is generally reserved for use if other drugs have failed. These drugs are effective for mild systemic lupus erythematosus, particularly involving cutaneous and joint manifestations. Chloroquine and hydroxychloroquine should not be used for psoriatic arthritis.

Chloroquine and hydroxychloroquine are better tolerated than gold or penicillamine. Retinopathy (see below) occurs rarely provided that the recommended doses are not exceeded; in the elderly it is difficult to distinguish drug-induced retinopathy from ageing changes.

**Mepacrine** (section 5.4.4) is sometimes used in discoid lupus erythematosus [unlicensed].

**Cautions** Chloroquine and hydroxychloroquine should be used with caution in hepatic impairment (Appendix 2) and in renal impairment (Appendix 3). Manufacturers recommend regular ophthalmological examination but the evidence of practical value is unsatisfactory (see advice of Royal College of Ophthalmologists, below). It is not necessary to withdraw an antimalarial during pregnancy (Appendix 4) if the rheumatic disease is well controlled. Chloroquine and hydroxychloroquine are present in breast milk and breast-feeding (Appendix 5) should be avoided when they are used to treat rheumatic disease; chloroquine can, however, be used for malaria during pregnancy and breast-feeding (section 5.4.1). Both should be used with caution in neurological disorders (especially in those with a history of epilepsy), in severe gastro-intestinal disorders, in G6PD deficiency (section 9.1.5), in porphyria, and in the elderly (see also above). Chloroquine and hydroxychloroquine may exacerbate psoriasis and aggravate myasthenia gravis. Concurrent use of hepatotoxic drugs should be avoided; other **interactions**: Appendix 1 (chloroquine and hydroxychloroquine).

**Screening for ocular toxicity**

A review group convened by the Royal College of Ophthalmologists has updated guidelines for screening to prevent ocular toxicity on long-term treatment with chloroquine, hydroxychloroquine, and mepacrine (*Ocular toxicity with hydroxychloroquine: guidelines for screening 2004*). Chloroquine should be considered (for treating chronic inflammatory conditions) **only** if other drugs have failed. All patients taking chloroquine should receive ocular examination according to a protocol arranged locally between the prescriber and the ophthalmologist. Mepacrine has negligible ocular toxicity. The following recommendations relate to hydroxychloroquine, which is only rarely associated with toxicity.

*Before treatment:*

- Assess renal and liver function (adjust dose if impaired)
- Ask patient about visual impairment (not corrected by glasses). If impairment or eye disease present, assessment by an optometrist is advised and any abnormality should be referred to an ophthalmologist
- Record near visual acuity of each eye (with glasses where appropriate) using a standard reading chart
- Initiate hydroxychloroquine treatment if no abnormality detected (at a dose not exceeding hydroxychloroquine sulphate 6.5 mg/kg daily)

*During treatment:*

- Ask patient about visual symptoms and monitor visual acuity annually using the standard reading chart
- Refer to ophthalmologist if visual acuity changes or if vision blurred and warn patient to stop treatment and seek prescribing doctor's advice
- A child treated for juvenile arthritis should receive slit-lamp examination routinely to check for uveitis
- If long-term treatment is required (more than 5 years), individual arrangement should be agreed with the local ophthalmologist

**Note** To avoid excessive dosage in obese patients, the dose of hydroxychloroquine and chloroquine should be calculated on the basis of lean body weight. Ocular toxicity is unlikely with chloroquine phosphate not exceeding 4 mg/kg daily (equivalent to chloroquine base approx. 2.5 mg/kg daily)

**Side-effects** The side-effects of chloroquine and hydroxychloroquine include gastro-intestinal disturbances, headache and skin reactions (rashes, pruritus); those occurring less frequently include ECG changes, convulsions, visual changes, retinal damage (see above), keratopathy, ototoxicity, hair depigmentation, hair loss, and discoloration of skin, nails, and mucous membranes. Side-effects that occur rarely include blood disorders (including thrombocytopenia, agranulocytosis, and aplastic anaemia), mental changes (including emotional disturbances and psychosis), myopathy (including cardiomyopathy and neuromyopathy), acute generalised exanthematous pustulosis, exfoliative dermatitis, Stevens-Johnson syndrome, photosensitivity, and hepatic damage. **Important**: very toxic in overdosage—immediate advice from poisons centres essential (see also p. 32).

## CHLOROQUINE

**Indications** active rheumatoid arthritis (including juvenile arthritis), systemic and discoid lupus erythematosus; malaria (section 5.4.1)

**Cautions** see notes above

**Side-effects** see notes above

**Dose**

- Administered on expert advice, by mouth, chloroquine (base) 150 mg daily; max. 2.5 mg/kg daily, see recommendations above; CHILD up to 3 mg/kg daily

**Note** Chloroquine base 150 mg ≡ chloroquine sulphate 200 mg ≡ chloroquine phosphate 250 mg (approx.).

**Preparations**

Section 5.4.1

## HYDROXYCHLOROQUINE SULPHATE

**Indications** active rheumatoid arthritis (including juvenile arthritis), systemic and discoid lupus erythematosus; dermatological conditions caused or aggravated by sunlight

**Cautions** see notes above

**Side-effects** see notes above

**Dose**

- Administered on expert advice, initially 400 mg daily in divided doses; maintenance 200–400 mg daily; max. 6.5 mg/kg daily (but not exceeding 400 mg daily), see recommendations above; CHILD, up to 6.5 mg/kg daily (max. 400 mg daily)

**Plaquenil®** (Sanofi-Synthelabo) PoM

Tablets, f/c, hydroxychloroquine sulphate 200 mg. Net price 60-tab pack = £4.55. Label: 5, 21

## Drugs affecting the immune response

**Methotrexate** is a disease-modifying antirheumatic drug suitable for moderate to severe rheumatoid arthritis. **Azathioprine**, **ciclosporin**, **cyclophosphamide**, **leflunomide**, and the **cytokine inhibitors** (adalimumab, anakinra, etanercept, and infliximab) are considered more toxic and they are used in cases that have not responded to other disease-modifying drugs.

**Methotrexate** is usually given in an initial dose of 7.5 mg by mouth once a week, adjusted according to response to a maximum of 15 mg once a week (occasionally 20 mg once a week). Regular full blood counts (including differential white cell count and platelet count), renal and liver-function tests are required. In patients who experience mucosal or gastro-intestinal side-effects with methotrexate, folic acid 5 mg every week may help to reduce the frequency of such side-effects.

**Azathioprine** is usually given in a dose of 1.5 to 2.5 mg/kg daily in divided doses. Blood counts are needed to detect possible neutropenia or thrombocytopenia (usually resolved by reducing the dose). Nausea, vomiting, and diarrhoea may occur, usually starting early during the course of treatment, and may necessitate withdrawal of the drug; herpes zoster infection may also occur.

**Leflunomide** acts on the immune system as a disease-modifying antirheumatic drug. Its therapeutic effect starts after 4–6 weeks and improvement may continue for a further 4–6 months. Leflunomide, which is similar in efficacy to sulfasalazine and methotrexate, may be chosen when these drugs cannot be used. The active metabolite of leflunomide persists for a long period; active procedures to wash the drug out are required in case of serious adverse effects, or before starting treatment with another disease-modifying antirheumatic drug, or, in men or women, before conception. Side-effects of leflunomide include bone-marrow toxicity; its immunosuppressive effects increase the risk of infection and malignancy.

**Ciclosporin** (cyclosporin) is licensed for severe active rheumatoid arthritis when conventional second-line therapy is inappropriate or ineffective. There is some evidence that ciclosporin may retard the rate of erosive progression and improve symptom control in those who respond only partially to methotrexate.

**Cyclophosphamide** (section 8.1.1) may be used at a dose of 1 to 1.5 mg/kg daily by mouth for rheumatoid arthritis with severe systemic manifestations [unlicensed indication]; it is toxic and regular blood counts (including platelet count) should be carried out. Cyclophosphamide may also be given intravenously in a dose of 0.5 to 1 g (with prophylactic mesna) for *severe systemic rheumatoid arthritis* and for other connective tissue diseases (especially with active vasculitis), repeated initially at fortnightly then at monthly intervals (according to clinical response and haematological monitoring).

Drugs that affect the immune response are also used in the management of severe cases of *systemic lupus erythematosus* and other connective tissue disorders. They are often given in conjunction with corticosteroids for patients with severe or progressive renal disease. They may be used in cases of *polymyositis* which are resistant to corticosteroids. They are used for their corticosteroid-sparing effect in patients whose corticosteroid requirements are excessive. **Azathioprine** is usually used.

Azathioprine and methotrexate are used in the treatment of *psoriatic arthropathy* [unlicensed indication] for severe or progressive cases which are not controlled with anti-inflammatory drugs.

## AZATHIOPRINE

**Indications** see notes above; transplantation rejection, see section 8.2.1

**Cautions** see section 8.2.1

**Contra-indications** see section 8.2.1

**Side-effects** see section 8.2.1

**Dose**

- By mouth, initially, rarely more than 3 mg/kg daily, reduced according to response; maintenance 1–3 mg/kg daily; consider withdrawal if no improvement within 3 months

**Preparations**
Section 8.2.1

## CICLOSPORIN
(Cyclosporin)

**Indications** severe active rheumatoid arthritis when conventional second-line therapy inappropriate or ineffective; graft-versus-host disease (section 8.2.2); atopic dermatitis and psoriasis (section 13.5.3).

**Cautions** see section 8.2.2

Additional cautions in rheumatoid arthritis *Contra-indicated* in abnormal renal function, uncontrolled hypertension (see also below), uncontrolled infections, and malignancy. Measure serum creatinine at least twice before treatment and monitor every 2 weeks for first 3 months, then every 4 weeks (or more frequently if dose increased or concomitant NSAIDs introduced or increased (see also *interactions:* Appendix 1 (ciclosporin)), reduce dose if serum creatinine increases more than 30% above baseline in more than 1 measurement; if above 50%, reduce dose by 50% (even if within normal range) and discontinue if reduction not successful within 1 month; monitor blood pressure (discontinue if hypertension develops that cannot be controlled by antihypertensive therapy); monitor hepatic function if concomitant NSAIDs given.

**Side-effects** see section 8.2.2

**Dose**

- By mouth, administered in accordance with expert advice, initially 2.5 mg/kg daily in 2 divided doses, if necessary increased gradually after 6 weeks; max. 4 mg/kg daily (discontinue if response insufficient after 3 months); dose adjusted according to response for maintenance and treatment reviewed after 6 months (continue only if benefits outweigh risks); CHILD and under 18 years, not recommended

Important For preparations and counselling and for advice on conversion between the preparations, see section 8.2.2

**Preparations**
Section 8.2.2

## LEFLUNOMIDE

**Indications** moderate to severe active rheumatoid arthritis; active psoriatic arthritis

**Cautions** renal impairment (Appendix 3); impaired bone-marrow function including anaemia, leucopenia or thrombocytopenia (avoid if significant and due to causes other than rheumatoid arthritis); recent treatment with other hepatotoxic or myelotoxic disease-modifying antirheumatic drugs (avoid concomitant use); history of tuberculosis; exclude pregnancy before treatment; effective contraception **essential** during treatment and for at least 2 years after treatment in women and at least 3 months after treatment in men (plasma concentration monitoring required; waiting time before conception may be reduced with washout procedures—consult product literature and see Washout Procedure below); monitor full blood count (including differential white cell count and platelet count) before treatment and every 2 weeks for 6 months then every 8 weeks; monitor liver function—(see Hepatotoxicity below); monitor blood pressure; washout procedures recommended for serious adverse effects and before switching to other disease-modifying antirheumatic drugs (consult product literature and see below); **interactions:** Appendix 1 (leflunomide)

Hepatotoxicity Potentially life-threatening hepatotoxicity reported usually in the first 6 months; monitor liver function before treatment and every 2 weeks for first 6 months then every 8 weeks. Discontinue treatment (and institute washout procedure—consult product literature and see Washout Procedure below) or reduce dose according to liver-function abnormality; if liver-function abnormality persists after dose reduction, discontinue treatment and institute washout procedure

Washout procedure To aid drug elimination in case of serious adverse effect, or before starting another disease-modifying antirheumatic drug, or before conception (see also Appendix 4), stop treatment and give *either* colestyramine 8 g 3 times daily for 11 days *or* activated charcoal 50 g 4 times daily for 11 days; the concentration of the active metabolite after washout should be less than 20 micrograms/litre (measured on 2 occasions 14 days apart) in men or women before conception—consult product literature

**Contra-indications** severe immunodeficiency; serious infection; hepatic impairment (Appendix 2); severe hypoproteinaemia; pregnancy (**important teratogenic risk:** see Cautions and Appendix 4); breast-feeding (Appendix 5)

**Side-effects** diarrhoea, nausea, vomiting, anorexia, oral mucosal disorders, abdominal pain, weight loss; increase in blood pressure; headache, dizziness, asthenia, paraesthesia; tenosynovitis; alopecia, eczema, dry skin, rash, pruritus; leucopenia; rarely taste disturbances, anxiety, tendon rupture, urticaria, anaemia, thrombocytopenia, eosinophilia, hyperlipidaemia, hypokalaemia, hypophosphataemia, hepatic dysfunction (see Hepatotoxicity above); also reported, pancreatitis, anaphylaxis, interstitial lung disease, severe infection, pancytopenia, vasculitis, Stevens-Johnson syndrome, toxic epidermal necrolysis (discontinue and initiate washout procedure—consult product literature)

**Dose**

- Rheumatoid arthritis, ADULT over 18 years, initially 100 mg once daily for 3 days then maintenance, 10–20 mg once daily
- Psoriatic arthritis, ADULT over 18 years, initially 100 mg once daily for 3 days then maintenance, 20 mg once daily

**Arava®** (Aventis Pharma) ▼ PoM
Tablets, f/c, leflunomide 10 mg, net price 30-tab pack = £51.13; 20 mg (ochre), 30-tab pack = £51.13; 100 mg, 3-tab pack = £25.56. Label: 4

## METHOTREXATE

**Indications** moderate to severe active rheumatoid arthritis; Crohn's disease (section 1.5); malignant disease (section 8.1.3); psoriasis (section 13.5.3)

**Cautions** section 8.1; see CSM advice below (blood count, liver and pulmonary toxicity); extreme caution in blood disorders (avoid if severe); renal impairment (avoid in moderate or severe—Appendix 3); peptic ulceration, ulcerative colitis, diarrhoea and ulcerative stomatitis (withdraw if stomatitis develops—may be first sign of gastro-intestinal toxicity); risk of accumulation in pleural effusion or ascites—drain before treatment; porphyria (section 9.8.2); **interactions:** see below and Appendix 1 (methotrexate)

**CSM advice**
In view of reports of blood dyscrasias (including fatalities) and liver cirrhosis with low-dose methotrexate, the CSM has advised:

- full blood count and renal and liver function tests before starting treatment and repeated weekly until therapy stabilised, thereafter patients should be monitored every 2–3 months
- that patients should be advised to report all symptoms and signs suggestive of infection, especially sore throat

Treatment with folinic acid (as calcium folinate, section 8.1) may be required in acute toxicity

**Blood count** Haematopoietic suppression may occur abruptly; factors likely to increase toxicity include advanced age, renal impairment and concomitant administration of another anti-folate drug. Any profound drop in white cell or platelet count calls for immediate withdrawal of methotrexate and introduction of supportive therapy

**Liver toxicity** Liver cirrhosis reported. Treatment should not be started or should be discontinued if any abnormality of liver function tests or liver biopsy is present or develops during therapy. Abnormalities may return to normal within 2 weeks after which treatment may be recommenced if judged appropriate

**Pulmonary toxicity** Pulmonary toxicity may be a special problem in rheumatoid arthritis (patient to seek medical attention if dyspnoea, cough or fever); monitor for symptoms at each visit—discontinue if pneumonitis suspected.

**Aspirin and other NSAIDs** If aspirin or other NSAIDs are given concurrently the dose of methotrexate should be carefully monitored. Patients should be advised to avoid self-medication with over-the-counter aspirin or ibuprofen

**Contra-indications** see Cautions above, hepatic impairment (Appendix 2), pregnancy (following administration to a woman or a man, avoid conception for **at least 3 months** after stopping—Appendix 4), breast-feeding (Appendix 5), active infection and immunodeficiency syndromes

**Side-effects** section 8.1; also anorexia, abdominal discomfort, intestinal ulceration and bleeding, diarrhoea, toxic megacolon, hepatotoxicity (see Cautions above); ecchymosis; pulmonary oedema, pleuritic pain, pulmonary fibrosis, interstitial pneumonitis (see Pulmonary Toxicity above); anaphylactic reactions, urticaria; dizziness, drowsiness, malaise, headache, mood changes, abnormal cranial sensations; precipitation of diabetes, osteoporosis; menstrual disturbances, vaginitis, impotence, loss of libido; haematuria, dysuria, renal failure; arthralgia, myalgia, vasculitis, blurred vision; rash, pruritus, Stevens-Johnson syndrome, toxic epidermal necrolysis, photosensitivity, changes of skin pigmentation, telangiectasia

**Dose**
- By mouth, 7.5 mg once weekly (as a single dose *or* divided into 3 doses of 2.5 mg given at intervals of 12 hours), adjusted according to response; max. total weekly dose 20 mg

**Important**
Note that the above dose is a **weekly** dose. The CSM has received reports of prescription and dispensing errors including fatalities. Attention should be paid to the **strength** of methotrexate tablets prescribed and the **frequency** of dosing.

**Methotrexate** (Non-proprietary) PoM
Tablets, yellow, methotrexate 2.5 mg, net price 28-tab pack = £3.27. Counselling, dose, NSAIDs
Brands include *Maxtrex®*

Tablets, yellow, methotrexate 10 mg, net price 20 (Mayne) = £11.01; (Pharmacia, *Maxtrex®*) = £9.03. Counselling, dose NSAIDs

## Cytokine inhibitors

Cytokine inhibitors should be used under specialist supervision.

Adalimumab, etanercept, and infliximab inhibit the activity of tumour necrosis factor.

**NICE guidance (etanercept and infliximab for rheumatoid arthritis).**
NICE has recommended (March 2002) the use of either etanercept or infliximab for highly active rheumatoid arthritis in adults who have failed to respond to at least 2 standard disease-modifying antirheumatic drugs, including methotrexate (unless methotrexate cannot be used because of intolerance or contra-indications). Etanercept and infliximab should be prescribed (according to the guidelines of the British Society for Rheumatology) and their use monitored by consultant rheumatologists specialising in their use. Infliximab should be given concomitantly with methotrexate.

Etanercept or infliximab should be withdrawn if severe side-effects develop or if there is no response after 3 months. There is no evidence to support treatment for longer than 4 years; a decision to continue therapy should be based on disease activity and clinical effectiveness in individual cases.

Consecutive use of etanercept and infliximab is not recommended.

Prescribers of etanercept and infliximab should register consenting patients with the Biologics Registry of the British Society for Rheumatology.

**NICE guidance (etanercept for juvenile idiopathic arthritis).**
NICE has recommended (March 2002) the use of etanercept in children aged 4–17 years with active polyarticular-course juvenile idiopathic arthritis who have not responded adequately to methotrexate or who are intolerant of it. Etanercept should be used under specialist supervision according to the guidelines of the British Society for Paediatric and Adolescent Rheumatology [previously the British Paediatric Rheumatology Group].

Etanercept should be withdrawn if severe side-effects develop or if there is no response after 6 months or if the initial response is not maintained. There is no evidence to support treatment for longer than 2 years; a decision to continue therapy should be based on disease activity and clinical effectiveness in individual cases.

Prescribers of etanercept and infliximab should register consenting patients with the Biologics Registry of the British Society for Paediatric and Adolescent Rheumatology [previously the British Paediatric Rheumatology Group].

**Adalimumab** is licensed for moderate to severe active rheumatoid arthritis when response to other disease-modifying antirheumatic drugs (including methotrexate) has been inadequate; it should be used in combination with methotrexate, but it may be given alone if methotrexate is inappropriate. Adalimumab is also licensed for the treatment of active and progressive psoriatic arthritis that has not responded adequately to other disease-modifying anti-rheumatic drugs.

**Etanercept** is licensed for the treatment of active *rheumatoid arthritis* either alone or in combination with methotrexate when the response to other disease-modifying antirheumatic drugs is inadequate (see also NICE guidelines). It is also licensed for the treatment of active and progressive *psoriatic arthritis* inadequately responsive to other disease-modifying antirheumatic drugs, and for severe *ankylosing spondylitis* inadequately responsive to conventional therapy. For the role of etanercept in psoriasis see section 13.5.3.

**Infliximab** is licensed for the treatment of active rheumatoid arthritis in combination with methotrexate when the response to other disease-modifying antirheumatic drugs is inadequate (see also NICE guidelines). It is also licensed for the treatment of *ankylosing spondylitis*, in patients with severe axial symptoms who have not responded adequately to conventional therapy and in combination with methotrexate for the treatment of active and progressive *psoriatic arthritis* which has not responded adequately to disease-modifying antirheumatic drugs. For the role of infliximab in psoriasis, see section 13.5.3.

Adalimumab, etanercept, and infliximab have been associated with infections, sometimes severe, including tuberculosis and septicaemia. Other side-effects include nausea, abdominal pain, worsening heart failure, hypersensitivity reactions, fever, headache, depression, lupus erythematosus-like syndrome, pruritus, injection-site reactions, and blood disorders (including anaemia, leucopenia, thrombocytopenia, pancytopenia, and aplastic anaemia).

**Anakinra** inhibits the activity of interleukin-1. Anakinra (in combination with methotrexate) is licensed for the treatment of *rheumatoid arthritis* which has not responded to methotrexate alone; it is not, however, recommended for routine management of *rheumatoid arthritis*, see NICE guidance below.

The *Scottish Medicines Consortium* has advised (October 2003) that anakinra is **not** recommended for rheumatoid arthritis.

> **NICE guidance (anakinra for rheumatoid arthritis).**
> NICE does not recommend (November 2003) anakinra for the treatment of rheumatoid arthritis except when used in a controlled long-term clinical study. Patients receiving anakinra for rheumatoid arthritis should continue treatment until they and their consultant consider it appropriate to stop.

## ADALIMUMAB

**Indications** see under Cytokine Inhibitors above; severe, active and progressive rheumatoid arthritis in patients not previously treated with methotrexate

**Cautions** hepatic impairment; renal impairment; monitor for infections before, during, and for 5 months after treatment (see also Tuberculosis below); not to be initiated until active (including chronic or local) infections controlled; predisposition to infections; heart failure (discontinue if symptoms develop or worsen; avoid in moderate or severe heart failure); demyelinating CNS disorders (risk of exacerbation); **interactions:** Appendix 1 (adalimumab)

**Tuberculosis** Patients should be evaluated for tuberculosis before treatment. Active tuberculosis should be treated with standard treatment (section 5.1.9) for at least 2 months before starting adalimumab. Patients who have previously received adequate treatment for tuberculosis can start adalimumab but should be monitored every 3 months for possible recurrence. In patients without active tuberculosis but who were previously not treated adequately, chemoprophylaxis should ideally be completed before starting adalimumab. Patients should be advised to seek medical attention if symptoms suggestive of tuberculosis (e.g. persistent cough, weight loss, and fever) develop

**Contra-indications** pregnancy (Appendix 4); breast-feeding (Appendix 5); severe infections (see also Cautions)

**Side-effects** see under Cytokine Inhibitors and Cautions above; also diarrhoea, constipation, vomiting, oesophagitis, dyspepsia, gastritis, dysphagia, taste disturbances, mouth ulceration, hypertension, vasodilatation, chest pain, ecchymosis, cough, sore throat, asthma, dyspnoea, asthenia, insomnia, drowsiness, dizziness, agitation, tremor, paraesthesia, hypoaesthesia, neuralgia, menorrhagia, urinary frequency, haematuria, proteinuria, arthralgia, myalgia, eye disorders, rash, alopecia, sweating, hyperlipidaemia, hypokalaemia, hyperuricaemia

**Dose**

- By subcutaneous injection

  Rheumatoid arthritis, ADULT over 18 years, 40 mg on alternate weeks; if necessary increased to 40 mg weekly in patients receiving adalimumab alone; discontinue if no response after 12 weeks

  Psoriatic arthritis, ADULT over 18 years, 40 mg on alternate weeks

**Humira®** (Abbott) ▼ PoM
Injection, adalimumab, net price 40-mg prefilled syringe = £357.50. Counselling, tuberculosis

## ANAKINRA

**Indications** see under Cytokine Inhibitors above

**Cautions** renal impairment (Appendix 3); predisposition to infections; history of asthma (risk of serious infection); **interactions:** Appendix 1 (anakinra)

**Blood disorders** Neutropenia reported commonly. Monitor neutrophil count before treatment, then every month for 6 months, then every 3 months—discontinue if neutropenia develops. Patients should be instructed to seek medical advice if symptoms suggestive of neutropenia (such as fever, sore throat, infection) develop

**Contra-indications** pregnancy (Appendix 4); breast-feeding (Appendix 5); neutropenia

**Side-effects** injection-site reactions, headache; infections, neutropenia (see also Cautions)

**Dose**

- By subcutaneous injection, ADULT over 18 years, 100 mg once daily

**Kineret®** (Amgen) ▼ PoM
Injection, anakinra, net price 100-mg prefilled syringe = £19.03. Counselling, blood disorder symptoms

## ETANERCEPT

**Indications** see under Cytokine Inhibitors above; severe, active and progressive rheumatoid arthritis in patients not previously treated with methotrexate; psoriasis (section 13.5.3)

**Cautions** predisposition to infection (avoid if predisposition to septicaemia); significant exposure to herpes zoster virus—interrupt treatment and consider varicella–zoster immunoglobulin; heart failure (risk of exacerbation); demyelinating CNS disorders (risk of exacerbation); history of blood disorders; **interactions:** Appendix 1 (etanercept)

Tuberculosis Patients should be evaluated for tuberculosis before treatment. Active tuberculosis should be treated with standard treatment (section 5.1.9) for at least 2 months before starting etanercept. Patients who have previously received adequate treatment for tuberculosis can start etanercept but should be monitored every 3 months for possible recurrence. In patients without active tuberculosis but who were previously not treated adequately, chemoprophylaxis should ideally be completed before starting etanercept. Patients should be advised to seek medical attention if symptoms suggestive of tuberculosis (e.g. persistent cough, weight loss, and fever) develop

Blood disorders Patients should be advised to seek medical attention if symptoms suggestive of blood disorders (such as fever, sore throat, bruising, or bleeding) develop.

**Contra-indications** pregnancy (Appendix 4); breast-feeding (Appendix 5); active infection

**Side-effects** see under Cytokine Inhibitors above; also vomiting, oesophagitis, cholecystitis, pancreatitis, gastro-intestinal haemorrhage, myocardial or cerebral ischaemia, venous thromboembolism, hypotension, hypertension, dyspnoea, demyelinating disorders, seizures, bone fracture, renal impairment, polymyositis, bursitis, lymphadenopathy

**Dose**

- By subcutaneous injection, rheumatoid arthritis ADULT over 18 years, 25 mg twice weekly *or* 50 mg once weekly

  Psoriatic arthritis, ankylosing spondylitis ADULT over 18 years, 25 mg twice weekly

  Polyarticular-course juvenile idiopathic arthritis, CHILD and ADOLESCENT 4–17 years, 400 micrograms/kg twice weekly (max. 25 mg twice weekly)

  Psoriasis, ADULT over 18 years, initially 25–50 mg twice weekly for up to 12 weeks then reduce to 25 mg twice weekly; max. treatment duration 24 weeks; discontinue if no response after 12 weeks

**Enbrel** (Wyeth) ▼ PoM

Injection, powder for reconstitution, etanercept, net price 25-mg vial = £89.38, 50-mg vial = £178.75

## INFLIXIMAB

**Indications** see under Cytokine Inhibitors above; severe, active and progressive rheumatoid arthritis in patients not previously treated with methotrexate; psoriasis; Crohn's disease (section 1.5)

**Cautions** hepatic impairment; renal impairment; monitor for infections before, during, and for 6 months after treatment (see also Tuberculosis below); heart failure (discontinue if symptoms develop or worsen; avoid in moderate or severe heart failure); demyelinating CNS disorders (risk of exacerbation); **interactions:** Appendix 1 (infliximab)

Tuberculosis Patients should be evaluated for tuberculosis before treatment. Active tuberculosis should be treated with standard treatment (section 5.1.9) for at least 2 months before starting infliximab. Patients who have previously received adequate treatment for tuberculosis can start infliximab but should be monitored every 3 months for possible recurrence. In patients without active tuberculosis but who were previously not treated adequately, chemoprophylaxis should ideally be completed before starting infliximab. Patients should be advised to seek medical attention if symptoms suggestive of tuberculosis (e.g. persistent cough, weight loss, and fever) develop

Hypersensitivity reactions Hypersensitivity reactions (including fever, chest pain, hypotension, hypertension, dyspnoea, pruritus, urticaria, serum sickness-like reactions, angioedema, anaphylaxis) reported during or within 1–2 hours after infusion (risk greatest during first or second infusion or in patients who discontinue other immunosuppressants. All patients should be observed carefully for 1–2 hours after infusion and resuscitation equipment should be available for immediate use. Prophylactic antipyretics, antihistamines, or hydrocortisone may be administered. Readministration not recommended after infliximab-free interval of more than 16 weeks—risk of delayed hypersensitivity reactions. Patients should be advised to keep Alert card with them at all times and seek medical advice if symptoms of delayed hypersensitivity develop

**Contra-indications** pregnancy (Appendix 4); breast-feeding (Appendix 5); severe infections (see also under Cautions)

**Side-effects** see under Cytokine Inhibitors and Cautions above; also dyspepsia, diarrhoea, constipation, hepatitis, cholecystitis, diverticulitis, gastro-intestinal haemorrhage, flushing, bradycardia, arrhythmias, palpitation, syncope, vasospasm, peripheral ischaemia, ecchymosis, haematoma, interstitial pneumonitis or fibrosis, fatigue, anxiety, drowsiness, dizziness, insomnia, confusion, agitation, amnesia, seizures, demyelinating disorders, vaginitis, myalgia, arthralgia, endophthalmitis, rash, sweating, hyperkeratosis, skin pigmentation, alopecia

**Dose**

- By intravenous infusion, rheumatoid arthritis (in combination with methotrexate), ADULT over 18 years, 3 mg/kg, repeated 2 weeks and 6 weeks after initial infusion, then every 8 weeks

  Ankylosing spondylitis, ADULT over 18 years, 5 mg/kg, repeated 2 weeks and 6 weeks after initial infusion, then every 6–8 weeks; discontinue if no response by 6 weeks of initial infusion

  Psoriatic arthritis (in combination with methotrexate), ADULT over 18 years, 5 mg/kg, repeated 2 weeks and 6 weeks after initial infusion, then every 8 weeks

  Psoriasis, ADULT over 18 years, 5 mg/kg, repeated 2 weeks and 6 weeks after initial infusion, then every 8 weeks; discontinue if no response by 14 weeks of initial infusion

**Remicade®** (Schering-Plough) ▼ PoM

Intravenous infusion, powder for reconstitution, infliximab, net price 100-mg vial = £419.62. Label: 10, alert card, counselling, tuberculosis and hypersensitivity reactions

## Sulfasalazine

**Sulfasalazine** (sulphasalazine) has a beneficial effect in suppressing the inflammatory activity of rheumatoid arthritis. Side-effects include rashes, gastro-intestinal intolerance and, especially in patients with rheumatoid arthritis, occasional leucopenia, neutropenia, and thrombocytopenia. These haematological abnormalities occur usually in the first 3 to 6 months of treatment and are reversible on cessation of treatment. Close monitoring of full blood counts (including differential white cell count and platelet count) is necessary initially, and at monthly intervals during the first 3 months (liver-function tests also being performed at monthly intervals for the first 3 months). Although the manufacturer recommends renal function tests, evidence of practical value is unsatisfactory.

## SULFASALAZINE
(Sulphasalazine)

**Indications** active rheumatoid arthritis; ulcerative colitis, see section 1.5 and notes above

**Cautions** see section 1.5 and notes above

The CSM has recommended that patients should be advised to report any unexplained bleeding, bruising, purpura, sore throat, fever or malaise. A blood count should be performed and the drug stopped immediately if there is suspicion of a blood dyscrasia.

**Contra-indications** see section 1.5 and notes above

**Side-effects** see section 1.5 and notes above

**Dose**

- By mouth, administered on expert advice, as enteric-coated tablets, initially 500 mg daily, increased by 500 mg at intervals of 1 week to a max. of 2–3 g daily in divided doses

**Sulfasalazine** (Non-proprietary) PoM

Tablets, e/c, sulfasalazine 500 mg. Net price 112-tab pack = £8.43. Label: 5, 14, 25, counselling, blood disorder symptoms (see CSM recommendation above), contact lenses may be stained

Brands include *Sulazine EC*®

**Salazopyrin EN-Tabs**® (Pharmacia) PoM

Tablets, e/c, yellow, f/c, sulfasalazine 500 mg. Net price 112-tab pack = £8.43. Label: 5, 14, 25, counselling, blood disorder symptoms (see CSM recommendation above), contact lenses may be stained



# 10.1.4 Gout and cytotoxic-induced hyperuricaemia

It is important to distinguish drugs used for the treatment of acute attacks of gout from those used in the long-term control of the disease. The latter exacerbate and prolong the acute manifestations if started during an attack.

## Acute attacks of gout

Acute attacks of gout are usually treated with high doses of **NSAIDs** such as diclofenac, etoricoxib, indometacin, ketoprofen, naproxen, piroxicam, or sulindac (section 10.1.1). Colchicine is an alternative. Aspirin is *not* indicated in gout. Allopurinol and uricosurics are not effective in treating an acute attack and may prolong it indefinitely if started during the acute episode.

**Colchicine** is probably as effective as NSAIDs. Its use is limited by the development of toxicity at higher doses, but it is of value in patients with heart failure since, unlike NSAIDs, it does not induce fluid retention; moreover, it can be given to patients receiving anticoagulants.

Intra-articular injection of a **corticosteroid** may be used in acute monoarticular gout [unlicensed indication]. A corticosteroid by intramuscular injection can be effective in podagra.

## COLCHICINE

**Indications** acute gout, short-term prophylaxis during initial therapy with allopurinol and uricosuric drugs; prophylaxis of familial Mediterranean fever (recurrent polyserositis) [unlicensed]

**Cautions** breast-feeding (Appendix 5), elderly, gastro-intestinal disease, cardiac, hepatic impairment, renal impairment (Appendix 3); **interactions**: Appendix 1 (colchicine)

**Contra-indications** pregnancy (Appendix 4)

**Side-effects** most common are nausea, vomiting, and abdominal pain; excessive doses may also cause profuse diarrhoea, gastro-intestinal haemorrhage, rashes, renal and hepatic damage. Rarely peripheral neuritis, myopathy, alopecia, inhibition of spermatogenesis, and with prolonged treatment blood disorders

**Dose**

- Treatment of gout, initially 1 mg, then 500 micrograms no more frequently than every 4 hours until pain relieved or vomiting or diarrhoea occur, max. 6 mg per course; course not to be repeated within 3 days
- Prevention of gout attacks during initial treatment with allopurinol or uricosuric drugs, 500 micrograms 2–3 times daily
- Prophylaxis of familial Mediterranean fever [unlicensed], 0.5–2 mg daily

**Colchicine** (Non-proprietary) PoM

Tablets, colchicine 500 micrograms, net price 20 = £3.32

## Long-term control of gout

Frequent recurrence of acute attacks of gout, the presence of tophi, or signs of chronic gouty arthritis may call for the initiation of long-term ('interval') treatment. For long-term control of gout the formation of uric acid from purines may be reduced with the xanthine-oxidase inhibitor allopurinol, or the uricosuric drug sulfinpyrazone may be used to increase the excretion of uric acid in the urine. Treatment should be continued indefinitely to prevent further attacks of gout by correcting the hyperuricaemia. These drugs should never be started during an acute attack; they are usually started 2–3 weeks after the attack has settled. The initiation of treatment may precipitate an acute attack therefore colchicine or an anti-inflammatory analgesic should be used as a prophylactic and continued for at least one month after the hyperuricaemia has been corrected (usually about 3 months of prophylaxis). However, if an acute attack develops during treatment, then the treatment should continue at the same dosage and the acute attack treated in its own right.

**Allopurinol** is a well tolerated drug which is widely used. It is especially useful in patients with renal impairment or urate stones where uricosuric drugs cannot be used; it is *not* indicated for the treatment of asymptomatic hyperuricaemia. It is usually given once daily, since the active metabolite of allopurinol has a long half-life, but doses over 300 mg daily should be divided. It may occasionally cause rashes.

**Sulfinpyrazone** (sulphinpyrazone) can be used instead of allopurinol, or in conjunction with it in cases that are resistant to treatment.

**Probenecid** (available on a named-patient basis) is a uricosuric drug used to prevent nephrotoxicity associated with cidofovir (section 5.3.2.2).

Crystallisation of urate in the urine may occur with the uricosuric drugs and it is important to ensure an adequate urine output especially in the first few weeks of treatment. As an additional precaution the urine may be rendered alkaline.

Aspirin and salicylates antagonise the uricosuric drugs; they do not antagonise allopurinol but are nevertheless *not* indicated in gout.

## ALLOPURINOL

**Indications** prophylaxis of gout and of uric acid and calcium oxalate renal stones; prophylaxis of hyperuricaemia associated with cancer chemotherapy

**Cautions** administer prophylactic colchicine or NSAID (*not* aspirin or salicylates) until at least 1 month after hyperuricaemia corrected; ensure adequate fluid intake (2–3 litres/day); for hyperuricaemia associated with cancer therapy, allopurinol treatment should be started before cancer therapy; hepatic impairment (Appendix 2); renal impairment (Appendix 3); pregnancy (Appendix 4); breast-feeding (Appendix 5); **interactions**: Appendix 1 (allopurinol)

**Contra-indications** not a treatment for acute gout but continue if attack develops when already receiving allopurinol, and treat attack separately (see notes above)

**Side-effects** rashes (**withdraw** therapy; if rash mild re-introduce cautiously but **discontinue** immediately if recurrence—hypersensitivity reactions occur rarely and include exfoliation, fever, lymphadenopathy, arthralgia, and eosinophilia resembling Stevens-Johnson or Lyell's syndrome, vasculitis, hepatitis, renal impairment, and very rarely seizures); gastro-intestinal disorders; rarely malaise, headache, vertigo, drowsiness, visual and taste disturbances, hypertension, alopecia, hepatotoxicity, paraesthesia and neuropathy, gynaecomastia, blood disorders (including leucopenia, thrombocytopenia, haemolytic anaemia and aplastic anaemia)

**Dose**

- Initially 100 mg daily, preferably after food, then adjusted according to plasma or urinary uric acid concentration; usual maintenance dose in mild conditions 100–200 mg daily, in moderately severe conditions 300–600 mg daily, in severe conditions 700–900 mg daily; doses over 300 mg daily given in divided doses; CHILD under 15 years, (in neoplastic conditions, enzyme disorders) 10–20 mg/kg daily (max. 400 mg daily)

**Allopurinol** (Non-proprietary) PoM
Tablets, allopurinol 100 mg, net price 28-tab pack = £1.22; 300 mg, 28-tab pack = £1.22. Label: 8, 21, 27
Brands include *Caplenal®*, *Cosuric®*, *Rimapurinol®*

**Zyloric®** (GSK) PoM
Tablets, allopurinol 100 mg, net price 100-tab pack = £10.19; 300 mg, 28-tab pack = £7.31. Label: 8, 21, 27

## PROBENECID

**Indications** prevention of nephrotoxicity associated with cidofovir (section 5.3.2.2)

**Cautions** ensure adequate fluid intake (about 2–3 litres daily) and render urine alkaline if uric acid overload is high; peptic ulceration, renal impairment (avoid if severe—Appendix 3); transient false-positive Benedict's test; G6PD-deficiency (section 9.1.5); **interactions**: Appendix 1 (probenecid)

**Contra-indications** history of blood disorders, nephrolithiasis, porphyria (section 9.8.2), acute gout attack; avoid aspirin and salicylates

**Side-effects** gastro-intestinal disturbances, urinary frequency, headache, flushing, dizziness, alopecia, anaemia, haemolytic anaemia, sore gums; hypersensitivity reactions including anaphylaxis, dermatitis, pruritus, urticaria, fever and Stevens-Johnson syndrome; rarely nephrotic syndrome, hepatic necrosis, leucopenia, aplastic anaemia; toxic epidermal necrolysis reported with concurrent colchicine

**Dose**

- Used with cidofovir, see section 5.3.2.2

**Probenecid** (Non-proprietary) PoM
Tablets, probenecid 500 mg. Label: 12, 21, 27
Available on named-patient basis from IDIS (*Benuryl®*, *Probecid®*)

## SULFINPYRAZONE
**(Sulphinpyrazone)**

**Indications** gout prophylaxis, hyperuricaemia

**Cautions** see under Probenecid; regular blood counts advisable; cardiac disease (may cause salt and water retention); renal impairment (Appendix 3); **interactions**: Appendix 1 (sulfinpyrazone)

**Contra-indications** see under Probenecid; avoid in hypersensitivity to NSAIDs

**Side-effects** gastro-intestinal disturbances, occasionally allergic skin reactions, salt and water retention; rarely blood disorders, gastro-intestinal ulceration and bleeding, acute renal failure, raised liver enzymes, jaundice and hepatitis

**Dose**

- Initially 100–200 mg daily with food (or milk) increasing over 2–3 weeks to 600 mg daily (rarely 800 mg daily), continued until serum uric acid concentration normal then reduced for maintenance (maintenance dose may be as low as 200 mg daily)

**Anturan®** (Amdipharm) PoM
Tablets, both yellow, s/c, sulfinpyrazone 100 mg, net price 84-tab pack = £4.72; 200 mg, 84-tab pack = £9.38. Label: 12, 21

## Hyperuricaemia associated with cytotoxic drugs

**Allopurinol** is used to prevent hyperuricaemia associated with cytotoxic drugs—see section 8.1 (Hyperuricaemia) and Allopurinol above.

**Rasburicase** is licensed for the prophylaxis and treatment of acute hyperuricaemia, before and during initiation of chemotherapy, in patients with haematological malignancy and a high tumour burden at risk of rapid lysis.

## RASBURICASE

**Indications** prophylaxis and treatment of acute hyperuricaemia with initial chemotherapy for haematological malignancy

**Cautions** monitor closely for hypersensitivity; atopic allergies; may interfere with test for uric acid—consult product literature

**Contra-indications** susceptibility to haemolytic anaemia including G6PD deficiency; pregnancy (Appendix 4); breast-feeding (Appendix 5)

**Side-effects** fever; nausea, vomiting; less frequently diarrhoea, headache, hypersensitivity reactions (including rash, bronchospasm and anaphylaxis); haemolytic anaemia, methaemoglobinaemia

**Dose**

- By intravenous infusion, 200 micrograms/kg once daily for 5–7 days

**Fasturtec** (Sanofi-Synthelabo) ▼ PoM

Intravenous infusion, powder for reconstitution, rasburicase, net price 1.5-mg vial (with solvent) = £48.24; 7.5-mg vial (with solvent) = £201.00



# 10.2 Drugs used in neuromuscular disorders

## 10.2.1 Drugs which enhance neuromuscular transmission

Anticholinesterases are used as first-line treatment in *ocular myasthenia gravis* and as an adjunct to immunosuppressant therapy for *generalised myasthenia gravis*.

Corticosteroids are used when anticholinesterases do not control symptoms completely. A second-line immunosuppressant such as azathioprine is frequently used to reduce the dose of corticosteroid.

Plasmapheresis or infusion of intravenous immunoglobulin [unlicensed indication] may induce temporary remission in severe relapses, particularly where bulbar or respiratory function is compromised or before thymectomy.

### Anticholinesterases

Anticholinesterase drugs enhance neuromuscular transmission in voluntary and involuntary muscle in myasthenia gravis. They prolong the action of acetylcholine by inhibiting the action of the enzyme acetylcholinesterase. Excessive dosage of these drugs may impair neuromuscular transmission and precipitate 'cholinergic crises' by causing a depolarising block. This may be difficult to distinguish from a worsening myasthenic state.

Muscarinic side-effects of anticholinesterases include increased sweating, salivary, and gastric secretion, also increased gastro-intestinal and uterine motility, and bradycardia. These parasympathomimetic effects are antagonised by atropine.

**Edrophonium** has a very brief action and it is therefore used mainly for the diagnosis of myasthenia gravis. However, such testing should be performed only by those experienced in its use; other means of establishing the diagnosis are available. A single test-dose usually causes substantial improvement in muscle power (lasting about 5 minutes) in patients with the disease (if respiration already impaired, *only* in conjunction with someone skilled at intubation).

Edrophonium can also be used to determine whether a patient with myasthenia is receiving inadequate or excessive treatment with cholinergic drugs. If treatment is excessive an injection of edrophonium will either have no effect or will intensify symptoms (if respiration already impaired, *only* in conjunction with someone skilled at intubation). Conversely, transient improvement may be seen if the patient is being inadequately treated. The test is best performed just before the next dose of anticholinesterase.

**Neostigmine** produces a therapeutic effect for up to 4 hours. Its pronounced muscarinic action is a disadvantage, and simultaneous administration of an antimuscarinic drug such as atropine or propantheline may be required to prevent colic, excessive salivation, or diarrhoea. In severe disease neostigmine may be given every 2 hours. The maximum that most patients can tolerate is 180 mg daily.

**Pyridostigmine** is less powerful and slower in action than neostigmine but it has a longer duration of action. It is preferable to neostigmine because of its smoother action and the need for less frequent dosage. It is particularly preferred in patients whose muscles are weak on waking. It has a comparatively mild gastrointestinal effect but an antimuscarinic drug may still be required. It is inadvisable to exceed a total daily dose of 450 mg in order to avoid acetylcholine receptor down-regulation. Immunosuppressant therapy is usually considered if the dose of pyridostigmine exceeds 360 mg daily.

**Distigmine** has the longest action but the danger of a 'cholinergic crisis' caused by accumulation of the drug is greater than with shorter-acting drugs; it is rarely used in the management of myasthenia gravis.

Neostigmine and edrophonium are also used to reverse the actions of the non-depolarising muscle relaxants (see section 15.1.6).

### NEOSTIGMINE

**Indications** myasthenia gravis; other indications (section 15.1.6)

**Cautions** asthma (*extreme* caution), bradycardia, arrhythmias, recent myocardial infarction, epilepsy, hypotension, parkinsonism, vagotonia, peptic ulceration, hyperthyroidism, renal impairment (Appendix 3), pregnancy (Appendix 4), breast-feeding (Appendix 5); atropine or other antidote to muscarinic effects may be necessary (particularly when neostigmine is given by injection), but not given routinely because it may mask signs of overdosage; **interactions:** Appendix 1 (parasympathomimetics)

**Contra-indications** intestinal or urinary obstruction

**Side-effects** nausea, vomiting, increased salivation, diarrhoea, abdominal cramps (more marked with higher doses); signs of overdosage include bronchoconstriction, increased bronchial secretions, lacrimation, excessive sweating, involuntary defaecation and micturition, miosis, nystagmus, bradycardia, heart block, arrhythmias, hypotension, agitation, excessive dreaming, and weakness eventually leading to fasciculation and paralysis

**Dose**
- By mouth, neostigmine bromide 15–30 mg at suitable intervals throughout day, total daily dose 75–300 mg (but see also notes above); NEONATE 1–5 mg every 4 hours, half an hour before feeds; CHILD up to 6 years initially 7.5 mg, 6–12 years initially 15 mg, usual total daily dose 15–90 mg
- By subcutaneous *or* intramuscular injection, neostigmine metilsulfate 1–2.5 mg at suitable intervals throughout day (usual total daily dose 5–20 mg); NEONATE 50–250 micrograms every 4 hours half an hour before feeds; CHILD 200–500 micrograms as required

**Neostigmine** (Non-proprietary) PoM
Tablets, scored, neostigmine bromide 15 mg. Net price 20 = £4.24
Injection, neostigmine metilsulfate 2.5 mg/mL. Net price 1-mL amp = 58p

## DISTIGMINE BROMIDE

**Indications** myasthenia gravis (but rarely used); urinary retention and other indications (section 7.4.1)
**Cautions** see under Neostigmine; also oesophagitis
**Contra-indications** see under Neostigmine; also severe constipation, severe postoperative shock, serious circulatory insufficiency
**Side-effects** see under Neostigmine
**Dose**
- Initially 5 mg daily half an hour before breakfast, increased at intervals of 3–4 days if necessary to a max. of 20 mg daily; CHILD up to 10 mg daily according to age

Preparations
Section 7.4.1

## EDROPHONIUM CHLORIDE

**Indications** see under Dose and notes above; reversal of non-depolarising neuromuscular blockade and diagnosis of dual block (section 15.1.6)
**Cautions** see under Neostigmine; have resuscitation facilities; *extreme* caution in respiratory distress (see notes above) and in asthma
**Note** Severe cholinergic reactions can be counteracted by injection of atropine sulphate (which should always be available)
**Contra-indications** see under Neostigmine
**Side-effects** see under Neostigmine
**Dose**
- Diagnosis of myasthenia gravis, by intravenous injection, 2 mg followed after 30 seconds (if no adverse reaction has occurred) by 8 mg; in adults without suitable veins, by intramuscular injection, 10 mg
- Detection of overdosage or underdosage of cholinergic drugs, by intravenous injection, 2 mg (best before next dose of anticholinesterase, see notes above)
- CHILD by intravenous injection, 20 micrograms/kg followed after 30 seconds (if no adverse reaction has occurred) by 80 micrograms/kg

**Edrophonium** (Cambridge) PoM
Injection, edrophonium chloride 10 mg/mL. Net price 1-mL amp = £4.76

## PYRIDOSTIGMINE BROMIDE

**Indications** myasthenia gravis
**Cautions** see under Neostigmine; weaker muscarinic action
**Contra-indications** see under Neostigmine
**Side-effects** see under Neostigmine
**Dose**
- By mouth, 30–120 mg at suitable intervals throughout day, total daily dose 0.3–1.2 g (but see also notes above); NEONATE 5–10 mg every 4 hours, 30–60 minutes before feeds; CHILD up to 6 years initially 30 mg, 6–12 years initially 60 mg, usual total daily dose 30–360 mg

**Mestinon®** (Valeant) PoM
Tablets, scored, pyridostigmine bromide 60 mg. Net price 20 = £4.81

## Immunosuppressant therapy

**Corticosteroids** (section 6.3) are established as treatment for myasthenia gravis; although they are commonly given on alternate days there is little evidence of benefit over daily administration. Corticosteroid treatment is usually initiated under in-patient supervision and all patients should receive osteoporosis prophylaxis (section 6.6).

In *generalised myasthenia gravis* small initial doses of prednisolone (10 mg on alternate days) are increased in steps of 10 mg on alternate days to 1–1.5 mg/kg (max. 100 mg) on alternate days. When given daily, prednisolone is started at 5 mg daily and then increased in steps of 5 mg daily to 60 mg daily or occasionally up to 80 mg daily (0.75–1 mg/kg daily). About 10% of patients experience a transient but very serious worsening of symptoms in the first 2–3 weeks, especially if the corticosteroid is started at a high dose. However, ventilated patients may be started on 1.5 mg/kg (max. 100 mg) on alternate days. Smaller doses of corticosteroid are usually required in *ocular myasthenia*. Once clinical remission has occurred (usually after 2–6 months), the dose of prednisolone should be reduced slowly to the minimum effective dose (usually 10–40 mg on alternate days).

In generalised myasthenia gravis **azathioprine** (section 8.2.1) is usually started at the same time as the corticosteroid and it allows a lower maintenance dose of the corticosteroid to be used; azathioprine is initiated at a low dose, which is increased over 3–4 weeks to 2–2.5 mg/kg daily. **Ciclosporin** (section 8.2.2), **methotrexate** (section 8.1.3), or **mycophenolate mofetil** (section 8.2.1) may be used in patients unresponsive or intolerant to other treatments [unlicensed indications].

# 10.2.2 Skeletal muscle relaxants

Drugs described below are used for the relief of chronic muscle spasm or spasticity associated with multiple sclerosis or other neurological damage; they are not indicated for spasm associated with minor injuries. They act principally on the central nervous system with the exception of dantrolene which has a peripheral site of action. They differ in action from the muscle relaxants used in anaesthesia (section 15.1.5) which block transmission at the neuromuscular junction.

The underlying cause of spasticity should be treated and any aggravating factors (e.g. pressure sores, infection) remedied. Skeletal muscle relaxants are effective in most forms of spasticity except the rare alpha variety. The major disadvantage of treatment with these drugs is that reduction in muscle tone can cause a loss of splinting action of the spastic leg and trunk muscles and sometimes lead to an increase in disability.

**Dantrolene** acts directly on skeletal muscle and produces fewer central adverse effects making it a drug of choice. The dose should be increased slowly.

**Baclofen** inhibits transmission at spinal level and also depresses the central nervous system. The dose should be increased slowly to avoid the major side-effects of sedation and muscular hypotonia (other adverse events are uncommon).

**Diazepam** may also be used. Sedation and, occasionally, extensor hypotonus are disadvantages. Other benzodiazepines also have muscle-relaxant properties. Muscle-relaxant doses of benzodiazepines are similar to anxiolytic doses (section 4.1.2).

**Tizanidine** is an $alpha_2$-adrenoceptor agonist indicated for spasticity associated with multiple sclerosis or spinal cord injury.



## BACLOFEN

**Indications** chronic severe spasticity resulting from disorders such as multiple sclerosis or traumatic partial section of spinal cord

**Cautions** renal impairment (Appendix 3); psychiatric illness, Parkinson's disease, cerebrovascular disease, elderly; respiratory impairment, epilepsy; history of peptic ulcer; diabetes; hypertonic bladder sphincter; pregnancy (Appendix 4); avoid abrupt withdrawal (risk of hyperactive state, may exacerbate spasticity, and precipitate autonomic dysfunction including hyperthermia, psychiatric reactions and convulsions, see also under Withdrawal below); porphyria (section 9.8.2); **interactions:** Appendix 1 (muscle relaxants)

Withdrawal CSM has advised that serious side-effects can occur on abrupt withdrawal; to minimise risk, discontinue by gradual dose reduction over at least 1–2 weeks (longer if symptoms occur)

Driving Drowsiness may affect performance of skilled tasks (e.g. driving); effects of alcohol enhanced

**Contra-indications** peptic ulceration

**Side-effects** frequently sedation, drowsiness, muscular hypotonia, nausea, urinary disturbances; occasionally lassitude, confusion, speech disturbance, dizziness, ataxia, hallucinations, nightmares, headache, euphoria, insomnia, depression, anxiety, agitation, tremor, nystagmus, paraesthesias, seizures, myalgia, fever, respiratory or cardiovascular depression, hypotension, dry mouth, gastro-intestinal disturbances, sexual dysfunction, visual disorders, rash, pruritus, urticaria, hyperhidrosis, angioedema; rarely taste alterations, blood sugar changes, and paradoxical increase in spasticity

**Dose**

- By mouth, 5 mg 3 times daily, preferably with or after food, gradually increased; max. 100 mg daily (discontinue if no benefit within 6 weeks); CHILD 0.75–2 mg/kg daily (over 10 years, max. 2.5 mg/kg daily) *or* 2.5 mg 4 times daily increased gradually according to age to maintenance: 1–2 years 10–20 mg daily, 2–6 years 20–30 mg daily, 6–10 years 30–60 mg daily
- By intrathecal injection, see preparation below

**Baclofen** (Non-proprietary) PoM

Tablets, baclofen 10 mg, net price 28-tab pack = 74p, 84-tab pack = £2.60. Label: 2, 8

Brands include *Baclospas®*

Oral solution, baclofen 5 mg/5 mL, net price 300 mL = £7.95. Label: 2, 8

Brands include *Lyflex®* (sugar-free)

**Lioresal®** (Novartis) PoM

Tablets, scored, baclofen 10 mg. Net price 84-tab pack = £10.84. Label: 2, 8

Excipients include gluten

Liquid, sugar-free, raspberry–flavoured, baclofen 5 mg/5 mL. Net price 300 mL = £8.95. Label: 2, 8

### By intrathecal injection

**Lioresal®** (Novartis) PoM

Intrathecal injection, baclofen, 50 micrograms/mL, net price 1-mL amp (for test dose) = £2.74; 500 micrograms/mL, 20-mL amp (for use with implantable pump) = £60.77; 2 mg/mL, 5-mL amp (for use with implantable pump) = £60.77

**Important:** consult product literature for details on dose testing and titration—important to monitor patients closely in appropriately equipped and staffed environment during screening and immediately after pump implantation, and to have resuscitation equipment available for immediate use

Dose by intrathecal injection, specialist use only, severe chronic spasticity unresponsive to oral antispastic drugs (or where side-effects of oral therapy unacceptable) *or* as alternative to ablative neurosurgical procedures, initial *test dose* 25–50 micrograms over at least 1 minute via catheter or lumbar puncture, increased in 25-microgram steps (not more often than every 24 hours) to max. 100 micrograms to determine appropriate dose *then dose-titration phase*, most often using infusion pump (implanted into chest wall or abdominal wall tissues) to establish *appropriate maintenance dose* (ranging from 12 micrograms to 2 mg daily for spasticity of spinal origin *or* 22 micrograms to 1.4 mg daily for spasticity of cerebral origin) retaining some spasticity to avoid sensation of paralysis; CHILD 4–18 years (spasticity of cerebral origin only), initial *test dose* 25 micrograms then titrated as for ADULT to *appropriate maintenance dose* (ranging from 24 micrograms to 1.2 mg daily in children under 12 years)

## DANTROLENE SODIUM

**Indications** chronic severe spasticity of voluntary muscle; malignant hyperthermia (section 15.1.8)

**Cautions** impaired cardiac and pulmonary function; test liver function before and at intervals during therapy; therapeutic effect may take a few weeks to develop but if treatment is ineffective it should be discontinued after 4–6 weeks; avoid when spasticity is useful, for example, locomotion; **interactions:** Appendix 1 (muscle relaxants).

Driving Drowsiness may affect performance of skilled tasks (e.g. driving); effects of alcohol enhanced

**Contra-indications** hepatic impairment (may cause severe liver damage); acute muscle spasm; pregnancy (Appendix 4); breast-feeding (Appendix 5)

**Side-effects** transient drowsiness, dizziness, weakness, malaise, fatigue, diarrhoea (withdraw if severe, discontinue treatment if recurs on re-introduction), anorexia, nausea, headache, rash; less frequently constipation, dysphagia, speech and visual disturbances, confusion, nervousness, insomnia, depression, seizures, chills, fever, increased urinary frequency; rarely, tachycardia, erratic blood pressure, dyspnoea, haematuria, possible crystalluria, urinary incontinence or retention, pleural effusion, pericarditis, dose-related hepatotoxicity (occasionally fatal) may be more common in women over 30 especially those taking oestrogens

**Dose**

- Initially 25 mg daily, may be increased at weekly intervals to max. of 100 mg 4 times daily; usual dose 75 mg 3 times daily; CHILD not recommended

**Dantrium®** (Procter & Gamble Pharm.) PoM

Capsules, both orange/brown, dantrolene sodium 25 mg, net price 20 = £2.46; 100 mg, 20 = £8.61. Label: 2

## DIAZEPAM

**Indications** muscle spasm of varied aetiology, including tetanus; other indications (section 4.1.2, section 4.8, section 15.1.4.1)

**Cautions** see section 4.1.2; special precautions for intravenous injection (section 4.8.2)

**Contra-indications** see section 4.1.2

**Side-effects** see section 4.1.2; also hypotonia

**Dose**

- Muscle spasm, by mouth, 2–15 mg daily in divided doses, increased if necessary in spastic conditions to 60 mg daily according to response

  Cerebral spasticity in selected cases, CHILD 2–40 mg daily in divided doses

  By intramuscular *or* by slow intravenous injection (into a large vein at a rate of not more than 5 mg/minute), in acute muscle spasm, 10 mg repeated if necessary after 4 hours

  **Note** Only use intramuscular route when oral and intravenous routes not possible; special precautions for intravenous injection see section 4.8.2

- Tetanus, ADULT and CHILD, by intravenous injection, 100–300 micrograms/kg repeated every 1–4 hours; by intravenous infusion (*or* by nasoduodenal tube), 3–10 mg/kg over 24 hours, adjusted according to response

**Preparations**

Section 4.1.2

## TIZANIDINE

**Indications** spasticity associated with multiple sclerosis or spinal cord injury or disease

**Cautions** elderly, renal impairment (Appendix 3), pregnancy (Appendix 4), breast-feeding (Appendix 5), monitor liver function monthly for first 4 months and in those who develop unexplained nausea, anorexia or fatigue; concomitant administration of drugs that prolong QT interval; **interactions**: Appendix 1 (muscle relaxants)

**Driving** Drowsiness may affect performance of skilled tasks (e.g. driving); effects of alcohol enhanced

**Contra-indications** severe hepatic impairment

**Side-effects** drowsiness, fatigue, dizziness, dry mouth, nausea, gastro-intestinal disturbances, hypotension; also reported, bradycardia, insomnia, hallucinations and altered liver enzymes (discontinue if persistently raised—consult product literature); rarely acute hepatitis

**Dose**

- Initially 2 mg daily as a single dose increased according to response at intervals of at least 3–4 days in steps of 2 mg daily (and given in divided doses) usually up to 24 mg daily in 3–4 divided doses; max. 36 mg daily; CHILD not recommended

**Tizanidine** (Non-proprietary) PoM

Tablets, tizanidine (as hydrochloride) 2 mg net price 120-tab pack = £33.14; 4 mg, 120-tab pack = £45.24. Label: 2

**Zanaflex®** (Zeneus) PoM

Tablets, scored, tizanidine (as hydrochloride) 2 mg, net price 120-tab pack = £63.00; 4 mg, 120-tab pack = £80.00. Label: 2

## Other muscle relaxants

The clinical efficacy of carisoprodol, meprobamate (section 4.1.2), and methocarbamol as muscle relaxants is **not** well established although they have been included in compound analgesic preparations.

## CARISOPRODOL

**Indications** short-term symptomatic relief of muscle spasm (but see notes above)

**Cautions** see under Meprobamate (section 4.1.2); breast-feeding (Appendix 5); **interactions**: Appendix 1 (muscle relaxants)

**Contra-indications** see under Meprobamate (section 4.1.2); porphyria (section 9.8.2)

**Side-effects** see under Meprobamate (section 4.1.2); drowsiness is common

**Dose**

- 350 mg 3 times daily; ELDERLY half adult dose or less

**Carisoma®** (Forest) PoM

Tablets, carisoprodol 125 mg, net price 100 = £6.65; 350 mg, 100 = £7.45. Label: 2

## METHOCARBAMOL

**Indications** short-term symptomatic relief of muscle spasm (but see notes above)

**Cautions** hepatic impairment (Appendix 2); renal impairment (Appendix 3); pregnancy (Appendix 4); breast-feeding (Appendix 5); **interactions**: Appendix 1 (muscle relaxants)

**Driving** Drowsiness may affect performance of skilled tasks (e.g. driving); effects of alcohol enhanced

**Contra-indications** coma or pre-coma, brain damage, epilepsy, myasthenia gravis

**Side-effects** nausea, vomiting, dyspepsia; hypersensitivity reactions (including urticaria, angioedema, anaphylaxis); fever, headache, drowsiness, dizziness, confusion, amnesia, restlessness, anxiety, tremor, seizures; blurred vision, nasal congestion; rash, pruritus; leucopenia, cholestatic jaundice

**Dose**

- 1.5 g 4 times daily; may be reduced to 750 mg 3 times daily; ELDERLY up to 750 mg 4 times daily may be sufficient; CHILD not recommended

**Robaxin®** (Shire) PoM

750 Tablets, f/c, scored, methocarbamol 750 mg, net price 20 = £2.53. Label: 2

## Nocturnal leg cramps

**Quinine** salts (section 5.4.1) 200–300 mg at bedtime are effective in reducing the frequency of nocturnal leg cramps by about 25% in ambulatory patients. It may take up to 4 weeks for improvement to become apparent and it is then given on a continuous basis if there is benefit. Patients should be monitored closely during the early stages for adverse effects as well as for benefit. Treatment should be interrupted at intervals of approximately 3 months to assess the need for further quinine treatment. Quinine is very toxic in overdosage and accidental fatalities have occurred in children (see also below).

### QUININE

**Indications** see notes above; malaria (section 5.4.1)
**Cautions** see section 5.4.1
**Contra-indications** see section 5.4.1
**Side-effects** see section 5.4.1; **important:** very toxic in **overdosage**—immediate advice from poison centres essential (see also p. 32)
**Dose**
- See notes above

**Preparations**
Section 5.4.1

10 Musculoskeletal and joint diseases

## 10.3 Drugs for the relief of soft-tissue inflammation


10.3.1 Enzymes
10.3.2 Rubefacients and other topical antirheumatics


### Extravasation

Local guidelines for the management of extravasation should be followed where they exist or specialist advice sought.

Extravasation injury follows leakage of drugs or intravenous fluids from the veins or inadvertent administration into the subcutaneous or subdermal tissue. It must be dealt with **promptly** to prevent tissue necrosis.

Acidic or alkaline preparations and those with an osmolarity greater than that of plasma can cause extravasation injury and excipients including alcohol and polyethylene glycol have also been implicated. Cytotoxic drugs commonly cause extravasation injury. In addition, certain patients such as the very young and the elderly are at increased risk. Those receiving anticoagulants are more likely to lose blood into surrounding tissues if extravasation occurs whilst those receiving sedatives or analgesics may not notice the early signs or symptoms of extravasation.

**Prevention of extravasation** Precautions should be taken to avoid extravasation; ideally, drugs liable to cause extravasation injury should be given through a central line and patients receiving repeated doses of hazardous drugs peripherally should have the cannula resited at regular intervals. Attention should be paid to the manufacturers' recommendations for administration. Placing a glyceryl trinitrate patch (section 2.6.1) distal to the cannula may improve the patency of the vessel in patients with small veins or in those whose veins are prone to collapse.

Patients should be asked to report any pain or burning at the site of injection immediately.

**Management of extravasation** If extravasation is suspected the infusion should be stopped immediately but the cannula should not be removed until after an attempt has been made to aspirate the area (through the cannula) in order to remove as much of the drug as possible. Aspiration is sometimes possible if the extravasation presents with a raised bleb or blister at the injection site and is surrounded by hardened tissue, but it is often unsuccessful if the tissue is soft or soggy. Corticosteroids are usually given to treat inflammation, although there is little evidence to support their use in extravasation. Hydrocortisone or dexamethasone (section 6.3.2) may be given either locally by subcutaneous injection or intravenously at a site distant from the injury. Antihistamines (section 3.4.1) and analgesics (section 4.7) may be required for symptom relief.

The management of extravasation beyond these measures is not well standardised and calls for specialist advice. Treatment depends on the nature of the offending substance; one approach is to localise and neutralise the substance whereas another is to spread and dilute it. The first method may be appropriate following extravasation of vesicant drugs and involves administration of an antidote (if available) and the application of cold compresses 3–4 times a day (consult specialist literature for details of specific antidotes). Spreading and diluting the offending substance involves infiltrating the area with physiological saline, applying warm compresses, elevating the affected limb, and administering hyaluronidase (section 10.3.1). A saline flush-out technique (involving flushing the subcutaneous tissue with physiological saline) may be effective but requires specialist advice. Hyaluronidase should **not** be administered following extravasation of vesicant drugs (unless it is either specifically indicated or used in the saline flush-out technique).

## 10.3.1 Enzymes

**Hyaluronidase** is used to render the tissues more easily permeable to injected fluids, e.g. for introduction of fluids by subcutaneous infusion (termed hypodermoclysis).

### HYALURONIDASE

**Indications** enhance permeation of subcutaneous or intramuscular injections, local anaesthetics and subcutaneous infusions; promote resorption of excess fluids and blood
**Cautions** infants or elderly (control speed and total volume and avoid overhydration especially in renal impairment)
**Contra-indications** do not apply direct to cornea; avoid sites where infection or malignancy; not for anaesthesia in unexplained premature labour; not to be used to reduce swelling of bites or stings; not for intravenous administration
**Side-effects** occasional severe allergy

**Dose**
- With subcutaneous or intramuscular injection, 1500 units dissolved directly in solution to be injected (ensure compatibility)
- With local anaesthetics, 1500 units mixed with local anaesthetic solution (ophthalmology, 15 units/mL)
- Hypodermoclysis, 1500 units dissolved in 1 mL water for injections or 0.9% sodium chloride injection, administered before start of 500–1000 mL infusion fluid
- Extravasation (see notes above) or haematoma, 1500 units dissolved in 1 mL water for injections or 0.9% sodium chloride injection, infiltrated into affected area (as soon as possible after extravasation)

**Hyalase®** (CP) PoM
Injection, powder for reconstitution, hyaluronidase (ovine). Net price 1500-unit amp = £7.60

## 10.3.2 Rubefacients and other topical antirheumatics

**Rubefacients** act by counter-irritation. Pain, whether superficial or deep-seated, is relieved by any method which itself produces irritation of the skin. Counter-irritation is comforting in painful lesions of the muscles, tendons, and joints, and in non-articular rheumatism. Rubefacients probably all act through the same essential mechanism and differ mainly in intensity and duration of action.

The use of a NSAID by mouth is effective for relieving musculoskeletal pain. **Topical NSAIDs** (e.g. felbinac, ibuprofen, ketoprofen and piroxicam) may provide some slight relief of pain in musculoskeletal conditions.

### Topical NSAIDs and counter-irritants

**Cautions** Apply with gentle massage only. Avoid contact with eyes, mucous membranes, and inflamed or broken skin; discontinue if rash develops. Hands should be washed immediately after use. Not for use with occlusive dressings. Topical application of large amounts may result in systemic effects including hypersensitivity and asthma (renal disease has also been reported). Not generally suitable for children. Patient packs carry a **warning** to avoid during **pregnancy** or **breast-feeding**.

**Hypersensitivity** For NSAID hypersensitivity and asthma warning, see p. 506 and p. 507

**Photosensitivity** Patients should be advised against excessive exposure to sunlight of area treated in order to avoid possibility of photosensitivity

**Ketoprofen** (Non-proprietary) PoM
Gel, ketoprofen 2.5%, net price 30 g = £2.59, 50 g = £3.06, 100 g = £5.87
Dose apply 2–4 times daily for up to 7 days (usual max. 15 g daily)

**Piroxicam** (Non-proprietary) PoM
Gel, piroxicam 0.5%, net price 60 g = £2.74; 112 g = £5.63
Dose apply 3–4 times daily

**Proprietary preparations**

**Feldene®** (Pfizer) PoM
Gel, piroxicam 0.5%. Net price 60 g = £6.00; 112 g = £9.41 (also 7.5 g starter pack, hosp. only)
Excipients include benzyl alcohol, propylene glycol
Dose apply 3–4 times daily; therapy should be reviewed after 4 weeks

**Fenbid® Forte Gel** (Goldshield) PoM
Gel, ibuprofen 10%, net price 100 g = £6.50
Excipients include benzyl alcohol
Dose apply up to 4 times daily; therapy should be reviewed after 14 days

**Ibugel® Forte** (Dermal) PoM
Forte gel, ibuprofen 10%, net price 100 g = £6.05
Excipients none as listed in section 13.1.3
Dose apply up to 3 times daily

**Oruvail®** (Rhône-Poulenc Rorer) PoM
Gel, ketoprofen 2.5%. Net price 100 g = £5.87
Excipients include fragrance
Dose apply 2–4 times daily for up to 7 days (usual recommended dose 15 g daily)

**Pennsaid®** (Dimethaid) PoM
Cutaneous solution, diclofenac sodium 16 mg/mL in dimethyl sulfoxide, net price 60 mL = £16.00
Excipients include propylene glycol
Dose pain in osteoarthritis of superficial joints, apply 0.5–1 mL 4 times daily

**Powergel®** (Menarini) PoM
Gel, ketoprofen 2.5%. Net price 50 g = £3.06; 100 g = £5.89
Excipients include hydroxybenzoates (parabens), fragrance
Dose apply 2–3 times daily for up to max. 10 days

**Traxam®** (Goldshield) PoM
Foam, felbinac 3.17%. Net price 100 g = £7.00. Label: 15
Excipients include cetostearyl alcohol

Gel, felbinac 3%. Net price 100 g = £7.00
Excipients none as listed in section 13.1.3
Dose apply 2–4 times daily; max. 25 g daily; therapy should be reviewed after 14 days
Note Felbinac is an active metabolite of the NSAID fenbufen

**Voltarol Emulgel®** (Novartis) PoM
Gel, diclofenac diethylammonium salt 1.16% (equivalent to diclofenac sodium 1%). Net price 20 g (hosp. only) = £1.55; 100 g = £7.00
Excipients include propylene glycol, fragrance
Dose apply 3–4 times daily; therapy should be reviewed after 14 days (or after 28 days for osteoarthritis)

**Voltarol Gel Patch®** (Novartis) PoM
Gel patch, diclofenac epolamine (equivalent to 140 mg diclofenac sodium per patch), net price 10-patch pack = £14.09
Dose ankle sprain, apply 1 patch daily for up to 3 days; epicondylitis, apply 1 patch twice daily for up to 14 days; CHILD under 15 years not recommended

**Preparations on sale to the public**

Many preparations on sale to the public contain topical NSAIDs and counter-irritants. To identify active ingredients in such preparations, consult the product literature or manufacturer.
**Note** The correct proprietary name should be ascertained—many products have very similar names but different active ingredients

## Capsaicin

**Cautions** Avoid contact with eyes, and inflamed or broken skin. Hands should be washed immediately after use. Not for use under tight bandages. Avoid taking a hot shower or bath just before or after applying capsaicin—burning sensation enhanced.

**Side-effects** Transient burning sensation may occur during initial treatment, particularly if too much cream is used, or if the frequency of administration is less than 3–4 times daily.

**Axsain®** (Zeneus) PoM

Cream, capsaicin 0.075%. net price 45 g = £12.15.

Excipients include benzyl alcohol, cetyl alcohol

Dose post-herpetic neuralgia (**important: after** lesions have healed), apply a small amount up to 3–4 times daily; for painful diabetic neuropathy, under supervision of hospital consultant, apply 3–4 times daily for 8 weeks then review

**Zacin®** (Zeneus) PoM

Cream, capsaicin 0.025%. net price 45 g = £15.04.

Excipients include benzyl alcohol, cetyl alcohol

Dose symptomatic relief in osteoarthritis, apply a small amount 4 times daily

## Poultices

**Kaolin Poultice**

Poultice, heavy kaolin 52.7%, thymol 0.05%, boric acid 4.5%, peppermint oil 0.05%, methyl salicylate 0.2%, glycerol 42.5%. Net price 200 g = £2.12

Dose warm and apply directly or between layers of muslin; avoid application of overheated poultice

**Kaolin Poultice K/L Pack®** (K/L)

Kaolin poultice Net price 4 × 100-g pouches = £6.40

# 11 Eye


**11.1** **Administration of drugs to the eye** 533

**11.2** **Control of microbial contamination** 534

**11.3** **Anti-infective eye preparations** 534

**11.3.1** Antibacterials 534

**11.3.2** Antifungals 536

**11.3.3** Antivirals 536

**11.4** **Corticosteroids and other anti-inflammatory preparations** 536

**11.4.1** Corticosteroids 536

**11.4.2** Other anti-inflammatory preparations 538

**11.5** **Mydriatics and cycloplegics** 539

**11.6** **Treatment of glaucoma** 540

**11.7** **Local anaesthetics** 545

**11.8** **Miscellaneous ophthalmic preparations** 545

**11.8.1** Tear deficiency, ocular lubricants, and astringents 545

**11.8.2** Ocular diagnostic and peri-operative preparations and photodynamic treatment 547

**11.9** **Contact lenses** 548


## 11.1 Administration of drugs to the eye

Drugs are most commonly administered to the eye by topical application as eye drops or eye ointments. Where a higher drug concentration is required within the eye, a local injection may be necessary.

Eye-drop dispenser devices are available to aid the instillation of eye drops from plastic bottles especially amongst the elderly, visually impaired, arthritic, or otherwise physically limited patients. Eye-drop dispensers are for use with plastic eye drop bottles, for repeat use by individual patients.

**Eye drops and eye ointments** Eye drops are generally instilled into the pocket formed by gently pulling down the lower eyelid and keeping the eye closed for as long as possible after application; one drop is all that is needed. A small amount of eye ointment is applied similarly; the ointment melts rapidly and blinking helps to spread it.

When two different eye-drop preparations are used at the same time of day, dilution and overflow may occur when one immediately follows the other. The patient should therefore leave an interval of at least 5 minutes between the two.

Systemic effects may arise from absorption of drugs into the general circulation from conjunctival vessels or from the nasal mucosa after the excess preparation has drained down through the tear ducts. The extent of systemic absorption following ocular administration is highly variable; nasal drainage of drugs is associated with eye drops much more often than with eye ointments.

For warnings relating to eye drops and contact lenses, see section 11.9.

**Eye lotions** These are solutions for the irrigation of the conjunctival sac. They act mechanically to flush out irritants or foreign bodies as a first-aid treatment. Sterile sodium chloride 0.9% solution (section 11.8.1) is usually used. Clean water will suffice in an emergency.

**Other preparations** Subconjunctival injection may be used to administer anti-infective drugs, mydriatics, or corticosteroids for conditions not responding to topical therapy. The drug diffuses through the cornea and sclera to the anterior and posterior chambers and vitreous humour. However, because the dose-volume is limited (usually not more than 1 mL), this route is suitable only for drugs which are readily soluble.

Drugs such as antimicrobials and corticosteroids may be administered systemically to treat an eye condition.

**Preservatives and sensitisers** Information on preservatives and on substances identified as skin sensitisers (see section 13.1.3) is provided under preparation entries.

## 11.2 Control of microbial contamination

Preparations for the eye should be sterile when issued. Eye drops in multiple-application containers include a preservative but care should nevertheless be taken to avoid contamination of the contents during use.

Eye drops in multiple-application containers for *domiciliary use* should not be used for more than 4 weeks after first opening (unless otherwise stated).

Eye drops for use in *hospital wards* are normally discarded 1 week after first opening. Individual containers should be provided for each patient. A separate bottle should be supplied for each eye only if there are special concerns about contamination. Containers used before an operation should be discarded at the time of the operation and fresh containers supplied. A fresh supply should also be provided upon discharge from hospital; in specialist ophthalmology units, it may be acceptable to issue eye-drop bottles that have been dispensed to the patient on the day of discharge.

In *out-patient departments* single-application packs should preferably be used; if multiple-application packs are used, they should be discarded at the end of each day. In clinics for eye diseases and in accident and emergency departments, where the dangers of infection are high, single-application packs should be used; if a multiple-application pack is used, it should be discarded after single use.

Diagnostic dyes (e.g. fluorescein) should be used only from single-application packs.

In *eye surgery* single-application containers should be used if possible; if a multiple-application pack is used, it should be discarded after single use. Preparations used during intra-ocular procedures and others that may penetrate into the anterior chamber must be isotonic and without preservatives and buffered if necessary to a neutral pH. Specially formulated fluids should be used for intra-ocular surgery; intravenous infusion preparations are not suitable for this purpose. For all surgical procedures, a previously unopened container is used for each patient.

## 11.3 Anti-infective eye preparations

11.3.1 Antibacterials
11.3.2 Antifungals
11.3.3 Antivirals

**Eye infections** Most acute superficial eye infections can be treated topically. Blepharitis and conjunctivitis are often caused by staphylococci; keratitis and endophthalmitis may be bacterial, viral, or fungal.

Bacterial *blepharitis* is treated by application of an antibacterial eye ointment to the conjunctival sac or to the lid margins. Systemic treatment may occasionally be required and is usually undertaken after culturing organisms from the lid margin and determining their antimicrobial sensitivity; antibiotics such as the tetracyclines given for 3 months or longer may be appropriate.

Most cases of acute bacterial conjunctivitis are self-limiting; where treatment is appropriate, antibacterial eye drops or an eye ointment are used. A poor response might indicate viral or allergic conjunctivitis. *Gonococcal conjunctivitis* is treated with systemic and topical antibacterials.

*Corneal ulcer* and *keratitis* require specialist treatment and may call for subconjunctival or systemic administration of antimicrobials.

*Endophthalmitis* is a medical emergency which also calls for specialist management and often requires parenteral, subconjunctival, or intra-ocular administration of antimicrobials.

For reference to the treatment of *crab lice of the eyelashes*, see section 13.10.4

### 11.3.1 Antibacterials

Bacterial infections are generally treated topically with eye drops and eye ointments. Systemic administration is sometimes appropriate in blepharitis. In intra-ocular infection, a variety of routes (intracorneal, intravitreal and systemic) may be used.

**Chloramphenicol** has a broad spectrum of activity and is the drug of choice for *superficial eye infections*. Chloramphenicol eye drops are well tolerated and the recommendation that chloramphenicol eye drops should be avoided because of an increased risk of aplastic anaemia is not well founded.

Other antibacterials with a broad spectrum of activity include the quinolones, **ciprofloxacin** and **ofloxacin**; **framycetin**, **gentamicin**, **neomycin**, and **polymixin B** are also active against a wide variety of bacteria. Gentamicin, ciprofloxacin, and ofloxacin are effective for infections caused by *Pseudomonas aeruginosa*.

**Ciprofloxacin** eye drops are licensed for *corneal ulcers*; intensive application (especially in the first 2 days) is required throughout the day and night.

*Trachoma* which results from chronic infection with *Chlamydia trachomatis* can be treated with **azithromycin** by mouth [unlicensed indication].

**Fusidic acid** is useful for staphylococcal infections.

**Propamidine isetionate** is of little value in bacterial infections but is specific for the rare but potentially devastating condition of *acanthamoeba keratitis* (see also section 11.9).

**With corticosteroids** Many antibacterial preparations also incorporate a corticosteroid but such mixtures should **not** be used unless a patient is under close specialist supervision. In particular they should not be prescribed for undiagnosed 'red eye' which is sometimes caused by the herpes simplex virus and may be difficult to diagnose (section 11.4).

#### Administration

**Eye drops** Apply 1 drop at least every 2 hours then reduce frequency as infection is controlled and continue for 48 hours after healing.

**Eye ointment** Apply *either* at night (if eye drops used during the day) *or* 3–4 times daily (if eye ointment used alone).

## CHLORAMPHENICOL

**Indications** see notes above
**Side-effects** transient stinging; see also notes above
**Dose**
- See notes above

[1]**Chloramphenicol** (Non-proprietary) PoM
Eye drops, chloramphenicol 0.5%. Net price 10 mL = £1.43
Eye ointment, chloramphenicol 1%. Net price 4 g = £1.59

1. Chloramphenicol 0.5% eye drops can be sold to the public (in max. pack size 10 mL) for treatment of acute bacterial conjunctivitis in adults and children over 2 years; max. duration of treatment 5 days; proprietary brands on sale to the public include *Optrex Infected Eyes®*

**Chloromycetin®** (Goldshield) PoM
Redidrops (= eye drops), chloramphenicol 0.5%. Net price 5 mL = £1.65; 10 mL = £2.01
Excipients include phenylmercuric acetate
Ophthalmic ointment (= eye ointment), chloramphenicol 1%. Net price 4 g = £2.01

**Single use**
**Minims® Chloramphenicol** (Chauvin) PoM
Eye drops, chloramphenicol 0.5%. Net price 20 × 0.5 mL = £4.92

## CIPROFLOXACIN

**Indications** superficial bacterial infections, see notes above; corneal ulcers
**Cautions** not recommended for children under 1 year; pregnancy (Appendix 4); breast-feeding (Appendix 5)
**Side-effects** local burning and itching; lid margin crusting; hyperaemia; taste disturbances; corneal staining, keratitis, lid oedema, lacrimation, photophobia, corneal infiltrates; nausea and visual disturbances reported
**Dose**
- Superficial bacterial infection, see notes above
- Corneal ulcer, apply *eye drops* throughout day and night, day 1 apply every 15 minutes for 6 hours then every 30 minutes, day 2 apply every hour, days 3–14 apply every 4 hours (max. duration of treatment 21 days)

  Apply *eye ointment* throughout day and night; apply 1.25 cm ointment every 1-2 hours for 2 days then every 4 hours for next 12 days

**Ciloxan®** (Alcon) PoM
Ophthalmic solution (= eye drops), ciprofloxacin (as hydrochloride) 0.3%. Net price 5 mL = £4.94
Excipients include benzalkonium chloride
Eye ointment, ciprofloxacin (as hydrochloride) 0.3%. Net price 3.5 g = £5.49

## FRAMYCETIN SULPHATE

**Indications** see notes above
**Dose**
- See notes above

**Soframycin®** (Florizel) PoM
Eye drops, framycetin sulphate 0.5%. Net price 10 mL = £4.30
Excipients include benzalkonium chloride

## FUSIDIC ACID

**Indications** see notes above
**Dose**
- See under preparation below

**Fucithalmic®** (LEO) PoM
Eye drops, m/r, fusidic acid 1% in gel basis (liquifies on contact with eye). Net price 5 g = £2.09
Excipients include benzalkonium chloride, disodium edetate
Dose apply twice daily

## GENTAMICIN

**Indications** see notes above
**Dose**
- See notes above

**Genticin®** (Roche) PoM
Drops (for ear or eye), gentamicin 0.3% (as sulphate). Net price 10 mL = £1.78
Excipients include benzalkonium chloride

**Single use**
**Minims® Gentamicin Sulphate** (Chauvin) PoM
Eye drops, gentamicin 0.3% (as sulphate). Net price 20 × 0.5 mL = £5.75

## NEOMYCIN SULPHATE

**Indications** see notes above
**Dose**
- See notes above

**Neomycin** (Non-proprietary) PoM
Eye drops, neomycin sulphate 0.5% (3500 units/mL). Net price 10 mL = £3.11
Eye ointment, neomycin sulphate 0.5% (3500 units/g). Net price 3 g = £2.44

**With antibacterials**
**Neosporin®** (PLIVA) PoM
Eye drops, gramicidin 25 units, neomycin sulphate 1700 units, polymyxin B sulphate 5000 units/mL. Net price 5 mL = £4.86
Excipients include thiomersal
Dose apply 2–4 times daily or more frequently if required

**With hydrocortisone**
Section 12.1.1

## OFLOXACIN

**Indications** see notes above
**Cautions** pregnancy (Appendix 4); breast-feeding (Appendix 5); not to be used for more than 10 days
**Side-effects** local irritation including photophobia; dizziness, numbness, nausea and headache reported
**Dose**
- See notes above

**Exocin®** (Allergan) PoM
Ophthalmic solution (= eye drops), ofloxacin 0.3%. Net price 5 mL = £2.17
Excipients include benzalkonium chloride

## POLYMYXIN B SULPHATE

**Indications** see notes above
**Side-effects** local irritation and dermatitis
**Dose**
- See notes above

**With antibacterials**

**Polyfax®** (PLIVA) PoM
Eye ointment, polymyxin B sulphate 10 000 units, bacitracin zinc 500 units/g. Net price 4 g = £3.26

**Polytrim®** (PLIVA) PoM
Eye drops, trimethoprim 0.1%, polymyxin B sulphate 10 000 units/mL. Net price 5 mL = £3.05
Excipients include benzalkonium chloride

Eye ointment, trimethoprim 0.5%, polymyxin B sulphate 10 000 units/g. Net price 4 g = £2.90

## PROPAMIDINE ISETIONATE

**Indications** local treatment of infections (but see notes above)
**Dose**
- See preparations

**Brolene®** (Aventis Pharma)
Eye drops, propamidine isetionate 0.1%. Net price 10 mL = £2.73
Excipients include benzalkonium chloride
Dose apply 4 times daily
Note Eye drops containing propamidine isetionate 0.1% also available from Typharm (*Golden Eye Drops*)

Eye ointment, dibromopropamidine isetionate 0.15%. Net price 5 g = £2.85
Dose apply 1–2 times daily
Note Eye ointment containing dibromopropamidine isetionate 0.15% also available from Typharm (*Golden Eye Ointment*)



# 11.3.2 Antifungals

Fungal infections of the cornea are rare but can occur after agricultural injuries, especially in hot and humid climates. Orbital mycosis is rarer, and when it occurs it is usually because of a direct spread of infection from the paranasal sinuses. Increasing age, debility, or immunosuppression may encourage fungal proliferation. The spread of infection through blood occasionally produces a metastatic endophthalmitis.

Many different fungi are capable of producing ocular infection; they may be identified by appropriate laboratory procedures.

Antifungal preparations for the eye are not generally available. Treatment will normally be carried out at specialist centres, but requests for information about supplies of preparations not available commercially should be addressed to the local Health Authority (or equivalent in Scotland or Northern Ireland), or to the nearest hospital ophthalmology unit, or to Moorfields Eye Hospital, City Road, London EC1V 2PD (tel. (020) 7253 3411).

# 11.3.3 Antivirals

Herpes simplex infections producing, for example, dendritic corneal ulcer can be treated with **aciclovir**. **Ganciclovir** eye drops are licensed for the treatment of acute herpetic keratitis.

Slow-release ocular implants containing **ganciclovir** may be inserted surgically to treat immediate sight-threatening CMV retinitis. Local treatments do not protect against systemic infection or infection in the other eye. For systemic treatment of CMV retinitis, see section 5.3.2.2.

## ACICLOVIR
(Acyclovir)

**Indications** local treatment of herpes simplex infections
**Side-effects** local irritation and inflammation reported
**Dose**
- Apply 5 times daily (continue for at least 3 days after complete healing)

**Zovirax®** (GSK) PoM
Eye ointment, aciclovir 3%. Net price 4.5 g = £9.92
Tablets, see section 5.3.2.1
Injection, see section 5.3.2.1
Cream, see section 13.10.3

## GANCICLOVIR

**Indications** acute herpetic keratitis
**Cautions** pregnancy (Appendix 4); breast-feeding (Appendix 5)
**Side-effects** ocular irritation, visual disturbances; superficial punctate keratitis
**Dose**
- Apply 5 times daily until complete corneal re-epithelialisation, then 3 times daily for 7 days (usual duration of treatment 21 days)

**Virgan®** (Chauvin) PoM
Eye drops, ganciclovir 0.15 % in gel basis, net price 5 g = £10.64
Excipients include benzalkonium chloride

# 11.4 Corticosteroids and other anti-inflammatory preparations

**11.4.1** Corticosteroids
**11.4.2** Other anti-inflammatory preparations

# 11.4.1 Corticosteroids

Corticosteroids administered locally (as eye drops, eye ointments or subconjunctival injection) or by mouth have an important place in treating anterior segment inflammation, including that which results from surgery.

*Topical corticosteroids* should normally only be used under expert supervision; three main dangers are associated with their use:

- a 'red eye', where the diagnosis is unconfirmed, may be due to herpes simplex virus, and a corticosteroid may aggravate the condition, leading to corneal ulceration, with possible damage to vision and even loss of the eye. Bacterial, fungal and amoebic infections pose a similar hazard;

- 'steroid glaucoma' may follow the use of corticosteroid eye preparations in susceptible individuals;
- a 'steroid cataract' may follow prolonged use.

Other side-effects include thinning of the cornea and sclera.

Use of a combination product containing a corticosteroid with an anti-infective is rarely justified.

*Systemic corticosteroids* (section 6.3.2) may be useful for ocular conditions. The risk of producing a 'steroid cataract' is very high (75%) if the equivalent of more than 15 mg prednisolone is given daily for several years.

## BETAMETHASONE

**Indications** local treatment of inflammation (short-term)

**Cautions** see notes above

**Side-effects** see notes above

**Dose**

- Apply eye drops every 1–2 hours until controlled then reduce frequency, eye ointment 2–4 times daily or at night when used with eye drops

**Betnesol®** (Celltech) PoM

Drops (for ear, eye, or nose), betamethasone sodium phosphate 0.1%. Net price 10 mL = £2.32

Excipients include benzalkonium chloride, disodium edetate

Eye ointment, betamethasone sodium phosphate 0.1%. Net price 3 g = £1.41

**Vista-Methasone®** (Martindale) PoM

Drops (for ear, eye, or nose), betamethasone sodium phosphate 0.1%. Net price 5 mL = £1.02; 10 mL = £1.16

Excipients include benzalkonium chloride

### With neomycin

**Betnesol-N®** (Celltech) PoM

Drops (for ear, eye, or nose), see section 12.1.1

Eye ointment, betamethasone sodium phosphate 0.1%, neomycin sulphate 0.5%. Net price 3 g = £1.28

Note May be difficult to obtain

**Vista-Methasone N®** (Martindale) PoM

Drops (for ear, eye, or nose), see section 12.1.1

## DEXAMETHASONE

**Indications** local treatment of inflammation (short-term)

**Cautions** see notes above

**Side-effects** see notes above

**Dose**

- Apply eye drops 4–6 times daily; severe conditions every 30–60 minutes until controlled then reduce frequency

**Maxidex®** (Alcon) PoM

Eye drops, dexamethasone 0.1%, hypromellose 0.5%. Net price 5 mL = £1.49; 10 mL = £2.95

Excipients include benzalkonium chloride, disodium edetate, polysorbate 80

### Single use

**Minims® Dexamethasone** (Chauvin) PoM

Eye drops, dexamethasone sodium phosphate 0.1%. Net price 20 × 0.5 mL = £6.95

Excipients include disodium edetate

### With antibacterials

**Maxitrol®** (Alcon) PoM

Eye drops, dexamethasone 0.1%, hypromellose 0.5%, neomycin 0.35% (as sulphate), polymyxin B sulphate 6000 units/mL. Net price 5 mL = £1.77

Excipients include benzalkonium chloride, polysorbate 20

Eye ointment, dexamethasone 0.1%, neomycin 0.35% (as sulphate), polymyxin B sulphate 6000 units/g. Net price 3.5 g = £1.52

Excipients include hydroxybenzoates (parabens), wool fat

**Sofradex®** (Florizel) PoM

Drops (for ear or eye), see section 12.1.1

**Tobradex®** (Alcon) PoM

Eye drops, dexamethasone 0.1%, tobramycin 0.3%. Net price 5 mL = £5.65

Excipients include benzalkonium chloride, disodium edetate

## FLUOROMETHOLONE

**Indications** local treatment of inflammation (short-term)

**Cautions** see notes above

**Side-effects** see notes above

**Dose**

- Apply eye drops 2–4 times daily (initially every hour for 24–48 hours then reduce frequency)

**FML®** (Allergan) PoM

Ophthalmic suspension (= eye drops), fluorometholone 0.1%, polyvinyl alcohol (*Liquifilm®*) 1.4%. Net price 5 mL = £1.71; 10 mL = £2.95

Excipients include benzalkonium chloride, disodium edetate, polysorbate 80

## HYDROCORTISONE ACETATE

**Indications** local treatment of inflammation (short-term)

**Cautions** see notes above

**Side-effects** see notes above

**Hydrocortisone** (Non-proprietary) PoM

Eye drops, hydrocortisone acetate 1%. Net price 10 mL = £3.21

Eye ointment, hydrocortisone acetate 0.5%, net price 3 g = £2.40; 1%, 3 g = £2.42; 2.5%, 3 g = £2.44

### With neomycin

**Neo-Cortef®** (PLIVA) PoM

Ointment (for ear or eye), see section 12.1.1

Note May be difficult to obtain

## PREDNISOLONE

**Indications** local treatment of inflammation (short-term)

**Cautions** see notes above

**Side-effects** see notes above

**Dose**

- Apply eye drops every 1–2 hours until controlled then reduce frequency

**Pred Forte®** (Allergan) PoM

Eye drops, prednisolone acetate 1%. Net price 5 mL = £1.52; 10 mL = £3.05

Excipients include benzalkonium chloride, disodium edetate, polysorbate 80

Dose apply 2–4 times daily

**Predsol®** (Celltech) PoM

Drops (for ear or eye), prednisolone sodium phosphate 0.5%. Net price 10 mL = £2.00

Excipients include benzalkonium chloride, disodium edetate

**Single use**

**Minims® Prednisolone Sodium Phosphate** (Chauvin) PoM

Eye drops, prednisolone sodium phosphate 0.5%. Net price 20 × 0.5 mL = £5.75

Excipients include disodium edetate

**With neomycin**

**Predsol-N®** (Celltech) PoM

Drops (for ear or eye), see section 12.1.1

## RIMEXOLONE

**Indications** local treatment of inflammation (short-term)

**Cautions** see notes above

**Side-effects** see notes above

**Dose**

- Postoperative inflammation, apply 4 times daily for 2 weeks, beginning 24 hours after surgery
- Steroid-responsive inflammation, apply at least 4 times daily for up to 4 weeks
- Uveitis, apply every hour during daytime in week 1, then every 2 hours in week 2, then 4 times daily in week 3, then twice daily for first 4 days of week 4, then once daily for remaining 3 days of week 4

**Vexol®** (Alcon) ▼ PoM

Eye drops, rimexolone 1%, net price 5 mL = £5.95

Excipients include benzalkonium chloride, disodium edetate, polysorbate 80

11 Eye

# 11.4.2 Other anti-inflammatory preparations

Other preparations used for the topical treatment of inflammation and allergic conjunctivitis include antihistamines, lodoxamide, and sodium cromoglicate.

Topical preparations of **antihistamines** such as eye drops containing **antazoline** (with xylometazoline as *Otrivine-Antistin®*), **azelastine**, **epinastine**, **ketotifen** and **olopatadine** may be used for allergic conjunctivitis.

**Sodium cromoglicate** (sodium cromoglycate) and **nedocromil sodium** eye drops may be useful for vernal keratoconjunctivitis and other allergic forms of conjunctivitis.

**Lodoxamide** eye drops are used for allergic conjunctival conditions including seasonal allergic conjunctivitis.

**Diclofenac** eye drops (section 11.8.2) and **emedastine** eye drops are also licensed for seasonal allergic conjunctivitis.

## ANTAZOLINE SULPHATE

**Indications** allergic conjunctivitis

**Otrivine-Antistin®** (Novartis Consumer Health)

Eye drops, antazoline sulphate 0.5%, xylometazoline hydrochloride 0.05%. Net price 10 mL = £2.35

Excipients include benzalkonium chloride, disodium edetate

Dose ADULT and CHILD over 5 years apply 2–3 times daily

Note Xylometazoline is a sympathomimetic; it should be avoided in angle-closure glaucoma; absorption of antazoline and xylometazoline may result in systemic side-effects and the possibility of interaction with other drugs

## AZELASTINE HYDROCHLORIDE

**Indications** allergic conjunctivitis

**Side-effects** mild transient irritation; bitter taste reported

**Dose**

- Seasonal allergic conjunctivitis, ADULT and CHILD over 4 years, apply twice daily, increased if necessary to 4 times daily
- Perennial conjunctivitis, ADULT and ADOLESCENT over 12 years, apply twice daily, increased if necessary to 4 times daily; max. duration of treatment 6 weeks

[1]**Optilast®** (Viatris) PoM

Eye drops, azelastine hydrochloride 0.05%. Net price 8 mL = £6.40

Excipients include benzalkonium chloride, disodium edetate

1. Azelastine 0.05% eye drops can be sold to the public (in max. pack size of 6 mL) for treatment of seasonal and perennial allergic conjunctivitis in adults and children over 12 years; proprietary brands on sale to the public include *Aller-eze®*

## EMEDASTINE

**Indications** seasonal allergic conjunctivitis

**Side-effects** transient burning or stinging; blurred vision, local oedema, keratitis, irritation, dry eye, lacrimation, corneal infiltrates (discontinue) and staining; photophobia; headache, and rhinitis occasionally reported

**Dose**

- ADULT and CHILD over 3 years, apply twice daily

**Emadine®** (Alcon) PoM

Eye drops, emedastine 0.05% (as difumarate), net price 5 mL = £7.69

Excipients include benzalkonium chloride

## EPINASTINE HYDROCHLORIDE

**Indications** seasonal allergic conjunctivitis

**Side-effects** burning; less commonly dry mouth, taste disturbance; nasal irritation, rhinitis; headache, blepharoptosis, conjunctival oedema and hyperaemia, dry eye, local irritation, photophobia, visual disturbance; pruritus

**Dose**

- ADULT and ADOLESCENT over 12 years, apply twice daily; max. duration of treatment 8 weeks

**Relestat®** (Allergan) ▼ PoM

Eye drops, epinastine hydrochloride 500 micrograms/mL, net price 5 mL = £14.50

Excipients include benzalkonium chloride, disodium edetate

## KETOTIFEN

**Indications** seasonal allergic conjunctivitis

**Side-effects** transient burning or stinging, punctate corneal epithelial erosion; less commonly dry eye, subconjunctival haemmorhage, photophobia; headache, drowsiness, skin reactions, and dry mouth also reported

**Dose**

- ADULT and CHILD over 3 years, apply twice daily

**Zaditen®** (Novartis) PoM
Eye drops, ketotifen (as fumarate) 250 micrograms/mL, net price 5 mL = £9.75
Excipients include benzalkonium chloride

## LODOXAMIDE

**Indications** allergic conjunctivitis

**Side-effects** mild transient burning, stinging, itching, and lacrimation; flushing and dizziness reported

**Dose**

- ADULT and CHILD over 4 years, apply eye drops 4 times daily

[1]**Alomide®** (Alcon) PoM
Ophthalmic solution (= eye drops), lodoxamide 0.1% (as trometamol). Net price 10 mL = £5.48
Excipients include benzalkonium chloride, disodium edetate

1. Lodoxamide 0.1% eye drops can be sold to the public for treatment of allergic conjunctivitis in adults and children over 4 years; proprietary brands on sale to the public include *Alomide Allergy®*

## NEDOCROMIL SODIUM

**Indications** allergic conjunctivitis; vernal keratoconjunctivitis

**Side-effects** transient burning and stinging; distinctive taste reported

**Dose**

- Seasonal and perennial conjunctivitis, ADULT and CHILD over 6 years, apply twice daily increased if necessary to 4 times daily; max. 12 weeks treatment for seasonal allergic conjunctivitis
- Vernal keratoconjunctivitis, ADULT and CHILD over 6 years, apply 4 times daily

**Rapitil®** (Aventis Pharma) PoM
Eye drops, nedocromil sodium 2%. Net price 5 mL = £5.12
Excipients include benzalkonium chloride, disodium edetate

## OLOPATADINE

**Indications** seasonal allergic conjunctivitis

**Side-effects** local irritation; less commonly keratitis, dry eye, local oedema, photophobia; headache, asthenia, dizziness; dry nose also reported

**Dose**

- ADULT and CHILD over 3 years, apply twice daily; max. duration of treatment 4 months

**Opatanol®** (Alcon) ▼ PoM
Eye drops, olopatadine (as hydrochloride) 1 mg/mL, net price 5 mL = £4.11
Excipients include benzalkonium chloride

## SODIUM CROMOGLICATE
### (Sodium cromoglycate)

**Indications** allergic conjunctivitis; vernal keratoconjunctivitis

**Side-effects** transient burning and stinging

**Dose**

- ADULT and CHILD apply eye drops 4 times daily

[1]**Sodium Cromoglicate** (Non-proprietary) PoM
Eye drops, sodium cromoglicate 2%. Net price 13.5 mL = £3.08
Brands include *Hay-Crom® Aqueous, Opticrom® Aqueous, Vividrin®*)

1. Sodium cromoglicate 2% eye drops can be sold to the public (in max. pack size of 10 mL) for treatment of acute seasonal and perennial allergic conjunctivitis; proprietary brands on sale to the public include *Boots Hayfever Relief, Clariteyes®, Opticrom® Allergy, Optrex® Allergy*, and *Vivicrom®*

# 11.5 Mydriatics and cycloplegics

Antimuscarinics dilate the pupil and paralyse the ciliary muscle; they vary in potency and duration of action.

Short-acting, relatively weak mydriatics, such as **tropicamide** 0.5%, facilitate the examination of the fundus of the eye. **Cyclopentolate** 1% or **atropine** are preferable for producing cycloplegia for refraction in young children. Atropine ointment 1% is sometimes preferred for children aged under 5 years because the ointment formulation reduces systemic absorption. Atropine, which has a longer duration of action, is also used for the treatment of anterior uveitis mainly to prevent posterior synechiae, often with phenylephrine 10% eye drops (2.5% in children, the elderly, and those with cardiac disease). **Homatropine** 1% is also used in the treatment of anterior segment inflammation, and may be preferred for its shorter duration of action.

**Cautions** Darkly pigmented iris is more resistant to pupillary dilatation and caution should be exercised to avoid overdosage. Mydriasis may precipitate acute angle-closure glaucoma in a very few patients, usually aged over 60 years and hypermetropic (long-sighted), who are predisposed to the condition because of a shallow anterior chamber. Phenylephrine may interact with systemically administered monoamine-oxidase inhibitors; other **interactions:** Appendix 1 (sympathomimetics).

Driving Patients should be warned not to drive for 1–2 hours after mydriasis.

**Side-effects** Ocular side-effects of mydriatics and cycloplegics include transient stinging and raised intra-ocular pressure; on prolonged administration, local irritation, hyperaemia, oedema and conjunctivitis may occur. Contact dermatitis (conjunctivitis) is not uncommon with the antimuscarinic mydriatic drugs, especially atropine.

Toxic systemic reactions to atropine and cyclopentolate may occur in the very young and the very old; see under Atropine Sulphate (section 1.2) for systemic side-effects of antimuscarinic drugs.

## Antimuscarinics

### ATROPINE SULPHATE

**Indications** refraction procedures in young children; anterior uveitis—see also notes above
**Cautions** risk of systemic effects with eye drops in infants under 3 months—eye ointment preferred; see also notes above
**Side-effects** see notes above

**Atropine** (Non-proprietary) PoM
Eye drops, atropine sulphate 0.5%, net price 10 mL = £2.32; 1%, 10 mL = 91p
Eye ointment, atropine sulphate 1%. Net price 3 g = £2.96

**Isopto Atropine®** (Alcon) PoM
Eye drops, atropine sulphate 1%, hypromellose 0.5%. Net price 5 mL = 99p
Excipients include benzalkonium chloride

**Single use**
**Minims® Atropine Sulphate** (Chauvin) PoM
Eye drops, atropine sulphate 1%. Net price 20 × 0.5 mL = £4.92

### CYCLOPENTOLATE HYDROCHLORIDE

**Indications** see notes above
**Cautions** see notes above
**Side-effects** see notes above

**Mydrilate®** (Intrapharm) PoM
Eye drops, cyclopentolate hydrochloride 0.5%, net price 5 mL = 97p; 1%, 5 mL = £1.19
Excipients include benzalkonium chloride

**Single use**
**Minims® Cyclopentolate Hydrochloride** (Chauvin) PoM
Eye drops, cyclopentolate hydrochloride 0.5 and 1%. Net price 20 × 0.5 mL (both) = £4.92

### HOMATROPINE HYDROBROMIDE

**Indications** see notes above
**Cautions** see notes above
**Side-effects** see notes above

**Homatropine** (Non-proprietary) PoM
Eye drops, homatropine hydrobromide 1%, net price 10 mL = £2.14; 2%, 10 mL = £2.26

### TROPICAMIDE

**Indications** see notes above
**Cautions** see notes above
**Side-effects** see notes above

**Mydriacyl®** (Alcon) PoM
Eye drops, tropicamide 0.5%, net price 5 mL = £1.36; 1%, 5 mL = £1.68
Excipients include benzalkonium chloride, disodium edetate

**Single use**
**Minims® Tropicamide** (Chauvin) PoM
Eye drops, tropicamide 0.5 and 1%. Net price 20 × 0.5 mL (both) = £5.75

## Sympathomimetics

### PHENYLEPHRINE HYDROCHLORIDE

**Indications** mydriasis; see also notes above
**Cautions** children and elderly (avoid 10% strength); cardiovascular disease (avoid or use 2.5% strength only); tachycardia; hyperthyroidism; diabetes; see also notes above
**Contra-indications** angle-closure glaucoma
**Side-effects** eye pain and stinging; blurred vision, photophobia; systemic effects include arrhythmias, hypertension, coronary artery spasm

**Phenylephrine** (Non-proprietary)
Eye drops, phenylephrine hydrochloride 10%. Net price 10 mL = £3.38
See also under Hypromellose (section 11.8.1)

**Single use**
**Minims® Phenylephrine Hydrochloride** (Chauvin)
Eye drops, phenylephrine hydrochloride 2.5%, net price 20 × 0.5 mL = £5.75; 10%, 20 × 0.5 mL = £5.75
Excipients include disodium edetate, sodium metabisulphite

# 11.6 Treatment of glaucoma

Glaucoma describes a group of disorders characterised by a loss of visual field associated with cupping of the optic disc and optic nerve damage. While glaucoma is generally associated with raised intra-ocular pressure, it can occur when the intra-ocular pressure is within the normal range.

The commonest form of glaucoma is *primary open-angle glaucoma* (chronic simple glaucoma; wide-angle glaucoma), where the obstruction is in the trabecular meshwork. The condition is often asymptomatic and the patient may present with significant loss of visual-field. *Primary angle closure glaucoma* (acute closed-angle glaucoma, narrow-angle glaucoma) results from blockage of aqueous humour flow into the anterior chamber and is a medical emergency.

Only drugs that reduce intra-ocular pressure are available for managing glaucoma; they act by a variety of mechanisms. A topical beta-blocker or a prostaglandin analogue is commonly the drug of first choice. It may be necessary to combine these drugs or add others such as miotics, sympathomimetics and carbonic anhydrase inhibitors to control intra-ocular pressure.

For urgent reduction of intra-ocular pressure and before surgery, mannitol 20% (up to 500 mL) is given by slow intravenous infusion until the intra-ocular pressure has been satisfactorily reduced. Acetazolamide by intravenous injection may also be used for the emergency management of raised intra-ocular pressure.

Standard antiglaucoma therapy is used if supplementary treatment is required after iridotomy, iridectomy or a drainage operation in either primary open-angle or acute closed-angle glaucoma.

## Beta-blockers

Topical application of a beta-blocker to the eye reduces intra-ocular pressure effectively in *primary open-angle glaucoma*, probably by reducing the rate of production of aqueous humour. Administration by mouth also reduces intra-ocular pressure but this route is not used since side-effects may be troublesome.

Beta-blockers used as eye drops include **betaxolol**, **carteolol**, **levobunolol**, **metipranolol**, and **timolol**.

**Cautions, contra-indications and side-effects** Systemic absorption may follow topical application therefore eye drops containing a beta-blocker are contra-indicated in patients with bradycardia, heart block, or uncontrolled heart failure. **Important:** for a warning to avoid in asthma see CSM advice below. Consider also other cautions, contra-indications and side-effects of beta-blockers (p. 83). Local side-effects of eye drops include ocular stinging, burning, pain, itching, erythema, dry eyes and allergic reactions including anaphylaxis and blepharoconjunctivitis; occasionally corneal disorders have been reported.

**CSM advice.** The CSM has advised that beta-blockers, even those with apparent cardioselectivity, should not be used in patients with asthma or a history of obstructive airways disease, unless no alternative treatment is available. In such cases the risk of inducing bronchospasm should be appreciated and appropriate precautions taken.

**Interactions** Since systemic absorption may follow topical application the possibility of interactions, in particular, with drugs such as verapamil should be borne in mind. See also Appendix 1 (beta-blockers).

## BETAXOLOL HYDROCHLORIDE

**Indications** see notes above
**Cautions** see notes above
**Contra-indications** see notes above
**Side-effects** see notes above
**Dose**
- Apply twice daily

**Betoptic®** (Alcon) PoM
Ophthalmic solution (= eye drops), betaxolol (as hydrochloride) 0.5%, net price 5 mL = £2.00
Excipients include benzalkonium chloride, disodium edetate

Ophthalmic suspension (= eye drops), m/r, betaxolol (as hydrochloride) 0.25%, net price 5 mL = £2.80
Excipients include benzalkonium chloride, disodium edetate

Unit dose eye drop suspension, m/r, betaxolol (as hydrochloride) 0.25%, net price 50 × 0.25 mL = £14.49

## CARTEOLOL HYDROCHLORIDE

**Indications** see notes above
**Cautions** see notes above
**Contra-indications** see notes above
**Side-effects** see notes above
**Dose**
- Apply twice daily

**Teoptic®** (Novartis) PoM
Eye drops, carteolol hydrochloride 1%, net price 5 mL = £4.60; 2%, 5 mL = £5.40
Excipients include benzalkonium chloride

## LEVOBUNOLOL HYDROCHLORIDE

**Indications** see notes above
**Cautions** see notes above
**Contra-indications** see notes above
**Side-effects** see notes above; anterior uveitis occasionally reported
**Dose**
- Apply once or twice daily

**Levobunolol** (Non-proprietary) PoM
Eye drops, levobunolol hydrochloride 0.5%. Net price 5 mL = £2.28

**Betagan®** (Allergan) PoM
Eye drops, levobunolol hydrochloride 0.5%, polyvinyl alcohol (*Liquifilm®*) 1.4%. Net price 5-mL = £2.85
Excipients include benzalkonium chloride, disodium edetate, sodium metabisulphite

Unit dose eye drops, levobunolol hydrochloride 0.5%, polyvinyl alcohol (*Liquifilm®*) 1.4%. Net price 30 × 0.4 mL = £9.98
Excipients include disodium edetate

## METIPRANOLOL

**Indications** see notes above but in chronic open-angle glaucoma **restricted** to patients allergic to preservatives or to those wearing soft contact lenses (in whom benzalkonium chloride should be avoided)
**Cautions** see notes above
**Contra-indications** see notes above
**Side-effects** see notes above; granulomatous anterior uveitis reported (discontinue treatment)
**Dose**
- Apply twice daily

**Minims® Metipranolol** (Chauvin) PoM
Eye drops, metipranolol 0.1%, net price 20 × 0.5 mL = £10.19; 0.3%, 20 × 0.5 mL = £11.09

## TIMOLOL MALEATE

**Indications** see notes above
**Cautions** see notes above
**Contra-indications** see notes above
**Side-effects** see notes above
**Dose**
- Apply twice daily; long-acting preparations, see under preparations below

**Timolol** (Non-proprietary) PoM
Eye drops, timolol (as maleate) 0.25%, net price 5 mL = £1.75; 0.5%, 5 mL = £1.69

**Timoptol®** (MSD) PoM
Eye drops, in *Ocumeter®* metered-dose unit, timolol (as maleate) 0.25%, net price 5 mL = £3.12; 0.5%, 5 mL = £3.12
Excipients include benzalkonium chloride

Unit dose eye drops, timolol (as maleate) 0.25%, net price 30 × 0.2 mL = £8.45; 0.5%, 30 × 0.2 mL = £9.65

### Once-daily preparations

**Nyogel®** (Novartis) PoM
Eye gel (= eye drops), timolol (as maleate) 0.1%, net price 5 g = £2.85
Excipients include benzalkonium chloride
Dose apply eye drops once daily

**Timoptol®-LA** (MSD) PoM
Ophthalmic gel-forming solution (= eye drops), timolol (as maleate) 0.25%, net price 2.5 mL = £3.12; 0.5%, 2.5 mL = £3.12
Excipients include benzododecinium bromide
Dose apply eye drops once daily

**With brimonidine**
See under Brimonidine

**With dorzolamide**
See under Dorzolamide

**With latanoprost**
See under Latanoprost

## Prostaglandin analogues

**Latanoprost** and **travoprost** are prostaglandin analogues which increase uveoscleral outflow; **bimatoprost** is a related drug. They are used to reduce intra-ocular pressure in ocular hypertension or in open-angle glaucoma. Patients receiving prostaglandin analogues should be monitored for any changes to eye coloration since an increase in the brown pigment in the iris may occur; particular care is required in those with mixed coloured irides and those receiving treatment to one eye only.

### BIMATOPROST

**Indications** raised intra-ocular pressure in open-angle glaucoma and ocular hypertension
**Cautions** see under Latanoprost and notes above
**Side-effects** see under Latanoprost; also ocular pruritus, allergic conjunctivitis, cataract, conjunctival oedema, eye discharge, photophobia, superficial punctate keratitis, headache; hypertension
**Dose**
- Apply once daily, preferably in the evening; CHILD and ADOLESCENT under 18 years, not recommended

**Lumigan®** (Allergan) ▼ PoM
Eye drops, bimatoprost 300 micrograms/mL, net price 3 mL = £11.46, triple pack (3 × 3 mL) = £32.66
Excipients include benzalkonium chloride

### LATANOPROST

**Indications** raised intra-ocular pressure in open-angle glaucoma and ocular hypertension
**Cautions** before initiating treatment, advise patients of possible change in eye colour; monitor for eye colour change; aphakia, or pseudophakia with torn posterior lens capsule or anterior chamber lenses; risk factors for cystoid macular oedema; brittle or severe asthma; not to be used within 5 minutes of use of thiomersal-containing preparations; pregnancy (Appendix 4); breast-feeding (Appendix 5)
**Side-effects** brown pigmentation particularly in those with mixed-colour irides; blepharitis, ocular irritation and pain; darkening, thickening and lengthening of eye lashes; conjunctival hyperaemia; transient punctate epithelial erosion; skin rash; *less commonly* eye lid oedema and rash; *rarely* dyspnoea, exacerbation of asthma, iritis, uveitis, local oedema, darkening of palpebral skin; *very rarely* chest pain, exacerbation of angina
**Dose**
- Apply once daily, preferably in the evening; CHILD not recommended

**Xalatan®** (Pharmacia) PoM
Eye drops, latanoprost 50 micrograms/mL, net price 2.5 mL = £11.95
Excipients include benzalkonium chloride

**With timolol**
For cautions, contra-indications, and side-effects of timolol, see section 11.6, Beta-blockers

**Xalacom®** (Pharmacia) ▼ PoM
Eye drops, latanoprost 50 micrograms, timolol (as maleate) 5 mg/mL, net price 2.5 mL = £15.07
Excipients include benzalkonium chloride
Dose for raised intra-ocular pressure in patients with open-angle glaucoma and ocular hypertension when beta-blocker alone not adequate; apply once daily

### TRAVOPROST

**Indications** raised intra-ocular pressure in open-angle glaucoma and ocular hypertension
**Cautions** see under Latanoprost and notes above
**Side-effects** see under Latanoprost; also headache, ocular pruritus, photophobia, and keratitis reported; rarely, hypotension, bradycardia, conjunctivitis, browache
**Dose**
- Apply once daily, preferably in the evening; CHILD and ADOLESCENT under 18 years, not recommended

**Travatan®** (Alcon) ▼ PoM
Eye drops, travoprost 40 micrograms/mL, net price 2.5 mL = £11.06
Excipients include benzalkonium chloride

## Sympathomimetics

**Dipivefrine** is a pro-drug of adrenaline. It is claimed to pass more rapidly than adrenaline through the cornea and is then converted to the active form.

Adrenaline (epinephrine) probably acts both by reducing the rate of production of aqueous humour and by increasing the outflow through the trabecular meshwork. It is contra-indicated in angle-closure glaucoma because it is a mydriatic, unless an iridectomy has been carried out. Side-effects include severe smarting and redness of the eye; adrenaline should be used with caution in patients with hypertension and heart disease.

**Brimonidine**, a selective $alpha_2$-adrenoceptor stimulant, is licensed for the reduction of intra-ocular pressure in open-angle glaucoma or ocular hypertension in patients for whom beta-blockers are inappropriate; it may also be used as adjunctive therapy when intra-ocular pressure is inadequately controlled by other anti-glaucoma therapy.

**Apraclonidine** (section 11.8.2) is another $alpha_2$-adrenoceptor stimulant. Eye drops containing apraclonidine 0.5% are used for a short term to delay laser treatment or surgery for glaucoma in patients not adequately controlled by another drug; eye drops containing 1% are used for control of intra-ocular pressure after anterior segment laser surgery.

## BRIMONIDINE TARTRATE

**Indications** raised intra-ocular pressure, see notes above

**Cautions** severe cardiovascular disease; cerebral or coronary insufficiency, Raynaud's syndrome, postural hypotension, depression, hepatic or renal impairment; pregnancy, breast-feeding; **interactions:** Appendix 1 (alpha$_2$-adrenoceptor stimulants)

Driving Drowsiness may affect performance of skilled tasks (e.g. driving)

**Side-effects** ocular reactions include hyperaemia, burning, stinging, blurring, pruritus, allergy, and conjunctival follicles; occasionally corneal erosion and staining, photophobia, eyelid inflammation, conjunctivitis; headache, dry mouth, taste alteration, fatigue, dizziness, drowsiness reported; rarely depression, nasal dryness, palpitation, and hypersensitivity reactions

**Dose**

- Apply twice daily

**Alphagan®** (Allergan) PoM

Eye drops, brimonidine tartrate 0.2%, net price 5 mL = £8.25

Excipients include benzalkonium chloride

### With timolol

For cautions, contra-indications, and side-effects of timolol, see section 11.6, Beta-blockers

**Combigan®** (Allergan) ▼ PoM

Eye drops, brimonidine tartrate 0.2%, timolol (as maleate) 0.5%, net price 5-mL = £10.00

Excipients include benzalkonium chloride

Dose for raised intra-ocular pressure in open-angle glaucoma or ocular hypertension when beta-blocker alone not adequate, apply twice daily

## DIPIVEFRINE HYDROCHLORIDE

**Indications** see notes above

**Contra-indications** see notes above

**Side-effects** see notes above

**Dose**

- Apply twice daily

**Propine®** (Allergan) PoM

Eye drops, dipivefrine hydrochloride 0.1%, net price 5 mL = £3.81, 10 mL = £4.77

Excipients include benzalkonium chloride, disodium edetate

## Carbonic anhydrase inhibitors and systemic drugs

The **carbonic anhydrase inhibitors**, acetazolamide and dorzolamide, reduce intra-ocular pressure by reducing aqueous humour production. Systemic use also produces weak diuresis.

**Acetazolamide** is given by mouth or by intravenous injection (intramuscular injections are painful because of the alkaline pH of the solution). It is used as an adjunct to other treatment for reducing intra-ocular pressure. Acetazolamide is a sulphonamide; blood disorders, rashes and other sulphonamide-related side-effects occur occasionally. It is not generally recommended for long-term use; electrolyte disturbances and metabolic acidosis that occur may be corrected by administering potassium bicarbonate (as effervescent potassium tablets, section 9.2.1.3).

**Dorzolamide** and **brinzolamide** are topical carbonic anhydrase inhibitors. They are licensed for use in patients resistant to beta-blockers or those in whom beta-blockers are contra-indicated. They are used alone or as an adjunct to a topical beta-blocker. Systemic absorption may rarely give rise to sulphonamide-like side-effects and may require discontinuation if severe.

The **osmotic diuretics**, intravenous hypertonic **mannitol** (section 2.2.5), or **glycerol** by mouth, are useful short-term ocular hypotensive drugs.

## ACETAZOLAMIDE

**Indications** reduction of intra-ocular pressure in open-angle glaucoma, secondary glaucoma, and peri-operatively in angle-closure glaucoma; diuresis (section 2.2.7); epilepsy

**Cautions** not generally recommended for prolonged use but if given monitor blood count and plasma electrolyte concentration; pulmonary obstruction (risk of acidosis); elderly; pregnancy (Appendix 4); avoid extravasation at injection site (risk of necrosis); **interactions:** Appendix 1 (diuretics)

**Contra-indications** hypokalaemia, hyponatraemia, hyperchloraemic acidosis; severe hepatic impairment; renal impairment (Appendix 3); sulphonamide hypersensitivity

**Side-effects** nausea, vomiting, diarrhoea, taste disturbance; loss of appetite, paraesthesia, flushing, headache, dizziness, fatigue, irritability, depression; thirst, polyuria; reduced libido; metabolic acidosis and electrolyte disturbances on long-term therapy; occasionally, drowsiness, confusion, hearing disturbances, urticaria, malaena, glycosuria, haematuria, abnormal liver function, renal calculi, blood disorders including agranulocytosis and thrombocytopenia, rashes including Stevens-Johnson syndrome and toxic epidermal necrolysis; rarely, photosensitivity, liver damage, flaccid paralysis, convulsions; transient myopia reported

**Dose**

- Glaucoma, by mouth *or* by intravenous injection, 0.25–1 g daily in divided doses
- Epilepsy, by mouth *or* by intravenous injection, 0.25–1 g daily in divided doses; CHILD 8–30 mg/kg daily, max. 750 mg daily

Note Dose by intramuscular injection, as for intravenous injection but preferably avoided because of alkalinity

**Diamox®** (Goldshield) PoM

Tablets, acetazolamide 250 mg. Net price 112-tab pack = £12.68. Label: 3

Sodium Parenteral (= injection), powder for reconstitution, acetazolamide (as sodium salt). Net price 500-mg vial = £14.76

**Diamox® SR** (Goldshield) PoM

Capsules, m/r, two-tone orange, enclosing orange f/c pellets, acetazolamide 250 mg. Net price 28-cap pack = £11.55. Label: 3, 25

Dose glaucoma, 1–2 capsules daily

## BRINZOLAMIDE

**Indications** adjunct to beta-blockers or used alone in raised intra-ocular pressure in ocular hypertension and in open-angle glaucoma if beta-blocker alone inadequate or inappropriate

**Cautions** hepatic impairment; pregnancy (Appendix 4); **interactions:** Appendix 1 (brinzolamide)

**Contra-indications** renal impairment (creatinine clearance less than 30 mL/minute), hyperchloraemic acidosis; breast-feeding

**Side-effects** local irritation, taste disturbance; less commonly nausea, dyspepsia, dry mouth, chest pain, epistaxis, haemoptysis, dyspnoea, rhinitis, pharyngitis, bronchitis, paraesthesia, depression, dizziness, headache, dermatitis, alopecia, corneal erosion

**Dose**

- Apply twice daily increased to 3 times daily if necessary

**Azopt®** (Alcon) PoM
Eye drops, brinzolamide 10 mg/mL, net price 5 mL = £6.90
Excipients include benzalkonium chloride, disodium edetate

## DORZOLAMIDE

**Indications** raised intra-ocular pressure in ocular hypertension, open-angle glaucoma, pseudo-exfoliative glaucoma *either* as adjunct to beta-blocker *or* used alone in patients unresponsive to beta-blockers or if beta-blockers contra-indicated

**Cautions** hepatic impairment; systemic absorption follows topical application; history of renal calculi; chronic corneal defects, history of intra-ocular surgery; **interactions:** Appendix 1 (dorzolamide)

**Contra-indications** severe renal impairment or hyperchloraemic acidosis; pregnancy and breast-feeding

**Side-effects** ocular burning, stinging and itching, blurred vision, lacrimation, conjunctivitis, superficial punctate keratitis, eyelid inflammation and crusting, anterior uveitis, transient myopia, corneal oedema, iridocyclitis; headache, dizziness, paraesthesia, asthenia, sinusitis, rhinitis, nausea; hypersensitivity reactions (including urticaria, angioedema, bronchospasm); bitter taste, epistaxis, urolithiasis

**Dose**

- Used alone, apply 3 times daily
- With topical beta-blocker, apply twice daily

**Trusopt®** (MSD) PoM
Ophthalmic solution (= eye drops), dorzolamide (as hydrochloride) 2%, net price 5 mL = £6.33
Excipients include benzalkonium chloride

### With timolol

For cautions, contra-indications, and side-effects of timolol, see section 11.6, Beta-blockers

**Cosopt®** (MSD) PoM
Ophthalmic solution (= eye drops), dorzolamide (as hydrochloride) 2%, timolol (as maleate) 0.5%, net price 5 mL = £10.05
Excipients include benzalkonium chloride
Dose for raised intra-ocular pressure in open-angle glaucoma, or pseudoexfoliative glaucoma when beta-blockers alone not adequate, apply twice daily

## Miotics

The small pupil is an unfortunate side-effect of these drugs (except when pilocarpine is used temporarily before an operation for *angle-closure glaucoma*). They act by opening up the inefficient drainage channels in the trabecular meshwork resulting from contraction or spasm of the ciliary muscle.

Miotics used in the management of raised intra-ocular pressure include pilocarpine.

**Cautions** A darkly pigmented iris may require higher concentration of the miotic or more frequent administration and care should be taken to avoid overdosage. Retinal detachment has occurred in susceptible individuals and those with retinal disease; therefore fundus examination is advised before starting treatment with a miotic. Care is also required in conjunctival or corneal damage. Intra-ocular pressure and visual fields should be monitored in those with chronic simple glaucoma and those receiving long-term treatment with a miotic. Miotics should be used with caution in cardiac disease, hypertension, asthma, peptic ulceration, urinary-tract obstruction, and Parkinson's disease.
Counselling Blurred vision may affect performance of skilled tasks (e.g. driving) particularly at night or in reduced lighting

**Contra-indications** Miotics are contra-indicated in conditions where pupillary constriction is undesirable such as acute iritis, anterior uveitis and some forms of secondary glaucoma. They should be avoided in acute inflammatory disease of the anterior segment.

**Side-effects** Ciliary spasm leads to headache and browache which may be more severe in the initial 2–4 weeks of treatment (a particular disadvantage in patients under 40 years of age). Ocular side-effects include burning, itching, smarting, blurred vision, conjunctival vascular congestion, myopia, lens changes with chronic use, vitreous haemorrhage, and pupillary block. Systemic side-effects (see under Parasympathomimetics, section 7.4.1) are rare following application to the eye.

## PILOCARPINE

**Indications** see notes above; dry mouth (section 12.3.5)

**Cautions** see notes above

**Contra-indications** see notes above

**Side-effects** see notes above

**Dose**

- Apply up to 4 times daily; long-acting preparations, see under preparations below

**Pilocarpine Hydrochloride** (Non-proprietary) PoM
Eye drops, pilocarpine hydrochloride 0.5%, net price 10 mL = £1.39; 1%, 10 mL = £2.29; 2%, 10 mL = £2.09; 3%, 10 mL = £1.44; 4%, 10 mL = £2.83

### Single use

**Minims® Pilocarpine Nitrate** (Chauvin) PoM
Eye drops, pilocarpine nitrate 2 and 4%, net price 20 × 0.5 mL (both) = £4.92

### Long acting

**Pilogel®** (Alcon) PoM
Ophthalmic gel, pilocarpine hydrochloride 4%, net price 5 g = £6.86
Excipients include benzalkonium chloride, disodium edetate
Dose apply 1–1.5 cm gel once daily at bedtime

# 11.7 Local anaesthetics

Oxybuprocaine and tetracaine (amethocaine) are probably the most widely used topical local anaesthetics. Proxymetacaine causes less initial stinging and is useful for children. Oxybuprocaine or a combined preparation of lidocaine (lignocaine) and fluorescein is used for tonometry. Tetracaine produces a more profound anaesthesia and is suitable for use before minor surgical procedures, such as the removal of corneal sutures. It has a temporary disruptive effect on the corneal epithelium. Lidocaine, with or without adrenaline (epinephrine), is injected into the eyelids for minor surgery, while retrobulbar or peribulbar injections are used for surgery of the globe itself. Local anaesthetics should never be used for the management of ocular symptoms.

## LIDOCAINE HYDROCHLORIDE
(Lignocaine hydrochloride)

**Indications** local anaesthetic

**Minims® Lignocaine and Fluorescein** (Chauvin) PoM
Eye drops, lidocaine hydrochloride 4%, fluorescein sodium 0.25%. Net price 20 × 0.5 mL = £6.93

## OXYBUPROCAINE HYDROCHLORIDE

**Indications** local anaesthetic

**Minims® Benoxinate (Oxybuprocaine) Hydrochloride** (Chauvin) PoM
Eye drops, oxybuprocaine hydrochloride 0.4%. Net price 20 × 0.5 mL = £4.92

## PROXYMETACAINE HYDROCHLORIDE

**Indications** local anaesthetic

**Minims® Proxymetacaine** (Chauvin) PoM
Eye drops, proxymetacaine hydrochloride 0.5%. Net price 20 × 0.5 mL = £6.95

With fluorescein

**Minims® Proxymetacaine and Fluorescein** (Chauvin) PoM
Eye drops, proxymetacaine hydrochloride 0.5%, fluorescein sodium 0.25%. Net price 20 × 0.5 mL = £7.95

## TETRACAINE HYDROCHLORIDE
(Amethocaine hydrochloride)

**Indications** local anaesthetic

**Minims® Amethocaine Hydrochloride** (Chauvin) PoM
Eye drops, tetracaine hydrochloride 0.5 and 1%. Net price 20 × 0.5 mL (both) = £5.75

# 11.8 Miscellaneous ophthalmic preparations

**11.8.1** Tear deficiency, ocular lubricants, and astringents
**11.8.2** Ocular diagnostic and peri-operative preparations and photodynamic treatment

Certain eye drops, e.g. amphotericin, ceftazidime, cefuroxime, colistin, desferrioxamine, dexamethasone, gentamicin and vancomycin may be prepared aseptically from material supplied for injection; for details on preparation of trisodium edetate eye drops see under *Limclair®* section 9.5.1.2.

## 11.8.1 Tear deficiency, ocular lubricants, and astringents

Chronic soreness of the eyes associated with reduced or abnormal tear secretion (e.g. in Sjögren's syndrome) often responds to tear replacement therapy or pilocarpine given by mouth (section 12.3.5). The severity of the condition and patient preference will often guide the choice of preparation.

**Hypromellose** is the traditional choice of treatment for tear deficiency. It may need to be instilled frequently (e.g. hourly) for adequate relief. Ocular surface mucin is often abnormal in tear deficiency and the combination of hypromellose with a mucolytic such as **acetylcysteine** can be helpful.

The ability of **carbomers** to cling to the eye surface may help reduce frequency of application to 4 times daily.

**Polyvinyl alcohol** increases the persistence of the tear film and is useful when the ocular surface mucin is reduced.

**Povidone** eye drops are also used in the management of tear deficiency.

**Sodium chloride 0.9%** drops are sometimes useful in tear deficiency, and can be used as 'comfort drops' by contact lens wearers, and to facilitate lens removal. Special presentations of sodium chloride 0.9% and other irrigation solutions are used routinely for intraocular surgery.

Eye ointments containing a **paraffin** may be used to lubricate the eye surface, especially in cases of recurrent corneal epithelial erosion. They may cause temporary visual disturbance and are best suited for application before sleep. Ointments should not be used during contact lens wear.

**Zinc sulphate** is a traditional astringent that is now little used.

## ACETYLCYSTEINE

**Indications** tear deficiency, impaired or abnormal mucus production

**Dose**
- Apply eye drops 3–4 times daily

**Ilube®** (Alcon) PoM
Eye drops, acetylcysteine 5%, hypromellose 0.35%. Net price 10 mL = £4.63
Excipients include benzalkonium chloride, disodium edetate

## CARBOMERS
### (Polyacrylic acid)

Note Synthetic high molecular weight polymers of acrylic acid cross-linked with either allyl ethers of sucrose or allyl ethers of pentaerithrityl

**Indications** dry eyes including keratoconjunctivitis sicca, unstable tear film

**Dose**

- Apply 3–4 times daily or as required

**GelTears®** (Chauvin)
Gel (= eye drops), carbomer 980 (polyacrylic acid) 0.2%, net price 10 g = £2.80
Excipients include benzalkonium chloride

**Liposic®** (Bausch & Lomb)
Gel (= eye drops), carbomer 980 (polyacrylic acid) 0.2%, net price 10 g = £2.96
Excipients include cetrimide

**Liquivisc®** (Allergan)
Gel (= eye drops), carbomer 974P (polyacrylic acid) 0.25%, net price 10 g = £1.99
Excipients include benzalkonium chloride

**Viscotears®** (Novartis)
Liquid gel (= eye drops), carbomer 980 (polyacrylic acid) 0.2%, net price 10 g = £3.12
Excipients include cetrimide, disodium edetate

Liquid gel (= eye drops), carbomer 980 (polyacrylic acid) 0.2%, net price 30 × 0.6-mL single-dose units = £5.75



## CARMELLOSE SODIUM

**Indications** dry eye conditions

**Dose**

- Apply as required

**Celluvisc®** (Allergan)
Eye drops, carmellose sodium 1%, net price 30 × 0.4 mL = £5.75, 60 × 0.4 mL = £10.99

## HYDROXYETHYLCELLULOSE

**Indications** tear deficiency

**Minims® Artificial Tears** (Chauvin)
Eye drops, hydroxyethylcellulose 0.44%, sodium chloride 0.35%. Net price 20 × 0.5 mL = £5.75

## HYPROMELLOSE

**Indications** tear deficiency

Note The Royal Pharmaceutical Society of Great Britain has stated that where it is not possible to ascertain the strength of hypromellose prescribed, the prescriber should be contacted to clarify the strength intended.

**Hypromellose** (Non-proprietary)
Eye drops, hypromellose 0.3%, net price 10 mL = £1.23

**Isopto Alkaline®** (Alcon)
Eye drops, hypromellose 1%, net price 10 mL = 99p
Excipients include benzalkonium chloride

**Isopto Plain®** (Alcon)
Eye drops, hypromellose 0.5%, net price 10 mL = 85p
Excipients include benzalkonium chloride

**Tears Naturale®** (Alcon)
Eye drops, dextran '70' 0.1%, hypromellose 0.3%, net price 15 mL = £1.68
Excipients include benzalkonium chloride, disodium edetate

**Single use**

**Artelac® SDU** (Pharma-Global)
Eye drops, hypromellose 0.32%, net price 30 × 0.5 mL = £11.88

**With phenylephrine**

Note Phenylephrine (section 11.5) acts to constrict conjunctival vessels, thus producing a whiter eye; it is not recommended for prolonged use

**Isopto Frin®** (Alcon)
Eye drops, phenylephrine hydrochloride 0.12%, hypromellose 0.5%, net price 10 mL = £1.14
Excipients include benzethonium chloride
Dose temporary relief of redness due to minor irritation, apply up to 4 times daily

## LIQUID PARAFFIN

**Indications** dry eye conditions

**Lacri-Lube®** (Allergan)
Eye ointment, white soft paraffin 57.3%, liquid paraffin 42.5%, wool alcohols 0.2%. Net price 3.5 g = £1.90, 5 g = £2.47

**Lubri-Tears®** (Alcon)
Eye ointment, white soft paraffin 60%, liquid paraffin 30%, wool fat 10%. Net price 5 g = £2.29

## PARAFFIN, YELLOW, SOFT

**Indications** see notes above

**Simple Eye Ointment**
Ointment, liquid paraffin 10%, wool fat 10%, in yellow soft paraffin. Net price 4 g = £2.68

## POLYVINYL ALCOHOL

**Indications** tear deficiency

**Liquifilm Tears®** (Allergan)
Ophthalmic solution (= eye drops), polyvinyl alcohol 1.4%. Net price 15 mL = £1.61
Excipients include benzalkonium chloride, disodium edetate

Ophthalmic solution (= eye drops), polyvinyl alcohol 1.4%, povidone 0.6%. Net price 30 × 0.4 mL = £5.35

**Sno Tears®** (Chauvin)
Eye drops, polyvinyl alcohol 1.4%. Net price 10 mL = £1.06
Excipients include benzalkonium chloride, disodium edetate

## POVIDONE

**Indications** dry eye conditions

**Dose**

- Apply 4 times daily or as required

**Oculotect®** (Novartis)
Eye drops, povidone 5%. Net price 20 × 0.4 mL = £3.40

## SODIUM CHLORIDE

**Indications** irrigation, including first-aid removal of harmful substances

**Sodium Chloride 0.9% Solutions**
See section 13.11.1

**Balanced Salt Solution**
Solution (sterile), sodium chloride 0.64%, sodium acetate 0.39%, sodium citrate 0.17%, calcium chloride 0.048%, magnesium chloride 0.03%, potassium chloride 0.075%
For intra-ocular or topical irrigation during surgical procedures
Brands include *Iocare®*

Single use

**Minims® Saline** (Chauvin)
Eye drops, sodium chloride 0.9%. Net price 20 × 0.5 mL = £4.92

## ZINC SULPHATE

**Indications** see notes above
**Cautions** see notes above

**Zinc Sulphate** (Non-proprietary)
Eye drops, zinc sulphate 0.25%. Net price 10 mL = £3.15

# 11.8.2 Ocular diagnostic and peri-operative preparations and photodynamic treatment

## Ocular diagnostic preparations

**Fluorescein sodium** and **rose bengal** are used in diagnostic procedures and for locating damaged areas of the cornea due to injury or disease. Rose bengal is more efficient for the diagnosis of conjunctival epithelial damage but it often stings excessively unless a local anaesthetic is instilled beforehand.

## FLUORESCEIN SODIUM

**Indications** detection of lesions and foreign bodies

**Minims® Fluorescein Sodium** (Chauvin)
Eye drops, fluorescein sodium 1 or 2%. Net price 20 × 0.5 mL (both) = £4.92

With local anaesthetic
Section 11.7

## ROSE BENGAL

**Indications** detection of lesions and foreign bodies

**Minims® Rose Bengal** (Chauvin)
Eye drops, rose bengal 1%. Net price 20 × 0.5 mL = £5.75

## Ocular peri-operative drugs

Drugs used to prepare the eye for surgery and drugs that are injected into the anterior chamber at the time of surgery are included here.

Sodium hyaluronate (*Ophthalin®*) is used during surgical procedures on the eye.

**Apraclonidine**, an $alpha_2$-adrenoceptor stimulant, reduces intra-ocular pressure possibly by reducing the production of aqueous humour. It is used for short-term treatment only.

Special presentations of **sodium chloride 0.9%** solution are used routinely in intra-ocular surgery (section 11.8.1).

## ACETYLCHOLINE CHLORIDE

**Indications** cataract surgery, penetrating keratoplasty, iridectomy, and other anterior segment surgery requiring rapid complete miosis

**Miochol-E®** (Novartis) PoM
Solution for intra-ocular irrigation, acetylcholine chloride 1%, mannitol 3% when reconstituted. Net price 2 mL-vial = £9.10

## APRACLONIDINE

**Note** Apraclonidine is a derivative of clonidine

**Indications** control of intra-ocular pressure

**Cautions** history of angina, severe coronary insufficiency, recent myocardial infarction, heart failure, cerebrovascular disease, vasovagal attack, chronic renal failure; depression; pregnancy and breast-feeding; monitor intra-ocular pressure and visual fields; loss of effect may occur over time; suspend treatment if reduction in vision occurs in end-stage glaucoma; monitor for excessive reduction in intra-ocular pressure following peri-operative use; **interactions:** Appendix 1 ($alpha_2$-adrenoceptor stimulants)
**Driving** Drowsiness may affect performance of skilled tasks (e.g. driving)

**Contra-indications** history of severe or unstable and uncontrolled cardiovascular disease

**Side-effects** dry mouth, taste disturbance; hyperaemia, ocular pruritus, discomfort and lacrimation (withdraw if ocular intolerance including oedema of lids and conjunctiva); headache, asthenia, dry nose; lid retraction, conjunctival blanching and mydriasis reported after peri-operative use; since absorption may follow topical application systemic effects (see Clonidine Hydrochloride, section 2.5.2) may occur

**Dose**
- See under preparations below

**Iopidine®** (Alcon) PoM
Ophthalmic solution (= eye drops), apraclonidine 1% (as hydrochloride). Net price 12 × 2 single use 0.25-mL units = £81.90
**Dose** control or prevention of postoperative elevation of intra-ocular pressure after anterior segment laser surgery, apply 1 drop 1 hour before laser procedure then 1 drop immediately after completion of procedure; CHILD not recommended

Iopidine 0.5% ophthalmic solution (= eye drops), apraclonidine 0.5% (as hydrochloride). Net price 5 mL = £11.45
**Excipients** include benzalkonium chloride
**Dose** short-term adjunctive treatment of chronic glaucoma in patients not adequately controlled by another drug (see note below), apply 1 drop 3 times daily usually for max. 1 month; CHILD not recommended
**Note** May not provide additional benefit if patient already using two drugs that suppress the production of aqueous humour

## DICLOFENAC SODIUM

**Indications** inhibition of intra-operative miosis during cataract surgery (but does not possess intrinsic mydriatic properties); postoperative inflammation in cataract surgery, strabismus surgery or argon laser trabeculoplasty; pain in corneal epithelial defects after photorefractive keratectomy, radial keratotomy or accidental trauma; seasonal allergic conjunctivitis (section 11.4.2)

**Voltarol® Ophtha Multidose** (Novartis) PoM
Eye drops, diclofenac sodium 0.1%, net price 5 mL = £6.68
Excipients include benzalkonium chloride, disodium edetate, propylene glycol

**Single use**

**Voltarol® Ophtha** (Novartis) PoM
Eye drops, diclofenac sodium 0.1%. Net price pack of 5 single-dose units = £4.00, 40 single-dose units = £32.00

## FLURBIPROFEN SODIUM

**Indications** inhibition of intra-operative miosis (but does not possess intrinsic mydriatic properties); anterior segment inflammation following postoperative and post-laser trabeculoplasty when corticosteroids contra-indicated

**Ocufen®** (Allergan) PoM
Ophthalmic solution (= eye drops), flurbiprofen sodium 0.03%, polyvinyl alcohol (*Liquifilm®*) 1.4%. Net price 40 × 0.4 mL = £37.15

## KETOROLAC TROMETAMOL

**Indications** prophylaxis and reduction of inflammation and associated symptoms following ocular surgery

**Acular®** (Allergan) PoM
Eye drops, ketorolac trometamol 0.5%. Net price 5 mL = £5.00
Excipients include benzalkonium chloride, disodium edetate

## Subfoveal choroidal neovascularisation

**Verteporfin** is licensed for use in the photodynamic treatment of age-related macular degeneration associated with predominantly classic subfoveal choroidal neovascularisation *or* with pathological myopia (see NICE guidance below). It is also licensed for occult subfoveal choroidal neovascularisation with disease progression. Following intravenous infusion, verteporfin is activated by local irradiation using non-thermal red light to produce cytotoxic derivatives. Only specialists experienced in the management of these conditions should use it.

**NICE guidance (photodynamic therapy for wet age-related macular degeneration)**
NICE has recommended (September 2003) photodynamic therapy for wet age-related macular degeneration with a confirmed diagnosis of classic (no occult) subfoveal choroidal neovascularisation and best-corrected visual acuity of 6/60 or better. Photodynamic therapy is **not** recommended for wet age-related macular degeneration with predominantly classic but partly occult subfoveal choroidal neovascularisation *except* in clinical studies.

## VERTEPORFIN

**Indications** see notes above—specialist use only
**Cautions** photosensitivity—avoid exposure of unprotected skin and eyes to bright light during infusion and for 48 hours afterwards; hepatic impairment (avoid if severe), biliary obstruction; avoid extravasation; pregnancy (Appendix 4)
**Contra-indications** porphyria; breast-feeding (Appendix 5)
**Side-effects** visual disturbances (including blurred vision, flashing lights, visual-field defects), nausea, back pain, asthenia, pruritus, hypercholesterolaemia, fever; rarely lacrimation disorder, subretinal or vitreous haemorrhage, hypersensitivity reactions (including chest pain, syncope, sweating, changes in blood pressure and in heart rate); injection-site reactions including pain, oedema, inflammation, haemorrhage, discoloration
**Dose**
- By intravenous infusion over 10 minutes, 6 mg/m²
  **Note** For information on administration and light activation, consult product literature

**Visudyne®** (Novartis) PoM
Injection, powder for reconstitution, verteporfin, net price 15-mg vial = £850.00

# 11.9 Contact lenses

**Note** Some recommendations in this section involve non-licensed indications.

For cosmetic reasons many people prefer to wear contact lenses rather than spectacles; contact lenses are also sometimes required for medical indications. Visual defects are corrected by either rigid ('hard' or gas permeable) lenses or soft (hydrogel) lenses; soft lenses are the most popular type, because they are the most comfortable, though they may not give the best vision. Lenses should usually be worn for a specified number of hours each day. Continuous (extended) wear involves much greater risks to eye health and is not recommended except where medically indicated.

Contact lenses require meticulous care. Poor compliance with directions for use, and with daily cleaning and disinfection, may result in complications which include ulcerative keratitis, conjunctival problems (such as purulent or papillary conjunctivitis). One-day disposable lenses, which are worn only once and therefore require no maintenance or storage, are becoming increasingly popular.

*Acanthamoeba keratitis*, a sight-threatening condition, is associated with ineffective lens cleaning and disinfection or the use of contaminated lens cases. The condition is especially associated with the use of soft lenses (including frequently replaced lenses). Acanthamoeba keratitis is treated by specialists with intensive use of polihexanide (polyhexamethylene biguanide), propamidine isetionate, chlorhexidine and neomycin drops, sometimes in combination.

**Contact lenses and drug treatment** Special care is required in prescribing eye preparations for contact lens users. Some drugs and preservatives in eye preparations can accumulate in hydrogel lenses and may induce toxic reactions. Therefore, unless medically indicated, the lenses should be removed before instillation and not worn during the period of treatment. Alternatively, unpreserved drops can be used. Eye drops may, however, be instilled over rigid corneal contact lenses. Ointment preparations should never be used in conjunction with contact lens wear; oily eye drops should also be avoided.

Many drugs given systemically can also have adverse effects on contact lens wear. These include oral contraceptives (particularly those with a higher oestrogen content), drugs which reduce blink rate (e.g. anxiolytics, hypnotics, antihistamines, and muscle relaxants), drugs which reduce lacrimation (e.g. antihistamines, antimuscarinics, phenothiazines and related drugs, some beta-blockers, diuretics, and tricyclic antidepressants), and drugs which increase lacrimation (including ephedrine and hydralazine). Other drugs that may affect contact lens wear are isotretinoin (may cause conjunctival inflammation), aspirin (salicylic acid appears in tears and may be absorbed by contact lenses—leading to irritation), and rifampicin and sulfasalazine (may discolour lenses).

# 12 Ear, nose, and oropharynx

**12.1 Drugs acting on the ear** 550
12.1.1 Otitis externa 550
12.1.2 Otitis media 553
12.1.3 Removal of ear wax 553
**12.2 Drugs acting on the nose** 554
12.2.1 Drugs used in nasal allergy 554
12.2.2 Topical nasal decongestants 556
12.2.3 Nasal preparations for infection 558
**12.3 Drugs acting on the oropharynx** 558
12.3.1 Drugs for oral ulceration and inflammation 558
12.3.2 Oropharyngeal anti-infective drugs 560
12.3.3 Lozenges and sprays 562
12.3.4 Mouthwashes, gargles, and dentifrices 562
12.3.5 Treatment of dry mouth 564

This chapter includes advice on the drug management of the following:
allergic rhinitis, p. 554
nasal polyps, p. 554
oropharyngeal infections, p. 560
periodontitis, p. 559



## 12.1 Drugs acting on the ear

**12.1.1 Otitis externa**
**12.1.2 Otitis media**
**12.1.3 Removal of ear wax**

### 12.1.1 Otitis externa

Otitis externa is an inflammatory reaction of the meatal skin. It is important to exclude an underlying chronic otitis media before treatment is commenced. Many cases recover after thorough cleansing of the external ear canal by suction or dry mopping. A frequent problem in resistant cases is the difficulty in applying lotions and ointments satisfactorily to the relatively inaccessible affected skin. The most effective method is to introduce a ribbon gauze dressing or sponge wick soaked with **corticosteroid** ear drops or with an astringent such as **aluminium acetate** solution. When this is not practical, the ear should be gently cleansed with a probe covered in cotton wool and the patient encouraged to lie with the affected ear uppermost for ten minutes after the canal has been filled with a liberal quantity of the appropriate solution.

If infection is present, a topical anti-infective which is not used systemically (such as **neomycin** or **clioquinol**) may be used, but for only about a week as excessive use may result in fungal infections; these may be difficult to treat and require expert advice. Sensitivity to the anti-infective or solvent may occur and resistance to antibacterials is a possibility with prolonged use. Aluminium acetate ear drops are also effective against bacterial infection and inflammation of the ear. **Chloramphenicol** may also be used but the ear drops contain propylene glycol and cause sensitivity in about 10% of patients. Solutions containing an anti-infective and a corticosteroid (such as *Locorten-Vioform®*) are used for treating cases where infection is present with inflammation and eczema. In view of reports of ototoxicity in patients with a perforated tympanic membrane (eardrum), the CSM has stated that treatment with a topical aminoglycoside antibiotic is contra-indicated in those with a tympanic perforation. However, many specialists do use these drops cautiously in the presence of a perforation in patients with otitis media (section 12.1.2) and where other measures have failed for otitis externa.

A solution of **acetic acid** 2% acts as an antifungal and antibacterial in the external ear canal. It may be used to treat mild otitis externa but in severe cases an anti-inflammatory preparation with or without an anti-infective drug is required. A proprietary preparation containing acetic acid 2% (*EarCalm®* spray) is on sale to the public.

An acute infection may cause severe pain and a systemic antibacterial is required with a simple analgesic such as paracetamol. When a resistant staphylococcal infection (a boil) is present in the external auditory meatus, **flucloxacillin** is the drug of choice (section 5.1, table 1); **ciprofloxacin** (or an aminoglycoside) may be needed in pseudomonal infections which may occur if the patient has diabetes or is immunocompromised.

The skin of the pinna adjacent to the ear canal is often affected by eczema. Topical corticosteroid creams and ointments (see section 13.4) are then required, but prolonged use should be avoided.

## Astringent preparations

### ALUMINIUM ACETATE

**Indications** inflammation in otitis externa (see notes above)

**Dose**

- Insert into meatus or apply on a ribbon gauze dressing or sponge wick which should be kept saturated with the ear drops

**Aluminium Acetate** (Non-proprietary)
Ear drops 13%, aluminium sulphate 2.25 g, calcium carbonate 1 g, tartaric acid 450 mg, acetic acid (33%) 2.5 mL, purified water 7.5 mL
Available from manufacturers of 'special order' products

Ear drops 8%, dilute 8 parts aluminium acetate ear drops (13%) with 5 parts purified water. Must be freshly prepared

## Anti-inflammatory preparations

### BETAMETHASONE SODIUM PHOSPHATE

**Indications** eczematous inflammation in otitis externa (see notes above)
**Cautions** avoid prolonged use
**Contra-indications** untreated infection
**Side-effects** local sensitivity reactions

**Betnesol®** (Celltech) PoM
Drops (for ear, eye, or nose), betamethasone sodium phosphate 0.1%. Net price 10 mL = £2.32
Excipients include benzalkonium chloride, disodium edetate
Dose ear, apply 2–3 drops every 2–3 hours; reduce frequency when relief obtained; eye, see section 11.4.1; nose, see section 12.2.1

**Vista-Methasone®** (Martindale) PoM
Drops (for ear, eye, or nose), betamethasone sodium phosphate 0.1%. Net price 5 mL = £1.10; 10 mL = £1.25
Excipients include benzalkonium chloride, disodium edetate
Dose ear, apply 2–3 drops every 3–4 hours; reduce frequency when relief obtained; eye, see section 11.4.1; nose, see section 12.2.1

#### With antibacterial

**Betnesol-N®** (Celltech) PoM
Drops (for ear, eye, or nose), betamethasone sodium phosphate 0.1%, neomycin sulphate 0.5%. Net price 10 mL = £2.39
Excipients include benzalkonium chloride, disodium edetate
Dose ear, apply 2–3 drops 3–4 times daily; eye, see section 11.4.1; nose, section 12.2.3

**Vista-Methasone N®** (Martindale) PoM
Drops (for ear, eye, or nose), betamethasone sodium phosphate 0.1%, neomycin sulphate 0.5%. Net price 5 mL = £1.09; 10 mL = £1.20
Excipients include thiomersal
Dose ear, apply 2–3 drops every 3–4 hours; reduce frequency when relief obtained; eye, see section 11.4.1; nose, section 12.2.3

### DEXAMETHASONE

**Indications** eczematous inflammation in otitis externa (see notes above)
**Cautions** avoid prolonged use
**Contra-indications** untreated infection
**Side-effects** local sensitivity reactions

#### With antibacterial

**Otomize®** (GSK Consumer Healthcare) PoM
Ear spray, dexamethasone 0.1%, neomycin sulphate 3250 units/mL, glacial acetic acid 2%. Net price 5-mL pump-action aerosol unit = £4.24
Excipients include hydroxybenzoates (parabens)
Dose apply 1 metered spray into the ear 3 times daily

**Sofradex®** (Florizel) PoM
Drops (for ear or eye), dexamethasone (as sodium metasulphobenzoate) 0.05%, framycetin sulphate 0.5%, gramicidin 0.005%. Net price 10 mL = £4.85
Excipients include polysorbate 80
Dose ear, apply 2–3 drops 3–4 times daily; eye, see section 11.4.1

### FLUMETASONE PIVALATE
(Flumethasone Pivalate)

**Indications** eczematous inflammation in otitis externa (see notes above)
**Cautions** avoid prolonged use
**Contra-indications** untreated infection
**Side-effects** local sensitivity reactions

#### With antibacterial

**Locorten-Vioform®** (Amdipharm) PoM
Ear drops, flumetasone pivalate 0.02%, clioquinol 1%. Net price 7.5 mL = £1.47
Contra-indications iodine sensitivity
Dose apply 2–3 drops into the ear twice daily for up to 7–10 days; not recommended for child under 2 years
Note Clioquinol stains skin and clothing

### HYDROCORTISONE

**Indications** eczematous inflammation in otitis externa (see notes above)
**Cautions** avoid prolonged use
**Contra-indications** untreated infection
**Side-effects** local sensitivity reactions

#### With antibacterial

**Gentisone® HC** (Roche) PoM
Ear drops, hydrocortisone acetate 1%, gentamicin 0.3% (as sulphate). Net price 10 mL = £3.69
Excipients include benzalkonium chloride, disodium edetate
Dose apply 2–4 drops into the ear 3–4 times daily and at night

**Neo-Cortef®** (PLIVA) PoM
Ointment (for ear or eye), hydrocortisone acetate 1.5%, neomycin sulphate 0.5%. Net price 3.9 g = £1.53
Excipients include wool fat
Dose ear, apply 1–2 times daily; eye, see section 11.4.1
Note May be difficult to obtain

**Otosporin**® (GSK) PoM
Ear drops, hydrocortisone 1%, neomycin sulphate 3400 units, polymyxin B sulphate 10 000 units/mL. Net price 5 mL = £2.00; 10 mL = £4.00
Excipients include cetostearyl alcohol, hydroxybenzoates (parabens), polysorbate 20
Dose ADULT and CHILD over 3 years, apply 3 drops into the ear 3–4 times daily

## PREDNISOLONE SODIUM PHOSPHATE

**Indications** eczematous inflammation in otitis externa (see notes above)
**Cautions** avoid prolonged use
**Contra-indications** untreated infection
**Side-effects** local sensitivity reactions

**Predsol**® (Celltech) PoM
Drops (for ear or eye), prednisolone sodium phosphate 0.5%. Net price 10 mL = £2.00
Excipients include benzalkonium chloride, disodium edetate
Dose ear, apply 2–3 drops every 2–3 hours; reduce frequency when relief obtained; eye, see section 11.4.1

**With antibacterial**
**Predsol-N**® (Celltech) PoM
Drops (for ear or eye), prednisolone sodium phosphate 0.5%, neomycin sulphate 0.5%. Net price 10 mL = £2.36
Excipients include benzalkonium chloride, disodium edetate
Dose ear, apply 2–3 drops 3–4 times daily; eye, see section 11.4.1

## TRIAMCINOLONE ACETONIDE

**Indications** eczematous inflammation in otitis externa (see notes above)
**Cautions** avoid prolonged use
**Contra-indications** untreated infection
**Side-effects** local sensitivity reactions

**With antibacterial**
**Tri-Adcortyl Otic**® (Squibb) PoM
Ear ointment, triamcinolone acetonide 0.1%, gramicidin 0.025%, neomycin 0.25% (as sulphate), nystatin 100 000 units/g in *Plastibase*®. Net price 10 g = £1.58
Dose apply into the ear 2–3 times daily; CHILD under 1 year not recommended

# Anti-infective preparations

## CHLORAMPHENICOL

**Indications** bacterial infection in otitis externa (but see notes above)
**Cautions** avoid prolonged use (see notes above)
**Side-effects** high incidence of sensitivity reactions to vehicle

**Chloramphenicol** (Non-proprietary) PoM
Ear drops, chloramphenicol in propylene glycol, net price 5%, 10 mL = £1.47; 10%, 10 mL = £1.40
Dose apply 2–3 drops into the ear 2–3 times daily

## CLIOQUINOL

**Indications** mild bacterial or fungal infections in otitis externa (see notes above)
**Cautions** avoid prolonged use (see notes above)
**Contra-indications** perforated tympanic membrane
**Side-effects** local sensitivity; stains skin and clothing

**With corticosteroid**
**Locorten-Vioform**®, see Flumetasone

## CLOTRIMAZOLE

**Indications** fungal infection in otitis externa (see notes above)
**Side-effects** occasional local irritation or sensitivity

**Canesten**® (Bayer Consumer Care)
Solution, clotrimazole 1% in polyethylene glycol 400 (macrogol 400). Net price 20 mL = £2.43
Dose ear, apply 2–3 times daily continuing for at least 14 days after disappearance of infection; skin, see section 13.10.2

## FRAMYCETIN SULPHATE

**Indications** see under Gentamicin
**Cautions** see under Gentamicin
**Contra-indications** perforated tympanic membrane (see notes above)
**Side-effects** local sensitivity

**With corticosteroid**
**Sofradex**®, see Dexamethasone

## GENTAMICIN

**Indications** bacterial infection in otitis externa (see notes above)
**Cautions** avoid prolonged use (see notes above)
**Contra-indications** perforated tympanic membrane (but see also notes above and section 12.1.2)
**Side-effects** local sensitivity

**Genticin**® (Roche) PoM
Drops (for ear or eye), gentamicin 0.3% (as sulphate). Net price 10 mL = £1.91
Excipients include benzalkonium chloride
Dose ear, apply 2–3 drops 3–4 times daily and at night; eye, see section 11.3.1

**With corticosteroid**
**Gentisone**® **HC** see Hydrocortisone

## NEOMYCIN SULPHATE

**Indications** bacterial infection in otitis externa (see notes above)
**Cautions** avoid prolonged use (see notes above)
**Contra-indications** perforated tympanic membrane (see notes above)
**Side-effects** local sensitivity

**With corticosteroid**

**Betnesol-N®** see Betamethasone

**Neo-Cortef®** see Hydrocortisone

**Otomize®** see Dexamethasone

**Otosporin®** see Hydrocortisone

**Predsol-N®** see Prednisolone

**Tri-Adcortyl Otic®** see Triamcinolone

**Vista-Methasone N®** see Betamethasone

## Other aural preparations

Choline salicylate is a mild analgesic but it is of doubtful value when applied topically.

**Audax®** (SSL) NHS

Ear drops, choline salicylate 21.6%, glycerol 12.6%. Net price 10 mL = £2.62

Excipients include propylene glycol

## 12.1.2 Otitis media

**Acute otitis media** Acute otitis media is the commonest cause of severe pain in small children. Many infections, especially those accompanying coryza, are caused by viruses. Most uncomplicated cases resolve without antibacterial treatment and a **simple analgesic**, such as paracetamol, may be sufficient. In children without systemic features, a **systemic antibacterial** may be started after 72 hours if there is no improvement, or earlier if there is deterioration (Table 1, section 5.1). Topical treatment of acute otitis media is ineffective and there is no place for drops containing a local anaesthetic. If the tympanic membrane has perforated, culture and sensitivity testing of any discharge is helpful in selecting an appropriate systemic antibacterial (Table 1, section 5.1).

In *recurrent* acute otitis media *either* a systemic antibacterial (Table 1, section 5.1) given at the first sign of an upper respiratory-tract infection *or*, in young children who live at home and do not attend a day centre, low-dose antibacterial prophylaxis (e.g. with amoxicillin) during the winter months may be tried. A full course of a systemic antibacterial is required if otitis media recurs.

**Otitis media with effusion** Otitis media with effusion ('glue ear') occurs in about 10% of children and in 90% of children with cleft palates. Systemic antibacterials are not usually required for otitis media with effusion. If 'glue ear' persists for more than a month or two, the child should be referred for assessment and follow up because of the risk of long-term hearing impairment which can delay language development. Untreated or resistant glue ear may be responsible for some types of *chronic otitis media*.

**Chronic otitis media** Opportunistic organisms are often present in the debris, keratin, and necrotic bone of the middle ear and mastoid in patients with chronic otitis media. The mainstay of treatment is thorough cleansing with aural microsuction which may completely resolve long-standing infection. Local cleansing of the meatal and middle ear may be followed by treatment with a sponge wick or ribbon gauze dressing soaked with corticosteroid ear drops or with an astringent such as aluminium acetate solution; this is particularly beneficial for discharging ears or infections of the mastoid cavity. An antibacterial ear ointment may also be used. Acute exacerbations of chronic infection may also require systemic treatment with amoxicillin (or erythromycin if penicillin-allergic); treatment is adjusted according to the results of sensitivity testing. Parenteral antibacterials are required if *Pseudomonas aeruginosa* and *Proteus* spp. are present.

The CSM has stated that topical treatment with ototoxic antibacterials is contra-indicated in the presence of a perforation (section 12.1.1). However, many specialists use ear drops containing **aminoglycosides** (e.g. neomycin) or **polymyxins** if the otitis media has failed to settle with systemic antibacterials; it is considered that the pus in the middle ear associated with otitis media carries a higher risk of ototoxicity than the drops themselves. Ciprofloxacin or ofloxacin ear drops [both unlicensed; available on named-patient basis from IDIS] or eye drops used in the ear [unlicensed indication] are an effective alternative to aminoglycoside ear drops for chronic otitis media in patients with perforation of the tympanic membrane.

## 12.1.3 Removal of ear wax

Wax is a normal bodily secretion which provides a protective film on the meatal skin and need only be removed if it causes deafness or interferes with a proper view of the ear drum. Syringing is generally best avoided in young children, in patients with a history of recurrent otitis externa, a history of ear-drum perforation, or previous ear surgery. A person who has hearing in one ear only should not have that ear syringed because even a very slight risk of damage is unacceptable in this situation.

Wax may be removed by syringing with water (warmed to body temperature). If necessary, wax can be softened using simple remedies such as **olive oil** ear drops or **almond oil** ear drops; **sodium bicarbonate** ear drops are also effective but may cause dryness of the ear canal. If the wax is hard and impacted the drops may be used twice daily for a few days before syringing; otherwise the wax may be softened on the day of syringing. The patient should lie with the affected ear uppermost for 5 to 10 minutes after a generous amount of the softening remedy has been introduced into the ear. Some proprietary preparations containing organic solvents can irritate the meatal skin, and in most cases the simple remedies indicated above are just as effective and less likely to cause irritation. Docusate sodium or urea–hydrogen peroxide are ingredients in a number of proprietary preparations for softening ear wax.

**Almond Oil** (Non-proprietary)

Ear drops, almond oil in a suitable container

Allow to warm to room temperature before use

**Olive Oil** (Non-proprietary)

Ear drops, olive oil in a suitable container

Allow to warm to room temperature before use

**Sodium Bicarbonate** (Non-proprietary)

Ear drops, sodium bicarbonate 5%, net price 10 mL = £1.25

**Cerumol®** (LAB)
Ear drops, chlorobutanol 5%, paradichlorobenzene 2%, arachis (peanut) oil 57.3%. Net price 11 mL = £1.60

**Exterol®** (Dermal)
Ear drops, urea–hydrogen peroxide complex 5% in glycerol. Net price 8 mL = £1.83

**Molcer®** (Wallace Mfg)
Ear drops, docusate sodium 5%. Net price 15 mL = £1.90
Excipients include propylene glycol

**Otex®** (DDD)
Ear drops, urea–hydrogen peroxide 5%. Net price 8 mL = £2.64

**Waxsol®** (Norgine)
Ear drops, docusate sodium 0.5%. Net price 10 mL = £1.26



# 12.2 Drugs acting on the nose

12.2.1 Drugs used in nasal allergy
12.2.2 Topical nasal decongestants
12.2.3 Nasal preparations for infection

Rhinitis is often self-limiting but bacterial sinusitis may require treatment with antibacterials (Table 1, section 5.1). There are few indications for nasal sprays and drops except in allergic rhinitis and perennial rhinitis (section 12.2.1). Many nasal preparations contain sympathomimetic drugs which may damage the nasal cilia (section 12.2.2). Some specialists use saline sniffs for a short period after endonasal surgery.

**Nasal polyps** Short-term use of corticosteroid nasal drops helps to shrink nasal polyps; to be effective, the drops must be administered with the patient in the 'head down' position. A short course of a systemic corticosteroid (section 6.3.2) may be required initially to shrink large polyps. A corticosteroid nasal spray can be used to maintain the reduction in swelling and also for the initial treatment of small polyps.

## 12.2.1 Drugs used in nasal allergy

Mild allergic rhinitis is controlled by **antihistamines** (see also section 3.4.1) or topical **nasal corticosteroids**; systemic nasal decongestants are of doubtful value (section 3.10). Topical nasal decongestants can be used for a short period to relieve congestion and allow penetration of a topical nasal corticosteroid.

More persistent symptoms and nasal congestion can be relieved by topical nasal **corticosteroids** and **cromoglicate** (cromoglycate); the topical antihistamine azelastine is useful for controlling breakthrough symptoms in allergic rhinitis. In seasonal allergic rhinitis (e.g. hay fever), treatment should begin 2 to 3 weeks before the season commences and may have to be continued for several months; continuous treatment may be required for years in perennial rhinitis.

In allergic rhinitis, topical preparations of corticosteroids and cromoglicate have a well-established role; although it may be less effective, cromoglicate is often the first choice in children. Topical antihistamines are considered less effective than topical corticosteroids but probably more effective than cromoglicate.

Sometimes allergic rhinitis is accompanied by vasomotor rhinitis. In this situation, the addition of topical nasal ipratropium bromide (section 12.2.2) can reduce watery rhinorrhoea.

Very disabling symptoms occasionally justify the use of **systemic corticosteroids** for short periods (section 6.3), for example, in students taking important examinations. They may also be used at the beginning of a course of treatment with a corticosteroid spray to relieve severe mucosal oedema and allow the spray to penetrate the nasal cavity.

**Pregnancy** If a pregnant woman cannot tolerate the symptoms of allergic rhinitis, treatment with nasal beclometasone or sodium cromoglicate may be considered.

### Antihistamines

#### AZELASTINE HYDROCHLORIDE

**Indications** allergic rhinitis
**Side-effects** irritation of nasal mucosa; bitter taste (if applied incorrectly)

[1]**Rhinolast®** (Viatris) PoM
Nasal spray, azelastine hydrochloride 140 micrograms (0.14 mL)/metered spray. Net price 22 mL (with metered pump) = £11.09
Excipients include sodium edetate
Dose ADULT and CHILD over 5 years, apply 140 micrograms (1 spray) into each nostril twice daily

1. Can be sold to the public for nasal administration in aqueous form (other than by aerosol) if supplied for the treatment of seasonal allergic rhinitis or perennial allergic rhinitis in adults and children over 5 years, subject to max. single dose of 140 micrograms per nostril, max. daily dose of 280 micrograms per nostril, and a pack size limit of 36 doses; a proprietary brand (*Aller-eze®*) is on sale to the public

### Corticosteroids

Nasal preparations containing corticosteroids (beclometasone, betamethasone, budesonide, flunisolide, fluticasone, mometasone, and triamcinolone) have a useful role in the prophylaxis and treatment of allergic rhinitis (see notes above).

**Cautions** Corticosteroid nasal preparations should be avoided in the presence of untreated nasal infections, and also after nasal surgery (until healing has occurred); they should also be avoided in pulmonary tuberculosis. Patients transferred from systemic corticosteroids may experience exacerbation of some symptoms. Systemic absorption may follow nasal administration particularly if high doses are used or if treatment is prolonged; for cautions and side-effects of systemic corticosteroids, see section 6.3.2. The risk of systemic effects may be greater with nasal drops than with nasal sprays; drops are administered incorrectly more often than sprays. The CSM recommends that the height of children receiving prolonged treatment with nasal corticosteroids is monitored; if growth is slowed, referral to a paediatrician should be considered.

**Side-effects** Local side-effects include dryness, irritation of nose and throat, epistaxis and rarely ulceration; nasal septal perforation (usually following nasal surgery) and raised intra-ocular pressure or glaucoma may also occur rarely. Headache, smell and taste disturbances may also occur. Hypersensitivity reactions, including bronchospasm, have been reported.

## BECLOMETASONE DIPROPIONATE
### (Beclomethasone Dipropionate)

**Indications** prophylaxis and treatment of allergic and vasomotor rhinitis
**Cautions** see notes above
**Side-effects** see notes above
**Dose**
- ADULT and CHILD over 6 years, apply 100 micrograms (2 sprays) into each nostril twice daily; max. total 400 micrograms (8 sprays) daily; when symptoms controlled, dose reduced to 50 micrograms (1 spray) into each nostril twice daily

[1]**Beclometasone** (Non-proprietary) PoM
Nasal spray, beclometasone dipropionate 50 micrograms/metered spray. Net price 200-spray unit = £3.49
Brands include *Nasobec Aqueous*®

1. Can be sold to the public for nasal administration (other than by aerosol) if supplied for the prevention and treatment of allergic rhinitis in adults over 18 years subject to max. single dose of 100 micrograms per nostril, max. daily dose of 200 micrograms per nostril for max. 3 months, and a pack size of 20 mg; proprietary brands on sale to the public include *Beclogen*®, *Beconase*® *Allergy*, *Beconase*® *Hayfever*, *Nasobec*® *Hayfever*, *Pollenase*® *Hayfever*, *Vivabec*®

**Beconase**® (A&H) PoM
Nasal spray (aqueous suspension), beclometasone dipropionate 50 micrograms/metered spray. Net price 200-spray unit with applicator = £2.19
Excipients include benzalkonium chloride, polysorbate 80

## BETAMETHASONE SODIUM PHOSPHATE

**Indications** non-infected inflammatory conditions of nose
**Cautions** see notes above
**Side-effects** see notes above

**Betnesol**® (Celltech) PoM
Drops (for ear, eye, or nose), betamethasone sodium phosphate 0.1%, net price 10 mL = £2.32
Excipients include benzalkonium chloride, disodium edetate
Dose nose, apply 2–3 drops into each nostril 2–3 times daily; ear, section 12.1.1; eye, see section 11.4.1

**Vista-Methasone**® (Martindale) PoM
Drops (for ear, eye, or nose), betamethasone sodium phosphate 0.1%. Net price 5 mL = £1.02, 10 mL = £1.16
Excipients include benzalkonium chloride, disodium edetate
Dose nose, apply 2–3 drops into each nostril twice daily; ear, section 12.1.1; eye, see section 11.4.1

## BUDESONIDE

**Indications** prophylaxis and treatment of allergic and vasomotor rhinitis; nasal polyps
**Cautions** see notes above; **interactions**: Appendix 1 (corticosteroids)
**Side-effects** see notes above
**Dose**
- See preparations

[1]**Budesonide** (Non-proprietary) PoM
Nasal spray, budesonide 100 micrograms/metered spray, net price 100-spray unit = £5.85
Dose rhinitis, ADULT and CHILD over 12 years, apply 2 sprays into each nostril once daily in the morning *or* 1 spray into each nostril twice daily; when control achieved reduce to 1 spray into each nostril once daily
Nasal polyps, ADULT and CHILD over 12 years, 1 spray into each nostril twice daily for up to 3 months

1. Can be sold to the public for nasal administration (other than by aerosol) if supplied for the prevention and treatment of seasonal allergic rhinitis in adults over 18 years subject to max. single dose of 200 micrograms per nostril, max. daily dose of 200 micrograms per nostril for max. period of 3 months, and a pack size of 10 mg

**Rhinocort Aqua**® (AstraZeneca) PoM
Nasal spray, budesonide 64 micrograms/metered spray. Net price 120-spray unit = £4.49
Excipients include disodium edetate, polysorbate 80, potassium sorbate
Dose rhinitis, ADULT and CHILD over 12 years, apply 2 sprays into each nostril once daily in the morning or 1 spray into each nostril twice daily; when control achieved reduce to 1 spray into each nostril once daily; max. duration of treatment 3 months
Nasal polyps, ADULT and CHILD over 12 years, 1 spray into each nostril twice daily for up to 3 months

## DEXAMETHASONE ISONICOTINATE

**Indications** treatment of allergic rhinitis
**Cautions** see notes above; avoid contact with eyes
**Side-effects** see notes above

### With sympathomimetic

For cautions and side-effects of sympathomimetics see Ephedrine Hydrochloride, section 12.2.2

**Dexa-Rhinaspray Duo**® (Boehringer Ingelheim) PoM
Nasal spray, dexamethasone isonicotinate 20 micrograms, tramazoline hydrochloride 120 micrograms/metered spray. Net price 110-dose unit = £2.15
Excipients include benzalkonium chloride, polysorbate 80
Dose allergic rhinitis, ADULT and CHILD over 12 years, apply 1 spray into each nostril 2–3 times daily, max. 6 times daily; max. duration 14 days; CHILD 5–12 years 1 spray into each nostril up to twice daily; under 5 years not recommended

## FLUNISOLIDE

**Indications** prophylaxis and treatment of allergic rhinitis
**Cautions** see notes above
**Side-effects** see notes above

**Syntaris**® (IVAX) PoM
Aqueous nasal spray, flunisolide 25 micrograms/metered spray. Net price 240-spray unit with pump and applicator = £5.05
Excipients include benzalkonium chloride, butylated hydroxytoluene, disodium edetate, polysorbate 20, propylene glycol
Dose ADULT, apply 50 micrograms (2 sprays) into each nostril twice daily, increased if necessary to max. 3 times daily then reduced for maintenance; CHILD 5–14 years initially 25 micrograms (1 spray) into each nostril up to 3 times daily

## FLUTICASONE PROPIONATE

**Indications** prophylaxis and treatment of allergic rhinitis and perennial rhinitis; nasal polyps

**Cautions** see notes above; **interactions:** Appendix 1 (corticosteroids)

**Side-effects** see notes above

**Dose**

- Rhinitis, apply 100 micrograms (2 sprays) into each nostril once daily, preferably in the morning, increased to max. twice daily if required; when control achieved reduce to 50 micrograms (1 spray) into each nostril once daily; CHILD 4–11 years, 50 micrograms (1 spray) into each nostril once daily, preferably in the morning, increased to max. twice daily if required
- Nasal polyps, see *Flixonase Nasule®* below

[1]**Flixonase®** (A&H) PoM

Aqueous nasal spray, fluticasone propionate 50 micrograms/metered spray. Net price 150-spray unit with applicator = £11.69

Excipients include benzalkonium chloride, polysorbate 80

1. Can be sold to the public for nasal administration (other than by pressurised nasal spray) if supplied for the prevention and treatment of allergic rhinitis in adults over 18 years, subject to max. single dose of 100 micrograms per nostril, max. daily dose of 200 micrograms per nostril for max. 3 months, and a pack size of 3 mg; proprietary brands on sale to the public include *Flixonase® Allergy*

**Flixonase Nasule®** (A&H) PoM

Nasal drops, fluticasone propionate 400 micrograms/unit dose, net price 28 × 0.4-mL units = £13.76

Excipients include polysorbate 20

Dose nasal polyps, ADULT and ADOLESCENT over 16 years, apply 200 micrograms (approx. 6 drops) into each nostril once or twice daily; consider alternative treatment if no improvement after 4–6 weeks

**Nasofan®** (IVAX) PoM

Aqueous nasal spray fluticasone propionate 50 micrograms/metered spray. Net price 150-spray unit = £10.52

Excipients include benzalkonium chloride, polysorbate 80

## MOMETASONE FUROATE

**Indications** see preparations

**Cautions** see notes above

**Side-effects** see notes above

**Nasonex®** (Schering-Plough) PoM

Nasal spray, mometasone furoate 50 micrograms/metered spray. Net price 140-spray unit = £7.83

Excipients include benzalkonium chloride, polysorbate 80

Dose prophylaxis and treatment of allergic rhinitis, ADULT and CHILD over 12 years, apply 100 micrograms (2 sprays) into each nostril once daily, increased if necessary to max. 200 micrograms (4 sprays) into each nostril once daily; when control achieved reduce to 50 micrograms (1 spray) into each nostril once daily; CHILD 6–11 years, 50 micrograms (1 spray) into each nostril once daily

Nasal polyps, ADULT over 18 years, apply 100 micrograms (2 sprays) into each nostril once daily, increased if necessary after 5–6 weeks to 100 micrograms (2 sprays) into each nostril twice daily (consider alternative treatment if no improvement after further 5–6 weeks); reduce dose when control achieved

## TRIAMCINOLONE ACETONIDE

**Indications** prophylaxis and treatment of allergic rhinitis

**Cautions** see notes above

**Side-effects** see notes above

[1]**Nasacort®** (Aventis Pharma) PoM

Aqueous nasal spray, triamcinolone acetonide 55 micrograms/metered spray. Net price 120-spray unit = £7.39

Excipients include benzalkonium chloride, disodium edetate, polysorbate 80

Dose ADULT and CHILD over 12 years apply 110 micrograms (2 sprays) into each nostril once daily; when control achieved, reduce to 55 micrograms (1 spray) into each nostril once daily; CHILD 6–12 years, 55 micrograms (1 spray) into each nostril once daily

1. Can be sold to the public for nasal administration as a non-pressurised nasal spray if supplied for the symptomatic treatment of seasonal allergic rhinitis in adults over 18 years, subject to max. daily dose of 110 micrograms per nostril for max. 3 months, and a pack size of 3.575 mg

### Cromoglicate

## SODIUM CROMOGLICATE
(Sodium Cromoglycate)

**Indications** prophylaxis of allergic rhinitis

**Side-effects** local irritation; rarely transient bronchospasm

**Rynacrom®** (Sanofi-Aventis)

4% aqueous nasal spray, sodium cromoglicate 4% (5.2 mg/squeeze). Net price 22 mL with pump = £17.76

Excipients include benzalkonium chloride, disodium edetate

Dose ADULT and CHILD, apply 1 squeeze into each nostril 2–4 times daily

**Vividrin®** (Pharma-Global)

Nasal spray, sodium cromoglicate 2%. Net price 15 mL = £8.56

Excipients include benzalkonium chloride, edetic acid, polysorbate 80

Dose ADULT and CHILD, apply 1 spray into each nostril 4–6 times daily

# 12.2.2 Topical nasal decongestants

The nasal mucosa is sensitive to changes in atmospheric temperature and humidity and these alone may cause slight nasal congestion. The nose and nasal sinuses produce a litre of mucus in 24 hours and much of this finds its way silently into the stomach via the nasopharynx. Slight changes in the nasal airway, accompanied by an awareness of mucus passing along the nasopharynx causes some patients to be inaccurately diagnosed as suffering from chronic sinusitis. These symptoms are particularly noticeable in the later stages of the common cold. **Sodium chloride** 0.9% given as nasal drops may relieve nasal congestion by helping to liquefy mucous secretions. Corticosteroid nasal drops produce shrinkage of nasal polyps (section 12.2).

Symptoms of nasal congestion associated with vasomotor rhinitis and the common cold can be relieved by the short-term use (usually not longer than 7 days) of decongestant nasal drops and sprays. These all contain sympathomimetic drugs which exert their effect by vasoconstriction of the mucosal blood vessels which in turn reduces oedema of the nasal mucosa. They are of limited value because they can give rise to a rebound congestion (rhinitis medicamentosa) on withdrawal, due to a secondary vasodilation with a subsequent temporary increase in nasal congestion. This in turn tempts the further use of the decongestant, leading to a vicious cycle of events. **Ephedrine nasal drops** is the safest sympathomimetic preparation and can give relief for several hours. The more potent sympathomimetic drugs oxymetazoline, and xylometazoline are more likely to cause a rebound effect. **All** of these preparations may cause a hypertensive crisis if used during treatment with a monoamine-oxidase inhibitor including moclobemide.

Non-allergic watery rhinorrhoea often responds well to treatment with the antimuscarinic **ipratropium bromide**.

Inhalation of **warm moist air** is useful in the treatment of symptoms of acute infective conditions. The addition of volatile substances such as menthol and eucalyptus may encourage the use of warm moist air (section 3.8).

Systemic nasal decongestants—see section 3.10.

**Sinusitis and oral pain** Sinusitis affecting the maxillary antrum can cause pain in the upper jaw. Where this is associated with blockage of the opening from the sinus into the nasal cavity, it may be helpful to relieve the congestion with inhalation of warm moist air (section 3.8) or with **ephedrine nasal drops** (see above). For antibacterial treatment of sinusitis, see Table 1, section 5.1.

## Sympathomimetics

### EPHEDRINE HYDROCHLORIDE

**Indications** nasal congestion

**Cautions** avoid excessive or prolonged use; caution in infants under 3 months (no good evidence of value—if irritation occurs might narrow nasal passage); **interactions:** Appendix 1 (sympathomimetics)

**Side-effects** local irritation, nausea, headache; after excessive use tolerance with diminished effect, rebound congestion; cardiovascular effects also reported

**Dose**

- See below

**Ephedrine** (Non-proprietary)

Nasal drops, ephedrine hydrochloride 0.5%, net price 10 mL = £1.33; 1%, 10 mL = £1.39

Note The BP directs that if no strength is specified 0.5% drops should be supplied

Dose instil 1–2 drops into each nostril up to 3 or 4 times daily when required; CHILD over 3 months, instil 1–2 drops of 0.5% solution into each nostril 3–4 times daily; max. duration 7 days

Dental prescribing on NHS Ephedrine nasal drops may be prescribed

### XYLOMETAZOLINE HYDROCHLORIDE

**Indications** nasal congestion

**Cautions** see under Ephedrine Hydrochloride and notes above

**Side-effects** see under Ephedrine Hydrochloride and notes above

**Dose**

- See below

**Xylometazoline** (Non-proprietary)

Nasal drops, xylometazoline hydrochloride 0.1%, net price 10 mL = £1.91

Dose instil 2–3 drops into each nostril 2–3 times daily when required; max. duration 7 days; not recommended for children under 12 years

Brands include *Otradrops*®, *Otrivine*® NHS

Paediatric nasal drops, xylometazoline hydrochloride 0.05%, net price 10 mL = £1.59

Dose CHILD over 3 months instil 1–2 drops into each nostril 1–2 times daily when required (not recommended for infants under 3 months of age, doctor's advice only under 2 years); max. duration 7 days

Brands include *Otradrops*®, *Otrivine*® NHS, *Tixycolds*®

Nasal spray, xylometazoline hydrochloride 0.1%, net price 10 mL = £1.91

Dose apply 1 spray into each nostril 2–3 times daily when required; max. duration 7 days; not recommended for children under 12 years

Brands include *Otraspray*®, *Otrivine*® NHS

**Preparations on Sale to the Public**

Many topical nasal preparations on sale to the public contain **sympathomimetics**. To identify the active ingredients in such preparations, consult the product literature or manufacturer.

Note The correct proprietary name should be ascertained—many products have very similar names but different active ingredients

## Antimuscarinic

### IPRATROPIUM BROMIDE

**Indications** rhinorrhoea associated with allergic and non-allergic rhinitis

**Cautions** see section 3.1.2; avoid spraying near eyes

**Side-effects** epistaxis, nasal dryness, and irritation; less frequently nausea, headache, and pharyngitis; *very rarely* antimuscarinic effects such as gastro-intestinal motility disturbances, palpitations, and urinary retention

**Dose**

- Apply 42 micrograms (2 sprays) into each nostril 2–3 times daily; CHILD under 12 years not recommended

**Rinatec**® (Boehringer Ingelheim) PoM

Nasal spray 0.03%, ipratropium bromide 21 micrograms/metered spray. Net price 180-dose unit = £4.55

Excipients include benzalkonium chloride, disodium edetate

## 12.2.3 Nasal preparations for infection

There is **no** evidence that topical anti-infective nasal preparations have any therapeutic value in rhinitis or sinusitis; for elimination of nasal staphylococci, see below.

Systemic treatment of sinusitis—see section 5.1, table 1.

**Betnesol-N®** (Celltech) PoM

Drops (for ear, eye, or nose), betamethasone sodium phosphate 0.1%, neomycin sulphate 0.5%. Net price 10 mL = £2.39

Excipients include benzalkonium chloride, disodium edetate

Dose nose, apply 2–3 drops into nostril 2–3 times daily; eye, see section 11.4.1; ear, see section 12.1.1

**Vista-Methasone N®** (Martindale) PoM

Drops (for ear, eye, or nose), betamethasone sodium phosphate 0.1%, neomycin sulphate 0.5%. Net price 5 mL = £1.09, 10 mL = £1.20

Excipients include thiomersal

Dose nose, apply 2–3 drops into each nostril twice daily; eye, see section 11.4.1; ear, see section 12.1.1

### Nasal staphylococci

Elimination of organisms such as staphylococci from the nasal vestibule can be achieved by the use of a cream containing **chlorhexidine and neomycin** (*Naseptin®*), but re-colonisation frequently occurs. Coagulase-positive staphylococci are present in the noses of 40% of the population.

A nasal ointment containing **mupirocin** is also available; it should probably be held in reserve for resistant cases. In hospital or in care establishments, mupirocin nasal ointment should be reserved for the eradication (in both patients and staff) of nasal carriage of meticillin-resistant *Staphylococcus aureus* (MRSA). The ointment should be applied 3 times daily for 5 days and a sample taken 2 days after treatment to confirm eradication. The course may be repeated if the sample is positive (and the throat is not colonised). To avoid the development of resistance, the treatment course should not exceed 7 days and the course should not be repeated on more than one occasion. If the MRSA strain is mupirocin-resistant or does not respond after 2 courses, consider alternative products such as chlorhexidine and neomycin cream.

**Bactroban Nasal®** (GSK) PoM

Nasal ointment, mupirocin 2% (as calcium salt) in white soft paraffin basis. Net price 3 g = £5.80

Dose for eradication of nasal carriage of staphylococci, including meticillin-resistant *Staphylococcus aureus* (MRSA), apply 2–3 times daily to the inner surface of each nostril

**Naseptin®** (Alliance) PoM

Cream, chlorhexidine hydrochloride 0.1%, neomycin sulphate 0.5%, net price 15 g = £1.58

Excipients include arachis (peanut) oil, cetostearyl alcohol

Dose for eradication of nasal carriage of staphylococci, apply to nostrils 4 times daily for 10 days; for preventing nasal carriage of staphylococci apply to nostrils twice daily

## 12.3 Drugs acting on the oropharynx

12.3.1 Drugs for oral ulceration and inflammation
12.3.2 Oropharyngeal anti-infective drugs
12.3.3 Lozenges and sprays
12.3.4 Mouthwashes, gargles, and dentifrices
12.3.5 Treatment of dry mouth

## 12.3.1 Drugs for oral ulceration and inflammation

Ulceration of the oral mucosa may be caused by trauma (physical or chemical), recurrent aphthae, infections, carcinoma, dermatological disorders, nutritional deficiencies, gastro-intestinal disease, haematopoietic disorders, and drug therapy. It is important to establish the diagnosis in each case as the majority of these lesions require specific management in addition to local treatment. Patients with an unexplained mouth ulcer of more than 3 weeks' duration require urgent referral to hospital to exclude oral cancer. Local treatment aims at protecting the ulcerated area, or at relieving pain, or reducing inflammation, or at controlling secondary infection.

**Simple mouthwashes** A **saline** mouthwash (section 12.3.4) may relieve the pain of traumatic ulceration. The mouthwash is made up with warm water and used at frequent intervals until the discomfort and swelling subsides.

**Antiseptic mouthwashes** Secondary bacterial infection may be a feature of any mucosal ulceration; it can increase discomfort and delay healing. Use of a **chlorhexidine** or **povidone–iodine** mouthwash (section 12.3.4) is often beneficial and may accelerate healing of recurrent aphthae.

**Mechanical protection** **Carmellose gelatin paste** may relieve some discomfort arising from ulceration by protecting the ulcer site. The paste adheres to dry mucosa, but is difficult to apply effectively to some parts of the mouth. *Gelclair®* is available for the management of oral lesions; it forms a film of povidone and sodium hyaluronate on the lesion.

**Corticosteroids** Topical corticosteroid therapy may be used for some forms of oral ulceration. In the case of aphthous ulcers it is most effective if applied in the 'prodromal' phase.

Thrush or other types of candidiasis are recognised complications of corticosteroid treatment.

**Hydrocortisone oromucosal tablets** are allowed to dissolve next to an ulcer and are useful in recurrent aphthae and erosive lichenoid lesions.

**Triamcinolone dental paste** is designed to keep the corticosteroid in contact with the mucosa for long enough to permit penetration of the lesion, but is difficult for patients to apply properly.

**Beclometasone dipropionate** inhaler 50–100 micrograms sprayed twice daily on the oral mucosa is used to manage oral ulceration [unlicensed indication]. Alternatively, **betamethasone** soluble tablet 500 micrograms dissolved in water, may be used as a mouthwash 4 times daily to treat oral ulceration [unlicensed indication]; the solution should not be swallowed in order to minimise the risk of systemic effects.

Systemic corticosteroid therapy (section 6.3.2) is reserved for severe conditions such as pemphigus vulgaris.

**Local analgesics** Local analgesics have a limited role in the management of oral ulceration. When applied topically their action is of a relatively short duration so that analgesia cannot be maintained continuously throughout the day. The main indication for a topical local analgesic is to relieve the pain of otherwise intractable oral ulceration particularly when it is due to major aphthae. For this purpose lidocaine (lignocaine) 5% ointment or lozenges containing a local anaesthetic are applied to the ulcer. Lidocaine 10% solution as spray, section 15.2) can be applied thinly to the ulcer [unlicensed indication] using a cotton bud. When local anaesthetics are used in the mouth care must be taken not to produce anaesthesia of the pharynx before meals as this might lead to choking.

**Benzydamine** mouthwash or spray may be useful in palliating the discomfort associated with a variety of ulcerative conditions. It has also been found to be effective in reducing the discomfort of post-irradiation mucositis. Some patients find the full-strength mouthwash causes some stinging and, for them, it should be diluted with an equal volume of water. **Flurbiprofen** lozenges are licensed for the relief of sore throat.

**Choline salicylate** dental gel has some analgesic action and may provide relief for recurrent aphthae, but excessive application or confinement under a denture irritates the mucosa and can itself cause ulceration. Benefit in teething may merely be due to pressure of application (comparable with biting a teething ring); excessive use can lead to salicylate poisoning.

**Other preparations** **Carbenoxolone** gel or mouthwash may be of some value for mild oral and perioral lesions. **Doxycycline** rinsed in the mouth may also be of value for recurrent aphthous ulceration.

**Periodontitis** Low-dose doxycycline (*Periostat®*) is licensed as an adjunct to scaling and root planing for the treatment of periodontitis; a low dose of doxycycline reduces collagenase activity without inhibiting bacteria associated with periodontitis. For anti-infectives used in the treatment of destructive (refractory) forms of periodontal disease, see section 12.3.2 and Table 1, section 5.1. For mouthwashes used for oral hygiene and plaque inhibition, see section 12.3.4.

## BENZYDAMINE HYDROCHLORIDE

**Indications** painful inflammatory conditions of oropharynx

**Side-effects** occasional numbness or stinging; rarely hypersensitivity reactions

**Difflam®** (3M)

Oral rinse, green, benzydamine hydrochloride 0.15%, net price 200 mL (*Difflam® Sore Throat Rinse*) = £2.63; 300 mL = £4.01

Dose rinse or gargle, using 15 mL (diluted with water if stinging occurs) every 1½–3 hours as required, usually for not more than 7 days; not suitable for children aged 12 years or under

Dental prescribing on NHS May be prescribed as Benzydamine Mouthwash 0.15%

Spray, benzydamine hydrochloride 0.15%. Net price 30-mL unit = £3.17

Dose ADULT, 4–8 sprays onto affected area every 1½–3 hours; CHILD under 6 years 1 spray per 4 kg body-weight to max. 4 sprays every 1½–3 hours; 6–12 years 4 sprays every 1½–3 hours

Dental prescribing on NHS May be prescribed as Benzydamine Oromucosal Spray 0.15%

## CARBENOXOLONE SODIUM

**Indications** mild oral and perioral lesions

**Bioplex®** (TEVA UK) PoM

Mouthwash granules, carbenoxolone sodium 1% (20 mg/sachet). Net price 24 × 2-g sachets = £7.23

Dose for mouth ulcers, rinse with 1 sachet in 30–50 mL of warm water 3 times daily and at bedtime

## CARMELLOSE SODIUM

**Indications** mechanical protection of oral and perioral lesions

**Orabase®** (ConvaTec)

Protective paste (= oral paste), carmellose sodium 16.7%, pectin 16.7%, gelatin 16.7%, in *Plastibase®*. Net price 30 g = £1.94; 100 g = £4.32

Dose apply a thin layer when necessary after meals

Dental prescribing on NHS May be prescribed as Carmellose Gelatin Paste

**Orahesive®** (ConvaTec)

Powder, carmellose sodium, pectin, gelatin, equal parts. Net price 25 g = £2.24

Dose sprinkle on the affected area

## CORTICOSTEROIDS

**Indications** oral and perioral lesions

**Contra-indications** untreated oral infection; manufacturer of triamcinolone contra-indicates use on tuberculous and viral lesions

**Side-effects** occasional exacerbation of local infection; thrush or other candidal infections

[1]**Adcortyl in Orabase®** (Squibb) PoM

Oral paste, triamcinolone acetonide 0.1% in adhesive basis. Net price 10 g = £1.27

Dose ADULT and CHILD, apply a thin layer 2–4 times daily; do not rub in; use limited to 5 days for children and short-term use also advised for elderly

Dental prescribing on NHS May be prescribed as Triamcinolone Dental Paste

1. A 5-g tube (*Adcortyl in Orabase® for Mouth Ulcers*) is on sale to the public for the treatment of common mouth ulcers for max. 5 days

**Corlan®** (Celltech)

Pellets (= oromucosal tablets), hydrocortisone 2.5 mg (as sodium succinate). Net price 20 = £2.54

Dose ADULT and CHILD, 1 lozenge 4 times daily, allowed to dissolve slowly in the mouth in contact with the ulcer

Dental prescribing on NHS May be prescribed as Hydrocortisone Oromucosal Tablets

## DOXYCYCLINE

**Indications** see preparations; oral herpes (section 12.3.2); other indications (section 5.1.3)

**Cautions** section 5.1.3; monitor for superficial fungal infection, particularly, if predisposition to oral candidiasis

**Contra-indications** section 5.1.3

**Side-effects** section 5.1.3; fungal superinfection

**Dose**

- See preparations

**Periostat®** (Alliance) PoM

Tablets, f/c, doxycycline (as hyclate) 20 mg, net price 56-tab pack = £16.50. Label: 6, 11, 27, counselling, posture

Dose periodontitis (as an adjunct to gingival scaling and root planing), 20 mg twice daily for 3 months; CHILD under 12 years not recommended

Counselling Tablets should be swallowed whole with plenty of fluid, while sitting or standing

Dental prescribing on NHS May be prescribed as Doxycycline Tablets 20 mg

### Local application

For recurrent aphthous ulceration, the contents of a 100 mg doxycycline capsule can be stirred into a small amount of water then rinsed around the mouth for 2–3 minutes 4 times daily usually for 3 days; it should preferably not be swallowed [unlicensed indication].

Note Doxycycline stains teeth; avoid in children under 12 years of age



## FLURBIPROFEN

**Indications** relief of sore throat

**Cautions** see section 10.1.1

**Contra-indications** see section 10.1.1

**Side-effects** taste disturbance, mouth ulcers (move lozenge around mouth); see also section 10.1.1

**Strefen®** (Crookes)

Lozenges, flurbiprofen 8.75 mg, net price 16 = £2.08

Dose allow 1 lozenge to dissolve slowly in the mouth every 3–6 hours, max. 5 lozenges in 24 hours, for max. 3 days; CHILD under 12 years not recommended

## LOCAL ANAESTHETICS

**Indications** relief of pain in oral lesions

**Cautions** avoid prolonged use; hypersensitivity; pregnancy (Appendix 4); avoid anaesthesia of the pharynx before meals—risk of choking

**Lidocaine** (Non-proprietary)

Ointment, lidocaine 5% in a water-miscible basis, net price 15 g = 80p

Dose rub sparingly and gently on affected areas

Dental prescribing on NHS Lidocaine 5% Ointment may be prescribed

### Other preparations

Local anaesthetics are included in some mouth ulcer preparations, for details see below

Local anaesthetics are also included in some throat lozenges and sprays, see section 12.3.3

## SALICYLATES

**Indications** mild oral and perioral lesions

**Cautions** not to be applied to dentures—leave at least 30 minutes before re-insertion of dentures; frequent application, especially in children, may give rise to salicylate poisoning

Note CSM warning on aspirin and Reye's syndrome does not apply to non-aspirin salicylates or to topical preparations such as teething gels

### Choline salicylate

**Choline Salicylate Dental Gel, BP**

Oral gel, choline salicylate 8.7% in a flavoured gel basis, net price 15 g = £1.79

Brands include *Bonjela®* (sugar-free)

Dose apply ½-inch of gel with gentle massage not more often than every 3 hours; CHILD over 4 months ¼-inch of gel not more often than every 3 hours; max. 6 applications daily

Dental prescribing on NHS Choline Salicylate Dental Gel may be prescribed

### Salicylic acid

**Pyralvex®** (Norgine)

Oral paint, brown, rhubarb extract (anthraquinone glycosides 0.5%), salicylic acid 1%. Net price 10 mL with brush = £1.69

Dose apply 3–4 times daily; CHILD under 12 years not recommended

### Preparations on Sale to the Public

Many topical preparations are on sale to the public for **mouth ulcers** and for **teething pain**. To identify the active ingredients in such preparations, consult the product literature or manufacturer.

Note The correct proprietary name should be ascertained—many products have very similar names but different active ingredients

# 12.3.2 Oropharyngeal anti-infective drugs

The most common cause of a sore throat is a viral infection which does not benefit from anti-infective treatment. Streptococcal sore throats require systemic **penicillin** therapy (Table 1, section 5.1). Acute ulcerative gingivitis (Vincent's infection) responds to systemic **metronidazole** (section 5.1.11).

Preparations administered in the dental surgery for the local treatment of periodontal disease include gels of metronidazole (*Elyzol®*, Colgate-Palmolive) and of minocycline (*Dentomycin®*, Blackwell).

## Oropharyngeal fungal infections

Fungal infections of the mouth are usually caused by *Candida* spp. (candidiasis or candidosis). Different types of oropharyngeal candidiasis are managed as follows:

**Thrush** Acute pseudomembranous candidiasis (thrush), is classically an acute infection but one which may persist for months in patients receiving inhaled corticosteroids, cytotoxics or broad-spectrum antibacterials. Thrush is also associated with serious systemic disease associated with reduced immunity such as leukaemia, other malignancies, and HIV infection. The predisposing cause should be dealt with. When associated with corticosteroid inhalers, rinsing the mouth with water (or cleaning a child's teeth) immediately after using the inhaler may avoid the problem. Treatment with **nystatin**, **amphotericin**, or **miconazole** may be needed. **Fluconazole** (section 5.2) is effective for unresponsive infections or if a topical antifungal drug cannot be used or if the patient has dry mouth.

**Acute erythematous candidiasis** Acute erythematous (atrophic) candidiasis is a relatively uncommon condition associated with corticosteroid and broad-spectrum antibacterial use and with HIV disease. It is usually treated with **fluconazole** (section 5.2).

**Denture stomatitis** Patients with denture stomatitis (chronic atrophic candidiasis), should cleanse their dentures thoroughly and leave them out as often as possible during the treatment period. To prevent recurrence of the problem, dentures should not normally be worn at night. New dentures may be required if these measures fail despite good compliance.

**Miconazole** oral gel can be applied to the fitting surface of the denture before insertion (for short periods only). Alternatively, **nystatin** pastilles or **amphotericin** lozenges can be allowed to dissolve slowly in the mouth but they are less effective at resolving the stomatitis. Denture stomatitis is not always associated with candidiasis and other factors such as mechanical or chemical irritation, bacterial infection, or rarely allergy to the dental base material, may be the cause.

**Chronic hyperplastic candidiasis** Chronic hyperplastic candidiasis (candidal leucoplakia) carries an increased risk of malignancy; biopsy is essential—this type of candidiasis may be associated with varying degrees of dysplasia, with oral cancer present in a high proportion of cases. Chronic hyperplastic candidiasis is treated with a systemic antifungal such as **fluconazole** (section 5.2) to eliminate candidal overlay. Patients should avoid the use of tobacco.

**Angular cheilitis** Angular cheilitis (angular stomatitis) is characterised by soreness, erythema and fissuring at the angles of the mouth. It is commonly associated with denture stomatitis but may represent a nutritional deficiency or it may be related to orofacial granulomatosis or HIV infection. Both yeasts (*Candida* spp.) and bacteria (*Staphylococcus aureus* and beta-haemolytic streptococci) are commonly involved as interacting, infective factors. A reduction in facial height related to ageing and tooth loss with maceration in the deep occlusive folds that may subsequently arise, predisposes to such infection. While the underlying cause is being identified and treated, it is often helpful to apply **miconazole** and **hydrocortisone** cream or ointment (see p. 573), **nystatin** ointment (see p. 599), or **sodium fusidate** ointment (see p. 598).

**Immunocompromised patients** For advice on prevention of fungal infections in immunocompromised patients see p. 309.

**Drugs used in oropharyngeal candidiasis** **Amphotericin** and **nystatin** are not absorbed from the gastro-intestinal tract and are applied locally (as lozenges or suspension) to the mouth for treating local fungal infections. Nystatin ointment is available for perioral lesions (see p. 599). **Miconazole** is used by local application (as an oral gel) in the mouth but it is also absorbed to the extent that potential interactions need to be considered. Miconazole may be more effective than amphotericin or nystatin for some types of candidiasis, particularly chronic hyperplastic candidiasis or chronic mucocutaneous candidiasis (chronic thrush). Miconazole also has some activity against Gram-positive bacteria including streptococci and staphylococci. **Fluconazole** and **itraconazole** (section 5.2) are absorbed when taken by mouth; they are used for oropharyngeal candidiasis that does not respond to topical therapy.

If candidal infection fails to respond to 1 to 2 weeks of treatment with antifungal drugs the patient should be sent for investigation to eliminate the possibility of underlying disease. Persistent infection may also be caused by reinfection from the genito-urinary or gastro-intestinal tract. The infection can be eliminated from these sources by appropriate anticandidal therapy but calls for referral to the patient's medical practitioner; the patient's partner may also require treatment to prevent reinfection.

For the role of antiseptic mouthwashes in the prevention of oral candidiasis in immunocompromised patients and treatment of denture stomatitis, see section 12.3.4.

## AMPHOTERICIN

**Indications** oral and perioral fungal infections

**Side-effects** mild gastro-intestinal disturbances reported

**Fungilin®** (Squibb) PoM

Lozenges, yellow, amphotericin 10 mg. Net price 60-lozenge pack = £3.67. Label: 9, 24, counselling, after food

**Dose** allow 1 lozenge to dissolve slowly in the mouth 4 times daily for 10–15 days (continued for 48 hours after lesions have resolved); increase to 8 daily if infection severe

**Dental prescribing on NHS** May be prescribed as Amphotericin Lozenges

Oral suspension, yellow, sugar-free, amphotericin 100 mg/mL. Net price 12 mL with pipette = £2.15. Label: 9, counselling, use of pipette, hold in mouth, after food

**Dose** place 1 mL in the mouth after food and retain near lesions 4 times daily for 14 days (continued for 48 hours after lesions have resolved)

**Dental prescribing on NHS** May be prescribed as Amphotericin Oral Suspension

## MICONAZOLE

**Indications** see under Preparations; intestinal fungal infections (section 5.2)

**Cautions** pregnancy (Appendix 4) and breast-feeding; avoid in porphyria (section 9.8.2); **interactions:** Appendix 1 (antifungals, imidazole)

**Contra-indications** hepatic impairment

**Side-effects** nausea and vomiting, diarrhoea (with long-term treatment); rarely allergic reactions; isolated reports of hepatitis

**Daktarin®**[1] (Janssen-Cilag) PoM
Oral gel, sugar-free, orange-flavoured, miconazole 24 mg/mL (20 mg/g). Net price 15-g tube = £2.45, 80-g tube = £4.75. Label: 9, counselling, hold in mouth, after food

Dose prevention and treatment of oral fungal infections, place 5–10 mL in the mouth after food and retain near lesions 4 times daily; CHILD under 2 years 2.5 mL twice daily, 2–6 years 5 mL twice daily, over 6 years 5 mL 4 times daily; treatment continued for 48 hours after lesions have resolved

Localised lesions, smear small amount on affected area with clean finger 4 times daily for 5–7 days (dental prostheses should be removed at night and brushed with gel)

Note Not licensed for use in NEONATES

Dental prescribing on NHS May be prescribed as Miconazole Oromucosal Gel

1. 15-g tube can be sold to the public

## NYSTATIN

**Indications** oral and perioral fungal infections

**Side-effects** oral irritation and sensitisation, nausea reported; see also section 5.2

**Dose**

Note Dose as pastilles or as suspension

- Treatment, ADULT and CHILD, 100 000 units 4 times daily after food, usually for 7 days (continued for 48 hours after lesions have resolved)

  Note Unlicensed for treating candidiasis in NEONATE under 1 month. Immunosuppressed ADULT and CHILD over 1 month may require higher doses (e.g. 500 000 units 4 times daily)
- Prophylaxis, NEONATE 100 000 units once daily

**Nystatin** (Non-proprietary) PoM
Oral suspension, nystatin 100 000 units/mL. Net price 30 mL = £1.95. Label: 9, counselling, hold in mouth, after food

Brands include *Nystamont®*, (sugar-free)

Note Sugar-free versions are available and can be ordered by specifying 'sugar-free' on the prescription

Dental prescribing on NHS Nystatin Oral Suspension may be prescribed

**Nystan®** (Squibb) PoM
Pastilles, yellow/brown, nystatin 100 000 units. Net price 28-pastille pack = £3.24. Label: 9, 24, counselling, after food

Dental prescribing on NHS May be prescribed as Nystatin Pastilles

Oral suspension, yellow, nystatin 100 000 units/mL. Net price 30 mL with pipette = £2.05. Label: 9, counselling, use of pipette, hold in mouth, after food

## Oropharyngeal viral infections

The management of primary herpetic gingivostomatitis is a soft diet, adequate fluid intake, and analgesics as required, including local use of **benzydamine** (section 12.3.1). The use of chlorhexidine mouthwash (section 12.3.4) will control plaque accumulation if toothbrushing is painful and will also help to control secondary infection in general.

In the case of severe herpetic stomatitis, a systemic antiviral such as aciclovir is required (section 5.3.2.1). Valaciclovir and famciclovir are suitable alternatives for oral lesions associated with herpes zoster. Aciclovir and valaciclovir are also used for the prevention of frequently recurring herpes simplex lesions of the mouth, particularly when implicated in the initiation of erythema multiforme. See section 13.10.3 for the treatment of labial herpes simplex infections.

Herpes infections of the mouth may also respond to rinsing the mouth with **doxycycline** (section 12.3.1).

# 12.3.3 Lozenges and sprays

There is no convincing evidence that antiseptic lozenges and sprays have a beneficial action and they sometimes irritate and cause sore tongue and sore lips. Some of these preparations also contain local anaesthetics which relieve pain but may cause sensitisation.

### Preparations on Sale to the Public

Many throat lozenges and throat sprays on sale to the public contain an **antiseptic** or a **local anaesthetic**. To identify the active ingredients in such preparations, consult the product literature or manufacturer.

Note The correct proprietary name should be ascertained—many products have very similar names but different active ingredients

# 12.3.4 Mouthwashes, gargles, and dentifrices

Superficial infections of the mouth are often helped by warm mouthwashes which have a mechanical cleansing effect and cause some local hyperaemia. However, to be effective, they must be used frequently and vigorously. A warm saline mouthwash is ideal and can be prepared either by dissolving half a teaspoonful of salt in a glassful of warm water or by diluting **compound sodium chloride mouthwash** with an equal volume of warm water. **Mouthwash solution-tablets** are used to remove unpleasant tastes.

Mouthwashes containing an oxidising agent, such as **hydrogen peroxide**, may be useful in the treatment of acute ulcerative gingivitis (Vincent's infection) since the organisms involved are anaerobes. It also has a mechanical cleansing effect arising from frothing when in contact with oral debris.

**Chlorhexidine** is an effective antiseptic which has the advantage of inhibiting plaque formation on the teeth. It does not, however, completely control plaque deposition and is not a substitute for effective toothbrushing. Moreover, chlorhexidine preparations do not penetrate significantly into stagnation areas and are therefore of little value in the control of dental caries or of periodontal disease once pocketing has developed. Chlorhexidine mouthwash is used in the treatment of denture stomatitis. It is also used in the prevention of oral candidiasis in immunocompromised patients. Chlorhexidine is used to prevent bacteraemia in patients undergoing dental procedures requiring antibacterial prophylaxis (see Table 2, section 5.1). Chlorhexidine mouthwash may also reduce the incidence of alveolar osteitis following removal of a wisdom tooth.

Chlorhexidine can be used as a mouthwash, spray or gel for secondary infection in mucosal ulceration and for controlling gingivitis, as an adjunct to other oral hygiene measures. These preparations may also be used instead of toothbrushing where there is a painful periodontal condition (e.g. primary herpetic stomatitis) or if the patient has a haemorrhagic disorder, or is disabled. Chlorhexidine preparations are of little value in the control of acute necrotising ulcerative gingivitis.

**Povidone–iodine** mouthwash is licensed for oral mucosal infections but does not inhibit plaque accumulation. It should not be used for longer than 14 days because a significant amount of iodine is absorbed. As with chlorhexidine, povidone–iodine mouthwash is of little value in the control of acute necrotising ulcerative gingivitis.

There is no convincing evidence that gargles are effective.

## CHLORHEXIDINE GLUCONATE

**Indications** see under preparations below

**Side-effects** mucosal irritation (if desquamation occurs, discontinue treatment or dilute mouthwash with an equal volume of water); taste disturbance; reversible brown staining of teeth, and of silicate or composite restorations; tongue discoloration; parotid gland swelling reported

**Note** Chlorhexidine gluconate may be incompatible with some ingredients in toothpaste; leave an interval of at least 30 minutes between using mouthwash and toothpaste

**Chlorhexidine** (Non-proprietary)

Mouthwash, chlorhexidine gluconate 0.2%, net price 300 mL = £1.86

**Dose** oral hygiene and plaque inhibition, rinse mouth with 10 mL for about 1 minute twice daily

Denture stomatitis, cleanse and soak dentures in mouthwash solution for 15 minutes twice daily

Prophylaxis of endocarditis for dental procedures (as adjunct to antibacterial prophylaxis), Table 2, section 5.1

**Dental prescribing on NHS** Chlorhexidine Mouthwash may be prescribed

**Chlorohex®** (Colgate-Palmolive)

Chlorohex 1200® mouthwash, chlorhexidine gluconate 0.12% (mint-flavoured). Net price 300 mL = £2.20

**Dose** oral hygiene and plaque inhibition, rinse mouth with 15 mL for about 30 seconds twice daily

**Corsodyl®** (GSK Consumer Healthcare)

Dental gel, chlorhexidine gluconate 1%. Net price 50 g = £1.21

**Dose** oral hygiene and plaque inhibition and gingivitis, brush on the teeth once or twice daily

Oral candidiasis and management of aphthous ulcers, apply to affected areas once or twice daily

Prophylaxis of endocarditis for dental procedures (as adjunct to antibacterial prophylaxis), Table 2, section 5.1

**Dental prescribing on NHS** May be prescribed as Chlorhexidine Gluconate Gel 1%

Mouthwash, chlorhexidine gluconate 0.2%. Net price 300 mL (original or mint) = £1.81, 600 mL (mint) = £3.62

**Dose** oral hygiene and plaque inhibition, oral candidiasis, gingivitis, and management of aphthous ulcers, rinse mouth with 10 mL for about 1 minute twice daily

Denture stomatitis, cleanse and soak dentures in mouthwash solution for 15 minutes twice daily

Prophylaxis of endocarditis for dental procedures (as adjunct to antibacterial prophylaxis), Table 2, section 5.1

Oral spray, chlorhexidine gluconate 0.2% (mint-flavoured). Net price 60 mL = £4.10

**Dose** oral hygiene and plaque inhibition, oral candidiasis, gingivitis, and management of aphthous ulcers, apply as required to tooth, gingival, or ulcer surfaces using up to 12 actuations (approx. 0.14 mL/actuation) twice daily

**Dental prescribing on NHS** May be prescribed as Chlorhexidine Oral Spray

### With chlorobutanol

**Eludril®** (Ceuta)

Mouthwash or *gargle*, chlorhexidine gluconate 0.1%, chlorobutanol 0.5% (mint-flavoured), net price 90 mL = £1.22, 250 mL = £2.56, 500 mL = £4.64

**Dose** oral hygiene and plaque inhibition, use 10–15 mL (diluted with warm water in measuring cup provided) 2–3 times daily

Denture disinfection, soak previously cleansed dentures in mouthwash (diluted with 2 volumes of water) for 60 minutes

## HEXETIDINE

**Indications** oral hygiene

**Side-effects** local irritation; *very rarely* taste disturbance and transient anaesthesia

**Oraldene®** (Warner Lambert)

Mouthwash or *gargle*, red, hexetidine 0.1%. Net price 100 mL = £1.31; 200 mL = £2.02

**Dose** ADULT and CHILD over 6 years, use 15 mL undiluted 2–3 times daily

## HYDROGEN PEROXIDE

**Indications** oral hygiene, see notes above

**Hydrogen Peroxide Mouthwash, BP**

Mouthwash, consists of Hydrogen Peroxide Solution 6% (= approx. 20 volume) BP

**Dose** rinse the mouth for 2–3 minutes with 15 mL diluted in half a tumblerful of warm water 2–3 times daily

**Dental prescribing on NHS** Hydrogen Peroxide Mouthwash may be prescribed

**Peroxyl®** (Colgate-Palmolive)

Mouthwash, hydrogen peroxide 1.5%, net price 300 mL = £2.81

**Dose** rinse the mouth with 10 mL for about 1 minute up to 4 times daily (after meals and at bedtime)

## POVIDONE–IODINE

**Indications** oral hygiene

**Cautions** pregnancy (Appendix 4); breast-feeding (Appendix 5); see also notes above

**Contra-indications** avoid regular use in patients with thyroid disorders or those receiving lithium therapy

**Side-effects** idiosyncratic mucosal irritation and hypersensitivity reactions; may interfere with thyroid-function tests and with tests for occult blood

**Betadine®** (Medlock)

Mouthwash or *gargle*, amber, povidone-iodine 1%. Net price 250 mL = £1.12

**Dose** adults and children over 6 years, up to 10 mL undiluted or diluted with an equal quantity of warm water for up to 30 seconds up to 4 times daily for up to 14 days

## SODIUM CHLORIDE

**Indications** oral hygiene, see notes above

**Sodium Chloride Mouthwash, Compound, BP**
Mouthwash, sodium bicarbonate 1%, sodium chloride 1.5% in a suitable vehicle with a peppermint flavour.
Dose extemporaneous preparations should be prepared according to the following formula: sodium chloride 1.5 g, sodium bicarbonate 1 g, concentrated peppermint emulsion 2.5 mL, double-strength chloroform water 50 mL, water to 100 mL
To be diluted with an equal volume of warm water
**Dental prescribing on NHS** Compound Sodium Chloride Mouthwash may be prescribed

## THYMOL

**Indications** oral hygiene, see notes above

**Mouthwash Solution-tablets**
Consist of tablets which may contain antimicrobial, colouring, and flavouring agents in a suitable soluble effervescent basis to make a mouthwash suitable for dental purposes.
Dose dissolve 1 tablet in a tumblerful of warm water
Note Mouthwash solution tablets may contain ingredients such as thymol
**Dental prescribing on NHS** Mouthwash Solution-tablets may be prescribed



# 12.3.5 Treatment of dry mouth

Dry mouth (xerostomia) may be caused by drugs with antimuscarinic (anticholinergic) side-effects (e.g. antispasmodics, tricyclic antidepressants, and some antipsychotics), by diuretics, by irradiation of the head and neck region or by damage to or disease of the salivary glands. Patients with a persistently dry mouth may develop a burning or scalded sensation and have poor oral hygiene; they may develop increased dental caries, periodontal disease, intolerance of dentures, and oral infections (particularly candidiasis). Dry mouth may be relieved in many patients by simple measures such as frequent sips of cool drinks or sucking pieces of ice or sugar-free fruit pastilles. Sugar-free chewing gum stimulates salivation in patients with residual salivary function.

**Artificial saliva** can provide useful relief of dry mouth. A properly balanced artificial saliva should be of a neutral pH and contain electrolytes (including fluoride) to correspond approximately to the composition of saliva. The pH of some artificial saliva products may be inappropriate. Of the proprietary preparations, *Luborant®* is licensed for any condition giving rise to a dry mouth; *Biotène Oralbalance®* *BioXtra®*, *Glandosane®*, *Saliva Orthana®*, and *Saliveze®*, have ACBS approval for dry mouth associated only with radiotherapy or sicca syndrome. *Salivix®* pastilles, which act locally as salivary stimulants, are also available and have similar ACBS approval. *SST* tablets may be prescribed for dry mouth in patients with salivary gland impairment (and patent salivary ducts). *Salinum®* may also be prescribed for relief of symptoms of dry mouth.

**Pilocarpine** tablets are licensed for the treatment of xerostomia following irradiation for head and neck cancer and for dry mouth and dry eyes (xerophthalmia) in Sjögren's syndrome. They are effective only in patients who have some residual salivary gland function, and therefore should be withdrawn if there is no response.

## Local treatment

**AS Saliva Orthana®** (AS Pharma)
Oral spray, gastric mucin (porcine) 3.5%, xylitol 2%, sodium fluoride 4.2 mg/litre, with preservatives and flavouring agents. Net price 50-mL bottle = £4.25; 450-mL refill = £29.69
Lozenges, mucin 65 mg, xylitol 59 mg, in a sorbitol basis. Net price 45-lozenge pack = £3.02
Dose ACBS: patients suffering from dry mouth as a result of having (or having undergone) radiotherapy, or sicca syndrome, spray 2–3 times onto oral and pharyngeal mucosa, when required
Note *AS Saliva Orthana®* lozenges do not contain fluoride
**Dental prescribing on NHS** *AS Saliva Orthana®* Oral Spray and Lozenges may be prescribed

**Glandosane®** (Fresenius Kabi)
Aerosol spray, carmellose sodium 500 mg, sorbitol 1.5 g, potassium chloride 60 mg, sodium chloride 42.2 mg, magnesium chloride 2.6 mg, calcium chloride 7.3 mg, and dipotassium hydrogen phosphate 17.1 mg/50 g. Net price 50-mL unit (neutral, lemon or peppermint flavoured) = £4.48
Dose ACBS: patients suffering from dry mouth as a result of having (or having undergone) radiotherapy, or sicca syndrome, spray onto oral and pharyngeal mucosa as required
**Dental prescribing on NHS** *Glandosane®* Aerosol Spray may be prescribed

**Luborant®** (Goldshield)
Oral spray, pink, sorbitol 1.8 g, carmellose sodium (sodium carboxymethylcellulose) 390 mg, dibasic potassium phosphate 48.23 mg, potassium chloride 37.5 mg, monobasic potassium phosphate 21.97 mg, calcium chloride 9.972 mg, magnesium chloride 3.528 mg, sodium fluoride 258 micrograms/60 mL, with preservatives and colouring agents. Net price 60-mL unit = £3.96
Dose saliva deficiency, 2–3 sprays onto oral mucosa up to 4 times daily, or as directed
Note May be difficult to obtain
**Dental prescribing on NHS** *Luborant®* Oral Spray may be prescribed as Artificial Saliva

**Biotène Oralbalance®** (Anglian)
Saliva replacement gel, lactoperoxidase, lactoferrin, lysozyme, glucose oxidase, xylitol in a gel basis, net price 50-g tube = £4.10, 24 × 12.4-mL tube = £30.40 (for hospital use)
Dose ACBS: patients suffering from dry mouth as a result of having (or having undergone) radiotherapy, or sicca syndrome, apply to gums and tongue as required
Note Avoid use with toothpastes containing detergents (including foaming agents)
**Dental prescribing on NHS** *Biotène Oralbalance®* Saliva Replacement Gel may be prescribed

**BioXtra®** (Molar)
Gel, lactoperoxidase, lactoferrin, lysozyme, whey colostrum, xylitol and other ingredients, net price 40-mL tube = £2.25
Dose ACBS: patients suffering from dry mouth as a result of having (or having undergone) radiotherapy, or sicca syndrome, apply to oral mucosa as required
**Dental prescribing on NHS** *BioXtra®* Gel may be prescribed

**Salinum®** (Crawford)
Liquid, sugar-free, linseed extract (containing polysaccharides) with dipotassium phosphate buffer and preservatives, net price 300-mL bottle = £13.50
Dose symptomatic treatment of dry mouth, approx. 2 mL rinsed around the mouth and then swallowed, when required

**Saliveze®** (Wyvern)

Oral spray, carmellose sodium (sodium carboxymethylcellulose), calcium chloride, magnesium chloride, potassium chloride, sodium chloride, and dibasic sodium phosphate. Net price 50-mL bottle (mint-flavoured) = £3.50

Dose ACBS: patients suffering from dry mouth as a result of having (or having undergone) radiotherapy, or sicca syndrome, 1 spray onto oral mucosa as required

Dental prescribing on NHS *Saliveze®* Oral Spray may be prescribed

**Salivix®** (Provalis)

Pastilles, sugar-free, reddish-amber, acacia, malic acid and other ingredients. Net price 50-pastille pack = £2.86

Dose ACBS: patients suffering from dry mouth as a result of having (or having undergone) radiotherapy, or sicca syndrome, suck 1 pastille when required

Dental prescribing on NHS *Salivix®* Pastilles may be prescribed

**SST** (Medac)

Tablets, sugar-free, citric acid, malic acid and other ingredients in a sorbitol base, net price 100-tab pack = £4.86

Dose symptomatic treatment of dry mouth in patients with impaired salivary gland function and patent salivary ducts, allow 1 tablet to dissolve slowly in the mouth when required

## Systemic treatment

### PILOCARPINE HYDROCHLORIDE

**Indications** xerostomia following irradiation for head and neck cancer (see also notes above); dry mouth and dry eyes in Sjögren's syndrome

**Cautions** asthma and chronic obstructive pulmonary disease (avoid if uncontrolled, see Contra-indications), cardiovascular disease (avoid if uncontrolled); cholelithiasis or biliary-tract disease, peptic ulcer, hepatic impairment (Appendix 2), renal impairment; risk of increased urethral smooth muscle tone and renal colic; maintain adequate fluid intake to avoid dehydration associated with excessive sweating; cognitive or psychiatric disturbances; angle-closure glaucoma; **interactions**: Appendix 1 (parasympathomimetics)

Counselling Blurred vision or dizziness may affect performance of skilled tasks (e.g. driving) particularly at night or in reduced lighting

**Contra-indications** uncontrolled asthma and chronic obstructive pulmonary disease (increased bronchial secretions and increased airways resistance); uncontrolled cardiorenal disease; acute iritis; pregnancy (Appendix 4); breast-feeding

**Side-effects** headache, influenza-like syndrome, increased urinary frequency, sweating; less frequently, nausea, vomiting, abdominal pain, dyspepsia, diarrhoea, constipation, flushing, hypertension, palpitations, rhinitis, dizziness, asthenia, lacrimation, conjunctivitis, visual disturbances, ocular pain, rash, pruritus; rarely, flatulence, urinary urgency

**Dose**

- Xerostomia following irradiation for head and neck cancer, 5 mg 3 times daily with or immediately after meals (last dose always with evening meal); if tolerated but response insufficient after 4 weeks, may be increased to max. 30 mg daily in divided doses; max. therapeutic effect normally within 4–8 weeks; discontinue if no improvement after 2–3 months; CHILD not recommended
- Dry mouth and dry eyes in Sjögren's syndrome, 5 mg 4 times daily (with meals and at bedtime); if tolerated but response insufficient, may be increased to max. 30 mg daily in divided doses; discontinue if no improvement after 2–3 months; CHILD not recommended

**Salagen®** (Novartis) PoM

Tablets, f/c, pilocarpine hydrochloride 5 mg. Net price 84-tab pack = £51.43. Label: 21, 27, counselling, driving

# 13 Skin


| | | |
|---|---|---|
| **13.1** | **Management of skin conditions** | **566** |
| 13.1.1 | Vehicles | 566 |
| 13.1.2 | Suitable quantities for prescribing | 567 |
| 13.1.3 | Excipients and sensitisation | 567 |
| **13.2** | **Emollient and barrier preparations** | **567** |
| 13.2.1 | Emollients | 567 |
| 13.2.1.1 | Emollient bath additives | 570 |
| 13.2.2 | Barrier preparations | 571 |
| **13.3** | **Topical local anaesthetics and antipruritics** | **571** |
| **13.4** | **Topical corticosteroids** | **572** |
| **13.5** | **Preparations for eczema and psoriasis** | **579** |
| 13.5.1 | Preparations for eczema | 579 |
| 13.5.2 | Preparations for psoriasis | 580 |
| 13.5.3 | Drugs affecting the immune response | 585 |
| **13.6** | **Acne and rosacea** | **586** |
| 13.6.1 | Topical preparations for acne | 587 |
| 13.6.2 | Oral preparations for acne | 589 |
| **13.7** | **Preparations for warts and calluses** | **591** |
| **13.8** | **Sunscreens and camouflagers** | **593** |
| 13.8.1 | Sunscreen preparations | 593 |
| 13.8.2 | Camouflagers | 594 |
| **13.9** | **Shampoos and other preparations for scalp and hair conditions** | **595** |
| **13.10** | **Anti-infective skin preparations** | **596** |
| 13.10.1 | Antibacterial preparations | 596 |
| 13.10.1.1 | Antibacterial preparations only used topically | 597 |
| 13.10.1.2 | Antibacterial preparations also used systemically | 598 |
| 13.10.2 | Antifungal preparations | 599 |
| 13.10.3 | Antiviral preparations | 601 |
| 13.10.4 | Parasiticidal preparations | 602 |
| 13.10.5 | Preparations for minor cuts and abrasions | 605 |
| **13.11** | **Skin cleansers and antiseptics** | **606** |
| 13.11.1 | Alcohols and saline | 606 |
| 13.11.2 | Chlorhexidine salts | 606 |
| 13.11.3 | Cationic surfactants and soaps | 607 |
| 13.11.4 | Iodine | 607 |
| 13.11.5 | Phenolics | 608 |
| 13.11.6 | Astringents, oxidisers, and dyes | 608 |
| 13.11.7 | Preparations for promotion of wound healing | 608 |
| **13.12** | **Antiperspirants** | **609** |
| **13.13** | **Wound management products and Elastic Hosiery** | **610** |
| **13.14** | **Topical circulatory preparations** | **610** |




## 13.1 Management of skin conditions

### 13.1.1 Vehicles

Both vehicle and active ingredients are important in the treatment of skin conditions; the vehicle alone may have more than a mere placebo effect. The vehicle affects the degree of hydration of the skin, has a mild anti-inflammatory effect, and aids the penetration of active drug.

**Applications** are usually viscous solutions, emulsions, or suspensions for application to the skin (including the scalp) or nails.

**Collodions** are painted on the skin and allowed to dry to leave a flexible film over the site of application.

**Creams** are emulsions of oil and water and are generally well absorbed into the skin. They may contain an antimicrobial preservative unless the active ingredient or basis is intrinsically bactericidal and fungicidal. Generally, creams are cosmetically more acceptable than ointments because they are less greasy and easier to apply.

**Gels** consist of active ingredients in suitable hydrophilic or hydrophobic bases; they generally have a high water content. Gels are particularly suitable for application to the face and scalp.

**Lotions** have a cooling effect and may be preferred to ointments or creams for application over a hairy area. Lotions in alcoholic basis can sting if used on broken skin. *Shake lotions* (such as calamine lotion) contain insoluble powders which leave a deposit on the skin surface.

**Ointments** are greasy preparations which are normally anhydrous and insoluble in water, and are more occlusive than creams. They are particularly suitable for chronic, dry lesions. The most commonly used ointment bases consist of soft paraffin or a combination of soft, liquid and hard paraffin. Some ointment bases have both *hydrophilic and lipophilic* properties; they may have occlusive properties on the skin surface, encourage hydration, and also be miscible with water; they often have a mild anti-inflammatory effect. *Water-soluble ointments* contain macrogols which are freely soluble in water and are therefore readily washed off; they have a limited but useful role where ready removal is desirable.

**Pastes** are stiff preparations containing a high proportion of finely powdered solids such as zinc oxide and starch suspended in an ointment. They are used for circumscribed lesions such as those which occur in lichen simplex, chronic eczema, or psoriasis. They are less occlusive than ointments and can be used to protect inflamed, lichenified, or excoriated skin.

**Dusting powders** are used only rarely. They reduce friction between opposing skin surfaces. Dusting powders should not be applied to moist areas because they can cake and abrade the skin. Talc is a lubricant but it does not absorb moisture whereas starch is less lubricant but absorbs water.

**Dilution** The BP directs that creams and ointments should **not** normally be diluted but that should dilution be necessary care should be taken, in particular, to prevent microbial contamination. The appropriate diluent should be used and heating should be avoided during mixing; excessive dilution may affect the stability of some creams. Diluted creams should normally be used within 2 weeks of their preparation.

## 13.1.2 Suitable quantities for prescribing

**Suitable quantities of dermatological preparations to be prescribed for specific areas of the body**

| | Creams and Ointments | Lotions |
|---|---|---|
| Face | 15–30 g | 100 mL |
| Both hands | 25–50 g | 200 mL |
| Scalp | 50–100 g | 200 mL |
| Both arms or both legs | 100–200 g | 200 mL |
| Trunk | 400 g | 500 mL |
| Groins and genitalia | 15–25 g | 100 mL |

These amounts are usually suitable for an adult for twice daily application for 1 week. The recommendations do not apply to corticosteroid preparations—for suitable quantities of corticosteroid preparations see section 13.4.

## 13.1.3 Excipients and sensitisation

Excipients in topical products rarely cause problems. If a patch test indicates allergy to an excipient, then products containing the substance should be avoided. The following excipients in topical preparations may rarely be associated with sensitisation; the presence of these excipients is indicated in the entries for topical products.

| | |
|---|---|
| Beeswax | Imidurea |
| Benzyl alcohol | Isopropyl palmitate |
| Butylated hydroxyanisole | *N*-(3-Chloroallyl)hexaminium chloride (quaternium 15) |
| Butylated hydroxytoluene | Polysorbates |
| Cetostearyl alcohol (including cetyl and stearyl alcohol) | Propylene glycol |
| Chlorocresol | Sodium metabisulphite |
| Edetic acid (EDTA) | Sorbic acid |
| Ethylenediamine | Wool fat and related substances including lanolin[1] |
| Fragrances | |
| Hydroxybenzoates (parabens) | |

# 13.2 Emollient and barrier preparations

13.2.1 Emollients
13.2.2 Barrier preparations

**Borderline substances** The preparations marked 'ACBS' are regarded as drugs when prescribed in accordance with the advice of the Advisory Committee on Borderline Substances for the clinical conditions listed. Prescriptions issued in accordance with this advice and endorsed 'ACBS' will normally not be investigated. See Appendix 7 for listing by clinical condition.

## 13.2.1 Emollients

**Emollients** soothe, smooth and hydrate the skin and are indicated for all dry or scaling disorders. Their effects are short-lived and they should be applied frequently even after improvement occurs. They are useful in dry and eczematous disorders, and to a lesser extent in psoriasis (section 13.5.2). Light emollients such as **aqueous cream** are suitable for many patients with dry skin but a wide range of more greasy preparations including **white soft paraffin**, **emulsifying ointment**, and **liquid and white soft paraffin ointment** are available; the severity of the condition, patient preference and site of application will often guide the choice of emollient; emollients should be applied in the direction of hair growth. Some ingredients may rarely cause sensitisation (section 13.1.3) and this should be suspected if an eczematous reaction occurs.

Preparations such as **aqueous cream** and **emulsifying ointment** can be used as soap substitutes for hand washing and in the bath; the preparation is rubbed on the skin before rinsing off completely. The addition of a bath oil (section 13.2.1.1) may also be helpful.

Preparations containing an antibacterial should be avoided unless infection is present (section 13.10) or is a frequent complication.

**Urea** is employed as a hydrating agent. It is used in scaling conditions and may be useful in elderly patients. It is occasionally used with other topical agents such as corticosteroids to enhance penetration.

1. Purified versions of wool fat have reduced the problem

**Non-proprietary emollient preparations**

**Aqueous Cream, BP**

Cream, emulsifying ointment 30%, [1]phenoxyethanol 1% in freshly boiled and cooled purified water, net price 100 g = 50p

Excipients include cetostearyl alcohol

1. The BP permits use of alternative antimicrobials provided their identity and concentration are stated on the label

**Emulsifying Ointment, BP**

Ointment, emulsifying wax 30%, white soft paraffin 50%, liquid paraffin 20%, net price 100 g = 57p

Excipients include cetostearyl alcohol

**Hydrous Ointment, BP**

Ointment, (oily cream), dried magnesium sulphate 0.5%, phenoxyethanol 1%, wool alcohols ointment 50%, in freshly boiled and cooled purified water, net price 100 g = 40p

**Liquid and White Soft Paraffin Ointment, NPF**

Ointment, liquid paraffin 50%, white soft paraffin 50%, net price 250 g = £3.24

**Paraffin, White Soft, BP**

White petroleum jelly, net price 100 g = 52p

**Paraffin, Yellow Soft, BP**

Yellow petroleum jelly, net price 100 g = 33p

**Proprietary emollient preparations**

**Aveeno®** (J&J)

Cream, colloidal oatmeal in emollient basis, net price 100 mL = £3.78

Excipients include benzyl alcohol, cetyl alcohol, isopropyl palmitate

ACBS: For endogenous and exogenous eczema, xeroderma, ichthyosis, and senile pruritus (pruritus of the elderly) associated with dry skin

Lotion, colloidal oatmeal in emollient basis, net price 400-mL pump pack = £6.42

Excipients include benzyl alcohol, cetyl alcohol, isopropyl palmitate

ACBS: as for *Aveeno® Cream*

**Cetraben®** (Sankyo)

Emollient cream, white soft paraffin 13.2%, light liquid paraffin 10.5%, net price 50 g = £1.17, 125 g = £2.38, 500-g pump pack = £5.61

Excipients include cetostearyl alcohol, hydroxybenzoates (parabens)

For inflamed, damaged, dry or chapped skin including eczema

**Decubal® Clinic** (Alpharma)

Cream, isopropyl myristate 17%, glycerol 8.5%, wool fat 6%, dimeticone 5%, net price 50 g = £1.02, 100 g = £1.98

Excipients include cetyl alcohol, polysorbates, sorbic acid, wool fat

For dry skin conditions including ichthyosis, psoriasis, dermatitis and hyperkeratosis

**Dermamist®** (Astellas)

Spray application, white soft paraffin 10% in a basis containing liquid paraffin, fractionated coconut oil, net price 250-mL pressurised aerosol unit = £9.22

Excipients none as listed in section 13.1.3

For dry skin conditions including eczema, ichthyosis, pruritus of the elderly

Note Flammable

**Diprobase®** (Schering-Plough)

Cream, cetomacrogol 2.25%, cetostearyl alcohol 7.2%, liquid paraffin 6%, white soft paraffin 15%, water-miscible basis used for *Diprosone®* cream, net price 50 g = £1.43; 500-g dispenser = £6.15

Excipients include cetostearyl alcohol, chlorocresol

For dry skin conditions

Ointment, liquid paraffin 5%, white soft paraffin 95%, basis used for *Diprosone®* ointment, net price 50 g = £1.54

Excipients none as listed in section 13.1.3

For dry skin conditions

**Doublebase®** (Dermal)

Gel, isopropyl myristate 15%, liquid paraffin 15%, net price 100 g = £2.77, 500 g = £6.09

Excipients none as listed in section 13.1.3

For dry chapped or itchy skin conditions

**Drapolene®**

Section 13.2.2

**E45®** (Crookes)

Cream, light liquid paraffin 12.6%, white soft paraffin 14.5%, hypoallergenic hydrous wool fat (hypoallergenic lanolin) 1% in self-emulsifying monostearin, net price 50 g = £1.18, 125 g = £2.39, 350 g = £4.14, 500-g pump pack = £6.20

Excipients include cetyl alcohol, hydroxybenzoates (parabens)

For dry skin conditions

Emollient Wash Cream, soap substitute, zinc oxide 5% in an emollient basis, net price 250-mL pump pack = £2.95

Excipients none as listed in section 13.1.3

ACBS: for endogenous and exogenous eczema, xeroderma, ichthyosis and senile pruritus (pruritus of the elderly) associated with dry skin

Lotion, light liquid paraffin 4%, cetomacrogol, white soft paraffin 10%, hypoallergenic anhydrous wool fat (hypoallergenic lanolin) 1% in glyceryl monostearate, net price 200 mL = £2.40, 500-mL pump pack = £4.50

Excipients include isopropyl palmitate, hydroxybenzoates (parabens), benzyl alcohol

ACBS: for symptomatic relief of dry skin conditions, such as those associated with atopic eczema and contact dermatitis

**Epaderm®** (Medlock)

Ointment, emulsifying wax 30%, yellow soft paraffin 30%, liquid paraffin 40%, net price 125 g = £3.48, 500 g = £5.90

Excipients include cetostearyl alcohol

For use as an emollient or soap substitute

**Gammaderm®** (Linderma)

Cream, evening primrose oil 20%, net price 50 g = £2.83, 250 g = £8.20

Excipients include beeswax, hydroxybenzoates (parabens), propylene glycol

Cautions epilepsy (but hazard unlikely with topical preparations)

For dry skin conditions

**Hewletts®** (Kestrel)

Cream, hydrous wool fat 4%, zinc oxide 8%, arachis (peanut) oil, oleic acid, white soft paraffin, net price 35 g = £1.43, 400 g = £6.69

Excipients include fragrance

For nursing hygiene and care of skin, and chapped hands

**Hydromol®** (Ferndale)

Cream, sodium pidolate 2.5%, net price 50 g = £2.04, 100 g = £3.80, 500 g = £12.60

Excipients include cetostearyl alcohol, hydroxybenzoates (parabens)

For dry skin conditions

Ointment, yellow soft paraffin 30%, emulsifying wax 30%, net price 125 g = £2.79, 500 g = £4.74

Excipients include cetostearyl alcohol

For use as an emollient or as a bath additive

**Kamillosan®** (Goldshield)

Ointment, chamomile extracts 10.5% in a basis containing wool fat, net price 50 g = £2.50, 100 g = £5.00

Excipients include beeswax, cetostearyl alcohol, hydroxybenzoates (parabens)

For nappy rash, sore nipples and chapped hands

**Keri®** (Bristol-Myers Squibb)
Lotion, mineral oil 16%, with lanolin oil, net price 190-mL pump pack = £3.56, 380-mL pump pack = £5.81
Excipients include fragrance, hydroxybenzoates (parabens), *N*-(3-chloroallyl)hexaminium chloride (quaternium 15), propylene glycol
For dry skin conditions and nappy rash

**LactiCare®** (Stiefel)
Lotion, lactic acid 5%, sodium pidolate 2.5%, net price 150 mL = £3.19
Excipients include cetostearyl alcohol, imidurea, isopropyl palmitate, fragrance
For dry skin conditions

**Lipobase®** (Astellas)
Cream, fatty cream basis used for *Locoid Lipocream®*, net price 50 g = £2.08
Excipients include cetostearyl alcohol, hydroxybenzoates (parabens)
For dry skin conditions, also for use during treatment with topical corticosteroid and as diluent for *Locoid Lipocream®*

**Neutrogena® Dermatological Cream** (J&J)
Cream, glycerol 40% in an emollient basis, net price 100 g = £3.77
Excipients include cetostearyl alcohol, hydroxybenzoates (parabens)
For dry skin conditions

**Oilatum®** (Stiefel)
Cream, light liquid paraffin 6%, white soft paraffin 15%, net price 40 g = £1.79, 150 g = £3.38
Excipients include benzyl alcohol, cetostearyl alcohol
For dry skin conditions

Shower emollient (gel), light liquid paraffin 70%, net price 150 g = £5.15
Excipients include fragrance
For dry skin conditions including dermatitis

**Ultrabase®** (Schering Health)
Cream, water-miscible, containing liquid paraffin and white soft paraffin, net price 50 g = 89p, 500-g dispenser = £6.44
Excipients include fragrance, hydroxybenzoates (parabens), disodium edetate, stearyl alcohol
For dry skin conditions

**Unguentum M®** (Crookes)
Cream, containing saturated neutral oil, liquid paraffin, white soft paraffin, net price 50 g = £1.59, 100 g = £3.13, 200-mL dispenser = £6.19, 500 g = £9.55
Excipients include cetostearyl alcohol, polysorbate 40, propylene glycol, sorbic acid
For dry skin conditions and nappy rash

**Vaseline Dermacare®** (Elida Fabergé)
Cream, dimeticone 1%, white soft paraffin 15%, net price 150 mL = £2.11
Excipients include hydroxybenzoates (parabens)
ACBS: for endogenous and exogenous eczema, xeroderma, ichthyosis and senile pruritus (pruritus of the elderly) associated with dry skin

Lotion, dimeticone 1%, liquid paraffin 4%, white soft paraffin 5% in an emollient basis, net price 75 mL = 78p, 200 mL = £1.49
Excipients include disodium edetate, hydroxybenzoates (parabens), wool fat
ACBS: as for *Vaseline Dermacare® Cream*

**Zerobase®** (Zeroderma)
Cream, liquid paraffin 11%, net price 500-g dispenser = £5.99
Excipients include cetostearyl alcohol, chlorocresol
For dry skin conditions

## ◢Preparations containing urea

**Aquadrate®** (Alliance)
Cream, urea 10%, net price 30 g = £1.37, 100 g = £3.64
Excipients none as listed in section 13.1.3
Dose for dry, scaling and itching skin, apply thinly and rub into area when required

**Balneum® Plus** (Crookes)
Cream, urea 5%, lauromacrogols 3%, net price 100 g = £5.58, 175-g pump pack = £7.81, 500-g pump pack = £19.50
Excipients include benzyl alcohol, polysorbates
Dose for dry, scaling and itching skin, apply twice daily

**Calmurid®** (Galderma)
Cream, urea 10%, lactic acid 5%. Diluent aqueous cream, life of diluted cream 14 days, net price 100 g = £6.84, 500-g dispenser = £25.78
Excipients none as listed in section 13.1.3
Dose for dry, scaling and itching skin, apply a thick layer for 3–5 minutes, massage into area, and remove excess, usually twice daily. Use half-strength cream for 1 week if stinging occurs

**E45® Itch Relief Cream** (Crookes)
Cream, urea 5%, macrogol lauryl ether 3%, net price 50 g = £2.16, 100 g = £3.47
Excipients include benzyl alcohol, polysorbates
Dose for dry, scaling, and itching skin, apply twice a day

**Eucerin®** (Beiersdorf)
Cream, urea 10%, net price 50 mL = £5.85, 150 mL = £9.23
Excipients include benzyl alcohol, isopropyl palmitate, wool fat
Dose for dry skin conditions including eczema, ichthyosis, xeroderma, hyperkeratosis, apply thinly and rub into area twice daily

Lotion, urea 10%, net price 250 mL = £7.69
Excipients include benzyl alcohol, isopropyl palmitate
Dose for dry skin conditions including eczema, ichthyosis, xeroderma, hyperkeratosis, apply sparingly and rub into area twice daily

**Nutraplus®** (Galderma)
Cream, urea 10%, net price 100 g = £4.37
Excipients include hydroxybenzoates (parabens), propylene glycol
Dose for dry, scaling and itching skin, apply 2–3 times daily

## ◢With antimicrobials

**Dermol®** (Dermal)
Cream, benzalkonium chloride 0.1%, chlorhexidine hydrochloride 0.1%, isopropyl myristate 10%, liquid paraffin 10%, net price 100-g tube = £3.22, 500-g bottle = £7.45
Excipients include cetostearyl alcohol
Dose for dry and pruritic skin conditions including eczema and dermatitis, apply to skin or use as soap substitute

Dermol® 500 Lotion, benzalkonium chloride 0.1%, chlorhexidine hydrochloride 0.1%, liquid paraffin 2.5%, isopropyl myristate 2.5%, net price 500-mL dispenser = £6.31
Excipients include cetostearyl alcohol
Dose for dry and pruritic skin conditions including eczema and dermatitis, apply to skin or use as soap substitute

Dermol® 200 Shower Emollient, benzalkonium chloride 0.1%, chlorhexidine hydrochloride 0.1%, liquid paraffin 2.5%, isopropyl myristate 2.5%, net price 200 mL = £3.71
Excipients include cetostearyl alcohol
Dose for dry and pruritic skin conditions including eczema and dermatitis, apply to skin or use as soap substitute

## 13.2.1.1 Emollient bath additives

Bath emollient additives should be added to bath water; some can be applied to wet skin undiluted and rinsed off. Hydration may be improved by soaking in the bath for 10–20 minutes. In dry skin conditions soap should be avoided (see section 13.2.1 for soap substitutes).

Note These preparations make skin and surfaces slippery—particular care is needed when bathing

**Alpha Keri Bath®** (Bristol-Myers Squibb)

Bath oil, liquid paraffin 91.7%, oil-soluble fraction of wool fat 3%, net price 240 mL = £3.45, 480 mL = £6.43

Excipients include fragrance

Dose for dry skin conditions including ichthyosis and pruritus of the elderly, add 10–20 mL/bath (INFANT 5 mL) or apply to wet skin and rinse

**Aveeno®** (J&J)

Aveeno® Bath oil, colloidal oatmeal, white oat fraction in emollient basis, net price 250 mL = £4.28

Excipients include beeswax, fragrance

Dose ACBS: for endogenous and exogenous eczema, xeroderma, ichthyosis, and senile pruritus (pruritus of the elderly) associated with dry skin, add 30 mL/bath

Aveeno Colloidal® Bath additive, oatmeal, white oat fraction in emollient basis, net price 10 × 50-g sachets = £7.33

Excipients none as listed in section 13.1.3

Dose ACBS: as for Aveeno® Bath oil; add 1 sachet/bath (INFANT half sachet)

**Balneum®** (Crookes)

Balneum® bath oil, soya oil 84.75%, net price 200 mL = £2.79, 500 mL = £6.06, 1 litre = £11.70

Excipients include butylated hydroxytoluene, propylene glycol, fragrance

Dose for dry skin conditions including those associated with dermatitis and eczema; add 20–60 mL/bath (INFANT 5–15 mL); do not use undiluted

Balneum Plus® bath oil, soya oil 82.95%, mixed lauromacrogols 15%, net price 500 mL = £7.50

Excipients include butylated hydroxytoluene, propylene glycol, fragrance

Dose for dry skin conditions including those associated with dermatitis and eczema where pruritus also experienced; add 20 mL/bath (INFANT 5 mL) or apply to wet skin and rinse

**Cetraben®** (Sankyo)

Emollient bath additive, light liquid paraffin 82.8%, net price 500 mL = £5.25

Dose for dry skin conditions, including eczema, add 1–2 capfuls/bath (CHILD ½–1 capful) or apply to wet skin and rinse

**Dermalo®** (Dermal)

Bath emollient, acetylated wool alcohols 5%, liquid paraffin 65%, net price 500 mL = £3.60

Excipients none as listed in section 13.1.3

Dose for dermatitis, dry skin conditions including ichthyosis and pruritus of the elderly; add 15–20 mL/bath (INFANT and CHILD 5–10 mL) or apply to wet skin and rinse

**Diprobath®** (Schering-Plough)

Bath additive, isopropyl myristate 39%, light liquid paraffin 46%, net price 500 mL = £6.97

Excipients none as listed in section 13.1.3

Dose for dry skin conditions including dermatitis and eczema; add 25–50 mL/bath (INFANT 10 mL); do not use undiluted

**E45®** (Crookes)

Emollient bath oil, cetyl dimeticone 5%, liquid paraffin 91%, net price 250 mL = £2.95, 500 mL = £4.70

Excipients none as listed in section 13.1.3

Dose ACBS: for endogenous and exogenous eczema, xeroderma, ichthyosis, and senile pruritus (pruritus of the elderly) associated with dry skin; add 15 mL/bath (CHILD 5–10 mL)

**Emollient Medicinal Bath Oil** (Ashbourne)

Emollient bath oil, liquid paraffin 65%, acetylated wool alcohols 5%, net price 250 mL = £2.75, 500 mL = £5.46

Dose for dry skin conditions including dermatitis, pruritus of the elderly, and ichthyosis, add 15–20 mL/bath (INFANT and CHILD 5–10 mL added to a small bath or washbasin); do not use undiluted

**Hydromol Emollient®** (Ferndale)

Bath additive, isopropyl myristate 13%, light liquid paraffin 37.8%, net price 350 mL = £3.80, 500 mL = £5.14, 1 litre = £9.00

Excipients none as listed in section 13.1.3

Dose for dry skin conditions including eczema, ichthyosis and pruritus of the elderly; add 1–3 capfuls/bath (INFANT ½–2 capfuls) or apply to wet skin and rinse

**Imuderm®** (Goldshield)

Bath oil, almond oil 30%, light liquid paraffin 69.6%, net price 250 mL = £3.75

Excipients include butylated hydroxyanisole

Dose for dry skin conditions including dermatitis, eczema, pruritus of the elderly, and ichthyosis, add 15–30 mL/bath (INFANT and CHILD 7.5–15 mL) or rub into dry skin until absorbed

**Oilatum®** (Stiefel)

Oilatum® Emollient bath additive (emulsion), acetylated wool alcohols 5%, liquid paraffin 63.4%, net price 250 mL = £2.75, 500 mL = £4.57

Excipients include isopropyl palmitate, fragrance

Dose for dry skin conditions including dermatitis, pruritus of the elderly and ichthyosis; add 1–3 capfuls/bath (INFANT 0.5–2 capfuls) or apply to wet skin and rinse

Oilatum® Fragrance Free Junior bath additive, light liquid paraffin 63.4%, net price 250 mL = £3.25, 500 mL = £5.75, 1 litre = £11.50

Excipients include wool fat, isopropyl palmitate

Dose for dry skin conditions including dermatitis, pruritus of the elderly and ichthyosis; add 1–3 capfuls/bath (INFANT 0.5–2 capfuls) or apply to wet skin and rinse

### With antimicrobials

**Dermol®** (Dermal)

Dermol® 600 Bath Emollient, benzalkonium chloride 0.5%, liquid paraffin 25%, isopropyl myristate 25%, net price 600 mL = £7.90

Excipients include polysorbate 60

Dose for dry and pruritic skin conditions including eczema and dermatitis, add up to 30 mL/bath (INFANT up to 15 mL); do not use undiluted

**Emulsiderm®** (Dermal)

Liquid emulsion, liquid paraffin 25%, isopropyl myristate 25%, benzalkonium chloride 0.5%, net price 300 mL (with 15-mL measure) = £4.03, 1 litre (with 30-mL measure) = £12.55

Excipients include polysorbate 60

Dose for dry skin conditions including eczema and ichthyosis; add 7–30 mL/bath or rub into dry skin until absorbed

**Oilatum®** (Stiefel)

Oilatum® Plus bath additive, benzalkonium chloride 6%, triclosan 2%, light liquid paraffin 52.5%, net price 500 mL = £6.98, 1 litre = £13.59

Excipients include wool fat, isopropyl palmitate

Dose for topical treatment of eczema including eczema at risk from infection; add 1–2 capfuls/bath (INFANT over 6 months 1 mL); do not use undiluted

### With coal tar

Section 13.5.2

## 13.2.2 Barrier preparations

Barrier preparations often contain water-repellent substances such as **dimeticone** (dimethicone) or other silicones. They are used on the skin around stomas, bedsores, and pressure areas in the elderly where the skin is intact. Where the skin has broken down, barrier preparations have a limited role in protecting adjacent skin. They are no substitute for adequate nursing care and it is doubtful if they are any more effective than the traditional compound **zinc ointments**.

**Nappy rash** Barrier creams and ointments are used for protection against nappy rash which is usually a local dermatitis. The first line of treatment is to ensure that nappies are changed frequently and that tightly fitting water-proof pants are avoided. The rash may clear when left exposed to the air and a barrier preparation may be helpful. If the rash is associated with a fungal infection, an antifungal cream such as clotrimazole cream (section 13.10.2) is useful. A mild corticosteroid such as hydrocortisone 1% may be useful but treatment should be limited to a week or less; the occlusive effect of nappies and water-proof pants may increase absorption (for cautions, see p. 573).

### Non-proprietary barrier preparations

**Zinc Cream, BP**

Cream, zinc oxide 32%, arachis (peanut) oil 32%, calcium hydroxide 0.045%, oleic acid 0.5%, wool fat 8%, in freshly boiled and cooled purified water, net price 50 g = 50p

For nappy and urinary rash and eczematous conditions

**Zinc Ointment, BP**

Ointment, zinc oxide 15%, in Simple Ointment BP 1988 (which contains wool fat 5%, hard paraffin 5%, cetostearyl alcohol 5%, white soft paraffin 85%), net price 25 g = 16p

For nappy and urinary rash and eczematous conditions

**Zinc and Castor Oil Ointment, BP**

Ointment, zinc oxide 7.5%, castor oil 50%, arachis (peanut) oil 30.5%, white beeswax 10%, cetostearyl alcohol 2%, net price 25 g = 14p

For nappy and urinary rash

### Proprietary barrier preparations

**Conotrane®** (Astellas)

Cream, benzalkonium chloride 0.1%, dimeticone '350' 22%, net price 100 g = 74p, 500 g = £3.51

Excipients include cetostearyl alcohol, fragrance

For nappy and urinary rash and pressure sores

**Drapolene®** (Warner Lambert)

Cream, benzalkonium chloride 0.01%, cetrimide 0.2% in a basis containing white soft paraffin, cetyl alcohol and wool fat, net price 100 g = £1.43, 200 g = £2.38, 350 g = £3.66

Excipients include cetyl alcohol, chlorocresol, wool fat

For nappy and urinary rash; minor wounds

**Medicaid®** (LPC)

Cream, cetrimide 0.5% in a basis containing light liquid paraffin, white soft paraffin, cetostearyl alcohol, glyceryl monostearate, net price 50 g = £1.69

Excipients include cetostearyl alcohol, fragrance, hydroxybenzoates (parabens), wool fat

For nappy rash, minor burns and abrasions

**Metanium®** (Ransom)

Ointment, titanium dioxide 20%, titanium peroxide 5%, titanium salicylate 3% in a basis containing dimeticone, light liquid paraffin, white soft paraffin, and benzoin tincture, net price 30 g = £2.01

Excipients none as listed in section 13.1.3

For nappy rash and related disorders

**Morhulin®** (Thornton & Ross)

Ointment, cod-liver oil 11.4%, zinc oxide 38%, in a basis containing liquid paraffin and yellow soft paraffin, net price 50 g = £1.62

Excipients include wool fat derivative

For minor wounds, varicose ulcers, pressure sores, eczema and nappy rash

**Siopel®** (Centrapharm)

Barrier cream, dimeticone '1000' 10%, cetrimide 0.3%, arachis (peanut) oil, net price 50 g = £1.66

Excipients include butylated hydroxytoluene, cetostearyl alcohol, hydroxybenzoates (parabens)

For protection against water-soluble irritants

**Sprilon®** (Ayrton Saunders)

Spray application, dimeticone 1.04%, zinc oxide 12.5%, in a basis containing wool alcohols, cetostearyl alcohol, dextran, white soft paraffin, liquid paraffin, propellants, net price 115-g pressurised aerosol unit = £3.54

Excipients include cetostearyl alcohol, hydroxybenzoates (parabens), wool fat

For urinary rash, pressure sores, leg ulcers, moist eczema, fissures, fistulae and ileostomy care

Note Flammable

**Sudocrem®** (Forest)

Cream, benzyl alcohol 0.39%, benzyl benzoate 1.01%, benzyl cinnamate 0.15%, hydrous wool fat (hypoallergenic lanolin) 4%, zinc oxide 15.25%, net price 30 g = £1.01, 60 g = £1.07, 125 g = £1.62, 250 g = £2.75, 400 g = £3.88

Excipients include beeswax (synthetic), propylene glycol, fragrance

For nappy rash and pressure sores

**Vasogen®** (Forest)

Barrier cream, dimeticone 20%, calamine 1.5%, zinc oxide 7.5%, net price 50 g = 80p, 100 g = £1.36

Excipients include hydroxybenzoates (parabens), wool fat

For nappy rash, pressure sores, ileostomy and colostomy care

## 13.3 Topical local anaesthetics and antipruritics

*Pruritus* may be caused by systemic disease (such as drug hypersensitivity, obstructive jaundice, endocrine disease, and certain malignant diseases), skin disease (e.g. psoriasis, eczema, urticaria, and scabies) or as a side-effect of opioid analgesics. Where possible the underlying causes should be treated. An **emollient** (section 13.2.1) may be of value where the pruritus is associated with dry skin. Pruritus that occurs in otherwise healthy elderly people can also be treated with an emollient. For advice on the treatment of pruritus in palliative care, see p. 16.

Preparations containing **crotamiton** are sometimes used but are of uncertain value. Preparations containing **calamine** are often ineffective.

A topical preparation containing **doxepin** 5% is licensed for the relief of pruritus in eczema; it can cause drowsiness and there may be a risk of sensitisation.

Pruritus is common in biliary obstruction, especially in primary biliary cirrhosis and drug-induced cholestasis. Oral administration of **colestyramine** (cholestyramine) is the treatment of choice (section 1.9.2).

Topical antihistamines and local anaesthetics are only marginally effective and may occasionally cause sensitisation. For *insect stings* and *insect bites*, a short course of a topical corticosteroid is appropriate. Short treatment with a **sedating antihistamine** (section 3.4.1) may help in insect stings and in intractable pruritus where sedation is desirable. Insect stings and bites should not be treated with calamine preparations.

For preparations used in *pruritus ani*, see section 1.7.1.

## CALAMINE

**Indications** pruritus

**Calamine** (Non-proprietary)

Aqueous cream, calamine 4%, zinc oxide 3%, liquid paraffin 20%, self-emulsifying glyceryl monostearate 5%, cetomacrogol emulsifying wax 5%, phenoxyethanol 0.5%, freshly boiled and cooled purified water 62.5%, net price 100 mL = 59p

Lotion (= cutaneous suspension), calamine 15%, zinc oxide 5%, glycerol 5%, bentonite 3%, sodium citrate 0.5%, liquefied phenol 0.5%, in freshly boiled and cooled purified water, net price 200 mL = 63p

Oily lotion (BP 1980), calamine 5%, arachis (peanut) oil 50%, oleic acid 0.5%, wool fat 1%, in calcium hydroxide solution, net price 200 mL = £1.57



## CROTAMITON

**Indications** pruritus (including pruritus after scabies—section 13.10.4); see notes above

**Cautions** avoid use near eyes and broken skin; use on doctor's advice for children under 3 years

**Contra-indications** acute exudative dermatoses

**Dose**

- Pruritus, apply 2–3 times daily; CHILD below 3 years, apply once daily

**Eurax®** (Novartis Consumer Health)

Cream, crotamiton 10%, net price 30 g = £2.27, 100 g = £3.95

Excipients include beeswax, fragrance, hydroxybenzoates (parabens), stearyl alcohol

Lotion, crotamiton 10%, net price 100 mL = £2.99

Excipients include cetyl alcohol, fragrance, propylene glycol, sorbic acid, stearyl alcohol

## DOXEPIN HYDROCHLORIDE

**Indications** pruritus in eczema; depressive illness (section 4.3.1)

**Cautions** glaucoma, urinary retention, severe liver impairment, mania; avoid application to large areas; pregnancy and breast-feeding; **interactions**: Appendix 1 (antidepressants, tricyclic)

**Driving** Drowsiness may affect performance of skilled tasks (e.g. driving); effects of alcohol enhanced

**Side-effects** drowsiness; local burning, stinging, irritation, tingling and rash; dry mouth and other systemic side-effects reported (section 4.3.1)

**Dose**

- Apply thinly 3–4 times daily; usual max. 3 g per application; usual total max. 12 g daily; coverage should be less than 10% of body surface area; CHILD under 12 years not recommended

**Xepin®** (CHS) PoM

Cream, doxepin hydrochloride 5%, net price 30 g = £11.70. Label: 2, 10, patient information leaflet

Excipients include benzyl alcohol

## TOPICAL LOCAL ANAESTHETICS

**Indications** relief of local pain, see notes above. See section 15.2 for use in surface anaesthesia

**Cautions** occasionally cause hypersensitivity

**Note** Topical local anaesthetic preparations may be absorbed, especially through mucosal surfaces, therefore excessive application should be avoided and they should preferably not be used for more than about 3 days; not generally suitable for young children

### Preparations on sale to the public

Many topical preparations on sale to the public contain **local anaesthetics**, often combined with **other ingredients**. To identify the active ingredients in such preparations, consult the product literature or manufacturer.

**Note** The correct proprietary name should be ascertained—many products have very similar names but different active ingredients

## TOPICAL ANTIHISTAMINES

**Indications** see notes above

**Cautions** may cause hypersensitivity; avoid in eczema; photosensitivity (diphenhydramine); not recommended for longer than 3 days

### Preparations on sale to the public

Many topical preparations on sale to the public contain **antihistamines**, often combined with **other ingredients**. To identify the active ingredients in such preparations, consult the product literature or manufacturer.

**Note** The correct proprietary name should be ascertained—many products have very similar names but different active ingredients

# 13.4 Topical corticosteroids

Topical corticosteroids are used for the treatment of inflammatory conditions of the skin (other than those arising from an infection) in particular eczema (section 13.5.1), contact dermatitis, insect stings (p. 36), and eczema of scabies (section 13.10.4). Corticosteroids suppress the inflammatory reaction during use; they are not curative and on discontinuation a rebound exacerbation of the condition may occur. They are generally used to relieve symptoms and suppress signs of the disorder when other measures such as emollients are ineffective.

Topical corticosteroids are of no value in the treatment of urticaria and they are **contra-indicated** in rosacea; they may worsen ulcerated or secondarily infected lesions. They should not be used indiscriminately in pruritus (where they will only benefit if inflammation is causing the itch) and are **not** recommended for acne vulgaris.

Systemic or potent topical corticosteroids should be avoided or given only under specialist supervision in *psoriasis* because, although they may suppress the psoriasis in the short term, relapse or vigorous rebound occurs on withdrawal (sometimes precipitating severe pustular psoriasis). Topical use of potent corticosteroids on widespread psoriasis can lead to systemic as well as to local side-effects. It is reasonable, however, to prescribe a mild to moderate topical corticosteroid for a short period (2–4 weeks) for *flexural* and *facial psoriasis*. In the case of scalp psoriasis it is reasonable to use a more potent corticosteroid such as betamethasone or fluocinonide (see below for cautions in psoriasis).

In general, the most potent topical corticosteroids should be reserved for recalcitrant dermatoses such as *chronic discoid lupus erythematosus, lichen simplex chronicus, hypertrophic lichen planus,* and *palmoplantar pustulosis.* Potent corticosteroids should generally be avoided on the face and skin flexures, but specialists occasionally prescribe them for these areas in certain circumstances.

When topical treatment has failed, intralesional corticosteroid injections (section 10.1.2.2) may be used. These are more effective than the very potent topical corticosteroid preparations and should be reserved for severe cases where there are localised lesions such as *keloid scars, hypertrophic lichen planus,* or *localised alopecia areata.*

**Perioral lesions** **Hydrocortisone** cream 1% can be used for up to 7 days to treat uninfected inflammatory lesions on the lips and on the skin surrounding the mouth. **Hydrocortisone and miconazole** cream or ointment is useful where infection by susceptible organisms and inflammation co-exist, particularly for initial treatment (up to 7 days) e.g. in angular cheilitis (see also p. 561). Organisms susceptible to miconazole include *Candida* spp. and many Gram-positive bacteria including streptococci and staphylococci.

**Children** Children, especially infants, are particularly susceptible to side-effects. However, concern about the safety of topical corticosteroids in children should not result in the child being undertreated. The aim is to control the condition as well as possible; inadequate treatment will perpetuate the condition. A mild corticosteroid such as hydrocortisone 1% ointment or cream is useful for treating nappy rash (section 13.2.2) and for atopic eczema in childhood (section 13.5.1). A moderately potent or potent corticosteroid may be appropriate for severe atopic eczema on the limbs, for 1–2 weeks only, switching to a less potent preparation as the condition improves. In an acute flare-up of atopic eczema, it may be appropriate to use more potent formulations of topical corticosteroids for a short period to regain control of the condition. Continuous daily application of a mild corticosteroid such as hydrocortisone 1% is equivalent to a potent corticosteroid such as betamethasone 0.1% applied intermittently. Carers of young children should be advised that treatment should **not** necessarily be reserved to 'treat only the worst areas' and they may need to be advised that patient information leaflets may contain inappropriate advice for the patient's condition.

**Choice of formulation** Water-miscible corticosteroid *creams* are suitable for moist or weeping lesions whereas *ointments* are generally chosen for dry, lichenified or scaly lesions or where a more occlusive effect is required. *Lotions* may be useful when minimal application to a large or hair-bearing area is required or for the treatment of exudative lesions. *Occlusive polythene or hydrocolloid dressings* increase absorption, but also increase the risk of side-effects; they are therefore used only under supervision on a short-term basis for areas of very thick skin (such as the palms and soles). The inclusion of urea or salicylic acid also increases the penetration of the corticosteroid.

In the BNF topical corticosteroids for the skin are categorised as 'mild', 'moderately potent', 'potent' or 'very potent' (see p. 574); the **least potent** preparation which is effective should be chosen but dilution should be avoided whenever possible.

**Cautions** Avoid prolonged use of a topical corticosteroid on the face (and keep away from eyes). In children avoid prolonged use and use potent or very potent corticosteroids under specialist supervision; extreme caution is required in dermatoses of infancy including nappy rash—treatment should be limited to 5–7 days.

Psoriasis The use of potent or very potent corticosteroids in psoriasis can result in rebound relapse, development of generalised pustular psoriasis, and local and systemic toxicity.

**Contra-indications** Topical corticosteroids are contra-indicated in untreated bacterial, fungal, or viral skin lesions, in acne rosacea, and in perioral dermatitis; potent corticosteroids are contra-indicated in widespread plaque psoriasis (see notes above).

**Side-effects** *Mild* and *moderately potent* topical corticosteroids are associated with few side-effects but care is required in the use of *potent* and *very potent* corticosteroids. Absorption through the skin can rarely cause adrenal suppression and even Cushing's syndrome (section 6.3.2), depending on the area of the body being treated and the duration of treatment. Absorption is greatest where the skin is thin or raw, and from intertriginous areas; it is increased by occlusion. Local side-effects include:

- spread and worsening of untreated infection;
- thinning of the skin which may be restored over a period after stopping treatment but the original structure may never return;
- irreversible striae atrophicae and telangiectasia;
- contact dermatitis;
- perioral dermatitis;
- acne, or worsening of acne or acne rosacea;
- mild depigmentation which may be reversible;
- hypertrichosis also reported

In order to minimise the side-effects of a topical corticosteroid, it is important to apply it **thinly** to affected areas **only**, no more frequently than **twice daily**, and to use the least potent formulation which is fully effective.

**Application** Topical corticosteroid preparations should be applied no more frequently than twice daily; once daily is often sufficient.

Topical corticosteroids are spread thinly on the skin; the length of cream or ointment expelled from a tube may be used to specify the quantity to be applied to a given area of skin. This length can be measured in terms of a *fingertip unit* (the distance from the tip of the adult index finger to the first crease). One fingertip unit (approximately 500 mg) is sufficient to cover an area that is twice that of the flat adult palm.

**Suitable quantities of corticosteroid preparations to be prescribed for specific areas of the body**

| | Creams and Ointments |
|---|---|
| Face and neck | 15 to 30 g |
| Both hands | 15 to 30 g |
| Scalp | 15 to 30 g |
| Both arms | 30 to 60 g |
| Both legs | 100 g |
| Trunk | 100 g |
| Groins and genitalia | 15 to 30 g |

These amounts are usually suitable for an adult for a single daily application for 2 weeks

Mixing topical preparations on the skin should be avoided where possible; at least 30 minutes should elapse between application of different preparations. The practice of using an emollient immediately before a topical corticosteroid is inappropriate.

**Compound preparations** The advantages of including other substances (such as antibacterials or antifungals) with corticosteroids in topical preparations are uncertain, but such combinations may have a place where inflammatory skin conditions are associated with bacterial or fungal infection, such as infected eczema. In these cases the antimicrobial drug should be chosen according to the sensitivity of the infecting organism and used regularly for a short period (typically twice daily for 1 week). Longer use increases the likelihood of resistance and of sensitisation.



## Topical corticosteroid preparation potencies

Potency of a topical corticosteroid preparation is a result of the formulation as well as the corticosteroid. Therefore, proprietary names are shown below.

**Mild**

Hydrocortisone 0.1–2.5%, *Dioderm*, *Efcortelan*, *Mildison*

- Mild with antimicrobials: *Canesten HC*, *Daktacort*, *Econacort*, *Fucidin H*, *Nystaform-HC*, *Synalar 1 in 10 Dilution*, *Timodine*, *Vioform-Hydrocortisone*
- Mild with crotamiton: *Eurax-Hydrocortisone*

**Moderate**

*Betnovate-RD*, *Eumovate*, *Haelan*, *Modrasone*, *Synalar 1 in 4 Dilution*, *Ultralanum Plain*

- Moderate with antimicrobials: *Trimovate*
- Moderate with urea: *Alphaderm*, *Calmurid HC*

**Potent**

Betamethasone valerate 0.1%, *Betacap*, *Bettamousse*, *Betnovate*, *Cutivate*, *Diprosone*, *Elocon*, *Locoid*, *Locoid Crelo*, *Metosyn*, *Nerisone*, *Propaderm*, *Synalar*

- Potent with antimicrobials: *Acorvio Plus*, *Aureocort*, *Betnovate-C*, *Betnovate-N*, *FuciBET*, *Locoid C*, *Lotriderm*, *Synalar C*, *Synalar N*, *Tri-Adcortyl*
- Potent with salicylic acid: *Diprosalic*

**Very potent**

*Dermovate*, *Halciderm Topical*, *Nerisone Forte*

- Very potent with antimicrobials: *Dermovate-NN*

## HYDROCORTISONE

**Indications** mild inflammatory skin disorders such as eczemas (but for over-the-counter preparations, see below); nappy rash, see notes above and section 13.2.2

**Cautions** see notes above

**Contra-indications** see notes above

**Side-effects** see notes above

**Dose**

- Apply thinly 1–2 times daily

**Hydrocortisone** (Non-proprietary) PoM

Cream, hydrocortisone 0.5%, net price, 15 g = 97p, 30 g = £1.52; 1%, 15 g = £1.41 Label: 28. Potency: mild

Dental prescribing on NHS Hydrocortisone Cream 1% 15 g may be prescribed

Ointment, hydrocortisone 0.5%, net price 15 g = £1.21, 30 g = £1.82; 1%, 15 g = £1.28. Label: 28. Potency: mild

When hydrocortisone cream or ointment is prescribed and no strength is stated, the 1% strength should be supplied

### Over-the-counter hydrocortisone preparations

Skin creams and ointments containing hydrocortisone (alone or with other ingredients) can be sold to the public for the treatment of allergic contact dermatitis, irritant dermatitis, insect bite reactions and mild to moderate eczema, to be applied sparingly over the affected area 1–2 times daily for max. 1 week. Over-the-counter hydrocortisone preparations should not be sold without medical advice for children under 10 years or for pregnant women; they should **not** be sold for application to the face, anogenital region, broken or infected skin (including cold sores, acne, and athlete's foot).

### Proprietary hydrocortisone preparations

Note The following preparations are PoM; those on sale to the public (with restrictions) are listed above

**Dioderm®** (Dermal) PoM

Cream, hydrocortisone 0.1%, net price 30 g = £2.50. Label: 28. Potency: mild

Excipients include cetostearyl alcohol, propylene glycol

Note Although this contains only 0.1% hydrocortisone, the formulation is designed to provide a clinical activity comparable to that of Hydrocortisone Cream 1% BP

**Efcortelan®** (GSK) PoM

Cream, hydrocortisone 0.5%, net price, 30 g = 61p; 1%, 30 g = 75p. Label: 28. Potency: mild

Excipients include cetostearyl alcohol, chlorocresol

Ointment, hydrocortisone 0.5%, net price, 30 g = 61p; 1%, 30 g = 75p; 2.5%, 30 g = £1.70. Label: 28. Potency: mild

Excipients none as listed in section 13.1.3

**Mildison®** (Astellas) PoM

Lipocream, hydrocortisone 1%, net price 30 g = £2.45. Label: 28. Potency: mild

Excipients include cetostearyl alcohol, hydroxybenzoates (parabens)

### Compound preparations

Compound preparations with coal tar see section 13.5.2

**Alphaderm®** (Alliance) PoM

Cream, hydrocortisone 1%, urea 10%, net price 30 g = £1.98; 100 g = £5.86. Label: 28. Potency: moderate

Excipients none as listed in section 13.1.3

**Calmurid HC®** (Galderma) PoM
Cream, hydrocortisone 1%, urea 10%, lactic acid 5%, net price 30 g = £2.80, 50 g = £4.67. Label: 28. Potency: moderate
Excipients none as listed in section 13.1.3
Note Manufacturer advises dilute to half-strength with aqueous cream for 1 week if stinging occurs then transfer to undiluted preparation (but see section 13.1.1 for advice to avoid dilution where possible)

[1]**Eurax-Hydrocortisone®** (Novartis Consumer Health) PoM
Cream, hydrocortisone 0.25%, crotamiton 10%, net price 30 g = 87p. Label: 28. Potency: mild
Excipients include fragrance, hydroxybenzoates (parabens), propylene glycol, stearyl alcohol
1. A 15-g tube is on sale to the public for treatment of contact dermatitis and insect bites (*Eurax Hc®*)

### With antimicrobials
See notes above for comment on compound preparations

[1]**Canesten HC®** (Bayer Consumer Care) PoM
Cream, hydrocortisone 1%, clotrimazole 1%, net price 30 g = £2.15. Label: 28. Potency: mild
Excipients include benzyl alcohol, cetostearyl alcohol
1. A 15-g tube is on sale to the public for the treatment of athlete's foot and fungal infection of skin folds with associated inflammation (*Canesten® Hydrocortisone*)

[1]**Daktacort®** (Janssen-Cilag) PoM
Cream, hydrocortisone 1%, miconazole nitrate 2%, net price 30 g = £2.13. Label: 28. Potency: mild
Excipients include butylated hydroxyanisole, disodium edetate
Ointment, hydrocortisone 1%, miconazole nitrate 2%, net price 30 g = £2.14. Label: 28. Potency: mild
Excipients none as listed in section 13.1.3
Dental prescribing on NHS May be prescribed as Hydrocortisone and Miconazole Cream or Ointment for max. 7 days
1. A 15-g tube is on sale to the public for the treatment of athlete's foot and candidal intertrigo (*Daktacort® HC*)

**Econacort®** (Squibb) PoM
Cream, hydrocortisone 1%, econazole nitrate 1%, net price 30 g = £2.25. Label: 28. Potency: mild
Excipients include butylated hydroxyanisole

**Fucidin H®** (LEO) PoM
Cream, hydrocortisone acetate 1%, fusidic acid 2%, net price 30 g = £5.30, 60 g = £10.60. Label: 28. Potency: mild
Excipients include butylated hydroxyanisole, cetyl alcohol, potassium sorbate
Ointment, hydrocortisone acetate 1%, sodium fusidate 2%, net price 30 g = £3.26, 60 g = £6.53. Label: 28. Potency: mild
Excipients include cetyl alcohol, wool fat

**Nystaform-HC®** (Typharm) PoM
Cream, hydrocortisone 0.5%, nystatin 100 000 units/g, chlorhexidine hydrochloride 1%, net price 30 g = £2.66. Label: 28. Potency: mild
Excipients include benzyl alcohol, cetostearyl alcohol, polysorbate '60'
Ointment, hydrocortisone 1%, nystatin 100 000 units/g, chlorhexidine acetate 1%, net price 30 g = £2.66. Label: 28. Potency: mild
Excipients none as listed in section 13.1.3

**Timodine®** (R&C) PoM
Cream, hydrocortisone 0.5%, nystatin 100 000 units/g, benzalkonium chloride solution 0.2%, dimeticone '350' 10%, net price 30 g = £2.38. Label: 28. Potency: mild
Excipients include butylated hydroxyanisole, cetostearyl alcohol, hydroxybenzoates (parabens), sodium metabisulphite, sorbic acid

**Vioform-Hydrocortisone®** (Novartis Consumer Health) PoM
Cream, hydrocortisone 1%, clioquinol 3%, net price 30 g = £1.46. Label: 28. Potency: mild
Excipients include cetostearyl alcohol
Ointment, hydrocortisone 1%, clioquinol 3%, net price 30 g = £1.46. Label: 28. Potency: mild
Excipients none as listed in section 13.1.3
Note Stains clothing

## HYDROCORTISONE BUTYRATE

**Indications** severe inflammatory skin disorders such as eczemas unresponsive to less potent corticosteroids; psoriasis, see notes above
**Cautions** see notes above
**Contra-indications** see notes above
**Side-effects** see notes above
**Dose**
- Apply thinly 1–2 times daily

**Locoid®** (Astellas) PoM
Cream, hydrocortisone butyrate 0.1%, net price 30 g = £2.29, 100 g = £7.05. Label: 28. Potency: potent
Excipients include cetostearyl alcohol, hydroxybenzoates (parabens)
Lipocream, hydrocortisone butyrate 0.1%, net price 30 g = £2.41, 100 g = £7.38. Label: 28. Potency: potent
Excipients include cetostearyl alcohol, hydroxybenzoates (parabens)
Note For bland cream basis see *Lipobase®*, section 13.2.1
Ointment, hydrocortisone butyrate 0.1%, net price 30 g = £2.29, 100 g = £7.05. Label: 28. Potency: potent
Excipients none as listed in section 13.1.3
Scalp lotion, hydrocortisone butyrate 0.1%, in an aqueous isopropyl alcohol basis, net price 100 mL = £9.76. Label: 15, 28. Potency: potent
Excipients none as listed in section 13.1.3

**Locoid Crelo®** (Astellas) PoM
Lotion (topical emulsion), hydrocortisone butyrate 0.1% in a water-miscible basis, net price 100 g (with applicator nozzle) = £8.44. Label: 28. Potency: potent
Excipients include butylated hydroxytoluene, cetostearyl alcohol, hydroxybenzoates (parabens), propylene glycol

### With antimicrobials
See notes above for comment on compound preparations

**Locoid C®** (Astellas) PoM
Cream, hydrocortisone butyrate 0.1%, chlorquinaldol 3%, net price 30 g = £3.00. Label: 28. Potency: potent
Excipients include cetostearyl alcohol
Note Stains clothing and can darken skin and hair
Ointment, ingredients as for cream, in a greasy basis, net price 30 g = £3.00. Label: 28. Potency: potent
Excipients none as listed in section 13.1.3
Note Stains clothing and can darken skin and hair

## ALCLOMETASONE DIPROPIONATE

**Indications** inflammatory skin disorders such as eczemas
**Cautions** see notes above
**Contra-indications** see notes above
**Side-effects** see notes above
**Dose**
- Apply thinly 1–2 times daily

**Modrasone®** (PLIVA) PoM
Cream, alclometasone dipropionate 0.05%, net price 50 g = £2.68. Label: 28. Potency: moderate
Excipients include cetostearyl alcohol, chlorocresol, propylene glycol

Ointment, alclometasone dipropionate 0.05%, net price 50 g = £2.68. Label: 28. Potency: moderate
Excipients include beeswax, propylene glycol

## BECLOMETASONE DIPROPIONATE
(Beclomethasone dipropionate)

**Indications** severe inflammatory skin disorders such as eczemas unresponsive to less potent corticosteroids; psoriasis, see notes above
**Cautions** see notes above
**Contra-indications** see notes above
**Side-effects** see notes above
**Dose**
- Apply thinly 1–2 times daily

**Propaderm®** (GSK) PoM
Cream, beclometasone dipropionate 0.025%, net price 30 g = £1.77. Label: 28. Potency: potent
Excipients include cetostearyl alcohol, chlorocresol

Ointment, beclometasone dipropionate 0.025%, net price 30 g = £1.77. Label: 28. Potency: potent
Excipients include propylene glycol

## BETAMETHASONE ESTERS

**Indications** severe inflammatory skin disorders such as eczemas unresponsive to less potent corticosteroids; psoriasis, see notes above
**Cautions** see notes above; use of more than 100 g per week of 0.1% preparation likely to cause adrenal suppression
**Contra-indications** see notes above
**Side-effects** see notes above
**Dose**
- Apply thinly 1–2 times daily

**Betamethasone Valerate** (Non-proprietary) PoM
Cream, betamethasone (as valerate) 0.1%, net price 30 g = £1.43. Label: 28. Potency: potent

Ointment, betamethasone (as valerate) 0.1%, net price 30 g = £1.68. Label: 28. Potency: potent

**Betacap®** (Dermal) PoM
Scalp application, betamethasone (as valerate) 0.1% in a water-miscible basis containing coconut oil derivative, net price 100 mL = £3.92. Label: 15, 28. Potency: potent
Excipients none as listed in section 13.1.3

**Betnovate®** (GSK) PoM
Cream, betamethasone (as valerate) 0.1% in a water-miscible basis, net price 30 g = £1.43, 100 g = £4.05. Label: 28. Potency: potent
Excipients include cetostearyl alcohol, chlorocresol

Ointment, betamethasone (as valerate) 0.1% in an anhydrous paraffin basis, net price 30 g = £1.43, 100 g = £4.05. Label: 28. Potency: potent
Excipients none as listed in section 13.1.3

Lotion, betamethasone (as valerate) 0.1%, net price 100 mL = £4.86. Label: 28. Potency: potent
Excipients include cetostearyl alcohol, hydroxybenzoates (parabens)

Scalp application, betamethasone (as valerate) 0.1% in a water-miscible basis, net price 100 mL = £5.30. Label: 15, 28. Potency: potent
Excipients none as listed in section 13.1.3

**Betnovate-RD®** (GSK) PoM
Cream, betamethasone (as valerate) 0.025% in a water-miscible basis (1 in 4 dilution of *Betnovate®* cream), net price 100 g = £3.34. Label: 28. Potency: moderate
Excipients include cetostearyl alcohol, chlorocresol

Ointment, betamethasone (as valerate) 0.025% in an anhydrous paraffin basis (1 in 4 dilution of *Betnovate®* ointment), net price 100 g = £3.34. Label: 28. Potency: moderate
Excipients none as listed in section 13.1.3

**Bettamousse®** (Celltech) PoM
Foam (= scalp application), betamethasone valerate 0.12% (≡ betamethasone 0.1%), net price 100 g = £9.75. Label: 28. Potency: potent
Excipients include cetyl alcohol, polysorbate 60, propylene glycol, stearyl alcohol
Note Flammable

**Diprosone®** (Schering-Plough) PoM
Cream, betamethasone (as dipropionate) 0.05%, net price 30 g = £2.24, 100 g = £6.36. Label: 28. Potency: potent
Excipients include cetostearyl alcohol, chlorocresol

Ointment, betamethasone (as dipropionate) 0.05%, net price 30 g = £2.24, 100 g = £6.36. Label: 28. Potency: potent
Excipients none as listed in section 13.1.3

Lotion, betamethasone (as dipropionate) 0.05%, net price 30 mL = £2.83, 100 mL = £8.10. Label: 28. Potency: potent
Excipients none as listed in section 13.1.3

### With salicylic acid
See notes above for comment on compound preparations

**Diprosalic®** (Schering-Plough) PoM
Ointment, betamethasone (as dipropionate) 0.05%, salicylic acid 3%, net price 30 g = £3.30, 100 g = £9.50. Label: 28. Potency: potent
Excipients none as listed in section 13.1.3
Dose apply thinly 1–2 times daily; max. 60 g per week

Scalp application, betamethasone (as dipropionate) 0.05%, salicylic acid 2%, in an alcoholic basis, net price 100 mL = £10.50. Label: 28. Potency: potent
Excipients include disodium edetate
Dose apply a few drops 1–2 times daily

### With antimicrobials
See notes above for comment on compound preparations

**Betnovate-C®** (GSK) PoM
Cream, betamethasone (as valerate) 0.1%, clioquinol 3%, net price 30 g = £1.76. Label: 28. Potency: potent
Excipients include cetostearyl alcohol, chlorocresol
Note Stains clothing

Ointment, betamethasone (as valerate) 0.1%, clioquinol 3%, net price 30 g = £1.76. Label: 28. Potency: potent
Excipients none as listed in section 13.1.3
Note Stains clothing

**Betnovate-N®** (GSK) PoM
Cream, betamethasone (as valerate) 0.1%, neomycin sulphate 0.5%, net price 30 g = £1.76, 100 g = £4.88. Label: 28. Potency: potent
Excipients include cetostearyl alcohol, chlorocresol

Ointment, betamethasone (as valerate) 0.1%, neomycin sulphate 0.5%, net price 30 g = £1.76, 100 g = £4.88. Label: 28. Potency: potent
Excipients none as listed in section 13.1.3

**FuciBET®** (LEO) PoM

Cream, betamethasone (as valerate) 0.1%, fusidic acid 2%, net price 30 g = £5.62, 60 g = £11.23. Label: 28. Potency: potent

Excipients include cetostearyl alcohol, chlorocresol

**Lotriderm®** (PLIVA) PoM

Cream, betamethasone dipropionate 0.064% (≡ betamethasone 0.05%), clotrimazole 1%, net price 30 g = £6.34. Label: 28. Potency: potent

Excipients include benzyl alcohol, cetostearyl alcohol, propylene glycol

## CLOBETASOL PROPIONATE

**Indications** short-term treatment only of severe resistant inflammatory skin disorders such as recalcitrant eczemas unresponsive to less potent corticosteroids; psoriasis, see notes above

**Cautions** see notes above

**Contra-indications** see notes above

**Side-effects** see notes above

**Dose**

- Apply thinly 1–2 times daily for up to 4 weeks; max. 50 g of 0.05% preparation per week

**Dermovate®** (GSK) PoM

Cream, clobetasol propionate 0.05%, net price 30 g = £2.86, 100 g = £8.39. Label: 28. Potency: very potent

Excipients include beeswax (or beeswax substitute), cetostearyl alcohol, chlorocresol, propylene glycol

Ointment, clobetasol propionate 0.05%, net price 30 g = £2.86, 100 g = £8.39. Label: 28. Potency: very potent

Excipients include propylene glycol

Scalp application, clobetasol propionate 0.05%, in a thickened alcoholic basis, net price 30 mL = £3.26, 100 mL = £11.06. Label: 15, 28. Potency: very potent

Excipients none as listed in section 13.1.3

### With antimicrobials

See notes above for comment on compound preparations

**Dermovate-NN®** (GSK) PoM

Cream, clobetasol propionate 0.05%, neomycin sulphate 0.5%, nystatin 100 000 units/g, net price 30 g = £3.91. Label: 28. Potency: very potent

Excipients include arachis (peanut) oil, beeswax substitute

## CLOBETASONE BUTYRATE

**Indications** eczemas and dermatitis of all types; maintenance between courses of more potent corticosteroids

**Cautions** see notes above

**Contra-indications** see notes above

**Side-effects** see notes above

**Dose**

- Apply thinly 1–2 times daily

[1]**Eumovate®** (GSK) PoM

Cream, clobetasone butyrate 0.05%, net price 30 g = £1.97, 100 g = £5.77. Label: 28. Potency: moderate

Excipients include beeswax substitute, cetostearyl alcohol, chlorocresol

Ointment, clobetasone butyrate 0.05%, net price 30 g = £1.97, 100 g = £5.77. Label: 28. Potency: moderate

Excipients none as listed in section 13.1.3

1. Cream can be sold to the public for short-term symptomatic treatment and control of patches of eczema and dermatitis (but not seborrhoeic dermatitis) in adults and children over 12 years provided pack does not contain more than 15 g

### With antimicrobials

See notes above for comment on compound preparations

**Trimovate®** (GSK) PoM

Cream, clobetasone butyrate 0.05%, oxytetracycline 3% (as calcium salt), nystatin 100 000 units/g, net price 30 g = £3.49. Label: 28. Potency: moderate

Excipients include cetostearyl alcohol, chlorocresol, sodium metabisulphite

Note Stains clothing

## DIFLUCORTOLONE VALERATE

**Indications** severe inflammatory skin disorders such as eczemas unresponsive to less potent corticosteroids; high strength (0.3%), short-term treatment of severe exacerbations; psoriasis, see notes above

**Cautions** see notes above

**Contra-indications** see notes above

**Side-effects** see notes above

**Dose**

- Apply thinly 1–2 times daily for up to 4 weeks (0.1% preparations) or 2 weeks (0.3% preparations), reducing strength as condition responds; max. 60 g of 0.3% per week

**Nerisone®** (Meadow) PoM

Cream, diflucortolone valerate 0.1%, net price 30 g = £1.59. Label: 28. Potency: potent

Excipients include disodium edetate, hydroxybenzoates (parabens), stearyl alcohol

Oily cream, diflucortolone valerate 0.1%, net price 30 g = £2.56. Label: 28. Potency: potent

Excipients include beeswax

Ointment, diflucortolone valerate 0.1%, net price 30 g = £1.59. Label: 28. Potency: potent

Excipients none as listed in section 13.1.3

**Nerisone Forte®** (Meadow) PoM

Oily cream, diflucortolone valerate 0.3%, net price 15 g = £2.09. Label: 28. Potency: very potent

Excipients include beeswax

Ointment, diflucortolone valerate 0.3%, net price 15 g = £2.09. Label: 28. Potency: very potent

Excipients none as listed in section 13.1.3

## FLUDROXYCORTIDE
(Flurandrenolone)

**Indications** inflammatory skin disorders such as eczemas

**Cautions** see notes above

**Contra-indications** see notes above

**Side-effects** see notes above

**Dose**

- Apply thinly 1–2 times daily

**Haelan®** (Typharm) PoM

Cream, fludroxycortide 0.0125%, net price 60 g = £3.26. Label: 28. Potency: moderate

Excipients include cetyl alcohol, propylene glycol

Ointment, fludroxycortide 0.0125%, net price 60 g = £3.26. Label: 28. Potency: moderate

Excipients include beeswax, cetyl alcohol, polysorbate

Tape, polythene adhesive film impregnated with fludroxycortide 4 micrograms /cm$^2$, net price 7.5 cm × 50 cm = £9.27, 7.5 cm × 200 cm = £24.95

Dose for chronic localised recalcitrant dermatoses (but not acute or weeping), cut tape to fit lesion, apply to clean, dry skin shorn of hair, usually for 12 of each 24 hours

## FLUOCINOLONE ACETONIDE

**Indications** inflammatory skin disorders such as eczemas; psoriasis, see notes above

**Cautions** see notes above

**Contra-indications** see notes above

**Side-effects** see notes above

**Dose**

- Apply thinly 1–2 times daily, reducing strength as condition responds

**Synalar®** (GP Pharma) PoM

Cream, fluocinolone acetonide 0.025%, net price 30 g = £2.26, 100 g = £6.42. Label: 28. Potency: potent
Excipients include benzyl alcohol, cetostearyl alcohol, polysorbates, propylene glycol

Gel, fluocinolone acetonide 0.025%, net price 30 g = £3.34. For use on scalp and other hairy areas. Label: 28. Potency: potent
Excipients include hydroxybenzoates (parabens), propylene glycol

Ointment, fluocinolone acetonide 0.025%, net price 30 g = £2.26, 100 g = £6.42. Label: 28. Potency: potent
Excipients include propylene glycol, wool fat

**Synalar 1 in 4 Dilution®** (GP Pharma) PoM

Cream, fluocinolone acetonide 0.00625%, net price 50 g = £2.64. Label: 28. Potency: moderate
Excipients include benzyl alcohol, cetostearyl alcohol, polysorbates, propylene glycol

Ointment, fluocinolone acetonide 0.00625%, net price 50 g = £2.64. Label: 28. Potency: moderate
Excipients include propylene glycol, wool fat

**Synalar 1 in 10 Dilution®** (GP Pharma) PoM

Cream, fluocinolone acetonide 0.0025%, net price 50 g = £2.50. Label: 28. Potency: mild
Excipients include benzyl alcohol, cetostearyl alcohol, polysorbates, propylene glycol

### With antibacterials

See notes above for comment on compound preparations

**Synalar C®** (GP Pharma) PoM

Cream, fluocinolone acetonide 0.025%, clioquinol 3%, net price 15 g = £1.46. Label: 28. Potency: potent
Excipients include cetostearyl alcohol, disodium edetate, hydroxybenzoates (parabens), polysorbates, propylene glycol

Ointment, ingredients as for cream, net price 15 g = £1.46. Label: 28. Potency: potent.
Note stains clothing
Excipients include propylene glycol, wool fat

**Synalar N®** (GP Pharma) PoM

Cream, fluocinolone acetonide 0.025%, neomycin sulphate 0.5%, net price 30 g = £2.38. Label: 28. Potency: potent
Excipients include cetostearyl alcohol, hydroxybenzoates (parabens), polysorbates, propylene glycol

Ointment, ingredients as for cream, in a greasy basis, net price 30 g = £2.38. Label: 28. Potency: potent
Excipients include propylene glycol, wool fat

## FLUOCINONIDE

**Indications** severe inflammatory skin disorders such as eczemas unresponsive to less potent corticosteroids; psoriasis, see notes above

**Cautions** see notes above

**Contra-indications** see notes above

**Side-effects** see notes above

**Dose**

- Apply thinly 1–2 times daily

**Metosyn®** (GP Pharma) PoM

FAPG cream, fluocinonide 0.05%, net price 25 g = £1.98, 100 g = £6.68. Label: 28. Potency: potent
Excipients include propylene glycol

Ointment, fluocinonide 0.05%, net price 25 g = £1.76, 100 g = £6.59. Label: 28. Potency: potent
Excipients include propylene glycol, wool fat

## FLUOCORTOLONE

**Indications** severe inflammatory skin disorders such as eczemas unresponsive to less potent corticosteroids; psoriasis, see notes above

**Cautions** see notes above

**Contra-indications** see notes above

**Side-effects** see notes above

**Dose**

- Apply thinly 1–2 times daily, reducing strength as condition responds

**Ultralanum Plain®** (Meadow) PoM

Cream, fluocortolone caproate 0.25%, fluocortolone pivalate 0.25%, net price 50 g = £2.95. Label: 28. Potency: moderate
Excipients include disodium edetate, fragrance, hydroxybenzoates (parabens), stearyl alcohol

Ointment, fluocortolone 0.25%, fluocortolone caproate 0.25%, net price 50 g = £2.95. Label: 28. Potency: moderate
Excipients include wool fat, fragrance

## FLUPREDNIDENE ACETATE

**Indications** see notes above

**Cautions** see notes above

**Contra-indications** see notes above

**Side-effects** see notes above

**Dose**

- See preparation below

### With antimicrobials

**Acorvio® Plus** (Ferndale) PoM

Cream, fluprednidene acetate 0.1%, miconazole nitrate 2%, net price 20 g = £5.25, 45 g = £ 8.10. Label: 28. Potency: potent
Excipients include propylene glycol, stearyl alcohol
Dose inflammatory dermatophyte, candidal and fungal skin conditions, apply thinly twice daily for up to 1 week (max. 2 weeks)

## FLUTICASONE PROPIONATE

**Indications** inflammatory skin disorders such as dermatitis and eczemas unresponsive to less potent corticosteroids

**Cautions** see notes above

**Contra-indications** see notes above

**Side-effects** see notes above

**Dose**

- Apply thinly 1–2 times daily

**Cutivate®** (GSK) PoM

Cream, fluticasone propionate 0.05%, net price 15 g = £2.41, 50 g = £7.11. Label: 28. Potency: potent
Excipients include cetostearyl alcohol, imidurea, propylene glycol

Ointment, fluticasone propionate 0.005%, net price 15 g = £2.41, 50 g = £7.11. Label: 28. Potency: potent
Excipients include propylene glycol

## HALCINONIDE

**Indications** short-term treatment only of severe resistant inflammatory skin disorders such as recalcitrant eczemas unresponsive to less potent corticosteroids; psoriasis, see notes above
**Cautions** see notes above
**Contra-indications** see notes above
**Side-effects** see notes above
**Dose**
- Apply thinly 1–2 times daily

**Halciderm Topical®** (Squibb) PoM
Cream, halcinonide 0.1%, net price 30 g = £3.16. Label: 28. Potency: very potent
Excipients include propylene glycol

## MOMETASONE FUROATE

**Indications** severe inflammatory skin disorders such as eczemas unresponsive to less potent corticosteroids; psoriasis, see notes above
**Cautions** see notes above
**Contra-indications** see notes above
**Side-effects** see notes above
**Dose**
- Apply thinly once daily (to scalp in case of lotion)

**Elocon®** (Schering-Plough) PoM
Cream, mometasone furoate 0.1%, net price 30 g = £4.54, 100 g = £13.07. Label: 28. Potency: potent
Excipients include stearyl alcohol

Ointment, mometasone furoate 0.1%, net price 30 g = £4.54, 100 g = £13.07. Label: 28. Potency: potent
Excipients none as listed in section 13.1.3

Scalp lotion, mometasone furoate 0.1% in an aqueous isopropyl alcohol basis, net price 30 mL = £4.54. Label: 28. Potency: potent
Excipients include propylene glycol

## TRIAMCINOLONE ACETONIDE

**Indications** severe inflammatory skin disorders such as eczemas unresponsive to less potent corticosteroids; psoriasis, see notes above
**Cautions** see notes above
**Contra-indications** see notes above
**Side-effects** see notes above
**Dose**
- Apply thinly 1–2 times daily

### With antimicrobials

See notes above for comment on compound preparations

**Aureocort®** (Lederle) PoM
Ointment, triamcinolone acetonide 0.1%, chlortetracycline hydrochloride 3%, in an anhydrous greasy basis containing wool fat and white soft paraffin, net price 15 g = £2.70. Label: 28. Potency: potent
Excipients include wool fat
Note Stains clothing

**Tri-Adcortyl®** (Squibb) PoM
Cream, triamcinolone acetonide 0.1%, gramicidin 0.025%, neomycin (as sulphate) 0.25%, nystatin 100 000 units/g, net price 30 g = £3.15. Label: 28. Potency: potent
Excipients include benzyl alcohol, ethylenediamine, propylene glycol, fragrance

Ointment, triamcinolone acetonide 0.1%, gramicidin 0.025%, neomycin (as sulphate) 0.25%, nystatin 100 000 units/g, net price 30 g = £3.15. Label: 28. Potency: potent
Excipients none as listed in section 13.1.3
Note Not recommended owing to presence of ethylenediamine in the cream and also because combination of antibacterial with antifungal not considered useful in either the cream or ointment

# 13.5 Preparations for eczema and psoriasis

13.5.1 Preparations for eczema
13.5.2 Preparations for psoriasis
13.5.3 Drugs affecting the immune response

## 13.5.1 Preparations for eczema

Eczema (dermatitis) has several causes, which may influence treatment. The main types of eczema are irritant, allergic contact, atopic, venous and discoid; different types may co-exist. Lichenification, due to scratching and rubbing, may complicate any chronic eczema. *Atopic eczema* is the most common type and it usually involves dry skin as well as infection and lichenification.

Management of eczema involves the removal or treatment of contributory factors including occupational and domestic irritants. Known or suspected contact allergens should be avoided. Rarely, ingredients in topical medicinal products may sensitise the skin; the BNF lists active ingredients together with excipients that have been associated with skin sensitisation.

Skin dryness and the consequent irritant eczema requires **emollients** (section 13.2.1) applied regularly and liberally to the affected area; this may be supplemented with bath or shower emollients. The use of emollients should continue even if the eczema improves or if other treatment is being used.

**Topical corticosteroids** (section 13.4) are also required in the management of eczema; the potency of the corticosteroid should be appropriate to the severity and site of the condition. Mild corticosteroids are generally used on the face and on flexures; potent corticosteroids are generally required for use on adults with discoid or lichenified eczema or with eczema on the scalp, limbs, and trunk. Treatment should be reviewed regularly, especially if a potent corticosteroid is required. Bandages (including those containing **zinc** and **ichthammol**) are sometimes applied over topical corticosteroids to treat eczema of the limbs.

**Infection** Bacterial infection (commonly with *Staphylococcus aureus* and occasionally with *Streptococcus pyogenes*) can exacerbate eczema and requires treatment with topical or systemic **antibacterial drugs** (section 13.10.1 and section 5.1). Antibacterial drugs, particularly fusidic acid, should be used in short courses (typically 1 week) to reduce the risk of drug resistance or skin sensitisation. Associated eczema is treated simultaneously with a topical corticosteroid usually of moderate or high potency.

Eczema involving widespread or recurrent infection requires the use of a systemic antibacterial that is active against the infecting organism. Products that combine an antiseptic with an emollient application (section 13.2.1) and with a bath emollient (section 13.2.1.1) may also be used; antiseptic shampoos (section 13.9) may be used on the scalp.

Intertriginous eczema commonly involves candida and bacteria; it is best treated with a mild or moderately potent topical corticosteroid and a suitable antimicrobial drug.

Widespread herpes simplex infection may complicate atopic eczema and treatment with a systemic antiviral drug (section 5.3.2.1) is indicated.

The management of *seborrhoeic dermatitis* is described below.

**Management of other features of eczema** *Lichenification*, which results from repeated scratching is treated initially with a potent corticosteroid. Bandages containing **ichthammol paste** (to reduce pruritus) and other substances such as **zinc oxide** may be applied over the corticosteroid. **Coal tar** (section 13.5.2) and **ichthammol** can be useful in some cases of *chronic eczema*.

**Antihistamines** (section 3.4.1) may be of some value in relieving the itch of eczema, usually because of their sedating effect.

*Exudative* ('*weeping*') *eczema* requires a potent corticosteroid initially; infection may also be present and require specific treatment (see above). **Potassium permanganate** solution (1 in 10 000) can be used in exudating eczema for its antiseptic and astringent effect; treatment should be stopped when exudation stops.

*Severe refractory eczema* is best managed under specialist supervision; it may require phototherapy, systemic corticosteroids (section 6.3.2), or other drugs acting on the immune system (section 13.5.3).

**Seborrhoeic dermatitis** *Seborrhoeic dermatitis* (*seborrhoeic eczema*) is associated with species of the yeast *Malassezia* and affects the scalp, paranasal areas, and eyebrows. Shampoos active against the yeast (including those containing ketoconazole and coal tar, section 13.9) and combinations of mild corticosteroids with suitable antimicrobials (section 13.4) are used.

### ICHTHAMMOL

**Indications** chronic lichenified eczema

**Side-effects** skin irritation

**Dose**

- Apply 1–3 times daily

**Ichthammol Ointment, BP 1980**

Ointment, ichthammol 10%, yellow soft paraffin 45%, wool fat 45%, net price 25 g = 53p

**Zinc and Ichthammol Cream, BP**

Cream, ichthammol 5%, cetostearyl alcohol 3%, wool fat 10%, in zinc cream, net price 100 g = 79p

**Zinc Paste and Ichthammol Bandage, BP 1993**

See Appendix 8 (section A8.2.9)

## 13.5.2 Preparations for psoriasis

Psoriasis is characterised by epidermal thickening and scaling. It commonly affects extensor surfaces and the scalp. For mild psoriasis, reassurance and treatment with an emollient may be all that is necessary.

Occasionally psoriasis is provoked or exacerbated by drugs such as lithium, chloroquine and hydroxychloroquine, beta-blockers, non-steroidal anti-inflammatory drugs, and ACE inhibitors. Psoriasis may not be seen until the drug has been taken for weeks or months.

**Emollients** (section 13.2.1), in addition to their effects on dryness, scaling and cracking, may have an antiproliferative effect in psoriasis. They are particularly useful in *inflammatory psoriasis* and in *plaque psoriasis of palms and soles*, in which irritant factors can perpetuate the condition. Emollients are useful adjuncts to other more specific treatment.

More specific treatment for *chronic stable plaque psoriasis* on extensor surfaces of trunk and limbs involves the use of **vitamin D analogues**, **coal tar**, **dithranol**, and the retinoid **tazarotene**. However, they can irritate the skin and they are not suitable for the more inflammatory forms of psoriasis; their use should be suspended during an inflammatory phase of psoriasis. The efficacy and the irritancy of each substance varies between patients. If a substance irritates significantly, it should be stopped or the concentration reduced; if it is tolerated, its effects should be assessed after 4 to 6 weeks and treatment continued if it is effective.

Widespread *unstable psoriasis* of erythrodermic or generalised pustular type requires urgent specialist assessment. Initial topical treatment should be limited to using emollients frequently and generously; emollients should be prescribed in quantities of 1 kg or more. More localised acute or subacute *inflammatory psoriasis* with hot, spreading or itchy lesions, should be treated topically with emollients or with a corticosteroid of medium potency.

**Calcipotriol** and **tacalcitol** are analogues of vitamin D that affect cell division and differentiation. **Calcitriol** is an active form of vitamin D. Vitamin D and its analogues do not smell or stain and they may be more acceptable than tar or dithranol products. Of the vitamin D analogues, tacalcitol and calcitriol are less likely to irritate.

**Coal tar** has anti-inflammatory properties that are useful in chronic plaque psoriasis; it also has antiscaling properties. Crude coal tar (coal tar, BP) is the most effective form, typically in a concentration of 1 to 10% in a soft paraffin base, but few outpatients tolerate the smell and mess. Cleaner extracts of coal tar included in proprietary preparations, are more practicable for home use but they are less effective and improvement takes longer. Contact of coal tar products with normal skin is not normally harmful and they can be used for widespread small lesions; however, irritation, contact allergy, and sterile folliculitis can occur. The milder tar extracts can be used on the face and flexures. Tar baths and tar shampoos are also helpful.

**Dithranol** is effective for chronic plaque psoriasis. Its major disadvantages are irritation (for which individual susceptibility varies) and staining of skin and of clothing. It should be applied to chronic extensor plaques only, carefully avoiding normal skin. Dithranol is not generally suitable for widespread small lesions nor should it be used in the flexures or on the face. Treatment should be started with a low concentration such as dithranol 0.1%, and the strength increased gradually every few days up to 3%, according to tolerance. Proprietary preparations are more suitable for home use; they are usually washed off after 5 to 60 minutes ('short contact'). Specialist nurses may apply intensive treatment with dithranol paste which is covered by stockinette dressings and usually retained overnight. Dithranol should be discontinued if even a low concentration causes acute inflammation; continued use can result in the psoriasis becoming unstable. When applying dithranol, hands should be protected by gloves or they should be washed thoroughly afterwards.

**Tazarotene**, a retinoid, is effective in psoriasis. It is clean and odourless. Irritation is common but it is minimised by applying tazarotene sparingly to the plaques and avoiding normal skin.

A topical **corticosteroid** (section 13.4) is not generally suitable as the sole treatment of extensive chronic plaque psoriasis; any early improvement is not usually maintained and there is a risk of the condition deteriorating or of precipitating an unstable form of psoriasis (e.g. erythrodermic psoriasis or generalised pustular psoriasis). However, it may be appropriate to treat psoriasis in specific sites such as the face and flexures usually with a mild corticosteroid, and psoriasis of the scalp, hands and feet with a potent corticosteroid.

Combining the use of a corticosteroid with another specific topical treatment may be beneficial in chronic plaque psoriasis; the drugs may be used separately at different times of the day or used together in a single formulation. *Eczema* co-existing with psoriasis may be treated with a corticosteroid, or coal tar, or both.

*Scalp psoriasis* is usually scaly, and the scale may be thick and adherent. This requires softening with an emollient ointment, cream, or oil and usually combined with **salicylic acid** as a keratolytic.

Some preparations prescribed for psoriasis affecting the scalp combine salicylic acid with coal tar or **sulphur**. Preparations containing salicylic acid, sulphur, and coal tar are available as proprietary products. The product should be applied generously and an adequate quantity should be prescribed. It should be left on for at least an hour, often more conveniently overnight, before washing it off. If a corticosteroid lotion or gel is required (e.g. for itch), it can be used in the morning.

**Phototherapy** **Phototherapy** is available in specialist centres under the supervision of a dermatologist. **Ultraviolet B** (UVB) radiation is usually effective for *chronic stable psoriasis* and for *guttate psoriasis*. It may be considered for patients with moderately severe psoriasis in whom topical treatment has failed, but it may irritate inflammatory psoriasis.

**Photochemotherapy** combining long-wave ultraviolet A radiation with a psoralen (PUVA) is available in specialist centres under the supervision of a dermatologist. The psoralen, which enhances the effect of irradiation, is administered either by mouth or topically. PUVA is effective in most forms of psoriasis, including *localised palmoplantar pustular psoriasis*. Early adverse effects include phototoxicity and pruritus. Higher cumulative doses exaggerate skin ageing, increase the risk of dysplastic and neoplastic skin lesions, especially squamous cancer, and pose a theoretical risk of cataracts.

Phototherapy combined with coal tar, dithranol, vitamin D or vitamin D analogues allows reduction of the cumulative dose of phototherapy required to treat psoriasis.

**Systemic treatment** **Systemic treatment** is required for severe, resistant, unstable or complicated forms of psoriasis, and it should be initiated only under specialist supervision. Systemic drugs for psoriasis include acitretin and drugs that act on the immune system (such as ciclosporin, hydroxycarbamide, and methotrexate, section 13.5.3).

Systemic corticosteroids should be used only rarely in psoriasis because rebound deterioration may occur on reducing the dose.

The main indication for **acitretin** is *psoriasis*, but it is also used in disorders of keratinisation such as severe *Darier's disease* (keratosis follicularis), and some forms of *ichthyosis*. Acitretin, a metabolite of etretinate, is a retinoid (vitamin A derivative). Although a minority of cases of psoriasis respond well to acitretin alone, it is only moderately effective in many cases and it is combined with other treatments. A therapeutic effect occurs after 2 to 4 weeks and the maximum benefit after 4 to 6 weeks or longer. Acitretin is prescribed by specialists and its availability is limited to hospital pharmacies or to a small number of specified retail pharmacies.

Apart from teratogenicity, which remains a risk for 2 years after stopping, acitretin is the least toxic systemic treatment for psoriasis; in women with a potential for child-bearing, the possibility of pregnancy must be excluded before treatment and pregnancy must be avoided during treatment and for a period of 2 years afterwards. Common side effects derive from its widespread but reversible effects on epithelia, such as dry and cracking lips, dry skin and mucosal surfaces, hair thinning, paronychia, and soft and sticky palms and soles. Liver function and blood lipid concentration should be monitored.



## Topical preparations for psoriasis

### Vitamin D and analogues

**Calcipotriol**, **calcitriol**, and **tacalcitol** are used for the management of *plaque psoriasis*. They should be avoided by those with calcium metabolism disorders, and used with caution in *generalised pustular* or *erythrodermic exfoliative psoriasis* (enhanced risk of hypercalcaemia). Local skin reactions (itching, erythema, burning, paraesthesia, dermatitis) are common. Hands should be washed thoroughly after application to avoid inadvertent transfer to other body areas. Aggravation of psoriasis has also been reported.

### CALCIPOTRIOL

**Indications** plaque psoriasis

**Cautions** see notes above; pregnancy (Appendix 4); avoid use on face; if used with UV treatment apply at least 2 hours before UV exposure

**Contra-indications** see notes above

**Side-effects** see notes above; also photosensitivity; rarely facial or perioral dermatitis, skin atrophy

**Dose**

- *cream* or *ointment* apply once or twice daily; max. 100 g weekly (less with *scalp solution*, see below); CHILD over 6 years, apply twice daily; 6–12 years max. 50 g weekly; over 12 years max. 75 g weekly

Note Patient information leaflets for *Dovonex®* cream and ointment advise liberal application (but note max. recommended weekly dose, above)

**Dovonex®** (LEO) PoM

Cream, calcipotriol 50 micrograms/g, net price 60 g = £13.04, 120 g = £26.07

Excipients include cetostearyl alcohol, disodium edetate

Ointment, calcipotriol 50 micrograms/g, net price 60 g = £12.02, 120 g = £26.07

Excipients include disodium edetate, propylene glycol

Scalp solution, calcipotriol 50 micrograms/mL, net price 60 mL = £13.04, 120 mL = £26.07

Excipients include propylene glycol

Dose scalp psoriasis, apply to scalp twice daily; max. 60 mL weekly (less with cream or ointment, see below); CHILD not recommended

Note When preparations used together max. total calcipotriol 5 mg in any one week (e.g. scalp solution 60 mL with cream or ointment 30 g *or* cream or ointment 60 g with scalp solution 30 mL)

### With betamethasone

For cautions, contra-indications, side-effects, and for comment on the limited role of corticosteroids in psoriasis, see section 13.4.

**Dovobet®** (LEO) PoM

Ointment, betamethasone 0.05% (as dipropionate), calcipotriol 50 micrograms/g, net price 60 g = £35.00. Label: 28

Excipients none as listed in section 13.1.3

Dose initial treatment of stable plaque psoriasis, apply once daily to max. 30% of body surface for up to 4 weeks; max. 15 g daily, max. 100 g weekly; CHILD and ADOLESCENT under 18 years not recommended

## CALCITRIOL
### (1,25-Dihydroxycholecalciferol)

**Indications** mild to moderate plaque psoriasis

**Cautions** see notes above; liver impairment (Appendix 2), renal impairment (Appendix 3); pregnancy (Appendix 4)

**Contra-indications** see notes above; do not apply under occlusion

**Side-effects** see notes above

**Dose**

- Apply twice daily; not more than 35% of body surface to be treated daily, max. 30 g daily; CHILD not recommended

**Silkis®** (Galderma) ▼ PoM

Ointment, calcitriol 3 micrograms/g, net price 30 g = £5.76, 100 g = £16.34

Excipients none as listed in section 13.1.3

## TACALCITOL

**Indications** plaque psoriasis

**Cautions** see notes above; pregnancy (Appendix 4), breast-feeding (Appendix 5); avoid eyes; monitor plasma calcium if risk of hypercalcaemia or in renal impairment; if used in conjunction with UV treatment, UV radiation should be given in the morning and tacalcitol applied at bedtime

**Contra-indications** see notes above

**Side-effects** see notes above

**Dose**

- Apply daily preferably at bedtime; max. 10 g daily; CHILD not recommended

**Curatoderm®** (Crookes) PoM

Ointment, tacalcitol (as monohydrate) 4 micrograms/g, net price 30 g = £15.09, 60 g = £26.06, 100 g = £34.75

Excipients none as listed in section 13.1.3

## Tazarotene

## TAZAROTENE

**Indications** mild to moderate plaque psoriasis affecting up to 10% of skin area

**Cautions** wash hands immediately after use, avoid contact with eyes, face, intertriginous areas, hair-covered scalp, eczematous or inflamed skin; avoid excessive exposure to UV light (including sunlight, solariums, PUVA or UVB treatment); do not apply emollients or cosmetics within 1 hour of application

**Contra-indications** pregnancy—advise women of child-bearing age to ensure adequate contraceptive protection; breast-feeding (Appendix 5)

**Side-effects** local irritation (more common with higher concentration and may require discontinuation), pruritus, burning, erythema, desquamation, non-specific rash, contact dermatitis, and worsening of psoriasis; rarely stinging and inflamed, dry or painful skin

**Dose**

- Apply once daily in the evening usually for up to 12 weeks; CHILD under 18 years not recommended

**Zorac®** (Allergan) PoM

Gel, tazarotene 0.05%, net price 30 g = £14.09; 0.1%, 30 g = £14.80

Excipients include benzyl alcohol, butylated hydroxyanisole, butylated hydroxytoluene, disodium edetate, polysorbate 40

## Coal tar

## COAL TAR

**Indications** psoriasis and occasionally chronic atopic eczema

**Cautions** avoid eyes, mucosa, genital or rectal areas, and broken or inflamed skin; use suitable chemical protection gloves for extemporaneous preparation

**Contra-indications** not for use in sore, acute, or pustular psoriasis or in presence of infection

**Side-effects** skin irritation and acne-like eruptions, photosensitivity; stains skin, hair, and fabric

**Dose**

- Apply 1–3 times daily starting with low-strength preparations

Note For shampoo preparations see section 13.9; impregnated dressings see Appendix 8 (section A8.2.9)

### Non-proprietary preparations

May be difficult to obtain—some patients may find newer proprietary preparations more acceptable

**Calamine and Coal Tar Ointment, BP**

Ointment, calamine 12.5 g, strong coal tar solution 2.5 g, zinc oxide 12.5 g, hydrous wool fat 25 g, white soft paraffin 47.5 g

Excipients include wool fat

Dose apply 1–2 times daily

**Coal Tar and Salicylic Acid Ointment, BP**
Ointment, coal tar 2 g, salicylic acid 2 g, emulsifying wax 11.4 g, white soft paraffin 19 g, coconut oil 54 g, polysorbate '80' 4 g, liquid paraffin 7.6 g
Excipients include cetostearyl alcohol
Dose apply 1–2 times daily

**Coal Tar Paste, BP**
Paste, strong coal tar solution 7.5%, in compound zinc paste
Dose apply 1–2 times daily

**Zinc and Coal Tar Paste, BP**
Paste, zinc oxide 6%, coal tar 6%, emulsifying wax 5%, starch 38%, yellow soft paraffin 45%
Excipients include cetostearyl alcohol
Dose apply 1–2 times daily

### Proprietary preparations

**Carbo-Dome®** (Sandoz)
Cream, coal tar solution 10%, in a water-miscible basis, net price 30 g = £4.77, 100 g = £16.38
Excipients include beeswax, hydroxybenzoates (parabens)
Dose psoriasis, apply to skin 2–3 times daily

**Clinitar®** (CHS)
Cream, coal tar extract 1%, net price 100 g = £10.99
Excipients include cetostearyl alcohol, isopropyl palmitate, propylene glycol
Dose psoriasis and eczema, apply to skin 1–2 times daily

**Cocois®** (Celltech)
Scalp ointment, coal tar solution 12%, salicylic acid 2%, precipitated sulphur 4%, in a coconut oil emollient basis, net price 40 g (with applicator nozzle) = £6.65, 100 g = £12.30
Excipients include cetostearyl alcohol
Dose scaly scalp disorders including psoriasis, eczema, seborrhoeic dermatitis and dandruff, apply to scalp once weekly as necessary (if severe use daily for first 3–7 days), shampoo off after 1 hour; CHILD 6–12 years, medical supervision required (not recommended under 6 years)

**Exorex®** (Forest)
Lotion, prepared coal tar 1% in an emollient basis, net price 100 mL = £8.11, 250 mL = £16.24
Excipients include hydroxybenzoates (parabens), polysorbate 80
Dose psoriasis, apply to skin or scalp 2–3 times daily; CHILD and ELDERLY, dilute with a few drops of water before applying

**Pragmatar®** (Alliance)
Cream, cetyl alcohol-coal tar distillate 4%, salicylic acid 3%, sulphur (precipitated) 3%, net price 25 g = £3.04, 100 g = £9.82
Excipients include cetyl alcohol, fragrance
Dose scaly skin disorders, apply thinly once daily; dandruff and other seborrhoeic conditions, apply to scalp once weekly or in severe cases daily; INFANT dilute with a few drops of water before application

**Psoriderm®** (Dermal)
Cream, coal tar 6%, lecithin 0.4%, net price 225 mL = £9.85
Excipients include isopropyl palmitate, propylene glycol
Dose psoriasis, apply to skin or scalp 1–2 times daily
Scalp lotion—section 13.9

**Sebco®** (Centrapharm)
Scalp ointment, coal tar solution 12%, salicylic acid 2%, precipitated sulphur 4%, in a coconut oil emollient basis, net price 40 g = £4.54, 100 g = £8.52
Excipients include cetostearyl alcohol
Dose scaly scalp disorders including psoriasis, eczema, seborrhoeic dermatitis and dandruff, apply to scalp as necessary (if severe use daily for first 3–7 days), shampoo off after 1 hour; CHILD 6–12 years, medical supervision required (not recommended under 6 years)

### Bath preparations

**Coal Tar Solution, BP**
Solution, coal tar 20%, polysorbate '80' 5%, in alcohol (96%), net price 100 mL = 91p
Excipients include polysorbates
Dose use 100 mL in a bath
Note Strong Coal Tar Solution BP contains coal tar 40%

**Pinetarsol®** (Crawford)
Bath oil, coal tar 2.3% in a light liquid paraffin basis, net price 200 mL = £4.75, 500 mL = £7.95
Excipients include fragrance
Dose eczema and psoriasis, use 15–30 mL in a bath or apply directly to wet skin and rinse after a few minutes; can be used as soap substitute
Gel, coal tar 1.6%, net price 100 g = £4.95
Dose eczema and psoriasis, apply directly to wet skin and rinse after a few minutes; can be used as soap substitute
Solution, coal tar 2.3%, net price 200 mL = £4.45, 500 mL = £7.45
Dose eczema and psoriasis, use 15–30 mL in a bath *or* dilute 15 mL with 3 litres of water and apply to affected areas *or* apply solution directly to wet skin and rinse after a few minutes; can be used as soap substitute

**Polytar Emollient®** (Stiefel)
Bath additive, coal tar solution 2.5%, arachis (peanut) oil extract of coal tar 7.5%, tar 7.5%, cade oil 7.5%, liquid paraffin 35%, net price 500 mL = £5.78
Excipients include isopropyl palmitate
Dose psoriasis, eczema, atopic and pruritic dermatoses, use 2–4 capfuls (15–30 mL) in bath and soak for 20 minutes

**Psoriderm®** (Dermal)
Bath emulsion, coal tar 40%, net price 200 mL = £2.87
Excipients include polysorbate 20
Dose psoriasis, use 30 mL in a bath and soak for 5 minutes

### With corticosteroids

**Alphosyl HC®** (GSK Consumer Healthcare) PoM
Cream, coal tar extract 5%, hydrocortisone 0.5%, allantoin 2%, net price 100 g = £3.54. Label: 28. Potency: mild
Excipients include beeswax, cetyl alcohol, hydroxybenzoates (parabens), isopropyl palmitate, wool fat
Dose psoriasis, apply thinly 1–2 times daily; CHILD under 5 years not recommended

## Dithranol

### DITHRANOL
**(Anthralin)**

**Indications** subacute and chronic psoriasis, see notes above

**Cautions** avoid use near eyes and sensitive areas of skin; see also notes above

**Contra-indications** hypersensitivity; acute and pustular psoriasis

**Side-effects** local burning sensation and irritation; stains skin, hair, and fabrics

**Dose**
- See notes above and under preparations

Note Some of these dithranol preparations also contain coal tar or salicylic acid—for cautions and side-effects see under Coal Tar (above) or under Salicylic Acid

**Non-proprietary preparations**

**[1]Dithranol Ointment, BP** (PoM)

Ointment, dithranol, in yellow soft paraffin; usual strengths 0.1–2%. Part of basis may be replaced by hard paraffin if a stiffer preparation is required. Label: 28

1. (PoM) if dithranol content more than 1%, otherwise may be sold to the public

**Dithranol Paste, BP**

Paste, dithranol in zinc and salicylic acid (Lassar's) paste. Usual strengths 0.1–1% of dithranol. Label: 28

**Proprietary preparations**

**Dithrocream®** (Dermal)

Cream, dithranol 0.1%, net price 50 g = £3.94; 0.25%, 50 g = £4.23; 0.5%, 50 g = £4.87; 1%, 50 g = £5.67; (PoM) 2%, 50 g = £7.10. Label: 28

Excipients include cetostearyl alcohol, chlorocresol

Dose for application to skin or scalp; 0.1–0.5% suitable for overnight treatment, 1–2% for max. 1 hour

**Micanol®** (GP Pharma)

Cream, dithranol 1% in a lipid-stabilised basis, net price 50 g = £10.37; (PoM) 3%, 50 g = £12.92. Label: 28

Excipients none as listed in section 13.1.3

Dose for application to skin, for up to 30 minutes, if necessary 3% cream may be used under medical supervision; apply to scalp for up to 30 minutes

Note At the end of contact time use plenty of lukewarm (not hot) water to rinse off cream; soap should not be used

**Psorin®** (LPC)

Ointment, dithranol 0.11%, coal tar 1%, salicylic acid 1.6%, net price 50 g = £8.20, 100 g = £16.35. Label: 28

Excipients include beeswax, wool fat

Dose for application to skin up to twice daily

Scalp gel, dithranol 0.25%, salicylic acid 1.6% in gel basis containing methyl salicylate, net price 50 g = £6.25. Label: 28

Excipients none as listed in section 13.1.3

Dose for application to scalp, initially apply on alternate days for 10–20 minutes; may be increased to daily application for max. 1 hour and then wash off

## Salicylic acid

### SALICYLIC ACID

For coal tar preparations containing salicylic acid, see under Coal Tar p. 582; for dithranol preparations containing salicylic acid see under Dithranol, above

**Indications** hyperkeratotic skin disorders; acne (section 13.6.1); warts and calluses (section 13.7); scalp conditions (section 13.9); fungal nail infections (section 13.10.2)

**Cautions** see notes above; avoid broken or inflamed skin

Salicylate toxicity If large areas of skin are treated, salicylate toxicity may be a hazard

**Side-effects** sensitivity, excessive drying, irritation, systemic effects after widespread use (see under Cautions)

**Zinc and Salicylic Acid Paste, BP**

Paste, (Lassar's Paste), zinc oxide 24%, salicylic acid 2%, starch 24%, white soft paraffin 50%, net price 25 g = 17p

Dose apply twice daily

## Oral retinoids for psoriasis

### ACITRETIN

Note Acitretin is a metabolite of etretinate

**Indications** severe extensive psoriasis resistant to other forms of therapy; palmoplantar pustular psoriasis; severe congenital ichthyosis; severe Darier's disease (keratosis follicularis)

**Cautions** exclude pregnancy before starting (test for pregnancy within 2 weeks before treatment and monthly thereafter; start treatment on day 2 or 3 of menstrual cycle)—women (including those with history of infertility) should avoid pregnancy for at least 1 month before, during, and for at least 2 years after treatment; patients should avoid concomitant tetracycline or methotrexate, high doses of vitamin A (more than 4000–5000 units daily) and use of keratolytics, and should not donate blood during or for at least 1 year after stopping therapy (teratogenic risk); check liver function at start, then every 1–2 weeks for 2 months, then every 3 months; monitor plasma lipids; diabetes (can alter glucose tolerance—initial frequent blood glucose checks); radiographic assessment on long-term treatment; investigate atypical musculoskeletal symptoms; in children use only in exceptional circumstances (premature epiphyseal closure reported); avoid excessive exposure to sunlight and unsupervised use of sunlamps; **interactions:** Appendix 1 (retinoids)

**Contra-indications** hepatic impairment (Appendix 2); renal impairment (Appendix 3); hyperlipidaemia, pregnancy (**important teratogenic risk:** see Cautions above); breast-feeding

**Side-effects** dryness of mucous membranes (sometimes erosion), of skin (sometimes scaling, thinning, erythema especially of face, and pruritus), and of conjunctiva (sometimes conjunctivitis and decreased tolerance of contact lenses); sticky skin, dermatitis; other side-effects reported include palmoplantar exfoliation, epistaxis, epidermal and nail fragility, oedema, paronychia, granulomatous lesions, bullous eruptions, reversible hair thinning and alopecia, myalgia and arthralgia, occasional nausea, headache, malaise, drowsiness, rhinitis, sweating, taste disturbance, and gingivitis; benign intracranial hypertension (discontinue if severe headache, vomiting, diarrhoea, abdominal pain, and visual disturbance occur; **avoid** concomitant tetracyclines); photosensitivity, corneal ulceration, raised liver enzymes, rarely jaundice and hepatitis (**avoid** concomitant methotrexate); raised triglycerides; decreased night vision reported; skeletal hyperostosis and extra-osseous calcification reported following long-term administration of etretinate (and premature epiphyseal closure in children, see Cautions)

**Dose**

- Under expert supervision, initially 25–30 mg daily (Darier's disease 10 mg daily) for 2–4 weeks, then adjusted according to response, usual range 25–50 mg daily (max. 75 mg daily) for further 6–8 weeks (in Darier's disease and ichthyosis not more than 50 mg daily for up to 6 months); CHILD (**important:** exceptional circumstances only, see Cautions), 500 micrograms/kg daily (occasionally up to 1 mg/kg daily to max. 35 mg daily for limited periods) with careful monitoring of musculoskeletal development

**Neotigason®** (Roche) PoM

Capsules, acitretin 10 mg (brown/white), net price 60-cap pack = £25.25; 25 mg (brown/yellow), 60-cap pack = £58.59 (hosp. or specified retail pharmacy only—consult product literature for details, specialist dermatological supervision). Label: 10, patient information leaflet, 21

## 13.5.3 Drugs affecting the immune response

Drugs affecting the immune response are used for eczema or psoriasis. Systemic drugs acting on the immune system are generally used by **specialists** in a hospital setting.

**Ciclosporin** (cyclosporin) by mouth can be used for *severe psoriasis* and for *severe eczema*. **Azathioprine** (section 8.2.1) or **mycophenolate mofetil** (section 8.2.1) are used for severe refractory eczema [unlicensed indication]. **Hydroxycarbamide** (hydroxyurea) (section 8.1.5) is used by mouth for severe psoriasis [unlicensed indication].

**Methotrexate** may be used for *severe psoriasis*, the dose being adjusted according to severity of the condition and haematological and biochemical measurements; the usual dose is methotrexate 10 to 25 mg **once weekly**, by mouth. Folic acid may be given to reduce the possibility of methotrexate toxicity. For *severe psoriasis* refractory to at least two systemic treatments and photochemotherapy or if other treatments are not tolerated, **efalizumab**, which inhibits T-cell activation and is licensed for moderate and severe *chronic plaque psoriasis*, or the cytokine inhibitors **etanercept** and **infliximab** (section 10.1.3) may be used; etanercept and infliximab are also licensed for *psoriatic arthritis*.

**Pimecrolimus** by topical application is licensed for *mild to moderate atopic eczema* for short-term use to treat signs and symptoms and for intermittent use to prevent flares. **Tacrolimus** is licensed for topical use in *moderate to severe atopic eczema*. Both are drugs whose long-term safety and place in therapy is still being evaluated and they should not usually be considered first-line treatments unless there is a specific reason to avoid or reduce the use of topical corticosteroids.

For the role of corticosteroids in eczema see section 13.5.1 and for comment on their limited role in psoriasis see section 13.4.

> **NICE guidance (tacrolimus and pimecrolimus for atopic eczema)**
> NICE has recommended (August 2004) that topical pimecrolimus and tacrolimus are options for atopic eczema not controlled by maximal topical corticosteroid treatment or if there is a risk of important corticosteroid side-effects (particularly skin atrophy).
> Topical pimecrolimus is recommended for moderate atopic eczema on the face and neck of children aged 2–16 years and topical tacrolimus is recommended for moderate to severe atopic eczema in adults and children over 2 years. Pimecrolimus and tacrolimus should be used within their licensed indications.

### CICLOSPORIN
(Cyclosporin)

**Indications** see under Dose; transplantation and graft-versus-host disease (section 8.2.2)

**Cautions** see section 8.2.2

**Additional cautions in atopic dermatitis and psoriasis** *Contra-indicated* in abnormal renal function, hypertension not under control (see also below), infections not under control, and malignancy (see also below). Dermatological and physical examination, including blood pressure and renal function measurements required at least twice before starting; discontinue if hypertension develops that cannot be controlled by dose reduction or antihypertensive therapy; avoid excessive exposure to sunlight and use of UVB or PUVA; *in atopic dermatitis*, also allow herpes simplex infections to clear before starting (if they occur during treatment withdraw if severe); *Staphylococcus aureus* skin infections not absolute contra-indication providing controlled (but avoid erythromycin unless no other alternative—see also **interactions**: Appendix 1 (ciclosporin)); monitor serum creatinine every 2 weeks during treatment; *in psoriasis*, also exclude malignancies (including those of skin and cervix) before starting (biopsy any lesions not typical of psoriasis) and treat patients with malignant or pre-malignant conditions of skin only after appropriate treatment (and if no other option); monitor serum creatinine every 2 weeks for first 3 months then every 2 months (monthly if dose more than 2.5 mg/kg daily), reducing dose by 25–50% if increases more than 30% above baseline (even if within normal range) and discontinuing if reduction not successful within 1 month; also discontinue if lymphoproliferative disorder develops

**Side-effects** see section 8.2.2

**Dose**

- Short-term treatment (max. 8 weeks) of severe atopic dermatitis where conventional therapy ineffective or inappropriate, administered in accordance with expert advice, by mouth, ADULT over 16 years, initially 2.5 mg/kg daily in 2 divided doses, if good initial response not achieved within 2 weeks, increase rapidly to max. 5 mg/kg daily; initial dose of 5 mg/kg daily in 2 divided doses if very severe; CHILD and ADOLESCENT under 16 years not recommended
- Severe psoriasis where conventional therapy ineffective or inappropriate, administered in accordance with expert advice, by mouth, ADULT over 16 years, initially 2.5 mg/kg daily in 2 divided doses, increased gradually to max. 5 mg/kg daily if no improvement within 1 month (discontinue if response still insufficient after 6 weeks); initial dose of 5 mg/kg daily justified if condition requires rapid improvement; CHILD and ADOLESCENT under 16 years not recommended

**Important** For preparations and counselling and for advice on conversion between the preparations, see section 8.2.2

**Preparations**
Section 8.2.2

### EFALIZUMAB

**Indications** moderate to severe chronic plaque psoriasis for those whose disease is unresponsive to, or who are intolerant of other systemic therapy or photochemotherapy

**Cautions** low platelet count (monitor platelet count before treatment, monthly during initial therapy then every 3 months), hepatic impairment, renal impairment; **interactions**: Appendix 1 (efalizumab)

**Contra-indications** immunodeficiency, severe infection, active tuberculosis; history of malignancy; pregnancy and breast-feeding (Appendix 5)

**Side-effects** influenza-like symptoms, leucocytosis, arthralgia, exacerbation of psoriasis or development of variant forms including psoriatic arthritis (discontinue treatment), *less commonly* thrombocytopenia and injection-site reactions

**Dose**

- By subcutaneous injection, initially 700 micrograms/kg then 1 mg/kg *weekly*; discontinue if inadequate response after 12 weeks; CHILD and ADOLESCENT not recommended

**Raptiva®** (Serono) ▼ PoM
Injection, powder for reconstitution, efalizumab, net price 125-mg vial = £169.20 (with 1.3 mL water for injections in prefilled syringe )
Note The Scottish Medicines Consortium has advised (January 2005) that *Raptiva®* is **not** recommended for the treatment of psoriasis

## METHOTREXATE

**Indications** severe psoriasis unresponsive to conventional therapy (specialist use only); Crohn's disease (section 1.5); malignant disease (section 8.1.3); rheumatoid arthritis (section 10.1.3)

**Cautions** section 10.1.3; also photosensitivity—psoriasis lesions aggravated by UV radiation (skin ulceration reported)

**Contra-indications** section 10.1.3

**Side-effects** section 10.1.3

**Dose**

- By mouth, 10–25 mg once weekly, adjusted according to response; ELDERLY consider dose reduction (extreme caution); CHILD not recommended

> Important
> Note that the above dose is a **weekly** dose. The CSM has received reports of prescription and dispensing errors including fatalities. Attention should be paid to the **strength** of methotrexate tablets prescribed and the **frequency** of dosing.

Preparations
Section 10.1.3

## PIMECROLIMUS

**Indications** acute treatment of mild to moderate atopic eczema (including flares)

**Cautions** UV light (avoid excessive exposure to sunlight and sunlamps), avoid other topical treatments except emollients at treatment site; alcohol consumption (risk of facial flushing and skin irritation)

**Contra-indications** contact with eyes and mucous membranes, application under occlusion, infection at treatment site; congenital epidermal barrier defects; generalised erythroderma

**Side-effects** burning sensation, pruritus, erythema, skin infections (including folliculitis and *less commonly* impetigo, herpes simplex and zoster, molluscum contagiosum); *less commonly* papilloma, local reactions including pain, paraesthesia, peeling, dryness, oedema, and worsening of eczema

**Dose**

- Apply twice daily until symptoms resolve; CHILD under 2 years not recommended

**Elidel®** (Novartis) ▼ PoM
Cream, pimecrolimus 1%, net price 30 g = £19.69, 60 g = £37.41, 100 g = £59.07. Label: 4, 28
Excipients include benzyl alcohol, cetyl alcohol, propylene glycol, stearyl alcohol

## TACROLIMUS

**Indications** moderate to severe atopic eczema unresponsive to conventional therapy (prescribed by physicians experienced in treating atopic eczema); other indications section 8.2.2

**Cautions** infection at treatment site, UV light (avoid excessive exposure to sunlight and sunlamps); alcohol consumption (risk of facial flushing and skin irritation)

**Contra-indications** avoid contact with eyes and mucous membranes, application under occlusion; congenital epidermal barrier defects; generalised erythroderma; pregnancy and breast-feeding

**Side-effects** application-site reactions including rash, irritation, pain and paraesthesia; herpes simplex infection, Kaposi's varicelliform eruption; *less commonly* acne; acne rosacea also reported

**Dose**

- ADULT and ADOLESCENT over 16 years initially apply 0.1% ointment thinly twice daily until lesion clears (consider other treatment options if no improvement after 2 weeks); reduce to once daily or switch to 0.03% ointment if clinical condition allows; CHILD 2–15 years, initially apply 0.03% ointment twice daily for up to 3 weeks then reduce to once daily until lesion clears

**Protopic®** (Astellas) ▼ PoM
Ointment, tacrolimus (as monohydrate) 0.03%, net price 30 g = £19.44, 60 g = £36.94; 0.1%, 30 g = £21.60, 60 g = £41.04. Label: 4, 11, 28
Excipients include beeswax

# 13.6 Acne and rosacea

**13.6.1** Topical preparations for acne
**13.6.2** Oral preparations for acne

**Acne** Treatment of acne should be commenced early to prevent scarring. Patients should be counselled that an improvement may not be seen for at least a couple of months. The choice of treatment depends on whether the acne is predominantly inflammatory or comedonal and its severity.

*Mild to moderate acne* is generally treated with topical preparations (section 13.6.1). Systemic treatment (section 13.6.2) with oral antibiotics is generally used for *moderate to severe acne* or where topical preparations are not tolerated or are ineffective or where application to the site is difficult. Another oral preparation used for acne is the hormone treatment co-cyprindiol (cyproterone acetate with ethinylestradiol); it is for women only.

*Severe acne*, acne unresponsive to prolonged courses of oral antibiotics, scarring, or acne associated with psychological problems calls for early referral to a consultant dermatologist who may prescribe isotretinoin for administration by mouth.

**Rosacea** Rosacea is not comedonal (but may exist with acne which may be comedonal). The pustules and papules of rosacea respond to topical metronidazole (section 13.10.1.2) or to oral administration of oxytetracycline or tetracycline 500 mg twice daily (section 5.1.3) or of erythromycin 500 mg twice daily (section 5.1.5); courses usually last 6–12 weeks and are repeated intermittently. Alternatively, doxycycline (section 5.1.3) in a dose of 100 mg once daily may be used [unlicensed indication] if oxytetracycline or tetracycline is inappropriate (e.g. in renal impairment). Isotretinoin is occasionally given in refractory cases [unlicensed indication]. Camouflagers (section 13.8.2) may be required for the redness.

## 13.6.1 Topical preparations for acne

Significant comedonal acne responds well to topical retinoids (see p. 588), whereas both comedones and inflamed lesions respond well to benzoyl peroxide or azelaic acid (see below). Alternatively, topical application of an antibiotic such as erythromycin or clindamycin may be effective for inflammatory acne. If topical preparations prove inadequate oral preparations may be needed (section 13.6.2).

### Benzoyl peroxide and azelaic acid

**Benzoyl peroxide** is effective in mild to moderate acne. Both comedones and inflamed lesions respond well to benzoyl peroxide. The lower concentrations seem to be as effective as higher concentrations in reducing inflammation. It is usual to start with a lower strength and to increase the concentration of benzoyl peroxide gradually. Adverse effects include local skin irritation, particularly when therapy is initiated, but the scaling and redness often subside with treatment continued at a reduced frequency of application. If the acne does not respond after 2 months then use of a topical antibacterial should be considered.

**Azelaic acid** has antimicrobial and anticomedonal properties. It may be an alternative to benzoyl peroxide or to a topical retinoid for treating mild to moderate comedonal acne, particularly of the face. Some patients prefer it because it is less likely to cause local irritation than benzoyl peroxide.

#### BENZOYL PEROXIDE

**Indications** acne vulgaris

**Cautions** avoid contact with eyes, mouth, and mucous membranes; may bleach fabrics and hair; avoid excessive exposure to sunlight

**Side-effects** skin irritation (reduce frequency or suspend use until irritation subsides and re-introduce at reduced frequency)

**Dose**

- Apply 1–2 times daily preferably after washing with soap and water, start treatment with lower-strength preparations

Note May bleach clothing

**Brevoxyl®** (Stiefel)

Cream, benzoyl peroxide 4% in an aqueous basis, net price 40 g = £3.30

Excipients include cetyl alcohol, fragrance, stearyl alcohol

**PanOxyl®** (Stiefel)

Aquagel (= aqueous gel), benzoyl peroxide 2.5%, net price 40 g = £1.76; 5%, 40 g = £1.92; 10%, 40 g = £2.07

Excipients include propylene glycol

Cream, benzoyl peroxide 5% in a non-greasy basis, net price 40 g = £1.51

Excipients include isopropyl palmitate, propylene glycol

Gel, benzoyl peroxide 5% in an aqueous alcoholic basis, net price 40 g = £1.51; 10%, 40 g = £1.69

Excipients include fragrance

Wash, benzoyl peroxide 10% in a detergent basis, net price 150 mL = £4.00

Excipients include imidurea

**With antimicrobials**

**Benzamycin®** (Schwarz) PoM

Gel, pack for reconstitution, providing erythromycin 3% and benzoyl peroxide 5% in an alcoholic basis, net price per pack to provide 46.6 g = £15.62

Excipients none as listed in section 13.1.3

Dose apply twice daily (very fair skin, initially once daily at night)

**Duac® Once Daily** (Stiefel) PoM

Gel, benzoyl peroxide 5%, clindamycin 1% (as phosphate) in an aqueous basis, net price 25 g = £9.95, 50 g = £19.90

Excipients include disodium edetate

Dose apply once daily in the evening

**Quinoderm®** (Ferndale)

Cream, benzoyl peroxide 5%, potassium hydroxyquinoline sulphate 0.5%, in an astringent vanishing-cream basis, net price 50 g = £2.21

Excipients include cetostearyl alcohol, edetic acid (EDTA)

Cream, benzoyl peroxide 10%, potassium hydroxyquinoline sulphate 0.5%, in an astringent vanishing-cream basis, net price 25 g = £1.30, 50 g = £2.49

Excipients include cetostearyl alcohol, edetic acid (EDTA)

#### AZELAIC ACID

**Indications** acne vulgaris

**Cautions** pregnancy, breast-feeding; avoid contact with eyes

**Side-effects** local irritation (reduce frequency or discontinue use temporarily); rarely photosensitisation

**Skinoren®** (Schering Health) PoM

Cream, azelaic acid 20%, net price 30 g = £3.74

Excipients include propylene glycol

Dose apply twice daily (sensitive skin, once daily for first week). Extended treatment may be required but manufacturer advises period of treatment should not exceed 6 months



### Topical antibacterials for acne

For many patients with mild to moderate inflammatory acne, topical antibacterials may be no more effective than topical benzoyl peroxide or tretinoin. Topical antibacterials are probably best reserved for patients who wish to avoid oral antibacterials or who cannot tolerate them. Topical preparations of **erythromycin** and **clindamycin** are effective for inflammatory acne; topical preparations of tetracycline may also be effective. Topical antibacterials can produce mild irritation of the skin, and on rare occasions cause sensitisation.

Antibacterial resistance of *Propionibacterium acnes* is increasing; there is cross-resistance between erythromycin and clindamycin. To avoid development of resistance:

- when possible use non-antibiotic antimicrobials (such as benzoyl peroxide or azelaic acid);
- avoid concomitant treatment with different oral and topical antibiotics;
- if a particular antibiotic is effective, use it for repeat courses if needed (short intervening courses of a

topical antibacterial, such as benzoyl peroxide or azelaic acid, may eliminate any resistant propionibacteria);
- do not continue treatment for longer than necessary (however, treatment with a topical preparation should be continued for at least 6 months)

## ANTIBIOTICS

**Indications** acne vulgaris

**Cautions** some manufacturers advise preparations containing alcohol are not suitable for use with benzoyl peroxide

**Benzamycin®** PoM

See under Benzoyl Peroxide above

**Dalacin T®** (Pharmacia) PoM

Topical solution, clindamycin 1% (as phosphate), in an aqueous alcoholic basis, net price (both with applicator) 30 mL = £4.34, 50 mL = £7.23

Excipients include propylene glycol

Dose apply twice daily

Lotion, clindamycin 1% (as phosphate) in an aqueous basis, net price 30 mL = £5.08, 50 mL = £8.47

Excipients include cetostearyl alcohol, hydroxybenzoates (parabens)

Dose apply twice daily

**Stiemycin®** (Stiefel) PoM

Solution, erythromycin 2% in an alcoholic basis, net price 50 mL = £8.00

Excipients include propylene glycol

Dose apply twice daily

**Topicycline®** (Shire) PoM

Solution, powder for reconstitution, tetracycline hydrochloride, 4-epitetracycline hydrochloride, providing tetracycline hydrochloride 2.2 mg/mL when reconstituted with solvent containing *n*-decyl methyl sulphoxide and citric acid in 40% alcohol. Net price per pack of powder and solvent to provide 70 mL = £6.15

Excipients none as listed in section 13.1.3

Dose apply twice daily

**Zindaclin®** (Strakan) PoM

Gel, clindamycin 1% (as phosphate), net price 30 g = £8.66

Excipients include propylene glycol

Dose apply once daily

**Zineryt®** (Astellas) PoM

Topical solution, powder for reconstitution, erythromycin 40 mg, zinc acetate 12 mg/mL when reconstituted with solvent containing ethanol, net price per pack of powder and solvent to provide 30 mL = £7.71, 90 mL = £22.24

Excipients none as listed in section 13.1.3

Dose apply twice daily

## Topical retinoids and related preparations for acne

**Tretinoin** and its isomer **isotretinoin** are useful in treating comedonal acne but patients should be warned that some redness and skin peeling might occur initially but settles with time. Several months of treatment may be needed to achieve an optimal response and the treatment should be continued until no new lesions develop.

Topical **isotretinoin** is licensed to treat non-inflammatory and inflammatory lesions in patients with mild to moderate acne. Isotretinoin is also given by mouth; see section 13.6.2 for **warnings** relating to use by mouth.

**Adapalene**, a retinoid-like drug, is licensed for mild to moderate acne. It is less irritant than topical retinoids.

**Cautions** Topical retinoids should be avoided in severe acne involving large areas. Contact with eyes, nostrils, mouth and mucous membranes, eczematous, broken or sunburned skin should be avoided. These drugs should be used with caution in sensitive areas such as the neck, and accumulation in angles of the nose should be avoided. Exposure to UV light (including sunlight, solariums) should be avoided; if sun exposure is unavoidable, an appropriate sunscreen or protective clothing should be used. Use of retinoids with abrasive cleaners, comedogenic or astringent cosmetics should be avoided. Allow peeling (e.g. resulting from use of benzoyl peroxide) to subside before using a topical retinoid; alternating a preparation that causes peeling with a topical retinoid may give rise to contact dermatitis (reduce frequency of retinoid application).

**Contra-indications** Topical retinoids are contra-indicated in pregnancy (Appendix 4); women of child-bearing age should take adequate contraceptive precautions. Tretinoin is contra-indicated in personal or familial history of cutaneous epithelioma.

**Side-effects** Local reactions include burning, erythema, stinging, pruritus, dry or peeling skin (discontinue if severe). Increased sensitivity to UVB light or sunlight occurs. Temporary changes of skin pigmentation have been reported. Eye irritation and oedema, and blistering or crusting of skin have been reported rarely.

## ADAPALENE

**Indications** mild to moderate acne

**Cautions** see notes above

**Contra-indications** see notes above

**Side-effects** see notes above

**Dose**

- Apply thinly once daily before retiring

**Differin®** (Galderma) PoM

Cream, adapalene 0.1%, net price 45 g = £11.40

Excipients include disodium edetate, hydroxybenzoates (parabens)

Gel, adapalene 0.1%, net price 45 g = £11.40

Excipients include disodium edetate, hydroxybenzoates (parabens), propylene glycol

## TRETINOIN

**Note** Tretinoin is the acid form of vitamin A

**Indications** see under preparations below; photodamage (section 13.8.1); malignant disease (section 8.1.5)

**Cautions** see notes above

**Contra-indications** see notes above

**Side-effects** see notes above

**Dose**

- See under preparations below

**Retin-A**® (Janssen-Cilag) PoM

Cream, tretinoin 0.025%, net price 60 g = £5.73
Excipients include butylated hydroxytoluene, sorbic acid, stearyl alcohol

Dose acne vulgaris, for dry or fair skin, apply thinly 1–2 times daily

Gel, tretinoin 0.01%, net price 60 g = £5.73; 0.025%, 60 g = £5.73
Excipients include butylated hydroxytoluene

Dose acne vulgaris and other keratotic conditions, apply thinly 1–2 times daily

Lotion, tretinoin 0.025%, net price 100 mL = £6.59
Excipients include butylated hydroxytoluene

Dose acne vulgaris, apply thinly 1–2 times daily

**With antibacterial**

**Aknemycin**® **Plus** (Crookes) PoM

Solution, tretinoin 0.025%, erythromycin 4% in an alcoholic basis, net price 25 mL = £7.94

Dose acne, apply thinly 1–2 times daily

Excipients none as listed in section 13.1.3

## ISOTRETINOIN

Note Isotretinoin is an isomer of tretinoin

Important For **indications, cautions, contra-indications** and **side-effects** of isotretinoin **when given by mouth**, see p. 590

**Indications** see notes above; oral treatment (see section 13.6.2)

**Cautions** (*topical application* **only**) see notes above

**Contra-indications** (*topical application* **only**) see notes above

**Dose**

- Apply thinly 1–2 times daily

**Isotrex**® (Stiefel) PoM

Gel, isotretinoin 0.05%, net price 30 g = £6.18
Excipients include butylated hydroxytoluene

**With antibacterial**

**Isotrexin**® (Stiefel) PoM

Gel, isotretinoin 0.05%, erythromycin 2% in ethanolic basis, net price 30 g = £7.78
Excipients include butylated hydroxytoluene

## Other topical preparations for acne

**Salicylic acid** is available in various preparations for sale direct to the public for the treatment of mild acne. Other products are more suitable for acne; salicylic acid is used mainly for its keratolytic effect.

Preparations containing **sulphur** and **abrasive agents** are not considered beneficial in acne.

Topical **corticosteroids** should **not** be used in acne.

A topical preparation of **nicotinamide** is available for inflammatory acne.

## ABRASIVE AGENTS

**Indications** acne vulgaris (but see notes above)

**Cautions** avoid contact with eyes; discontinue use temporarily if skin becomes irritated

**Contra-indications** superficial venules, telangiectasia

**Brasivol**® (Stiefel)

Paste No. 1, aluminium oxide 38.09% in fine particles, in a soap-detergent basis, net price 75 g = £2.21
Excipients include fragrance, *N*-(3-Chloroallyl)hexaminium chloride (quaternium 15)

Dose use instead of soap 1–3 times daily

## CORTICOSTEROIDS

**Indications** use in acne not recommended (see notes above)

**Cautions** see section 13.4 and notes above

**Contra-indications** see section 13.4 and notes above

**Side-effects** see section 13.4 and notes above

**Actinac**® (Peckforton) PoM

Lotion (powder for reconstitution with solvent), chloramphenicol 40 mg, hydrocortisone acetate 40 mg, allantoin 24 mg, butoxyethyl nicotinate 24 mg, precipitated sulphur 320 mg/g. Discard 21 days after reconstitution, net price 2 × 6.25-g bottles powder with 2 × 20-mL bottles solvent = £16.28. Label: 28. Potency: mild
Excipients none as listed in section 13.1.3

## NICOTINAMIDE

**Indications** see under preparation

**Cautions** avoid contact with eyes and mucous membranes (including nose and mouth); reduce frequency of application if excessive dryness, irritation or peeling

**Side-effects** dryness of skin; also pruritus, erythema, burning and irritation

**Nicam**® (Dermal)

Gel, nicotinamide 4%, net price 60 g = £7.42
Excipients none as listed in section 13.1.3

Dose inflammatory acne vulgaris, apply twice daily; reduce to once daily or on alternate days if irritation occurs

Note Formerly marketed as *Papulex*®

## SALICYLIC ACID

**Indications** acne; psoriasis (section 13.5.2); warts and calluses (section 13.7); fungal nail infections (section 13.10.2)

**Cautions** avoid contact with mouth, eyes, mucous membranes; systemic effects after excessive use (see Aspirin and the salicylates, section 10.1.1)

**Side-effects** local irritation

**Acnisal**® (Alliance)

Topical solution, salicylic acid 2% in a detergent and emollient basis, net price 177 mL = £4.03.
Excipients include benzyl alcohol

Dose use up to 3 times daily

## SULPHUR

**Cautions** avoid contact with eyes, mouth, and mucous membranes; causes skin irritation

**With resorcinol**

Prolonged application of resorcinol may interfere with thyroid function, therefore not recommended

**Eskamel**® (Goldshield) NHS

Cream, resorcinol 2%, sulphur 8%, in a non-greasy flesh-coloured basis, net price 25 g = £3.03
Excipients include propylene glycol, fragrance

# 13.6.2 Oral preparations for acne

## Oral antibacterials for acne

Systemic antibacterial treatment is useful for inflammatory acne if topical treatment is not adequately effective or if it is inappropriate. Anticomedonal treatment (e.g. with topical benzoyl peroxide) may also be required.

Either **oxytetracycline** or **tetracycline** (section 5.1.3) is usually given for acne in a dose of 500 mg twice daily. If there is no improvement after the first 3 months another oral antibacterial should be used. Maximum improvement usually occurs after 4 to 6 months but in more severe cases treatment may need to be continued for 2 years or longer.

**Doxycycline** and **minocycline** (section 5.1.3) are alternatives to tetracycline. Doxycycline may be used in a dose of 100 mg daily. Minocycline offers less likelihood of bacterial resistance but may sometimes cause irreversible pigmentation; it is given in a dose of 100 mg daily (in one or two divided doses).

**Erythromycin** (section 5.1.5) in a dose of 500 mg twice daily is an alternative for the management of acne but propionibacteria strains resistant to erythromycin are becoming widespread and this may explain poor response.

**Trimethoprim** (section 5.1.8) in a dose of 300 mg twice daily may be used for acne resistant to other antibacterials [unlicensed indication]. Prolonged treatment with trimethoprim may depress haematopoiesis; it should generally be initiated by specialists.

Concomitant use of different topical and systemic antibacterials is undesirable owing to the increased likelihood of the development of bacterial resistance.



## Hormone treatment for acne

**Co-cyprindiol** (cyproterone acetate with ethinylestradiol) contains an anti-androgen. It is no more effective than an oral broad-spectrum antibacterial but is useful in women who also wish to receive oral contraception.

Improvement of acne with co-cyprindiol probably occurs because of decreased sebum secretion which is under androgen control. Some women with moderately severe hirsutism may also benefit because hair growth is also androgen-dependent. Contra-indications of co-cyprindiol include pregnancy and a predisposition to thrombosis.

> **CSM advice**
> Venous thromboembolism occurs more frequently in women taking co-cyprindiol than those taking a low-dose combined oral contraceptive. The CSM has reminded prescribers that co-cyprindiol is licensed for use in women with severe acne which has not responded to oral antibacterials and for moderately severe hirsutism; it should not be used solely for contraception. It is contra-indicated in those with a personal or close family history of venous thromboembolism. Women with severe acne or hirsutism may have an inherently increased risk of cardiovascular disease.

### CO-CYPRINDIOL

A mixture of cyproterone acetate and ethinylestradiol in the mass proportions 2000 parts to 35 parts, respectively

**Indications** severe acne in women refractory to prolonged oral antibacterial therapy (but see notes above); moderately severe hirsutism

**Cautions** see under Combined Hormonal Contraceptives, section 7.3.1

**Contra-indications** see under Combined Hormonal Contraceptives, section 7.3.1

**Side-effects** see under Combined Hormonal Contraceptives, section 7.3.1

**Dose**

- 1 tablet daily for 21 days starting on day 1 of menstrual cycle and repeated after a 7-day interval, usually for several months; withdraw when acne or Hirsutism completely resolved (repeat courses may be given if recurrence)

**Co-cyprindiol** (Non-proprietary) PoM
Tablets, co-cyprindiol 2000/35 (cyproterone acetate 2 mg, ethinylestradiol 35 micrograms), net price 21-tab pack = £3.70
Brands include *Acnocin®*, *Cicafem®*, *Diva®*

**Dianette®** (Schering Health) PoM
Tablets, beige, s/c, co-cyprindiol 2000/35 (cyproterone acetate 2 mg, ethinylestradiol 35 micrograms), net price 21-tab pack = £3.11

## Oral retinoid for acne

The retinoid **isotretinoin** (*Roaccutane®*) reduces sebum secretion. It is used for the systemic treatment of nodulo-cystic and conglobate acne, severe acne, scarring, acne which has not responded to an adequate course of a systemic antibacterial, or acne which is associated with psychological problems. It is also useful in women who develop acne in the third or fourth decades of life, since late onset acne is frequently unresponsive to antibacterials.

Isotretinoin is a toxic drug that should be prescribed **only** by, or under the supervision of, a consultant dermatologist. It is given for at least 16 weeks; repeat courses are not normally required.

Side-effects of isotretinoin include severe dryness of the skin and mucous membranes, nose bleeds, and joint pains. The drug is **teratogenic** and must **not** be given to women of child-bearing age unless they practise effective contraception and then only after detailed assessment and explanation by the physician and they are registered with a pregnancy prevention programme (see under Cautions below).

Although a causal link between isotretinoin use and psychiatric changes (including suicidal ideation) has not been established, the possibility should be considered before initiating treatment; if psychiatric changes occur during treatment, isotretinoin should be stopped, the prescriber informed, and specialist psychiatric advice should be sought.

### ISOTRETINOIN

Note Isotretinoin is an isomer of tretinoin

**Indications** see notes above

**Cautions** exclude pregnancy before starting (perform pregnancy test 2–3 days before expected menstruation, start treatment on day 2 or 3 of menstrual cycle)—effective contraception must be practised at least 1 month before, during, and for at least 1 month after treatment; avoid blood donation during treatment and for at least 1 month after treatment; history of depression; measure hepatic function before treatment, 1 month after starting and then every 3 months (reduce dose or discontinue if transaminase raised above normal); measure serum lipids before treatment, 1 month after starting, then at end of treatment (reduce dose or discontinue if raised), discontinue if uncontrolled hypertriglyceridaemia or pancreatitis; diabetes; dry eye syndrome (associated with risk of keratitis); avoid keratolytics; renal impairment (Appendix 3) **interactions:** Appendix 1 (retinoids)

Counselling Warn patient to avoid wax epilation (risk of epidermal stripping), dermabrasion, and laser skin treatments (risk of scarring) during treatment and for at least 6 months after stopping; patient should avoid exposure to UV light (including sunlight) and use sunscreen and emollient (including lip balm) preparations from the start of treatment.

**Contra-indications** pregnancy (**important teratogenic risk:** see Cautions above); breast-feeding; hepatic impairment (Appendix 2); hypervitaminosis A, hyperlipidaemia

**Side-effects** dryness of skin (with dermatitis, scaling, thinning, erythema, pruritus), epidermal fragility (trauma may cause blistering), dryness of lips (sometimes cheilitis), dryness of eyes (with blepharitis and conjunctivitis), dryness of pharyngeal mucosa (with hoarseness), dryness of nasal mucosa (with epistaxis), headache, myalgia and arthralgia, raised plasma concentration of triglycerides, of glucose, of serum transaminases, and of cholesterol (risk of pancreatitis if triglycerides above 8 g/litre), haematuria and proteinuria, thrombocytopenia, thrombocytosis, neutropenia and anaemia; *rarely* irreversible mood changes (depression, suicidal ideation, aggressive behaviour, anxiety)—expert referral required, exacerbation of acne, acne fulminans, allergic skin reactions, and hypersensitivity, alopecia; *very rarely* nausea, inflammatory bowel disease, diarrhoea (discontinue if severe), benign intracranial hypertension (avoid concomitant tetracyclines), convulsions, malaise, drowsiness, lymphadenopathy, increased sweating, hyperuricaemia, raised serum creatinine concentration and glomerulonephritis, hepatitis, tendonitis, bone changes (including reduced bone density, early epiphyseal closure, and skeletal hyperostosis following long-term administration), visual disturbances (papilloedema, corneal opacities, cataracts, decreased night vision, photophobia, blurred vision, colour blindness)—expert referral required and consider withdrawal, decreased tolerance to contact lenses and keratitis, impaired hearing, Gram-positive infections of skin and mucous membranes, allergic vasculitis and granulomatous lesions, paronychia, hirsutism, nail dystrophy, skin hyperpigmentation, photosensitivity

**Dose**

- 500 micrograms/kg daily increased if necessary to 1 mg/kg (in 1–2 divided doses) for 16–24 weeks (8 weeks if failure or relapse after first course); max. cumulative dose 150 mg/kg per course; CHILD not recommended

**Isotretinoin** (Non-proprietary) PoM

Capsules, isotretinoin 5 mg, net price 56-cap pack = £15.00; 20 mg, 56-cap pack = £40.00 (hosp. only). Label: 10, patient information leaflet, 11, 21

**Roaccutane®** (Roche) PoM

Capsules, isotretinoin 5 mg (red-violet/white), net price 30-cap pack = £9.08; 20 mg (red-violet/white), 30-cap pack = £25.02 (hosp. or specified retail pharmacy only). Label: 10, patient information card, 11, 21

Excipients include arachis (peanut) oil

## 13.7 Preparations for warts and calluses

Warts (verrucas) are caused by a human papillomavirus, which most frequently affects the hands, feet (plantar warts), and the anogenital region (see below); treatment usually relies on local tissue destruction. Warts may regress on their own and treatment is required only if the warts are painful, unsightly, persistent, or cause distress.

Preparations of **salicylic acid, formaldehyde, gluteraldehyde** or **silver nitrate** are available for purchase by the public; they are suitable for the removal of warts on hands and feet. **Salicylic acid** is a useful keratolytic which may be considered first; it is also suitable for the removal of *corns and calluses.* Preparations of salicylic acid in a collodion basis are available but some patients may develop an allergy to colophony in the formulation. An ointment combining **salicylic acid** with **podophyllum resin** (*Posalfilin®*) is available for treating plantar warts. Cryotherapy causes pain, swelling, and blistering and may be no more effective than topical salicylic acid in the treatment of warts.

### SALICYLIC ACID

**Indications** see under preparations; psoriasis (section 13.5.2); acne (section 13.6.1); fungal nail infections (section 13.10.2)

**Cautions** significant peripheral neuropathy, patients with diabetes at risk of neuropathic ulcers; protect surrounding skin and avoid broken skin; not suitable for application to face, anogenital region, or large areas

**Side-effects** skin irritation, see notes above

**Dose**

- See under preparations; advise patient to apply carefully to wart and to protect surrounding skin (e.g. with soft paraffin or specially designed plaster); rub wart surface gently with file or pumice stone once weekly; treatment may need to be continued for up to 3 months

**Cuplex®** (Crawford)

Gel, salicylic acid 11%, lactic acid 4%, in a collodion basis, net price 5 g = £2.23. Label: 15

Dose for plantar and mosaic warts, corns, and calluses, apply twice daily

Note Contains colophony (see notes above)

**Duofilm®** (Stiefel)

Paint, salicylic acid 16.7%, lactic acid 16.7%, in flexible collodion, net price 15 mL (with applicator) = £1.74. Label: 15

Dose for plantar and mosaic warts, apply daily

**Occlusal®** (Alliance)

Cutaneous solution, salicylic acid 26% in polyacrylic solution, net price 10 mL (with applicator) = £3.39. Label: 15

Dose for common and plantar warts, apply daily

**Salactol®** (Dermal)

Paint, salicylic acid 16.7%, lactic acid 16.7%, in flexible collodion, net price 10 mL (with applicator) = £1.79. Label: 15

Dose for warts, particularly plantar warts, verrucas, corns, and calluses, apply daily

Note Contains colophony (see notes above)

**Salatac®** (Dermal)
Gel, salicylic acid 12%, lactic acid 4% in a collodion basis, net price 8 g (with applicator) = £3.12. Label: 15
Dose for warts, verrucas, corns, and calluses, apply daily

**Verrugon®** (Pickles)
Ointment, salicylic acid 50% in a paraffin basis, net price 6 g = £2.83
Dose for plantar warts, apply daily

■With podophyllum
**Posalfilin®** (Norgine)
Ointment, podophyllum resin 20%, salicylic acid 25%, net price 10 g = £3.51
Dose for plantar warts apply daily
Note Owing to the salicylic acid content, not suitable for anogenital warts; owing to the podophyllum content also contra-indicated in pregnancy and breast-feeding

## FORMALDEHYDE

**Indications** see under preparations
**Cautions** see under Salicylic Acid
**Side-effects** see under Salicylic Acid

**Veracur®** (Typharm)
Gel, formaldehyde 0.75% in a water-miscible gel basis, net price 15 g = £2.41.
Dose for warts, particularly plantar warts, apply twice daily

## GLUTARALDEHYDE

**Indications** warts, particularly plantar warts
**Cautions** protect surrounding skin; not for application to face, mucosa, or anogenital areas
**Side-effects** rashes, skin irritation (discontinue if severe); stains skin brown
**Dose**
- Apply twice daily (see also under Salicylic acid)

**Glutarol®** (Dermal)
Solution (= application), glutaraldehyde 10%, net price 10 mL (with applicator) = £2.17

## SILVER NITRATE

**Indications** see under preparation
**Cautions** protect surrounding skin and avoid broken skin; not suitable for application to face, ano-genital region, or large areas
**Side-effects** stains skin and fabric
**Dose**
- See under preparation; instructions in proprietary packs generally incorporate advice to remove dead skin before use by gentle filing and to cover with adhesive dressing after application

**AVOCA®** (Bray)
Caustic pencil, tip containing silver nitrate 95%, potassium nitrate 5%, net price, treatment pack (including emery file, 6 adhesive dressings and protector pads) = £1.89.
Dose for common warts and verrucas, apply moistened caustic pencil tip for 1–2 minutes; repeat after 24 hours up to max. 3 applications for warts *or* max. 6 applications for verrucas

## Anogenital warts

The treatment of anogenital warts (condylomata acuminata) should be accompanied by screening for other sexually transmitted diseases. **Podophyllum** and **podophyllotoxin** (the major active ingredient of podophyllum) may be used for *soft, non-keratinised* external anogenital warts; these preparations can cause considerable irritation of the treated area. They can also cause severe systemic toxicity on excessive application including gastro-intestinal, renal, haematological, and CNS effects. Patients with a limited number of external warts or *keratinised* lesions may be better treated with cryotherapy or other forms of physical ablation.

**Imiquimod** cream is licensed for the treatment of external anogenital warts; it may be used for both keratinised and non-keratinised lesions. It is also licensed for the treatment of superficial basal cell carcinoma.

Inosine pranobex (section 5.3.2.1) is licensed for adjunctive treatment of genital warts but it has been superseded by more effective drugs.

## IMIQUIMOD

**Indications** external genital and perianal warts; superficial basal cell carcinoma
**Cautions** avoid normal skin, inflamed skin and open wounds; not suitable for internal genital warts; uncircumcised males (risk of phimosis or stricture of foreskin); pregnancy
**Side-effects** local reactions including itching, pain, erythema, erosion, oedema, and excoriation; less commonly local ulceration and scabbing; permanent hypopigmentation or hyperpigmentation and dysuria in women reported
**Dose**
- Warts, apply thinly 3 times a week at night until lesions resolve (max. 16 weeks)
- Superficial basal cell carcinoma, apply to lesion (and 1 cm beyond it) on 5 days each week for 6 weeks; assess response after a further 12 weeks
- CHILD not recommended

Important Should be rubbed in and allowed to stay on the treated area for 6–10 hours for warts or for 8 hours for basal cell carcinoma then washed off with mild soap and water (uncircumcised males treating warts under foreskin should wash the area daily). The cream should be washed off before sexual contact

**Aldara®** (3M) PoM
Cream, imiquimod 5%, net price 12-sachet pack = £51.32. Label: 10, patient information leaflet
Excipients include benzyl alcohol, cetyl alcohol, hydroxybenzoates (parabens), polysorbate 60, stearyl alcohol
Condoms may damage latex condoms and diaphragms

## PODOPHYLLUM

**Indications** see under preparations
**Cautions** avoid normal skin and open wounds; keep away from face; very irritant to eyes; **important**: see also warnings below
**Contra-indications** pregnancy and breast-feeding; children
**Side-effects** see notes above

**Podophyllin Paint, Compound, BP** PoM
(podophyllum resin 15% in compound benzoin tincture), podophyllum resin 1.5 g, compound benzoin tincture to 10 mL; 5 mL to be dispensed unless otherwise directed. Label: 15
Dose external genital warts, applied weekly in genitourinary clinic (or at a general practitioner's surgery by trained nurses after screening for other sexually transmitted diseases)
Important Should be allowed to stay on the treated area for not longer than 6 hours and then washed off. Care should be taken to

avoid splashing the surrounding skin during application (which must be covered with soft paraffin as a protection). Where there are a large number of warts only a few should be treated at any one time as **severe toxicity** caused by absorption of podophyllin has been reported

### Podophyllotoxin

**Condyline®** (Ardern) PoM

Solution, podophyllotoxin 0.5% in alcoholic basis, net price 3.5 mL (with applicators) = £14.49. Label: 15

**Dose** condylomata acuminata affecting the penis or the female external genitalia, apply twice daily for 3 consecutive days; treatment may be repeated at weekly intervals if necessary for a total of five 3-day treatment courses; direct medical supervision for lesions in the female and for lesions greater than 4 cm² in the male; max. 50 single applications ('loops') per session (consult product literature)

**Warticon®** (Stiefel) PoM

Cream, podophyllotoxin 0.15%, net price 5 g (with mirror) = £15.46

**Excipients** include butylated hydroxyanisole, cetyl alcohol, hydroxybenzoates (parabens), sorbic acid, stearyl alcohol

**Dose** condylomata acuminata affecting the penis or the female external genitalia, apply twice daily for 3 consecutive days; treatment may be repeated at weekly intervals if necessary for a total of four 3-day treatment courses; direct medical supervision for lesions greater than 4 cm²

Solution, blue, podophyllotoxin 0.5% in alcoholic basis, net price 3 mL (with applicators— *Warticon®* [for men]; with applicators and mirror—*Warticon Fem®* [for women]) = £12.88. Label: 15

**Dose** condylomata acuminata affecting the penis or the female external genitalia, apply twice daily for 3 consecutive days; treatment may be repeated at weekly intervals if necessary for a total of four 3-day treatment courses; direct medical supervision for lesions greater than 4 cm²; max. 50 single applications ('loops') per session (consult product literature)

# 13.8 Sunscreens and camouflagers

13.8.1 Sunscreen preparations
13.8.2 Camouflagers

## 13.8.1 Sunscreen preparations

Solar ultraviolet irradiation can be harmful to the skin. It is responsible for disorders such as *polymorphic light eruption, solar urticaria,* and it provokes the various *cutaneous porphyrias.* It also provokes (or at least aggravates) skin lesions of *lupus erythematosus* and may aggravate *rosacea* and some other *dermatoses.* Sunlight may also cause photosensitivity in patients taking some drugs such as demeclocycline, phenothiazines, or amiodarone. All these conditions (as well as *sunburn*) may occur after relatively short periods of exposure to the sun. Solar ultraviolet irradiation may provoke attacks of recurrent herpes labialis (but it is not known whether the effect of sunlight exposure is local or systemic).

The effects of exposure over longer periods include *ageing changes* and more importantly the initiation of *skin cancer.*

Solar ultraviolet radiation is approximately 200–400 nm in wavelength. The medium wavelengths (290–320 nm, known as UVB) cause sunburn and contribute to the long-term changes responsible for skin cancer and ageing. The long wavelengths (320–400 nm, known as UVA) do not cause sunburn but are responsible for many *photosensitivity reactions* and *photodermatoses.* Both UVA and UVB contribute to long-term *photodamage* and to the pathogenesis of *skin cancer.*

Sunscreen preparations contain substances that protect the skin against UVB and hence against sunburn, but they are no substitute for covering the skin and avoiding sunlight. The sun protection factor (SPF, usually indicated in the preparation title) provides guidance on the degree of protection offered against UVB; it indicates the multiples of protection provided against burning, compared with unprotected skin; for example, an SPF of 8 should enable a person to remain 8 times longer in the sun without burning. However, in practice users do not apply sufficient sunscreen product and the protection is lower than that found in experimental studies. Sunscreen preparations, do not prevent long-term damage associated with UVA, which might not become apparent for 10 to 20 years. Preparations that also contain reflective substances, such as titanium dioxide, provide the most effective protection against UVA. Some products use a star rating system to indicate the protection against UVA relative to protection against UVB for the same product. Four stars indicate that the product offers balanced UVA and UVB protection; products with 3, 2, or 1 star rating indicate that greater protection is offered against UVB than against UVA. However, the usefulness of the star rating system remains controversial.

Sunscreen preparations, may rarely cause allergic reactions.

> For optimum photoprotection, sunscreen preparations should be applied **thickly** and **frequently** (approximately 2 hourly). In photodermatoses, they should be used from spring to autumn. As maximum protection from sunlight is desirable, preparations with the highest SPF should be prescribed.

**Borderline substances** The preparations marked 'ACBS' are regarded as drugs when prescribed for skin protection against ultraviolet radiation in abnormal cutaneous photosensitivity resulting from genetic disorders or photodermatoses, including vitiligo and those resulting from radiotherapy; chronic or recurrent herpes simplex labialis. Preparations with SPF less than 15 are not prescribable. See also Appendix 7.

**Delph®** (Fenton)

Lotion, (UVA and UVB protection; UVB-SPF 15), ethylhexyl *p*-methoxycinnamate 7.5%, oxybenzone 3%, titanium dioxide 0.6%, net price 200 mL = £1.99. ACBS

**Excipients** include cetostearyl alcohol, fragrance, hydroxybenzoates (parabens), imidurea

Lotion, (UVA and UVB protection; UVB-SPF 20), ethylhexyl *p*-methoxycinnamate 7.5%, oxybenzone 3%, titanium dioxide 1.6%, net price 200 mL = £1.99. ACBS

**Excipients** include cetostearyl alcohol, fragrance, hydroxybenzoates (parabens), imidurea

Lotion, (UVA and UVB protection; UVB-SPF 25), avobenzone 4%, ethylhexyl *p*-methoxycinnamate 3.5%, titanium dioxide 2.1%, oxybenzone 1.3%, net price 200 mL = £2.85. ACBS

**Excipients** include cetostearyl alcohol, fragrance, hydroxybenzoates (parabens), imidurea

Lotion, (UVA and UVB protection; UVB-SPF 30), ethylhexyl *p*-methoxycinnamate 4.8%, avobenzone 4%, titanium dioxide 2.5%, oxybenzone 1.5%, net price 200 mL = £2.85. ACBS

**Excipients** include cetostearyl alcohol, fragrance, hydroxybenzoates (parabens), imidurea

**E45 Sun®** (Crookes)
Reflective Sunscreen (UVA and UVB protection; UVB-SPF 25), waterproof, titanium dioxide 3.6%, zinc oxide 13.9%, net price 150 mL = £6.56. ACBS
Excipients include hydroxybenzoates (parabens), isopropyl palmitate
Reflective Sunscreen (UVA and UVB protection; UVB-SPF 50), waterproof, titanium dioxide 6.4%, zinc oxide 16%, net price 150 mL = £7.09. ACBS
Excipients include hydroxybenzoates (parabens), isopropyl palmitate

**RoC Sante Soleil®** (J&J)
Cream (UVA and UVB protection; UVB-SPF 25), containing avobenzone 2%, ethylhexyl *p*-methoxycinnamate 7.5%, titanium dioxide 5.5%, net price 50 mL = £4.06. ACBS
Excipients include beeswax, cetostearyl alcohol, disodium edetate, hydroxybenzoates (parabens)

**SpectraBan®** (Stiefel)
Lotion (UVB protection; UVB-SPF 25), aminobenzoic acid 5%, padimate-O 3.2%, in an alcoholic basis, net price 150 mL = £3.45. ACBS
Excipients include fragrance
Note Flammable; stains clothing
Ultra lotion (UVA and UVB protection; UVB-SPF 28), water resistant, avobenzone 2%, oxybenzone 3%, padimate-O 8%, titanium dioxide 2%, net price 150 mL = £5.45. ACBS
Excipients include benzyl alcohol, disodium edetate, sorbic acid, fragrance

**Sunsense® Ultra** (Typharm)
Lotion (UVA and UVB protection; UVB-SPF 60), ethylhexyl *p*-methoxycinnamate 7.5% oxybenzone 3%, titanium dioxide 3.5%, net price 50-mL bottle with roll-on applicator = £3.11, 125 mL = £5.10. ACBS
Excipients include butylated hydroxytoluene, cetyl alcohol, fragrance, hydroxybenzoates (parabens), propylene glycol

**Uvistat®** (LPC)
Cream (UVA and UVB protection; UVB-SPF 22 but marketed as 'factor 20'), water-resistant, ethylhexyl *p*-methoxycinnamate 7%, avobenzone 4%, titanium dioxide 4.5%, net price 125 g = £5.10. ACBS
Excipients include disodium edetate, fragrance, hydroxybenzoates (parabens)
Ultrablock cream (UVA and UVB protection; UVB-SPF 30), water-resistant, ethylhexyl *p*-methoxycinnamate 7.5%, avobenzone 4%, titanium dioxide 6.5%, net price 125 g = £5.10. ACBS
Excipients include disodium edetate, fragrance, hydroxybenzoates (parabens)

## Photodamage

**Diclofenac** gel is licensed for *actinic keratosis.* Treatment should continue for 60 to 90 days (optimal therapeutic effect may not be seen until 30 days after stopping). **Fluorouracil** cream (section 8.1.3) is also licensed for actinic keratosis. **Methyl-5-aminolevulinate** cream (*Metvix®*, available from Galderma), followed by irradiation with red light, is licensed for treating thin non-hyperkeratotic actinic keratoses of the face and scalp when other treatments are less appropriate, or for treating superficial or nodular basal cell carcinoma that is considered unsuitable for other therapies; it is used in specialist centres.

Application of **tretinoin** 0.05% cream is reported to be associated with gradual improvement in *photodamaged skin* (usually within 3–4 months of starting).

### DICLOFENAC SODIUM

**Indications** actinic keratosis
**Cautions** as for topical NSAIDs, see section 10.3.2
**Contra-indications** as for topical NSAIDs, see section 10.3.2
**Side-effects** as for topical NSAIDs, see section 10.3.2; also paraesthesia; application of large amounts may result in systemic effects, see section 10.1
**Dose**
- Apply thinly twice daily for 60–90 days; max. 8 g daily

**Solaraze®** (Shire) PoM
Gel, diclofenac sodium 3%, net price 25 g = £16.65
Excipients include benzyl alcohol

### TRETINOIN

Note Tretinoin is the acid form of vitamin A

**Indications** mottled hyperpigmentation, roughness and fine wrinkling of photodamaged skin due to chronic sun exposure; acne vulgaris (section 13.6); malignant disease (section 8.1.5)
**Cautions** see section 13.6.1
**Contra-indications** see section 13.6.1
**Side-effects** see section 13.6.1
**Dose**
- Apply thinly at night, then reduce to 1–3 nights weekly

**Retinova®** (Janssen-Cilag) PoM NHS
Cream, tretinoin 0.05%, net price 20 g = £13.75.
Excipients include fragrance

## 13.8.2 Camouflagers

Disfigurement of the skin can be very distressing to patients and may have a marked psychological effect. In skilled hands, or with experience, camouflage cosmetics can be very effective in concealing scars and birthmarks. The depigmented patches in vitiligo are also very disfiguring and camouflage creams are of great cosmetic value.

**Borderline substances** The preparations marked 'ACBS' are regarded as drugs when prescribed for postoperative scars and other deformities and as an adjunctive therapy in the relief of emotional disturbances due to disfiguring skin disease, such as vitiligo. See also Appendix 7.

**Covermark®** (Epiderm)
Classic foundation (masking cream), net price 15 mL (10 shades) = £10.75. ACBS
Excipients include beeswax, hydroxybenzoates (parabens), fragrance
Finishing powder, net price 60 g = £10.55. ACBS
Excipients include beeswax, hydroxybenzoates (parabens), fragrance

**Dermacolor®** (Fox)
Camouflage creme, (100 shades), net price 25 g = £8.10. ACBS
Excipients include beeswax, butylated hydroxytoluene, fragrance, propylene glycol, stearyl alcohol, wool fat
Fixing powder, (7 shades), net price 60 g = £6.55. ACBS
Excipients include fragrance

**Keromask®** (Network)
Masking cream, (2 shades), net price 15 mL = £5.67. ACBS
Excipients include butylated hydroxyanisole, hydroxybenzoates (parabens), wool fat, propylene glycol
Finishing powder, net price 20 g = £5.67. ACBS
Excipients include butylated hydroxytoluene, hydroxybenzoates (parabens)

**Veil®** (Blake)
Cover cream, (20 shades), net price 19 g = £8.23, 44 g = £13.90, 70 g = £18.44. ACBS
Excipients include hydroxybenzoates (parabens), wool fat derivative
Finishing powder, translucent, net price 35 g = £8.79. ACBS
Excipients include butylated hydroxyanisole, hydroxybenzoates (parabens)

# 13.9 Shampoos and other preparations for scalp and hair conditions

*Dandruff* is considered to be a mild form of seborrhoeic dermatitis (see also section 13.5.1). Shampoos containing antimicrobial agents such as **pyrithione zinc** (which are widely available) and **selenium sulphide** may have beneficial effects. Shampoos containing **tar** extracts may be useful and they are also used in *psoriasis.* **Ketoconazole** shampoo should be considered for more persistent or severe dandruff or for seborrhoeic dermatitis of the scalp.

**Corticosteroid** gels and lotions (section 13.4) can also be used.

Shampoos containing **coal tar** and **salicylic acid** may also be useful. A cream or an ointment containing coal tar and salicylic acid is very helpful in *psoriasis* that affects the scalp (section 13.5.2). Patients who do not respond to these treatments may need to be referred to exclude the possibility of other skin conditions.

*Cradle cap* in infants may be treated with **olive oil** or **arachis oil** (ground-nut oil, peanut oil) applications followed by shampooing.

See below for male-pattern baldness and also section 13.5 (psoriasis and eczema), section 13.10.4 (lice), and section 13.10.2 (ringworm).

## Shampoos

[1]**Ketoconazole** (Non-proprietary) PoM

Cream—section 13.10.2

Shampoo, ketoconazole 2%, net price 120 mL = £4.19

Excipients include imidurea

Brands include *Dandrazol® 2% Shampoo, Nizoral®*

Dose treatment of seborrhoeic dermatitis and dandruff apply twice weekly for 2–4 weeks (prophylaxis apply once every 1–2 weeks); treatment of pityriasis versicolor apply once daily for max. 5 days (prophylaxis apply once daily for up to 3 days before sun exposure); leave preparation on for 3–5 minutes before rinsing

1. Can be sold to the public for the prevention and treatment of dandruff and seborrhoeic dermatitis of the scalp as a shampoo formulation containing ketoconazole max. 2%, in a pack containing max. 120 mL and labelled to show a max. frequency of application of once every 3 days; brands on sale to the public include *Dandrazol® Antidandruff 2% Shampoo, Nizoral® Dandruff Shampoo,* and *Nizoral® Anti-Dandruff Shampoo*

**Alphosyl 2 in 1®** (GSK Consumer Healthcare)

Shampoo, alcoholic coal tar extract 5%, net price 125 mL = £1.81, 250 mL = £3.43

Excipients include hydroxybenzoates (parabens), fragrance

Dose dandruff, use once or twice weekly as necessary; psoriasis, seborrhoeic dermatitis, scaling and itching, use every 2–3 days

**Betadine®** (Medlock)

Skin disinfectants—section 13.11.4

Shampoo, povidone–iodine 4%, in a surfactant solution, net price 250 mL = £2.32

Excipients include fragrance

Dose seborrhoeic scalp conditions associated with excessive dandruff, pruritus, scaling, exudation and erythema, infected scalp lesions (recurrent furunculosis, infective folliculitis, impetigo), apply 1–2 times weekly; CHILD under 2 years not recommended

*Cautions; Contra-indications; Side-effects:* section 13.11.4, Povidone-Iodine

**Capasal®** (Dermal)

Shampoo, coal tar 1%, coconut oil 1%, salicylic acid 0.5%, net price 250 mL = £4.91

Excipients none as listed in section 13.1.3

Dose scaly scalp disorders including psoriasis, seborrhoeic dermatitis, dandruff, and cradle cap, apply daily as necessary

**Ceanel Concentrate®** (Ferndale)

Shampoo, cetrimide 10%, undecenoic acid 1%, phenylethyl alcohol 7.5%, net price 150 mL = £3.40, 500 mL = £9.80

Excipients none as listed in section 13.1.3

Dose scalp psoriasis, seborrhoeic dermatitis, dandruff, apply 3 times in first week then twice weekly

**Clinitar®** (CHS)

Shampoo, coal tar extract 2%, net price 100 g = £2.50

Excipients include polysorbates, fragrance

Dose scalp psoriasis, seborrhoeic dermatitis, and dandruff, apply up to 3 times weekly

**Meted®** (Alliance)

Shampoo, salicylic acid 3%, sulphur 5%, net price 120 mL = £3.80

Excipients include fragrance

Dose scaly scalp disorders including psoriasis, seborrhoeic dermatitis, and dandruff, apply at least twice weekly

**Pentrax®** (Alliance)

Shampoo, coal tar 4.3%, net price 120 mL = £3.80

Excipients none as listed in section 13.1.3

Dose scaly scalp disorders including psoriasis, seborrhoeic dermatitis, and dandruff, apply at least twice weekly

**Polytar AF®** (Stiefel)

Shampoo, arachis (peanut) oil extract of coal tar 0.3%, cade oil 0.3%, coal tar solution 0.1%, pine tar 0.3%, pyrithione zinc 1%, net price 150 mL = £3.91

Excipients include fragrance, imidurea

Dose scaly scalp disorders including psoriasis, seborrhoeic dermatitis, and dandruff, apply 2–3 times weekly for at least 3 weeks

**Psoriderm®** (Dermal)

Scalp lotion (= shampoo), coal tar 2.5%, lecithin 0.3%, net price 250 mL = £4.96

Excipients include disodium edetate

Dose scalp psoriasis, use as necessary

**Selsun®** (Abbott)

Shampoo, selenium sulphide 2.5%, net price 50 mL = £1.44, 100 mL = £1.96, 150 mL = £2.75

Excipients include fragrance

Dose seborrhoeic dermatitis and dandruff, apply twice weekly for 2 weeks then once weekly for 2 weeks and then as necessary; CHILD under 5 years not recommended; pityriasis versicolor, section 13.10.2 [unlicensed indication]

Cautions avoid using 48 hours before or after applying hair colouring, straightening or waving preparations

**T/Gel®** (Neutrogena)

Shampoo, coal tar extract 2%, net price 125 mL = £3.18, 250 mL = £4.78

Excipients include fragrance, hydroxybenzoates (parabens), imidurea, tetrasodium edetate

Dose scalp psoriasis, seborrhoeic dermatitis, dandruff, apply as necessary

## Other scalp preparations

**Cocois®**

Section 13.5.2

**Polytar®** (Stiefel)

Liquid, arachis (peanut) oil extract of coal tar 0.3%, cade oil 0.3%, coal tar solution 0.1%, oleyl alcohol 1%, tar 0.3%, net price 250 mL = £2.23

Excipients include fragrance, imidurea, polysorbate 80

Dose scalp disorders including psoriasis, seborrhoea, eczema, pruritus, and dandruff, apply 1–2 times weekly

**Polytar Plus®** (Stiefel)

Liquid, ingredients as *Polytar®* liquid with hydrolysed animal protein 3%, net price 500 mL = £3.91

Excipients include fragrance, imidurea, polysorbate 80

Dose scalp disorders including psoriasis, seborrhoea, eczema, pruritus, and dandruff, apply 1–2 times weekly

**Pragmatar®**

Section 13.5.2

## Hirsutism

Hirsutism may result from hormonal disorders or as a side-effect of drugs such as minoxidil, corticosteroids, anabolic steroids, androgens, danazol, and progestogens.

When hirsutism co-exists with acne (e.g. in polycystic ovary syndrome) co-cyprindiol (section 13.6.2) may be effective.

Eflornithine, an antiprotozoal drug, inhibits the enzyme ornithine decarboxylase in hair follicles and topical application can reduce the growth of unwanted facial hair. It must be used indefinitely to prevent regrowth. Continuous use for 8 weeks is required before benefit is seen. Eflornithine should be discontinued in the absence of improvement after treatment for 4 months.

### EFLORNITHINE

**Indications** facial hirsutism in women

**Contra-indications** pregnancy (Appendix 4); breast-feeding (Appendix 5)

**Side-effects** acne, application site reactions including burning and stinging sensation, rash

**Dose**

- Apply thinly twice daily; CHILD under 12 years not recommended

Note Preparation must be rubbed in thoroughly; cosmetics may be applied over treated area 5 minutes after eflornithine; do not wash treated area for 4 hours after application

**Vaniqa®** (Shire) ▼ PoM

Cream, eflornithine (as hydrochloride) 11.5%, net price 30 g = £26.04

Excipients include cetostearyl alcohol, hydroxybenzoates, stearyl alcohol

Note The *Scottish Medicines Consortium* has advised (September 2005) that eflornithine for facial hirsutism be restricted for use in women in whom alternative drug treatment cannot be used

## Male-pattern baldness

**Finasteride** is licensed for the treatment of male-pattern baldness in men. Continuous use for 3–6 months is required before benefit is seen, and effects are reversed 6–12 months after treatment is discontinued.

Topical application of **minoxidil** may stimulate limited hair growth in a small proportion of adults but only for as long as it is used.

### FINASTERIDE

**Indications** male-pattern baldness in men

**Cautions** see section 6.4.2

**Side-effects** see section 6.4.2

**Dose**

- 1 mg daily

**Propecia®** (MSD) PoM NHS

Tablets, f/c, beige, finasteride 1 mg, net price 28-tab pack = £26.99

### MINOXIDIL

**Indications** male-pattern baldness (men and women)

**Cautions** section 2.5.1 (only about 1.4–1.7% absorbed); avoid contact with eyes, mouth and mucous membranes, broken, infected, shaved, or inflamed skin; avoid inhalation of spray mist; avoid occlusive dressings and topical drugs which enhance absorption

**Contra-indications** section 2.5.1

**Side-effects** section 2.5.1; irritant dermatitis, allergic contact dermatitis, discontinue if hair loss persists for more than 2 weeks

**Dose**

- Apply 1 mL twice daily to dry hair and scalp (discontinue if no improvement after 1 year); 5% strength for use in men only

**Regaine®** (Pharmacia) NHS

Regaine® Regular Strength topical solution, minoxidil 2% in an aqueous alcoholic basis, net price 60-mL bottle with applicators = £14.16

Excipients include propylene glycol

Regaine® Extra Strength topical solution, minoxidil 5% in an aqueous alcoholic basis, net price 60-mL bottle with applicators = £17.00, 3 × 60-mL bottles = £34.03

Excipients include propylene glycol

Cautions flammable; wash hands after application

# 13.10 Anti-infective skin preparations

13.10.1 Antibacterial preparations
13.10.2 Antifungal preparations
13.10.3 Antiviral preparations
13.10.4 Parasiticidal preparations
13.10.5 Preparations for minor cuts and abrasions

## 13.10.1 Antibacterial preparations

13.10.1.1 Antibacterial preparations only used topically
13.10.1.2 Antibacterial preparations also used systemically

*Cellulitis*, a rapidly spreading deeply seated inflammation of the skin and subcutaneous tissue, requires systemic antibacterial treatment (see Table 1, section 5.1); it often involves staphylococcal infection. Lower leg infections or infections spreading around wounds are almost always cellulitis. *Erysipelas*, a superficial infection with clearly defined edges (and often affecting the face), is also treated with a systemic antibacterial (see Table 1, section 5.1); it usually involves streptococcal infection.

In the community acute *impetigo* on small areas of the skin may be treated by short-term topical application of **fusidic acid**; **mupirocin** should be used only to treat methicillin-resistant *Staphylococcus aureus*. If the impetigo is extensive or longstanding, an oral antibacterial such as **flucloxacillin** (or **erythromycin** in penicillin-allergy) (section 5.1, Table 1) should be used. Mild antiseptics such as **povidone–iodine** (section 13.11.4) are used to soften crusts and exudate.

Although there are a great many antibacterial drugs presented in topical preparations some are potentially hazardous and frequently their use is not necessary if adequate hygienic measures can be taken. Moreover, not all skin conditions that are oozing, crusted, or characterised by pustules are actually infected. Topical antibacterials should be **avoided** on *leg ulcers* unless used in short courses for defined infections; treatment of bacterial colonisation is generally inappropriate.

To minimise the development of resistant organisms it is advisable to limit the choice of antibacterials applied topically to those not used systemically. Unfortunately some of these, for example neomycin, may cause sensitisation, and there is cross-sensitivity with other aminoglycoside antibiotics, such as gentamicin. If *large areas of skin* are being treated, ototoxicity may also be a hazard with aminoglycoside antibiotics (and also with polymyxins), particularly in children, in the elderly, and in those with renal impairment. *Resistant organisms* are more common in hospitals, and whenever possible swabs should be taken for bacteriological examination before beginning treatment.

**Mupirocin** is not related to any other antibacterial in use; it is effective for skin infections, particularly those due to Gram-positive organisms but it is not indicated for pseudomonal infection. Although *Staphylococcus aureus* strains with low-level resistance to mupirocin are emerging, it is generally useful in infections resistant to other antibacterials. To avoid the development of resistance, mupirocin or fusidic acid should not be used for longer than 10 days and local microbiology advice should be sought before using it in hospital. In the presence of mupirocin-resistant MRSA infection, a polymyxin or an antiseptic like povidone-iodine, chlorhexidine, and alcohol can be used; their use should be discussed with the local microbiologist.

**Silver sulfadiazine** (silver sulphadiazine) is used in the treatment of infected burns.

## 13.10.1.1 Antibacterial preparations only used topically

### MUPIROCIN

**Indications** bacterial skin infections (see also notes above)

**Side-effects** local reactions including urticaria, pruritus, burning sensation, rash

**Dose**

- Apply up to 3 times daily for up to 10 days; INFANT under 1 year not recommended

**Bactroban®** (GSK) PoM

Cream, mupirocin (as mupirocin calcium) 2%, net price 15 g = £4.38

Excipients include benzyl alcohol, cetyl alcohol, stearyl alcohol

Ointment, mupirocin 2%, net price 15 g = £4.38

Excipients none as listed in section 13.1.3

Note Contains macrogol and manufacturer advises caution in renal impairment; may sting

Nasal ointment—section 12.2.3

### NEOMYCIN SULPHATE

**Indications** bacterial skin infections

**Cautions** large areas, see below

Large areas If large areas of skin are being treated ototoxicity may be a hazard, particularly in children, in the elderly, and in those with renal impairment

**Contra-indications** neonates

**Side-effects** sensitisation (see also notes above)

**Neomycin Cream BPC** PoM

Cream, neomycin sulphate 0.5%, cetomacrogol emulsifying ointment 30%, chlorocresol 0.1%, disodium edetate 0.01%, in freshly boiled and cooled purified water, net price 15 g = £2.17

Excipients include cetostearyl alcohol, edetic acid (EDTA)

Dose apply up to 3 times daily (short-term use)

**Cicatrin®** (GSK) PoM

Cream, neomycin sulphate 3300 units, bacitracin zinc 250 units, cysteine 2 mg, glycine 10 mg, threonine 1 mg/g, net price 15 g = 92p, 30 g = £1.84

Excipients include wool fat derivative, polysorbates

Dose superficial bacterial infection of skin, ADULT and CHILD over 2 years, apply up to 3 times daily (short-term use)

Dusting powder, neomycin sulphate 3300 units, bacitracin zinc 250 units, cysteine 2 mg, glycine 10 mg, threonine 1 mg/g, net price 15 g = 92p, 50 g = £3.07

Excipients none as listed in section 13.1.3

Dose superficial bacterial infection of skin, ADULT and CHILD over 2 years, apply up to 3 times daily (short-term use)

**Graneodin®** (Squibb) PoM

Ointment, neomycin sulphate 0.25%, gramicidin 0.025%, net price 25 g = £1.37

Excipients none as listed in section 13.1.3

Dose superficial bacterial infection of skin, apply 2–4 times daily (for max. 7 days—possibly longer for sycosis barbae)

### POLYMYXINS

(Includes colistin sulphate and polymyxin B sulphate)

**Indications** bacterial skin infections

**Cautions** large areas, see below

Large areas If large areas of skin are being treated nephrotoxicity and neurotoxicity may be a hazard, particularly in children, in the elderly, and in those with renal impairment

**Side-effects** sensitisation (see also notes above)

**Polyfax®** (PLIVA) PoM

Ointment, polymyxin B sulphate 10 000 units, bacitracin zinc 500 units/g, net price 20 g = £4.62

Excipients none as listed in section 13.1.3

Dose apply twice daily or more frequently if required

### SILVER SULFADIAZINE
(Silver sulphadiazine)

**Indications** prophylaxis and treatment of infection in burn wounds; as an adjunct to short-term treatment of infection in leg ulcers and pressure sores; as an adjunct to prophylaxis of infection in skin graft donor sites and extensive abrasions; for conservative management of finger-tip injuries

**Cautions** hepatic and renal impairment; G6PD deficiency; pregnancy and breast-feeding (avoid in late pregnancy and in neonate—see also Appendix 4); may inactivate enzymatic debriding agents—concomitant use may be inappropriate; for large amounts see also **interactions:** Appendix 1 (sulphonamides)

Large areas Plasma-sulfadiazine concentrations may approach therapeutic levels with *side-effects* and *interactions* as for sulphonamides (see section 5.1.8) if large areas of skin are treated. Owing to the association of sulphonamides with severe blood and skin disorders treatment should be stopped immediately if blood disorders or rashes develop—but leucopenia developing 2–3 days after starting treatment of burns patients is reported usually to be self-limiting and silver sulfadiazine need not usually be discontinued provided blood counts are monitored carefully to ensure return to normality within a few days. Argyria may also occur if large areas of skin are treated (or if application is prolonged).

**Contra-indications** pregnancy (Appendix 4) and breast-feeding (Appendix 5); sensitivity to sulphonamides; not recommended for neonates (see also Appendix 4)

**Side-effects** allergic reactions including burning, itching and rashes; argyria reported following prolonged use; leucopenia reported (monitor blood levels)

**Flamazine®** (S&N Hlth.) PoM

Cream, silver sulfadiazine 1%, net price 20 g = £2.91, 50 g = £3.85, 250 g = £10.32, 500 g = £18.27

Excipients include cetyl alcohol, polysorbates, propylene glycol

Dose apply with sterile applicator; burns, apply daily or more frequently if very exudative; leg ulcers or pressure sores, apply daily or on alternate days (not recommended if ulcer very exudative); finger-tip injuries, apply every 2–3 days; consult product literature for details



## 13.10.1.2 Antibacterial preparations also used systemically

**Sodium fusidate** is a narrow-spectrum antibacterial used for staphylococcal infections. For the role of sodium fusidate in the treatment of impetigo see p. 597.

**Metronidazole** is used topically for acne rosacea and to reduce the odour associated with anerobic infections; oral metronidazole (section 5.1.11) is used to treat wounds infected with anaerobic bacteria.

**Angular cheilitis** An ointment containing sodium fusidate is used in the fissures of angular cheilitis when associated with staphylococcal infection. For further information on angular cheilitis, see section 12.3.2.

### FUSIDIC ACID

**Indications** staphylococcal skin infections; penicillin-resistant staphylococcal infections (section 5.1.7); staphylococcal eye infections (section 11.3.1)

**Cautions** see notes above; avoid contact with eyes

**Side-effects** rarely hypersensitivity reactions

**Dose**

- Apply 3–4 times daily

**Fucidin®** (LEO) PoM

Cream, fusidic acid 2%, net price 15 g = £2.00, 30 g = £3.79

Excipients include butylated hydroxyanisole, cetyl alcohol

Ointment, sodium fusidate 2%, net price 15 g = £2.23, 30 g = £3.79

Excipients include cetyl alcohol, wool fat

Dental prescribing on NHS May be prescribed as Sodium Fusidate ointment

### METRONIDAZOLE

**Indications** see preparations; *Helicobacter pylori* eradication (section 1.3); anaerobic infections (section 5.1.11 and section 7.2.2); protozoal infections (section 5.4.2)

**Cautions** avoid exposure to strong sunlight or UV light

**Side-effects** skin irritation

**Dose**

- See preparations

#### Rosacea (see also section 13.6)

**Metrogel®** (Novartis) PoM

Gel, metronidazole 0.75%, net price 40 g = £19.90. Label: 10, patient information leaflet

Excipients include hydroxybenzoates (parabens), propylene glycol

Dose acute inflammatory exacerbations of acne rosacea, apply thinly twice daily for 8–9 weeks

**Metrosa®** (Linderma) PoM

Gel, metronidazole 0.75%, net price 40 g = £19.90. Label: 10, patient information leaflet

Excipients include propylene glycol

Dose acute exacerbation of acne rosacea, apply thinly twice daily for up to 8 weeks

**Noritate®** (Aventis Pharma) PoM

Cream, metronidazole 1%, net price 30 g = £19.08. Label: 10, patient information leaflet

Excipients include hydroxybenzoates (parabens)

Dose acne rosacea, apply once daily for 8 weeks

**Rozex®** (Galderma) PoM

Cream, metronidazole 0.75%, net price 40 g = £15.28. Label: 10, patient information leaflet

Excipients include benzyl alcohol, isopropyl palmitate

Gel, metronidazole 0.75%, net price 40 g = £15.28. Label: 10, patient information leaflet

Excipients include disodium edetate, hydroxybenzoates (parabens), propylene glycol

Dose inflammatory papules, pustules and erythema of acne rosacea, apply twice daily for 3–4 months

**Zyomet®** (Goldshield) PoM

Gel, metronidazole 0.75%, net price 30 g = £12.00. Label: 10, patient information leaflet

Excipients include benzyl alcohol, disodium edetate, propylene glycol

Dose acute inflammatory exacerbations of acne rosacea, apply thinly twice daily for 8–9 weeks

#### Malodorous tumours and skin ulcers

**Anabact®** (CHS) PoM

Gel, metronidazole 0.75%, net price 15 g = £4.47, 30 g = £7.89

Excipients include hydroxybenzoates (parabens), propylene glycol

Dose malodorous fungating tumours and malodorous gravitational and decubitus ulcers, apply to clean wound 1–2 times daily and cover with non-adherent dressing

**Metrotop®** (Medlock) PoM

Gel, metronidazole 0.8%, net price 15 g = £4.73, 30 g = £8.36

Excipients none as listed in section 13.1.3

Dose malodorous fungating tumours and malodorous gravitational and decubitus ulcers, apply to clean wound 1–2 times daily and cover (flat wounds, apply liberally; cavities, smear on paraffin gauze and pack loosely)

## 13.10.2 Antifungal preparations

Most localised fungal infections are treated with topical preparations. Systemic therapy (section 5.2) is necessary for nail or scalp infection or if the skin infection is widespread, disseminated or intractable. Skin scrapings should be examined if systemic therapy is being considered or where there is doubt about the diagnosis.

**Dermatophytoses** Ringworm infection can affect the scalp (tinea capitis), body (tinea corporis), groin (tinea cruris), hand (tinea manuum), foot (tinea pedis, athlete's foot), or nail (tinea unguium). Scalp infection requires systemic treatment (section 5.2); additional topical application of an antifungal may reduce the risk of transmission. Most other local ringworm infections can be treated adequately with topical antifungal preparations (including shampoos, section 13.9). The imidazole antifungals **clotrimazole, econazole, ketoconazole, miconazole**, and **sulconazole** are all effective. **Terbinafine** cream is also effective but it is more expensive. Other topical antifungals include **amorolfine**, **griseofulvin**, and the **undecenoates**. **Compound benzoic acid ointment** (Whitfield's ointment) has been used for ringworm infections but it is cosmetically less acceptable than proprietary preparations. Topical preparations for athlete's foot containing **tolnaftate** are on sale to the public.

Antifungal dusting powders are of little therapeutic value in the treatment of fungal skin infections and may cause skin irritation; they may have some role in preventing re-infection.

Tinea infection of the nail is almost always treated systemically (section 5.2); topical application of **amorolfine** or **tioconazole** may be effective for treating early onychomycosis when involvement is limited to mild distal disease in up to 2 nails.

**Pityriasis versicolor** Pityriasis (tinea) versicolor may be treated with **ketoconazole** shampoo (section 13.9). Alternatively, **selenium sulphide** shampoo [unlicensed indication] (section 13.9) may be used as a lotion (diluted with water to reduce irritation) and left on for at least 30 minutes or overnight; it is applied 2–7 times over a fortnight and the course repeated if necessary.

Topical imidazole antifungals **clotrimazole**, **econazole**, **ketoconazole**, **miconazole**, and **sulconazole** and topical **terbinafine** are alternatives but large quantities may be required.

If topical therapy fails, or if the infection is widespread, pityriasis versicolor is treated systemically with an azole antifungal (section 5.2). Relapse is common, especially in the immunocompromised.

**Candidiasis** Candidal skin infections may be treated with topical imidazole antifungals **clotrimazole**, **econazole**, **ketoconazole**, **miconazole**, and **sulconazole**; topical terbinafine is an alternative. Topical application of **nystatin** is also effective for candidiasis but it is ineffective against dermatophytosis. Refractory candidiasis requires systemic treatment (section 5.2) generally with a triazole such as fluconazole; systemic treatment with terbinafine is **not appropriate** for refractory candidiasis.

**Angular cheilitis** Nystatin ointment is used in the fissures of angular cheilitis when associated with *Candida*. For further information on angular cheilitis, see p. 561.

**Compound topical preparations** Combination of an imidazole and a mild corticosteroid (such as hydrocortisone 1%) (section 13.4) may be of value in the treatment of eczematous intertrigo and, in the first few days only, of a severely inflamed patch of ringworm. Combination of a mild corticosteroid with either an imidazole or nystatin may be of use in the treatment of intertrigo associated with candida.

**Cautions** Contact with eyes and mucous membranes should be avoided.

**Side-effects** Occasional local irritation and hypersensitivity reactions include mild burning sensation, erythema, and itching. Treatment should be discontinued if these are severe.

### AMOROLFINE

**Indications** see under preparations
**Cautions** see notes above; also avoid contact with ears; pregnancy and breast-feeding
**Side-effects** see notes above

**Loceryl®** (Galderma) PoM
Cream, amorolfine (as hydrochloride) 0.25%, net price 20 g = £4.83. Label: 10, patient information leaflet
Excipients include cetostearyl alcohol, disodium edetate
Dose fungal skin infections, apply once daily after cleansing in the evening for at least 2–3 weeks (up to 6 weeks for foot infection) continuing for 3–5 days after lesions have healed

Nail lacquer, amorolfine (as hydrochloride) 5%, net price 5-mL pack (with nail files, spatulas and cleansing swabs) = £21.43. Label: 10, patient information leaflet
Excipients none as listed in section 13.1.3
Dose fungal nail infections, apply to infected nails 1–2 times weekly after filing and cleansing; allow to dry (approx. 3 minutes); treat finger nails for 6 months, toe nails for 9–12 months (review at intervals of 3 months); avoid nail varnish or artificial nails during treatment

### BENZOIC ACID

**Indications** ringworm (tinea), but see notes above

**Benzoic Acid Ointment, Compound, BP (Whitfield's ointment)**
Ointment, benzoic acid 6%, salicylic acid 3%, in emulsifying ointment
Dose apply twice daily
Excipients include cetostearyl alcohol

### CLOTRIMAZOLE

**Indications** fungal skin infections; vaginal candidiasis (section 7.2.2); otitis externa (section 12.1.1)
**Cautions** see notes above
**Side-effects** see notes above
**Dose**
- Apply 2–3 times daily

**Clotrimazole** (Non-proprietary)
Cream, clotrimazole 1%, net price 20 g = £2.12

[1]**Canesten®** (Bayer Consumer Care)

Cream, clotrimazole 1%, net price 20 g = £2.14, 50 g = £3.80. On sale to the public as *Canesten® AF* cream
Excipients include benzyl alcohol, cetostearyl alcohol, polysorbate 60

Powder, clotrimazole 1%, net price 30 g = £1.52. On sale to the public as *Canesten® AF* powder
Excipients none as listed in section 13.1.3

Solution, clotrimazole 1% in macrogol 400 (polyethylene glycol 400), net price 20 mL = £2.43. For hairy areas
Excipients none as listed in section 13.1.3

Spray, clotrimazole 1%, in 30% isopropyl alcohol, net price 40-mL atomiser = £4.99. Label: 15. For large or hairy areas. On sale to the public as *Canesten® AF* spray
Excipients include propylene glycol

1. The brand name *Canesten® AF Once Daily* is used for bifonazole

## ECONAZOLE NITRATE

**Indications** fungal skin infections; vaginal candidiasis (section 7.2.2)

**Cautions** see notes above

**Side-effects** see notes above

**Dose**

- Skin infections apply twice daily; nail infections, apply once daily under occlusive dressing

**Ecostatin®** (Squibb)

Cream, econazole nitrate 1%, net price 15 g = £1.49; 30 g = £2.75
Excipients include butylated hydroxyanisole, fragrance

**Pevaryl®** (Janssen-Cilag)

Cream, econazole nitrate 1%, net price 30 g = £2.65
Excipients include butylated hydroxyanisole, fragrance

## GRISEOFULVIN

**Indications** tinea pedis; resistant fungal infections (section 5.2)

**Cautions** see notes above

**Side-effects** see notes above

**Dose**

- Apply 400 micrograms (1 spray) to an area approx. 13 cm² once daily, increased to 1.2 mg (3 sprays, allowing each spray to dry between applications) once daily if necessary; max. treatment duration 4 weeks

**Grisol®** (Transdermal)

Spray, griseofulvin 400 micrograms/metered spray, net price 20-mL (400-dose) spray = £4.00. Label: 15
Excipients include benzyl alcohol

## KETOCONAZOLE

**Indications** fungal skin infections; systemic or resistant fungal infections (section 5.2); vulval candidiasis (section 7.2.2)

**Cautions** see notes above; do **not** use within 2 weeks of a topical corticosteroid for seborrhoeic dermatitis—risk of skin sensitisation

**Side-effects** see notes above

**Dose**

- Tinea pedis, apply twice daily; other fungal infections, apply 1–2 times daily

[1]**Nizoral®** (Janssen-Cilag) PoM

[2]Cream, ketoconazole 2%, net price 30 g = £3.62
Excipients include cetyl alcohol, polysorbates, propylene glycol, stearyl alcohol

Shampoo—section 13.9

1. A 15-g tube is available for sale to the public for the treatment of tinea pedis, tinea cruris, and candidal intertrigo (*Daktarin® Gold*)
2. NHS except for seborrhoeic dermatitis and pityriasis versicolor and endorsed 'SLS'

## MICONAZOLE NITRATE

**Indications** fungal skin infections; intestinal fungal infections (section 5.2); oral fungal infections (section 12.3.2); vaginal candidiasis (section 7.2.2)

**Cautions** see notes above

**Side-effects** see notes above

**Dose**

- Apply twice daily continuing for 10 days after lesions have healed; nail infections, apply 1–2 times daily

**Miconazole** (Non-proprietary)

Cream, miconazole nitrate 2%, net price 20 g = £2.05, 45 g = £1.97
Brands include *Acorvio®* (*excipients: include* cetostearyl alcohol, polysorbate 40, propylene glycol)

**Daktarin®** (Janssen-Cilag)

Cream, miconazole nitrate 2%, net price 30 g = £1.97. Also on sale to the public as *Daktarin® Dual Action cream* for athlete's foot
Excipients include butylated hydroxyanisole
Note A 15-g tube NHS is on sale to the public.

Powder NHS, miconazole nitrate 2%, net price 20 g = £1.81. Also on sale to the public as *Daktarin® Dual Action powder* for athlete's foot
Excipients include none as listed in section 13.1.3

Dual Action Spray powder, miconazole nitrate 0.16%, in an aerosol basis, net price 100 g = £2.27
Excipients none as listed in section 13.1.3

## NYSTATIN

**Indications** skin infections due to *Candida* spp.; intestinal candidiasis (section 5.2); vaginal candidiasis (section 7.2.2); oral fungal infections (section 12.3.2)

**Cautions** see notes above

**Side-effects** see notes above

**Nystaform®** (Typharm) PoM

Cream, nystatin 100 000 units/g, chlorhexidine hydrochloride 1%, net price 30 g = £2.62
Excipients include benzyl alcohol, cetostearyl alcohol, polysorbate 60
Dose apply 2–3 times daily continuing for 7 days after lesions have healed.

**Nystan®** (Squibb) PoM

Cream, nystatin 100 000 units/g, net price 30 g = £2.18
Excipients include benzyl alcohol, propylene glycol, fragrance
Dose apply 2–4 times daily

Ointment, nystatin 100 000 units/g, in *Plastibase®*, net price 30 g = £1.75
Excipients none as listed in section 13.1.3
Dose apply 2–4 times daily
Dental prescribing on NHS May be prescribed as Nystatin Ointment

**Tinaderm-M**® (Schering-Plough) PoM

Cream, nystatin 100 000 units/g, tolnaftate 1%, net price 20 g = £1.83

**Excipients** include butylated hydroxytoluene, cetostearyl alcohol, hydroxybenzoates (parabens), fragrance

**Dose** apply 2–3 times daily

## SALICYLIC ACID

**Indications** fungal nail infections, particularly tinea; hyperkeratotic skin disorders (section 13.5.2); acne vulgaris (section 13.6.1); warts and calluses (section 13.7)

**Contra-indications** pregnancy

**Side-effects** see notes above

**Dose**

- Apply twice daily; CHILD under 5 years not recommended

**Phytex**® (Wynlit)

Paint, salicylic acid 1.46% (total combined), tannic acid 4.89% and boric acid 3.12% (as borotannic complex), in a vehicle containing alcohol and ethyl acetate, net price 25 mL (with brush) = £1.56

**Excipients** none as listed in section 13.1.3

**Note** Flammable

## SULCONAZOLE NITRATE

**Indications** fungal skin infections

**Cautions** see notes above

**Side-effects** see notes above; also blistering

**Dose**

- Apply 1–2 times daily continuing for 2–3 weeks after lesions have healed

**Exelderm**® (Centrapharm)

Cream, sulconazole nitrate 1%, net price 30 g = £3.00

**Excipients** include cetyl alcohol, polysorbates, propylene glycol, stearyl alcohol

## TERBINAFINE

**Indications** fungal skin infections

**Cautions** pregnancy, breast-feeding; avoid contact with eyes

**Side-effects** redness, itching, or stinging; *rarely* allergic reactions (discontinue)

[1]**Lamisil**® (Novartis) PoM

Cream, terbinafine hydrochloride 1%, net price 15 g = £4.86, 30 g = £8.76

**Dose** apply thinly 1–2 times daily for up to 1 week in tinea pedis, 1–2 weeks in tinea corporis and tinea cruris, 2 weeks in cutaneous candidiasis and pityriasis versicolor; review after 2 weeks; CHILD not recommended

**Excipients** include benzyl alcohol, cetyl alcohol, polysorbate 60, stearyl alcohol

Tablets—section 5.2

1. Can be sold to the public for external use for the treatment of tinea pedis and tinea cruris as a cream containing terbinafine hydrochloride max. 1% in a pack containing max. 15 g (*Lamisil*® *AT* cream); also for the treatment of tinea pedis, tinea cruris, and tinea corporis as a spray containing terbinafine hydrochloride max. 1% in a pack containing max. 30 mL (*Lamisil*® *AT* spray) or max. 30 g (*Lamisil*® *AT* gel)

## TIOCONAZOLE

**Indications** fungal nail infections

**Cautions** see notes above

**Contra-indications** pregnancy

**Side-effects** see notes above; also local oedema, dry skin, nail discoloration, periungual inflammation, nail pain, rash, exfoliation

**Dose**

- Apply to nails and surrounding skin twice daily for up to 6 months (may be extended to 12 months)

**Trosyl**® (Pfizer) PoM

Cutaneous solution, tioconazole 28%, net price 12 mL (with applicator brush) = £27.38

**Excipients** none as listed in section 13.1.3

## UNDECENOATES

**Indications** see under preparations below

**Side-effects** see notes above

**Dose**

- See under preparations below

**Monphytol**® (LAB)

Paint, methyl undecenoate 5%, propyl undecenoate 0.7%, salicylic acid 3%, methyl salicylate 25%, propyl salicylate 5%, chlorobutanol 3%, net price 18 mL (with brush) = £1.77

**Excipients** none as listed in section 13.1.3

**Dose** fungal skin and nail infections, apply twice daily

**Mycota**® (Thornton & Ross)

Cream, zinc undecenoate 20%, undecenoic acid 5%, net price 25 g = £1.31

**Excipients** include fragrance

**Dose** treatment of athlete's foot, apply twice daily continuing for 7 days after lesions have healed

Prevention of athlete's foot, apply once daily

Powder, zinc undecenoate 20%, undecenoic acid 2%, net price 70 g = £1.87

**Excipients** include fragrance

**Dose** treatment of athlete's foot, apply twice daily continuing for 7 days after lesions have healed

Prevention of athlete's foot, apply once daily

Spray application, undecenoic acid 2.5%, dichlorophen 0.25% (pressurised aerosol pack), net price 100 mL = £2.13

**Excipients** include fragrance

**Dose** treatment of athlete's foot, apply twice daily continuing for 7 days after lesions have healed

Prevention of athlete's foot, apply once daily

# 13.10.3 Antiviral preparations

**Aciclovir** cream is licensed for the treatment of initial and recurrent labial and genital *herpes simplex infections*; treatment should begin as early as possible. Systemic treatment is necessary for buccal or vaginal infections and for *herpes zoster (shingles)* (for details of systemic use see section 5.3.2.1).

**Idoxuridine** solution (5% in dimethyl sulfoxide) is of little value.

**Herpes labialis** **Aciclovir** cream can be used for the treatment of initial and recurrent labial herpes simplex infections (cold sores). It is best applied at the earliest possible stage, usually when prodromal changes of sensation are felt in the lip and before vesicles appear.

**Penciclovir** cream is also licensed for the treatment of herpes labialis; it needs to be applied more frequently than aciclovir cream. These creams should not be used in the mouth.

Systemic treatment is necessary if cold sores recur frequently or for infections in the mouth (see p. 322).

## ACICLOVIR
(Acyclovir)

**Indications** see notes above; herpes simplex and varicella–zoster infections (section 5.3.2.1); eye infections (section 11.3.3)

**Cautions** avoid contact with eyes and mucous membranes

**Side-effects** transient stinging or burning; occasionally erythema, itching or drying of the skin

**Dose**

- Apply to lesions every 4 hours (5 times daily) for 5–10 days, starting at first sign of attack

[1]**Aciclovir** (Non-proprietary) PoM
Cream, aciclovir 5%, net price 2 g = £1.81, 10 g = £4.74
Excipients include propylene glycol
Brands include *Zuvogen®* (*excipients* also include cetyl alcohol, propylene glycol)
Dental prescribing on NHS Aciclovir Cream may be prescribed

1. A 2-g tube and a pump pack are on sale to the public for the treatment of cold sores (*Zovirax® Cold Sore Cream*); other brands on sale to the public include *Action® Cold Sore, Aviral®, Boots Cold Sore®, Clearsore®, Herpetad®, Soothelip®, Viralief®*, and *Virasorb®*

**Zovirax®** (GSK) PoM
Cream, aciclovir 5%, net price 2 g = £4.92, 10 g = £14.82
Excipients include cetostearyl alcohol, propylene glycol
Eye ointment—section 11.3.3
Tablets—section 5.3.2.1

## PENCICLOVIR

**Indications** see notes above

**Cautions** avoid contact with eyes and mucous membranes

**Side-effects** transient stinging, burning, numbness

**Vectavir®** (Novartis Consumer Health) PoM
Cream, penciclovir 1%, net price 2 g = £4.20
Excipients include cetostearyl alcohol, propylene glycol
Dose herpes labialis, apply to lesions every 2 hours during waking hours for 4 days, starting at first sign of attack; CHILD under 12 years, not recommended
Dental prescribing on NHS May be prescribed as Penciclovir Cream

## IDOXURIDINE IN DIMETHYL SULFOXIDE

**Indications** herpes simplex and herpes zoster infection but of little value

**Cautions** avoid contact with the eyes, mucous membranes, and textiles; breast-feeding (Appendix 5)

**Contra-indications** pregnancy (Appendix 4); **not** to be used in mouth

**Side-effects** stinging on application, changes in taste; overuse may cause maceration

**Herpid®** (Astellas) PoM
Application, idoxuridine 5% in dimethyl sulfoxide, net price 5 mL (with applicator) = £6.33
Dose apply to lesions 4 times daily for 4 days, starting at first sign of attack; CHILD under 12 years, not recommended

# 13.10.4 Parasiticidal preparations

**Suitable quantities of parasiticidal preparations**

| | Skin creams | Lotions | Cream rinses |
|---|---|---|---|
| Scalp (headlice) | — | 50–100 mL | 50–100 mL |
| Body (scabies) | 30–60 g | 100 mL | — |
| Body (crab lice) | 30–60 g | 100 mL | — |

These amounts are usually suitable for an adult for single application.

## Scabies

**Permethrin** is effective for the treatment of *scabies* (*Sarcoptes scabiei*); **malathion** can be used if permethrin is inappropriate.

Aqueous preparations are preferable to alcoholic lotions, which are not recommended owing to irritation of excoriated skin and the genitalia.

Older preparations include **benzyl benzoate**, which is an irritant and should be avoided in children; it is less effective than malathion and permethrin.

**Ivermectin** (available on a named patient basis from IDIS) in a single dose of 200 micrograms/kg by mouth has been used, in combination with topical drugs, for the treatment of hyperkeratotic (crusted or 'Norwegian') scabies that does not respond to topical treatment alone.

**Application** Although acaricides have traditionally been applied after a hot bath, this is **not** necessary and there is even evidence that a hot bath may increase absorption into the blood, removing them from their site of action on the skin.

All members of the affected household should be treated simultaneously. Treatment should be applied to the whole body including the scalp, neck, face, and ears. Particular attention should be paid to the webs of the fingers and toes and lotion brushed under the ends of nails. It is now recommended that malathion and permethrin should be applied twice, one week apart; in the case of benzyl benzoate up to 3 applications on consecutive days may be needed. It is important to warn users to reapply treatment to the hands if they are washed. Patients with hyperkeratotic scabies may require 2 or 3 applications of acaricide on consecutive days to ensure that enough penetrates the skin crusts to kill all the mites.

**Itching** The *itch* and *eczema* of scabies persists for some weeks after the infestation has been eliminated and treatment for pruritus and eczema (section 13.5.1) may be required. Application of **crotamiton** can be used to control itching after treatment with more effective acaricides. A topical corticosteroid may help to reduce itch and inflammation after scabies has been treated successfully; however, persistent symptoms suggest that scabies eradication was not successful. Oral administration of a **sedating antihistamine** (section 3.4.1) at night may also be useful.

## Head lice

**Carbaryl**, **malathion**, and the **pyrethroids** (permethrin and phenothrin) are effective against head lice (*Pediculus humanus capitis*) but lice in some districts have developed resistance; resistance to two or more parasiticidal preparations has also been reported. Careful application of **dimeticone**, which acts on the surface of head lice, is also effective. Benzyl benzoate is licensed for the treatment of head lice but it is less effective than other drugs.

Head lice infestation (pediculosis) should be treated using lotion or liquid formulations. Shampoos are diluted too much in use to be effective. Alcoholic formulations are effective but aqueous formulations are preferred in severe eczema, for patients with asthma, and small children. A contact time of 12 hours or overnight treatment is recommended for lotions and liquids; a 2-hour treatment is not sufficient to kill eggs.

In general, a course of treatment for head lice should be 2 applications of product 7 days apart to prevent lice emerging from any eggs that survive the first application.

The policy of rotating insecticides on a district-wide basis is now considered outmoded. To overcome the development of resistance, a mosaic strategy is required whereby, if a course of treatment fails to cure, a different insecticide is used for the next course. If a course of treatment with either permethrin or phenothrin fails, then a non-pyrethroid parasiticidal product should be used for the next course.

**Wet combing methods** Head lice may be mechanically removed by combing wet hair meticulously with a plastic detection comb (probably for at least 30 minutes each time) over the whole scalp at 4-day intervals for a minimum of 2 weeks; hair conditioner or vegetable oil may be used to facilitate the process. Several products are available and some are prescribable on the NHS.

## Crab lice

**Carbaryl** [unlicensed for crab lice], **permethrin**, **phenothrin**, and **malathion** are effective for *crab lice* (*Pthirus pubis*). An aqueous preparation should be applied, allowed to dry naturally and washed off after 12 hours; a second treatment is needed after 7 days to kill lice emerging from surviving eggs. All surfaces of the body should be treated, including the scalp, neck, ears, and face (paying particular attention to the eyebrows and any beard). A different insecticide should be used if a course of treatment fails. Alcoholic lotions are not recommended (owing to irritation of excoriated skin and the genitalia).

Aqueous **malathion** lotion is effective for *crab lice of the eye lashes* [unlicensed use].

## Benzyl benzoate

**Benzyl benzoate** is effective for *scabies* but is not a first-choice for *scabies* (see notes above).

### BENZYL BENZOATE

**Indications** scabies (but see notes above)

**Cautions** children (not recommended, see also under Dose, below), avoid contact with eyes and mucous membranes; do not use on broken or secondarily infected skin; breast-feeding (suspend feeding until product has been washed off)

**Side-effects** skin irritation, burning sensation especially on genitalia and excoriations, occasionally rashes

**Dose**

- Apply over the whole body; repeat without bathing on the following day and wash off 24 hours later; a third application may be required in some cases

  **Note** Not recommended for children—dilution to reduce irritant effect also reduces efficacy. Some manufacturers recommend application to the body but to exclude the head and neck. However, application should be extended to the scalp, neck, face, and ears

**Benzyl Benzoate Application, BP** (Non-proprietary)

Application, benzyl benzoate 25% in an emulsion basis, net price 500 mL = £2.47

Brands include *Ascabiol®* (*excipients: include* triethanolamine)

## Carbaryl

**Carbaryl** is recommended for *head lice*; an aqueous preparation is recommended for *crab lice* (see notes above) but a suitable product is not currently licensed for this indication. In the light of experimental data in *animals* it would be prudent to consider carbaryl as a potential human carcinogen and it has been restricted to prescription only use. The Department of Health has emphasised that the risk is a theoretical one and that any risk from the intermittent use of head lice preparations is likely to be exceedingly small.

### CARBARYL
(Carbaril)

**Indications** see notes above and under preparations

**Cautions** avoid contact with eyes; do not use on broken or secondarily infected skin; do not use more than once a week for 3 consecutive weeks; children under 6 months, medical supervision required; alcoholic lotion **not** recommended for pediculosis in asthma, in severe eczema or in small children

**Side-effects** skin irritation

**Dose**

- Head lice, rub into dry hair and scalp, allow to dry naturally, shampoo after 12 hours, and comb wet hair (see also notes above); repeat application after 7 days [unlicensed use]
- Crab lice [unlicensed indication], apply aqueous solution over whole body (see notes above), allow to dry naturally and wash off after 12 hours or overnight; repeat application after 7 days

**Carylderm®** (SSL) PoM

Liquid, carbaryl 1% in an aqueous basis, net price 50 mL = £2.28

Excipients include cetostearyl alcohol, hydroxybenzoates (parabens)

Lotion, carbaryl 0.5%, in an alcoholic basis, net price 50 mL = £2.28. Label: 15

Excipients include fragrance

## Dimeticone

**Dimeticone** coats head lice and interferes with water balance in lice by preventing the excretion of water; it is less active against eggs and treatment should be repeated after 7 days.

### DIMETICONE

**Indications** head lice

**Cautions** avoid contact with eyes; children under 6 months, medical supervision required

**Side-effects** skin irritation

**Dose**

- Rub into dry hair and scalp, allow to dry naturally, shampoo after minimum 8 hours (or overnight); repeat application after 7 days

**Hedrin®** (Thornton & Ross)

Lotion, dimeticone 4%, net price 50 mL = £2.98, 150 mL = £6.83

## Malathion

**Malathion** is recommended for *scabies*, *head lice* and *crab lice* (for details see notes above).

The risk of systemic effects associated with 1–2 applications of malathion is considered to be very low; however, applications of lotion repeated at intervals of less than 1 week *or* application for more than 3 consecutive weeks should be **avoided** since the likelihood of eradication of lice is not increased.

### MALATHION

**Indications** see notes above and under preparations

**Cautions** avoid contact with eyes; do not use on broken or secondarily infected skin; do not use lotion more than once a week for 3 consecutive weeks; children under 6 months, medical supervision required; alcoholic lotions **not** recommended for head lice in severe eczema, asthma or in small children, or for scabies or crab lice

**Side-effects** skin irritation

**Dose**

- Head lice, rub 0.5% preparation into dry hair and scalp, allow to dry naturally, remove by washing after 12 hours (see also notes above); repeat application after 7 days [unlicensed use]
- Crab lice, apply 0.5% aqueous preparation over whole body, allow to dry naturally, wash off after 12 hours or overnight; repeat application after 7 days [unlicensed use]
- Scabies, apply 0.5% preparation over whole body, and wash off after 24 hours; if hands are washed with soap within 24 hours, they should be retreated; see also notes above; repeat application after 7 days [unlicensed use]

  **Note** For scabies, manufacturer recommends application to the body but not necessarily to the head and neck. However, application should be extended to the scalp, neck, face, and ears

**Derbac-M®** (SSL)

Liquid, malathion 0.5% in an aqueous basis, net price 50 mL = £2.22, 200 mL = £5.70

Excipients include cetostearyl alcohol, fragrance, hydroxybenzoates (parabens)

For crab lice, head lice, and scabies

**Prioderm®** (SSL)

Lotion, malathion 0.5%, in an alcoholic basis, net price 50 mL = £2.22, 200 mL = £5.70. Label: 15

Excipients include fragrance

For head lice (alcoholic formulation, see notes above)

Cream shampoo NHS, malathion 1%, net price 40 g = £2.77

Excipients include cetostearyl alcohol, fragrance, hydroxybenzoates (parabens), sodium edetate, wool fat

**Dose** head and crab lice, not recommended, therefore no dose stated (product too diluted in use and insufficient contact time)

**Quellada M®** (GSK Consumer Healthcare)

Liquid, malathion 0.5% in an aqueous basis, net price 50 mL = £1.85, 200 mL = £4.62

Excipients include cetostearyl alcohol, fragrance, hydroxybenzoates (parabens)

For crab lice, head lice, and scabies

Cream shampoo, malathion 1%, net price 40 g = £2.18

Excipients include cetostearyl alcohol, fragrance, hydroxybenzoates (parabens), sodium edetate, wool fat

**Dose** head and crab lice, not recommended, therefore no dose stated (product too diluted in use and insufficient contact time)

**Suleo-M®** (SSL)

Lotion, malathion 0.5%, in an alcoholic basis, net price 50 mL = £2.22, 200 mL = £5.70. Label: 15

Excipients include fragrance

For head lice (alcoholic formulation, see notes above)

## Permethrin

**Permethrin** is effective for *scabies* and *crab lice* (for details see notes above). Permethrin is active against *head lice* but the formulation and licensed methods of application of the current products make them unsuitable for the treatment of head lice.

### PERMETHRIN

**Indications** see notes above and under Dose

**Cautions** avoid contact with eyes; do not use on broken or secondarily infected skin; children under 6 months, medical supervision required for cream rinse (head lice); children aged 2 months–2 years, medical supervision required for dermal cream (scabies)

**Side-effects** pruritus, erythema, and stinging; rarely rashes and oedema

**Dose**

- Scabies, apply 5% preparation over whole body and wash off after 8–12 hours; CHILD (see also Cautions, above) apply over whole body including face, neck, scalp and ears; if hands washed with soap within 8 hours of application, they should be treated again with cream (see notes above); repeat application after 7 days

  **Note** Manufacturer recommends application to the body but to exclude head and neck. However, application should be extended to the scalp, neck, face, and ears

  Larger patients may require up to two 30-g packs for adequate treatment
- Crab lice, ADULT over 18 years, apply 5% cream over whole body, allow to dry naturally and wash off after

12 hours or after leaving on overnight; repeat application after 7 days

**Permethrin** (Non-proprietary)
Cream, permethrin 5%, net price 30 g = £5.52

**Lyclear® Creme Rinse** (Chefaro UK)
Cream rinse, permethrin 1% in basis containing isopropyl alcohol 20%, net price 59 mL = £2.38, 2 × 59-mL pack = £4.32
Excipients include cetyl alcohol
Dose head lice, not recommended, therefore no dose stated (insufficient contact time)

**Lyclear® Dermal Cream** (Chefaro UK)
Dermal cream, permethrin 5%, net price 30 g = £5.52. Label: 10, patient information leaflet
Excipients include butylated hydroxytoluene, wool fat derivative

## Phenothrin

**Phenothrin** is recommended for *head lice* and *crab lice* (for details see notes above).

### PHENOTHRIN

**Indications** see notes above and under preparations
**Cautions** avoid contact with eyes; do not use on broken or secondarily infected skin; do not use more than once a week for 3 weeks at a time; children under 6 months, medical supervision required; alcoholic preparations **not** recommended for head lice in severe eczema, in asthma, in small children, or for crab lice (see notes above)
**Side-effects** skin irritation
**Dose**
- See under preparations

**Full Marks®** (SSL)
Liquid, phenothrin 0.5% in an aqueous basis, net price 50 mL = £2.22, 200 mL = £5.70
Excipients include cetostearyl alcohol, fragrance, hydroxybenzoates (parabens)
Dose head lice, apply to dry hair, allow to dry naturally; shampoo after 12 hours or next day, comb wet hair; repeat application after 7 days [unlicensed use]

Lotion, phenothrin 0.2% in basis containing isopropyl alcohol 69.3%, net price 50 mL = £2.22, 200 mL = £5.70. Label: 15
Excipients include fragrance
Dose crab lice and head lice (alcoholic formulation, see notes above), apply to dry hair, allow to dry naturally; shampoo after 12 hours [unlicensed contact duration], comb wet hair; repeat application after 7 days [unlicensed use]

Mousse (= foam application), phenothrin 0.5% in an alcoholic basis, net price 50 g = £2.44, 150 g = £6.11. Label: 15
Excipients include cetostearyl alcohol
Dose head lice (alcoholic formulation, see notes above), apply to dry hair, shampoo after 30 minutes, comb wet hair—but product not recommended because contact time insufficient (longer contact time not recommended because of risk of irritation)

# 13.10.5 Preparations for minor cuts and abrasions

Some of the preparations listed are used in minor burns, and abrasions. They are applied as necessary but should not be used on large wounds or for prolonged periods because of the possibility of hypersensitivity. The effervescent effect of hydrogen peroxide (section 13.11.6) is used to clean minor cuts and abrasions. Preparations containing camphor and sulphonamides should be **avoided**. Preparations such as magnesium sulphate paste are also listed but are now rarely used to treat carbuncles and boils as these are best treated with antibiotics (section 5.1.1.2).

**Cetrimide Cream, BP**
Cream, cetrimide 0.5% in a suitable water-miscible basis such as cetostearyl alcohol 5%, liquid paraffin 50% in freshly boiled and cooled purified water, net price 50 g = 76p

**Proflavine Cream, BPC**
Cream, proflavine hemisulphate 0.1%, yellow beeswax 2.5%, chlorocresol 0.1%, liquid paraffin 67.3%, freshly boiled and cooled purified water 25%, wool fat 5%, net price 100 mL = 85p
Excipients include beeswax, wool fat
Note Stains clothing

Preparations for boils
**Magnesium Sulphate Paste, BP**
Paste, dried magnesium sulphate 45 g, glycerol 55 g, phenol 500 mg, net price 25 g = 59p, 50 g = 72p
Note Should be stirred before use
Dose apply under dressing

## Collodion

**Flexible collodion** may be used to seal minor cuts and wounds that have partially healed.

**Collodion, Flexible, BP**
Collodion, castor oil 2.5%, colophony 2.5% in a collodion basis, prepared by dissolving pyroxylin (10%) in a mixture of 3 volumes of ether and 1 volume of alcohol (90%), net price 10 mL = 27p. Label: 15

## Skin tissue adhesive

Tissue adhesives are used for closure of minor skin wounds and for additional suture support. They should be applied by an appropriately trained healthcare professional.

**Dermabond®** (Ethicon)
Topical skin adhesive, sterile, ocrilate, net price 0.5 mL = £10.18

**Epiglu®** (Valeant)
Tissue adhesive, sterile, ethyl-2-cyanoacrylate 954.5 mg/g, polymethylmethacrylate, net price 4 × 3-g vials = £95.00 (with dispensing pipettes and pallete)

**Indermil®** (Tyco)
Tissue adhesive, sterile, enbucrilate, net price 5 × 500-mg units = £32.50, 20 × 500-mg units = £130.00

**Histoacryl®** (Braun)
Tissue adhesive, sterile, enbucrilate, net price 5 × 200-mg unit (blue) = £32.00, 10 × 200-mg unit (blue) = £67.20, 5 × 500-mg unit (clear or blue) = £34.65, 10 × 500-mg unit (blue) = £69.30

**LiquiBand®** (MedLogic)
Tissue adhesive, sterile, enbucrilate, net price 0.5-g amp = £5.50

# 13.11 Skin cleansers and antiseptics


13.11.1 Alcohols and saline
13.11.2 Chlorhexidine salts
13.11.3 Cationic surfactants and soaps
13.11.4 Iodine
13.11.5 Phenolics
13.11.6 Astringents, oxidisers, and dyes
13.11.7 Preparations for promotion of wound healing


Soap or detergent is used with water to cleanse intact skin; emollient preparations such as aqueous cream or emulsifying ointment (section 13.2.1) that do not irritate the skin are best used for cleansing dry skin.

An antiseptic is used for skin that is infected or that is susceptible to recurrent infection. Detergent preparations containing **chlorhexidine**, **triclosan**, or **povidone–iodine**, which should be thoroughly rinsed off, are used. Emollients may also contain antiseptics (section 13.2.1).

Antiseptics such as **chlorhexidine** or **povidone–iodine** are used on intact skin before surgical procedures; their antiseptic effect is enhanced by an alcoholic solvent. **Cetrimide** solution may be used if a detergent effect is also required.

For irrigating ulcers or wounds, lukewarm sterile sodium chloride 0.9% solution is used but tap water is often appropriate.

**Potassium permanganate** solution 1 in 10 000, a mild antiseptic with astringent properties, can be used for exudative eczematous areas; it should be stopped when the skin becomes dry. It can stain skin and nails especially with prolonged use.



## 13.11.1 Alcohols and saline

### ALCOHOL

**Indications** skin preparation before injection

**Cautions** flammable; avoid broken skin; patients have suffered severe burns when diathermy has been preceded by application of alcoholic skin disinfectants

**Industrial Methylated Spirit, BP**
Solution, 19 volumes of ethanol and 1 volume approved wood naphtha, net price '66 OP' (containing 95% by volume alcohol) 100 mL = 32p; '74 OP' (containing 99% by volume alcohol) 100 mL = 32p. Label: 15

**Surgical Spirit, BP**
Spirit, methyl salicylate 0.5 mL, diethyl phthalate 2%, castor oil 2.5%, in industrial methylated spirit, net price 100 mL = 20p. Label: 15

### SODIUM CHLORIDE

**Indications** see notes above; nebuliser diluent (section 3.1.5); sodium depletion (section 9.2.1.2); electrolyte imbalance (section 9.2.2.1); eye (section 11.8.1); oral hygiene (section 12.3.4)

**Sodium Chloride** (Non-proprietary)
Solution (sterile), sodium chloride 0.9%, net price 10 × 10-mL unit = £3.60, 10 × 20-mL unit = £10.36, 10 × 30-mL unit = £3.00, 200-mL can = £2.65

**Flowfusor®** (Fresenius Kabi)
Solution (sterile), sodium chloride 0.9%, net price 120-mL Bellows Pack = £1.55

**Irriclens®** (ConvaTec)
Solution in aerosol can (sterile), sodium chloride 0.9%, net price 240-mL can = £3.00

**Irripod®** (C D Medical)
Solution (sterile), sodium chloride 0.9%, net price 25 × 20-mL sachet = £5.50

**Miniversol®** (Aguettant)
Solution (sterile), sodium chloride 0.9%, net price 30 × 45-mL unit = £15.00; 30 × 100-mL unit = £21.30

**Normasol®** (Medlock)
Solution (sterile), sodium chloride 0.9%, net price 25 × 25-mL sachet = £5.95; 10 × 100-mL sachet = £7.28

**Stericlens®** (C D Medical)
Solution in aerosol can (sterile), sodium chloride 0.9%, net price 100-mL can = £1.94, 240-mL can = £2.95

**Steripod® Sodium Chloride** (Medlock)
Solution (sterile), sodium chloride 0.9%, net price 25 × 20-mL sachet = £6.95

## 13.11.2 Chlorhexidine salts

### CHLORHEXIDINE

**Indications** see under preparations; bladder irrigation and catheter patency solutions (see section 7.4.4)

**Cautions** avoid contact with eyes, brain, meninges and middle ear; not for use in body cavities; alcoholic solutions not suitable before diathermy

**Side-effects** occasional sensitivity

**Chlorhexidine 0.05%** (Baxter)
2000 Solution (sterile), pink, chlorhexidine acetate 0.05%, net price 500 mL = 72p, 1000 mL = 77p
For cleansing and disinfecting wounds and burns

**Cepton®** (LPC)
Skin wash (= solution), red, chlorhexidine gluconate 1%, net price 150 mL = £1.99
For use as skin wash in acne

Lotion, blue, chlorhexidine gluconate 0.1%, net price 150 mL = £1.99
For skin disinfection in acne

**CX Antiseptic Dusting Powder®** (Adams Hlth.)
Dusting powder, sterile, chlorhexidine acetate 1%, net price 15 g = £2.52
For skin disinfection

**Hibiscrub®** (SSL)
Cleansing solution, red, chlorhexidine gluconate solution 20% (≡ 4% chlorhexidine gluconate), per-

fumed, in a surfactant solution, net price 250 mL = £1.10, 500 mL = £1.60, 5 litres = £12.70
**Excipients** include fragrance
Use instead of soap for pre-operative hand and skin preparation and for general hand and skin disinfection

**Hibisol®** (SSL)
Solution, chlorhexidine gluconate solution 2.5% (≡ 0.5% chlorhexidine gluconate), in isopropyl alcohol 70% with emollients, net price 500 mL = £1.70
To be used undiluted for hand and skin disinfection

**Hibitane Obstetric®** (Centrapharm)
Cream, chlorhexidine gluconate solution 5% (≡ 1% chlorhexidine gluconate), in a pourable water-miscible basis, net price 250 mL = £2.89
For use in obstetrics and gynaecology as an antiseptic and lubricant (for application to skin around vulva and perineum and to hands of midwife or doctor)

**Hydrex®** (Adams Hlth.)
Solution, chlorhexidine gluconate solution 2.5% (≡ chlorhexidine gluconate 0.5%), in an alcoholic solution, net price 600 mL (clear) = £1.94; 600 mL (pink) = £1.94, 200-mL spray = £1.77, 500-mL spray = £3.01; 600 mL (blue) = £2.12
For pre-operative skin disinfection
**Note** Flammable

Surgical scrub, chlorhexidine gluconate 4% in a surfactant solution, net price 250 mL = £1.82, 500 mL = £1.92
For pre-operative hand and skin preparation and for general hand disinfection

**Unisept®** (Medlock)
Solution (sterile), pink, chlorhexidine gluconate 0.05%, net price 25 × 25-mL sachet = £5.59; 10 × 100-mL sachet = £6.84
For cleansing and disinfecting wounds and burns and swabbing in obstetrics

**With cetrimide**

**Tisept®** (Medlock)
Solution (sterile), yellow, chlorhexidine gluconate 0.015%, cetrimide 0.15%, net price 25 × 25-mL sachet = £5.59; 10 × 100-mL sachet = £6.84
To be used undiluted for general skin disinfection and wound cleansing

**Travasept 100®** (Baxter)
Solution (sterile), yellow, chlorhexidine acetate 0.015%, cetrimide 0.15%, net price 500 mL = 72p, 1 litre = 77p
To be used undiluted in skin disinfection such as wound cleansing and obstetrics

## Concentrates

**Hibitane 5% Concentrate®** (SSL)
Solution, red, chlorhexidine gluconate solution 25% (≡ 5% chlorhexidine gluconate), in a perfumed aqueous solution, net price 5 litres = £11.50
**Dose** to be used diluted 1 in 10 (0.5%) with alcohol 70% for pre-operative skin preparation, or 1 in 100 (0.05%) with water for general skin disinfection
**Note** Alcoholic solutions not suitable before diathermy (see Alcohol, p. 606)

**With cetrimide**

**Hibicet Hospital Concentrate®** (SSL)
Solution, orange, chlorhexidine gluconate solution 7.5% (≡ chlorhexidine gluconate 1.5%), cetrimide 15%, net price 5 litres = £8.55
**Dose** to be used diluted 1 in 100 (1%) to 1 in 30 with water for skin disinfection and wound cleansing, and diluted 1 in 30 in alcohol 70% for pre-operative skin preparation
**Note** Alcoholic solutions not suitable before diathermy (see Alcohol, p. 606)

## 13.11.3 Cationic surfactants and soaps

### CETRIMIDE

**Indications** skin disinfection
**Cautions** avoid contact with eyes; avoid use in body cavities
**Side-effects** skin irritation and occasionally sensitisation

**Preparations**
Ingredient of *Hibicet Hospital Concentrate®*, *Tisept®*, and *Travasept® 100*, see above

## 13.11.4 Iodine

### POVIDONE–IODINE

**Indications** skin disinfection; vaginal infections (section 7.2.2); oral hygiene (section 12.3.4)
**Cautions** pregnancy (Appendix 4), breast-feeding (Appendix 5); broken skin (see below); renal impairment (Appendix 3)
**Large open wounds** The application of povidone–iodine to large wounds or severe burns may produce systemic adverse effects such as metabolic acidosis, hypernatraemia and impairment of renal function.
**Contra-indications** avoid regular use in patients with thyroid disorders or those receiving lithium therapy
**Side-effects** rarely sensitivity; may interfere with thyroid function tests

**Betadine®** (Medlock)
Antiseptic paint, povidone–iodine 10% in an alcoholic solution, net price 8 mL (with applicator brush) = £1.01
**Dose** apply undiluted to minor wounds and infections, twice daily

Alcoholic solution, povidone–iodine 10%, net price 500 mL = £1.91
**Dose** apply undiluted in pre- and post-operative skin disinfection; NEONATE not recommended for regular use (contra-indicated if birth-weight below 1.5 kg)
**Note** Flammable—caution in procedures involving hot wire cautery and diathermy

Antiseptic solution, povidone–iodine 10% in aqueous solution, net price 500 mL = £1.75
**Dose** apply undiluted in pre- and post-operative skin disinfection; NEONATE not recommended for regular use (contra-indicated if birth-weight below 1.5 kg)
**Note** Not for body cavity irrigation

Dry powder spray, povidone–iodine 2.5% in a pressurised aerosol unit, net price 150-g unit = £2.79
For skin disinfection, particularly minor wounds and infections; INFANT under 2 years not recommended
Note Not for use in serous cavities

Ointment, povidone–iodine 10%, in a water-miscible basis, net price 20 g = £1.39, 80 g = £2.79
Excipients none as listed in section 13.1.3
For skin disinfection, particularly minor wounds and infections; INFANT under 2 years not recommended

Skin cleanser solution, povidone–iodine 4%, in a surfactant basis, net price 250 mL = £2.14
Dose for infective conditions of the skin. Retain on skin for 3–5 minutes before rinsing; repeat twice daily; INFANT under 2 years max. treatment duration 3 days

Surgical scrub, povidone–iodine 7.5%, in a non-ionic surfactant basis, net price 500 mL = £1.58
To be used as a pre-operative scrub for hands and skin; NEONATE not recommended for regular use (contra-indicated if birth-weight below 1.5 kg)

**Savlon® Dry Antiseptic** (Novartis Consumer Health)
Powder spray, povidone–iodine 1.14% in a pressurised aerosol unit, net price 50-mL unit = £2.39
For minor wounds

**Videne®** (Adams Hlth.)
Alcoholic tincture, povidone–iodine 10%, net price 500 mL = £2.35
To be applied undiluted in pre-operative skin disinfection

Antiseptic solution, povidone–iodine 10% in aqueous solution, net price 500 mL = £2.35
To be applied undiluted in pre-operative skin disinfection and general antisepsis

Surgical scrub, povidone–iodine 7.5% in aqueous solution, net price 500 mL = £2.35
To be used as a pre-operative scrub for hand and skin disinfection

## 13.11.5 Phenolics

### TRICLOSAN

**Indications** skin disinfection
**Cautions** avoid contact with eyes

**Aquasept®** (Medlock)
Skin cleanser, blue, triclosan 2%, net price 250 mL = £1.10, 500 mL = £1.68
Excipients include chlorocresol, propylene glycol, fragrance, tetrasodium edetate
For disinfection and pre-operative hand preparation

**Manusept®** (Medlock)
Antibacterial hand rub, triclosan 0.5%, isopropyl alcohol 70%, net price 250 mL = £1.07, 500 mL = £1.56
Excipients none as listed in section 13.1.3
For disinfection and pre-operative hand preparation
Note Flammable

**Ster-Zac Bath Concentrate®** (Medlock)
Solution, triclosan 2%, net price 28.5 mL = 40p, 500 mL = £2.24
Dose for prevention of cross-infection use 28.5 mL/bath
Excipients include trisodium edetate

## 13.11.6 Astringents, oxidisers, and dyes

### HYDROGEN PEROXIDE

**Indications** see under preparations below
**Cautions** large or deep wounds; avoid on healthy skin and eyes; bleaches fabric; incompatible with products containing iodine or potassium permanganate

**Hydrogen Peroxide Solution, BP**
Solution 6% (20 vols), net price 100 mL = 17p
Solution 3% (10 vols), net price 100 mL = 18p
For skin disinfection, particularly cleansing and deodorising wounds and ulcers
Note The BP directs that when hydrogen peroxide is prescribed, hydrogen peroxide solution 6% (20 vols) should be dispensed.
Important Strong solutions of hydrogen peroxide which contain 27% (90 vols) and 30% (100 vols) are only for the preparation of weaker solutions

**Crystacide®** (GP Pharma)
Cream, hydrogen peroxide 1%, net price 10 g = £3.71, 25 g = £6.21
Dose superficial bacterial skin infection, apply 2-3 times daily for up to 3 weeks
Excipients include edetic acid (EDTA), propylene glycol

**Hioxyl®**
Section 13.11.7

### POTASSIUM PERMANGANATE

**Indications** cleansing and deodorising suppurating eczematous reactions and wounds
**Cautions** irritant to mucous membranes
**Dose**

- Wet dressings or baths, approx. 0.01% solution
  Note Stains skin and clothing

**Potassium Permanganate Solution**
Solution, potassium permanganate 0.1% (1 in 1000) in water
Dose to be diluted 1 in 10 to provide a 0.01% (1 in 10 000) solution

**Permitabs®** (Centrapharm)
Solution tablets, for preparation of topical solution, potassium permanganate 400 mg, net price 30-tab pack = £6.22
Note 1 tablet dissolved in 4 litres of water provides a 0.01% (1 in 10 000) solution

## 13.11.7 Preparations for promotion of wound healing

### Desloughing agents

Alginate, hydrogel and hydrocolloid dressings (Appendix 8) are effective at wound debridement. Sterile larvae (maggots) (*LarvE®*, Zoobiotic) are also used for managing sloughing wounds and are prescribable on the NHS. Dextranomer beads are designed for applying to sloughing ulcers but they are less effective than dressings and are rarely used nowadays.

Desloughing solutions and creams are also of little clinical value and are rarely used nowadays. Substances applied to an open area are easily absorbed and perilesional skin is easily sensitised; gravitational dermatitis may be complicated by superimposed contact sensitivity to substances such as neomycin or lanolin.

The enzyme preparation streptokinase–streptodornase, which removes slough, can provoke hypersensitivity reactions; furthermore, antibodies against streptokinase may reduce the thrombolytic effectiveness of parenteral streptokinase.

**Aserbine®** (Goldshield)
Solution, benzoic acid 0.15%, malic acid 2.25%, propylene glycol 40%, salicylic acid 0.0375%, net price 500 mL = £3.61
Excipients include fragrance
Dose use as wash before each application of cream (or use as wet dressing)

**Hioxyl®** (Ferndale)
Cream, hydrogen peroxide (stabilised) 1.5%, net price 25 g = £2.16, 100 g = £6.76
Excipients include cetostearyl alcohol
For leg ulcers and pressure sores
Dose apply when necessary and if necessary cover with a dressing

**Varidase Topical®** (Wyeth) PoM
Powder, streptokinase 100 000 units, streptodornase 25 000 units. For preparing solutions for topical use, net price with sterile physiological saline 20 mL (combi-pack) = £10.06
Excipients none as listed in section 13.1.3
Dose reconstitute with 20 mL sterile physiological saline (or water for injections) and apply as wet dressing 1–2 times daily; cover with semi-occlusive dressing; irrigate lesion thoroughly with physiological saline and remove loosened material before next application; also used to dissolve clots in the bladder or urinary catheters
Contra-indications active haemorrhage, severe hypertension
Side-effects infrequent allergic reactions (reduced by careful and frequent removal of exudate and thorough irrigation with physiological saline); fever, transient burning, haemorrhage, and hypersensitivity reactions including shock reported

## Growth factor

A topical preparation of **becaplermin** (recombinant human platelet-derived growth factor) is licensed as an adjunct treatment of full-thickness, neuropathic, diabetic ulcers.

**Regranex®** (Janssen-Cilag) PoM
Gel, becaplermin (recombinant human platelet-derived growth factor) 0.01%, net price 15 g = £275
Excipients include hydroxybenzoates
Dose full-thickness, neuropathic, diabetic ulcers (no larger than 5 cm²), apply thin layer daily and cover with gauze dressing moistened with physiological saline; max. duration of treatment 20 weeks (reassess if no healing after first 10 weeks)
Cautions malignant disease; avoid on sites with infection, malignancy, peripheral arteriopathy, or osteomyelitis
Side-effects irritation, rarely bullous eruption, oedema

# 13.12 Antiperspirants

**Aluminium chloride** is a potent antiperspirant used in the treatment of hyperhidrosis. Aluminium salts are also incorporated in preparations used for minor fungal skin infections associated with hyperhidrosis.

In more severe cases specialists use **glycopyrronium bromide** as a 0.05% solution in the iontophoretic treatment of hyperhidrosis of plantar and palmar areas. **Botulinum A toxin-haemagglutinin complex** (section 4.9.3) is licensed for use intradermally for severe hyperhidrosis of the axillae unresponsive to topical antiperspirant or other antihidrotic treatment.

## ALUMINIUM SALTS

**Indications** see under Dose below

**Cautions** avoid contact with eyes or mucous membranes; avoid use on broken or irritated skin; do not shave axillae or use depilatories within 12 hours of application; avoid contact with clothing

**Side-effects** skin irritation

**Dose**
- Hyperhidrosis affecting axillae, hands or feet, apply liquid formulation at night to dry skin, wash off the following morning, initially daily then reduce frequency as condition improves—do not bathe immediately before use
- Hyperhidrosis, bromidrosis, intertrigo, and prevention of tinea pedis and related conditions, apply powder to dry skin

**Anhydrol Forte®** (Dermal)
Solution (= application), aluminium chloride hexahydrate 20% in an alcoholic basis, net price 60-mL bottle with roll-on applicator = £2.62. Label: 15
Excipients none as listed in section 13.1.3

[1]**Driclor®** (Stiefel)
Application, aluminium chloride hexahydrate 20% in an alcoholic basis, net price 60-mL bottle with roll-on applicator = £2.82. Label: 15
Excipients none as listed in section 13.1.3

1. A 30-mL pack is on sale to the public (*Driclor® Solution*)

**ZeaSORB®** (Stiefel)
Dusting powder, aldioxa 0.22%, chloroxylenol 0.5%, net price 50 g = £2.15
Excipients include fragrance

## GLYCOPYRRONIUM BROMIDE

**Indications** iontophoretic treatment of hyperhidrosis; other indications section 15.1.3

**Cautions** see section 15.1.3 (but poorly absorbed and systemic effects unlikely)

**Contra-indications** see section 15.1.3 (but poorly absorbed and systemic effects unlikely), infections affecting the treatment site

**Side-effects** see section 15.1.3 (but poorly absorbed and systemic effects unlikely), tingling at administration site

**Dose**
- Consult product literature; only 1 site to be treated at a time, max. 2 sites treated in any 24 hours, treatment not to be repeated within 7 days

**Robinul®** (Antigen) PoM
Powder, glycopyrronium bromide, net price 3 g = £110.00

# 13.13 Wound management products and Elastic Hosiery

**Preparations**
See Appendix 8

# 13.14 Topical circulatory preparations

These preparations are used to improve circulation in conditions such as bruising, superficial thrombophlebitis, chilblains and varicose veins but are of little value. Chilblains are best managed by avoidance of exposure to cold; neither systemic nor topical vasodilator therapy is established as being effective. Sclerotherapy of varicose veins is described in section 2.13.

Rubefacients are described in section 10.3.2.

**Hirudoid®** (Sankyo)
Cream, heparinoid 0.3% in a vanishing-cream basis, net price 50 g = £1.39
Excipients include cetostearyl alcohol, hydroxybenzoates (parabens)

Gel, heparinoid 0.3%, net price 50 g = £1.39
Excipients include propylene glycol, fragrance

Dose apply up to 4 times daily in superficial soft-tissue injuries and superficial thrombophlebitis

**Lasonil®** (Bayer Consumer Care)
Ointment, heparinoid 0.8% in white soft paraffin, net price 40 g = £1.08
Excipients include wool fat derivative

Dose apply 2–3 times daily in superficial soft-tissue injuries

# 14 Immunological products and vaccines


14.1 Active immunity 611
14.2 Passive immunity 612
14.3 Storage and use 613
14.4 Vaccines and antisera 613
14.5 Immunoglobulins 627
14.6 International travel 630


## 14.1 Active immunity

**Vaccines** may consist of:

1. a *live attenuated* form of a virus (e.g. rubella or measles vaccine) or bacteria (e.g. BCG vaccine)
2. *inactivated* preparations of the virus (e.g. influenza vaccine) or bacteria, or
3. *extracts of* or *detoxified exotoxins* produced by a micro-organism (e.g. tetanus vaccine).

They stimulate production of antibodies and other components of the immune mechanism.

**Live attenuated vaccines** usually produce a durable immunity but not always as long-lasting as that of the natural infection. When two live virus vaccines are required (and are not available as a combined preparation) they should be given either simultaneously at different sites or separated by an interval of at least 3 weeks.

**Inactivated** vaccines may require a primary series of injections of vaccine to produce adequate antibody response and in most cases booster (reinforcing) injections are required; the duration of immunity varies from months to many years. Some inactivated vaccines are adsorbed onto an adjuvant (such as aluminium hydroxide) to enhance the antibody response.

Advice in this chapter reflects that in the handbook *Immunisation against Infectious Disease* (1996), which in turn reflects the guidance of the Joint Committee on Vaccination and Immunisation (JCVI).
Chapters from the handbook are available at www.dh.gov.uk
The advice incorporates changes announced by the Chief Medical Officer and Health Department Updates.

**Side-effects** Some vaccines (e.g. poliomyelitis) produce very few reactions, while others (e.g. measles and rubella) may produce a very mild form of the disease. Some vaccines may produce discomfort at the site of injection and mild fever and malaise. Occasionally there are more serious untoward reactions and these should always be reported to the CSM. Anaphylactic reactions are very rare but can be fatal (see section 3.4.3 for management). The product literature should be consulted for full details of side-effects.

**Post-immunisation pyrexia in infants**
The parent should be advised that if pyrexia develops after childhood immunisation, the infant can be given a dose of paracetamol and, if necessary, a second dose given 6 hours later; ibuprofen may be used if paracetamol is unsuitable. The parent should be warned to seek medical advice if the pyrexia persists.
For post-immunisation pyrexia in an infant aged 2–3 months, the dose of paracetamol is 60 mg; the dose of ibuprofen is 50 mg (on doctor's advice). An oral syringe can be obtained from any pharmacy to give the small volume required.

**Contra-indications** Most vaccines have some basic contra-indication to their use, and the product literature and *Immunisation against Infectious Disease* should be consulted for details. In general, vaccination should be postponed if the individual is suffering from an *acute illness*. Minor illnesses without fever or systemic upset are not contra-indications. Anaphylaxis with a preceding dose of a vaccine (or vaccine component) is a contra-indication to further doses.

*Hypersensitivity to egg* contra-indicates influenza vaccine and tick-borne encephalitis vaccine (residual egg protein present) and, if evidence of previous anaphylactic reaction, also yellow fever vaccine. Some viral vaccines contain small quantities of antibacterials; such vaccines may need to be withheld from individuals who are *extremely sensitive to the antibacterial*. Other excipients in vaccines may also rarely cause allergic reactions. The presence of the following excipients in vaccines and immunological products has been noted under the relevant entries:

| | |
|---|---|
| Gelatin | Penicillins |
| Gentamicin | Polymyxin B |
| Kanamycin | Streptomycin |
| Neomycin | Thiomersal |

Live vaccines should not be administered routinely to *pregnant women* because of possible harm to the fetus but where there is a significant risk of exposure (e.g. to yellow fever), the need for vaccination usually outweighs any possible risk to the fetus. Live vaccines should not be given to individuals with *impaired immune response*, whether caused by disease (for special reference to *HIV infection*, see below) or treatment with high doses of corticosteroids or other immunosuppressive drugs. They should not be given to those being treated for *malignant conditions* with chemotherapy or generalised radiotherapy[1,2]. The response to vaccines may be

1. Live vaccines should be postponed until at least 3 months after stopping corticosteroids or other immunosuppressive drugs and 6 months after stopping chemotherapy or generalised radiotherapy.
2. Use of normal immunoglobulin should be considered after exposure to measles (see p. 628) and varicella–zoster immunoglobulin considered after exposure to chickenpox or herpes zoster (see p. 628).

reduced and there is risk of generalised infection with live vaccines.

The Royal College of Paediatrics and Child Health has produced a statement, *Immunisation of the Immunocompromised Child (2002)* (available at www.rcpch.ac.uk).

The intramuscular route should not be used in patients with bleeding disorders such as haemophilia or thrombocytopenia. Vaccines that are usually given by the intramuscular route may be given by subcutaneous injection in those with bleeding disorders.

**Note** The Department of Health has advised *against the use of jet guns* for vaccination owing to the risk of transmitting blood-borne infections, such as HIV.

**Vaccines and HIV infection** HIV-positive individuals with or without symptoms can receive the following live vaccines:

MMR (but not whilst severely immunosuppressed), varicella-zoster (but avoid if immunity significantly impaired—consult product literature);[1,2]

and the following inactivated vaccines:

cholera (oral), diphtheria, haemophilus influenzae type b, hepatitis A, hepatitis B, influenza, meningococcal, pertussis, pneumococcal, poliomyelitis[3], rabies, tetanus, typhoid (injection).

HIV-positive individuals should **not** receive:

BCG, yellow fever[4]

**Note** The above advice differs from that for other immunocompromised patients.

**Vaccines and asplenia** The following vaccines are recommended for asplenic patients or those with splenic dysfunction:

haemophilus influenzae type b, meningococcal group C, pneumococcal, influenza.

For antibiotic prophylaxis in asplenia see p. 272.

## Immunisation schedule

Vaccines for the childhood immunisation schedule should be obtained from **local health authorities** or **direct from Farillon**—not to be prescribed on FP10 (HS21 in Northern Ireland; GP10 in Scotland; WP10 in Wales).

### During first year of life

**Diphtheria, Tetanus, Pertussis (Acellular, Component), Poliomyelitis (Inactivated) and Haemophilus Type b Conjugate Vaccine (Adsorbed)**

3 doses at intervals of 4 weeks; first dose at 2 months of age

*plus*

**Meningococcal Group C Conjugate Vaccine**

3 doses at intervals of 4 weeks; first dose at 2 months of age

**BCG Vaccine** (for neonates at risk only)

See section 14.4, BCG Vaccines

**Important.** Late change, see p. viii

1. Use of normal immunoglobulin should be considered after exposure to measles (see p. 628) and varicella–zoster immunoglobulin considered after exposure to chickenpox or herpes zoster (see p. 628).
2. The Royal College of Paediatrics and Child Health recommends that MMR is not given to a child with HIV infection whilst severely immunosuppressed.
3. Inactivated poliomyelitis vaccine is now used instead of oral poliomyelitis vaccine for routine immunisation of children.
4. Because insufficient evidence of safety.

### During second year of life

**Measles, Mumps and Rubella Vaccine, Live** (MMR)

Single dose at 12–15 months of age

### Before school or nursery school entry

**Adsorbed Diphtheria** [low dose], **Tetanus, Pertussis (Acellular, Component) and Inactivated Poliomyelitis Vaccine**

or

**Adsorbed Diphtheria, Tetanus, Pertussis (Acellular, Component) and Inactivated Poliomyelitis Vaccine**

Single booster dose

Preferably allow interval of at least 3 years after completing basic course; can be given at same session as MMR Vaccine but use separate syringe and needle, and give in different limb

*plus*

**Measles, Mumps and Rubella Vaccine, Live** (MMR)

Single booster dose

Can be given at same session as Adsorbed Diphtheria [low dose], Tetanus, Pertussis (Acellular, Component) and Inactivated Poliomyelitis Vaccine but use separate syringe and needle, and use different limb

### Before leaving school or before employment or further education

**Adsorbed Diphtheria** [low dose], **Tetanus and Inactivated Poliomyelitis Vaccine**

Single booster dose

### During adult life

**Measles, Mumps and Rubella Vaccine, Live** (MMR) (for women of child-bearing age susceptible to rubella)

Single dose

Women of child-bearing age should be tested for rubella antibodies and sero-negative women offered rubella immunisation (using the MMR vaccine)—exclude pregnancy before immunisation, but see also section 14.4, Measles, Mumps and Rubella Vaccine

**Adsorbed Diphtheria** [low dose], **Tetanus and Inactivated Poliomyelitis Vaccine** (if not previously immunised)

3 doses at intervals of 4 weeks

Booster dose at least 1 year after primary course and again 5–10 years later

### High-risk groups

For information on high-risk groups, see section 14.4 under individual vaccines

**BCG Vaccines**

**Hepatitis A Vaccine**

**Hepatitis B Vaccine**

**Influenza Vaccine**

**Pneumococcal Vaccines**

**Tetanus Vaccines**

## 14.2 Passive immunity

Immunity with immediate protection against certain infective organisms can be obtained by injecting preparations made from the plasma of immune individuals with adequate levels of antibody to the disease for which protection is sought (see under Immunoglobulin section 14.5). This passive immunity lasts only a few weeks; where necessary passive immunisation can be repeated.

Antibodies of human origin are usually termed *immunoglobulins*. The term *antiserum* is applied to material prepared in animals. Because of serum sickness and other allergic-type reactions that may follow injections of antisera, this therapy has been replaced wherever possible by the use of immunoglobulins. Reactions are theoretically possible after injection of human immunoglobulins but reports of such reactions are very rare.

# 14.3 Storage and use

Care must be taken to store all vaccines and other immunological products under the conditions recommended in the product literature, otherwise the preparation may become ineffective. **Refrigerated storage** is usually necessary; many vaccines need to be stored at 2–8°C and not allowed to freeze. Vaccines should be protected from light. Unused vaccine in multidose vials without preservative (most live virus vaccines) should be discarded within 1 hour of first use; those containing a preservative (including oral poliomyelitis vaccine) should be discarded within 3 hours or at the end of a session. Unused vaccines should be disposed of by incineration at a registered disposal contractor.

Particular attention must be paid to instructions on the use of diluents. Vaccines which are liquid suspensions or are reconstituted before use should be adequately mixed to ensure uniformity of the material to be injected.

# 14.4 Vaccines and antisera

**Availability** Anthrax and yellow fever vaccines, botulism antitoxin, diphtheria antitoxin, and snake and spider venom antitoxins are available from local designated holding centres.

For antivenom, see Emergency Treatment of Poisoning, p. 36.

Enquiries for vaccines not available commercially can also be made to:

Immunisation and Communicable Diseases Branch
Department of Health
Skipton House
80 London Road
London, SE1 6LH
Tel: (020) 7972 1522

In Scotland information about availability of vaccines can be obtained from a Specialist in Pharmaceutical Public Health. In Wales enquiries should be directed to:

Welsh Medicines Information Centre
University Hospital of Wales
Cardiff, CF14 4XW
Tel: (029) 2074 2979

and in Northern Ireland:

Regional Pharmacist (procurement co-ordination)
United Hospitals Trust Pharmacy Dept
Whiteabbey Hospital
Doagh Road
Newtownabbey, BT37 9RH
Tel: (028) 9086 5181 ext 2386

For further details of availability, see under individual vaccines.

## Anthrax vaccine

Anthrax immunisation is indicated for individuals who handle infected animals, for those exposed to imported infected animal products, and for laboratory staff who work with *Bacillus anthracis*.

In the event of possible contact with *B. anthracis*, post-exposure immunisation may be indicated, in addition to antimicrobial prophylaxis (section 5.1.12). Advice on the use of anthrax vaccine must be obtained from the Communicable Disease Surveillance Centre, Health Protection Agency (CDSC) (tel. 020 8200 6868)

The vaccine is derived from antigens from *B. anthracis* and, following the primary course of injections, booster doses should be given at about yearly intervals.

**Anthrax Vaccine** PoM

Dose initial course 3 doses of 0.5 mL by intramuscular injection at intervals of 3 weeks followed by a fourth dose after an interval of 6 months

Booster doses: 0.5 mL annually

Note Advice on post-exposure prophylaxis must be obtained from CDSC

Available from CDSC (*excipients include* thiomersal)

## BCG vaccines

BCG (Bacillus Calmette-Guérin) is a live attenuated strain derived from *Mycobacterium bovis* which stimulates the development of hypersensitivity to *M. tuberculosis*. BCG vaccine should be given intradermally by operators skilled in the technique (see below).

The expected reaction to successful BCG vaccination is induration at the site of injection followed by a local lesion which starts as a papule 2 or more weeks after vaccination; the lesion may ulcerate then subside over several weeks or months, leaving a small, flat scar. A dry dressing may be used if the ulcer discharges, but air should **not** be excluded.

Serious reactions with BCG are uncommon and most often consist of prolonged ulceration or subcutaneous abscess formation due to faulty injection technique. Anaphylaxis and disseminated BCG complications, such as osteitis or osteomyelitis, are rare.

BCG is recommended for the following groups if BCG immunisation has not previously been carried out and they are negative for tuberculoprotein hypersensitivity:

- all neonates and infants (0–12 months) living in areas where the incidence of tuberculosis is greater than 40 per 100 000;
- neonates, infants, and children under 16 years with a parent or grandparent born in a country with an incidence of tuberculosis greater than 40 per 100 000;
- previously unvaccinated new immigrants aged under 16 years who were born in, or lived for more than 3 months in a country with an incidence of tuberculosis greater than 40 per 100 000;
- contacts of those with active respiratory tuberculosis;
- individuals at occupational risk aged under 35 years[1] including healthcare workers and laboratory staff who are likely to have contact with patients, clinical materials or derived isolates, veterinary and other staff who handle animal species susceptible to tuberculosis, and staff working directly with prison-

ers, in care homes for the elderly, or in hostels or facilities for the homeless or refugees;

- individuals aged under 35 years[1] intending to live or work with local people for more than 1 month in a country with an incidence of tuberculosis greater than 40 per 100 000 (section 14.6).

Apart from children under 6 years, any person being considered for BCG immunisation must first be given a skin test for hypersensitivity to tuberculoprotein (see under Diagnostic agents, below). A skin test is not necessary for a child under 6 years provided that the child has not stayed for longer than 1 month in a country with an incidence of tuberculosis of greater than 40 per 100 000, or had contact with a person with tuberculosis.

BCG vaccine may be given simultaneously with another live vaccine (see also section 14.1), but if they are not given at the same time, an interval of 4 weeks should normally be allowed between them. When BCG is given to infants, there is no need to delay routine primary immunisations.

See section 14.1 for general contra-indications. BCG is also contra-indicated in individuals with generalised septic skin conditions (in the case of eczema, a vaccination site free from lesions should be chosen).

Bladder instillations of BCG are licensed for the management of bladder carcinoma (section 8.2.4).

For advice on chemoprophylaxis against tuberculosis, see section 5.1.9.



### Intradermal

**Bacillus Calmette-Guérin Vaccine** ▼ PoM

**BCG Vaccine, Dried/Tub/BCG**

A freeze-dried preparation of live bacteria of a strain derived from the bacillus of Calmette and Guérin.

**Dose** by intradermal injection, 0.1 mL (NEONATE and INFANT under 12 months 0.05 mL)

Available from health authorities or direct from Farillon (SSI brand, multidose vial with diluent)

**Intradermal injection technique** Skin is stretched between thumb and forefinger and needle (size 25G or 26G) inserted (bevel upwards) for about 3 mm into superficial layers of dermis (almost parallel with surface). Needle should be short with short bevel (can usually be seen through epidermis during insertion). Tense raised blanched bleb showing tips of hair follicles is sign of correct injection; 7 mm bleb ≡ 0.1 mL injection, 3 mm bleb ≡ 0.05 mL injection; if considerable resistance not felt, needle too deep and should be removed and reinserted before giving more vaccine.

To be injected at insertion of deltoid muscle onto humerus (keloid formation more likely with sites higher on arm); tip of shoulder should be **avoided**.

## Diagnostic agents

The *Mantoux test* is recommended for tuberculin skin testing, but no licensed preparation is currently available. Guidance for healthcare professionals is available at www.immunisation.nhs.uk.

In the Mantoux test, the diagnostic dose is by intradermal injection of Tuberculin Purified Protein Derivative (PPD).

The *Heaf test* (involving the use of multiple-puncture apparatus) is no longer available.

**Note** Tuberculin testing should not be carried out within 4 weeks of receiving a live viral vaccine since response to tuberculin may be inhibited.

1. There is inadequate evidence of protection by BCG vaccine in adults aged over 35 years

## Botulism antitoxin

A trivalent botulism antitoxin is available for the post-exposure prophylaxis of botulism and for the treatment of persons thought to be suffering from botulism. It specifically neutralises the toxins produced by *Clostridium botulinum* types A, B, and E. It is not effective against infantile botulism as the toxin (type A) is seldom, if ever, found in the blood in this type of infection.

Hypersensitivity reactions are a problem. It is essential to read the contra-indications, warnings, and details of sensitivity tests on the package insert. Prior to treatment checks should be made regarding previous administration of any antitoxin and history of any allergic condition, e.g. asthma, hay fever, etc. All patients should be tested for sensitivity (diluting the antitoxin if history of allergy).

**Botulism Antitoxin** PoM

A preparation containing the specific antitoxic globulins that have the power of neutralising the toxins formed by types A, B, and E of *Clostridium botulinum*.

**Note** The BP title Botulinum Antitoxin is not used because the preparation currently in use may have a different specification.

**Dose** prophylaxis, consult product literature

Available from local designated centres, for details see TOXBASE (requires registration) www.spib.axl.co.uk. For supplies outside working hours apply to other designated centres and, as a last resort, to Department of Health Duty Officer (Tel (020) 7210 3000).

## Cholera vaccine

**Cholera vaccine** (oral) contains inactivated Inaba (including El-Tor biotype) and Ogawa strains of *Vibrio cholerae*, serotype O1 together with recombinant B-subunit of the cholera toxin produced in Inaba strains of *V. cholerae*, serotype O1.

Oral cholera vaccine is licensed for travellers to endemic or epidemic areas on the basis of current recommendations (see also section 14.6). Immunisation should be completed at least 1 week before potential exposure. However, there is no requirement for cholera vaccination for international travel.

Immunisation with cholera vaccine does not provide complete protection and all travellers to a country where cholera exists should be warned that scrupulous attention to food, water, and personal hygiene is **essential**.

**Cautions and side-effects** Food, drink, and other oral medicines should be avoided 1 hour before and after vaccination. Side-effects of oral cholera vaccine include diarrhoea, abdominal pain, headache; rarely nausea, vomiting, loss of appetite, dizziness, fever, and respiratory symptoms can also occur.

See section 14.1 for general contra-indications.

**Injectable cholera vaccine** provides unreliable protection and is no longer available in the UK

**Dukoral®** (Chiron) ▼ PoM

Oral suspension, for dilution with solution of effervescent sodium bicarbonate granules, heat- and formaldehyde-inactivated Inaba (including El-Tor biotype) and Ogawa strains of *Vibrio cholerae* bacteria and recombinant cholera toxin B-subunit produced in *V. cholerae*, net price 2-dose pack = £16.00

**Dose** ADULT and CHILD over 6 years 2 doses separated by an interval of 1 week; CHILD 2–6 years 3 doses each separated by an interval of 1 week (consult product literature for dilution and administration)

Booster dose can be given after 2 years for adults and children over 6 years, and after 6 months for children 2–6 years

## Diphtheria vaccines

Diphtheria vaccines are prepared from the toxin of *Corynebacterium diphtheriae* and adsorption on aluminium hydroxide or aluminium phosphate improves antigenicity. The vaccine stimulates the production of the protective antitoxin. Single-antigen diphtheria vaccine is not available and adsorbed diphtheria vaccine is given as a combination product containing other vaccines.

For primary immunisation *of children aged between 2 months and 10 years* vaccination is recommended usually in the form of 3 doses (separated by 1-month intervals) of **diphtheria, tetanus, pertussis (acellular, component), poliomyelitis (inactivated) and haemophilus type b conjugate vaccine (adsorbed)** (see schedule, section 14.1). In unimmunised individuals aged *over 10 years* the primary course comprises of 3 doses of **adsorbed diphtheria** [low dose], **tetanus and inactivated poliomyelitis vaccine**.

A booster dose should be given 3 years after the primary course. Children *under 10 years* should receive *either* **adsorbed diphtheria, tetanus, pertussis (acellular, component) and inactivated poliomyelitis vaccine** *or* **adsorbed diphtheria** [low dose], **tetanus, pertussis (acellular, component) and inactivated poliomyelitis vaccine**. Individuals aged *over 10 years* should receive **adsorbed diphtheria** [low dose], **tetanus, and inactivated poliomyelitis vaccine**.

A second booster dose of adsorbed diphtheria [low dose], tetanus and inactivated poliomyelitis vaccine should be given 10 years after the previous booster dose.

Those intending to travel to areas with a risk of diphtheria infection should be fully immunised according to the UK schedule. If more than 10 years have lapsed since completion of the UK schedule, a dose of **adsorbed diphtheria** [low dose], **tetanus and inactivated poliomyelitis vaccine** should be administered.

Staff in contact with diphtheria patients or with potentially pathogenic clinical specimens or working directly with *C. diphtheriae* or *C. ulcerans* should receive a booster dose if fully immunised (with 5 doses of diphtheria-containing vaccine given at appropriate intervals); further doses should be given at 10-year intervals if risk persists. Individuals at risk who are not fully immunised should complete the primary course; a booster dose should be given after 5 years and then at 10-year intervals. **Adsorbed diphtheria** [low dose], **tetanus and inactivated poliomyelitis vaccine** is used for this purpose; immunity should be checked by antibody testing at least 3 months after completion of immunisation.

Advice on the management of cases, carriers, contacts and outbreaks must be sought from health protection units. The immunisation history of infected individuals and their contacts should be determined; those who have been incompletely immunised should complete their immunisation and fully immunised individuals should receive a reinforcing dose. For advice on antibacterial treatment to prevent a secondary case of diphtheria in a non-immune individual, see Table 2, section 5.1.

See section 14.1 for general contra-indications.

### Diphtheria vaccines for children under 10 years

**Important Not** recommended for persons *aged 10 years or over* (see Diphtheria Vaccines for Children over 10 years and Adults, below)

**Diphtheria, Tetanus, Pertussis (Acellular, Component), Poliomyelitis (Inactivated) and Haemophilus Type b Conjugate Vaccine (Adsorbed)** (PoM)

Injection, suspension of diphtheria toxoid, tetanus toxoid, acellular pertussis (5 component), inactivated poliomyelitis and *Haemophilus influenzae* type b (conjugated to tetanus protein), net price 0.5-mL vial = £19.94

**Excipients** include neomycin, polymyxin B and streptomycin

**Dose** CHILD up to 10 years, by intramuscular injection 0.5 mL; primary immunisation, 3 doses at intervals of 1 month (see schedule, section 14.1)

Available as part of childhood immunisation schedule, from health authorities or Farillon; brands include ▼*Pediacel*®

**Important.** Late change, see p. viii

**Adsorbed Diphtheria, Tetanus, Pertussis (Acellular, Component) and Inactivated Poliomyelitis Vaccine** (PoM)

Injection, suspension of diphtheria toxoid, tetanus toxoid, acellular pertussis (3 component) and inactivated poliomyelitis vaccine components adsorbed on a mineral carrier, net price 0.5-mL prefilled syringe = £17.56

**Excipients** include neomycin and polymyxin B

**Dose** CHILD 3–10 years, by intramuscular injection, 0.5 mL (see schedule, section 14.1)

Available as part of childhood immunisation schedule, from health authorities or Farillon; brands include ▼ *Infanrix-IPV*®

**Adsorbed Diphtheria [low dose], Tetanus, Pertussis (Acellular, Component) and Inactivated Poliomyelitis Vaccine** (PoM)

Injection, suspension of diphtheria toxoid [low dose], tetanus toxoid, acellular pertussis (5 component) and inactivated poliomyelitis vaccine components adsorbed on a mineral carrier, net price 0.5-mL prefilled syringe = £11.98

**Excipients** include neomycin, polymyxin B and streptomycin

**Dose** CHILD 3–10 years, by intramuscular injection, 0.5 mL (see schedule, section 14.1)

Available as part of childhood immunisation schedule, from health authorities or Farillon; brands include ▼*Repevax*®

### Diphtheria vaccines for children over 10 years and adults

A low dose of diphtheria toxoid is sufficient to recall immunity in individuals previously immunised against diphtheria but whose immunity may have diminished with time; it is insufficient to cause serious reactions that may occur when a higher-dose vaccine is used in an individual who is already immune. Preparations containing low dose diphtheria should be used for adults and children *over 10 years*, whether for primary immunisation or for booster doses.

**Adsorbed Diphtheria [low dose], Tetanus and Inactivated Poliomyelitis Vaccine** (PoM)

Injection, suspension of diphtheria toxoid [low dose], tetanus toxoid and inactivated poliomyelitis vaccine

components adsorbed on a mineral carrier, net price 0.5-mL prefilled syringe = £6.74
Excipients include neomycin, polymyxin B and streptomycin
Dose primary immunisation in ADULT and CHILD over 10 years, by intramuscular injection, 3 doses each of 0.5 mL separated by intervals of 4 weeks; booster, 0.5 mL after 5 years, repeated 10 years later (see schedule, section 14.1)
Available as part of childhood schedule, from health authorities or Farillon; brands include ▼*Revaxis*®

**Adsorbed Diphtheria [low dose] and Tetanus Vaccine for Adults and Adolescents** PoM
DT/Vac/Ads(Adult)
Injection, suspension of diphtheria formol toxoid and tetanus formol toxoid adsorbed on a mineral carrier, net price 0.5-mL prefilled syringe = £2.48
Note Not recommended for routine use (vaccines which also protect against poliomyelitis should be used for primary immunisation and for boosters)
Brands include *Diftavax*®

### Diphtheria antitoxin

**Diphtheria antitoxin** is used for passive immunisation. It is derived from horse serum and reactions are common after administration; resuscitation facilities should be available immediately.

It is now only used in suspected cases of diphtheria (without waiting for bacteriological confirmation); tests for hypersensitivity should be first carried out.

It is no longer used for prophylaxis because of the risk of hypersensitivity; unimmunised contacts should be promptly investigated and given antibacterial prophylaxis (section 5.1, table 2) and vaccine (see notes above).

**Diphtheria Antitoxin** PoM
Dip/Ser
Dose prophylaxis, not recommended therefore no dose stated (see notes above)
Treatment, by intravenous infusion, nasal diphtheria, 10 000–20 000 units; tonsillar diphtheria, 15 000–25 000 units; pharyngeal or laryngeal diphtheria, 20 000–40 000 units; combined types or delayed diagnosis, 40 000–60 000 units; severe diphtheria, 40 000–100 000 units; CHILD under 10 years half adult dose
Available from Communicable Disease Surveillance Centre (Tel (020) 8200 6868) or in Northern Ireland from Public Health Laboratory, Belfast City Hospital (Tel (028) 9032 9241)

## Haemophilus influenzae type B vaccine

**Haemophilus influenzae type b (Hib) vaccine** is made from capsular polysaccharide; it is conjugated with a protein such as tetanus toxoid to increase immunogenicity, especially in young children. Haemophilus influenzae type b vaccine is a component of the primary course of childhood immunisation (see schedule, section 14.1); it is combined with diphtheria, tetanus, pertussis (acellular, component) and inactivated poliomyelitis vaccine (see under Diphtheria Vaccines). For infants under 1 year, the course consists of 3 doses of a vaccine containing haemophilus influenzae type b component with an interval of 1 month between doses. Unimmunised children over 12 months need receive only 1 dose of the vaccine, but for full protection against other diseases, 3 doses should be given of diphtheria, tetanus, pertussis (acellular, component), poliomyelitis (inactivated) and haemophilus type b conjugate vaccine (adsorbed). The risk of infection falls sharply in older children and the vaccine is not normally required for children over 10 years.

**Important.** Late change, see p. viii

Haemophilus influenzae type b vaccine may be given to those over 10 years who are considered to be at increased risk of invasive *H. influenzae* type b disease (such as those with sickle-cell disease and those receiving treatment for malignancy). Also, children and adults with asplenia or splenic dysfunction, irrespective of age or the time laspsed since splenectomy, should receive a single dose of haemophilus influenzae type b vaccine; those under 1 year should be given 3 doses. Individuals vaccinated in infancy who have had a splenectomy or develop splenic dysfunction should receive a single booster dose of haemophilus influenzae type b vaccine after the age of 1 year. For elective splenectomy, the vaccine should ideally be given at least 2 weeks before surgery.

Side-effects of haemophilus influenzae type b vaccine include fever, restlessness, prolonged crying, loss of appetite, vomiting, and diarrhoea; hypersensitivity reactions (including anaphylaxis) and collapse have been reported.

See section 14.1 for general contra-indications.

#### Single component

**Hiberix**® (GSK) PoM
Injection, powder for reconstitution, capsular polysaccharide of *Haemophilus influenzae* type b (conjugated to tetanus protein), net price single-dose vial = £8.97
Dose children and adults at risk because of asplenia (and where combination vaccination not required), by intramuscular injection, 0.5 mL

#### Combined vaccines

See Diphtheria vaccines

## Hepatitis A vaccine

**Hepatitis A vaccine** is prepared from formaldehyde-inactivated hepatitis A virus grown in human diploid cells.

Immunisation is recommended for:

- laboratory staff who work directly with the virus;
- staff and residents of homes for those with severe learning difficulties;
- workers at risk of exposure to untreated sewage;
- individuals who work with primates;
- patients with haemophilia treated with plasma-derived clotting factors;
- patients with severe liver disease;
- travellers to high-risk areas (see p. 631);
- individuals who are at risk due to their sexual behaviour;
- parenteral drug abusers.

Immunisation should be considered for :

- patients with chronic liver disease including chronic hepatitis B or chronic hepatitis C;
- prevention of secondary cases in close contacts of confirmed cases of hepatitis A, within 7 days of onset of disease in the primary case.

Side-effects of hepatitis A vaccine, usually mild, include transient soreness, erythema, and induration at the injection site. Less common effects include fever, malaise, fatigue, headache, nausea, diarrhoea, and loss of appetite; arthralgia, myalgia, and, generalised rashes are occasionally reported.

See section 14.1 for general contra-indications.

### Single component

**Avaxim®** (Sanofi Pasteur) PoM

Injection, suspension of formaldehyde-inactivated hepatitis A virus (GBM grown in human diploid cells) 320 antigen units/mL adsorbed onto aluminium hydroxide, net price 0.5-mL prefilled syringe = £19.19

**Excipients** include neomycin

**Dose** by intramuscular injection (see note below), 0.5 mL as a single dose; booster dose 0.5 mL 6–12 months after initial dose; further booster doses, 0.5 mL every 10 years; CHILD under 16 years, not recommended

**Note** Booster dose may be delayed by up to 3 years if not given after recommended interval following primary dose with *Avaxim®*. The deltoid region is the preferred site of injection. The subcutaneous route may be used for patients with bleeding disorders

**Epaxal®** (MASTA) PoM

Injection, suspension of formaldehyde-inactivated hepatitis A virus (RG-SB grown in human diploid cells) at least 48 units/mL, net price 0.5-mL prefilled syringe = £23.81

**Dose** by intramuscular injection (see note below), ADULT and CHILD over 1 year, 0.5 mL as a single dose; booster dose 0.5 mL 6–12 months after initial dose (1–6 months if splenectomised)

**Note** Booster dose may be delayed by up to 4 years in adults if not given after recommended interval following primary dose. The deltoid region is the preferred site of injection. The subcutaneous route may be used for patients with bleeding disorders

**Important** *Epaxal®* contains influenza virus haemagglutinin grown in the allantoic cavity of chick embryos, therefore contra-indicated in those hypersensitive to eggs or chicken protein.

**Havrix Monodose®** (GSK) PoM

Injection, suspension of formaldehyde-inactivated hepatitis A virus (HM 175 grown in human diploid cells) 1440 ELISA units/mL adsorbed onto aluminium hydroxide, net price 1-mL prefilled syringe = £22.14, 0.5-mL (720 ELISA units) prefilled syringe (*Havrix Junior Monodose®*) = £16.77

**Excipients** include neomycin

**Dose** by intramuscular injection (see note below), 1 mL as a single dose; booster dose, 1 mL 6–12 months after initial dose; CHILD 1–15 years 0.5 mL; booster dose, 0.5 mL 6–12 months after initial dose

**Note** Booster dose may be delayed by up to 3 years if not given after recommended interval following primary dose with *Havrix Monodose®*. The deltoid region is the preferred site of injection. The subcutaneous route may be used for patients with bleeding disorders

**Vaqta® Paediatric** (Sanofi Pasteur) PoM

Injection, suspension of formaldehyde-inactivated hepatitis A virus (grown in human diploid cells) 50 antigen units/mL adsorbed onto aluminium hydroxyphosphate sulphate, net price 0.5-mL vial = £14.55

**Excipients** include neomycin

**Dose** by intramuscular injection (see note below) CHILD and ADOLESCENT 1–17 years, 0.5 mL as a single dose; booster dose 0.5 mL 6–18 months after initial dose; under 1 year, not recommended

**Note** The deltoid region is the preferred site of injection. The subcutaneous route may be used for patients with bleeding disorders

### With hepatitis B vaccine

**Twinrix®** (GSK) PoM

Injection, inactivated hepatitis A virus 720 ELISA units and recombinant (DNA) hepatitis B surface antigen 20 micrograms/mL adsorbed onto aluminium hydroxide and aluminium phosphate, net price 1-mL prefilled syringe (*Twinrix® Adult*) = £27.76, 0.5-mL prefilled syringe (*Twinrix® Paediatric*) = £20.79

**Excipients** include neomycin and thiomersal

**Dose** by intramuscular injection (see note below); primary course of 3 doses of 1 mL, the second 1 month and the third 6 months after the first dose; CHILD 1–15 years by intramuscular injection, 3 doses of 0.5 mL

Accelerated schedule (e.g. for travellers departing within 1 month), ADULT, second dose 7 days after first dose, third dose after further 14 days and a fourth dose after 12 months

**Note** Primary course should be completed with *Twinrix®* (single component vaccines given at appropriate intervals may be used for booster dose); the deltoid region is the preferred site of injection in adults and older children; anterolateral thigh is preferred site in infants; not to be injected into the buttock (vaccine efficacy reduced); subcutaneous route used for patients with bleeding disorders (but immune response may be reduced).

**Important** *Twinrix®* **not** recommended for post-exposure prophylaxis following percutaneous (needle-stick), ocular or mucous membrane exposure to hepatitis B virus.

### With typhoid vaccine

**Hepatyrix®** (GSK) PoM

Injection, suspension of inactivated hepatitis A virus (grown in human diploid cells) 1440 ELISA units/mL adsorbed onto aluminium hydroxide, combined with typhoid vaccine containing 25 micrograms/mL virulence polysaccharide antigen of *Salmonella typhi*, net price 1-mL prefilled syringe = £32.08

**Excipients** include neomycin

**Dose** by intramuscular injection (see note below), ADULT and ADOLESCENT over 15 years, 1 mL as a single dose; booster doses, see under single component hepatitis A vaccine and under polysaccharide typhoid vaccine

**Note** The deltoid region is the preferred site of injection. The subcutaneous route may be used for patients with bleeding disorders

**ViATIM®** (Sanofi Pasteur) PoM

Injection, suspension of inactivated hepatitis A virus (grown in human diploid cells) 160 antigen units/mL adsorbed onto aluminium hydroxide, combined with typhoid vaccine containing 25 micrograms/mL virulence polysaccharide antigen of *Salmonella typhi*, net price 1-mL prefilled syringe = £30.22

**Excipients** include neomycin

**Dose** by intramuscular injection (see note below), ADULT and ADOLESCENT over 16 years, 1 mL as a single dose; booster doses, see under single component hepatitis A vaccine and under polysaccharide typhoid vaccine

**Note** The deltoid region is the preferred site of injection. The subcutaneous route may be used for patients with bleeding disorders

## Hepatitis B vaccine

**Hepatitis B vaccine** contains inactivated hepatitis B virus surface antigen (HBsAg) adsorbed on aluminium hydroxide adjuvant. It is made biosynthetically using recombinant DNA technology. The vaccine is used in individuals at high risk of contracting hepatitis B.

In the UK, groups at high-risk of hepatitis B include:

- parenteral drug abusers, their sexual partners, and household contacts;
- individuals who change sexual partners frequently;
- close family contacts of a case or carrier;
- babies whose mothers have had hepatitis B during pregnancy *or* are positive for hepatitis B surface antigen (regardless of e-antigen markers); hepatitis B vaccination is started immediately on delivery and *hepatitis B immunoglobulin* (see p. 628) given at the same time (but preferably at a different site). Babies whose mothers are

positive for hepatitis B surface antigen and for e-antigen antibody should receive the vaccine only (but babies weighing 1.5 kg or less should also receive the immunoglobulin regardless of the mother's e-antigen antibody status);

- individuals with haemophilia, those receiving regular blood transfusions or blood products, and carers responsible for the administration of such products;
- patients with chronic renal failure including those on haemodialysis. Haemodialysis patients should be monitored for antibodies annually and re-immunised if necessary. Home carers (of dialysis patients) who are negative for hepatitis B surface antigen should be vaccinated;
- individuals with chronic liver disease;
- healthcare personnel (including trainees) who have direct contact with blood or blood-stained body fluids or with patients' tissues;
- other occupational risk groups such as morticians and embalmers;
- staff and patients of day-care or residential accommodation for those with severe learning difficulties;
- staff and inmates of custodial institutions;
- those travelling to areas of high or intermediate prevalence who are at increased risk or who plan to remain there for lengthy periods (see p. 631);
- families adopting children from countries with a high or intermediate prevalence of hepatitis B;
- foster carers.

Immunisation may take up to 6 months to confer adequate protection; the duration of immunity is not known precisely, but a single booster 5 years after the primary course may be sufficient to maintain immunity for those who continue to be at risk.

More detailed guidance is given in the memorandum *Immunisation against Infectious Disease*. Immunisation does not eliminate the need for commonsense precautions for avoiding the risk of infection from known carriers by the routes of infection which have been clearly established, consult *Guidance for Clinical Health Care Workers: Protection against Infection with Blood-borne Viruses* (available at www.dh.gov.uk). Accidental inoculation of hepatitis B virus-infected blood into a wound, incision, needle-prick, or abrasion may lead to infection, whereas it is unlikely that indirect exposure to a carrier will do so.

Specific **hepatitis B immunoglobulin** ('HBIG') is available for use with the vaccine in those accidentally infected and in neonates at special risk of infection (section 14.5).

A combined hepatitis A and hepatitis B vaccine is also available.

See section 14.1 for general contra-indications.

### Single component

**Engerix B®** (GSK) PoM

Injection, suspension of hepatitis B surface antigen (rby, prepared from yeast cells by recombinant DNA technique) 20 micrograms/mL adsorbed onto aluminium hydroxide, net price 0.5-mL (paediatric) vial = £9.16, 0.5-mL (paediatric) prefilled syringe = £9.67, 1-mL vial = £12.34, 1-mL prefilled syringe = £12.99

Excipients include thiomersal

Dose by intramuscular injection (see note below), 3 doses of 1 mL (20 micrograms), the second 1month and the third 6 months after the first dose; CHILD birth to 15 years 3 doses of 0.5 mL (10 micrograms); if compliance likely to be low in CHILD 10–15 years increase dose to 1 mL (20 micrograms)

Accelerated schedule, third dose 2 months after first dose and a fourth dose at 12 months; exceptionally (e.g. for travellers departing within 1 month), ADULT, second dose 7 days after first dose, third dose after a further 14 days and a fourth dose after 12 months

NEONATE born to hepatitis B surface antigen-positive mother (see also notes above), 4 doses of 0.5 mL (10 micrograms), first dose at birth with hepatitis B immunoglobulin injection (separate site) the second 1 month, the third 2 months and the fourth 12 months after the first dose

Chronic haemodialysis patients, by intramuscular injection (see note below) 4 doses of 2 mL (40 micrograms), the second 1 month, the third 2 months and the fourth 6 months after the first dose; immunisation schedule and booster doses may need to be adjusted in those with low antibody concentration

Note Deltoid muscle is preferred site of injection in adults and older children; anterolateral thigh is preferred site in neonates, infants and young children; not to be injected into the buttock (vaccine efficacy reduced); subcutaneous route used for patients with bleeding disorders

**Fendrix®** (GSK) ▼ PoM

Injection, suspension of hepatitis B surface antigen (prepared from yeast cells by recombinant DNA technique) 40 micrograms/mL adsorbed onto aluminium phosphate, net price 0.5-mL prefilled syringe = £38.10

Dose ADULT and CHILD over 15 years with renal insufficiency (including pre-haemodialysis and haemodialysis patients), by intramuscular injection (see note below) 4 doses of 0.5 mL (20 micrograms), the second 1 month, the third 2 months and the fourth 6 months after the first dose; immunisation schedule and booster doses may need to be adjusted in those with low antibody concentration

Note Deltoid muscle is preferred site of injection; not to be injected into the buttock (vaccine efficacy reduced); subcutaneous route used for patients with bleeding disorders

**HBvaxPRO®** (Sanofi Pasteur) PoM

Injection, suspension of hepatitis B surface antigen (prepared from yeast cells by recombinant DNA technique) 10 micrograms/mL adsorbed onto aluminium hydroxyphosphate sulphate, net price 0.5-mL (5-microgram) vial = £9.02, 1-mL (10-microgram) vial = £12.00; 40 micrograms/mL, 1-mL (40-microgram) vial = £29.30

Dose by intramuscular injection (see note below), ADULT and ADOLESCENT over 16 years, 3 doses of 10 micrograms, the second 1 month and the third 6 months after the first dose; CHILD under 16 years, 3 doses of 5 micrograms

Accelerated schedule, third dose 2 months after first dose with fourth dose at 12 months

Booster doses may be required in immunocompromised patients with low antibody concentration

NEONATE born to hepatitis B surface antigen-positive mother (see also notes above), 0.5 mL (5 micrograms), first dose at birth with hepatitis B immunoglobulin injection (separate site), the second 1 month, the third 2 months and the fourth 12 months after the first dose

Chronic haemodialysis patients, by intramuscular injection (see note below) 3 doses of 40 micrograms, the second 1 month and the third 6 months after the first dose; booster doses may be required in those with low antibody concentration

Note Deltoid muscle is preferred site of injection in adults and older children; anterolateral thigh is preferred site in neonates and infants; not to be injected into the buttock (vaccine efficacy reduced); subcutaneous route used for patients with bleeding disorders

### With hepatitis A vaccine

See Hepatitis A Vaccine

## Influenza vaccine

While most viruses are antigenically stable, the influenza viruses A and B (especially A) are constantly altering their antigenic structure as indicated by changes in the haemagglutinins (H) and neuraminidases (N) on the surface of the viruses. It is essential that influenza vaccines in use contain the H and N components of the prevalent strain or strains. Every year the World Health Organization recommends which strains should be included.

The recommended strains are grown in the allantoic cavity of chick embryos (therefore **contra-indicated** in those with anaphylactic hypersensitivity to eggs).

Since **influenza vaccines** will not control epidemics they are recommended *only for persons at high risk.* Annual immunisation is strongly recommended for individuals aged over 6 months with the following conditions:

- chronic respiratory disease, including asthma;
- chronic heart disease;
- chronic liver disease;
- chronic renal disease;
- diabetes mellitus;
- immunosuppression because of disease (including asplenia or splenic dysfunction) or treatment (including prolonged corticosteroid treatment);
- HIV infection (regardless of immune status).

Influenza immunisation is also recommended for all persons aged over 65 years, for residents of nursing or residential homes for the elderly and other long-stay facilities, and for carers of persons whose welfare may be at risk if the carer falls ill.

As part of the winter planning, NHS employers should offer vaccination to healthcare workers directly involved in patient care. Employers of social care workers should consider similar action.

**Interactions:** Appendix 1 (vaccines).

See section 14.1 for general contra-indications.

**Inactivated Influenza Vaccine (Split Virion)** (Non-proprietary) PoM

**Flu**

Injection, suspension of formaldehyde-inactivated influenza virus (split virion), net price 0.25-mL prefilled syringe = £6.29; 0.5-mL prefilled syringe = £6.29

Excipients may include neomycin and polymyxin

Dose by intramuscular injection, ADULT and CHILD over 13 years 0.5 mL as a single dose; CHILD 6–35 months 0.25–0.5 mL, 3–12 years 0.5 mL, in children dose repeated after 4–6 weeks if not previously vaccinated

Note Subcutaneous route used for patients with bleeding disorders

**Inactivated Influenza Vaccine (Surface Antigen)** (Non-proprietary) PoM

**Flu or Flu(adj)**

Injection, suspension of propiolactone-inactivated influenza virus (surface antigen), net price 0.5-mL prefilled syringe = £3.98

Excipients may include neomycin, polymyxin B and thiomersal

Dose by intramuscular injection, ADULT and CHILD over 13 years 0.5 mL as a single dose; CHILD 6–35 months 0.25–0.5 mL, 3–12 years 0.5 mL, in children dose repeated after 4–6 weeks if not previously vaccinated

Note Subcutaneous route used for patients with bleeding disorders

**Agrippal®** (Wyeth) PoM

Injection, suspension of formaldehyde-inactivated influenza virus (surface antigen), net price 0.5-mL prefilled syringe = £5.03

Excipients include kanamycin, neomycin

Dose by intramuscular injection, ADULT and CHILD over 13 years 0.5 mL as a single dose; CHILD 6–35 months 0.25–0.5 mL, 3–12 years 0.5 mL, in children dose repeated after 4–6 weeks if not previously vaccinated

Note Subcutaneous route used for patients with bleeding disorders

**Begrivac®** (Wyeth) PoM

Injection, suspension of formaldehyde-inactivated influenza virus (split virion), net price 0.5-mL prefilled syringe = £5.03

Excipients include polymyxin B

Dose by intramuscular injection, ADULT and CHILD over 13 years 0.5 mL as a single dose; CHILD 6–35 months 0.25–0.5 mL, 3–12 years 0.5 mL, in children dose repeated after 4–6 weeks if not previously vaccinated

Note Subcutaneous route used for patients with bleeding disorders

**Enzira®** (Chiron Vaccines) ▼ PoM

Injection, suspension of inactivated influenza virus (split virion), net price 0.5-mL prefilled syringe = £6.59

Excipients include neomycin and polymyxin B

Dose by intramuscular injection, ADULT and CHILD over 13 years 0.5 mL as a single dose; CHILD 6–35 months 0.25–0.5 mL, 3–12 years 0.5 mL, in children dose repeated after 4–6 weeks if not previously vaccinated

Note Subcutaneous route used for patients with bleeding disorders

**Fluarix®** (GSK) PoM

Injection, suspension of formaldehyde-inactivated influenza virus (split virion), net price 0.5-mL prefilled syringe = £4.49

Excipients include gentamicin and traces of thiomersal

Dose by intramuscular injection, ADULT and CHILD over 13 years 0.5 mL as a single dose; CHILD 6–35 months 0.25–0.5 mL, 3–12 years 0.5 mL, in children dose repeated after 4–6 weeks if not previously vaccinated

Note Subcutaneous route used for patients with bleeding disorders

**Inflexal® V** (Sanofi Pasteur) PoM

Injection, suspension of inactivated influenza virus (surface antigen), net price 0.5-mL prefilled syringe = £6.13

Excipients include neomycin and polymyxin B

Dose by intramuscular injection, ADULT and CHILD over 13 years 0.5 mL as a single dose; CHILD 6–35 months 0.25–0.5 mL, 3–12 years 0.5 mL, in children dose repeated after 4–6 weeks if not previously vaccinated

Note Subcutaneous route used for patients with bleeding disorders

**Influvac Sub-unit®** (Solvay) PoM

Injection, suspension of formaldehyde-inactivated influenza virus (surface antigen), net price 0.5-mL prefilled syringe = £5.22

Excipients include gentamicin

Dose by intramuscular injection, ADULT and CHILD over 13 years 0.5 mL as a single dose; CHILD 6–35 months 0.25–0.5 mL, 3–12 years 0.5 mL, in children dose repeated after 4–6 weeks if not previously vaccinated

Note Subcutaneous route used for patients with bleeding disorders

**Invivac®** (Solvay) PoM

Injection, suspension of inactivated influenza virus (surface antigen), net price 0.5-mL prefilled syringe = £6.59

Excipients include gentamicin

Dose by intramuscular injection, ADULT 0.5 mL as a single dose

Note Subcutaneous route used for patients with bleeding disorders

**Mastaflu®** (MASTA) PoM

Injection, suspension of formaldehyde-inactivated influenza virus (surface antigen), net price 0.5-mL prefilled syringe = £6.50

**Excipients** include gentamicin

**Dose** by intramuscular injection, ADULT and CHILD over 13 years 0.5 mL as a single dose; CHILD 6–35 months 0.25–0.5 mL, 3–12 years 0.5 mL, in children dose repeated after 4–6 weeks if not previously vaccinated

**Note** Subcutaneous route used for patients with bleeding disorders

## Measles vaccine

**Measles vaccine** has been replaced by a combined live measles, mumps and rubella vaccine (MMR vaccine) for all eligible children.

Administration of a measles-containing vaccine to children may be associated with a mild measles-like syndrome with a measles-like rash and pyrexia about a week after injection. Much less commonly, convulsions and, very rarely, encephalitis have been reported. Convulsions in infants are much less frequently associated with measles vaccines than with other conditions leading to febrile episodes.

MMR vaccine may be used in the control of outbreaks of measles (see under MMR Vaccine).

### Single antigen vaccine

No longer available in the UK

### Combined vaccines

See MMR vaccine

## Measles, Mumps and Rubella (MMR) vaccine

A combined live **measles, mumps, and rubella vaccine** (MMR vaccine) aims to eliminate measles, mumps, and rubella (and congenital rubella syndrome). Every child should receive two doses of MMR vaccine by entry to primary school, unless there is a valid contra-indication (see below) or parental refusal. MMR vaccine should be given irrespective of previous measles, mumps or rubella infection.

The first dose of MMR vaccine is given to children aged 12–15 months. A second (booster) dose is given before starting school at 3–5 years of age (see schedule, section 14.1). Children presenting for pre-school booster who have not received the first dose of MMR vaccine should be given a dose of MMR vaccine followed 3 months later by a second dose. At school-leaving age or at entry into further education, MMR immunisation should be offered to individuals of both sexes who have not received both doses. In a young adult who has received only a single dose of MMR in childhood, a second dose is recommended to acheive full protection.

MMR vaccine should be used to protect against rubella in *seronegative women of child-bearing age* (see schedule, section 14.1); unimmunised healthcare workers who might put pregnant women at risk of rubella should be vaccinated. MMR vaccine may also be offered to previously *unimmunised and seronegative post-partum women*. Vaccination a few days after delivery is important because about 60% of congenital abnormalities from rubella infection occur in babies of women who have borne more than one child. Immigrants arriving after the age of school immunisation are particularly likely to require immunisation.

MMR vaccine may also be used in the control of outbreaks of measles and should be offered to susceptible children aged over 6 months who are contacts of a case, within 3 days of exposure to infection; these children should still receive routine MMR vaccinations at the recommended ages. Household contacts of a case, aged between 6 and 9 months may receive normal immunoglobulin (section 14.5). MMR vaccine is **not suitable** for prophylaxis following exposure to mumps or rubella since the antibody response to the mumps and rubella components is too slow for effective prophylaxis.

Children with impaired immune response should not receive live vaccines (for advice on HIV see section 14.1). If they have been exposed to measles infection they should be given normal immunoglobulin (section 14.5).

Fever or a rash may occur after the first dose of MMR vaccine, most commonly about a week after vaccination and lasting about 2 to 3 days (section 14.1). Leaflets are available for parents on advice for reducing fever (including the use of paracetamol). Parotid swelling occurs occasionally, usually in the third week. Adverse reactions are considerably less common after the second dose of MMR vaccine than after the first dose.

Idiopathic thrombocytopenic purpura has occurred rarely following MMR vaccination, usually within 6 weeks of the first dose. The risk of developing idiopathic thrombocytopenic purpura after MMR vaccine is much less than the risk of developing it after infection with wild measles, mumps or rubella virus. The CSM has recommended that children who develop idiopathic thrombocytopenic purpura within 6 weeks of the first dose of MMR should undergo serological testing before the second dose is due; if the results suggest incomplete immunity against measles, mumps or rubella then a second dose of MMR is recommended. The Specialist and Reference Microbiology Division, Health Protection Agency offers free serological testing for children who develop idiopathic thrombocytopenic purpura *within 6 weeks* of the first dose of MMR.

Post-vaccination meningoencephalitis was reported (rarely and with complete recovery) following vaccination with MMR vaccine containing Urabe mumps vaccine, which has now been discontinued; no cases have been confirmed in association with the currently used Jeryl Lynn mumps vaccine. Children with post-vaccination symptoms are not infectious.

Reviews undertaken on behalf of the CSM and the Medical Research Council have not found any evidence of a link between MMR vaccination and bowel disease or autism. The Chief Medical Officers have advised that the MMR vaccine is the safest and best way to protect children against measles, mumps, and rubella. Information (including fact sheets and a list of references) may be obtained from:
www.immunisation.nhs.uk and
www.mmrthefacts.nhs.uk

Contra-indications to MMR include:

- children with untreated malignant disease or altered immunity (for advice on vaccines and HIV see section 14.1), and those receiving immunosuppressive drugs or radiotherapy, or high-dose corticosteroids;
- children who have received another live vaccine by injection within 3 weeks;
- children with allergies to excipients such as gelatin and neomycin;
- children with acute febrile illness (vaccination should be deferred);
- if given to women, pregnancy should be avoided for 1 month;
- should not be given within 3 months of an immunoglobulin injection.

The Department of Health recommends avoiding rubella vaccination during pregnancy. However, if given inadvertently during pregnancy, then termination is not recommended because extensive studies have failed to link rubella vaccination in early pregnancy with fetal damage.

**Note** Children with a personal or close family history of convulsions should be given MMR vaccine, provided the parents understand that there may be a febrile response; doctors should seek specialist paediatric advice rather than withhold vaccination; there is increasing evidence that MMR vaccine can be given safely even when the child has had an anaphylactic reaction to food containing egg (dislike of egg or refusal to eat egg is not a contra-indication).

**Measles, Mumps and Rubella Vaccine, Live** PoM
**MMR(live)**

Live measles, mumps, and rubella vaccine

**Dose** by deep subcutaneous *or* by intramuscular injection, 0.5 mL (see schedule, section 14.1)

Available from health authorities or direct from Farillon as *MMR II*® (*excipients include* gelatin and neomycin) or *Priorix*® (*excipients include* neomycin)

## Meningococcal vaccines

Almost all childhood meningococcal disease in the UK is caused by *Neisseria meningitidis* serogroups B and C. **Meningococcal Group C conjugate vaccine** protects only against infection by serogroup C; it can be given from 2 months of age. After early adulthood the risk of meningococcal disease declines, and immunisation is not generally recommended after the age of 25 years.

**Childhood immunisation** **Meningococcal Group C conjugate vaccine** provides long-term protection against infection by serogroup C of *Neisseria meningitidis* in children from 2 months of age; it is now a component of the primary course of childhood immunisation. The recommended schedule consists of 3 doses starting at 2 months of age with an interval of 1 month between each dose (see schedule, section 14.1). Infants aged 5–12 months not previously vaccinated should receive 2 doses, with an interval of 1 month between doses. It is recommended that meningococcal group C conjugate vaccine be given to anyone aged under 25 years who has not been vaccinated previously with this vaccine; those over 1 year receive a single dose.

Meningococcal group C conjugate vaccine is also recommended for individuals with a dysfunctional or absent spleen.

**Immunisation for travellers** Individuals travelling to countries of risk (see below) should be immunised with a meningococcal polysaccharide vaccine that covers serotypes **A, C, W135 and Y**. Vaccination is particularly important for those living or working with local people or visiting an area of risk during outbreaks.

Outbreaks of infection with the W135 strain of meningococcus have occurred in Burkina Faso, West Africa and there have been cases in a number of other African countries. Countries with risk in Africa are listed below but outbreaks may also occur in countries not listed:

> Angola, Benin, Burkina Faso, Burundi, Cameroon, Central African Republic, Chad, Democratic Republic of Congo, Eritrea, Ethiopia, Gambia, Ghana, Guinea, Guinea Bissau, Ivory Coast, Kenya, Mali, Mozambique, Namibia, Niger, Nigeria, Rwanda, Senegal, Sierra Leone, Somalia, Sudan, Tanzania, Togo, Uganda, and Zambia

Proof of vaccination with the tetravalent (A, C, W135 and Y) meningococcal vaccine is required for those travelling to Saudi Arabia during the Hajj and Umrah pilgrimages (where outbreaks of the W135 strain have occurred).

Travellers should be immunised with the meningococcal polysaccharide vaccine that covers serogroups A, C, W135 and Y, even if they have already received meningococcal group C conjugate vaccine. The response to serotype C in unconjugated meningococcal polysaccharide vaccines given to children aged under 18 months is not as good as in adults.

**Contacts of infected individuals and laboratory workers** For advice on the immunisation of *close contacts* of cases of meningococcal disease in the UK and on the role of the vaccine in the control of *local outbreaks*, consult Guidelines for Public Health Management of Meningococcal Disease in the UK in *Commun Dis Public Health* 2002; **5**: 187–204. See section 5.1 Table 2 for antibacterial prophylaxis to prevent a secondary case of meningococcal meningitis

The need for immunisation of laboratory staff who work directly with *Neisseria meningitidis* should be considered.

**Side-effects** Side-effects of meningococcal Group C conjugate vaccine include redness, swelling, and pain at the site of the injection, mild fever, irritability, drowsiness, dizziness, nausea, vomiting, diarrhoea, anorexia in children, headache, myalgia, rash, urticaria, pruritus, malaise, lymphadenopathy, hypotonia, paraesthesia, hypoaesthesia, and syncope. Hypersensitivity reactions (including anaphylaxis, bronchospasm, and angioedema) and seizures have been reported rarely. Symptoms of meningism have also been reported rarely, but there is no evidence that the vaccine causes meningococcal C meningitis. There have been very rare reports of Stevens-Johnson syndrome. The CSM has advised that vaccination provides benefit in terms of lives saved and disabilities prevented.

Meningococcal polysaccharide A, C, W135 and Y vaccine is associated with injection-site reactions and very rarely headache, fatigue, fever, and drowsiness. Hypersensitivity reactions including anaphylaxis have been reported.

See section 14.1 for general contra-indications.

◢Meningococcal Group C conjugate vaccine

**Important.** Late change, see p. viii

**Meningitec®** (Wyeth) PoM
Injection, suspension of capsular polysaccharide antigen of *Neisseria meningitidis* group C (conjugated to *Corynebacterium diphtheriae* protein), adsorbed onto aluminium phosphate, net price 0.5-mL vial = £17.95
**Dose** by intramuscular injection, ADULT and CHILD over 1 year 0.5 mL as a single dose; for routine immunisation in INFANT under 1 year, 3 doses (each of 0.5 mL) at intervals of 1 month (but see notes above and schedule, section 14.1)
Available as part of childhood immunisation schedule from Farillon
**Note** Subcutaneous route used for patients with bleeding disorders

**Menjugate®** (Chiron) PoM
Injection, powder for reconstitution, capsular polysaccharide antigen of *Neisseria meningitidis* group C (conjugated to *Corynebacterium diphtheriae* protein), adsorbed onto aluminium hydroxide, single-dose and 10-dose vials
**Dose** by intramuscular injection, ADULT and CHILD over 1 year 0.5 mL as a single dose; for routine immunisation in INFANT under 1 year, 3 doses (each of 0.5 mL) at intervals of 1 month (but see notes above and schedule, section 14.1)
**Note** Subcutaneous route used for patients with bleeding disorders

**NeisVac-C®** (Baxter) PoM
Injection, suspension of polysaccharide antigen of *Neisseria meningitidis* group C (conjugated to tetanus toxoid protein), adsorbed onto aluminium hydroxide, 0.5-mL prefilled syringe
**Dose** by intramuscular injection, ADULT and CHILD over 1 year 0.5 mL as a single dose; for routine immunisation in INFANT under 1 year, 3 doses (each of 0.5 mL) at intervals of 1 month (but see notes above and schedule, section 14.1)
Available from Farillon
**Note** Subcutaneous route used for patients with bleeding disorders

◢Meningococcal polysaccharide A, C, W135 and Y vaccine

**ACWY Vax®** (GSK) PoM
Injection, powder for reconstitution, capsular polysaccharide antigens of *Neisseria meningitidis* groups A, C, W135 and Y, net price single-dose vial (with syringe containing diluent) = £16.73
**Dose** by deep subcutaneous injection, ADULT and CHILD over 2 years 0.5 mL
**Note** May be given to INFANT 2 months–2 years [unlicensed] but antibody response may be suboptimal

## Mumps vaccine

◢Single antigen vaccine
No longer available in the UK

◢Combined vaccine
See MMR Vaccine

## Pertussis vaccine

**Pertussis vaccine** is usually given as a combination preparation containing other vaccines (see under Diphtheria Vaccines). Acellular vaccines are derived from highly purified components of *Bordetella pertussis.*

For the routine immunisation of infants, primary immunisation with pertussis (whooping cough) vaccine is recommended in the form of 3 doses (separated by 1-month intervals) of **diphtheria, tetanus, pertussis (acellular, component), poliomyelitis (inactivated) and haemophilus type b conjugate vaccine (adsorbed)** (see schedule, section 14.1).

A booster dose should be given 3 years after the primary course; children *under 10 years* should receive *either* **adsorbed diphtheria, tetanus, pertussis (acellular, component) and inactivated poliomyelitis vaccine** *or* **adsorbed diphtheria** [low dose], **tetanus, pertussis (acellular, component) and inactivated poliomyelitis vaccine**.

The incidence of local and systemic effects is lower with vaccines containing acellular pertussis components than with the whole-cell pertussis vaccine used previously.

The vaccine should not be withheld from children with a history to a preceding dose of:

- fever, irrespective of severity;
- persistent crying or screaming for more than 3 hours;
- severe local reaction, irrespective of extent.

These side-effects were associated with whole-cell pertussis vaccine.

**Predisposition to neurological problems** When there is a personal or family history of *febrile* convulsions, there is an increased risk of these occurring during fever from any cause including immunisation. In such children, immunisation is *recommended* but advice on the *prevention of fever* (see Post-immunisation pyrexia, p. 611) should be given before immunisation.

When a child has had a convulsion not associated with fever and the neurological condition is not deteriorating, immunisation is *recommended.*

Where there is a *still evolving neurological problem* including poorly controlled epilepsy, immunisation should be *deferred* and the child referred to a specialist. Immunisation is recommended if a cause for the neurological disorder is found. If a cause is not found, immunisation should be deferred until the condition is stable.

Children with stable neurological disorders (e.g. spina bifida, congenital brain abnormality, and perinatal hypoxic ischaemic encephalopathy) should be immunised according to the recommended schedule.

**Older children** All children up to the age of 10 years should receive primary immunisation with diphtheria, tetanus, pertussis (acellular, component), poliomyelitis (inactivated) and haemophilus type b conjugate vaccine (adsorbed). Primary immunisation against pertussis is not currently recommended in individuals over 10 years of age.

◢Combined vaccines
Combined vaccines, see under Diphtheria vaccines

## Pneumococcal vaccines

Pneumococcal vaccines protect against infection with *Streptococcus pneumoniae* (pneumococcus); the vaccines contain polysaccharide from capsular pneumococci. Pneumococcal polysaccharide vaccine contains purified polysaccharide from 23 capsular types of pneumococci whereas pneumococcal polysaccharide conjugated vaccine contains polysaccharide from 7 capsular types, the polysaccharide being conjugated to protein.

Pneumococcal vaccination is recommended for individuals at special risk as follows:

- age over 65 years;
- asplenia or splenic dysfunction (including homozygous sickle cell disease and coeliac disease which could lead to splenic dysfunction);
- chronic respiratory disease (includes asthma treated with continuous or frequent use of a systemic corticosteroid);
- chronic heart disease;
- chronic renal disease;
- chronic liver disease;
- diabetes mellitus;
- immune deficiency because of disease (e.g. HIV infection) or treatment (including prolonged systemic corticosteroid treatment);
- presence of cochlear implant;
- presence of CSF shunt or other condition where leakage of cerebrospinal fluid may occur;
- child under 5 years with a history of invasive pneumococcal disease.

Where possible, the vaccine should be given at least 2 weeks before splenectomy, surgery to insert a CSF shunt, cochlear implant surgery, and chemotherapy; patients should be given advice about increased risk of pneumococcal infection. A patient card and information leaflet for patients with asplenia are available from the Department of Health or in Scotland from the Scottish Executive, Public Health Division 1 (Tel (0131) 244 2501). Prophylactic antibacterial therapy against pneumococcal infection should not be stopped after immunisation.

**Choice of vaccine** A single dose of the 23-valent unconjugated **pneumococcal polysaccharide vaccine** is used to immunise individuals over 5 years who are at special risk of pneumococcal disease. Children under 5 years who are at special risk should receive the 7-valent **pneumococcal polysaccharide conjugated vaccine** as follows:

- infants from 2 months to under 6 months should receive 3 doses (separated by 1-month intervals) of pneumococcal polysaccharide conjugated vaccine, starting at 2 months of age; a further dose is given after the first birthday;
- unimmunised infants 6–11 months should receive 2 doses (separated by 1 month) of pneumococcal polysaccharide conjugated vaccine; a further dose is given after the first birthday and at least 1 month after the previous dose;
- children 1–5 years should receive 2 doses (separated by 2 months) of pneumococcal polysaccharide conjugated vaccine.

All children who have received the pneumococcal polysaccharide conjugated vaccine should receive a single dose of the 23-valent pneumococcal polysaccharide vaccine after their second birthday and at least 2 months after the final dose of the 7-valent pneumococcal polysaccharide conjugated vaccine.

**Revaccination** In individuals with higher concentrations of antibodies to pneumococcal polysaccharides, revaccination with the 23-valent pneumococcal polysaccharide vaccine more commonly produces adverse reactions. Revaccination is therefore not recommended, except every 5 years in individuals in whom the antibody concentration is likely to decline rapidly (e.g. asplenia, splenic dysfunction and nephrotic syndrome). If there is doubt, the need for revaccination should be discussed with a haematologist, immunologist, or microbiologist.

See section 14.1 for general contra-indications.

### ◢Pneumococcal polysaccharide vaccines

**Pneumovax® II** (Sanofi Pasteur) PoM

Polysaccharide from each of 23 capsular types of pneumococcus, net price 0.5-mL vial = £8.83

**Dose** by intramuscular injection, 0.5 mL; revaccination, see notes above; INFANT under 2 years, not recommended (suboptimal response and also safety and efficacy not established)

### ◢Pneumococcal polysaccharide conjugated vaccine

**Important.** Late change, see p. viii

**Prevenar®** (Wyeth) ▼ PoM

Polysaccharide from each of 7 capsular types of pneumococcus (conjugated to diphtheria toxoid) adsorbed onto aluminium phosphate, net price 0.5-mL prefilled syringe = £34.50

**Dose** by intramuscular injection, INFANT 2–6 months 3 doses each of 0.5 mL separated by intervals of 1 month and a further dose in second year of life; 6–11 months 2 doses each of 0.5 mL separated by an interval of 1 month and a further dose in second year of life; CHILD 1–5 years 2 doses each of 0.5 mL separated by an interval of 2 months

**Note** Deltoid muscle is preferred site of injection in young children; anterolateral thigh is preferred site in infants

The dose in the BNF may differ from that in product literature

## Poliomyelitis vaccines

There are two types of poliomyelitis vaccine, inactivated poliomyelitis vaccine and live (oral) poliomyelitis vaccine. **Inactivated poliomyelitis vaccine** is now recommended for routine immunisation; it is given by injection and contains inactivated strains of human poliovirus types 1, 2 and 3.

A course of primary immunisation consists of 3 doses of a combined preparation containing inactivated poliomyelitis vaccine (see under Diphtheria Vaccines), starting at 2 months of age with intervals of 1 month between doses (see schedule, section 14.1). A course of 3 doses should also be given to all unimmunised adults; no adult should remain unimmunised against poliomyelitis.

Two booster doses of a preparation containing inactivated poliomyelitis vaccine are recommended, the first before school entry and the second before leaving school (see schedule, section 14.1). Booster doses for adults are not necessary except for those at special risk such as travellers to endemic areas, or laboratory staff likely to be exposed to the viruses, or healthcare workers in possible contact with cases; booster doses should be given to such individuals every 10 years.

Preparations containing inactivated poliomyelitis vaccine may be used to complete an immunisation course initiated with the live (oral) poliomyelitis vaccine.

Live (oral) poliomyelitis vaccine is available only for use during outbreaks. The live (oral) vaccine poses a very rare risk of vaccine-associated paralytic polio because the attenuated strain of the virus can revert to a virulent form. For this reason the live (oral) vaccine must **not** be used for immunosuppressed individuals or their household contacts. The use of inactivated poliomyelitis vaccine removes the risk of vaccine-associated paralytic polio altogether.

**Travellers** Unimmunised travellers to areas with a high incidence of poliomyelitis should receive a full course of a preparation containing inactivated poliomyelitis vaccine. Those who have not been vaccinated in the last 10 years should receive a booster dose of adsorbed diphtheria [low dose], tetanus and inactivated poliomyelitis vaccine. A list of countries with a high incidence of poliomyelitis can be obtained from www.travax.scot.nhs.uk or by contacting the National Travel Health Network and Centre.

### Inactivated (Salk)

Combined vaccines, see under Diphtheria Vaccines

**Inactivated Poliomyelitis Vaccine** (Non-proprietary)
▼ PoM

IPV

Injection, inactivated suspension of suitable strains of poliomyelitis virus, types 1, 2, and 3, net price 0.5-mL prefilled syringe = £10.35

Excipients may include neomycin, polymyxin B and streptomycin

Note Not recommended for routine use—combination vaccines are recommended for primary immunisation and for boosters (see schedule, section 14.1)

### Live (oral) (Sabin)

**Poliomyelitis Vaccine, Live (Oral)** (GSK) PoM

OPV

A suspension of suitable live attenuated strains of poliomyelitis virus, types 1, 2, and 3. Available in single-dose and 10-dose containers

Excipients include neomycin and polymyxin B

Dose control of outbreaks, 3 drops; may be given on a lump of sugar; not to be given with foods which contain preservatives

Note Live poliomyelitis vaccine loses potency once the container has been opened—any vaccine remaining at the end of an immunisation session should be discarded; whenever possible sessions should be arranged to avoid undue wastage.

## Rabies vaccine

The licensed rabies vaccines, the human diploid cell vaccine and the purified chick embryo cell vaccine are both cell-derived.

**Pre-exposure prophylaxis** Immunisation should be offered to those at high risk of exposure to rabies—laboratory staff who handle the rabies virus, those working in quarantine stations, animal handlers, veterinary surgeons and field workers who are likely to be bitten by infected wild animals, certain port officials, and bat handlers. Transmission of rabies by humans has not been recorded but it is advised that those caring for patients with the disease should be vaccinated.

Immunisation against rabies is also recommended where there is limited access to prompt medical care for those living in areas where rabies is enzootic, for those travelling to such areas for longer than 1 month, and for those on shorter visits who may be exposed to unusual risk.

Immunisation against rabies is indicated during pregnancy if there is substantial risk of exposure to rabies and rapid access to post-exposure prophylaxis is likely to be limited.

Up-to-date country-by-country information on the incidence of rabies can be obtained from the National Travel Health Network and Centre (www.nathnac.org) and, in Scotland, from Health Protection Scotland (www.hps.scot.nhs.uk).

Immunisation against rabies requires 3 doses of rabies vaccine, with further booster doses for those who remain at continued risk (see under preparations below for details of regimens). To ensure protection in persons at high risk (e.g. laboratory workers), the concentration of antirabies antibodies in plasma is used to determine the intervals between doses.

**Post-exposure prophylaxis** Following potential exposure to rabies, the wound or site of exposure (e.g. mucous membrane) should be cleansed under running water and washed for several minutes with soapy water as soon as possible after exposure. Disinfectant and a simple dressing may be applied, but suturing should be delayed because it may increase the risk of introducing rabies virus into the nerves.

Post-exposure prophylaxis against rabies depends on the level of risk in the country, the nature of exposure, and the individual's immunity. In each case, expert risk assessment and advice on appropriate management should be obtained from the Health Protection Agency Virus Reference Department, Colindale, London (tel. (020) 8200 4400) or the Communicable Disease Surveillance Centre (tel. (020) 8200 6868), in Scotland from the Scottish Centre for Infection and Environmental Health (tel. (0141) 300 1100), in Northern Ireland from the Public Health Laboratory, Belfast City Hospital (tel. (028) 9032 9241).

There are no specific contra-indications to the use of rabies vaccine for post-exposure prophylaxis and its use should be considered whenever a patient has been attacked by an animal in a country where rabies is enzootic, even if there is no direct evidence of rabies in the attacking animal. Because of the potential consequences of untreated rabies exposure and because rabies vaccination has not been associated with fetal abnormalities, pregnancy is not considered a contra-indication to post-exposure prophylaxis.

For post-exposure prophylaxis of *fully immunised* individuals (who have previously received pre-exposure or post-exposure prophylaxis with cell-derived rabies vaccine), 2 doses of cell-derived vaccine, separated by 3 days, are likely to be sufficient. Rabies immunoglobulin is not necessary in such cases.

Post-exposure treatment for *unimmunised individuals* (or those whose prophylaxis is possibly incomplete) comprises 5 doses of rabies vaccine given over 1 month (on days 0, 3, 7, 14, and 30); also, depending on the level of risk (determined by factors such as the nature of the bite and the country where it was sustained), rabies immunoglobulin is given on day 0 (section 14.5). The course may be discontinued if it is proved that the individual was not at risk.

**Rabies Vaccine** (Sanofi Pasteur) PoM
**Rab**
Freeze-dried inactivated Wistar rabies virus strain PM/WI 38 1503-3M cultivated in human diploid cells, net price single-dose vial with syringe containing diluent = £22.15
**Excipients** include neomycin
**Dose** prophylactic, by deep subcutaneous *or* intramuscular injection in the deltoid region, 1 mL on days 0, 7, and 28; also booster doses every 2–3 years to those at continued risk
Post-exposure, by deep subcutaneous *or* intramuscular injection in the deltoid region, 1 mL, see notes above
Also available from local designated centres (special workers and post-exposure treatment)

**Rabipur®** (Chiron Vaccines) PoM
Freeze-dried inactivated Flury LEP rabies virus strain cultivated in chick embryo cells, net price single-dose vial = £22.15
**Excipients** include neomycin
**Dose** prophylactic, by intramuscular injection in the deltoid muscle or anterolateral thigh in small children, 1 mL on days 0, 7 and 21 or 28; also booster doses every 2–5 years for those at continued risk
Post-exposure, by intramuscular injection in the deltoid muscle or anterolateral thigh in small children, 1 mL, see notes above

## Rubella vaccine

A combined measles, mumps and rubella vaccine (MMR vaccine) aims to eliminate rubella (German measles) and congenital rubella syndrome. MMR vaccine is used for childhood vaccination as well as for vaccinating adults (including women of child-bearing age) who do not have immunity against rubella.

### Single antigen vaccine

No longer available in the UK; the combined live measles, mumps and rubella vaccine is a suitable alternative (see MMR vaccine, p. 620)

### Combined vaccines

see MMR vaccine

## Smallpox vaccine

Limited supplies of **smallpox vaccine** are held at the Specialist and Reference Microbiology Division, Health Protection Agency (Tel. (020) 8200 4400) for the exclusive use of workers in laboratories where pox viruses (such as vaccinia) are handled.

If a wider use of the vaccine is being considered, *Guidelines for smallpox response and management in the post-eradication era* should be consulted at www.dh.gov.uk

## Tetanus vaccines

**Tetanus vaccines** stimulate production of a protective antitoxin. In general, adsorption on aluminium hydroxide or aluminium phosphate improves antigenicity.

Primary immunisation for children under 10 years consists of 3 doses of a combined preparation containing adsorbed tetanus vaccine, with an interval of 1 month between doses (see schedule, section 14.1).

The recommended schedule of tetanus vaccination not only gives protection against tetanus in childhood but also gives the basic immunity for subsequent booster doses (see schedule, section 14.1).

For primary immunisation of adults and children over 10 years previously unimmunised against tetanus, 3 doses of adsorbed diphtheria [low dose], tetanus and inactivated poliomyelitis vaccine are given with an interval of 1 month between doses (see under Diphtheria Vaccines).

Following routine childhood vaccination, 2 booster doses of a preparation containing adsorbed tetanus vaccine are recommended, the first before school entry and the second before leaving school.

If an individual presents for a booster dose but has been vaccinated following a tetanus-prone wound, the vaccine preparation administered at the time of injury should be determined. If this is not possible, the booster should still be given to ensure adequate protection against all antigens in the booster vaccine. An adult who has received 5 doses of tetanus vaccine is likely to have life-long immunity. Active immunisation is important for individuals who may not have completed a course of immunisation. Adults and children over 10 years may be given a course of adsorbed diphtheria [low dose], tetanus and inactivated poliomyelitis vaccine.

Very rarely, tetanus has developed after abdominal surgery; patients awaiting elective surgery should be asked about tetanus immunisation and immunised if necessary. Parenteral drug abuse is also associated with tetanus; those abusing drugs by injection should be vaccinated if unimmunised. Booster doses should be given if there is any doubt about the immunisation status. All laboratory staff should be offered a primary course if unimmunised.

For travel recommendations see section 14.6.

**Wounds** Wounds are considered to be tetanus-prone if they are sustained more than 6 hours before surgical treatment *or* at any interval after injury and are puncture-type (particularly if contaminated with soil or manure) *or* show much devitalised tissue *or* are septic *or* are compound fractures *or* contain foreign bodies. All wounds should receive thorough cleansing.

- For *clean wounds*, fully immunised individuals (those who have received a total of 5 doses of a tetanus-containing vaccine at appropriate intervals) and those whose primary immunisation is complete (with boosters up to date), do not require tetanus vaccine; individuals whose primary immunisation is incomplete or whose boosters are not up to date require a reinforcing dose of a tetanus-containing vaccine (followed by further doses as required to complete the schedule); non-immunised individuals (or whose immunisation status is not known or who have been fully immunised but are now immunocompromised) should be given a dose of the appropriate tetanus-containing vaccine immediately (followed by completion of the full course of the vaccine if records confirm the need).
- For *tetanus-prone wounds*, management is as for clean wounds with the addition of a dose of tetanus immunoglobulin (section 14.5) given at a different site; in fully immunised individuals and those whose primary immunisation is complete (see above) the immunoglobulin is needed only if the risk of infection is especially high (e.g. contamination with manure). Antibacterial prophylaxis (with benzylpenicillin, co-amoxiclav, or metronidazole) may also be required for tetanus-prone wounds.

See section 14.1 for general contra-indications.

### Combined vaccines

See Diphtheria Vaccines

## Tick-borne encephalitis vaccine

Tick-borne encephalitis vaccine is licensed for immunisation of those in high-risk areas based on official recommendations (see section 14.6). Those working, walking or camping in warm forested areas of Central and Eastern Europe and Scandinavia, particularly from April to October when ticks are most prevalent, are at greatest risk of tick-borne encephalitis. Ideally, immunisation should be completed at least one month before travel.

Fever exceeding 40°C may occur, particularly after the first dose of tick-borne encephalitis vaccine. Other side effects include arrhythmias; the vaccine should be used with caution in those with cardiovascular disease. Tick-borne encephalitis vaccine is **contra-indicated** in those with acute febrile infection and severe hypersensitivity to egg protein. See section 14.1 for general contra-indications and side-effects.

**FSME-IMMUN®** (MASTA) PoM

Injection, suspension, inactivated Neudörfl tick-borne encephalitis virus strain, cultivated in chick embryo cells, net price 0.5-mL prefilled syringe = £32.00

Excipients include gentamicin and neomycin

Dose ADULT and ADOLESCENT over 16 years by intramuscular injection in deltoid muscle, 3 doses each of 0.5 mL, second dose after 1–3 months and third dose after further 5–12 months; ELDERLY over 60 years and immunocompromised (including those receiving immunosuppressants), antibody concentration may be measured 4 weeks after second dose and dose repeated if protective levels not achieved

Note To achieve more rapid protection, second dose may be given 14 days after first dose

First booster dose given within 3 years after third dose, subsequent boosters after 3–5 years

## Typhoid vaccines

Typhoid immunisation is advised for travellers to areas where sanitation standards may be poor, although it is not a substitute for scrupulous personal hygiene (see p. 631). Immunisation is also advised for laboratory workers handling specimens from suspected cases.

Capsular **polysaccharide typhoid vaccine** is usually given by *intramuscular injection*. Young children may respond suboptimally to the vaccine, but children aged between 12 and 18 months should be immunised if the risk of typhoid fever is considered high (immunisation is not recommended for infants under 12 months). Booster doses are needed every 3 years on continued exposure. Local reactions, including pain, swelling or erythema, may appear 48–72 hours after administration.

For general contra-indications to vaccines, see section 14.1.

### Polysaccharide vaccine for injection

**Typherix®** (GSK) PoM

Injection, Vi capsular polysaccharide typhoid vaccine, 50 micrograms/mL virulence polysaccharide antigen of *Salmonella typhi*, net price 0.5-mL prefilled syringe = £9.93

Dose by intramuscular injection, 0.5 mL; CHILD under 2 years may show suboptimal response (see notes above)

Note Subcutaneous route used for patients with bleeding disorders

**Typhim Vi®** (Sanofi Pasteur) PoM

Injection, Vi capsular polysaccharide typhoid vaccine, 50 micrograms/mL virulence polysaccharide antigen of *Salmonella typhi*, net price 0.5-mL prefilled syringe = £9.49

Dose by intramuscular injection, 0.5 mL; CHILD under 18 months may show suboptimal response (see notes above)

Note Subcutaneous route used for patients with bleeding disorders

### Polysaccharide vaccine with hepatitis A vaccine

See Hepatitis A Vaccine

## Varicella–zoster vaccine

Varicella–zoster vaccine (live) is licensed for immunisation against varicella in seronegative individuals. It is not recommended for routine use in children but may be given to seronegative healthy children over 1 year who come into close contact with individuals at high risk of severe varicella infections. The Department of Health recommends varicella–zoster vaccine for seronegative healthcare workers who come into direct contact with patients. Those with a history of chickenpox or shingles can be considered immune, but healthcare workers with a negative or uncertain history should be tested.

Varicella–zoster vaccine is contra-indicated in pregnancy (avoid pregnancy for 3 months after vaccination) and during breast-feeding. It must not be given to individuals with primary or acquired immunodeficiency or to individuals receiving immunosuppressive therapy. For further contra-indications, see section 14.1.

Rarely, the varicella–zoster vaccine virus has been transmitted from the vaccinated individual to close contacts. Therefore, contact with the following should be avoided if a vaccine-related cutaneous rash develops within 4–6 weeks of the first or second dose:

- varicella-susceptible pregnant women;
- individuals at high risk of severe varicella, including those with immunodeficiency or those receiving immunosuppressive therapy.

Healthcare workers who develop a generalised papular or vesicular rash on vaccination should avoid contact with patients until the lesions have crusted. Those who develop a localised rash after vaccination should cover the lesions and be allowed to continue working unless in contact with patients at high risk of severe varicella.

For reference to specific **varicella–zoster immunoglobulin** see section 14.5.

**Varilrix®** (GSK) ▼ PoM

Injection, powder for reconstitution, live attenuated varicella–zoster virus (Oka strain) propagated in human diploid cells, net price 0.5-mL vial (with diluent) = £27.31

Excipients include neomycin

Dose by subcutaneous injection preferably into deltoid region, ADULT and ADOLESCENT over 13 years (see notes above), 2 doses of 0.5 mL separated by an interval of 8 weeks (minimum 6 weeks); CHILD 1–12 years (but see notes above), 0.5 mL as a single dose

**Varivax®** (Sanofi Pasteur) ▼ PoM

Injection powder for reconstitution, live attenuated varicella-zoster virus (Oka/Merck strain) propagated in human diploid cells, net price 0.5-mL vial (with diluent) = £32.14

Excipients include gelatin and neomycin

Dose by subcutaneous injection into deltoid region or higher anterolateral thigh, ADULT and ADOLESCENT over 13 years (see notes above), 2 doses of 0.5 mL separated by 4–8 weeks; CHILD 1–12 years (but see notes above), 0.5 mL as a single dose (2 doses separated by 12 weeks in children with asymptomatic HIV infection)

## Yellow fever vaccine

Live yellow fever vaccine is indicated for those travelling or living in areas where infection is endemic (see p. 630) and for laboratory staff who handle the virus or who handle clinical material from suspected cases. Infants under 9 months of age should be vaccinated only if the risk of yellow fever is unavoidable because there is a small risk of encephalitis. The immunity which probably lasts for life is officially accepted for 10 years starting from 10 days after primary immunisation and for a further 10 years immediately after revaccination.

The vaccine should not be given to those with impaired immune responsiveness, or who have had an anaphylactic reaction to egg; it should not be given during pregnancy but if a significant risk of exposure cannot be avoided then vaccination should be delayed to the third trimester if possible (but the need for immunisation usually outweighs risk to the fetus). See section 14.1 for further contra-indications.

Headache, fever, tiredness, and stiffness may occur 4–7 days after vaccination. Other side-effects include myalgia, asthenia, lymphadenopathy, rash, urticaria, and injection-site reactions; very rarely, neurological disorders such as meningoencephalitis have been reported.

**Yellow Fever Vaccine, Live** (PoM)

**Yel(live)**

Injection, powder for reconstitution, preparation of 17D strain of yellow fever virus grown in fertilized hens eggs

Dose by deep subcutaneous injection, 0.5 mL

Available (only to designated Yellow Fever Vaccination centres) as *Arilvax®* (*excipients: include* gelatin) and *Stamaril®*

# 14.5 Immunoglobulins

Human immunoglobulins have replaced immunoglobulins of animal origin (antisera) which were frequently associated with hypersensitivity. Injection of immunoglobulins produces immediate protection lasting for several weeks.

Immunoglobulins are produced from pooled human plasma or serum, and are tested and found non-reactive for hepatitis B surface antigen and for antibodies against hepatitis C virus and human immunodeficiency virus (types 1 and 2)

The two types of human immunoglobulin preparation are **normal immunoglobulin** and **specific immunoglobulins**.

Further information about immunoglobulins is included in *Immunisation against Infectious Disease* (see section 14.1) and in the Health Protection Agency's *Immunoglobulin Handbook* www.hpa.org.uk.

**Availability** **Normal immunoglobulin** is available from Health Protection and microbiology laboratories only for contacts and the control of outbreaks. It is available commercially for other purposes.

**Specific immunoglobulins** are available from Health Protection and microbiology laboratories with the exception of **tetanus immunoglobulin** which is distributed through BPL to hospital pharmacies or blood transfusion departments and is also available to general medical practitioners. **Rabies immunoglobulin** is available from the Specialist and Reference Microbiology Division, Health Protection Agency. The large amounts of **hepatitis B immunoglobulin** required by transplant centres should be obtained commercially.

In Scotland all immunoglobulins are available from the *Blood Transfusion Service*. **Tetanus immunoglobulin** is distributed by the *Blood Transfusion Service* to hospitals and general medical practitioners on demand.

## Normal immunoglobulin

Human **normal immunoglobulin** ('HNIG') is prepared from pools of at least 1000 donations of human plasma; it contains antibody to measles, mumps, varicella, hepatitis A, and other viruses that are currently prevalent in the general population.

**Cautions and side-effects** Side-effects of immunoglobulins include malaise, chills, fever, and rarely anaphylaxis. Normal immunoglobulin is **contra-indicated** in patients with known class specific antibody to immunoglobulin A (IgA).

Normal immunoglobulin may **interfere with the immune response to live virus vaccines** which should therefore only be given **at least 3 weeks before or 3 months after** an injection of normal immunoglobulin (this does not apply to yellow fever vaccine since normal immunoglobulin does not contain antibody to this virus). For travellers, if there is insufficient time, the recommended interval may have to be ignored.

**Uses** Normal immunoglobulin is administered by intramuscular injection for the protection of susceptible contacts against **hepatitis A** virus (infectious hepatitis), **measles** and, to a lesser extent, **rubella**.

Special formulations of immunoglobulins for intravenous administration are available for *replacement therapy* for patients with congenital agammaglobulinaemia and hypogammaglobulinaemia, for the treatment of idiopathic thrombocytopenic purpura and Kawasaki syndrome, and for the prophylaxis of infection following bone-marrow transplantation and in children with symptomatic HIV infection who have recurrent bacterial infections. Normal immunoglobulin may also be given intramuscularly or subcutaneously for replacement therapy, but intravenous formulations are normally preferred.

Intravenous immunoglobulin is also used in the treatment of Guillain-Barré syndrome in preference to plasma exchange.

**Hepatitis A** **Hepatitis A vaccine** is preferred for individuals at risk of infection (see p. 616) including those visiting areas where the disease is highly endemic (all countries excluding Northern and Western Europe, North America, Japan, Australia, and New Zealand). In unimmunised individuals, transmission of hepatitis A is reduced by good hygiene. Intramuscular normal immunoglobulin is no longer recommended for routine prophylaxis in travellers but it may be indicated for immunocompromised patients if their antibody response to vaccine is unlikely to be adequate.

Intramuscular normal immunoglobulin is of value in the prevention of infection in close contact of confirmed cases of hepatitis A where there has been a delay in identifying cases or for individuals at high risk of severe disease.

**Measles** Intramuscular normal immunoglobulin may be given to prevent or attenuate an attack of measles in individuals who do not have adequate immunity. Children and adults with compromised immunity who have come into contact with measles should receive intramuscular normal immunoglobulin as soon as possible after exposure. It is most effective if given within 72 hours but can be effective if given within 6 days. For individuals receiving intravenous immunoglobulin, 100 mg/kg given within 3 weeks before measles exposure should prevent measles. Intramuscular normal immunoglobulin should also be considered for the following individuals if they have been in contact with a confirmed case of measles or with a person associated with a local outbreak:

- non-immune pregnant women
- infants under 9 months

Further advice should be sought from the Communicable Disease Surveillance Centre, Health Protection Agency (tel. (020) 8200 6868).

Individuals with normal immunity who are not in the above categories and who have not been fully immunised against measles, can be given MMR vaccine (section 14.4) for prophylaxis following exposure to measles.

**Rubella** Intramuscular immunoglobulin after exposure to rubella does **not** prevent infection in non-immune contacts and is **not** recommended for protection of pregnant women exposed to rubella. It may, however, reduce the likelihood of a clinical attack which may possibly reduce the risk to the fetus. It should be used only if termination of pregnancy would be unacceptable to the pregnant woman, when it should be given as soon as possible after exposure. Serological follow-up of recipients is essential. For routine prophylaxis, see MMR vaccine (p. 620).

### For intramuscular use

**Normal Immunoglobulin** PoM

Normal immunoglobulin injection. 250-mg vial; 750-mg vial

**Dose** by deep intramuscular injection, to control outbreaks of hepatitis A (see notes above), 500 mg; CHILD under 10 years 250 mg

Measles prophylaxis, CHILD under 1 year 250 mg, 1–2 years 500 mg, 3 years and over 750 mg; to allow attenuated attack, CHILD under 1 year 100 mg, 1 year and over 250 mg

Rubella in pregnancy, prevention of clinical attack, 750 mg

Available from the Communicable Disease Surveillance Centre and other regional Health Protection Agency offices (for contacts and control of outbreaks only, see above) and from SNBTS (as *Liberim® IM*, 250-mg strength only)

### For subcutaneous use

**Subcuvia®** (Baxter BioScience) PoM

Normal immunoglobulin injection, net price 5-mL vial = £29.60, 10-mL vial = £59.20

**Dose** by subcutaneous injection, antibody deficiency syndromes, consult product literature

**Note** May be administered by intramuscular injection (if subcutaneous route not possible) but **not** for patients with thrombocytopenia or other bleeding disorders

**Subgam®** (BPL) PoM

Normal immunoglobulin injection, net price 2-mL vial = £11.20, 5-mL vial = £28.00, 10-mL vial = £56.00

**Dose** by subcutaneous injection, antibody deficiency syndromes, consult product literature

**Note** May be administered by intramuscular injection (if subcutaneous route not possible) but **not** for patients with thrombocytopenia or other bleeding disorders

**Vivaglobin®** (ZLB Behring) PoM

Normal immunoglobulin injection, net price 10-mL vial = £59.20

**Dose** by subcutaneous injection, antibody deficiency syndromes, consult product literature

### For intravenous use

**Normal Immunoglobulin for Intravenous Use** PoM

Brands include *Flebogamma® 5%* (0.5 g, 2.5 g, 5 g, 10 g); *Gammagard® S/D* (0.5 g, 2.5 g, 5 g, 10 g); Human Immunoglobulin (3 g, 5 g, 10 g); *Octagam®* (2.5 g, 5 g, 10 g); *Sandoglobulin®* (1 g, 3 g, 6 g, 12 g); *Sandoglobulin®* NF Liquid (6 g, 12 g); *Vigam® S* (2.5 g, 5 g); *Vigam® Liquid* (2.5 g, 5 g, 10 g)

**Dose** consult product literature

## Specific immunoglobulins

Specific immunoglobulins are prepared by pooling the plasma of selected donors with high levels of the specific antibody required.

Although a hepatitis B vaccine is now available for those at high risk of infection, specific **hepatitis B immunoglobulin** ('HBIG') is available for use in association with hepatitis B vaccine for the prevention of infection in laboratory and other personnel who have been accidentally inoculated with hepatitis B virus, and in infants born to mothers who have become infected with this virus in pregnancy or who are high-risk carriers (see Hepatitis B Vaccine, p. 617).

Following exposure of an unimmunised individual to an animal in or from a high-risk country, the site of the bite should be washed with soapy water and specific **rabies immunoglobulin** of human origin administered; as much of the dose as possible should be injected in and around the cleansed wound. Rabies vaccine should also be given (for details see Rabies Vaccine, p. 624).

For the management of tetanus-prone wounds, **tetanus immunoglobulin** of human origin ('HTIG') should be used in addition to wound cleansing and, where appropriate, antibacterial prophylaxis and a tetanus-containing vaccine (section 14.4). Tetanus immunoglobulin, together with metronidazole (section 5.1.11) and wound cleansing, should also be used for the treatment of established cases of tetanus.

**Varicella–zoster immunoglobulin** (VZIG) is recommended for individuals who are at increased risk of severe varicella *and* who have no antibodies to varicella–zoster virus *and* who have significant exposure to chickenpox or herpes zoster. Those at increased risk include neonates of women who develop chickenpox in the period 7 days before to 7 days after delivery, women exposed at any stage of pregnancy (but when supplies of VZIG are short, only issued to those exposed in the first 20 weeks' gestation or to those near term), and the immunosuppressed including those who have received corticosteroids in the previous 3 months at the following dose equivalents of prednisolone: *children* 2 mg/kg daily for at least 1 week or 1 mg/kg daily for 1 month; *adults* about 40 mg daily for more than 1 week. (**Important:** for full details consult *Immunisation against Infectious*

*Disease*). **Varicella–zoster vaccine** is available—see section 14.4

**Cytomegalovirus (CMV) immunoglobulin** (available on a named-patient basis from SNBTS) is indicated for prophylaxis in patients receiving immunosuppressive treatment.

### Hepatitis B

**Hepatitis B Immunoglobulin** PoM

See notes above

Dose by intramuscular injection (as soon as possible after exposure), ADULT and CHILD over 10 years 500 units; CHILD under 5 years 200 units, 5–9 years 300 units; NEONATE 200 units as soon as possible after birth; for full details consult *Immunisation against Infectious Disease*

Available from selected Health Protection Agency and NHS laboratories (except for Transplant Centres, see p. 627), also available from BPL and SNBTS (as *Liberim® HB*)

Note Hepatitis B immunoglobulin for intravenous use is available from BPL and SNBTS on a named-patient basis.

### Rabies

**Rabies Immunoglobulin** PoM
**(Antirabies Immunoglobulin Injection)**

See notes above

Dose 20 units/kg by infiltration in and around the cleansed wound; if wound not visible or healed or if infiltration of whole volume not possible, give remainder by intramuscular injection into anterolateral thigh (remote from vaccination site)

Available from Specialist and Reference Microbiology Division, Health Protection Agency (also from BPL and SNBTS)

### Tetanus

**Tetanus Immunoglobulin** PoM
**(Antitetanus Immunoglobulin Injection)**

See notes above

Dose by intramuscular injection, prophylactic 250 units, increased to 500 units if more than 24 hours have elapsed or there is risk of heavy contamination or following burns

Therapeutic, 150 units/kg (multiple sites)

Available from BPL and from SNBTS (as *Liberim® T*, licensed only for tetanus prophylaxis)

**Tetabulin®** (Baxter BioScience) PoM

Tetanus immunoglobulin, net price 250-unit prefilled syringe = £14.80

Dose by intramuscular injection, prophylactic, 250 units, increased to 500 units if wound older than 12 hours or if risk of heavy contamination or if patient weighs more than 90 kg; second dose of 250 units given after 3–4 weeks if patient immunosuppressed or if active immunisation with tetanus vaccine contra-indicated

Therapeutic, 150 units/kg (multiple sites)

**Tetanus Immunoglobulin for Intravenous Use** PoM

Used for proven or suspected clinical tetanus

Dose by intravenous infusion, 5000–10 000 units

Available from BPL and SNBTS on a named-patient basis and from the Northern Ireland Blood Transfusion Service

### Varicella–zoster

**Varicella–Zoster Immunoglobulin** PoM
**(Antivaricella–zoster Immunoglobulin)**

See notes above

Dose by deep intramuscular injection, prophylaxis (as soon as possible—not later than 10 days after exposure), NEONATE, INFANT and CHILD up to 5 years 250 mg, 6–10 years 500 mg, 11–14 years 750 mg, over 15 years 1 g; give second dose if further exposure occurs more than 3 weeks after first dose

Note No evidence that effective in treatment of severe disease. Normal immunoglobulin for intravenous use may be used to provide an immediate source of antibody.

Available from selected Health Protection Agency and NHS laboratories (also from BPL, and SNBTS as *Liberim® Z*)

## Anti-D ($Rh_0$) immunoglobulin

Anti-D ($Rh_0$) immunoglobulin is available to prevent a rhesus-negative mother from forming antibodies to fetal rhesus-positive cells which may pass into the maternal circulation. The objective is to protect any subsequent child from the hazard of haemolytic disease of the newborn.

Anti-D immunoglobulin should be administered following any sensitising episode (e.g. abortion, miscarriage and birth); it should be injected within 72 hours of the episode but even if a longer period has elapsed it may still give protection and should be administered. The dose of anti-D immunoglobulin is determined according to the level of exposure to rhesus-positive blood.

For routine antenatal prophylaxis (see also NICE guidance below), two doses of at least 500 units of anti-D immunoglobulin should be given, the first at 28 weeks' gestation and the second at 34 weeks.

> **NICE Guidance (routine antenatal anti-D prophylaxis for rhesus-negative women)**
> NICE has recommended (May 2002) that routine antenatal anti-D prophylaxis be offered to all non-sensitised pregnant women who are rhesus negative.
> Use of routine *antenatal* anti-D prophylaxis should not be affected by previous anti-D prophylaxis for a sensitising event early in the same pregnancy. Similarly, *postpartum* anti-D prophylaxis should not be affected by previous routine antenatal anti-D prophylaxis or by antenatal anti-D prophylaxis for a sensitising event.

> **Note**
> MMR vaccine may be given in the postpartum period with anti-D ($Rh_0$) immunoglobulin injection provided that separate syringes are used and the products are administered into different limbs. If blood is transfused, the antibody response to the vaccine may be inhibited—measure rubella antibodies after 8 weeks and revaccinate if necessary.

**Anti-D ($Rh_0$) Immunoglobulin** (Non-proprietary) PoM

Injection, anti-D ($Rh_0$) immunoglobulin, net price 250-unit vial = £14.95, 500-unit vial = £19.50, 2500-unit vial = £94.40

Dose by deep intramuscular injection, to rhesus-negative woman for prevention of $Rh_0$(D) sensitisation:

Following birth of rhesus-positive infant, 500 units immediately or within 72 hours; for transplacental bleed of over 4 mL fetal red cells, extra 100–125 units per mL fetal red cells

Following any potentially sensitising episode (e.g. stillbirth, abortion, amniocentesis) up to 20 weeks' gestation 250 units per episode (after 20 weeks, 500 units) immediately or within 72 hours

Antenatal prophylaxis, 500 units given at weeks 28 and 34 of pregnancy; a further dose is still needed immediately or within 72 hours of delivery

Note Some UK authorities recommend different doses for antenatal prophylaxis (see notes above)

Following $Rh_0$(D) incompatible blood transfusion, 100–125 units per mL transfused rhesus-positive red cells

Available from Blood Centres and from BPL (*D-Gam®*) and SNBTS (as *Liberim® D250, Liberim® D500*)

**Partobulin SDF®** (Baxter BioScience) PoM

Injection, anti-D ($Rh_0$) immunoglobulin 1250 units/mL (250 micrograms/mL), net price 1-mL prefilled syringe = £35.00

**Dose** by intramuscular injection, to rhesus-negative woman for prevention of $Rh_0$ (D) sensitisation:

Following birth of rhesus-positive infant, 1000–1650 units immediately or within 72 hours; for large transplacental blood loss, 50–125 units per mL of fetal red cells

Antenatal prophylaxis, 1000–1650 units given at weeks 28 and 34 of pregnancy; if infant rhesus-positive, further dose is needed immediately or within 72 hours of delivery

Following abortion, ectopic pregnancy or hydatidiform mole up to 12 weeks' gestation, 600–750 units (after 12 weeks, 1250–1650 units) immediately or within 72 hours

Following amniocentesis or chorionic villous sampling, 1250–1650 units immediately or within 72 hours

**Note** Some UK authorities recommend different doses for antenatal prophylaxis (see notes above)

Following $Rh_0$ (D) incompatible blood or red cell transfusion, 1250 units per 10 mL of transfused rhesus-positive red cells immediately or within 72 hours

**Rhophylac®** (ZLB Behring) PoM

Injection, anti-D ($Rh_0$) immunoglobulin 750 units/mL (150 micrograms/mL), net price 2-mL (1500-unit) prefilled syringe = £46.50.

**Dose** by intramuscular *or* intravenous injection, to rhesus-negative woman for prevention of $Rh_0$(D) sensitisation:

Following birth of rhesus-positive infant, 1000–1500 units immediately or within 72 hours; for large transplacental bleed, extra 100 units per mL fetal red cells (preferably by intravenous injection)

Following any potentially sensitising episode (e.g. abortion, amniocentesis, chorionic villous sampling) up to 12 weeks' gestation 1000 units per episode (after 12 weeks, higher doses may be required) immediately or within 72 hours

Antenatal prophylaxis, 1500 units given between weeks 28–30 of pregnancy; a further dose is still needed immediately or within 72 hours of delivery

**Note** Some UK authorities recommend different doses for antenatal prophylaxis (see notes above)

Following $Rh_0$(D) incompatible blood transfusion, by intravenous injection, 50 units per mL transfused rhesus-positive blood (or 100 units per mL of erythrocyte concentrate)

**WinRho SDF®** (Baxter BioScience) PoM

Injection, anti-D ($Rh_0$) immunoglobulin, powder for reconstitution, net price 1500-unit (300-microgram) vial (with diluent) = £313.50, 5000-unit (1-mg) vial (with diluent) = £1045.00

**Dose** to rhesus-negative woman for prevention of $Rh_0$(D) sensitisation:

Following birth of rhesus-positive infant, by intramuscular injection, 1500 units *or* by intravenous injection, 600 units immediately or within 72 hours; for transplacental bleed of over 25 mL fetal blood, by intramuscular injection, extra 50 units per mL fetal blood

Following any potentially sensitising episode (e.g. abortion, amniocentesis, chorionic villous sampling) up to 12 weeks' gestation, by intramuscular injection, 600 units per episode (after 12 weeks, 1500 units) immediately or within 72 hours

Antenatal prophylaxis, by intramuscular *or* intravenous injection, 1500 units given at week 28 of pregnancy; a further dose is still needed immediately or within 72 hours of delivery

Following $Rh_0$(D) incompatible thrombocyte transfusion in rhesus-negative woman of child-bearing age, by intravenous injection, 1500 units

**Note** Some UK authorities recommend different doses for antenatal prophylaxis (see notes above)

Following $Rh_0$(D) incompatible blood transfusion, by intramuscular injection, at least 600 units per 10 mL transfused rhesus-positive blood, given in divided doses over several days

Autoimmune (idiopathic) thrombocytopenic purpura, consult product literature

## Interferons

**Interferon gamma-1b** is licensed to reduce the frequency of serious infection in chronic granulomatous disease and in severe malignant osteopetrosis.

### INTERFERON GAMMA-1b
**(Immune interferon)**

**Indications** see notes above

**Cautions** severe hepatic impairment (Appendix 2) or severe renal impairment (Appendix 3); seizure disorders (including seizures associated with fever); cardiac disease (including ischaemia, congestive heart failure, and arrhythmias); monitor before and during treatment: haematological tests (including full blood count, differential white cell count, and platelet count), blood chemistry tests (including renal and liver function tests) and urinalysis; avoid simultaneous administration of foreign proteins including immunological products (risk of exaggerated immune response); pregnancy (Appendix 4); breast-feeding (Appendix 5); **interactions:** Appendix 1 (interferons)

**Driving** May impair ability to drive or operate machinery; effects may be enhanced by alcohol

**Side-effects** fever, headache, chills, myalgia, fatigue; nausea, vomiting, arthralgia, rashes and injection-site reactions reported

**Dose**

- See under Preparations

**Immukin®** (Boehringer Ingelheim) PoM

Injection, recombinant human interferon gamma-1b 200 micrograms/mL, net price 0.5-mL vial = £88.00

**Dose** by subcutaneous injection, 50 micrograms/m² 3 times a week; patients with body surface area of 0.5 m² or less, 1.5 micrograms/kg 3 times a week; not yet recommended for children under 6 months with chronic granulomatous disease

## 14.6 International travel

**Note** For advice on **malaria chemoprophylaxis**, see section 5.4.1.

No special immunisation is required for travellers to the United States, Europe, Australia, or New Zealand although all travellers should have immunity to tetanus and poliomyelitis (and childhood immunisations should be up to date). Certain special precautions are required in non-European areas surrounding the Mediterranean, in Africa, the Middle East, Asia, and South America.

Long-term travellers to areas that have a high incidence of **poliomyelitis** or **tuberculosis** should be immunised with the appropriate vaccine; in the case of poliomyelitis previously immunised adults may be given a booster dose of a preparation containing inactivated poliomyelitis vaccine. BCG immunisation is recommended for travellers aged under 35 years[1] proposing to stay for longer than one month (or in close contact with the local population) in Asia, Africa, or Central and South America; it should preferably be given three months or more before departure.

**Yellow fever** immunisation is recommended for travel to the endemic zones of Africa and South America. Many countries require an International Certificate of

1. There is inadequate evidence of protection by BCG vaccine in adults aged over 35 years

14 Immunological products and vaccines

Vaccination from individuals arriving from, or who have been travelling through, endemic areas, whilst other countries require a certificate from all entering travellers (consult the Department of Health handbook, *Health Information for Overseas Travel*, www.dh.gov.uk).

Immunisation against **meningococcal meningitis** is recommended for a number of areas of the world (for details, see p. 621).

Protection against **hepatitis A** is recommended for travellers to high-risk areas outside Northern and Western Europe, North America, Japan, Australia and New Zealand. Hepatitis A vaccine (see p. 616) is preferred and it is likely to be effective even if given shortly before departure; normal immunoglobulin is no longer given routinely but may be indicated in the immunocompromised (see p. 627). Special care must also be taken with food hygiene (see below).

**Hepatitis B** vaccine (see p. 617) is recommended for those travelling to areas of high or intermediate prevalence who intend to seek employment as healthcare workers or who plan to remain there for lengthy periods and who may therefore be at increased risk of acquiring infection as the result of medical or dental procedures carried out in those countries. Short-term tourists or business travellers are not generally at increased risk of infection but may place themselves at risk by their sexual behaviour when abroad.

Prophylactic immunisation against **rabies** (see p. 624) is recommended for travellers to enzootic areas on long journeys or to areas out of reach of immediate medical attention.

Travellers who have not had a **tetanus** booster in the last 10 years and are visiting areas where medical attention may not be accessible should receive a booster dose of adsorbed diphtheria [low dose], tetanus and inactivated poliomyelitis vaccine (see p. 615), even if they have received 5 doses of a tetanus-containing vaccine previously.

**Typhoid vaccine** is indicated for travellers to those countries where typhoid is endemic but the vaccine is no substitute for personal precautions (see below).

There is no requirement for cholera vaccination as a condition for entry into any country, but **oral cholera vaccine** (see p. 614) may be considered for backpackers and those travelling to situations where the risk is greatest (e.g. refugee camps). Regardless of vaccination, travellers to areas where cholera is endemic should take special care with food hygiene (see below).

Advice on **diphtheria**, on **Japanese encephalitis** (NHS vaccine available on named-patient basis from Sanofi Pasteur and MASTA) and on **tick-borne encephalitis** is included in *Health Information for Overseas Travel*, see below.

**Food hygiene** In areas where sanitation is poor, good food hygiene is important to help prevent hepatitis A, typhoid, cholera, and other diarrhoeal diseases (including travellers' diarrhoea). Food should be freshly prepared and hot, and uncooked vegetables (including green salads) should be avoided; only fruits which can be peeled should be eaten. Only suitable bottled water, or tap water that has been boiled, or treated with sterilising tablets should be used for drinking.

**Information on health advice for travellers**

The Department of Health booklet, *Health Advice For Travellers* (code: T6) includes information on immunisation requirements (or recommendations) around the world. The booklet can be obtained from travel agents, post-offices or by telephoning 0800 555 777 (24-hour service); also available on the Internet at:
www.dh.gov.uk

The Department of Health handbook, *Health Information for Overseas Travel* (2001), which draws together essential information *for healthcare professionals* regarding health advice for travellers, can be obtained from
The Stationery Office
PO Box 29, Norwich NR3 1GN
Telephone orders, 0870 600 5522
Fax: 0870 600 5533
www.tso.co.uk

Immunisation requirements change from time to time, and information on the current requirements for any particular country may be obtained from:

National Travel Health Network and Centre
Hospital for Tropical Diseases
Mortimer Market Centre
Capper Street, off Tottenham Court Road
London, WC1E 6AU
Tel: (020) 7380 9234
(9 a.m.–noon, 2–4.30 p.m. weekdays for healthcare professionals **only**)
www.nathnac.org

Scottish Centre for Infection and Environmental Health
Clifton House
Clifton Place
Glasgow, G3 7LN
Tel: (0141) 300 1130
(14.00–16.00 hours weekdays)
www.travax.scot.nhs.uk (registration required. Annual fee may be payable for users outside NHS Scotland)

Welsh Medicines Information Centre
University Hospital of Wales
Cardiff, CF14 4XW
Tel: (029) 2074 2979 (for health professionals **only**)

Department of Health and Social Services
Castle Buildings
Stormont
Belfast, BT4 3PP
Tel: (028) 9052 0000

or from the embassy or legation of the appropriate country.

# 15 Anaesthesia


15.1 General anaesthesia 632
15.1.1 Intravenous anaesthetics 633
15.1.2 Inhalational anaesthetics 635
15.1.3 Antimuscarinic drugs 637
15.1.4 Sedative and analgesic peri-operative drugs 638
15.1.4.1 Anxiolytics and neuroleptics 638
15.1.4.2 Non-opioid analgesics 640
15.1.4.3 Opioid analgesics 641
15.1.5 Muscle relaxants 642
15.1.6 Anticholinesterases used in anaesthesia 645
15.1.7 Antagonists for central and respiratory depression 646
15.1.8 Drugs for malignant hyperthermia 646
15.2 Local anaesthesia 647




## 15.1 General anaesthesia


15.1.1 Intravenous anaesthetics
15.1.2 Inhalational anaesthetics
15.1.3 Antimuscarinic drugs
15.1.4 Sedative and analgesic peri-operative drugs
15.1.5 Muscle relaxants
15.1.6 Anticholinesterases used in anaesthesia
15.1.7 Antagonists for central and respiratory depression
15.1.8 Drugs for malignant hyperthermia


**Note** The drugs in section 15.1 should be used only by experienced personnel and where adequate resuscitation equipment is available.

It is common practice to administer several drugs with different actions during surgery. An intravenous anaesthetic is usually used for induction, followed by maintenance with an inhalational anaesthetic, often supplemented by other drugs administered intravenously. Specific drugs are often used to produce muscle relaxation; these drugs interfere with spontaneous respiration and intermittent positive-pressure ventilation is commonly employed.

**Surgery and long-term medication** The risk of losing disease control on stopping long-term medication before surgery is often greater than the risk posed by continuing it during surgery. It is vital that the anaesthetist knows about **all** drugs that a patient is (or has been) taking.

Patients with adrenal atrophy resulting from long-term corticosteroid use (section 6.3.2) may suffer a precipitous fall in blood pressure unless corticosteroid cover is provided during anaesthesia and in the immediate post-operative period. Anaesthetists must therefore know whether a patient is, or has been, receiving corticosteroids (including high-dose inhaled corticosteroids).

Other drugs that should normally not be stopped before surgery include antiepileptics, antiparkinsonian drugs, antipsychotics, anxiolytics, bronchodilators, cardiovascular drugs, glaucoma drugs, immunosuppressants, drugs of dependence, and thyroid or antithyroid drugs. Expert advice is required for patients receiving antivirals for HIV infection. For general advice on surgery in diabetic patients see section 6.1.1.

Patients taking aspirin or an oral anticoagulant present an increased risk for surgery. In these circumstances, the anaesthetist and surgeon should assess the relative risks and decide jointly whether the aspirin or anticoagulant should be stopped or replaced with heparin therapy.

Drugs that are stopped before surgery include combined oral contraceptives (see Surgery, section 7.3.1

for details); for advice on hormone replacement therapy, see section 6.4.1.1. If antidepressants need to be stopped, they should be withdrawn gradually to avoid withdrawal symptoms. In view of their hazardous interactions MAOIs should normally be stopped 2 weeks before surgery. Tricyclic antidepressants need not be stopped, but there may be an increased risk of arrhythmias and hypotension (and dangerous interaction with vasopressor drugs); therefore, the anaesthetist should be informed if they are not stopped. Lithium should be stopped 24 hours before major surgery but the normal dose can be continued for minor surgery (with careful monitoring of fluids and electrolytes). Potassium-sparing diuretics may need to be withheld on the morning of surgery because hyperkalaemia may develop if renal perfusion is impaired or if there is tissue damage.

**Anaesthesia and driving** Patients given sedatives and analgesics during minor outpatient procedures should be very carefully warned about the risk of driving afterwards. For intravenous benzodiazepines and for a short general anaesthetic the risk extends to **at least 24 hours** after administration. Responsible persons should be available to take patients home. The dangers of taking **alcohol** should also be emphasised.

**Prophylaxis of acid aspiration** Regurgitation and aspiration of gastric contents (Mendelson's syndrome) is an important complication of general anaesthesia, particularly in obstetrics and emergency surgery.

An **$H_2$-receptor antagonist** (section 1.3.1) or a **proton pump inhibitor** (section 1.3.5) such as omeprazole may be used before surgery to increase the pH and reduce the volume of gastric fluid. They do not affect the pH of fluid already in the stomach and this limits their value in emergency procedures; oral $H_2$-receptor antagonists can be given 1–2 hours before the procedure but omeprazole must be given at least 12 hours earlier. Antacids are frequently used to neutralise the acidity of the fluid already in the stomach; 'clear' (non-particulate) antacids such as sodium citrate are preferred. Sodium citrate 300 mmol/litre (88.2 mg/mL) oral solution is licensed for use before general anaesthesia for caesarean section.

## Anaesthesia, sedation and resuscitation in dental practice

> Anaesthesia, sedation and resuscitation in dental practice
>
> For details see *A Conscious Decision: A review of the use of general anaesthesia and conscious sedation in primary dental care*; report by a group chaired by the Chief Medical Officer and Chief Dental Officer, July 2000 and associated documents.
> Further details can also be found in *Conscious Sedation in the Provision of Dental Care*; report of an Expert Group on Sedation for Dentistry (commissioned by the Department of Health), 2003. Both documents are available at www.dh.gov.uk.
> Guidance is also included in *Standards for Dental Professionals*, London, General Dental Council, May 2005 (and as amended subsequently).

## Gas cylinders

Each gas cylinder bears a label with the name of the gas contained in the cylinder. The name or chemical symbol of the gas appears on the shoulder of the cylinder and is also clearly and indelibly stamped on the cylinder valve.

The colours on the valve end of the cylinder extend down to the shoulder; in the case of mixed gases the colours for the individual gases are applied in four segments, two for each colour.

Gas cylinders should be stored in a cool well-ventilated room, free from flammable materials.

**No lubricant of any description should be used on the cylinder valves.**

# 15.1.1 Intravenous anaesthetics

Intravenous anaesthetics may be used either to induce anaesthesia or for maintenance of anaesthesia throughout surgery. Intravenous anaesthetics nearly all produce their effect in one arm-brain circulation time and can cause apnoea and hypotension, and so adequate resuscitative facilities **must** be available. They are **contra-indicated** if the anaesthetist is not confident of being able to maintain the airway (e.g. in the presence of a tumour in the pharynx or larynx). Extreme care is required in surgery of the mouth, pharynx, or larynx and in patients with acute circulatory failure (shock) or fixed cardiac output.

Individual requirements vary considerably and the recommended dosage is only a guide. Smaller dosage is indicated in ill, shocked, or debilitated patients and in significant hepatic impairment, while robust individuals may require more. To facilitate tracheal intubation, induction is followed by a neuromuscular blocking drug (section 15.1.5).

**Total intravenous anaesthesia** This is a technique in which major surgery is carried out with all anaesthetic drugs given intravenously. Respiration is controlled, the lungs being inflated with oxygen-enriched air. Muscle relaxants are used to provide relaxation and prevent reflex muscle movements. The main problem to be overcome is the assessment of depth of anaesthesia.

**Anaesthesia and driving** See section 15.1.

## Barbiturates

**Thiopental sodium** (thiopentone sodium) is used widely, but it has no analgesic properties. Induction is generally smooth and rapid, but owing to its potency, overdosage with cardiorespiratory depression may occur.

Awakening from a moderate dose of thiopental is rapid due to redistribution of the drug into other tissues. However, metabolism is slow and some sedative effects may persist for 24 hours. Repeated doses have a cumulative effect.

### THIOPENTAL SODIUM
(Thiopentone sodium)

**Indications** induction of general anaesthesia; anaesthesia of short duration; reduction of raised intracranial pressure if ventilation controlled; status epilepticus (see also section 4.8.2)

**Cautions** see notes above; cardiovascular disease; hepatic impairment (Appendix 2); reconstituted solution is highly alkaline—extravasation causes tissue necrosis and severe pain; avoid intra-arterial injection; pregnancy (Appendix 4); **interactions:** Appendix 1 (anaesthetics, general)

**Contra-indications** see notes above; porphyria (section 9.8.2); myotonic dystrophy; breast-feeding (Appendix 5)

**Side-effects** arrhythmias, myocardial depression, laryngeal spasm, cough, sneezing, hypersensitivity reactions, rash, injection-site reactions

**Dose**

- Induction of general anaesthesia, by intravenous injection usually as a 2.5% (25 mg/mL) solution, in fit premedicated adults, initially 100–150 mg (reduced in elderly or debilitated) over 10–15 seconds (longer in elderly or debilitated), followed by further quantity if necessary according to response after 30–60 seconds; *or* up to 4 mg/kg (max. 500mg); CHILD induction 2–7 mg/kg
- Raised intracranial pressure, by intravenous injection, 1.5–3 mg/kg, repeated as required
- Status epilepticus (only if other measures fail, see section 4.8.2), by intravenous injection as a 2.5% (25 mg/mL) solution, 75–125 mg as a single dose

**Thiopental** (Link) PoM

Injection, powder for reconstitution, thiopental sodium, net price 500-mg vial = £3.06

## Other intravenous anaesthetics

**Etomidate** is an induction agent associated with rapid recovery without a hangover effect. It causes less hypotension than other drugs used for induction. It produces a high incidence of extraneous muscle movement, which can be minimised by an opioid analgesic or a short-acting benzodiazepine given just before induction. Pain on injection can be reduced by injecting into a larger vein or by giving an opioid analgesic just before induction. Etomidate may suppress adrenocortical function, particularly on continuous administration, and it should not be used for maintenance of anaesthesia.

**Propofol** is associated with rapid recovery without a hangover effect and it is very widely used. There is sometimes pain on intravenous injection and significant extraneous muscle movements may occur. Convulsions, anaphylaxis, and delayed recovery from anaesthesia can occur after propofol administration; since the onset of convulsions can be delayed the CSM has advised special caution after day surgery. Propofol has been associated with bradycardia, occasionally profound; intravenous administration of an antimuscarinic drug may be necessary to prevent this.

**Ketamine** is used rarely now. It has good analgesic properties at sub-anaesthetic dosage. It is used mainly for paediatric anaesthesia, particularly when repeated administration is required; recovery is relatively slow. There is a high incidence of extraneous muscle movements; also cardiovascular stimulation, tachycardia, and raised arterial pressure may occur. The main disadvantage of ketamine is the high incidence of hallucinations, nightmares, and other transient psychotic effects; these can be reduced when drugs such as diazepam are also used. Ketamine is **contra-indicated** in patients with hypertension and is best avoided in those prone to hallucinations or nightmares. It also has abuse potential and may itself cause dependence.

## ETOMIDATE

**Indications** induction of anaesthesia

**Cautions** see notes above; avoid in porphyria (section 9.8.2); pregnancy (Appendix 4); breast-feeding (Appendix 5); **interactions:** Appendix 1 (anaesthetics, general)

**Contra-indications** see notes above

**Side-effects** see notes above

**Dose**

- See under preparations

**Etomidate-Lipuro®** (Braun) PoM

Injection (emulsion), etomidate 2 mg/mL, net price 10-mL amp = £1.53

Dose ADULT and CHILD, by slow intravenous injection, 150–300 micrograms/kg; CHILD under 10 years may need up to 400 micrograms/kg; ELDERLY 150–200 micrograms/kg

**Hypnomidate®** (Janssen-Cilag) PoM

Injection, etomidate 2 mg/mL, net price 10-mL amp = £1.50

Excipients include propylene glycol (see Excipients, p. 2)

Dose ADULT and CHILD, by slow intravenous injection, 300 micrograms/kg; ELDERLY 150–200 micrograms/kg; max. total dose 60 mg

## KETAMINE

**Indications** induction and maintenance of anaesthesia

**Cautions** see notes above; pregnancy (Appendix 4); **interactions:** Appendix 1 (anaesthetics, general)

**Contra-indications** see notes above; also porphyria (section 9.8.2)

**Side-effects** see notes above

**Dose**

- By intramuscular injection, short procedures, initially 6.5–13 mg/kg (10 mg/kg usually produces 12–25 minutes of surgical anaesthesia)

  Diagnostic manoeuvres and procedures not involving intense pain, initially 4 mg/kg
- By intravenous injection over at least 60 seconds, short procedures, initially 1–4.5 mg/kg (2 mg/kg usually produces 5–10 minutes of surgical anaesthesia)
- By intravenous infusion of a solution containing 1 mg/mL, longer procedures, induction, total dose of 0.5–2 mg/kg; maintenance, 10–45 micrograms/kg/minute, rate adjusted according to response

**Ketalar®** (Pfizer) PoM

Injection, ketamine (as hydrochloride) 10 mg/mL, net price 20-mL vial = £4.22; 50 mg/mL, 10-mL vial = £8.77; 100 mg/mL, 10-mL vial = £16.10

## PROPOFOL

**Indications** see under dose

**Cautions** see notes above; monitor blood-lipid concentration if risk of fat overload or if sedation longer than 3 days; pregnancy (Appendix 4); **interactions:** Appendix 1 (anaesthetics, general)

**Contra-indications** see notes above; not to be used for sedation of ventilated children and adolescents under 17 years (risk of potentially fatal effects including metabolic acidosis, cardiac failure, rhabdomyolysis, hyperlipidaemia and hepatomegaly)

**Side-effects** see notes above; also flushing; transient apnoea during induction; *less commonly* thrombosis, phlebitis; *very rarely* pancreatitis, pulmonary oedema, sexual disinhibition, and discoloration of urine; serious and sometimes fatal side-effects reported with prolonged infusion of doses exceeding 5 mg/kg/hour, including metabolic acidosis, rhabdomyolysis, hyperkalaemia, and cardiac failure

**Dose**

- 1% injection
- Induction of anaesthesia, by intravenous injection *or* infusion, 1.5–2.5 mg/kg (less in those over 55 years) at a rate of 20–40 mg every 10 seconds; CHILD over 1 month, administer slowly until response (usual dose in child over 8 years 2.5 mg/kg, may need more in younger child e.g. 2.5–4 mg/kg)
- Maintenance of anaesthesia, by intravenous injection, 25–50 mg repeated according to response *or* by intravenous infusion, 4–12 mg/kg/hour; CHILD over 3 years, by intravenous infusion, 9–15 mg/kg/hour

  Note *Propofol-Lipuro*® may be used for maintenance of anaesthesia in CHILD over 1 month, by intravenous infusion, 9–15 mg/kg/hour
- Sedation in intensive care, by intravenous infusion, ADULT over 17 years, 0.3–4 mg/kg/hour
- Sedation for surgical and diagnostic procedures, initially by intravenous injection over 1–5 minutes, 0.5–1 mg/kg; maintenance, by intravenous infusion, 1.5–4.5 mg/kg/hour (additionally, if rapid increase in sedation required, by intravenous injection, 10–20 mg); those over 55 years may require lower dose; CHILD and ADOLESCENT under 17 years not recommended

- 2% injection
- Induction of anaesthesia, by intravenous infusion, 1.5–2.5 mg/kg (less in those over 55 years) at a rate of 20–40 mg every 10 seconds; CHILD over 3 years, administer slowly until response (usual dose in child over 8 years 2.5 mg/kg, may need more in younger child e.g. 2.5–4 mg/kg)
- Maintenance of anaesthesia, by intravenous infusion, 4–12 mg/kg/hour; CHILD over 3 years, by intravenous infusion, 9–15 mg/kg/hour
- Sedation in intensive care, by intravenous infusion, ADULT over 17 years, 0.3–4 mg/kg/hour

**Propofol** (Non-proprietary) PoM

1% injection (emulsion), propofol 10 mg/mL, net price 20-mL amp = £2.33, 50-mL bottle = £5.82, 100-mL bottle = £11.64

2% injection (emulsion), propofol 20 mg/mL, net price 50-mL vial = £11.64

Brands include *Propofol-Lipuro*®

**Diprivan**® (AstraZeneca) PoM

1% injection (emulsion), propofol 10 mg/mL, net price 20-mL amp = £3.88, 50-mL vial = £9.70, 50-mL prefilled syringe (for use with *Diprifusor*® *TCI* system) = £10.67, 100-mL vial = £19.40

2% injection (emulsion), propofol 20 mg/mL, net price 50-mL vial = £19.40, 50-mL prefilled syringe (for use with *Diprifusor*® *TCI* system) = £20.37

Note *Diprifusor*® *TCI* ('target controlled infusion') system is for use **only** for induction and maintenance of general anaesthesia in adults

## 15.1.2 Inhalational anaesthetics

Inhalational anaesthetics may be gases or volatile liquids. They can be used both for induction and maintenance of anaesthesia and may also be used following induction with an intravenous anaesthetic (section 15.1.1).

*Gaseous anaesthetics* require suitable equipment for storage and administration. They may be supplied via hospital pipelines or from metal cylinders. *Volatile liquid anaesthetics* are administered using calibrated vaporisers, using air, oxygen, or nitrous oxide–oxygen mixtures as the carrier gas. It should be noted that they can all trigger malignant hyperthermia (section 15.1.8).

To prevent hypoxia inhalational anaesthetics must be given with concentrations of oxygen greater than in air.

**Anaesthesia and driving** See section 15.1.

### Volatile liquid anaesthetics

**Halothane** is a volatile liquid anaesthetic. Its advantages are that it is potent, induction is smooth, the vapour is non-irritant, pleasant to inhale, and seldom induces coughing or breath-holding. Despite these advantages, however, halothane is much less widely used than previously owing to its association with *severe hepatotoxicity* (**important:** see CSM advice, below).

Halothane causes cardiorespiratory depression. Respiratory depression results in elevation of arterial carbon dioxide tension and perhaps ventricular arrhythmias. Halothane also depresses the cardiac muscle fibres and may cause bradycardia. The result is diminished cardiac output and fall of arterial pressure. Adrenaline (epinephrine) infiltrations should be avoided in patients anaesthetised with halothane as ventricular arrhythmias may result.

Halothane produces moderate muscle relaxation, but this may be inadequate for major abdominal surgery and specific muscle relaxants are then used.

**CSM advice (halothane hepatotoxicity)**

In a publication on findings confirming that *severe hepatotoxicity* can follow halothane anaesthesia the CSM has reported that this occurs more frequently after repeated exposures to halothane and has a high mortality. The risk of severe hepatotoxicity appears to be increased by repeated exposures within a short time interval, but even after a long interval (sometimes of several years) susceptible patients have been reported to develop jaundice. Since there is no reliable way of identifying susceptible patients the CSM recommends the following precautions prior to use of halothane:

1. a careful anaesthetic history should be taken to determine previous exposure and previous reactions to halothane;
2. repeated exposure to halothane within a period of **at least** 3 months should be **avoided** unless there are **overriding** clinical circumstances;
3. a history of unexplained jaundice or pyrexia in a patient following exposure to halothane is an absolute **contra-indication** to its future use in that patient.

**Isoflurane** is a less potent anaesthetic than halothane. Heart rhythm is generally stable during isoflurane anaesthesia, but heart-rate may rise, particularly in younger patients. Systemic arterial pressure may fall, owing to a decrease in systemic vascular resistance and with less decrease in cardiac output than occurs with halothane. Respiration is depressed. Muscle relaxation is produced and muscle relaxant drugs potentiated. Isoflurane may also cause hepatotoxicity in those sensitised to halogenated anaesthetics but the risk is appreciably smaller than with halothane.

**Desflurane** is reported to have about one-fifth the potency of isoflurane. Owing to limited experience it is not recommended in neurosurgical patients. It is not recommended for induction in children because cough, breath-holding, apnoea, laryngospasm and increased secretions can occur. The risk of hepatotoxicity with desflurane in those sensitised to halogenated anaesthetics appears to be remote.

**Sevoflurane** is a rapid acting volatile liquid anaesthetic. Patients may require early postoperative pain relief as emergence and recovery are particularly rapid. Sevoflurane can interact with carbon dioxide absorbents to form compound A, a potentially nephrotoxic vinyl ether. However, in spite of extensive use, no cases of sevoflurane-induced permanent renal injury have been reported and the carbon dioxide absorbents used in the UK produce very low concentrations of compound A, even in low-flow anaesthetic systems.

## DESFLURANE

**Indications** see notes above

**Cautions** see notes above; hepatic impairment (Appendix 2); renal impairment (Appendix 3); pregnancy (Appendix 4); **interactions:** Appendix 1 (anaesthetics, general)

**Contra-indications** see notes above; susceptibility to malignant hyperthermia

**Side-effects** see notes above

**Dose**

- Using a specifically calibrated vaporiser, *induction*, 4–11%; CHILD not recommended for induction

  *Maintenance*, 2–6% in nitrous oxide; 2.5–8.5% in oxygen or oxygen-enriched air; max. 17%

**Suprane®** (Baxter) PoM
Desflurane, net price 240 mL = £44.41

## HALOTHANE

**Indications** see notes above

**Cautions** see notes above (**important:** CSM advice, see notes above); avoid for dental procedures in those under 18 years unless treated in hospital (high risk of arrhythmia); avoid in porphyria (section 9.8.2); pregnancy (Appendix 4); breast-feeding (Appendix 5); **interactions:** Appendix 1 (anaesthetics, general)

**Contra-indications** see notes above; susceptibility to malignant hyperthermia

**Side-effects** see notes above

**Dose**

- Using a specifically calibrated vaporiser, *induction*, increased gradually to 2–4% in oxygen or nitrous oxide–oxygen; CHILD (see cautions) 1.5–2%

  *Maintenance*, 0.5–2%

**Halothane** (Concord)
Halothane, net price 250 mL = £20.57

## ISOFLURANE

**Indications** see notes above

**Cautions** see notes above; pregnancy (Appendix 4); **interactions:** Appendix 1 (anaesthetics, general)

**Contra-indications** susceptibility to malignant hyperthermia

**Side-effects** see notes above

**Dose**

- Using a specifically calibrated vaporiser, *induction*, increased gradually from 0.5% to 3%, in oxygen or nitrous oxide–oxygen

  *Maintenance*, 1–2.5% in nitrous oxide–oxygen; an additional 0.5–1% may be required when given with oxygen alone; caesarean section, 0.5–0.75% in nitrous oxide–oxygen

**Isoflurane** (Abbott)
Isoflurane, net price 250 mL = £47.50

**Aerrane®** (Baxter)
Isoflurane, net price 100 mL = £7.98, 250 mL = £30.00

## SEVOFLURANE

**Indications** see notes above

**Cautions** see notes above; renal impairment (Appendix 3); pregnancy (Appendix 4); **interactions:** Appendix 1 (anaesthetics, general)

**Contra-indications** see notes above; susceptibility to malignant hyperthermia

**Side-effects** see notes above; also agitation occurs frequently in children

**Dose**

- Using a specifically calibrated vaporiser, *induction*, up to 5% in oxygen or nitrous oxide–oxygen; CHILD up to 7%

  *Maintenance*, 0.5–3%

**Sevoflurane** (Abbott) PoM
Sevoflurane, net price 250 mL = £123.00

## Nitrous oxide

**Nitrous oxide** is used for maintenance of anaesthesia and, in sub-anaesthetic concentrations, for analgesia. For anaesthesia it is commonly used in a concentration of 50 to 70% in oxygen as part of a balanced technique in association with other inhalational or intravenous agents. Nitrous oxide is unsatisfactory as a sole anaesthetic owing to lack of potency, but is useful as part of a combination of drugs since it allows a significant reduction in dosage.

A mixture of nitrous oxide and oxygen containing 50% of each gas (*Entonox®*, *Equanox®*) is used to produce analgesia without loss of consciousness. Self-administration using a demand valve is popular in obstetric practice, for changing painful dressings, as an aid to postoperative physiotherapy, and in emergency ambulances.

Nitrous oxide may have a deleterious effect if used in patients with an air-containing closed space since nitrous oxide diffuses into such a space with a resulting increase in pressure. This effect may be dangerous in the presence of a pneumothorax which may enlarge to compromise respiration.

Special care is needed to avoid hypoxia if an anaesthetic machine is being used; machines should incorporate an anti-hypoxia device. Exposure of patients to nitrous oxide for prolonged periods, either by continuous or by intermittent administration, may result in megaloblastic anaemia owing to interference with the action of vitamin $B_{12}$. For the same reason, exposure of theatre staff to nitrous oxide should be minimised. Depression of white cell formation may also occur.

### NITROUS OXIDE

**Indications** see notes above

**Cautions** see notes above; pregnancy (Appendix 4); **interactions:** Appendix 1 (anaesthetics, general)

**Side-effects** see notes above

**Dose**

- Using suitable anaesthetic apparatus, *maintenance* of light anaesthesia, as a mixture with 25–30% oxygen
  *Analgesic*, as a mixture with 50% oxygen, according to the patient's needs

## 15.1.3 Antimuscarinic drugs

Antimuscarinic drugs are used (less commonly nowadays) as premedicants to dry bronchial and salivary secretions which are increased by intubation, by surgery to the upper airways, and by some inhalational anaesthetics. They are also used before or with neostigmine (section 15.1.6) to prevent bradycardia, excessive salivation, and other muscarinic actions of neostigmine. They also prevent bradycardia and hypotension associated with drugs such as halothane, propofol, and suxamethonium.

**Atropine** is now rarely used for premedication but still has an emergency role in the treatment of vagotonic side-effects. For its role in acute arrhythmias after myocardial infarction, see section 2.3.1; see also cardiopulmonary resuscitation, section 2.7.3.

**Hyoscine** reduces secretions and also provides a degree of amnesia, sedation and anti-emesis. Unlike atropine it may produce bradycardia rather than tachycardia. In some patients, especially the elderly, hyoscine may cause the central anticholinergic syndrome (excitement, ataxia, hallucinations, behavioural abnormalities, and drowsiness).

**Glycopyrronium** reduces salivary secretions. When given intravenously it produces less tachycardia than atropine. It is widely used with neostigmine for reversal of non-depolarising muscle relaxants (section 15.1.5).

**Phenothiazines** do not effectively reduce secretions when used alone.

### ATROPINE SULPHATE

**Indications** drying secretions; reversal of excessive bradycardia; with neostigmine for reversal of non-depolarising neuromuscular block; antidote to organophosphorous poisoning (see Emergency Treatment of Poisoning p. 36), antispasmodic (section 1.2); bradycardia (section 2.3.1); cardiopulmonary resuscitation (section 2.7.3); eye (section 11.5)

**Cautions** cardiovascular disease; see also section 1.2; **interactions:** Appendix 1 (antimuscarinics)

Duration of action Since atropine has a shorter duration of action than neostigmine, late unopposed bradycardia may result; close monitoring of the patient is necessary

**Contra-indications** see section 1.2

**Side-effects** see section 1.2

**Dose**

- Premedication, by intravenous injection, 300–600 micrograms immediately before induction of anaesthesia; CHILD 20 micrograms/kg (max. 600 micrograms)
  By subcutaneous or intramuscular injection, 300–600 micrograms 30–60 minutes before induction; CHILD 20 micrograms/kg (max. 600 micrograms)
- Intra-operative bradycardia, by intravenous injection, 300–600 micrograms (larger doses in emergencies); CHILD [unlicensed indication] 1–12 years 10–20 micrograms/kg
- Control of muscarinic side-effects of neostigmine in reversal of competitive neuromuscular block, by intravenous injection, 0.6–1.2 mg; CHILD under 12 years (but rarely used) 20 micrograms/kg (max. 600 micrograms) with neostigmine 50 micrograms/kg
- Arrhythmias after myocardial infarction, see section 2.3.1; see also cardiopulmonary resuscitation algorithm, inside back cover

[1]**Atropine** (Non-proprietary) PoM

Injection, atropine sulphate 600 micrograms/mL, net price 1-mL amp = 50p

Note Other strengths also available

Injection, prefilled disposable syringe, atropine sulphate 100 micrograms/mL, net price 5 mL = £4.16, 10 mL = £4.66, 30 mL = £8.52

Brands include *Minijet® Atropine Sulphate*

Injection, prefilled disposable syringe, atropine sulphate 200 micrograms/mL, net price 5 mL = £4.67; 300 micrograms/mL, 10 mL = £4.67; 600 micrograms/mL, 1 mL = £4.67

1. PoM restriction does not apply where administration is for saving life in emergency

### GLYCOPYRRONIUM BROMIDE
(Glycopyrrolate)

**Indications** drying secretions; reversal of excessive bradycardia; with neostigmine for reversal of non-depolarising neuromuscular block; hyperhidrosis (section 13.12)

**Cautions** cardiovascular disease; see also Atropine sulphate (section 1.2); **interactions:** Appendix 1 (antimuscarinics)

**Side-effects** see under Atropine Sulphate

**Dose**

- Premedication, by intramuscular *or* intravenous injection, 200–400 micrograms, *or* 4–5 micrograms/kg to a max. of 400 micrograms; CHILD by intramuscular *or* preferably by intravenous injection, 4–8 micrograms/kg to a max. of 200 micrograms
- Intra-operative use, by intravenous injection, as for premedication, repeated if necessary
- Control of muscarinic side-effects of neostigmine in reversal of non-depolarising neuromuscular block, by intravenous injection, 200 micrograms per 1 mg of neostigmine, *or* 10–15 micrograms/kg with neostigmine 50 micrograms/kg; CHILD 10 micrograms/kg with neostigmine 50 micrograms/kg

**Robinul®** (Anpharm) PoM
Injection, glycopyrronium bromide 200 micrograms/mL, net price 1-mL amp = 60p; 3-mL amp = £1.01
Available as a generic from Antigen

**With neostigmine metilsulphate**
Section 15.1.6

## HYOSCINE HYDROBROMIDE
**(Scopolamine hydrobromide)**

**Indications** drying secretions, amnesia; other indications (section 4.6)
**Cautions** see under Hyoscine Hydrobromide (section 4.6); also paralytic ileus, myasthenia gravis, epilepsy, prostatic enlargement; avoid in the elderly (see notes above)
**Contra-indications** porphyria (section 9.8.2); angle-closure glaucoma
**Side-effects** see under Atropine Sulphate; bradycardia
**Dose**
- Premedication, by subcutaneous *or* intramuscular injection, 200–600 micrograms 30–60 minutes before induction of anaesthesia; CHILD 15 micrograms/kg

**Hyoscine** (Non-proprietary) PoM
Injection, hyoscine hydrobromide 400 micrograms/mL, net price 1-mL amp = £2.71; 600 micrograms/mL, 1-mL amp = £2.81

**With papaveretum**
See under papaveretum (section 4.7.2)



# 15.1.4 Sedative and analgesic peri-operative drugs

15.1.4.1 Anxiolytics and neuroleptics
15.1.4.2 Non-opioid analgesics
15.1.4.3 Opioid analgesics

These drugs are given to allay the apprehension of the patient in the pre-operative period (including the night before operation), to relieve pain and discomfort when present, and to augment the action of subsequent anaesthetic agents. A number of the drugs used also provide some degree of pre-operative amnesia. The choice will vary with the individual patient, the nature of the operative procedure, the anaesthetic to be used and other prevailing circumstances such as outpatients, obstetrics, recovery facilities etc. The choice would also vary in elective and emergency operations.

**Premedication in children** Oral administration is preferred where possible but it is not altogether satisfactory; the rectal route should only be used in exceptional circumstances. Oral alimemazine (trimeprazine, section 3.4.1) is still used but when given alone it may cause postoperative restlessness in the presence of pain.

Atropine or hyoscine is often given orally to children, but may be given intravenously immediately before induction.

The use of a suitable local anaesthetic cream (section 15.2) should be considered to avoid pain at injection site.

**Anaesthesia and driving** See section 15.1.

## 15.1.4.1 Anxiolytics and neuroleptics

Anxiolytic benzodiazepines are widely used for premedication; neuroleptics such as **chlorpromazine** are rarely used. **Alimemazine (trimeprazine)** (section 3.4.1) is still occasionally used as a premedicant for children (but see section 15.1.4).

### Benzodiazepines

Benzodiazepines possess useful properties for premedication including relief of anxiety, sedation, and amnesia; short-acting benzodiazepines taken by mouth are the most common premedicants. They have no analgesic effect so an opioid analgesic may sometimes be required for pain.

Benzodiazepines can alleviate anxiety at doses that do not necessarily cause excessive sedation and they are of particular value during short procedures or during operations under local anaesthesia (including dentistry). Amnesia reduces the likelihood of any unpleasant memories of the procedure (although benzodiazepines, particularly when used for more profound sedation, can sometimes induce sexual fantasies). Benzodiazepines are also used in intensive care units for sedation, particularly in those receiving assisted ventilation.

Benzodiazepines may occasionally cause marked respiratory depression and facilities for its treatment are essential; flumazenil (section 15.1.7) is used to antagonise the effects of benzodiazepines. They are best avoided in myasthenia gravis, especially peri-operatively.

**Diazepam** is used to produce mild sedation with amnesia. It is a long-acting drug with active metabolites and a second period of drowsiness can occur several hours after its administration. Peri-operative use of diazepam in children is not generally recommended; its effect and timing of response are unreliable and paradoxical effects may occur.

Diazepam is relatively insoluble in water and preparations formulated in organic solvents are painful on intravenous injection and give rise to a high incidence of venous thrombosis (which may not be noticed for several days after the injection). Intramuscular injection of diazepam is painful and absorption is erratic. An emulsion preparation for intravenous injection is less irritant and is followed by a negligible incidence of venous thrombosis; it is not suitable for intramuscular injection. Diazepam is also available as a rectal solution but this preparation is not used for premedication or sedation.

**Temazepam** is given by mouth and has a shorter duration of action and a more rapid onset than diazepam given by mouth. It has been used as a premedicant in inpatient and day-case surgery; anxiolytic and sedative effects last about 90 minutes although there may be residual drowsiness.

**Lorazepam** produces more prolonged sedation than temazepam and it has marked amnesic effects. It is used as a premedicant the night before major surgery; a further, smaller dose may be required the following morning if any delay in starting surgery is anticipated. Alternatively the first dose may be given early in the morning on the day of operation.

**Midazolam** is a water-soluble benzodiazepine which is often used in preference to intravenous diazepam; recovery is faster than from diazepam. Midazolam is associated with profound sedation when high doses are given intravenously or when used with certain other drugs.

**Dental procedures** Anxiolytics diminish anxiety and panic, and may benefit anxious patients. However, their use is no substitute for sympathy and reassurance.

Diazepam and temazepam are effective anxiolytics for dental treatment in adults, but they are less suitable for children. Diazepam has a longer duration of action than temazepam. When given at night diazepam is associated with more residual effects the following day; patients should be very carefully warned **not** to drive (**important**: for general advice on anaesthesia and driving see p. 633). For further information on hypnotics and anxiolytics, see section 4.1. For further information on hypnotics used for dental procedures, see section 4.1.1.

## DIAZEPAM

**Indications** premedication; sedation with amnesia, and in conjunction with local anaesthesia; other indications (section 4.1.2, section 4.8.2, and section 10.2.2)

**Cautions** see notes above and section 4.1.2 and section 4.8.2

**Contra-indications** see notes above and section 4.1.2

**Side-effects** see notes above and section 4.1.2

**Dose**

- By mouth, 5 mg on night before minor or dental surgery then 5 mg 2 hours before procedure; ELDERLY (or debilitated), half adult dose
- By intravenous injection, into a large vein 10–20 mg over 2–4 minutes as sedative cover for minor surgical and medical procedures; premedication 100–200 micrograms/kg

**Preparations**
Section 4.1.2

## LORAZEPAM

**Indications** sedation with amnesia; premedication; other indications (section 4.1.2 and section 4.8.2)

**Cautions** see notes above and section 4.1.2; **interactions**: Appendix 1 (anxiolytics and hypnotics)

**Contra-indications** see notes above and under Diazepam (section 4.1.2)

**Side-effects** see notes above and under Diazepam (section 4.1.2)

**Dose**

- By mouth, 2–3 mg the night before operation; 2–4 mg 1–2 hours before operation
- By slow intravenous injection, preferably diluted with an equal volume of sodium chloride intravenous infusion 0.9% or water for injections, 50 micrograms/kg 30–45 minutes before operation
- By intramuscular injection, diluted as above, 50 micrograms/kg 60–90 minutes before operation

**Preparations**
Section 4.1.2

## MIDAZOLAM

**Indications** sedation with amnesia; sedation in intensive care; premedication, induction of anaesthesia; status epilepticus [unlicensed use], section 4.8.2

**Cautions** hepatic impairment (Appendix 2); renal impairment (Appendix 3); pregnancy (Appendix 4) and breast-feeding (Appendix 5); cardiac disease; respiratory disease; myasthenia gravis; children (particularly if cardiovascular impairment); history of drug or alcohol abuse; reduce dose in elderly and debilitated; avoid prolonged use (and abrupt withdrawal thereafter); concentration of midazolam in children under 15 kg not to exceed 1 mg/mL; **interactions**: Appendix 1 (anxiolytics and hypnotics)

**Contra-indications** marked neuromuscular respiratory weakness including unstable myasthenia gravis; severe respiratory depression; acute pulmonary insufficiency

**Side-effects** gastro-intestinal disturbances, increased appetite, jaundice; hypotension, cardiac arrest, heart rate changes, anaphylaxis, thrombosis; laryngospasm, bronchospasm, respiratory depression and respiratory arrest (particularly with high doses or on rapid injection); drowsiness, confusion, ataxia, amnesia, headache, euphoria, hallucinations, fatigue, dizziness, vertigo, involuntary movements, paradoxical excitement and aggression (especially in children and elderly), dysarthria; urinary retention, incontinence, changes in libido; blood disorders; muscle weakness; visual disturbances; salivation changes; skin reactions; on intravenous injection, pain, thrombophlebitis

**Dose**

- Conscious sedation, by slow intravenous injection (approx. 2 mg/minute), initially 2–2.5 mg (ELDERLY 0.5–1 mg), increased if necessary in steps of 1 mg (ELDERLY 0.5–1 mg); usual range 3.5–7.5 mg, ELDERLY max. 3.5 mg; CHILD by intravenous injection over 2–3 minutes, 6 months–5 years initially 50–100 micrograms/kg, dose increased if necessary in small steps (max. total dose 6 mg), 6–12 years initially 25–50 micrograms/kg, dose increased if necessary in small steps (max. total dose 10 mg)

  By intramuscular injection, CHILD 1–15 years 50–150 micrograms/kg; max. 10 mg
- Sedative in combined anaesthesia, by intravenous injection, 30–100 micrograms/kg repeated as required or by intravenous infusion, 30–100 micrograms/kg/hour (ELDERLY lower doses needed); CHILD not recommended
- Premedication, by deep intramuscular injection, 70–100 micrograms/kg (ELDERLY 25–50 micrograms/kg) 20–60 minutes before induction, usual dose 2–3 mg; CHILD 1–15 years 80–200 micrograms/kg
- Induction, by slow intravenous injection, with premedication, 150–200 micrograms/kg (ELDERLY 100–200 micrograms/kg); without premedication, 300–350 micrograms/kg (ELDERLY 150–300 micrograms/kg); doses increased in steps not greater than 5 mg every 2 minutes; max. 600 micrograms/kg; CHILD over 7 years 150 micrograms/kg
- Sedation of patients receiving intensive care, by slow intravenous injection, initially 30–300 micrograms/kg given in steps of 1–2.5 mg every 2 minutes, then by slow intravenous injection *or* by intravenous infusion, 30–200 micrograms/kg/hour; reduce dose (or omit initial dose) in hypovolaemia, vasoconstriction, or hypothermia; lower doses may be adequate if opioid analgesic also used; NEONATE under 32 weeks gestational age by intravenous infusion, 30 micrograms/kg/hour, NEONATE over 32 weeks gestational age and CHILD under 6 months 60 micrograms/kg/hour, CHILD over 6 months by slow intravenous injection, initially

50–200 micrograms/kg, then by intravenous infusion, 60–120 micrograms/kg/hour

**Midazolam** (Non-proprietary) PoM
Injection, midazolam (as hydrochloride) 1 mg/mL, net price 50-mL vial = £6.30; 5 mg/mL, 2-mL amp = 79p, 5-mL amp = 91p, 10-mL amp = £4.70, 18-mL amp = £6.80

**Hypnovel®** (Roche) PoM
Injection, midazolam (as hydrochloride) 2 mg/mL, net price 5-mL amp = 75p; 5 mg/mL, 2-mL amp = 90p

## TEMAZEPAM

**Indications** premedication before surgery; anxiety before investigatory procedures; hypnotic (section 4.1.1)

**Cautions** see notes above and under Diazepam (section 4.1.2 and section 4.8.2); **interactions:** Appendix 1 (anxiolytics and hypnotics)

**Contra-indications** see notes above and under Diazepam (section 4.1.2)

**Side-effects** see notes above and under Diazepam (section 4.1.2)

**Dose**

- By mouth, premedication, 20–40 mg (elderly, 10–20 mg) 1 hour before operation; CHILD 1 mg/kg (max. 30 mg)

**Preparations**
Section 4.1.1



## 15.1.4.2 Non-opioid analgesics

Since non-steroidal anti-inflammatory drugs (NSAIDs) do not depress respiration, do not impair gastro-intestinal motility, and do not cause dependence, they may be useful alternatives (or adjuncts) to the use of opioids for the relief of postoperative pain. NSAIDs may be inadequate for the relief of severe pain.

**Acemetacin**, **diclofenac**, **flurbiprofen**, **ibuprofen**, **ketoprofen**, (section 10.1.1), **parecoxib**, and **ketorolac** are licensed for postoperative use. Diclofenac, ketoprofen, and ketorolac can be given by injection as well as by mouth. Intramuscular injections of diclofenac and ketoprofen are given deep into the gluteal muscle to minimise pain and tissue damage; diclofenac can also be given by intravenous infusion for the treatment or prevention of postoperative pain. Ketorolac is less irritant on intramuscular injection but pain has been reported; it can also be given by intravenous injection.

Parecoxib (a selective inhibitor of cyclo-oxygenase-2) can be given by intramuscular or intravenous injection (but see also Cyclo-oxygenase-2 inhibitors and Cardiovascular Events, section 10.1.1). The *Scottish Medicines Consortium* has advised (January 2003) that parecoxib should **not** be used because there is no evidence of a reduction in postoperative haemorrhagic or gastro-intestinal complications compared with non-selective NSAIDs.

Suppositories of diclofenac and ketoprofen may be effective alternatives to the parenteral use of these drugs. Flurbiprofen is also available as suppositories.

## KETOROLAC TROMETAMOL

**Indications** short-term management of moderate to severe acute postoperative pain **only**

**Cautions** see section 10.1.1; avoid in porphyria (section 9.8.2); **interactions:** Appendix 1 (NSAIDs)

**Contra-indications** see section 10.1.1; also history of asthma, complete or partial syndrome of nasal polyps, angioedema or bronchospasm; history of peptic ulceration or gastro-intestinal bleeding; haemorrhagic diatheses (including coagulation disorders) and following operations with high risk of haemorrhage or incomplete haemostasis; confirmed or suspected cerebrovascular bleeding; moderate or severe renal impairment; hypovolaemia or dehydration; pregnancy (including labour and delivery); breast-feeding

**Side-effects** see section 10.1.1; also anaphylaxis, dry mouth, excessive thirst, psychotic reactions, convulsions, myalgia, hyponatraemia, hyperkalaemia, flushing or pallor, bradycardia, hypertension, palpitations, chest pain, purpura, postoperative wound haemorrhage, haematoma, epistaxis; pain at injection site

**Dose**

- By mouth, 10 mg every 4–6 hours (ELDERLY every 6–8 hours); max. 40 mg daily; max. duration of treatment 7 days; CHILD under 16 years, not recommended
- By intramuscular injection *or* by intravenous injection over not less than 15 seconds, initially 10 mg, then 10–30 mg every 4–6 hours when required (every 2 hours in initial postoperative period); max. 90 mg daily (ELDERLY and patients weighing less than 50 kg max. 60 mg daily); max. duration of treatment 2 days by either route; CHILD under 16 years, not recommended

**Note** Pain relief may not occur for over 30 minutes after intravenous or intramuscular injection. When converting from parenteral to oral administration, total combined dose on the day of converting should not exceed 90 mg (60 mg in the elderly and patients weighing less than 50 kg) of which the oral component should not exceed 40 mg; patients should be converted to oral route as soon as possible

**Toradol®** (Roche) PoM
Tablets, ivory, f/c, ketorolac trometamol 10 mg, net price 20-tab pack = £5.79. Label: 17, 21
Injection, ketorolac trometamol 10 mg/mL, net price 1-mL amp = 94p; 30 mg/mL, 1-mL amp = £1.14

## PARECOXIB

**Indications** short-term management of acute post-operative pain

**Cautions** see section 10.1.1; dehydration; following coronary artery bypass graft surgery; **interactions:** Appendix 1 (NSAIDs)

**Contra-indications** see section 10.1.1; sulphonamide hypersensitivity, inflammatory bowel disease; severe congestive heart failure

**Side-effects** see section 10.1.1; also flatulence; hypertension, hypotension, peripheral oedema; pharyngitis, respiratory insufficiency; hypoaesthesia; alveolar osteitis; oliguria; postoperative anaemia, hypokalaemia; back pain; pruritus; *less commonly* bradycardia, cerebrovascular disorders, increased blood urea nitrogen, ecchymosis, thrombocytopenia, rash (discontinue—risk of serious reactions including Stevens-Johnson syndrome and toxic epidermal necrolysis)

**Dose**

- By deep intramuscular injection *or* by intravenous injection, initially 40 mg, then 20–40 mg every 6–12 hours when required; max. 80 mg daily; ELDERLY weighing less than 50 kg, initially 20 mg, then max. 40 mg daily; CHILD and ADOLESCENT under 18 years, not recommended

**Dynastat®** (Pharmacia) ▼ PoM
Injection, powder for reconstitution, parecoxib (as sodium salt), net price 40-mg vial = £4.96, 40-mg vial (with solvent) = £5.67

## 15.1.4.3 Opioid analgesics

Opioid analgesics are now rarely used as premedicants; they are more likely to be administered at induction. Pre-operative use of opioid analgesics is generally limited to those patients who require control of existing pain. The main side-effects of opioid analgesics are respiratory depression, cardiovascular depression, nausea, and vomiting; for general notes on opioid analgesics and their use in postoperative pain, see section 4.7.2.

For the management of opioid-induced respiratory depression, see section 15.1.7.

**Intra-operative analgesia** Opioid analgesics given in small doses before or with induction reduce the dose requirement of some drugs used during anaesthesia. Pethidine and morphine have been used for this purpose, but shorter-acting and more potent drugs such as alfentanil, fentanyl, and remifentanil are now preferred.

**Alfentanil**, **fentanyl** and **remifentanil** are particularly useful because they act within 1–2 minutes. The initial doses of alfentanil or fentanyl are followed either by successive intravenous injections or by an intravenous infusion; prolonged infusions increase the duration of effect. Repeated intra-operative doses of alfentanil or fentanyl should be given with care since the respiratory depression can persist into the postoperative period and occasionally it may become apparent for the first time postoperatively when monitoring of the patient might be less intensive.

In contrast to other opioids which are metabolised in the liver, remifentanil undergoes rapid metabolism by non-specific blood and tissue esterases; its short duration of action allows prolonged administration at high dosage, without accumulation, and with little risk of residual postoperative respiratory depression. Remifentanil should not be given as a bolus injection intra-operatively, but it is well suited to continuous infusion; a supplementary analgesic will often be required after stopping the infusion.

### ALFENTANIL

**Indications** analgesia especially during short operative procedure and outpatient surgery; enhancement of anaesthesia; analgesia and suppression of respiratory activity in patients receiving intensive care, with assisted ventilation, for up to 4 days

**Cautions** see under Morphine Salts (section 4.7.2) and notes above

**Contra-indications** see section 4.7.2 and notes above

**Side-effects** see section 4.7.2 and notes above; also hypertension, myoclonic movements; *less commonly* arrhythmias, cough, hiccup, laryngospasm, visual disturbances

**Dose**

> To avoid excessive dosage in obese patients, dose may need to be calculated on the basis of ideal body-weight

- By intravenous injection, spontaneous respiration, ADULT, initially up to 500 micrograms over 30 seconds; supplemental, 250 micrograms
  With assisted ventilation, ADULT and CHILD, initially 30–50 micrograms/kg; supplemental, 15 micrograms/kg
- By intravenous infusion, with assisted ventilation, ADULT and CHILD, initially 50–100 micrograms/kg over 10 minutes *or* as a bolus, followed by maintenance of 0.5–1 micrograms/kg/minute
  Analgesia and suppression of respiratory activity during intensive care, with assisted ventilation, by intravenous infusion, initially 2 mg/hour subsequently adjusted according to response (usual range 0.5–10 mg/hour); more rapid initial control may be obtained with an intravenous dose of 5 mg given in divided portions over 10 minutes (slowing if hypotension or bradycardia occur); additional doses of 0.5–1 mg may be given by intravenous injection during short painful procedures

**Rapifen®** (Janssen-Cilag) CD
Injection, alfentanil (as hydrochloride) 500 micrograms/mL. Net price 2-mL amp = 69p; 10-mL amp = £3.14
Intensive care injection, alfentanil (as hydrochloride) 5 mg/mL. To be diluted before use. Net price 1-mL amp = £2.52

### FENTANYL

**Indications** analgesia during operation, enhancement of anaesthesia; respiratory depressant in assisted respiration; analgesia in other situations (section 4.7.2)

**Cautions** see under Morphine Salts (section 4.7.2) and notes above

**Contra-indications** see section 4.7.2 and notes above

**Side-effects** see section 4.7.2 and notes above

**Dose**

- By intravenous injection, with spontaneous respiration, 50–200 micrograms, then 50 micrograms as required; CHILD 3–5 micrograms/kg, then 1 microgram/kg as required
  With assisted ventilation, 0.3–3.5 mg, then 100–200 micrograms as required; CHILD 15 micrograms/kg, then 1–3 micrograms/kg as required
- By intravenous infusion, with spontaneous respiration, ADULT and CHILD, 50–80 nanograms/kg/minute adjusted according to response
  With assisted ventilation, ADULT and CHILD, initially 10 micrograms/kg over 10 minutes then 100 nanograms/kg/minute; up to 3 micrograms/kg/minute may be required in cardiac surgery

**Fentanyl** (Non-proprietary) CD
Injection, fentanyl (as citrate) 50 micrograms/mL, net price 2-mL amp = 54p, 10-mL amp = £1.65

**Sublimaze®** (Janssen-Cilag) CD
Injection, fentanyl (as citrate) 50 micrograms/mL, net price 2-mL amp = 23p, 10-mL amp = £1.11

## REMIFENTANIL

**Indications** supplementation of general anaesthesia during induction and analgesia during maintenance of anaesthesia (consult product literature for use in patients undergoing cardiac surgery); analgesia and sedation in ventilated, intensive care patients

**Cautions** see under Morphine Salts (section 4.7.2, but no dose adjustment necessary in renal impairment) and notes above

**Contra-indications** see under Morphine Salts (section 4.7.2) and notes above; left ventricular dysfunction

**Side-effects** see under Morphine Salts (section 4.7.2) and notes above

**Dose**

To avoid excessive dosage in obese patients, dose should be calculated on the basis of ideal body-weight

- Induction, ADULT and CHILD over 12 years, by intravenous infusion, 0.5–1 micrograms/kg/minute, *with or without* an initial dose by intravenous injection over not less than 30 seconds, 1 microgram/kg
  Note If patient to be intubated more than 8 minutes after start of intravenous infusion, initial intravenous injection dose is not necessary
- Maintenance in ventilated patients, ADULT and CHILD over 12 years, by intravenous infusion, 0.05–2 micrograms/kg/minute according to anaesthetic technique and adjusted according to response; in light anaesthesia supplemental doses by intravenous injection every 2–5 minutes
- Maintenance in spontaneous respiration anaesthesia, ADULT and CHILD over 12 years, by intravenous infusion, initially 40 nanograms/kg/minute adjusted according to response, usual range 25–100 nanograms/kg/minute
- Maintenance, CHILD 1–12 years, by intravenous infusion, 0.05–1.3 micrograms/kg/minute (*with or without* an initial dose by intravenous injection over not less than 30 seconds, 1 microgram/kg/minute) according to anaesthetic technique and adjusted according to response
- Analgesia and sedation in ventilated, intensive care patients, by intravenous infusion, ADULT over 18 years initially 100–150 nanograms/kg/minute adjusted according to response in steps of 25 nanograms/kg/minute (allow at least 5 minutes between dose adjustments); usual range 6–740 nanograms/kg/minute; if an infusion rate of 200 nanograms/kg/minute does not produce adequate sedation add another sedative (consult product literature for details)
- Additional analgesia during stimulating or painful procedures in ventilated, intensive care patients, by intravenous infusion, ADULT over 18 years maintain infusion rate of at least 100 nanograms/kg/minute for at least 5 minutes before procedure and adjust every 2–5 minutes according to requirements, usual range 250–750 nanograms/kg/minute

**Ultiva®** (GSK) CD
Injection, powder for reconstitution, remifentanil (as hydrochloride), net price 1-mg vial = £5.50; 2-mg vial = £11.00; 5-mg vial = £27.50

## 15.1.5 Muscle relaxants

Muscle relaxants used in anaesthesia are also known as **neuromuscular blocking drugs**. By specific blockade of the neuromuscular junction they enable light levels of anaesthesia to be employed with adequate relaxation of the muscles of the abdomen and diaphragm. They also relax the vocal cords and allow the passage of a tracheal tube. Their action differs from the muscle relaxants acting on the spinal cord or brain which are used in musculoskeletal disorders (section 10.2.2).

Patients who have received a muscle relaxant should **always** have their respiration assisted or controlled until the drug has been inactivated or antagonised (section 15.1.6).

### Non-depolarising muscle relaxants

Non-depolarising muscle relaxants (also known as competitive muscle relaxants) compete with acetylcholine for receptor sites at the neuromuscular junction and their action may be reversed with anticholinesterases such as neostigmine (section 15.1.6). Non-depolarising muscle relaxants may be divided into the **aminosteroid** group comprising pancuronium, rocuronium, and vecuronium, and the **benzylisoquinolinium** group comprising atracurium, cisatracurium, gallamine, and mivacurium.

Non-depolarising muscle relaxants have a slower onset of action than suxamethonium. These drugs can be classified by their duration of action as short-acting (15–30 minutes), intermediate-acting (30–40 minutes) and long-acting (60–120 minutes), although duration of action is dose-dependent. Drugs with a shorter or intermediate duration of action, such as atracurium and vecuronium, are more widely employed than those with a longer duration of action such as pancuronium.

Non-depolarising muscle relaxants have no sedative or analgesic effects and are not considered to be a triggering factor for malignant hyperthermia.

For patients receiving intensive care and who require tracheal intubation and mechanical ventilation, a non-depolarising muscle relaxant is chosen according to its onset of effect, duration of action and side-effects. Rocuronium, with a rapid onset of effect, may facilitate intubation. Atracurium or cisatracurium may be suitable for long-term muscle relaxation since their duration of action is not dependent on elimination by the liver or the kidneys.

**Cautions** Allergic cross-reactivity between neuromuscular blocking agents has been reported; caution is advised in cases of hypersensitivity to these drugs. Their activity is prolonged in patients with myasthenia gravis and in hypothermia, therefore lower doses are required. Resistance may develop in patients with burns who may require increased doses; low plasma cholinesterase activity in these patients requires dose titration for mivacurium. **Interactions:** Appendix 1 (muscle relaxants).

**Side-effects** Benzylisoquinolinium non-depolarising muscle relaxants (except cisatracurium) are associated with histamine release which can cause skin flushing, hypotension, tachycardia, bronchospasm and rarely, anaphylactoid reactions. Most aminosteroid muscle relaxants produce minimal histamine release. Drugs possessing vagolytic activity can counteract any bradycardia that occurs during surgery.

**Atracurium**, a mixture of 10 isomers, is a benzylisoquinolinium muscle relaxant with an intermediate duration of action. It undergoes non-enzymatic metabolism which is independent of liver and kidney function, thus allowing its use in patients with hepatic or renal impairment. Cardiovascular effects are associated with significant histamine release.

**Cisatracurium** is a single isomer of atracurium. It is more potent and has a slightly longer duration of action than atracurium and provides greater cardiovascular stability because cisatracurium lacks histamine-releasing effects.

**Mivacurium**, a benzylisoquinolinium muscle relaxant, has a short duration of action. It is metabolised by plasma cholinesterase and muscle paralysis is prolonged in individuals deficient in this enzyme. It is not associated with vagolytic activity or ganglionic blockade although histamine release may occur, particularly with rapid injection.

**Pancuronium**, an aminosteroid muscle relaxant, has a long duration of action and is often used in patients receiving long-term mechanical ventilation in intensive care units. It lacks a histamine-releasing effect, but vagolytic and sympathomimetic effects can cause tachycardia and hypertension.

**Rocuronium** exerts an effect within 2 minutes and has the most rapid onset of any of the competitive muscle relaxants. It is an aminosteroid muscle relaxant with an intermediate duration of action. It is reported to have minimal cardiovascular effects; high doses produce mild vagolytic activity.

**Vecuronium**, an aminosteroid muscle relaxant, has an intermediate duration of action. It does not generally produce histamine release and lacks cardiovascular effects.

**Gallamine** has vagolytic and sympathomimetic properties and frequently increases pulse rate and blood pressure. It is rarely used since the other neuromuscular blocking drugs have a more predictable response and it should be avoided in patients with renal impairment.

## ATRACURIUM BESILATE
**(Atracurium besylate)**

**Indications** muscle relaxation (short to intermediate duration) for surgery or during intensive care

**Cautions** see notes above; pregnancy (Appendix 4); breast-feeding (Appendix 5)

**Side-effects** see notes above

**Dose**

> To avoid excessive dosage in obese patients, dose should be calculated on the basis of ideal body-weight

- Surgery or intubation, ADULT and CHILD over 1 month, by intravenous injection, initially 300–600 micrograms/kg; maintenance, by intravenous injection, 100–200 micrograms/kg as required *or* by intravenous infusion, 5–10 micrograms/kg/minute (300–600 micrograms/kg/hour)
- Intensive care, ADULT and CHILD over 1 month, by intravenous injection, initially 300–600 micrograms/kg (optional) then by intravenous infusion 4.5–29.5 micrograms/kg/minute (usual dose 11–13 micrograms/kg/minute)

**Atracurium** (Non-proprietary) PoM

Injection, atracurium besilate 10 mg/mL, net price 2.5-mL amp = £1.85; 5-mL amp = £3.37; 25-mL amp = £14.45

**Tracrium®** (GSK) PoM

Injection, atracurium besilate 10 mg/mL, net price 2.5-mL amp = £1.66; 5-mL amp = £3.00; 25-mL amp = £12.91

## CISATRACURIUM

**Indications** muscle relaxation (intermediate duration) for surgery or during intensive care

**Cautions** see notes above; pregnancy (Appendix 4)

**Side-effects** see notes above

**Dose**

> To avoid excessive dosage in obese patients, dose should be calculated on the basis of ideal body-weight

- Intubation, by intravenous injection, ADULT and CHILD over 1 month, initially 150 micrograms/kg; maintenance, by intravenous injection, 30 micrograms/kg approx. every 20 minutes; CHILD 2–12 years, 20 micrograms/kg approx. every 9 minutes; or maintenance, by intravenous infusion, ADULT and CHILD over 2 years, initially, 3 micrograms/kg/minute, *then after stabilisation*, 1–2 micrograms/kg/minute; dose reduced by up to 40% if used with isoflurane
- Intensive care, by intravenous infusion, ADULT 0.5–10.2 micrograms/kg/minute (usual dose 3 micrograms/kg/minute)

**Note** Lower doses can be used for children over 2 years when *not* for intubation

**Nimbex®** (GSK) PoM

Injection, cisatracurium (as besilate) 2 mg/mL, net price 2.5-mL amp = £2.04, 5-mL amp = £3.91, 10-mL amp = £7.55

Forte injection, cisatracurium (as besilate) 5 mg/mL, net price 30-mL vial = £31.09

## GALLAMINE TRIETHIODIDE

**Indications** muscle relaxation (intermediate duration) for surgery

**Cautions** see notes above

**Contra-indications** renal impairment (Appendix 3)

**Side-effects** see notes above

**Dose**

> To avoid excessive dosage in obese patients, dose should be calculated on the basis of ideal body-weight

- By intravenous injection, 80–120 mg, then 20–40 mg as required; NEONATE 600 micrograms/kg; CHILD 1.5 mg/kg

**Gallamine** (Concord) PoM

Injection, gallamine triethiodide 40 mg/mL, net price 2-mL amp = £4.97

## MIVACURIUM

**Indications** muscle relaxation (short duration) for surgery

**Cautions** see notes above; low plasma cholinesterase activity; elderly; hepatic impairment (Appendix 2); renal impairment (Appendix 3); pregnancy (Appendix 4)

**Side-effects** see notes above

**Dose**

> To avoid excessive dosage in obese patients, dose should be calculated on the basis of ideal body-weight

- By intravenous injection, 70–250 micrograms/kg; maintenance 100 micrograms/kg every 15 minutes; CHILD 2–6 months initially 150 micrograms/kg, 7 months–12 years initially 200 micrograms/kg; maintenance (CHILD 2 months–12 years) 100 micrograms/kg every 6–9 minutes

  **Note** Doses up to 150 micrograms/kg may be given over 5–15 seconds, higher doses should be given over 30 seconds. In patients with asthma, cardiovascular disease or those who are sensitive to falls in arterial blood pressure give over 60 seconds
- By intravenous infusion, maintenance of block, 8–10 micrograms/kg/minute, adjusted if necessary every 3 minutes by 1 microgram/kg/minute to usual dose of 6–7 micrograms/kg/minute; CHILD 2 months–12 years, usual dose 11–14 micrograms/kg/minute

**Mivacron®** (GSK) PoM

Injection, mivacurium (as chloride) 2 mg/mL, net price 5-mL amp = £2.79; 10-mL amp = £4.51

## PANCURONIUM BROMIDE

**Indications** muscle relaxation (long duration) for surgery or during intensive care

**Cautions** see notes above; hepatic impairment (Appendix 2); renal impairment (Appendix 3); pregnancy (Appendix 4) and breast-feeding (Appendix 5)

**Side-effects** see notes above

**Dose**

> To avoid excessive dosage in obese patients, dose should be calculated on the basis of ideal body-weight

- Intubation, by intravenous injection, initially 50–100 micrograms/kg then 10–20 micrograms/kg as required; CHILD initially 60–100 micrograms/kg, then 10–20 micrograms/kg, NEONATE 30–40 micrograms/kg initially then 10–20 micrograms/kg
- Intensive care, by intravenous injection, 60 micrograms/kg every 60–90 minutes

**Pancuronium** (Non-proprietary) PoM

Injection, pancuronium bromide 2 mg/mL, net price 2-mL amp = 65p

## ROCURONIUM BROMIDE

**Indications** muscle relaxation (intermediate duration) for surgery or during intensive care

**Cautions** see notes above; hepatic impairment (Appendix 2); renal impairment (Appendix 3); pregnancy (Appendix 4) and breast-feeding (Appendix 5)

**Side-effects** see notes above

**Dose**

> To avoid excessive dosage in obese patients, dose should be calculated on the basis of ideal body-weight

- Intubation, ADULT and CHILD over 1 month, by intravenous injection, initially 600 micrograms/kg; maintenance by intravenous injection, 150 micrograms/kg (ELDERLY 75–100 micrograms/kg) *or* maintenance by intravenous infusion, 300–600 micrograms/kg/hour (ELDERLY up to 400 micrograms/kg/hour)
- Intensive care, by intravenous injection, ADULT initially 600 micrograms/kg; maintenance by intravenous infusion, 300–600 micrograms/kg/hour for first hour, then adjusted according to response

**Esmeron®** (Organon) PoM

Injection, rocuronium bromide 10 mg/mL, net price 5-mL vial = £3.01, 10-mL vial = £6.01

## VECURONIUM BROMIDE

**Indications** muscle relaxation (intermediate duration) for surgery

**Cautions** see notes above; pregnancy (Appendix 4)

**Side-effects** see notes above

**Dose**

> To avoid excessive dosage in obese patients, dose should be calculated on the basis of ideal body-weight

- By intravenous injection, intubation, 80–100 micrograms/kg; maintenance 20–30 micrograms/kg according to response; NEONATE and INFANT up to 4 months, initially 10–20 micrograms/kg then incremental doses to achieve response; CHILD over 5 months, as adult dose (up to 1 year onset more rapid and high intubation dose may not be required)
- By intravenous infusion, 0.8–1.4 micrograms/kg/minute (after initial intravenous injection of 40–100 micrograms/kg)

**Norcuron®** (Organon) PoM

Injection, powder for reconstitution, vecuronium bromide, net price 10-mg vial = £3.95 (with water for injections)

### Depolarising muscle relaxants

**Suxamethonium** has the most rapid onset of action of any of the muscle relaxants and is ideal if fast onset and brief duration of action are required e.g. with tracheal intubation. Its duration of action is about 2 to 6 minutes following intravenous doses of about 1 mg/kg; repeated doses can be used for longer procedures.

Suxamethonium acts by mimicking acetylcholine at the neuromuscular junction but hydrolysis is much slower than for acetylcholine; depolarisation is therefore prolonged, resulting in neuromuscular blockade. Unlike the non-depolarising muscle relaxants, its action cannot be reversed and recovery is spontaneous; anticholinesterases such as neostigmine potentiate the neuromuscular block.

Suxamethonium should be given after anaesthetic induction because paralysis is usually preceded by painful muscle fasciculations. While tachycardia occurs with single use, bradycardia may occur with repeated doses in adults and with the first dose in children. Premedication with atropine reduces bradycardia as well as the excessive salivation associated with suxamethonium use.

Prolonged paralysis may occur in **dual block**, which occurs with high or repeated doses of suxamethonium and is caused by the development of a non-depolarising block following the initial depolarising block; edrophonium (section 15.1.6) may be used to confirm the diagnosis of dual block. Individuals with myasthenia gravis are resistant to suxamethonium but can develop dual block resulting in delayed recovery. Prolonged paralysis may also occur in those with low or atypical plasma cholinesterase. Assisted ventilation should be continued until muscle function is restored.

### SUXAMETHONIUM CHLORIDE

**Indications** muscle relaxation (rapid onset, short duration)

**Cautions** see notes above; pregnancy (Appendix 4); patients with cardiac, respiratory or neuromuscular disease; raised intra-ocular pressure (avoid in penetrating eye injury); severe sepsis (risk of hyperkalaemia); **interactions:** Appendix 1 (muscle relaxants)

**Contra-indications** family history of malignant hyperthermia, low plasma cholinesterase activity (including severe liver disease) (Appendix 2), hyperkalaemia; major trauma, severe burns, neurological disease involving acute wasting of major muscle, prolonged immobilisation—risk of hyperkalaemia, personal or family history of congenital myotonic disease, Duchenne muscular dystrophy

**Side-effects** see notes above; also postoperative muscle pain, myoglobinuria, myoglobinaemia; tachycardia, arrhythmias, cardiac arrest, hypertension, hypotension; bronchospasm, apnoea, prolonged respiratory depression, anaphylactic reactions; hyperkalaemia; hyperthermia; increased gastric pressure; rash, flushing

**Dose**

- By intravenous injection, initially 1 mg/kg; maintenance, usually 0.5–1 mg/kg at 5–10 minute intervals; max. 500 mg/hour; NEONATE and INFANT under 1 year, 2 mg/kg; CHILD over 1 year, 1 mg/kg
- By intravenous infusion of a solution containing 1–2 mg/mL (0.1–0.2%), 2.5–4 mg/minute; max. 500 mg/hour; CHILD reduce infusion rate according to body-weight
- By intramuscular injection, INFANT under 1 year, up to 4–5 mg/kg; CHILD over 1 year, up to 4 mg/kg; max. 150 mg

**Suxamethonium Chloride** (Non-proprietary) PoM
Injection, suxamethonium chloride 50 mg/mL, net price 2-mL amp = 70p, 2-mL prefilled syringe = £7.35

**Anectine®** (GSK) PoM
Injection, suxamethonium chloride 50 mg/mL, net price 2-mL amp = 71p

## 15.1.6 Anticholinesterases used in anaesthesia

Anticholinesterases reverse the effects of the non-depolarising (competitive) muscle relaxant drugs such as pancuronium but they prolong the action of the depolarising muscle relaxant drug suxamethonium.

**Edrophonium** has a transient action and may be used in the diagnosis of suspected dual block due to suxamethonium.

**Neostigmine** has a longer duration of action than edrophonium. It is the specific drug for reversal of non-depolarising (competitive) blockade. It acts within one minute of intravenous injection and lasts for 20 to 30 minutes; a second dose may then be necessary. Atropine or preferably glycopyrronium (section 15.1.3) should be given before or with neostigmine in order to prevent bradycardia, excessive salivation, and other muscarinic actions of neostigmine.

### EDROPHONIUM CHLORIDE

**Indications** see under Dose; myasthenia gravis (section 10.2.1)

**Cautions** see section 10.2.1 and notes above; atropine should also be given

**Contra-indications** see section 10.2.1 and notes above

**Side-effects** see section 10.2.1 and notes above

**Dose**

- Brief reversal of non-depolarising neuromuscular blockade, by intravenous injection over several minutes, 500–700 micrograms/kg (after or with atropine sulphate 600 micrograms)
- Diagnosis of dual block, by intravenous injection, 10 mg

**Edrophonium** (Cambridge) PoM
Injection, edrophonium chloride 10 mg/mL, net price 1-mL amp = £4.76

### NEOSTIGMINE METILSULFATE
**(Neostigmine methylsulphate)**

**Indications** see under Dose

**Cautions** see section 10.2.1 and notes above; atropine should also be given

**Contra-indications** see section 10.2.1 and notes above

**Side-effects** see section 10.2.1 and notes above

**Dose**

- Reversal of non-depolarising neuromuscular blockade, by intravenous injection over 1 minute, 50–70 micrograms/kg (max. 5 mg) after or with atropine sulphate 0.6–1.2 mg
- Myasthenia gravis, see section 10.2.1

**Neostigmine** (Non-proprietary) PoM
Injection, neostigmine metilsulfate 2.5 mg/mL, net price 1-mL amp = 58p

With glycopyrronium

**Robinul-Neostigmine®** (Anpharm) PoM
Injection, neostigmine metilsulfate 2.5 mg, glycopyrronium bromide 500 micrograms/mL, net price 1-mL amp = £1.01
Dose reversal of non-depolarising neuromuscular blockade by intravenous injection over 10–30 seconds, 1–2 mL *or* 0.02 mL/kg, dose may be repeated if required (total max. 2 mL); CHILD 0.02 mL/kg (*or* 0.2 mL/kg of a 1 in 10 dilution using water for injections or sodium chloride injection 0.9%), dose may be repeated if required (total max. 2 mL)

## 15.1.7 Antagonists for central and respiratory depression

Respiratory depression is a major concern with opioid analgesics and it may be treated by artificial ventilation or be reversed by **naloxone**. Naloxone will immediately reverse opioid-induced respiratory depression but the dose may have to be repeated because of the short duration of action of naloxone; however, naloxone will also antagonise the analgesic effect.

**Flumazenil** is a benzodiazepine antagonist for the reversal of the central sedative effects of benzodiazepines after anaesthetic and similar procedures. Flumazenil has a shorter half-life than that of diazepam and midazolam (and there is a risk that patients may become resedated).

**Doxapram** (section 3.5.1) is a central and respiratory stimulant but is of limited value.

### FLUMAZENIL

**Indications** reversal of sedative effects of benzodiazepines in anaesthetic, intensive care, and diagnostic procedures

**Cautions** short-acting (repeat doses may be necessary—benzodiazepine effects may persist for at least 24 hours); benzodiazepine dependence (may precipitate withdrawal symptoms); prolonged benzodiazepine therapy for epilepsy (risk of convulsions); history of panic disorders (risk of recurrence); ensure neuromuscular blockade cleared before giving; avoid rapid injection in high-risk or anxious patients and following major surgery; hepatic impairment; head injury (rapid reversal of benzodiazepine sedation may cause convulsions); elderly, children, pregnancy (Appendix 4), breast-feeding

**Contra-indications** life-threatening condition (e.g. raised intracranial pressure, status epilepticus) controlled by benzodiazepines

**Side-effects** nausea, vomiting, and flushing; if wakening too rapid, agitation, anxiety, and fear; transient increase in blood pressure and heart-rate in intensive care patients; very rarely convulsions (particularly in epileptics)

**Dose**

- By intravenous injection, 200 micrograms over 15 seconds, then 100 micrograms at 60-second intervals if required; usual dose range, 300–600 micrograms; max. total dose 1 mg (2 mg in intensive care); question aetiology if no response to repeated doses
- By intravenous infusion, if drowsiness recurs after injection, 100–400 micrograms/hour, adjusted according to level of arousal

**Flumazenil** (Non-proprietary) PoM
Injection, flumazenil 100 micrograms/mL, net price 5-mL amp = £14.49

**Anexate®** (Roche) PoM
Injection, flumazenil 100 micrograms/mL, net price 5-mL amp = £14.49

### NALOXONE HYDROCHLORIDE

**Indications** reversal of opioid-induced respiratory depression; reversal of neonatal respiratory depression resulting from opioid administration to mother during labour; overdosage with opioids (see Emergency Treatment of Poisoning)

**Cautions** cardiovascular disease or those receiving cardiotoxic drugs (serious adverse cardiovascular effects reported); physical dependence on opioids (precipitates withdrawal); pain (see also under Titration of Dose, below); has short duration of action (repeated doses or infusion may be necessary to reverse effects of opioids with longer duration of action); pregnancy (Appendix 4)

**Titration of dose** In postoperative use, the dose should be titrated for each patient in order to obtain sufficient respiratory response; however, naloxone antagonises analgesia

**Side-effects** hypotension, hypertension, ventricular tachycardia and fibrillation, cardiac arrest; hyperventilation, dyspnoea, pulmonary oedema; *less commonly* agitation, excitement, paraesthesia

**Dose**

- By intravenous injection, 100–200 micrograms (1.5–3 micrograms/kg); if response inadequate, increments of 100 micrograms every 2 minutes; further doses by intramuscular injection after 1–2 hours if required; CHILD by intravenous injection, 10 micrograms/kg; subsequent dose of 100 micrograms/kg if no response; if intravenous route not possible, may be given in divided doses by intramuscular *or* subcutaneous injection
- NEONATE, reversal of respiratory depression resulting from opioid administration to mother, by subcutaneous, intramuscular, *or* intravenous injection, 10 micrograms/kg, repeated every 2–3 minutes; alternatively by intramuscular injection, 200 micrograms (60 micrograms/kg) as a single dose at birth

**Naloxone** PoM
See under Emergency Treatment of Poisoning p. 31

## 15.1.8 Drugs for malignant hyperthermia

Malignant hyperthermia is a rare but potentially lethal complication of anaesthesia. It is characterised by a rapid rise in temperature, increased muscle rigidity, tachycardia, and acidosis. The most common triggers of malignant hyperthermia are the volatile anaesthetics. Suxamethonium has also been implicated, but malignant hyperthermia is more likely if it is given following a volatile anaesthetic. Volatile anaesthetics and suxamethonium should be avoided during anaesthesia in patients at high risk of malignant hyperthermia.

**Dantrolene** is used in the treatment of malignant hyperthermia. It acts on skeletal muscle cells by interfering with calcium efflux, thereby stopping the contractile process.

### DANTROLENE SODIUM

**Indications** malignant hyperthermia; chronic severe spasticity of voluntary muscle (section 10.2.2)

**Cautions** avoid extravasation; pregnancy (Appendix 4); **interactions:** Appendix 1 (muscle relaxants)

**Contra-indications** breast-feeding (Appendix 5)

**Dose**

- By rapid intravenous injection, 1 mg/kg, repeated as required to a cumulative max. of 10 mg/kg

**Dantrium Intravenous®** (Procter & Gamble Pharm.) PoM
Injection, powder for reconstitution, dantrolene sodium, net price 20-mg vial = £15.08 (hosp. only)

## 15.2 Local anaesthesia

The use of local anaesthetics by injection or by application to mucous membranes to produce local analgesia is discussed in this section.

See also section 1.7 (anus), section 11.7 (eye), section 12.3 (oropharynx), and section 13.3 (skin).

**Use of local anaesthetics** Local anaesthetic drugs act by causing a reversible block to conduction along nerve fibres. The drugs used vary widely in their potency, toxicity, duration of action, stability, solubility in water, and ability to penetrate mucous membranes. These variations determine their suitability for use by various routes, e.g. topical (surface), infiltration, intravenous regional anaesthesia (Bier's block), plexus, epidural (extradural) or spinal block. Local anaesthetics may also be used for postoperative pain relief, thereby reducing the need for analgesics such as opioids.

**Administration** In estimating the safe dosage of these drugs it is important to take account of the rate at which they are absorbed and excreted as well as their potency. The patient's age, weight, physique, and clinical condition, the degree of vascularity of the area to which the drug is to be applied, and the duration of administration are other factors which must be taken into account.

Local anaesthetics do not rely on the circulation to transport them to their sites of action, but uptake into the systemic circulation is important in terminating their action and producing toxicity. Following most regional anaesthetic procedures, maximum arterial plasma concentrations of anaesthetic develop within about 10 to 25 minutes, so **careful surveillance** for toxic effects is necessary during the first 30 minutes after injection. Great care must be taken to avoid accidental intravascular injection. Local anaesthesia around the oral cavity may impair swallowing and therefore increase the risk of aspiration.

Epidural anaesthesia is commonly used during surgery, often combined with general anaesthesia, because of its protective effect against the stress response of surgery. It is often used when good postoperative pain relief is essential (e.g. aortic aneurysm surgery or major gut surgery).

**Toxicity** Toxic effects associated with local anaesthetics usually result from excessively high plasma concentrations; single application of topical lidocaine preparations does not generally cause systemic side-effects. Effects initially include a feeling of inebriation and lightheadedness followed by sedation, circumoral paraesthesia and twitching; convulsions can occur in severe reactions. On intravenous injection convulsions and cardiovascular collapse may occur very rapidly. Hypersensitivity reactions occur mainly with the ester-type local anaesthetics such as benzocaine, cocaine, procaine, and tetracaine (amethocaine); reactions are less frequent with the amide types such as lidocaine (lignocaine), bupivacaine, prilocaine, and ropivacaine.

When prolonged analgesia is required, a long-acting local anaesthetic is preferred to minimise the likelihood of cumulative systemic toxicity. Local anaesthetic injections should be given slowly in order to detect inadvertent intravascular administration. Local anaesthetics should **not** be injected into inflamed or infected tissues nor should they be applied to the traumatised urethra. In such cases absorption into the blood may increase the possibility of systemic side-effects. The local anaesthetic effect may also be reduced by the altered local pH.

**Use of vasoconstrictors** Most local anaesthetics, with the exception of cocaine, cause dilation of blood vessels. The addition of a vasoconstrictor such as **adrenaline (epinephrine)** diminishes local blood flow, slows the rate of absorption of the local anaesthetic, and prolongs its local effect. Adrenaline must be used in a low concentration (e.g. 1 in 200 000) for this purpose and it should **not** be given with a local anaesthetic injection in digits and appendages; it may produce ischaemic necrosis.

When adrenaline is included the final concentration should be 1 in 200 000 (5 micrograms/mL). In dental surgery, up to 1 in 80 000 (12.5 micrograms/mL) of adrenaline is used with local anaesthetics. There is no justification for using higher concentrations.

The total dose of adrenaline should **not** exceed 500 micrograms and it is essential not to exceed a concentration of 1 in 200 000 (5 micrograms/mL) if more than 50 mL of the mixture is to be injected. For general cautions associated with the use of adrenaline, see section 2.7.3. For drug interactions, see Appendix 1 (sympathomimetics).

**Dental anaesthesia** **Lidocaine** (lignocaine) is widely used in dental procedures; it is most often used in combination with **adrenaline** (epinephrine). Lidocaine 2% with adrenaline 1 in 80 000 is a safe and effective preparation that has been used for many years.

The local anaesthetics **articaine** (carticaine) and **mepivacaine** are also used in dentistry; they are available in cartridges suitable for dental use. Mepivacaine is available with or without adrenaline (as *Scandonest®*) and articaine is available with adrenaline (as *Septanest®*).

In patients with severe hypertension or unstable cardiac rhythm, the use of adrenaline in a local anaesthetic may be hazardous. For these patients **prilocaine** with or without felypressin can be used but there is no evidence that it is any safer.

Great care should be taken to avoid inadvertent intravenous administration of a preparation containing adrenaline.

There is no clinical evidence of dangerous interactions between adrenaline-containing local anaesthetics and monoamine-oxidase inhibitors (MAOIs) or tricyclic antidepressants.

## Lidocaine

**Lidocaine** (lignocaine) is effectively absorbed from mucous membranes and is a useful surface anaesthetic in concentrations up to 10%. Except for surface anaesthesia and dental anaesthesia, solutions should **not** usually exceed 1% in strength. The duration of the block (with adrenaline) is about 90 minutes.

## LIDOCAINE HYDROCHLORIDE
**(Lignocaine hydrochloride)**

**Indications** see under Dose; also dental anaesthesia (see below); ventricular arrhythmias (section 2.3.2)

**Cautions** epilepsy, respiratory impairment, impaired cardiac conduction, bradycardia, severe shock; porphyria (section 9.8.2); myasthenia gravis; reduce dose in elderly or debilitated; resuscitative equipment should be available; see section 2.3.2 for effects on heart; hepatic impairment (Appendix 2); renal impairment (Appendix 3); pregnancy (Appendix 4); **interactions**: Appendix 1 (lidocaine)

**Contra-indications** hypovolaemia, complete heart block; do not use solutions containing adrenaline for anaesthesia in appendages

**Side-effects** CNS effects include confusion, respiratory depression and convulsions; hypotension and bradycardia (may lead to cardiac arrest); hypersensitivity reported; see also notes above and section 2.3.2

**Dose**
- Infiltration anaesthesia, by injection, according to patient's weight and nature of procedure, max. 200 mg (or 500 mg if given in solutions containing adrenaline)—see also Administration on p. 647 and see also **important** warning below
- Intravenous regional anaesthesia and nerve blocks, seek expert advice
- Surface anaesthesia, usual strengths 2–4%, see preparations below

> Important The licensed doses stated above may not be appropriate in some settings and expert advice should be sought

### Lidocaine hydrochloride injections

**Lidocaine** (Non-proprietary) PoM

Injection 0.5%, lidocaine hydrochloride 5 mg/mL, net price 10-mL amp = 35p

Injection 1%, lidocaine hydrochloride 10 mg/mL, net price 2-mL amp = 21p; 5-mL amp = 22p; 10-mL amp = 35p; 10-mL prefilled syringe = £4.53; 20-mL amp = 63p

Injection 2%, lidocaine hydrochloride 20 mg/mL, net price 2-mL amp = 28p; 5-mL amp = 25p

**Xylocaine®** (AstraZeneca) PoM

Injection 1% with adrenaline 1 in 200 000, anhydrous lidocaine hydrochloride 10 mg/mL, adrenaline 1 in 200 000 (5 micrograms/mL), net price 20-mL vial = 76p

Injection 2% with adrenaline 1 in 200 000, anhydrous lidocaine hydrochloride 20 mg/mL, adrenaline 1 in 200 000 (5 micrograms/mL), net price 20-mL vial = 81p

### Lidocaine injections for dental use

**Note** Consult expert dental sources for specific advice in relation to dose of lidocaine for dental anaesthesia

A variety of lidocaine injections with adrenaline is available in dental cartridges; brands include *Lignospan Special®*, *Rexocaine®* and *Xylocaine®*

### Lidocaine for surface anaesthesia

**Important**. Rapid and extensive absorption may result in systemic side-effects

**Lidocaine** (Non-proprietary)

Gel, lidocaine hydrochloride 1%, net price 15 mL = £1.30; 2%, 15 mL = £1.30

Dose urethral catheterisation, into urethra at least 5 minutes before catheter insertion, MEN 10 mL followed by further 3–5 mL; WOMEN 3–5 mL; CHILD 1–5 mL

Mucocutaneous anaesthesia, 2–3 mL applied when necessary; CHILD 1–2 mL

Major aphthae in immunocompromised patients, 2–3 mL applied when necessary, max. 15 mL in 24 hours; CHILD 1–2 mL, max. 8 mL in 24 hours

Ointment, lidocaine hydrochloride 5%, net price 15 g = 88p

Dose dental practice, rub gently into dry gum

Sore nipples from breast-feeding, apply using gauze and wash off immediately before feed

Pain relief (in anal fissures, haemorrhoids, pruritus ani, pruritus vulvae, herpes zoster, or herpes labialis), 1–2 mL applied when necessary; avoid long-term use

Solution, lidocaine hydrochloride 4%, net price 25 mL = £1.35

Dose biopsy in mouth, 3–4 mL with suitable spray *or* swab (with adrenaline if necessary); max. 5 mL, ELDERLY lower max. dose, CHILD max. 3 mg/kg

Puncture of maxillary sinus or polypectomy, apply with swab for 2–3 minutes (with adrenaline); max. 5 mL, ELDERLY lower max. dose, CHILD max. 3 mg/kg

Bronchoscopy and bronchography, 2–3 mL with suitable spray; max. 5 mL, ELDERLY lower max. dose, CHILD max. 3 mg/kg

**Lidocaine and chlorhexidine** (Non-proprietary)

Gel, lidocaine hydrochloride 1%, chlorhexidine gluconate solution 0.25%, net price 15 mL = 70p; lidocaine hydrochloride 2%, chlorhexidine gluconate solution 0.25%, 15 mL = 70p

Dose urethral catheterisation, into urethra at least 5 minutes before catheter insertion, MEN 10 mL followed by further 3–5 mL; WOMEN 3–5 mL; CHILD 1–5 mL

Mucocutaneous anaesthesia, 2–3 mL applied when necessary; CHILD 1–2 mL

Major aphthae in immunocompromised patients, 2–3 mL applied when necessary, max. 15 mL in 24 hours; CHILD 1–2 mL, max. 8 mL in 24 hours

**EMLA®** (AstraZeneca)

Drug Tariff cream, lidocaine 2.5%, prilocaine 2.5%, net price 5-g tube = £1.73

Surgical pack cream, lidocaine 2.5%, prilocaine 2.5%, net price 30-g tube = £10.25

Premedication pack cream, lidocaine 2.5%, prilocaine 2.5%, net price 5 × 5-g tube with 12 occlusive dressings = £9.75

Cautions not for wounds, mucous membranes (except genital warts in adults), or atopic dermatitis; avoid use near eyes or middle ear; although systemic absorption low, caution in anaemia, in congenital or acquired methaemoglobinaemia or in G6PD deficiency (see also Prilocaine, p. 650)

Side-effects include transient paleness, redness, and oedema

Dose anaesthesia before minor skin procedures including venepuncture, apply thick layer under occlusive dressing 1–5 hours before procedure (2–5 hours before procedures on large areas e.g. split skin grafting); INFANT 1–12 months [unlicensed use] single application on intact skin under specialist supervision, under 1 month not recommended (risk of methaemoglobinaemia, see Cautions above)

Removal of warts from genital mucosa in adults, apply up to 10 g 5–10 minutes before removal

**Instillagel®** (CliniMed)

Gel, lidocaine hydrochloride 2%, chlorhexidine gluconate solution 0.25%, in a sterile lubricant basis in disposable syringe, net price 6-mL syringe = £1.41, 11-mL syringe = £1.58

**Excipients** include hydroxybenzoates (parabens)

**Dose** 6–11 mL into urethra

**Laryngojet®** (Celltech) PoM

Jet spray 4% (disposable kit for laryngotracheal anaesthesia), lidocaine hydrochloride 40 mg/mL, net price per unit (4-mL vial and disposable sterile cannula with cover and vial injector) = £5.10

**Cautions** may be rapidly and almost completely absorbed from respiratory tract and systemic side-effects may occur; extreme caution if mucosa has been traumatised or if sepsis present

**Dose** usually 160 mg (4 mL) as a single dose instilled as jet spray to larynx and trachea or applied with a swab (reduce dose according to size, age and condition of patient), max. 200 mg (5 mL); CHILD up to 3 mg/kg

**Xylocaine®** (AstraZeneca)

Spray (= pump spray), lidocaine 10% (100 mg/g) supplying 10 mg lidocaine/dose; 500 spray doses per container. Net price 50-mL bottle = £3.13

**Dose** dental practice, 1–5 doses

Maxillary sinus puncture, 3 doses

During delivery in obstetrics, up to 20 doses

Procedures in pharynx, larynx, and trachea, up to 20 doses

Lidocaine can damage plastic cuffs of endotracheal tubes

Topical 4%, anhydrous lidocaine hydrochloride 40 mg/mL, net price 30-mL bottle = £1.21

**Excipients** include hydroxybenzoates (parabens)

**Dose** bronchoscopy, laryngoscopy, oesophagoscopy, endotracheal intubation, 1–7.5 mL with suitable spray; max. 5 mL when applied to larynx, trachea, or bronchi (max. 7.5 mL when applied to oesophagus); max. 10 mL when nebulised or when used for prolonged procedures (over 5 minutes); CHILD under 12 years, max. 0.075 mL/kg (3 mg/kg)

Biopsy in mouth, 3–4 mL with suitable spray *or* swab (with adrenaline if necessary)

### Lidocaine for ear, nose, and oropharyngeal use

**Lidocaine with Phenylephrine** (Non-proprietary)

Topical solution, lidocaine hydrochloride 5%, phenylephrine hydrochloride 0.5%, net price 2.5 mL (with nasal applicator) = £8.73. For cautions, contra-indications and side-effects of phenylephrine, see section 2.7.2

## Bupivacaine

The advantage of bupivacaine over other local anaesthetics is its longer duration of action. It has a slow onset of action, taking up to 30 minutes for full effect. It is often used in lumbar epidural blockade and is particularly suitable for continuous epidural analgesia in labour. It is the principal drug used for spinal anaesthesia.

### BUPIVACAINE HYDROCHLORIDE

**Indications** see under Dose

**Cautions** see under Lidocaine Hydrochloride and notes above; myocardial depression may be more severe and more resistant to treatment; **interactions**: Appendix 1 (bupivacaine)

**Contra-indications** see under Lidocaine Hydrochloride and notes above; intravenous regional anaesthesia (Bier's block)

**Side-effects** see under Lidocaine Hydrochloride and notes above

**Dose**

**Note** Doses should be adjusted according to patient's physical status and nature of procedure—**important**: see also under Administration, above

- *Local infiltration*, max. 60 mL, using a 2.5 mg/mL (0.25%) solution
- *Peripheral nerve block*, max. 60 mL, using a 2.5 mg/mL (0.25%) solution; max. 30 mL, using a 5 mg/mL (0.5%) solution
- *Epidural block*

  Surgery, *lumbar*, max. 20 mL, using a 5 mg/mL (0.5%) solution

  Surgery, *caudal*, max. 30 mL, using a 5 mg/mL (0.5%) solution; CHILD (up to 10 years) using a 2.5 mg/mL (0.25%) solution, up to lower-thoracic (T10) 0.3–0.4 mL/kg, up to mid-thoracic (T6) 0.4–0.8 mL/kg

  Labour, *lumbar*, max. 12 mL using a 2.5 mg/mL (0.25%) or 5 mg/mL (0.5%) solution; *caudal* (but rarely used) max. 20 mL using a 2.5 mg/mL (0.25%) or 5 mg/mL (0.5%) solution
- *Sympathetic block*, max. 50 mL, using a 2.5 mg/mL (0.25%) solution
- *Intrathecal anaesthesia*, see under preparations

> Important The licensed doses stated above may not be appropriate in some settings and expert advice should be sought

**Bupivacaine** (Non-proprietary) PoM

Injection, anhydrous bupivacaine hydrochloride 2.5 mg/mL (0.25%), net price 10 mL = 82p; 5 mg/mL (0.5%), 10 mL = 94p

**Note** Bupivacaine hydrochloride injection 0.25% and 0.5% are available in glass or plastic ampoules, and sterile-wrapped glass ampoules

Infusion, anhydrous bupivacaine hydrochloride 1 mg/mL (0.1%), net price 100 mL = £8.41, 250 mL = £10.59; 1.25 mg/mL (0.125%), 250 mL = £10.80

**Dose** Continuous lumbar epidural infusion during labour (once epidural block established), 10–15 mg/hour of 0.1% or 0.125% solution; max. 2 mg/kg over 4 hours and total of 400 mg in 24 hours

Continuous thoracic, upper abdominal, or lower abdominal epidural infusion for post-operative pain (once epidural block established), 4–15 mg/hour of 0.1% or 0.125% solution; max. 2 mg/kg over 4 hours and total of 400 mg in 24 hours; not recommended for use in children

**Marcain®** (AstraZeneca) PoM

Injection, anhydrous bupivacaine hydrochloride 2.5 mg/mL (*Marcain® 0.25%*), net price 10-mL *Polyamp®* = £1.06; 5 mg/mL (*Marcain® 0.5%*), 10-mL *Polyamp®* = £1.21

**Marcain Heavy®** (AstraZeneca) PoM

Injection, anhydrous bupivacaine hydrochloride 5 mg, glucose 80 mg/mL, net price 4-mL amp = 93p

**Dose** intrathecal anaesthesia for surgery, 2–4 mL (dose may need to be reduced in elderly and in late pregnancy)

### With adrenaline

**Bupivacaine and Adrenaline** (Non-proprietary) PoM

Injection, anhydrous bupivacaine hydrochloride 2.5 mg/mL (0.25%), adrenaline 1 in 200 000 (5 micrograms/mL), net price 10-mL amp = £1.23

Injection, anhydrous bupivacaine hydrochloride 5 mg/mL (0.5%), adrenaline 1 in 200 000 (5 micrograms/mL), net price 10-mL amp = £1.40

## Levobupivacaine

Levobupivacaine, an isomer of bupivacaine, has anaesthetic and analgesic properties similar to bupivacaine, but is thought to have fewer adverse efffects.

### LEVOBUPIVACAINE

Note Levobupivacaine is an isomer of bupivacaine

**Indications** see under Dose

**Cautions** see under Lidocaine Hydrochloride and notes above; **interactions:** Appendix 1 (levobupivacaine)

**Contra-indications** see under Lidocaine Hydrochloride and notes above; intravenous regional anaesthesia (Bier's block); paracervical block in obstetrics

**Side-effects** see under Lidocaine Hydrochloride and notes above

**Dose**

Note Doses should be adjusted according to patient's physical status and nature of procedure—**important:** see also under Administration, above

- Surgical anaesthesia

  *lumbar epidural*, 10–20 mL (50–150 mg) of 5 mg/mL or 7.5 mg/mL solution over 5 minutes; caesarean section, 15–30 mL (75–150 mg) of 5 mg/mL solution over 15–20 minutes

  *intrathecal*, 3 mL (15 mg) of 5 mg/mL solution

  *peripheral nerve block*, 1–40 mL of 2.5 mg/mL or 5 mg/mL solution (max. 150 mg)

  *ilioinguinal/iliohypogastric block*, CHILD 0.25–0.5 mL/kg (0.625–2.5 mg/kg) of a 2.5 mg/mL or 5 mg/mL solution

  *peribulbar block*, 5–15 mL (37.5–112.5 mg) of 7.5 mg/mL solution

  *local infiltration*, 1–60 mL (max. 150 mg) of 2.5 mg/mL solution

- Acute pain

  *Lumbar epidural*, labour pain, 6–10 mL (15–25 mg) of 2.5 mg/mL solution at intervals of at least 15 minutes *or* 5–12.5 mg/hour as a continuous epidural infusion, postoperative pain, 12.5–18.75 mg/hour as a continuous epidural infusion

  Note 7.5 mg/mL **contra-indicated** for use in obstetrics; for 1.25 mg/mL concentration dilute standard solutions with sodium chloride 0.9%.

> *Important* The licensed doses stated above may not be appropriate in some settings and expert advice should be sought

**Chirocaine®** (Abbott) ▼ PoM

Injection, levobupivacaine (as hydrochloride) 2.5 mg/mL, net price 10-mL amp = £1.66; 5 mg/mL, 10-mL amp = £1.90; 7.5 mg/mL, 10-mL amp = £2.85

Infusion, levobupivacaine (as hydrochloride) 625 micrograms/mL, net price 100 mL = £7.80, 200 mL = £10.40; 1.25 mg/mL, net price 100 mL = £8.54, 200 mL = £12.20

## Prilocaine

Prilocaine is a local anaesthetic of low toxicity which is similar to lidocaine (lignocaine). If used in high doses, methaemoglobinaemia may occur which can be treated with intravenous injection of methylthioninium chloride (methylene blue) 1% using a dose of 1 mg/kg. Infants under 6 months are particularly susceptible to methaemoglobinaemia.

### PRILOCAINE HYDROCHLORIDE

**Indications** infiltration anaesthesia (higher strengths for dental use only), nerve block

**Cautions** see under Lidocaine Hydrochloride and notes above; severe or untreated hypertension, severe heart disease; concomitant drugs which cause methaemoglobinaemia; reduce dose in elderly or debilitated; hepatic impairment; renal impairment; pregnancy (Appendix 4); **interactions:** Appendix 1 (prilocaine)

**Contra-indications** see under Lidocaine Hydrochloride and notes above; anaemia or congenital or acquired methaemoglobinaemia

**Side-effects** see under Lidocaine Hydrochloride and notes above; ocular toxicity (including blindness) reported with excessively high strengths used for ophthalmic procedures

**Dose**

- See under preparations

**Citanest®** (AstraZeneca) PoM

Injection 1%, prilocaine hydrochloride 10 mg/mL, net price 50-mL multidose vial = £2.01

Dose adjusted according to site of administration and response, 100–200 mg/minute, or in incremental doses, to max. total dose 400 mg; CHILD over 6 months up to 5 mg/kg

**For dental use**

**Citanest®** (Dentsply) PoM

Injection 4%, prilocaine hydrochloride 40 mg/mL, net price 2-mL cartridge = 16p

Dose dental infiltration and dental nerve block, adjusted according to response, ADULT, 1–2 mL (max. 10 mL); CHILD under 10 years, 1 mL

**Citanest with Octapressin®** (Dentsply) PoM

Injection 3%, prilocaine hydrochloride 30 mg/mL, felypressin 0.03 unit/mL, net price 2-mL cartridge and self-aspirating cartridge (both) = 16p

Dose dental infiltration and dental nerve block, adjusted according to response 1–5 mL (max. 10 mL); CHILD under 10 years, 1–2 mL

## Procaine

Procaine is now seldom used. It is as potent as lidocaine (lignocaine) but has a shorter duration of action. It provides less intense analgesia because of reduced spread through the tissues. It is of no value as a surface anaesthetic.

### PROCAINE HYDROCHLORIDE

**Indications** local anaesthesia by infiltration and regional routes (but see notes above)

**Cautions** see notes above; pregnancy (Appendix 4)

**Side-effects** see notes above

**Dose**

Note Doses should be adjusted according to site of operation and patient's response

- By injection, up to 1 g (200 mL of 0.5% solution or 100 mL of 1%) with adrenaline 1 in 200 000

**Procaine** (Martindale) PoM
Injection, procaine hydrochloride 2% (20 mg/mL) in sodium chloride intravenous infusion, net price 2-mL amp = 95p

## Ropivacaine

Ropivacaine is an amide-type local anaesthetic agent similar to bupivacaine. It is less cardiotoxic than bupivacaine, but also less potent.

### ROPIVACAINE HYDROCHLORIDE

**Indications** see under Dose

**Cautions** see Lidocaine Hydrochloride and notes above; **interactions:** Appendix 1 (ropivacaine)

**Contra-indications** see Lidocaine Hydrochloride and notes above; intravenous regional anaesthesia (Bier's block); paracervical block in obstetrics

**Side-effects** see Lidocaine Hydrochloride and notes above

**Dose**

Note Doses should be adjusted according to patient's physical status and nature of procedure—see also under Administration on p. 647

- Surgical anaesthesia

  *lumbar epidural*, 15–20 mL of 10 mg/mL solution *or* 15–25 mL of 7.5 mg/mL solution; caesarean section, 15–20 mL of 7.5 mg/mL solution in incremental doses (max. total dose 150 mg)

  *thoracic epidural* (to establish block for postoperative pain), 5–15 mL of 7.5 mg/mL solution

  *major nerve block* (brachial plexus block), 30–40 mL of 7.5 mg/mL solution

  *field block*, up to 30 mL of 7.5 mg/mL solution

- Acute pain

  *lumbar epidural*, 10–20 mL of 2 mg/mL solution followed by 10–15 mL of 2 mg/mL solution at intervals of at least 30 minutes *or* 6–10 mL/hour of 2 mg/mL solution as a continuous epidural infusion for labour pain *or* 6–14 mL/hour of 2 mg/mL solution as a continuous epidural infusion for postoperative pain

  *thoracic epidural*, 6–14 mL/hour of 2 mg/mL solution as a continuous infusion

  *field block*, up to 100 mL of 2 mg/mL solution

  *peripheral nerve block*, 5–10 mL/hour of 2 mg/mL solution as a continuous infusion *or* by intermittent injection

  CHILD over 1 year (body-weight up to 25 kg), *caudal epidural* (for pre- and post-operative pain only), 2 mg/kg of 2 mg/mL solution

**Naropin®** (AstraZeneca) PoM
Injection, ropivacaine hydrochloride 2 mg/mL, net price 10-mL *Polyamp®* = £1.37; 7.5 mg/mL, 10-mL *Polyamp®* = £2.65; 10 mg/mL, 10-mL *Polyamp®* = £3.20

Epidural infusion, ropivacaine hydrochloride 2 mg/mL, net price 200-mL *Polybag®* = £14.45

## Tetracaine

**Tetracaine** (amethocaine) is an effective local anaesthetic for topical application; a 4% gel is indicated for anaesthesia prior to venepuncture or venous cannulation. It is rapidly absorbed from mucous membranes and should **never** be applied to inflamed, traumatised, or highly vascular surfaces. It should **never** be used to provide anaesthesia for bronchoscopy or cystoscopy, as lidocaine (lignocaine) is a safer alternative. It is used in ophthalmology (section 11.7) and in skin preparations (section 13.3). Hypersensitivity to tetracaine has been reported.

### TETRACAINE
(Amethocaine)

**Indications** see under preparation below

**Cautions** see notes above

**Contra-indications** see notes above

**Side-effects** see notes above; also erythema, oedema and pruritus; very rarely blistering

**Important.** Rapid and extensive absorption may result in systemic side-effects (see also notes above)

**Ametop®** (S&N Hlth.)
Gel, tetracaine 4%, net price 1.5-g tube = £1.08
Dose apply contents of tube to site of venepuncture or venous cannulation and cover with occlusive dressing; remove gel and dressing after 30 minutes for venepuncture and after 45 minutes for venous cannulation; PRETERM NEONATE and INFANT under 1 month not recommended

## Other local anaesthetics

**Benzocaine** is a local anaesthetic of low potency and toxicity. It is used in concentrations of up to 20% for topical anaesthesia of the oral mucosa before injection. It is an ingredient of some proprietary topical preparations for musculoskeletal conditions (section 10.3.2), mouth-ulcer preparations (section 12.3.1), and throat lozenges (section 12.3.3).

**Cocaine** readily penetrates mucous membranes and is an effective surface anaesthetic with an intense vasoconstrictor action. However, apart from its use in otolaryngology (see below), it has now been replaced by less toxic alternatives. It has marked sympathomimetic activity and should **never** be given by injection because of its toxicity. As a result of its intense stimulant effect it is a drug of addiction. In otolaryngology cocaine is applied to the nasal mucosa in concentrations of 4 to 10% (40–100 mg/mL); an oromucosal solution and nasal spray both containing cocaine hydrochloride 10% are available (Aurum). In order to avoid systemic effects, the maximum dose recommended for application to the nasal mucosa in fit adults is a total of 1.5 mg/kg, which is equivalent to a total topical dose of approximately 100 mg for an adult male; this dose relates to direct application of cocaine (application on gauze may reduce systemic absorption). It should be used only by those skilled in the precautions needed to *minimise absorption* and the *consequent risk of arrhythmias.* Although cocaine interacts with other drugs liable to induce arrhythmias, including adrenaline, some otolaryngologists consider that combined use of topical cocaine with topical adrenaline (in the form of a paste or a solution) improves the operative field and may possibly reduce absorption. Cocaine is a mydriatic as well as a local anaesthetic but owing to corneal toxicity it is now little used in ophthalmology. Cocaine should be avoided in porphyria (section 9.8.2).

# A1 Interactions

Two or more drugs given at the same time may exert their effects independently or may interact. The interaction may be potentiation or antagonism of one drug by another, or occasionally some other effect. Adverse drug interactions should be reported to the CSM as for other adverse drug reactions.

Drug interactions may be **pharmacodynamic** or **pharmacokinetic**.

## Pharmacodynamic interactions

These are interactions between drugs which have similar or antagonistic pharmacological effects or side-effects. They may be due to competition at receptor sites, or occur between drugs acting on the same physiological system. They are usually predictable from a knowledge of the pharmacology of the interacting drugs; in general, those demonstrated with one drug are likely to occur with related drugs. They occur to a greater or lesser extent in most patients who receive the interacting drugs.

## Pharmacokinetic interactions

These occur when one drug alters the absorption, distribution, metabolism, or excretion of another, thus increasing or reducing the amount of drug available to produce its pharmacological effects. They are not easily predicted and many of them affect only a small proportion of patients taking the combination of drugs. Pharmacokinetic interactions occurring with one drug cannot be assumed to occur with related drugs unless their pharmacokinetic properties are known to be similar.

Pharmacokinetic interactions are of several types:



**Affecting absorption** The rate of absorption or the total amount absorbed can both be altered by drug interactions. Delayed absorption is rarely of clinical importance unless high peak plasma concentrations are required (e.g. when giving an analgesic). Reduction in the total amount absorbed, however, may result in ineffective therapy.

**Due to changes in protein binding** To a variable extent most drugs are loosely bound to plasma proteins. Protein-binding sites are non-specific and one drug can displace another thereby increasing its proportion free to diffuse from plasma to its site of action. This only produces a detectable increase in effect if it is an extensively bound drug (more than 90%) that is not widely distributed throughout the body. Even so displacement rarely produces more than transient potentiation because this increased concentration of free drug results in an increased rate of elimination.

Displacement from protein binding plays a part in the potentiation of warfarin by sulphonamides and tolbutamide but the importance of these interactions is due mainly to the fact that warfarin metabolism is also inhibited.

**Affecting metabolism** Many drugs are metabolised in the liver. Induction of the hepatic microsomal enzyme system by one drug can gradually increase the rate of metabolism of another, resulting in lower plasma concentrations and a reduced effect. On withdrawal of the inducer plasma concentrations increase and toxicity may occur. Barbiturates, griseofulvin, many antiepileptics, and rifampicin are the most important enzyme inducers. Drugs affected include warfarin and the oral contraceptives.

Conversely when one drug inhibits the metabolism of another higher plasma concentrations are produced, rapidly resulting in an increased effect with risk of toxicity. Some drugs which potentiate warfarin and phenytoin do so by this mechanism.

Isoenzymes of the hepatic cytochrome P450 system interact with a wide range of drugs. Drugs may be substrates, inducers or inhibitors of the different isoenzymes. A great deal of *in-vitro* information is available on the effect of drugs on the isoenzymes; however, since drugs are eliminated by a number of different metabolic routes as well as renal excretion, the clinical effects of interactions cannot be predicted accurately from laboratory data on the cytochrome P450 isoenzymes. Except where a combination of drugs is specifically contra-indicated, the BNF presents only interactions that have been reported in clinical practice. In all cases the possibility of an interaction must be considered if toxic effects occur or if the activity of a drug diminishes.

**Affecting renal excretion** Drugs are eliminated through the kidney both by glomerular filtration and by active tubular secretion. Competition occurs between those which share active transport mechanisms in the proximal tubule. For example, salicylates and some other NSAIDs delay the excretion of methotrexate; serious methotrexate toxicity is possible.

## Relative importance of interactions

Many drug interactions are harmless and many of those which are potentially harmful only occur in a small proportion of patients; moreover, the severity of an interaction varies from one patient to another. Drugs with a small therapeutic ratio (e.g. phenytoin) and those which require careful control of dosage (e.g. anticoagulants, antihypertensives, and antidiabetics) are most often involved.

Patients at increased risk from drug interactions include the elderly and those with impaired renal or liver function.

**Hazardous interactions** The symbol • has been placed against interactions that are **potentially hazardous** and where combined administration of the drugs involved should be **avoided** (or only undertaken with caution and appropriate monitoring).

Interactions that have no symbol do not usually have serious consequences.

## List of drug interactions

The following is an alphabetical list of drugs and their interactions; to avoid excessive cross-referencing each drug or group is listed twice: in the alphabetical list and also against the drug or group with which it interacts; changes in the interactions lists since BNF No. 50 (September 2005) are underlined.

For explanation of symbol • see above

**Abacavir**
- Analgesics: abacavir possibly reduces plasma concentration of methadone
- Antibacterials: plasma concentration of abacavir possibly reduced by rifampicin
- Antiepileptics: plasma concentration of abacavir possibly reduced by phenytoin
- • Antivirals: plasma concentration of abacavir reduced by •tipranavir
- Barbiturates: plasma concentration of abacavir possibly reduced by phenobarbital

**Acarbose** *see* Antidiabetics

**ACE Inhibitors**
- Alcohol: enhanced hypotensive effect when ACE inhibitors given with alcohol
- Aldesleukin: enhanced hypotensive effect when ACE inhibitors given with aldesleukin
- Allopurinol: increased risk of toxicity when captopril given with allopurinol especially in renal impairment
- Alpha-blockers: enhanced hypotensive effect when ACE inhibitors given with alpha-blockers
- Anaesthetics, General: enhanced hypotensive effect when ACE inhibitors given with general anaesthetics
- Analgesics: increased risk of renal impairment when ACE inhibitors given with NSAIDs, also hypotensive effect antagonised; increased risk of hyperkalaemia when ACE inhibitors given with ketorolac; risk of renal impairment when ACE inhibitors given with aspirin (in doses over 300 mg daily), also hypotensive effect antagonised
- Angiotensin-II Receptor Antagonists: enhanced hypotensive effect when ACE inhibitors given with angiotensin-II receptor antagonists
- Antacids: absorption of ACE inhibitors possibly reduced by antacids; absorption of captopril, enalapril and fosinopril reduced by antacids
- Anti-arrhythmics: increased risk of toxicity when captopril given with procainamide especially in renal impairment
- Antibacterials: plasma concentration of active metabolite of imidapril reduced by rifampicin (reduced antihypertensive effect); quinapril tablets reduce absorption of tetracyclines (quinapril tablets contain magnesium carbonate)
- Anticoagulants: increased risk of hyperkalaemia when ACE inhibitors given with heparins
- Antidepressants: hypotensive effect of ACE inhibitors possibly enhanced by MAOIs
- Antidiabetics: ACE inhibitors possibly enhance hypoglycaemic effect of insulin, metformin and sulphonylureas
- Antipsychotics: enhanced hypotensive effect when ACE inhibitors given with antipsychotics
- Anxiolytics and Hypnotics: enhanced hypotensive effect when ACE inhibitors given with anxiolytics and hypnotics
- Beta-blockers: enhanced hypotensive effect when ACE inhibitors given with beta-blockers

**ACE Inhibitors** *(continued)*
- Calcium-channel Blockers: enhanced hypotensive effect when ACE inhibitors given with calcium-channel blockers
- Cardiac Glycosides: captopril possibly increases plasma concentration of digoxin
- • Ciclosporin: increased risk of hyperkalaemia when ACE inhibitors given with •ciclosporin
- Clonidine: enhanced hypotensive effect when ACE inhibitors given with clonidine; antihypertensive effect of captopril possibly delayed by previous treatment with clonidine
- Corticosteroids: hypotensive effect of ACE inhibitors antagonised by corticosteroids
- Cytotoxics: increased risk of leucopenia when captopril given with azathioprine
- Diazoxide: enhanced hypotensive effect when ACE inhibitors given with diazoxide
- • Diuretics: enhanced hypotensive effect when ACE inhibitors given with •diuretics; increased risk of severe hyperkalaemia when ACE inhibitors given with •potassium-sparing diuretics and aldosterone antagonists (monitor potassium concentration with low-dose spironolactone in heart failure)
- Dopaminergics: enhanced hypotensive effect when ACE inhibitors given with levodopa
- Epoetin: antagonism of hypotensive effect and increased risk of hyperkalaemia when ACE inhibitors given with epoetin
- • Lithium: ACE inhibitors reduce excretion of •lithium (increased plasma concentration)
- Methyldopa: enhanced hypotensive effect when ACE inhibitors given with methyldopa
- Moxisylyte (thymoxamine): enhanced hypotensive effect when ACE inhibitors given with moxisylyte
- Moxonidine: enhanced hypotensive effect when ACE inhibitors given with moxonidine
- Muscle Relaxants: enhanced hypotensive effect when ACE inhibitors given with baclofen or tizanidine
- Nitrates: enhanced hypotensive effect when ACE inhibitors given with nitrates
- Oestrogens: hypotensive effect of ACE inhibitors antagonised by oestrogens
- • Potassium Salts: increased risk of severe hyperkalaemia when ACE inhibitors given with •potassium salts
- Probenecid: excretion of captopril reduced by probenecid
- Progestogens: risk of hyperkalaemia when ACE inhibitors given with drospirenone (monitor serum potassium during first cycle)
- Prostaglandins: enhanced hypotensive effect when ACE inhibitors given with alprostadil
- Vasodilator Antihypertensives: enhanced hypotensive effect when ACE inhibitors given with hydralazine, minoxidil or nitroprusside

**Acebutolol** *see* Beta-blockers

**Aceclofenac** *see* NSAIDs

**Acemetacin** *see* NSAIDs

**Acenocoumarol (nicoumalone)** *see* Coumarins

**Acetazolamide** *see* Diuretics

**Aciclovir**

*Note.* Interactions do not apply to topical aciclovir preparations

*Note.* Valaciclovir interactions as for aciclovir

- Ciclosporin: increased risk of nephrotoxicity when aciclovir given with ciclosporin
- Cytotoxics: plasma concentration of aciclovir increased by mycophenolate mofetil, also plasma concentration of inactive metabolite of mycophenolate mofetil increased
- Probenecid: excretion of aciclovir reduced by probenecid (increased plasma concentration)

**Acitretin** *see* Retinoids
**Acrivastine** *see* Antihistamines
**Adalimumab**
- • Anakinra: avoid concomitant use of adalimumab with •anakinra
- • Vaccines: avoid concomitant use of adalimumab with live •vaccines (see p. 611)

**Adenosine**
*Note.* Possibility of interaction with drugs tending to impair myocardial conduction
- Anaesthetics, Local: increased myocardial depression when anti-arrhythmics given with bupivacaine, levobupivacaine or prilocaine
- • Anti-arrhythmics: increased myocardial depression when anti-arrhythmics given with other •anti-arrhythmics
- • Antipsychotics: increased risk of ventricular arrhythmias when anti-arrhythmics that prolong the QT interval given with •antipsychotics that prolong the QT interval
- • Beta-blockers: increased myocardial depression when anti-arrhythmics given with •beta-blockers
- • Dipyridamole: effect of adenosine enhanced and extended by •dipyridamole (important risk of toxicity)
- $5HT_3$ Antagonists: caution with anti-arrhythmics advised by manufacturer of tropisetron (risk of ventricular arrhythmias)
- Theophylline: anti-arrhythmic effect of adenosine antagonised by theophylline

**Adrenaline (epinephrine)** *see* Sympathomimetics
**Adrenergic Neurone Blockers**
- Alcohol: enhanced hypotensive effect when adrenergic neurone blockers given with alcohol
- Alpha-blockers: enhanced hypotensive effect when adrenergic neurone blockers given with alpha-blockers
- • Anaesthetics, General: enhanced hypotensive effect when adrenergic neurone blockers given with •general anaesthetics
- Analgesics: hypotensive effect of adrenergic neurone blockers antagonised by NSAIDs
- Angiotensin-II Receptor Antagonists: enhanced hypotensive effect when adrenergic neurone blockers given with angiotensin-II receptor antagonists
- Antidepressants: enhanced hypotensive effect when adrenergic neurone blockers given with MAOIs; hypotensive effect of adrenergic neurone blockers antagonised by tricyclics
- Antipsychotics: hypotensive effect of adrenergic neurone blockers antagonised by haloperidol; hypotensive effect of adrenergic neurone blockers antagonised by higher doses of chlorpromazine; enhanced hypotensive effect when adrenergic neurone blockers given with phenothiazines
- Anxiolytics and Hypnotics: enhanced hypotensive effect when adrenergic neurone blockers given with anxiolytics and hypnotics
- Beta-blockers: enhanced hypotensive effect when adrenergic neurone blockers given with beta-blockers
- Calcium-channel Blockers: enhanced hypotensive effect when adrenergic neurone blockers given with calcium-channel blockers
- Clonidine: enhanced hypotensive effect when adrenergic neurone blockers given with clonidine
- Corticosteroids: hypotensive effect of adrenergic neurone blockers antagonised by corticosteroids
- Diazoxide: enhanced hypotensive effect when adrenergic neurone blockers given with diazoxide
- Diuretics: enhanced hypotensive effect when adrenergic neurone blockers given with diuretics

**Adrenergic Neurone Blockers** *(continued)*
- Dopaminergics: enhanced hypotensive effect when adrenergic neurone blockers given with levodopa
- Methyldopa: enhanced hypotensive effect when adrenergic neurone blockers given with methyldopa
- Moxisylyte (thymoxamine): enhanced hypotensive effect when adrenergic neurone blockers given with moxisylyte
- Moxonidine: enhanced hypotensive effect when adrenergic neurone blockers given with moxonidine
- Muscle Relaxants: enhanced hypotensive effect when adrenergic neurone blockers given with baclofen or tizanidine
- Nitrates: enhanced hypotensive effect when adrenergic neurone blockers given with nitrates
- Oestrogens: hypotensive effect of adrenergic neurone blockers antagonised by oestrogens
- Pizotifen: hypotensive effect of adrenergic neurone blockers antagonised by pizotifen
- Prostaglandins: enhanced hypotensive effect when adrenergic neurone blockers given with alprostadil
- • Sympathomimetics: hypotensive effect of adrenergic neurone blockers antagonised by •ephedrine, •isometheptene, •metaraminol, •methylphenidate, •noradrenaline (norepinephrine), •oxymetazoline, •phenylephrine, •phenylpropanolamine, •pseudoephedrine and •xylometazoline
- Vasodilator Antihypertensives: enhanced hypotensive effect when adrenergic neurone blockers given with hydralazine, minoxidil or nitroprusside

**Adsorbents** *see* Kaolin
**Agalsidase Beta**
- Anti-arrhythmics: effects of agalsidase beta possibly inhibited by amiodarone (manufacturer of agalsidase beta advises avoid concomitant use)
- Antibacterials: effects of agalsidase beta possibly inhibited by gentamicin (manufacturer of agalsidase beta advises avoid concomitant use)
- Antimalarials: effects of agalsidase beta possibly inhibited by chloroquine and hydroxychloroquine (manufacturer of agalsidase beta advises avoid concomitant use)

**Alcohol**
- ACE Inhibitors: enhanced hypotensive effect when alcohol given with ACE inhibitors
- Adrenergic Neurone Blockers: enhanced hypotensive effect when alcohol given with adrenergic neurone blockers
- Alpha-blockers: increased sedative effect when alcohol given with indoramin; enhanced hypotensive effect when alcohol given with alpha-blockers
- Analgesics: enhanced hypotensive and sedative effects when alcohol given with opioid analgesics
- Angiotensin-II Receptor Antagonists: enhanced hypotensive effect when alcohol given with angiotensin-II receptor antagonists
- • Antibacterials: disulfiram-like reaction when alcohol given with metronidazole; possibility of disulfiram-like reaction when alcohol given with tinidazole; increased risk of convulsions when alcohol given with •cycloserine
- • Anticoagulants: major changes in consumption of alcohol may affect anticoagulant control with •coumarins or •phenindione
- • Antidepressants: some beverages containing alcohol and some dealcoholised beverages contain tyramine which interacts with •MAOIs (hypertensive crisis)—if no tyramine, enhanced

**Alcohol**

- Antidepressants *(continued)*
  hypotensive effect; sedative effects possibly increased when alcohol given with SSRIs; increased sedative effect when alcohol given with •mirtazapine, •tricyclic-related antidepressants or •tricyclics

Antidiabetics: alcohol enhances hypoglycaemic effect of antidiabetics; increased risk of lactic acidosis when alcohol given with metformin; flushing, in susceptible subjects, when alcohol given with chlorpropamide

Antiepileptics: alcohol possibly increases CNS side-effects of carbamazepine; increased sedative effect when alcohol given with primidone

Antifungals: effects of alcohol possibly enhanced by griseofulvin

Antihistamines: increased sedative effect when alcohol given with antihistamines (possibly less effect with non-sedating antihistamines)

Antimuscarinics: increased sedative effect when alcohol given with hyoscine

Antipsychotics: increased sedative effect when alcohol given with antipsychotics

Anxiolytics and Hypnotics: increased sedative effect when alcohol given with anxiolytics and hypnotics

Barbiturates: increased sedative effect when alcohol given with barbiturates

Beta-blockers: enhanced hypotensive effect when alcohol given with beta-blockers

Calcium-channel Blockers: enhanced hypotensive effect when alcohol given with calcium-channel blockers; plasma concentration of alcohol possibly increased by verapamil

Clonidine: enhanced hypotensive effect when alcohol given with clonidine

Cytotoxics: disulfiram-like reaction when alcohol given with procarbazine

Diazoxide: enhanced hypotensive effect when alcohol given with diazoxide

Disulfiram: disulfiram reaction when alcohol given with disulfiram (see p. 260)

Diuretics: enhanced hypotensive effect when alcohol given with diuretics

Dopaminergics: alcohol reduces tolerance to bromocriptine

Levamisole: possibility of disulfiram-like reaction when alcohol given with levamisole

Lofexidine: increased sedative effect when alcohol given with lofexidine

Methyldopa: enhanced hypotensive effect when alcohol given with methyldopa

Moxonidine: enhanced hypotensive effect when alcohol given with moxonidine

Muscle Relaxants: increased sedative effect when alcohol given with baclofen, methocarbamol or tizanidine

Nabilone: increased sedative effect when alcohol given with nabilone

Nicorandil: alcohol possibly enhances hypotensive effect of nicorandil

Nitrates: enhanced hypotensive effect when alcohol given with nitrates

- Paraldehyde: increased sedative effect when alcohol given with •paraldehyde

Retinoids: presence of alcohol causes etretinate to be formed from acitretin

Vasodilator Antihypertensives: enhanced hypotensive effect when alcohol given with hydralazine, minoxidil or nitroprusside

**Aldesleukin**

ACE Inhibitors: enhanced hypotensive effect when aldesleukin given with ACE inhibitors

Alpha-blockers: enhanced hypotensive effect when aldesleukin given with alpha-blockers

Angiotensin-II Receptor Antagonists: enhanced hypotensive effect when aldesleukin given with angiotensin-II receptor antagonists

Beta-blockers: enhanced hypotensive effect when aldesleukin given with beta-blockers

Calcium-channel Blockers: enhanced hypotensive effect when aldesleukin given with calcium-channel blockers

Clonidine: enhanced hypotensive effect when aldesleukin given with clonidine

Diazoxide: enhanced hypotensive effect when aldesleukin given with diazoxide

Diuretics: enhanced hypotensive effect when aldesleukin given with diuretics

Methyldopa: enhanced hypotensive effect when aldesleukin given with methyldopa

Moxonidine: enhanced hypotensive effect when aldesleukin given with moxonidine

Nitrates: enhanced hypotensive effect when aldesleukin given with nitrates

Vasodilator Antihypertensives: enhanced hypotensive effect when aldesleukin given with hydralazine, minoxidil or nitroprusside

**Alendronic Acid** *see* Bisphosphonates

**Alfentanil** *see* Opioid Analgesics

**Alfuzosin** *see* Alpha-blockers

**Alimemazine (trimeprazine)** *see* Antihistamines

**Alkylating Drugs** *see* Busulfan, Cyclophosphamide, Ifosfamide, Melphalan, and Thiotepa

**Allopurinol**

ACE Inhibitors: increased risk of toxicity when allopurinol given with captopril especially in renal impairment

Antibacterials: increased risk of rash when allopurinol given with amoxicillin or ampicillin

Anticoagulants: allopurinol possibly enhances anticoagulant effect of coumarins

Antivirals: allopurinol possibly increases plasma concentration of didanosine

Ciclosporin: allopurinol possibly increases plasma concentration of ciclosporin (risk of nephrotoxicity)

- Cytotoxics: allopurinol enhances effects and increases toxicity of •azathioprine and •mercaptopurine (reduce dose of azathioprine and mercaptopurine); avoidance of allopurinol advised by manufacturer of •capecitabine

Diuretics: increased risk of hypersensitivity when allopurinol given with thiazides and related diuretics especially in renal impairment

Theophylline: allopurinol possibly increases plasma concentration of theophylline

**Almotriptan** *see* $5HT_1$ Agonists

**$Alpha_2$-adrenoceptor Stimulants**

Antidepressants: manufacturer of apraclonidine and brimonidine advises avoid concomitant use with MAOIs; manufacturer of apraclonidine and brimonidine advises avoid concomitant use with tricyclic-related antidepressants; manufacturer of apraclonidine and brimonidine advises avoid concomitant use with tricyclics

**Alpha-blockers**

ACE Inhibitors: enhanced hypotensive effect when alpha-blockers given with ACE inhibitors

**Alpha-blockers** *(continued)*
- Adrenergic Neurone Blockers: enhanced hypotensive effect when alpha-blockers given with adrenergic neurone blockers
- Alcohol: enhanced hypotensive effect when alpha-blockers given with alcohol; increased sedative effect when indoramin given with alcohol
- Aldesleukin: enhanced hypotensive effect when alpha-blockers given with aldesleukin
- • Anaesthetics, General: enhanced hypotensive effect when alpha-blockers given with •general anaesthetics
- Analgesics: hypotensive effect of alpha-blockers antagonised by NSAIDs
- Angiotensin-II Receptor Antagonists: enhanced hypotensive effect when alpha-blockers given with angiotensin-II receptor antagonists
- • Antidepressants: enhanced hypotensive effect when alpha-blockers given with MAOIs; manufacturer of indoramin advises avoid concomitant use with •MAOIs
- Antipsychotics: enhanced hypotensive effect when alpha-blockers given with antipsychotics
- Anxiolytics and Hypnotics: enhanced hypotensive and sedative effects when alpha-blockers given with anxiolytics and hypnotics
- • Beta-blockers: enhanced hypotensive effect when alpha-blockers given with •beta-blockers, also increased risk of first-dose hypotension with post-synaptic alpha-blockers such as prazosin
- • Calcium-channel Blockers: enhanced hypotensive effect when alpha-blockers given with •calcium-channel blockers, also increased risk of first-dose hypotension with post-synaptic alpha-blockers such as prazosin
- Cardiac Glycosides: prazosin increases plasma concentration of digoxin
- Clonidine: enhanced hypotensive effect when alpha-blockers given with clonidine
- Corticosteroids: hypotensive effect of alpha-blockers antagonised by corticosteroids
- Diazoxide: enhanced hypotensive effect when alpha-blockers given with diazoxide
- • Diuretics: enhanced hypotensive effect when alpha-blockers given with •diuretics, also increased risk of first-dose hypotension with post-synaptic alpha-blockers such as prazosin
- Dopaminergics: enhanced hypotensive effect when alpha-blockers given with levodopa
- Methyldopa: enhanced hypotensive effect when alpha-blockers given with methyldopa
- • Moxisylyte (thymoxamine): possible severe postural hypotension when alpha-blockers given with •moxisylyte
- Moxonidine: enhanced hypotensive effect when alpha-blockers given with moxonidine
- Muscle Relaxants: enhanced hypotensive effect when alpha-blockers given with baclofen or tizanidine
- Nitrates: enhanced hypotensive effect when alpha-blockers given with nitrates
- Oestrogens: hypotensive effect of alpha-blockers antagonised by oestrogens
- Prostaglandins: enhanced hypotensive effect when alpha-blockers given with alprostadil
- • Sildenafil: enhanced hypotensive effect when alpha-blockers given with •sildenafil (avoid alpha-blockers for 4 hours after sildenafil)
- • Sympathomimetics: avoid concomitant use of tolazoline with •adrenaline (epinephrine) or •dopamine
- • Tadalafil: enhanced hypotensive effect when alpha-blockers given with •tadalafil—avoid concomitant use
- • Ulcer-healing Drugs: effects of tolazoline antagonised by •cimetidine and •ranitidine
- • Vardenafil: enhanced hypotensive effect when alpha-blockers (excludes tamsulosin) given with •vardenafil—avoid vardenafil for 6 hours after alpha-blockers
- Vasodilator Antihypertensives: enhanced hypotensive effect when alpha-blockers given with hydralazine, minoxidil or nitroprusside

**Alpha-blockers (post-synaptic)** *see* Alpha-blockers
**Alprazolam** *see* Anxiolytics and Hypnotics
**Alprostadil** *see* Prostaglandins
**Aluminium Hydroxide** *see* Antacids

**Amantadine**
- Antimuscarinics: increased risk of antimuscarinic side-effects when amantadine given with antimuscarinics
- Antipsychotics: increased risk of extrapyramidal side-effects when amantadine given with antipsychotics
- Bupropion: increased risk of side-effects when amantadine given with bupropion
- Domperidone: increased risk of extrapyramidal side-effects when amantadine given with domperidone
- • Memantine: increased risk of CNS toxicity when amantadine given with •memantine (manufacturer of memantine advises avoid concomitant use); effects of dopaminergics possibly enhanced by memantine
- Methyldopa: increased risk of extrapyramidal side-effects when amantadine given with methyldopa; antiparkinsonian effect of dopaminergics antagonised by methyldopa
- Metoclopramide: increased risk of extrapyramidal side-effects when amantadine given with metoclopramide
- Tetrabenazine: increased risk of extrapyramidal side-effects when amantadine given with tetrabenazine

**Amikacin** *see* Aminoglycosides
**Amiloride** *see* Diuretics

**Aminoglycosides**
- Agalsidase Beta: gentamicin possibly inhibits effects of agalsidase beta (manufacturer of agalsidase beta advises avoid concomitant use)
- Analgesics: plasma concentration of amikacin and gentamicin in neonates possibly increased by indometacin
- Antibacterials: neomycin reduces absorption of phenoxymethylpenicillin; increased risk of nephrotoxicity when aminoglycosides given with colistin or polymyxins; increased risk of nephrotoxicity and ototoxicity when aminoglycosides given with capreomycin, teicoplanin or vancomycin
- • Anticoagulants: experience in anticoagulant clinics suggests that INR possibly altered when neomycin (given for local action on gut) is given with •coumarins or •phenindione
- Antidiabetics: neomycin possibly enhances hypoglycaemic effect of acarbose, also severity of gastro-intestinal effects increased
- Antifungals: increased risk of nephrotoxicity when aminoglycosides given with amphotericin
- Bisphosphonates: increased risk of hypocalcaemia when aminoglycosides given with bisphosphonates
- Cardiac Glycosides: gentamicin possibly increases plasma concentration of digoxin; neomycin reduces absorption of digoxin
- • Ciclosporin: increased risk of nephrotoxicity when aminoglycosides given with •ciclosporin

**Aminoglycosides** *(continued)*
- Cytotoxics: neomycin possibly reduces absorption of methotrexate; increased risk of nephrotoxicity and possibly of ototoxicity when aminoglycosides given with •platinum compounds
- Diuretics: increased risk of otoxicity when aminoglycosides given with •loop diuretics
- Muscle Relaxants: aminoglycosides enhance effects of •non-depolarising muscle relaxants and •suxamethonium

Oestrogens: antibacterials that do not induce liver enzymes possibly reduce contraceptive effect of oestrogens (risk probably small, see p. 408)
- Parasympathomimetics: aminoglycosides antagonise effects of •neostigmine and •pyridostigmine
- Tacrolimus: increased risk of nephrotoxicity when aminoglycosides given with •tacrolimus

Vitamins: neomycin possibly reduces absorption of vitamin A

**Aminophylline** *see* Theophylline

**Aminosalicylates**

Cardiac Glycosides: sulfasalazine possibly reduces absorption of digoxin

Cytotoxics: possible increased risk of leucopenia when aminosalicylates given with azathioprine or mercaptopurine

Folates: sulfasalazine possibly reduces absorption of folic acid

**Amiodarone**

*Note.* Amiodarone has a long half-life; there is a potential for drug interactions to occur for several weeks (or even months) after treatment with it has been stopped

Agalsidase Beta: amiodarone possibly inhibits effects of agalsidase beta (manufacturer of agalsidase beta advises avoid concomitant use)

Anaesthetics, Local: increased myocardial depression when anti-arrhythmics given with bupivacaine, levobupivacaine or prilocaine
- Anti-arrhythmics: increased myocardial depression when anti-arrhythmics given with other •anti-arrhythmics; increased risk of ventricular arrhythmias when amiodarone given with •disopyramide—avoid concomitant use; amiodarone increases plasma concentration of •flecainide (halve dose of flecainide); amiodarone increases plasma concentration of •procainamide and •quinidine (increased risk of ventricular arrhythmias—avoid concomitant use)
- Antibacterials: increased risk of ventricular arrhythmias when amiodarone given with parenteral •erythromycin—avoid concomitant use; increased risk of ventricular arrhythmias when amiodarone given with •moxifloxacin—avoid concomitant use; increased risk of ventricular arrhythmias when amiodarone given with •sulfamethoxazole and •trimethoprim (as co-trimoxazole)—avoid concomitant use of co-trimoxazole
- Anticoagulants: amiodarone inhibits metabolism of •coumarins and •phenindione (enhanced anticoagulant effect)
- Antidepressants: increased risk of ventricular arrhythmias when amiodarone given with •tricyclics—avoid concomitant use
- Antiepileptics: amiodarone inhibits metabolism of •phenytoin (increased plasma concentration)
- Antihistamines: increased risk of ventricular arrhythmias when amiodarone given with •mizolastine—avoid concomitant use
- Antimalarials: avoidance of amiodarone advised by manufacturer of •artemether/lumefantrine (risk of ventricular arrhythmias); increased risk of ventricular arrhythmias when amiodarone given

**Amiodarone**
- Antimalarials *(continued)* with •chloroquine and hydroxychloroquine, •mefloquine or •quinine—avoid concomitant use
- Antipsychotics: increased risk of ventricular arrhythmias when anti-arrhythmics that prolong the QT interval given with •antipsychotics that prolong the QT interval; increased risk of ventricular arrhythmias when amiodarone given with •amisulpride, •haloperidol, •phenothiazines, •pimozide or •sertindole—avoid concomitant use
- Antivirals: plasma concentration of amiodarone possibly increased by •amprenavir (increased risk of ventricular arrhythmias—avoid concomitant use); plasma concentration of amiodarone possibly increased by •atazanavir; increased risk of ventricular arrhythmias when amiodarone given with •nelfinavir—avoid concomitant use; plasma concentration of amiodarone increased by •ritonavir (increased risk of ventricular arrhythmias—avoid concomitant use)
- Beta-blockers: increased risk of bradycardia, AV block and myocardial depression when amiodarone given with •beta-blockers; increased myocardial depression when anti-arrhythmics given with •beta-blockers; increased risk of ventricular arrhythmias when amiodarone given with •sotalol—avoid concomitant use
- Calcium-channel Blockers: increased risk of bradycardia, AV block and myocardial depression when amiodarone given with •diltiazem or •verapamil
- Cardiac Glycosides: amiodarone increases plasma concentration of •digoxin (halve dose of digoxin)

Ciclosporin: amiodarone possibly increases plasma concentration of ciclosporin

Diuretics: increased cardiac toxicity with amiodarone if hypokalaemia occurs with acetazolamide, loop diuretics or thiazides and related diuretics; amiodarone increases plasma concentration of eplerenone (reduce dose of eplerenone)
- Dolasetron: increased risk of ventricular arrhythmias when amiodarone given with •dolasetron—avoid concomitant use

$5HT_3$ Antagonists: caution with anti-arrhythmics advised by manufacturer of tropisetron (risk of ventricular arrhythmias)
- Ivabradine: increased risk of ventricular arrhythmias when amiodarone given with •ivabradine
- Lipid-regulating Drugs: increased risk of myopathy when amiodarone given with •simvastatin
- Lithium: manufacturer of amiodarone advises avoid concomitant use with •lithium (risk of ventricular arrhythmias)

Orlistat: plasma concentration of amiodarone possibly reduced by orlistat
- Pentamidine Isetionate: increased risk of ventricular arrhythmias when amiodarone given with •pentamidine isetionate—avoid concomitant use

Thyroid Hormones: for concomitant use of amiodarone and thyroid hormones see p. 79

Ulcer-healing Drugs: plasma concentration of amiodarone increased by cimetidine

**Amisulpride** *see* Antipsychotics

**Amitriptyline** *see* Antidepressants, Tricyclic

**Amlodipine** *see* Calcium-channel Blockers

**Amobarbital** *see* Barbiturates

**Amoxapine** *see* Antidepressants, Tricyclic

**Amoxicillin** *see* Penicillins

**Amphotericin**

*Note.* Close monitoring required with concomitant administration of nephrotoxic drugs or cytotoxics

Antibacterials: increased risk of nephrotoxicity when amphotericin given with aminoglycosides or polymyxins; possible increased risk of nephrotoxicity when amphotericin given with vancomycin

Antifungals: amphotericin reduces renal excretion and increases cellular uptake of flucytosine (toxicity possibly increased); effects of amphotericin possibly antagonised by imidazoles and triazoles

• Cardiac Glycosides: hypokalaemia caused by amphotericin increases cardiac toxicity with •cardiac glycosides

• Ciclosporin: increased risk of nephrotoxicity when amphotericin given with •ciclosporin

• Corticosteroids: increased risk of hypokalaemia when amphotericin given with •corticosteroids—avoid concomitant use unless corticosteroids needed to control reactions

Diuretics: increased risk of hypokalaemia when amphotericin given with loop diuretics or thiazides and related diuretics

Pentamidine Isetionate: possible increased risk of nephrotoxicity when amphotericin given with pentamidine isetionate

• Tacrolimus: increased risk of nephrotoxicity when amphotericin given with •tacrolimus

**Ampicillin** *see* Penicillins

**Amprenavir**

*Note.* Fosamprenavir is a prodrug of amprenavir—see also Amprenavir

Analgesics: amprenavir reduces plasma concentration of methadone

Antacids: absorption of amprenavir possibly reduced by antacids

• Anti-arrhythmics: amprenavir possibly increases plasma concentration of •amiodarone, •flecainide, •propafenone and •quinidine (increased risk of ventricular arrhythmias—avoid concomitant use); amprenavir possibly increases plasma concentration of •lidocaine (lignocaine)—avoid concomitant use

• Antibacterials: plasma concentration of both drugs increased when amprenavir given with erythromycin; amprenavir increases plasma concentration of •rifabutin (reduce dose of rifabutin); plasma concentration of amprenavir significantly reduced by •rifampicin—avoid concomitant use; amprenavir possibly increases plasma concentration of dapsone

Anticoagulants: amprenavir may enhance or reduce anticoagulant effect of coumarins

• Antidepressants: plasma concentration of amprenavir reduced by •St John's wort—avoid concomitant use; amprenavir possibly increases side-effects of tricyclics

Antiepileptics: amprenavir possibly increases plasma concentration of carbamazepine; plasma concentration of amprenavir possibly reduced by phenytoin

Antifungals: amprenavir increases plasma concentration of ketoconazole; amprenavir possibly increases plasma concentration of itraconazole

Antihistamines: amprenavir possibly increases plasma concentration of loratadine

• Antimalarials: avoidance of amprenavir advised by manufacturer of •artemether/lumefantrine

Antimuscarinics: avoidance of amprenavir advised by manufacturer of tolterodine

• Antipsychotics: amprenavir possibly inhibits metabolism of •aripiprazole (reduce dose of aripiprazole); amprenavir possibly increases plasma concentration of clozapine; amprenavir increases plasma concentration of •pimozide and •sertindole (increased risk of ventricular arrhythmias—avoid concomitant use)

• Antivirals: plasma concentration of amprenavir reduced by efavirenz and •tipranavir; plasma concentration of amprenavir reduced by lopinavir, effect on lopinavir plasma concentration not predictable; plasma concentration of amprenavir possibly reduced by nevirapine; plasma concentration of amprenavir increased by ritonavir

• Anxiolytics and Hypnotics: increased risk of prolonged sedation and respiratory depression when amprenavir given with •alprazolam, clonazepam, •diazepam, •flurazepam or •midazolam

Barbiturates: plasma concentration of amprenavir possibly reduced by phenobarbital

Calcium-channel Blockers: amprenavir possibly increases plasma concentration of diltiazem, nicardipine, nifedipine and nimodipine

• Cilostazol: amprenavir possibly increases plasma concentration of •cilostazol—avoid concomitant use

• Ergot Alkaloids: increased risk of ergotism when amprenavir given with •ergotamine and methysergide—avoid concomitant use

• Lipid-regulating Drugs: possible increased risk of myopathy when amprenavir given with atorvastatin; possible increased risk of myopathy when amprenavir given with •simvastatin—avoid concomitant use

Oestrogens: amprenavir possibly reduces contraceptive effect of oestrogens

Progestogens: amprenavir possibly reduces contraceptive effect of progestogens

Sildenafil: amprenavir possibly increases plasma concentration of sildenafil— reduce initial dose of sildenafil

Ulcer-healing Drugs: amprenavir possibly increases plasma concentration of cimetidine

Vardenafil: amprenavir possibly increases plasma concentration of vardenafil

**Anabolic Steroids**

• Anticoagulants: anabolic steroids enhance anticoagulant effect of •coumarins and •phenindione

Antidiabetics: anabolic steroids possibly enhance hypoglycaemic effect of antidiabetics

**Anaesthetics, General**

*Note. See also* Surgery and Long-term Medication, p. 632

ACE Inhibitors: enhanced hypotensive effect when general anaesthetics given with ACE inhibitors

• Adrenergic Neurone Blockers: enhanced hypotensive effect when general anaesthetics given with •adrenergic neurone blockers

• Alpha-blockers: enhanced hypotensive effect when general anaesthetics given with •alpha-blockers

Angiotensin-II Receptor Antagonists: enhanced hypotensive effect when general anaesthetics given with angiotensin-II receptor antagonists

Antibacterials: general anaesthetics possibly potentiate hepatotoxicity of isoniazid; effects of thiopental enhanced by sulphonamides; hypersensitivity-like reactions can occur when general anaesthetics given with intravenous vancomycin

• Antidepressants: Because of hazardous interactions between general anaesthetics and •MAOIs, MAOIs should normally be stopped 2 weeks before surgery; increased risk of arrhythmias and hypotension when general anaesthetics given with tricyclics

**Anaesthetics, General** *(continued)*
- • Antipsychotics: enhanced hypotensive effect when general anaesthetics given with •antipsychotics
- Anxiolytics and Hypnotics: increased sedative effect when general anaesthetics given with anxiolytics and hypnotics
- Beta-blockers: enhanced hypotensive effect when general anaesthetics given with beta-blockers
- • Calcium-channel Blockers: enhanced hypotensive effect when general anaesthetics or isoflurane given with calcium-channel blockers; general anaesthetics enhance hypotensive effect of •verapamil (also AV delay)
- Clonidine: enhanced hypotensive effect when general anaesthetics given with clonidine
- • Cytotoxics: nitrous oxide increases antifolate effect of •methotrexate—avoid concomitant use
- Diazoxide: enhanced hypotensive effect when general anaesthetics given with diazoxide
- Diuretics: enhanced hypotensive effect when general anaesthetics given with diuretics
- • Dopaminergics: increased risk of arrhythmias when volatile liquid general anaesthetics given with •levodopa
- Ergot Alkaloids: halothane reduces effects of ergometrine on the parturient uterus
- • Memantine: increased risk of CNS toxicity when ketamine given with •memantine (manufacturer of memantine advises avoid concomitant use)
- Methyldopa: enhanced hypotensive effect when general anaesthetics given with methyldopa
- Moxonidine: enhanced hypotensive effect when general anaesthetics given with moxonidine
- Muscle Relaxants: volatile liquid general anaesthetics enhance effects of non-depolarising muscle relaxants and suxamethonium
- Nitrates: enhanced hypotensive effect when general anaesthetics given with nitrates
- Oxytocin: oxytocic effect possibly reduced, also enhanced hypotensive effect and risk of arrhythmias when volatile liquid general anaesthetics given with oxytocin
- • Sympathomimetics: increased risk of arrhythmias when volatile liquid general anaesthetics given with •adrenaline (epinephrine); increased risk of hypertension when volatile liquid general anaesthetics given with •methylphenidate
- Theophylline: increased risk of convulsions when ketamine given with theophylline; increased risk of arrhythmias when halothane given with theophylline
- Vasodilator Antihypertensives: enhanced hypotensive effect when general anaesthetics given with hydralazine, minoxidil or nitroprusside

**Anaesthetics, General (intravenous)** *see* Anaesthetics, General

**Anaesthetics, General (volatile liquids)** *see* Anaesthetics, General

**Anaesthetics, Local** *see* Bupivacaine, Levobupivacaine, Lidocaine (lignocaine), Prilocaine, and Ropivacaine

**Anagrelide**
- • Cilostazol: manufacturer of anagrelide advises avoid concomitant use with •cilostazol
- • Phosphodiesterase Inhibitors: manufacturer of anagrelide advises avoid concomitant use with •enoximone and •milrinone

**Anakinra**
- • Adalimumab: avoid concomitant use of anakinra with •adalimumab
- • Etanercept: increased risk of side-effects when anakinra given with •etanercept—avoid concomitant use

**Anakinra** *(continued)*
- • Infliximab: avoid concomitant use of anakinra with •infliximab
- • Vaccines: avoid concomitant use of anakinra with live •vaccines (see p. 611)

**Analgesics** *see* Aspirin, Nefopam, NSAIDs, Opioid Analgesics, and Paracetamol

**Angiotensin-II Receptor Antagonists**
- ACE Inhibitors: enhanced hypotensive effect when angiotensin-II receptor antagonists given with ACE inhibitors
- Adrenergic Neurone Blockers: enhanced hypotensive effect when angiotensin-II receptor antagonists given with adrenergic neurone blockers
- Alcohol: enhanced hypotensive effect when angiotensin-II receptor antagonists given with alcohol
- Aldesleukin: enhanced hypotensive effect when angiotensin-II receptor antagonists given with aldesleukin
- Alpha-blockers: enhanced hypotensive effect when angiotensin-II receptor antagonists given with alpha-blockers
- Anaesthetics, General: enhanced hypotensive effect when angiotensin-II receptor antagonists given with general anaesthetics
- Analgesics: increased risk of renal impairment when angiotensin-II receptor antagonists given with NSAIDs, also hypotensive effect antagonised; increased risk of hyperkalaemia when angiotensin-II receptor antagonists given with ketorolac; risk of renal impairment when angiotensin-II receptor antagonists given with aspirin (in doses over 300 mg daily), also hypotensive effect antagonised
- Anticoagulants: increased risk of hyperkalaemia when angiotensin-II receptor antagonists given with heparin
- Antidepressants: hypotensive effect of angiotensin-II receptor antagonists possibly enhanced by MAOIs
- Antipsychotics: enhanced hypotensive effect when angiotensin-II receptor antagonists given with antipsychotics
- Anxiolytics and Hypnotics: enhanced hypotensive effect when angiotensin-II receptor antagonists given with anxiolytics and hypnotics
- Beta-blockers: enhanced hypotensive effect when angiotensin-II receptor antagonists given with beta-blockers
- Calcium-channel Blockers: enhanced hypotensive effect when angiotensin-II receptor antagonists given with calcium-channel blockers
- • Cardiac Glycosides: telmisartan increases plasma concentration of •digoxin
- • Ciclosporin: increased risk of hyperkalaemia when angiotensin-II receptor antagonists given with •ciclosporin
- Clonidine: enhanced hypotensive effect when angiotensin-II receptor antagonists given with clonidine
- Corticosteroids: hypotensive effect of angiotensin-II receptor antagonists antagonised by corticosteroids
- Diazoxide: enhanced hypotensive effect when angiotensin-II receptor antagonists given with diazoxide
- • Diuretics: enhanced hypotensive effect when angiotensin-II receptor antagonists given with •diuretics; increased risk of hyperkalaemia when angiotensin-II receptor antagonists given with •potassium-sparing diuretics and aldosterone antagonists

**Angiotensin-II Receptor Antagonists** *(continued)*
- Dopaminergics: enhanced hypotensive effect when angiotensin-II receptor antagonists given with levodopa
- Epoetin: antagonism of hypotensive effect and increased risk of hyperkalaemia when angiotensin-II receptor antagonists given with epoetin
- • Lithium: angiotensin-II receptor antagonists reduce excretion of •lithium (increased plasma concentration)
- Methyldopa: enhanced hypotensive effect when angiotensin-II receptor antagonists given with methyldopa
- Moxisylyte (thymoxamine): enhanced hypotensive effect when angiotensin-II receptor antagonists given with moxisylyte
- Moxonidine: enhanced hypotensive effect when angiotensin-II receptor antagonists given with moxonidine
- Muscle Relaxants: enhanced hypotensive effect when angiotensin-II receptor antagonists given with baclofen or tizanidine
- Nitrates: enhanced hypotensive effect when angiotensin-II receptor antagonists given with nitrates
- Oestrogens: hypotensive effect of angiotensin-II receptor antagonists antagonised by oestrogens
- • Potassium Salts: increased risk of hyperkalaemia when angiotensin-II receptor antagonists given with •potassium salts
- Progestogens: risk of hyperkalaemia when angiotensin-II receptor antagonists given with drospirenone (monitor serum potassium during first cycle)
- Prostaglandins: enhanced hypotensive effect when angiotensin-II receptor antagonists given with alprostadil
- Vasodilator Antihypertensives: enhanced hypotensive effect when angiotensin-II receptor antagonists given with hydralazine, minoxidil or nitroprusside

**Anion-exchange Resins** *see* Colestipol and Colestyramine

**Antacids**

*Note.* Antacids should preferably not be taken at the same time as other drugs since they may impair absorption

- ACE Inhibitors: antacids possibly reduce absorption of ACE inhibitors; antacids reduce absorption of captopril, enalapril and fosinopril
- Analgesics: antacids reduce absorption of diflunisal; alkaline urine due to some antacids increases excretion of aspirin
- Anti-arrhythmics: alkaline urine due to some antacids reduces excretion of quinidine (plasma concentration of quinidine occasionally increased)
- Antibacterials: antacids reduce absorption of azithromycin, cefaclor, cefpodoxime, ciprofloxacin, isoniazid, levofloxacin, moxifloxacin, norfloxacin, ofloxacin, rifampicin and tetracyclines; oral magnesium salts (as magnesium trisilicate) reduce absorption of nitrofurantoin
- Antiepileptics: antacids reduce absorption of gabapentin and phenytoin
- Antifungals: antacids reduce absorption of itraconazole and ketoconazole
- Antihistamines: antacids reduce absorption of fexofenadine
- Antimalarials: antacids reduce absorption of chloroquine and hydroxychloroquine; oral magnesium salts (as magnesium trisilicate) reduce absorption of proguanil
- Antipsychotics: antacids reduce absorption of phenothiazines and sulpiride

**Antacids** *(continued)*
- Antivirals: antacids possibly reduce absorption of amprenavir; antacids possibly reduce plasma concentration of atazanavir; antacids reduce absorption of tipranavir and zalcitabine
- Bile Acids: antacids possibly reduce absorption of bile acids
- Bisphosphonates: antacids reduce absorption of bisphosphonates
- Cardiac Glycosides: antacids possibly reduce absorption of digoxin
- Corticosteroids: antacids reduce absorption of deflazacort
- Cytotoxics: antacids reduce absorption of mycophenolate mofetil
- Dipyridamole: antacids possibly reduce absorption of dipyridamole
- Iron: oral magnesium salts (as magnesium trisilicate) reduce absorption of *oral* iron
- Lipid-regulating Drugs: antacids reduce absorption of rosuvastatin
- Lithium: sodium bicarbonate increases excretion of lithium (reduced plasma concentration)
- Penicillamine: antacids reduce absorption of penicillamine
- Ulcer-healing Drugs: antacids possibly reduce absorption of lansoprazole

**Antazoline** *see* Antihistamines

**Anti-arrhythmics** *see* Adenosine, Amiodarone, Bretylium, Disopyramide, Flecainide, Lidocaine (lignocaine), Mexiletine, Procainamide, Propafenone, and Quinidine

**Antibacterials** *see* individual drugs

**Antibiotics (cytotoxic)** *see* Bleomycin, Doxorubicin, Epirubicin

**Anticoagulants** *see* Coumarins, Heparins, and Phenindione

**Antidepressants** *see* Antidepressants, SSRI; Antidepressants, Tricyclic; Antidepressants, Tricyclic (related); MAOIs; Mirtazapine; Moclobemide; Reboxetine; St John's Wort; Tryptophan; Venlafaxine

**Antidepressants, Noradrenaline Re-uptake Inhibitors** *see* Reboxetine

**Antidepressants, SSRI**
- Alcohol: sedative effects possibly increased when SSRIs given with alcohol
- Anaesthetics, Local: fluvoxamine inhibits metabolism of ropivacaine—avoid prolonged administration of ropivacaine
- • Analgesics: increased risk of bleeding when SSRIs given with •NSAIDs or •aspirin; fluvoxamine possibly increases plasma concentration of methadone; increased risk of CNS toxicity when SSRIs given with •tramadol
- • Anti-arrhythmics: fluoxetine increases plasma concentration of flecainide; fluvoxamine inhibits metabolism of •mexiletine (increased risk of toxicity); paroxetine possibly inhibits metabolism of propafenone (increased risk of toxicity)
- • Anticoagulants: SSRIs possibly enhance anticoagulant effect of •coumarins
- • Antidepressants: avoidance of fluvoxamine advised by manufacturer of •reboxetine; possible increased serotonergic effects when SSRIs given with duloxetine; fluvoxamine inhibits metabolism of •duloxetine—avoid concomitant use; sertraline should not be started until 2 weeks after stopping •MAOIs, also MAOIs should not be started until at least 2 weeks after stopping sertraline; citalopram, escitalopram, fluvoxamine or paroxetine should not be started until 2 weeks after stopping •MAOIs, also MAOIs should not be started until at least 1 week after stopping

**Antidepressants, SSRI**

- Antidepressants *(continued)*
  citalopram, escitalopram, fluvoxamine or paroxetine; fluoxetine should not be started until 2 weeks after stopping •MAOIs, also MAOIs should not be started until at least 5 weeks after stopping fluoxetine; CNS effects of SSRIs increased by •MAOIs (risk of serious toxicity); increased risk of CNS toxicity when escitalopram given with •moclobemide, preferably avoid concomitant use; after stopping citalopram, fluvoxamine or paroxetine do not start •moclobemide for at least 1 week; after stopping fluoxetine do not start •moclobemide for 5 weeks; after stopping sertraline do not start •moclobemide for 2 weeks; increased serotonergic effects when SSRIs given with •St John's wort—avoid concomitant use; SSRIs increase plasma concentration of some •tricyclics; agitation and nausea may occur when SSRIs given with •tryptophan
- Antiepileptics: SSRIs antagonise anticonvulsant effect of •antiepileptics (convulsive threshold lowered); fluoxetine and fluvoxamine increase plasma concentration of •carbamazepine; plasma concentration of paroxetine reduced by carbamazepine, phenytoin and primidone; fluoxetine and fluvoxamine increase plasma concentration of •phenytoin

Antihistamines: antidepressant effect of SSRIs possibly antagonised by cyproheptadine

- Antimalarials: avoidance of antidepressants advised by manufacturer of •artemether/lumefantrine

Antimuscarinics: paroxetine increases plasma concentration of procyclidine

- Antipsychotics: fluoxetine increases plasma concentration of •clozapine, •haloperidol, risperidone, •sertindole and •zotepine; paroxetine inhibits metabolism of perphenazine (reduce dose of perphenazine); fluoxetine and paroxetine possibly inhibit metabolism of •aripiprazole (reduce dose of aripiprazole); fluvoxamine, paroxetine and sertraline increase plasma concentration of •clozapine; citalopram possibly increases plasma concentration of clozapine (increased risk of toxicity); fluvoxamine increases plasma concentration of olanzapine; sertraline increases plasma concentration of •pimozide (increased risk of ventricular arrhythmias—avoid concomitant use); paroxetine possibly increases plasma concentration of risperidone (increased risk of toxicity); paroxetine increases plasma concentration of •sertindole
- Antivirals: plasma concentration of sertraline reduced by efavirenz; plasma concentration of SSRIs possibly increased by •ritonavir

Anxiolytics and Hypnotics: fluvoxamine increases plasma concentration of some benzodiazepines; sedative effects possibly increased when sertraline given with zolpidem

Barbiturates: SSRIs antagonise anticonvulsant effect of barbiturates (convulsive threshold lowered); plasma concentration of paroxetine reduced by phenobarbital

Beta-blockers: paroxetine possibly increases plasma concentration of metoprolol (enhanced effect); citalopram and escitalopram increase plasma concentration of metoprolol; fluvoxamine increases plasma concentration of propranolol

- Dopaminergics: caution with paroxetine advised by manufacturer of entacapone; increased risk of CNS toxicity when SSRIs given with •rasagiline; fluvoxamine should not be started until 2 weeks after stopping •rasagiline; fluoxetine should not be started until 2 weeks after stopping •rasagiline, also rasagiline should not be started until at least 5 weeks after stopping fluoxetine; increased risk of hypertension and CNS excitation when fluoxetine given with •selegiline (selegiline should not be started until 5 weeks after stopping fluoxetine, avoid fluoxetine for 2 weeks after stopping selegiline); theoretical risk of serotonin syndrome if citalopram given with selegiline (especially if dose of selegiline exceeds 10 mg daily); manufacturer of escitalopram advises caution with selegiline; increased risk of hypertension and CNS excitation when paroxetine or sertraline given with •selegiline (selegiline should not be started until 2 weeks after stopping paroxetine or sertraline, avoid paroxetine or sertraline for 2 weeks after stopping selegiline); increased risk of hypertension and CNS excitation when fluvoxamine given with •selegiline (selegiline should not be started until 1 week after stopping fluvoxamine, avoid fluvoxamine for 2 weeks after stopping selegiline)
- $5HT_1$ Agonists: fluvoxamine inhibits the metabolism of frovatriptan; possible increased serotonergic effects when SSRIs given with frovatriptan; increased risk of CNS toxicity when citalopram, escitalopram, fluoxetine, fluvoxamine or paroxetine given with •sumatriptan; increased risk of CNS toxicity when sertraline given with •sumatriptan (manufacturer of sertraline advises avoid concomitant use); fluvoxamine possibly inhibits metabolism of zolmitriptan (reduce dose of zolmitriptan)
- Lithium: Increased risk of CNS effects when SSRIs given with •lithium (lithium toxicity reported)

Parasympathomimetics: paroxetine increases plasma concentration of galantamine

- Sibutramine: increased risk of CNS toxicity when SSRIs given with •sibutramine (manufacturer of sibutramine advises avoid concomitant use)

Sympathomimetics: metabolism of SSRIs possibly inhibited by methylphenidate

- Theophylline: fluvoxamine increases plasma concentration of •theophylline (concomitant use should usually be avoided, but where not possible halve theophylline dose and monitor plasma-theophylline concentration)

Ulcer-healing Drugs: plasma concentration of citalopram, escitalopram and sertraline increased by cimetidine; plasma concentration of escitalopram increased by omeprazole

**Antidepressants, SSRI (related)** *see* Duloxetine and Venlafaxine

**Antidepressants, Tricyclic**

Adrenergic Neurone Blockers: tricyclics antagonise hypotensive effect of adrenergic neurone blockers

- Alcohol: increased sedative effect when tricyclics given with •alcohol

$Alpha_2$-adrenoceptor Stimulants: avoidance of tricyclics advised by manufacturer of apraclonidine and brimonidine

Anaesthetics, General: increased risk of arrhythmias and hypotension when tricyclics given with general anaesthetics

- Analgesics: increased risk of CNS toxicity when tricyclics given with •tramadol; side-effects possibly increased when tricyclics given with nefopam; sedative effects possibly increased when tricyclics given with opioid analgesics

**Antidepressants, Tricyclic** *(continued)*

- Anti-arrhythmics: increased risk of ventricular arrhythmias when tricyclics given with •amiodarone—avoid concomitant use; increased risk of ventricular arrhythmias when tricyclics given with •disopyramide, •flecainide, •procainamide or •quinidine; increased risk of arrhythmias when tricyclics given with •propafenone
- Antibacterials: increased risk of ventricular arrhythmias when tricyclics given with •moxifloxacin—avoid concomitant use; plasma concentration of tricyclics possibly reduced by rifampicin
- Anticoagulants: tricyclics may enhance or reduce anticoagulant effect of •coumarins
- Antidepressants: possible increased serotonergic effects when amitriptyline or clomipramine given with duloxetine; increased risk of hypertension and CNS excitation when tricyclics given with •MAOIs, tricyclics should not be started until 2 weeks after stopping MAOIs (3 weeks if starting clomipramine or imipramine), also MAOIs should not be started for at least 1–2 weeks after stopping tricyclics (3 weeks in the case of clomipramine or imipramine); after stopping tricyclics do not start •moclobemide for at least 1 week; plasma concentration of some tricyclics increased by •SSRIs; plasma concentration of amitriptyline reduced by St John's wort
- Antiepileptics: tricyclics antagonise anticonvulsant effect of •antiepileptics (convulsive threshold lowered); metabolism of tricyclics accelerated by •carbamazepine (reduced plasma concentration and reduced effect); plasma concentration of tricyclics possibly reduced by •phenytoin; tricyclics antagonises anticonvulsant effect of •primidone (convulsive threshold lowered), also metabolism of tricyclics possibly accelerated (reduced plasma concentration)

Antifungals: plasma concentration of imipramine and nortriptyline possibly increased by terbinafine

Antihistamines: increased antimuscarinic and sedative effects when tricyclics given with antihistamines

- Antimalarials: avoidance of antidepressants advised by manufacturer of •artemether/lumefantrine

Antimuscarinics: increased risk of antimuscarinic side-effects when tricyclics given with antimuscarinics

- Antipsychotics: plasma concentration of tricyclics increased by •antipsychotics—possibly increased risk of ventricular arrhythmias; possibly increased antimuscarinic side-effects when tricyclics given with clozapine; increased risk of antimuscarinic side-effects when tricyclics given with phenothiazines; increased risk of ventricular arrhythmias when tricyclics given with •pimozide—avoid concomitant use
- Antivirals: side-effects of tricyclics possibly increased by amprenavir; plasma concentration of tricyclics possibly increased by •ritonavir

Anxiolytics and Hypnotics: increased sedative effect when tricyclics given with anxiolytics and hypnotics

- Barbiturates: tricyclics antagonises anticonvulsant effect of •barbiturates (convulsive threshold lowered), also metabolism of tricyclics possibly accelerated (reduced plasma concentration)
- Beta-blockers: increased risk of ventricular arrhythmias when tricyclics given with •sotalol

**Antidepressants, Tricyclic** *(continued)*

Calcium-channel Blockers: plasma concentration of tricyclics possibly increased by diltiazem and verapamil; plasma concentration of imipramine increased by diltiazem and verapamil

- Clonidine: tricyclics antagonise hypotensive effect of •clonidine, also increased risk of hypertension on clonidine withdrawal

Disulfiram: metabolism of tricyclics inhibited by disulfiram (increased plasma concentration); concomitant amitriptyline reported to increase disulfiram reaction with alcohol

Diuretics: increased risk of postural hypotension when tricyclics given with diuretics

- Dopaminergics: caution with tricyclics advised by manufacturer of entacapone; increased risk of CNS toxicity when tricyclics given with •rasagiline; CNS toxicity reported when tricyclics given with •selegiline

Lithium: risk of toxicity when tricyclics given with lithium

Muscle Relaxants: tricyclics enhance muscle relaxant effect of baclofen

Nicorandil: tricyclics possibly enhance hypotensive effect of nicorandil

Nitrates: tricyclics reduce effects of sublingual tablets of nitrates (failure to dissolve under tongue owing to dry mouth)

Oestrogens: antidepressant effect of tricyclics antagonised by oestrogens (but side-effects of tricyclics possibly increased due to increased plasma concentration)

- Sibutramine: increased risk of CNS toxicity when tricyclics given with •sibutramine (manufacturer of sibutramine advises avoid concomitant use)
- Sympathomimetics: increased risk of hypertension and arrhythmias when tricyclics given with •adrenaline (epinephrine) (but local anaesthetics with adrenaline appear to be safe); metabolism of tricyclics possibly inhibited by methylphenidate; increased risk of hypertension and arrhythmias when tricyclics given with •noradrenaline (norepinephrine)

Thyroid Hormones: effects of tricyclics possibly enhanced by thyroid hormones; effects of amitriptyline and imipramine enhanced by thyroid hormones

Ulcer-healing Drugs: plasma concentration of tricyclics possibly increased by cimetidine; metabolism of amitriptyline, doxepin, imipramine and nortriptyline inhibited by cimetidine (increased plasma concentration)

**Antidepressants, Tricyclic (related)**

- Alcohol: increased sedative effect when tricyclic-related antidepressants given with •alcohol

Alpha$_2$-adrenoceptor Stimulants: avoidance of tricyclic-related antidepressants advised by manufacturer of apraclonidine and brimonidine

- Antidepressants: tricyclic-related antidepressants should not be started until 2 weeks after stopping •MAOIs, also MAOIs should not be started until at least 1–2 weeks after stopping tricyclic-related antidepressants; after stopping tricyclic-related antidepressants do not start •moclobemide for at least 1 week
- Antiepileptics: tricyclic-related antidepressants possibly antagonise anticonvulsant effect of •antiepileptics (convulsive threshold lowered); plasma concentration of mianserin reduced by •carbamazepine and •phenytoin; metabolism of mianserin accelerated by •primidone (reduced plasma concentration)

**Antidepressants, Tricyclic (related)** *(continued)*

Antihistamines: possible increased antimuscarinic and sedative effects when tricyclic-related antidepressants given with antihistamines

• Antimalarials: avoidance of antidepressants advised by manufacturer of •artemether/lumefantrine

Antimuscarinics: possibly increased antimuscarinic side-effects when tricyclic-related antidepressants given with antimuscarinics

• Antipsychotics: increased risk of ventricular arrhythmias when maprotiline given with •pimozide—avoid concomitant use

Anxiolytics and Hypnotics: increased sedative effect when tricyclic-related antidepressants given with anxiolytics and hypnotics

• Barbiturates: tricyclic-related antidepressants possibly antagonise anticonvulsant effect of •barbiturates (convulsive threshold lowered); metabolism of mianserin accelerated by •phenobarbital (reduced plasma concentration)

Diazoxide: enhanced hypotensive effect when tricyclic-related antidepressants given with diazoxide

Dopaminergics: caution with maprotiline advised by manufacturer of entacapone

Nitrates: tricyclic-related antidepressants possibly reduce effects of sublingual tablets of nitrates (failure to dissolve under tongue owing to dry mouth)

• Sibutramine: increased risk of CNS toxicity when tricyclic-related antidepressants given with •sibutramine (manufacturer of sibutramine advises avoid concomitant use)

Vasodilator Antihypertensives: enhanced hypotensive effect when tricyclic-related antidepressants given with hydralazine or nitroprusside

**Antidiabetics**

ACE Inhibitors: hypoglycaemic effect of insulin, metformin and sulphonylureas possibly enhanced by ACE inhibitors

Alcohol: hypoglycaemic effect of antidiabetics enhanced by alcohol; increased risk of lactic acidosis when metformin given with alcohol; flushing, in susceptible subjects, when chlorpropamide given with alcohol

Anabolic Steroids: hypoglycaemic effect of antidiabetics possibly enhanced by anabolic steroids

• Analgesics: effects of sulphonylureas possibly enhanced by •NSAIDs

Anti-arrhythmics: hypoglycaemic effect of gliclazide, insulin and metformin possibly enhanced by disopyramide

• Antibacterials: hypoglycaemic effect of acarbose possibly enhanced by neomycin, also severity of gastro-intestinal effects increased; effects of repaglinide enhanced by clarithromycin; effects of glibenclamide possibly enhanced by ciprofloxacin and norfloxacin; plasma concentration of nateglinide and repaglinide reduced by rifampicin; plasma concentration of rosiglitazone reduced by •rifampicin—consider increasing dose of rosiglitazone; effects of sulphonylureas enhanced by •chloramphenicol; metabolism of sulphonylureas possibly accelerated by •rifamycins (reduced effect); metabolism of chlorpropamide and tolbutamide accelerated by •rifamycins (reduced effect); effects of sulphonylureas rarely enhanced by sulphonamides and trimethoprim

• Anticoagulants: hypoglycaemic effect of sulphonylureas possibly enhanced by •coumarins, also possible changes to anticoagulant effect

**Antidiabetics** *(continued)*

Antidepressants: hypoglycaemic effect of insulin, metformin and sulphonylureas enhanced by MAOIs; hypoglycaemic effect of antidiabetics possibly enhanced by MAOIs

Antiepileptics: tolbutamide transiently increases plasma concentration of phenytoin (possibility of toxicity)

• Antifungals: plasma concentration of sulphonylureas increased by •fluconazole and •miconazole; hypoglycaemic effect of gliclazide and glipizide enhanced by •miconazole— avoid concomitant use; hypoglycaemic effect of nateglinide possibly enhanced by fluconazole; plasma concentration of sulphonylureas possibly increased by voriconazole

Antihistamines: thrombocyte count depressed when metformin given with ketotifen

Antipsychotics: hypoglycaemic effect of sulphonylureas possibly antagonised by phenothiazines

Antivirals: plasma concentration of tolbutamide possibly increased by ritonavir

Aprepitant: plasma concentration of tolbutamide reduced by aprepitant

Beta-blockers: warning signs of hypoglycaemia (such as tremor) with antidiabetics may be masked when given with beta-blockers; hypoglycaemic effect of insulin enhanced by beta-blockers

• Bosentan: plasma concentration of both drugs reduced when glibenclamide given with •bosentan (avoid concomitant use)

Calcium-channel Blockers: glucose tolerance occasionally impaired when insulin given with nifedipine

Cardiac Glycosides: acarbose possibly reduces plasma concentration of digoxin

Corticosteroids: hypoglycaemic effect of antidiabetics antagonised by corticosteroids

Cytotoxics: metabolism of rosiglitazone possibly inhibited by paclitaxel

Diazoxide: hypoglycaemic effect of antidiabetics antagonised by diazoxide

Diuretics: hypoglycaemic effect of antidiabetics antagonised by loop diuretics and thiazides and related diuretics; increased risk of hyponatraemia when chlorpropamide given with potassium-sparing diuretics and aldosterone antagonists plus thiazide; increased risk of hyponatraemia when chlorpropamide given with thiazides and related diuretics plus potassium-sparing diuretic

Hormone Antagonists: requirements for insulin, metformin, repaglinide and sulphonylureas possibly reduced by lanreotide; requirements for insulin, metformin, repaglinide and sulphonylureas possibly reduced by octreotide

Leflunomide: hypoglycaemic effect of tolbutamide possibly enhanced by leflunomide

• Lipid-regulating Drugs: hypoglycaemic effect of acarbose possibly enhanced by colestyramine; hypoglycaemic effect of nateglinide possibly enhanced by gemfibrozil; increased risk of severe hypoglycaemia when repaglinide given with •gemfibrozil—avoid concomitant use; plasma concentration of rosiglitazone increased by •gemfibrozil (consider reducing dose of rosiglitazone); may be improved glucose tolerance and an additive effect when insulin or sulphonylureas given with fibrates

Oestrogens: hypoglycaemic effect of antidiabetics antagonised by oestrogens

Orlistat: avoidance of acarbose advised by manufacturer of orlistat

**Antidiabetics** *(continued)*

Pancreatin: hypoglycaemic effect of acarbose antagonised by pancreatin

Probenecid: hypoglycaemic effect of chlorpropamide possibly enhanced by probenecid

Progestogens: hypoglycaemic effect of antidiabetics antagonised by progestogens

• Sulfinpyrazone: effects of sulphonylureas enhanced by •sulfinpyrazone

Testosterone: hypoglycaemic effect of antidiabetics possibly enhanced by testosterone

Ulcer-healing Drugs: excretion of metformin reduced by cimetidine (increased plasma concentration); hypoglycaemic effect of sulphonylureas enhanced by cimetidine

**Antiepileptics** *see* Carbamazepine, Ethosuximide, Gabapentin, Lamotrigine, Levetiracetam, Oxcarbazepine, Phenytoin, Primidone, Tiagabine, Topiramate, Valproate, Vigabatrin, and Zonisamide

**Antifungals** *see* Amphotericin; Antifungals, Imidazole; Antifungals, Triazole; Caspofungin; Flucytosine; Griseofulvin; Terbinafine

**Antifungals, Imidazole**

• Analgesics: ketoconazole inhibits metabolism of alfentanil (risk of prolonged or delayed respiratory depression); ketoconazole inhibits metabolism of •buprenorphine (reduce dose of buprenorphine)

Antacids: absorption of ketoconazole reduced by antacids

• Anti-arrhythmics: miconazole increases plasma concentration of •quinidine (increased risk of ventricular arrhythmias—avoid concomitant use)

• Antibacterials: metabolism of ketoconazole accelerated by •rifampicin (reduced plasma concentration), also plasma concentration of rifampicin may be reduced by ketoconazole; plasma concentration of ketoconazole possibly reduced by isoniazid

• Anticoagulants: ketoconazole enhances anticoagulant effect of •coumarins; miconazole enhances anticoagulant effect of •coumarins (miconazole oral gel and possibly vaginal formulations absorbed)

• Antidepressants: avoidance of imidazoles advised by manufacturer of •reboxetine; ketoconazole increases plasma concentration of mirtazapine

• Antidiabetics: miconazole enhances hypoglycaemic effect of •gliclazide and •glipizide— avoid concomitant use; miconazole increases plasma concentration of •sulphonylureas

• Antiepileptics: miconazole possibly increases plasma concentration of carbamazepine; miconazole enhances anticonvulsant effect of •phenytoin (plasma concentration of phenytoin increased); plasma concentration of ketoconazole reduced by •phenytoin

Antifungals: imidazoles possibly antagonise effects of amphotericin

• Antihistamines: manufacturer of loratadine advises ketoconazole possibly increases plasma concentration of loratadine; imidazoles possibly inhibit metabolism of •mizolastine (avoid concomitant use); ketoconazole inhibits metabolism of •mizolastine—avoid concomitant use

• Antimalarials: avoidance of imidazoles advised by manufacturer of •artemether/lumefantrine

Antimuscarinics: absorption of ketoconazole reduced by antimuscarinics; ketoconazole increases plasma concentration of solifenacin; avoidance of ketoconazole advised by manufacturer of tolterodine

• Antipsychotics: ketoconazole inhibits metabolism of •aripiprazole (reduce dose of aripiprazole); increased risk of ventricular arrhythmias when imidazoles given with •pimozide—avoid concomitant use; imidazoles possibly increase plasma concentration of quetiapine (reduce dose of quetiapine); possible increased risk of ventricular arrhythmias when imidazoles given with •sertindole—avoid concomitant use; increased risk of ventricular arrhythmias when ketoconazole given with •sertindole—avoid concomitant use

• Antivirals: plasma concentration of ketoconazole increased by amprenavir; ketoconazole inhibits the metabolism of indinavir; plasma concentration of ketoconazole reduced by •nevirapine—avoid concomitant use; combination of ketoconazole with •ritonavir may increase plasma concentration of either drug (or both); imidazoles possibly increase plasma concentration of saquinavir; ketoconazole increases plasma concentration of saquinavir

• Anxiolytics and Hypnotics: ketoconazole increases plasma concentration of •midazolam (risk of prolonged sedation)

Aprepitant: ketoconazole increases plasma concentration of aprepitant

Bosentan: ketoconazole possibly increases plasma concentration of bosentan

• Calcium-channel Blockers: ketoconazole inhibits metabolism of •felodipine (increased plasma concentration); avoidance of ketoconazole advised by manufacturer of lercanidipine; ketoconazole possibly inhibits metabolism of dihydropyridines (increased plasma concentration)

• Ciclosporin: ketoconazole inhibits metabolism of •ciclosporin (increased plasma concentration); miconazole possibly inhibits metabolism of •ciclosporin (increased plasma concentration)

• Cilostazol: ketoconazole possibly increases plasma concentration of •cilostazol—avoid concomitant use

Cinacalcet: ketoconazole inhibits metabolism of cinacalcet (increased plasma concentration)

Corticosteroids: ketoconazole possibly inhibits metabolism of corticosteroids; ketoconazole increases plasma concentration of inhaled budesonide and mometasone; ketoconazole inhibits the metabolism of methylprednisolone

Cytotoxics: *in vitro* studies suggest a possible interaction between ketoconazole and docetaxel (consult docetaxel product literature); ketoconazole inhibits metabolism of erlotinib (increased plasma concentration); ketoconazole increases plasma concentration of imatinib

• Diuretics: ketoconazole increases plasma concentration of •eplerenone—avoid concomitant use

• Ergot Alkaloids: increased risk of ergotism when imidazoles given with •ergotamine and methysergide—avoid concomitant use

• $5HT_1$ Agonists: ketoconazole increases plasma concentration of almotriptan (increased risk of toxicity); ketoconazole increases plasma concentration of •eletriptan (risk of toxicity)—avoid concomitant use

• Ivabradine: ketoconazole increases plasma concentration of •ivabradine—avoid concomitant use

• Lipid-regulating Drugs: possible increased risk of myopathy when imidazoles given with atorvastatin or simvastatin; increased risk of myopathy when ketoconazole given with •simvastatin (avoid concomitant use); possible

**Antifungals, Imidazole**

- Lipid-regulating Drugs *(continued)* increased risk of myopathy when miconazole given with •simvastatin—avoid concomitant use

  Oestrogens: anecdotal reports of contraceptive failure when imidazoles or ketoconazole given with oestrogens

  Parasympathomimetics: ketoconazole increases plasma concentration of galantamine

  Sildenafil: ketoconazole increases plasma concentration of sildenafil—reduce initial dose of sildenafil

- Sirolimus: ketoconazole increases plasma concentration of •sirolimus—avoid concomitant use; miconazole increases plasma concentration of •sirolimus
- Tacrolimus: imidazoles possibly increase plasma concentration of •tacrolimus; ketoconazole increases plasma concentration of •tacrolimus

  Tadalafil: ketoconazole increases plasma concentration of tadalafil

- Theophylline: ketoconazole possibly increases plasma concentration of •theophylline

  Ulcer-healing Drugs: absorption of ketoconazole reduced by histamine $H_2$-antagonists, proton pump inhibitors and sucralfate

- Vardenafil: ketoconazole increases plasma concentration of •vardenafil—avoid concomitant use

**Antifungals, Polyene** *see* Amphotericin

**Antifungals, Triazole**

*Note.* In general, fluconazole interactions relate to multiple-dose treatment

- Analgesics: fluconazole increases plasma concentration of celecoxib (halve dose of celecoxib); fluconazole increases plasma concentration of parecoxib (reduce dose of parecoxib); fluconazole inhibits metabolism of alfentanil (risk of prolonged or delayed respiratory depression); itraconazole possibly inhibits metabolism of alfentanil; voriconazole increases plasma concentration of •methadone (consider reducing dose of methadone)

  Antacids: absorption of itraconazole reduced by antacids

- Anti-arrhythmics: itraconazole and voriconazole increase plasma concentration of •quinidine (increased risk of ventricular arrhythmias—avoid concomitant use)
- Antibacterials: plasma concentration of itraconazole increased by clarithromycin; triazoles possibly increase plasma concentration of •rifabutin (increased risk of uveitis—reduce rifabutin dose); voriconazole increases plasma concentration of •rifabutin, also rifabutin reduces plasma concentration of voriconazole (increase dose of voriconazole and also monitor for rifabutin toxicity); fluconazole increases plasma concentration of •rifabutin (increased risk of uveitis—reduce rifabutin dose); plasma concentration of itraconazole reduced by •rifabutin—avoid concomitant use; plasma concentration of voriconazole reduced by •rifampicin—avoid concomitant use; metabolism of fluconazole and itraconazole accelerated by •rifampicin (reduced plasma concentration)
- Anticoagulants: fluconazole, itraconazole and voriconazole enhance anticoagulant effect of •coumarins
- Antidepressants: avoidance of triazoles advised by manufacturer of •reboxetine
- Antidiabetics: fluconazole possibly enhances hypoglycaemic effect of nateglinide; voriconazole possibly increases plasma concentration of sulphonylureas; fluconazole increases plasma concentration of •sulphonylureas
- Antiepileptics: plasma concentration of itraconazole possibly reduced by carbamazepine; plasma concentration of voriconazole possibly reduced by •carbamazepine and •primidone—avoid concomitant use; fluconazole increases plasma concentration of •phenytoin (consider reducing dose of phenytoin); voriconazole increases plasma concentration of •phenytoin, also phenytoin reduces plasma concentration of voriconazole (increase dose of voriconazole and also monitor for phenytoin toxicity); plasma concentration of itraconazole reduced by •phenytoin—avoid concomitant use

  Antifungals: triazoles possibly antagonise effects of amphotericin

- Antihistamines: itraconazole inhibits metabolism of •mizolastine—avoid concomitant use
- Antimalarials: avoidance of triazoles advised by manufacturer of •artemether/lumefantrine

  Antimuscarinics: itraconazole increases plasma concentration of solifenacin; avoidance of itraconazole advised by manufacturer of tolterodine

- Antipsychotics: itraconazole possibly inhibits metabolism of •aripiprazole (reduce dose of aripiprazole); increased risk of ventricular arrhythmias when triazoles given with •pimozide—avoid concomitant use; triazoles possibly increase plasma concentration of quetiapine (reduce dose of quetiapine); increased risk of ventricular arrhythmias when itraconazole given with •sertindole—avoid concomitant use; possible increased risk of ventricular arrhythmias when triazoles given with •sertindole—avoid concomitant use
- Antivirals: plasma concentration of itraconazole possibly increased by amprenavir; plasma concentration of voriconazole reduced by •efavirenz, also plasma concentration of efavirenz increased (avoid concomitant use); itraconazole increases plasma concentration of •indinavir (consider reducing dose of indinavir); fluconazole increases plasma concentration of •nevirapine, ritonavir and tipranavir; plasma concentration of voriconazole reduced by •ritonavir—avoid concomitant use; combination of itraconazole with •ritonavir may increase plasma concentration of either drug (or both); triazoles possibly increase plasma concentration of saquinavir; fluconazole increases plasma concentration of •zidovudine (increased risk of toxicity)
- Anxiolytics and Hypnotics: itraconazole increases plasma concentration of alprazolam; fluconazole and itraconazole increase plasma concentration of •midazolam (risk of prolonged sedation); itraconazole increases plasma concentration of buspirone (reduce dose of buspirone)
- Barbiturates: plasma concentration of voriconazole possibly reduced by •phenobarbital—avoid concomitant use; plasma concentration of itraconazole possibly reduced by phenobarbital
- Bosentan: fluconazole increases plasma concentration of •bosentan—avoid concomitant use; itraconazole possibly increases plasma concentration of bosentan
- Calcium-channel Blockers: negative inotropic effect possibly increased when itraconazole given with calcium-channel blockers; itraconazole inhibits metabolism of •felodipine (increased plasma concentration); avoidance of itraconazole advised

**Antifungals, Triazole**

- Calcium-channel Blockers *(continued)* by manufacturer of lercanidipine; itraconazole possibly inhibits metabolism of dihydropyridines (increased plasma concentration)
- Cardiac Glycosides: itraconazole increases plasma concentration of •digoxin
- Ciclosporin: fluconazole, itraconazole and voriconazole inhibit metabolism of •ciclosporin (increased plasma concentration)

Corticosteroids: itraconazole possibly inhibits metabolism of corticosteroids and methylprednisolone; itraconazole increases plasma concentration of inhaled budesonide

- Cytotoxics: itraconazole inhibits metabolism of busulfan (increased risk of toxicity); itraconazole possibly inhibits metabolism of •vincristine (increased risk of neurotoxicity)
- Diuretics: fluconazole increases plasma concentration of eplerenone (reduce dose of eplerenone); itraconazole increases plasma concentration of •eplerenone—avoid concomitant use; plasma concentration of fluconazole increased by hydrochlorothiazide
- Ergot Alkaloids: increased risk of ergotism when triazoles given with •ergotamine and methysergide—avoid concomitant use
- $5HT_1$ Agonists: itraconazole increases plasma concentration of •eletriptan (risk of toxicity)—avoid concomitant use
- Ivabradine: fluconazole increases plasma concentration of ivabradine—reduce initial dose of ivabradine; itraconazole possibly increases plasma concentration of •ivabradine—avoid concomitant use
- Lipid-regulating Drugs: possible increased risk of myopathy when triazoles given with atorvastatin or simvastatin; increased risk of myopathy when itraconazole given with •atorvastatin or •simvastatin (avoid concomitant use)

Oestrogens: anecdotal reports of contraceptive failure when fluconazole or itraconazole given with oestrogens

Sildenafil: itraconazole increases plasma concentration of sildenafil—reduce initial dose of sildenafil

- Sirolimus: itraconazole and voriconazole increase plasma concentration of •sirolimus—avoid concomitant use
- Tacrolimus: triazoles possibly increase plasma concentration of •tacrolimus; fluconazole and voriconazole increase plasma concentration of •tacrolimus

Tadalafil: itraconazole possibly increases plasma concentration of tadalafil

- Theophylline: fluconazole possibly increases plasma concentration of •theophylline

Ulcer-healing Drugs: voriconazole increases plasma concentration of omeprazole (reduce dose of omeprazole); absorption of itraconazole reduced by histamine $H_2$-antagonists and proton pump inhibitors

- Vardenafil: itraconazole possibly increases plasma concentration of •vardenafil—avoid concomitant use

**Antihistamines**

*Note.* Sedative interactions apply to a lesser extent to the non-sedating antihistamines. Interactions do not generally apply to antihistamines used for topical action (including inhalation)

Alcohol: increased sedative effect when antihistamines given with alcohol (possibly less effect with non-sedating antihistamines)

**Antihistamines** *(continued)*

Antacids: absorption of fexofenadine reduced by antacids

- Anti-arrhythmics: increased risk of ventricular arrhythmias when mizolastine given with •amiodarone, •disopyramide, •flecainide, •mexiletine, •procainamide, •propafenone or •quinidine—avoid concomitant use
- Antibacterials: manufacturer of loratadine advises plasma concentration possibly increased by erythromycin; metabolism of mizolastine inhibited by •erythromycin—avoid concomitant use; increased risk of ventricular arrhythmias when mizolastine given with •moxifloxacin—avoid concomitant use; metabolism of mizolastine possibly inhibited by •macrolides (avoid concomitant use)

Antidepressants: increased antimuscarinic and sedative effects when antihistamines given with MAOIs or tricyclics; cyproheptadine possibly antagonises antidepressant effect of SSRIs; possible increased antimuscarinic and sedative effects when antihistamines given with tricyclic-related antidepressants

Antidiabetics: thrombocyte count depressed when ketotifen given with metformin

- Antifungals: manufacturer of loratadine advises plasma concentration possibly increased by ketoconazole; metabolism of mizolastine inhibited by •itraconazole or •ketoconazole—avoid concomitant use; metabolism of mizolastine possibly inhibited by •imidazoles (avoid concomitant use)

Antimuscarinics: increased risk of antimuscarinic side-effects when antihistamines given with antimuscarinics

Antivirals: plasma concentration of loratadine possibly increased by amprenavir; plasma concentration of chlorphenamine (chlorpheniramine) possibly increased by lopinavir; plasma concentration of non-sedating antihistamines possibly increased by ritonavir

Anxiolytics and Hypnotics: increased sedative effect when antihistamines given with anxiolytics and hypnotics

- Beta-blockers: increased risk of ventricular arrhythmias when mizolastine given with •sotalol—avoid concomitant use

Betahistine: antihistamines theoretically antagonise effect of betahistine

Ulcer-healing Drugs: manufacturer of loratadine advises plasma concentration possibly increased by cimetidine

**Antihistamines, Non-sedating** *see* Antihistamines

**Antihistamines, Sedating** *see* Antihistamines

**Antimalarials** *see* Artemether with Lumefantrine, Chloroquine and Hydroxychloroquine, Mefloquine, Primaquine, Proguanil, and Quinine

**Antimetabolites** *see* Cytarabine, Fludarabine, Fluorouracil, Mercaptopurine, Methotrexate, and Tioguanine

**Antimuscarinics**

*Note.* Many drugs have antimuscarinic effects; concomitant use of two or more such drugs can increase side-effects such as dry mouth, urine retention, and constipation; concomitant use can also lead to confusion in the elderly. Interactions do not generally apply to antimuscarinics used by inhalation

Alcohol: increased sedative effect when hyoscine given with alcohol

Analgesics: increased risk of antimuscarinic side-effects when antimuscarinics given with nefopam

Anti-arrhythmics: increased risk of antimuscarinic side-effects when antimuscarinics given with

**Antimuscarinics**

Anti-arrhythmics *(continued)* disopyramide; atropine delays absorption of mexiletine

Antibacterials: manufacturer of tolterodine advises avoid concomitant use with clarithromycin and erythromycin

Antidepressants: plasma concentration of procyclidine increased by paroxetine; increased risk of antimuscarinic side-effects when antimuscarinics given with MAOIs or tricyclics; possibly increased antimuscarinic side-effects when antimuscarinics given with tricyclic-related antidepressants

Antifungals: antimuscarinics reduce absorption of ketoconazole; plasma concentration of solifenacin increased by itraconazole and ketoconazole; manufacturer of tolterodine advises avoid concomitant use with itraconazole and ketoconazole

Antihistamines: increased risk of antimuscarinic side-effects when antimuscarinics given with antihistamines

Antipsychotics: antimuscarinics possibly reduce effects of haloperidol; increased risk of antimuscarinic side-effects when antimuscarinics given with clozapine; antimuscarinics reduce plasma concentration of phenothiazines, but risk of antimuscarinic side-effects increased

Antivirals: manufacturer of tolterodine advises avoid concomitant use with amprenavir, indinavir, lopinavir, nelfinavir, ritonavir and saquinavir; plasma concentration of solifenacin increased by nelfinavir and ritonavir

Domperidone: antimuscarinics antagonise effects of domperidone on gastro-intestinal activity

Dopaminergics: increased risk of antimuscarinic side-effects when antimuscarinics given with amantadine; antimuscarinics possibly reduce absorption of levodopa

Memantine: effects of antimuscarinics possibly enhanced by memantine

Metoclopramide: antimuscarinics antagonise effects of metoclopramide on gastro-intestinal activity

Nitrates: antimuscarinics possibly reduce effects of sublingual tablets of nitrates (failure to dissolve under tongue owing to dry mouth)

Parasympathomimetics: antimuscarinics antagonise effects of parasympathomimetics

**Antipsychotics**

*Note.* Increased risk of toxicity with myelosuppressive drugs

*Note.* Avoid concomitant use of clozapine with drugs that have a substantial potential for causing agranulocytosis

ACE Inhibitors: enhanced hypotensive effect when antipsychotics given with ACE inhibitors

Adrenergic Neurone Blockers: enhanced hypotensive effect when phenothiazines given with adrenergic neurone blockers; higher doses of chlorpromazine antagonise hypotensive effect of adrenergic neurone blockers; haloperidol antagonises hypotensive effect of adrenergic neurone blockers

Adsorbents: absorption of phenothiazines possibly reduced by kaolin

Alcohol: increased sedative effect when antipsychotics given with alcohol

Alpha-blockers: enhanced hypotensive effect when antipsychotics given with alpha-blockers

• Anaesthetics, General: enhanced hypotensive effect when antipsychotics given with •general anaesthetics

Analgesics: possible severe drowsiness when haloperidol given with indometacin; increased risk of convulsions when antipsychotics given with tramadol; enhanced hypotensive and sedative effects when antipsychotics given with opioid analgesics

Angiotensin-II Receptor Antagonists: enhanced hypotensive effect when antipsychotics given with angiotensin-II receptor antagonists

Antacids: absorption of phenothiazines and sulpiride reduced by antacids

• Anti-arrhythmics: increased risk of ventricular arrhythmias when antipsychotics that prolong the QT interval given with •anti-arrhythmics that prolong the QT interval; increased risk of ventricular arrhythmias when amisulpride, haloperidol, phenothiazines, pimozide or sertindole given with •amiodarone—avoid concomitant use; increased risk of ventricular arrhythmias when phenothiazines given with •disopyramide, •procainamide or •quinidine; increased risk of ventricular arrhythmias when amisulpride, pimozide or sertindole given with •disopyramide—avoid concomitant use; increased risk of arrhythmias when clozapine given with •flecainide; increased risk of ventricular arrhythmias when amisulpride, pimozide or sertindole given with •procainamide—avoid concomitant use; increased risk of ventricular arrhythmias when amisulpride, pimozide or sertindole given with •quinidine—avoid concomitant use; metabolism of aripiprazole inhibited by •quinidine (reduce dose of aripiprazole)

• <u>Antibacterials</u>: increased risk of ventricular arrhythmias when pimozide given with •clarithromycin, •moxifloxacin or •telithromycin—avoid concomitant use; increased risk of ventricular arrhythmias when sertindole given with •erythromycin or •moxifloxacin—avoid concomitant use; increased risk of ventricular arrhythmias when amisulpride given with parenteral •erythromycin—avoid concomitant use; plasma concentration of clozapine possibly increased by •erythromycin (possible increased risk of convulsions); possible increased risk of ventricular arrhythmias when pimozide given with •erythromycin—avoid concomitant use; plasma concentration of olanzapine possibly increased by ciprofloxacin; increased risk of ventricular arrhythmias when haloperidol or phenothiazines given with •moxifloxacin—avoid concomitant use; plasma concentration of aripiprazole possibly reduced by •rifabutin and •rifampicin—increase dose of aripiprazole; plasma concentration of clozapine possibly reduced by rifampicin; metabolism of haloperidol accelerated by •rifampicin (reduced plasma concentration); avoid concomitant use of clozapine with •chloramphenicol or •sulphonamides (increased risk of agranulocytosis); possible increased risk of ventricular arrhythmias when sertindole given with •macrolides—avoid concomitant use; plasma concentration of quetiapine possibly increased by macrolides (reduce dose of quetiapine)

• <u>Antidepressants</u>: plasma concentration of clozapine possibly increased by citalopram (increased risk of toxicity); metabolism of aripiprazole possibly inhibited by •fluoxetine and •paroxetine (reduce dose of aripiprazole); plasma concentration of clozapine, haloperidol, risperidone, sertindole and zotepine increased by •fluoxetine; plasma concentration of clozapine and olanzapine increased by •fluvoxamine; plasma concen-

**Antipsychotics**

- Antidepressants *(continued)* tration of clozapine and sertindole increased by •paroxetine; plasma concentration of risperidone possibly increased by paroxetine (increased risk of toxicity); metabolism of perphenazine inhibited by paroxetine (reduce dose of perphenazine); plasma concentration of clozapine increased by •sertraline and •venlafaxine; plasma concentration of pimozide increased by •sertraline (increased risk of ventricular arrhythmias—avoid concomitant use); plasma concentration of haloperidol increased by venlafaxine; increased risk of ventricular arrhythmias when pimozide given with •maprotiline or •tricyclics—avoid concomitant use; clozapine possibly increases CNS effects of •MAOIs; plasma concentration of aripiprazole possibly reduced by •St John's wort—increase dose of aripiprazole; possibly increased antimuscarinic side-effects when clozapine given with tricyclics; antipsychotics increase plasma concentration of •tricyclics—possibly increased risk of ventricular arrhythmias; increased risk of antimuscarinic side-effects when phenothiazines given with tricyclics

Antidiabetics: phenothiazines possibly antagonise hypoglycaemic effect of sulphonylureas

- Antiepileptics: antipsychotics antagonise anticonvulsant effect of •carbamazepine, •ethosuximide, •oxcarbazepine, •phenytoin, •primidone and •valproate (convulsive threshold lowered); metabolism of haloperidol, olanzapine, quetiapine, risperidone and sertindole accelerated by carbamazepine (reduced plasma concentration); metabolism of clozapine accelerated by •carbamazepine (reduced plasma concentration), also avoid concomitant use of drugs with substantial potential for causing agranulocytosis; plasma concentration of aripiprazole reduced by •carbamazepine—increase dose of aripiprazole; metabolism of clozapine, quetiapine and sertindole accelerated by phenytoin (reduced plasma concentration); plasma concentration of aripiprazole possibly reduced by •phenytoin and •primidone—increase dose of aripiprazole; metabolism of haloperidol accelerated by primidone (reduced plasma concentration); increased risk of neutropenia when olanzapine given with •valproate
- Antifungals: metabolism of aripiprazole inhibited by •ketoconazole (reduce dose of aripiprazole); increased risk of ventricular arrhythmias when sertindole given with •itraconazole or •ketoconazole—avoid concomitant use; metabolism of aripiprazole possibly inhibited by •itraconazole (reduce dose of aripiprazole); possible increased risk of ventricular arrhythmias when sertindole given with •imidazoles or •triazoles—avoid concomitant use; plasma concentration of quetiapine possibly increased by imidazoles and triazoles (reduce dose of quetiapine); increased risk of ventricular arrhythmias when pimozide given with •imidazoles or •triazoles—avoid concomitant use
- Antimalarials: avoidance of antipsychotics advised by manufacturer of •artemether/lumefantrine; increased risk of ventricular arrhythmias when pimozide given with •mefloquine or •quinine—avoid concomitant use

Antimuscarinics: increased risk of antimuscarinic side-effects when clozapine given with antimuscarinics; plasma concentration of phenothiazines reduced by antimuscarinics, but risk of antimuscarinic side-effects increased; effects of haloperidol possibly reduced by antimuscarinics

- Antipsychotics: avoid concomitant use of clozapine with depot formulation of •flupentixol, •fluphenazine, •haloperidol, •pipotiazine, •risperidone or •zuclopenthixol as cannot be withdrawn quickly if neutropenia occurs; increased risk of ventricular arrhythmias when sertindole given with •amisulpride—avoid concomitant use; increased risk of ventricular arrhythmias when pimozide given with •phenothiazines—avoid concomitant use
- Antivirals: metabolism of aripiprazole possibly inhibited by •amprenavir, •atazanavir, •indinavir, •lopinavir, •nelfinavir, •ritonavir and •saquinavir (reduce dose of aripiprazole); plasma concentration of pimozide and sertindole increased by •amprenavir (increased risk of ventricular arrhythmias—avoid concomitant use); plasma concentration of clozapine possibly increased by amprenavir; plasma concentration of pimozide possibly increased by •atazanavir—avoid concomitant use; plasma concentration of pimozide possibly increased by •efavirenz, •indinavir, •nelfinavir and •saquinavir (increased risk of ventricular arrhythmias—avoid concomitant use); plasma concentration of aripiprazole possibly reduced by •efavirenz and •nevirapine—increase dose of aripiprazole; plasma concentration of sertindole increased by •indinavir, •lopinavir, •nelfinavir, •ritonavir and •saquinavir (increased risk of ventricular arrhythmias—avoid concomitant use); plasma concentration of pimozide increased by •ritonavir (increased risk of ventricular arrhythmias—avoid concomitant use); plasma concentration of clozapine increased by •ritonavir (increased risk of toxicity)—avoid concomitant use; plasma concentration of antipsychotics possibly increased by •ritonavir
- Anxiolytics and Hypnotics: increased sedative effect when antipsychotics given with anxiolytics and hypnotics; plasma concentration of zotepine increased by diazepam; increased risk of hypotension, bradycardia and respiratory depression when intramuscular olanzapine given with parenteral •benzodiazepines; plasma concentration of haloperidol increased by buspirone
- Aprepitant: avoidance of pimozide advised by manufacturer of •aprepitant
- Barbiturates: antipsychotics antagonise anticonvulsant effect of •barbiturates (convulsive threshold lowered); plasma concentration of aripiprazole possibly reduced by •phenobarbital—increase dose of aripiprazole; metabolism of haloperidol accelerated by phenobarbital (reduced plasma concentration)
- Beta-blockers: enhanced hypotensive effect when phenothiazines given with beta-blockers; plasma concentration of both drugs may increase when chlorpromazine given with •propranolol; increased risk of ventricular arrhythmias when amisulpride, phenothiazines, pimozide or sertindole given with •sotalol

Calcium-channel Blockers: enhanced hypotensive effect when antipsychotics given with calcium-channel blockers

Clonidine: enhanced hypotensive effect when phenothiazines given with clonidine

- Cytotoxics: avoid concomitant use of clozapine with •cytotoxics (increased risk of agranulocytosis)

Antipsychotics *(continued)*

Desferrioxamine: manufacturer of levomepromazine (methotrimeprazine) advises avoid concomitant use with desferrioxamine; avoidance of prochlorperazine advised by manufacturer of desferrioxamine

Diazoxide: enhanced hypotensive effect when phenothiazines given with diazoxide

• Diuretics: risk of ventricular arrhythmias with amisulpride or sertindole increased by hypokalaemia caused by •diuretics; risk of ventricular arrhythmias with pimozide increased by hypokalaemia caused by •diuretics (avoid concomitant use); enhanced hypotensive effect when phenothiazines given with diuretics

Dopaminergics: increased risk of extrapyramidal side-effects when antipsychotics given with amantadine; antipsychotics antagonise effects of apomorphine, levodopa, lisuride and pergolide; antipsychotics antagonise hypoprolactinaemic and antiparkinsonian effects of bromocriptine and cabergoline; manufacturer of amisulpride advises avoid concomitant use of levodopa (antagonism of effect); avoidance of antipsychotics advised by manufacturer of pramipexole and ropinirole (antagonism of effect)

• Ivabradine: increased risk of ventricular arrhythmias when pimozide or sertindole given with •ivabradine

• Lithium: increased risk of ventricular arrhythmias when sertindole given with •lithium—avoid concomitant use; increased risk of extrapyramidal side-effects and possibly neurotoxicity when clozapine, haloperidol or phenothiazines given with lithium; increased risk of extrapyramidal side-effects when sulpiride given with lithium

Memantine: effects of antipsychotics possibly reduced by memantine

Methyldopa: enhanced hypotensive effect when antipsychotics given with methyldopa (also increased risk of extrapyramidal effects)

Metoclopramide: increased risk of extrapyramidal side-effects when antipsychotics given with metoclopramide

Moxonidine: enhanced hypotensive effect when phenothiazines given with moxonidine

Muscle Relaxants: promazine possibly enhances effects of suxamethonium

Nitrates: enhanced hypotensive effect when phenothiazines given with nitrates

• Penicillamine: avoid concomitant use of clozapine with •penicillamine (increased risk of agranulocytosis)

• Pentamidine Isetionate: increased risk of ventricular arrhythmias when amisulpride given with •pentamidine isetionate—avoid concomitant use

• Sibutramine: increased risk of CNS toxicity when antipsychotics given with •sibutramine (manufacturer of sibutramine advises avoid concomitant use)

Sodium Benzoate: haloperidol possibly reduces effects of sodium benzoate

Sodium Phenylbutyrate: haloperidol possibly reduces effects of sodium phenylbutyrate

Sympathomimetics: antipsychotics antagonise hypertensive effect of sympathomimetics

Tetrabenazine: increased risk of extrapyramidal side-effects when antipsychotics given with tetrabenazine

• Ulcer-healing Drugs: effects of antipsychotics, chlorpromazine and clozapine possibly enhanced by cimetidine; increased risk of ventricular arrhythmias when sertindole given with •cimetidine—avoid concomitant use; plasma concentration of clozapine possibly reduced by omeprazole; absorption of sulpiride reduced by sucralfate

Vasodilator Antihypertensives: enhanced hypotensive effect when phenothiazines given with hydralazine, minoxidil or nitroprusside

Antivirals *see* Abacavir, Aciclovir, Amprenavir, Atazanavir, Cidofovir, Didanosine, Efavirenz, Emtricitabine, Famciclovir, Foscarnet, Ganciclovir, Indinavir, Lamivudine, Lopinavir, Nelfinavir, Nevirapine, Ribavirin, Ritonavir, Saquinavir, Stavudine, Tenofovir, Tipranavir, Valaciclovir, Zalcitabine, and Zidovudine

Anxiolytics and Hypnotics

ACE Inhibitors: enhanced hypotensive effect when anxiolytics and hypnotics given with ACE inhibitors

Adrenergic Neurone Blockers: enhanced hypotensive effect when anxiolytics and hypnotics given with adrenergic neurone blockers

Alcohol: increased sedative effect when anxiolytics and hypnotics given with alcohol

Alpha-blockers: enhanced hypotensive and sedative effects when anxiolytics and hypnotics given with alpha-blockers

Anaesthetics, General: increased sedative effect when anxiolytics and hypnotics given with general anaesthetics

Analgesics: increased sedative effect when anxiolytics and hypnotics given with opioid analgesics

Angiotensin-II Receptor Antagonists: enhanced hypotensive effect when anxiolytics and hypnotics given with angiotensin-II receptor antagonists

• Antibacterials: metabolism of midazolam inhibited by •clarithromycin, •erythromycin, •quinupristin/dalfopristin and •telithromycin (increased plasma concentration with increased sedation); plasma concentration of buspirone increased by erythromycin (reduce dose of buspirone); metabolism of zopiclone inhibited by erythromycin and quinupristin/dalfopristin; metabolism of benzodiazepines possibly accelerated by rifampicin (reduced plasma concentration); metabolism of diazepam accelerated by rifampicin (reduced plasma concentration); metabolism of buspirone and zaleplon possibly accelerated by rifampicin; metabolism of zolpidem accelerated by rifampicin (reduced plasma concentration and reduced effect); metabolism of diazepam inhibited by isoniazid

Anticoagulants: chloral and triclofos may transiently enhance anticoagulant effect of coumarins

Antidepressants: plasma concentration of some benzodiazepines increased by fluvoxamine; sedative effects possibly increased when zolpidem given with sertraline; manufacturer of buspirone advises avoid concomitant use with MAOIs; increased sedative effect when anxiolytics and hypnotics given with mirtazapine, tricyclic-related antidepressants or tricyclics

Antiepileptics: plasma concentration of clonazepam often reduced by carbamazepine, phenytoin and primidone; benzodiazepines possibly increase or decrease plasma concentration of phenytoin; diazepam increases or decreases plasma concentration of phenytoin

• Antifungals: plasma concentration of midazolam increased by •fluconazole, •itraconazole and •ketoconazole (risk of prolonged sedation); plasma concentration of alprazolam increased by

**Anxiolytics and Hypnotics**
- Antifungals *(continued)*
  itraconazole; plasma concentration of buspirone increased by itraconazole (reduce dose of buspirone)
  Antihistamines: increased sedative effect when anxiolytics and hypnotics given with antihistamines
- Antipsychotics: increased sedative effect when anxiolytics and hypnotics given with antipsychotics; buspirone increases plasma concentration of haloperidol; increased risk of hypotension, bradycardia and respiratory depression when parenteral benzodiazepines given with intramuscular •olanzapine; diazepam increases plasma concentration of zotepine
- Antivirals: increased risk of prolonged sedation and respiratory depression when alprazolam, clonazepam, diazepam, flurazepam or midazolam given with •amprenavir; increased risk of prolonged sedation when midazolam given with •efavirenz, •indinavir or •nelfinavir—avoid concomitant use; increased risk of prolonged sedation when alprazolam given with •indinavir—avoid concomitant use; plasma concentration of alprazolam, diazepam, flurazepam, midazolam and zolpidem possibly increased by •ritonavir (risk of extreme sedation and respiratory depression —avoid concomitant use); plasma concentration of anxiolytics and hypnotics possibly increased by •ritonavir; plasma concentration of buspirone increased by ritonavir (increased risk of toxicity); plasma concentration of midazolam increased by •saquinavir (risk of prolonged sedation)
  Barbiturates: plasma concentration of clonazepam often reduced by phenobarbital
  Beta-blockers: enhanced hypotensive effect when anxiolytics and hypnotics given with beta-blockers
  Calcium-channel Blockers: enhanced hypotensive effect when anxiolytics and hypnotics given with calcium-channel blockers; midazolam increases absorption of lercanidipine; metabolism of midazolam inhibited by diltiazem and verapamil (increased plasma concentration with increased sedation); plasma concentration of buspirone increased by diltiazem and verapamil (reduce dose of buspirone)
  Cardiac Glycosides: alprazolam increases plasma concentration of digoxin (increased risk of toxicity)
  Clonidine: enhanced hypotensive effect when anxiolytics and hypnotics given with clonidine
  Diazoxide: enhanced hypotensive effect when anxiolytics and hypnotics given with diazoxide
  Disulfiram: metabolism of benzodiazepines inhibited by disulfiram (increased sedative effects); increased risk of temazepam toxicity when given with disulfiram
  Diuretics: enhanced hypotensive effect when anxiolytics and hypnotics given with diuretics; administration of chloral or triclofos with parenteral furosemide (frusemide) may displace thyroid hormone from binding sites
  Dopaminergics: benzodiazepines possibly antagonise effects of levodopa
  Grapefruit Juice: plasma concentration of buspirone increased by grapefruit juice
  Lofexidine: increased sedative effect when anxiolytics and hypnotics given with lofexidine
  Methyldopa: enhanced hypotensive effect when anxiolytics and hypnotics given with methyldopa

Appendix 1

**Anxiolytics and Hypnotics** *(continued)*
  Moxonidine: enhanced hypotensive effect when anxiolytics and hypnotics given with moxonidine; sedative effects possibly increased when benzodiazepines given with moxonidine
  Muscle Relaxants: increased sedative effect when anxiolytics and hypnotics given with baclofen or tizanidine
  Nabilone: increased sedative effect when anxiolytics and hypnotics given with nabilone
  Nitrates: enhanced hypotensive effect when anxiolytics and hypnotics given with nitrates
  Theophylline: effects of benzodiazepines possibly reduced by theophylline
  Ulcer-healing Drugs: metabolism of benzodiazepines, clomethiazole and zaleplon inhibited by cimetidine (increased plasma concentration); metabolism of diazepam possibly inhibited by esomeprazole and omeprazole (increased plasma concentration)
  Vasodilator Antihypertensives: enhanced hypotensive effect when anxiolytics and hypnotics given with hydralazine, minoxidil or nitroprusside

**Apomorphine**
  Antipsychotics: effects of apomorphine antagonised by antipsychotics
  Dopaminergics: effects of apomorphine possibly enhanced by entacapone
  Memantine: effects of dopaminergics possibly enhanced by memantine
  Methyldopa: antiparkinsonian effect of dopaminergics antagonised by methyldopa
  Nitrates: sublingual apomorphine enhances hypotensive effect of nitrates

**Apraclonidine** *see* Alpha$_2$-adrenoceptor Stimulants

**Aprepitant**
  Antibacterials: plasma concentration of aprepitant possibly increased by clarithromycin and telithromycin; plasma concentration of aprepitant reduced by rifampicin
  Anticoagulants: aprepitant possibly reduces anticoagulant effect of warfarin
- Antidepressants: manufacturer of aprepitant advises avoid concomitant use with •St John's wort
  Antidiabetics: aprepitant reduces plasma concentration of tolbutamide
  Antiepileptics: plasma concentration of aprepitant possibly reduced by carbamazepine and phenytoin
  Antifungals: plasma concentration of aprepitant increased by ketoconazole
- Antipsychotics: manufacturer of aprepitant advises avoid concomitant use with •pimozide
  Antivirals: plasma concentration of aprepitant possibly increased by ritonavir
  Barbiturates: plasma concentration of aprepitant possibly reduced by phenobarbital
  Corticosteroids: aprepitant inhibits metabolism of dexamethasone and methylprednisolone (reduce dose of dexamethasone and methylprednisolone)
- Oestrogens: aprepitant possibly causes contraceptive failure of hormonal contraceptives containing •oestrogens (alternative contraception recommended)
- Progestogens: aprepitant possibly causes contraceptive failure of hormonal contraceptives containing •progestogens (alternative contraception recommended)

**Aripiprazole** *see* Antipsychotics

**Artemether with Lumefantrine**
- Anti-arrhythmics: manufacturer of artemether/lumefantrine advises avoid concomitant use with •amiodarone, •disopyramide, •flecainide,

**Artemether with Lumefantrine**

- Anti-arrhythmics *(continued)*
  •procainamide or •quinidine (risk of ventricular arrhythmias)
- Antibacterials: manufacturer of artemether/lumefantrine advises avoid concomitant use with •macrolides and •quinolones
- Antidepressants: manufacturer of artemether/lumefantrine advises avoid concomitant use with •antidepressants
- Antifungals: manufacturer of artemether/lumefantrine advises avoid concomitant use with •imidazoles and •triazoles
- Antimalarials: manufacturer of artemether/lumefantrine advises avoid concomitant use with •antimalarials
- Antipsychotics: manufacturer of artemether/lumefantrine advises avoid concomitant use with •antipsychotics
- Antivirals: manufacturer of artemether/lumefantrine advises avoid concomitant use with •amprenavir, •atazanavir, •indinavir, •lopinavir, •nelfinavir, •ritonavir and •saquinavir; possible increased risk of ventricular arrhythmias when artemether/lumefantrine given with •tipranavir—avoid concomitant use
- Beta-blockers: manufacturer of artemether/lumefantrine advises avoid concomitant use with •metoprolol and •sotalol
- Grapefruit Juice: metabolism of artemether/lumefantrine possibly inhibited by •grapefruit juice (avoid concomitant use)
- Ulcer-healing Drugs: manufacturer of artemether/lumefantrine advises avoid concomitant use with •cimetidine

**Aspirin**

ACE Inhibitors: risk of renal impairment when aspirin (in doses over 300 mg daily) given with ACE inhibitors, also hypotensive effect antagonised

Adsorbents: absorption of aspirin possibly reduced by kaolin

- Analgesics: avoid concomitant use of aspirin with •NSAIDs (increased side-effects); antiplatelet effect of aspirin possibly reduced by ibuprofen

Angiotensin-II Receptor Antagonists: risk of renal impairment when aspirin (in doses over 300 mg daily) given with angiotensin-II receptor antagonists, also hypotensive effect antagonised

Antacids: excretion of aspirin increased by alkaline urine due to some antacids

- Anticoagulants: increased risk of bleeding when aspirin given with •coumarins or •phenindione (due to antiplatelet effect); aspirin enhances anticoagulant effect of •heparins
- Antidepressants: increased risk of bleeding when aspirin given with •SSRIs or •venlafaxine

Antiepileptics: aspirin enhances effects of phenytoin and valproate

Cilostazol: manufacturer of cilostazol recommends dose of aspirin should not exceed 80 mg daily when given with cilostazol

Clopidogrel: increased risk of bleeding when aspirin given with clopidogrel

Corticosteroids: increased risk of gastro-intestinal bleeding and ulceration when aspirin given with corticosteroids, also corticosteroids reduce plasma concentration of salicylate

- Cytotoxics: aspirin reduces excretion of •methotrexate (increased risk of toxicity)—but for concomitant use in rheumatic disease see p. 520

Diuretics: aspirin antagonises diuretic effect of spironolactone; increased risk of toxicity when high-dose aspirin given with carbonic anhydrase inhibitors

Iloprost: increased risk of bleeding when aspirin given with iloprost

Leukotriene Antagonists: aspirin increases plasma concentration of zafirlukast

Metoclopramide: rate of absorption of aspirin increased by metoclopramide (enhanced effect)

Mifepristone: avoidance of aspirin advised by manufacturer of mifepristone

Probenecid: aspirin antagonises effects of probenecid

Sibutramine: increased risk of bleeding when aspirin given with sibutramine

Sulfinpyrazone: aspirin antagonises effects of sulfinpyrazone

**Atazanavir**

Antacids: plasma concentration of atazanavir possibly reduced by antacids

- Anti-arrhythmics: atazanavir possibly increases plasma concentration of •amiodarone and •lidocaine (lignocaine); atazanavir possibly increases plasma concentration of •quinidine—avoid concomitant use
- Antibacterials: plasma concentration of both drugs increased when atazanavir given with clarithromycin; atazanavir increases plasma concentration of •rifabutin (reduce dose of rifabutin); plasma concentration of atazanavir reduced by •rifampicin—avoid concomitant use

Anticoagulants: atazanavir may enhance or reduce anticoagulant effect of warfarin

- Antidepressants: plasma concentration of atazanavir reduced by •St John's wort—avoid concomitant use
- Antimalarials: avoidance of atazanavir advised by manufacturer of •artemether/lumefantrine
- Antipsychotics: atazanavir possibly inhibits metabolism of •aripiprazole (reduce dose of aripiprazole); atazanavir possibly increases plasma concentration of •pimozide—avoid concomitant use
- Antivirals: plasma concentration of atazanavir reduced by efavirenz—increase dose of atazanavir; avoid concomitant use of atazanavir with •indinavir; plasma concentration of atazanavir possibly reduced by •nevirapine—avoid concomitant use; plasma concentration of atazanavir reduced by tenofovir
- Calcium-channel Blockers: atazanavir increases plasma concentration of •diltiazem (reduce dose of diltiazem); atazanavir possibly increases plasma concentration of verapamil
- Ciclosporin: atazanavir possibly increases plasma concentration of •ciclosporin
- Cytotoxics: atazanavir possibly inhibits metabolism of •irinotecan (increased risk of toxicity)
- Ergot Alkaloids: atazanavir possibly increases plasma concentration of •ergot alkaloids—avoid concomitant use
- Lipid-regulating Drugs: possible increased risk of myopathy when atazanavir given with atorvastatin; increased risk of myopathy when atazanavir given with •simvastatin (avoid concomitant use)
- Oestrogens: atazanavir increases plasma concentration of •ethinylestradiol—avoid concomitant use
- Sildenafil: atazanavir possibly increases side-effects of •sildenafil
- Sirolimus: atazanavir possibly increases plasma concentration of •sirolimus

**Atazanavir** *(continued)*
- Tacrolimus: atazanavir possibly increases plasma concentration of •tacrolimus
- Ulcer-healing Drugs: plasma concentration of atazanavir significantly reduced by •omeprazole—avoid concomitant use; plasma concentration of atazanavir possibly reduced by histamine $H_2$-antagonists; plasma concentration of atazanavir possibly reduced by •proton pump inhibitors—avoid concomitant use

**Atenolol** *see* Beta-blockers

**Atomoxetine**
- Antidepressants: atomoxetine should not be started until 2 weeks after stopping •MAOIs, also MAOIs should not be started until at least 2 weeks after stopping atomoxetine

Sympathomimetics, Beta$_2$: Increased risk of cardiovascular side-effects when atomoxetine given with parenteral salbutamol

**Atorvastatin** *see* Statins

**Atovaquone**
- Antibacterials: plasma concentration of atovaquone reduced by •rifabutin and •rifampicin (possible therapeutic failure of atovaquone); plasma concentration of atovaquone reduced by tetracycline

Antivirals: atovaquone possibly reduces plasma concentration of indinavir; atovaquone possibly inhibits metabolism of zidovudine (increased plasma concentration)

Metoclopramide: plasma concentration of atovaquone reduced by metoclopramide

**Atracurium** *see* Muscle Relaxants

**Atropine** *see* Antimuscarinics

**Azathioprine**

ACE Inhibitors: increased risk of leucopenia when azathioprine given with captopril
- Allopurinol: enhanced effects and increased toxicity of azathioprine when given with •allopurinol (reduce dose of azathioprine)

Aminosalicylates: possible increased risk of leucopenia when azathioprine given with aminosalicylates
- Antibacterials: increased risk of haematological toxicity when azathioprine given with •sulfamethoxazole (as co-trimoxazole); increased risk of haematological toxicity when azathioprine given with •trimethoprim (also with co-trimoxazole)
- Anticoagulants: azathioprine possibly reduces anticoagulant effect of •coumarins

Antiepileptics: cytotoxics possibly reduce absorption of phenytoin
- Antipsychotics: avoid concomitant use of cytotoxics with •clozapine (increased risk of agranulocytosis)

**Azelastine** *see* Antihistamines

**Azithromycin** *see* Macrolides

**Aztreonam**
- Anticoagulants: aztreonam possibly enhances anticoagulant effect of •coumarins

Oestrogens: antibacterials that do not induce liver enzymes possibly reduce contraceptive effect of oestrogens (risk probably small, see p. 408)

**Baclofen** *see* Muscle Relaxants

**Balsalazide** *see* Aminosalicylates

**Bambuterol** *see* Sympathomimetics, Beta$_2$

**Barbiturates**

Alcohol: increased sedative effect when barbiturates given with alcohol

Anti-arrhythmics: barbiturates accelerate metabolism of disopyramide and quinidine (reduced plasma concentration)

**Barbiturates** *(continued)*
- Antibacterials: barbiturates accelerate metabolism of •chloramphenicol, doxycycline and metronidazole (reduced plasma concentration); phenobarbital reduces plasma concentration of •telithromycin (avoid during and for 2 weeks after phenobarbital)
- Anticoagulants: barbiturates accelerate metabolism of •coumarins (reduced anticoagulant effect)
- Antidepressants: phenobarbital reduces plasma concentration of paroxetine; phenobarbital accelerates metabolism of •mianserin (reduced plasma concentration); anticonvulsant effect of barbiturates possibly antagonised by MAOIs and •tricyclic-related antidepressants (convulsive threshold lowered); anticonvulsant effect of barbiturates antagonised by SSRIs (convulsive threshold lowered); plasma concentration of phenobarbital reduced by •St John's wort—avoid concomitant use; anticonvulsant effect of barbiturates antagonised by •tricyclics (convulsive threshold lowered), also metabolism of tricyclics possibly accelerated (reduced plasma concentration)

Antiepileptics: phenobarbital reduces plasma concentration of carbamazepine, lamotrigine, tiagabine and zonisamide; phenobarbital possibly reduces plasma concentration of ethosuximide; plasma concentration of phenobarbital increased by oxcarbazepine, also plasma concentration of an active metabolite of oxcarbazepine reduced; plasma concentration of phenobarbital often increased by phenytoin, plasma concentration of phenytoin often reduced but may be increased; increased sedative effect when barbiturates given with primidone; plasma concentration of phenobarbital increased by valproate (also plasma concentration of valproate reduced); plasma concentration of phenobarbital possibly reduced by vigabatrin
- Antifungals: phenobarbital possibly reduces plasma concentration of itraconazole; phenobarbital possibly reduces plasma concentration of •voriconazole—avoid concomitant use; phenobarbital reduces absorption of griseofulvin (reduced effect)
- Antipsychotics: anticonvulsant effect of barbiturates antagonised by •antipsychotics (convulsive threshold lowered); phenobarbital accelerates metabolism of haloperidol (reduced plasma concentration); phenobarbital possibly reduces plasma concentration of •aripiprazole—increase dose of aripiprazole
- Antivirals: phenobarbital possibly reduces plasma concentration of abacavir, amprenavir and •lopinavir; barbiturates possibly reduce plasma concentration of •indinavir, •nelfinavir and •saquinavir

Anxiolytics and Hypnotics: phenobarbital often reduces plasma concentration of clonazepam

Aprepitant: phenobarbital possibly reduces plasma concentration of aprepitant
- Calcium-channel Blockers: barbiturates reduce effects of •felodipine and •isradipine; barbiturates probably reduce effects of •dihydropyridines, •diltiazem and •verapamil

Cardiac Glycosides: barbiturates accelerate metabolism of digitoxin (reduced effect)
- Ciclosporin: barbiturates accelerate metabolism of •ciclosporin (reduced effect)
- Corticosteroids: barbiturates accelerate metabolism of •corticosteroids (reduced effect)

**Barbiturates** *(continued)*
Cytotoxics: phenobarbital possibly reduces plasma concentration of etoposide
• Diuretics: phenobarbital reduces plasma concentration of •eplerenone—avoid concomitant use; increased risk of osteomalacia when phenobarbital given with carbonic anhydrase inhibitors
Folates: plasma concentration of phenobarbital possibly reduced by folates
Hormone Antagonists: barbiturates accelerate metabolism of gestrinone (reduced plasma concentration); barbiturates possibly accelerate metabolism of toremifene (reduced plasma concentration)
$5HT_3$ Antagonists: phenobarbital reduces plasma concentration of tropisetron
Leukotriene Antagonists: phenobarbital reduces plasma concentration of montelukast
Memantine: effects of barbiturates possibly reduced by memantine
• Oestrogens: barbiturates accelerate metabolism of •oestrogens (reduced contraceptive effect—see p. 408)
• Progestogens: barbiturates accelerate metabolism of •progestogens (reduced contraceptive effect—see p. 408)
Sympathomimetics: plasma concentration of phenobarbital possibly increased by methylphenidate
Theophylline: barbiturates accelerate metabolism of theophylline (reduced effect)
Thyroid Hormones: barbiturates accelerate metabolism of thyroid hormones (may increase requirements for thyroid hormones in hypothyroidism)
Tibolone: barbiturates accelerate metabolism of tibolone (reduced plasma concentration)
Vitamins: barbiturates possibly increase requirements for vitamin D

**Beclometasone** *see* Corticosteroids
**Belladonna Alkaloids** *see* Antimuscarinics
**Bendroflumethiazide (bendrofluazide)** *see* Diuretics
**Benperidol** *see* Antipsychotics
**Benzatropine (benztropine)** *see* Antimuscarinics
**Benzodiazepines** *see* Anxiolytics and Hypnotics
**Benzthiazide** *see* Diuretics
**Benzylpenicillin** *see* Penicillins

**Beta-blockers**
*Note.* Since systemic absorption may follow topical application of beta-blockers to the eye the possibility of interactions, in particular, with drugs such as verapamil should be borne in mind
ACE Inhibitors: enhanced hypotensive effect when beta-blockers given with ACE inhibitors
Adrenergic Neurone Blockers: enhanced hypotensive effect when beta-blockers given with adrenergic neurone blockers
Alcohol: enhanced hypotensive effect when beta-blockers given with alcohol
Aldesleukin: enhanced hypotensive effect when beta-blockers given with aldesleukin
• Alpha-blockers: enhanced hypotensive effect when beta-blockers given with •alpha-blockers, also increased risk of first-dose hypotension with post-synaptic alpha-blockers such as prazosin
Anaesthetics, General: enhanced hypotensive effect when beta-blockers given with general anaesthetics
• Anaesthetics, Local: propranolol increases risk of •bupivacaine toxicity
Analgesics: hypotensive effect of beta-blockers antagonised by NSAIDs; plasma concentration of esmolol possibly increased by morphine

**Beta-blockers** *(continued)*
Angiotensin-II Receptor Antagonists: enhanced hypotensive effect when beta-blockers given with angiotensin-II receptor antagonists
• Anti-arrhythmics: increased myocardial depression when beta-blockers given with •anti-arrhythmics; increased risk of ventricular arrhythmias when sotalol given with •amiodarone, •disopyramide, •procainamide or •quinidine—avoid concomitant use; increased risk of bradycardia, AV block and myocardial depression when beta-blockers given with •amiodarone; increased risk of myocardial depression and bradycardia when beta-blockers given with •flecainide; propranolol increases risk of •lidocaine (lignocaine) toxicity; plasma concentration of metoprolol and propranolol increased by propafenone
• Antibacterials: increased risk of ventricular arrhythmias when sotalol given with •moxifloxacin—avoid concomitant use; metabolism of bisoprolol and propranolol accelerated by rifampicin (plasma concentration significantly reduced)
• Antidepressants: plasma concentration of metoprolol increased by citalopram and escitalopram; plasma concentration of propranolol increased by fluvoxamine; plasma concentration of metoprolol possibly increased by paroxetine (enhanced effect); enhanced hypotensive effect when beta-blockers given with MAOIs; increased risk of ventricular arrhythmias when sotalol given with •tricyclics
Antidiabetics: beta-blockers may mask warning signs of hypoglycaemia (such as tremor) with antidiabetics; beta-blockers enhance hypoglycaemic effect of insulin
• Antihistamines: increased risk of ventricular arrhythmias when sotalol given with •mizolastine—avoid concomitant use
• Antimalarials: avoidance of metoprolol and sotalol advised by manufacturer of •artemether/lumefantrine; increased risk of bradycardia when beta-blockers given with mefloquine
• Antipsychotics: plasma concentration of both drugs may increase when propranolol given with •chlorpromazine; increased risk of ventricular arrhythmias when sotalol given with •amisulpride, •phenothiazines, •pimozide or •sertindole; enhanced hypotensive effect when beta-blockers given with phenothiazines
Anxiolytics and Hypnotics: enhanced hypotensive effect when beta-blockers given with anxiolytics and hypnotics
• Calcium-channel Blockers: enhanced hypotensive effect when beta-blockers given with calcium-channel blockers; possible severe hypotension and heart failure when beta-blockers given with •nifedipine or •nisoldipine; increased risk of AV block and bradycardia when beta-blockers given with •diltiazem; asystole, severe hypotension and heart failure when beta-blockers given with •verapamil (see p. 114)
Cardiac Glycosides: increased risk of AV block and bradycardia when beta-blockers given with cardiac glycosides
• Ciclosporin: carvedilol increases plasma concentration of •ciclosporin
• Clonidine: increased risk of withdrawal hypertension when beta-blockers given with •clonidine (withdraw beta-blockers several days before slowly withdrawing clonidine)
Corticosteroids: hypotensive effect of beta-blockers antagonised by corticosteroids

**Beta-blockers** *(continued)*
Diazoxide: enhanced hypotensive effect when beta-blockers given with diazoxide
• Diuretics: enhanced hypotensive effect when beta-blockers given with diuretics; risk of ventricular arrhythmias with sotalol increased by hypokalaemia caused by •loop diuretics or •thiazides and related diuretics
• Dolasetron: increased risk of ventricular arrhythmias when sotalol given with •dolasetron—avoid concomitant use
Dopaminergics: enhanced hypotensive effect when beta-blockers given with levodopa
Ergot Alkaloids: increased peripheral vasoconstriction when beta-blockers given with ergotamine and methysergide
$5HT_1$ Agonists: propranolol possibly increases plasma concentration of rizatriptan (reduce dose of rizatriptan)
$5HT_3$ Antagonists: caution with beta-blockers advised by manufacturer of tropisetron (risk of ventricular arrhythmias)
• Ivabradine: increased risk of ventricular arrhythmias when sotalol given with •ivabradine
Methyldopa: enhanced hypotensive effect when beta-blockers given with methyldopa
• Moxisylyte (thymoxamine): possible severe postural hypotension when beta-blockers given with •moxisylyte
Moxonidine: enhanced hypotensive effect when beta-blockers given with moxonidine
Muscle Relaxants: propranolol enhances effects of muscle relaxants; enhanced hypotensive effect when beta-blockers given with baclofen; possible enhanced hypotensive effect and bradycardia when beta-blockers given with tizanidine
Nitrates: enhanced hypotensive effect when beta-blockers given with nitrates
Oestrogens: hypotensive effect of beta-blockers antagonised by oestrogens
Parasympathomimetics: propranolol antagonises effects of neostigmine and pyridostigmine; increased risk of arrhythmias when beta-blockers given with pilocarpine
Prostaglandins: enhanced hypotensive effect when beta-blockers given with alprostadil
• Sympathomimetics: severe hypertension when beta-blockers given with •adrenaline (epinephrine) or •noradrenaline (norepinephrine) especially with non-selective beta-blockers; possible severe hypertension when beta-blockers given with •dobutamine especially with non-selective beta-blockers
Ulcer-healing Drugs: plasma concentration of labetalol, metoprolol and propranolol increased by cimetidine
Vasodilator Antihypertensives: enhanced hypotensive effect when beta-blockers given with hydralazine, minoxidil or nitroprusside

**Betahistine**
Antihistamines: effect of betahistine theoretically antagonised by antihistamines

**Betamethasone** *see* Corticosteroids
**Betaxolol** *see* Beta-blockers
**Bethanechol** *see* Parasympathomimetics

**Bexarotene**
Antiepileptics: cytotoxics possibly reduce absorption of phenytoin
• Antipsychotics: avoid concomitant use of cytotoxics with •clozapine (increased risk of agranulocytosis)
• Lipid-regulating Drugs: plasma concentration of bexarotene increased by •gemfibrozil—avoid concomitant use

**Bezafibrate** *see* Fibrates

**Bicalutamide**
Anticoagulants: bicalutamide possibly enhances anticoagulant effect of coumarins

**Biguanides** *see* Antidiabetics
**Bile Acids** *see* Ursodeoxycholic Acid
**Bisoprolol** *see* Beta-blockers

**Bisphosphonates**
Analgesics: bioavailability of tiludronic acid increased by indometacin
Antacids: absorption of bisphosphonates reduced by antacids
Antibacterials: increased risk of hypocalcaemia when bisphosphonates given with aminoglycosides
Calcium Salts: absorption of bisphosphonates reduced by calcium salts
Iron: absorption of bisphosphonates reduced by *oral* iron

**Bleomycin**
Antiepileptics: cytotoxics possibly reduce absorption of phenytoin
• Antipsychotics: avoid concomitant use of cytotoxics with •clozapine (increased risk of agranulocytosis)
• Cytotoxics: increased pulmonary toxicity when bleomycin given with •cisplatin

**Bosentan**
Anticoagulants: manufacturer of bosentan recommends monitoring anticoagulant effect of coumarins
• Antidiabetics: plasma concentration of both drugs reduced when bosentan given with •glibenclamide (avoid concomitant use)
• Antifungals: plasma concentration of bosentan possibly increased by itraconazole and ketoconazole; plasma concentration of bosentan increased by •fluconazole—avoid concomitant use
Antivirals: plasma concentration of bosentan possibly increased by ritonavir
• Ciclosporin: plasma concentration of bosentan increased by •ciclosporin (also plasma concentration of ciclosporin reduced—avoid concomitant use)
Lipid-regulating Drugs: bosentan reduces plasma concentration of simvastatin
• Oestrogens: bosentan possibly causes contraceptive failure of hormonal contraceptives containing •oestrogens (alternative contraception recommended)
• Progestogens: bosentan possibly causes contraceptive failure of hormonal contraceptives containing •progestogens (alternative contraception recommended)

**Brimonidine** *see* $Alpha_2$-adrenoceptor Stimulants
**Brinzolamide** *see* Diuretics

**Bromocriptine**
Alcohol: tolerance of bromocriptine reduced by alcohol
Antibacterials: plasma concentration of bromocriptine increased by erythromycin (increased risk of toxicity); plasma concentration of bromocriptine possibly increased by macrolides (increased risk of toxicity)
Antipsychotics: hypoprolactinaemic and antiparkinsonian effects of bromocriptine antagonised by antipsychotics
Domperidone: hypoprolactinaemic effect of bromocriptine possibly antagonised by domperidone
Hormone Antagonists: plasma concentration of bromocriptine increased by octreotide

**Bromocriptine** *(continued)*
- Memantine: effects of dopaminergics possibly enhanced by memantine
- Methyldopa: antiparkinsonian effect of dopaminergics antagonised by methyldopa
- Metoclopramide: hypoprolactinaemic effect of bromocriptine antagonised by metoclopramide
- • Sympathomimetics: risk of toxicity when bromocriptine given with •isometheptene or •phenylpropanolamine

**Buclizine** *see* Antihistamines

**Budesonide** *see* Corticosteroids

**Bumetanide** *see* Diuretics

**Bupivacaine**
- Anti-arrhythmics: increased myocardial depression when bupivacaine given with anti-arrhythmics
- • Beta-blockers: increased risk of bupivacaine toxicity when given with •propranolol

**Buprenorphine** *see* Opioid Analgesics

**Bupropion**

*Note.* Bupropion should be administered with extreme caution to patients receiving other medication known to lower the seizure threshold—see CSM advice p. 261 and Cautions, Contra-indications and Side-effects of individual drugs
- • Antidepressants: manufacturer of bupropion advises avoid for 2 weeks after stopping •MAOIs; manufacturer of bupropion advises avoid concomitant use with •moclobemide
- Antiepileptics: plasma concentration of bupropion reduced by carbamazepine and phenytoin; metabolism of bupropion inhibited by valproate
- • Antivirals: plasma concentration of bupropion increased by •ritonavir (risk of toxicity)—avoid concomitant use
- Dopaminergics: increased risk of side-effects when bupropion given with amantadine or levodopa

**Buspirone** *see* Anxiolytics and Hypnotics

**Busulfan**
- Analgesics: metabolism of *intravenous* busulfan possibly inhibited by paracetamol (manufacturer of *intravenous* busulfan advises caution within 72 hours of paracetamol)
- Antiepileptics: cytotoxics possibly reduce absorption of phenytoin
- Antifungals: metabolism of busulfan inhibited by itraconazole (increased risk of toxicity)
- • Antipsychotics: avoid concomitant use of cytotoxics with •clozapine (increased risk of agranulocytosis)
- Cytotoxics: increased risk of hepatotoxicity when busulfan given with tioguanine

**Butobarbital** *see* Barbiturates

**Butyrophenones** *see* Antipsychotics

**Cabergoline**
- Antibacterials: plasma concentration of cabergoline increased by erythromycin (increased risk of toxicity); plasma concentration of cabergoline possibly increased by macrolides (increased risk of toxicity)
- Antipsychotics: hypoprolactinaemic and antiparkinsonian effects of cabergoline antagonised by antipsychotics
- Domperidone: hypoprolactinaemic effect of cabergoline possibly antagonised by domperidone
- Memantine: effects of dopaminergics possibly enhanced by memantine
- Methyldopa: antiparkinsonian effect of dopaminergics antagonised by methyldopa
- Metoclopramide: hypoprolactinaemic effect of cabergoline antagonised by metoclopramide

**Calcium Salts**

*Note. see also* Antacids
- Antibacterials: calcium salts reduce absorption of ciprofloxacin and tetracycline
- Bisphosphonates: calcium salts reduce absorption of bisphosphonates
- Cardiac Glycosides: large intravenous doses of calcium salts can precipitate arrhythmias when given with cardiac glycosides
- Corticosteroids: absorption of calcium salts reduced by corticosteroids
- Diuretics: increased risk of hypercalcaemia if calcium salts given with thiazides and related diuretics
- Fluorides: calcium salts reduce absorption of fluorides
- Iron: calcium salts reduce absorption of *oral* iron
- Thyroid Hormones: calcium salts reduce absorption of levothyroxine (thyroxine)
- Zinc: calcium salts reduce absorption of zinc

**Calcium-channel Blockers**

*Note.* Dihydropyridine calcium-channel blockers include amlodipine, felodipine, isradipine, lacidipine, lercanidipine, nicardipine, nifedipine, nimodipine, and nisoldipine
- ACE Inhibitors: enhanced hypotensive effect when calcium-channel blockers given with ACE inhibitors
- Adrenergic Neurone Blockers: enhanced hypotensive effect when calcium-channel blockers given with adrenergic neurone blockers
- Alcohol: enhanced hypotensive effect when calcium-channel blockers given with alcohol; verapamil possibly increases plasma concentration of alcohol
- Aldesleukin: enhanced hypotensive effect when calcium-channel blockers given with aldesleukin
- • Alpha-blockers: enhanced hypotensive effect when calcium-channel blockers given with •alpha-blockers, also increased risk of first-dose hypotension with post-synaptic alpha-blockers such as prazosin
- • Anaesthetics, General: enhanced hypotensive effect when calcium-channel blockers given with general anaesthetics or isoflurane; hypotensive effect of verapamil enhanced by •general anaesthetics (also AV delay)
- Analgesics: hypotensive effect of calcium-channel blockers antagonised by NSAIDs; diltiazem inhibits metabolism of alfentanil (risk of prolonged or delayed respiratory depression)
- Angiotensin-II Receptor Antagonists: enhanced hypotensive effect when calcium-channel blockers given with angiotensin-II receptor antagonists
- • Anti-arrhythmics: increased risk of bradycardia, AV block and myocardial depression when diltiazem or verapamil given with •amiodarone; increased risk of myocardial depression and asystole when verapamil given with •disopyramide or •flecainide; verapamil increases plasma concentration of •quinidine (extreme hypotension may occur); nifedipine reduces plasma concentration of quinidine
- • Antibacterials: metabolism of verapamil possibly inhibited by •clarithromycin and •erythromycin (increased risk of toxicity); metabolism of felodipine possibly inhibited by erythromycin (increased plasma concentration); manufacturer of lercanidipine advises avoid concomitant use with erythromycin; metabolism of diltiazem, nifedipine, nimodipine and verapamil accelerated by •rifampicin (plasma concentration significantly reduced); metabolism of isradipine, nicardipine and nisoldipine possibly accelerated by •rifampicin (possible significantly reduced

**Calcium-channel Blockers**

- Antibacterials *(continued)* plasma concentration); plasma concentration of nifedipine increased by •quinupristin/dalfopristin
  Antidepressants: diltiazem and verapamil increase plasma concentration of imipramine; enhanced hypotensive effect when calcium-channel blockers given with MAOIs; diltiazem and verapamil possibly increase plasma concentration of tricyclics
  Antidiabetics: glucose tolerance occasionally impaired when nifedipine given with insulin
- Antiepileptics: effects of dihydropyridines, nicardipine and nifedipine probably reduced by carbamazepine; effects of felodipine and isradipine reduced by carbamazepine; diltiazem and verapamil enhance effects of •carbamazepine; effects of felodipine, isradipine and verapamil reduced by phenytoin; effects of dihydropyridines, nicardipine and nifedipine probably reduced by •phenytoin; diltiazem increases plasma concentration of •phenytoin but also effect of diltiazem reduced; plasma concentration of nisoldipine reduced by phenytoin; effects of felodipine and isradipine reduced by •primidone; effects of dihydropyridines, diltiazem and verapamil probably reduced by •primidone
- Antifungals: metabolism of dihydropyridines possibly inhibited by itraconazole and ketoconazole (increased plasma concentration); metabolism of felodipine inhibited by •itraconazole and •ketoconazole (increased plasma concentration); manufacturer of lercanidipine advises avoid concomitant use with itraconazole and ketoconazole; negative inotropic effect possibly increased when calcium-channel blockers given with itraconazole
  Antimalarials: possible increased risk of bradycardia when calcium-channel blockers given with mefloquine
  Antipsychotics: enhanced hypotensive effect when calcium-channel blockers given with antipsychotics
- Antivirals: plasma concentration of diltiazem, nicardipine, nifedipine and nimodipine possibly increased by amprenavir; plasma concentration of diltiazem increased by •atazanavir (reduce dose of diltiazem); plasma concentration of verapamil possibly increased by atazanavir; manufacturer of lercanidipine advises avoid concomitant use with ritonavir; plasma concentration of calcium-channel blockers possibly increased by •ritonavir
  Anxiolytics and Hypnotics: enhanced hypotensive effect when calcium-channel blockers given with anxiolytics and hypnotics; diltiazem and verapamil inhibit metabolism of midazolam (increased plasma concentration with increased sedation); absorption of lercanidipine increased by midazolam; diltiazem and verapamil increase plasma concentration of buspirone (reduce dose of buspirone)
- Barbiturates: effects of dihydropyridines, diltiazem and verapamil probably reduced by •barbiturates; effects of felodipine and isradipine reduced by •barbiturates
- Beta-blockers: enhanced hypotensive effect when calcium-channel blockers given with beta-blockers; increased risk of AV block and bradycardia when diltiazem given with •beta-blockers; asystole, severe hypotension and heart failure when verapamil given with •beta-blockers (see p. 114); possible severe hypotension and heart failure

**Calcium-channel Blockers**

- Beta-blockers *(continued)* when nifedipine or nisoldipine given with •beta-blockers
  Calcium-channel Blockers: plasma concentration of both drugs may increase when diltiazem given with nifedipine
- Cardiac Glycosides: nifedipine possibly increases plasma concentration of •digoxin; diltiazem, lercanidipine and nicardipine increase plasma concentration of •digoxin; verapamil increases plasma concentration of •digoxin, also increased risk of AV block and bradycardia
- Ciclosporin: diltiazem, nicardipine and verapamil increase plasma concentration of •ciclosporin; combination of lercanidipine with •ciclosporin may increase plasma concentration of either drug (or both)—avoid concomitant use; plasma concentration of nifedipine possibly increased by ciclosporin (increased risk of toxicity including gingival hyperplasia)
- Cilostazol: diltiazem increases plasma concentration of •cilostazol—avoid concomitant use
  Clonidine: enhanced hypotensive effect when calcium-channel blockers given with clonidine
  Corticosteroids: hypotensive effect of calcium-channel blockers antagonised by corticosteroids
  Cytotoxics: nifedipine possibly inhibits metabolism of vincristine
  Diazoxide: enhanced hypotensive effect when calcium-channel blockers given with diazoxide
  Diuretics: enhanced hypotensive effect when calcium-channel blockers given with diuretics; diltiazem and verapamil increase plasma concentration of eplerenone (reduce dose of eplerenone)
  Dopaminergics: enhanced hypotensive effect when calcium-channel blockers given with levodopa
  Grapefruit Juice: plasma concentration of felodipine, isradipine, lacidipine, lercanidipine, nicardipine, nifedipine, nimodipine, nisoldipine and verapamil increased by grapefruit juice
  Hormone Antagonists: diltiazem and verapamil increase plasma concentration of dutasteride
- Ivabradine: diltiazem and verapamil increase plasma concentration of •ivabradine—avoid concomitant use
- Lipid-regulating Drugs: possible increased risk of myopathy when diltiazem given with simvastatin; increased risk of myopathy when verapamil given with •simvastatin
  Lithium: neurotoxicity may occur when diltiazem or verapamil given with lithium without increased plasma concentration of lithium
- Magnesium (parenteral): profound hypotension reported with concomitant use of nifedipine and •parenteral magnesium in pre-eclampsia
  Methyldopa: enhanced hypotensive effect when calcium-channel blockers given with methyldopa
  Moxisylyte (thymoxamine): enhanced hypotensive effect when calcium-channel blockers given with moxisylyte
  Moxonidine: enhanced hypotensive effect when calcium-channel blockers given with moxonidine
  Muscle Relaxants: verapamil enhances effects of non-depolarising muscle relaxants and suxamethonium; enhanced hypotensive effect when calcium-channel blockers given with baclofen or tizanidine; risk of arrhythmias when diltiazem given with intravenous dantrolene; hypotension, myocardial depression, and hyperkalaemia when verapamil given with intravenous dantrolene;

**Calcium-channel Blockers**
Muscle Relaxants *(continued)*
nifedipine enhances effects of non-depolarising muscle relaxants
Nitrates: enhanced hypotensive effect when calcium-channel blockers given with nitrates
Oestrogens: hypotensive effect of calcium-channel blockers antagonised by oestrogens
Prostaglandins: enhanced hypotensive effect when calcium-channel blockers given with alprostadil
Sildenafil: enhanced hypotensive effect when amlodipine given with sildenafil
• Sirolimus: diltiazem increases plasma concentration of •sirolimus; plasma concentration of both drugs increased when verapamil given with •sirolimus
• Tacrolimus: diltiazem and nifedipine increase plasma concentration of •tacrolimus; felodipine possibly increases plasma concentration of tacrolimus
• Theophylline: calcium-channel blockers possibly increase plasma concentration of •theophylline (enhanced effect); diltiazem increases plasma concentration of theophylline; verapamil increases plasma concentration of •theophylline (enhanced effect)
Ulcer-healing Drugs: metabolism of calcium-channel blockers possibly inhibited by cimetidine (increased plasma concentration)
Vardenafil: enhanced hypotensive effect when nifedipine given with vardenafil
Vasodilator Antihypertensives: enhanced hypotensive effect when calcium-channel blockers given with hydralazine, minoxidil or nitroprusside

**Calcium-channel Blockers (dihydropyridines)** *see* Calcium-channel Blockers
**Candesartan** *see* Angiotensin-II Receptor Antagonists
**Capecitabine** *see* Fluorouracil
**Capreomycin**
Antibacterials: increased risk of nephrotoxicity when capreomycin given with colistin or polymyxins; increased risk of nephrotoxicity and ototoxicity when capreomycin given with aminoglycosides or vancomycin
Cytotoxics: increased risk of nephrotoxicity and ototoxicity when capreomycin given with platinum compounds
Oestrogens: antibacterials that do not induce liver enzymes possibly reduce contraceptive effect of oestrogens (risk probably small, see p. 408)
**Captopril** *see* ACE Inhibitors
**Carbamazepine**
Alcohol: CNS side-effects of carbamazepine possibly increased by alcohol
• Analgesics: effects of carbamazepine enhanced by •dextropropoxyphene; carbamazepine reduces plasma concentration of methadone; carbamazepine reduces effects of tramadol
• Antibacterials: plasma concentration of carbamazepine increased by •clarithromycin and •erythromycin; plasma concentration of carbamazepine reduced by •rifabutin; carbamazepine accelerates metabolism of doxycycline (reduced effect); plasma concentration of carbamazepine increased by •isoniazid (also possibly increased isoniazid hepatotoxicity); carbamazepine reduces plasma concentration of •telithromycin (avoid during and for 2 weeks after carbamazepine)
• Anticoagulants: carbamazepine accelerates metabolism of •coumarins (reduced anticoagulant effect)

**Carbamazepine** *(continued)*
• Antidepressants: plasma concentration of carbamazepine increased by •fluoxetine and •fluvoxamine; carbamazepine reduces plasma concentration of •mianserin, mirtazapine and paroxetine; manufacturer of carbamazepine advises avoid for 2 weeks after stopping •MAOIs, also antagonism of anticonvulsant effect; anticonvulsant effect of antiepileptics possibly antagonised by MAOIs and •tricyclic-related antidepressants (convulsive threshold lowered); anticonvulsant effect of antiepileptics antagonised by •SSRIs and •tricyclics (convulsive threshold lowered); plasma concentration of carbamazepine reduced by •St John's wort—avoid concomitant use; carbamazepine accelerates metabolism of •tricyclics (reduced plasma concentration and reduced effect)
Antiepileptics: carbamazepine possibly reduces plasma concentration of ethosuximide; carbamazepine often reduces plasma concentration of lamotrigine, also plasma concentration of an active metabolite of carbamazepine sometimes raised (but evidence is conflicting); plasma concentration of carbamazepine sometimes reduced by oxcarbazepine (but concentration of an active metabolite of carbamazepine may be increased), also plasma concentration of an active metabolite of oxcarbazepine often reduced; plasma concentration of both drugs often reduced when carbamazepine given with phenytoin, also plasma concentration of phenytoin may be increased; plasma concentration of carbamazepine often reduced by primidone, also plasma concentration of primidone sometimes reduced (but concentration of an active metabolite of primidone often increased); carbamazepine reduces plasma concentration of tiagabine; carbamazepine often reduces plasma concentration of topiramate; carbamazepine reduces plasma concentration of valproate, also plasma concentration of active metabolite of carbamazepine increased; carbamazepine reduces plasma concentration of zonisamide, effect on carbamazepine plasma concentration not predictable
• Antifungals: plasma concentration of carbamazepine possibly increased by miconazole; carbamazepine possibly reduces plasma concentration of itraconazole; carbamazepine possibly reduces plasma concentration of •voriconazole—avoid concomitant use; carbamazepine possibly reduces plasma concentration of caspofungin—consider increasing dose of caspofungin
• Antimalarials: possible increased risk of convulsions when antiepileptics given with chloroquine and hydroxychloroquine; anticonvulsant effect of antiepileptics and carbamazepine antagonised by •mefloquine
• Antipsychotics: anticonvulsant effect of carbamazepine antagonised by •antipsychotics (convulsive threshold lowered); carbamazepine accelerates metabolism of haloperidol, olanzapine, quetiapine, risperidone and sertindole (reduced plasma concentration); carbamazepine reduces plasma concentration of •aripiprazole—increase dose of aripiprazole; carbamazepine accelerates metabolism of •clozapine (reduced plasma concentration), also avoid concomitant use of drugs with substantial potential for causing agranulocytosis
• Antivirals: plasma concentration of carbamazepine possibly increased by amprenavir and •ritonavir; carbamazepine possibly reduces plasma concen-

**Carbamazepine**

- Antivirals *(continued)*
  tration of indinavir, lopinavir, nelfinavir and saquinavir
  Anxiolytics and Hypnotics: carbamazepine often reduces plasma concentration of clonazepam
  Aprepitant: carbamazepine possibly reduces plasma concentration of aprepitant
  Barbiturates: plasma concentration of carbamazepine reduced by phenobarbital
  Bupropion: carbamazepine reduces plasma concentration of bupropion
- Calcium-channel Blockers: carbamazepine reduces effects of felodipine and isradipine; carbamazepine probably reduces effects of dihydropyridines, nicardipine and nifedipine; effects of carbamazepine enhanced by •diltiazem and •verapamil
  Cardiac Glycosides: carbamazepine accelerates metabolism of digitoxin (reduced effect)
- Ciclosporin: carbamazepine accelerates metabolism of •ciclosporin (reduced plasma concentration)
- Corticosteroids: carbamazepine accelerates metabolism of •corticosteroids (reduced effect)
- Diuretics: increased risk of hyponatraemia when carbamazepine given with diuretics; plasma concentration of carbamazepine increased by •acetazolamide; carbamazepine reduces plasma concentration of •eplerenone—avoid concomitant use
- Hormone Antagonists: metabolism of carbamazepine inhibited by •danazol (increased risk of toxicity); carbamazepine accelerates metabolism of gestrinone (reduced plasma concentration); carbamazepine possibly accelerates metabolism of toremifene (reduced plasma concentration)
  $5HT_3$ Antagonists: carbamazepine accelerates metabolism of ondansetron (reduced effect)
  Lithium: neurotoxicity may occur when carbamazepine given with lithium without increased plasma concentration of lithium
  Muscle Relaxants: carbamazepine antagonises muscle relaxant effect of non-depolarising muscle relaxants (accelerated recovery from neuromuscular blockade)
- Oestrogens: carbamazepine accelerates metabolism of •oestrogens (reduced contraceptive effect—see p. 408)
- Progestogens: carbamazepine accelerates metabolism of •progestogens (reduced contraceptive effect—see p. 408)
  Retinoids: plasma concentration of carbamazepine possibly reduced by isotretinoin
  Theophylline: carbamazepine accelerates metabolism of theophylline (reduced effect)
  Thyroid Hormones: carbamazepine accelerates metabolism of thyroid hormones (may increase requirements for thyroid hormones in hypothyroidism)
  Tibolone: carbamazepine accelerates metabolism of tibolone (reduced plasma concentration)
- Ulcer-healing Drugs: metabolism of carbamazepine inhibited by •cimetidine (increased plasma concentration)
  Vitamins: carbamazepine possibly increases requirements for vitamin D

**Carbapenems** *see* Ertapenem, Imipenem with Cilastatin, and Meropenem
**Carbonic Anhydrase Inhibitors** *see* Diuretics
**Carboplatin** *see* Platinum Compounds
**Carboprost** *see* Prostaglandins

**Cardiac Glycosides**

  ACE Inhibitors: plasma concentration of digoxin possibly increased by captopril
  Alpha-blockers: plasma concentration of digoxin increased by prazosin
  Aminosalicylates: absorption of digoxin possibly reduced by sulfasalazine
  Analgesics: plasma concentration of cardiac glycosides possibly increased by NSAIDs, also possible exacerbation of heart failure and reduction of renal function
- Angiotensin-II Receptor Antagonists: plasma concentration of digoxin increased by •telmisartan
  Antacids: absorption of digoxin possibly reduced by antacids
- Anti-arrhythmics: plasma concentration of digoxin increased by •amiodarone, •propafenone and •quinidine (halve dose of digoxin)
  Antibacterials: plasma concentration of digoxin possibly increased by gentamicin, telithromycin and trimethoprim; absorption of digoxin reduced by neomycin; plasma concentration of digoxin possibly reduced by rifampicin; plasma concentration of digoxin increased by macrolides (increased risk of toxicity); metabolism of digitoxin accelerated by rifamycins (reduced effect)
- Antidepressants: plasma concentration of digoxin reduced by •St John's wort—avoid concomitant use
  Antidiabetics: plasma concentration of digoxin possibly reduced by acarbose
  Antiepileptics: metabolism of digitoxin accelerated by carbamazepine, phenytoin and primidone (reduced effect); plasma concentration of digoxin possibly reduced by phenytoin
- Antifungals: increased cardiac toxicity with cardiac glycosides if hypokalaemia occurs with •amphotericin; plasma concentration of digoxin increased by •itraconazole
- Antimalarials: plasma concentration of digoxin possibly increased by •chloroquine and hydroxychloroquine; possible increased risk of bradycardia when digoxin given with mefloquine; plasma concentration of digoxin increased by •quinine
  Anxiolytics and Hypnotics: plasma concentration of digoxin increased by alprazolam (increased risk of toxicity)
  Barbiturates: metabolism of digitoxin accelerated by barbiturates (reduced effect)
  Beta-blockers: increased risk of AV block and bradycardia when cardiac glycosides given with beta-blockers
  Calcium Salts: arrhythmias can be precipitated when cardiac glycosides given with large intravenous doses of calcium salts
- Calcium-channel Blockers: plasma concentration of digoxin increased by •diltiazem, •lercanidipine and •nicardipine; plasma concentration of digoxin possibly increased by •nifedipine; plasma concentration of digoxin increased by •verapamil, also increased risk of AV block and bradycardia
- Ciclosporin: plasma concentration of digoxin increased by •ciclosporin (increased risk of toxicity)
  Corticosteroids: increased risk of hypokalaemia when cardiac glycosides given with corticosteroids
- Diuretics: increased cardiac toxicity with cardiac glycosides if hypokalaemia occurs with •aceta-

**Cardiac Glycosides**
- Diuretics *(continued)*
  zolamide, •loop diuretics or •thiazides and related diuretics; plasma concentration of digitoxin possibly affected by spironolactone; plasma concentration of digoxin increased by •spironolactone
  Lipid-regulating Drugs: absorption of cardiac glycosides possibly reduced by colestipol and colestyramine; plasma concentration of digoxin possibly increased by atorvastatin
  Muscle Relaxants: risk of ventricular arrhythmias when cardiac glycosides given with suxamethonium; possible increased risk of bradycardia when cardiac glycosides given with tizanidine
  Penicillamine: plasma concentration of digoxin possibly reduced by penicillamine
  Sympathomimetics, $Beta_2$: plasma concentration of digoxin possibly reduced by salbutamol
  Ulcer-healing Drugs: plasma concentration of digoxin possibly slightly increased by proton pump inhibitors; absorption of cardiac glycosides possibly reduced by sucralfate

**Carisoprodol** *see* Muscle Relaxants
**Carteolol** *see* Beta-blockers
**Carvedilol** *see* Beta-blockers
**Caspofungin**
  Antibacterials: plasma concentration of caspofungin initially increased and then reduced by rifampicin (consider increasing dose of caspofungin)
  Antiepileptics: plasma concentration of caspofungin possibly reduced by carbamazepine and phenytoin—consider increasing dose of caspofungin
  Antivirals: plasma concentration of caspofungin possibly reduced by efavirenz and nevirapine—consider increasing dose of caspofungin
- Ciclosporin: plasma concentration of caspofungin increased by •ciclosporin (manufacturer of caspofungin recommends monitoring liver enzymes)
  Corticosteroids: plasma concentration of caspofungin possibly reduced by dexamethasone—consider increasing dose of caspofungin
- Tacrolimus: caspofungin reduces plasma concentration of •tacrolimus

**Cefaclor** *see* Cephalosporins
**Cefadroxil** *see* Cephalosporins
**Cefalexin** *see* Cephalosporins
**Cefixime** *see* Cephalosporins
**Cefotaxime** *see* Cephalosporins
**Cefpirome** *see* Cephalosporins
**Cefpodoxime** *see* Cephalosporins
**Cefprozil** *see* Cephalosporins
**Cefradine** *see* Cephalosporins
**Ceftazidime** *see* Cephalosporins
**Ceftriaxone** *see* Cephalosporins
**Cefuroxime** *see* Cephalosporins
**Celecoxib** *see* NSAIDs
**Celiprolol** *see* Beta-blockers
**Cephalosporins**
  Antacids: absorption of cefaclor and cefpodoxime reduced by antacids
- Anticoagulants: cephalosporins possibly enhance anticoagulant effect of •coumarins
  Oestrogens: antibacterials that do not induce liver enzymes possibly reduce contraceptive effect of oestrogens (risk probably small, see p. 408)
  Probenecid: excretion of cephalosporins reduced by probenecid (increased plasma concentration)
  Ulcer-healing Drugs: absorption of cefpodoxime reduced by histamine $H_2$-antagonists

**Cetirizine** *see* Antihistamines
**Chloral** *see* Anxiolytics and Hypnotics
**Chloramphenicol**
  Antibacterials: metabolism of chloramphenicol accelerated by rifampicin (reduced plasma concentration)
- Anticoagulants: chloramphenicol enhances anticoagulant effect of •coumarins
- Antidiabetics: chloramphenicol enhances effects of •sulphonylureas
- Antiepileptics: chloramphenicol increases plasma concentration of •phenytoin (increased risk of toxicity); metabolism of chloramphenicol accelerated by •primidone (reduced plasma concentration)
- Antipsychotics: avoid concomitant use of chloramphenicol with •clozapine (increased risk of agranulocytosis)
- Barbiturates: metabolism of chloramphenicol accelerated by •barbiturates (reduced plasma concentration)
- Ciclosporin: chloramphenicol possibly increases plasma concentration of •ciclosporin
  Hydroxocobalamin: chloramphenicol reduces response to hydroxocobalamin
  Oestrogens: antibacterials that do not induce liver enzymes possibly reduce contraceptive effect of oestrogens (risk probably small, see p. 408)
- Tacrolimus: chloramphenicol possibly increases plasma concentration of •tacrolimus

**Chlordiazepoxide** *see* Anxiolytics and Hypnotics
**Chloroquine and Hydroxychloroquine**
  Adsorbents: absorption of chloroquine and hydroxychloroquine reduced by kaolin
  Agalsidase Beta: chloroquine and hydroxychloroquine possibly inhibit effects of agalsidase beta (manufacturer of agalsidase beta advises avoid concomitant use)
  Antacids: absorption of chloroquine and hydroxychloroquine reduced by antacids
- Anti-arrhythmics: increased risk of ventricular arrhythmias when chloroquine and hydroxychloroquine given with •amiodarone—avoid concomitant use
- Antibacterials: increased risk of ventricular arrhythmias when chloroquine and hydroxychloroquine given with •moxifloxacin—avoid concomitant use
  Antiepileptics: possible increased risk of convulsions when chloroquine and hydroxychloroquine given with antiepileptics
- Antimalarials: avoidance of antimalarials advised by manufacturer of •artemether/lumefantrine; increased risk of convulsions when chloroquine and hydroxychloroquine given with •mefloquine
- Cardiac Glycosides: chloroquine and hydroxychloroquine possibly increase plasma concentration of •digoxin
- Ciclosporin: chloroquine and hydroxychloroquine increase plasma concentration of •ciclosporin (increased risk of toxicity)
  Laronidase: chloroquine and hydroxychloroquine possibly inhibit effects of laronidase (manufacturer of laronidase advises avoid concomitant use)
  Parasympathomimetics: chloroquine and hydroxychloroquine have potential to increase symptoms of myasthenia gravis and thus diminish effect of neostigmine and pyridostigmine
  Ulcer-healing Drugs: metabolism of chloroquine and hydroxychloroquine inhibited by cimetidine (increased plasma concentration)

**Chlorothiazide** *see* Diuretics

**Chlorphenamine (chlorpheniramine)** *see* Antihistamines
**Chlorpromazine** *see* Antipsychotics
**Chlorpropamide** *see* Antidiabetics
**Chlortalidone** *see* Diuretics
**Chlortetracycline** *see* Tetracyclines
**Ciclesonide** *see* Corticosteroids
**Ciclosporin**
- ACE Inhibitors: increased risk of hyperkalaemia when ciclosporin given with •ACE inhibitors
- Allopurinol: plasma concentration of ciclosporin possibly increased by allopurinol (risk of nephrotoxicity)
- Analgesics: increased risk of nephrotoxicity when ciclosporin given with •NSAIDs; ciclosporin increases plasma concentration of •diclofenac (halve dose of diclofenac)
- Angiotensin-II Receptor Antagonists: increased risk of hyperkalaemia when ciclosporin given with •angiotensin-II receptor antagonists
- Anti-arrhythmics: plasma concentration of ciclosporin possibly increased by amiodarone and propafenone
- Antibacterials: metabolism of ciclosporin inhibited by •clarithromycin and •erythromycin (increased plasma concentration); metabolism of ciclosporin accelerated by •rifampicin (reduced plasma concentration); plasma concentration of ciclosporin possibly reduced by •sulfadiazine; plasma concentration of ciclosporin possibly increased by •chloramphenicol, •doxycycline and •telithromycin; increased risk of nephrotoxicity when ciclosporin given with •aminoglycosides, •polymyxins, •quinolones, •sulphonamides or •vancomycin; metabolism of ciclosporin possibly inhibited by •macrolides (increased plasma concentration); plasma concentration of ciclosporin increased by •quinupristin/dalfopristin; increased risk of nephrotoxicity when ciclosporin given with •trimethoprim, also plasma concentration of ciclosporin reduced by intravenous trimethoprim
- Antidepressants: plasma concentration of ciclosporin reduced by •St John's wort—avoid concomitant use
- Antiepileptics: metabolism of ciclosporin accelerated by •carbamazepine and •phenytoin (reduced plasma concentration); plasma concentration of ciclosporin possibly reduced by oxcarbazepine; metabolism of ciclosporin accelerated by •primidone (reduced effect)
- Antifungals: metabolism of ciclosporin inhibited by •fluconazole, •itraconazole, •ketoconazole and •voriconazole (increased plasma concentration); metabolism of ciclosporin possibly inhibited by •miconazole (increased plasma concentration); increased risk of nephrotoxicity when ciclosporin given with •amphotericin; ciclosporin increases plasma concentration of •caspofungin (manufacturer of caspofungin recommends monitoring liver enzymes); plasma concentration of ciclosporin possibly reduced by griseofulvin
- Antimalarials: plasma concentration of ciclosporin increased by •chloroquine and hydroxychloroquine (increased risk of toxicity)
- Antivirals: increased risk of nephrotoxicity when ciclosporin given with aciclovir; plasma concentration of ciclosporin possibly increased by •atazanavir, •nelfinavir and •ritonavir; plasma concentration of both drugs increased when ciclosporin given with •saquinavir
- Barbiturates: metabolism of ciclosporin accelerated by •barbiturates (reduced effect)

**Ciclosporin** *(continued)*
- Beta-blockers: plasma concentration of ciclosporin increased by •carvedilol
- Bile Acids: absorption of ciclosporin increased by •ursodeoxycholic acid
- Bosentan: ciclosporin increases plasma concentration of •bosentan (also plasma concentration of ciclosporin reduced—avoid concomitant use)
- Calcium-channel Blockers: combination of ciclosporin with •lercanidipine may increase plasma concentration of either drug (or both)—avoid concomitant use; plasma concentration of ciclosporin increased by •diltiazem, •nicardipine and •verapamil; ciclosporin possibly increases plasma concentration of nifedipine (increased risk of toxicity including gingival hyperplasia)
- Cardiac Glycosides: ciclosporin increases plasma concentration of •digoxin (increased risk of toxicity)
- Colchicine: possible increased risk of nephrotoxicity and myotoxicity when ciclosporin given with •colchicine (increased plasma concentration of ciclosporin)
- Corticosteroids: plasma concentration of ciclosporin increased by high-dose •methylprednisolone (risk of convulsions); ciclosporin increases plasma concentration of prednisolone
- Cytotoxics: increased risk of nephrotoxicity when ciclosporin given with •melphalan; increased risk of neurotoxicity when ciclosporin given with •doxorubicin; risk of toxicity when ciclosporin given with •methotrexate; *in vitro* studies suggest a possible interaction between ciclosporin and docetaxel (consult docetaxel product literature); ciclosporin possibly increases plasma concentration of etoposide (increased risk of toxicity)
- Diuretics: increased risk of hyperkalaemia when ciclosporin given with •potassium-sparing diuretics and aldosterone antagonists; increased risk of nephrotoxicity and possibly hypermagnesaemia when ciclosporin given with thiazides and related diuretics
- Grapefruit Juice: plasma concentration of ciclosporin increased by •grapefruit juice (increased risk of toxicity)
- Hormone Antagonists: metabolism of ciclosporin inhibited by •danazol (increased plasma concentration); plasma concentration of ciclosporin reduced by lanreotide and •octreotide
- Lipid-regulating Drugs: increased risk of renal impairment when ciclosporin given with fenofibrate; increased risk of myopathy when ciclosporin given with •rosuvastatin (avoid concomitant use); plasma concentration of both drugs may increase when ciclosporin given with •ezetimibe; increased risk of myopathy when ciclosporin given with •statins
- Metoclopramide: plasma concentration of ciclosporin increased by •metoclopramide
- Modafinil: plasma concentration of ciclosporin reduced by •modafinil
- Oestrogens: plasma concentration of ciclosporin possibly increased by oestrogens
- Orlistat: absorption of ciclosporin possibly reduced by •orlistat
- Potassium Salts: increased risk of hyperkalaemia when ciclosporin given with •potassium salts
- Progestogens: metabolism of ciclosporin inhibited by •progestogens (increased plasma concentration)
- Sirolimus: ciclosporin increases plasma concentration of sirolimus

**Ciclosporin** *(continued)*
- • Tacrolimus: plasma concentration of ciclosporin increased by •tacrolimus (increased risk of toxicity)—avoid concomitant use
- • Ulcer-healing Drugs: plasma concentration of ciclosporin possibly increased by •cimetidine; plasma concentration of ciclosporin possibly affected by omeprazole

**Cidofovir**
- Antivirals: combination of cidofovir with tenofovir may increase plasma concentration of either drug (or both)

**Cilazapril** *see* ACE Inhibitors

**Cilostazol**
- • Anagrelide: avoidance of cilostazol advised by manufacturer of •anagrelide
- Analgesics: manufacturer of cilostazol recommends dose of concomitant aspirin should not exceed 80 mg daily
- • Antibacterials: plasma concentration of cilostazol increased by •erythromycin (also plasma concentration of erythromycin reduced)—avoid concomitant use
- • Antifungals: plasma concentration of cilostazol possibly increased by •ketoconazole—avoid concomitant use
- • Antivirals: plasma concentration of cilostazol possibly increased by •amprenavir, •indinavir, •lopinavir, •nelfinavir, •ritonavir and •saquinavir—avoid concomitant use
- • Calcium-channel Blockers: plasma concentration of cilostazol increased by •diltiazem—avoid concomitant use
- • Ulcer-healing Drugs: plasma concentration of cilostazol possibly increased by •cimetidine and •lansoprazole—avoid concomitant use; plasma concentration of cilostazol increased by •omeprazole (risk of toxicity)—avoid concomitant use

**Cimetidine** *see* Histamine $H_2$-antagonists

**Cinacalcet**
- Antifungals: metabolism of cinacalcet inhibited by ketoconazole (increased plasma concentration)
- Tobacco: metabolism of cinacalcet increased by tobacco smoking (reduced plasma concentration)

**Cinnarizine** *see* Antihistamines

**Ciprofibrate** *see* Fibrates

**Ciprofloxacin** *see* Quinolones

**Cisatracurium** *see* Muscle Relaxants

**Cisplatin** *see* Platinum Compounds

**Citalopram** *see* Antidepressants, SSRI

**Clarithromycin** *see* Macrolides

**Clemastine** *see* Antihistamines

**Clindamycin**
- • Muscle Relaxants: clindamycin enhances effects of •non-depolarising muscle relaxants and •suxamethonium
- Oestrogens: antibacterials that do not induce liver enzymes possibly reduce contraceptive effect of oestrogens (risk probably small, see p. 408)
- Parasympathomimetics: clindamycin antagonises effects of neostigmine and pyridostigmine

**Clobazam** *see* Anxiolytics and Hypnotics

**Clomethiazole** *see* Anxiolytics and Hypnotics

**Clomipramine** *see* Antidepressants, Tricyclic

**Clonazepam** *see* Anxiolytics and Hypnotics

**Clonidine**
- ACE Inhibitors: enhanced hypotensive effect when clonidine given with ACE inhibitors; previous treatment with clonidine possibly delays antihypertensive effect of captopril
- Adrenergic Neurone Blockers: enhanced hypotensive effect when clonidine given with adrenergic neurone blockers

**Clonidine** *(continued)*
- Alcohol: enhanced hypotensive effect when clonidine given with alcohol
- Aldesleukin: enhanced hypotensive effect when clonidine given with aldesleukin
- Alpha-blockers: enhanced hypotensive effect when clonidine given with alpha-blockers
- Anaesthetics, General: enhanced hypotensive effect when clonidine given with general anaesthetics
- Analgesics: hypotensive effect of clonidine antagonised by NSAIDs
- Angiotensin-II Receptor Antagonists: enhanced hypotensive effect when clonidine given with angiotensin-II receptor antagonists
- • Antidepressants: enhanced hypotensive effect when clonidine given with MAOIs; hypotensive effect of clonidine antagonised by •tricyclics, also increased risk of hypertension on clonidine withdrawal
- Antipsychotics: enhanced hypotensive effect when clonidine given with phenothiazines
- Anxiolytics and Hypnotics: enhanced hypotensive effect when clonidine given with anxiolytics and hypnotics
- • Beta-blockers: increased risk of withdrawal hypertension when clonidine given with •beta-blockers (withdraw beta-blockers several days before slowly withdrawing clonidine)
- Calcium-channel Blockers: enhanced hypotensive effect when clonidine given with calcium-channel blockers
- Corticosteroids: hypotensive effect of clonidine antagonised by corticosteroids
- Diazoxide: enhanced hypotensive effect when clonidine given with diazoxide
- Diuretics: enhanced hypotensive effect when clonidine given with diuretics
- Dopaminergics: enhanced hypotensive effect when clonidine given with levodopa
- Methyldopa: enhanced hypotensive effect when clonidine given with methyldopa
- Moxisylyte (thymoxamine): enhanced hypotensive effect when clonidine given with moxisylyte
- Moxonidine: enhanced hypotensive effect when clonidine given with moxonidine
- Muscle Relaxants: enhanced hypotensive effect when clonidine given with baclofen or tizanidine
- Nitrates: enhanced hypotensive effect when clonidine given with nitrates
- Oestrogens: hypotensive effect of clonidine antagonised by oestrogens
- Prostaglandins: enhanced hypotensive effect when clonidine given with alprostadil
- • Sympathomimetics: possible risk of hypertension when clonidine given with adrenaline (epinephrine) or noradrenaline (norepinephrine); serious adverse events reported with concomitant use of clonidine and •methylphenidate (causality not established)
- Vasodilator Antihypertensives: enhanced hypotensive effect when clonidine given with hydralazine, minoxidil or nitroprusside

**Clopamide** *see* Diuretics

**Clopidogrel**
- Analgesics: increased risk of bleeding when clopidogrel given with NSAIDs or aspirin
- • Anticoagulants: manufacturer of clopidogrel advises avoid concomitant use with •warfarin; antiplatelet action of clopidogrel enhances anticoagulant effect of •coumarins and •phenindione; increased risk of bleeding when clopidogrel given with heparins

**Clopidogrel** *(continued)*
Dipyridamole: increased risk of bleeding when clopidogrel given with dipyridamole
Iloprost: increased risk of bleeding when clopidogrel given with iloprost
**Clotrimazole** *see* Antifungals, Imidazole
**Clozapine** *see* Antipsychotics
**Co-amoxiclav** *see* Penicillins
**Co-beneldopa** *see* Levodopa
**Co-careldopa** *see* Levodopa
**Codeine** *see* Opioid Analgesics
**Co-fluampicil** *see* Penicillins
**Colchicine**
• Antibacterials: increased risk of colchicine toxicity when given with •clarithromycin or •erythromycin
• Ciclosporin: possible increased risk of nephrotoxicity and myotoxicity when colchicine given with •ciclosporin (increased plasma concentration of ciclosporin)
**Colestipol**
*Note.* Other drugs should be taken at least 1 hour before or 4-6 hours after colestipol to reduce possible interference with absorption
Bile Acids: colestipol possibly reduces absorption of bile acids
Cardiac Glycosides: colestipol possibly reduces absorption of cardiac glycosides
Diuretics: colestipol reduces absorption of thiazides and related diuretics (give at least 2 hours apart)
Thyroid Hormones: colestipol reduces absorption of thyroid hormones
**Colestyramine**
*Note.* Other drugs should be taken at least 1 hour before or 4-6 hours after colestyramine to reduce possible interference with absorption
Analgesics: colestyramine increases the excretion of meloxicam; colestyramine reduces absorption of paracetamol
Antibacterials: colestyramine antagonises effects of oral vancomycin
• Anticoagulants: colestyramine may enhance or reduce anticoagulant effect of •coumarins and •phenindione
Antidiabetics: colestyramine possibly enhances hypoglycaemic effect of acarbose
Antiepileptics: colestyramine possibly reduces absorption of valproate
Bile Acids: colestyramine possibly reduces absorption of bile acids
Cardiac Glycosides: colestyramine possibly reduces absorption of cardiac glycosides
Cytotoxics: colestyramine reduces absorption of mycophenolate mofetil
Diuretics: colestyramine reduces absorption of thiazides and related diuretics (give at least 2 hours apart)
Leflunomide: colestyramine significantly decreases effect of leflunomide (enhanced elimination)—avoid unless drug elimination desired
Raloxifene: colestyramine reduces absorption of raloxifene (manufacturer of raloxifene advises avoid concomitant administration)
Thyroid Hormones: colestyramine reduces absorption of thyroid hormones
**Colistin** *see* Polymyxins
**Contraceptives, oral** *see* Oestrogens and Progestogens
**Corticosteroids**
*Note.* Interactions do not generally apply to corticosteroids used for topical action (including inhalation) unless specified
ACE Inhibitors: corticosteroids antagonise hypotensive effect of ACE inhibitors

**Corticosteroids** *(continued)*
Adrenergic Neurone Blockers: corticosteroids antagonise hypotensive effect of adrenergic neurone blockers
Alpha-blockers: corticosteroids antagonise hypotensive effect of alpha-blockers
Analgesics: increased risk of gastro-intestinal bleeding and ulceration when corticosteroids given with NSAIDs; increased risk of gastro-intestinal bleeding and ulceration when corticosteroids given with aspirin, also corticosteroids reduce plasma concentration of salicylate
Angiotensin-II Receptor Antagonists: corticosteroids antagonise hypotensive effect of angiotensin-II receptor antagonists
Antacids: absorption of deflazacort reduced by antacids
• Antibacterials: plasma concentration of methylprednisolone possibly increased by clarithromycin; metabolism of corticosteroids possibly inhibited by erythromycin; metabolism of methylprednisolone inhibited by erythromycin; metabolism of corticosteroids accelerated by •rifamycins (reduced effect)
• Anticoagulants: corticosteroids may enhance or reduce anticoagulant effect of •coumarins (high-dose corticosteroids enhance anticoagulant effect)
Antidiabetics: corticosteroids antagonise hypoglycaemic effect of antidiabetics
• Antiepileptics: metabolism of corticosteroids accelerated by •carbamazepine, •phenytoin and •primidone (reduced effect)
• Antifungals: metabolism of corticosteroids possibly inhibited by itraconazole and ketoconazole; plasma concentration of inhaled budesonide and mometasone increased by ketoconazole; metabolism of methylprednisolone inhibited by ketoconazole; increased risk of hypokalaemia when corticosteroids given with •amphotericin—avoid concomitant use unless amphotericin needed to control reactions; plasma concentration of inhaled budesonide increased by itraconazole; metabolism of methylprednisolone possibly inhibited by itraconazole; dexamethasone possibly reduces plasma concentration of caspofungin—consider increasing dose of caspofungin
• Antivirals: dexamethasone possibly reduces plasma concentration of indinavir, lopinavir and saquinavir; plasma concentration of corticosteroids, dexamethasone and prednisolone possibly increased by ritonavir; plasma concentration of inhaled and intranasal budesonide and fluticasone increased by •ritonavir
Aprepitant: metabolism of dexamethasone and methylprednisolone inhibited by aprepitant (reduce dose of dexamethasone and methylprednisolone)
• Barbiturates: metabolism of corticosteroids accelerated by •barbiturates (reduced effect)
Beta-blockers: corticosteroids antagonise hypotensive effect of beta-blockers
Calcium Salts: corticosteroids reduce absorption of calcium salts
Calcium-channel Blockers: corticosteroids antagonise hypotensive effect of calcium-channel blockers
Cardiac Glycosides: increased risk of hypokalaemia when corticosteroids given with cardiac glycosides
• Ciclosporin: high-dose methylprednisolone increases plasma concentration of •ciclosporin

**Corticosteroids**

- Ciclosporin *(continued)* (risk of convulsions); plasma concentration of prednisolone increased by ciclosporin
  Clonidine: corticosteroids antagonise hypotensive effect of clonidine
- Cytotoxics: increased risk of haematological toxicity when corticosteroids given with •methotrexate
  Diazoxide: corticosteroids antagonise hypotensive effect of diazoxide
  Diuretics: corticosteroids antagonise diuretic effect of diuretics; increased risk of hypokalaemia when corticosteroids given with acetazolamide, loop diuretics or thiazides and related diuretics
  Methyldopa: corticosteroids antagonise hypotensive effect of methyldopa
  Mifepristone: effect of corticosteroids (including inhaled corticosteroids) may be reduced for 3–4 days after mifepristone
  Moxonidine: corticosteroids antagonise hypotensive effect of moxonidine
  Nitrates: corticosteroids antagonise hypotensive effect of nitrates
  Oestrogens: plasma concentration of corticosteroids increased by oral contraceptives containing oestrogens
  Sodium Benzoate: corticosteroids possibly reduce effects of sodium benzoate
  Sodium Phenylbutyrate: corticosteroids possibly reduce effects of sodium phenylbutyrate
  Somatropin: corticosteroids may inhibit growth-promoting effect of somatropin
  Sympathomimetics: metabolism of dexamethasone accelerated by ephedrine
  Sympathomimetics, Beta$_2$: increased risk of hypokalaemia when corticosteroids given with high doses of beta$_2$ sympathomimetics—for CSM advice (hypokalaemia) see p. 145
  Theophylline: increased risk of hypokalaemia when corticosteroids given with theophylline
- Vaccines: high doses of corticosteroids impair immune response to •vaccines, avoid concomitant use with live vaccines (see p. 611)
  Vasodilator Antihypertensives: corticosteroids antagonise hypotensive effect of hydralazine, minoxidil and nitroprusside

**Cortisone** *see* Corticosteroids

**Co-trimoxazole** *see* Trimethoprim and Sulfamethoxazole

**Coumarins**

*Note.* Change in patient's clinical condition, particularly associated with liver disease, intercurrent illness, or drug administration, necessitates more frequent testing. Major changes in diet (especially involving salads and vegetables) and in alcohol consumption may also affect anticoagulant control

- Alcohol: anticoagulant control with coumarins may be affected by major changes in consumption of •alcohol
  Allopurinol: anticoagulant effect of coumarins possibly enhanced by allopurinol
- Anabolic Steroids: anticoagulant effect of coumarins enhanced by •anabolic steroids
- <u>Analgesics</u>: anticoagulant effect of coumarins possibly enhanced by •NSAIDs, •celecoxib, •dextropropoxyphene, •diflunisal, •etodolac, •etoricoxib, •flurbiprofen, •ibuprofen, •lumiracoxib, •mefenamic acid, •meloxicam, •parecoxib, •piroxicam and •sulindac; anticoagulant effect of coumarins possibly enhanced by •diclofenac, also increased risk of haemorrhage with intravenous diclofenac (avoid concomitant use); increased risk of bleeding when coumarins given with •ketorolac (avoid concomitant use); anticoagulant effect of coumarins enhanced by •tramadol; increased risk of bleeding when coumarins given with •aspirin (due to antiplatelet effect); anticoagulant effect of coumarins possibly enhanced by prolonged regular use of paracetamol
- Anti-arrhythmics: metabolism of coumarins inhibited by •amiodarone (enhanced anticoagulant effect); anticoagulant effect of coumarins enhanced by •propafenone; anticoagulant effect of coumarins possibly enhanced by •quinidine
- Antibacterials: experience in anticoagulant clinics suggests that INR possibly altered when coumarins are given with •neomycin (given for local action on gut); anticoagulant effect of coumarins enhanced by •chloramphenicol, •ciprofloxacin, •clarithromycin, •erythromycin, •metronidazole, •nalidixic acid, •norfloxacin, •ofloxacin and •sulphonamides; anticoagulant effect of coumarins possibly enhanced by •aztreonam, •cephalosporins, levofloxacin, •macrolides, •tetracyclines and trimethoprim; studies have failed to demonstrate an interaction with coumarins, but common experience in anticoagulant clinics is that INR can be altered by a course of broad-spectrum penicillins such as ampicillin; metabolism of coumarins accelerated by •rifamycins (reduced anticoagulant effect)
- <u>Antidepressants</u>: anticoagulant effect of warfarin possibly enhanced by •venlafaxine; anticoagulant effect of coumarins possibly enhanced by •SSRIs; anticoagulant effect of coumarins reduced by •St John's wort (avoid concomitant use); anticoagulant effect of warfarin enhanced by mirtazapine; anticoagulant effect of coumarins may be enhanced or reduced by •tricyclics
- Antidiabetics: coumarins possibly enhance hypoglycaemic effect of •sulphonylureas, also possible changes to anticoagulant effect
- Antiepileptics: metabolism of coumarins accelerated by •carbamazepine and •primidone (reduced anticoagulant effect); metabolism of coumarins accelerated by •phenytoin (possibility of reduced anticoagulant effect, but enhancement also reported); anticoagulant effect of coumarins possibly enhanced by valproate
- Antifungals: anticoagulant effect of coumarins enhanced by •fluconazole, •itraconazole, •ketoconazole and •voriconazole; anticoagulant effect of coumarins enhanced by •miconazole (miconazole oral gel and possibly vaginal formulations absorbed); anticoagulant effect of coumarins reduced by •griseofulvin
  Antimalarials: isolated reports that anticoagulant effect of warfarin may be enhanced by proguanil
- <u>Antivirals</u>: anticoagulant effect of coumarins may be enhanced or reduced by amprenavir; anticoagulant effect of warfarin may be enhanced or reduced by atazanavir, •nevirapine and •ritonavir; anticoagulant effect of coumarins possibly enhanced by •ritonavir; anticoagulant effect of warfarin possibly enhanced by saquinavir
  Anxiolytics and Hypnotics: anticoagulant effect of coumarins may transiently be enhanced by chloral and triclofos
  Aprepitant: anticoagulant effect of warfarin possibly reduced by aprepitant
- Barbiturates: metabolism of coumarins accelerated by •barbiturates (reduced anticoagulant effect)

**Coumarins** *(continued)*
Bosentan: monitoring anticoagulant effect of coumarins recommended by manufacturer of bosentan
• Clopidogrel: anticoagulant effect of coumarins enhanced due to antiplatelet action of •clopidogrel; avoidance of warfarin advised by manufacturer of •clopidogrel
• Corticosteroids: anticoagulant effect of coumarins may be enhanced or reduced by •corticosteroids (high-dose corticosteroids enhance anticoagulant effect)
• Cranberry Juice: anticoagulant effect of coumarins possibly enhanced by •cranberry juice—avoid concomitant use
• Cytotoxics: anticoagulant effect of coumarins possibly enhanced by •etoposide, •fluorouracil and •ifosfamide; anticoagulant effect of coumarins possibly reduced by •azathioprine and •mercaptopurine; increased risk of bleeding when coumarins given with •erlotinib; replacement of warfarin with a heparin advised by manufacturer of imatinib (possibility of enhanced warfarin effect)
• Dipyridamole: anticoagulant effect of coumarins enhanced due to antiplatelet action of •dipyridamole
• Disulfiram: anticoagulant effect of coumarins enhanced by •disulfiram
• Dopaminergics: anticoagulant effect of warfarin enhanced by •entacapone
• Enteral Foods: anticoagulant effect of coumarins antagonised by vitamin K (present in some •enteral feeds )
• Hormone Antagonists: anticoagulant effect of coumarins possibly enhanced by bicalutamide and •toremifene; metabolism of coumarins inhibited by •danazol (enhanced anticoagulant effect); anticoagulant effect of coumarins enhanced by •flutamide and •tamoxifen
Iloprost: anticoagulant effect of coumarins possibly enhanced by iloprost
Leflunomide: anticoagulant effect of warfarin possibly enhanced by leflunomide
Leukotriene Antagonists: anticoagulant effect of warfarin enhanced by zafirlukast
• Levamisole: anticoagulant effect of warfarin possibly enhanced by •levamisole
• Lipid-regulating Drugs: anticoagulant effect of coumarins may be enhanced or reduced by •colestyramine; anticoagulant effect of warfarin may be transiently reduced by atorvastatin; anticoagulant effect of coumarins enhanced by •fibrates, •fluvastatin and simvastatin; anticoagulant effect of coumarins possibly enhanced by •rosuvastatin; anticoagulant effect of warfarin possibly enhanced by ezetimibe
• Oestrogens: anticoagulant effect of coumarins antagonised by •oestrogens
Orlistat: monitoring anticoagulant effect of coumarins recommended by manufacturer of orlistat
• Progestogens: anticoagulant effect of coumarins antagonised by •progestogens
Raloxifene: anticoagulant effect of coumarins antagonised by raloxifene
• Retinoids: anticoagulant effect of coumarins possibly reduced by •acitretin
Sibutramine: increased risk of bleeding when anticoagulants given with sibutramine
• Sulfinpyrazone: anticoagulant effect of coumarins enhanced by •sulfinpyrazone
• Sympathomimetics: anticoagulant effect of coumarins possibly enhanced by •methylphenidate



**Coumarins** *(continued)*
Terpene Mixture: anticoagulant effect of coumarins possibly reduced by Rowachol®
• Testolactone: anticoagulant effect of coumarins enhanced by •testolactone
• Testosterone: anticoagulant effect of coumarins enhanced by •testosterone
• Thyroid Hormones: anticoagulant effect of coumarins enhanced by •thyroid hormones
• Ulcer-healing Drugs: metabolism of coumarins inhibited by •cimetidine (enhanced anticoagulant effect); anticoagulant effect of coumarins possibly enhanced by •esomeprazole and •omeprazole; absorption of coumarins possibly reduced by •sucralfate (reduced anticoagulant effect)
Vaccines: anticoagulant effect of warfarin possibly enhanced by influenza vaccine
• Vitamins: anticoagulant effect of coumarins antagonised by •vitamin K

**Cranberry Juice**
• Anticoagulants: cranberry juice possibly enhances anticoagulant effect of •coumarins—avoid concomitant use

**Cyclizine** *see* Antihistamines

**Cyclopenthiazide** *see* Diuretics

**Cyclopentolate** *see* Antimuscarinics

**Cyclophosphamide**
Antiepileptics: cytotoxics possibly reduce absorption of phenytoin
• Antipsychotics: avoid concomitant use of cytotoxics with •clozapine (increased risk of agranulocytosis)
• Cytotoxics: increased toxicity when high-dose cyclophosphamide given with •pentostatin—avoid concomitant use
Muscle Relaxants: cyclophosphamide enhances effects of suxamethonium

**Cycloserine**
• Alcohol: increased risk of convulsions when cycloserine given with •alcohol
Antibacterials: increased risk of CNS toxicity when cycloserine given with isoniazid
Oestrogens: antibacterials that do not induce liver enzymes possibly reduce contraceptive effect of oestrogens (risk probably small, see p. 408)

**Cyproheptadine** *see* Antihistamines

**Cytarabine**
Antiepileptics: cytotoxics possibly reduce absorption of phenytoin
Antifungals: cytarabine possibly reduces plasma concentration of flucytosine
• Antipsychotics: avoid concomitant use of cytotoxics with •clozapine (increased risk of agranulocytosis)
Cytotoxics: intracellular concentration of cytarabine increased by fludarabine

**Cytotoxics** *see* individual drugs

**Dairy Products**
Antibacterials: dairy products reduces absorption of ciprofloxacin and norfloxacin; dairy products reduces absorption of tetracyclines (except doxycycline and minocycline)

**Dalteparin** *see* Heparins

**Danazol**
• Anticoagulants: danazol inhibits metabolism of •coumarins (enhanced anticoagulant effect)
• Antiepileptics: danazol inhibits metabolism of •carbamazepine (increased risk of toxicity)
• Ciclosporin: danazol inhibits metabolism of •ciclosporin (increased plasma concentration)
• Lipid-regulating Drugs: possible increased risk of myopathy when danazol given with •simvastatin
Tacrolimus: danazol possibly increases plasma concentration of tacrolimus

**Dantrolene** *see* Muscle Relaxants
**Dapsone**
Antibacterials: plasma concentration of dapsone reduced by rifamycins; plasma concentration of both drugs may increase when dapsone given with trimethoprim
Antivirals: plasma concentration of dapsone possibly increased by amprenavir
Oestrogens: antibacterials that do not induce liver enzymes possibly reduce contraceptive effect of oestrogens (risk probably small, see p. 408)
Probenecid: excretion of dapsone reduced by probenecid (increased risk of side-effects)
**Darbepoetin** *see* Epoetin
**Deflazacort** *see* Corticosteroids
**Demeclocycline** *see* Tetracyclines
**Desferrioxamine**
Antipsychotics: avoidance of desferrioxamine advised by manufacturer of levomepromazine (methotrimeprazine); manufacturer of desferrioxamine advises avoid concomitant use with prochlorperazine
**Desflurane** *see* Anaesthetics, General
**Desloratadine** *see* Antihistamines
**Desmopressin**
Analgesics: effects of desmopressin enhanced by indometacin
Loperamide: plasma concentration of *oral* desmopressin increased by loperamide
**Desogestrel** *see* Progestogens
**Dexamethasone** *see* Corticosteroids
**Dexamfetamine** *see* Sympathomimetics
**Dexibuprofen** *see* NSAIDs
**Dexketoprofen** *see* NSAIDs
**Dextromethorphan** *see* Opioid Analgesics
**Dextropropoxyphene** *see* Opioid Analgesics
**Diamorphine** *see* Opioid Analgesics
**Diazepam** *see* Anxiolytics and Hypnotics
**Diazoxide**
ACE Inhibitors: enhanced hypotensive effect when diazoxide given with ACE inhibitors
Adrenergic Neurone Blockers: enhanced hypotensive effect when diazoxide given with adrenergic neurone blockers
Alcohol: enhanced hypotensive effect when diazoxide given with alcohol
Aldesleukin: enhanced hypotensive effect when diazoxide given with aldesleukin
Alpha-blockers: enhanced hypotensive effect when diazoxide given with alpha-blockers
Anaesthetics, General: enhanced hypotensive effect when diazoxide given with general anaesthetics
Analgesics: hypotensive effect of diazoxide antagonised by NSAIDs
Angiotensin-II Receptor Antagonists: enhanced hypotensive effect when diazoxide given with angiotensin-II receptor antagonists
Antidepressants: enhanced hypotensive effect when diazoxide given with MAOIs or tricyclic-related antidepressants
Antidiabetics: diazoxide antagonises hypoglycaemic effect of antidiabetics
Antiepileptics: diazoxide reduces plasma concentration of phenytoin, also effect of diazoxide may be reduced
Antipsychotics: enhanced hypotensive effect when diazoxide given with phenothiazines
Anxiolytics and Hypnotics: enhanced hypotensive effect when diazoxide given with anxiolytics and hypnotics
Beta-blockers: enhanced hypotensive effect when diazoxide given with beta-blockers

**Diazoxide** *(continued)*
Calcium-channel Blockers: enhanced hypotensive effect when diazoxide given with calcium-channel blockers
Clonidine: enhanced hypotensive effect when diazoxide given with clonidine
Corticosteroids: hypotensive effect of diazoxide antagonised by corticosteroids
Diuretics: enhanced hypotensive effect when diazoxide given with diuretics
Dopaminergics: enhanced hypotensive effect when diazoxide given with levodopa
Methyldopa: enhanced hypotensive effect when diazoxide given with methyldopa
Moxisylyte (thymoxamine): enhanced hypotensive effect when diazoxide given with moxisylyte
Moxonidine: enhanced hypotensive effect when diazoxide given with moxonidine
Muscle Relaxants: enhanced hypotensive effect when diazoxide given with baclofen or tizanidine
Nitrates: enhanced hypotensive effect when diazoxide given with nitrates
Oestrogens: hypotensive effect of diazoxide antagonised by oestrogens
Prostaglandins: enhanced hypotensive effect when diazoxide given with alprostadil
Vasodilator Antihypertensives: enhanced hypotensive effect when diazoxide given with hydralazine, minoxidil or nitroprusside
**Diclofenac** *see* NSAIDs
**Dicycloverine (dicyclomine)** *see* Antimuscarinics
**Didanosine**
*Note.* Antacids in tablet formulation may affect absorption of other drugs
Allopurinol: plasma concentration of didanosine possibly increased by allopurinol
• Antivirals: plasma concentration of didanosine possibly increased by ganciclovir; increased risk of side-effects when didanosine given with •stavudine; plasma concentration of didanosine increased by •tenofovir (increased risk of toxicity)—avoid concomitant use; plasma concentration of didanosine reduced by •tipranavir
• Cytotoxics: increased risk of toxicity when didanosine given with •hydroxycarbamide—avoid concomitant use
**Diflunisal** *see* NSAIDs
**Digitoxin** *see* Cardiac Glycosides
**Digoxin** *see* Cardiac Glycosides
**Dihydrocodeine** *see* Opioid Analgesics
**Diltiazem** *see* Calcium-channel Blockers
**Dimercaprol**
• Iron: avoid concomitant use of dimercaprol with •iron
**Dinoprostone** *see* Prostaglandins
**Diphenoxylate** *see* Opioid Analgesics
**Diphenylpyraline** *see* Antihistamines
**Dipipanone** *see* Opioid Analgesics
**Dipivefrine** *see* Sympathomimetics
**Dipyridamole**
Antacids: absorption of dipyridamole possibly reduced by antacids
• Anti-arrhythmics: dipyridamole enhances and extends the effects of •adenosine (important risk of toxicity)
• Anticoagulants: antiplatelet action of dipyridamole enhances anticoagulant effect of •coumarins and •phenindione; dipyridamole enhances anticoagulant effect of heparins
Clopidogrel: increased risk of bleeding when dipyridamole given with clopidogrel
Cytotoxics: dipyridamole possibly reduces effects of fludarabine
**Disodium Etidronate** *see* Bisphosphonates

**Disodium Pamidronate** *see* Bisphosphonates

**Disopyramide**

Anaesthetics, Local: increased myocardial depression when anti-arrhythmics given with bupivacaine, levobupivacaine or prilocaine

• Anti-arrhythmics: increased myocardial depression when anti-arrhythmics given with other •anti-arrhythmics; increased risk of ventricular arrhythmias when disopyramide given with •amiodarone—avoid concomitant use

• Antibacterials: plasma concentration of disopyramide possibly increased by •clarithromycin (increased risk of toxicity); plasma concentration of disopyramide increased by •erythromycin (increased risk of toxicity); increased risk of ventricular arrhythmias when disopyramide given with •moxifloxacin or •quinupristin/dalfopristin—avoid concomitant use; metabolism of disopyramide accelerated by •rifamycins (reduced plasma concentration)

• Antidepressants: increased risk of ventricular arrhythmias when disopyramide given with •tricyclics

Antidiabetics: disopyramide possibly enhances hypoglycaemic effect of gliclazide, insulin and metformin

Antiepileptics: plasma concentration of disopyramide reduced by phenytoin; metabolism of disopyramide accelerated by primidone (reduced plasma concentration)

• Antihistamines: increased risk of ventricular arrhythmias when disopyramide given with •mizolastine—avoid concomitant use

• Antimalarials: avoidance of disopyramide advised by manufacturer of •artemether/lumefantrine (risk of ventricular arrhythmias)

Antimuscarinics: increased risk of antimuscarinic side-effects when disopyramide given with antimuscarinics

• Antipsychotics: increased risk of ventricular arrhythmias when anti-arrhythmics that prolong the QT interval given with •antipsychotics that prolong the QT interval; increased risk of ventricular arrhythmias when disopyramide given with •amisulpride, •pimozide or •sertindole—avoid concomitant use; increased risk of ventricular arrhythmias when disopyramide given with •phenothiazines

• Antivirals: plasma concentration of disopyramide possibly increased by •ritonavir (increased risk of toxicity)

Barbiturates: metabolism of disopyramide accelerated by barbiturates (reduced plasma concentration)

• Beta-blockers: increased myocardial depression when anti-arrhythmics given with •beta-blockers; increased risk of ventricular arrhythmias when disopyramide given with •sotalol—avoid concomitant use

• Calcium-channel Blockers: increased risk of myocardial depression and asystole when disopyramide given with •verapamil

• Diuretics: increased cardiac toxicity with disopyramide if hypokalaemia occurs with •acetazolamide, •loop diuretics or •thiazides and related diuretics

• Dolasetron: increased risk of ventricular arrhythmias when disopyramide given with •dolasetron—avoid concomitant use

$5HT_3$ Antagonists: caution with anti-arrhythmics advised by manufacturer of tropisetron (risk of ventricular arrhythmias)

**Disopyramide** *(continued)*

• Ivabradine: increased risk of ventricular arrhythmias when disopyramide given with •ivabradine

Nitrates: disopyramide reduces effects of sublingual tablets of nitrates (failure to dissolve under tongue owing to dry mouth)

**Distigmine** *see* Parasympathomimetics

**Disulfiram**

Alcohol: disulfiram reaction when disulfiram given with alcohol (see p. 260)

Antibacterials: psychotic reaction reported when disulfiram given with metronidazole

• Anticoagulants: disulfiram enhances anticoagulant effect of •coumarins

Antidepressants: increased disulfiram reaction with alcohol reported with concomitant amitriptyline; disulfiram inhibits metabolism of tricyclics (increased plasma concentration)

• Antiepileptics: disulfiram inhibits metabolism of •phenytoin (increased risk of toxicity)

Anxiolytics and Hypnotics: disulfiram increases risk of temazepam toxicity; disulfiram inhibits metabolism of benzodiazepines (increased sedative effects)

• Paraldehyde: risk of toxicity when disulfiram given with •paraldehyde

Theophylline: disulfiram inhibits metabolism of theophylline (increased risk of toxicity)

**Diuretics**

*Note.* Since systemic absorption may follow topical application of brinzolamide to the eye, the possibility of interactions should be borne in mind

*Note.* Since systemic absorption may follow topical application of dorzolamide to the eye, the possibility of interactions should be borne in mind

• ACE Inhibitors: enhanced hypotensive effect when diuretics given with •ACE inhibitors; increased risk of severe hyperkalaemia when potassium-sparing diuretics and aldosterone antagonists given with •ACE inhibitors (monitor potassium concentration with low-dose spironolactone in heart failure)

Adrenergic Neurone Blockers: enhanced hypotensive effect when diuretics given with adrenergic neurone blockers

Alcohol: enhanced hypotensive effect when diuretics given with alcohol

Aldesleukin: enhanced hypotensive effect when diuretics given with aldesleukin

Allopurinol: increased risk of hypersensitivity when thiazides and related diuretics given with allopurinol especially in renal impairment

• Alpha-blockers: enhanced hypotensive effect when diuretics given with •alpha-blockers, also increased risk of first-dose hypotension with post-synaptic alpha-blockers such as prazosin

Anaesthetics, General: enhanced hypotensive effect when diuretics given with general anaesthetics

• Analgesics: possibly increased risk of hyperkalaemia when potassium-sparing diuretics and aldosterone antagonists given with NSAIDs; diuretics increase risk of nephrotoxicity of NSAIDs, also antagonism of diuretic effect; effects of diuretics antagonised by indometacin and ketorolac; increased risk of hyperkalaemia when potassium-sparing diuretics and aldosterone antagonists given with indometacin; occasional reports of reduced renal function when triamterene given with •indometacin—avoid concomitant use; increased risk of toxicity when carbonic anhydrase inhibitors given with high-dose aspirin; diuretic effect of spironolactone antagonised by aspirin

Diuretics *(continued)*

- Angiotensin-II Receptor Antagonists: enhanced hypotensive effect when diuretics given with •angiotensin-II receptor antagonists; increased risk of hyperkalaemia when potassium-sparing diuretics and aldosterone antagonists given with •angiotensin-II receptor antagonists
- Anti-arrhythmics: plasma concentration of eplerenone increased by amiodarone (reduce dose of eplerenone); hypokalaemia caused by acetazolamide, loop diuretics or thiazides and related diuretics increases cardiac toxicity with amiodarone; hypokalaemia caused by acetazolamide, loop diuretics or thiazides and related diuretics increases cardiac toxicity with •disopyramide; hypokalaemia caused by acetazolamide, loop diuretics or thiazides and related diuretics increases cardiac toxicity with •flecainide; hypokalaemia caused by acetazolamide, loop diuretics or thiazides and related diuretics antagonises action of •lidocaine (lignocaine); hypokalaemia caused by acetazolamide, loop diuretics or thiazides and related diuretics antagonises action of •mexiletine; hypokalaemia caused by loop diuretics or thiazides and related diuretics increases cardiac toxicity with •quinidine; acetazolamide possibly reduces excretion of •quinidine (increased plasma concentration), also cardiotoxicity of quinidine increased in hypokalaemia
- Antibacterials: plasma concentration of eplerenone increased by •clarithromycin and •telithromycin—avoid concomitant use; plasma concentration of eplerenone increased by erythromycin (reduce dose of eplerenone); plasma concentration of eplerenone reduced by •rifampicin—avoid concomitant use; avoidance of diuretics advised by manufacturer of lymecycline; increased risk of otoxicity when loop diuretics given with •aminoglycosides, •polymyxins or •vancomycin; acetazolamide antagonises effects of •methenamine; increased risk of hyperkalaemia when eplerenone given with trimethoprim
- Antidepressants: possible increased risk of hypokalaemia when loop diuretics or thiazides and related diuretics given with reboxetine; enhanced hypotensive effect when diuretics given with MAOIs; plasma concentration of eplerenone reduced by •St John's wort—avoid concomitant use; increased risk of postural hypotension when diuretics given with tricyclics

Antidiabetics: loop diuretics and thiazides and related diuretics antagonise hypoglycaemic effect of antidiabetics; increased risk of hyponatraemia when thiazides and related diuretics plus potassium-sparing diuretic given with chlorpropamide; increased risk of hyponatraemia when potassium-sparing diuretics and aldosterone antagonists plus thiazide given with chlorpropamide

- Antiepileptics: acetazolamide increases plasma concentration of •carbamazepine; plasma concentration of eplerenone reduced by •carbamazepine and •phenytoin—avoid concomitant use; increased risk of hyponatraemia when diuretics given with carbamazepine; increased risk of osteomalacia when carbonic anhydrase inhibitors given with phenytoin or primidone; acetazolamide possibly reduces plasma concentration of primidone
- Antifungals: plasma concentration of eplerenone increased by •itraconazole and •ketoconazole—avoid concomitant use; increased risk of hypokalaemia when loop diuretics or thiazides and related diuretics given with amphotericin; hydrochlorothiazide increases plasma concentration of fluconazole; plasma concentration of eplerenone increased by fluconazole (reduce dose of eplerenone)
- Antipsychotics: hypokalaemia caused by diuretics increases risk of ventricular arrhythmias with •amisulpride or •sertindole; enhanced hypotensive effect when diuretics given with phenothiazines; hypokalaemia caused by diuretics increases risk of ventricular arrhythmias with •pimozide (avoid concomitant use)
- Antivirals: plasma concentration of eplerenone increased by •nelfinavir and •ritonavir—avoid concomitant use; plasma concentration of eplerenone increased by saquinavir (reduce dose of eplerenone)

Anxiolytics and Hypnotics: enhanced hypotensive effect when diuretics given with anxiolytics and hypnotics; administration of parenteral furosemide (frusemide) with chloral or triclofos may displace thyroid hormone from binding sites

- Barbiturates: increased risk of osteomalacia when carbonic anhydrase inhibitors given with phenobarbital; plasma concentration of eplerenone reduced by •phenobarbital—avoid concomitant use
- Beta-blockers: enhanced hypotensive effect when diuretics given with beta-blockers; hypokalaemia caused by loop diuretics or thiazides and related diuretics increases risk of ventricular arrhythmias with •sotalol

Calcium Salts: increased risk of hypercalcaemia when thiazides and related diuretics given with calcium salts

Calcium-channel Blockers: enhanced hypotensive effect when diuretics given with calcium-channel blockers; plasma concentration of eplerenone increased by diltiazem and verapamil (reduce dose of eplerenone)

- Cardiac Glycosides: hypokalaemia caused by acetazolamide, loop diuretics or thiazides and related diuretics increases cardiac toxicity with •cardiac glycosides; spironolactone possibly affects plasma concentration of digitoxin; spironolactone increases plasma concentration of •digoxin
- Ciclosporin: increased risk of nephrotoxicity and possibly hypermagnesaemia when thiazides and related diuretics given with ciclosporin; increased risk of hyperkalaemia when potassium-sparing diuretics and aldosterone antagonists given with •ciclosporin

Clonidine: enhanced hypotensive effect when diuretics given with clonidine

Corticosteroids: diuretic effect of diuretics antagonised by corticosteroids; increased risk of hypokalaemia when acetazolamide, loop diuretics or thiazides and related diuretics given with corticosteroids

Cytotoxics: increased risk of nephrotoxicity and ototoxicity when diuretics given with platinum compounds

Diazoxide: enhanced hypotensive effect when diuretics given with diazoxide

Diuretics: increased risk of hypokalaemia when loop diuretics or thiazides and related diuretics given with acetazolamide; profound diuresis possible when metolazone given with furosemide (frusemide); increased risk of hypokalaemia when

**Diuretics**

Diuretics *(continued)*
thiazides and related diuretics given with loop diuretics

Dopaminergics: enhanced hypotensive effect when diuretics given with levodopa

Hormone Antagonists: increased risk of hypercalcaemia when thiazides and related diuretics given with toremifene; increased risk of hyperkalaemia when potassium-sparing diuretics and aldosterone antagonists given with trilostane

Lipid-regulating Drugs: absorption of thiazides and related diuretics reduced by colestipol and colestyramine (give at least 2 hours apart)

• Lithium: loop diuretics and thiazides and related diuretics reduce excretion of •lithium (increased plasma concentration and risk of toxicity)—loop diuretics safer than thiazides; potassium-sparing diuretics and aldosterone antagonists reduce excretion of •lithium (increased plasma concentration and risk of toxicity); acetazolamide increases the excretion of •lithium

Methyldopa: enhanced hypotensive effect when diuretics given with methyldopa

Moxisylyte (thymoxamine): enhanced hypotensive effect when diuretics given with moxisylyte

Moxonidine: enhanced hypotensive effect when diuretics given with moxonidine

Muscle Relaxants: enhanced hypotensive effect when diuretics given with baclofen or tizanidine

Nitrates: enhanced hypotensive effect when diuretics given with nitrates

Oestrogens: diuretic effect of diuretics antagonised by oestrogens

• Potassium Salts: increased risk of hyperkalaemia when potassium-sparing diuretics and aldosterone antagonists given with •potassium salts

Progestogens: risk of hyperkalaemia when potassium-sparing diuretics and aldosterone antagonists given with drospirenone (monitor serum potassium during first cycle)

Prostaglandins: enhanced hypotensive effect when diuretics given with alprostadil

Sympathomimetics, $Beta_2$: increased risk of hypokalaemia when acetazolamide, loop diuretics or thiazides and related diuretics given with high doses of $beta_2$ sympathomimetics—for CSM advice (hypokalaemia) see p. 145

• Tacrolimus: increased risk of hyperkalaemia when potassium-sparing diuretics and aldosterone antagonists given with •tacrolimus

Theophylline: increased risk of hypokalaemia when acetazolamide, loop diuretics or thiazides and related diuretics given with theophylline

Vasodilator Antihypertensives: enhanced hypotensive effect when diuretics given with hydralazine, minoxidil or nitroprusside

Vitamins: increased risk of hypercalcaemia when thiazides and related diuretics given with vitamin D

**Diuretics, Loop** *see* Diuretics

**Diuretics, Potassium-sparing and Aldosterone Antagonists** *see* Diuretics

**Diuretics, Thiazide and related** *see* Diuretics

**Dobutamine** *see* Sympathomimetics

**Docetaxel**

Antibacterials: *in vitro* studies suggest a possible interaction between docetaxel and erythromycin (consult docetaxel product literature)

Antiepileptics: cytotoxics possibly reduce absorption of phenytoin

**Docetaxel** *(continued)*

Antifungals: *in vitro* studies suggest a possible interaction between docetaxel and ketoconazole (consult docetaxel product literature)

• Antipsychotics: avoid concomitant use of cytotoxics with •clozapine (increased risk of agranulocytosis)

Ciclosporin: *in vitro* studies suggest a possible interaction between docetaxel and ciclosporin (consult docetaxel product literature)

**Dolasetron**

• Anti-arrhythmics: increased risk of ventricular arrhythmias when dolasetron given with •amiodarone, •disopyramide, •flecainide, •lidocaine (lignocaine), •mexiletine, •procainamide or •propafenone—avoid concomitant use

• Beta-blockers: increased risk of ventricular arrhythmias when dolasetron given with •sotalol—avoid concomitant use

**Domperidone**

Analgesics: effects of domperidone on gastro-intestinal activity antagonised by opioid analgesics

Antimuscarinics: effects of domperidone on gastro-intestinal activity antagonised by antimuscarinics

Dopaminergics: increased risk of extrapyramidal side-effects when domperidone given with amantadine; domperidone possibly antagonises hypoprolactinaemic effects of bromocriptine and cabergoline

**Donepezil** *see* Parasympathomimetics

**Dopamine** *see* Sympathomimetics

**Dopaminergics** *see* Amantadine, Apomorphine, Bromocriptine, Cabergoline, Entacapone, Levodopa, Lisuride, Pergolide, Pramipexole, Quinagolide, Ropinirole, Rasagiline, Selegiline, and Tolcapone

**Dopexamine** *see* Sympathomimetics

**Dorzolamide** *see* Diuretics

**Dosulepin (dothiepin)** *see* Antidepressants, Tricyclic

**Doxapram**

Antidepressants: effects of doxapram enhanced by MAOIs

Sympathomimetics: increased risk of hypertension when doxapram given with sympathomimetics

Theophylline: increased CNS stimulation when doxapram given with theophylline

**Doxazosin** *see* Alpha-blockers

**Doxepin** *see* Antidepressants, Tricyclic

**Doxorubicin**

Antiepileptics: cytotoxics possibly reduce absorption of phenytoin

• Antipsychotics: avoid concomitant use of cytotoxics with •clozapine (increased risk of agranulocytosis)

Antivirals: doxorubicin possibly inhibits effects of stavudine

• Ciclosporin: increased risk of neurotoxicity when doxorubicin given with •ciclosporin

**Doxycycline** *see* Tetracyclines

**Drospirenone** *see* Progestogens

**Drotrecogin Alfa**

• Anticoagulants: manufacturer of drotrecogin alfa advises avoid concomitant use with high doses of •heparin—consult product literature

**Duloxetine**

Analgesics: possible increased serotonergic effects when duloxetine given with pethidine or tramadol

• Antibacterials: metabolism of duloxetine inhibited by •ciprofloxacin—avoid concomitant use

• Antidepressants: metabolism of duloxetine inhibited by •fluvoxamine—avoid concomitant use; possible increased serotonergic effects when

**Duloxetine**
- Antidepressants *(continued)* duloxetine given with SSRIs, St John's wort, amitriptyline, clomipramine, •moclobemide, tryptophan or venlafaxine; duloxetine should not be started until 2 weeks after stopping •MAOIs, also MAOIs should not be started until at least 5 days after stopping duloxetine; after stopping SSRI-related antidepressants do not start •moclobemide for at least 1 week
- Antimalarials: avoidance of antidepressants advised by manufacturer of •artemether/lumefantrine

5HT$_1$ Agonists: possible increased serotonergic effects when duloxetine given with 5HT$_1$ agonists
- Sibutramine: increased risk of CNS toxicity when SSRI-related antidepressants given with •sibutramine (manufacturer of sibutramine advises avoid concomitant use)

**Dutasteride**

Calcium-channel Blockers: plasma concentration of dutasteride increased by diltiazem and verapamil

**Dydrogesterone** *see* Progestogens

**Edrophonium** *see* Parasympathomimetics

**Efalizumab**
- Vaccines: discontinue efalizumab 8 weeks before and until 2 weeks after vaccination with live or live-attenuated •vaccines

**Efavirenz**

Analgesics: efavirenz reduces plasma concentration of methadone

Antibacterials: increased risk of rash when efavirenz given with clarithromycin; efavirenz reduces plasma concentration of rifabutin—increase dose of rifabutin; plasma concentration of efavirenz reduced by rifampicin—increase dose of efavirenz
- Antidepressants: efavirenz reduces plasma concentration of sertraline; plasma concentration of efavirenz reduced by •St John's wort—avoid concomitant use
- Antifungals: efavirenz reduces plasma concentration of •voriconazole, also plasma concentration of efavirenz increased (avoid concomitant use); efavirenz possibly reduces plasma concentration of caspofungin—consider increasing dose of caspofungin
- Antipsychotics: efavirenz possibly reduces plasma concentration of •aripiprazole—increase dose of aripiprazole; efavirenz possibly increases plasma concentration of •pimozide (increased risk of ventricular arrhythmias—avoid concomitant use)

Antivirals: efavirenz reduces plasma concentration of amprenavir, indinavir and lopinavir; efavirenz reduces plasma concentration of atazanavir—increase dose of atazanavir; plasma concentration of efavirenz reduced by nevirapine; toxicity of efavirenz increased by ritonavir, monitor liver function tests; efavirenz significantly reduces plasma concentration of saquinavir
- Anxiolytics and Hypnotics: increased risk of prolonged sedation when efavirenz given with •midazolam—avoid concomitant use
- Ergot Alkaloids: increased risk of ergotism when efavirenz given with •ergot alkaloids—avoid concomitant use

Grapefruit Juice: plasma concentration of efavirenz possibly increased by grapefruit juice

Oestrogens: efavirenz possibly reduces contraceptive effect of oestrogens

**Eletriptan** *see* 5HT$_1$ Agonists

**Emtricitabine**

Antivirals: manufacturer of emtricitabine advises avoid concomitant use with lamivudine and zalcitabine

**Enalapril** *see* ACE Inhibitors

**Enoxaparin** *see* Heparins

**Enoximone** *see* Phosphodiesterase Inhibitors

**Entacapone**
- Anticoagulants: entacapone enhances anticoagulant effect of •warfarin
- Antidepressants: manufacturer of entacapone advises caution with maprotiline, moclobemide, paroxetine, tricyclics and venlafaxine; avoid concomitant use of entacapone with non-selective •MAOIs

Dopaminergics: entacapone possibly enhances effects of apomorphine; entacapone possibly reduces plasma concentration of rasagiline; manufacturer of entacapone advises max. dose of 10 mg selegiline if used concomitantly

Iron: absorption of entacapone reduced by *oral* iron

Memantine: effects of dopaminergics possibly enhanced by memantine

Methyldopa: entacapone possibly enhances effects of methyldopa; antiparkinsonian effect of dopaminergics antagonised by methyldopa

Sympathomimetics: entacapone possibly enhances effects of adrenaline (epinephrine), dobutamine, dopamine and noradrenaline (norepinephrine)

**Enteral Foods**
- Anticoagulants: the presence of vitamin K in some enteral feeds can antagonise the anticoagulant effect of •coumarins and •phenindione

Antiepileptics: enteral feeds possibly reduce absorption of phenytoin

**Ephedrine** *see* Sympathomimetics

**Epinephrine (adrenaline)** *see* Sympathomimetics

**Epirubicin**

Antiepileptics: cytotoxics possibly reduce absorption of phenytoin
- Antipsychotics: avoid concomitant use of cytotoxics with •clozapine (increased risk of agranulocytosis)
- Ulcer-healing Drugs: plasma concentration of epirubicin increased by •cimetidine

**Eplerenone** *see* Diuretics

**Epoetin**

ACE Inhibitors: antagonism of hypotensive effect and increased risk of hyperkalaemia when epoetin given with ACE inhibitors

Angiotensin-II Receptor Antagonists: antagonism of hypotensive effect and increased risk of hyperkalaemia when epoetin given with angiotensin-II receptor antagonists

**Eprosartan** *see* Angiotensin-II Receptor Antagonists

**Eptifibatide**

Iloprost: increased risk of bleeding when eptifibatide given with iloprost

**Ergometrine** *see* Ergot Alkaloids

**Ergot Alkaloids**

Anaesthetics, General: effects of ergometrine on the parturient uterus reduced by halothane
- Antibacterials: increased risk of ergotism when ergotamine and methysergide given with •macrolides or •telithromycin—avoid concomitant use; avoidance of ergotamine and methysergide advised by manufacturer of •quinupristin/dalfopristin; increased risk of ergotism when ergotamine and methysergide given with tetracyclines

**Ergot Alkaloids** *(continued)*

Antidepressants: possible risk of hypertension when ergotamine and methysergide given with reboxetine

- Antifungals: increased risk of ergotism when ergotamine and methysergide given with •imidazoles or •triazoles—avoid concomitant use
- Antivirals: increased risk of ergotism when ergotamine and methysergide given with •amprenavir, •indinavir, •nelfinavir, •ritonavir or •saquinavir—avoid concomitant use; plasma concentration of ergot alkaloids possibly increased by •atazanavir—avoid concomitant use; increased risk of ergotism when ergot alkaloids given with •efavirenz—avoid concomitant use

Beta-blockers: increased peripheral vasoconstriction when ergotamine and methysergide given with beta-blockers

- $5HT_1$ Agonists: increased risk of vasospasm when ergotamine and methysergide given with •almotriptan, •rizatriptan, •sumatriptan or •zolmitriptan (avoid ergotamine and methysergide for 6 hours after almotriptan, rizatriptan, sumatriptan or zolmitriptan, avoid almotriptan, rizatriptan, sumatriptan or zolmitriptan for 24 hours after ergotamine and methysergide); increased risk of vasospasm when ergotamine and methysergide given with •eletriptan or •frovatriptan (avoid ergotamine and methysergide for 24 hours after eletriptan or frovatriptan, avoid eletriptan or frovatriptan for 24 hours after ergotamine and methysergide)

Sympathomimetics: increased risk of ergotism when ergotamine and methysergide given with sympathomimetics

- Ulcer-healing Drugs: increased risk of ergotism when ergotamine and methysergide given with •cimetidine—avoid concomitant use

**Ergotamine and Methysergide** *see* Ergot Alkaloids

**Erlotinib**

- Analgesics: increased risk of bleeding when erlotinib given with •NSAIDs

Antibacterials: metabolism of erlotinib accelerated by rifampicin (reduced plasma concentration)

- Anticoagulants: increased risk of bleeding when erlotinib given with •coumarins

Antiepileptics: cytotoxics possibly reduce absorption of phenytoin

Antifungals: metabolism of erlotinib inhibited by ketoconazole (increased plasma concentration)

- Antipsychotics: avoid concomitant use of cytotoxics with •clozapine (increased risk of agranulocytosis)

**Ertapenem**

Antiepileptics: ertapenem possibly reduces plasma concentration of valproate

Oestrogens: antibacterials that do not induce liver enzymes possibly reduce contraceptive effect of oestrogens (risk probably small, see p. 408)

**Erythromycin** *see* Macrolides

**Erythropoietin** *see* Epoetin

**Escitalopram** *see* Antidepressants, SSRI

**Esmolol** *see* Beta-blockers

**Esomeprazole** *see* Proton Pump Inhibitors

**Estradiol** *see* Oestrogens

**Estriol** *see* Oestrogens

**Estrone** *see* Oestrogens

**Estropipate** *see* Oestrogens

**Etanercept**

- Anakinra: increased risk of side-effects when etanercept given with •anakinra—avoid concomitant use
- Vaccines: avoid concomitant use of etanercept with live •vaccines (see p. 611)

**Ethinylestradiol** *see* Oestrogens

**Ethosuximide**

- Antibacterials: metabolism of ethosuximide inhibited by •isoniazid (increased plasma concentration and risk of toxicity)
- Antidepressants: anticonvulsant effect of antiepileptics possibly antagonised by MAOIs and •tricyclic-related antidepressants (convulsive threshold lowered); anticonvulsant effect of antiepileptics antagonised by •SSRIs and •tricyclics (convulsive threshold lowered)
- Antiepileptics: plasma concentration of ethosuximide possibly reduced by carbamazepine and primidone; plasma concentration of ethosuximide possibly reduced by •phenytoin, also plasma concentration of phenytoin possibly increased; plasma concentration of ethosuximide possibly increased by valproate
- Antimalarials: possible increased risk of convulsions when antiepileptics given with chloroquine and hydroxychloroquine; anticonvulsant effect of antiepileptics antagonised by •mefloquine
- Antipsychotics: anticonvulsant effect of ethosuximide antagonised by •antipsychotics (convulsive threshold lowered)

Barbiturates: plasma concentration of ethosuximide possibly reduced by phenobarbital

**Etodolac** *see* NSAIDs

**Etomidate** *see* Anaesthetics, General

**Etonogestrel** *see* Progestogens

**Etoposide**

- Anticoagulants: etoposide possibly enhances anticoagulant effect of •coumarins

Antiepileptics: cytotoxics possibly reduce absorption of phenytoin; plasma concentration of etoposide possibly reduced by phenytoin

- Antipsychotics: avoid concomitant use of cytotoxics with •clozapine (increased risk of agranulocytosis)

Barbiturates: plasma concentration of etoposide possibly reduced by phenobarbital

Ciclosporin: plasma concentration of etoposide possibly increased by ciclosporin (increased risk of toxicity)

**Etoricoxib** *see* NSAIDs

**Etynodiol** *see* Progestogens

**Exemestane**

Antibacterials: plasma concentration of exemestane possibly reduced by rifampicin

**Ezetimibe**

Anticoagulants: ezetimibe possibly enhances anticoagulant effect of warfarin

- Ciclosporin: plasma concentration of both drugs may increase when ezetimibe given with •ciclosporin
- Lipid-regulating Drugs: manufacturer of ezetimibe advises avoid concomitant use with •fibrates

**Famciclovir**

Probenecid: excretion of famciclovir possibly reduced by probenecid (increased plasma concentration)

**Famotidine** *see* Histamine $H_2$-antagonists

**Felodipine** *see* Calcium-channel Blockers

**Fenbufen** *see* NSAIDs

**Fenofibrate** *see* Fibrates

**Fenoprofen** *see* NSAIDs

**Fenoterol** *see* Sympathomimetics, $Beta_2$

**Fentanyl** *see* Opioid Analgesics

**Ferrous Salts** *see* Iron

**Fexofenadine** *see* Antihistamines

**Fibrates**
- • Anticoagulants: fibrates enhance anticoagulant effect of •coumarins and •phenindione
- • Antidiabetics: gemfibrozil increases plasma concentration of •rosiglitazone (consider reducing dose of rosiglitazone); fibrates may improve glucose tolerance and have an additive effect with insulin or sulphonylureas; gemfibrozil possibly enhances hypoglycaemic effect of nateglinide; increased risk of severe hypoglycaemia when gemfibrozil given with •repaglinide—avoid concomitant use
- Ciclosporin: increased risk of renal impairment when fenofibrate given with ciclosporin
- • Cytotoxics: gemfibrozil increases plasma concentration of •bexarotene—avoid concomitant use
- • Lipid-regulating Drugs: avoidance of fibrates advised by manufacturer of •ezetimibe; increased risk of myopathy when fibrates given with •statins; increased risk of myopathy when gemfibrozil given with •statins (preferably avoid concomitant use)

**Filgrastim**

*Note.* Pegfilgrastim interactions as for filgrastim
- Cytotoxics: neutropenia possibly exacerbated when filgrastim given with fluorouracil

**Flavoxate** *see* Antimuscarinics

**Flecainide**
- Anaesthetics, Local: increased myocardial depression when anti-arrhythmics given with bupivacaine, levobupivacaine or prilocaine
- • Anti-arrhythmics: increased myocardial depression when anti-arrhythmics given with other •anti-arrhythmics; plasma concentration of flecainide increased by •amiodarone (halve dose of flecainide)
- • Antidepressants: plasma concentration of flecainide increased by fluoxetine; increased risk of ventricular arrhythmias when flecainide given with •tricyclics
- • Antihistamines: increased risk of ventricular arrhythmias when flecainide given with •mizolastine—avoid concomitant use
- • Antimalarials: avoidance of flecainide advised by manufacturer of •artemether/lumefantrine (risk of ventricular arrhythmias); plasma concentration of flecainide increased by •quinine
- • Antipsychotics: increased risk of ventricular arrhythmias when anti-arrhythmics that prolong the QT interval given with •antipsychotics that prolong the QT interval; increased risk of arrhythmias when flecainide given with •clozapine
- • Antivirals: plasma concentration of flecainide possibly increased by •amprenavir (increased risk of ventricular arrhythmias—avoid concomitant use); plasma concentration of flecainide increased by •ritonavir (increased risk of ventricular arrhythmias—avoid concomitant use)
- • Beta-blockers: increased risk of myocardial depression and bradycardia when flecainide given with •beta-blockers; increased myocardial depression when anti-arrhythmics given with •beta-blockers
- • Calcium-channel Blockers: increased risk of myocardial depression and asystole when flecainide given with •verapamil
- • Diuretics: increased cardiac toxicity with flecainide if hypokalaemia occurs with •acetazolamide, •loop diuretics or •thiazides and related diuretics
- • Dolasetron: increased risk of ventricular arrhythmias when flecainide given with •dolasetron—avoid concomitant use

**Flecainide** *(continued)*
- $5HT_3$ Antagonists: caution with anti-arrhythmics advised by manufacturer of tropisetron (risk of ventricular arrhythmias)
- Ulcer-healing Drugs: metabolism of flecainide inhibited by cimetidine (increased plasma concentration)

**Flucloxacillin** *see* Penicillins

**Fluconazole** *see* Antifungals, Triazole

**Flucytosine**
- Antifungals: renal excretion of flucytosine decreased and cellular uptake increased by amphotericin (toxicity possibly increased)
- Cytotoxics: plasma concentration of flucytosine possibly reduced by cytarabine

**Fludarabine**
- Antiepileptics: cytotoxics possibly reduce absorption of phenytoin
- • Antipsychotics: avoid concomitant use of cytotoxics with •clozapine (increased risk of agranulocytosis)
- • Cytotoxics: fludarabine increases intracellular concentration of cytarabine; increased pulmonary toxicity when fludarabine given with •pentostatin (unacceptably high incidence of fatalities)
- Dipyridamole: effects of fludarabine possibly reduced by dipyridamole

**Fludrocortisone** *see* Corticosteroids

**Flunisolide** *see* Corticosteroids

**Fluorides**
- Calcium Salts: absorption of fluorides reduced by calcium salts

**Fluorouracil**

*Note.* Capecitabine is a prodrug of fluorouracil

*Note.* Tegafur is a prodrug of fluorouracil
- • Allopurinol: manufacturer of capecitabine advises avoid concomitant use with •allopurinol
- Antibacterials: metabolism of fluorouracil inhibited by metronidazole (increased toxicity)
- • Anticoagulants: fluorouracil possibly enhances anticoagulant effect of •coumarins
- Antiepileptics: fluorouracil possibly inhibits metabolism of phenytoin (increased risk of toxicity); cytotoxics possibly reduce absorption of phenytoin
- • Antipsychotics: avoid concomitant use of cytotoxics with •clozapine (increased risk of agranulocytosis)
- Filgrastim: neutropenia possibly exacerbated when fluorouracil given with filgrastim
- • Temoporfin: increased skin photosensitivity when topical fluorouracil used with •temoporfin
- Ulcer-healing Drugs: metabolism of fluorouracil inhibited by cimetidine (increased plasma concentration)

**Fluoxetine** *see* Antidepressants, SSRI

**Flupentixol** *see* Antipsychotics

**Fluphenazine** *see* Antipsychotics

**Flurazepam** *see* Anxiolytics and Hypnotics

**Flurbiprofen** *see* NSAIDs

**Flutamide**
- • Anticoagulants: flutamide enhances anticoagulant effect of •coumarins

**Fluticasone** *see* Corticosteroids

**Fluvastatin** *see* Statins

**Fluvoxamine** *see* Antidepressants, SSRI

**Folates**
- Aminosalicylates: absorption of folic acid possibly reduced by sulfasalazine
- Antiepileptics: folates possibly reduce plasma concentration of phenytoin and primidone
- Barbiturates: folates possibly reduce plasma concentration of phenobarbital

**Folic Acid** *see* Folates
**Folinic Acid** *see* Folates
**Formoterol (eformoterol)** *see* Sympathomimetics, $Beta_2$
**Fosamprenavir** *see* Amprenavir
**Foscarnet**
Antivirals: avoidance of foscarnet advised by manufacturer of lamivudine
**Fosinopril** *see* ACE Inhibitors
**Fosphenytoin** *see* Phenytoin
**Framycetin** *see* Aminoglycosides
**Frovatriptan** *see* $5HT_1$ Agonists
**Furosemide (frusemide)** *see* Diuretics
**Fusidic Acid**
Antivirals: plasma concentration of both drugs may increase when fusidic acid given with ritonavir
Lipid-regulating Drugs: possible increased risk of myopathy when fusidic acid given with atorvastatin or simvastatin
Oestrogens: antibacterials that do not induce liver enzymes possibly reduce contraceptive effect of oestrogens (risk probably small, see p. 408)
**Gabapentin**
Antacids: absorption of gabapentin reduced by antacids
• Antidepressants: anticonvulsant effect of antiepileptics possibly antagonised by MAOIs and •tricyclic-related antidepressants (convulsive threshold lowered); anticonvulsant effect of antiepileptics antagonised by •SSRIs and •tricyclics (convulsive threshold lowered)
• Antimalarials: possible increased risk of convulsions when antiepileptics given with chloroquine and hydroxychloroquine; anticonvulsant effect of antiepileptics antagonised by •mefloquine
**Galantamine** *see* Parasympathomimetics
**Ganciclovir**
*Note.* Increased risk of myelosuppression with other myelosuppressive drugs—consult product literature
*Note.* Valganciclovir interactions as for ganciclovir
• Antibacterials: increased risk of convulsions when ganciclovir given with •imipenem with cilastatin
• Antivirals: ganciclovir possibly increases plasma concentration of didanosine; avoidance of intravenous ganciclovir advised by manufacturer of lamivudine; profound myelosuppression when ganciclovir given with •zidovudine (if possible avoid concomitant administration, particularly during initial ganciclovir therapy)
Cytotoxics: plasma concentration of ganciclovir possibly increased by mycophenolate mofetil, also plasma concentration of inactive metabolite of mycophenolate mofetil possibly increased
Probenecid: excretion of ganciclovir reduced by probenecid (increased plasma concentration and risk of toxicity)
**Gemeprost** *see* Prostaglandins
**Gemfibrozil** *see* Fibrates
**Gentamicin** *see* Aminoglycosides
**Gestodene** *see* Progestogens
**Gestrinone**
Antibacterials: metabolism of gestrinone accelerated by rifampicin (reduced plasma concentration)
Antiepileptics: metabolism of gestrinone accelerated by carbamazepine, phenytoin and primidone (reduced plasma concentration)
Barbiturates: metabolism of gestrinone accelerated by barbiturates (reduced plasma concentration)
**Glibenclamide** *see* Antidiabetics
**Gliclazide** *see* Antidiabetics
**Glimepiride** *see* Antidiabetics
**Glipizide** *see* Antidiabetics
**Gliquidone** *see* Antidiabetics
**Glyceryl Trinitrate** *see* Nitrates
**Glycopyrronium** *see* Antimuscarinics
**Grapefruit Juice**
• Antimalarials: grapefruit juice possibly inhibits metabolism of •artemether/lumefantrine (avoid concomitant use)
Antivirals: grapefruit juice possibly increases plasma concentration of efavirenz
Anxiolytics and Hypnotics: grapefruit juice increases plasma concentration of buspirone
Calcium-channel Blockers: grapefruit juice increases plasma concentration of felodipine, isradipine, lacidipine, lercanidipine, nicardipine, nifedipine, nimodipine, nisoldipine and verapamil
• Ciclosporin: grapefruit juice increases plasma concentration of •ciclosporin (increased risk of toxicity)
Ivabradine: grapefruit juice increases plasma concentration of ivabradine
• Lipid-regulating Drugs: grapefruit juice increases plasma concentration of •simvastatin—avoid concomitant use
Sildenafil: grapefruit juice possibly increases plasma concentration of sildenafil
• Sirolimus: grapefruit juice increases plasma concentration of •sirolimus—avoid concomitant use
• Tacrolimus: grapefruit juice increases plasma concentration of •tacrolimus
Tadalafil: grapefruit juice possibly increases plasma concentration of tadalafil
• Vardenafil: grapefruit juice possibly increases plasma concentration of •vardenafil—avoid concomitant use
**Griseofulvin**
Alcohol: griseofulvin possibly enhances effects of alcohol
• Anticoagulants: griseofulvin reduces anticoagulant effect of •coumarins
Antiepileptics: absorption of griseofulvin reduced by primidone (reduced effect)
Barbiturates: absorption of griseofulvin reduced by phenobarbital (reduced effect)
Ciclosporin: griseofulvin possibly reduces plasma concentration of ciclosporin
• Oestrogens: griseofulvin accelerates metabolism of •oestrogens (reduced contraceptive effect—see p. 408)
• Progestogens: griseofulvin accelerates metabolism of •progestogens (reduced contraceptive effect—see p. 408)
**Guanethidine** *see* Adrenergic Neurone Blockers
**Haloperidol** *see* Antipsychotics
**Halothane** *see* Anaesthetics, General
**Heparin** *see* Heparins
**Heparins**
ACE Inhibitors: increased risk of hyperkalaemia when heparins given with ACE inhibitors
• Analgesics: possible increased risk of bleeding when heparins given with NSAIDs; increased risk of haemorrhage when heparins given with intravenous •diclofenac (avoid concomitant use, including low-dose heparin); increased risk of haemorrhage when heparins given with •ketorolac (avoid concomitant use, including low-dose heparin); anticoagulant effect of heparins enhanced by •aspirin
Angiotensin-II Receptor Antagonists: increased risk of hyperkalaemia when heparin given with angiotensin-II receptor antagonists
Clopidogrel: increased risk of bleeding when heparins given with clopidogrel

**Heparins** *(continued)*

Dipyridamole: anticoagulant effect of heparins enhanced by dipyridamole

• Drotrecogin Alfa: avoidance of concomitant use of high doses of heparin with drotrecogin alfa advised by manufacturer of •drotrecogin alfa—consult product literature

Iloprost: anticoagulant effect of heparins possibly enhanced by iloprost

• Nitrates: anticoagulant effect of heparins reduced by infusion of •glyceryl trinitrate

Sibutramine: increased risk of bleeding when anticoagulants given with sibutramine

**Histamine $H_2$-antagonists**

• Alpha-blockers: cimetidine and ranitidine antagonise effects of •tolazoline

Analgesics: cimetidine inhibits metabolism of opioid analgesics (increased plasma concentration)

• Anti-arrhythmics: cimetidine increases plasma concentration of amiodarone, •procainamide, •propafenone and •quinidine; cimetidine inhibits metabolism of flecainide (increased plasma concentration); cimetidine increases plasma concentration of •lidocaine (lignocaine) (increased risk of toxicity)

Antibacterials: histamine $H_2$-antagonists reduce absorption of cefpodoxime; cimetidine increases plasma concentration of erythromycin (increased risk of toxicity, including deafness); cimetidine inhibits metabolism of metronidazole (increased plasma concentration); metabolism of cimetidine accelerated by rifampicin (reduced plasma concentration); ranitidine bismuth citrate reduces absorption of tetracyclines

• Anticoagulants: cimetidine inhibits metabolism of •coumarins (enhanced anticoagulant effect)

Antidepressants: cimetidine increases plasma concentration of citalopram, escitalopram, mirtazapine and sertraline; cimetidine inhibits metabolism of amitriptyline, doxepin, imipramine and nortriptyline (increased plasma concentration); cimetidine increases plasma concentration of moclobemide (halve dose of moclobemide); cimetidine possibly increases plasma concentration of tricyclics

Antidiabetics: cimetidine reduces excretion of metformin (increased plasma concentration); cimetidine enhances hypoglycaemic effect of sulphonylureas

• Antiepileptics: cimetidine inhibits metabolism of •carbamazepine, •phenytoin and •valproate (increased plasma concentration)

Antifungals: histamine $H_2$-antagonists reduce absorption of itraconazole and ketoconazole; cimetidine increases plasma concentration of terbinafine

Antihistamines: manufacturer of loratadine advises cimetidine possibly increases plasma concentration of loratadine

• Antimalarials: avoidance of cimetidine advised by manufacturer of •artemether/lumefantrine; cimetidine inhibits metabolism of chloroquine and hydroxychloroquine and quinine (increased plasma concentration)

• Antipsychotics: cimetidine possibly enhances effects of antipsychotics, chlorpromazine and clozapine; increased risk of ventricular arrhythmias when cimetidine given with •sertindole—avoid concomitant use

Antivirals: plasma concentration of cimetidine possibly increased by amprenavir; histamine $H_2$-antagonists possibly reduce plasma concentration of atazanavir; cimetidine possibly increases plasma concentration of zalcitabine

Anxiolytics and Hypnotics: cimetidine inhibits metabolism of benzodiazepines, clomethiazole and zaleplon (increased plasma concentration)

Beta-blockers: cimetidine increases plasma concentration of labetalol, metoprolol and propranolol

Calcium-channel Blockers: cimetidine possibly inhibits metabolism of calcium-channel blockers (increased plasma concentration)

• Ciclosporin: cimetidine possibly increases plasma concentration of •ciclosporin

• Cilostazol: cimetidine possibly increases plasma concentration of •cilostazol—avoid concomitant use

• Cytotoxics: cimetidine increases plasma concentration of •epirubicin; cimetidine inhibits metabolism of fluorouracil (increased plasma concentration)

Dopaminergics: cimetidine reduces excretion of pramipexole (increased plasma concentration)

• Ergot Alkaloids: increased risk of ergotism when cimetidine given with •ergotamine and methysergide—avoid concomitant use

Hormone Antagonists: absorption of cimetidine possibly delayed by octreotide

$5HT_1$ Agonists: cimetidine inhibits metabolism of zolmitriptan (reduce dose of zolmitriptan)

Mebendazole: cimetidine possibly inhibits metabolism of mebendazole (increased plasma concentration)

Sildenafil: cimetidine increases plasma concentration of sildenafil (reduce initial dose of sildenafil)

• Theophylline: cimetidine inhibits metabolism of •theophylline (increased plasma concentration)

Thyroid Hormones: cimetidine reduces absorption of levothyroxine (thyroxine)

**Homatropine** *see* Antimuscarinics

**Hormone Antagonists** *see* Bicalutamide, Danazol, Dutasteride, Exemestane, Flutamide, Gestrinone, Lanreotide, Octreotide, Tamoxifen, Toremifene, and Trilostane

**$5HT_1$ Agonists**

• Antibacterials: plasma concentration of eletriptan increased by •clarithromycin and •erythromycin (risk of toxicity)—avoid concomitant use; metabolism of zolmitriptan possibly inhibited by quinolones (reduce dose of zolmitriptan)

• Antidepressants: increased risk of CNS toxicity when sumatriptan given with •citalopram, •escitalopram, •fluoxetine, •fluvoxamine or •paroxetine; metabolism of frovatriptan inhibited by fluvoxamine; metabolism of zolmitriptan possibly inhibited by fluvoxamine (reduce dose of zolmitriptan); increased risk of CNS toxicity when sumatriptan given with •sertraline (manufacturer of sertraline advises avoid concomitant use); possible increased serotonergic effects when $5HT_1$ agonists given with duloxetine; risk of CNS toxicity when rizatriptan or sumatriptan given with •MAOIs (avoid rizatriptan or sumatriptan for 2 weeks after MAOIs); increased risk of CNS toxicity when zolmitriptan given with •MAOIs; risk of CNS toxicity when rizatriptan or sumatriptan given with •moclobemide (avoid rizatriptan or sumatriptan for 2 weeks after moclobemide); risk of CNS toxicity when zolmitriptan given with •moclobemide (reduce dose of

**5HT$_1$ Agonists**
- Antidepressants *(continued)*
  zolmitriptan); possible increased serotonergic effects when frovatriptan given with SSRIs; increased serotonergic effects when 5HT$_1$ agonists given with •St John's wort—avoid concomitant use
- Antifungals: plasma concentration of eletriptan increased by •itraconazole and •ketoconazole (risk of toxicity)—avoid concomitant use; plasma concentration of almotriptan increased by ketoconazole (increased risk of toxicity)
- Antivirals: plasma concentration of eletriptan increased by •indinavir, •nelfinavir and •ritonavir (risk of toxicity)—avoid concomitant use
  Beta-blockers: plasma concentration of rizatriptan possibly increased by propranolol (reduce dose of rizatriptan)
- Ergot Alkaloids: increased risk of vasospasm when eletriptan or frovatriptan given with •ergotamine and methysergide (avoid ergotamine and methysergide for 24 hours after eletriptan or frovatriptan, avoid eletriptan or frovatriptan for 24 hours after ergotamine and methysergide); increased risk of vasospasm when almotriptan, rizatriptan, sumatriptan or zolmitriptan given with •ergotamine and methysergide (avoid ergotamine and methysergide for 6 hours after almotriptan, rizatriptan, sumatriptan or zolmitriptan, avoid almotriptan, rizatriptan, sumatriptan or zolmitriptan for 24 hours after ergotamine and methysergide)
  Ulcer-healing Drugs: metabolism of zolmitriptan inhibited by cimetidine (reduce dose of zolmitriptan)

**5HT$_3$ Antagonists** *see* Ondansetron and Tropisetron
**Hydralazine** *see* Vasodilator Antihypertensives
**Hydrochlorothiazide** *see* Diuretics
**Hydrocortisone** *see* Corticosteroids
**Hydroflumethiazide** *see* Diuretics
**Hydromorphone** *see* Opioid Analgesics
**Hydrotalcite** *see* Antacids

**Hydroxocobalamin**
  Antibacterials: response to hydroxocobalamin reduced by chloramphenicol

**Hydroxycarbamide**
  Antiepileptics: cytotoxics possibly reduce absorption of phenytoin
- Antipsychotics: avoid concomitant use of cytotoxics with •clozapine (increased risk of agranulocytosis)
- Antivirals: increased risk of toxicity when hydroxycarbamide given with •didanosine and •stavudine—avoid concomitant use

**Hydroxychloroquine** *see* Chloroquine and Hydroxychloroquine
**Hydroxyzine** *see* Antihistamines
**Hyoscine** *see* Antimuscarinics
**Ibandronic Acid** *see* Bisphosphonates
**Ibuprofen** *see* NSAIDs

**Ifosfamide**
- Anticoagulants: ifosfamide possibly enhances anticoagulant effect of •coumarins
  Antiepileptics: cytotoxics possibly reduce absorption of phenytoin
- Antipsychotics: avoid concomitant use of cytotoxics with •clozapine (increased risk of agranulocytosis)

**Iloprost**
  Analgesics: increased risk of bleeding when iloprost given with NSAIDs or aspirin
  Anticoagulants: iloprost possibly enhances anticoagulant effect of coumarins and heparins; increased risk of bleeding when iloprost given with phenindione
  Clopidogrel: increased risk of bleeding when iloprost given with clopidogrel
  Eptifibatide: increased risk of bleeding when iloprost given with eptifibatide
  Tirofiban: increased risk of bleeding when iloprost given with tirofiban

**Imatinib**
- Antibacterials: plasma concentration of imatinib reduced by •rifampicin—avoid concomitant use
  Anticoagulants: manufacturer of imatinib advises replacement of warfarin with a heparin (possibility of enhanced warfarin effect)
- Antiepileptics: plasma concentration of imatinib reduced by •phenytoin—avoid concomitant use; cytotoxics possibly reduce absorption of phenytoin
  Antifungals: plasma concentration of imatinib increased by ketoconazole
- Antipsychotics: avoid concomitant use of cytotoxics with •clozapine (increased risk of agranulocytosis)
  Lipid-regulating Drugs: imatinib increases plasma concentration of simvastatin

**Imidapril** *see* ACE Inhibitors

**Imipenem with Cilastatin**
- Antivirals: increased risk of convulsions when imipenem with cilastatin given with •ganciclovir
  Oestrogens: antibacterials that do not induce liver enzymes possibly reduce contraceptive effect of oestrogens (risk probably small, see p. 408)

**Imipramine** *see* Antidepressants, Tricyclic

**Immunoglobulins**
*Note.* For advice on immunoglobulins and live virus vaccines, see under Normal Immunoglobulin, p. 627

**Immunosuppressants (antiproliferative)** *see* Azathioprine and Mycophenolate Mofetil
**Indapamide** *see* Diuretics

**Indinavir**
- Antibacterials: indinavir increases plasma concentration of •rifabutin, also plasma concentration of indinavir decreased (reduce dose of rifabutin and increase dose of indinavir); metabolism of indinavir accelerated by •rifampicin (reduced plasma concentration—avoid concomitant use)
- Antidepressants: plasma concentration of indinavir reduced by •St John's wort—avoid concomitant use
- Antiepileptics: plasma concentration of indinavir possibly reduced by carbamazepine, phenytoin and •primidone
- Antifungals: metabolism of indinavir inhibited by ketoconazole; plasma concentration of indinavir increased by •itraconazole (consider reducing dose of indinavir)
- Antimalarials: avoidance of indinavir advised by manufacturer of •artemether/lumefantrine
  Antimuscarinics: avoidance of indinavir advised by manufacturer of tolterodine
- Antipsychotics: indinavir possibly inhibits metabolism of •aripiprazole (reduce dose of aripiprazole); indinavir possibly increases plasma concentration of •pimozide (increased risk of ventricular arrhythmias—avoid concomitant use); indinavir increases plasma concentration of •sertindole (increased risk of ventricular arrhythmias—avoid concomitant use)
- Antivirals: avoid concomitant use of indinavir with •atazanavir; plasma concentration of indinavir reduced by efavirenz and nevirapine; combina-

**Indinavir**
- Antivirals *(continued)* tion of indinavir with nelfinavir may increase plasma concentration of either drug (or both); plasma concentration of indinavir increased by ritonavir; indinavir increases plasma concentration of saquinavir
- Anxiolytics and Hypnotics: increased risk of prolonged sedation when indinavir given with •alprazolam or •midazolam—avoid concomitant use

  Atovaquone: plasma concentration of indinavir possibly reduced by atovaquone
- Barbiturates: plasma concentration of indinavir possibly reduced by •barbiturates
- Cilostazol: indinavir possibly increases plasma concentration of •cilostazol—avoid concomitant use

  Corticosteroids: plasma concentration of indinavir possibly reduced by dexamethasone
- Ergot Alkaloids: increased risk of ergotism when indinavir given with •ergotamine and methysergide—avoid concomitant use
- $5HT_1$ Agonists: indinavir increases plasma concentration of •eletriptan (risk of toxicity)—avoid concomitant use
- Lipid-regulating Drugs: possible increased risk of myopathy when indinavir given with atorvastatin; increased risk of myopathy when indinavir given with •simvastatin (avoid concomitant use)

  Sildenafil: indinavir increases plasma concentration of sildenafil—reduce initial dose of sildenafil
- Vardenafil: indinavir increases plasma concentration of •vardenafil—avoid concomitant use

**Indometacin** *see* NSAIDs

**Indoramin** *see* Alpha-blockers

**Infliximab**
- Anakinra: avoid concomitant use of infliximab with •anakinra
- Vaccines: avoid concomitant use of infliximab with live •vaccines (see p. 611)

**Influenza Vaccine** *see* Vaccines

**Insulin** *see* Antidiabetics

**Interferon Alfa** *see* Interferons

**Interferon Gamma** *see* Interferons

**Interferons**

*Note.* Peginterferon alfa interactions as for interferon alfa

Theophylline: interferon alfa inhibits metabolism of theophylline (increased plasma concentration)

Vaccines: manufacturer of interferon gamma advises avoid concomitant use with vaccines

**Ipratropium** *see* Antimuscarinics

**Irbesartan** *see* Angiotensin-II Receptor Antagonists

**Irinotecan**

Antiepileptics: cytotoxics possibly reduce absorption of phenytoin
- Antipsychotics: avoid concomitant use of cytotoxics with •clozapine (increased risk of agranulocytosis)
- Antivirals: metabolism of irinotecan possibly inhibited by •atazanavir (increased risk of toxicity)

**Iron**

Antacids: absorption of *oral* iron reduced by oral magnesium salts (as magnesium trisilicate)

Antibacterials: *oral* iron reduces absorption of ciprofloxacin, levofloxacin, moxifloxacin, norfloxacin and ofloxacin; *oral* iron reduces absorption of tetracyclines, also absorption of *oral* iron reduced by tetracyclines

Bisphosphonates: *oral* iron reduces absorption of bisphosphonates

Calcium Salts: absorption of *oral* iron reduced by calcium salts

**Iron** *(continued)*
- Dimercaprol: avoid concomitant use of iron with •dimercaprol

  Dopaminergics: *oral* iron reduces absorption of entacapone; *oral* iron possibly reduces absorption of levodopa

  Methyldopa: *oral* iron antagonises hypotensive effect of methyldopa

  Penicillamine: *oral* iron reduces absorption of penicillamine

  Thyroid Hormones: *oral* iron reduces absorption of levothyroxine (thyroxine) (give at least 2 hours apart)

  Trientine: absorption of *oral* iron reduced by trientine

  Zinc: *oral* iron reduces absorption of zinc, also absorption of *oral* iron reduced by zinc

**Isocarboxazid** *see* MAOIs

**Isoflurane** *see* Anaesthetics, General

**Isometheptene** *see* Sympathomimetics

**Isoniazid**

Anaesthetics, General: hepatotoxicity of isoniazid possibly potentiated by general anaesthetics

Antacids: absorption of isoniazid reduced by antacids

Antibacterials: increased risk of CNS toxicity when isoniazid given with cycloserine
- Antiepileptics: isoniazid increases plasma concentration of •carbamazepine (also possibly increased isoniazid hepatotoxicity); isoniazid inhibits metabolism of •ethosuximide (increased plasma concentration and risk of toxicity); isoniazid inhibits metabolism of •phenytoin (increased plasma concentration)

  Antifungals: isoniazid possibly reduces plasma concentration of ketoconazole

  Anxiolytics and Hypnotics: isoniazid inhibits the metabolism of diazepam

  Oestrogens: antibacterials that do not induce liver enzymes possibly reduce contraceptive effect of oestrogens (risk probably small, see p. 408)

  Theophylline: isoniazid possibly increases plasma concentration of theophylline

**Isosorbide Dinitrate** *see* Nitrates

**Isosorbide Mononitrate** *see* Nitrates

**Isotretinoin** *see* Retinoids

**Isradipine** *see* Calcium-channel Blockers

**Itraconazole** *see* Antifungals, Triazole

**Ivabradine**
- Anti-arrhythmics: increased risk of ventricular arrhythmias when ivabradine given with •amiodarone, •disopyramide or •quinidine
- Antibacterials: plasma concentration of ivabradine possibly increased by •clarithromycin and •telithromycin—avoid concomitant use; increased risk of ventricular arrhythmias when ivabradine given with •erythromycin—avoid concomitant use

  Antidepressants: plasma concentration of ivabradine reduced by St John's wort—avoid concomitant use
- Antifungals: plasma concentration of ivabradine increased by •ketoconazole—avoid concomitant use; plasma concentration of ivabradine increased by fluconazole—reduce initial dose of ivabradine; plasma concentration of ivabradine possibly increased by •itraconazole—avoid concomitant use
- Antimalarials: increased risk of ventricular arrhythmias when ivabradine given with •mefloquine
- Antipsychotics: increased risk of ventricular arrhythmias when ivabradine given with •pimozide or •sertindole

**Ivabradine** *(continued)*
- • Antivirals: plasma concentration of ivabradine possibly increased by •nelfinavir and •ritonavir—avoid concomitant use
- • Beta-blockers: increased risk of ventricular arrhythmias when ivabradine given with •sotalol
- • Calcium-channel Blockers: plasma concentration of ivabradine increased by •diltiazem and •verapamil—avoid concomitant use
- Grapefruit Juice: plasma concentration of ivabradine increased by grapefruit juice
- • Pentamidine Isetionate: increased risk of ventricular arrhythmias when ivabradine given with •pentamidine isetionate

**Kaolin**
- Analgesics: kaolin possibly reduces absorption of aspirin
- Anti-arrhythmics: kaolin possibly reduces absorption of quinidine
- Antibacterials: kaolin possibly reduces absorption of tetracyclines
- Antimalarials: kaolin reduces absorption of chloroquine and hydroxychloroquine
- Antipsychotics: kaolin possibly reduces absorption of phenothiazines

**Ketamine** *see* Anaesthetics, General
**Ketoconazole** *see* Antifungals, Imidazole
**Ketoprofen** *see* NSAIDs
**Ketorolac** *see* NSAIDs
**Ketotifen** *see* Antihistamines
**Labetalol** *see* Beta-blockers
**Lacidipine** *see* Calcium-channel Blockers

**Lamivudine**
- Antibacterials: plasma concentration of lamivudine increased by trimethoprim (as co-trimoxazole)—avoid concomitant use of high-dose co-trimoxazole
- Antivirals: avoidance of lamivudine advised by manufacturer of emtricitabine; manufacturer of lamivudine advises avoid concomitant use with foscarnet; manufacturer of lamivudine advises avoid concomitant use of intravenous ganciclovir; lamivudine possibly inhibits effects of zalcitabine (manufacturers advise avoid concomitant use)

**Lamotrigine**
- • Antibacterials: plasma concentration of lamotrigine reduced by •rifampicin
- • Antidepressants: anticonvulsant effect of antiepileptics possibly antagonised by MAOIs and •tricyclic-related antidepressants (convulsive threshold lowered); anticonvulsant effect of antiepileptics antagonised by •SSRIs and •tricyclics (convulsive threshold lowered)
- Antiepileptics: plasma concentration of lamotrigine often reduced by carbamazepine and oxcarbazepine, also plasma concentration of an active metabolite of carbamazepine and oxcarbazepine sometimes raised (but evidence is conflicting); plasma concentration of lamotrigine reduced by phenytoin and primidone; plasma concentration of lamotrigine increased by valproate
- • Antimalarials: possible increased risk of convulsions when antiepileptics given with chloroquine and hydroxychloroquine; anticonvulsant effect of antiepileptics antagonised by •mefloquine
- Barbiturates: plasma concentration of lamotrigine reduced by phenobarbital
- • Oestrogens: plasma concentration of lamotrigine reduced by •oestrogens
- • Progestogens: plasma concentration of lamotrigine reduced by •progestogens

**Lanreotide**
- Antidiabetics: lanreotide possibly reduces requirements for insulin, metformin, repaglinide and sulphonylureas
- Ciclosporin: lanreotide reduces plasma concentration of ciclosporin

**Lansoprazole** *see* Proton Pump Inhibitors

**Laronidase**
- Anaesthetics, Local: effects of laronidase possibly inhibited by procaine (manufacturer of laronidase advises avoid concomitant use)
- Antimalarials: effects of laronidase possibly inhibited by chloroquine and hydroxychloroquine (manufacturer of laronidase advises avoid concomitant use)

**Leflunomide**

*Note.* Increased risk of toxicity with other haematotoxic and hepatotoxic drugs

- Anticoagulants: leflunomide possibly enhances anticoagulant effect of warfarin
- Antidiabetics: leflunomide possibly enhances hypoglycaemic effect of tolbutamide
- Antiepileptics: leflunomide possibly increases plasma concentration of phenytoin
- Lipid-regulating Drugs: the effect of leflunomide is significantly decreased by colestyramine (enhanced elimination)—avoid unless drug elimination desired
- • Vaccines: avoid concomitant use of leflunomide with live •vaccines (see p. 611)

**Lercanidipine** *see* Calcium-channel Blockers

**Leukotriene Antagonists**
- Analgesics: plasma concentration of zafirlukast increased by aspirin
- Antibacterials: plasma concentration of zafirlukast reduced by erythromycin
- Anticoagulants: zafirlukast enhances anticoagulant effect of warfarin
- Antiepileptics: plasma concentration of montelukast reduced by primidone
- Barbiturates: plasma concentration of montelukast reduced by phenobarbital
- Theophylline: zafirlukast possibly increases plasma concentration of theophylline, also plasma concentration of zafirlukast reduced

**Levamisole**
- Alcohol: possibility of disulfiram-like reaction when levamisole given with alcohol
- • Anticoagulants: levamisole possibly enhances anticoagulant effect of •warfarin
- Antiepileptics: levamisole possibly increases plasma concentration of phenytoin

**Levetiracetam**
- • Antidepressants: anticonvulsant effect of antiepileptics possibly antagonised by MAOIs and •tricyclic-related antidepressants (convulsive threshold lowered); anticonvulsant effect of antiepileptics antagonised by •SSRIs and •tricyclics (convulsive threshold lowered)
- • Antimalarials: possible increased risk of convulsions when antiepileptics given with chloroquine and hydroxychloroquine; anticonvulsant effect of antiepileptics antagonised by •mefloquine

**Levobunolol** *see* Beta-blockers

**Levobupivacaine**
- Anti-arrhythmics: increased myocardial depression when levobupivacaine given with anti-arrhythmics

**Levocetirizine** *see* Antihistamines

**Levodopa**
- ACE Inhibitors: enhanced hypotensive effect when levodopa given with ACE inhibitors

**Levodopa** *(continued)*
Adrenergic Neurone Blockers: enhanced hypotensive effect when levodopa given with adrenergic neurone blockers
Alpha-blockers: enhanced hypotensive effect when levodopa given with alpha-blockers
• Anaesthetics, General: increased risk of arrhythmias when levodopa given with •volatile liquid general anaesthetics
Angiotensin-II Receptor Antagonists: enhanced hypotensive effect when levodopa given with angiotensin-II receptor antagonists
• Antidepressants: risk of hypertensive crisis when levodopa given with •MAOIs, avoid levodopa for at least 2 weeks after stopping MAOIs; increased risk of side-effects when levodopa given with moclobemide
Antiepileptics: effects of levodopa possibly reduced by phenytoin
Antimuscarinics: absorption of levodopa possibly reduced by antimuscarinics
Antipsychotics: effects of levodopa antagonised by antipsychotics; avoidance of levodopa advised by manufacturer of amisulpride (antagonism of effect)
Anxiolytics and Hypnotics: effects of levodopa possibly antagonised by benzodiazepines
Beta-blockers: enhanced hypotensive effect when levodopa given with beta-blockers
Bupropion: increased risk of side-effects when levodopa given with bupropion
Calcium-channel Blockers: enhanced hypotensive effect when levodopa given with calcium-channel blockers
Clonidine: enhanced hypotensive effect when levodopa given with clonidine
Diazoxide: enhanced hypotensive effect when levodopa given with diazoxide
Diuretics: enhanced hypotensive effect when levodopa given with diuretics
Dopaminergics: enhanced effects and increased toxicity of levodopa when given with selegiline (reduce dose of levodopa)
Iron: absorption of levodopa possibly reduced by *oral* iron
Memantine: effects of dopaminergics possibly enhanced by memantine
Methyldopa: enhanced hypotensive effect when levodopa given with methyldopa; antiparkinsonian effect of dopaminergics antagonised by methyldopa
Moxonidine: enhanced hypotensive effect when levodopa given with moxonidine
Muscle Relaxants: possible agitation, confusion and hallucinations when levodopa given with baclofen
Nitrates: enhanced hypotensive effect when levodopa given with nitrates
Vasodilator Antihypertensives: enhanced hypotensive effect when levodopa given with hydralazine, minoxidil or nitroprusside
Vitamins: effects of levodopa reduced by pyridoxine when given without dopa-decarboxylase inhibitor

**Levofloxacin** *see* Quinolones
**Levomepromazine (methotrimeprazine)** *see* Antipsychotics
**Levonorgestrel** *see* Progestogens
**Levothyroxine (thyroxine)** *see* Thyroid Hormones
**Lidocaine (lignocaine)**
*Note.* Interactions less likely when lidocaine used topically
Anaesthetics, Local: increased myocardial depression when anti-arrhythmics given with bupivacaine, levobupivacaine or prilocaine

**Lidocaine (lignocaine)** *(continued)*
• Anti-arrhythmics: increased myocardial depression when anti-arrhythmics given with other •anti-arrhythmics
• Antibacterials: increased risk of ventricular arrhythmias when lidocaine (lignocaine) given with •quinupristin/dalfopristin—avoid concomitant use
• Antipsychotics: increased risk of ventricular arrhythmias when anti-arrhythmics that prolong the QT interval given with •antipsychotics that prolong the QT interval
• Antivirals: plasma concentration of lidocaine (lignocaine) possibly increased by •amprenavir—avoid concomitant use; plasma concentration of lidocaine (lignocaine) possibly increased by •atazanavir and lopinavir
• Beta-blockers: increased myocardial depression when anti-arrhythmics given with •beta-blockers; increased risk of lidocaine (lignocaine) toxicity when given with •propranolol
• Diuretics: action of lidocaine (lignocaine) antagonised by hypokalaemia caused by •acetazolamide, •loop diuretics or •thiazides and related diuretics
• Dolasetron: increased risk of ventricular arrhythmias when lidocaine (lignocaine) given with •dolasetron—avoid concomitant use
$5HT_3$ Antagonists: caution with anti-arrhythmics advised by manufacturer of tropisetron (risk of ventricular arrhythmias)
Muscle Relaxants: neuromuscular blockade enhanced and prolonged when lidocaine (lignocaine) given with suxamethonium
• Ulcer-healing Drugs: plasma concentration of lidocaine (lignocaine) increased by •cimetidine (increased risk of toxicity)

**Linezolid**
*Note.* Linezolid is a reversible, non-selective MAO inhibitor—see interactions of MAOIs
Oestrogens: antibacterials that do not induce liver enzymes possibly reduce contraceptive effect of oestrogens (risk probably small, see p. 408)

**Liothyronine** *see* Thyroid Hormones
**Lipid-regulating Drugs** *see* Colestipol, Colestyramine, Ezetimibe, Fibrates, Nicotinic Acid, and Statins
**Lisinopril** *see* ACE Inhibitors
**Lisuride**
Antipsychotics: effects of lisuride antagonised by antipsychotics
Memantine: effects of dopaminergics possibly enhanced by memantine
Methyldopa: antiparkinsonian effect of dopaminergics antagonised by methyldopa

**Lithium**
• ACE Inhibitors: excretion of lithium reduced by •ACE inhibitors (increased plasma concentration)
• Analgesics: excretion of lithium probably reduced by •NSAIDs (increased risk of toxicity); excretion of lithium reduced by •diclofenac, •ibuprofen, •indometacin, •mefenamic acid, •naproxen, •parecoxib and •piroxicam (increased risk of toxicity); excretion of lithium reduced by •ketorolac (increased risk of toxicity)—avoid concomitant use
• Angiotensin-II Receptor Antagonists: excretion of lithium reduced by •angiotensin-II receptor antagonists (increased plasma concentration)
Antacids: excretion of lithium increased by sodium bicarbonate (reduced plasma concentration)
• Anti-arrhythmics: avoidance of lithium advised by manufacturer of •amiodarone (risk of ventricular arrhythmias)

**Lithium** *(continued)*
- Antibacterials: increased risk of lithium toxicity when given with metronidazole
- • Antidepressants: increased risk of CNS effects when lithium given with •SSRIs (lithium toxicity reported); risk of toxicity when lithium given with tricyclics
- Antiepileptics: neurotoxicity may occur when lithium given with carbamazepine or phenytoin without increased plasma concentration of lithium
- • Antipsychotics: increased risk of extrapyramidal side-effects and possibly neurotoxicity when lithium given with clozapine, haloperidol or phenothiazines; increased risk of ventricular arrhythmias when lithium given with •sertindole—avoid concomitant use; increased risk of extrapyramidal side-effects when lithium given with sulpiride
- Calcium-channel Blockers: neurotoxicity may occur when lithium given with diltiazem or verapamil without increased plasma concentration of lithium
- • Diuretics: excretion of lithium increased by •acetazolamide; excretion of lithium reduced by •loop diuretics and •thiazides and related diuretics (increased plasma concentration and risk of toxicity)—loop diuretics safer than thiazides; excretion of lithium reduced by •potassium-sparing diuretics and aldosterone antagonists (increased plasma concentration and risk of toxicity)
- • Methyldopa: neurotoxicity may occur when lithium given with •methyldopa without increased plasma concentration of lithium
- Muscle Relaxants: lithium enhances effects of muscle relaxants; hyperkinesis caused by lithium possibly aggravated by baclofen
- Parasympathomimetics: lithium antagonises effects of neostigmine and pyridostigmine
- Theophylline: excretion of lithium increased by theophylline (reduced plasma concentration)

**Lofepramine** *see* Antidepressants, Tricyclic

**Lofexidine**
- Alcohol: increased sedative effect when lofexidine given with alcohol
- Anxiolytics and Hypnotics: increased sedative effect when lofexidine given with anxiolytics and hypnotics

**Loperamide**
- Desmopressin: loperamide increases plasma concentration of *oral* desmopressin

**Lopinavir**

*Note.* In combination with ritonavir as Kaletra® (ritonavir is present to inhibit lopinavir metabolism and increase plasma-lopinavir concentration)—see also Ritonavir

- Anti-arrhythmics: lopinavir possibly increases plasma concentration of lidocaine (lignocaine)
- • Antibacterials: plasma concentration of lopinavir reduced by •rifampicin—avoid concomitant use
- • Antidepressants: plasma concentration of lopinavir reduced by •St John's wort—avoid concomitant use
- • Antiepileptics: plasma concentration of lopinavir possibly reduced by carbamazepine, phenytoin and •primidone
- Antihistamines: lopinavir possibly increases plasma concentration of chlorphenamine (chlorpheniramine)
- • Antimalarials: avoidance of lopinavir advised by manufacturer of •artemether/lumefantrine
- Antimuscarinics: avoidance of lopinavir advised by manufacturer of tolterodine

**Lopinavir** *(continued)*
- • Antipsychotics: lopinavir possibly inhibits metabolism of •aripiprazole (reduce dose of aripiprazole); lopinavir increases plasma concentration of •sertindole (increased risk of ventricular arrhythmias—avoid concomitant use)
- • Antivirals: lopinavir reduces plasma concentration of amprenavir, effect on lopinavir plasma concentration not predictable; plasma concentration of lopinavir reduced by efavirenz and •tipranavir; plasma concentration of lopinavir reduced by nelfinavir, also plasma concentration of active metabolite of nelfinavir increased; plasma concentration of lopinavir possibly reduced by nevirapine; lopinavir increases plasma concentration of saquinavir and tenofovir
- • Barbiturates: plasma concentration of lopinavir possibly reduced by •phenobarbital
- • Cilostazol: lopinavir possibly increases plasma concentration of •cilostazol—avoid concomitant use
- Corticosteroids: plasma concentration of lopinavir possibly reduced by dexamethasone
- • Lipid-regulating Drugs: possible increased risk of myopathy when lopinavir given with atorvastatin; possible increased risk of myopathy when lopinavir given with •simvastatin—avoid concomitant use
- Sirolimus: lopinavir possibly increases plasma concentration of sirolimus

**Loprazolam** *see* Anxiolytics and Hypnotics

**Loratadine** *see* Antihistamines

**Lorazepam** *see* Anxiolytics and Hypnotics

**Lormetazepam** *see* Anxiolytics and Hypnotics

**Losartan** *see* Angiotensin-II Receptor Antagonists

**Lumefantrine** *see* Artemether with Lumefantrine

**Lumiracoxib** *see* NSAIDs

**Lymecycline** *see* Tetracyclines

**Macrolides**

*Note. See also* Telithromycin

*Note.* Interactions do not apply to small amounts of erythromycin used topically

- Analgesics: erythromycin increases plasma concentration of alfentanil
- Antacids: absorption of azithromycin reduced by antacids
- • Anti-arrhythmics: increased risk of ventricular arrhythmias when parenteral erythromycin given with •amiodarone—avoid concomitant use; clarithromycin possibly increases plasma concentration of •disopyramide (increased risk of toxicity); erythromycin increases plasma concentration of •disopyramide (increased risk of toxicity); increased risk of ventricular arrhythmias when parenteral erythromycin given with •quinidine; increased risk of ventricular arrhythmias when clarithromycin given with •quinidine
- • Antibacterials: increased risk of ventricular arrhythmias when parenteral erythromycin given with •moxifloxacin—avoid concomitant use; macrolides possibly increase plasma concentration of •rifabutin (increased risk of uveitis—reduce rifabutin dose); clarithromycin increases plasma concentration of •rifabutin (increased risk of uveitis—reduce rifabutin dose); plasma concentration of clarithromycin reduced by rifamycins
- • Anticoagulants: macrolides possibly enhance anticoagulant effect of •coumarins; clarithromycin and erythromycin enhance anticoagulant effect of •coumarins
- • Antidepressants: avoidance of macrolides advised by manufacturer of •reboxetine
- Antidiabetics: clarithromycin enhances effects of repaglinide

**Macrolides** *(continued)*

- • Antiepileptics: clarithromycin and erythromycin increase plasma concentration of •carbamazepine; clarithromycin inhibits metabolism of phenytoin (increased plasma concentration); erythromycin possibly inhibits metabolism of valproate (increased plasma concentration)
- Antifungals: clarithromycin increases plasma concentration of itraconazole
- • Antihistamines: manufacturer of loratadine advises erythromycin possibly increases plasma concentration of loratadine; macrolides possibly inhibit metabolism of •mizolastine (avoid concomitant use); erythromycin inhibits metabolism of •mizolastine—avoid concomitant use
- • Antimalarials: avoidance of macrolides advised by manufacturer of •artemether/lumefantrine
- Antimuscarinics: avoidance of clarithromycin and erythromycin advised by manufacturer of tolterodine
- • Antipsychotics: increased risk of ventricular arrhythmias when parenteral erythromycin given with •amisulpride—avoid concomitant use; erythromycin possibly increases plasma concentration of •clozapine (possible increased risk of convulsions); increased risk of ventricular arrhythmias when clarithromycin given with •pimozide—avoid concomitant use; possible increased risk of ventricular arrhythmias when erythromycin given with •pimozide—avoid concomitant use; macrolides possibly increase plasma concentration of quetiapine (reduce dose of quetiapine); possible increased risk of ventricular arrhythmias when macrolides given with •sertindole—avoid concomitant use; increased risk of ventricular arrhythmias when erythromycin given with •sertindole—avoid concomitant use
- • Antivirals: plasma concentration of both drugs increased when erythromycin given with amprenavir; plasma concentration of both drugs increased when clarithromycin given with atazanavir; increased risk of rash when clarithromycin given with efavirenz; plasma concentration of azithromycin and erythromycin possibly increased by ritonavir; plasma concentration of clarithromycin increased by •ritonavir (reduce dose of clarithromycin in renal impairment); plasma concentration of clarithromycin increased by •tipranavir (reduce dose of clarithromycin in renal impairment), also clarithromycin increases plasma concentration of tipranavir; clarithromycin tablets reduce absorption of zidovudine
- • Anxiolytics and Hypnotics: clarithromycin and erythromycin inhibit metabolism of •midazolam (increased plasma concentration with increased sedation); erythromycin increases plasma concentration of buspirone (reduce dose of buspirone); erythromycin inhibits the metabolism of zopiclone
- Aprepitant: clarithromycin possibly increases plasma concentration of aprepitant
- • Calcium-channel Blockers: erythromycin possibly inhibits metabolism of felodipine (increased plasma concentration); avoidance of erythromycin advised by manufacturer of lercanidipine; clarithromycin and erythromycin possibly inhibit metabolism of •verapamil (increased risk of toxicity)
- Cardiac Glycosides: macrolides increase plasma concentration of digoxin (increased risk of toxicity)
- • Ciclosporin: macrolides possibly inhibit metabolism of •ciclosporin (increased plasma concentration); clarithromycin and erythromycin inhibit metabolism of •ciclosporin (increased plasma concentration)
- • Cilostazol: erythromycin increases plasma concentration of •cilostazol (also plasma concentration of erythromycin reduced)—avoid concomitant use
- • Colchicine: clarithromycin or erythromycin increase risk of •colchicine toxicity
- Corticosteroids: erythromycin possibly inhibits metabolism of corticosteroids; erythromycin inhibits the metabolism of methylprednisolone; clarithromycin possibly increases plasma concentration of methylprednisolone
- • Cytotoxics: *in vitro* studies suggest a possible interaction between erythromycin and docetaxel (consult docetaxel product literature); erythromycin increases toxicity of •vinblastine—avoid concomitant use
- • Diuretics: clarithromycin increases plasma concentration of •eplerenone—avoid concomitant use; erythromycin increases plasma concentration of eplerenone (reduce dose of eplerenone)
- Dopaminergics: macrolides possibly increase plasma concentration of bromocriptine and cabergoline (increased risk of toxicity); erythromycin increases plasma concentration of bromocriptine and cabergoline (increased risk of toxicity)
- • Ergot Alkaloids: increased risk of ergotism when macrolides given with •ergotamine and methysergide—avoid concomitant use
- • $5HT_1$ Agonists: clarithromycin and erythromycin increase plasma concentration of •eletriptan (risk of toxicity)—avoid concomitant use
- • Ivabradine: clarithromycin possibly increases plasma concentration of •ivabradine—avoid concomitant use; increased risk of ventricular arrhythmias when erythromycin given with •ivabradine—avoid concomitant use
- Leukotriene Antagonists: erythromycin reduces plasma concentration of zafirlukast
- • Lipid-regulating Drugs: clarithromycin increases plasma concentration of atorvastatin; possible increased risk of myopathy when erythromycin given with atorvastatin; erythromycin reduces plasma concentration of rosuvastatin; increased risk of myopathy when clarithromycin or erythromycin given with •simvastatin (avoid concomitant use)
- Oestrogens: antibacterials that do not induce liver enzymes possibly reduce contraceptive effect of oestrogens (risk probably small, see p. 408)
- Parasympathomimetics: erythromycin increases plasma concentration of galantamine
- Sildenafil: erythromycin increases plasma concentration of sildenafil—reduce initial dose of sildenafil
- • Sirolimus: clarithromycin increases plasma concentration of •sirolimus—avoid concomitant use; plasma concentration of both drugs increased when erythromycin given with •sirolimus
- • Tacrolimus: clarithromycin and erythromycin increase plasma concentration of •tacrolimus
- Tadalafil: clarithromycin and erythromycin possibly increase plasma concentration of tadalafil
- • Theophylline: azithromycin possibly increases plasma concentration of theophylline; clarithromycin inhibits metabolism of •theophylline (increased plasma concentration); erythromycin inhibits metabolism of •theophylline (increased

**Macrolides**

- Theophylline *(continued)* plasma concentration), if erythromycin given by mouth, also decreased plasma-erythromycin concentration
- Ulcer-healing Drugs: plasma concentration of erythromycin increased by cimetidine (increased risk of toxicity, including deafness); plasma concentration of both drugs increased when clarithromycin given with omeprazole
- Vardenafil: erythromycin increases plasma concentration of vardenafil (reduce dose of vardenafil)

**Magnesium (parenteral)**

- • Calcium-channel Blockers: profound hypotension reported with concomitant use of parenteral magnesium and •nifedipine in pre-eclampsia
- Muscle Relaxants: parenteral magnesium enhances effects of non-depolarising muscle relaxants and suxamethonium

**Magnesium Salts (oral)** *see* Antacids

**MAOIs**

*Note.* For interactions of reversible MAO-A inhibitors (RIMAs) see Moclobemide, and for interactions of MAO-B inhibitors see Rasagiline and Selegiline; the antibacterial Linezolid is a reversible, non-selective MAO inhibitor

- ACE Inhibitors: MAOIs possibly enhance hypotensive effect of ACE inhibitors
- Adrenergic Neurone Blockers: enhanced hypotensive effect when MAOIs given with adrenergic neurone blockers
- • Alcohol: MAOIs interact with tyramine found in some beverages containing •alcohol and some dealcoholised beverages (hypertensive crisis)—if no tyramine, enhanced hypotensive effect
- $Alpha_2$-adrenoceptor Stimulants: avoidance of MAOIs advised by manufacturer of apraclonidine and brimonidine
- • Alpha-blockers: avoidance of MAOIs advised by manufacturer of •indoramin; enhanced hypotensive effect when MAOIs given with alpha-blockers
- • Anaesthetics, General: Because of hazardous interactions between MAOIs and •general anaesthetics, MAOIs should normally be stopped 2 weeks before surgery
- • Analgesics: CNS excitation or depression (hypertension or hypotension) when MAOIs given with •pethidine—avoid concomitant use and for 2 weeks after stopping MAOIs; avoidance of MAOIs advised by manufacturer of •nefopam; possible CNS excitation or depression (hypertension or hypotension) when MAOIs given with •opioid analgesics—avoid concomitant use and for 2 weeks after stopping MAOIs
- Angiotensin-II Receptor Antagonists: MAOIs possibly enhance hypotensive effect of angiotensin-II receptor antagonists
- • Antidepressants: increased risk of hypertension and CNS excitation when MAOIs given with •reboxetine (MAOIs should not be started until 1 week after stopping reboxetine, avoid reboxetine for 2 weeks after stopping MAOIs); after stopping MAOIs do not start •citalopram, •escitalopram, •fluvoxamine or •paroxetine for 2 weeks, also MAOIs should not be started until at least 1 week after stopping citalopram, escitalopram, fluvoxamine or paroxetine; after stopping MAOIs do not start •fluoxetine for 2 weeks, also MAOIs should not be started until at least 5 weeks after stopping fluoxetine; after stopping MAOIs do not start •mirtazapine or •sertraline for 2 weeks, also MAOIs should not be started until at least 2 weeks after stopping mirtazapine or sertraline;

**MAOIs**

- • Antidepressants *(continued)* after stopping MAOIs do not start •duloxetine for 2 weeks, also MAOIs should not be started until at least 5 days after stopping duloxetine; enhanced CNS effects and toxicity when MAOIs given with •venlafaxine (venlafaxine should not be started until 2 weeks after stopping MAOIs, avoid MAOIs for 1 week after stopping venlafaxine); MAOIs can cause increased risk of hypertension and CNS excitation when given with other •MAOIs (avoid for at least 2 weeks after stopping previous MAOIs and then start at a reduced dose); after stopping MAOIs do not start •moclobemide for at least 1 week; MAOIs increase CNS effects of •SSRIs (risk of serious toxicity); after stopping MAOIs do not start •tricyclic-related antidepressants for 2 weeks, also MAOIs should not be started until at least 1–2 weeks after stopping tricyclic-related antidepressants; increased risk of hypertension and CNS excitation when MAOIs given with •tricyclics, tricyclics should not be started until 2 weeks after stopping MAOIs (3 weeks if starting clomipramine or imipramine), also MAOIs should not be started for at least 1–2 weeks after stopping tricyclics (3 weeks in the case of clomipramine or imipramine); CNS excitation and confusion when MAOIs given with •tryptophan (reduce dose of tryptophan)
- Antidiabetics: MAOIs possibly enhance hypoglycaemic effect of antidiabetics; MAOIs enhance hypoglycaemic effect of insulin, metformin and sulphonylureas
- • Antiepileptics: MAOIs possibly antagonise anticonvulsant effect of antiepileptics (convulsive threshold lowered); avoidance for 2 weeks after stopping MAOIs advised by manufacturer of •carbamazepine, also antagonism of anticonvulsant effect; avoidance of MAOIs advised by manufacturer of •oxcarbazepine
- Antihistamines: increased antimuscarinic and sedative effects when MAOIs given with antihistamines
- • Antimalarials: avoidance of antidepressants advised by manufacturer of •artemether/lumefantrine
- Antimuscarinics: increased risk of antimuscarinic side-effects when MAOIs given with antimuscarinics
- • Antipsychotics: CNS effects of MAOIs possibly increased by •clozapine
- Anxiolytics and Hypnotics: avoidance of MAOIs advised by manufacturer of buspirone
- • Atomoxetine: after stopping MAOIs do not start •atomoxetine for 2 weeks, also MAOIs should not be started until at least 2 weeks after stopping atomoxetine
- Barbiturates: MAOIs possibly antagonise anticonvulsant effect of barbiturates (convulsive threshold lowered)
- Beta-blockers: enhanced hypotensive effect when MAOIs given with beta-blockers
- • Bupropion: avoidance of bupropion for 2 weeks after stopping MAOIs advised by manufacturer of •bupropion
- Calcium-channel Blockers: enhanced hypotensive effect when MAOIs given with calcium-channel blockers
- Clonidine: enhanced hypotensive effect when MAOIs given with clonidine
- Diazoxide: enhanced hypotensive effect when MAOIs given with diazoxide

**MAOIs** *(continued)*
Diuretics: enhanced hypotensive effect when MAOIs given with diuretics
• Dopaminergics: avoid concomitant use of non-selective MAOIs with •entacapone; risk of hypertensive crisis when MAOIs given with •levodopa, avoid levodopa for at least 2 weeks after stopping MAOIs; risk of hypertensive crisis when MAOIs given with •rasagiline, avoid MAOIs for at least 2 weeks after stopping rasagiline; enhanced hypotensive effect when MAOIs given with selegiline; avoid concomitant use of MAOIs with tolcapone
Doxapram: MAOIs enhance effects of doxapram
• $5HT_1$ Agonists: risk of CNS toxicity when MAOIs given with •rizatriptan or •sumatriptan (avoid rizatriptan or sumatriptan for 2 weeks after MAOIs); increased risk of CNS toxicity when MAOIs given with •zolmitriptan
• Methyldopa: avoidance of MAOIs advised by manufacturer of •methyldopa
Moxonidine: enhanced hypotensive effect when MAOIs given with moxonidine
Muscle Relaxants: phenelzine enhances effects of suxamethonium
Nicorandil: enhanced hypotensive effect when MAOIs given with nicorandil
Nitrates: enhanced hypotensive effect when MAOIs given with nitrates
• Sibutramine: increased CNS toxicity when MAOIs given with •sibutramine (manufacturer of sibutramine advises avoid concomitant use), also avoid sibutramine for 2 weeks after stopping MAOIs
• Sympathomimetics: risk of hypertensive crisis when MAOIs given with •dexamfetamine, •dopamine, •dopexamine, •ephedrine, •isometheptene, •methylphenidate, •phenylephrine, •phenylpropanolamine, •pseudoephedrine or •sympathomimetics
• Tetrabenazine: risk of CNS excitation and hypertension when MAOIs given with •tetrabenazine
Vasodilator Antihypertensives: enhanced hypotensive effect when MAOIs given with hydralazine, minoxidil or nitroprusside

**MAOIs, reversible** *see* Moclobemide
**Maprotiline** *see* Antidepressants, Tricyclic (related)
**Mebendazole**
Ulcer-healing Drugs: metabolism of mebendazole possibly inhibited by cimetidine (increased plasma concentration)
**Meclozine** *see* Antihistamines
**Medroxyprogesterone** *see* Progestogens
**Mefenamic Acid** *see* NSAIDs
**Mefloquine**
• Anti-arrhythmics: increased risk of ventricular arrhythmias when mefloquine given with •amiodarone—avoid concomitant use; increased risk of ventricular arrhythmias when mefloquine given with •quinidine
• Antibacterials: increased risk of ventricular arrhythmias when mefloquine given with •moxifloxacin—avoid concomitant use
• Antiepileptics: mefloquine antagonises anticonvulsant effect of •antiepileptics, •carbamazepine and •valproate
• Antimalarials: avoidance of antimalarials advised by manufacturer of •artemether/lumefantrine; increased risk of convulsions when mefloquine given with •chloroquine and hydroxychloroquine; increased risk of convulsions when mefloquine given with •quinine (but should not prevent the use of intravenous quinine in severe cases)

**Mefloquine** *(continued)*
• Antipsychotics: increased risk of ventricular arrhythmias when mefloquine given with •pimozide—avoid concomitant use
Beta-blockers: increased risk of bradycardia when mefloquine given with beta-blockers
Calcium-channel Blockers: possible increased risk of bradycardia when mefloquine given with calcium-channel blockers
Cardiac Glycosides: possible increased risk of bradycardia when mefloquine given with digoxin
• Ivabradine: increased risk of ventricular arrhythmias when mefloquine given with •ivabradine
**Megestrol** *see* Progestogens
**Meloxicam** *see* NSAIDs
**Melphalan**
Antibacterials: increased risk of melphalan toxicity when given with nalidixic acid
Antiepileptics: cytotoxics possibly reduce absorption of phenytoin
• Antipsychotics: avoid concomitant use of cytotoxics with •clozapine (increased risk of agranulocytosis)
• Ciclosporin: increased risk of nephrotoxicity when melphalan given with •ciclosporin
**Memantine**
• Anaesthetics, General: increased risk of CNS toxicity when memantine given with •ketamine (manufacturer of memantine advises avoid concomitant use)
• Analgesics: increased risk of CNS toxicity when memantine given with •dextromethorphan (manufacturer of memantine advises avoid concomitant use)
Antiepileptics: memantine possibly reduces effects of primidone
Antimuscarinics: memantine possibly enhances effects of antimuscarinics
Antipsychotics: memantine possibly reduces effects of antipsychotics
Barbiturates: memantine possibly reduces effects of barbiturates
• Dopaminergics: memantine possibly enhances effects of dopaminergics and selegiline; increased risk of CNS toxicity when memantine given with •amantadine (manufacturer of memantine advises avoid concomitant use)
Muscle Relaxants: memantine possibly modifies effects of baclofen and dantrolene
**Mepacrine**
Antimalarials: mepacrine increases plasma concentration of primaquine (increased risk of toxicity)
**Meprobamate** *see* Anxiolytics and Hypnotics
**Meptazinol** *see* Opioid Analgesics
**Mercaptopurine**
• Allopurinol: enhanced effects and increased toxicity of mercaptopurine when given with •allopurinol (reduce dose of mercaptopurine)
Aminosalicylates: possible increased risk of leucopenia when mercaptopurine given with aminosalicylates
• Antibacterials: increased risk of haematological toxicity when mercaptopurine given with •sulfamethoxazole (as co-trimoxazole); increased risk of haematological toxicity when mercaptopurine given with •trimethoprim (also with co-trimoxazole)
• Anticoagulants: mercaptopurine possibly reduces anticoagulant effect of •coumarins
Antiepileptics: cytotoxics possibly reduce absorption of phenytoin

**Mercaptopurine** *(continued)*
- • Antipsychotics: avoid concomitant use of cytotoxics with •clozapine (increased risk of agranulocytosis)

**Meropenem**
- Antiepileptics: meropenem reduces plasma concentration of valproate
- Oestrogens: antibacterials that do not induce liver enzymes possibly reduce contraceptive effect of oestrogens (risk probably small, see p. 408)
- Probenecid: excretion of meropenem reduced by probenecid (manufacturers of meropenem advise avoid concomitant use)

**Mesalazine** *see* Aminosalicylates
**Mestranol** *see* Oestrogens
**Metaraminol** *see* Sympathomimetics
**Metformin** *see* Antidiabetics
**Methadone** *see* Opioid Analgesics
**Methenamine**
- • Antibacterials: increased risk of crystalluria when methenamine given with •sulphonamides
- • Diuretics: effects of methenamine antagonised by •acetazolamide
- Oestrogens: antibacterials that do not induce liver enzymes possibly reduce contraceptive effect of oestrogens (risk probably small, see p. 408)
- Potassium Salts: avoid concomitant use of methenamine with potassium citrate

**Methocarbamol** *see* Muscle Relaxants
**Methotrexate**
- • Anaesthetics, General: antifolate effect of methotrexate increased by •nitrous oxide—avoid concomitant use
- • Analgesics: excretion of methotrexate probably reduced by •NSAIDs (increased risk of toxicity)—but for concomitant use in rheumatic disease see p. 520; excretion of methotrexate reduced by •aspirin, •diclofenac, •ibuprofen, •indometacin, •ketoprofen, •meloxicam and •naproxen (increased risk of toxicity)—but for concomitant use in rheumatic disease see p. 520
- • Antibacterials: absorption of methotrexate possibly reduced by neomycin; excretion of methotrexate possibly reduced by ciprofloxacin (increased risk of toxicity); increased risk of haematological toxicity when methotrexate given with •sulfamethoxazole (as co-trimoxazole); increased risk of methotrexate toxicity when given with doxycycline, sulphonamides or tetracycline; excretion of methotrexate reduced by penicillins (increased risk of toxicity); increased risk of haematological toxicity when methotrexate given with •trimethoprim (also with co-trimoxazole)
- Antiepileptics: antifolate effect of methotrexate increased by phenytoin; cytotoxics possibly reduce absorption of phenytoin
- • Antimalarials: antifolate effect of methotrexate increased by •pyrimethamine
- • Antipsychotics: avoid concomitant use of cytotoxics with •clozapine (increased risk of agranulocytosis)
- • Ciclosporin: risk of toxicity when methotrexate given with •ciclosporin
- • Corticosteroids: increased risk of haematological toxicity when methotrexate given with •corticosteroids
- • Cytotoxics: increased pulmonary toxicity when methotrexate given with •cisplatin
- • Probenecid: excretion of methotrexate reduced by •probenecid (increased risk of toxicity)
- • Retinoids: plasma concentration of methotrexate increased by •acitretin (also increased risk of hepatotoxicity)—avoid concomitant use



**Methotrexate** *(continued)*
- Theophylline: methotrexate possibly increases plasma concentration of theophylline
- Ulcer-healing Drugs: excretion of methotrexate possibly reduced by omeprazole (increased risk of toxicity)

**Methoxamine** *see* Sympathomimetics
**Methyldopa**
- ACE Inhibitors: enhanced hypotensive effect when methyldopa given with ACE inhibitors
- Adrenergic Neurone Blockers: enhanced hypotensive effect when methyldopa given with adrenergic neurone blockers
- Alcohol: enhanced hypotensive effect when methyldopa given with alcohol
- Aldesleukin: enhanced hypotensive effect when methyldopa given with aldesleukin
- Alpha-blockers: enhanced hypotensive effect when methyldopa given with alpha-blockers
- Anaesthetics, General: enhanced hypotensive effect when methyldopa given with general anaesthetics
- Analgesics: hypotensive effect of methyldopa antagonised by NSAIDs
- Angiotensin-II Receptor Antagonists: enhanced hypotensive effect when methyldopa given with angiotensin-II receptor antagonists
- • Antidepressants: manufacturer of methyldopa advises avoid concomitant use with •MAOIs
- Antipsychotics: enhanced hypotensive effect when methyldopa given with antipsychotics (also increased risk of extrapyramidal effects)
- Anxiolytics and Hypnotics: enhanced hypotensive effect when methyldopa given with anxiolytics and hypnotics
- Beta-blockers: enhanced hypotensive effect when methyldopa given with beta-blockers
- Calcium-channel Blockers: enhanced hypotensive effect when methyldopa given with calcium-channel blockers
- Clonidine: enhanced hypotensive effect when methyldopa given with clonidine
- Corticosteroids: hypotensive effect of methyldopa antagonised by corticosteroids
- Diazoxide: enhanced hypotensive effect when methyldopa given with diazoxide
- Diuretics: enhanced hypotensive effect when methyldopa given with diuretics
- Dopaminergics: methyldopa antagonises antiparkinsonian effect of dopaminergics; increased risk of extrapyramidal side-effects when methyldopa given with amantadine; effects of methyldopa possibly enhanced by entacapone; enhanced hypotensive effect when methyldopa given with levodopa
- Iron: hypotensive effect of methyldopa antagonised by *oral* iron
- • Lithium: neurotoxicity may occur when methyldopa given with •lithium without increased plasma concentration of lithium
- Moxisylyte (thymoxamine): enhanced hypotensive effect when methyldopa given with moxisylyte
- Moxonidine: enhanced hypotensive effect when methyldopa given with moxonidine
- Muscle Relaxants: enhanced hypotensive effect when methyldopa given with baclofen or tizanidine
- Nitrates: enhanced hypotensive effect when methyldopa given with nitrates
- Oestrogens: hypotensive effect of methyldopa antagonised by oestrogens
- Prostaglandins: enhanced hypotensive effect when methyldopa given with alprostadil

**Methyldopa** *(continued)*
- • Sympathomimetics, Beta$_2$: acute hypotension reported when methyldopa given with infusion of •salbutamol
- Vasodilator Antihypertensives: enhanced hypotensive effect when methyldopa given with hydralazine, minoxidil or nitroprusside

**Methylphenidate** *see* Sympathomimetics
**Methylprednisolone** *see* Corticosteroids
**Methysergide** *see* Ergot Alkaloids
**Metipranolol** *see* Beta-blockers
**Metoclopramide**
- Analgesics: metoclopramide increases rate of absorption of aspirin (enhanced effect); effects of metoclopramide on gastro-intestinal activity antagonised by opioid analgesics; metoclopramide increases rate of absorption of paracetamol
- Antimuscarinics: effects of metoclopramide on gastro-intestinal activity antagonised by antimuscarinics
- Antipsychotics: increased risk of extrapyramidal side-effects when metoclopramide given with antipsychotics
- Atovaquone: metoclopramide reduces plasma concentration of atovaquone
- • Ciclosporin: metoclopramide increases plasma concentration of •ciclosporin
- Dopaminergics: increased risk of extrapyramidal side-effects when metoclopramide given with amantadine; metoclopramide antagonises hypoprolactinaemic effects of bromocriptine and cabergoline; metoclopramide antagonises antiparkinsonian effect of pergolide; metoclopramide antagonises antiparkinsonian effect of ropinirole (manufacturers of ropinirole advise avoid concomitant use)
- Muscle Relaxants: metoclopramide enhances effects of suxamethonium
- Tetrabenazine: increased risk of extrapyramidal side-effects when metoclopramide given with tetrabenazine

**Metolazone** *see* Diuretics
**Metoprolol** *see* Beta-blockers
**Metronidazole**
- Alcohol: disulfiram-like reaction when metronidazole given with alcohol
- • Anticoagulants: metronidazole enhances anticoagulant effect of •coumarins
- • Antiepileptics: metronidazole inhibits metabolism of •phenytoin (increased plasma concentration); metabolism of metronidazole accelerated by primidone (reduced plasma concentration)
- Barbiturates: metabolism of metronidazole accelerated by barbiturates (reduced plasma concentration)
- Cytotoxics: metronidazole inhibits metabolism of fluorouracil (increased toxicity)
- Disulfiram: psychotic reaction reported when metronidazole given with disulfiram
- Lithium: metronidazole increases risk of lithium toxicity
- Oestrogens: antibacterials that do not induce liver enzymes possibly reduce contraceptive effect of oestrogens (risk probably small, see p. 408)
- Ulcer-healing Drugs: metabolism of metronidazole inhibited by cimetidine (increased plasma concentration)

**Mexiletine**
- Anaesthetics, Local: increased myocardial depression when anti-arrhythmics given with bupivacaine, levobupivacaine or prilocaine
- Analgesics: absorption of mexiletine delayed by opioid analgesics

**Mexiletine** *(continued)*
- • Anti-arrhythmics: increased myocardial depression when anti-arrhythmics given with other •anti-arrhythmics
- Antibacterials: metabolism of mexiletine accelerated by rifampicin (reduced plasma concentration)
- • Antidepressants: metabolism of mexiletine inhibited by •fluvoxamine (increased risk of toxicity)
- Antiepileptics: metabolism of mexiletine accelerated by phenytoin (reduced plasma concentration)
- • Antihistamines: increased risk of ventricular arrhythmias when mexiletine given with •mizolastine—avoid concomitant use
- Antimuscarinics: absorption of mexiletine delayed by atropine
- • Antipsychotics: increased risk of ventricular arrhythmias when anti-arrhythmics that prolong the QT interval given with •antipsychotics that prolong the QT interval
- • Antivirals: plasma concentration of mexiletine possibly increased by •ritonavir (increased risk of toxicity)
- • Beta-blockers: increased myocardial depression when anti-arrhythmics given with •beta-blockers
- • Diuretics: action of mexiletine antagonised by hypokalaemia caused by •acetazolamide, •loop diuretics or •thiazides and related diuretics
- • Dolasetron: increased risk of ventricular arrhythmias when mexiletine given with •dolasetron—avoid concomitant use
- $5HT_3$ Antagonists: caution with anti-arrhythmics advised by manufacturer of tropisetron (risk of ventricular arrhythmias)
- Theophylline: mexiletine increases plasma concentration of theophylline

**Mianserin** *see* Antidepressants, Tricyclic (related)
**Miconazole** *see* Antifungals, Imidazole
**Midazolam** *see* Anxiolytics and Hypnotics
**Mifepristone**
- Analgesics: manufacturer of mifepristone advises avoid concomitant use with NSAIDs and aspirin
- Corticosteroids: mifepristone may reduce effect of corticosteroids (including inhaled corticosteroids) for 3–4 days

**Milrinone** *see* Phosphodiesterase Inhibitors
**Minocycline** *see* Tetracyclines
**Minoxidil** *see* Vasodilator Antihypertensives
**Mirtazapine**
- • Alcohol: increased sedative effect when mirtazapine given with •alcohol
- Anticoagulants: mirtazapine enhances anticoagulant effect of warfarin
- • Antidepressants: mirtazapine should not be started until 2 weeks after stopping •MAOIs, also MAOIs should not be started until at least 2 weeks after stopping mirtazapine; after stopping mirtazapine do not start •moclobemide for at least 1 week
- Antiepileptics: plasma concentration of mirtazapine reduced by carbamazepine and phenytoin
- Antifungals: plasma concentration of mirtazapine increased by ketoconazole
- • Antimalarials: avoidance of antidepressants advised by manufacturer of •artemether/lumefantrine
- Anxiolytics and Hypnotics: increased sedative effect when mirtazapine given with anxiolytics and hypnotics
- • Sibutramine: increased risk of CNS toxicity when mirtazapine given with •sibutramine (manufacturer of sibutramine advises avoid concomitant use)

**Mirtazapine** *(continued)*
Ulcer-healing Drugs: plasma concentration of mirtazapine increased by cimetidine
**Mivacurium** *see* Muscle Relaxants
**Mizolastine** *see* Antihistamines
**Moclobemide**
• Analgesics: possible CNS excitation or depression (hypertension or hypotension) when moclobemide given with •dextromethorphan or •pethidine—avoid concomitant use; possible CNS excitation or depression (hypertension or hypotension) when moclobemide given with •opioid analgesics
• Antidepressants: moclobemide should not be started for at least 1 week after stopping •MAOIs, •SSRI-related antidepressants, •citalopram, •fluvoxamine, •mirtazapine, •paroxetine, •tricyclic-related antidepressants or •tricyclics; increased risk of CNS toxicity when moclobemide given with •escitalopram, preferably avoid concomitant use; moclobemide should not be started until 5 weeks after stopping •fluoxetine; moclobemide should not be started until 2 weeks after stopping •sertraline; possible increased serotonergic effects when moclobemide given with •duloxetine
• Antimalarials: avoidance of antidepressants advised by manufacturer of •artemether/lumefantrine
• Bupropion: avoidance of moclobemide advised by manufacturer of •bupropion
• Dopaminergics: caution with moclobemide advised by manufacturer of entacapone; increased risk of side-effects when moclobemide given with levodopa; avoid concomitant use of moclobemide with •selegiline
• $5HT_1$ Agonists: risk of CNS toxicity when moclobemide given with •rizatriptan or •sumatriptan (avoid rizatriptan or sumatriptan for 2 weeks after moclobemide); risk of CNS toxicity when moclobemide given with •zolmitriptan (reduce dose of zolmitriptan)
• Sibutramine: increased CNS toxicity when moclobemide given with •sibutramine (manufacturer of sibutramine advises avoid concomitant use), also avoid sibutramine for 2 weeks after stopping moclobemide
• Sympathomimetics: risk of hypertensive crisis when moclobemide given with •dexamfetamine, •dopamine, •dopexamine, •ephedrine, •isometheptene, •methylphenidate, •phenylephrine, •phenylpropanolamine, •pseudoephedrine or •sympathomimetics
Ulcer-healing Drugs: plasma concentration of moclobemide increased by cimetidine (halve dose of moclobemide)
**Modafinil**
Antiepileptics: modafinil possibly increases plasma concentration of phenytoin
• Ciclosporin: modafinil reduces plasma concentration of •ciclosporin
• Oestrogens: modafinil accelerates metabolism of •oestrogens (reduced contraceptive effect—see p. 408)
**Moexipril** *see* ACE Inhibitors
**Mometasone** *see* Corticosteroids
**Monobactams** *see* Aztreonam
**Montelukast** *see* Leukotriene Antagonists
**Morphine** *see* Opioid Analgesics
**Moxifloxacin** *see* Quinolones
**Moxisylyte (thymoxamine)**
ACE Inhibitors: enhanced hypotensive effect when moxisylyte given with ACE inhibitors

**Moxisylyte (thymoxamine)** *(continued)*
Adrenergic Neurone Blockers: enhanced hypotensive effect when moxisylyte given with adrenergic neurone blockers
• Alpha-blockers: possible severe postural hypotension when moxisylyte given with •alpha-blockers
Angiotensin-II Receptor Antagonists: enhanced hypotensive effect when moxisylyte given with angiotensin-II receptor antagonists
• Beta-blockers: possible severe postural hypotension when moxisylyte given with •beta-blockers
Calcium-channel Blockers: enhanced hypotensive effect when moxisylyte given with calcium-channel blockers
Clonidine: enhanced hypotensive effect when moxisylyte given with clonidine
Diazoxide: enhanced hypotensive effect when moxisylyte given with diazoxide
Diuretics: enhanced hypotensive effect when moxisylyte given with diuretics
Methyldopa: enhanced hypotensive effect when moxisylyte given with methyldopa
Moxonidine: enhanced hypotensive effect when moxisylyte given with moxonidine
Nitrates: enhanced hypotensive effect when moxisylyte given with nitrates
Vasodilator Antihypertensives: enhanced hypotensive effect when moxisylyte given with hydralazine, minoxidil or nitroprusside
**Moxonidine**
ACE Inhibitors: enhanced hypotensive effect when moxonidine given with ACE inhibitors
Adrenergic Neurone Blockers: enhanced hypotensive effect when moxonidine given with adrenergic neurone blockers
Alcohol: enhanced hypotensive effect when moxonidine given with alcohol
Aldesleukin: enhanced hypotensive effect when moxonidine given with aldesleukin
Alpha-blockers: enhanced hypotensive effect when moxonidine given with alpha-blockers
Anaesthetics, General: enhanced hypotensive effect when moxonidine given with general anaesthetics
Analgesics: hypotensive effect of moxonidine antagonised by NSAIDs
Angiotensin-II Receptor Antagonists: enhanced hypotensive effect when moxonidine given with angiotensin-II receptor antagonists
Antidepressants: enhanced hypotensive effect when moxonidine given with MAOIs
Antipsychotics: enhanced hypotensive effect when moxonidine given with phenothiazines
Anxiolytics and Hypnotics: enhanced hypotensive effect when moxonidine given with anxiolytics and hypnotics; sedative effects possibly increased when moxonidine given with benzodiazepines
Beta-blockers: enhanced hypotensive effect when moxonidine given with beta-blockers
Calcium-channel Blockers: enhanced hypotensive effect when moxonidine given with calcium-channel blockers
Clonidine: enhanced hypotensive effect when moxonidine given with clonidine
Corticosteroids: hypotensive effect of moxonidine antagonised by corticosteroids
Diazoxide: enhanced hypotensive effect when moxonidine given with diazoxide
Diuretics: enhanced hypotensive effect when moxonidine given with diuretics
Dopaminergics: enhanced hypotensive effect when moxonidine given with levodopa

**Moxonidine** *(continued)*
Methyldopa: enhanced hypotensive effect when moxonidine given with methyldopa
Moxisylyte (thymoxamine): enhanced hypotensive effect when moxonidine given with moxisylyte
Muscle Relaxants: enhanced hypotensive effect when moxonidine given with baclofen or tizanidine
Nitrates: enhanced hypotensive effect when moxonidine given with nitrates
Oestrogens: hypotensive effect of moxonidine antagonised by oestrogens
Prostaglandins: enhanced hypotensive effect when moxonidine given with alprostadil
Vasodilator Antihypertensives: enhanced hypotensive effect when moxonidine given with hydralazine, minoxidil or nitroprusside

**Muscle Relaxants**
ACE Inhibitors: enhanced hypotensive effect when baclofen or tizanidine given with ACE inhibitors
Adrenergic Neurone Blockers: enhanced hypotensive effect when baclofen or tizanidine given with adrenergic neurone blockers
Alcohol: increased sedative effect when baclofen, methocarbamol or tizanidine given with alcohol
Alpha-blockers: enhanced hypotensive effect when baclofen or tizanidine given with alpha-blockers
Anaesthetics, General: effects of non-depolarising muscle relaxants and suxamethonium enhanced by volatile liquid general anaesthetics
Analgesics: excretion of baclofen possibly reduced by NSAIDs (increased risk of toxicity); excretion of baclofen reduced by ibuprofen (increased risk of toxicity)
Angiotensin-II Receptor Antagonists: enhanced hypotensive effect when baclofen or tizanidine given with angiotensin-II receptor antagonists
• Anti-arrhythmics: neuromuscular blockade enhanced and prolonged when suxamethonium given with lidocaine (lignocaine); effects of muscle relaxants enhanced by •procainamide and •quinidine
• Antibacterials: effects of non-depolarising muscle relaxants and suxamethonium enhanced by piperacillin; effects of non-depolarising muscle relaxants and suxamethonium enhanced by •aminoglycosides; effects of non-depolarising muscle relaxants and suxamethonium enhanced by •clindamycin; effects of non-depolarising muscle relaxants and suxamethonium enhanced by •polymyxins; effects of suxamethonium enhanced by •vancomycin
Antidepressants: effects of suxamethonium enhanced by phenelzine; muscle relaxant effect of baclofen enhanced by tricyclics
Antiepileptics: muscle relaxant effect of non-depolarising muscle relaxants antagonised by carbamazepine and phenytoin (accelerated recovery from neuromuscular blockade)
Antimalarials: effects of suxamethonium possibly enhanced by quinine
Antipsychotics: effects of suxamethonium possibly enhanced by promazine
Anxiolytics and Hypnotics: increased sedative effect when baclofen or tizanidine given with anxiolytics and hypnotics
Beta-blockers: enhanced hypotensive effect when baclofen given with beta-blockers; possible enhanced hypotensive effect and bradycardia when tizanidine given with beta-blockers; effects of muscle relaxants enhanced by propranolol
Calcium-channel Blockers: enhanced hypotensive effect when baclofen or tizanidine given with calcium-channel blockers; effects of non-depolarising muscle relaxants enhanced by nifedipine and verapamil; risk of arrhythmias when intravenous dantrolene given with diltiazem; hypotension, myocardial depression, and hyperkalaemia when intravenous dantrolene given with verapamil; effects of suxamethonium enhanced by verapamil
Cardiac Glycosides: possible increased risk of bradycardia when tizanidine given with cardiac glycosides; risk of ventricular arrhythmias when suxamethonium given with cardiac glycosides
Clonidine: enhanced hypotensive effect when baclofen or tizanidine given with clonidine
Cytotoxics: effects of suxamethonium enhanced by cyclophosphamide and thiotepa
Diazoxide: enhanced hypotensive effect when baclofen or tizanidine given with diazoxide
Diuretics: enhanced hypotensive effect when baclofen or tizanidine given with diuretics
Dopaminergics: possible agitation, confusion and hallucinations when baclofen given with levodopa
Lithium: effects of muscle relaxants enhanced by lithium; baclofen possibly aggravates hyperkinesis caused by lithium
Magnesium (parenteral): effects of non-depolarising muscle relaxants and suxamethonium enhanced by parenteral magnesium
Memantine: effects of baclofen and dantrolene possibly modified by memantine
Methyldopa: enhanced hypotensive effect when baclofen or tizanidine given with methyldopa
Metoclopramide: effects of suxamethonium enhanced by metoclopramide
Moxonidine: enhanced hypotensive effect when baclofen or tizanidine given with moxonidine
Nitrates: enhanced hypotensive effect when baclofen or tizanidine given with nitrates
Parasympathomimetics: effects of suxamethonium possibly enhanced by donepezil; effects of non-depolarising muscle relaxants possibly antagonised by donepezil; effects of suxamethonium enhanced by edrophonium, galantamine, neostigmine, pyridostigmine and rivastigmine; effects of non-depolarising muscle relaxants antagonised by edrophonium, neostigmine, pyridostigmine and rivastigmine
Sympathomimetics, $Beta_2$: effects of suxamethonium enhanced by bambuterol
Vasodilator Antihypertensives: enhanced hypotensive effect when baclofen or tizanidine given with hydralazine; enhanced hypotensive effect when baclofen or tizanidine given with minoxidil; enhanced hypotensive effect when baclofen or tizanidine given with nitroprusside

**Muscle Relaxants, depolarising** *see* Muscle Relaxants

**Muscle Relaxants, non-depolarising** *see* Muscle Relaxants

**Mycophenolate Mofetil**
Antacids: absorption of mycophenolate mofetil reduced by antacids
Antiepileptics: cytotoxics possibly reduce absorption of phenytoin
• Antipsychotics: avoid concomitant use of cytotoxics with •clozapine (increased risk of agranulocytosis)
Antivirals: mycophenolate mofetil increases plasma concentration of aciclovir, also plasma concentration of inactive metabolite of myco-

**Mycophenolate Mofetil**
Antivirals *(continued)*
phenolate mofetil increased; mycophenolate mofetil possibly increases plasma concentration of ganciclovir, also plasma concentration of inactive metabolite of mycophenolate mofetil possibly increased
Lipid-regulating Drugs: absorption of mycophenolate mofetil reduced by colestyramine

**Nabilone**
Alcohol: increased sedative effect when nabilone given with alcohol
Anxiolytics and Hypnotics: increased sedative effect when nabilone given with anxiolytics and hypnotics

**Nabumetone** *see* NSAIDs
**Nadolol** *see* Beta-blockers
**Nalidixic Acid** *see* Quinolones
**Nandrolone** *see* Anabolic Steroids
**Naproxen** *see* NSAIDs
**Naratriptan** *see* $5HT_1$ Agonists
**Nateglinide** *see* Antidiabetics
**Nebivolol** *see* Beta-blockers

**Nefopam**
- Antidepressants: manufacturer of nefopam advises avoid concomitant use with •MAOIs; side-effects possibly increased when nefopam given with tricyclics

Antimuscarinics: increased risk of antimuscarinic side-effects when nefopam given with antimuscarinics

**Nelfinavir**
Analgesics: nelfinavir reduces plasma concentration of methadone
- Anti-arrhythmics: increased risk of ventricular arrhythmias when nelfinavir given with •amiodarone or •quinidine—avoid concomitant use
- Antibacterials: nelfinavir increases plasma concentration of •rifabutin (halve dose of rifabutin); plasma concentration of nelfinavir significantly reduced by •rifampicin—avoid concomitant use
- Antidepressants: plasma concentration of nelfinavir reduced by •St John's wort—avoid concomitant use
- Antiepileptics: plasma concentration of nelfinavir possibly reduced by carbamazepine and •primidone; nelfinavir reduces plasma concentration of phenytoin
- Antimalarials: avoidance of nelfinavir advised by manufacturer of •artemether/lumefantrine

Antimuscarinics: nelfinavir increases plasma concentration of solifenacin; avoidance of nelfinavir advised by manufacturer of tolterodine
- Antipsychotics: nelfinavir possibly inhibits metabolism of •aripiprazole (reduce dose of aripiprazole); nelfinavir possibly increases plasma concentration of •pimozide (increased risk of ventricular arrhythmias—avoid concomitant use); nelfinavir increases plasma concentration of •sertindole (increased risk of ventricular arrhythmias—avoid concomitant use)

Antivirals: combination of nelfinavir with indinavir, ritonavir or saquinavir may increase plasma concentration of either drug (or both); nelfinavir reduces plasma concentration of lopinavir, also plasma concentration of active metabolite of nelfinavir increased
- Anxiolytics and Hypnotics: increased risk of prolonged sedation when nelfinavir given with •midazolam—avoid concomitant use
- Barbiturates: plasma concentration of nelfinavir possibly reduced by •barbiturates

**Nelfinavir** *(continued)*
- Ciclosporin: nelfinavir possibly increases plasma concentration of •ciclosporin
- Cilostazol: nelfinavir possibly increases plasma concentration of •cilostazol—avoid concomitant use

Cytotoxics: nelfinavir increases plasma concentration of paclitaxel
- Diuretics: nelfinavir increases plasma concentration of •eplerenone—avoid concomitant use
- Ergot Alkaloids: increased risk of ergotism when nelfinavir given with •ergotamine and methysergide—avoid concomitant use
- $5HT_1$ Agonists: nelfinavir increases plasma concentration of •eletriptan (risk of toxicity)—avoid concomitant use
- Ivabradine: nelfinavir possibly increases plasma concentration of •ivabradine—avoid concomitant use
- Lipid-regulating Drugs: possible increased risk of myopathy when nelfinavir given with atorvastatin; increased risk of myopathy when nelfinavir given with •simvastatin (avoid concomitant use)
- Oestrogens: nelfinavir accelerates metabolism of •oestrogens (reduced contraceptive effect—see p. 408)

Progestogens: nelfinavir possibly reduces contraceptive effect of progestogens
Sildenafil: nelfinavir possibly increases plasma concentration of sildenafil— reduce initial dose of sildenafil
- Tacrolimus: nelfinavir possibly increases plasma concentration of •tacrolimus

**Neomycin** *see* Aminoglycosides
**Neostigmine** *see* Parasympathomimetics
**Netilmicin** *see* Aminoglycosides

**Nevirapine**
Analgesics: nevirapine possibly reduces plasma concentration of methadone
- Antibacterials: plasma concentration of nevirapine reduced by •rifampicin—avoid concomitant use
- Anticoagulants: nevirapine may enhance or reduce anticoagulant effect of •warfarin
- Antidepressants: plasma concentration of nevirapine reduced by •St John's wort—avoid concomitant use
- Antifungals: nevirapine reduces plasma concentration of •ketoconazole—avoid concomitant use; plasma concentration of nevirapine increased by •fluconazole; nevirapine possibly reduces plasma concentration of caspofungin—consider increasing dose of caspofungin
- Antipsychotics: nevirapine possibly reduces plasma concentration of •aripiprazole—increase dose of aripiprazole
- Antivirals: nevirapine possibly reduces plasma concentration of amprenavir and lopinavir; nevirapine possibly reduces plasma concentration of •atazanavir—avoid concomitant use; nevirapine reduces plasma concentration of efavirenz, indinavir and saquinavir
- Oestrogens: nevirapine accelerates metabolism of •oestrogens (reduced contraceptive effect—see p. 408)
- Progestogens: nevirapine accelerates metabolism of •progestogens (reduced contraceptive effect—see p. 408)

**Nicardipine** *see* Calcium-channel Blockers

**Nicorandil**
Alcohol: hypotensive effect of nicorandil possibly enhanced by alcohol
Antidepressants: enhanced hypotensive effect when nicorandil given with MAOIs; hypotensive

**Nicorandil**
Antidepressants *(continued)*
effect of nicorandil possibly enhanced by tricyclics
- • Sildenafil: hypotensive effect of nicorandil significantly enhanced by •sildenafil (avoid concomitant use)
- • Tadalafil: hypotensive effect of nicorandil significantly enhanced by •tadalafil (avoid concomitant use)
- • Vardenafil: possible increased hypotensive effect when nicorandil given with •vardenafil—avoid concomitant use

Vasodilator Antihypertensives: possible enhanced hypotensive effect when nicorandil given with hydralazine, minoxidil or nitroprusside

**Nicotinic Acid**
*Note.* Interactions apply to lipid-regulating doses of nicotinic acid
- • Lipid-regulating Drugs: increased risk of myopathy when nicotinic acid given with •statins (applies to lipid regulating doses of nicotinic acid)

**Nifedipine** *see* Calcium-channel Blockers
**Nimodipine** *see* Calcium-channel Blockers
**Nisoldipine** *see* Calcium-channel Blockers

**Nitrates**
ACE Inhibitors: enhanced hypotensive effect when nitrates given with ACE inhibitors
Adrenergic Neurone Blockers: enhanced hypotensive effect when nitrates given with adrenergic neurone blockers
Alcohol: enhanced hypotensive effect when nitrates given with alcohol
Aldesleukin: enhanced hypotensive effect when nitrates given with aldesleukin
Alpha-blockers: enhanced hypotensive effect when nitrates given with alpha-blockers
Anaesthetics, General: enhanced hypotensive effect when nitrates given with general anaesthetics
Analgesics: hypotensive effect of nitrates antagonised by NSAIDs
Angiotensin-II Receptor Antagonists: enhanced hypotensive effect when nitrates given with angiotensin-II receptor antagonists
Anti-arrhythmics: effects of sublingual tablets of nitrates reduced by disopyramide (failure to dissolve under tongue owing to dry mouth)
- • Anticoagulants: infusion of glyceryl trinitrate reduces anticoagulant effect of •heparins

Antidepressants: enhanced hypotensive effect when nitrates given with MAOIs; effects of sublingual tablets of nitrates possibly reduced by tricyclic-related antidepressants (failure to dissolve under tongue owing to dry mouth); effects of sublingual tablets of nitrates reduced by tricyclics (failure to dissolve under tongue owing to dry mouth)
Antimuscarinics: effects of sublingual tablets of nitrates possibly reduced by antimuscarinics (failure to dissolve under tongue owing to dry mouth)
Antipsychotics: enhanced hypotensive effect when nitrates given with phenothiazines
Anxiolytics and Hypnotics: enhanced hypotensive effect when nitrates given with anxiolytics and hypnotics
Beta-blockers: enhanced hypotensive effect when nitrates given with beta-blockers
Calcium-channel Blockers: enhanced hypotensive effect when nitrates given with calcium-channel blockers
Clonidine: enhanced hypotensive effect when nitrates given with clonidine

**Nitrates** *(continued)*
Corticosteroids: hypotensive effect of nitrates antagonised by corticosteroids
Diazoxide: enhanced hypotensive effect when nitrates given with diazoxide
Diuretics: enhanced hypotensive effect when nitrates given with diuretics
Dopaminergics: hypotensive effect of nitrates enhanced by sublingual apomorphine; enhanced hypotensive effect when nitrates given with levodopa
Methyldopa: enhanced hypotensive effect when nitrates given with methyldopa
Moxisylyte (thymoxamine): enhanced hypotensive effect when nitrates given with moxisylyte
Moxonidine: enhanced hypotensive effect when nitrates given with moxonidine
Muscle Relaxants: enhanced hypotensive effect when nitrates given with baclofen or tizanidine
Oestrogens: hypotensive effect of nitrates antagonised by oestrogens
Prostaglandins: enhanced hypotensive effect when nitrates given with alprostadil
- • Sildenafil: hypotensive effect of nitrates significantly enhanced by •sildenafil (avoid concomitant use)
- • Tadalafil: hypotensive effect of nitrates significantly enhanced by •tadalafil (avoid concomitant use)
- • Vardenafil: possible increased hypotensive effect when nitrates given with •vardenafil—avoid concomitant use

Vasodilator Antihypertensives: enhanced hypotensive effect when nitrates given with hydralazine, minoxidil or nitroprusside

**Nitrazepam** *see* Anxiolytics and Hypnotics

**Nitrofurantoin**
Antacids: absorption of nitrofurantoin reduced by oral magnesium salts (as magnesium trisilicate)
Oestrogens: antibacterials that do not induce liver enzymes possibly reduce contraceptive effect of oestrogens (risk probably small, see p. 408)
Probenecid: excretion of nitrofurantoin reduced by probenecid (increased risk of side-effects)
Sulfinpyrazone: excretion of nitrofurantoin reduced by sulfinpyrazone (increased risk of toxicity)

**Nitroimidazoles** *see* Metronidazole and Tinidazole
**Nitroprusside** *see* Vasodilator Antihypertensives
**Nitrous Oxide** *see* Anaesthetics, General
**Nizatidine** *see* Histamine $H_2$-antagonists
**Noradrenaline (norepinephrine)** *see* Sympathomimetics
**Norelgestromin** *see* Progestogens
**Norepinephrine (noradrenaline)** *see* Sympathomimetics
**Norethisterone** *see* Progestogens
**Norfloxacin** *see* Quinolones
**Norgestimate** *see* Progestogens
**Norgestrel** *see* Progestogens
**Nortriptyline** *see* Antidepressants, Tricyclic

**NSAIDs**
*Note. See also* Aspirin. Interactions do not generally apply to topical NSAIDs
ACE Inhibitors: increased risk of renal impairment when NSAIDs given with ACE inhibitors, also hypotensive effect antagonised; increased risk of hyperkalaemia when ketorolac given with ACE inhibitors
Adrenergic Neurone Blockers: NSAIDs antagonise hypotensive effect of adrenergic neurone blockers
Alpha-blockers: NSAIDs antagonise hypotensive effect of alpha-blockers

**NSAIDs** *(continued)*

- Analgesics: avoid concomitant use of NSAIDs with •NSAIDs or •aspirin (increased side-effects); avoid concomitant use of NSAIDs with •ketorolac (increased side-effects and haemorrhage); ibuprofen possibly reduces antiplatelet effect of aspirin
- Angiotensin-II Receptor Antagonists: increased risk of renal impairment when NSAIDs given with angiotensin-II receptor antagonists, also hypotensive effect antagonised; increased risk of hyperkalaemia when ketorolac given with angiotensin-II receptor antagonists
- Antacids: absorption of diflunisal reduced by antacids
- • Antibacterials: indometacin possibly increases plasma concentration of amikacin and gentamicin in neonates; plasma concentration of etoricoxib reduced by rifampicin; possible increased risk of convulsions when NSAIDs given with •quinolones
- • Anticoagulants: celecoxib, diflunisal, etodolac, etoricoxib, flurbiprofen, ibuprofen, lumiracoxib, mefenamic acid, meloxicam, parecoxib, piroxicam and sulindac possibly enhance anticoagulant effect of •coumarins; diclofenac possibly enhances anticoagulant effect of •coumarins, also increased risk of haemorrhage with intravenous diclofenac (avoid concomitant use); NSAIDs possibly enhance anticoagulant effect of •coumarins and •phenindione; increased risk of bleeding when ketorolac given with •coumarins (avoid concomitant use); increased risk of haemorrhage when intravenous diclofenac given with •heparins (avoid concomitant use, including low-dose heparin); possible increased risk of bleeding when NSAIDs given with heparins; increased risk of haemorrhage when ketorolac given with •heparins (avoid concomitant use, including low-dose heparin); diclofenac enhances anticoagulant effect of •phenindione, also increased risk of haemorrhage with intravenous diclofenac (avoid concomitant use); ketorolac enhances anticoagulant effect of •phenindione (increased risk of haemorrhage—avoid concomitant use)
- • Antidepressants: increased risk of bleeding when NSAIDs given with •SSRIs or •venlafaxine
- • Antidiabetics: NSAIDs possibly enhance effects of •sulphonylureas
- • Antiepileptics: NSAIDs possibly enhance effects of •phenytoin
- Antifungals: plasma concentration of parecoxib increased by fluconazole (reduce dose of parecoxib); plasma concentration of celecoxib increased by fluconazole (halve dose of celecoxib)
- Antipsychotics: possible severe drowsiness when indometacin given with haloperidol
- • Antivirals: plasma concentration of piroxicam increased by •ritonavir (risk of toxicity)—avoid concomitant use; plasma concentration of NSAIDs possibly increased by ritonavir; increased risk of haematological toxicity when NSAIDs given with zidovudine
- Beta-blockers: NSAIDs antagonise hypotensive effect of beta-blockers
- Bisphosphonates: indometacin increases bioavailability of tiludronic acid
- Calcium-channel Blockers: NSAIDs antagonise hypotensive effect of calcium-channel blockers
- Cardiac Glycosides: NSAIDs possibly increase plasma concentration of cardiac glycosides, also possible exacerbation of heart failure and reduction of renal function
- • Ciclosporin: increased risk of nephrotoxicity when NSAIDs given with •ciclosporin; plasma concentration of diclofenac increased by •ciclosporin (halve dose of diclofenac)
- Clonidine: NSAIDs antagonise hypotensive effect of clonidine
- Clopidogrel: increased risk of bleeding when NSAIDs given with clopidogrel
- Corticosteroids: increased risk of gastro-intestinal bleeding and ulceration when NSAIDs given with corticosteroids
- • Cytotoxics: NSAIDs probably reduce excretion of •methotrexate (increased risk of toxicity)—but for concomitant use in rheumatic disease see p. 520; diclofenac, ibuprofen, indometacin, ketoprofen, meloxicam and naproxen reduce excretion of •methotrexate (increased risk of toxicity)—but for concomitant use in rheumatic disease see p. 520; increased risk of bleeding when NSAIDs given with •erlotinib
- Desmopressin: indometacin enhances effects of desmopressin
- Diazoxide: NSAIDs antagonise hypotensive effect of diazoxide
- • Diuretics: risk of nephrotoxicity of NSAIDs increased by diuretics, also antagonism of diuretic effect; indometacin and ketorolac antagonise effects of diuretics; occasional reports of reduced renal function when indometacin given with •triamterene—avoid concomitant use; possibly increased risk of hyperkalaemia when NSAIDs given with potassium-sparing diuretics and aldosterone antagonists; increased risk of hyperkalaemia when indometacin given with potassium-sparing diuretics and aldosterone antagonists
- Iloprost: increased risk of bleeding when NSAIDs given with iloprost
- Lipid-regulating Drugs: excretion of meloxicam increased by colestyramine
- • Lithium: NSAIDs probably reduce excretion of •lithium (increased risk of toxicity); diclofenac, ibuprofen, indometacin, mefenamic acid, naproxen, parecoxib and piroxicam reduce excretion of •lithium (increased risk of toxicity); ketorolac reduces excretion of •lithium (increased risk of toxicity)—avoid concomitant use
- Methyldopa: NSAIDs antagonise hypotensive effect of methyldopa
- Mifepristone: avoidance of NSAIDs advised by manufacturer of mifepristone
- Moxonidine: NSAIDs antagonise hypotensive effect of moxonidine
- Muscle Relaxants: NSAIDs possibly reduce excretion of baclofen (increased risk of toxicity); ibuprofen reduces excretion of baclofen (increased risk of toxicity)
- Nitrates: NSAIDs antagonise hypotensive effect of nitrates
- Oestrogens: etoricoxib increases plasma concentration of ethinylestradiol
- Penicillamine: possible increased risk of nephrotoxicity when NSAIDs given with penicillamine
- • Pentoxifylline (oxpentifylline): possible increased risk of bleeding when NSAIDs given with pentoxifylline (oxpentifylline); increased risk of bleeding when ketorolac given with •pentoxifylline (oxpentifylline) (avoid concomitant use)
- • Probenecid: excretion of indometacin, ketoprofen and naproxen reduced by •probene-

Appendix 1

NSAIDs
- Probenecid *(continued)*
  cid (increased plasma concentration); excretion of ketorolac reduced by •probenecid (increased plasma concentration)—avoid concomitant use
  Progestogens: risk of hyperkalaemia when NSAIDs given with drospirenone (monitor serum potassium during first cycle)
  Sibutramine: increased risk of bleeding when NSAIDs given with sibutramine
- Tacrolimus: possible increased risk of nephrotoxicity when NSAIDs given with tacrolimus; increased risk of nephrotoxicity when ibuprofen given with •tacrolimus
  Vasodilator Antihypertensives: NSAIDs antagonise hypotensive effect of hydralazine, minoxidil and nitroprusside

Octreotide
  Antidiabetics: octreotide possibly reduces requirements for insulin, metformin, repaglinide and sulphonylureas
- Ciclosporin: octreotide reduces plasma concentration of •ciclosporin
  Dopaminergics: octreotide increases plasma concentration of bromocriptine
  Ulcer-healing Drugs: octreotide possibly delays absorption of cimetidine

Oestrogens
*Note.* Interactions of combined oral contraceptives may also apply to combined contraceptive patches; in case of hormone replacement therapy low dose unlikely to induce interactions
  ACE Inhibitors: oestrogens antagonise hypotensive effect of ACE inhibitors
  Adrenergic Neurone Blockers: oestrogens antagonise hypotensive effect of adrenergic neurone blockers
  Alpha-blockers: oestrogens antagonise hypotensive effect of alpha-blockers
  Analgesics: plasma concentration of ethinylestradiol increased by etoricoxib
  Angiotensin-II Receptor Antagonists: oestrogens antagonise hypotensive effect of angiotensin-II receptor antagonists
- Antibacterials: contraceptive effect of oestrogens possibly reduced by antibacterials that do not induce liver enzymes (risk probably small, see p. 408); metabolism of oestrogens accelerated by •rifamycins (reduced contraceptive effect—see p. 408)
- Anticoagulants: oestrogens antagonise anticoagulant effect of •coumarins and •phenindione
- Antidepressants: contraceptive effect of oestrogens reduced by •St John's wort (avoid concomitant use); oestrogens antagonise antidepressant effect of tricyclics (but side-effects of tricyclics possibly increased due to increased plasma concentration)
  Antidiabetics: oestrogens antagonise hypoglycaemic effect of antidiabetics
- Antiepileptics: metabolism of oestrogens accelerated by •carbamazepine, •oxcarbazepine, •phenytoin, •primidone and •topiramate (reduced contraceptive effect—see p. 408); oestrogens reduce plasma concentration of •lamotrigine
- Antifungals: anecdotal reports of contraceptive failure when oestrogens given with fluconazole, imidazoles, itraconazole or ketoconazole; metabolism of oestrogens accelerated by •griseofulvin (reduced contraceptive effect—see p. 408); occasional reports of breakthrough bleeding when oestrogens (used for contraception) given with terbinafine

Oestrogens *(continued)*
- Antivirals: contraceptive effect of oestrogens possibly reduced by amprenavir and efavirenz; plasma concentration of ethinylestradiol increased by •atazanavir—avoid concomitant use; metabolism of oestrogens accelerated by •nelfinavir, •nevirapine and •ritonavir (reduced contraceptive effect—see p. 408)
- Aprepitant: possible contraceptive failure of hormonal contraceptives containing oestrogens when given with •aprepitant (alternative contraception recommended)
- Barbiturates: metabolism of oestrogens accelerated by •barbiturates (reduced contraceptive effect—see p. 408)
  Beta-blockers: oestrogens antagonise hypotensive effect of beta-blockers
  Bile Acids: elimination of cholesterol in bile increased when oestrogens given with bile acids
- Bosentan: possible contraceptive failure of hormonal contraceptives containing oestrogens when given with •bosentan (alternative contraception recommended)
  Calcium-channel Blockers: oestrogens antagonise hypotensive effect of calcium-channel blockers
  Ciclosporin: oestrogens possibly increase plasma concentration of ciclosporin
  Clonidine: oestrogens antagonise hypotensive effect of clonidine
  Corticosteroids: oral contraceptives containing oestrogens increase plasma concentration of corticosteroids
  Diazoxide: oestrogens antagonise hypotensive effect of diazoxide
  Diuretics: oestrogens antagonise diuretic effect of diuretics
  Dopaminergics: oestrogens increase plasma concentration of ropinirole; oestrogens increase plasma concentration of selegiline (increased risk of toxicity)
  Lipid-regulating Drugs: plasma concentration of ethinylestradiol increased by rosuvastatin
  Methyldopa: oestrogens antagonise hypotensive effect of methyldopa
- Modafinil: metabolism of oestrogens accelerated by •modafinil (reduced contraceptive effect—see p. 408)
  Moxonidine: oestrogens antagonise hypotensive effect of moxonidine
  Nitrates: oestrogens antagonise hypotensive effect of nitrates
  Somatropin: oestrogens (when used as oral replacement therapy) may increase dose requirements of somatropin
  Tacrolimus: contraceptive effect of oestrogens possibly reduced by tacrolimus
  Theophylline: oestrogens reduce excretion of theophylline (increased plasma concentration)
  Vasodilator Antihypertensives: oestrogens antagonise hypotensive effect of hydralazine, minoxidil and nitroprusside

Oestrogens, conjugated *see* Oestrogens
Ofloxacin *see* Quinolones
Olanzapine *see* Antipsychotics
Olmesartan *see* Angiotensin-II Receptor Antagonists
Olsalazine *see* Aminosalicylates
Omeprazole *see* Proton Pump Inhibitors

Ondansetron
  Analgesics: ondansetron possibly antagonises effects of tramadol
  Antibacterials: metabolism of ondansetron accelerated by rifampicin (reduced effect)

**Ondansetron** *(continued)*
Antiepileptics: metabolism of ondansetron accelerated by carbamazepine and phenytoin (reduced effect)

**Opioid Analgesics**
Alcohol: enhanced hypotensive and sedative effects when opioid analgesics given with alcohol
Anti-arrhythmics: opioid analgesics delay absorption of mexiletine
Antibacterials: plasma concentration of alfentanil increased by erythromycin; avoidance of premedication with opioid analgesics advised by manufacturer of ciprofloxacin (reduced plasma concentration of ciprofloxacin) when ciprofloxacin used for surgical prophylaxis; metabolism of methadone accelerated by rifampicin (reduced effect)
• Anticoagulants: tramadol enhances anticoagulant effect of •coumarins; dextropropoxyphene possibly enhances anticoagulant effect of •coumarins
• Antidepressants: plasma concentration of methadone possibly increased by fluvoxamine; possible increased serotonergic effects when pethidine or tramadol given with duloxetine; CNS excitation or depression (hypertension or hypotension) when pethidine given with •MAOIs—avoid concomitant use and for 2 weeks after stopping MAOIs; possible CNS excitation or depression (hypertension or hypotension) when opioid analgesics given with •MAOIs—avoid concomitant use and for 2 weeks after stopping MAOIs; possible CNS excitation or depression (hypertension or hypotension) when opioid analgesics given with •moclobemide; possible CNS excitation or depression (hypertension or hypotension) when dextromethorphan or pethidine given with •moclobemide—avoid concomitant use; increased risk of CNS toxicity when tramadol given with •SSRIs or •tricyclics; sedative effects possibly increased when opioid analgesics given with tricyclics
• Antiepileptics: effects of tramadol reduced by carbamazepine; plasma concentration of methadone reduced by carbamazepine; dextropropoxyphene enhances effects of •carbamazepine; metabolism of methadone accelerated by phenytoin (reduced effect and risk of withdrawal effects)
• Antifungals: metabolism of alfentanil inhibited by fluconazole and ketoconazole (risk of prolonged or delayed respiratory depression); metabolism of buprenorphine inhibited by •ketoconazole (reduce dose of buprenorphine); metabolism of alfentanil possibly inhibited by itraconazole; plasma concentration of methadone increased by •voriconazole (consider reducing dose of methadone)
Antipsychotics: enhanced hypotensive and sedative effects when opioid analgesics given with antipsychotics; increased risk of convulsions when tramadol given with antipsychotics
• Antivirals: plasma concentration of methadone possibly reduced by abacavir and nevirapine; plasma concentration of methadone reduced by amprenavir, efavirenz, nelfinavir and ritonavir; plasma concentration of fentanyl increased by •ritonavir; plasma concentration of dextropropoxyphene increased by •ritonavir (risk of toxicity)—avoid concomitant use; plasma concentration of opioid analgesics (except methadone) possibly increased by •ritonavir; plasma concentration of pethidine reduced by •ritonavir, but plasma concentration of toxic pethidine metabolite increased (avoid concomitant use); methadone possibly increases plasma concentration of zidovudine
Anxiolytics and Hypnotics: increased sedative effect when opioid analgesics given with anxiolytics and hypnotics
Beta-blockers: morphine possibly increases plasma concentration of esmolol
Calcium-channel Blockers: metabolism of alfentanil inhibited by diltiazem (risk of prolonged or delayed respiratory depression)
Domperidone: opioid analgesics antagonise effects of domperidone on gastro-intestinal activity
• Dopaminergics: risk of CNS toxicity when pethidine given with •rasagiline (avoid pethidine for 2 weeks after rasagiline); avoid concomitant use of dextromethorphan with •rasagiline; hyperpyrexia and CNS toxicity reported when pethidine given with •selegiline (avoid concomitant use); caution with tramadol advised by manufacturer of selegiline
$5HT_3$ Antagonists: effects of tramadol possibly antagonised by ondansetron
• Memantine: increased risk of CNS toxicity when dextromethorphan given with •memantine (manufacturer of memantine advises avoid concomitant use)
Metoclopramide: opioid analgesics antagonise effects of metoclopramide on gastro-intestinal activity
Ulcer-healing Drugs: metabolism of opioid analgesics inhibited by cimetidine (increased plasma concentration)

**Orciprenaline** *see* Sympathomimetics

**Orlistat**
Anti-arrhythmics: orlistat possibly reduces plasma concentration of amiodarone
Anticoagulants: manufacturer of orlistat recommends monitoring anticoagulant effect of coumarins
Antidiabetics: manufacturer of orlistat advises avoid concomitant use with acarbose
• Ciclosporin: orlistat possibly reduces absorption of •ciclosporin

**Orphenadrine** *see* Antimuscarinics

**Oxaliplatin** *see* Platinum Compounds

**Oxandrolone** *see* Anabolic Steroids

**Oxazepam** *see* Anxiolytics and Hypnotics

**Oxcarbazepine**
• Antidepressants: anticonvulsant effect of antiepileptics possibly antagonised by MAOIs and •tricyclic-related antidepressants (convulsive threshold lowered); manufacturer of oxcarbazepine advises avoid concomitant use with •MAOIs; anticonvulsant effect of antiepileptics antagonised by •SSRIs and •tricyclics (convulsive threshold lowered)
Antiepileptics: oxcarbazepine sometimes reduces plasma concentration of carbamazepine (but concentration of an active metabolite of carbamazepine may be increased), also plasma concentration of an active metabolite of oxcarbazepine often reduced; oxcarbazepine often reduces plasma concentration of lamotrigine, also plasma concentration of an active metabolite of oxcarbazepine sometimes raised (but evidence is conflicting); oxcarbazepine increases plasma concentration of phenytoin, also plasma concentration of an active metabolite of oxcarbazepine reduced; oxcarbazepine increases plasma concentration of an active metabolite of primidone, also plasma concentra-

**Oxcarbazepine**
Antiepileptics *(continued)* tion of an active metabolite of oxcarbazepine reduced; plasma concentration of an active metabolite of oxcarbazepine sometimes reduced by valproate
• Antimalarials: possible increased risk of convulsions when antiepileptics given with chloroquine and hydroxychloroquine; anticonvulsant effect of antiepileptics antagonised by •mefloquine
• Antipsychotics: anticonvulsant effect of oxcarbazepine antagonised by •antipsychotics (convulsive threshold lowered)
Barbiturates: oxcarbazepine increases plasma concentration of phenobarbital, also plasma concentration of an active metabolite of oxcarbazepine reduced
Ciclosporin: oxcarbazepine possibly reduces plasma concentration of ciclosporin
• Oestrogens: oxcarbazepine accelerates metabolism of •oestrogens (reduced contraceptive effect—see p. 408)
• Progestogens: oxcarbazepine accelerates metabolism of •progestogens (reduced contraceptive effect—see p. 408)

**Oxprenolol** *see* Beta-blockers
**Oxybutynin** *see* Antimuscarinics
**Oxycodone** *see* Opioid Analgesics
**Oxymetazoline** *see* Sympathomimetics
**Oxytetracycline** *see* Tetracyclines

**Oxytocin**
Anaesthetics, General: oxytocic effect possibly reduced, also enhanced hypotensive effect and risk of arrhythmias when oxytocin given with volatile liquid general anaesthetics
Prostaglandins: uterotonic effect of oxytocin potentiated by prostaglandins
Sympathomimetics: risk of hypertension when oxytocin given with vasoconstrictor sympathomimetics (due to enhanced vasopressor effect)

**Paclitaxel**
Antidiabetics: paclitaxel possibly inhibits metabolism of rosiglitazone
Antiepileptics: cytotoxics possibly reduce absorption of phenytoin
• Antipsychotics: avoid concomitant use of cytotoxics with •clozapine (increased risk of agranulocytosis)
Antivirals: plasma concentration of paclitaxel increased by nelfinavir and ritonavir

**Pancreatin**
Antidiabetics: pancreatin antagonises hypoglycaemic effect of acarbose

**Pancuronium** *see* Muscle Relaxants
**Pantoprazole** *see* Proton Pump Inhibitors
**Papaveretum** *see* Opioid Analgesics

**Paracetamol**
Anticoagulants: prolonged regular use of paracetamol possibly enhances anticoagulant effect of coumarins
Cytotoxics: paracetamol possibly inhibits metabolism of *intravenous* busulfan (manufacturer of *intravenous* busulfan advises caution within 72 hours of paracetamol)
Lipid-regulating Drugs: absorption of paracetamol reduced by colestyramine
Metoclopramide: rate of absorption of paracetamol increased by metoclopramide

**Paraldehyde**
• Alcohol: increased sedative effect when paraldehyde given with •alcohol

**Paraldehyde** *(continued)*
• Disulfiram: risk of toxicity when paraldehyde given with •disulfiram

**Parasympathomimetics**
Anti-arrhythmics: effects of neostigmine and pyridostigmine antagonised by procainamide; effects of neostigmine and pyridostigmine possibly antagonised by propafenone; effects of neostigmine and pyridostigmine antagonised by quinidine
• Antibacterials: plasma concentration of galantamine increased by erythromycin; effects of neostigmine and pyridostigmine antagonised by •aminoglycosides; effects of neostigmine and pyridostigmine antagonised by clindamycin; effects of neostigmine and pyridostigmine antagonised by •polymyxins
Antidepressants: plasma concentration of galantamine increased by paroxetine
Antifungals: plasma concentration of galantamine increased by ketoconazole
Antimalarials: effects of neostigmine and pyridostigmine may be diminished because of potential for chloroquine and hydroxychloroquine to increase symptoms of myasthenia gravis
Antimuscarinics: effects of parasympathomimetics antagonised by antimuscarinics
Beta-blockers: increased risk of arrhythmias when pilocarpine given with beta-blockers; effects of neostigmine and pyridostigmine antagonised by propranolol
Lithium: effects of neostigmine and pyridostigmine antagonised by lithium
Muscle Relaxants: donepezil possibly enhances effects of suxamethonium; edrophonium, galantamine, neostigmine, pyridostigmine and rivastigmine enhance effects of suxamethonium; donepezil possibly antagonises effects of non-depolarising muscle relaxants ; edrophonium, neostigmine, pyridostigmine and rivastigmine antagonise effects of non-depolarising muscle relaxants

**Parecoxib** *see* NSAIDs
**Paroxetine** *see* Antidepressants, SSRI
**Pegfilgrastim** *see* Filgrastim
**Peginterferon Alfa** *see* Interferons

**Penicillamine**
Analgesics: possible increased risk of nephrotoxicity when penicillamine given with NSAIDs
Antacids: absorption of penicillamine reduced by antacids
• Antipsychotics: avoid concomitant use of penicillamine with •clozapine (increased risk of agranulocytosis)
Cardiac Glycosides: penicillamine possibly reduces plasma concentration of digoxin
Iron: absorption of penicillamine reduced by *oral* iron
Zinc: penicillamine reduces absorption of zinc, also absorption of penicillamine reduced by zinc

**Penicillins**
Allopurinol: increased risk of rash when amoxicillin or ampicillin given with allopurinol
Antibacterials: absorption of phenoxymethylpenicillin reduced by neomycin
Anticoagulants: common experience in anticoagulant clinics is that INR can be altered by a course of broad-spectrum penicillins such as ampicillin, although studies have failed to demonstrate an interaction with coumarins or phenindione
Cytotoxics: penicillins reduce excretion of methotrexate (increased risk of toxicity)

**Penicillins** *(continued)*
Muscle Relaxants: piperacillin enhances effects of non-depolarising muscle relaxants and suxamethonium
Oestrogens: antibacterials that do not induce liver enzymes possibly reduce contraceptive effect of oestrogens (risk probably small, see p. 408)
Probenecid: excretion of penicillins reduced by probenecid (increased plasma concentration)
Sulfinpyrazone: excretion of penicillins reduced by sulfinpyrazone

**Pentamidine Isetionate**
• Anti-arrhythmics: increased risk of ventricular arrhythmias when pentamidine isetionate given with •amiodarone—avoid concomitant use
• Antibacterials: increased risk of ventricular arrhythmias when pentamidine isetionate given with •moxifloxacin—avoid concomitant use
Antifungals: possible increased risk of nephrotoxicity when pentamidine isetionate given with amphotericin
• Antipsychotics: increased risk of ventricular arrhythmias when pentamidine isetionate given with •amisulpride—avoid concomitant use
• Ivabradine: increased risk of ventricular arrhythmias when pentamidine isetionate given with •ivabradine

**Pentazocine** *see* Opioid Analgesics

**Pentostatin**
Antiepileptics: cytotoxics possibly reduce absorption of phenytoin
• Antipsychotics: avoid concomitant use of cytotoxics with •clozapine (increased risk of agranulocytosis)
• Cytotoxics: increased toxicity when pentostatin given with high-dose •cyclophosphamide—avoid concomitant use; increased pulmonary toxicity when pentostatin given with •fludarabine (unacceptably high incidence of fatalities)

**Pentoxifylline (oxpentifylline)**
• Analgesics: possible increased risk of bleeding when pentoxifylline (oxpentifylline) given with NSAIDs; increased risk of bleeding when pentoxifylline (oxpentifylline) given with •ketorolac (avoid concomitant use)
Theophylline: pentoxifylline (oxpentifylline) increases plasma concentration of theophylline

**Pergolide**
Antipsychotics: effects of pergolide antagonised by antipsychotics
Memantine: effects of dopaminergics possibly enhanced by memantine
Methyldopa: antiparkinsonian effect of dopaminergics antagonised by methyldopa
Metoclopramide: antiparkinsonian effect of pergolide antagonised by metoclopramide

**Pericyazine** *see* Antipsychotics
**Perindopril** *see* ACE Inhibitors
**Perphenazine** *see* Antipsychotics
**Pethidine** *see* Opioid Analgesics
**Phenazocine** *see* Opioid Analgesics
**Phenelzine** *see* MAOIs

**Phenindione**
*Note.* Change in patient's clinical condition particularly associated with liver disease, intercurrent illness, or drug administration, necessitates more frequent testing. Major changes in diet (especially involving salads and vegetables) and in alcohol consumption may also affect anticoagulant control
• Alcohol: anticoagulant control with phenindione may be affected by major changes in consumption of •alcohol
• Anabolic Steroids: anticoagulant effect of phenindione enhanced by •anabolic steroids

**Phenindione** *(continued)*
• Analgesics: anticoagulant effect of phenindione possibly enhanced by •NSAIDs; anticoagulant effect of phenindione enhanced by •diclofenac, also increased risk of haemorrhage with intravenous diclofenac (avoid concomitant use); anticoagulant effect of phenindione enhanced by •ketorolac (increased risk of haemorrhage—avoid concomitant use); increased risk of bleeding when phenindione given with •aspirin (due to antiplatelet effect)
• Anti-arrhythmics: metabolism of phenindione inhibited by •amiodarone (enhanced anticoagulant effect)
• Antibacterials: experience in anticoagulant clinics suggests that INR possibly altered when phenindione is given with •neomycin (given for local action on gut); anticoagulant effect of phenindione possibly enhanced by levofloxacin and •tetracyclines; studies have failed to demonstrate an interaction with phenindione, but common experience in anticoagulant clinics is that INR can be altered by a course of broad-spectrum penicillins such as ampicillin
• Antivirals: anticoagulant effect of phenindione possibly enhanced by •ritonavir
• Clopidogrel: anticoagulant effect of phenindione enhanced due to antiplatelet action of •clopidogrel
• Dipyridamole: anticoagulant effect of phenindione enhanced due to antiplatelet action of •dipyridamole
• Enteral Foods: anticoagulant effect of phenindione antagonised by vitamin K (present in some •enteral feeds )
Iloprost: increased risk of bleeding when phenindione given with iloprost
• Lipid-regulating Drugs: anticoagulant effect of phenindione may be enhanced or reduced by •colestyramine; anticoagulant effect of phenindione possibly enhanced by •rosuvastatin; anticoagulant effect of phenindione enhanced by •fibrates
• Oestrogens: anticoagulant effect of phenindione antagonised by •oestrogens
• Progestogens: anticoagulant effect of phenindione antagonised by •progestogens
Sibutramine: increased risk of bleeding when anticoagulants given with sibutramine
• Testolactone: anticoagulant effect of phenindione enhanced by •testolactone
• Testosterone: anticoagulant effect of phenindione enhanced by •testosterone
• Thyroid Hormones: anticoagulant effect of phenindione enhanced by •thyroid hormones
• Vitamins: anticoagulant effect of phenindione antagonised by •vitamin K

**Phenobarbital** *see* Barbiturates
**Phenoperidine** *see* Opioid Analgesics
**Phenothiazines** *see* Antipsychotics
**Phenoxybenzamine** *see* Alpha-blockers
**Phenoxymethylpenicillin** *see* Penicillins
**Phentolamine** *see* Alpha-blockers
**Phenylephrine** *see* Sympathomimetics
**Phenylpropanolamine** *see* Sympathomimetics

**Phenytoin**
• Analgesics: effects of phenytoin possibly enhanced by •NSAIDs; phenytoin accelerates metabolism of methadone (reduced effect and risk of withdrawal effects); effects of phenytoin enhanced by aspirin
Antacids: absorption of phenytoin reduced by antacids

**Phenytoin** *(continued)*

- Anti-arrhythmics: metabolism of phenytoin inhibited by •amiodarone (increased plasma concentration); phenytoin reduces plasma concentration of disopyramide; phenytoin accelerates metabolism of mexiletine and •quinidine (reduced plasma concentration)
- Antibacterials: metabolism of phenytoin inhibited by clarithromycin, •isoniazid and •metronidazole (increased plasma concentration); plasma concentration of phenytoin increased or decreased by ciprofloxacin; phenytoin accelerates metabolism of doxycycline (reduced plasma concentration); plasma concentration of phenytoin increased by •chloramphenicol (increased risk of toxicity); metabolism of phenytoin accelerated by •rifamycins (reduced plasma concentration); plasma concentration of phenytoin possibly increased by sulphonamides; phenytoin reduces plasma concentration of •telithromycin (avoid during and for 2 weeks after phenytoin); plasma concentration of phenytoin increased by •trimethoprim (also increased antifolate effect)
- Anticoagulants: phenytoin accelerates metabolism of •coumarins (possibility of reduced anticoagulant effect, but enhancement also reported)
- Antidepressants: plasma concentration of phenytoin increased by •fluoxetine and •fluvoxamine; phenytoin reduces plasma concentration of •mianserin, mirtazapine and paroxetine; anticonvulsant effect of antiepileptics possibly antagonised by MAOIs and •tricyclic-related antidepressants (convulsive threshold lowered); anticonvulsant effect of antiepileptics antagonised by •SSRIs and •tricyclics (convulsive threshold lowered); plasma concentration of phenytoin reduced by •St John's wort—avoid concomitant use; phenytoin possibly reduces plasma concentration of •tricyclics

Antidiabetics: plasma concentration of phenytoin transiently increased by tolbutamide (possibility of toxicity)

- Antiepileptics: plasma concentration of both drugs often reduced when phenytoin given with carbamazepine, also plasma concentration of phenytoin may be increased; plasma concentration of phenytoin possibly increased by •ethosuximide, also plasma concentration of ethosuximide possibly reduced; phenytoin reduces plasma concentration of lamotrigine, tiagabine and zonisamide; plasma concentration of phenytoin increased by oxcarbazepine, also plasma concentration of an active metabolite of oxcarbazepine reduced; phenytoin possibly reduces plasma concentration of primidone (but concentration of an active metabolite increased), plasma concentration of phenytoin often reduced but may be increased; plasma concentration of phenytoin increased by •topiramate (also plasma concentration of topiramate reduced); plasma concentration of phenytoin increased or possibly reduced when given with valproate, also plasma concentration of valproate reduced; plasma concentration of phenytoin reduced by vigabatrin
- Antifungals: phenytoin reduces plasma concentration of •ketoconazole; anticonvulsant effect of phenytoin enhanced by •miconazole (plasma concentration of phenytoin increased); plasma concentration of phenytoin increased by •fluconazole (consider reducing dose of phenytoin); phenytoin reduces plasma concentration of •itraconazole—avoid concomitant use; plasma concentration of phenytoin increased by •voriconazole, also phenytoin reduces plasma concentration of voriconazole (increase dose of voriconazole and also monitor for phenytoin toxicity); phenytoin possibly reduces plasma concentration of caspofungin—consider increasing dose of caspofungin
- Antimalarials: possible increased risk of convulsions when antiepileptics given with chloroquine and hydroxychloroquine; anticonvulsant effect of antiepileptics antagonised by •mefloquine; anticonvulsant effect of phenytoin antagonised by •pyrimethamine, also increased antifolate effect
- Antipsychotics: anticonvulsant effect of phenytoin antagonised by •antipsychotics (convulsive threshold lowered); phenytoin possibly reduces plasma concentration of •aripiprazole—increase dose of aripiprazole; phenytoin accelerates metabolism of clozapine, quetiapine and sertindole (reduced plasma concentration)

Antivirals: phenytoin possibly reduces plasma concentration of abacavir, amprenavir, indinavir, lopinavir and saquinavir; plasma concentration of phenytoin reduced by nelfinavir; plasma concentration of phenytoin increased or decreased by zidovudine

Anxiolytics and Hypnotics: phenytoin often reduces plasma concentration of clonazepam; plasma concentration of phenytoin increased or decreased by diazepam; plasma concentration of phenytoin possibly increased or decreased by benzodiazepines

Aprepitant: phenytoin possibly reduces plasma concentration of aprepitant

Barbiturates: phenytoin often increases plasma concentration of phenobarbital, plasma concentration of phenytoin often reduced but may be increased

Bupropion: phenytoin reduces plasma concentration of bupropion

- Calcium-channel Blockers: phenytoin reduces effects of felodipine, isradipine and verapamil; phenytoin probably reduces effects of dihydropyridines, nicardipine and •nifedipine; phenytoin reduces plasma concentration of nisoldipine; plasma concentration of phenytoin increased by •diltiazem but also effect of diltiazem reduced

Cardiac Glycosides: phenytoin accelerates metabolism of digitoxin (reduced effect); phenytoin possibly reduces plasma concentration of digoxin

- Ciclosporin: phenytoin accelerates metabolism of •ciclosporin (reduced plasma concentration)
- Corticosteroids: phenytoin accelerates metabolism of •corticosteroids (reduced effect)
- Cytotoxics: metabolism of phenytoin possibly inhibited by fluorouracil (increased risk of toxicity); phenytoin increases antifolate effect of methotrexate; absorption of phenytoin possibly reduced by cytotoxics; phenytoin possibly reduces plasma concentration of etoposide; phenytoin reduces plasma concentration of •imatinib—avoid concomitant use

Diazoxide: plasma concentration of phenytoin reduced by diazoxide, also effect of diazoxide may be reduced

- Disulfiram: metabolism of phenytoin inhibited by •disulfiram (increased risk of toxicity)
- Diuretics: phenytoin reduces plasma concentration of •eplerenone—avoid concomitant use; increased risk of osteomalacia when phenytoin given with carbonic anhydrase inhibitors

**Phenytoin** *(continued)*
Dopaminergics: phenytoin possibly reduces effects of levodopa
Enteral Foods: absorption of phenytoin possibly reduced by enteral feeds
Folates: plasma concentration of phenytoin possibly reduced by folates
Hormone Antagonists: phenytoin accelerates metabolism of gestrinone (reduced plasma concentration); phenytoin possibly accelerates metabolism of toremifene
$5HT_3$ Antagonists: phenytoin accelerates metabolism of ondansetron (reduced effect)
Leflunomide: plasma concentration of phenytoin possibly increased by leflunomide
Levamisole: plasma concentration of phenytoin possibly increased by levamisole
Lipid-regulating Drugs: combination of phenytoin with fluvastatin may increase plasma concentration of either drug (or both)
Lithium: neurotoxicity may occur when phenytoin given with lithium without increased plasma concentration of lithium
Modafinil: plasma concentration of phenytoin possibly increased by modafinil
Muscle Relaxants: phenytoin antagonises muscle relaxant effect of non-depolarising muscle relaxants (accelerated recovery from neuromuscular blockade)
• Oestrogens: phenytoin accelerates metabolism of •oestrogens (reduced contraceptive effect—see p. 408)
• Progestogens: phenytoin accelerates metabolism of •progestogens (reduced contraceptive effect—see p. 408)
• Sulfinpyrazone: plasma concentration of phenytoin increased by •sulfinpyrazone
Sympathomimetics: plasma concentration of phenytoin increased by methylphenidate
• Theophylline: plasma concentration of both drugs reduced when phenytoin given with •theophylline
Thyroid Hormones: phenytoin accelerates metabolism of thyroid hormones (may increase requirements in hypothyroidism), also plasma concentration of phenytoin possibly increased
Tibolone: phenytoin accelerates metabolism of tibolone
• Ulcer-healing Drugs: metabolism of phenytoin inhibited by •cimetidine (increased plasma concentration); effects of phenytoin enhanced by •esomeprazole; effects of phenytoin possibly enhanced by omeprazole; absorption of phenytoin reduced by •sucralfate
Vaccines: effects of phenytoin enhanced by influenza vaccine
Vitamins: phenytoin possibly increases requirements for vitamin D

**Phosphodiesterase Inhibitors**
• Anagrelide: avoidance of enoximone and milrinone advised by manufacturer of •anagrelide

**Physostigmine** *see* Parasympathomimetics
**Pilocarpine** *see* Parasympathomimetics
**Pimozide** *see* Antipsychotics
**Pindolol** *see* Beta-blockers
**Pioglitazone** *see* Antidiabetics
**Piperacillin** *see* Penicillins
**Pipotiazine** *see* Antipsychotics
**Piroxicam** *see* NSAIDs
**Pivmecillinam** *see* Penicillins

**Pizotifen**
Adrenergic Neurone Blockers: pizotifen antagonises hypotensive effect of adrenergic neurone blockers

**Platinum Compounds**
• Antibacterials: increased risk of nephrotoxicity and possibly of ototoxicity when platinum compounds given with •aminoglycosides or •polymyxins; increased risk of nephrotoxicity and ototoxicity when platinum compounds given with capreomycin; increased risk of nephrotoxicity and possibly of ototoxicity when cisplatin given with vancomycin
Antiepileptics: cytotoxics possibly reduce absorption of phenytoin
• Antipsychotics: avoid concomitant use of cytotoxics with •clozapine (increased risk of agranulocytosis)
• Cytotoxics: increased pulmonary toxicity when cisplatin given with •bleomycin and •methotrexate
Diuretics: increased risk of nephrotoxicity and ototoxicity when platinum compounds given with diuretics

**Polymyxin B** *see* Polymyxins

**Polymyxins**
Antibacterials: increased risk of nephrotoxicity when colistin or polymyxins given with aminoglycosides; increased risk of nephrotoxicity when colistin or polymyxins given with capreomycin; increased risk of nephrotoxicity and ototoxicity when colistin given with teicoplanin or vancomycin; increased risk of nephrotoxicity when polymyxins given with vancomycin
Antifungals: increased risk of nephrotoxicity when polymyxins given with amphotericin
• Ciclosporin: increased risk of nephrotoxicity when polymyxins given with •ciclosporin
• Cytotoxics: increased risk of nephrotoxicity and possibly of ototoxicity when polymyxins given with •platinum compounds
• Diuretics: increased risk of otoxicity when polymyxins given with •loop diuretics
• Muscle Relaxants: polymyxins enhance effects of •non-depolarising muscle relaxants and •suxamethonium
Oestrogens: antibacterials that do not induce liver enzymes possibly reduce contraceptive effect of oestrogens (risk probably small, see p. 408)
• Parasympathomimetics: polymyxins antagonise effects of •neostigmine and •pyridostigmine

**Potassium Aminobenzoate**
Antibacterials: potassium aminobenzoate inhibits effects of sulphonamides

**Potassium Bicarbonate** *see* Potassium Salts
**Potassium Chloride** *see* Potassium Salts
**Potassium Citrate** *see* Potassium Salts

**Potassium Salts**
*Note.* Includes salt substitutes
• ACE Inhibitors: increased risk of severe hyperkalaemia when potassium salts given with •ACE inhibitors
• Angiotensin-II Receptor Antagonists: increased risk of hyperkalaemia when potassium salts given with •angiotensin-II receptor antagonists
Antibacterials: avoid concomitant use of potassium citrate with methenamine
• Ciclosporin: increased risk of hyperkalaemia when potassium salts given with •ciclosporin
• Diuretics: increased risk of hyperkalaemia when potassium salts given with •potassium-sparing diuretics and aldosterone antagonists
• Tacrolimus: increased risk of hyperkalaemia when potassium salts given with •tacrolimus

**Pramipexole**
Antipsychotics: manufacturer of pramipexole advises avoid concomitant use of antipsychotics (antagonism of effect)

Appendix 1

Pramipexole *(continued)*
Memantine: effects of dopaminergics possibly enhanced by memantine
Methyldopa: antiparkinsonian effect of dopaminergics antagonised by methyldopa
Ulcer-healing Drugs: excretion of pramipexole reduced by cimetidine (increased plasma concentration)

Pravastatin *see* Statins

Prazosin *see* Alpha-blockers

Prednisolone *see* Corticosteroids

Prilocaine
Anti-arrhythmics: increased myocardial depression when prilocaine given with anti-arrhythmics
Antibacterials: increased risk of methaemoglobinaemia when prilocaine given with sulphonamides

Primaquine
- Antimalarials: avoidance of antimalarials advised by manufacturer of •artemether/lumefantrine
Mepacrine: plasma concentration of primaquine increased by mepacrine (increased risk of toxicity)

Primidone
Alcohol: increased sedative effect when primidone given with alcohol
Anti-arrhythmics: primidone accelerates metabolism of disopyramide and quinidine (reduced plasma concentration)
- Antibacterials: primidone accelerates metabolism of •chloramphenicol, doxycycline and metronidazole (reduced plasma concentration); primidone reduces plasma concentration of •telithromycin (avoid during and for 2 weeks after primidone)
- Anticoagulants: primidone accelerates metabolism of •coumarins (reduced anticoagulant effect)
- Antidepressants: primidone reduces plasma concentration of paroxetine; primidone accelerates metabolism of •mianserin (reduced plasma concentration); anticonvulsant effect of antiepileptics possibly antagonised by MAOIs and •tricyclic-related antidepressants (convulsive threshold lowered); anticonvulsant effect of antiepileptics antagonised by •SSRIs and •tricyclics (convulsive threshold lowered); plasma concentration of active metabolite of primidone reduced by •St John's wort—avoid concomitant use; anticonvulsant effect of primidone antagonised by •tricyclics (convulsive threshold lowered), also metabolism of tricyclics possibly accelerated (reduced plasma concentration)
- Antiepileptics: primidone often reduces plasma concentration of carbamazepine, also plasma concentration of primidone sometimes reduced (but concentration of an active metabolite of primidone often increased); primidone possibly reduces plasma concentration of ethosuximide; primidone reduces plasma concentration of lamotrigine and tiagabine; plasma concentration of an active metabolite of primidone increased by oxcarbazepine, also plasma concentration of an active metabolite of oxcarbazepine reduced; plasma concentration of primidone possibly reduced by phenytoin (but concentration of an active metabolite increased), plasma concentration of phenytoin often reduced but may be increased; plasma concentration of primidone possibly increased by •valproate (plasma concentration of active metabolite of primidone increased), also plasma concentration of valproate reduced; plasma concentration of primidone possibly reduced by vigabatrin
- Antifungals: primidone possibly reduces plasma concentration of •voriconazole—avoid concomitant use; primidone reduces absorption of griseofulvin (reduced effect)
- Antimalarials: possible increased risk of convulsions when antiepileptics given with chloroquine and hydroxychloroquine; anticonvulsant effect of antiepileptics antagonised by •mefloquine
- Antipsychotics: anticonvulsant effect of primidone antagonised by •antipsychotics (convulsive threshold lowered); primidone accelerates metabolism of haloperidol (reduced plasma concentration); primidone possibly reduces plasma concentration of •aripiprazole—increase dose of aripiprazole
- Antivirals: primidone possibly reduces plasma concentration of •indinavir, •lopinavir, •nelfinavir and •saquinavir
Anxiolytics and Hypnotics: primidone often reduces plasma concentration of clonazepam
Barbiturates: increased sedative effect when primidone given with barbiturates
- Calcium-channel Blockers: primidone reduces effects of •felodipine and •isradipine; primidone probably reduces effects of •dihydropyridines, •diltiazem and •verapamil
Cardiac Glycosides: primidone accelerates metabolism of digitoxin (reduced effect)
- Ciclosporin: primidone accelerates metabolism of •ciclosporin (reduced effect)
- Corticosteroids: primidone accelerates metabolism of •corticosteroids (reduced effect)
Diuretics: plasma concentration of primidone possibly reduced by acetazolamide; increased risk of osteomalacia when primidone given with carbonic anhydrase inhibitors
Folates: plasma concentration of primidone possibly reduced by folates
Hormone Antagonists: primidone accelerates metabolism of gestrinone and toremifene (reduced plasma concentration)
$5HT_3$ Antagonists: primidone reduces plasma concentration of tropisetron
Leukotriene Antagonists: primidone reduces plasma concentration of montelukast
Memantine: effects of primidone possibly reduced by memantine
- Oestrogens: primidone accelerates metabolism of •oestrogens (reduced contraceptive effect—see p. 408)
- Progestogens: primidone accelerates metabolism of •progestogens (reduced contraceptive effect—see p. 408)
Sympathomimetics: plasma concentration of primidone possibly increased by methylphenidate
Theophylline: primidone accelerates metabolism of theophylline (reduced effect)
Thyroid Hormones: primidone accelerates metabolism of thyroid hormones (may increase requirements for thyroid hormones in hypothyroidism)
Tibolone: primidone accelerates metabolism of tibolone (reduced plasma concentration)
Vitamins: primidone possibly increases requirements for vitamin D

Probenecid
ACE Inhibitors: probenecid reduces excretion of captopril
- Analgesics: probenecid reduces excretion of •indometacin, •ketoprofen and •naproxen (increased plasma concentration); probenecid reduces excretion of •ketorolac (increased

**Probenecid**

- Analgesics *(continued)*
  plasma concentration)—avoid concomitant use; effects of probenecid antagonised by aspirin
- Antibacterials: probenecid reduces excretion of meropenem (manufacturers of meropenem advise avoid concomitant use); probenecid reduces excretion of cephalosporins, ciprofloxacin, nalidixic acid, norfloxacin and penicillins (increased plasma concentration); probenecid reduces excretion of dapsone and nitrofurantoin (increased risk of side-effects); effects of probenecid antagonised by pyrazinamide
- Antidiabetics: probenecid possibly enhances hypoglycaemic effect of chlorpropamide
- Antivirals: probenecid reduces excretion of aciclovir (increased plasma concentration); probenecid possibly reduces excretion of famciclovir and zalcitabine (increased plasma concentration); probenecid reduces excretion of ganciclovir and zidovudine (increased plasma concentration and risk of toxicity)
- • Cytotoxics: probenecid reduces excretion of •methotrexate (increased risk of toxicity)
- Sodium Benzoate: probenecid possibly reduces excretion of conjugate formed by sodium benzoate
- Sodium Phenylbutyrate: probenecid possibly reduces excretion of conjugate formed by sodium phenylbutyrate

**Procainamide**

- ACE Inhibitors: increased risk of toxicity when procainamide given with captopril especially in renal impairment
- Anaesthetics, Local: increased myocardial depression when anti-arrhythmics given with bupivacaine, levobupivacaine or prilocaine
- • Anti-arrhythmics: increased myocardial depression when anti-arrhythmics given with other •anti-arrhythmics; plasma concentration of procainamide increased by •amiodarone (increased risk of ventricular arrhythmias—avoid concomitant use)
- • Antibacterials: increased risk of ventricular arrhythmias when procainamide given with •moxifloxacin—avoid concomitant use; plasma concentration of procainamide increased by trimethoprim
- • Antidepressants: increased risk of ventricular arrhythmias when procainamide given with •tricyclics
- • Antihistamines: increased risk of ventricular arrhythmias when procainamide given with •mizolastine—avoid concomitant use
- • Antimalarials: avoidance of procainamide advised by manufacturer of •artemether/lumefantrine (risk of ventricular arrhythmias)
- • Antipsychotics: increased risk of ventricular arrhythmias when anti-arrhythmics that prolong the QT interval given with •antipsychotics that prolong the QT interval; increased risk of ventricular arrhythmias when procainamide given with •amisulpride, •pimozide or •sertindole—avoid concomitant use; increased risk of ventricular arrhythmias when procainamide given with •phenothiazines
- • Beta-blockers: increased myocardial depression when anti-arrhythmics given with •beta-blockers; increased risk of ventricular arrhythmias when procainamide given with •sotalol—avoid concomitant use

**Procainamide** *(continued)*

- • Dolasetron: increased risk of ventricular arrhythmias when procainamide given with •dolasetron—avoid concomitant use
- $5HT_3$ Antagonists: caution with anti-arrhythmics advised by manufacturer of tropisetron (risk of ventricular arrhythmias)
- • Muscle Relaxants: procainamide enhances effects of •muscle relaxants
- Parasympathomimetics: procainamide antagonises effects of neostigmine and pyridostigmine
- • Ulcer-healing Drugs: plasma concentration of procainamide increased by •cimetidine

**Procaine**

- Laronidase: procaine possibly inhibits effects of laronidase (manufacturer of laronidase advises avoid concomitant use)

**Procarbazine**

- Alcohol: disulfiram-like reaction when procarbazine given with alcohol
- Antiepileptics: cytotoxics possibly reduce absorption of phenytoin
- • Antipsychotics: avoid concomitant use of cytotoxics with •clozapine (increased risk of agranulocytosis)

**Prochlorperazine** *see* Antipsychotics

**Procyclidine** *see* Antimuscarinics

**Progesterone** *see* Progestogens

**Progestogens**

*Note.* Interactions of combined oral contraceptives may also apply to combined contraceptive patches

- ACE Inhibitors: risk of hyperkalaemia when drospirenone given with ACE inhibitors (monitor serum potassium during first cycle)
- Analgesics: risk of hyperkalaemia when drospirenone given with NSAIDs (monitor serum potassium during first cycle)
- Angiotensin-II Receptor Antagonists: risk of hyperkalaemia when drospirenone given with angiotensin-II receptor antagonists (monitor serum potassium during first cycle)
- • Antibacterials: metabolism of progestogens accelerated by •rifamycins (reduced contraceptive effect—see p. 408)
- • Anticoagulants: progestogens antagonise anticoagulant effect of •coumarins and •phenindione
- • Antidepressants: contraceptive effect of progestogens reduced by •St John's wort (avoid concomitant use)
- Antidiabetics: progestogens antagonise hypoglycaemic effect of antidiabetics
- • Antiepileptics: metabolism of progestogens accelerated by •carbamazepine, •oxcarbazepine, •phenytoin, •primidone and •topiramate (reduced contraceptive effect—see p. 408); progestogens reduce plasma concentration of •lamotrigine
- • Antifungals: metabolism of progestogens accelerated by •griseofulvin (reduced contraceptive effect—see p. 408); occasional reports of breakthrough bleeding when progestogens (used for contraception) given with terbinafine
- • Antivirals: contraceptive effect of progestogens possibly reduced by amprenavir and nelfinavir; metabolism of progestogens accelerated by •nevirapine (reduced contraceptive effect—see p. 408)
- • Aprepitant: possible contraceptive failure of hormonal contraceptives containing progestogens when given with •aprepitant (alternative contraception recommended)
- • Barbiturates: metabolism of progestogens accelerated by •barbiturates (reduced contraceptive effect—see p. 408)

**Progestogens** *(continued)*

- • Bosentan: possible contraceptive failure of hormonal contraceptives containing progestogens when given with •bosentan (alternative contraception recommended)
- • Ciclosporin: progestogens inhibit metabolism of •ciclosporin (increased plasma concentration)
- Diuretics: risk of hyperkalaemia when drospirenone given with potassium-sparing diuretics and aldosterone antagonists (monitor serum potassium during first cycle)
- Dopaminergics: progestogens increase plasma concentration of selegiline (increased risk of toxicity)
- Lipid-regulating Drugs: plasma concentration of norgestrel increased by rosuvastatin
- • Retinoids: efficacy of low dose progestogens may be reduced by •tretinoin but need not affect prescribing of combined oral contraceptives, there is no compelling evidence of interaction between isotretinoin and combined oral contraceptives
- Tacrolimus: contraceptive effect of progestogens possibly reduced by tacrolimus

**Proguanil**

- Antacids: absorption of proguanil reduced by oral magnesium salts (as magnesium trisilicate)
- Anticoagulants: isolated reports that proguanil may enhance anticoagulant effect of warfarin
- • Antimalarials: avoidance of antimalarials advised by manufacturer of •artemether/lumefantrine; increased antifolate effect when proguanil given with pyrimethamine

**Promazine** *see* Antipsychotics

**Promethazine** *see* Antihistamines

**Propafenone**

- Anaesthetics, Local: increased myocardial depression when anti-arrhythmics given with bupivacaine, levobupivacaine or prilocaine
- • Anti-arrhythmics: increased myocardial depression when anti-arrhythmics given with other •anti-arrhythmics; plasma concentration of propafenone increased by quinidine
- • Antibacterials: metabolism of propafenone accelerated by •rifampicin (reduced effect)
- • Anticoagulants: propafenone enhances anticoagulant effect of •coumarins
- • Antidepressants: metabolism of propafenone possibly inhibited by paroxetine (increased risk of toxicity); increased risk of arrhythmias when propafenone given with •tricyclics
- • Antihistamines: increased risk of ventricular arrhythmias when propafenone given with •mizolastine—avoid concomitant use
- • Antipsychotics: increased risk of ventricular arrhythmias when anti-arrhythmics that prolong the QT interval given with •antipsychotics that prolong the QT interval
- • Antivirals: plasma concentration of propafenone possibly increased by •amprenavir (increased risk of ventricular arrhythmias—avoid concomitant use); plasma concentration of propafenone increased by •ritonavir (increased risk of ventricular arrhythmias—avoid concomitant use)
- • Beta-blockers: increased myocardial depression when anti-arrhythmics given with •beta-blockers; propafenone increases plasma concentration of metoprolol and propranolol
- • Cardiac Glycosides: propafenone increases plasma concentration of •digoxin (halve dose of digoxin)
- Ciclosporin: propafenone possibly increases plasma concentration of ciclosporin

**Propafenone** *(continued)*

- • Dolasetron: increased risk of ventricular arrhythmias when propafenone given with •dolasetron—avoid concomitant use
- $5HT_3$ Antagonists: caution with anti-arrhythmics advised by manufacturer of tropisetron (risk of ventricular arrhythmias)
- Parasympathomimetics: propafenone possibly antagonises effects of neostigmine and pyridostigmine
- Theophylline: propafenone increases plasma concentration of theophylline
- • Ulcer-healing Drugs: plasma concentration of propafenone increased by •cimetidine

**Propantheline** *see* Antimuscarinics

**Propiverine** *see* Antimuscarinics

**Propofol** *see* Anaesthetics, General

**Propranolol** *see* Beta-blockers

**Prostaglandins**

- ACE Inhibitors: enhanced hypotensive effect when alprostadil given with ACE inhibitors
- Adrenergic Neurone Blockers: enhanced hypotensive effect when alprostadil given with adrenergic neurone blockers
- Alpha-blockers: enhanced hypotensive effect when alprostadil given with alpha-blockers
- Angiotensin-II Receptor Antagonists: enhanced hypotensive effect when alprostadil given with angiotensin-II receptor antagonists
- Beta-blockers: enhanced hypotensive effect when alprostadil given with beta-blockers
- Calcium-channel Blockers: enhanced hypotensive effect when alprostadil given with calcium-channel blockers
- Clonidine: enhanced hypotensive effect when alprostadil given with clonidine
- Diazoxide: enhanced hypotensive effect when alprostadil given with diazoxide
- Diuretics: enhanced hypotensive effect when alprostadil given with diuretics
- Methyldopa: enhanced hypotensive effect when alprostadil given with methyldopa
- Moxonidine: enhanced hypotensive effect when alprostadil given with moxonidine
- Nitrates: enhanced hypotensive effect when alprostadil given with nitrates
- Oxytocin: prostaglandins potentiate uterotonic effect of oxytocin
- Vasodilator Antihypertensives: enhanced hypotensive effect when alprostadil given with hydralazine, minoxidil or nitroprusside

**Proton Pump Inhibitors**

- Antacids: absorption of lansoprazole possibly reduced by antacids
- Antibacterials: plasma concentration of both drugs increased when omeprazole given with clarithromycin
- • Anticoagulants: esomeprazole and omeprazole possibly enhance anticoagulant effect of •coumarins
- Antidepressants: omeprazole increases plasma concentration of escitalopram
- • Antiepileptics: esomeprazole enhances effects of •phenytoin; omeprazole possibly enhances effects of phenytoin
- Antifungals: proton pump inhibitors reduce absorption of itraconazole and ketoconazole; plasma concentration of omeprazole increased by voriconazole (reduce dose of omeprazole)
- Antipsychotics: omeprazole possibly reduces plasma concentration of clozapine
- • Antivirals: proton pump inhibitors possibly reduce plasma concentration of •atazanavir—avoid concomitant use; omeprazole significantly

**Proton Pump Inhibitors**
- Antivirals *(continued)*
  reduces plasma concentration of •atazanavir—avoid concomitant use
  Anxiolytics and Hypnotics: esomeprazole and omeprazole possibly inhibit metabolism of diazepam (increased plasma concentration)
  Cardiac Glycosides: proton pump inhibitors possibly slightly increase plasma concentration of digoxin
  Ciclosporin: omeprazole possibly affects plasma concentration of ciclosporin
- Cilostazol: omeprazole increases plasma concentration of •cilostazol (risk of toxicity)—avoid concomitant use; lansoprazole possibly increases plasma concentration of •cilostazol—avoid concomitant use
  Cytotoxics: omeprazole possibly reduces excretion of methotrexate (increased risk of toxicity)
  Tacrolimus: omeprazole possibly increases plasma concentration of tacrolimus
  Ulcer-healing Drugs: absorption of lansoprazole possibly reduced by sucralfate

**Pseudoephedrine** *see* Sympathomimetics

**Pyrazinamide**
  Oestrogens: antibacterials that do not induce liver enzymes possibly reduce contraceptive effect of oestrogens (risk probably small, see p. 408)
  Probenecid: pyrazinamide antagonises effects of probenecid
  Sulfinpyrazone: pyrazinamide antagonises effects of sulfinpyrazone

**Pyridostigmine** *see* Parasympathomimetics

**Pyridoxine** *see* Vitamins

**Pyrimethamine**
- Antibacterials: increased antifolate effect when pyrimethamine (includes Fansidar®) given with •sulphonamides; increased antifolate effect when pyrimethamine given with •trimethoprim
- Antiepileptics: pyrimethamine antagonises anticonvulsant effect of •phenytoin, also increased antifolate effect
- Antimalarials: avoidance of antimalarials advised by manufacturer of •artemether/lumefantrine; increased antifolate effect when pyrimethamine given with proguanil
  Antivirals: increased antifolate effect when pyrimethamine given with zidovudine
- Cytotoxics: pyrimethamine increases antifolate effect of •methotrexate

**Quetiapine** *see* Antipsychotics

**Quinagolide**
  Memantine: effects of dopaminergics possibly enhanced by memantine
  Methyldopa: antiparkinsonian effect of dopaminergics antagonised by methyldopa

**Quinapril** *see* ACE Inhibitors

**Quinidine**
  Adsorbents: absorption of quinidine possibly reduced by kaolin
  Anaesthetics, Local: increased myocardial depression when anti-arrhythmics given with bupivacaine, levobupivacaine or prilocaine
  Antacids: excretion of quinidine reduced by alkaline urine due to some antacids (plasma concentration of quinidine occasionally increased)
- Anti-arrhythmics: increased myocardial depression when anti-arrhythmics given with other •anti-arrhythmics; plasma concentration of quinidine increased by •amiodarone (increased risk of ventricular arrhythmias—avoid concomitant use); quinidine increases plasma concentration of propafenone

**Quinidine** *(continued)*
- Antibacterials: increased risk of ventricular arrhythmias when quinidine given with •clarithromycin; increased risk of ventricular arrhythmias when quinidine given with parenteral •erythromycin; increased risk of ventricular arrhythmias when quinidine given with •moxifloxacin or •quinupristin/dalfopristin—avoid concomitant use; metabolism of quinidine accelerated by •rifamycins (reduced plasma concentration)
- Anticoagulants: quinidine possibly enhances anticoagulant effect of •coumarins
- Antidepressants: increased risk of ventricular arrhythmias when quinidine given with •tricyclics
- Antiepileptics: metabolism of quinidine accelerated by •phenytoin and primidone (reduced plasma concentration)
- Antifungals: plasma concentration of quinidine increased by •itraconazole, •miconazole and •voriconazole (increased risk of ventricular arrhythmias—avoid concomitant use)
- Antihistamines: increased risk of ventricular arrhythmias when quinidine given with •mizolastine—avoid concomitant use
- Antimalarials: avoidance of quinidine advised by manufacturer of •artemether/lumefantrine (risk of ventricular arrhythmias); increased risk of ventricular arrhythmias when quinidine given with •mefloquine
- Antipsychotics: increased risk of ventricular arrhythmias when anti-arrhythmics that prolong the QT interval given with •antipsychotics that prolong the QT interval; increased risk of ventricular arrhythmias when quinidine given with •amisulpride, •pimozide or •sertindole—avoid concomitant use; quinidine inhibits metabolism of •aripiprazole (reduce dose of aripiprazole); increased risk of ventricular arrhythmias when quinidine given with •phenothiazines
- Antivirals: plasma concentration of quinidine possibly increased by •amprenavir (increased risk of ventricular arrhythmias—avoid concomitant use); plasma concentration of quinidine possibly increased by •atazanavir—avoid concomitant use; increased risk of ventricular arrhythmias when quinidine given with •nelfinavir—avoid concomitant use; plasma concentration of quinidine increased by •ritonavir (increased risk of ventricular arrhythmias—avoid concomitant use)
  Barbiturates: metabolism of quinidine accelerated by barbiturates (reduced plasma concentration)
- Beta-blockers: increased myocardial depression when anti-arrhythmics given with •beta-blockers; increased risk of ventricular arrhythmias when quinidine given with •sotalol—avoid concomitant use
- Calcium-channel Blockers: plasma concentration of quinidine reduced by nifedipine; plasma concentration of quinidine increased by •verapamil (extreme hypotension may occur)
- Cardiac Glycosides: quinidine increases plasma concentration of •digoxin (halve dose of digoxin)
- Diuretics: excretion of quinidine possibly reduced by •acetazolamide (increased plasma concentration), also cardiotoxicity of quinidine increased in hypokalaemia; increased cardiac toxicity with quinidine if hypokalaemia occurs with •loop diuretics or •thiazides and related diuretics
  $5HT_3$ Antagonists: caution with anti-arrhythmics advised by manufacturer of tropisetron (risk of ventricular arrhythmias)
- Ivabradine: increased risk of ventricular arrhythmias when quinidine given with •ivabradine

Quinidine *(continued)*
- • Muscle Relaxants: quinidine enhances effects of •muscle relaxants
- Parasympathomimetics: quinidine antagonises effects of neostigmine and pyridostigmine
- • Ulcer-healing Drugs: plasma concentration of quinidine increased by •cimetidine

Quinine
- • Anti-arrhythmics: increased risk of ventricular arrhythmias when quinine given with •amiodarone—avoid concomitant use; quinine increases plasma concentration of •flecainide
- • Antibacterials: increased risk of ventricular arrhythmias when quinine given with •moxifloxacin—avoid concomitant use
- • Antimalarials: avoidance of antimalarials advised by manufacturer of •artemether/lumefantrine; increased risk of convulsions when quinine given with •mefloquine (but should not prevent the use of intravenous quinine in severe cases)
- • Antipsychotics: increased risk of ventricular arrhythmias when quinine given with •pimozide—avoid concomitant use
- • Cardiac Glycosides: quinine increases plasma concentration of •digoxin
- Muscle Relaxants: quinine possibly enhances effects of suxamethonium
- Ulcer-healing Drugs: metabolism of quinine inhibited by cimetidine (increased plasma concentration)

Quinolones
- • Analgesics: possible increased risk of convulsions when quinolones given with •NSAIDs; manufacturer of ciprofloxacin advises avoid premedication with opioid analgesics (reduced plasma concentration of ciprofloxacin) when ciprofloxacin used for surgical prophylaxis
- Antacids: absorption of ciprofloxacin, levofloxacin, moxifloxacin, norfloxacin and ofloxacin reduced by antacids
- • Anti-arrhythmics: increased risk of ventricular arrhythmias when moxifloxacin given with •amiodarone, •disopyramide, •procainamide or •quinidine—avoid concomitant use
- • Antibacterials: increased risk of ventricular arrhythmias when moxifloxacin given with parenteral •erythromycin—avoid concomitant use
- • Anticoagulants: ciprofloxacin, nalidixic acid, norfloxacin and ofloxacin enhance anticoagulant effect of •coumarins; levofloxacin possibly enhances anticoagulant effect of coumarins and phenindione
- • Antidepressants: ciprofloxacin inhibits metabolism of •duloxetine—avoid concomitant use; increased risk of ventricular arrhythmias when moxifloxacin given with •tricyclics—avoid concomitant use
- Antidiabetics: ciprofloxacin and norfloxacin possibly enhance effects of glibenclamide
- Antiepileptics: ciprofloxacin increases or decreases plasma concentration of phenytoin
- • Antihistamines: increased risk of ventricular arrhythmias when moxifloxacin given with •mizolastine—avoid concomitant use
- • Antimalarials: avoidance of quinolones advised by manufacturer of •artemether/lumefantrine; increased risk of ventricular arrhythmias when moxifloxacin given with •chloroquine and hydroxychloroquine, •mefloquine or •quinine—avoid concomitant use
- • <u>Antipsychotics</u>: increased risk of ventricular arrhythmias when moxifloxacin given with •haloperidol, •phenothiazines, •pimozide or •sertindole—avoid concomitant use; ciprofloxacin possibly increases plasma concentration of olanzapine
- • Beta-blockers: increased risk of ventricular arrhythmias when moxifloxacin given with •sotalol—avoid concomitant use
- Calcium Salts: absorption of ciprofloxacin reduced by calcium salts
- • Ciclosporin: increased risk of nephrotoxicity when quinolones given with •ciclosporin
- Cytotoxics: nalidixic acid increases risk of melphalan toxicity; ciprofloxacin possibly reduces excretion of methotrexate (increased risk of toxicity)
- Dairy Products: absorption of ciprofloxacin and norfloxacin reduced by dairy products
- $5HT_1$ Agonists: quinolones possibly inhibit metabolism of zolmitriptan (reduce dose of zolmitriptan)
- Iron: absorption of ciprofloxacin, levofloxacin, moxifloxacin, norfloxacin and ofloxacin reduced by *oral* iron
- <u>Oestrogens</u>: antibacterials that do not induce liver enzymes possibly reduce contraceptive effect of oestrogens (risk probably small, see p. 408)
- • Pentamidine Isetionate: increased risk of ventricular arrhythmias when moxifloxacin given with •pentamidine isetionate—avoid concomitant use
- Probenecid: excretion of ciprofloxacin, nalidixic acid and norfloxacin reduced by probenecid (increased plasma concentration)
- Strontium Ranelate: absorption of quinolones reduced by strontium ranelate (manufacturer of strontium ranelate advises avoid concomitant use)
- • Theophylline: possible increased risk of convulsions when quinolones given with •theophylline; ciprofloxacin and norfloxacin increase plasma concentration of •theophylline
- Ulcer-healing Drugs: absorption of ciprofloxacin, levofloxacin, moxifloxacin, norfloxacin and ofloxacin reduced by sucralfate
- Zinc: absorption of ciprofloxacin, levofloxacin, moxifloxacin, norfloxacin and ofloxacin reduced by zinc

Quinupristin with Dalfopristin
- • Anti-arrhythmics: increased risk of ventricular arrhythmias when quinupristin/dalfopristin given with •disopyramide, •lidocaine (lignocaine) or •quinidine—avoid concomitant use
- Antibacterials: manufacturer of quinupristin/dalfopristin recommends monitoring liver function when given with rifampicin
- Antivirals: quinupristin/dalfopristin possibly increases plasma concentration of saquinavir
- • Anxiolytics and Hypnotics: quinupristin/dalfopristin inhibits metabolism of •midazolam (increased plasma concentration with increased sedation); quinupristin/dalfopristin inhibits the metabolism of zopiclone
- • Calcium-channel Blockers: quinupristin/dalfopristin increases plasma concentration of •nifedipine
- • Ciclosporin: quinupristin/dalfopristin increases plasma concentration of •ciclosporin
- • Ergot Alkaloids: manufacturer of quinupristin/dalfopristin advises avoid concomitant use with •ergotamine and methysergide
- <u>Oestrogens</u>: antibacterials that do not induce liver enzymes possibly reduce contraceptive effect of oestrogens (risk probably small, see p. 408)
- • Tacrolimus: quinupristin/dalfopristin increases plasma concentration of •tacrolimus

**Rabeprazole** *see* Proton Pump Inhibitors
**Raloxifene**
Anticoagulants: raloxifene antagonises anticoagulant effect of coumarins
Lipid-regulating Drugs: absorption of raloxifene reduced by colestyramine (manufacturer of raloxifene advises avoid concomitant administration)
**Ramipril** *see* ACE Inhibitors
**Ranitidine** *see* Histamine $H_2$-antagonists
**Ranitidine Bismuth Citrate** *see* Histamine $H_2$-antagonists
**Rasagiline**
*Note.* Rasagiline is a MAO-B inhibitor
• Analgesics: avoid concomitant use of rasagiline with •dextromethorphan; risk of CNS toxicity when rasagiline given with •pethidine (avoid pethidine for 2 weeks after rasagiline)
• Antidepressants: after stopping rasagiline do not start •fluoxetine for 2 weeks, also rasagiline should not be started until at least 5 weeks after stopping fluoxetine; after stopping rasagiline do not start •fluvoxamine for 2 weeks; risk of hypertensive crisis when rasagiline given with •MAOIs, avoid MAOIs for at least 2 weeks after stopping rasagiline; increased risk of CNS toxicity when rasagiline given with •SSRIs or •tricyclics
Dopaminergics: plasma concentration of rasagiline possibly reduced by entacapone
Memantine: effects of dopaminergics possibly enhanced by memantine
Methyldopa: antiparkinsonian effect of dopaminergics antagonised by methyldopa
• Sympathomimetics: avoid concomitant use of rasagiline with •sympathomimetics
**Reboxetine**
• Antibacterials: manufacturer of reboxetine advises avoid concomitant use with •macrolides
• Antidepressants: manufacturer of reboxetine advises avoid concomitant use with •fluvoxamine; increased risk of hypertension and CNS excitation when reboxetine given with •MAOIs (MAOIs should not be started until 1 week after stopping reboxetine, avoid reboxetine for 2 weeks after stopping MAOIs)
• Antifungals: manufacturer of reboxetine advises avoid concomitant use with •imidazoles and •triazoles
• Antimalarials: avoidance of antidepressants advised by manufacturer of •artemether/lumefantrine
Diuretics: possible increased risk of hypokalaemia when reboxetine given with loop diuretics or thiazides and related diuretics
Ergot Alkaloids: possible risk of hypertension when reboxetine given with ergotamine and methysergide
• Sibutramine: increased risk of CNS toxicity when noradrenaline re-uptake inhibitors given with •sibutramine (manufacturer of sibutramine advises avoid concomitant use)
**Remifentanil** *see* Opioid Analgesics
**Repaglinide** *see* Antidiabetics
**Retinoids**
Alcohol: etretinate formed from acitretin in presence of alcohol
• Antibacterials: possible increased risk of benign intracranial hypertension when retinoids given with •tetracyclines (avoid concomitant use)
• Anticoagulants: acitretin possibly reduces anticoagulant effect of •coumarins
Antiepileptics: isotretinoin possibly reduces plasma concentration of carbamazepine

**Retinoids** *(continued)*
• Cytotoxics: acitretin increases plasma concentration of •methotrexate (also increased risk of hepatotoxicity)—avoid concomitant use
• Progestogens: oral tretinoin may reduce contraceptive efficacy of low dose •progestogens but need not affect prescribing of combined oral contraceptives, there is no compelling evidence of interaction between isotretinoin and combined oral contraceptives
Vitamins: risk of hypervitaminosis A when retinoids given with vitamin A
**Reviparin** *see* Heparins
**Ribavirin**
• Antivirals: ribavirin possibly inhibits effects of •stavudine; ribavirin possibly inhibits effects of •zidovudine (manufacturer of zidovudine advises avoid concomitant use)
**Rifabutin** *see* Rifamycins
**Rifampicin** *see* Rifamycins
**Rifamycins**
ACE Inhibitors: rifampicin reduces plasma concentration of active metabolite of imidapril (reduced antihypertensive effect)
Analgesics: rifampicin reduces plasma concentration of etoricoxib; rifampicin accelerates metabolism of methadone (reduced effect)
Antacids: absorption of rifampicin reduced by antacids
• Anti-arrhythmics: rifamycins accelerate metabolism of •disopyramide and •quinidine (reduced plasma concentration); rifampicin accelerates metabolism of mexiletine (reduced plasma concentration); rifampicin accelerates metabolism of •propafenone (reduced effect)
• Antibacterials: rifamycins reduce plasma concentration of clarithromycin and dapsone; plasma concentration of rifabutin increased by •clarithromycin (increased risk of uveitis—reduce rifabutin dose); rifampicin accelerates metabolism of chloramphenicol (reduced plasma concentration); plasma concentration of rifabutin possibly increased by •macrolides (increased risk of uveitis—reduce rifabutin dose); monitoring of liver function with rifampicin recommended by manufacturer of quinupristin/dalfopristin; rifampicin reduces plasma concentration of •telithromycin (avoid during and for 2 weeks after rifampicin)
• Anticoagulants: rifamycins accelerate metabolism of •coumarins (reduced anticoagulant effect)
Antidepressants: rifampicin possibly reduces plasma concentration of tricyclics
• Antidiabetics: rifamycins accelerate metabolism of •chlorpropamide and •tolbutamide (reduced effect); rifampicin reduces plasma concentration of •rosiglitazone—consider increasing dose of rosiglitazone; rifampicin reduces plasma concentration of nateglinide and repaglinide; rifamycins possibly accelerate metabolism of •sulphonylureas (reduced effect)
• Antiepileptics: rifabutin reduces plasma concentration of •carbamazepine; rifampicin reduces plasma concentration of •lamotrigine; rifamycins accelerate metabolism of •phenytoin (reduced plasma concentration)
• Antifungals: rifampicin accelerates metabolism of •ketoconazole (reduced plasma concentration), also plasma concentration of rifampicin may be reduced by ketoconazole; plasma concentration of rifabutin increased by •fluconazole (increased risk of uveitis—reduce rifabutin dose); rifampicin accelerates metabolism of •fluconazole and

Appendix 1

Rifamycins
- Antifungals *(continued)*
  •itraconazole (reduced plasma concentration); rifabutin reduces plasma concentration of •itraconazole—avoid concomitant use; plasma concentration of rifabutin increased by •voriconazole, also rifabutin reduces plasma concentration of voriconazole (increase dose of voriconazole and also monitor for rifabutin toxicity); rifampicin reduces plasma concentration of •voriconazole—avoid concomitant use; rifampicin initially increases and then reduces plasma concentration of caspofungin (consider increasing dose of caspofungin); rifampicin reduces plasma concentration of terbinafine; plasma concentration of rifabutin possibly increased by •triazoles (increased risk of uveitis—reduce rifabutin dose)
- Antipsychotics: rifampicin accelerates metabolism of •haloperidol (reduced plasma concentration); rifabutin and rifampicin possibly reduce plasma concentration of •aripiprazole—increase dose of aripiprazole; rifampicin possibly reduces plasma concentration of clozapine
- Antivirals: rifampicin possibly reduces plasma concentration of abacavir; rifampicin significantly reduces plasma concentration of •amprenavir, •nelfinavir and •saquinavir—avoid concomitant use; plasma concentration of rifabutin increased by •amprenavir, •atazanavir and •tipranavir (reduce dose of rifabutin); rifampicin reduces plasma concentration of •atazanavir, •lopinavir and •nevirapine—avoid concomitant use; plasma concentration of rifabutin reduced by efavirenz—increase dose of rifabutin; rifampicin reduces plasma concentration of efavirenz—increase dose of efavirenz; rifampicin accelerates metabolism of •indinavir (reduced plasma concentration—avoid concomitant use); plasma concentration of rifabutin increased by •indinavir, also plasma concentration of indinavir decreased (reduce dose of rifabutin and increase dose of indinavir); plasma concentration of rifabutin increased by •nelfinavir (halve dose of rifabutin); plasma concentration of rifabutin increased by •ritonavir (risk of uveitis—avoid concomitant use); rifabutin significantly reduces plasma concentration of •saquinavir—avoid concomitant use unless another protease inhibitor also given e.g. ritonavir; rifampicin possibly reduces plasma concentration of •tipranavir—avoid concomitant use; avoidance of rifampicin advised by manufacturer of zidovudine

  Anxiolytics and Hypnotics: rifampicin accelerates metabolism of diazepam (reduced plasma concentration); rifampicin possibly accelerates metabolism of benzodiazepines (reduced plasma concentration); rifampicin possibly accelerates metabolism of buspirone and zaleplon; rifampicin accelerates metabolism of zolpidem (reduced plasma concentration and reduced effect)

  Aprepitant: rifampicin reduces plasma concentration of aprepitant
- Atovaquone: rifabutin and rifampicin reduce plasma concentration of •atovaquone (possible therapeutic failure of atovaquone)

  Beta-blockers: rifampicin accelerates metabolism of bisoprolol and propranolol (plasma concentration significantly reduced)
- Calcium-channel Blockers: rifampicin possibly accelerates metabolism of •isradipine, •nicardipine and •nisoldipine (possible significantly reduced plasma concentration); rifampicin accelerates metabolism of •diltiazem, •nifedipine, •nimodipine and •verapamil (plasma concentration significantly reduced)

  Cardiac Glycosides: rifamycins accelerate metabolism of digitoxin (reduced effect); rifampicin possibly reduces plasma concentration of digoxin
- Ciclosporin: rifampicin accelerates metabolism of •ciclosporin (reduced plasma concentration)
- Corticosteroids: rifamycins accelerate metabolism of •corticosteroids (reduced effect)
- Cytotoxics: rifampicin accelerates metabolism of erlotinib (reduced plasma concentration); rifampicin reduces plasma concentration of •imatinib—avoid concomitant use
- Diuretics: rifampicin reduces plasma concentration of •eplerenone—avoid concomitant use

  Hormone Antagonists: rifampicin possibly reduces plasma concentration of exemestane; rifampicin accelerates metabolism of gestrinone (reduced plasma concentration)

  $5HT_3$ Antagonists: rifampicin accelerates metabolism of ondansetron (reduced effect); rifampicin reduces plasma concentration of tropisetron

  Lipid-regulating Drugs: rifampicin accelerates metabolism of fluvastatin (reduced effect)
- Oestrogens: rifamycins accelerate metabolism of •oestrogens (reduced contraceptive effect—see p. 408); antibacterials that do not induce liver enzymes possibly reduce contraceptive effect of oestrogens (risk probably small, see p. 408)
- Progestogens: rifamycins accelerate metabolism of •progestogens (reduced contraceptive effect—see p. 408)
- Sirolimus: rifabutin and rifampicin reduce plasma concentration of •sirolimus—avoid concomitant use
- Tacrolimus: rifampicin reduces plasma concentration of •tacrolimus

  Tadalafil: rifampicin reduces plasma concentration of tadalafil

  Theophylline: rifampicin accelerates metabolism of theophylline (reduced plasma concentration)

  Thyroid Hormones: rifampicin accelerates metabolism of levothyroxine (thyroxine) (may increase requirements for levothyroxine (thyroxine) in hypothyroidism)

  Tibolone: rifampicin accelerates metabolism of tibolone (reduced plasma concentration)

  Ulcer-healing Drugs: rifampicin accelerates metabolism of cimetidine (reduced plasma concentration)

**Risedronate Sodium** *see* Bisphosphonates

**Risperidone** *see* Antipsychotics

**Ritodrine** *see* Sympathomimetics, $Beta_2$

**Ritonavir**
- Analgesics: ritonavir possibly increases plasma concentration of NSAIDs; ritonavir increases plasma concentration of •dextropropoxyphene and •piroxicam (risk of toxicity)—avoid concomitant use; ritonavir increases plasma concentration of •fentanyl; ritonavir reduces plasma concentration of methadone; ritonavir reduces plasma concentration of •pethidine, but increases plasma concentration of toxic metabolite of pethidine (avoid concomitant use); ritonavir possibly increases plasma concentration of •opioid analgesics (except methadone)
- Anti-arrhythmics: ritonavir increases plasma concentration of •amiodarone, •flecainide, •propafenone and •quinidine (increased risk of

**Ritonavir**

- Anti-arrhythmics *(continued)* ventricular arrhythmias—avoid concomitant use); ritonavir possibly increases plasma concentration of •disopyramide and •mexiletine (increased risk of toxicity)
- Antibacterials: ritonavir possibly increases plasma concentration of azithromycin and erythromycin; ritonavir increases plasma concentration of •clarithromycin (reduce dose of clarithromycin in renal impairment); ritonavir increases plasma concentration of •rifabutin (risk of uveitis—avoid concomitant use); plasma concentration of both drugs may increase when ritonavir given with fusidic acid
- Anticoagulants: ritonavir may enhance or reduce anticoagulant effect of •warfarin; ritonavir possibly enhances anticoagulant effect of •coumarins and •phenindione
- Antidepressants: ritonavir possibly increases plasma concentration of •SSRIs and •tricyclics; plasma concentration of ritonavir reduced by •St John's wort—avoid concomitant use

Antidiabetics: ritonavir possibly increases plasma concentration of tolbutamide

- Antiepileptics: ritonavir possibly increases plasma concentration of •carbamazepine
- Antifungals: combination of ritonavir with •itraconazole or •ketoconazole may increase plasma concentration of either drug (or both); plasma concentration of ritonavir increased by fluconazole; ritonavir reduces plasma concentration of •voriconazole—avoid concomitant use

Antihistamines: ritonavir possibly increases plasma concentration of non-sedating antihistamines

- Antimalarials: avoidance of ritonavir advised by manufacturer of •artemether/lumefantrine

Antimuscarinics: ritonavir increases plasma concentration of solifenacin; avoidance of ritonavir advised by manufacturer of tolterodine

- Antipsychotics: ritonavir possibly increases plasma concentration of •antipsychotics; ritonavir possibly inhibits metabolism of •aripiprazole (reduce dose of aripiprazole); ritonavir increases plasma concentration of •clozapine (increased risk of toxicity)—avoid concomitant use; ritonavir increases plasma concentration of •pimozide and •sertindole (increased risk of ventricular arrhythmias—avoid concomitant use)
- Antivirals: ritonavir increases plasma concentration of amprenavir, indinavir and •saquinavir; ritonavir increases toxicity of efavirenz, monitor liver function tests; combination of ritonavir with nelfinavir may increase plasma concentration of either drug (or both)
- Anxiolytics and Hypnotics: ritonavir possibly increases plasma concentration of •anxiolytics and hypnotics; ritonavir possibly increases plasma concentration of •alprazolam, •diazepam, •flurazepam, •midazolam and •zolpidem (risk of extreme sedation and respiratory depression — avoid concomitant use); ritonavir increases plasma concentration of buspirone (increased risk of toxicity)

Aprepitant: ritonavir possibly increases plasma concentration of aprepitant

Bosentan: ritonavir possibly increases plasma concentration of bosentan

- Bupropion: ritonavir increases plasma concentration of •bupropion (risk of toxicity)—avoid concomitant use

**Ritonavir** *(continued)*

- Calcium-channel Blockers: ritonavir possibly increases plasma concentration of •calcium-channel blockers; avoidance of ritonavir advised by manufacturer of lercanidipine
- Ciclosporin: ritonavir possibly increases plasma concentration of •ciclosporin
- Cilostazol: ritonavir possibly increases plasma concentration of •cilostazol—avoid concomitant use
- Corticosteroids: ritonavir possibly increases plasma concentration of corticosteroids, dexamethasone and prednisolone; ritonavir increases plasma concentration of inhaled and intranasal budesonide and •fluticasone

Cytotoxics: ritonavir increases plasma concentration of paclitaxel

- Diuretics: ritonavir increases plasma concentration of •eplerenone—avoid concomitant use
- Ergot Alkaloids: increased risk of ergotism when ritonavir given with •ergotamine and methysergide—avoid concomitant use
- $5HT_1$ Agonists: ritonavir increases plasma concentration of •eletriptan (risk of toxicity)—avoid concomitant use
- Ivabradine: ritonavir possibly increases plasma concentration of •ivabradine—avoid concomitant use
- Lipid-regulating Drugs: possible increased risk of myopathy when ritonavir given with atorvastatin; increased risk of myopathy when ritonavir given with •simvastatin (avoid concomitant use)
- Oestrogens: ritonavir accelerates metabolism of •oestrogens (reduced contraceptive effect—see p. 408)
- Sildenafil: ritonavir significantly increases plasma concentration of •sildenafil—avoid concomitant use

Sympathomimetics: ritonavir possibly increases plasma concentration of dexamfetamine

- Tacrolimus: ritonavir possibly increases plasma concentration of •tacrolimus

Tadalafil: ritonavir increases plasma concentration of tadalafil

- Theophylline: ritonavir accelerates metabolism of •theophylline (reduced plasma concentration)
- Vardenafil: ritonavir possibly increases plasma concentration of •vardenafil—avoid concomitant use

**Rivastigmine** *see* Parasympathomimetics

**Rizatriptan** *see* $5HT_1$ Agonists

**Rocuronium** *see* Muscle Relaxants

**Ropinirole**

Antipsychotics: manufacturer of ropinirole advises avoid concomitant use of antipsychotics (antagonism of effect)

Memantine: effects of dopaminergics possibly enhanced by memantine

Methyldopa: antiparkinsonian effect of dopaminergics antagonised by methyldopa

Metoclopramide: antiparkinsonian effect of ropinirole antagonised by metoclopramide (manufacturers of ropinirole advise avoid concomitant use)

Oestrogens: plasma concentration of ropinirole increased by oestrogens

**Ropivacaine**

Antidepressants: metabolism of ropivacaine inhibited by fluvoxamine—avoid prolonged administration of ropivacaine

**Rosiglitazone** *see* Antidiabetics

**Rosuvastatin** *see* Statins

**Rowachol®**
  Anticoagulants: Rowachol® possibly reduces anticoagulant effect of coumarins

**St John's Wort**
- • Antibacterials: St John's wort reduces plasma concentration of •telithromycin (avoid during and for 2 weeks after St John's wort)
- • Anticoagulants: St John's wort reduces anticoagulant effect of •coumarins (avoid concomitant use)
- • Antidepressants: possible increased serotonergic effects when St John's wort given with duloxetine; St John's wort reduces plasma concentration of amitriptyline; increased serotonergic effects when St John's wort given with •SSRIs—avoid concomitant use
- • Antiepileptics: St John's wort reduces plasma concentration of •carbamazepine and •phenytoin—avoid concomitant use; St John's wort reduces plasma concentration of active metabolite of •primidone—avoid concomitant use
- • Antimalarials: avoidance of antidepressants advised by manufacturer of •artemether/lumefantrine
- • Antipsychotics: St John's wort possibly reduces plasma concentration of •aripiprazole—increase dose of aripiprazole
- • Antivirals: St John's wort reduces plasma concentration of •amprenavir, •atazanavir, •efavirenz, •indinavir, •lopinavir, •nelfinavir, •nevirapine, •ritonavir and •saquinavir—avoid concomitant use; St John's wort possibly reduces plasma concentration of •tipranavir—avoid concomitant use
- • Aprepitant: avoidance of St John's wort advised by manufacturer of •aprepitant
- • Barbiturates: St John's wort reduces plasma concentration of •phenobarbital—avoid concomitant use
- • Cardiac Glycosides: St John's wort reduces plasma concentration of •digoxin—avoid concomitant use
- • Ciclosporin: St John's wort reduces plasma concentration of •ciclosporin—avoid concomitant use
- • Diuretics: St John's wort reduces plasma concentration of •eplerenone—avoid concomitant use
- • $5HT_1$ Agonists: increased serotonergic effects when St John's wort given with •$5HT_1$ agonists—avoid concomitant use
- Ivabradine: St John's wort reduces plasma concentration of ivabradine—avoid concomitant use
- Lipid-regulating Drugs: St John's wort reduces plasma concentration of simvastatin
- • Oestrogens: St John's wort reduces contraceptive effect of •oestrogens (avoid concomitant use)
- • Progestogens: St John's wort reduces contraceptive effect of •progestogens (avoid concomitant use)
- • Tacrolimus: St John's wort reduces plasma concentration of •tacrolimus—avoid concomitant use
- • Theophylline: St John's wort reduces plasma concentration of •theophylline—avoid concomitant use

**Salbutamol** *see* Sympathomimetics, $Beta_2$

**Salmeterol** *see* Sympathomimetics, $Beta_2$

**Saquinavir**
- • Antibacterials: plasma concentration of saquinavir significantly reduced by •rifabutin—avoid concomitant use unless another protease inhibitor also given e.g. ritonavir; plasma concentration of saquinavir significantly reduced by •rifampicin—avoid concomitant use; plasma concentration of saquinavir possibly increased by quinupristin/dalfopristin
- Anticoagulants: saquinavir possibly enhances anticoagulant effect of warfarin
- • Antidepressants: plasma concentration of saquinavir reduced by •St John's wort—avoid concomitant use
- • Antiepileptics: plasma concentration of saquinavir possibly reduced by carbamazepine, phenytoin and •primidone
- Antifungals: plasma concentration of saquinavir increased by ketoconazole; plasma concentration of saquinavir possibly increased by imidazoles and triazoles
- • Antimalarials: avoidance of saquinavir advised by manufacturer of •artemether/lumefantrine
- Antimuscarinics: avoidance of saquinavir advised by manufacturer of tolterodine
- • Antipsychotics: saquinavir possibly inhibits metabolism of •aripiprazole (reduce dose of aripiprazole); saquinavir possibly increases plasma concentration of •pimozide (increased risk of ventricular arrhythmias—avoid concomitant use); saquinavir increases plasma concentration of •sertindole (increased risk of ventricular arrhythmias—avoid concomitant use)
- • Antivirals: plasma concentration of saquinavir significantly reduced by efavirenz; plasma concentration of saquinavir increased by indinavir, lopinavir and •ritonavir; combination of saquinavir with nelfinavir may increase plasma concentration of either drug (or both); plasma concentration of saquinavir reduced by nevirapine and •tipranavir
- • Anxiolytics and Hypnotics: saquinavir increases plasma concentration of •midazolam (risk of prolonged sedation)
- • Barbiturates: plasma concentration of saquinavir possibly reduced by •barbiturates
- • Ciclosporin: plasma concentration of both drugs increased when saquinavir given with •ciclosporin
- • Cilostazol: saquinavir possibly increases plasma concentration of •cilostazol—avoid concomitant use
- Corticosteroids: plasma concentration of saquinavir possibly reduced by dexamethasone
- Diuretics: saquinavir increases plasma concentration of eplerenone (reduce dose of eplerenone)
- • Ergot Alkaloids: increased risk of ergotism when saquinavir given with •ergotamine and methysergide—avoid concomitant use
- • Lipid-regulating Drugs: possible increased risk of myopathy when saquinavir given with atorvastatin; increased risk of myopathy when saquinavir given with •simvastatin (avoid concomitant use)
- Sildenafil: saquinavir possibly increases plasma concentration of sildenafil— reduce initial dose of sildenafil
- • Tacrolimus: saquinavir increases plasma concentration of •tacrolimus (consider reducing dose of tacrolimus)
- Tadalafil: saquinavir possibly increases plasma concentration of tadalafil— reduce initial dose of tadalafil
- Vardenafil: saquinavir possibly increases plasma concentration of vardenafil— reduce initial dose of vardenafil

**Secobarbital** *see* Barbiturates

**Selegiline**

*Note.* Selegiline is a MAO-B inhibitor

- Analgesics: hyperpyrexia and CNS toxicity reported when selegiline given with •pethidine (avoid concomitant use); manufacturer of selegiline advises caution with tramadol
- Antidepressants: theoretical risk of serotonin syndrome if selegiline given with citalopram (especially if dose of selegiline exceeds 10 mg daily); caution with selegiline advised by manufacturer of escitalopram; increased risk of hypertension and CNS excitation when selegiline given with •fluoxetine (selegiline should not be started until 5 weeks after stopping fluoxetine, avoid fluoxetine for 2 weeks after stopping selegiline); increased risk of hypertension and CNS excitation when selegiline given with •fluvoxamine or •venlafaxine (selegiline should not be started until 1 week after stopping fluvoxamine or venlafaxine, avoid fluvoxamine or venlafaxine for 2 weeks after stopping selegiline); increased risk of hypertension and CNS excitation when selegiline given with •paroxetine or •sertraline (selegiline should not be started until 2 weeks after stopping paroxetine or sertraline, avoid paroxetine or sertraline for 2 weeks after stopping selegiline); enhanced hypotensive effect when selegiline given with MAOIs; avoid concomitant use of selegiline with •moclobemide; CNS toxicity reported when selegiline given with •tricyclics

Dopaminergics: max. dose of 10 mg selegiline advised by manufacturer of entacapone if used concomitantly; selegiline enhances effects and increases toxicity of levodopa (reduce dose of levodopa)

Memantine: effects of dopaminergics and selegiline possibly enhanced by memantine

Methyldopa: antiparkinsonian effect of dopaminergics antagonised by methyldopa

Oestrogens: plasma concentration of selegiline increased by oestrogens (risk of toxicity)

Progestogens: plasma concentration of selegiline increased by progestogens (increased risk of toxicity)

- Sympathomimetics: risk of hypertensive crisis when selegiline given with •dopamine

**Sertindole** *see* Antipsychotics

**Sertraline** *see* Antidepressants, SSRI

**Sevoflurane** *see* Anaesthetics, General

**Sibutramine**

Analgesics: increased risk of bleeding when sibutramine given with NSAIDs or aspirin

Anticoagulants: increased risk of bleeding when sibutramine given with anticoagulants

- Antidepressants: increased CNS toxicity when sibutramine given with •MAOIs or •moclobemide (manufacturer of sibutramine advises avoid concomitant use), also avoid sibutramine for 2 weeks after stopping MAOIs or moclobemide; increased risk of CNS toxicity when sibutramine given with •SSRI-related antidepressants, •SSRIs, •mirtazapine, •noradrenaline re-uptake inhibitors, •tricyclic-related antidepressants, •tricyclics or •tryptophan (manufacturer of sibutramine advises avoid concomitant use)
- Antipsychotics: increased risk of CNS toxicity when sibutramine given with •antipsychotics (manufacturer of sibutramine advises avoid concomitant use)

**Sildenafil**

- Alpha-blockers: enhanced hypotensive effect when sildenafil given with •alpha-blockers (avoid alpha-blockers for 4 hours after sildenafil)

**Sildenafil** *(continued)*

Antibacterials: plasma concentration of sildenafil increased by erythromycin—reduce initial dose of sildenafil

Antifungals: plasma concentration of sildenafil increased by itraconazole and ketoconazole—reduce initial dose of sildenafil

- Antivirals: plasma concentration of sildenafil possibly increased by amprenavir, nelfinavir and saquinavir— reduce initial dose of sildenafil; side-effects of sildenafil possibly increased by •atazanavir; plasma concentration of sildenafil increased by indinavir—reduce initial dose of sildenafil; plasma concentration of sildenafil significantly increased by •ritonavir—avoid concomitant use

Calcium-channel Blockers: enhanced hypotensive effect when sildenafil given with amlodipine

Grapefruit Juice: plasma concentration of sildenafil possibly increased by grapefruit juice

- Nicorandil: sildenafil significantly enhances hypotensive effect of •nicorandil (avoid concomitant use)
- Nitrates: sildenafil significantly enhances hypotensive effect of •nitrates (avoid concomitant use)

Ulcer-healing Drugs: plasma concentration of sildenafil increased by cimetidine (reduce initial dose of sildenafil)

**Simvastatin** *see* Statins

**Sirolimus**

- Antibacterials: plasma concentration of sirolimus increased by •clarithromycin and •telithromycin—avoid concomitant use; plasma concentration of both drugs increased when sirolimus given with •erythromycin; plasma concentration of sirolimus reduced by •rifabutin and •rifampicin—avoid concomitant use
- Antifungals: plasma concentration of sirolimus increased by •itraconazole, •ketoconazole and •voriconazole—avoid concomitant use; plasma concentration of sirolimus increased by •miconazole
- Antivirals: plasma concentration of sirolimus possibly increased by •atazanavir and lopinavir
- Calcium-channel Blockers: plasma concentration of sirolimus increased by •diltiazem; plasma concentration of both drugs increased when sirolimus given with •verapamil

Ciclosporin: plasma concentration of sirolimus increased by ciclosporin

- Grapefruit Juice: plasma concentration of sirolimus increased by •grapefruit juice—avoid concomitant use

**Sodium Benzoate**

Antiepileptics: effects of sodium benzoate possibly reduced by valproate

Antipsychotics: effects of sodium benzoate possibly reduced by haloperidol

Corticosteroids: effects of sodium benzoate possibly reduced by corticosteroids

Probenecid: excretion of conjugate formed by sodium benzoate possibly reduced by probenecid

**Sodium Bicarbonate** *see* Antacids

**Sodium Clodronate** *see* Bisphosphonates

**Sodium Phenylbutyrate**

Antiepileptics: effects of sodium phenylbutyrate possibly reduced by valproate

Antipsychotics: effects of sodium phenylbutyrate possibly reduced by haloperidol

Corticosteroids: effects of sodium phenylbutyrate possibly reduced by corticosteroids

Probenecid: excretion of conjugate formed by sodium phenylbutyrate possibly reduced by probenecid

**Sodium Polystyrene Sulphonate**
Thyroid Hormones: sodium polystyrene sulphonate reduces absorption of levothyroxine (thyroxine)
**Sodium Valproate** *see* Valproate
**Solifenacin** *see* Antimuscarinics
**Somatropin**
Corticosteroids: growth-promoting effect of somatropin may be inhibited by corticosteroids
Oestrogens: increased doses of somatropin may be needed when given with oestrogens (when used as oral replacement therapy)
**Sotalol** *see* Beta-blockers
**Spironolactone** *see* Diuretics
**Statins**
Antacids: absorption of rosuvastatin reduced by antacids
• Anti-arrhythmics: increased risk of myopathy when simvastatin given with •amiodarone
• Antibacterials: plasma concentration of atorvastatin increased by clarithromycin; increased risk of myopathy when simvastatin given with •clarithromycin, •erythromycin or •telithromycin (avoid concomitant use); plasma concentration of rosuvastatin reduced by erythromycin; possible increased risk of myopathy when atorvastatin given with erythromycin or fusidic acid; metabolism of fluvastatin accelerated by rifampicin (reduced effect); possible increased risk of myopathy when simvastatin given with fusidic acid; increased risk of myopathy when atorvastatin given with •telithromycin (avoid concomitant use)
• Anticoagulants: atorvastatin may transiently reduce anticoagulant effect of warfarin; rosuvastatin possibly enhances anticoagulant effect of •coumarins and •phenindione; fluvastatin and simvastatin enhance anticoagulant effect of •coumarins
Antidepressants: plasma concentration of simvastatin reduced by St John's wort
Antiepileptics: combination of fluvastatin with phenytoin may increase plasma concentration of either drug (or both)
• Antifungals: increased risk of myopathy when simvastatin given with •itraconazole or •ketoconazole (avoid concomitant use); possible increased risk of myopathy when simvastatin given with •miconazole—avoid concomitant use; increased risk of myopathy when atorvastatin given with •itraconazole (avoid concomitant use); possible increased risk of myopathy when atorvastatin or simvastatin given with imidazoles; possible increased risk of myopathy when atorvastatin or simvastatin given with triazoles
• Antivirals: possible increased risk of myopathy when atorvastatin given with amprenavir, atazanavir, indinavir, lopinavir, nelfinavir, ritonavir or saquinavir; possible increased risk of myopathy when simvastatin given with •amprenavir or •lopinavir—avoid concomitant use; increased risk of myopathy when simvastatin given with •atazanavir, •indinavir, •nelfinavir, •ritonavir or •saquinavir (avoid concomitant use)
Bosentan: plasma concentration of simvastatin reduced by bosentan
• Calcium-channel Blockers: possible increased risk of myopathy when simvastatin given with diltiazem; increased risk of myopathy when simvastatin given with •verapamil
Cardiac Glycosides: atorvastatin possibly increases plasma concentration of digoxin

**Statins** *(continued)*
• Ciclosporin: increased risk of myopathy when statins given with •ciclosporin; increased risk of myopathy when rosuvastatin given with •ciclosporin (avoid concomitant use)
Cytotoxics: plasma concentration of simvastatin increased by imatinib
• Grapefruit Juice: plasma concentration of simvastatin increased by •grapefruit juice—avoid concomitant use
• Hormone Antagonists: possible increased risk of myopathy when simvastatin given with •danazol
• Lipid-regulating Drugs: increased risk of myopathy when statins given with •gemfibrozil (preferably avoid concomitant use); increased risk of myopathy when statins given with •fibrates; increased risk of myopathy when statins given with •nicotinic acid (applies to lipid regulating doses of nicotinic acid)
Oestrogens: rosuvastatin increases plasma concentration of ethinylestradiol
Progestogens: rosuvastatin increases plasma concentration of norgestrel
**Stavudine**
• Antivirals: increased risk of side-effects when stavudine given with •didanosine; effects of stavudine possibly inhibited by •ribavirin; effects of stavudine possibly inhibited by •zidovudine (manufacturers advise avoid concomitant use)
• Cytotoxics: effects of stavudine possibly inhibited by doxorubicin; increased risk of toxicity when stavudine given with •hydroxycarbamide—avoid concomitant use
**Streptomycin** *see* Aminoglycosides
**Strontium Ranelate**
Antibacterials: strontium ranelate reduces absorption of quinolones and tetracyclines (manufacturer of strontium ranelate advises avoid concomitant use)
**Sucralfate**
Antibacterials: sucralfate reduces absorption of ciprofloxacin, levofloxacin, moxifloxacin, norfloxacin, ofloxacin and tetracyclines
• Anticoagulants: sucralfate possibly reduces absorption of •coumarins (reduced anticoagulant effect)
• Antiepileptics: sucralfate reduces absorption of •phenytoin
Antifungals: sucralfate reduces absorption of ketoconazole
Antipsychotics: sucralfate reduces absorption of sulpiride
Cardiac Glycosides: sucralfate possibly reduces absorption of cardiac glycosides
Thyroid Hormones: sucralfate reduces absorption of levothyroxine (thyroxine)
Ulcer-healing Drugs: sucralfate possibly reduces absorption of lansoprazole
**Sulfadiazine** *see* Sulphonamides
**Sulfadoxine** *see* Sulphonamides
**Sulfamethoxazole** *see* Sulphonamides
**Sulfasalazine** *see* Aminosalicylates
**Sulfinpyrazone**
Analgesics: effects of sulfinpyrazone antagonised by aspirin
Antibacterials: sulfinpyrazone reduces excretion of nitrofurantoin (increased risk of toxicity); sulfinpyrazone reduces excretion of penicillins; effects of sulfinpyrazone antagonised by pyrazinamide
• Anticoagulants: sulfinpyrazone enhances anticoagulant effect of •coumarins
• Antidiabetics: sulfinpyrazone enhances effects of •sulphonylureas

**Sulfinpyrazone** *(continued)*
- • Antiepileptics: sulfinpyrazone increases plasma concentration of •phenytoin
- Theophylline: sulfinpyrazone reduces plasma concentration of theophylline

**Sulindac** *see* NSAIDs

**Sulphonamides**
- Anaesthetics, General: sulphonamides enhance effects of thiopental
- Anaesthetics, Local: increased risk of methaemoglobinaemia when sulphonamides given with prilocaine
- • Anti-arrhythmics: increased risk of ventricular arrhythmias when sulfamethoxazole (as co-trimoxazole) given with •amiodarone—avoid concomitant use of co-trimoxazole
- • Antibacterials: increased risk of crystalluria when sulphonamides given with •methenamine
- • Anticoagulants: sulphonamides enhance anticoagulant effect of •coumarins
- Antidiabetics: sulphonamides rarely enhance the effects of sulphonylureas
- Antiepileptics: sulphonamides possibly increase plasma concentration of phenytoin
- • Antimalarials: increased antifolate effect when sulphonamides given with •pyrimethamine (includes Fansidar®)
- • Antipsychotics: avoid concomitant use of sulphonamides with •clozapine (increased risk of agranulocytosis)
- • Ciclosporin: increased risk of nephrotoxicity when sulphonamides given with •ciclosporin; sulfadiazine possibly reduces plasma concentration of •ciclosporin
- • Cytotoxics: increased risk of haematological toxicity when sulfamethoxazole (as co-trimoxazole) given with •azathioprine, •mercaptopurine or •methotrexate; sulphonamides increase risk of methotrexate toxicity
- Oestrogens: antibacterials that do not induce liver enzymes possibly reduce contraceptive effect of oestrogens (risk probably small, see p. 408)
- Potassium Aminobenzoate: effects of sulphonamides inhibited by potassium aminobenzoate

**Sulphonylureas** *see* Antidiabetics

**Sulpiride** *see* Antipsychotics

**Sumatriptan** *see* $5HT_1$ Agonists

**Suxamethonium** *see* Muscle Relaxants

**Sympathomimetics**
- • Adrenergic Neurone Blockers: ephedrine, isometheptene, metaraminol, methylphenidate, noradrenaline (norepinephrine), oxymetazoline, phenylephrine, phenylpropanolamine, pseudoephedrine and xylometazoline antagonise hypotensive effect of •adrenergic neurone blockers
- • Alpha-blockers: avoid concomitant use of adrenaline (epinephrine) or dopamine with •tolazoline
- • Anaesthetics, General: increased risk of arrhythmias when adrenaline (epinephrine) given with •volatile liquid general anaesthetics; increased risk of hypertension when methylphenidate given with •volatile liquid general anaesthetics
- • Anticoagulants: methylphenidate possibly enhances anticoagulant effect of •coumarins
- • Antidepressants: risk of hypertensive crisis when dexamfetamine, dopamine, dopexamine, ephedrine, isometheptene, methylphenidate, phenylephrine, phenylpropanolamine, pseudoephedrine or sympathomimetics given with •MAOIs; risk of hypertensive crisis when dexamfetamine, dopamine, dopexamine, ephedrine, isometheptene, methylphenidate, phenylephrine, phenylpropanolamine,

**Sympathomimetics**
- • Antidepressants *(continued)* pseudoephedrine or sympathomimetics given with •moclobemide; methylphenidate possibly inhibits metabolism of SSRIs and tricyclics; increased risk of hypertension and arrhythmias when noradrenaline (norepinephrine) given with •tricyclics; increased risk of hypertension and arrhythmias when adrenaline (epinephrine) given with •tricyclics (but local anaesthetics with adrenaline appear to be safe)
- Antiepileptics: methylphenidate increases plasma concentration of phenytoin; methylphenidate possibly increases plasma concentration of primidone
- Antipsychotics: hypertensive effect of sympathomimetics antagonised by antipsychotics
- Antivirals: plasma concentration of dexamfetamine possibly increased by ritonavir
- Barbiturates: methylphenidate possibly increases plasma concentration of phenobarbital
- • Beta-blockers: severe hypertension when adrenaline (epinephrine) or noradrenaline (norepinephrine) given with •beta-blockers especially with non-selective beta-blockers; possible severe hypertension when dobutamine given with •beta-blockers especially with non-selective beta-blockers
- • Clonidine: possible risk of hypertension when adrenaline (epinephrine) or noradrenaline (norepinephrine) given with clonidine; serious adverse events reported with concomitant use of methylphenidate and •clonidine (causality not established)
- Corticosteroids: ephedrine accelerates metabolism of dexamethasone
- • Dopaminergics: risk of toxicity when isometheptene or phenylpropanolamine given with •bromocriptine; effects of adrenaline (epinephrine), dobutamine, dopamine and noradrenaline (norepinephrine) possibly enhanced by entacapone; avoid concomitant use of sympathomimetics with •rasagiline; risk of hypertensive crisis when dopamine given with •selegiline
- Doxapram: increased risk of hypertension when sympathomimetics given with doxapram
- Ergot Alkaloids: increased risk of ergotism when sympathomimetics given with ergotamine and methysergide
- Oxytocin: risk of hypertension when vasoconstrictor sympathomimetics given with oxytocin (due to enhanced vasopressor effect)
- • Sympathomimetics: effects of adrenaline (epinephrine) possibly enhanced by •dopexamine; dopexamine possibly enhances effects of •noradrenaline (norepinephrine)
- Theophylline: avoidance of ephedrine in children advised by manufacturer of theophylline

**Sympathomimetics, Beta$_2$**
- Atomoxetine: Increased risk of cardiovascular side-effects when parenteral salbutamol given with atomoxetine
- Cardiac Glycosides: salbutamol possibly reduces plasma concentration of digoxin
- Corticosteroids: increased risk of hypokalaemia when high doses of beta$_2$ sympathomimetics given with corticosteroids—for CSM advice (hypokalaemia) see p. 145
- Diuretics: increased risk of hypokalaemia when high doses of beta$_2$ sympathomimetics given with acetazolamide, loop diuretics or thiazides and

**Sympathomimetics, Beta$_2$**
Diuretics *(continued)*
related diuretics—for CSM advice (hypokalaemia) see p. 145
- Methyldopa: acute hypotension reported when infusion of salbutamol given with •methyldopa

Muscle Relaxants: bambuterol enhances effects of suxamethonium
Theophylline: increased risk of hypokalaemia when high doses of beta$_2$ sympathomimetics given with theophylline—for CSM advice (hypokalaemia) see p. 145

**Tacrolimus**
- Analgesics: possible increased risk of nephrotoxicity when tacrolimus given with NSAIDs; increased risk of nephrotoxicity when tacrolimus given with •ibuprofen
- Antibacterials: plasma concentration of tacrolimus increased by •clarithromycin, •erythromycin and •quinupristin/dalfopristin; plasma concentration of tacrolimus reduced by •rifampicin; increased risk of nephrotoxicity when tacrolimus given with •aminoglycosides; plasma concentration of tacrolimus possibly increased by •chloramphenicol and •telithromycin
- Antidepressants: plasma concentration of tacrolimus reduced by •St John's wort—avoid concomitant use
- Antifungals: plasma concentration of tacrolimus increased by •fluconazole, •ketoconazole and •voriconazole; increased risk of nephrotoxicity when tacrolimus given with •amphotericin; plasma concentration of tacrolimus reduced by •caspofungin; plasma concentration of tacrolimus possibly increased by •imidazoles and •triazoles
- Antivirals: plasma concentration of tacrolimus possibly increased by •atazanavir, •nelfinavir and •ritonavir; plasma concentration of tacrolimus increased by •saquinavir (consider reducing dose of tacrolimus)
- Calcium-channel Blockers: plasma concentration of tacrolimus possibly increased by felodipine; plasma concentration of tacrolimus increased by •diltiazem and •nifedipine
- Ciclosporin: tacrolimus increases plasma concentration of •ciclosporin (increased risk of toxicity)—avoid concomitant use
- Diuretics: increased risk of hyperkalaemia when tacrolimus given with •potassium-sparing diuretics and aldosterone antagonists
- Grapefruit Juice: plasma concentration of tacrolimus increased by •grapefruit juice

Hormone Antagonists: plasma concentration of tacrolimus possibly increased by danazol
Oestrogens: tacrolimus possibly reduces contraceptive effect of oestrogens
- Potassium Salts: increased risk of hyperkalaemia when tacrolimus given with •potassium salts

Progestogens: tacrolimus possibly reduces contraceptive effect of progestogens
Ulcer-healing Drugs: plasma concentration of tacrolimus possibly increased by omeprazole

**Tadalafil**
- Alpha-blockers: enhanced hypotensive effect when tadalafil given with •alpha-blockers—avoid concomitant use

Antibacterials: plasma concentration of tadalafil possibly increased by clarithromycin and erythromycin; plasma concentration of tadalafil reduced by rifampicin
Antifungals: plasma concentration of tadalafil increased by ketoconazole; plasma concentration of tadalafil possibly increased by itraconazole

**Tadalafil** *(continued)*
Antivirals: plasma concentration of tadalafil increased by ritonavir; plasma concentration of tadalafil possibly increased by saquinavir—reduce initial dose of tadalafil
Grapefruit Juice: plasma concentration of tadalafil possibly increased by grapefruit juice
- Nicorandil: tadalafil significantly enhances hypotensive effect of •nicorandil (avoid concomitant use)
- Nitrates: tadalafil significantly enhances hypotensive effect of •nitrates (avoid concomitant use)

**Tamoxifen**
- Anticoagulants: tamoxifen enhances anticoagulant effect of •coumarins

**Tamsulosin** *see* Alpha-blockers
**Taxanes** *see* Docetaxel and Paclitaxel
**Tegafur with uracil** *see* Fluorouracil
**Teicoplanin**
Antibacterials: increased risk of nephrotoxicity and ototoxicity when teicoplanin given with aminoglycosides or colistin
Oestrogens: antibacterials that do not induce liver enzymes possibly reduce contraceptive effect of oestrogens (risk probably small, see p. 408)

**Telithromycin**
- Antibacterials: plasma concentration of telithromycin reduced by •rifampicin (avoid during and for 2 weeks after rifampicin)
- Antidepressants: plasma concentration of telithromycin reduced by •St John's wort (avoid during and for 2 weeks after St John's wort)
- Antiepileptics: plasma concentration of telithromycin reduced by •carbamazepine, •phenytoin and •primidone (avoid during and for 2 weeks after carbamazepine, phenytoin and primidone)
- Antipsychotics: increased risk of ventricular arrhythmias when telithromycin given with •pimozide—avoid concomitant use
- Anxiolytics and Hypnotics: telithromycin inhibits metabolism of •midazolam (increased plasma concentration with increased sedation)

Aprepitant: telithromycin possibly increases plasma concentration of aprepitant
- Barbiturates: plasma concentration of telithromycin reduced by •phenobarbital (avoid during and for 2 weeks after phenobarbital)

Cardiac Glycosides: telithromycin possibly increases plasma concentration of digoxin
- Ciclosporin: telithromycin possibly increases plasma concentration of •ciclosporin
- Diuretics: telithromycin increases plasma concentration of •eplerenone—avoid concomitant use
- Ergot Alkaloids: increased risk of ergotism when telithromycin given with •ergotamine and methysergide—avoid concomitant use
- Ivabradine: telithromycin possibly increases plasma concentration of •ivabradine—avoid concomitant use
- Lipid-regulating Drugs: increased risk of myopathy when telithromycin given with •atorvastatin or •simvastatin (avoid concomitant use)

Oestrogens: antibacterials that do not induce liver enzymes possibly reduce contraceptive effect of oestrogens (risk probably small, see p. 408)
- Sirolimus: telithromycin increases plasma concentration of •sirolimus—avoid concomitant use
- Tacrolimus: telithromycin possibly increases plasma concentration of •tacrolimus

**Telmisartan** *see* Angiotensin-II Receptor Antagonists
**Temazepam** *see* Anxiolytics and Hypnotics

**Temoporfin**
- Cytotoxics: increased skin photosensitivity when temoporfin given with topical •fluorouracil

**Temozolomide**
Antiepileptics: cytotoxics possibly reduce absorption of phenytoin; plasma concentration of temozolomide increased by valproate
- Antipsychotics: avoid concomitant use of cytotoxics with •clozapine (increased risk of agranulocytosis)

**Tenofovir**
- Antivirals: tenofovir reduces plasma concentration of atazanavir; combination of tenofovir with cidofovir may increase plasma concentration of either drug (or both); tenofovir increases plasma concentration of •didanosine (increased risk of toxicity)—avoid concomitant use; plasma concentration of tenofovir increased by lopinavir

**Tenoxicam** *see* NSAIDs
**Terazosin** *see* Alpha-blockers
**Terbinafine**
Antibacterials: plasma concentration of terbinafine reduced by rifampicin
Antidepressants: terbinafine possibly increases plasma concentration of imipramine and nortriptyline
Oestrogens: occasional reports of breakthrough bleeding when terbinafine given with oestrogens (when used for contraception)
Progestogens: occasional reports of breakthrough bleeding when terbinafine given with progestogens (when used for contraception)
Ulcer-healing Drugs: plasma concentration of terbinafine increased by cimetidine

**Terbutaline** *see* Sympathomimetics, $Beta_2$
**Terpene Mixture** *see* Rowachol®
**Testolactone**
- Anticoagulants: testolactone enhances anticoagulant effect of •coumarins and •phenindione

**Testosterone**
- Anticoagulants: testosterone enhances anticoagulant effect of •coumarins and •phenindione

Antidiabetics: testosterone possibly enhances hypoglycaemic effect of antidiabetics

**Tetrabenazine**
- Antidepressants: risk of CNS excitation and hypertension when tetrabenazine given with •MAOIs

Antipsychotics: increased risk of extrapyramidal side-effects when tetrabenazine given with antipsychotics
Dopaminergics: increased risk of extrapyramidal side-effects when tetrabenazine given with amantadine
Metoclopramide: increased risk of extrapyramidal side-effects when tetrabenazine given with metoclopramide

**Tetracosactide** *see* Corticosteroids
**Tetracycline** *see* Tetracyclines
**Tetracyclines**
ACE Inhibitors: absorption of tetracyclines reduced by quinapril tablets (quinapril tablets contain magnesium carbonate)
Adsorbents: absorption of tetracyclines possibly reduced by kaolin
Antacids: absorption of tetracyclines reduced by antacids
- Anticoagulants: tetracyclines possibly enhance anticoagulant effect of •coumarins and •phenindione

Antiepileptics: metabolism of doxycycline accelerated by carbamazepine (reduced effect); metabolism of doxycycline accelerated by phenytoin and primidone (reduced plasma concentration)

**Tetracyclines**
Antiepileptics *(continued)*
Atovaquone: tetracycline reduces plasma concentration of atovaquone
Barbiturates: metabolism of doxycycline accelerated by barbiturates (reduced plasma concentration)
Calcium Salts: absorption of tetracycline reduced by calcium salts
- Ciclosporin: doxycycline possibly increases plasma concentration of •ciclosporin

Cytotoxics: doxycycline or tetracycline increase risk of methotrexate toxicity
Dairy Products: absorption of tetracyclines (except doxycycline and minocycline) reduced by dairy products
Diuretics: manufacturer of lymecycline advises avoid concomitant use with diuretics
Ergot Alkaloids: increased risk of ergotism when tetracyclines given with ergotamine and methysergide
Iron: absorption of tetracyclines reduced by *oral* iron, also absorption of *oral* iron reduced by tetracyclines
<u>Oestrogens</u>: antibacterials that do not induce liver enzymes possibly reduce contraceptive effect of oestrogens (risk probably small, see p. 408)
- Retinoids: possible increased risk of benign intracranial hypertension when tetracyclines given with •retinoids (avoid concomitant use)

Strontium Ranelate: absorption of tetracyclines reduced by strontium ranelate (manufacturer of strontium ranelate advises avoid concomitant use)
Ulcer-healing Drugs: absorption of tetracyclines reduced by ranitidine bismuth citrate, sucralfate and tripotassium dicitratobismuthate
Zinc: absorption of tetracyclines reduced by zinc, also absorption of zinc reduced by tetracyclines

**Theophylline**
Allopurinol: plasma concentration of theophylline possibly increased by allopurinol
Anaesthetics, General: increased risk of convulsions when theophylline given with ketamine; increased risk of arrhythmias when theophylline given with halothane
Anti-arrhythmics: theophylline antagonises anti-arrhythmic effect of adenosine; plasma concentration of theophylline increased by mexiletine and propafenone
- Antibacterials: plasma concentration of theophylline possibly increased by azithromycin and isoniazid; metabolism of theophylline inhibited by •clarithromycin (increased plasma concentration); metabolism of theophylline inhibited by •erythromycin (increased plasma concentration), if erythromycin given by mouth, also decreased plasma-erythromycin concentration; plasma concentration of theophylline increased by •ciprofloxacin and •norfloxacin; metabolism of theophylline accelerated by rifampicin (reduced plasma concentration); possible increased risk of convulsions when theophylline given with •quinolones
- Antidepressants: plasma concentration of theophylline increased by •fluvoxamine (concomitant use should usually be avoided, but where not possible halve theophylline dose and monitor plasma-theophylline concentration); plasma concentration of theophylline reduced by •St John's wort—avoid concomitant use

**Theophylline** *(continued)*

- Antiepileptics: metabolism of theophylline accelerated by carbamazepine and primidone (reduced effect); plasma concentration of both drugs reduced when theophylline given with •phenytoin
- Antifungals: plasma concentration of theophylline possibly increased by •fluconazole and •ketoconazole
- Antivirals: metabolism of theophylline accelerated by •ritonavir (reduced plasma concentration)

Anxiolytics and Hypnotics: theophylline possibly reduces effects of benzodiazepines

Barbiturates: metabolism of theophylline accelerated by barbiturates (reduced effect)

- Calcium-channel Blockers: plasma concentration of theophylline possibly increased by •calcium-channel blockers (enhanced effect); plasma concentration of theophylline increased by diltiazem; plasma concentration of theophylline increased by •verapamil (enhanced effect)

Corticosteroids: increased risk of hypokalaemia when theophylline given with corticosteroids

Cytotoxics: plasma concentration of theophylline possibly increased by methotrexate

Disulfiram: metabolism of theophylline inhibited by disulfiram (increased risk of toxicity)

Diuretics: increased risk of hypokalaemia when theophylline given with acetazolamide, loop diuretics or thiazides and related diuretics

Doxapram: increased CNS stimulation when theophylline given with doxapram

Interferons: metabolism of theophylline inhibited by interferon alfa (increased plasma concentration)

Leukotriene Antagonists: plasma concentration of theophylline possibly increased by zafirlukast, also plasma concentration of zafirlukast reduced

Lithium: theophylline increases excretion of lithium (reduced plasma concentration)

Oestrogens: excretion of theophylline reduced by oestrogens (increased plasma concentration)

Pentoxifylline (oxpentifylline): plasma concentration of theophylline increased by pentoxifylline (oxpentifylline)

Sulfinpyrazone: plasma concentration of theophylline reduced by sulfinpyrazone

Sympathomimetics: manufacturer of theophylline advises avoid concomitant use with ephedrine in children

Sympathomimetics, $Beta_2$: increased risk of hypokalaemia when theophylline given with high doses of $beta_2$ sympathomimetics—for CSM advice (hypokalaemia) see p. 145

Tobacco: metabolism of theophylline increased by tobacco smoking (reduced plasma concentration)

- Ulcer-healing Drugs: metabolism of theophylline inhibited by •cimetidine (increased plasma concentration)

Vaccines: plasma concentration of theophylline possibly increased by influenza vaccine

**Thiazolidinediones** *see* Antidiabetics

**Thiopental** *see* Anaesthetics, General

**Thiotepa**

Antiepileptics: cytotoxics possibly reduce absorption of phenytoin

- Antipsychotics: avoid concomitant use of cytotoxics with •clozapine (increased risk of agranulocytosis)

Muscle Relaxants: thiotepa enhances effects of suxamethonium

**Thioxanthenes** *see* Antipsychotics

**Thyroid Hormones**

Anti-arrhythmics: for concomitant use of thyroid hormones and amiodarone see p. 79

Antibacterials: metabolism of levothyroxine (thyroxine) accelerated by rifampicin (may increase requirements for levothyroxine (thyroxine) in hypothyroidism)

- Anticoagulants: thyroid hormones enhance anticoagulant effect of •coumarins and •phenindione

Antidepressants: thyroid hormones enhance effects of amitriptyline and imipramine; thyroid hormones possibly enhance effects of tricyclics

Antiepileptics: metabolism of thyroid hormones accelerated by carbamazepine and primidone (may increase requirements for thyroid hormones in hypothyroidism); metabolism of thyroid hormones accelerated by phenytoin (may increase requirements in hypothyroidism), also plasma concentration of phenytoin possibly increased

Barbiturates: metabolism of thyroid hormones accelerated by barbiturates (may increase requirements for thyroid hormones in hypothyroidism)

Calcium Salts: absorption of levothyroxine (thyroxine) reduced by calcium salts

Iron: absorption of levothyroxine (thyroxine) reduced by *oral* iron (give at least 2 hours apart)

Lipid-regulating Drugs: absorption of thyroid hormones reduced by colestipol and colestyramine

Sodium Polystyrene Sulphonate: absorption of levothyroxine (thyroxine) reduced by sodium polystyrene sulphonate

Ulcer-healing Drugs: absorption of levothyroxine (thyroxine) reduced by cimetidine and sucralfate

**Tiagabine**

- Antidepressants: anticonvulsant effect of antiepileptics possibly antagonised by MAOIs and •tricyclic-related antidepressants (convulsive threshold lowered); anticonvulsant effect of antiepileptics antagonised by •SSRIs and •tricyclics (convulsive threshold lowered)

Antiepileptics: plasma concentration of tiagabine reduced by carbamazepine, phenytoin and primidone

- Antimalarials: possible increased risk of convulsions when antiepileptics given with chloroquine and hydroxychloroquine; anticonvulsant effect of antiepileptics antagonised by •mefloquine

Barbiturates: plasma concentration of tiagabine reduced by phenobarbital

**Tiaprofenic Acid** *see* NSAIDs

**Tibolone**

Antibacterials: metabolism of tibolone accelerated by rifampicin (reduced plasma concentration)

Antiepileptics: metabolism of tibolone accelerated by carbamazepine and primidone (reduced plasma concentration); metabolism of tibolone accelerated by phenytoin

Barbiturates: metabolism of tibolone accelerated by barbiturates (reduced plasma concentration)

**Ticarcillin** *see* Penicillins

**Tiludronic Acid** *see* Bisphosphonates

**Timolol** *see* Beta-blockers

**Tinidazole**

Alcohol: possibility of disulfiram-like reaction when tinidazole given with alcohol

Oestrogens: antibacterials that do not induce liver enzymes possibly reduce contraceptive effect of oestrogens (risk probably small, see p. 408)

**Tinzaparin** *see* Heparins

**Tioguanine**
Antiepileptics: cytotoxics possibly reduce absorption of phenytoin
• Antipsychotics: avoid concomitant use of cytotoxics with •clozapine (increased risk of agranulocytosis)
Cytotoxics: increased risk of hepatotoxicity when tioguanine given with busulfan

**Tiotropium** *see* Antimuscarinics

**Tipranavir**
Antacids: absorption of tipranavir reduced by antacids
• Antibacterials: tipranavir increases plasma concentration of •clarithromycin (reduce dose of clarithromycin in renal impairment), also plasma concentration of tipranavir increased by clarithromycin; tipranavir increases plasma concentration of •rifabutin (reduce dose of rifabutin); plasma concentration of tipranavir possibly reduced by •rifampicin—avoid concomitant use
• Antidepressants: plasma concentration of tipranavir possibly reduced by •St John's wort—avoid concomitant use
Antifungals: plasma concentration of tipranavir increased by fluconazole
• Antimalarials: possible increased risk of ventricular arrhythmias when tipranavir given with •artemether/lumefantrine—avoid concomitant use
• Antivirals: tipranavir reduces plasma concentration of •abacavir, •amprenavir, •didanosine, •lopinavir, •saquinavir and •zidovudine

**Tirofiban**
Iloprost: increased risk of bleeding when tirofiban given with iloprost

**Tizanidine** *see* Muscle Relaxants

**Tobacco**
Cinacalcet: tobacco smoking increases cinacalcet metabolism (reduced plasma concentration)
Theophylline: tobacco smoking increases theophylline metabolism (reduced plasma concentration)

**Tobramycin** *see* Aminoglycosides

**Tolazoline** *see* Alpha-blockers

**Tolbutamide** *see* Antidiabetics

**Tolcapone**
Antidepressants: avoid concomitant use of tolcapone with MAOIs
Memantine: effects of dopaminergics possibly enhanced by memantine
Methyldopa: antiparkinsonian effect of dopaminergics antagonised by methyldopa

**Tolfenamic Acid** *see* NSAIDs

**Tolterodine** *see* Antimuscarinics

**Topiramate**
• Antidepressants: anticonvulsant effect of antiepileptics possibly antagonised by MAOIs and •tricyclic-related antidepressants (convulsive threshold lowered); anticonvulsant effect of antiepileptics antagonised by •SSRIs and •tricyclics (convulsive threshold lowered)
• Antiepileptics: plasma concentration of topiramate often reduced by carbamazepine; topiramate increases plasma concentration of •phenytoin (also plasma concentration of topiramate reduced)
• Antimalarials: possible increased risk of convulsions when antiepileptics given with chloroquine and hydroxychloroquine; anticonvulsant effect of antiepileptics antagonised by •mefloquine
• Oestrogens: topiramate accelerates metabolism of •oestrogens (reduced contraceptive effect—see p. 408)

**Topiramate** *(continued)*
• Progestogens: topiramate accelerates metabolism of •progestogens (reduced contraceptive effect—see p. 408)

**Torasemide** *see* Diuretics

**Toremifene**
• Anticoagulants: toremifene possibly enhances anticoagulant effect of •coumarins
Antiepileptics: metabolism of toremifene possibly accelerated by carbamazepine (reduced plasma concentration); metabolism of toremifene possibly accelerated by phenytoin; metabolism of toremifene accelerated by primidone (reduced plasma concentration)
Barbiturates: metabolism of toremifene possibly accelerated by barbiturates (reduced plasma concentration)
Diuretics: increased risk of hypercalcaemia when toremifene given with thiazides and related diuretics

**Tramadol** *see* Opioid Analgesics

**Trandolapril** *see* ACE Inhibitors

**Tranylcypromine** *see* MAOIs

**Trazodone** *see* Antidepressants, Tricyclic (related)

**Tretinoin** *see* Retinoids

**Triamcinolone** *see* Corticosteroids

**Triamterene** *see* Diuretics

**Triclofos** *see* Anxiolytics and Hypnotics

**Trientine**
Iron: trientine reduces absorption of *oral* iron
Zinc: trientine reduces absorption of zinc, also absorption of trientine reduced by zinc

**Trifluoperazine** *see* Antipsychotics

**Trihexyphenidyl (benzhexol)** *see* Antimuscarinics

**Trilostane**
Diuretics: increased risk of hyperkalaemia when trilostane given with potassium-sparing diuretics and aldosterone antagonists

**Trimethoprim**
• Anti-arrhythmics: increased risk of ventricular arrhythmias when trimethoprim (as co-trimoxazole) given with •amiodarone—avoid concomitant use of co-trimoxazole; trimethoprim increases plasma concentration of procainamide
Antibacterials: plasma concentration of both drugs may increase when trimethoprim given with dapsone
Anticoagulants: trimethoprim possibly enhances anticoagulant effect of coumarins
Antidiabetics: trimethoprim rarely enhances the effects of sulphonylureas
• Antiepileptics: trimethoprim increases plasma concentration of •phenytoin (also increased antifolate effect)
• Antimalarials: increased antifolate effect when trimethoprim given with •pyrimethamine
Antivirals: trimethoprim (as co-trimoxazole) increases plasma concentration of lamivudine—avoid concomitant use of high-dose co-trimoxazole; trimethoprim possibly increases plasma concentration of zalcitabine
Cardiac Glycosides: trimethoprim possibly increases plasma concentration of digoxin
• Ciclosporin: increased risk of nephrotoxicity when trimethoprim given with •ciclosporin, also plasma concentration of ciclosporin reduced by intravenous trimethoprim
• Cytotoxics: increased risk of haematological toxicity when trimethoprim (also with co-trimoxazole) given with •azathioprine, •mercaptopurine or •methotrexate
Diuretics: increased risk of hyperkalaemia when trimethoprim given with eplerenone

Appendix 1

**Trimethoprim** *(continued)*
Oestrogens: antibacterials that do not induce liver enzymes possibly reduce contraceptive effect of oestrogens (risk probably small, see p. 408)
**Trimipramine** *see* Antidepressants, Tricyclic
**Tripotassium Dicitratobismuthate**
Antibacterials: tripotassium dicitratobismuthate reduces absorption of tetracyclines
**Tropicamide** *see* Antimuscarinics
**Tropisetron**
Anti-arrhythmics: manufacturer of tropisetron advises caution with anti-arrhythmics (risk of ventricular arrhythmias)
Antibacterials: plasma concentration of tropisetron reduced by rifampicin
Antiepileptics: plasma concentration of tropisetron reduced by primidone
Barbiturates: plasma concentration of tropisetron reduced by phenobarbital
Beta-blockers: manufacturer of tropisetron advises caution with beta-blockers (risk of ventricular arrhythmias)
**Trospium** *see* Antimuscarinics
**Tryptophan**
• Antidepressants: possible increased serotonergic effects when tryptophan given with duloxetine; CNS excitation and confusion when tryptophan given with •MAOIs (reduce dose of tryptophan); agitation and nausea may occur when tryptophan given with •SSRIs
• Antimalarials: avoidance of antidepressants advised by manufacturer of •artemether/lumefantrine
• Sibutramine: increased risk of CNS toxicity when tryptophan given with •sibutramine (manufacturer of sibutramine advises avoid concomitant use)
**Ulcer-healing Drugs** *see* Carbenoxolone, Histamine $H_2$-antagonists, Proton Pump Inhibitors, Sucralfate, and Tripotassium Dicitratobismuthate
**Ursodeoxycholic Acid**
Antacids: absorption of bile acids possibly reduced by antacids
• Ciclosporin: ursodeoxycholic acid increases absorption of •ciclosporin
Lipid-regulating Drugs: absorption of bile acids possibly reduced by colestipol and colestyramine
Oestrogens: elimination of cholesterol in bile increased when bile acids given with oestrogens
**Vaccines**
*Note.* For a general warning on live vaccines and high doses of corticosteroids or other immunosuppressive drugs, see p. 611; for advice on live vaccines and immunoglobulins, see under Normal Immunoglobulin, p. 627
• Adalimumab: avoid concomitant use of live vaccines with •adalimumab (see p. 611)
• Anakinra: avoid concomitant use of live vaccines with •anakinra (see p. 611)
Anticoagulants: influenza vaccine possibly enhances anticoagulant effect of warfarin
Antiepileptics: influenza vaccine enhances effects of phenytoin
• Corticosteroids: immune response to vaccines impaired by high doses of •corticosteroids, avoid concomitant use with live vaccines (see p. 611)
• Efalizumab: live or live-attenuated vaccines should be given 2 weeks before •efalizumab or withheld until 8 weeks after discontinuation
• Etanercept: avoid concomitant use of live vaccines with •etanercept (see p. 611)
• Infliximab: avoid concomitant use of live vaccines with •infliximab (see p. 611)
Interferons: avoidance of vaccines advised by manufacturer of interferon gamma

**Vaccines** *(continued)*
• Leflunomide: avoid concomitant use of live vaccines with •leflunomide (see p. 611)
Theophylline: influenza vaccine possibly increases plasma concentration of theophylline
**Valaciclovir** *see* Aciclovir
**Valganciclovir** *see* Ganciclovir
**Valproate**
Analgesics: effects of valproate enhanced by aspirin
Antibacterials: plasma concentration of valproate possibly reduced by ertapenem; plasma concentration of valproate reduced by meropenem; metabolism of valproate possibly inhibited by erythromycin (increased plasma concentration)
Anticoagulants: valproate possibly enhances anticoagulant effect of coumarins
• Antidepressants: anticonvulsant effect of antiepileptics possibly antagonised by MAOIs and •tricyclic-related antidepressants (convulsive threshold lowered); anticonvulsant effect of antiepileptics antagonised by •SSRIs and •tricyclics (convulsive threshold lowered)
• Antiepileptics: plasma concentration of valproate reduced by carbamazepine, also plasma concentration of active metabolite of carbamazepine increased; valproate possibly increases plasma concentration of ethosuximide; valproate increases plasma concentration of lamotrigine; valproate sometimes reduces plasma concentration of an active metabolite of oxcarbazepine; valproate increases or possibly decreases plasma concentration of phenytoin, also plasma concentration of valproate reduced; valproate possibly increases plasma concentration of •primidone (plasma concentration of active metabolite of primidone increased), also plasma concentration of valproate reduced
• Antimalarials: possible increased risk of convulsions when antiepileptics given with chloroquine and hydroxychloroquine; anticonvulsant effect of antiepileptics and valproate antagonised by •mefloquine
• Antipsychotics: anticonvulsant effect of valproate antagonised by •antipsychotics (convulsive threshold lowered); increased risk of neutropenia when valproate given with •olanzapine
Antivirals: valproate possibly increases plasma concentration of zidovudine (increased risk of toxicity)
Barbiturates: valproate increases plasma concentration of phenobarbital (also plasma concentration of valproate reduced)
Bupropion: valproate inhibits the metabolism of bupropion
Cytotoxics: valproate increases plasma concentration of temozolomide
Lipid-regulating Drugs: absorption of valproate possibly reduced by colestyramine
Sodium Benzoate: valproate possibly reduces effects of sodium benzoate
Sodium Phenylbutyrate: valproate possibly reduces effects of sodium phenylbutyrate
• Ulcer-healing Drugs: metabolism of valproate inhibited by •cimetidine (increased plasma concentration)
**Valsartan** *see* Angiotensin-II Receptor Antagonists
**Vancomycin**
Anaesthetics, General: hypersensitivity-like reactions can occur when intravenous vancomycin given with general anaesthetics
Antibacterials: increased risk of nephrotoxicity and ototoxicity when vancomycin given with aminoglycosides, capreomycin or colistin; increased

**Vancomycin**
Antibacterials *(continued)*
risk of nephrotoxicity when vancomycin given with polymyxins
Antifungals: possible increased risk of nephrotoxicity when vancomycin given with amphotericin
• Ciclosporin: increased risk of nephrotoxicity when vancomycin given with •ciclosporin
Cytotoxics: increased risk of nephrotoxicity and possibly of ototoxicity when vancomycin given with cisplatin
• Diuretics: increased risk of otoxicity when vancomycin given with •loop diuretics
Lipid-regulating Drugs: effects of oral vancomycin antagonised by colestyramine
• Muscle Relaxants: vancomycin enhances effects of •suxamethonium
Oestrogens: antibacterials that do not induce liver enzymes possibly reduce contraceptive effect of oestrogens (risk probably small, see p. 408)

**Vardenafil**
• Alpha-blockers: enhanced hypotensive effect when vardenafil given with •alpha-blockers (exludes tamsulosin)—avoid vardenafil for 6 hours after alpha-blockers
Antibacterials: plasma concentration of vardenafil increased by erythromycin (reduce dose of vardenafil)
• Antifungals: plasma concentration of vardenafil increased by •ketoconazole—avoid concomitant use; plasma concentration of vardenafil possibly increased by •itraconazole—avoid concomitant use
• Antivirals: plasma concentration of vardenafil possibly increased by amprenavir; plasma concentration of vardenafil increased by •indinavir—avoid concomitant use; plasma concentration of vardenafil possibly increased by •ritonavir—avoid concomitant use; plasma concentration of vardenafil possibly increased by saquinavir—reduce initial dose of vardenafil
Calcium-channel Blockers: enhanced hypotensive effect when vardenafil given with nifedipine
• Grapefruit Juice: plasma concentration of vardenafil possibly increased by •grapefruit juice—avoid concomitant use
• Nicorandil: possible increased hypotensive effect when vardenafil given with •nicorandil—avoid concomitant use
• Nitrates: possible increased hypotensive effect when vardenafil given with •nitrates—avoid concomitant use



**Vasodilator Antihypertensives**
ACE Inhibitors: enhanced hypotensive effect when hydralazine, minoxidil or nitroprusside given with ACE inhibitors
Adrenergic Neurone Blockers: enhanced hypotensive effect when hydralazine, minoxidil or nitroprusside given with adrenergic neurone blockers
Alcohol: enhanced hypotensive effect when hydralazine, minoxidil or nitroprusside given with alcohol
Aldesleukin: enhanced hypotensive effect when hydralazine, minoxidil or nitroprusside given with aldesleukin
Alpha-blockers: enhanced hypotensive effect when hydralazine, minoxidil or nitroprusside given with alpha-blockers
Anaesthetics, General: enhanced hypotensive effect when hydralazine, minoxidil or nitroprusside given with general anaesthetics

**Vasodilator Antihypertensives** *(continued)*
Analgesics: hypotensive effect of hydralazine, minoxidil and nitroprusside antagonised by NSAIDs
Angiotensin-II Receptor Antagonists: enhanced hypotensive effect when hydralazine, minoxidil or nitroprusside given with angiotensin-II receptor antagonists
Antidepressants: enhanced hypotensive effect when hydralazine, minoxidil or nitroprusside given with MAOIs; enhanced hypotensive effect when hydralazine or nitroprusside given with tricyclic-related antidepressants
Antipsychotics: enhanced hypotensive effect when hydralazine, minoxidil or nitroprusside given with phenothiazines
Anxiolytics and Hypnotics: enhanced hypotensive effect when hydralazine, minoxidil or nitroprusside given with anxiolytics and hypnotics
Beta-blockers: enhanced hypotensive effect when hydralazine, minoxidil or nitroprusside given with beta-blockers
Calcium-channel Blockers: enhanced hypotensive effect when hydralazine, minoxidil or nitroprusside given with calcium-channel blockers
Clonidine: enhanced hypotensive effect when hydralazine, minoxidil or nitroprusside given with clonidine
Corticosteroids: hypotensive effect of hydralazine, minoxidil and nitroprusside antagonised by corticosteroids
Diazoxide: enhanced hypotensive effect when hydralazine, minoxidil or nitroprusside given with diazoxide
Diuretics: enhanced hypotensive effect when hydralazine, minoxidil or nitroprusside given with diuretics
Dopaminergics: enhanced hypotensive effect when hydralazine, minoxidil or nitroprusside given with levodopa
Methyldopa: enhanced hypotensive effect when hydralazine, minoxidil or nitroprusside given with methyldopa
Moxisylyte (thymoxamine): enhanced hypotensive effect when hydralazine, minoxidil or nitroprusside given with moxisylyte
Moxonidine: enhanced hypotensive effect when hydralazine, minoxidil or nitroprusside given with moxonidine
Muscle Relaxants: enhanced hypotensive effect when hydralazine, minoxidil or nitroprusside given with baclofen; enhanced hypotensive effect when hydralazine, minoxidil or nitroprusside given with tizanidine
Nicorandil: possible enhanced hypotensive effect when hydralazine, minoxidil or nitroprusside given with nicorandil
Nitrates: enhanced hypotensive effect when hydralazine, minoxidil or nitroprusside given with nitrates
Oestrogens: hypotensive effect of hydralazine, minoxidil and nitroprusside antagonised by oestrogens
Prostaglandins: enhanced hypotensive effect when hydralazine, minoxidil or nitroprusside given with alprostadil
Vasodilator Antihypertensives: enhanced hypotensive effect when hydralazine given with minoxidil or nitroprusside; enhanced hypotensive effect when minoxidil given with nitroprusside

**Vecuronium** *see* Muscle Relaxants

**Venlafaxine**
• Analgesics: increased risk of bleeding when venlafaxine given with •NSAIDs or •aspirin

**Venlafaxine** *(continued)*
- Anticoagulants: venlafaxine possibly enhances anticoagulant effect of •warfarin
- Antidepressants: possible increased serotonergic effects when venlafaxine given with duloxetine; enhanced CNS effects and toxicity when venlafaxine given with •MAOIs (venlafaxine should not be started until 2 weeks after stopping MAOIs, avoid MAOIs for 1 week after stopping venlafaxine); after stopping SSRI-related antidepressants do not start •moclobemide for at least 1 week
- Antimalarials: avoidance of antidepressants advised by manufacturer of •artemether/lumefantrine
- Antipsychotics: venlafaxine increases plasma concentration of •clozapine and haloperidol
- Dopaminergics: caution with venlafaxine advised by manufacturer of entacapone; increased risk of hypertension and CNS excitation when venlafaxine given with •selegiline (selegiline should not be started until 1 week after stopping venlafaxine, avoid venlafaxine for 2 weeks after stopping selegiline)
- Sibutramine: increased risk of CNS toxicity when SSRI-related antidepressants given with •sibutramine (manufacturer of sibutramine advises avoid concomitant use)

**Verapamil** *see* Calcium-channel Blockers

**Vigabatrin**
- Antidepressants: anticonvulsant effect of antiepileptics possibly antagonised by MAOIs and •tricyclic-related antidepressants (convulsive threshold lowered); anticonvulsant effect of antiepileptics antagonised by •SSRIs and •tricyclics (convulsive threshold lowered)

Antiepileptics: vigabatrin reduces plasma concentration of phenytoin; vigabatrin possibly reduces plasma concentration of primidone
- Antimalarials: possible increased risk of convulsions when antiepileptics given with chloroquine and hydroxychloroquine; anticonvulsant effect of antiepileptics antagonised by •mefloquine

Barbiturates: vigabatrin possibly reduces plasma concentration of phenobarbital

**Vinblastine**
- Antibacterials: toxicity of vinblastine increased by •erythromycin—avoid concomitant use

Antiepileptics: cytotoxics possibly reduce absorption of phenytoin
- Antipsychotics: avoid concomitant use of cytotoxics with •clozapine (increased risk of agranulocytosis)

**Vincristine**

Antiepileptics: cytotoxics possibly reduce absorption of phenytoin
- Antifungals: metabolism of vincristine possibly inhibited by •itraconazole (increased risk of neurotoxicity)
- Antipsychotics: avoid concomitant use of cytotoxics with •clozapine (increased risk of agranulocytosis)

Calcium-channel Blockers: metabolism of vincristine possibly inhibited by nifedipine

**Vitamin A** *see* Vitamins

**Vitamin D** *see* Vitamins

**Vitamin K (Phytomenadione)** *see* Vitamins

**Vitamins**

Antibacterials: absorption of vitamin A possibly reduced by neomycin
- Anticoagulants: vitamin K antagonises anticoagulant effect of •coumarins and •phenindione

**Vitamins** *(continued)*

Antiepileptics: vitamin D requirements possibly increased when given with carbamazepine, phenytoin or primidone

Barbiturates: vitamin D requirements possibly increased when given with barbiturates

Diuretics: increased risk of hypercalcaemia when vitamin D given with thiazides and related diuretics

Dopaminergics: pyridoxine reduces effects of levodopa when given without dopa-decarboxylase inhibitor

Retinoids: risk of hypervitaminosis A when vitamin A given with retinoids

**Voriconazole** *see* Antifungals, Triazole

**Warfarin** *see* Coumarins

**Xipamide** *see* Diuretics

**Xylometazoline** *see* Sympathomimetics

**Zafirlukast** *see* Leukotriene Antagonists

**Zalcitabine**

*Note.* Clinical data limited. Avoid use with other drugs which have a potential to cause peripheral neuropathy or pancreatitis—for further details consult product literature

Antacids: absorption of zalcitabine reduced by antacids

Antibacterials: plasma concentration of zalcitabine possibly increased by trimethoprim

Antivirals: avoidance of zalcitabine advised by manufacturer of emtricitabine; effects of zalcitabine possibly inhibited by lamivudine (manufacturers advise avoid concomitant use)

Probenecid: excretion of zalcitabine possibly reduced by probenecid (increased plasma concentration)

Ulcer-healing Drugs: plasma concentration of zalcitabine possibly increased by cimetidine

**Zaleplon** *see* Anxiolytics and Hypnotics

**Zidovudine**

*Note.* Increased risk of toxicity with nephrotoxic and myelosuppressive drugs - for further details consult product literature

Analgesics: increased risk of haematological toxicity when zidovudine given with NSAIDs; plasma concentration of zidovudine possibly increased by methadone

Antibacterials: absorption of zidovudine reduced by clarithromycin tablets; manufacturer of zidovudine advises avoid concomitant use with rifampicin

Antiepileptics: zidovudine increases or decreases plasma concentration of phenytoin; plasma concentration of zidovudine possibly increased by valproate (increased risk of toxicity)
- Antifungals: plasma concentration of zidovudine increased by •fluconazole (increased risk of toxicity)

Antimalarials: increased antifolate effect when zidovudine given with pyrimethamine
- Antivirals: profound myelosuppression when zidovudine given with •ganciclovir (if possible avoid concomitant administration, particularly during initial ganciclovir therapy); effects of zidovudine possibly inhibited by •ribavirin (manufacturer of zidovudine advises avoid concomitant use); zidovudine possibly inhibits effects of •stavudine (manufacturers advise avoid concomitant use); plasma concentration of zidovudine reduced by •tipranavir

Atovaquone: metabolism of zidovudine possibly inhibited by atovaquone (increased plasma concentration)

Probenecid: excretion of zidovudine reduced by probenecid (increased plasma concentration and risk of toxicity)

**Zinc**

Antibacterials: zinc reduces absorption of ciprofloxacin, levofloxacin, moxifloxacin, norfloxacin and ofloxacin; zinc reduces absorption of tetracyclines, also absorption of zinc reduced by tetracyclines

Calcium Salts: absorption of zinc reduced by calcium salts

Iron: absorption of zinc reduced by *oral* iron, also absorption of *oral* iron reduced by zinc

Penicillamine: absorption of zinc reduced by penicillamine, also absorption of penicillamine reduced by zinc

Trientine: absorption of zinc reduced by trientine, also absorption of trientine reduced by zinc

**Zoledronic Acid** *see* Bisphosphonates

**Zolmitriptan** *see* $5HT_1$ Agonists

**Zolpidem** *see* Anxiolytics and Hypnotics

**Zonisamide**

• Antidepressants: anticonvulsant effect of antiepileptics possibly antagonised by MAOIs and •tricyclic-related antidepressants (convulsive threshold lowered); anticonvulsant effect of antiepileptics antagonised by •SSRIs and •tricyclics (convulsive threshold lowered)

Antiepileptics: plasma concentration of zonisamide reduced by carbamazepine, effect on carbamazepine plasma concentration not predictable; plasma concentration of zonisamide reduced by phenytoin

• Antimalarials: possible increased risk of convulsions when antiepileptics given with chloroquine and hydroxychloroquine; anticonvulsant effect of antiepileptics antagonised by •mefloquine

Barbiturates: plasma concentration of zonisamide reduced by phenobarbital

**Zopiclone** *see* Anxiolytics and Hypnotics

**Zotepine** *see* Antipsychotics

**Zuclopenthixol** *see* Antipsychotics

# A2 Liver disease

Liver disease may alter the response to drugs in several ways as indicated below, and drug prescribing should be kept to a minimum in all patients with severe liver disease. The main problems occur in patients with jaundice, ascites, or evidence of encephalopathy.

**Impaired drug metabolism** Metabolism by the liver is the main route of elimination for many drugs, but the hepatic reserve appears to be large and liver disease has to be severe before important changes in drug metabolism occur. Routine liver-function tests are a poor guide to the capacity of the liver to metabolise drugs, and in the individual patient it is not possible to predict the extent to which the metabolism of a particular drug may be impaired.

A few drugs, e.g. rifampicin and fusidic acid, are excreted in the bile unchanged and may accumulate in patients with intrahepatic or extrahepatic obstructive jaundice.

**Hypoproteinaemia** The hypoalbuminaemia in severe liver disease is associated with reduced protein binding and increased toxicity of some highly protein-bound drugs such as phenytoin and prednisolone.

**Reduced clotting** Reduced hepatic synthesis of blood-clotting factors, indicated by a prolonged prothrombin time, increases the sensitivity to oral anticoagulants such as warfarin and phenindione.

**Hepatic encephalopathy** In severe liver disease many drugs can further impair cerebral function and may precipitate hepatic encephalopathy. These include all sedative drugs, opioid analgesics, those diuretics that produce hypokalaemia, and drugs that cause constipation.

**Fluid overload** Oedema and ascites in chronic liver disease may be exacerbated by drugs that give rise to fluid retention, e.g. NSAIDs, corticosteroids, and carbenoxolone.

**Hepatotoxic drugs** Hepatotoxicity is either dose-related or unpredictable (idiosyncratic). Drugs causing dose-related toxicity may do so at lower doses than in patients with normal liver function, and some drugs producing reactions of the idiosyncratic kind do so more frequently in patients with liver disease. These drugs should be avoided or used very carefully.

## Table of drugs to be avoided or used with caution in liver disease

The list of drugs given below is not comprehensive and is based on current information concerning the use of these drugs in therapeutic dosage. Products introduced or amended since publication of BNF No. 50 (September 2005) are underlined.

| Drug | Comment |
|---|---|
| Abacavir | Avoid in moderate hepatic impairment unless essential; avoid in severe hepatic impairment |
| Abciximab | Avoid in severe liver disease—increased risk of bleeding |
| Acamprosate | Avoid in severe liver disease |
| Acarbose | Avoid |
| ACE inhibitors | Use of prodrugs such as cilazapril, enalapril, fosinopril, imidapril, moexipril, perindopril, quinapril, ramipril, and trandolapril requires close monitoring in patients with impaired liver function |
| Aceclofenac | *see* NSAIDs |
| Acemetacin | *see* NSAIDs |
| Acenocoumarol (nicoumalone) | *see* Anticoagulants, Oral |
| Acitretin | Avoid—further impairment of liver function may occur |
| Alfentanil | *see* Opioid Analgesics |
| Alfuzosin | Reduce dose in mild to moderate liver disease; avoid if severe |
| Alimemazine (trimeprazine) | Avoid—may precipitate coma in severe liver disease; hepatotoxic |
| Allopurinol | Reduce dose |
| Almotriptan | Manufacturer advises caution in mild to moderate liver disease; avoid in severe liver disease |
| Alprazolam | *see* Anxiolytics and Hypnotics |
| Alteplase | Avoid in severe hepatic impairment |
| Amfebutamone | *see* Bupropion |
| Aminophylline | *see* Theophylline |
| Amitriptyline | *see* Antidepressants, Tricyclic (and related) |
| Amlodipine | Half-life prolonged—may need dose reduction |
| Amoxapine | *see* Antidepressants, Tricyclic (and related) |
| Amprenavir | Avoid oral solution due to high propylene glycol content; reduce dose of capsules to 450 mg every 12 hours in moderate hepatic impairment and reduce dose to 300 mg every 12 hours in severe impairment |
| Amsacrine | Reduce dose |

| Drug | Comment |
|---|---|
| Anabolic steroids | Preferably avoid—dose-related toxicity |
| Anagrelide | Manufacturer advises caution in mild hepatic impairment; avoid in moderate to severe impairment |
| Analgesics | *see* Aspirin, NSAIDs, Opioid Analgesics and Paracetamol |
| Anastrozole | Avoid in moderate to severe liver disease |
| Androgens | Preferably avoid—dose-related toxicity with some, and produce fluid retention |
| Antacids | In patients with fluid retention, avoid those containing large amounts of sodium, e.g. magnesium trisilicate mixture, *Gaviscon*® Avoid those causing constipation—can precipitate coma |
| Anticoagulants, oral | Avoid in severe liver disease, especially if prothrombin time already prolonged |
| Antidepressants, MAOI | May cause idiosyncratic hepatotoxicity; see also Moclobemide |
| Antidepressants, SSRI | Reduce dose or avoid; *see also* Escitalopram |
| Antidepressants, tricyclic (and related) | Tricyclics preferable to MAOIs but sedative effects increased (avoid in severe liver disease) |
| Antihistamines | *see* individual entries |
| Antipsychotics | All can precipitate coma; phenothiazines are hepatotoxic; *see also* Aripiprazole, Clozapine, Olanzapine, Quetiapine, Risperidone and Sertindole |
| Anxiolytics and hypnotics | All can precipitate coma; small dose of oxazepam or temazepam probably safest; reduce oral dose of clomethiazole; reduce dose of zaleplon to 5 mg (avoid if severe); reduce dose of zolpidem to 5 mg (avoid if severe); reduce dose of zopiclone (avoid if severe); *see also* Chloral Hydrate and Clonazepam |
| Apomorphine | Manufacturer of *APO-go*® advises avoid; low sublingual doses of *Uprima*® may be used with caution for erectile dysfunction |
| Aprepitant | Manufacturer advises caution in moderate to severe hepatic impairment |
| Aripiprazole | Manufacturer advises use with caution in severe impairment |
| Artemether [ingredient] | *see Riamet*® |
| Aspirin | Avoid in severe hepatic impairment—increased risk of gastro-intestinal bleeding |
| Atazanavir | Manufacturer advises caution in mild hepatic impairment; avoid in moderate to severe hepatic impairment |
| Atomoxetine | Halve dose in moderate liver disease; quarter dose in severe liver disease |
| Atorvastatin | *see* Statins |
| Atosiban | No information available |
| Atovaquone | Manufacturer advises caution—monitor more closely |
| Auranofin | Caution in mild to moderate liver disease; avoid in severe liver disease |
| Azathioprine | May need dose reduction |
| Azithromycin | Avoid; jaundice reported |
| Bambuterol | Avoid in severe liver disease |
| Bemiparin | Manufacturer advises avoid in severe liver disease |
| Bendrofluazide | *see* Thiazides and Related Diuretics |
| Bendroflumethiazide (bendrofluazide) | *see* Thiazides and Related Diuretics |
| Benperidol | *see* Antipsychotics |
| Benzthiazide | *see* Thiazides and Related Diuretics |
| Bexarotene | Avoid |
| Bezafibrate | Avoid in severe liver disease |
| Bicalutamide | Increased accumulation possible in moderate to severe hepatic impairment |
| Bisoprolol | Max. 10 mg daily in severe liver impairment |
| Bortezomib | Manufacturer advises caution in mild to moderate hepatic impairment—consider dose reduction; avoid in severe hepatic impairment |
| Bosentan | Avoid in moderate and severe hepatic impairment |
| Bromocriptine | Dose reduction may be necessary |
| Buclizine | Sedation inappropriate in severe liver disease—avoid |
| Budesonide | Plasma-budesonide concentration may increase on oral administration |
| Bumetanide | *see* Loop Diuretics |
| Bupivacaine | *see* Lidocaine |
| Buprenorphine | *see* Opioid Analgesics |
| Bupropion | Manufacturer recommends 150 mg daily; avoid in severe hepatic cirrhosis |
| Buspirone | Reduce dose in mild to moderate liver disease; avoid in severe liver disease |
| Cabergoline | Reduce dose in severe hepatic impairment |
| Calcitriol | Manufacturer of topical calcitriol advises avoid in severe liver disease |
| Candesartan | For hypertension, initially 2 mg once daily in mild or moderate hepatic impairment (no initial dose adjustment necessary in heart failure); avoid in severe hepatic impairment |
| Capecitabine | Manufacturer advises avoid in severe hepatic impairment |
| Carbamazepine | Metabolism impaired in advanced liver disease |
| Carvedilol | Avoid |

Appendix 2

| Drug | Comment |
|---|---|
| Caspofungin | 70 mg on first day then 35 mg once daily in moderate hepatic impairment; no information available for severe hepatic impairment |
| Ceftriaxone | Reduce dose and monitor plasma concentration if both hepatic and severe renal impairment |
| Celecoxib | *see* NSAIDs |
| Cetrorelix | Manufacturer advises avoid in moderate or severe liver impairment |
| Chloral hydrate | Reduce dose in mild to moderate hepatic impairment; avoid in severe impairment; *see also* Anxiolytics and Hypnotics |
| Chlorambucil | Manufacturer advises consider dose reduction in severe hepatic impairment—limited information available |
| Chloramphenicol | Avoid if possible—increased risk of bone-marrow depression; reduce dose and monitor plasma-chloramphenicol concentration |
| Chlordiazepoxide | *see* Anxiolytics and Hypnotics |
| Chlorphenamine (chlorpheniramine) | Sedation inappropriate in severe liver disease—avoid |
| Chlorpheniramine | *see* Chlorphenamine |
| Chlorpromazine | *see* Antipsychotics |
| Chlorpropamide | *see* Sulphonylureas |
| Chlortalidone | *see* Thiazides and Related Diuretics |
| Chlortetracycline | *see* Tetracyclines |
| Ciclosporin | May need dose adjustment |
| Cilazapril | *see* ACE Inhibitors |
| Cilostazol | Avoid in moderate or severe liver disease |
| Cimetidine | Increased risk of confusion; reduce dose |
| Cinacalcet | Manufacturer advises caution in moderate to severe hepatic impairment—monitor closely especially when increasing dose |
| Cinnarizine | Sedation inappropriate in severe liver disease—avoid |
| Ciprofibrate | Avoid in severe liver disease |
| Citalopram | Use doses at lower end of range |
| Cladribine | Regular monitoring recommended |
| Clarithromycin | Hepatic dysfunction including jaundice reported |
| Clavulanic acid [ingredient] | *see* Co-amoxiclav, below and *Timentin*®, p. 743 |
| Clemastine | Sedation inappropriate in severe liver disease—avoid |
| Clindamycin | Reduce dose |
| Clobazam | *see* Anxiolytics and Hypnotics |
| Clomethiazole | *see* Anxiolytics and Hypnotics |
| Clomifene | Avoid in severe liver disease |
| Clomipramine | *see* Antidepressants, Tricyclic (and related) |
| Clonazepam | Reduce dose in mild to moderate impairment; avoid in severe liver impairment; *see also* Anxiolytics and Hypnotics |
| Clopamide | *see* Thiazides and Related Diuretics |
| Clopidogrel | Manufacturer advises caution (risk of bleeding); avoid in severe hepatic impairment |
| Clozapine | Monitor hepatic function regularly; avoid in symptomatic or progressive liver disease or hepatic failure |
| Co-amoxiclav | Monitor liver function in liver disease. Cholestatic jaundice, *see* p. 277 |
| Codeine | *see* Opioid Analgesics |
| Colestyramine | Interferes with absorption of fat-soluble vitamins and may aggravate malabsorption in primary biliary cirrhosis; likely to be ineffective in complete biliary obstruction |
| Contraceptives, oral | Avoid in active liver disease and if history of pruritus or cholestasis during pregnancy |
| Co-trimoxazole | Manufacturer advises avoid in severe liver disease |
| Cyclizine | Sedation inappropriate in severe liver disease—avoid |
| Cyclopenthiazide | *see* Thiazides and Related Diuretics |
| Cyclophosphamide | Reduce dose |
| Cyclosporin | *see* Ciclosporin |
| Cyproheptadine | Sedation inappropriate in severe liver disease—avoid |
| Cyproterone acetate | Dose-related toxicity; *see also* side-effects of cyproterone, section 8.3.4.2 |
| Cytarabine | Reduce dose |
| Dacarbazine | Dose reduction may be required in mild to moderate liver disease; avoid if severe |
| Dalfopristin [ingredient] | *see Synercid*® |
| Dalteparin | *see* Heparin |
| Danaparoid | Use with caution in moderate hepatic impairment (increased risk of bleeding); avoid in severe hepatic impairment unless patient has heparin-induced thrombocytopenia and no alternative |
| Dantrolene | Avoid oral use—may cause severe liver damage; injection may be used in emergency for malignant hyperthermia |
| Darbepoetin | Manufacturer advises caution |
| Daunorubicin | Reduce dose |
| Deferiprone | Manufacturer advises monitor liver function—interrupt treatment if persistent elevation in serum alanine aminotransferase |
| Demeclocycline | *see* Tetracyclines |
| Desflurane | Reduce dose |
| Desogestrel | Avoid; *see also* Contraceptives, Oral |
| Deteclo® | *see* Tetracyclines |
| Dexibuprofen | *see* NSAIDs |
| Dexketoprofen | *see* NSAIDs |
| Dextromethorphan | *see* Opioid Analgesics |
| Dextropropoxyphene | *see* Opioid Analgesics |
| Diamorphine | *see* Opioid Analgesics |

| Drug | Comment |
|---|---|
| Diazepam | *see* Anxiolytics and Hypnotics |
| Diclofenac | *see* NSAIDs |
| Didanosine | Insufficient information but monitor for toxicity |
| Diethylstilbestrol | Avoid; *see also* Contraceptives, Oral |
| Diflunisal | *see* NSAIDs |
| Dihydrocodeine | *see* Opioid Analgesics |
| Diltiazem | Reduce dose |
| Diphenoxylate | *see* Opioid Analgesics |
| Dipipanone | *see* Opioid Analgesics |
| Disodium pamidronate | Manufacturer advises caution in severe hepatic impairment—no information available |
| Disopyramide | Half-life prolonged—may need dose reduction |
| Docetaxel | Monitor liver function—reduce dose according to liver enzymes; avoid in severe hepatic impairment |
| Domperidone | Avoid |
| Dosulepin (dothiepin) | *see* Antidepressants, Tricyclic (and related) |
| Dothiepin | *see* Antidepressants, Tricyclic (and related) |
| Doxazosin | No information—manufacturer advises caution |
| Doxepin | *see* Antidepressants, Tricyclic (and related) |
| Doxorubicin | Reduce dose according to bilirubin concentration |
| Doxycycline | *see* Tetracyclines |
| Drotrecogin alfa (activated) | Avoid in chronic severe liver disease |
| Duloxetine | Manufacturer advises avoid |
| Dutasteride | Manufacturer advises avoid in severe liver impairment—no information available |
| Dydrogesterone | Avoid; *see also* Contraceptives, Oral |
| Efavirenz | In mild to moderate liver disease, monitor for dose related side-effects (e.g. CNS effects) and monitor liver function; avoid in severe hepatic impairment |
| Eformoterol | *see* Formoterol |
| Eletriptan | Manufacturer advises avoid in severe hepatic impairment |
| Enalapril | *see* ACE Inhibitors |
| Enfuvirtide | Manufacturer advises caution—no information available |
| Enoxaparin | *see* Heparin |
| Entacapone | Avoid |
| Epirubicin | Reduce dose according to bilirubin concentration |
| Eplerenone | Avoid in severe liver disease |
| Epoetin | Manufacturers advise caution in chronic hepatic failure |
| Eprosartan | Halve initial dose in mild or moderate liver disease; avoid if severe |
| Eptifibatide | Avoid in severe liver disease—increased risk of bleeding |
| Ergometrine | Avoid in severe liver disease |
| Ergotamine | Avoid in severe liver disease—risk of toxicity increased |
| Erlotinib | Manufacturer advises caution in mild to moderate impairment; avoid in severe impairment |
| Erythromycin | May cause idiosyncratic hepatotoxicity |
| Escitalopram | Initial dose 5 mg daily in mild to moderate hepatic impairment (for 2 weeks), increased to 10 mg daily according to response; manufacturer advises caution in severe hepatic impairment |
| Esomeprazole | In severe liver disease dose should not exceed 20 mg daily |
| Estradiol | Avoid; *see also* Contraceptives, Oral |
| Estramustine | Manufacturer advises caution and regular liver function tests; avoid in severe liver disease |
| Estriol | Avoid; *see also* Contraceptives, Oral |
| Estrone | Avoid; *see also* Contraceptives, Oral |
| Estropipate | Avoid; *see also* Contraceptives, Oral |
| Ethinylestradiol | Avoid; *see also* Contraceptives, Oral |
| Etodolac | *see* NSAIDs |
| Etoposide | Avoid in severe hepatic impairment |
| Etynodiol diacetate | Avoid; *see also* Contraceptives, Oral |
| Exemestane | Manufacturer advises caution |
| Ezetimibe | Avoid in moderate and severe hepatic impairment—may accumulate |
| Famciclovir | Usual dose in well compensated liver disease (information not available on decompensated) |
| Felodipine | Reduce dose |
| Fenbufen | *see* NSAIDs |
| Fenofibrate | Avoid in severe liver disease |
| Fenoprofen | *see* NSAIDs |
| Fentanyl | *see* Opioid Analgesics |
| Flecainide | Avoid (or reduce dose) in severe liver disease |
| Flucloxacillin | Caution in hepatic impairment (risk of cholestatic jaundice and hepatitis, *see* p. 275) |
| Fluconazole | Toxicity with related drugs |
| Fluorouracil | Manufacturer advises caution |
| Fluoxetine | *see* Antidepressants, SSRI |
| Flupentixol | *see* Antipsychotics |
| Fluphenazine | *see* Antipsychotics |
| Flurazepam | *see* Anxiolytics and Hypnotics |
| Flurbiprofen | *see* NSAIDs |
| Flutamide | Use with caution (hepatotoxic) |
| Fluvastatin | *see* Statins |
| Fluvoxamine | *see* Antidepressants, SSRI |
| Fondaparinux sodium | Caution in severe hepatic impairment (increased risk of bleeding) |
| Formoterol (eformoterol) | Metabolism possibly reduced in severe cirrhosis |

| Drug | Comment |
|---|---|
| Fosamprenavir | Manufacturer advises caution in mild to moderate hepatic impairment; avoid in severe hepatic impairment |
| Fosinopril | *see* ACE Inhibitors |
| Fosphenytoin | Consider 10–25% reduction in dose or infusion rate (except initial dose for status epilepticus) |
| Frovatriptan | Avoid in severe hepatic impairment |
| Frusemide | *see* Loop Diuretics |
| Fulvestrant | Manufacturer advises caution in mild to moderate hepatic impairment; avoid in severe hepatic impairment |
| Furosemide (frusemide) | *see* Loop Diuretics |
| Fusidic acid | *see* Sodium Fusidate |
| Galantamine | Reduce dose in moderate hepatic impairment; avoid in severe impairment |
| Ganirelix | Manufacturer advises avoid in moderate or severe hepatic impairment |
| Gemcitabine | Manufacturer advises caution |
| Gemfibrozil | Avoid in liver disease |
| Gestodene | Avoid; *see also* Contraceptives, Oral |
| Gestrinone | Avoid in severe liver disease |
| Glibenclamide | *see* Sulphonylureas |
| Gliclazide | *see* Sulphonylureas |
| Glimepiride | Manufacturer advises avoid in severe hepatic impairment |
| Glipizide | *see* Sulphonylureas |
| Gliquidone | *see* Sulphonylureas |
| Glyceryl trinitrate | *see* Nitrates |
| Griseofulvin | Avoid in severe liver disease |
| Haloperidol | *see* Antipsychotics |
| Halothane | Avoid if history of unexplained pyrexia or jaundice following previous exposure to halothane |
| Heparin | Reduce dose in severe liver disease |
| Hydralazine | Reduce dose |
| Hydrochlorothiazide | *see* Thiazides and Related Diuretics |
| Hydroflumethiazide | *see* Thiazides and Related Diuretics |
| Hydromorphone | *see* Opioid Analgesics |
| Hydroxyzine | Sedation inappropriate in severe liver disease—avoid |
| Hyoscine hydrobromide | Manufacturer advises caution |
| Hypnotics | *see* Anxiolytics and Hypnotics |
| Ibuprofen | *see* NSAIDs |
| Idarubicin | Reduce dose according to bilirubin concentration |
| Ifosfamide | Avoid |
| Iloprost | Elimination reduced in hepatic impairment—initially 2.5 micrograms no more frequently than every 3 hours (max. 6 times daily), adjusted according to response (consult product literature) |
| Imidapril | *see* ACE Inhibitors |
| Imipramine | *see* Antidepressants, Tricyclic (and related) |
| Indapamide | *see* Thiazides and Related Diuretics |
| Indinavir | Increased risk of nephrolithiasis; reduce dose to 600 mg every 8 hours in mild to moderate hepatic impairment; not studied in severe impairment |
| Indometacin | *see* NSAIDs |
| Indoramin | Manufacturer advises caution |
| Interferon alfa | Close monitoring in mild to moderate hepatic impairment; avoid if severe |
| Interferon beta | Avoid in decompensated liver disease |
| Interferon gamma-1b | Manufacturer advises caution in severe liver disease |
| Irinotecan | Monitor closely for neutropenia if plasma-bilirubin concentration up to 1.5 times upper limit of normal range; avoid if plasma-bilirubin concentration greater than 1.5 times upper limit of normal range |
| Iron dextran | Avoid in severe hepatic impairment |
| Iron sucrose | Avoid |
| Isocarboxazid | *see* Antidepressants, MAOI |
| Isometheptene [ingredient] | *see* *Midrid®* |
| Isoniazid | Use with caution; monitor liver function regularly and particularly frequently in the first 2 months; *see also* p. 300 |
| Isosorbide dinitrate | *see* Nitrates |
| Isosorbide mononitrate | *see* Nitrates |
| Isotretinoin | Avoid—further impairment of liver function may occur |
| Isradipine | Reduce dose |
| Itraconazole | Use only if potential benefit outweighs risk of hepatotoxicity (*see* p. 312); dose reduction may be necessary |
| Ivabradine | Manufacturer advises caution in moderate hepatic impairment; avoid in severe hepatic impairment |
| *Kaletra®* | Avoid oral solution because of propylene glycol content; manufacturer advises avoid capsules in severe hepatic impairment |
| Ketoconazole | Avoid |
| Ketoprofen | *see* NSAIDs |
| Ketorolac | *see* NSAIDs |
| Ketotifen | Sedation inappropriate in severe liver disease—avoid |
| Labetalol | Avoid—severe hepatocellular injury reported |
| Lacidipine | Antihypertensive effect possibly increased |
| Lamotrigine | Halve dose in moderate liver disease; quarter dose in severe liver disease |
| Lansoprazole | In severe liver disease dose should not exceed 30 mg daily |

| Drug | Comment |
|---|---|
| Leflunomide | Avoid—active metabolite may accumulate |
| Lepirudin | No information—manufacturer advises that cirrhosis may affect renal excretion |
| Lercanidipine | Avoid in severe liver disease |
| Levetiracetam | Halve dose in severe hepatic impairment if creatinine clearance less than 70 mL/minute |
| Levobupivacaine | Manufacturer advises caution in liver disease |
| Levomepromazine (methotrimeprazine) | *see* Antipsychotics |
| Levonorgestrel | Avoid; *see also* Contraceptives, Oral |
| Lidocaine (lignocaine) | Manufacturer advises caution—increased risk of side-effects |
| Lignocaine | *see* Lidocaine |
| Linezolid | In severe hepatic impairment manufacturer advises use only if potential benefit outweighs risk |
| Lofepramine | *see* Antidepressants, Tricyclic (and related) |
| Loop diuretics | Hypokalaemia may precipitate coma (use potassium-sparing diuretic to prevent this); increased risk of hypomagnesaemia in alcoholic cirrhosis |
| Lopinavir [ingredient] | *see Kaletra®* |
| Loprazolam | *see* Anxiolytics and Hypnotics |
| Lorazepam | *see* Anxiolytics and Hypnotics |
| Lormetazepam | *see* Anxiolytics and Hypnotics |
| Losartan | Consider lower dose |
| Lumefantrine [ingredient] | *see Riamet®* |
| Lumiracoxib | *see* NSAIDs |
| Lymecycline | *see* Tetracyclines |
| Magnesium salts | Avoid in hepatic coma if risk of renal failure |
| Maprotiline | *see* Antidepressants, Tricyclic (and related) |
| Meclozine | Sedation inappropriate in severe liver disease—avoid |
| Medroxyprogesterone | Avoid; *see also* Contraceptives, Oral |
| Mefenamic acid | *see* NSAIDs |
| Mefloquine | Avoid for prophylaxis in severe liver disease |
| Megestrol | Avoid; *see also* Contraceptives, Oral |
| Meloxicam | *see* NSAIDs |
| Meprobamate | *see* Anxiolytics and Hypnotics |
| Meptazinol | *see* Opioid Analgesics |
| Mercaptopurine | May need dose reduction |
| Meropenem | Monitor transaminase and bilirubin concentrations |
| Mesterolone | *see* Androgens |
| Mestranol | Avoid; *see also* Contraceptives, Oral |
| Metformin | Withdraw if tissue hypoxia likely—manufacturers advise avoid |
| Methadone | *see* Opioid Analgesics |
| Methenamine | Avoid |
| Methionine | May precipitate coma |
| Methocarbamol | Manufacturer advises caution; half-life may be prolonged |
| Methotrexate | Dose-related toxicity—avoid in non-malignant conditions (e.g. psoriasis); avoid for all indications in severe hepatic impairment |
| Methotrimeprazine | *see* Antipsychotics |
| Methoxsalen | Avoid or reduce dose |
| Methyldopa | Manufacturer advises caution in history of liver disease; avoid in active liver disease |
| Methysergide | Avoid |
| Metoclopramide | Reduce dose |
| Metolazone | *see* Thiazides and Related Diuretics |
| Metoprolol | Reduce oral dose |
| Metronidazole | In severe liver disease reduce total daily dose to one-third, and give once daily |
| Mexiletine | Avoid (or reduce dose) in severe liver disease |
| Mianserin | *see* Antidepressants, Tricyclic (and related) |
| Miconazole | Avoid |
| Midazolam | *see* Anxiolytics and Hypnotics |
| *Midrid®* | Avoid in severe liver disease; *see also* Paracetamol |
| Miglustat | No information available—manufacturer advises caution |
| Minocycline | *see* Tetracyclines |
| Mirtazapine | Manufacturer advises caution |
| Mitotane | Manufacturer advises caution in mild to moderate impairment—monitoring of plasma-mitotane concentration recommended; avoid in severe impairment |
| Mitoxantrone | Manufacturer advises caution in severe hepatic impairment |
| Mivacurium | Reduce dose in severe liver impairment |
| Mizolastine | Manufacturer recommends avoid in significant hepatic impairment |
| Moclobemide | Reduce dose in severe liver disease |
| Modafinil | Halve dose in severe liver disease |
| Moexipril | *see* ACE Inhibitors |
| Morphine | *see* Opioid Analgesics |
| Moxifloxacin | Manufacturer advises avoid in severe hepatic impairment |
| Moxonidine | Avoid in severe liver disease |
| Nabilone | Avoid in severe liver disease |
| Nabumetone | *see* NSAIDs |
| Nalbuphine | *see* Opioid Analgesics |
| Nalidixic acid | Manufacturer advises caution in liver disease |
| Nandrolone | *see* Anabolic Steroids |
| Naproxen | *see* NSAIDs |
| Naratriptan | Max. 2.5 mg in 24 hours in moderate hepatic impairment; avoid if severe |
| Nateglinide | Manufacturer advises caution in moderate hepatic impairment; avoid in severe impairment—no information available |

| Drug | Comment |
|---|---|
| Nebivolol | No information available—manufacturer advises avoid |
| Nelfinavir | No information available—manufacturer advises caution |
| Neomycin | Absorbed from gastro-intestinal tract in liver disease—increased risk of ototoxicity |
| Nevirapine | Manufacturer advises caution in moderate hepatic impairment; avoid in severe hepatic impairment; *see also* p. 321 |
| Nicardipine | Half-life prolonged in severe hepatic impairment—may need dose reduction |
| Nicotine | Manufacturers advise caution in moderate to severe hepatic impairment |
| Nicotinic acid | Manufacturer advises monitor liver function in mild to moderate hepatic impairment and avoid in severe impairment; discontinue if severe abnormalities in liver function tests |
| Nicoumalone | *see* Anticoagulants, Oral |
| Nifedipine | Reduce dose in severe liver disease |
| Nimodipine | Elimination reduced in cirrhosis—monitor blood pressure |
| Nisoldipine | Formulation not suitable in hepatic impairment |
| Nitrates | Caution in severe hepatic impairment |
| Nitrazepam | *see* Anxiolytics and Hypnotics |
| Nitrofurantoin | Cholestatic jaundice and chronic active hepatitis reported |
| Nitroprusside | *see* Sodium Nitroprusside |
| Nizatidine | Manufacturer advises caution |
| Norethisterone | Avoid; *see also* Contraceptives, Oral |
| Norgestimate | Avoid; *see also* Contraceptives, Oral |
| Norgestrel | Avoid; *see also* Contraceptives, Oral |
| Nortriptyline | *see* Antidepressants, Tricyclic (and related) |
| NSAIDs | Increased risk of gastro-intestinal bleeding and can cause fluid retention; avoid in severe liver disease; aceclofenac, initially 100 mg daily; celecoxib, halve initial dose in moderate liver disease; etoricoxib, max. 60 mg daily in mild hepatic impairment (max. 60 mg on alternate days in moderate hepatic impairment); parecoxib, halve dose in moderate hepatic impairment (max. 40 mg daily) |
| Oestrogens | Avoid; *see also* Contraceptives, Oral |
| Ofloxacin | Elimination may be reduced in severe hepatic impairment |
| Olanzapine | Consider initial dose of 5 mg daily |
| Olmesartan | No information available—manufacturer advises avoid |
| Omalizumab | Manufacturer advises caution—no information available |

| Drug | Comment |
|---|---|
| Omega-3-acid ethyl esters | Monitor liver function |
| Omeprazole | In liver disease not more than 20 mg daily should be needed |
| Ondansetron | Reduce dose; not more than 8 mg daily in severe liver disease |
| Opioid analgesics | Avoid or reduce dose—may precipitate coma |
| Oral contraceptives | *see* Contraceptives, Oral |
| Oxazepam | *see* Anxiolytics and Hypnotics |
| Oxcarbazepine | Manufacturer advises caution in severe hepatic impairment—no information available |
| Oxprenolol | Reduce dose |
| Oxybutynin | Manufacturer advises caution |
| Oxycodone | *see* Opioid Analgesics |
| Oxytetracycline | *see* Tetracyclines |
| Paclitaxel | Avoid in severe liver disease |
| Pancuronium | Possibly slower onset, higher dose requirement and prolonged recovery time |
| Pantoprazole | Max. 20 mg daily in severe hepatic impairment and cirrhosis—monitor liver function (discontinue if deterioration) |
| Papaveretum | *see* Opioid Analgesics |
| Paracetamol | Dose-related toxicity—avoid large doses |
| Parecoxib | *see* NSAIDs |
| Paroxetine | *see* Antidepressants, SSRI |
| Peginterferon alfa | Avoid in severe hepatic impairment |
| Pentazocine | *see* Opioid Analgesics |
| Pericyazine | *see* Antipsychotics |
| Perindopril | *see* ACE Inhibitors |
| Perphenazine | *see* Antipsychotics |
| Pethidine | *see* Opioid Analgesics |
| Phenazocine | *see* Opioid Analgesics |
| Phenelzine | *see* Antidepressants, MAOI |
| Phenindione | *see* Anticoagulants, Oral |
| Phenobarbital | May precipitate coma |
| Phenothiazines | *see* Antipsychotics |
| Phenytoin | Reduce dose to avoid toxicity |
| Pholcodine | *see* Opioid Analgesics |
| Pilocarpine | Reduce initial oral dose in moderate or severe cirrhosis |
| Pimozide | *see* Antipsychotics |
| Pioglitazone | Avoid |
| Piperazine | Manufacturer advises avoid |
| Pipotiazine | *see* Antipsychotics |
| Piracetam | Avoid |
| Piroxicam | *see* NSAIDs |
| Pravastatin | *see* Statins |
| Prazosin | Initially 500 micrograms daily; increased with caution |
| Prednisolone | Side-effects more common |
| Primidone | Reduce dose; may precipitate coma |
| Procainamide | Avoid or reduce dose |
| Procarbazine | Avoid in severe hepatic impairment |
| Prochlorperazine | *see* Antipsychotics |
| Progesterone | Avoid; *see also* Contraceptives, Oral |
| Progestogens | Avoid; *see also* Contraceptives, Oral |

| Drug | Comment |
|---|---|
| Promazine | *see* Antipsychotics |
| Promethazine | Avoid—may precipitate coma in severe liver disease; hepatotoxic |
| Propafenone | Reduce dose |
| Propantheline | Manufacturer advises caution |
| Propiverine | Avoid |
| Propranolol | Reduce oral dose |
| Propylthiouracil | Reduce dose |
| Pyrazinamide | Monitor hepatic function—idiosyncratic hepatotoxicity more common; avoid in severe hepatic impairment; *see also* p. 300 |
| Pyrimethamine | Manufacturer advises caution |
| Quetiapine | Manufacturer advises initial dose of 25 mg daily, increased daily in steps of 25–50 mg |
| Quinagolide | Manufacturer advises avoid—no information available |
| Quinapril | *see* ACE Inhibitors |
| Quinupristin [ingredient] | *see Synercid®* |
| Rabeprazole | Manufacturer advises caution in severe hepatic dysfunction |
| Raloxifene | Manufacturer advises avoid |
| Raltitrexed | Caution in mild or moderate disease; avoid if severe |
| Ramipril | *see* ACE Inhibitors |
| Rasagiline | Manufacturer advises caution in mild hepatic impairment; avoid in moderate to severe impairment |
| Reboxetine | Initial dose 2 mg twice daily, increased according to tolerance |
| Remifentanil | *see* Opioid Analgesics |
| Repaglinide | Manufacturer advises avoid in severe liver disease |
| Reteplase | Avoid in severe hepatic impairment |
| Reviparin | Manufacturer advises avoid in severe hepatic impairment |
| *Riamet®* | Manufacturer advises caution in severe hepatic impairment—monitor ECG and plasma potassium concentration |
| Ribavirin | No dosage adjustment required; avoid oral administration in severe hepatic dysfunction or decompensated cirrhosis |
| Rifabutin | Reduce dose in severe hepatic impairment |
| Rifampicin | Impaired elimination; monitor liver function; avoid or do not exceed 8 mg/kg daily; *see also* p. 301 |
| Riluzole | Avoid |
| Risperidone | Manufacturer advises initial oral dose of 500 micrograms twice daily increased in steps of 500 micrograms twice daily to 1–2 mg twice daily; if an oral dose of at least 2 mg daily tolerated, 25 mg as a depot injection can be given every 2 weeks |
| Ritonavir | Avoid in severe hepatic impairment |
| Rivastigmine | No information available—manufacturer advises avoid in severe liver disease |
| Rizatriptan | Reduce dose to 5 mg in mild to moderate liver disease; avoid in severe liver disease |
| Rocuronium | Reduce dose |
| Ropinirole | Avoid in severe hepatic impairment |
| Ropivacaine | Manufacturer advises caution in severe liver disease |
| Rosiglitazone | Avoid |
| Rosuvastatin | *see* Statins |
| Saquinavir | Manufacturer advises caution in moderate hepatic impairment; avoid in severe impairment |
| Sertindole | Slower titration and lower maintenance dose in mild to moderate hepatic impairment; avoid in severe hepatic impairment; *see also* Antipsychotics |
| Sertraline | *see* Antidepressants, SSRI |
| Sibutramine | Increased plasma-sibutramine concentration; manufacturer advises caution in mild to moderate hepatic impairment; avoid if severe impairment |
| Sildenafil | Initial dose 25 mg; manufacturer advises avoid in severe hepatic impairment |
| Simvastatin | *see* Statins |
| Sirolimus | Monitor blood-sirolimus trough concentration |
| Sodium aurothiomalate | Caution in mild to moderate liver disease; avoid in severe liver disease |
| Sodium bicarbonate | *see* Antacids |
| Sodium fusidate | Impaired biliary excretion; possibly increased risk of hepatotoxicity; avoid or reduce dose |
| Sodium nitroprusside | Avoid in severe liver disease |
| Sodium phenylbutyrate | Manufacturer advises caution |
| Sodium valproate | *see* Valproate |
| Solifenacin | Max. 5 mg daily in moderate liver disease; avoid if severe |
| Statins | Avoid in active liver disease or unexplained persistent elevations in serum transaminases |
| Stilboestrol (diethylstilbestrol) | Avoid; *see also* Contraceptives, Oral |
| Streptokinase | Avoid in severe hepatic impairment |
| Sulindac | *see* NSAIDs |
| Sulphonylureas | Increased risk of hypoglycaemia in severe liver disease; avoid or use small dose; can produce jaundice; *see also* Glimepiride |
| Sulpiride | *see* Antipsychotics |
| Sumatriptan | Manufacturer advises 50 mg oral dose in hepatic impairment; avoid in severe hepatic impairment |

| Drug | Comment |
|---|---|
| Suxamethonium | Prolonged apnoea may occur in severe liver disease due to reduced hepatic synthesis of pseudocholinesterase |
| *Synercid®* | Consider reducing dose to 5 mg/kg every 8 hours in moderate hepatic impairment, adjusted according to clinical response; avoid in severe hepatic impairment or if plasma-bilirubin concentration greater than 3 times upper limit of reference range |
| Tacrolimus | Reduce dose |
| Tadalafil | Max. dose 10 mg; manufacturer advises monitor patient in severe hepatic impairment |
| Tamsulosin | Avoid in severe hepatic impairment |
| Tegafur with uracil | *see Uftoral®* |
| Telmisartan | 20–40 mg once daily in mild or moderate impairment; avoid in severe hepatic impairment or biliary obstruction |
| Temazepam | *see* Anxiolytics and Hypnotics |
| Tenecteplase | Avoid in severe hepatic impairment |
| Tenoxicam | *see* NSAIDs |
| Terbinafine | Manufacturer advises avoid—elimination reduced |
| Testosterone and esters | *see* Androgens |
| Tetracyclines | Avoid (or use with caution); tetracycline, demeclocycline, and *Deteclo®* max. 1 g daily in divided doses |
| Theophylline | Reduce dose |
| Thiazides and related diuretics | Avoid in severe liver disease; hypokalaemia may precipitate coma (potassium-sparing diuretic can prevent); increased risk of hypomagnesaemia in alcoholic cirrhosis |
| Thiopental | Reduce dose for induction in severe liver disease |
| Tiagabine | Maintenance dose 5–10 mg 1–2 times daily initially in mild to moderate hepatic impairment; avoid in severe impairment |
| Tiaprofenic acid | *see* NSAIDs |
| Tibolone | Avoid in severe liver disease |
| Ticarcillin [ingredient] | *see* Timentin® |
| *Timentin®* | Cholestatic jaundice, *see* under Co-amoxiclav p. 277 |
| Timolol | Dose reduction may be necessary |
| Tinzaparin | *see* Heparin |
| Tipranavir | Manufacturer advises monitor liver function in mild hepatic impairment (*see* p. 320); avoid in moderate or severe hepatic impairment —no information available |
| Tirofiban | Caution in mild to moderate liver disease; avoid in severe liver disease—increased risk of bleeding |
| Tizanidine | Avoid in severe liver disease |
| Tolbutamide | *see* Sulphonylureas |
| Tolcapone | Avoid |
| Tolfenamic acid | *see* NSAIDs |
| Tolterodine | Reduce dose to 1 mg twice daily |
| Topiramate | Use with caution in hepatic impairment—clearance may be decreased |
| Topotecan | Avoid in severe hepatic impairment |
| Torasemide | *see* Loop Diuretics |
| Toremifene | Elimination decreased in hepatic impairment—avoid if severe |
| Tramadol | *see* Opioid Analgesics |
| Trandolapril | *see* ACE Inhibitors |
| Tranylcypromine | *see* Antidepressants, MAOI |
| Trazodone | *see* Antidepressants, Tricyclic (and related) |
| Tretinoin (oral) | Reduce dose |
| Tribavirin | *see* Ribavirin |
| Triclofos | *see* Anxiolytics and Hypnotics |
| Trifluoperazine | *see* Antipsychotics |
| Trimeprazine | *see* Alimemazine |
| Trimetrexate | Manufacturer advises caution; interrupt treatment if severe abnormalities in liver function tests (consult product literature) |
| Trimipramine | *see* Antidepressants, Tricyclic (and related) |
| Trospium | Manufacturer advises avoid—no information available |
| *Uftoral®* | Manufacturer advises monitor liver function in mild to moderate hepatic impairment and avoid in severe impairment |
| Ursodeoxycholic acid | Avoid in chronic liver disease (but used in primary biliary cirrhosis) |
| Valaciclovir | Manufacturer advises caution with high doses used for preventing cytomegalovirus disease—no information available |
| Valproate | Avoid if possible—hepatotoxicity and hepatic failure may occasionally occur (usually in first 6 months); *see also* p. 245 |
| Valproic acid | *see* Valproate |
| Valsartan | Halve dose in mild to moderate hepatic impairment; avoid if severe |
| Vardenafil | Initial dose 5 mg in mild to moderate hepatic impairment, increased subsequently according to response (max. 10 mg in moderate hepatic impairment); manufacturer advises avoid in severe hepatic impairment |
| Venlafaxine | Halve dose in moderate hepatic impairment; avoid if severe |
| Verapamil | Reduce oral dose |
| Verteporfin | Avoid in severe hepatic impairment |
| Vinblastine | Dose reduction may be necessary |
| Vincristine | Dose reduction may be necessary |
| Vindesine | Dose reduction may be necessary |

| Drug | Comment |
|---|---|
| Vinorelbine | Dose reduction may be required in significant hepatic impairment |
| Voriconazole | In mild to moderate hepatic cirrhosis use normal loading dose then halve normal maintenance dose; no information available for severe hepatic cirrhosis—manufacturer advises use only if potential benefit outweighs risk |
| Warfarin | *see* Anticoagulants, Oral |
| Xipamide | *see* Thiazides and Related Diuretics |
| Zafirlukast | Manufacturer advises avoid |
| Zalcitabine | Further impairment of liver function may occur |
| Zaleplon | *see* Anxiolytics and Hypnotics |
| Zidovudine | Accumulation may occur |
| Zoledronic acid | Manufacturer advises caution in severe hepatic impairment—limited information available |
| Zolmitriptan | Max. 5 mg in 24 hours in moderate or severe hepatic impairment |
| Zolpidem | *see* Anxiolytics and Hypnotics |
| Zonisamide | Initially, increase dose at 2-week intervals if mild or moderate hepatic impairment; avoid in severe impairment |
| Zopiclone | *see* Anxiolytics and Hypnotics |
| Zotepine | Initial dose 25 mg twice daily, increased gradually according to response (max. 75 mg twice daily); monitor liver function at weekly intervals for first 3 months |
| Zuclopenthixol | *see* Antipsychotics |

# A3 Renal impairment

The use of drugs in patients with reduced renal function can give rise to problems for several reasons:

- failure to excrete a drug or its metabolites may produce toxicity;
- sensitivity to some drugs is increased even if elimination is unimpaired;
- many side-effects are tolerated poorly by patients in renal failure;
- some drugs cease to be effective when renal function is reduced.

Many of these problems can be avoided by reducing the dose or by using alternative drugs.

## Principles of dose adjustment in renal impairment

The level of renal function below which the dose of a drug must be reduced depends on whether the drug is eliminated entirely by renal excretion or is partly metabolised, and on how toxic it is.

For many drugs with only minor or no dose-related side-effects very precise modification of the dose regimen is unnecessary and a simple scheme for dose reduction is sufficient.

For more toxic drugs with a small safety margin dose regimens based on glomerular filtration rate should be used. For those where both efficacy and toxicity are closely related to plasma concentrations recommended regimens should be seen only as a guide to initial treatment; subsequent treatment must be adjusted according to clinical response and plasma concentration.

The total daily maintenance dose of a drug can be reduced either by reducing the size of the individual doses or by increasing the interval between doses. For some drugs, if the size of the maintenance dose is reduced it will be important to give a loading dose if an immediate effect is required. This is because when a patient is given a regular dose of any drug it takes more than five times the half-life to achieve steady-state plasma concentrations. As the plasma half-life of drugs excreted by the kidney is prolonged in renal failure it may take many days for the reduced dosage to achieve a therapeutic plasma concentration. The loading dose should usually be the same size as the initial dose for a patient with normal renal function.

**Nephrotoxic drugs** should, if possible, be avoided in patients with renal disease because the consequences of nephrotoxicity are likely to be more serious when the renal reserve is already reduced.

## Use of dosage table

Dose recommendations are based on the severity of renal impairment. This is expressed in terms of glomerular filtration rate (GFR), usually measured by the **creatinine clearance** (best calculated from a 24-hour urine collection). The serum-creatinine concentration is sometimes used instead as a measure of renal function but is only a **rough guide** even when corrected for age, weight, and sex. Nomograms are available for making the correction and should be used where accuracy is important.

For *prescribing purposes* renal impairment is arbitrarily divided into 3 grades (definitions vary for grades of renal impairment; therefore, where the product literature does not correspond with this grading, values for creatinine clearance or another measure of renal function are included):

**Grades of renal impairment**

| *Grade* | *GFR* | *Serum creatinine (approx.)* (but see above) |
|---|---|---|
| Mild | 20–50 mL/minute | 150–300 micromol/litre |
| Moderate | 10–20 mL/minute | 300–700 micromol/litre |
| Severe | < 10 mL/minute | > 700 micromol/litre |

**Note** Conversion factors are:
Litres/24 hours = mL/minute × 1.44
mL/minute = Litres/24 hours × 0.69

**Dialysis**
For prescribing in patients on continuous ambulatory peritoneal dialysis (CAPD) or haemodialysis, consult specialist literature.

Renal function declines with age; many elderly patients have a glomerular filtration rate below 50 mL/minute which, because of reduced muscle mass, may not be indicated by a raised serum creatinine. It is wise to assume at least mild impairment of renal function when prescribing for the elderly.

The following table may be used as a guide to drugs which are known to require a reduction in dose in renal impairment, and to those which are potentially harmful or are ineffective. Drug prescribing should be kept to the minimum in all patients with severe renal disease.

If even mild renal impairment is considered likely on clinical grounds, renal function should be checked before prescribing **any** drug which requires dose modification.



## Table of drugs to be avoided or used with caution in renal impairment

Products introduced or amended since publication of BNF No.50 (September 2005) are underlined.

| Drug and degree of impairment | Comment |
|---|---|
| Abacavir | |
| Severe | Manufacturer advises avoid |
| Abciximab | |
| Severe | Avoid—increased risk of bleeding |
| Acamprosate | |
| Mild | Avoid; excreted in urine |

| Drug and degree of impairment | Comment |
|---|---|
| Acarbose | |
| Moderate to severe | Manufacturer advises avoid—no information available |
| ACE inhibitors | |
| Mild to moderate | Use with caution and monitor response (see also p. 97). Hyperkalaemia and other side-effects more common. *Initial doses*: captopril 12.5 mg twice daily, cilazapril 500 micrograms once daily, enalapril 2.5 mg once daily if creatinine clearance less than 30 mL/minute, imidapril 2.5 mg once daily (avoid if creatinine clearance less than 30 mL/minute), lisinopril 2.5–5 mg, moexipril 3.75 mg once daily, perindopril 2 mg once daily (2 mg once daily on alternate days in moderate impairment), quinapril 2.5 mg once daily, ramipril 1.25 mg once daily, trandolapril 500 micrograms once daily (max. 2 mg daily if creatinine clearance less than 10 mL/minute) |
| Acebutolol | *see* Beta-blockers |
| Aceclofenac | *see* NSAIDs |
| Acemetacin | *see* NSAIDs |
| Acenocoumarol (nicoumalone) | *see* Anticoagulants, Oral |
| Acetazolamide | |
| Mild | Avoid; metabolic acidosis |
| Aciclovir | Use normal intravenous dose every 12 hours if creatinine clearance 25–50 mL/minute (every 24 hours if creatinine clearance 10–25 mL/minute); consult product literature for intravenous dose if creatinine clearance less than 10 mL/minute; for herpes zoster, use normal oral dose every 8 hours if creatinine clearance 10–25 mL/minute (every 12 hours if creatinine clearance less than 10 mL/minute); for herpes simplex, use normal oral dose every 12 hours if creatinine clearance less than 10 mL/minute |
| Acipimox | Reduce dose if creatinine clearance 30–60 mL/minute; avoid if creatinine clearance less than 30 mL/minute |
| Acitretin | |
| Mild | Avoid; increased risk of toxicity |
| Acrivastine | |
| Moderate | Avoid; excreted by kidney |
| Adefovir dipivoxil | |
| Mild | 10 mg every 48 hours |
| Moderate | 10 mg every 72 hours |
| Severe | No information available |
| Alendronic acid | |
| Mild | Manufacturer advises avoid if creatinine clearance less than 35 mL/minute |
| Alfentanil | *see* Opioid Analgesics |
| Alfuzosin | Start at 2.5 mg twice daily and adjust according to response |
| Alimemazine (trimeprazine) | |
| Severe | Avoid |
| Allopurinol | |
| Moderate | 100–200 mg daily; increased toxicity; rashes; also monitor liver function |
| Severe | 100 mg on alternate days (max. 100 mg daily); also monitor liver function |
| Almotriptan | |
| Severe | Max. 12.5 mg in 24 hours |
| Alprazolam | *see* Anxiolytics and Hypnotics |
| Alteplase | |
| Moderate | Risk of hyperkalaemia |
| Aluminium salts | |
| Severe | Aluminium is absorbed and may accumulate<br>**Note** Absorption of aluminium from aluminium salts is increased by citrates, which are contained in many effervescent preparations (such as effervescent analgesics) |
| Amantadine | Reduce dose; avoid if creatinine clearance less than 15 mL/minute (60 mL/minute in elderly) |
| Amfebutamone | *see* Bupropion |
| Amikacin | *see* Aminoglycosides |
| Amiloride | *see* Potassium-sparing Diuretics |
| Aminoglycosides | |
| Mild | Reduce dose; monitor serum concentrations; *see also* section 5.1.4 |
| Amisulpride | Halve dose if creatinine clearance 30–60 mL/minute; use one-third dose if creatinine clearance 10–30 mL/minute; manufacturers advise intermittent treatment with a reduced dose if creatinine clearance less than 10 mL/minute |
| Amoxicillin | |
| Mild to moderate | Risk of crystalluria with high doses (particularly during parenteral therapy) |
| Severe | Reduce dose; rashes more common and risk of crystalluria |
| Amphotericin | |
| Mild | Use only if no alternative; nephrotoxicity may be reduced with use of lipid formulations |
| Ampicillin | |
| Severe | Reduce dose; rashes more common |
| Amprenavir | |
| Mild to moderate | Use oral solution with caution due to high propylene glycol content |
| Severe | Avoid oral solution |
| Amsacrine | Reduce dose |
| Anagrelide | Manufacturer advises avoid if creatinine clearance less than 50 mL/minute |

Appendix 3

| Drug and degree of impairment | Comment |
|---|---|
| Anakinra | Manufacturer advises caution if creatinine clearance 30–50 mL/minute; avoid if creatinine clearance less than 30 mL/minute |
| Analgesics | *see* Opioid Analgesics and NSAIDs |
| Anastrozole | |
| Moderate to severe | Avoid—no information available |
| *Angeliq®* | |
| Severe | Manufacturer advises avoid |
| Anticoagulants, oral | |
| Severe | Avoid |
| Antipsychotics | |
| Severe | Start with small doses; increased cerebral sensitivity; *see also* Amisulpride, Clozapine, Olanzapine, Quetiapine, Risperidone and Sulpiride |
| Anxiolytics and hypnotics | |
| Severe | Start with small doses; increased cerebral sensitivity; *see also* chloral hydrate |
| Apomorphine | |
| Severe | Use with caution; max. sublingual dose 2 mg |
| Arsenic trioxide | Manufacturer advises caution |
| Artemether [ingredient] | *see Riamet®* |
| Aspirin | |
| Severe | Avoid; sodium and water retention; deterioration in renal function; increased risk of gastro-intestinal bleeding |
| Atenolol | *see* Beta-blockers |
| Atosiban | No information available |
| Atovaquone | Manufacturer advises caution—monitor more closely |
| Auranofin | *see* Sodium Aurothiomalate |
| Azathioprine | |
| Severe | Reduce dose |
| Aztreonam | If creatinine clearance 10–30 mL/minute, usual initial dose, then half normal dose; if creatinine clearance less than 10 mL/minute usual initial dose, then one-quarter normal dose |
| Baclofen | |
| Mild | Use smaller doses (e.g. 5 mg daily); excreted by kidney |
| Balsalazide | |
| Moderate to severe | Manufacturer advises avoid |
| Bambuterol | |
| Mild | Reduce dose |
| Barbiturates | |
| Severe | Reduce dose; *see also* Phenobarbital |
| Bemiparin | *see* Heparin |
| Bendrofluazide | *see* Thiazides and Related Diuretics |
| Bendroflumethiazide (bendrofluazide) | *see* Thiazides and Related Diuretics |
| Benperidol | *see* Antipsychotics |
| Benzodiazepines | *see* Anxiolytics and Hypnotics |
| Benzylpenicillin | |
| Moderate to severe | Max. 6 g daily; neurotoxicity—high doses may cause convulsions |
| Beta-blockers | |
| Mild | Atenolol 50 mg daily (10 mg on alternate days *intravenously*) if creatinine clearance 15–35 mL/minute; start with 2.5 mg of nebivolol; reduce dose of celiprolol if creatinine clearance less than 40 mL/minute; halve dose of sotalol if creatinine clearance 30–60 mL/minute |
| Moderate | Start with small dose of acebutolol (active metabolite accumulates); reduce dose of atenolol (see above), bisoprolol, nadolol, pindolol (all excreted unchanged); avoid celiprolol if creatinine clearance less than 15 mL/minute; use one-quarter normal dose of sotalol if creatinine clearance 10–30 mL/minute |
| Severe | Start with small dose; may reduce renal blood flow and adversely affect renal function in severe impairment; manufacturer advises avoid celiprolol and sotalol; atenolol 25 mg daily (10 mg every 4 days *intravenously*) if creatinine clearance less than 15 mL/minute |
| Bezafibrate | Reduce dose to 400 mg daily if creatinine clearance 40–60 mL/minute; reduce dose to 200 mg every 1–2 days if creatinine clearance 15–40 mL/minute; avoid if creatinine clearance less than 15 mL/minute |
| Bisoprolol | *see* Beta-blockers |
| Bivalirudin | Reduce dose of infusion to 1.4 mg/kg/hour if creatinine clearance 30–60 mL/minute; avoid if creatinine clearance less than 30 mL/minute |
| Bleomycin | |
| Moderate | Reduce dose |
| Bortezomib | Manufacturer advises caution—consider dose reduction |
| Bumetanide | |
| Moderate | May need high doses |
| Buprenorphine | *see* Opioid Analgesics |
| Bupropion | Manufacturer recommends 150 mg daily |
| Buspirone | |
| Mild | Reduce dose |
| Moderate to severe | Avoid |
| Calcitriol | |
| Severe | Manufacturer of topical calcitriol advises avoid—no information available |
| Candesartan | Initially 4 mg daily |

Appendix 3

| Drug and degree of impairment | Comment |
|---|---|
| Capecitabine | |
| Mild | Use three-quarters of starting dose if creatinine clearance 30–50 mL/minute; avoid if creatinine clearance less than 30 mL/minute |
| Capreomycin | |
| Mild | Reduce dose; nephrotoxic; ototoxic |
| Captopril | *see* ACE Inhibitors |
| Carbamazepine | Manufacturer advises caution |
| Carboplatin | |
| Mild | Reduce dose and monitor haematological parameters and renal function |
| Moderate to severe | Avoid |
| Cefaclor | No dose adjustment required—manufacturer advises caution |
| Cefadroxil | |
| Moderate | Reduce dose |
| Cefalexin | Max. 3 g daily if creatinine clearance 40–50 mL/minute; max. 1.5 g daily if creatinine clearance 10–40 mL/minute; max. 750 mg daily if creatinine clearance less than 10 mL/minute |
| Cefixime | |
| Moderate | Reduce dose |
| Cefotaxime | If creatinine clearance less than 5 mL/minute, initial dose of 1 g then use half normal dose |
| Cefpirome | |
| Mild | Usual initial dose, then use half normal dose |
| Moderate to severe | Usual initial dose, then use one-quarter normal dose |
| Cefpodoxime | |
| Mild | Reduce dose |
| Cefprozil | Usual initial dose, then use half normal dose |
| Cefradine | |
| Moderate to severe | Reduce dose |
| Ceftazidime | |
| Mild | Reduce dose |
| Ceftriaxone | |
| Severe | Max. 2 g daily; also monitor plasma concentration if both hepatic and severe renal impairment |
| Cefuroxime | |
| Moderate to severe | Reduce parenteral dose |
| Celecoxib | *see* NSAIDs |
| Celiprolol | *see* Beta-blockers |
| Cetirizine | |
| Moderate | Use half normal dose |
| Cetrorelix | |
| Moderate to severe | Manufacturer advises avoid |
| Chloral hydrate | |
| Severe | Avoid |
| Chloramphenicol | |
| Severe | Avoid unless no alternative; dose-related depression of haematopoiesis |
| Chlordiazepoxide | *see* Anxiolytics and Hypnotics |

| Drug and degree of impairment | Comment |
|---|---|
| Chloroquine | |
| Mild to moderate | Reduce dose (but for malaria prophylaxis see section 5.4.1) |
| Severe | Avoid (but for malaria prophylaxis see section 5.4.1) |
| Chlorpromazine | *see* Antipsychotics |
| Chlorpropamide | Avoid |
| Chlortalidone | *see* Thiazides and Related Diuretics |
| Chlortetracycline | *see* Tetracyclines |
| Ciclosporin | *see* p. 449 (*see also* p. 585 if used in atopic dermatitis or psoriasis and p. 520 if used in rheumatoid arthritis) |
| Cidofovir | |
| Mild | Avoid; nephrotoxic |
| Cilastatin [ingredient] | *see Primaxin®* |
| Cilazapril | *see* ACE Inhibitors |
| Cilostazol | Avoid if creatinine clearance less than 25 mL/minute |
| Cimetidine | |
| Mild to moderate | 600–800 mg daily; occasional risk of confusion |
| Severe | 400 mg daily |
| Ciprofibrate | |
| Moderate | 100 mg on alternate days |
| Severe | Avoid |
| Ciprofloxacin | |
| Moderate | Use half normal dose |
| Cisplatin | |
| Mild | Avoid if possible; nephrotoxic and neurotoxic |
| Citalopram | |
| Moderate to severe | No information available |
| *Citramag®* | |
| Severe | Avoid—risk of hypermagnesaemia |
| Citrates | Absorption of aluminium from aluminium salts is increased by citrates, which are contained in many effervescent preparations (such as effervescent analgesics) |
| Cladribine | Regular monitoring recommended |
| Clarithromycin | Use half normal dose if creatinine clearance less than 30 mL/minute; avoid *Klaricid XL®* if creatinine clearance less than 30 mL/minute |
| Clavulanic acid [ingredient] | *see* Co-amoxiclav and *Timentin®* |
| Clobazam | *see* Anxiolytics and Hypnotics |
| Clodronate sodium | *see* Sodium Clodronate |
| Clomethiazole | *see* Anxiolytics and Hypnotics |
| Clopamide | *see* Thiazides and Related Diuretics |
| Clopidogrel | Manufacturer advises caution |
| Clozapine | |
| Severe | Avoid |
| Co-amoxiclav | Risk of crystalluria with high doses (particularly during parenteral therapy); reduce dose if creatinine clearance less than 30 mL/minute |
| Codeine | *see* Opioid Analgesics |

| Drug and degree of impairment | Comment |
|---|---|
| Colchicine | |
| Moderate | Reduce dose |
| Severe | Avoid or reduce dose if no alternative |
| Colistin | |
| Mild | Monitor plasma-colistin concentration during parenteral treatment |
| Moderate to severe | Reduce parenteral dose; monitor plasma-colistin concentration |
| Co-trimoxazole | Use half normal dose if creatinine clearance 15–30 mL/minute; avoid if creatinine clearance less than 15 mL/minute and if plasma-sulfamethoxazole concentration cannot be monitored |
| Cyclopenthiazide | *see* Thiazides and Related Diuretics |
| Cyclophosphamide | Reduce dose |
| Cycloserine | |
| Mild to moderate | Reduce dose |
| Severe | Avoid |
| Cyclosporin | *see* Ciclosporin |
| Dacarbazine | |
| Mild to moderate | Dose reduction may be required |
| Severe | Avoid |
| Dalteparin | *see* Heparin |
| Danaparoid | |
| Moderate | Increased risk of bleeding (monitor anti-Factor Xa activity) |
| Severe | Avoid unless patient has heparin-induced thrombocytopenia and no alternative |
| Daunorubicin | |
| Mild to moderate | Reduce dose |
| Deferiprone | Manufacturer advises caution—no information available |
| Demeclocycline | *see* Tetracyclines |
| Desflurane | |
| Moderate | Reduce dose |
| Desloratadine | |
| Severe | Manufacturer advises caution |
| Desmopressin | Antidiuretic effect may be reduced |
| Dexibuprofen | *see* NSAIDs |
| Dexketoprofen | *see* NSAIDs |
| Dextromethorphan | *see* Opioid Analgesics |
| Dextropropoxyphene | *see* Opioid Analgesics |
| Diamorphine | *see* Opioid Analgesics |
| Diazepam | *see* Anxiolytics and Hypnotics |
| Diazoxide | |
| Severe | 75–150 mg i/v; increased sensitivity to hypotensive effect |
| Diclofenac | *see* NSAIDs |
| Didanosine | |
| Mild | Reduce dose; consult product literature |
| Diflunisal | see NSAIDs (excreted by kidney) |
| Digitoxin | |
| Severe | Max. 100 micrograms daily |
| Digoxin | |
| Mild | Reduce dose; toxicity increased by electrolyte disturbances |

| Drug and degree of impairment | Comment |
|---|---|
| Dihydrocodeine | *see* Opioid Analgesics |
| Diltiazem | Start with smaller dose |
| Diphenoxylate | *see* Opioid Analgesics |
| Dipipanone | *see* Opioid Analgesics |
| Disodium etidronate | |
| Mild | Reduce dose |
| Moderate to severe | Avoid |
| Disodium pamidronate | Max. infusion rate 20 mg/hour; except in life-threatening hypercalcaemia, manufacturer advises avoid if creatinine clearance less than 30 mL/minute; if renal function deteriorates in patients with bone metastases, withhold dose until serum creatinine returns to within 10% of baseline value |
| Disopyramide | |
| Mild | 100 mg every 8 hours *or* 150 mg every 12 hours |
| Moderate | 100 mg every 12 hours |
| Severe | 150 mg every 24 hours<br>Note Sustained-release preparations may be unsuitable; monitor plasma-disopyramide concentrations |
| Diuretics, potassium-sparing | *see* Potassium-sparing Diuretics |
| Domperidone | Manufacturer advises reduce dose |
| Doxycycline | *see* Tetracyclines |
| Drospirenone [ingredient] | *see Angeliq®* and *Yasmin®* |
| Duloxetine | Avoid if creatinine clearance less than 30 mL/minute |
| Efavirenz | |
| Severe | Manufacturer advises caution—no information available |
| Eletriptan | Reduce initial dose to 20 mg; max. 40 mg in 24 hours; avoid if creatinine clearance less than 30 mL/minute |
| Emtricitabine | |
| Mild | Reduce dose; consult product literature; *see also Truvada®* |
| Enalapril | *see* ACE Inhibitors |
| Enfuvirtide | Manufacturer advises caution if creatinine clearance less than 35 mL/minute—no information available |
| Enoxaparin | Consider switching to heparin if creatinine clearance less than 30 mL/minute; alternatively adjust dose according to plasma concentration of anti-factor Xa |
| Enoximone | Consider dose reduction |
| Ephedrine | |
| Severe | Avoid; increased CNS toxicity |
| Eplerenone | Increased risk of hyperkalaemia—close monitoring required; avoid if creatinine clearance less than 50 mL/minute |
| Eprosartan | |
| Mild | Halve initial dose |
| Eptifibatide | Avoid if creatinine clearance less than 30 mL/minute |

| Drug and degree of impairment | Comment |
|---|---|
| Ergometrine | |
| Severe | Manufacturer advises avoid |
| Ergotamine | |
| Moderate | Avoid; nausea and vomiting; risk of renal vasoconstriction |
| Erlotinib | Manufacturer advises avoid if creatinine clearance less than 15 mL/minute—no information available |
| Ertapenem | Manufacturer advises avoid if creatinine clearance less than 30 mL/minute |
| Erythromycin | |
| Severe | Max. 1.5 g daily (ototoxicity) |
| Escitalopram | Manufacturer advises caution if creatinine clearance less than 30 mL/minute |
| Esmolol | *see* Beta-blockers |
| Esomeprazole | |
| Severe | Manufacturer advises caution |
| Estramustine | Manufacturer advises caution |
| Ethambutol | |
| Mild | Reduce dose; if creatinine clearance less than 30 mL/minute monitor plasma-ethambutol concentration; optic nerve damage |
| Etidronate disodium | *see* Disodium Etidronate |
| Etodolac | *see* NSAIDs |
| Etoposide | Consider dose reduction |
| Etoricoxib | *see* NSAIDs |
| Exemestane | Manufacturer advises caution |
| Famciclovir | Reduce dose; consult product literature |
| Famotidine | |
| Severe | Max. 20 mg at night |
| Fenbufen | *see* NSAIDs |
| Fenofibrate | |
| Mild | 134 mg daily |
| Moderate | 67 mg daily |
| Severe | Avoid |
| Fenoprofen | *see* NSAIDs |
| Fentanyl | *see* Opioid Analgesics |
| Flecainide | |
| Mild | Max. initial dose 100 mg daily |
| *Fleet Phospho-soda®* | Avoid |
| Severe | |
| Flucloxacillin | |
| Severe | Reduce dose |
| Fluconazole | |
| Mild to moderate | Usual initial dose then halve subsequent doses |
| Flucytosine | Reduce dose and monitor plasma-flucytosine concentration—consult product literature |
| Fludarabine | |
| Mild | Reduce dose; avoid if creatinine clearance less than 30 mL/minute |
| Flupentixol | *see* Antipsychotics |
| Fluphenazine | *see* Antipsychotics |
| Flurazepam | *see* Anxiolytics and Hypnotics |
| Flurbiprofen | *see* NSAIDs |
| Fluvoxamine | |
| Moderate | Start with smaller dose |
| Fondaparinux | Increased risk of bleeding; use with caution if creatinine clearance 30–50 mL/minute; for treatment avoid if creatinine clearance less than 30 mL/minute; for prophylaxis reduce dose to 1.5 mg daily if creatinine clearance 20–30 mL/minute, avoid if less than 20 mL/minute |
| Foscarnet | |
| Mild | Reduce dose; consult product literature |
| Fosinopril | *see* ACE Inhibitors |
| Fosphenytoin | Consider 10–25% reduction in dose or infusion rate (except initial dose for status epilepticus) |
| Frusemide | *see* Furosemide |
| Furosemide (frusemide) | |
| Moderate | May need high doses; deafness may follow rapid i/v injection |
| *Fybogel Mebeverine®* | |
| Severe | Avoid; contains 7 mmol potassium per sachet |
| Gabapentin | Reduce dose if creatinine clearance less than 80 mL/minute; consult product literature |
| Galantamine | |
| Severe | Avoid |
| Gallamine | |
| Moderate | Avoid; prolonged paralysis |
| Ganciclovir | |
| Mild | Reduce dose; consult product literature |
| Ganirelix | |
| Moderate to severe | Manufacturer advises avoid |
| *Gaviscon®* | |
| Severe | Avoid; high sodium content |
| Gemcitabine | Manufacturer advises caution |
| Gemeprost | Manufacturer advises avoid |
| Gemfibrozil | Start with 900 mg daily if creatinine clearance 30–80 mL/minute; avoid if creatinine clearance less than 30 mL/minute |
| Gentamicin | *see* Aminoglycosides |
| Gestrinone | |
| Severe | Avoid |
| Glatiramer | No information available—manufacturer advises caution |
| Glibenclamide | |
| Severe | Avoid |
| Gliclazide | |
| Mild to moderate | Reduce dose |
| Severe | Avoid if possible; if no alternative reduce dose and monitor closely |
| Glimepiride | |
| Severe | Avoid |
| Glipizide | |
| Mild to moderate | Increased risk of hypoglycaemia; avoid if hepatic impairment also present |
| Severe | Avoid |
| Gliquidone | Avoid in renal failure |
| Glyceryl trinitrate | *see* Nitrates |

| Drug and degree of impairment | Comment |
|---|---|
| Guanethidine | Reduce dose if creatinine clearance less than 65 mL/minute, avoid if creatinine clearance less than 40 mL/minute |
| Haloperidol | *see* Antipsychotics |
| Heparin | |
| Severe | Risk of bleeding increased |
| Hetastarch | |
| Severe | Avoid; excreted by kidney |
| Hydralazine | Reduce dose if creatinine clearance less than 30 mL/minute |
| Hydrochlorothiazide | *see* Thiazides and Related Diuretics |
| Hydroflumethiazide | *see* Thiazides and Related Diuretics |
| Hydromorphone | *see* Opioid Analgesics |
| Hydroxychloroquine | |
| Mild to moderate | Reduce dose; only on prolonged use |
| Severe | Avoid |
| Hydroxyzine | Use half normal dose |
| Hyoscine hydrobromide | Manufacturer advises caution |
| Hypnotics | *see* Anxiolytics and Hypnotics |
| Ibandronic acid | For repeated doses, if creatinine clearance less than 30 mL/minute, reduce intravenous dose to 2 mg every 3–4 weeks and in bone metastasis, change oral dose to 50 mg once weekly |
| Ibuprofen | *see* NSAIDs |
| Idarubicin | |
| Mild | Reduce dose |
| Ifosfamide | |
| Mild | Avoid if serum creatinine concentration greater than 120 micromol/litre |
| Imidapril | *see* ACE Inhibitors |
| Imipenem [ingredient] | *see Primaxin®* |
| Indapamide | *see* Thiazides and Related Diuretics |
| Indometacin | *see* NSAIDs |
| Indoramin | Manufacturer advises caution |
| Inosine pranobex | |
| Mild | Avoid; metabolised to uric acid |
| Insulin | |
| Severe | May need dose reduction; insulin requirements fall; compensatory response to hypoglycaemia is impaired |
| Interferon alfa | |
| Mild to moderate | Close monitoring required |
| Severe | Avoid |
| Interferon beta | No information available—monitoring advised |
| Interferon gamma-1b | |
| Severe | Manufacturer advises caution |
| Irinotecan | No information available |
| Iron dextran | Avoid in acute renal failure |
| Isometheptene [ingredient] | see Midrid® |
| Isoniazid | |
| Severe | Max. 200 mg daily; peripheral neuropathy |

| Drug and degree of impairment | Comment |
|---|---|
| Isosorbide dinitrate | *see* Nitrates |
| Isosorbide mononitrate | *see* Nitrates |
| Isotretinoin | |
| Severe | Start with 10 mg daily and increased if necessary to max. 1 mg/kg daily |
| Itraconazole | Risk of congestive heart failure; bioavailability of oral formulations possibly reduced; use intravenous infusion with caution if creatinine clearance 30–50 mL/minute (monitor renal function); avoid intravenous infusion if creatinine clearance less than 30 mL/minute |
| Ivabradine | Manufacturer advises caution if creatinine clearance less than 15 mL/minute |
| *Kaletra®* | Avoid oral solution due to propylene glycol content; use capsules with caution in severe impairment |
| Ketoprofen | *see* NSAIDs |
| Ketorolac | *see* NSAIDs |
| Lamivudine | |
| Mild | Reduce dose; consult product literature |
| Lamotrigine | |
| Moderate to severe | Metabolite may accumulate |
| Leflunomide | |
| Moderate to severe | Manufacturer advises avoid—no information available |
| Lepirudin | |
| Mild to moderate | Manufacturer advises reducing initial dose by 50% and subsequent doses by 50–85% |
| Severe | Avoid or stop infusion (unless APTT is below therapeutic levels when alternate day administration may be considered) |
| Lercanidipine | |
| Severe | Avoid |
| Levetiracetam | Max. 2 g daily if creatinine clearance 50–80 mL/minute; max. 1.5 g daily if creatinine clearance 30–50 mL/minute; max. 1 g daily if creatinine clearance less than 30 mL/minute |
| Levocetirizine | 5 mg on alternate days if creatinine clearance 30–50 mL/minute; 5 mg every 3 days if creatinine clearance 10–30 mL/minute; avoid if creatinine clearance less than 10 mL/minute |
| Levofloxacin | |
| Mild | Usual initial dose, then use half normal dose |
| Moderate to severe | Reduce dose; consult product literature |
| Levomepromazine (methotrimeprazine) | *see* Antipsychotics |
| Lidocaine | |
| Severe | Caution |

| Drug and degree of impairment | Comment |
|---|---|
| Linezolid | Manufacturer advises metabolites may accumulate if creatinine clearance less than 30 mL/minute |
| Lisinopril | *see* ACE Inhibitors |
| Lithium salts | |
| Mild | Avoid if possible or reduce dose and monitor plasma concentration carefully |
| Moderate | Avoid |
| Lofepramine | |
| Severe | Avoid |
| Lopinavir [ingredient] | *see Kaletra®* |
| Loprazolam | *see* Anxiolytics and Hypnotics |
| Lorazepam | *see* Anxiolytics and Hypnotics |
| Lormetazepam | *see* Anxiolytics and Hypnotics |
| Losartan | |
| Moderate to severe | Start with 25 mg once daily |
| Lumefantrine [ingredient] | *see Riamet®* |
| Lumiracoxib | Avoid if creatinine clearance less than 50 mL/minute |
| Lymecycline | *see* Tetracyclines |
| Magnesium salts | |
| Moderate | Avoid or reduce dose; increased risk of toxicity; magnesium carbonate mixture and magnesium trisilicate mixture also have high sodium content |
| *Malarone®* | Avoid for malaria prophylaxis (and if possible for malaria treatment) if creatinine clearance less than 30 mL/minute |
| Mefenamic acid | *see* NSAIDs |
| Meloxicam | *see* NSAIDs |
| Melphalan | Reduce dose initially; avoid high doses in moderate to severe impairment |
| Memantine | Reduce dose to 10 mg daily if creatinine clearance 40–60 mL/minute; manufacturer advises avoid if creatinine clearance less than 10 mL/minute |
| Meprobamate | *see* Anxiolytics and Hypnotics |
| Meptazinol | *see* Opioid Analgesics |
| Mercaptopurine | |
| Moderate | Reduce dose |
| Meropenem | |
| Mild | Increase dose interval to every 12 hours |
| Moderate | Use half normal dose every 12 hours |
| Severe | Use half normal dose every 24 hours |
| Mesalazine | |
| Moderate | Use with caution |
| Severe | Manufacturers advise avoid |
| Metformin | |
| Mild | Avoid; increased risk of lactic acidosis |
| Methadone | *see* Opioid Analgesics |
| Methenamine | |
| Severe | Avoid—risk of hippurate crystalluria |
| Methocarbamol | Manufacturer advises caution |
| Methotrexate | |
| Mild | Reduce dose; accumulates; nephrotoxic |
| Moderate | Avoid |
| Methotrimeprazine | *see* Antipsychotics |
| Methyldopa | |
| Moderate | Start with small dose; increased sensitivity to hypotensive and sedative effect |
| Methysergide | Avoid |
| Metoclopramide | |
| Severe | Avoid or use small dose; increased risk of extrapyramidal reactions |
| Metolazone | *see* Thiazides and Related Diuretics |
| Metoprolol | *see* Beta-blockers |
| Midazolam | *see* Anxiolytics and Hypnotics |
| *Midrid®* | |
| Severe | Avoid |
| Miglustat | Initially 100 mg twice daily if creatinine clearance 50–70 mL/minute; initially 100 mg once daily if creatinine clearance 30–50 mL/minute; avoid if creatinine clearance less than 30 mL/minute |
| Milrinone | |
| Mild | Reduce dose and monitor response |
| Minocycline | *see* Tetracyclines |
| Mirtazapine | Manufacturer advises caution |
| Mitotane | Manufacturer advises caution if creatinine clearance 30–80 mL/minute—monitoring of plasma-mitotane concentration recommended; avoid if creatinine clearance less than 30 mL/minute |
| Mivacurium | |
| Severe | Reduce dose; prolonged paralysis |
| Modafinil | |
| Severe | Use half normal dose |
| Moexipril | *see* ACE Inhibitors |
| Morphine | *see* Opioid Analgesics |
| Moxonidine | |
| Mild | Max. single dose 200 micrograms and max. daily dose 400 micrograms |
| Moderate to severe | Avoid |
| Nabumetone | *see* NSAIDs |
| Nadolol | *see* Beta-blockers |
| Nalbuphine | *see* Opioid Analgesics |
| Nalidixic acid | |
| Moderate to severe | Use half normal dose; ineffective in renal failure because concentration in urine is inadequate |
| Naproxen | *see* NSAIDs |
| Naratriptan | |
| Moderate | Max. 2.5 mg in 24 hours |
| Severe | Avoid |
| Narcotic analgesics | *see* Opioid Analgesics |
| Nebivolol | *see* Beta-blockers |
| Nelfinavir | No information available—manufacturer advises caution |

| Drug and degree of impairment | Comment |
|---|---|
| Neomycin | |
| Mild | Avoid; ototoxic; nephrotoxic |
| Neostigmine | |
| Moderate | May need dose reduction |
| Netilmicin | *see* Aminoglycosides |
| Nicardipine | |
| Moderate | Start with small dose |
| Nicotine | |
| Severe | Manufacturers advise caution |
| Nicoumalone | *see* Anticoagulants, Oral |
| Nimodipine | Manufacturer advises caution with intravenous administration |
| Nitrates | |
| Severe | Use with caution |
| Nitrazepam | *see* Anxiolytics and Hypnotics |
| Nitrofurantoin | |
| Mild | Avoid; peripheral neuropathy; ineffective because of inadequate urine concentrations |
| Nitroprusside | *see* Sodium Nitroprusside |
| Nizatidine | |
| Mild | Use half normal dose |
| Moderate | Use one-quarter normal dose |
| Norfloxacin | Use half normal dose if creatinine clearance less than 30 mL/minute |
| NSAIDs | |
| Mild | Use lowest effective dose and monitor renal function; sodium and water retention; deterioration in renal function possibly leading to renal failure; deterioration also reported after topical use; *see also* Lumiracoxib |
| Moderate to severe | Avoid if possible |
| Ofloxacin | |
| Mild | Usual initial dose, then use half normal dose |
| Moderate | Usual initial dose, then 100 mg every 24 hours |
| Olanzapine | Consider initial dose of 5 mg daily |
| Olmesartan | Max. 20 mg daily if creatinine clearance 20–60 mL/minute; avoid if creatinine clearance less than 20 mL/minute |
| Olsalazine | |
| Moderate | Use with caution |
| Severe | Manufacturer advises avoid |
| Omalizumab | Manufacturer advises caution—no information available |
| Opioid analgesics | |
| Moderate to severe | Reduce doses or avoid; increased and prolonged effect; increased cerebral sensitivity; no dose adjustment necessary with remifentanil |
| Oseltamivir | Reduce dose if creatinine clearance 10–30 mL/minute; avoid if creatinine clearance less than 10 mL/minute |
| Oxaliplatin | |
| Mild | Manufacturer advises avoid if creatinine clearance less than 30 mL/minute |
| Oxazepam | *see* Anxiolytics and Hypnotics |
| Oxcarbazepine | Use half initial dose if creatinine clearance less than 30 mL/minute; increase according to response at intervals of at least 1 week |
| Oxpentifylline | *see* Pentoxifylline |
| Oxprenolol | *see* Beta-blockers |
| Oxybutynin | Manufacturer advises caution |
| Oxycodone | *see* Opioid Analgesics |
| Oxytetracycline | *see* Tetracyclines |
| Pamidronate disodium | *see* Disodium Pamidronate |
| Pancuronium | |
| Severe | Prolonged duration of block |
| Pantoprazole | Max. oral dose 40 mg daily |
| Papaveretum | *see* Opioid Analgesics |
| Paracetamol | Increase *infusion* dose interval to every 6 hours if creatinine clearance less than 30 mL/minute |
| Parecoxib | *see* NSAIDs |
| Paroxetine | Reduce dose if creatinine clearance less than 30 mL/minute |
| Peginterferon alfa | Close monitoring required—reduce dose if necessary |
| Penicillamine | |
| Mild | Reduce dose and monitor renal function (consult product literature) |
| Moderate to severe | Avoid |
| Pentamidine | |
| Mild | Reduce dose; consult product literature |
| Pentazocine | *see* Opioid Analgesics |
| Pentoxifylline (oxpentifylline) | Reduce dose by 30–50% if creatinine clearance less than 30 mL/minute |
| Pericyazine | *see* Antipsychotics |
| Perindopril | *see* ACE Inhibitors |
| Perphenazine | *see* Antipsychotics |
| Pethidine | *see* Opioid Analgesics |
| Phenazocine | *see* Opioid Analgesics |
| Phenindione | *see* Anticoagulants, Oral |
| Phenobarbital | |
| Severe | Avoid large doses |
| Phenothiazines | *see* Antipsychotics |
| Pholcodine | *see* Opioid Analgesics |
| *Picolax*® | |
| Severe | Avoid—risk of hypermagnesaemia |
| Pilocarpine | Manufacturer advises caution with tablets |
| Pimozide | *see* Antipsychotics |
| Pindolol | *see* Beta-blockers |
| Piperacillin [ingredient] | *see* *Tazocin*® |
| Piperazine | |
| Severe | Avoid—neurotoxic |
| Pipotiazine | *see* Antipsychotics |

| Drug and degree of impairment | Comment |
|---|---|
| Piracetam | Use two-thirds of normal dose if creatinine clearance 50–80 mL/minute; use one-third of normal dose in 2 divided doses if creatinine clearance 30–50 mL/minute; use one-sixth normal dose as a single dose if creatinine clearance 20–30 mL/minute; avoid if creatinine clearance less than 20 mL/minute |
| Piroxicam | *see* NSAIDs |
| Potassium salts | |
| Moderate | Avoid routine use; high risk of hyperkalaemia |
| Potassium-sparing diuretics | |
| Mild | Monitor plasma $K^+$; high risk of hyperkalaemia in renal impairment; amiloride excreted by kidney unchanged |
| Moderate | Avoid |
| Povidone–iodine | |
| Severe | Avoid regular application to inflamed or broken mucosa |
| Pramipexole | |
| Mild | Initially 88 micrograms twice daily; if renal function declines, reduce dose further |
| Moderate to severe | Initially 88 micrograms daily; if renal function declines, reduce dose further |
| Pravastatin | |
| Moderate to severe | Start at lower end of dosage range |
| Prazosin | |
| Moderate to severe | Initially 500 micrograms daily; increased with caution |
| Pregabalin | |
| Mild | Reduce dose; consult product literature |
| *Primaxin*® | |
| Mild | Reduce dose |
| Primidone | *see* Phenobarbital |
| Probenecid | |
| Moderate | Avoid; ineffective and toxicity increased |
| Procainamide | |
| Mild | Avoid or reduce dose |
| Procarbazine | |
| Severe | Avoid |
| Prochlorperazine | *see* Antipsychotics |
| Proguanil | |
| Mild | 100 mg once daily |
| Moderate | 50 mg on alternate days |
| Severe | 50 mg once weekly; increased risk of haematological toxicity |
| Promazine | *see* Antipsychotics |
| Propantheline | Manufacturer advises caution |
| Propiverine | |
| Severe | Avoid |
| Propranolol | *see* Beta-blockers |
| Propylthiouracil | |
| Mild to moderate | Use three-quarters normal dose |
| Severe | Use half normal dose |
| Pseudoephedrine | |
| Severe | Avoid; increased CNS toxicity |

| Drug and degree of impairment | Comment |
|---|---|
| Pyridostigmine | |
| Moderate | Reduce dose; excreted by kidney |
| Pyrimethamine | Manufacturer advises caution |
| Quetiapine | Manufacturer advises initial dose of 25 mg daily, increased daily in steps of 25–50 mg |
| Quinagolide | Manufacturer advises avoid—no information available |
| Quinapril | *see* ACE Inhibitors |
| Quinine | Reduce parenteral maintenance dose for malaria treatment, *see* section 5.4.1 |
| Raloxifene | |
| Severe | Avoid |
| Raltitrexed | |
| Mild | Reduce dose and increase dosing interval |
| Moderate to severe | Avoid |
| Ramipril | *see* ACE Inhibitors |
| Ranitidine | |
| Severe | Use half normal dose; occasional risk of confusion |
| Ranitidine bismuth citrate | Avoid if creatinine clearance less than 25 mL/minute |
| Reboxetine | Initial dose 2 mg twice daily, increased according to tolerance |
| Remifentanil | *see* Opioid Analgesics |
| Reviparin | |
| Severe | Manufacturer advises avoid |
| *Riamet*® | Manufacturer advises caution in severe renal impairment—monitor ECG and plasma potassium concentration |
| Ribavirin | |
| Mild | Plasma-ribavirin concentration increased; manufacturer advises avoid oral ribavirin unless essential—monitor haemoglobin concentration closely |
| Rifabutin | Use half normal dose if creatinine clearance less than 30 mL/minute |
| Riluzole | No information available—manufacturer advises avoid |
| Risedronate sodium | Manufacturer advises avoid if creatinine clearance less than 30 mL/minute |
| Risperidone | Manufacturer advises initial oral dose of 500 micrograms twice daily increased in steps of 500 micrograms twice daily to 1–2 mg twice daily; if an oral dose of at least 2 mg daily tolerated, 25 mg as a depot injection can be given every 2 weeks |
| Ritonavir [ingredient] | *see Kaletra*® |
| Rivastigmine | Manufacturer advises caution |
| Rizatriptan | |
| Mild to moderate | Reduce dose to 5 mg |
| Severe | Avoid |
| Rocuronium | |
| Moderate | Reduce dose; prolonged paralysis |
| Ropinirole | |
| Severe | Avoid |

| Drug and degree of impairment | Comment |
|---|---|
| Rosiglitazone | Manufacturer advises caution, if creatinine clearance less than 30 mL/minute |
| Rosuvastatin | Initially 5 mg once daily and avoid dose of 40 mg daily if creatinine clearance less than 60 mL/minute; avoid if creatinine clearance less than 30 mL/minute |
| Saquinavir | |
| Severe | Dose adjustment possibly required |
| Sertraline | Manufacturer advises caution |
| Sevoflurane | Manufacturer advises caution |
| Sibutramine | |
| Mild to moderate | Manufacturer advises caution |
| Severe | Avoid |
| Sildenafil | Initial dose 25 mg if creatinine clearance less than 30 mL/minute |
| Simvastatin | Doses above 10 mg daily should be used with caution if creatinine clearance less than 30 mL/minute |
| Sirolimus | Adjust immunosuppressant regimen in patients with raised serum creatinine |
| Sodium aurothiomalate | Caution; nephrotoxic |
| Sodium bicarbonate | |
| Severe | Avoid; specialised role in some forms of renal disease |
| Sodium clodronate | |
| Mild to moderate | Use half normal dose and monitor serum creatinine |
| Severe | Avoid |
| Sodium nitroprusside Moderate | Avoid prolonged use |
| Sodium valproate | *see* Valproate |
| Solifenacin | Max. 5 mg daily if creatinine clearance less than 30 mL/minute |
| *Solpadeine*® | |
| Severe | Avoid effervescent tablet preparations; contains 18.5 mmol sodium per tablet |
| *Solpadol*® | |
| Severe | Avoid effervescent tablets; contains 16.9 mmol sodium per tablet |
| Sotalol | *see* Beta-blockers |
| Spironolactone | *see* Potassium-sparing Diuretics |
| Stavudine | 20 mg every 12 hours (15 mg every 12 hours if body-weight under 60 kg) if creatinine clearance 25–50 mL/minute; 20 mg once daily (15 mg once daily if body-weight under 60 kg) if creatinine clearance less than 25 mL/minute |
| Streptomycin | *see* Aminoglycosides |
| Strontium ranelate | Manufacturer advises no dose adjustment required if creatinine clearance 30–70 mL/minute; avoid if creatinine clearance less than 30 mL/minute |
| Sucralfate | |
| Severe | Avoid; aluminium is absorbed and may accumulate |
| Sulfadiazine | |
| Severe | Avoid; high risk of crystalluria |
| Sulfasalazine | |
| Moderate | Risk of toxicity including crystalluria—ensure high fluid intake |
| Severe | Avoid |
| Sulfinpyrazone | |
| Moderate | Avoid; ineffective as uricosuric |
| Sulindac | *see* NSAIDs |
| Sulphonamides | |
| Moderate | Ensure high fluid intake; rashes and blood disorders; crystalluria a risk |
| Sulphonylureas | *see under* individual drugs |
| Sulpiride | |
| Moderate | Avoid if possible, or reduce dose |
| Tacalcitol | Monitor serum calcium concentration |
| Tadalafil | Max. dose 10 mg if creatinine clearance less than 30 mL/minute |
| Tamsulosin | |
| Severe | Manufacturer advises caution |
| Tazobactam [ingredient] | *see Tazocin*® |
| *Tazocin*® | Max. 4.5 g every 8 hours if creatinine clearance 20–80 mL/minute; max. 4.5 g every 12 hours if creatinine clearance less than 20 mL/minute; child under 12 years: Consult product literature |
| Teicoplanin | On day 4 use half normal dose if creatinine clearance is 40–60 mL/minute and use one-third normal dose if creatinine clearance is less than 40 mL/minute |
| Telithromycin | Use half normal dose if creatinine clearance less than 30 mL/minute |
| Telmisartan | |
| Severe | Initially 20 mg once daily |
| Temazepam | *see* Anxiolytics and Hypnotics |
| Tenofovir | Monitor renal function —interrupt treatment if further deterioration; 245 mg every 2 days if creatinine clearance 30–50 mL/minute; 245 mg every 3–4 days if creatinine clearance 10–30 mL/minute; *see also Truvada*® |
| Tenoxicam | *see* NSAIDs |
| Terbinafine | |
| Mild | Use half normal dose |
| Tetracyclines | |
| Mild | Avoid tetracyclines except doxycycline or minocycline which may be used cautiously (avoid excessive doses) |

| Drug and degree of impairment | Comment |
|---|---|
| Thiazides and related diuretics | Avoid if creatinine clearance less than 30 mL/minute—ineffective (metolazone remains effective but risk of excessive diuresis) |
| Tiaprofenic acid | *see* NSAIDs |
| Ticarcillin [ingredient] | *see Timentin®* |
| Tiludronic acid | |
| Moderate to severe | Avoid |
| *Timentin®* | |
| Mild | Reduce dose |
| Timolol | *see* Beta-blockers |
| Tinzaparin | |
| Severe | May need dose reduction |
| Tioguanine | |
| Moderate | Reduce dose |
| Tiotropium | Plasma-tiotropium concentration raised; manufacturer advises caution |
| Tirofiban | Use half normal dose if creatinine clearance less than 30 mL/minute |
| Tizanidine | Initially 2 mg once daily if creatinine clearance less than 25 mL/minute; increase once-daily dose gradually according to response before increasing frequency |
| Tobramycin | *see* Aminoglycosides |
| Tolbutamide | |
| Mild to moderate | Reduce dose |
| Severe | Avoid if possible; if no alternative reduce dose and monitor closely |
| Tolfenamic acid | *see* NSAIDs |
| Tolterodine | Reduce dose to 1 mg twice daily if creatinine clearance less than 30 mL/minute |
| Topiramate | |
| Moderate to severe | Longer time to steady-state plasma concentrations |
| Topotecan | |
| Moderate | Reduce dose |
| Severe | Avoid |
| Torasemide | |
| Moderate | May need high doses |
| Tramadol | *see* Opioid Analgesics |
| Trandolapril | *see* ACE Inhibitors |
| Tranexamic acid | |
| Mild to moderate | Reduce dose |
| Severe | Avoid |
| Tretinoin (oral) | |
| Mild | Reduce dose |
| Triamterene | *see* Potassium-sparing Diuretics |
| Tribavirin | *see* Ribavirin |
| Triclofos | *see* Anxiolytics and Hypnotics |
| Trifluoperazine | *see* Antipsychotics |
| Trimeprazine | *see* Alimemazine |
| Trimethoprim | Use half normal dose after 3 days if creatinine clearance 15–30 mL/minute; use half normal dose if creatinine clearance less than 15 mL/minute; (monitor plasma-trimethoprim concentration if creatinine clearance less than 10 mL/minute) |
| Tripotassium dicitratobismuthate | |
| Severe | Avoid |
| Trisodium edetate | |
| Mild | Avoid |
| Trospium | |
| Mild to moderate | Reduce dose to 20 mg once daily or 20 mg on alternate days if creatinine clearance 10–30 mL/minute |
| Severe | Avoid |
| *Truvada®* | Monitor renal function; use normal dose every 48 hours if creatinine clearance 30–50 mL/minute; avoid if creatinine clearance less than 30 mL/minute |
| *Tylex®* | |
| Moderate to severe | Avoid effervescent tablets; contain 13.6 mmol sodium per tablet |
| *Ultramol®* | Avoid; contains 15.7 mmol sodium per tablet |
| Valaciclovir | |
| Mild | Reduce treatment dose for herpes zoster; reduce dose according to creatinine clearance for cytomegalovirus prophylaxis following renal transplantation |
| Moderate to severe | Reduce dose for all indications |
| Valganciclovir | Reduce dose; consult product literature |
| Valproate | |
| Mild to moderate | Reduce dose |
| Severe | Alter dosage according to free serum valproic acid concentration |
| Valproic acid | *see* Valproate |
| Valsartan | Initially 40 mg once daily if creatinine clearance less than 20 mL/minute |
| Vancomycin | |
| Mild | Reduce dose—monitor plasma-vancomycin concentration and renal function regularly |
| Vardenafil | Initial dose 5 mg if creatinine clearance less than 30 mL/minute; avoid in endstage renal disease requiring dialysis |
| Venlafaxine | Use half normal dose if creatinine clearance 10–30 mL/minute; avoid if creatinine clearance less than 10 mL/minute |
| Vigabatrin | |
| Mild | Excreted by kidney—lower maintenance dose may be required |
| Voriconazole | Intravenous vehicle may accumulate if creatinine clearance less than 50 mL/minute—manufacturer advises use intravenous infusion only if potential benefit outweighs risk, and monitor renal function; alternatively, use tablets or oral suspension (no dose adjustment required) |

| Drug and degree of impairment | Comment |
|---|---|
| Warfarin | *see* Anticoagulants, Oral |
| Xipamide | *see* Thiazides and Related Diuretics |
| *Yasmin®* | |
| Severe | Manufacturer advises avoid |
| Zafirlukast | |
| Moderate to severe | Manufacturer advises caution |
| Zalcitabine | |
| Mild to moderate | 750 micrograms every 12 hours |
| Severe | 750 micrograms daily |
| Zidovudine | |
| Severe | Reduce dose; manufacturer advises oral dose of 300–400 mg daily in divided doses or intravenous dose of 1 mg/kg 3–4 times daily |
| Zoledronic acid | Avoid if serum creatinine above 400 micromol/litre in tumor-induced hypercalcaemia; in cancer and bone metastases, if creatinine clearance 50–60 mL/minute reduce dose to 3.5 mg every 3–4 weeks, if creatinine clearance 40–50 mL/minute reduce dose to 3.3 mg every 3–4 weeks, if creatinine clearance 30–40 mL/minute reduce dose to 3 mg every 3–4 weeks, and avoid if creatinine clearance below 30 mL/minute (or if serum creatinine above 265 micromol/litre); if renal function deteriorates in patients with bone metastases, withhold dose until serum creatinine returns to within 10% of base-line value |
| Zonisamide | Initially increase dose at 2-week intervals; discontinue if renal function deteriorates |
| Zopiclone | *see* Anxiolytics and Hypnotics |
| Zotepine | Initial dose 25 mg twice daily, increased gradually according to response (max. 75 mg twice daily) |
| Zuclopenthixol | *see* Antipsychotics |

# A4 Pregnancy

Drugs can have harmful effects on the fetus at any time during pregnancy. It is important to bear this in mind when prescribing for a woman of *childbearing age* or for men *trying* to *father* a child.

During the *first trimester* drugs may produce congenital malformations (teratogenesis), and the period of greatest risk is from the third to the eleventh week of pregnancy.

During the *second* and *third trimesters* drugs may affect the growth and functional development of the fetus or have toxic effects on fetal tissues; and drugs given shortly before term or during labour may have adverse effects on labour or on the neonate after delivery.

The following list includes drugs which:

- may have harmful effects in pregnancy and indicates the trimester of risk
- are not known to be harmful in pregnancy

The list is based on human data but information on *animal* studies has been included for some drugs when its omission might be misleading.

> Drugs should be prescribed in pregnancy only if the expected benefit to the mother is thought to be greater than the risk to the fetus, and all drugs should be avoided if possible during the first trimester. Drugs which have been extensively used in pregnancy and appear to be usually safe should be prescribed in preference to new or untried drugs; and the smallest effective dose should be used.
> Few drugs have been shown conclusively to be teratogenic in man but no drug is safe beyond all doubt in early pregnancy. Screening procedures are available where there is a known risk of certain defects.
> Absence of a drug from the list does not imply safety.
> It should be noted that the BNF provides independent advice and may not always agree with the product literature.
> Information on drugs and pregnancy is also available from the National Teratology Information Service Telephone: (0191) 232 1525
> (0191) 223 1307 (out of hours emergency only)
> www.nyrdtc.nhs.uk/Services/teratology/teratology.html

Appendix 4

## Table of drugs to be avoided or used with caution in pregnancy

Products introduced or amended since publication of BNF No. 50 (September 2005) are underlined.

| Drug (trimester of risk) | Comment |
|---|---|
| Abacavir | Manufacturer advises avoid (toxicity in *animal* studies); *see also* p. 314 |
| Abciximab | Manufacturer advises use only if potential benefit outweighs risk—no information available |
| Acamprosate | Manufacturer advises avoid |
| Acarbose | Manufacturer advises avoid; insulin is normally substituted in all diabetics |
| ACE inhibitors (1, 2, 3) | Avoid; may adversely affect fetal and neonatal blood pressure control and renal function; also possible skull defects and oligohydramnios; toxicity in *animal* studies |
| Acebutolol | *see* Beta-blockers |
| Aceclofenac | *see* NSAIDs |
| Acemetacin | *see* NSAIDs |
| Acenocoumarol (nicoumalone) | *see* Anticoagulants, Oral |
| Acetazolamide | *see* Diuretics |
| Aciclovir | Not known to be harmful—manufacturers advise use only when potential benefit outweighs risk; limited absorption from topical aciclovir preparations |
| Acipimox | Manufacturer advises avoid |
| Acitretin (1, 2, 3) | Teratogenic; effective contraception must be used for at least 1 month before treatment, during treatment, and for at least 2 years after stopping |
| Acrivastine | *see* Antihistamines |
| Adalimumab | Avoid; manufacturer advises adequate contraception during and for at least 5 months after last dose |
| Adapalene | Manufacturer advises teratogenicity in *animal* studies and recommends effective contraception during treatment |
| Adefovir dipivoxil | Toxicity in *animal* studies—manufacturer advises use only if potential benefit outweighs risk; effective contraception required during treatment |
| Agalsidase beta | Manufacturer advises avoid unless essential—no information available |
| Alclometasone | *see* Corticosteroids |

| Drug (trimester of risk) | Comment |
|---|---|
| Alcohol | |
| (1, 2) | Regular daily drinking is teratogenic (fetal alcohol syndrome) and may cause growth restriction; occasional single drinks are probably safe |
| (3) | Withdrawal syndrome may occur in babies of alcoholic mothers |
| Alemtuzumab | Avoid; manufacturer advises effective contraception during and for 6 months after administration to men or women |
| Alendronic acid | *see* Bisphosphonates |
| Alfentanil | *see* Opioid Analgesics |
| Alimemazine (trimeprazine) | *see* Antihistamines |
| Allopurinol | Toxicity not reported; manufacturer advises avoid; use only if no safer alternative and disease carries risk for mother or child |
| Almotriptan | *see* $5HT_1$ Agonists |
| Alpha-blockers, post-synaptic | No evidence of teratogenicity; manufacturers advise use only when potential benefit outweighs risk |
| Alprazolam | *see* Benzodiazepines |
| Alprostadil (urethral application only) | Manufacturer advises barrier contraception if partner pregnant |
| Alteplase | *see* Streptokinase |
| Amantadine | Avoid; toxicity in *animal* studies |
| Amfebutamone | *see* Bupropion |
| Amikacin | *see* Aminoglycosides |
| Amiloride | *see* Diuretics |
| Aminoglycosides | |
| (2, 3) | Auditory or vestibular nerve damage; risk greatest with streptomycin; probably very small with gentamicin and tobramycin, but avoid unless essential (if given, serum-aminoglycoside concentration monitoring essential) |
| Aminophylline | *see* Theophylline |
| Amiodarone | |
| (2, 3) | Possible risk of neonatal goitre; use only if no alternative |
| Amisulpride | Manufacturer advises avoid |
| Amitriptyline | *see* Antidepressants, Tricyclic (and related) |
| Amlodipine | No information available—manufacturer advises avoid, but risk to fetus should be balanced against risk of uncontrolled maternal hypertension |
| Amobarbital | *see* Barbiturates |
| Amorolfine | Systemic absorption very low, but manufacturer advises avoid—no information available |
| Amoxapine | *see* Antidepressants, Tricyclic (and related) |
| Amoxicillin | *see* Penicillins |
| Amphotericin | Not known to be harmful but manufacturers advise avoid unless potential benefit outweighs risk |
| Ampicillin | *see* Penicillins |
| Amprenavir | Avoid oral solution due to high propylene glycol content; manufacturer advises use capsules only if potential benefit outweighs risk |
| Amsacrine | Avoid (teratogenic and toxic in *animal* studies); may reduce fertility; *see also* section 8.1 |
| Anabolic steroids | |
| (1, 2, 3) | Masculinisation of female fetus |
| Anaesthetics, general | |
| (3) | Depress neonatal respiration; dose of thiopental should not exceed 250 mg |
| Anaesthetics, local | |
| (3) | With large doses, neonatal respiratory depression, hypotonia, and bradycardia after paracervical or epidural block; neonatal methaemoglobinaemia with prilocaine and procaine; lower doses of bupivacaine for intrathecal use during late pregnancy |
| Anagrelide | Manufacturer advises avoid (toxicity in *animal* studies) |
| Anakinra | Manufacturer advises avoid; effective contraception must be used during treatment |
| Analgesics | *see* Opioid Analgesics, Nefopam, NSAIDs, and Paracetamol |
| Androgens | |
| (1, 2, 3) | Masculinisation of female fetus |
| Anticoagulants, oral | |
| (1, 2, 3) | Congenital malformations; fetal and neonatal haemorrhage; *see also* section 2.8.2 |
| Antidepressants, MAOI | |
| (1, 2, 3) | No evidence of harm but manufacturers advise avoid unless compelling reasons |
| Antidepressants, SSRI | Manufacturers advise use only if potential benefit outweighs risk; risk of neonatal withdrawal, particularly with fluoxetine and paroxetine; toxicity in *animal* studies with escitalopram and paroxetine |
| Antidepressants, tricyclic (and related) | |
| (3) | Tachycardia, irritability, and muscle spasms in neonate reported with imipramine |
| Antiepileptics | Benefit of treatment outweighs risk to fetus; risk of teratogenicity greater if more than one drug used; **important:** *see also* Carbamazepine, Ethosuximide, Levetiracetam, Phenobarbital, Phenytoin, Topiramate, Valproate, Vigabatrin, and p. 238 |

Appendix 4

| Drug (trimester of risk) | Comment |
|---|---|
| Antihistamines | No evidence of teratogenicity; embryotoxicity in *animal* studies with high doses of hydroxyzine and loratadine; manufacturers of cetirizine, desloratadine, hydroxyzine, loratadine, mizolastine and terfenadine advise avoid |
| Antimalarials (1, 3) | Benefit of prophylaxis and treatment in malaria outweighs risk; **important:** *see also* individual drugs and p. 330 and p. 331 |
| Antipsychotics | *See also* Amisulpride, Clozapine, Olanzapine, Quetiapine, Risperidone, Sertindole, Zotepine |
| (3) | Extrapyramidal effects in neonate occasionally reported |
| Apomorphine | Avoid |
| Aprepitant (1, 2, 3) | Manufacturer advises avoid unless potential benefit outweighs risk—no information available |
| Aprotonin | Manufacturer advises use only if potential benefit outweighs risk; possibly reduced fibrinolytic activity in newborn |
| Aripiprazole (1, 2, 3) | Manufacturer advises use only if potential benefit outweighs risk—no information available |
| Arsenic trioxide | Avoid (teratogenic and embryotoxic in *animal* studies); manufacturer advises effective contraception during administration to men or women; *see also* section 8.1 |
| Artemether [ingredient] | *see Riamet®* |
| Aspirin (3) | Impaired platelet function and risk of haemorrhage; delayed onset and increased duration of labour with increased blood loss; avoid analgesic doses if possible in last few weeks (low doses probably not harmful); with high doses, closure of fetal ductus arteriosus *in utero* and possibly persistent pulmonary hypertension of newborn; kernicterus in jaundiced neonates |
| Atazanavir | Manufacturer advises use only if potential benefit outweighs risk; theoretical risk of hyperbilirubinaemia in neonate if used at term |
| Atenolol | *see* Beta-blockers |
| Atomoxetine | Manufacturer advises avoid unless potential benefit outweighs risk—no information available |
| Atorvastatin | *see* Statins |
| Atosiban | For use in premature labour *see* section 7.1.3 |
| Atovaquone | Manufacturer advises avoid unless potential benefit outweighs risk—no information available |
| Atracurium | Does not cross placenta in significant amounts but manufacturer advises use only if potential benefit outweighs risk |
| Atropine | Not known to be harmful; manufacturer advises caution |
| Auranofin | Manufacturer advises avoid (effective contraception should be used during and for at least 6 months after treatment) but limited data suggests usually not necessary to withdraw if condition well controlled—consider reducing dose and frequency |
| Azathioprine | *see* p. 447 |
| Azelastine | *see* Antihistamines |
| Azithromycin | Manufacturer advises use only if adequate alternatives not available |
| Aztreonam | Manufacturer advises avoid—no information available |
| Baclofen | Manufacturer advises use only if potential benefit outweighs risk (toxicity in *animal* studies) |
| Balsalazide | Manufacturer advises avoid |
| Bambuterol | *see* section 3.1 |
| Barbiturates (3) | Withdrawal effects in neonate; *see also* Phenobarbital |
| Basiliximab | Avoid; adequate contraception must be used during treatment and for 8 weeks after last dose |
| Beclometasone | *see* Corticosteroids |
| Bemiparin | Manufacturer advises avoid unless essential—no information available |
| Bendrofluazide | *see* Diuretics |
| Bendroflumethiazide (bendrofluazide) | *see* Diuretics |
| Benperidol | *see* Antipsychotics |
| Benzodiazepines | Avoid regular use (risk of neonatal withdrawal symptoms); use only if clear indication such as seizure control (high doses during late pregnancy or labour may cause neonatal hypothermia, hypotonia and respiratory depression) |
| Benzylpenicillin | *see* Penicillins |
| Beta-blockers | May cause intra-uterine growth restriction, neonatal hypoglycaemia, and bradycardia; risk greater in severe hypertension; *see also* section 2.5 |
| Betamethasone | *see* Corticosteroids |
| Bethanechol | Manufacturer advises avoid—no information available |

Appendix 4

| Drug (trimester of risk) | Comment |
|---|---|
| Bevacizumab | Manufacturer advises avoid—toxicity in *animal* studies; effective contraception required during and for at least 6 months after treatment in women (*see also* section 8.1) |
| Bexarotene | Avoid; manufacturer advises effective contraception during and for at least 1 month after administration to men or women; *see also* section 8.1 |
| Bezafibrate | *see* Fibrates |
| Bimatoprost | Manufacturer advises use only if potential benefit outweighs risk |
| Bisoprolol | *see* Beta-blockers |
| Bisphosphonates | Manufacturers advise avoid |
| Bivalirudin | Manufacturer advises avoid unless potential benefit outweighs risk—no information available |
| Bleomycin | Avoid (teratogenic and carcinogenic in *animal* studies); *see also* section 8.1 |
| Bortezomib | Manufacturer advises effective contraception during and for 3 months after treatment in men or women—no information available; *see also* section 8.1 |
| Bosentan | Avoid (teratogenic in *animal* studies); effective contraception required during and for at least 3 months after administration |
| Botulinum toxin | Manufacturers advise avoid unless essential—toxicity in *animal* studies |
| Brinzolamide | Manufacturer advises avoid unless essential |
| Buclizine | *see* Anthistamines |
| Budesonide | *see* Corticosteroids |
| Bumetanide | *see* Diuretics |
| Bupivacaine | *see* Anaesthetics, Local |
| Buprenorphine | *see* Opioid Analgesics |
| Bupropion | Manufacturer advises avoid—no information available |
| Buserelin | Avoid |
| Buspirone | Manufacturer advises avoid |
| Busulfan | Avoid (teratogenic in *animals*); manufacturer advises effective contraception during administration to men or women; *see also* section 8.1 |
| Cabergoline | No evidence of harm; manufacturer advises discontinuation one month before intended conception and avoidance during pregnancy; *see also* section 6.7.1 |
| Calcipotriol | Manufacturer advises avoid if possible |
| Calcitonin (salmon) (salcatonin) | Manufacturer advises avoid unless potential benefit outweighs risk (toxicity in *animal* studies) |
| Calcitriol | *see* Vitamin D |
| Calcium folinate | Manufacturer advises use only if potential benefit outweighs risk |
| Calcium levofolinate | *see* Calcium Folinate |
| Candesartan | *As for* ACE Inhibitors |
| Capecitabine | Avoid (teratogenic in animal studies); *see also* section 8.1 |
| Capreomycin | Manufacturer advises use only if potential benefit outweighs risk—teratogenic in *animal* studies |
| Captopril | *see* ACE Inhibitors |
| Carbamazepine | |
| (1) | Risk of teratogenesis including increased risk of neural tube defects (counselling and screening and adequate folate supplements advised, e.g. 5 mg daily); *see also* Antiepileptics and p. 238 |
| (3) | May possibly cause vitamin K deficiency and risk of neonatal bleeding; if vitamin K not given at birth, neonate should be monitored closely for signs of bleeding |
| Carbimazole | |
| (2, 3) | Neonatal goitre and hypothyroidism; has been associated with aplasia cutis of the neonate |
| Carbocisteine | |
| (1) | Manufacturer advises avoid |
| Carboplatin | Avoid (teratogenic and embryotoxic in *animal* studies); *see also* section 8.1 |
| Carglumic acid | Manufacturer advises avoid unless essential—no information available |
| Carmustine | Avoid (teratogenic and embryotoxic in *animals*); manufacturer advises effective contraception during administration to men or women; *see also* section 8.1 |
| Carnitine | No evidence of teratogenicity in *animal* studies; consider serious consequence of discontinuing treatment |
| Carvedilol | *see* Beta-blockers |
| Caspofungin | Manufacturer advises avoid unless essential—toxicity in *animal* studies |
| Cefaclor | Not known to be harmful |
| Cefadroxil | Not known to be harmful |
| Cefalexin | Not known to be harmful |
| Cefixime | Not known to be harmful |
| Cefotaxime | Not known to be harmful |
| Cefpirome | Manufacturer advises avoid |
| Cefpodoxime | Not known to be harmful |
| Cefprozil | Not known to be harmful |
| Cefradine | Not known to be harmful |
| Ceftazidime | Not known to be harmful |
| Ceftriaxone | Not known to be harmful |
| Cefuroxime | Not known to be harmful |
| Celecoxib | Manufacturer advises avoid (teratogenic in *animal* studies); *see also* NSAIDs |

| Drug (trimester of risk) | Comment |
|---|---|
| Celiprolol | *see* Beta-blockers |
| Cetirizine | *see* Antihistamines |
| Cetrorelix | Manufacturer advises avoid in confirmed pregnancy |
| Cetuximab | Manufacturer advises use only if potential benefit outweighs risk—no information available |
| Chloral hydrate | Avoid |
| Chlorambucil | Avoid; manufacturer advises effective contraception during administration to men or women; *see also* section 8.1 |
| Chloramphenicol (3) | Neonatal 'grey' syndrome |
| Chlordiazepoxide | *see* Benzodiazepines |
| Chloroquine | *see* Antimalarials |
| Chlorphenamine (chlorpheniramine) | *see* Anthistamines |
| Chlorpheniramine | *see* Antihistamines |
| Chlorpromazine | *see* Antipsychotics |
| Chlorpropamide | *see* Sulphonylureas |
| Chlortalidone | *see* Diuretics |
| Chlortetracycline | *see* Tetracyclines |
| Ciclesonide | *see* Corticosteroids |
| Ciclosporin | *see* p. 447 |
| Cidofovir | Avoid (toxicity in *animal* studies); effective contraception required during and for 1 month after treatment; also men should avoid fathering a child during and for 3 months after treatment |
| Cilastatin [ingredient] | *see Primaxin®* |
| Cilazapril | *see* ACE Inhibitors |
| Cilostazol | Avoid—toxicity in *animal* studies |
| Cimetidine | Manufacturer advises avoid unless essential |
| Cinacalcet | Manufacturer advises use only if potential benefit outweighs risk—no information available |
| Cinnarizine | *see* Anthistamines |
| Ciprofibrate | *see* Fibrates |
| Ciprofloxacin | *see* Quinolones |
| Cisatracurium | Manufacturer advises avoid—no information available |
| Cisplatin | Avoid (teratogenic and toxic in *animal* studies); *see also* section 8.1 |
| Citalopram | *see* Antidepressants, SSRI |
| Cladribine | Avoid (teratogenic in *animal* studies); *see also* section 8.1 |
| Clarithromycin | Manufacturer advises avoid unless potential benefit outweighs risk |
| Clavulanic acid [ingredient] | *see* Co-amoxiclav, *Timentin®* |
| Clemastine | *see* Anthistamines |
| Clindamycin | Not known to be harmful |
| Clobazam | *see* Benzodiazepines |
| Clobetasol | *see* Corticosteroids |
| Clobetasone | *see* Corticosteroids |
| Clodronate sodium | *see* Bisphosphonates |
| Clomethiazole | Avoid if possible—especially during first and third trimesters |
| Clomifene | Possible effects on fetal development |
| Clomipramine | *see* Antidepressants, Tricyclic (and related) |
| Clonazepam | *see* Benzodiazepines |
| Clonidine | May lower fetal heart rate, but risk should be balanced against risk of uncontrolled maternal hypertension; avoid intravenous injection |
| Clopidogrel | Manufacturer advises avoid—no information available |
| Clozapine | Manufacturer advises caution |
| Co-amoxiclav | *see* Penicillins |
| Co-beneldopa | *see* Levodopa |
| Co-careldopa | *see* Levodopa |
| Co-cyprindiol (1, 2, 3) | Feminisation of male fetus (due to cyproterone) |
| Codeine | *see* Opioid Analgesics |
| Co-fluampicil | *see* Penicillins |
| Colchicine | Avoid—teratogenicity in animal studies |
| Colistin (2, 3) | Avoid—possible risk of fetal toxicity |
| Contraceptives, oral | Epidemiological evidence suggests no harmful effects on fetus |
| Corticosteroids | Benefit of treatment, e.g. in asthma, outweighs risk (*see also* CSM advice, section 6.3.2); risk of intra-uterine growth restriction on prolonged or repeated systemic treatment; corticosteroid cover required by mother during labour; monitor closely if fluid retention |
| Co-trimoxazole (1) | Teratogenic risk (trimethoprim a folate antagonist) |
| (3) | Neonatal haemolysis and methaemoglobinaemia; fear of increased risk of kernicterus in neonates appears to be unfounded |
| Crisantaspase | Avoid; *see also* section 8.1 |
| Cromoglicate | *see* Sodium Cromoglicate |
| Cyclizine | *see* Antihistamines |
| Cyclopenthiazide | *see* Diuretics |
| Cyclophosphamide | Avoid (manufacturer advises effective contraception during and for at least 3 months after administration to men or women); *see also* section 8.1 |
| Cycloserine | Manufacturer advises use only if potential benefit outweighs risk—crosses the placenta |
| Cyclosporin | *see* p. 447 |
| Cyproheptadine | *see* Antihistamines |
| Cyproterone [ingredient] | *see* Co-cyprindiol |
| Cytarabine | Avoid (teratogenic in *animal* studies); *see also* section 8.1 |

Appendix 4

| Drug (trimester of risk) | Comment |
|---|---|
| Dacarbazine | Avoid (carcinogenic and teratogenic in *animal* studies); ensure effective contraception during and for at least 6 months after administration to men or women; *see also* section 8.1 |
| Daclizumab | Avoid |
| Dactinomycin | Avoid (teratogenic in *animal* studies); *see also* section 8.1 |
| Dalfopristin [ingredient] | *see Synercid®* |
| Dalteparin | Not known to be harmful |
| Danaparoid | Limited information available but not known to be harmful—manufacturer advises avoid |
| Danazol | |
| (1, 2, 3) | Avoid; has weak androgenic effects and virilisation of female fetus reported |
| Dantrolene | Use only for malignant hyperthermia if potential benefit outweighs risk; avoid use in chronic spasticity—embryotoxic in *animal* studies |
| Dantron (danthron) | Manufacturer advises avoid—no information available |
| Dapsone | |
| (3) | Neonatal haemolysis and methaemoglobinaemia; folic acid 5 mg daily should be given to mother |
| Darbepoetin | No evidence of harm in *animal* studies—manufacturer advises caution |
| Daunorubicin | Avoid (teratogenic and carcinogenic in *animal* studies); *see also* section 8.1 |
| Deferiprone | Manufacturer advises avoid before intended conception and during pregnancy—teratogenic and embryotoxic in *animal* studies; contraception advised in women of child-bearing potential |
| Deflazacort | *see* Corticosteroids |
| Demeclocycline | *see* Tetracyclines |
| Desferrioxamine | Teratogenic in *animal* studies; manufacturer advises use only if potential benefit outweighs risk |
| Desflurane | *see* Anaesthetics, General |
| Desloratadine | *see* Antihistamines |
| Desmopressin | |
| (3) | Small oxytocic effect in third trimester; increased risk of pre-eclampsia |
| Desogestrel | *see* Contraceptives, Oral |
| Dexamethasone | *see* Corticosteroids |
| Dexamfetamine | Manufacturer advises avoid (retrospective evidence of uncertain significance suggesting possible embryotoxicity) |
| Dexibuprofen | *see* NSAIDs |
| Dexketoprofen | *see* NSAIDs |
| Dextran | Avoid—reports of anaphylaxis in mother causing fetal anoxia, neurological damage and death |
| Dextromethorphan | *see* Opioid Analgesics |
| Dextropropoxyphene | *see* Opioid Analgesics |
| Diamorphine | *see* Opioid Analgesics |
| Diazepam | *see* Benzodiazepines |
| Diazoxide | |
| (2, 3) | Prolonged use may produce alopecia and impaired glucose tolerance in neonate; inhibits uterine activity during labour |
| Diclofenac | *see* NSAIDs |
| Didanosine | Manufacturer advises use only if potential benefit outweighs risk—no information available |
| Diethylstilbestrol | |
| (1) | High doses associated with vaginal carcinoma, urogenital abnormalities, and reduced fertility in female offspring; increased risk of hypospadias in male offspring |
| Diflucortolone | *see* Corticosteroids |
| Diflunisal | *see* NSAIDs |
| Digoxin | May need dosage adjustment |
| Dihydrocodeine | *see* Opioid Analgesics |
| Diloxanide | Manufacturer advises avoid—no information available |
| Diltiazem | Avoid |
| Diphenoxylate | *see* Opioid Analgesics |
| Dipipanone | *see* Opioid Analgesics |
| Dipyridamole | Not known to be harmful |
| Disodium etidronate | *see* Bisphosphonates |
| Disodium pamidronate | *see* Bisphosphonates |
| Disopyramide | |
| (3) | May induce labour |
| Distigmine | Manufacturer advises avoid (may stimulate uterine contractions) |
| Disulfiram | |
| (1) | High concentrations of acetaldehyde which occur in presence of alcohol may be teratogenic |
| Diuretics | Not used to treat hypertension in pregnancy |
| (1) | Manufacturers advise avoid acetazolamide and torasemide (toxicity in *animal* studies) |
| (3) | Thiazides may cause neonatal thrombocytopenia |
| Dobutamine | No information available |
| Docetaxel | Avoid (toxicity and reduced fertility in *animal* studies); manufacturer advises effective contraception during and for at least 3 months after administration; *see also* section 8.1 |
| Docusate sodium | Not known to be harmful—manufacturer advises caution |
| Dolasetron | Manufacturer advises avoid unless potential benefit outweighs risk—no information available |
| Domperidone | Manufacturer advises avoid |
| Dopamine | Manufacturer advises use only if potential benefit outweighs risk |

| Drug (trimester of risk) | Comment |
|---|---|
| Dopexamine | No information available—manufacturer advises avoid |
| Dornase alfa | No evidence of teratogenicity; manufacturer advises use only if potential benefit outweighs risk |
| Dosulepin (dothiepin) | *see* Antidepressants, Tricyclic (and related) |
| Dothiepin | *see* Antidepressants, Tricyclic (and related) |
| Doxazosin | *see* Alpha-blockers, Post-synaptic |
| Doxepin | *see* Antidepressants, Tricyclic (and related) |
| Doxorubicin | Avoid (teratogenic and toxic in *animal* studies); manufacturer of liposomal product advises effective contraception during and for at least 6 months after administration to men or women; *see also* section 8.1 |
| Doxycycline | *see* Tetracyclines |
| Drotrecogin alfa (activated) | Manufacturer advises avoid unless benefit outweighs risk—no information available |
| Duloxetine | Toxicity in *animal* studies—manufacturer advises avoid in patients with stress urinary incontinence and use only if potential benefit outweighs risk in depression; risk of neonatal withdrawal symptoms if used near term |
| Dutasteride (1, 2, 3) | Avoid unprotected intercourse (*see* section 6.4.2). May cause feminisation of male fetus |
| Dydrogesterone | Not known to be harmful |
| Econazole | Not known to be harmful |
| Edrophonium | Manufacturer advises use only if potential benefit outweighs risk |
| Efalizumab | Manufacturer advises avoid |
| Efavirenz | Manufacturer advises avoid unless no alternative available |
| Eflornithine | Toxicity in *animal* studies—manufacturer advises avoid |
| Eformoterol | *see* Formoterol |
| Eletriptan | *see* $5HT_1$ Agonists |
| Emtricitabine | No information available—manufacturer advises use only if essential |
| Enalapril | *see* ACE Inhibitors |
| Enfuvirtide | Manufacturer advises use only if potential benefit outweighs risk |
| Enoxaparin | Manufacturer advises avoid unless no safer alternative |
| Enoximone | Manufacturer advises use only if potential benefit outweighs risk |
| Entacapone | Manufacturer advises avoid—no information available |
| Ephedrine | Increased fetal heart rate reported with parenteral ephedrine |
| Epinastine | *see* Antihistamines |
| Epirubicin | Avoid (carcinogenic in *animal* studies); *see also* section 8.1 |
| Eplerenone | Manufacturer advises caution—no information available |
| Epoetin | No evidence of harm; benefits probably outweigh risk of anaemia and of transfusion in pregnancy |
| Epoprostenol | Manufacturer advises use with caution—no information available |
| Eprosartan | *As for* ACE Inhibitors |
| Eptifibatide | Manufacturer advises use only if potential benefit outweighs risk—no information available |
| Ergotamine (1, 2, 3) | Oxytocic effects on the pregnant uterus |
| Erlotinib | Manufacturer advises avoid—toxicity in *animal* studies; effective contraception required during and for at least 2 weeks after treatment; *see also* section 8.1 |
| Ertapenem | Manufacturer advises avoid unless potential benefit outweighs risk |
| Erythromycin | Not known to be harmful |
| Escitalopram | *see* Antidepressants, SSRI |
| Esmolol | *see* Beta-blockers |
| Esomeprazole | Manufacturer advises caution—no information available |
| Etanercept | Manufacturer advises avoid—no information available |
| Ethambutol | Not known to be harmful; *see also* p. 298 |
| Ethinylestradiol | *see* Contraceptives, Oral |
| Ethionamide (1) | May be teratogenic |
| Ethosuximide (1) | May possibly be teratogenic; *see* Antiepileptics |
| Etidronate disodium | *see* Bisphosphonates |
| Etodolac | *see* NSAIDs |
| Etomidate | *see* Anaesthetics, General |
| Etoposide | Avoid (teratogenic in *animal* studies); *see also* section 8.1 |
| Etoricoxib | *see* NSAIDs |
| Etynodiol | *see* Contraceptives, Oral |
| Ezetimibe | Manufacturer advises use only if potential benefit outweighs risk—no information available |
| Famciclovir | *see* Aciclovir |
| Famotidine | Manufacturer advises avoid unless potential benefit outweighs risk |
| *Fansidar®* (1) | Possible teratogenic risk (pyrimethamine a folate antagonist) |
| (3) | Neonatal haemolysis and methaemoglobinaemia; fear of increased risk of kernicterus in neonates appears to be unfounded |
| | *see also* Antimalarials |
| Felodipine | Avoid; toxicity in *animal* studies; may inhibit labour |

Appendix 4

| Drug (trimester of risk) | Comment |
|---|---|
| Fenbufen | *see* NSAIDs |
| Fenofibrate | *see* Fibrates |
| Fenoprofen | *see* NSAIDs |
| Fenoterol | *see* section 3.1 |
| Fentanyl | *see* Opioid Analgesics |
| Fexofenadine | *see* Antihistamines |
| Fibrates | Embryotoxicity in *animal* studies—manufacturers advise avoid |
| Filgrastim | Toxicity in *animal* studies; manufacturer advises use only if potential benefit outweighs risk |
| Finasteride (1, 2, 3) | Avoid unprotected intercourse (*see* section 6.4.2). May cause feminisation of male fetus |
| Flavoxate | Manufacturer advises avoid unless no safer alternative |
| Flecainide | Manufacturer advises toxicity in *animal* studies |
| Flucloxacillin | *see* Penicillins |
| Fluconazole | Manufacturer advises avoid—multiple congenital abnormalities reported with long-term high doses |
| Flucytosine | Teratogenic in *animal* studies; manufacturer advises use only if potential benefit outweighs risk |
| Fludarabine | Avoid (embryotoxic and teratogenic in *animal* studies); manufacturer advises effective contraception during and for at least 6 months after administration to men or women; *see also* section 8.1 |
| Fludrocortisone | *see* Corticosteroids |
| Fludroxycortide (flurandrenolone) | *see* Corticosteroids |
| Flumazenil | May cross placenta in small amounts—manufacturer advises avoid unless potential benefit outweighs risk |
| Flunisolide | *see* Corticosteroids |
| Fluocinolone | *see* Corticosteroids |
| Fluocinonide | *see* Corticosteroids |
| Fluocortolone | *see* Corticosteroids |
| Fluorometholone | *see* Corticosteroids |
| Fluorouracil | Avoid (teratogenic); *see also* section 8.1 |
| Fluoxetine | *see* Antidepressants, SSRI |
| Flupentixol | *see* Antipsychotics |
| Fluphenazine | *see* Antipsychotics |
| Flurandrenolone | *see* Corticosteroids |
| Flurazepam | *see* Benzodiazepines |
| Flurbiprofen | *see* NSAIDs |
| Fluticasone | *see* Corticosteroids |
| Fluvastatin | *see* Statins |
| Fluvoxamine | *see* Antidepressants, SSRI |
| Follitropin alfa and beta | Avoid |
| Fondaparinux | Manufacturer advises avoid unless potential benefit outweighs possible risk—no information available |
| Formoterol (eformoterol) | Manufacturers advise use only if potential benefit outweighs risk; *see also* section 3.1 |
| Fosamprenavir | Toxicity in *animal* studies; manufacturer advises use only if potential benefit outweighs risk |
| Foscarnet | Manufacturer advises avoid |
| Fosinopril | *see* ACE Inhibitors |
| Fosphenytoin | *see* Phenytoin |
| Framycetin | *see* Aminoglycosides |
| Frovatriptan | *see* $5HT_1$ Agonists |
| Frusemide | *see* Diuretics |
| Fulvestrant | Manufacturer advises avoid—increased incidence of fetal abnormalities and death in *animal* studies |
| Furosemide (frusemide) | *see* Diuretics |
| Fusidic acid | *see* Sodium Fusidate |
| Gabapentin | *see* Antiepileptics |
| Galantamine | Developmental delay in *animal* studies |
| Ganciclovir | Avoid—teratogenic risk; *see also* p. 325 |
| Ganirelix | Manufacturer advises avoid in confirmed pregnancy—toxicity in *animal* studies |
| Gemcitabine | Avoid (teratogenic in *animal* studies); *see also* section 8.1 |
| Gemfibrozil | *see* Fibrates |
| Gentamicin | *see* Aminoglycosides |
| Gestodene | *see* Contraceptives, Oral |
| Gestrinone (1, 2, 3) | Avoid |
| Glatiramer | Manufacturer advises avoid—no information available |
| Glibenclamide | *see* Sulphonylureas |
| Gliclazide | *see* Sulphonylureas |
| Glimepiride | *see* Sulphonylureas |
| Glipizide | *see* Sulphonylureas |
| Gliquidone | *see* Sulphonylureas |
| Glyceryl trinitrate | Not known to be harmful but most manufacturers advise avoid unless potential benefit outweighs risk |
| Goserelin | Manufacturer advises avoid in pregnancy—exclude pregnancy before treatment and use non-hormonal contraceptives during treatment |
| Granisetron | Manufacturer advises use only when compelling reasons—no information available |
| Griseofulvin | Avoid (fetotoxicity and teratogenicity in *animals*); effective contraception required during and for at least 1 month after administration (**important:** effectiveness of oral contraceptives reduced, see p. 408); also men should avoid fathering a child during and for at least 6 months after administration |

| Drug (trimester of risk) | Comment |
|---|---|
| Guanethidine (3) | Postural hypotension and reduced uteroplacental perfusion; should not be used to treat hypertension in pregnancy |
| Haem arginate | Manufacturer advises avoid unless essential |
| Halcinonide | *see* Corticosteroids |
| Haloperidol | *see* Antipsychotics |
| Halothane | *see* Anaesthetics, General |
| Heparin (1, 2, 3) | Maternal osteoporosis reported after prolonged use; multidose vials may contain benzyl alcohol—some manufacturers advise avoid; *see also* Bemiparin, Dalteparin, Enoxaparin, Reviparin, and Tinzaparin |
| $5HT_1$ agonists | Limited experience—manufacturers advise avoid unless potential benefit outweighs risk |
| Human menopausal gonadotrophins | Avoid |
| Hydralazine (1, 2) | Manufacturer advises avoid before third trimester; no reports of serious harm following use in third trimester |
| Hydrochlorothiazide | *see* Diuretics |
| Hydrocortisone | *see* Corticosteroids |
| Hydroflumethiazide | *see* Diuretics |
| Hydromorphone | *see* Opioid Analgesics |
| Hydroxycarbamide (hydroxyurea) | Avoid (teratogenic in *animal* studies); manufacturer advises effective contraception before and during administration; *see also* section 8.1 |
| Hydroxychloroquine | Manufacturer advises avoid but see p. 518 |
| Hydroxyurea | *see* Hydroxycarbamide |
| Hydroxyzine | *see* Antihistamines |
| Hyoscine butylbromide | Manufacturer advises use only if potential benefit outweighs risk |
| Hyoscine hydrobromide | Manufacturer advises use only if potential benefit outweighs risk; injection may depress neonatal respiration |
| Ibandronic acid | *see* Bisphosphonates |
| Ibuprofen | *see* NSAIDs |
| Idarubicin | Avoid (teratogenic and toxic in *animal* studies); *see also* section 8.1 |
| Idoxuridine | Teratogenic in *animal* studies—manufacturer advises avoid |
| Ifosfamide | Avoid (teratogenic and carcinogenic in *animals*); manufacturer advises adequate contraception during and for at least 6 months after administration to men or women; *see also* section 8.1 |
| Iloprost | Manufacturer advises avoid (toxicity in *animal* studies); effective contraception must be used during treatment |
| Imatinib | Manufacturer advises avoid unless potential benefit outweighs risk; *see also* section 8.1 |
| Imidapril | *see* ACE Inhibitors |
| Imiglucerase | Manufacturer advises use only if potential benefit outweighs risk—no information available |
| Imipenem [ingredient] | *see Primaxin®* |
| Imipramine | *see* Antidepressants, Tricyclic (and related) |
| Imiquimod | No evidence of teratogenicity or toxicity in *animal* studies; manufacturer advises caution |
| Indapamide | *see* Diuretics |
| Indinavir | Toxicity in *animal* studies; manufacturer advises use only if potential benefit outweighs risk; theoretical risk of hyperbilirubinaemia and renal stones in neonate if used at term |
| Indometacin | *see* NSAIDs |
| Infliximab | Avoid; manufacturer advises adequate contraception during and for at least 6 months after last dose |
| Influenza vaccine | Not known to be harmful |
| Inosine | Manufacturer advises avoid |
| Inositol nicotinate | No information available—manufacturer advises avoid unless potential benefit outweighs risk |
| Insulin (1, 2, 3) | Insulin requirements should be assessed frequently by an experienced diabetes physician; limited evidence of safety of newer insulin analogues |
| Interferons | Manufacturers recommend avoid unless compelling reasons; effective contraception to be used by men and women receiving treatment |
| Iodine and iodides (2, 3) | Neonatal goitre and hypothyroidism |
| Iodine, radioactive (1, 2, 3) | Permanent hypothyroidism—avoid |
| Iodoform | *see* Povidone–iodine |
| Ipratropium | Not known to be harmful; *see* section 3.1 |
| Irbesartan | *As for* ACE Inhibitors |
| Irinotecan | Avoid (teratogenic and toxic in *animal* studies); manufacturer advises effective contraception during and for at least 3 months after administration; *see also* section 8.1 |
| Iron (parenteral) | Avoid in first trimester |
| Iron dextran | *see* Iron (parenteral) |
| Iron sucrose | *see* Iron (parenteral) |
| Isocarboxazid | *see* Antidepressants, MAOI |
| Isoflurane | *see* Anaesthetics, General |
| Isometheptene [ingredient] | *see* Midrid® |

Appendix 4

| Drug (trimester of risk) | Comment |
|---|---|
| Isoniazid | Not known to be harmful; *see also* p. 298 |
| Isosorbide dinitrate | May cross placenta—manufacturers advise avoid unless potential benefit outweighs risk |
| Isosorbide mononitrate | Manufacturers advise avoid unless potential benefit outweighs risk |
| Isotretinoin | |
| (1, 2, 3) | Teratogenic; effective contraception must be used for at least 1 month before oral treatment, during treatment and for at least 1 month after stopping; also avoid topical treatment |
| Isradipine | May inhibit labour; risk to fetus should be balanced against risk of uncontrolled maternal hypertension |
| Itraconazole | Manufacturer advises use only in life-threatening situations (toxicity at high doses in *animal* studies); ensure effective contraception during treatment and until the next menstrual period following end of treatment |
| Ivabradine | Manufacturer advise avoid—toxicity in *animal* studies |
| *Kaletra*® | Avoid oral solution due to high propylene glycol content; manufacturer advises use capsules only if potential benefit outweighs risk (toxicity in *animal* studies) |
| Ketamine | *see* Anaesthetics, General |
| Ketoconazole | Manufacturer advises teratogenicity in *animal* studies; packs carry a warning to avoid in pregnancy |
| Ketoprofen | *see* NSAIDs |
| Ketorolac | *see* NSAIDs |
| Ketotifen | *see* Antihistamines |
| Labetalol | *see* Beta-blockers |
| Lacidipine | Manufacturer advises avoid; may inhibit labour |
| Lactulose | Not known to be harmful |
| Lamivudine | |
| (1) | Manufacturer advises avoid during first trimester—no information available |
| Lamotrigine | *see* Antiepileptics |
| Lanreotide | Manufacturer advises use only if potential benefit outweighs risk |
| Lansoprazole | Manufacturer advises avoid |
| Laronidase | Manufacturer advises avoid unless essential—no information available |
| Latanoprost | Manufacturer advises avoid |
| Leflunomide | Avoid—active metabolite teratogenic in *animal* studies; effective contraception essential during treatment and for at least 2 years after treatment in women and at least 3 months after treatment in men (*see also* Leflunomide section 10.1.3) |
| Lenograstim | Toxicity in *animal* studies; manufacturer advises use only if potential benefit outweighs risk |
| Lepirudin | Avoid |
| Lercanidipine | Manufacturer advises avoid—no information available |
| Leuprorelin | Avoid—teratogenic in *animal* studies |
| Levetiracetam | Toxicity in *animal* studies—manufacturer advises use only if potential benefit outweighs risk; *see also* Antiepileptics |
| Levobupivacaine | |
| (1) | Manufacturer advises avoid if possible—toxicity in *animal* studies; *see also* Anaesthetics, Local |
| Levocetirizine | *see* Antihistamines |
| Levodopa | Manufacturers advise toxicity in *animal* studies |
| Levofloxacin | *see* Quinolones |
| Levomepromazine (methotrimeprazine) | *see* Antipsychotics |
| Levonorgestrel | *see* Contraceptives, Oral |
| Levothyroxine (thyroxine) | Monitor maternal serum-thyrotrophin concentration—levothyroxine may cross the placenta and excessive maternal concentration can be detrimental to fetus |
| Lidocaine (lignocaine) | *see* Anaesthetics, Local |
| Lignocaine | *see* Anaesthetics, Local |
| Linezolid | Manufacturer advises use only if potential benefit outweighs risk—no information available |
| Liothyronine | Does not cross the placenta in significant amounts; monitor maternal thyroid function tests—dosage adjustment may be necessary |
| Lisinopril | *see* ACE Inhibitors |
| Lithium salts | |
| (1) | Avoid if possible (risk of teratogenicity, including cardiac abnormalities) |
| (2, 3) | Dose requirements increased (but on delivery return to normal abruptly); close monitoring of serum-lithium concentration advised (risk of toxicity in neonate) |
| Lofepramine | *see* Antidepressants, Tricyclic (and related) |
| Loperamide | Manufacturers advise avoid—no information available |
| Lopinavir [ingredient] | *see Kaletra*® |
| Loprazolam | *see* Benzodiazepines |
| Loratadine | Embryotoxic in *animal* studies; *see also* Antihistamines |
| Lorazepam | *see* Benzodiazepines |
| Lormetazepam | *see* Benzodiazepines |
| Losartan | *As for* ACE Inhibitors |

| Drug (trimester of risk) | Comment |
|---|---|
| Lumefantrine [ingredient] | *see Riamet®* |
| Lumiracoxib | *see* NSAIDs |
| Lymecycline | *see* Tetracyclines |
| Magnesium sulphate (3) | Not known to be harmful for short-term intravenous administration in eclampsia but excessive doses cause neonatal respiratory depression |
| *Malarone®* | Manufacturer advises avoid unless essential |
| Maprotiline | *see* Antidepressants, Tricyclic (and related) |
| Mebendazole | Manufacturer advises toxicity in *animal* studies |
| Mebeverine | Not known to be harmful; manufacturers advise caution |
| Medroxyprogesterone | Avoid—genital malformations and cardiac defects reported in male and female fetuses |
| Mefenamic acid | *see* NSAIDs |
| Mefloquine (1) | Manufacturer advises teratogenicity in *animal* studies, but *see* p. 330, and p. 331 |
| Meloxicam | *see* NSAIDs |
| Melphalan | Avoid (manufacturer advises adequate contraception during administration to men or women); *see also* section 8.1 |
| Memantine | Manufacturer advises avoid unless essential—intra-uterine growth restriction in *animal* studies |
| Menadiol (3) | Neonatal haemolytic anaemia, hyperbilirubinaemia and increased risk of kernicterus in jaundiced infants |
| Menotrophin | Avoid |
| Meprobamate | Manufacturer advises avoid if possible |
| Meptazinol | *see* Opioid Analgesics |
| Mercaptamine | Manufacturer advises avoid |
| Mercaptopurine | Avoid (teratogenic); *see also* section 8.1 |
| Meropenem | Manufacturer advises use only if potential benefit outweighs risk—no information available |
| Mesalazine | Negligible quantities cross placenta |
| Mesna | Not known to be harmful; *see also* section 8.1 |
| Mesterolone | *see* Androgens |
| Mestranol | *see* Contraceptives, Oral |
| Metaraminol | May reduce placental perfusion—manufacturer advises use only if potential benefit outweighs risk |
| Metformin (1, 2, 3) | Avoid; insulin is normally substituted in all diabetics |
| Methadone | *see* Opioid Analgesics |
| Methocarbamol | Manufacturer advises avoid unless potential benefit outweighs risk |
| Methotrexate | Avoid (teratogenic; fertility may be reduced during therapy but this may be reversible); manufacturer advises effective contraception during and for at least 3 months after administration to men or women; *see also* section 8.1 |
| Methotrimeprazine | *see* Antipsychotics |
| Methyldopa | Not known to be harmful |
| Methylphenidate | Limited experience—manufacturer advises avoid unless potential benefit outweighs risk; toxicity in *animals* |
| Methylprednisolone | *see* Corticosteroids |
| Methysergide | Manufacturer advises avoid |
| Metoclopramide | Not known to be harmful but manufacturer advises use only when compelling reasons |
| Metolazone | *see* Diuretics |
| Metoprolol | *see* Beta-blockers |
| Metronidazole | Manufacturer advises avoidance of high-dose regimens |
| Metyrapone | Avoid (may impair biosynthesis of fetal-placental steroids) |
| Mexiletine | Manufacturer advises avoid unless potential benefit outweighs risk |
| Mianserin | *see* Antidepressants, Tricyclic (and related) |
| Miconazole | Manufacturer advises avoid unless essential |
| Midazolam | *see* Benzodiazepines |
| *Midrid®* | Manufacturer advises avoid |
| Mifepristone | Manufacturer advises that if treatment fails, essential that pregnancy be terminated by another method |
| Miglustat | Manufacturer advises avoid (toxicity in *animal* studies)—effective contraception must be used during treatment; also men should avoid fathering a child during and for 3 months after treatment |
| Milrinone | Manufacturer advises use only if potential benefit outweighs risk |
| Minocycline | *see* Tetracyclines |
| Minoxidil (3) | Neonatal hirsutism reported |
| Mirtazapine | Manufacturers advise avoid—toxicity in *animal* studies |
| Misoprostol (1, 2, 3) | Avoid—potent uterine stimulant (has been used to induce abortion) and may be teratogenic |
| Mitomycin | Avoid (teratogenic in *animal* studies); *see also* section 8.1 |
| Mitotane | Manufacturer advises avoid—women of childbearing age should use effective contraception during and after treatment; *see also* section 8.1 |

Appendix 4

| Drug (trimester of risk) | Comment |
|---|---|
| Mitoxantrone (mitozantrone) | Avoid; manufacturer advises effective contraception during and for at least 6 months after administration to men or women; *see also* section 8.1 |
| Mitozantrone | *see* Mitoxantrone |
| Mivacurium | Manufacturer advises avoid—no information available |
| Mizolastine | Manufacturer advises avoid; *see also* Antihistamines |
| Moclobemide | *see* Antidepressants, MAOI |
| Modafinil | Manufacturer advises avoid |
| Moexipril | *see* ACE Inhibitors |
| Montelukast | Manufacturer advises avoid unless essential |
| Morphine | *see* Opioid Analgesics |
| *Movicol®* | Manufacturer advises use only if essential—no information available |
| Moxifloxacin | *see* Quinolones |
| Moxisylyte (thymoxamine) | Manufacturer advises avoid |
| Moxonidine | Manufacturer advises avoid—no information available |
| Mupirocin | Manufacturer advises avoid unless potential benefit outweighs risk—no information available |
| Mycophenolate mofetil | Manufacturer advises avoid—toxicity in *animal* studies; effective contraception required during and for 6 weeks after discontinuation of treatment |
| Nabilone | Manufacturer advises avoid unless essential |
| Nabumetone | *see* NSAIDs |
| Nadolol | *see* Beta-blockers |
| Nafarelin | Avoid |
| Nalbuphine | *see* Opioid Analgesics |
| Nalidixic acid | *see* Quinolones |
| Naloxone | Manufacturer advises use only if potential benefit outweighs risk |
| Nandrolone | *see* Anabolic Steroids |
| Naproxen | *see* NSAIDs |
| Naratriptan | *see* $5HT_1$ Agonists |
| Narcotic analgesics | *see* Opioid Analgesics |
| Nateglinide | Manufacturer advises avoid—toxicity in *animal* studies; insulin is normally substituted in all diabetics |
| Nebivolol | *see* Beta-blockers |
| Nedocromil | *see* section 3.1 |
| Nefopam | No information available—manufacturer advises avoid unless no safer treatment |
| Nelfinavir | No information available—manufacturer advises use only if potential benefit outweighs risk |
| Neomycin | *see* Aminoglycosides |
| Neostigmine | Manufacturer advises use only if potential benefit outweighs risk |
| Netilmicin | *see* Aminoglycosides |
| Nevirapine | Although manufacturers advise avoid, may be appropriate to use if clearly indicated; *see also* p. 314 |
| Nicardipine | May inhibit labour; manufacturer advises avoid, but risk to fetus should be balanced against risk of uncontrolled maternal hypertension |
| Nicorandil | Manufacturer advises use only if potential benefit outweighs risk—no information available |
| Nicotine | Use only if smoking cessation without nicotine replacement fails; avoid liquorice-flavoured nicotine products; patient information for some products contra-indicates use |
| Nicotinic acid | No information available—manufacturer advises avoid unless potential benefit outweighs risk |
| Nicoumalone | *see* Anticoagulants, Oral |
| Nifedipine | May inhibit labour; manufacturer advises avoid, but risk to fetus should be balanced against risk of uncontrolled maternal hypertension |
| Nimodipine | Manufacturer advises use only if potential benefit outweighs risk |
| Nisoldipine | Avoid (toxicity in *animal* studies) |
| Nitrazepam | *see* Benzodiazepines |
| Nitrofurantoin | |
| (3) | May produce neonatal haemolysis if used at term |
| Nitroprusside | *see* Sodium Nitroprusside |
| Nitrous oxide | *see* Anaesthetics, General |
| Nizatidine | Manufacturer advises avoid unless essential |
| Noradrenaline (norepinephrine) (1, 2, 3) | Avoid—may reduce placental perfusion |
| Norethisterone | Masculinisation of female fetuses and other defects reported; *see also* Contraceptives, Oral |
| Norfloxacin | *see* Quinolones |
| Norgestimate | *see* Contraceptives, Oral |
| Norgestrel | *see* Contraceptives, Oral |
| Nortriptyline | *see* Antidepressants, Tricyclic (and related) |
| NSAIDs | Most manufacturers advise avoid (or avoid unless potential benefit outweighs risk); ketorolac contra-indicated during pregnancy, labour and delivery |
| (3) | With regular use closure of fetal ductus arteriosus *in utero* and possibly persistent pulmonary hypertension of the newborn. Delayed onset and increased duration of labour |
| Nystatin | No information available, but absorption from gastro-intestinal tract negligible |

| Drug (trimester of risk) | Comment |
|---|---|
| Octreotide | |
| (1, 2, 3) | Possible effect on fetal growth; manufacturer advises use only if potential benefit outweighs risk |
| Oestrogens | *see* Contraceptives, Oral |
| Ofloxacin | *see* Quinolones |
| Olanzapine | |
| (3) | Manufacturer advises use only if potential benefit outweighs risk; neonatal lethargy, tremor, and hypertonia reported |
| Olmesartan | *As for* ACE inhibitors |
| Olsalazine | Manufacturer advises avoid unless potential benefit outweighs risk |
| Omalizumab | Manufacturer advises avoid unless essential; no evidence of teratogenicity in *animal* studies |
| Omega-3-acid ethyl esters | Manufacturer advises use only if potential benefit outweighs risk—no information available |
| Omeprazole | Not known to be harmful |
| Ondansetron | No information available; manufacturer advises avoid unless potential benefit outweighs risk |
| Opioid analgesics | |
| (3) | Depress neonatal respiration; withdrawal effects in neonates of dependent mothers; gastric stasis and risk of inhalation pneumonia in mother during labour; *see also* Tramadol |
| Oral contraceptives | *see* Contraceptives, Oral |
| Orlistat | Manufacturer advises caution |
| Orphenadrine | Manufacturer advises caution |
| Oseltamivir | Manufacturer advises avoid unless potential benefit outweighs risk |
| Oxaliplatin | Manufacturer advises avoid—no information available; *see also* section 8.1 |
| Oxazepam | *see* Benzodiazepines |
| Oxcarbazepine | |
| (1) | Risk of teratogenesis including increased risk of neural tube defects (counselling and screening and adequate folate supplements advised, e.g. 5 mg daily); *see also* Antiepileptics and p. 238 |
| (3) | Because of neonatal bleeding tendency associated with some antiepileptics, manufacturer advises prophylactic vitamin $K_1$ for mother before delivery (as well as for neonate) |
| Oxprenolol | *see* Beta-blockers |
| Oxybutynin | Manufacturer advises avoid unless potential benefit outweighs risk—toxicity in *animal* studies |
| Oxycodone | *see* Opioid Analgesics |
| Oxytetracycline | *see* Tetracyclines |

| Drug (trimester of risk) | Comment |
|---|---|
| Paclitaxel | Avoid (toxicity in *animal* studies); ensure effective contraception during and for at least 6 months after administration to men or women; *see also* section 8.1 |
| Palonosetron | Manufacturer advises avoid—no information available |
| Pamidronate disodium | *see* Bisphosphonates |
| Pancreatin | Not known to be harmful |
| Pancuronium | Manufacturer advises avoid unless potential benefit outweighs risk—no information available |
| Pantoprazole | Manufacturer advises avoid unless potential benefit outweighs risk—fetotoxic in *animals* |
| Papaveretum | *see* Opioid Analgesics |
| Paracetamol | Not known to be harmful |
| Paraldehyde | Manufacturer advises avoid unless essential—crosses the placenta |
| Parecoxib | *see* NSAIDS |
| Paricalcitol | Toxicity in *animal* studies—manufacturer advises avoid unless potential benefit outweighs risk; *see also* Vitamin D |
| Paroxetine | *see* Antidepressants, SSRI |
| Pegfilgrastim | Toxicity in *animal* studies; manufacturer advises use only if potential benefit ouweighs risk |
| Pemetrexed | Avoid (toxicity in *animal* studies); manufacturer advises effective contraception during treatment; men must avoid fathering a child during and for at least 6 months after treatment; *see also* section 8.1 |
| Penicillamine | |
| (1, 2, 3) | Fetal abnormalities reported rarely; avoid if possible |
| Penicillins | Not known to be harmful |
| Pentamidine isetionate | Manufacturer advises avoid unless essential |
| Pentazocine | *see* Opioid Analgesics |
| Pentostatin | Avoid (teratogenic in *animal* studies); manufacturer advises that men should not father children during and for 6 months after administration; *see also* section 8.1 |
| Pergolide | Manufacturer advises use only if potential benefit outweighs risk |
| Pericyazine | *see* Antipsychotics |
| Perindopril | *see* ACE Inhibitors |
| Perphenazine | *see* Antipsychotics |
| Pethidine | *see* Opioid Analgesics |
| Phenelzine | *see* Antidepressants, MAOI |
| Phenindione | *see* Anticoagulants, Oral |

Appendix 4

| Drug (trimester of risk) | Comment |
|---|---|
| Phenobarbital | |
| (1, 3) | Congenital malformations. May possibly cause vitamin K deficiency and risk of neonatal bleeding; if vitamin K not given at birth, neonate should be monitored closely for signs of bleeding; *see also* Antiepileptics |
| Phenothiazines | *see* Antipsychotics |
| Phenoxybenzamine | Hypotension may occur in newborn |
| Phenoxymethylpenicillin | *see* Penicillins |
| Phentolamine | Use with caution—may cause marked decrease in maternal blood pressure with resulting fetal anoxia |
| Phenylephrine | |
| (1) | Malformations reported |
| (3) | Avoid if possible—fetal hypoxia and bradycardia reported in late pregnancy and labour |
| Phenytoin | |
| (1, 3) | Congenital malformations (screening advised); adequate folate supplements should be given to mother (e.g. folic acid 5 mg daily). May possibly cause vitamin K deficiency and risk of neonatal bleeding; if vitamin K not given at birth, neonate should be monitored closely for signs of bleeding. Caution in interpreting plasma concentrations—bound may be reduced but free (i.e. effective) unchanged; *see also* Antiepileptics |
| Pholcodine | *see* Opioid Analgesics |
| Phytomenadione | Manufacturer advises use only if potential benefit outweighs risk—no specific information available |
| Pilocarpine | Avoid—smooth muscle stimulant; toxicity in *animal* studies |
| Pimozide | *see* Antipsychotics |
| Pindolol | *see* Beta-blockers |
| Pioglitazone | Manufacturer advises avoid—toxicity in *animal* studies; insulin is normally substituted in all diabetics |
| Piperacillin [ingredient] | *see Tazocin®* |
| Piperazine | Not known to be harmful but manufacturer advises avoid in first trimester |
| Pipotiazine | *see* Antipsychotics |
| Piracetam | Manufacturer advises avoid |
| Piroxicam | *see* NSAIDs |
| Pivmecillinam | *see* Penicillins |
| Pizotifen | Manufacturer advises avoid unless potential benefit outweighs risk |
| Podophyllum | Avoid—neonatal death and teratogenesis have been reported |
| Polystyrene sulphonate resins | Manufacturers advise use only if potential benefit outweighs risk—no information available |
| Porfimer | Manufacturer advises avoid unless essential |
| Povidone–iodine | |
| (2, 3) | Sufficient iodine may be absorbed to affect the fetal thyroid |
| Pramipexole | Manufacturer advises use only if potential benefit outweighs risk—no information available |
| Pravastatin | *see* Statins |
| Prazosin | *see* Alpha-blockers, Post-synaptic |
| Prednisolone | *see* Corticosteroids |
| Pregabalin | Toxicity in *animal* studies—manufacturer advises use only if potential benefit outweighs risk |
| Prilocaine | |
| (3) | Neonatal methaemoglobinaemia reported after paracervical block or pudendal block; *see also* Anaesthetics, Local |
| Primaquine | |
| (3) | Neonatal haemolysis and methaemoglobinaemia; *see also* Antimalarials |
| *Primaxin®* | Manufacturer advises avoid unless potential benefit outweighs risk (toxicity in *animal* studies) |
| Primidone | *see* Phenobarbital |
| Procainamide | Manufacturer advises avoid unless potential benefit outweighs risk |
| Procaine | |
| (3) | Neonatal methaemoglobinaemia; *see also* Anaesthetics, Local |
| Procarbazine | Avoid (teratogenic in *animal* studies and isolated reports in humans); *see also* section 8.1 |
| Prochlorperazine | *see* Antipsychotics |
| Progesterone | Not known to be harmful |
| Proguanil | Adequate folate supplements should be given to mother; *see also* Antimalarials |
| Promazine | *see* Antipsychotics |
| Promethazine | *see* Antihistamines |
| Propafenone | Manufacturer advises avoid—no information available |
| Propantheline | Manufacturer advises avoid—no information available |
| Propiverine | Manufacturer advises avoid (restriction of skeletal development in *animals*) |
| Propofol | *see* Anaesthetics, General |
| Propranolol | *see* Beta-blockers |
| Propylthiouracil | |
| (2, 3) | Neonatal goitre and hypothyroidism |
| Protionamide | |
| (1) | May be teratogenic |
| Pseudoephedrine | Not known to be harmful |

| Drug (trimester of risk) | Comment |
|---|---|
| Pyrazinamide | Manufacturer advises use only if potential benefit outweighs risk; see also p. 298 |
| Pyridostigmine | Manufacturer advises use only if potential benefit outweighs risk |
| Pyrimethamine | |
| (1) | Theoretical teratogenic risk (folate antagonist); adequate folate supplements should be given to mother; *see also* Antimalarials |
| Quetiapine | Manufacturer advises use only if potential benefit outweighs risk |
| Quinagolide | Manufacturer advises discontinue when pregnancy confirmed unless medical reason for continuing |
| Quinapril | *see* ACE Inhibitors |
| Quinidine | Not known to be harmful at therapeutic doses but manufacturer advises avoid |
| Quinine | |
| (1) | High doses are teratogenic; but in malaria benefit of treatment outweighs risk |
| Quinolones | |
| (1, 2, 3) | Avoid—arthropathy in *animal* studies; safer alternatives available |
| Quinupristin [ingredient] | *see Synercid®* |
| Rabeprazole | Manufacturer advises avoid—no information available |
| Raltitrexed | Pregnancy must be excluded before treatment; ensure effective contraception during and for at least 6 months after administration to men or women; *see also* section 8.1 |
| Ramipril | *see* ACE Inhibitors |
| Ranitidine | Manufacturer advises avoid unless essential, but not known to be harmful |
| Ranitidine bismuth citrate | Safety not established |
| Rasagiline | Manufacturer advises caution |
| Rasburicase | Manufacturer advises avoid—no information available |
| Reboxetine | Manufacturer advises avoid (and discontinue if pregnancy occurs)—no information available |
| Remifentanil | No information available; *see also* Opioid Analgesics |
| Repaglinide | Manufacturer advises avoid; insulin is normally substituted in all diabetics |
| Reteplase | *see* Streptokinase |
| Reviparin | Manufacturer advises avoid—no information available |
| *Riamet®* | Toxicity in *animal* studies with artemether; manufacturer advises use only if potential benefit outweighs risk |
| Ribavirin | Avoid; teratogenicity in *animal* studies; ensure effective contraception during oral administration and for 6 months after treatment in women and in men; *see also* Ribavirin section 5.3.5 |
| Rifabutin | Manufacturer advises avoid—no information available |
| Rifampicin | |
| (1) | Manufacturers advise very high doses teratogenic in *animal* studies; *see also* p. 298 |
| (3) | Risk of neonatal bleeding may be increased |
| Riluzole | No information available; manufacturer advises avoid |
| Risedronate sodium | *see* Bisphosphonates |
| Risperidone | Manufacturer advises use only if potential benefit outweighs risk |
| Ritodrine | For use in premature labour *see* section 7.1.3 |
| Ritonavir | Manufacturer advises use only if potential benefit outweighs risk—no information available |
| Rituximab | Avoid unless potential benefit to mother outweighs risk of B-lymphocyte depletion in fetus—effective contraception required during and for 12 months after treatment |
| Rivastigmine | Manufacturer advises use only if potential benefit outweighs risk |
| Rizatriptan | *see* $5HT_1$ Agonists |
| Rocuronium | Manufacturer advises avoid unless potential benefit outweighs risk |
| Ropivacaine | Safety not established but not known to be harmful |
| Rosiglitazone | Manufacturer advises avoid—toxicity in *animal* studies; insulin is normally substituted in all diabetics |
| Rosuvastatin | *see* Statins |
| Salbutamol | For use in asthma *see* section 3.1 |
| (3) | For use in premature labour *see* section 7.1.3 |
| Salcatonin | *see* Calcitonin (salmon) |
| Salmeterol | *see* section 3.1 |
| Saquinavir | Manufacturer advises use only if potential benefit outweighs risk |
| Selegiline | Manufacturer advises avoid—no information available |
| Sertindole | Manufacturer advises avoid |
| Sertraline | *see* Antidepressants, SSRI |
| Sevelamer | Manufacturer advises use only if potential benefit outweighs risk |
| Sevoflurane | *see* Anaesthetics, General |
| Sibutramine | Manufacturer advises avoid—toxicity in *animal* studies |
| Silver sulfadiazine | *see* Sulphonamides |
| Simvastatin | *see* Statins |

Appendix 4

| Drug (trimester of risk) | Comment |
|---|---|
| Sirolimus | Manufacturer advises avoid (toxicity in *animal* studies); effective contraception must be used during treatment and for 12 weeks after stopping |
| Sodium aurothiomalate | Manufacturer advises avoid but limited data suggests usually not necessary to withdraw if condition well controlled—consider reducing dose and frequency |
| Sodium clodronate | *see* Bisphosphonates |
| Sodium cromoglicate | Not known to be harmful; *see also* section 3.1 |
| Sodium fusidate | Not known to be harmful; manufacturer advises use only if potential benefit outweighs risk |
| Sodium nitroprusside | Potential for accumulation of cyanide in fetus—avoid prolonged use |
| Sodium phenylbutyrate | Avoid (toxicity in *animal* studies); manufacturer advises adequate contraception during administration |
| Sodium valproate | *see* Valproate |
| Solifenacin | Manufacturer advises caution—no information available |
| Somatropin | Discontinue if pregnancy occurs—no information available but theoretical risk |
| Sotalol | *see* Beta-blockers |
| Spironolactone | Manufacturers advise toxicity in *animal* studies |
| Statins | Avoid—congenital anomalies reported; decreased synthesis of cholesterol possibly affects fetal development |
| Stavudine | Manufacturer advises use only if potential benefit outweighs risk |
| Streptokinase | |
| (1, 2, 3) | Possibility of premature separation of placenta in first 18 weeks; theoretical possibility of fetal haemorrhage throughout pregnancy; risk of maternal haemorrhage on post-partum use |
| Streptomycin | *see* Aminoglycosides |
| Strontium ranelate | Avoid—toxicity in *animal* studies |
| Sulfadiazine | *see* Sulphonamides |
| Sulfadoxine | *see* Sulphonamides |
| Sulfasalazine | |
| (3) | Theoretical risk of neonatal haemolysis; adequate folate supplements should be given to mother |
| Sulindac | *see* NSAIDs |
| Sulphonamides | |
| (3) | Neonatal haemolysis and methaemoglobinaemia; fear of increased risk of kernicterus in neonates appears to be unfounded |
| Sulphonylureas | |
| (3) | Neonatal hypoglycaemia; insulin is normally substituted in all diabetics; if oral drugs are used therapy should be stopped at least 2 days before delivery |
| Sulpiride | *see* Antipsychotics |
| Sumatriptan | *see* $5HT_1$ Agonists |
| Suxamethonium | Mildly prolonged maternal paralysis may occur |
| *Synercid®* | Manufacturer advises avoid unless potential benefit outweighs risk—no information available |
| Tacalcitol | Manufacturer advises avoid unless no safer alternative—no information available |
| Tacrolimus | Avoid; manufacturer advises toxicity in *animal* studies following systemic administration |
| Tamoxifen | Avoid—possible effects on fetal development; effective contraception must be used during treatment and for 2 months after stopping |
| Tazarotene | Avoid; effective contraception required |
| Tazobactam [ingredient] | *see Tazocin®* |
| *Tazocin®* | Manufacturer advises use only if potential benefit outweighs risk |
| Tegafur with uracil | *see Uftoral®* |
| Teicoplanin | Manufacturer advises use only if potential benefit outweighs risk |
| Telithromycin | Toxicity in animal studies—manufacturer advises use only if potential benefit outweighs risk |
| Telmisartan | *As for* ACE Inhibitors |
| Temazepam | *see* Benzodiazepines |
| Temozolomide | Avoid (teratogenic and embryotoxic in *animal* studies); manufacturer advises adequate contraception during administration; *see also* section 8.1; also men should avoid fathering a child during and for at least 6 months after treatment |
| Tenecteplase | *see* Streptokinase |
| Tenofovir | No information available—manufacturer advises use only if potential benefit outweighs risk |
| Tenoxicam | *see* NSAIDs |
| Terazosin | *see* Alpha-blockers, Post-synaptic |
| Terbinafine | Manufacturer advises use only if potential benefit outweighs risk—no information available |
| Terbutaline | For use in asthma *see* section 3.1 |
| (3) | For use in premature labour *see* section 7.1.3 |
| Testosterone | *see* Androgens |

| Drug (trimester of risk) | Comment |
|---|---|
| Tetrabenazine | Inadequate information but no evidence of harm |
| Tetracyclines | |
| (1) | Effects on skeletal development in *animal* studies |
| (2, 3) | Dental discoloration; maternal hepatotoxicity with large parenteral doses |
| Theophylline | |
| (3) | Neonatal irritability and apnoea have been reported |
| Thiazides and related diuretics | *see* Diuretics |
| Thiopental | *see* Anaesthetics, General |
| Thiotepa | Avoid (teratogenic and embryotoxic in *animals*); *see also* section 8.1 |
| Thymoxamine | *see* Moxisylyte |
| Thyroxine | *see* Levothyroxine |
| Tiagabine | Manufacturer advises avoid unless potential benefit outweighs risk |
| Tiaprofenic acid | *see* NSAIDs |
| Ticarcillin [ingredient] | *see* Penicillins |
| Tiludronic acid | *see* Bisphosphonates |
| *Timentin®* | *see* Penicillins |
| Timolol | *see* Beta-blockers |
| Tinidazole | Manufacturer advises avoid in first trimester |
| Tinzaparin | Manufacturer advises avoid unless no safer alternative |
| Tioconazole | Manufacturer advises avoid |
| Tioguanine | Avoid (teratogenicity reported when men receiving tioguanine have fathered children); ensure effective contraception during administration to men or women; *see also* section 8.1 |
| Tiotropium | Toxicity in *animal* studies—manufacturer advises use only if potential benefit outweighs risk |
| Tipranavir | Manufacturer advises use only if potential benefit outweighs risk—toxicity in *animal* studies |
| Tirofiban | Manufacturer advises use only if potential benefit outweighs risk—no information available |
| Tizanidine | Manufacturer advises use only if potential benefit outweighs risk—no information available |
| Tobramycin | *see* Aminoglycosides |
| Tocopheryl acetate | |
| (1, 2, 3) | No evidence of safety of high doses |
| Tolbutamide | *see* Sulphonylureas |
| Tolcapone | Toxicity in *animal* studies—manufacturer advises use only if potential benefit outweighs risk |
| Tolfenamic acid | *see* NSAIDs |
| Tolterodine | Manufacturer advises avoid—toxicity in *animal* studies |
| Topiramate | Manufacturer advises avoid unless potential benefit outweighs risk—toxicity in *animal* studies; *see also* Antiepileptics |
| Topotecan | Avoid (teratogenicity and fetal loss in *animal* studies); *see also* section 8.1 |
| Torasemide | *see* Diuretics |
| Tramadol | Embryotoxic in animal studies—manufacturers advise avoid; *see also* Opioid Analgesics |
| Trandolapril | *see* ACE Inhibitors |
| Tranexamic acid | No evidence of teratogenicity in *animal* studies; manufacturer advises use only if potential benefit outweighs risk—crosses the placenta |
| Tranylcypromine | *see* Antidepressants, MAOI |
| Trastuzumab | Avoid unless potential benefit outweighs risk |
| Travoprost | Manufacturer advises use only if potential benefit outweighs risk |
| Trazodone | *see* Antidepressants, Tricyclic (and related) |
| Treosulfan | Avoid; *see also* section 8.1 |
| Tretinoin | |
| (1, 2, 3) | Teratogenic; effective contraception must be used for at least 1 month before oral treatment, during treatment and for at least 1 month after stopping; also avoid topical treatment |
| Triamcinolone | *see* Corticosteroids |
| Triamterene | *see* Diuretics |
| Tribavirin | *see* Ribavirin |
| Triclofos | Avoid |
| Trientine | Manufacturer advises use only if potential benefit outweighs risk; monitor maternal and neonatal serum-copper concentration; teratogenic in *animal* studies |
| Trifluoperazine | *see* Antipsychotics |
| Trilostane | |
| (1, 2, 3) | Interferes with placental sex hormone production |
| Trimeprazine | *see* Antihistamines |
| Trimethoprim | |
| (1) | Teratogenic risk (folate antagonist); manufacturers advise avoid |
| Trimipramine | *see* Antidepressants, Tricyclic (and related) |
| Tripotassium dicitratobismuthate | Manufacturer advises avoid on theoretical grounds |
| Triptorelin | Manufacturers advise avoid |
| Tropisetron | Manufacturer advises toxicity in *animal* studies |
| Trospium | Manufacturer advises caution—no information available |
| *Uftoral®* | Avoid; manufacturer advises effective contraception during and for 3 months after administration to men or women |

| Drug (trimester of risk) | Comment |
|---|---|
| Ursodeoxycholic acid | No evidence of harm but manufacturer advises avoid |
| Vaccines (live) (1) | Theoretical risk of congenital malformations, but need for vaccination may outweigh possible risk to fetus (*see also* p. 611); avoid MMR vaccine but *see* p. 621 |
| Valaciclovir | *see* Aciclovir |
| Valganciclovir | *see* Ganciclovir |
| Valproate (1, 3) | Increased risk of congenital malformations and developmental delay (counselling and screening advised—**important:** *see also* Antiepileptics and p. 238); neonatal bleeding (related to hypofibrinaemia) and neonatal hepatotoxicity also reported |
| Valproic acid | *see* Valproate |
| Valsartan | *As for* ACE Inhibitors |
| Vancomycin | Manufacturer advises use only if potential benefit outweighs risk—plasma-vancomycin concentration monitoring essential to reduce risk of fetal toxicity |
| Vasopressin | Oxytocic effect in third trimester |
| Vecuronium | Manufacturer advises avoid unless potential benefit outweighs risk—no information available |
| Venlafaxine | Manufacturer advises avoid—no information available |
| Verapamil | May reduce uterine blood flow with fetal hypoxia; manufacturer advises avoid in first trimester unless absolutely necessary; may inhibit labour |
| Verteporfin | Manufacturer advises use only if potential benefit outweighs risk (teratogenic in *animal* studies) |
| Vigabatrin | Congenital anomalies reported—manufacturer advises avoid unless potential benefit outweighs risk; *see also* Antiepileptics |
| Vinblastine | Avoid (limited experience suggests fetal harm; teratogenic in *animal* studies); *see also* section 8.1 |
| Vincristine | Avoid (teratogenicity and fetal loss in *animal* studies); *see also* section 8.1 |
| Vindesine | Avoid (teratogenic in *animal* studies); *see also* section 8.1 |
| Vinorelbine | Avoid (teratogenicity and fetal loss in *animal* studies); *see also* section 8.1 |
| Vitamin A (1) | Excessive doses may be teratogenic; *see also* p. 494 |
| Vitamin D | High systemic doses teratogenic in *animals* but therapeutic doses unlikely to be harmful; manufacturer of *topical* calcitriol advises avoid; *see also* Calcipotriol and Tacalcitol |
| Voriconazole | Toxicity in *animal* studies—manufacturer advises avoid unless potential benefit outweighs risk; effective contraception required during treatment |
| Warfarin | *see* Anticoagulants, Oral |
| Xipamide | *see* Diuretics |
| Zafirlukast | Manufacturer advises use only if potential benefit outweighs risk |
| Zalcitabine | Manufacturer advises use only if potential benefit outweighs risk—toxicity in *animal* studies; women of childbearing age should use effective contraception during treatment |
| Zaleplon | Manufacturer advises avoid in early pregnancy—no information available; risk of neonatal withdrawal symptoms if used in late pregnancy |
| Zanamivir | Manufacturer advises use only if potential benefit outweighs risk—no information available |
| Zidovudine | Limited information available; manufacturer advises use only if clearly indicated; *see also* p. 314 |
| Zinc acetate | Usual dose 25 mg 3 times daily adjusted according to plasma-copper concentration and urinary copper excretion |
| Zinc sulphate | Safety not established—crosses placenta |
| Zoledronic acid | Manufacturer advises avoid—toxicity in *animal* studies |
| Zolmitriptan | *see* $5HT_1$ Agonists |
| Zolpidem | *see* Benzodiazepines |
| Zonisamide | Toxicity in *animal* studies—manufacturer advises use only if potential benefit outweighs risk |
| Zopiclone | *see* Benzodiazepines |
| Zotepine | Manufacturer advises avoid unless potential benefit outweighs risk |
| Zuclopenthixol | *see* Antipsychotics |

# A5 Breast-feeding

Administration of some drugs (e.g. ergotamine) to nursing mothers may harm the infant, whereas administration of others (e.g. digoxin) has little effect. Some drugs inhibit lactation (e.g. bromocriptine).

Toxicity to the infant can occur if the drug enters the milk in pharmacologically significant quantities. The concentration in milk of some drugs (e.g. iodides) may exceed the concentration in maternal plasma so that therapeutic doses in the mother may cause toxicity to the infant. Some drugs inhibit the infant's sucking reflex (e.g. phenobarbital). Drugs in breast milk may, at least theoretically, cause hypersensitivity in the infant even when concentration is too low for a pharmacological effect. The following table lists drugs:

- which should be used with caution or which are contra-indicated in breast-feeding for the reasons given above;
- which, on present evidence, may be given to the mother during breast-feeding, because they appear in milk in amounts which are too small to be harmful to the infant;
- which are not known to be harmful to the infant although they are present in milk in significant amounts.

For many drugs insufficient evidence is available to provide guidance and it is advisable to administer only essential drugs to a mother during breast-feeding. Because of the inadequacy of information on drugs in breast milk the following table should be used only as a guide; absence from the table does not imply safety.

## Table of drugs present in breast milk

Products introduced or amended since publication of BNF No. 50 (September 2005) are underlined.

| Drug | Comment |
|---|---|
| Abacavir | Breast-feeding not advised in HIV infection |
| Abciximab | Manufacturer advises avoid—no information available |
| Acamprosate | Manufacturer advises avoid |
| Acarbose | Manufacturer advises avoid |
| Acebutolol | *see* Beta-blockers |
| Aceclofenac | Manufacturer advises avoid—no information available |
| Acemetacin | Manufacturer advises avoid |
| Acenocoumarol (nicoumalone) | *see* Anticoagulants, Oral |
| Acetazolamide | Amount too small to be harmful |
| Aciclovir | Significant amount in milk after systemic administration—not known to be harmful but manufacturer advises caution |
| Acipimox | Manufacturer advises avoid |
| Acitretin | Avoid |
| Acrivastine | *see* Antihistamines |
| Adalimumab | Avoid; manufacturer advises avoid for at least 5 months after last dose |
| Adapalene | Manufacturer advises avoid (if used, avoid application to chest)—no information available |
| Adefovir dipivoxil | Manufacturer advises avoid—no information available |
| Agalsidase beta | Manufacturer advises avoid—no information available |
| Alcohol | Large amounts may affect infant and reduce milk consumption |
| Alemtuzumab | Avoid; manufacturer advises avoid breast-feeding for at least 4 weeks after administration |
| Alendronic acid | No information available |
| Alfacalcidol | *see* Vitamin D |
| Alfentanil | Present in milk—manufacturer advises withhold breast-feeding for 24 hours |
| Alimemazine (trimeprazine) | *see* Antihistamines |
| Allopurinol | Present in milk—not known to be harmful |
| Almotriptan | Present in milk in *animal* studies—withhold breast-feeding for 24 hours |
| Alprazolam | *see* Benzodiazepines |
| Alverine | Manufacturer advises avoid—little information available |
| Amantadine | Avoid; present in milk; toxicity in infant reported |
| Amethocaine | *see* Tetracaine |
| Amfebutamone | *see* Bupropion |
| Amiloride | Manufacturer advises avoid—no information available |
| Aminophylline | *see* Theophylline |
| Amiodarone | Avoid; present in milk in significant amounts; theoretical risk from release of iodine; *see also* Iodine |
| Amisulpride | Manufacturer advises avoid—no information available |
| Amitriptyline | *see* Antidepressants, Tricyclic (and related) |
| Amlodipine | Manufacturer advises avoid—no information available |
| Amobarbital | *see* Barbiturates |
| Amorolfine | Manufacturer advises avoid—no information available |
| Amoxapine | *see* Antidepressants, Tricyclic (and related) |
| Amoxicillin | *see* Penicillins |
| Amphetamines | Significant amount in milk. Avoid |
| Amphotericin | No information available |
| Ampicillin | *see* Penicillins |
| Amprenavir | Breast-feeding not advised in HIV infection |

| Drug | Comment |
|---|---|
| Amsacrine | *see* Cytotoxic Drugs |
| Anagrelide | Manufacturer advises avoid—no information available |
| Anakinra | Manufacturer advises avoid—no information available |
| Analgesics | *see* Aspirin, NSAIDs, Opioid Analgesics and Paracetamol |
| Androgens | Avoid; may cause masculinisation in the female infant or precocious development in the male infant; high doses suppress lactation |
| Anticoagulants, oral | Risk of haemorrhage; increased by vitamin-K deficiency; warfarin appears safe but phenindione should be avoided; manufacturer of acenocoumarol (nicoumalone) recommends prophylactic vitamin K for the infant (consult product literature) |
| Antidepressants, SSRI | *see* individual entries |
| Antidepressants, tricyclic (and related) | Amount of tricyclic antidepressants (including related drugs such as mianserin and trazodone) too small to be harmful but most manufacturers advise avoid; accumulation of doxepin metabolite may cause sedation and respiratory depression |
| Antihistamines | Significant amount of some antihistamines present in milk; although not known to be harmful manufacturers of alimemazine, cetirizine, cyproheptadine, desloratadine, fexofenadine, hydroxyzine, loratadine, mizolastine and terfenadine advise avoid; adverse effects in infant reported with clemastine |
| Antipsychotics | Although amount present in milk probably too small to be harmful, *animal* studies indicate possible adverse effects of these drugs on developing nervous system therefore avoid unless absolutely necessary; *see also* Amisulpride, Chlorpromazine, Clozapine, Olanzapine, Quetiapine, Risperidone, Sertindole, Sulpiride, Zotepine |
| Apomorphine | Manufacturer advises avoid—no information available |
| Aprepitant | Manufacturer advises avoid—present in milk in *animal* studies |
| Aripiprazole | Manufacturer advises avoid—present in milk in *animal* studies |
| Arsenic trioxide | *see* Cytotoxic Drugs |
| Artemether [ingredient] | *see Riamet®* |
| Aspirin | Avoid—possible risk of Reye's syndrome; regular use of high doses could impair platelet function and produce hypoprothrombinaemia in infant if neonatal vitamin K stores low |
| Atazanavir | Breast-feeding not advised in HIV infection |

| Drug | Comment |
|---|---|
| Atenolol | *see* Beta-blockers |
| Atomoxetine | Manufacturer advises avoid—present in milk in *animal* studies |
| Atorvastatin | *see* Statins |
| Atosiban | Small amounts present in milk |
| Atovaquone | Manufacturer advises avoid—no information available |
| Atracurium | Breast-feeding unlikely to be harmful following recovery from neuromuscular block; some manufacturers advise avoiding breast-feeding for 24 hours after administration |
| Atropine | Small amount present in milk—manufacturer advises caution |
| Auranofin | Present in milk; manufacturer advises avoid |
| Azathioprine | *see* Cytotoxic Drugs |
| Azithromycin | Present in milk; manufacturer advises use only if no suitable alternative |
| Aztreonam | Amount probably too small to be harmful—manufacturer advises avoid |
| Baclofen | Amount too small to be harmful |
| Balsalazide | Manufacturer advises avoid |
| Barbiturates | Avoid if possible (*see also* Phenobarbital); large doses may produce drowsiness |
| Basiliximab | Avoid |
| Beclometasone | *see* Corticosteroids |
| Bemiparin | Manufacturer advises avoid—no information available |
| Bendrofluazide | *see* Thiazides and Related Diuretics |
| Bendroflumethiazide (bendrofluazide) | *see* Thiazides and Related Diuretics |
| Benperidol | *see* Antipsychotics |
| Benzodiazepines | Present in milk—avoid if possible |
| Benzylpenicillin | *see* Penicillins |
| Beta-blockers | Monitor infant; possible toxicity due to beta-blockade but amount of most beta-blockers present in milk too small to affect infant; acebutolol, atenolol, nadolol, and sotalol are present in greater amounts than other beta-blockers; manufacturers advise avoid celiprolol and nebivolol |
| Betamethasone | *see* Corticosteroids |
| Bethanechol | Manufacturer advises avoid |
| Bevacizumab | Manufacturer advises avoid breast-feeding during and for at least 6 months after treatment |
| Bexarotene | *see* Cytotoxic Drugs |
| Bezafibrate | Manufacturer advises avoid—no information available |
| Bimatoprost | Manufacturer advises avoid |
| Bisoprolol | *see* Beta-blockers |
| Bivalirudin | Manufacturer advises caution—no information available |
| Bleomycin | *see* Cytotoxic Drugs |
| Bortezomib | *see* Cytotoxic Drugs |
| Bosentan | Manufacturer advises avoid—no information available |

| Drug | Comment |
|---|---|
| Botulinum toxin | Manufacturers advise avoid (or avoid unless essential)—no information available |
| Bromocriptine | Suppresses lactation |
| Buclizine | *see* Antihistamines |
| Budesonide | *see* Corticosteroids |
| Bumetanide | Manufacturer advises avoid if possible—no information available |
| Bupivacaine | Amount too small to be harmful |
| Buprenorphine | Avoid unless essential—may inhibit lactation; manufacturer advises contra-indicated in the treatment of opioid dependence |
| Bupropion | Present in milk—manufacturer advises avoid |
| Buserelin | Small amount present in milk—manufacturer advises avoid |
| Buspirone | Manufacturer advises avoid |
| Busulfan | *see* Cytotoxic Drugs |
| Butobarbital | *see* Barbiturates |
| Cabergoline | Suppresses lactation |
| Caffeine | Regular intake of large amounts can affect infant |
| Calciferol | *see* Vitamin D |
| Calcipotriol | No information available |
| Calcitonin (salmon) (salcatonin) | Avoid; inhibits lactation in *animals* |
| Calcitriol | *see* Vitamin D |
| Calcium folinate | Manufacturer advises caution—no information available |
| Calcium levofolinate | *see* Calcium Folinate |
| Candesartan | Manufacturer advises avoid—no information available |
| Capecitabine | Discontinue breast-feeding |
| Capreomycin | Manufacturer advises caution—no information available |
| Captopril | Present in milk— manufacturers advise avoid |
| Carbamazepine | Amount probably too small to be harmful but severe skin reaction reported in 1 infant |
| Carbimazole | Amounts in milk may be sufficient to affect neonatal thyroid function therefore lowest effective dose should be used (*see also* section 6.2.2) |
| Carbocisteine | No information available |
| Carboplatin | *see* Cytotoxic Drugs |
| Carglumic acid | Manufacturer advises avoid unless essential—no information available |
| Carisoprodol | Concentrated in milk; no adverse effects reported but best avoided |
| Carmustine | *see* Cytotoxic Drugs |
| Carvedilol | *see* Beta-blockers |
| Caspofungin | Present in milk in *animal* studies—manufacturer advises avoid |
| Cefaclor | Present in milk in low concentration |
| Cefadroxil | Present in milk in low concentration |
| Cefalexin | Present in milk in low concentration |
| Cefixime | Manufacturer advises avoid—no information available |
| Cefotaxime | Present in milk in low concentration |
| Cefpirome | Present in milk—manufacturer advises avoid |
| Cefpodoxime | Present in milk in low concentration |
| Cefprozil | Present in milk in low concentration |
| Cefradine | Present in milk in low concentration |
| Ceftazidime | Present in milk in low concentration |
| Ceftriaxone | Present in milk in low concentration |
| Cefuroxime | Present in milk in low concentration |
| Celecoxib | Manufacturer advises avoid—no information available |
| Celiprolol | *see* Beta-blockers |
| Cetirizine | *see* Antihistamines |
| Cetrorelix | Manufacturer advises avoid |
| Cetuximab | Manufacturer advises avoid breast-feeding during and for one month after treatment—no information available |
| Chloral hydrate | Sedation in infant—manufacturer advises avoid |
| Chlorambucil | *see* Cytotoxic Drugs |
| Chloramphenicol | Use another antibiotic; may cause bone-marrow toxicity in infant; concentration in milk usually insufficient to cause 'grey syndrome' |
| Chlordiazepoxide | *see* Benzodiazepines |
| Chloroquine | Amount probably too small to be harmful when used for malaria prophylaxis; inadequate for reliable protection against malaria, *see* section 5.4.1; avoid breast-feeding when used for rheumatic diseases |
| Chlorphenamine (chlorpheniramine) | *see* Antihistamines |
| Chlorpheniramine | *see* Antihistamines |
| Chlorpromazine | Drowsiness in infant reported; *see* Antipsychotics |
| Chlorpropamide | *see* Sulphonylureas |
| Chlortalidone | *see* Thiazides and Related Diuretics |
| Chlortetracycline | *see* Tetracyclines |
| Ciclesonide | *see* Corticosteroids |
| Ciclosporin | Present in milk—manufacturer advises avoid |
| Cidofovir | Manufacturer advises avoid |
| Cilastatin [ingredient] | *see Primaxin*® |
| Cilazapril | No information available—manufacturer advises avoid |
| Cilostazol | Present in milk in *animal* studies—manufacturer advises avoid |
| Cimetidine | Significant amount—not known to be harmful but manufacturer advises avoid |
| Cinacalcet | Manufacturer advises avoid—present in milk in *animal* studies |
| Ciprofibrate | Manufacturer advises avoid—present in milk in *animal* studies |

Appendix 5

| Drug | Comment |
|---|---|
| Ciprofloxacin | Avoid—high concentrations in breast milk |
| Cisatracurium | No information available |
| Cisplatin | *see* Cytotoxic Drugs |
| Citalopram | Present in milk—manufacturer advises avoid |
| Cladribine | *see* Cytotoxic Drugs |
| Clarithromycin | Manufacturer advises avoid unless potential benefit outweighs risk—present in milk |
| Clavulanic acid [ingredient] | see Co-amoxiclav, *Timentin*® |
| Clemastine | *see* Antihistamines |
| Clindamycin | Amount probably too small to be harmful but bloody diarrhoea reported in 1 infant |
| Clobazam | *see* Benzodiazepines |
| Clodronate sodium | *see* Sodium Clodronate |
| Clomethiazole | Amount too small to be harmful |
| Clomifene | May inhibit lactation |
| Clomipramine | *see* Antidepressants, Tricyclic (and related) |
| Clonazepam | *see* Benzodiazepines |
| Clonidine | Present in milk—manufacturer advises avoid |
| Clopidogrel | Manufacturer advises avoid |
| Clozapine | Manufacturer advises avoid |
| Co-amoxiclav | *see* Penicillins |
| Co-beneldopa | *see* Levodopa |
| Co-careldopa | *see* Levodopa |
| Codeine | Amount too small to be harmful |
| Co-fluampicil | *see* Penicillins |
| Colchicine | Present in milk but no adverse effects reported; manufacturers advise avoid because of risk of cytotoxicity |
| Colecalciferol | *see* Vitamin D |
| Colistin | Present in milk but poorly absorbed from gut; manufacturers advise avoid (or use only if potential benefit outweighs risk) |
| Contraceptives, oral | Avoid combined oral contraceptives until weaning or for 6 months after birth (adverse effects on lactation); progestogen-only contraceptives do not affect lactation (start 3 weeks after birth or later) |
| Corticosteroids | Systemic effects in infant unlikely with maternal dose of prednisolone up to 40 mg daily; monitor infant's adrenal function with higher doses—the amount of inhaled drugs in breast milk is probably too small to be harmful |
| Cortisone acetate | *see* Corticosteroids |
| Co-trimoxazole | Small risk of kernicterus in jaundiced infants and of haemolysis in G6PD-deficient infants (due to sulfamethoxazole) |
| Crisantaspase | *see* Cytotoxic Drugs |
| Cromoglicate | *see* Sodium Cromoglicate |
| Cyclopenthiazide | *see* Thiazides and Related Diuretics |
| Cyclophosphamide | Discontinue breast-feeding during and for 36 hours after stopping treatment |
| Cycloserine | Amount too small to be harmful |
| Cyclosporin | *see* Ciclosporin |
| Cyproheptadine | *see* Antihistamines |
| Cyproterone | Caution; possibility of anti-androgen effects in neonate |
| Cytarabine | *see* Cytotoxic Drugs |
| Cytotoxic drugs | Discontinue breast-feeding |
| Daclizumab | Avoid |
| Dactinomycin | *see* Cytotoxic Drugs |
| Dalfopristin [ingredient] | *see Synercid*® |
| Dalteparin | No information available |
| Danaparoid | Amount probably too small to be harmful but manufacturer advises avoid |
| Danazol | No data available but avoid because of possible androgenic effects in infant |
| Dantrolene | Present in milk—manufacturer advises avoid |
| Dapsone | Haemolytic anaemia; although significant amount in milk, risk to infant very small unless infant is G6PD deficient |
| Darbepoetin | Manufacturer advises avoid—no information available |
| Daunorubicin | *see* Cytotoxic Drugs |
| Deferiprone | Manufacturer advises avoid—no information available |
| Deflazacort | *see* Corticosteroids |
| Demeclocycline | *see* Tetracyclines |
| Desferrioxamine | Manufacturer advises use only if potential benefit outweighs risk—no information available |
| Desloratadine | *see* Antihistamines |
| Desmopressin | Not known to be harmful |
| Desogestrel | *see* Contraceptives, Oral |
| Dexamethasone | *see* Corticosteroids |
| Dexamfetamine | *see* Amphetamines |
| Dexibuprofen | Present in milk—but risk to infant minimal |
| Dexketoprofen | Manufacturer advises avoid—no information available |
| Dextropropoxyphene | Amount too small to be harmful |
| Diamorphine | Therapeutic doses unlikely to affect infant; withdrawal symptoms in infants of dependent mothers; breast-feeding not best method of treating dependence in offspring |
| Diazepam | *see* Benzodiazepines |
| Diclofenac | Amount too small to be harmful |
| Didanosine | Breast-feeding not advised in HIV infection |
| Diflunisal | Manufacturer advises avoid |
| Digoxin | Amount too small to be harmful |
| Dihydrocodeine | Manufacturer advises use only if potential benefit outweighs risk |
| Dihydrotachysterol | *see* Vitamin D |
| Diloxanide | Manufacturer advises avoid |
| Diltiazem | Significant amount present in milk—no evidence of harm but avoid unless no safer alternative |

| Drug | Comment |
|---|---|
| Dipyridamole | Small amount present in milk—manufacturer advises caution |
| Disodium etidronate | No information available |
| Disodium pamidronate | Manufacturer advises avoid |
| Disopyramide | Present in milk—use only if essential and monitor infant for antimuscarinic effects |
| Distigmine | No information available |
| Disulfiram | Manufacturer advises avoid—no information available |
| Docetaxel | *see* Cytotoxic Drugs |
| Docusate sodium | Present in milk following oral administration—manufacturer advises caution; rectal administration not known to be harmful |
| Dolasetron | Not known to be harmful but manufacturer advises avoid |
| Domperidone | Amount probably too small to be harmful |
| Dornase alfa | Amount probably too small to be harmful—manufacturer advises caution |
| Dosulepin (dothiepin) | *see* Antidepressants, Tricyclic (and related) |
| Dothiepin | *see* Antidepressants, Tricyclic (and related) |
| Doxazosin | Accumulates in milk—manufacturer advises avoid |
| Doxepin | *see* Antidepressants, Tricyclic (and related) |
| Doxorubicin | *see* Cytotoxic Drugs |
| Doxycycline | *see* Tetracyclines |
| Drotrecogin alfa (activated) | Manufacturer advises avoid—no information available |
| Duloxetine | Present in milk in *animal* studies—avoid |
| Dydrogesterone | Present in milk—no adverse effects reported |
| Edrophonium | Amount probably too small to be harmful |
| Efalizumab | May be present in milk—manufacturer advises avoid |
| Efavirenz | Breast-feeding not advised in HIV infection |
| Eflornithine | Manufacturer advises avoid—no information available |
| Eformoterol | *see* Formoterol |
| Eletriptan | Present in milk—avoid breast-feeding for 24 hours |
| Emtricitabine | Breast-feeding not advised in HIV infection |
| Enalapril | Amount probably too small to be harmful |
| Enfuvirtide | Breast-feeding not advised in HIV infection |
| Enoxaparin | Manufacturer advises avoid—no information available |
| Enoximone | Manufacturer advises caution—no information available |
| Entacapone | Manufacturer advises avoid—present in milk in *animal* studies |
| Ephedrine | Irritability and disturbed sleep reported |
| Epinastine | Present in milk in *animal* studies—manufacturer advises caution |
| Epirubicin | *see* Cytotoxic Drugs |
| Eplerenone | Manufacturer advises use only if potential benefit outweighs risk |
| Epoetin | Unlikely to be present in milk; risk to infant minimal |
| Eprosartan | Manufacturer advises avoid unless potential benefit outweighs risk |
| Eptifibatide | No information available—manufacturer advises avoid |
| Ergocalciferol | *see* Vitamin D |
| Ergotamine | Avoid; ergotism may occur in infant; repeated doses may inhibit lactation |
| Erlotinib | Manufacturer advises avoid—no information available |
| Ertapenem | Present in milk—manufacturer advises avoid |
| Erythromycin | Only small amounts in milk—not known to be harmful |
| Escitalopram | Manufacturer advises avoid—no information available |
| Esmolol | *see* Beta-blockers |
| Esomeprazole | Manufacturer advises avoid—no information available |
| Etamsylate | Significant amount but not known to be harmful |
| Etanercept | Manufacturer advises avoid—no information available |
| Ethambutol | Amount too small to be harmful |
| Ethinylestradiol | *see* Oestrogens |
| Ethosuximide | Present in milk but unlikely to be harmful; manufacturer advises avoid |
| Etidronate disodium | *see* Disodium Etidronate |
| Etodolac | Manufacturer advises avoid |
| Etomidate | Avoid breast-feeding for 24 hours after administration |
| Etoposide | *see* Cytotoxic Drugs |
| Etoricoxib | Manufacturer advises avoid—present in milk in *animal* studies |
| Etynodiol | *see* Contraceptives, Oral |
| Ezetimibe | Present in milk in *animal* studies—manufacturer advises avoid |
| Famciclovir | Manufacturer advises avoid unless potential benefit outweighs risk—present in milk in *animal* studies |
| Famotidine | Present in milk—not known to be harmful but manufacturer advises avoid |
| *Fansidar*® | Small risk of kernicterus in jaundiced infants and of haemolysis in G6PD-deficient infants (due to sulfadoxine) |
| Felodipine | Present in milk |
| Fenbufen | Small amount present in milk—manufacturer advises avoid |
| Fenofibrate | Manufacturer advises avoid—no information available |
| Fenoprofen | Amount too small to be harmful |
| Fentanyl | Amount too small to be harmful |
| Fexofenadine | *see* Antihistamines |
| Filgrastim | No information available—manufacturer advises avoid |
| Flavoxate | Manufacturer advises caution—no information available |

Appendix 5

| Drug | Comment |
|---|---|
| Flecainide | Significant amount but not known to be harmful |
| Flucloxacillin | *see* Penicillins |
| Fluconazole | Manufacturer advises avoid—present in milk |
| Flucytosine | Manufacturer advises avoid |
| Fludarabine | *see* Cytotoxic Drugs |
| Fluorouracil | *see* Cytotoxic Drugs |
| Fluoxetine | Present in milk—manufacturer advises avoid |
| Flupentixol | *see* Antipsychotics |
| Fluphenazine | *see* Antipsychotics |
| Flurazepam | *see* Benzodiazepines |
| Flurbiprofen | Amount too small to be harmful |
| Fluticasone | *see* Corticosteroids |
| Fluvastatin | *see* Statins |
| Fluvoxamine | Present in milk—manufacturer advises avoid |
| Follitropin alfa and beta | Avoid |
| Fomepizole | Manufacturer advises caution—no information available |
| Fondaparinux | Present in milk in *animal* studies—manufacturer advises avoid |
| Formoterol (eformoterol) | Amount in milk probably too small to be harmful but manufacturers advise avoid |
| Fosamprenavir | Breast-feeding not advised in HIV infection |
| Foscarnet | Avoid—present in milk in *animal* studies |
| Fosinopril | Present in milk—manufacturer advises avoid |
| Fosphenytoin | *see* Phenytoin |
| Frovatriptan | Present in milk in *animal* studies—withhold breast-feeding for 24 hours |
| Frusemide | *see* Furosemide |
| Fulvestrant | Manufacturer advises avoid—present in milk in *animal* studies |
| Furosemide (frusemide) | Amount too small to be harmful |
| Fusidic acid | *see* Sodium Fusidate |
| Gabapentin | Present in milk—manufacturer advises avoid |
| Galantamine | Manufacturer advises avoid—no information available |
| Ganciclovir | Avoid—no information available |
| Ganirelix | Manufacturer advises avoid—no information available |
| Gemcitabine | *see* Cytotoxic Drugs |
| Gemfibrozil | Manufacturer advises avoid—no information available |
| Gestodene | *see* Contraceptives, Oral |
| Gestrinone | Manufacturer advises avoid |
| Glatiramer | Manufacturer advises caution—no information available |
| Glibenclamide | *see* Sulphonylureas |
| Gliclazide | *see* Sulphonylureas |
| Glimepiride | *see* Sulphonylureas |
| Glipizide | *see* Sulphonylureas |
| Gliquidone | *see* Sulphonylureas |
| Glyceryl trinitrate | No information available—manufacturers advise use only if potential benefit outweighs risk |
| Goserelin | Manufacturer advises avoid |
| Granisetron | Not known to be harmful but manufacturer advises avoid |
| Griseofulvin | Avoid—no information available |
| Haem arginate | Manufacturer advises avoid unless essential—no information available |
| Haloperidol | *see* Antipsychotics |
| Halothane | Present in milk |
| Hepatitis A vaccine | No information available |
| Human menopausal gonadotrophins | Avoid |
| Hydralazine | Present in milk but not known to be harmful; monitor infant |
| Hydrochlorothiazide | *see* Thiazides and Related Diuretics |
| Hydrocortisone | *see* Corticosteroids |
| Hydroflumethiazide | *see* Thiazides and Related Diuretics |
| Hydromorphone | Manufacturer advises avoid—no information available |
| Hydroxocobalamin | Present in milk but not known to be harmful |
| Hydroxycarbamide (hydroxyurea) | *see* Cytotoxic Drugs |
| Hydroxychloroquine | Avoid—risk of toxicity in infant |
| Hydroxyurea | *see* Cytotoxic Drugs |
| Hydroxyzine | *see* Antihistamines |
| Hyoscine | Amount too small to be harmful |
| Ibandronic acid | Manufacturer advises caution—present in milk in *animal* studies |
| Ibuprofen | Amount too small to be harmful but some manufacturers advise avoid (including topical use) |
| Idarubicin | *see* Cytotoxic Drugs |
| Idoxuridine | May make milk taste unpleasant |
| Ifosfamide | *see* Cytotoxic Drugs |
| Iloprost | Manufacturer advises avoid—no information available |
| Imatinib | *see* Cytotoxic Drugs |
| Imidapril | Manufacturer advises avoid—no information available |
| Imiglucerase | No information available |
| Imipenem [ingredient] | *see Primaxin®* |
| Imipramine | *see* Antidepressants, Tricyclic (and related) |
| Imiquimod | Manufacturer advises no information available |
| Indapamide | No information available—manufacturer advises avoid |
| Indinavir | Breast-feeding not advised in HIV infection |
| Indometacin | Amount probably too small to be harmful but convulsions reported in one infant—manufacturers advise avoid |
| Infliximab | Avoid; manufacturer advises avoid for at least 6 months after last dose |
| Influenza vaccine | Not known to be harmful |
| Insulin | Amount too small to be harmful |
| Interferons | Manufacturers advise avoid—no information available |

| Drug | Comment |
|---|---|
| Iodine and iodides | Stop breast-feeding; danger of neonatal hypothyroidism or goitre; appears to be concentrated in milk |
| Iodine, radioactive | Breast-feeding contra-indicated after therapeutic doses. With diagnostic doses withhold breast-feeding for at least 24 hours |
| Ipratropium | Amount probably too small to be harmful |
| Irbesartan | Manufacturer advises avoid—no information available |
| Irinotecan | *see* Cytotoxic Drugs |
| Isoniazid | Monitor infant for possible toxicity; theoretical risk of convulsions and neuropathy; prophylactic pyridoxine advisable in mother and infant |
| Isosorbide dinitrate | No information available—manufacturers advise use only if potential benefit outweighs risk |
| Isosorbide mononitrate | No information available—manufacturers advise use only if potential benefit outweighs risk |
| Isotretinoin | Avoid |
| Isradipine | Manufacturer advises avoid—present in milk in *animal* studies |
| Itraconazole | Small amounts present in milk—may accumulate; manufacturer advises avoid unless potential benefit outweighs risk |
| Ivabradine | Present in milk in *animal* studies—manufacturer advises avoid |
| *Kaletra*® | Breast-feeding not advised in HIV infection |
| Ketoconazole | Manufacturer advises avoid |
| Ketoprofen | Amount probably too small to be harmful but manufacturer advises avoid unless essential |
| Ketorolac | Avoid |
| Ketotifen | *see* Antihistamines |
| Labetalol | *see* Beta-blockers |
| Lacidipine | Manufacturer advises avoid—no information available |
| Lamivudine | Present in milk—manufacturer advises avoid; breast-feeding not advised in HIV infection |
| Lamotrigine | Present in milk but limited data suggest no harmful effects on infants |
| Lanreotide | Manufacturer advises avoid unless potential benefit outweighs risk—no information available |
| Lansoprazole | Manufacturer advises avoid unless essential—present in milk in *animal* studies |
| Laronidase | Manufacturer advises avoid—no information available |
| Latanoprost | May be present in milk—manufacturer advises avoid |
| Leflunomide | Present in milk—manufacturer advises avoid |
| Lenograstim | Manufacturer advises avoid—no information available |
| Lepirudin | Avoid |
| Lercanidipine | Manufacturer advises avoid |
| Leuprorelin | Manufacturer advises avoid |
| Levetiracetam | Present in milk—manufacturer advises avoid |
| Levobupivacaine | Likely to be present in milk but risk to infant minimal |
| Levocetirizine | *see* Antihistamines |
| Levodopa | May suppress lactation; present in milk—manufacturers advise avoid |
| Levofloxacin | Manufacturer advises avoid |
| Levomepromazine (methotrimeprazine) | *see* Antipsychotics |
| Levonorgestrel | *see* Contraceptives, Oral |
| Levothyroxine (thyroxine) | Amount too small to affect tests for neonatal hypothyroidism |
| Lidocaine (lignocaine) | Amount too small to be harmful |
| Lignocaine | *see* Lidocaine |
| Linezolid | Manufacturer advises avoid—present in milk in *animal* studies |
| Liothyronine | Amount too small to affect tests for neonatal hypothyroidism |
| Lisinopril | No information available—manufacturer advises caution |
| Lisuride | May suppress lactation |
| Lithium salts | Present in milk and risk of toxicity in infant—manufacturers advise avoid |
| Lofepramine | *see* Antidepressants, Tricyclic (and related) |
| Loperamide | Amount probably too small to be harmful |
| Lopinavir [ingredient] | *see Kaletra*® |
| Loprazolam | *see* Benzodiazepines |
| Loratadine | *see* Antihistamines |
| Lorazepam | *see* Benzodiazepines |
| Lormetazepam | *see* Benzodiazepines |
| Losartan | Manufacturer advises avoid—no information available |
| Lumefantrine [ingredient] | *see Riamet*® |
| Lumiracoxib | Manufacturer advises avoid—present in milk in *animal* studies |
| Lymecycline | *see* Tetracyclines |
| Macrogols | Manufacturers advise use only if essential—no information available |
| *Malarone*® | Manufacturer advises avoid; *see also* Atovaquone and Proguanil |
| Maprotiline | *see* Antidepressants, Tricyclic (and related) |
| Mebendazole | Amount too small to be harmful but manufacturer advises avoid |
| Mebeverine | Amount too small to be harmful |
| Medroxyprogesterone | Present in milk—no adverse effects reported |
| Mefenamic acid | Amount too small to be harmful but manufacturer advises avoid |
| Mefloquine | Present in milk but risk to infant minimal |
| Meloxicam | No information available—manufacturer advises avoid |
| Melphalan | *see* Cytotoxic Drugs |
| Memantine | Manufacturer advises avoid—no information available |

| Drug | Comment |
|---|---|
| Menotrophin | Avoid |
| Meprobamate | Avoid; concentration in milk may exceed maternal plasma concentrations fourfold and may cause drowsiness in infant |
| Meptazinol | Manufacturer advises use only if potential benefit outweighs risk |
| Mercaptamine | Manufacturer advises avoid |
| Mercaptopurine | *see* Cytotoxic Drugs |
| Meropenem | Unlikely to be absorbed (however, manufacturer advises avoid unless potential benefit justifies potential risk) |
| Mesalazine | Diarrhoea reported but manufacturers advise negligible amounts detected in breast milk |
| Mesterolone | *see* Androgens |
| Mestranol | *see* Oestrogens |
| Metaraminol | Manufacturer advises caution—no information available |
| Metformin | Manufacturer advises avoid; present in milk |
| Methadone | Withdrawal symptoms in infant; breast-feeding permissible during maintenance but dose should be as low as possible and infant monitored to avoid sedation |
| Methenamine | Amount too small to be harmful |
| Methocarbamol | Present in milk in *animal* studies—manufacturer advises caution |
| Methotrexate | *see* Cytotoxic Drugs |
| Methotrimeprazine | *see* Antipsychotics |
| Methyldopa | Amount too small to be harmful |
| Methylphenidate | No information available—manufacturer advises avoid |
| Methylprednisolone | *see* Corticosteroids |
| Methysergide | Manufacturer advises avoid |
| Metoclopramide | Small amount present in milk; manufacturer advises avoid |
| Metolazone | *see* Thiazides and Related Diuretics |
| Metoprolol | *see* Beta-blockers |
| Metronidazole | Significant amount in milk; manufacturer advises avoid large single doses |
| Metyrapone | Manufacturer advises avoid—no information available |
| Mexiletine | Amount too small to be harmful |
| Mianserin | *see* Antidepressants, Tricyclic (and related) |
| Miconazole | Manufacturer advises caution—no information available |
| Midazolam | *see* Benzodiazepines |
| Mifepristone | No information available—manufacturer advises stop breast-feeding for 14 days after administration |
| Miglustat | Manufacturer advises avoid—no information available |
| Milrinone | Manufacturer advises caution—no information available |
| Minocycline | *see* Tetracyclines |
| Minoxidil | Present in milk but not known to be harmful |
| Mirtazapine | Manufacturer advises avoid—present in milk in *animal* studies |
| Misoprostol | No information available—manufacturer advises avoid |
| Mitomycin | *see* Cytotoxic Drugs |
| Mitotane | *see* Cytotoxic Drugs |
| Mitoxantrone (mitozantrone) | *see* Cytotoxic Drugs |
| Mitozantrone | *see* Cytotoxic Drugs |
| Mizolastine | *see* Antihistamines |
| Moclobemide | Amount too small to be harmful, but patient leaflet advises avoid |
| Modafinil | Manufacturer advises avoid—no information available |
| Moexipril | Manufacturer advises avoid—no information available |
| Montelukast | Manufacturer advises avoid unless essential |
| Morphine | Therapeutic doses unlikely to affect infant; withdrawal symptoms in infants of dependent mothers; breast-feeding not best method of treating dependence in offspring |
| Moxifloxacin | Manufacturer advises avoid—present in milk in *animal* studies |
| Moxonidine | Present in milk—manufacturer advises avoid |
| Mupirocin | Manufacturer advises avoid unless potential benefit outweighs risk—no information available |
| Mycophenolate mofetil | Manufacturer advises avoid—present in milk in *animal* studies |
| Nabilone | Manufacturer advises avoid—no information available |
| Nabumetone | No information available—manufacturer advises avoid |
| Nadolol | *see* Beta-blockers |
| Nafarelin | Manufacturer advises avoid—no information available |
| Nalbuphine | Manufacturer advises caution—no information available |
| Nalidixic acid | Risk to infant very small but one case of haemolytic anaemia reported |
| Naloxone | No information available |
| Naproxen | Amount too small to be harmful but manufacturer advises avoid |
| Naratriptan | Manufacturer advises caution—no information available |
| Nateglinide | Manufacturer advises avoid—present in milk in *animal* studies |
| Nebivolol | *see* Beta-blockers |
| Nedocromil | Unlikely to be present in milk |
| Nelfinavir | Breast-feeding not advised in HIV infection |
| Neostigmine | Amount probably too small to be harmful; monitor infant |
| Nevirapine | Breast-feeding not advised in HIV infection |
| Nicardipine | Manufacturer advises avoid—no information available |
| Nicorandil | No information available—manufacturer advises avoid |
| Nicotine | Present in milk; use only if smoking cessation without nicotine replacement fails; patient information for some products contra-indicates use |

| Drug | Comment |
|---|---|
| Nicotinic acid | Present in milk—avoid |
| Nicoumalone | *see* Anticoagulants, Oral |
| Nifedipine | Amount too small to be harmful but manufacturers advise avoid |
| Nimodipine | No information available |
| Nisoldipine | Manufacturer advises avoid—no information available |
| Nitrazepam | *see* Benzodiazepines |
| Nitrofurantoin | Only small amounts in milk but could be enough to produce haemolysis in G6PD-deficient infants |
| Nitroprusside | *see* Sodium Nitroprusside |
| Nizatidine | Amount too small to be harmful |
| Nonoxynol-9 | Present in milk in *animal* studies |
| Norethisterone | Higher doses may suppress lactation and alter milk composition—use lowest effective dose; *see also* Contraceptives, Oral |
| Norfloxacin | No information available—manufacturer advises avoid |
| Norgestimate | *see* Contraceptives, Oral |
| Norgestrel | *see* Contraceptives, Oral |
| Nortriptyline | *see* Antidepressants, Tricyclic (and related) |
| NSAIDs | *see* individual entries |
| Nystatin | No information available, but absorption from gastro-intestinal tract negligible |
| Octreotide | Manufacturer advises avoid unless essential—no information available |
| Oestrogens | Avoid; adverse effects on lactation; *see also* Contraceptives, Oral |
| Ofloxacin | Manufacturer advises avoid |
| Olanzapine | Manufacturer advises avoid—present in milk |
| Olmesartan | Manufacturer advises avoid—present in milk in *animal* studies |
| Olsalazine | Manufacturer advises avoid |
| Omalizumab | Manufacturer advises avoid—present in milk in *animal* studies |
| Omega-3-acid ethyl esters | Manufacturer advises avoid—no information available |
| Omeprazole | Present in milk but not known to be harmful |
| Ondansetron | Not known to be harmful but manufacturer advises avoid |
| Opioid analgesics | *see* individual entries |
| Oral contraceptives | *see* Contraceptives, Oral |
| Orlistat | Manufacturer advises avoid—no information available |
| Orphenadrine | Present in milk—manufacturer advises avoid |
| Oseltamivir | Manufacturer advises use only if potential benefit outweighs risk—present in milk in *animal* studies |
| Oxaliplatin | *see* Cytotoxic Drugs |
| Oxazepam | *see* Benzodiazepines |
| Oxcarbazepine | Present in milk—manufacturer advises avoid |
| Oxprenolol | *see* Beta-blockers |
| Oxybutynin | Present in milk—manufacturers advise avoid |
| Oxycodone | Present in milk—manufacturer advises avoid |
| Oxytetracycline | *see* Tetracyclines |
| Paclitaxel | *see* Cytotoxic Drugs |
| Palonosetron | Manufacturer advises avoid—no information available |
| Pamidronate disodium | *see* Disodium Pamidronate |
| Pancuronium | Manufacturer advises avoid unless potential benefit outweighs possble risk—no information available |
| Pantoprazole | Manufacturer advises avoid unless potential benefit outweighs risk—small amount present in milk in *animal* studies |
| Papaveretum | *see* Morphine |
| Paracetamol | Amount too small to be harmful |
| Paraldehyde | Manufacturer advises avoid unless essential—present in milk |
| Parecoxib | Manufacturer advises avoid—present in milk in animal studies |
| Paricalcitol | Manufacturer advises caution—no information available; *see also* Vitamin D |
| Paroxetine | Present in milk but amount too small to be harmful |
| Pegfilgrastim | No information available—manufacturer advises avoid |
| Peginterferon alfa | *see* Interferons |
| Pemetrexed | *see* Cytotoxic Drugs |
| Penicillamine | Manufacturer advises avoid unless potential benefit outweighs risk—no information available |
| Penicillins | Trace amounts in milk |
| Pentamidine isetionate | Manufacturer advises avoid unless essential |
| Pentazocine | Small amount present in milk—manufacturer advises caution |
| Pentostatin | *see* Cytotoxic Drugs |
| Pergolide | May suppress lactation |
| Pericyazine | *see* Antipsychotics |
| Perindopril | Manufacturer advises avoid—no information available |
| Perphenazine | *see* Antipsychotics |
| Pethidine | Present in milk but not known to be harmful |
| Phenindione | *see* Anticoagulants, Oral |
| Phenobarbital | Avoid when possible; drowsiness may occur but risk probably small; one report of methaemoglobinaemia with phenobarbital and phenytoin |
| Phenoxybenzamine | May be present in milk |
| Phenoxymethylpenicillin | *see* Penicillins |
| Phentolamine | Manufacturer advises avoid—no information available |
| Phenytoin | Small amount present in milk; manufacturer advises avoid—but *see* section 4.8.1 |
| Phytomenadione | Present in milk |
| Pilocarpine | Manufacturer advises avoid—no information available |
| Pimozide | *see* Antipsychotics |

| Drug | Comment |
|---|---|
| Pindolol | *see* Beta-blockers |
| Pioglitazone | Manufacturer advises avoid—present in milk in *animal* studies |
| Piperacillin [ingredient] | *see Tazocin®* |
| Piperazine | Present in milk—manufacturer advises avoid breast-feeding for 8 hours after dose (express and discard milk during this time) |
| Piracetam | Manufacturer advises avoid |
| Piroxicam | Amount too small to be harmful |
| Pizotifen | Amount probably too small to be harmful, but manufacturer advises avoid |
| Podophyllum | Avoid |
| Porfimer | No information available—manufacturer advises avoid |
| Povidone–iodine | Avoid; iodine absorbed from vaginal preparations is concentrated in milk |
| Pramipexole | May suppress lactation; manufacturer advises avoid—present in milk in *animal* studies |
| Pravastatin | Small amount present in milk—manufacturer advises avoid |
| Prazosin | Amount probably too small to be harmful |
| Prednisolone | *see* Corticosteroids |
| Pregabalin | Present in milk in *animal* studies—manufacturer advises avoid |
| Prilocaine | Present in milk but not known to be harmful |
| *Primaxin®* | Present in milk but unlikely to be absorbed (however, manufacturer advises avoid) |
| Primidone | *see* Phenobarbital |
| Probenecid | No information available |
| Procainamide | Present in milk—manufacturer advises avoid |
| Procarbazine | *see* Cytotoxic Drugs |
| Prochlorperazine | *see* Antipsychotics |
| Progesterone | Manufacturers advise avoid—present in milk |
| Proguanil | Amount probably too small to be harmful when used for malaria prophylaxis; inadequate for reliable protection against malaria in breast-fed infant, see p. 331 |
| Promazine | *see* Antipsychotics |
| Promethazine | *see* Antihistamines |
| Propafenone | Manufacturer advises avoid—no information available |
| Propantheline | May suppress lactation |
| Propiverine | Manufacturer advises avoid—present in milk in *animal* studies |
| Propofol | Present in milk but amount probably too small to be harmful |
| Propranolol | *see* Beta-blockers |
| Propylthiouracil | Monitor infant's thyroid status but amounts in milk probably too small to affect infant; high doses might affect neonatal thyroid function |
| Protirelin | Breast enlargement and leaking of milk reported |
| Pseudoephedrine | Amount too small to be harmful |
| Pyrazinamide | Amount too small to be harmful |
| Pyridostigmine | Amount probably too small to be harmful |
| Pyrimethamine | Significant amount—avoid administration of other folate antagonists to infant; avoid breast-feeding during toxoplasmosis treatment |
| Quetiapine | Manufacturer advises avoid—no information available |
| Quinagolide | Suppresses lactation |
| Quinapril | No information available—manufacturer advises caution |
| Quinidine | Significant amount but not known to be harmful |
| Quinupristin [ingredient] | *see Synercid®* |
| Rabeprazole | Manufacturer advises avoid—no information available |
| Raltitrexed | *see* Cytotoxic Drugs |
| Ramipril | Manufacturer advises avoid—no information available |
| Ranitidine | Significant amount but not known to be harmful |
| Ranitidine bismuth citrate | Manufacturer advises avoid—no information available |
| Rasagiline | Manufacturer advises caution—may suppress lactation |
| Rasburicase | Manufacturer advises avoid—no information available |
| Reboxetine | Manufacturer advises avoid—no information available |
| Remifentanil | Manufacturer advises caution—present in milk in *animal* studies |
| Repaglinide | Manufacturer advises avoid—present in milk in *animal* studies |
| Reteplase | Manufacturer advises avoid breast-feeding for 24 hours after dose (express and discard milk during this time) |
| Reviparin | No information available |
| *Riamet®* | Manufacturer advises avoid breast-feeding for at least 1 week after last dose; present in milk in *animal* studies |
| Ribavirin | Avoid—no information available |
| Rifabutin | Manufacturer advises avoid—no information available |
| Rifampicin | Amount too small to be harmful |
| Riluzole | Manufacturer advises avoid—no information available |
| Risedronate sodium | Manufacturer advises avoid |
| Risperidone | Present in milk—manufacturer advises avoid |
| Ritonavir | Breast-feeding not advised in HIV infection |
| Rituximab | Avoid |
| Rivastigmine | Present in milk in *animal* studies—manufacturer advises avoid |
| Rizatriptan | Present in milk in *animal* studies—withhold breast-feeding for 24 hours |
| Rocuronium | Manufacturer advises avoid unless potential benefit outweighs risk—present in milk in *animal* studies |

| Drug | Comment |
|---|---|
| Rosiglitazone | Manufacturer advises avoid—present in milk in *animal* studies |
| Rosuvastatin | *see* Statins |
| Salbutamol | Probably present in milk; manufacturer advises avoid unless potential benefit outweighs risk—the amount of inhaled drugs in breast milk is probably too small to be harmful |
| Salcatonin | *see* Calcitonin (salmon) |
| Saquinavir | Breast-feeding not advised in HIV infection |
| Secobarbital | *see* Barbiturates |
| Selegiline | Manufacturer advises avoid—no information available |
| Senna | Not known to be harmful |
| Sertindole | Manufacturer advises avoid—no information available |
| Sertraline | Present in milk but not known to be harmful in short-term use |
| Sevelamer | Manufacturer advises use only if potential benefit outweighs risk |
| Sibutramine | Manufacturer advises avoid—no information available |
| Silver sulfadiazine | *see* Sulphonamides |
| Simvastatin | *see* Statins |
| Sirolimus | Discontinue breast-feeding |
| Sodium aurothiomalate | Caution—present in milk; theoretical possibility of rashes and idiosyncratic reactions |
| Sodium clodronate | No information available |
| Sodium cromoglicate | Unlikely to be present in milk |
| Sodium fusidate | Present in milk—manufacturer advises caution |
| Sodium nitroprusside | Manufacturer advises caution—no information available |
| Sodium phenylbutyrate | Manufacturer advises avoid—no information available |
| Sodium picosulfate | Not known to be present in milk but manufacturer advises avoid |
| Sodium valproate | *see* Valproate |
| Solifenacin | Manufacturer advises avoid—present in milk in *animal* studies |
| Somatropin | No information available |
| Sotalol | *see* Beta-blockers |
| Spironolactone | Amount probably too small to be harmful but manufacturer advises avoid |
| Statins | Manufacturers of atorvastatin, fluvastatin, rosuvastatin and simvastatin advise avoid—no information available; *see also* pravastatin |
| Stavudine | Breast-feeding not advised in HIV infection |
| Strontium ranelate | Avoid |
| Sulfadiazine | *see* Sulphonamides |
| Sulfasalazine | Small amounts in milk (1 report of bloody diarrhoea and rashes); theoretical risk of neonatal haemolysis especially in G6PD-deficient infants |
| Sulfinpyrazone | No information available |
| Sulindac | No information available |
| Sulphonamides | Small risk of kernicterus in jaundiced infants particularly with long-acting sulphonamides, and of haemolysis in G6PD-deficient infants |
| Sulphonylureas | Theoretical possibility of hypoglycaemia in infant |
| Sulpiride | Best avoided; present in milk; *see also* Antipsychotics |
| Sumatriptan | Present in milk—withhold breast-feeding for 24 hours |
| Suxamethonium | No information available |
| *Synercid®* | Manufacturer advises avoid—no information available |
| Tacalcitol | Manufacturer advises avoid application to breast area—no information available |
| Tacrolimus | Avoid—present in milk following systemic administration |
| Tamoxifen | Supresses lactation; manufacturer advises avoid unless potential benefit outweighs risk |
| Tazarotene | Manufacturer advises avoid—present in milk in *animal* studies |
| Tazobactam [ingredient] | *see Tazocin®* |
| *Tazocin®* | Present in milk—manufacturer advises use only if potential benefit outweighs risk |
| Tegafur with uracil | *see* Cytotoxic Drugs |
| Teicoplanin | No information available |
| Telithromycin | Manufacturer advises avoid—present in milk in *animal* studies |
| Telmisartan | Manufacturer advises avoid—no information available |
| Temazepam | *see* Benzodiazepines |
| Temozolomide | *see* Cytotoxic Drugs |
| Tenecteplase | Manufacturer advises avoid breast-feeding for 24 hours after dose (express and discard milk during this time) |
| Tenofovir | Breast-feeding not advised in HIV infection |
| Tenoxicam | No information available |
| Terazosin | No information available |
| Terbinafine | Present in milk—manufacturer advises avoid |
| Terbutaline | Amount too small to be harmful |
| Terlipressin | Not known to be harmful |
| Testosterone | *see* Androgens |
| Tetrabenazine | Manufacturer advises avoid |
| Tetracaine (amethocaine) | No information available |
| Tetracyclines | Avoid (although absorption and therefore discoloration of teeth in infant probably usually prevented by chelation with calcium in milk) |
| Theophylline | Present in milk—irritability in infant reported; modified-release preparations preferable |
| Thiamine | Severely thiamine-deficient mothers should avoid breast-feeding as toxic methyl-glyoxal present in milk |
| Thiazides and related diuretics | Amount too small to be harmful; large doses may suppress lactation |

| Drug | Comment |
|---|---|
| Thiopental | Present in milk—manufacturer advises avoid |
| Thiotepa | *see* Cytotoxic Drugs |
| Thyroxine | *see* Levothyroxine |
| Tiagabine | Manufacturer advises avoid unless potential benefit outweighs risk |
| Tiaprofenic acid | Amount too small to be harmful |
| Ticarcillin [ingredient] | *see* Penicillins |
| Tiludronic acid | Manufacturer advises avoid—no information available |
| *Timentin*® | *see* Penicillins |
| Timolol | *see* Beta-blockers |
| Tinidazole | Present in milk—manufacturer advises avoid breast-feeding during and for 3 days after stopping treatment |
| Tinzaparin | Manufacturer advises avoid—no information available |
| Tioguanine | *see* Cytotoxic Drugs |
| Tiotropium | Amount in milk probably too small to be harmful (present in milk in *animal* studies)—manufacturer advises use only if potential benefit outweighs risk |
| Tipranavir | Breast-feeding not advised in HIV infection |
| Tirofiban | Manufacturer advises avoid—no information available |
| Tizanidine | Manufacturer advises use only if potential benefit outweighs risk—no information available |
| Tolbutamide | *see* Sulphonylureas |
| Tolcapone | Manufacturer advises avoid—present in milk in *animal* studies |
| Tolfenamic acid | Amount too small to be harmful |
| Tolterodine | Manufacturer advises avoid—no information available |
| Topiramate | Manufacturer advises avoid—present in milk |
| Topotecan | *see* Cytotoxic Drugs |
| Torasemide | No information available |
| Tramadol | Amount probably too small to be harmful, but manufacturer advises avoid |
| Trandolapril | Manufacturers advise avoid |
| Tranexamic acid | Small amount present in milk—antifibrinolytic effect in infant unlikely |
| Trastuzumab | Avoid breast-feeding during treatment and for six months after |
| Travoprost | Present in milk in animal studies; manufacturer advises avoid |
| Trazodone | *see* Antidepressants, Tricyclic (and related) |
| Treosulfan | *see* Cytotoxic Drugs |
| Tretinoin | Avoid |
| Triamcinolone | *see* Corticosteroids |
| Triamterene | Present in milk—manufacturer advises avoid |
| Tribavirin | *see* Ribavirin |
| Triclofos | Avoid |
| Trifluoperazine | *see* Antipsychotics |
| Trimeprazine | *see* Antihistamines |
| Trimethoprim | Present in milk—short-term use not known to be harmful |
| Trimipramine | *see* Antidepressants, Tricyclic (and related) |
| Triptorelin | Manufacturers advise avoid |
| Tropisetron | No information available |
| Trospium | Manufacturer advises caution—no information available |
| Ursodeoxycholic acid | Not known to be harmful but manufacturer advises avoid |
| Valaciclovir | No information available; *see also* Aciclovir |
| Valganciclovir | *see* Ganciclovir |
| Valproate | Amount too small to be harmful |
| Valproic acid | *see* Valproate |
| Valsartan | Manufacturer advises avoid—no information available |
| Vancomycin | Present in milk—significant absorption following oral administration unlikely |
| Vasopressin | Not known to be harmful |
| Vecuronium | No information available |
| Venlafaxine | Present in milk—manufacturer advises avoid |
| Verapamil | Amount too small to be harmful |
| Verteporfin | No information available—manufacturer advises avoid breast-feeding for 48 hours after administration |
| Vigabatrin | Present in milk—manufacturer advises avoid |
| Vinblastine | *see* Cytotoxic Drugs |
| Vincristine | *see* Cytotoxic Drugs |
| Vindesine | *see* Cytotoxic Drugs |
| Vinorelbine | *see* Cytotoxic Drugs |
| Vitamin A | Theoretical risk of toxicity in infants of mothers taking large doses |
| Vitamin D | Caution with high systemic doses; may cause hypercalcaemia in infant; manufacturer of *topical* calcitriol advises avoid; *see also* Calcipotriol and Tacalcitol |
| Voriconazole | Manufacturer advises avoid—no information available |
| Warfarin | *see* Anticoagulants, Oral |
| Xipamide | No information available |
| Zafirlukast | Present in milk—manufacturer advises avoid |
| Zalcitabine | Breast-feeding not advised in HIV infection |
| Zaleplon | Present in milk—manufacturer advises avoid |
| Zanamivir | Manufacturer advises avoid—present in milk in *animal* studies |
| Zidovudine | Breast-feeding not advised in HIV infection |
| Zoledronic acid | Manufacturer advises avoid—no information available |
| Zolmitriptan | Manufacturer advises caution—present in milk in *animal* studies |
| Zolpidem | Small amounts present in milk—manufacturer advises avoid |
| Zonisamide | Avoid; manufacturer advises avoid breast-feeding for 4 weeks after administration |

| Drug | Comment |
| --- | --- |
| Zopiclone | Present in milk—manufacturer advises avoid |
| Zotepine | Manufacturer advises avoid |
| Zuclopenthixol | *see* Antipsychotics |

# A6 Intravenous additives

**Intravenous additives policies** A local policy on the addition of drugs to intravenous fluids should be drawn up by a multi-disciplinary team in each Health Authority and issued as a document to the members of staff concerned.

Centralised additive services are provided in a number of hospital pharmacy departments and should be used in preference to making additions on wards.

The information that follows should be read in conjunction with local policy documents.

## Guidelines

1. Drugs should only be added to infusion containers when constant plasma concentrations are needed or when the administration of a more concentrated solution would be harmful.
2. In general, only one drug should be added to any infusion container and the components should be compatible. Ready-prepared solutions should be used whenever possible. Drugs should not normally be added to blood products, mannitol, or sodium bicarbonate. Only specially formulated additives should be used with fat emulsions or amino-acid solutions (section 9.3).
3. Solutions should be thoroughly mixed by shaking and checked for absence of particulate matter before use.
4. Strict asepsis should be maintained throughout and in general the giving set should not be used for more than 24 hours (for drug admixtures).
5. The infusion container should be labelled with the patient's name, the name and quantity of additives, and the date and time of addition (and the new expiry date or time). Such additional labelling should not interfere with information on the manufacturer's label that is still valid. When possible, containers should be retained for a period after use in case they are needed for investigation.
6. It is good practice to examine intravenous infusions from time to time while they are running. If cloudiness, crystallisation, change of colour, or any other sign of interaction or contamination is observed the infusion should be discontinued.

## Problems

**Microbial contamination** The accidental entry and subsequent growth of micro-organisms converts the infusion fluid pathway into a potential vehicle for infection with micro-organisms, particularly species of Candida, Enterobacter, and Klebsiella. Ready-prepared infusions containing the additional drugs, or infusions prepared by an additive service (when available) should therefore be used in preference to making extemporaneous additions to infusion containers on wards etc. However, when this is necessary strict aseptic procedure should be followed.

**Incompatibility** Physical and chemical incompatibilities may occur with loss of potency, increase in toxicity, or other adverse effect. The solutions may become opalescent or precipitation may occur, but in many instances there is no visual indication of incompatibility. Interaction may take place at any point in the infusion fluid pathway, and the potential for incompatibility is increased when more than one substance is added to the infusion fluid.

**Common incompatibilities.** Precipitation reactions are numerous and varied and may occur as a result of pH, concentration changes, 'salting-out' effects, complexation or other chemical changes. Precipitation or other particle formation must be avoided since, apart from lack of control of dosage on administration, it may initiate or exacerbate adverse effects. This is particularly important in the case of drugs which have been implicated in either thrombophlebitis (e.g. diazepam) or in skin sloughing or necrosis caused by extravasation (e.g. sodium bicarbonate and certain cytotoxic drugs). It is also especially important to effect solution of colloidal drugs and to prevent their subsequent precipitation in order to avoid a pyrogenic reaction (e.g. amphotericin).

It is considered undesirable to mix beta-lactam antibiotics, such as semi-synthetic penicillins and cephalosporins, with proteinaceous materials on the grounds that immunogenic and allergenic conjugates could be formed.

A number of preparations undergo significant loss of potency when added singly or in combination to large volume infusions. Examples include ampicillin in infusions that contain glucose or lactates. The breakdown products of dacarbazine have been implicated in adverse effects.

**Blood.** Because of the large number of incompatibilities, drugs should not normally be added to blood and blood products for infusion purposes. Examples of incompatibility with blood include hypertonic mannitol solutions (irreversible crenation of red cells), dextrans (rouleaux formation and interference with cross-matching), glucose (clumping of red cells), and oxytocin (inactivated).

If the giving set is not changed after the administration of blood, but used for other infusion fluids, a fibrin clot may form which, apart from blocking the set, increases the likelihood of microbial growth.

**Intravenous fat emulsions** may break down with coalescence of fat globules and separation of phases when additions such as antibacterials or electrolytes are made, thus increasing the possibility of embolism. Only specially formulated products such as *Vitlipid N®* (section 9.3) may be added to appropriate intravenous fat emulsions.

**Other infusions** that frequently give rise to incompatibility include amino acids, mannitol, and sodium bicarbonate.

**Bactericides** such as chlorocresol 0.1% or phenylmercuric nitrate 0.001% are present in some injection solutions. The total volume of such solutions added to a container for infusion on one occasion should not exceed 15 mL.

## Method

Ready-prepared infusions should be used whenever available. **Potassium chloride** is usually available in concentrations of 20, 27, and 40 mmol/litre in sodium chloride intravenous infusion (0.9%), glucose intravenous infusion (5%) or sodium chloride and glucose intravenous infusion. **Lidocaine hydrochloride** (lignocaine hydrochloride) is usually available in concentrations of 0.1 or 0.2% in glucose intravenous infusion (5%).

When addition is required to be made extemporaneously, any product reconstitution instructions such as those relating to concentration, vehicle, mixing, and handling precautions should be strictly followed using an aseptic technique throughout. Once the product has been reconstituted, addition to the infusion fluid should be made immediately in order to minimise microbial contamination and, with certain products, to prevent degradation or other formulation change which may occur; e.g. reconstituted ampicillin injection degrades rapidly on standing, and also may form polymers which could cause sensitivity reactions.

It is also important in certain instances that an infusion fluid of specific pH be used (e.g. **furosemide** (frusemide) injection requires dilution in infusions of pH greater than 5.5).

When drug additions are made it is important to mix thoroughly; additions should not be made to an infusion container that has been connected to a giving set, as mixing is hampered. If the solutions are not thoroughly mixed a concentrated layer of the additive may form owing to differences in density. **Potassium chloride** is particularly prone to this 'layering' effect when added without adequate mixing to infusions packed in non-rigid infusion containers; if such a mixture is administered it may have a serious effect on the heart.

A time limit between addition and completion of administration must be imposed for certain admixtures to guarantee satisfactory drug potency and compatibility. For admixtures in which degradation occurs without the formation of toxic substances, an acceptable limit is the time taken for 10% decomposition of the drug. When toxic substances are produced stricter limits may be imposed. Because of the risk of microbial contamination a maximum time limit of 12 hours may be appropriate for additions made elsewhere than in hospital pharmacies offering central additive service.

Certain injections must be protected from light during continuous infusion to minimise oxidation, e.g. amphotericin, dacarbazine, and sodium nitroprusside.

Dilution with a small volume of an appropriate vehicle and administration using a motorised infusion pump is advocated for preparations such as heparin where strict control over administration is required. In this case the appropriate dose may be dissolved in a convenient volume (e.g. 24 to 48 mL) of sodium chloride intravenous infusion (0.9%).



## Use of table

The table lists preparations given by three methods:

- continuous infusion,
- intermittent infusion, and
- addition via the drip tubing.

Drugs for **continuous infusion** must be diluted in a large volume infusion. Penicillins and cephalosporins are not usually given by continuous infusion because of stability problems and because adequate plasma and tissue concentrations are best obtained by intermittent infusion. Where it is necessary to administer them by continuous infusion, detailed literature should be consulted.

Drugs that are both compatible and clinically suitable may be given by **intermittent infusion** in a relatively small volume of infusion over a short period of time, e.g. 100 mL in 30 minutes. The method is used if the product is incompatible or unstable over the period necessary for continuous infusion; the limited stability of ampicillin or amoxicillin in large volume glucose or lactate infusions may be overcome in this way.

Intermittent infusion is also used if adequate plasma and tissue concentrations are not produced by continuous infusion as in the case of drugs such as dacarbazine, gentamicin, and ticarcillin.

An in-line burette may be used for intermittent infusion techniques in order to achieve strict control over the time and rate of administration, especially for infants and children and in intensive care units. Intermittent infusion may also make use of the 'piggy-back' technique provided that no additions are made to the primary infusion. In this method the drug is added to a small secondary container connected to a Y-type injection site on the primary infusion giving set; the secondary solution is usually infused within 30 minutes.

**Addition *via* the drip tubing** is indicated for a number of cytotoxic drugs in order to minimise extravasation. The preparation is added aseptically *via* the rubber septum of the injection site of a fast-running infusion. In general, drug preparations intended for a bolus effect should be given directly into a separate vein where possible. Failing this, administration may be made *via* the drip tubing provided that the preparation is compatible with the infusion fluid when given in this manner.

## Table of drugs given by intravenous infusion

Covers addition to *Glucose intravenous infusion* 5 and 10%, *Sodium chloride intravenous infusion* 0.9%, *Compound sodium chloride intravenous infusion* (Ringer's solution), and *Compound sodium lactate intravenous infusion* (Hartmann's solution). Compatibility with glucose 5% and with sodium chloride 0.9% indicates compatibility with *Sodium chloride and glucose intravenous infusion*. Infusion of a large volume of hypotonic solution should be avoided therefore care should be taken if water for injections is used. The information in the Table relates to the proprietary preparations indicated; for other preparations suitability should be checked with the manufacturer

**Abciximab** (*ReoPro®*)

Continuous *in* Glucose 5% *or* Sodium chloride 0.9%

Dilute requisite dose in infusion fluid and give *via* infusion pump through a non-pyrogenic low protein-binding 0.2, 0.22 or 5 micron filter

**Acetylcysteine** (*Parvolex®*)

Continuous *in* Glucose 5% or Sodium chloride 0.9%

Glucose 5% is preferable—see Emergency Treatment of Poisoning

**Aciclovir (as sodium salt)** (*Zovirax IV®*; *Aciclovir IV*, Mayne; *Aciclovir IV*, Genus; *Aciclovir Sodium*, Zurich)

Intermittent *in* Sodium chloride 0.9% *or* Sodium chloride and glucose *or* Compound sodium lactate

For *Zovirax IV®*, *Aciclovir IV* (Genus) initially reconstitute to 25 mg/mL in water for injections or sodium chloride 0.9% then dilute to not more than 5 mg/mL with the infusion fluid; to be given over 1 hour; alternatively, may be administered in a concentration of 25 mg/mL using a suitable infusion pump and given over 1 hour; for *Aciclovir IV* (Mayne) dilute to not more than 5 mg/mL with infusion fluid; give over 1 hour

**Agalsidase beta** (*Fabrazyme®*)

Intermittent *in* Sodium chloride 0.9%

Reconstitute initially with water for injections (35 mg in 7.2 mL, 5 mg in 1.1 mL) to give 5 mg/mL solution; dilute requisite dose to 500 mL with infusion fluid and give over at least 2 hours

**Alemtuzumab** (*MabCampath®*)

Intermittent in Glucose 5% *or* Sodium chloride 0.9%

Add requisite dose to 100 mL infusion fluid; infuse over 2 hours

**Alfentanil (as hydrochloride)** (*Rapifen® preparations*)

Continuous *or* intermittent *in* Glucose 5% *or* Sodium chloride 0.9% *or* Compound sodium lactate

**Alprostadil** (*Prostin VR®*)

Continuous *in* Glucose 5% *or* Sodium chloride 0.9%

Add directly to the infusion solution avoiding contact with the walls of plastic containers

**Alteplase** (*Actilyse®*)

Continuous *or* intermittent *in* Sodium chloride 0.9%

Dissolve in water for injections to a concentration of 1 mg/mL and infuse intravenously; alternatively dilute the solution further in the infusion fluid to a concentration of not less than 200 micrograms/mL; not to be infused in glucose solution

**Amikacin sulphate** (*Amikin®*)

Intermittent *in* Glucose 5% *or* Sodium chloride 0.9% *or* Compound sodium lactate

To be given over 30 minutes

**Aminophylline**

Continuous *in* Glucose 5% *or* Sodium chloride 0.9% *or* Compound sodium lactate

**Amiodarone hydrochloride** (*Cordarone X®*)

Continuous *or* intermittent *in* Glucose 5%

Suggested initial infusion volume 250 mL given over 20–120 minutes; for repeat infusions up to 1.2 g in max. 500 mL; infusion in extreme emergency see section 2.7.3; should not be diluted to less than 600 micrograms/mL; incompatible with sodium chloride infusion; avoid equipment containing the plasticizer di-2-ethylhexyphthalate (DEHP)

**Amoxicillin (as sodium salt)** (*Amoxil®*)

Intermittent *in* Glucose 5% *or* Sodium chloride 0.9%

Reconstituted solutions diluted and given without delay; suggested volume 100 mL given over 30–60 minutes

*via* drip tubing *in* Glucose 5% *or* Sodium chloride 0.9%

Continuous infusion not usually recommended

**Amphotericin (colloidal)** (*Amphocil®*)

Intermittent *in* Glucose 5%

Initially reconstitute with water for injections (50 mg in 10 mL, 100 mg in 20 mL), shaking gently to dissolve (fluid may be opalescent) then dilute to a concentration of 625 micrograms/mL (1 volume of reconstituted solution with 7 volumes of infusion fluid); give at a rate of 1–2 mg/kg/hour or slower if not tolerated (initial test dose 2 mg of a 100 microgram/mL solution over 10 minutes); incompatible with sodium chloride or other electrolyte solutions, flush existing intravenous line with glucose 5% or use separate line

**Amphotericin (lipid complex)** (*Abelcet®*)

Intermittent *in* Glucose 5%

Allow suspension to reach room temperature, shake gently to ensure no yellow settlement, withdraw requisite dose (using 17–19 gauge needle) into one or more 20-mL syringes; replace needle on syringe with a 5-micron filter needle provided (fresh needle for each syringe) and dilute to a concentration of 1 mg/mL (2 mg/mL in fluid restriction); preferably give *via* an infusion pump at a rate of 2.5 mg/kg/hour (initial test dose of 1 mg given over 15 minutes); an in-line filter (pore size no less than 15 micron) may be used; do not use sodium chloride or other electrolyte solutions, flush existing intravenous line with glucose 5% or use separate line

**Amphotericin (liposomal)** (*AmBisome®*)

Intermittent *in* Glucose 5%

Reconstitute each vial with 12 mL water for injections and shake vigorously to produce a preparation containing 4 mg/mL; withdraw requisite dose from vial and introduce into infusion fluid through the 5 micron filter provided to produce a final concentration of 0.2–2 mg/mL; infuse over 30–60 minutes (initial test dose 1 mg over 10 minutes); incompatible with sodium chloride solutions, flush existing intravenous line with glucose 5% or use separate line

**Amphotericin (as sodium deoxycholate complex)** (*Fungizone®*)

Intermittent *in* Glucose 5%

Reconstitute each vial with 10 mL water for injections and shake immediately to produce a 5 mg/mL colloidal solution; dilute further in infusion fluid to a concentration of 100 micrograms/mL; pH of the glucose must not be below 4.2 (check each container—consult product literature for details of buffer); infuse over 2–4 hours, or longer if not tolerated (initial test dose 1 mg over 20–30 minutes); begin infusion immediately after dilution and protect from light; incompatible with sodium chloride solutions, flush existing intravenous line with glucose 5% or use separate line; an in-line filter (pore size no less than 1 micron) may be used

**Ampicillin sodium** (*Penbritin®*)

Intermittent *in* Glucose 5% *or* Sodium chloride 0.9%

Reconstituted solutions diluted and given without delay; suggested volume 100 mL given over 30–60 minutes

*via* drip tubing *in* Glucose 5% *or* Sodium chloride 0.9% *or* Ringer's solution *or* Compound sodium lactate

Continuous infusion not usually recommended

**Amsacrine** (*Amsidine®*)

Intermittent in Glucose 5%

Reconstitute with diluent provided and dilute to suggested volume 500 mL; give over 60–90 minutes; use glass syringes; incompatible with sodium chloride infusion

**Arsenic trioxide** (*Trisenox®*)

Intermittent *in* Glucose 5% *or* Sodium chloride 0.9%

Dilute requisite dose with 100–250 mL infusion fluid; infuse over 1–2 hours (up to 4 hours if vasomotor reactions observed)

**Atenolol** (*Tenormin®*)

Intermittent *in* Glucose 5% *or* Sodium chloride 0.9%

Suggested infusion time 20 minutes

**Atosiban** (*Tractocile®*)

Continuous *in* Glucose 5% *or* Sodium chloride 0.9% *or* Compound sodium lactate

Withdraw 10 mL infusion fluid from 100-mL bag and replace with 10 mL atosiban concentrate (7.5 mg/mL) to produce a final concentration of 750 micrograms/mL

**Atracurium besilate** (*Tracrium®*; *Atracurium besilate injection*, Mayne; *Atracurium injection/infusion*, Genus)
Continuous *in* Glucose 5% *or* Sodium chloride 0.9% *or* Compound sodium lactate
Stability varies with diluent; dilute requisite dose with infusion fluid to a concentration of 0.5–5 mg/mL

**Azathioprine (as sodium salt)** (*Imuran®*)
Intermittent *in* Sodium chloride 0.9% *or* Sodium chloride and glucose
Reconstitute 50 mg with 5–15 mL water for injections; dilute with 20–200 mL infusion fluid

**Aztreonam** (*Azactam®*)
Intermittent *in* Glucose 5% *or* Sodium chloride 0.9% *or* Ringer's solution *or* Compound sodium lactate
Dissolve initially in water for injections (1 g per 3 mL) then dilute to a concentration of less than 20 mg/mL; to be given over 20–60 minutes

**Basiliximab** (*Simulect®*)
Intermittent in Glucose 5% or Sodium chloride 0.9%
Reconstitute 10 mg with 5 mL water for injections then dilute to at least 25 mL with infusion fluid; reconstitute 20 mg with 10 mL water for injections then dilute to at least 50 mL with infusion fluid; give over 20–30 minutes

**Benzylpenicillin sodium** (*Crystapen®*)
Intermittent *in* Glucose 5% *or* Sodium chloride 0.9%
Suggested volume 100 mL given over 30–60 minutes
Continuous infusion not usually recommended

**Betamethasone (as sodium phosphate)** (*Betnesol®*)
Continuous *or* intermittent *or via* drip tubing *in* Glucose 5% *or* Sodium chloride 0.9%

**Bevacizumab** (*Avastin®*)
Intermittent in Sodium chloride 0.9%
Dilute requisite dose in infusion fluid to 100 mL and give over 90 minutes; if initial dose well tolerated give second dose over 60 minutes; if second dose well tolerated give subsequent doses over 30 minutes; incompatible with glucose solutions

**Bivalirudin** (*Angiox®*)
Continuous *in* Glucose 5% *or* Sodium chloride 0.9%
Reconstitute each 250-mg vial with 5 mL water for injections then withdraw 5 mL and dilute to 50 mL with infusion fluid

**Bleomycin sulphate**
Intermittent *in* Sodium chloride 0.9%
To be given slowly; suggested volume 200 mL

**Bumetanide** (*Burinex®*)
Intermittent *in* Glucose 5% *or* Sodium chloride 0.9%
Suggested volume 500 mL given over 30–60 minutes

**Busulfan** (*Busilvex®*)
Intermittent in Glucose 5% or Sodium chloride 0.9%
Dilute to a concentration of 500 micrograms/mL; give through a central venous catheter over 2 hours

**Calcitonin (salmon)/Salcatonin** (*Miacalcic®*)
Intermittent *in* Sodium chloride 0.9%
Diluted solution given without delay; dilute in 500 mL and give over at least 6 hours; glass or hard plastic containers should not be used; some loss of potency on dilution and administration

**Calcium folinate** (*Calcium Leucovorin®*, *Refolinon®*)
Intermittent *in* Sodium chloride 0.9%
*Calcium Leucovorin®* can also be infused in Glucose 5 and 10% or Compound sodium lactate
Protect from light

**Calcium gluconate**
Continuous *in* Glucose 5% *or* Sodium chloride 0.9%
Avoid bicarbonates, phosphates, or sulphates

**Calcium levofolinate** (*Isovorin®*)
Intermittent *in* Glucose 5 and 10% *or* Sodium chloride 0.9% *or* Compound sodium lactate
Protect from light

**Carboplatin** (*Paraplatin®*)
Intermittent *in* Glucose 5% *or* Sodium chloride 0.9%
Final concentration as low as 500 micrograms/mL; give over 15–60 minutes

**Carmustine** (*BiCNU®*)
Intermittent *in* Glucose 5% *or* Sodium chloride 0.9%
Reconstitute with solvent provided; give over 1–2 hours

**Caspofungin**
Intermittent *in* Sodium chloride 0.9% *or* Compound sodium lactate
Allow vial to reach room temperature; initially reconstitute each vial with 10.5 mL water for injections, mixing gently to dissolve then dilute requisite dose in 250 mL infusion fluid (35- or 50-mg doses may be diluted in 100 mL infusion fluid if necessary); give over 60 minutes; incompatible with glucose solutions

**Cefotaxime (as sodium salt)** (*Claforan®*; *Cefotaxime Injection*, Genus)
Intermittent *in* Glucose 5% *or* Sodium chloride 0.9% *or* Compound sodium lactate *or* Water for injections
Suggested volume 40–100 mL given over 20–60 minutes

**Cefradine** (*Velosef®*)
Continuous *or* intermittent *in* Glucose 5 and 10% *or* Sodium chloride 0.9% *or* Ringer's solution *or* Compound sodium lactate
Reconstitute 500 mg with 5 mL water for injections or glucose 5% or sodium chloride 0.9% then dilute with infusion fluid

**Ceftazidime (as pentahydrate)** (*Fortum®*, *Kefadim®*)
Intermittent *or via* drip tubing *in* Glucose 5 and 10% *or* Sodium chloride 0.9% *or* Compound sodium lactate
Dissolve 2 g initially in 10 mL (3 g in 15 mL) infusion fluid; for *Fortum®* dilute further to a concentration of 40 mg/mL; for *Kefadim®* dilute further to a concentration of 20 mg/mL; give over up to 30 minutes

**Ceftriaxone (as sodium salt)** (*Rocephin®*; *Ceftriaxone Injection*, Genus)
Intermittent *or via* drip tubing *in* Glucose 5 and 10% *or* Sodium chloride 0.9%
Reconstitute 2-g vial with 40 mL infusion fluid; give intermittent infusion over at least 30 minutes (60 minutes in neonates); not to be given with infusion fluids containing calcium

**Cefuroxime (as sodium salt)** (*Zinacef®*)
Intermittent *or via* drip tubing *in* Glucose 5% *or* Sodium chloride 0.9% *or* Compound sodium lactate
Dissolve initially in water for injections (at least 2 mL for each 250 mg, 15 mL for 1.5 g); suggested volume 50–100 mL given over 30 minutes

**Chloramphenicol (as sodium succinate)** (*Kemicetine®*)
Intermittent *or via* drip tubing *in* Glucose 5% *or* Sodium chloride 0.9%

**Chloroquine sulphate** (*Nivaquine®*)
Continuous *in* Sodium chloride 0.9%
See also section 5.4.1

**Ciclosporin** (*Sandimmun®*)
Continuous *in* Glucose 5% *or* Sodium chloride 0.9%
Dilute to a concentration of 50 mg in 20–100 mL; give over 2–6 hours; not to be used with PVC equipment

**Cidofovir** (*Vistide®*)
Intermittent *in* Sodium chloride 0.9%
Dilute requisite dose with 100 mL infusion fluid; infuse over 1 hour

**Cimetidine** (*Tagamet®*)
Continuous *or* intermittent *in* Glucose 5% *or* Sodium chloride 0.9%
For intermittent infusion suggested volume 100 mL given over 30–60 minutes

**Cisatracurium** (*Nimbex®*, *Nimbex Forte®*)
Continuous *in* Glucose 5% *or* Sodium chloride 0.9%
Solutions of 2 mg/mL and 5 mg/mL may be infused undiluted; alternatively dilute with infusion fluid to a concentration of 0.1–2 mg/mL

**Cisplatin** (*Cisplatin*, Pharmacia; *Cisplatin injection solution*, Mayne)
Intermittent *in* Sodium chloride 0.9% *or* Sodium chloride and glucose
Reconstitute initially with water for injections to produce 1 mg/mL solution then dilute in 2 litres infusion fluid; give over 6–8 hours

**Cladribine** (*Leustat®*)
Continuous *in* Sodium chloride 0.9%
Dilute with 100–500 mL; glucose solutions are unsuitable

**Clarithromycin** (*Klaricid® I.V.*)
Intermittent *in* Glucose 5% *or* Sodium chloride 0.9% *or* Ringer's solution *or* Compound sodium lactate
Dissolve initially in water for injections (500 mg in 10 mL) then dilute to a concentration of 2 mg/mL; give over 60 minutes

**Clindamycin (as phosphate)** (*Dalacin® C Phosphate*)
Continuous *or* intermittent *in* Glucose 5% *or* Sodium chloride 0.9%
Dilute to not more than 18 mg/mL and give over 10–60 minutes at a rate not exceeding 30 mg/minute (1.2 g over at least 60 minutes; higher doses by continuous infusion)

**Clonazepam** (*Rivotril®*)
Intermittent *in* Glucose 5 and 10% *or* Sodium chloride 0.9%
Suggested volume 250 mL

**Co-amoxiclav** (*Augmentin®*; *Co-amoxiclav Injection*, CP)
Intermittent *in* Sodium chloride 0.9% *or* Water for injections; see also package leaflet
Suggested volume 50–100 mL given over 30–40 minutes and completed within 4 hours of reconstitution
*via* drip tubing *in* Glucose 5% *or* Sodium chloride 0.9%

**Co-fluampicil (as sodium salts)** (*Magnapen®*)
Intermittent *in* Glucose 5% *or* Sodium chloride 0.9%
Reconstituted solutions diluted and given without delay; suggested volume 100 mL given over 30–60 minutes
*via* drip tubing *in* Glucose 5% *or* Sodium chloride 0.9% *or* Ringer's solution *or* Compound sodium lactate

**Colistimethate sodium** (*Colomycin®*)
Intermittent *in* Sodium chloride 0.9% *or* Water for injections
Dilute with 50 mL infusion fluid and give over 30 minutes

**Co-trimoxazole** (*Septrin® for infusion*)
Intermittent *in* Glucose 5 and 10% *or* Sodium chloride 0.9% *or* Ringer's solution
Dilute contents of 1 ampoule (5 mL) to 125 mL, 2 ampoules (10 mL) to 250 mL or 3 ampoules (15 mL) to 500 mL; suggested duration of infusion 60–90 minutes (but may be adjusted according to fluid requirements); if fluid restriction necessary, 1 ampoule (5 mL) may be diluted with 75 mL glucose 5% and infused over max. 60 minutes

**Cyclophosphamide** (*Endoxana®*)
*via* drip tubing *in* Glucose 5% *or* Sodium chloride 0.9%
Reconstitute with sodium chloride 0.9%

**Cyclosporin** *see* Ciclosporin

**Cytarabine** (*Cytosar®*)
Continuous *or* intermittent *or via* drip tubing *in* Glucose 5% *or* Sodium chloride 0.9%
Reconstitute *Cytosar®* with water for injections or with infusion fluid; check container for haze or precipitate during administration

**Dacarbazine** (*DTIC-Dome®*; *Dacarbazine*, Medac)
Intermittent *in* Glucose 5% *or* Sodium chloride 0.9%
Reconstitute initially with water for injections then for *DTIC-Dome®* dilute in 125–250 mL infusion fluid; for *Dacarbazine* (Medac) dilute in 200–300 mL infusion fluid; give over 15–30 minutes; protect infusion from light

**Daclizumab** (*Zenapax®*)
Intermittent *in* Sodium chloride 0.9%
Dilute requisite dose in 50 mL infusion fluid; infuse over 15 minutes

**Dactinomycin** (*Cosmegen Lyovac®*)
Intermittent *or via* drip tubing *in* Glucose 5% *or* Sodium chloride 0.9%
Reconstitute with water for injections

**Danaparoid sodium** (*Orgaran®*)
Continuous *in* Glucose 5% *or* Sodium chloride 0.9%

**Daunorubicin (as hydrochloride)** (*Cerubidin®*)
*via* drip tubing *in* Sodium chloride 0.9%
Reconstitute vial with 4 mL water for injections to give 5 mg/mL solution; dilute requisite dose with infusion fluid to a concentration of 1 mg/mL; give over 20 minutes

**Daunorubicin (liposomal)** (*DaunoXome®*)
Intermittent *in* Glucose 5%
Dilute to a concentration of 0.2–1 mg/mL; give over 30–60 minutes; incompatible with sodium chloride solutions; in-line filter not recommended (if used, pore size should be no less than 5 micron)

**Desferrioxamine mesilate** (*Desferal®*)
Continuous *or* intermittent *in* Glucose 5% *or* Sodium chloride 0.9%
Dissolve initially in water for injections (500 mg in 5 mL) then dilute with infusion fluid

**Desmopressin** (*DDAVP®*, *Octim®*)
Intermittent *in* Sodium chloride 0.9%
Dilute with 50 mL and give over 20 minutes

**Dexamethasone sodium phosphate** (*Dexamethasone*, Mayne; *Dexamethasone*, Organon)
Continuous *or* intermittent *or via* drip tubing *in* Glucose 5% *or* Sodium chloride 0.9%
*Dexamethasone* (Organon) can also be infused in Ringer's solution *or* Compound sodium lactate

**Diamorphine hydrochloride** (*Diamorphine Injection*, CP)
Continuous *in* Glucose 5% *or* Sodium chloride 0.9%
Glucose is preferred as infusion fluid

**Diazepam (solution)** (*Diazepam*, CP)
Continuous *in* Glucose 5% *or* Sodium chloride 0.9%
Dilute to a concentration of not more than 10 mg in 200 mL; adsorbed to some extent by the plastics of bags and infusion sets

**Diazepam (emulsion)** (*Diazemuls®*)
Continuous *in* Glucose 5 and 10%
May be diluted to a max. concentration of 200 mg in 500 mL; max. 6 hours between addition and completion of administration; adsorbed to some extent by the plastics of the infusion set
*via* drip tubing *in* Glucose 5 and 10% *or* Sodium chloride 0.9%
Adsorbed to some extent by the plastics of the infusion set

**Diclofenac sodium** (*Voltarol*®)

Continuous *or* intermittent *in* Glucose 5% *or* Sodium chloride 0.9%

Dilute 75 mg with 100–500 mL infusion fluid (previously buffered with 0.5 mL sodium bicarbonate 8.4% solution *or* with 1 mL sodium bicarbonate 4.2% solution); for intermittent infusion give 25–50 mg over 15–60 minutes or 75 mg over 30–120 minutes; for continuous infusion give at a rate of 5 mg/hour

**Digoxin** (*Lanoxin*®)

Intermittent *in* Glucose 5% *or* Sodium chloride 0.9%

To be given over at least 2 hours

**Digoxin-specific antibody fragments** (*Digibind*®)

Intermittent *in* Sodium chloride 0.9%

Dissolve initially in water for injections (4 mL/vial) then dilute with the sodium chloride 0.9% and give through a 0.22 micron sterile, disposable filter over 30 minutes

**Dinoprostone** (*Prostin E2*®)

Continuous *or* intermittent *in* Glucose 5% *or* Sodium chloride 0.9%

**Disodium folinate** (*Sodiofolin*®)

Intermittent *in* Sodium chloride 0.9%

Protect from light

Avoid bicarbonate containing infusions

**Disodium pamidronate** (*Aredia*®; *Disodium pamidronate*, Britannia, Mayne, Medac)

Intermittent *in* Glucose 5% *or* Sodium chloride 0.9%

For *Aredia*® and *Pamidronate disodium* (Britannia), reconstitute initially with water for injections (15 mg in 5 mL, 30 mg or 90 mg in 10 mL); for *Aredia*®, *Pamidronate disodium* (Britannia), *Disodium pamidronate* (Mayne), dilute with infusion fluid to a concentration of not more than 60 mg in 250 mL; for *Disodium pamidronate* (Medac) dilute with infusion fluid to a concentration of not more than 90 mg in 250 mL; give at a rate not exceeding 1 mg/minute; not to be given with infusion fluids containing calcium

**Disopyramide (as phosphate)** (*Rythmodan*®)

Continuous *or* intermittent *in* Glucose 5% *or* Sodium chloride 0.9% *or* Ringer's solution *or* Compound sodium lactate

Max. rate by continuous infusion 20–30 mg/hour (or 400 micrograms/kg/hour)

**Dobutamine (as hydrochloride)** (*Dobutrex*®, *Posiject*®)

Continuous *in* Glucose 5% *or* Sodium chloride 0.9%

Dilute to a concentration of 0.5–1 mg/mL and give *via* a controlled infusion device; give higher concentration (max. 5 mg/mL) with infusion pump; incompatible with bicarbonate

**Docetaxel** (*Taxotere*®)

Intermittent *in* Glucose 5% *or* Sodium chloride 0.9%

Stand docetaxel vials and diluent at room temperature for 5 minutes; add diluent to produce a concentrate containing 10 mg/mL and allow to stand for a further 5 minutes; dilute the requisite dose with at least 250 mL infusion fluid to a final concentration not exceeding 740 micrograms/mL; infuse over 1 hour

**Dolasetron mesilate** (*Anzemet*®)

Intermittent *in* Glucose 5% *or* Sodium chloride 0.9% *or* Compound sodium lactate

Suggested volume 50 mL given over 30 seconds–15 minutes

**Dopamine hydrochloride**

Continuous *in* Glucose 5% *or* Sodium chloride 0.9% *or* Compound sodium lactate

Dilute to max concentration of 3.2 mg/mL; incompatible with bicarbonate

**Dopexamine hydrochloride** (*Dopacard*®)

Continuous *in* Glucose 5% *or* Sodium chloride 0.9%

Dilute to a concentration of 400 or 800 micrograms/mL; max. concentration *via* large peripheral vein 1 mg/mL, concentrations up to 4 mg/mL may be infused *via* central vein; give *via* infusion pump or other device which provides accurate control of rate; contact with metal should be minimised; incompatible with bicarbonate

**Doxorubicin hydrochloride** (*Doxorubicin Rapid Dissolution*, *Doxorubicin Solution*) (both Pharmacia)

*via* drip tubing *in* Glucose 5% *or* Sodium chloride 0.9%

Reconstitute *Doxorubicin Rapid Dissolution* with water for injections or sodium chloride 0.9% (10 mg in 5 mL, 50 mg in 25 mL); give over 2–3 minutes

**Doxorubicin hydrochloride (liposomal)** (*Caelyx*®)

*via* drip tubing *in* Glucose 5%

Dilute up to 90 mg in 250 mL infusion fluid and over 90 mg in 500 mL infusion fluid

**Enoximone** (*Perfan*®)

Continuous *or* intermittent *in* Sodium chloride 0.9% *or* Water for injections

Dilute to a concentration of 2.5 mg/mL; incompatible with glucose solutions; use only plastic containers or syringes

**Epirubicin hydrochloride** (*Pharmorubicin*® *Rapid Dissolution*, *Pharmorubicin*® *Solution*)

*via* drip tubing *in* Sodium chloride 0.9%

Reconstitute *Pharmorubicin*® *Rapid Dissolution* with sodium chloride 0.9% or with water for injections (10 mg in 5 mL, 20 mg in 10 mL, 50 mg in 25 mL); give over 3–5 minutes

**Epoprostenol** (*Flolan*®)

Continuous *in* Sodium chloride 0.9% (but see also below)

Reconstitute using the filter and solvent (glycine buffer diluent) provided to make a concentrate; may be diluted further (consult product literature); for *pulmonary hypertension* dilute further with glycine buffer diluent only, for *renal dialysis* may be diluted further with sodium chloride 0.9%

**Ertapenem** (*Invanz*®)

Intermittent *in* Sodium chloride 0.9%

Reconstitute 1 g with 10 mL water for injections or sodium chloride 0.9%; dilute requisite dose in infusion fluid to a final concentration not exceeding 20 mg/mL; give over 30 minutes; incompatible with glucose solutions

**Erythromycin (as lactobionate)**

Continuous *or* intermittent *in* Glucose 5% (neutralised with sodium bicarbonate) *or* Sodium chloride 0.9%

Dissolve initially in water for injections (1 g in 20 mL) then dilute to a concentration of 1 mg/mL for continuous infusion and 1–5 mg/mL for intermittent infusion; give intermittent infusion over 20–60 minutes

**Esmolol hydrochloride** (*Brevibloc*®)

Continuous *or* intermittent *in* Glucose 5% *or* Sodium chloride 0.9%

Dilute to a concentration of 10 mg/mL; for continuous infusion use a suitable infusion control device; incompatible with bicarbonate

**Esomeprazole (as sodium salt)** (*Nexium*®)

Intermittent *in* Sodium chloride 0.9%

Reconstitute 40 mg with 5 mL sodium chloride 0.9% then dilute with up to 100 mL infusion fluid, give requisite dose over 10–30 minutes

**Ethanol**

Continuous *in* Glucose 5% *or* Sodium chloride 0.9% *or* Ringer's solution *or* Compound sodium lactate

Dilute to a concentration of 5–10%

**Etoposide** (*Eposin®*; *Vepesid®*; *Etoposide*, TEVA UK and Mayne)

Intermittent *in* Sodium chloride 0.9%

For *Vepesid®* dilute to a concentration of not more than 250 micrograms/mL and give over not less than 30 minutes; for *Etoposide* (TEVA UK) dilute with either sodium chloride 0.9% or glucose 5% to a concentration of 200 micrograms/mL and give over 30–60 minutes; for *Etoposide* (Mayne) dilute with either sodium chloride 0.9% or glucose 5% to a concentration of not more than 250 micrograms/mL and give over not less than 30 minutes; for *Eposin®* dilute with either sodium chloride 0.9% or glucose 5% to a concentration of 200–400 micrograms/mL and give over at least 30 minutes; check container for haze or precipitate during infusion

**Etoposide (as phosphate)** (*Etopophos®*)

Intermittent *in* Glucose 5% *or* Sodium chloride 0.9%

Reconstitute with 5–10 mL of either water for injections *or* with infusion fluid then dilute further with infusion fluid to a concentration as low as 100 micrograms/mL and give over 5 minutes to 3.5 hours

**Fentanyl** (*Sublimaze®*)

Continuous *or* intermittent *in* Glucose 5% *or* Sodium chloride 0.9%

**Filgrastim** (*Neupogen®*)

Continuous *or* intermittent *in* Glucose 5%

For a filgrastim concentration of less than 1 500 000 units/mL (15 micrograms/mL) albumin solution (human serum albumin) is added to produce a final albumin concentration of 2 mg/mL; should not be diluted to a filgrastim concentration of less than 200 000 units/mL (2 micrograms/mL) and should not be diluted with sodium chloride solution

**Flecainide acetate** (*Tambocor®*)

Continuous *or* intermittent *in* Glucose 5% *or* Sodium chloride 0.9% *or* Compound sodium lactate

Minimum volume in infusion fluids containing chlorides 500 mL

**Flucloxacillin (as sodium salt)** (*Floxapen®*)

Intermittent *in* Glucose 5% *or* Sodium chloride 0.9%

Suggested volume 100 mL given over 30–60 minutes

*via* drip tubing *in* Glucose 5% *or* Sodium chloride 0.9% *or* Ringer's solution *or* Compound sodium lactate

Continuous infusion not usually recommended

**Fludarabine phosphate** (*Fludara®*)

Intermittent *in* Sodium chloride 0.9%

Reconstitute each 50 mg with 2 mL water for injections and dilute requisite dose in 100 mL; give over 30 minutes

**Flumazenil** (*Anexate®*)

Continuous *in* Glucose 5% *or* Sodium chloride 0.9%

**Fluorouracil (as sodium salt)**

Continuous *or* intermittent *or via* drip tubing *in* Glucose 5% *or* Sodium chloride 0.9%

Give intermittent infusion over 30–60 minutes or over 4 hours

**Foscarnet sodium** (*Foscavir®*)

Intermittent *in* Glucose 5% *or* Sodium chloride 0.9%

Dilute to a concentration of 12 mg/mL for infusion into peripheral vein (undiluted solution *via* central venous line only); infuse over at least 1 hour

**Fosphenytoin Sodium** (*Pro-Epanutin®*)

Intermittent *in* Glucose 5% *or* Sodium chloride 0.9%

Dilute to a concentration of 1.5–25 mg (phenytoin sodium equivalent)/mL

**Furosemide/Frusemide (as sodium salt)** (*Lasix®*)

Continuous *in* Sodium chloride 0.9% *or* Ringer's solution

Infusion pH must be above 5.5 and rate should not exceed 4 mg/minute; glucose solutions are unsuitable

**Fusidic acid (as sodium salt)**

Continuous *in* Glucose 5% (but see below) *or* Sodium chloride 0.9%

Reconstitute with the buffer solution provided and dilute to 500 mL; give through central venous line over 2 hours (or over 6 hours if superficial vein used); incompatible in solution of pH less than 7.4

**Ganciclovir (as sodium salt)** (*Cymevene®*)

Intermittent *in* Glucose 5% *or* Sodium chloride 0.9% *or* Ringer's solution *or* Compound sodium lactate

Reconstitute initially in water for injections (500 mg/10 mL) then dilute to not more than 10 mg/mL with infusion fluid (usually 100 mL); give over 1 hour

**Gemcitabine** (*Gemzar®*)

Intermittent *in* Sodium chloride 0.9%

Reconstitute initially with sodium chloride 0.9% (200 mg in at least 5 mL, 1 g in at least 25 mL); may be diluted further with infusion fluid; give over 30 minutes

**Gentamicin (as sulphate)** (*Cidomycin®*; *Gentamicin Paediatric Injection*, Beacon; *Gentamicin Injection*, Mayne)

Intermittent *or via* drip tubing *in* Glucose 5% *or* Sodium chloride 0.9%

Suggested volume for intermittent infusion 50–100 mL given over 20–30 minutes

**Glyceryl trinitrate** (*Nitrocine®*, *Nitronal®*, *Tridil®*)

Continuous *in* Glucose 5% *or* Sodium chloride 0.9%

For *Tridil®* dilute to a concentration of not more than 400 micrograms/mL; for *Nitrocine®* suggested infusion concentration 100 micrograms/mL; incompatible with polyvinyl chloride infusion containers such as *Viaflex®* or *Steriflex®*; use glass or polyethylene containers or give *via* a syringe pump

**Granisetron (as hydrochloride)** (*Kytril®*)

Intermittent *in* Glucose 5% *or* Sodium chloride 0.9% *or* Compound sodium lactate

Dilute 3 mL in 20–50 mL infusion fluid (up to 3 mL in 10–30 mL for children); give over 5 minutes

**Haem arginate** (*Normosang®*)

Intermittent *in* Sodium chloride 0.9%

Dilute requisite dose in 100 mL infusion fluid in glass bottle and give over at least 30 minutes *via* large antebrachial vein; administer within 1 hour after dilution

**Heparin sodium**

Continuous *in* Glucose 5% *or* Sodium chloride 0.9%

Administration with a motorised pump advisable

**Hydralazine hydrochloride** (*Apresoline®*)

Continuous *in* Sodium chloride 0.9% *or* Ringer's solution

Suggested infusion volume 500 mL

**Hydrocortisone (as sodium phosphate)** (*Efcortesol®*)

Continuous *or* intermittent *or via* drip tubing *in* Glucose 5% *or* Sodium chloride 0.9%

**Hydrocortisone (as sodium succinate)** (*SoluCortef®*)

Continuous *or* intermittent *or via* drip tubing *in* Glucose 5% *or* Sodium chloride 0.9%

**Ibandronic acid** (*Bondronat®*)

Intermittent *in* Glucose 5% *or* Sodium chloride 0.9%

Dilute requisite dose in 500 mL infusion fluid and give over 1–2 hours

**Idarubicin hydrochloride** (*Zavedos®*)

*via* drip tubing *in* Sodium chloride 0.9%

Reconstitute with water for injections; give over 5–10 minutes

**Ifosfamide** (*Mitoxana*®)

Continuous *or* intermittent *or via* drip tubing *in* Glucose 5% *or* Sodium chloride 0.9%

For continuous infusion, suggested volume 3 litres given over 24 hours; for intermittent infusion, give over 30–120 minutes

**Imiglucerase** (*Cerezyme*®)

Intermittent *in* Sodium chloride 0.9%

Initially reconstitute with 5.1 mL water for injections to give 40 units/mL solution; dilute requisite dose in 100–200 mL infusion fluid and give over 1–2 hours *or* at a rate not exceeding 1 unit/kg/minute; administer within 3 hours after reconstitution

**Imipenem with cilastatin (as sodium salt)** (*Primaxin*®)

Intermittent *in* Sodium chloride 0.9% *or* Sodium chloride and Glucose

Dilute to a concentration of 5 mg (as imipenem)/mL; infuse 250–500 mg (as imipenem) over 20–30 minutes, 1 g over 40–60 minutes

Continuous infusion not usually recommended

**Infliximab** (*Remicade*®)

Intermittent *in* Sodium chloride 0.9%

Reconstitute each 100-mg vial with 10 mL water for injections; gently swirl vial without shaking to dissolve; allow to stand for 5 minutes; dilute requisite dose with infusion fluid to a final volume of 250 mL and give through a low protein-binding filter (1.2 micron or less) over at least 2 hours; start infusion within 3 hours of reconstitution

**Insulin (soluble)**

Continuous *in* Sodium chloride 0.9% *or* Compound sodium lactate

Adsorbed to some extent by plastics of infusion set; see also section 6.1.3; ensure insulin is not injected into 'dead space' of injection port of the infusion bag

**Insulin aspart**

Continuous *in* Sodium chloride 0.9% *or* Glucose 5%

Dilute to 0.05–1 unit/mL with infusion fluid; adsorbed to some extent by plastics of infusion set

**Insulin lispro**

Continuous *in* Sodium chloride 0.9% *or* Glucose 5%

**Interferon alfa-2b** (*IntronA*®)

Intermittent *in* Sodium chloride 0.9%

For *IntronA*® solution, dilute requisite dose in 50 mL infusion fluid and administer over 20 minutes; not to be diluted to less than 300 000 units/mL

For *IntronA*® powder, reconstitute with 1 mL water for injections; dilute requisite dose in 100 mL infusion fluid and administer over 20 minutes; not to be diluted to less than 100 000 units/mL



**Irinotecan hydrochloride** (*Campto*®)

Intermittent *in* Glucose 5% *or* Sodium chloride 0.9%

Dilute requisite dose in 250 mL infusion fluid; give over 30–90 minutes

**Iron dextran** (*Cosmofer*®)

Intermittent *in* Glucose 5% *or* Sodium chloride 0.9%

Dilute 100–200 mg in 100 mL infusion fluid; give 25 mg over 15 minutes as a test dose initially, then give at a rate not exceeding 3.33 mL/minute; *total dose infusion* diluted in 500 mL infusion fluid and given over 4–6 hours (initial test dose 25 mg over 15 minutes)

**Iron sucrose** (*Venofer*®)

Intermittent *in* Sodium chloride 0.9%

Dilute 100 mg in up to 100 mL infusion fluid; give 25 mg over 15 minutes as a test dose initially, then give at a rate not exceeding 3.33 mg/minute

**Isosorbide dinitrate** (*Isoket 0.05%*®, *Isoket 0.1%*®)

Continuous *in* Glucose 5% *or* Sodium chloride 0.9%

Adsorbed to some extent by polyvinyl chloride infusion containers; preferably use glass or polyethylene containers or give *via* a syringe pump; *Isoket 0.05%*® can alternatively be administered undiluted using a syringe pump with a glass or rigid plastic syringe

**Itraconazole** (*Sporanox*®)

Intermittent *in* Sodium chloride 0.9%

Dilute 250 mg in 50 mL infusion fluid and infuse only **60 mL** through an in-line filter (0.2 micron) over 60 minutes

**Ketamine (as hydrochloride)** (*Ketalar*®)

Continuous *in* Glucose 5% *or* Sodium chloride 0.9%

Dilute to 1 mg/mL; microdrip infusion for maintenance of anaesthesia

**Labetalol hydrochloride** (*Trandate*®)

Intermittent *in* Glucose 5% *or* Sodium chloride and glucose

Dilute to a concentration of 1 mg/mL; suggested volume 200 mL; adjust rate with in-line burette

**Laronidase** (*Aldurazyme*®)

Intermittent *in* Sodium chloride 0.9%

Body-weight under 20 kg, use 100 mL infusion fluid; body-weight over 20 kg use 250 mL infusion fluid; withdraw volume of infusion fluid equivalent to volume of laronidase concentrate being added; give through an in-line filter (0.22 micron) at an initial rate of 2 units/kg/hour then increasing gradually every 15 minutes to max. 43 units/kg/hour

**Lenograstim** (*Granocyte*®)

Intermittent *in* Sodium chloride 0.9%

Initially reconstitute with 1 mL water for injection provided (do not shake vigorously) then dilute with up to 50 mL infusion fluid for each vial of *Granocyte-13* or up to 100 mL infusion fluid for *Granocyte-34*; give over 30 minutes

**Lepirudin** (*Refludan*®)

Continuous *in* Glucose 5% *or* Sodium chloride 0.9%

Reconstitute initially with water for injections *or* sodium chloride 0.9% then dilute to a concentration of 2 mg/mL with infusion fluid

**Magnesium sulphate**

Continuous *in* Glucose 5% *or* Sodium chloride 0.9%

Suggested concentration up to 200 mg/mL

**Melphalan** (*Alkeran*®)

Intermittent *or via* drip tubing *in* Sodium chloride 0.9%

Reconstitute with the solvent provided then dilute with infusion fluid; max. 90 minutes between addition and completion of administration; incompatible with glucose infusion

**Meropenem** (*Meronem*®)

Intermittent *in* Glucose 5 and 10% *or* Sodium chloride 0.9%

Dilute in 50–200 mL infusion fluid and give over 15–30 minutes

**Mesna** (*Uromitexan*®)

Continuous *or via* drip tubing *in* Glucose 5% *or* Sodium chloride 0.9%

**Metaraminol (as tartrate)** (*Aramine*®)

Continuous *or via* drip tubing *in* Glucose 5% *or* Sodium chloride 0.9%

Suggested volume 500 mL

**Methotrexate (as sodium salt)** (*Methotrexate*, Lederle)

Continuous *or via* drip tubing *in* Glucose 5% *or* Sodium chloride 0.9% *or* Compound sodium lactate *or* Ringer's solution

Dilute in a large-volume infusion; max. 24 hours between addition and completion of administration

**Methylprednisolone (as sodium succinate)** (*Solu-Medrone*®)

Continuous *or* intermittent *or via* drip tubing *in* Glucose 5% *or* Sodium chloride 0.9%

Reconstitute initially with water for injections; doses up to 250 mg should be given over at least 5 minutes, high doses over at least 30 minutes

**Metoclopramide hydrochloride** (*Maxolon High Dose®*)

Continuous *or* intermittent *in* Glucose 5% *or* Sodium chloride 0.9% *or* Compound sodium lactate

Continuous infusion recommended; loading dose, dilute with 50–100 mL and give over 15–20 minutes; maintenance dose, dilute with 500 mL and give over 8–12 hours; for intermittent infusion dilute with at least 50 mL and give over at least 15 minutes

**Mexiletine hydrochloride** (*Mexitil®*)

Continuous *in* Glucose 5% *or* Sodium chloride 0.9%

**Midazolam** (*Hypnovel®*)

Continuous *in* Glucose 5% *or* Sodium chloride 0.9%

For neonates and children under 15 kg dilute to a max. concentration of 1 mg/mL

**Milrinone** (*Primacor®*)

Continuous *in* Glucose 5% *or* Sodium chloride 0.9%

Dilute to a suggested concentration of 200 micrograms/mL

**Mitoxantrone/Mitozantrone (as hydrochloride)** (*Novantrone®*, *Onkotrone®*)

Intermittent *or via* drip tubing *in* Glucose 5% *or* Sodium chloride 0.9%

For administration *via* drip tubing suggested volume at least 50 mL given over at least 3–5 minutes; for intermittent infusion (*Onkotrone®* only), dilute with 50–100 mL and give over 15–30 minutes

**Mivacurium (as chloride)** (*Mivacron®*)

Continuous *in* Glucose 5% *or* Sodium chloride 0.9%

Dilute to a concentration of 500 micrograms/mL; may also be given undiluted

**Mycophenolate mofetil (as hydrochloride)** (*CellCept®*)

Intermittent *in* Glucose 5%

Reconstitute each 500-mg vial with 14 mL glucose 5% and dilute the contents of 2 vials in 140 mL infusion fluid; give over 2 hours

**Naloxone** (*Min-I-Jet® Naloxone Hydrochloride*, *Narcan®*)

Continuous *in* Glucose 5% *or* Sodium chloride 0.9%

Reversal of opioid-induced respiratory depression, dilute to a concentration of 4 micrograms/mL; opioid overdose only, dilute 10 mg in 50 mL glucose 5%, see Emergency Treatment of Poisoning

**Netilmicin (as sulphate)** (*Netillin®*)

Intermittent *or via* drip tubing *in* Glucose 5 and 10% *or* Sodium chloride 0.9%

For intermittent infusion suggested volume 50–200 mL given over 30–120 minutes

**Nimodipine** (*Nimotop®*)

*via* drip tubing *in* Glucose 5% *or* Sodium chloride 0.9% *or* Ringer's solution

Not to be added to infusion container; administer *via* an infusion pump through a Y-piece into a central catheter; incompatible with polyvinyl chloride giving sets or containers; protect infusion from light

**Nizatidine** (*Axid®*)

Continuous *or* intermittent *in* Glucose 5% *or* Sodium chloride 0.9% *or* Compound sodium lactate

For continuous infusion, dilute 300 mg in 150 mL and give at a rate of 10 mg/hour; for intermittent infusion, dilute 100 mg in 50 mL and give over 15 minutes

**Noradrenaline acid tartrate/Norepinephrine bitartrate**

Continuous *in* Glucose 5% *or* Sodium chloride and glucose

Give *via* controlled infusion device; for administration *via* syringe pump, dilute 4 mg noradrenaline acid tartrate (2 mL solution) with 48 mL; for administration *via* drip counter dilute 40 mg (20 mL solution) with 480 mL; give through a central venous catheter; incompatible with alkalis

**Omeprazole (as sodium salt)** (*Losec®*)

Intermittent *in* Glucose 5% *or* Sodium chloride 0.9%

Reconstitute with infusion fluid and dilute to 100 mL; give over 20–30 minutes

**Ondansetron (as hydrochloride)** (*Zofran®*)

Continuous *or* intermittent *in* Glucose 5% *or* Sodium chloride 0.9% *or* Ringer's solution

For intermittent infusion, dilute 32 mg in 50–100 mL and give over at least 15 minutes

**Oxaliplatin** (*Eloxatin®*)

Continuous *in* Glucose 5%

Reconstitute with water for injections or glucose 5% to a concentration of 5 mg/mL; dilute with 250–500 mL infusion fluid and give over 2–6 hours

**Oxycodone hydrochloride** (*OxyNorm®*)

Continuous *or* intermittent *in* Glucose 5% *or* Sodium chloride 0.9%

Dilute to a concentration of 1 mg/mL

**Oxytocin** (*Syntocinon®*)

Continuous *in* Glucose 5% *or* Sodium chloride 0.9% or Compound sodium lactate *or* Ringer's solution

Preferably given *via* a variable-speed infusion pump in a concentration appropriate to the pump; if given by drip infusion for *induction or enhancement of labour*, dilute 5 units in 500 mL infusion fluid; for *postpartum uterine haemorrhage* dilute 5–30 units in 500 mL; if high doses given for prolonged period (e.g. for inevitable or missed abortion or for postpartum haemorrhage), use low volume of an electrolyte-containing infusion fluid (not Glucose 5%) given at higher concentration than for induction or enhancement of labour; close attention to patient's fluid and electrolyte status essential

**Paclitaxel** (*Taxol®*)

Continuous *in* Glucose 5% *or* Sodium chloride 0.9%

Dilute to a concentration of 0.3–1.2 mg/mL and give through an in-line filter (0.22 micron or less) over 3 hours; not to be used with PVC equipment (short PVC inlet or outlet on filter may be acceptable)

**Pantoprazole (as sodium sesquihydrate)** (*Protium®*)

Intermittent *in* Glucose 5 and 10% *or* Sodium chloride 0.9%

Reconstitute 40 mg with 10 mL sodium chloride 0.9% and dilute to 100 mL with infusion fluid

**Pemetrexed** (*Alimta®*)

Intermittent *in* Sodium chloride 0.9%

Reconstitute 500-mg vial with 20 mL sodium chloride 0.9% to produce a 25 mg/mL solution; dilute requisite dose with infusion fluid to 100 mL; give over 10 minutes

**Pentamidine isetionate** (*Pentacarinat®*)

Intermittent *in* Glucose 5% *or* Sodium chloride 0.9%

Dissolve initially in water for injections (300 mg in 3–5 mL) then dilute in 50–250 mL; give over at least 60 minutes

**Pentostatin** (*Nipent®*)

Intermittent *in* Glucose 5% *or* Sodium chloride 0.9%

Reconstitute initially with 5 mL water for injections to produce a 2 mg/mL solution; dilute requisite dose in 25–50 mL infusion fluid (final concentration 180–330 micrograms/mL) and give over 20–30 minutes

**Phenoxybenzamine hydrochloride**

Intermittent *in* Sodium chloride 0.9%

Dilute in 200–500 mL infusion; give over at least 2 hours; max. 4 hours between dilution and completion of administration

**Phentolamine mesilate** (*Rogitine®*)

Intermittent *in* Glucose 5% *or* Sodium chloride 0.9%

**Phenylephrine hydrochloride**

Intermittent *in* Glucose 5% *or* Sodium chloride 0.9%

Dilute 10 mg in 500 mL infusion fluid

**Phenytoin sodium** (*Epanutin®*)

Intermittent *in* Sodium chloride 0.9%

Flush intravenous line with Sodium chloride 0.9% before and after infusion; dilute in 50–100 mL infusion fluid (final concentration not to exceed 10 mg/mL) and give through an in-line filter (0.22–0.50 micron) at a rate not exceeding 50 mg/minute (neonates, give at a rate of 1–3 mg/kg/minute); complete administration within 1 hour of preparation

**Phytomenadione (in mixed micelles vehicle)** (*Konakion® MM*)

Intermittent *in* Glucose 5%

Dilute with 55 mL; may be injected into lower part of infusion apparatus

**Piperacillin with tazobactam (as sodium salts)** (*Tazocin®*)

Intermittent *in* Glucose 5% *or* Sodium chloride 0.9% *or* Water for injections

Reconstitute initially with water for injections or sodium chloride infusion 0.9% (2.25 g in 10 mL, 4.5 g in 20 mL) then dilute to at least 50 mL with infusion fluid; give over 20–30 minutes

**Potassium chloride**

Continuous *in* Glucose 5% *or* Sodium chloride 0.9%

Dilute in a large-volume infusion; mix thoroughly to avoid 'layering', especially in non-rigid infusion containers; use ready-prepared solutions when possible

**Procainamide hydrochloride** (*Pronestyl®*)

Continuous *or* intermittent *in* Glucose 5%

For maintenance, dilute to a concentration of *either* 2 mg/mL and give at a rate of 1–3 mL/minute *or* 4 mg/mL and give at a rate of 0.5–1.5 mL/minute



**Propofol (emulsion)** (*Diprivan®*; Abbott; Baxter; *Propofol-Lipuro®*, Braun; Mayne; Fresenius Kabi; Zurich)

**1% or 2% emulsion**

*via* drip tubing *in* Glucose 5% *or* Sodium chloride 0.9%

To be administered *via* a Y-piece close to injection site; microbiological filter not recommended

**1% emulsion only**

Continuous *in* Glucose 5% (*or* Sodium chloride 0.9% for *Propofol-Lipuro®*, Braun, Fresenius Kabi, and Zurich brands only)

Dilute to a concentration not less than 2 mg/mL; microbiological filter not recommended; administer using suitable device to control infusion rate; use glass or PVC containers (if PVC bag used it should be full—withdraw volume of infusion fluid equal to that of propofol to be added); give within 6 hours of preparation; propofol may alternatively be infused undiluted using a suitable infusion pump

**Quinine dihydrochloride**

Continuous *in* Glucose 5% *or* Sodium chloride 0.9%

To be given over 4 hours; see also section 5.4.1

**Quinupristin with dalfopristin** (*Synercid®*)

Intermittent *in* Glucose 5%

Reconstitute 500 mg with 5 mL water for injections or glucose 5%; gently swirl vial without shaking to dissolve; allow to stand for at least 2 minutes until foam disappears; dilute requisite dose in 100 mL infusion fluid and give over 60 minutes *via* central venous catheter (in an emergency, first dose may be diluted in 250 mL infusion fluid and given over 60 minutes *via* peripheral line); flush line with glucose 5% before and after infusion; incompatible with sodium chloride solutions

**Raltitrexed** (*Tomudex®*)

Intermittent *in* Glucose 5% *or* Sodium chloride 0.9%

Reconstitute with water for injections; dilute requisite dose in 50–250 mL infusion fluid and give over 15 minutes

**Ranitidine (as hydrochloride)** (*Zantac®*)

Intermittent *in* Glucose 5% *or* Sodium chloride 0.9% *or* Compound sodium lactate

**Rasburicase** (*Fasturtec®*)

Intermittent *in* Sodium chloride 0.9%

Reconstitute with solvent provided; gently swirl vial without shaking to dissolve; dilute requisite dose to 50 mL with infusion fluid and give over 30 minutes

**Remifentanil** (*Ultiva®*)

Intermittent *or via* drip tubing *in* Glucose 5% *or* Sodium chloride 0.9% *or* Water for injections

Reconstitute with infusion fluid to a concentration of 1 mg/mL then dilute further to a concentration of 20–250 micrograms/mL (50 micrograms/mL recommended for general anaesthesia, 20–25 micrograms/mL recommended for children over 1 year; 20–50 micrograms/mL recommended when used with target controlled infusion (TCI) device)

**Rifampicin** (*Rifadin®*, *Rimactane®*)

Intermittent *in* Glucose 5 and 10% *or* Sodium chloride 0.9% *or* Ringer's solution

Reconstitute with solvent provided then dilute with 250 mL (*Rimactane®*) or 500 mL (*Rifadin®*) infusion fluid; give over 2–3 hours

**Ritodrine hydrochloride** (*Yutopar®*)

Continuous *in* Glucose 5%

Give *via* controlled infusion device, preferably a syringe pump; if syringe pump available dilute to a concentration of 3 mg/mL; if syringe pump not available dilute to a concentration of 300 micrograms/mL; close attention to patient's fluid and electrolyte status essential

**Rituximab** (*MabThera®*)

Intermittent *in* Glucose 5% *or* Sodium chloride 0.9%

Dilute to 1–4 mg/mL and gently invert bag to avoid foaming

**Rocuronium bromide** (*Esmeron®*)

Continuous *or via* drip tubing *in* Glucose 5% *or* Sodium chloride 0.9%

**Salbutamol (as sulphate)** (*Ventolin® For Intravenous Infusion*)

Continuous *in* Glucose 5%

For *bronchodilatation* dilute 5 mg with 500 mL glucose 5% or sodium chloride 0.9%; for *premature labour* dilute with glucose 5% to a concentration of 200 micrograms/mL for use in a syringe pump *or* for other infusion methods (preferably *via* controlled infusion device), dilute to a concentration of 20 micrograms/mL; close attention to patient's fluid and electrolyte status essential

**Sodium calcium edetate** (*Ledclair®*)

Continuous *in* Glucose 5% *or* Sodium chloride 0.9%

Dilute to a concentration of not more than 3%; suggested volume 250–500 mL given over at least 1 hour

**Sodium clodronate** (*Bonefos® Concentrate*)

Continuous *in* Glucose 5% *or* Sodium chloride 0.9%

Dilute 300 mg in 500 mL and give over at least 2 hours or 1.5 g in 500 mL and give over at least 4 hours

**Sodium nitroprusside** (Mayne)
Continuous *in* Glucose 5%
Reconstitute 50 mg with 2–3 mL glucose 5% then dilute immediately with 250–1000 mL infusion fluid; preferably infuse *via* infusion device to allow precise control; protect infusion from light

**Sodium valproate** (*Epilim®*)
Continuous *or* intermittent *in* Glucose 5% *or* Sodium chloride 0.9%
Reconstitute with solvent provided then dilute with infusion fluid

**Sotalol hydrochloride** (*Sotacor®*)
Continuous *or* intermittent *in* Glucose 5% *or* Sodium chloride 0.9%
Dilute to a concentration of between 0.01–2 mg/mL

**Streptokinase** (*Streptase®*; *Streptokinase*, Braun)
Continuous *or* intermittent *in* Glucose 5% *or* Sodium chloride 0.9%
Reconstitute *Streptase®* with sodium chloride 0.9%, and *Streptokinase* (Braun) with either water for injections or sodium chloride 0.9% then dilute further with infusion fluid

**Sulfadiazine sodium**
Continuous *in* Sodium chloride 0.9%
Suggested volume 500 mL; ampoule solution has a pH of over 10

**Suxamethonium chloride** (*Anectine®*)
Continuous *in* Glucose 5% *or* Sodium chloride 0.9%

**Tacrolimus** (*Prograf®*)
Continuous *in* Glucose 5% *or* Sodium chloride 0.9%
Dilute concentrate in infusion fluid to a final concentration of 4–100 micrograms/mL; give over 24 hours; incompatible with PVC

**Teicoplanin** (*Targocid®*)
Intermittent *in* Glucose 5% *or* Sodium chloride 0.9% *or* Compound sodium lactate
Reconstitute initially with water for injections provided; infuse over 30 minutes
Continuous infusion not usually recommended

**Terbutaline sulphate** (*Bricanyl®*)
Continuous *in* Glucose 5%
For *bronchodilatation* dilute 1.5–2.5 mg with 500 mL glucose 5% or sodium chloride 0.9% and give over 8–10 hours; for *premature labour* dilute in glucose 5% and give *via* controlled infusion device preferably a syringe pump; if syringe pump available dilute to a concentration of 100 micrograms/mL; if syringe pump not available dilute to a concentration of 10 micrograms/mL; close attention to patient's fluid and electrolyte status essential

**Ticarcillin sodium with clavulanic acid** (*Timentin®*)
Intermittent *in* Glucose 5% *or* Water for injections
Suggested volume (depending on dose) glucose 5% 100–150 mL or water for injections 50–100 mL; given over 30–40 minutes

**Tirofiban** (*Aggrastat®*)
Continuous *in* Glucose 5% *or* Sodium chloride 0.9%
Withdraw 50 mL infusion fluid from 250-mL bag and replace with 50 mL tirofiban concentrate (250 micrograms/mL) to give a final concentration of 50 micrograms/mL

**Tobramycin (as sulphate)** (*Nebcin®*)
Intermittent *or via* drip tubing *in* Glucose 5% *or* Sodium chloride 0.9%
For adult intermittent infusion suggested volume 50–100 mL (children proportionately smaller volume) given over 20–60 minutes

**Topotecan (as hydrochloride)** (*Hycamtin®*)
Intermittent *in* Glucose 5% *or* Sodium chloride 0.9%
Reconstitute 4 mg with 4 mL water for injections then dilute to a final concentration of 25–50 micrograms/mL; give over 30 minutes

**Tramadol hydrochloride** (*Zydol®*)
Continuous *or* intermittent *in* Glucose 5% *or* Sodium chloride 0.9% *or* Ringer's solution *or* Compound sodium lactate

**Tranexamic acid** (*Cyklokapron®*)
Continuous *in* Glucose 5% *or* Sodium chloride 0.9% *or* Ringer's solution

**Trastuzumab** (*Herceptin ®*)
Intermittent *in* Sodium chloride 0.9%
Reconstitute each 150-mg vial with 7.2 mL water for injections to produce 21 mg/mL solution, swirl vial gently to avoid excessive foaming and allow to stand for approximately 5 minutes; dilute requisite dose in 250 mL infusion fluid

**Treosulfan** (*Treosulfan*) (Medac)
Intermittent *in* Water for injections
Infusion suggested for doses above 5 g; dilute to a concentration of 5 g in 100 mL

**Trisodium edetate** (*Limclair®*)
Continuous *in* Glucose 5% *or* Sodium chloride 0.9%
Dilute to a concentration of 10 mg/mL; give over 2–3 hours

**Tropisetron (as hydrochloride)** (*Navoban®*)
Intermittent *or via* drip tubing *in* Glucose 5% *or* Sodium chloride 0.9% *or* Ringer's solution
Suggested concentration for infusion 50 micrograms/mL

**Vancomycin (as hydrochloride)** (*Vancocin®*)
Intermittent *in* Glucose 5% *or* Sodium chloride 0.9%
Reconstitute each 500 mg with 10 mL water for injections and dilute with infusion fluid to a concentration of up to 5 mg/mL (10 mg/mL in fluid restriction but increased risk of infusion-related effects); give over at least 60 minutes (rate not to exceed 10 mg/minute for doses over 500 mg); use continuous infusion only if intermittent not feasible

**Vasopressin, synthetic** (*Pitressin®*)
Intermittent *in* Glucose 5%
Suggested concentration 20 units/100 mL given over 15 minutes

**Vecuronium bromide** (*Norcuron®*)
Continuous *in* Glucose 5% *or* Sodium chloride 0.9% *or* Ringer's solution

**Verteporfin** (*Visudyne®*)
Intermittent *in* Glucose 5%
Reconstitute each 15 mg with 7 mL water for injections to produce a 2 mg/mL solution then dilute requisite dose with infusion fluid to a final volume of 30 mL and give over 10 minutes; protect from light and administer within 4 hours of reconstitution. Incompatible with sodium chloride infusion

**Vinblastine sulphate** (*Velbe®*)
*via* drip tubing *in* Sodium chloride 0.9%
Reconstitute with sodium chloride 0.9%; give over approx. 1 minute

**Vincristine sulphate** (*Oncovin®*)
*via* drip tubing *in* Glucose 5% *or* Sodium chloride 0.9%

**Vindesine sulphate** (*Eldisine®*)
*via* drip tubing *in* Glucose 5% *or* Sodium chloride 0.9%
Reconstitute with sodium chloride 0.9%; give over 1–3 minutes

**Vinorelbine** (*Navelbine®*)
Intermittent *in* Glucose 5% *or* Sodium chloride 0.9%
Dilute in 125 mL infusion fluid; give over 20–30 minutes

**Vitamins B & C** (*Pabrinex® I/V High potency*)
Intermittent *or via* drip tubing *in* Glucose 5% *or* Sodium chloride 0.9%
Ampoule contents should be mixed, diluted, and administered without delay; give over 10 minutes (see CSM advice, section 9.6.2)

**Vitamins, multiple**

(*Cernevit®*)

Intermittent *in* Glucose 5% *or* Sodium chloride 0.9%

Dissolve initially in 5 mL water for injections (or infusion fluid)

(*Solivito N®*)

Intermittent *in* Glucose 5 and 10%

Suggested volume 500–1000 mL given over 2–3 hours; see also section 9.3

**Voriconazole** (*Vfend®*)

Intermittent *in* Glucose 5% *or* Sodium chloride 0.9% *or* Compound sodium lactate

Reconstitute each 200 mg with 19 mL water for injections to produce a 10 mg/mL solution; dilute dose in infusion fluid to concentration of 0.5–5 mg/mL; give at a rate not exceeding 3 mg/kg/hour

**Zidovudine** (*Retrovir®*)

Intermittent *in* Glucose 5%

Dilute to a concentration of 2 mg/mL or 4 mg/mL and give over 1 hour

**Zoledronic acid** (*Zometa®*)

Intermittent *in* Glucose 5% *or* Sodium chloride 0.9%

Dilute requisite dose with 100 mL infusion fluid; infuse over at least 15 minutes

# A7 Borderline substances

In certain conditions some foods (and toilet preparations) have characteristics of drugs and the Advisory Committee on Borderline Substances advises as to the circumstances in which such substances may be regarded as drugs. Prescriptions issued in accordance with the Committee's advice and endorsed 'ACBS' will normally not be investigated.

> General Practitioners are reminded that the ACBS recommends products on the basis that they may be regarded as drugs for the management of specified conditions. Doctors should satisfy themselves that the products can safely be prescribed, that patients are adequately monitored and that, where necessary, expert hospital supervision is available.

## Foods which may be prescribed on FP10, GP10 (Scotland), or when available WP10 (Wales)

**Note** This is a list of food products which the ACBS has approved. The clinical condition for which the product has approval follows each entry.

Foods included in this Appendix may contain cariogenic sugars and patients should be advised to take appropriate oral hygiene measures.

**Alcoholic Beverages**
*see under* Rectified Spirit

**Alembicol D®** (Alembic Products)
Fractionated coconut oil. Net price 5 kg = £125.55.
For steatorrhoea associated with cystic fibrosis of the pancreas, intestinal lymphangiectasia, surgery of the intestine, chronic liver disease, liver cirrhosis, other proven malabsorption syndromes; in a ketogenic diet in the management of epilepsy; type 1 hyperlipoproteinaemia

**Aminex®** (Gluten Free Foods Ltd)
Low-protein. Biscuits, net price 200 g = £3.75. Cookies, 150 g = £3.75. Rusks, 200 g = £3.75.
For inherited metabolic disorders, renal or liver failure requiring a low-protein diet

**Amino Acid Modules** (SHS)
*see XLEU Faladon, XMET Homidon, XMTVI Asadon, XPHEN TYR Tyrosidon,* or *XPTM Tyrosidon*

**Aminogran®** (UCB Pharma)
Food Supplement, powder, containing all essential amino acids except phenylalanine, net price 500 g = £39.78. Aminogran PKU tablet (≡ 1 g powder), net price 150-tab pack = £30.00.
For the dietary management of phenylketonuria. Tablets not to be prescribed for any child under 8 years

**Analog®** (SHS)
*see MSUD Analog, XLEU Analog, XLYS Analog, XLYS Low TRY Analog, XMET Analog, XMTVI Analog, XP Analog, XP LCP Analog, XPHEN TYR Analog, XPTM Analog*
**Note** Analog products are generally intended for use in children up to 1 year

**Aproten®** (Ultrapharm)
Gluten-free. Flour. Net price 500 g = £4.99.
For gluten-sensitive enteropathies including steatorrhoea due to gluten sensitivity, coeliac disease, and dermatitis herpetiformis

Low protein. Low $Na^+$ and $K^+$. Net prices: biscuits 180 g (36) = £2.88; bread mix 250 g = £2.17; cake mix 300 g = £2.10; crispbread 260 g = £4.06; pasta (anellini, ditalini, rigatini, spaghetti) 500 g = £4.06; tagliatelle 250 g = £2.16.
For inherited metabolic disorders, renal or liver failure requiring a low-protein diet

**L-Arginine** (SHS)
Powder, net price 100 g = £8.39.
For use as a supplement in urea cycle disorders other than arginase deficiency, such as hyperammonaemia types I and II, citrullaemia, arginosuccinic aciduria, and deficiency of N-acetyl glutamate synthetase

**Arnott®** (Ultrapharm)
Rice Cookies, gluten-free. Net price 200 g = £2.06.
For gluten-sensitive enteropathies including steatorrhoea due to gluten sensitivity, coeliac disease, and dermatitis herpetiformis

**Baker's Delight®**
Gluten-free. Bread, net price 100 g = 80p.
For established gluten enteropathy

**Barkat®** (Gluten Free Foods Ltd)
Gluten-free. Bread mix, net price 500 g = £4.12. Multi Grain Bread, 450 g = £2.99. Rice bread (sliced), brown or white, 450 g = £2.99. Rice pizza crust, brown or white, 150 g = £2.21.
For gluten-sensitive enteropathies including steatorrhoea due to gluten sensitivity, coeliac disease, and dermatitis herpetiformis

**Bi-Aglut®** (Novartis Consumer Health)
Gluten-free. Biscuits, net price 180 g = £2.89. Crackers, 150 g = £2.36. Cracker toast, 240 g = £4.18. Pasta (fusilli, macaroni, penne, spaghetti), 500 g = £5.23.
For gluten-sensitive enteropathies including steatorrhoea due to gluten sensitivity, coeliac disease, and dermatitis herpetiformis

**Calogen®** (SHS)
Emulsion, arachis oil (peanut oil) 50% in water, net price, 250 mL = £4.45; 500 mL = £8.73 (natural, banana, strawberry or butterscotch flavour).
For disease-related malnutrition, malabsorption states or other conditions requiring fortification with a high-fat supplement with or without fluid and electrolyte restrictions

**Caloreen®** (Nestlé Clinical)
Powder, water-soluble dextrins, 390 kcal/100 g, with less than 1.8 mmol of $Na^+$ and 0.3 mmol of $K^+$/100 g. Gluten-, lactose-, and fructose-free. Net price 500 g = £3.02.
For disease-related malnutrition, malabsorption states or other conditions requiring fortification with a high or readily available carbohydrate supplement

**Calshake®** (Fresenius Kabi)
Powder, protein 4 g, carbohydrate 58 g, fat 20.4 g, energy 1809 kJ (432 kcal)/87 g. Gluten-free. Strawberry, vanilla, neutral, and banana flavours, net price 87-g sachet = £1.82; also available chocolate flavour (protein 4 g, carbohydrate 58 g, fat 20.4 g, fibre 1.6 g, energy 1809 kJ (432 kcal)/90 g = £1.82.
For disease-related malnutrition, malabsorption states or other conditions requiring fortification with a fat/carbohydrate supplement

**Caprilon®** (SHS)
Powder, protein 11.8%, carbohydrate 55.1%, fat 28.3% (medium chain triglycerides 21.3%). Low in lactose, gluten- and sucrose-free. Used as a 12.7% solution. Net price 420 g = £12.46.
For disorders in which a high intake of MCT is beneficial

**Carobel, Instant®** (Cow & Gate)
Powder, carob seed flour. Net price 135 g = £2.63.
For thickening feeds in the treatment of vomiting

**Casilan 90®** (Heinz)
Powder, whole protein, containing all essential amino acids, 90% with less than 0.1% $Na^+$. Net price 250 g = £4.69.
For biochemically proven hypoproteinaemia

**Clinutren® 1.5** (Nestlé Clinical)
Liquid, protein 11 g, carbohydrate 42 g, fat 10 g, energy 1260 kJ (300 kcal)/200 mL with vitamins and minerals. Gluten-free; clinically lactose-free. Flavours: apricot, banana, chocolate, coffee, strawberry-raspberry or vanilla, net price 4 × 200-mL pot = £5.60.
For indications see *Clinutren Fruit*

**Clinutren® 1.5 Fibre** (Nestlé Clinical)
Liquid, protein 5.7 g, carbohydrate 19 g, fat 5.9 g, fibre 2.6 g, energy 630 kJ (150 kcal)/100 mL with vitamins, minerals and trace elements. Gluten-free; clinically lactose-free. Flavours: vanilla or plum, net price 4 × 200-mL pot = £5.60.
For use as the sole source of nutrition or as a necessary nutritional supplement prescribed on medical grounds for: short-bowel syndrome, intractable malabsorption, pre-operative preparation of undernourished patients, proven inflammatory bowel disease, following total gastrectomy, dysphagia, bowel fistulas, disease-related malnutrition. Not suitable for any child under 3 years; not suitable as a sole source of nutrition for patients under 6 years

**Clinutren® Dessert** (Nestlé Clinical)
Semi-solid, protein 12 g, carbohydrate 19 g, fat 3.3 g, energy 650 kJ (160 kcal)/ 125 g with vitamins and minerals. Gluten-free. Flavours: caramel, chocolate, peach or vanilla, net price 4 × 125-g pot = £4.20.
For use as a nutritional supplement prescribed on medical grounds for: short-bowel syndrome, intractable malabsorption, pre-operative preparation of undernourished patients, proven inflammatory bowel disease, following total gastrectomy, dysphagia, bowel fistulas, disease-related malnutrition, continuous ambulatory peritoneal dialysis (CAPD), haemodialysis. Not suitable for any child under 3 years; maximum of 3 units daily for children aged 3 to 6 years

**Clinutren® Fruit** (Nestlé Clinical)
Liquid, protein 8 g, carbohydrate 54 g, fat less than 0.4 g, energy 1040 kJ (250 kcal)/200 mL with vitamins and minerals. Gluten-free. Low-lactose. Flavours: grapefruit, orange, pear-cherry, or raspberry-blackcurrant, net price 4 × 200-mL cup = £6.00.
For use as a nutritional supplement prescribed on medical grounds for: short-bowel syndrome, intractable malabsorption, pre-operative preparation of undernourished patients, proven inflammatory bowel disease, following total gastrectomy, dysphagia, bowel fistulas, disease-related malnutrition. Not suitable for any child under 3 years; maximum of 3 units daily for children aged 3 to 6 years

**Clinutren® ISO** (Nestlé Clinical)
Liquid, protein 7.6 g, carbohydrate 28 g, fat 6.6 g, energy 840 kJ (200 kcal)/200 mL with vitamins and minerals. Gluten-free. Flavours: chocolate or vanilla, net price 4 × 200-mL pot = £4.72.
For use as a sole source of nutrition or as a necessary nutritional supplement prescribed on medical grounds for: short-bowel syndrome, intractable malabsorption, pre-operative preparation of undernourished patients, proven inflammatory bowel disease, following total gastrectomy, dysphagia, bowel fistulas, disease-related malnutrition. Not suitable for any child under 3 years; not suitable as a sole source of nutrition for patients under 6 years; maximum of 3 units daily for children aged 3 to 6 years

**Clinutren Junior®** (Nestlé Clinical)
Powder, protein 13.9 g, carbohydrate 62.2 g, fat 18.3 g, energy 1950 kJ (467 kcal)/100 g with vitamins, minerals and trace elements. Gluten-free; clinically lactose-free. Flavour: vanilla, net price 400 g = £9.72.
For use as a sole source of nutrition or as a nutritional supplement prescribed on medical grounds for: short bowel syndrome, intractable malabsorption, pre-operative preparation of undernourished patients, proven inflammatory bowel disease, following total gastrectomy, dysphagia, bowel fistulas, disease-related malnutrition, and growth failure in children aged 1 to 10 years.

**Clinutren® Thickened Drinks** (Nestlé Clinical)
Liquid, modified maize starch, gluten-free. Flavours: orange, peppermint, and tea, net price 4 × 125 g = £1.96.
Thickening of foods and fluids in dysphagia. Not to be used for children under 3 years

**Clinutren® Thickener** (Nestlé Clinical)
Powder, modified maize starch, gluten-free, net price 300 g = £4.53.
Thickening of foods and fluids in dysphagia. Not to be used for children under 3 years

**Colief®** (Britannia)
Liquid, lactase 50 000 units/g, net price 7-mL dropper bottle = £7.00
For the relief of symptoms associated with lactose intolerance in infants, provided that lactose intolerance is confirmed by the presence of reducing substances and/or excessive acid in stools, a low concentration of the corresponding disaccharide enzyme on intestinal biopsy or by breath hydrogen test or lactose intolerance test. For dosage and administration details, consult product literature

**Comminuted Chicken Meat** (SHS)
Suspension (aqueous). Net price 150 g = £2.56.
For carbohydrate intolerance in association with possible or proven intolerance of milk; glucose and galactose intolerance

**Corn flour and corn starch**
For hypoglycaemia associated with glycogen-storage disease

**Dextrose**
*see* Glucose

**Dialamine®** (SHS)
Powder, essential amino acids 30%, with carbohydrate 62%, energy 1500 kJ (360 kcal)/100 g, with ascorbic acid, minerals, and trace elements. Flavour: orange. Net price 200 g = £25.11.
For oral feeding where essential amino acid supplements are required; e.g. chronic renal failure, hypoproteinaemia, wound fistula leakage with excessive protein loss, conditions requiring a controlled nitrogen intake, and haemodialysis

**Dietary Specials** (Nutrition Point)
Gluten-free. Bread. Loaf, sliced (brown, white or multigrain) 400 g = £2.50; bread rolls, long (white) 3 = £1.55. Bread mix, net price 500 g = £4.75; cracker bread, 150 g = £1.80; cake mix (white), 750 g = £4.75; white mix, 500 g = £4.75; digestive biscuits, 150 g = £1.70. Tea biscuits, 220 g = £2.00. Pasta (spaghetti, penne, fusilli), 500 g = £3.20
For gluten-sensitive enteropathies including steatorrhoea due to gluten sensitivity, coeliac disease, and dermatitis herpetiformis

**Duobar®** (SHS)
Bar, protein-free (phenylalanine nil added), carbohydrate 49.9 g, fat 49.9 g, energy 2692 kJ (648 kcal)/100 g. Low sodium and potassium. Strawberry, toffee, or neutral flavours. Net price 45-g bar = £1.34.
For disease-related malnutrition, malabsorption states or other conditions requiring fortification with fat/carbohydrate supplement

**Duocal®** (SHS)
Liquid, emulsion providing carbohydrate 23.4 g, fat 7.1 g, energy 661 kJ (158 kcal)/100 mL. Low-electrolyte, gluten-, lactose-, and protein-free. Net price 250 mL = £2.74; 1 litre = £9.77
MCT Powder, carbohydrate 74 g, fat 23.2 g (of which MCT 83%), energy 2042 kJ (486 kcal)/100 g. Low electrolyte, gluten-, protein- and lactose-free. Net price 400 g = £14.69
Super Soluble Powder, carbohydrate 72.7 g, fat 22.3 g, energy 2061 kJ (492 kcal)/100 g. Low electrolyte, gluten-, protein-, and lactose-free. Net price 400 g = £12.36
All for disease-related malnutrition, malabsorption states or other conditions requiring fortification with fat/carbohydrate supplement

**Easiphen®** (SHS)
Liquid, protein (containing essential and non-essential amino acids, phenylalanine-free) 6.7 g, carbohydrate 5.1 g, fat 2 g, energy 275 kJ (65 kcal)/100 mL with vitamins, minerals, and trace elements. Forest berries or grapefruit flavour, net price 250-mL carton = £6.60.
For the dietary management of proven phenylketonuria. Not to be prescribed for children under 8 years

**Elemental 028®** (SHS)
028 Powder, amino acids 12%, carbohydrate 70.5–72%, fat 6.64%, energy 1544–1568 kJ (364–370 kcal)/100 g with vitamins and minerals. For preparation with water before use. Net price 100-g box (orange flavoured or plain) = £4.03
For use as the sole source of nutrition or as a nutritional supplement prescribed on medical grounds for: short-bowel syndrome, intractable malabsorption, proven inflammatory bowel disease, bowel fistulas. Not to be prescribed for any child under 1 year; use with caution for children up to 5 years
Note See also Flavour Sachets, for use with unflavoured amino acid and peptide products from SHS

**Elemental 028® Extra** (SHS)
Liquid, amino acids 3 g, carbohydrate 11 g, fat 3.48 g, energy 358 kJ (86 kcal)/100 mL, with vitamins, minerals, and trace elements. Flavours: grapefruit, orange and pineapple, summer fruits. Net price 250-mL carton = £2.51
Powder, amino acids 15%, carbohydrate 59%, fat 17.45%, energy 1860 kJ (443 kcal)/100 g, with vitamins, minerals, and trace elements. For preparation with water before use. Net price 100 g (plain) = £4.88; also available in banana, citrus, or orange flavours (carbohydrate 55%, energy 1793 kJ (427 kcal)/100 g), 100 g = £4.88
All for use as the sole source of nutrition or as a nutritional supplement prescribed on medical grounds for: short-bowel syndrome, intractable malabsorption, proven inflammatory bowel disease, bowel fistulas. Not to be prescribed for any child under 1 year; use with caution for children up to 5 years
Note see also Flavour Sachets, for use with unflavoured amino acid and peptide products from SHS

**Emsogen®** (SHS)
Powder, amino acids 15%, carbohydrate 60%, fat 16.4%, energy 1839 kJ (438 kcal)/100 g, with vitamins, minerals, and trace elements. For preparation with water before use. Net price 100 g = £5.03; also available orange-flavoured (carbohydrate 55%, energy 1754 kJ (418 kcal)/100 g), 100 g = £5.03.
For use as the sole source of nutrition or as a nutritional supplement prescribed on medical grounds for short-bowel syndrome, intractable malabsorption, proven inflammatory bowel disease, bowel fistulas. Not to be prescribed for any child under 1 year; use with caution for children up to 5 years

**Ener-G®** (General Dietary)
Gluten-free. Cookies (vanilla flavour), net price 435 g = £4.88. Dinner Rolls (× 6), 280 g = £2.90. Rice bread (sliced), brown, 474 g = £4.28; white, 456 g = £4.28. Rice loaf (sliced), 612 g = £4.28. Seattle brown loaf, 600 g = £4.93. Tapioca bread (sliced), 480 g = £4.28. Rice pasta (macaroni, shells, small shells, and lasagne), 454 g = £3.98; spaghetti, 447 g = £3.98; tagliatelle, 400 g = £3.98; vermicelli, 300 g = £3.98; cannelloni, 335 g = £3.98. Brown rice pasta: lasagne, 454 g = £3.98; macaroni, 454 g = £3.98; spaghetti, 447 g = £3.98. Xanthan gum, 170 g = £6.76.
For gluten-sensitive enteropathies including steatorrhoea due to gluten sensitivity, coeliac disease, and dermatitis herpetiformis
Gluten-free. Pizza bases, 372 g = £3.75. Six flour bread loaf, 576 g = £3.60. Seattle brown rolls (round or long), 4 x 119 g = £3.00
For established gluten enteropathy with coexisting established wheat sensitivity only
Low protein egg replacer, carbohydrate 94 g, energy 1574 kJ (376 kcal)/100 g. Egg-, gluten- and lactose-free, net price 454 g = £4.05.
For phenylketonuria, similar amino acid abnormalities, renal failure, liver failure and liver cirrhosis.
Low protein pasta (lasagne, macaroni, large shells, small shells, spaghetti), net price 454 g = £5.05.
For phenylketonuria, similar amino acid abnormalities, renal failure, liver failure requiring a low-protein diet
Low protein rice bread, net price 600 g = £4.39.
For inherited metabolic disorders, renal or liver failure requiring a low-protein diet

**Energivit®** (SHS)
Powder, protein-free, carbohydrate 66.7 g, fat 25 g, energy 2059 kJ, (492 kcal)/100 g with vitamins, minerals and trace elements, net price 400 g = £15.04.
For infants requiring additional enegy, vitamins, minerals and trace elements following a protein restricted diet

**Enfamil AR®** (Mead Johnson)
AR (Anti-Reflux), powder, protein 1.7 g, fat 3.5 g, carbohydrate 7.6 g, energy 285 kJ (68 kcal)/100 mL, with vitamins, minerals and trace elements, net price 400 g = £2.76.
For significant reflux disease. For use not in excess of a 6-month period. Not to be used in conjunction with any other thickener or antacid product.

**Enfamil Lactofree®** (Mead Johnson)
Powder, protein 1.42 g, fat 3.7 g, carbohydrate 7.2 g, energy 280 kJ (68 kcal)/100 mL with vitamins, minerals and trace elements. Lactose- and sucrose-free, net price 400 g = £2.76.
For proven lactose intolerance

**Enlive Plus®** (Abbott)
Liquid, protein 4.8 g, carbohydrate 32.7 g, energy 638 kJ (150 kcal)/100 mL, with vitamins, minerals and trace elements. Fat- and gluten-free; clinically lactose-free. Flavours: apple, fruit punch, grapefruit, lemon and lime, orange, peach, pineapple, strawberry, net price 220-mL Tetrapak® = £1.66.
For use as a nutritional supplement prescribed on medical grounds for: short-bowel syndrome, intractable malabsorption, pre-operative preparation of undernourished patients, proven inflammatory bowel disease, following total gastrectomy, dysphagia, bowel fistulas, disease-related malnutrition. Not for use in galactosaemia. Not to be prescribed for any child under 1 year; use with caution for children up to 5 years

**Enmix Plus Commence®** (Abbott)
Starter pack, contains: *Ensure Plus* milkshake-style (4 flavours), yoghurt-style (2 flavours); *Enlive Plus* (4 flavours) – see *Ensure Plus®* and *Enlive Plus®* for product information, net price 1 pack (10 × 220 mL) = £16.18.
Intended as an initial 5- to 10-day supply to establish patient preferences. For use as a nutritional supplement prescribed on medical grounds for: short-bowel syndrome, intractable malabsorption, pre-operative preparation of undernourished patients, proven inflammatory bowel disease, following total gastrectomy, dysphagia, bowel fistulas, disease-related malnutrition. Not to be prescribed for any child under 1 year; use with caution for children up to 5 years

**Enrich®** (Abbott)
Liquid with dietary fibre, providing protein 3.8 g, carbohydrate 14 g, fat 3.5 g, fibre 1.4 g, energy 432 kJ (102 kcal)/100 mL with vitamins and minerals. Lactose- and gluten-free. Vanilla flavour. Net price 250-mL can = £2.24.
For use as the sole source of nutrition or as a nutritional supplement prescribed on medical grounds for: short-bowel syndrome, intractable malabsorption, pre-operative preparation of patients who are undernourished, proven inflammatory bowel disease, following total gastrectomy, dysphagia, disease-related malnutrition. Not to be prescribed for any child under 1 year; use with caution for children up to 5 years

**Enrich Plus®** (Abbott)
Liquid with dietary fibre, providing protein 6.25 g, carbohydrate 20.2 g, fat 4.92 g, fibre 1.25 g, energy 642 kJ (153 kcal)/100 mL with vitamins and minerals. Lactose- and gluten-free. Vanilla, chocolate, fruits of the forest, raspberry, strawberry and banana flavours. Net price 200-mL Tetrapak® = £1.71.
For use as a nutritional supplement for patients with disease-related malnutrition, continuous ambulatory peritoneal dialysis (CAPD), short-bowel syndrome, intractable malabsorption, dysphagia, proven inflammatory bowel disease, bowel fistulas, gastrectomy, and pre-operative preparation of undernourished patients. Not to be prescribed for any child under 1 year; use with caution for children up to 5 years

**Enshake®** (Abbott)
Powder, protein 16 g, carbohydrate 78.4 g, fat 24.7 g, energy 2519 kJ (600 kcal)/310 mL serving (serving = 1 sachet reconstituted with 240mL whole milk), with vitamins, minerals and trace elements. Gluten-free. Flavours: banana, chocolate, strawberry, vanilla, net price 96.5-g sachet = £1.82.
For use as a nutritional supplement prescribed on medical grounds for: disease-related malnutrition, malabsorption states or other conditions requiring fortification with a fat/carbohydrate supplement. Not suitable for children under 1 year

**Ensure®** (Abbott)
Liquid, protein 4 g, fat 3.4 g, carbohydrate 13.6 g, energy 423 kJ (100 kcal)/100 mL with minerals and vitamins, lactose- and gluten-free. Vanilla, coffee, eggnog, nut, chicken, mushroom, and asparagus flavours. Net price 250-mL can = £1.92; 500-mL ready-to-hang (vanilla) = £3.74

For use as the sole source of nutrition or as a nutritional supplement prescribed on medical grounds for: short-bowel syndrome, intractable malabsorption, pre-operative preparation of patients who are undernourished, proven inflammatory bowel disease, following total gastrectomy, dysphagia, bowel fistulas, disease-related malnutrition. Not to be prescribed for any child under 1 year; use with caution for children up to 5 years

**Ensure Plus®** (Abbott)
Liquid, protein 6.3 g, fat 4.9 g, carbohydrate 20.2 g, with vitamins and minerals, lactose- and gluten-free, energy 632 kJ (150 kcal)/100 mL. Vanilla flavour, (formulations may vary slightly). Net price 220-mL Tetrapak® = £1.59; 250-mL can = £2.10; 500-mL ready-to-hang (unflavoured) = £3.91; 1-litre ready-to-hang (unflavoured) = £7.63; 1.5-litre ready-to-hang (unflavoured) = £11.44. Caramel, chocolate, strawberry, banana, fruit of the forest, raspberry, orange, coffee, blackcurrant, peach, vanilla or neutral flavours. Net price 220-mL Tetrapak® = £1.59.

Yoghurt Style, protein 6.3 g, fat 4.9 g, carbohydrate 20.2 g, with vitamins, minerals and trace elements, gluten-free, clinically lactose-free, energy 632 kJ (150 kcal)/100 mL. Orange, peach, pineapple, or strawberry flavour, net price 220-mL Tetrapak® = £1.59.

Both as nutritional supplements prescribed on medical grounds for: short-bowel syndrome, intractable malabsorption, pre-operative preparation of patients who are undernourished, proven inflammatory bowel disease, following total gastrectomy, dysphagia, bowel fistulas, disease-related malnutrition, continuous ambulatory peritoneal dialysis (CAPD), and haemodialysis. Not to be prescribed for any child under 1 year; use with caution for children up to 5 years

**Farley's Soya Formula** (Heinz)
Powder, providing protein 2%, carbohydrate 7%, fat 3.8% with vitamins and minerals when reconstituted. Gluten-, sucrose-, and lactose-free. Net price 450 g = £3.38.

For proven lactose and associated sucrose intolerance in pre-school children, galactokinase deficiency, galactosaemia, and cow's milk protein intolerance

**Fate®** (Fate)
Low protein. All-purpose mix, net price 500 g = £5.63; Cake mix, 2 × 250 g = £5.63; Chocolate-flavour cake mix, 2 × 250 g = £5.63.

For inherited metabolic disorders, renal or liver failure requiring a low-protein diet

**FlavourPac®** (Vitaflo)
Powder, flavours: blackcurrant, lemon, orange, tropical or raspberry, net price 4 × 30 × 4-g sachets = £40.12

For use in conjuntion with Vitaflo's Inborn Error range of protein substitutes

**Flavour Sachets** (SHS)
Powder, flavours: cherry-vanilla, grapefruit, lemon-lime, net price 20 × 5-g sachets = £8.32.

For use with SHS unflavoured amino acid and peptide products

**Foodlink Complete** (Foodlink)
Powder, protein 21.9 g, carbohydrate 57.3 g, fat 13.3 g, energy 1838 kJ (436.5 kcal)/100 g with vitamins and minerals, Flavours: banana, chocolate, natural, or strawberry, net price 450-g carton = £3.19; also available, vanilla with fibre, protein 19.5 g, carbohydrate 60.2 g, fat 12.3 g, fibre 8 g, energy 1804 kJ (428 kcal)/100 g = £3.75.

As a nutritional supplement prescribed on medical grounds for: short-bowel syndrome, intractable malabsorption, pre-operative preparation of undernourished patients, proven inflammatory bowel disease, following total gastrectomy, dysphagia, bowel fistulas, disease-related malnutrition. Not to be prescribed for any child under 1 year; use with caution for children up to 5 years

**Formance®** (Abbott)
Semi-solid, protein 4 g, carbohydrate 27 g, fat 5 g, energy 703 kJ (167 kcal)/113 g with vitamins and minerals. Gluten-free. Vanilla and butterscotch flavours. Net price 113-g pot = £1.40.

As a nutritional supplement prescribed on medical grounds for: short-bowel syndrome, intractable malabsorption, pre-operative preparation of patients who are undernourished, proven inflammatory bowel disease, following total gastrectomy, dysphagia, bowel fistulas, disease-related malnutrition, continuous ambulatory peritoneal dialysis (CAPD), and haemodialysis. Not to be prescribed for any child under 1 year; use with caution for children up to 5 years

**Forticreme®** (Nutricia Clinical)
Semi-solid, protein 10 g, carbohydrate 19 g, fat 5 g, energy 680 kJ (160 kcal)/100 g with vitamins and minerals. Gluten-free. Vanilla, chocolate, coffee, banana, and forest fruit flavours, net price 4 × 125-g pot = £6.37.

As a nutritional supplement prescribed on medical grounds for: short-bowel syndrome, intractable malabsorption, pre-operative preparation of patients who are undernourished, proven inflammatory bowel disease, following total gastrectomy, dysphagia, bowel fistulas, disease-related malnutrition, continuous ambulatory peritoneal dialysis (CAPD) and haemodialysis. Not to be prescribed for any child under 3 years; use with caution for children aged 3 to 5 years

**Fortifresh®** (Nutricia Clinical)
Liquid, protein 12 g, carbohydrate 37.4 g, fat 11.6 g, energy 1260 kJ (300 kcal)/200 mL with vitamins, minerals and trace elements. Gluten-free. Flavours: blackcurrant, peach and orange, pineapple, raspberry, and vanilla and lemon, net price 200 mL carton = £1.64.

For use as a sole source of nutrition or as a nutritional supplement prescribed on medical grounds for: short-bowel syndrome, intractable malabsorption, pre-operative preparation of patients who are undernourished, inflammatory bowel disease, following total gastrectomy, bowel fistulas, dysphagia, disease-related malnutrition. Not to be prescribed for any child under 3 years; use with caution for children aged 3 to 5 years

**Fortijuce®** (Nutricia Clinical)
Liquid, protein 4 g, carbohydrate 33.5 g, energy 630 kJ (150 kcal)/100 mL, with vitamins, minerals and trace elements. Fat-free. Flavours: apple and pear, apricot, blackcurrant, forest fruits, lemon and lime, peach and orange, pineapple. Net price 200-mL carton = £1.64.

As a nutritional supplement prescribed on medical grounds for: short-bowel syndrome, intractable malabsorption, pre-operative preparation of patients who are undernourished, proven inflammatory bowel disease, following total gastrectomy, dysphagia, bowel fistulas, disease-related malnutrition. Not to be prescribed for any child under 3 years; use with caution for children up to 5 years

**Fortimel®** (Nutricia Clinical)
Liquid, protein 20 g, carbohydrate 20.8 g, fat 4.2 g, energy 840 kJ (200 kcal)/200 mL with vitamins and minerals. Gluten-free. Vanilla, strawberry, coffee, chocolate, and forest fruits flavours. Net price 200-mL carton = £1.39.

As a nutritional supplement prescribed on medical grounds for: short-bowel syndrome, intractable malabsorption, pre-operative preparation of patients who are undernourished, proven inflammatory bowel disease, following total gastrectomy, dysphagia, bowel fistulas, disease-related malnutrition. Not to be prescribed for any child under 3 years; use with caution for children up to 5 years

**Fortini®** (Nutricia Clinical)
Liquid, protein 3.4 g, carbohydrate 18.8 g, fat 6.8 g, energy 630 kJ (150 kcal)/100 mL with vitamins, minerals, and trace elements. Gluten- and lactose-free. Flavours: strawberry or vanilla, net price 200 mL = £2.38.

For use as a nutritional supplement prescribed on medical grounds for: disease-related malnutrition, and growth failure. For children between 8–20 kg body-weight

**Fortini Multifibre®** (Nutricia Clinical)
Liquid, protein 3.4 g, carbohydrate 18.8 g, fat 6.8 g, fibre 1.5 g, energy 630 kJ (150 kcal)/ 100 mL with vitamins, minerals, and trace elements. Gluten- and lactose-free. Flavours: banana, chocolate, strawberry, and vanilla, net price 200-mL = £2.50.

For indications see Fortini liquid

**Fortisip® Bottle** (Nutricia Clinical)

Liquid, protein 12 g, carbohydrate 36.8 g, fat 11.6 g, energy 1260 kJ (300 kcal)/200 mL, with vitamins, minerals and trace elements. Gluten-free; clinically lactose-free. Vanilla, banana, chocolate, orange, strawberry, tropical fruits, toffee, and neutral flavours, net price 200 mL = £1.63.

As a nutritional supplement prescribed on medical grounds for: short-bowel syndrome, intractable malabsorption, pre-operative preparation of patients who are undernourished, proven inflammatory bowel disease, following total gastrectomy, dysphagia, bowel fistulas, disease-related malnutrition. Not to be prescribed for any child under 3 years; use with caution for children aged 3 to 5 years

**Fortisip® Multi Fibre** (Nutricia Clinical)

Liquid, protein 12 g, carbohydrate 36.8 g, fat 11.6 g, fibre 4.5 g, energy 1260 kJ (300 kcal)/200 mL, with vitamins, minerals and trace elements. Gluten-free, clinically lactose-free. Banana, chicken, orange, strawberry, tomato, vanilla flavours; also available chocolate flavour (protein 10 g, carbohydrate 36 g, fat 13 g, fibre 4.5 g, energy 1260 kJ (300 kcal)/200 mL, net price 200 mL = £1.69.

As a nutritional supplement prescribed on medical grounds for: short-bowel syndrome, intractable malabsorption, pre-operative preparation of undernourished patients, proven inflammatory bowel disease, following total gastrectomy, dysphagia, disease-related malnutrition. Not to be prescribed for any child under 3 years; use with caution for children aged 3 to 5 years

**Fortisip® Protein** (Nutricia Clinical)

Liquid, protein 10 g, carbohydrate 14.7 g, fat 3.5 g, energy 550 kJ (130 kcal)/100 mL, with vitamins, minerals and trace elements. Gluten-free. Chocolate, forest fruits, strawberry, and vanilla flavour, net price 200 mL = £1.54.

As a nutritional supplement prescribed on medical grounds for: short-bowel syndrome, intractable malabsorption, pre-operative preparation of undernourished patients, proven inflammatory bowel disease, following total gastrectomy, dysphagia, bowel fistulas, disease-related malnutrition. Not to be prescribed for any child under 6 years

**Frebini® Energy** (Fresenius Kabi)

Sip feed, protein 3.75 g, carbohydrate 18.8 g, fat 6.65 g, energy 630 kJ (150 kcal)/100 mL, with vitamins, minerals and trace elements. Gluten-free; clinically lactose-free. Flavours: banana or strawberry. Net price 200-mL carton = £2.16.

Tube feed, protein 3.75 g, carbohydrate 18.75 g, fat 6.7 g, energy 630 kJ (150 kcal)/100 mL, with vitamins, minerals and trace elements. Gluten-free; clinically lactose-free. Flavour: neutral, net price 500-mL EasyBag® = £5.70.

For use as a sole source of nutrition or as a nutritional supplement for children aged 1 to 10 years or 8–30kg with disease-related malnutrition and/or growth failure, proven inflammatory bowel disease, following total gastrectomy, short-bowel syndrome, intractable malabsorption, dysphagia, bowel fistulas, and for pre-operative preparation of malnourished patients. Not to be prescribed for any child under 1 year

**Frebini® Energy Fibre** (Fresenius Kabi)

Sip feed, protein 3.75 g, carbohydrate 18.8 g, fat 6.65 g, fibre 1.1 g, energy 630 kJ (150 kcal)/100 mL, with vitamins, minerals and trace elements. Gluten-free; clinically lactose-free. Chocolate flavour, net price 200-mL carton = £2.21.

Tube feed, protein 3.75 g, carbohydrate 18.75 g, fat 6.7 g, fibre 1.13 g, energy 630 kJ (150 kcal)/100 mL, with vitamins, minerals and trace elements. Gluten-free, clinically lactose-free. Flavour: neutral, net price 500-mL EasyBag® = £6.10.

For indications see *Frebini Energy®*

**Frebini® Original** (Fresenius Kabi)

Liquid, tube feed, protein 2.5 g, carbohydrate 13.5 g, fat 4 g, energy 420 kJ (100 kcal)/100 mL, with vitamins, minerals and trace elements. Flavour: neutral, net price 500-mL EasyBag® = £4.55

For use as the sole source of nutrition or as a nutritional supplement for children aged 1–10 years or 8–30 kg with short-bowel syndrome, intractable malabsorption, pre-operative preparation of patients who are undernourished, proven inflammatory bowel disease, following total gastrectomy, dysphagia, bowel fistulas, disease-related malnutrition and/or growth failure. Not to be prescribed for any child under 1 year

**Frebini® Original Fibre** (Fresenius Kabi)

Tube feed, protein 2.5 g, carbohydrate 12.5 g, fat 4.4 g, fibre 750 mg, energy 420 kJ (100 kcal)/100 mL, with vitamins, minerals and trace elements. Gluten-free, clinically lactose-free. Neutral flavour, net price 500-mL EasyBag® = £5.05

For use as a sole source of nutrition or as a nutritional supplement for children aged 1–10 years or 8–30 kg with disease-related malnutrition and/or growth failure, proven inflammatory bowel disease, following total gastrectomy, short-bowel syndrome, intractable malabsorption, dysphagia, bowel fistulas, and pre-operative preparation of malnourished patients. Not to be prescribed for any child under 1 year

**Fresubin® Energy** (Fresenius Kabi)

Liquid, protein 5.65 g, carbohydrate 18.8 g, fat 5.83 g, energy 630 kJ (150 kcal)/100 mL, with vitamins and minerals. Net price 200-mL carton = £1.55 (flavours: vanilla, strawberry, butterscotch, blackcurrant, banana, orange, pineapple, chocolate-mint, vegetable cream, and neutral): 500-mL bottle = £3.80 (flavour: neutral); 500-mL EasyBag® = £3.88; 1-litre EasyBag® = £7.70; 1.5-litre EasyBag® = £9.60.

For use as sole source of nutrition or as a nutritional supplement prescribed on medical grounds for: short-bowel syndrome, intractable malabsorption, pre-operative preparation of undernourished patients, proven inflammatory bowel disease, following total gastrectomy, dysphagia, bowel fistulas, disease-related malnutrition. Not to be prescribed for any child under 1 year; use with caution for children under 5 years

**Fresubin® Energy Fibre** (Fresenius Kabi)

Sip feed, protein 5.65 g, carbohydrate 18.8 g, fat 5.83 g, fibre 2.5 g, energy 630 kJ (150 kcal)/100 mL, with vitamins, minerals and trace elements. Gluten-free; clinically lactose-free. Flavours: banana, cappucino, chocolate, lemon, strawberry, vanilla. Net price 200-mL carton = £1.70.

For indications see *Fresubin® Energy*

Tube feed, protein 5.6 g, carbohydrate 18.8 g, fat 5.8 g, fibre 2 g, energy 630 kJ (150 kcal)/100 mL, with vitamins, minerals and trace elements. Gluten-free; clinically lactose-free. Unflavoured, net price 500-mL EasyBag® = £4.00; 1-litre EasyBag® = £7.99; 1.5-litre EasyBag® = £10.60.

For indications see *Fresubin® Energy*

**Fresubin HP Energy®** (Fresenius Kabi)

Liquid, protein 7.5 g, carbohydrate 17 g, fat 6 g, energy 630 kJ (150 kcal)/100 mL with vitamins, minerals, and trace elements. Gluten-free and low lactose. Vanilla flavour. Net price 500-mL bottle = £3.67; 500-mL EasyBag® = £3.72; 1-litre EasyBag® = £7.44.

As a nutritional supplement prescribed on medical grounds for: short-bowel syndrome, intractable malabsorption, pre-operative preparation of patients who are undernourished, proven inflammatory bowel disease, following total gastrectomy, dysphagia, bowel fistulas, disease-related malnutrition, continuous ambulatory peritoneal dialysis (CAPD), and haemodialysis. Not to be prescribed for any child under 1 year; use with caution for children up to 5 years

**Fresubin® 1000 Complete** (Fresenius Kabi)

Liquid, tube feed, protein 5.5 g, carbohydrate 12.5 g, fat 3.1 g, fibre 2 g, energy 420 kJ (100 kcal)/100mL with vitamins, minerals and trace elements. Gluten-free, clinically lactose-free, net price 1-litre EasyBag® = £8.20.

For use as the sole source of nutrition or as a nutritional supplement prescribed on medical grounds for: short-bowel syndrome, intractable malabsorption, pre-operative preparation of undernourished patients, proven inflammatory bowel disease, following total gastrectomy, dysphagia, bowel fistulas, disease-related malnutrition. Not to be prescribed for any child under 1 year; use with caution for children up to 5 years

**Fresubin® 1200 Complete** (Fresenius Kabi)

Liquid, tube feed, protein 4 g, carbohydrate 10 g, fat 2.7 g, fibre 2 g, energy 336 kJ (80 kcal)/100 mL with vitamins, minerals and trace elements. Gluten-free, clinically lactose-free, net price 1.5-litre EasyBag® = £10.20.

For use as the sole source of nutrition or as a nutritional supplement prescribed on medical grounds for: short-bowel syndrome, intractable malabsorption, pre-operative preparation of undernourished patients, proven inflammatory bowel disease, following total gastrectomy, bowel fistulas, disease-related malnutrition. Not to be prescribed for any child under 5 years

**Fresubin® Original** (Fresenius Kabi)
Liquid, protein 3.8 g, carbohydrate 13.8 g, fat 3.4 g, energy 420 kJ (100 kcal)/100 mL with vitamins and minerals. Gluten-free, low lactose and cholesterol. Net price 200-mL carton (nut, peach, blackcurrant, chocolate, mocha, and vanilla flavours) = £1.55; 500-mL bottle (neutral flavour) = £3.08; 500-mL EasyBag® = £2.99; 1-litre EasyBag® = £5.97; 1.5-litre EasyBag® = £8.96

For use as the sole source of nutrition or as a nutritional supplement prescribed on medical grounds for: short-bowel syndrome, intractable malabsorption, pre-operative preparation of patients who are undernourished, proven inflammatory bowel disease, following total gastrectomy, dysphagia, bowel fistulas, disease-related malnutrition. Not to be prescribed for any child under 1 year; use with caution for children up to 5 years

**Fresubin® Original Fibre** (Fresenius Kabi)
Liquid with dietary fibre, protein 3.8 g, carbohydrate 13.8 g, fat 3.4 g, energy 420 kJ (100 kcal)/100 mL, with vitamins and minerals. Flavour: neutral. Net price 500-mL bottle = £3.48; 500-mL EasyBag® = £3.62; 1-litre EasyBag® = £7.24; 1.5-litre EasyBag® = £10.20.

For use as sole source of nutrition or as a nutritional supplement prescribed on medical grounds for: short-bowel syndrome, intractable malabsorption, pre-operative preparation of patients who are undernourished, proven inflammatory bowel disease, following total gastrectomy, dysphagia, disease-related malnutrition. Not to be prescribed for any child under 2 years; use with caution for children up to 5 years

**Fresubin Protein Energy Drink** (Fresenius Kabi)
Liquid, protein 10 g, carbohydrate 12.4 g, fat 6.7 g, energy 630 kJ (150 kcal)/100 mL, with vitamins, minerals and trace elements. Gluten- and lactose-free. Chocolate, strawberry, and vanilla flavours, net price 200-mL = £1.58.

As a necessary nutritional supplement prescribed on medical grounds for: short-bowel syndrome, intractable malabsorption, pre-operative preparation of undernourished patients, proven inflammatory bowel disease, following total gastrectomy, dysphagia, bowel fistulas, disease-related malnutrition, continuous ambulatory peritoneal dialysis (CAPD), haemodialysis. Not to be prescribed for any child under 1 year; use with caution for children up to 5 years of age

**Fructose**
**(Laevulose)**

For proven glucose/galactose intolerance

**Gadsby's**
Gluten-free. White bread flour, net price 1 kg = £4.99. White sliced bread, 400 g = £2.50. White bread rolls, 4 × 75 g = £2.00

For established gluten enteropathy

**Galactomin® 17** (SHS)
Powder, protein 14.5 g, fat 25.9 g, carbohydrate 56.9 g, mineral salts 3.4 g/100 g. Used as a 13.1% solution with additional vitamins in place of milk. Net price 400 g = £11.48.

For proven lactose intolerance in preschool children, galactosaemia and galactokinase deficiency

**Galactomin® 19** (SHS)
Powder, protein 14.6 g, fat 30.8 g, carbohydrate 49.7 g (fructose as carbohydrate source), mineral salts 2.1 g/100 g, with vitamins. Used as a 12.9% solution in place of milk. Net price 400 g = £30.24.

For glucose plus galactose intolerance

**Generaid®** (SHS)
Powder, whey protein and additional branched-chain amino acids (protein equivalent 81%). Net price 200 g (unflavoured) = £20.92. See also Flavour Sachets.

For patients with chronic liver disease and/or porto-hepatic encephalopathy

**Generaid Plus®** (SHS)
Powder, whey protein and additional branched-chain amino acids (protein equivalent 11%) carbohydrate 62%, fat 19% with vitamins, minerals and trace elements. Net price 400 g = £14.96.

For children over 1 year with hepatic disorders

**Glucose**
**(Dextrose monohydrate)**
Net price 100 g = 39p.

For glycogen storage disease and sucrose/isomaltose intolerance

**Glutafin®** (Nutricia Dietary)
Gluten-free. Biscuits, savoury, 125 g = £1.70; 150 g = £2.32. Biscuits, digestive, sweet or tea, 150 g = £1.70. Biscuits, 200 g = £3.31. Biscuits, shortbread, 125 g = £1.47. Cake mix, 500 g = £5.31. Crackers, 200 g = £2.76. High fibre crackers, 200 g = £2.31. Pasta (penne, shells, spirals, spaghetti), 500 g = £5.36; (lasagne, tagliatelle), 250 g = £2.81. Pizza bases, 2 × 110 g = £3.83.

Select Gluten-free. Fibre loaf (sliced or unsliced), 400 g = £2.73; part-baked, 400 g = £3.06. Fresh Bread, white loaf, (sliced), 400 g = £2.94 Seeded loaf, 400 g = £2.97. White loaf (sliced or unsliced), 400 g = £2.73; part-baked, 400 g = £3.06. Fibre rolls, 4 = £3.06; (part-baked), 4 = £2.97; long, 2 = £3.06. White rolls, 4 = £2.76; (part-baked), 4 = £3.06; long, 2 = £3.06. Mixes (bread, cake, fibre, fibre bread, pastry, and white), 500 g = £5.31

For gluten-sensitive enteropathies including steatorrhoea due to gluten sensitivity, coeliac disease, and dermatitis herpetiformis

Gluten-free, wheat-free, crisp bread, 2 × 125 g = £3.61; crisp roll, 220 g = £3.72. Fibre loaf (sliced or unsliced), 400 g = £2.73. Fibre rolls, 4 = £2.97. White loaf (sliced or unsliced), 400 g = £3.06. White rolls, 4 = £2.97. Mixes (fibre bread, bread, white or fibre), 500 g = £5.31; cake or pastry mix, 500 g = £5.31.

For gluten-sensitive enteropathy with co-existing established wheat sensitivity

**Glutano®** (Gluten Free Foods Ltd)
Gluten-free, wheat-free. Tea biscuits, net price 125 g = £1.58; wheat-free digestive biscuit, 200 g = £1.58. Shortcake rings, 125 g = £1.12. Crispbread, 125 g = £1.58. Crackers, 150 g = £1.58. Flour mix, 750 g = £4.12. Pasta (animal shapes, spaghetti, spirals, tagliatelle), 250 g = £1.58; macaroni, 500 g = £3.16. White sliced bread (par-baked), 300 g = £1.86. Wholemeal bread (sliced), 500 g = £2.24. Baguette or rolls (par-baked), 200 g = £1.49.

For gluten-sensitive enteropathies including steatorrhoea due to gluten sensitivity, coeliac disease, and dermatitis herpetiformis

**HCU Express®** (Vitaflo)
Powder, protein (essential and non-essential amino acids except methionine) 15 g, carbohydrate 3.8 g, fat 0.03 g, energy 315 kJ (75.3 kcal)/25 g with vitamins, minerals and trace elements. Unflavoured, net price 30 × 25-g sachets = £225.00

A methionine-free protein substitute for use as a nutritional supplement in patients over 8 years of age with homocystinuria

**HCU gel®** (Vitaflo)
Powder, protein (essential and non-essential amino acids except methionine) 8.4 g, carbohydrate 8.6 g, fat 0.03 g, energy 286 kJ (68 kcal)/20 g with vitamins, minerals and trace elements. Unflavoured, net price 30 × 20- g sachets = £129.50

For the dietary management of homocystinuria in children between 12 months and 10 years of age

**InfaSoy®** (Cow & Gate)
Powder, carbohydrate 7.1%, fat 3.6%, and protein 1.8% with vitamins and minerals when used as a 12.7% solution. Net price 450 g = £3.77; 900 g = £7.23.

For proven lactose and associated sucrose intolerance in pre-school children, galactokinase deficiency, galactosaemia, and proven whole cow's milk sensitivity

**Infatrini®** (Nutricia Clinical)
Liquid, protein 2.6 g, carbohydrate 10.3 g, fat 5.4 g, energy 420 kJ (100 kcal)/100 mL with vitamins, minerals and trace elements. Gluten-free. Net price 100 mL = 88p, 200-mL Tetrapak® = £1.75

For use as a sole source of nutrition or as a nutritional supplement prescribed on medical grounds for: failure to thrive, disease-related malnutrition and malabsorption. Manufacturer advises suitable for infants between 1–8 kg body weight

**Instant Carobel®**
*see* **Carobel, Instant®**

**Isoleucine Amino Acid Supplement** (Vitaflo)
Powder, isoleucine 0.05 g, carbohydrate 4 g, fat nil, energy 64 kJ (15 kcal)/4 g, net price 30 × 4-g sachets = £37.50
For use in conjunction with a protein supplement for maple syrup urine disease in children over 1 year

**Isomil®** (Abbott)
Powder, protein 1.8%, carbohydrate 6.9%, fat 3.7% with vitamins and minerals when reconstituted. Lactose-free. Net price 400 g = £3.38.
For proven lactose intolerance in preschool children, galactokinase deficiency, galactosaemia, and proven whole cow's milk sensitivity

**Isosource® Energy** (Novartis Consumer Health)
Liquid, protein 5.7 g, carbohydrate 20 g, fat 6.2 g, energy 660 kJ (160 kcal)/100 mL with vitamins, minerals and trace elements. Gluten-free; clinically lactose-free. Net price 500-mL flexible pouch = £3.72, 1-litre flexible pouch = £7.44.
For indications see *Isosource Standard*

**Isosource® Energy Fibre** (Novartis Consumer Health)
Liquid, tube feed, protein 4.9 g, carbohydrate 20.2 g, fat 5.5 g, fibre, 1.5 g, energy 630 kJ (150 kcal)/100 mL with vitamins, minerals and trace elements. Gluten-free; clinically lactose-free. Net price 500-mL flexible pouch = £4.04, 1-litre flexible pouch = £8.08.
For use as the sole source of nutrition or as a nutritional supplement prescribed on medical grounds for: short-bowel syndrome, intractable malabsorption, pre-operative preparation of undernourished patients, proven inflammatory bowel disease, following total gastrectomy, dysphagia, disease-related malnutrition. Not to be prescribed for any child under 1 year; use with caution for children up to 5 years

**Isosource® Fibre** (Novartis Consumer Health)
Liquid, protein 3.8 g, carbohydrate 13.6 g, fat 3.4 g, fibre 1.4 g, energy 422 kJ (100 kcal)/100 mL with vitamins, minerals and trace elements. Gluten-free; clinically lactose-free. Net price 500-mL flexible pouch = £3.45, 1-litre flexible pouch = £6.90.
For indications see *Isosource Standard*

**Isosource® Junior** (Novartis Consumer Health)
Liquid, protein 2.7 g, carbohydrate 17 g, fat 4.7 g, energy 512 kJ (122 kcal)/100 mL with vitamins, minerals and trace elements. Gluten-free; clinically lactose-free. Net price 500-mL flexible pouch = £5.17.
Nutritionally complete feed for disease-related malnutrition, short-bowel syndrome, intractable malabsorption, pre-operative preparation of undernourished patients, proven inflammatory bowel disease, following total gastrectomy, dysphagia, bowel fistulas, growth failure, for children aged 1 to 6 years or 8 to 20 kg

**Isosource® Standard** (Novartis Consumer Health)
Liquid, protein 4.1 g, carbohydrate 14.2 g, fat 3.5 g, energy 441 kJ (105 kcal)/100 mL with vitamins, minerals and trace elements. Gluten-free; clinically lactose-free. Net price 500-mL flexible pouch = £3.03, 1-litre flexible pouch = £6.06.
For use as a sole source of nutrition or as a nutritional supplement prescribed on medical grounds for: short-bowel syndrome, intractable malabsorption, pre-operative preparation of undernourished patients, proven inflammatory bowel disease, following total gastrectomy, dysphagia, bowel fistulas, disease-related malnutrition. Not to be prescribed for any child under 1 year; use with caution for children up to 5 years

**Jevity®** (Abbott)
Liquid, protein 4 g, fat 3.5 g, carbohydrate 14.8 g, dietary fibre 1.1 g, energy 441 kJ (106 kcal)/100 mL, with vitamins and minerals. Gluten-, lactose-, and sucrose-free. Net price 500-mL ready-to-hang = £3.53, 1-litre ready-to-hang = £6.82, 1.5-litre ready-to-hang = £10.23.
For use as the sole source of nutrition or as a nutritional supplement prescribed on medical grounds for: short-bowel syndrome, intractable malabsorption, pre-operative preparation of patients who are undernourished, proven inflammatory bowel disease, bowel fistulas, following total gastrectomy, dysphagia, disease-related malnutrition. Not to be prescribed for any child under 2 years; use with caution for children up to 5 years

**Jevity 1.5 kcal®** (Abbott)
Liquid, tube feed, protein 6.38 g, carbohydrate 21.1 g, fat 4.9 g, fibre 1.2 g, energy 640 kJ (152 kcal)/100 mL, with vitamins, minerals and trace elements. Gluten- and lactose-free. Net price 500-mL ready-to-hang = £4.42, 1-litre ready-to-hang = £8.20, 1.5-litre ready-to-hang = £12.80.
For use as the sole source of nutrition or as a nutritional supplement prescribed on medical grounds for: short-bowel syndrome, intractable malabsorption, pre-operative preparation of undernourished patients, proven inflammatory bowel disease, bowel fistulas, following total gastrectomy, dysphagia, disease-related malnutrition. Not to be prescribed for any child under 2 years; use with caution for children up to 10 years

**Jevity Plus®** (Abbott)
Liquid, protein 5.6 g, carbohydrate 16.1 g, fat 3.9 g, dietary fibre 1.2 g, energy 504 kJ (120 kcal)/100 mL, with vitamins and minerals. Gluten- and lactose-free. Net price 500-mL ready-to-hang = £4.00, 1-litre ready-to-hang = £8.18, 1.5-litre ready-to-hang = £12.28.
For indications see under *Jevity®*.

**Juvela®** (SHS)
Gluten-free. Harvest mix, fibre mix, and flour mix, net price 500 g = £5.47. Bread (whole or sliced), 400-g loaf = £2.72; part-baked loaf (with or without fibre), 400g = £2.83. Fibre bread (sliced and unsliced), 400-g loaf = £2.64. Bread rolls, 5 × 85 g = £3.56, fibre bread rolls, 5 × 85 g = £3.56, part-baked rolls (with or without fibre), 5 × 75 g = £3.67. Crispbread, 210 g = £3.45. Pasta (fusilli, macaroni, spaghetti), 500 g = £5.36; lasagne, 250 g = £2.47; tagliatelle, 250 g = £2.74. Pizza bases, 2 × 180 g = £6.53. Digestive biscuits, 160 g = £2.27. Savoury biscuits, 150 g = £2.84. Tea biscuits, 160 g = £2.27.
For gluten-sensitive enteropathies including steatorrhoea due to gluten sensitivity, coeliac disease, and dermatitis herpetiformis
Low Protein. Mix, net price 500 g = £5.81. Bread (whole or sliced), 400-g loaf = £2.72. Bread rolls, 5 × 70 g = £3.38. Biscuits, orange and cinnamon flavour, 125 g = £5.68; chocolate chip, 130 g = £4.89.
For inherited metabolic disorders, renal or liver failure requiring a low-protein diet

**Kindergen®** (SHS)
Powder, protein 7.5 g, carbohydrate 60.5 g, fat 26.1 g, energy 2060 kJ (492 kcal)/100 g with vitamins and minerals. Net price 400 g = £19.86.
For complete nutritional support or supplementary feeding for infants and children with chronic renal failure who are receiving peritoneal rapid overnight dialysis

**Leucine-Free Amino Acid Mix**
*see* Amino Acid Modules, Xleu Faladon

**Lifestyle®** (Ultrapharm)
Gluten-free. Brown bread (sliced and unsliced), net price 400 g = £2.63. White bread (sliced and unsliced), 400 g = £2.63. High fibre bread (unsliced), 400 g = £2.63. Bread rolls, 400 g = £2.63.
For gluten-sensitive enteropathies including steatorrhoea due to gluten sensitivity, coeliac disease, and dermatitis herpetiformis

**Liquigen®** (SHS)
Emulsion, medium chain triglycerides 52%. Net price 250 mL = £6.34; 1 litre = £26.60.
For steatorrhoea associated with cystic fibrosis of the pancreas; intestinal lymphangiectasia, surgery of the intestine; chronic liver disease and liver cirrhosis; other proven malabsorption syndromes; ketogenic diet in the management of epilepsy; type I hyperlipoproteinaemia

**Locasol®** (SHS)
Powder, protein 14.6 g, carbohydrate 56.5 g, fat 26.1 g, mineral salts 1.9 g, not more than 55 mg of $Ca^{2+}$/100 g and vitamins. Used as a 13.1% solution in place of milk. Net price 400 g = £15.96.
For calcium intolerance

**Lophlex®** (SHS)
Powder, protein (containing essential and non-essential amino acids, phenylalanine-free) 20 g, carbohydrate 1.4 g, fat 60 mg, fibre 220 mg, energy 366 kJ (86 kcal)/27.8 g with vitamins, minerals, and trace elements. Flavours: berry, orange or unflavoured, net price 30 x 27.8-g sachets = £198.00.
For use in the dietary management of proven phenylketonuria in older children (over 8 years) and adults (includes use in pregnant women)

**Loprofin®** (SHS)

Low protein. Sweet biscuits, net price 150 g = £1.82; chocolate cream-filled biscuits, 125 g = £1.82; cookies (chocolate chip or cinnamon), 100 g = £4.82; crunch bar, 8 × 41 g = £11.09; wafers (orange, vanilla, or chocolate), 100 g = £1.76. Breakfast cereal, 375 g = £5.65. Egg replacer, 500 g = £10.59. Egg-white replacer, 100 g = £6.82. Bread (sliced or whole), 400-g loaf = £2.72. Rolls (part-baked) 4 × 65 g = £2.86. Mix, 500 g = £5.78. Crackers, 150 g = £2.48. Herb crackers, 150 g = £2.48. Pasta (lasagne, macaroni, pasta spirals, spaghetti), 500 g = £6.03. Pasta (vermicelli), 250 g = £3.00. Snack Pot, 47 g = £3.20.

For inherited metabolic disorders, renal or liver failure requiring a low-protein diet

PKU Drink, protein 0.4 g (phenylalanine 10 mg), lactose 9.4 g, fat 2 g, energy 165 kJ (40 kcal)/100 mL. Net price 200-mL Tetrapak® = 52p.

For phenylketonuria

**Low protein drink** (Milupa)

Powder, protein 0.4%, carbohydrate 5.1%, fat 2% when reconstituted. Net price 400 g = £7.23.

For inherited disorders of amino acid metabolism in childhood

Note Termed *Milupa® lpd* by manufacturer

**Mapleflex®** (SHS)

Powder, essential and non-essential amino acids 35% except isoleucine, leucine, and valine, with carbohydrate 38%, fat 13.5%, vitamins, minerals, and trace elements. Unflavoured. Net price 30 × 29-g sachets = £142.10.

For maple syrup urine disease in children aged 1–10 years

**Maxamaid®** (SHS)

*see MSUD Maxamaid, XLEU Maxamaid, XLYS Maxamaid, XLYS Low TRY Maxamaid, XMET Maxamaid, XMTVI Maxamaid, XP Maxamaid, XP Maxamaid Concentrate, XPHEN TYR Maxamaid*

**Note** Maxamaid products are generally intended for use in children aged 1 to 8 years, see also Flavour Sachets, for use with unflavoured amino acid and peptide products from SHS

**Maxamum®** (SHS)

*see MSUD Maxamum, XMET Maxamum, XMTVI Maxamum, XP Maxamum*

**Note** Maxamum products are generally intended for use in children over 8 years

**Maxijul®** (SHS)

Liquid, carbohydrate 50%, with potassium 0.004%, sodium 0.023%. Gluten-, lactose-, and fructose-free. Flavours: blackcurrant, lemon and lime, orange, and natural. Net price 200 mL = £1.12

LE Powder, modification of *Maxijul®* with lower concentrations of sodium and potassium. Net price 200 g = £3.82, 2 kg = £26.62

Super Soluble Powder, glucose polymer, potassium 0.004%, sodium 0.046%. Gluten-, lactose-, and fructose-free. Net price 4 × 132-g sachet pack = £4.41, 200 g = £1.78, 2.5 kg = £15.66, 25 kg = £106.35

All for disease-related malnutrition; malabsorption states or other conditions requiring fortification with high or readily available carbohydrate supplement

**Maxipro Super Soluble®** (SHS)

Powder, whey protein and additional amino acids (protein equivalent 80%). Net price 200 g = £8.64; 1 kg = £34.66.

For biochemically proven hypoproteinaemia. Not to be prescribed for any child under 1 year; unsuitable as a sole source of nutrition

**Maxisorb®** (SHS)

Powder, protein 12 g, carbohydrate 9 g, fat 6 g, energy 579 kJ (138 kcal)/30 g with minerals. Vanilla, strawberry and chocolate flavours. Net price 5 × 30-g sachets = £3.63.

For biochemically proven hypoproteinaemia. Not to be prescribed for any child under 1 year; use with caution for children up to 5 years

**MCT Oil**

Triglycerides from medium chain fatty acids. For steatorrhoea associated with cystic fibrosis of the pancreas; intestinal lymphangiectasia; surgery of the intestine; chronic liver disease and liver cirrhosis; other proven malabsorption syndromes; in a ketogenic diet in the management of epilepsy; in type I hyperlipoproteinaemia

Available from SHS (net price 500 mL = £9.79)

**MCT Pepdite®** (SHS)

Powder, essential and non-essential amino acids, peptides, medium chain triglycerides, monoglyceride of sunflower oil, with carbohydrate, fat, vitamins, minerals, and trace elements. Flavour Sachets available.

*MCT Pepdite*. Net price 400 g = £13.96

*MCT Pepdite 1+*. Net price 400 g = £13.96

Both for disorders in which a high intake of medium chain triglyceride is beneficial

**Metabolic Mineral Mixture®** (SHS)

Powder, essential mineral salts. Net price 100 g = £8.67.

For mineral supplementation in synthetic diets

**Methionine-Free Amino Acid Mix**

*see* Amino Acid Modules, XMET Homidon

**Methionine, Threonine, Valine-Free and Isoleucine-Low Amino Acid Mix**

*see* Amino Acid Modules, XMTVI Asadon

**Milupa® lpd**

*see under* Low Protein Drink

**Milupa® PKU2 and PKU3**

*see under* PKU2 and PKU3

**Minaphlex®** (SHS)

Liquid, protein equivalent 8.4 g, carbohydrate 9.9 g, fat 3.9 g, energy 455 (108 kcal)/29-g sachet, with vitamins, minerals, and trace elements. Phenylalanine-free. Chocolate, pineapple, and vanilla. Unflavoured version also available (contains an extra 5 kcal of carbohydrate per sachet), net price 30 × 29 g sachets = £86.33.

For the dietary management of phenylketonuria. Not recommended for children under 1 year

**Modulen IBD®** (Nestlé)

Powder, protein 18 g, carbohydrate 54 g, fat 23 g, energy 2040 kJ (500 kcal)/100 g with vitamins, minerals and trace elements. Net price 400 g = £9.72.

For use as the sole source of nutrition during the active phase of Crohn's disease and for nutritional support during the remission phase in patients who are malnourished. Not to be prescribed for any child under one year; use with caution for children up to 5 years

May be flavoured with Nestlé Nutrition Flavour Mix (see under *Peptamen*)

**Monogen®** (SHS)

Powder, protein 11.4 g, carbohydrate 68 g, fat 11.4 g (of which MCT 93%), energy 1772 kJ (420 kcal)/100 g, with vitamins, minerals and trace elements. Net price 400 g = £13.89.

For long-chain acyl-CoA dehydrogenase deficiency (LCAD), carnitine palmitoyl transferase deficiency (CPTD), primary and secondary lipoprotin lipase deficiency

**MSUD Aid III®** (SHS)

Powder, containing full range of amino acids except isoleucine, leucine, and valine, with vitamins, minerals, and trace elements. Net price 500 g = £127.20.

For maple syrup urine disease and related conditions where it is necessary to limit the intake of branched chain amino acids

**MSUD Analog** (SHS)

Powder, essential and non-essential amino acids 15.5% except isoleucine, leucine and valine, with carbohydrate, fat, vitamins, minerals, and trace elements. Net price 400 g = £24.62.

For maple syrup urine disease

**Note** Analog products are generally intended for use in children up to 1 year

**MSUD express®** (Vitaflo)

Powder, protein equivalent (essential and non-essential amino acids except leucine, isoleucine, and valine) 15 g, carbohydrate 3.8 g, fat less than 0.1 g, energy 315 kJ (75 kcal)/25 g with vitamins, minerals, and trace elements. Unflavoured (see FlavourPac® for available flavouring sachets), net price 30 × 25-g sachets = £231.75.

For maple syrup urine disease in children over 8 years and adults

**MSUD Gel®** (Vitaflo)
Powder, protein equivalent (essential and non-essential amino acids except leucine, isoleucine, and valine) 8.4 g, carbohydrate 8.6 g, fat less than 0.1 g, energy 286 kJ (68 kcal)/20 g with vitamins, minerals, and trace elements. Unflavoured (see FlavourPac® for available flavouring sachets), net price 30 × 20-g sachets = £129.50.
For maple syrup urine disease in children aged 1 to 10 years

**MSUD Maxamaid®** (SHS)
Powder, essential and non-essential amino acids 30% except isoleucine, leucine, and valine, with carbohydrate, fat less than 0.5%, vitamins, minerals, and trace elements. Net price 500 g = £67.15.
For maple syrup urine disease
**Note** Maxamaid products are generally intended for use in children aged 1 to 8 years, see also Flavour Sachets, for use with unflavoured amino acid and peptide products from SHS

**MSUD Maxamum®** (SHS)
Powder, essential and non-essential amino acids 47% except isoleucine, leucine, and valine, with carbohydrate, fat less than 0.5%, vitamins, minerals, and trace elements. Flavours: orange, unflavoured, see also Flavour Sachets. Net price 500 g = £107.65.
For maple syrup urine disease
**Note** Maxamum products are generally intended for use in children over 8 years

**Neocate®** (SHS)
Powder, essential and non-essential amino acids, maltodextrin, fat, vitamins, minerals, and trace elements. Net price 400 g = £19.98.
For proven whole protein intolerance, short-bowel syndrome, intractable malabsorption, and other gastrointestinal disorders where an elemental diet is specifically indicated; for use in children under 1 year

**Neocate Advance®** (SHS)
Powder, essential and non-essential amino acids, carbohydrate, fat, vitamins, minerals and trace elements. Milk protein-, soy- and lactose-free. Net price 100 g = £4.10; banana-vanilla flavour 15 x 50 g = £33.24.
For proven whole protein intolerance, short-bowel syndrome, intractable malabsorption, and other gastrointestinal disorders where an elemental diet is specifically indicated; for use in children over 1 year

**Nepro®** (Abbott)
Liquid, protein 7 g, carbohydrate 20.6 g, fat 9.6 g, energy 840 kJ (200 kcal)/100 mL with vitamins and minerals. Net price 237-mL can = £2.28; 500–mL ready-to-hang = £4.81.
For patients with chronic renal failure who are on haemodialysis or continuous ambulatory peritoneal dialysis (CAPD), or patients with cirrhosis or other conditions requiring a high energy, low fluid, low electrolyte diet

**Nestargel®** (Nestlé)
Powder, carob seed flour 96.5%, calcium lactate 3.5%. Net price 125 g = £2.99.
For thickening feeds in the treatment of vomiting

**Novasource® Forte** (Novartis Consumer Health)
Liquid, protein 6 g, carbohydrate 18.3 g, fat 5.9 g, fibre 2.2 g, energy 631 kJ (150 kcal)/100 mL with vitamins, minerals and trace elements. Gluten-free; low-lactose, net price 500-mL flexible pouch = £4.36.
For use as a sole source of nutrition or as a nutritional supplement prescribed on medical grounds for: short-bowel syndrome, intractable malabsorption, pre-operative preparation of undernourished patients, proven inflammatory bowel disease, following total gastrectomy, dysphagia, bowel fistulas, disease-related malnutrition, neoplasia-related cachexia. Not to be prescribed for any child under 1 year; use with caution for children up to 5 years

**Novasource GI Control®** (Novartis Consumer Health)
Liquid, protein 4.1 g, carbohydrate 14.2 g, fat 3.5 g, fibre 2.2 g, energy 440 kJ (100 kcal)/100 mL with vitamins minerals and trace elements. Gluten-free; clinically lactose-free, net price 500-mL bottle = £4.39, 500-mL flexible pouch = £4.70.
For use as a sole source of nutrition or as a nutritional supplement prescribed on medical grounds for: short-bowel syndrome, intractable malabsorption, pre-operative preparation of undernourished patients, proven inflammatory bowel disease, following total gastrectomy, dysphagia, bowel fistulas, disease-related malnutrition. Not to be prescribed for any child under 1 year; use with caution for children up to 5 years

**Nutilis®** (Nutricia Clinical)
Powder, modified maize starch, gluten- and lactose-free, net price 20 × 9-g sachets = £5.00; 225 g = £3.88.
For thickening of foods in dysphagia. Not to be prescribed for children under 3 years

**Nutramigen® 1** (Mead Johnson)
Powder, protein 1.9 g, carbohydrate 7.5 g, fat 3.4 g, energy 280 kJ (68 kcal)/100 mL with vitamins and minerals. Gluten-, sucrose-, and lactose-free. Net price 400 g = £7.81.
For disaccharide and/or whole protein intolerance where additional medium chain triglyceride is not indicated

**Nutramigen® 2** (Mead Johnson)
Powder, protein 2.3 g, carbohydrate 7.8 g, fat 3.5 g energy 301 kJ (72 kcal) per 100 mL when normal dilution used, with vitamins, minerals and trace elements. Gluten-, sucrose-, and lactose-free, net price 400 g = £7.81.
For disaccharide and/or whole protein intolerance where additional medium chain triglyceride is not indicated. Not suitable for infants under 6 months

**Nutrini®** (Nutricia Clinical)
Liquid, protein 2.75 g, carbohydrate 12.3 g, fat 4.4 g, energy 420 kJ (100 kcal)/100 mL. Gluten- and sucrose-free; clinically lactose-free. Net price 200-mL bottle = £1.93, 500-mL = £4.83.
For use as the sole source of nutrition or as a nutritional supplement prescribed on medical grounds for: short-bowel syndrome, intractable malabsorption, pre-operative preparation of undernourished patients, dysphagia, bowel fistulas, disease-related malnutrition and/or growth failure. For children aged 1 to 6 years or between 8–20 kg body-weight

**Nutrini® Energy** (Nutricia Clinical)
Liquid, protein 4.1 g, carbohydrate 18.5 g, fat 6.7 g, energy 630 kJ (150 kcal)/100 mL. Gluten- and sucrose-free; clinically lactose-free. Net price 200-mL bottle = £2.38, 500-mL = £5.95.
For use as the sole source of nutrition or as a nutritional supplement prescribed on medical grounds for: short-bowel syndrome, intractable malabsorption, pre-operative preparation of undernourished patients, following total gastrectomy, dysphagia, bowel fistulas, disease-related malnutrition and growth failure. For children aged 1 to 6 years or between 8–20 kg body-weight

**Nutrini® Energy Multi Fibre** (Nutricia Clinical)
Liquid, tube feed, protein 4.1 g, carbohydrate 18.5 g, fat 6.7 g, fibre 0.75 g, energy 630 kJ (150 kcal)/100 mL with vitamins, minerals and trace elements. Gluten- and lactose-free, net price 200-mL bottle = £2.58, 500-mL pack = £6.44.
For short-bowel syndrome, intractable malabsorption, pre-operative preparation of undernourished patients, total gastrectomy, dysphagia, disease-related malnutrition, and growth failure. For children aged 1 to 6 years or between 8–20 kg body-weight

**Nutrini® Low Energy Multi Fibre** (Nutricia Clinical)
Liquid, tube feed, protein 2.06 g, carbohydrate 9.3 g, fat 3.3 g, fibre 0.75 g, energy 315 kJ (75 kcal)/100 mL with vitamins, minerals and trace elements. Gluten- and lactose-free, net price 200-mL bottle = £1.87, 500-mL pack = £4.71
For indications see *Nutrini Multi Fibre*

**Nutrini® Multi Fibre** (Nutricia Clinical)
Liquid, protein 2.75 g, carbohydrate 12.3 g, fat 4.4 g, fibre 750 mg, energy 420 kJ (100 kcal)/100 mL. Gluten- and sucrose-free; clinically lactose-free. Net price 200-mL bottle = £2.14, 500-mL pack = £5.35.
For use as a sole source of nutrition or as a nutritional supplement prescribed on medical grounds for: short-bowel syndrome, intractable malabsorption, pre-operative preparation of undernourished patients, total gastrectomy, dysphagia, disease-related malnutrition and growth failure. For children aged 1 to 6 years or 8–20 kg body-weight

**Nutriprem 2®** (Cow & Gate)
Liquid, protein 2 g, carbohydrate 7.5 g, fat 4.1 g, energy 310 kJ (75 kcal)/100 mL, with vitamins, minerals, and trace elements, net price 200-mL Tetrapak® = £1.32. Also available to hospitals-only as a sterilised prepared feed in 100-mL bottles

Powder, protein 2 g, carbohydrate 7.4 g, fat 4.1 g, energy 310 kJ (75 kcal) per 100 mL when reconstituted, with vitamins and minerals. Net price 900 g = £8.80.

For catch-up growth in pre-term infants (less than 35 weeks at birth), and small-for-gestational-age infants, until 6 months corrected age

**Nutrison® Energy** (Nutricia Clinical)
Liquid, protein 6 g, carbohydrate 18.5 g, fat 5.8 g, energy 630 kJ (150 kcal)/100 mL with vitamins, minerals and trace elements. Gluten- and sucrose-free; clinically lactose-free. Net price 500-mL bottle = £3.77; 500-mL pack = £4.04; 1-litre pack = £7.55; 1.5-litre pack = £11.32.

As a nutritional supplement prescribed on medical grounds for: short-bowel syndrome, intractable malabsorption, pre-operative preparation of undernourished patients, proven inflammatory bowel disease, following total gastrectomy, dysphagia, bowel fistulas, disease-related malnutrition. Not to be prescribed for any child under 1 year; use with caution for children aged 1 to 6 years

**Nutrison® Energy Multi Fibre** (Nutricia Clinical)
Liquid, protein 6 g, carbohydrate 18.5 g, fat 5.8 g, fibre 1.5 g, energy 630 kJ (150 kcal)/100 mL with vitamins, minerals, and trace elements. Gluten-free and clinically lactose-free. Net price 500-mL bottle = £4.20; 500-mL pack = £4.48; 1-litre pack = £8.39; 1.5-litre pack = £13.45.

For use as the sole source of nutrition or as a nutritional supplement prescribed on medical grounds for: short-bowel syndrome, intractable malabsorption, pre-operative preparation of undernourished patients, proven inflammatory bowel disease, following total gastrectomy, dysphagia, disease-related malnutrition. Not to be prescribed for any child under 1 year; use with caution for children aged 1 to 6 years

**Nutrison MCT®** (Nutricia Clinical)
Liquid, protein 5 g, carbohydrate 12.6 g, fat 3.3 g, energy 420 kJ (100 kcal)/100 mL with vitamins, minerals and trace elements. Gluten- and fructose-free, clinically lactose-free. Net price 1-litre pack = £7.05.

For indications see *Nutrison Energy*. Not to be prescribed for any child under 1 year; use with caution for children aged 1 to 6 years

**Nutrison® Multi Fibre** (Nutricia Clinical)
Liquid, protein 4 g, carbohydrate 12.3 g, fat 3.9 g, fibre 1.5 g, energy 420 kJ (100 kcal)/100 mL with vitamins, minerals and trace elements. Gluten- and sucrose-free; clinically lactose-free. Net price 500-mL bottle = £3.40; 500-mL pack = £3.63; 1-litre pack = £6.79; 1.5-litre pack = £10.19.

For indications see *Nutrison Standard* excluding bowel fistulas. Not to be prescribed for any child under 1 year; use with caution for children aged 1 to 6 years

**Nutrison® Protein Plus** (Nutricia Clinical)
Liquid, protein 6.3 g, carbohydrate 14.2 g, fat 4.9 g, energy 525 kJ (125 kcal)/100 mL, with vitamins, minerals and trace elements. Gluten- and lactose-free. Net price l-litre pack = £7.45.

For use in the dietary management of disease-related malnutrition. Not suitable for infants under 1 year; use with caution in children aged 1 to 6 years

**Nutrison® Protein Plus Multi Fibre** (Nutricia Clinical)
Liquid, protein 6.3 g, carbohydrate 14.2 g, fat 4.9 g, fibre 1.5 g, energy 525 kJ (125 kcal)/100 mL, with vitamins, minerals and trace elements. Gluten- and lactose-free. Net price l-litre pack = £8.29.

For use in the dietary management of disease-related malnutrition. Not suitable for infants under 1 year; use with caution in children aged 1 to 6 years

**Nutrison® Soya** (Nutricia Clinical)
Liquid, protein 4 g, carbohydrate 12.3 g, fat 3.9 g, energy 420 kJ (100 kcal)/100 mL, with vitamins, minerals and trace elements. Gluten- and sucrose-free; clinically lactose-free. Net price 500-mL bottle = £3.75; 1-litre pack = £7.50.

For use as the sole source of nutrition or as a nutritional supplement prescribed on medical grounds for: cow's milk protein and lactose intolerance, short-bowel syndrome, intractable malabsorption, pre-operative preparation of undernourished patients, proven inflammatory bowel disease, following total gastrectomy, dysphagia, bowel fistulas, disease-related malnutrition. Not to be prescribed for any child under 1 year; use with caution for children aged 1 to 6 years

**Nutrison® Standard** (Nutricia Clinical)
Liquid, protein 4 g, carbohydrate 12.3 g, fat 3.9 g, energy 425 kJ (100 kcal)/100 mL, with vitamins, minerals and trace elements. Gluten- and sucrose-free; clinically lactose-free. Net price 500-mL bottle = £3.12; 500-mL pack = £3.36; 1-litre pack = £6.09; 1.5-litre pack = £9.14.

For use as the sole source of nutrition or as a nutritional supplement prescribed on medical grounds for: short-bowel syndrome, intractable malabsorption, pre-operative preparation of undernourished patients, proven inflammatory bowel disease, following total gastrectomy, dysphagia, bowel fistulas, disease-related malnutrition. Not to be prescribed for any child under 1 year; use with caution for children aged 1 to 6 years

**Nutrison® 1200 Complete Multi Fibre** (Nutricia Clinical)
Liquid, protein 5.5 g, carbohydrate 15 g, fat 4.3 g, energy 505 kJ (120 kcal)/100 mL, with vitamins, minerals and trace elements. Gluten- and lactose-free, net price 500-mL bottle = £4.03; l-litre pack = £8.05; 1.5-litre pack = £12.08.

As a sole source of nutrition or as a nutritional supplement prescribed on medical grounds for: short-bowel syndrome, intractable malabsorption, pre-operative preparation of undernourished patients, proven inflammatory bowel disease, following total gastrectomy, dysphagia, disease-related malnutrition. Not to be prescribed for any child under 1 year; use with caution for children aged 1 to 6 years

**Orgran®** (Community)
Gluten-free. Pasta: lasagne (corn, rice and maize), 150 g = £2.89; shells (split pea and soya), 200 g = £2.25; spaghetti (corn, rice, rice and maize), 250 g = £2.25; spirals (buckwheat, corn, rice, rice and millet, rice and maize), 250 g = £2.25, spirals (organic brown rice), 250 g = £2.60. Crispbread (corn or rice), 200 g = £2.39. Pizza and pastry mix, 375 g = £3.33.

For gluten-sensitive enteropathies including steatorrhoea due to gluten sensitivity, coeliac disease, and dermatitis herpetiformis

**Osmolite®** (Abbott)
Liquid, protein 4 g, carbohydrate 13.56 g, fat 3.4 g, energy 424 kJ (100 kcal)/100 mL with vitamins and minerals. Gluten- and lactose-free. Net price 250-mL can = £1.69; 500-mL bottle = £3.10, 1-litre bottle = £5.99, 1.5-litre bottle = £8.99.

For use as the sole source of nutrition or as a nutritional supplement prescribed on medical grounds for: short-bowel syndrome, intractable malabsorption, pre-operative preparation of undernourished patients, proven inflammatory bowel disease, following total gastrectomy, bowel fistulas, disease-related malnutrition, dysphagia. Not to be prescribed for any child under 1 year; use with caution for children up to 5 years

**Osmolite Plus®** (Abbott)
Liquid, protein 5.6 g, carbohydrate 15.8 g, fat 3.9 g, energy 508 kJ (121 kcal)/100 mL with vitamins, minerals and trace elements. Gluten-free and clinically lactose-free. Net price 500-mL ready-to-hang = £3.73, 1-litre ready-to-hang = £7.20, 1.5-litre ready-to-hang = £10.79.

For indications see *Osmolite*

**Paediasure®** (Abbott)
Liquid, protein 2.8 g, carbohydrate 11 g, fat 5 g, energy 422 kJ (101 kcal)/100 mL with vitamins and minerals. Gluten-free, clinically lactose-free. Flavours: vanilla (can, ready-to-hang and Tetrapak®), strawberry, chocolate and banana (Tetrapak®). Net price 250-mL can = £2.34, 500-mL ready-to-hang = £4.69, 200-mL Tetrapak® = £1.88.

For use as the sole source of nutrition or as a nutritional supplement prescribed on medical grounds for children aged 1 to 10 years for short-bowel syndrome, intractable malabsorption, pre-operative preparation of undernourished patients, dysphagia, bowel fistulas, and disease-related malnutrition and/or growth failure. Not to be prescribed for any child under 1 year

**Paediasure® Fibre** (Abbott)
Liquid, protein 2.8 g, carbohydrate 11.16 g, fat 5 g, fibre 520 mg, energy 422 kJ (101 kcal)/100 mL with vitamins and minerals. Gluten-free, clinically lactose-free. Flavours: vanilla (can, ready-to-hang and Tetrapak®), banana (Tetrapak®),

strawberry (Tetrapak®). Net price 250-mL can = £2.60, 500-mL ready-to-hang = £5.20, 200-mL Tetrapak® = £2.08.

For indications see *Paediasure*

**Paediasure® Plus** (Abbott)

Liquid, protein 4.2 g, carbohydrate 16.7 g, fat 7.5 g, energy 632 kJ (151 kcal)/100 mL with vitamins and minerals. Gluten-free, clinically lactose-free. Flavours: vanilla (ready-to-hang and Tetrapak®), strawberry (Tetrapak®). Net price 200-mL Tetrapak® = £2.30, 500-mL ready-to-hang = £5.87.

For indications see *Paediasure liquid*

**Paediasure® Plus Fibre** (Abbott)

Sip feed, protein 4.2 g, carbohydrate 16.4 g, fat 7.47 g, fibre 1.1g, energy 626 kJ (150 kcal)/100 mL with vitamins and minerals. Gluten-free, clinically lactose-free, net price 200-mL Tetrapak® = £2.50.

Tube feed, protein 4.2 g, carbohydrate 16.7 g, fat 7.5 g, fibre 1.1g, energy 629 kJ (150 kcal)/100 mL with vitamins and minerals. Gluten-free, clinically lactose-free, net price 500-mL ready-to-hang = £6.25.

As a sole source of nutrition, or as a nutritional supplement for children aged 1 to 10 years, or 8–30 kg body-weight, with disease-related malnutrition and/or growth failure, short-bowel syndrome, intractable malabsorption, dysphagia, bowel fistulas, pre-operative preparation of undernourished patients. Not to be prescribed for any child under 1 year.

**Paediatric Seravit®** (SHS)

Powder, vitamins, minerals, low sodium and potassium, and trace elements. Net price 200 g (unflavoured) = £12.24; pineapple flavour, 200 g = £13.04.

For vitamin and mineral supplementation in restrictive therapeutic diets in infants and children

**Pepdite®** (SHS)

Powder, peptides, essential and non-essential amino acids, with carbohydrate, fat, vitamins, minerals, and trace elements. Flavour Sachets available.

*Pepdite* (birth to 1 year). Providing 1925 kJ (472 kcal)/100 g. Net price 400 g = £12.83

*Pepdite 1+*. Providing 1787 kJ (439 kcal)/100 g. Net price 400 g = £13.48; 15 x 57 g (banana flavour) = £32.70

Both for disaccharide and/or whole protein intolerance, or where amino acids or peptides are indicated in conjunction with medium chain triglycerides

**Peptamen®** (Nestlé Clinical)

Liquid, protein 4 g, carbohydrate 12.7 g, fat 3.7 g, energy 420 kJ (100 kcal)/100 mL, with vitamins, minerals and trace elements. Lactose- and gluten-free. Flavours: unflavoured (can), vanilla (cup, see also *Flavour Sachets*). Net price 375-mL can = £3.88, 200-mL cup = £2.25; 500-mL (Dripac-Flex) = £4.57, 1-litre = £8.23.

For use as the sole source of nutrition or as a nutritional supplement prescribed on medical grounds for: short-bowel syndrome, intractable malabsorption, proven inflammatory bowel disease, bowel fistulas. Not to be prescribed for any child under 1 year; use with caution for children up to 5 years

Nestlé Nutrition Flavour Mix for use with *Peptamen Liquid* 200-mL cup and *Modulen IBD*. Flavours: banana, chocolate, coffee, lemon and lime, strawberry. Net price 60 g = £5.62

**Pepti®** (Cow & Gate)

Powder, protein equivalent 12.4 g, fat 28.5 g, carbohydrate 54.2 g, energy 2185 kJ (522 kcal)/100 g, with vitamins, minerals, and trace elements. Used as a solution in place of milk, net price 900 g = £15.98.

For the dietary management of established cows' milk protein intolerance with or without proven secondary lactose intolerance

**Pepti-Junior®** (Cow & Gate)

Powder, protein 15.3 g, fat 28.3 g, carbohydrate 55.1 g, energy 2140 kJ (507 kcal)/100 g with vitamins and minerals. Used as a 13.1% solution in place of milk. Net price 450 g = £8.80.

For disaccharide and/or whole protein intolerance or where amino acids and peptides are indicated in conjunction with medium chain triglycerides

**Peptisorb®** (Nutricia Clinical)

Liquid, protein 4 g, carbohydrate 17.6 g, fat 1.7 g, energy 425 kJ (100 kcal)/100 mL with vitamins, minerals and trace elements. Gluten-free. Net price 500-mL bottle = £4.86; 500-mL pack = £5.34; 1-litre pack = £9.65.

For use as the sole source of nutrition or as a nutritional supplement prescribed on medical grounds for: short-bowel syndrome, intractable malabsorption, proven inflammatory bowel disease, bowel fistulas. Not to be prescribed for any child under 1 year; use with caution for children up to 5 years

**Perative®** (Abbott)

Liquid, providing protein 6.67 g, carbohydrate 17.7 g, fat 3.7 g, energy 552 kJ (131 kcal)/100 mL, with vitamins and minerals. Gluten-free, unflavoured. Net price 500-mL ready-to-hang = £5.36, 1-litre ready-to-hang = £10.72.

For use as a nutritional supplement prescribed on medical grounds for: short-bowel syndrome, intractable malabsorption, pre-operative preparation of patients who are undernourished, proven inflammatory bowel disease, following total gastrectomy, bowel fistulas, disease-related malnutrition. Not to be prescribed for any child under 5 years

**Phenylalanine, Tyrosine and Methionine-Free Amino Acid Mix**

*see* Amino Acid Modules, XPTM Tyrosidon

**Phlexy-10® Exchange System** (SHS)

Bar, essential and non-essential amino acids except phenylalanine 8.33 g, carbohydrate 20.5 g, fat 4.5 g/42-g bar. Citrus fruit flavour. Net price per bar = £4.16

Capsules, essential and non-essential amino acids except phenylalanine 500 mg/capsule. Net price 200-cap pack = £29.09

Tablets, essential and non-essential amino acids except phenylalanine, 1 g tablet. Net price 75-tab pack = £18.85

Drink Mix, powder, containing essential and non-essential amino acids except phenylalanine 10 g, carbohydrate 8.8 g/20-g sachet. Apple and blackcurrant, citrus, or tropical flavour. Net price 20-g sachet = £2.92

All for phenylketonuria

**Phlexyvits®** (SHS)

Powder, vitamins, minerals and trace elements, net price 30 × 7-g sachets = £48.94.

For use as a vitamin and mineral component of restricted therapeutic diets in older children from the age of around 11 years and over and adults with phenylketonuria and similar amino acid abnormalities

**PK Aid 4®** (SHS)

Powder, containing essential and non-essential amino acids except phenylalanine. Net price 500 g = £97.78.

For phenylketonuria

**PK Foods** (Gluten Free Foods Ltd)

Bread, white (sliced), 550 g = £4.00. Crispbread, 75 g = £2.00. Pasta (spirals), 250 g = £2.00.

For phenylketonuria and similar amino acid abnormalities

Cookies (chocolate chip, orange, or cinnamon), 150 g = £3.75. Egg replacer, 350 g = £3.75. Flour mix, 750 g = £6.99. Jelly (orange or cherry flavour), 4 × 80 g = £5.76.

For phenylketonuria

**PKU 2®** (Milupa)

Granules, containing essential and non-essential amino acids except phenylalanine; with vitamins, minerals, trace elements, 7.1% sucrose. Flavour: vanilla. Net price 500 g = £44.75.

For phenylketonuria

**PKU 3®** (Milupa)

Granules, containing essential and non-essential amino acids except phenylalanine, vitamins, minerals, and trace elements, with 3.4% sucrose. Flavour: vanilla. Net price 500 g = £44.75.

For phenylketonuria, not recommended for child under 8 years

**PKU express®** (Vitaflo)

Powder, protein (containing essential and non-essential amino acids, phenylalanine-free) 72 g, carbohydrate 15.1 g, energy 1260 kJ (301.5 kcal)/100 g with vitamins, minerals, and trace elements. Lemon, orange, tropical or unflavoured, net price 30 x 25 g sachets = £140.50.

For phenylketonuria, not recommended for children under 8 years

**PKU express cooler®** (Vitaflo)
Liquid, protein equivalent 15 g, carbohydrate 7.8 g, energy 386 kJ (92 kcal)/130-mL pouch, with vitamins, minerals, and trace elements. Phenylalanine-free. Orange or purple option, net price 30 x 130 mL = £151.93.
For the dietary management of phenylketonuria, not recommended for children under 8 years

**PKU gel®** (Vitaflo)
Powder, protein (containing essential and non-essential amino acids, phenylalanine-free) 8.4 g, carbohydrate 8.6 g, fat 0.03 g, energy 285.5 kJ (68 kcal)/20 g with vitamins, minerals and trace elements. Orange or unflavoured, net price 30 × 20-g sachets = £80.85.
For use as part of the low-protein dietary management of phenylketonuria in children aged 1 to 10 years. Not recommended for children under 1 year

**Pleniday®** (TOL)
Gluten-free. Bread: loaf (sliced) net price 350 g = £1.80; country loaf (sliced), 500 g = £2.85; rustic loaf (par-baked baguette), 400 g = £2.09; petit pain, 2 × 150 g = £2.02. Pasta (penne), 250 g = £1.27; (rigate), 250 g = £1.50
For gluten-sensitive enteropathies including steatorrhoea due to gluten sensitivity, coeliac disease, and dermatitis herpetiformis

**Polial®** (Ultrapharm)
Biscuits. Gluten- and lactose-free. Net price 200-g pack = £2.85.
For gluten-sensitive enteropathies including steatorrhea due to gluten sensitivity, coeliac disease, and dermatitis herpetiformis

**Polycal®** (Nutricia Clinical)
Powder, glucose, maltose, and polysaccharides, providing 1630 kJ (384 kcal)/100 g. Net price 400 g = £3.24
Liquid, glucose polymers providing carbohydrate 61.9 g/100 mL. Low-electrolyte, protein-free. Flavours: orange and neutral. Net price 200 mL = £1.29
Both for disease-related malnutrition; malabsorption states or other conditions requiring fortification with a high or readily available carbohydrate supplement

**Polycose®** (Abbott)
Powder, glucose polymers, providing carbohydrate 94 g, energy 1598 kJ (376 kcal)/100 g. Net price 350-g can = £3.30.
For disease-related malnutrition; malabsorption states or other conditions requiring fortification with a high or readily available carbohydrate supplement

**Pregestimil®** (Mead Johnson)
Powder, protein 12.8%, carbohydrate 61.6%, fat 18.3% with vitamins and minerals. Gluten-, sucrose-, and lactose-free. Net price 400 g = £8.91.
For disaccharide and/or whole protein intolerance or where amino acids or peptides are indicated in conjunction with medium chain triglycerides

**Prejomin®** (Milupa)
Granules, protein 13.5 g, carbohydrate 57 g, fat 24 g, energy 2085 kJ (497 kcal)/100 g, with vitamins and minerals. Gluten-free. For preparation with water before use. Net price 400 g = £9.44.
For disaccharide and/or whole protein intolerance where additional medium chain triglyceride is not indicated

**PremCare®** (Heinz)
Powder, protein 1.85 g, carbohydrate 7.24 g, fat 3.96 g, energy 301 kJ (72 kcal) per 100 mL when reconstituted, with vitamins and minerals. Gluten-, sucrose-, and lactose-free. Net price 450 g = £3.29.
For catch-up growth in pre-term infants (less than 35 weeks at birth), and small-for-gestational-age infants, until 6 months postnatal age

**Pro-Cal®** (Vitaflo)
Powder, protein 13.5 g, carbohydrate 26.8 g, fat 56.2 g, energy 2788 kJ (667 kcal)/100 g, net price 25 x 15 g sachets = £11.73, 510 g = £10.86, 1.5 kg = £21.15, 12.5 kg = £140, 25 kg = £250.
For disease-related malnutrition, malabsorption states or other conditions requiring fortification with a fat/carbohydrate supplement. Not to be prescribed for any child under 1 year; use with caution for young children up to 5 years

Appendix 7

**Promin®** (Firstplay Dietary)
Low protein. Cous Cous, 500 g = £5.70. Pasta (alphabets, macaroni, shells, shortcut spaghetti, spirals); Pasta tricolour (alphabets, shells, spirals), net price 500 g = £5.70; Lasagne sheets, 200 g = £2.45. Pasta shells in tomato, pepper and herb sauce, 4 x 72-g sachets = £6.30; Pasta elbows in cheese and broccoli sauce, 4 x 66- g sachets = £6.20. Pasta meal, 500 g = £5.70. Pasta imitation rice, 500 g = £5.70.
For inherited metabolic disorders, renal or liver failure requiring a low-protein diet

**ProMod®** (Abbott)
Powder, protein 75 g, carbohydrate 7.5 g, fat 6.9 g/100 g. Gluten-free. Net price 275-g can = £8.82.
For biochemically proven hypoproteinaemia

**Prosobee®** (Mead Johnson)
Powder, protein 1.76 g, carbohydrate 6.8 g, fat 3.7 g, energy 285 kJ (68 kcal)/100 mL with vitamins and minerals. Gluten-, sucrose-, and lactose-free. Net price 400 g = £3.51.
For proven lactose and associated sucrose intolerance in preschool children, galactokinase deficiency, galactosaemia, and proven whole cow's milk sensitivity

**ProSure®** (Abbott)
Liquid, protein 6.65 g, carbohydrate 19.4 g, fat 2.56 g, fibre 0.97 g, energy 528 kJ (125 kcal)/100 mL with vitamins, minerals, and trace elements. Gluten-free, clinically lactose-free. Vanilla, orange, or banana flavour, net price, 240-mL Tetrapak® = £2.70; 500-mL ready-to-hang = £5.63 (vanilla only).
As a nutritional supplement for patients with cancer cachexia. Not to be prescribed for children under 1 year; use with caution in children under 4 years

**Protifar®** (Nutricia Clinical)
Powder, protein 88.5%. Low lactose, gluten- and sucrose-free. Net price 225 g = £6.58.
For biochemically proven hypoproteinaemia

**Provide Xtra®** (Fresenius Kabi)
Liquid, protein 3.75 g, carbohydrate 27.5 g, energy 525 kJ (125 kcal)/100 mL with vitamins, minerals and trace elements. Gluten-free. Apple, blackcurrant, carrot-apple, cherry, citrus cola, lemon & lime, melon, orange & pineapple, or tomato flavour. Net price 200-mL carton = £1.58.
As a nutritional supplement prescribed on medical grounds for: short-bowel syndrome, intractable malabsorption, pre-operative preparation of patients who are undernourished, proven inflammatory bowel disease, following total gastrectomy, dysphagia, bowel fistulas, disease-related malnutrition. Not to be prescribed for any child under 1 year; use with caution for children up to 5 years

**QuickCal®** (Vitaflo)
Powder, protein 4.6 g, carbohydrate 17 g, fat 77 g, energy 3260 kJ (780 kcal)/100 g, net price 25 × 13-g sachets = £10.55.
For disease-related malnutrition, malabsorption states or other conditions requiring fortification with a fat/carbohydrate supplement. Not to be prescribed for any child under 1 year; use with caution for young children up to 5 years

**Rectified Spirit**
Where the therapeutic qualities of alcohol are required rectified spirit (suitably flavoured and diluted) should be prescribed

**Renamil®** (KoRa)
Powder, protein 4.7 g, carbohydrate 70.2 g, fat 18.7 g, 1984 kJ (468 kcal)/100 g, with vitamins and minerals. Net price 1 kg = £25.40.
For chronic renal failure. Not suitable for infants and children under 1 year

**Renapro®** (KoRa)
Powder, whey protein providing protein 92 g, carbohydrate less than 300 mg, fat 500 mg, 1562 kJ (367 kcal)/100 g. Net price 20-g sachet = £2.32.
For dialysis and hypoproteinaemia. Not suitable for infants and children under 1 year

**Resource® Benefiber®** (Novartis Consumer Health)
Powder, soluble dietary fibre, carbohydrate 19 g, fibre 78 g, energy 323 kJ (76 kcal)/100 g with minerals. Gluten-free; low

lactose, net price 250 g pack = £8.76, 16 x 8-g sachets = £5.72.

As a nutritional supplement prescribed on medical grounds for: short-bowel syndrome, intractable malabsorption, pre-operative preparation of undernourished patients, proven inflammatory bowel disease, following total gastrectomy, bowel fistulas, disease-related malnutrition. Not to be prescribed for children under 5 years

**Resource® Energy Dessert** (Novartis Consumer Health)
Semi-solid, protein 4.8 g, carbohydrate 21.2 g, fat 6.24 g, energy 671 kJ (160 kcal)/100 g with vitamins, minerals, and trace elements. Gluten-free; low lactose. Flavours: caramel, chocolate, or vanilla, net price 125-g cup = £1.35.

For use as a nutritional supplement prescribed on medical grounds for: disease-related malnutrition, short-bowel syndrome, intractable malabsorption, proven inflammatory bowel disease, bowel fistulas, dysphagia, pre-operative preparation of undernourished patients, after total gastrectomy, continuous ambulatory peritoneal dialysis (CAPD), haemodialysis. Not to be prescribed for any child under 1 year; use with caution for children up to 5 years

**Resource® Fruit Flavour Drink** (Novartis Consumer Health)
Liquid, protein 4 g, carbohydrate 33.5 g, energy 638 kJ (150 kcal)/100 mL with vitamins, minerals, and trace elements. Fat- and gluten-free; low lactose. Flavours: apple, orange, or pineapple, net price 125-g carton = £1.49.

For use as a nutritional supplement prescribed on medical grounds for: disease-related malnutrition, short-bowel syndrome, intractable malabsorption, proven inflammatory bowel disease, bowel fistulas, dysphagia, pre-operative preparation of undernourished patients, after total gastrectomy. Not to be prescribed for any child under 3 years; use with caution for children up to 5 years

**Resource® Junior** (Novartis Consumer Health)
Liquid, protein 3 g, carbohydrate 20.6 g, fat 6.2 g, energy 631 kJ (150 kcal)/100 mL with vitamins, minerals, and trace elements. Gluten-free; clinically lactose-free. Flavours: chocolate, strawberry, or vanilla, net price 200-mL carton = £1.69.

For use as a sole source of nutrition or as a nutritional supplement prescribed on medical grounds for: disease-related malnutrition, short-bowel syndrome, intractable malabsorption, pre-operative preparation of undernourished patients, proven inflammatory bowel disease, following total gastrectomy, bowel fistulas, and dysphagia. Not to be prescribed for any child under 1 year

**Resource® Protein Extra** (Novartis Consumer Health)
Liquid, protein 9.4 g, carbohydrate 14 g, fat 3.5 g, energy 530 kJ (125 kcal)/100 mL with vitamins, minerals and trace elements. Gluten-free; low lactose. Flavours: apricot, chocolate, summer fruits, or vanilla. Net price 200-mL carton = £1.29.

For use as a nutritional supplement prescribed on medical grounds for: disease-related malnutrition, short-bowel syndrome, intractable malabsorption, proven inflammatory bowel disease, bowel fistulas, dysphagia, pre-operative preparation of undernourished patients, after total gastrectomy. Not to be prescribed for any child under 1 year; use with caution for children up to 5 years

**Resource® Shake** (Novartis Consumer Health)
Liquid, protein 5.1 g, carbohydrate 22.6 g, fat 7 g, energy 731 kJ (174 kcal)/100 mL with vitamins, minerals and trace elements. Gluten-free; low lactose. Flavours: banana, chocolate, lemon, strawberry, summer fruits, toffee, or vanilla. Net price 175-mL carton = £1.46.

For use as a nutritional supplement prescribed on medical grounds for: disease-related malnutrition, short-bowel syndrome, intractable malabsorption, proven inflammatory bowel disease, bowel fistulas, dysphagia, pre-operative preparation of undernourished patients, after total gastrectomy. Not to be prescribed for any child under 1 year; use with caution for children up to 5 years

**Resource® Thickened Drink** (Novartis Consumer Health)
Liquid, carbohydrate 22 g, energy: orange 383 kJ (89 kcal); apple 375 kJ (89 kcal)/100 mL. Syrup and custard consistencies. Gluten-free; clinically lactose free, net price 12 × 114-mL cups = £7.08.

For dysphagia. Not suitable for children under 1 year

**Resource® Thickened Squash** (Novartis Consumer Health)
Liquid, syrup consistency: carbohydrate 16.9 g, energy 287 kJ (68 kcal)/100 mL; custard consistency: carbohydrate 17.8 g, energy 303 kJ (71 kcal)/100 mL. Gluten-free; clinically lactose-free. Orange and lemon flavour, net price 1.89-litre bottle = £3.99.

For dysphagia. Not suitable for children under 1 year

**Resource® ThickenUp®** (Novartis Consumer Health)
Powder, modified maize starch. Gluten- and lactose-free, net price 227 g = £3.90; 75 × 6.4-g sachet = £15.75.

For thickening of foods in dysphagia. Not to be prescribed for children under 1 year

**Rite-Diet® Gluten-free** (Nutricia Dietary)
Gluten-free. White bread (sliced or unsliced), 400 g = £2.75. White loaf (part-baked), 400 g = £3.09. Fibre bread (sliced or unsliced), 400 g = £2.75. Fibre loaf (part-baked), 400 g = £3.09. White rolls, 4 = £2.72; (part-baked) long, 2 = £3.04. Fibre rolls, 4 = £2.72 (part-baked) long, 2 = £2.95. Flour mix (white or fibre), 500 g = £5.22.

For gluten-sensitive enteropathies including steatorrhoea due to gluten sensitivity, coeliac disease, and dermatitis herpetiformis

**Rite-Diet® Low-protein** (SHS)
Low protein. Baking mix. Net price 500 g = £5.78. Flour mix. 400 g = £4.95.

For inherited metabolic disorders, renal or liver failure requiring a low-protein diet

**Scandishake® Mix** (Nutricia Clinical)
Powder, protein 11.7 g, carbohydrate 66.8 g, fat 30.4 g, energy 2457 kJ (588 kcal)/unflavoured serving (serving = 1 sachet reconstituted with 240 mL whole milk; protein, carbohydrate and energy values vary with flavour). Flavours: banana, caramel, chocolate, strawberry, vanilla, and unflavoured. Net price 85-g sachet = £1.90.

For disease-related malnutrition; malabsorption states or other conditions requiring fortification with a fat/carbohydrate supplement

**Schar®** (Nutrition Point)
Gluten-free. Bread.(white, sliced), net price 2 x 200 g = £2.65. Baguette (french bread), 400 g = £2.90. Bread rolls, 150 g = £1.60. Lunch rolls, 150 g = £1.85. White bread buns, 200 g = £2.30. Bread mix, 1 kg = £4.75. Ertha brown bread, 2 x 250 g = £3.00. Cake mix, 500 g = £4.50. Flour mix, 1 kg = £4.75. Breadsticks (Grissini), 150 g = £1.95. Cracker toast, 150 g = £2.10. Crackers, 200 g = £2.35. Crispbread, 250 g = £3.50. Pasta (fusilli, penne), 500 g = £3.30; lasagne, 250 g = £3.30; macaroni pipette, 500 g = £3.30; spaghetti, 500 g = £3.30. Pizza bases, 300 g (2 × 150 g) = £4.75. Biscuits, 200 g = £2.00. Savoy biscuits, 200 g = £2.25.

For gluten-sensitive enteropathies including steatorrhoea due to gluten sensitivity, coeliac disease, and dermatitis herpetiformis

**SHS Modjul® Flavour System** (SHS)
Powder, blackcurrant, orange, and pineapple flavours. Net price 100 g = £8.32.

For use with any unflavoured products based on peptides or amino acids

**SMA High Energy®** (SMA Nutrition)
Liquid, protein 2 g, carbohydrate 9.8 g, fat 4.9 g, energy 382 kJ (91 kcal)/100mL, with vitamins and minerals. Net price 250 mL = £1.80.

For disease-related malnutrition, malabsorption, and growth failure

**SMA LF®** (SMA Nutrition)
Powder, protein 1.5 g, carbohydrate 7.2 g, fat 3.6 g, energy 282 kJ (67 kcal)/100 mL, with vitamins and minerals. Net price 430 g = £3.99.

For proven lactose intolerance

**SMA Staydown®** (SMA Nutrition)
Powder, protein 12.4 g, fat 27.9 g, carbohydrate 54.3 g, energy 2166 kJ (518 kcal)/100g, with vitamins, minerals, and trace elements. Net price 900 g = £5.74.

For significant reflux disease. Not to be used for more than 6 months or in conjunction with any other thickener or antacid product

**Sno-Pro®** (SHS)
Drink, protein 220 mg (phenylalanine 12.5 mg), carbohydrate 8 g, fat 3.8 g, energy 280 kJ (67 kcal)/100 mL. Net price 200 mL = 85p.
For phenylketonuria, chronic renal failure, and other inborn errors of metabolism

**Sunnyvale®** (Everfresh)
Mixed grain bread, gluten-free. Net price 400 g = £1.79.
For gluten-sensitive enteropathies including steatorrhoea due to gluten sensitivity, coeliac disease and dermatitis herpetiformis

**Suplena®** (Abbott)
Liquid, protein 3 g, carbohydrate 25.5 g, fat 9.6 g, energy 841 kJ (201 kcal)/100 mL. Flavour: vanilla. Net price 237-mL can = £2.28.
For patients with chronic or acute renal failure who are not undergoing dialysis; chronic or acute liver disease with fluid restriction; other conditions requiring a high-energy, low-protein, low-electrolyte, low-volume enteral feed

**Survimed OPD®** (Fresenius Kabi)
Liquid, protein 4.5 g, carbohydrate 15 g, fat 2.6 g, energy 420 kJ (100 kcal)/100 mL, with vitamins, minerals, and trace elements. Gluten-free, and low lactose. Net price 500-mL EasyBag® = £5.00.
As a nutritional supplement prescribed on medical grounds for: short-bowel syndrome, intractable malabsorption, pre-operative preparation of patients who are undernourished, proven inflammatory bowel disease, following total gastrectomy, dysphagia, bowel fistulas, disease-related malnutrition. Not to be prescribed for any child under 1 year; use with caution for children up to 5 years

**Tentrini®** (Nutricia Clinical)
Liquid, tube feed, protein 3.3 g, carbohydrate 12.3 g, fat 4.2 g, energy 420 kJ (100 kcal)/100 mL, with vitamins, minerals and trace elements. Gluten- and lactose-free. Unflavoured, net price 500-mL bottle or pack = £4.24
For short-bowel syndrome, intractable malabsorption, pre-operative preparation of undernourished patients, inflammatory bowel disease, total gastrectomy, dysphagia, bowel fistulas, disease-related malnutrition, and growth failure. For children between 21–45 kg body-weight

**Tentrini® Energy** (Nutricia Clinical)
Liquid, tube feed, protein 4.9 g, carbohydrate 18.5 g, fat 6.3 g, energy 630 kJ (150 kcal)/100 mL, with vitamins, minerals and trace elements. Gluten- and lactose-free. Unflavoured, net price 500-mL bottle or pack = £5.25
For indications see *Tentrini*

**Tentrini® Energy Multi Fibre** (Nutricia Clinical)
Liquid, tube feed, protein 4.9 g, carbohydrate 18.5 g, fat 6.3 g, fibre 1.12 g, energy 630 kJ (150 kcal)/100 mL, with vitamins, minerals and trace elements. Gluten- and lactose-free. Unflavoured, net price 500-mL bottle or pack = £5.79
For indications see *Tentrini Multi Fibre*

**Tentrini® Multi Fibre** (Nutricia Clinical)
Liquid, tube feed, protein 3.3 g, carbohydrate 12.3 g, fat 4.2 g, fibre 1.12 g, energy 420 kJ (100 kcal)/100 mL, with vitamins, minerals and trace elements. Gluten- and lactose-free. Unflavoured, net price 500-mL bottle or pack = £4.66
For short-bowel syndrome, intractable malabsorption, pre-operative preparation of undernourished patients, inflammatory bowel disease, total gastrectomy, dysphagia, disease-related malnutrition, and growth failure. Not to be prescribed for any child under 1 year; use with caution for children under 7 years or 21 kg

**Thick and Easy®** (Fresenius Kabi)
Powder. Modified maize starch, net price 225-g can = £3.99; 100 × 9-g sachets = £26.35; 4.54 kg = £70.53.
Dairy. Pre-thickened milk, net price 250 mL = £1.38
Thickened Juices, liquid, modified food starch. Flavours: apple, blackcurrant, cranberry, kiwi-strawberry, and orange, net price 118-mL pot = 52p; 1.42-litre bottle = £3.61.
For thickening of foods in dysphagia. Not to be prescribed for children under 1 year except in cases of failure to thrive

**Thixo-D®** (Sutherland)
Powder, modified maize starch, gluten-free. Net price 375-g tub = £5.79.
For thickening of foods in dysphagia. Not to be prescribed for children under 1 year except in cases of failure to thrive

**Tinkyada®** (General Dietary)
Gluten-free. Brown rice pasta (elbows, fettucini, fusilli, penne, shells, spaghetti, spirals). Net price 454 g = £3.00.
For gluten-sensitive enteropathies including steatorrhoea due to gluten-sensitivity, coeliac disease and dermatitis herpetiformis

**Tritamyl®** (Gluten Free Foods Ltd)
Gluten-free. Flour, net price 1 kg = £5.60. Brown bread mix, 1 kg = £5.60. White bread mix, 1 kg = £5.60.
For gluten-sensitive enteropathies including steatorrhoea due to gluten sensitivity, coeliac disease and dermatitis herpetiformis

**TYR Gel®** (Vitaflo)
Gel, essential and non-essential amino acids (except tyrosine and phenylalanine) 10.1 g, protein equivalent 8.4 g, carbohydrate 8.6 g, fat 0.03 g, energy 285.5 kJ (68 kcal)/20 g, with vitamins, minerals and trace elements. Unflavoured, net price 30 × 20-g sachets = £129.50
A tyrosine- and phenylalanine-free protein substitute for use in the dietary management of tyrosinaemia in children between 12 months and 10 years

**L-Tyrosine** (SHS)
Powder, net price 100 g = £12.53.
For use as a supplement in maternal phenylketonurics who have low plasma tyrosine concentrations

**Ultra®** (Ultrapharm)
Gluten-free. Baguette, net price 400 g = £2.46. Bread, net price 400 g = £2.46. High-fibre bread, 500 g = £3.26. Crackerbread, 100 g = £1.77. Pizza base, net price 400 g = £2.65.
For gluten-sensitive enteropathies including steatorrhoea due to gluten sensitivity, coeliac disease and dermatitis herpetiformis
Low protein. PKU bread, 400 g = £2.16. PKU flour, 500 g = £3.07. PKU biscuits, 200 g = £2.21. PKU cookies, 250 g = £2.31. PKU pizza base, 400 g = £2.21. PKU savoy biscuits, 150 g = £2.06.
For inherited metabolic disorders, renal or liver failure requiring a low-protein diet

**Valine Amino Acid Supplement** (Vitaflo)
Powder, valine 0.05 g, carbohydrate 4 g, fat nil, energy 64 kJ (15 kcal)/4 g, net price 30 × 4-g sachets = £37.50
For use in conjunction with a protein supplement for maple syrup urine disease in children over 1 year

**Valpiform®** (Gluten Free Foods Ltd)
Gluten-free. Bread mix, 2 × 500 g = £6.74; country loaf (sliced), 400 g = £3.74. Crac'form toast, 2 × 125 g = £3.52. Crisp rolls, 220 g = £3.60; Maxi baguettes, 2 × 200 g = £4.49. Pastry mix, 2 × 500 g = £6.74. Petites baguettes, 2 × 160 g = £2.99.
For gluten-sensitive enteropathies including steatorrhoea due to gluten sensitivity, coeliac disease and dermatitis herpetiformis

**Vita Bite®** (Vitaflo)
Bar, protein 30 mg (less than 2.5 mg phenylalanine), carbohydrate 15.35 g, fat 8.4 g, energy 572 kJ (137 kcal)/25 g. Chocolate flavoured, net price 25 g = 88p.
For inherited metabolic disorders, renal or liver failure requiring a low-protein diet. Not recommended for any child under 1 year

**Vitajoule®** (Vitaflo)
Powder, glucose polymers, providing carbohydrate 96 g, energy 1610 kJ (380 kcal)/100 g. Net price 500 g = £3.24, 2.5 kg = £16.15, 25 kg = £99.00.
For disease-related malnutrition; malabsorption states or other conditions requiring fortification with a high or readily available carbohydrate supplement

**Vitamins and Minerals**
Only for use in the management of actual or potential vitamin or mineral deficiency; not to be prescribed as dietary supplements or 'pick-me-ups'

**Vitapro®** (Vitaflo)
Powder, whole milk proteins, containing all essential amino acids, 75%. Net price 250 g = £6.49, 2 kg = £50.90.
For biochemically proven hypoproteinaemia

**Vitaquick®** (Vitaflo)
Powder. Modified maize starch. Net price 300 g = £5.85; 2 kg = £30.72; 6 kg = £78.60.
For thickening of foods in dysphagia. Not to be prescribed for children under 1 year except in cases of failure to thrive

**Vitasavoury®** (Vitaflo)
Powder, protein 12 g, carbohydrate 24 g, fat 54 g, energy 2610 kJ (630 kcal)/100 g, net price 10 x 50-g sachets = £14.63, 24 × 33-g ready cups = £24.28. Flavours: chicken, leek and potato, mushroom, vegetable.
As a nutritional supplement for disease-related malnutrition, malabsorption states or other conditions requiring fortification with a fat/carbohydrate supplement. Not to be prescribed for any child under 1 year; use with caution for young children up to 5 years

**Wysoy®** (Wyeth)
Powder, carbohydrate 6.9%, fat 3.6%, and protein 2.1% with vitamins and minerals when reconstituted. Net price 430 g = £3.98; 860 g = £7.58.
For proven lactose and associated sucrose intolerance in pre-school children, galactokinase deficiency, galactosaemia and proven whole cow's milk sensitivity

**XLEU Analog** (SHS)
Powder, essential and non-essential amino acids 15.5% except leucine, with carbohydrate, fat, vitamins, minerals, and trace elements. Net price 400 g = £24.62.
For isovaleric acidaemia
*Ingredients: include* arachis oil (peanut oil)
**Note** Analog products are generally intended for use in children up to 1 year

**XLEU Faladon** (SHS)
Powder, essential and non-essential amino acids 93%, except leucine. Net price 200 g = £50.87.
For isovaleric acidaemia

[1]**XLEU Maxamaid** (SHS)
Powder, essential and non-essential amino acids 28.6% except leucine, with carbohydrate, fat less than 0.5%, vitamins, minerals, and trace elements. Net price 500 g = £67.15.
For isovaleric acidaemia

**XLYS Analog** (SHS)
Powder, essential and non-essential amino acids 15.5% except lysine, with carbohydrate, fat, vitamins, minerals, and trace elements. Net price 400 g = £24.62.
For hyperlysinaemia
**Note** Analog products are generally intended for use in children up to 1 year

**XLYS, Low TRY, Analog** (SHS)
Powder, essential and non-essential amino acids 15.5% except lysine, and low tryptophan, with carbohydrate, fat, vitamins, minerals, and trace elements. Net price 400 g = £24.62.
For type 1 glutaric aciduria
**Note** Analog products are generally intended for use in children up to 1 year

[1]**XLYS, Low TRY, Maxamaid** (SHS)
Powder, essential and non-essential amino acids 30% except lysine, with carbohydrate, fat less than 0.5%, vitamins, minerals, and trace elements. Net price 500 g = £67.15.
For type 1 glutaric aciduria

[1]**XLYS Maxamaid** (SHS)
Powder, essential and non-essential amino acids 30% except lysine, with carbohydrate, fat less than 0.5%, vitamins, minerals, and trace elements. Net price 500 g = £67.15.
For hyperlysinaemia

1. Maxamaid products are generally intended for use in children aged 1 to 8 years, see also Flavour Sachets, for use with unflavoured amino acid and peptide products from SHS
2. Maxamum products are generally intended for use in children aged over 8 years

**XMET Analog** (SHS)
Powder, essential and non-essential amino acids 15.5% except methionine, with carbohydrate, fat, vitamins, minerals, and trace elements. Net price 400 g = £24.62.
For hypermethioninaemia; homocystinuria
**Note** Analog products are generally intended for use in children up to 1 year

**XMET Homidon** (SHS)
Powder, essential and non-essential amino acids 93%, except methionine. Net price 200 g = £49.59.
For homocystinuria or hypermethioninaemia

[1]**XMET Maxamaid** (SHS)
Powder, essential and non-essential amino acids 30% except methionine, with carbohydrate, fat less than 0.5%, vitamins, minerals, and trace elements. Net price 500 g = £67.15
For hypermethioninaemia, homocystinuria

[2]**XMET Maxamum®** (SHS)
Powder, essential and non-essential amino acids 47% except methionine, with carbohydrate, fat less than 0.5%, vitamins, minerals, and trace elements. Unflavoured, see also Flavour Sachets. Net price 500 g = £107.65.
For hypermethioninaemia, homocystinuria

**XMTVI Analog** (SHS)
Powder, essential and non-essential amino acids 15.5% except methionine, threonine, valine and low isoleucine, with carbohydrate, fat, vitamins, minerals, and trace elements. Net price 400 g = £24.62.
For methylmalonic acidaemia or propionic acidaemia
**Note** Analog products are generally intended for use in children up to 1 year

**XMTVI Asadon** (SHS)
Powder, essential and non-essential amino acids 93%, except methionine, threonine, and valine, with trace amounts of isoleucine. Net price 200 g = £50.87.
For methylmalonic acidaemia or propionic acidaemia

[1]**XMTVI Maxamaid** (SHS)
Powder, essential and non-essential amino acids 30% except methionine, threonine, valine and low isoleucine, with carbohydrate, fat less than 0.5%, vitamins, minerals, and trace elements. Net price 500 g = £67.15.
For methylmalonic acidaemia or propionic acidaemia

[2]**XMTVI Maxamum®** (SHS)
Powder, essential and non-essential amino acids 47% except methionine, threonine, valine, and low isoleucine, with carbohydrate, fat less than 0.5%, vitamins, minerals, and trace elements. Unflavoured, see also Flavour Sachets. Net price 500 g = £107.65.
For methylmalonic acidaemia or propionic acidaemia

**XP Analog** (SHS)
Powder, essential and non-essential amino acids 15.5% except phenylalanine, with carbohydrate, fat, vitamins, minerals, and trace elements. Net price 400 g = £19.67.
For phenylketonuria
**Note** Analog products are generally intended for use in children up to 1 year

**XP LCP Analog** (SHS)
Powder, essential and non-essential amino acids except phenylalanine 15.5%, with carbohydrate, fat, vitamins, minerals and trace elements. Gluten- and lactose-free. Net price 400 g = £22.38.
For phenylketonuria in infants and children under 2 years of age

[1]**XP Maxamaid** (SHS)
Powder, essential and non-essential amino acids 30% except phenylalanine, with carbohydrate, vitamins, minerals, and trace elements. Net price powder (unflavoured), 500 g = £39.73; (orange-flavoured), 500 g = £39.73.
For phenylketonuria. Not to be prescribed for children under 2 years

[1]**XP Maxamaid Concentrate** (SHS)

Powder, essential and non-essential amino acids 65% except phenylalanine, with carbohydrate, fat less than 0.5%, vitamins, minerals, and trace elements. Unflavoured. Net price 500 g = £101.72.

For phenylketonuria. Not to be prescribed for children under 2 years

**Note** See also Flavour Sachets, for use with unflavoured amino acid and peptide products from SHS

[2]**XP Maxamum®** (SHS)

Powder, essential and non-essential amino acids 47% except phenylalanine, with carbohydrates, vitamins, minerals, and trace elements. Flavours: orange, unflavoured, see also Flavour Sachets. Net price 30 × 50-g sachets = £190.17, 500 g = £61.42.

For phenylketonuria. Not to be prescribed for children under 8 years

**XPHEN TYR Analog** (SHS)

Powder, essential and non-essential amino acids 15.5% except phenylalanine and tyrosine, with carbohydrate, fat, vitamins, minerals and trace elements. Net price 400 g = £24.62.

For tyrosinaemia

**Note** Analog products are generally intended for use in children up to 1 year

[1]**XPHEN TYR Maxamaid** (SHS)

Powder, essential and non-essential amino acids 30% except phenylalanine and tyrosine, with carbohydrate, fat less than 0.5%, vitamins, minerals, and trace elements. Unflavoured. Net price 500 g = £67.15.

For tyrosinaemia

**XPHEN TYR Tyrosidon** (SHS)

Powder, essential and non-essential amino acids 93%, except phenylalanine and tyrosine. Net price 500 g = £127.20

For tyrosinaemia where plasma methionine concentrations are normal

**XPTM Analog** (SHS)

Powder, essential and non-essential amino acids 15.5% except phenylalanine, tyrosine and methionine, with carbohydrate, fat, vitamins, minerals and trace elements. Net price 400 g = £24.62.

For tyrosinaemia

**Note** Analog products are generally intended for use in children up to 1 year

**XPTM Tyrosidon** (SHS)

Powder, essential and non-essential amino acids 93%, except methionine, phenylalanine, and tyrosine. Net price 500 g = £127.20.

For tyrosinaemia type I where plasma concentrations are above normal

## Conditions for which foods may be prescribed on FP10, GP10 (Scotland), or when available, WP10 (Wales)

**Note** This is a list of clinical conditions for which the ACBS has approved food products. It is essential to check the list of products (above) for availability.

**Amino acid metabolic disorders and similar protein disorders**

See histidinaemia; homocystinuria; maple syrup urine disease; phenylketonuria; low-protein products; synthetic diets; tyrosinaemia.

**Bowel fistulas**

*Complete foods*: Clinutren 1.5 Fibre and Clinutren ISO; Elemental 028 and 028 Extra; Emsogen; Enrich and Enrich Plus; Ensure; Ensure Powder; Foodlink Complete; Frebini, Frebini Energy, Frebini Energy Fibre; Fresubin Energy, Fresubin Original Liquid and Sip feeds, Fresubin 1000, and Fresubin 1200 Complete; Isosource Energy, Standard; Jevity; Modulen IBD; Novasource Forte and GI Control; Nutrini, Nutrini Energy and Fibre; Nutrison Standard and Multifibre; Osmolite Liquid and Plus; Paediasure Liquid and Plus; Peptamen; Peptisorb; Clinutren Junior; Tentrini and Energy.

*Nutritional supplements*: Clinutren Dessert, Fruit, and 1.5; Enlive Plus; Ensure Plus; Formance; Forticreme; Fortifresh; Fortijuce; Fortimel; Fortisip Bottle; Fortisip Multi Fibre, Protein; Fresubin HP Energy; Nutrison Energy, and MCT; Perative; Provide Xtra; Resource Benefiber, Energy, Dessert, Protein Extra, Shake; Survimed OPD.

**Calcium intolerance**

Locasol.

**Carbohydrate malabsorption**

See also synthetic diets; malabsorption states.

(a) *Disaccharide intolerance*: Caloreen; Duocal Super Soluble and Duocal Liquid; Maxijul LE, Liquid, Super Soluble; Nutramigen 1 and 2; Nutrison Soya; Pepdite; Pepti-Junior; Polycal liquid and powder; Polycose powder; Prejomin; Pro-Cal; QuickCal; Vitajoule; Vitasavoury. See also lactose intolerance; lactose with associated sucrose intolerance.

(b) *Isomaltose intolerance*: Glucose (dextrose).

(c) *Glucose and galactose intolerance*: Comminuted Chicken Meat (Cow & Gate); Fructose; Galactomin 19 (fructose formula).

(d) *Lactose intolerance*: Colief; Comminuted Chicken Meat (SHS); Enfamil Lactofree; Farley's Soya Formula; Galactomin 17; InfaSoy; Isomil powder; Nutramigen 1; Nutrison Soya; Pepdite; Prejomin; Prosobee; SMA LF; Wysoy.

(e) *Lactose with associated sucrose intolerance*: Comminuted Chicken Meat (SHS); Farley's Soya Formula; Galactomin 17; InfaSoy; Nutramigen 1; Nutrison Soya; Pepti-Junior; Prejomin; Prosobee; Wysoy.

(f) *Sucrose intolerance*: Glucose (dextrose) and see also synthetic diets; malabsorption states; lactose with associated sucrose intolerance.

**Note** Lactose or sucrose intolerance is defined as a condition of intolerance to an intake of the relevant disaccharide confirmed by demonstrated clinical benefit of the effectiveness of the disaccharide-free diet, and presence of reducing substances and/or excessive acid in the stools, a low concentration of the corresponding disaccharidase enzyme on intestinal biopsy, or by breath tests or lactose tolerance tests

**Carnitine palmitoyl transferase deficiency (CPTD)**

Monogen

**Coeliac disease**

See gluten-sensitive enteropathies.

**Continuous Ambulatory Peritoneal Dialysis (CAPD)**

See dialysis.

**Cystic fibrosis**

See malabsorption states.

**Dermatitis Herpetiformis**

See gluten-sensitive enteropathies.

**Dialysis**

Nutritional supplements for haemodialysis or continuous ambulatory peritoneal dialysis (CAPD) patients: Clinutren Dessert; Enrich Plus; Ensure Plus; Formance; Forticreme; Fresubin HP Energy, and Fresubin Protein Energy Drink; Kindergen; Nepro; Renapro; Resource Energy Dessert; Suplena.

1. Maxamaid products are generally intended for use in children aged 1 to 8 years, see also Flavour Sachets, for use with unflavoured amino acid and peptide products from SHS
2. Maxamum products are generally intended for use in children aged over 8 years

**Disaccharide intolerance**
See carbohydrate malabsorption.

**Dysphagia**
*Complete foods*: Clinutren 1.5 Fibre and Clinutren ISO; Enfamil AR; Enrich and Enrich Plus; Ensure; Ensure Powder; Foodlink Complete; Frebini Original, Energy Fibre and Energy; Fresubin Energy, Fresubin Energy Fibre (sip and tube feed), Fresubin Original Fibre, Fresubin Original Liquid and Sip Feeds, Fresubin Protein Energy Drink; Fresubin 1000, and Fresubin 1200 Complete; Isosource Energy, Fibre Junior and Standard; Jevity; Novasource GI Control and Forte; Nutrini Fibre and Standard; Nutrison Multi Fibre, Energy Multi Fibre, Soya, Standard and 1200 Complete Multifibre; Osmolite Liquid and Plus; Paediasure Liquid, Liquid with fibre and Plus; SMA Staydown; Clinutren Junior; Tentrini, Energy, Energy Multi Fibre, Multi Fibre.
*Nutritional supplements*: Clinutren Dessert, Fruit, and 1.5; Clinutren Thickened Drinks, Enlive Plus; Ensure Plus and Yoghurt style; Formance; Forticreme; Fortifresh; Fortijuce; Fortimel; Fortisip Bottle, Multi Fibre, Protein; Fresubin HP Energy, and Fresubin Protein Energy Drink; Nutrison Energy and MCT; Provide Xtra; Resource Energy Dessert, Resource Benefiber, Protein Extra, ThickenUp, Thickened Squash, and Shake; Survimed OPD.
*Thickeners*: Clinutren Thickener, Nutilis; Thick & Easy powder and thickened juices; Thixo-D; Vitaquick.
**Note** Dysphagia is defined as that associated with intrinsic disease of the oesophagus, e.g. oesophagitis; neuromuscular disorders, e.g. multiple sclerosis and motor neurone disease; major surgery and/or radiotherapy for cancer of the upper digestive tract; protracted severe inflammatory disease of the upper digestive tract, e.g. Stevens-Johnson syndrome and epidermolysis bullosa

**Epilepsy (ketogenic diet in)**
Alembicol D; Liquigen; Medium-Chain Triglyceride Oil (MCT).

**Flavouring**
For use with any unflavoured SHS product based on peptides or amino acids: SHS Flavour Modjul; Flavour Sachets

**Galactokinase deficiency and galactosaemia**
Farley's Soya Formula; Galactomin 17; InfaSoy; Isomil powder; Prosobee; Wysoy

**Gastrectomy (total)**
*Complete foods*: Clinutren 1.5 Fibre and Clinutren ISO; Enrich; Enrich Plus; Ensure; Ensure Powder; Foodlink Complete; Frebini Original; Fresubin Energy, Fresubin Energy Fibre (sip and tube feed), Fresubin Original Fibre, Fresubin Original Liquid and Sip Feeds, Fresubin 1000, and Fresubin 1200 Complete; Isosource Energy, Fibre and Standard; Jevity and Plus; Novasource GI Control, and Forte; Nutrison Multi Fibre, Energy Multi Fibre, Soya and Standard; Osmolite Liquid and Plus; Clinutren Junior; Tentrini, Energy, Energy Multi Fibre, Multi Fibre.
*Nutritional supplements*: Clinutren Dessert, Fruit, and 1.5; Enlive Plus; Ensure Plus; Formance; Fortijuce; Fortimel; Fortipudding; Fortisip Bottle, Multi Fibre, Protein; Fresubin HP Energy, and Fresubin Protein Energy Drink; Nutrison Energy and MCT; Perative; Provide Xtra; Resource Benefiber, Resource Energy Dessert, Protein Extra, and Shake; Survimed OPD.

**Glucose/galactose intolerance**
See carbohydrate malabsorption.

**Glutaric aciduria**
XLYS, Low Try Analog; XLYS, Low Try Maxamaid

**Gluten-sensitive enteropathies**
Aproten flour; Arnott gluten-free rice cookies; Baker's Delight wheat-, gluten- and dairy-free bread; Barkat gluten-free bread mix, brown or white rice bread, Brown or white rice pizza crust; Bi-Aglut biscuits, crackers, cracker toast, lasagne, pasta (fusilli, macaroni, penne, spaghetti); DS Dietary Specials Mixes: brown or white bread, white cake, white or fibre; Ener-G brown and white rice bread, gluten-free tapioca bread, rice loaf, Seattle brown loaf, cookies (vanilla), xanthum gum, gluten-free rice pasta (cannelloni, lasagna, macaroni, shells, small shells, spaghetti, tagliatelli, vermicelli); brown rice pasta (lasagna, macaroni, spaghetti); Gadsby's white bread (sliced or unsliced), white bread flour, white bread rolls; Glutafin bread, multigrain white loaf (sliced or unsliced, white or part-baked), rolls (white or part-baked), fibre bread, mixes (white, multigrain white, fibre, multigrain fibre), biscuits (digestive, savoury, sweet (without chocolate or sultanas), tea), crackers, high fibre crackers and pasta (lasagne, penne, spirals, spaghetti), pizza bases; Glutano gluten-free tea biscuits, crackers, crispbread, flour mix, pastas (animal shapes, macaroni, spaghetti, spirals, tagliatelle), wholemeal bread (sliced or par-baked), baguette or rolls (par-baked), white sliced bread (par-baked); Juvela gluten-free harvest mix, loaf and high-fibre loaf (sliced and unsliced), bread rolls, fibre bread rolls, part-baked rolls with or without fibre, crispbread, mix and fibre mix; digestive biscuits, savoury biscuits and tea biscuits, pizza bases; Lifestyle gluten-free bread rolls, brown and white bread, high-fibre bread or rolls; Pleniday bread and pastas; Polial gluten-free biscuits; Rite-Diet gluten-free fibre rolls, high-fibre bread (sliced and unsliced), white bread (sliced and unsliced), white rolls, part-baked fibre loaf and long rolls; Schar gluten-free bread, bread mix, ertha brown bread, bread rolls and buns, crackers, cake mix, cracker toast, crispbread, flour mix, french bread (baguette), pasta (fusilli, lasagne, macaroni pipette penne, rigati, rings, shells, spaghetti), pizza base, biscuits, savoy biscuits, white bread buns, wholemeal flour mix; Sunnyvale gluten-free bread; Tinkyada gluten-free brown rice pasta (elbows, fettucini, fusilli, penne, shells, spaghetti, spirals); Tritamyl flour, brown bread mix and white bread mix; Ultra gluten-free baguette, bread, bread rolls, high-fibre bread, cracker-bread, pizza base; Valpiform bread mix, country loaf, pastry mix, petites baguettes

**Gluten-sensitive enteropathies with coexisting established wheat sensitivity**
Ener-G pizza bases, Seattle brown rolls (round or long), Six flour loaf; Glutafin Crisp Bread, Crisp Roll

**Glycogen storage disease**
Caloreen; Corn Flour or Corn Starch; Glucose (dextrose); Maxijul LE, Liquid (orange flavour), and Super Soluble; Polycal; Polycal Liquid and powder; Polycose; Pro-Cal; QuickCal; Vitajoule; Vitasavoury.

**Growth Failure (disease related)**
Enrich Plus ready-to-hang; Fortini, Fortini Multifibre; Frebini Original; Infatrini; Nutrini Extra, Multifibre and Standard; Paediasure Liquid and Liquid with fibre and Plus; SMA High Energy; Clinutren Junior; Survimed OPD; Tentrini, Energy, Energy Multi Fibre, Multi Fibre.

**Haemodialysis**
See dialysis.

**Histidinaemia**
See low-protein products; synthetic diets.

**Homocystinuria**
Analog XMet; Methionine-Free Amino Acid Mix; Vitaflo Flavour Pac; HCU Express; HCU gel; XMet Homidon; XMet Maxamaid; XMet Maxamum, and see also low-protein products; synthetic diets.

**Hyperlipoproteinaemia type 1**
Alembicol D; Liquigen; Medium Chain Triglyceride Oil.

**Hyperlysinaemia**
Analog XLys; XLys Maxamaid

**Hypermethioninaemia**
XMET Analog; Methionine-Free Amino Acid Mix; XMET Homidon; XMET Maxamaid; XMET Maxamum.

**Hypoglycaemia**
Corn Flour or Corn Starch; and see also glycogen storage disease.

**Hypoproteinaemia**
Casilan 90; Dialamine; Maxipro Super Soluble; Maxisorb; ProMod; Protifar; Renapro; Vitapro.

**Inflammatory Bowel Disease**
*Complete foods*: Clinutren 1.5 Fibre, and Clinutren ISO; Elemental 028; Elemental 028 Extra; Emsogen; Enrich; Ensure; Ensure Powder; Foodlink Complete; Frebini Original; Fresubin Energy, Fresubin Energy Fibre (sip and tube feed) Fresubin Original Liquid and Sip Feeds, Fresubin 1000, and Fresubin 1200 Complete; Isosource Energy, Fibre and Standard; Jevity and Plus; Novasource GI Control, and Forte; Nutini Extra, and Fibre; Nutrison Multi Fibre, Energy Multi Fibre, Soya and Standard; Osmolite Liquid and Plus; Peptamen, Clinutren Junior; Tentrini, Energy, Energy Multi Fibre, Multi Fibre.
*Nutritional supplements*: Clinutren Dessert, Fruit and 1.5; Enlive Plus; Ensure Plus; Formance; Forticreme; Fortifresh; Fortijuce; Fortimel; Fortipudding; Fortisip Bottle, Multi Fibre, Protein; Fresubin HP Energy, and Fresubin Protein Energy Drink; Nutrison Energy, MCT and Pepti Powder; Perative; Provide Xtra; Resource Benefiber, Dessert Energy, Protein Extra, and Shake; Survimed OPD.

**Intestinal lymphangiectasia**
See malabsorption states.

**Intestinal surgery**
See malabsorption states

**Isomaltose intolerance**
See carbohydrate malabsorption.

**Isovaleric acidaemia**
XLEU Analog; XLEU Faladon; XLEU Maxamaid.

**Lactose intolerance**
See carbohydrate malabsorption.

**Lipoprotein lipase deficiency (primary and secondary)**
Monogen

**Liver failure**
Alembicol D; Aminex low-protein biscuits, cookies and rusks; Aproten products (anellini, biscuits, bread mix, cake mix, crispbread, ditalini, rigatini, spaghetti, tagliatelle); Ener-G low protein egg replacer, rice bread; Generaid; Generaid Plus; Juvela low-protein (chocolate chip, orange, and cinnamon flavour) cookies, loaf (sliced and unsliced), bread rolls, mix; Liquigen; Loprofin egg replacer, egg white replacer; Loprofin low-protein bread (sliced and unsliced), bread rolls (part-baked), white rolls, fibre bread (sliced and unsliced), mix, breakfast cereal, pasta (macaroni, penne, spaghetti long, pasta spirals, vermicelli), sweet biscuits, chocolate cream-filled biscuits, crackers, cookies (chocolate chip, cinnamon), wafers (orange, chocolate, vanilla); Medium Chain Triglyceride Oil; Nepro; Promin low-protein pasta (alphabets, macaroni, shells, shortcut spaghetti, spirals), pasta tricolour (alphabets, shells, spirals), pasta meal, Rite-Diet low-protein baking mix, flour mix; Suplena; Ultra low-protein, canned bread (brown and white); Ultra PKU biscuits, bread, cookies, flour, pizza base and savoy biscuits; Valpiform cookies with chocolate nuggets, shortbread biscuits; Vita-Bite.

**Long chain acyl-CoA dehydrogenase deficiency (LCAD)**
Monogen

**Low-protein products**
Aminex low-protein biscuits, cookies and rusks; Aproten products (anellini, biscuits, bread mix, cake mix, crispbread, ditalini, rigatini, spaghetti, tagliatelle); Ener-G low protein egg replacer, rice bread; Juvela low-protein (chocolate chip, orange, and cinnamon flavour) cookies, loaf (sliced and unsliced), mix, bread rolls; Loprofin egg replacer, egg white replacer; Loprofin low-protein bread (sliced and unsliced), mix, rolls (part-baked), fibre bread (sliced or unsliced), herb crackers, pasta (macaroni, spaghetti long, pasta spirals, vermicelli); sweet biscuits, chocolate cream-filled biscuits, crackers, cookies (chocolate chip, cinnamon), wafers (orange, chocolate, vanilla), breakfast cereal; PK Foods bread (sliced), crispbread, pasta (spirals); PKU gel; Promin low-protein pasta (alphabets, macaroni, shells, shortcut spaghetti, spirals), pasta tricolour (alphabets, shells, spirals), pasta meal, pasta imitation rice; Rite-Diet low-protein flour mix, baking mix; Ultra low-protein, canned bread (brown and white); Ultra PKU biscuits, bread, cookies, flour, pizza base and savoy biscuits; Valpiform cookies with chocolate nuggets, shortbread biscuits; Vita-Bite.

**Malabsorption states**
(see also gluten-sensitive enteropathies; liver failure; carbohydrate malabsorption; intestinal lymphangiectasia; milk intolerance and synthetic diets); includes short-bowel syndrome. It should be noted that hyperosmolar feeds should be **avoided** if the short bowel ends in a stoma or the short bowel is anastomosed to the colon.

(a) *Protein sources*: Caprilon; Comminuted Chicken Meat (SHS); Maxipro Super Soluble; Maxisorb; MCT Pepdite; Neocate; Neocate Advance; Pepdite.

(b) *Fat sources*: Alembicol D; Calogen; Caprilon; Liquigen; MCT Pepdite; Medium Chain Triglyceride Oil; Pro-Cal; QuickCal; Vitasavoury.

(c) *Carbohydrate*: Caloreen; Maxijul LE, Liquid, and Super Soluble; Novasource GI Control, and Forte; Nutini Extra and Multifibre, Polycal Liquid and Powder; Polycose; Pro-Cal; QuickCal; Resource Benefiber; Vitajoule; Vitasavoury.

(d) *Fat/carbohydrate sources*: Calshake; Duobar; Duocal Liquid, MCT and Super Soluble; Scandishake; SPS Energy Bar.

(e) *Complete Feeds*: For use as the sole source of nutrition or as a nutritional supplement prescribed on medical grounds: Caprilon; Clinutren 1.5 Fibre and Clinutren ISO; Elemental 028; Elemental 028 Extra; Emsogen; Enrich; Ensure; Ensure Powder; Foodlink Complete; Frebini Original; Fresubin Energy, Fresubin Energy Fibre (sip and tube feed), Fresubin Original Liquid and Sip Feeds, Fresubin 1000, and Fresubin 1200 Complete; Isosource Energy, Fibre and Standard; Jevity, and Plus; MCT Pepdite; Novasource GI Control, and Forte; Nutrini, Extra and Fibre; Nutrison Multi Fibre, Energy Multi Fibre, Soya, Standard, 1200 Complete Multi Fibre; Osmolite Liquid and Plus; Paediasure Liquid, Liquid with fibre and Plus; Pepdite; Peptamen; Pepti-Junior; SMA High Energy; Clinutren Junior; Tentrini, Energy, Energy Multi Fibre, Multi Fibre.

(f) *Nutritional supplements*: Nutritional supplements prescribed on medical grounds: Clinutren Dessert, Fruit, Junior, and 1.5; Enlive Plus; Enrich Plus; Ensure Bar and Plus; Formance; Forticreme; Fortifresh; Fortijuce; Fortimel; Fortisip Bottle, Multi Fibre, Protein; Fresubin HP Energy, and Fresubin Protein Energy Drink; Nutrison Energy, MCT, and Pepti Powder; Perative; Provide Xtra; Resource Shake and Benefiber; Survimed OPD.

(g) *Minerals*: Aminogran Mineral Mixture; Metabolic Mineral Mixture.

(h) *Vitamins*: As appropriate, and see synthetic diets.

(i) *Vitamins and Minerals*: Energivit; Paediatric Seravit

**Malnutrition (disease-related)**

*Complete foods*: Calogen; Caloreen; Calshake; Duobar; Duocal Liquid, MCT, and Super Soluble; Enrich and Plus; Ensure; Ensure Powder; Foodlink Compete; Frebini Original; Fresubin Energy, Fresubin Energy Fibre (sip and tube feed), Fresubin Original Liquid and Sip Feeds, Fresubin 1000, and Fresubin 1200 Complete; Infatrini; Isosource Energy, Fibre and Standard; Jevity and Plus; Maxijul LE, Liquid and Super Soluble; Novasource GI Control and Forte; Nutrini Extra, Fibre and Standard; Nutrison Multi Fibre, Energy Multi Fibre, Soya, Standard, 1200 Complete Multi Fibre; Osmolite Liquid and Plus; Paediasure Liquid, Liquid with fibre and Plus; Polycal Liquid and Powder; Polycose; Scandishake; SMA High Energy; Tentrini, Energy, Energy Multi Fibre, Multi Fibre; Vitajoule.

*Nutritional supplements*: Clinutren Dessert, Fruit, ISO and 1.5; Enlive Plus; Ensure Plus; Formance; Forticreme; Fortifresh; Fortijuce; Fortimel; Fortini, Fortini Multifibre, Fortipudding; Fortisip Bottle, Multi Fibre, Protein; Fresubin HP Energy; Nutrison Energy and MCT; Perative; ProSure, Provide Xtra; Pro-Cal; Quickcal; Resource Benefiber, Dessert Energy, Protein Xtra, and Shake; Clinutren Junior; Survimed OPD; Vitasavoury.

**Maple syrup urine disease**

Mapleflex; MSUD Analog; MSUD Maxamaid; MSUD Maxamum; MSUD Aid III, and see also low-protein products; synthetic diets.

**Methylmalonic acidaemia**

XMTVI Analog; XMTVI Asadon; XMTVI Maxamaid; XMTVI Maxamum.

**Milk protein sensitivity**

Comminuted Chicken Meat (SHS); Farley's Soya Formula; InfaSoy; Isomil powder; Nutramigen; Prosobee; Wysoy, and see also synthetic diets.

**Nutritional support for adults**

(a) **Nutritionally complete feeds.** For use as the sole source of nutrition or as a necessary nutritional supplement prescribed on medical grounds:

(i) Gluten-Free: Foodlink Complete; Fortifresh; Fresubin Liquid and Sip Feeds; Nutrison Multi Fibre, Energy Multi Fibre and Standard; Clinutren Junior.

(ii) Lactose- and Gluten-Free: Enrich; Ensure, Ensure Powder; Fresubin Original Fibre; Nutrison Soya; Osmolite Liquid and Plus.

(iii) Containing fibre: Enrich; Fresubin Energy Fibre (tube and sip feed), Fresubin Original Fibre; Isosource Fibre; Jevity; Novasource GI Control, and Forte; Nutrini Extra, and Fibre; Nutrison Multi Fibre, Energy Multi Fibre; Paediasure with Fibre.

(iv) Elemental Feeds: Elemental 028; Elemental 028 Extra; Emsogen; Peptamen; Peptisorb.

(b) **Nutritional source supplements**: see synthetic diets; malabsorption states.

(i) General supplements. Necessary nutritional supplements prescribed on medical grounds: Clinutren range; Enlive Plus; Enrich Plus; Ensure Plus; Foodlink Complete; Formance; Forticreme; Fortijuce; Fortimel; Fortini, Fortini MultiFibre; Fortisip; Fortisip Multi Fibre; Fresubin HP Energy; Fresubin 1000, and 1200 Complete; Maxisorb; Nutrison Energy and MCT; Perative; Provide Xtra; Resource Shake; Survimed OPD.

(ii) Carbohydrates; lactose-free and gluten-free; [1]Caloreen; [1]Maxijul LE Liquid, and Super Soluble; [1]Polycal; [1]Polycal Liquid; Polycose; Pro-Cal; QuickCal; Resource Benefiber; Vitajoule; Vitasavoury.

(iii) Fat: Alembicol D; Calogen; Liquigen; MCT Oil.

(iv) Fat/carbohydrate sources: Calshake; Duobar; Duocal Liquid, MCT Powder and Super Soluble (low-electrolyte content); Scandishake, SPS Energy Bar.

(v) Nitrogen sources: Casilan 90 (whole protein based, low-sodium); Maxipro Super Soluble (whey protein based, low-sodium); Maxisorb; Pro-Mod (whey protein based, low-sodium).

(vi) Minerals: Aminogran Mineral Mixture; Metabolic Mineral Mixture.

**Phenylketonuria**

Aminex low-protein biscuits, cookies and rusks; Aminogran Food Supplement (powder and tablets) and Mineral Mixture; Analog LCP; Analog XP; Aproten products (annellini, biscuits, bread mix, cake mix, crispbread, ditalini, rigatini, spaghetti, tagliatelle); Ener-G low protein egg replacer; Juvela low-protein loaf (sliced and unsliced), bread rolls, cookies (chocolate chip, orange, and cinnamon flavour), mix; Lofenalac; Loprofin egg replacer; Loprofin low-protein bread (sliced and unsliced), breakfast cereal, rolls (part-baked), rolls (white), fibre bread (sliced and unsliced), mix and pasta (macaroni, penne, spaghetti long, pasta spirals, vermicelli), sweet biscuits, chocolate cream-filled biscuits, crackers, cookies (chocolate chip, cinnamon), wafers (orange, chocolate, vanilla); Loprofin PKU drink; Metabolic Mineral Mixture; Milupa PKU2 and PKU3; Phlexy-10 exchange system; Phlexyvits; PK Aid 4; PK Foods bread (sliced), crispbread, pasta (spirals), cookies (chocolate chip, orange, cinnamon), egg replacer, flour mix, jelly (orange, cherry); PKU gel; Promin low-protein pasta (alphabets, macaroni, shells, shortcut spaghetti, spirals), pasta tricolour (alphabets, shells, spirals), pasta meal; Rite-Diet low-protein baking mix, flour mix; Sno-Pro; L-Tyrosine supplement; Ultra low-protein, canned white bread; Ultra PKU biscuits, bread, cookies, flour, pizza base, savoy biscuits; Valpiform cookies, shortbread biscuits; XP Maxamaid XP Concentrate Maxamaid; XP Maxamum; and see low-protein products and synthetic diets

**Propionic acidaemia**

XMTVI Analog; XMTVI Asadon; XMTVI Maxamaid; XMTVI Maxamum.

**Protein intolerance**

See amino acid metabolic disorders, low-protein products, milk protein sensitivity, synthetic diets, and whole protein sensitivity.

**Renal dialysis**

See Dialysis.

**Renal failure**

Aminex low-protein biscuits, cookies and rusks; Aproten products (annellini, biscuits, bread mix, cake mix, crispbread, ditalini, rigatini, spaghetti, tagliatelle); Dialamine; Ener-G low protein egg replacer, rice bread; Juvela low-protein (chocolate chip, orange, and cinnamon flavour) cookies, loaf (sliced and unsliced), bread rolls and flour mix; Kindergen; Loprofin egg replacer, egg white replacer, Loprofin bread (sliced and unsliced), breakfast cereal, rolls (part-baked), rolls (white), fibre

1. Have low electrolyte content

bread (sliced and unsliced), mix and pasta (macaroni, penne, spaghetti long, pasta spirals, vermicelli), sweet biscuits, chocolate cream-filled biscuits, crackers, cookies (chocolate chip, cinnamon), wafers (orange, chocolate, vanilla); Nepro; Promin low-protein pasta (alphabets, macaroni, shells, shortcut spaghetti, spirals), pasta tricolour (alphabets, shells, spirals), pasta meal; Renamil; Rite-Diet low-protein flour mix, baking mix, Sno-Pro Drink; Suplena; Ultra low-protein, canned bread (brown and white); Ultra PKU bread, biscuits, cookies, flour, pizza base and savoy biscuits; Valpiform cookies with chocolate nuggets, shortbread biscuits, Vita-Bite

**Short-bowel syndrome**

See Malabsorption states.

**Sicca Syndrome**

Bioxtra Moisturising Gel; Glandosane; Luborant; Oral-balance; Saliva Orthana; Salivace; Saliveze; Salivix.

**Sucrose intolerance**

See Carbohydrate malabsorption.

**Synthetic diets**

(a) *Fat*: Alembicol D; Calogen; Liquigen; Medium Chain Triglyceride Oil; Pro-Cal; QuickCal; Vitasavoury.

(b) *Carbohydrate*: Caloreen; Maxijul LE, Liquid, Super Soluble; Polycal; Polycal Liquid; Polycose powder; Pro-Cal; QuickCal; Vitasavoury.

(c) *Fat/carbohydrate sources*: Calshake; Duobar; Duocal Liquid, MCT Powder and Super Soluble (low-electrolyte content); Scandishake.

(d) *Minerals*: Aminogran Mineral Mixture; Metabolic Mineral Mixture.

(e) *Protein sources*: see malabsorption states, complete feeds.

(f) *Vitamins*: as appropriate and see malabsorption states, nutritional support for adults.

(g) *Vitamins and Minerals*: Paediatric Seravit; Phlexyvits.

**Tyrosinaemia**

Analog XPhen, Tyr; Analog XPhen, Tyr, Met; XPhen, Tyr Maxamaid; XPTM Tyrosidon; XPT Tyrosidon.

**Urea cycle disorders**

L-Arginine supplement

**Vomiting in infancy**

Instant Carobel, Nestargel.

**Whole protein sensitivity**

Caprilon; MCT Pepdite; Neocate; Neocate Advance; Nutramigen; Pepdite; Pepti-Junior; Prejomin.

**Note** Defined as intolerance to whole protein, proven by at least two withdrawal and challenge tests, as suggested by an accurate dietary history

**Xerostomia**

Bioxtra Moisturising Gel; Glandosane; Luborant; Bio-tene Oralbalance Dry Mouth Saliva Replacement Gel; Saliva Orthana; Saliveze; Salivix.



## Conditions for which toilet preparations may be prescribed on FP10, GP10 (Scotland), WP10 (Wales)

**Note** This is a list of clinical conditions for which the ACBS has approved toilet preparations. For details of the preparations see Chapter 13.

**Birthmarks**

See disfiguring skin lesions.

**Dermatitis**

Aveeno Bath Oil; Aveeno Cream; Aveeno Colloidal; Aveeno Baby Colloidal ; E45 Emollient Bath Oil; E45 Emollient Wash Cream; E45 Lotion; Vaseline Dermacare Cream and Lotion

**Dermatitis herpetiformis**

See gluten-sensitive enteropathies.

**Disfiguring skin lesions (birthmarks, mutilating lesions, scars, vitiligo)**

Covermark classic foundation and finishing powder; Dermacolor Camouflage cream and fixing powder; Keromask masking cream and finishing powder; Veil Cover cream and Finishing Powder. (Cleansing Creams, Cleansing Milks, and Cleansing Lotions are excluded)

**Disinfectants (antiseptics)**

May be prescribed on an FP10 only when ordered in such quantities and with such directions as are appropriate for the treatment of patients, but not for general hygenic purposes.

**Eczema**

See dermatitis.

**Photodermatoses (skin protection in)**

Coppertone Ultrashade 23; Delph Sun Lotion SPF 15, SPF 20, SPF 25, and SPF 30; E45 Sun Block SPF 25, and 50; RoC Total Sunblock Cream SPF 25; Spectraban 25, and Ultra; Sunsense Ultra; Uvistat Sun Block Cream Factor 20, and Ultrablock Suncream Factor 30.

**Pruritus**

See dermatitis.

# A8 Wound management products and elastic hosiery


**A8.1 Wound dressings** 821
A8.1.1 Alginate dressings 822
A8.1.2 Foam dressings 823
A8.1.3 Hydrogel dressings 824
A8.1.4 Hydrocolloid dressings 825
A8.1.5 Vapour-permeable films and membranes 826
A8.1.6 Low adherence dressing and wound contact materials 827
A8.1.7 Odour absorbent dressings 828
A8.1.8 Dressing packs 829
A8.1.9 Surgical absorbents 829
A8.1.10 Capillary dressings 829
**A8.2 Bandages and adhesives** 830
A8.2.1 Non-extensible bandages 830
A8.2.2 Light-weight conforming bandages 830
A8.2.3 Tubular bandages 830
A8.2.4 Support bandages 831
A8.2.5 High compression bandages 831
A8.2.6 Extra-high performance compression bandages 832
A8.2.7 Adhesive bandages 832
A8.2.8 Cohesive bandages 833
A8.2.9 Medicated bandages 833
A8.2.10 Multi-layer compression bandaging 833
A8.2.11 Surgical adhesive tapes 833
A8.2.12 Adhesive dressings 834
A8.2.13 Skin closure dressings 835
**A8.3 Elastic hosiery** 835
A8.3.1 Graduated compression hosiery 835
A8.3.2 Accessories 835
A8.3.3 Anklets 835
A8.3.4 Knee caps 835


## A8.1 Wound dressings

An overview of the management of *chronic wounds* (including venous ulcers and pressure sores) and the role of different dressings is given below as is the NICE guidance on difficult-to-heal surgical wounds; the notes do not deal with the management of clean surgical wounds which usually heal very rapidly. The correct dressing for wound management depends not only on the type of wound but also on the stage of the healing process. The principal stages of healing are:

- cleansing, removal of debris;
- granulation, vascularisation;
- epithelialisation.

Greater understanding of the requirements of a surgical dressing, including recognition of the benefits of maintaining a moist environment for wound healing, has improved the management of chronic wounds.

The ideal dressing needs to ensure that the wound remains:

- moist with exudate, but not macerated;
- free of clinical infection and excessive slough;
- free of toxic chemicals, particles or fibres;
- at the optimum temperature for healing;
- undisturbed by the need for frequent changes;
- at the optimum pH value.

As wound healing passes through its different stages, variations in dressing type may be required to satisfy better one or other of these requirements. The type of dressing depends on the type of wound or the stage of the healing process.

**Functions of dressings**

| Type of wound | Role of dressing |
|---|---|
| Dry, necrotic, black | Moisture retention or rehydration |
| Yellow, sloughy | If dry, moisture retention or rehydration<br>If moist, fluid absorption<br>Possibly odour absorption<br>Possibly antimicrobial activity |
| Clean, exuding (granulating) | Fluid absorption<br>Thermal insulation<br>Possibly odour absorption<br>Possibly antimicrobial activity |
| Dry, low exudate (epithelialising) | Moisture retention or rehydration<br>Low adherence<br>Thermal insulation |

Appendix 8

A decrease in pain and reduction in healing time is achieved to a marked extent with **alginate**, **foam**, **hydrogel** and **hydrocolloid** dressings and also to an important extent with **vapour-permeable films** and **membranes**; dressings such as dry gauze have little place. Practices such as the use of irritant cleansers may be harmful and are largely obsolete; removal of debris and dressing remnants should need minimal irrigation with physiological saline.

**Alginate**, **foam**, **hydrogel** and **hydrocolloid** dressings are designed to absorb wound exudate and thus to control the state of hydration of a wound. All are claimed to be effective, but as yet there have been few trials able to establish a clear advantage for any particular product. The choice between different dressings may therefore often depend not only on the type and stage of the wound, but also on personal experience, availability of the dressing, patient preference or tolerance and site of the wound.

**NICE guidance (debriding agents for difficult-to-heal surgical wounds)**
The National Institute for Health and Clinical Excellence has stated (April 2001) that alginate, foam, hydrocolloid, hydrogel, and polysaccharide (as beads or paste) dressings as well as maggots may reduce pain from difficult-to-heal surgical wounds. There is insufficient evidence to support one debriding agent over another and choice should be based on patient acceptability (including factors such as comfort and odour control), type and location of the wound, and total cost (including time for changing the dressings).

## A8.1.1 Alginate dressings

The gelling characteristics of alginate dressings vary according to the product used. Some products only gel to a limited extent to form a partially gelled sheet that can be lifted off; others form an amorphous gel that can be rinsed off with water or physiological saline. A secondary covering is needed. They are highly absorbent and are therefore suitable for moderately or heavily exuding wounds, but not for eschars or for dry wounds.



**ActivHeal® Alginate** (MedLogic)
Calcium sodium alginate dressing, sterile, net price 5 cm × 5 cm = 57p, 10 cm × 10 cm = £1.11, 10 cm × 20 cm = £2.73
Uses moderately to heavily exuding wounds
ActivHeal® *Alginate cavity dressing*, net price 2 cm × 30 cm = £2.05
Uses moderately to heavily exuding cavity wounds

**Algisite® M** (S&N Hlth.)
Calcium alginate fibre, sterile, flat non-woven dressing, net price 5 cm × 5 cm = 80p, 10 cm × 10 cm = £1.66, 15 cm × 20 cm = £4.44
Uses moderately to heavily exuding wounds
Algisite® *M Rope*, net price 2 cm × 30 cm = £3.00
Uses moderately to heavily exuding cavity wounds

**Algosteril®** (Beiersdorf)
Calcium alginate dressing. Net price 5 cm × 5 cm = 79p, 10 cm × 10 cm = £1.81, 10 cm × 20 cm = £3.07
Uses moderately to heavily exuding wounds
Algosteril® Rope, net price 2 g, 30 cm = £3.28
Uses moderately to heavily exuding cavity wounds

**Curasorb®** (Tyco)
Calcium alginate dressing, net price 5 cm × 5 cm = 69p, 10 cm × 10 cm = £1.46, 10 cm × 14 cm = £2.36, 10 cm × 20 cm = £2.87, 15 cm × 25 cm = £5.05, 30 cm × 61 cm = £26.50 (other sizes NHS)
Curasorb® Plus, calcium alginate dressing, 10 cm × 10 cm = £2.00
Curasorb® Zn, calcium alginate and zinc dressing, 5 cm × 5 cm = 78p, 10 cm × 10 cm = £1.65, 10 cm × 20 cm = £3.24 (other sizes NHS)

**Kaltostat®** (ConvaTec)
(Alginate Dressing, BP 1993, type C). Calcium alginate fibre, flat non-woven pads, 5 cm × 5 cm, net price = 83p, 7.5 cm × 12 cm = £1.80, 10 cm × 20 cm = £3.50, 15 cm × 25 cm = £6.01, (NHS) 30 cm × 60 cm = £25.13
Uses moderately to heavily exuding wounds
Kaltostat® Wound Packing, net price 2 g = £3.28
Uses moderately to heavily exuding cavity wounds

**Melgisorb®** (Mölnlycke)
Calcium sodium alginate fibre, sterile, highly absorbent, gelling dressing, flat non-woven pads, net price 5 cm × 5 cm = 79p, 10 cm × 10 cm = £1.64, 10 cm × 20 cm = £3.09
Uses moderately to heavily exuding wounds including leg ulcers, dermal lesions and traumatic wounds
Melgisorb® Cavity, calcium sodium alginate fibre, sterile, highly absorbent, gelling filler ribbon, net price 32 cm × 2.2 cm, 3 pieces (2 g) = £3.11
Uses moderately to heavily exuding cavity wounds, fistulas, sinuses, pressure sores and deep leg ulcers

**SeaSorb®** (Coloplast)
SeaSorb® Soft, alginate containing hydrocolloid dressing, sterile, highly absorbent, gelling dressing, 5 cm × 5 cm = 85p, 10 cm × 10 cm = £2.02, 15 cm × 15 cm = £3.83
Uses heavily exuding wounds including leg ulcers and pressure sores
SeaSorb® Soft Filler, calcium sodium alginate fibre, highly absorbent, gelling filler, 44 cm = £2.38
Uses moderately to heavily exuding cavity wounds, fistulas, sinus drainage, decubitus and deep leg ulcers

**Sorbalgon®** (Hartmann)
Calcium alginate dressing, net price 5 cm × 5 cm = 73p, 10 cm × 10 cm = £1.52
Uses for medium to heavily exuding wounds
Sorbalgon T®, calcium alginate cavity dressing, net price 2 g, 32 cm = £3.11
Uses for medium to heavily exuding wounds

**Sorbsan®** (Unomedical)
(Alginate Dressing, BP 1993, type A). Calcium alginate fibre, highly absorbent, flat non-woven pads, 5 cm × 5 cm, net price = 74p, 10 cm × 10 cm = £1.55, 10 cm × 20 cm = £2.90
Uses moderately to heavily exuding wounds
Sorbsan® Plus, alginate dressing bonded to a secondary absorbent viscose pad, net price 7.5 cm × 10 cm = £1.57, 10 cm × 15 cm = £2.77, 10 cm × 20 cm = £3.53, 15 cm × 20 cm = £4.90
Uses moderately to heavily exuding shallow wounds and ulcers
Sorbsan® Surgical Packing, 30 cm (2 g) = £3.22
Sorbsan® Ribbon, 40 cm (with 12.5-cm probe) = £1.88
Uses moderately to heavily exuding cavity wounds
Sorbsan® SA NHS calcium alginate fibre, highly absorbent flat non-woven pads for wound contact bonded to adhesive semi-permeable polyurethane foam. Net price 9 cm × 11 cm = £2.24
Uses moderately to lightly exuding shallow wounds

**Suprasorb A®** (Vernon-Carus)
Calcium alginate dressing, sterile, net price 5 cm × 5 cm = 56p, 10 cm × 10 cm = £1.10
Suprasorb A® Rope, net price 2 g × 30 cm = £2.04
Uses moderate to heavily exuding wounds

**Tegagen®** (3M)
(Alginate Dressing, BP 1993, type B). Net price 5 cm × 5 cm = 75p, 10 cm × 10 cm = £1.58
Uses for leg ulcers, pressure sores, second degree burns, post-operative wounds, fungating carcinomas
Tegagen® Rope, net price 2 cm × 30 cm = £2.63
Uses moderately to heavily exuding cavity wounds

**Urgosorb®** (Urgo)

Alginate containing hydrocolloid dressing without adhesive border, sterile, net price 10 cm × 10 cm = £1.83, 10 cm × 20 cm = £3.35

*Urgosorb Rope* cavity dressing, net price 30 cm = £2.44

## A8.1.2 Foam dressings

Foam dressings vary from products that are suitable for lightly exuding wounds to highly absorbent structures for heavily exuding wounds. They may also be used as secondary dressings. In hypergranulating (or overgranulating) tissue (which may arise from the use of occlusive dressings such as hydrocolloids), changing to a more permeable product such as a foam dressing may be beneficial.

**Polyurethane Foam Dressing, BP 1993**

Absorbent foam dressing of low adherence, sterile

Lyofoam®, net price 7.5 cm × 7.5 cm = 97p, 10 cm × 10 cm = £1.14, 10 cm × 17.5 cm = £1.78, 15 cm × 20 cm = £2.40, other sizes (NHS) 10 cm × 25 cm = £4.79 (hosp. only), 25 cm × 30 cm = £11.35 (Medlock)

Uses treatment of burns, decubitus ulcers, donor sites, granulating wounds

**Polyurethane Foam Film Dressing, Sterile, with Adhesive Border**

(Drug Tariff specification 47)

Allevyn® Lite Island, net price 9.75 cm × 16.5 cm = £1.71; 13.5 cm × 13.5 cm = £2.23; 16 cm × 16 cm = £2.65; 13.5 cm × 23.5 cm = £3.41 (S & N Hlth)

Lyofoam® Extra Adhesive, net price 9 cm × 9 cm = £1.20; 15 cm × 15 cm = £2.25; 22 cm × 22 cm = £4.44; 30 cm × 30 cm = £6.45; sacral, 15 cm × 13 cm = £1.84; 22 cm × 26 cm = £3.49 (Medlock)

Suprasorb P®, net price 7.5 cm × 7.5 cm = £1.16, 10 cm × 10 cm = £1.25, 15 cm × 15 cm = £2.24 (Vernon-Carus)

Tielle®, net price 11 cm × 11 cm = £2.24; 15 cm × 15 cm = £3.66; 18 cm × 18 cm = £4.67; 7 cm × 9 cm = £1.21; 15 cm × 20 cm = £4.59; *Tielle® Sacrum* 18 cm × 18 cm = £3.39 (J&J)

Trufoam®, net price 7 cm × 9 cm = £1.07; 11 cm × 11 cm = £2.04 (Unomedical)

Uses light to moderately exuding wounds, not recommended for dry superficial wounds

**Polyurethane Foam Film Dressing, Sterile, without Adhesive Border**

(Drug Tariff specification 47)

Allevyn® Lite, net price 5 cm × 5 cm = 98p; 10 cm × 10 cm = £1.77; 10 cm × 20 cm = £3.04; 15 cm × 20 cm = £3.79 (S&N Hlth)

Allevyn® Thin (with adhesive border), net price 5 cm × 6 cm = 92p, 10 cm × 10 cm = £1.87, 15 cm × 15 cm = £3.08, 15 cm × 20 cm = £3.73

FlexiPore®, net price 10 cm × 10 cm = £1.73; 10 cm × 30 cm = £3.60 (MedLogic)

Lyofoam® Extra, net price 10 cm × 10 cm = £1.91; 17.5 cm × 10 cm = £3.23; 20 cm × 15 cm = £4.19; 25 cm × 10 cm = £3.84; (NHS) 30 cm × 25 cm = £14.35 (Medlock)

Suprasorb M®, net price 10 cm × 10 cm = £1.72, 10 cm × 20 cm = £3.03, 20 cm × 20 cm = £5.05 (Vernon-Carus)

Suprasorb P®, net price 5 cm × 5 cm = 90p, 7.5 cm × 7.5 cm = 96p, 10 cm × 10 cm = £1.13, 15 cm × 15 cm = £3.01 (Vernon-Carus)

Transorbent®, net price 5 cm × 7 cm = 94p; 10 cm × 10 cm = £1.78; 15 cm × 15 cm = £3.27; 20 cm × 20 cm = £5.23 (Unomedical)

Uses light to moderately exuding wounds, not recommended for dry superficial wounds

**Polyurethane Foam Film Dressing, Sterile, with Adhesive Border**

Tielle® Lite, net price 11 cm × 11 cm = £2.15; 7 cm × 9 cm = £1.14; 8 cm × 15 cm = £2.65; 8 cm × 20 cm = £2.80 (J&J)

Uses light to non-exuding wounds

ActivHeal® Foam Island, net price 10 cm × 10 cm = £1.57, 12.5 cm × 12.5 cm = £1.50, 15 cm × 15 cm = £1.92, 20 cm × 20 cm = £4.34 (MedLogic)

Uses moderate to heavily exuding wounds

Allevyn® Adhesive, net price 7.5 cm × 7.5 cm = £1.32, 10 cm × 10 cm = £1.93, 12.5 cm × 12.5 cm = £2.37, 17.5 cm × 17.5 cm = £4.66, 12.5 cm × 22.5 cm = £3.68, 22.5 cm × 22.5 cm = £6.79 (S&N Hlth)

Allevyn® Plus Adhesive, net price 12.5 cm × 12.5 cm = £2.90; 17.5 cm × 17.5 cm = £5.60; 12.5 cm × 22.5 cm = £5.14

Allevyn® Sacrum shaped, net price 17 cm × 17 cm = £3.49, 22 cm × 22 cm = £5.02

Uses light to moderately exuding sacral wounds

Biatain® Adhesive, net price 12 cm × 12 cm = £2.25, 18 cm × 18 cm = £4.50, 18 cm × 28 cm = £6.79, 23 cm × 23 cm (sacral) = £3.85, 19 cm × 20 cm (heel) = £4.49; 6 cm diameter = £1.50 (Coloplast)

Uses moderate to heavily exuding wounds

Comfifoam®, net price 7.5 cm × 7.5 cm = £1.13, 10 cm × 10 cm = £1.65, 12.5 cm × 12.5 cm = £2.03, 17.5 cm × 17.5 cm = £4.01 (Shiloh)

Curafoam® Island, net price 10 cm × 10 cm = £1.21, 15 cm × 15 cm = £2.19, 20 cm × 20 cm = £4.34 (Tyco)

Uses moderate to heavily exuding wounds

PermaFoam®, net price concave 16.5 cm × 18 cm = £ 3.60; sacral 18 cm × 18 cm = £2.96, 22 cm × 22 cm = £3.40; *PermaFoam Comfort®* 8 cm × 8 cm = £1.00, 10 cm × 20 cm = £3.00, 11 cm × 11 cm = £1.90, 15 cm × 15 cm = £3.10, 20 cm × 20 cm = £4.50 (Hartmann)

Tielle® Plus, net price 11 cm × 11 cm = £2.48; 15 cm × 15 cm = £4.05; 15 cm × 20 cm = £5.08; 15 cm × 15 cm (sacrum) = £2.95; *Tielle® Plus Heel Hydropolymer Adhesive Dressing* 20 cm × 26.5 cm = £4.20 (J&J)

Uses moderate to heavily exuding wounds

Trufoam®, net price 15 cm × 15 cm = £3.41, 15 cm × 20 cm = £4.28 (Unomedical)

Uses moderate to heavily exuding wounds

**Polyurethane Foam Film Dressing, Sterile, without Adhesive Border**

ActivHeal® Foam Non-Adhesive, net price 5 cm × 5 cm = 72p, 10 cm × 10 cm = £1.09, 10 cm × 17.8 cm = £2.26, 20 cm × 20 cm = £3.78 (MedLogic)

Uses heavily exuding wounds

Advazorb®, net price 5 cm × 7.5 cm = 45p, 10 cm × 10 cm = 80p (Advancis)

Allevyn®, net price 5 cm × 5 cm = £1.11, 9 cm × 9 cm = £3.49 (NHS), 10 cm × 10 cm = £2.21, 10 cm × 20 cm = £3.55, 20 cm × 20 cm = £5.92, 10.5 cm × 13.5 cm (heel) = £4.43 (S&N Hlth)

Allevyn® Compression, net price 5 cm × 6 cm = £1.08; 10 cm × 10 cm = £2.23; 15 cm × 15 cm = £3.78, 15 cm × 20 cm = £4.24 (S&N Hlth)

Uses moderately exuding wounds, burns, decubitus ulcers, and leg ulcers

Biatain® Non-Adhesive, net price 10 cm × 10 cm = £2.07, 10 cm × 20 cm = £3.49, 15 cm × 15 cm = £3.82, 20 cm × 20 cm = £5.68, circular, 5 cm diameter = £1.07, 8 cm diameter = £1.50 (Coloplast)

Comfifoam®, net price 5 cm × 5 cm = 96p, 10 cm × 10 cm = £1.90, 10 cm × 20 cm = £3.05, 20 cm × 20 cm = £5.09 (Shiloh)

Curafoam® Plus, net price 6 cm × 6 cm = £1.06, 10 cm × 10 cm = £1.65, 10 cm × 13 cm = £2.05, 10 cm × 20 cm = £3.20, 20 cm × 20 cm = £5.04 (Tyco)

Hydrafoam®, net price 10 cm × 10 cm = £1.73, 10 cm × 20 cm = £3.10, 15 cm × 15 cm = £3.32, 20 cm × 20 cm = £5.15 (Tyco)

3M®, net price 8.9 cm × 8.9 cm (fenestrated) = £2.13, 10 cm × 10 cm = £2.09, 10 cm × 20 cm = £3.54, 20 cm × 20 cm = £5.65, 10 cm × 60 cm = £11.96 (3M)

PermaFoam®, net price 10 cm × 10 cm = £1.90, 10 cm × 20 cm = £3.25, 15 cm × 15 cm = £3.60, 20 cm × 20 cm = £5.50; 6 cm diameter = 98p; *PermaFoam® Cavity®* 10 cm × 10 cm = £1.80 (Hartmann)

Tielle® Plus Borderless, net price 11 cm × 11 cm = £2.98; 15 cm × 20 cm = £5.40 (J&J)

Trufoam® NA, net price 5 cm × 5 cm = £1.02, 10 cm × 10 cm = £1.93, 15 cm × 15 cm = £3.56 (Unomedical)

Uses moderate to heavily exuding wounds

**Allevyn®** (S&N Hlth.)

Hydrophilic polyurethane dressing, foam sheets with trilaminate structure, non-adherent wound contact layer, foam based central layer, bacteria- and water-proof outer layer

Allevyn® Plus Cavity Sterile, highly absorbent polyurethane dressing consisting of a vapour-permeable foam matrix, net price 1.5 cm × 20 cm = £1.61, 5 cm × 6 cm = £1.64; 10 cm × 10 cm = £2.73; 15 cm × 20 cm = £5.46

Uses heavily exuding deep wounds, including deep leg ulcers, decubitus ulcers, abscesses; management of post-operative wounds including pilonidal sinus excision

Allevyn® Cavity, net price circular, 5 cm diameter = £3.64, 10 cm = £8.69, tubular 9 cm × 2.5 cm = £3.53, 12 cm × 4 cm = £6.22

Uses moderately to heavily exuding cavity wounds including deep pressure sores and leg ulcers, surgical incisions and excisions such as pilonidal sinus excisions

**Avance®** (Medlock)

Silver impregnated polyurethane foam film dressing

Avance® (without adhesive border), net price 10 cm × 10 cm = £2.59, 10 cm × 17 cm = £4.13, 15 cm × 20 cm = £5.71

Avance® A (with adhesive border), net price 9 cm × 9 cm = £2.18, 12 cm × 12 cm = £3.61, 15 cm × 15 cm = £4.42, 15 cm × 13 cm (sacral) = £3.25

Uses for exuding wounds

**Cavi-Care®** (S&N Hlth.)

Soft, conforming cavity wound dressing prepared by mixing thoroughly for 15 seconds immediately before use and allowing to expand its volume within the cavity. Net price 20 g = £17.13

Uses in the management of open post-operative granulating cavity wounds (with no underlying tracts or sinuses) such as pilonidal sinus excision, dehisced surgical wounds, hydradenitis suppurativa wounds, perianal wounds, perineal wounds, pressure sores

**Contreet Foam®** (Coloplast)

Silver impregnated, polyurethane foam film dressing with adhesive border, net price 12.5 cm × 12.5 cm = £8.22, 18 cm × 18 cm = £16.49, 19 cm × 20 cm (heel) = £15.95, 23 cm × 23 cm (sacral) = £16.95; without adhesive border 10 cm × 10 cm = £7.18, 10 cm × 20 cm = £12.95, 15 cm × 15 cm = £14.42, 20 cm × 20 cm = £19.95, 5 cm diameter = £2.95

Uses moderate to heavily exuding or malodorous wounds



## A8.1.3 Hydrogel dressings

Hydrogel dressings are most commonly supplied as an amorphous, cohesive material that can take up the shape of a wound. A secondary covering is needed. These dressings are generally used to donate liquid to dry sloughy wounds and facilitate autolytic debridement but they may also have the ability to absorb limited amounts of exudate. Hydrogel sheets are also available which have a fixed structure; such products have limited fluid handling capacity. Hydrogel sheets are best avoided in the presence of infection.

**ActiFormCool®** (Activa)

Net price 5 cm × 6.5 cm = £1.59, 10 cm × 10 cm = £2.33, 10 cm × 15 cm = £3.35

**ActivHeal® Hydrogel** (MedLogic)

Net price 15 g = £1.36

Uses pressure sores, cavity wounds, leg ulcers, skin donor sites, diabetic foot ulcers

**Aquaform®** (Unomedical)

(Drug Tariff specification 50) Hydrogel containing modified starch copolymer, net price 8 g = £1.48, 15 g = £1.80

Uses for dry, sloughy or necrotic wounds, lightly exuding wounds, granulating wounds

**Aquaflo®** (Tyco)

Net price 3.8 cm diameter = £2.41, 7.5 cm = £2.50, 12 cm = £5.16

**Coolie®** (Zeroderma)

Sterile, hydrogel dressing with lint backing, net price 7 cm diameter = £2.47

Uses for dry, sloughy or necrotic wounds, lightly exuding wounds, granulating wounds

**Curagel®** (Tyco)

Net price 5 cm × 7.5 cm = £1.74, 10 cm × 10 cm = £2.71

Curagel Island (with adhesive border), net price 7.5 cm × 10 cm = £2.47, 12.5 cm × 12.5 cm = £3.58

**Geliperm®** (Geistlich)

Gel sheets in wet form, 10 cm × 10 cm = £2.23, 12 cm × 13cm = £4.88 (NHS); 12 cm × 26 cm = £8.73 (NHS)

Uses wound and ulcer dressing, burns, donor sites

**GranuGel®** (ConvaTec)

(Drug Tariff Specification 50). Net price 15 g = £2.01

Uses dry, sloughy or necrotic wounds, lightly exuding wounds, granulating wounds

**Hydrosorb®** (Hartmann)

Absorbent, transparent, hydrogel sheets containing polyurethane polymers covered with a semi-permeable film

Hydrosorb®, 5 cm × 7.5 cm = £1.80; 10 cm × 10 cm = £2.84; 20 cm × 20 cm = £6.84

Hydrosorb® comfort (with adhesive border, waterproof), 4.5 cm × 6.5 cm = £1.66; 7.5 cm × 10 cm = £2.59; 12.5 cm × 12.5 cm = £3.73

Uses second degree burns, donor sites; chronic wounds where granulation is unsatisfactory, including leg ulcers, pressure sores

**Intrasite Conformable®** (S&N Hlth.)

(Drug Tariff specification 50). Soft and easily moulded non-woven dressing impregnated with Intrasite gel, net price 10 cm × 10 cm = £1.56; 10 cm × 20 cm = £2.11; 10 cm × 40 cm = £3.77

Uses for dry, sloughy or necrotic wounds, lightly exuding wounds; granulating wounds

**Intrasite® Gel** (S&N Hlth.)

(Drug Tariff specification 50). A ready-mixed hydrogel containing modified carmellose polymer applied directly into the wound. Net price 8-g sachet = £1.56, 15-g sachet = £2.09, 25-g sachet = £3.10

Uses for dry, sloughy or necrotic wounds; lightly exuding wounds; granulating wounds

**Iodoflex®** (S&N Hlth.)

Paste, iodine 0.9% as cadexomer–iodine in a paste basis with gauze backing, net price 5-g unit = £3.65; 10 g = £7.32; 17 g = £11.58

Uses for treatment of chronic exuding wounds, such as leg ulcers, apply to wound surface, remove gauze backing and cover; renew when saturated (usually 2–3 times weekly, daily for heavily exuding wounds); max. single application 50 g, max. weekly application 150 g; max. duration up to 3 months in any single course of treatment

Cautions caution in patients with severe renal impairment or history of thyroid disorders; iodine may be absorbed particularly if large wounds treated

Contra-indications avoid in thyroid disorders, in those receiving lithium, in pregnancy and breast-feeding and use in children

**Iodosorb®** (S&N Hlth.)

Ointment, iodine 0.9% as cadexomer–iodine in an ointment basis, net price 10 g = £4.04; 20 g = £8.09

Powder, iodine 0.9% as cadexomer–iodine microbeads, net price 3-g sachet = £1.73

Uses for treatment of chronic exuding wounds, such as leg ulcers, apply to wound surface to depth of approx. 3 mm and cover; renew when saturated (usually 2–3 times weekly, daily for heavily exuding wounds); max. single application 50 g, max. weekly application 150 g; max. duration up to 3 months in any single course of treatment

Cautions caution in patients with severe renal impairment or history of thyroid disorders; iodine may be absorbed particularly if large wounds treated

Contra-indications avoid in thyroid disorders, in those receiving lithium, in pregnancy and breast-feeding, and use in children

**Novogel®** (Ford)

Sterile, glycerol-based hydrogel sheets, net price 10 cm × 10 cm = £2.95; 30 cm × 30 cm, standard = £12.50, thin = £11.80; 5 cm × 7.5 cm = £1.88; 15 cm × 20 cm = £5.63; 20 cm × 40 cm = £10.73; 7.5 cm diameter = £2.68

Uses diabetic wounds, burns, leg ulcers, decubitus ulcers, donor sites

**Nu-Gel®** (J&J)

(Drug Tariff Specification 50). A ready-mixed hydrogel containing alginate, applied directly into wound and covered with secondary dressing. Net price 15 g = £1.97

Uses dry, sloughy or necrotic, lightly exuding or granulating wounds

**Purilon® Gel** (Coloplast)

(Drug Tariff specification 50). Net price 8 g = £1.52, 15 g = £1.98

Uses for dry, sloughy or necrotic wounds; lightly exuding wounds; granulating wounds

### Protease modulating matrix

**Cadesorb®** (S&N Hlth.)

Sterile, matrix dressing, net price 20 g = £7.98

**Promogran®** (J&J)

Sterile, collagen and oxidised regenerated cellulose matrix, applied directly to wound and covered with secondary dressing, net price 28 cm² (hexagonal) = £4.80, 123 cm² (hexagonal) = £14.73

Uses chronic wounds free of necrotic tissue and infection, e.g. leg ulcers, pressure sores, diabetic foot ulcers

**Suprasorb C®** (Vernon-Carus)

Net price 4 cm × 6 cm = £2.55, 6 cm × 8 cm = £3.90, 8 cm × 12 cm = £7.65

## A8.1.4 Hydrocolloid dressings

Hydrocolloid dressings are usually presented as an absorbent layer on a vapour-permeable film or foam. Because of their impermeable nature, hydrocolloid dressings facilitate rehydration and autolytic debridement of dry, sloughy, or necrotic wounds; they are also suitable for promoting granulation. Fibrous dressings made from modified carmellose fibres resemble alginate dressings (e.g. *Aquacel®*); these are not occlusive.

**ActivHeal® Hydrocolloid** (MedLogic)

Sterile, semi-permeable polyurethane film backing, hydrocolloid wound contact layer, net price 10 cm × 10 cm = £1.52, 15 cm × 15 cm = £3.31, 15 cm × 18 cm (sacral) = £3.84

Uses light to moderately exuding wounds

**Alione®** (Coloplast)

Sterile, semi-permeable hydrocolloid dressing with adhesive border, net price 10 cm × 10 cm = £2.79, 12.5 cm × 12.5 cm = £3.83, 12 cm × 20 cm = £5.04, 15 cm × 15 cm = £4.85, 20 cm × 20 cm = £7.26; without adhesive border 10 cm × 10 cm = £2.79, 12.5 cm × 12.5 cm = £3.83, 12 cm × 20 cm = £5.04, 15 cm × 15 cm = £4.85, 20 cm × 20 cm = £7.26

Uses chronic and exuding wounds

**Aquacel®** (ConvaTec)

Soft sterile non-woven pad containing hydrocolloid fibres, net price 5 cm × 5 cm = £1.01; 10 cm × 10 cm = £2.40; 15 cm × 15 cm = £4.51

Uses moderately to heavily exuding wounds

Aquacel® Ribbon, 2 cm × 45 cm = £2.40

Uses moderately to heavily exuding cavity wounds

Aquacel® Ag (silver impregnated), net price 5 cm × 5 cm = £1.68, 10 cm × 10 cm = £4.00, 15 cm × 15 cm = £7.54, 20 cm × 30 cm = £18.70

Uses moderately to heavily exuding wounds

Aquacel® Ag Ribbon (silver impregnated), net price 2 cm × 45 cm = £4.02

Uses moderately to heavily exuding cavity wounds

**Askina® Biofilm Transparent** (Braun)

Sterile, semi-permeable, polyurethane film dressing with hydrocolloid adhesive, net price, 10 cm × 10 cm = £1.00, 15 cm × 15 cm = £2.27, 20 cm × 20 cm = £2.96

**Biofilm S®** (Braun) NHS

Hydrocolloid dressing with polyurethane-polyester backing; also in powder form for direct application into wound, net price 10 cm × 10 cm = £1.65, 20 cm × 20 cm = £5.70

Biofilm® powder, 1 sachet = £1.82

**CombiDERM®** (ConvaTec)

Dressing with hydrocolloid adhesive border and absorbent wound contact pad, net price 10 cm × 10 cm = £1.42; 14 cm × 14 cm = £1.97; 15 cm × 18 cm (triangular) = £3.40; 20 cm × 20 cm = £3.78; 20 cm × 23 cm (triangular) = £4.56

Uses chronic exuding wounds such as leg ulcers, pressure sores; postoperative wounds

CombiDERM N® Hydrocolloid absorbent dressing, net price 7.5 cm × 7.5 cm = £1.11; 14 cm × 14 cm = £1.98; 15 cm × 25 cm = £4.03

Uses chronic wounds (e.g. leg ulcers and diabetic ulcers) and exuding wounds (e.g. biopsies), and surgical wounds

**Comfeel®** (Coloplast)

Soft elastic pad consisting of carmellose sodium particles embedded in adhesive mass; smooth outer layer and polyurethane film backing; available as sheets, powder in plastic blister units and paste for direct application into the wound: ulcer dressing, net price 10 cm × 10 cm = £2.41; 15 cm × 15 cm = £4.83; 20 cm × 20 cm = £7.39; other sizes (NHS): 4 cm × 6 cm = £1.19; powder 6 g = £4.04; paste 12-g sachet = £1.56; 50 g = £5.98

**Comfeel® Plus** (Coloplast)

Hydrocolloid dressings containing carmellose sodium and calcium alginate. Contour dressing, net price 6 cm × 8 cm = £1.92, 9 cm × 11 cm = £3.34; Ulcer Dressing, 4 cm × 6 cm = 83p, 10 cm × 10 cm = £2.13, 15 cm × 15 cm = £4.56, 18 cm × 20 cm (triangular) = £4.96, 20 cm × 20 cm = £6.56; Transparent Dressing, 5 cm × 7 cm = 58p, 5 cm × 15 cm = £1.37, 5 cm × 25 cm = £2.24, 9 cm × 14 cm = £2.11, 9 cm × 25 cm = £3.00, 10 cm × 10 cm = £1.11, 15 cm × 15 cm = £2.89, 15 cm × 20 cm = £2.93, 20 cm × 20 cm = £2.95; Pressure Relieving Dressing, 7 cm diameter = £3.00, 10 cm = £4.02, 15 cm = £6.06

**Contreet® Hydrocolloid** (Coloplast)

Semi-permeable, antimicrobial barrier dressing with ionic silver (silver sodium thiosulphate). Net price 10 cm × 10 cm = £6.46, 15 cm × 15 cm = £12.92

Uses low to moderate exuding venous leg ulcers

**Cutinova®** (Beiersdorf)

Cutinova® Hydro Border Sterile, highly absorbent semi-transparent two-layered polyurethane dressing with vapour-permeable foam matrix on a semi-permeable film backing, net price 5 cm × 6 cm = £1.09; 10 cm × 10 cm = £2.20; 15 cm × 20 cm = £4.66

Uses moderately to heavily exuding wounds including burns and decubitus ulcers

Cutinova® Thin NHS Sterile, highly absorbent, semi-transparent two-layered polyurethane dressing with two-layered vapour-permeable foam matrix on a semi-permeable film backing, net price 5 cm × 6 cm = £1.16; 10 cm × 10 cm = £1.87; 15 cm × 20 cm = £5.13

Uses lightly exuding wounds including abrasions, burns, decubitus ulcers, donor sites, skin protection and post-operative wounds

**DuoDERM®** (ConvaTec)

Extra Thin (formerly *Granuflex® Extra Thin*), net price 5 cm × 10 cm = 66p, 7.5 cm × 7.5 cm = 69p, 10 cm × 10 cm = £1.14, 9 cm × 15 cm = £1.54, 9 cm × 25 cm = £2.46, 9 cm × 35 cm = £3.44, 15 cm × 15 cm = £2.46, NHS 5 cm × 20 cm = £1.38

Uses minimally exuding wounds, such as abrasions, minor burns or minor surgery

Signal, hydrocolloid dressing with 'Time to change' indicator net price 10 cm × 10 cm = £1.82, 14 cm × 14 cm = £3.20, 20 cm × 20 cm = £6.35, 11 cm × 19 cm (oval) = £2.77, 18.5 cm × 19.5 cm (heel) = £4.47, 22.5 cm × 20 cm (sacral) = £5.22

Uses leg ulcers, pressure sores, diabetic ulcers, burns, post-operative wounds

**Granuflex®** (ConvaTec)

Hydrocolloid wound contact layer bonded to plastic foam layer, with outer semi-permeable polyurethane film, net price 10 cm × 10 cm = £2.42, 15 cm × 15 cm = £4.59, 15 cm × 20 cm = £4.97, 20 cm × 20 cm = £6.91, NHS 20 cm × 30 cm = £11.36

Granuflex® Paste (NHS), net price 30 g = £2.73

Granuflex® Bordered Dressing, net price 6 cm × 6 cm = £1.51, 10 cm × 10 cm = £2.88, 15 cm × 15 cm = £5.45, triangular dressing, 10 cm × 13 cm = £3.40, 15 cm × 18 cm = £5.30

Uses chronic ulcers, pressure sores, open wounds, debridement of wounds; powders, gel, and pastes used with sheet dressings to fill deep or heavily exuding wounds

**Hydrocoll®** (Hartmann)

Hydrocolloid dressing with adhesive border and absorbent wound contact pad, net price 5 cm × 5 cm = 90p, 7.5 cm × 7.5 cm = £1.48, 10 cm × 10 cm = £2.15, 15 cm × 15 cm = £4.05; Concave dressing, 8 cm × 12 cm = £1.90; Sacral dressing, 12 cm × 18 cm = £3.22; Basic dressing without adhesive border, 10 cm × 10 cm = £2.19; Thin film dressing, 7.5 cm × 7.5 cm = 62p, 10 cm × 10 cm = £1.03, 15 cm × 15 cm = £2.32

Uses light to medium exuding wounds

**NU DERM®** (J&J)

Sterile, semi permeable hydrocolloid dressing without adhesive border, net price 5 cm × 5 cm = 80p, 10 cm × 10 cm = £1.50, 15 cm × 15 cm = £3.00, 20 cm × 20 cm = £6.00, 8 cm × 12 cm (heel/elbow) = £3.00, 15 cm × 18 cm (sacral) = £4.20; without adhesive border, thin, 10 cm × 10 cm = £1.00

**Replicare Ultra®** (S&N Hlth.)

Sterile, adhesive hydrocolloid dressing with outer semi-permeable polyurethane film backing, net price 10 cm × 10 cm = £2.25, 15 cm × 15 cm = £4.48, 20 cm × 20 cm = £6.61; Sacral dressing, 15 cm × 18 cm = £4.24

Uses lightly to moderately exuding wounds such as leg ulcers, pressure sores; postoperative wounds; superficial burns

**Suprasorb H®** (Vernon-Carus)

Sterile, semi permeable hydrocolloid dressing, with adhesive border net price 14 cm × 14 cm = £2.23; without adhesive border 10 cm × 10 cm = £1.51, 15 cm × 15 cm = £3.30; without adhesive border, thin 5 cm × 10 cm = 65p, 10 cm × 10 cm = 99p, 15 cm × 15 cm = £2.26

Uses lightly to moderately exuding wounds

**Tegasorb®** (3M)

Hydrocolloid dressing with adhesive border, net price 10 cm × 12 cm (oval) = £2.20; 13 cm × 15 cm (oval) = £4.11; without adhesive border 10 cm × 10 cm = £2.24; 15 cm × 15 cm = £4.34

Uses chronic wounds such as leg ulcers and pressure sores

Tegasorb® Thin Sterile, semi-permeable, clear film dressing with hydrocolloid and adhesive border, net price 10 cm × 12 cm (oval) = £1.46; 13 cm × 15 cm (oval) = £2.74; without adhesive border 10 cm × 10 cm = £1.47

Uses low to moderately exuding wounds including leg ulcers, abrasions, burns, and donor sites

**Ultec Pro®** (Tyco)

Sterile, semi-permeable hydrocolloid dressing with adhesive border, net price 10.5 cm × 10.5 cm = £1.39, 14 cm × 14 cm = £2.24, 21 cm × 21 cm = £4.49, 15 cm × 18 cm (sacral) = £3.17, 19.5 cm × 23 cm (sacral) = £4.88; without adhesive border 10 cm × 10 cm = £2.19, 15 cm × 15 cm = £4.27, 20 cm × 20 cm = £6.43

Uses lightly to moderately exuding wounds

**Versiva®** (ConvaTec)

Sterile, semi-permeable hydrocolloid dressing with adhesive border, net price 9 cm × 9 cm = £2.26, 11 cm × 19 cm (oval) = £4.00, 14 cm × 14 cm = £4.22, 19 cm × 19 cm = £6.57, 19 cm × 24 cm = £7.93, 19 cm × 17.7 cm (sacral) = £5.59, 21 cm × 22.5 cm (sacral) = £7.93, 19.5 cm × 18.5 cm (heel) = £6.74

Uses chronic and acute exudating wounds

### Keloid dressings

Silicone gel and gel sheets are used to reduce and prevent hypertrophic and keloid scarring. They should not be used on open wounds. Application times should be increased gradually. Silicone sheets can be washed and reused.

**Cica-Care®** (S&N Hlth.)

Soft, self-adhesive, semi-occlusive silicone gel sheet with backing. Net price, 6 cm × 12 cm = £12.66; 15 cm × 12 cm = £24.68

**Dermatix®** (Valeant)

Silicone gel, net price 15 g = £19.00, 60 g = £57.00

**Mepiform®** (Mölnlycke)

Self-adhesive silicone gel sheet with polyurethane film backing, net price 5 cm × 7.5 cm = £3.24, 10 cm × 18 cm = £13.15, 4 cm × 30 cm = £9.26

**Silgel®** (Nagor)

Silicone gel sheet, net price 10 cm × 10 cm = £13.50; 20 cm × 20 cm = £40.00; 40 cm × 40 cm = £144.00; 10 cm × 5 cm = £7.50; 15 cm x 10 cm = £19.50; 30 cm × 5 cm = £19.50; 10 cm × 30 cm = £31.50; 25 cm × 15 cm (submammary) = £21.12; 46 cm × 8.5 cm (abdominal) = £39.46; 5 cm diameter (circular) = £4.00

Silgel® STC-SE silicone gel, net price, 20-mL tube = £19.00

### Hyaluronic acid

**Hyalofill®** (ConvaTec)

Hyalofill-F, NHS flat, non-woven, absorbent fibrous fleece of *Hyaff* (an ester of hyaluronic acid), net price 5 cm × 5 cm = £9.98, 10 cm × 10 cm = £27.68

Uses for treatment of chronic or acute wounds, place on surface of lesion and cover with sterile dressing, renew daily or when saturated (at least every 2–3 days)

Hyalofill-R, NHS absorbent fibrous rope of *Hyaff* (an ester of hyaluronic acid), net price 500 mg = £27.68

Uses for treatment of chronic or acute wounds, position gently inside cavity and cover with sterile dressing, renew daily or when saturated (at least every 2–3 days)

## A8.1.5 Vapour-permeable films and membranes

Vapour-permeable films and membranes allow the passage of water vapour and oxygen but not of water or micro-organisms, and are suitable for mildly exuding wounds. They are highly conformable, convenient to use, provide a moist healing environment, and some may permit constant observation of the wound. However, water vapour loss may occur at a slower rate than exudate is generated, so that fluid accumulates under the dressing, which can lead to tissue maceration and to wrinkling at the adhesive contact site (with risk of bacterial entry). Newer versions have increased moisture vapour permeability; some also contain water-soluble antimicrobials. Despite these advances vapour-permeable films and membranes remain less suitable for large heavily exuding wounds and are probably not suitable for chronic leg ulcers. They are most commonly used as secondary dressings over alginates or gels; they are also sometimes used to protect fragile skin of patients at risk of developing minor skin damage.

**Vapour-permeable Adhesive Film Dressing, BP 1993 (Semi-permeable Adhesive Dressing)**

Sterile, extensible, waterproof, water vapour-permeable polyurethane film coated with synthetic adhesive mass; transparent. Supplied in single-use pieces.

ActivHeal® Film, net price 6 cm × 7 cm = 31p, 10 cm × 12.7 cm = 73p, 15 cm × 17.8 cm = £1.78 (MedLogic)

Alldress®, net price 10 cm × 10 cm = 83p, 15 cm × 15 cm = £1.82, 15 cm × 20 cm = £2.25 (Mölnlycke)

Bioclusive®, net price 10.2 cm × 12.7 cm = £1.45 (J&J)

Blisterfilm®, net price 5 cm × 8 cm = 40p, 9 cm × 10 cm = 70p, 10 cm × 13 cm = 90p, 14 cm × 15 cm = £1.23 (Tyco)

C-View®, net price 6 cm × 7 cm = 37p, 10 cm × 12 cm = £1.02, 12 cm × 12 cm = £1.18, 15 cm × 20 cm = £2.33, 20 cm × 30 cm = £3.53 (NHS) (Unomedical)

Hydrofilm®, net price 6 cm × 9 cm = 50p, 10 cm × 15 cm = £1.32, 12 cm × 25 cm = £2.37 (Hartmann)

Mefilm®, net price 6 cm × 7 cm = 40p, 10 cm × 12.7 cm = £1.08, 10 cm × 25 cm = £2.11, 15 cm × 21.5 cm = £2.67 (Mölnlycke)

Mepore® Ultra, net price 6 cm × 7 cm = 27p, 9 cm × 10 cm = 58p, 9 cm × 15 cm = 87p, 9 cm × 20 cm = £1.31, 9 cm × 25 cm = £1.45, 9 cm × 30 cm = £2.39 (Mölnlycke)

OpSite® Flexigrid, net price 6 cm × 7 cm = 34p, 12 cm × 12 cm = 98p, 15 cm × 20 cm = £2.47, 12 cm × 25 cm = £3.20 (NHS), 10 cm × 12 cm = £2.06 (NHS), *OpSite® Plus*, 5 cm × 5 cm = 27p, 9.5 cm × 8.5 cm = 76p, 10 cm × 12 cm = £1.04, 10 cm × 20 cm = £1.75, 35 cm × 10 cm = £2.89 (S&N Hlth)

Polyskin® II, net price 4 cm × 4 cm = 35p, 5 cm × 7 cm = 38p, 10 cm × 12 cm = 99p, 10 cm × 20 cm = £1.96, 15 cm × 20 cm = £2.26, 20 cm × 25 cm = £3.95 (Tyco)

Polyskin® MR, net price 5 cm × 7 cm = 40p, 10 cm × 12 cm = £1.08, 15 cm × 20 cm = £2.53 (Tyco)

Suprasorb F®, net price 5 cm × 7 cm = 30p, 10 cm × 12 cm = 72p, 15 cm × 20 cm = £2.25, 10 cm × 25 cm = £3.44 NHS (Vernon-Carus)

Tegaderm®, net price 6 cm × 7 cm = 38p, 12 cm × 12 cm = £1.23, 15 cm × 20 cm = £2.34 (3M)

Uses postoperative dressing, donor sites, superficial decubitus ulcers, amputation stumps, stoma care; protective cover to prevent skin breakdown

**Omiderm®** (Chemical Search) NHS

Sterile, water-vapour permeable polyurethane film (plain and meshed versions). Net price 5 cm × 7 cm = £2.00; 8 cm × 10 cm = £3.50, meshed = £4.75; 18 cm × 10 cm = £6.40, meshed = £9.50; 60 cm × 10 cm = £23.50; 21 cm × 31 cm = £24.00, meshed = £32.00; meshed 23 cm × 39 cm = £48.75

Uses ulcers; donor sites; superficial and partial thickness burns; meshed: donor sites, skin grafts

## A8.1.6 Low adherence dressing and wound contact materials

Low adherence dressings and wound contact materials are used as interface layers under secondary absorbent dressings.

**Tulle dressings** are manufactured from cotton or viscose fibres which are impregnated with white or yellow soft paraffin to prevent the fibres from sticking, but this is only partly successful and it may be necessary to change the dressings frequently. The paraffin reduces absorbency of the dressing. Dressings with a reduced content of soft paraffin (i.e. *Paratulle®* and *Unitulle®*) are less liable to interfere with absorption; those containing the traditional amount (such as *Jelonet®*) have been considered more suitable for skin graft transfer.

Medicated tulle dressings are not generally recommended for wound care. Although hypersensitivity is unlikely with **chlorhexidine gauze dressing**, its antibacterial efficacy has not been established.

**Povidone–iodine fabric dressing** is a knitted viscose dressing with povidone–iodine incorporated in a hydrophilic polyethylene glycol basis; this facilitates diffusion of the iodine into the wound and permits removal of the dressing by irrigation. The iodine has a wide spectrum of antimicrobial activity but it is rapidly deactivated by wound exudate; systemic absorption of iodine may occur.

**Perforated film absorbent dressings** partially overcome the problems of adherence but they are suitable only for wounds with mild to moderate amounts of exudate; they are **not** appropriate for leg ulcers or for other lesions that produce large quantities of viscous exudate.

**Knitted viscose primary dressing** is an alternative to tulle dressings for exuding wounds; it is sometimes used as the initial layer of multi-layer compression bandaging.

**Absorbent Cellulose Dressing with Fluid Repellent Backing**

Exu-Dry®, net price 10 cm × 15 cm = 97p, 15 cm × 23 cm = £1.99, 23 cm × 38 cm = £4.62 (S&N Hlth)

Uses primary or secondary dressing for medium to heavily exuding wounds

Mesorb® cellulose wadding pad with gauze wound contact layer and non-woven repellent backing, net price 10 cm × 10 cm = 55p, 10 cm × 15 cm = 71p, 10 cm × 20 cm = 87p, 15 cm × 20 cm = £1.24, 20 cm × 25 cm = £1.97, 20 cm × 30 cm = £2.23 (Mölnlycke)

Uses post-operative use for heavily exuding wounds

**Absorbent Perforated Dressing with Adhesive Border**

Low adherence dressing consisting of viscose and rayon absorbent pad with adhesive border.

Cosmopor E®, net price 5 cm × 7.2 cm = 7p, 6 cm × 10 cm = 13p, 8 cm × 10 cm = 15p, 6 cm × 15 cm = 17p, 8 cm × 15 cm = 24p, 8 cm × 20 cm = 33p, 10 cm × 20 cm = 40p, 10 cm × 25 cm = 49p, 10 cm × 35 cm = 69p (Hartmann)

Medipore® + Pad, net price 5 cm × 7.2 cm = 7p, 10 cm × 10 cm = 15p, 10 cm × 15 cm = 23p, 10 cm × 20 cm = 36p, 10 cm × 25 cm = 44p, 10 cm × 35 cm = 61p (3M)

Medisafe®, net price 6 cm × 8 cm = 12p, 8 cm × 10 cm = 13p, 8 cm × 12 cm = 23p, 9 cm × 15 cm = 29p, 9 cm × 20 cm = 34p, 9 cm × 25 cm = 36p (GP Supplies)

Mepore®, net price 7 cm × 8 cm = 9p, 10 cm × 11 cm = 19p, 11 cm × 15 cm = 32p, 9 cm × 20 cm = 39p, 9 cm × 25 cm = 53p, 9 cm × 30 cm = 61p, 9 cm × 35 cm = 67p (Mölnlycke)

Neosafe®, net price 9 cm × 10 cm = 16p, 9 cm × 20 cm = 34p (Neomedic)

Primapore®, net price 6 cm × 8.3 cm = 16p, 8 cm × 10 cm = 17p, 8 cm × 15 cm = 29p, 10 cm × 20 cm = 37p, 10 cm × 25 cm = 42p, 10 cm × 30 cm = 54p, 10 cm × 35 cm = 85p (S&N Hlth)

Sterifix®, net price 5 cm × 7 cm = 18p, 7 cm × 10 cm = 29p, 10 cm × 14 cm = 52p (Hartmann)

Telfa® Island, net price 5 cm × 10 cm = 8p, 10 cm × 12.5 cm = 26p, 10 cm × 20 cm = 34p, 10 cm × 25.5 cm = 43p, 10 cm × 35 cm = 60p (Tyco)

Uses lightly exuding and post-operative wounds

**Absorbent Perforated Plastic Film Faced Dressing**

(Drug Tariff specification 9). Low-adherence dressing consisting of 3 layers.

Cutilin®, net price 5 cm × 5 cm = 13p, 10 cm × 10 cm = 21p, 10 cm × 20 cm = 40p (Beiersdorf)

Interpose®, net price 5 cm × 5 cm = 9p, 10 cm × 10 cm = 15p, 10 cm × 20 cm = 32p (Frontier)

Melolin®, net price 5 cm × 5 cm = 15p, 10 cm × 10 cm = 24p, 20 cm × 10 cm = 46p (S&N Hlth)

Release®, net price 5 cm × 5 cm = 14p, 10 cm × 10 cm = 22p, 20 cm × 10 cm = 42p (J&J)

Skintact®, net price 5 cm × 5 cm = 10p, 10 cm × 10 cm = 17p, 20 cm × 10 cm = 34p (Robinson)

Solvaline N®, net price 5 cm × 5 cm = 9p, 10 cm × 10 cm = 16p, 10 cm × 20 cm = 32p (Vernon-Carus)

Telfa®, net price 5 cm × 7.5 cm = 12p, 10 cm × 7.5 cm = 15p, 15 cm × 7.5 cm = 17p, 20 cm × 7.5 cm = 28p (Tyco)

Where no size specified by the prescriber, the 5 cm × 5 cm size to be supplied

Uses dressing for post-operative and low exudate wounds; low adherence property and low absorption capacity

**Knitted Viscose Primary Dressing, BP 1993**

Warp knitted fabric manufactured from a bright viscose monofilament.

N-A Dressing®, net price 9.5 cm × 9.5 cm = 33p, 9.5 cm × 19 cm = 63p (J&J)

N-A Ultra® (silicone-coated), net price 9.5 cm × 9.5 cm = 32p, 9.5 cm × 19 cm = 60p (J&J)

Paratex®, net price 9.5 cm × 9.5 cm = 25p (Urgo)

Robinson Primary®, net price 12.5 cm × 14.5 cm = 39p (Robinsons)

Tricotex®, net price 9.5 cm × 9.5 cm = 29p (S&N Hlth)

Uses low adherence wound contact layer for use on ulcerative and other granulating wounds with superimposed absorbent pad

**Paraffin Gauze Dressing, BP 1993**

(Tulle Gras). Fabric of leno weave, weft and warp threads of cotton and/or viscose yarn, impregnated with white or yellow soft paraffin, sterile, 10 cm × 10 cm, net price (light loading) = 27p; (normal loading) = 35p (most suppliers including Vernon-Carus—*Paranet*® (light loading); Aventis Pharma—*Unitulle*® (light loading); S&N Hlth—*Jelonet*® (normal loading))

Uses treatment of abrasions, burns, and other injuries of skin, and ulcerative conditions; postoperatively as penile and vaginal dressing and for sinus packing; heavier loading for skin graft transfer

**Chlorhexidine Gauze Dressing, BP 1993** ▲

Fabric of leno weave, weft and warp threads of cotton and/or viscose yarn, impregnated with ointment containing chlorhexidine acetate, sterile, 5 cm × 5 cm, net price = 25p; 10 cm × 10 cm = 53p(S&N Hlth—*Bactigras*®)

**Povidone–iodine Fabric Dressing**

(Drug Tariff specification 43). Knitted viscose primary dressing impregnated with povidone–iodine ointment 10%, net price 5 cm × 5 cm = 30p; 9.5 cm × 9.5 cm = 45p (J&J—*Inadine*®)

Uses wound contact layer for abrasions and superficial burns

**Atrauman®** (Hartmann)

Non-adherent knitted polyester primary dressing impregnated with neutral triglycerides, 5 cm × 5 cm = 24p, 7.5 cm × 10 cm = 25p, 10 cm × 20 cm = 56p

Uses abrasions, burns, and other injuries of skin, and ulcerative conditions; postoperatively for granulating wounds

**Mepilex®** (Mölnlycke)

Absorbent soft silicone dressing with polyurethane foam film backing, net price 10 cm × 10 cm = £2.33, 10 cm × 20 cm = £3.84, 15 cm × 15 cm = £4.33, 20 cm × 20 cm = £6.41

Mepilex® Border, with soft silicone adhesive border, net price 7.5 cm × 7.5 cm = £1.35, 10 cm × 10 cm = £2.45, 15 cm × 15 cm = £4.00, 15 cm × 20 cm = £5.01

Mepilex® Lite, thin absorbent soft silicone dressing, net price 6 cm × 8.5 cm = £1.60, 10 cm × 10 cm = £1.91, 15 cm × 15 cm = £3.71

Mepilex® Transfer, soft silicone exudate transfer dressing, net price, 15 cm × 20 cm = £9.33, 20 cm × 50 cm = £23.84

**Mepitel®** (Mölnlycke)

Soft silicone wound contact dressing. Net price 5 cm × 7 cm = £1.44, 8 cm × 10 cm = £2.88, 12 cm × 15 cm = £5.83, 20 cm × 30 cm = £14.99

Uses leg ulcers, decubitus ulcers, burns, fixation of skin grafts; should be covered with simple absorbent secondary dressing



**Physiotulle®** (Coloplast)

Non-adherent soft polymer wound contact dressing, net price 10 cm × 10 cm = £1.98, 15 cm × 20 cm = £6.02

Uses leg ulcers, pressure sores, burns, postoperative wounds, donor sites, skin abrasions

[1] **Surgipad®** (J&J) NHS

Absorbent pad of absorbent cotton and viscose in sleeve of non-woven viscose fabric, sterile, net price pouch 12 cm × 10 cm = 18p, 20 cm × 10 cm = 25p, 20 cm × 20 cm = 30p, 40 cm × 20 cm = 41p; non-sterile, net price pack 12 cm × 10 cm = 5p, 20 cm × 10 cm = 10p, 20 cm × 20 cm = 17p, 40 cm × 20 cm = 28p

Uses for heavily exuding wounds requiring frequent dressing changes

1. NHS Except in Sterile Dressing Pack with Non-woven Pads

**Tegapore®** (3M)

Non-adherent soft polymer wound contact dressing, net price 7.5 cm × 10 cm = £2.13, 7.5 cm × 20 cm = £4.17, 20 cm × 25 cm = £10.16

**Urgotul®** (Urgo)

Non-adherent soft polymer wound contact dressing, net price 10 cm × 12 cm = £2.86, 10 cm × 40 cm = £9.34, 15 cm × 20 cm = £7.23

Urgotul® SSD (silver impregnated), net price 10 cm × 12 cm = £2.84, 15 cm × 20 cm = £7.17

UrgoCell® (with polyurethane foam film backing), net price 10 cm × 12 cm = £4.20, 15 cm × 20 cm = £8.50; with adhesive border 13 cm × 13 cm = £4.20, 15 cm × 20 cm = £8.50

## A8.1.7 Odour absorbent dressings

These dressings have an important role in absorbing the odour of infected wounds. Some dressings may also benefit wound healing by binding bacteria, but this effect awaits confirmation.

**Actisorb® Silver 200** (J&J)

(formerly Actisorb® Plus) Knitted fabric of activated charcoal, with one-way stretch, with silver residues, within spun-bonded nylon sleeve. Net price 6.5 cm × 9.5 cm = £1.55, 10.5 cm × 10.5 cm = £2.44, 10.5 cm × 19 cm = £4.43

**CarboFLEX®** (ConvaTec)

Dressing in 5 layers: wound-facing absorbent layer containing alginate and hydrocolloid; water-resistant second layer; third layer containing activated charcoal; non-woven absorbent fourth layer; water-resistant backing layer. Net price 10 cm × 10 cm = £2.74, 8 cm × 15 cm = £3.29, 15 cm × 20 cm = £6.23

**Carbonet®** (S&N Hlth.) NHS

Activated charcoal dressing, net price 10 cm × 10 cm = £3.13, 10 cm × 20 cm = £6.10

**Carbopad® VC** (Vernon-Carus)

Activated charcoal non-absorbent dressing, net price 10 cm × 10 cm = £1.59, 10 cm × 20 cm = £2.15

**CliniSorb® Odour Control Dressings** (CliniMed)

Layer of activated charcoal cloth between viscose rayon with outer polyamide coating. Net price 10 cm × 10 cm = £1.65, 10 cm × 20 cm = £2.20, 15 cm × 25 cm = £3.54

**Lyofoam C®** (Medlock)

Lyofoam sheet with layer of activated charcoal cloth and additional outer envelope of polyurethane foam. Net price 10 cm × 10 cm = £2.69, 15 cm × 20 cm = £6.11, 25 cm × 10 cm = £5.39

## A8.1.8 Dressing packs

The role of dressing packs is very limited. They are used to provide a clean or sterile working surface; packs shown below include cotton wool balls, but they are not recommended for use on wounds.

**Non-Drug Tariff Specification Sterile Dressing Pack**
Contains paper towel, disposable bag, softswabs, dressing pad, softdrape, net price = 60p (Richardson — *Dress-it*®)

**Sterile Dressing Pack**
(Drug Tariff specification 10). Contains gauze and cotton tissue pad, gauze swabs, absorbent cotton wool balls, absorbent paper towel, water repellent inner wrapper. Net price per pack = 79p (Vernon-Carus—*Vernaid*®)

**Sterile Dressing Pack with Non-woven Pads**
(Drug Tariff specification 35). Contains non-woven fabric covered dressing pad, non-woven fabric swabs, absorbent cotton wool balls, absorbent paper towel, water repellent inner wrapper. Net price per pack = 78p (Vernon-Carus—*Vernaid*®)

## A8.1.9 Surgical absorbents

Surgical absorbent dressings, applied directly to the wound, have many disadvantages, since they adhere to the wound, shed fibres into it, and dehydrate it; they also permit leakage of exudate ('strike through') with an associated risk of infection. Surgical absorbents may be used as secondary absorbent layers in the management of heavily exuding wounds.

**Absorbent Cotton, BP**
Carded cotton fibres of not less than 10 mm average staple length, available in rolls and balls, 25 g, net price = 65p; 100 g = £1.49; 500 g = £5.01 (most suppliers). 25-g pack to be supplied when weight not stated
Uses general purpose cleansing and swabbing, pre-operative skin preparation, application of medicaments; supplementary absorbent pad to absorb excess wound exudate

**Absorbent Cotton, Hospital Quality**
As for absorbent cotton but lower quality materials, shorter staple length etc. 100 g, net price = £1.03; 500 g = £3.26 (most suppliers)
Drug Tariff specifies to be supplied only where specifically ordered
Uses suitable only as general purpose absorbent, for swabbing, and routine cleansing of incontinent patients; not for wound cleansing

**Gauze and Cotton Tissue, BP 1988**
Consists of absorbent cotton enclosed in absorbent cotton gauze type 12 or absorbent cotton and viscose gauze type 2. 500 g, net price = £6.35 (most suppliers, includingRobinsons—*Gamgee Tissue*® (blue label))
Uses absorbent and protective pad, as burns dressing on non-adherent layer

**Gauze and Cotton Tissue**
(Drug Tariff specification 14). Similar to above. 500 g, net price = £4.64 (most suppliers, including Robinsons—*Gamgee Tissue*® (pink label))
Drug Tariff specifies to be supplied only where specifically ordered
Uses absorbent and protective pad, as burns dressing on non-adherent layer

**Absorbent Lint, BPC**
Cotton cloth of plain weave with nap raised on one side from warp yarns. 25 g, net price = 81p; 100 g = £2.48; 500 g = £10.44 (most suppliers). 25-g pack supplied where no quantity stated
Note Not recommended for wound management

**Absorbent Cotton Gauze, BP 1988**
Cotton fabric of plain weave, in rolls and as swabs (see below), usually Type 13 light, sterile. 90 cm (all) × 1 m, net price = 98p; 3 m = £2.04; 5 m = £3.19; 10 m = £6.10 (most suppliers). 1-m packet supplied when no size stated
Uses pre-operative preparation, for cleansing and swabbing
Note Drug Tariff also includes unsterilised absorbent cotton gauze, 25 m roll, net price = £13.98

**Absorbent Muslin, BP 1988** NHS
Fabric of plain weave, warp threads of cotton, weft threads of cotton and/or viscose
Uses wet dressing, soaked in 0.9% sterile sodium chloride solution

**Absorbent Cotton Ribbon Gauze, BP 1993** NHS
Cotton fabric of plain weave in ribbon form with fast selvedge edges
Uses post-surgery cavity packing for sinus, dental, throat cavities etc.

**Absorbent Cotton and Viscose Ribbon Gauze, BP 1993**
Woven fabric in ribbon form with fast selvedge edges, warp threads of cotton, weft threads of viscose or combined cotton and viscose yarn, sterile. 5 m (both) × 1.25 cm, net price = 74p; 2.5 cm = 82p
Uses post-surgery cavity packing for sinus, dental, throat cavities etc.

**Gauze Swab, BP 1988**
Consists of absorbent cotton gauze type 13 light or absorbent cotton and viscose gauze type 1 folded into squares or rectangles of 8-ply with no cut edges exposed, net price sterile, 7.5 cm × 7.5 cm 5-pad packet = 36p; non-sterile, 10 cm × 10 cm 100-pad packet = £5.73 (most suppliers)

**Filmated Gauze Swab, BP 1988**
As for Gauze Swab, but with thin layer of Absorbent Cotton enclosed within, net price non-sterile, 10 cm × 10 cm, 100-pad packet = £7.87 (Vernon-Carus—*Cotfil*®)
Uses general swabbing and cleansing

**Non-woven Fabric Swab**
(Drug Tariff specification 28). Consists of non-woven fabric folded 4-ply; alternative to gauze swabs, type 13 light, net price sterile, 7.5 cm × 7.5 cm, 5-pad packet = 23p; non-sterile, 10 cm × 10 cm, 100-pad packet = £2.69 (J & J—*Topper 8*®); 100-pad pack = £2.74 (CliniMed)
Uses general purpose swabbing and cleansing; absorbs more quickly than gauze

**Filmated Non-woven Fabric Swab**
(Drug Tariff specification 29). Film of viscose fibres enclosed within non-woven viscose fabric folded 8-ply, net price non-sterile, 10 cm × 10 cm, 100-pad packet = £5.82 (J & J—*Regal*®)
Uses general purpose swabbing and cleansing

## A8.1.10 Capillary dressings

Capillary dressings consist of an absorbent core of hydrophilic fibres sandwiched between two low-adherent wound-contact layers. Wound exudate is taken up by the dressing and retained within the highly absorbent central layer.

The dressing may be applied intact to relatively superficial areas, but for deeper wounds or cavities it may be cut to shape to ensure good contact with the wound base. Multiple layers may be applied to heavily exuding wounds to further increase the fluid-absorbing capacity of the dressing.

Capillary dressings can be applied to a variety of wounds but they are contra-indicated for heavily bleeding wounds or arterial bleeding.

**Advadraw®** (Advancis)

Non-adherent, sterile dressing consisting of a soft viscose and polyester absorbent pad with central wicking layer between two perforated permeable wound contact layers. Net price 5 cm × 7.5 cm = 55p, 10 cm × 10 cm = 85p, 10 cm × 15 cm = £1.15

Advadraw Spiral®, net price 0.5 cm × 40 cm = 79p

**Vacutex®** (Hybrand)

Low-adherent dressing consisting of two external polyester wound contact layers with central wicking polyester/cotton mix absorbent layer. Net price 5 cm × 5 cm = 94p, 10 cm × 10 cm = £1.66, 10 cm × 15 cm = £2.23, 10 cm × 20 cm = £2.68, 15 cm × 20 cm = £3.14, 20 cm × 20 cm = £4.28

## A8.2 Bandages and adhesives

According to their structure and performance bandages are used for dressing retention, for support, and for compression.

### A8.2.1 Non-extensible bandages

Bandages made from non-extensible woven fabrics have generally been replaced by more conformable products, therefore their role is now extremely limited. Triangular calico bandage has a role as a sling.

**Open-wove Bandage, BP 1988**

Cotton cloth, plain weave, warp of cotton, weft of cotton, viscose, or combination, one continuous length. Type 1, 5 m (all): 2.5 cm, net price = 32p; 5 cm = 53p; 7.5 cm = 75p; 10 cm = 98p (most suppliers) 5 m × 5 cm supplied when size not stated

Uses protection and retention of absorbent dressings; support for minor strains, sprains; securing splints

**Triangular Calico Bandage, BP 1980**

Unbleached calico right-angled triangle. 90 cm × 90 cm × 1.27 m, net price = £1.17 (most suppliers)

Uses sling

**Domette Bandage, BP 1988** NHS

Fabric, plain weave, cotton warp and wool weft (hospital quality also available, all cotton). Net price 5 m (all): 5 cm = 54p; 7.5 cm = 81p; 10 cm = £1.08; 15 cm = £1.61 (Bailey, Robert)

Uses protection and support where warmth required

**Multiple Pack Dressing No. 1**

(Drug Tariff). Contains absorbent cotton, absorbent cotton gauze type 13 light (sterile), open-wove bandages (banded). Net price per pack = £3.71

### A8.2.2 Light-weight conforming bandages

Lightweight conforming bandages are used for dressing retention, with the aim of keeping the dressing close to the wound without inhibiting movement or restricting blood flow. The elasticity of **conforming-stretch bandages** (also termed contour bandages) is greater than that of **cotton conforming bandages**.

**Cotton Conforming Bandage, BP 1988**

Cotton fabric, plain weave, treated to impart some elasticity to warp and weft. Net price 3.5 m (all): type A, 5 cm = 67p, 7.5 cm = 83p, 10 cm = £1.02, 15 cm = £1.39 (S&N Hlth—*Crinx®*)

**Knitted Polyamide and Cellulose Contour Bandage, BP 1988**

Fabric, knitted warp of polyamide filament, weft of cotton or viscose, fast edges, one continuous length. 4 m stretched (all):

K-Band®, net price 5 cm = 19p, 7 cm = 25p, 10 cm = 27p, 15 cm = 47p (Urgo)

Knit-Band®, net price 5 cm = 11p, 7 cm = 16p, 10 cm = 18p, 15 cm = 33p (CliniMed)

Knit Fix®, net price 5 cm = 13p, 7 cm = 18p, 10 cm = 19p, 15 cm = 36p (Bailey, Robert)

**Polyamide and Cellulose Contour Bandage, BP 1988 (formerly Nylon and Viscose Stretch Bandage)**

Fabric, plain weave, warp of polyamide filament, weft of cotton or viscose, fast edges, one continuous length. 4 m stretched (all):

Acti-Wrap®, net price cohesive, 6 cm = 39p, 8 cm = 57p, 10 cm = 68p; latex-free 6 cm = 45p, 8 cm = 65p, 10 cm = 77p (Activa)

Stayform®, net price 5 cm = 31p, 7.5 cm = 39p, 10 cm = 44p, 15 cm = 74p (Robinsons)

Slinky®, net price 5 cm = 41p, 7.5 cm = 59p, 10 cm = 71p, 15 cm = £1.01 (Medlock)

Easifix®, net price 5 cm = 36p, 7.5 cm = 44p, 10 cm = 51p, 15 cm = 87p (S&N Hlth)

**Conforming Bandage (Synthetic)**

Fabric, plain weave, warp of polyamide, weft of viscose. 4 m stretched (all):

Hospiform® (formerly *Peha Crepp®* E), net price 6 cm = 13p, 8 cm = 16p, 10 cm = 19p, 12 cm = 23p (Hartmann)

### A8.2.3 Tubular bandages

Tubular bandages are available in different forms, according to the function required of them. Some are used under orthopaedic casts and some are suitable for protecting areas to which creams or ointments (other than those containing potent corticosteroids) have been applied. The conformability of the elasticated versions makes them particularly suitable for retaining dressings on difficult parts of the body or for soft tissue injury, but their use as the only means of applying pressure to an oedematous limb or to a varicose ulcer is not appropriate, since the pressure they exert is inadequate. Compression hosiery (section A8.3.1) reduces the recurrence of venous leg ulcers and should be considered after wound healing.

**Cotton Stockinette, Bleached, BP 1988**

Knitted fabric, cotton yarn, tubular, net price 1 m × 2.5 cm = 32p; 5 cm = 48p; 7.5 cm = 59p; 6 m × 10 cm = £3.99 (J&J, Medlock)

Uses 1 m lengths, basis (with wadding) for Plaster of Paris bandages etc.; 6 m length, compression bandage

**Elasticated Tubular Bandage, BP 1993**

(formerly Elasticated Surgical Tubular Stockinette). Knitted fabric, elasticated threads of rubber-cored polyamide or polyester with cotton or cotton and viscose yarn, tubular. Lengths 50 cm and 1 m, widths 6.25 cm, 6.75 cm, 7.5 cm, 8.75 cm, 10 cm, 12 cm (other sizes NHS); Shiloh—*Comfigrip®*; Easigrip—*EasiGRIP®*; Sallis—*Eesiban®*; Sigma—*Sigma ETB®*; S&N Hlth—*Tensogrip®* NHS; JLB—*Textube®*; Medlock—*Tubigrip®*. Where no size stated by prescriber the 50 cm length should be supplied and width endorsed

Uses retention of dressings on limbs, abdomen, trunk

**Elasticated Surgical Tubular Stockinette, Foam padded**

(Drug Tariff specification 25). Fabric as for Elasticated Tubular Bandage with polyurethane foam lining. Net price heel, elbow, knee, small = £2.63, medium = £2.83, large = £3.03;

Appendix 8

sacral, small, medium, and large (all) = £13.55 (Medlock—*Tubipad*®)

Uses relief of pressure and elimination of friction in relevant area; porosity of foam lining allows normal water loss from skin surface

**Elasticated Viscose Stockinette**

(Drug Tariff specification 46). Lightweight plain-knitted elasticated tubular bandage.

*Acti-Fast*®, net price 3.5 cm red line (small limb), length 1 m = 74p; 5 cm green line (medium limb), length 1 m = 80p, 3 m = £2.27, 5 m = £3.89; 7.5 cm blue line (large limb), length 1 m = £1.06, 3 m = £2.99, 5 m = £5.22; 10.75 cm yellow line (child trunk), length 1 m = £1.70, 3 m = £4.86, 5 m = £8.36; 17.5 cm beige line (adult trunk), length 1 m = £2.15 (Activa)

*Comfifast*®, net price 3.5 cm red line (small limb), length 1 m = 64p; 5 cm green line (medium limb), length 1 m = 68p, 3 m = £1.94, 5 m = £3.33; 7.5 cm blue line (large limb), length 1 m = 92p, 3 m = £2.56, 5 m = £ 4.47; 10.75 cm yellow line (child trunk), length 1 m = £1.46, 3 m = £4.17, 5 m = £7.16; 17.5 cm beige line (adult trunk), length 1 m = £1.84 (Shiloh)

*Coverflex*®, net price 3.5 cm red line (small limb), length 1 m = 73p; 5 cm green line (medium limb), length 1 m = 76p, 3 m = £2.24, 5 m = £3.87; 7.5 cm blue line (large limb), length 1 m = £1.07, 3 m = £2.54, 5 m = £ 5.04; 10.75 cm yellow line (child trunk), length 1 m = £1.68, 3 m = £4.83, 5 m = £8.50; 17.5 cm beige line (adult trunk), length 1 m = £2.24 (Hartmann)

*Tubifast*®, net price 3.5 cm red line (small limb), length 1 m = 80p; 5 cm green line (medium limb), length 1 m = 87p, 3 m = £2.48, 5 m = £4.23; 7.5 cm blue line (large limb), length 1 m = £1.16, 3 m = £3.26, 5 m = £5.68; 10.75 cm yellow line (child trunk), length 1 m = £1.85, 3 m = £5.30, 5 m = £9.11; 17.5 cm beige line (adult trunk), length 1 m = £2.34; vest, 6–24 months = £10.07, 2–5 years = £13.43, 5–8 years = £15.10, 8–11 years = £16.78, 11–14 years = £16.78; tights (pair) 6–24 months = £10.07; leggings (pair) 2–5 years = £13.43, 5–8 years = £15.10, 8–11 years = £16.78, 11–14 years = £16.78; socks (pair) = £4.20 (Medlock)

Uses retention of dressings

**Ribbed Cotton and Viscose Surgical Tubular Stockinette, BP 1988**

Knitted fabric of 1:1 ribbed structure, singles yarn spun from blend of two-thirds cotton and one-third viscose fibres, tubular. Length 5 m (all):

type A (lightweight): net price arm/leg (child), arm (adult) 5 cm = £2.26; arm (OS adult), leg (adult) 7.5 cm = £2.97; leg (OS adult) 10 cm = £3.94; trunk (child) 15 cm = £5.68; trunk (adult) 20 cm = £6.55; trunk (OS adult) 25 cm = £7.84 (SSL)

type B (heavyweight): sizes as for type A, net price £2.26–£7.84 (Sallis—*Eesiban*®)

Drug Tariff specifies various combinations of sizes to provide sufficient material for part or full body coverage

Uses protective dressings with tar-based and other non-steroid ointments

**Tubular Gauze Bandage, Seamless** NHS

Unbleached cotton yarn, positioned with applicators. Net price 20 m roll (all): 00 = £2.95; 01 = £3.55; 12 = £4.60; 34 = £6.75; 56 = £9.35; 78 = £10.75; T1 = £14.75; T2 = £19.00 (Medlock—*Tubegauz*®)

Uses retention of dressings on limbs, abdomen, trunk

## A8.2.4 Support bandages

Light support bandages, which include the various forms of crepe bandage, are used in the prevention of oedema; they are also used to provide support for mild sprains and joints but their effectiveness has not been proven for this purpose. Since they have limited extensibility, they are able to provide light support without exerting undue pressure. For a warning against injudicious compression see section A8.2.5.

**Crepe Bandage, BP 1988**

Fabric, plain weave, warp of wool threads and crepe-twisted cotton threads, weft of cotton threads; stretch bandage. Net price 4.5 m stretched (all): 5 cm = 93p; 7.5 cm = £1.31; 10 cm = £1.72; 15 cm = £2.49 (most suppliers)

Uses light support system for strains, sprains, compression over paste bandages for varicose veins

**Cotton Crepe Bandage**

light support bandage, net price 4.5 m stretched (all): 5 cm = 48p; 7.5 cm = 67p; 10 cm = 87p; 15 cm = £1.27 (Bailey, Robert– *Hospicrepe 239*)

**Cotton Crepe Bandage, BP 1988**

Fabric, plain weave, warp of crepe-twisted cotton threads, weft of cotton and/or viscose threads; stretch bandage. Net price 4.5 m stretched (both): 7.5 cm = £2.93; 10 cm = £3.77; other sizes NHS (most suppliers)

Uses light support system for strains, sprains, compression over paste bandages for varicose ulcers

**Cotton, Polyamide and Elastane Bandage**

Fabric, cotton, polyamide, and elastane; light support bandage (Type 2). 4.5 m stretched (all): 5 cm, net price = 59p, 7.5 cm = 79p, 10 cm = 99p (Neomedic—*Neosport*®); 5 cm, net price = 68p, 7.5 cm = 97p, 10 cm = £1.24, 15 cm = £1.78 (S&N Hlth —*Soffcrepe*®); 10 cm, net price = £1.18 (Medlock—*Setocrepe*®)

Uses light support for sprains and strains; retention of dressings

**Cotton Stretch Bandage, BP 1988**

Fabric, plain weave, warp of crepe-twisted cotton threads, weft of cotton threads; stretch bandage, lighter than cotton crepe. Net price 4.5 m stretched (all): 5 cm = 56p; 7.5 cm = 78p; 10 cm = £1.04; 15 cm = £1.48 (Bailey, Robert—*Hospicrepe 233*)

Uses light support system for strains, sprains, compression over paste bandages for varicose veins

**Cotton Suspensory Bandage**

(Drug Tariff). Type 1: cotton net bag with draw tapes and webbing waistband; net price small, medium, and large (all) = £1.62, extra large = £1.72. Type 2: cotton net bag with elastic edge and webbing waistband; small = £1.79, medium = £1.85, large = £1.91, extra large = £1.99. Type 3: cotton net bag with elastic edge and webbing waistband with elastic insertion; small, medium, and large (all) = £1.94; extra large = £2.00. Type supplied to be endorsed

Uses support of scrotum

**Knitted Elastomer and Viscose Bandage**

Knitted fabric, viscose and elastomer yarn. Type 2 (light support bandage) 4.5 m stretched (all):

K-Lite®, net price 5 cm = 53p, 7 cm = 74p, 10 cm = 72p, 15 cm = £1.40 (Urgo)

Knit-Firm®, net price 5 cm = 39p, 7 cm = 55p, 10 cm = 72p, 15 cm = £1.04 (Bailey, Robert)

Ultra Lite®, net price 5 cm = 52p, 7 cm = 73p, 10 cm = 95p, 15 cm = £1.37 (Robinson)

Uses light support for sprains and strains

Type 3a (light compression bandage):

Elset®, 6 m stretched, net price 10 cm = £2.55, 15 cm = £2.76; 8 m stretched, 10 cm = £3.26 (Medlock)

Elset® S, 12 m stretched, net price 15 cm = £5.48 (Medlock)

K-Plus®, net price 6 m = £1.34, 8.7 m = £2.17 (Urgo)

Mill Plus®, 6 m stretched, net price 10 cm = £1.34; 8.7 m stretched, 10 cm = £1.81 (Bailey, Robert)

Ultra Plus®, net price 8.7 m stretched, 10 cm = £2.05 (Robinson)

## A8.2.5 High compression bandages

High compression products are used to provide the high compression needed for the management of gross varices, post-thrombotic venous insufficiency, venous leg ulcers, and gross oedema in average-sized limbs. Their use calls for an expert knowledge of the elastic properties of the products and experience in the technique of providing careful graduated compression. Inappropriate application can lead to uneven and inadequate pressures or to hazardous levels of pressure. In particular, injudicious use of compression in limbs with arterial disease has been reported to cause severe skin and tissue necrosis (in some instances calling for amputation). Doppler testing is required before treatment with compression. Pentoxifylline (section 2.6.4.1) may be of benefit if a chronic venous leg ulcer does not respond to compression bandaging [unlicensed indication].

### High compression bandages

**PEC High Compression Bandage**

(Drug Tariff specification 52). Polyamide, elastane, and cotton compression (high) extensible bandage, 3.5 m unstretched (both): net price 7.5 cm = £2.68; 10 cm = £3.46 (Medlock—*Setopress®*)

**VEC High Compression Bandage**

(Drug Tariff specification 52). Viscose, elastane, and cotton compression (high) extensible bandage, 3 m unstretched (both); net price 7.5 cm = £2.70; 10 cm = £3.47 (S&N—*Tensopress®*)

**High Compression Bandage**

(Drug Tariff specification 52). Cotton, viscose, nylon, and Lycra® extensible bandage, 3 m (unstretched), 10 cm = £3.41 (ConvaTec—*SurePress®*); 3.5 m (unstretched), 10 cm = £1.95 (Advancis—*Adva-Co®*)

**ProGuide®** (S&N Hlth.)

Two layer system, pack containing wound contact layer, absorbent padding (ProGuide® #1), and a high compression bandage (ProGuide® #2), for ankle circumference 18–22 cm (red), net price = £9.23, 22–28 cm (yellow) = £9.74, 28–32 cm (green) = £10.24

Note Second layer is orthopaedic padding; to be used with any High Compression bandage

### Short Stretch Compression Bandage

Short stretch bandages help to reduce oedema and promote healing of venous leg ulcers. They are also used to reduce swelling associated with lymphoedema. They are applied at full stretch over padding (*see* Sub-compression Wadding Bandage below) which protects areas of high pressure and sites at high risk of pressure damage.

**Actiban®** (Activa)

Net price (all 5 m), 8 cm = £3.22; 10 cm = £3.46; 12 cm = £4.21

**Actico®** (Activa)

Cohesive, net price (all 6 m) 4 cm = £2.49, 6 cm = £2.69, 8 cm = £3.09, 10 cm = £3.21, 12 cm = £4.09

**Comprilan®** (Beiersdorf)

Net price (all 5 m) 6 cm = £2.68; 8 cm = £3.15; 10 cm = £3.39; 12 cm = £4.13

**Rosidal K®** (Vernon-Carus)

Net price (all 5 m) 8 cm = £3.08; 10 cm = £3.36; 12 cm = £4.08; NHS 6 cm = £2.58

**Silkolan®** (Urgo)

Net price (all 5 m) 8 cm = £3.20; 10 cm = £3.62

### Sub-compression Wadding Bandage

**Advasoft®** (Advancis)

Net price 3.5 m unstretched, 10 cm = 39p

**Cellona® Undercast Padding** (Vernon-Carus)

Net price 2.75 m unstretched (all): 7.5 cm = 37p; 10 cm = 46p; 15 cm = 59p

**Flexi-Ban®** (Activa)

Padding, net price 3.5 m unstretched, 10cm = 48p

**K-Soft®** (Urgo)

Net price 3.5 m unstretched, 10 cm = 43p

**Ortho-Band Plus®** (Bailey, Robert)

Net price 10 cm × 3.5 cm unstretched = 40p

**Profore® #1** (S&N Hlth.)

Natural fleece, net price 3.5 m unstretched, 10 cm = 66p (Formerly *Soffban® Natural*)

**Softexe®** (Medlock)

Net price 3.5 m unstretched, 10 cm = 62p

**SurePress®** (ConvaTec)

Absorbent padding, net price 3 m unstretched, 10 cm = 52p

**Ultra Soft®** (Robinsons)

Soft absorbent bandage, net price 3.5 m unstretched, 10 cm = 42p

**Velband®** (J&J)

Absorbent padding, net price 4.5 m unstretched, 10 cm = 72p

## A8.2.6 Extra-high performance compression bandages

These bandages are capable of applying pressures even higher than those of high compression bandages, therefore the same stringent warnings apply. Their use is reserved for the largest and most oedematous limbs. Extra-high performance compression bandages are poorly tolerated by patients.

**Elastic Web Bandage, BP 1993**

(Also termed Blue Line Webbing). Characteristic fabric woven ribbon fashion, warp threads of cotton and rubber with mid-line threads coloured blue, weft threads of cotton or combined cotton and viscose; may be dyed skin colour; with or without foot loop. Per m (both) 7.5 cm, net price = 80p; 10 cm = £1.15; with foot loop (Drug Tariff specification 2a) 7.5 cm = £4.62

Uses provision of support and high compression over large surface

**Elastic Web Bandage without Foot Loop**

(Also termed Red Line Webbing) (Drug Tariff specification 2b) (Scott-Curwen). Characteristic fabric woven ribbon fashion, warp threads of cotton and rubber with mid-line threads coloured red, weft threads of cotton or combined cotton and viscose. 7.5 cm × 2.75 m (2.5 m unstretched), net price = £3.65; 7.5 cm × 3.75 m (3.5 m unstretched) = £4.41

Uses provision of support and high compression over large surfaces

**Heavy Cotton and Rubber Elastic Bandage, BP 1993**

Heavy version of above with one end folded as foot loop; fastener also supplied. 1.8 m unstretched × 7.5 cm, net price = £12.40 (SSL, S&N Hlth—*Elastoweb®*).

Uses provision of high even compression over large surface

## A8.2.7 Adhesive bandages

**Elastic adhesive bandages** are used to provide compression in the treatment of varicose veins and for the support of injured joints; they should no longer be used for the support of fractured ribs and clavicles. They have also been used with **zinc paste bandage** in the treatment of venous ulcers, but they can cause skin reactions in susceptible patients and may not produce sufficient pressures for healing (significantly lower than those provided by other compression bandages).

**Elastic Adhesive Bandage, BP 1993**

Woven fabric, elastic in warp (crepe-twisted cotton threads), weft of cotton and/or viscose threads spread with adhesive mass containing zinc oxide. 4.5 m stretched (all): 5 cm, net price = £3.46; 7.5 cm = £5.00; 10 cm = £6.65 (Robinsons—

*Flexoplast*®; S&N Hlth—*Elastoplast*® Bandage). 7.5 cm width supplied when size not stated

Uses compression for chronic leg ulcers; compression and support for swollen or sprained joints

## A8.2.8 Cohesive bandages

**Cohesive bandages** adhere to themselves, but not to the skin, and are useful for providing support for sports use where ordinary stretch bandages might become displaced and adhesive bandages are inappropriate. Care is needed in their application, however, since the loss of ability for movement between turns of the bandage to equalise local areas of high tension carries the potential for creating a tourniquet effect. They should not be used if arterial disease is suspected.

### Cohesive extensible bandages

These elastic bandages adhere to themselves and not to skin; this prevents slipping during use.

*Uses:* support of sprained joints; outer layer of multi-layer compression bandaging

**Coban®** (3M)

Net price 6 m stretched, 10 cm = £2.95; other sizes NHS 4.5 m stretched (all): 2.5 cm = £1.29; 5 cm = £1.81; 7.5 cm = £2.74; 10 cm = £3.61; 15 cm = £5.33

**Ultra Fast®** (Robinsons)

Latex-free, net price 6.3 m stretched, 10 cm = £2.82

## A8.2.9 Medicated bandages

**Zinc Paste Bandage** remains one of the standard treatments for leg ulcers and can be left on undisturbed for up to a week; it is often used in association with compression for treatment of venous ulcers.

Zinc paste bandages are also used with **coal tar** or **ichthammol** in chronic lichenified skin conditions such as chronic eczema (ichthammol often being preferred since its action is considered to be milder). They are also used with **calamine** in milder eczematous skin conditions (but the inclusion of **clioquinol** may lead to irritation in susceptible subjects).

**Zinc Paste Bandage, BP 1993**

Cotton fabric, plain weave, impregnated with suitable paste containing zinc oxide; requires additional bandaging. Net price 6 m × 7.5 cm = £3.28 (Medlock—*Steripaste*® (15%), *excipients: include* polysorbate 80); £3.23 (Medlock—*Zincaband*® (15%), *excipients: include* hydroxybenzoates); £3.37 (S&N Hlth—*Viscopaste PB7*® (10%), *excipients: include* hydroxybenzoates)

**Zinc Paste and Calamine Bandage**

(Drug Tariff specification 5). Cotton fabric, plain weave, impregnated with suitable paste containing calamine and zinc oxide; requires additional bandaging. Net price 6 m × 7.5 cm = £3.33 (Medlock—*Calaband*®)

**Zinc Paste and Ichthammol Bandage, BP 1993**

Cotton fabric, plain weave, impregnated with suitable paste containing zinc oxide and ichthammol; requires additional bandaging. Net price 6 m × 7.5 cm = £3.24 (Medlock—*Icthaband*® (15/2%), *excipients: include* hydroxybenzoates; S&N Hlth—*Ichthopaste*® (6/2%)

Excipients none as listed in section 13.1.3

Uses see section 13.5

### Medicated stocking

**Zipzoc®** (S&N Hlth.)

Sterile rayon stocking impregnated with ointment containing zinc oxide 20%. Net price 4-pouch carton = £12.50; 10-pouch carton = £31.26

Uses chronic leg ulcers; can be used under appropriate compression bandages or hosiery in chronic venous insufficiency

## A8.2.10 Multi-layer compression bandaging

Multi-layer compression bandaging systems are an alternative to High Compression Bandages (section A8.2.5) for the treatment of venous leg ulcers. Compression is achieved by the combined effects of two or three extensible bandages applied over a layer of orthopaedic wadding.

**Hospifour®** (Bailey, Robert)

*Hospifour*® # 1 (Ortho-Band Plus®—see Sub-compression Wadding Bandage); *Hospifour*® # 2 (*Hospicrepe 239*®—see Cotton Crepe Bandage); *Hospifour*® # 3 (*Mill Plus*® —see Knitted Elastomer and Viscose Bandage); *Hospifour*® # 4 (*AAA-Flex*®), net price 10 cm × 6.3 m (stretched) = £1.93

**K-Four®** (Urgo)

*K-Four*® # 1 (*K-Soft*®—see Sub-compression Wadding Bandage); *K-Four*® # 2 (*Ultra Lite*®—see Knitted Elastomer and Viscose Bandage); *K-Four*® # 3 (*Ultra Plus*®—see Knitted Elastomer and Viscose Bandage); *K-Four*® # 4 (*Ko-Flex*®), net price 10 cm × 6 m (unstretched) = £2.90

Multi-layer compression bandaging kit, four layer system, for ankle circumference 18–25 cm, net price = £6.67

**Profore®** (S&N Hlth.)

*Profore*® wound contact layer (*Tricotex*®—see Knitted Viscose Primary Dressing); *Profore*® *#1* (see Sub-compression Wadding bandage); *Profore*® *#2* (*Soffcrepe*®—see Cotton, Polyamide and Elastane Bandage); *Profore*® *#3* (*Litepress*® NHS—see Knitted Elastomer and Viscose Bandage); *Profore*® *#4* (*Co-Plus*® NHS—see Cohesive bandages); *Profore*® *Plus* = £3.46

Multi-layer compression bandaging kit, four layer system, for ankle circumference up to 18 cm, net price = £9.58, 18–25 cm = £8.92, 25–30 cm = £7.40, above 30 cm = £11.09

**System 4®** (Medlock)

*System 4*® wound contact layer (*Setoprime*® 9.5 cm × 9.5 cm; *System 4*® *#1* (*Softexe*®—see Sub-compression Wadding Bandage), *System 4*® *#2* (*Setocrepe*®—see Cotton, Polyamide and Elastane Bandage); *System 4*® *#3* (*Elset*®—see Knitted Elastomer and Viscose Bandage); *System 4*® *#4* (*Coban*®—see Cohesive bandages)

Multi-layer compression bandaging kit, four layer system, for ankle circumference 18–25 cm, net price = £8.29

**Ultra Four®** (Robinsons)

*Ultra Four*® wound dressing 14.5 cm × 12.5 cm; *Ultra Four*® *#1* (Robinsons—*Ultra Soft*®—see Sub-compression Wadding Bandage); *Ultra Four*® *#2* (Robinsons—*Ultra Lite*®—see Knitted Elastomer and Viscose Bandage); *Ultra Four*® *#3* (Robinsons—*Ultra Plus*®—see Knitted Elastomer and Viscose Bandage); *Ultra Four*® *#4* (Robinsons—*Ultra Fast*®—see Cohesive bandages)

Multi-layer compression bandaging kit, four layer system, for ankle circumference 18–25 cm, net price = £6.16

## A8.2.11 Surgical adhesive tapes

Adhesive tapes are useful for retaining dressings on joints or awkward body parts. These tapes, particularly those containing rubber, can cause irritant and allergic reactions in susceptible patients; synthetic adhesives have been developed to overcome this problem, but they, too, may sometimes be associated with reactions. Adhesive tapes that are occlusive may cause skin maceration. Care is needed not to apply these tapes under tension, to avoid creating a tourniquet effect. If applied over joints they need to be orientated so that the area of maximum extensibility of the fabric is in the direction of movement of the limb.

## Permeable adhesive tapes

**Elastic Adhesive Tape, BP 1988**
(Elastic Adhesive Plaster). Woven fabric, elastic in warp (crepe-twisted cotton threads), weft of cotton and/or viscose threads, spread with adhesive mass containing zinc oxide. Net price 4.5 m stretched × 2.5 cm = £1.55 (Robinsons—*Flexoplast®*; S&N—*Elastoplast®*)
Uses securing dressings
For 5 cm width, see Elastic Adhesive Bandage

**Permeable, Apertured Non-Woven Synthetic Adhesive Tape, BP 1988**
Non-woven fabric with a polyacrylate adhesive.
*Hypafix®*, net price 10 m (all): 2.5 cm = £1.51, 5 cm = £2.39, 10 cm = £4.18, 15 cm = £6.19, 20 cm = £8.21, 30 cm = £11.87 (BSN Medical)
*Mefix®*, net price 5 m (all): 2.5 cm = 90p, 5 cm = £1.58; 10 cm = £2.53, 15 cm = £3.45, 20 cm = £4.42, 30 cm = £6.34 (Mölnlycke)
*Omnifix®*, net price 10 m (all): 5 cm = £2.15, 10 cm = £3.62, 15 cm = £5.34 (Hartmann)
Uses securing dressings

**Permeable Non-woven Synthetic Adhesive Tape, BP 1988**
Backing of paper-based or non-woven textile material spread with a polymeric adhesive mass. 5 m (all):
Clinipore®, net price 1.25 cm = 35p, 2.5 cm = 59p, 5 cm = 99p (Clinisupplies)
Leukofix®, net price 1.25 cm = 51p, 2.5 cm = 81p, 5 cm = £1.42 (BSN Medical)
Leukopor®, net price 1.25 cm = 45p, 2.5 cm = 70p, 5 cm = £1.23 (Beiersdorf)
Mediplast®, net price 1.25 cm = 30p, 2.5 cm = 50p (Neomedic)
Micropore®, net price 1.25 cm = 60p, 2.5 cm = 89p, 5 cm = £1.57 (3M)
Scanpor®, net price 1.25 cm = 40p, 2.5 cm = 64p, 5 cm = £1.11 (BioDiagnostics)
Where no brand stated by prescriber, net price of tape supplied not to exceed 35p (1.25 cm), 59p (2.5 cm), 99p (5 cm)
Uses securing dressings; skin closures for small incisions for patients with skin reactions to other plasters and strapping, which require use for long periods

**Permeable Woven Synthetic Adhesive Tape, BP 1988**
Non-extensible closely woven fabric, spread with a polymeric adhesive. Net price 5 m (all): 1.25 cm = 72p; 2.5 cm = £1.06; 5 cm = £1.84 (Beiersdorf—*Leukosilk®*)
Uses securing dressings for patients with skin reactions to other plasters and strapping, which require use for long periods

**Zinc Oxide Adhesive Tape, BP 1988**
(Zinc Oxide Plaster). Fabric, plain weave, warp and weft of cotton and /or viscose, spread with an adhesive containing zinc oxide. 5 m (all): 1.25 cm, net price = 88p; 2.5 cm = £1.27; 5 cm = £2.15; 7.5 cm = £3.23 (most suppliers)
Uses securing dressings and immobilising small areas

**Mepitac®** (Mölnlycke)
Soft silicone, water-resistant, knitted fabric, polyurethane film tape, net price 2 cm × 3 m = £6.04, 4 cm × 1.5 m = £6.04
Uses securing dressing and appliances, skin protection under devices

**Strappal®** (BSN Medical)
Zinc oxide adhesive tape. Net price 5 m (all): 1.25 cm = 86p, 2.5 cm = £1.24, 5 cm = £2.10, 7.5 cm = £3.15; other sizes NHS

## Occlusive adhesive tapes

**Impermeable Plastic Adhesive Tape, BP 1988**
Extensible water-impermeable plastic film spread with an adhesive mass. Net price 2.5 cm × 3 m = £1.23; 2.5 cm × 5 m = £1.84; 5 cm × 5 m = £2.33; 7.5 cm × 5 m = £3.39 (Robinsons; Medlock—*Setoplast®*; S&N Hlth)
Uses securing dressings; covering site of infection where exclusion of air, water, and water vapour is required

**Impermeable Plastic Synthetic Adhesive Tape, BP 1988**
Extensible water-impermeable plastic film spread with a polymeric adhesive mass. Net price 5 m (both): 2.5 cm = £1.72; 5 cm = £3.27 (3M—*Blenderm®*)
Uses isolating wounds from external environment; covering sites where total exclusion of water and water vapour required; securing dressings and appliances

# A8.2.12 Adhesive dressings

Adhesive dressings (also termed 'island dressings') have a limited role for minor wounds only. The inclusion of an antiseptic is not particularly useful and may cause skin irritation in susceptible subjects.

## Permeable adhesive dressings

**Elastic Adhesive Dressing, BP 1993** NHS
Wound dressing or dressing strip, pad attached to piece of extension plaster, leaving suitable adhesive margin; both pad and margin covered with suitable protector; pad may be dyed yellow and may be impregnated with suitable antiseptic (see below); extension plaster may be perforated or ventilated
Uses general purpose wound dressing
Note Permitted antiseptics are aminoacridine hydrochloride (aminacrine hydrochloride), chlorhexidine hydrochloride (both 0.07–0.13%), chlorhexidine gluconate (0.11–0.20%); domiphen bromide (0.05–0.25%)

**Permeable Plastic Wound Dressing, BP 1993** NHS
Consisting of an absorbent pad, which may be dyed and impregnated with a suitable antiseptic (see under Elastic Adhesive Dressing), attached to a piece of permeable plastic surgical adhesive tape, to leave a suitable adhesive margin; both pad and margin covered with suitable protector (most suppliers)
Uses general purpose wound dressing, permeable to air and water

## Vapour permeable adhesive dressings

**Vapour-permeable Waterproof Plastic Wound Dressing, BP 1993**
(former Drug Tariff title: Semipermeable Waterproof Plastic Wound Dressing). Consists of absorbent pad, may be dyed and impregnated with suitable antiseptic (see under Elastic Adhesive Dressing), attached to piece of semi-permeable waterproof surgical adhesive tape, to leave suitable adhesive margin; both pad and margin covered with suitable protector. 8.5 cm × 6 cm, net price = 34p (S&N Hlth—*Elastoplast Airstrip®*)
Uses general purpose waterproof wound dressing, permeable to air and water vapour

## Occlusive adhesive dressings

**Impermeable Plastic Wound Dressing, BP 1993** NHS
Consists of absorbent pad, may be dyed and impregnated with suitable antiseptic (see under Elastic Adhesive Dressing), attached to piece of impermeable plastic surgical

Appendix 8

adhesive tape, to leave suitable adhesive margin; both pad and margin covered with suitable protector (most suppliers)
*Uses:* protective covering for wounds requiring an occlusive dressing

## A8.2.13 Skin closure dressings

Skin closure strips are used as an alternative to sutures for minor cuts and lacerations.

**Skin closure strips, sterile**

Leukostrip®, 6.4 mm × 76 mm, 3 strips per envelope. Net price 10 envelopes = £5.46 (Beiersdorf)

Steri-strip®, 6 mm × 75 mm, 3 strips per envelope. Net price 12 envelopes = £8.52; ~~NHS~~ 3 mm × 75 mm, 12 envelopes = £8.32; 12 mm × 100 mm, 12 envelopes = £8.52 (3M)

Drug Tariff specifies that these are specifically for personal administration by the prescriber

# A8.3 Elastic hosiery

Before elastic hosiery can be dispensed, the quantity (single or pair), article (including accessories), and compression class (I, II or III) must be specified by the prescriber; all dispensed articles must state on the packaging that they conform with Drug Tariff technical specification No. 40, for further details see Drug Tariff.

**Note** Graduated compression tights are ~~NHS~~

## A8.3.1 Graduated compression hosiery

**Class 1 Light Support**

Hosiery, compression at ankle 14–17 mm Hg, thigh length or below knee with knitted in heel. Net price per pair, circular knit (standard), thigh length = £7.02, below knee = £6.41; light weight elastic net (made-to-measure), thigh length = £18.79, below knee = £14.67

Uses superficial or early varices, varicosis during pregnancy

**Class 2 Medium Support**

Hosiery, compression at ankle 18–24 mm Hg, thigh length or below knee with knitted in heel. Net price per pair, circular knit (standard), thigh length = £10.43, below knee = £9.37, (made-to-measure), thigh length = £34.85, below knee = £21.80; net (made-to-measure), thigh length = £18.79, below knee = £14.67; flat bed (made-to-measure, only with closed heel and open toe), thigh length = £34.85, below knee = £21.80

Uses varices of medium severity, ulcer treatment and prophylaxis, mild oedema, varicosis during pregnancy

**Class 3 Strong Support**

Hosiery, compression at ankle 25–35 mm Hg, thigh length or below knee with open or knitted in heel. Net price per pair, circular knit (standard), thigh length = £12.36, below knee = £10.63, (made-to-measure) thigh length = £34.85, below knee = £21.80; flat bed (made-to-measure, only with open heel and open toe), thigh length = £34.85, below knee = £21.80

Uses gross varices, post thrombotic venous insufficiency, gross oedema, ulcer treatment and prophylaxis

## A8.3.2 Accessories

**Suspender**

Suspender, for thigh stockings, net price = 61p, belt (specification 13), = £4.68, fitted (additional price) = 61p

## A8.3.3 Anklets

**Class 2 Medium Support**

Anklets, compression 18–24 mm Hg, circular knit (standard and made-to-measure), net price per pair = £6.14; flat bed (standard and made-to-measure) = £12.76; made-to-measure = £12.76

Uses soft tissue support

**Class 3 Strong Support**

Anklets, compression 25–35 mm Hg, circular knit (standard and made-to-measure), net price per pair = £8.57; flat bed (standard) = £8.57; made-to-measure = £12.76

Uses soft tissue support

## A8.3.4 Knee caps

**Class 2 Medium Support**

Kneecaps, compression 18–24 mm Hg, circular knit (standard and made-to-measure), net price per pair = £6.14; flat bed (standard and made-to-measure) = £12.76; net made-to-measure = £10.03

Uses soft tissue support

**Class 3 Strong Support**

Kneecaps, compression 25–35 mm Hg, circular knit (standard and made-to-measure), net price per pair = £8.19; flat bed (standard) = £8.19; made-to-measure = £12.76

Uses soft tissue support

# A9 Cautionary and advisory labels for dispensed medicines

Numbers following the preparation entries in the BNF correspond to the code numbers of the cautionary labels that pharmacists are recommended to add when dispensing. It is also expected that pharmacists will counsel patients when necessary.

Counselling needs to be related to the age, experience, background, and understanding of the individual patient. The pharmacist should ensure that the patient understands how to take or use the medicine and how to follow the correct dosage schedule. Any effects of the medicine on driving or work, any foods or medicines to be avoided, and what to do if a dose is missed should also be explained. Other matters, such as the possibility of staining of the clothes or skin by a medicine should also be mentioned.

For some preparations there is a special need for counselling, such as an unusual method or time of administration or a potential interaction with a common food or domestic remedy, and this is indicated where necessary.

**Original packs** Most preparations are now dispensed in unbroken original packs (see Patient Packs, p. vii) that include further advice for the patient in the form of patient information leaflets. Label 10 may be of value where appropriate. More general leaflets advising on the administration of preparations such as eye drops, eye ointments, inhalers, and suppositories are also available.



**Scope of labels** In general no label recommendations have been made for injections on the assumption that they will be administered by a healthcare professional or a well-instructed patient. The labelling is not exhaustive and pharmacists are recommended to use their professional discretion in labelling new preparations and those for which no labels are shown.

Individual labelling advice is not given on the administration of the large variety of antacids. In the absence of instructions from the prescriber, and if on enquiry the patient has had no verbal instructions, the directions given under 'Dose' should be used on the label.

It is recognised that there may be occasions when pharmacists will use their knowledge and professional discretion and decide to omit one or more of the recommended labels for a particular patient. In this case counselling is of the utmost importance. There may also be an occasion when a prescriber does not wish additional cautionary labels to be used, in which case the prescription should be endorsed 'NCL' (no cautionary labels). The exact wording that is required instead should then be specified on the prescription.

Pharmacists label medicines with various wordings in addition to those directions specified on the prescription. Such labels include 'Shake the bottle', 'For external use only', and 'Store in a cool place', as well as 'Discard . . . . days after opening' and 'Do not use after . . . .', which apply particularly to antibiotic mixtures, diluted liquid and topical preparations, and to eye-drops. Although not listed in the BNF these labels should continue to be used when appropriate; indeed, 'For external use only' is a legal requirement on external liquid preparations, while 'Keep out of the reach of children' is a legal requirement on all dispensed medicines. Care should be taken not to obscure other relevant information with adhesive labelling.

It is the usual practice for patients to take standard tablets with water or other liquid and for this reason no separate label has been recommended.

The label wordings recommended by the BNF apply to medicines dispensed against a prescription. Patients should be aware that a dispensed medicine should never be taken by, or shared with, anyone other than for whom the prescriber intended it. Therefore, the BNF does not include warnings against the use of a dispensed medicine by persons other than for whom it was specifically prescribed.

The label or labels for each preparation are recommended after careful consideration of the information available. However, it is recognised that in some cases this information may be either incomplete or open to a different interpretation. The Executive Editor will therefore be grateful to receive any constructive comments on the labelling suggested for any preparation.

## Recommended label wordings

Wordings which can be given as separate warnings are labels 1-19 and labels 29-33. Wordings which can be incorporated in an appropriate position in the directions for dosage or administration are labels 21-28. A label has been omitted for number 20.

If separate labels are used it is recommended that the wordings be used without modification. If changes are made to suit computer requirements, care should be taken to retain the sense of the original.

1 **Warning. May cause drowsiness**
To be used on *preparations for children* containing antihistamines, or other preparations given to children where the warnings of label 2 on driving or alcohol would not be appropriate.

2 **Warning. May cause drowsiness. If affected do not drive or operate machinery. Avoid alcoholic drink**
To be used on *preparations for adults that can cause drowsiness*, thereby affecting the ability to drive and operate hazardous machinery; label 1 is more appropriate for children. *It is an offence to drive while under the influence of drink or drugs.*

Some of these preparations only cause drowsiness in the first few days of treatment and some only cause drowsiness in higher doses.
In such cases the patient should be told that the advice applies until the effects have worn off. However many of these preparations can produce a slowing of reaction time and a loss of mental concentration that can have the same effects as drowsiness.
Avoidance of alcoholic drink is recommended because the effects of CNS depressants are enhanced by alcohol. Strict prohibition however could lead to some patients not taking the medicine. Pharmacists should therefore explain the risk and encourage compliance, particularly in patients who may think they already tolerate the effects of alcohol (see also label 3).
Queries from patients with epilepsy regarding fitness to drive should be referred back to the patient's doctor.
Side-effects unrelated to drowsiness that may affect a patient's ability to drive or operate machinery safely include *blurred vision, dizziness, or nausea*. In general, no label has been recommended to cover these cases, but the patient should be suitably counselled.

3 **Warning. May cause drowsiness. If affected do not drive or operate machinery**
To be used on *preparations containing monoamine-oxidase inhibitors*; the warning to avoid alcohol and dealcoholised (low alcohol) drink is covered by the patient information leaflet.
Also to be used as for label 2 but where alcohol is not an issue.

4 **Warning. Avoid alcoholic drink**
To be used on *preparations where a reaction such as flushing may occur if alcohol is taken* (e.g. metronidazole and chlorpropamide). Alcohol may also enhance the hypoglycaemia produced by some oral antidiabetic drugs but routine application of a warning label is not considered necessary.

5 **Do not take indigestion remedies at the same time of day as this medicine**
To be used with label 25 on *preparations coated to resist gastric acid* (e.g. enteric-coated tablets). This is to avoid the possibility of premature dissolution of the coating in the presence of an alkaline pH.
Label 5 also applies to drugs such as ketoconazole *where the absorption is significantly affected by antacids*; the usual period of avoidance recommended is 2 to 4 hours.

6 **Do not take indigestion remedies or medicines containing iron or zinc at the same time of day as this medicine**
To be used on *preparations containing ofloxacin and some other quinolones, doxycycline, lymecycline, minocycline, and penicillamine*. These drugs chelate calcium, iron and zinc and are less well absorbed when taken with calcium-containing antacids or preparations containing iron or zinc. These incompatible preparations should be taken 2-3 hours apart.

7 **Do not take milk, indigestion remedies, or medicines containing iron or zinc at the same time of day as this medicine**
To be used on *preparations containing ciprofloxacin, norfloxacin or tetracyclines that chelate, calcium, iron, magnesium, and zinc* and are thus less available for absorption; these incompatible preparations should be taken 2-3 hours apart. Doxycycline, lymecycline and minocycline are less liable to form chelates and therefore only require label 6 (see above).

8 **Do not stop taking this medicine except on your doctor's advice**
To be used on *preparations that contain a drug which is required to be taken over long periods without the patient necessarily perceiving any benefit* (e.g. antituberculous drugs).
Also to be used on *preparations that contain a drug whose withdrawal is likely to be a particular hazard* (e.g. clonidine for hypertension). Label 10 (see below) is more appropriate for corticosteroids.

9 **Take at regular intervals. Complete the prescribed course unless otherwise directed**
To be used on *preparations where a course of treatment should be completed* to reduce the incidence of relapse or failure of treatment.
The preparations are antimicrobial drugs given by mouth. Very occasionally, some may have severe side-effects (e.g. diarrhoea in patients receiving clindamycin) and in such cases the patient may need to be advised of reasons for stopping treatment quickly and returning to the doctor.

10 **Warning. Follow the printed instructions you have been given with this medicine**
To be used particularly on *preparations containing anticoagulants, lithium and oral corticosteroids*. The appropriate treatment card should be given to the patient and any necessary explanations given.
This label may also be used on other preparations to remind the patient of the instructions that have been given.

11 **Avoid exposure of skin to direct sunlight or sun lamps**
To be used on *preparations that may cause phototoxic or photoallergic reactions* if the patient is exposed to ultraviolet radiation. Many drugs other than those listed in Appendix 9 (e.g. phenothiazines and sulphonamides) may, on rare occasions, cause reactions in susceptible patients. Exposure to high intensity ultraviolet radiation from sunray lamps and sunbeds is particularly likely to cause reactions.

12 **Do not take anything containing aspirin while taking this medicine**
To be used on *preparations containing probenecid and sulfinpyrazone* whose activity is reduced by aspirin.
Label 12 should not be used for anticoagulants since label 10 is more appropriate.

13 **Dissolve or *mix with water* before taking**
To be used on *preparations that are intended to be dissolved in water* (e.g. soluble tablets) or *mixed with water* (e.g. powders, granules) before use. In a few cases other liquids such as fruit juice or milk may be used.

14 **This medicine may colour the urine**
To be used on *preparations that may cause the patient's urine to turn an unusual colour*. These include phenolphthalein (alkaline urine pink), triamterene (blue under some lights), levodopa (dark reddish), and rifampicin (red).

15 **Caution flammable: keep away from fire or flames**
To be used on *preparations containing sufficient flammable solvent to render them flammable if exposed to a naked flame*.

16 **Allow to dissolve under the tongue. Do not transfer from this container. Keep tightly closed. Discard eight weeks after opening**
To be used on *glyceryl trinitrate tablets* to remind the patient not to transfer the tablets to plastic or less suitable containers.

17 **Do not take more than . . . in 24 hours**
To be used on *preparations for the treatment of acute migraine* except those containing ergotamine, for which label 18 is used. The dose form should be specified, e.g. tablets or capsules.
It may also be used on preparations for which no dose has been specified by the prescriber.

18 **Do not take more than . . . in 24 hours or . . . in any one week**
To be used on preparations containing ergotamine. The dose form should be specified, e.g. tablets or suppositories.

19 **Warning. Causes drowsiness which may continue the next day. If affected do not drive or operate machinery. Avoid alcoholic drink**
To be used on *preparations containing hypnotics (or some other drugs with sedative effects) prescribed to be taken at night*. On the rare occasions (e.g. nitrazepam in epilepsy) when hypnotics are prescribed for

daytime administration this label would clearly not be appropriate. Also to be used as an *alternative to the label 2 wording* (the choice being at the discretion of the pharmacist) *for anxiolytics prescribed to be taken at night.*
It is hoped that this wording will convey adequately the problem of residual morning sedation after taking 'sleeping tablets'.

21 **. . . with or after food**
To be used on *preparations that are liable to cause gastric irritation, or those that are better absorbed with food.*
Patients should be advised that a *small amount of food is sufficient.*

22 **. . . half to one hour before food**
To be used on some preparations *whose absorption is thereby improved.*
Most oral antibacterials require label 23 instead (see below).

23 **. . . an hour before food or on an empty stomach**
To be used on *oral preparations whose absorption may be reduced by the presence of food and acid in the stomach.*

24 **. . . sucked or chewed**
To be used on *preparations that should be sucked or chewed.*
The pharmacist should use discretion as to which of these words is appropriate.

25 **. . . swallowed whole, not chewed**
To be used on *preparations that are enteric-coated or designed for modified-release.*
Also to be used on *preparations that taste very unpleasant or may damage the mouth* if not swallowed whole.

26 **. . . dissolved under the tongue**
To be used on *preparations designed for sublingual use.* Patients should be advised to hold under the tongue and avoid swallowing until dissolved. The buccal mucosa between the gum and cheek is occasionally specified by the prescriber.

27 **. . . with plenty of water**
To be used on *preparations that should be well diluted* (e.g. chloral hydrate), *where a high fluid intake is required* (e.g. sulphonamides), or *where water is required to aid the action* (e.g. methylcellulose). The patient should be advised that 'plenty' means at least 150 mL (about a tumblerful). In most cases fruit juice, tea, or coffee may be used.

28 **To be spread thinly . . .**
To be used on *external preparations* that should be applied sparingly (e.g. corticosteroids, dithranol).

29 **Do not take more than 2 at any one time. Do not take more than 8 in 24 hours**
To be used on containers of dispensed *solid dose preparations containing paracetamol for adults when the instruction on the label indicates that the dose can be taken on an 'as required' basis.* The dose form should be specified, e.g. tablets or capsules.
This label has been introduced because of the serious consequences of overdosage with paracetamol.

30 **Do not take with any other paracetamol products**
To be used on all containers of dispensed *preparations containing paracetamol.*

31 **Contains aspirin and paracetamol. Do not take with any other paracetamol products**
To be used on all containers of dispensed *preparations containing aspirin and paracetamol.*

32 **Contains aspirin**
To be used on containers of dispensed *preparations containing aspirin when the name on the label does not include the word 'aspirin'.*

33 **Contains an aspirin-like medicine**
To be used on containers of dispensed *preparations containing aspirin derivatives.*

# Products and their labels

Products introduced or amended since publication of BNF No. 50 (September 2005) are underlined.
Proprietary names are in *italic.*
C = counselling advised; see BNF = consult product entry in BNF




Abacavir, C, hypersensitivity reactions, see BNF
*Abilify*, C, driving
Acamprosate, 21, 25
Acarbose, C, administration, see BNF
*Accolate*, 23
Acebutolol, 8
Aceclofenac, 21
Acemetacin, 21, C, driving
Acenocoumarol, 10, anticoagulant card
Acetazolamide, 3
Acetazolamide m/r, 3, 25
Aciclovir susp and tabs, 9
Acipimox, 21
Acitretin, 10, patient information leaflet 21
*Acorvio Plus*, 28
Acrivastine, C, driving, alcohol, see BNF
*Actinac*, 28
*Actiq*, 2
*Actonel*, C, administration, food and calcium, see BNF
*Acupan*, 2, 14, (urine pink)
*Adalat LA*, 25
*Adalat Retard*, 25
Adalimumab, C, tuberculosis
*Adcal*, 24
*Adcal-D$_3$*, 24
*Adcortyl with Graneodin*, 28
*Adipine MR*, 21, 25
*Adipine XL*, 25
*Adizem preps*, 25
*AeroBec*, 8, C, dose
*AeroBec Forte*, 8, 10, steroid card C, dose
*Agenerase caps*, 5
*Agenerase oral solution*, 4, 5
*Airomir*, C, dose, change to CFC-free inhaler, see BNF
Albendazole, 9
Alclometasone external preps, 28
*Aldara*, 10, patient information leaflet
*Aldomet*, 3, 8
Alendronic acid, C, administration, see BNF
Alfuzosin, 3, C, dose, see BNF
Alfuzosin m/r, 3, 21, 25, C, dose, see BNF
Alimemazine, 2
*Allegron*, 2
Allopurinol, 8, 21, 27
*Almogran*, 3
Almotriptan, 3
*Alphosyl HC*, 28
*Alphaderm*, 28
Alprazolam, 2
*Alvedon*, 30
*Alvesco*, 8, C, dose
*Alvercol*, 25, 27, C, administration, see BNF
Amantadine, C, driving
Aminophylline m/r, see preps
Amiodarone, 11
Amisulpride, 2
Amitriptyline, 2
Amitriptyline m/r, 2, 25
Amobarbital, 19
Amorolfine, 10, patient information leaflet
Amoxapine, 2

Amoxicillin, 9
Amoxicillin chewable tabs, 9, 10, patient information leaflet
Amoxicillin dispersible sachets, 9, 13
*Amoxil*, 9
*Amoxil dispersible sachets*, 9, 13
*Amoxil paed susp*, 9, C, use of pipette
Amphotericin loz, 9, 24, C, after food
Amphotericin mixt (g.i.), 9, C, use of pipette
Amphotericin mixt (mouth), 9, C, use of pipette, hold in mouth, after food
Amphotericin tabs, 9
Ampicillin, 9, 23
Amprenavir caps, 5
Amprenavir oral solution, 4, 5
*Amytal*, 19
*Anafranil*, 2
*Anafranil m/r*, 2, 25
Anagrelide, C, driving
Anakinra, C, blood disorder symptoms
*Androcur*, 21
*Andropatch*, C, administration, see BNF
*Angettes-75*, 32
*Angiopine 40 LA*, 21, 25
*Angitil SR*, 25
*Angitil XL*, 25
*Anhydrol Forte*, 15
*Anquil*, 2
*Antabuse*, 2, C, alcohol reaction, see BNF
Antacids, see BNF dose statements
*Antepsin*, 5
*Anthranol preps*, 28
Anticoagulants, oral, 10, anticoagulant card
Antihistamines, (see individual preparations)
*Anturan*, 12, 21
Apomorphine sublingual tabs, C, driving
*Aptivus*, 21
*Arava*, 4
Aripiprazole, C, driving
*Aromasin*, 21
*Arpicolin*, C, driving
*Artane*, C, before or after food, driving, see BNF
Artemether with lumefantrine, 21, C, driving
*Arythmol*, 21, 25
*Arthrotec*, 21, 25
*Asacol MR tabs*, 5, 25, C, blood disorder symptoms, see BNF
*Asacol enema and supps*, C, blood disorder symptoms, see BNF
*Asasantin Retard*, 21, 25
Ascorbic acid, effervescent, 13
Ascorbic acid tabs (500mg), 24
*Asendis*, 2
*Asmabec preps*, 8, 10, steroid card (high-dose preparations only), C, dose
*Asmanex*, 8, 10, steroid card C, dose
*Asmasal*, C, dose, see BNF
*Aspav*, 2, 13, 21, 32
Aspirin and papaveretum dispersible tabs, 2, 13, 21, also 32 (if 'aspirin' not on label)
Aspirin dispersible tabs, 13, 21, also 32 (if 'aspirin' not on label)
Aspirin effervescent, 13, also 32 (if 'aspirin' not on label)
Aspirin e/c, 5, 25, also 32 (if 'aspirin' not on label)
Aspirin m/r, 25, also 32 (if 'aspirin' not on label)
Aspirin supps, 32, (if 'aspirin' not on label)
Aspirin tabs, 21, also 32 (if 'aspirin' not on label)
Aspirin, paracetamol and codeine tabs, 21, 29, also 31 (if 'aspirin' and 'paracetamol' not on label)
*Atarax*, 2
Atazanavir, 5, 21
Atenolol, 8
Atomoxetine, 3
Atorvastatin, C, muscle effects, see BNF
Atovaquone, 21
*Atrovent inhalations*, C, dose, see BNF
*Augmentin susp and tabs*, 9
*Augmentin Duo*, 9
*Augmentin dispersible tabs*, 9, 13
Auranofin, 21, C, blood disorder symptoms, see BNF
*Aureocort*, 28
*Avandamet*, 21
*Avelox*, 6, 9, C, driving
*Avloclor*, 5, C, malaria prophylaxis, see BNF
*Avodart*, 25
*Avomine*, 2
Azathioprine, 21
Azithromycin caps, 5, 9, 23
Azithromycin susp, 5, 9

Baclofen, 2, 8
Balsalazide, 21, 25
*Baratol*, 2
*Baxan*, 9
*Beclazone*, 8, 10, steroid card (250-microgram only), C, dose
*Becloforte preps*, 8, 10, steroid card C, dose
Beclometasone external preps, 28
Beclometasone inhalations, 8, 10, steroid card (high-dose preparations only), C, dose
*Becodisks*, 8, 10, steroid card (high-dose preparation only), C, dose
*Becotide preps*, 8, C, dose
*Benemid*, 12, 21, 27
Benperidol, 2
Benzatropine, 2
Benzoin tincture, cpd, 15
*Beta-Adalat*, 8, 25
*Betacap*, 15, 28
*Beta-Cardone*, 8
Betahistine, 21
*Betaloc*, 8
*Betaloc-SA*, 8, 25
Betamethasone inj, 10, steroid card
Betamethasone tab, 10, steroid card, 21
Betamethasone external preps, 28
Betamethasone scalp application, 15, 28
Bethanechol, 22
*Betim*, 8
*Betnelan*, 10, steroid card, 21
*Betnesol injection*, 10, steroid card
*Betnesol tabs*, 10, steroid card, 13, 21
*Betnovate external preps*, 28
*Betnovate scalp application*, 15, 28
*Betnovate-RD*, 28
*Bettamousse*, 28
Bezafibrate, 21
*Bezalip*, 21
*Bezalip-Mono*, 21, 25
*Biorphen*, C, driving
Bisacodyl tabs, 5, 25
Bisoprolol, 8
*Bondronat tabs*, C, administration, see BNF
*Bonefos caps and tabs*, C, food and calcium, see BNF
*Bonviva tabs*, C, administration, see BNF
*Brexidol*, 21
*Bricanyl inhalations*, C, dose, see BNF
*Bricanyl SA*, 25
*Britlofex*, 2
*Broflex*, C, before or after food, driving, see BNF
Bromocriptine, 21, C, hypotensive reactions, see BNF
*Brufen*, 21
*Brufen gran*, 13, 21
*Brufen Retard*, 25, 27
*Buccastem*, 2, C, administration, see BNF
*Budenofalk*, 5, 10, steroid card 22, 25
Budesonide inhalations, 8, 10, steroid card (high-dose preparations only), C, dose
Budesonide caps, 5, 10, steroid card 22, 25
Buprenorphine, 2, 26
Bupropion, 25
*Burinex K*, 25, 27, C, posture, see BNF

Buserelin nasal spray, C, nasal decongestants, see BNF
*Buspar*, C, driving
Buspirone, C, driving
Butobarbital, 19
*BuTrans*, 2

*Cabaser*, 21, C, driving, hypotensive reactions, see BNF
Cabergoline, 21, C, driving, hypotensive reactions, see BNF
*Cacit*, 13
*Cacit D3*, 13
*Cafergot*, 18, C, dosage
*Calceos*, 24
*Calcicard CR*, 25
*Calcichew preps*, 24
*Calcisorb*, 13, 21, C, may be sprinkled on food
*Calcium-500*, 25
Calcium acetate tabs, 21, 25
Calcium carbonate tabs, chewable, 24
Calcium carbonate tabs and gran effervescent, 13
Calcium gluconate tabs, 24
Calcium phosphate sachets, 13
*Calcium Resonium*, 13
Calcium and ergocalciferol tabs, C, administration, see BNF
*Calcort*, 5, 10, steroid card
*Calfovit D3*, 13, 21
*Calmurid HC*, 28
*Calpol susp*, 30
*Camcolit 250 tabs*, 10, lithium card, C, fluid and salt intake, see BNF
*Camcolit 400 tabs*, 10, lithium card, 25, C, fluid and salt intake, see BNF
*Campral EC*, 21, 25
*Canesten HC*, 28
*Canesten spray*, 15
Capecitabine, 21
*Caprin*, 5, 25, 32
*Carbaglu*, 13
Carbamazepine chewable, 3, 8, 21, 24, C, blood, hepatic or skin disorder symptoms (see BNF), driving (see BNF)
Carbamazepine liq, supps and tabs, 3, 8, C, blood, hepatic or skin disorder symptoms (see BNF), driving (see BNF)
Carbamazepine m/r, 3, 8, 25, C, blood, hepatic or skin disorder symptoms (see BNF), driving (see BNF)
Carbimazole, C, blood disorder symptoms, see BNF
*Cardene SR*, 25
*Cardilate MR*, 25
*Cardinol*, 8
*Cardura XL*, 25
Carglumic acid, 13
*Carisoma*, 2
Carisoprodol, 2
Carvedilol, 8
*Carylderm lotion*, 15
*Catapres*, 3, 8
*Cedocard Retard*, 25
*Cefaclor*, 9
*Cefaclor m/r*, 9, 21, 25
Cefadroxil, 9
Cefalexin, 9
Cefixime, 9
Cefpodoxime, 5, 9, 21
Cefprozil, 9
Cefradine, 9
Cefuroxime susp, 9, 21
Cefuroxime sachets, 9, 13, 21
Cefuroxime tab, 9, 21, 25
*Cefzil*, 9
*Celance*, C, driving, hypotensive reactions, see BNF
*Celectol*, 8, 22
*Celevac (constipation or diarrhoea)*, C, administration, see BNF
*Celevac tabs (anorectic)*, C, administration, see BNF
Celiprolol, 8, 22
*Centyl K*, 25, 27, C, posture, see BNF
*Ceporex caps, mixts, and tabs*, 9
Cerivastatin, C, muscle effects, see BNF
Cetirizine, C, driving, alcohol, see BNF
*Chemydur 60XL*, 25
Chloral hydrate, 19, 27
Chloral paed elixir, 1, 27
Chloral mixt, 19, 27
Chlordiazepoxide, 2
Chloroquine, 5, C, malaria prophylaxis, see BNF
Chlorphenamine, 2
Chlorpromazine mixts and supps, 2, 11
Chlorpromazine tabs, 2, 11
Chlorpropamide, 4
Cholera vaccine (oral), C, administration
Ciclesonide, 8, C, dose
Ciclosporin, C, administration, see BNF
Cimetidine chewable tabs, C, administration, see BNF
*Cinacalcet*, 21
Cinnarizine, 2
*Cipralex*, C, driving
*Cipramil drops*, C, driving, administration
*Cipramil tabs*, C, driving
Ciprofloxacin, 7, 9, 25, C, driving
*Ciproxin susp and tabs*, 7, 9, 25, C, driving
Citalopram drops, C, driving, administration
Citalopram tabs, C, driving
*Citramag*, 10, patient information leaflet 13, C, administration
Clarithromycin, 9
Clarithromycin m/r, 9, 21, 25
Clarithromycin sachets, 9, 13
Clarithromycin straws, 9, C, administration
*Clarosip*, 9, C, administration
Clemastine, 2
Clindamycin, 9, 27, C, diarrhoea, see BNF
*Clinoril*, 21
Clobazam, 2 or 19, 8, C, driving (see BNF)
Clobetasol external preps, 28
Clobetasol scalp application, 15, 28
Clofazimine, 8, 14, (urine red) 21
Clomethiazole, 19
Clomipramine, 2
Clomipramine m/r, 2, 25
Clonazepam, 2, 8, C, driving (see BNF)
Clonidine, see Catapres
*Clopixol*, 2
Clotrimazole spray, 15
Clozapine, 2, 10, patient information leaflet
*Clozaril*, 2, 10, patient information leaflet
Coal tar paint, 15
Co-amoxiclav, 9
Co-amoxiclav dispersible tabs, 9, 13
*Cobadex*, 28
Co-beneldopa, 14, (urine reddish), C, driving
Co-beneldopa dispersible tabs, 14, (urine reddish), C, administration, driving, see BNF
Co-beneldopa m/r, 14, (urine reddish), 25, C, driving
*Co-Betaloc*, 8
Co-careldopa, 14, (urine reddish), C, driving
Co-careldopa intestinal gel, 14, (urine reddish), C, driving
Co-careldopa m/r, 14, (urine reddish), 25, C, driving
Co-codamol, see preps
Co-codaprin dispersible tabs, 13, 21, 32
*Codalax*, 14, (urine red)
Co-danthramer, 14, (urine red)
Co-danthrusate, 14, (urine red)
Codeine phosphate syr and tabs, 2
*Codipar*, 2, 29, 30
Co-dydramol, 21, 29, 30
Co-fluampicil, 9, 22
*Cogentin*, 2
*Colazide*, 21, 25
*Colestid*, 13, C, avoid other drugs at same time, see BNF
Colestipol preps, 13, C, avoid other drugs at same time, see BNF
Colestyramine, 13, C, avoid other drugs at same time, see BNF
Collodion, flexible, 15
*Colofac*, C, administration, see BNF
*Colofac MR*, 25, C, administration, see BNF
*Colpermin*, 5, 25
*Combivent*, C, dose

Appendix 9

Co-methiamol, 29, 30
*Comtess*, 14, (urine reddish-brown) C, driving
*Concerta XL*, 25
*Condyline*, 15
*Convulex*, 8, 25, C, blood or hepatic disorder symptoms (see BNF), driving (see BNF)
*Copegus*, 21
Co-prenozide, 8, 25
Co-proxamol, 2, 10, patient information leaflet, 29, 30
*Coracten preps*, 25
*Cordarone X*, 11
*Corgard*, 8
Corticosteroid external preps, 28
Corticosteroid tabs, 10, steroid card, 21
Corticosteroid injections (systemic), 10, steroid card
Cortisone tab, 10, steroid card, 21
*Cosalgesic*, 2, 10, patient information leaflet, 29, 30
Co-tenidone, 8
Co-triamterzide, 14, (urine blue in some lights) 21
Co-trimoxazole mixts and tabs, 9
Co-trimoxazole dispersible tabs, 9, 13
*Creon preps*, C, administration, see BNF
*Crixivan*, 27, C, administration, see BNF
*Cromogen Easi-Breathe*, 8
*Cuplex*, 15
Cyclizine, 2
Cyclophosphamide, 27
Cycloserine caps, 2, 8
*Cymbalta*, 2
*Cymevene*, 21
Cyproheptadine, 2
*Cyprostat*, 21
Cyproterone, 21
*Cystrin*, 3

*Daktacort*, 28
*Daktarin oral gel*, 9, C, hold in mouth, after food
*Dalacin C*, 9, 27, C, diarrhoea, see BNF
*Dalmane*, 19
*Dantrium*, 2
Dantrolene, 2
Dapsone, 8
*DDAVP tabs and intranasal*, C, fluid intake, see BNF
Deferiprone, 14, C, blood disorders
Deflazacort, 5, 10, steroid card
*Deltacortril e/c*, 5, 10, steroid card 25
*Deltastab inj*, 10, steroid card
Demeclocycline, 7, 9, 11, 23
*De-Noltab*, C, administration, see BNF
*Denzapine*, 2, 10, patient information leaflet
*Depakote*, 25
*Depixol*, 2
*Depo-Medrone (systemic)*, 10, steroid card
*Dermestril*, C, administration, see BNF
*Dermovate cream and oint*, 28
*Dermovate scalp application*, 15, 28
*Dermovate-NN*, 28
*Deseril*, 2, 21
Desmopressin tabs and intranasal, C, fluid intake, see BNF
*Desmospray*, C, fluid intake, see BNF
*Desmotabs*, C, fluid intake, see BNF
*Destolit*, 21
*Deteclo*, 7, 9, 11, 23, C, posture
*Detrunorm*, 3
*Detrusitol m/r*, 25
Dexamethasone inj, 10, steroid card
Dexamethasone tabs and solution, 10, steroid card, 21
Dexamfetamine, C, driving
*Dexedrine*, C, driving
Dexibuprofen, 21
Dexketoprofen, 22
Dextropropoxyphene, 2
*DF118 Forte*, 2, 21
*DHC Continus*, 2, 25
*Diamicron MR*, 25
Diamorphine preps, 2
*Diamox tabs*, 3
*Diamox SR*, 3, 25
Diazepam, 2 or 19
Diclofenac dispersible tabs, 13, 21
Diclofenac e/c, 5, 25
Diclofenac m/r, 21, 25
*Dicloflex Retard*, 21, 25
*Diclomax 75 mg SR and Retard*, 21, 25
*Diconal*, 2
Didanosine e/c caps, 25, C, administration
Didanosine tabs, 23, C, administration
*Didronel*, C, food and calcium, see BNF
*Didronel PMO*, 10, patient leaflet, C, food and calcium, see BNF
*Diflucan 50 and 200mg*, 9
*Diflucan susp*, 9
Diflucortolone external preps, 28
Diflunisal, 21, 25, C, avoid aluminium hydroxide
Digoxin elixir, C, use of pipette
Dihydrocodeine, 2, 21
Dihydrocodeine m/r, 2, 25
*Dilcardia SR*, 25
Diloxanide, 9
Diltiazem, 25
*Dilzem preps*, 25
*Dindevan*, 10, anticoagulant card 14, (urine pink or orange)
*Dioderm*, 28
*Dipentum*, 21, C, blood disorder symptoms, see BNF
Diphenhydramine, 2
*Diprosalic*, 28
*Diprosone*, 28
Dipyridamole, 22
Dipyridamole m/r, 21, 25
*Disipal*, C, driving
Disodium etidronate, C, food and calcium, see BNF
Disopyramide m/r, 25
*Disprin CV*, 25, 32
*Disprol*, 30
*Distaclor*, 9
*Distaclor MR*, 9, 21, 25
*Distalgesic*, 2, 10, patient information leaflet, 29, 30
*Distamine*, 6, 22, C, blood disorder symptoms, see BNF
Distigmine, 22
Disulfiram, 2, C, alcohol reaction, see BNF
Dithranol preps, 28
*Dithrocream preps*, 28
*Dithrolan*, 28
*Ditropan*, 3
*Dolmatil*, 2
*Dolobid*, 21, 25, C, avoid aluminium hydroxide
*Doloxene*, 2
*Doloxene Compound*, 2, 21, 32
*Domperamol*, 17, 30
*Doralese*, 2
*Dostinex*, 21, C, hypotensive reactions, see BNF
Dosulepin, 2
*Dovobet*, 28
Doxazosin m/r, 25
Doxepin, 2
Doxepin topical, 2, 10, patient information leaflet
Doxycycline caps, 6, 9, 11, 27, C, posture, see BNF
Doxycycline dispersible tabs, 6, 9, 11, 13
Doxycycline tabs, 6, 11, 27, C, posture, see BNF
*Dozic*, 2
*Driclor*, 15
*Droleptan*, 2
*Dromadol XL*, 2, 25
*Dukoral*, C, administration
*Dulcolax tabs*, 5, 25
Duloxetine, 2
*Dumicoat*, 10, patient information leaflet
*Duodopa*, 14, (urine reddish), C, driving
*Duofilm*, 15
*Duovent inhalations*, C, dose
*Duraphat toothpaste*, C, administration
*Durogesic*, 2
Dutasteride, 25
*Dutonin*, 3

*Dyazide*, 14, (urine blue in some lights) 21
*Dyspamet tabs*, C, administration, see BNF
*Dytac*, 14, (urine blue in some lights) 21
*Dytide*, 14, (urine blue in some lights) 21

*Econacort*, 28
*Edronax*, C, driving
Efavirenz tabs, 23
*Efcortelan external preps*, 28
*Efcortesol*, 10, steroid card
*Efexor*, 3, 21, C, driving
*Efexor XL*, 3, 21, 25, C, driving
*Elantan preps*, 25
*Elidel*, 4, 28
*Elleste Solo MX patches*, C, administration, see BNF
*Elocon*, 28
*Emcor preps*, 8
*Emeside*, 8, C, blood disorder symptoms (see BNF), driving (see BNF)
*Emflex*, 21, C, driving
*En-De-Kay mouthwash*, C, food and drink, see BNF
*Endoxana*, 27
Enfuvirtide, C, hypersensitivity reactions, see BNF
Entacapone, 14, (urine reddish-brown) C, driving, avoid iron-containing preparations at the same time of day
*Entocort CR*, 5, 10, steroid card 22, 25
*Epanutin caps*, 8, 27, C, administration, blood or skin disorder symptoms (see BNF), driving (see BNF)
*Epanutin Infatabs*, 8, 24, C, blood or skin disorder symptoms (see BNF), driving (see BNF)
*Epanutin susp*, 8, C, administration, blood or skin disorder symptoms (see BNF), driving (see BNF)
*Epilim Chrono*, 8, 25, C, blood or hepatic disorder symptoms (see BNF), driving (see BNF)
*Epilim e/c tabs*, 5, 8, 25, C, blood or hepatic disorder symptoms (see BNF), driving (see BNF)
*Epilim crushable tabs, liquid and syrup*, 8, C, blood or hepatic disorder symptoms (see BNF), driving (see BNF)
Eprosartan, 21
*Equanil*, 2
*Equasym XL*, 25
Ergotamine, 18, C, dosage
Erlotinib, 23
*Erymax*, 5, 9, 25
*Erythrocin*, 9
Erythromycin caps, 5, 9, 25
Erythromycin ethyl succinate, 9
Erythromycin ethyl succinate gran, 9, 13
Erythromycin stearate tabs, 9
Erythromycin tabs, 5, 9, 25
*Erythroped*, 9
*Erythroped A tabs*, 9
Escitalopram, C, driving
Esomeprazole, C, administration, see BNF
*Estracombi*, C, administration, see BNF
*Estracyt*, 23, C, dairy products, see BNF
*Estraderm MX*, C, administration, see BNF
*Estraderm TTS*, C, administration, see BNF
Estradiol vaginal ring, 10, patient information leaflet
*Estradot*, C, administration, see BNF
*Estrapak-50*, C, administration, see BNF
Estramustine, 23, C, dairy products, see BNF
*Estring*, 10, patient information leaflet
Estriol, 25
Ethambutol, 8
Ethosuximide, 8, C, blood disorder symptoms (see BNF), driving (see BNF)
Etidronate, C, food and calcium, see BNF
Etodolac m/r, 25
Etonogestrel implant, C, see patient information leaflet
Etoposide caps, 23
*Eucardic*, 8
*Eumovate external preps*, 28
*Eurax-Hydrocortisone*, 28
*Evorel preps*, C, administration, see BNF
*Exelon caps*, 21, 25
*Exelon solution*, 21
Exemestane, 21

Famciclovir, 9
*Famvir*, 9
*Farlutal 500-mg tabs*, 27
*Fasigyn*, 4, 9, 21, 25
*Faverin*, C, driving, see BNF
*Fefol*, 25
*Fefol-Vit*, 25
Felbinac foam, 15
*Feldene caps*, 21
*Feldene dispersible tabs*, 13, 21
*Feldene Melt*, 10, patient information leaflet 21
Felodipine m/r, 25
*Fematrix*, C, administration, see BNF
*Femapak*, C, administration, see BNF
*FemSeven*, C, administration, see BNF
*Fenbid*, 25
Fenbufen, 21
Fenofibrate, 21
Fenofibrate m/r, 21, 25
*Fenogal*, 21
Fenoprofen, 21
*Fenopron*, 21
Fentanyl patches and lozenges, 2
*Fentazin*, 2
*Feospan*, 25
*Ferriprox*, 14, C, blood disorders
*Ferrograd*, 25
*Ferrograd C*, 25
*Ferrograd Folic*, 25
Ferrous salts m/r, see preps
Ferrous sulphate paed mixt, 27
Fexofenadine, C, driving, see BNF
*Fibrelief*, 13, C, administration, see BNF
*Flagyl S*, 4, 9, 23
*Flagyl supps*, 4, 9
*Flagyl tabs*, 4, 9, 21, 25, 27
*Fleet Phospho-soda*, 10, patient information leaflet C, administration
*Flixotide*, 8, 10, steroid card (high-dose preparations only), C, dose
*Flixotide Evohaler*, 8, C, dose, change to CFC-free inhaler (see BNF), 10, steroid card (250-Evohaler only)
*Flomax MR*, 25
*Florinef*, 10, steroid card
*Floxapen*, 9, 23
*Fluanxol*, 2, C, administration, driving, see BNF
Flucloxacillin, 9, 23
Fluconazole 50 and 200mg, 9
Fluconazole susp, 9
Fludrocortisone, 10, steroid card
Fludroxycortide external preps, 28
Fluocinolone external preps, 28
Fluocinonide external preps, 28
Fluocinonide scalp lotion, 15, 28
Fluocortolone external preps, 28
*Fluorigard mouthwash*, C, food and drink, see BNF
Fluoxetine, C, driving, see BNF
Flupentixol, see preps
Fluphenazine, 2
Fluprednidene, 28
Flurazepam, 19
Flurbiprofen, 21
Flurbiprofen m/r, 21, 25
Fluticasone inhalations, 8, 10, steroid card (high-dose preparations only), C, dose
Fluticasone inhalations (CFC-free), 8, C, dose, change to CFC-free inhaler (see BNF), 10, steroid card (high-dose preparations only)
Fluvastatin, C, muscle effects, see BNF
Fluvastatin m/r, 25, C, muscle effects, see BNF
Fluvoxamine, C, driving, see BNF
*Foradil*, C, dose, see BNF

Formoterol fumarate, C, dose, see BNF
*Fortipine LA 40*, 21, 25
*Fortral caps and tabs*, 2, 21
*Fortral supps*, 2
*Fosamax*, C, administration, see BNF
*Fosavance*, C, administration, see BNF
*Franol*, 21
*Franol Plus*, 21
*Frisium*, 2 or 19, 8, C, driving (see BNF)
*Froben*, 21
*Froben SR*, 21, 25
Frovatriptan, 3
*Frusene*, 14, (urine blue in some lights) 21
*Fucibet*, 28
*Fucidin susp*, 9, 21
*Fucidin tabs*, 9
*Fucidin H*, 28
*Full Marks lotion, mousse*, 15
*Fungilin loz*, 9, 24, C, after food
*Fungilin susp (g.i.)*, 9, C, use of pipette
*Fungilin susp (mouth)*, 9, C, use of pipette, hold in mouth, after food
*Fungilin tabs*, 9
*Furadantin*, 9, 14, (urine yellow or brown), 21
*Furamide*, 9
*Fuzeon*, C, hypersensitivity reactions, see BNF
*Fybogel*, 13, C, administration, see BNF
*Fybogel Mebeverine*, 13, 22, C, administration, see BNF

Gabapentin, 3, 5, 8, C, driving (see BNF)
*Gabitril*, 21
*Galake*, 21, 29, 30
Galantamine, 3, 21
Galantamine m/r, 3, 21, 25
*Gamanil*, 2
Ganciclovir, 21
*Gastrobid Continus*, 25
Gemfibrozil, 22
*Gliclazide m/r*, 25
*Glucobay*, C, administration, see BNF
*Glucophage*, 21
*Glucophage SR*, 21, 25
Glyceryl trinitrate patch, see preps
Glyceryl trinitrate m/r, 25
Glyceryl trinitrate tabs, 16
Griseofulvin spray, 15
Griseofulvin tabs, 9, 21, C, driving
*Grisol*, 15
*Grisovin*, 9, 21, C, driving
*GTN 300 mcg*, 16

*Haelan*, 28
*Halciderm Topical*, 28
Halcinonide external preps, 28
*Haldol*, 2
*Half-Inderal LA*, 8, 25
*Half-Securon SR*, 25
*Half-Sinemet CR*, 14, (urine reddish), 25
Haloperidol, 2
*HeliClear*, 5, 9, 25
*Heminevrin*, 19
*Hiprex*, 9
*Humira*, C, tuberculosis
Hydrocortisone inj, 10, steroid card
Hydrocortisone external preps, 28
Hydrocortisone tabs, 10, steroid card, 21
Hydrocortisone butyrate external preps, 28
Hydrocortisone butyrate scalp lotion, 15, 28
*Hydrocortistab inj*, 10, steroid card
*Hydrocortone*, 10, steroid card, 21
Hydromorphone caps, 2, C, administration, see BNF
Hydromorphone m/r, 2, C, administration, see BNF
Hydroxychloroquine, 5, 21
Hydroxyzine, 2
Hyoscine hydrobromide, 2, (patches 19)
*Hypolar Retard*, 25
*Hypovase*, 3, C, initial dose, see BNF
*Hytrin*, 3, C, dose, see BNF

Ibandronic acid tabs, C, administration, see BNF
*Ibumousse*, 15
Ibuprofen, 21
Ibuprofen gran, 13, 21
Ibuprofen m/r, 25, 27
*Ibuspray*, 15
Idarubicin caps, 25
*Idrolax*, 13
*Imdur*, 25
*Imigran*, 3, 10, patient information leaflet
*Imigran RADIS*, 3, 10, patient information leaflet
Imipramine, 2
Imiquimod, 10, patient information leaflet
*Imodium Plus*, 24
*Implanon*, C, see patient information leaflet
*Imunovir*, 9
*Imuran*, 21
Indapamide m/r, 25
*Inderal-LA*, 8, 25
Indinavir, 27, C, administration, see BNF
*Indolar SR*, 21, 25, C, driving
Indometacin caps and mixt, 21, C, driving
Indometacin m/r, see preps
Indometacin supps, C, driving
*Indomod*, 25, C, driving
Indoramin, 2
Industrial methylated spirit, 15
*Inegy*, C, muscle effects, see BNF
*Infacol*, C, use of dropper
Infliximab, 10, Alert card, C, tuberculosis and hypersensitivity reactions
Inosine pranobex, 9
*Insulin*, C, see BNF
*Intal Spincaps and inhalers*, 8
*Invirase*, 21
Iodine Solution, Aqueous, 27
*Ionamin*, 25, C, driving
*Ipocol*, 5, 25, C, blood disorder symptoms, see BNF
Ipratropium inhalations, C, dose, see BNF
*Isib 60XL*, 25
*Ismo Retard*, 25
*Ismo tabs*, 25
Isocarboxazid, 3, 10, patient information leaflet
*Isodur XL*, 25
*Isogel*, 13, C, administration, see BNF
*Isoket Retard*, 25
*Isomide CR*, 25
Isoniazid elixir and tabs, 8, 22
Isosorbide dinitrate m/r, 25
Isosorbide mononitrate, 25
Isosorbide mononitrate m/r, 25
*Isotard XL*, 25
Isotretinoin, 10, patient information leaflet 11, 21
Isotretinoin gel, 10, patient information leaflet
*Isotrex*, 10, patient information leaflet
*Isotrexin*, 10, patient information leaflet
*Ispagel*, 13, C, administration, see BNF
Ispaghula, 13, C, administration, see BNF
Itraconazole caps, 5, 9, 21, 25
Itraconazole liq, 9, 23

*Junifen*, 21

*Kaletra*, 21
*Kalspare*, 14, (urine blue in some lights) 21
*Kalten*, 8
*Kapake caps and tabs*, 2, 29, 30
*Kapake effervescent*, 2, 13, 29, 30
*Kay-Cee-L*, 21
*Keflex*, 9
*Kemadrin*, C, driving
*Kenalog (systemic)*, 10, steroid card
*Kentera*, C, administration, see BNF
*Keppra*, 3, 8
*Keral*, 22
*Ketek*, 9

Ketoconazole tabs and susp, 5, 9, 21
Ketoprofen caps, 21
Ketoprofen CR, 21, 25
Ketoprofen m/r caps, 21, 25
Ketotifen, 2, 8, 21
Ketorolac tabs, 17, 21
*Ketovail*, 21, 25
*Kineret*, C, blood disorder symptoms
*Kinidin Durules*, 25
*Kivexa*, C, hypersensitivity reactions, see BNF
*Klaricid*, 9
*Klaricid sachets*, 9, 13
*Klaricid XL*, 9, 21, 25
*Klean-Prep*, C, administration, see BNF
*Kloref*, 13, 21
*Konakion tabs*, 24

Labetalol, 8, 21
*Lamictal dispersible tabs*, 8, 13, C, driving (see BNF), skin reactions
*Lamictal tabs*, 8, C, driving (see BNF), skin reactions
*Lamisil*, 9
Lamotrigine dispersible tabs, 8, 13, C, driving (see BNF), skin reactions
Lamotrigine tabs, 8, C, driving (see BNF), skin reactions
*Lanoxin-PG elixir*, C, use of pipette
Lansoprazole caps, 5, 25
Lansoprazole oro-dispersible tabs, 5, C, administration, see BNF
Lansoprazole susp, 5, 13
*Larapam SR*, 2, 25
*Largactil*, 2, 11
*Lariam*, 21, 25, 27, C, driving, malaria prophylaxis, see BNF
*Lasikal*, 25, 27, C, posture, see BNF
*Lasix + K*, 25, 27, C, posture, see BNF
*Lederfen*, 21
*Ledermycin*, 7, 9, 11, 23
Leflunomide, 4
Lercanidipine, 22
*Lescol*, C, muscle effects, see BNF
*Lescol XL*, 25, C, muscle effects, see BNF
Levetiracetam, 3, 8
Levocetirizine, C, driving
Levodopa, 14, (urine reddish), 21, C, driving
Levofloxacin, 6, 9, 25, C, driving
Levomepromazine, 2
*Librium*, 2
*Li-Liquid*, 10, lithium card, C, fluid and salt intake, see BNF
Linezolid susp and tabs, 9, 10, patient information leaflet
*Lioresal*, 2, 8
*Lipantil*, 21
*Lipitor*, C, muscle effects, see BNF
*Lipostat*, C, muscle effects, see BNF
Liquid paraffin, C, administration, see BNF
*Liskonum*, 10, lithium card, 25, C, fluid and salt intake, see BNF
Lisuride, 21, C, hypotensive reactions, see BNF
*Litarex*, 10, lithium card, 25, C, fluid and salt intake, see BNF
Lithium carbonate, 10, lithium card, C, fluid and salt intake, see BNF
Lithium carbonate m/r, 10, lithium card, 25, C, fluid and salt intake, see BNF
Lithium citrate liq, 10, lithium card, C, fluid and salt intake, see BNF
Lithium citrate m/r, 10, lithium card, 25, C, fluid and salt intake, see BNF
*Lithonate*, 10, lithium card, 25, C, fluid and salt intake, see BNF
*Loceryl*, 10, patient information leaflet
*Locoid cream, oint, and topical emulsion*, 28
*Locoid scalp lotion*, 15, 28
*Locoid C*, 28
Lofepramine, 2
Lofexidine, 2
Lopid, 22
Loprazolam, 19
*Lopresor*, 8
*Lopresor SR*, 8, 25
Loratadine, C, driving, alcohol, see BNF
Lorazepam, 2 or 19
Lormetazepam, 19
*Loron tabs*, 10, patient information leaflet C, food and calcium, see BNF
*Losec*, C, administration, see BNF
*Lotriderm*, 28
*Ludiomil*, 2
Lugol's solution, 27
*Lustral*, C, driving, see BNF
*Lyclear Dermal cream*, 10, patient information leaflet
Lymecycline, 6, 9
*Lyrica*, 3, 8, C, driving
*Lysodren*, 2, 21
*Lysovir*, C, driving

*Macrobid*, 9, 14, (urine yellow or brown), 21, 25
*Macrodantin*, 9, 14, (urine yellow or brown), 21
*Madopar*, 14, (urine reddish), C, driving
*Madopar dispersible tabs*, 14, (urine reddish), C, administration, driving, see BNF
*Madopar CR*, 5, 14, (urine reddish) 25, C, driving
*Magnapen*, 9, 22
Magnesium citrate effervescent pdr, 10, patient information leaflet 13, C, administration
Magnesium sulphate, 13, 23
*Malarivon*, 5, C, malaria prophylaxis
*Malarone*, 21
*Manerix*, 10, patient information leaflet 21
*Manevac*, 25, 27
Maprotiline, 2
*Marevan*, 10, anticoagulant card
*Maxalt*, 3
*Maxalt Melt*, 3, C, administration
*Maxepa*, 21
*Maxolon paed liquid*, C, use of pipette
*Maxolon SR*, 25
*Maxtrex (methotrexate)*, C, NSAIDs (see BNF)
Mebeverine, C, administration, see BNF
Mecysteine, 5, 22, 25
*Medrone tabs*, 10, steroid card, 21
Mefenamic acid caps, paed susp, and tabs, 21
Mefloquine, 21, 25, 27, C, driving, malaria prophylaxis, see BNF
Meloxicam tabs, 21
*Menoring 50*, 10, patient information leaflet
Mepacrine, 4, 9, 14, 21
Meprobamate, 2
Meptazinol, 2
*Meptid*, 2
Mesalazine e/c, see preps
Mesalazine m/r, see preps
Mesalazine enema and supps, C, blood disorder symptoms, see BNF
Mesalazine gran, see preps
*Mesren MR*, 5, 25, C, blood disorder symptoms, see BNF
Metformin, 21
Metformin m/r, 21, 25
Methadone, 2
*Methadose*, 2
Methenamine, 9
Methocarbamol, 2
Methotrexate tabs, C, NSAIDs (see BNF)
Methylcellulose (constipation or diarrhoea), C, administration, see BNF
Methylcellulose tabs (anorectic), C, administration, see BNF
Methyldopa, 3, 8
Methylphenidate m/r, 25
Methylprednisolone external preps, 28
Methylprednisolone inj, 10, steroid card
Methylprednisolone tabs, 10, steroid card, 21

Methysergide, 2, 21
Metirosine, 2
Metoclopramide paed liquid, C, use of pipette
Metoclopramide m/r, see preps
Metopirone, 21, C, driving
Metoprolol, 8
Metoprolol m/r, see preps
*Metosyn cream and oint*, 28
*Metosyn scalp lotion*, 15, 28
*Metrogel*, 10, patient information leaflet
*Metrolyl supps*, 4, 9
Metronidazole gel, see preps
Metronidazole mixt, 4, 9, 23
Metronidazole supps, 4, 9
Metronidazole tabs, 4, 9, 21, 25, 27
Metyrapone, 21, C, driving
Mianserin, 2, 25
*Micanol*, 28
Miconazole denture lacquer, 10, patient information leaflet
Miconazole oral gel, 9, C, hold in mouth, after food
Miconazole tabs, 9, 21
*Midrid*, 30, C, dosage
*Mifegyne*, 10, patient information leaflet
Mifepristone, 10, patient information leaflet
*Migard*, 3
*Migraleve*, 2, (pink tablets), 17, 30
*Migravess*, 13, 17, 32
*Migravess Forte*, 13, 17, 32
*Migril*, 2, 18, C, dosage
*Mildison*, 28
*Mimpara*, 21
*Minocin*, 6, 9, C, posture, see BNF
*Minocin MR*, 6, 25
Minocycline, 6, 9, C, posture, see BNF
Minocycline m/r, 6, 25
*Mintec*, 5, 22, 25
*Mintezol*, 3, 21, 24
*Mirapexin*, C, hypotensive reactions, driving, see BNF
Mirtazapine oral solution, 2
Mirtazapine orodispersible tablets, 2, C, administration, see BNF
Mirtazapine tabs, 2, 25
Mitotane, 2, 21
Mizolastine, 25, C, driving
*Mizollen*, 25, C, driving
*Mobic tabs*, 21
*Mobiflex*, 21
Moclobemide, 10, patient information leaflet, 21
*Modisal LA*, 25
*Modisal XL*, 25
*Moditen*, 2
*Modrasone*, 28
*Modrenal*, 21
*Moducren*, 8
*Mogadon*, 19
*Molipaxin*, 2, 21
Mometasone cream, 28
Mometasone inhaler, 8, 10, steroid card C, dose
Mometasone ointment, 28
Mometasone scalp lotion, 28
*Mono-Cedocard*, 25
*Monomax SR*, 25
*Monomax XL*, 25
*Monomil XL*, 25
*Monosorb XL*, 25
*Monotrim*, 9
*Montelukast chewable tabs*, 24
*Morcap SR*, 2, C, administration, see BNF
Morphine preps, 2
Morphine m/r susp, 2, 13
Morphine m/r caps and tabs, see preps
*Motifene*, 25
*Motival*, 2
*Movicol*, 13
*Movicol-Half*, 13
Moxifloxacin, 6, 9, C, driving
Moxisylyte, 21
Moxonidine, 3
*MST Continus susp*, 2, 13
*MST Continus tabs*, 2, 25
*MXL*, 2, C, administration, see BNF
*Myambutol*, 8
*Mycobutin*, 8, 14, (urine orange-red) C, soft lenses
*Mynah*, 8, 23
*Myocrisin inj*, C, blood disorder symptoms, see BNF
*Myotonine Chloride*, 22
*Mysoline*, 2, 8, C, driving (see BNF)

Nabilone, 2, C, behavioural effects, see BNF
Nabumetone, 21
Nabumetone dispersible tabs, 13, 21
Nabumetone susp, 21
Nadolol, 8
Nafarelin spray, 10, patient information leaflet C, nasal decongestants, see BNF
Naftidrofuryl, 25, 27
*Nalcrom*, 22, C, administration, see BNF
Nalidixic acid, 9, 11
*Napratec*, 21
*Naprosyn EC*, 5, 25
*Naprosyn tabs and susp*, 21
Naproxen e/c, 5, 25
Naproxen tabs and susp, 21
*Naramig*, 3
Naratriptan, 3
*Nardil*, 3, 10, patient information leaflet
*Natrilix SR*, 25
*Navelbine caps*, 21, 25
*Navoban*, 23
*Nebilet*, 8
Nebivolol, 8
Nedocromil sodium inhalation, 8, C, change to CFC-free inhaler
Nefopam, 2, 14, (urine pink)
Nelfinavir tabs, 21
Nelfinavir powder, 21, C, administration, see BNF
*Neo-Medrone*, 28
*Neo-Mercazole*, C, blood disorder symptoms, see BNF
*Neo-NaClex-K*, 25, 27, C, posture, see BNF
*Neoral*, C, administration, see BNF
*Neotigason*, 10, patient information leaflet 21
*Nerisone*, 28
*Nerisone Forte*, 28
*Neulactil*, 2
*Neurontin*, 3, 5, 8, C, driving (see BNF)
Nevirapine, C, hypersensitivity reactions, see BNF
*Nexium*, C, administration, see BNF
*Niaspan*, 21, 25
Nicardipine m/r, 25
*Nicorette Microtab*, 26
Nicotine (sublingual), 26
*Nicotinell lozenges*, 24
Nicotinic acid tabs, 21
Nicotinic acid m/r, see preps
*Nidazol*, 4, 9, 21, 25, 27
Nifedipine m/r, see preps
*Nifedipress MR*, 25
*Nifedotard*, 25
*Nifelease*, 25
*Niferex elixir*, C, infants, use of dropper
*NiQuitin CQ lozenges*, 24
Nisoldipine, 22, 25
Nitrazepam, 19
Nitrofurantoin, 9, 14, (urine yellow or brown), 21
Nitrofurantoin m/r, 9, 14, (urine yellow or brown), 21, 25
*Nivaquine*, 5, C, malaria prophylaxis, see BNF
*Nizoral*, 5, 9, 21
*Nocutil*, C, fluid intake, see BNF
*Nootropil*, 3
Norfloxacin, 7, 9, 23, C, driving
Noritate, 10, patient information leaflet
*Normacol preps*, 25, 27, C, administration, see BNF
Normax, 14, (urine red)
*Norprolac*, 21, C, hypotensive reactions, see BNF
Nortriptyline, 2
*Norvir*, 21, C, administration, see BNF
*Nozinan*, 2
*Nuelin SA preps*, 25
*Nurofen for children*, 21
*Nu-Seals Aspirin*, 5, 25, 32
*Nycopren*, 5, 25
*Nystadermal*, 28
*Nystaform-HC*, 28
*Nystan pastilles*, 9, 24, C, after food

*Nystan susp (g.i.)*, 9, C, use of pipette
*Nystan susp (mouth)*, 9, C, use of pipette, hold in mouth, after food
*Nystan tabs*, 9
Nystatin mixt (g.i.), 9, C, use of pipette
Nystatin mixt (mouth), 9, C, use of pipette, hold in mouth, after food
Nystatin pastilles, 9, 24, C, after food
Nystatin tabs, 9

*Occlusal*, 15
*Octim*, C, fluid intake, see BNF
*Ocusert Pilo*, C, method of use
*Oestrogel*, C, administration, see BNF
Ofloxacin, 6, 9, 11, C, driving
Olanzapine tabs, 2
Olanzapine orodispersible tabs, 2, C, administration, see BNF
*Olbetam*, 21
Olsalazine, 21, C, blood disorder symptoms, see BNF
*Omacor*, 21
Omega-3-acid ethyl esters, 21
Omeprazole caps, 5, C, administration, see BNF
Omeprazole tabs, 25
Ondansetron (freeze-dried tablets), C, administration, see BNF
*Opilon*, 21
*Optimax*, 3
*Oramorph preps*, 2
*Oramorph SR*, 2, 25
*Orap*, 2
*Orbenin*, 9, 23
*Orelox*, 5, 9, 21
*Orovite Complement B6*, 25
Orphenadrine, C, driving
*Orudis caps*, 21
*Oruvail*, 21, 25
Oseltamivir, 9
*Ovestin*, 25
Oxazepam, 2
Oxcarbazepine, 3, 8, C, see BNF
Oxerutins, 21
*Oxis*, C, dose, see BNF
Oxprenolol, 8
Oxprenolol m/r, 8, 25
Oxybutynin tabs and elixir, 3
Oxybutynin patch, C, administration, see BNF
Oxycodone caps and liq, 2
Oxycodone m/r, 2, 25
*OxyContin*, 2, 25
*OxyNorm*, 2
Oxytetracycline, 7, 9, 23

*Palladone*, 2, C, administration, see BNF
*Palladone SR*, 2, C, administration, see BNF
*Paludrine*, 21, C, malaria prophylaxis, see BNF
*Panadeine*, 29, 30
*Panadeine effervescent*, 13, 29, 30
*Panadol tabs*, 29, 30
*Panadol Soluble*, 13, 29, 30
*Panadol susp*, 30
*Pancrease preps*, C, administration, see BNF
Pancreatin, C, administration, see BNF
*Pancrex gran*, 25, C, dose, see BNF
*Pancrex V Forte tabs*, 5, 25, C, dose, see BNF
*Pancrex V caps, 125 caps and pdr*, C, administration, see BNF
*Pancrex V tabs*, 5, 25, C, dose, see BNF
Pantoprazole, 25
Paracetamol liq and supps, 30
Paracetamol tabs, 29, 30
Paracetamol tabs, soluble, 13, 29, 30
*Paracodol*, 13, 29, 30
*Paradote*, 29, 30
*Paramax sachets*, 13, 17, 30
*Paramax tabs*, 17, 30
*Pariet*, 25
*Parlodel*, 21, C, hypotensive reactions, see BNF
*Paroven*, 21
Paroxetine, 21, C, driving, see BNF
*Penbritin caps*, 9, 23
Penicillamine, 6, 22, C, blood disorder symptoms, see BNF
*Pentasa tabs and gran*, C, administration, blood disorder symptoms, see BNF
*Pentasa enema and supps*, C, blood disorder symptoms, see BNF
Pentazocine caps and tabs, 2, 21
Pentazocine supps, 2
Pentoxifylline m/r, 21, 25
Peppermint oil caps, 5, 22, 25
*Percutol*, C, administration, see BNF
Pergolide, C, driving, hypotensive reactions, see BNF
*Periactin*, 2
Pericyazine, 2
*Periostat*, 6, 11, 27, C, posture, see BNF
Permethrin dermal cream, 10, patient information leaflet
Perphenazine, 2
*Persantin*, 22
*Persantin Retard*, 21, 25
Pethidine, 2
Phenelzine, 3, 10, patient information leaflet
*Phenergan*, 2
Phenindione, 10, anticoagulant card 14, (urine pink or orange)
Phenobarbital elixir and tabs, 2, 8, C, driving (see BNF)
Phenothrin lotion, mousse, 15
Phenoxymethylpenicillin, 9, 23
Phentermine m/r, 25, C, driving
Phenytoin caps and tabs, 8, 27, C, administration, blood or skin disorder symptoms (see BNF), driving (see BNF)
Phenytoin chewable tabs, 8, 24, C, blood or skin disorder symptoms (see BNF), driving (see BNF)
Phenytoin susp, 8, C, administration, blood or skin disorder symptoms (see BNF), driving (see BNF)
*Phosex*, 21, 25
*Phosphate-Sandoz*, 13
*Phyllocontin Continus*, 25
*Physeptone*, 2
*Physiotens*, 3
Phytomenadione, 24
*Picolax*, 10, patient information leaflet 13, C, solution, see BNF
Pilocarpine tabs, 21, 27, C, driving
Pimecrolimus, 4, 28
Pimozide, 2
Pindolol, 8
Piperazine powder, 13
Piracetam, 3
*Piriton*, 2
Piroxicam caps and tabs, 21
Piroxicam dispersible tabs, 13, 21
Pivmecillinam, 9, 21, 27, C, posture, see BNF
Pizotifen, 2
*Plaquenil*, 5, 21
*Plendil*, 25
Podophyllin paint cpd, 15, C, application, see BNF
*Ponstan*, 21
*Potaba caps and tabs*, 21
*Potaba Envules*, 13, 21
Potassium chloride m/r, see preps
Potassium citrate mixt, 27
Potassium effervescent tabs, 13, 21
Pramipexole, C, hypotensive reactions, driving, see BNF
*Pranoxen Continus*, 25
Pravastatin, C, muscle effects, see BNF
*Praxilene*, 25, 27
Prazosin, 3, C, initial dose, see BNF
*Prednesol*, 10, steroid card, 13, 21
Prednisolone inj, 10, steroid card
Prednisolone tabs, 10, steroid card, 21
Prednisolone e/c, 5, 10, steroid card 25
*Pregabalin*, 3, 8, C, driving
*Preservex*, 21
*Prestim*, 8
*Priadel liq*, 10, lithium card, C, fluid and salt intake, see BNF

*Priadel tabs*, 10, lithium card, 25, C, fluid and salt intake, see BNF
Primidone, 2, 8, C, driving (see BNF)
*Prioderm lotion*, 15
*Pripsen*, 13
*Pro-Banthine*, 23
Probenecid, 12, 21, 27
Procarbazine, 4
Prochlorperazine, 2
Prochlorperazine buccal tabs, 2, C, administration, see BNF
Prochlorperazine sachets, 2, 13
Procyclidine, C, driving
*Prograf*, 23, C, driving, see BNF
Proguanil, 21, C, malaria prophylaxis, see BNF
*Progynova TS preps*, C, administration, see BNF
Promazine, 2
Promethazine, 2
*Propaderm*, 28
Propafenone, 21, 25
Propantheline, 23
Propiverine hydrochloride, 3
Propranolol, 8
Propranolol m/r, 8, 25
*Protelos*, 5, 13, C, administration, see BNF
*Prothiaden*, 2
Protionamide, 8, 21
*Protium*, 25
*Protopic*, 4, 11, 28
*Prozac*, C, driving, see BNF
*Psorin*, 28
*Pulmicort*, 8, 10, steroid card C, dose
*Pulmicort LS*, 8, C, dose
*Pulmicort Respules*, 8, 10, steroid card C, dose
*Pylorid*, C, discoloration (tongue and faeces), see BNF
Pyrazinamide, 8

*Questran preps*, 13, C, avoid other drugs at same time, see BNF
Quetiapine, 2
Quinagolide, 21, C, hypotensive reactions, see BNF
Quinidine m/r, 25
Quinocort, 28
*Quinoderm with Hydrocortisone*, 28
*Qvar preps*, 8, 10, steroid card (high-dose preparations only), C, dose

Rabeprazole, 25
Ranitidine bismuth citrate, C, discoloration (tongue and faeces), see BNF
Ranitidine effervescent tabs, 13
*Rapamune*, C, administration
*Rebetol*, 21
*Reboxetine*, C, driving
*Regulan*, 13, C, administration, see BNF
*Regurin*, 23
*Relifex*, 21
*Relifex dispersible tablets*, 13, 21
*Relifex susp*, 21
*Remedeine*, 2, 21, 29, 30
*Remedeine effervescent tabs*, 2, 13, 21, 29, 30
*Remicade*, 10, Alert card, C, tuberculosis and hypersensitivity reactions
*Reminyl*, 3, 21
*Reminyl XL*, 3, 21, 25
*Renagel*, 25, C, with meals
*Requip*, 21, C, driving, see BNF
*Resonium A*, 13
*Restandol*, 21, 25
*Retrovir syrup*, C, use of oral syringe
*Revanil*, 21, C, hypotensive reactions, see BNF
*Reyataz*, 5, 21
*Rheumacin SR*, 21, 25, C, driving
*Rhumalgan*, 5, 25
*Riamet*, 21, C, driving
Ribavirin caps and tabs, 21
*Ridaura*, 21, C, blood disorder symptoms, see BNF
Rifabutin, 8, 14, (urine orange-red) C, soft lenses
*Rifadin*, 8, 14, (urine orange-red) 22, C, soft lenses
Rifampicin caps and mixt, 8, 14, (urine orange-red) 22, C, soft lenses
*Rifater*, 8, 14, (urine orange-red) 22, C, soft lenses
*Rifinah*, 8, 14, (urine orange-red) 22, C, soft lenses
*Rilutek*, C, blood disorders, driving
*Rimactane*, 8, 14, (urine orange-red) 22, C, soft lenses
*Rimactazid*, 8, 14, (urine orange-red) 22, C, soft lenses
Risedronate sodium, C, administration, food and calcium, see BNF
*Risperdal*, 2
Risperidone, 2
Ritonavir, 21, C, administration, see BNF
Rivastigmine, 21, 25
*Rivotril*, 2, 8, C, driving (see BNF)
Rizatriptan tabs, 3
Rizatriptan wafers, 3, C, administration
*Roaccutane*, 10, patient information leaflet 11, 21
*Robaxin*, 2
Ropinirole, 21, C, driving, see BNF
*Rowachol*, 22
*Rowatinex caps*, 25
*Rozex*, 10, patient information leaflet
*Rythmodan Retard*, 25
*Sabril sachets*, 3, 8, 13, C, driving (see BNF)
*Sabril tabs*, 3, 8, C, driving (see BNF)
*Safapryn*, 5, 25
*Safapryn-Co*, 5, 25
*Salactol*, 15
*Salagen*, 21, 27, C, driving
*Salatac*, 15
*Salazopyrin*, 14, (urine orange-yellow) C, blood disorder symptoms and soft lenses, see BNF
*Salazopyrin EN-tabs*, 5, 14, (urine orange-yellow) 25, C, blood disorder symptoms and soft lenses, see BNF
*Salbulin*, C, dose, change to CFC-free inhaler, see BNF
Salbutamol inhalations, C, dose, see BNF
Salbutamol inhalations (CFC-free), C, dose, change to CFC-free inhaler, see BNF
Salbutamol m/r, 25
Salicylic acid collodion, 15
Salicylic acid lotion, 15
Salmeterol, C, dose, see BNF
*Salofalk enema and supps*, C, blood disorder symptoms, see BNF
*Salofalk gran*, C, administration, blood disorder symptoms, see BNF
*Salofalk tabs*, 5, 25, C, blood disorder symptoms, see BNF
*Sandimmun*, C, administration, see BNF
*Sandrena*, C, administration, see BNF
*Sando-K*, 13, 21
*Sandocal*, 13
*Sanomigran*, 2
Saquinavir, 21
*Scopoderm TTS*, 19, C, administration, see BNF
*Sebomin MR*, 6, 25
Secobarbital, 19
*Seconal*, 19
*Sectral*, 8
*Securon SR*, 25
Selegiline (freeze-dried tablets), C, administration, see BNF
*Selexid*, 9, 21, 27, C, posture, see BNF
*Semprex*, C, driving, alcohol, see BNF
*Septrin susp and tabs*, 9
*Septrin dispersible tabs*, 9, 13
*Seractil*, 21
*Serc*, 21
*Serenace*, 2
*Seretide*, 8, 10, steroid card (250- and 500-Accuhaler only), C, dose
*Seretide Evohaler*, 8, C, dose, change to CFC-free inhaler (see BNF), 10, steroid card (125- and 250-Evohaler only)

*Serevent*, C, dose, see BNF
*Seroquel*, 2
*Seroxat liq and tabs*, 21, C, driving, see BNF
Sertraline, C, driving, see BNF
Sevelamer, 21
*Sevredol*, 2
Simeticone, see paediatric prep
Simvastatin, C, muscle effects, see BNF
*Sinemet CR*, 14, (urine reddish), 25, C, driving
*Sinemet preps*, 14, (urine reddish), C, driving
*Sinequan*, 2
*Singulair chewable tabs*, 24
*Sinthrome*, 10, anticoagulant card
Sirolimus, C, administration
*Skelid*, C, food and calcium
*Slofedipine XL*, 25
*Slo-Indo*, 21, 25, C, driving
*Slo-Phyllin*, 25 or C, administration, see BNF
*Sloprolol*, 8, 25
*Slow Sodium*, 25
*Slow-Fe*, 25
*Slow-Fe Folic*, 25
*Slow-K*, 25, 27, C, posture, see BNF
*Slow-Trasicor*, 8, 25
*Slozem*, 25
*Sodium Amytal*, 19
Sodium aurothiomalate, C, blood disorder symptoms, see BNF
Sodium cellulose phosphate, 13, 21, C, may be sprinkled on food
Sodium chloride m/r, 25
Sodium chloride tabs, 13
Sodium chloride and glucose oral pdr, cpd, 13
Sodium chloride solution-tabs, 13
Sodium clodronate, C, food and calcium, see BNF
Sodium cromoglicate (oral), 22, C, administration, see BNF
Sodium cromoglicate inhalations, 8
Sodium fusidate susp, 9, 21
Sodium fusidate tabs, 9
Sodium picosulfate pdr, 10, patient information leaflet 13, C, see BNF
Sodium valproate e/c, 5, 8, 25, C, blood or hepatic disorder symptoms (see BNF), driving (see BNF)
Sodium valproate m/r, 8, 25, C, blood or hepatic disorder symptoms (see BNF), driving (see BNF)
Sodium valproate crushable tabs, liquid and syrup, 8, C, blood or hepatic disorder symptoms (see BNF), driving (see BNF)
*Solian*, 2
Solifenacin, 3
*Solpadol caps and caplets*, 2, 29, 30
*Solpadol Effervescent*, 2, 13, 29, 30
*Solu-Cortef*, 10, steroid card
*Solu-Medrone*, 10, steroid card
*Solvazinc*, 13, 21
*Somnite*, 19
*Sonata*, 2
*Soneryl*, 19
*Sotacor*, 8
*Sotalol*, 8
*Sporanox caps*, 5, 9, 21, 25
*Sporanox liq*, 9, 23
*Stalevo*, 14, (urine reddish-brown) C, driving, avoid iron-containing preparations at the same time of day
*Stelazine syrup and tabs*, 2
*Stelazine Spansule*, 2, 25
*Stemetil*, 2
*Stemetil Eff*, 2, 13
Sterculia, C, administration, see BNF
*Stilnoct*, 19
*Strattera*, 3
*Striant SR*, C, administration, see BNF
Strontium, 5, 13, C, administration, see BNF
*Stugeron*, 2
*Stugeron Forte*, 2
*Subutex*, 2, 26
Sucralfate, 5
*Sudafed Plus*, 2
*Suleo-M*, 15
Sulfadiazine, 9, 27
Sulfasalazine, 14, (urine orange-yellow) C, blood disorder symptoms and soft lenses, see BNF
Sulfasalazine e/c, 5, 14, (urine orange-yellow) 25, C, blood disorder symptoms and soft lenses, see BNF
Sulfinpyrazone, 12, 21
Sulindac, 21
Sulpiride, 2
*Sulpitil*, 2
*Sulpor*, 2
Sumatriptan, 3, 10, patient information leaflet
*Suprax*, 9
*Supralip*, 21, 25
*Suprecur*, C, nasal decongestants, see BNF
*Suprefact nasal spray*, C, nasal decongestants, see BNF
*Surgam tabs*, 21
*Surgam SA*, 25
Surgical spirit, 15
*Surmontil*, 2
*Suscard Buccal*, C, administration, see BNF
*Sustac*, 25
*Sustiva tabs*, 23
*Symbicort*, C, dose, 10, steroid card
*Symmetrel*, C, driving
*Synalar external preps*, 28
*Synarel*, 10, patient information leaflet C, nasal decongestants, see BNF
*Synflex*, 21
*Syscor MR*, 22, 25

Tacrolimus caps, 23, C, driving, see BNF
Tacrolimus topical, 4, 11, 28
*Tamiflu*, 9
Tamsulosin m/r, 25
*Tarceva*, 23
*Tarivid*, 6, 9, 11, C, driving
*Tarka*, 25
*Tasmar*, 14, 25
*Tavanic*, 6, 9, 25, C, driving
*Tavegil*, 2
*Tegretol Chewtabs*, 3, 8, 21, 24, C, blood, hepatic or skin disorder symptoms (see BNF), driving (see BNF)
*Tegretol liq, supps and tabs*, 3, 8, C, blood, hepatic or skin disorder symptoms (see BNF), driving (see BNF)
*Tegretol Retard*, 3, 8, 25, C, blood, hepatic or skin disorder symptoms (see BNF), driving (see BNF)
*Telfast*, C, driving, see BNF
Telithromycin, 9
Temazepam, 19
*Temgesic*, 2, 26
*Temodal*, 23, 25
Temozolomide, 23, 25
*Tenben*, 8
*Tenif*, 8, 25
Tenofovir, 21, C, administration, see BNF
*Tenoret 50*, 8
*Tenoretic*, 8
*Tenormin*, 8
Tenoxicam tabs, 21
*Tensipine MR*, 21, 25
Terazosin, 3, C, dose, see BNF
Terbinafine, 9
Terbutaline inhalations, C, dose, see BNF
Terbutaline m/r, 25
*Testim*, C, administration, see BNF
*Testogel*, C, administration, see BNF
Testosterone buccal tablets, C, administration, see BNF
Testosterone gel, C, administration, see BNF
Testosterone patch, C, administration, see BNF
Testosterone undecanoate caps, 21, 25
Tetrabenazine, 2
Tetracycline, 7, 9, 23, C, posture
Tetracycline mouthwash, see BNF
*Tetralysal preps*, 6, 9
*Teveten*, 21

Theophylline, 21
Theophylline m/r, see preps
Tiabendazole, 3, 21, 24
Tiagabine, 21
Tiaprofenic acid m/r, 25
Tiaprofenic acid tabs, 21
*Tilade*, 8, C, change to CFC-free inhaler
*Tildiem preps*, 25
*Tilolec*, 14, 25, C, driving (see BNF)
Tiludronic acid, C, food and calcium
*Timodine*, 28
Timolol, 8
Tinidazole tabs, 4, 9, 21, 25
Tipranavir, 21
Tizanidine, 2
Tolcapone, 14, 25
Tolterodine m/r, 25
*Topamax Sprinkle*, 3, 8, C, administration, driving (see BNF)
*Topamax tabs*, 3, 8, C, driving (see BNF)
Topiramate Sprinkle caps, 3, 8, C, administration, driving (see BNF)
Topiramate tabs, 3, 8, C, driving (see BNF)
*Toradol tabs*, 17, 21
*Tramacet*, 2, 25, 29, 30
Tramadol, 2
Tramadol m/r, 2, 25
Tramadol sachets, 2, 13
Tramadol soluble, 2, 13
*Tramake*, 2
*Tramake Insts*, 2, 13
*Trandate*, 8, 21
*Trasicor*, 8
*Trasidrex*, 8, 25
*Traxam foam*, 15
Trazodone, 2, 21
Trazodone m/r, 2, 21, 25
*Trental m/r*, 21, 25
Treosulfan, 25
Tretinoin caps, 21
*Tri-Adcortyl external preps*, 28
Triamcinolone inj, 10, steroid card
Triamcinolone tabs, 10, steroid card, 21
Triamterene, 14, (urine blue in some lights) 21
*Triapin preps*, 25
Triclofos sodium, 19
Trientine, 6, 22
Trifluoperazine, 2
Trihexyphenidyl, C, before or after food, driving, see BNF
*Trileptal*, 3, 8, C, see BNF
Trilostane, 21
Trimethoprim mixt and tabs, 9
Trimipramine, 2
*Trimopan*, 9
*Trimovate*, 28
Tripotassium dicitratobismuthate, C, administration, see BNF
Triprolidine m/r, 2, 25
*Triptafen preps*, 2
*Trizivir*, C, hypersensitivity reactions, see BNF
Tropisetron, 23
*Tropium*, 2
Trospium chloride, 23
Truvada, 21, C, administration, see BNF
*Tryptophan*, 3
*Tuinal*, 19
*Tylex caps*, 2, 29, 30
*Tylex effervescent tabs*, 2, 13, 29, 30
Typhoid vaccine, oral, 23, 25, C, administration, see BNF

*Ubretid*, 22
*Ucerax*, 2
*Ultralanum Plain*, 28
*Uniphyllin Continus*, 25
*Univer*, 25
*Uprima*, C, driving
*Urdox*, 21
*Uriben*, 9, 11
Ursodeoxycholic acid, 21
*Ursogal*, 21
*Ursofalk*, 21
*Utinor*, 7, 9, 23, C, driving

Valaciclovir, 9
*Valcyte*, 21
Valganciclovir, 21
*Valium*, 2 or 19
*Vallergan*, 2
*Valoid*, 2
Valproic acid, see individual preparations
*Valtrex*, 9
*Vancocin caps*, 9
Vancomycin caps, 9
*Velosef*, 9
Venlafaxine, 3, 21, C, driving
Venlafaxine m/r, 3, 21, 25, C, driving
*Ventmax SR*, 25
*Ventodisks*, C, dose, see BNF
*Ventolin Evohaler*, C, dose, change to CFC-free inhaler, see BNF
*Ventolin inhalations*, C, dose, see BNF
*Vepesid caps*, 23
Verapamil m/r, 25
*Verapress*, 25
*Vertab SR*, 25
*Vesanoid*, 21
*Vesicare*, 3
*Vfend*, 11, 23
*Viazem XL*, 25
*Vibramycin caps*, 6, 9, 11, 27, C, posture, see BNF
*Vibramycin-D*, 6, 9, 11, 13
*Videx*, 23, C, administration, see BNF
*Videx e/c caps*, 25, C, administration
*Videx tabs*, 23, C, administration
Vigabatrin sachets, 3, 8, 13, C, driving (see BNF)
Vigabatrin tabs, 3, 8, C, driving (see BNF)
Vinorelbine caps, 21, 25
*Vioform-Hydrocortisone*, 28
*Viracept powder*, 21, C, administration, see BNF
*Viracept tabs*, 21
*Viramune*, C, hypersensitivity reactions, see BNF
*Viread*, 21, C, administration, see BNF
*Visclair*, 5, 22, 25
*Viskaldix*, 8
*Visken*, 8
*Volmax*, 25
*Voltarol dispersible tabs*, 13, 21
*Voltarol 75mg SR and Retard*, 21, 25
*Voltarol tabs*, 5, 25
Voriconazole, 11, 23

Warfarin, 10, anticoagulant card
*Warfarin WBP*, 10, anticoagulant card
*Warticon*, 15
*Welldorm*, 19, 27
*Wellvone*, 21

*Xagrid*, C, driving
*Xanax*, 2
*Xatral*, 3, C, dose, see BNF
*Xatral XL*, 3, 21, 25, C, dose, see BNF
*Xeloda*, 21
*Xepin*, 2, 10, patient information leaflet
*Xismox XL*, 25
*Xyzal*, C, driving

*Yentreve*, 2

*Zaditen*, 2, 8, 21
*Zadstat supps*, 4, 9
Zafirlukast, 23
*Zaleplon*, 2
*Zamadol*, 2
*Zamadol 24hr*, 2, 25
*Zamadol SR*, 2, 25
*Zanaflex*, 2
*Zanidip*, 22
*Zantac effervescent tabs*, 13
*Zaponex*, 2, 10, patient information leaflet
*Zarontin*, 8, C, blood disorder symptoms (see BNF), driving (see BNF)
*Zavedos caps*, 25
*Zelapar*, C, administration, see BNF
*Zemon XL*, 25
*Zemtard XL*, 25
*Ziagen*, C, hypersensitivity reactions, see BNF
Zidovudine syrup, C, use of oral syringe
*Zimovane*, 19

*Zinamide*, 8
Zinc sulphate, see preps
*Zinnat susp*, 9, 21
*Zinnat tabs*, 9, 21, 25
*Zispin SolTab*, 2
*Zithromax caps*, 5, 9, 23
*Zithromax susp*, 5, 9
*Zocor*, C, muscle effects, see BNF
*Zofran Melt*, C, administration, see BNF
*Zoleptil*, 2
Zolmitriptan orodispersible tabs, C, administration, see BNF
*Zolpidem*, 19
*Zomig Rapimelt*, C, administration, see BNF
*Zomorph*, 2, 25
*Zonegran*, 3
Zonisamide, 3
Zopiclone, 19
Zotepine, 2
*Zoton caps*, 5, 25
*Zoton FasTab*, 5, C, administration, see BNF
*Zoton susp*, 5, 13
*Zovirax susp and tabs*, 9
Zuclopenthixol, 2
*Zyban*, 25
*Zydol*, 2
*Zydol soluble*, 2, 13
*Zydol SR*, 2, 25
*Zydol XL*, 2, 25
*Zyloric*, 8, 21, 27
*Zyomet*, 10, patient information leaflet
*Zyprexa tabs*, 2
*Zyprexa Velotab*, 2, C, administration, see BNF
*Zyvox susp and tabs*, 9, 10, patient information leaflet

# Dental Practitioners' Formulary

## List of Dental Preparations

The following list has been approved by the appropriate Secretaries of State, and the preparations therein may be prescribed by dental practitioners on form FP10D (GP14 in Scotland, WP10D in Wales).

**Sugar-free** versions, where available, are preferred.

Aciclovir Cream, BP
Aciclovir Oral Suspension, BP, 200 mg/5 mL
Aciclovir Tablets, BP, 200 mg
Amoxicillin Capsules, BP
Amoxicillin Oral Powder, DPF[1]
Amoxicillin Oral Suspension, BP
Amphotericin Lozenges, BP
Amphotericin Oral Suspension, BP
Ampicillin Capsules, BP
Ampicillin Oral Suspension, BP
Artificial Saliva, DPF[2]
Artificial Saliva Substitutes as listed below (to be prescribed only for indications approved by ACBS[3]):
- AS Saliva Orthana®
- Glandosane®
- Biotene Oralbalance®
- BioXtra®
- Saliveze®
- Salivix®

Ascorbic Acid Tablets, BP
Aspirin Tablets, Dispersible, BP[4]
Azithromycin Oral Suspension, 200 mg/5 mL, DPF
Benzydamine Mouthwash, BP 0.15%
Benzydamine Oromucosal Spray, BP 0.15%
Carbamazepine Tablets, BP
Carmellose Gelatin Paste, DPF
Cefalexin Capsules, BP
Cefalexin Oral Suspension, BP
Cefalexin Tablets, BP
Cefradine Capsules, BP
Cefradine Oral Solution, DPF
Chlorhexidine Gluconate 1% Gel, DPF
Chlorhexidine Mouthwash, BP
Chlorhexidine Oral Spray, DPF
Chlorphenamine Tablets, BP
Choline Salicylate Dental Gel, BP
Clindamycin Capsules, BP
Diazepam Oral Solution, BP, 2 mg/5 mL
Diazepam Tablets, BP
Diflunisal Tablets, BP
Dihydrocodeine Tablets, BP, 30 mg
Doxycycline Capsules, BP, 100 mg
Doxycycline Tablets, 20 mg, DPF
Ephedrine Nasal Drops, BP
Erythromycin Ethyl Succinate Oral Suspension, BP
Erythromycin Ethyl Succinate Tablets, BP
Erythromycin Stearate Tablets, BP
Erythromycin Tablets, BP
Fluconazole Capsules, 50 mg, DPF
Fluconazole Oral Suspension, 50 mg/5 mL, DPF
Hydrocortisone Cream, BP, 1%
Hydrocortisone Oromucosal Tablets, BP
Hydrocortisone and Miconazole Cream, DPF
Hydrocortisone and Miconazole Ointment, DPF
Hydrogen Peroxide Mouthwash, BP
Ibuprofen Oral Suspension, BP, sugar-free
Ibuprofen Tablets, BP
Lidocaine 5% Ointment, DPF
Menthol and Eucalyptus Inhalation, BP 1980[5]
Metronidazole Oral Suspension, DPF
Metronidazole Tablets, BP
Miconazole Oromucosal Gel, BP
Mouthwash Solution-tablets, DPF
Nitrazepam Tablets, BP
Nystatin Ointment, BP
Nystatin Oral Suspension, BP
Nystatin Pastilles, BP
Oxytetracycline Tablets, BP
Paracetamol Oral Suspension, BP[6]
Paracetamol Tablets, BP
Paracetamol Tablets, Soluble, BP
Penciclovir Cream, DPF
Pethidine Tablets, BP
Phenoxymethylpenicillin Oral Solution, BP
Phenoxymethylpenicillin Tablets, BP
Promethazine Hydrochloride Tablets, BP
Promethazine Oral Solution, BP
Sodium Chloride Mouthwash, Compound, BP
Sodium Fluoride Mouthwash, BP
Sodium Fluoride Oral Drops, BP
Sodium Fluoride Tablets, BP
Sodium Fluoride Toothpaste 0.619%, DPF
Sodium Fusidate Ointment, BP
Temazepam Oral Solution, BP
Temazepam Tablets, BP
Tetracycline Tablets, BP
Triamcinolone Dental Paste, BP
Vitamin B Tablets, Compound, Strong, BPC

Preparations in this list which are not included in the BP or BPC are described on p. 852

1. Amoxicillin Dispersible Tablets are no longer available
2. Supplies may be difficult to obtain
3. Indications approved by the ACBS are: patients suffering from dry mouth as a result of having (or having undergone) radiotherapy or sicca syndrome
4. The BP directs that when soluble aspirin tablets are prescribed, dispersible aspirin tablets should be dispensed
5. This preparation does not appear in subsequent editions of the BP
6. The BP directs that when Paediatric Paracetamol Oral Suspension or Paediatric Paracetamol Mixture is prescribed and no strength stated Paracetamol Oral Suspension 120 mg/5 mL should be dispensed

## Details of DPF preparations

Preparations on the List of Dental Preparations which are specified as DPF are described as follows in the DPF.

Although brand names have sometimes been included for identification purposes preparations on the list should be prescribed by non-proprietary name.

**Amoxicillin Oral Powder** PoM

(proprietary product: *Amoxil Sachets SF*), amoxicillin (as trihydrate) 750 mg[1] and 3 g sachet

1. 750-mg sachets are no longer available

**Artificial Saliva**

(proprietary product: *Luborant*) consists of sorbitol 1.8 g, carmellose sodium (sodium carboxymethylcellulose) 390 mg, dibasic potassium phosphate 48.23 mg, potassium chloride 37.5 mg, monobasic potassium phosphate 21.97 mg, calcium chloride 9.972 mg, magnesium chloride 3.528 mg, sodium fluoride 258 micrograms/60 mL, with preservatives and colouring agents

**Azithromycin Oral Suspension 200 mg/5 mL** PoM

(proprietary product: *Zithromax*); azithromycin (as dihydrate) 200 mg/5 mL when reconstituted with water

**Carmellose Gelatin Paste**

(proprietary product: *Orabase Oral Paste*), gelatin, pectin, carmellose sodium, 16.58% of each in a suitable basis

**Cefradine Oral Solution** PoM

(proprietary product: *Velosef Syrup*), cefradine 250 mg/5mL when reconstituted with water

**Chlorhexidine Gluconate 1% Gel**

(proprietary product: *Corsodyl Dental Gel*), chlorhexidine gluconate 1%

**Chlorhexidine Oral Spray**

(proprietary product: *Corsodyl Oral Spray*), chlorhexidine gluconate 0.2%

**Doxycycline Tablets 20 mg** PoM

(proprietary product: *Periostat*), doxycycline (as hyclate) 20 mg

**Fluconazole Capsules 50 mg** PoM

(proprietary product: *Diflucan*), fluconazole 50 mg

**Fluconazole Oral Suspension 50 mg/5 mL** PoM

(proprietary product: *Diflucan*), fluconazole 50 mg/5 mL when reconstituted with water

**Hydrocortisone and Miconazole Cream** PoM

(proprietary product: *Daktacort Cream*), hydrocortisone 1%, miconazole nitrate 2%

**Hydrocortisone and Miconazole Ointment** PoM

(proprietary product: *Daktacort Ointment*), hydrocortisone 1%, miconazole nitrate 2%

**Lidocaine 5% Ointment**

lidocaine 5% in a suitable basis

**Metronidazole Oral Suspension** PoM

(proprietary product: *Flagyl S*), metronidazole (as benzoate) 200 mg/5mL

**Mouthwash Solution-tablets**

consist of tablets which may contain antimicrobial, colouring and flavouring agents in a suitable soluble effervescent basis to make a mouthwash suitable for dental purposes

**Penciclovir Cream** PoM

(proprietary product: *Vectavir Cream*), penciclovir 1%

**Sodium Fluoride Toothpaste 0.619%** (Non-proprietary) PoM

(proprietary product: *Duraphat Toothpaste*), sodium fluoride 0.619%

## Changes to Dental Practitioners Formulary since September 2005

### Addition

Sodium Fluoride Mouthwash, BP
Sodium Fluoride Toothpaste 0.619%, DPF

# Nurse Prescribers' Formulary

## Nurse Prescribers' Formulary for Community Practitioners

**Nurse Prescribers' Formulary Appendix** (Appendix NPF). List of preparations approved by the Secretary of State which may be prescribed on form FP10P (form HS21(N) in Northern Ireland, form GP10(N) in Scotland, forms FP10(CN) and FP10(PN) in Wales or, when available, WP10CN and WP10PN in Wales) by Nurses for National Health Service patients.

Community practitioners who have completed the necessary training may only prescribe items appearing in the nurse prescribers' list set out below.

### Medicinal Preparations

Preparations on this list which are not included in the BP or BPC are described on p. 856

Almond Oil Ear Drops, BP
Arachis Oil Enema, NPF
[1] Aspirin Tablets, Dispersible, 300 mg, BP
Bisacodyl Suppositories, BP (includes 5-mg and 10-mg strengths)
Bisacodyl Tablets, BP
Cadexomer-Iodine Ointment, NPF
Cadexomer-Iodine Paste, NPF
Cadexomer-Iodine Powder, NPF
Catheter Maintenance Solution, Chlorhexidine, NPF
Catheter Maintenance Solution, Sodium Chloride, NPF
Catheter Maintenance Solution, 'Solution G', NPF
Catheter Maintenance Solution, 'Solution R', NPF
Chlorhexidine Gluconate Alcoholic Solutions containing at least 0.05%
Chlorhexidine Gluconate Aqueous Solutions containing at least 0.05%
Choline Salicylate Dental Gel, BP
Clotrimazole Cream 1%, BP
Co-danthramer Capsules, NPF
Co-danthramer Capsules, Strong, NPF
Co-danthramer Oral Suspension, NPF
Co-danthramer Oral Suspension, Strong, NPF
Co-danthrusate Capsules, BP
Co-danthrusate Oral Suspension, NPF
Crotamiton Cream, BP
Crotamiton Lotion, BP
Dimeticone barrier creams containing at least 10%
Docusate Capsules, BP
Docusate Enema, NPF
Docusate Enema, Compound, BP
Docusate Oral Solution, BP
Docusate Oral Solution, Paediatric, BP
Econazole Cream 1%, BP

1. Max. 96 tablets; max. pack size 32 tablets

Emollients as listed below:
- Aqueous Cream, BP
- Arachis Oil, BP
- Cetraben® Emollient Cream
- Decubal® Clinic
- Dermamist®
- Diprobase® Cream
- Diprobase® Ointment
- Doublebase®
- E45® Cream
- Emulsifying Ointment, BP
- [2] Epaderm®
- Gammaderm® Cream
- Hydromol® Cream
- Hydromol® Ointment
- Hydrous Ointment, BP
- Keri® Therapeutic Lotion
- LactiCare® Lotion
- Lipobase®
- Liquid and White Soft Paraffin Ointment, NPF
- Neutrogena® Dermatological Cream
- Oilatum® Cream
- Paraffin, White Soft, BP
- Paraffin, Yellow Soft, BP
- Ultrabase®
- Unguentum M®
- Zerobase® Cream

Emollient Bath Additives as listed below:
- Alpha Keri® Bath Oil
- Ashbourne Emollient Medicinal Bath Oil
- [3] Balneum®
- Cetraben® Emollient Bath Additive
- Dermalo® Bath Emollient
- Diprobath®
- Hydromol® Emollient
- Imuderm® Bath Oil
- Oilatum® Emollient
- Oilatum® Fragrance Free Junior
- Oilatum® Gel

Folic Acid 400 micrograms/5 mL Oral Solution, NPF
Folic Acid Tablets 400 micrograms, BP
Glycerol Suppositories, BP
[4] Ibuprofen Oral Suspension, BP
[4] Ibuprofen Tablets, BP
Ispaghula Husk Granules, BP
Ispaghula Husk Granules, Effervescent, BP
Ispaghula Husk Oral Powder, BP
Lactulose Solution, BP
Lidocaine Gel, BP
Lidocaine Ointment, BP

2. Included in the Drug Tariff, Scottish Drug Tariff, and Northern Ireland Drug Tariff
3. Except pack sizes that are not to be prescribed under the NHS (see Part XVIIIA of the Drug Tariff, Part XI of the Northern Ireland Drug Tariff)
4. Except for indications and doses that are PoM

Lidocaine and Chlorhexidine Gel, BP
Macrogol Oral Powder, NPF
Macrogol Oral Powder, Compound, NPF
Macrogol Oral Powder, Compound, Half-strength, NPF
Magnesium Hydroxide Mixture, BP
Magnesium Sulphate Paste, BP
Malathion alcoholic lotions containing at least 0.5%
Malathion aqueous lotions containing at least 0.5%
Mebendazole Oral Suspension, NPF
Mebendazole Tablets, NPF
Methylcellulose Tablets, BP
Miconazole Cream 2%, BP
Miconazole Oromucosal Gel, BP
Mouthwash Solution-tablets, NPF
Nicotine Inhalation Cartridge for Oromucosal Use, NPF
Nicotine Lozenge, NPF
Nicotine Medicated Chewing Gum, NPF
Nicotine Nasal Spray, NPF
Nicotine Sublingual Tablets, NPF
Nicotine Transdermal Patches, NPF
Nystatin Oral Suspension, BP
Nystatin Pastilles, BP
Olive Oil Ear Drops, BP
Paracetamol Oral Suspension, BP (includes 120 mg/5 mL and 250 mg/5 mL strengths—both of which are available as sugar-free formulations)
[1] Paracetamol Tablets, BP
[1] Paracetamol Tablets, Soluble, BP (includes 120-mg and 500-mg tablets)
Permethrin Cream, NPF
Phenothrin Alcoholic Lotion, NPF
Phenothrin Aqueous Lotion, NPF
Phosphate Suppositories, NPF
Phosphates Enema, BP
Piperazine and Senna Powder, NPF
Povidone–Iodine Solution, BP
Senna Granules, Standardised, BP
Senna Oral Solution, NPF
Senna Tablets, BP
Senna and Ispaghula Granules, NPF
Sodium Chloride Solution, Sterile, BP
Sodium Citrate Compound Enema, NPF
Sodium Picosulfate Capsules, NPF
Sodium Picosulfate Elixir, NPF
Spermicidal contraceptives as listed below:
  Ortho-Creme® Cream
  Orthoforms® Pessaries
Sterculia Granules, NPF
Sterculia and Frangula Granules, NPF
Streptokinase and Streptodornase Topical Powder, NPF
Titanium Ointment, BP
Water for Injections, BP
Zinc and Castor Oil Ointment, BP
Zinc Cream, BP
Zinc Ointment, BP
Zinc Oxide and Dimeticone Spray, NPF
Zinc Oxide Impregnated Medicated Stocking, NPF
Zinc Paste Bandage, BP 1993
Zinc Paste and Calamine Bandage
Zinc Paste, Calamine and Clioquinol Bandage BP 1993
Zinc Paste and Ichthammol Bandage, BP 1993

1. Max. 96 tablets; max. pack size 32 tablets



## Appliances and Reagents (including Wound Management Products)

> In the Drug Tariff Appliances and Reagents which may **not** be prescribed by Nurses are annotated Ⓝ (**Nx** in the Scottish Drug Tariff and N̸ in the Northern Ireland Drug Tariff)

**Applicators, Vaginal** as listed in Part IXA of the Drug Tariff (Part 3 of the Scottish Drug Tariff, not prescribable by nurses in Northern Ireland)
**Atomizers, Hand Operated** as listed in Part IXA of the Drug Tariff (Part 3 of the Scottish Drug Tariff, not prescribable by nurses in Northern Ireland)
**Auto Inflation Device** (for treatment of glue ear) as listed in Part IXA of the Drug Tariff (Part 3 of the Scottish Drug Tariff, Part III of the Northern Ireland Drug Tariff)
**Breast Reliever** as listed in Part IXA of the Drug Tariff (Part 3 of the Scottish Drug Tariff, not prescribable by nurses in Northern Ireland)
**Breast Shields** as listed in Part IXA of the Drug Tariff (not prescribable by nurses in Scotland or Northern Ireland)
**Catheter Accessories** as listed in Part IXA of the Drug Tariff (Part 3 of the Scottish Drug Tariff, Part III of the Northern Ireland Drug Tariff)
**Catheter Maintenance Solutions** as listed in Part IXA of the Drug Tariff (Part 3 of the Scottish Drug Tariff, Part III of the Northern Ireland Drug Tariff)
**Catheters, Urethral Sterile** as listed under Catheters in Part IXA of the Drug Tariff (Part 3 of the Scottish Drug Tariff, Part III of the Northern Ireland Drug Tariff)
**Cervical Collar, Soft Foam** as listed in Part IXA of the Drug Tariff (Part 3 of the Scottish Drug Tariff, not prescribable by nurses in Northern Ireland)
**Chemical Reagents**
The following as listed in Part IXR of the Drug Tariff (Part 9 of the Scottish Drug Tariff, Part II of the Northern Ireland Drug Tariff):
  Detection Strips for Glycosuria
  Detection Strips for Ketonuria
  Detection Strips for Proteinuria
  Detection Strips for Blood Glucose
  Detection Strips for Blood Ketones (not prescribable by nurses in Northern Ireland)
  Detection Strips for Determination of International Normalised Ratio (INR) (not prescribable by nurses in Northern Ireland)
**Chiropody Appliances** as listed in Part IXA of the Drug Tariff (Part 2 of the Scottish Drug Tariff (except for Corn Plasters), not prescribable by nurses in Northern Ireland)
**Contraceptive Devices** as listed in Part IXA of the Drug Tariff (Part 3 of the Scottish Drug Tariff, Part III of the Northern Ireland Drug Tariff (fertility (ovulation) thermometers only))
**Douches** (with vaginal and rectal fittings) as listed in Part IXA of the Drug Tariff (Part 3 of the Scottish Drug Tariff, not prescribable by nurses in Northern Ireland)
**Droppers** as listed in Part IXA of the Drug Tariff (Part 3 of the Scottish Drug Tariff, not prescribable by nurses in Northern Ireland)
**Dry Mouth Products** as listed in part IXA of the Drug Tariff (Part 3 of the Scottish Drug Tariff, not prescribable by nurses in Northern Ireland)
**Ear Wax Softening Medical Devices** as listed in Part IXA of the Drug Tariff (Part 3 of the Scottish Drug Tariff, Part III of the Northern Ireland Drug Tariff)

**Elastic Hosiery** including accessories as listed in Part IXA of the Drug Tariff (Part 4 of the Scottish Drug Tariff, Part III of the Northern Ireland Drug Tariff)
**Emollients** as listed in Part IXA of the Drug Tariff (Part 3 of the Scottish Drug Tariff, Part III of the Northern Ireland Drug Tariff)
**Eye Baths** as listed in Part IXA of the Drug Tariff (Part 3 of the Scottish Drug Tariff, not prescribable by nurses in Northern Ireland)
**Eye-drop Dispensers** as listed in Part IXA of the Drug Tariff (Part 3 of the Scottish Drug Tariff, Part III of the Northern Ireland Drug Tariff)
**Eye Shades** as listed in Part IXA of the Drug Tariff (Part 3 of the Scottish Drug Tariff, not prescribable by nurses in Northern Ireland)
**Finger Cots** as listed in Part IXA of the Drug Tariff (Part 3 of the Scottish Drug Tariff, not prescribable by nurses in Northern Ireland)
**Finger Stalls** as listed in Part IXA of the Drug Tariff (Part 3 of the Scottish Drug Tariff, not prescribable by nurses in Northern Ireland)
**Head Lice Device** as listed in Part IXA of the Drug Tariff (Part 3 of the Scottish Drug Tariff, Part III of the Northern Ireland Drug Tariff)
**Hypodermic Equipment** as listed in Part IXA of the Drug Tariff (Part 3 of the Scottish Drug Tariff, Part III of the Northern Ireland Drug Tariff (with some exceptions))
**Incontinence Appliances** as listed in Part IXB of the Drug Tariff (Part 5 of the Scottish Drug Tariff, Part III of the Northern Ireland Drug Tariff)
**Inhaler, Spare Tops** as listed in Part IXA of the Drug Tariff (Part 3 of the Scottish Drug Tariff, not prescribable by nurses in Northern Ireland)
**Insufflators** as listed in Part IXA of the Drug Tariff (Part 3 of the Scottish Drug Tariff, not prescribable by nurses in Northern Ireland)
**Irrigation Fluids** as listed in Part IXA of the Drug Tariff (Part 2 of the Scottish Drug Tariff, Part III of the Northern Ireland Drug Tariff)
**Latex Foam, Adhesive** as listed in Part IXA of the Drug Tariff (not prescribable by nurses in Scotland or Northern Ireland)
**Lubricating Jelly** as listed in Part IXA of the Drug Tariff (Part 2 of the Scottish Drug Tariff, not prescribable by nurses in Northern Ireland)
**Nasal Device** (nasal dilator) as listed in Part IXA of the Drug Tariff (Part 3 of the Scottish Drug Tariff, Part III of the Northern Ireland Drug Tariff)
**Nasal Drops, Sodium Chloride 0.9%** as listed in Part IXA of the Drug Tariff (Part 3 of the Scottish Drug Tariff)
**Nipple Shields, Plastic** as listed in Part IXA of the Drug Tariff (Part 3 of the Scottish Drug Tariff, not prescribable by nurses in Northern Ireland)
**Oral Film Forming Agents** as listed in Part IXA of the Drug Tariff (Part 3 of the Scottish Drug Tariff, not prescribable by nurses in Northern Ireland)
**Peak Flow Meters** as listed in Part IXA of the Drug Tariff (Part 3 of the Scottish Drug Tariff, not prescribable by nurses in Northern Ireland)
**Pessaries** as listed in Part IXA of the Drug Tariff (Part 3 of the Scottish Drug Tariff, Part III of the Northern Ireland Drug Tariff (with some exceptions))
**Protectives** as listed in Part IXA of the Drug Tariff (Part 2 of the Scottish Drug Tariff, Part III of the Northern Ireland Drug Tariff (EMA Disposable Film Gloves only))
**Stoma Appliances and Associated Products** as listed in Part IXC of the Drug Tariff (Part 6 of the Scottish Drug Tariff, Part III of the Northern Ireland Drug Tariff)
**Suprapubic Belts** (replacements only) as listed in Part IXA of the Drug Tariff (Part 3 of the Scottish Drug Tariff, not prescribable by nurses in Northern Ireland)
**Suprapubic Catheters** as listed in Part IXA of the Drug Tariff (Part 3 of the Scottish Drug Tariff, not prescribable by nurses in Northern Ireland)
**Synovial Fluid** as listed in Part IXA of the Drug Tariff (Part 3 of the Scottish Drug Tariff, not prescribable by nurses in Northern Ireland)
**Syringes** (Bladder/Irrigating, Ear, Enema, Spare Vaginal Pipes) as listed in Part IXA of the Drug Tariff (Part 3 of the Scottish Drug Tariff, not prescribable by nurses in Northern Ireland)
**Test Tubes** as listed in Part IXA of the Drug Tariff (Part 3 of the Scottish Drug Tariff, not prescribable by nurses in Northern Ireland)
**Tracheostomy and Laryngectomy Appliances** as listed in Part IXA of the Drug Tariff (Part 2 of the Scottish Drug Tariff, not prescribable by nurses in Northern Ireland)
**Trusses** as listed in Part IXA of the Drug Tariff (Part 3 of the Scottish Drug Tariff, not prescribable by nurses in Northern Ireland)
**Vacuum Pumps and Constrictor Rings for Erectile Dysfunction** as listed in Part IXA of the Drug Tariff (Part 3 of the Scottish Drug Tariff, Part III of the Northern Ireland Drug Tariff)—prescribing restrictions may apply (see Drug Tariff)
**Vaginal Moisturisers** as listed in Part IXA of the Drug Tariff (Part 3 of the Scottish Drug Tariff)
**Wound Management and Related Products** (including bandages, dressings, gauzes, lint, stockinette, etc)
The following as listed in Part IXA of the Drug Tariff (Part 2 of the Scottish Drug Tariff, Part III of the Northern Ireland Drug Tariff):

- Absorbent Cellulose Dressing with Fluid Repellent Backing
- Absorbent Cottons
- Absorbent Cotton Gauzes
- Absorbent Cotton and Viscose Ribbon Gauze, BP 1988
- Absorbent Dressing Pads, Sterile
- Absorbent Lint, BPC
- Absorbent Perforated Dressing with Adhesive Border
- Absorbent Perforated Plastic Film Faced Dressing
- Arm Slings
- Belladonna Adhesive Plaster BP 1980
- Boil Dressing Pack
- Cellulose Wadding, BP 1988
- Chlorhexidine Gauze Dressing, BP
- Conforming Bandage (Synthetic)
- Cotton Conforming Bandage, BP 1988
- Cotton Crêpe Bandage, BP 1988
- Cotton Crêpe Bandage, Hospicrepe 239
- Cotton, Polyamide and Elastane Bandage
- Cotton Stretch Bandage, BP 1988
- Crêpe Bandage, BP 1988
- Elastic Adhesive Bandage, BP
- Elastic Web Bandages
- Elastomer and Viscose Bandage, Knitted
- Gauze and Cotton Tissues
- Gauze Dressings (Impregnated)
- Heavy Cotton and Rubber Elastic Bandage, BP
- High Compression Bandages (Extensible)

- Knitted Polyamide and Cellulose Contour Bandage, BP 1988
- Knitted Viscose Primary Dressing, BP, Type 1
- Multi-layer Compression Bandaging
- Multiple Pack Dressing No. 1
- Open-wove Bandage, BP 1988, Type 1
- Paraffin Gauze Dressing, BP
- Plaster of Paris Bandage BP 1988
- Polyamide and Cellulose Contour Bandage, BP 1988
- Polyester Primary Dressing with Neutral Triglycerides, Knitted
- Povidone–Iodine Fabric Dressing, Sterile
- Short Stretch Compression Bandage
- Skin Adhesive, Sterile
- Skin Closure Strips, Sterile
- Standard Dressings
- Sterile Dressing Packs
- Stockinettes
- Sub-compression Wadding Bandage
- Surgical Adhesive Tapes
- Surgical Sutures (absorbable and non-absorbable)
- Suspensory Bandages, Cotton
- Swabs
- Triangular Calico Bandage, BP 1980
- Vapour-permeable Adhesive Film Dressing, BP (including with absorbent pad)
- Vapour-permeable Waterproof Plastic Wound Dressing, BP, Sterile
- Venous Ulcer Compression System
- Wound Drainage Pouch
- Wound Management Dressings (including activated charcoal, alginate, capillary-action, cavity, collagen, honey-based application, hydrocolloid, hydrogel, foam, polyurethane matrix, protease modulating matrix, silicone, silver-coated and silver-impregnated, and soft polymer dressings)
- Zinc Paste Bandages (including both plain and with additional ingredients)—see also under Medicinal Preparations

> In the Drug Tariff Appliances and Reagents which may **not** be prescribed by Nurses are annotated Ⓝ (**Nx** in the Scottish Drug Tariff and N̶ in the Northern Ireland Drug Tariff)

## Details of NPF preparations

Preparations on the Nurse Prescribers' Formulary which are not included in the BP or BPC are described as follows in the Nurse Prescribers' Formulary.

Although brand names have sometimes been included for identification purposes, it is recommended that non-proprietary names should be used for prescribing medicinal preparations in the NPF except where a non-proprietary name is not available.

**Arachis Oil Enema**
(proprietary product: *Fletchers' Arachis Oil Retention Enema*), arachis oil

**Cadexomer–Iodine Ointment**
(proprietary product: *Iodosorb Ointment*), cadexomer–iodine containing iodine 0.9% in an ointment basis

**Cadexomer–Iodine Paste** PoM
(proprietary product: *Iodoflex*), cadexomer–iodine containing iodine 0.9% in a paste basis

**Cadexomer–Iodine Powder** PoM
(proprietary product: *Iodosorb Powder*), cadexomer–iodine containing iodine 0.9%

**Catheter Maintenance Solution, Chlorhexidine**
(proprietary products: *Uro-Tainer Chlorhexidine*; *Uriflex C*), chlorhexidine 0.02%

**Catheter Maintenance Solution, Sodium Chloride**
(proprietary products: *Uro-Tainer Sodium Chloride*; *Uriflex-S*), sodium chloride 0.9%

**Catheter Maintenance Solution, 'Solution G'**
(proprietary products: *Uro-Tainer Suby G*, *Uriflex G*), citric acid 3.23%, magnesium oxide 0.38%, sodium bicarbonate 0.7%, disodium edetate 0.01%

**Catheter Maintenance Solution, 'Solution R'**
(proprietary products: *Uro-Tainer Solution R*, *Uriflex R*), citric acid 6%, gluconolactone 0.6%, magnesium carbonate 2.8%, disodium edetate 0.01%

**Chlorhexidine gluconate alcoholic solutions**
chlorhexidine gluconate at least 0.05% in alcoholic solution

**Chlorhexidine gluconate aqueous solutions**
(proprietary product: *Unisept*) chlorhexidine gluconate in aqueous solution

**Co-danthramer Capsules** PoM
co-danthramer 25/200 (dantron 25 mg, poloxamer '188' 200 mg)

**Co-danthramer Capsules, Strong** PoM
co-danthramer 37.5/500 (dantron 37.5 mg, poloxamer '188' 500 mg)

**Co-danthramer Oral Suspension** PoM
(proprietary product: *Codalax*), co-danthramer 25/200 in 5 mL (dantron 25 mg, poloxamer '188' 200 mg/5 mL)

**Co-danthramer Oral Suspension, Strong** PoM
(proprietary product: *Codalax Forte*), co-danthramer 75/1000 in 5 mL (dantron 75 mg, poloxamer '188' 1 g/5 mL)

**Co-danthrusate Oral Suspension** PoM
(proprietary product: *Normax*), co-danthrusate 50/60 (dantron 50 mg, docusate sodium 60 mg/5 mL)

**Dimeticone barrier creams**
(proprietary products: *Conotrane Cream*, dimeticone '350' 22%; *Siopel Barrier Cream*, dimeticone '1000' 10%; *Vasogen Barrier Cream*, dimeticone 20%), dimeticone 10–22%

**Docusate Enema**
(proprietary product: *Norgalax Micro-enema*) docusate sodium 120 mg in 10 g

**Folic Acid Oral Solution 400 micrograms/5 mL**
(proprietary product: *Folicare*), folic acid 400 micrograms/5 mL

**Liquid and White Soft Paraffin Ointment**
liquid paraffin 50%, white soft paraffin 50%

**Macrogol Oral Powder**
(proprietary product: *Idrolax*), macrogol '4000' (polyethylene glycol '4000') 10 g/sachet

**Macrogol Oral Powder, Compound**
(proprietary product: *Movicol*), macrogol '3350' (polyethylene glycol '3350') 13.125 g, sodium bicarbonate 178.5 mg, sodium chloride 350.7 mg, potassium chloride 46.6 mg/sachet

**Macrogol Oral Powder, Compound, Half-strength**
(proprietary product: *Movicol-Half*), macrogol '3350' (polyethylene glycol '3350') 6.563 g, sodium bicarbonate 89.3 g, sodium chloride 175.4 mg, potassium chloride 23.3 mg/sachet

**Malathion alcoholic lotions**
(proprietary products: *Prioderm Lotion*; *Suleo-M Lotion*), malathion 0.5% in an alcoholic basis

**Malathion aqueous lotions**
(proprietary products: *Derbac-M Liquid*; *Quellada M Liquid*), malathion 0.5% in an aqueous basis

**Mebendazole Oral Suspension** PoM
(proprietary product: *Vermox*), mebendazole 100 mg/5 mL

[1]**Mebendazole Tablets** PoM
(proprietary products: *Ovex*, *Vermox*), mebendazole 100 mg

**Mouthwash Solution-tablets**
consist of tablets which may contain antimicrobial, colouring and flavouring agents in a suitable soluble effervescent basis to make a mouthwash

[2]**Nicotine Inhalation Cartridge for Oromucosal Use**
(proprietary products: *Nicorette Inhalator*, *Boots Nicotine Inhalator*), nicotine 10 mg

**Nicotine Lozenge**
nicotine (as bitartrate) 1 mg (proprietary product: *Nicotinell Mint Lozenge*) or nicotine (as polacrilex) 2 mg or 4 mg (proprietary product: *NiQuitin CQ Lozenges*)

**Nicotine Medicated Chewing Gum**
(proprietary products: *Nicorette Gum*, *Nicorette Plus Gum*, *Nicotinell Gum*, *Nicotinell Plus Gum*, *NiQuitin CQ Gum*, *Boots Nicotine Gum*), nicotine 2 mg or 4 mg

**Nicotine Nasal Spray**
(proprietary product: *Nicorette Nasal Spray*), nicotine 500 micrograms/metered spray

[3]**Nicotine Sublingual Tablets**
(proprietary product: *Nicorette Microtab*), nicotine (as a cyclodextrin complex) 2 mg

[4]**Nicotine Transdermal Patches**
releasing in each 16 hours, nicotine approx. 5 mg, 10 mg, or 15 mg (proprietary product: *Nicorette Patch*) or releasing in each 24 hours nicotine approx. 7 mg, 14 mg, or 21 mg (proprietary products: *Nicotinell TTS*, *NiQuitin CQ*, *Boots NRT Patch*)

**Permethrin Cream**
(proprietary product: *Lyclear Dermal Cream*), permethrin 5%

1. For PoM exemption, see p. 340
2. For use with inhalation mouthpiece; to be prescribed as either a starter pack (6 cartridges with inhalator device and holder) or refill pack (42 cartridges with inhalator device)
3. To be prescribed as either a starter pack (2 x 15-tablet discs with dispenser) or refill pack (7 x 15-tablet discs)
4. Prescriber should specify the brand to be dispensed

**Phenothrin Alcoholic Lotion**
(proprietary product: *Full Marks Lotion*), phenothrin 0.2% in a basis containing isopropyl alcohol

**Phenothrin Aqueous Lotion**
(proprietary product: *Full Marks Liquid*), phenothrin 0.5% in an aqueous basis

**Phosphate Suppositories**
(proprietary product: *Carbalax*), sodium acid phosphate (anhydrous) 1.3 g, sodium bicarbonate 1.08 g

**Piperazine and Senna Powder**
(proprietary product: *Pripsen Oral Powder*), piperazine phosphate 4 g, sennosides 15.3 mg/sachet

**Senna Oral Solution**
(proprietary product: *Senokot Syrup*), sennosides 7.5 mg/5 mL

**Senna and Ispaghula Granules**
(proprietary product: *Manevac Granules*), senna fruit 12.4%, ispaghula 54.2%

**Sodium Citrate Compound Enema**
(proprietary products: *Micolette Micro-enema*; *Micralax Micro-enema*; *Relaxit Micro-enema*), sodium citrate 450 mg with glycerol, sorbitol and an anionic surfactant

**Sodium Picosulfate Capsules**
(proprietary products: *Dulco-lax Perles*), sodium picosulfate 2.5 mg

**Sodium Picosulfate Elixir**
(proprietary products: *Dulco-lax Liquid*, *Laxoberal* NHS), sodium picosulfate 5 mg/5 mL

**Sterculia Granules**
(proprietary product: *Normacol Granules*), sterculia 62%

**Sterculia and Frangula Granules**
(proprietary product: *Normacol Plus Granules*), sterculia 62%, frangula (standardised) 8%

**Streptokinase and Streptodornase Topical Powder** PoM
(proprietary product: *Varidase Topical*), streptokinase 100 000 units, streptodornase 25 000 units

**Zinc Oxide and Dimeticone Spray**
(proprietary product: *Sprilon*), dimeticone 1.04%, zinc oxide 12.5% in a pressurised aerosol unit

**Zinc Oxide Impregnated Medicated Stocking**
(proprietary product: *Zipzoc*), sterile rayon stocking impregnated with ointment containing zinc oxide 20%

## Nurse Prescribers' Extended Formulary

**List of preparations which may be prescribed by Extended Formulary Nurse Prescribers on Form FP10P, for NHS patients in England (Form HS21(N) in Northern Ireland, Form GP10(N2) in Scotland).**

Independent nurse prescribers who have completed the necessary training and are authorised to prescribe from the Nurse Prescribers' Extended Formulary list may prescribe all General Sales List and Pharmacy medicines currently prescribable by GPs, together with specified Prescription Only Medicines. In addition they may prescribe all items in the nurse prescribing list for Community Practitioners on p. 853. Until legislative changes take place in Spring 2006, Extended Formulary Nurse Prescribers should prescribe medicines (including pharmacy-only and general sales list medicines) **only** for the medical conditions specified below. Nurses should **not** prescribe independently for conditions other than those on the list. However, it is expected that from April/May 2006, following legislative changes, Extended Formulary Nurse Prescribers will be able to prescribe *any* licensed medicine, with the exception of some controlled drugs, for *any* medical condition within their competence. (Up-to-date information is available on the Department of Health website, www.dh.gov.uk)

## Medical Conditions

| | BNF section[1] |
|---|---|
| **Central Nervous System** | |
| Acute dystonias | 4.9.2 |
| Acute severe pain after trauma | 4.7.2 |
| Changing painful dressings | 15.2 |
| Nausea and vomiting | 4.6 |
| Prophylaxis and treatment of nausea and vomiting in the postoperative period | 4.6 |
| Recurrent generalised tonic-clonic seizures | 4.8.2 |
| **Circulatory** | |
| Acute myocardial infarction | 2.10 |
| Acute pulmonary oedema associated with cardiac failure | 2.2.2 |
| Angina pectoris | 2.6 |
| Fluid replacement and potassium replacement (hypovolaemia and dehydration) | 9.2.2.1 |
| Haemorrhoids | 1.7.1, 1.7.2 |
| Phlebitis, superficial | - |
| Plasma substitutes for patients with a low blood volume | 9.2.2.2 |
| Thromboprophylaxis—defined as prophylaxis against venous thrombosis (including congestive heart failure, in bed-bound patients, and perioperatively) and for acute coronary syndrome | 2.8.1 |
| Ventricular fibrillation or pulseless ventricular tachycardia | 2.7.3 |
| **Ear** | |
| Furuncle | - |
| Otitis externa | 12.1.1 |
| Otitis media | 12.1.2 |
| Wax in ear | 12.1.3 |
| **Endocrine** | |
| Hyperglycaemia | 6.1.1 |
| Hypoglycaemia | 6.1.4 |
| **Eye** | |
| Blepharitis | 11.3.1 |
| Conjunctivitis, allergic | 11.4.2 |
| Conjunctivitis, infective | 11.3.1 |
| Corneal trauma | 11.7 |
| Diagnostic use in ophthalmology | 11.5 |
| Local anaesthetic for ophthalmic conditions | 11.7 |
| Tear deficiency | 11.8.1 |
| **Gastro-intestinal conditions** | |
| Constipation | 1.6 |
| Gastro-enteritis | 1.4 |
| Heartburn | 1.1 |
| Infantile colic | 1.1.1 |
| Pre-surgery prophylaxis against acid aspiration | 1.3.1, 1.3.5 |
| Worms, threadworms | 5.5.1 |
| **Immunisations** | |
| Routine childhood and specific vaccinations | 14.1, 14.4 |
| **Infections** | |
| Emergency treatment of suspected meningococcal septicaemia or meningococcal meningitis | 5.1 (table 1) |
| Spreading cellulitis usually of a limb with a risk of, or an established lymphangitis | 5.1 (table 1) |
| Tetanus prophylaxis and treatment | 14.4, 14.5 |
| **Musculoskeletal** | |
| Back pain, acute uncomplicated | 4.7.1, 10.1.1 |
| Neck pain, acute uncomplicated | 4.7.1, 10.1.1 |
| Pain and inflammation | 10.1.1 |
| Soft tissue injuries | 4.7.1, 10.1.1, 10.3.2 |
| Sprains | 4.7.1, 10.1.1, 10.3.2 |
| **Oral conditions** | |
| Aphthous ulcer | 12.3.1 |
| Candidiasis, oral | 12.3.2 |
| Dental abscess | 4.7.1, 10.1.1 |
| Dental infections | 5.1 (table 1) |
| Gingivitis | 12.3.4 |
| Stomatitis | - |
| **Poisoning** | |
| Poisoning | Emergency treatment of poisoning |
| **Respiratory** | |
| Acute attacks of asthma | 3.1 |
| Acute exacerbation of chronic bronchitis | 5.1 (table 1) |
| Acute nasopharyngitis (coryza) | 12.2.2 |
| Acute reversible airways obstruction (acute severe asthma or acute exacerbation of chronic obstructive pulmonary disease) | 3.1 |
| Anaphylaxis | 3.4.3 |
| Conditions requiring oxygen supplementation (e.g. hypoxaemia) | 3.6 |
| Croup | 3.1 |
| Laryngitis | 12.3.1 |
| Pharyngitis | 12.3.1 |
| Rhinitis, allergic | 3.4.1, 12.2.1, 12.2.2 |

1. BNF sections appropriate to the listed conditions are shown. However, not all drugs in these sections are prescribable by nurses. Also, in some cases preparations (including General Sales List and Pharmacy medicines) in other BNF sections may be suitable. Before choosing a Prescription Only Medicine, nurses need to check the Nurse Prescribers' Extended Formulary list and to satisfy themselves that the product is licensed for the condition they wish to prescribe for and that the condition falls within the remit of the Nurse Prescribers' Extended Formulary.

| | |
|---|---|
| Sinusitis, acute | 12.2.2 |
| Tonsillitis | 12.3.1 |
| **Skin** | |
| Abrasions | 13.10.5 |
| Acne | 13.6 |
| Animal and human bites | 5.1 (table 1) |
| Boil/carbuncle | 13.10.5 |
| Burn/scald | 13.11, App. 8 |
| Candidiasis, skin | 13.10.2 |
| Chronic skin ulcer | 13.11.7, 13.10.1 |
| Dermatitis, atopic | 13.5.1 |
| Dermatitis, contact | 13.5.1 |
| Dermatitis, seborrhoeic | 13.5.1 |
| Dermatophytosis of the skin (ringworm) | 13.10.2 |
| Herpes labialis | 13.10.3 |
| Impetigo | 5.1 (table 1), 13.10.1 |
| Insect bite/sting | 13.3 |
| Lacerations | 13.11, App. 8 |
| Local anaesthetic for occasions when procedure requires it | 15.2 |
| Local anaesthetic for suturing of lacerations | 15.2 |
| Molluscum contagiosum | - |
| Nappy rash | 13.2.2 |
| Pediculosis (head lice) | 13.10.4 |
| Pruritus in chicken pox | 13.3 |
| Psoriasis | 13.5.2 |
| Scabies | 13.10.4 |
| Urticaria | 3.4.1 |
| Warts (including verrucas) | 13.7 |
| **Substance Dependence** | |
| Acute alcohol withdrawal | 4.10 |
| Smoking cessation | 4.10 |
| **Urinary system** | |
| Urinary tract infection (women)—lower, uncomplicated | 5.1 (table 1), 7.4.3 |
| **Female genital system** | |
| Bacterial vaginosis | 5.1.11, 7.2.2 |
| Candidiasis, vulvovaginal | 7.2.2 |
| Contraception | 7.3 |
| Dysmenorrhoea | 4.7.1, 10.1.1 |
| Emergency contraception | 7.3 |
| Laboratory-confirmed uncomplicated genital chlamydia infection (and the sexual partners of these patients) | 5.1 (table 1) |
| Menopausal vaginal atrophy | 7.2.1 |
| Preconceptual counselling | 9.1.2 |
| *Trichomonas vaginalis* infection (and the sexual partners of these patients) | 5.4.3 |
| **Male genital system** | |
| Balanitis | 13.10.2 |
| **Palliative Care** of patients with advanced progressive illness | |
| Anxiety | 4.1.2 |
| Bowel colic | Prescribing in palliative care |
| Candidiasis, oral | 12.3.2 |
| Confusion | Prescribing in palliative care |
| Constipation | Prescribing in palliative care |
| Convulsions and restlessness | Prescribing in palliative care |
| Cough | Prescribing in palliative care |
| Dry mouth | Prescribing in palliative care |
| Excessive respiratory secretions | Prescribing in palliative care |
| Fungating malodorous tumours | 13.10.1.2 |
| Muscle spasm | Prescribing in palliative care |
| Nausea and vomiting | Prescribing in palliative care |
| Neuropathic pain in palliative care | Prescribing in palliative care |
| Pain control | Prescribing in palliative care |

## Nurse Prescribers' Extended Formulary

1. All licensed P and GSL Medicines prescribable on the NHS
2. Prescription Only Medicines from the list below by the route or form specified
3. See above for the list of those medical conditions for which nurses may prescribe independently

### List of prescription only medicines for prescribing by extended formulary nurse prescribers

Oral antibacterials marked *—see separate list below for indications

| Drug | Route of administration, use or pharmaceutical form |
|---|---|
| Acetylcysteine | Parenteral |
| Aciclovir | External |
| Acrivastine | Oral |
| Adapalene | External |
| Adrenaline | Parenteral |
| Alclometasone dipropionate | External |
| Alimemazine tartrate (trimeprazine tartrate) | Oral |
| Alteplase | Parenteral |
| Amiodarone | Parenteral |
| Amitriptyline hydrochloride | Palliative care—oral |
| Amorolfine hydrochloride | External |
| Amoxicillin trihydrate* | Oral |
| Aspirin | Oral |
| Azelaic acid | External |
| Azelastine hydrochloride | Ophthalmic, nasal |
| Azithromycin dihydrate* | Oral |
| Baclofen | Palliative care—oral |
| Beclometasone dipropionate | External, inhalation, nasal |
| Bemiparin sodium | Parenteral |
| Benzatropine mesilate | Parenteral |
| Benzylpenicillin sodium | Parenteral |
| Betamethasone sodium phosphate | Aural, nasal |
| Betamethasone valerate | External, rectal |
| Budesonide | Inhalation, nasal |
| Buprenorphine | Palliative care—transdermal |
| Calcipotriol | External |
| Calcitriol | External |
| Carbamazepine | Palliative care—oral, rectal |

Footnotes—see p. 862

| | |
|---|---|
| Carbaryl | External |
| Carbenoxolone sodium | Mouthwash |
| Cefotaxime sodium | Parenteral |
| Ceftriaxone sodium | Parenteral |
| Certoparin sodium | Parenteral |
| Cetirizine hydrochloride | Oral |
| Chloramphenicol | Ophthalmic |
| Chlordiazepoxide hydrochloride | Oral for acute alcohol withdrawal |
| Chlorphenamine maleate | Parenteral |
| Cimetidine | Oral, parenteral |
| Cinchocaine hydrochloride | Rectal |
| [1]Clavulanic acid | Oral |
| Clindamycin phosphate | External, vaginal |
| Clobetasone butyrate | External |
| Clotrimazole | External |
| Codeine phosphate | Oral |
| Conjugated oestrogens (equine) | External |
| Co-phenotrope | Oral |
| Cyclizine hydrochloride | Oral |
| Cyclizine lactate | Parenteral |
| Dalteparin sodium | Parenteral |
| Dantrolene sodium | Palliative care—oral |
| Dantron | Oral |
| [2]Desogestrel | Oral |
| Desoximetasone | External |
| Dexamethasone | Aural |
| Dexamethasone isonicotinate | Nasal |
| Dexamethasone sodium phosphate | Oral |
| Dextran 70 | Parenteral |
| Diamorphine hydrochloride | Oral, parenteral for pain relief in palliative care, myocardial infarction, acute or severe pain after trauma or surgery |
| Diazepam | Oral, parenteral, rectal |
| Diclofenac diethylammonium | External |
| Diclofenac potassium | Oral |
| Diclofenac sodium | Oral, rectal, ophthalmic |
| Dihydrocodeine tartrate | Oral |
| Dolasetron mesilate | Oral,parenteral |
| Domperidone | Oral, rectal |
| Domperidone maleate | Oral |
| Doxycycline* | Oral |
| Doxycycline hyclate* | Oral |
| Econazole nitrate | External, vaginal |
| Emedastine | Ophthalmic |
| Enoxaparin | Parenteral |
| Erythromycin* | External, oral |
| Erythromycin ethyl succinate* | Oral |
| Erythromycin stearate* | Oral |
| Estradiol | External |
| Estriol | External |
| [2]Ethinylestradiol | Oral |
| Etonogestrel | Implant |
| [2]Etynodiol diacetate | Oral |
| Famotidine | Oral |
| Felbinac | External |
| Fentanyl | Palliative care—transdermal |
| Fenticonazole nitrate | Vaginal |
| Fexofenadine hydrochloride | Oral |
| Flucloxacillin magnesium* | Oral |
| Flucloxacillin sodium* | Oral, parenteral |
| Fluconazole | Oral |
| Fludroxycortide (flurandrenolone) | External |

| | |
|---|---|
| Flumazenil | Parenteral |
| Flumetasone pivalate | Aural |
| Flunisolide | Nasal |
| Fluocinolone acetonide | External |
| Fluocinonide | External |
| Fluocortolone hexanoate | External, rectal |
| Fluocortolone pivalate | External, rectal |
| Flurbiprofen | Lozenges |
| Fluticasone propionate | External, nasal |
| Furosemide | Oral, parenteral |
| Fusidic acid | External |
| Gabapentin | Palliative care—oral |
| Gelatin 3.5–4% | Parenteral |
| Gentamicin sulphate | Aural |
| [2]Gestodene | Oral |
| Glucagon hydrochloride | Parenteral |
| Glucose intravenous infusion | Parenteral |
| Glucose 5% intravenous infusion | Parenteral |
| Granisetron hydrochloride | Parenteral |
| Heparin | Parenteral |
| Heparin sodium | Parenteral for the purpose of cannulae flushing |
| Hexastarch | Parenteral |
| Human soluble insulin | Parenteral |
| Hydrocortisone | External including rectal |
| Hydrocortisone acetate | Aural, external |
| Hydrocortisone butyrate | External |
| Hydrocortisone sodium succinate | Lozenges, parenteral |
| Hydroxyethyl starch | Parenteral |
| Hyoscine | Palliative care—transdermal |
| Hyoscine butylbromide | Palliative care—parenteral |
| Hyoscine hydrobromide | Palliative care—oral, parenteral |
| Ibuprofen | External, oral |
| Ibuprofen lysine | Oral |
| Imipramine hydrochloride | Palliative care—oral |
| Ipratropium bromide | Inhalation, nasal |
| Isotretinoin | External |
| Ketoconazole | External |
| Ketoprofen | External |
| Levocabastine hydrochloride | Nasal, ophthalmic |
| Levomepromazine (including levomepromazine (methotrimeprazine) maleate and levomepromazine (methotrimeprazine) hydrochloride) | Oral, parenteral |
| [2]Levonorgestrel | Oral |
| Lidocaine hydrochloride | External, parenteral |
| Lithium succinate | External |
| Lodoxamide trometamol | Ophthalmic |
| Loperamide hydrochloride | Oral |
| Loratadine | Oral |
| Lorazepam | Oral, parenteral |
| Lymecycline* | Oral |
| Mebendazole | Oral |
| [2]Medroxyprogesterone acetate | Injection |
| [2]Mestranol | Oral |
| Metoclopramide hydrochloride | Oral, parenteral |
| Metronidazole* | Oral, external, vaginal, rectal |
| Metronidazole benzoate* | Oral |
| Miconazole | Dental lacquer |
| Miconazole nitrate | External, vaginal |
| Midazolam | Parenteral |

Footnotes—see p. 862

| | |
|---|---|
| Minocycline hydrochloride* | Oral |
| Mizolastine | Oral |
| Mometasone furoate | External, nasal |
| Morphine hydrochloride | Rectal for pain relief in palliative care, myocardial infarction, acute or severe pain after trauma or surgery |
| Morphine sulphate | Oral, parenteral, rectal for pain relief in palliative care, myocardial infarction, acute or severe pain after trauma or surgery |
| Naloxone | Parenteral |
| Nedocromil sodium | Ophthalmic |
| Nefopam hydrochloride | Oral |
| Neomycin sulphate | Aural |
| Neomycin undecanoate | Aural |
| Nitrofurantoin* | Oral |
| Nizatidine | Oral |
| [2]Norethisterone | Oral |
| [2]Norethisterone acetate | Oral |
| [2]Norethisterone enanthate | Parenteral |
| [2]Norgestimate | Oral |
| [2]Norgestrel | Oral |
| Nortriptyline hydrochloride | Palliative care—oral |
| Nystatin | External, local mouth treatment, vaginal |
| Omeprazole | Oral |
| Omeprazole sodium | Parenteral |
| Ondansetron hydrochloride | Oral, parenteral |
| Oxybuprocaine hydrochloride | Ophthalmic |
| Oxycodone hydrochloride | Palliative care—oral, parenteral |
| Oxytetracycline dihydrate* | Oral |
| Paracetamol | Oral |
| Penciclovir | External |
| Pentastarch | Parenteral |
| Piroxicam | External |
| Potassium chloride 0.3% and glucose 5% intravenous infusion ($K^+$ 40 mmol/litre) | Parenteral |
| Potassium chloride 0.3% and sodium chloride 0.9% intravenous infusion | Parenteral |
| Potassium chloride 0.3%, sodium chloride 0.45% and glucose 5% intravenous infusion ($K^+$ 40 mmol/litre) | Parenteral |
| Prednisolone | Oral |
| Prednisolone hexanoate | Rectal |
| Prednisolone sodium phosphate | Aural, oral |
| Prilocaine | External, parenteral |
| Prochlorperazine mesilate | Oral, rectal |
| Prochlorperazine maleate | Oral, rectal, buccal |
| Proxymetacaine hydrochloride | Ophthalmic |
| Ranitidine hydrochloride | Oral, parenteral |
| Reteplase | Parenteral |
| Salbutamol sulphate | Inhalation |
| Silver sulfadiazine | External |
| Sodium chloride 0.9% | Parenteral, for reconstitution of injections and for the purpose of cannulae flushing |
| Sodium chloride 0.45% and glucose 5% intravenous infusion | Parenteral |
| Sodium chloride 0.9% and glucose 5% intravenous infusion | Parenteral |
| Sodium cromoglicate | Ophthalmic |
| Sodium fusidate | External |
| Streptodornase | External |
| Streptokinase | External, parenteral |
| Sulconazole nitrate | External |
| Tacalcitol | External |
| Tenecteplase | Parenteral |
| Terbinafine hydrochloride | External |
| Terbutaline sulphate | Inhalation |
| Tetanus immunoglobulin | Parenteral |
| Tetracaine | External |
| Tetracycline hydrochloride* | External, oral |
| Tinzaparin sodium | Parenteral |
| Tretinoin | External |
| Triamcinolone acetonide | Aural, external, nasal, oral paste |
| Trimethoprim* | Oral |
| Tropicamide | Ophthalmic |
| Tropisetron hydrochloride | Parenteral |
| [3]Tuberculin PPD | Injection |
| [3]Vaccine, Adsorbed Diphtheria | Injection |
| [3]Vaccine, Adsorbed Diphtheria and Tetanus | Injection |
| [3]Vaccine, Adsorbed Diphtheria and Tetanus for Adults and Adolescents | Injection |
| [3]Vaccine, Adsorbed Diphtheria for Adults and Adolescents | Injection |
| [3]Vaccine, Adsorbed Diphtheria, Tetanus and Pertussis | Injection |
| [3]Vaccine, Adsorbed Diphtheria, Tetanus Toxoid and Pertussis (Acellular Component) | Injection |
| [3]Vaccine, BCG | Injection |
| [3]Vaccine, BCG Percutaneous | Injection |
| Vaccine, Combined Tetanus, Diphtheria, Acellular Pertussis, Inactivated Poliomyelitis and Haemophilus Influenza Type B | Parenteral |
| [3]Vaccine, Haemophilus Influenzae Type B (Hib) | Injection |
| [3]Vaccine, Haemophilus Influenzae Type B (Hib) with Diphtheria, Tetanus and Pertussis | Injection |
| [3]Vaccine, Haemophilus Influenzae Type B, (Hib) with Diphtheria, Tetanus and Acellular Pertussis | Injection |
| [4]Vaccine, Hepatitis A | Injection |
| [4]Vaccine, Hepatitis A with Typhoid | Injection |
| [4]Vaccine, Hepatitis A, Inactivated, with recombinant (DNA) Hepatitis B | Injection |
| [4]Vaccine, Hepatitis B | Injection |
| Vaccine, Inactivated Poliomyelitis | Parenteral |
| [4]Vaccine, Influenza | Injection |
| [3]Vaccine, Live Measles, Mumps and Rubella (MMR) | Injection |
| [3]Vaccine, Meningococcal Group C Conjugate | Injection |
| [3 or 4]Vaccine, Meningococcal Polysaccharide A and C | Injection |
| Vaccine, Meningococcal Polysaccharide A, C, W135 and Y | Injection |
| [4]Vaccine, Pneumococcal | Injection |
| [3]Vaccine, Poliomyelitis, Live (Oral) | Oral |
| [3]Vaccine, Rubella, Live | Injection |
| [4]Vaccine, Tetanus, Adsorbed | Injection |
| Vaccine, Typhoid, Live Attenuated (Oral) | Oral |
| [4]Vaccine, Typhoid, Polysaccharide | Injection |
| Water for Injections | Parenteral |

Footnotes—see p. 862

*** Oral antibacterials and indications considered suitable for nurse prescribing**

| Drug | Indication |
|---|---|
| [5]Amoxicillin trihydrate | Lower urinary-tract infection (women), animal and human bites, acute exacerbation of chronic bronchitis, dental infections |
| Azithromycin dihydrate | Laboratory-confirmed uncomplicated genital chlamydial infection, plus sexual partners of these patients |
| Doxycycline hyclate | Acne, animal and human bites, laboratory-confirmed uncomplicated genital chlamydial infection, plus sexual partners of these patients |
| Doxycycline monohydrate | Acne, animal and human bites, laboratory-confirmed uncomplicated genital chlamydial infection, plus sexual partners of these patients |
| Erythromycin | Impetigo, animal and human bites, laboratory-confirmed uncomplicated genital chlamydial infection, plus sexual partners of these patients, spreading cellulitis usually of a limb with a risk of, or an established lymphangitis, dental infections |
| Erythromycin ethyl succinate | Impetigo, animal and human bites, laboratory-confirmed uncomplicated genital chlamydial infection, plus sexual partners of these patients, spreading cellulitis usually of a limb with a risk of, or an established lymphangitis, dental infections |
| Erythromycin stearate | Impetigo, animal and human bites, laboratory-confirmed uncomplicated genital chlamydial infection, plus sexual partners of these patients, spreading cellulitis usually of a limb with a risk of, or an established lymphangitis, dental infections |
| Flucloxacillin magnesium | Impetigo, spreading cellulitis usually of a limb with a risk of, or an established lymphangitis |
| Flucloxacillin sodium | Impetigo, spreading cellulitis usually of a limb with a risk of, or an established lymphangitis |
| Lymecycline | Acne |
| Metronidazole | Animal and human bites; fungating malodorous tumours; bacterial vaginosis; *trichomonas vaginalis* infection plus sexual partners of these patients, dental infections |
| Metronidazole benzoate | Animal and human bites, dental infections |
| Minocycline hydrochloride | Acne |
| Nitrofurantoin | Lower urinary-tract infection (women) |
| Oxytetracycline dihydrate | Acne, animal and human bites, acute exacerbation of chronic bronchitis |
| Tetracycline hydrochloride | Acne |
| Trimethoprim | Lower urinary-tract infection (women) |

1 Present as potassium clavulanate in co-amoxiclav

2 Nurse Prescribers in Family Planning Clinics—where it is not appropriate for nurse prescribers in family planning clinics to prescribe contraceptive drugs using form FP10(P) (forms FP10(CN) and FP10(PN), or when available WP10CN and WP10PN, in Wales), they may prescribe using the same system as doctors in the clinic.

3 Centrally supplied vaccine excluded from reimbursement via prescription route

4 High Volume Personally Administered Vaccine. Claims for these vaccines should be ordered on form FP34D

5 With Clavulanic acid (as co-amoxiclav) for animal and human bites

# Index of manufacturers

**3M**
3M Health Care Ltd
3M House
Morley St
Loughborough
Leics, LE11 1EP.
tel: (01509) 611611
fax: (01509) 237288

**A&H**
Allen & Hanburys Ltd
See GSK

**Abbott**
Abbott Laboratories Ltd
Abbott House
Norden Rd, Maidenhead
Berks, SL6 4XE.
tel: (01628) 773 355
fax: (01628) 644 185
ukmedinfo@abbott.com

**Acorus**
Acorus Therapeutics Ltd
High Crane Lodge
Hamsterley, Bishop Auckland
Durham, DL13 3QS.
tel: (01388) 710 505
fax: (01388) 710 770
enquiries@acorus-therapeutics.com

**Actelion**
Actelion Pharmaceuticals UK Ltd
BSi Building, 13th Floor
389 Chiswick High Rd,
London, W4 4AL.
tel: (020) 8987 3333
fax: (020) 8987 3322

**Activa**
Activa Healthcare
1 Lancaster Park
Newborough Rd, Needwood
Burton-upon-Trent, Staffs, DE13 9PD.
tel: (0845) 060 6707
fax: (01283) 576 808
advice@activahealthcare.co.uk

**Adams Hlth.**
Adams Healthcare Ltd
Lotherton Way
Garforth, Leeds, LS25 2JY.
tel: (0113) 232 0066
fax: (0113) 287 1317
enquiries@adams-healthcare.co.uk

**Advancis**
Advancis Medical Ltd
Lowmoor Business Park
Kirkby-in-Ashfield,
Nottingham, NG17 7JZ.
tel: (01623) 751 500
fax: (01623) 757 636
info@advancis.co.uk

**Aguettant**
Aguettant Ltd
Bishops House
Bishops Rd, Claverham
Somerset, BS49 4NF.
tel: (01934) 835 694
fax: (01934) 876 790
info@aguettant.co.uk

**Air Products**
Air Products plc
Medical Group
2 Millennium Gate
Westmere Drive, Crewe
Cheshire, CW1 6AP.
tel: (0800) 373 580
fax: (0800) 214 709

**Alcon**
Alcon Laboratories (UK) Ltd
Pentagon Park
Boundary Way
Hemel Hempstead, Herts, HP2 7UD.
tel: (01442) 341 234
fax: (01442) 341 200

**Alembic Products**
Alembic Products Ltd
River Lane
Saltney, Chester, Cheshire, CH4 8RQ.
tel: (01244) 680 147
fax: (01244) 680 155

**ALK-Abelló**
ALK-Abelló (UK) Ltd
1 Tealgate
Hungerford, Berks, RG17 0YT.
tel: (01488) 686 016
fax: (01488) 685 423
info@uk.alk-abello.com

**Allergan**
Allergan Ltd
1st Floor Marlow International
The Parkway
Marlow
Bucks, SL7 1YL.
tel: (01628) 494 026
fax: (01628) 497 057

**Allergy**
Allergy Therapeutics Ltd
Dominion Way
Worthing, West Sussex, BN14 8SA.
tel: (01903) 844 702
fax: (01903) 844 744
infoservices@allergytherapeutics.com

**Alliance**
Alliance Pharmaceuticals Ltd
Avonbridge House
2 Bath Rd
Chippenham, Wilts, SN15 2BB.
tel: (01249) 466 966
fax: (01249) 466 977
info@alliancepharma.co.uk

**Alpharma**
Alpharma Ltd
Whiddon Valley
Barnstaple, Devon, EX32 8NS.
tel: (01271) 311 257
fax: (01271) 346 106
med.info@alpharma.co.uk

**Alphashow**
Alphashow Ltd
PO Box 1009
Hemel Hempstead, HP3 OXN.
tel: (0870) 240 2775
fax: (0870) 240 2775
info@alphashow.co.uk

**Altana**
Altana Pharma Ltd
Three Globeside Business Park
Fieldhouse Lane
Marlow, Bucks, SL7 1HZ.
tel: (01628) 646 400
fax: (01628) 646 401
medinfo@altanapharma.co.uk

**Amdipharm**
Amdipharm plc
Regency House
Miles Gray Rd
Basildon, Essex, SS14 3AF.
tel: (0870) 777 7675
fax: (0870) 777 7875
info@amdipharm.com

**Amgen**
Amgen Ltd
240 Cambridge Science Park
Milton Rd, Cambridge, CB4 0WD.
tel: (01223) 420 305
fax: (01223) 426 314
infoline@uk.amgen.com

**Anglian**
Anglian Pharma Sales & Marketing
Titmore Court
Titmore Green
Little Wymondley, Hitchin
Herts, SG4 7XJ.
tel: (01438) 743 070
fax: (01438) 743 080
mail@anglianpharma.com

**Anpharm**
See Goldshield

**Antigen**
See Goldshield

**APS**
See TEVA UK

**Ardana**
Ardana Bioscience Ltd
58 Queen St
Edinburgh, EH2 3NS.
tel: (0131) 226 8550
fax: (0131) 226 8551
info@ardana.co.uk

**Ardern**
Ardern Healthcare Ltd
Pipers Brook Farm
Eastham
Tenbury Wells, Worcs, WR15 8NP.
tel: (01584) 781 777
fax: (01584) 781 788
info@ardernhealthcare.com

**AS Pharma**
AS Pharma Ltd
PO Box 181
Polegate, East Sussex, BN26 6WD.
tel: (08700) 664 117
fax: (08700) 664 118
info@aspharma.co.uk

**Ashbourne**
Ashbourne Pharmaceuticals Ltd
Victors Barns
Northampton Rd
Brixworth, Northampton, NN6 9DQ.
tel: (01604) 883 100
fax: (01604) 881 640

**Astellas**
Astellas Pharma Ltd
Lovett House, Lovett Rd
Staines, TW18 3AZ.
tel: (01784) 419 615
fax: (01784) 419 401

**AstraZeneca**
AstraZeneca UK Ltd
Horizon Place
600 Capability Green
Luton, Beds, LU1 3LU.
tel: 0800 7830 033
fax: (01582) 838 003
medical.informationuk@astrazeneca.com

**Auden Mckenzie**
Auden Mckenzie (Pharma Division) Ltd
30 Stadium Business Centre
North End Rd
Wembley, Middx, HA9 0AT.
tel: (020) 8900 2122
fax: (020) 8903 9620

**Aurum**
Aurum Pharmaceuticals Ltd
Hubert Rd
Brentwood
Essex, CM14 4LZ.
tel: (01277) 266600
fax: (01277) 848 976
info@martindalepharma.co.uk

**Aventis Pasteur**
Aventis Pasteur MSD Ltd
See Sanofi Pasteur
tel: (01628) 785 291
fax: (01628) 671 722

**Aventis Pharma**
See Sanofi-Aventis

**Ayrton Saunders**
Ayrton Saunders Ltd
Ayrton House
Commerce Way
Parliament Business Park
Liverpool, Merseyside, L8 7BA.
tel: (0151) 709 2074
fax: (0151) 709 7336
info@ayrtons.com

**Bailey, Robert**
Robert Bailey Healthcare Ltd
Unit 6
Heapham Rd Industrial Estate
Gainsborough, Lincs, DN21 1RZ.
tel: (01427) 677 559
fax: (01427) 677 654
rbsales@cottonwool.uk.com

**Bard**
Bard Ltd
Forest House
Brighton Rd
Crawley, West Sussex, RH11 9BP.
tel: (01293) 527 888
fax: (01293) 552 428

**Bausch & Lomb**
Bausch & Lomb UK Ltd
106 London Rd
Kingston-upon-Thames
Surrey, KT2 6TN.
tel: (020) 8781 2900
fax: (01344) 8781 2901

**Baxter**
Baxter Healthcare Ltd
Wallingford Rd
Compton
Newbury
Berks, RG20 7QW.
tel: (01635) 206 345
fax: (01635) 206 071
surecall@baxter.com

**Baxter BioScience**
See Baxter

**Bayer**
Bayer plc
Pharmaceutical Division
Bayer House, Strawberry Hill
Newbury, Berks, RG14 1JA.
tel: (01635) 563 000
fax: (01635) 563 393
medical.science@bayer.co.uk

**Bayer Consumer Care**
See Bayer

**Bayer Diagnostics**
See Bayer

**BCM Specials**
BCM Specials Manufacturing
D10 First 114
Nottingham, NG90 2PR.
tel: 0800 952 1010
fax: 0800 085 0673
bcm-specials@bcm-ltd.co.uk

**Beacon**
Beacon Pharmaceuticals Ltd
85 High St
Tunbridge Wells, TN1 1YG.
tel: (01892) 506 958
fax: (01892) 610 397
info@beaconpharma.co.uk

**Becton Dickinson**
Becton Dickinson UK Ltd
Between Towns Rd
Cowley, Oxford, Oxon, OX4 3LY.
tel: (01865) 748 844
fax: (01865) 717 313

**Beiersdorf**
Beiersdorf UK Ltd
2010 Solihull Parkway
Birmingham Business Park
Birmingham, B37 7YS.
tel: (0121) 329 8800
fax: (0121) 329 8801

**Bell and Croyden**
John Bell and Croyden
50-54 Wigmore St
London, W1U 2AU.
tel: (020) 7935 5555
fax: (020) 7935 9605
jbc@johnbellcroyden.co.uk

**Berk**
See TEVA UK

**BHR**
BHR Pharmaceuticals Ltd
41 Centenary Business Centre
Hammond Close
Attleborough Fields, Nuneaton
Warwickshire, CV11 6RY.
tel: (024) 7635 3742
fax: (024) 7632 7812
info@bhr.co.uk

**Bioaccelerate**
Bioaccelerate Ltd
11-12 Charles II St
Savanah House
London, SW1Y 4QU.
tel: (020) 7451 2488
fax: (020) 7451 2469
info@bioaccelerate.com

**Biogen**
Biogen Ltd
5d Roxborough Way
Foundation Park
Maidenhead
Berks, SL6 3UD.
tel: (01628) 501 000
fax: (01628) 501 010

**Biolitec**
Biolitec Pharma Ltd
Unit 2, Broomhill Business Park
Broomhill Rd
Tallaght
Dublin 24, Ireland.
tel: (00353) 14637415
fax: (00353) 14637411
medical.info@biolitec.com

**Biosurgical Research**
Biosurgical Research Unit
See ZooBiotic

**Blackwell**
Blackwell Supplies Ltd
Medcare House
Centurion Close
Gillingham Business Park, Gillingham
Kent, ME8 0SB.
tel: (01634) 877 620
fax: (01634) 877 621

**Blake**
Thomas Blake & Co
The Byre House
Fearby
Nr. Masham
North Yorks, HG4 4NF.
tel: (01765) 689 042
fax: (01765) 689 042
sales@veilcover.com

**BOC**
BOC Medical
The Priestley Centre,
10 Priestley Rd
Surrey Research Park
Guildford, Surrey, GU2 7XY.
tel: 0800 111 333
fax: 0800 111 555

**Boehringer Ingelheim**
Boehringer Ingelheim Ltd
Ellesfield Ave
Bracknell
Berks, RG12 8YS.
tel: (01344) 424 600
fax: (01344) 741 444
medinfo@bra.boehringer-ingelheim.com

**Boots**
Boots The Chemists
Medical Services
Thane Rd
D90 East S10
Nottingham, NG90 1BS.
tel: (0115) 959 5168
fax: (0115) 959 2565

**Borg**
Borg Medicare
PO Box 99
Hitchin
Herts, SG5 2GF.
tel: (01462) 442 993
fax: (01462) 441 293

**BPC 100**
The Bolton Pharmaceutical 100 Ltd
2 Chapel Drive
Ambrosden
Oxfordshire, OX25 2RS.
tel: (0845) 602 3907
fax: (0845) 602 3908
info@bpc100.com

**BPL**
Bio Products Laboratory
Dagger Lane
Elstree, Herts, WD6 3BX.
tel: (020) 8258 2200
fax: (020) 8258 2601

**Braun**
B Braun (Medical) Ltd
Brookdale Rd
Thorncliffe Park Estate
Chapeltown, Sheffield, S35 2PW.
tel: (0114) 225 9000
fax: (0114) 225 9111
enquiry@bbmuk.demon.co.uk

**Braun Biotrol**
See Braun

**Bray**
Bray Health & Leisure
1 Regal Way
Faringdon
Oxon, SN7 7BX.
tel: (01367) 240 736
fax: (01367) 242 625
info@bray.co.uk

**Bristol**
Bristol Laboratories Ltd
Unit 3, Canalside
Northbridge Rd
Berkhamsted
Herts, HP4 1EG.
tel: (01442) 200 922
fax: (01442) 873 717
info@bristol-labs.co.uk

**Bristol-Myers Squibb**
Bristol-Myers Squibb Pharmaceuticals Ltd
Uxbridge Business Park
Sanderson Rd
Uxbridge
Middx, UB8 1DH.
tel: (01895) 523 000
fax: (01895) 523 010
medical.information@bms.com

**Britannia**
Britannia Pharmaceuticals Ltd
41-51 Brighton Rd
Redhill
Surrey, RH1 6YS.
tel: (01737) 773 741
fax: (01737) 762 672
medicalservices@forumgroup.co.uk

**British Biocell**
British Biocell International
Golden Gate, Ty Glas Avenue
Llanishen, Cardiff, CF14 5DX.
tel: (02920) 747 232
fax: (02920) 747 242
info@bbigold.co.uk

**BSIA**
See Torbet

**BSN Medical**
BSN Medical Ltd
PO Box 258
Willerby
Hull, HU10 6WT.
tel: (0845) 1223 600
fax: (0845) 1223 666

**C D Medical**
C D Medical Ltd
Aston Grange
Oker, Matlock, DE4 2JJ.
tel: (01629) 733 860
fax: (01629) 733 414

**Cambridge**
Cambridge Laboratories
Deltic House, Kingfisher Way
Silverlink Business Park, Wallsend
Tyne & Wear, NE28 9NX.
tel: (0191) 296 9369
fax: (0191) 296 9368
enquries@camb-labs.com

**Cardinal**
Cardinal Health Martindale Products
Hubert Rd
Brentwood
Essex, CM14 4JY.
tel: (01277) 266 600
fax: (01277) 848 976
info@martindalepharma.co.uk

**Castlemead**
Castlemead Healthcare Ltd
2nd Floor
The Maltings
Bridge St
Hitchin, Herts, SG5 2DE.
tel: (01462) 454 452
fax: (01462) 435 684

**Cell Therapeutics**
Cell Therapeutics (UK) Ltd
100 Pall Mall
London, SW1Y 5HP.
tel: (0031) 6 5164 1765
fax: (0031) 24360 8075
celltherapeuticseurope@vwbintermedical.com

**Celltech**
See UCB Pharma

**Centrapharm**
Centrapharm Ltd
Dale House
Suckley Rd
Knightwick
Worcs, WR6 5QE.
tel: (01886) 822 116
fax: (01886) 822 125
info@centrapharm.co.uk

**Cephalon**
Cephalon UK Ltd
11-13 Frederick Sanger Rd
Surrey Research Park
Guildford
Surrey, GU2 7YD.
tel: 0800 783 4869
fax: (01483) 453 324
ukmedinfo@cephalon.com

**Ceuta**
Ceuta Healthcare Ltd
Hill House
41 Richmond Hill
Bournemouth
Dorset, BH2 6HS.
tel: (01202) 780 558
fax: (01202) 780 559

**Chauvin**
Chauvin Pharmaceuticals Ltd
106 London Rd
Kingston-Upon-Thames
Surrey, KT2 6TN.
tel: (020) 8781 2900
fax: (020) 8781 2901

**Chefaro UK**
Chefaro UK Ltd
Unit 1, Tower Close
St. Peter's Industrial Park
Huntingdon
Cambs, PE29 7DH.
tel: (01480) 421 800
fax: (01480) 434 861

**Chemical Search**
Chemical Search International Ltd
29th floor
1 Canada Square
Canary Wharf
London, E14 5DY.
tel: (020) 7712 1758
fax: (020) 7712 1759
info@chemicalsearch.co.uk

**Chemidex**
Chemidex Pharma Ltd
Chemidex House
Egham Business Village
Crabtree Rd, Egham
Surrey, TW20 8RB.
tel: (01784) 477 167
fax: (01784) 471 776
info@chemidex.co.uk

**Chiron**
Chiron Corporation Ltd
Symphony House
7 Cowley Business Park
High St, Cowley
Uxbridge, UB8 2AD.
tel: (020) 8580 4000
fax: (020) 8580 4001
medicalinfo-europe@chiron.com

**Chiron Vaccines**
Chiron Vaccines Ltd
Gaskill Rd
Speke
Liverpool, L24 9GR.
tel: (08457) 451 500
fax: (0151) 7055 669
serviceuk@chiron.com

**CHS**
Cambridge Healthcare Supplies Ltd
14D Wendover Rd
Rackheath Industrial Estate
Rackheath
Norwich, NR13 6LH.
tel: (01603) 735 200
fax: (01603) 735 217
customerservices@typharm.com

**Chugai**
Chugai Pharma UK Ltd
Mulliner House, Flanders Rd
Turnham Green
London, W4 1NN.
tel: (020) 8987 5680
fax: (020) 8987 5661

**Clement Clarke**
Clement Clarke International Ltd
Edinburgh Way
Harlow
Essex, CM20 2TT.
tel: (01279) 414 969
fax: (01279) 456 304
resp@clement-clarke.com

**CliniMed**
CliniMed Ltd
Cavell House, Knaves Beech Way
Loudwater
High Wycombe
Bucks, HP10 9QY.
tel: (01628) 850 100
fax: (01628) 850 331
enquires@clinimed.co.uk

**Clinisupplies**
Clinisupplies Ltd
9 Crystal Way
Elmgrove Rd
Harrow
Middx, HA1 2HP.
tel: (020) 8863 4168
fax: (020) 8426 0768
info@clinisupplies.co.uk

**Clonmel**
Clonmel Healthcare Ltd
Waterford Rd
Clonmel
Co. Tipperary
Ireland
tel: (00353) 52 77777
fax: (00353) 52 77799
info@clonmelhealthcare.com

**Colgate-Palmolive**
Colgate-Palmolive Ltd
Guildford Business Park
Middleton Rd
Guildford
Surrey, GU2 5LZ.
tel: (01483) 302 222
fax: (01483) 303 003

**Coloplast**
Coloplast Ltd
Peterborough Business Park
Peterborough, PE2 6FX.
tel: (01733) 392 000
fax: (01733) 233 348
gbcareteam@coloplast.com

**Community**
Community Foods Ltd
Micross, Brent Terrace
London, NW2 1LT.
tel: (020) 8450 9411
fax: (020) 8208 1803
email@communityfoods.co.uk

**Concord**
Concord Pharmaceuticals Ltd
Bishops Weald House
Albion Way
Horsham, RH12 1AH.
tel: (0870) 241 2330
fax: 0870 241 2335
enquiries@concordpharma.com

**ConvaTec**
ConvaTec Ltd
Harrington House, Milton Rd
Ickenham
Uxbridge
Middx, UB10 8PU.
tel: (01895) 628 400
fax: (01895) 628 456

**Cow & Gate**
See Nutricia Clinical
tel: (01225) 768 381
fax: (01225) 768 847

**CP**
See Wockhardt

**Crawford**
Crawford Pharmaceuticals
Furtho House
20 Towcester Rd
Milton Keynes, MK19 6AQ.
tel: (01908) 262 346
fax: (01908) 567 730

**Crookes**
Crookes Healthcare Ltd
D6 Building
Nottingham, NG90 6BH.
tel: (0115) 968 8922
fax: (0115) 968 8722
medicalinfo@crookes.co.uk

**DDD**
DDD Ltd
94 Rickmansworth Rd
Watford
Herts, WD18 7JJ.
tel: (01923) 229 251
fax: (01923) 220 728

**De Vilbiss**
De Vilbiss Health Care UK Ltd
High Street
Wollaston
West Midlands, DY8 4PS.
tel: (01384) 446 688
fax: (01384) 446 699

**De Witt**
E C De Witt & Co Ltd
Tudor Rd
Manor Park
Runcorn
Cheshire, WA7 1SZ.
tel: (01928) 579 029
fax: (01928) 579 712
ecdewitt@ecdewitt.com

**Denfleet**
Denfleet Pharmaceuticals Ltd
260 Centennial Park
Elstree Hill South
Elstree
Herts, WD6 3SR.
tel: (020) 8236 0000
fax: (020) 8236 3501
medical.information@denfleet.com

**Dental Health**
Dental Health Products Ltd
60 Boughton Lane
Maidstone
Kent, ME15 9QS.
tel: (01622) 749 222
fax: (01622) 744 672

**Dentsply**
Dentsply Ltd
Hamm Moor Lane
Addlestone
Weybridge
Surrey, KT15 2SE.
tel: (01932) 837 279
fax: (01932) 858 970

**Dermal**
Dermal Laboratories Ltd
Tatmore Place
Gosmore
Hitchin
Herts, SG4 7QR.
tel: (01462) 458 866
fax: (01462) 420 565

**Dexcel**
Dexcel-Pharma Ltd
1 Cottesbrooke Park
Heartlands Business Park
Daventry
Northamptonshire, NN11 5YL.
tel: (01327) 312 266
fax: (01327) 312 262
office@dexcelpharma.co.uk

**DiagnoSys**
DiagnoSys Medical
Cams Hall
Fareham
Hants, PO16 8AB.
tel: 0800 085 8808
fax: (01329) 227 599

**Dimethaid**
Dimethaid International
c/o Benoliel Partners
Linden House, Ewelme
Oxfordshire, OX10 6HQ.
tel: (01491) 825 016
fax: (01491) 834 592
medinfo@dimethaid.com

**Dista**
Dista Products Ltd
See Lilly

**Dr Falk**
Dr Falk Pharma UK Ltd
Bourne End Business, Cores End Rd
Bourne End, Bucks, SL8 5AS.
tel: (01628) 536 600

**DuPont**
See Bristol-Myers Squibb

**Durbin**
Durbin plc
180 Northolt Rd
South Harrow
Middx, HA2 0LT.
tel: (020) 8869 6500
fax: (020) 8869 6565
info@durbin.co.uk

**Easigrip**
Easigrip Ltd
Unit 13, Scar Bank
Millers Rd
Warwick
Warwickshire, CV34 5DB.
tel: (01926) 497 108
fax: (01926) 497 109
enquiry@easigrip.co.uk

**Egis**
Egis Pharmaceuticals UK Ltd
127 Shirland Rd
London, W9 2EP.
tel: (020) 7266 2669
fax: (020) 7266 2702
enquiries@medimpexuk.com

**Eisai**
Eisai Ltd
3 Shortlands
Hammersmith
London, W6 8EE.
tel: (020) 8600 1400
fax: (020) 8600 1401
Lmedinfo@eisai.net

**Elida Fabergé**
Elida Fabergé Ltd
Coal Rd
Seacroft
Leeds, LS14 2AR.
tel: (0113) 222 5000
fax: (0113) 222 5362

**ENTACO**
ENTACO Ltd
Royal Victoria Works,
Birmingham Rd, Studley
Warwickshire, B80 7AP.
tel: (01527) 852 306
fax: (01527) 857 447
sales@entaco.com

**Epiderm**
Epiderm Ltd
Wass Lane
Sotby
Market Rasen, LN8 5LR.
tel: (01507) 343 091
fax: (01507) 343 092
djjcovermarkcryo@aol.com

**Espire**
Espire Healthcare Ltd
The Search Offices
Main Gate Road
The Historic Dockyard
Chatham, ME4 4TE.
tel: (01634) 812 144
fax: (01634) 813 601
info@espirehealth.com

**Essential Generics**
Essential Generics
7 Egham Business Village
Thorpe Industrial Estate
Egham
Surrey, TW20 8RB.
tel: (01784) 477 167
fax: (01784) 471 776

**Ethicon**
Ethicon Ltd
P.O. Box 1988
Simpson Parkway
Kirkton Campus
Livingston, EH54 0AB.
tel: (01506) 594 500
fax: (01506) 460 714

**Eumedica**
Eumedica S.A.
Winston Churchill Avenue 67
1180 Brussels
Belgium
tel: (0208) 444 3377
fax: (0208) 444 6866
enquiries@eumedica.com

**Everfresh**
Everfresh Natural Foods
Gatehouse Close
Aylesbury
Bucks, HP19 3DE.
tel: (01296) 425 333
fax: (01296) 422 545

**Exelgyn**
Exelgyn Laboratories
PO Box 4511
Henley-on-Thames
Oxon, RG9 5ZQ.
tel: (01491) 642 137
fax: (0800) 731 6120

**Fabre**
Pierre Fabre Ltd
Hyde Abbey House
23 Hyde St
Winchester
Hampshire, SO23 7DR.
tel: (01962) 856 956
fax: (01962) 874 413
PFabreUK@aol.com

**Farillon**
Farillon Ltd
Ashton Rd
Harold Hill
Romford
Essex, RM3 8UE.
tel: (01708) 379 000
fax: (01708) 376 554

**Fate**
Fate Special Foods
Unit E2
Brook Street Business Centre
Brook St, Tipton
West Midlands, DY4 9DD.
tel: (01215) 224 433
fax: (01215) 224 433

**Fenton**
Fenton Pharmaceuticals Ltd
4J Portman Mansions
Chiltern St
London, W1U 6NS.
tel: (020) 7224 1388
fax: (020) 7486 7258
mail@Fent-Pharm.co.uk

**Ferndale**
Ferndale Pharmaceuticals Ltd
Unit 605, Thorp Arch Estate
Wetherby
West Yorks, LS23 7BJ.
tel: (01937) 541 122
fax: (01937) 849 682
info@ferndalepharma.co.uk

**Ferraris**
Ferraris Medical Ltd
4 Harforde Court
John Tate Rd
Hertford
Herts, SG13 7NW.
tel: (01992) 526 300
fax: (01992) 526 320
info@fre.ferrarisgroup.com

**Ferring**
Ferring Pharmaceuticals (UK)
The Courtyard
Waterside Drive
Langley
Berks, SL3 6EZ.
tel: (01753) 214 800
fax: (01753) 214 801

**Firstplay Dietary**
Firstplay Dietary Foods Ltd
338 Turncroft Lane
Offerton
Stockport
Cheshire, SK1 4BP.
tel: (0161) 474 7576
fax: (0161) 474 7576

**Florizel**
Florizel Ltd
PO Box 138
Stevenage, SG2 8YN.
tel: (01462) 436 156
fax: (01462) 457 402

**Flynn**
Flynn Pharma Ltd
2nd Floor, The Maltings
Bridge St
Hitchin
Herts, SG5 2DE.
tel: (01462) 458 974
fax: (01462) 450 755

**Foodlink**
Foodlink (UK) Ltd
2B Plymouth Rd
Plympton
Plymouth, PL7 4JR.
tel: (01752) 344 544
fax: (01752) 342 412
info@foodlinkltd.co.uk

**Ford**
Ford Medical Associates Ltd
8 Wyndham Way
Orchard Heights
Ashford
Kent, TN25 4PZ.
tel: (01233) 633 224
fax: (01223) 646 595
enquiries@fordmedical.co.uk

**Forest**
Forest Laboratories UK Ltd
Bourne Rd
Bexley
Kent, DA5 1NX.
tel: (01322) 550 550
fax: (01322) 555 469
medinfo@forest-labs.co.uk

**Fournier**
See Solvay

**Fox**
C. H. Fox Ltd
22 Tavistock St
London, WC2E 7PY.
tel: (020) 7240 3111
fax: (020) 7379 3410

**FP**
Family Planning Sales Ltd
28 Kelburne Rd
Cowley
Oxford, OX4 3SZ.
tel: (01865) 772 486
fax: (01865) 748 746

**Fresenius Kabi**
Fresenius Kabi Ltd
Hampton Court
Tudor Rd
Manor Park, Runcorn
Cheshire, WA7 1UF.
tel: (01928) 594 200
fax: (01928) 594 314
med.info-uk@fresenius-kabi.com

**Frontier**
Frontier Multigate
Newbridge Rd Industrial Estate
Blackwood
South Wales, NP12 2YL.
tel: (01495) 233 050
fax: (01495) 233 055
multigate@frontier-group.co.uk

**Fujisawa**
See Astellas

**Galderma**
Galderma (UK) Ltd
Galderma House
Church lane
Kings Langley
Herts, WD4 8JP.
tel: (01923) 291 033
fax: (01923) 291 060

**Galen**
Galen Ltd
Seagoe Industrial Estate
Craigavon
Northern Ireland, BT63 5UA.
tel: (028) 3833 4974
fax: (028) 3835 0206

**Garnier**
Laboratoires Garnier
255 Hammersmith Rd,
London, W6 8AZ.
tel: (020) 8762 4000
fax: (020) 8762 4001

**GBM**
GBM Healthcare Ltd
Beechlawn House
Hurtmore Rd
Godalming
Surrey, GU7 2RA.
tel: (01483) 860 881
fax: (01483) 425 715
mba_gbm@compuserve.com

**GE Healthcare**
GE Healthcare
The Grove Centre, White Lion Rd
Amersham, Bucks, HP7 9LL.
tel: (01494) 544 000

**Geistlich**
Geistlich Pharma
Newton Bank
Long Lane
Chester, CH2 2PF.
tel: (01244) 347 534
fax: (01244) 319 327

**General Dietary**
General Dietary Ltd
PO Box 38
Kingston upon Thames
Surrey, KT2 7YP.
tel: (020) 8336 2323
fax: (020) 8942 8274

**Generics**
Generics (UK) Ltd
Albany Gate
Darkes Lane
Potters Bar
Herts, EN6 1AG.
tel: (01707) 853 000
fax: (01707) 643 148

**Genus**
Genus Pharmaceuticals
Benham Valence
Newbury
Berks, RG20 8LU.
tel: (01635) 568 400
fax: (01635) 568 401
enquiries@genuspharma.com

**Genzyme**
Genzyme Biosurgery
4620 Kingsgate
Cascade Way
Oxford Business Park South
Oxford, OX4 2SU.
tel: (01865) 405 200
fax: (01865) 774 172

**Gilead**
Gilead Sciences
The Flowers Building
Granta Park
Great Abington
Cambs, CB1 6GT.
tel: (01223) 897 300
fax: (01223) 897 282
ukmedinfo@gilead.com

**GlaxoSmithKline**
See GSK

**Glenwood**
Glenwood Laboratories Ltd
Jenkins Dale
Chatham
Kent, ME4 5RD.
tel: (01634) 830 535
fax: (01634) 831 345
g.wooduk@virgin.net

**Gluten Free Foods Ltd**
Gluten Free Foods Ltd
Unit 270 Centennial Park
Centennial Ave
Elstree, Borehamwood
Herts, WD6 3SS.
tel: (020) 8953 4444
fax: (020) 8953 8285
info@glutenfree-foods.co.uk

**Goldshield**
Goldshield Pharmaceuticals Ltd
NLA Tower
12-16 Addiscombe Rd
Croydon, CR0 0XT.
tel: (020) 8649 8500
fax: (020) 8686 0807

**GP Pharma**
GP Pharma
ARC Progress
Beckerings Park Rd
Lidlington
Beds, MK43 0RD.
tel: (01525) 288 588
fax: (01525) 289 339
info@gppharma.co.uk

**Grünenthal**
Grünenthal Ltd
Aston Court
Kingsmead Business Park
Frederick Place
High Wycombe, Bucks, HP11 1LA.
tel: (0870) 351 8960

**Grifols**
Grifols UK Ltd
72 St Andrew's Rd
Cambs, CB4 1GS.
tel: (01223) 446 900
fax: (01223) 446 911
reception.uk@grifols.com

**GSK**
GlaxoSmithKline
Stockley Park West
Uxbridge
Middx, UB11 1BT.
tel: 0800 221 441
fax: (020) 8990 4328
customercontactuk@gsk.com

**GSK Consumer Healthcare**
GlaxoSmithKline Consumer Healthcare
GSK House
980 Great West Rd
Brentford
Middx, TW8 9GS.
tel: (0500) 888 878
fax: (020) 8047 6860
customer.relations@gsk.com

**Hameln**
Hameln Pharmaceuticals Ltd
Nexus
Gloucester Business Park
Gloucester, GL3 4AG.
tel: (01452) 621 661
fax: (01452) 632 732
enquiries@hameln.co.uk

**Hartmann**
Paul Hartmann Ltd
Unit P2, Parklands
Heywood Distribution Park
Pilsworth Rd, Heywood
Lancs, OL10 2TT.
tel: (01706) 363 200
fax: (01706) 363 201
info@uk.hartmann.info

**Hawgreen**
Hawgreen Ltd
The Maltings, 2nd Floor
Bridge St
Hitchin
Herts, SG5 2DE.
tel: (01462) 441 831
fax: (01462) 435 868

**Heinz**
H. J. Heinz Company Ltd
South Building
Hayes Park
Hayes, UB4 8AL.
tel: (020) 8573 7757
fax: (020) 8848 2325
Farleys_Heinz@Heinz.co.uk

**Henleys**
Henleys Medical Supplies Ltd
Brownfields
Welwyn Garden City
Herts, AL7 1AN.
tel: (01707) 333 164
fax: (01707) 334 795

**Hillcross**
AAH Pharmaceuticals Ltd
Sapphire Court
Walsgrave Triangle
Coventry, CV2 2TX.
tel: (024) 7643 2000
fax: (024) 7643 2001

**HK Pharma**
HK Pharma Ltd
PO Box 105
Hitchin
Herts, SG5 2GG.
tel: (01462) 433 993
fax: (01462) 450 755

**Hoechst Marion Roussel**
See Sanofi-Aventis

**HRA Pharma**
Laboratoire HRA Pharma
15 rue Beranger 75003
Paris
France
tel: (0033) 1 40 33 11 30
fax: (0033) 1 40 33 12 31
info@lysodren-europe.com

**Hybrand**
Hybrand Ltd
Eagle House, The Ring
Bracknell, Berks, RG12 1HB.
tel: (08700) 114 545
fax: (08700) 114 646
customer.services@hybrand.com

**Hypoguard**
Hypoguard Ltd
Dock Lane
Melton
Woodbridge
Suffolk, IP12 1PE.
tel: (01394) 387 333
fax: (01394) 380 152
enquiries@hypoguard.com

**IDIS**
IDIS World Medicines
IDIS House
Churchfield Rd
Weybridge
Surrey, KT13 8DB.
tel: (01932) 824 000
fax: (01932) 824 200
idis@idispharma.com

**Infai**
Infai UK Ltd
Innovation Centre
University of York Science Park
University Rd
Heslington, York, YO10 5DG.
tel: (01904) 435 228
fax: (01904) 435 229
paul@infai.co.uk

**Intrapharm**
Intrapharm Laboratories Ltd
60 Boughton Lane
Maidstone
Kent, ME15 9QS.
tel: (01622) 749 222
fax: (01622) 744 672
sales@intraphamlabs.com

**Invicta**
See Pfizer

**Ipsen**
Ipsen Ltd
190 Bath Rd
Slough
Berks, SL1 3XE.
tel: (01753) 627 777
fax: (01753) 627 778
medical.information@ipsen.com

**IVAX**
IVAX Pharmaceuticals UK Ltd
IVAX Quay, Albert Basin
Royal Docks
London, E16 2QJ.
tel: (08705) 020 304
fax: (08705) 323 334

**J&J**
Johnson & Johnson Ltd
Foundation Park
Roxborough Way
Maidenhead
Berks, SL6 3UG.
tel: (01628) 822 222
fax: (01628) 821 222

**J&J Medical**
Johnson & Johnson Medical
Coronation Rd
Ascot
Berks, SL5 9EY.
tel: (01344) 871 000
fax: (01344) 872 599

**J&J MSD**
Johnson & Johnson MSD
See McNeil
tel: (01494) 450 778
fax: (01494) 450 487

**Janssen-Cilag**
Janssen-Cilag Ltd
PO Box 79
Saunderton
High Wycombe
Bucks, HP14 4HJ.
tel: (01494) 567 567
fax: (01494) 567 568

**JHC**
JHC Healthcare Ltd
The Maltings, 2nd Floor
Bridge St
Hitchin
Herts, SG5 2DE.
tel: (01462) 432 533
fax: (01462) 432 535

**JLB**
B. Braun JLB Ltd
Unit 2A
St Columb Industrial Estate
St Columb Major
Cornwall, TR9 6SF.
tel: (01637) 880 065
fax: (01637) 881 549

**K/L**
K/L Pharmaceuticals Ltd
21 Macadam Place
South Newmoor
Irvine
Ayrshire, KA11 4HP.
tel: (01294) 215 951
fax: (01294) 221 600

**Kestrel**
Kestrel Ltd
Ashfield House
Resolution Rd
Ashby de la Zouch
Leics, LE65 1HW.
tel: (01530) 562 301
fax: (01530) 562 430
kestrel@ventiv.co.uk

**King**
King Pharmaceuticals Ltd
3 Ash Street
Leicester, LE5 0DA.
tel: (01462) 434 366
fax: (01462) 450 755

**KoRa**
KoRa Healthcare Ltd
Frans Maas House
Swords Business Park, Swords
Co. Dublin
Ireland
tel: (00353) 1890 0406
fax: (00353) 1890 3016
Kora@ireland.com

**Kyowa Hakko**
Kyowa Hakko UK Ltd
258 Bath Rd
Slough
Berks, SL1 4DX.
tel: (01753) 566 020
fax: (01753) 566 030

**LAB**
Laboratories for Applied Biology
91 Amhurst Park
London, N16 5DR.
tel: (020) 8800 2252
fax: (020) 8809 6884
enquiries@cerumol.com

**Lederle**
See Wyeth

**LEO**
LEO Pharma
Longwick Rd
Princes Risborough
Bucks, HP27 9RR.
tel: (01844) 347 333
fax: (01844) 342 278
medical-info.uk@leo-pharma.com

**LifeScan**
LifeScan
50-100 Holmers Farm Way
High Wycombe
Bucks, HP12 4DP.
tel: (01494) 658 750
fax: (01494) 658 751

**Lilly**
Eli Lilly & Co Ltd
Lilly House
Priestley Rd
Basingstoke
Hampshire, RG24 9NL.
tel: (01256) 315 999
fax: (01256) 775 858

**Linderma**
Linderma Ltd
Canon Bridge House
Canon Bridge
Madley
Hereford, HR2 9JF.
tel: (01981) 250 124
fax: (01981) 251 412
linderma@virgin.net

**Link**
Link Pharmaceuticals Ltd
Bishops Weald House
Albion Way
Horsham
West Sussex, RH12 1AH.
tel: (01403) 272 451
fax: (01403) 272 455
medical.information@linkpharm.co.uk

**LPC**
LPC Medical (UK) Ltd
30 Chaul End Lane
Luton, Beds, LU4 8EZ.
tel: (01582) 560 393
fax: (01582) 560 395
info@lpcpharma.com

**Lundbeck**
Lundbeck Ltd
Lundbeck House
Caldecotte Lake Business Park
Caldecotte, Milton Keynes
Bucks, MK7 8LF.
tel: (01908) 649 966
fax: (01908) 647 888
ukmedicalinformation@lundbeck.com

**Mölnlycke**
Mölnlycke Health Care Ltd
The Arenson Centre
Arenson Way
Dunstable
Beds, LU5 5UL.
tel: (0870) 606 0766
fax: (0870) 608 1888
info.uk@molnlycke.net

**Mandeville**
Mandeville Medicines
Stoke Mandeville Hospital
Ayelsbury
Bucks, HP21 8AL.
tel: (01296) 394 142
fax: (01296) 397 223

**Manx**
Manx Healthcare
Taylor Group House
Wedgnock Lane
Warwick, CV34 5YA.
tel: (01926) 482 511
fax: (01926) 498 711
info@manxhealthcare.com

**Martindale**
Martindale Pharmaceuticals Ltd
Hubert Rd
Brentwood
Essex, CM14 4LZ.
tel: (01277) 266 600
fax: (01277) 848 976
info@martindalepharma.co.uk

**MASTA**
MASTA
Moorfield Rd
Yeadon
Leeds, LS19 7BN.
tel: (0113) 238 7500
fax: (0113) 238 7501
medical@masta.org

**Mayne**
Mayne Pharma plc
Queensway
Royal Leamington Spa
Warwickshire, CV31 3RW.
tel: (01926) 820 820
fax: (01926) 821 041
medinfouk@uk.maynepharma.com

**McNeil**
McNeil Ltd
Enterprise House, Station Rd
Loadwater, High Wycombe, Bucks,
HP10 9UF.
tel: (01494) 450 778
fax: (01494) 450 487

**MDE**
MDE Diagnostics Europe Ltd
The Surrey Technology Centre
40 Occam Rd
Surrey Research Park, Guildford
Surrey, GU2 7YG.
tel: (01483) 688 400
info@mdediagnostic.co.uk

**Mead Johnson**
Mead Johnson Nutritionals
Uxbridge Business Park
Sanderson Rd
Uxbridge
Middx, UB8 1DH.
tel: (00800) 8834 2568
fax: (01895) 523 103

**Meadow**
Meadow Laboratories Ltd
18 Avenue Rd
Chadwell Heath
Romford
Essex, RM6 4JF.
tel: (020) 8597 1203
enquiries@meadowlabs.fsnet.co.uk

**Meda**
Meda Pharmaceuticals Ltd
Regus House, Herald Way
Pegasus Business Park
Castle Donnington
Derbyshire, DE74 2TZ.
tel: (01332) 638 033
fax: (01332) 638 192
information@uk.meda.se

**Medac**
Medac (UK)
Scion House, Stirling University
Stirling, FK9 4NF.
tel: (01786) 458 086
fax: (01786) 458 032
info@medac-uk.co.uk

**Medical House**
The Medical House plc
199 Newhall Rd
Sheffield, S9 2QJ.
tel: (0114) 261 9011
fax: (0114) 243 1597
info@themedicalhouse.com

**Medigas**
Medigas Ltd
Enterprise Drive
Four Ashes
Wolverhampton, WV10 7DF.
tel: (01902) 791 944
fax: (01902) 791 125

**MediSense**
MediSense
Abbott Laboratories Ltd
Mallory House
Vanwall Business Park
Maidenhead, Berks, SL6 4UD.
tel: (01628) 678 900
fax: (01628) 678 805

**Medix**
See Clement Clarke

**Medlock**
Medlock Medical Ltd
Tubiton House
Medlock St.
Oldham, OL1 3HS.
tel: (0161) 621 2100
fax: (0161) 627 0932
medical.information@
medlockmedical.com

**MedLogic**
MedLogic Global Ltd
Western Wood Way
Langage Science Park
Plympton
Plymouth, Devon, PL7 5BG.
tel: (01752) 209 955
fax: (01752) 209 956
enquiries@mlgl.co.uk

**Menarini**
A. Menarini Pharma UK SRL
Menarini House
Mercury Park
Wycombe Lane, Wooburn Green
Bucks, HP10 0HH.
tel: (01628) 856 400
fax: (01628) 856 402

**Menarini Diagnostics**
A. Menarini Diagnostics
Wharfedale Rd
Winnersh
Wokingham
Berks, RG41 5RA.
tel: (0118) 944 4100
fax: (0118) 944 4111

**Merck**
Merck Pharmaceuticals
Harrier House
High St
West Drayton
Middx, UB7 7QG.
tel: (01895) 452 307
fax: (01895) 452 296
medinfo@merckpharma.co.uk

**Merck Consumer Health**
See Seven Seas

**Merck Sharp & Dohme**
See MSD

**Micro Medical**
Micro Medical Ltd
Quayside
Chatham Maritime
Chatham
Kent, ME4 4QY.
tel: (01634) 893 500
fax: (01634) 893 600
sales@micromedical.co.uk

**Milupa**
Milupa Ltd
White Horse Business Park
Trowbridge
Wilts, BA14 0XQ.
tel: (01225) 711 511
fax: (01225) 711 970

**Molar**
Molar Ltd
The Borough Yard
The Borough
Wedmore
Somerset, BS28 4EB.
tel: (01934) 710 022
fax: (01934) 710 033
info@molar.ltd.uk

**MSD**
Merck Sharp & Dohme Ltd
Hertford Rd
Hoddesdon
Herts, EN11 9BU.
tel: (01992) 467 272
fax: (01992) 451 066

**Myogen**
Myogen GmbH
PO Box 122
Richmond
North Yorks, DL10 5YA.
tel: (01748) 828 812
fax: (01748) 828 801
info@myogen.de

**Nagor**
Nagor Ltd
PO Box 21, Global House
Isle of Man Business Park
Douglas
Isle of Man, IM99 1AX.
tel: (01624) 625 556
fax: (01624) 661 656
enquiries@nagor.com

**Napp**
Napp Pharmaceuticals Ltd
Cambridge Science Park
Milton Rd
Cambs, CB4 0GW.
tel: (01223) 424 444
fax: (01223) 424 441

**Neolab**
Neolab Ltd
57 High St
Odiham, Hampshire, RG29 1LF.
tel: (01256) 704 110
fax: (01256) 701 144
info@neolab.co.uk

**Neomedic**
Neomedic Ltd
2a Crofters Rd
Northwood
Middx, HA6 3ED.
tel: (01923) 836 379
fax: (01923) 840 160
marketing@neomedic.co.uk

**Nestlé**
Nestlé UK Ltd
St. George's House
Park Lane
Croydon
Surrey, CR9 1NR.
tel: (020) 8686 3333
fax: (020) 8686 6072

**Nestlé Clinical**
Nestlé Clinical Nutrition
St George's House
Park Lane
Croydon
Surrey, CR9 1NR.
tel: (020) 8667 5130
fax: (020) 8667 6061
nutrition@uk.nestle.com

**Network**
Network Health & Beauty
Network House
41 Invincible Rd
Farnborough
Hants, GU14 7QU.
tel: (01252) 533 333
fax: (01252) 533 344
networkm@globalnet.co.uk

**Neutrogena**
See J&J

**Nordic**
Nordic Pharma UK Ltd
Abbey House
1650 Arlington Business Park
Theale
Reading, RG7 4SA.
tel: (0118) 929 8233
fax: (0118) 929 8234
info@nordicpharma.co.uk

**Norgine**
Norgine Pharmaceuticals Ltd
Chaplin House
Moorhall Rd
Harefield
Middx, UB9 6NS.
tel: (01895) 826 600
fax: (01895) 825 865

**Nova**
Nova Laboratories Ltd
Martin House
Gloucester Crescent
Wigston
Leicester, LE18 4YL.
tel: (0116) 223 0099
fax: (0116) 223 0120
sales@novalabs.co.uk

**Novartis**
Novartis Pharmaceuticals UK Ltd
Frimley Business Park
Frimley
Camberley
Surrey, GU16 7SR.
tel: (01276) 692 255
fax: (01276) 692 508

**Novartis Consumer Health**
Novartis Consumer Health
Wimblehurst Rd
Horsham
West Sussex, RH12 5AB.
tel: (01403) 210 211
fax: (01403) 323 939
medicalaffairs.uk@ch.novartis.com

**Novo Nordisk**
Novo Nordisk Ltd
Broadfield Park
Brighton Rd
Crawley
West Sussex, RH11 9RT.
tel: (01293) 613 555
fax: (01293) 613 535
customercareuk@novonordisk.com

**Nutricia Clinical**
Nutricia Clinical Care
Nutricia Ltd
White Horse Business Park
Trowbridge
Wilts, BA14 0XQ.
tel: (01225) 711 688
fax: (01225) 711 798
cndirect@nutricia.co.uk

**Nutricia Dietary**
Nutricia Dietary Care
see Nutricia Clinical
tel: (01225) 711 801
fax: (01225) 711 567

**Nutrition Point**
Nutrition Point Ltd
13 Taurus Park
Westbrook
Warrington
Cheshire, WA5 7ZT.
tel: (07041) 544 044
fax: (07041) 544 055
info@nutritionpoint.co.uk

**Nycomed**
Nycomed UK Ltd
The Magdalen Centre
Oxford Science Park,
Oxford, UX4 4GA.
tel: (01865) 784 500
fax: (01865) 784 501
nycomed.uk@nycomed.com

**Octapharma**
Octapharma Ltd
6 Elm Court
Copse Drive, Meriden Green
Coventry, CV5 9RG.
tel: (01676) 521 000
fax: (01676) 521 200
octapharma@octapharma.co.uk

**Omron**
Omron Healthcare (UK) Ltd
Opal Drive
Fox Milne
Milton Keynes, MK15 0DG.
tel: (0870) 750 2771
fax: (0870) 750 2772
info.omronhealthcare.uk@eu.omron.com

**OPi**
OPi Ltd
2nd Floor, Titan Court
3 Bishop Square
Hatfield
Herts, AL10 9NA.
tel: (01707) 226 094
fax: (01707) 226 194
OPi.UK@orphan-opi.com

**Opus**
See Trinity-Chiesi

**Oral B Labs**
Oral B Laboratories Ltd
Gillette Corner
Great West Rd
Isleworth
Middx, TW7 5NP.
tel: (020) 8847 7800
fax: (020) 8847 7828

**Organon**
Organon Laboratories Ltd
Cambridge Science Park
Milton Rd
Cambs, CB4 0FL.
tel: (01223) 432 700
fax: (01223) 424 368
medrequest@organon.co.uk

**Orion**
Orion Pharma (UK) Ltd
Leat House, Overbridge Square
Hambridge Lane
Newbury
Berks, RG14 5UX.
tel: (01635) 520 300
fax: (01635) 520 319
medicalinformation@orionpharma.com

**Orphan Europe**
Orphan Europe (UK) Ltd
Isis House
43 Station Rd
Henley-on-Thames
Oxon, RG9 1AT.
tel: (01491) 414 333
fax: (01491) 414 443
info.uk@orphan-europe.com

**Ortho Biotech**
Ortho Biotech
PO Box 79
Saunderton
High Wycombe
Bucks, HP14 4HJ.
tel: (0800) 389 2926
fax: (01494) 567 568

**Otsuka**
Otsuka Pharmaceutical (UK) Ltd
BSi Tower
389 Chiswick High Rd,
London, W4 4AJ.
tel: (020) 8742 4300
fax: (020) 8994 8548
medinfo@otsuka.co.uk

**Owen Mumford**
Owen Mumford Ltd
Brook Hill
Woodstock
Oxford, OX20 1TU.
tel: (01993) 812 021
fax: (01993) 813 466
customerservices@owenmumford.co.uk

**Paines & Byrne**
Paines & Byrne Ltd
Lovett House
Lovett Rd
Staines
Middx, TW18 3AZ.
tel: (01784) 419 620
fax: (01784) 419 401

**Parema**
See Urgo

**Pari**
PARI Medical Ltd
Enterprise House
Station Approach
West Byfleet
Surrey, KT14 6NE.
tel: (01932) 341 122
fax: (01932) 341 134
parimedical@compuserve.com

**Parke-Davis**
See Pfizer

**Parkside**
Parkside Healthcare
12 Parkside Ave
Salford, M7 4HB.
tel: (0161) 795 2792
fax: (0161) 795 4076

**Peckforton**
Peckforton Pharmaceuticals Ltd
Crewe Hall
Crewe
Cheshire, CW1 6UL.
tel: (01270) 582 255
fax: (01270) 582 299
info@peckforton.com

**Penn**
Penn Pharmaceuticals Services Ltd
Unit 23 & 24, Tafarnaubach Industrial Estate
Tredegar
Gwent, NP22 3AA.
tel: (01495) 711 222
fax: (01495) 711 225
penn@pennpharm.co.uk

**Pfizer**
Pfizer Ltd
Walton Oaks
Dorking Rd
Walton-on-the-Hill
Surrey, KT20 7NS.
tel: (01304) 616 161
fax: (01304) 656 221

**Pfizer Consumer**
See Pfizer

**Pharma-Global**
Pharma-Global Ltd
SEQ Ltd, Nerin House
26 Ridgeway St
Douglas, Isle of Man, IM1 1EL.
tel: (01624) 692 999
fax: (01624) 613 998

**Pharmacia**
see Pfizer

**Pharmasol**
Pharmasol Ltd
North Way, Walworth Industrial Estate
Andover, Hampshire, SP10 5AZ.
tel: (01264) 363 117
fax: (01264) 332 223
info@pharmasol.co.uk

**Pharmion**
Pharmion Ltd
Riverside House
Riverside Walk
Windsor
Berks, SL4 1NA.
tel: (01753) 240 600
fax: (01753) 240 656
info-UK@pharmion.com

**Pickles**
J. Pickles Healthcare
Beech House
62 High St
Knaresborough
N. Yorks, HG5 0EA.
tel: (01423) 867 314
fax: (01423) 869 177

**Pinewood**
Pinewood Healthcare
Ballymacabry
Clonmel, Co Tipperary, Eire
tel: (00353) 523 6253
fax: (00353) 523 6311
info@pinewood.ie

**PLIVA**
PLIVA Pharma Ltd
Vision House
Bedford Rd
Petersfield
Hampshire, GU32 3QB.
tel: (01730) 710900
fax: (01730) 710901
medinfo@pliva-pharma.co.uk

**Procter & Gamble**
Procter & Gamble UK
The Heights
Brooklands
Weybridge
Surrey, KT13 0XP.
tel: (01932) 896 000
fax: (01932) 896 200

**Procter & Gamble Pharm.**
Procter & Gamble Technical Centres
Medical Dept
Rusham Park
Whitehall Lane
Egham, Surrey, TW20 9NW.
tel: (01784) 474 900
fax: (01784) 474 705

**Profile**
Profile Pharma Ltd
Heath Place
Bognor Regis
West Sussex, PO22 9SL.
tel: (0870) 770 2025
fax: (0870) 770 2224
info@profilepharma.com

**Profile Respiratory**
Profile Respiratory Systems Ltd
Heath Place
Bognor Regis
West Sussex, PO22 9SL.
tel: (0870) 770 3434
fax: (0870) 770 3433
info@profilehs.com

**Provalis**
Provalis Healthcare Ltd
Newtech Square
Deeside Industrial Park
Deeside
Flintshire, CH5 2NT.
tel: (01244) 288 888
fax: (01244) 280 342
enquiries@provalis.plc.uk

**R&C**
See Reckitt Benckiser

**Ransom**
Ransom Consumer Healthcare
104 Bancroft
Hitchin
Herts, SG5 1LY.
tel: (01462) 437 615
fax: (01462) 443 512
info@williamransom.com

**Reckitt Benckiser**
Reckitt Benckiser Healthcare
Dansom Lane
Hull, HU8 7DS.
tel: (01482) 326 151
fax: (01482) 582 526
miu@reckittbenckiser.com

**Recordati**
Recordati Pharmaceuticals Ltd
Ash House
Fairfield Avenue
Staines
Middx, TW18 4AB.
tel: (01784) 224 237
fax: (01784) 224 312

**Rhône-Poulenc Rorer**
See Sanofi-Aventis

**Richardson**
Richardson Healthcare
Richardson House
Crondal Rd
Coventry
Warwickshire, CV7 9NH.
tel: (08700) 111 126
fax: (08700) 111 127

**Robinsons**
Robinson Healthcare Ltd
Lawn Rd
Carlton-in-Lindrick Industrial Estate
Worksop
Notts, S81 9LB.
tel: (01909) 735 001
fax: (01909) 731 103
enquiries@robinsoncare.com

**Roche**
Roche Products Ltd
Hexagon Place
6 Falcon Way, Shire Park
Welwyn Garden City
Herts, AL7 1TW.
tel: (0800) 328 1629
fax: (01707) 384 555
medinfo.uk@roche.com

**Roche Consumer Health**
See Bayer

**Roche Diagnostics**
Roche Diagnostics Ltd
Bell Lane
Lewes
East Sussex, BN7 1LG.
tel: (01273) 480 444
fax: (01273) 480 266

**Rosemont**
Rosemont Pharmaceuticals Ltd
Rosemont House
Yorkdale Industrial Park
Braithwaite St
Leeds, LS11 9XE.
tel: (0113) 244 1999
fax: (0113) 246 0738
infodesk@rosemontpharma.com

**Rowa**
Rowa Pharmaceuticals Ltd
Bantry
Co Cork
Ireland
tel: (00 353 27) 50077
fax: (00 353 27) 50417
rowa@rowa-pharma.ie

**Rybar**
See Shire

**S&N Hlth.**
Smith & Nephew Healthcare Ltd
Healthcare House
Goulton St
Hull, HU3 4DJ.
tel: (01482) 222 200
fax: (01482) 222 211
advice@smith-nephew.com

**Sallis**
Sallis Healthcare Ltd
Vernon Works
Waterford St
Basford
Nottingham, NG6 0DH.
tel: (0115) 978 7841
fax: (0115) 942 2272

**Sandoz**
Sandoz Ltd
Unit 37
Woolmer Way
Bordon
Hants, GU35 9QE.
tel: (01420) 478 301
fax: (01420) 474 427

**Sankyo**
Sankyo Pharma UK Ltd
Sankyo House
Repton Place
White Lion Rd, Amersham
Bucks, HP7 9LP.
tel: (01494) 766 866
fax: (01494) 766 557
medinfo@sankyo.co.uk

**Sanochemia**
Sanochemia Diagnostics UK Ltd
Argentum
510 Bristol Business Park
Coldharbour Lane
Bristol, BS16 1EJ.
tel: (0117) 906 3562
fax: (0117) 906 3709

**Sanofi Pasteur**
Sanofi Pasteur MSD Ltd
Mallards Reach
Bridge Avenue
Maidenhead
Berks, SL6 1QP.
tel: (01628) 785 291
fax: (01628) 671 722

**Sanofi-Aventis**
Sanofi-Aventis Ltd
1 Onslow St
Guildford
Surrey, GU1 4YS.
tel: (01483) 505 515
fax: (01483) 535 432
uk-medicalinformation@
sanofi-aventis.com

**Sanofi-Synthelabo**
See Sanofi-Aventis

**Schering Health**
Schering Health Care Ltd
The Brow
Burgess Hill
West Sussex, RH15 9NE.
tel: (0845) 609 6767
fax: (01444) 465 878
customer.care@schering.co.uk

**Schering-Plough**
Schering-Plough Ltd
Shire Park
Welwyn Garden City
Herts, AL7 1TW.
tel: (01707) 363 636
fax: (01707) 363 763
medical.info@spcorp.com

**Schwarz**
Schwarz Pharma Ltd
Schwarz House
East St
Chesham
Bucks, HP5 1DG.
tel: (01494) 797 500
fax: (01494) 774 960
medinfo@schwarzpharma.co.uk

**Searle**
See Pfizer

**Serono**
Serono Pharmaceuticals Ltd
Bedfont Cross
Stanwell Rd
Feltham
Middx, TW14 8NX.
tel: (020) 8818 7200
fax: (020) 8818 7222
serono_uk@serono.com

**Servier**
Servier Laboratories Ltd
Gallions
Wexham Springs
Framewood Rd
Wexham, SL3 6RL.
tel: (01753) 662 744
fax: (01753) 663 456

**Seven Seas**
Seven Seas Ltd
Hedon Rd
Marfleet
Hull, HU9 5NJ.
tel: (01482) 375 234
fax: (01482) 374 345

**Shiloh**
Shiloh Healthcare Ltd
Lion Mill
Fitton St
Royton
Oldham, OL2 5JX.
tel: (0161) 624 5641
fax: (0161) 627 0902
enquiry@shiloh.co.uk

**Shire**
Shire Pharmaceuticals Ltd
Hampshire International Business Park
Chineham
Basingstoke
Hants, RG24 8EP.
tel: (01256) 894 000
fax: (01256) 894 708

**SHS**
SHS International Ltd
100 Wavertree Boulevard
Wavertree Technology Park
Liverpool, L7 9PT.
tel: (0151) 228 8161
fax: (0151) 230 5365
seve@shsint.co.uk

**Sigma**
Sigma Pharmaceuticals plc
PO Box 233
Unit 1-7 Colonial Way
Watford
Herts, WD24 4YR.
tel: (01923) 444 999
fax: (01923) 444 998
info@sigpharm.co.uk

**Sinclair**
Sinclair Pharmaceuticals Ltd
Borough Rd
Godalming
Surrey, GU7 2AB.
tel: (01483) 426 644
fax: (01483) 860 927
info@sinclairpharma.com

**SMA Nutrition**
See Wyeth

**SNBTS**
Scottish National Blood Transfusion
Service
Protein Fractionation Centre
Ellen's Glen Rd
Edinburgh, EH17 7QT.
tel: (0131) 536 5700
fax: (0131) 536 5781

**Solvay**
Solvay Healthcare Ltd
Mansbridge Rd
West End
Southampton, SO18 3JD.
tel: (023) 8046 7000
fax: (023) 8046 5350
medinfo.shl@solvay.com

**Sovereign**
Sovereign Medical
Sovereign House
Miles Gray Rd
Basildon
Essex, SS14 3FR.
tel: (01268) 535 200
fax: (01268) 535 299

**Special Products**
Special Products Ltd
Unit 25
Boundary Business Centre
Surrey, GU21 5DH.
tel: (01483) 736 950
fax: (01483) 721 926
graham.march@specprod.co.uk

**Specials Laboratory**
The Specials Laboratory Ltd
Unit 1, Regents Drive
Lower Prudhoe Industrial Estate
Northumberland, NE42 6PX.
tel: (0800) 028 4925
fax: (0800) 083 4222

**Squibb**
See Bristol-Myers Squibb

**SSL**
SSL International plc
Venus, 1 Old Park Lane
Trafford Park
Urmston
Manchester, M41 7HA.
tel: (08701) 222 690
fax: (08701) 222 692
medical.information@ssl-international.com

**STD Pharmaceutical**
STD Pharmaceutical Products Ltd
Plough Lane
Hereford, HR4 0EL.
tel: (01432) 373 555
fax: (01432) 373 556
enquiries@stdpharm.co.uk

**Sterling Health**
See GSK Consumer Healthcare

**Sterwin**
See Winthrop

**Stiefel**
Stiefel Laboratories (UK) Ltd
Holtspur Lane
Wooburn Green
High Wycombe
Bucks, HP10 0AU.
tel: (01628) 524 966
fax: (01628) 810 021
general@stiefel.co.uk

**Strakan**
Strakan Ltd
Buckholm Mill
Galashiels, TD1 2HB.
tel: (01896) 668 060
fax: (01896) 668 061
medinfo@strakan.com

**Sutherland**
Sutherland Health Ltd
Unit 1, Rivermead
Pipers Way
Thatcham
Berks, RG19 4EP.
tel: (01635) 874 488
fax: (01635) 877 622

**Swedish Orphan**
Swedish Orphan International (UK) Ltd
The White House
Wilderspool Park, Greenalls Ave
Stockton Heath, Warrington
Cheshire, WA4 6HL.
tel: (01925) 438 028
fax: (01925) 438 001

**Syner-Med**
Syner-Med (Pharmaceutical Products) Ltd
Beech House
840 Brighton Rd
Purley, CR8 2BH.
tel: (0845) 634 2100
fax: (0845) 634 2101
mail@syner-med.com

**Takeda**
Takeda UK Ltd
Takeda House, Mercury Park
Wycombe Lane
Wooburn Green
High Wycombe, Bucks, HP10 0HH.
tel: (01628) 537 900
fax: (01628) 526 615

**Taro**
Taro Pharmaceuticals (UK) Ltd
1st Floor, Prince of Wales House
3 Bluecoats Ave
Hertford, SG14 1PB.
tel: (01992) 557 445
fax: (01992) 557 447
customerservice@taropharma.co.uk

**Tarus**
See Chemidex

**Teva**
Teva Pharmaceuticals Ltd
The Gate House
Gatehouse Way
Aylesbury
Bucks, HP19 8DB.
tel: (01296) 719 768
fax: (01296) 719 769
info@tevapharma.co.uk

**TEVA UK**
TEVA UK Ltd
Brampton Rd
Hampden Park, Eastbourne
East Sussex, BN22 9AG.
tel: (01323) 501 111
fax: (01323) 520 306

**TheraSense**
TheraSense UK
Centaur House
Ancells Business Park, Ancells Rd
Fleet
Hants, GU51 2UJ.
tel: (01252) 761 392
fax: (01252) 761 393

**Thornton & Ross**
Thornton & Ross Ltd
Linthwaite Laboratories
Huddersfield, HD7 5QH.
tel: (01484) 842 217
fax: (01484) 847 301
mail@thorntonross.com

**Tillomed**
Tillomed Laboratories Ltd
3 Howard Rd
Eaton Socon, St Neots
Cambs, PE19 3ET.
tel: (01480) 402 400
fax: (01480) 402 402
info@tillomed.co.uk

**TOL**
Tree of Life
Coaldale Rd
Lymedale Business Park
Newcastle Under Lyme
Staff, ST5 9QX.
tel: (01782) 567 100
fax: (01782) 567 199
health@tol-europe.com

**Torbet**
Torbet Laboratories Ltd
14D Wendover Rd
Rackheath Industrial Estate
Rackheath
Norwich, NR13 6LH.
tel: (01603) 735 200
fax: (01603) 735 217
torbet@typharm.com

**Transdermal**
Transdermal Ltd
35 Grimwade Ave
Croydon
Surrey, CR0 5DJ.
tel: (020) 8654 2251
fax: (020) 8654 2252
transdermal@transdermal.co.uk

**Trinity**
Trinity Pharmaceuticals Ltd
See Trinity-Chiesi

**Trinity-Chiesi**
Trinity-Chiesi Pharmaceuticals Ltd
Cheadle Royal Business Park
Highfield
Cheadle, SK8 3GY.
tel: (0161) 488 5555
fax: (0161) 488 5565

**TSL**
Tissue Science Laboratories plc
Victoria House
Victoria Rd
Aldershot
Hants, GU11 1EJ.
tel: (01252) 333 002
fax: (01252) 333 010
enquiries@tissuescience.com

**Tyco**
Tyco Healthcare
154 Fareham Rd
Gosport
Hants, PO13 0AS.
tel: (01329) 224 000

**Typharm**
Typharm Ltd
14D Wendover Rd
Rackheath Industrial Estate
Rackheath
Norwich, NR13 6LH.
tel: (01603) 735 200
fax: (01603) 735 217
customerservices@typharm.com

**UCB Pharma**
UCB Pharma Ltd
208 Bath Rd
Slough, SL1 3WE.
tel: (01753) 534 655
fax: (01753) 536 632
medicalinformationuk@ucb-group.com

**Ultrapharm**
Ultrapharm Ltd
Centenary Business Park
Henley-on-Thames
Oxon, RG9 1DS.
tel: (01491) 578 016
fax: (01491) 570 001
orders@glutenfree.co.uk

**Univar**
Univar Ltd
International House
Zenith, Paycocke Rd
Basildon
Essex, SS14 3DW.
tel: (01268) 594 400
fax: (01268) 594 481
trientine@univareurope.com

**Unomedical**
Unomedical Ltd
Thornhill Rd
Redditch, B98 7NL.
tel: (01527) 587 700
fax: (01527) 592 111

**Urgo**
Urgo Ltd
Sullington Rd
Shepshed
Loughborough
Leics, LE12 9JJ.
tel: (01509) 502 051
fax: (01509) 650 898
medical@parema.com

**Valeant**
Valeant Pharmaceuticals Ltd
Cedarwood
Chineham Business Park
Crockford Lane, Basingstoke
Hants, RG24 8WD.
tel: (01256) 707 744
fax: (01256) 707 334
valeantuk@valeant.com

**Vernon-Carus**
Vernon-Carus Ltd
Penwortham Mills
Preston
Lancs, PR1 9SN.
tel: (01772) 744 493
fax: (01772) 748 754
mail@vernon-carus.co.uk

**Viatris**
Viatris Pharmaceuticals Ltd
Building 2000, Beach Drive
Cambridge Research Park
Waterbeach, Cambs, CB5 9PD.
tel: (01223) 205 999
fax: (01223) 205 998
info@viatrisuk.co.uk

**Viridian**
Viridian Pharma Ltd
Seales Barn
School Lane
Shuttington, Tamworth
Staffs, B79 0DX.
tel: (01827) 896 996
fax: (0870) 705 8153
info@viridianpharma.co.uk

**Vitaflo**
Vitaflo Ltd
11 Century Building
Brunswick Business Park
Liverpool, L3 4BL.
tel: (0151) 709 9020
fax: (0151) 709 9727
vitaflo@vitaflo.co.uk

**Vitaline**
Vitaline Pharmaceuticals UK Ltd
8 Ridge Way
Drakes Drive
Crendon Business Park
Long Crendon, Bucks, HP18 9BF.
tel: (01844) 202 044
fax: (01844) 202 077
vitalineinfo@aol.com

**Vitalograph**
Vitalograph Ltd
Maids Moreton
Buckingham, MK18 1SW.
tel: (01280) 827 110
fax: (01280) 823 302
sales@vitalograph.co.uk

**W-L**
Warner Lambert UK Ltd
See Pfizer

**Wallace Mfg**
Wallace Manufacturing Chemists Ltd
Wallace House
New Abbey Court
51-53 Stert St, Abingdon
Oxon, OX14 3JF.
tel: (01235) 538 700
fax: (01235) 538 800
info@alinter.co.uk

**Wanskerne**
Wanskerne Ltd
44 Broomfield Drive
Billingshurst, RH4 9TN.
tel: (01403) 783 214
fax: (01403) 783 214

**Warner Lambert**
See Pfizer

**Winthrop**
Winthrop Pharmaceuticals UK Ltd
PO Box 611
Guildford, Surrey, GU1 4YS.
tel: (01483) 554 101
fax: (01483) 554 810
sterwin.sales@sterwin.com

**Wockhardt**
Wockhardt UK Ltd
Ash Rd North
Wrexham Industrial Estate
Wrexham, LL13 9UF.
tel: (01978) 661 261
fax: (01978) 660 130

**Wyeth**
Wyeth Pharmaceuticals
Huntercombe Lane South
Taplow
Maidenhead
Berks, SL6 0PH.
tel: (01628) 604 377
fax: (01628) 666 368
ukmedinfo@wyeth.com

**Wynlit**
Wynlit Laboratories
153 Furzehill Rd
Borehamwood
Herts, WD6 2DR.
tel: (07903) 370 130
fax: (020) 8292 6117

**Wyvern**
Wyvern Medical Ltd
PO Box 17
Ledbury
Herefordshire, HR8 2ES.
tel: (01531) 631 105
fax: (01531) 634 844

**Yamanouchi**
See Astellas

**Zeal**
G. H. Zeal Ltd
Deer Park Rd
London, SW19 3UU.
tel: (020) 8542 2283
fax: (020) 8543 7840
scientific@zeal.co.uk

**Zeneus**
Zeneus Pharma Ltd
Abel Smith House
Gunnels Wood Rd
Stevenage, Herts, SG1 2BT.
tel: (01438) 731 731
fax: (01438) 765 080
medinfo@zeneuspharma.com

**Zeroderma**
Zeroderma Ltd
The Manor House
Victor Barns
Northampton Rd, Brixworth
Northampton, NN6 9DQ.
tel: (01604) 889 855
fax: (01604) 883 199
info@ixlpharma.com

**ZLB Behring**
ZLB Behring UK Ltd
Hayworth House
Market Place
Haywards Heath
West Sussex, RH16 1DB.
tel: (01444) 447 400
fax: (01444) 447 401
medinfo@zlbbehring.com

**ZooBiotic**
ZooBiotic Ltd
Biosurgical Research Unit
Surgical Materials Testing Laboratory
Princess of Wales Hospital, Coity Rd
Brigend, Mid Glamorgan, South Wales,
CF31 1RQ.
tel: (0845) 230 1810
fax: (01656) 752 830
maggots@smtl.co.uk

**Zurich**
See Trinity-Chiesi

# Special-order manufacturers

The following **companies** manufacture 'special-order' products: BCM Specials, Fresenius, Mandeville Medicines, Martindale, Nova Laboratories, Phoenix, Rosemont, Special Products, The Specials Laboratory (see Index of Manufacturers for contact details).

**Hospital manufacturing units** also manufacture 'special-order' products, details may be obtained from any of the centres listed below.

> It should be noted that when a product has a licence the *Department of Health recommends that the licensed product should be ordered* unless a specific formulation is required

## England

### East Anglian and Oxford

Mr G. Hanson
Production Manager
Pharmacy Manufacturing Unit
Ipswich Hospital NHS Trust
Heath Rd
Ipswich, IP4 5PD.
tel: (01473) 703 603
fax: (01473) 703 609
con.hanson@ipswichhospital.nhs.uk

### London

Mr M. Lillywhite
Director of Technical Services
Barts and the London NHS Trust, St. Bartholomew's Hospital
West Smithfield
London, EC1A 7BE.
tel: (020) 7601 7491
fax: (020) 7601 7486
mike.lillywhite@bartsandthelondon.nhs.uk

Mr P. Forsey
Production Manager
Guy's and St. Thomas' Hospital Trust
St. Thomas' Hospital
Lambeth Palace Rd
London, SE1 7EH.
tel: (020) 7118 4992
fax: (020) 7118 5013
paul.forsey@gstt.sthames.nhs.uk

Mr C. Evans
Production Manager
Pharmacy Department
St. George's Hospital
Blackshaw Rd
Tooting
London, SW17 0QT.
tel: (020) 8725 1770
fax: (020) 8725 3690
chris.evans@stgeorges.nhs.uk

Mr A. Krol
Director of Commercial Services
Pharmaceutical Manufacturing Unit
Moorfields Eye Hospital NHS Trust
34 Nile St
London, N1 7LX.
tel: (020) 7684 8561 / 8562
fax: 0800 328 8191
alan.krol@moorfields.nhs.uk

### North West

Mr M.D. Booth
Production & Aseptic Services Manager
Stockport Pharmaceuticals
Stepping Hill Hospital
Poplar Grove
Stockport, Cheshire, SK2 7JE.
tel: (0161) 419 5657
fax: (0161) 419 5664
mike.booth@stockport-tr.nwest.nhs.uk

### Northern

Mr Ian Smeaton
Production and Quality Control Unit
Royal Victoria Infirmary
Queen Victoria Rd
Newcastle-upon-Tyne, NE1 4LP.
tel: (0191) 282 0377
fax: (0191) 282 0376
pharmacy.tpn@nuth.northy.nhs.uk

### South East

Mr F. Brown
Production Manager
Pharmacy Production Unit
St Peter's Hospital
Guildford Rd
Chertsey, Surrey, KT16 OPZ.
tel: (01932) 722 520
fax: (01932) 873 632
fraser.brown@asph.nhs.uk

Ms G. Middlehurst
Production Manager
Pharmacy Manufacturing Unit
Queen Alexandra Hospital
Cosham
Portsmouth, Hants , PO6 3LY.
tel: (02392) 286 335
fax: (02392) 378 288
gillian.middlehurst@porthosp.nhs.uk

### South Western

Mr P. S. Bendell
Principal Pharmacist
Unit Manager, Torbay PMU
South Devon Healthcare
Long Rd
Paignton, Devon , TQ4 7TW.
tel: (01803) 664 707
fax: (01803) 664 354
phil.bendell@sdevonhc-tr.swest.nhs.uk

### Trent

Mr R.W. Brookes
Production Pharmacist
Royal Hallamshire Hospital
Glossop Rd
Sheffield, S10 2JF.
tel: (0114) 271 3104
fax: (0114) 271 2783
roger.brookes@sth.nhs.uk

### West Midlands

Mr A. Broad
Principal Pharmacist
Sterile Fluids Manufacturing Unit
Queen Elizabeth Medical Centre
Edgbaston
Birmingham, B15 2TH.
tel: (0121) 627 2326
fax: (0121) 627 2168
alan.broad@uhb.nhs.uk

Mr P.G. Williams
Principal Pharmacist
Pharmacy Manufacturing Unit
Queens Hospital
Burton Hospitals NHS Trust
Belvedere Rd
Burton-on-Trent, DE13 0RB.
tel: (01283) 566 333/511 511 Extn 5138
fax: (01283) 593 036
paul.williams@burtonh-tr.wmids.nhs.uk

### Yorkshire

Dr J. Harwood
Production Manager
Pharmacy Manufacturing Unit
Huddersfield Royal Infirmary
Lindley
Huddersfield
West Yorks, HD3 3EA.
tel: (01484) 342 421
fax: (01484) 342 074
john.harwood@cht.nhs.uk

## Northern Ireland

Principal Pharmacist
Victoria Pharmaceuticals
The Royal Hospitals
77 Boucher Cres
Belfast, BT12 6HU.
tel: (028) 9055 3407
fax: (028) 9055 3498

## Scotland

Mr J.A. Cook
Principal Pharmacist—Production
Tayside Pharmaceuticals
Ninewells Hospital
Dundee, DD1 9SY.
tel: (01382) 632 273
fax: (01382) 632 060
jon.a.cook@tuht.scot.nhs.uk

## Wales

Mr P. Spark
Principal Pharmacist
Pharmacy Department
Cardiff and Vale NHS Trust
Heath Park
Cardiff, CF14 4XW..
tel: (029) 2074 4828
fax: (029) 2074 3114
paul.spark@cardiffandvale.wales.nhs.uk

# Index

Principal page references are printed in **bold** type. Proprietary (trade) names and names of organisms are printed in *italic* type; where the BNF does not include a full entry for a branded product, the non-proprietary name is shown in brackets.

## A


Abacavir, **315**, 316
  lamivudine and zidovudine with, 316
  lamivudine with, 316
Abbreviations, *inside back cover*
  Latin, *inside back cover*, 488
  of units, 4
  Symbols, *inside back cover*, 487
*Abcare*, 351
Abciximab, **126**, 127
  infusion table, 791
Abdominal surgery, antibacterial prophylaxis, 271, 272
*Abelcet*, *309*, 310
*Abidec*, 498
*Abilify*, 188
*Able Spacer*, 151
Abortion
  habitual *see* Miscarriage, recurrent, 375
  haemorrhage, 399
  induction, 398
Abrasive agents, acne, 589
Abscess
  amoebic, 337
  periapical, 270
  periodontal, 270
Absence seizures, 238
  atypical, 238
Absorbent cotton, 829
  gauze, 829
  hospital quality, 829
  ribbon gauze, 829
  viscose ribbon gauze and, 829
Absorbent dressing, perforated, 827
Absorbent lint, 829
Absorbent muslin, 829
Absorbent pads, 829
*AC 2000 HI FLO*, 153
*AC 4000*, 153
Acamprosate, **260**
Acanthamoeba keratitis, 534, 548
Acarbose, **354**
Acaricides, 602
ACBS, 801
  alcoholic beverages, 812
  foods, 801
  toilet preparations, 820
*Accolate*, 160
*Accu-Chek* preparations, 358
*Accuhaler*
  *Flixotide*, 158
  *Seretide*, 158
  *Serevent*, 147
  *Ventolin*, 146
*Accupro*, 102
*Accuretic*, 102
ACE inhibitors, 97
  heart failure, 97
  myocardial infarction, 129
  renal function, 98
Acebutolol, **85**
  *see also* Beta-adrenoceptor blocking drugs
Aceclofenac, 505, **507**
Acemetacin, 507, 508
  postoperative pain, 640
Acenocoumarol, 124, **125**
*Acepril* (captopril), 99
Acetaminophen *see* Paracetamol
Acetazolamide, 238, **543**
  diuretic, 77
  epilepsy, 238, 247
  glaucoma, 540, 543
Acetic acid
  otitis externa, 550
Acetomenaphthone [ingredient], 499
Acetylcholine, eye, 547
Acetylcholine chloride, 547
Acetylcysteine
  eye, 545, 546
  infusion table, 791
  poisoning, 29, **30**, 31
Acetylsalicylic acid *see* Aspirin
*Acezide* (co-zidocapt), 99
Aciclovir, 322, **323**
  herpes simplex, 322
    buccal, 562
    eye, 322, **536**
    genital, 322, 406, 601
    labialis, 601
  herpes zoster, 322
  infusion table, 791
  preparations, 323
    cream, 602
    eye ointment, 536
Acid aspiration, 45
  surgery, 633
*Acidex*, 40
Acidification of urine, 422
Acidosis, metabolic, 477
*Aci-Jel*—discontinued, ix
Acipimox, **138**
Acitretin, 581, **584**, 585
Acknowledgements, iv
Aclometasone dipropionate, 576
Acne, 285, **587**
Acne rosacea *see* Rosacea, 586, 598
*Acnisal*, 589
*Acnocin* (co-cyprindiol), 590
*Acoflam* preparations, 508, 509
*Acorvio* (miconazole), 600
*Acorvio Plus*, 578
Acrivastine, **162**
Acrolein, 430
Acromegaly, 383, 391, 461
ACTH *see* Corticotropin, 380
*Actiban*, 832
*Actico*, 832
*Actidose-Aqua Advance*, 28
*Acti-Fast*, 831
*ActiFormCool*, 824
*Actilyse*, 130
*Actinac*, 589
Actinic keratosis, 594
Actinomycin D *see* Dactinomycin
*Action Cold Sore*, 602
*Actiq*, 227
*Actisorb Plus*, 828
*Actisorb Silver*, 828
*Active*, 358
*ActivHeal* products, 822, 823, 824, 825, 827
*Acti-Wrap*, 830
*Actonel* preparations, 390
*Actos*, 355
*Actrapid* preparations p. 346
  Pork, 346
*Acular*, 548
*Acupan*, 222
  injection—discontinued, ix
Acute coronary syndrome, 126
*ACWY Vax*, 622
Acyclovir *see* Aciclovir
Acyl-CoA dehydrogenase deficiency, 818
*Adalat* preparations, 112, 113
Adalimumab, 521, **522**
Adapalene, **588**
*Adcal*, 489
*Adcal-D$_3$*, 496
*Adcortyl*
  *Intra-articular/Intradermal*, 515
  *in Orabase*, 559
Addicts, notification of, 9
*Addiphos*, 483
Addison's disease, 361
Additives *see* Excipients
*Additrace*, 483
Adefovir, **326**
*Adenocor*, 79
*Adenoscan* (adenosine), 79
Adenosine, 78, **79**
ADH *see* Antidiuretic hormone
ADHD *see* Attention deficit hyperactivity disorder, 206
Adhesive
  dressings, 834
  films, 826, 827
  tissue, 605
*Adipine* preparations, 113
*Adizem* preparations, 110
Adrenal
  function test, 380
  hyperplasia, 364
  insufficiency, 361
    dental practice, 20
  suppression
    metyrapone, 396
  systemic corticosteroids, 362
  topical corticosteroids, 572
Adrenaline, 119, 166, 167
  anaphylaxis, 165, **166**
  cardiopulmonary resuscitation, 119
  croup, 143
  eye, 542
  local anaesthesia, 647, 649
  palliative care, 16
Adrenergic neurone blocking drugs, 95
Adrenoceptor agonists, 144
*Adriamycin* (doxorubicin), 434
ADROIT, 10
Adsorbed Diphtheria [low dose] and Tetanus Vaccine for Adults and Adolescents, 616
Adsorbents
  gastro-intestinal, 51
  poisoning, 28

*Adva-Co*, 832
*Advadraw* products, 830
*Advantage Plus*, 358
*Advasoft*, 832
*Advate* (factor VIII fraction), 132
*Advazorb*, 823
Adverse reactions, reporting, 10
Advisory Committee on Borderline Substances *see* ACBS
Advisory labels *see* Cautionary and advisory labels, 836, 838
*AeroBec* preparations, 156
*AeroChamber*, 151
*Aerodiol*, 372
*Aerrane*, 636
Agalsidase beta, 500, **501**
infusion table, 791
Agammaglobulinaemia, congenital, 627
*Agenerase*, 319
Age-related macular degeneration, 548
*Aggrastat*, 128
*Agrippal*, 619
AIDS, 314
vaccines and, 612
*Airomir* preparations, 146
*Airstrip*, *834*
*Aknemin* (minocycline), 287
*Aknemycin Plus*, 589
*ALBA* preparations (albumin solution), 480
Albendazole
hydatid disease, 341
strongyloidiasis, 342
Albumin solution, **480**
*Albustix*, 359
*Albutein* preparations (albumin solution), 480
Alclometasone dipropionate, 575
Alcohol
ACBS, 812
dependence, 260
hypnotic, 177
infusion table, 794
nutrition, 483
poisoning by, 29
skin, 606
withdrawal, 260
Alcoholism, 260
vitamin B, 494
*Aldactide* preparations (co-flumactone), 77
*Aldactone*, 76
*Aldara*, 592
Aldesleukin, 454
Aldioxa, 609
*Aldomet*, 94
Aldosterone antagonists, 75
*Aldurazyme*, 501
*Alembicol D*, 801
Alemtuzumab, **452**
infusion table, 791
Alendronate sodium *see* Alendronic acid
Alendronic acid, 386, 388
colecalciferol with, 388
Alfacalcidol, 496, **497**
Alfentanil, 222, **641**
infusion table, 791
Alfuzosin, 417, **418**
*Algicon*, 40
Alginates
antacids, 38, 40
dressings, 822, 823
*Algisite M* products, 822
*Algosteril* products, 822
Alimemazine
allergic disorders, 161, **163**
premedication, 163, 638
*Alimta*, 438
*Alione*, 825
Alkalinisation of urine, 422
*Alkeran*, 432
Alkylating drugs, 430
*Alldress*, 827
*Allegron*, 199
Aller-eze, *554*
*Aller-eze* preparations
eye, 538
Allergen extract vaccines, 164
Allergy, 364
angiodema, 165
anaphylaxis, 165
conjunctivitis, 538
food, 57
rhinitis, 554
*Allevyn* products, 823, 824
*All-Flex* diaphragm, 417
Allopurinol, 524, **525**
*Almogran*, 232
Almond oil, ear, 553
Almotriptan, **232**
*Alomide*, 539
*Alomide* preparations, 539
Alopecia
cytotoxic drugs, 429
male-pattern, 596
*Aloxi*, 216
*Alpha Keri Bath Oil*, 570
Alpha tocopheryl acetate, 498
Alpha$_2$-adrenoceptor stimulants
cardiovascular, 94
eye, 542, 543, 547
migraine, 236
Alpha-adrenoceptor blocking drugs, 95
cardiovascular, 95
urinary tract, 417
Alpha-blockers *see* Alpha-adrenoceptor blocking drugs
*Alphaderm*, 574
*Alphagan*, 543
*Alphanate* (factor VIII fraction), 132
*AlphaNine* (factor IX fraction), 132
*Alphosyl 2 in 1*, 595
*Alphosyl HC*, 583
Alprazolam, 178, **179**
Alprostadil
ductus arteriosus, 401
erectile dysfunction, **424**, 425
infusion table, 791
*Altacite* preparations (hydrotalcite), 39
Alteplase, 129, **130**
infusion table, 791
Alternative medicine, 1
*Alu-Cap*
antacid, 39
hyperphosphataemia, 491
Aluminium acetate, **551**
ear, 550, 551
Aluminium chloride, 609
Aluminium hydroxide, 39
antacid, 39, 40
diarrhoea, 51
hyperphosphataemia, 491
Aluminium oxide, 589
*Alupent* preparations, 148
*Alvedon* (paracetamol), 220
Alverine, **42**
*Alvesco*, 158
Alzheimer's disease, 264
Amantadine, 253, 327
parkinsonism, 251, **253**
viral infections, **327**
*Amaryl*, 352
AmBisome, *309*, 310
Amethocaine *see* Tetracaine
*Ametop*, 651
Amfebutamone *see* Bupropion, 261
Amfetamine *see* Amphetamines
*Amias*, 103
Amikacin, **288**, 289, 299
infusion table, 791
*Amikin*, 289
*Amilamont* (amiloride), 75
*Amil-Co* (co-amilozide), 76
Amiloride, 74, **75**
bumetanide with, 76
cyclopenthiazide with, 76
furosemide with, 76
hydrochlorothiazide with, 76
*Aminex*, 801
Amino acids
ACBS, 815, 816
intravenous nutrition, 482
Aminobenzoic acid, 494, **495**, 594
Aminoglycosides, 287
ear, 550, 553
eye, 534
skin, 597
systemic, 287
*Aminogran*, 801
Aminophylline, 149, **150**
infusion table, 791
*see also* Theophylline
*Aminoplasmal* preparations, 484
Aminosalicylates, 53, 54
*Aminoven* preparations, 484
Amiodarone, 79, **80**
cardiopulmonary resuscitation, 119
infusion table, 791
Amisulpride, 187, **188**
Amitriptyline, **197**
neuropathic pain, 230
perphenazine with, 197
postherpetic neuralgia, 231
*Amix* (amoxicillin), 276
Amlodipine, **109**, 110
*see also* Calcium-channel blockers
*Amlostin* (amlodipine), 110
*Ammonaps*, 502
Ammonia and ipecacuanha mixture, 172
Ammonia, poisoning by, 35
Ammonium chloride
acidification of urine, 422
*Amnivent 225 SR* (aminophylline), 150
Amobarbital, 180
secobarbital with, 180
Amoebiasis, 337
Amoebic abscess, 337

Amoebic dysentery, 337
Amoebicides, 337
*Amoram* (amoxicillin), 276
Amorolfine, **599**
Amoxapine, 196, **197**, 198
Amoxicillin, 275, **276**, 307
  infusion table, 791
*Amoxident* (amoxicillin), 276
*Amoxil* preparations, 276
Amoxycillin *see* Amoxicillin
Amphetamines, 206
  abuse, 7
  poisoning by, 33
*Amphocil*, 309, 310
Amphotericin, 308, **309**, 561
  bladder infections, 422
  infusion table, 791
  leishmaniasis, 338
  liposomal, 308, 309
  mouth, 561
  preparations, 310
    eye drops, 545
    lozenges, 561
    oral suspension, 561
Ampicillin, 275, **276**, 277
  flucloxacillin with [co-fluampicil], 276, **278**
  infusion table, 791
Amprenavir, 315, **318**, 319
Amsacrine, **439**, 440
  infusion table, 791
*Amsidine*, 440
*Amyben* (amiodarone), 80
Amylobarbitone *see* Amobarbital
Amyotrophic lateral sclerosis, 258
*Amytal*, 180
*Anabact*, 598
Anabolic steroids, 379
  anaemias, 468
Anaemias, 463
  aplastic, 468
  chronic renal failure, 468
  haemolytic, 468
  hypoplastic, 468
  iron-deficiency, 463
  megaloblastic, 466
  pernicious, 466
  sideroblastic, 468
Anaesthesia
  analgesics, 640
  antimuscarinics, 637
  corticosteroids, 362, 632
  dental practice, 633
  driving, 633
  general, 632
    inhalational, 635
    intravenous, 633
  local, 647
    dental practice, 647
    eye, 545
    mouth, 559
    rectal, 64
    skin, 571
  muscle relaxants, 642
*Anafranil* preparations, 198
Anagrelide, **471**, 472
*Ana-Guard, 166*
Anakinra, **522**
*Ana-Kit, 166*
Anal fissure, 65
Analeptics, 167
Analgesics, 217
  compound, 219
  non-opioid, 217
  NSAIDs, 217, 505
    anaesthesia, 640
    dental pain, 506
    elderly, 19
    orofacial pain, 506
    poisoning by, 29
    rheumatic diseases, 505
    topical, 531
  opioid, 222
    anaesthesia, 641
    cough suppressants, 171
    dependence on, 7
    diabetic neuropathy, 357
    diarrhoea, 51
    equivalent doses, 14
    neuropathic pain, 230
    palliative care, 14, 17
    poisoning by, 31
*Analog* preparations, 808, 815, 816
Anapen, *166*, 167
Anaphylaxis, 165
Anastrozole, 456, **457**
*Ancotil*, 311
Ancylostomiasis, 341
*Androcur*, 378
Androgens, 377
  malignant disease, 456
*Andropatch*, 378
*Anectine*, 645
*Anexate*, 646
*Angeliq*, 370
*Angeze* (isosorbide mononitrate) preparations, 108
*Angilol* (propranolol), 85
Angina
  aspirin, 105
  beta-blockers, 84
  calcium-channel blockers, 109
  dental practice, 21
  heparins, 105
  nitrates, 105
  potassium-channel activators, 115
  stable, 105
  statins, 105
  unstable, 105
Angioedema, 165, 364
  hereditary, 131, 165, 393
Angiotensin-converting enzyme inhibitors *see* ACE inhibitors
Angiotensin-II receptor antagonists, 103
*Angiox*, 123
*Angiozem CR* (diltiazem), 110
*Angitak*, 107
*Angitil* preparations, 110
Angular cheilitis, 561, 573, 598, 599
*Anhydrol Forte*, 609
Anistreplase, 130
Ankylosing spondylitis, 522
Anogenital warts, 592
Anorectics, 208
*Anquil*, 183
*Antabuse*, 260
Antacids
  alginates and, 38
  aluminium, 38
  bismuth, 38
  calcium, 38
  magnesium, 38
  simeticone and, 38
  sodium, 38
Antazoline, **538**
*Antepsin*, 48
Anterior uveitis, 539
Anthelmintics, 340
Anthracyclines, 432
Anthralin *see* Dithranol
Anthraquinones, 59
Anthrax, 273
  prophylaxis, 304
  treatment, 304
  vaccine, 613
Anti-androgens, 378
Anti-arrhythmic drugs, 77
Antibacterial policies, 267
Antibacterials, 266
  acne, 587, 589
  choice, 266
  diarrhoea, 51
  ear, 550
  eczema, 579
  eye, 534
  oral infections, 267
  prophylaxis, 272
  skin, 596
  summary of therapy, 268
  vaginal, 405
Antibiotic policies *see* Antibacterial policies, 267
Antibiotic sensitivity, 267
Antibiotic-associated colitis, **54**, 268, 291, 293, 303
Antibiotics *see* Antibacterials
Anticholinergic drugs *see* Antimuscarinics
Anticholinergic syndrome, 637
Anticholinesterases, 526
  anaesthesia, 645
Anticoagulant treatment booklets, 125
Anticoagulants
  oral, 124
    dental practice, 24
    reversal, 124
    surgery, 632
  parenteral, 119
Anticonvulsants *see* Antiepileptics
Anti-D ($Rh_0$) immunoglobulin, 629, 630
Antidepressants, 195
  choice, 196
  compound, 196
  panic disorders, 196
  poisoning by, 31
  *see also* Monoamine-oxidase inhibitors
  serotonin re-uptake inhibitors, 202
  surgery, 633
  tricyclic, 196
    diabetic neuropathy, 357
    enuresis, 421
    MAOIs with, 200
    migraine, 235
    urinary incontinence, 419
  withdrawal, 196

Antidiabetic drugs, 343
 insulin, 344
 oral, 351
Antidiarrhoeal drugs *see* Diarrhoea, 51, 476
Antidiuretic hormone, 384
 antagonist, 386
 inappropriate secretion, 386
Anti-emetics, 210
 cytotoxic therapy and, 428
 migraine, 235
Antiepileptics, 238
 surgery, 632
Antifibrinolytic drugs, 131
Antifungal drugs, 308
 anogenital, 405
 oropharyngeal, 560
 skin, 599
Antigiardial drugs, 337
Antihaemophilic fraction, human, 132
Antihepatitis B immunoglobulin, 629
Antihistamines, 161
 allergic emergencies, 165
 allergy, 161
 cough preparations, 171
 dental, 161
 eczema, 580
 eye, 538
 nasal allergy, 554
 nasal decongestants, 172
 nausea and vertigo, 210, **211**
 skin, 572
Antihypertensives, 97
 ACE inhibitors, 97
 adrenergic neurone blockers, 95
 alpha-blockers, 95
 angiotensin-II receptor antagonists, 103
 beta-blockers, 83
 calcium-channel blockers, 109
 centrally-acting, 94
 vasodilator, 92
Anti-inflammatory analgesics *see* Analgesics, NSAIDs
Antileprotic drugs, 302
Antilymphocyte globulin, 468
Antimalarials, 329, 518
Antimanic drugs, 193
Antimetabolites, 435
Antimigraine drugs, 231
Antimotility drugs, 51
Antimuscarinics
 antipsychotics and, 182
 bronchodilator, 148
 diabetic neuropathy, 357
 eye, 539
 gastro-intestinal, 41
 parkinsonism, 257
 premedication, 637
 quaternary ammonium, 41
 urinary tract, 419
Antineoplastic drugs, 427
 *see also* Cytotoxic drugs
Anti-oestrogens, 379, 456
Antiperspirants, 609
Antiplatelet drugs, 126
Antiprotozoal drugs, 329
Antipruritics, topical, 572
Antipsychotics, 181
 depot injections, 191
 equivalent doses
  depot, 191
  oral, 183
 high doses, 181
 mania, 193
 withdrawal, 181
Antipyretics, 218
Antirabies immunoglobulin, 629
Antiretrovirals, 314, 322
Antiseptics, 606
 ACBS, 820
 lozenges, 562
 mouthwashes, 562
 sprays, oropharynx, 562
 vaginal preparations, 406
Antiserum, 613, 627
Antispasmodics, 41
Antitetanus immunoglobulin, 629
Antithrombin III concentrate, **132**
Antithrombin III, Dried, 132
Antithyroid drugs, 360
Antituberculous drugs, 297
Antitussives, 171
Antivaricella-zoster immunoglobulin, 629
Antivenoms, 36
Antiviral drugs, 314
 eye, 536
 mouth, 562
 skin, 601
*Antizol*, 34
*Anturan*, 525
*Anugesic-HC*, 64
*Anusol* preparations, 65
Anxiety, 177
 antipsychotics, 181
 chronic, 196
Anxiolytics, 173, **177**
 anaesthesia, 638
 benzodiazepines, 178
 poisoning by, 32
 withdrawal, 173
*Anzemet*, 215
APD *see* Disodium pamidronate
Aphthous ulcers, 558
*Apidra*, 347
Aplastic anaemia, 468
*APO-go*, 254
Apomorphine, 254
 erectile dysfunction, **425**
 Parkinson's disease, 250, 251, **253**
Appetite stimulants, 499
Appetite suppressants, 208
Applications, definition, 566
Apraclonidine, 542, **547**
Aprepitant, 211, **216**, 428
*Apresoline*, 93
*Aprinox* (bendroflumethiazide), 72
*Aproten*, 801
Aprotinin, **131**
*Aprovel*, 103
*Aptivus*, 321
*Aquacel* products, 825
*Aquadrate*, 569
*Aquaflo*, 824
*Aquaform*, 824
*Aquasept*, 608
Aqueous cream, 568
*Aquilon*, 153
Arachis oil, 61
 cradle cap, 595
 enema, 61
 presence of, 2, 165
*Aranesp* preparations, 469
*Arava*, 520
*Arcoxia*, 510
*Aredia Dry Powder*, 389
Arginine supplement, 801
Argipressin *(Pitressin)*, 385
*Aricept*, 264
*Aridil* (co-amilofruse), 76
*Arilvax*, 627
*Arimidex*, 457
Aripiprazole, 187, **188**
*Arixtra*, 124
*Arnott*, 801
*Aromasin*, 458
Aromatase inhibitors, 457
*Arpicolin*, 257
*Arret* (loperamide), 52
Arrhythmias, 77
 beta-blockers, 84
 dental practice, 23
 poisoning and, 27
 supraventricular, 69, 78
 ventricular, 78
Arsenic trioxide, **440**
 infusion table, 791
*Artelac SDU*, 546
Artemether, 329
 lumefantrine with, **333**
Arterial occlusion, 124
Arteritis, giant cell, 514
Arteritis, temporal, 514
Artesunate, 329
*Arthrease*, 505
Arthritis, 504
 juvenile idiopathic, 516
 psoriatic, 516
 rheumatoid, 504
 septic, 270
*Arthrofen* (ibuprofen), 507
*Arthrotec* preparations, 509
*Arthroxen* (naproxen), 512
Articaine, 647
Artificial saliva, 564
*Arythmol*, 82
*AS Saliva Orthana*, 564
5-ASA, 54
*Asacol* preparations, 54, 55
*Asasantin Retard*, 128
*Ascabiol* (benzyl benzoate), 603
Ascaricides, 341
Ascaris, 341
*Ascensia* products, 350, 358
Ascorbic acid, **495**, 496
 acidification of urine, 422
 iron excretion, 470
*Asendis*, 198
*Aserbine*, 609
*Ashbourne Emollient Medicinal Bath Oil*, 570
*Asilone* preparations, 39
*Askina*, 825
*Asmabec* preparations, 156
*Asmanex*, 159
*Asmasal* preparations, 146
Asparaginase, 441
Aspartame, 487
 presence of, 2

Index

*Aspav*, 220
Aspergillosis, 308
Aspirin, 218
 analgesia, 219, 506
 angina, 105
 antiplatelet, 126, **127**
 cerebrovascular, 127
 dipyridamole with, 128
 metoclopramide with, 231
 migraine, 231
 myocardial infarction, 126, 129
 papaveretum with, 220
 preparations, 219
  antiplatelet, 127
  compound, 220
 rheumatic disease, **514**
Asplenia
 *Haemophilus influenzae* type b (Hib)
  prophylaxis, 272
  vaccine, 616
 influenza vaccine, 619
 malaria, 331
 meningococcal vaccine, 621
 pneumococcal infection, 272
 pneumococcal vaccine, 623
 vaccines and, 612
Asthma, 140, 144
 $beta_2$ agonists, 144
 emergency treatment, 143
  dental practice, 21
 exercise-induced, 144
 nocturnal, 144
 pregnancy, 143
 prophylaxis, 154, 159
Astringents
 ear, 550
 skin, 606
*AT-10*, 497
*Atarax*, 164
Atazanavir, 315, **319**
*Atenix* (atenolol) preparations, 85
*AtenixCo* (co-tenidone), 86
Atenolol, **85**
 chlortalidone with, 86
 co-amilozide with, 86
 infusion table, 791
 nifedipine with, 86
 *see also* Beta-adrenoceptor blocking drugs
Athlete's foot, 599
*Atimos Modulite*, 147
*Ativan* (lorazepam), 179
Atomoxetine, 206, **207**
Atonic seizures, 238
Atorvastatin, 135, **136**
Atosiban, 402, **403**
 infusion table, 791
Atovaquone, **339**
 malaria, 329, 335
 pneumocystis pneumonia, 339
 proguanil with, 335
Atracurium, **643**
 infusion table, 792
*Atrauman*, 828
Atrial fibrillation, 69, **77**, 124
Atrial flutter, 78
Atropine sulphate, 41, 637
 anticholinesterases and, 645
 antispasmodic, 41
 bradycardia, 78, 637
 cardiopulmonary resuscitation, 119
 eye, 540
 myocardial infarction, 78
 organophosphorus poisoning, 36
 premedication, 637
*Atrovent* preparations, 149
Attention deficit hyperactivity disorder, 206
Atypical antipsychotics, 187
 prolactin elevation, 187
*Audax*, 553
*Augmentin* preparations, 277, 278
Auranofin, 516, **517**
*Aureocort*, 579
Aurothiomalate, 516, **517**
*Autolet* devices, 350
*Autopen*, 350
*Avance* products, 824
*Avandamet*, 355
*Avandia*, 355
*Avastin*, 440
*Avaxim*, 617
*Aveeno* preparations, 568, 570
*Avelox*, 306
*Aviral*, 602
*Avloclor*, 334
Avobenzone, 593, 594
*Avoca*, 592
*Avodart*, 379
*Avomine*, 212
*Avonex*, 454
*Axid*, 46
*Axsain*, 532
*Azactam*, 284
*Azamune* (azathioprine), 448
Azathioprine, 436, **447**, 448
 eczema, 585
 inflammatory bowel disease, 53
 infusion table, 792
 myasthenia gravis, 527
 preparations, 448
 rheumatic disease, 519
 transplant rejection, 448
Azelaic acid, 587
Azelastine, **538**
 eye, 538
 nose, 554
Azidothymidine, 318
*Azilect*, 256
Azithromycin, 289, **290**, 291, 534
*Azopt*, 544
AZT, 318
Aztreonam, 283, **284**
 infusion table, 792

# B

*Babyhaler*, 152
Bacillus Calmette-Guérin
 bladder instillation, 454
 vaccines, 613, 614
Bacitracin
 eye, 536
 neomycin with, 597
 polymyxin with, 597
Back pain, 505
Baclofen, **528**
 palliative care, 15
*Baclospas* (baclofen), 528
Bacterial vaginosis, 302
*Bacteroides fragilis* infections, 278, 292, 303
*Bactigras*, 828
*Bactroban*, 597
*Bactroban Nasal*, 558
*Baker's Delight*, 801
BAL, 34
Balanced Salt Solution, 547
Baldness
 cytotoxic drugs, 429
 male-pattern, 596
*Balneum* preparations, 569, 570
Balsalazide, 53, **54**
*Bambec*, 147
Bambuterol, 147
Bandages, 830
 Adhesive, 832
 Cohesive, 833
 Compression, 831, 832, 833
 Conforming, 830
 Medicated, 833
 Non-extensible, 830
 Support, 831
 Tubular, 830
*Baratol*, 95
Barbiturates, **180**
 anaesthesia, 633
 regulations, 7
*Barkat*, 801
Barrier preparations, 571
Basal cell carcinoma, 592, 594
Basiliximab, **449**
 infusion table, 792
Bath additives
 antimicrobial with, 570
 coal tar, 583
 emollient, 570
*Baxan*, 280
BCG bladder instillation, 454
BCG vaccines, 613
*B-D Lancer*, 350
*BD Micro-Fine* products, 350, 351
*BD Safe-clip*, 351
Becaplermin, 609
*Beclazone* (beclometasone) preparations, 155, 156, 157
*Becloforte* preparations, 157
Beclogen, *555*
Beclometasone dipropionate
 asthma, 154, 155, 156, 157
 nasal allergy, 555
 skin, 576
Beclomethasone dipropionate *see* Beclometasone dipropionate
*Becodisks*, 156, 157
*Beconase* preparations, 555
*Becotide* preparations, 156
*Bedranol SR* (propranolol), 85
Bedsores, 571
Bee sting allergy preparations, 165
Beeswax, excipient, 567
*Begrivac*, 619
Belladonna, 41
Bemiparin, **121**
*Benadryl* preparations, 162

Bendrofluazide *see* Bendroflumethiazide, 72
Bendroflumethiazide, **72**
  hypercalciuria, 489
  potassium with, 77
  timolol with, 89
*BeneFIX* (factor IX fraction), 132
*Benerva* (thiamine), 494
Benign fibrocystic breast disease, 393
Benoxinate *see* Oxybuprocaine, **545**
Benperidol, **183**
*Benquil*, 183
*Benuryl* (probenecid), 525
Benzalkonium
  cetrimide with, 571
  chlorhexidine with, 569
  dimeticone with, 571
*Benzamycin*, 587
Benzatropine, **257**
Benzhexol *see* Trihexyphenidyl
Benzocaine, 651
Benzodiazepines, 173
  anaesthesia, 638
  antagonist, 646
  anxiolytics, 178
  epilepsy, 247
  hypnotics, 174
  mania, 193
  muscle spasm, 528
  poisoning by, 32
  withdrawal, 173
Benzoic acid ointment, compound, 599
Benzoin tincture, compound, 170
Benzoyl peroxide
  acne, 587
    clindamycin with, 587
    erythromycin with, 587
    hydroxyquinoline with, 587
Benzthiazide, 72
  triamterene with, 76
Benztropine *see* Benzatropine, **257**
Benzydamine, 559
  mouth, 559
Benzyl alcohol, presence of, 2, 567
Benzyl benzoate, 602, **603**
Benzylpenicillin, 273, **274**
  infusion table, 792
  injection, 274
Beractant, **168**
*Beriate P* (factor VIII fraction), 132
$Beta_2$ agonists, 144
*Beta-Adalat*, 86
Beta-adrenoceptor blocking drugs, 83
  angina, 84
  anxiety, 180
  arrhythmias, 79, 84
  eye, **540**
  heart failure, 84, 97
  hypertension, 83
  migraine, 235
  myocardial infarction, 84, 129
  poisoning by, 32
  thyrotoxicosis, 84, 360
  verapamil and, 114
Beta-adrenoceptor stimulants
  asthma, 144
  premature labour, 402
Beta-blockers *see* Beta-adrenoceptor blocking drugs
*Betacap*, 576
*Beta-Cardone*, 89
*Betadine*
  mouthwash, 563
  shampoo, 595
  skin, 607
  vaginal, 406
*Betaferon*, 454
*Betagan*, 541
Betahistine, 211, **217**
*Betaject Light* (interferon beta-1b), 454
Beta-lactamases, 273
*Betaloc* preparations, 88
Betamethasone, 362, 364, **365**
Betamethasone dipropionate, 576
  calcipotriol with, 582
  clotrimazole with, 577
  salicylic acid with, 576
Betamethasone sodium phosphate, 551, 555
  infusion table, 792
  preparations, 365
    ear, 551
    eye, 537
    nose, 555, 558
Betamethasone valerate
  skin, 576
    fusidic acid with, 577
    neomycin with, 576
*Beta-Prograne*, 85
Betaxolol, eye, 541
Bethanechol
  laxative, 59
  urinary retention, 418, **419**
*Betim*, 89
*Betnelan*, 365
*Betnesol*, 365
  ear, 551
  eye, 537
  nose, 555
*Betnesol-N*
  ear, 551
  eye, 537
  nose, 558
*Betnovate* preparations
  skin, 576
*Betoptic*, 541
*Bettamousse*, 576
Bevacizumab, **440**
  infusion table, 792
Bexarotene, **440**
Bezafibrate, **134**, 135
*Bezalip* preparations, 135
*Bi-Aglut*, 801
*Biatain* products, 823
Bicalutamide, **459**
Bicarbonate
  intravenous, 479
  oral, 477
  *see also* Sodium bicarbonate
*BiCNU*, 431
Bifonazole, 600
Biguanides, 353
Bilharziasis, 341
Biliary-tract infection, 268
Bimatoprost, **542**
*BiNovum*, 411
*Bioclusive*, 827
*Biofilm S*, 825
*Bioplex*, 559
*Biorphen*, 257
*Biotène Oralbalance*, 564
Biotin, 13, 494
*BioXtra*, 564
Biphosphonates *see* Bisphosphonates
Bipolar disorder, 193
*Bipranix* (bisoprolol), 86
Birthmarks, ACBS, 820
Bisacodyl, 59
Bismuth chelate, 47
Bismuth subgallate, 64
Bisoprolol, **86**
  *see also* Beta-adrenoceptor blocking drugs
Bisphosphonates, 386, 388
  breast cancer, 457
  hypercalcaemia, 489
Bites
  animal, 270
  human, 270
  snake, 36
Bitters, 499
Bivalirudin, **123**
  infusion table, 792
Bladder
  blood clot dissolution, 423
  irrigations, 422
    cytotoxic, 423
*Blenderm*, 834
*Bleo-Kyowa* (bleomycin), 433
Bleomycin, **433**
  infusion table, 792
Blepharitis, 534
Blepharospasm, 259
*Blisterfilm*, 827
Blood incompatibilities, 789
Blood products, 132, 133
Blue line webbing, 832
*BM-Accutest*, 358
Body-surface, dosage and, 13
Body-weight, dosage and, 13
Boils, 605
*Bondronat*, 390
Bone metabolism, drugs affecting, 386
Bone tumours, analgesia, 218
*Bonefos*, 390
Bone-marrow suppression, cytotoxic drugs, 429
*Bonjela* preparations (choline salicylate), 560
*Bonviva*, 390
*Boots:* Threadworm Treatment (mebendazole), 340
Borderline substances *see* ACBS
Bortezomib, **440**
Bosentan, **92**
*Botox*, 259
Botulinum A toxin, 259
Botulinum A toxin-haemagglutinin complex, 259
  hyperhidrosis, 609
Botulinum antitoxin, 614
Botulinum B toxin, **259**
Botulism antitoxin, 614
Bowel
  cleansing solutions, 63
  fistulas, ACBS, 816
  irrigation, 28
  sterilisation, 288
Bradycardia, 78
  anaesthesia, 637
Bran, 58
Brand names, symbol, 1
*Brasivol*, 589

- Breast cancer, 433, 436, 446, **456**
  - bone metastases, 388
- Breast disease, benign, 391
- Breast pain, 392, **396**
- Breast-feeding, prescribing during, 776
- *Brevibloc*, 87
- *Brevinor*, 411
- *Brevoxyl*, 587
- *Brexidol*, 513
- *Bricanyl* preparations, 146, 147
- Brimonidine, 542, **543**
  - timolol with, 543
- Brinzolamide, **543**, 544
- *BritLofex*, 263
- *Broflex*, 258
- *Brolene*, 536
- Bromocriptine, 391, **392**
  - acromegaly, 391
  - breast disease, benign, 391
  - breast pain, 396
  - galactorrhoea, 391
  - hypogonadism, 392
  - lactation suppression, 392
  - neuroleptic malignant syndrome, 182
  - parkinsonism, 250, **254**
  - preparations, 392
  - prolactinoma, 392
- Bronchiectasis, 170
- Bronchitis, 170, 268
  - bronchodilators, 143
- Bronchodilators
  - adrenoceptor agonist, 144
  - antimuscarinic, 148
  - surgery, 632
  - sympathomimetic, 144
  - theophylline, 149
- Bronchospasm, 144
- Brucellosis, 285, 301
- *Brufen* preparations, 507
- Brugia malayi, *342*
- Bruxism, 218
- BSA, 13
- *Buccastem*, 213
- Buclizine, 231
- *Budenofalk*, 56
- Budesonide, 157
  - asthma, 154, **157**
  - Crohn's disease, 56
  - croup, 143
  - inflammatory bowel disease, 53
  - nasal allergy, 555
  - nasal polyps, 555
  - with formoterol, 157
- Bumetanide, 73, **74**
  - amiloride with, 76
  - infusion table, 792
  - potassium with, 77
- Bupivacaine, **649**
  - adrenaline with, 649
- Buprenorphine, 225, 263
  - intra-operative analgesia, 225
  - opioid dependence, 263
  - pain, 222, **225**
  - premedication, 225
- Bupropion, 261
- *Burinex* preparations, 74, 76, 77
- Burns, infected, 597
- *Buscopan* preparations (hyoscine butylbromide), 42
- Buserelin, 395, 459
  - endometriosis, 395
  - IVF, 395
  - prostate cancer, 458, **459**
- *Busilvex*, 431
- *Buspar*, 180
- Buspirone, **179**, 180
- Busulfan, 430, **431**
  - infusion table, 792
- Busulphan *see* Busulfan
- Butobarbital, 180
- Butobarbitone *see* Butobarbital, 180
- *BuTrans*, 225
- Butylated hydroxyanisole, excipient, 567
- Butylated hydroxytoluene, excipient, 567
- Butyrophenones, 182


# C


- $C_1$ esterase inhibitor, 165
- *Cabaser*, 254
- Cabergoline, 254, 393
  - hyperprolactinaemia, 391, **392**
  - parkinsonism, 250, **254**
- *Cacit*, 389, 489
- *Cacit D3*, 496
- *Cadesorb*, 825
- Cadexomer–iodine, 824
- *Caelyx*, 434
- *Cafergot*, 235
- Caffeine, 206, 219
- *Calaband*, 833
- Calamine, 572
  - coal tar with, 582
- *Calceos*, 496
- *Calcicard CR*, 110
- *Calcichew*, 489
- *Calcichew D3*, 496
- *Calcichew D3 Forte*, 496
- Calciferol, 496
- *Calcijex*, 497
- *Calciparine*, 120
- Calcipotriol, 580, **581**, 582
  - betamethasone dipropionate with, 582
- Calcitonin (salmon), 386, **387**, 489
  - infusion table, 792
- Calcitriol, 386, 496, **497**
  - psoriasis, 580, 581, **582**
- Calcium
  - colecalciferol with, 496
- Calcium acetate, 492
- Calcium alginate dressings, 822
- Calcium and ergocalciferol tablets, **496**
- Calcium and vitamin D tablets, 496
- Calcium balance, maintenance, 387
- Calcium carbonate, 389, 491, 492
  - antacid, 38
- Calcium chloride, 488, 489
- Calcium folinate, **429**, 467
  - infusion table, 792
- Calcium gluconate, 489
  - infusion table, 792
- Calcium intolerance, ACBS, 816
- Calcium lactate tablets, 489
- Calcium leucovorin *see* Calcium folinate
- Calcium levofolinate, **429**, 430
  - infusion table, 792
- Calcium phosphate, 496
- Calcium polystyrene sulphonate, 475
- *Calcium Resonium*, 475
- Calcium salts, 488, 491
- Calcium supplements, 489
  - vitamin D and, 496
- *Calcium-500*, 489
- Calcium-channel blockers, 109
  - angina, 109
  - hypertension, 109
  - poisoning by, 32
- *Calcium-Sandoz*, 489
- *Calcort*, 366
- *Calfovit D3*, 496
- Calluses, 591
- *Calmurid*, 569
- *Calmurid HC*, 575
- *Calogen*, 801
- *Caloreen*, 801
- *Calpol* (paracetamol) preparations, 220
- *Calprofen* (ibuprofen), 507
- *Calshake*, 801
- *Camcolit* preparations, 194
- Camouflaging preparations, 594
- *Campral EC*, 260
- *Campto*, 446
- Campylobacter enteritis, 268, 289
- *Cancidas*, 310
- Candesartan, 103
- Candidiasis, 308
  - intestinal, 309
  - oropharyngeal, 308, 560
  - perianal, 64
  - skin, 599
  - systemic, 308
  - vaginal, **405**
  - vulval, 405
- Candidosis see Candidiasis
- *Canesten*
  - *AF*, 600
  - anogenital, 405
  - ear, 552
  - *HC*, 575
  - *Oral* (fluconazole), 311
  - skin, 600
- Cannabis, regulations, 7
- *Canusal*, 123
- *Capasal*, 595
- *Capastat*, 299
- Capecitabine, 435, **436**
- *Caplenal* (allopurinol), 525
- *Capoten*, 99
- *Capozide*, 99
- Capreomycin, **299**
- *Caprilon*, 801
- *Caprin*
  - analgesia, 219
  - cardiovascular, 127
- Caps, contraceptive, 417
- Capsaicin, 532
  - diabetic neuropathy, 357, 532
  - neuropathic pain, 230
  - osteoarthritis, 505, 532
  - postherpetic neuralgia, 231, 532
- *Capsuvac*, 60
- *Capto-co* (co-zidocapt), 99


Index

Captopril, **99**
hydrochlorothiazide with, 99
*see also* ACE inhibitors
*Carace* preparations, 101
*Caralpha* preparations, 101
Carbachol
glaucoma, 544
*Carbagen SR*, 239
*Carbaglu*, 502
*Carbalax*, 63
Carbamazepine
bipolar disorder, 193
diabetes insipidus, 384
diabetic neuropathy, 357
epilepsy, **238**, 239
poisoning, elimination, 28
preparations, 239
trigeminal neuralgia, 231
Carbaryl, **603**, 604
Carbenoxolone
mouth, **559**
Carbimazole, 360, **361**
Carbocisteine, **170**
*Carbo-Dome*, 583
*CarboFLEX*, 828
Carbohydrate malabsorption, ACBS, 816
Carbomers, 546
*Carbomix*, 28
Carbon monoxide poisoning, 35
*Carbonet*, 828
Carbonic anhydrase inhibitors, 77
glaucoma, 543
*Carbopad VC*, 828
Carboplatin, **443**
infusion table, 792
Carboprost, 399
Carbuncle, 605
Carcinoid tumour, 452, 461
*Cardene* preparations, 112
Cardiac arrest, **119**, 479
Cardiac arrest chart, inside back cover
Cardiac glycosides, 69
arrhythmias, 78
Cardiac problems, dental practice, 21
Cardiac *see also* Heart
*Cardicor*, 86
*Cardilate MR*, 113
*Cardioplen XL* (felodipine), 111
Cardiopulmonary resuscitation, 119
*Cardura* preparations, 95
Carglumic acid, 502
*Carisoma*, 529
Carisoprodol, **529**
Carmellose, 558, **559**
eye, **546**
gelatin preparations, 559
Carmustine, **431**
infusion table, 792
Carnitine, 500
Carnitine palmitoyl transferase deficiency, ACBS, 816
*Carnitor*, 500
*Carobel, Instant*, 801
Carpal tunnel syndrome, 515
Carteolol, **541**
Carticaine *see* Articaine, 647
Carvedilol, 83, **86**
*see also* Beta-adrenoceptor blocking drugs
*Carylderm*, 604
Cascara, 59
*Casilan-90*, 802
*Casodex*, 459
Caspofungin, 308, 309, **310**
infusion table, 792
Castor oil, 59
*Catapres*, 94
Catarrh, vernal, 538
Catheter maintenance, 423
Catheter patency solutions
chlorhexidine, 423
sodium chloride, 423
solution G, 423
solution R, 423
Cautionary and advisory labels, 836 *inside back cover*
counselling, 836
list of products, 838
NCL, 836
original packs, 836
*Caverject* preparations, 424
*Cavi-Care*, 824
*CCNU* (lomustine), 432
*Ceanel Concentrate*, 595
*Cedocard Retard*, 107
Cefaclor, **280**
Cefadroxil, **280**
Cefalexin, **280**, 281
Cefixime, 280, **281**
Cefotaxime, 279, **281**
infusion table, 792
Cefpirome, 280, **281**
Cefpodoxime, 280, **281**, 282
Cefprozil, 280, **282**
Cefradine, 279, 280, **282**
infusion table, 792
*Cefrom*, 281
Ceftazidime, 279, **282**, 283
eye drops, 545
infusion table, 792
Ceftriaxone, 279, **283**
infusion table, 792
Cefuroxime, 279, **283**
eye drops, 545
infusion table, 792
Cefuroxime axetil, 280, 283
*Cefzil*, 282
*Celance*, 255
*Celebrex*, 508
Celecoxib, 506, **508**
*Celectol*, 87
*Celevac*, 59
Celiprolol, 83, **87**
*see also* Beta-adrenoceptor blocking drugs
*CellCept*, 448
*Cellona*, 832
Cellulitis, 270
*Celluvisc*, 546
Central nervous system stimulants, 206
*Centyl K*, 77
Ceph... *see also* Cef...
Cephalosporins, 279
*Ceporex*, 281
*Ceprotin* (protein C concentrate), 133
*Cepton*, 606
*Cerazette*, 414
Cerebral oedema, 364
*Cerezyme*, 501
*Cernevit*, 483
*Cerubidin* (daunorubicin), 433
*Cerumol*, 554
Cetirizine, 161, **162**
Cetostearyl alcohol, excipient, 567
*Cetraben*, 568, 570
Cetrimide, 571, 605, 606, **607**
benzalkonium with, 571
chlorhexidine with, 607
dimeticone with, 571
Cetrorelix, **393**
*Cetrotide*, 393
Cetuximab, **441**
Cetyl alcohol, excipient, 567
CFCs, 144, 154
Chamomile extract, 568
Charcoal, activated
dressings, 828
poisoning, 28
*Charcodote*, 28
CHD *see* Coronary heart disease
Cheilitis, angular, 561, 573, 598, 599
*Chemydur*, 108
Chicken meat, comminuted, 802
Chickenpox, 322, 628
Chilblains, 610
Children
adverse reactions, 12
medicine storage, 3
prescribing for, 12
Child-resistant containers, 3
*Chirocaine*, 650
Chlamydia, 285
eye, 534
genital, 269
*Chloractil* (chlorpromazine), 183
Chloral betaine *see* Cloral betaine, 177
Chloral hydrate, **176**
Chlorambucil, 430, **431**
Chloramphenicol, **292**, 293
ear, 550, **552**
eye, 534, **535**
infusion table, 792
skin, hydrocortisone with, 589
Chlordiazepoxide, 178, **179**
Chlorhexidine, 606
benzalkonium with, 569
bladder infections, 422
cetrimide with, 607
dressing, gauze, 828
hydrocortisone and nystatin with, 575
mouth, 558, 562, **563**
neomycin with, 558
nose, 558
skin disinfection, 606, 607
dressing, 827
dusting powder, 606
Chlorine poisoning, 35
Chlormethiazole *see* Clomethiazole
Chlorocresol, excipient, 567
Chlorofluorocarbon propellants, 144, 154
*Chlorohex*, 563
*Chloromycetin*, 535
Chloroquine
infusion table, 792
malaria prophylaxis, 331–332, **333**
malaria treatment, 328, **333**
preparations, 334
rheumatic disease, 516, 519
Chloroquine phosphate, 334


Index

Chloroquine sulphate, 334
Chloroxylenol, 609
Chlorphenamine, 161, **163**
Chlorpheniramine *see* Chlorphenamine, 161, **163**
Chlorpromazine, 182, **183**
hiccup, 183
nausea, **212**
nausea and vertigo, 210
preparations, 183
psychosis, 182
Chlorpropamide, **352**
diabetes insipidus, 384
Chlorquinaldol
hydrocortisone with, 575
Chlortalidone, **72**
atenolol with, 86
diabetes insipidus, 384
triamterene with, 76
Chlorthalidone *see* Chlortalidone
Cholecalciferol *see* Colecalciferol
Cholera vaccine, 614
travel, 631
Cholestyramine *see* Colestyramine
Choline, 494
Choline salicylate
dental gel, 559, **560**
ear drops, 553
Cholinergic crises, 526
Cholinesterase inhibitors, 526, 645
*Choragon*, 381
Choreas, 258
Choriocarcinoma, 435
Choriogonadotropin alfa, **381**
Chorionic gonadotrophin, **380**, 381
Chronic obstructive pulmonary disease, 143, 148, 154, 167
oxygen, 168, 169
*Cialis*, 426
*Cica-Care*, 826
*Cicafem*, 590
*Cicatrin* preparations, 597
Ciclesonide, **158**
Ciclosporin, **449**, 450
aplastic anaemia, 468
eczema, **585**
immunosuppression, **449**, 450
infusion table, 792
nephrotic syndrome, 449
psoriasis, **585**
rheumatic disease, 519, **520**
ulcerative colitis, 53
Cidofovir, **324**, 325
infusion table, 792
*Cidomycin*, 288
Cigarette smoking, 260
Cilastatin, 284
imipenem with, 284
infusion table, 796
Cilazapril, **99**
*see also* ACE inhibitors
*Cilest*, 411
Cilostazol, 115, **116**
*Ciloxan*, 535
Cimetidine, **45**
infusion table, 793
preparations, 45
Cinacalcet, 387, 489, **490**
*Cinaziere* (cinnarizine), 212
Cinchocaine, 64, 65
Cinnarizine, 116, 212
nausea and vertigo, 211
vascular disease, 116
*Cipralex*, 203
*Cipramil*, 202
Ciprofibrate, 134, **135**
Ciprofloxacin, 304, **305**
ear, 553
eye, 534, **535**
travellers' diarrhoea, 51
*Ciproxin*, 305
Cisatracurium, **643**
infusion table, 793
Cisplatin, 443, **444**
infusion table, 793
Citalopram, **202**
*Citanest*, 650
*Citanest with Octapressin*, 650
*Citramag*, 63
Cladribine, 435, **436**
infusion table, 793
*Claforan*, 281
Clariteyes, *539*
Clarithromycin, 289, **291**
infusion table, 793
*Clarosip*, 291
Classification changes, ix
Clavulanic acid, 275
amoxicillin with, 275, 277
infusion table (co-amoxiclav), 793
ticarcillin with, 278, 279
infusion table, 799
*Cleanlet Fine*, 350
Cleansers, skin, 606
*Clearsore*, 602
Clemastine, **163**
*Clexane* preparations, 122
*Climagest*, 370
*Climaval*, 372
*Climesse*, 370
Clindamycin, 291, **292**
acne, 587, 588
infusion table, 793
benzoyl peroxide with, 587
malaria treatment, 328
oral infections, 292
pneumocystis pneumonia, 339
vaginal infections, 406
*Clinimix* preparations, 484
*ClinOleic*, 484
*Clinipak* syringe, 351
*Clinipore*, 834
*Clinisorb*, 828
*Clinistix*, 359
*Clinitar*, 583
shampoo, 595
*Clinitek Microalbumin*, 359
*Clinitest*, 359
*Clinoril*, 513
*Clinutren* preparations, 802
Clioquinol
ear, 550, 551, **552**
skin
betamethasone with, 576
fluocinolone with, 578
hydrocortisone with, 575
*Clivarine*, 122
CLL *see* Leukaemia
chronic lymphocytic
Clobazam, 178, 238, **247**
epilepsy, 247
Clobetasol propionate, 577
neomycin with, 577
nystatin with, 577
Clobetasone butyrate
skin, 577
tetracycline with, 577
Clodronate sodium *see* Sodium clodronate
Clofazimine, **302**
Clomethiazole, **177**
alcohol withdrawal, 177, 260
*Clomid*, 380
Clomifene, 379, **380**
Clomiphene *see* Clomifene, 379, **380**
Clomipramine, 196, **198**
Clonazepam, 238, 247, 248
epilepsy, **247**
status epilepticus, 247, **248**
infusion table, 793
Clonidine, **94**, 236
hypertension, 94
menopausal flushing, 236, 368
migraine, 235, **236**
Tourette syndrome, 258
Clopamide, 72
pindolol with, 89
Clopidogrel, 126, **127**
*Clopixol*, 187, 193
*Clopixol Acuphase*, 187
*Clopixol Conc.*, 193
Cloral betaine, 177
*Clostridium botulinum*, 614
*Clostridium difficile*, 54
*Clotam*, 232
Clotrimazole, 309, 599
anogenital, 405
betamethasone dipropionate with, 577
ear, 552
hydrocortisone with, 575
skin, **599**, 600
Clozapine, 187, **188**, 189
*Clozaril*, 189
Cluster headache, 236
CMV, 324
Coal tar, 580, **582**
preparations, 582, 583
calamine with, 582
dithranol with, 584
hydrocortisone with, 583
salicylic acid with, 583
scalp, 583, 595, 596
zinc with, 583
Co-amilofruse, 76
Co-amilozide, 76
atenolol with, 86
timolol with, 89
Co-amoxiclav, 275, **277**, 278, 307
infusion table, 793
*CoAprovel*, 103
*Cobalin-H* (hydroxocobalamin), 467
*Coban*, 833
Co-beneldopa, **252**
*Co-Betaloc* preparations, 88
COC *see* Contraception, oral, combined, 407
Cocaine, 208
local anaesthesia, 651
poisoning by, 33

Co-careldopa, **252**, 253
 with entacapone, 253
Co-codamol preparations, 220, 221
Co-codaprin preparations, 220
*Cocois*, 583
Co-cyprindiol, **590**
Cod liver oil
 zinc oxide with, 571
*Codafen Continus*—discontinued, ix
*Codalax* preparations, 60
Co-danthramer preparations, 60
Co-danthrusate preparations, 60
Codeine, 52, 226
 cough suppressant, **171**
 diabetic neuropathy, 357
 diarrhoea, 51
 pain, 222, **226**
 preparations, 52, 226
  compound, 220, 231
  linctuses, 171
*Co-Diovan*, 104
*Codipar*, 221
Co-dydramol, 221
Coeliac disease, 488
 ACBS, 816
Co-fluampicil, 276, **278**
 infusion table, 793
Co-flumactone, 77
*Cogentin*, 257
*Colazide*, 54
Colchicine, **524**
Cold sores, 601
Colds
 decongestants, iii
  systemic nasal, 172
  topical nasal, 495
Colecalciferol, 496, **497**
 alendronic acid with, 388
*Colestid*, 134
Colestipol, 133, **134**
Colestyramine, **133**
 diarrhoea, 51, **67**
 hypercholesterolaemia, 133
 hyperlipidaemias, 133
 preparations, 134
 pruritus, 67
*Colief*, 802
*Colifoam*, 56
Colistimethate sodium
 infusion table, 793
Colistin, **295**, 296
 eye drops, 545
Colitis
 antibiotic-associated (pseudo-membranous), 54, 268, 293, 303
 ulcerative, 53
Collodion, 566
 flexible, 605
Colloid dressings, 825
Colloidal oatmeal, 568, 570
*Colofac* preparations (mebeverine), 42
*Colomycin*, 296
 powder—discontinued, ix
*Colpermin*, 43
Coma
 hyperglycaemic, 355
 hyperosmolar nonketotic, 355
 hypoglycaemic, 356
 hypothyroid, 359
 insulin, 355
 ketoacidotic, 355
Co-magaldrox, 39
*CombiDERM* products, 825
*Combigan*, 543
Combined hormonal contraceptives, 409
 *see also* Contraception
*Combivent*, 150
*Combivir*, 318
*Combur-3 Test*, 359
Co-methiamol, 221
*Comfeel* products, 825
*Comfifast*, 831
*Comfifoam*, 823
*Comfigrip*, 830
*Compact*, 358
Complementary medicine, 1
*Compleven*, 484
Compliance, 1
*Comprilan*, 832
*Comtess*, 254
*Concerta XL*, 208
Concordance, 1
*Condyline*, 593
Condylomata acuminata, 592, 593
Conforming bandage (synthetic), 830
Conjugated oestrogens
 HRT, 369, 370, 372
 vaginal, 404
Conjunctivitis, 270, 534
 allergic, 538
Conn's syndrome, 75
*Conotrane*, 571
Contact lenses, 548
Containers, child-resistant, 3
Contents, iii
*Contigen*, 419
Contraception, 407
 devices, 416
  contraceptive caps, 417
  contraceptive diaphragms, 417
 implants, 414, 415
 intra-uterine system, 415
 oral, 407
  combined, 407
  emergency, 412
  missed pill, 408, 413
  progestogen-only, 413
  starting routines, 410, 413
  surgery, **409**, 413, 632
  travel, 408
 parenteral, **414**
 perimenopausal, 369
 spermicidal, 415
 transdermal, 407, 410
  detached patch, 408
  starting routines, 410
*Contreet Foam* products, 824, 825
Controlled drugs, 7
 *see also* preparations identified by CD throughout BNF
 travel abroad, 8
Conversions, *inside back cover*
*Convulex*, 246
Convulsions
 dental practice, 22
 febrile, 250
 poisoning and, 28
 *see also* Epilepsy
*Coolie*, 824
*Copaxone*, 455
COPD *see* Chronic obstructive pulmonary disease
*Copegus*, 328
Co-phenotrope, 52
Co-prenozide, 88
Co-proxamol, 219, 221
 poisoning, 31
*Coracten* preparations, 113
*Cordarone X*, 80
*Cordilox* preparations, 114, 115
*Corgard*, 88
*Corlan*, 559
Corn flour, 802
Corn starch, 802
Corneal ulcers, 534, 536
Coronary heart disease
 angina, 105
 dental practice, 23
 myocardial infarction, 129
 prevention
  antiplatelet therapy, 126
  diabetes, 91
  dyslipidaemia, 136
  hypertension, 90
  non-drug treatment, 90
  obesity, 90
 risk assessment, *inside back cover*, 136
*Coro-Nitro Pump Spray*, 106
*Corsodyl* preparations, 563
Corticosteroids, 361, 362
 adrenal suppression, 362
 allergic emergencies, 165
 allergy, 364
  nasal, 554
 anaesthesia, 362, 632
 anaphylactic shock, 364
 aphthous ulcers, 558, **559**
 asthma, 154
  acute severe (table), 142
 blood disorders, 468
 breast-feeding, 364
 cancer, 448
 croup, 143
 ear, 550
 equivalent doses, 362
 eye, 534, 536
 gout, 524
 haemorrhoids, 64
 hypercalcaemia, 489
 immunosuppression, 448
 infections, 363
 inflammatory bowel disease, 53
 myasthenia gravis, 526, 527
 nose, 554
 neuropathic pain, 230
 osteoarthritis, 505
 pregnancy, 364
 proctitis, 56
 proctosigmoiditis, 56
 replacement therapy, 361
 rheumatic disease, 514
 septic shock, 364
 skin
  acne, 589
  eczema, 572, 579
  psoriasis, 573
  suitable quantities, 574
 surgery, 362
 thrombocytopenic purpura, 471
 ulcerative colitis, 56, 57


Index

Corticotrophin *see* Corticotropin, 380
Corticotropin, 380
Cortisol, 361
Cortisone acetate, 366
*Cosalgesic* (co-proxamol), 222
Co-simalcite [ingredient], 39
*Cosmegen Lyovac*, 433
*CosmoFer*, 466
*Cosmopor E*, 827
*Cosopt*, 544
*Cosuric* (allopurinol), 525
Co-tenidone, 86
*Cotfil*, 829
Co-triamterzide, 76
Co-trimoxazole, **296**
  infusion table, 793
  pneumocystis pneumonia, 339
Cotton,
  absorbent, 829
  bandages, 830, 831
Cough suppressants, 171
Coumarins, 124
Counter-irritants, 531
*Coverflex*, 831
Covering creams, 594
*Covermark* preparations, 594
*Coversyl* preparations, 101
*Cow & Gate Pepti see Pepti*, 811
*Cozaar* preparations, 104
Co-zidocapt, 99
Crab lice, 603
Cradle cap, 595
Cramps, nocturnal, 529
Creams
  definition, 566
  suitable quantities, 567
Creatinine clearance, dosage and, 745
*Creon* preparations, 67, 68
Crepe bandage, 831
  cotton, 831
*Crestor*, 137
Cretinism *see* Hypothyroidism, neonatal, 359
*Crinone*, 376
*Crinx*, 830
Crisantaspase, **441**
*Crixivan*, 319
Crohn's disease, 53
  ACBS, 818
*Cromogen* preparations, 159
Cromoglicate (*or* cromoglycate) *see* Sodium cromoglicate
Crotamiton, 572
  hydrocortisone with, 575
  scabies, 602
Croup, 143
Cryptococcosis, 308
*Crystacide*, 608
*Crystapen*, 274
CS gas *see* CS spray, 35
CS spray, 35
*Cuplex*, 591
*Curafoam* products, 823
*Curagel* products, 824
*Curasorb* products, 822
*Curatoderm*, 582
*Curosurf*, 168
Cushing's syndrome, 396
  corticosteroid-induced, 362
Cutaneous larva migrans, 342
*Cutilin*, 827
*Cutinova* products, 825
*Cutivate*, 578
*C-View*, 827
*CX Antiseptic Dusting Powder*, 606
Cyanides, poisoning by, 33
Cyanocobalamin, 467
Cyanokit, *34*
*Cyclimorph*, 225
Cyclizine, 211, **212**
*Cyclocaps*
  beclometasone, 156
  budesonide, 157
  salbutamol, 146
*Cyclogest*, 376
*Cyclohaler*
  beclometasone, 156
  budesonide, 157
  salbutamol, 146
Cyclopenthiazide, **72**, 73
  amiloride with, 76
  oxprenolol with, 88
Cyclopentolate, **540**
Cyclophosphamide, 430, **431**
  infusion table, 793
  rheumatic disease, 519
Cycloplegics, 539
*Cyclo-Progynova*, 370
Cycloserine, **299**, 300
Cyclosporin *see* Ciclosporin
*Cyklokapron*, 132
*Cymalon* (sodium citrate), 422
*Cymbalta*, 205
*Cymevene*, 325
Cyproheptadine, **163**
  migraine, 235
*Cyprostat*, 460
Cyproterone acetate, 378, 460
  acne, 590
  male hypersexuality, **378**
  malignant disease, **459**
*Cystagon*, 502
Cysteamine *see* Mercaptamine, **501**, 502
Cystic fibrosis, 67
  ACBS, 816
*Cysticide*, 341, 342
Cystinuria, 500
Cystitis, 422
  haemorrhagic, 430
  interstitial, 423
*Cystopurin* (potassium citrate), 422
*Cystrin*, 420
*Cytacon* (cyanocobalamin), 467
*Cytamen* (cyanocobalamin), 467
Cytarabine, 435, **436**
  infusion table, 793
Cytokine inhibitors
  Crohn's disease, 57
  rheumatoid arthritis, 521
Cytomegalovirus
  immunoglobulin, 629
  infections, 324, 536
*Cytotec*, 48
Cytotoxic drugs, 427
  alopecia, 429
  bladder instillation, 423
  bone-marrow suppression, 429
  dosage, 428
  extravasation, 428
  handling guidelines, 427
  hyperuricaemia, 428
  nausea and vomiting, 428
  pregnancy, 429
  regimens, 428
  thromboembolism, 429

# D

Dacarbazine, **441**
  infusion table, 793
Daclizumab, 449, **450**
  infusion table, 793
Dactinomycin, **433**
  infusion table, 793
*Daktacort*, 575
*Daktacort HC*, 575
*Daktarin*, 313
  *Gold*, 600
  oral gel, 562
  skin, 600
*Dalacin* preparations, 292
  acne, 588
  vaginal, 406
Dalfopristin, **295**
  quinupristin with
    infusion table, 798
*Dalivit*, 499
*Dalmane*, 175
Dalteparin, **121**
Danaparoid, **122**
  infusion table, 793
Danazol, **393**, 394, 396
*Dandrazol* preparations, 595
Dandruff, 595
*Danlax*, 60
*Danol*, 394
Danthron *see* Dantron, 59, 60
*Dantrium*, 529
  *Intravenous*, 647
Dantrolene, **528**, 529
  malignant hyperthermia, **646**
  muscle spasm, 528
  neuroleptic malignant syndrome, 183
Dantron, 59, 60
*Daonil*, 352
Dapsone, **302**
  dermatitis herpetiformis, 302
  leprosy, 302
  pneumocystis pneumonia, 339
  poisoning, elimination, 28
*Daraprim*, 336
Darbepoetin, **468**
Darbepoetin alfa, **468**, 469
Darier's disease, 581
Daunorubicin, **433**, 434
  infusion table, 793
*DaunoXome*, 434
*DDAVP*, 386
DDC *see* Zalcitabine, **317**, 318
DDI *see* Didanosine, **316**
De Vilbiss nebulisers, 153
*Deca-Durabolin*, 379

*Decan*, 483
*Decapeptyl SR*, 460
Decongestants
nasal, 557
*Decubal Clinic*, 568
Deep-vein thrombosis, 120, 124
DEET *see* Diethyltoluamide, 331
Defective medicines, 12
*Defenac* preparations, 508, 509
Deferiprone, **470**, 471
Deferoxamine *see* Desferrioxamine
Deflazacort, 362, **366**
*Delph*, 593
*Deltacortril Enteric* (prednisolone), 365
Deltaprim, *332*
*Deltastab*, 515
Demeclocycline, **286**
hyponatraemia, 386
Dementia, 264
*Demser*, 96
Demulcent cough preparations, 172
Dendritic ulcer, 536
*De-Nol* preparations, 47
Dental caries, 492
Dental Practitioners' Formulary, 851
Dental prescribing
anaesthesia
general, 633
local, 647
vasoconstrictors, 647
angular cheilitis, 561
anxiety, 174, 639
chronic facial pain, 231
denture stomatitis, 561
dry mouth, 564
endocarditis prophylaxis, 23, 271
fluoride, 492
herpes labialis, 322, 601
herpetic gingivostomatitis, 322
hypnotic, 174, 639
infections
bacterial, 267, 270, 598
fungal, 560, 599
prophylaxis, 271
viral, 322, 562, 601
medical emergencies, 20
medical problems, 23
nausea and vomiting, 161
neuropathic pain, 230
oral hygiene, 562
oral side-effects, 11
oral ulceration, 558
orofacial pain, 230
pain, 217, 218, 223, 506
postoperative, 218
panic attacks, 174, 639
postherpetic neuralgia, 231
premedication, 174, 639
sinusitis, 557
temporomandibular, dysfunction, 218
trigeminal neuralgia, 231
vitamin deficiency, 494
*Dentinox*
colic drops, 40
Dentomycin, *560*
Denture stomatitis, 561
*Denzapine*, 189
*Depakote*, 193
Dependence *see* Drug dependence
*Depixol* preparations, 184, 192
*DepoCyte*, 436
Depolarising muscle relaxants *see* Muscle relaxants
*Depo-Medrone*, 367, 515
*with Lidocaine*, 515
*Deponit*, 107
*Depo-Provera*, 414
contraception, 414
Depression, 195
antipsychotics, 181
manic, 193
*Derbac-M*, 604
*Dermabond*, 605
*Dermacare, Vaseline*, 569
*Dermacolor* preparations, 594
*Dermalo*, 570
*Dermamist*, 568
Dermatitis
ACBS, 820
herpetiformis, 302
*see also* Eczema
*Dermatix*, 826
Dermatophyte infections, 309
*Dermol* preparations, 569, 570
*Dermovate* preparations, 577
*Dermovate-NN*
ointment—discontinued, ix
*Deseril*, 236
*Desferal*, 471
Desferrioxamine, 32, **471**
eye, 545
infusion table, 793
iron overload, 470
poisoning, 32
Desflurane, **636**
Desloratadine, 161, **162**
Desloughing agents, 609
Desmopressin, 384, **385**, 386
fibrinolytic response, 384
haemophilia, 131
infusion table, 793
nocturnal enuresis, **385**, 421
von Willebrand's disease, 384
*Desmospray*, 386
*Desmotabs*, 386
Desogestrel contraception, 410, 411, 414
*Destolit*, 67
*Deteclo*, 285, 286
*Detrunorm*, 421
*Detrusitol* preparations, 421
Dexamethasone, 362, 364, **366**
croup, 143
ear, 551
eye, 537, 545
infusion table, 793
nausea and vertigo, 211
nausea and vomiting, 428
nose, 555
palliative care, 15, 16
rheumatic disease, 515
suppression test, 364
Dexamfetamine, 206, **207**
Dexamphetamine *see* Dexamfetamine
*Dexa-Rhinaspray Duo*, 555
*Dexedrine*, 207
Dexfenfluramine, 209
Dexibuprofen, 505, **508**
Dexketoprofen, 505, **508**
*Dexomon* preparations, 509
*Dexsol* (dexamethasone), 366
Dextran
eye, 546
intravenous infusions, 481
Dextromethorphan, 171
Dextropropoxyphene, 219
paracetamol with, 221
poisoning by, 31
Dextrose monohydrate *see* Glucose
*DF-118 Forte*, 226
*D-Gam*, 629
*DHC Continus*, 226
*diabact UBT*, 43
Diabetes insipidus, 384
diagnosis, 384
Diabetes mellitus, 344
diagnosis, 359
monitoring, 345
meters, 358
test strips, 358
Diabetic ketoacidosis, **355**, 477, 478
Diabetic nephropathy, 357
Diabetic neuropathy, 357
skin ulcers, 609
*Diabur Test-5000*, 359
*DIAGLYK* (gliclazide), 352
*Dialamine*, 802
*Dialar* (diazepam), 178
Dialysis, ACBS, 816
*Diamicron* preparations, 352
Diamorphine, 222, **226**
infusion table, 793
pain, 222
chronic, 15, 222
myocardial infarction, 129, 226
preparations, 226
pulmonary oedema, 226
*Diamox* preparations, 543
*Dianette*, 590
Diaphragms, contraceptive, 417
Diarrhoea, 51, 476
*Diasorb* (loperamide), 52
*Diastix*, 359
*Diazemuls* (diazepam), 179, 248
Diazepam, **178**
anaesthesia, 638, **639**
anxiety, 178
febrile convulsions, 250
hypnotic, 175
infusion table, 793
muscle spasm, 218, 528, 529
palliative care, 15
preparations, 178, 248
status epilepticus, 247, **248**
temporomandibular joint pain, 218
*Diazepam Rectubes*, 179, 248
Diazoxide, **92**
hypertension, 92
hypoglycaemia, **356**, 357
*Dibenyline*, 96
Diclofenac, 508
actinic keratosis, 594
eye, 548
gout, 524
infusion table, 794
postoperative pain, 640
preparations, 508, 509
misoprostol with, 509
topical, 531, 594
rheumatic disease, 505, **508**
ureteric colic, 422, 508

Index

*Dicloflex* preparations, 508, 509
*Diclomax* preparations, 509
*Diclovol* preparations, 508, 509
*Diclozip* (diclofenac), 508
Dicobalt edetate, 33, **34**
*Diconal*, 227
Dicyclomine *see* Dicycloverine
Dicycloverine, **41**
*Dicynene*, 131
Didanosine, **316**
*Didronel* preparations, 389
*Dietary Specialities*, 802
Diethylcarbamazine, 342
Diethylstilbestrol, **455**, 459
Diethyltoluamide, 331
*Differin*, 588
*Difflam*
  oral rinse, 559
  spray, 559
*Diflucan* preparations, 311
Diflucortolone valerate, 577
Diflunisal, 509
  pain, 505, 506
  rheumatic disease, 505, **509**
*Diftavax*, 616
*Digibind*, 71
Digitoxin, **70**
Digoxin, 69, **70**
  heart failure, 97
  infusion table, 794
  poisoning, 70
Digoxin-specific antibody fragments, **70**, 71
  infusion table, 794
Dihydrocodeine, 222, **226**
  paracetamol with, 221
  preparations, 226
Dihydropyridine calcium-channel blockers, 109
Dihydrotachysterol, 496, **497**
Dihydroxycholecalciferol, 496, 497, 582
*Dilcardia SR*, 110
Diloxanide furoate, **337**
Diltiazem, 109, **110**, 111
  poisoning by, 32
  *see also* Calcium-channel blockers
*Dilzem* preparations, 110, 111
Dimercaprol, **34**
Dimethicone, activated *see* Simeticone, 38, 39, 40
Dimethyl sulfoxide
  idoxuridine with, 602
  interstitial cystitis, 423
Dimethyl sulphoxide *see* Dimethyl sulfoxide
Dimeticone, 603, **604**
  benzalkonium with, 571
  cetrimide with, 571
  zinc oxide with, 571
Dimeticone, activated *see* Simeticone, 38, 39, 40
*Dimetriose*, 394
Dinoprostone, 398, 399, 400
  infusion table, 794
*Diocalm Ultra* (loperamide), 52
*Dioctyl*, 60
Dioctyl sodium sulphosuccinate *see* Docusate sodium
*Dioderm*, 574
*Dioralyte* preparations, 476
*Diovan*, 104
*Dipentum*, 55
*Dipeptiven*, 483
Diphenoxylate, 52, 222
  *see also* Analgesics, opioid
Diphenylbutylpiperidines, 182
Diphosphonates *see* Bisphosphonates
Diphtheria, 273, 615
  antibacterial prophylaxis, 272
  antitoxin, 616
  immunisation
    travel, 615
    vaccines, 615, 616
Dipipanone, 222, **226**
  cyclizine with, 227
Dipivefrine, 542, **543**
*Diprivan*, 635
*Diprobase*, 568
*Diprobath*, 570
*Diprosalic*, 576
*Diprosone*, 576
Dip/Ser, 616
Dipyridamole, 126, **127**, 128
  aspirin with, 128
Disaccharide intolerance, ACBS, 816
Discontinued preparations, ix
Disease-modifying antirheumatic drugs *see* DMARDs, 504, 516
Disfiguring skin lesions, ACBS, 820
Disinfectants, 606
  ACBS, 820
*Disipal*, 257
*Diskhaler*
  *Becodisks*, 156
  *Flixotide*, 158
  *Relenza*, 327
  *Serevent*, 148
  *Ventodisks*, 146
Disodium clodronate *see* Sodium clodronate
Disodium cromoglicate *see* Sodium cromoglicate
Disodium etidronate, 386, 388, 389
Disodium folinate, 429, **430**
  infusion table, 794
Disodium pamidronate, 389
  infusion table, 794
*Disogram SR* (diltiazem), 110
Disopyramide, 79, **80**, 81
  infusion table, 794
*Disprol* (paracetamol) preparations, 220
*Distaclor* preparations, 280
*Distalgesic* (co-proxamol), 222
*Distamine*, 518
Distigmine, 526
  laxative, 59
  myasthenia gravis, 527
  urinary retention, 418, **419**
Disulfiram, **260**
Dithranol, 580, **583**, 584
  preparations
    coal tar with, 584
    salicylic acid with, 584
*Dithrocream*, 584
*Ditropan*, 420
Diuretics
  carbonic anhydrase inhibitors, 77
  heart failure, 97
  loop, 73
  mercurial, 77
  osmotic, 77
  potassium with, 77, 474
  potassium-sparing, 74
    with other diuretics, 76
  *see also* Thiazides
*Diurexan*, 73
*Diva*, 590
Diverticular disease, 41, **54**
*Dixarit*, 236
DMARDs (disease-modifying anti-rheumatic drugs), 504, 516
DMPS *see* Unithiol, 34
DMSA *see* Succimer, 34
Dobutamine, **117**
  infusion table, 794
Docetaxel, 445
  infusion table, 794
Docusate sodium, 60
  ear, 553, 554
  laxative, 59
*Docusol*, 60
Dolasetron, 211, **214**, 215
  infusion table, 794
*Dolmatil*, 186
*Dolobid*, 509
Domette bandage, 830
*Domperamol*, 231
Domperidone, 213, 214
  diabetic neuropathy, 357
  gastro-intestinal, 43
  migraine, 235
  nausea and vomiting, 210, 428
  palliative care, 15
  paracetamol with, 231
Donepezil, **264**
*Dopacard*, 118
Dopamine, **117**, 118
  infusion table, 794
Dopamine receptor agonists
  parkinsonism, 250
Dopaminergic drugs
  endocrine, 391
  parkinsonism, 250
Dopexamine, 117, **118**
  infusion table, 794
*Dopram*, 167
*Doralese*, 418
Dornase alfa, 170
Dorzolamide, 543, **544**
Dose changes, viii
Doses, 2
  children, 13
  elderly, 19
  liver disease, 735
  renal impairment, 745
*Dostinex*, 393
Dosulepin, 196, **198**
DOT, 298
*Dothapax* (dosulepin), 198
Dothiepin *see* Dosulepin, 196, **198**
*Doublebase*, 568
*Dovobet*, 582
*Dovonex* preparations, 582
*Doxadura* (doxazosin), 95
Doxapram, **167**

Doxazosin
cardiovascular, **95**
urinary tract, 417, **418**
Doxepin
depression, 196, 198
topical, 572
Doxorubicin, 432, **434**
bladder, 423
infusion table, 794
Doxycycline, 276, **286**
acne, 589
aphthous ulcers, 559, **560**
malaria
prophylaxis, 331–2, 333, **336**
treatment, 329
oral infections, 285, 559, **560**
rosacea, 586
*Doxylar* (doxycycline), 286
*Dozic*, 184
*Drapolene*, 571
Dressing packs, 829, 830
Dressings, 821
*Dress-it*, 829
*Driclor*, 609
Driver and Vehicle Licensing Agency, *inside front cover*
Driving and drugs, 2
*Drogenil*, 460
*Dromadol* preparations, 230
Drospirenone
contraception, 412
HRT, 370
Drotrecogin alfa (activated), **132**
Drug allergy, 161
Drug dependence, 7
management, 259
Drug interactions, 652
Drug misusers, notification of, 9
Dry mouth, 564
d4T *see* Stavudine, 315, **317**
*DTIC-Dome*, 441
DT/Vac/Ads(Adult), 616
*Duac*, 587
Dual block, 645
Ductus arteriosus
closure, 401
patency, 401
*Dukoral*, 614
*Dulco-lax* (bisacodyl), 59
*Dulco-lax* (sodium picosulfate), 59, 61
Duloxetine, 204
depression, **205**
diabetic neuropathy, **205**, 357
urinary incontinence, 419, **420**
*Dumas Vault Cap*, 417
*Duobar*, 802
*Duocal*, 802
*DuoDERM* products, 826
*Duodopa*, 253
*Duofilm*, 591
*Duovent* preparations, 150
*Duphalac* (lactulose), 62
*Duphaston* preparations, 376
*Duraphat* preparations, 493
*Durogesic DTrans*, 227
*Durolane*, 505
Dusting powders, 567
Dutasteride, 378, **379**
DVLA, *inside front cover*
*Dyazide*, 76
Dydrogesterone, **375**
HRT, 371, 376
menstrual disorders, 376
*Dymotil* (co-phenotrope), 52
*Dynamin* (isosorbide mononitrate), 108
*Dynastat*, 641
Dysentery
amoebic, 337
bacillary *see* Shigellosis, 268
Dysmenorrhoea, 218
*Dyspamet*, 45
Dyspepsia, 37, 38
Dysphagia, ACBS, 817
*Dysport*, 259
Dystonias, drug-induced, 257
*Dytac*, 75
*Dytide*, 76

# E

E numbers *inside back cover*
*E45* preparations, 568, 570
*Itch Relief*, 569
*Sun*, 594
Ear
infections, 550
wax, removal, 553
*EarCalm*, 550
*Easi-Breathe*
*Beclazone*, 156, 157
*Cromogen*, 159
*Salamol*, 146
*Easifix*, 830
*EasiGRIP*, 830
*Easiphen*, 802
*Easyhaler* (salbutamol), 146
*Easyhaler Beclometasone Dipropionate*, 156
*Ebixa*, 265
*Ebufac* (ibuprofen), 507
*Eccoxolac* (etodolac), 509
Echinococcosis, 341
Eclampsia, 490
*Econac* (diclofenac), 508
*Econacort*, 575
Econazole, 309
anogenital, 405, 406
skin, 599, **600**
hydrocortisone with, 575
vaginal, 405, 406
*Econoneb*, 153
*Ecopace* (captopril), 99
*Ecostatin*
anogenital, 405
skin, 600
Ecstacy, liquid (sodium oxybate), 33
Ecstasy
controlled drug, 8
poisoning by, 33
Ectopic beats, 77
Eczema, 579
ACBS, 820
ear, 551
Edetic acid, excipient, 567
*Ednyt* (enalapril), 100
*Edronax*, 205
Edrophonium, 527, 645
anaesthesia, **645**
myasthenia gravis, 526, 527
*Eesiban*, 830, 831
Efalizumab, **585**, 586
Efavirenz, 315, **321**
*Efcortelan* preparations, 574
*Efcortesol*, 366
*Efexor* preparations, 206
*Effercitrate* (potassium citrate), 422
*Effico*, 499
Eflornithine, **596**
Eformoterol *see* Formoterol
*Efudix*, 437
*Elantan* preparations, 108
Elastic adhesive
bandages, 832
dressing, 834
plaster, 834
Elastic web bandage, 832
Elasticated
surgical tubular stockinette, 830
foam padded, 830
tubular bandage, 830
viscose stockinette, 831
*Elastoplast* products, 833, 834
*Elastoweb*, 832
*Eldepryl*, 256
Elderly
diuretics and, 19
hypertension in, 91
prescribing for, 18
*Eldisine*, 439
Electroconvulsive therapy, 195
*Electrolade*, 476
Electrolyte and water replacement
intravenous, 477
oral, 474
Electrolyte concentrations, 474
*Elemental-028* preparations, 803
Eletriptan, **232**
*Elidel*, 586
*Elleste Duet* preparations, 370
*Elleste Solo*, 372
*Elleste Solo MX*, 372
*Elocon*, 579
*eloHAES*, 482
*Eloxatin*, 444
*Elset* products, 831
*Eltroxin* (levothyroxine), 360
*Eludril* preparations, 563
*Elyzol*, 560
*Emadine*, 538
*Emcor*, 86
Emedastine, **538**
*Emend*, 216
Emergencies, dental practice, 20
Emergency contraception, 412
Emergency supply, 6
*Emeside*, 240
capsules—discontinued, ix
Emesis, in poisoning, 28
*Emflex*, 508
*Emla*, 648
Emollients, 567
eczema, 579
psoriasis, 580
Emphysema, 143
*Emsogen*, 803

Index

Emtricitabine, 315, **316**
tenofovir with, 317
*Emtriva*, 316
*Emulsiderm*, 570
Emulsifying ointment, 568
Enalapril, **99**, 100
hydrochlorothiazide with, 100
*see also* ACE inhibitors
*Enbrel*, 523
Enbucrilate, 605
Encephalopathy, hepatic, 62, 735
*En-De-Kay* preparations, 492, 493
Endocarditis, 268, 287
prophylaxis, 271
dental practice, 23, 271
Endometrial cancer, 455
Endometriosis, 375, 393
Endophthalmitis, 534
*Endoxana*, 431
*Ener-G*, 803
*Energivit*, 803
Energy, intravenous nutrition, 483
*Enfamil* preparations, 803
Enfuvirtide, 315, **322**
*Engerix B*, 618
*Enlive Plus*, 803
*Enmix Plus Commence*, 803
Enoxaparin, **121**, 122
Enoximone, **71**
infusion table, 794
*Enrich* preparations, 803
*Enshake*, 803
*Ensure* preparations, 804
Entacapone, 251, **254**
*Entamoeba histolytica*, 337
Enteric infections, 268
Enterobiasis, 340
*Entocort* preparations, 56
*Entonox*, *636*
Enuresis, nocturnal, 421
*Enzira*, 619
Enzyme induction, 652
Enzymes
fibrinolytic, 129
ulcers, 609
*Epaderm*, 568
*Epanutin* preparations, 243
*Ready Mixed Parenteral*, 250
*Epaxal*, 617
Ephedrine, 118, 148
anaesthesia, 118
bronchospasm, 148
diabetic neuropathy, 357
nasal congestion, **557**
*Ephynal* (tocopheryl acetate), 498
Epiglottitis, 268, 292
*Epiglu*, 605
Epilepsy, 238
dental practice, 22
driving, 237
ketogenic diet, ACBS, 817
pregnancy, 238
status, 247
*Epilim* preparations, 245
*Epimaz* (carbamazepine), 239
Epinastine, **538**
eye, 538
Epinephrine *see* Adrenaline
*EpiPen*, 166, 167
Epirubicin, 433, **434**
bladder, 423
infusion table, 794
*Epivir*, 317
Eplerenone, **75**
Epoetin, **469**
alfa, 469
beta, 470
Epoprostenol, 92, **123**
infusion table, 794
*Eposin*, 439
*Eprex*, 469
Eprosartan, **103**
Epsom salts, 63
Eptacog alfa (activated), 132
Eptifibatide, 105, 126, **128**
*Equanox*, 636
*Equasym* (methylphenidate), 208
*Equasym XL*, 208
*Erbitux*, 441
Erectile dysfunction, 423, 425, 426
Ergocalciferol, **496**
Ergometrine, 399, **400**
oxytocin with, 400
Ergot alkaloids, 234
Ergotamine, 234
caffeine with, 235
cluster headache, 236
cyclizine and caffeine with, 235
Erlotinib, **441**, 442
Ertapenem, **284**
infusion table, 794
*Erwinase*, 441
*Erymax*, 290
Erysipelas, 270
*Erythrocin*, 290
Erythromycin, 289, **290**
acne, 587, 588, 589
benzoyl peroxide with, 587
tretinoin with, 589
infusion table, 794
topical, 589
rosacea, 586
*Erythroped* preparations, 290
Erythropoietin, 468
Escitalopram, 202, **203**
*Eskamel*, 589
*Esmeron*, 644
Esmolol, 84, **87**
infusion table, 794
*see also* Beta-adrenoceptor blocking drugs
Esomeprazole, 48, **49**
infusion table, 794
*Estracombi*, 370
*Estracyt*, 432
*Estraderm MX*, 372
*Estraderm TTS*, 372
Estradiol, 370, 373
HRT, 370, 371, 372, 373, 374
implants, 372
nasal spray, 372
vaginal, 404
vaginal ring, 373
Estradiol valerate, 370, 371, 372, 373
*Estradot*, 373
*Estragest TTS*, 370
Estramustine, **431**, 432
*Estring*, 404
Estriol
HRT, 374
vaginal, 404
Estrone, 374
Estropipate, 374
Etamsylate, **131**
Etanercept, 521, **522**, 523
psoriasis, 585
Ethambutol, 297, 298, 299, **300**
Ethamsylate *see* Etamsylate, **131**
Ethanol, 483
infusion table, 794
*see also* Alcohol
Ethanolamine oleate, **139**
Ethinylestradiol, **374**
acne *see* Co-cyprindiol, **590**
contraception, 407, 410, 411, 412
HRT, 374
malignant disease, 455
menstrual disorders, 374
Ethinyloestradiol *see* Ethinylestradiol
*Ethmozine*, *82*
Ethosuximide, 238, **240**
Ethyl-2-cyanoacrylate, 605
Ethylene glycol, poisoning by, 34
Ethylenediamine, excipient, 567
Ethylhexyl *p*-methoxycinnamate, 593, 594
Ethynodiol *see* Etynodiol, 414
Etidronate disodium *see* Disodium etidronate, 386, 388, 389
Etodolac, 505, **509**
Etomidate, **634**
*Etomidate-Lipuro*, 634
Etonogestrel, 414, 415
*Etopophos*, 439
Etoposide, **438**, 439
infusion table, 795
Etoricoxib, 506, **510**
gout, 524
Etretinate, 581
Etynodiol, 414
*Eucardic*, 86
*Eucerin*, 569
*Eudemine*, 92, 357
*Euglucon*, 352
*Eumovate*, 577
*Eurax* preparations, 572, 575
European viper venom antiserum, 36
Evening primrose oil, 568
*Evista*, 375
*Evohaler*
*Flixotide*, 158
*Ventolin*, 146
*Evorel* preparations, 370, 373
*Evra*, 410
Excipients
details provided, 2
skin preparations and, 567
*Exelderm*, 601
*Exelon*, 265
Exemestane, 456, **457**, 458
Exfoliative dermatitis, 363
*Exocin*, 535
*Exorex*, 583
Expectorants, 172
*Exterol*, 554
Extrapyramidal symptoms
antipsychotics and, 181
treatment, 257
Extravasation, 530

*Exu-Dry*, 827
Eye
antibacterial, 534
antifungal, 536
anti-inflammatory, 536, 538
antiviral, 536
contact lenses, 549
cycloplegics, 539
drops, 533
glaucoma, 540
lotions, 533
microbial contamination, 534
miotics, 544
mydriatics, 539
ointments, 533
*E-Z Spacer*, 152
Ezetimibe, **134**
simvastatin with, 138
*Ezetrol*, 134

# F

*F16 Wave*, 154
*Fabrazyme*, 501
Fabry's Disease, 500, 501
Factor VIIa (recombinant), 132
Factor VIII fraction, 132
Factor VIII inhibitor bypassing fraction, 132
Factor IX fraction, 132
Factor XIII fraction, 132
Faecal softeners, 61
Fainting
dental practice, 22
Famciclovir, 322, **323**, 324, 406
Familial Mediterranean fever, 524
Famotidine, **46**
*Famvir*, 324
*Fanhdi* (factor VIII fraction), 132
*Fansidar*, 336
*Fareston*, 458
*Farley's Soya Formula*, 804
*Farlutal*, 455
*Fasigyn*, 304
*Faslodex*, 458
*Fasturtec*, 526
Fat emulsions, intravenous, 483, 789
*Fate*, 804
*Faverin*, 203
Favism, 472
Febrile convulsions, 250
*Fectrim* (co-trimoxazole), 297
*Fefol*, 465
*FEIBA*, 132
Felbinac, 531
*Feldene* preparations, 513
gel, 531
*Melt*, 513
Felodipine, 109, **111**
ramipril with, 102
*see also* Calcium-channel blockers
*Felogen XL* (felodipine), 111
*Felotens XL* (felodipine), 111
Felypressin, 647, 650
*Femapak*, 371
*Femara*, 458
*Fematrix*, 373
*Femidom*, 407
*Femodene* preparations, 412
*Femodette*, 410
*Femoston* preparations, 371
*FemSeven* preparations, 371, 373
*FemTab* preparations, 371, 373
*Femulen*, 414
*Fenactol* preparations, 508, 509
*Fenbid* preparations
*Spansules*, 507
topical, 531
Fenbufen, 505, **510**
*Fendrix*, 618
Fenfluramine, 209
Fenofibrate, 134, **135**
*Fenogal* (fenofibrate), 135
Fenoprofen, **510**
pain, 505
rheumatic disease, 505, **510**
*Fenopron* preparations, 510
Fenoterol, 144, **147**
ipratropium, with, 150
*Fenpaed* (ibuprofen), 507
Fentanyl, 641
infusion table, 795
injection, **641**
lozenge, 227
patch, 14, 222, **227**
*Fentazin*, 185
*Feospan*, 464
*Feprapax* (lofepramine), 199
*Ferfolic SV*, 465
*Fermathron*, 505
Ferric ammonium citrate, folic acid with, 465
Ferric salts, 463
*Ferriprox*, 471
*Ferrograd* preparations, 464, 465
Ferrous fumarate, 464
compound preparations, 465
folic acid with, 465
Ferrous gluconate, 465
ascorbic acid with, 465
folic acid with, 465
Ferrous salts, 463
Ferrous sulphate, **464**
compound preparations, 465
folic acid with, 465
*Fersaday*, 464
*Fersamal*, 464
Fertility
female, 379, 380, 383
male, 380
thermometer, 417
Fexofenadine, 161, **162**
Fibrates, 134
*Fibrelief*, 58
Fibrinolytic drugs, 129
*Fibrogammin P* (factor XIII fraction), 132
Fibrosing alveolitis, 168
*Fibro-Vein*, 139
*Filair* (beclometasone), 155
*Filair Forte* (beclometasone), 156
Filaricides, 342
Filgrastim, 472, **473**
infusion table, 795
Finasteride, 378, **379**
baldness, **596**
*Finepoint*, 350
Fingertip unit, 573
*Fisonair*, 159
Fits *see* Epilepsy
*Flagyl* preparations, 303
*Flamatak* preparations, 509
*Flamazine*, 598
*Flamrase* preparations, 508, 509
*Flavour Sachets*, 804
Flavouring, ACBS, 817
*FlavourPac*, 804
Flavoxate, 419, 420
*Flebogamma*, 628
Flecainide, 80, **81**
infusion table, 795
*Fleet*
*Phospho-soda*, 63
*Ready-to-use enema*, 63
*Fletchers'* enemas, 61, 63
*Flexi-Ban*, 832
Flexible collodion, 605
*Flexin Continus* (indometacin m/r), 511
*FlexiPore*, 823
*Flexi-T 300*, 416
*Flexoplast*, 832, 834
*Flexotard MR*, 509
*Flixonase* preparations, 556
*Flixotide* preparations, 158
*Flolan*, 123
*Flomaxtra* XL, 418
*Florinef*, 361
*Flowfusor*, 606
*Floxapen*, 275
*Flu-Amp* (co-fluampicil), 278
*Fluanxol*, 205
*Fluarix*, 619
*Fluclomix* (flucloxacillin), 275
Flucloxacillin, 274, **275**
ampicillin with [co-fluampicil], 276, **278**
ear, 551
infusion table, 795
Fluconazole, 308, 309, **310**, 311
mouth, 561
Flucytosine, 308, 309, **311**
*Fludara*, 437
Fludarabine, 435, **437**
infusion table, 795
Fludrocortisone, **361**
diabetic neuropathy, 357
Fludroxycortide, **577**
Fluid and electrolyte replacement, 474
Fluid overload, liver disease, 735
Flumazenil, 32, **646**
infusion table, 795
Flumetasone, **551**
Flumethasone *see* Flumetasone, **551**
Flunisolide, **555**
Fluocinolone acetonide, 578
clioquinol with, 578
neomycin with, 578
Fluocinonide, 578
Fluocortolone, 65, **578**
*Fluor-a-day*, 492
Fluorescein, 545, **547**
Fluoride, 492, 493
*FluoriGard* preparations, 492, 493
Fluorometholone, 537
Fluorouracil, 436, **437**, 594
infusion table, 795
Fluoxetine, 202, **203**
Flupenthixol *see* Flupentixol, 205
Flupentixol
depot injections, **191**, 192
depression, 204, 205
psychoses, 182, **184**, **191**

Index

Fluphenazine, 182, **184**, **192**
depot injections, 192
nortriptyline with, 199
tablets, 184
Fluphenazine decanoate, 192
Fluprednidene, **578**
Flurandrenolone *see* Fludroxycortide, **577**
Flurazepam, 174, **175**
Flurbiprofen, 510
diabetic neuropathy, 357
eye, 548
postoperative pain, 640
rheumatic disease, 505, **510**
sore throat, 559, 560
Flutamide, 459, **460**
Fluticasone propionate
asthma, 154, **158**
nasal allergy, 556
nasal polyps, 556
salmeterol with, 158
skin, 578
Fluvastatin, 135, **137**
Fluvoxamine, 202, **203**
*FML*, 537
Foam dressings, 823
Folate deficiency, 466
Folate rescue, 429
Folic acid, 466, **467**
pregnancy, 465, 467
preparations
iron and, 465
*Folicare* (folic acid), 467
Folinic acid rescue, 429
Folinic acid *see* Calcium folinate
Folinic acid *see* Disodium folinate
Follicle-stimulating hormone, 380
Follitropin, 381
Follitropin alfa, 381
Follitropin beta, 381
Fomepizole, 34
Fondaparinux, 123, **124**
*Foodlink Complete*, 804
Foods for special diets, 487, 488
ACBS, 801
vitamin supplements, 499
*Foradil*, 147
*Forceval*, 488, 499
Formaldehyde, 591, 592
*Formance*, 804
Formoterol, 144, **147**
budesonide with, 157
Formulary
Dental, 851
Nurse, 853
*Forsteo*, 388
*Forticreme*, 804
*Fortifresh*, 804
*Fortijuce*, 804
*Fortimel*, 804
*Fortini* preparations, 804
*Fortipine LA 40*, 113
*Fortisip* preparations, 805
*Fortovase*—discontinued, ix
*Fortral* (pentazocine), 229
*Fortum*, 282
*Fosamax* preparations, 388
Fosamprenavir, 315, **319**
*Fosavance*, 388
*Foscan*, 444
Foscarnet, 324, **325**
infusion table, 795
*Foscavir*, 325
Fosinopril, **100**
*see also* ACE inhibitors
Fosphenytoin, 247, 248, 249
infusion table, 795
*Fragmin*, 121
Fragrances, excipient, 567
Framycetin
ear, 551
eye, 534, **535**
Frangula, 59
*Frebini* preparations, 805
*FreeStyle* products, 350, 358
*Freeway Freedom*, 153
Fresh frozen plasma, 132
*Fresubin* preparations, 805, 806
Friars' Balsam, 170
*Frisium* (clobazam), 247
*Froben* preparations, 510
*Froop* (furosemide), 74
*Froop-Co* (co-amilofruse), 76
Frovatriptan, 232, **233**
*Fru-Co* (co-amilofruse), 76
Fructose, 483
ACBS, 806
presence of, 2
*Frumil* preparations (co-amilofruse), 76
Frusemide *see* Furosemide
*Frusene*, 76
*Frusid* (furosemide), 74
*Frusol* (furosemide), 74
FSH *see* Follicle-stimulating hormone, 380
*FSME-IMMUN*, 626
FTU *see* Fingertip unit, 573
*Fucibet*, 577
*Fucidin*, 293
skin, 598
*Fucidin H*, 575
*Fucithalmic*, 535
*Full Marks*, 605
Fulvestrant, 456, **458**
Fungal infections, 308
anogenital, 405
eye, 536
oral, 308, 560
skin, 599
*Fungilin*, 310
mouth, 561
*Fungizone*, 310
*Furadantin*, 308
Furosemide, 73, **74**
amiloride with, 76
infusion table, 795
potassium with, 77
spironolactone with, 77
triamterene with, 76
Fusidic acid, 293
eye, 534, **535**
infusion table, 795
skin, 597, **598**
angular cheilitis, 561
betamethasone valerate with, 577
hydrocortisone with, 575
*Fuzeon*, 322
*Fybogel*, 58
*Fybogel Mebeverine*, 42

# G

G6PD deficiency, 472
drugs to be avoided in, 472
Gabapentin, 238, **240**, 241
diabetic neuropathy, 357
neuropathic pain, 230
postherpetic neuralgia, 231
trigeminal neuralgia, 231
*Gabitril*, 244
*Gadsby's*, 806
Galactokinase deficiency, ACBS, 817
*Galactomin* preparations, 806
Galactorrhoea, 392
Galactosaemia, ACBS, 817
Galactose intolerance, ACBS, 816
Galantamine, 264, **265**
*Galcodine* preparations, 171
*Galenamox* (amoxicillin), 276
*Galenphol*, 171
*Galfer*, 464
*Galfer FA*, 465
*Galfloxin* (flucloxacillin), 275
Gallamine, **643**
Gallstones, 66
*Galprofen* (ibuprofen), 507
*Galpseud*, 172
*Gamanil*, 199
*Gamgee Tissue*, blue label, 829
*Gamgee Tissue*, pink label, 829
*Gammaderm*, 568
*Gammagard S/D*, 628
Gamma-hydroxybutyrate (sodium oxybate), 33
Ganciclovir, 324, **325**
eye, 536
infusion table, 795
Ganirelix, 393, **394**
*Gardnerella vaginalis*, 303
Gargles, 563
Gas cylinders, 633
Gas-gangrene, 273
prophylaxis, 272
Gastrectomy
ACBS, 817
iron therapy, 463
vitamin $B_{12}$, 466
Gastric emptying, poisoning and, 28
*Gastrobid Continus*, 214
*Gastrocote*, 40
Gastro-enteritis, 51, 268
Gastro-intestinal procedures, anti-bacterial prophylaxis, 272
Gastro-intestinal system, electrolytes, 474
Gastro-oesophageal reflux disease, **37**
Gaucher's disease, 501
Gauze and cotton tissue, 829
Gauze swabs, 829
filmated, 829
Gauze, cotton ribbon, absorbent, 829
viscose and, 829
*Gavilast-P* (ranitidine), 47
*Gaviscon*
tablets—discontinued, ix
*Gaviscon* preparations, 40
infant, 40
G-CSF, 473
Gelatin
infusion, **481**
succinylated, 481, 482

- *Gelclair*, 558
- *Geliperm*, 824
- *Gelofusine*, 481
- Gels, definition, 566
- *GelTears*, 546
- Gemcitabine, 435, **437**
  - infusion table, 795
- Gemeprost, 398, **400**, 402
- Gemfibrozil, 134, **135**
- *Gemzar*, 437
- *Gencardia* (aspirin), 127
- *Generaid* preparations, 806
- General anaesthesia *see* Anaesthesia, general
- Generic prescribing, 1
- Genital warts, 592
- *Genotropin* preparations, 382
- Gentamicin, 287, **288**
  - ear, 551, 552
  - eye, 534, **535**, 545
  - infusion table, 795
  - injections, 288
- Gentian mixture, alkaline, 499
- *Genticin*, 288
  - ear, 552
  - eye, 535
- *Gentisone HC*, 551
- *Geref-50*, 384
- German measles *see* Rubella
- *Germoloids* preparations, 65
- Gestodene, contraception, 410, 412
- *Gestone*, 376
- Gestrinone, 393, **394**
- GHB (sodium oxybate), 33
- GHRH *see* Somatorelin, 384
- Giant cell arteritis, 514
- *Giardia lamblia*, 337
- Giardiasis, 337
- Gilles de la Tourette syndrome *see* Tourette syndrome, 258
- Gingivitis, 562
  - acute necrotising ulcerative
    - antibacterial treatment, 270, 303
    - mouthwashes, 562
- *Givitol*, 465
- *Glamin*, 484
- *Glandosane*, 564
- Glatiramer, **454**, 455
- Glaucoma, 540
  - steroid, 537
- *Gliadel*, 431
- Glibenclamide, 351, **352**
- *Glibenese*, 352
- Gliclazide, 351, **352**
- Glimepiride, **352**
- Glipizide, 352
- Gliquidone, 352, 353
- *Glivec*, 442
- Glomerular filtration rate, dosage and, 745
- Glossopharyngeal neuralgia, 231
- *GlucaGen HypoKit*, 356
- Glucagon, **356**
  - injection, 356
- *Glucobay*, 354
- Glucocorticoids
  - equivalent doses, 362
  - replacement therapy, 361
- *GlucoGel*, 356
- *Glucolet*, 350
- *GlucoMen* products, 350, 358
- *Glucophage*, 353
- Glucose, 478, 479
  - hypoglycaemia, 356
  - infusion, 479
    - potassium and, 479
    - sodium and, 478
  - intravenous nutrition, 483
  - oral rehydration, 476
  - presence of, 2
  - special diets, 806
  - tests
    - blood, 357
    - tolerance, 359
    - urine, 358, 359
- Glucose 6-phosphate dehydrogenase deficiency, 472
  - drugs to be avoided in, 472
- Glucose intolerance, ACBS, 816
- Glucose syrup, hydrogenated, presence of, 2
- *Glucotide*, 358
- Glue ear, 553
- *Glurenorm*, 353
- *Glutafin*, 806
- *Glutano*, 806
- Glutaraldehyde, 591, 592
- Glutaric aciduria, ACBS, 817
- *Glutarol*, 592
- Gluten enteropathy, ACBS, 817
- Gluten, presence of, 2
- Gluten-free products, ACBS, 817
- Glycerin suppositories, 60
- Glycerol, 60
  - glaucoma, 543
  - suppositories, 59, 60
- Glyceryl trinitrate, 105, **106**, 107
  - anal fissure, **65**, 66
  - infusion table, 795
- Glycine, **423**
- Glycine irrigation solution, 423
- Glycogen storage disease, ACBS, 817
- Glycopeptide antibiotics, 293
- *Glycophos* , 483
- Glycoprotein IIb/IIIa inhibitors, 126
- Glycopyrrolate *see* Glycopyrronium bromide
- Glycopyrronium bromide, 609, 638
  - hyperhidrosis, 609
  - neostigmine with, 645
  - palliative care, 17
  - premedication, 637
- *Glypressin*, 386
- *Glytrin Spray*, 106
- GnRH *see* Gonadorelin, 383, **384**
- Goitre, 359
- Gold, 516
- *Golden Eye Drops* (propamidine), 536
- *Golden Eye Ointment* (dibromopropamidine), 536
- Golfer's elbow, 515
- Gonadorelin, 383, **384**
- Gonadorelin analogues, 394
  - malignant disease, 458
- Gonadotrophin-releasing hormone *see* Gonadorelin, 383, **384**
- Gonadotrophins, 380
- *Gonal-F*, 381
- *Gonapeptyl Depot*, 461
- Gonorrhoea, 269, 273
  - pharyngeal, 269
- *Gopten*, 102
- GORD *see* Gastro-oesophageal reflux disease, 37
- Goserelin
  - endometriosis, 395
  - IVF, 395
  - malignant disease, 457, 458, **460**
- Gout, 524
- Gramicidin, 535
  - ear, 551
  - neomycin with, 597
- Gramicidin [ingredient], 552
- *Gramoxone*, poisoning by, 35
- Grand mal, 238
- *Graneodin*, 597
- Granisetron, 211, **215**
  - infusion table, 795
- *Granocyte*, 473
- *Granuflex* products, 826
- *GranuGel*, 824
- Granulocyte-colony stimulating factor, 472, 473
- Grass pollen allergy preparations, 165
- Griseofulvin, 309, **311**, 312
  - topical, 599, **600**
- *Grisol*, 600
- *Grisovin*, 312
- Ground-nut oil *see* Arachis oil
- Group A streptococcal infection
  - antibacterial prophylaxis, 272
- Growth factor, platelet derived, 609
- Growth failure, ACBS, 817
- Growth hormone, 382
- Growth hormone receptor antagonists, 383
- Growth hormone test, 384
- Guanethidine, **95**
- Guillain-Barré syndrome, 627
- *Gyne T*, 416
- GyneFix, 416
- *Gyno-Daktarin* preparations, 405, 406
- *Gynol II*—discontinued, ix
- *Gyno-Pevaryl* preparations, 406


# H


- *Haelan* preparations, 577
- Haem arginate, **502**
  - infusion table, 795
- *Haemaccel*, 481
- *Haemate P* (factor VIII fraction), 132
- Haemodialysis, 29
  - ACBS, 816
- Haemolytic anaemia, 468
  - G6PD deficiency, 472
- Haemolytic disease of newborn, prevention, 629
- Haemophilia, 132
  - mild to moderate, 384
- *Haemophilus influenzae* type b (Hib), 616
  - immunisation, 616
    - vaccines, viii, 615, 616
  - prophylaxis, 270
- Haemorrhage, 131
  - abortion, 399
  - gastro-intestinal, 45
  - postpartum, 399
- Haemorrhoids, 64
- Haemostatics, 131
- *HAES-steril*, 482
- *Halciderm Topical*, 579

- Halcinonide, 579
- *Haldol*, 184
- *Haldol Decanoate*, 192
- *Haleraid*, 152
- *Half-Beta-Prograne* (propranolol), 85
- *Half-Inderal LA*, 85
- *Half-Securon SR*, 114
- *Half-Sinemet CR*, 253
- Halibut-liver oil capsules, 494
- Haloperidol, **184**, 192
  - hiccup, 183
  - movement disorders, **258**
  - nausea and vertigo, 210
  - palliative care, 15, 17
  - preparations, 184
    - depot, 192
  - psychoses, 182, **184**, **192**
- Haloperidol decanoate, 192
- Halothane, 635, **636**
- *Halycitrol*, 494
- Hansen's disease, 302
- *Harmogen*, 374
- Hartmann's solution *see* Sodium lactate, intravenous infusion, compound, 478
- *Havrix* preparations, 617
- Hay fever, 161, 554
- *Hay-Crom* preparations (sodium cromoglicate), 539
- HBIG *see* Hepatitis B immunoglobulin
- *HBvaxPRO*, 618
- HCG *see* Chorionic gonadotrophin, **380**, 381
- *HCU Express*, 806
- *HCU gel*, 806
- Head lice, 603
- Headache, 218
  - cluster, 236
  - migraine, 231
- Heaf test, 614
- Heart failure, 97
  - ACE inhibitors, 97
  - beta-blockers, 84
  - vasodilators, 97
- Heart *see also* Cardiac
- *Hedrin*, 604
- Height-weight charts, 13
- *HeliClear*, 49
- *Helicobacter pylori*, 37, **43**
  - test, 43, 44
- *Helixate NexGen* (factor VIII fraction), 132
- Helminth infections, 340
- *Hemabate*, 399
- *Heminevrin*, 177
- *Hemohes*, 482
- Heparin, 119, **120**, 121
  - flushes, 123
  - infusion table, 795
  - low molecular weight, 121
  - myocardial infarction, 129
- Heparinoids
  - thrombosis prophylaxis, 122
  - topical, 610
- Hepatic encephalopathy, 288, 735
- Hepatic *see also* Liver
- Hepatitis A, 616
  - immunisation
    - immunoglobulin, normal, 627
    - travel, 631
    - vaccine, 616, 617
- Hepatitis B, 617
  - auto-immune, 364
  - chronic, 317, 326, 452, 453
  - chronic active, 500
  - immunisation
    - immunoglobulin, 628, **629**
    - vaccine, 617, 618
  - travel, 631
- Hepatitis C
  - chronic, 326, 452, 453
- Hepatolenticular degeneration *see* Wilson's disease, 499
- Hepatotoxicity, 735
- *Hepatyrix*, 617
- *Hepsal*, 123
- *Hepsera*, 326
- Herbal medicines, 1
- *Herceptin*, 446
- Hereditary angioedema *see* Angioedema, hereditary, 131, 165, 393
- Heroin *see* Diamorphine
- Herpes infections, 322
  - eye, 536
  - genital, 322, 406
  - immunoglobulin, 629
  - mouth, 562
  - skin, 601
- *Herpetad*, 602
- *Herpid*, 602
- *Hewletts*, 568
- Hexamine *see* Methenamine, 307, **308**
- Hexastarch, **482**
- Hexetidine, 563
- *Hexopal*, 116
- HFAs, 144, 154
- HGH *see* Somatropin, 382, 383
- Hib, 616
- *Hiberix*, 616
- *Hibicet Hospital Concentrate*, 607
- *Hibiscrub*, 606
- *Hibisol*, 607
- *Hibitane* preparations, 607
- Hiccup, 183, 258
- *Hioxyl*, 609
- *Hipfix* (factor IX fraction), 132
- *Hiprex*, 308
- Hirsutism, 590, 596
- Hirudins, 122
- *Hirudoid*, 610
- Histamine $H_1$-antagonists, 161
- Histamine $H_2$-antagonists, 44
- Histidinaemia, ACBS, 817
- *Histoacryl*, 605
- Histoplasmosis, 308
- HIV infection, 314
- *Hivid*, 318
- HNIG *see* Immunoglobulins, normal, 627, 628
- Hodgkin's disease, 430, 441, 448
- Homatropine
  - eye drops, 540
- Homocystinuria, ACBS, 817
- Hookworm infections, 341
- Hormone antagonists
  - hypersexuality, 378
  - malignant disease, 456
- Hormone replacement
  - androgens, 377
  - oestrogens, 367, **369**
    - vaginal, 404
  - progestogens, 367, 375
  - surgery, 369
- *Hormonin*, 374
- Hosiery, elastic, 835
- *Hospicrepe* products, 831
- *Hospiform*, 830
- *Hospifour* products, 833
- *HRF*, 384
- HRT, 367, 386
- $5HT_1$ agonists, 231, **232**
- $5HT_3$ antagonists, 211, 215, 216, 428
- *HT-Defix* (factor IX fraction), 132
- HTIG *see* Immunoglobulins, tetanus, 628, **629**
- *Humalog* preparations, 347, 349
- Human antihaemophilic fraction, 132
- Human chorionic gonadotrophin *see* Chorionic gonadotrophin, **380**, 381
- Human factor VIII fraction, 132
- Human factor IX fraction, 132
- Human factor XIII fraction, 132
- Human luteinising hormone *see* Lutropin alfa, 381
- Human menopausal gonadotrophins, 381
- Human normal immunoglobulin *see* Immunoglobulins, normal, 628
- *HumaPen Ergo*, 350
- *HumaPen Luxura*, 350
- *Humatrope*, 383
- *Humira*, 522
- *Humulin I*, 348
- *Humulin M3*, 350
- *Humulin S*, 347
- Huntington's chorea, 258
- Hyaff, *826*
- *Hyalase*, 531
- *Hyalgan*, 505
- Hyaline membrane disease, 167
- *Hyalofill* products, 826
- Hyaluronic acid, 505
  - wounds, 826
- Hyaluronidase, **530**, 531
- *Hycamtin*, 446
- Hycanthone, 342
- Hydatid disease, 341
- *Hydrafoam*, 823
- Hydralazine, **92**, 93
  - infusion table, 795
- *Hydrea*, 442
- *Hydrex*, 607
- Hydrochlorothiazide, 72
  - amiloride with, 76
  - captopril with, 99
  - enalapril with, 100
  - irbesartan with, 103
  - lisinopril with, 101
  - losartan with, 104
  - metoprolol with, 88
  - quinapril with, 102
  - telmisartan with, 104
  - triamterene with, 76
  - valsartan with, 104
- *Hydrocoll*, 826
- Hydrocolloid dressings, 825, 826

Hydrocortisone, 364, **366**
colitis, 56
ear, 551, 552
emergency use
dental practice, 20
eye, 537
haemorrhoids, 64, 65
mouth, 558, 559
rectal, 64, 65
rheumatic disease, 515
skin, 574, 575
chloramphenicol with, 589
chlorhexidine and nystatin with, 575
clioquinol with, 575
coal tar with, 583
crotamiton with, 575
econazole with, 575
fusidic acid with, 575
miconazole with, 575
nystatin with, 575
urea with, 574, 575
replacement therapy, 361
Hydrocortisone butyrate, 575
chlorquinaldol with, 575
Hydrocortisone sodium phosphate, 366
infusion table, 795
Hydrocortisone sodium succinate, 366
infusion table, 795
*Hydrocortistab*, 515
*Hydrocortone*, 366
*Hydrofilm*, 827
Hydroflumethiazide, 72
spironolactone with, 77
Hydrofluoroalkane propellants, 144, 154
Hydrogel dressings, 824, 825
Hydrogen peroxide, **563**, **608**, 609
cream, 608
mouthwash, 562, 563
solution, 608
*Hydromol* preparations, 568, 570
Hydromorphone, 14, **227**
*Hydrosorb* products, 824
Hydrotalcite, 38, **39**
Hydrous ointment, 568
Hydroxocobalamin, 466, **467**
cyanide poisoning, 33
Hydroxybenzoates, excipient, 567
Hydroxycarbamide, **442**
psoriasis, 585
sickle cell disease, 468
Hydroxychloroquine, 516, **519**
Hydroxycholecalciferol, 496, 497
Hydroxyethyl starch *see* Starch, etherified, 482
Hydroxyethylcellulose, 546
Hydroxyquinoline
benzoyl peroxide with, 587
Hydroxyurea *see* Hydroxycarbamide
Hydroxyzine, **163**, 164
*Hygroton*, 72
Hyoscine butylbromide, **41**, 42
Hyoscine hydrobromide, 638
nausea and vertigo, 211, **217**
palliative care, 17
premedication, 637, **638**
*Hypafix*, 834
Hyperactive children, 206
Hyperaldosteronism, 396
*Hyperamine*, 484
Hypercalcaemia, 387, 388, 489
Hypercalciuria, 489
Hypercholesterolaemia, 133, 134, 136
Hyperemesis gravidarum, 211
Hyperglycaemia, 344
coma, 355
*HyperHAES*, 482
Hyperhidrosis, 609
*Hypericum perforatum*, 195
Hyperkalaemia, 475, 478, 480, 488
Hyperlipidaemia, 133
Hyperlipoproteinaemia, ACBS, 817
Hyperlysinaemia, ACBS, 817
Hypermethioninaemia, ACBS, 818
Hyperparathyroidism, 489
Hyperphosphataemia, 491
Hypersensitivity *see* Allergic disorders
Hypersexuality, 378
Hypertension, 72, 83, 90, 98, 109
crisis, 91
diabetes, 91
elderly, 91
malignant, 91
poisoning and, 27
pregnancy, 91
pulmonary, 92, 123
renal disease, 91
systolic, 91
Hyperthermia
malignant, 646
poisoning and, 28
Hyperthyroidism *see* Thyrotoxicosis
Hyperuricaemia, 428, 524, 525
Hyperventilation, dental practice, 23
*Hypnomidate*, 634
Hypnotics, 174
poisoning by, 32
withdrawal, 173
*Hypnovel*, 640
Hypocalcaemia, 488
Hypodermic equipment, insulin, 350
Hypodermoclysis, 477, 530
Hypogammaglobulinaemia, 627
Hypoglycaemia, 345, 356
ACBS, 818
acute, 356
chronic, 356
dental practice, 22
Hypogonadism, 377
*Hypoguard* products, 350, 358
Hypokalaemia, 479
diuretics and, 71
*Hypolar Retard 20*, 113
Hypomagnesaemia, 490
Hyponatraemia, 477
Hypoparathyroidism, 496
Hypopituitarism, 361, 377, 380
Hypoproteinaemia
ACBS, 818
liver disease, 735
Hyposensitisation, 164
*Hypostop Gel*, 356
Hypotension
poisoning and, 27
sympathomimetics, 118
Hypothalamic hormones, 383
Hypothermia
antipsychotics and, 182
poisoning and, 28
Hypothyroidism, 359
neonatal, 359
*Hypovase*, 96
Hypovolaemia, 480
Hypoxaemia, 168
Hypromellose, 546
*Hypurin Isophane*, 348
biphasic, 349
*Hypurin Lente*, 348
*Hypurin Neutral*, 346
*Hypurin Protamine Zinc*, 349
*Hytrin* preparations
cardiovascular, 96
prostatic hyperplasia, 418


# I


Ibandronic acid, **389**, 390
infusion table, 795
*Ibugel*, 531
Ibuprofen, 507
pain, 505, 506, 507
postoperative, 640
post-immunisation pyrexia, 611
preparations, 507
topical, 531
rheumatic disease, 505, **507**
Ichthammol, 579, **580**
zinc with, 580
*Ichthopaste*, 833
Ichthyosis, 567
*Icthaband*, 833
Idarubicin, 433, **434**
infusion table, 795
Idoxuridine, 323
dimethyl sulfoxide with, 601, **602**
*Idrolax*, 62
Ifosfamide, 430, **432**
infusion table, 796
*Ikorel*, 115
Iloprost, 92, **93**
*Ilube*, 546
Imatinib, 442
*Imazin XL*—discontinued, ix
*Imdur*, 108
Imidapril, **100**
*see also* ACE inhibitors
Imidazole antifungal drugs, 309
Imidurea, excipient, 567
Imiglucerase, **501**
infusion table, 796
*Imigran* preparations, 234
Imipenem, **284**, 285
cilastatin with
infusion table, 796
Imipramine, 196, **198**, 419
Imiquimod, **592**
*ImmuCyst*, 454
*Immukin*, 630
Immune interferon *see* Interferons, gamma-1b
Immunisation, 611
international travel, 630
schedule, viii, 612
Immunity
active, 611
passive, 612


Index

Immunodeficiency, 627, 628
  syndrome, acquired, 314
Immunoglobulins, 613, **627**
  anti-D ($Rh_0$), 629, 630
  aplastic anaemia, 468
  cytomegalovirus, 629
  hepatitis B, 628, 629
  myasthenia gravis, 526
  normal, 627, 628
  rabies, 628, 629
  tetanus, 628, **629**
  thrombocytopenic purpura, autoimmune, 471
  varicella-zoster, 628, 629
*Immunoprin* (azathioprine), 448
Immunostimulants, 451
Immunosuppressants
  malignant disease, 448
  myasthenia gravis, 527
  rheumatic disease, 516, 519
  skin disease, 585
  transplant rejection, 447
*Imodium* preparations, 52
*Imodium* preparations (loperamide), 52
Impetigo, 597
  systemic treatment, 270
  topical treatment, 597
Implanon, *414*, 415
Impotence *see* Erectile dysfunction
*Imuderm*, 570
*Imunovir*, 324
*Imuran*, 448
*Inadine*, 828
Incontinence, urinary, 419
Indapamide, 72, **73**
  perindopril with, 101
*Inderal* preparations, 85
*Indermil*, 605
Indian hemp *see* Cannabis, 7
Indinavir, 315, **319**
*Indivina* preparations, 371
*Indocid PDA*, 402
*Indolar SR* (indometacin m/r), 511
*Indomax 75 SR* (indometacin m/r), 511
Indometacin, 401, 510
  ductus closure, 401, 402
  gout, 524
  premature labour, 402
  rheumatic disease, 505, **510**
Indomethacin *see* Indometacin
Indoramin
  cardiovascular, **95**
  urinary tract, 417, **418**
*Inegy*, 138
*Infacol*, 40
*InfaSoy*, 806
*Infatrini*, 806
Infections
  amoebic, 337
  antisera, 613, 627
  bladder, 307
    mycotic, 422
  ear, 550
  eye, 534
  fungal, 308
  helminth, 340
  immunoglobulins, 627
  nail, fungal, 309, 599
  notifiable diseases, 266
Infections (*continued*)—
    oropharyngeal, 560
      bacterial, 267, 270
  protozoal, 329
  skin, 596
  trichomonal, 337
  vaccines, 611
  vaginal, 405
  viral, 314
  vulval, 405
Infertility
  female, 379, 380, 383
  male, 380
Inflammation, oral, 558
Inflammatory bowel disease, 53
  ACBS, 818
*Inflexal V*, 619
Infliximab, 57, **523**
  Crohn's disease, 53, **57**
  infusion table, 796
  psoriasis, 585
  rheumatic disease, 521, 522
Influenza
  immunisation
    vaccines, 619, 620
  prophylaxis, 326, 327
  treatment, 326
*Influvac Sub-unit*, 619
Information services
  poisons, 27
*Infukoll*, 482
Inhalations
  aromatic, 170
  steam, 170, 557
Inhaler devices, 151
*Innohep*, 122
*Innovace*, 100
*Innovo*, 350
*Innozide*, 100
Inosine pranobex, 323, **324**
  anogenital warts, 592
Inositol, 494
Inositol nicotinate, **116**
Inotropic drugs, positive, 69, 117
Insect stings, 36, 161
Insecticides, poisoning by, 35
Insomnia, 174
*Inspra*, 75
*Instillagel*, 649
*Insulatard* preparations, 348
Insulin, 344
  analogues, 346
  aspart, 346, **347**
    biphasic, 347, **349**
  detemir, 347, **348**
  glargine, 347, **348**
  glulisine, 346, **347**
  human, 344
  hypodermic equipment, 350
  infusion table, 796
  injection devices, 350
  isophane, 347, **348**
    biphasic, 347, **349**, 350
  lispro, 346, **347**
    biphasic, 347, **349**
  protamine zinc, 347, **349**
  soluble, **346**, 347
  subcutaneous infusion, 345
  zinc suspension, 347, **348**
    crystalline, 347
    mixed, 348
*Insuman Basal*, 348
*Insuman Comb* preparations, 350
*Insuman Rapid*, 347
*Insupak*, 351
*Intal*
  nebuliser solution—discontinued
*Intal* preparations, 159
*Integrilin*, 128
Interactions, 652
Interferons
  alfa, 452, 453
    chronic hepatitis B, 326
    chronic hepatitis C, 326
    infusion table, 796
    peginterferon, 326, 452
  beta, 453, **454**
  gamma, 630
  peginterferon alfa , 453
Interleukin-2 *see* Aldesleukin, 454
Intermittent claudication, 115
International travel, immunisation for, 630
*Interpose*, 827
*Intersurgical* masks, 168
Intestinal lymphangiectasia, ACBS, 818
Intracranial pressure, raised, 364
*Intrafusin* preparations, 484
*Intralipid* preparations, 484
*Intrasite* products, 824
Intra-uterine devices, 416
  copper-bearing, 416
  progestogen-releasing, 415
Intravenous infusions, 477
  addition to, 789
Intravenous nutrition, 482
*IntronA*, 452
*Invanz*, 284
*Invirase*, 320
*Invivac*, 619
*Iocare*, 547
Iodine, 360, **361**
  preparations
    oral solution, 361
    skin, 607, 608
  radioactive, 360
*Iodoflex*, 824
*Iodosorb* products, 824
*Iopidine*, 547
Ipecacuanha mixture, 28
*Ipocol*, 55
Ipratropium, **148**, 149
  asthma, 148
  rhinorrhoea, **557**
  *Steri-Neb*, 149
  with fenoterol, 150
  with salbutamol, 150
Irbesartan, 103
  hydrochlorothiazide with, 103
Iridocyclitis *see* Anterior uveitis, 539
Irinotecan, 445, **446**
  infusion table, 796
Iron
  deficiency, 463
  folic acid and, 465
  overload, 470
  poisoning by, 32
  preparations, 464, 465, 466
  therapy
    oral, 463
    parenteral, 466

Iron dextran, **466**
infusion table, 796
Iron sucrose, **466**
infusion table, 796
*Ironorm*, 464
*Irriclens*, 606
*Irripod*, 606
Irritable bowel syndrome, 41, **53**
Ischaemic attacks, 124
Ischaemic disease of limbs, 481
*Isib 60XL*, 108
Island dressings, 834
*Ismelin*, 95
*Ismo* preparations, 108
Isocarboxazid, 200, **201**
*Isodur* preparations, 108
Isoflurane, 635, **636**
*Isogel*, 58
*Isoket* preparations, 107, 108
Isoleucine Amino Acid Supplement, 807
Isomaltose intolerance, ACBS, 816
Isometheptene, 235
paracetamol with, 235
*Isomil*, 807
Isoniazid, 297, 298, 299, **300**
Isophane protamine insulin *see* Insulin, isophane
Isoprenaline, 117
Isopropyl palmitate, excipient, 567
*Isopto*
Alkaline, 546
Atropine, 540
Frin, 546
Plain, 546
Isosorbide dinitrate, 106, **107**, 108
infusion table, 796
Isosorbide mononitrate, 106, **108**, 109
*Isosource* preparations, 807
*Isotard* preparations, 108
Isotretinoin, 586, **590**
acne
oral, **590**, 591
topical, 588, 589
topical, erythromycin with, 589
rosacea, 587
*Isotrex*, 589
*Isotrexin*, 589
Isovalearic acidaemia, ACBS, 818
*Isovorin*, 430
*Ispagel Orange*, 59
Ispaghula, 42, 58, 59
constipation, 58
diarrhoea, 51
Isradipine, 109, **111**
*see also* Calcium-channel blockers
*Istin*, 110
Itraconazole, 308, 309, **312**
infusion table, 796
mouth, 561
IUDs *see* Intra-uterine devices, 416
Ivabradine, **115**
*Ivelip* preparations, 484
Ivermectin
larva migrans, 342
onchocerciasis, 342
scabies, 602
strongyloidiasis, 342
IZS *see* Insulin, zinc suspension


# J


Japanese encephalitis, 631
*Jelonet*, 828
Jet nebulisers, 152
*Jevity* preparations, 807
Joint prostheses
endocarditis prophylaxis, 271
*Joy-rides* (hyoscine hydrobromide), 217
*Juvela* preparations, 807


# K


*Kabiven* preparations, 484, 485
Kala-azar, 338
*Kaletra*, 320
*Kalspare*, 76
*Kalten*, 86
*Kaltostat* products, 822
*Kamillosan*, 568
*Kaodene*, 52
Kaolin, 51, 52
preparations, 51
morphine and, 52
poultices, 532
*Kapake*, 221
*Kaplon* (captopril), 99
*Karvol* preparations, 170
Kawasaki syndrome, 627
*Kay-Cee-L*, 475
*K-Band*, 830
*Kefadim*, 283
*Keflex*, 281
*Keftid* (cefaclor), 280
*Keloc SR* (felodipine), 111
Keloid dressings, 826
*Kemadrin* preparations, 257
*Kemicetine*, 293
*Kenalog Intra-articular/Intramuscular*, 367, 516
*Kentera*, 420
*Keppra*, 242
*Keral*, 508
Keratitis, 534
Keratolytics, 591
Keratosis follicularis, 581
*Keri*, 569
*Keromask* preparations, 594
*Ketalar*, 634
Ketamine, **634**
infusion table, 796
neuropathic pain, 230
*Ketek*, 291
*Ketocid*, 511
Ketoconazole, 308, 309, **312**, 313
anogenital, 406
Cushing's syndrome, 396
scalp, 595
skin, 599, 600
*Ketodiastix*, 359
Ketolides, 290
Ketoprofen, 511
gout, 524
pain, 511
postoperative, 640
rheumatic disease, 505, **511**
topical, 531
Ketorolac, 506, **640**
eye, 548
*Ketostix*, 359
Ketotifen, 160
eye, 538, **539**
*Ketovail*, 511
*Ketovite*, 499
*Ketpron*, 511
*Ketur Test*, 359
*K-Four* products, 833
Kidney *see* Renal
*Kindergen*, 807
*Kineret*, 522
*Kinidin Durules*, 82
*Kivexa*, 316
*Klaricid* preparations, 291
*Klean-Prep*, 64
*Kliofem*, 371
*Kliovance*, 371
*K-Lite*, 831
*Kloref* preparations, 475
*Knit Fix*, 830
*Knit-Band*, 830
*Knit-Firm*, 831
Knitted Elastomer and Viscose Bandage, 831
Knitted viscose dressing, primary, 828
*Ko-Flex*, 833
*Kogenate Bayer* (factor VIII fraction), 132
*Kolanticon*, 41
*Konakion Neonatal*—discontinued, ix
*Konakion* preparations, 498
Korsakoff's psychosis, 494
*K-Plus*, 831
*K-Soft*, 832, 833
*Kwells* (hyoscine hydrobromide), 217
*Kytril*, 215


# L


Labelling, cautionary and advisory *see* Cautionary and advisory labels, 836, 838
Labetalol, 83, **87**
infusion table, 796
*see also* Beta-adrenoceptor blocking drugs
*Labiton*, 499
Labour
analgesia, 223
induction, 398
premature, 402
Labyrinthine disorders, 211
Lacidipine, 109, **111**, 112
*see also* Calcium-channel blockers
*Lacri-Lube*, 546
Lactation, suppression, 367, 392
Lactic acid
hydrocortisone with, 575
salicylic acid with, 591, 592
sodium pidolate with, 569
*LactiCare*, 569
Lactose intolerance, ACBS, 816
with sucrose intolerance, 816
*Lactugal* (lactulose), 62
Lactulose, 61, **62**
*Ladropen* (flucloxacillin), 275
Laevulose *see* Fructose
*Lamictal*, 242
*Lamisil*, 313
cream, 601
gel, 601
spray, 601


Index

Lamivudine, **316**, 317
abacavir and zidovudine with, 316
abacavir with, 316
chronic hepatitis B, 326
HIV infection, 315
zidovudine with, 318
Lamotrigine, 238, **241**, 242
trigeminal neuralgia, 231
Lancets sterile, 350
Lanolin, excipient, 567, 568
*Lanoxin* preparations, 70
Lanreotide, **461**, 462
Lansoprazole, 48, **49**
*Lantus*, 348
*Lanvis*, 438
*Larafen CR*, 511
*Larapam SR*, 230
*Largactil*, 183
*Lariam*, 335
Laronidase, **501**
infusion table, 796
*LarvE*, 608
*Laryngojet*, 649
*Lasikal*, 77
*Lasilactone*, 77
*Lasix*, 74
*Lasonil*, 610
*Lasoride* (co-amilofruse), 76
Lassar's paste, 584
Latanoprost, **542**
Latin abbreviations, *see inside back cover*
Laxatives, 57
bulk-forming, 58
faecal softeners, 61
osmotic, 61
stimulant, 59
*Laxoberal* (sodium picosulfate), 61
*Ledclair*, 35
*Lederfen* preparations, 510
*Lederfolin* (calcium folinate), 429
*Ledermycin*, 286
Leflunomide, **520**
rheumatic disease, 519
Left ventricular failure *see* Heart failure
Legionnaires' disease, 289
Leishmaniacides, 338
Leishmaniasis, 338
Lenograstim, 472, **473**
infusion table, 796
Lepirudin, 122, **123**
infusion table, 796
Lepra reactions, 302
Leprosy, 302
Leptospirosis, 273, 285
Lercanidipine, 109, **112**
*see also* Calcium-channel blockers
*Lescol* preparations, 137
Letrozole, 456, 457, **458**
Leucovorin *see* Calcium folinate
Leukaemia
acute, 432
lymphoblastic, 435, 441, 448
chronic lymphocytic, 430, 435
chronic myeloid, 430, 442, 452, 453
CNS, prophylaxis, 435
hairy cell, 452, 453
lymphoid, 468
*Leukeran*, 431
*Leukofix*, 834
*Leukopor*, 834
*Leukosilk*, 834
*Leukostrip*, 835
Leukotriene receptor antagonists, 160
Leuprorelin, 394
endometriosis, 395
prostate cancer, 458, **460**
*Leustat*, 436
Levamisole, 341
*Levemir*, 348
Levetiracetam, 238, **242**
*Levitra*, 426
Levobunolol, **541**
Levobupivacaine, **650**
Levocabastine—discontinued, ix
Levocetirizine, 161, **162**
Levodopa, 251
dopa-decarboxylase inhibitor, 252
entacapone with, 253
Levofloxacin, 304, **305**
Levofolinic acid *see* Calcium levofolinate
Levomenthol, 170
Levomepromazine, **185**
nausea and vertigo, 210
palliative care, 15, 17, 185
psychosis, 185
*Levonelle 1500*, 413
*Levonelle One Step*, 412
*Levonelle-2*—discontinued, ix
Levonorgestrel, **412**, 415
contraception, 411, 414
emergency, 412, 413
intra-uterine, 415
HRT, 370, 371
Levothyroxine, 359, 360
*Lexpec* (folic acid), 467
*Lexpec with Iron*, 465
*Lexpec with Iron-M*, 465
LH *see* Luteinising hormone, 380
LH-RH *see* Gonadorelin, 383, **384**
*Liberate* (factor VIII fraction), 132
*Liberim HB*, 629
*Liberim T*, 629
*Liberim Z*, 629
*Liberty* nebuliser, 154
*Librium* (chlordiazepoxide), 179
Lice, 603
Lidocaine, 65, 648
arrhythmias, **82**
chlorhexidine, with, 648
dental, 647, 648
eye, **545**
local anaesthesia, 647, **648**, 649
urethral pain, 422
mouth, 560
neuropathic pain, 230
phenylephrine, with, 649
rectal, 65
*Lifestyle* preparations, 807
Lignocaine *see* Lidocaine
*Lignospan Special* , 648
*Lignostab A*—discontinued, ix
*Li-Liquid*, 194
*Limclair*, 490
Linezolid, **294**, 295
Lint, absorbent, 829
*Lioresal*, 528
Liothyronine, 359, **360**
resistant depression, 196
*Lipantil* preparations, 135
Lipid-regulating drugs, 133
*Lipitor*, 136
*Lipobase*, 569
Lipodystrophy syndrome, 315
*Lipofundin* preparations, 485
*Lipofundin N*—discontinued, ix
Lipoprotein lipase deficiency, 818
*Liposic*, 546
*Lipostat*, 137
*LiquiBand*, 605
Liquid and White Soft Paraffin Ointment, 568
Liquid paraffin, 61
emulsion, 61
magnesium hydroxide and, 62
eye, 546
*Liquifilm Tears*, 546
*Liquigen*, 807
*Liquivisc*, 546
*Lisicostad* preparations, 101
Lisinopril, **100**, 101
hydrochlorothiazide with, 101
*see also* ACE inhibitors
*Liskonum*, 194
Lisuride, 250, **254**, 255
Lithium, 193–5
cluster headache, 236
mania, 194
poisoning by, 32
recurrent depression, 194
surgery, 633
Lithium carbonate, 194
Lithium citrate, 194
*Lithonate* (lithium carbonate), 194
Liver disease, prescribing in, 735
Liver failure, ACBS, 818
*Livial*, 374
Loa loa, *342*
*Load 375*, 416
*Locabiotal*—discontinued, ix
Local anaesthetics *see* Anaesthesia, local
*Locasol*, 807
*Loceryl*, 599
*Locoid* preparations, 575
*Locorten-Vioform*, 551
*Lodine SR*, 509
Lodoxamide, 538, **539**
*Loestrin-20*, 410
*Loestrin-30*, 411
*Lofensaid* (diclofenac) preparations, 508
Lofepramine, 196, **199**
Lofexidine, **263**
*Logynon* preparations, 411
*Lomont* (lofepramine), 199
*Lomotil*, 52
Lomustine, 431, **432**
*Loniten*, 93
Loop diuretics *see* Diuretics, loop, 73
*Lopace* (ramipril), 102
Loperamide, 52
palliative care, 15
Lophlex, *807*
*Lopid*, 135
Lopinavir, 315, **319**
ritonavir with, 320
*Lopranol LA* (propranolol), 85
Loprazolam, 174, **175**
*Lopresor* preparations, 88
*Loprofin*, 808

Loratadine, 161, **162**
Lorazepam, 178, **179**
- anaesthesia, 638, **639**
- nausea and vomiting, 428
- status epilepticus, 247, **249**

Lormetazepam, 174, **175**
*Loron*, 390
Losartan, 103, **104**
- hydrochlorothiazide with, 104

*Losec*, 50
Lotions
- definition, 566
- eye, 533
- suitable quantities, 567

*Lotriderm*, 577
*Low protein drink*, 808
Low protein products, ACBS, 818
Low sodium content (antacids), 38
LSD *see* Lysergide, 7
*Luborant*, 564
*Lubri-Tears*, 546
Lucanthone, 342
*Ludiomil*, 199
Lugol's solution, 361
Lumefantrine, 329, **333**
- artemether with, 333

*Lumigan*, 542
Lumiracoxib, 506, **511**
Lupus erythematosus
- discoid, 516
- systemic, 364, 514, 516, 519

*Lustral*, 204
Luteinising hormone, 380
Lutropin alfa, **381**
*Luveris*, 381
*Lyclear*, 605
*Lyflex* (baclofen), 528
Lyme disease, 276, 285
Lymecycline, **286**
Lymphangiectasia, intestinal, ACBS, 818
Lymphogranuloma venereum, 285
*Lyofoam* products, 823, 828
*Lyrica*, 241
*Lyrinel XL*, 420
Lysergic acid diethylamide *see* Lysergide, 7
Lysergide, regulations, 7
*Lysodren*, 443
Lysosomal storage disorder, 501
*Lysovir*, 327
Lysuride *see* Lisuride, 250, **254**, 255


Index

# M


*Maalox* preparations, 39, 40
*MabCampath*, 452
*MabThera*, 452
*Macrobid*, 308
*Macrodantin*, 308
Macrogol Oral Powder, Compound, NPF, 854, 857
Macrogol Oral Powder, NPF, 854, 856
Macrogols, 62, 64
Macrolides, 289
Macular degeneration, age-related, 548
*Madopar* preparations, 252
*Magnapen*, 278
Magnesium carbonate, 38, **39**
Magnesium citrate, 64
Magnesium glycerophosphate, 490
Magnesium hydroxide, 40, 62
- liquid paraffin, 62

Magnesium sulphate, 63, **491**
- arrhythmias, 490
- asthma, 143
- eclampsia, 490
- infusion table, 796
- injection, 491
- laxative, 63
- myocardial infarction, 490
- paste, 605

Magnesium trisilicate, 38, **39**
Malabsorption syndromes, 53
- ACBS, 818
- electrolytes, 474
- vitamin K, 498

Malaria, 329
- prophylaxis, 328
- treatment, 329

*Malarivon*, 334
*Malarone*, 335
- malaria prophylaxis, 331, 332, 333, 335
- malaria treatment, 329, 335

*Malarone Paediatric*, 335
Malathion, 602, 603, **604**
Malignant disease, 427
- bladder, 423
- gonadorelin analogues, 458
- hormone antagonists, 456
- pain, 222
  - bone, 218
- sex hormones, 455

Malignant effusions, 431
Malignant hyperthermia, 646
- antagonists, 646

Malnutrition, disease-related, ACBS, 819
*Manerix*, 202
*Manevac*, 60
Mania, 181, 193
Manic depression *see* Bipolar disorder, 193
Mannitol, **77**
- glaucoma, 540
- presence of, 2

Mantoux test, 614
Manufacturers, special order, 876
*Manusept*, 608
MAOIs *see* Monoamine-oxidase inhibitors
Maple syrup urine disease, ACBS, 819
*Mapleflex*, 808
Maprotiline, 196, **199**
*Marcain* preparations, 649
*Marevan* (warfarin), 125
Marine stings, 36
Marketing authorisation, 1
*Marvelon*, 411
*Mastaflu*, 620
Mastalgia, 392, **396**
*Maxalt*, 233
*Maxamaid* preparations, 809, 815, 816
*Maxamum* preparations, 809, 815, 816
*Maxepa*, 139
*Maxidex*, 537
*Maxijul* preparations, 808
*Maxipro Super Soluble*, 808
*Maxisorb*, 808
*Maxitrol*, 537
*Maxolon* preparations, 214
*Maxtrex* (methotrexate), 521
MCT Oil, 808
*MCT Pepdite*, 808
MDMA *see* Methylenedioxymethamfetamine
Measles, 620
- immunisation
  - immunoglobulin, 628
  - vaccines, 620

Measles, mumps and rubella vaccine, 621
Mebendazole, 340
- hookworm infections, 341
- roundworm infections, 341
- threadworm infections, 340
- whipworm infections, 340

Mebeverine, **42**
Mecillinam, 279
Meclozine, 212
Mecysteine, 170
*Medicaid*, 571
Medicated bandages, 833
Medicines information services, *inside front cover*
*Medinol* (paracetamol) preparations, 220
*Mediplast*, 834
*Medipore+Pad*, 827
*Medisafe*, 827
*MediSense* products, 350, 358
Mediterranean fever, familial, 524
*Medi-Test* products, 359
*Medix* nebulisers, 153
*Medocodene* (co-codamol 30/500), 221
*Medrone*, 367
Medroxyprogesterone
- contraception, 414
- HRT, 369, 371, 372, 376
- malignant disease, **455**
- menstrual disorders, 375, **376**

Mefenamic acid, 512
- menorrhagia, 511
- pain, 505, **511**
- rheumatic disease, 505, **511**

*Mefilm*, 827
*Mefix*, 834
Mefloquine, **334**, 335
- malaria prophylaxis, 331–3
- malaria treatment, 329

*Megace*, 456
Megestrol, **455**, 456
Melanoma, 441, 452
*Melgisorb* products, 822
*Melolin*, 827
Meloxicam, 505, **512**
Melphalan, 430, **432**
- infusion table, 796

Memantine, 264, **265**
Menadiol sodium phosphate, **498**
Mendelson's syndrome, 45, 633
Meniere's disease, 211
Meningeal carcinoma, 435
*Meningitec*, 622

Meningitis
  cryptococcal, 311
  haemophilus, 269, 292
  initial therapy, 269
  listerial, 269
  meningococcal, 269
    immunisation, 621, 622
    prophylaxis, 270
    travel, 621, 631
    vaccine, viii, 621
  pneumococcal, 269
*Menjugate*, 622
*Menogon*, 381
Menopausal symptoms, 236, 367
*Menopur*, 381
*Menoring 50*, 373
Menorrhagia, 375, 415
  antifibrinolytics, 131
  NSAIDS, 511
Menotrophin *see* Human menopausal gonadotrophins, 381
Menthol and eucalyptus inhalation, 170
Mepacrine, **337**, 338
  rheumatic disease, 518
*Mepiform*, 826
*Mepilex* products, 828
*Mepitac*, 834
*Mepitel*, 828
Mepivacaine, 647
*Mepore* products, 827
Meprobamate, **180**
  muscle spasm, 529
Meptazinol, 223, **227**, 228
*Meptid*, 228
*Merbentyl* preparations, 41
Mercaptamine (cysteamine), **501**, 502
Mercaptopurine, 436, **437**
  inflammatory bowel disease, 53
*Mercilon*, 410
*Meronem*, 285
Meropenem, 284, **285**
  infusion table, 796
Mesalazine, 53, **54**, 55
Mesna, **430**
  infusion fluid, 796
*Mesorb*, 827
*Mesren MR*, 55
Mesterolone, **378**
*Mestinon*, 527
Mestranol, contraception, 412
Metabolic Mineral Mixture, *808*
Metals, poisoning by, 34
*Metalyse*, 131
*Metanium*, 571
Metaraminol, **118**
  infusion table, 796
*Metastron*, 14
*Metatone*, 499
*Meted*, 595
*Metenix-5*, 73
Metformin, **353**
  rosiglitazone with, 355
Methadone, 14, 228, 263
  cough, 171
  opioid dependence, **263**
  pain, 222, **228**
  poisoning by, 31
  preparations, 228
    linctus, 171
    oral solution (1 mg/mL), 263
*Methadose*, 263
Methaemoglobinaemia, 650
Methanol, poisoning by, 34
*Metharose* (methadone), 263
Methenamine, 307, **308**
Methicillin *see* Meticillin, 274, 294, 295
Methionine, 29, **31**
Methocarbamol, **529**
Methotrexate, 437
  Crohn's disease, 53
  infusion table, 796
  malignant disease, 435, 437
  preparations, 521
  psoriasis, 585, 586
  rheumatic disease, 516, 519, **520**
Methotrimeprazine *see* Levomepromazine
Methyl alcohol *see* Methanol, 34
Methyl cysteine *see* Mecysteine, 170
Methyl salicylate, 601, 606
  dithranol and salicylic acid with, 584
Methyl-5-aminolevulinate, 594
Methylated spirit, industrial, 606
Methylcellulose, 59, 209
  constipation, 58
  diarrhoea, 51
  obesity, 59, 209
Methylcysteine *see* Mecysteine, 170
Methyldopa, **94**
Methylene blue *see* Methylthioninium chloride, 650
Methylenedioxymethamfetamine
  controlled drug, 8
  poisoning by, 33
Methylmalonic acidaemia, 819
Methylphenidate, 206, **207**, 208
Methylprednisolone, **367**
  lidocaine with, 515
  rheumatic disease, 515
Methylprednisolone acetate, 367
Methylprednisolone sodium succinate, 367
  infusion table, 796
Methylthioninium chloride, 650
Methysergide, 235, **236**
  cluster headache, 236
Meticillin-resistant *Staphylococcus aureus*, 274, 294, 295
Metipranolol, **541**
Metirosine, 96
Metoclopramide, 211
  aspirin with, 231
  diabetic neuropathy, 357
  gastro-intestinal, 43
  infusion table, 797
  migraine, 235
  nausea and vomiting, 210, **214**, 428
  palliative care, 15
  paracetamol with, 232
  preparations, 214
Metolazone, 72, **73**
*Metopirone*, 397
Metoprolol, **87**, 88
  hydrochlorothiazide with, 88
  migraine, 235
  *see also* Beta-adrenoceptor blocking drugs
*Metosyn*, 578
*Metrogel*, 598
*Metrolyl*, 303
Metronidazole, 302, **303**
  amoebiasis, 337
  Crohn's disease, 53
  giardiasis, 337
  preparations, 303
    topical, 598
    vaginal, 407
  protozoal infections, 337
  skin, 598
  trichomoniasis, 337
  ulcerative gingivitis, 303, 560
*Metrosa*, 598
*Metrotop*, 598
Metvix, *594*
Metyrapone, **396**, 397
Mexiletine, 82, **83**
  infusion table, 797
*Mexitil*, 83
*mhi-500*, 350
*Miacalcic*, 387
Mianserin, 196, **199**, 200
*Micanol*, 584
*Micardis* preparations, 104
*Micolette Micro-enema*, 63
Miconazole, 309, **313**
  mouth, 561
  preparations, 600
    oral gel, 562
  skin, 599, **600**
    fluprednidene with, 578
    hydrocortisone, with, 575
  vaginal, 405
*Micralax Micro-enema*, 63
*Micral-Test II*, 359
*Microalbustik*, 359
*Microbumintest*, 359
*Microgynon preparations*, 411
*Microlance*, 350
*Micronor*, 414
*Micronor HRT*, 376
*MicroPeak*, 151
*Micropirin* (aspirin), 127
*Micropore*, 834
*Microval*—discontinued, ix
Midazolam, 638, **639**, 640
  infusion table, 797
  palliative care, 17
  status epilepticus, 247
*Midrid*, 235
*Mifegyne*, 402
Mifepristone, 398, 402
*Migard*, 233
Miglustat, **501**
Migraine, 231
  acute attack, 231
  prophylaxis, 235
*Migraleve*, 231
*MigraMax*, 231
*Migril*, 235
*Mildison*, 574
Milk intolerance, ACBS, 819
Milk, drugs in, 776
Milk-alkali syndrome, 38
*Mill Plus*, 831
*Milpar* (liquid paraffin emulsion and magnesium hydroxide), 62
Milrinone, **71**
  infusion table, 797
*Milupa Low Protein Drink*, 808
*Milupa lpd*, 808
*Milupa PKU* preparations, 811

- *Milward Steri-Let*, 350
- *Mimpara*, 490
- *Minaphlex*, 808
- Mineralocorticoids, 361
  - replacement therapy, 361
- *Minijet*
  - *Adrenaline*, 119, 166, 167
  - *Aminophylline*, 150
  - *Atropine Sulphate*, 637
  - *Calcium Chloride*, 489
  - *Furosemide*, 74
  - *Glucose*, 479
  - *Lignocaine*, 83
  - Magnesium Sulphate, 491
  - *Morphine Sulphate*, 225
  - *Naloxone*, 31
  - *Sodium Bicarbonate*, 480
- *Minims*
  - Amethocaine, 545
  - Artificial Tears, 546
  - Atropine Sulphate, 540
  - Benoxinate (Oxybuprocaine), 545
  - Chloramphenicol, 535
  - Cyclopentolate, 540
  - Dexamethasone, 537
  - Fluorescein Sodium, 547
  - Gentamicin, 535
  - Lignocaine and Fluorescein, 545
  - Metipranolol, 541
  - Phenylephrine, 540
  - Pilocarpine Nitrate, 544
  - Prednisolone, 538
  - Proxymetacaine, 545
  - Proxymetacaine and Fluorescein, 545
  - Rose Bengal, 547
  - Saline, 547
  - Tropicamide, 540
- *MiniQuick*, 382
- *Minitran*, 107
- *Miniversol*, 606
- *Mini-Wright*, 151
- *Minocin* preparations, 287
- Minocycline, 285, **286**
  - acne, 589
  - preparations, 287
- *Minodiab*, 352
- Minoxidil
  - hypertension, 92, **93**
  - scalp, 596
- *Mintec*, 43
- Mintezol, 342
- *Minulet*, 412
- *Miochol-E*, 547
- *Mirapexin*, 255
- *Mirena*, 415
- Mirtazapine, 204, **205**
- Miscarriage, recurrent, 375
- Misoprostol, 48
  - diclofenac with, 509
  - naproxen with, 512
  - obstetrics, 398
- Misuse of drugs
  - Act, 8
  - Regulations 2001, 8
- Mitobronitol, 431
- Mitomycin, 433, **434**
  - bladder, 423
- *Mitomycin C Kyowa*, 434
- Mitotane, **442**, 443
- *Mitoxana*, 432
- Mitoxantrone, 433, **434**
  - infusion table, 797
- Mitozantrone *see* Mitoxantrone
- *Mivacron*, 644
- Mivacurium, 643, **644**
  - infusion table, 797
- *Mixtard* preparations, 349, 350
- Mizolastine, 161, **162**, 163
- *Mizollen*, 163
- MMR vaccine, 620, 621
- *MMR-II*, 621
- *Mobic*, 512
- *Mobiflex*, 513
- Moclobemide, **201**, 202
- Modafinil, 207, **208**
- *Modalim*, 135
- *Modecate* preparations, 192
- *Modisal* preparations, 108
- *Modisal XL*, 108
- *Moditen*, 184
- *Modrasone*, 576
- *Modrenal*, 397
- *Moducren*, 89
- *Modulen IBD*, 808
- *Moduret-25* (co-amilozide), 76
- *Moduretic* (co-amilozide), 76
- Moexipril, **101**
  - *see also* ACE inhibitors
- *Mogadon* (nitrazepam), 175
- *Molcer*, 554
- *Molipaxin*, 200
- Mometasone
  - asthma, 159
  - nasal allergy, 556
  - skin, 579
- Mometasone furoate
  - asthma, 154
- *Monigen XL* (isosorbide mononitrate), 109
- Monoamine-oxidase inhibitors, 200
  - reversible, 201
  - surgery, 633
  - type A, 201
  - type B, 251
- *Monocor*—discontinued, ix
- Monoethanolamine oleate *see* Ethanolamine oleate, **139**
- Monofluorophosphate, 492
- *Monogen*, 808
- *Monoject*, 350
- *Monoject Ultra*, 351
- *Monojector*, 350
- *Monolet*, 350
- *Monomax* preparations, 108
- *Monomil XL*, 109
- *Mononine* (factor IX fraction), 132
- *Monoparin* preparations, 121
- *Monosorb XL*, 109
- *Monotard*—discontinued, ix
- *Monotrim*, 297
- *Monovent*—discontinued, ix
- *Monphytol*, 601
- Montelukast, **160**
- Moracizine, 82
- *Morcap SR*, 224
  - palliative care, 14
- *Morhulin*, 571
- *Morphgesic SR*, 224
- Morphine, 52, **223**
  - cough, 171
  - pain, 222
    - chronic, 14, 222
  - palliative care, 14
  - preparations, 224, 225
    - cyclizine with, 225
    - kaolin and, 52
- *Motens*, 112
- *Motifene*, 509
- *Motilium*, 214
- Motion sickness, 211
- *Motival*, 199
- Motor neurone disease, amyotrophic lateral sclerosis, 258
- Mountain sickness, 77
- Mouth ulceration, 558
- Mouthwash solution-tablets, 564
- Mouthwashes, 562
- Movement disorders, 258
- *Movicol* preparations, 62
- Moxifloxacin, 304, **306**
- Moxisylyte, 115, **116**
- Moxonidine, **94**
- MRSA, 274, 295
- *MST Continus*, 224
  - palliative care, 14
- *MSUD Aid*, 808
- *MSUD Analog*, 808
- *MSUD express*, 808
- *MSUD Gel*, 809
- *MSUD Maxamaid*, 809
- *MSUD Maxamum*, 809
- *Mucodyne*, 170
- *Mucogel*, 39
- Mucolytics, 170
  - eye, 545
- Mucopolysaccharidosis I, 501
- Mucosa, oral, side-effects on, 11
- Mucositis, oral, 428
- *Multiload* IUDs, 416
- *Multiparin*, 121
- Multiple myeloma, 440, 452, 468
- Multiple sclerosis, 453, 454, 528, 529
- Multivitamin preparations, 498, 499
- Mumps
  - vaccines, 620, **622**
- Mupirocin, **597**
  - nose, 558
  - skin, 597
- Muscle relaxants
  - anaesthesia, 642
    - depolarising, 644
    - non-depolarising, 642
  - skeletal, 527
- Muscle spasm, 527
  - temporomandibular joint pain, 218
- Musculoskeletal disorders, rheumatic, 504
- *MUSE*, 425
- Muslin, absorbent, 829
- *MXL*, 224
  - palliative care, 14
- Myasthenia gravis, 526
  - corticosteroids, 527
  - diagnosis, 526
  - immunosuppressants, 527
- *Mycobacterium avium* complex infections, 298, 300
- *Mycobutin*, 301

Mycophenolate mofetil, 447, 448
eczema, 585
infusion table, 797
Mycophenolic acid, 448
Mycoplasma infections, 285
*Mycota*, 601
*Mydriacyl*, 540
Mydriatics, 539
*Mydrilate*, 540
*Myelobromol*, 431
Myeloma, multiple *see* Multiple myeloma, 440, 452, 468
*Myfortic*, 448
*Myleran*, 431
Myocardial infarction, 129
analgesia, 224, 226
arrhythmias, 78
beta-blockers, 84
dental practice, 21
magnesium sulphate, 490
secondary prevention, 139
thrombolytics, 129
*Myocet*, 434
Myoclonic seizures, 238
*Myocrisin*, 517
Myometrial relaxants, 402
*Myotonine*, 419
*Mysoline*, 243
Myxoedema, 359

# N

*N-A Dressing*, 828
*N-A Ultra*, 828
Nabilone, 211, **216**, 217
Nabumetone, 505, **512**
Nadolol, **88**
cardiovascular, 88
migraine, 235
*see also* Beta-adrenoceptor blocking drugs
thyrotoxicosis, 360
Nafarelin, 395, 396
Naftidrofuryl, 115, **116**
*Nalcrom*, 57
Nalidixic acid, 304, **306**, 307
*Nalorex*, 264
Naloxone
anaesthesia, **646**
infusion table, 797
poisoning, 31
preparations, 31
Naltrexone, 263, **264**
Name changes, x
Nandrolone decanoate, 379
Nappy rash, 571
*Napratec*, 512
*Naprosyn* preparations, 512
Naproxen, 512
gout, 524
pain, 505
preparations, 512
misoprostol with, 512
rheumatic disease, 505, **512**
*Naramig*, 233
Naratriptan, 232, **233**
*Narcan*—discontinued, ix
Narcolepsy, 206
Narcotic analgesics *see* Analgesics, opioid
Narcotic antagonists *see* Opioid antagonists
*Nardil*, 201
*Naropin*, 651
*Nasacort*, 556
Nasal
allergy, 554
congestion, 554, 557
decongestants
infection, 558
systemic, 161, 172
topical, 556
polyps, 554
*Naseptin*, 558
*Nasobec* preparations, 555
*Nasofan*, 556
*Nasonex*, 556
Nateglinide, **354**
National Institute for Health and Clinical Excellence, 3
*Natrilix* preparations, 73
Nausea, 211
cytotoxic drugs, 428
motion sickness, 211
palliative care, 16
postoperative, 211
pregnancy, 211
*Navelbine*, 439
*Navidrex*, 73
*Navispare*, 76
*Navoban*, 216
*Nebcin*—discontinued, ix
*Nebido*, 377
*Nebilet*, 88
Nebivolol, 83, **88**
*see also* Beta-adrenoceptor blocking drugs
*Nebuchamber*, 152
*Nebuhaler*, 152
Nebulisers, 152
Necatoriasis, 341
Nedocromil
asthma, 159
eye, 538, **539**
Needles, insulin, 350
clipping device, 351
Nefopam, 218, **222**
*Negaban*, ix
*Negram*—discontinued, ix
*NeisVac-C*, 622
Nelfinavir, 315, **320**
*Neocate* preparations, 809
*Neoclarityn*, 162
*Neo-Cortef*
ear, 551
eye, 537
*Neo-Cytamen* (hydroxocobalamin), 467
*Neofel XL* (felodipine), 111
*Neo-Mercazole*, 361
Neomycin, 288, **289**
chlorhexidine with, 558
ear, 550, 551, **552**
eye, 534, **535**, 537
nose, 558
skin, **597**
betamethasone valerate with, 576
clobetasol propionate with, 577
fluocinolone acetonide with, 578
gramicidin with, 597
*Neo-NaClex* preparations, 72, 77
*Neoral*, 450
*NeoRecormon*, 470
*Neosafe*, 827
*Neosporin*, 535
*Neosport*, 831
Neostigmine, 526, 645
anaesthesia, **645**
glycopyrronium bromide with, 645
laxative, 59
myasthenia gravis, 526, 527
*Neotigason*, 585
Nephrotic syndrome, 364
*Nepro*, 809
*Nerisone* preparations, 577
Nerve agent, poisoning by, 35
*Nestargel*, 809
*Netillin*, 289
Netilmicin, 288, **289**
infusion table, 797
*Neulactil*, 185
*Neulasta*, 474
*Neupogen*, 473
Neural tube defects, prevention, 467
Neuralgia, 196, 230
glossopharyngeal, 231
*NeuroBloc*, 259
Neuroleptic malignant syndrome, 182
Neuroleptics *see* Antipsychotics
Neuromuscular blocking drugs, 642
Neuromuscular disorders, 526
*Neurontin*, 241
Neuropathic pain, 230
Neuropathy, compression, 515
Neutral insulin *see* Insulin, soluble, **346**, 347
*Neutrogena Dermatological Cream*, 569
Neutropenias, 468, 472
Nevirapine, 315, **321**
New preparations, ix
*Nexium*, 49
*Niaspan*, 139
NHS Direct *inside front cover*
*Nicam*, 589
Nicardipine, 109, **112**
*see also* Calcium-channel blockers
NICE *see* National Institute for Health and Clinical Excellence, 3
*Nicef* (cefradine), 282
Niclosamide, 341
Nicorandil, **115**
*Nicorette* preparations, 262
Nicotinamide, 494
tablets, 495
topical, 589
Nicotine
replacement therapy, 260
smoking cessation products, 261, 262
*Nicotinell* preparations, 262
Nicotinic acid, 138, 139
hyperlipidaemia, **138**
Nicoumalone *see* Acenocoumarol, 124, **125**
Nifedipine, 109, **112**, 113, 115, 402
atenolol with, 86
palliative care, 15
*see also* Calcium-channel blockers
*Nifedipress MR*, 113
*Niferex* preparations, 465
*Nifopress Retard*, 113
*Nimbex*, 643

Nimodipine, 109, **113**, 114
infusion table, 797
*Nimotop*, 114
*Nindaxa-2.5* (indapamide), 73
*Nipent*, 443
*Niquitin CQ* preparations, 262
Niridazole, 342
Nisoldipine, 109, **114**
*see also* Calcium-channel blockers
Nitrates
angina, 105
heart failure, 106
myocardial infarction, 129
tolerance to, 106
Nitrazepam, 174, **175**
*Nitrocine*, 107
*Nitro-Dur*, 107
Nitrofurantoin, **307**, 308
*Nitrolingual Pumpspray*, 106
*Nitromin*, 106
*Nitronal*, 107
Nitroprusside, 92, **93**
infusion table, 799
Nitrous oxide, 636, **637**
Nitrous oxide-oxygen, 636
*Nivaquine*, 334
*Nivemycin* (neomycin), 289
Nizatidine, **46**
infusion table, 797
*Nizoral*, 313
anogenital, 406
scalp, 595
skin, 600
Nocturnal enuresis, 421
*Nocutil*, 386
*Nolvadex* preparations, 457
Nonacog alfa, 132
Non-depolarising muscle relaxants *see* Muscle relaxants
Non-nucleoside reverse transcriptase inhibitors, 314, 315
Nonoxinol, 415, 416
Non-woven swabs, fabric, 829
filmated, 829
*Nootropil*, 258
Noradrenaline, **118**, 119
infusion table, 797
*Norcuron*, 644
*Norditropin*, 383
Norelgestromin, 410
Norepinephrine *see* Noradrenaline
Norethisterone
contraception, 411, 412, 414
HRT, 370, 376
malignant disease, 456
menstrual disorders, **376**
Norethisterone acetate
contraception, 410, 411
HRT, 370, 371, 372
Norethisterone enantate, 414
contraception, 415
Norfloxacin, 304, **306**
*Norgalax Micro-enema*, 60
Norgestimate, 411
*Norgeston*, 414
Norgestrel
HRT, 370
*see also* Levonorgestrel
*Noriday*, 414
*Norimin*, 411
*Norimode* (loperamide), 52
*Norinyl-1*, 412
Noristerat, *414*, 415
*Noritate*, 598
*Normacol* preparations, 59
Normal immunoglobulin *see* Immunoglobulins, normal, 627, 628
'Normal saline', 478
*Normaloe* (loperamide), 52
*Normasol*, 606
*Normax*, 60
*Normosang*, 502
*Norphyllin SR* (aminophylline), 150
*Norprolac*, 393
Nortriptyline, 196, **199**
fluphenazine with, 199
neuropathic pain, 230
*Norvir*, 320
*Norzol* (metronidazole), 303
Nose *see* Nasal, 554
Notifiable diseases, 266
*Novantrone*, 434
*Novasource* preparations, 809
*Nova-T*, 416
*Novofem*, 371
*NovoFine*, 350
*Novogel*, 825
*Novolizer*, 157
*NovoMix 30*, 349
*NovoNorm*, 355
*NovoPen*, 350
*NovoRapid*, 347
*NovoSeven* (factor VIIa fraction), 132
*Nozinan*, 185
NPH *see* Insulin, isophane
NSAIDs (non-steroidal anti-inflammatory drugs) *see* Analgesics
*NU DERM*, 826
Nucleoside analogues *see* Nucleoside reverse transcriptase inhibitors, 314, 315
Nucleoside reverse transcriptase inhibitors, 314, 315
*Nuelin SA*, 150
*Nu-Gel*, 825
Nurse Prescribers' Extended Formulary, 857, 859
Nurse Prescribers' Formulary, 853
*Nu-Seals Aspirin*
analgesia, 219
cardiovascular, 127
*Nutilis*, 809
*Nutracel* preparations, 485
*Nutramigen* preparations, 809
*Nutraplus*, 569
*Nutriflex* preparations, 485
*Nutriflex Basal*—discontinued, ix
*Nutriflex Peri*—discontinued, ix
*Nutriflex Plus*—discontinued, ix
*Nutriflex Special*—discontinued, ix
*Nutrini* preparations, 809
*Nutriprem* preparations, 810
*Nutrison* preparations, 810
Nutrition, 482
ACBS, 801
enteral, 487, 488
intravenous, 482
oral, 487, 488
total parenteral, 482
Nutritional supplements, ACBS, 819
*Nutrizym* preparations, 68
*NutropinAq*, 383
*Nuvelle* preparations, 371, 372
Nylon and viscose stretch bandage, 830
*Nyogel*, 541
*Nystaform*, 600
*Nystaform-HC*, 575
*Nystamont* (nystatin), 313, 562
*Nystan*, 313
anogenital, 406
mouth, 562
skin, 600
Nystatin, 309, **313**
anogenital
perianal, 64
vaginal, 406
vulval, 406
ear, 552
mouth, 561, 562
skin, 599, **600**
chlorhexidine and hydrocortisone with, 575
clobetasol propionate with, 577
hydrocortisone with, 575
tolnaftate with, 601

# O

Obesity, 208
Obidoxime, 35
Obstetric and gynaecological surgery, antibacterial prophylaxis, 273
Obstructive pulmonary disease *see* Chronic obstructive pulmonary disease
*Occlusal*, 591
Ocrilate, 605
*Octagam*, 628
*Octalbin* preparations (albumin solution), 480
*Octaplas* (fresh frozen plasma), 133
*Octim*, 386
Octocog alfa, 132
Octreotide, **461**
palliative care, 17
*Ocufen*, 548
*Oculotect*, 546
*Odrik*—discontinued, ix
Oedema
cerebral, 77
pulmonary, 73
Oesophageal varices, 384
Oesophagitis *see* Gastro-oesophageal reflux disease, 37, 38
Oestradiol *see* Estradiol
Oestriol *see* Estriol
*Oestrogel*, 373
Oestrogens, 367
conjugated
HRT, 369, 370, 372
HRT, 367, **369**
malignant disease, 455
oral contraceptives, 407
vaginal, 404
Oestrone *see* Estrone, 374
Ofloxacin, 304, **306**
ear, 553
eye, **535**
*Oilatum*
cream, 569
*Emollient*, 570
*Fragrance Free*, 570
*Plus*, 570
shower emollient, 569

Oily cream, 568
Ointments
definition, 566
eye, 533
suitable quantities, 567
Olanzapine, 187, **189**
*Olbetam*, 138
*OliClinomel* preparations, 486
Olive oil
cradle cap, 595
ear, 553
Olmesartan, 103, **104**
*Olmetec*, 104
Olopatadine, 538, **539**
Olsalazine, 53, 54, **55**
*Omacor*, 139
Omalizumab, 160, **161**
Omega-3 fatty acid compounds, 139
Omega-3-acid ethyl esters, **139**
Omega-3-marine triglycerides, **139**
Omeprazole, 48, **50**
infusion table, 797
*Omiderm*, 827
*Omnifix*, 834
*Omnikan*, 351
*Omnopon* (papaveretum), 228
*Omron* nebulisers, 154
Onchocerciasis, 342
*OncoTice*, 454
*Onco-vial* preparations, 436, 443
*Oncovin*, 439
Ondansetron, 211, **215**
infusion table, 797
*One Touch* products, 350, 358
*One-Alpha*, 497
*Onkotrone*, 434
Onychomycosis see Fungal infections
*Opatanol*, 539
Open-wove bandage, 830
Ophthalin, *547*
*Opilon*, 116
Opioid analgesics *see* Analgesics, opioid
Opioid antagonists, 646
poisoning, 31
*OpSite* products, 827
*Opticrom* preparations, 539
*OptiFlo* preparations, 423
*Optil* (diltiazem), 110
*Optilast*, 538
*Optimax*, 206
*OptiPen Pro*, 350
*Optivate*, 132
Optrex Allergy, *539*
*Optrex Infected Eyes*, 535
*Orabase*, 559
*Orahesive*, 559
*Oral balance* see *Biotène Oralbalance*
Oral contraceptives *see* Contraception, oral
Oral Film Forming Agents, 855
Oral hypoglycaemic drugs *see* Antidiabetic drugs, oral, 351
Oral rehydration, 476
WHO formula, 477
Oral rehydration salts, 476
Oral syringes, 2
*Oraldene*, 563
*Oramorph* preparations, 224
*Orap*, 185
*Orbifen* (ibuprofen), 507
Orciprenaline, 148
*Orelox*, 282
*Orgalutran*, 394
Organophosphorus insecticides, poisoning by, 35
*Orgaran*, 122
*Orgran*, 810
*Orimeten*—discontinued, ix
*Orlept* (sodium valproate), 245
Orlistat, **209**
Oropharynx, 558
anti-infective drugs, 560
Orphenadrine, **257**
Orphenadrine hydrochloride, 257
ORS, 476
ORT, 476
*Ortho* diaphragm, 417
*Ortho-Band Plus*, 832
*Ortho-Creme*, 415
*Orthoforms*, 416
*Ortho-Gynest*, 404
Orthopaedic surgery
antibacterial prophylaxis, 272
*Orthovisc*, 505
*Orudis*, 511
*Oruvail* preparations, 511
gel, 531
Oseltamivir, 326, **327**
*Osmolite* preparations, 810
*Ostenil*, 505
Osteoarthritis, 504, 505
Osteomyelitis, 269, 292, 293
Osteonecrosis
jaw, 389, 391
Osteoporosis, 386
anabolic steroids, 379
bisphosphonates, 386, 388
calcitonin, 386
calcitriol, 386, 496
calcium, 386, 488
corticosteroid-induced, 387
HRT, 386
postmenopausal, 386
raloxifene, 387
strontium ranelate, 386
teriparatide, 386
*Otex*, 554
Otitis externa, 550
systemic treatment, 270
topical treatment, 550
Otitis media, 553
systemic treatment, 270
with effusion, 553
*Otomize*, 551
*Otosporin*, 552
*Otradrops* (xylometazoline), 557
*Otraspray* (xylometazoline), 557
*Otrivine* (xylometazoline), 557
*Otrivine-Antistin*, 538
*Ovestin*
cream, 404
tablets, 374
*Ovex* (mebendazole), 340
*Ovitrelle*, 381
*Ovranette*, 411
*Ovysmen*, 411
*Oxactin* (fluoxetine), 203
Oxaliplatin, 443, **444**
infusion table, 797
Oxamniquine, 342
Oxazepam, 178, **179**
Oxazolidinone antibacterials, 294
Oxcarbazepine, 238, **239**, 240
trigeminal neuralgia, 231
Oxerutins, 117
Oxidising agents *see* Hydrogen peroxide
*Oxis*, 147
Oxpentifylline *see* Pentoxifylline, 116
Oxprenolol, **88**
cyclopenthiazide with, 88
*see also* Beta-adrenoceptor blocking drugs
Oxybenzone, 593, 594
Oxybuprocaine, **545**
Oxybutynin, 419, **420**
Oxycodone, 14, 222, **228**
infusion table, 797
*OxyContin*, 228
Oxygen, 168
acute asthma, 168
allergic emergencies, 165
anaphylaxis, 165
chronic obstructive pulmonary disease, 169
cluster headache, 236
concentrators, 169
cylinders, 168
long-term therapy, 169
myocardial infarction, 129
Oxymetazoline, 557
Oxymetholone, 468
*Oxymycin* (oxytetracycline), 287
*OxyNorm*, 228
Oxytetracycline, **287**
acne, 589
oral infections, 285
rosacea, 586
*Oxytetramix* (oxytetracycline), 287
Oxytocin, 399, **400**, 401
ergometrine with, 400
infusion table, 797

# P

P2S, 36
*Pabrinex*, 494
Pacemakers
dental practice, 24
Paclitaxel, **445**
infusion table, 797
PACT, vii
Padimate-O, 594
*Paediasure* preparations, 810, 811
Paediatric doses, 13
*Paediatric Seravit*, 811
Paget's disease, 387
Pain, 217
bone, 218
dental, 217, 218, 223, 506
dressings, 636
musculoskeletal, 218, 531
neuropathic, 230
obstetric, 636
orofacial, 217, 218, 223, 230, 506
palliative care, 14, 17, 222
perioperative, 223, 640
rheumatic, 504
sickle-cell disease, 217
trigeminal neuralgia, 231
urethral, 422
visceral, 222

*Paldesic* (paracetamol) preparations, 220
Palivizumab, **328**
*Palladone* preparations, 227
Palliative care
 analgesic solutions, 224
 prescribing, 14
 subcutaneous infusion, 16
Palonosetron, 211, **216**
*Paludrine*, 335
*Paludrine/Avloclor*, 334
*Pamergan-P100*, 229
Pamidronate disodium *see* Disodium pamidronate
*Panadeine* (co-codamol 8/500), 220
*Panadol* (paracetamol) preparations, 220
*Pancrease* preparations, 68
Pancreatin, **67**, 68
Pancreatitis, chronic, 67
*Pancrex* preparations, 68
Pancuronium, 643, **644**
Panic disorders, 196
*Panoxyl* preparations, 587
Panthenol, 494
Pantoprazole, 48, **50**, 51
 infusion table, 797
Pantothenic acid, 494
Papaveretum, 228
 anaesthesia, **228**
 aspirin with, 220
 hyoscine with, 228
Papaverine, impotence, 426
*Papulex*, 589
Parabens, excipient, 567
Paracetamol, 218, **220**
 dextropropoxyphene with, 221
 dihydrocodeine with, 221
 domperidone with, 231
 febrile convulsions, 250
 isometheptene with, 235
 metoclopramide with, 232
 migraine, 231
 poisoning by, 29
 post-immunisation pyrexia, 611
 preparations, 220
  compound, 220, 231
 tramadol with, 230
*Paracodol* (co-codamol 8/500), 220
*Paradote*, 221
Paraffin
 gauze dressing, 828
 liquid
  eye, 546
  oral emulsion, 61
  white soft, with, 568
 white soft, 568
  eye, 546
 yellow soft, 568
  eye, 546
Paraldehyde, 247, **249**
*Paramax*, 232
*Paramol* (co-dydramol), 221
*Paranet*, 828
*Paraplatin*, 443
Paraproteinaemias, 468
Paraquat, poisoning by, 35
Parasiticidal preparations, 602
 suitable quantities, 602
Parasympathomimetics
 anaesthesia, 645
 eye, 544
 laxatives, 59
 myasthenia gravis, 526
 urinary retention, 418
*Paratex*, 828
*Paratulle*, 828
*Pardelprin* (indometacin m/r), 511
Parecoxib, 506, **640**, 641
Parenteral nutrition, 482
 preparations, 483
*PARI*
 nebulisers, 153
 *Vortex Spacer*, 152
Paricalcitol, 496, **497**
*Pariet*, 51
Parkinsonism, 250
 drug-induced, 182, 257
 idiopathic, 250
*Parlodel*, 392
Paromomycin, 338
*Paroven*, 117
Paroxetine, 202, **204**
Partial seizures, 238
*Partobulin SDF*, 630
*Parvolex*, 31
Pastes, definition, 567
Patents, 3
Patient group direction, 3
Patient packs, vii
*Pavacol-D* (pholcodine), 171
Peak flow meters, 151
Peanut oil *see* Arachis oil
PEC high compression bandage, 832
*Pediacel*, 615
Pediculosis, 603
*Peditrace*, 483
*Pegasys*, 453
Pegfilgrastim, 472, **474**
Peginterferon alfa, 326, **453**
*PegIntron*, 453
Pegvisomant, **383**
*Peha Crepp E*, 830
Pelvic inflammatory disease, 269
Pemetrexed, 436, **438**
 infusion table, 797
Pemphigus, 364
*Penbritin*, 277
Penciclovir, 322, **602**
*Penfine*, 350
Penicillamine, 499, 516, **517**, 518
 autoimmune hepatitis, 500
 cystinuria, 500
 poisoning, **34**
 rheumatic disease, 516, **517**
 Wilson's disease, 500
Penicillin G *see* Benzylpenicillin
Penicillin V *see* Phenoxymethylpenicillin, 273, **274**
Penicillin VK *see* Phenoxymethylpenicillin, 273, **274**
Penicillinases, 274
Penicillins, 273
 antipseudomonal, 278
 broad spectrum, 275
 penicillinase-resistant, 274
 penicillinase-sensitive, 273
*Penlet II*, 350
*Pennsaid*, 531
*Pentacarinat*, 340
Pentamidine isetionate, **339**, 340
 infusion table, 797
 leishmaniasis, 338
 pneumocystis pneumonia, 339
*Pentasa*, 55
Pentastarch, **481**, 482
Pentazocine, 223, **229**
*Pentostam*, 338
Pentostatin, **443**
 infusion table, 797
Pentoxifylline, **116**, 117, 832
Pentrax, 595
*Pepcid* (famotidine) preparations, 46
*Pepdite*, 811
Peppermint oil, **42**, 43
*Peptac*, 40
*Peptamen*, 811
*Pepti*, 811
*Pepti-Junior*, 811
*Peptimax* (cimetidine), 45
*Peptisorb*, 811
*Perative*, 811
*Percutol*, 107
*Perdix*, 101
*Perfalgan*, 220
*Perfan*, 71
Perforated plastic absorbent dressing, 827
Pergolide, 250, **255**
*Periactin*, 163
Pericoronitis, 270
Pericyazine, **185**
*Perinal*, 65
Perindopril, **101**
 indapamide with, 101
 *see also* ACE inhibitors
Periodontitis, 559
 antibacterial treatment, 270
Periostat, 559, 560
Peripheral vascular disease, 115
Peritonitis, 268
*PermaFoam* products, 823
Permeable adhesive tape, 834
Permethrin, 602, **604**, 605
Permitabs, 608
*Peroxyl*, 563
Perphenazine, 182, **185**
 amitriptyline with, 197
 nausea and vertigo, 210, 212
 psychoses, 185
*Persantin* preparations, 128
Pertussis
 immunisation
  vaccines, 615, **622**
 prophylaxis, 272
Pethidine, 223
 anaesthesia, 229
 analgesia, 223, **229**
 preparations, 229
 promethazine with, 229
Petit mal, 238
Petroleum jelly, 568
Petroleum products, poisoning by, 28
*Pevaryl*, 600
 anogenital, 406
Peyronie's disease, 495
PGD *see* Patient group direction, 3
Phaeochromocytoma, 84, **96**
Pharma-Ject Morphine Sulphate, *223*
*Pharmalgen*, 165
*Pharmorubicin* preparations, 434

Index

Pharyngitis *see* Throat infections
Pharynx *see* Oropharynx
Phenelzine, **200**, 201
*Phenergan* preparations, 164
Phenindione, 124, **125**
Phenobarbital, **242**
    epilepsy, 238, **242**
    poisoning, elimination, 28
    preparations, 243
Phenobarbital sodium, **249**
    status epilepticus, 247, 249
Phenobarbitone *see* Phenobarbital
Phenol, 65
    haemorrhoids, 65
    injection, oily, 65
Phenothiazines, 182
    classification, 182
    nausea and vertigo, 210, 211
    poisoning by, 33
    psychoses, 182
Phenothrin, **605**
Phenoxybenzamine, **96**
    infusion table, 798
Phenoxymethylpenicillin, 273, **274**
Phentermine, 209
Phentolamine, 96, **97**
    impotence, 426
    infusion table, 798
    papaverine with, 426
    preparations, 97
Phenylephrine
    eye, **540**, 546
    hypotension, 119
    infusion table, 798
    injection, 119
    lidocaine with, 649
Phenylketonuria, 487
    ACBS, 819
Phenylpropanolamine—discontinued
Phenytoin, 243
    diabetic neuropathy, 357
    epilepsy, 238, **243**
        status, **249**
        status epilepticus, 247
    infusion table, 798
    preparations, 243, 250
    trigeminal neuralgia, 231
*Phlexy-10*, 811
*Phlexyvits*, 811
Phobia, 200
Pholcodine, **171**
*Phosex*, 492
Phosgene, poisoning by, 35
Phosphate supplements, 491
Phosphate-binding agents, 491
Phosphates, 63, 491
    enemas, 62
    intravenous, 491
    rectal, 63
*Phosphate-Sandoz*, 491
Phosphodiesterase inhibitors, 71
Phosphodiesterase type 5 inhibitors, 425
Phosphorus, 491
Photodamage, skin, 594
Photodermatoses, 593
    ACBS, 820
Photodynamic therapy, 444
*Photofrin*, 444
Phototherapy, psoriasis, 581
*Phyllocontin Continus*, 150
    *Paediatric*—discontinued, ix
*Physeptone* (methadone), 228, 263
Physiological saline, 478
*Physiotens*, 94
*Physiotulle*, 828
*Phytex*, 601
Phytomenadione, 498
    infusion table, 798
Phytosterolaemia, 134
*Picolax*, 64
Piggy-back technique, 790
Pilocarpine, **544**
    dry eyes, 564, **565**
    dry mouth, 564, **565**
    eye preparations, 544
*Pilogel*, 544
Pimecrolimus, 585, **586**
Pimozide, 182, **185**
    Tourette syndrome, 258
Pindolol, **89**
    clopamide with, 89
    *see also* Beta-adrenoceptor blocking drugs
*Pinetarsol*, 583
Pinworm infections, 340
Pioglitazone, **354**, 355
Piperacillin, **278**
    tazobactam with, 278
        infusion table, 798
Piperazine, **341**
    roundworm infections, 341
    threadworm infections, 340
Piperazine oestrone sulphate *see* Estropipate, 374
*Piportil Depot*, 192
Pipothiazine *see* Pipotiazine, **192**
Pipotiazine, **192**
Piracetam, 247, **258**
Pirenzepine, 47
*Piriton*, 163
Piroxicam, 512
    gout, 524
    preparations, 513
        topical, 531
    rheumatic disease, 505, **512**
*Pitressin*, 385
Pituitary function test, 396
Pituitary hormones, 380
    anterior, 380
    posterior, 384
Pityriasis versicolor, 309, 599
Pivmecillinam, **279**
Pizotifen, **235**, 236
*PK Aid 4*, 811
*PK Foods* preparations, 811
*PKU* preparations, 811, 812
Plaque, 562
*Plaquenil*, 519
Plasma concentrations, electrolytes, 474
*Plasma-Lyte* preparations, 486
Plasma substitutes, 480
Plasma, fresh frozen, 132
Plasmapheresis, myasthenia gravis, 526
Plasters, 834
Plastic wound dressing
    impermeable, 834
    permeable, 834
*Plastipak*, 351
*Platinex* (cisplatin), 444
*Plavix*, 127
*Plendil*, 111
*Pleniday*, 812
*Plesmet*—discontinued, ix
*Pletal*, 116
Pneumococcal infection
    antibacterial prophylaxis, 272
    immunisation
        vaccines, viii, 622, 623
Pneumocystis pneumonia, 338
Pneumonia, 168, 268
    pneumococcal, 623
*Pneumovax II*, 623
*Pocket Chamber*, 152
*Pocketpeak*, 151
*PocketScan* products, 358
Podagra, 524
Podophyllin, 591, **592**
Podophyllotoxin, 592, 593
Podophyllum resin *see also* Podophyllin
    *see also* Podophyllotoxin
Poisoning, 27
    active elimination, 28
    adsorbents, 28
    hospital admission, 27
*Polial*, 812
Polihexanide, 549
Poliomyelitis, 623
    immunisation
        travel, 624, 630
        vaccines, 615, 623, 624
Pollenase Hayfever, *555*
*Pollinex*, 165
Polyacrylic acid *see* Carbomers, 546
Polyamide and cellulose contour bandage, 830
    knitted, 830
Polyamide, elastane, and cotton compression bandage, 832
Polyarteritis nodosa, 364, 514
*Polycal*, 812
    glucose tolerance test, 359
*Polycose*, 812
Polycystic ovary syndrome, 353
Polyene antifungal drugs, 309
Polyethoxylated castor oil *see* Polyoxyl castor oil, 2
Polyethylene glycols, 62, 64
Polyfax, 597
    eye, 536
Polygeline, 481
Polyhexamethylene biguanide, 549
Polyhexanide *see* Polihexanide
Polymethylmethacrylate, 605
Polymyalgia rheumatica, 514
Polymyositis, 514, 519
Polymyxin B
    ear, 552
    eye, 534, 535, 536, 537
    skin, 597
Polymyxins, 295
    ear, 553
    skin, 597
Polyoxyl castor oil, presence of, 2
Polyps, nasal, 554
Polysaccharide-iron complex, 465
Polyserositis, 524
*Polyskin* products, 827
Polysorbates, excipient, 567
Polystyrene sulphonate resins, 475

*Polytar*
- *AF*, 595
- *Emollient*, 583
- *Liquid*, 595
- *Plus*, 596

*Polytrim*, 536
Polyurethane foam dressing, 823, 824
Polyvinyl alcohol, 546
*Ponstan*, 512
*Ponstan Forte*, 512
POP *see* Progestogens, contraceptives, oral, 407, **413**
Poractant alfa, 168
Porfimer sodium, 444
*Pork Actrapid*, 346
*Pork Insulatard*, 348
*Pork Mixtard-30*, 349
Porphyrias, acute, 502
- drugs to be avoided in, 502, 503

Portal hypertension, 85
*Porta-Neb*, 153
*Posalfilin*, 592
Postherpetic neuralgia, 231, 322
*Potaba*, 495
Potable water, 2
Potassium aminobenzoate, 495
Potassium bicarbonate, **477**
- tablets, effervescent, 477

Potassium chloride, 475, 479
- concentrate, sterile, 479
- effervescent, 477
- infusion
  - glucose and, 479
  - sodium chloride and, 479
  - sodium chloride, glucose and, 479
- infusion table, 798
- oral preparations, 475

Potassium citrate, 422
Potassium permanganate, 580, 606, **608**
Potassium supplements, 474
- diuretic with, 77

Potassium-channel activators, 115
- angina, 105

Povidone, eye, 546
Povidone-iodine
- mouth, 558, 563
- mouthwash, 563
- oropharynx, 563
- skin, 606, **607**, 608
  - dressing, 827, 828
  - shampoo, 595
- vaginal, 406

*Powergel*, 531
Prader-Willi syndrome, 382
*Pragmatar*, 583
Pralidoxime mesilate, 35, **36**
Pramipexole, 250, **255**
Pramocaine [ingredient], 64, 65
Pramoxine *see* Pramocaine, 64, 65
Pravastatin, 135, **137**
*Praxilene*, 116
Praziquantel, 341, 342
Prazosin, **95**
- cardiovascular, 95
- preparations, 96
- urinary tract, 417, **418**

Precocious puberty, 394, 461
*Preconceive* (folic acid), 468
*Pred Forte*, 538
*Predenema*, 57
*Predfoam*, 57
Prednisolone, 362, **365**
- anorexia (palliative care), 16
- asthma
  - acute (dose), 143
  - chronic, 141
- ear, 552
- eye, 537, 538
- haemorrhoids, 65
- Inflammatory bowel disease, 57
- injection (local), 515
- lepra reactions, 302
- malignant disease, 448
- myasthenia gravis, 527
- palliative care, 16
- pneumocystis pneumonia, 339
- rectal, 57, 65
- rheumatic diseases, 514, 515
- withdrawal of, 365

Prednisolone sodium phosphate, 365
- ear, 552
- tablets, soluble, 365

*Predsol*
- ear, 552
- eye, 538
- rectal, 57

*Predsol-N*
- ear, 552
- eye, 538

Pre-eclampsia, 91, 490
Preface, iii
Pregabalin, **241**
- epilepsy, 240
- neuropathic pain, 230

*Pregaday*, 465
*Pregestimil*, 812
Pregnancy
- anticoagulants, 125
- asthma, 143
- epilepsy and, 238
- folate supplements, 465, 467
- hypertension in, 91
- iron, 463
  - folic acid and, 465
- nausea and vomiting, 211
- prescribing in, 758
- termination, 398

*Pregnyl*, 381
*Prejomin*, 812
*Premarin* cream, 404
*Premarin* tablets, 372
*PremCare*, 812
Premedication, 637
- children, 638
- dental procedures, 174, 639

Premenstrual syndrome, 375, 494
*Premique* preparations, 369
*Prempak-C*, 370
*Prentif Cervical Cap*, 417
*Prepadine* (dosulepin), 198
*Prescal*, 111
Prescribing, vii
- ACBS, 801
- addicts, 9
- analyses and cost, vii
- breast-feeding, 776
- children, 12
- computer-generated, 5
- controlled drugs, 7

Prescribing (*continued*)—
- dental practice, 4
- drug misusers, 9
- elderly, 18
- generic, 1
- instalments, 7
- liver disease, 735
- non-proprietary, 1
- palliative care, 14
- patient packs, vii
- pregnancy, 758
- renal impairment, 745

Prescription forms
- controlled drugs, 7
- dental, 4
- nurses, 853, 857
- security, 3

Prescription only medicines *see* preparations identified by PoM throughout BNF, *4*
Prescription writing, 4
*Preservex*, 507
*Presinex* (desmopressin), 385
Pressure sores, 571
*Prestige Smart System*, 358
*Prestim*, 89
*Prevenar*, 623
*Prexige*, 511
*Priadel*, 194, 195
Priapism, 423
Prices, vii
Prilocaine, **650**
- felypressin with, 647, 650

*Primacine* (erythromycin), 290
*Primacor*, 71
*Primapore*, 827
Primaquine, 328, **335**
- pneumocystis pneumonia, 339

*Primaxin*, 285, 796
*Primene*, 486
Primidone, 238, 242, **243**
*Primolut N*, 376
*Prioderm*, 604
*Priorix*, 621
*Pripsen*, 341
*Pripsen Mebendazole*, 340
*Pro-Banthine*, 42
*Probecid* (probenecid), 525
Probenecid, 524, **525**
Procainamide, 80, **81**
- infusion table, 798

Procaine, **650**, 651
Procaine benzylpenicillin, 273
Procaine penicillin *see* Procaine benzylpenicillin, 273
*Pro-Cal*, 812
Procarbazine, **444**
Prochlorperazine, 213
- nausea and vertigo, 210, 211, **213**
- preparations, 213
- psychoses, **186**

*Procoralan*, 115
*Proctofoam HC*, 65
*Proctosedyl*, 65
Procyclidine, **257**
*Prodose*, 93, 296
Product licence, 1
*Pro-Epanutin*, 249
Proflavine cream, 605
*Profore* products, 832, 833
Progesterone, 375, **376**

Progestogen-only pill *see* Progestogens, contraceptives, oral, 407, **413**
Progestogens, 375, 456
contraceptives
intra-uterine, **415**
oral, 407, **413**
parenteral, **414**
HRT and, 375
malignant disease, 455
*Prograf*, 451
Proguanil, 331, 332, 333, 334, **335**
atovaquone with, 329, 335
*ProGuide* products, 832
*Progynova*, 373
*Progynova TS*, 373
Proleukin, *454*
Promazine, 182, **186**
Promethazine, 164
allergic disorders, 161, **164**
hypnotic, **177**
nausea and vertigo, 211, **212**
premedication, 164
Promethazine teoclate, 212
*Promin*, 812
*Promixin*, 296
*ProMod*, 812
*Promogran*, 825
*Pronestyl*, 81
*Propaderm*, 576
Propafenone, 80, **81**, 82
Propamidine isetionate, 534, **536**
Propantheline, 42, 419
gastro-intestinal, 41, 42
urinary tract, 421
*Propecia*, 596
*Propess*, 400
Prophylaxis, antibacterial, 270
*Propine*, 543
*Propionibacterium acnes*, 587
Propionic acidaemia, ACBS, 819
Propiverine, 419, 421
Propofol, **634**, 635
infusion table, 798
*Propofol-Lipuro*, 635
Propranolol, **84**, 85
cardiovascular, 84
migraine, 235
*see also* Beta-adrenoceptor blocking drugs
thyrotoxicosis, 360
tremor, 258
Proprietary names, symbol, 1
Propylene glycol, presence of, 2, 567
Propylthiouracil, 360, **361**
*Proscar*, 379
*Prosobee*, 812
Prostacyclin *see* Epoprostenol
Prostaglandins
anticoagulant, 123
ductus arteriosus, 401
eye, 540, 542
gastro-intestinal, 48
obstetrics, 398, 399, 400, 401
*Prostap SR*, 460
*Prostap-3*, 460
Prostate cancer, 431, **458**, 460
Prostatic hyperplasia, benign, 379, 417
Prostatitis, 269, 307
*Prostin E2* preparations, 400
*Prostin VR*, 401
*Prosulf*, 126
*ProSure*, 812
Protamine sulphate, 120, **125**, 126
Protease inhibitors, 314, 315
Protease modulating matrix, 825
Proteasome inhibitors, 440
Protein C concentrate, 133
Protein intolerance, ACBS, 819
Protein sensitivity, ACBS, 820
Protein, intravenous nutrition, 482
*Protelos*, 391
*Prothiaden*, 198
Prothionamide *see* Protionamide, 299
*Protifar*, 812
Protionamide, 299
Protirelin, 383, **384**
*Protium*, 51
Proton pump inhibitors, 48
*Protopic*, 586
Protozoal infections, 329
*Provera*
gynaecology, 376
malignant disease, 455
*Provide*, 812
*Provigil*, 208
*Pro-Viron*, 378
Proxymetacaine, **545**
*Prozac*, 203
*Proziere* (prochlorperazine), 213
Pruritus, 161, 571
ACBS, 820
Pruritus ani, 64
Pseudoephedrine, **172**
Pseudomembranous colitis, 54, 268, 293, 303
*Pseudomonas aeruginosa* infections, 278, 279, 283, 287, 295
eye, 534
Psittacosis, 285
Psoriasis, 580
corticosteroids, 573
Psoriatic arthropathy, 519
*Psoriderm* preparations, 583
scalp, 595
*Psorin* preparations, 584
Psychoses, 181
Puberty
delayed, 377, 380
precocious, 394, 396, 461
Pubic lice, 603
*Pulmicort* preparations, 157
Pulmonary embolism, 120, 129, 168
Pulmonary hypertension, 92, 123, 169
Pulmonary oedema, 73
Pulmonary surfactants, 167
*Pulmozyme*, 170
*Pulvinal Beclometasone Dipropionate*, 156
*Pulvinal Salbutamol*, 146
*Puregon*, 381
*Purilon*, 825
*Puri-Nethol*, 437
Purpura, thrombocytopenic, 471
Pyelonephritis, 269, 307
Pylobactell, *44*
*Pylorid*, 47
*Pyralvex*, 560
Pyrazinamide, 297, 298, 299, **300**
Pyrexia, 218
post immunisation, 611
Pyridostigmine, 526, **527**
laxative, 59
Pyridoxine, 494, **495**
anaemias, 468
preparations, 495
status epilepticus, 247
Pyrimethamine, **336**
malaria, 336
sulfadoxine with, 336
toxoplasmosis, 338
Pyrithione zinc shampoos, 595

# Q

Q-fever, 285
Quaternary ammonium compounds, 41
Quaternium 15, excipient, 567
*Quellada M*, 604
*Questran* preparations, 134
Quetiapine, 187, **190**
*QuickCal*, 812
Quinagolide, 391, **393**
Quinalbarbitone *see* Secobarbital
Quinapril, **101**, 102
hydrochlorothiazide with, 102
*see also* ACE inhibitors
Quinidine, **82**
*Quinil* (quinapril), 102
Quinine, **336**
infusion table, 798
malaria, 329, 330, 336
nocturnal cramps, 529
poisoning, 32
elimination, 28
*Quinoderm*, 587
Quinolones, 304
eye, 534
Quinupristin, **295**
dalfopristin with
infusion table, 798
*Qvar* preparations, 156

# R

Rabeprazole, 48, **51**
Rabies, 624, 625
immunisation, 624
travel, 631
immunoglobulin, 628, **629**
vaccine, 624, 625
*Rabipur*, 625
Raloxifene, **374**, 375, 387
Raltitrexed, 436, 438
infusion table, 798
Ramipril, **102**
felodipine with, 102
*see also* ACE inhibitors
*Ranitic* (ranitidine), 47
Ranitidine, **46**, 47
infusion table, 798
Ranitidine bismuth citrate, 47
Ranitidine bismutrex, 47
*Rantec* (ranitidine), 47
*Ranzac* (ranitidine), 47
*Rapamune*, 451
*Rapifen*, 641
*Rapilysin*, 130
*Rapitil*, 539
*Rapolyte*, 476
*Raptiva*, 586
Rasagiline, 251, **255**, 256

Rasburicase, 428, **525**, 526
infusion table, 798
Rashes, urticarial, 161
Raynaud's syndrome, 96, 112, 115
*Rebetol*, 329
*Rebif*, 454
Reboxetine, 204, **205**
Recently prepared, 2
Recombinant activated protein C, **132**
*Rectogesic*, 66
Red eye, 534, 536
Red line webbing, 832
*Redoxon* (ascorbic acid), 496
*Reductil*, 210
*ReFacto* (factor VIII fraction), 132
*Reflexions*, 417
*Refludan*, 123
Reflux oesophagitis *see* Gastro-oesophageal reflux disease, 37, 38
*Refolinon* (calcium folinate), 429
*Regaine*, 596
*Regal*, 829
*Regranex*, 609
*Regulan*, 59
*Regulose* (lactulose), 62
*Regurin*, 421
Rehydration
oral, 476
parenteral, 478
*Relaxit*, 63
*Release*, 828
*Relenza*, 327
*Relestat*, 538
*Relifex*, 512
*Relpax*, 232
*Remedeine*, 221
*Remicade*, 523
Remifentanil, 222, 641, **642**
infusion table, 798
*Reminyl* preparations, 265
*Remnos* (nitrazepam), 175
*Renagel*, 492
Renal colic *see* Ureteric colic, 422
Renal excretion, interactions affecting, 652
Renal impairment
ACBS, 819
prescribing in, 745
*Renamil*, 812
*Renapro*, 812
*Rennie Duo*, 40
*ReoPro*, 127
Repaglinide, 354, **355**
*Repevax*, 615
*Replenate* (factor VIII fraction), 132
*Replenine-VF* (factor IX fraction), 132
*Replens*, 405
*Replicare*, 826
*Requip*, 256
*RescueFlow*, 481
*Resonium A*, 475
Resorcinol, sulphur with, 589
*Resource* preparations, 812, 813
Respiratory depression
poisoning, 27
postoperative, 646
Respiratory distress syndrome, 167
Respiratory failure, 167
Respiratory stimulants, 167
Respiratory syncytial virus infections, 328
*Respontin*, 149
*Resprin*, 219
*Restandol*, 377
Resuscitation
cardiopulmonary, 119
dental practice, 633
Reteplase, 129, **130**
*Retin-A*, 589
Retinoids
acne
oral, 590
topical, 588
hyperpigmentation, 594
leukaemia, 446
psoriasis, 581, **584**
Retinol *see* Vitamin A
*Retinova*, 594
*Retrovir*, 318
*Revaxis*, 616
Reviparin, 121, **122**
*Rexocaine*, 648
*Reyataz*, 319
Reye's syndrome, aspirin and, 219
Rhesus incompatibility, 629
*Rheumacin LA* (indometacin m/r), 511
*Rheumatac Retard*, 509
Rheumatic diseases, 504, 514
corticosteroid injections, 515
rubefacients, 531
Rheumatic fever
prophylaxis, 272
Rheumatism, palindromic, 516
Rheumatoid arthritis, 364, 504
Rhinitis
allergic, 161, 554
medicamentosa, 557
vasomotor, 161, 557
*Rhinocort Aqua*, 555
*Rhinolast* preparations, 554
*Rhophylac*, 630
*Rhumalgan* preparations, 509
*Riamet*, 329, 333
Ribavirin, **328**, 329
chronic hepatitis C, 326, 328
respiratory syncytial virus, 328
Riboflavin, 494
Rickets, hypophosphataemic, 491
Rickettsia, 285
*Ridaura*, *517*
Rifabutin, 299, **300**, 301
*Rifadin*, 301
Rifampicin, **301**
compound preparations, 301
infusion table, 798
leprosy, 302
tuberculosis, 297, 298, 299
Rifamycins, 297, 298, 299, 300, 301
Rifater, *298*, 301
*Rifinah* preparations, 298, 301
*Rilutek*, 259
Riluzole, **258**, 259
RIMA, 201
*Rimacid* (indometacin), 511
*Rimacillin* (ampicillin), 277
*Rimactane*, 301
*Rimactazid* preparations, 298, 301
*Rimafen* (ibuprofen), 507
*Rimapam* (diazepam), 178
*Rimapurinol* (allopurinol), 525
Rimexolone, **538**
*Rimoxallin* (amoxicillin), 276
Rimso-50, *423*
*Rinatec*, 557
Ringer's solution, 478
Ringer-Lactate solution, 478
Ringworm infection *see* Dermatophyte infection, 309
Risedronate sodium, 386, **390**
*Risperdal* preparations, 190, 192
Risperidone, 187, **190**
depot injections, 192
injection, 192
*Ritalin*, 208
*Rite-Diet* preparations, 813
Ritodrine, 403
infusion table, 798
Ritonavir, 315, **320**
lopinavir with, 320
*see also Kaletra*
Rituximab, 451, 452
infusion table, 798
Rivastigmine, 264, 265
*Rivotril*, 247, 248
Rizatriptan, 232, **233**
*Roaccutane*, 591
*Robaxin*, 529
*Robinson Primary*, 828
*Robinul*, 609, 638
*Robinul-Neostigmine*, 645
*RoC Total Sunblock*, 594
*Rocaltrol*, 497
*Rocephin*, 283
Rocuronium, 643, **644**
infusion table, 798
*Roferon-A*, 453
*Rogitine*, 97
*Rommix* (erythromycin), 290
Ropinirole, 250, **256**
Ropivacaine, **651**
Rosacea, 586, 598
Rose bengal, **547**
*Rosidal K*, 832
Rosiglitazone, 354, **355**
metformin with, 355
Rosuvastatin, 135, **137**
Roundworm infections, 341
*Rowachol*, 67
*Rowatinex*, 422
*Rozex*, 598
rt-PA *see* Alteplase
Rubefacients, 531
Rubella, 625
immunisation
immunoglobulin, 628
vaccines, 625
*Rusyde* (furosemide), 74
Rutosides, 117
*Rynacrom* preparations, 556
*Rythmodan* preparations, 81

# S

*Sabril*, 246
*Saizen* preparations, 383
*Salactol*, 591
*Salagen*, 565
*Salamol* (salbutamol) preparations, 146
*Salapin* (salbutamol), 145
Salatac, 592

Index

*Salazopyrin*, 56, 524
Salbutamol, 145
  asthma, 144
  infusion table, 798
  premature labour, 403
  preparations, 145, 146
  with ipratropium, 150
Salcatonin *see* Calcitonin
Salicylates
  aphthous ulcers, 560
  rheumatic disease, 514
    topical, 531
Salicylic acid, 584
  acne, 589
  betamethasone with, 576
  fungal infections, 601
    undecenoates with, 601
  hyperkeratoses, 591
  podophyllum with, 592
  psoriasis, 581
    coal tar with, 583, 595
    dithranol with, 584
    sulphur with, 595
    zinc with, 584
  scalp, 595
  warts and calluses, 591, 592
Saline
  physiological, 478, 606
  purgatives, 62
  *Steri-Neb*, 154
  *Steripoule*, 154
*Salinum*, 564
Saliva, artificial, 564
*Saliveze*, 565
*Salivix*, 565
Salmeterol, 144, **147**
  with fluticasone, 158
Salmonellosis, 268
*Salofalk* preparations, 55
Salpingitis, 285
Salt substitutes, 475
*Sandimmun*, 450
*Sandocal* preparations, 489
*Sandoglobulin* preparations, 628
*Sando-K*, 475
*Sandostatin*, 461
*Sandostatin LAR*, 461
*Sandrena*, 373
*Sanomigran*, 236
Saquinavir, 315, **320**
*Savlon Dry* powder, 608
Scabies, 602
*Scandishake*, 813
*Scandonest*, 647
*Scanpor*, 834
*Schar*, 813
*Scheriproct*, 65
Schistosoma, 341
Schistosomicides, 341
Schizophrenia, 181
Scleroderma, 495
Sclerosants, 139
*Scopoderm* preparations, 217
Scopolamine *see* Hyoscine, **41**, 42
Scottish Medicines Consortium, 3
Scottish Prescribing Analysis, vii
Scurvy, 495
*Sea-legs* (meclozine), 212
*SeaSorb*, 822
*Sebco*, 583
*Sebomin*, 287
Seborrhoeic
  dermatitis, 580
  eczema, 580
*Secadrex*—discontinued, ix
Secobarbital, 180
  amobarbital with, 180
*Seconal Sodium*, 180
*Sectral*, 85
*Securon* preparations, 114
Sedation, anaesthesia, 638
Sedatives, 173
  *see also* Anxiolytics
*Select-A-Jet Dopamine*, 118
Selegiline, 251, **256**
Selenium sulphide, 595, 599
*Selexid*, 279
*Selsun*, 595
*Semi-Daonil*, 352
Semi-permeable adhesive film, 827
Semisodium valproate *see* Valproate
Senna, **60**, 61
*Senokot*, 60, 61
*Septanest*, 647
Septic arthritis, 270
Septicaemia
  catheter-related, 269
  community-acquired, 269
  hospital-acquired, 269
  meningococcal, 269
*Septrin*, 297
*Seractil*, 508
*Seravit, Paediatric*, 811
*Serc*, 217
*Serdolect*, 190
*Serenace*, 184
*Seretide*, 158
*Serevent*, 147
Sermorelin, **384**
*Seroquel*, 190
Serotonin re-uptake inhibitor antidepressants *see* Antidepressants
*Seroxat*, 204
Sertindole, 187, 190
Sertraline, 202, **204**
Sesame oil, presence of, 2
*Setocrepe*, 831
*Setoplast*, 834
*Setopress*, 832
Sevelamer, 491, **492**
Sevoflurane, **636**
*Sevredol*, 224
Sex hormones, 367, 377
  androgens, 377
    antagonists, 378
  malignant disease, 455
  oestrogens, 367
    antagonists, 379
  progestogens, 375
Sexual deviation, 183, 378
Shampoos, 595
Shared care, 4
Sharpsbin, 351
Shigellosis, 268
Shingles, 322
Shock, 117, 364, 481
  anaphylactic, 165
    dental practice, 20
  cardiogenic, 117
  septic, 117, 364
Short-bowel syndrome, ACBS, 818, 820
*SHS Modjul Flavour*, 813
Sibutramine, 209, **210**
Sicca syndrome, 564
  ACBS, 820
Sickle-cell disease, pain, 217
*Sidestream Durable*, 153
*Sigma ETB*, 830
Significant changes, viii
Sildenafil, 425, **426**
*Silgel*, 826
Silicone gel products, 826
*Silkis*, 582
*Silkolan*, 832
Silver nitrate, 591, **592**
Silver sulfadiazine, **597**, 598
Silver sulphadiazine *see* Silver sulfadiazine, **597**
Simeticone, 38, 39, 40
Simple eye ointment, 546
Simple linctus, 172
  paediatric, 172
*SimpleXx*, 383
*Simulect*, 449
*Simvador* (simvastatin), 138
Simvastatin, 135, **137**, 138
  ezetimibe with, 138
*Simzal* (simvastatin), 138
*Sinemet* preparations, 252, 253
*Sinequan*, 198
*Singulair*, 160
*Sinthrome*, 125
Sinusitis, 557
  antibacterial treatment, 270
  inhalation, 170
*Siopel*, 571
Sirolimus, 449, **450**, 451
Sitosterolaemia, 134
*Skelid*, 391
Skin preparations
  anaesthetic, 571
  antibacterials, 596
  antipruritic, 572
  antiviral, 601
  barrier, 571
  cleansing, 606
  corticosteroids, 572
  emollient, 567
  excipients, 567
  ulcers, 608
*Skinoren*, 587
*Skintact*, 828
*Slinky*, 830
*Slofedipine* preparations, 113
*Slofenac* preparations, 509
*Slo-Indo* (indometacin m/r), 511
*Slo-Phyllin*, 150
*Slo-Pro* (propranolol), 85
*Slow-K*, 475
*Slow-Sodium*, 476
*Slow-Trasicor*, 88
*Slozem*, 111
*SMA* preparations, 813
Smallpox vaccine, 625
SMC *see* Scottish Medicines Consortium, 3
Smoking cessation, 260
Snake bites, 36
  antivenom, 36
*Sno Tears*, 546
*Sno-Pro*, 814
*Sodiofolin*, 430

Sodium acid phosphate, 491
Sodium alendronate *see* Alendronic acid
*Sodium Amytal*, 180
Sodium aurothiomalate, 516, **517**
Sodium benzoate, 13
Sodium bicarbonate, 477, 479, 480
  antacid preparations, 38
  capsules, 477
  ear drops, 553
  injection, 480
  intravenous infusion, 480
  tablets, 477
  urine alkalinisation, 422
Sodium calcium edetate, **34**, 35
  infusion table, 798
Sodium calciumedetate *see* Sodium calcium edetate
Sodium carboxymethylcellulose *see* Carmellose
Sodium chloride, 476, 477, 478
  bladder irrigation, 423, 606
  eye, 533, **547**
  infusion, 478
    glucose and, 478
    hypercalcaemia, 489
    potassium chloride and, 479
    potassium chloride, glucose and, 479
  mouthwash, compound, 562, **564**
  nebuliser solution, 154
  nose, 556
  oropharynx, 564
  solution
    eye, 547
    nose, 556
    skin cleansing, **606**
  tablets, 476
Sodium citrate
  acid aspiration prophylaxis, 633
  bladder irrigation, **423**
  rectal, 63
  urine alkalinisation, 422
Sodium clodronate, 390
  infusion table, 798
Sodium content, antacids, 38
Sodium cromoglicate, 57
  asthma, **159**
  eye, 538, **539**
  food allergy, 57
  nose, 554, **556**
Sodium cromoglycate *see* Sodium cromoglicate
Sodium feredetate, 465
Sodium fluoride, **492**, 493
Sodium fusidate, **293**
  angular cheilitis, 561
  skin, 598
Sodium ironedetate *see* Sodium feredetate, 465
Sodium lactate, 480
  intravenous infusion, 480
    compound, 478
Sodium metabisulphite, excipient, 567
Sodium nitrite, 33, **34**
Sodium nitroprusside *see* Nitroprusside
Sodium oxybate, 33
Sodium phenylbutyrate, 502
Sodium picosulfate, **61**, 64
Sodium picosulphate *see* Sodium picosulfate, **61**, 64
Sodium pidolate, 568
  lactic acid with, 569
Sodium polystyrene sulphonate, 475
Sodium risedronate *see* Risedronate sodium, 386, **390**
Sodium stibocaptate, 342
Sodium stibogluconate, **338**
Sodium tetradecyl sulphate, **139**
Sodium thiosulphate, 33, **34**
Sodium valproate *see* Valproate
*Soffban*, 832
*Soffcrepe*, 831
*Sofradex*
  ear, 551
  eye, 537
*Soframycin*, 535
  eye ointment—discontinued, ix
Soft tissue disorders, 504
*Soft Touch*, 350
*Softclix* products, 350
*Softexe*, 832
*Solian*, 188
Solifenacin, 419, **421**
*Solivito N*, 483
*Soloc* (bisoprolol), 86
*Solpadol*, 221
*Soltamox* (tamoxifen), 457
*Solu-Cortef*, 366
*Solu-Medrone*, 367
*Solvaline N*, 828
*Solvazinc*, 493
Solvents, ear wax removal, 553
Somatorelin, 384
Somatostatin analogues, 461
Somatotrophin *see* Somatropin, 382, 383
Somatropin, 382, 383
*Somatuline Autogel*, 462
*Somatuline LA*, 461
*Somavert*, 383
*Somnite* (nitrazepam), 175
*Sonata*, 176
*Soneryl*, 180
*Soothelip*, 602
*Sorbalgon*, 822
Sorbic acid, excipient, 567
Sorbitol, 483
  presence of, 2
*Sorbsan* products, 822
*Sotacor*, 89
Sotalol, **89**
  cardiovascular, 84
  infusion table, 799
  *see also* Beta-adrenoceptor blocking drugs
Soya oil, 570
SPA, vii
Spacer devices, 151
*Spasmonal* preparations, 42
Spasticity, 527
*SpectraBan*, 594
Spermicides, 415
SPF, 593
*Spinhaler*, 152, 159
Spiramycin, 289, 338
Spirit
  industrial methylated, 606
  surgical, 606
*Spiriva*, 149
Spironolactone, **75**, 76
  furosemide with, 77
  heart failure, 97
  hydroflumethiazide with, 77
*Spirospare* (spironolactone), 76
Splenectomy *see* Asplenia
*Sporanox*, 312
*Sporanox-Pulse*, 312
Sports card, 26
*Sprilon*, 571
SSRIs *see* Antidepressants, serotonin re-uptake inhibitor, 202
*SST*, 565
St John's Wort, 195
*Stalevo*, 253
*Stamaril*, 627
Stannous fluoride, 493
Starch, etherified, 482
*Staril*, 100
*Starlix*, 354
Statins, 135
  angina, 105
Status epilepticus, 247
Stavudine, 315, **317**
*Stayform*, 830
*STD injection* see *Fibro-Vein*
Steam inhalations, 557
Stearyl alcohol, excipient, 567
*Stelazine*, 186
*Stemetil*, 213
Sterculia, 59
  constipation, 58
  diarrhoea, 51
*Stericlens*, 606
*Sterifix*, 827
Sterile larvae, 608
*Steri-Neb*
  *Salamol*, 146
  sodium chloride, 154
*Steripaste*, 833
*Steripod*
  sodium chloride, 606
*Steripoule* (sodium chloride), 154
*Steri-strip*, 835
Steroid cards, 363
*Ster-Zac Bath Concentrate*, 608
*Stesolid* (diazepam), 179, 248
Stibocaptate *see* Sodium stibocaptate, 342
*Stiemycin*, 588
Stilboestrol *see* Diethylstilbestrol, **455**, 459
Still's disease *see* Arthritis, juvenile idiopathic, 516
*Stilnoct*, 176
Stimulants
  central nervous system, 206
  respiratory, 167
Stings, 36
Stockinette
  cotton, 830
  elasticated, 830
    viscose, 831
    foam padded, 830
  ribbed cotton and viscose, 831
Stoma, drugs and, 66
Stomatitis, 562
  denture, 561
  herpetic, 562
*Strappal*, 834
*Strattera*, 207
*Strefen*, 560

Index

*Streptase*, 131
Streptogramin antibiotics, 295
Streptokinase, 129, **130**, 131
  infusion table, 799
Streptokinase-streptodornase, 609
Streptomycin, 297, 299, **301**
Stretch bandage, cotton, 831
*Striant SR*, 377
Strongyloidiasis, 342
Strontium ranelate, 386, 388, **390**, 391
*StructoKabiven* preparations, 486
*Structolipid*, 487
*Stugeron*, 212
*Stugeron Forte*, 116
*Subcuvia*, 628
*Subgam*, 628
*Sublimaze*, 641
*Subutex*, 263
Succimer, 34
Sucralfate, 47, **48**
Sucrose intolerance, ACBS, 816
Sucrose, presence of, 2
*Sudafed* preparations, 172
*Sudocrem*, 571
Sugar, 2
Sugar-free liquid medicines *see* preparations identified by 'sugar-free' throughout BNF
Sugar-free, definition, 2
*Sulazine EC* (sulfasalazine), 56, 524
Sulconazole, 309, 599, **601**
*Suleo-M*, 604
Sulfa... *see also* Sulpha...
Sulfabenzamide, 406
Sulfacetamide
  vaginal, 406
Sulfadiazine, **297**
  infusion table, 799
  preparations, 297
  toxoplasmosis, 338
Sulfadiazine, silver, 597
Sulfadoxine
  malaria, 336
  pyrimethamine with, 336
  pyrimethamine with, *see Fansidar*
Sulfamethoxazole, trimethoprim with, *see* Co-trimoxazole
Sulfasalazine, 53, 54, **55**, 56, 524
  Crohn's disease, 55
  preparations, 56, 524
  rheumatic disease, 516, 523, 524
  ulcerative colitis, 54
Sulfathiazole, 406
Sulfinpyrazone, 524, **525**
Sulindac, 505, **513**
  gout, 524
  preparations, 513
Sulpha... *see also* Sulfa...
Sulphadiazine *see* Sulfadiazine
Sulphasalazine *see* Sulfasalazine
Sulphinpyrazone *see* Sulfinpyrazone, 524, **525**
Sulphonamides, 296
  vaginal, 406
Sulphonylureas, 351
Sulphur, 581, **589**
  coal tar with, 583
  resorcinol with, 589
  salicylic acid with, 595
Sulphur dioxide, poisoning, 35
Sulpiride, 182, **186**
  Tourette syndrome, 258
*Sulpitil*, 186
*Sulpor*, 186
*Sultrin*, 406
Sumatriptan, 232, **233**, 234
  cluster headache, 236
  migraine, 232
Sun protection factor, 593
*Sunnyvale*, 814
Sunscreens, 593
  ACBS, 820
*Sunsense Ultra*, 594
Superinfection, 268
*Suplasyn*, 505
*Suplena*, 814
Supplementary preparations, 483
*Supralip*, 135
*Suprane*, 636
*Suprasorb* products, 822, 825–827
*Suprax*, 281
*Suprecur*, 395
*Suprefact*, 459
Suramin, 342
*SurePress*, 832
*Surgam* preparations, 513, 514
Surgery
  antibacterial prophylaxis, 271, 272, 273
  diabetes and, 345
  long-term medication and, 632
  tetanus vaccine, 625
Surgical adhesive tapes, 834
Surgical spirit, 606
*Surgipad*, 828
*Surmontil*, 199
*Survanta*, 168
*Survimed OPD*, 814
*Suscard*, 106
Suspensory bandage, cotton, 831
*Sustac*, 107
*Sustanon* preparations, 377
*Sustiva*, 321
Suxamethonium, 644, **645**
  infusion table, 799
Swabs, 829
*Symbicort*, 157
Symbols, *inside back cover*
*Symmetrel*, 253
Sympathomimetics
  asthma, 144
  decongestants, 557
  eye, 540, 542
  inotropic, 117
  premature labour, 402
  vasoconstrictor, 118
*Synacthen*, 380
*Synacthen Depot*, 380
*Synagis*, 328
*Synalar* preparations, 578
*Synarel*, 396
*Synastone* (methadone), 228, 263
Syncope, dental practice, 22
*Synercid*, 295
*Synflex*, 512
*Synphase*, 411
*Syntaris*, 555
*Synthamin* preparations, 487
Synthetic diets, ACBS, 820
*Syntocinon*, 398, 401
*Syntometrine*, 399, 400
*Synvisc*, 505
Syphilis, 269
*Syprol* (propranolol), 85
Syringe drivers, palliative care, 16
Syringes
  insulin, 351
    blind patients, 351
  oral, 2
*Syscor MR*, 114
*System 4* products, 833
*System 22 nebulisers*, 154
*Sytron*, 465

# T

Tacalcitol, 580, 581, **582**
Tachycardias *see* Arrhythmias
Tacrolimus, 449, **451**
  eczema, 585, **586**
  infusion table, 799
Tadalafil, 425, **426**
Taenicides, 341
*Tagamet* preparations, 45
*Tambocor*, 81
*Tamiflu*, 327
Tamoxifen, 456, **457**
  breast pain, 396
  infertility, 379
Tamsulosin, 417, **418**
*Tanatril*, 100
Tapes, surgical adhesive, 834
Tapeworm infections, 341
Tar *see* Coal tar
*Tarceva*, 442
Tardive dyskinesia, 182
*Targocid*, 294
*Targretin*, 440
*Tarivid*, 306
*Tarka*, 102
Tartrazine, presence of, 2
*Tasmar*, 257
*Tavanic*, 305
*Tavegil*, 163
Taxanes, 445
*Taxol*, 445
*Taxotere*, 445
Tazarotene, 581, 582
Tazobactam, 278
  piperacillin with, 278
    infusion table, 798
*Tazocin*, 278, 798
3TC *see* Lamivudine
Tear deficiency, 545
Tear gas, 35
*Tears Naturale*, 546
Tears, artificial, 545
*Tegaderm*, 827
Tegafur, 436, 438
  uracil with, 438
*Tegagen* products, 822
*Tegapore*, 828
*Tegasorb* products, 826
*Tegretol* preparations, 239
Teicoplanin, 293, **294**
  infusion table, 799
Telangiectasia, hereditary haemorrhagic, 374
*Telfa* products, 827, 828
*Telfast*, 162
Telithromycin, 290, **291**
Telmisartan, 103, **104**
  hydrochlorothiazide with, 104
*Telzir*, 319

Temazepam, 174, **175**
anaesthesia, 638, **640**
*Temgesic*, 225
Temocillin, ix
*Temodal*, 441
Temoporfin, **444**
Temozolomide, **441**
Temporomandibular joint pain, 218
Tendinitis, 515
Tenecteplase, 129, **131**
*Tenif*, 86
Tennis elbow, 515
Tenofovir, 315, **317**
emtricitibine with, 317
*Tenoret-50*, 86
*Tenoretic*, 86
*Tenormin* preparations, 85
Tenoxicam, 505, **513**
TENS, 15
*Tensipine MR*, 113
*Tensium* (diazepam), 178
*Tensogrip*, 830
*Tensopress*, 832
*Tensopril* (captopril), 99
*Tentrini* preparations, 814
*Teoptic*, 541
Teratogenesis, 758
Terazosin, **96**, **418**
cardiovascular, 95, 96
urinary tract, 417, 418
Terbinafine, 309, **313**
topical, 599, **601**
Terbutaline, **146**
asthma, 144
infusion table, 799
premature labour, 403
preparations, 146, 147
Terfenadine—discontinued, ix
Teriparatide, 386, **387**, 388
Terlipressin, 386
Terminal care *see* Palliative care
Terpenes, gall bladder, 67
*Tertroxin*, 360
*Testim*, 378
*Testogel*, 378
Testosterone
buccal tablets, 377
enantate, 377
gel, 378
implants, 378
injection, 377
oral, 377
patches, 378
propionate, 377
undecanoate, 377
Testosterone esters, 377
malignant disease, 456
*Tetabulin*, 629
Tetanus, 273
immunisation
immunoglobulin, 628, **629**
vaccines, 615, 616, **625**
muscle spasm, 529
travel, 631
Tetany, hypocalcaemic, 488
Tetrabenazine, 258, **259**
Tetracaine, 64, **651**
eye, **545**
Tetracosactide, **380**
Tetracosactrin *see* Tetracosactide, **380**
Tetracycline, 285, 286
acne, 587, 588, 589
diabetic neuropathy, 357
oral infections, 285
skin, 588
clobetasone with, 577
rosacea, 586
*Tetralysal-300*, 286
*Teveten*, 103
*Textube*, 830
*T-Gel*, 595
Thalassaemia, 470
Thalidomide, 449
lepra reactions, 302
Theophylline, **149**, 150
poisoning, 33
elimination, 28
*see also* Aminophylline
Thermometer, fertility, 417
Thiamine, 494
Thiazides, 72
diabetes insipidus, 384
*see also* Diuretics
Thiazolidinediones, 354
*Thick and Easy*, 814
Thioguanine *see* Tioguanine, 436, **438**
Thiopental, **633**, 634
Thiopentone *see* Thiopental, **633**, 634
Thiopurine methyltransferase, 447
Thiotepa, 423, 431, **432**
Thioxanthenes, 182
*Thixo-D*, 814
Threadworm infections, 340
Throat infections, 270
gonorrhoea, 269
Thrombocytopenia, 468
Thrombocytopenic purpura, 471, 627
Thromboembolism, 124
pulmonary, 120, 129, 168
Thrombolytics, 129
Thrombosis
antiplatelet drugs, 126
deep-vein, 120, 124
prophylaxis, 120
venous, 129
Thrush see Candidiasis
Thymol, 564
Thymoxamine *see* Moxisylyte, 115, **116**
*Thyrogen*, 383
Thyroid
antagonists, 360
carcinoma, 359
function test, 383
hormones, 359
stimulating hormone, 383
storm, 361
Thyroidectomy, 360
Thyrotoxic crisis, 361
Thyrotoxicosis, 360
beta-blockers, 84, 360
Thyrotrophin, 383
Thyrotrophin-releasing hormone *see* Protirelin, 383, **384**
Thyrotropin alfa, **383**
Thyroxine *see* Levothyroxine, 359, 360
Tiabendazole, 342
Tiagabine, 238, **244**
Tiaprofenic acid, 505, **513**, 514
Tibolone, 367, **374**
Ticarcillin, 278, **279**
clavulanic acid with, 278, 279
infusion table, 799
Tick-borne encephalitis, 631
immunisation
vaccine, 626
Tics, 258
*Tielle* products, 823
*Tilade CFC-free Inhaler*, 159
*Tilade*—discontinued, ix
*Tildiem* preparations, 110, 111
*Tiloket CR*, 511
*Tilolec*, 253
*Tiloryth* (erythromycin), 290
Tiludronic acid, 391
*Timentin*, 279
infusion table, 799
*Timodine*, 575
Timolol
bendroflumethiazide with, 89
cardiovascular, **89**
co-amilozide with, 89
eye, **541**, 542, 544
brimonidine with, 543
migraine, 235
*see also* Beta-adrenoceptor blocking drugs
*Timoptol*, 541
*Timoptol LA*, 542
*Tinaderm-M*, 601
Tinea infections, 308, 599
Tinidazole, 303, **304**
amoebiasis, 337
giardiasis, 337
protozoal infections, 337
trichomoniasis, 337
*Tinkyada*, 814
Tinzaparin, 121, **122**
Tioconazole, 309, 599, 601
Tioguanine, 436, **438**
Tiotropium, 148, **149**
Tipranavir, 315, **320**, 321
Tirofiban, 105, 126, **128**
infusion table, 799
*Tisept*, 607
Tissue adhesive, 605
Titanium dioxide, 571, 593, 594
*Tixycolds* preparations, 557
Tizanidine, 528, **529**
*Tobi*, 289
*Tobradex*, 537
Tobramycin, 288, **289**
eye, 537
infusion table, 799
Tocopherols, 497
Tocopheryl, 498
*Tofranil*—discontinued, ix
Toilet preparations, ACBS, 820
Tolbutamide, 351, **353**
Tolcapone, 251, **256**, 257
Tolfenamic acid, **232**, 506
Tolnaftate, 599, 601
Tolterodine, 419, **421**
*Tomudex*, 438
Tonic seizures, 238
Tonic-clonic seizures, 238
Tonics, 499
Tonsillitis *see* Throat infections
*Topal*, 40
*Topamax*, 244
*Topicycline*, 588

Topiramate, 235, 238, **244**
Topotecan, 445, **446**
infusion table, 799
*Topper-8*, 829
*Toradol*, 640
Torasemide, 73, **74**
*Torem*, 74
Toremifene, 457, **458**
Torsades de pointes, **78**, 490
magnesium sulphate, 490
Torsion dystonias, 259
Total parenteral nutrition, 482
*Totaretic* (co-tenidone), 86
*Tourer*, 153
Tourette syndrome, 258
TOXBASE, 27
Toxoplasma choroidoretinitis, 338
Toxoplasmosis, 338
TPA *see* Alteplase
TPN, 482
Trachoma, 285, 534
*Tracleer*, 92
*Tracrium*, 643
*Tractocile*, 403
Trade marks, symbol, 1
*Tramacet*, 230
Tramadol, 223, **229**, 230
infusion table, 799
paracetamol with, 230
*Tramake* preparations, 229
Tramazoline, 555
*Trandate*, 87
Trandolapril, **102**
*see also* ACE inhibitors
verapamil with, 102
Tranexamic acid, **131**, 132
infusion table, 799
*Trangina XL* (isosorbide mononitrate), 109
Tranquillisers, 173
Transcutaneous electrical nerve stimulation, 15
Transfusion reactions, 468
*Transiderm-Nitro*, 107
*Transorbent*, 823
Transplant rejection, 447, 449
*Transtec*, 225
*Tranxene*—discontinued, ix
Tranylcypromine, 200, **201**
*Trasicor*, 88
*Trasidrex*, 88
Trastuzumab, **446**
infusion table, 799
*Trasylol*, 131
*Travasept-100*, 607
*Travatan*, 542
Travel, vaccination for, 630
Travellers' diarrhoea, 631
Travoprost, **542**
*Traxam* preparations, 531
Trazodone, 196, **200**
Treatment cards, anticoagulant, 125
Tree pollen allergy preparations, 165
Tremors, 258
*Trental*, 117
Treosulfan, 431, **432**
infusion table, 799
Tretinoin, 447
acne, 588, 589
erythromycin with, 589
hyperpigmentation, 594
leukaemia, 446
TRH *see* Protirelin
*Tri-Adcortyl*, 579
*Tri-Adcortyl Otic*, 552
*Triadene*, 412
Triamcinolone acetonide, **367**
dental paste, 559
ear, 552
injection, 367
nasal allergy, 556
rheumatic disease, 515, 516
skin, 579
Triamcinolone hexacetonide, 515
*Triam-Co* (co-triamterzide), 76
Triamterene, 74, **75**
benzthiazide with, 76
chlortalidone with, 76
furosemide with, 76
hydrochlorothiazide with, 76
Triangular calico bandage, 830
*Triapin* preparations, 102
Triasox, *342*
Triazole antifungal drugs, 309
Tribavirin *see* Ribavirin
Trichomonacides, 337
Trichomonal infections, 337
Triclofos, 176, **177**
Triclosan, 606, 608
*Tricotex*, 828
Tricyclic antidepressants *see* Antidepressants, tricyclic
*Tridestra*, 372
Trientine, **500**
Trifluoperazine, 186
nausea and vertigo, 210, **213**
preparations, 186
psychoses, 182, **186**
Trigeminal neuralgia, 231
Trihexyphenidyl, **257**
movement disorders, 258
preparations, 258
Tri-iodothyronine, 360
*Trileptal*, 240
Trilostane, 396, **397**
malignant disease, 457
Trimeprazine *see* Alimemazine
Trimethoprim, 296, **297**, 307
acne, 590
eye, 536
pneumocystis pneumonia, 339
preparations, 297
co-trimoxazole, 297
sulfamethoxazole with, *see* Co-trimoxazole
*Tri-Minulet*, 412
Trimipramine, 196, **199**
*Trimopan* (trimethoprim), 297
*Trimovate*, 577
*Trinordiol*, 411
*TriNovum*, 411
*Trintek*, 107
Tripotassium dicitratobismuthate, **47**
*Triptafen* preparations, 197
Triptans *see* $5HT_1$ agonists, 231, **232**, **232**
Triptorelin, 394, 458, 460, 461
endometriosis, 396
prostate cancer, 460
uterine fibroids, 394, 396
*Trisenox*, 440
*Trisequens* preparations, 372
Trisodium edetate, 489, **490**
eye, 490, 545
infusion table, 799
*Tritace*, 102
*Tritamyl*, 814
*Trizivir*, 316
Tropical diseases, advice, 329
Tropicamide, 539, **540**
Tropisetron, 211, **216**
infusion table, 799
*Tropium* (chlordiazepoxide), 179
Trospium, 419, **421**
*Trosyl*, 601
*Trufoam* products, 823, 824
*Trusopt*, 544
*Truvada*, 317
Trypanocides, 338
Trypanosomiasis, 338
Tryptophan, 204, **206**
*T-Safe CU 380 A*, 416
*TT 380 Slimline*, 417
*Tubegauz*, 831
Tuberculin, 614
Tuberculosis, 297
diagnosis, 614
immunisation
travel, 630
vaccines, 613
prophylaxis, 272
*Tubifast*, 831
*Tubigrip*, 830
*Tubipad*, 831
Tubular gauze bandage, seamless, 831
Tub/Vac/BCG, Dried, 614
*Tuinal*, 180
Tulle dressings, 828
Tumour lysis syndrome, 428
*Turbohaler*
*Bricanyl*, 147
*Oxis*, 147
*Pulmicort*, 157
*Symbicort*, 157
*Turboneb*, 154
Turner's syndrome, 382
*Twinrix Adult*, 617
*Twinrix Paediatric*, 617
*Tylex*, 221
*Typherix*, 626
*Typhim Vi*, 626
Typhoid
fever, 268
immunisation
travel, 631
vaccines, 626
*TYR gel*, 814
Tyrosinaemia, ACBS, 820
Tyrosine supplement, 814


# U


*Ubretid*, 419
*Ucerax*, 164
*Uftoral*, 438
Ulcerative colitis, 53
ACBS, 818

Ulcerative gingivitis
  antibacterial treatment, 270, 303
  mouthwashes, 562
Ulcer-healing drugs, 43
Ulcers
  aphthous, 558
  corneal, 534, 536
  duodenal, 43, 44
  gastric, 43, 44
  Hunner's, 423
  mouth, 558
  NSAID-associated, 44
  skin, 608, 609
*Ultec Pro*, 826
*Ultima*, 153
*Ultiva*, 642
*Ultra Fast*, 833
*Ultra* foods, 814
*Ultra Four*, 833
*Ultra Lite*, 831, 833
*Ultra Neb-2000*, 154
*Ultra Plus*, 831, 833
*Ultra Soft*, 832
*Ultrabase*, 569
Ultralanum Plain, 578
*Ultraproct*, 65
Ultrasonic nebulisers, 154
*Ultratard*—discontinued, ix
Ultraviolet radiation, 593
Undecenoates, **601**
*Unguentum M*, 569
*Unifine* products, 350, 351
*Unilet* products, 350
*Uniphyllin Continus*, 150
*Uniroid-HC*, 65
*Unisept*, 607
Unithiol, 34
*Unitulle*, 828
*Univer*, 114
*Uprima*, 425
Uracil, tegafur with, 438
*Urdox*, 67
Urea, 567, 569
  hydrocortisone with, 574, 575
Urea cycle disorders, 502, 820
Ureteric colic, 422
Urethritis, non-gonococcal, 269, 285
*Urgosorb* products, 823
*Urgotul* products, 828
*Uriben*, 306
Uricosuric drugs, 524
*Uriflex* preparations, 423
Urinary
  frequency, 419
  incontinence, 419
  infections, 269, 307
  pH adjustment, 422
  retention, 417
Urine tests
  glucose, 358, 359
  ketones, 358, 359
  protein, 358, 359
*Urispas-200*, 420
*Uristix*, 359
Urofollitrophin *see* Urofollitropin, 380
Urofollitropin, 380
Urological procedures
  antibacterial prophylaxis, 272
*Uromitexan*, 430
*Uro-Tainer* preparations, 423
Urothelial toxicity, 430
Ursodeoxycholic acid, **66**, 67
*Ursofalk*, 67
*Ursogal*, 67
Urticaria, 161
*UT 380 Short*, 417
*UT 380 Standard*, 417
  bleeding, 399
  relaxants, 402
  stimulants, 398
*Utinor*, 306
*Utovlan*, 376
UVB, psoriasis, 581
*Uvistat* preparations, 594


# V


Vaccination
  HIV-positive subjects, 612
  schedule, 612
  travel, 630
Vaccines, 611
  allergen extract, 164
  contra-indications, 611
  post-immunisation pyrexia, 611
  pregnancy, 611
  side-effects, 611
  storage and use, 613
*Vacutex*, 830
*Vagifem*, 404
Vaginitis
  candidal, 405
  menopausal, 367, 404
  non-specific *see* Vaginosis, bacterial, 302
Vaginosis, bacterial, 302
*Vaginyl* (metronidazole), 303
Valaciclovir, 322, **324**, 406
*Valclair* (diazepam), 179
*Valcyte*, 326
Valganciclovir, 324, 326
Valine Amino Acid Supplement, 814
*Vallergan*, 163
*Valoid*, 212
*Valpiform*, 814
Valproate, 238
  bipolar disorder, **193**
  epilepsy, 244, **245**, 246
  infusion table, 799
  migraine, 235
Valproic acid *see* Valproate
Valsartan, 103, **104**
  hydrochlorothiazide with, 104
*Valtrex*, 324
*Vancocin*, 294
*Vamin* preparations, 487
*Vaminolact*, 487
Vancomycin, **293**, 294
  eye, 545
  infusion table, 799
Vancomycin-resistant enterococci, 294
*Vaniqa*, 596
Vapour-permeable adhesive film, 827
*Vaqta*, 617
Vardenafil, 425, **426**
Variceal bleeding, 384, 461
Varicella-zoster, 322
  immunisation
    vaccine, 626, 629
  immunoglobulin, 628, **629**
Varicose veins, 139, 610
*Varidase Topical*, 609
*Varilrix*, 626
*Varivax*, 626
*Vascace*, 99
*Vascalpha* (felodipine), 111
Vascular surgery
  antibacterial prophylaxis, 273
*Vaseline Dermacare*, 569
Vasoconstrictors
  local anaesthesia, 647
    dental practice, 647
  sympathomimetic, 118
Vasodilators
  antihypertensive, 92
  peripheral, 115
*Vasogen*, 571
Vasopressin, **384**
  infusion table, 799
VEC high compression bandage, 832
*Vectavir*, 602
Vecuronium, 643, **644**
  infusion table, 799
*Veil* preparations, 594
*Velband*, 832
*Velbe*, 439
*Velcade*, 440
*Velosef*, 282
*Velosulin*, 347
Venlafaxine, 204, **206**
*Venofer*, 466
*Venta-Neb*, 93
*Ventavis*, 93
*Venticaire* masks, 168
Ventilatory failure, 167
Ventimask, *168*
*Ventmax SR*, 145
*Ventodisks*, 146
*Ventolin* preparations, 145, 146
*Ventstream*, 153
*Vepesid*, 439
*Veracur*, 592
Verapamil, **114**, 115
  angina, 109
  arrhythmias, 78
  beta-blockers and, 114
  cluster headache, 236
  hypertension, 109
  poisoning by, 32
  *see also* Calcium-channel blockers
  trandolapril with, 102
*Verapress MR*, 115
*Vermox*, 340
*Vernaid*, 829
Verrucas, 591
*Verrugon*, 592
*Versiva*, 826
*Vertab SR 240*, 115
Verteporfin, **548**
  infusion table, 799
*Vesanoid*, 447
*Vesicare*, 421
Vestibular disorders, 211
*Vexol*, 538
*Vfend*, 314
*Viagra*, 426
*ViATIM*, 617
*Viazem XL*, 111
*Vibramycin* preparations, 286
*Videne*, 608
*Videx* preparations, 316
Vigabatrin, 238, **246**

*Vigam* preparations, 628
*Vigranon B*, 495
*Vimule Cap*, 417
Vinblastine, 438, **439**
  infusion table, 799
Vinca alkaloids, 438
Vincent's infection
  antibacterial treatment, 270, 303
  mouthwashes, 562
Vincristine, 438, **439**
  infusion table, 799
Vindesine, 438, **439**
  infusion table, 799
Vinorelbine, 438, **439**
  infusion table, 799
*Vioform-Hydrocortisone*, 575
*Viracept*, 320
*Viraferon*, 453
*ViraferonPeg*, 453
*Viralief*, 602
*Viramune*, 321
*Virasorb*, 602
*Virazole*, 329
*Viread*, 317
*Virgan*, 536
*Viridal Duo*, 425
*Virormone* injection, 377
*Virovir* (aciclovir), 323
Virus infections, 314
*Visclair*, 170
*Viscopaste PB7*, 833
Viscose, elastane, and cotton compression bandage, 832
*Viscotears*, 546
*Viskaldix*, 89
*Visken*, 89
*Vista-Methasone*
  ear, 551
  eye, 537
  nose, 555
*Vista-Methasone N*
  ear, 551
  eye, 537
  nose, 558
*Vistide*, 325
*Visudyne*, 548
*Vita Bite*, 814
*Vitajoule*, 814
Vitalograph peak flow meters, 151
Vitamin
  multivitamin preparations, 499
Vitamin A, **494**
  vitamin D and, 494
Vitamin B group, 494
  preparations, 494, 495
    B and C injection, 494, 799
Vitamin $B_{12}$, 466, 467
Vitamin C *see* Ascorbic acid
Vitamin D, 496
  psoriasis, 580
Vitamin deficiency, 493
Vitamin E, 497, 498
Vitamin K, 498
Vitamins, 493
  multivitamin preparations, 498, 499
  parenteral, 483
    infusion table, 800
Vitamins capsules, 498
*Vitapro*, 814
*Vitaquick*, 814
*Vitasavoury*, 815
Vitiligo, 594
  ACBS, 820
*Vitlipid N*, 483
*Vitrex* products, 350
*Vitrimix*, 487
Vivabec, *555*
*Vivacor* (bisoprolol), 86
*Vivaglobin*, 628
Vivicrom, *539*
*Vividrin* (sodium cromoglicate), 539, 556
*Vivioptal*, 499
*Volmax*, 145
*Volplex*, 482
*Volraman* (diclofenac), 508
*Volsaid* preparations, 509
*Voltarol* preparations, 509
  *Emulgel*, 531
  eye, 548
  gel patch, 531
  *Ophtha*, 548
  *Rapid*, 509
*Volumatic*, 152
Volume expansion, 480
*Voluven*, 482
Vomiting, 210
  cytotoxic drugs, 428
  in infancy, ACBS, 820
  palliative care, 16
  postoperative, 211
  pregnancy, 211
von Willebrand's disease, 385
Voriconazole, 308, 309, **313**, 314
  infusion table, 800
Vulvitis, candidal, 405
VZIG *see* Immunoglobulins, varicella-zoster, 628, 629

# W

Waldenstrom's macroglobulinaemia, 430
Warfarin, 124, **125**
*Warticon* preparations, 593
Warts, 591
Wasp sting allergy preparations, 165
Water
  for injections, 480
  potable, 2
*Waxsol*, 554
Webbing, blue line, 832
Webbing, red line, 832
*Welldorm*, 177
*Wellvone*, 339
Wernicke's encephalopathy, 494
West's syndrome, 246
Whooping cough *see* Pertussis
Wilson's disease, 499
*Wilzin*, 500
*WinRho SDF*, 630
Withdrawal
  alcohol, 260
  anxiolytics, 173
  hypnotics, 173
  nicotine, 260
  opioids, 263
Wolff-Parkinson-White syndrome, 79
Wool fat, excipient, 567
Wool fat, hydrous, 568
*World Traveller HI FLO*, 153
Worm infestation, 340
Wound dressings, 821
  pads, 827
Wuchereria bancrofti, *342*
*Wysoy*, 815

# X

*Xagrid*, 472
*Xalacom*, 542
*Xalatan*, 542
*Xanax*, 179
Xanthine bronchodilators *see* Theophylline
Xanthine-oxidase inhibitor, 524
*Xatral* preparations, 418
*Xeloda*, 436
*Xenazine*, 259
*Xenical*, 209
*Xepin*, 572
Xerostomia, 564
  ACBS, 820
*Xigris* (drotrecogin alfa (activated)), 132
Xipamide, 72, **73**
*Xismox XL* (isosorbide mononitrate), 109
*XLEU Analog*, 815
*XLEU Faladon*, 815
*XLEU Maxamaid*, 815
*XLYS Analog*, 815
*XLYS Low TRY Analog*, 815
*XLYS Low TRY Maxamaid*, 815
*XLYS Maxamaid*, 815
*XMET Analog*, 815
*XMET Homidon*, 815
*XMET Maxamaid*, 815
*XMET Maxamum*, 815
*XMTVI Analog*, 815
*XMTVI Asadon*, 815
*XMTVI Maxamaid*, 815
*XMTVI Maxamum*, 815
*Xolair*, 161
*XP Analog*, 815
*XP LCP Analog*, 815
*XP Maxamaid Concentrate*, 816
*XP Maxamaid*, 815
*XP Maxamum*, 816
*XPHEN TYR Analog*, 816
*XPHEN TYR Maxamaid*, 816
*XPHEN TYR Tyrosidon*, 816
*XPTM Analog*, 816
*XPTM Tyrosidon*, 816
Xylitol, presence of, 2
*Xylocaine*, 648, 649
Xylometazoline
  eye, 538
  nose, **557**
*Xyloproct*, 65
*Xyzal*, 162

# Y

*8Y* (factor VIII fraction), 132
*Yasmin*, 412
Yeasts, 309

Yel/Vac, 627
Yellow cards, *inside back cover*, 10
Yellow fever
immunisation
travel, 630
vaccine, 627
*Yentreve*, 420
*Yutopar*, 403

# Z

*Zacin*, 532
*Zaditen*, 160, 539
Zafirlukast, **160**
Zalcitabine, **317**, 318
Zaleplon, **175**, 176
*Zamadol* preparations, 230
*Zanaflex*, 529
Zanamivir, 326, **327**
*Zanidip*, 112
*Zanprol* (omeprazole), 50
*Zantac*, 47
*Zantac* (ranitidine), 47
*Zapain* (co-codamol 30/500), 221
*Zaponex*, 189
*Zarontin*, 240
capsules—discontinued, ix
*Zavedos*, 434
*Zavesca*, 501
*ZeaSORB*, 609
*Zeffix*, 317
*Zelapar*, 256
*Zemon* preparations, 109
*Zemplar*, 497
*Zemtard* preparations, 111
*Zenalb* preparations (albumin solution), 480
*Zenapax*, 450
*Zentel*, 341, *342*
*Zerit*, 317
*Zerobase*, 569
*Zestoretic* preparations, 101
*Zestril*, 101
*Ziagen*, 316
*Zibor*, 121
*Zidoval*, 407
Zidovudine, **318**
abacavir and lamivudine with, 316
infusion table, 800
lamivudine with, 318
*Zileze* (zopiclone), 176
*Zimbacol XL* (bezafibrate), 135
*Zimovane*, 176
*Zinacef*, 283
Zinc
acetate, 500
bandages, 580, 833
calamine and, 833
ichthammol and, 579, 580, 833
stocking, 833
deficiency, 493
eye, 545, **547**
injection, 493
oral preparations
deficiency, 493
Wilson's disease (zinc acetate), 500
skin, 594
barrier preparations, 571
castor oil with, 571
coal tar with, 583
cod liver oil with, 571
cream, 571
dimeticone with, 571
dithranol and salicylic acid with, 584
erythromycin with, 588
ichthammol with, 580
ointment, 571
plaster, 834
salicylic acid with, 584
tape adhesive, 834
sulphate, 493
Wilson's disease (zinc acetate), 500
Zinc acetate, **500**
Zinc eye preparations, 545
Zinc oxide
bandages, 833
plaster, 834
stocking, 833
tape, adhesive, 834
Zinc paste bandage, 833
calamine and, 833
ichthammol and, 833
Zinc sulphate preparations
eye drops, 547
*Zincaband*, 833
*Zindaclin*, 588
*Zineryt*, 588
*Zinnat*, 283
*Zipzoc*, 833
*Zispin* preparations, 205
*Zithromax*, 291
*Zocor*, 138
*Zocor Heart-Pro* (simvastatin), 138
*Zofran*, 215
*Zoladex* preparations, 460
endometriosis, 395
IVF, 395
Zoledronic acid, **391**
infusion table, 800
*Zoleptil*, 191
Zollinger–Ellison syndrome, 44, 48
Zolmitriptan, 232, **234**
Zolpidem, 175, **176**
*Zolvera* (verapamil), 114
*Zomacton*, 383
*Zometa*, 391
*Zomig* preparations, 234
*Zomorph*, 224
palliative care, 14
*Zonegran*, 247
Zonisamide, **246**, 247
Zopiclone, 175, **176**
*Zorac*, 582
Zoster *see* Herpes infections
Zotepine, 187, **190**, 191
*Zoton*, 49
*Zovirax* preparations, 323
cold sore cream, 602
cream, 602
eye ointment, 536
Zuclopenthixol, 182, 187, 191, 192
depot injections, 193
tablets, 187
Zuclopenthixol acetate, **187**
Zuclopenthixol decanoate, **192**
Zuclopenthixol dihydrochloride, **187**
*Zumenon*, 373
*Zuvogen*, 602
*Zyban*, 261
*Zydol* preparations, 230
*Zyloric*, 525
*Zyomet*, 598
*Zyprexa*, 189
*Zyvox*, 295


Index

Yellowcard

In Confidence

MHRA

## SUSPECTED ADVERSE DRUG REACTIONS

If you suspect that an adverse reaction may be related to a drug, or a combination of drugs, you should complete this Yellow Card or complete a report on the website at www.yellowcard.gov.uk. For *intensively monitored medicines* (identified by ▼) report **all** suspected reactions (including any considered not to be serious). For *established drugs* and *herbal remedies* report **all serious** adverse reactions in adults; report **all serious and minor** adverse reactions in **children** (under 18 years). You do not have to be certain about causality: if in doubt, please report. Do not be put off reporting just because some details are not known. See BNF (page 10) or the MHRA website (www.mhra.gov.uk) for additional advice.

**PATIENT DETAILS** Patient Initials: ________ Sex: M / F Weight if known (kg): ________

Age (at time of reaction): ________ Identification (Your Practice / Hospital Ref.)*: ________

**SUSPECTED DRUG(S)**

| Give brand name of drug and batch number if known | Route | Dosage | Date started | Date stopped | Prescribed for |
|---|---|---|---|---|---|
| | | | | | |
| | | | | | |

**SUSPECTED REACTION(S)**

**Please describe the reaction(s) and any treatment given:**

**Outcome**

- Recovered ☐
- Recovering ☐
- Continuing ☐
- Other ☐

Date reaction(s) started: ________ Date reaction(s) stopped: ________

Do you consider the reaction to be serious? Yes / No

If *yes*, please indicate why the reaction is considered to be serious (please tick all that apply):

- Patient died due to reaction ☐
- Life threatening ☐
- Congenital abnormality ☐
- Involved or prolonged inpatient hospitalisation ☐
- Involved persistent or significant disability or incapacity ☐
- Medically significant; please give details:

* This is to enable you to identify the patient in any future correspondence concerning this report

*Please attach additional pages if necessary*

**Please list other drugs taken in the last 3 months prior to the reaction (including self-medication & herbal remedies)**

Was the patient on any other medication? Yes / No

If *yes*, please give the following information if known:

| Drug (Brand, if known) | Route | Dosage | Date started | Date stopped | Prescribed for |
|---|---|---|---|---|---|
| | | | | | |
| | | | | | |
| | | | | | |
| | | | | | |

**Additional relevant information** e.g. medical history, test results, known allergies, rechallenge (if performed), suspected drug interactions. For congenital abnormalities please state all other drugs taken during pregnancy and the date of the last menstrual period.

**REPORTER DETAILS**

Name and Professional Address: ______

Post code: ______ Tel No: ______

Speciality: ______

Signature: Date:

**CLINICIAN (if not the reporter)**

Name and Professional Address: ______

Post code: ______

Tel No: ______ Speciality: ______

If you would like information about other adverse reactions associated with the suspected drug, please tick this box ☐

Send to **Medicines and Healthcare Products Regulatory Agency, CHM FREEPOST, LONDON SW8 5BR** or if you are in one of the following NHS regions:

to **CHM Mersey, FREEPOST, Liverpool L3 3AB**
or **CHM Northern, FREEPOST 1085, Newcastle upon Tyne NE1 1BR**
or **CHM West Midlands, FREEPOST SW2991, Birmingham B18 7BR**
or **CHM Scotland, CARDS, FREEPOST NAT3271, Edinburgh EH16 4BR**
or **CHM Wales, FREEPOST, Cardiff CF4 1ZZ**

**Yellowcard** In Confidence MHRA

## SUSPECTED ADVERSE DRUG REACTIONS

If you suspect that an adverse reaction may be related to a drug, or a combination of drugs, you should complete this Yellow Card or complete a report on the website at www.yellowcard.gov.uk. For *intensively monitored medicines* (identified by ▼) report **all** suspected reactions (including any considered not to be serious). For *established drugs* and *herbal remedies* report **all serious** adverse reactions in adults; report **all serious and minor** adverse reactions in **children** (under 18 years). You do not have to be certain about causality: if in doubt, please report. Do not be put off reporting just because some details are not known. See BNF (page 10) or the MHRA website (www.mhra.gov.uk) for additional advice.

**PATIENT DETAILS** Patient Initials: ______ Sex: M / F Weight if known (kg): ______

Age (at time of reaction): ______ Identification (Your Practice / Hospital Ref.)*: ______

**SUSPECTED DRUG(S)**

| Give brand name of drug and batch number if known | Route | Dosage | Date started | Date stopped | Prescribed for |
|---|---|---|---|---|---|
| | | | | | |
| | | | | | |

**SUSPECTED REACTION(S)**

**Please describe the reaction(s) and any treatment given:**

**Outcome**

- Recovered ☐
- Recovering ☐
- Continuing ☐
- Other ☐

Date reaction(s) started: ______ Date reaction(s) stopped: ______

Do you consider the reaction to be serious? Yes / No

If *yes*, please indicate why the reaction is considered to be serious (please tick all that apply):

- Patient died due to reaction ☐
- Life threatening ☐
- Congenital abnormality ☐
- Involved or prolonged inpatient hospitalisation ☐
- Involved persistent or significant disability or incapacity ☐
- Medically significant; please give details:

* This is to enable you to identify the patient in any future correspondence concerning this report

*Please attach additional pages if necessary*

**Please list other drugs taken in the last 3 months prior to the reaction (including self-medication & herbal remedies)**

Was the patient on any other medication? Yes / No

If *yes*, please give the following information if known:

| Drug (Brand, if known) | Route | Dosage | Date started | Date stopped | Prescribed for |
|---|---|---|---|---|---|
| | | | | | |
| | | | | | |
| | | | | | |
| | | | | | |

**Additional relevant information** e.g. medical history, test results, known allergies, rechallenge (if performed), suspected drug interactions. For congenital abnormalities please state all other drugs taken during pregnancy and the date of the last menstrual period.

**REPORTER DETAILS**

Name and Professional Address: ______

Post code: ______ Tel No: ______

Speciality: ______

Signature: Date:

**CLINICIAN (if not the reporter)**

Name and Professional Address: ______

Post code: ______

Tel No: ______ Speciality: ______

If you would like information about other adverse reactions associated with the suspected drug, please tick this box ☐

Send to **Medicines and Healthcare Products Regulatory Agency, CHM FREEPOST, LONDON SW8 5BR** or if you are in one of the following NHS regions:

to **CHM Mersey, FREEPOST, Liverpool L3 3AB**

or **CHM Northern, FREEPOST 1085, Newcastle upon Tyne NE1 1BR**

or **CHM West Midlands, FREEPOST SW2991, Birmingham B18 7BR**

or **CHM Scotland, CARDS, FREEPOST NAT3271, Edinburgh EH16 4BR**

or **CHM Wales, FREEPOST, Cardiff CF4 1ZZ**

**Yellowcard** In Confidence **MHRA**

## SUSPECTED ADVERSE DRUG REACTIONS

If you suspect that an adverse reaction may be related to a drug, or a combination of drugs, you should complete this Yellow Card or complete a report on the website at www.yellowcard.gov.uk. For *intensively monitored medicines* (identified by ▼) report **all** suspected reactions (including any considered not to be serious). For *established drugs* and *herbal remedies* report **all serious** adverse reactions in adults; report **all serious and minor** adverse reactions in **children** (under 18 years). You do not have to be certain about causality: if in doubt, please report. Do not be put off reporting just because some details are not known. See BNF (page 10) or the MHRA website (www.mhra.gov.uk) for additional advice.

**PATIENT DETAILS** Patient Initials: ____________ Sex: M / F Weight if known (kg): ____________

Age (at time of reaction): ____________ Identification (Your Practice / Hospital Ref.)*: ____________

**SUSPECTED DRUG(S)**

| Give brand name of drug and batch number if known | Route | Dosage | Date started | Date stopped | Prescribed for |
|---|---|---|---|---|---|
| | | | | | |
| | | | | | |

**SUSPECTED REACTION(S)**

**Please describe the reaction(s) and any treatment given:**

**Outcome**

- Recovered ☐
- Recovering ☐
- Continuing ☐
- Other ☐

Date reaction(s) started: ____________ Date reaction(s) stopped: ____________

Do you consider the reaction to be serious? Yes / No

If *yes*, please indicate why the reaction is considered to be serious (please tick all that apply):

- Patient died due to reaction ☐
- Life threatening ☐
- Congenital abnormality ☐
- Involved or prolonged inpatient hospitalisation ☐
- Involved persistent or significant disability or incapacity ☐
- Medically significant; please give details:

* This is to enable you to identify the patient in any future correspondence concerning this report

*Please attach additional pages if necessary*

**Please list other drugs taken in the last 3 months prior to the reaction (including self-medication & herbal remedies)**

Was the patient on any other medication? Yes / No

If *yes*, please give the following information if known:

| Drug (Brand, if known) | Route | Dosage | Date started | Date stopped | Prescribed for |
|---|---|---|---|---|---|
| | | | | | |
| | | | | | |
| | | | | | |
| | | | | | |

**Additional relevant information** e.g. medical history, test results, known allergies, rechallenge (if performed), suspected drug interactions. For congenital abnormalities please state all other drugs taken during pregnancy and the date of the last menstrual period.

**REPORTER DETAILS**

Name and Professional Address: ______

Post code: ______ Tel No: ______

Speciality: ______

Signature: Date:

**CLINICIAN (if not the reporter)**

Name and Professional Address: ______

Post code: ______

Tel No: ______ Speciality: ______

If you would like information about other adverse reactions associated with the suspected drug, please tick this box ☐

Send to **Medicines and Healthcare Products Regulatory Agency, CHM FREEPOST, LONDON SW8 5BR** or if you are in one of the following NHS regions:

to **CHM Mersey, FREEPOST, Liverpool L3 3AB**
or **CHM Northern, FREEPOST 1085, Newcastle upon Tyne NE1 1BR**
or **CHM West Midlands, FREEPOST SW2991, Birmingham B18 7BR**
or **CHM Scotland, CARDS, FREEPOST NAT3271, Edinburgh EH16 4BR**
or **CHM Wales, FREEPOST, Cardiff CF4 1ZZ**

Yellowcard

In Confidence

MHRA

# SUSPECTED ADVERSE DRUG REACTIONS

If you suspect that an adverse reaction may be related to a drug, or a combination of drugs, you should complete this Yellow Card or complete a report on the website at www.yellowcard.gov.uk. For *intensively monitored medicines* (identified by ▼) report **all** suspected reactions (including any considered not to be serious). For *established drugs* and *herbal remedies* report **all serious** adverse reactions in adults; report **all serious and minor** adverse reactions in **children** (under 18 years). You do not have to be certain about causality: if in doubt, please report. Do not be put off reporting just because some details are not known. See BNF (page 10) or the MHRA website (www.mhra.gov.uk) for additional advice.

**PATIENT DETAILS** Patient Initials: ____________ Sex: M / F Weight if known (kg): ____________

Age (at time of reaction): ____________ Identification (Your Practice / Hospital Ref.)*: ____________

**SUSPECTED DRUG(S)**

| Give brand name of drug and batch number if known | Route | Dosage | Date started | Date stopped | Prescribed for |
|---|---|---|---|---|---|
| | | | | | |
| | | | | | |

**SUSPECTED REACTION(S)**

**Please describe the reaction(s) and any treatment given:**

Date reaction(s) started: ____________ Date reaction(s) stopped: ____________

**Outcome**

Recovered ☐
Recovering ☐
Continuing ☐
Other ☐

Do you consider the reaction to be serious? Yes / No

If *yes*, please indicate why the reaction is considered to be serious (please tick all that apply):

Patient died due to reaction ☐
Life threatening ☐
Congenital abnormality ☐
Involved or prolonged inpatient hospitalisation ☐
Involved persistent or significant disability or incapacity ☐
Medically significant; please give details:

* This is to enable you to identify the patient in any future correspondence concerning this report

*Please attach additional pages if necessary*

**Please list other drugs taken in the last 3 months prior to the reaction (including self-medication & herbal remedies)**

Was the patient on any other medication? Yes / No

If *yes*, please give the following information if known:

| Drug (Brand, if known) | Route | Dosage | Date started | Date stopped | Prescribed for |
|---|---|---|---|---|---|
| | | | | | |
| | | | | | |
| | | | | | |
| | | | | | |

**Additional relevant information** e.g. medical history, test results, known allergies, rechallenge (if performed), suspected drug interactions. For congenital abnormalities please state all other drugs taken during pregnancy and the date of the last menstrual period.

**REPORTER DETAILS**

Name and Professional Address: ______

Post code: ______ Tel No: ______

Speciality: ______

Signature: Date:

**CLINICIAN (if not the reporter)**

Name and Professional Address: ______

Post code: ______

Tel No: ______ Speciality: ______

If you would like information about other adverse reactions associated with the suspected drug, please tick this box ☐

Send to **Medicines and Healthcare Products Regulatory Agency, CHM FREEPOST, LONDON SW8 5BR** or if you are in one of the following NHS regions:

to **CHM Mersey, FREEPOST, Liverpool L3 3AB**
or **CHM Northern, FREEPOST 1085, Newcastle upon Tyne NE1 1BR**
or **CHM West Midlands, FREEPOST SW2991, Birmingham B18 7BR**
or **CHM Scotland, CARDS, FREEPOST NAT3271, Edinburgh EH16 4BR**
or **CHM Wales, FREEPOST, Cardiff CF4 1ZZ**

# Cardiovascular Risk Prediction Charts

*J Hum Hypertens* 2004; **18**: 139–85

## How to use the Cardiovascular Risk Prediction Charts for Primary Prevention

These charts are for estimating cardiovascular disease (CVD) risk (non-fatal myocardial infarction and stroke, coronary and stroke death and new angina pectoris) for individuals who have **not** already developed coronary heart disease (CHD) or other major atherosclerotic disease. They are an aid to making clinical decisions about how intensively to intervene on lifestyle and whether to use antihypertensive, lipid lowering and anti-platelet medication, but should **not replace clinical judgment**.

- The use of these charts is **not appropriate** for patients who have existing diseases which already put them at high risk such as:
  - coronary heart disease or other major atherosclerotic disease;
  - familial hypercholesterolaemia or other inherited dyslipidaemias;
  - renal dysfunction including diabetic nephropathy;
  - type 1 and 2 diabetes mellitus.
- The charts should **not** be used to decide whether to introduce antihypertensive medication when blood pressure is persistently at or above 160/100 mmHg or when target organ damage due to hypertension is present. In both cases antihypertensive medication is recommended regardless of CVD risk. Similarly the charts should **not** be used to decide whether to introduce lipid-lowering medication when the ratio of serum total to HDL cholesterol exceeds 7. Such medication is generally then indicated regardless of estimated CVD risk.
- To estimate an individual's absolute 10-year risk of developing CVD choose the chart for his or her gender, lifetime smoking status and age. Within this square identify the level of risk according to the point where the coordinates for systolic blood pressure and the ratio of total cholesterol to high density lipoprotein (HDL) cholesterol meet. If no HDL cholesterol result is available, then assume this is 1.0 mmol/litre and the lipid scale can be used for total cholesterol alone.
- Higher risk individuals (red areas) are defined as those whose 10-year CVD risk exceeds 20%, which is approximately equivalent to the coronary heart disease risk of > 15% over the same period.
- The chart also assists in identifying individuals whose 10-year CVD risk is moderately increased in the range 10–20% (orange areas) and those in whom risk is lower than 10% over 10 years (green areas).
- Smoking status should reflect lifetime exposure to tobacco and not simply tobacco use at the time of assessment. For example, those who have given up smoking within 5 years should be regarded as current smokers for the purposes of the charts.
- The initial blood pressure and the first random (non-fasting) total cholesterol and HDL cholesterol can be used to estimate an individual's risk. However, the decision on using drug therapy should generally be based on repeat risk factor measurements over a period of time.

(Continued over)

- Men and women do not reach the level of risk predicted by the charts for the three age bands until they reach the ages 49, 59, and 69 years respectively. The charts will overestimate current risk most in the under 40s. Clinical judgement must be exercised in deciding on treatment in younger patients. However, it should be recognised that blood pressure and cholesterol tend to rise most and HDL cholesterol to decline most in younger people already with adverse levels. Left untreated, their risk at the age 49 years is likely to be higher than the projected risk shown on the age-under-50-years chart. From age 70 years the CVD risk, especially for men, is usually $\geq$ 20% over 10 years and the charts will underestimate true total CVD risk.

- These charts (and all other currently available methods of CVD risk prediction) are based on groups of people with **untreated** levels of blood pressure, total cholesterol and HDL cholesterol. In patients already receiving antihypertensive therapy in whom the decision is to be made about whether to introduce lipid-lowering medication, or vice versa, the charts can only act as a guide. Unless recent pre-treatment risk factor values are available it is generally safest to assume that CVD risk is higher than that predicted by current levels of blood pressure or lipids on treatment.

- CVD risk is also higher than indicated in the charts for:

  - those with a family history of premature CVD or stroke (male first-degree relatives aged < 55 years and female first-degree relatives aged < 65 years) which increases the risk by a factor of approximately 1.5;

  - those with raised triglyceride levels (> 1.7 mmol/litre);

  - women with premature menopause;

  - those who are not yet diabetic, but have impaired fasting glycaemia (6.1–6.9 mmol/litre) or impaired glucose tolerance (2 hour glucose $\geq$ 7.8 mmol/litre but < 11.1 mmol/litre in an oral glucose tolerance test).

- The charts have not been validated in ethnic minorities and in some may underestimate CVD risk. For example, in people originating from the Indian subcontinent it is safest to assume that the CVD risk is higher than predicted from the charts (1.5 times).

- An individual can be shown on the chart the direction in which his or her risk of CVD can be reduced by changing smoking status, blood pressure, or cholesterol, but it should be borne in mind that the estimate of risk is for a group of people with similar risk factors and that within that group there will be considerable variation in risk. It should also be pointed out in younger people that the estimated risk will generally not be reached before the age of 50, if their current blood pressure and lipid levels remain unchanged. The charts are primarily to assist in directing intervention to those who typically stand to benefit most.

(Continued over)

# NONDIABETIC MEN

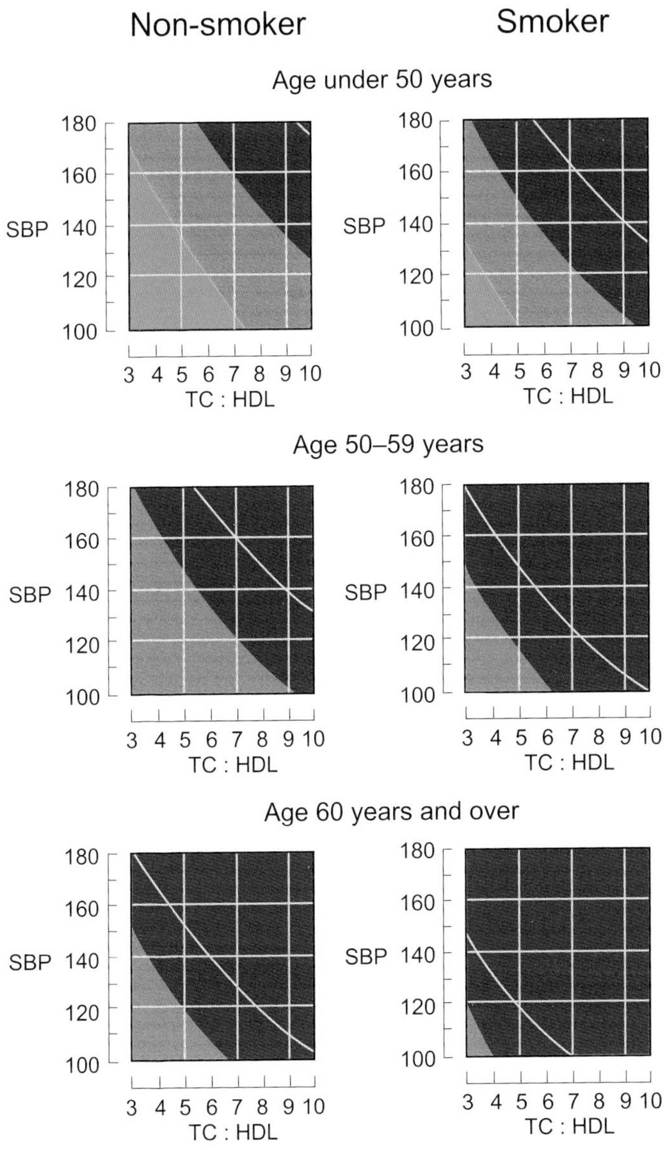


CVD risk <10% over next 10 years

CVD risk 10-20% over next 10 years

CVD risk >20% over next 10 years

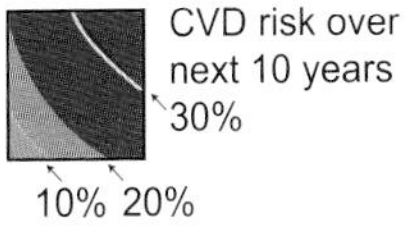


SBP = systolic blood pressure mmHg

TC : HDL = serum total cholesterol to HDL cholesterol ratio

(Continued over)

# NONDIABETIC WOMEN

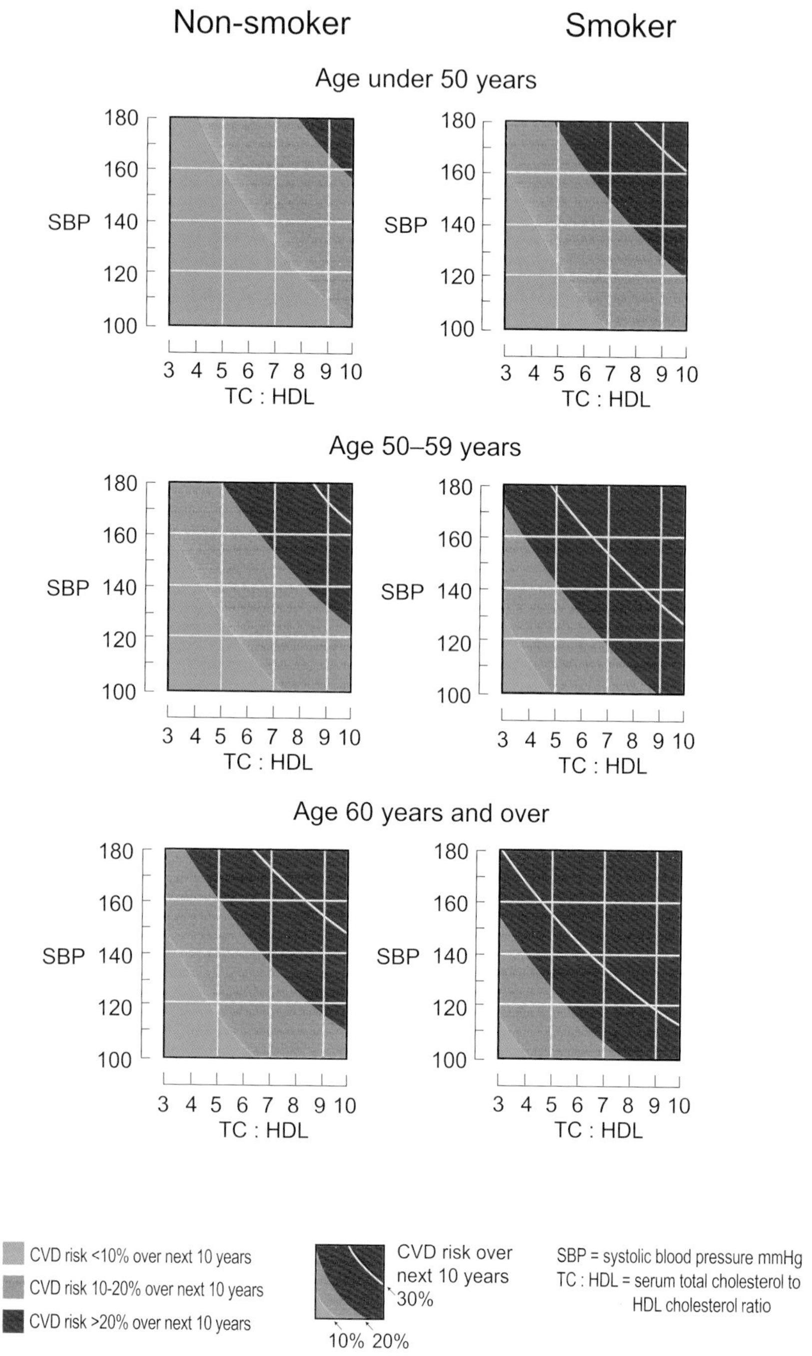

Non-smoker
Smoker
Age under 50 years
Age 50–59 years
Age 60 years and over
SBP
180
160
140
120
100
3 4 5 6 7 8 9 10
TC : HDL
CVD risk <10% over next 10 years
CVD risk 10-20% over next 10 years
CVD risk >20% over next 10 years
CVD risk over next 10 years
30%
10% 20%
SBP = systolic blood pressure mmHg
TC : HDL = serum total cholesterol to HDL cholesterol ratio

# ADULT ADVANCED LIFE SUPPORT ALGORITHM

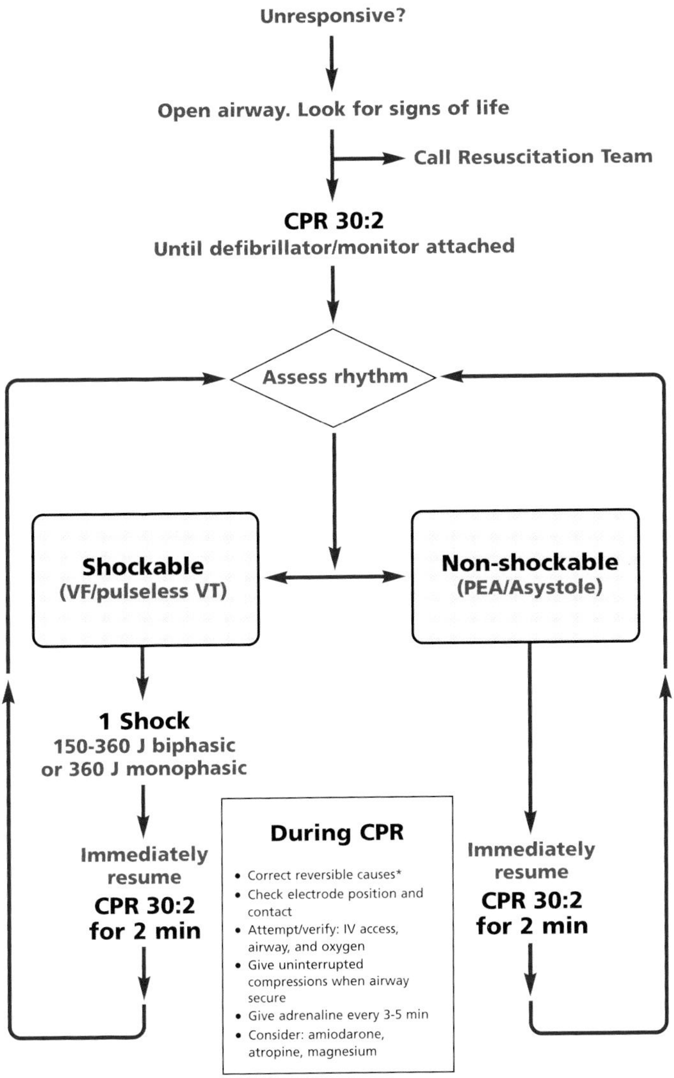

Unresponsive?
Open airway. Look for signs of life
Call Resuscitation Team
CPR 30:2
Until defibrillator/monitor attached
Assess rhythm
Shockable
(VF/pulseless VT)
Non-shockable
(PEA/Asystole)
1 Shock
150-360 J biphasic
or 360 J monophasic
Immediately resume
CPR 30:2
for 2 min
During CPR
• Correct reversible causes*
• Check electrode position and contact
• Attempt/verify: IV access, airway, and oxygen
• Give uninterrupted compressions when airway secure
• Give adrenaline every 3-5 min
• Consider: amiodarone, atropine, magnesium
Immediately resume
CPR 30:2
for 2 min

***Reversible causes**

| | |
|---|---|
| Hypoxia | Tension pneumothorax |
| Hypovolaemia | Tamponade, cardiac |
| Hypo/hyperkalaemia/metabolic | Toxins |
| Hypothermia | Thrombosis (coronary or plumonary) |

European Resuscitation Council

Resuscitation Council (UK)

## pproximate conversions and units

| kg | stones | kg |
|---|---|---|
| 0.45 | 1 | 6.35 |
| 0.91 | 2 | 12.70 |
| 1.36 | 3 | 19.05 |
| 1.81 | 4 | 25.40 |
| 2.27 | 5 | 31.75 |
| 2.72 | 6 | 38.10 |
| 3.18 | 7 | 44.45 |
| 3.63 | 8 | 50.80 |
| 4.08 | 9 | 57.15 |
| 4.54 | 10 | 63.50 |
| 4.99 | 11 | 69.85 |
| 5.44 | 12 | 76.20 |
| 5.90 | 13 | 82.55 |
| 6.35 | 14 | 88.90 |
| | 15 | 95.25 |

| mL | fl oz |
|---|---|
| 50 | 1.8 |
| 100 | 3.5 |
| 150 | 5.3 |
| 200 | 7.0 |
| 500 | 17.6 |
| 1000 | 35.2 |

## ength

| | | |
|---|---|---|
| etre (m) | | = 1000 millimetres (mm) |
| entimetre (cm) | | = 10 mm |
| ch (in) | | = 25.4 mm |
| ot (ft) | =12 inches | = 304.8 mm |

## ass

| | |
|---|---|
| logram (kg) | = 1000 grams (g) |
| am (g) | = 1000 milligrams (mg) |
| illigram (mg) | = 1000 micrograms |
| icrogram | = 1000 nanograms |
| anogram | = 1000 picograms |

## olume

| | |
|---|---|
| tre | = 1000 millilitres (mL) |
| illilitre (1 mL) | = 1000 microlitres |
| int | ≈ 568 mL |

## ther units

| | |
|---|---|
| ilocalorie (kcal) | = 4186.8 joules (J) |
| 0 kilocalories (kcal) | = 4.1868 megajoules (MJ) |
| egajoule (MJ) | = 238.8 kilocalories (kcal) |
| illimetre of mercury mmHg) | = 133.3 pascals (Pa) |
| ilopascal (kPa) | = 7.5 mmHg (pressure) |

**asma-drug concentrations** in the BNF are xpressed in mass units per litre (e.g. mg/litre). The pproximate equivalent in terms of amount of sub-ance units (e.g. micromol/litre) is given in brackets.

## Prescribing in children

| Age | Ideal body-weight kg | Ideal body-weight lb | Height cm | Height inch | Body-surface $m^2$ |
|---|---|---|---|---|---|
| Newborn* | 3.5 | 7.7 | 50 | 20 | 0.23 |
| 1 month* | 4.2 | 9 | 55 | 22 | 0.26 |
| 3 months* | 5.6 | 12 | 59 | 23 | 0.32 |
| 6 months | 7.7 | 17 | 67 | 26 | 0.40 |
| 1 year | 10 | 22 | 76 | 30 | 0.47 |
| 3 years | 15 | 33 | 94 | 37 | 0.62 |
| 5 years | 18 | 40 | 108 | 42 | 0.73 |
| 7 years | 23 | 51 | 120 | 47 | 0.88 |
| 12 years | 39 | 86 | 148 | 58 | 1.25 |
| Adult | | | | | |
| Male | 68 | 150 | 173 | 68 | 1.80 |
| Female | 56 | 123 | 163 | 64 | 1.60 |

* The figures relate to full term and not preterm infants who may need reduced dosage according to their clinical condition.

## Recommended wording of cautionary and advisory labels

For details see Appendix 9

1 Warning. May cause drowsiness
2 Warning. May cause drowsiness. If affected do not drive or operate machinery. Avoid alcoholic drink
3 Warning. May cause drowsiness. If affected do not drive or operate machinery
4 Warning. Avoid alcoholic drink
5 Do not take indigestion remedies at the same time of day as this medicine
6 Do not take indigestion remedies or medicines containing iron or zinc at the same time of day as this medicine
7 Do not take milk, indigestion remedies, or medicines containing iron or zinc at the same time of day as this medicine
8 Do not stop taking this medicine except on your doctor's advice
9 Take at regular intervals. Complete the prescribed course unless otherwise directed
10 Warning. Follow the printed instructions you have been given with this medicine
11 Avoid exposure of skin to direct sunlight or sun lamps
12 Do not take anything containing aspirin while taking this medicine
13 Dissolve or mix with water before taking
14 This medicine may colour the urine
15 Caution flammable: keep away from fire or flames
16 Allow to dissolve under the tongue. Do not transfer from this container. Keep tightly closed. Discard 8 weeks after opening
17 Do not take more than ... in 24 hours
18 Do not take more than ... in 24 hours or ... in any one week
19 Warning. Causes drowsiness which may continue the next day. If affected do not drive or operate machinery. Avoid alcoholic drink
21 ... with or after food
22 ... half to one hour before food
23 ... an hour before food or on an empty stomach
24 ... sucked or chewed
25 ... swallowed whole, not chewed
26 ... dissolved under the tongue
27 ... with plenty of water
28 To be spread thinly ...
29 Do not take more than 2 at any one time. Do not take more than 8 in 24 hours
30 Do not take with any other paracetamol products
31 Contains aspirin and paracetamol. Do not take with any other paracetamol products
32 Contains aspirin
33 Contains an aspirin-like medicine